DICTIONARY OF CATHOLIC BIOGRAPHY

DICTIONARY OF
CATHOLIC
BIOGRAPHY

JOHN J. DELANEY

AND

JAMES EDWARD TOBIN

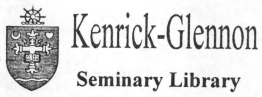
DOUBLEDAY & COMPANY, INC.
GARDEN CITY, NEW YORK

Imprimatur: ✠ FRANCIS CARDINAL SPELLMAN
Archbishop of New York
September 28, 1961

Library of Congress Catalog Card Number: 62–7620
Copyright © 1961 by John J. Delaney and James Edward Tobin
Printed in the United States of America
All Rights Reserved
First Edition

TO ANN
AND
TO LORRAINE

CONTENTS

FOREWORD

FOR MANY YEARS the authors have felt the need of a single reference volume of biographical information on outstanding Catholics from the time of the apostles to the present day. There is, to the best of our knowledge, none in existence. The purpose of this *Dictionary*, then, is to make such reference material readily accessible.

We have tried to present the salient facts of the life of each person included: date and place of birth, educational background, important positions held, and place and date of death. Where the significance of a subject's work warrants, a short summary is given of his contribution to a particular field of endeavor; major works of literature, art, and music are given for each author, artist, and composer, as are the major contributions in ecclesiastical, philosophical, medical, legal, and other professional worlds. As complete a picture as possible is thus presented of each individual's life and significance.

In the course of almost 2000 years there have been hundreds of thousands of persons who have played a role in the history and development of the Catholic Church. It obviously has not been possible, nor would it be feasible, to include them all. Among the more difficult tasks in preparing this work has been that of selecting the almost 15,000 names which are presently included. We have tried to include all who made a significant contribution to the Church, sometimes by virtue of office, or by virtue of a major action, where nothing further could be learned. We have also included Catholic men and women who have made a substantial contribution to the many areas of human endeavor. In some instances, we have included individuals whose actions may have been inimical to the welfare of the Church or whose personal lives may have left much to be desired. Such persons have been included because they were Catholics, because their actions did have an effect on human history or culture, and, most obviously, because it is not within our province to pass such moral judgment.

Using such broad criteria, we undoubtedly have passed over some figures who readers will feel should have been included. In some cases the omissions were deliberate (on the theory that some selection had to be made to keep the volume within bounds); in other cases, significant figures who should have been included have been unintentionally missed. We apologize in advance. With one hand we beg indulgence in the light of the magnitude of the past; with the other hand we welcome suggestions for additions.

The inclusion of those figures whose presence may be questioned should not need further comment. We have taken the traditional position that any figure recognized by the Church as a Catholic, by reason of Church burial services or interment in consecrated ground, can be accepted in a Catholic biographical work. We have been inclined in all cases to give the benefit of doubt to the individual, and to follow authority in so doing.

A word should be said about the sources for the material we have used. We have drawn on biographies and historical studies, existing reference works, studies of art, literature, and science, annual lists of obituaries and other annual chronicles, and newspaper reports. Primary sources are often sparse, as the serious reader knows. Destruction of documents by time or disaster, original inaccuracy or incompleteness, even lack of interest in keeping records—these are part of the thousand and one obstacles which historians have encountered in their own research. We have made every effort to screen out errors, discrepancies, and, sometimes, amazing contradictions, in the sources at hand. It is still probable that some errors have crept into our work, although we have made every effort to be accurate.

Whenever dates and facts are uncertain we have so indicated. The reader will notice that many of the birth and death dates at the beginning of biographical entries have question marks after them. The reason for this is that the date has not definitely been established and that this is generally accepted at the present time; or that the date is still a matter of lively debate among scholars and that the one given seems the most likely (in most cases, no more definite dates will ever be assigned). One more word about dates. In the case of saints, the date of death is usually identical with the feast day (abbreviated as F. D. throughout this book); when the date of death is different from the feast day, references to both dates should make this fact clear.

No living figures are included. Information about prominent contemporaries is generally available in a number of reference works of a Who's Who nature.

Several suggestions may be made about the most effective way to use this *Dictionary*. Many of them are obvious, but we will risk mentioning them. Names are arranged alphabetically. When there is a series of persons with the same name, the names within such a sequence are usually arranged chronologically (by date of death). But when there is an exceptionally long series of the same basic name, difficulties arise. This sample illustration, and the explanation which follows it, should help.

> John I, pope
> John XXII, pope
> John XXIII, antipope
> John I, king of Aragon
> John, king of England
> John I, king of Portugal
> John, St., d. 303
> John, St., d. 1342
> John, Dudley (or modern figures whose last
>   name is John)
> John Achaius
> John of Austria
> John de Balbi
> John of Capistrano
> John Cassian
> John the Evangelist
> John Joseph of the Cross
> John of Segovia
> John the Silent
> John de Trokelowe

The arrangement above is standard practice in many libraries, and does help a reader to locate the figure he is searching for. Names of the popes are listed first, in numerical order (including antipopes). Names of emperors follow (there is none in the list given above). Then come the names of kings (alphabetically by country—Aragon, England, France, Poland, Portugal, etc.). Then come individual figures, saints and others, whose only name is John (these are arranged chronologically, by date of death). After them, in most series, are listed modern figures whose last names belong in the series. Finally, the series continues with all those persons who have the name John followed by an identifying phrase. Notice in this last listing, that articles and prepositions (à, de, della, di, of, the, von) are totally disregarded in the alphabetizing. As a final bit of advice, the reader should remember that John sometimes takes the form Johan, Johannes, Juan, etc.

In the modern period of history (roughly, the years after 1300), surnames have been used in the alphabetical arrangement, except in the case of certain prominent figures (chiefly saints, artists, and a few mediaeval writers and scholars) who are known principally by their first names. For example, St. Thérèse of Lisieux is best known by this name, and she is so listed; there is however a cross reference under Martin, Marie Françoise Thérèse, her family name. Similarly, full information is given in the entry under Greco, El; there is a cross-reference listing under Theotocopuli, Domenico.

Other cross-reference entries serve obvious purposes. For example:

> **ABLEBERT.** *See* Emebert. A book the reader is using may refer to a person named Ablebert, but that person is usually known as Emebert. Full information is given in this *Dictionary* under Emebert, but the reader can be helped by the other type of reference.
>
> **POTAMIA, ST.** (d. 302), martyr. *See* Felix, St. This entry means that St. Potamia was a fellow martyr with, or one of a group of martyrs slain at the same time as, St. Felix. The date is included in the cross reference, since there are more than fifty Felixes in the *Dictionary*.
>
> **AYSCOUGH, JOHN.** *See* Bickerstaffe-Drew, Francis. This is the usual form of cross reference for a pen name, one well known from its use on many title pages.

Bibliographical references have been kept to a minimum and are given only for major figures. In many cases, no bibliographical titles are provided, either because there is no strictly biographical study in existence or because available lives are inadequate or unreliable; in other instances, biographies exist, but are out of print or otherwise generally unavailable.

As one of the appendices to the *Dictionary* we have compiled a list of rulers of major powers, from the Roman emperors and Christian popes of the first years of the present era to kings and presidents of the present moment. Perhaps many historical events referred to in several entries will become clearer if the reader checks the date of an event against the names of persons who directed government at that particular time. Another appendix brings together the names of certain saints and the places of which they are patron, and the activity or profession with which they have become associated. Another lists the symbols by which they are often represented in art (sculpture, stained-glass windows, heraldry, and other allegorical representations). It is hoped that such lists prove of some service.

Again we emphasize that the main purpose of this work is for quick, handy popular (yet intelligently thorough) reference: the scholar or specialist already knows sources for advanced study and probably has them on his own shelves.

JOHN J. DELANEY
JAMES EDWARD TOBIN

DICTIONARY OF CATHOLIC BIOGRAPHY

A

AARON, ST. (d. 304?), martyr. A Briton who, according to tradition, was executed with St. Julius and others at Caerleon in Monmouthshire, England, during the persecution of Diocletian. F. D. July 3 (sometimes, July 1).

AARON, ST. (6th century). He crossed from his homeland to live as a recluse in Brittany, where he was joined by other Britons and by St. Malo of Wales; the latter's name later became attached to the settlement. F. D. June 22.

AARON, BL. (d. 1059). The first abbot of the Benedictine monastery at Tyniec, Poland, to which he may have come from Cluny, he became first archbishop of Cracow in 1046. He died on May 15. F. D. Oct. 9.

ABACHUM, ST. (d. 260?), martyr. *See* Marius, St.

ABARCA, PEDRO (1619–1693), theologian. Born in Aragon, he became a Jesuit in 1641, taught at Salamanca, and wrote on the Incarnation, grace, and the sacraments, and two historical studies. He died at Palencia, Spain.

ABBADIE, ANTOINE D' (1810–1897), explorer. He and his brother Arnauld (1815–93) worked on expeditions to Ethiopia, where he wrote on geology, physics, and philology. His will provided for the establishment of an observatory there and gave his estate in southern France to the Paris Academy of Sciences. The brothers persuaded Pope Gregory XVI to enlarge the missionary endeavors in Ethiopia.

ABBAN, ST. An Irishman, he lived in solitude at Abington, England, before the time of St. Patrick. The name is also spelled Ewen. F. D. May 13.

ABBAN, ST. (5th century). Nephew of St. Ibar, he founded the abbey of Kill-Abban in Leinster, Ireland. F. D. Mar. 16.

ABBAN, ST. (6th century). A nephew of St. Kevin, he founded and was abbot of several monasteries in southern Ireland. F. D. Oct. 27.

ABBAN, ST. Founder of Ros-mic-treoin (New Ross), he died in County Wexford, Ireland. His name was corrupted to Stephen, Neville, and Nevin. F. D. Dec. 22.

ABBELOOS, JEAN BAPTISTE (1836–1906), educator. Born on Jan. 15 in Goyck, Belgium, he was educated at Malines, ordained there in 1860, received his doctorate at Louvain in 1867, and became professor of scripture at Malines. He was pastor at Duffel in 1876, vicar general to Cardinal Dechamps in 1883–87, and rector of Louvain in 1887–1900.

He wrote studies on the Church in the Near East.

ABBO, ST. (d. 860?). Abbot of the Benedictine monastery of St. Germain at Auxerre, France, he was bishop of that city from 857 to 859, when he resigned. F. D. Dec. 3.

ABBO, ST. (945?–1004), martyr. Born near Orléans, France, he became a Benedictine monk at Fleury, studied at Paris, Rheims, and Orléans, and was widely recognized as a scholar in astronomy, mathematics, and philosophy. In 986, at the invitation of St. Oswald of York, he took charge of the monastery of Ramsey in Huntingdonshire, England. In 988 he returned to Fleury, was elected abbot, and installed the Cluniac observance. He was active at synods, strove to exempt monasteries from episcopal control, and acted as mediator between the papacy and the king of France. He was much in demand to arbitrate monastic disputes; while reforming the monastery of La Réole, Gascony, he was killed when he attempted to separate two groups of quarreling monks. F. D. Nov. 13.

ABBO CERNUUS (d. 921?). A Benedictine monk at Paris, he wrote (about 896) a Latin verse description of the siege of the city by the Normans, and a number of sermons.

ABBOT, BL. HENRY (d. 1596), martyr. *See* Knight, Ven. William.

ABBOT, JOHN (d. 1597), martyr. An English layman, he was hanged at York with three others on July 4, having been charged with hiding priests.

ABDECHALAS, ST. (d. 341), martyr. *See* Simeon Barsabae, St.

ABDIAS (1st century). He is said to have been first bishop of Babylon. An account of the labors and death of the apostles, long attributed to him, probably originated in sixth-century Europe.

ABDIESUS, ST. (d. 342?), martyr. He and another deacon named Azadanes, Abrosimus a priest, Mareas a bishop, Azades a royal official, Aithalas, and many others were put to death during the persecution of King Sapor II of Persia. F. D. Apr. 22.

ABDISHO (d. 1567), bishop. He succeeded Sulaga as Catholic patriarch of Chaldea, having been consecrated at Rome in 1562 by Pope Pius IV. He declined an invitation to attend the Council of Trent, sent a profession of faith, and died at Seert while serving his Nestorian-persecuted flock.

ABDON, ST. (d. 303?), martyr. He and St. Sennen were Persian nobles, brought to Rome during the persecution of Diocletian (or of Decius) and hacked to death by gladiators after refusing to sacrifice to the pagan gods. F. D. July 30.

ABDULLAH, ACHMED (1881–1945), author. Born in Yalta, Russia, on May 12, also known as the Moslem Prince Nadir Khan Durani, he studied at Eton, Oxford, and Paris, and took his doctorate in Koranic law at El Azhar, Cairo. He served seventeen years with the British army in the East and as interpreter on an expedition to Tibet. He wrote *The Honourable Gentleman* (1919), a novel on China, several collections of short stories, the autobiographical *The Cat Had Nine Lives* (1933), and *Never without You* (1934). In *Lute and Scimitar* (1928) he translated the poetry of Afghanistan and Turkestan. After his conversion he wrote *Deliver Us from Evil* (1939) and, with Fulton Oursler, *The Shadow of the Master* (1940). The name Achmed Abdullah was a nom de plume. He died in New York City on May 12.

ABEL, ST. (d. 751?), bishop. He went with St. Boniface from the British Isles to the Continent, was chosen archbishop of Rheims in 744, was unable to occupy his see because it was usurped by Milo, and retired to the Benedictine abbey of Lobbes, where he served as abbot. F. D. Aug. 5.

ABEL, BL. THOMAS (1497?–1540), martyr. A graduate of Oxford and a secular priest, he became chaplain to Queen Catherine of Aragon. When sent to Spain by Henry VIII to secure from Emperor Charles V the original papal brief of dispensation for Henry's marriage, he persuaded the emperor to refuse to give it up. The king suspected that the action was prompted by the queen; when Fr. Abel wrote *Invicta veritas*, expressing opposition to university support of Henry's attempts to end his marriage, he was imprisoned in the Tower. Released, he was rearrested in 1533, kept a prisoner for six years, released briefly, then ordered hanged, drawn, and quartered at Smithfield for refusing to acknowledge Henry's claim of ecclesiastical supremacy. He was beatified in 1886. F. D. July 30.

ABELARD, PETER (1079–1142), philosopher. Born in Le Pallet, Brittany, where his father, Berengar, was lord, he became a wandering scholar instead of a soldier, as he was expected to become, and studied under the nominalist Roscelin at Locmenach and under the realist William of Champeaux at the cathedral school in Paris. About 1101, differing from his teachers, he set up a school of his own at Melun and then at Corbeil, returned briefly to Paris and study under William, then established his school of rhetoric and dialectic on Mt. Ste. Geneviève in 1108. He studied exegesis at Laon under Anselm, quarreled with him and his students, and returned to Paris in 1113 to occupy the chair of theology at the cathedral school. There he gave lectures to crowds of students, fell in love with Heloise, niece of Canon Fulbert, who was responsible for the subsequent attack which mutilated Abelard, and fled with her to Pallet, where their son Astrolabus was born. Abelard, in minor orders, married Heloise, who then retired to a convent at Argenteuil. He gave up his teaching career, became a Benedictine monk at St. Denis, quarreled with the monks there, erred in his discussions on the Trinity, and was brought before a papal inquiry board. He himself was not condemned, but his work was ordered burned and he was confined at St. Médard. He escaped to the wilderness near Troyes, built an oratory, and became the center of increasing crowds of admirers. Abbot Suger removed the Benedictine censure against Abelard and the latter became abbot of St. Gildas in Brittany; Heloise, whose community had been dispersed, took over the oratory near Troyes as abbess. The monks at St. Gildas found him too strict and, according to the account in his highly dramatic autobiography, *Historia calamitatum*, tried to poison him and finally drove him out of the monastery. He lived at Nantes, returned to Paris about 1136 to teach, and had as pupils John of Salisbury and Arnold of Brescia. His Trinitarian views were still suspect and were denounced by St. Bernard; Abelard demanded a meeting; a council of bishops met at Sens in 1141 (with Bernard but not Abelard present), condemned his writings, and their decision was sustained by Pope Innocent II. Abelard set out for Rome to appeal, but accepted the hospitality of Peter of Cluny, who reconciled him with Bernard and gave him the hospitality of his monastery. Abelard remained there in his last years, taught quietly in the monastery, and died on Apr. 21 in Châlon-sur-Saône. His body and that of Heloise were later taken to Paris and buried together there in 1817 during the height of the romantic movement. Abelard wrote dialectic discussions of philosophy besides his works on the Trinity, and popularized the "*Sic et non*" method of presenting the arguments for and against particular propositions and inviting debate. The method was developed by Alexander of Hales and St. Thomas Aquinas. He opposed obscurantism, developed scholasticism, had a direct effect on Peter Lombard, also his pupil, and seems to have erred more in lack of accurate phrasing than in unorthodoxy of position.

ÉTIENNE GILSON, *Heloise and Abelard* (Chicago, Regnery, 1951).

ABELLÓN, BL. ANDREW (1375–1450). Born in St. Maximin in Provence, France, he became Dominican prior of the monastery of St. Mary Magdalen there. He was active as a missioner and decorated many Dominican churches in southern France. His cult was confirmed in 1902. F. D. May 17.

ABELLY, LOUIS (1603–1691), bishop. After holding offices in Bayonne and Paris, he was bishop of Rodez in 1664–66, when he became associated with St. Vincent de Paul at St. Lazare. He wrote on theological problems, against Jansenism, on the hierarchy, on the Virgin Mary, and a biography of St. Vincent.

ABENNER, king. See Josaphat.

ABERCROMBY, JOHN (d. 1561), martyr. He is said to have been a Benedictine priest and writer who was slain during the Reformation in Scotland.

ABERCROMBY, ROBERT (1532–1613). A Jesuit missioner in Scotland, he converted Anne of Denmark, wife of King James VI, about 1598, and became her confessor and royal falconer. When the monarch went to England as James I, Fr. Abercromby found there was a price on his head in both countries and went to Braunsberg in East Prussia, where he died.

ABERICIUS MARCELLUS, ST. (2nd century), bishop. A resident of Phrygia Salutaris, he was imprisoned for his activity against paganism, freed, and, after a pilgrimage to Rome at seventy-two, following the route of St. Paul's third mission, he wrote a lengthy epitaph for his tomb, on which he referred to the Eucharist, the seal of baptism, the divinity of Christ, and the supremacy of the pope. The authenticity of the writing was established by the British archaeologist, W. M. Ramsay, who unearthed stones at Kelendres and at Hieropolis, his see city; these are now in the Lateran Museum. F. D. Oct. 22.

ABERLE, MORITZ VON (1819–1875), theologian. Born in Rottum, Swabia, on Apr. 25, he taught at Ehingen and the University of Tübingen, where he was professor of scripture. He helped the Church regain some freedom in Würtemberg. His view of the basically apologetic aims of the four evangelists is erroneous.

ABGAR (1st century), king. He is called the author of a legendary correspondence with Christ, recorded as actual by the historian Eusebius.

ABGAR IX (3rd century). He was the first king of Edessa, Mesopotamia, to embrace Christianity and helped its spread there after 206.

ABIBAS, ST. (1st century). The second son of Gamaliel (Acts 5:34, 22:3), he became a Christian and lived to be eighty. F. D. Aug. 3.

ABIBUS, ST. (d. 297), martyr. See Hipparchus, St.

ABIBUS, ST. (4th century), martyr. A deacon in Edessa, Syria, he was burned alive during the reign of Licinius. F. D. Nov. 15.

ABILIUS, ST. (d. 98?), bishop. He succeeded St. Anianus about 84 as the third bishop of Alexandria, Egypt. F. D. Feb. 22.

ABLEBERT. See Emebert, St.

ABRA DE RACONIS, CHARLES FRANÇOIS D' (1580–1646), bishop. A convert at twelve from Calvinism, he taught philosophy at Plessis and theology at Navarre, became royal almoner and preacher in 1618, bishop of Lavaur in 1643, and spent the rest of his life at Paris writing against Jansenists and against the heresy of Martin de Barcos which called SS. Peter and Paul "equal heads" of the Church. He was a friend of St. Vincent de Paul, but aroused hostility among some French bishops who attributed to him a complaining letter to the pope which he claimed he did not write.

ABRAHAM, ST. (d. 339), martyr. See Sapor, St.

ABRAHAM, ST. (d. 345?), martyr. Bishop of Arbela, Assyria, he was put to death during the persecution of King Sapor II of Persia. F. D. Feb. 5.

ABRAHAM, ST. (d. 367). Known as "the Child," he was born in Menuf, Egypt, became a follower of St. Pachomius and a hermit at twenty-three, and spent seventeen years in a cave. F. D. Oct. 27.

ABRAHAM, ST. (d. 422?), bishop. A Syrian hermit, he became a missioner in the region of Mt. Lebanon, gained many converts, and was made bishop of Carrae (once called Haran), Mesopotamia, and died at Constantinople while spiritual adviser to Emperor Theodosius II. F. D. Feb. 14.

ABRAHAM, ST. (474–558?), bishop. Born in Emesa, Syria, he became a monk there, fled to Constantinople when the monastery was raided, and at twenty-six became abbot at Kratia, Bithynia, retiring to Palestine about 513 to seek seclusion. Recalled, he served as bishop, then about 528 fled permanently to a monastery in the Holy Land. F. D. Dec. 6.

ABRAHAM, ST. (d. 480?). Born in Asia Minor, he was captured and held prisoner for five years by bandits in Egypt, escaped to Gaul, and became a hermit near Clermont. He later was ordained and placed in charge of the monastery of St. Cyriacus. F. D. June 15.

ABRAHAM, ST. (6th century), archbishop. He built monasteries in Constantinople and in Jerusalem, for followers who took the name Abrahamites, and became archbishop of Ephesus. F. D. Oct. 28.

ABRAHAM, ST. (d. 1121). Born at Smolensk, Russia, he was orphaned at an early age and became a priest at Bogoroditskaya monastery. Although a popular preacher, he incurred the enmity of other monks and was forbidden by his abbot to continue teaching. He then went to Holy Cross monastery, but was accused of immorality and heresy, and tried and acquitted by two courts. Sent back to Bogoroditskaya, he was forbidden by the bishop of Smolensk to say mass. After five years, during which Abraham patiently suffered insults, the bishop re-examined the case, declared him innocent, begged forgiveness, and sent him as abbot to the monastery of the Mother of God, which he directed until his death. F. D. Aug. 21.

ABRAHAM, ST. (12th century). Born near Galich, of pagan parents, he was converted and became a monk. He built two churches in Rostov, Russia, and founded a community of monks there. F. D. Oct. 29.

ABRAHAM ECCELENSIS (1600–1664), scholar. Born in Hekel on Mt. Lebanon, he studied at the Maronite college in Rome, taught Syriac and Arabic at the College of Propaganda there and at Paris, worked on Le Jay's polyglot Bible, wrote a *Synopsis of Arab Philosophy* (1641), a life of St. Antony, and detailed studies of the use of the name "pope," on Eastern rites, and canons.

ABRAHAM KIDUNAIA, ST. (6th century). Born in Mesopotamia, he fled to the desert to escape an arranged marriage, ordered his wealth given to the poor when his parents died, was ordained by the bishop of Edessa and directed to preach to a settlement of idolaters near his hermitage. He destroyed their images, was stoned almost to death, but after three years won them over to Christianity. F. D. Mar. 16.

ABRAHAM A SANCTA CLARA. *See* Megerlin, John.

ABRAM, NICHOLAS (1589–1655), theologian. Born in Xaronval, Lorraine, he did missionary work as a Jesuit, taught theology at Pont-à-Mousson for seventeen years, and wrote biblical and classical commentaries.

ABREAU, BL. EMMANUELE D' (d. 1737), martyr. *See* Alvarez, Bl. Bartholomew.

ABROSIMUS, ST. (d. 342?), martyr. *See* Abdiesus, St.

ABSALON. *See* Axel.

ABUCARA, THEODORE (d. 770?). He was bishop of Caria, Syria, and a disciple of St. John of Damascus, who sent him three discourses in defense of icons.

ABUDIMUS, ST. (4th century), martyr. A native of the island of Tenedos, he was put to death during the persecution of Diocletian. F. D. July 15.

ABUNDANTIUS, ST. (d. 304?), martyr. *See* Abundius, St.

ABUNDIUS, ST. (d. 258?), martyr. He and St. Irenaeus were put to death by drowning in a Roman sewer during the Valerian persecution. F. D. Aug. 26.

ABUNDIUS, ST. (d. 283), martyr. He and St. Justus were burned and beheaded in Spain during the persecution of Numerian. F. D. Dec. 14.

ABUNDIUS, ST. (d. 300?), martyr. *See* Carpophorus, St.

ABUNDIUS, ST. (d. 304?), martyr. Unreliable sources call him a priest in Rome who, with his deacon, Abundantius, Marcian, a senator, and the latter's son John, was beheaded during the persecution of Diocletian. F. D. Sept. 16.

ABUNDIUS, ST. (d. 469), bishop. Born in Thessalonica, he was fourth bishop of Como, Italy, attended the Council of Constantinople in 450, represented Pope Leo the Great at the General Council of Chalcedon in 451, and also refuted the Eutychian heresy while at the Council of Milan in 452. F. D. Apr. 2.

ABUNDIUS, ST. (d. 564?). Sacristan of St. Peter's in Rome, he was memorialized by St. Gregory the Great for his humility and piety. F. D. Apr. 14.

ABUNDIUS, ST. (d. 854), martyr. A priest stationed in the parish of Ananelos, near Cordova, Spain, he was brought before the Moorish caliph there, refused to give up his religion, and was beheaded. F. D. July 11.

ACACIUS, ST. (d. 251?). Called bishop of Melitene, Armenia, though this is questioned, he seems to have been charged as a Christian at Antioch during the persecution of Decius, but to have been pardoned because of the effective arguments he used in his defense. F. D. Mar. 31.

ACACIUS, ST. (d. 303?), martyr. A centurion from Cappadocia, he was tortured and beheaded at Constantinople when his Christianity became known during the Diocletian persecution. F. D. May 8.

ACACIUS, ST. (d. 305?), martyr. A priest at Sebaste, Armenia, he was slain with seven women and Hirenarchus, who witnessed their courage and accepted Christianity. F. D. Nov. 27.

ACACIUS, ST. (d. 310?), martyr. He was put to death at Miletus during the reign of Licinius. F. D. July 28.

ACACIUS, ST. (d. 425?), bishop. When he sold the sacred vessels of his church in Mesopotamia to aid the victims of Persian persecution, the bishop of Amida so impressed King Bahram V that he ordered the attacks brought to an end. F. D. Apr. 9.

ACACIUS (322?–432?), bishop. Born in Syria, he became a recluse outside Antioch, suffered during Arian persecution, was consecrated bishop of Beroea by Eusebius of Samosata, and began a career of contradictions. He was sent to Rome as a deputy explaining the heresy of Apollinaris to Pope Damasus and spoke against the Macedonians at the first General Council of Constantinople in 381. He was excommunicated from about 381 to 392 because he took part in the schismatical consecration of Flavian as bishop of Antioch. In 398 he went to Rome to inform Pope Siricius of the election of St. John Chrysostom as patriarch of Constantinople and won considerable favor. Then he turned against St. John, sought violently at four synods to remove him, and again suffered excommunication (403–14). In his last years—he lived to be 110—he worked actively against Cyril of Alexandria and in favor of tolerance for Nestorius, then tried to erase the scars which Nestorianism had left.

ACARIE, BARBARA. *See* Mary of the Incarnation, Bl.

ACCA, ST. (660?–740?), bishop. A native of Northumbria, England, he served in the household of St. Bosa and became the companion of St. Wilfrid on trips to the Continent. He was appointed abbot of the Benedictine monastery of St. Andrew, Hexham, by Wilfrid, and in 709 succeeded the latter to that see. He encouraged learning, was a patron of scholars, and was noted for his knowledge of scripture. Bede, who admired him, dedicated several works to him. In 732, for reasons unknown, he was exiled to Withern, where he died. F. D. Oct. 20.

ACCIAJUOLI, ANGELO (1349–1408), cardinal. Born in Florence, Italy, he was made its archbishop in 1383 and a cardinal in 1385 by Pope Urban VI, whom he supported vigorously against the antipope Clement VII. He won half the votes at the next conclave, but threw his support to Boniface IX. He became governor of Naples, reconciled the pope with the Orsini, and directly settled Church difficulties in Germany and the Balkans.

ACCIAJUOLI, FILIPPO (1700–1766), cardinal. Born in Rome, he was papal nuncio to Portugal, was expelled for his support of the Jesuits, and in 1759 was made cardinal-bishop of Ancona, Italy, by Pope Clement XIII.

ACCIAJUOLI, NICCOLÒ (1630–1719), cardinal. Born in Florence, he was cardinal-bishop of Ostia, and died in Rome.

ACCOLTI, BENEDETTO (1415–1466), jurist. Born in Arezzo, Italy, he was professor of law at Florence, wrote a history of the crusades, *De bello a Christianis contra barbaros* (1572), which was a source of Tasso's *Jerusalem Delivered*, and became chancellor of the Florentine republic. He died in Florence.

ACCOLTI, BERNARDO (1465–1536), poet. Son of Benedetto, he was born in Arezzo, Italy, wrote such popular poetry that business and government closed down when he gave readings, and was flattered as "the Unique" in his lifetime. *Virginia, comedia, capitoli, e strambotti* was published in 1513.

ACCORSO, MARIANGELO (1490?–1544), critic. Born in Aquila, Naples, he served in the court of Emperor Charles V for thirty-three years, went on diplomatic missions, and unearthed and published significant manuscripts. He edited Ammianus Marcellinus, the *Epistolae* of Cassiodorus, and published *Diatribae in Ausonium, Solinum, et Ovidium.*

ACCURSIUS, FRANCESCO (1182–1260), jurist. Born in Florence, Italy, he became a lawyer, taught at Bologna, and compiled a monumental commentary on law. His son Francesco (1225–93), also a lawyer, went to England with King Edward I, and returned in 1282 to practice law in Bologna with two sons and a daughter. Noted for his tactlessness, the younger Francesco was condemned by Dante (*Inferno* 15:110).

ACCURSORIO, ST. (d. 1220), martyr. *See* Berard, St.

ACEOLUS, ST. (d. 303?), martyr. *See* Acius, St.

ACEPSIMAS, ST. (d. 376), martyr. The aged bishop of Hnaita, Persia, was tortured and beaten to death on Oct. 10, during the persecution of Sapor II. F. D. Apr. 22.

ACEPSIMAS, ST. (5th century). He lived for sixty years as a hermit near Cyrrhus, Syria, during the reign of Theodosius I and died soon after his ordination. F. D. Nov. 3.

ACESTES, ST. (1st century), martyr. Legend calls him one of the soldiers who led St. Paul to his death and who, converted, was executed at that same time. F. D. July 2.

ACHAICUS (1st century). A Christian, he carried a letter from the Corinthians to St. Paul, and returned to his homeland with one from the latter (I Cor. 16:15–17). His companions were Fortunatus and Stephanas.

ACHAICUS, ST. (4th century), martyr. *See* Domninus, St.

ACHARIUS, ST. (d. 640). He was a monk at Luxeuil under St. Eustace and in 621 became bishop of Noyon-Tournai, France. F. D. Nov. 27.

ACHÉRY, LUCAS D' (1609–1685), scholar. Born in St. Quentin, Picardy, France, he was professed as a Benedictine in 1632, and stationed at St. Germain-des-Prés at Paris for nearly fifty years, where he published bibliographies as well as editions of the works of Lanfranc, Guibert of Nogent, Grimlaic, and laid the groundwork for Mabillon's edition of St. Benedict.

ACHILLAS, ST. (d. 313), bishop. He succeeded the martyred St. Peter as bishop of Alexandria, ordained the later heretic, Arius, and was attacked by the Meletians. F. D. Nov. 7.

ACHILLAS, ST. (4th century). He and St. Amoes were Egyptian recluses, mentioned by Rufinus and praised in the Greek liturgy. F. D. Jan. 17.

ACHILLES, ST. (d. 330?), bishop. He became metropolitan of Larissa, Thessaly, and attended the first Council of Nicaea. F. D. May 15.

ACHILLEUS, ST. (1st century), martyr. *See* Nereus, St.

ACHILLEUS, ST. (d. 212), martyr. *See* Felix, St.

ACHILLINI, ALESSANDRO (1463–1512). Born in Bologna, Italy, he studied at Paris, began to teach at Bologna in 1485, and in 1506 became a professor of medicine and philosophy at Padua. After three years there he returned to Bologna, where he remained until his death. He was famed for his anatomical researches and writings, was the first to describe the small bones of the ear, and was a pioneer in intestinal research.

ACHLER, BL. ELIZABETH (1386–1420). Born in Waldsee, Würtemberg, of poor parents, she became a Franciscan tertiary at fourteen and joined a small community in Reute, where she lived the rest of her life in obscurity but undergoing many supernatural experiences. Her cult was approved in 1766. F. D. Nov. 17.

ACHTERFELDT, JOHANN HEINRICH (1788–1877). Born in Wesel, Germany, he was professor of theology at Bonn, and published the philosophical writings of George Hermes, which were then condemned by Pope Gregory XVI. Achterfeldt refused to submit to ecclesiastical authority, was suspended in 1848, but returned to teaching in 1862; official censure was lifted in 1873.

ACHTERMAN, THEODORE WILLIAM (1799–1884), sculptor. Born in Münster, Westphalia, he became a cabinetmaker, studied sculpture in Berlin, and moved to Rome in 1839. He completed a *Pietà* for the Münster cathedral and a monumental altar for the cathedral in Prague.

ACIDALIUS, VALENS (1567–1595), critic. Born in Wittstock, Brandenburg, he studied in the universities of Germany and Italy, took a medical degree at Bologna, but became a classical scholar who published several commentaries on the Latin poets, and was converted in 1593. He died in Neisse on May 25.

ACINDYNUS, ST. (d. 345), martyr. He and SS. Anempodistus, Aphthonius, Elpidephorus, and Pegasius were put to death by King Sapor II of Persia. F. D. Nov. 2.

ACISCLUS, ST. (4th century?), martyr. He and his sister Victoria are said to have been natives of Cordova, Spain, who were tortured and slain there: he by beheading and Victoria by being riddled with arrows. F. D. Nov. 17.

ACIUS, ST. (d. 303?), martyr. A deacon, he was put to death with Aceolus, a subdeacon, near Amiens, Gaul, during the Diocletian persecution. F. D. May 1.

ACOSTA, JOSÉ DE (1540–1600). Born in Medina del Campo, Spain, he was one of five brothers who became Jesuits, taught theology at Ocana, Spain, and, in 1569, was sent to Lima, Peru. He founded five colleges, served as provincial, and wrote widely on the history and nature of the Indians of South America. Recalled to Spain in 1585, he died while rector of Salamanca.

ACQUAVIVA, CLAUDIUS (1543–1615). Son of Prince Giovanni Acquaviva, duke of Atri, he was born in the Abruzzi, Italy, in Oct. and became a Jesuit at twenty-five, served as provincial at Naples and at Rome, and in 1581 became the fifth general of the Society of Jesus, the youngest to hold the post. He faced a major schism which began in Spain under Vasquez, attacks by the Inquisition, hostility from Pope Sixtus V (who died just before he was to suppress the Society), the persecutions in England, France, and Japan, and a nine-year-long doctrinal controversy with the Dominicans on grace. His rule was the period of such great Jesuits as Bellarmine, Campion, Clavius, Gonzaga, Persons, Ricci, and Southwell, and of missionary and educational foundations in Canada, China, Poland, Russia, and Turkey. The Reductions in Paraguay were begun and the counter-Reformation in Germany completed. He directed the preparation and wrote much of the detailed plan of Jesuit education known as the *Ratio studiorum*, revised a guide to the *Spiritual Exercises* of St. Ignatius, and wrote a great many administrative counsels. He died on Jan. 31.

ACQUAVIVA, FRANCESCO (1665–1723), cardinal. Born in Naples, Italy, he entered the papal service under Innocent XI and was made a cardinal and bishop of Sabina by Pope Clement XI.

ACQUAVIVA, GIOVANNI VINCENZO (d. 1566), cardinal. He became bishop of Melfi and Rapolla, Italy, in 1537 and a cardinal in 1542.

ACQUAVIVA, GIULIO (1546–1574), cardinal. Born in Naples, Italy, of the Atri family, he was papal nuncio to Philip II of Spain, and created cardinal by Pope Pius V.

ACQUAVIVA, OTTAVIO (1560–1612), cardinal. Born in Naples, Italy, he served Popes Sixtus V, Gregory XIV, and Clement VIII, was legate at Avignon, aided in the conversion of King Henry IV, and died as archbishop of Naples.

ACQUAVIVA, OTTAVIO (1608–1674), cardinal. Born in Naples, Italy, of the Atri family, he was made a cardinal in 1654 by Pope Innocent IX, served as legate at Viterbo and in Romagna, and died at Rome.

ACQUAVIVA, PASQUALE (1719–1788), cardinal. Born in Naples, Italy, he was made a cardinal in 1773 by Pope Clement XIV.

ACQUAVIVA, TROIANO (1694–1747), cardinal. Born in Naples, Italy, of the Atri family, he served Pope Benedict XIII, was made cardinal in 1732 by Clement XII, and became archbishop of Toledo and then of Montereale.

ACTINEA, ST. (4th century), martyr. She was beheaded at Volterra in Etruria during the Diocletian persecution. F. D. June 16.

ACTON, CHARLES JANUARIUS (1803–

1847), cardinal. Born in Naples, Italy, on March 6, he was educated in London and at Cambridge after the death in 1811 of his father, Sir John Francis Acton, of Shropshire, England. He studied for the priesthood at Rome, served as a papal attaché in Paris, legate in Bologna, assistant judge of the civil court in Rome, papal auditor in 1837, and cardinal in 1842. He died at Naples on June 23.

ACTON, JOHN (d. 1350), canonist. A student of John Stratford, archbishop of Canterbury, he became a canon of Lincoln cathedral in 1329, and wrote glosses to the constitutions of Cardinals Otho and Ottobone, papal legates to England. They were published in William Lyndewood's *Provinciale* (1496) by Wynken de Worde. His name is also spelled Aton, Ayton and Eaton.

ACTON, JOHN EMERICH (1834–1902), historian. Born in Naples, Italy, on Jan. 10, son of the English diplomat, Sir Richard Acton, he studied at Oscott, Birmingham, under Nicholas Wiseman, and at Munich under Döllinger. He returned to Shropshire in 1859, was a Liberal party member of parliament for six years, and succeeded John Henry Newman as editor of *The Rambler* (called *Home and Foreign Review* from 1862 to 1864), which he discontinued when serious ecclesiastical hostility arose. He objected bitterly to the strictures of the Syllabus of Pope Pius IX and actively opposed the definition of papal infallibility, although he never left the Church, as his friend Döllinger did. In 1895 Lord Acton became professor of history at Cambridge, where he helped to organize the *Cambridge Modern History*. Among the many books he published are *Historical Essays and Freedom, History of Freedom, Lectures on Modern History, Lectures on the French Revolution*, and *Essays on Church and State*. He died in Tegernsee, Bavaria, on June 19.

ACTON, JOHN FRANCIS (1736–1811). Born in Besançon, France, son of a Shropshire, England, physician, he fought for Tuscany against Algiers, reorganized the navy of Naples, and became that kingdom's prime minister. He was forced to flee at the advent of the French, and died at Palermo, Sicily.

ACUÑA, CRISTOBAL DE (1597–1675?), missioner. Born in Burgos, Spain, he became a Jesuit at fifteen, was sent to South America, served as rector of the college at Cuenca, Ecuador, accompanied Teixeira on his trip along the Amazon, and returned to Spain in 1641 with a report of the expedition. He became provincial in Rome, censor at Madrid, and returned to Lima, Peru, where he died.

ACUTIUS, ST. (d. 305?), martyr. *See* Januarius, St.

ACYLLINUS, ST. (d. 180), martyr. *See* Speratus, St.

ADA, ST. (7th century). Niece of St. Engebert, she became abbess of St. Julien-des-Prés at Le Mans, France. F. D. Dec. 4.

ADACTUS, ST. (d. 304?), martyr. *See* Felix, St.

ADALAR, ST. (d. 755), martyr. A Benedictine priest, he was put to death at Dokkum, Frisia, with St. Boniface. F. D. June 5.

ADALBALD OF OSTREVANT, ST. (d. 652). Grandson of St. Gertrude and brother-in-law of St. Bertha, he served in the court of King Dagobert I of France and fought in the wars against the Gascons, one of whom, St. Rictrudis, he married. Their four children (Adalsindis, Clotsindis, Eusebia, and Mauront) also were canonized; the family was widely known for its care of the sick, the poor, and criminals. On a later visit to Gascony he was waylaid and slain by his wife's relatives, who had not forgiven the Franks. F. D. Feb. 2.

ADALBALD OF UTRECHT (10th century). He wrote a biography of Emperor Henry II and a commentary on Boethius.

ADALBERO, BL. (d. 909), bishop. Uncle of St. Ulric, he became a Benedictine monk at Dillingen in 850, then abbot of Ellwangen and of Lorsch. He was bishop of Augsburg after 887, chief adviser to Emperor Arnulf, and tutor to and regent of Prince Louis. F. D. Apr. 28.

ADALBERO, BL. (d. 1128), bishop. He was a canon at Metz before he became bishop of Liège, and the founder of the monastery of St. Giles. F. D. Jan. 1.

ADALBERO, BL. (1045–1090), bishop. Son of Count Arnold of Lambach, he studied at Paris, became bishop of Würzburg, and defended Pope Gregory VII against Emperor Henry IV. Driven from his see as a result, he retired to the Benedictine abbey of Lambach, Austria, which he had helped to endow, and died there. His cult was approved in 1883. F. D. Oct. 6.

ADALBERT, ST. (d. 705?). A native of Northumbria, he went to Ireland with St. Egbert and then joined the mission of St. Willibrord in Friesland, where he served as archdeacon of Utrecht. F. D. June 25.

ADALBERT, ST. (d. 981), archbishop. A Benedictine monk at St. Maximin in Trèves, he led a group of missioners to Russia in 961 at the request of the aged convert, Princess Olga. The latter's son proved hostile, the group was scattered, some were slain near Kiev, and Adalbert went to Mainz. He served as abbot of Weissenburg, directed the continuation of the *Chronicle* of Reginald von Prüm, and was papally approved in 962 as first archbishop of Magdeburg, Saxony, with jurisdiction over the Slavs. The creation of the new see was objected to by the archbishop of Mainz, but Adalbert labored strongly among the Wends, making many converts, strengthening religious discipline, and encouraging learning. F. D. June 20.

ADALBERT, ST. (956–997), bishop and martyr. Born in Bohemia and educated by St. Adalbert of Magdeburg, he took the latter's name at confirmation, became a subdeacon, and, in 982, bishop of Prague. In 990, under political pressure, he left for Rome, where he became a Benedictine. He twice went back to Prague, but returned to Rome, the second time when nobles violated the law of sanctuary and seized a prisoner in his cathedral; their hostility led them later to kill his relatives. At the request of Duke Boleslaus of Poland he led a mission to convert the pagans of Pomerania and Danzig, also visiting Hungary and perhaps Russia. He and SS. Benedict and Gaudentius were put to death when seized by pagans along the Nogat River. F. D. Apr. 23.

ADALBERT (1000?–1072), archbishop. Son of Count Friedrich von Goseck, he held several ecclesiastical posts before he was royally appointed archbishop of Hamburg-Bremen in Germany about 1043; he may have been Emperor Henry III's chancellor for Italy in 1045. He developed successful missions among the Wends, created three new bishoprics (Oldenburg, Mecklenburg, and Ratzenburg), and sought long and unsuccessfully to become patriarch of Scandinavia. This quest was ended in 1103 when Pope Paschal II appointed Archbishop Lund the metropolitan, with jurisdiction over the northern churches. Adalbert's extreme tolerance of Emperor Henry IV, whom he won to his side after a struggle with Anno, archbishop of Cologne, and whom he defended against the papacy, had unfortunate effects. Contemporary biographies note his generosity and religious zeal, as well as his personal cleverness and pride.

ADALBERT (d. 1137), archbishop. Of the family of the counts Saarbrücken, he blindly served Emperors Henry IV and Henry V as chancellor, tricked Pope Paschal II in diplomatic intrigue, stood by when Henry V briefly imprisoned the pontiff, and was rewarded by royal appointment as archbishop of Mainz. He reformed suddenly, became an ardent churchman, and in 1112 announced the papal excommunication of the emperor. Henry then locked Adalbert in a dungeon for three years until a popular riot freed him. Pope Callistus II made Adalbert his legate, and a civil war was avoided and the difficult question of investitures solved at the Council of Worms (1122). When Henry died without issue, Adalbert called a meeting of princes which transferred the empire from the house of Franconia to Lothair II of the house of Saxony.

ADALGER (10th century). Possibly bishop of Augsburg, Bavaria, but certainly a cleric, he wrote a tract on virtue, *Admonitio ad nonsvindam.*

ADALGIS, ST. (d. 686). An Irish monk, he went to France to evangelize the Arras and Laon areas, then founded a monastery at Thiérarche in Picardy. F. D. June 2.

ADALGIS, ST. (d. 850), bishop. He governed the see of Novara, Italy, from about 830 until his death. F. D. Oct. 7.

ADALGOTT, BL. (d. 1031). A Benedictine monk at Einsiedeln, Switzerland, he became abbot of Dissentis in 1012. F. D. Oct. 26.

ADALGOTT, BL. (d. 1165), bishop. He became a Cistercian monk at Clairvaux under St. Bernard and in 1150 became Benedictine abbot at Dissentis and bishop of Chur, where he founded a hospital. F. D. Oct. 3.

ADALHARD, ST. (753–827). Grandson of Charles Martel and cousin of Charlemagne, he became a Benedictine at Corbie in Picardy when he was twenty and later its abbot. He served in the emperor's court and was chief minister to Pepin II and tutor of his son, Bernard of Italy. After the emperor's death, Adalhard was a political exile for five years, then was cleared and returned to Corbie. He wrote a rule for that monastery and for New Corbie in Paderborn, promoted the study of the vernacular languages, and exerted great cultural influence on SS. Paschasius Radbertus and Anskar. He himself probably studied under Alcuin. He is also called Alard. F. D. Jan. 2.

ADALRIC, ST. (d. 888), martyr. *See* Ageranus, St.

ADAM, ST. (13th century). A hermit, he became a Benedictine monk and later abbot of the monastery of San Sabino near Fermo, Italy. F. D. May 16.

ADAM, JEAN (1608–1684). Born in Limoges, France, he became a Jesuit in 1622, wrote sermons, two books on the Eucharist, and tracts against Calvinism and Jansenism. He clashed with Cardinal Noris over interpretations of St. Augustine. He died in Bordeaux.

ADAM, NICHOLAS (1716–1792). Born in Paris, he taught rhetoric at Lisieux, wrote a quinlingual grammar, translated Joseph Addison, Samuel Johnson, Alexander Pope, and Edward Young, and served as French ambassador to Venice.

ADAM OF BREMEN (11th century), historian. Possibly a Saxon, he became a canon of the cathedral of Bremen about 1066, directed its schools, and wrote a geographical and historical study of the diocese of Hamburg and the German missions in Scandinavia and Iceland from 788 to 1072. He relied heavily on primary sources as well as on the direct testimony of Archbishop Adalbert.

ADAM OF DRYBURGH (13th century). He authored a number of theological works, including De *quadripartito exercicio cellae.*

ADAM OF FULDA (1450?–1540?), composer. A monk in Franconia, he became a master of contrapuntal music, composed much, and wrote a treatise on music in 1490.

ADAM DE LA BASSÉE (d. 1286), poet. A canon at Lille, France, he wrote *Ludus super Anticlaudianum*, a fantasy influenced by Alan de Lille.

ADAM OF MURIMUTH (14th century), historian. A canon of St. Paul's, London, he wrote a chronicle of English history for the years 1302–43, based on direct observation or careful reporting; the work was continued anonymously to 1380.

ADAM OF PERSEIGNE (12th century). Believed to have been a canon regular, he became a Benedictine at Marmoutier, France, then a Cistercian at the monastery of Perseigne, near Le Mans, and its abbot, and helped to preach the fourth crusade. His sermons were published in 1662.

ADAM OF ST. VICTOR (1130–1192). Educated in Paris, he entered the suburban monastery of St. Victor when quite young, and wrote more than 100 hymns and sequences. Whether he wrote a dictionary of biblical terms and a commentary on the prologues of St. Jerome is debated.

ADAM SCOTUS (12th century), theologian. Born in Scotland or England, he became a Premonstratensian, probably was abbot-bishop of Whithorn, Scotland, and wrote sermons, a commentary on the rule of St. Augustine, a history of his order, and mystical works.

ADAM OF USK (1352?–1430), historian. Born in Usk, Monmouthshire, England, he became a doctor of canon law at Oxford, served at Canterbury from 1390 to 1397, was pastor at Bangor, and wrote in Latin a chronicle of English history for the years 1377–1404. His sharp criticism of King Richard II resulted in his exile to Rome and prevented him from assuming the sees of Hereford and St. David's to which he was nominated.

ADAMI DA BOLSENA, ANDREA (1663–1742). Born in Bolsena, Italy, in Oct., he became master of the Vatican choir, wrote its history, and was a distinguished musician. He died in Rome on July 22.

ADAMNAN, ST. (624?–704). Born in Drumhome, Donegal, Ireland, he became a monk there, entered the monastery of Iona and became abbot in 679. He gave shelter to Aldfrid, on his father's death, and when Aldfrid became king of Northumbria, Adamnan visited him to secure the release of Irish prisoners in 686. He visited several English monasteries in 688 from which he took home but was unable to impose on his monks the Roman observance of Easter. He was an outstanding scholar and the author of a life of St. Columba, an extremely important biography of the early Middle Ages, and

De locis sanctis. He is also known as Adam, Eunan, and Aunan. F. D. Sept. 23.

ADAMNAN OF COLDINGHAM (d. 680?). Mentioned by Bede, he is said to have been an Irish monk at Coldingham, England, near Berwick, who had visionary powers. His cult was confirmed in 1898. F. D. Jan. 31.

ADAMS, JAMES (1737–1802). Born in England, he became a Jesuit at Watten in 1756, wrote a history of Rome and a study of English pronunciation, and died in Dublin.

ADAMS, VEN. JOHN (d. 1586), martyr. A Protestant minister in England, he became a convert, was ordained at Rheims, and sent in 1581 on the missions in Winchester and Hampshire. He was imprisoned in 1584 and exiled with seventy-two others in 1585. When he returned he was executed, for being a priest against Elizabethan law, with Ven. Robert Dibdale and John Lowe.

ADAUCTUS, ST. (d. 304?), martyr. See Felix, St. (d. Aug. 30).

ADAUCTUS, ST. (d. 312?), martyr. He was put to death at Ephesus during the persecution of Maximinus Daza; his daughter Callisthene continued to distinguish herself by her charities there. F. D. Oct. 4.

ADAUCUS, ST. (d. 303), martyr. An Italian high public official, he was killed at the command of Emperor Galerian Maximian when an entire Phrygian town of Christians was put to the torch. F. D. Feb. 7.

ADDA, FERDINANDO D' (1649–1719), cardinal. Born in Milan, Italy, he served as papal nuncio to the court of James II of England, tried at the request of Pope Innocent XI to lessen the hostility of Louis XIV of France toward Protestants, and was made a cardinal in 1690 and bishop of Albano in 1715.

ADDAI, ST. (d. 180?), bishop. A Mesopotamanian, he is said to have been sent as a missioner to Edessa with St. Mari; they are called the "holy apostles" of Syria and Persia. F. D. Aug. 5.

ADDAI (d. 1617). A Chaldean archimandrite, he headed a group sent to Rome in 1612 to object to charges by the Franciscans in the Holy Land that the non-Roman Christians under Elias II were heretical. At a synod at Amid he was made a bishop and may have served as patriarch of Jerusalem. His profession of faith was considered genuine.

ADELA (d. 734?). Daughter of St. Dagobert II, king of the Franks, she became a Benedictine nun on her husband's death and founded the monastery of Pfalzel near Trèves, of which she was abbess. Her cult has never been confirmed, though she is honored on Dec. 24.

ADELAIDE (931–999), empress. Daughter of King Rudolf II of Upper Burgundy, she was betrothed at two to Lothair II, son of Hugh of Provence, and married him in 947. On the death of Lothair in 950, Berengarius Ivrea succeeded to the throne and imprisoned Adelaide. Escaping four months later, she married the German king, Otto the Great, in Italy and became tremendously popular in Germany. On his death in 973, she was harshly treated and exiled both by her son Otto and by his Byzantine wife, Theophano. When her daughter-in-law died in 991, Adelaide returned as regent. During her last years she encouraged the building of convents and monasteries (she had long been devoted to Cluny) and labored to convert the pagans. Though she was never canonized, her feast is celebrated in several German dioceses on Dec. 16.

ADELAIDE, ST. (d. 1015?). She was abbess of the Benedictine convents of Bellich, near Bonn, and at Cologne. F. D. Feb. 5.

ADELAIDE, ST. See Aleydis, St.

ADELAIDE OF BELLICH, ST. (d. 1015). Daughter of Megengose, count of Guelder, she was abbess of the Benedictine convents at Bellich and at Cologne (St. Mary's), both of which her father had built. F. D. Feb. 5.

ADELARD OF BATH (12th century), philosopher. Born in England, he studied at Tours and Laon, taught at the latter and at Paris, traveled across Europe, Asia Minor, and northern Africa, and translated and wrote treatises on mathematics and medicine which show Arabic influence. His *Perdifficiles quaestiones naturales* was printed in the late fifteenth century; his allegory of the struggle of materialism and wisdom struggling for the soul of man, *De eodem et diverso*, was written before 1116; he also made a Latin translation of Euclid.

ADELELMUS, ST. (d. 1100). A French soldier, he was making a pilgrimage to Rome when he encountered St. Robert, abbot of Chaise-Dieu. On his return, he entered that monastery and may have succeeded his preceptor as abbot; later, he moved to a monastery near Burgos in Spain. He is also called Aleaume. F. D. Jan. 30.

ADELHAM, JOHN PLACID (d. 1685?). Born in Wiltshire, England, he became a Protestant minister, was converted and professed a Benedictine at Paris in 1652, stationed at Somerset House from 1661 to 1675, exiled, and, on his return, arrested and in 1679 condemned to death during the Titus Oates hysteria. He died in prison either two or six years later.

ADELHEIM. See Hadelin, St.

ADELINA, ST. (d. 1125). Sister of St. Vitalis of Savigny, she became abbess of the Benedictine convent of La Blanche at Moriton, Normandy, which he had founded. F. D. Oct. 20.

ADELOGA, ST. (d. 745?). A Frankish princess, she founded and became first abbess of the Benedictine convent of Kitzingen in Franconia. F. D. Feb. 2.

ADELPHUS, ST. (5th century). The Roman Martyrology lists him as bishop of Metz. F. D. Aug. 29.

ADELPHUS, ST. (d. 670?). He succeeded his godfather, St. Romaricus, as Benedictine abbot of Remiremont in 653 and died at Luxeuil, France. F. D. Sept. 11.

ADEODAT. See Deodatus, St.

ADEODATUS, pope. See Deusdedit, St.

ADEODATUS, (d. 676), pope. A native Roman and a monk at the cloister of St. Erasmus, Rome, he was elected pope on Apr. 11, 672, and sought to better monastic discipline and to end the Monothelite heresy. His letters to the abbeys of St. Martin of Tours and St. Peter of Canterbury are extant. He is sometimes called Adeodatus II, since Deusdedit is a variant spelling of his name and there was an earlier pope called Deusdedit. He died on June 17.

ADEODATUS (372–389). The illegitimate son of St. Augustine and an unnamed Carthaginian woman, he accepted Christianity at the time of his father's baptism, joined the latter, Alypius, St. Monica, and others at Cassiciacum, near Milan, Italy, and participated in the discussions there which resulted in the writing of Augustine's *The Happy Life* and *The Teacher*.

ADERALD, ST. (d. 1004). An archdeacon at Troyes, France, he led a pilgrimage to Palestine, and on his return with several relics built the Benedictine abbey of St. Sepulchre at Samblières. F. D. Oct. 20.

ADHEMAR (d. 1098). Bishop of Puy, and papal legate, he accompanied the French forces on the first crusade (1096–99).

ADHEMAR DE CHABANNES (998?–1034). Born in Chabannes, France, he studied at St. Martial in Limoges, became a monk, and wrote a history of France to the year 1028, to which later writers added legendary material. He also wrote on his abbey; he died in Jerusalem while on a pilgrimage.

ADHERITUS, ST. (2nd century?). He is said to have succeeded St. Apollinaris as bishop of Ravenna, Italy. F. D. Sept. 27.

ADILIA. See Odilia, St.

ADJUTOR, ST. (d. 1220), martyr. See Berard, St.

ADJUTOR, ST. (5th century), bishop. See Priscus, St.

ADJUTOR, ST. (d. 1131). A Norman, he fought in the crusade as lord of Vernon, became a monk at Tiron, and later a hermit at Vernon. He is also called Ayutre. F. D. Apr. 30.

ADO, ST. (799?–876?), archbishop. Born in the diocese of Sens, Burgundy, he was educated and became a Benedictine monk at Ferrières. He was head of the monastic school at Prüm for several years until disagreements arose with some of the monks. After a pilgrimage to Rome he became pastor of a church at Lyons and in

859 was chosen archbishop of Vienne, where he instituted widespread reforms. He opposed King Lothair II of Lorraine when the king tried to put aside his lawful wife, Theutberga, and it was Ado's protests to Pope St. Nicholas I which caused the decision (the result of royal bribery) of the synod of Metz to sanction Lothair's marriage to his mistress to be reversed. Although a good bishop, he had no historical sense. While at Ravenna he had discovered the *Martyrologium romanum parvum* (completely spurious) on which he based his own *Martyrology* (c. 858). He also wrote lives of SS. Desiderius and Theuderius and a "chronicle" of world history. F. D. Dec. 16.

ADOLF I (d. 1220). He became archbishop of Cologne in 1194, was a leading opponent of the Hohenstaufen dynasty, and defiantly nominated Otto IV of Brunswick and crowned him emperor in 1198. He withstood the papal faction until 1205, when Otto lost to the incursions of Philip of Swabia; Adolf was then excommunicated and deposed.

ADOLF, ST. (1185?–1224), bishop. Born in Westphalia, he became a canon at Cologne, then joined the Cistercians at the monastery of Camp. He became bishop of Osnabrück in 1216, and was widely respected for his piety and charity. He died on June 30. F. D. Feb. 14.

ADOLF I (1353–1390). He became bishop of Speyer in 1371 and archbishop of Mainz in 1373. The landgrave of Thuringia sought to remove him and Emperor Charles IV supported his position at the papal court. Adolf refused to give up his see and was supported by the antipope Clement VII and Urban VI.

ADOLF OF NASSAU (1255?–1298), emperor, German king. Son of Count Walram of Nassau, he succeeded to his father's lands in 1276, became noted for his military ability, and in 1292 was elected German king to succeed Rudolf I. He made an alliance with Edward I of England against Philip IV of France, though he never fought against the French, claimed Meissen, and in 1294–96 fought the sons of Landgrave Albert II for Thuringia, which he had purchased from Albert. Unable to fulfill the many promises he had made to secure election, he was deserted by his followers and in 1298 was deposed; Albert of Austria was elected in his place. He marched against Albert and was killed at the battle of Göllheim, near Worms, on July 2.

ADOLPHUS, ST. (d. 850?), martyr. He and his brother John, born of a Moorish father and Christian mother at Seville, Spain, were put to death at Cordova. F. D. Sept. 27.

ADRIA, ST. (d. 254?), martyr. *See* Eusebius, St.

ADRIAN I (d. 795), pope. A Roman, he served Popes Paul I and Stephen IV, and was unanimously acclaimed as pope on Feb. 1, 772, by the clergy and people of the city in spite of the presence of the hostile Lombard chamberlain, Paul Afiarta, and consecrated on Feb. 9. When the new pontiff released from prison the victims of the chamberlain's tyranny and even charged him with murder, King Desiderius of the Lombards prepared to seize all Italy. Adrian fortified the city, brought in his neighbors to help, and sent an urgent call to Charlemagne. The emperor crossed the Alps, took Verona and, later, Pavia. A meeting in Rome with Adrian resulted in the "Donation of Charlemagne" which defined the temporal power of the popes and which the emperor personally, and out of deep friendship and regard, defended during his lifetime. Adrian worked with Empress Irene to repair the damages caused in the East by the Iconoclastic heresy, called the seventh General Council of Nicaea to define the veneration of images, and opposed the new heresy of Adoptionism. He died on Dec. 25.

ADRIAN II (792–872), pope. A Roman cardinal, of the family of Stephen III and Sergius II, he was elected to the papacy on Dec. 14, 867, at the age of seventy-five. He sought to keep the descendants of Charlemagne at peace, lifted the condemnation of King Lothaire of Lorraine after the latter abandoned his mistress, and worked for reunion with the East by convening the eighth General Council of Constantinople (869). Though he aided SS. Cyril and Methodius and approved the use of the Slavonic liturgy, Bulgaria was lost to the Church during his reign; the western Slavs remained faithful. He died on Dec. 14.

ADRIAN III, ST. (d. 885), pope. Of Roman descent, he became pope on May 17, 884. The next year he was asked by Emperor Charles the Fat to attend the Diet of Worms and discuss the rising Saracen power, but fell ill on the way, died near Modena, and was buried at Nonantula. His cult was approved in 1891. F. D. July 8.

ADRIAN IV (1100?–1159), pope. Nicholas Breakspear is said to have been born near St. Albans, England, educated in France as a youth, and to have joined the Augustinians at the monastery of St. Rufus, near Avignon. Sent on a mission to Rome, he was retained there by Pope Eugenius III, who is said to have made him cardinal-bishop of Albano in 1146. In 1152 he went to Scandinavia as papal legate, reformed widespread clerical abuses, and established the see of Trondhjem. On his return he was elected pope on Dec. 4, 1154, and took office the next day. William I of Sicily and the barons of Campagna were in active military opposition, as was the city of Rome itself, under Arnold of Brescia, and Frederick Barbarossa was restive; travel anywhere was unsafe. The new pope placed the city under interdict until submission was made; Arnold escaped to Campagna, but was later surrendered and executed. Frederick came to Italy and was crowned emperor after considerable unpleasantness, but his army caused havoc during a Roman riot and on his retirement to the north Frederick reduced Spoleto to ashes. William, who had great military success, capturing and enslaving many wealthy Greeks, was acknowledged as king when the pope made peace in 1156. William became a liege of the pope, and Adrian gave him rule over Naples and Salerno. The territorial grants immediately brought an end to Emperor Frederick's so-called friendship and the emperor began an attack which continued into the reign of Alexander III, who excommunicated him. One other major problem of Adrian's reign was the so-called "Donation of Ireland." John of Salisbury records that he was successful in his request to the pope that Ireland, a papal fief, be given over to young Henry II of England. Although the transfer, if it were really made, became invalid when Henry was excommunicated, later historians are at complete odds about the intention of the wording of extant documents. Adrian died in Rome on Sept. 1.

ADRIAN V (d. 1276), pope. Ottobuono Fieschi, born in Genoa, Italy, and nephew of Innocent IV, was elected pope at Viterbo on July 11, 1276, and died a month later, on Aug. 18. As a cardinal he had worked to end the quarrel between King Henry III and the English barons.

ADRIAN VI (1459–1523), pope. Adrian Florensz was born in Utrecht, Holland, on March 2 and educated by the Brothers of the Common Life and at Louvain, where he became a doctor of divinity in 1491. His lectures on theology were published by students; later he became vice-chancellor of the university. In 1506 Emperor Maximilian made him tutor to his grandson, later Charles V; he soon became the associate of Bishop Ximenes and was made a cardinal and regent of Spain. He was unanimously chosen pope on Jan. 9, 1522, and consecrated on Aug. 31. The papal treasury had been almost emptied by extravagance; the clergy and curia were corrupt and hostile to any reform, especially from a non-Italian; Germany was in revolt; the Turks held Belgrade and, despite Adrian's call for aid, captured Rhodes and swept the Mediterranean. An almost singlehanded battle against such opposition ruined his health; he died in Rome a year later, on Sept. 14.

ADRIAN, ST. (d. 290?), martyr. He, St. Hermes, and twenty-four other Christians died at Marula in Numidia, Africa, and were praised in a discourse by St. Augustine. F. D. Mar. 1.

ADRIAN, ST. (d. 304?), martyr. A pagan officer at the imperial court in Nicomedia, he was so impressed by the behavior of twenty-three Christians who were being tortured that he became a Christian and was hacked to death with them on Mar. 4. His wife Natalia and others were able to save their relics. Shortly after, she fled to Constantinople to escape the attentions of an imperial officer and died there on Dec. 1. The Adrian separately listed in Roman Martyrology as slain in Nicomedia and honored on Aug. 26 may be identical. F. D. Sept. 8.

ADRIAN, ST. (d. 309), martyr. When he refused to sacrifice to pagan gods during the Diocletian persecution he was tortured, mangled by wild beasts, and then beheaded at Caesarea in Palestine. F. D. Mar. 5.

ADRIAN, ST. (d. 688), martyr. A follower of St. Landoald, pastor of the mission church of Wintershoven in the Netherlands, he was set upon and slain by outlaws at Maestricht as he was carrying a royal contribution from King Childeric II. F. D. Mar. 19.

ADRIAN, ST. (d. 710). Born in North Africa, he became abbot of Nerida, near Naples, Italy, then proceeded to England as assistant to Archbishop Theodore. There he was abbot of the Benedictine monastery of SS. Peter and Paul at Canterbury, and taught Greek and Latin. During the thirty-nine years he was its director, the school became famous for its achievements in Roman law and the vernacular languages, and attracted St. Anselm and others from Britain and Ireland. F. D. Jan. 9.

ADRIAN, ST. (d. 875), martyr. One of a number, which varies from 100 to 6602, of Christians who were massacred by the Danes on the Isle of May in the Firth of Forth. Once believed to be a missionary bishop from Hungary, he possibly is identical with the Irish St. Odhran. F. D. Mar. 4.

ADRIAN, BL. (13th century), martyr. A Dominican, he was put to death with twenty-seven others by Mohammedans in Dalmatia. F. D. Dec. 21.

ADRIAN DE CORNETO (1460?–1521?). Born in Tuscany, he became a priest and in 1488 was sent to Scotland as papal nuncio, returned to Rome as agent of King Henry VII of England, became a rector in London and collector of charitable gifts for the papacy, and wrote a number of poems and philosophical treatises. In 1502 he became bishop of Hereford (later of Bath and Wells) and in 1503 a cardinal. He was deeply involved in politics and in 1517 was implicated in the attempted murder of Pope Leo X. Though the latter forgave him, Adrian fled to Venice and was stripped of all his offices and titles.

ADRICHEM, CHRISTIAN KRUIK VAN (1533–1585). Born in Delft, Holland, he was ordained in 1566, directed the convent of St. Barbara until removed by the Reformation, wrote on the antiquities and history of the Holy Land, and died at Cologne.

ADSO (d. 992). Educated at Luxeuil, France, he became Benedictine abbot at Moutier-en-Der in 960 and wrote hymns and a metrical version of Book 2 of Gregory the Great's *Dialogues*, a life of St. Mansuetus, and, probably, *De antichristo* (also attributed to Alcuin and Rhabanus Maurus). He died on pilgrimage to Jerusalem.

ADUARTE, DIEGO FRANCISCO (1566–1635?), historian. Born in Saragossa, Spain, he was educated at Alcalá, became a Dominican, and in 1594 was sent to the Philippine missions, working with Chinese residents. After serving as rector of the College of San Tomás, he went to Siam and Cochin China, suffering from great hostility. Later stationed in the Philippines, he was recalled to Spain in 1608 to spend his remaining years writing several volumes on mission history, recording the exceptional cruelty and evil of the Spaniards who controlled the islands, Dominican success abroad, and lives of martyrs in the East.

ADULF, ST. (7th century), bishop. *See* Botulf, St.

ADVENTOR, ST. (d. 287?), martyr. *See* Maurice, St.

ADVENTOR, ST. (d. 297), martyr. He and SS. Octavius and Solutor were slain at Turin, Italy, of which they are the patrons. F. D. Nov. 20.

AEDBERT, ST. (d. 698), bishop. He succeeded St. Cuthbert as bishop of Lindisfarne, England, and ruled for eleven years, restoring the cathedral and devoting himself to the care of the poor. Bede comments on his knowledge of scripture. F. D. May 6.

AEDESIUS, ST. (d. 306), martyr. Brother of St. Apphian, he was severely tortured and put to death by drowning at Alexandria because he objected to judges sending consecrated Christian virgins into prostitution. F. D. Apr. 8.

AEDH DUBH, ST. (d. 639). King of Leinster, Ireland, he gave up his crown in 592, entered the monastery of Kildare, and became its bishop in 630. F. D. Jan. 4.

AEDH FINN (7th century). King of Ossory, Ireland, he gave up his crown to become a monk. Fair-featured, he is not to be confused with Aedh the Dark, king of Leinster.

AEDH MacBRICC, ST. (d. 589), bishop. A disciple of St. Illathan of Rathlihen, Offaly, Ireland, he worked in Meath, particularly at Cill-áir in Westmeath, where he became bishop. F. D. Nov. 10.

AEDILBERCT. *See* Ethelbert, St. (d. 616).

AEDISIUS (4th century). *See* Frumentius, St.

AEGIDIUS. *See* Giles.

AEGIDIUS ROMANUS. *See* Colonna, Egidio.

AEGIDIUS OF VITERBO (d. 1532). Born in Viterbo, Italy, he became an Augustinian, later served as general of that order, made a name for himself at the fifth General Council at the Lateran (1512), and was made a cardinal by Pope Leo X. He worked hard to reform the Church, was a member of the pontifical senate, wrote a universal history, a commentary on Peter Lombard, a treatise on Lutheranism, a volume on Hebrew philology, and a large body of correspondence on the affairs of his order.

AELFRIC (955?–1020), author. A monk at the monastery in Winchester, England, he studied under St. Athelwold, whose Latin biography he wrote, was ordained, and in 987 was sent to the abbey of Cerne in Dorsetshire, where he served as master of novices. In 1005 he became abbot of Eynsham, near Oxford. He became the most significant writer in English before the Norman Conquest as a result of his decision to cast his two sets of *Homilies* (990–95) in the vernacular instead of in Latin. They are sermons on the creation, fall, flood, Mosaic law, and other Old Testament highlights, and on the life of Christ. The second collection discussed the apostolic succession, the origins of monasticism, and the development of the Church in England under Gregory the Great and Cuthbert. One sermon, on the Eucharist, long was considered an attack on transubstantiation by sixteenth-century writers, but careful study of the language has resulted in modern acceptance of Aelfric's orthodoxy. His diction is poetical, highly symbolic, and heavily marked by alliteration. Aelfric also wrote a Latin grammar, vocabulary, and colloquy (method of teaching); *Lives of the Saints*, a third set of homilies (about 996), developing the story of St. Swithin from local tradition; questions on Genesis, presented as being asked by Bishop Sigewulf; a paraphrase of the first seven books of the Bible (possibly with assistance); a pastoral on clerical shortcomings, composed about 998; a scriptural treatise, *De veteri et de novo testamento*, based on Augustine's *De doctrina christiana*; and a pastoral, composed about 1015, for Bishop Wulfstan. In all his work Aelfric, as he admitted, relied heavily on his predecessors, particularly Alcuin, Augustine, Bede, Gregory, Jerome, Rufinus, and Smaragdus.

AELIA FLACCILLA (d. 385?), empress. Of Spanish descent, perhaps the daughter of Claudius Antonius, prefect of Gaul, she married Theodosius about 376, and had three children: Arcadius and Honorius, who became emperors, and Pulcheria, who died young. She was a firm supporter of the Nicene Creed, strengthened her husband in his stand against Arian inroads, and was highly praised by SS. Ambrose and Gregory of Nyssa. Her career was marked by great charities and by work with cripples. She died in Constantinople and is venerated as a saint in the Greek Church on Sept. 14.

AELNOTH (12th century), biographer. A native of Canterbury, England, he probably was sent to Denmark in 1085, and became attached to the Benedictine monastery of St. Canute the Martyr at Odense, whose life he wrote in 1109.

AELRED, ST. (1109–1167). Born in Hexham, England, he entered the service of King David of Scotland, then at twenty-four became a Cistercian in Yorkshire, abbot of Revesby in 1142, and of Rievaulx in 1147. There he ruled 300 monks with charity and humility, wrote some poetry, and many ascetical works, including *Spiritual Friendship* and *Mirror of Love*. He is also called Ethelred. F. D. Mar. 3.

AEMILIUS, ST. (d. 250), martyr. He and St. Castus were North African Christians who lapsed under intense torture, but repented and were burned to death for their faith during the persecution of Decius. They are praised by St. Cyprian, and St. Augustine preached a sermon on their actions. F. D. May 22.

AENEAS OF GAZA (5th century), philosopher. A Neoplatonist, he was converted to Christianity and wrote on the relationship of body and soul.

AENGUS THE CULDEE, ST. (d. 824?). Born in Ulster, Ireland, he entered the monastery of Clonenagh in Leix, then became a hermit, and finally a servant for seven years at the monastery of Tallacht under St. Maelruain. When his identity was discovered, he was welcomed into the community and there composed the *Félire*, a metrical hymn to the saints. After the death of Maelruain in 787, he returned to Clonenagh, where he became abbot and bishop. He is also known as Oengus. F. D. Mar. 11.

AENGUS McNISSE. *See* Macansius, St.

AETHERIUS, ST. (4th century), bishop and martyr. He and SS. Agathadorus, Basil, Capiton, Elpidius, Ephrem, and Eugene were missionary bishops in Crimea and southern Russia, where they were put to death. F. D. Mar. 4.

AFAN, ST. (6th century?), bishop. He was probably a Welshman who lived in Brecknock, became a bishop, and is buried in Llanafan. F. D. Nov. 16.

AFFRE, DENIS AUGUSTE (1793–1848), bishop. Born in St. Rome-de-Tarn, France, on Sept. 27, he entered the seminary of St. Sulpice at fourteen, taught at Nantes, was ordained in 1818, and became a Sulpician, holding several major offices in the order. He became archbishop of Paris in 1840 and wrote several philosophical and pastoral studies. As he was pleading for peace during the insurrection of 1848, he was fired on and slain. He died on June 27.

AFRA, ST. (d. 304), martyr. She was put to death in Augsburg, Germany, during the Diocletian persecution. Accounts of her origin in Cyprus and death with three others, called converted prostitutes, are fiction. F. D. Aug. 5.

AFRICANUS, ST. (d. 250), martyr. With SS. Pompeius, Terence, and nearly fifty others, he was beheaded at Carthage after torture during the reign of Decius. F. D. Apr. 10.

AFRICUS, ST. (7th century). His shrine at Comminges, France, was destroyed by Calvinists; it is unlikely that he was a bishop. F. D. Nov. 16.

AGABIUS, ST. (d. 250?). He was bishop of Verona, Italy. F. D. Aug. 4.

AGABUS, ST. (1st century). He is mentioned as a prophet in the Acts of the Apostles (11:28; 21:10–12). He is said traditionally to have come from Palestine and to have died a martyr at Antioch. F. D. Feb. 13.

AGAMUND, ST. (d. 870), martyr. *See* Theodore, St.

AGAPE, ST., martyr. She is said to have been put to death at Terni, Italy, at the time of Bishop St. Valentine, but it is more likely that she died at Antioch. There were a number of martyrs of this name, which makes dating impossible. F. D. Feb. 15.

AGAPE, ST. (d. 304), martyr. Sister of SS. Chionia and Irene, she was burned to death at Thessalonica during the Diocletian persecution for possessing copies of scripture and for refusing to eat food sacrificed to the gods. Chionia died with her; Irene, later. F. D. Apr. 3.

AGAPES, ST. (d. 303), martyr. He and SS. Domna, Indes, and Theophila were slain at Nicomedia during the Diocletian persecution. F. D. Dec. 28.

AGAPETUS I, ST. (d. 536), pope. Born in Rome, son of Gordian, a priest, he became pope on May 13, 535, and went to Constantinople to oppose Justinian and the Monophysites, replaced the heretic patriarch Anthimus with St. Mennas, and died there on Apr. 22 before he had been in office a year. F. D. Apr. 23 (formerly, Sept. 20).

AGAPETUS II (d. 955), pope. A Roman, he became pope on May 10, 946, and had no temporal power since Rome was in the grip of the tyrannical senator, Albericht, who announced that his son Octavian would succeed Agapetus. The pope worked to restore ecclesiastical discipline, ended a quarrel in the see of Rheims, and gave support to Emperor Otto for evangelizing northern Europe. He died in Rome in Dec.

AGAPITUS (6th century). A deacon at St. Sophia, Constantinople, said to have been a tutor of Justinian, he wrote a popular treatise on the duties of rulers which was popular for more than ten centuries.

AGAPITUS, ST. (d. 118?), martyr. *See* Eustace, St.

AGAPITUS, ST. (d. 258), martyr. *See* Sixtus II, St.

AGAPITUS, ST. (d. 274?), martyr. According to legend, he was a fifteen-year-old boy who was tortured and beheaded at Palestrina, near Rome, during Aurelian's reign. Pope Felix III dedicated a church to him there in the fifth century. F. D. Aug. 18.

AGAPITUS, ST. (3rd century). He was bishop of Synnada, Smyrna. F. D. Mar. 24.

AGAPITUS, ST. (4th century). He was bishop of Ravenna, Italy. F. D. Mar. 16.

AGAPIUS, ST. (d. 259), martyr. He and St. Secundinus, Spanish priests banished to Africa, were among the Christians slaughtered by the sword at Citra, Algeria, during the persecution of Valerian. With them died Emilian, a soldier, and Antonia and Tertulla. F. D. Apr. 29.

AGAPIUS, ST. (d. 303), martyr. He and SS. Pausis, Romulus, Timolaus, two named Alexander, and two named Dionysius were beheaded at Caesarea in Palestine during the Diocletian persecution. F. D. Mar. 24.

AGAPIUS, ST. (d. 304), martyr. *See* Bassa, St.

AGAPIUS, ST. (d. 306?), martyr. Arrested and tortured on three occasions, he was put to death by drowning at Caesarea, Palestine, during the Diocletian persecution. F. D. Nov. 20 (also, Aug. 19).

AGAPIUS, ST. (d. 315?), martyr. He, SS. Carterius, Eudoxius, Styriacus, Tobias, and five other soldiers were burned to death at Sebaste, Armenia. F. D. Nov. 2.

AGAPIUS, ST. (d. 420?), bishop. He succeeded St. Gaudentius as bishop of Novara, Italy, about 400. F. D. Sept. 10.

AGATHA, ST., martyr. Put to death sometime before 530 at Catania, though nothing else is known for certain about her, she is said to have suffered the grossest insults because of her persistence in virtue, to have been tortured to incredible lengths by a consul named Quintian, racked, torn, and burned before she died in prison. Because her breasts were said to have been mutilated, they are often portrayed on a salver in mediaeval art. F. D. Feb. 5.

AGATHADORUS, ST. (2nd or 3rd century), martyr. *See* Carpus, St.

AGATHADORUS, ST. (4th century), bishop and martyr. *See* Aetherius, St.

AGATHANGELOS. This probably is a pen name assumed by the author of a life of Gregory the Illuminator, the first apostle of Armenia, who died about 332; he is said to have been secretary to King Tiridates II.

AGATHANGELUS, ST. (d. 308?), martyr. Said to have been a convert of St. Clement, bishop of Ancyra, when the latter was exhibited as a prisoner in Rome, he became a deacon and shared the other's martyrdom at Ancyra. F. D. Jan. 23.

AGATHO, ST. (d. 681), pope. A Sicilian, he had been married for twenty years before he became a monk. He held office in Rome under Pope Donus, whom he succeeded on June 27, 678. His short pontificate was marked by his opposition to the Monothelite heresy, by his clear definition of the power and succession of the papacy, and by a great plague which probably took him as a victim. F. D. Jan. 10.

AGATHO, ST. (d. 306?), martyr. He and St. Triphina were put to death in Sicily during the Diocletian persecution. F. D. July 5.

AGATHO, ST. (4th century). One of the desert fathers, he was abbot of a hermitage in Egypt. F. D. Oct. 21.

AGATHO, ST. A name given by error, and listed in the Roman Martyrology under Dec. 7; he has since been identified as St. Besas.

AGATHONICE, ST. (2nd or 3rd century), martyr. *See* Carpus, St.

AGATHONICUS, ST. (3rd century), martyr. A patrician, he was put to death at Constantinople during the persecution of Maximian Herculius. Zoticus, a philosopher from Bithynia, and followers of his were slain about the same time. F. D. Aug. 22.

AGATHOPEDES, ST. (d. 303), martyr. A deacon at Thessalonica, he was tortured and executed by drowning, with St. Theodulus, a lector, during the persecution under Maximian Herculius, for owning copies of scripture. F. D. Apr. 4.

AGATHOPUS, ST. (d. 150?). He and St. Philo were deacons who accompanied St. Ignatius of Antioch on his journey to Rome and probably wrote the account of his martyrdom. F. D. Apr. 25.

AGATHOPUS, ST. (d. 250), martyr. *See* Theodulus, St.

AGAZZARI, AGOSTINI (1578–1640), composer. Born in Siena, Italy, he served Emperor Matthias, then went to Rome in 1600 as choirmaster of the German College. He later was at the Roman seminary, then at the Siena cathedral. He wrote masses, motets, magnificats, madrigals, and a pamphlet on church music.

AGERANUS, ST. (d. 888), martyr. A Benedictine monk at Bèze, he remained in Burgundy during the Norman invasion, and was slain with four other monks—Berard, Genesius, Sifrard, and Rodron—a priest named Ansuinus, and Adalric, a boy. F. D. May 21.

AGERICUS, ST. (521?–588), bishop. Born near Verdun where he became a priest, he succeeded St. Desiderius as bishop there about 554, was a friend of King Sigebert I and adviser to his son and successor, Childebert. He is also called Airy. F. D. Dec. 1.

AGGAEUS, ST. (d. 300?), martyr. He and SS. Caius and Hermes were put to death, probably at Bononia on the Danube River; they were earlier listed as martyrs at Bologna. F. D. Jan. 4.

AGIA, ST. (d. 714?). Wife of St. Hydulphus of Hainault, she became a nun at Mons, France, and her husband entered religious life at the same time as a monk at Lobbes. She is also called Austegildis. F. D. Apr. 18.

AGILBERT, ST., martyr. With St. Agoard and others he was put to death at Creteil, near Paris, at an uncertain date between the first and seventh centuries. F. D. June 24.

AGILBERT, ST. (d. 685), bishop. A Frankish monk from the Benedictine monastery of Jouarre, he preached in Wessex and was invited to stay as a bishop by Coenwalh, king of the West Saxons. He became famed for his missionary activities and ordained St. Wilfrid, whom he designated to speak on behalf of the Roman party at the Synod of Whitby called to resolve the conflict between Roman and Celtic customs. When King Coenwalh divided his diocese and appointed an English bishop, named Wine, to the better half, he resigned and returned to France. In 668 he was made bishop of Paris and, when asked to return to Wessex by the king, declined and sent his nephew Eleutherius in his stead. F. D. Oct. 11.

AGILBERTA, ST. (d. 680?). She was elected second abbess of the Benedictine convent of Jouarre, France, in 660, and was related to SS. Ado, Agilbert, and Ebrigisil. F. D. Aug. 10.

AGILES, RAYMOND D' (11th century). A canon at Puy-en-Velay, France, he went with the count of Toulouse on the first crusade, led an attack at Antioch, reached Jerusalem, and wrote an extravagant history of the expedition.

AGILEUS, ST. (d. 300?), martyr. A North African, he was slain at Carthage and honored by St. Augustine in a sermon. F. D. Oct. 15.

AGILULF, ST. (8th century), bishop and martyr. He was abbot of the Benedictine monastery of Stavelot-Malmédy before he became archbishop of Cologne. He was slain because of his ecclesiastical zeal, allegedly through the plotting of Charles Martel. F. D. July 9.

AGILUS, ST. (580?–650). A Frankish nobleman, he became a monk at Luxeuil, under St. Columbanus, did mission work in Bavaria, and served as abbot of Rebais, near Paris. He is also called Ayeul. F. D. Aug. 30.

AGLIARDI, ANTONIO (1832–1915), cardinal. Born in Cologno, Italy, he studied theology and canon law in Rome, was ordained, sent to Canada as bishop, appointed archbishop of Caesarea, Palestine, in 1884, then sent as apostolic delegate to Goa to settle the controversy in Portuguese India. In 1889 he was papal nuncio at Munich and in 1893 in Vienna. He was made a cardinal in 1896, became bishop of Albano, and chancellor of the Church.

AGNELLI, GIUSEPPE (1621–1706). Born in Naples, Italy, he became a Jesuit in 1637 and rector of the society's colleges of Montepulciano, Macerata, and Ancona. His last thirty-three years were spent at Rome, where he wrote sermons, treatises on the *Spiritual Exercises*, and a commentary on the Sunday gospels.

AGNELLI, GUGLIELMO (1238?–1313?), sculptor. Probably a native of Pisa, Italy, he studied sculpture under Niccolò Pisano, became a Dominican laybrother in 1257, worked on several buildings for his order, executed a series of reliefs for the tomb of St. Dominic at Bologna and others for the cathedral in Orvieto and the church of San Michele in Pisa.

AGNELLO, BL. (1194–1236). Born in Pisa, Italy, Agnello was accepted as a Friar Minor there by St. Francis himself, sent to Paris as guardian of the order and then to England as first provincial. He landed in 1224 with Fr. Richard of Ingworth and six others, founded a house at Canterbury, was well received by Archbishop Stephen Langton and in London by King Henry III. He established a school and infirmary at Oxford and from this early Franciscan center grew the later university. His cult was confirmed in 1892. F. D. May 7.

AGNELLUS, ST. (d. 596?). A recluse, he became abbot of the Benedictine monastery of San Gaudioso, near Naples, Italy. F. D. Dec. 14.

AGNELLUS, ANDREAS (805–846?). A secular priest at Ravenna, Italy, possibly titular abbot of St. Mary's and St. Bartholomew's there, he wrote a history of that see, accurate in its physical descriptions, but anti-papal when he treats of major issues.

AGNES, ST. (d. 304), martyr. A thirteen-year-old Roman, she was executed, probably by stabbing, and buried in the cemetery given her name, where Constantina erected a basilica. The stories of the angry suitors who sought her in marriage and then demanded her death, when she said she was dedicated to virginity, and of the numerous tortures, insults, and romantic miracles, associated with many biographies of her, are pious fictions. F. D. Jan. 21.

AGNES, ST. (1196?–1253). She followed her older sister, St. Clare, to the Benedictine convent of Sant' Angelo at Ponso in 1212, despite violent objections by her father, Count Favorini Scifi. After she received the habit from St. Francis of Assisi, she and Clare were sent to San Damiano. In 1219 she became abbess of the convent of Monticelli, Florence, and from there founded houses at Padua, Venice, and Mantua. In 1253 she was recalled to Assisi and died three months after St. Clare. F. D. Nov. 16.

AGNES OF AUSTRIA (1281–1364), queen. Daughter of Emperor Albrecht I of Germany, she married King Andreas III of Hungary, and after her father was murdered in 1308 lived at the convent of Königsfelden, which her mother had built. She was active in contemporary politics and often was mediator in disputes between the Swiss Confederacy and Austria.

AGNES OF BAGNO, BL. (d. 1105). She was a Camaldolese nun at the convent of Santa Lucia, near Bagno di Romagna, Tuscany; her cult was confirmed in 1823. F. D. Sept. 4.

AGNES OF BENIGNAM. *See* Albiniana, Bl. Ines.

AGNES OF BOHEMIA, BL. (1205–1282). Daughter of King Ottokar I and cousin of St. Elizabeth of Hungary, she evaded a series of arranged engagements and in 1236 became a Poor Clare in the Prague center she and her brother King Wenceslaus built and to which St. Clare had sent five nuns. A hundred girls joined her and she served briefly as abbess at the request of Pope Gregory IX. F. D. Mar. 1 (also, June 8).

AGNES OF MERAN (d. 1201), queen. Daughter of the Duke of Meran in Tyrol, she was married to Philip Augustus of France in 1196 after he was granted a divorce by his bishops from Ingeborg of Denmark. Pope Innocent III refused to recognize the divorce and placed France under an interdict. Agnes died in 1201; her two children were legitimized in 1213 when Philip was reconciled to Ingeborg.

AGNES OF MONTE PULCIANO, ST. (1268–1317). Born in Tuscany, she entered a convent at nine, was housekeeper at fourteen, and abbess at Procena the next year. She fasted for fifteen years and enjoyed exceptional supernatural gifts. Her village built her a convent, to which she returned about 1300 and to which she introduced the Dominican rule. Her shrine was a popular one, and St. Catherine of Siena's visit to it inspired several painters. She was canonized by Pope Benedict XIII in 1726. F. D. Apr. 20.

AGNES OF POITIERS, ST. (d. 588). She was abbess of the convent of the Holy Cross at Poitiers, France, and a friend of the poet Venantius Fortunatus. F. D. May 13.

AGNES OF POITIERS (1025?–1077), queen. Daughter of Duke William IV of Aquitaine, she married Henry III of Germany in 1043. She was regent of the empire after his death in 1056; when rebellious nobles seized young Henry IV in 1063, Agnes fled to Italy. She had been interested in the Cluniac reform and at Rome aided Pope Gregory VII in his stand against the German leaders.

AGNESI, MARIA GAETANA (1718–1799). Daughter of a mathematician in Bologna, Italy, she mastered Latin, Greek, Hebrew, and many modern languages before she was thirteen, and published a defense of the liberal arts for women. She wrote widely on philosophy and mathematics, taught at the University of Bologna in 1750, later turned to the study of theology and patristics, and became a member of the Blue Nuns and director of their hospice at Milan.

AGNEW, WILLIAM HENRY (1881–1931), educator. Born in Westphalia, Kansas, on Oct. 12, he studied at St. Louis and was ordained a Jesuit in 1915. He was head of the department of science at Loyola (Chicago) and St. Louis, was president of Loyola in 1921–27, did parish work in Chicago, edited *Queen's Work*, and was president of Creighton University when he died in Rochester, Minnesota, on Feb. 13.

AGNOLO, ANDREA D'. *See* Andrea del Sarto.

AGNOLO OF SIENA (14th century), sculptor. Son of Ventura, he worked with Agostino on the monument to Bishop Tarlati at Arezzo, Italy, on that to Pino de Sinibaldi in the Pistoia cathedral, and on sculptural and architectural designs in Siena, including the Castello Grosseto and the city gates. He flourished between 1310 and 1350.

AGOARD, ST., martyr. *See* Agilbert, St.

AGOBARD, ST. (769?–840), bishop. Born in Spain, he escaped a Moorish invasion as a youth, studied and was ordained in France, became archbishop of Lyons in 813, wrote on theology and liturgy, and played an important role in contemporary affairs. F. D. June 6.

AGOFRID, ST. (8th century). He succeeded his brother, St. Leutfrid, in 738 as abbot of the Benedictine monastery of the Holy Cross in Évreux, Normandy. F. D. June 21.

AGOSTINI, ALBERTO DE (d. 1960), missionary. Born in Italy where he became a Salesian priest in 1909, he was sent to Argentina as a missionary, and traveled widely through unexplored areas on a dozen expeditions. He made the first accurate map of Tierra del Fuego, was first to cross the southern Cordillera of the Andes and first to climb the Sarmiento peak in the Cordillera. He wrote numerous books on his explorations which earned him the nickname Padre Patagonia. He died in Turin, Italy, on Dec. 25.

AGOSTINI, CARLO (1888–1952), bishop. Born in San Martino di Lupari, Italy, on Apr. 22, he was ordained at twenty-two by special permission of Pope Pius X, became bishop of Padua in 1932, patriarch of Venice in 1949, and was a cardinal-designate at the time of his death in Venice on Dec. 28.

AGOSTINI, PAOLO (1593–1629), composer. Following the Venetian and Roman schools, he composed for grouped choirs and published psalms, magnificats, and masses. He became master of the Vatican chapel in 1627.

AGOSTINO OF SIENA (14th century), sculptor. Son of Giovanni, he worked with Agnolo of Siena on the monument to Bishop Tarlati at Arezzo, Italy, on that to Pino de Sinibaldi in the Pistoia cathedral, and on sculptural architectural designs in Siena. He worked before 1350 on the tower of the Palazzo Communale and the fortress of Massa, with the assistance of his son Giovanni.

AGOULT, CHARLES D' (1747–1824), bishop. Born in Grenoble, France, he studied at St. Sulpice in Paris and became bishop of Pamiers in 1787. He surrendered his post, went into exile during the revolution, returned in 1801, and wrote studies on politics and a national bank.

AGRARIUS, ST. (d. 413), martyr. *See* Marcellinus, St.

AGRECIUS, ST. (d. 329?), bishop. In spite of many legends about his transfer to Germany of major relics from the hands of St. Helena, mother of Constantine, all that is known is that Agrecius attended the Council of Arles (314) as a bishop of Trèves. F. D. Jan. 13.

AGRICOLA, ST. (d. 304?), martyr. *See* Vitalis, St.

AGRICOLA, ST. (d. 305?), martyr. *See* Valentine, St.

AGRICOLA, ST. (d. 420), bishop. He is listed as the eleventh to occupy the see of Tongres, Gaul. F. D. Feb. 5.

AGRICOLA, ST. (497?–580), bishop. Praised highly by his contemporary, St. Gregory of Tours, he was bishop of Châlon-sur-Saône, France, for forty-eight years, attending several councils, and living a life of notable asceticism. F. D. Mar. 17.

AGRICOLA, ST. (d. 594?). He is said to have become bishop of Nevers, France, in 570. F. D. Feb. 26.

AGRICOLA, ALEXANDER (1446?–1506), composer. Of Belgian or German origin, he studied in the Netherlands and was a member of the choir of the ducal chapel at Milan before 1474, later serving the dukes of Mantua and Austria. He died at Vallodolid, Spain. Songs, motets, and five masses have been published; a large corpus of his work is in manuscript.

AGRICOLA, GEORGE (1494–1555), scientist. George Bauer (Latinized to Agricola, under which name he wrote) was born in Glauchau, Saxony, studied in Germany and Italy, practiced medicine in Bohemia, became historiographer to Elector Maurice of Saxony, studied geology and wrote *De re metallica*, which gained him the title of "Father of Mineralogy." He briefly was sympathetic toward Luther, but study of the Fathers of the Church and the writing of papers on the apostolic tradition strenuously established his orthodoxy. He died at Chemnitz, Saxony.

AGRICOLA, RUDOLPH (1442?–1485). Rudolph Huysmann was born in Bafflo, Holland, studied classics at Louvain and Paris, went to Rome and Ferrara for seven years, then returned to Germany. In 1482 he began to lecture at Heidelberg on the invitation of John

Dalberg, bishop of Worms, studied Hebrew, and published a translation of the Psalms. He also wrote, using the name Agricola, *Da nativitate Christi*, poems, discourses, and a treatise on dialectics.

AGRICOLUS, ST. (630?–700?), bishop. Son of St. Magnus, bishop of Avignon, France, he became a monk at Lérins when about sixteen, was recalled to Avignon when about thirty to be consecrated as coadjutor, and in 670 succeeded his father to that see, of which he is patron. F. D. Sept. 2.

AGRIPPA, HEINRICH CORNELIUS (1486–1534?). Born in Cologne on Sept. 14, he studied there, at Paris, and in Spain, taught in England in 1510, and became a knight in Italy in the army of Emperor Maximilian. He wrote widely on cabalism and the occult, a commentary on Ramón Lull, a defense of women, and strong attacks on scholasticism, canon law, and the hierarchy. In his last years he was exiled from Cologne as a debtor and was openly in support of Luther, though he stated he was attacking abuses only and died nominally a Catholic. He died in either Grenoble or Lyons, France.

AGRIPPINA, ST. (3rd century), martyr. She is said to have been beheaded or scourged to death at Rome during the Valerian or Diocletian persecutions. Details are confused; even her relics are claimed by two places: Mineo (Sicily) and Constantinople. F. D. June 23.

AGRIPPINUS (3rd century). Bishop of Carthage at the turn of the century, he became involved in the problem of converts, contending that those previously baptized outside the Church had to be baptized again, absolutely, not conditionally, on the ground that heretics and schismatics did not have the power to absolve from sin. The problem had not been clarified up to his time and, though he was incorrect, he acted in good faith and was later praised by St. Augustine.

AGRIPPINUS, ST. (d. 180?), bishop. He is said to have been the ninth to occupy the Alexandria, Egypt, see after St. Mark. F. D. Jan. 30.

AGRIPPINUS, ST. He was bishop of Naples in the second or third century. F. D. Nov. 9.

AGRIPPINUS, ST. (d. 538). He was bishop of Autun in Gaul and ordained St. Germanus of Paris. F. D. July 9.

AGUIRRE, JOSEPH SAENZ DE (1630–1699), cardinal. Born in Logrono, Old Castile, Spain, on Mar. 24, he became a Benedictine at Monte Cassino, director of studies at the monastery of St. Vincent at Salamanca and its abbot, and professor of theology and of scripture at the university there. After his active part against the Declaration of the Gallican clergy in 1682, he was made a cardinal by Pope Innocent XI. He wrote commentaries on Aristotle and SS. Anselm and Thomas, against Jansenism and Quietism, a treatise on guardian angels, and one supporting John Gerson as author of the *Imitation of Christ*. He died in Rome on Aug. 19.

AGUIRRE, ST. MARTIN DE (d. 1597), martyr. *See* Peter Baptist, St.

AHERN, MICHAEL JOSEPH (1877–1951), educator. Born in New York City on May 25, he studied at St. Francis Xavier, became a Jesuit in 1896, was at Innsbruck in 1907–11, and taught at Canisius and Boston College. He set up the seismograph station at the latter and gained attention as a radio commentator on the "Catholic Truth Period" program, of which he was director from 1929 to 1950. He also had taught at Holy Cross and was president of Canisius from 1919 to 1923. He died in Boston on June 5.

AIBLINGER, JOHANN CASPAR (1779–1867), composer. Born in Wasserberg, Bavaria, on Feb. 23, he studied piano and organ at Munich and Landshut, as well as theology, then went to Vicenza, Italy, for eleven years. At Venice in 1811 he met Meyerbeer, who appointed him to the conservatory; he later directed the ballet at Milan. In the service of King Maximilian I of Bavaria he directed opera at Munich, became organist at All Saints' church, and wrote several unsuccessful operas and much church music. He died in Munich on May 6.

AICHARD, ST. (d. 687?). Son of one of Clotaire II's officers, he was born in Poitiers, educated at the abbey of St. Hilaire there, and became a Benedictine monk in Ansion, where he spent the next thirty-nine years of his life. He then was made abbot of St. Benedict's priory in Quinçay by St. Philibert, whom he succeeded at Jumièges. F. D. Sept. 15.

AICHINGER, GREGOR (1565–1628), composer. Born probably at Ratisbon, he was organist to Jacob Fugger of Augsburg from 1590 to 1599, visited Rome, fell under the influence of Gabrieli, and returned to the service of the Fuggers in 1601 to direct their choir. He was a priest at his death; when he was ordained is not known. He died in Augsburg on Jan. 21.

AIDAN, ST. (d. 626), bishop. Born probably in Connaught, Ireland, he went to study scripture in Wales with St. David, returned to Ireland, and built a monastery in Wexford, where he later became bishop of Ferns. Many legends have become associated with his name, which is also written Maedoc. He died in Bamborough and is represented in art by a stag. F. D. Jan. 31.

AIDAN, ST. (d. 651), bishop. A native of Ireland, he became a monk at Iona and served in the missions of Northumbria. He made his headquarters the island of Lindisfarne, where he established the monastery which became a

great missionary center, and became bishop. He was greatly aided in his evangelizing work by Kings St. Oswald and Oswin. F. D. Aug. 31.

AIGUILLON, DUCHESSE D'. *See* Roure, Marie de.

AIGULF, ST. (630?–676?), martyr. Born in Blois, France, he became a Benedictine monk at Fleury when twenty. According to a ninth-century biography, he was in charge of a group sent to Monte Cassino to rescue St. Benedict's relics from the Lombards. About 670, he was sent to Lérins as abbot. His attempts to reform the monastery occasioned opposition which led to interference in the dispute by the local governor, whose soldiers kidnaped Aigulf and four of his supporters and took them to Capraia (near Corsica), where the abbot was slain. He is also called Aieul and Aout. F. D. Sept. 3.

AIGULF, ST. (d. 836), bishop. A hermit, he was brought in to his native city of Bourges, France, by the populace and made its bishop about 812. F. D. May 22.

AIKENHEAD, MARY (1787–1858), foundress. Born in Cork, Ireland, on Jan. 19, to David and Mary Stacpole Aikenhead, she entered the Church in 1802 after the death of her physician father, a deathbed convert. She became a novice at a York convent in 1812; three years later she was appointed superior general of the Irish Sisters of Charity as Sister M. Augustine. As head of that order, which she founded at the direction of Archbishop Murray of Dublin, she sent missions to France and Australia, built hospitals, and performed heroic service during the plague of 1832. She died in Dublin on July 22.

AILBHE, ST. (d. 526?), bishop. He is said to have been an Irishman who preached successfully through Ireland, first bishop of Emly, and the author of a monastic rule. F. D. Sept. 12.

AILERAN, ST. (d. 664), scholar. Attracted to the monastery of Clonard, Ireland, by the work of St. Finnian, he became rector there in 650, and wrote lives of SS. Brigid, Fechin, and Patrick, a commentary on the genealogy of Christ according to St. Matthew, and other studies. F. D. Dec. 29.

AILLEBOUST, BARBE D' (d. 1685), foundress. Wife of Louis, sieur de Coulanges, Barbe de Boulogne was born in France, went to Canada, mastered Algonquin, and taught the language to the Sulpician missioners. After her husband's death in 1660 she devoted herself to a life of prayer and in 1663, with Fr. Chaumonot, S.J., founded the Confraternity of the Holy Family, canonically approved in 1664 by Bishop Laval. She died at the Hôtel Dieu, Quebec, to which she had given her wealth.

AILLEBOUST, LOUIS D' (d. 1660), governor. Born in France, he was sent to Canada in 1643, helped Maisonneuve to found Montreal, became commandant (1646–47), and was third governor general of Canada (1648–51) at Quebec. During this time the Jesuit martyrs were slain and he set up a refuge for the Hurons on the island of Orleans. The governor then retired as a farmer at Montreal, became sieur de Coulanges, and introduced Sulpician and other missions. In 1658 he laid the first stone of the shrine of St. Anne de Beaupré. He died in Montreal on May 31.

AILLY, PIERRE D' (1350–1420?), cardinal. Born in Compiègne, France, he became a doctor of theology at Paris in 1380, director of the College of Navarre there in 1383, and chancellor of the university in 1389. He wrote and preached widely, was appointed bishop of Le Puy in 1395 and of Cambrai in 1397. He tried to bring an end to the Western schism, was made a cardinal by the antipope John XXIII, and in 1414 Martin V made him a papal legate at Avignon. His writings were varied: he supported an astrological interpretation of history; maintained that the pope was subordinate to a general council, denied papal infallibility, denied scriptural sources for the doctrine of the Trinity, and followed Occam and the Nominalists quite closely. However, he persuaded Pope Clement VII to remain firm in condemning John of Monzon for denying the Immaculate Conception. D'Ailly's proposal for reforming the calendar (1411) was completed and put into actuality by Pope Gregory XIII, and a copy of his *Imago mundi*, pointing to a western route to the Indies, was owned and annotated by Columbus. He died in Avignon, France.

AIMERICH, MATEO (1715–1799), philologian. Born in Bordil, Spain, he became a Jesuit at eighteen, taught in several colleges, was rector at Barcelona and Cervera, and chancellor of the University of Gandia. When the Jesuits were exiled he went to Ferrara, Italy, and wrote ascetical and philosophical works and a critical and historical lexicon of Latin literature. He died in Ferrara.

AIMO, ST. (d. 1173). Born in Rennes, France, he became a Benedictine at Savigny. When he was thought to be a leper, he served two monks who actually were, was subsequently ordained, and had several supernatural gifts. F. D. Apr. 30.

AIMOIN (960?–1010?), historian. Born in Villefranche de Longchapt, France, he became a monk at Fleury, wrote a study of that abbey and its abbots, Books 2–3 of *Miracula sancti Benedicti*, and *Historia francorum*.

AIROLI, GIACOMO MARIA (1660–1721). Born in Genoa, Italy, he became a Jesuit, taught Hebrew at the Roman College, and wrote more than a dozen studies on the chronology of the Bible. He died in Rome on Mar. 27.

AIRY. *See* Agericus, St.

AITHALAS, ST. (d. 342?), martyr. *See* Abdiesus, St.

AIZAN, ST. (d. 400?). He and his brother Sazan were Abyssinian chiefs, friends of St. Athanasius, and helped to spread Christianity there. F. D. Oct. 1.

AKHTAL, GHIYATH AL (640?–710?), poet. Born in Hira, son of a Christian mother, Laila, who belonged to the Yad tribe, he became a court poet at Damascus, Syria, and was highly regarded as a poet in later times; his contemporaries scorned him for his religion and his failure to cater to contemporary taste.

AKOMINATOS, MICHAEL (d. 1215). A native of Chonia, Greece, he tutored his younger brother Nicetas at Constantinople, became a priest and, in 1175, archbishop of Athens, and went into exile on Chios when the crusaders occupied the East. He wrote letters, poems, an historical account of contemporary Attica, and a detailed description of Athenian art objects destroyed by Latin Christians.

AKOMINATOS, NICETAS (d. 1206). Born in Chonia, Greece, he studied history, law, and theology and became governor of the province of Philoppopolis. After the area was ravaged by Frederick Barbarossa and the crusaders in 1189, he fled to Nicaea. He wrote against heresy in *Treasure of Orthodoxy*, as well as a history of Constantinople, ending with an account of its pillage by Latin Christians in 1204.

ALACCI, LEO (1586–1669), scholar. Born on the Greek island of Chios, he studied at Rome, took his medical degree at Sapienza in 1616, and taught rhetoric at the Greek College in Rome for two years. Pope Gregory XV sent him to Germany to oversee the transfer of the library at Heidelberg which Maximilian had given the Vatican; in 1661 Alexander VII made him custodian of the Vatican Library. He edited or translated into Latin a number of Greek writers, wrote a study on the Eastern Church in the hope of ending the schism, and was an editor of *Corpus Byzantinorum*.

ALACOQUE, ST. MARGARET MARY (1647–1690). Born in L'Hautecourt, France, fifth of seven children of a notary, she was sent to the Poor Clares' school at Charolles when her father died in 1655, was stricken at ten with rheumatism that kept her bedridden for five years, and in 1671 entered the Order of the Visitation at Paray-le-Monial. She took her final vows the next year and eventually served as mistress of novices and as assistant superior. From the time she was twenty she experienced visions; in one, which occurred in 1675, she was directed to establish widespread devotion to the Sacred Heart of Jesus. She encountered great opposition, particularly from Jansenists, and her visions were dismissed as delusions. When Claude la Columbière became confessor to the nuns at Paray, he approved her claims as genuine and helped to spread the devotion. She was canonized in 1920. F. D. Oct. 17.

MARGARET YEO, *These Three Hearts* (Milwaukee, Bruce, 1940).

ALACRINUS, BL. (d. 1216). Cistercian prior at Casamari, Italy, he served Popes Innocent III and Honorius III as legate to Germany. F. D. Jan. 5.

ALADIUS, ST. (d. 520?). He was bishop of Toul, France. F. D. Oct. 1.

ALAGONA, PIETRO (1549–1624). Born in Syracuse, Sicily, he became a Jesuit, made a compendium of the works of Martin Aspelcueta, uncle of St. Francis Xavier; of the *Summa* of Thomas Aquinas, which ran through more than a score of editions; of canon law; and wrote the popular *Enchiridion, seu manuale confessariorum*. He died in Rome on Oct. 19.

ALAIN DE L'ISLE (1128?–1203?), philosopher. Born in Lille, France, he probably studied and taught at Paris, attended the third Lateran Council in 1179, and became a Cistercian at Cîteaux, where he died. He was a rationalist, and wrote *Ars fidei catholicae, Tractatus contra haereticos*, and *Theologicae regulae*, as well as satirical poems. His style reveals a mysticism comparable to that of John Scotus Erigena; he was strongly Platonic (through the writings of Martianus Capella Apuleius and Boethius), to which he added eclectically some of Aristotle on logic and the Pythagoreanism of Asclepius. His synthesis is not successful and his colorfully poetic diction reveals more imagination than theological precision. He was an influence on Dante. He is also known as Alanus ab Insulis.

ALAMAN, LUCAS (1792–1853), historian. Born in Guanajuato, Mexico, of Spanish parentage, on Oct. 18, he studied there and in Spain and France, returned to Mexico in 1815, and in 1824 became secretary of state of the republic. He was opposed by the extremists in the government, forced to take flight in 1835 and to remain in hiding for a year, and thereafter devoted himself to writing. He published a *History of the Mexican Republic* (1844) and a *History of Mexico* (1849), both valuable studies of the country (except as to his ignorance of the Indians). He was recalled by Santa Anna in 1851 to serve as secretary of state and died in Mexico City on June 2.

ALAMANNI, NICCOLÒ (1583–1626). Born in Ancona, Italy, on Jan. 12, he studied at the Greek College, Rome, was ordained, and became secretary to Cardinal Borghese and custodian of the Vatican Library. He wrote on papal coins and on the restoration of the church of St. John Lateran, and edited the *Secret History* of Procopius. He died in Rome.

ALAN OF TEWKSBURY (d. 1202). An Englishman, he became a Benedictine at Canterbury, prior there in 1179, and close friend of St. Thomas à Becket, whose life he wrote. During the quarrel between the archbishop and Henry II, the king had Alan removed to Tewksbury, where he became abbot.

ALAN OF WALSINGHAM (d. 1364?), architect. A monk at Ely, England, in 1314, he was a skilled goldsmith who studied architecture, constructed St. Mary's chapel and other buildings, and repaired the cathedral by designing the great octagonal rotunda after its Norman tower had fallen. He became prior in 1341 and twice was named bishop of Ely, but each time the election was overruled by Avignon.

ALANUS, ST. (5th century). He was bishop of Quimper, Brittany. F. D. Oct. 26.

ALANUS, ST. (7th century). He was abbotfounder of the Benedictine monastery of Lavaur, Gascony. F. D. Nov. 25.

ALANUS AB INSULIS. *See* Alain de L'Isle.

ALANUS DE RUPE. *See* Roche, Bl. Alain de la.

ALARCÓN, PEDRO ANTONIO DE (1833–1891), novelist. Born in Guadox, Spain, on Mar. 10, he studied at Granada, and was editor of *El látigo*, an anti-royalist newspaper, when revolution broke out in 1854. His account of service with O'Donnell's army in Africa in 1859–60 was published in 1860; historical sketches, poems, plays, and much fiction followed. His best novels were *El sombrero de tres picos* (which inspired Manuel de Falla's ballet, *The Three-cornered Hat*), *El escándalo*, and *El niño de la bola*. He died on July 20.

ALARD. *See* Adalhard, St.

ALARICUS, BL. (d. 975). Son of Duke Burchard II of Swabia, he became a Benedictine monk at Einsiedeln, Switzerland, then a recluse on an island near Zurich. F. D. Sept. 29.

ALBA, JUAN DE (d. 1591). He was a Carthusian at Val-Christ, near Segovia, Spain, and a Hebrew and Oriental scholar, who published a biblical commentary. He died on Dec. 27.

ALBAN, ST. (d. 304?), martyr. A leading citizen of Verulam, Hertfordshire, he hid a Christian priest (possibly during the Diocletian persecution) and was converted during his guest's stay. He then exchanged clothes, sent the priest off safely, was himself captured and was beheaded at Verulam, probably the first English martyr. These and other details are found in Bede's *Ecclesiastical History*; some writers say he was slain at Caerleon, Wales. F. D. June 22.

ALBAN, ST. (d. 400?), martyr. A Greek from Naxos, he was exiled during an Arian persecution, preached in Germany, particularly in the region of Mainz, where a Benedictine abbey was later named after him, and was put to death there by Arians. F. D. June 21.

ALBANI, ALESSANDRO (1692–1779), cardinal. Brother of Annibale, and born in Urbino, Italy, on Oct. 19, he became a priest at the insistence of his cousin, Pope Clement XI, but followed a worldly life. Pope Innocent XII made him a cardinal in 1721, but he sided with the opponents of Pope Clement XIV. In 1761 he became librarian of the Vatican. His great collection of classical art at the Villa Albani was dispersed by the conquering Napoleon. Alessandro died on Dec. 11.

ALBANI, ANNIBALE (1682–1751), cardinal. Born in Urbino, Italy, on Aug. 15, cousin of Clement XI, he edited that pope's writings in 1724, issued a history of Urbino, was a patron of letters, and amassed a valuable collection of books, coins, and art objects which he left to the Vatican. He was made cardinal-bishop of Sabina in 1711 and died on Sept. 21.

ALBANI, GIAN GIROLAMO (1504–1591), cardinal. Born in Bergamo, Italy, on Jan. 3, he was a soldier in the Venetian army, became inquisitor at Bergamo, was made a cardinal by Pope Pius V and sent to Turkey on papal diplomatic missions. He was famed as a canonist and wrote on the Donation of Charlemagne and on the power of the pope. He died on April 25.

ALBANI, GIOVANNI FRANCESCO (1727–1803), cardinal. Born in Rome on Feb. 26, nephew of Pope Clement XI, he was at twenty-seven made cardinal-bishop of Ostia, Italy.

ALBANI, GIUSEPPE (1750–1834), cardinal. A nephew of Giovanni, he was born in Rome, was made a cardinal in 1801, lived in Austria from 1796 to 1814, and returned to hold administrative positions in the Vatican.

ALBAUD. *See* Aladius, St.

ALBERGATI, BL. NICCOLÒ (1375–1443), cardinal. Born in Bologna, he became a Carthusian in 1394, served as prior at several charterhouses, and was forced to become bishop of Bologna in 1417. He was a patron of learning (aiding Aeneas Sylvius) and a papal diplomat on six missions to France and Lombardy. He was made a cardinal in 1426, attended the Councils of Basle, Ferrara, and Florence as papal legate, was protector of the Augustinian order, confessor to Pope Eugenius IV, a patron of letters, and wrote theological treatises. He died at Siena. His cult was confirmed in 1744. F. D. May 9.

ALBERIC, ST. (d. 784). A scholarly Benedictine and friend of Alcuin, he succeeded his uncle, St. Gregory, as bishop of St. Martin, Utrecht, in 775, and was a successful missioner among the Teutons. He died on Aug. 21. F. D. Nov. 14.

ALBERIC, ST. (d. 1050?). He was a Camaldolese monk who lived as a hermit at Orci, Italy. F. D. Aug. 29.

ALBERIC (d. 1088), cardinal. A Benedictine at Monte Cassino, possibly from Trèves, France, he defended Pope Gregory VII, attacked Berengarius, wrote on theology, the

saints, and a treatise on letter writing, *De dictamine*. He was made a cardinal in 1057.

ALBERIC, ST. (d. 1109), founder. A hermit at Collan, he became prior in 1075 of a group of monks near Molesmes under Abbot Robert. Internal strike broke out, Robert left, and the monks beat and imprisoned their prior, who also moved away. After a promise of penitent reform, the monks reorganized, Robert and Alberic returned, but rebellion broke out again. Seeking an arrangement which would exist under a much stricter regimen, twenty-one monks moved to Cîteaux in 1098, and set up what was to be the Cistercian order. The English Stephen Harding became sub-prior and, when Robert returned to Molesmes, Alberic succeeded him as abbot. The new superior developed a rule close to that of the original Benedictine one, but with added austerity, introduced the white habit with black hood, and created a class of laybrothers to allow the monks more time for private devotions. Much of his planning was carried to fruition by his successor, St. Stephen. F. D. Jan. 26.

ALBERIC (1080–1147), cardinal. Born in Beauvais, France, he became a Benedictine at Cluny, was prior of St. Martin-des-Champs, and returned to Cluny in 1126 to reform the monastery at the direction of Peter the Venerable. From 1131 to 1138 he was abbot at Vezelay. He then was made cardinal-bishop of Ostia by Innocent II and was sent to England as papal legate. He ended the war between Stephen of Blois and David I of Scotland, consecrated Thibaut of Bec as archbishop of Canterbury, and returned to Rome. In 1140 he presided at a council of Eastern clerics which deposed Rodolph, patriarch of Antioch. He helped St. Bernard in 1147 to lessen some of the effects of the Albigensian heresy at Toulouse, then arranged with King Louis VII of France to support the second crusade. He died at Verdun.

ALBERICO DE ROSATE (d. 1354), jurist. Born in Rosate (Rosciate), Bergamo, Italy, of poor parents, he studied law at Padua, where he received his doctorate, and practiced in Bergamo. He acted as the bishop of Novara's envoy to Pope Benedict XII at Avignon in 1340 and wrote several commentaries on the codex and digests, *Opus statutorum* and *Dictionarium*.

ALBERO (12th century). Bishop of Liège, Belgium, he founded in 1124 the Premonstratensian abbey of Cornillon, three years after the order was founded by St. Norbert.

ALBERO DE MONTREUIL (1080–1152), archbishop. Born in Toul, Lorraine, he was ordained and served churches there and at Verdun and Metz. He was active as a reformer, brought about papal deposition of Bishop Adalbero IV and aided in the election of Stephen of Bar. In 1130 Albero was consecrated archbishop of Trèves, France, by Pope Innocent II, continued his reforms, with the help of SS. Bernard and Norbert, supported the pope against the antipope Anacletus II, and was made primate of Belgium and papal delegate in Germany. Long a supporter of Emperor Lothair II, he was active in arranging the succession by Conrad III. He died at Coblenz on Jan. 18.

ALBERONI, GIULIO (1664–1752), cardinal. Born in Firenzuola, Parma, Italy, on May 30, he was a farmer and bell ringer until fifteen, studied for the priesthood, and became a canon at Piacenza. The duke of Vendôme became his patron and used his diplomatic capabilities in France and Spain; he then served at Madrid for the duke of Parma and in 1714 arranged a marriage between the latter's daughter, Elisabetta Farnese, and the widowed Philip V. He then was made a duke, prime minister of Spain, and bishop of Malaga. In 1717 he was made a cardinal at the king's insistence. Alberoni introduced some reforms in government, but strengthened the monarchy, sought the crown of France for his master, approved the unwarranted and oath-breaking invasion of Sardinia and Sicily, and had a hand in the attempt to restore the Stuarts to the English throne. When faced with a European war in 1719, Philip dismissed his minister, who was imprisoned in Genoa by Pope Clement XI. Alberoni escaped, was cleared by Pope Innocent XIII in 1723, and later became legate at Ravenna and at Bologna. His last years were spent in retirement at the College of San Lazzaro at Piacenza, which he had founded, and where he died on June 26.

ALBERT I (1250?–1308), emperor, German king. Son of King Rudolf I, who vested him with the duchies of Austria and Styria in 1282, he was obliged to accept the election of Adolf of Nassau as king in 1292, but in 1298 defeated Adolf at Göllheim, near Worms, and was elected king soon after and crowned emperor on Aug. 24. He was not recognized as emperor until 1303 by Pope Boniface VIII, made his son Rudolph king of Bohemia in 1306, was unsuccessful in an attempt to annex Thuringia in 1307, and put down an uprising (1300-2) by the count palatine of the Rhine and Rhenish archbishops, who objected to his abolition of tolls on the Rhine. He was murdered by his nephew John at Windisch, Switzerland, on May 1, while on the way to Swabia to put down a revolt.

ALBERT II (1397–1439), emperor, German king. Son of Albert IV, duke of Austria, he was born on Aug. 10, inherited Austria on Albert's death in 1404, was elected German king and emperor in 1438 to succeed his father-in-law Emperor Sigismund, was crowned king of Hungary and Bohemia, though he never occupied the latter, and spent his short reign fighting against the Turks in Hungary. He died at Langendorf, Germany, on Oct. 27, while on a campaign against the Turks.

ALBERT I (1875–1934), king of Belgium. Born in Brussels, Belgium, on Apr. 8, son of Count Philip of Flanders and Princess Marie of Hohenzollern-Sigmaringen, he attended military school and became a member of the senate. On visits to the United States he became interested in industrial methods and technical colleges and introduced new methods in Belgium, established industrial training schools, and helped to develop the nation's shipping. He succeeded to the throne in 1909 (his older brother Baudouin had died in 1891), visited the Congo and recommended social and economic reforms (which others failed to carry out), and sought to keep Belgium neutral in the European war already shaping up. When he realized that this was impossible in the light of long-range German plans, he threw in his fortune with the Allies and in 1914 took the field as commander in chief. Although outnumbered, he withstood the Germans long enough at Liège to allow the French to build up forces along the Marne. He led the reconstruction of a country with a billion dollars in damages and saw the nation restored to an almost normal economy by 1922. He also worked to stabilize the currency in a 1926 crisis and to prevent civil strife between Flemings and Walloons over collaboration charges. Long an enthusiastic mountain climber, he died while scaling a height near Namur, Belgium, on Feb. 17.

ALBERT, ST. (7th century). A courtier, he became abbot-founder of Gambron sur-l'Authion, which followed the Rules of St. Benedict and of Columban. F. D. Dec. 29.

ALBERT, ST. (d. 1073). He was abbot-founder of the Benedictine monastery of Butrio, Italy. F. D. Sept. 5.

ALBERT, ST. (d. 1092), bishop. He was a hermit at Rho, and abbot of San Carpoforo, Italy, before he became bishop of Como. F. D. June 3.

ALBERT, BL. (d. 1095). After being wounded in battle, he became a Benedictine and founded the Cluniac abbey of Pontida, near Bergamo, Italy, his birthplace. He died on May 1. F. D. Sept. 5.

ALBERT, BL. (11th century). He was an associate of St. John Gualbert at Vallombrosa; his cult was approved in 1600. F. D. Aug. 1.

ALBERT, ST. (d. 1127), bishop. Born of a Norman family which settled in Apulia, Italy, he became bishop of Monte Corvino and served his diocese well until he became blind in his old age. His coadjutor Crescentius treated him with great cruelty in an attempt to succeed the old man, but Albert sustained the ill-treatment with great tolerance. F. D. Apr. 5.

ALBERT, ST. (1166?–1192), bishop. Born at Mt. César, Louvain, son of Duke Godfrey III of Brabant, he was made a canon of Liège at twelve but renounced his benefices and in 1187 became a knight under Count Baldwin V of Hainault. In 1191, though not a priest, he was chosen bishop of Liège, but the election was protested by Albert of Rethel to Emperor Henry VI, his nephew by marriage. Henry turned the see over to Lothaire, provost of Bonn, and, although Albert of Louvain was upheld by Pope Celestine III, he was barred from his see. On Nov. 24 he was murdered at Rheims, where he had been consecrated and where he was living in retirement, by a group of Henry's knights. His cult was confirmed in 1613. F. D. Nov. 21.

ALBERT, ST. (1149?–1214), patriarch. Born in Parma, Italy, he became a canon regular at Holy Cross Abbey in Mortara, Lombardy. About 1184 he was made bishop of Bobbio, but was immediately translated to Vercelli. He was made legate for northern Italy by Pope Gregory III, settled the dispute between Parma and Piacenza, acted as mediator between the pope and Frederick Barbarossa, and in 1205 was appointed patriarch and legate at Palestine. At his see in Akka (the Turks had recaptured Jerusalem) he devoted himself to maintaining peaceful relations between the various Christian factions and the natives. Between 1205 and 1210, at the request of St. Brocard, prior of the hermits on Mt. Carmel, he wrote a rule for them which became the basic rule of the Carmelites. He was murdered by a man he had deposed as head of the Holy Ghost Hospital in Akka. F. D. Sept. 25 (also, Apr. 8).

ALBERT, ST. (d. 1307?). Born in Trapani, Sicily, he joined the Carmelites there and after ordination was sent to their priory at Messina, where he was most successful in the conversion of Jews. His last years were spent in solitary prayer. His cult was approved in 1476. F. D. Aug. 9.

ALBERT OF AACHEN (12th century). A canon, at either Aix-la-Chapelle or Aix-en-Provence, he wrote an enthusiastic, emotional report of the first crusade (1095–1121) to arouse interest for the ideals which chivalry swore by; the work is often inaccurate as to time and place.

ALBERT THE BEAVER (1100?–1170), margrave. A vassal of Emperor Lothair II, he was invested with the East Mark in 1123, was given the North Mark in 1134 for his aid to Lothair in the latter's Italian campaign, and used it as a base for several campaigns against the Wends. He was made duke of Saxony by Conrad III in 1138 but was driven from his duchy by Henry the Lion, and in 1147 participated in the Wendish crusade. His conciliatory attitude toward the Wends led to his receiving Brandenburg from them. He became its first margrave in 1150, and founder of the house of Brandenburg, and was successful in Christianizing and civilizing northeast Germany during the rest of his life. He is also called Albert the Bear.

ALBERT OF BERGAMO, BL. (d. 1279). Born in Ogna, Italy, he was a farmer who became a Dominican tertiary, gave so much to the poor that his wife and relatives scolded him all too frequently, and eventually retired to a life of prayer in Cremona. His cult was approved in 1748. F. D. May 11.

ALBERT OF BRANDENBURG (1490–1545), cardinal. A humanistic supporter of renaissance thought, he was born on June 28 and was attached to the cathedral of Mainz, Germany, before he became archbishop of Magdeburg in 1513, of Mainz in 1514, and a cardinal in 1518. Publication of anti-Catholic books in the latter see, largely because of the bishop's friendship with Ulrich von Hutten, brought censure from Pope Leo X. Earlier (1517) the pope had given Albert the task of explaining the indulgence granted for aid in building St. Peter's in Rome; the bishop was careful in his instructions, but one of his emissaries, Tetzel, helped to undermine the faith throughout Europe by misrepresenting indulgences. Luther was Albert's loudest enemy; Peter Faber and other Jesuits, among his closest friends. At the Diet of Nuremburg he made effective suggestions for the spread of religious instruction. He also served as elector of the Holy Roman Empire. He died on Sept. 24.

ALBERT OF CASHEL, ST. (7th century), bishop. Patron of Cashel, he came to Ireland from Britain, then is said to have gone to Bavaria as a missioner and to have died at Ratisbon. Biographical details are unreliable. F. D. Jan. 8.

ALBERT OF CASTILE (1460?–1522), historian. A Dominican stationed at Venice, he wrote biographical accounts of the popes and of leaders of his order, edited its rules and studies by his predecessors, and compiled a biblical concordance.

ALBERT OF GENOA, ST. (d. 1239). Born in Genoa, Italy, he became a Cistercian laybrother at the nearby abbey of Sestri da Ponente, and later a hermit. F. D. July 8.

ALBERT THE GREAT, ST. (1206?–1280), bishop and Doctor of the Church. Eldest son of the count of Bollstädt, he was born in Lauingen, Swabia, studied at Padua, where he became a Dominican in 1223, and taught at Hildesheim, Freiburg im Breisgau, Ratisbon, Strassburg, and Cologne. His scholarly reputation brought him to the University of Paris for about five years; in 1248 he was regent of the new Dominican school in Cologne. St. Thomas Aquinas, whose genius he early recognized and proclaimed, was one of his students at Paris and Cologne. In 1254 he became provincial of Germany and in 1256 went to Rome, where he successfully defended the mendicant orders against William of St. Armour, whom Pope Alexander IV subsequently condemned. In 1259, with St. Thomas and Peter of Tarentasia, he drew up a new study curriculum for the Dominicans. In 1260, despite his opposition, he was named bishop of Ratisbon, but resigned after two years to resume teaching. He was prominent at the Council of Lyons (1274), despite the death of Thomas Aquinas, who had become his close intellectual associate, and in 1277, at Paris, he denounced Stephen Tempier and others who sought to condemn Thomas' writings. In 1278 he suffered a loss of mental powers which hastened his death at Cologne. He was a deep student of Arabic learning and a direct observer of natural phenomena and scientific fact. He wrote encyclopedically on logic, metaphysics, exegesis, astronomy, biology, entomology, mineralogy, and psychology. Particularly important were his treatises in philosophy and theology, to which studies he gave a form and method they still retain. By applying Aristotelian methods and principles to revealed doctrine he was the pioneer in the scholastic method which his pupil, Thomas Aquinas, developed. He was the leading commentator on Aristotle (after Averroës, against whose unorthodox interpretations he wrote two treatises), the adoption of whose principles for systematizing theology led to such bitter opposition. Although he was beatified in 1622 by Pope Gregory XV, he was not canonized until 1931, when Pius XI proclaimed him a Doctor of the Church, automatically proclaiming him a saint. He is the patron of natural scientists. F. D. Nov. 15.

ALBERT OF HELMSTÄDT (14th century), philosopher. Probably from Saxony, he studied at Paris, became procurator of the English "nation" in 1351, rector of the university in 1353, and represented the English nation in 1358 in the concordat with the Picard nation. He wrote tracts on logic and physics, among them *De caelo et mundo*, *Tractatus proportionum*, and *Quaestiones in libros de generatione et corruptione*. He is often known as Albert of Saxony (and confused with Albert of Ricmerstorp, who was also called Albert of Saxony), and also Albertus Parvus, Albertutius, and Albertilla. All writings attributed to Albert of Saxony are by Albert of Helmstädt.

ALBERT PARISI, BL. (d. 1245), abbot. Born in Bologna, Italy, he became a monk and later abbot at the Vallambrosan abbey there which later was named after him. F. D. May 20.

ALBERT OF RICMERSTORP (14th cen-

tury), bishop. Son of Bernard the Rich of Ricmerstorp, he was a master at Paris in 1362 and became its rector in 1363. In 1365, he was ambassador to Pope Urban V from Duke Rudolf of Austria, who appointed him first rector of the newly established university of Vienna, became a canon at Hildesheim, and in 1366 bishop of Halberstädt. He is often confused with Albert of Helmstädt, since both men were also known as Albert of Saxony.

ALBERT OF SASSOFERRATO, BL. (d. 1330). He was a Benedictine monk at Santa Croce di Tripozzi; he died on Aug. 7. His cult was confirmed in 1837. F. D. Oct. 25.

ALBERT OF STADE (13th century), historian. Abbot of the Benedictine monastery of Stade, near Hamburg, Germany, in 1232, he became a Franciscan in 1240, and began a chronicle of events from the creation to 1256 (perhaps through 1265), based in part on Bede and Ekkehard of Ayra and in part on contemporary testimony. He also wrote *Troilus*, a long Latin epic.

ALBERTA, ST. (d. 286?), martyr. She was put to death at Agen in southern Gaul during the Diocletian persecution. F. D. Mar. 11.

ALBERTI, LEANDRO (1479–1552?), historian. A native of Bologna, Italy, he became a Dominican in 1493. He wrote lives of the saints, of leaders of his order, and of famous Venetians, and a chronicle of the city of Bologna to 1273 and of Italian history from 1499 to 1552. His *Descrizione d'Italia* (1550) is valuable for its topographical and archaeological material, but the historical sources he used were inaccurate.

ALBERTI, LEONE BATTISTA (1404–1472), architect. Born on Feb. 18, he became a canon at Florence, Italy, in 1447 and later was abbot of San Sovino, Pisa. He completed the Pitti palace at Florence and built several churches, including that of St. Francis at Rimini. His *De re aedificatoria* was published in 1485.

ALBERTINI, NICCOLÒ (1250?–1321), cardinal. Born in Prato, Italy, he became a Dominican at Florence when sixteen, preached throughout Italy, became procurator general of his order and later its provincial in Rome. Boniface VIII made him bishop of Spoleto in 1299 and sent him as papal legate to reconcile Philip IV of France and Edward I of England, a task in which he succeeded. Pope Benedict XI made him cardinal-bishop of Ostia in 1303 and for ten years he served as dean of the Sacred College; he also was master of the Sacred Palace. He brought peace to several disturbed areas in Italy, but was unable to reconcile the Guelphs and Ghibellines and placed Florence under interdict. He crowned Henry VII of Luxembourg and Robert of Sicily, dispensed charities widely, and established a community of Dominican nuns at Avignon, where he died on Apr. 27.

ALBERTINUS, ST. (d. 1294). A Benedictine monk at the abbey of the Holy Cross, Fonte Avellana, Italy, he served as prior general and ended a quarrel between the bishop of Gubbio and his flock. His cult was confirmed by Pope Pius VI. F. D. Aug. 31.

ALBERTINUS, BRO. *See* Juge, Gabriel.

ALBERTONI, BL. LODOVICA DEGLI (1473-1533). Born in Rome and married to Jacopo de Cithara, to whom she bore three daughters, she became a Franciscan tertiary on his death in 1506, giving away her fortune and devoting herself to the care of the poor. She died on Jan. 31 and was beatified in 1671. F. D. Feb. 28.

ALBERTRANDI, JOHN BAPTIST (1731-1808), historian. Born in Warsaw, Poland, on Dec. 7, of Italian ancestry, he became a Jesuit in 1748 and taught literature for twelve years; he is missing from the records of the society after its suppression in 1769, but seems to have remained a cleric and become bishop of Zenopolis. He was in charge of King Stanislaus Royal Library, founded by Zaluski and later seized by Russia, and published a ten-volume annotated catalogue. He traveled through Europe and collected 110 folio volumes of copied manuscript material for a history of Poland, plus ninety more of personal summary. He published an abridged *Annals of Poland*, a history of Stephen Bori, a work on coins and medals, edited a periodical, and founded the Academy of Warsaw.

ALBERTUS, ST. (d. 711), martyr. Bishop of Città di Castello, Italy, he was put to death with his deacon Britius by the Arian Lombards.

ALBERTUS BOHEMUS (1180-1260). From 1205 to 1237 Albert von Behaim was a lawyer at the papal court; that year he went to Germany to aid in the formation of the league against Emperor Frederick II and to make the sentence of excommunication against him effective. Serving as papal legate until 1253, he excommunicated a number of bishops and nobles, but could not stem the emperor's power. Albertus was present at the Council of Lyons (1245) when Frederick was again excommunicated.

ALBERTUS MAGNUS. *See* Albert the Great, St.

ALBICUS, SIGISMUND (1347-1427), archbishop. Born in Mährisch-Neustadt, he took a degree in medicine at Prague and in civil and canon law at Padua (1404). He taught medicine at Prague for twenty years, was royal physician, and became archbishop there from 1409 to 1413. He was then given the priory at Wissehrad and called archbishop of Caesarea. Accused of favoring John Hus, he went to Hungary, where he died.

ALBINA, ST. (d. 250), martyr. She was slain at Caesarea, or at Gaeta, Italy, during the Decian persecution. F. D. Dec. 16.

ALBINI, CHARLES DOMINIQUE (1790-1839). Born in Menton, France, on Nov. 26, he studied in Cimiez, where he was ordained in 1815, later became rector of its seminary, and in 1824 became an Oblate at Aix. He labored in Marseilles and Italy, and died in Corsica on May 21.

ALBINIANA, BL. INES (1625-1696). Born of a poor family near Valencia, Spain, she became a Benedictine hermit at Benignam, as Sr. Josepha-Maria-of-St.-Agnes, and was so widely known for her devout life that her days were interrupted by great numbers who came to seek spiritual counsel. She is also known as Josepha of Benignam. She was beatified in 1888. F. D. Jan. 21.

ALBINUS, ST. (d. 390?). He succeeded St. Justus as bishop of Lyons, France, in 380. The name is also spelled Alban, Alvitus, and Aubin. F. D. Sept. 15.

ALBINUS, ST. (5th century), martyr. He is said to have been a priest from Greece or Albania who came to Milan with St. Ursus and continued on with him to the German missions at the request of St. Ambrose. Ursus was killed in the Val d'Aosta; Albinus went to Mainz, worked with Bishop St. Aureus, and was beheaded at Hunum, probably in a Vandal raid before 451. F. D. June 21.

ALBINUS (d. 732). Follower of Archbishop Theodore and Adrian of Canterbury, whom he succeeded as abbot, he was the chief inspirer and one of the major sources of Bede's *Ecclesiastical History of the English People*.

ALBINUS, ST. (8th century). An Anglo-Saxon named Witta, he became a Benedictine monk, went with St. Boniface to Germany, and in 741 became bishop of Buraburg. He was alive in 760. F. D. Oct. 26.

ALBINUS, ST. (11th century). He was bishop of Brixen, Austria. F. D. Feb. 5.

ALBINUS. *See* Aubin, St.; Conogan, St.

ALBISI, BARTOLOMMEO (14th century). An Italian Franciscan, he wrote a *Vita B. Gerardi* long attributed to Bartolommeo Riconico.

ALBIZZESCHI, BERNARDINO DEGLI. *See* Bernardino of Siena, St.

ALBORNOZ, GIL ALVAREZ CARILLO DE (1300?-1367), cardinal. Born in Cuenca, Castile, Spain, of royal lineage, he studied law at Toulouse, and became royal almoner, archdeacon of Calatrava, and in 1338 archbishop of Toledo and chancellor of Castile. He accompanied Alfonso XI in the 1340-44 wars against the Moors and saved the king's life on the battlefield; when Pedro the Cruel succeeded his father in 1350, the archbishop was forced to flee to Avignon. There, Pope Clement VI made him a cardinal-priest. In 1353 Innocent VI sent him to Italy to restore papal authority; as vicar general of the Papal States he led an army against Giovanni di Vico, prefect of Rome, and defeated him at Orvieto in 1354. In a mild peace treaty, Vico was named governor of Corneto. This displeased the pope, and the latter's trust in Cola di Rienzi upset the cardinal. After Rienzi, who was supposed to have aided Albornoz, took over Rome and introduced cruelty and excessive taxation, the mob rose and killed him in 1354. The cardinal brought peace to the city, moved northward with great success; only Oredelaffi of Romagna remained unconquered by 1357. Under Pope Urban V, Bernabò of Milan sought to seize Bologna and was bought off by the pope, whose chief interest was now a crusade against the Turks. Albornoz was the author of the Egidian *Constitutions* for the Papal States, which would become one of the first books printed in Italy (1473), and founded the College of St. Clement in 1365 at Bologna for Spanish students. He died near Viterbo, Italy, on Aug. 23 shortly after he received the pope on his way back to Rome. He is sometimes known as Aegidius de Albornoz.

ALBRECHT (d. 1229), bishop. In 1200 he led a military crusade against the Livonians, who had twice lapsed into paganism, founded the city of Riga, Latvia, and became its bishop, and reconverted the country by 1206. He established three other sees and founded the Order of Knights of the Sword (1202), who served as his standing army.

ALBRECHT II (d. 1232), archbishop. Son of Count Gunther III of Saxony, he studied at Hildesheim, Paris, and Bologna, and was appointed by Pope Innocent III to the cathedral chapter at Magdeburg, Germany. He succeeded Bishop Ludolph in 1206 as eighteenth archbishop there. He rebuilt his city after a totally destructive fire and brought the Dominicans and Franciscans to his see. His later years were taken up with the politics of the imperial succession. He shifted his support from the Swabian line to Otto IV, whom he saw crowned at Rome, then had to announce the latter's excommunication after the seizure of papal territories, and transferred his allegiance to Frederick II.

ALBRECHTSBERGER, JOHANN (1736–1809), musician. Born in Klosterneuberg, Austria, on Feb. 3, he was a choirboy there and studied music under the pastor of St. Martin's church. He then studied at the Benedictine abbey at Melk, became an organist and choirmaster, took further lessons in the organ from the court organist, Mann, at Vienna, and succeeded him from 1772 to 1792. He also served as choirmaster at the Carmelite church and at the cathedral of St. Stephen. He published

treatises on harmony and composition and is known as teacher of Ludwig von Beethoven and Johann Hummel, among others. He died in Vienna on Mar. 7.

ALBRIZZI, BL. MAGDALENA (d. 1465). A native of Como, Italy, she entered a convent in Brunate after the death of her parents, and by her holy example increased the size of the community, of which she became superior and which she affiliated with the Augustinians. She built a hospice at Como, took care of the sick, and received many supernatural gifts. Her cult was approved in 1907. F. D. May 15.

ALBUQUERQUE, AFONZO DE (1453–1515). He attended King Alfonso V of Portugal on his journey to Otranto, Italy, in 1480, and after other voyages went to India in 1506 with Tristão da Cunha. He established trading monopolies in the East and in 1509 succeeded Almeida as viceroy. He destroyed Calcutta in 1510 and seized Goa, Malacca (1511), and Aden (1513). Court intrigue led the crown to replace him by Lope Suarez, and he died soon after at Goa.

ALBURGA, ST. (d. 800?). Sister of King Egbert of Wessex, she founded and entered Wilton abbey, near Salisbury, after the death of her husband, Wulfstan. F. D. Dec. 25.

ALCEDO, ANTONIO DE (d. 1755), general. Born in Quito, Ecuador, he became in 1792 a brigadier general in the Spanish army and wrote a five volume history of the West Indies; its English translation by G. A. Thompson (1812) is filled with errors.

ALCIATI, ANDREA (1492–1550), jurist. Born in Alzano, Italy, son of the Milanese ambassador to Venice, he studied law at Pavia and Bologna, taught at Avignon, Bourges, Pavia, and other Italian universities. His works include a study of Greek terms in Roman law, six volumes on jurisprudence and two of epigrams.

ALCMUND, ST. (d. 781), bishop. He began his rule of the English see of Hexham in 767 as its seventh bishop. F. D. Sept. 7.

ALCMUND (d. 792?). He was of the family of King Alhred of Northumbria, who had been driven from his throne in 774. When Osred attempted to regain the crown and lost his life, his brother Alcmund may have fought by his side. The latter was venerated as a martyr on Mar. 19 at Lilleshall and Derby.

ALCOBER, BL. JOHN (1694–1748), martyr. Born in Gerona, Spain, he became a Dominican, was sent to China in 1728, was captured in 1746, and strangled in prison at Fu-tsheu. He was beatified in 1893. F. D. Dec. 30.

ALCOCK, JOHN (1430–1500), bishop. Born in Beverly, England, he studied at Cambridge, was associated with two London parishes, became master of the rolls in 1462, and was attached to St. Paul's in 1468. He became privy councilor in 1470, tutored King Edward V, and designed a chapel for Ely cathedral, in which he was buried. He founded Jesus College, Cambridge, endowed Peterhouse, and became bishop of Rochester. He wrote sermons on the gospel of St. Luke, a metrical reflection on the penitential Psalms, a translation, from the French, of *The Castle of Labor*, and *Spousage of a Virgin to Christ* (1486) and *The Hill of Perfection* (1491).

ALCUIN (735?–804), scholar. Born probably near York, England, he studied at the cathedral school there under Archbishop Egbert, succeeded Aelbert as its master in 767, taught for fifteen years, and built up its library and reputation. In 782, at the request of Charlemagne, he moved to France and became master of the palace school, chiefly at Aachen. He went to England on ecclesiastical or royal missions in 786 and 790, attended the synod at Frankfort in 794, and in 796 was made abbot of St. Martin's in Tours. There he developed another famous school and died on May 19. He usually signed himself deacon, but may have been ordained in his last years; he may also have been a Benedictine, but probably was not at the time Charlemagne made him abbot. His work in Northumbria is vividly described in his poem, *On the Saints of the Church of York*, including an outline of the course of studies and a defense of academic life. Other poems are epigrammatic, historical, or occasional. He had wide influence in Europe, drew great numbers of young men to his schools, and wrote texts, often in dialogue form and borrowing heavily from earlier scholars, on astronomy, dialectics, grammar, orthography, and rhetoric. He was primarily a teacher, a preserver and distributor of wisdom, and passed his enthusiasm and breadth of outlook on to such pupils as Arno, Adelhard, Fridugis, Theodulf, and Rhabanus Maurus. He probably had much to do with Charlemagne's successful plan for establishing primary schools for the common people in every city and village in his realm, and thus was responsible for a lasting interest in learning. He also wrote nine biblical commentaries and began a revision of the text of the Vulgate in the attempt to establish a more acceptable single text. Biographies of SS. Martin of Tours, Willibrord, and others, paraphrases of St. Augustine on the soul and on virtue, an explanation of confession, and several doctrinal works against the heresy of adoptionism were published. Both in England and in France he was interested in the Roman liturgy and was a major force in the liturgical reform sponsored by Charlemagne. He prepared a list of epistles for Sunday reading, and a sacramentary or missal (drawn from the Gregorian and other models) which became widely used and established much-needed uniformity. He also compiled *De psalmorum usu*, a breviary for laymen. Al-

though his cult was never confirmed, he is often listed as Blessed, with a feast on May 19.
ELEANOR S. DUCKETT, *Alcuin, Friend of Charlemagne* (New York, Macmillan, 1951).

ALDA, ST. (1249–1309). Born in Siena, she gave up her possessions at the death of her husband, devoted herself to work in a hospital for the sick poor, and was given exceptional supernatural gifts, some of which brought ridicule upon her. When she forgave her tormentors, they changed their scorn to respect. She is also known as Aldobrandesca and Aude. F. D. Apr. 26.

ALDATE, ST. (5th century). He is said to have roused the Britons of western England to resist the pagan invasions; in some accounts he is called bishop of Gloucester; all details are questionable. F. D. Feb. 4.

ALDEBRANDUS. *See* Hildebrand, St.

ALDEGUNDIS, ST. (630–684). Born in Hainault of SS. Walbert and Bertilia, she first lived in retirement near her sister Waldetrudis, who had founded a convent at Mons, and then at an even more private hermitage. She was founder-abbess of the Benedictine convent of Mauberge, Flanders, where she died. Her patience during the ravages of cancer was widely noted. F. D. Jan. 30.

ALDEMAR, ST. (d. 1080?). A native of Capua, Italy, he studied at Monte Cassino and founded several houses which he directed from his monastery at Bocchignano. F. D. Mar. 24.

ALDERICUS, ST. (790–841), bishop. Born in the Gatinais, he became a Benedictine at Ferrières, France, served the archbishop of Sens, became chancellor, and was raised to that see in 828. He is also known as Audry. F. D. Oct. 10.

ALDERICUS. *See* Aldric, St.

ALDETRUDIS, ST. (d. 696?). She succeeded her aunt, St. Aldegundis, as abbess of the Benedictine convent of Mauberge. F. D. Feb. 25.

ALDFRITH (d. 705), king. Son of King Oswin, he was educated in Ireland, and succeeded his brother Egfrid as king of Northumberland. He built up the area in the peace which followed war with the Picts, was known for his learning, and supported the Irish faction in the Church against his early friend, Bishop Wilfrid of York, who favored the Roman rule of administration.

ALDHELM, ST. (639?–709), bishop. Born in Wessex, England, he studied under the Irish scholar Mailduib at Malmesbury, where he became a Benedictine monk, and about 671 at Canterbury, under St. Adrian, to whom he owed his literary training. On Mailduib's death Aldhelm returned to direct the school at Malmesbury and became its abbot. He was adviser to his relative, King Ine of the West Saxons, taught the poor of the nation, composed hymns and ballads in English, now lost, and built a number of churches. He was made bishop of Sherborne in 705 and died at Doulting. Letters, a text on metrics (including 100 riddles), Latin poems, a prose treatise on virginity and a poetic version are all that remain of his writing. The last were written for a group of nuns at Barking under Abbess Hildelitha. The number of allusions indicate that Aldhelm had recourse to a library of considerable size; their continuing popularity indicate his influence. F. D. May 25.

ALDO, BL. (8th century). Count of Ostrevant, he succeeded his brother John as second abbot of the Benedictine monastery of Hasnon, Belgium. F. D. Mar. 31.

ALDOBRANDESCA. See Alda, St.

ALDOBRANDINI, PIETRO (1571–1621), cardinal. Nephew of Pope Clement VIII, he became archbishop of Ravenna, Italy, and was a noted patron of science.

ALDOBRANDINI, SILVESTRO (1499–1558). Born in Florence, Italy, on Nov. 23, he became a teacher of law at Pisa, led a revolt in Florence against the Medici, defended the city against Charles V and was condemned to death on its capture, and was banished in 1530. He became papal vice-legate and vice-regent at Bologna in 1538, lived briefly at Ferrara, and served Pope Paul III in Rome as fiscal adviser. His son Ippolito became Pope Clement VIII. He died in Rome on Jan. 6.

ALDRED (d. 1069), archbishop. He became abbot of Tavistock, England, about 1027, bishop of Worcester in 1044, made a pilgrimage to Jerusalem in 1058, and was elected archbishop of York in 1060. He served Edward the Confessor on diplomatic missions, crowned William the Conqueror, helped to initiate reforms, and was noted for his extensive charities. He died on Sept. 11.

ALDRIC, ST. (800?–856), bishop. A noble who served in the court of Charlemagne and was ordained after study at Metz, he became chaplain to Louis the Pious. In 832 he became bishop of Le Mans. Though he ran into difficulty over his claim to the monastery of St. Calais, supported by forged documents of unknown authorship, and was removed from his see, he was later restored to office. He established many religious foundations and was honored for his work with the poor. F. D. Jan. 7.

ALDROVANI, ULISSI (1522–1602), naturalist. Born in Bologna, Italy, on Sept. 11, he studied there, took his medical degree at Padua, and became professor of natural history at Bologna. On his recommendation the city set up a botanical garden and made him director in 1568, and also inspector of pharmacies. He had Popes Gregory XIII and Sixtus V as patrons, spent his fortune on collections which later were the foundation of the Bologna museum, published fourteen volumes of studies,

and was praised by Cuvier and Buffon. He died in Bologna on Nov. 10.

ALEA, LEONARD (d. 1812). Of a family of French bankers, he wrote against atheism (1801) in refutation of Sylvien Maréchal (who acknowledged his opponent's quiet logic) and against divorce (1802).

ALEANDER, GIROLAMO (1480–1542), cardinal. Born in Motta, Italy, on Feb. 13, he studied medicine, theology, and languages, taught at the University of Paris from 1508, entered the service of Bishop Eberhard of Liège in 1514, became librarian of the Vatican in 1519, and in 1520 was papal legate to Germany, charged with the task of stemming the advance of Lutheranism. He may have been the author of the edict of Charles V against Luther, the writing of which he at least directed, and was appointed bishop of Brindisi in 1524. He failed to prevent the Peace of Nuremberg in 1532. He was named by Pope Paul III as a member of the reform commission directed by the Contarini, was made a cardinal in 1538, and returned to Germany. He wrote historically significant reports, letters, and *De concilio habendo*. He died in Rome on Jan. 31.

ALEAUME. See Adelelmus, St.

ALEGAMBE, PHILIPPE (1592–1652). Born in Brussels, Belgium, on Jan. 22, he served the duke of Osuna in Spain and Sicily, and in 1613 became a Jesuit, studied at Rome, and taught in Austria. He continued Fr. Ribadeneira's catalogue of Jesuit writers from 1608 to 1642. He died in Rome on Sept. 6.

ALEGRE, FRANCESCO XAVIER (1729–1788). Born in Vera Cruz, Mexico, on Nov. 12, he became a Jesuit in 1747 and taught classics at Havana, Mérida, and Bologna, Italy. He published Spanish translations of Homer, Horace, and Boileau and wrote a valuable *History of the Society of Jesus in New Spain* (1841). He died in Bologna on Aug. 16.

ALEMANY, JOSÉ SADOC (1814–1888), archbishop. Born in Vich, Catalonia, Spain, on July 13, he joined the Dominicans, studied in Spain and Italy, and was ordained in Viterbo in 1837. He was sent as a missionary to the United States in 1841, served in Kentucky and Ohio, was elected provincial of the American Dominicans in 1848, and in 1850 was appointed bishop of Monterey, California. He was transferred to San Francisco as the newly created see's first archbishop in 1853, successfully negotiated the Church's claim to a fund which the Mexican government had confiscated, and in 1884 resigned and retired to Spain. He died in Valencia on Apr. 14.

ALENA, ST. (d. 640?), martyr. Born near Brussels, she secretly became a Christian and was slain when she slipped from the home of her pagan parents to attend mass. F. D. June 24.

ALENCASTRE, STEPHEN PETER (1876–

1940), bishop. Born in Porto Santo, Madeira, on Nov. 3, he went to Hawaii in 1883, studied at St. Louis College, Honolulu, and the Louvain, joined the Congregation of the Fathers of the Sacred Heart, and was ordained in Honolulu in 1902. He engaged in missionary work, became rector of Sacred Heart Church in Honolulu in 1913, and was consecrated titular bishop of Arabissus and vicar apostolic of the Hawaiian Islands in 1924, a position he occupied until his death on Nov. 9.

ALENIO, GIULIO (1582–1644). Born in Brescia, Italy, he became a Jesuit in 1600 and served as a missioner in China from 1610 until his death at Fou-Tcheou. A mathematician, he published an account of the 1612 eclipse, observed at Macao; he also wrote a number of apologetical works in Chinese.

ALER, PAUL (1656–1727). Born in St. Veit, Luxembourg, he became a Jesuit, taught at Cologne and Trèves, and after 1703 was regent of gymnasia in several cities. He wrote philosophy, philology, eleven tragedies in Latin or German, and the popular *Gradus ad Parnassum* (1702).

ALERDING, HERMAN JOSEPH (1845–1924), bishop. Born in Westphalia, Germany, on Apr. 13, he studied at St. Gabriel seminary, Vincennes, Indiana, St. Thomas, Kentucky, and St. Meinrad's abbey, Indiana, where he was ordained in 1868. He did parish work in the Vincennes diocese the next three decades, was consecrated bishop of Fort Wayne, Indiana, in 1900, and died there on Dec. 6. He wrote histories of the Church in the dioceses of Vincennes and Fort Wayne, and in Maryland.

ALERIC (d. 1102), antipope. Elected by the imperialists to succeed antipope Theodoric in 1102, he quickly submitted to Pope Paschal II, was remanded to a monastery, and died soon after.

ALESSI, GALEAZZO (1512?–1572), architect. He studied architecture under Giambattista Caporali of Perugia, Italy, where he was born, built palaces, and completed the fortress. At Genoa he repaired the cathedral, built the church of the Madonna, and designed the elaborate harbor; at Milan, the church of San Vittore, the palace of Marino, and other structures. He also completed works at Ferrara, Bologna, Naples, and in France, Germany, Flanders, and Spain. His design for the monastery and church of the Escorial was selected as the best submitted, but Alessi died before he could build it.

ALETH, BL. (d. 1105). She was the wife of Tecelin and mother of St. Bernard of Clairvaux. F. D. Apr. 4.

ALEXANDER I, ST. (d. 115), pope. He is said to have been a Roman who became pope in 105 and ruled during the reign of Emperor Trajan. He introduced the practice of blessing homes with holy water and salt and may have made additions to the liturgy. Traditionally, he is said to have been decapitated on the Via Nomentana, Rome, and his remains transferred to Freising, Bavaria, in 834. F. D. May 3.

ALEXANDER II (d. 1073), pope. Anselm was born in Baggio, near Milan, Italy. With Hildebrand, he had been inspired by the Cluniac reform and was loud in his condemnation of simony and clerical disregard for celibacy. His opponent, Archbishop Guido, had him sent to the court of Emperor Henry III, but that led to equally successful preaching in Germany. He was appointed bishop of Lucca, Italy, in 1057 and was papal legate to Milan in that year and in 1059. As a result of the new method of electing a pope directly by the college of cardinals, Alexander was chosen on Oct. 1, 1061, and enthroned on Sept. 30. Cadalus, bishop of Parma, who was strongly opposed to reforming contemporary vices, was elected pope by a dissident faction headed by Roman nobles at an assembly called by Empress Agnes at Basle on Oct. 28; he had the backing of Roman nobles, who objected to losing the privilege of voting, and of a number of Lombard bishops. Cadalus took the name Honorius II. Alexander was supported politically (there was no question of the legality of his election) by Tuscany and the Normans in Italy and in 1064 by Germany, after Anno of Cologne displaced Agnes as regent. Alexander removed a number of bishops, ordered others to do public penance, prevented the young emperor, Henry IV, from divorcing Bertha of Turin, and bettered Church conditions in many areas. Politically, he approved the invasion of Sicily by Robert and of England by William the Norman. He died on Apr. 21, a year after the excommunicated antipope.

ALEXANDER III (d. 1181), pope. Orlando Bandinelli was born in Siena, Italy, was professor of canon law at Bologna, and published a commentary on the *Decretum* of Gratian. He was called to Rome in 1150, where Pope Eugene III made him a cardinal and chancellor; he also was an adviser to Pope Adrian IV. At the Diet of Besançon (1057), Cardinal Bandinelli told Emperor Frederick Barbarossa that his crown was a papal favor (but not a feudal grant), and almost lost his life under the ax of Otto of Wittelsbach. Otto joined with Rainald von Dassel, whose claim to the archbishopric of Cologne was not papally approved, in trying to undermine Bandinelli. They obtained three votes at the papal election on Sept. 7, 1159; twenty-two cardinals voted for Bandinelli in the hope of freeing the papacy from German pressure. Alexander was consecrated on Sept. 20 at the Volscian town of Nympha, after a mob hired by Otto broke up the conclave. The imperialist faction of three then chose as antipope one of their number, Cardinal Octavien of Monticello, who took the name Victor IV. Frederick further supported his choice at a directed trial at Pavia in 1160. The schism lasted until 1177, when Frederick surrendered in Venice (the expression, with the pope's foot on his neck, which is used in legend, is figurative, not literal). Victor IV died in 1164 and was succeeded by Guy of Cremona, who held the title Paschal II until 1168; and by John, abbot of Sturmi, who claimed the title Callistus III, until 1178. A fourth antipope, Landus of Sezze, followed in 1179–80. Alexander III, driven into France from 1162 to 1165 by the forces of Otto, had to call on the greatest diplomacy in the quarrel between Henry II of England and Thomas à Becket, handling the strong-willed English cardinal, whom he canonized in 1173, with some success and receiving the penance of Henry after Thomas' murder. He supported educational strides which led to the establishment of the great universities, and helped to banish slavery. In 1179 the pope called the third Lateran (eleventh Ecumenical) Council, one of the decisions of which was that henceforth the pope was to be elected by a direct two-thirds vote of the cardinals and not by the bishops and people of Rome. He died at Città Castellana on Aug. 30.

ALEXANDER IV (d. 1261), pope. Rinaldo, count of Segni, was born in Anagni, Italy, was made a cardinal-deacon in 1227 by his uncle, Gregory IV, and in 1231 cardinal-bishop of Ostia. He was an old man at the death of Innocent IV, was elected pope on Dec. 12, 1254, and consecrated on Dec. 20. Personally a religious man, with great regard for the Franciscans (he defended them in quarrels which arose at Paris, and canonized St. Clare), he was a poor political figure. One disaster followed another when he allowed his advisers to sway him to abandon Conradin, son of Emperor Frederick II. The power of the remaining heir, Manfred, rose; he invaded Italy and, in spite of excommunication, had himself crowned king at Palermo and took over the leadership of the Ghibelline faction in northern Italy. Sicily had already been handed over by treaty to Edmund of Lancaster, son of King Henry III of England, and its loss alienated the English. There were threats of war throughout Europe and the great danger of a Tatar invasion from the East. Without power of any value, even in the city of Rome, he died on May 25.

ALEXANDER V (1339?–1410), antipope. Pietro Filargo was a homeless beggar on Crete who was raised by the Capuchins and became a Franciscan, later studying at Paris and Oxford. He tutored the sons of Giovanni Galeazzo of Milan, who had him made bishop of Piacenza, of Vicenza, of Navoya, and, in 1402, archbishop of Milan. Innocent VII made him a cardinal in 1405, as well as papal legate to Lombardy. Filargo turned against Pope Gregory XII, who stripped him of his cardinalate and removed him as archbishop. Filargo and the cardinals supporting him met in an illegal council at Pisa, at which he presided and declared his opposition to be heretics. He was hailed as pope by the rebellious cardinals on June 26, 1409, and died ten months later on May 3.

ALEXANDER VI (1431–1503), pope. Rodrigo Borgia was born in Xantiva, near Valencia, Spain, on Jan. 1, son of Jofre and Isabella Borja Lançol, and nephew of Cardinal Alfonso Borja, whose name he adopted and whose official family he joined; the cardinal became Pope Callistus III. Rodrigo received several rich benefices, studied law briefly at Bologna, became cardinal-deacon in 1456, vice-chancellor in 1457, cardinal-bishop of Albano in 1471 and of Porto in 1476. He held an astonishing number of other offices, became a very wealthy man, fond of card playing, and notorious as a rake. Ordination in 1468 did not change his ways; he had four children (Juan, Cesare, Lucrezia, and Jofre) by Vanozza Catanei between 1474 and 1482 and others (Girolama, Pedro Luis, and another Juan) by other affairs. He was elected pope on Aug. 11, 1492, by the barest majority (his own vote tipped the scales in his favor); the charge was that he had also paved the way by promises to those who, like Cardinal Ascanio Sforza, expected and received high office as a result of their support. Alexander was hailed with delight by the Romans, was consecrated on Aug. 26, and prepared to restore order to the crime-infested capital. He appointed four judges to direct judicial needs, then turned to the beautification of the physical city. Palaces, national churches (German, French, Spanish), fortifications, the approach to St. Peter's, and other building changed the face of the city. Culturally, he rebuilt the Roman University, encouraged musical and dramatic composition, was protective toward the Jews (which made Spain hostile toward him), declared a successful holy year in 1500, sent missionaries to the New World, and ruled with a strong administrative sense. In other directions, Alexander failed. When Charles marched on Rome and demanded he be crowned king of Naples, Alexander's cardinals deserted him; others took sides with Cardinal della Rovere; Virginio Orsini (his commander in chief) defected; and the pope faced a foreign army alone. Alexander refused to yield, in spite of the overwhelming foreign force outside Rome, and Charles left the capital to take Naples in 1495 and crown himself king. Eventually, the French and their leader withdrew from the peninsula, and the pope was temporarily victorious. Alexander then made the mistake of trying to protect himself against hostile nobles and rebellious cardinals by placing his children and other relatives in positions of power and of trust (though he was optimistic in relying on such flagrant nepotism). Through his son Duke Juan he crushed the Orsino and imposed heavy reparations; he used Gonsalvo de Cordova's Spanish army to bring della Rovere into line. When Juan was slain and thrown in the Tiber on June 16, 1497, the pope felt that reform of his life and outlook was necessary, established a commission which prepared decrees preshadowing those of the Council of Trent, was properly contrite, but all too often lost his sense of determination. Cesare, the pope's oldest son, was dispensed from his cardinalate, became a secular prince, and between 1498 and 1503 conquered most of northern Italy and routed and slew the Orsini leaders and forces. Before he could enjoy the political security of this success, Alexander caught a fever at an outdoor party in Rome and died within two weeks, on Aug. 18. One of the major crises of his reign was his struggle with Savonarola, who strongly attacked Alexander as a major evil of the times, particularly his simony. The pope tolerated the attacks briefly, sought to have the reformer's energies pointed in other directions, and finally ordered him put to death.

ALEXANDER VII (1599–1667), pope. Fabio Chigi was born in Siena, Italy, on Feb. 13, grandnephew of Pope Paul V, was tutored at home, received his doctorate at Siena, and served the papacy as vice-legate at Ferrara and as inquisitor on Malta. In 1639 he was nuncio to Cologne; Pope Innocent X made him envoy extraordinary in 1644, and he helped to write the Peace of Westphalia after the Thirty Years' War. He was papal secretary of state in 1651 and a cardinal in 1652. He was elected pope on Apr. 7, 1655, consecrated on Apr. 18, and began a career which seemed to sound the death knell of nepotism. Within a year, however, advisers assured him that the strength of the papal court would fade without family support, and he brought his brother and nephews to Rome. They soon directed political policy; other advisers also proved unfortunate; and the pope devoted himself more and more to literature. His relations with Louis XIV of France were made difficult by the machinations of Cardinal Mazarin, the French prime minister. As a theologian, Alexander condemned a number of contemporary errors and was extremely firm toward the powerful Jansenists. He aided Venice against the Turks and secured the return of the Jesuits to that city; confirmed Queen Christina of Sweden, who came to Rome after her abdication; founded the Sapienza in Rome and gave a library to that university; made great additions to the Vatican Library; and beautified Rome by sweeping changes in civic architec-

ture and landscaping. He died on May 22 in Rome.

ALEXANDER VIII (1610–1691), pope. Pietro Ottoboni, son of Marco, the chancellor of Venice, was born in that city on April 22, studied at Padua, and took his doctorate in law in 1627. During the pontificate of Urban VIII he served as governor of Terni, Rieti, and Spoleto, and as auditor of the rota. Pope Innocent X made him a cardinal in 1652 and bishop of Brescia in 1654. He was elected pope on Oct. 6, 1689, and consecrated on Oct. 16; he died in Rome sixteen months later on Feb. 1. Although Louis XIV of France restored Avignon to him, the pope condemned as invalid the Declaration of Gallican Liberties drawn up in 1682. He spent much for the books and manuscripts of Queen Christina of Sweden, which he brought to the Vatican Library, but he also helped to subsidize the wars of his native city against the Turks. While with one hand he gave widely to the tax-impoverished Italians, he revived the custom of sinecure offices which had been avoided by his predecessor, showered wealth upon his relatives, and made twenty-two-year-old Pietro Ottoboni a cardinal and his secretary of state.

ALEXANDER (d. 1506), king of Poland. Son of Casimir IV and younger brother of John Albert, he became grand duke of Lithuania in 1492 and king of Poland in 1501. He fought a disastrous war with Ivan the Great of Russia and agreed in 1505 to the Constitution of Radom, which made the diet of nobles the chief legislative body.

ALEXANDER I (1078?–1124), king of Scotland. The fourth son of Malcolm Canmore, he succeeded his brother Edgar as king of Scotland in 1107. He fought against the northern clans, who objected to the introduction of English customs, but also sought to free the Church in Scotland from subservience to Canterbury and York. He had been educated in England, worked for peace between the two nations, endowed the abbeys of Scone and Incholm, and was notably charitable toward Church institutions. He died on Apr. 27.

ALEXANDER II (1198–1249), king of Scotland. Son of William the Lion, he succeeded his father as king of Scotland in 1214 and joined the English barons who sought to gain respect and consideration from King John, was excommunicated with them when the pope was led to support the English monarch, and waited for the ban to be lifted, as it was. He worked so amicably with Henry III that the warfare between the two countries came to an end, and won for himself the name "the Peaceful." He married Henry's sister Joan in 1221, but on her death in 1238 married a French noblewoman. Henry then invaded Scotland to force Alexander to swear fealty, but peace was arranged before the countries resorted to arms. Alexander died of fever on the island of Kerrera.

ALEXANDER III (1241-1285), king of Scotland. Son of Alexander II of Scotland, he succeeded his father as king in 1249, married Margaret, daughter of Henry III of England, in 1251, but prevented the English king from making him his vassal. In 1263 he successfully thwarted an invasion by Haakon of Norway, added the Hebrides and Isle of Man to areas allied with him, and soon arranged peace with Norway by marrying his daughter Margaret to King Eric of Norway. The balance of his reign was marked by peace and notable examples of justice and generosity.

ALEXANDER (1st century). He was son of Simon of Cyrene who helped Jesus to carry the cross (Mark 15:21). Some identify him with the Alexander (Acts 19:33-34) who tried to defend St. Paul at Ephesus.

ALEXANDER, ST. (d. 113?), martyr. He and SS. Eventius and Theodulus were tortured and put to death, possibly during the persecution of Hadrian; they were buried on the Via Nomentana, Rome. For centuries Alexander was erroneously identified with Pope Alexander I. F. D. May 3.

ALEXANDER, ST. (d. 150?), martyr. He and SS. Martial and Vitalis were beheaded at Rome during Antoninus' persecution when they refused to sacrifice to the pagan gods. Legend has incorrectly made them and four others the sons of St. Felicitas and has blossomed into the story of the Seven Brothers. F. D. July 10.

ALEXANDER, ST. (d. 172?), martyr. He was slain for his faith, with St. Caius, at Apamea, Phrygia, during the reign of Marcus Aurelius. F. D. Mar. 10.

ALEXANDER, ST. (d. 177), martyr. A native of Greece, he was associated with St. Epipodius before he was tortured and put to death at Lyons with thirty-four other early Christians. F. D. Apr. 24.

ALEXANDER, ST. (2nd century), martyr. Bishop of a settlement near Rome, he was captured twenty miles from the capital and put to death. Pope St. Damasus enshrined his relics in the city. F. D. Sept. 21.

ALEXANDER, ST. (d. 250), bishop and martyr. Probably a man of good birth and education who gave over his wealth to the poor and became a charcoal burner, he was made bishop of Comana on the recommendation of St. Gregory Thaumaturgus. He was burned at the stake for his faith. F. D. Aug. 11.

ALEXANDER, ST. (d. 250?), bishop and martyr. Born in Fermo, he became bishop there before he was put to death during the persecution of Decius. F. D. Jan. 11.

ALEXANDER, ST. (d. 250), martyr. See Epimachus, St.

ALEXANDER, ST. (d. 251), bishop and

martyr. A bishop in Cappadocia, he was imprisoned for some time during the persecution of Severus. When released, he made a pilgrimage to Jerusalem, where he was chosen coadjutor bishop in 212, the first recorded example of coadjutorship and of translation of see. He was censured by Bishop Demetrius of Alexandria for encouraging Origen, with whom he had gone to school and whom he received as an exile. Alexander founded a great library in Jerusalem, of which Eusebius was to make use. He was captured during the reign of Decius and died in prison in Caesarea. F. D. Mar. 18.

ALEXANDER, ST. (d. 260), martyr. He and SS. Malchus and Priscus were slain by wild beasts in an arena at Caesarea in Palestine during the persecution of Valerian. F. D. Mar. 28.

ALEXANDER, ST. (d. 260), martyr. He was burned to death at Alexandria, Egypt, during the reign of Decius. F. D. May 10 (also, Dec. 12).

ALEXANDER, ST. (d. 284?), martyr. See Thalelaeus, St.

ALEXANDER, ST. (d. 287?), martyr. See Maurice, St.

ALEXANDER, ST. (d. 300?), martyr. He, SS. Attius and Leontius, and six others were put to death at Perge, Pamphylia, for destroying a pagan shrine. F. D. Aug. 1.

ALEXANDER, ST. (d. 303), martyr. See Agapius, St.; also, Mark, St.

ALEXANDER, ST. (d. 304), martyr. He and SS. Diocletius and Florentius were stoned to death at Osimo, Italy, during the persecution of Diocletian. F. D. May 11.

ALEXANDER, ST. (d. 290?), martyr. See Victor, St.

ALEXANDER, ST. (d. 313), martyr. A soldier, he was tortured and burned to death at Constantinople, during the persecution of Maximian, with St. Antonina, whom he had tried to save by exchanging robes. F. D. May 3.

ALEXANDER, ST. (250?-328), bishop. Trying at first to win Arius back to orthodoxy by gentle persuasion, he was soon forced to summon him for excommunication. The sentence was upheld by the Council of Alexandria, from which Alexander, bishop of Alexandria, Egypt, wrote explanatory letters to Bishop Alexander of Constantinople and the hierarchy of the Church. The Council of Nicaea (325), which Alexander and his deacon St. Athanasius attended, further defined the errors of Arianism. F. D. Feb. 26.

ALEXANDER, ST. (244?-340), patriarch. Elected patriarch of Constantinople when he was seventy-three, he participated in the first Council of Nicaea (325), where he spoke against Arianism. He fought actively against Arius and his heresy for twenty-three years. F. D. Aug. 28.

ALEXANDER, ST. (d. 361), martyr. He was

put to death at Corinth during the persecution of Julian the Apostate. F. D. Nov. 24.

ALEXANDER, ST. (d. 397), martyr. *See* Sisinius, St.

ALEXANDER, ST. (4th century), martyr. He died at Salonica during the persecution of Maximian Herculius. F. D. Nov. 9.

ALEXANDER, ST. (590). Bishop of Fiesole, Italy, he defended the Church in Tuscany against heavy opposition from Lombard leaders and was ambushed and drowned near Bologna. F. D. June 6.

ALEXANDER, ST. (8th century). He was bishop of Verona, Italy. F. D. June 4.

ALEXANDER, ST., martyr. *See* Amantius, St.

ALEXANDER AKIMETES, ST. (d. 430?). Born in Asia, he studied and was converted at Constantinople and became a hermit in Syria. He then became a successful missioner in Mesopotamia and founded two monasteries near the Bosphorus, at one of which he introduced the continuous singing of the divine office by relays of his 400 monks. F. D. Jan. 15 (sometimes, Feb. 23, July 3).

ALEXANDER OF ANTIOCH (5th century). As thirty-eighth bishop of Antioch (413–21) he brought an end to the Meletian heresy there, restored to honor the name of St. John Chrysostom, and was praised by Theodoret.

ALEXANDER OF BASILINOPOLIS (5th century). He was appointed bishop in Bithynia by St. John Chrysostom and at the latter's fall retired to Ptolemais, Egypt, and suffered attacks by Theophilus of Antioch.

ALEXANDER OF BYZANTIUM (4th century). He was seventy-three when appointed bishop of Byzantium in 313 or 317 and ruled that city for twenty-three years during the Arian heresy, under frequent attack and threat of exile. He supported Alexander of Alexandria at the Council of Nicaea and died soon after Arius himself.

ALEXANDER OF HALES (1175?–1245), theologian. Born in Hailes, Gloucestershire, England, he was educated there and at Oxford and Paris. He took degrees in philosophy and in theology at Paris, taught there as early as 1210, and became a Franciscan in 1231. His *Summa universae theologiae*, begun that year, was the first attempt at a systematic presentation of Catholic dogma in relation to Aristotle's metaphysical and physical works. In manner his method of argumentation followed that of Peter Abelard and prepared for that of St. Thomas Aquinas. The matter considers God and the Trinity in Part 1 (in which Alexander relied on SS. Augustine, Anselm, and Hugh of St. Victor, as well as Aristotle); men and sin in Part 2; Christ and redemption in Part 3; and the sacraments in Part 4. Alexander died at Paris before the work was finished; the sections, *Summa virtutum* was written by another Franciscan, William of Melitona, and the *Commentaries* on Aristotle's *Metaphysics* and *De anima* by Alexander of Bonini.

ALEXANDER OF HIERAPOLIS (5th century). Bishop of Hierapolis (Euphratensis), he opposed St. Cyril at the Council of Ephesus in 431, supported Nestorius, and died in exile in the Egyptian mines.

ALEXANDER OF LUGO, BL. (d. 1645). He was a Spanish Dominican who was put to death by the Turks. F. D. Feb. 10.

ALEXANDER NATALIS. *See* Natalis, Alexandre.

ALEXANDER OF NECKHAM (1157–1217), a scholar. Born in Hertfordshire, England, he studied at St. Albans and at Petit Pons, Paris, taught there in 1180–86, and returned to England to teach at Dunstable and St. Albans. He then became an Augustinian and in 1213 was elected abbot of Cirencester. He wrote theological treatises, sermons, commentaries on scripture and Aristotle, and a grammar. Only *De naturis rerum* and *De laudibus divinae sapientiae* (a poem) have been printed. He died in Kempsey, Worcestershire.

ALEXANDRA, ST. (d. 300), martyr. She and SS. Claudia, Derphuta, Euphemia, Euphrasia, Juliana, Matrona, and Theodosia were burned at Amisus during the persecution of Diocletian. F. D. Mar. 20.

ALEXANDRE, JACQUES (1653–1734). Born in Orléans, France, on Jan. 24, he became a Benedictine monk at Vendôme in 1673, was stationed at the monastery of Bonne Nouvelle, became sub-prior, and died there on June 23. He published a theoretical work on the cause of tides and wrote on the construction of clocks and several papers on mathematics.

ALEXANDRE NOEL. *See* Natalis, Alexandre.

ALEXANDRE DE VILLEDIEU (13th century). A canon of Avranches, France, he wrote a Latin grammar which had wide usage.

ALEXIS, ST. (5th century?). Legend calls him the son of a wealthy Roman senator, Euphemian, who left home on his wedding day, went to Syria, and lived for seventeen years as a hermit. He is then said to have returned to Rome and to have worked, in disguise, as a servant in his father's house for another seventeen years. Factually, he was a holy citizen of Edessa, poor and well loved. F. D. July 17.

ALEYDIS, ST. (d. 1250). Born in Schaerbeek, near Brussels, Belgium, she was placed in a Cistercian convent at seven, joined the order, but later contracted leprosy, became blind and paralyzed, and was segregated from the community. She was particularly devoted to the Eucharist, offered her sufferings for the souls in purgatory, and had several supernatural gifts. Her cult was approved by Pope Pius X in 1907. F. D. June 15.

ALFELD, AUGUSTIN VON (d. 1532?), theologian. Born near Hildesheim, Prussia, he became a Franciscan and defended the monastic pattern of life at the 1521 public disputation at Weimar, with Langer and Mechler as opponents. In 1523 he was in charge of the monastery at Halle and in 1529 provincial in Saxony. He wrote much on scripture and on the contemporary religious quarrels.

ALFERIUS, ST. (930–1050). Born at Salerno, Italy, he was sent by Duke Gisulf as ambassador to France, fell ill, and on his recovery entered the monastery of Cluny. Recalled by the duke to reform local monasteries, he worked at this task, then retired as a recluse, later accepting disciples and establishing the Benedictine abbey of La Cava. From this mother house thirty foundations were developed within a few years after his death. F. D. Apr. 12.

ALFIELD, BL. THOMAS (d. 1585), martyr. Born at Gloucester, England, and educated at Eton and Cambridge, he became a convert and was ordained at Douai in 1581. On the English mission he was associated with Edmund Campion, was arrested in 1582, tortured, and recanted. After his release he went to Rheims and returned to the Church. Back in England, he was arrested for distributing Cardinal Allen's *True and Modest Defence*, tortured, and hanged at Tyburn. He was beatified in 1929. F. D. July 6.

ALFIERI, PIETRO (1801–1863). Born in Rome, he was ordained, taught singing at the English College there, and published studies on plain chant and collections of earlier music, most important of which were seven volumes of sixteenth-century church music by Palestrina and others. He died in Rome on June 12.

ALFIERI, VITTORIO (1749–1803), dramatist. Born in Asti, Italy, on Jan. 17, he led a life of reckless debauchery, climaxed by his liaison with Louisa von Stolberg-Gedern, wife of the profligate Charles Stuart. In 1778 he began the writing of twenty-two tragedies (*Rosamunda, Ottavia, Timoleone, Merope, Saul* are among his best), often on the theme of tyranny. Early an enthusiastic supporter of the French Revolution, he later opposed it and wrote *Misogallo*, a bitter diatribe against the French. He became a Catholic at Florence on his deathbed, on Oct. 8.

ALFONSO I (d. 1134), king of Aragon and Navarre. Son of Sancho Ramirez, he succeeded Pedro I to the two crowns in 1104. Known as "the Warrior," he married Urraca of Castile in an attempt to get control of that country, fought the Castilians until the Moorish danger became too great, battled the Moors at the Ebro, captured Saragossa about 1118, and won the battle of Cutanda (1120) and pushed on to the Mediterranean. On his death the two kingdoms again became separate.

ALFONSO II (1152–1196), king of Aragon. Son of Ramón Berenguer IV and Queen Petronila, he became king in 1164, made a treaty with Alfonso VIII of Castile, and joined him against the Moors in besieging Cuenca in 1177. He also was a patron of the troubadour poets.

ALFONSO III (1265–1291), king of Aragon. Son of Pedro III, he became king in 1285 and was forced by the nobility to reaffirm the General Privilege of 1293. He fought against Venice and the Papal States on behalf of his brother, James II, who claimed Sicily, but was forced to withdraw his support by the Treaty of Tarascon in 1291. He also fought Castile and against James I of Majorca.

ALFONSO IV (1299–1336), king of Aragon. Son of James II, he became king in 1327, aroused the nobles to rebellion when he tried to establish a dynasty for his son Ferdinand (by his second wife, Leonor of Castile), and also was embroiled in a long and tax-draining war with Genoa over Sardinia.

ALFONSO V (1396?–1458), king of Aragon, Naples, and Sicily. Son of Ferdinand I of Aragon and called "the Magnanimous," he became king of Aragon and Sicily in 1416, and set out to conquer Naples in 1435. He was captured by the Genoese as he landed, released by Filippo of Milan, and recognized as king (instead of Louis XIII of Anjou) by the papacy in 1442. He gave over the rule of Aragon to his brother, John II, who ruled as viceroy and bequeathed Naples to his son Ferrante. He was an enthusiast of Renaissance culture.

ALFONSO I (693?–757), king of Asturias. Called "the Catholic," and son-in-law of the Gothic chieftain Pelayo, whom he succeeded in 739, he captured segments of Galicia, Santander, and León from the Moors.

ALFONSO II (d. 842), king of Asturias. Called "the Chaste," he became king in 791, recaptured territory from the Moors, but lost favor with the nobles by his alliances with Charlemagne and Louis the Pious. The shrine of St. James (Santiago) of Compostela was set up during his reign; he also built the cathedral of Oviedo.

ALFONSO III (d. 912?), king of Asturias and León. Son of Ordoño I and called "the Great," he became king in 866, suffered in civil war involving attacks by the nobles and his own children, captured parts of Portugal and Castile from the Moors, and built Burgos. His sons forced his abdication in 909.

ALFONSO IV (d. 933?), king of Asturias and León. Son of Ordoño II and called "the Monk," he became king in 925, abdicated in 931 in favor of his brother Ramiro, and entered the monastery of Sahagún. He then left the monastery, attempted to regain the crown, and was defeated.

ALFONSO V (994–1027), king of Asturias and León. Son of Bermudo II and called "the

Noble," he became king at the age of five. He gave León its law code, and died in battle against the Moors at the siege of Viseo.

ALFONSO VI (1030–1109), king of Castile and León. Son of Ferdinand I, he became king of León in 1065, was captured by his brother, Sancho II of Castile, escaped to the Moorish court at Toledo, and succeeded Sancho as king of Castile in 1072. He captured Galicia from his brother García in 1073, took Toledo from the Moors in 1085, and was defeated by a large invading force at Zalaca in 1086. Yusuf, the Moslem leader, had considerable success and defeated him again at Uclès in 1108, but when he was recalled to Morocco the Spaniards retook some territory. Alfonso was aided by Rodrigo Diaz de Bivar, the Cid.

ALFONSO VII (1104–1157), king of Castile and León. Son of Urraca and Raymond of Burgundy, he became ruler of both Spanish kingdoms in 1126 and, after defeating his stepfather, Alfonso I of Aragon, was crowned in 1135. He had wide success in the reconquest of Spain (1144–47) and made many raids into Andalusia, but his gains were not lasting.

ALFONSO VIII (1155–1214), king of Castile. Son of Sancho III, he became king in 1158, faced grave internal struggles during his minority, went to war against the Moors, and was badly beaten at Alarcos in 1195. León and Navarre took advantage of the situation and invaded Castile. Alfonso was able to defeat Ferdinand II of León and push the invaders out, with the help of the Church leaders. He then turned once more against the Moors and defeated them decisively at Las Navas de Tolosa (1212).

ALFONSO X (1221–1284), king of Castile and León. Son of Ferdinand III and Beatrix (of the Hohenstaufens) and called "the Learned" or "the Wise," he became king in 1252. He was a patron of letters, introduced oriental literature to Spain, and wrote a vernacular chronicle and, perhaps, *Songs to the Virgin*. He was an astronomer and invited fifty astronomers to Toledo, who issued about 1252 the revision of the Ptolemaic tables which became known as the Alfonsine tables. He also codified Roman law (*Siete Partidas*). To avoid civil war he made such great concessions to the nobility after 1271 that he undid the centralized government he preferred; to gain new income he debased the currency. Later in his reign he had trouble with the Moors at Granada. With the help of James I of Aragon he regained the kingdom of Murcia and added it to Castile in 1266. He failed to take Gascony from England, fought unsuccessfully from 1257 to 1275 to become Holy Roman emperor, and was unable to gain control of Portugal. When the burden of taxation became intolerable, the Cortes deposed him and gave the throne to his son Sancho.

ALFONSO XI (1311–1350), king of Castile. Son of Ferdinand IV, he became king in 1312, and decisively defeated a combined force of Moors from Gibraltar (which they had captured in 1333) and Morocco at Tarifa on the Rio Salado in 1340. He then won the battle of Algeciras and was attacking Gibraltar when he died. His campaigns lessened the threat of invasion from North Africa.

ALFONSO IX (d. 1230), king of León. Son of Ferdinand II, he married in succession his close cousins, Teresa of Portugal and Berenguela of Castile, but the unions were annulled by the pope. He fought against Alfonso VIII of Castile and won the battle of Mérida against the Moors.

ALFONSO I (1111?–1185), king of Portugal. Son of Henry of Burgundy and the dissolute Teresa of Castile, he became count of Portugal at two, had to wrest his territory from his mother, who was regent, and her favorite, Fernando Perez, whom he defeated at São Mamede in 1128, and spent the next fifteen years fighting Castile for Portuguese freedom. He defeated a huge Moorish force at Ourique in 1139 (legend says 200,000 Moslems were slain) and declared himself king of Portugal. In 1143, he succeeded in establishing the independence of Portugal when he was recognized as king; he then offered his kingdom to the Holy See and became the vassal of Pope Lucius II, an agreement later confirmed by Alexander III. He then devoted himself to fighting the Moors, pushed them below the Tagus River in a number of raids, and captured Santarem and Lisbon in 1147; he captured Alcacer do Sal in 1158. He went to war against Ferdinand II of León in 1169 and though he won other cities was unable to hold his gains and met several defeats in his last years at the hands of Ferdinand. He successfully defended Santarem in 1184 against heavy Moorish attack. Although his moral reputation was not high, he was generous to religious orders; he founded and endowed the monastery of Alcobaça for the Cistercians and of Santa Cruz for the Augustinians. He died in Coimbra, Portugal, on Dec. 6.

ALFONSO II (1185–1223), king of Portugal. *See* Alfonso III.

ALFONSO III (1210–1279), king of Portugal. Alfonso II (1185–1223), who had become king in 1211, erased clerical immunities, fought the Church throughout his reign, and died excommunicated; Sancho II (d. 1246), who became king as a boy, heavily taxed the religious orders, continued to fight the Church, had his nation placed under interdict, and fled to Spain, where he died. Alfonso III succeeded his brother in 1245 at the people's request. He was successful against the Moors in North Africa, but became involved with Alfonso X of Castile, whose illegitimate daughter Beatrice he married, though he was already married to the mother of their son Diniz. His first wife died soon after, and the bishops persuaded Pope Urban IV to legitimize his relationship with Beatrice. Alfonso called the Cortes of Leiria (1254), the first with representatives from the cities, tried to debase the currency, reorganized administration, tried to crush corruption, regained crown lands which had been given away, and battled with the clergy over taxes.

ALFONSO IV (1291–1357), king of Portugal. Son of Diniz, he succeeded his father in 1325, treated his half-brothers (his father's favorites) with great cruelty, and led an army against Alfonso XI of Castile to vindicate his daughter, whom the Spanish monarch had mistreated. The queen mother, St. Isabel, who had entered a convent, went to the battlefield and prevented the war and brought the two monarchs together; they then joined forces to defeat the Moors at Salado in 1340. Late in his reign he agreed to the murder of Inés de Castro, his son Pedro's mistress.

ALFONSO V (1432–1481), king of Portugal. He became king as a child in 1438, with his uncle Pedro as regent. His mother, Leonor, was not accepted by the populace, sought to gain the regency, and had Alfonso declare war on his uncle; this resulted in the latter's death and the queen's excommunication. Alfonso received enormous grants from Popes Nicholas V and Sixtus IV: sole protection of West African ports, exclusive dominion over waters between Africa and India, and sole right of exploration in that area. Colonizing expeditions were frequent during his reign and he invaded North Africa in 1458, 1464, and 1471; although success was great and gained him the title "the African," he could not maintain his conquests. He sought the throne of Castile, but was defeated by the troops of Ferdinand V and Isabella and forced to surrender all claim. He was particularly pious during his late years, retired to a monastery, and was planning to abdicate when he died.

ALFONSO (d. 1489), bishop. Born in Burgos, Spain, he became a Dominican, was chosen by Ferdinand and Isabella as royal confessor, became bishop of Cordova in 1477, and was transferred to the sees of Cuenca and, in 1486, of Palencia. He was counselor to the throne and president of the council of Castile, was successful in gaining large grants for outfitting the fleet of Columbus, built the Dominican convent of St. Vincent Ferrer, Palencia, and completed the College of St. Gregory at Valladolid. He died at Palencia on Dec. 8.

ALFORD, MICHAEL. See Griffith, Michael.

ALFRED OF BEVERLEY (12th century), historian. Treasurer and sacrist of a church in Beverley, Yorkshire, England, he compiled from existing sources his *Annales*, a Latin chronicle of Britain from its legendary beginnings to 1129.

ALFRED THE GREAT (849–899), king of England. Born in Wantage, Berkshire, England, to Aethelwulf, king of Wessex, and Osburgh, a Jutish noblewoman, he went to Rome with his father in 855. In 858 his father died and the kingdom was governed by his three sons until 871, when Alfred took over. He had married Ealhswith in 868. The early years of his reign were marked by invasions by the Danes, who made peace, then broke their pledges. Alfred smashed the largest invasion, led by Guthrum, at Ethandun in 878; results were fifteen years of peace (the Danes were lastingly defeated in another attempt in 903), the conversion of Guthrum, and the unification of the small, individual Saxon kingdoms under the supremacy of Wessex. Fanciful and historical legend became attached to his name as years went on: that he was consecrated at four by the pope, that he founded a school which later became Oxford, that he established trial by jury, that he scouted the camp of the Danes in the disguise of a harper. Factually, he codified English law, enforced it with respected justice, removed the ruins of war, founded monasteries, and brought many scholars to his court. He was interested in the vernacular as well as Latin, studied Latin in his middle age, and made a translation of Orosius' *World History* (into which he inserted his own accounts of the voyages to the Arctic and Baltic of Othere and Wulfstan), Boethius' *Consolation of Philosophy* (with personal adaptations), the *Pastoral Rule* of St. Gregory the Great, and Bede's *Ecclesiastical History*. Under his inspiration the monks at Winchester and elsewhere began to gather together annals of English history and to add yearly records of outstanding events; this was the *Anglo-Saxon Chronicle*, which gives a detailed account of life during the struggle with the Danes, and which was continued (showing changes in language) until 1154. He died on Oct. 26.

ELEANOR SHIPLEY DUCKETT, *Alfred the Great* (University of Chicago Press, 1956).

ALFRICK, ST. (d. 1005), bishop. Benedictine abbot of Abingdon, he was bishop of Wilton in 990 and archbishop of Canterbury in 995 during the Danish invasion of England. F. D. Nov. 16.

ALFWOLD, ST. (d. 1058?), bishop. A Benedictine monk at Winchester, England, greatly devoted to SS. Swithun and Cuthbert, he was widely respected for his asceticism and became bishop of Sherborne in 1045. F. D. Mar. 25.

ALGER (1055?–1132). Born in Liège, Belgium, he studied there, became deacon at St. Bartholomew's, was canon of the cathedral of St. Lambert from about 1100 to 1120, then retired to the monastery at Cluny, France, where he died. He wrote on the mass, free will, mercy and justice, and on the Eucharist in opposition to the heresy of Berengarius.

ALGOTSSÖN, BRYNIOLF (1248?–1317). He studied at Paris, became dean of Linköping, and in 1278 was appointed bishop of Skara, Sweden. He issued statutes in 1281, wrote hymns, and completed a life of St. Helena of Sköffde. He died on Feb. 6, and was formally praised, though never officially canonized, by Pope Alexander VI in 1499.

ALIGHIERI, DANTE. *See* Dante Alighieri.

ALIPRANDUS, ST. (8th century). Also known as Leuprandus, of royal Lombard descent, he was abbot of the monastery of St. Augustine, Pavia, Italy. F. D. July 24.

ALLARMET, JEAN. *See* Brogny, Jean Allarmet de.

ALLEGRANZA, JOSEPH (1715–1785). Born in Milan, Italy, on Oct. 16, he became a Dominican, was in charge of the Royal Library at Milan and catalogued its holdings (1775), and published antiquarian studies. He died there on Dec. 18.

ALLEGRI, ANTONIO. *See* Correggio, Antonio Allegri da.

ALLEGRI, GREGORIO (1582–1652), composer. Born in Rome, he was a priest at the cathedral in Fermo, studied music under Nanini, and was invited in 1629 by Pope Urban VIII to sing in the papal choir. He spent the rest of his life in this position, aiding prisoners and the poor, and publishing two volumes of *Concertini* and two of *Motetti*. A number of magnificats and lamentations exist in manuscript. He died in Rome on Feb. 18.

ALLEMAND, BL. LOUIS (1380?–1450), cardinal. Born in Arbent, France, he studied law at Avignon and attended the Synod of Pisa in 1409 and the Council of Constance in 1414. In 1416 he was vice-chamberlain of the conclave that elected Pope Martin V. The latter named him, in 1418, bishop of Maguelonne; in 1423 he was made governor of Bologna, Ravenna, and Romagna, and archbishop of Arles, and, in 1426, cardinal. Driven from Bologna, by a revolt, he went to Rome. When Martin died in 1431, Eugene IV was elected, and dissolved the general Council of Basle, called by his predecessor. Louis, a long-time opponent of Eugene, fled from Rome, and by 1454 had become leader of the conciliar forces which had ignored Eugene's order to dissolve, and his later command to reassemble at Ferrara. Led by Louis, they declared Eugene deposed in 1439 and elected Amadeus of Savoy as Felix V (the last antipope), whereupon Eugene excommunicated Louis. In 1447, Eugene died, and Nicholas V was elected pope, revoked all excommunications and penalties against the rebellious council members, and restored Louis as cardinal. He retired to his diocese and lived the balance of his life in prayer. His cult was approved by Pope Clement VII in 1527. F. D. Sept. 16.

ALLEN, EDWARD PATRICK (1853–1926), bishop. Born in Lowell, Massachusetts, on Mar. 17, he studied at Mt. St. Mary's College, Maryland, was ordained in 1881, and taught at St. Mary's in 1881–82. After parish work in the Boston area, he was president of St. Mary's in 1884 to 1897, became fifth bishop of Mobile, Alabama, in 1897 and died there on Oct. 21.

ALLEN, FRANCES (1784–1819). Born in Sunderland, Vermont, on Nov. 13, daughter of Gen. Ethan Allen, she went to Montreal at twenty-one and studied under the Sisters of the Congregation of Notre Dame. She became a convert, was recalled to the home of her mother who had remarried, but returned to Canada and made her religious profession at the Hôtel Dieu in 1810. She died in Montreal on Sept. 10.

ALLEN, GEORGE (1808–1876), educator. Born in Milton, Vermont, on Dec. 17, he graduated from the University of Vermont in 1827, was admitted to the bar in 1831, studied theology and was rector of the Episcopal church in St. Albans from 1834 to 1837, then taught classics at Delaware College and at the University of Pennsylvania. He became a convert in 1847 and died in Worcester, Massachusetts, on May 28.

ALLEN, JOHN (d. 1538), martyr. He was executed at Tyburn when he refused to take the oath of supremacy in favor of King Henry VIII.

ALLEN, WILLIAM (1532–1594), cardinal. Son of John Allen of Rossall, Lancashire, England, he studied at Oxford, became principal of St. Mary's Hall in 1556 and a canon at York, and in 1561, when he opposed Elizabeth's accession, was forced into exile at Louvain. In 1562 he returned to organize a missionary center near Oxford and evaded capture for three years, leaving the country in 1565 for Mechlin, where he was ordained. In 1568 he founded the English College at Douai, from which issued not only missioners for his homeland but a stream of publications in English in defense of Catholicism. There, too, was completed the English translation of the New Testament (published in 1582 at Rheims, to which the college was transferred after anti-English riots in 1578) and of the Old Testament (published at Douai in 1609, two years before the King James version). In 1575, Allen went to Rome and helped Pope Gregory XIII establish the English College there. In the last years of the century Allen became associated with the unsuccessful attempt to inspire support in England for an invasion by Spain. He was created a cardinal in 1587, helped the Jesuit leader, Robert Persons, in founding the English College at Valladolid in 1589, then returned to

Rome, where he died on Oct. 16. His writings dealt with the priesthood, the sacraments, and martyrdom (160 priests from Douai died in England); he also published an account of the death of Edmund Campion and an explanation of the papal deposition of Queen Elizabeth.

ALLERSTEIN, AUGUST (d. 1777?). Born in Germany, he became a Jesuit and was assigned to the China mission, where his skill as astronomer and scientist won him the post of chief of the department of mathematics at the Peking court of Emperor Kiang-long. His census of China for two years of the latter's reign reached Europe in 1779 and was of considerable value.

ALLIES, THOMAS WILLIAM (1813–1903), historian. Born in Midsomer Norton, Somersetshire, England, on Feb. 12, son of an Anglican curate, he attended Eton and Oxford, where he took his M.A. in 1832. He entered the Anglican ministry in 1838, served in London for two years, then retired to an Oxford parsonage with his new wife, Eliza Newman. In 1850 he became a convert. He served as secretary to the primary school committee of the Catholic bishops from 1853 to 1900, lectured in history at the Catholic University of Ireland, and helped to establish the Training College for Women in Liverpool. His apologia, A Life's Decision, appeared in 1880 and his eight-volume Formation of Christendom, covering the period from St. Peter to Charlemagne, was published from 1861 to 1905. He died on June 17.

ALLIOLI, JOSEPH FRANZ (1793–1873). Born in Sulzbach, Germany, on Aug. 10, he was ordained at Ratisbon in 1816, studied at Vienna, Rome, and Paris, taught at Landshut and Munich but gave up teaching because of a throat ailment, and was dean of the chapter at Augsburg from 1838 until his death there on May 22. He wrote a number of biblical studies and commentaries.

ALLISON, WILLIAM (d. 1680?). An English priest, he was seized during the Titus Oates Plot hysteria and died as a prisoner in York Castle.

ALLORI, ALESSANDRO (1536–1607). Born in Florence, Italy, he was a painter under the patronage of Duke Francesco and the nephew of Angiolo. His son, Cristofani (1577–1621), who studied under him and wasted himself by dissipation, achieved some fame as a figure and landscape artist at Florence.

ALLORI, ANGIOLO (1502–1572), painter. Born in Florence, Italy, Il Bronzino was a pupil of Raffaelino del Garbo and of Jacopo da Pontormo, completing many of the latter's works. He became court painter to Duke Cosimo I and drew portraits of Dante, Petrarch, and Boccaccio. His religious, allegorical, and historical paintings are in many Italian and other European museums.

ALLOT, WILLIAM (d. 1590?). Born in England, he attended Cambridge, went into exile at Louvain, where he was ordained, and returned to serve in the English mission. He was imprisoned, then banished, and became a canon at St. Quentin, Picardy, at the request of Mary of Scotland, whom he had visited in prison. His Thesaurus bibliorum was published at Antwerp in 1577.

ALLOUEZ, CLAUDE JEAN (1622–1689). Born in St. Didier, Haute Loire, France, he graduated from Le Puy at seventeen, became a Jesuit in 1639, and was ordained in 1655. He went to Canada in 1658 and labored among the Indians, preaching to twenty different tribes and baptizing more than 10,000. He was appointed vicar general of the Northwest in 1663, prepared a prayerbook in Illinois and French, and explored thousands of miles of unknown territory. He died near Niles, Michigan, on Aug. 27.

ALLOWIN. See Bavo, St.

ALLUCIO, BL. (d. 1134). A shepherd in Pescia, Tuscany, he was director of an almshouse in Val di Nievole, built hospices, bridges, and shelters, and staffed them with followers who became known as the Brothers of St. Allucio. His cult was confirmed by Pope Pius IX. F. D. Oct. 23.

ALLYRE. See Illidius, St.

ALMACHIUS, ST. (d. 400?), martyr. Sometimes called Telemachus, this holy easterner sought to end a gladiatorial contest at Rome. Although he was stoned to death on the spot, the incident so affected Emperor Honorius that he banned such games. F. D. Jan. 1.

ALMADURA, PIETRO (d. 1482), theologian. Born in Bergamo, Italy, where he became a Dominican, he studied at Bologna, held several offices in his order, and wrote treatises on St. Thomas Aquinas. He died in Placentia and was widely revered for his sanctity. He is also known as Peter of Bergamo.

ALMATÓ, BL. PEDRO (1828–1861), martyr. A native of Sassera, Spain, he became a Dominican and was sent to the Philippines and in 1855 to Tonkin. He was beheaded with Bl. Valentine Berrio-Ochoa and Bl. Jerome Hermosilla, and beatified in 1906. F. D. Nov. 1.

ALMEDHA, ST. (6th century). Welsh legend makes her a daughter of King Brychan, who fled her home to avoid an arranged marriage; the enraged suitor is said to have found her in a hillside refuge and to have beheaded her in a rage. She is also called Aled, Eiluned, Eled, and Elevetha. F. D. Aug. 1.

ALMEIDA, JOHN (1571–1653). Born in London as John Meade, he was sent at ten to Portugal, gained a Portuguese name, was adopted by the family of Benedict de Rocha, a merchant, with whom at seventeen he went to Brazil. In 1592 he joined the Jesuits, became a disciple of the missioner Joseph Anchieta, was ordained in 1602, and devoted himself to extreme austerities. He was particularly successful among the cannibals near Santo Spirito, and died at Rio de Janeiro on Sept. 24.

ALMEIDA, JOSÉ CORRÊA DE (1820–1905), poet. Born in Barbacena, Brazil, on Sept. 4, he published twenty-three volumes of poetry, also attained fame as a historian, and died in his native town on Apr. 5.

ALMICI, CAMILLO (1714–1779). Born in Brescia, Italy, on Nov. 2, he became a member of the Congregation of the Oratory and was highly regarded as theologian, scripture scholar, linguist, and historian. His critical examination of Sarpi's inaccurate history of the Council of Trent was published in 1765, and a criticism of Voltaire appeared at Brescia in 1770. He died on Dec. 30.

ALMOND, JOHN (d. 1585). Born in Cheshire, England, he was a monk at an unidentified abbey during the reign of Henry VIII and suffered long in prison and died on Apr. 18 at Hull of neglect in extreme old age.

ALMOND, BL. JOHN (1577–1612), martyr. Born in Allerton, England, he was raised in Ireland, studied at Rheims and at Rome, where he was ordained in 1598. In 1602 he was sent on the English mission and worked successfully until 1612 when he was arrested, convicted of high treason for being a priest, and hanged, drawn, and quartered at Tyburn. He was beatified in 1929. F. D. Dec. 5.

ALMOND, OLIVER (17th century). Educated at the English College at Rome and that of Valladolid between 1582 and 1587, he became a missioner to England and may have been the author of *The Uncasing of Heresies*, published in 1623 (probably at Louvain).

ALNOTH, ST. (d. 700?). A cowherd at the monastery of Weedon, England, who was saved from a beating by the interference of St. Werburga, he became a recluse at Stowe and was killed by bandits. F. D. Feb. 27 (sometimes, Nov. 25).

ALODIA, ST. (d. 851), martyr. *See* Nunilo, St.

ALORUS, ST. (5th century). He was bishop of Quimper, Brittany. F. D. Oct. 26.

ALPAIS, ST. (1150?–1211). Born in Cudot, France, of peasant parents, she contracted what seems to have been leprosy, remained bedridden, and fasted for a great number of years, receiving only the Eucharist. Great crowds were attracted by accounts of her visions and of her extraordinary patience under suffering. Her cult was confirmed by Pope Pius IX in 1874. F. D. Nov. 3.

ALPHAEUS, ST. (1st century). He was the father of St. James the Less (Matt. 10:3). F. D. May 26.

ALPHAEUS, ST. (d. 303), martyr. A native of Eleutheropolis, and a lector and exorcist in Caesarea, Palestine, he was beheaded there with his cousin Zachaeus, a deacon from Gadara, during the Diocletian persecution. F. D. Nov. 17.

ALPHAGE. *See* Elphege, St.

ALPHIUS (d. 251). He and Philadelphus and Cyrinus, said to have been his brothers, were put to death in Lentini, Sicily, during the Decian persecution. Though they were honored on May 10, their story is apparently a pious fiction.

ALPHIUS, ST. (d. 303?), martyr. *See* Mark, St.

ALPHONSE (1220–1271). Son of King Louis VII of France, he was count of Poitiers and Toulouse, and was captured with his brother, St. Louis, during the sixth crusade. He became ill and died in Tunis while accompanying his brother on the seventh crusade. He was known as a skilled and just administrator.

ALPHONSUS, ST. (9th century), bishop. He retired from the see of Astorga in Spanish Galicia to spend his last years as a Benedictine in the monastery of St. Stephen. F. D. Jan. 26.

ALPHONSUS ABULENSIS. *See* Tostado, Alonso.

ALPHONSUS MARY DE' LIGUORI, ST. (1696–1787), bishop, Doctor of the Church. Born in Marianella, near Naples, Italy, on Sept. 27, he began to study law at thirteen, became a lawyer by acclamation at sixteen, and within eight years was a most successful barrister. He then decided to become a priest and was ordained in 1726. While giving a retreat to nuns at Scala he became convinced that the revelations of one of them, Sr. Mary Celeste, of a new rule, were genuine, reorganized her convent, and founded the Redemptorines in 1731. At Bishop Thomas Falcoia's invitation he came to stay at Scala and to found a new congregation, that of the Most Holy Redeemer, especially for mission work among the peasants. This was approved and he was elected superior general in 1749. In 1762, Pope Clement XIII appointed him, against his wishes, bishop of Sant' Agata dei Goti, a small diocese racked by spiritual laxity, which he proceeded to reform. From 1770 to 1783 he was engaged in defending the Redemptorists in the courts on charges of being disguised Jesuits (an order suppressed in Spanish territories). Ill health led to his resignation from his see in 1775, though he remained otherwise active. In 1777, when attempting to obtain the sanction of the king of Naples, he was betrayed into submitting a falsified constitution; the temporal powers approved it, but, since it was different from that approved by the papacy, Pope Pius VI denounced it and excluded Alphonsus from his own order. The latter was seriously shaken by these events, but regained his equanimity and had many supernatural gifts before his death on Aug. 1 at Nocera de' Pagani, Italy. He wrote many ascetical, theological, and historical works (his *Moral Theology*, published in 1748, went through nine editions in his lifetime); engaged in controversy concerning "probabilism"; fought Jansenism and rampant anticlericalism; and in his *Glories of Mary* (1750) was particularly effective in combating those who maintained that Marian devotion was superstition. He was canonized in 1839 and was declared a Doctor of the Church in 1871. F. D. Aug. 2.

ALPHONSUS RODRIGUEZ, ST. (1533?-1617). Born in Segovia, Spain, on July 25, of a well-to-do wool merchant whose business he tried to carry on, he married Mary Suarez at twenty-three. When his trade failed and his wife, children, and mother died, he tried to join the Jesuits. Refused at first, he was accepted in 1571 as a laybrother. He was sent to Majorca and from 1580 to 1604 served as porter at the College of Montesión. His sanctity and devotion to the Immaculate Conception became famous. He did not compose the Little Office of the Immaculate Conception, as was believed, but popularized it. He encouraged St. Peter Claver in his plans for missionary labors and South America. He died on Nov. 1 on Majorca and was canonized in 1888. F. D. Oct. 30.

ALPINI, PROSPERO (1553-1617), botanist. Born in Marostica, Venice, on Nov. 23, he took his medical degree at Padua in 1578, became physician to the consul general in Egypt in 1580, and on his return in 1586 similarly served Prince Andrea Doria. He held the chair of botany at Padua from 1593 and wrote a number of medical and botanical works, particularly on Egypt. He died in Padua on Feb. 6.

ALPINIAN, BL. (3rd century). *See* Martial, St.

ALTAMIRANO, DIEGO FRANCISCO (1625-1715), historian. Born in Madrid on Oct. 26, he became a Jesuit, was sent to Peru, and wrote two historical studies of the work of his Society there. He died at Lima on Nov. 22.

ALTFRID, ST. (d. 874), bishop. A Benedictine monk, he was headmaster of the school at Corbie, Saxony, and became bishop of Hildesheim in 851. F. D. Aug. 15.

ALTHAM, JOHN (1589-1640). A native of Warwickshire, England, he became a Jesuit in 1623, labored in Devonshire and London, and in 1633 joined, with Fr. Andrew White, the colonizing expedition to Maryland headed by Leonard Calvert. Though plagued by ill health, he preached to the Indians, successfully converting several chieftains before his death at St. Mary's, Maryland, on Nov. 5. He is sometimes referred to as Gravenor or Grosvenor.

ALTHOFF, HENRY (1873-1947), bishop.

Born in Aviston, Illinois, on Aug. 28, he studied at St. Joseph's and St. Francis Solanus colleges in Illinois and at Innsbruck, Austria, where he was ordained in 1902. He did parish work in Illinois until 1913, when he was appointed bishop of Belleville, Illinois, and died on July 3.

ALTIGIANUS, ST. (d. 731), martyr. He and a fellow Benedictine monk, Hilarinus, were killed by Saracens at St. Seine, France. F. D. Aug. 23.

ALTINUS, ST. (1st century?). He is called an early disciple of Christ, who founded churches in Orléans and Chartres in Gaul, and also is listed as a fourth-century martyr. F. D. Oct. 19.

ALTMAN, ST. (1020?-1091), bishop. Born in Paderborn, Westphalia, he studied at Paris and after ordination became master of the cathedral school in Paderborn and chaplain to Emperor Henry III. In 1065 he became bishop of Passau and sought to correct grave abuses. In 1074 the diocese was split over papal condemnation of simony and married clergy, and he was forced to flee to Rome under pressure from Henry IV. Although he returned to his see in 1081, he was immediately forced out again and spent the rest of his life at the Benedictine abbey of Gottweig, Austria, which he had founded and from which he continued to exert great influence on the Germanic world. F. D. Aug. 8.

ALTO, ST. (d. 760?). Believed to be Irish, he appeared in Germany in 743 as a hermit, when word of his holiness moved King Pepin to give him land in Bavaria on which to build the monastery later called Altomünster, whose church St. Boniface dedicated in 750. F. D. Feb. 9.

ALUNNO, NICCOLÒ. *See* Liberatore, Niccolò di.

ALVA, FERNANDO ALVAREZ DE TOLEDO DE (1508-1582), general. Born in Castile, Spain, he was a soldier at sixteen, fought against France and the Turks, and began a military career which never saw defeat. In 1567 he was sent to the Netherlands by Emperor Charles V with orders to crush the rebellion against the Spanish regent there. Although loyal to monarch and Church, Alva set no limits to his methods. He executed twenty-two nobles who had led the army attempting to stay the invasion, directed the death of 6,000 others (generally on the mere suspicion of heresy and without trial), and drained the nation by excessive taxation. His own financial policy defeated him, and he withdrew to Spain in 1573. An adulterous scandal involving his son, Don Frederic, put the family in royal disgrace, and Alva remained in seclusion until 1580, when he led an army against Portugal, quickly conquered the country, and annexed it to Spain. In this, as in his campaign against Pope Paul IV, he was consistent with his military upbringing: the purpose of war, once entered into, was to bring the enemy into complete submission as early as possible. His methods were obviously censurable, but the bias of most biographers, written in support of the house of Orange, deny him any character at all. He died in Thomar on Jan. 12.

ALVA Y ASTORGA, PEDRO D' (d. 1667), theologian. Born in Carbajales, Spain, he became a Franciscan of the Strict Observance in Peru, was procurator general of his order at Rome, and was a violent opponent of the Dominicans. His *Nodus indissolubilis* (1661) is on the Index; his defense of the doctrine of the Immaculate Conception of Mary (1648) is approved and significant. He died in Belgium.

ALVARADO, ALONZO DE (d. 1559). Born near Burgos, Spain, he accompanied Pedro de Alvarado (no relative) to Peru in 1534. He conquered the Chachapoyas there in 1535-36, commanded Pizarro's army in 1537, was defeated and captured by Almagro, but escaped to rejoin Pizarro. He also was defeated in 1554 by rebel forces under Francisco Giron at Chuquinga.

ALVARADO, FRANCISCO DE (16th century). Born in Mexico, he became a Dominican in 1574 and in 1593 published a dictionary of the Mistecan language of the state of Oaxaca.

ALVARADO, PEDRO DE (1485?-1541), general. Born in Badajóz, Spain, he came to America in 1510, served with Grijalva during the exploration of Yucatan in 1518, and was second in command to Cortés during the conquest of Mexico. In 1524 he conquered Guatemala and became its governor. Ten years later he went to Quito, Ecuador, to seize it for Pizarro but found it already occupied by one of the latter's followers; Diego de Almagro prevented a civil war between the explorers, and Alvarado returned to Guatemala. A brave military commander, he was a failure as an administrator, became the dupe of the viceroy, Antonio de Mendoza, whom he joined in the Mixtón War, and lost his life in an attack on an Indian camp at Nochistlán, in northern Mexico on June 24.

ALVAREZ, BALTHAZAR (1533-1580). Born in Cervera, Spain, he studied at Alcalá, became a Jesuit there in 1555, was ordained in 1558, and was spiritual director of St. Teresa of Avila for seven years. He helped her in her Carmelite reforms and in framing the rule for her order. In 1574 he became rector at Salamanca and was noted for his power of advanced contemplation. He died in Belmonte on July 25.

ALVAREZ, BL. BARTHOLOMEW (d. 1737), martyr. Born near Braganza, Portugal, he became a Jesuit in 1723 and was sent to the mission in Tonkin, Indochina, where he was seized in 1736 and beheaded the following year with three other Jesuits, Bl. Emmanuele d'Abreau, John Gaspard Cratz, and Vincent da Cunha. F. D. Jan. 12.

ALVAREZ, DIEGO (1550?-1635), archbishop. Born in Media, Spain, he became a Dominican there, and taught at Burgos, Valladolid, and Rome, among other places. He opposed the interpretation of free will maintained by the Jesuit Louis Molina, and wrote commentaries on Thomistic philosophy, on Isaias, on the Pelagian heresy, and a manual for preachers. In 1606 he was appointed archbishop of Trani, Kingdom of Naples, by Pope Paul V, a position he held until his death there.

ALVAREZ, MANOEL (1526-1582), educator. Born on the Island of Madeira, he became a Jesuit in 1546, taught classical languages at Coimbra and Evora, at each of which he served as rector, and wrote a Latin grammar which ran into more than 400 editions. He died in Evora, Portugal, on Dec. 30.

ALVAREZ OF CORDOVA, BL. (d. 1430?). He entered the Dominican monastery of St. Paul at Cordova, Spain, in 1368, preached in Spain and Italy, became confessor of Queen Catherine of Castile (daughter of John of Gaunt) and tutor of King John II. He established a priory at Escalaceli, under strict discipline, successfully opposed the false claims of Peter de Luna to the papacy as Benedict XIII, and spent his last years begging publicly for his associates, teaching, and observing the most extreme austerities. His cult was confirmed in 1741. F. D. Feb. 19.

ALVAREZ DE PAZ (1560-1620). Born in Toledo, Spain, he became a Jesuit in 1578, taught at Lima, Peru, and served as provincial in that country. He wrote three volumes on mysticism and was known throughout South America for his spiritual gifts. He died at Potosí, Bolivia, on Jan. 17.

ALVAREZ DE PEREIRA, BL. NUÑEZ (1360-1431). Born in Bomjardin, Portugal, he joined the army, fought in the Portuguese war of independence, and after his wife's death became a Carmelite laybrother in Lisbon. His cult was confirmed in 1918. F. D. Nov. 6.

ALVITUS, ST. (d. 1063?), bishop. Born in Spanish Galicia, he became a Benedictine at Sahagún, followed the Cluniac reform, and in 1057 was appointed bishop of León by King Ferdinand I. F. D. Sept. 5.

ALYPIUS, ST. (360?-430?), bishop. Born in Tagaste, North Africa, he was from childhood a close friend of St. Augustine, studied under him at Carthage, was a fellow Manichaean, and joined him in Rome in 383 for the study of law. There he became a wastrel devotee of theatrical diversions and the circus, but gradually became more serious and was baptized a Christian in 387 by St. Ambrose. He was with Augustine at Cassiciacum and is featured in the dialogues written there; he returned to Africa with him in 388 and spent three years in prayer and penance. He then went to Hippo, became a priest, made a pilgrimage to Palestine, and on his return in 393, became bishop of Tagaste. He was Augustine's assistant in the latter's public activities during the remainder of his life. F. D. Aug. 18.

ALZATE, JOSÉ ANTONIO (1738–1799). Born in Oxumba, Mexico, he became a priest and served as a corresponding member of the French Academy, writing on astronomy, physics, metallurgy, on silk growing, and on the use of ammonia against gases in mines. He directed several scientific missions for the government and the Church, made extensive maps of Mexico, and in 1768 founded the newspaper *Diario literario*.

ALZOG, JOHANN BAPTIST (1808–1878), historian. Born in Ohlau, Silesia, on June 29, he studied at Breslau and Bonn, was ordained in 1834, taught at Posen in 1836 and defended its archbishop against the Prussian government, was professor at Hildesheim in 1845, and held the chair of church history at Freiburg (Breisgau) in 1853. He edited the *Oratio Apologetica* of Gregory of Nazianzen and wrote *Manual of Church History, Patrology*, and theological studies. He died in Freiburg, Germany, on Mar. 1.

ALZON, EMMANUEL JOSEPH MARIE MAURICE D' (1810–1880), founder. Born in Le Vigan, France, on Aug. 30, he studied at Montpellier, was ordained in Rome in 1834, and became vicar general of Nîmes in 1835, a position he held the next forty-five years. He founded the College of the Assumption in 1843, the *Revue de l'enseignement chrétien*, the Association of St. Francis de Sales, and began the practice of national pilgrimages to Rome. From his college, established for the education of the nobility, stemmed fifteen schools for boys of poor means who had vocations to the priesthood, as well as the organization of the Augustinian Congregation of the Assumption (Assumptionists). This group was papally approved in 1864, with Fr. d'Alzon as first superior general. He also created an auxiliary association of Our Lady of Vocations, and was sent to Constantinople in 1863 by Pope Pius IX to establish a branch of his mission there. He died in Nîmes, France, on Nov. 21.

AMADEO, GIOVANNI ANTONIO (1447–1522), sculptor. Born near Pavia, Italy, he became a sculptor with his brother Protasio, followed the style of Bramantino of Milan, worked on the façade of the Certosa at Pavia, became chief architect of the Certosa in 1490, and designed a new façade. He executed the tomb of Medea, daughter of Bartolomeo Colleoni, at Basella, near Bergamo, as well as that of Colleoni himself; the Borromeo monuments originally at Milan; much work on the cathedrals of Pavia and Milan; and statues of Eve and St. George in Venice. He died in Milan on Aug. 27.

AMADEUS, BL. (1110–1159), bishop. Son of Amadeus, lord of Hauterive, he was educated at Bonnevaux, served at the court of Emperor Henry V, then became a Cistercian at Clairvaux; his father had entered Cluny in 1118. The son completed the reform of the monastery at Hautecombe, where he became abbot in 1139, was appointed bishop of Lausanne in 1144, and later became chancellor of Burgundy. His cult was approved in 1910. F. D. Jan. 28.

AMADEUS OF PORTUGAL. *See* Mendes de Silva, João.

AMADEUS IX OF SAVOY, BL. (1435–1472). Born in Thonon, son of Duke Louis I and Anne of Cyprus, he married Yolande, daughter of Charles VII of France, in 1451 and became a wise and charitable administrator, enemy of those who oppressed the poor, and a peacemaker in the quarrels with Milan. Because he suffered from epilepsy, he resigned his rule to his wife in his last years. He was beatified in 1677. F. D. Mar. 30.

AMALARIUS OF METZ (d. 850?). Born in Metz in the eighth century, he was a disciple of Alcuin, and probably became bishop of Trèves, France, in 811, resigning in 813 to go as envoy to Constantinople. He attended synods at Aix-la-Chapelle and Paris, was French ambassador to Pope Gregory IV, and directed the see of Lyons during the exile of Bishop Agobard. The writings of Amalarius on liturgical subjects, though marked by excessive symbolism, had a great effect on the establishment of the Roman liturgy (with many Gallican borrowings) in western Europe.

AMALBURGA, ST. (d. 690). Born in Brabant, a relative of Pepin of Landen, she married Count Witger; their children were SS. Emebert, Gudula, and Reineldis. She became a Benedictine nun at Mauberge, Flanders, and her husband a Benedictine monk at Lobbes. A false legend makes her a beauty whom Pepin's son Charles pursued ardently, only to be spurned. The name is also spelled Amalia, Amelberga, and Amelia. F. D. July 10.

AMALRICUS AGGERII (14th century). He received his doctorate from Montpellier and became prior of an Augustinian monastery and in 1362 chaplain to Urban V. He wrote on the papacy and church history.

AMAND, ST. (584?–679?), bishop. Born near Nantes, Lower Poitou, he became a recluse at twenty, was ordained at Tours, then lived for fifteen years in a cell under the direction of Bishop Austregisilus of Bourges. In 629 he was made a missionary bishop, preaching in Flanders and Carinthia. He was banished for censuring King Dagobert I, recalled, sent on a mission to the hostile region around Ghent, where he was badly treated physically before eventual success, and went on to found a great many monasteries. He retired to one of them, Elnon, as abbot four years before his death. F. D. Feb. 6.

AMANDUS, ST. (d. 346). He was the first bishop of Strassburg. F. D. Oct. 26.

AMANDUS, ST. (4th century). He was bishop of Worms, Germany. F. D. Oct. 26.

AMANDUS, ST. (4th century). He was bishop of Rennes, France. F. D. Nov. 13.

AMANDUS, ST. (d. 431?), bishop. He was ordained by St. Delphinus, whom he succeeded as bishop of Bordeaux about 400, prepared St. Paulinus of Nola for baptism, and gave over the direction of the Gallic see to St. Severinus. When the latter died, St. Amandus was persuaded to return to office. F. D. June 18.

AMANDUS, ST. (6th century). He was abbot-founder of the monastery of St. Amand de Coly, Limoges, France. F. D. June 25.

AMANDUS, ST. (d. 644). He was abbot-founder of the monastery of Moissac. F. D. Feb. 6.

AMANDUS, ST. (d. 679?). *See* Amand, St.

AMANDUS, ST. (7th century). He was abbot-founder of the monastery of St. Amand de Boixe, France. F. D. May 22.

AMANDUS, ST. (d. 708). He succeeded St. Aigulf as Benedictine abbot of Lérins in 676. F. D. Nov. 18.

AMANIEU, GUILLAUME (d. 1226). He was made archbishop of Bordeaux, France, in 1207, was seneschal over French property for Henry III of England, and served in Spain in the wars against the Moors.

AMANNI, BL. MARCOLINO (1317?–1397). Born at Forlì, Italy, and known as Marcolino of Forlì, he is said to have become a Dominican novice at ten and to have lived as a rigorous ascetic and penitent. He was beatified in 1750. F. D. Jan. 24.

AMANTIUS, ST. (d. 120), martyr. He, SS. Hyacinth, Irenaeus, Zoticus, and six other soldiers were put to death at Rome when their Christianity was discovered. F. D. Feb. 10.

AMANTIUS, ST. (d. 120?), martyr. *See* Getulius, St.

AMANTIUS, ST. (d. 440). He succeeded St. Providus as bishop of Como, Italy. F. D. Apr. 8.

AMANTIUS, ST. (d. 600?). He was a priest at Città di Castello near Perugia, Italy, highly venerated by Pope St. Gregory the Great. F. D. Sept. 26.

AMANTIUS, ST. (7th century). A deacon sent from Rome to assist St. Amand in evangelizing the Netherlands, he built a church at Wintershoven with St. Landoald. F. D. Mar. 19.

AMANTIUS, ST., bishop and martyr. He is said to have been bishop of Noyon, France, and put to death at Cannes with his three brothers,

Alexander and two others, all priests. F. D. June 6.

AMARAND, ST. (8th century). He was Benedictine abbot of Moissac and was bishop of Albi, France, sometime between 689 and 722. F. D. Nov. 7.

AMARANTHUS, ST. (3rd century), martyr. He died in the neighborhood of Albi, France, and was praised by St. Gregory of Tours. F. D. Nov. 7.

AMARINUS, ST. (d. 676), martyr. Abbot of a Benedictine monastery in the Vosges region of France, he was slain with St. Praejectus; St. Amaria, Alsace, is named for him. F. D. Jan. 25.

AMASIUS, ST. (d. 356), bishop. A Greek, he was driven from his home during an Arian persecution, settled in Italy, and became second bishop of Teano in 346. F. D. Jan. 23.

AMASWINTHUS, ST. (d. 982). He was abbot of the Benedictine monastery at Silva de Málaga, Andalusia, Spain, for forty-two years. F. D. Dec. 22.

AMAT, THADDEUS (1810–1878), bishop. Born in Barcelona, Spain, on Dec. 31, he was ordained a Lazarist in 1838 at Paris and that year was sent to Louisiana. He served as master of novices in Lazarist houses in Missouri and Pennsylvania and was consecrated bishop of Monterey, California, in 1854; the see was transferred to Los Angeles in 1859. The Lazarists opened St. Vincent's College there, and Bishop Amat brought in Franciscan brothers for work in parochial schools and Sisters of Charity and Sisters of the Immaculate Heart of Mary. He died in Los Angeles on May 12.

AMATOR, ST. (3rd century). He was bishop of Autun, France. F. D. Nov. 26.

AMATOR, ST. (d. 418), bishop. Married against his will to a wealthy girl who later was venerated locally as St. Martha, he entered the priesthood and she, a convent. He is believed to have ordained St. Patrick in the lower orders and to have reformed St. Germanus, wastrel governor of the area, and appointed him his successor as bishop of Auxerre, France. F. D. May 1.

AMATOR, ST. (d. 855), martyr. Born in Martos, near Cordova, Spain, and ordained there, he was slain by the Moors for his faith, with Peter, a monk, and Louis, a layman. F. D. Apr. 30.

AMATOR, ST. Supposedly the first Christian hermit in Gaul, he is reputed to have founded the shrine of Our Lady of Rocamadour. One pious fiction makes him a servant of the Holy Family, who married Veronica and with her evangelized Gaul; another identifies him with the publican Zacchaeus. F. D. Aug. 20.

AMATUS, ST. (567?–630?), abbot. Born in Grenoble, France, he entered the abbey of St. Maurice at Agaunum, Switzerland, as a child, became a Benedictine monk, and lived there for thirty years, the last few as a hermit. In 614, at St. Eustace's request, he went to Luxeuil, where he converted St. Romaric. About 620 the latter founded a double monastery at Habendum (later called Remiremont), of which Amatus became first abbot and where he died. F. D. Sept. 13.

AMATUS, ST. (d. 690?), bishop. The Benedictine abbot of St. Maurice at Agaunum, Switzerland, he became tenth bishop of Sion in Valais about 660. Some sixteen years later, King Thierry III, acting on false information, banished him to Peronne. He lived there and at Breuil, Flanders, for the rest of his life. F. D. Sept. 13.

AMATUS, ST. (12th century), bishop. A Benedictine priest, he was bishop of Nusco and died in either 1093 or 1193. F. D. Aug. 31.

AMBARACH, PETER (1663–1742), scholar. Born in Gusta, Syria, he was educated by the Jesuits at the Maronite college in Rome, was ordained in Syria in 1685, taught Hebrew at Pisa, and set up an oriental printing house at Florence. In 1708 he became a Jesuit, translated two volumes of St. Ephrem from Syriac into Latin, and served on a papal commission working on a corrected edition of the Septuagint. He died in Rome on Aug. 25.

AMBICUS, ST. (4th century), martyr. He was slain at Nicomedia, during the Diocletian persecution, with SS. Julius and Victor. F. D. Dec. 3.

AMBOISE, BL. FRANÇOISE D' (1427–1485). Daughter of Louis d'Amboise, she was raised in the court of the duke of Brittany from the age of four; she married the duke's son Peter when she was fifteen. When he succeeded to the dukedom in 1450, she founded a convent at Nantes and was active in charities. Peter died in 1457, and in 1463 she founded a Carmelite convent at Vannes, became a nun there in 1468, and prioress in 1472. She also founded a convent at Couëts, where she died. Through her aid Bl. John Soreth introduced the Carmelite nuns to France. Her cult was confirmed in 1863. F. D. Nov. 4.

AMBOISE, GEORGE D' (1460–1510), cardinal. Born in Chaumont-sur-Loire, France, he was at fourteen named bishop of Montauban, though he did not take office until he was twenty-four; at thirty-three he was archbishop of Rouen. King Louis XII made him prime minister in 1498 and Pope Alexander VI made him a cardinal in 1499. He approved the conquest of Milan by the French king, reformed the nation's judicial and financial policies, and reduced taxes. He campaigned violently to become pope both at the death of Alexander VI and of Paul III and opposed Pope Julius II to the point of trying to separate France and Rome. He died in Lyons on May 25.

AMBROGINI, ANGELO DE' (1454–1494), scholar. Born in Monte Pulciano, from which he took the name Politian, he went to Florence in 1464, where he studied under leading humanists and became tutor to Lorenzo de' Medici's children in 1477 and a member of the academy. He was professor of classical literature at Florence in 1480, translated Epictetus, Hippocrates, Homer, Plato, and Plutarch, and wrote *Miscellanea* (1489) and Latin and Italian poetry. He died in Florence, where he was canon of the cathedral, having taken orders late in life.

AMBROGIO DI LORENZO. *See* Lorenzetti, Ambrogio.

AMBROS, AUGUST WILHELM (1816–1876), critic. Born in Mauth, Bohemia, on Nov. 17, he took his doctor's degree in law and became councilor of state, but turned to music and served as a governor of the royal conservatory, Prague. He wrote several overtures, heavily influenced by Schumann, a four-volume history of music, and an elaborate study of the interrelationship of the arts, *Die Grenzen der Musik und Poesie*. He died in Vienna on June 28.

AMBROSE, ST. (d. 250?). A wealthy resident of Alexandria, Egypt, he aided Origen early in his career; later he suffered imprisonment but not death during the persecution of Maximinus. F. D. Mar. 17.

AMBROSE, ST. (d. 303), martyr. A centurion at Ferentino, Italy, he was put to death during the Diocletian persecution. F. D. Aug. 16.

AMBROSE, ST. (340?–397), bishop and Doctor of the Church. Born probably in Trèves, son of the Roman prefect of Gaul, he was educated at Rome, studied law, and about 370 was appointed consular governor of Liguria and Aemilia by Emperor Valentinian, ruling from Milan with justice and ability. On Dec. 7, 374, despite lack of ecclesiastical training and his vigorous objections (he had not yet even been baptized), he was elected bishop of Milan by popular acclamation. He gave away his possessions, devoted himself to study, and soon became known as the most eloquent preacher of his day. He eliminated Arianism from his diocese and resisted attempts of the imperial authorities to encroach upon the domain of the Church. In 377 he wrote *De fide* for Emperor Gratian's guidance in combating Arianism and in 379 persuaded the emperor to issue a decree outlawing the heresy in the West. Ambrose acted as envoy between Theodosius in the East and Maximus (who killed Gratian in battle in 383) in the West over the division of the empire, Valentinian becoming emperor of Italy and Maximus emperor of the rest of the West. In 385, Empress Justina (Valentinian's mother), who had been secretly an Arian, induced her son to demand several basilicas for the Arians. Ambrose refused and, when the conflict became intensified, Maximus invaded Italy. Justina and Valentinian fled. Theodosius defeated and executed Maximus in Pannonia and made Valentinian emperor in the West. In 390, Theodosius massacred some 7,000 Thessalonians in retaliation for the assassination of his governor there. Ambrose upbraided the emperor and Theodosius did public penance for his crime. In 393, Valentinian II was slain by Arbogastes in Gaul, and the latter's candidate for the throne, the usurper Eugenius, attempted to restore paganism over Ambrose's vigorous objections. Theodosius intervened, defeated and slew Arbogastes at Aquileia in 394, and finally eliminated heathenism from the empire. Theodosius died a few months later. Ambrose was one of the greatest teachers in the history of the Church; his writings reveal him as the vigorous, active expounder of Catholicism rather than as a reflective philosopher. He was an eloquent exponent of virginity and wrote several treatises (among them his famous *On Virgins*, addressed to his sister, St. Marcellina). Other writings include scriptural commentaries, particularly on the gospel of St. Luke; treatises on the duties of Christian ecclesiastics, on the sacraments and the mass, and on the divinity of Christ and the Incarnation; sermons; and letters. He also introduced, about 386, the practice of having his congregation sing hymns and psalms; his hymns (although only six are definitely his) became standard in Western hymnody. He baptized St. Augustine in 387. Ambrose died in Milan on Apr. 4 and is honored on Dec. 7.

FREDERICK HOMES DUDDEN, *Life and Times of St. Ambrose*, 2 vols. (New York, Oxford, 1935); PIERRE CHAMPAGNE DE LABRIOLLE, *Life and Times of St. Ambrose* (St. Louis, Herder, 1928).

AMBROSE, ST. (d. 455?). He was bishop of Sens, France. F. D. Sept. 3.

AMBROSE, ST. (5th century). He was bishop of Saintes, France, for about fourteen years and was alive in 475. F. D. Aug. 28.

AMBROSE, ST. (d. 523). As abbot of the monastery of Agaunum (now St. Maurice), Switzerland, he introduced to the West the perpetual psalmody (*laus perennis*) in 522 or 523. This practice of unbroken recitation of the office by successive choirs spread throughout Gaul. F. D. Nov. 2.

AMBROSE, ST. (d. 752?). He was thirteenth bishop of Cahors, France, and resigned to live as a recluse. F. D. Oct. 16.

AMBROSE (12th century), poet. A Norman, he wrote *L'Estoire de la guerre sainte*, a poetic chronicle of the career of King Richard I of England as a crusader in the Holy Land in 1190–92.

AMBROSE AUTPERT, ST. (d. 778?). He left the court of King Pepin the Short, where he had been Charlemagne's tutor, and became a Benedictine monk in Benevento, Italy, and later the abbot of the monastery of St. Vincent there. He wrote a long-popular commentary on the Apocalypse. F. D. July 19.

AMBROSE OF CAMALDOLI. See Traversari, Ambrosio.

AMBROSE OF SIENA. See Sansedoni, Bl. Ambrose.

AMELBERGA, ST. (d. 772?). She became a Benedictine nun at Munsterbilsen, Flanders, at the hands of St. Willibrord, and is honored at Ghent. F. D. July 10. She is often confused with St. Amalburga.

AMELBURGA, ST. (10th century). She was abbess of Susteren, where she taught the daughters of the king of Lorraine. F. D. Nov. 21.

AMELIA. See Amalburga, St.

AMELOTE, DENIS (1609–1678). Born in Saintes, France, he was ordained in 1631, wrote on scripture and against Jansenism, and published a four-volume translation of the New Testament (1666–70). He died at Paris on Oct. 7.

AMERBACH, VEIT (1503–1557). Born in Wembdingen, Germany, he studied at Eichstätt and Wittenberg, taught theology at the latter university during the rise of Luther, engaged in controversy with Melancthon, and became a Catholic in 1543. He wrote classical studies and on the religious controversy of his day and became professor of philosophy at Ingolstadt, where he died.

AMERIGHI, MICHELANGELO. See Caravaggio, Michelangelo.

AMETTE, LÉON ADOLPHE (1850–1920), cardinal. Born in Douville, France, on Sept. 6, he studied at Évreux and St. Sulpice, was ordained in 1873, and was stationed at Évreux, where he became secretary to the bishop and vicar general. He was consecrated bishop of Bayeux in 1899, titular archbishop of Sida and coadjutor of Paris in 1906, and succeeded to the latter see in 1908. He was made cardinal-priest in 1911, gained an admirable reputation during World War I for his relief work and, afterward, for his championing labor. He consecrated the basilica of the Sacred Heart, Montmartre, Paris, in 1919 and died in Paris on Aug. 29.

AMHERST, FRANCIS KERRIL (1819–1883). Born in London on Mar. 21, he graduated from Oscott College in 1838, was ordained in 1846, taught at Oscott, and became bishop of Northampton in 1858. He resigned his see in 1879 because of ill health and died in Warwick on Aug. 21.

AMIAS, BL. JOHN (d. 1589), martyr. Born near Wakefield, England, he went to Rheims after the death of his wife, was ordained in 1581, labored in the English underground mission for several years, and was hanged, drawn, and quartered at York for his priesthood. He was beatified in 1929. F. D. Mar. 16.

AMIATA, BL. (13th century). *See* Diana, Bl.

AMICI, BL. BERNARDINO (1420–1503). Born in Fossa, Italy, he studied at Aquila and then law at Perugia, and became a Franciscan in 1445. He was a well-known preacher, successfully united Dalmatia and Bosnia in 1464, and continued in mission work until his death at Aquila. His writings include a biography of St. Bernardino of Siena and *Chronicle of the Friars Minor of the Observance*. His cult was approved in 1828. F. D. Nov. 27.

AMICO, ANTONIO (d. 1641). A canon at Palermo, he wrote on Sicilian royalty, naval affairs, and the Church there.

AMICO, BERNARDINO (d. 1590). A Franciscan at Naples, he became prior in Jerusalem and wrote an important description of the shrines of the Holy Land in his day.

AMICO, FRANCESCO (b. 1578), theologian. Born in Cosenza, Italy, on Apr. 2, he became a Jesuit in 1596 and taught for twenty-four years at Naples, Aquila, and Gratz. He published studies of the Trinity, the Incarnation, the sacraments, the nature of angels, the purpose of life, and faith, hope, and charity. His *De justitia et jure* was condemned, but a corrected edition (1649) was approved.

AMICUS, ST. (925?–1045?). A priest of his native Camerino, he became a hermit, a Benedictine monk at St. Peter's in Fonteavellana, and a hermit again in the Abruzzi, where he attracted many disciples. His last years were spent at St. Peter's. F. D. Nov. 3.

AMICUS, ST. (11th century). He was abbot of the Benedictine monastery of Rambara. F. D. Nov. 2.

AMIDEI, ST. BARTHOLOMEW (13th century), founder. *See* Monaldo, St. Buonfiglio.

AMIGO, PETER EMMANUEL (1864–1949), archbishop. Born in Gibraltar on May 26, he was ordained in 1888, consecrated bishop in 1904, and made archbishop of Southwark, England, in 1937. He was well known for his charities and his work with the poor of his parish, St. George's, which was heavily bombed during World War I. He died in London on Oct. 1.

AMIOT, JOSEPH MARIA (1718–1793), missioner. Born in Toulon, France, on Feb. 8, he became a Jesuit in 1737, went to China as a missioner in 1740, and won the confidence of Emperor Kien Long. He mastered Chinese and Tatar, compiled a chronological history of the emperors, prepared a Tatar-Manchu grammar and dictionary, and wrote extensively on Chinese music, geography, history, and thought. He died in Peking on Oct. 8 or 9.

AMIRANTE, CARLO (1852–1934). Born in Italy, he was an officer in the revolutionary army which defeated the papal Zouaves in Rome, brought an end to the Papal States in 1870, and made the popes "prisoners of the Vatican." He later begged forgiveness of Pope Pius IX, entered a seminary at twenty-five, and was ordained in 1877. He was known as a poet, musician, and teacher, served as pastor in Naples, and died on Jan. 30.

AMMEN, DANIEL (1820–1898), admiral. Born in Brown County, Ohio on May 16, he became a midshipman in 1836, also studied briefly at West Point under his brother Jacob Ammen (later a brigadier general), and served at sea for several years, including blockade duty during the Civil War. He was chief of the bureau of yards and docks in 1868–71 and of the bureau of navigation in 1871–78, and served on the commission approving the plan for a canal through Nicaragua, and also on that which met in Paris in 1879 to discuss at water passage through Central America. He worked on harbor defenses, became a rear admiral in 1877, designed a life raft named after him, and published *The Old Navy and the New* (1891), an autobiography. He died in Washington, D.C., on July 11.

AMMIA, ST. (d. 270?), martyr. *See* Theodotus, St.

AMMIANUS, ST. (3rd century), martyr. *See* Isidore of Chios, St.

AMMIANUS, ST. (d. 310?), martyr. He and SS. Julian, Occanus, and Theodore were burned at the stake, probably during the reign of Maximian. F. D. Sept. 4.

AMMIRATO, SCIPIONE (1531–1601), historian. Born in Lecce, Naples, he lived principally in Venice, where he issued an edition of Ariosto, and in Florence. He was commissioned by Duke Cosimo I to write the history of Tuscany from its beginnings to 1574; he worked on this *Istorie fiorentine* for four years, drawing accurately on original sources. He also wrote on Tacitus and on Florentine and Neapolitan families. He became a canon of the cathedral in Florence in 1595.

AMMON, ST. (d. 250), martyr. He and four other soldiers—Ingenes, Ptolemy, Theophilus, and Zeno—encouraged a Christian under torture in Alexandria, Egypt; all were promptly beheaded. F. D. Dec. 20.

AMMON, ST. (288?–350?). When he retired to the Nitrian desert of Egypt as a hermit, his wife organized a community of religious women and directed them. Ammon attracted so many disciples that, on St. Anthony's advice, he established a loosely organized monastery, of which he was superior over thousands of monks. F. D. Oct. 4.

AMMON, ST. (d. 322?), martyr. A deacon, he and forty young women he had converted were put to death at Heraclea, Thrace. F. D. Sept. 1.

AMMONARIA, ST. (d. 250), martyr. See Epimachus, St.

AMMONIUS, ST. (d. 250), martyr. With a fellow soldier, Moseus, he was condemned to life imprisonment in the mines of Bithynia because they were discovered as Christians; they later were burned alive at Astas. F. D. Jan. 18.

AMMONIUS, ST. (d. 310), martyr. See Theodore, St.

AMMONIUS, ST. (d. 311?), martyr. See Hesychius, St.

AMO, ST. (4th century). He was the second bishop of Toul, France, succeeding St. Mansuetus. F. D. Oct. 23.

AMOES, ST. (4th century), hermit. See Achillas, St.

AMOR, ST. (d. 767?). A companion of St. Pirminius in mission work in Germany and also known as Amator, he became abbot-founder of the Benedictine monastery of Amorbach, Franconia. F. D. Aug. 17.

AMOR, ST. (9th century). Born in Aquitaine, he was a hermit at Maastricht, and founded Münsterbilsen, near Liège, Belgium. F. D. Oct. 8.

AMORETTI, CARLO (1741–1816), naturalist. Born near Genoa, Italy, he became an Augustinian, taught at Parma, and was curator of the Ambrosian Library, Milan. He wrote a life of Leonardo da Vinci (1784) and treatises on natural science, including A Journey from Milan to the Three Lakes (1794), a detailed study of the Como, Maggiore, and Lugano area. He died in Milan.

AMORT, EUSEBIUS (1692–1775), theologian. Born in Bibermühle, Bavaria, on Nov. 15, he was educated at Munich, became an Augustinian at Polling, and taught philosophy, theology, and canon law there for most of his life. In 1722 he founded the review Parnassus Biocus; he wrote seventy books on his three interests and on the saints; corresponded extensively with Popes Benedict XIII and XIV and St. Alphonsus Liguori; opposed the mysticism of Maria de Agreda; and supported Thomas à Kempis as author of the Imitation against the new choice of Jean Gerson. He died in Polling on Feb. 5.

AMPELIUS, ST. (d. 302?), martyr. He and St. Caius were put to death at Messina, Italy, during the Diocletian persecution. F. D. Nov. 20.

AMPELIUS, ST. (d. 304), martyr. See Saturninus, St.

AMPELIUS, ST. (d. 672?), bishop. He directed the see of Milan, Italy, during its invasion by the Lombards, over whom he wielded considerable influence. F. D. July 7.

AMPÈRE, ANDRÉ MARIE (1775–1836), physicist. Born in Lyons, France, on Jan. 22, he early was directed in Latin and mathematical studies by his father, a merchant. When the latter was executed after the siege of Lyons in 1793, André suffered a breakdown, recovered, became a teacher, and gained attention by his writings on mathematics. In 1805, a year after the death of his wife, Julie Carron, he was invited to the faculty of L'École Polytechnique at Paris, where he was made professor of analysis in 1809. In 1820, on the heels of electrodynamic findings by the Danish scholar Oersted, he showed the French Academy how two parallel wires carrying electric currents could be mutually attracted or repelled as currents flowed in the same or opposite directions. His findings were published in 1822 and developed in his Mathematical Theory of the Phenomena of Electrodynamics (1830). He planned an electric telegraph, with a different wire for each letter, and continued to write widely on magnetism, light, curves, calculus, as well as on zoology and philosophy. His Journal and Correspondence was published in 1872, and in 1881 the Paris Conference of Electricians perpetuated his name by calling the practical unit of electrical current an ampere. He died in Marseilles on June 10.

AMPHIBALUS, ST. (d. 304?), martyr. An Englishman, he was arrested while wearing the cloak (amphibalus) of St. Alban of Verulam, whom he had hidden in his home, and was put to death. F. D. June 24.

AMPHILOCHIUS, ST. (d. 121?), martyr. See Philetus, St.

AMPHILOCHIUS, ST. (d. 400?), bishop. A fellow student at Constantinople with St. Basil, later a hermit, he was appointed bishop of Iconium by Basil. He wrote a book on the Holy Spirit against the Arian heretics of Macedonia and presided at a synod at Sidon which condemned the Messalians, who held that only through prayer could man attain salvation. F. D. Nov. 23.

AMPHILOCHIUS (5th century). Bishop of Sida, Pamphylis, he attended the Council of Ephesus (431) where he was firm in his condemnation of Nestorius, but was sympathetic toward the condemned Dioscorus of Alexandria at the Council of Chalcedon. He wrote to Leo I in 458 that he did not acknowledge the power of that council, although he had accepted the exactions of the Tome that pope had issued.

AMPHION, ST. (4th century), bishop. He was bishop of Epiphania in Cilicia, was elected to the see of Nicomedia at the beginning of the Arian heresy, attended the Council of Nicaea (325), and was highly praised by St. Athanasius. F. D. June 12.

AMPLIATUS, ST. (1st century). Mentioned by St. Paul (Rom. 16:8–9), he traditionally became a bishop and with his associates, SS. Narcissus and Urban, preached with St. Andrew in the Balkans, where they were martyred. F. D. Oct. 31.

AMULWINUS, ST. (d. 750?), bishop. He was abbot-bishop of Lobbes, France, succeeding St. Erminus in 737. F. D. Feb. 7.

AMYOT, JACQUES (1513–1593), bishop. Born in Melun, France, on Oct. 30, he studied at Paris, was tutor to Marguerite, sister of King Francis I, and taught classics at Bourges. He also tutored the sons of Henry II. Charles IX made him bishop of Auxerre in 1570, almoner, and curator of the University of Paris. He contributed much to the French language by his translations of Heliodorus, Diodorus Siculus, and Plutarch's *Lives* and *Morals*. His *Lives* was a source for Sir Thomas North's translation of Plutarch, on which Shakespeare relied. Amyot died in Auxerre, France, on Feb. 6.

ANA DE JESUS, VEN. *See* Lobera, Ven. Ana.

ANACHARIUS. *See* Aunacharius.

ANACLETUS, pope. *See* Cletus.

ANACLETUS II (d. 1138), antipope. Pietro Pierleoni, born in Rome to a senatorial family, studied in Paris, became a monk at Cluny, and was called to Rome by Pope Paschal II and made a cardinal-deacon. He fled to France with Pope Gelasius and began, by careful gifts of great wealth, to secure the papal throne for himself. When Pope Honorius II died on Feb. 13, 1130, Anacletus was sure of the votes of thirty cardinals from all ranks of the nobility except the Frangipani. To try to assure a worthy election, the decision was left to eight cardinals; they forced the papacy on Cardinal Gregory of San Georgio, who was proclaimed pope the next day as Innocent II. Later the same day, other cardinals chose Pierleoni, who had been one of the eight who met to elect Innocent (though he voted against him), at a conclave at the church of St. Mark and accepted him as Anacletus II. He had the majority of the cardinals and the city of Rome on his side; even the Frangipani refused to back what they thought was a losing cause and abandoned Innocent II. Anacletus spent lavishly from plunder taken from churches and endeared himself to the populace; he made Duke Roger of Apulia the first king of the Two Sicilies in 1130; and scorned the small army which came with Lothair to be crowned emperor by Innocent in the Lateran, since St. Peter's was closed to him. Anacletus finally lost all favor through the efforts of St. Bernard, who had opposed him from the day of his election and who preached everywhere against him. Anacletus died in Rome on Jan. 25; his successor as antipope, Victor IV, ended the schism within two months.

ANANIAS, ST. (1st century), martyr. The disciple who baptized St. Paul (Acts 9), he is believed to have continued his preaching in Damascus and Eleutheropolis and to have been put to death for his work. F. D. Jan. 25.

ANANIAS, ST. (d. 298?), martyr. A priest in Phoenicia he converted his jailer and seven guards and was put to death with them during the Diocletian persecution. F. D. Feb. 25.

ANANIAS, ST. (d. 341), martyr. *See* Simeon Barsabae, St.

ANANIAS, ST., martyr. *See* Demetrius, St.

ANASTASIA, ST. (d. 68?), martyr. She and St. Basilissa were convert noblewomen who are said to have buried SS. Peter and Paul in Rome and to have been tortured and beheaded on Nero's orders. The account, however, is not authenticated. F. D. Apr. 15.

ANASTASIA, ST. (3rd century), martyr. According to the Roman Martyrology, she was tortured and beheaded during the Valerian persecution. When Cyril offered her a drink of water during her sufferings he, too, was martyred. The story is probably a pious fiction. F. D. Oct. 28.

ANASTASIA, ST. (304?), martyr. According to tradition, she was the daughter of a Roman noble, Praetextatus, married a pagan, Publius, and on his death went to Aquileia during the Diocletian persecution to help the imprisoned Christians there. She was imprisoned and eventually burned alive on the island of Palmaria (another legend has her martyred at Sirmium, Pannonia). F. D. Dec. 25.

ANASTASIA PATRICIA. Supposed to have fled from Constantinople to the desert near Alexandria to escape the attentions of Emperor Justinian, and to have lived as a hermit who never left her cave for twenty-eight years, she is probably a pious fiction.

ANASTASIUS I, ST. (d. 401), pope. A native of Rome, he became pope on Nov. 27, 399, condemned the Donatists and, in 400, the works of Origen and their translator Rufinus. SS. Jerome, Augustine, and Paulinus of Nola spoke warmly of his poverty and saintly qualities. F. D. Dec. 19.

ANASTASIUS II (d. 498), pope. A Roman, he was elected pope on Nov. 24, 496; declared valid the sacramental acts of Acacius, patriarch of Constantinople, though he condemned him; and condemned the heresy of Traducianism. His letter congratulating Clovis on the latter's conversion is now considered a seventeenth-century forgery. He died on Nov. 19.

ANASTASIUS III (d. 913), pope. A Roman, he was elected pope in April, 911, determined the ecclesiastical divisions of Germany, and died two years later, in June.

ANASTASIUS IV (d. 1154), pope. A Roman, Corrado della Subarra was vicar general of Rome and cardinal-bishop of Sabina when he was crowned pope on July 12, 1153. He restored the Pantheon, gave special privileges to the Knights Hospitallers, and wrote a treatise on the Trinity. He died on Dec. 3.

ANASTASIUS, ST. (d. 251), martyr. A

tribune in the army of Decius, he became a Christian because of admiration of the courage of those he was putting to death, and was thereupon beheaded with his family. F. D. May 11.

ANASTASIUS, ST. (d. 274), martyr. He was a Roman missioner who was scourged to death near Bourges in Gaul for preaching Christianity. His companion, St. Marcellus, was beheaded. F. D. June 29.

ANASTASIUS, ST. (d. 303), martyr. He, SS. Cyriacus, Paulillus, Secundus, and Sindimius, and others were slain at Nicomedia during the Diocletian persecution. F. D. Dec. 19.

ANASTASIUS, ST. (d. 304?), martyr. He worked as a fuller in Aquileia, near Venice, Italy, then moved to Salona, Dalmatia. He refused to conceal his faith and even painted a cross on his door, whereupon he was put to death by drowning. F. D. Sept. 7. There is some confusion between this Anastasius and others of the same name: a third-century Roman officer, said to have been tortured to death with other Christians during the reign of Decius (May 11, 251), and a tribune slain (Aug. 21, 274) at Salone, near Rome.

ANASTASIUS, ST. (d. 553?), martyr. He is said to have been a Syrian who lived near Perugia, Italy, and was put to death during the invasion by Totila; he seems to have been listed erroneously as bishop of Terni. F. D. Aug. 17.

ANASTASIUS, ST. (d. 570?). He became a monk and abbot at the Benedictine monastery of Suppentonia, near Mt. Soracte, north of Rome, and is spoken of by St. Gregory the Great. F. D. Jan. 11.

ANASTASIUS I, ST. (d. 599), patriarch. A vigorous opponent of imperial support of theological vagaries as patriarch of Alexandria, Egypt, he was banished for twenty-three years by Justin II, and was restored to his see by Emperor Maurice. F. D. Apr. 21.

ANASTASIUS II, ST. (d. 609), patriarch. Successor of St. Anastasius I to the patriarchate of Antioch in 599, he was tortured and put to death by Syrian Jews during riots in protest against their forced conversions by Emperor Phocas. As a result, he was popularly considered a martyr. F. D. Dec. 21.

ANASTASIUS, ST. (d. 610), bishop. He was successful in converting many Lombards from Arianism during his reign as bishop of Brescia, Italy. F. D. May 20.

ANASTASIUS, ST. (d. 680), bishop. A convert from Arianism, he became bishop of Pavia, Italy, in 668. F. D. May 30.

ANASTASIUS, ST. (d. 797?), martyr. He was superior of a group of hermits at St. Sabas, Jerusalem, slain with his followers in a bandit raid. F. D. Mar. 20.

ANASTASIUS, ST. (d. 853), martyr. A deacon at Cordova, Spain, he became a Benedictine monk at Tábanos and was beheaded by the Moorish emir with SS. Felix and Digna. The former, born in Alcalá, became a monk in Asturias and was transferred to Tábanos; Digna was a nun in the double monastery outside Cordova. F. D. June 14.

ANASTASIUS (810?–880?), antipope. Born in Rome, nephew of Bishop Arsenius of Orta, he studied under Greek monks and became abbot of the monastery of the Blessed Virgin at Trastevere, Rome. Often surnamed Bibliothecarius, he is said to be the Anastasius who fled from Rome in 848, was excommunicated in 850, and as cardinal of Graz was elected antipope in 855 by the faction supporting Emperor Louis II. He then seized the Lateran palace and imprisoned Pope Benedict III for two days, was removed and pardoned. He served under Pope Nicholas I in several offices, was papal librarian under Nicholas II and John VIII, and acted as mediator between the Eastern patriarch, Photius, and Rome in the difficulties over defining the procession of the Holy Spirit. In 869 Emperor Louis II sent him to Constantinople to arrange the marriage between his daughter and the Eastern emperor's son. While there, Anastasius defended papal supremacy at the last session (869) of the eighth Ecumenical Council. He translated the acts of this and of the seventh council into Latin, edited documents relating to Pope Honorius, and wrote *Chronographia Tripartita*, and saints' lives.

ANASTASIUS, ST. (d. 977). He became archbishop of Sens, France, in 968 and began the erection of its cathedral. F. D. Jan. 7.

ANASTASIUS, ST. (d. 1040?), archbishop. Probably a Bohemian named Astrik Radla, and also known as Astericus, he became a monk at Brevnov, taking the name Anastasius, and accompanied St. Adalbert on his mission to convert the Bohemians. When this failed, Anastasius worked among the Magyars and became first abbot of Pannonhalma, Hungary, founded by Duke Geza. When Geza died, St. Stephen succeeded to the throne and sent Anastasius to Rome to secure papal recognition of the Hungarian kingdom. With Emperor Otto I's approval Stephen was crowned in 1001 and Anastasius became archbishop of Esztergom. The rest of his life was devoted to evangelizing the Magyars. F. D. Nov. 12.

ANASTASIUS, ST. (1020?–1085). A learned Venetian, he became a monk at Mont-St.-Michel, Normandy, then lived as a hermit, and about 1066 joined the Benedictine community at Cluny. In 1073 he was sent by Pope St. Gregory VII to preach to the Moors in Spain; about 1080 he returned, lived as a recluse near Toulouse, and was on his way back to Cluny when he died. F. D. Oct. 16.

ANASTASIUS THE PERSIAN, ST. (d. 628), martyr. A soldier named Magundat, he was converted after he saw the relics of the true cross brought back from the sack of Jerusalem in 614, became a monk in 621, and was arrested and tortured in Caesarea for refusing to renounce his faith and worship the sun. Sent to Bethsaloe in Assyria, he attracted such crowds by his fortitude that King Chrosroës had him strangled to death after sixty-eight other Christians had met a similar fate in his presence. F. D. Jan. 22.

ANASTASIUS THE SINAITE, ST. (7th century). He lived on Mt. Sinai, wrote against the Monophysite heresy, and had wide influence in Egypt and Syria about 675. F. D. Apr. 21.

ANATHLON, ST. (1st century). He is listed as first bishop of Milan, Italy, sent there by St. Barnabas. He died at Brescia. F. D. Sept. 24.

ANATOLIA, ST. (d. 250?), martyr. According to legend, she refused to marry her suitor Aurelius and convinced her sister Victoria to reject her suitor Eugenius; when they persisted in their refusal, they were denounced as Christians, tortured, and put to death. Their guard, Audax, was converted as a result. Although the details are probably fictional, they did actually live. Anatolia is mentioned with Audax in the Roman Martyrology on July 9. F. D. Dec. 23.

ANATOLIANUS, ST. (d. 267?), martyr. He and SS. Cassius, Maximus, Liminius, and Victorinus were put to death at Auvergne, Gaul, during the persecution of Valerian and Galienus. F. D. Feb. 6.

ANATOLIUS, ST. (d. 235), martyr. He and SS. Eustace and Thespesius were put to death at Nicaea during the persecution of Emperor Maximinus the Thracian. F. D. Nov. 20.

ANATOLIUS, ST. (d. 283?), bishop. When a rebellion broke out in Alexandria, where he had been born and was head of an Aristotelian school, he persuaded the rebels to allow the non-combatants to leave unmolested. He later went to Palestine, became assistant to the bishop of Caesarea, and succeeded Eusebius as bishop of Laodicea about 269. His work as philosopher, mathematician, and physical scientist was highly praised by St. Jerome. F. D. July 3.

ANATOLIUS, ST. (d. 458), patriarch. A native of Alexandria, Egypt, he succeeded St. Flavian as patriarch there and was consecrated by Dioscorus the heretic in 449. Pope St. Leo I recognized the legitimacy of his accession after Anatolius accepted Leo's *Tome*. He took a prominent part in the Council of Chalcedon and unequivocally recognized the authority of the papacy. F. D. July 3.

AÑAZCO, PEDRO DE (1550–1605), son of Pedro de Añazco, an army captain, he was born in Chachapoyas, Peru, became a Jesuit at twenty-two, worked as a missioner in Paraguay, and wrote nine grammars and catechisms in Chaco and other Indian languages. He died in Asunción, Paraguay.

ANCHIETA, VEN. JOSEPH (1533–1597). Known as the "Apostle of Brazil," he was born on the Island of Tenerife, studied at Coimbra, Portugal, became a Jesuit at seventeen, and began a life of extreme austerity, marked by many supernatural manifestations. Sent to Brazil in 1553 for his health, he established the first classical school in the New World, compiled a dictionary and grammar, wrote plays and poems for the purpose of instructing the colonists and natives, traveled widely with the missioners, and, twice left as a hostage with cannibal tribes, was unexpectedly spared. He was ordained later and in his last years was rector of the College of St. Vincent and provincial of Brazil. He died at Reritigbá (now Anchieta), Brazil, on June 9.

ANCINA, BL. JUVENAL (1545–1604), bishop. Born in Fossano, Italy, he studied at Montpellier, Savoy, Padua, and Turin, received doctorates in philosophy and medicine, and in 1569 became professor of medicine at Turin. In 1575 he went to Rome as the private physician of the ambassador of Savoy to the papacy, studied theology under St. Robert Bellarmine, joined the Oratorians under St. Philip Neri in 1578, and four years later was ordained and sent to Naples. He devoted himself to the care of the poor and the ill, became known for his great preaching ability, was recalled to the Oratory in Rome, and in 1602 was appointed bishop of Saluzzo. He was poisoned by a friar whom he had rebuked for his scandalous living. He was beatified in 1869. F. D. Aug. 31.

ANDALO, BL. DIANA D' (1201?–1236). Born near Bologna, Italy, she took private vows from St. Dominic, joined the Augustinians at Roxana, and was violently captured and brought home. Bl. Jordan of Saxony quieted her family and they built a Dominican convent for her and seven others, including Amata and Cecilia, two nuns from Rome. Diana and the latter were beatified in 1891. F. D. June 9.

ANDEOLUS, ST. (d. 208), martyr. A subdeacon sent from Smyrna to France, he is said to have been slain near Viviers. F. D. May 1.

ANDERDON, WILLIAM (1816–1890). Born in London on Dec. 26, he graduated from Oxford in 1840, was ordained an Anglican minister, and was vicar at Withyam and Reigate in 1846–50. He became a convert in 1850 at Paris and was ordained at Oscott in 1853. He was a lecturer at Ushaw College, chaplain at the Catholic University of Dublin, and from 1856 to 1872, when he joined the Jesuits, was secretary to his uncle, Cardinal Manning. Earlier, he had written a number of popular novels, among them *Antoine de Bonneval*, *Surgeon's Mate*, and *Bracton*. Thereafter, while stationed at Manchester, he wrote magazine articles, pamphlets, and a score of controversial and apologetical works. He died in Roehampton on July 28.

ANDERLEDY, ANTHONY MARIA (1819–1892). Born in Berisal, Switzerland, on June 3, he became a Jesuit in 1839, taught at Freiburg, and, when the society was expelled in 1848, went to St. Louis, Missouri, where he was ordained. He was pastor at Green Bay, Wisconsin, for two years, returned to the German mission, directed Jesuit studies at Cologne and at Paderborn, and became provincial in 1859. He purchased the mediaeval abbey of Maria-Laach, taught moral theology there from 1865 to 1870, became vicar general of his society at Rome, and succeeded Fr. Beck as general in 1887. He died at Fiesole, Italy, on Jan. 18.

ANDERSON, HENRY JAMES (1799–1875), scientist. Born in New York City on Feb. 6, he studied at Columbia, obtained a degree in medicine, then taught mathematics and astronomy at Columbia from 1841 to 1866. In 1848 he was a member of the United States expedition to the Dead Sea. He became a convert in 1849, served as head of the supreme council of the St. Vincent de Paul Society, and established and helped to build the New York Catholic Protectory. He died in Lahore, India, on Oct. 19, and is buried in Fort Lee, New Jersey.

ANDERSON, JOSEPH GAUDENTIUS (1865–1927), bishop. Born in Boston, Massachusetts, on Sept. 30, he studied at Boston College and St. John's seminary and was ordained in 1892. He served as a curate, was chaplain of the state prison in 1894–1904, and director of Catholic charities in 1903–8. He became a pastor of St. Paul's and monsignor in 1909, was named auxiliary bishop of Boston, and founded the bureau for the care of neglected children. He died in Dorchester, as pastor of St. Peter's, on July 2.

ANDERSON, LIONEL ALBERT (1620?–1710). Born in Lincolnshire, England, he was a convert, became a Dominican at Paris in 1638, was ordained in 1665, and entered the English mission under the name of Munson. He was arrested at the time of the Titus Oates Plot and condemned to death about 1679, imprisoned for at least a year, then exiled. He returned to England under James II, fled to France with the king, and came home in 1698. He died on Oct. 21.

ANDERSON, PATRICK (1575–1624). Born in Elgin, Scotland, nephew of Bishop Leslie of Ross, he took his degree at Edinburgh, became a Jesuit at Rome in 1597, and worked underground in Scotland from 1609 to 1611. He brought 100 young men from Scotland to the continental seminaries, became rector of the Scots College in Rome in 1615, returned to his homeland, and was imprisoned. His life was spared at the request, it is believed, of the French ambassador. He wrote lives of Scots saints and a defense of Catholicism (1623). He died in London on Sept. 24.

ANDERTON, LAWRENCE (17th century). He became a Jesuit and is believed to be the author of *The Protestant's Apologie*, published as by "John Brereley, priest."

ANDERTON, BL. ROBERT (d. 1586), martyr. Born in Chorley, Lancashire, England, he was educated at Oxford, ordained at Rheims in 1585, and sent to the English mission. His ship was driven ashore on the Isle of Wight, where, after the court's pretense at legal consultation with London, he and Bl. William Marsden, whose career was the same as that of his fellow Lancashireman, were hanged for being priests. F. D. Apr. 25.

ANDERTON, ROGER (d. 1640?). Uncle of Lawrence and brother of James Anderton, he was a leading Catholic in Lancashire, England. He is believed to have established an underground press at Lostock, which he later moved to Birchley.

ANDERTON, THOMAS (1611–1671). Born in Lancashire, England, to William Anderton and Isabel Hancock, both of whom were persecuted for their faith, he became a Benedictine at Paris in 1630 and was ordained in 1636. He held several high positions in the order and was prior of St. Edmund's monastery, St. Malo, and twice of St. Edmund's, Paris. He was sent to the English mission in 1669. His *History of the Iconoclasts* was published in 1671. He died on Oct. 9.

ANDLAW, HEINRICH BERNHARD VON (1802–1871). Born in Freiburg im Breisgau, Germany, on Aug. 20, son of Baron Konrad Karl, he studied at Landshut and Freiburg, served in the army, and entered the state department of Baden. In 1830 he returned to his home; in 1835 he was elected to the lower house of the legislature, where he served, except for two short terms, until he was sixty. He strongly opposed bureaucracy and the liberal flavor of the 1848 revolutions, and sought long and with success to see that German Catholics were legally allowed to participate in economic and political affairs, writing much on these themes. He died in Freiburg on May 3.

ANDLEBY, BL. WILLIAM (d. 1597), martyr. Born in Etton, Yorkshire, England, he studied at Cambridge, fought against the Dutch, visited Dr. Allen at Douai to engage him in debate, was converted, ordained in 1577, and returned to the English mission to serve in Lincolnshire. He was captured and was hanged, drawn, and quartered at York. He was beatified in 1929. F. D. July 4.

ANDOCHIUS, ST. (2nd century), martyr. A priest, he was sent to Gaul with Thyrsus, a deacon from Smyrna, lived at Autun in the home of Felix, a merchant, whom he converted, and was put to death with them. F. D. Sept. 24.

ANDRADA, ALONSO (1590–1672), biographer. Born in Toledo, Spain, he became a Jesuit in 1612, served as rector at Plasencia, and wrote some thirty-four volumes, including a continuation of Nuremberg's lives of famous members of his society. He died in Madrid on June 20.

ANDRADA, ANTONIO DE (1580–1634), explorer. Born in Oleiros, Portugal, he became a Jesuit in 1596 and served on the Indian mission from 1600 to 1624. In that year he penetrated Tibet, was well received, and was allowed to bring other missioners from Agra, India. His account of his observations was published at Paris in 1629. He later was recalled to Goa, Portuguese India, where he served as superior for the Indies, and died of poisoning on Mar. 19.

ANDRADA, THOMAS DE (1529–1582). Born in Lisbon, Portugal, he was educated by the Augustinian Hermits, whom he joined in 1534 with the name Thomas of Jesus, studied at Coimbra, became novice-master, and attempted unsuccessfully to reform the order (a separate congregation for the Discalced Augustinians was authorized in 1622). He became influential in court circles, accompanied King Sebastian on his expedition to Africa, where he was captured at Alcacer in 1578, and spent the rest of his life in prison. He died at Sagena, Morocco, on Apr. 17. While in prison he wrote *Os trabalhos de Jesus*.

ANDRADA DE PAYVA, DIEGO (1528–1575), theologian. Born in Coimbra, Portugal, he studied and was ordained there and became professor of theology. King Sebastian then appointed him theologian at the Council of Trent (1561), where he was active in support of papal authority and of the dogma of the Immaculate Conception, and after which he engaged in long published controversy with Chemnitz. He also published three volumes of sermons. He died in Lisbon on Dec. 1.

ANDRÉ, BERNARD (15th century), historian. Born in Toulouse, France, he became an Augustinian friar and was a tutor at Oxford and also of the two sons of King Henry VII of England: Arthur and Henry VIII. His Latin chronicle of his royal patron's reign was published as late as 1858.

ANDRÉ, YVES MARIE (1675–1764), mathematician. Born in Chateaulin, France, he became a Jesuit in 1693 and taught mathematics at Caen for thirty-nine years. He issued many works on physics, optics, architecture, an *Essay on the Beautiful,* a *Treatise on Man,* and a poem, *The Art of Conversation.* He had been at odds with his Society quite early because of his Jansenism and criticized them after the suppression of the Society secularized him. He became a canon regular at Caen, was a close friend of Malebranche, whose biography he may have written, and received a government pension.

ANDREA, GIOVANNI D' (1275?–1348). Born in Mugello, near Florence, Italy, he studied at Bologna and taught canon law there after teaching at Padua and Pisa. He wrote widely on canon law, was highly praised by Bellarmine, and died a victim of the great plague.

ANDREA, MIGUEL DE (1877–1960), bishop. Born in Navarro, Buenos Aires, Argentina, on July 5, of Italian immigrant parents, he studied there and at the Latin American College and the Gregorian in Rome, and was ordained in 1899. He was appointed pastor of San Miguel church in Buenos Aires in 1913, retaining his pastorate until his death, became titular bishop of Temnos in 1919, and was known as the "poor man's bishop" for his lifelong devotion to the working class and championship of social and economic reforms. He helped build low-rent housing, founded the Federation of Women Workers' Catholic Association in 1924, which included twenty-six groups, and built a hotel for working girls in Buenos Aires in 1932. He steadfastly opposed Perón's encroachments on the rights of the Church and was arrested for his opposition during the 1955 revolt, but was quickly released by a regime which feared his popularity. He died in Buenos Aires on June 23.

ANDREA DI CASTELLANA. *See* Scalimoli, Andrea.

ANDREA PISANO (1270–1349), sculptor. Andrea da Pontadera was a pupil of Giovanni Pisano, worked as a goldsmith, and helped his master with the sculpture of Santa Maria della Spina in Pisa and of St. Mark's and the doge's palace in Venice. He himself designed the bronze door on the south side of the baptistery of the Duomo in Florence, and continued the Campanile, probably from Giotto's plans, after the latter's death. Andrea's two sons, Nino and Tomasso, also were sculptors.

ANDREA DA PONTADERA. *See* Pisano, Andrea.

ANDREA DEL SANSOVINO. *See* Contucci, Andrea.

ANDREA DEL SARTO (1486–1531), painter. Andrea d'Agnolo was born in Florence, Italy, on July 14, son of a tailor, from which fact he received his surname, studied under Giovanni Basile, and in 1498 became a pupil of Piero di Cosimo. He became famed for his religious paintings and easel pictures, was a master of design and composition, but above all was noted for his superb coloring. Most of his life was spent in Florence, where he became a member of the painters' guild in 1508, but he visited Rome briefly and Paris, where he was invited by Francis I, for whom he painted the dauphin and *Holy Family and Charity.* He was commissioned by Francis to purchase paintings on his return to Florence but spent the money (on a house for his model and wife, Lucrezia, in Browning's poem) and never returned to Paris. Among his masterpieces are five frescoes in the Servites' Santa Annunziata church in Florence depicting the life of St. Philip Benizi (1509–14), to which he later added *Madonna del Sacco* (perhaps his greatest work), *Adoration of the Magi*, and *Nativity of the Virgin*; ten frescoes depicting the life of St. John the Baptist for the Scalzo in Florence; *The Last Supper* for the San Salvi convent outside Florence; and among his easel pictures *Madonna of the Harpies*, several of the Holy Family, the Annunciation, and Assumption, *Sacrifice of Abraham*, *Marriage of St. Catherine*, and self-portraits. He died in Florence of the plague on Jan. 22.

ANDREAS (15th century), historian. He was ordained at Eichstätt, Germany, in 1405, became an Augustinian at Ratisbon in 1410, and wrote three chronicles of the city of Ratisbon up to 1452.

ANDREASI, BL. OSANNA (1449–1505). Born in Mantua, Italy, on Jan. 17, eldest daughter of Nicholas Andreasi and Louisa Gonzaga, she is said to have received supernatural gifts as early as five years of age. She became a Dominican tertiary at about seventeen (though she was not professed until thirty-seven years later), devoted herself to great austerities and constant devotions, and at thirty directed the family of Duke Frederick of Mantua during the war with Tuscany. She greatly influenced Girolamo de Monte Oliveto, who published their joint *Spiritual Colloquies* after her death, and was herself deeply influenced by Savonarola, whose dismay over the spiritual degradation of Italy she shared. Her cult was approved by Popes Leo X and Innocent XIII. F. D. June 20.

ANDREIS, FELIX DE (1778–1820). Born in Demonte, Piedmont, Italy, on Dec. 13, he became a member of the Congregation of the Mission (Lazarists) in 1797 and was ordained in 1801. He directed missions from 1806 until 1815, then lectured on theology to clerical students after the suppression of religious houses. In 1816, at the invitation of Bishop Dubourg, he went to the United States, taught at Bardstown, Kentucky, and in 1818 set up two schools in St. Louis, Missouri. He died there on Oct. 15, worn out by missionary labors.

ANDRÉS, JUAN (16th century). Of Moorish descent, he was born at Xativa, Spain, became a Christian in 1587, was ordained, and went to Granada at the request of King Ferdinand to labor for the conversion of other Moors. He translated the Koran into Spanish and wrote an attack on Mohammedan errors and a work on mathematics.

ANDRÉS, JUAN (1740–1817), historian.

Born in Planes, Spain, he became a Jesuit in 1754, went to Italy when the Society was suppressed in Spain in 1767, and taught philosophy at Ferrara; when the Society was completely suppressed in 1773 he toured Europe for materials for his history of universal literature (1782–99). He also wrote on the philosophy of Galileo, served Joseph Bonaparte as royal librarian, rejoined the Society at sixty-four when it was restored in Naples, and died at Rome.

ANDREW I (d. 1060), king of Hungary. After the great pagan uprising under Vatha in 1046 which overthrew King Peter had subsided, Andrew gained the throne in 1047 and restored the royal power. During his reign he fought against three invasions by Emperor Henry III, but in 1058 secured the emperor's recognition of Hungary's independence. He was killed in a war with his brother Béla.

ANDREW II (1176?–1235), king of Hungary. Son of King Béla III, he became king in 1205, participated in the fifth crusade in 1217, and by his reckless extravagances weakened the royal power by surrendering crown lands to the greater nobles to raise funds. In 1222 he was forced by the lesser nobles to issue the "golden bull," a document which set limits on the royal power. It provided for an annual diet, no tax on nobles and the Church, guaranteed them against arbitrary imprisonment and confiscation of their property, allowed them to dispose of their property as they willed, directed that no foreigners could hold office without permission of the diet, that offices could not be granted *in perpetuum*, and finally that, in the event the king violated any of these provisions, the nobles would have the right to resist him. Alarmed by the growing influence of non-Christians on Andrew and his policies, and his failure to observe Church rights, Archbishop Robert of Gran placed Hungary under an interdict in 1232, which was later lifted on the king's promise to reform his ways. St. Elizabeth of Hungary was the daughter of Andrew and his first wife, Gertrude of Meran, who was murdered by rebellious nobles in 1213.

ANDREW III (d. 1301), king of Hungary. Grandson of King Andrew II, he was born in Venice, Italy, ascended the throne in 1290, and spent his regime fighting the domination of the aristocracy and against foreign claimants to the throne. He resisted Rudolf of Hapsburg, who attempted to secure the throne for his son, had Hungary presented to Charles Martel of Naples by the pope, who claimed it as a fief, and in 1291 defeated Charles at the battle of Agram. Andrew was the last of the Arpád dynasty of Hungarian kings.

ANDREW, ST. (1st century), apostle. A native of Bethsaida, Galilee, son of Jona, a fisherman, and brother of St. Peter, he became a disciple of St. John the Baptist, was attracted to Christ when St. John baptized Him, and was the first of the apostles. He brought Peter to Christ, and they both gave up everything when He called them, saying He would make them "fishers of men." Andrew was present at the miracle of the loaves and the fishes (John 6:8–9) and when the Gentiles spoke to Christ (John 12:20–22). He is reputed (by Eusebius) to have preached in Scythia; (by Theodoret) in Greece; (by St. Gregory Nazianzen) in Epirus; (by St. Jerome) in Achaia. According to tradition he was crucified in Patras, Achaia, on an X-shaped cross. He is the patron of Russia (because of a legend that he preached there), of Scotland (a legend says St. Rule brought the apostle's relics there as a result of a dream), and of Greece. F. D. Nov. 30.

I. G. CAPALD, *Andrew of Galilee* (New York, Longmans, 1955).

ANDREW, ST. (1st century), martyr. He and St. Aponius were put to death at Bethlehem during the persecution which took the life of St. James the Greater. F. D. Feb. 10.

ANDREW, ST. (d. 235?). He is listed as the twelfth bishop of Trèves, in Gaul. F. D. Jan. 13.

ANDREW, ST. (d. 251), martyr. *See* Peter, St.

ANDREW, ST. (d. 300?), martyr. A tribune in the Roman army sent against the Persians, he became a Christian with several companions, was relieved of his command, and forced to flee with them to the Taurus mountains. Seleucus, military governor of Cilicia, captured and executed them when they refused to renounce their faith. F. D. Aug. 19.

ANDREW, ST. (d. 364), martyr. *See* Gaudentius, St.

ANDREW, ST. (d. 407?). He was bishop of Florence, Italy. F. D. Feb. 26.

ANDREW (6th century). Bishop of Caesarea, Cappadocia, and author of a commentary on the Apocalypse, he has also been listed as living in the fifth and in the ninth century.

ANDREW, ST. (d. 690?), abbot. He succeeded St. Amandus as abbot of the Benedictine monastery of Elnone. F. D. Feb. 6.

ANDREW, ST. (d. 735), martyr. A priest, born in Lydia, he was killed with his deacon, St. Hypatius, at Constantinople, during the Iconoclast persecution of Leo the Isaurian. F. D. Aug. 29.

ANDREW, ST. (d. 764), martyr. *See* Stephen, St.

ANDREW, ST. (d. 880?). Legend makes him a young Scotsman who accompanied St. Donatus on a pilgrimage to Rome and who became a deacon in Fiesole when Donatus was made its bishop. Andrew later restored the Benedictine abbey of San Martino at Mensula. F. D. Aug. 22.

ANDREW, ST. (d. 900?), martyr. Deported by the Saracens from Syracuse, Sicily, he and SS. Antony, John, and Peter were put to death in Africa. F. D. Sept. 23.

ANDREW, ST. (d. 1020?), martyr. He and St. Benedict went from Poland to live as hermits in Moravia, became Camaldolese monks at Zobor abbey in Hungary, and were slain by bandits. F. D. July 17.

ANDREW OF ANAGNI, BL. (d. 1302). A relative of Popes Alexander IV and Boniface VIII, he became a Franciscan brother, refusing a cardinalate to devote himself to simpler tasks. He was beatified in 1724. F. D. Feb. 17.

ANDREW OF ANTIOCH, BL. (1268?–1348?). Of Norman descent, he was born in Antioch and became an Augustinian at the basilica of the Holy Sepulcher in Jerusalem. He spent the last few years of his life touring Europe to raise funds to support the canons at the basilica and died in Annecy, Savoy, on Mar. 27. His cult was approved in 1360. F. D. Nov. 30.

ANDREW AVELLINO. *See* Avellino, St. Lorenzo.

ANDREW CACCIOLI, BL. (d. 1254). Born in Spello, Italy, he served as a diocesan priest in Spoleto and at twenty-nine became a Franciscan at the hands of the founder. He served in Spain, then returned to Italy to work to maintain strict observance of the rule; his opposition to the reforms of Bro. Elias led to active opposition and, twice, to imprisonment. He directed the Poor Clares, lived a life of notable devotion at the friary of Carceri, near Assisi, and died at the house which he had founded in Spello. F. D. June 3.

ANDREW THE CALABYTE, ST. (d. 766), martyr. A native of Crete, he went as a monk to Constantinople to oppose the Iconoclastic heresy of Emperor Constantine Copronymus. When he protested the ill-treatment of Christians he was seized, tortured, and stabbed to death by the surrounding mob. F. D. Oct. 20.

ANDREW OF CRETE, ST. (660?–740?), archbishop. Born in Damascus, he went to Jerusalem at fifteen and became a monk under St. Sabas. He was put in charge of an orphanage and old-men's home in Constantinople and later made bishop of Gortyna, Crete. He became involved in the final stages of the Monothelite heresy, but explained that his participation was forced. He was distinguished as a preacher and writer of hymns, saints' lives, and homilies, and is reputed to have initiated the *kanon* in the Byzantine liturgy. F. D. July 4.

ANDREW DE' GALLERANI, BL. (d. 1251), founder. A soldier in Siena, Italy, he killed a blasphemer, fled to escape vengeance, and returned later to devote himself to prayer and good works. He built a hospital and founded the Society of Mercy for the care of the sick. The group merged with the Dominicans in 1308. F. D. Mar. 19.

ANDREW OF LONJUMEAU (d. 1253?), missioner. Born in Paris, he was sent to the East in 1228 by Bl. Jordanus of Saxony and was one of those delegated to bring the Crown of Thorns from Constantinople to Venice and then to King Louis IX, who enshrined it at Aix. In 1245, Andrew was sent by Innocent IV as papal ambassador to seek an end to the Eastern schism, had considerable success in converting a number in Palestine, but failed to sway the Orthodox patriarchs.

ANDREW OF MONTEREALE, BL. (1397–1480). Born in Mascioni, Italy, he became an Augustinian at fourteen, was ordained, and preached widely in France and Italy. He served as provincial in Umbria and was known for his severe asceticism. His cult was confirmed in 1764. F. D. Apr. 12.

ANDREW OF PESCHIERA, BL. (d. 1485). Born of Greek descent near Verona, Italy, he entered the Dominican monastery in Brescia, studied at San Marco in Florence, then served for forty-five years as a missioner to the heretics along the Italian and Swiss borders in the Valtelline district. His cult was confirmed in 1820. F. D. Jan. 19.

ANDREW OF RHODES (d. 1440), bishop. A Greek, he became a theologian, was converted from his schismatic church, became a Dominican, and devoted his life to working for religious unity. In 1413 he was made archbishop of Rhodes and was active at the councils of Basle and Ferrara-Florence. Pope Eugene IV sent him to Cyprus, where he brought an end to fragments of Nestorianism, persuaded the local bishops to accept the leadership of Rome, and established peace.

ANDREW OF STRUMI, BL. (d. 1097). Born in Parma, Italy, he supported the faction of St. Arialdo which was attacking Archbishop Guido of Milan for tolerating simony and other evils. When Arialdo was murdered by Guido, Andrew rescued and buried the body of the murdered saint, Andrew became a Vallombrosan monk, abbot of San Fedele, peacemaker between Florence and Arezzo, and biographer of SS. Arialdo and John Gualbert. F. D. Mar. 10.

ANDREW OF WYNTOUN (14th century), historian. A native of Scotland, he was a canon regular of St. Andrew's priory who became prior of Lochleven monastery around 1395 and wrote his *Orygynale Cronykil of Scotland* in rhyme and in the Scots dialect, the first attempt to present history in Scotland accurately and scientifically. Much of the material is by an unknown author which Andrew included in his text.

ANDRONICUS, ST. (1st century). He and St. Junias are mentioned as fellow prisoners by St. Paul (Rom. 16:7). F. D. May 17.

ANDRONICUS, ST. (d. 304), martyr. *See* Tarachus, St.

ANDRONICUS, ST. (5th century). Born in Alexandria, Egypt, he became a silversmith at Antioch, married Athanasia and had two children who died in their parents' twelfth year of marriage. The bereaved couple then went to Egypt where, under the direction of St. Daniel, they lived in separate cells in a large monastic settlement at Tabenna. F. D. Oct. 9.

ANEMPODISTUS, ST. (d. 345), martyr. *See* Acindynus, St.

ANERIO, FELICE (1560?–1614), composer. Brother of Giovanni and born in Rome, he was a boy soprano in the papal choir in 1575–79, studied under Nanini, became a choirmaster in Rome, and in 1594 succeeded Palestrina as composer for the papal choir, a position he held until 1602. He published three collections of church music, but much of his work remains in manuscript. He died in Rome on Sept. 27.

ANERIO, GIOVANNI FRANCESCO (1567?–1620?), composer. A native Roman, and brother of Felice, he served four years in the papal choir under Palestrina, became choirmaster to Sigismund III of Poland about 1609 and later in churches at Verona and Rome. He became a priest in 1616. He was one of the first Italian composers to use the eighth note, or quaver, and the solo with figured bass. Several collections of his work exist; one of the more famous is his arrangement for four voices of Palestrina's six-voice *Mass for Pope Marcellus*.

ANEURIN, ST. (6th century). *See* Gwinoc, St.

ANFOSSI, FILIPPO (d. 1825). Born at Taggia, Italy, he became a Dominican, vicar general of his order, and from 1815 to 1825 was master of the sacred palace under Pope Pius VII. He was active as a controversialist against Gallicanism and arranged with Lamennais the corrections to be made in the latter's *Essai sur l'indifférence*. He died in Rome on May 14.

ANGADRISMA, ST. (615?–695?). A cousin of St. Lambert of Lyons, she became a nun, despite her father's attempt to have her married, and became abbess of the Benedictine convent of Oroër near Beauvais, France. F. D. Oct. 14.

ANGE DE ST. JOSEPH. *See* Brosse, Joseph de la.

ANGE DE STE. ROSALIE. *See* Vaffard, François.

ANGELA OF FOLIGNO, BL. (1248?–1309). From a selfish and sinful early life, even though she was married and the mother of several sons, she reformed suddenly and completely in 1385. She became a Franciscan tertiary and, after the death of her family, the even more active leader of a group which served the poor and sick. She was given numerous spiritual gifts, and died on Jan. 4. She was beatified in 1693 by Pope Innocent XII. F. D. Feb. 28.

ANGELI, FRANCESCO DEGLI (1567–1628), missioner. Born in Sorrento, Italy, he became a Jesuit in 1583, served two years on the Indian mission, then was stationed in Ethiopia from 1604 until his death. He was particularly successful in missionary work among the idolatrous Agazi, into whose language he translated spiritual works and biblical commentaries. He died in Colela, Ethiopia, on Dec. 21.

ANGELI, GIROLAMO DEGLI (1567–1623), martyr. Born in Castro Giovanni, Sicily, he became a Jesuit in 1585 and was sent in 1602 to Japan. He was the first missioner to penetrate the Yezo, Jasu, and Cai regions, where he was so successful that the authorities began a persecution, in which he and others were put to death on Dec. 4 at Yezo, Japan.

ANGELICO, FRA (1387–1455), painter. Christened Guido, he was born in Vicchio, Tuscany, Italy, became a Dominican in 1407 (taking the name Giovanni) with his brother Benedetto (d. 1448), and is also known as Guidolino di Pietro and Giovanni da Fiesole. He worked with Benedetto in illuminating manuscripts. In 1409 the brothers were exiled to Foligno during the papal wars; Giovanni came under the influence of Giotto and produced sincerely pious and brilliantly colored religious studies (*Madonna and Four Saints, St. Dominic, Annunciation*). In 1414 plague drove them out and they stayed in Cortona until 1418, then returned to Fiesole until 1434. Transferred to Florence in 1436, they decorated the cloister and chapter house of their order, San Marco. Invited to Rome in 1445, Fra Angelico painted frescoes in two chapels for Popes Eugenius IV and Nicholas V, began work on a chapel in the Orvieto cathedral, and on his return to Rome in 1447 did miniatures in antiphonaries. San Marco has his *Crucifixion* and a series of Dominican saints; he did many other scenes from the life of Christ, madonnas, *St. Peter Martyr*, and several studies of SS. Cosmas and Damian. His *Christ in Glory Surrounded by Saints and Angels* contains 266 figures. From such designs and the twelve musician angels with which he surrounded his *Madonna of the Linen Weavers* (Uffizi, 1431) comes one interpretation of his nickname, Angelico. Others attribute its origin to his excellence of character. He developed steadily until he became one of the greatest of the Renaissance religious painters, effective in color and composition; he was a pioneer in the use of identifiable landscape and one of the

first to paint the Christ Child as a simple baby. In 1449 he became prior at Fiesole. He died in Rome and is buried there in the Minerva.

ANGELINA OF MARSCIANO, BL. *See* Angioballi, Bl. Angelina.

ANGELIS, BL. JEROME DE (d. 1623), martyr. Born in Castrogiovanni, Sicily, he became a Jesuit at Messina and served as a missioner in Japan for twenty-two years. He was burned to death at Tokyo with Bl. Simon Yempo, a former Buddhist monk, and Pedro Galvez. They were beatified in 1867. F. D. Dec. 5.

ANGELO, ST. (1145–1220), martyr. Son of Jewish converts in Jerusalem, he became a Carmelite at eighteen, then was sent from Mt. Carmel to Rome to obtain the approval of Pope Honorius III for the order's rule. In Sicily his preaching at Palermo and Leocata reformed many sinners and converted hundreds from Judaism. When he publicly rebuked a notorious figure in the latter city he was stabbed to death. F. D. May 5.

ANGELO, ST. (d. 1227), martyr. *See* Daniel, St.

ANGELO, BL. (1226–1312). Born in Foligno, Italy, son of Count Bernard of Torre and Vignole, he became an Augustinian friar at Botriolo in 1246. He founded houses at Foligno, Gualdo Cattanco, and Montefalco, of which he was prior until 1292. He then retired to Foligno for the rest of his life. His cult was approved in 1891. F. D. Aug. 27.

ANGELO, BL. (1669–1739). Born in Acri, Italy, he became a Capuchin in 1690. After early failure, he became a most successful preacher in Naples and Calabria. He was beatified in 1825. F. D. Oct. 30.

ANGELO OF FURCIO, BL. (1246–1327). Born in the Abruzzi, he became an Augustinian when quite young, was brought back to his home at eighteen, and then re-entered religious life. He studied at Paris, then became professor of theology at the Augustinian college in Naples, where he died. His cult was confirmed in 1888. F. D. Feb. 6.

ANGELO OF GUALDO, BL. (1265?–1325). Born in the diocese of Nocera, Italy, he became a Camaldolese laybrother, living his last forty years as a recluse. He died on Jan. 25. His cult was confirmed in 1825. F. D. Feb. 14.

ANGELO OF MASSACCIO, BL. (d. 1458), martyr. A Camaldolese monk at Santa Maria di Serra in Ancona, Italy, he was put to death by the Fraticelli heretics. F. D. May 8.

ANGELUS, BL. (1271–1313). A Camaldolese laybrother at the monastery of San Salvatore at Acquapagana, Italy, he suffered from consumption with exceptional patience. His cult was approved in 1815. F. D. Aug. 19.

ANGELUS SILESIUS. *See* Scheffler, Johannes.

ANGELUS SINESIUS, BL. (d. 1385?). Born in Catania, he became a Benedictine and was abbot of San Martino at Palermo and restored monastic discipline throughout Sicily. F. D. Nov. 27.

ANGILBERT, ST. (740?–814). A member of Charlemagne's court, he served as secretary, privy councilor, and ambassador, pleased many by his Latin verse, enjoyed the high regard of the emperor, whose daughter Bertha he may (or may not) have married. Of their two children, Nithard became a monk. Late in life, the layman Angilbert also became a monk at the monastery of Centula, near Amiens. As abbot, he introduced the practice of the continuous chanting of the divine office by his 300 monks and built up a rich library as well as the foundation itself. F. D. Feb. 18.

ANGIOBALLI, BL. ANGELINA (1377–1435). Daughter of the lord of Marsciano, she was born in Montegiove, near Orvieto, Italy. Married at fifteen to John of Terni, count of Civitella, she was widowed at seventeen. She then became a Franciscan tertiary and made her castle a community of secular tertiaries who went about preaching the desirability of virginity. They were so effective that she was denounced as a sorcerer and a Manichaean heretic. King Ladislaus of Naples dismissed the charges but exiled her shortly after. She and her companions went to Assisi; in 1397 she founded at Foligno, an enclosed convent (the first with vows and enclosures) of the third order regular of St. Francis. Many such convents were established during her lifetime. Her cult was approved in 1825. F. D. July 21.

ANGIOLINI, FRANCESCO (1750–1788). Born in Piacenza, Italy, he became a Jesuit in 1765 and went to Polotsk after the suppression of his Society. There he wrote an Italian-Polish grammar; several plays and a translation of Sophocles in Polish; translations of Josephus Flavius, Thucydides, and Sophocles into Italian; and poems in four languages.

ANGLIN, TIMOTHY WARREN (1822–1896). Born in Clonakilty, Cork, Ireland, he went to St. John, New Brunswick, in 1849, wrote for the Catholic press, and founded the *Morning Freeman* in 1851. As a member of parliament he opposed the confederation of Canada and fought successfully for the right of Catholics to maintain their own schools. He was out of office during the Fenian revolts initiated from the United States in 1866 and 1870 by Gen. John O'Neil, in which he played no part, but after the confederation was elected to the House of Commons and served as its speaker from 1874 to 1877. In his last years he was on the staff of the Toronto *Globe* and also edited the Catholic weekly, the Toronto *Tribune*. He died in Toronto on May 3.

ANGLINUS, ST. (d. 768?). He was tenth abbot of the Benedictine monastery of Stavelot-Malmédy, Belgium. F. D. Oct. 28.

ANGULO, PEDRO (d. 1561), bishop. Born in Burgos, Spain, he came to America as a soldier, became a Dominican in 1529, and went with Las Casas to Central America and Santo Domingo. After a term as provincial he was made bishop of Vera Paz. He labored with the Nahuatl and Zutuhil tribes, wrote tracts in the latter language, and used pictures, charts, and other visual aids with great success on his missions.

ANIAN (1267–1305), bishop. Rebuilder of the cathedral in Bangor, Wales, he baptized King Edward II and wrote several liturgical works for use in his see.

ANIANUS, ST. (1st century), bishop. According to tradition he was the successor to St. Mark as bishop of Alexandria, Egypt, having occupied the see earlier during the Evangelist's absences. F. D. Apr. 25.

ANIANUS, ST. (d. 453?), bishop. Born in Vienne, France, he lived as a hermit there for a while and then went to Orléans, where he was ordained and became its fifth bishop. In 451, Attila and his Huns laid siege to the city, which was saved only through Anianus' efforts. F. D. Nov. 17.

ANIANUS, ST. (5th century). He was fifth bishop of Chartres, France. F. D. Dec. 7.

ANICETUS, ST. (d. 166), pope. A Syrian, he succeeded Pius I in 155, worked against the Marcionites and Gnostics, and discussed with St. Polycarp of Smyrna the involved question of defining the date of Easter. He suffered such tribulations that he is listed as a martyr. F. D. Apr. 17.

ANICETUS, ST. (d. 305?), martyr. He and a relative, Photinus, were put to death at Nicomedia during the Diocletian persecution. F. D. Aug. 12.

ANIMUCCIA, GIOVANNI (1500?–1571), composer. He was born in Florence, Italy, was choirmaster at the Vatican (as predecessor to Palestrina) from 1555 until his death, and sought to blend melody and text in harmonic clarity at the time of counterpoint experimentation. He later was music master under St. Philip Neri, for whose congregation he composed two volumes of *laudi*. He wrote many masses and psalms, published between 1548 and 1568; most of his work is in manuscript in the Sistine Chapel. Often called "father of the oratorio," he died in Rome in Mar. His brother Paolo (d. 1563) was choirmaster at the Lateran in 1550–52 and composed madrigals and a motet. He, too, died in Rome.

ANIMUCCIA, PAOLO. *See* Animuccia, Giovanni.

ANNA, ST. (1st century). Daughter of Phanuel, she was devoted to fasting and prayer, and spoke of Christ, at the time of His Presentation in the Temple, as the Redeemer of Israel (Luke 2:36–38). A widow for eighty-four years, she lived in the Temple. F. D. Sept. 1 (in the East, Feb. 3).

ANNABRING, JOSEPH JOHN (1900–1959), bishop. Born in Hungary, he was brought to the United States as a child and brought up in Turtle Neck, Wisconsin. He was ordained in 1927, served on the staff of the Superior, Wisconsin, cathedral, and became its rector in 1936. He was diocesan superintendent of schools in 1944–45, became a domestic prelate in 1946, and was consecrated bishop of Superior in 1954. He died there on Aug. 27.

ANNAT, FRANÇOIS (1590–1670), theologian. Born in Rodez, France, he became a Jesuit in 1607 and taught thirteen years at Toulouse, where he became rector. He held other offices, including that of provincial at Paris, and was confessor to Louis XIV but resigned when the king took the duchesse de la Vallière as mistress. He defended the Jesuit interpretation of grace against the Oratorian Bigeuf and against the theologians of Port Royal, for which he was attacked by Pascal. His *Works* were published in three volumes at Paris in 1666.

ANNE, ST. (1st century). Nothing certain is known of the mother of the Virgin Mary, not even her name. According to tradition, she was the daughter of a nomad named Akar, was born in Nazareth, and educated (as her daughter was to be) in the Temple at Jerusalem. When about twenty she married a Nazarene, said to have been named Joachim; twenty years later she gave birth to Mary, possibly at Nazareth. She was widowed just after the birth of Christ and died at an advanced age. F. D. July 26.

FRANCES P. KEYES, *St. Anne, Grandmother of Our Saviour* (New York, Messner, 1955).

ANNE, ST. (840?–918?). Born of a wealthy family, she chose to live a monastic life. Many suitors desired her; when she was twenty-eight and Emperor Basil of Macedonia ordered her to take a husband of his choosing, she fled to Leucadia in Epirus to live in prayerful solitude. F. D. July 23.

ANNE OF ST. BARTHOLOMEW. See García, Bl. Anne.

ANNEGARN, JOSEPH (1794–1843), historian. Born in Ostbevern, Westphalia, he taught history at Braunsberg, East Prussia, and wrote a popular and polemic eight-volume *Universal History* (1827–29) and a *Handbook of Patrology* (1839).

ANNEMUND, ST. (d. 658), archbishop. Son of a Gallo-Roman prefect in Lyons, he was educated at the court of Dagobert and became archbishop of Lyons and an adviser to Clovis II. He was friend and patron of the young St. Wilfrid of York. Annemund was attacked and murdered at Châlons-sur-Saône by a group of soldiers sent from the court of queen-regent St.

Bathildis, probably by Ebroin, mayor of the palace. He is also known as Chamond. F. D. Sept. 28.

ANNIBALDI, ANNIBALE D' (d. 1271), cardinal. Born in Rome of a senatorial family, he became a Dominican, studied at Paris, where he was a friend of St. Thomas Aquinas, and served three popes as master of the palace. Urban IV made him a cardinal in 1262. Annibaldi directed the arrangements which made Charles I of Anjou the king of the Two Sicilies and formally crowned that monarch at the Lateran. He served on other papal missions and wrote commentaries on the *Sentences* and *Quodlibeta* ascribed to St. Thomas; the latter dedicated his *Catena aurea* to the cardinal.

ANNIBALE, GIUSEPPE D' (1815–1892), cardinal. Born in Borbona, near Rieta, Italy, he taught at the seminary there, was vicar general of the diocese, was made a bishop in 1881 and a cardinal in 1889 by Pope Leo XIII. He served as prefect of the Congregation of Indulgences and wrote on moral theology, canon law, and the papacy.

ANNIUS OF VITERBO. See Nanni, Giovanni.

ANNO, ST. (d. 780). Born in Verona, Italy, he became bishop of that see. F. D. May 13.

ANNO, ST. (1010–1075), archbishop. Son of a poor Swabian knight, he studied at the cathedral school at Bamberg and became its master and one of Emperor Henry III's chaplains. In 1056 he was appointed archbishop of Cologne and Chancellor. On the death of Henry III, Agnes of Poitou became regent for Henry IV; when the youngster was kidnaped in 1062, Anno became regent with Adalbert, bishop of Bremen. When he became of age, Henry dismissed Anno. Anno led the German bishops in support of Pope Alexander II against the antipope Honorius II. He also became embroiled in a dispute with Count Theodoric when Anno appointed a nephew, Conrad, as bishop of Trèves. The count claimed the right of investiture, and Conrad was murdered when he attempted to occupy the see. Though constantly engaged in political matters, sometimes unfortunately, Anno reformed his see, built monasteries and churches, and cared for the sick and poor. He died at the Benedictine abbey of Siegburg which he had built and to which he had retired for a year of penance. F. D. Dec. 4.

ANNOBERT, ST. (d. 690?), bishop. A Benedictine monk at the abbey of Almenèches, he was appointed bishop of Séez, France, about 685. F. D. May 16.

ANQUETIL, LOUIS PIERRE (1723–1806), historian. Born in Paris on Jan. 21, he became a priest, of the congregation of Ste. Geneviève, taught at Paris and Rheims, was prior of two houses and rector of the college at Senlis. He wrote a history of Rheims and other works but from 1766 to the revolution devoted himself only to the work of his order. Imprisoned, he began his *Universal History* (1797) and finished it and a *History of France* (1805) begun at the direction of Napoleon. He died in Paris on Sept. 6.

ANSALDI, CASTO INNOCENZIO (1710–1780), theologian. Born in Piacenza, Italy, he became a Dominican in 1728, studied at Rome, taught philosophy at Naples, and from 1737 to 1745 held the chair of theology which the king established for him at the university. He also taught at Brescia, Ferrara, and for twenty years at Turin. He wrote on Old and New Testament subjects, the natural law, the early martyrs, revelation, the sacraments, the historicity of the Fathers of the Church, and moral theology. One of his brothers, Carlo Agostino, published a study (1765) on Christians before Constantine; another, Pietro Tommaso, wrote on the divinity of Christ (1754).

ANSALONI, BL. GIORDANI (d. 1634), martyr. Born in San Angelo, Sicily, he became a Dominican, wrote a series of Dominican biographies while in Mexico, studied at Salamanca, and was sent in 1625 to the Philippines. He went to Japan in 1632, escaped detection for two years, was seized and tortured for seven days, then suffocated after he had witnessed the execution of Thomas of St. Hyacinth and sixty-nine other Christians. F. D. Nov. 17.

ANSANUS, ST. (d. 304?), martyr. Born in Rome, of the famous Anician family, he became a Christian at twelve, was denounced by his father, but escaped and was so successful in securing converts in Bagnorea and Siena that he was called "the Baptizer." He was tortured and beheaded during Diocletian's persecution. F. D. Dec. 1.

ANSBALD, ST. (d. 886). Descended from the Luxembourg counts of Querry, he became a Benedictine monk at Prüm, abbot at St. Hubert, and in 860 abbot of Prüm. His monastery was burned by the Normans in 882, and he spent his last years restoring it. F. D. July 12.

ANSBERT OF CHAUSSY, ST. (d. 695), bishop. Chancelor of King Clotaire III, he became a monk at Fontenelle under St. Wandregilsus, whom he succeeded as abbot. He served King Theodoric III as confessor, succeeded St. Ouen as bishop of Rouen in 684, and was banished, apparently for political reasons, to the monastery of Hautmont a few years before his death. F. D. Feb. 9.

ANSEGISUS, ST. (770?–833). Born in the Lyonnaise, France, he became a Benedictine monk at eighteen at Fontenelle and later was chosen to direct the material and spiritual restoration of the abbeys of St. Sixtus at Rheims, St. Meuge near Châlons, St. Germer at Beauvais, Luxeuil, and Fontenelle. The last became widely known for its library and scriptorium. Ansegisus

was an adviser of Charlemagne and of Louis the Debonair; his capitulary of the laws and decrees of the Frankish kings became the official collection for the empire. F. D. July 20.

ANSELM, ST. (1036–1086), bishop. Born in Mantua, Italy, and offered the succession when his uncle Pope Alexander II went from Lucca to Rome, he refused on the grounds that he would have to accept the office from a secular power, Emperor Henry IV. He later accepted the see of Lucca at the insistence of Pope St. Gregory VII but withdrew to the Cluniac monastery in Polirone where he became a Benedictine. The pope asked him to return to Lucca, which needed reformation, but when he introduced changes the canons rebelled. Countess Matilda of Tuscany tried to banish them, the pope excommunicated them, but Henry came to their support and removed Anselm in 1079. The bishop continued to support the papacy's attack on lay investiture, which caused him to suffer much, but he persevered, became legate to Lombardy under Pope Victor III, wrote a collection of ecclesiastical rules and a commentary on the Psalms, and established a reputation as a scholar of scripture and of the Church Fathers. F. D. Mar. 18.

ANSELM, ST. (1033–1109), archbishop and Doctor of the Church. Born in Aosta, Piedmont, Italy, he sought to enter a monastery at fifteen, was rejected, and followed a worldly and subsequently much-regretted way of life. He left home, studied in Burgundy, where he became a student under Lanfranc, and joined the Benedictines at Bec as a monk at twenty-seven. He became prior there in 1063, its abbot in 1078, and, still in Lanfranc's footsteps, archbishop of Canterbury, England, in 1093. King William II had been hostile to the appointment, since he wished to keep the revenues for himself, demanded payment of 1000 marks, and would not permit the calling of needed synods. Anselm refused to pay the levy and would not bend under attacks by William and several opportunistic bishops. In 1097, Anselm left for Rome, where his position was sustained but where he also saved the king from being excommunicated by Pope Urban II. At William's death, Anselm returned but met new opposition from Henry I, who demanded that the archbishop be reappointed and that a number of royal friends be appointed bishops. Anselm refused to countenance lay investiture, went again to Rome. Henry ordered him to stay out of the country and confiscated church revenues; Pope Paschal II threatened excommunication. The men were reconciled at a meeting in Normandy: the king agreed not to appoint bishops and Anselm permitted the bishops to give service for their temporal possessions. Henry even made Anselm regent of the nation in 1108 when he was absent on the

Continent. Anselm is called the "father of scholasticism" and was one of the great theologians. At Bec he wrote *Monologium*, on the existence of God; *Proslogium*, on His attributes, which influenuced Alexander of Hales, Duns Scotus, Descartes, and Hegel; studies on evil, free will, and predestination; prayers and meditations; and a text on logic. During his first journey to Rome, and while staying in Campania, he wrote *Cur Deus Homo*, on the Incarnation. Because of its clarity he was asked to attend the Council of Bari (1098) to resolve the difficulties of some Italo-Greek bishops. Four years later, at a domestic council at Westminster, he made one of the first and strongest attacks on the slave trade. He died and was buried in Canterbury and was declared a Doctor of the Church in 1720. F. D. Apr. 21. EADMER, *Vita Anselmi*, ed., Martin Rule (London, Rolls Series, 1884); JOSEPH CLAYTON, *St. Anselm* (Milwaukee, Bruce, 1933).

ANSELM OF LAON (d. 1117), theologian. Educated at Bec, France, under St. Anselm of Canterbury, he taught at Paris and aided William of Champeaux in setting up the university there. He then established a school of theology at Laon, which Abelard attended. Anselm was called *Doctor scholasticus*. His principal work is *Glossa interlinearis*, published at Antwerp in 1634, a commentary on the Vulgate. He died on July 15.

ANSELM OF LIÈGE (1008–1056?), historian. Educated at the episcopal school in Liège, he was ordained and became dean of the cathedral there. He worked zealously for Church reform and continued the chronicle of the bishops of the city (begun by Heriger) from 680 to his contemporary, Bishop Wazo.

ANSELM OF NONANTULA, ST. (d. 803?). This duke of Friuli fought in the army of the Lombard King Aistulf and founded a hospital and monastery at Fanano. He became a Benedictine at Rome and returned to rule over 1000 monks at the monastery of Nonantula, which he had founded and near which he built another hospital. He was banished to Monte Cassino for seven years by King Desiderius but restored by Charlemagne. F. D. Mar. 3.

ANSELME, ANTOINE (1652–1737). Born at L'Isle-Jourdain, France, he studied at Toulouse, was ordained, and served in Paris as tutor to the son of Marquis d'Antin. He preached at court, before the French Academy, and became so popular that his speaking schedule was booked three years in advance. He published seven volumes of sermons, a collection of odes, and papers for the Academy of Inscriptions, to which he was elected in 1710. He died at the abbey of St. Sever, which King Louis XIV had given him in 1699.

ANSFRIDUS, ST. (d. 1010), archbishop. Count of Brabant, he served Emperors Otto III and Henry II, built a convent at Thorn, which his wife and daughter entered, intending to become a monk, instead he was appointed archbishop of Utrecht. Later he founded the abbey of Heiligenberg and retired there as a Benedictine in his blind old age. F. D. May 3.

ANSKAR, ST. (800?–865), archbishop. Born near Amiens, he studied at both Old Corbie, where he became a monk, and New Corbie, and accepted the request of the converted King Harold of Denmark to return to his country as a missioner. For the next fifteen years he labored successfully in Norway, Sweden, and North Germany, was named abbot of New Corbie and first archbishop of Hamburg in 831 and papal legate to Scandinavia. When the Norsemen overran the area in 845, its inhabitants lapsed into paganism; Anskar was made archbishop of Bremen and returned later to his mission territory to reclaim the people from idolatry. F. D. Feb. 3.

ANSLO, REYER (1622–1669), poet. Born in Amsterdam, Holland, of Mennonite parents, he won many prizes for occasional poems and was honored for them by his own country and by Sweden. He became a convert in 1651, was secretary to Cardinal Capponi at Rome, and was honored for further poetic achievement by Pope Innocent X. He died in Perugia, Italy.

ANSOVINUS, ST. (d. 840), bishop. Born in Umbria, Italy, he became a hermit at Castel Raimondo, near Torcello, after his ordination served as chaplain to Louis the Pious while the emperor was in Italy, and was raised by him to the see of Camerino. F. D. Mar. 13.

ANSTEY, THOMAS CHISHOLM (1816–1873). Born in London, he was educated at University College there, passed the bar, was one of the first converts during the Oxford Movement, championed the restitution of rights to Catholics in England, and taught law at Prior Park College, near Bath. From 1847 to 1852 he served in parliament, opposing Palmerston's foreign policy and advocating currency reforms. In 1854 he became attorney general of Hong Kong but was suspended after four years because of his demands for reforms. He then was a lawyer and judge in Bombay, but again had to resign when his attack on commercial abuses caused a collision with powerful interests. Returning to England, he wrote and spoke out strongly for better treatment of natives, espoused the cause of universal suffrage, and attacked Disraeli's reform bill. He returned to India in 1868 and died in Bombay on Aug. 12.

ANSTRUDIS, ST. (d. 700?). Daughter of SS. Blandinus and Salaberga, she became a Benedictine nun at the convent of St. John the Baptist at Laon, which had been founded by her mother, whom she succeeded as abbess. She was persecuted by Ebroin, mayor of the palace, until Bl. Pepin of Landen became her protector. She is also called Austru. F. D. Oct. 17.

ANSTRUTHER, GEORGE ELLIOT (1870–1940), editor. Born in London, he married Lydia Richardson in 1896, served as secretary of the Catholic Truth Society from 1909 to 1920, of the Historical Research Society, and of the permanent committee of the national Catholic congresses. He edited the *Universe* in 1906–9, was assistant editor of the *Tablet* in 1920–36, and associate editor of the *Catholic Herald* until his death on Mar. 20. He wrote a study of William Hogarth, *A Hundred Years of Catholic Progress,* and numerous pamphlets.

ANSUERUS, ST. (11th century), martyr. A noble in Schleswig, he became abbot of a Benedictine monastery near Ratzenburg, and was stoned to death with twenty-eight monks when the Wends rose against Christianity after the death of Emperor Henry III. F. D. July 17.

ANSUINUS, ST. (d. 888), martyr. *See* Ageranus, St.

ANSURIUS, ST. (d. 925). Bishop of Orense, in Spanish Galicia, from 915 to 922, he helped to found the Benedictine abbey of Ribas de Sil, and retired there as a monk for his last three years. He is also known as Isauri. F. D. Jan. 26.

ANTELLA, ST. BENEDICT DELL' (13th century). *See* Monaldo, St. Buonfiglio.

ANTERUS, ST. (d. 236), pope and martyr. A Greek, he is listed as the successor of St. Pontian, elevated on Nov. 21, 235, with a brief pontificate of only forty-three days. He was put to death for attempting to obtain official records of the martyrdom of other Christians, and buried in the catacombs at St. Callistus, F. D. Jan. 3.

ANTHELM, ST. (1107–1178), bishop. Born near Chambéry, he became a Carthusian at twenty, followed Hugh I as seventh prior of the Grande Chartreuse, restored the buildings destroyed by an avalanche, and enlarged the settlement. He brought the charterhouses together by his labors before and after the first general chapter of the order (they formerly were individually subject to local bishops), directed Bl. John the Spaniard to write a constitution for women who wished to live under the Carthusian rule, and saw the order advance in all ways. In 1154 he became prior at Portes, returned to simple retirement at the mother house in 1156, then had to become active, with Geoffrey, abbot of Cistercian Hautecomb, in supporting Pope Alexander III against the antipope Victor IV. In 1163, against his earnest pleas, he was forced to accept the bishopric of Belley. Once consecrated, he reformed the diocese thoroughly, restored a celibate clergy, punished oppressors of the people, and excommunicated Humbert III, a powerful papal supporter, for interference and murder. In spite of a serious quarrel over this, Pope Alexander chose Anthelm to reconcile Henry II with Thomas à Becket, but the bishop

was unable to go to England. In his last years he worked directly with lepers and with the victims of drought. He was distributing food to the famished when Humbert came to him and obtained forgiveness; his charitable exertions proved too great, and he died of fever and exhaustion. F. D. June 26.

ANTHELMI, CHARLES (17th century). Bishop of Grasse, he collected and published a number of historical papers written by his brother Joseph.

ANTHELMI, JOSEPH (1648–1697), historian. Born in Fréjus, France, he was ordained at Lyons, became a canon of the cathedral at Fréjus, published a history of his diocese (1680), engaged in controversy with Quesnel (defending Prosper of Aquitaine over Leo the Great as author of several works, and preferring Vincent of Lérins over Bishop Vigilius as author of the Athanasian Creed), wrote a life of St. Martin of Tours, and became vicar general to the bishop of Pamiers.

ANTHEMIUS (5th century). A magistrate at Constantinople, he was a major official in the city at the time that his close friend St. John Chrysostom was deposed in 404; under pressure from the saint's enemies he supplied troops to disperse those faithful to the bishop, but censured those who forced his hand. He became consul in 405, and was prefect of the East until 417. He was counselor to Theodosius the Younger; his daughter married Procopius, and he became grandfather of Emperor Anthemius.

ANTHES, ST. (d. 303), martyr. He and SS. Caius and Fortunatus were put to death near Salerno, Italy, during the Diocletian persecution. F. D. Aug. 28.

ANTHIMUS, ST. (d. 303), bishop. During the extremes of the persecution of Diocletian and Maximian, most of the Christians in Nicomedia were put to death. On one day its bishop, Anthimus, was beheaded with eleven associates. F. D. Apr. 27.

ANTHIMUS, ST. (d. 303), martyr. A priest in Rome, he was ordered drowned for converting the prefect-husband of the Christian matron Lucina; the waters of the Tiber carried him away, but he was recaptured and beheaded. F. D. May 11.

ANTHIMUS, ST. (d. 303?), martyr. *See* Cosmas, St.

ANTHONY OF PADUA, ST. (1190?–1231), Doctor of the Church. Born in Lisbon, Fernando de Bulhões, when about sixteen, joined the canons regular of St. Augustine, went to Coimbra for eight years to avoid the closeness of friends, was ordained in 1219 or 1220, and about 1220 became a Franciscan, taking the name Anthony. He went to the Morocco missions but became so ill he had to sail for Rome. His ship was driven by storms to Sicily, and he went north as far as Assisi, where he attended the general chapter of 1221, at which Brother Elias and St. Francis were present. He served briefly at the hermitage of San Paoli near Forlì, then was sent to preach, with astonishing success, as a confessor and convert-maker, to great crowds throughout northern Italy. He also was the first of his order to be appointed lector in theology. After 1226 he was stationed in Padua, where he continued to preach, boldly and brilliantly, sparing neither civil nor ecclesiastical figures in his attacks on corruption and worthlessness, worked for the abolishment of debtors' prisons, and remained devoted to prisoners, the poor, and heretics. He was canonized in 1232 by Pope Gregory IX and declared a Doctor of the Church in 1946 by Pope Pius XII. The story that St. Anthony once held the Christ Child, depicted in popular art since the seventeenth century, is of late origin; his concern with lost objects seems to have originated from a posthumous legend. F. D. June 13.

MARY PURCELL, *St. Anthony and His Times* (Carden City, N. Y., Hanover House, 1960).

ANTHONY OF SIENA (d. 1585). Born near Braga, Portugal, he became a Dominican and studied at Lisbon, Coimbra, and Louvain. At the last university he taught for several years, became doctor of theology in 1571, and in 1574 was placed in charge of the Dominican college. Banished for political reasons, he traveled in England, France, and Italy and published annotated editions of the work of St. Thomas Aquinas. He also was one of the collaborators on the Roman edition of that saint's works, published in 1570–71 under the patronage of Pope Pius V. He had great devotion to St. Catherine of Siena, hence his added name; he also is known as Antoninus Luistanus. He died in Nantes, France, on Jan. 2.

ANTHONY OF STRONCONE. *See* Vici, Bl. Antonio.

ANTHUSA, ST. (8th century). A hermit, she later took charge of a convent near Constantinople, was tortured by Emperor Constantine Copronymus because she refused to destroy icons, and spared through the efforts of the empress. F. D. July 27.

ANTHUSIA, ST. (d. 280?). *See* Athanasius, St. (d. 257?).

ANTIDE-THOURET, ST. JOAN (1765–1826), foundress. Born in Sancey-le-Long, near Besançon, France, the daughter of a tanner, she joined the Sisters of Charity of St. Vincent de Paul at Paris in 1787. In 1793, during the revolution, the order was dispersed and she returned home before she had made her profession. There she opened a free school, nursed the sick, and sheltered priests, for which last she was forced to flee to Switzerland in 1796. She returned in 1799 and established the Institute of the Daughters of Charity, which in 1807 received the approval of the archbishop of Besan-

çon. The group spread to Switzerland, Savoy, and Naples (where she directed a 1000-bed hospital) and in 1818 was approved by Pope Pius VII. Her later years were marred when Archbishop de Pressigny of Besançon refused to acknowledge papal permission for each convent to be under the jurisdiction of the bishop where it was located; he then forbade all in his area even to write to the members of the order in Italy. Before her death Mother Joan was directing charitable work in 126 units outside France. She was canonized in 1934. F. D. Aug. 25.

ANTIDIUS, ST. (d. 265?), bishop and martyr. The successor to Froninus as bishop of Besançon in Gaul, and also known as Tude, was put to death by Vandals at Ruffey. F. D. June 17.

ANTIMUS, ST. (8th century). He was abbot of the Benedictine monastery of Brantôme, founded by Charlemagne in 769. F. D. Jan. 28.

ANTINOGENES, ST. (4th century), martyr. *See* Victor, St.

ANTIOCHUS, ST. (d. 110?), martyr. He was slain on Sulta, a small island off Sardinia, now named after him, during the reign of Hadrian. F. D. Dec. 13.

ANTIOCHUS, ST. (3rd century), martyr. A physician, he was slain at Sebaste during the reign of Hadrian; Cyriacus, his executioner, converted at the scene, was also put to death. F. D. July 15.

ANTIOCHUS, ST. (d. 303), martyr. *See* Nicostratus, St.

ANTIOCHUS, ST. (5th century). A priest at Lyons, France, he was sent to Egypt to ask Bishop Justus to give up his life as a hermit, returned alone, and was chosen to direct the vacant see. F. D. Oct. 15.

ANTIOCHUS OF PALESTINE (7th century). Born near Ancyra (now Ankara, Turkey), he became a monk at the laura of St. Saba in Jerusalem, whose members were scattered after the Persian conquest of 619. Between that date and 628 he wrote, at the request of Abbot Eustathius, the *Pandects of Holy Scripture*, a series of moral sentences, and *Exmologesis*, a prayerful lament for the miseries of the Holy Land. The *Pandects* records the martyrdom of forty-four monks at St. Sabas, lists the heresies from Simon Magus to the Monophysites, and preserves selections from many non-extant early writings.

ANTIPAS, ST. (d. 90?), bishop and martyr. The bishop of Pergamos was spoken of by St. John the Evangelist and was burned to death in Asia Minor during the persecution of Domitian. F. D. Apr. 11.

ANTIPATER OF BOSTRA (5th century), bishop. He succeeded Constantine as bishop of Bostra in Arabia about 460 and wrote a refutation of Eusebius' *Apology for Origen* which was of such authority it was ordered read in the Eastern churches to check the spread of Origen's doctrines. The seventh General Council (787) recorded sections of it. He also wrote strongly against the Apollinarists. He is honored in the East on June 13.

ANTOINE, PAUL GABRIEL (1678–1743), theologian. Born in Lunéville, France, he became a Jesuit in 1693, taught at Pont-à-Mousson, and published a series of theological texts and ascetical treatises.

ANTON ULRICH (1633–1714). He succeeded to the throne in the duchy of Brunswick-Lünenburg-Wolfenbüttel in 1704, made a serious study of the Fathers of the Church, and became a convert in 1710. He published a history of his conversion, several historical romances, dramas, and hymns. His daughters, Henrietta and Augusta, also were converts.

ANTONELLI, GIACOMO (1806–1876), cardinal. Born in Sonnino in the Papal States on Apr. 2, he took his law degree at the Sapienza, served in the diplomatic service of Pope Gregory XVI, became minister of the interior in 1841, treasurer of the Apostolic Camera in 1845, and, though not a priest, was made a cardinal by Pius IX in 1847. He held numerous papal offices, including that of secretary of state from 1848 until his death in Rome on Nov. 6.

ANTONELLI, LEONARDO (1730–1811), cardinal. Born in Sinigaglia, Italy, on Nov. 6, nephew of Cardinal Nicolò, he became a canon in the Vatican basilica, held numerous papal offices, was made cardinal-priest in 1775 by Pope Pius V, and later served as bishop of Ostia. He supported the French Civil Constitution of the Clergy in the hope of preventing the end of church services, later helped to prepare the concordat between France and the Vatican, accompanied Pope Pius VII to Paris, and was banished by the French from Rome in 1808. He died in his native town on Jan. 23.

ANTONELLI, NICOLÒ MARIA (1698–1767), cardinal. Born in Sinigaglia, Italy, on July 8, he wrote a study of parish life in early Rome, and edited the commentary on the psalms by St. Athanasius and the sermons by St. James of Nisibis. He died on Sept. 24.

ANTONIA, ST. (d. 259), martyr. See Agapius, St.

ANTONIA OF FLORENCE, BL. (1400–1472). Born in Florence and widowed when quite young, she became a Franciscan tertiary and later took charge of the convents at Foligno and at Aquila. When she asked St. John Capistran to permit her to follow a stricter rule, she was placed in charge of a house which followed that of St. Clare. Her patience was outstanding through years of extreme illness and family quarrels, primarily those led by her wastrel son. F. D. Feb. 28.

ANTONIANO, GIOVANNI (d. 1588), patrologist. Born in Nimejen, Holland, he became a Dominican, served as prior in his native city in 1566 and in 1587, and succeeded Henry Gravius as editor of the works of the Fathers of the Church. His special contributions were editions of SS. Basil, Gregory of Nyssa, Jerome, and Paulinus of Nola.

ANTONIANO, SILVIO (1540–1603), cardinal. Born in Rome on Dec. 31, he took his law degree at Ferrara, taught the classics there, and from 1563 to 1566 held the chair of belles-lettres founded by Pope Pius IV at the Sapienza. He studied theology under St. Philip Neri, was ordained in 1568, and at the suggestion of St. Charles Borromeo wrote on the Christian education of children (1583). He was made a cardinal in 1599 by Pope Clement VIII. He also was one of the authors of the Roman catechism and worked on the revision of the breviary. He died in Rome on Aug. 16.

ANTONIEWICZ, CHARLES (1807–1852). Born in Lwow, Poland, on Nov. 6, he studied at home; his father, Joseph, was a prominent lawyer and noble. After the latter's death in 1823 he studied law and philology at Lwow, wrote poetry in German and Polish, and gathered materials for the history of Armenians in his homeland. After service in the army he married and had five children. When his wife died he became a Jesuit in 1839, was ordained in 1844, and preached in the Sandec region and throughout Silesia. Some seventy volumes of poems, sermons, and devotional works were written in his last years, before his death of cholera at Posen, Poland, on Nov. 14.

ANTONINA, ST. (d. 304?), martyr. She was tortured and put to death, possibly at Nicomedia, during the persecution of Diocletian. There is no question of her existence, but she is claimed for Cea in Bithynia, Cea in the Aegean, and Ceja in Spanish Galicia, and honored on Mar. 1, May 4, and June 12.

ANTONINA, ST. (d. 313), martyr. See Alexander, St.

ANTONINUS, ST. (d. 186), martyr. An executioner in Rome, he became a Christian after the trial of St. Eusebius and was beheaded during the reign of Commodus. F. D. Aug. 22.

ANTONINUS, ST. (d. 297), martyr. He and SS. Germanus and Zebinas were beheaded at Caesarea in Palestine during the reign of Galerius; St. Ennatha was burned to death at the same time. F. D. Nov. 13.

ANTONINUS, ST. (3rd century), martyr. A soldier in the Theban legion, he was put to death near Piacenza, Italy. F. D. Sept. 30.

ANTONINUS, ST. (d. 304), martyr. He and SS. Claudius and Cyrinus were put to death in Rome with Pope St. Marcellinus. F. D. Oct. 25.

ANTONINUS, ST. (d. 360), martyr. See Melasippus, St.

ANTONINUS, ST. (4th century), martyr. He is said to have been a stonemason who was killed by a mob of pagans at Apomaea, Syria, for building a church; the place has also been listed as Pamiers, France. F. D. Sept. 2.

ANTONINUS OF FLORENCE, ST. *See* Pierozzi, St. Antoninus.

ANTONINUS FONTANA, ST. (d. 660). He became archbishop of Milan, Italy, in 659. F. D. Oct. 31.

ANTONINUS OF SORRENTO, ST. (d. 830), abbot. Born probably at Picenum, Italy, he lived under Benedictine rule, then retired to join St. Catellus in building the oratory of St. Michael. He later became abbot of the monastery of St. Agrippinus in Sorrento, serving the citizens while their bishop was in prison. F. D. Feb. 14.

ANTONIO DA MURANO. *See* Vivarini, Antonio.

ANTONIO OF VICENZA (1834–1884). Born in Vicenza, Italy, he became a reformed Minorite, was ordained in 1856, and published editions of St. Bonaventure's *Breviloquium* (1874), *Lexicon Bonaventurianum* (1880), and lives of nineteen Franciscan saints. He died in Rovigno on June 22.

ANTONIUS (3rd century). Although the poem *Carmen adversus gentes* published in Migne's *Patrologia latina* is attributed to him, it probably was written by St. Paulinus of Nola.

ANTONIUS, RICHARD. *See* Champs, Étienne.

ANTONIUS OF HOORNAER, BL. (d. 1572), martyr. *See* Antonius of Weert, Bl.

ANTONIUS OF WEERT, BL. (d. 1572), martyr. He and Bl. Antonius of Hoornaer were Franciscans at Gorkum, Brabant, when the community was seized by a mob of Calvinists. They were tortured and hanged at Briel, Holland. The group was beatified in 1867. F. D. July 9.

ANTONY, ST. (d. 258?), martyr. He, SS. Irenaeus, Saturninus, Theodore, Victor, and seventeen others were put to death during the reign of Valerian. F. D. Dec. 15.

ANTONY, ST. (251–356). Orphaned before he was twenty, he distributed his inherited wealth, placed his sister in a community of holy maidens, and entered the Egyptian desert to live a life which became known through Christendom for its devotion, prayer, fasting, and simplicity. In 305 he came out of retirement to found a monastery in the Fayum, with isolated cells for the many men who had followed his ascetic example. There he gave instruction to the monks; later, he entered Alexandria at the height of the persecution of Maximian to give solace to sufferers; and, still later, entered the city in 355 to preach against the Arians. Letters and visitors came to him from all over the Christian world, and he informed and converted many by his conversation and preaching.

He died, still exceptionally active at 105, at a hermitage on Mt. Kolzim, near the Red Sea. His biography was written by St. Athanasius, and there are important details in Palladius and Cassian. F. D. Jan. 17.

HENRI QUEFFELEC, *St. Anthony of the Desert* (New York, Dutton, 1954).

ANTONY, ST. (6th century). He and SS. John and Merulus were Benedictine monks at St. Andrew's abbey, Rome, when Pope St. Gregory the Great was abbot there. F. D. Jan. 17.

ANTONY, ST. (d. 900?), martyr. *See* Andrew, St.

ANTONY, ST. (983–1073). Born at Lubech, near Chernigov, Ukraine, he tried living as an anchorite but then became a hermit attached to the monastery of Esphigmenou on Mt. Athos. Several years later he returned to his native land and lived in a cave at Kiev on the Dnieper River. People came to see him because of his reputation for holiness, and gradually a community grew up—the famous Caves of Kiev, the first Russian monastery. After a land gift from Prince Syaslav a monastery and church were built. He gave up the rule of the community to Barlaam, established a monastery at Chernigov, but came back to die in his cave at the age of ninety. F. D. July 10.

ANTONY, ST. (d. 1342), martyr. He and his brother John were serving Duke Olgierd of Lithuania, became converted with Eustace, another official, and were tortured and put to death for their faith. The three are patron saints of the city of Vilna. F. D. Apr. 14.

ANTONY OF AMANDOLA, BL. (1260?–1350). Born near Ascoli Piceno, Italy, he became an Augustinian in 1306, and was noted for his great devotion to the poor and his exemplary imitation of the career of St. Nicholas of Tolentino. His cult was confirmed in 1759. F. D. Jan. 28.

ANTONY KAULEAS, ST. (829–901), patriarch. Abbot of a monastery near Constantinople, he became patriarch of Constantinople in 893 and devoted himself to repairing some of the ravages of the Iconoclast heresy. F. D. Feb. 12.

ANTONY OF LÉRINS, ST. (468?–520?). Born in Valeria, Lower Pannonia, he was raised by St. Severinus at Favia and later by his uncle, the bishop of Lorch, Bavaria. He became a monk in 488 and lived as a recluse on the shores of Lake Como, but was so besieged by disciples that he went to Gaul where he spent the last two years of his life as a monk at Lérins. F. D. Dec. 28.

ANTONY OF PADUA, ST. *See* Anthony, St.

ANTONY THE PILGRIM. *See* Manzi, Bl. Antony.

ANTONY OF ST. BONAVENTURE, BL.

(1588–1628), martyr. Born in Tuy, Galicia, Spain, he studied at Salamanca, became a Franciscan, and was sent to the Philippine mission. He was ordained in Manila, went to Japan, reconciled 2700 apostates, and was burned to death at Nagasaki. He was beatified in 1867. F. D. Sept. 8.

ANTONY OF SAXONY, BL. (d. 1369). A Franciscan friar, he was betrayed by an apostate monk and put to death for his faith at Widdin, Yugoslavia, during the persecution of King Bazarath. With him died four companions, Bl. Gregory of Tragurio, Ladislaus of Hungary, Nicholas of Hungary, and Thomas of Foligno. They were honored locally on Feb. 12.

ANTONY OF STRONCONE, BL. *See* Vici, Bl. Antonio dei.

ANTONY, FRANZ JOSEPH (1790–1837). Born in Münster, Westphalia, he was a priest and organist at the cathedral there and published songs, masses, and a study of Gregorian chant (1829).

ANYSIA, ST. (d. 304?), martyr. A native of Thessalonica, she was stabbed by a soldier when she refused his attempt to drag her to sacrifice to the gods. F. D. Dec. 30.

ANYSIUS, ST. (d. 410?), bishop. He succeeded to the see of Thessalonica in 383, was appointed vicar apostolic in Illyricum by Pope St. Damasus, and in 404, with fifteen other Macedonian bishops, appealed to Pope Innocent to come to the support of the censured St. John Chrysostom. F. D. Dec. 30.

AOUT. *See* Aigulf, St.

APARICIO, BL. SEBASTIAN (1502–1600). Born in Gudina, Spanish Galicia, he was a farm laborer at Salamanca, then went to Mexico. He became wealthy from success in cartage, road building, and a mail route, but lived simply, making large charitable gifts. At seventy he gave all his wealth to the Poor Clares, joined the Franciscans in Mexico City, and spent his last years begging for the friars. He was beatified in 1787. F. D. Feb. 25.

APARISI Y GUIJARRO, ANTONIO (1815–1872), poet. Born in Valencia, Spain, on Mar. 28, he became a criminal lawyer in 1839, edited several Catholic newspapers at Valencia and Madrid, and served both in the house of representatives and the senate. He worked for the union of the families of Isabel II and Charles of Bourbon, engaging in political conferences at Paris and London; he also was active in the Carlist movement in 1870. He wrote on royalty, Catholic union, and composed a large body of poetry. He was elected to the Spanish Royal Academy shortly before his death on Nov. 5.

APELLES, ST. (1st century), martyr. He and St. Lucius, mentioned by St. Paul (Rom. 16:10, 21), were among the first disciples of Christ; Apelles is traditionally known as bishop of Smyrna. F. D. Apr. 22.

APHRAATES (4th century), bishop. Born a pagan in Syria near the Persian border late in the third century, he was converted, entered religious life, and became bishop of the monastery of Mar Mattai, Mesopotamia. Because he took the name Jacob, he long was confused with Bishop Jacob of Nisibis (d. 338). Between 337 and 345 he wrote *Demonstrations*, twenty-three homilies or epistles, the oldest extant document from the Church in Syria. The comments are of great importance as to the continuity of the early Church, the virginity and maternity of Mary, the sacraments, particularly penance, and the popularity of scripture. The name is listed as that of a martyr during the persecution of King Sapor. F. D. Apr. 7.

APHRODISIUS, ST. (5th century), martyr. He and St. Peter were killed by Arian Vandals in northern Africa. F. D. Mar. 14.

APHTHONIUS, ST. (d. 345), martyr. *See* Acindynus, St.

APODEMIUS, ST. (d. 304), martyr. He is one of twenty Christians tortured and slain for their faith at Saragossa during the Diocletian persecution, and honored later by the poet Prudentius. They were Caecilian, Eventius, Felix, Fronto, Julia, Lupercus, Martial, Optatus, Primitvus, Publius, Quintilian, four called Saturninus, Successus, and Urban. F. D. Apr. 16. Two others, Caius and Crementius, died later from the effects of torture.

APOLLINARIS, ST. (1st century?), bishop and martyr. The first bishop of Ravenna, Italy, is said to have been banished four times from his see, tortured each time, and beaten to death by a mob during the persecution of Vespasian. Legend makes him a native of Antioch who was sent to the Italian city by St. Peter. F. D. July 23.

APOLLINARIS, ST. (d. 179?), bishop. He wrote a study of the sources of early heresies and tracts against the Montanists, but all his manuscripts have been lost. His defense of the Christian religion and of the power of prayer, addressed to Emperor Marcus Aurelius, has been preserved by Eusebius. Because of this, Claudius Apollinaris, bishop of Hierapolis, is called "the Apologist" by the Church Fathers. F. D. Jan. 8

APOLLINARIS, ST. (d. 290?), martyr. He was executioner at Rheims, France, who became a Christian after observing the courage of St. Timothy under torture and was beheaded with him. F. D. Aug. 23.

APOLLINARIS, ST. (453?–520?), bishop. The elder son of St. Hesychius, bishop of Vienne, he was educated by St. Mamertus and consecrated by his own brother, St. Avitus. He was exiled for a year by King Sigismund of Burgundy for joining other bishops in condemning the incestuous marriage of a royal official, but later was recalled. He died at Valence, of which he is patron, after more than a quarter century as its bishop. F. D. Oct. 4.

APOLLINARIS SYNCLETICA. She is a legendary fifth-century hermit who donned boy's clothing to live in the desert. Her name has been confused with that of St. Syncletica.

APOLLO, ST. (1st century). After St. Paul left Corinth, Greece, where he had stayed at the home of Aquila and Priscilla (Acts 18:1), Apollo became bishop, having been sent to Corinth from Ephesus by Priscilla.

APOLLO, ST. (d. 302?), martyr. A servant of Alexandra, wife of Emperor Diocletian, he and St. Isacius were starved to death in prison for their faith; a third servant, St. Codratus, was beheaded. F. D. Apr. 21.

APOLLO, ST. (306?-395?). A hermit until about eighty, he then established and directed at Hermopolis, a community of 500 monks who, unusually for the times, received Communion daily with their abbot for at least the next eleven years. F. D. Jan. 25.

APOLLONIA, ST. (d. 249), martyr. An aged deaconess, she was tortured and burned to death at Alexandria, Egypt, during the persecutions of Emperor Philip. Because her teeth were knocked out by the rioters, she is represented in art by pincers or a gold tooth. Three others died with her: St. Metras was stoned to death, St. Quinta dragged through the streets and scourged to death, and St. Serapion thrown from the roof of his house by the rioting mobs. F. D. Feb. 9.

APOLLONIUS, ST. (305?), martyr. A deacon at Antinoë, he converted the entertainer Philemon, with whom he was put to death by drowning at Alexandria, Egypt, during the persecution of Diocletian. F. D. Mar. 8.

APOLLONIUS, ST. (4th century). He was bishop of Benevento, Italy, in 326 during the last persecution of Diocletian. F. D. July 8.

APOLLONIUS, ST. (4th century). Born in Sardis in Asia Minor, he was put to death by crucifixion at Iconium. F. D. July 10.

APOLLONIUS THE APOLOGIST, ST. (d. 185?). A Roman senator who was denounced as a Christian by his own slaves, he debated his convictions with the prefect Perennis in the senate chamber and was put to death by the sword. F. D. Apr. 18.

APOLLONIUS OF EPHESUS (3rd century), apologist. Probably from Asia Minor, he may have been bishop of Ephesus. Between 180 and 210 he wrote a now-lost refutation of the Montanist heresy, and was highly praised by Eusebius and St. Jerome and attacked by Tertullian.

APONIUS, ST. (1st century), martyr. *See* Andrew, St.

APORTI, FERRANTE (1791-1858), educator. Born in San Martino dell'Argine, Italy, he was ordained, studied at Vienna, and became

professor of church history at Cremona and superintendent of schools there. He opened a primary school for the poor and lectured and published manuals for instruction in such schools. He also introduced a course in methods at the University of Turin, where he became rector in 1855, and was honored for his work with children by the governments of France and Italy.

APPHIA, ST. (1st century). *See* Philemon, St.

APPHIAN, ST. (d. 306), martyr. Born in Lycia and educated in Phoenicia, he became a convert at eighteen and two years later was beaten, burned, and finally slain by drowning for objecting to the public sacrifice of idols demanded of all citizens of Caesarea during the persecution of Maximian. F. D. Apr. 2.

APPIAN, ST. (d. 483?), martyr. He, SS. Donatus, Honorius, Mansuetus, Severus, and five others suffered at Alexandria, Egypt, during the Monophysite heresy. F. D. Dec. 30.

APPIAN, ST. (d. 800?). A native of Liguria, he became a Benedictine at the abbey of St. Peter at Pavia, Italy, and later a missioner along the Adriatic. F. D. Nov. 6.

APPONYI, ALBERT GYÖRGY (1846-1943), statesman. Born in Pest, Hungary, on May 29, son of Chancellor György Apponyi and Countess Julia Sztáry, he studied at the Jesuit seminary in Kalksburg, Vienna, and Pest, and became a member of parliament in 1872, and served in it until his death. At first a member of the Liberal party, he was president of the *Reichstag* in 1901 and speaker in 1902-4 but left the Liberal group to reorganize and lead the conservative National party in 1904. He was minister of education in 1906-10, succeeded Kossuth as leader of the Hungarian nationalists, retired during the October 1918 revolution, but returned to public life to lead the Hungarian delegation to the Paris peace conference in 1919. He represented Hungary in the League of Nations in 1924-25, and died on Feb. 7 at Geneva, Switzerland.

APRONIAN, ST. (d. 304?), martyr. An executioner, he became a convert as a result of the courage of St. Sisinnius, whom he was taking to trial, and was put to death near Ancona, Italy, during the persecution of Diocletian. F. D. Feb. 2.

APRUS, ST. (d. 507). Born near Trèves, he became bishop of Toul, France. He is also known as Epvre. F. D. Sept. 15.

AQUAVIVA, BL. RUDOLPH (1550-1583), martyr. Son of the duke of Atri and nephew of Claudio Aquaviva, fifth general of the Jesuits, he became a Jesuit in 1568 and was sent to Goa in Portuguese India. In 1579 he went to the court of the Great Mogul Akbar, whom he tried, without success, to convert. When he and other Jesuits attempted to build a church in Cuncolim, north of Bombay, they were attacked by Hindu natives and put to death. They were beatified in 1893. F. D. July 27.

AQUILA, ST. (1st century). A tentmaker and husband of St. Priscilla, he was forced to leave Rome by the decree of Claudius forbidding Jews in Rome. He and his wife took a house at Corinth, where St. Paul stayed (Acts 18:3); they accompanied him to Ephesus, and he used their home on his third missionary journey. Later they returned to Rome (Rom. 16:3–4), then went to Ephesus, and probably died in Asia Minor, although there is a tradition that they were martyred in Rome. F. D. July 8.

AQUILA, ST. (d. 311), martyr. She was torn to pieces during the persecution of Maximinus Daja. Arianus, governor of Thebes, who ordered her execution, became a convert and martyr. F. D. May 20.

AQUILA, ST. (d. 361), martyr. *See* Domitius, St.

AQUILINA, ST. (d. 293), martyr. Born in Byblus, Phoenicia, she was arrested as a child of twelve, tortured, and beheaded during the persecution of Diocletian. F. D. June 13.

AQUILINUS, ST. (d. 180), martyr. *See* Speratus, St.

AQUILINUS, ST. (3rd century), martyr. He and SS. Donatus, Gelasius, Geminus, and Magnus were put to death in Fossombrone, Italy. F. D. Feb. 4.

AQUILINUS, ST. (d. 303), martyr. He was put to death with SS. Heradius, Paul, and two other Christians at Nyon, near Geneva, during the Diocletian persecution. F. D. May 17.

AQUILINUS, ST. (d. 484?), martyr. He and SS. Eugene, Geminus, Marcian, Quintus, Theodotus, and Tryphon were put to death in Africa during the persecution of the Vandal Hunneric. F. D. Jan. 4.

AQUILINUS, ST. (d. 650), martyr. A native of Bavaria, who left his native land to avoid being chosen bishop, he became so forceful a preacher in northern Italy against Arianism that he was assassinated in Milan. F. D. Jan. 29.

AQUILINUS, ST. (620?–695?), bishop. Born in Bayeux, France, he fought under Clovis II against the Visigoths until about 660, when he retired to Évreux with his wife. He lived there quietly until 670, when he succeeded St. Aeternus as bishop of Évreux, spending much of his time as a hermit in a cell built near his cathedral. F. D. Oct. 19.

ARANDA, PHILIP (1642–1695). Born in Moneva, Spain, he became a Jesuit in 1658, taught at Saragossa, wrote on the Incarnation and Redemption, predestination and grace, human conduct, and a life of Isabel Pobar.

ARANHA, BL. FRANCIS (d. 1583), martyr. A native of Braga, Portugal, he went to Goa, Portuguese India, and joined the Jesuits there as a coadjutor. He was mission architect at Goa and had been in India for twenty-three years

when he joined Bl. Rudolph Aquaviva and three others in an attempt to build a church at Cuncolim, north of Bombay. They were attacked by a Hindu mob on July 25; he died the following day. They were beatified in 1893. F. D. July 27.

ARASON, JÓN (1484–1550), bishop and martyr. A native of Iceland, he was consecrated bishop of Hólar at Trondhjem, Norway, in 1524, but married in spite of the law of celibacy. As other Catholic bishops of the island became apostates or were imprisoned by Christian III of Denmark, Arason fought to preserve Catholic sees. He was captured and beheaded, with two of his sons, on Nov. 7. Although the Catholics elected another son, Jón, as his successor, the action could not be confirmed and Protestantism was imposed on the nation.

ARATOR (6th century), poet. Probably a Ligurian, he studied under Ennodius at Milan, Italy, became a lawyer at Ravenna, and entered the service of the Gothic leader, Theodoric. Pope Vigilius made him a subdeacon. His long poem, *De actibus apostolorum*, praises St. Peter at the expense of St. Paul and was read in Rome at the pope's request; the reading took four days. Highly allegorical, it was quite popular during the Middle Ages.

ARAUJO, ANTONIO DE (d. 1632). Born in the Azores, he became a Jesuit missioner, was superior of the missions in Brazil, and wrote a native catechism later published in Lisbon.

ARAUJO, FRANCISCO DE (1580–1664), bishop. Born in Verin, Spain, he became a Dominican, taught at Burgos, and held the chair of theology at Salamanca from 1623 to 1648. He then was appointed bishop of Sevogia, but resigned in 1658 to return to his order's house in Madrid. He wrote commentaries on Aristotle and St. Thomas and other studies in theology.

ARBIETO, IGNACIO DE (1585–1676). Born in Madrid, Spain, he became a Jesuit in 1603, was ordained in 1612 at Lima, Peru, taught philosophy briefly in Ecuador, then for twenty-five years in Peru, and wrote an unpublished history of the latter country.

ARBOGAST, ST. (d. 678?), bishop. Probably born in Aquitaine (not in Scotland or Ireland), he was a hermit in Alsace when Dagobert II made him bishop of Strassburg in gratitude for curing the king's son. F. D. July 21.

ARBUÉS, ST. PEDRO (1442–1485), martyr. Born in Epila, Aragon, he studied at Huesca and Bologna. In 1478 he became an Augustinian at Saragossa and in 1484 was appointed inquisitor of Aragon. He has been accused by some writers of great cruelty in this post, but none of the alleged charges has been proved. He was murdered in the cathedral of St. Savior in Saragossa on Sept. 14 and was canonized in 1867. F. D. Sept. 17.

ARCADELT, JACOB (1505?–1567?), composer. Born probably at Liège, Belgium, where he later became a canon, he was trained as a singer at the court in Florence, was singing master of the Julian Chapel in Rome, and a member of the Vatican choir for ten years. He became court musician to Charles of Lorraine, at Paris, in 1555 and published some 200 madrigals (which had a great influence on Palestrina) in three and four parts, chansons, motets, and masses.

ARCADIUS, ST. (d. 304?), martyr. A Christian who defied orders to sacrifice to the gods during the persecution of Valerian or of Diocletian, he was put to death in Africa by mutilation of each of his limbs but talked persuasively to the throngs present at his torture. The account, however, is believed to be a pious legend. F. D. Jan. 12.

ARCADIUS, ST. (4th century), bishop and martyr. He and St. Nestor were missionary bishops slain on Cyprus. F. D. Mar. 4.

ARCADIUS, ST. (d. 437), martyr. With his fellow Spaniards, SS. Eutychian, Paschasius, and Probus, he was exiled by Arian Vandal King Genseric to Africa when they refused to embrace Arianism, tortured, and slain. St. Paulillus, young brother of Paschasius, and Eutychian were beaten, sold into slavery, and died of exposure. F. D. Nov. 13.

ARCANGIA. See Cione, Andrea de'

ARCE Y OCHOTORENA, MANUEL (1879–1948), cardinal. Born in Pamplona, Spain, he studied at Saragossa and Rome, took doctorates in philosophy and canon law, and became bishop of Zamora in 1928. He was named archbishop of Tarragona in 1938, created cardinal in 1946, and died in Barcelona on Sept. 16.

ARCHANGELUS OF CALAFATIMI, BL. (d. 1460). Born in Calafatimi, Sicily, he was a hermit, then became a Franciscan of the Observance and was active in spreading that group in Sicily. His cult was confirmed in 1836. F. D. July 30.

ARCHDEACON, RICHARD (1620–1693). Born in Kilkenny, Ireland, on Mar. 30, he became a Jesuit at Mechlin in 1642 and taught at Antwerp and Louvain. He wrote a life of St. Patrick, a commentary on the prophecy of St. Malachy, and a treatise (in English and Irish) on miracles. His volume on theology (1671), which had thirteen editions, was placed on the Index, though corrected editions appeared after his death on Aug. 31.

ARCHELAIS, ST. (d. 293), martyr. She and SS. Susanna and Thecla were tortured and beheaded at Salerno, Italy. F. D. Jan. 18.

ARCHELAUS, ST. (3rd century), martyr. See Quiriacus, St.

ARCHELAUS, ST. He is reputed to have been a third-century bishop of Kashkar, Mesopotamia, and long was honored with Dec. 26 as his feast day. Although St. Jerome says he wrote a record of a debate with the founder of Manichaeism, it is believed that this was written long after the death of Manes, by one Hegemonius, who possibly invented the debate and the name Archelaus as well.

ARCHER, JAMES (1751–1832). While working in an inn in London, where he was born on Nov. 17, he attracted the attention of Bishop Challoner and was sent to Douai. Ordained in 1780, he returned and was appointed vicar general of London. He wrote on religious persecution and marriage, as well as six volumes of sermons. He died on Aug. 22.

ARCHINIMUS OF MASCULA (4th century). See Armogastes, St.

ARCHINTO, FILIPPO (1500–1558), bishop. Born in Milan, Italy, he took his law degree at Padua, then served Pope Paul III as governor of Rome, bishop of the Holy Sepulcher, and presiding officer at the Council of Trent. He was transferred to Bologna as bishop, wrote *De fide et sacramentis*, and was a friend and supporter of St. Ignatius Loyola. He was appointed archbishop of Milan by Pope Paul IV but died before he could occupy the see.

ARCHIPPUS, ST. (1st century). An associate of St. Paul (Col. 4:17), he is traditionally known as the first bishop of Colossae. F. D. Mar. 20.

ARCONTIUS, ST., bishop and martyr. An early bishop of Viviers, Gaul, he was mobbed and slain for upholding ecclesiastical rights. The date, eighth or tenth century, is uncertain. F. D. Feb. 5.

ARCOVERDE DE ALBUQUERQUE CAVALCANTI, JOACHIN (1850–1930), cardinal. Born in Pernambuco, Brazil, on Jan. 17, he was ordained, became archbishop of Rio de Janeiro, was made cardinal-priest in 1905, and died in his see city on Apr. 18.

ARCULF (7th century), bishop. A Frankish bishop (possibly of Périgueux, but more likely of a monastery), he landed in Scotland after a pilgrimage to the Holy Land, and gave so detailed a report of his travels to Adamnan, abbot of Iona, that the latter wrote a study which he presented to King Aldfrith of Northumbria in 698. St. Bede relied upon it for his own *De locis sanctis*.

ARDALION, ST. (d. 300?), martyr. An actor who, while mockingly impersonating a Christian martyr facing death, was himself so moved that he announced himself a Christian and was ordered burned at the stake. The story may be a pious fiction. F. D. Apr. 14.

ARDANUS, ST. (d. 1058). He was in charge of the Benedictine monastery at Tournus, near Autun. F. D. Feb. 11.

ARDEN, EDWARD (1542?–1583). Born in Warwickshire, son of a cousin of Mary Arden, Shakespeare's mother, he was high sheriff of the country in 1575 and was arrested in 1583 with his wife, and Fr. Hugh Hall, his chaplain whom he disguised as a gardener, and his son-in-law, John Somerville, and charged with plotting against the life of Queen Elizabeth. They had been named by Somerville after he had been arrested and tortured for his defense of Mary Stuart and attack on Elizabeth in public expression. It also has been charged that Somerville, who may have been feeble-minded, had been paid by followers of the earl of Leicester, whom Arden had openly censured for his immorality, to implicate his father-in-law. Mrs. Arden and Fr. Hall were released, but Arden was hanged at Smithfield on Dec. 30.

ARDO. *See* Smaragdus, St.

AREDIUS, ST. (d. 591). Born in Limoges, France, he served at court, then became abbot-founder of the monastery of Atane, in the Limousin, where the village of St. Yrieix was named for him. He is also known as Yrieix. F. D. Aug. 25.

AREMBERG, CHARLES D' (d. 1669). A prince, he became definitor general of the Capuchins, wrote a series of biographies of members eminent in the order from 1525 to 1612 and a defense of the *Annales* of Boverius.

ARETAS, ST. (d. 523), martyr. A chieftain named Abdullah ibn Kaab, he was the leader of some 300 Christians massacred at Najran in southwestern Arabia. F. D. Oct. 24.

ARETHAS (860?–932?), bishop. Born in Patrae, Greece, he was a follower of Photius, became archbishop of Caesarea early in the tenth century, and compiled the oldest extant Greek commentary on the Apocalypse. He also wrote commentaries on Plato and Lucian and preserved numerous writings in Greek, copied by his scriptors.

ARETINO, CARLO. *See* Marsuppini, Carlo.

ARETINO, LEONARDO. *See* Bruni, Leonardo.

ARÉVALO, FAUSTINO (1747–1824), patrologist. Born in Campanario, Spain, on July 23, he became a Jesuit in 1761, went to Italy in 1767 when his Society was suppressed in Spain, and published a collection of ancient Spanish hymns (1786) under the patronage of Cardinal Lorenzana. The latter's wealth also helped him to issue editions of Prudentius, St. Isidore of Seville, Caelius Sedulius, the works of the fifth-century African poet, Draco, and a Gothic missal. Recalled to Spain by King Ferdinand in 1815, he became provincial at Castile of the restored Society. He died in Madrid on Jan. 7.

ARÉVALO, RODRIGUEZ SANCHEZ DE (1404–1470), bishop. Born in Segovia, Spain, he studied law at Salamanca, became secretary to Kings John II and Henry IV of Castile, and served on several diplomatic missions. Pope Callistus III made him bishop of Oviedo and

commander of Sant' Angelo in Rome; Paul II transferred him to the Spanish sees of Zamorra, Calahorra, and Palencia. He wrote a popular reflection on human conduct, *Speculum vitae humanae* (1468); a history of Spain to 1469 (1470); and *De monarchia orbis* (1521), on the power of the papacy to punish kings. He died on Oct. 4.

AREZZO, BL. PAOLO BURALI D' (1511–1578), cardinal. Born in Itri, Italy, he was a well-known lawyer in Naples and served as royal counselor from 1549 to 1558. He then became a Theatine, was superior of houses in Naples and Rome, was made a cardinal by Pope Pius V and bishop of Piacenza and later of Naples. He was beatified in 1772. F. D. June 17.

ARGENSEN, PIERRE DE VOYER D' (1626–1710), governor. Born in Touraine, France, son of René de Voyer, ambassador to Venice, he served in the army, rose to high office under the crown, and in 1657 was appointed governor of Canada. He had only 100 soldiers to protect Quebec but gave brave example to the colonists and had some success with the Iroquois. Although his relations with the Jesuit missioners were good, he ran into difficulties at the arrival of Bishop Laval in 1689. Too much stress on continental formality created Church-state tension; too much tolerance of liquor sales to Indians invited numerous attacks. Requests to France to allow more self-government to the colony and for more soldiers to protect it met with disregard, and in 1661 the vicomte d'Argensen asked to be recalled and returned to his estate at Mouzé, where he died.

ARGENTRÉ, CHARLES DU PLESSIS D' (1673–1740), bishop. Born near Vitré, France, on May 16, he was educated at St. Sulpice, Paris, and the Sorbonne, ordained in 1699, and became vicar general to the bishop of Tréguier in 1707, royal almoner, and in 1723 bishop of Tulle. He wrote on faith, the supernatural, and scripture, edited the theological works of Martin Grandin, and compiled a three-volume collection of documents on theological controversies from the twelfth century, on papal decisions, and on the government of Oxford, Paris, and other universities. He died on Oct. 17.

ARGEUS, ST. (d. 320), martyr. He and his brothers, Marcellinus and Narcissus, were soldiers who were beheaded at Tomi in Pontus when their Christianity was discovered during the persecution of Licinius. F. D. Jan. 2.

ARGÜELLO, JOSÉ DARÍO (19th century), governor. A Mexican noble, he was acting governor of California from 1814 to 1815 and of Lower California until 1822. His son Luis succeeded him.

ARGÜELLO, LUIS ANTONIO (1784–1830), governor. Born in San Francisco of a distinguished family, he became commandant of California in 1806, led an expedition to the Columbia River in 1821, and served as governor from 1822 to 1825, the first native of the area to hold that post.

ARGYMIRUS, ST. (d. 858), martyr. A Mohammedan official at Cordova, Spain, he was converted, became a monk after his post was taken from him, and was later seized and beheaded. F. D. June 28.

ARGYROPOULOS, JOHN (1416–1486?). Born in Constantinople, he taught at Padua in 1434, returned to the East in 1441, and returned to Italy with other scholars after the Turks captured Constantinople in 1453. He taught Aristotelian philosophy at Florence and tutored the sons of Cosimo de' Medici; when plague broke out in 1471, he went to Rome and taught there, publishing translations of Aristotle, commentaries on the latter's *Ethics* and *Politics*, and a treatise on the Holy Spirit. He died in Rome.

ARIADNE, ST. (d. 130?), martyr. She is described as the Christian slave of a Phrygian prince, who was scourged when she refused to celebrate pagan rites, fled to a chasm, and was buried when a rock which was said to have opened to receive her closed over her body. F. D. Sept. 17.

ARIALDUS, ST. (d. 1066), martyr. A deacon, he so forcefully opposed the practice of simony in the diocese of Milan that he long was persecuted and was finally slain by associates of the archbishop. His cult was approved in 1904. F. D. June 27.

ARIANUS, ST. (d. 311?), martyr. Governor of Thebes, he was converted with Theotinus and three others as they observed the courage of SS. Apollonius and Philemon under martyrdom; they themselves were put to death in Egypt by drowning. F. D. Mar. 8.

ARIAS, BENEDICTUS (MONTANUS), (1527–1598). Born in Fregenal, Spain, he studied at Seville and Alcalá, mastered oriental languages, and became a priest. He attended the Council of Trent, went into retirement at Aracena, then was recalled by King Philip II to prepare a polyglot bible at Antwerp. This was published in eight volumes by Plantin (1569–73) and was widely hailed, but charges of heresy raised by the Jesuits sent him to Rome, where he was cleared. Philip then gave him a pension and made him court chaplain and librarian at the Escorial. He wrote Latin poems, a natural history, and studies of Hebrew and biblical antiquities before his death at Seville.

ARIAS, FRANCIS (1533–1605). Born in Seville, Spain, he became a Jesuit at twenty-six, taught at Cordova, was rector at Trigueros and at Cadiz, worked with Moors and Negroes, cared for the sick and prisoners, and wrote a great number of ascetical treatises. He died in Seville on May 15 and was popularly hailed as a saint by the thousands who attended his funeral.

ARIAS DE AVILA, PEDRO (d. 1530). A native of Segovia, Spain, he married a friend of Queen Isabella, became a soldier, and in 1514, when nearly seventy, led an expedition to Colombia. At Darien he displaced Balboa and then had him murdered, even though the latter had become his son-in-law. In 1519 he founded Panama City, Panama. He died at León, Nicaragua, in his eighties, after a career of great cruelty.

ARIBO (d. 1032), bishop. Son of Count Arbo, he was successively deacon at Salzburg, chaplain to Emperor Henry II, and in 1021 archbishop of Mainz, Prussia. At the emperor's death the Saxon succession came to an end; Aribo arranged the election of Conrad II and served as his chancellor. He ably administered his see, called the Council of Seligenstadt to improve discipline, brought Ekkehard IV from St. Gall to better his schools, won the right to issue coinage, attended the Lateran Council at Rome in 1027, and wrote a treatise on the Psalms. He died on Apr. 6.

ARIOSTO, LUDOVICO (1474–1533), poet. Born in Reggio, Italy, on Sept. 8, son of Nicolò, its governor, and the eldest of ten children, he studied law and the classics and took over the direction of the family in 1500 when his father died. He was in the service of Cardinal Ippolito d'Este from about 1503 to 1518, then of Duke Alfonso d'Este, and from 1522 to 1525 was governor of the district of Garfagnana. About 1530 he married Alessandra Benucci, a widow from Florence. He wrote considerable poetry in the style of Petrarch, five comedies (the first of which, *La Cassaria*, was produced in 1509), and seven long satires on the confusion of his own day. His most famous work is the epical treatment of chivalry, *Orlando Furioso*, begun about 1505, first published in 1516, revised and reissued in 1532. The poem tells of the siege of Paris by the Moors; the madness of Orlando (Roland) after he was spurned by Angelica; and the love of the once-pagan Ruggiero and Bradamante (from whose marriage mythically descended the d'Este dynasty). The poem began its somewhat confused narrative at the point where the poet Boiardo had left off in his *Orlando innamorato*. Ariosto's last years were spent in leisurely study at Ferrara, where he died on June 6.

ARISTARCHUS, ST. (1st century). Born in Salonika, Greece, he accompanied St. Paul (Acts 20:4; 27:2) and was arrested and imprisoned with him at Ephesus. He is traditionally said to have been first bishop of Salonika and to have been beheaded with St. Paul at Rome. F. D. Aug. 4.

ARISTIDES, ST. (d. 123?), apologist. During a persecution at Athens while Hadrian was there, he wrote a defense of Christianity which is said to have been given to the emperor in 126; some claim that the apologia was written later, during the reign of Antoninus Pius. It was praised by St. Jerome, recorded by Eusebius, and discovered in a Syriac version in the late nineteenth century. F. D. Aug. 31.

ARISTION, ST. (1st century), martyr. One of the seventy-two disciples of Christ, he was put to death either at Salamis on Cyprus or at Alexandria. F. D. Feb. 22.

ARISTOBULUS, ST. (1st century). He was one of the seventy-two disciples of Christ; no further identification is certain. F. D. Mar. 15.

ARISTON, ST. (d. 285?), martyr. He and SS. Crescentian, Eutychian, Felicissimus, Felix, Justus, Marcia, Symphorosa, Urban, and Vitalis were put to death at Campagna, Italy, during the persecution of Diocletian. F. D. July 2.

ARLEGUI, JOSÉ (18th century). Born in Biscay, Spain, he became a Franciscan, was sent as a missioner to Mexico, and published a valuable study (1737) of the Zacatecas Indians.

ARMAGILLUS, ST. (d. 570?). Born in southern Wales, he was a cousin of St. Samson. He went to Brittany, where he founded St. Armel des Boscheaux and Ploermel. He also is known as Armel, Arthmael, and Arzel. F. D. Aug. 16.

ARMAGNAC, GEORGES D' (1501?–1585), cardinal. Protégé of Cardinal d'Amboise in his youth, he was soon introduced to Francis I, was named bishop of Rodez, France, in 1529, and served as French ambassador to Venice in 1536–38. He fought for Francis against Charles V in 1538, became ambassador to Rome, and in 1544 was created a cardinal. He was made lieutenant general of the king in 1552, archbishop of Toulouse in 1560, and papal legate at Avignon in 1565. In this position he smoothed relationships between Catholics and Huguenots and between the populace of Avignon and that of Orange and Languedoc. He was made archbishop of Avignon in 1576, and died on June 2.

ARMANET, CRESCENT (1879–1955), educator. Born in France, he became an Assumptionist, was provincial of North America for his order, served as president of Assumption College, Worcester, Massachusetts, and died in Marseilles, France, on Dec. 22.

ARMEL. See Armagillus, St.

ARMELLINO, MARIANO (1657–1737). Born, perhaps in Ancona, Italy, he became a Benedictine at Rome, studied at Monte Cassino, taught philosophy for eight years, then preached widely from 1697 to 1722. He served as abbot of Siena, Assisi, and Foligno, where he died. He prepared a biographical dictionary of the Benedictines of the Cassinese congregation.

ARMENTARIUS, ST. (5th century). He was bishop of Antibes, Provence, about 450. F. D. Jan. 30.

ARMENTARIUS, ST. (d. 711?). He was bishop of Pavia, Italy. F. D. Jan. 30.

ARMOGASTES, ST. (d. 455?). A palace officer in the service of Theodoric the Vandal, he was cruelly tortured for his faith, condemned to labor in the mines at Byzacena, and then publicly disgraced by being made a cowherd at Carthage. It is possible that another official, Archinimus of Mascula, underwent the same disgrace. F. D. Mar. 29.

ARMSTRONG, ROBERT JOHN (1884–1957), bishop. Born in San Francisco on Nov. 17, he studied at Gonzaga University, Spokane, and the Grand seminary, Montreal, was ordained in 1910, served as curate in Spokane, and was pastor of St. Paul's in Yakima from 1914 to 1929. He was consecrated bishop of Sacramento in 1929 and reigned there until his death on Jan. 14. He founded the diocesan paper, the Sacramento *Register*, in 1930.

ARNAUD (12th century). He became abbot of Bonneval, Chartres, and wrote the mystical treatise *Traité de l'oeuvre des six jours* and a biography of St. Bernard.

ARNE, THOMAS AUGUSTINE (1710–1778). Born in London, England, on Mar. 12, he was educated at Eton, became a lawyer, and married Cecilia Young, a singer. He wrote the music for *Alfred*, a masque by James Thomson and David Mallett (which celebrated the Protestant succession and contained *Rule Britannia*), produced his oratorio *Abel* and his operas *Britannia* and *Comus* while in Dublin, then returned to Drury Lane Theatre and the London music halls. Oxford gave him the degree of doctor of music in 1759. *Artaxerxes*, an opera, and *Judith*, an oratorio, followed; he was the first to use women's voices in the choruses of oratorios. He wrote incidental music for a number of dramatic presentations and for the Shakespeare jubilee of 1769. He died on Mar. 5.

ARNI THORLAKSSON (1237–1297), bishop. Born in Iceland, he went to Norway in 1262 as a deacon, was ordained, served as administrator of the see of Holar, and became bishop of Skalholt in 1269. Iceland, previously a republic, had come under the political control of the king of Norway in 1264. The bishop worked both with the local council and with the king to protect Church interests, to clarify land problems, and to arrange for ecclesiastical investiture. He died in Bergen, Norway.

ARNOBIUS (3rd century). A rhetorician at Sicca, Africa, he became a Christian and wrote a defense of monotheism, on the divinity of Christ, the nature of the soul, and the extent and forms of idolatry. He made a number of major errors as to the actual existence of pagan gods and as to the divine origin of the soul.

ARNOLD (12th century). Abbot of the Benedictine monastery of Bonneval, near Chartres, France, from 1144 to 1156, he wrote a number of spiritual works and a life of St. Bernard.

ARNOLD (d. 1466). He was bishop of Lübeck, Germany, from 1449 to 1466, was skilled in canon law, and established peace in 1465 between Poland and the Teutonic Order.

ARNOLD, THOMAS (1823–1900). Son of Thomas Arnold, headmaster at Rugby, and brother of the critic Matthew Arnold, he was born in Laleham, Staines, England, on Nov. 30 and attended Winchester, Rugby, and Oxford. He was a friend of John Henry Newman, became a convert, and was selected as professor of literature for the Catholic University of Dublin but was barred by hostile Irish bishops. Arnold taught classics at the Oratory School, left the Church after the attack on Liberalism by Pope Pius IX, but returned and died a Catholic. His daughter was the novelist, Mrs. Humphry Ward. Thomas wrote on the history of English literature and published editions of *Beowulf*, Wyclif, and Henry of Huntington. He died in Dublin, Ireland, on Dec. 12.

ARNOLD AMALRICUS (d. 1225), archbishop. Cistercian abbot of Cîteau in 1201, he became papal legate and inquisitor in southern France in 1204 and was made archbishop of Narbonne in 1212. His alleged order to execute Catholics and Albigensians alike at the siege of Béziers has been historically refuted.

ARNOLD DE' CATTENEI, BL. (1184–1254), Italian abbot. Born in Padua, he became a Benedictine at the monastery of St. Justina there, was captured while abbot, and kept in chains for eight years by the tyrant Ezzelino. He died in prison at Asola, Italy. F. D. Mar. 14.

ARNOLD OF COLOGNE (14th century). He succeeded Meister Gerhard in 1301 as master architect of the cathedral of Cologne and with his son John completed the upper apse and the choir. He suggested the change from three to five naves.

ARNOLD OF CORBIE (11th century). He was abbot of the Benedictine monastery of St. Matthias, near Trèves, France, in 1063 and wrote a treatise on the calculation of Easter and a Latin poetical paraphrase of the book of Proverbs.

ARNOLD OF HARFF (1400?–1499?). Born in the duchy of Jülich, he wrote an account of a pilgrimage to the Holy Land during 1496–99.

ARNOLD OF LÜBECK (d. 1211?). A Benedictine abbot, he supported the papacy in the Hohenstaufen quarrel and was the author of *Chronica Slavorum* (1172–1200).

ARNOLD OF MADETO (d. 1536). Dominican prior at Limoux, France, he was inquisitor general at Toulouse in 1531, wrote against heresy, and published *Breviarium de mirabilis mundi* (1499) at Avignon.

ARNOLD OF MONTANERI (14th century).

A Franciscan, he was condemned for his extreme teachings on the poverty of Christ and the apostles.

ARNOLD OF TONGRES (d. 1540). A canon at the cathedral of Cologne, he became dean of the faculty of arts and taught theology there, wrote a commentary on Juvenal, a treatise on celibacy, and was satirized by Ullrich von Hutten.

ARNOLDI, ALBERTO (14th century). An architect, he directed the building of the cathedral in Florence, his native city, about 1358. In 1364 he completed the massive statue of the *Virgin and Child* (formerly attributed to Andrea Pisano) for the church of Santa Maria del Bigallo there.

ARNOLDI, BARTHOLOMEW (1463–1532). Born in Usingen, Germany, he became an Augustinian and taught philosophy and theology for thirty years at Erfurt, where Luther was one of his students. He preached against the attacks on the Church in 1521 and 1522, predicted the Peasants' War, attended the Diet of Augsburg (1530), and died at Würzburg, to which he had been transferred in 1526, on Sept. 9.

ARNOLFO DI CAMBIO (1232?–1300?), architect. Born in Florence, Italy, he seems to have begun his career at Siena under Nicolò Pisano, and went with his master to Pisa, Perugia, Cortona, Orvieto, and Rome. He had also studied with his father and with Cimabue. He built the outer wall, the corn market, the piazza of the Priori and the chapel of the Badia at Florence, designed the Franciscan church of Santa Croce and the cathedral of Santa Maria del Fiore, and erected the Palazzo Publico. He died in Florence.

ARNOUL. *See* Arnulf, St.

ARNPECK, VEIT (1440–1505). Born in Landshut, Bavaria, he studied at Amberg and Vienna, was a priest in his native city, and wrote a *History of Austria* (to 1488) and a chronicle of the bishops of Freising.

ARNULF (850?–899), emperor. Illegitimate son of Carloman of Bavaria, he led the East Franks in rebellion against his uncle, Charles III, in 887 and ruled as their king from that year until his death. He defeated the Normans in 891, was successful against the Moravians, and in 894 made a weak incursion into Italy at the request of Pope Formosus, but stopped at Piacenza. He invaded with more strength in 896, took Rome, and was crowned emperor. He was stricken with paralysis and returned to his homeland. He was the last of the Carolingian emperors.

ARNULF, ST. (d. 640?), bishop. He served at the court of King Theodebert II of Austrasia and married Doda, by whom he had two sons, Clodulf and Ansegisel. She entered a convent and he was about to become a monk at Lérins, when he was induced in 610 to become bishop of Metz and continued to take a prominent part in the affairs of state. He persuaded Clotaire of Neustria to accept the throne of Austrasia and then served for many years as counselor to Clotaire's son, Dagobert. In his last years Arnulf resigned the bishopric and retired with St. Romaricus to a hermitage near the abbey of Remiremont. The name is also spelled Arnoul. F. D. July 18.

ARNULF, ST. (d. 840?), martyr. A monk at Novalese, Piedmont, Italy, he was slain by Saracens. F. D. Oct. 31.

ARNULF, ST. (d. 871). He became bishop of Toul in 847 and strongly opposed the divorce of King Lothair. F. D. Nov. 15.

ARNULF, ST. (d. 1070). Born in Vendôme, France, he became a Benedictine there, was made bishop of Gap, and restored its cathedral. F. D. Sept. 19.

ARNULF, ST. (1040?–1087), bishop. Born in Flanders, he served in the armies of Kings Robert and Henry I of France, then became a Benedictine monk at the monastery of St. Médard at Soissons, where he lived as a recluse. In 1082 he was appointed bishop of Soissons against his will; he later resigned and founded a monastery in Oudenbourg. F. D. Aug. 16.

ARNULF, ST. (d. 1160), archbishop. He succeeded to the see of Mainz, Germany, in 1153 and was murdered by his own diocesans. F. D. July 1.

ARNULF (d. 1184), bishop. Educated by his brother, the bishop of Séez, France, he studied canon law at Rome, defended Pope Innocent II against the antipope Anacletus II, and in 1141 was made bishop of Lisieux. He went on the crusade in 1147 with King Louis VII, defended Henry II of England before the pope after the murder of Thomas à Becket, lost favor, and spent his last three years in retirement at Paris, where he died on Aug. 31.

ARNULF THE BAD (d. 937). He became duke of Bavaria in 907 when his father Luitpold fell in battle, with most of the Bavarian nobility, during the invasion by the Magyars. Arnulf defeated the conquerors twice, in 909 and 913, then became embroiled in strife with his stepfather, King Conrad of Swabia. He twice had to flee the country, but while he occupied it he despoiled eight major monasteries and most of the churches and controlled the bishops. When Henry I succeeded Conrad, Arnulf submitted to the Synod of Regensburg in 932, restored monastic land, and began to rebuild some of the churches. He died on July 14.

ARNULF CORNEBOUT, BL. (1180?–1228). Born near Brussels, he became a Cistercian laybrother at Villers, Brabant, at twenty-two and devoted himself to extreme mortification and austerities. F. D. June 30.

ARONTIUS, ST. (d. 303?), martyr. *See* Honoratus, St.

ARPE, AGOSTINO (d. 1704). A supporter of the theological views of Egidio Colonna, he published a *Summa* of the latter's works in 1701 at Bologna.

ARRIAGA, PABLO JOSÉ (1564–1622), missioner. Born in Vergara, Spain, he became a Jesuit in 1579, was ordained in Peru in 1585, and was three times rector of the College of San Martin at Lima. He also was rector of Arequipa, founded a college for Indians, and worked zealously in rooting out native idolatry (on which he wrote an elaborate study). He died in a shipwreck while on the way back to Europe.

ARRICITIVA, JUAN (18th century). A Mexican Franciscan, he was prefect of the College of Propaganda at Querétaro and wrote the second volume of the *Chronicles* of Querétaro on mission work in Arizona and California.

ARRIGHETTI, NICOLA (d. 1639), mathematician. Born in Florence, he became a disciple of Galileo and a member of the Florentine Academy. He was one of the founders of the Platonic Academy and was translating the *Dialogues* into Tuscan at the time of his death in Florence.

ARRIGHETTI, NICOLÒ (1709–1767). Born in Florence on Mar. 17, he became a Jesuit in 1724, taught philosophy at Spoleto, Prato, and Sienna, and wrote treatises on heat, light, electricity, and barometric pressure. He died on Jan. 31.

ARRIGHI, ST. BIAGIO (1676–1740). Born in Corte, Corsica, he became a Franciscan in 1693 and took the name Theophilus. He studied at Rome and Naples, was ordained in 1700, and after five years as teacher of philosophy began a brilliant career as missioner in Italy and Corsica. He was canonized in 1930. F. D. May 21.

ARROWSMITH, BL. EDMUND (1585–1628), martyr. Born in Haydock, Lancashire, England, of farming parents, he saw his family persecuted for their faith, went to Douai in 1605, was ordained in 1612, and was sent back to England for ten years. He was arrested in the winter of 1622–23, released, and became a Jesuit. He was recaptured in 1628, condemned for his priesthood, and hanged, drawn, and quartered at Lancaster. He was beatified in 1929. F. D. Aug. 28.

ARS, CURÉ D'. *See* Vianney, St. John Baptist.

ARSACIUS, ST. (d. 358). A Persian in the Roman army, he became a Christian and after his term of service lived as a recluse on a tower in Nicomedia. He warned the inhabitants of the city of its impending destruction, and asked them to pray and repent, but was ignored. An earthquake destroyed the area but spared his tower; survivors found him dead, in a posture of prayer. F. D. Aug. 16.

ARSENIUS, ST. (d. 250), martyr. With Heron and Isidore he was tortured and burned at the stake during Decius' persecution. Dioscorus, a boy of fifteen, also was tortured, but freed. F. D. Dec. 14.

ARSENIUS, ST. (d. 950?), martyr. He and two other hermits, Pelagius and Sylvanus, were slain by Moors near Burgos, Spain. The Benedictine abbey of Artanza was later built on the spot. F. D. Aug. 30.

ARSENIUS, ST. (d. 959), bishop. A native of Constantinople, he became first bishop of the Island of Corfu, of which he is the chief patron. F. D. Jan. 19.

ARSENIUS AUTORIANOS (d. 1273), patriarch. He joined a monastery in Nicaea, without taking orders, changed his name from George to Gennadius to Arsenius, became abbot and, in 1255, patriarch of Constantinople. He had great difficulty during the reign of Michael Palaelogus (who killed George Mouzalon, regent of John, son of John III, and then blinded the boy). Arsenius excommunicated the emperor, but was deposed in 1264 and died in exile on the island of Proconnesus. When Germanus, bishop of Adrianople, who followed him as patriarch, attempted to lift the sentence of excommunication, many of the court and people withdrew their allegiance, thus beginning the Arsenian schism, which was not healed until 1315.

ARSENIUS THE GREAT, ST. (d. 450?). A Roman deacon, he was appointed tutor to Emperor Theodosius' children, Arcadius and Honorius, about 383, at the recommendation of Pope Damasus. He left Constantinople, after ten years of court life, to join a group of monks at Alexandria. On the death of Theodosius he went into the desert at Skete and lived there for forty years of great austerity. About 434, a barbarian attack forced him to flee to various refuges until his death at Troë, near Memphis. F. D. July 19.

ARTALDUS, ST. (1101–1206), bishop. Born in Savoy, he served at the court of Duke Amadeus III of Saxony and in 1120 became a Carthusian at Portes, where he was ordained. He established charterhouses at Valromey and, after that burned down, on the Avrières River in 1140, and was widely consulted because of his sageness. When over eighty he was made bishop of Belley, against his wishes, and two years later, in 1190, was allowed to resign and retire to Avrières, where he died at 105. His cult was approved in 1834. F. D. Oct. 7.

ARTEMAS, ST. (1st century). He is mentioned by St. Paul (Titus 3:12) and is traditionally called bishop of Lystra. F. D. Oct. 30.

ARTEMIUS, ST. (d. 302), martyr. A jailer in Rome, he was converted with his wife Candida

and daughter Paulina by St. Peter the exorcist and baptized by St. Marcellinus. Artemius was beheaded and the others buried alive. F. D. June 6.

ARTEMIUS (d. 363). The Arian imperial prefect of Egypt under Constantine the Great, he persecuted Catholics and pagans alike. When Julian the Apostate became emperor, Artemius was beheaded for destroying idols. He is listed in the Roman Martyrology despite his Arianism.

ARTEMIUS, ST. (d. 396), bishop. An imperial legate, he became ill on his way to Spain, remained in the Auvergne region of Gaul, and later was chosen as bishop of Clermont. F. D. Jan. 24.

ARTEMIUS, ST. (d. 609). He was bishop of Sens, France. F. D. Apr. 28.

ARTEMON, ST. (d. 305?), martyr. A priest at Laodicea, Phrygia, he was burned to death during the Diocletian persecution. F. D. Oct. 8.

ARTHELAIS, ST. (d. 560?). Daughter of the proconsul Lucius of Constantinople, she was secretly sent to join her uncle in Benevento when Emperor Justinian had claimed her. In gratitude over her escape, she dedicated herself to a life of fasting, but died of fever at sixteen. F. D. Mar. 3.

ARTHMAEL. *See* Armagillus, St.

ARTHUR, JAMES (d. 1670?). Born in Limerick, Ireland, he became a Dominican and taught at Salamanca and, in 1640, at Coimbra. He lost the chair of theology there when he refused to agree to defend the doctrine of the Immaculate Conception, retired to a Dominican house in Lisbon, where he was preparing a commentary on the *Summa* of St. Thomas Aquinas when he died there.

ARTHUR, THOMAS (1593–1666?). Born in Limerick, Ireland, he studied at Bordeaux and at Paris, where he took his degree in medicine, and began practice in Limerick in 1619, moving to Dublin in 1624. He wrote a manuscript diary, in Latin, of his medical cases.

ARUNDEL, THOMAS (1353–1414), archbishop. Son of Richard Fitzalan, earl of Arundel, and Eleanor, daughter of Henry Plantagenet, he was born at Arundel Castle, Sussex, and rose quickly in the Church through his family's power. He was archdeacon at Taunton in 1374 when he was made bishop of Ely, became royal chancellor in 1386–88 through the regency of Richard II, and gained the forcefully vacated see of York in 1388. He was again named chancellor in 1391, moved the royal court from London to York, and in 1396 became archbishop of Canterbury and resigned as chancellor. He was most active against Wyclif and the Lollards, held a synod in 1397, but lost political favor. In 1397, King Richard persuaded the archbishop to bring his brother, Richard Arundel, to the royal palace for a conference, broke faith as a host and arrested the earl, and later publicly dishonored Thomas before parliament. Richard Arundel was tried for treason and executed; the archbishop was ordered banished, escaped to Rome, and stripped of his honors at the king's demands. Arundel was given the empty title of archbishop of St. Andrew's but later joined the forces of Henry of Lancaster in the invasion of Wales and England. He regained his see at Canterbury in 1399, was present in the House of Lords when Richard abdicated, and crowned Henry IV in Westminster in 1399. He continued his active opposition to Lollardry, and the defense of the papacy, served as chancellor in 1407 and 1412, and died on Feb. 19.

ARUNDELL, HENRY (1606–1694). He succeeded Thomas as third Lord Arundell of Qardour in 1643. He fought against Cromwell, who had imprisoned his family, blew up his castle (occupied by parliamentary troops), was wounded in battle, and forced into exile. He returned in 1660, arranged the preliminaries of the treaty between Louis XIV and Charles II, was imprisoned in 1678 on perjured evidence during the Titus Oates Plot, and was released after five years. While in prison he wrote *Five Little Meditations in Verse*. He became keeper of the privy seal under James II, and worked for fellow Catholics after the revolution of 1688.

ARUNDELL, JOHN (d. 1433). Called "the Magnificent," he was a wealthy landowner in Cornwall, a noted church benefactor, member of parliament in 1422–23, sheriff of Cornwall four times, and a naval officer of distinction, knighted by the crown.

ARUNDELL, JOHN (d. 1591?). A descendant of the Cornwall Arundells, Sir John was converted by Fr. Cornelius of Bodmin and, as a result of defending the latter, lost his title and property during the Elizabethan persecution and was imprisoned for nine years in Holborn. He died in Ideworth in 1589 or 1591.

ARUNDELL, THOMAS (1560–1639). Son of Sir Matthew Arundell of Wardour castle, Wiltshire, England, he opposed the Elizabethan religious changes, was imprisoned in 1580, and, when freed, joined the Austrian army under Archduke Matthias. For his valor at the battle of Gran, Hungary, against the Ottomans, he was made count of the Holy Roman Empire in 1595. When he returned to England he was created first Lord Arundell of Wardour by King James I. He died in Oxford on Nov. 7.

ARUNDELL, THOMAS (d. 1643). He succeeded to his father's title as second Lord Arundell of Wardour in 1639, raised a company of cavalry, fought for King Charles I, and died of wounds at Oxford. His wife, Lady Blanche, daughter of Edward, earl of Worcester, de-

fended the family castle with twenty-five men against 1,300 rebels under Sir Edward Hungerford, reducing it to uselessness before she was forced to surrender after an eight-day siege. She died at Winchester in 1649.

ARZEL. *See* Armagillus, St.

ASAPH, ST. (d. 600?), bishop. A monk, he may have succeeded St. Kentigern as abbot and bishop in Denbighshire, then founded the monastery of Llanasa in Flintshire, Wales. F. D. May 1 (sometimes, May 11).

ASCALESI, ALESSIO (1872–1952), cardinal. Born in Castelnuovo, Italy, he was ordained, was created a cardinal in 1916, became archbishop of Naples in 1938, and frequently made pleas for peace in 1938 over the Vatican radio. He died in Naples on May 11.

ASCELIN (d. 1255). He became a Dominican at Paris about 1221, and was sent by Pope Innocent IV with three other Dominicans to attempt to convert Sultan Melik Saleh, then in Persia. They were imprisoned and maltreated, but later released and allowed to preach. The mission returned to Rome in 1248. Ascelin returned to the East, where he died, but probably not as a martyr.

ASCENSIANUS, JODOCUS. *See* Badius, Jodocus.

ASCHBACH, JOSEPH VON (1801–1882), historian. Born in Höcht, Hesse-Nassau, on Apr. 29, he studied at Heidelberg and became professor of history at Bonn and at Vienna. In 1855 he became a member of the Academy of Sciences, received a title in 1870, and wrote on the Goths, the Moors in Spain, the Roman emperors, histories of Portugal and of the University of Vienna, and the four-volume *Allgemeine Kirchenlexicon*. He died in Vienna on Apr. 25.

ASCLAS, ST. (3rd century), martyr. An Egyptian, he is said to have been tortured, imprisoned, and put to death by drowning during the Diocletian persecution. F. D. Jan. 23 (in the East, May 20).

ASCLEPIADES, ST. (d. 217). He succeeded St. Serapion as bishop of Antioch in 211 and suffered much during the persecution of Severus. F. D. Oct. 18.

ASCLEPIODOTUS, ST. (d. 310?), martyr. He and SS. Maximus and Theodore were Bulgarians slain at Adrianopolis. F. D. Sept. 15.

ASELLA, ST. (d. 406?). She became a nun at ten and a recluse at twelve; Palladius mentioned her community of anchoresses at Rome. F. D. Dec. 6.

ASHBY, GEORGE (d. 1537), martyr. A Cistercian monk at Jervaulx, Yorkshire, England, he was among the many whom Henry VIII ordered hanged for the favors shown those who made the Pilgrimage of Grace in 1537; he may have been executed in June, with his abbot and others, or may have been the

Astbebe slain on Mar. 10 with the abbot of Sawley at Lancaster.

ASHLEY, BL. RALPH (d. 1606), martyr. An Englishman, he served as cook at Douai College, went to Valladolid, Spain, in 1590, became a Jesuit laybrother, and returned to England in 1598. He served and was captured in 1604 with Fr. Edward Oldcorne. He was frightfully tortured during two years of imprisonment in the Tower of London, then was executed at Worcester on Apr. 7. He was beatified in 1929.

ASHTON, JOHN (1742–1814?). Born in Ireland, he became a Jesuit in 1759, was a missionary in Yorkshire, and went as one of the first priests to Baltimore, Maryland, sometime between 1776 and 1784, serving a congregation totaling forty, mostly Acadian refugees. In 1788 he was chosen to begin building Georgetown University. He died in Maryland.

ASHTON, VEN. ROGER (d. 1592), martyr. Son of Richard Ashton of Croston, Lancashire, England, he had fought in 1585 under the earl of Leicester in the Low Countries, but with Sir William Stanley turned the town of Deventer over to the Spaniards and was declared a traitor. In 1587 he returned to England, was imprisoned in the Tower and Marshalsea prisons, escaped, was recaptured near Newcastle, and hanged, drawn, and quartered at Tyburn on June 23 after he refused to give up his religion.

ASICUS. *See* Tassach, St.

ASKE, ROBERT (d. 1537). Of an old Yorkshire family, he became an attorney and fellow of Gray's Inn. He was the leader of the Catholics in northern England on the Pilgrimage of Grace who rose to defend the monasteries in 1536, demanded the suppression of Lutheran books, the dismissal of heretical bishops, and the formation of a parliament at York. The rebels numbered 30,000; Henry VIII promised complete pardon if they would disband and also gave assurance that grievances would be discussed when a northern parliament was established. Aske and his associates believed the king, dismissed their followers, and were disregarded. When they attempted to re-form their scattered forces, they were defeated by the duke of Monmouth. Aske and his associates were executed at York in July. He was hung in chains from July 15 until his death on July 22. He is the central figure in H. F. M. Prescott's novel, *The Man on the Donkey*.

ASKEGA, ST. (d. 870), martyr. *See* Theodore, St.

ASPASIUS, ST. (d. 560?), bishop. He directed the present see of Auch, held a council there in 551, and attended three earlier councils in Orléans. F. D. Jan. 2.

ASPELCUETA, MARTIN (1491–1586), theologian. Born in Navarre, Spain, on Dec. 13, he studied at Alcalá and in France, and taught canon law at Toulouse, Cahors, Salamanca, and Coimbra. Known also as Navarrus, he wrote on the breviary, canons regular, ecclesiastical property, revenues from benefices, and penance. He died in Rome on June 1.

ASPERMONT, FLUGI D' (d. 1627). Appointed bishop of Chur, Switzerland, in 1601, under the name John V, he was driven out of his see by Protestants in 1607, 1612, and 1617 and saw the area torn by bloodshed during his reign.

ASPREN, ST. (1st century). Long-established tradition calls him first bishop of Naples, baptized and consecrated by St. Peter. F. D. Aug. 3.

ASSEMANI, JOSEPH ALOYSIUS (1710–1782), scholar. Born in Tripoli, Syria, he studied under his brother, Joseph Simeon, in Rome, became professor of Syriac at the Sapienza, and was appointed a member of Pope Benedict XIV's committee for historical research. He published numerous treatises, notably Codex liturgicus ecclesiae and a study of the Chaldean patriarchs. He died in Rome.

ASSEMANI, JOSEPH SIMEON (1687–1768), scholar. Born in Tripoli, Syria, he studied at the Maronite college, Rome, was ordained, became custodian of oriental manuscripts at the Vatican Library, made large additions from Syria and Egypt, and in 1738 became titular bishop of Tyre and Vatican librarian. He wrote on the Vatican collections, edited the works of St. Ephraem, and issued numerous bibliographical studies. His chief work is *Bibliotheca orientalis Clementino-Vaticana*. He died in Rome in Jan.

ASSEMANI, STEFANO EVODIO (1707–1782), scholar. An orientalist, he was born in Syria and succeeded his uncle, Joseph Simeon, as custodian of manuscripts in the Vatican Library and worked with him on bibliographical projects and on research aids of his own. He also compiled the *Acta* of the martyrs of the Near East. He became titular archbishop of Apamaea, Syria, and died in Rome.

ASSER, JOHN (d. 910?), bishop. Born in Pembrokeshire, Wales, he was educated at St. David's and attained such a reputation for learning that King Alfred invited him to court about 885; he spent half of each year there. He became bishop of Sherborne before 900 and wrote a life of Alfred which also chronicles English history from 849 to 887.

ASSMAYER, IGNAZ (1790–1862), musician. Born in Salzburg, Austria, on Feb. 11, he became choirmaster at the Schotten-Kirche, Vienna, in 1815 and imperial organist in 1825. He wrote fifteen masses and several oratorios, overtures, pastorales, and requiems. He died in Vienna on Aug. 31.

ASSONENSIS, JOHANNES (15th century), bishop. A priest stationed at St. Peter's, Rome, he founded a brotherhood of Germans living in the city, whose purpose was to arrange burial for their poor nationalists who died in the plague of 1448. The group built a church, a hospice for German pilgrims, and cared for Campo Santo de' Tedeschi, south of the cathedral. Johannes later became coadjutor bishop of Würzburg, Germany.

ASTERIA, ST. (d. 307?), martyr. She was beheaded near Bergamo, Lombardy, during the Diocletian persecution. F. D. Aug. 10.

ASTERICUS. *See* Anastasius, St. (d. 1040).

ASTERIUS, ST. (d. 223?), martyr. A priest at Rome, he secretly buried the body of Pope St. Callistus and was put to death by drowning in the Tiber at the command of Emperor Alexander. F. D. Oct. 21.

ASTERIUS, ST. (d. 284?), martyr. *See* Thalelaeus, St.

ASTERIUS, ST. (d. 303?), martyr. He and his brothers, SS. Claudius and Neon, were denounced at Aegea by their stepmother during the Diocletian persecution, tortured, and crucified. Two women, Domnina and Theonilla, were tortured and scourged to death on the same occasion. F. D. Aug. 23.

ASTERIUS OF AMASEA, ST. (d. 410?), bishop. Born in Pontus, he was educated at Antioch, became bishop of Amasea, and attained fame as a preacher. He wrote twenty-one homilies, on penance, fasting, and scriptural themes; they also are significant for their archaeological references. He may also have written a life of St. Basil. F. D. Oct. 30.

ASTERIUS OF PETRA, ST. (d. 365?), bishop. At the Council of Sardica (347) the bishop of Petra, Arabia, was harshly treated by the supporters of Arius, whom he had renounced, exiled to Egypt, and not recalled until 362, when he attended the Council of Alexandria. This dealt with the Meletian schism, supported by Lucifer of Cagliari, to whom Asterius carried a letter from the bishops but which Lucifer disregarded. Asterius then went to Antioch to report on the council's conclusions, and died soon after. F. D. June 10.

ASTIUS, ST. (d. 120?), bishop and martyr. Bishop of Durazzo, Macedonia, he was crucified during the persecution of Trajan. A number of Italian exiles, SS. Germanus, Hesychius, Lucian, Papias, Peregrinus, Pompeius, and Saturninus, were seized for their support of the bishop and put to death by drowning. F. D. July 7.

ASTON, SIR ARTHUR (d. 1649). Governor of Oxford, England, and then of Drogheda, Ireland, for King Charles I, he was beaten to death on Sept. 10 by the soldiers of Oliver Cromwell as the siege of the Irish city ended.

ASTON, HERBERT (b. 1614), poet. Born in Chelsea, England, son of Walter, Baron Aston, he accompanied his father to Spain in 1635 and published *Tixall Poetry* in 1658.

ASTON, WALTER (1584–1639), ambassador. Born in Tixall, Staffordshire, England, son of Sir Edward, he was ambassador to Spain in 1620–25 and 1635–38. He became a convert during his first stay there, was made first baron of Forfar, Scotland, in 1637, and became patron of the poet Michael Drayton. He died on Aug. 13.

ASTON, WILLIAM (1735–1800), educator. Born on Apr. 22, he was educated on the continent, became a Jesuit in 1751, and taught at St. Omer, Watten, and Bruges. He became canon of the cathedral in Liège, Belgium, and died there on Mar. 15. He writings include *Le cosmopolite* and *Lettres ultramontaines*.

ASTRIK RADLA. *See* Anastasius, St. (d. 1040).

ASTROS, PAUL THÉRÈSE DAVID D' (1772–1851), cardinal. Born in Tourves, France, he worked on the concordat of 1804, became administrator of the diocese of Paris, published the bull excommunicating Napoleon in 1808, and was consequently imprisoned for six years. He then became bishop of Bayonne and in 1830 archbishop of Toulouse. He was made a cardinal in 1850 by Pope Pius IX. He died on Sept. 29.

ASTRUC, JEAN (1684–1766). Born in Sauve, France, on Mar. 19, he taught medicine at Montpellier and Paris, became physician to the king about 1728, published *De morba veneris* (1736), and anonymously issued a tract questioning the Mosaic authorship of Genesis, which originated some of the so-called higher criticism of scripture. He died in Paris on May 5.

ASTYRIUS, ST. (3rd century). A Roman senator in Caesarea in Palestine, he witnessed the martyrdom of St. Marinus, buried him with honor, and is said to have been martyred as a result. F. D. Mar. 3.

ASYNCRITUS, ST. (1st century), martyr. Mentioned by St. Paul (Rom. 16:11), he became bishop of Marathon and was put to death. SS. Herodion, Paul's relative, who became bishop of Patras, and Phlegon, mentioned in the same scriptural passage, who became bishop of Hyrcania, also were martyred. F. D. Apr. 8.

ATHANASIA, ST. (5th century). *See* Andronicus, St.

ATHANASIA, ST. (d. 860). Born on the Island of Aegina, she married and was widowed after only sixteen days, when her husband was killed fighting Arab invaders. She married a second time, then separated from her husband when he expressed his wish to become a monk, and converted her home into a convent. She spent her last seven years in a cell at Constantinople as an adviser to Empress Theodora, and died at Timia, to which her convent was moved. F. D. Aug. 14.

ATHANASIUS, ST. (d. 257?), martyr. Bishop of Tarsus, Cilicia, he was put to death with SS. Charisius and Neophytus, two slaves of Anthusia whom he had converted, during the reign of Valerian. Anthusia lived a holy life at Seleucia for twenty-three further years. F. D. Aug. 22.

ATHANASIUS, ST. (d. 303), martyr. He and St. Zosimus are listed as martyrs in Cilicia, Asia Minor, during the Diocletian persecution; another account says that they survived torture and became hermits. F. D. Jan. 3.

ATHANASIUS, ST. (297?–373), Doctor of the Church. Born of Christian parents in Alexandria, Egypt, he was well educated, especially in scripture and theology, consulted the desert monks, including St. Antony, and in 318 became a deacon and secretary to Bishop Alexander. In 325 the two clerics attended the Council of Nicaea, which condemned and excommunicated Arius for teaching that Christ was created in time and was only symbolically the Son of God, thus attacking the full meaning of the Incarnation and Redemption. On the death of Alexander a few months later, Athanasius was chosen bishop of Alexandria and began the direction not only of the great city, but of all the hermit fathers and also of Ethiopia. Ariansim had already gained a foothold in Egypt, with the support of the schismatic Meletians, and spread quickly through the entire Mediterranean world. The Arian forces were led by the exiled bishop, Eusebius of Nicomedia, who directed the Meletians to remove Athanasius by any possible means. The latter countered every charge they raised against him at a series of Arian councils, including those of sorcery and of the murder of an Arian bishop; Athanasius knew where the alleged victim was in hiding but failed to produce him at the trial. In the face of an obviously predirected sentence by a packed council at Tyre, he went to Constantinople to seek out the emperor. During his absence Athanasius was deposed. Strangely, Constantine supported the decision and exiled the bishop to Trèves in 335. Constantine II, Constans, and Constantius divided the kingdom on their father's death; the first restored Athanasius to his see, in 338; the last supported the Arians and approved Pistus, who had the backing of Eusebius, as the new archbishop of Alexandria. A third faction placed Gregory of Cappadocia in power, and Athanasius went to Rome in 341 to bring an end to the violence which was sweeping his city. The Catholic bishops sent a letter of approval and explanation to Pope Julius, who agreed to a demand by Eusebius for a synod to clarify the situation. The Arians then refused to attend; Athanasius was cleared, but could not return to his see until Gregory died, violently, in 345. Athanasius went to Egypt in 346, with the begrudging permission of Constantius, but, when Constans was murdered, his brother ordered three councils to condemn the saint; the third also drove Pope Liberius into exile. Athanasius lived in the desert from 356 to 362, while the Arian George of Cappadocia held the see. The latter was murdered in 361 and was briefly succeeded by Pistus. Athanasius regained his office early the next year with the permission of Julian the Apostate, who, however, ordered him deposed after a few months. He again came out of the desert at Julian's death, was banished in 363 for the fifth time, by Emperor Valens, then restored. His last seven years were comparatively peaceful. His first defense of the Incarnation and Redemption, *Contra gentes*, and *De incarnatione verbi Dei* were written about 318–23 when he still was a deacon. His major works were apparently produced in exile: *Apologia to Constantius*, *Defense of Flight*, *Letter to the Monks*, and *History of the Arians*. While the author of the Athanasian Creed was probably an obscure and unknown cleric, its tenets are those reiterated by Athanasius in letters, sermons, and books. F. D. May 2.

WILLIAM THOMAS WALSH, *Saints in Action* (Garden City, N. Y., Hanover House, 1961).

ATHANASIUS, ST. (d. 452), martyr. A deacon in Jerusalem, he was beheaded when he objected to the heretic Theodosius replacing St. Juvenal as bishop. F. D. July 5.

ATHANASIUS, ST. (d. 818?). Born near Constantinople, he became abbot of a monastery near Nicomedia and suffered during the Iconoclast heresy led by Emperor Leo the Armenian. F. D. Feb. 22.

ATHANASIUS, ST. (d. 872), bishop. Son of the duke of Naples, he became bishop of Naples at eighteen and devoted himself to repairing the damages to the city caused by Saracen invaders and ransoming their captives. Because he denounced his nephew, Duke Sergius II of Naples, for immorality and simony, he was imprisoned at Sorrento, was freed when the populace murmured, but was exiled in 871 to Veroli, near Monte Cassino, where he died. F. D. July 15.

ATHANASIUS, ST. (d. 885?), bishop. Born in Sicily, he went to Patras in Greece when the Saracens invaded his homeland, became a Basilian monk, and, later, bishop of Modon. F. D. Jan. 31.

ATHANASIUS THE ATHONITE, ST. (920?–1000?). Born at Trebizond and baptized Abraham, he studied at Constantinople and became a professor. As a monk at St. Michael's in Bithynia he took the name Athanasius. To avoid becoming abbot he fled to a cave, but was persuaded to organize an expedition against the Saracens. It was successful and with the large sum of money donated by the victors he built the monastery of Mt. Athos in 961–63. By the time of his death he ruled over sixty communities, which later became, and still are, in schism. F. D. July 5.

ATHELBERT (d. 794?). King of the East Angles, he was slain shortly after he asked to marry Alfreda, daughter of King Offa and Queen Cynethryth of Mercia; the latter is blamed for the murder. He was listed as a martyr for some time, with a feast day of May 20.

ATHELM, ST. (d. 923). Uncle of St. Dunstan, he was Benedictine abbot at Glastonbury, became first bishop of Wells in 909, and in 914 was made bishop of Canterbury. F. D. Jan. 8.

ATHELSTAN (d. 940), king of England. Possibly the illegitimate son of King Edward the Elder, and a favorite grandson of Alfred the Great, he became king of England in 924, conquered Northumbria, defeated his enemies at Brunanburh in 937, invaded Cornwall, then settled down to rule a unified kingdom with justice and charity toward all estates. He became more power-conscious with age, however, and clashed with his nobles when he sought to assume more control than laws allowed.

ATHENAGORAS (2nd century), apologist. An Athenian philosopher who became a convert, he wrote an *Embassy for the Christians* (176 or 177) to Emperor Marcus Aurelius and his son Commodus against the slanders on his co-religionists, on monotheism and against atheism. His *Resurrection of the Body* is the first such tract on the subject.

ATHENAIS. *See* Eudocia.

ATHENODORUS, ST. (d. 269?), martyr. Born in Neo-Caesarea, Cappadocia, brother of St. Gregory Thaumaturgus, he became bishop of a see in Pontus and was put to death during the reign of Aurelian. F. D. Oct. 18.

ATHENODORUS, ST. (d. 304?), martyr. He died after undergoing numerous tortures in Mesopotamia during the Diocletian persecution. F. D. Nov. 11.

ATHENOGENES, ST. (d. 305?), bishop and martyr. He was put to death in Sebaste, in Armenia, with other Christians during the persecution of Diocletian. F. D. July 16. He is the same person, apparently, as honored on Jan. 18.

ATIENZA, JUAN DE (1546–16—?). Born in Tordehumos, Spain, he studied law at Salamanca, then became a Jesuit, and served at the colleges of Avila, Villa García, and Valladolid. Sent to Peru, he became rector of the College of San Pablo, Lima, in 1581, and founded the College of San Martín. He became provincial in 1585, set up a press to produce primers and religious textbooks, and enlarged the mission territory of Ecuador and Paraguay.

ATKINSON, MATTHEW (d. 1729). Born in Yorkshire, he became a Franciscan at Douai in 1673 as Fr. Paul of St. Francis, served in England, was captured and, in 1699, condemned to life imprisonment on the charge of being a priest. He died in Hurst castle on the Solent after thirty years as a prisoner.

ATKINSON, SARAH (1823–1893), writer. Born in Athlone, Ireland, on Oct. 13 to John and Anne Gaynor, she was educated at Dublin, married George Atkinson, editor of *Freeman's Journal*, translated *Annals of the Propagation of the Faith* from the French, and wrote a life of Mary Aikenhead and biographical and historical essays. She died in Dublin on July 8.

ATKINSON, VEN. THOMAS (1546–1616), martyr. Born in Yorkshire, England, he was ordained at Rheims and entered the underground mission in 1588, working with great success until captured at seventy, and hanged, drawn, and quartered at York on Mar. 11.

ATTALAS, ST. (d. 627). Born in Burgundy, he became a monk at Lérins, moved to the stricter monastery of Luxeuil and on to Bobbio in Lombardy in the company of St. Columban, whom he succeeded as abbot in 615. He was successful against the objections of the monks to the strictness of their rule and against the Arian heretics near Milan. F. D. Mar. 10.

ATTALUS, ST. (d. 177), martyr. *See* Pothinus, St.

ATTAVANTE (1452–1518?), artist. Born in Castel Fiorentino, Italy, he studied the art of the miniaturist and was influenced by Verocchio and Ghirlandaio. He decorated antiphonaries for the cathedrals of Florence and Prato, books for the libraries of the Medici, the duke of Urbino, and King Matthias Corvinus of Hungary, and a number of missals.

ATTAVANTI, PAOLO (d. 1499), canonist. A Servite in Italy, he wrote *Breviiarum totius juris canonici*.

ATTICUS, ST. (d. 425). He was falsely set up as bishop of Constantinople during the second banishment of St. John Chrysostom, but later repented and lived a virtuous life. He died on Oct. 10. F. D. Jan. 8.

ATTILANUS, ST. (939?–1009), bishop. Born in Tarazona, near Saragossa, Spain, he became a Benedictine under St. Froilan in Moruela, Old Castile, when fifteen. He was appointed to the see of Zamora in 990. He was canonized in 1089. F. D. Oct. 5.

ATTIRET, JEAN DENIS (1702–1768), painter. Born in Dole, France, on July 31, he studied art at Rome, then became a Jesuit laybrother and went to China in 1737. Made a mandarin by Emperor Kien-Lung, he painted portraits of court personages on silk and glass and helped to complete sixteen panoramic battle scenes recounting victories over the Tatars. He died in Peking on Dec. 8.

ATTIUS, ST. (d. 300?), martyr. *See* Alexander, St.

ATTO, ST. (d. 1044?), bishop. He was a Benedictine monk at Oña, Spain, before he was appointed bishop of Oca-Valpuesta. F. D. June 1.

ATTO, ST. (11th century). He was first abbot of the Benedictine abbey at Teramo, Italy, which was set up in 1004. F. D. Nov. 19.

ATTO (11th century), cardinal. A supporter of Pope Gregory VII in his attempt to root out simony, he attended a synod in Rome in 1079 as cardinal of Milan. He may also have been bishop of Praeneste.

ATTO, ST. (1070–1155), bishop. Born in Badajoz, Spain (or in Florence, Italy), he became a Vallambrosan in Tuscany, was abbot general in 1105, and bishop of Pistoia in 1135. He wrote biographies of SS. John Gualbert and Bernard of Parma, and an account of the shrine at Compostela. F. D. May 22.

ATTO OF VERCELLI (10th century), bishop. Chancellor of King Lothaire II of France in 933, he was known also as a theologian and preacher. Letters, sermons, a commentary on St. Paul, and notes on moral philosophy are among his extant writings. He was bishop of Vercelli, Italy, from 924 to 961.

ATTRACTA, ST. (6th century?). Daughter of a noble Irish family, she was a recluse at Lough Gara, founded a hospice at Killaraght, then lived at Drum. According to tradition, she was a friend of St. Patrick, from whom she received the veil in the fifth century; but names associated with her career suggest that she lived a century later. F. D. Aug. 11.

AUBAREDE, JEAN MICHEL (1639–1692). Educated in Toulouse, France, he was assigned to the cathedral in the diocese of Pamiers after ordination. When he became administrator he so vigorously fought royal attempts to make parish appointments, even excommunicating the king's selections, that he was imprisoned at Caen, where he died six years later on Aug. 4.

AUBERMONT, JEAN ANTOINE D' (d. 1686), theologian. Born in Bois-le-Duc, France, he became a Dominican in 1633 and, after study in his native city, wrote in defense of papal infallibility and Thomism and against Gallicanism. He died on Nov. 22.

AUBERY, JOSEPH (1673–1755), missioner. Born in Gisors, Normandy, on May 10, he became a Jesuit at seventeen, was transferred to Canada, and ordained at Quebec in 1700. He directed the Abenaki missions at St. François from 1708 until his death, on July 2, writing diligently to support French claims against the English in Acadia and preparing a map to establish boundaries. He is the original of the missioner in Chateaubriand's novel, *Athalie.*

AUBIERGE. *See* Ethelburga, St.

AUBIGNAC, FRANÇOIS HÉDELIN, D' (1604–1676), critic. Born in Paris on Aug. 4, he took his name from an abbey granted to him by Richelieu, to whose nephew he was tutor. He was active in the critical battle between the ancients, led by Boileau, and the moderns, led by Perrault, supporting those who preferred contemporary literature. He wrote a tragedy, *Zénobie*, a study of the stage, and an attack on the theory that Homer was an actual person; he proposed that the Greek epics were compilations of long-familiar individual narratives. He died in Nemours on July 27.

AUBIN, ST. (d. 554?), bishop. Born in Vannes, Brittany, he entered the monastery of Tincillac and became its abbot at thirty-five, but was called to Angers as bishop in 529. He was active as a preacher, helper of the sick and poor, and ransomer of captives. He is also called Albinus. F. D. Mar. 1.

AUBUSSON, PIERRE D' (1423–1503), cardinal. After fighting for Charles VII against the Swiss in 1444, he became a Knight Hospitaller about 1450 at Rhodes, where he was captain general and, by 1476, grand master of the order of St. John of Jerusalem. He had 2450 men at his disposal when Mohammed II attacked in 1480; in three months the Turks lost 25,000 men, the siege was lifted, and d'Aubusson was rewarded with a cardinalate. In 1501 he was selected as captain general of a league of Christian princes formed to fight the Moslems, but internal dissension caused its failure.

AUDARD. *See* Theodard, St. (d. 893).

AUDAS, ST. (d. 420), bishop and martyr. He and seven priests, nine deacons, and seven holy women were put to death at the outbreak of a persecution of Christians in Persia. He is also called Abdas. F. D. May 16.

AUDAX, ST. (d. 250?), martyr. *See* Anatolia, St.

AUDEMAR. *See* Othmar.

AUDIFAX, ST. (d. 260?), martyr. *See* Marius, St.

AUDIFFREDI, GIOVANNI BATTISTA (1734–1794), bibliographer. Born in Saorgio, Italy, he became a Dominican, was placed in charge of the Bibliotheca Casanetensis, founded in 1700, and began a never-completed catalogue of its holdings. Death also prevented the completion of a list of all books published in the major Italian cities. He also was an archaeologist, mathematician, and astronomer, writing on the transits of Venus and on the comets of 1769. He died in Rome in July.

AUDIN, J. M. VINCENT (1793–1851), historian. Born in Lyons, France, he studied at the Argentière seminary, gave up law and interested himself in literature, and after he went to Paris wrote history, chiefly on the Reformation and the reigns of Leo X and Henry VIII. His work was criticized for its inaccuracies and as leaning toward Protestantism, though Audin vigorously proclaimed his Catholicism. He died in Paris on Feb. 21.

AUDISIO, GUGLIELMO (1801–1882). Born in Bra, Piedmont, Italy, he taught at the seminary there, was president of the Superga Academy in Turin, but was expelled for his criticism in the newspaper *Armonia*, which he had helped to found, of the Piedmontese government's hostility toward religion. He then became a canon at the Vatican basilica and taught at the Roman University. His historical works were severely criticized as unorthodox and inaccurate; his political and religious writings were condemned; and at the Vatican Council he was accused of Gallicanism. He submitted and accepted correction. He died in Rome on Sept. 27.

AUDOENUS. *See* Ouen, St.

AUDOMARUS. *See* Omer, St.

AUDRAN, CHARLES (1594–1674), engraver. A student of art at Rome, he set up engraving establishments at Lyons and at Paris, producing numerous original portraits and hundreds of reproductions of Titian and other Italian masters.

AUDRAN, CLAUDE (1639–1684), painter. Son of Claude Audran (1597–1677, professor of engraving at Lyons and brother or cousin of Charles), he studied at Rome and at Paris under Charles Lebrun. His frescoes adorn the Tuileries grand gallery and the Versailles great staircase. Two brothers, Gérard and Germain, also were engravers; and four of the latter's sons (Claude, Benoit, Jean, and Louis) carried on the family tradition: the first two as painters, the others as engravers.

AUDREY. *See* Ethelreda, St.

AUDRY. *See* Aldericus, St.

AUENBRUGER, LEOPOLD (1722–1807), physician. Born in Graz, Austria, on Nov. 19, he studied at Vienna and served on the staff of the Spanish Military Hospital there for ten years. He discovered percussion as a way of ascertaining changes in the heart, signs of pneumonia, and lung cavities. His report on his percussion experiments, published as *Inventum novum*, established him as one of the pioneers of modern medicine. He died on May 17, and his work was continued by Laennec.

AUERSPERG, ANTON ALEXANDER VON (1806–1876), poet. Born in Laibach, Austria, he studied at Vienna and Graz, traveled extensively, and married Countess Attems in 1839. In 1848 he was elected to the national assembly, retired to the management of his estates, and in 1860 was appointed a life member of the Austrian *Reichsrat*. In 1830, two col-

lections of poetry appeared anonymously, and in 1831 a collection of political poems attacking Metternich and his rule, *Spaziergänge eines Wiener Poeten*, caused a furor. His lyric poetry, written under the pseudonym Anastasius Grün, gained a wider audience; he also edited Slovenic folk songs and old English ballads. He died in Graz, Austria, on Sept. 12.

AUFSEES, JOBST BERNHARD VON (1671–1738). Born on the family estate in Mengersdorf, Bavaria, on Mar. 28, he became a convert and later a parish priest at Bamberg and Würzburg. As provost of Bamberg he worked to establish a seminary, to which he contributed $200,000 in 1728 for the education of poor boys. He died on Apr. 2.

AUGEBERT, ST. (7th century), martyr. *See* Felix, St.

AUGER, EDMOND (1530–1591), educator. Born in Troyes, France, he became a Jesuit, preached effectively against the Calvinists, founded a college at Lyons, was confessor and military chaplain to King Henry III, and held several administrative posts within his Society. He wrote a catechism in Latin and Greek, a commentary on the Eucharist, advice for soldiers, and several translations and rules for congregations. He died at Como, Italy, on Jan. 31.

AUGOUARD, PHILIPPE PROSPER (1852–1921), archbishop. Born in Poitiers, France, on Sept. 16, he studied in Séez, fought during the Franco-Prussian War, became a member of the Congregation of the Holy Ghost, and was sent to East Africa in 1877. He directed schools in Upper Congo, aided French explorers, and was named vicar apostolic in 1890. He was honored by the French and Belgian governments and was made titular archbishop of Cassiope by Pope Benedict XV in 1915. He was highly regarded as engineer, doctor, teacher, and administrator as well as missioner, and died in Paris on Oct. 3.

AUGULUS, ST. (d. 303?), martyr. He is said to have died at London during the persecution of Diocletian; St. Jerome lists him as a bishop; the French call him St. Aule of Normandy. F. D. Feb. 7.

AUGURIUS, ST. (d. 259), martyr. *See* Fructuosus, St.

AUGUSTA, ST., martyr. Daughter of the Teuton duke of Friuli, Italy, she was killed by her father when she was converted to Christianity. F. D. Mar. 27.

AUGUSTALIS, ST. (d. 450?). He was a bishop in Gaul, probably of Arles. F. D. Sept. 7.

AUGUSTINE, ST. (d. 273), martyr. He and SS. Beata and Sanctian went from Spain to Gaul during a persecution and were put to death near Sens. F. D. Sept. 6.

AUGUSTINE, ST. (d. 300?), martyr. *See* Flavius, St.

AUGUSTINE, ST. (354–430), bishop, Doctor

of the Church. Born at Tagaste, northern Africa, on Nov. 13, son of St. Monica and Patricius, a pagan Roman official, he went to school at Madaura and, in 370, at Carthage. There he began a period of extravagant and licentious living, acquired a mistress with whom he lived for the next fifteen years and by whom he had a son, Adeodatus, and became a disciple of Manichaeism, though he never was a priest in the heretical sect. He taught grammar at Tagaste in 373–74 and rhetoric at Carthage from 374 to 383, when he went to Rome and opened a school there. Disillusioned by the students in Rome, he in 384 accepted the chair of rhetoric at Milan, where he met St. Ambrose. After three years of study, interest in Neoplatonism, and attention to the sermons of Ambrose and the arguments of Simplicianus, Augustine became a Christian and retired with Monica, his brother Navigius, Adeodatus, Alypius, and several others to Cassiciacum. There they lived a community life and Augustine wrote on happiness, providence, and skepticism. Adeodatus, Alypius, and he were baptized by St. Ambrose. Soon after, as they were on their way to Africa, St. Monica died at Ostia; a year later, 388, Augustine returned to Tagaste, where he founded a sort of monastery and led a life of retirement, prayer, and meditation. Adeodatus died, at seventeen or eighteen, in 389. In 391, Augustine was ordained at Hippo and established a religious community with Alypius, Evodius, Possidius, and others. He continued his interest in this monastic community, eventually developing it into a kind of theological seminary; many of its members became famous bishops. At Bishop Valerius' request (at the time, only bishops were allowed to preach), Augustine began preaching and his success was phenomenal. In 393 he participated in the Plenary Council of Africa, the first of many at which he assisted (in 398, 401, 407, and 419 at Carthage; at Mileve in 416 and 418). Late in 395 or early in 396 he was consecrated coadjutor to Bishop Valerius, whom he succeeded as bishop of Hippo. His public disputes with Manichaeans and Donatists had become increasingly numerous, and sometimes bitter, but Augustine proved victorious and helped to drain the strength from both heresies. He then turned to do battle with Pelagius, a task which occupied him for the rest of his life. When Rome was plundered by the Goths in 410, the Pelagians ascribed the decline of the empire to the debilitating effect of Christianity, and in 413 Augustine began his masterly answer, not to be finished until 426, the City of God. In 426, also, he had Heraclius chosen his coadjutor so that he could devote more time to his writings, but the last years were overcast by the dire threat of a Vandal invasion of Africa under Genseric

(who with his Arian leaders and allied Goths landed in 429). Augustine died during the siege of Hippo, but before the city fell. Long before his death he had come to dominate the thought of Christian Europe, particularly as defender of the faith and expositor on the origin, doctrine, marks, authority, and divine mission of the Church. More than 200 works, some 300 letters, and nearly 400 sermons testify to the energy, range, and timelessness of his teaching. With his extraordinary intellectual gifts he also possessed great love of his fellow men, humility, and loyalty. Besides the City of God and his autobiographical Confessions (397–401?), his works include writings against the major heresies, major studies like The Trinity (400–16), Literal Commentary on Genesis (401–15), Tractates on the Gospel of St. John (416–17), Faith, Hope, and Charity (421), and shorter considerations on the immortality of the soul, free will, teaching, belief, lying, government, music, marriage, baptism, demonology, grace, and the Psalms. F. D. Aug. 28.

ST. AUGUSTINE, Confessions, trans. JOHN K. RYAN (Garden City, N.Y., Image Books, 1960); HUGH POPE, St. Augustine of Hippo (Garden City, N.Y., Image Books, 1961); M. D'ARCY, ed., Monument to St. Augustine (New York, Sheed, 1931).

AUGUSTINE, ST. (d. 605?), archbishop. Sent from Rome by Pope St. Gregory the Great with monks from the abbey of St. Andrew where he was prior, Augustine arrived in England in 597. From the Isle of Thanet he sent envoys to King Ethelbert, received permission to preach through Kent, and baptized the monarch and thousands of his subjects. When Augustine sent Laurence and Peter to Rome with his report, the pope sent back SS. Justus, Mellitus, and Paulinus with books, vestments, church furnishings, and a plan for developing the English hierarchy. On the land the king gave him at Canterbury he rebuilt a church and set up the Benedictine monastery of SS. Peter and Paul. From there he established new sees in London and Rochester. He failed to bring the bishops in other parts of Britain and Wales into administrative agreement or even to accept current Western practices, but was most successful in leading the Anglo-Saxons from their pagan practices to Christianity, preserving or purifying older customs and festivals. He died on May 26. F. D. May 28 (in England, May 26).

AUGUSTINE, DOM. See Lestrange, Louis Henri de.

AUGUSTINE OF BIELLA. See Fangi, Bl. Agostino.

AUGUSTINE NOVELLO. See Matthew de Termini, Bl.

AUGUSTINUS, ANTONIUS (1517–1586), archbishop. Born in Saragossa, Spain, on Feb.

26, he studied at Salamanca and in Italy, becoming a doctor of civil and of canon law and serving on the rota for Pope Paul III in 1544. In 1555 he went to England as counselor to Cardinal Pole; the next year he became bishop of Alife, in Naples, and returned to Lérida, Spain, in 1561. He was active at the Council of Trent for three years and became archbishop of Tarragona in 1576. His most important writings include a revision and modernization of Gratian's law code, an edition of the imperial constitutions of Byzantium, of the Greek texts of early councils, and a treatise on the penitential canons. He died in Tarragona, Spain, on May 31.

AUGUSTINUS TRIUMPHUS (d. 1328). A contemporary of Egidio Colonna at Paris, where he also taught theology, he was a leading member of the Aegidian "school" of thought.

AUGUSTUS, ST. (d. 300?), martyr. *See* Flavius, St.

AUGUSTUS, ST. (5th century), bishop. *See* Priscus, St.

AUGUSTUS, ST. (6th century). He was abbot of Bourges, France, and a friend of St. Germanus. F. D. Oct. 7.

AULAF CUARANN (10th century). Son of Sitric, king of the Danes (who briefly accepted Christianity) and the daughter of King Athelstan of England, he became a convert in 943, went on a pilgrimage to Iona, and died soon after. Aulaf's conversion led to the conversion of the Danes in Dublin as the result of the labors of monks he brought to Ireland from Northumbria.

AULAIRE. *See* Eulalia of Barcelona, St.

AUNACHARIUS, ST. (d. 605), bishop. Born in Orléans, France, he spent his youth at the court of King Guntram of Burgundy, then left it to serve Bishop St. Syagrius of Autun, who ordained him. In 561 he was elected bishop of Auxerre and became most influential in French civil and ecclesiastical affairs. He attended the synods of Paris in 573 and of Mâcon in 583 and 585, held two synods in Auxerre, and was active in promoting Christianity and improving his diocese. He ordered the recitation of the divine office in all his churches and the litanies of the saints to be sung in rotation in the larger churches. At his direction, biographies of SS. Amatus and Germanus, his predecessors, were written. He is also known as Anacharius and Aunaire. F. D. Sept. 25.

AUNGERVILLE, RICHARD. *See* Richard de Bury.

AUREA, ST. (d. 260?), martyr. A Roman, she helped imprisoned Christians and was seized and drowned at Ostia during the reign of Claudius. F. D. Aug. 24.

AUREA, ST. (d. 666). A Syrian, she was placed in charge of the convent of St. Martial

at Paris in 633 by St. Eligius. She and 160 nuns of her community died of plague. F. D. Oct. 4.

AUREA, ST. (8th century). A native of Amiens, France, she founded a hermitage and attracted so many followers that she built a convent for them at Boves. F. D. Oct. 6.

AUREA, ST. (d. 856), martyr. Born in Cordova, Spain, she became a convert after the death of her husband, and had been a nun at Cuteclara for over twenty years when her family denounced her as a Christian; she was seized and beheaded. F. D. July 19.

AUREA, ST. (1042?–1069?). A recluse in Villavelayo, Spain, during the Moorish occupation, she became attached to a Benedictine convent at San Millán and lived a life of solitary meditation. F. D. Mar. 11.

AURELIA, ST. (d. 254?), martyr. *See* Eusebius, St.

AURELIA, ST. (d. 1027). A French princess, she lived fifty-five years in a hermitage near the Benedictine monastery at Strassburg. F. D. Oct. 15.

AURELIAN, ST. (d. 551), bishop. He was appointed bishop of Arles in 546, was made papal vicar in Gaul by Pope Vigilius, and founded a monastery and convent, for which he wrote the rules. F. D. June 16.

AURELIAN, ST. (d. 895), archbishop. He was abbot of the Benedictine monastery of Ainay before he was appointed to the see of Lyons, France. F. D. July 4.

AURELIUS, ST. (2nd century), martyr. He and another bishop, Publius, opposed the Cataphrygian heresy and were slain either in Asia Minor or North Africa. F. D. Nov. 12.

AURELIUS, ST. (d. 429), bishop. A deacon at Carthage, he was appointed its bishop in 392. During the thirty-seven years of his episcopacy he was occupied with the two great heresies of Donatism and Pelagianism. He called several synods to combat these evils and traveled widely in his efforts to expel them from his see. He was a friend of St. Augustine; it was because of his complaint about a monastic settlement that led the latter to write *The Work of Monks.* F. D. July 20.

AURELIUS, ST. (d. 852?), martyr. Son of a Moor and a Spanish woman, he was orphaned when young and secretly raised as a Christian by his aunt in Cordova, Spain. He married Natalia, whom he had converted, and with a relative named Felix, and the latter's wife, Liliosa, cared for Christians in prison. After George, a monk from the monastery of St. Sabas in Jerusalem, arrived in the city, they tried to practice their religion openly, were arrested while at mass in Aurelius' house, and beheaded. F. D. July 27 (also, Oct. 20).

AUREUS, ST., bishop and martyr. He was slain while saying mass in his see of Mainz, with his sister Justine and others of the congregation, at an unspecified date during invasion by a force of Huns. F. D. June 14.

AURISPA, GIOVANNI (1369?–1459), humanist. Born in Noto, Sicily, he went to Constantinople in 1418 to study Greek and returned to Venice in 1423 with nearly 300 volumes of Aeschylus, Demosthenes, Homer, Plato, Sophocles, Xenophon, and others. He held the chair of Greek at Bologna, Florence, and Ferrara, then served as secretary to Popes Eugene IV and Nicholas V. His writings include epigrams and poems. He died in Ferrara.

AUROROFF, CONSTANTINE (d. 1960). Born in Moscow, he studied at Petrograd and St. Vladimir seminary, participated in anti-czarist demonstrations and a seminarians' strike in 1906 to protest Czarist rule, and was ordained a Russian Orthodox priest in the United States in 1914. He became a Catholic priest of the Byzantine rite in 1916, did parish work in Michigan, Ohio, and Pennsylvania, and then taught Russian at Pennsylvania State College. He was sent to Danbury, Connecticut, in 1955, became pastor of St. Nicholas church, organized a Russian-language course at Danbury State College in 1958, and died in Danbury on June 23.

AUSONIUS, ST. (3rd century?). He is listed as first bishop of Angoulême, Gaul, and a follower of St. Martial of Limoges, although he may have lived earlier. F. D. May 22.

AUSONIUS, DECIMUS MAGNUS (310?–394?), poet. Born in Bordeaux, France, he studied there and at Toulouse, taught grammar and rhetoric at his birthplace, probably was a catechumen, and became tutor of Gratian, son of Emperor Valentinian I. He was made prefect of the Gauls, prefect of the West, jointly with his son Hesperius, and in 379 consul. After the death of Gratian in 383 he retired to Bordeaux and wrote a large body of poetry, including eclogues, epigrams, epistles, prayers, commemorative verse, a description of the Moselle River, and translations and rhetorical debates.

AUSPICIUS, ST. (d. 475?). He is listed as bishop of Toul, France. Another St. Auspicius, said to have succeeded St. Maternus in 130 as fourth bishop of Trèves, probably was a first-century bishop of Toul. They are both honored on July 8.

AUSTEGILDIS. See Agia, St.

AUSTELL, ST. (6th century). He was a follower of St. Mewan of Cornwall, whose name persists as the Welsh town of Hawystill; some writers say Austell may have been a woman, daughter of Brychan of Wales. F. D. June 28.

AUSTIN, JOHN (1613–1669), apologist. Born in Walpole, Norfolk, England, he studied at Cambridge and Lincoln's Inn and became

a convert in 1640. He wrote *The Christian Moderator* (1652), asking for equal rights with other dissenting groups; *The Catholique's Plea* (1659), an exposition of Church beliefs; and *Reflections upon the Oaths of Supremacy and Allegiance* (1661). The first two were under the pseudonym William Birchley. Several collections of prayers, published after his death in London, contain doctrinal errors.

AUSTINDUS, ST. (d. 1068), bishop. Born in Bordeaux, France, he became a Benedictine monk and as abbot of St. Orens introduced the Cluniac observance. He became archbishop of Auch in 1041. F. D. Sept. 25.

AUSTREBERTA, ST. (630–704). Daughter of Count Palatine Badefrid and St. Framechildis, she was born in Artois. She was received into religious life by St. Omer and stationed at the convent of Port (Abbeville), where she became abbess. At the suggestion of St. Philibert she later went to bring discipline to the convent of Pavilly, where she was almost murdered by the father of one of the discontented nuns. F. D. Feb. 10.

AUSTREGISILUS, ST. (551–624), bishop. He left the court of King Guntramnus to become a monk at the abbey of St. Nizier in Lyons, France, where he was made abbot. He became bishop of Bourges in 612. He is also known as Aoustrille. F. D. May 20.

AUSTREMONIUS, ST., bishop. According to St. Gregory of Tours, he was one of seven missioners sent from Rome to evangelize Gaul, in the third or fourth century, and is venerated as first bishop of Clermont-Ferrand. He is also known as Stremoine. F. D. Nov. 1.

AUSTRICLINIAN, BL. (3rd century). See Martial, St.

AUTBERT, ST. (d. 669?), bishop. He became bishop of Cambrai about 633 and built several monasteries, among them St. Vedastus at Arras. F. D. Dec. 13.

AUTBERT, ST. (d. 725?). Bishop of Avranches, France, he founded the church and monastery of Mont-St.-Michel during his rule. F. D. Sept. 10.

AUTBODUS, ST. (d. 690). An Irish missioner, he preached in northern France and died as a recluse near Laon. F. D. Nov. 20.

AUTHAIRE, ST. (7th century). He served in the court of King Dagobert of France and was the father of St. Ouen. He is also known as Oye. F. D. Apr. 24.

AUTONOMUS, ST. (d. 300?), martyr. He is said to have been an Italian bishop who fled to Bithynia, where he made many converts before he was put to death. F. D. Sept. 12.

AUTOR, ST. (5th century). He was thirteenth bishop of Metz. F. D. Aug. 9.

AUTPERT, AMBROSE (d. 778?), abbot. A writer and monastic leader, one of Charlemagne's advisers, he became abbot of the

Benedictine monastery of St. Vincent, near Beneventum, Italy, a year before his death.

AUTRAN, JOSEPH (1813–1877), poet. Born in Marseilles, France, on June 20, he studied at the Jesuit college in Aix, became a teacher, and began writing about 1835. Several volumes followed between *La Mer* (1835) and *La Légende des Paladins* (1875). A tragedy, *La Fille d'Achille* (1848), and *Vie rurale* (1856) were honored by the French Academy, to which he was elected in 1868. He died in Marseilles on Mar. 6.

AUXANUS, ST. (d. 568). He was bishop of Milan, Italy, and is often called Sant' Ansano. F. D. Sept. 3.

AUXENTIUS, ST. (4th century), bishop. A soldier in the imperial army of Licinius, he survived persecution, was ordained, and became bishop of Mopsuestia, Cilicia. F. D. Dec. 18.

AUXENTIUS, ST. (d. 473). A soldier in the service of Theodosius the Younger, he often visited the hermits of Bithynia and soon retired to the desert near Constantinople and then to a more remote refuge near Chalcedon. He directed many followers, among them a group of holy women who set up a convent at Mt. Skopa. F. D. Feb. 14.

AUXENTIUS, ST. (4th century), martyr. *See* Eustratius, St.

AUXIBIUS, ST. (1st century). He is traditionally listed as first bishop of Soli, Cyprus, baptized by St. Peter and consecrated by St. Paul. F. D. Feb. 19.

AUXILIUS, ST. (5th century), bishop. He and SS. Isserninus and Secundinus worked in Ireland with St. Patrick; the four signed an extant decree informing the Irish clergy that they might appeal beyond Armagh directly to Rome. F. D. Dec. 6.

AUXILIUS (10th century). A Frank living near Naples, Italy, he was ordained as priest or as deacon by Pope Formosus, whose name and honor he defended in three works written about 910 during the political turmoil which had been dishonoring the papacy from Stephen (896) through Sergius III (911). He may be identical with a Benedictine monk and deacon at Monte Cassino, or his name may have been the pseudonym of an unknown ecclesiastic.

AVA, ST. (d. 850?). Niece of King Pepin, she was cured of blindness by St. Rainfredis and became a Benedictine nun and abbess at Dinart, Hainault, France. F. D. Apr. 29.

AVA (d. 1127), poet. Author of a number of simple verses on New Testament themes and of a metrical life of St. John the Baptist, written in the assonantal and alliterative style of earlier German poetry, she died near Melk, Austria.

AVANCINI, NICOLA (1612–1686), theologian. Born in the Tyrol, he became a Jesuit, taught rhetoric and philosophy at Graz, and

served as provincial of Austria and assistant for the German provinces of the Society. He wrote many sermons, school dramas, and, in Latin, *Meditations on the Life and Doctrines of Jesus Christ*, a popular ascetical work translated into the vernacular throughout Europe. He died on Dec. 6.

AVAUGOUR, PIERRE DU BOIS D' (d. 1664), governor. Born in Brittany, he served in the French army for forty years, ranging as far as Persia and Russia. The baron was sixth governor general of Canada from 1661 to 1663, made the sale of liquor to Indians a capital offense, advised the fortifying of Quebec, the destruction of the Dutch at Albany who were supplying the Iroquois with arms, and the need of sending veteran soldiers from Europe who could settle as colonists. After serious disagreement with Bishop Laval and the Jesuits over the extent of his powers, he was recalled to Paris, where he presented his military and colonization plans to Louis XIV. He died in battle while defending Zrin, Austria, against the Turks.

AVELLINO, ST. LORENZO (1521–1608). A native of Castelnuovo, Italy, he studied law, was ordained, and practiced ecclesiastical law. In 1556 he was sent to Baiano to reform the convent of Sant' Angelo and was almost killed by those who objected (the house was later suppressed). In that year he joined the Theatines, took the name Andrew, and later became superior of their Naples house. In 1570 he was sent to Lombardy, where he met and became a friend and adviser of St. Charles Borromeo, became a successful preacher, and established houses at Milan and Piacenza. He returned to Naples in 1582 and labored there until his death. F. D. Nov. 10.

AVENDANO, FERNANDO (d. 1665), bishop. Born in Lima, he was a student of Peruvian culture and primitive religion and folklore. His sermons on Catholic belief, preached in Quichua, are also of great value to students of language. He was appointed bishop of Santiago, Chile, a few years before his death at Lima.

AVENTINUS, ST. (d. 520?), bishop. He succeeded his brother, St. Solemnis, as bishop of Chartres, France. F. D. Feb. 4.

AVENTINUS, ST. (d. 538?). Almoner to St. Lupus, bishop of Troyes, he later became a recluse. F. D. Feb. 4.

AVENTINUS, ST. (d. 732), martyr. Born in Bagnères in the Pyrenees, he became a hermit in Larboush, where he was captured and put to death by Moors. F. D. June 7.

AVERTANUS, BL. (d. 1380). Born in Limoges, France, where he became a Carmelite laybrother, he died of the plague while outside Lucca on a pilgrimage to the Holy Land with Bl. Romaeus. F. D. Feb. 25.

AVILA, DIAZ SANCHEZ DE (1564–1627), theologian. Born in Baeza, Andalusia, Spain, he studied the humanities and law at Salamanca, joined the Discalced Carmelites, taking the name Thomas à Jesu, in 1586, became prior at Saragossa and then provincial of Old Castile. When his term expired, he went to an eremetical convent, the Desert of Las Batuecas, near Alberca, one of four he had established during his provincialship, became prior, was called to Rome by Pope Paul V for a project to send missionaries to the Congo, and, when the plan failed, established a missionary branch of the Carmelites, the Congregation of St. Paul, in 1608. When the Spanish and Italian superiors disapproved, the pope withdrew his consent and he was sent in 1610 as a missionary to the Netherlands, where he founded numerous convents. He became provincial of Flanders in 1617, and definitor general in Rome in 1621. His *De procuranda salute omnium gentium* (1613), outlining the organization and functions of a papal congregation, was so closely followed by Pope Gregory XV in establishing the Propaganda in 1622 that he is often called the father of the Congregation of Propaganda. He wrote other treatises, including *Stimulus missionum* (1610), *De contemplatione divina* (1620), and *Divinae orationis methodus.* (1623). He died in Rome on May 24 or 27.

AVILA, FRANCISCO (17th century), scholar. Orphaned in Peru, he became a priest, and in his last years was stationed in La Plata, Bolivia. He made major studies, in 1608 and 1611, of the beliefs of the Peruvian Indians.

AVILA Y ZÚÑIGA, LUIS DE (1500–1564), historian. Born in Plasencia, Estremadura, Spain, he was attached to the court of Charles V, fought with him in Africa and against the Schmalkald League, and was his ambassador to Popes Paul IV and Pius IV. He wrote a history of the military campaign of 1546–47, valuable as eye-witness testimony, though very flattering to the emperor.

AVITUS (5th century). A priest at Braga, Portugal, he was sent on a mission to St. Augustine, helped to make known the finding of the body of St. Stephen the martyr, translated the encyclical letter of Lucian of Caphar Gamala from Greek to Latin, and attended the Council of Jerusalem (415) which condemned Pelagianism.

AVITUS, ST. (d. 530?). According to St. Gregory of Tours, he directed a monastery in Perche, France, tried without success to prevent the killing of St. Sigismund of Burgundy by King Clodomir, and died at Orléans. F. D. June 17.

AVITUS, ST. (d. 600?). He was eighteenth bishop of Clermont, France, and ordained St. Gregory of Tours a deacon. F. D. Aug. 21.

AVITUS, ST. (d. 689), bishop. He directed the French see of Clermont from 676 until his death. F. D. Feb. 21.

AVITUS, ST. ALCIMUS ECDICIUS (d. 519?). Born in Auvergne, Gaul, brother of St. Apollinaris, he succeeded their father, St. Hesychius, as bishop of Vienne in 490, and ransomed and converted King Sigismund of Bavaria. He wrote *De spiritualis historiae gestae,* an allegorical epic on the creation of man, and *De laude virginitatis,* a poem on chastity. F. D. Feb. 5.

AVRIL, PHILIPPE (1654–1698), missioner. Born in Angoulême, France, on Sept. 16, he became a Jesuit, taught philosophy and mathematics at Paris, traveled overland six years on his way to China, which he never reached, and returned to record the details of his journeys. He was lost at sea while on a second attempt to reach his missionary goal.

AXEL (1128?–1201), archbishop. Born in Finnestoe, Denmark, he studied and taught at Paris, became bishop of Roskilde in 1158, served as papal legate to Scandinavia, and after 1178 was archbishop of Lund. He laid out the city of Copenhagen, served as counselor to Waldemar I and Canute VI, doing much to arrange wise legislation, was a patron of the arts, and encouraged Saxo Grammaticus to write the history of Denmark. Also known as Absalon, he founded a monastery at Soro, Denmark, where he is buried.

AYALA, BL. FERDINAND (d. 1617), martyr. Born in Ballesteros, near Toledo, Spain, he became an Augustinian in 1603, and was sent to the missions in Mexico and Japan, where in 1605 he became vicar provincial. He was captured at Omura with Fr. Navarette, and beheaded at the outbreak of a major persecution. He was beatified in 1867. F. D. June 1.

AYBERT, ST. (1060–1140). Born in Espain, France, he became a hermit when quite young and, on his return from a pilgrimage to Rome, a Benedictine at the abbey of Crépin, serving as procurator and cellarer for twenty-five years. He then retired to twenty-two years of solitary life, still under the abbot, was ordained, and became famous as a confessor and counselor. F. D. Apr. 7.

AYETA, FRANCISCO DE (17th century), missioner. Franciscan visitor of the province of New Mexico and of the area south to Yucatán, he wrote a number of defenses of his order, printed about 1690. As early as 1678 he had warned Madrid that the Pueblo Indians were ready for war, but was unheeded; they swarmed over the area in 1680 and occupied it for fourteen years. Fr. Ayeta took care of more than 2000 refugees at El Paso at the beginning of hostilities.

AYEUL. *See* Agilus, St.

AYLLÓN, LUCAS VÁSQUEZ DE (1475?–1526), explorer. Born in Spain, he went to

Santo Domingo in 1502, became a member of the supreme council there, and in 1520 sent out an exploring expedition which discovered the coast of South Carolina. He returned to Spain, was authorized to continue his explorations, and was appointed governor of any colony he might found. In 1526 he set out with 500 men and women and established a settlement, San Miguel de Guandape, probably on the Cape Fear River, eighty years before the British founded Jamestown. He died of ship fever on Oct. 18 at the colony, whereupon the survivors, no more than 150, abandoned the settlement and returned to Santo Domingo. He was the first European to discover Chesapeake Bay.

AYLWARD, JAMES AMBROSE (1813–1872), theologian. Born in Leeds, England, on Apr. 4, he became a Dominican at Hinckley and was ordained in 1836. He served twice as provincial and became prior of Woodchester in 1854. He wrote a number of translations, particularly of Latin hymns, several pious manuals, and a significant study of ancient and modern spiritism. He died at Hinckley on Oct. 5.

AYMARD, BL. (d. 965). He was Benedictine abbot at Cluny from 942 to about 952, when he became blind. F. D. Oct. 5.

AYMERIC OF PIACENZA (d. 1327), theologian. Born in Lombardy, he became a Dominican, studied at Milan, and taught philosophy and theology for twenty-four years before he became provincial of Greece. He became master general in 1304, made sure that the members of his order in the areas polluted by the Fraticelli were particularly strong, and encouraged the study of science and oriental languages. He died at Bologna on Aug. 19.

AYRALD, BL. (d. 1146?). Son of William II of Burgundy and brother of Pope Callistus II, he became a Carthusian at Portes and later prior there, and probably was appointed bishop of Maurienne at a youthful age. He was beatified in 1863. There are, however, three bishops of Maurienne with this name in the twelfth century, and biographical details are confused. F. D. Jan. 2.

AYSCOUGH, JOHN. See Bickerstaffe-Drew, Francis.

AYTON, JOHN. See Acton, John.

AYUTRE. See Adjutor, St.

AZADANES, ST. (d. 342?), martyr. See Abdiesus, St.

AZADES, ST. (d. 342?), martyr. See Abdiesus, St.

AZARA, FÉLIZ DE (1746–1811), naturalist. Born in Barbunales, Aragon, Spain, on May 18, he became a military engineer and brigadier general and was sent to South America in 1781 to settle a border dispute between Spanish and Portuguese colonies. He remained for twenty years, making a study of the habits of mammals and birds, and sending his notes to Paris, where his brother was ambassador. Three studies of the natural history of Paraguay were published in 1801–2. A commentary on life and people in the area, issued in 1809, revealed an ignorance which was absent from his scientific works. He died in Aragon.

AZARIA, ARISTACES (1782–1854). Born in Constantinople on July 18, he studied in Rome until a French invasion, then became a Mechitarist priest at Trieste in 1801. He and his monks went to Vienna in 1810, setting up a printing press and educating the Armenian colony. He was made abbot in 1826, spread the order to other cities, founded the journal *Europa*, and opened a bookshop, a library, and an academy for his co-patriots. He was appointed titular archbishop of Caesarea and died in Vienna on May 6.

AZARIAS, BROTHER. See Mullany, Patrick.

AZAS, ST. (d. 304?) martyr. He was one of 150 soldiers put to death in Isauria, Asia Minor, during the Diocletian persecution. F. D. Nov. 19.

AZEVEDO, BL. DIEGO DE (d. 1207), bishop. He served on the staff of the cathedral of Osma, Spain, before he became its bishop in 1201, accompanied St. Dominic to southern France and Rome at the time of the formation of the Dominican order, became a Cistercian, and crusaded against the Albigensian heresy. He died on Dec. 30. F. D. Feb. 6.

AZEVEDO, BL. IGNATIUS DE (1528–1570), martyr. Born at Oporto, Portugal, he became a Jesuit in 1548 and was rector of St. Anthony's College in Lisbon at twenty-five and of the college in Braga at thirty-two. In 1566 he went to Brazil as inspector of Jesuit missions. As a result of the report he made on his return to Rome, St. Francis Borgia sent him back to Brazil as superior of a group of thirty-nine missionaries. Their ship was attacked near the Canary Islands by a ship captained by a French Huguenot, Jacques Sourie, who massacred them all. Their cult was confirmed in 1854. F. D. July 15.

AZEVEDO, LUIZ DE (1573–1634), scholar. Born in Carrazedo Montenegro, Portugal, he became a Jesuit in 1588. In 1605 he began missionary work in Ethiopia, reclaiming many schismatics, translating a number of scriptural commentaries into Chaldaic and the New Testament into Ethiopic, and writing a Portuguese catechism and an Ethiopic grammar. He died in Ethiopia.

AZOR, JUAN (1535–1603), theologian. Born in Lorca, Spain, he became a Jesuit in 1559, taught philosophy and theology at Piacenza, Alcalá, and Rome, and prepared a monumental three-volume work on moral theology (1600–11), later praised by Pope Clement VIII,

Bossuet, and St. Alphonsus Liguori. Fr. Azor was also a member of the commission which drew up the *Ratio studiorum* of Jesuit education. He died in Rome on Feb. 19.

B

BABENSTUBER, LUDWIG (1660–1726), theologian. Born in Teining, Bavaria, he became a Benedictine at the monastery at Ettal in 1681, and taught philosophy and later directed the scholasticate at Salzburg. From 1695 to 1717 he was professor of philosophy at the university there, serving as vice-chancellor for six years. He published a four-volume study of Thomism in 1704 and died in Ettal, Bavaria, on Apr. 5.

BABINET, JACQUES (1794–1872), physicist. Born in Lusignan, France, on Mar. 5, he studied science under Binet, taught mathematics, physics, and meteorology at various schools, joined the faculty of the Collège de France in 1838 and two years later was elected to the Academy of Sciences. He invented a compensator for use in the study of polarized light, and an improved air pump, and made contributions to the study of diffraction of light, magnetism, and the planet Mercury. He died in Paris on Oct. 21.

BABINGTON, ANTHONY (1561–1586). Born in Dethick, Derbyshire, England, he was orphaned at ten, became a page in the service of Mary Stuart during her imprisonment at Sheffield, and was persuaded by Ballard and others to join the conspiracy to free the queen. His letters to Mary were intercepted, revealed details, and allegedly evoked a reply in which the queen approved of the murder of Elizabeth I. Babington and his fellow conspirators were hanged, drawn, and quartered in London on Sept. 20.

BABOLENUS, ST. (d. 640?). He was fourth abbot of Bobbio, Italy, where he replaced the rule of St. Columban with the Benedictine. F. D. Aug. 31.

BABOLENUS, ST. (d. 677?). He served as a monk at Luxeuil under St. Columban, was first abbot of the monastery of St. Peter near Paris, and worked with St. Fursey in establishing churches and hospitals in that area. F. D. June 26.

BABYLAS, ST. (d. 250?), bishop and martyr. He succeeded Zebinus in 240 as bishop of Antioch and was captured there during the persecution of Decius. SS. Epolonius, Prilidian, and Urban, younger men, were beheaded; Babylas died in prison while awaiting execution. A seventh-century account, in prose and poetry, was written by Aldhelm of Sherborne. F. D. Jan. 24.

BACCHUS, ST. (d. 303?), martyr. *See* Sergius, St.

BACCHYLUS (2nd century), bishop. He supported Pope Victor I in the attempt to establish universal acceptance of the date of Easter and may have convened a synod at Corinth about 195 for this purpose.

BACHELOT, ALEXIS (d. 1837). A native of France, and a member of the Congregation of the Sacred Hearts of Jesus and Mary (Society of Picpus), he was appointed prefect apostolic of the Sandwich Islands and in 1827 was one of the first three priests to arrive in Honolulu. They were opposed by the Protestant missionaries on the islands and Fr. Bachelot, with Fr. Patrick Short, was exiled to Lower California. They returned in 1836, but Fr. Bachelot was again exiled in 1837 and died at sea on Dec. 5.

BACHIARIUS (5th century). Possibly a Spanish abbot, who may have been exiled, he wrote two letters from Rome: one on his orthodoxy, against any suspicion of Priscillianist leanings; the other, a plea for charitable treatment of a penitent monk.

BACHMAN, PAUL (b. 1466), apologist. Born in Chemnitz, Saxony, he became a Cistercian at the monastery of Altenzelle, Saxony, and its abbot in 1522 after study and teaching at Leipzig. He was one of the most active opponents of Lutheranism, defending the veneration of saints and demanding wide monastic reforms. He wrote a number of poems and prose devotions, but most of his work was pamphlet warfare with enemies of Catholicism.

BACICCIO, IL. *See* Gaulli, Giovanni Battista.

BACKER, AUGUSTIN DE (1809–1873), bibliographer. Born in Antwerp on July 18, he studied there and at Fribourg, became a Jesuit in 1835, trained at Nivelles, taught at Namur, and was ordained at Louvain. With his brother Aloysius, he published *La bibliothèque des écrivains de la compagnie de Jesus*, the second edition of which (1869–76) contained the names of 11,000 Jesuit writers. The work drew on the uncompleted list by Nathaniel Bacon and led to the later bibliography by Charles Sommervogel, who collaborated on the third and posthumous volume. Fr. de Backer died in Liège on Dec. 1.

BACKHOUSE, EDWARD TRELAWNY (1873–1944), historian. Born in Middleton Tyas, Yorkshire, England, on Oct. 20, son of Sir Jonathan and Florence Salusbury Backhouse, he studied at Winchester and Oxford, and mastered foreign languages. He went to the British legation in Peking, China, in 1897, taught at its university, after the Boxer Rebellion, from 1903 to 1913, and built up a library of 27,000 Chinese books and manuscripts which he left to Oxford. With J. Bland he wrote *China under the Empress Dowager* and *Annals and Memoirs of the Court of Peking* and with Sidney Barton a revision of Hillier's *English-Chinese* [Peking] *Dictionary*. He continued translating for the British legation and the London *Times*, became second baronet in 1918, worked on histories of the Manchu emperors, and became a scholarly recluse. All his manuscript notes were burned by the Japanese when they invaded in 1937. He became a convert in 1941, remained in the city during World War II, and died in Peking on Jan. 8.

BACKX, PETER HUBERT EVERMODE (1805–1868). Born in Tilburg, Holland, on Dec. 10, he was ordained in 1832, the first Premonstratensian novice in the area since the suppression of Catholicism in 1796. He was able to repurchase, repair, and enlarge the original abbey of Tongerloo, Belgium, where he had become abbot in 1839 and where he died twenty-nine years later on Oct. 28.

BACON, DAVID WILLIAM (1813–1874), bishop. Born in New York City on Sept. 15, he studied at Montreal and at Mt. St. Mary's, Maryland, was ordained at Baltimore in 1838, served in upper New York State, and was pastor of a Brooklyn parish from 1841 to 1855, when he became first bishop of Portland, Maine. The diocese included the entire state, had six priests and eight parishes, and was plagued by Know-Nothing propaganda; by the time of his death there were sixty-three parishes with 80,000 Catholics. He died in New York on Nov. 5.

BACON, JOHN (d. 1346), theologian. Born in Norfolk, England, he became a Carmelite at Snitterly, studied at Oxford and Paris, and became master in 1325. He was provincial of England from 1329 to 1333 and wrote more than 120 volumes, including commentaries on the New Testament. As a philosopher he was a realist, and followed Averroës rather than St. Thomas Aquinas. He is also known as Johannes Anglicus and Johannes de Baconthorpe.

BACON, NATHANIEL (1598–1676), bibliographer. Born in Norfolk, he was educated at St. Omer, and the English College in Rome. He was ordained in 1622 and sent on the English mission. He then became a Jesuit at Rome and from 1647 to 1668 was secretary to five successive generals of the Society. He began a compilation of Jesuit writings, basing his work on that of Frs. Ribadeneira and Alegambe, which he revised, annotated, and expanded. Since he adopted the name Fr. Southwell, he

is often so listed. He died in Rome on Dec. 2.

BACON, ROGER. *See* Roger Bacon.

BADELEY, EDWARD LOUTH (1808–1868), lawyer. A graduate of Oxford, he became a member of the English bar in 1841 and was converted during the Oxford Movement. He wrote *The Privilege of Religious Confessions in English Courts of Justice* (1865). John Henry Newman consulted him about his proposed answer to Charles Kingsley, which became the *Apologia*, and also relied on him as counsel in the libel suit brought by Achilli.

BADEMUS, ST. (d. 376?), martyr. Founder and abbot of a monastery near Beth-Lapat, he was captured with several monks and tortured and imprisoned during the persecution of King Sapor II of Persia. He was stabbed to death by a renegade Christian who had been promised his own life for the act of murder. F. D. Apr. 10.

BADEN, OLAF MORTENSEN (d. 1485). He became bishop of Roskilde, Denmark, in 1461, and consecrated the restored cathedral in 1464. He became first chancellor of the University of Copenhagen, founded in 1479 by King Christian I with the approval of Pope Sixtus IV.

BADIA, TOMASSO (1483–1547), cardinal. Born in Modena, Italy, he became a Dominican, taught theology, and served on the commission which compiled the abuses to be considered at the Council of Trent. He attended the Diet of Worms in 1540 as a disputant and was made cardinal and papal legate by Paul III on his return, after his evaluation of the findings at Trent. It was on his recommendation that the Society of Jesus was given formal approval. He died in Rome on Sept. 6.

BADILO, ST. (d. 870?). A Benedictine monk at Vezelay, France, he became abbot of Leuze in Hainault. F. D. Oct. 8.

BADIN, STEPHEN THEODORE (1768–1853), missioner. The first priest to be ordained in the new United States was born in Orléans, France, on July 17, studied at Paris until the Sulpician seminary was closed by the revolutionists, and arrived in Philadelphia in 1792. He was ordained at Baltimore a year later by Bishop Carroll. Later that year he had become settled at White Sulphur, Kentucky, riding dutifully to care for a 120-mile parish. In 1806 he was joined by Fr. Charles Nerinckx and in 1811 by Bishop Flaget. Difficulties arose over real estate, and Fr. Badin returned to parish work in France from 1819 to 1828. Returning to the United States, he worked in Michigan, Ohio, and Kentucky. He died in Cincinnati on Apr. 21 and is buried on the campus of the University of Notre Dame, inasmuch as in 1841 he had given some farm property to Fr. Sorin of Indiana, who was to be one of the founders of the university.

BADIUS, JODOCUS (1462–1535), printer.

Born in Asche, near Brussels, he studied at Brussels and Ferrara, taught Greek at Lyons, settled in Paris about 1500, and set up a printing press where he issued a life of Thomas à Kempis; *Navicula stultarum mulierum,* a satire on women; and editions of the classics with his own annotation. His colophon is the oldest known representation of a printing press. He also is known as Jodocus Ascensianus.

BADIUS, RAPHAEL (17th century), antiquarian. A Dominican who knew the history and hagiography of Florence and Tuscany, and aided the Jesuits in their work on the *Acta Sanctorum,* he was dean of the University of Florence, Italy, in 1681.

BADOUR. *See* Badulf, St.

BADUARIO BONAVENTURE (1332–1386), cardinal. Born in Peraga, near Padua, he became an Augustinian, studied at Paris, held the chair of theology there, and in 1377 became prior general. He preached the funeral sermon for his friend, the poet Petrarch, was made cardinal in 1378, and served as ambassador for Pope Urban VI. The cardinal was assassinated in Rome by a bowman, probably in the pay of his relative, Francis, Prince of Carrara, with whom he had clashed over the rights of the Church in Padua.

BADULF, ST. (d. 850?). Also known as Badour, he was Benedictine abbot of Ainay, Lyons, France. F. D. Aug. 19.

BAEGERT, JOHN JACOB (1717–1777), scholar. Born in Schlettstadt, Alsace, on Dec. 23, he became a Jesuit in 1736, taught at Mannheim, and was ordained in 1749. He served as a missioner in Lower California until the Society was expelled in 1767 and he was sent back to Europe. During his last years, at the Jesuit college in Neustadt, he wrote a detailed study of the language and customs of the people of his mission, which the Smithsonian Institution of Washington, D.C., published in 1863. He died in Neustadt-on-the-Haardt, Rhenish Palatinate, on Sept. (or Dec.) 29.

BAERT, FRANÇOIS (1651–1719), scholar. Born at Ypres, Belgium, on Aug. 25, he became a Jesuit at Mechlin in 1667 and was ordained in 1680. He worked with the Bollandist, Fr. Daniel Papebroch, and edited nine volumes of the *Acta Sanctorum.* He died in Antwerp on Oct. 27.

BAEUMER, SUITBERT (1845–1894), patrologist. Born in Leuchtenberg, Germany, on Mar. 28, he studied at Bonn and Tübingen, became a Benedictine at Beuron, and was ordained in 1869. He wrote on liturgy and the creed, a history of the breviary, a life of Mabillon, and supervised the publication at Tournai of modern missals and breviaries. He died in Freiburg, Germany, on Aug. 12.

BAGLIONI, BACCIO D'AGNOLO (1462–1543), architect. A Florentine, he helped Cronaca in constructing the Palazzo Vecchio, imitated this master but introduced more simplicity, and created the courts of the Teddei and Ginori palaces. He designed the Bartonini palace in 1520 and several nearby villas. His four sons became artists and architects; Domenico (d. 1511) designed the Buturlin palace.

BAGLIONI, GIOVANNI (1571–1644), painter. An art student of Francesco Morelli, this Roman executed work for the churches of Santa Maria dell' Orto in Rome, San Nicolo in Carcere, and the cathedrals of Perugia and Loretto. He wrote *Lives of the Painters, Sculptors, and Architects,* covering those who flourished in Rome from 1573 to 1642. He died in Rome. He is known as Il Sordo del Barozzo.

BAGNACAVALLO. *See* Ramenghi, Bartolommeo.

BAGNESI, BL. MARIA BARTHOLOMEA (1511–1577). Born in Florence, Italy, she was an invalid from seventeen to thirty-two, became a Dominican tertiary and briefly regained her strength, then became bedridden again and suffered intensely. She had many supernatural gifts and exerted great influence on hundreds who visited her for advice and consolation. Her cult was approved by Pope Pius VII. F. D. May 27.

BAGNUS. *See* Bain, St.

BAGOT, JEAN (1591–1664), theologian. Born in Rennes, France, on July 9, he became a Jesuit in 1611, and wrote a major study of theology and treatises on grace, penance, and free will. One work on penance met with ecclesiastical censure at Paris, but this was overruled at Rome. He died in Paris on Aug. 23 as superior of the Congregation of the Blessed Virgin there.

BAGSHAW, CHRISTOPHER (d. 1625?). Born in Derbyshire, England, he attended Cambridge and Oxford (where he helped to expel Bl. Robert Persons), became a teacher, and traveled on the Continent. There he became a convert and was ordained in 1582. Sent to England, he was captured and imprisoned for at least ten years, during which he seems to have been the leader of a rebellious faction against the Jesuits and to have attempted to prevent the plan for a Catholic successor to Queen Elizabeth. Freed, he became rector of Ave Maria College in Paris, where he died sometime after 1625.

BAILEY, THOMAS (d. 1657?). Born in Bangor, England, son of an Anglican bishop, he was educated at Cambridge, ordained, and served King Charles I during the civil war. While in Europe after Charles's death, he became a Catholic and wrote so favorably of royalty that Oliver Cromwell imprisoned him on his return to England. He died in Italy, probably while secretary to Cardinal Ottoboni of Ferrara.

BAILLARGEON, CHARLES FRANÇOIS (1798–1870), archbishop. Serving in many parishes during an era of great plagues, this Quebec-born priest was consecrated bishop in 1851, became administrator of that Canadian diocese in 1855, archbishop in 1867, and published a French translation of the New Testament. He died on Oct. 13.

BAILLOQUET, PIERRE (1612–1692), missioner. Born in Saintes, France, he became a Jesuit in 1631, was sent to Canada in 1647, and labored with zealous disregard for danger among the Indian tribes in an area extending from Acadia to Illinois. He died on the Ottawa missions on June 7.

BAILLY, EMMANUEL (1842–1917). Born in Paris on Aug. 4, he became an Augustinian of the Assumption in 1861, was ordained in 1865, held several posts at Nîmes, and became superior general in 1903. He visited America and the Orient, served as consultant to the Congregation of Seminaries and Studies, and died in Paris on Nov. 23.

BAILLY, VINCENT DE PAUL (1832–1912), editor. Born in Berteaucourt-les-Thennes, France, on Dec. 2, he studied in Paris, took a position with the telegraph bureau there and at Nîmes, and also taught mathematics at the Augustinian college, Nîmes. In 1860 he joined the Congregation of the Assumption, was ordained in 1863, and directed their college at Nîmes from 1863 to 1867. He was chaplain of the French forces defending the papacy in Rome and on his return was chaplain at the siege of Metz. After the war with Prussia he edited *La Pélerin* and *La Croix*, speaking strongly against rising anti-clericalism until his order was exiled in 1900. He lived in Rome until 1906, founded houses in Belgium and England, and returned to Paris, where he died on Dec. 2.

BAILY, THOMAS (d. 1591), educator. Born in Yorkshire, England, he studied at Cambridge, became a fellow there, but lost his mastership of Clare Hall on Elizabeth's accession. In exile he became a doctor of divinity at Louvain, and administered the English College at Douai as assistant to Cardinal Allen. He died in Douai on Oct. 7.

BAIN, ST. (d. 710?), bishop. He was a Benedictine monk at Fontenelle under St. Wandregisilus, became bishop of Thérouanne about 689, and made many converts in the region of Calais (of which he is chief patron). After twelve years he resigned, returned to Fontenelle, and became its abbot and also abbot of Fleury about 704. He was also known as Bagnus. F. D. June 20.

BAINBRIDGE, CHRISTOPHER (1464?–1514), cardinal. Born in Hilton, Westmoreland, England, he studied at Oxford, became a provost, then treasurer of the diocese of London, master of the rolls under Henry VII, and, in 1507, bishop of Durham. He was transferred to York in 1508, became special ambassador of Henry VIII to Rome in 1509, and was made cardinal in 1511 by Pope Julius II, who appointed him head of a military expedition against Ferrara. He was poisoned by an Italian priest, allegedly at the instigation of the resident English ambassador, Bishop Sylvester de Giglis, and died in Rome on July 14.

BAINES, PETER AUGUSTINE (1787–1843), bishop. Born in Kirkby, Lancashire, on Jan. 25, he studied at monasteries in Germany and Yorkshire and became a Benedictine. He gained a reputation as preacher and controversialist, became coadjutor to Bishop Collingridge and titular bishop of Siga in 1823, and was appointed vicar apostolic in 1829. He later became secularized, and established a short-lived college at Prior Park, outside Bath, where he died on July 6.

BAINES, RALPH (d. 1559), bishop. Born in Knowsthorp, Yorkshire, England, he attended Cambridge, was ordained in 1519, and served as pastor in Hardwicke until 1544. For nine years he was professor of Hebrew at Paris, where he published three scriptural studies. Returning to England, he was consecrated bishop of Lichfield and Coventry in 1554, but with ten other bishops was removed from office and subjected to house arrest when Elizabeth became queen. He died, still a prisoner, on Nov. 18.

BAINI, GIUSEPPE (1775–1844), musician. Born in Rome on Oct. 21, he became a member of the Sistine Chapel choir, serving as its director from 1818 until his death. He wrote a number of musical compositions and a discussion of rhythm, but his greatest contribution was a critical biography of Palestrina (1828), which created such interest that the latter's complete works were put into print. He died in Rome on May 21.

BAIRRE. *See* Finbar, St. (d. 633).

BAITHEN, ST. (536–599?). Son of Brenaron, he was a staunch supporter of St. Columcille, whom he succeeded as abbot of Iona in 596 at the latter's death. He had served as abbot of Tiree. He wrote a life of his predecessor and some poetry, now lost. F. D. Oct. 6. Another St. Baithin (F. D. May 22) is patron of Ennisboyne, and another (Feb. 19) of Tibohin. There are six other saints of the same name.

BAIUS, MICHEL (1513–1589). Born in Melun, France, and a graduate of Louvain, he taught philosophy, became president of Adrian College and taught scripture there. During the absence of better scholars, who were attending the Council of Trent, he and John Hessels introduced extreme philosophical interpretations, which were published in 1564 and papally censured in part. He defended his position and accepted correction of unclear passages on man's primitive innocence, grace, and redemption. His views, which occasionally reappeared after his complete recantation, were Pelagian and Calvinistic. He died at Louvain on Sept. 16 in good favor, but his interpretations had unfortunate influence on the later Jansenists, on the immanence theory of French philosophers, and on Russian writings on original sin.

BAKACS, TAMÁS. *See* Bakócz, Tamás.

BAKER, DAVID AUGUSTINE (1575-1641), apologist. Born in Abergavenny, Wales, on Dec. 9, he was educated at Oxford and the Middle Temple, and lost and regained his faith. In 1605 he became a Benedictine at Padua, returned to his father's deathbed to win him back to the Church, continued his own studies, and was professed in England. He made a study of the independence from Cluny of the original Benedictine foundation in England, becoming associated with such antiquarians as Sir Robert Cotton and William Camden. In 1624 he became spiritual adviser to a convent at Cambrai, where he wrote a number of ascetical treatises, went to Douai in 1633, then returned to London, where he died of the plague on Aug. 9.

BAKER, FRANCIS ASBURY (1820-1865). Son of Sam Baker, a famous Baltimore, Maryland, physician, he was born in Baltimore on Mar. 30, graduated from Princeton in 1839, became an Episcopalian minister, and served in two Baltimore churches. In 1853, influenced by the Oxford Movement, he became a convert, was ordained three years later, joined a Redemptorist mission group, then with Fr. Hecker and others left to establish the Paulists. He died in New York City on Apr. 4.

BAKER, NELSON H. (1841-1936). Born in Buffalo, New York, on Feb. 16, he studied at Canisius and Niagara, was ordained in 1876, and was attached to St. Joseph's orphanage in Buffalo for five years. After pastoral work he was placed in charge of an orphanage in Lackawanna, and between 1892 and 1915 built an industrial school, maternity hospital, and infants' home. In 1926 he completed the shrine of Our Lady of Victory. More than 25,000 boys were given shelter and work under his direction. He became a monsignor in 1905, received an honorary degree from Canisius, and died in Lackawanna, New York, on July 29.

BAKÓCZ, TAMÁS (1442?-1521), cardinal. Born in Erdoed, Hungary, he studied at Cracow, Ferrara, and Padua, returned to Hungary as a doctor of divinity about 1470, became secretary and vice-chancellor to King Matthias, and in 1486 bishop of Raab. On the accession in 1490 of King Ladislaus II, whose selection he had arranged, he became chancellor and a

year later bishop of Erlau as well, being transferred to Gran, Hungary, in 1497. He became a cardinal in 1500 and patriarch of Constantinople in 1507, and attended the Lateran Council in 1521, where he contributed to reform plans. As papal legate of Leo X, he helped to raise an army of 100,000 for a crusade, but civil war broke out when the nobles attacked and defeated this army in 1514. Two years later Ladislaus died and the chancellor, once a most powerful director of international policies, who had showered his enormous wealth upon his family, lost all influence. In spite of his Renaissance princeliness, he was a religious and acknowledgedly honest man. He died on June 15. His name is also spelled Bakacs.

BALBOA, VASCO NÚÑEZ DE (1475?-1517?), explorer. Born in Badajoz (or Jerez de los Caballeros), Spain, he went to Central America in 1501 with Rodrigo de Bastidas, settled in Cuba, and in 1510 joined Martín Fernández de Enciso, became a leader in the Panama area, and by 1511 had proclaimed himself governor of Darien and exiled Enciso. With a few companions he crossed the isthmus and discovered the Pacific Ocean on Sept. 25, thus establishing the fact that America was a continent. In 1514, Pedro Arias de Ávila arrived as governor of territory claimed in part by Balboa, married his daughter to Balboa to hide his enmity, and, while Balboa was exploring further, undermined his character. Actually, Balboa was easygoing, friendly with the Indians, and generous; he was staunchly defended by Bishop Quevedo of Castilla de Oro. When the bishop was recalled to Spain, Ávila struck. Balboa was swiftly charged with high treason and executed at Darien.

BALBUENA, BERNARDO DE (1568-1627), bishop. Born in Val de Peñas, Spain, he was taken as a child to Mexico, returned to Spain for ordination, spent twelve years as a priest in Jamaica, and in 1620 became bishop of Puerto Rico. He wrote a history of Mexico in the sixteenth century, a collection of eclogues, and *Bernardo o la victoria de Roncesvalles*, a long poem based on the romantic legend of Bernardo del Carpio. He died in Puerto Rico.

BALBUS, HIERONYMUS (1450?-1535?), bishop. Born in Venice, Italy, he studied under Pomponius Laetus, founder of the Roman Academy, mastered the classics, literature, and law, fell into a dissolute way of life, and became so vain and contentious that professorships at the University of Paris lasted only from 1485 to 1491, at Vienna from 1494 to 1497, and at Prague for less than a year. He then retired to Fünfkirchen, Hungary, for fifteen years, reformed his conduct, took orders, was attached to several cathedrals, and became secretary to King Ladislaus VI and tutor of the princes. He was an opponent of Lutheranism at the

Diet of Worms in 1521, became bishop of Gurk in 1522, working to reform his Carinthian diocese, but was often absent in the court of Clement VII in Rome or Emperor Charles V in Bologna. Of his writings, *De coronatione principum* was placed on the Index in 1611, and his early poems are coarse and realistically boastful. He probably died in Venice.

BALDE, JACOB (1604–1668), poet. Born in Ensisheim, Alsace, on Jan. 4, he studied there and at Ingolstadt, becoming a Jesuit in 1624, and teaching at Munich and Innsbruck before his ordination in 1633. He wrote much lyric poetry, highly praised by Herder, who translated some from the Latin; satires and drama; and the mock-heroic *Batrachomyomachia*, which influenced the eighteenth-century Irish poet, Thomas Parnell. He died in Neuburg, Germany, on Aug. 9.

BALDERIC, ST. (7th century). Son of King Sigisbert I of Austrasia, he became abbot-founder of the monastery of Montfaucon in Champagne and founded a convent at Rheims for his sister, St. Bova. He is also known as Baudry. F. D. Oct. 16.

BALDERIC (1050?–1130), bishop. A student at Angers, France, he entered the abbey of Bourgueil, Anjou, where he became abbot in 1079. He was made bishop of Dol in 1107, traveled to Rome and England, reformed monastic discipline, and wrote many poems and biographies, and a detailed history of the fourth crusade. He died on Jan. 7.

BALDERIC (d. 1157?), educator. A monk born in Florennes, Belgium, he served in the court of Pope Eugene III, attended the Synod of Paris (1147), and there met Archbishop Albers of Trèves, France, who placed him in charge of his cathedral school and whose biography he wrote.

BALDI, BERNARDINO (1553–1617), poet. Born in Urbino, Italy, on June 5, he studied at Padua and Rome and established a reputation as mathematician and classical and oriental linguist. He became abbot of Guastalla at Mantua, and wrote georgics, epigrams and dialogues in Italian, as well as lyrics in Latin, prose biographies, and studies of Aristotle, Musaeus, and Vitruvius. He died in Urbino on Oct. 10.

BALDINUCCI, BL. ANTONIO (1665–1717). Born in Florence, son of a painter and author, he joined the Jesuits when sixteen, was ordained at thirty and sent to Viterbo, where his unconventional methods of attracting converts (he often formed processions in which he carried a cross and scourged himself) brought many back to the faith. He wrote many Lenten sermons and hundreds of conferences. He was beatified in 1893 by Pope Leo XIII. F. D. Nov. 7.

BALDOMERUS, ST. (d. 660?). A locksmith of Lyons, France, he aided the poor and gave

such time to earnest prayer that Abbot Viventius invited him to the monastery of St. Justus, where he became a subdeacon. He is also known as Galmier. F. D. Feb. 27.

BALDOVINETTI, ALESSO (1427–1499), painter. Born in Florence on Oct. 14, he became a pupil of Paolo Uccelli at twenty-one, experimented with oils, and gained a reputation for his mosaics in the churches of Santa Maria Nuova and San Miniato. Portraits and religious scenes are in the galleries of Bergamo and the Uffizi and the Academy at Florence. He died in the latter city on Aug. 29.

BALDRED, ST. (d. 756). Born in southern Scotland, he became a recluse at Tyningham and on an island in the Firth of Forth. He is sometimes confused with a Balther of Durham. F. D. Mar. 6.

BALDUNG, HANS (1476?–1545), painter. Born in Gmünd, Swabia, he was a friend, admirer, and imitator of Albrecht Dürer. He executed altarpieces for a monastery at Freiburg, Germany, and the convent of Lichenthal. Other work came into the possession of museums in Berlin, Munich, Stuttgart, Frankfort, Prague, and Basle. He died in Strassburg shortly after he had become a senator.

BALDWIN, ST. (d. 1140). Born in Italy, he became a Cistercian at Clairvaux, a close follower of St. Bernard, and abbot of San Pastore in the diocese of Rieti, of which he is chief patron. F. D. July 15.

BALDWIN (d. 1190), archbishop. Born and ordained in Exeter, England, he became a Cistercian at the abbey of Ford in Devonshire, and later its abbot. In 1180 he was elected bishop of Worcester by the English bishops, and later that year archbishop of Canterbury, but the choice was disputed by the monks. He was finally approved, on the condition that later elections were to be by the monks of Canterbury. In 1188 he preached a crusade, outfitted a force of 500, left for the Holy Land two years later, and died on Nov. 19 at the siege of Acre.

BALDWIN (1285–1354), archbishop. Son of Count Henry III of Luxembourg and a brother of Emperor Henry VII, he was orphaned at three, studied at Paris, and was papally appointed archbishop of Trèves when he was only twenty-two, with the additional title of elector of the Holy Roman Empire. A powerful political figure, he fought the papacy and supported the election of his brother Henry, Louis of Bavaria (whom he defended in an eight-year civil war, but abandoned soon after papal excommunication), and his grandnephew Charles IV. Thereafter, the electors would accept no papal part in any choice; Baldwin was equally strong against the barons of his realm and forced them into submission by destroying their castles.

BALDWIN, CHARLES SEARS (1867–1935), critic. Born in New York City, he did his undergraduate and doctoral work at Columbia, taught at Yale from 1895 to 1911, and from then until his death in New York at Columbia and Barnard. He wrote texts, essays, poems, and three scholarly studies: *Ancient Rhetoric and Poetic, Medieval Rhetoric and Poetic, Renaissance Literary Theory and Practice*.

BALDWIN, FRANCIS (1520–1573), jurist. Born in Arras, France, on Jan. 1, he studied law at Louvain, served in the court of Emperor Charles V at Brussels, taught in several French and German cities, and wrote widely on Constantine the Great, several Church Fathers, and legal topics. Won over to Calvinism, he returned to Catholicism before his death in Paris on Oct. 24.

BALES, BL. CHRISTOPHER (d. 1590), martyr. Born in Coniscliffe, Durham, England, he was educated at Rome and Douai, ordained, entered the English underground mission as Mr. Rivers, and two years later was captured, tortured, and hanged, drawn, and quartered in London. He was beatified in 1929. His name is also spelled Bayles. F. D. Mar. 4.

BALL, FRANCES (1794–1861), educator. Born in Dublin, Ireland, on Jan. 9 to John Ball and Mary Clare Bennet, she studied at York under the Sisters of the Institute of the Blessed Virgin Mary, entering its novitiate in 1814. In 1821, at the invitation of Archbishop David Murray of Dublin, she and two novices established an Irish branch of that institute for the instruction of children. She died at Rathfarnam House, near Dublin, which she had founded, on May 19.

BALLACHI, BL. SIMON (1250?–1319). Born in Sant' Arcangelo, near Rimini, Italy, he became a Dominican laybrother at twenty-seven, and was noted for exceptional austerities. His cult was confirmed in 1821. F. D. Nov. 3.

BALLANTYNE, JOHN. *See* Bellenden, John.

BALLERINI, GIROLAMO (1702–1781). Born in Verona, Italy, on Jan. 29, he studied at the Jesuit college there and was ordained a parish priest. With his brother Pietro he edited the theological and historical writings of Cardinal Noris of Verona (1729–33), and of Bishop Giberti of Verona (1733), and the sermons of St. Zeno (1739). He died on Apr. 23.

BALLERINI, PIETRO (1698–1769), scholar. Born in Verona, Italy, on Sept. 7, he became principal of the classical school there after his ordination and in 1724 began a long writing career. He edited several collections with his brother Girolamo, issued a treatise on St. Augustine's method of study, a treatise against usury, and editions of the *Summa* of St. Antoninus (1740) and of the *Summa* of St. Raymond of Peñafort (1744). Venice sent him to Rome as a canonist in 1748, and at the request of Pope Benedict XIV he spent nine years on an edition of Pope St. Leo the Great. He died on Mar. 28.

BALLESTREM, FRANZ XAVER (1834–1910). Born in Plawniowitz, Upper Silesia, he served with the Prussian army in 1866–71, rose to the rank of captain, was elected to the *Reichstag* in 1872 and played an important role in the Centre party. He became vice-president of the *Reichstag* in 1890–93 and president in 1898–1906. He was decorated by Pope Pius IX for his opposition to the Kulturkampf and in 1903 became a member of the Prussian upper house.

BALME, HENRI (d. 1439). Born in Geneva, Switzerland, and also known as Hugh, he became a Friar Minor in Burgundy and was confessor to St. Colette, whose biography he wrote but destroyed at her request. He wrote *Theologia mystica*, long attributed to St. Bonaventure. He died on Feb. 23.

BALMES, JAIME LUCIANO (1810–1848), philosopher. Born in Vich, Spain, on Aug. 28, he was educated at Cervera, ordained, and returned to Vich to teach mathematics and physics. Poetry, a tract on clerical celibacy, a translation of maxims of St. Francis de Sales, and a school text on religion were published between 1834 and 1844, but the decade was climaxed by his *Protestantism, Catholicism and European Culture*, begun as an answer to the historian Guizot. The *Art of Thinking* and *Letters of a Skeptic* followed, then work on magazines and newspapers, an *Elementary Philosophy* and a *Basic Philosophy* (both of which are open to very serious criticism), a defense of Pope Pius IX's liberalism, some linguistic and political studies, and an inaugural address for the Royal Spanish Academy. He died at Vich on July 9.

BALSAMUS, BL. (d. 1232). He was tenth abbot of the Benedictine monastery of La Cava, Italy, appointed in 1208. His cult was approved in 1928. F. D. Nov. 24.

BALTES, PETER JOSEPH (1820–1886), bishop. Born in Ensheim, Bavaria, on Apr. 7, he was brought by his parents to Oswego, New York, at the age of six, attended Holy Cross College, and was ordained at Montreal in 1853. He worked in Illinois parishes and became vicar general and theologian to Bishop Juncker at the Second Plenary Council at Baltimore (1866). He was consecrated second bishop of Alton, Illinois, in 1870, at the Belleville cathedral, which he had built, and was active in exactness of liturgical ceremony, ecclesiastical discipline, and church property law. He died in Alton on Feb. 15.

BALTHASAR (1st century). This name is commonly attributed to one of the three wise men (magi) from the East who came to acknowledge the infant Jesus in Bethlehem; the others were called Melchior and Caspar and according to tradition were kings. On their way they stopped to ask Herod where the newborn king could be found and were told to report back when they found Him. Warned in a dream, they left by another route, whereupon Herod ordered a massacre of infants (Matt. 2:1–12). F. D. Jan. 6.

BALTIMORE, LORD. *See* Calvert.

BALTO. *See* Walto, Bl.

BALTUS, JEAN FRANÇOIS (1667–1743), theologian. Born in Metz on June 8, he entered the Jesuits in 1682, taught at Dijon and Strassburg, and became rector of several French houses and president of the college at Strassburg. Among his writings are a commentary on Fontenelle's work on pagan oracles and four studies of the Church Fathers. He died in Rheims on Mar. 9.

BALUE, JEAN (1421?–1491), cardinal. A lawyer from Poitou, he became executor of the bishop of Poitiers and was accused of misappropriating a trust fund for the poor. He then attached himself to Bishop Beauvau of Angers, climbed into favor with King Louis XI, who made him his almoner in 1464, gained control of several abbeys and priories, was appointed bishop of Évreux in 1465, deposed Beauvau and in 1467 took over his see, and maneuvered a cardinalate. He was arrested for high treason and imprisoned for eleven years by Louis XI. On his release in 1480 he went to Rome, managed to become bishop of Albans and Pope Julius II's legate to France, and then King Charles VIII's ambassador to Rome. He died on Oct. 5 in Ripatransone, Italy, in widespread disrepute.

BALUZE, ÉTIENNE (1630–1718), scholar. Born in Tulle, France, on Dec. 24, he studied there and at Toulouse, where he became secretary to the scholar, Archbishop Pierre de Marca, in 1650. In 1662 he published a history of Catalonia, which gained him a position as Colbert's librarian for thirty years; then editions of Mercator, of a number of unpublished capitularies, of a selection of Innocent III's letters, and biographies of the Avignon popes and a history of Tulle. He became professor of canon law and director at the Collège de France in 1670, but fell out of royal favor and was exiled to Tours. He died near Paris on July 28.

BANCEL, LOUIS (1628–1685), theologian. Born in Valence, France, he became a Dominican at Avignon, where he taught philosophy, and became the first to hold the chair of theology at its university, from 1654 until his death there. He wrote an introduction to theology and a study of St. Thomas Aquinas.

BANDARINUS, ST. (d. 566). He became bishop of Soissons in 540, founded Crépin abbey, was banished for seven years by Clo-

taire I, and recalled when he was discovered working as a gardener in England. He is also known as Banderik. F. D. Aug. 9.

BANDELLI, BL. STEFANO (1369–1450). Born in Castelnuovo, Piacenza, Italy, he became a Dominican, studied canon law at Pavia, and became a professor there. He died at Saluzzo after nearly fifty years in which his fame as preacher and confessor became widespread. His cult was confirmed in 1856. F. D. June 13.

BANDELLO, MATTEO (1480–1565), bishop. Born in Piedmont, Italy, he became a Dominican and died as bishop of Agen, France. Religious life, however, seems to have had little influence upon him; his *novelle* were tales of immorality in which vice is presented as amusing, centering on scandal, hypocrisy, cruelty, and indecency. They were deplored by the serious, served as witnesses for the reformers on the eve of the Council of Trent, but, translated by William Painter and others, were among the sources of Shakespeare's *Romeo and Juliet* and John Webster's tragedies.

BANDERIK. *See* Bandarinus, St.

BANDURI, ANSELMO (1671–1743), archaeologist. Born in Ragusa, Italy, he became a Benedictine, studied at Naples and Florence, joined the scholar Montfaucon in searching for materials for an edition of St. John Chrysostom, then worked for the Maurists at Paris, and published a history of the Byzantine Empire and a study of Roman coinage. He died in Paris on Jan. 4.

BAÑEZ, DOMINGO (1528–1604), theologian. Born in Medina del Campo, Spain, on Feb. 29, he studied at Salamanca, was professed a Dominican in 1547, preached for several years, held the chair of theology at Alcalá in 1567, and succeeded Bartolomé Medina as professor of theology at Salamanca in 1581. While rector of St. Gregory's at Valladolid, he was confessor of St. Teresa and contributed to the Carmelite reform. Besides writing a number of commentaries on St. Thomas Aquinas, to the study of whom these gave great impetus, he was involved in the long debate (1582–98) with the Jesuit Luis Molina and others on the questions of grace and redemption. His summation of the Dominican position won papal approval of the teaching of several interpretations which had been questioned by the inquisition. He died at Medina del Campo on Oct. 22.

BANIM, JOHN (1798–1842), writer. Born in Kilkenny, Ireland, on Apr. 3, he entered the college there in 1810, studied art in Dublin, and returned to teach it at home in 1815. He wrote *Damon and Pythias* in 1821, which was produced in London for Charles Kemble, and in the next fourteen years wrote in London a great deal of journalism and some twenty novels, operas, and plays. He returned to Ireland in 1835, was granted a pension, and died after a lifetime of suffering on Aug. 31. With his brother Michael he wrote *Tales of the O'Hara Family*; alone, he wrote *Soggarth Aroon* and *Aileen*, volumes of verse; and such novels as *The Mayor of Windgap* and *The Boyne Water*.

BANIM, MICHAEL (1796–1874), novelist. Born in Kilkenny, Ireland, on Aug. 5, he became a lawyer, and, to support his father after economic failure, wrote thirteen of the twenty-four novels of the *Tales of the O'Hara Family*, (*The Ghost Hunter* and *The Croppy* stand out) which he undertook with his brother John in imitation of Sir Walter Scott's *Waverley*. In his later years he became postmaster and died in Booterstown, near Dublin, on Aug. 30.

BAPST, JOHN (1815–1887), educator. Born in La Roche, Switzerland, on Dec. 17, he studied at Fribourg and became a Jesuit in 1835. In 1848 he was sent to an Indian mission in Old Town, Maine, which had been without a priest for twenty years. He founded temperance societies through the state and was quite successful in making converts while stationed at Eastport and Ellsworth. During the Know-Nothing campaign of 1854 he was tarred and feathered, almost burned to death, and driven out of his parish. He was transferred to Bangor, where he built the first church, then went to Massachusetts to become rector of the new Boston College for Jesuit scholastics, and later served as superior of the New England and Canadian area. He died at Mt. Hope, Maryland, on Nov. 2, after his mind had failed, apparently the result of his earlier mistreatment.

BAPTISTA MANTUANUS. *See* Spanuolo, Bl. Baptista.

BARACHISIUS, ST. (d. 327), martyr. *See* Jonas, St.

BARADATES, ST. (d. 460?). A learned hermit in Syria, consulted in correspondence by Emperor Leo I about the fourth General Council of Chalcedon, he devoted himself to years of austere living. F. D. Feb. 22.

BARAGA, FREDERIC (1797–1868), bishop. Born in Malavas, Austria, on June 29, he studied law at Vienna, entered the seminary at Laibach, and was ordained in 1823. He sailed for America seven years later and worked with great success among the Ottawas and Chippewas of Ohio, Michigan, and Wisconsin. In 1853 northern Michigan was made a vicariate apostolic and Baraga its first bishop; in 1865 the see was transferred from Sault Ste. Marie to Marquette. During his thirty-seven years of traveling he found time to write a Chippewa grammar, a dictionary, a prayer book, sermons, instructions on the sacraments; and, earlier, a prayer book and an *Imitation of Mary* in Slovenian. He died in Marquette on Jan. 19.

BARAT, ST. MADELEINE SOPHIE (1779–1865), foundress. Born on Dec. 12 in Joigny, Burgundy, France, she followed a strict but broad plan of education directed by an older, ordained brother, Louis. On his recommendation and that of Fr. Varin, her confessor, she entered religious life in 1800 with three companions, dedicated her group to the Sacred Heart, and devoted herself to the education of girls at Amiens. Such educational opportunities had been denied since the outbreak of the French Revolution. For sixty-three years she was superior of the Society of the Sacred Heart (formally approved by Pope Leo XII in 1826). In 1804 they absorbed a community of Visitation nuns at Grenoble, including Bl. Rose Philippine Duchesne. Convents and boarding schools were set up throughout France; Mother Duchesne was sent to the United States in 1818; when the novitiate was closed by the revolution of 1830, Mother Barat went to Switzerland. Before her death in Paris the order was established in twelve countries. She was canonized in 1925. F. D. May 25.

MOTHER MAUD MONAHAN, *Saint Madeleine Sophie* (New York, Longmans, 1925).

BARAT, NICHOLAS (d. 1706), scholar. A student of the biblical and oriental scholar, Richard Simon, while teaching at the Mazarin college in Paris, France, he wrote and collaborated in the preparation of several studies in both fields.

BARBA, ALVARO ALONZO (17th century), metallurgist. Of Andalusian origin, he worked effectively as a parish priest in Potosi, and wrote on the mineral deposits of Bolivia and on new methods of refining silver.

BARBADIGO, ANGELO (14th century), cardinal. He was made a cardinal by antipope Nicholas V, was in Rome at the coronation of Emperor Louis IV, and became bishop of Cisamus, Crete, and later of Verona, Italy.

BARBARA, ST., martyr. Although widely popular during the Middle Ages, her entire story is probably a pious legend. She was called the daughter of a wealthy man, Dioscorus, refused to marry as he commanded, became a Christian, was imprisoned in a tower, tried, and slain, with St. Juliana, by her father, who was thereupon struck dead by lightning. She is variously reported to have been martyred at Antioch, Heliopolis, Nicomedia, and Rome. She is revered as patron of many callings, among them gunners, architects, miners, builders, masons, and gravediggers, and protector against lightning, sudden death, and impenitence. F. D. Dec. 4.

BARBARIGO, GIOVANNI FRANCESCO (1658–1730), cardinal. Born in Venice, he represented that city at the court of Louis XIV of France, then entered orders and became pastor of St. Mark's, Venice, bishop of Verona in

1697, of Brescia in 1714, a cardinal in 1720, and bishop of Padua in 1723. He also was a patron of letters.

BARBARIGO, ST. GREGORIO LUIGI (1625–1697), cardinal. Born and educated in Venice, Italy, he served in the diplomatic service at twenty, attended the Congress of Münster which brought an end to the Thirty Years' War, and there met the papal nuncio, Fabio Chigi. Gregory became bishop of Bergamo in 1657, cardinal in 1660, and was transferred to Padua in 1664. He founded a college and seminary, established a library and press, and dispensed an enormous fortune to the needy. He was particularly noted for his efforts to reunite separated Christians with the Church. He was canonized in 1960. F. D. June 18.

BARBAS. *See* Barbatus, St.

BARBASYMAS, ST. (d. 346), martyr. The metropolitan of Seleucia-Ctesiphon and sixteen of his fellow priests were tortured, imprisoned for nearly a year, and then beheaded because they refused the command of King Sapor II of Persia to worship the sun. F. D. Jan. 14.

BARBATIAN, ST. (5th century). A priest at Antioch, he came to Rome as abbot of a monastery at Ravenna which Empress Placidia built for him and from which he served as her spiritual and political adviser. F. D. Dec. 31.

BARBATUS, ST. (612?–682), bishop. He is said to have been a priest at Morcona, Italy, also known as Barbas, and to have preached long but unsuccessfully to bring back the Lombards from their lapse into idolatry. They finally turned to him for help when Emperor Constans II laid siege to Benevento in 663, renounced paganism, and, when Bishop Hildebrand of Benevento died, elected him as successor. Barbatus attended the sixth General Council at Constantinople in 680 which condemned the Monothelites. F. D. Feb. 19.

BARBEA, ST. (d. 101), martyr. *See* Sarbelius, St.

BARBELIN, FELIX JOSEPH (1808–1869), educator. Born in Lunéville, Lorraine, on May 30, he was educated in French schools and seminaries, then became a Jesuit in Maryland in 1831 and a teacher at Georgetown University. Transferred to Philadelphia in 1838, he was pastor of St. Joseph's, built a hospital, was active in the care of the young, and became the first president of St. Joseph's College in 1852. He died there on June 8.

BARBER, DANIEL (1756–1834). Born in Simsbury, Connecticut, on Oct. 2, of Congregationalist parents, he fought in the American Revolution, and became an Episcopalian minister at thirty, preaching in churches in Schenectady, New York, and Claremont, New Hampshire. He became a convert in 1819, following his wife and four children, as a result of

the influence of Bishop Cheverus and of Frances, daughter of Gen. Ethan Allen. He wrote *History of My Own Times* (1827) and *Catholic Worships and Piety Explained* (1821) before his death at St. Inigoes, Maryland.

BARBER, VIRGIL (1782–1847). Born in Claremont, New Hampshire, on May 9, son of Daniel Barber, he was an Episcopalian minister and principal of Fairfield Academy near Utica, New York, when he decided to become a convert, with his wife Jerusha (1789–1860) and five young children. Virgil became a Jesuit, serving Indian missions in Maine and teaching at Georgetown University; his wife was professed as a Visitation nun, working at St. Louis and Mobile. Their four daughters became Ursulines and their son a Jesuit. Virgil died at Georgetown on Mar. 25.

BARBERI, DOMINIC (1792–1849). Born near Viterbo, Italy, on June 22, he became a Passionist in 1814, taking the name Dominic of the Mother of God, was ordained in 1818, taught for ten years, filled several posts in his order, and eventually became provincial. He founded the first Passionist retreat in Belgium, at Ere, in 1840, and in 1842 established his group in England, at Aston Hall, Staffordshire. He published sermons, theological and ascetical works, established two other Passionist houses in England, received John Henry Newman and three others of the Oxford Movement into the Church, and died at Reading, England, on Aug. 27.

BARBIERI, GIOVANNI (1591–1666), painter. Born in Cento, Italy, on Feb. 2, he studied under Bertozzi, Gennari the Elder, and Cremonini, produced portraits at Venice and Ferrara, and, at Rome, had Pope Gregory XV as his patron. He later returned to establish an academy at Cento, then settled at Bologna, where he died on Dec. 22. He was nicknamed Il Guercino.

BARBOSA, AGOSTINO (1589–1649), bishop. Born in Guimaraens, Portugal, he studied canon law there and at Rome, then devoted himself to writing, from 1632 to 1648, at Madrid. He was consecrated bishop of Ugento, Italy, the year of his death; his canonical works were published eight years later in nineteen volumes.

BARBOSA-MACHADO, DIEGO (1682–1772), critic. Brother of Ignacio, and also a priest, he compiled the monumental *Bibliotheca Lusitana, historica, critica e chronologica* (1741–59).

BARBOSA-MACHADO, IGNACIO (1686–1734), historian. Born in Lisbon, Portugal, he studied at Coimbra, went to Brazil as a judge, and became a priest after the death of his wife. He wrote several historical works, the most important of which is a study of the relationship between Brazil and Portugal.

BARBOUR, JOHN (1320?–1395), poet. Archdeacon of Aberdeen, Scotland, he was a commissioner in 1357 at Edinburgh to negotiate the ransom of King David II from the English, and in 1373 was an auditor of the exchequer. Several times between these dates he left the country, presumably for study in England or France. Of his poetry, only *The Bruce*, of more than 12,000 lines, is extant. Written in Scots, the last Western vernacular, it is a chronicle in couplets, describing the battles of Bannockburn and Berwick; the characters of Bruce, Douglas, Stewart, and ordinary soldiers; the countryside, customs, and culture of the past. The poem gained him pensions from the city and the crown. It was an influence on Sir Walter Scott's *Castle Dangerous* and *Tales of a Grandfather*.

BARBUS, PAULUS (d. 1494), philosopher. A Dominican, born in Soncino, Lombardy, he taught at Milan, Ferrara, and Bologna, wrote on Aristotle and on contemporary philosophical problems, and was prior at Cremona at the time of his death there on Aug. 4. He is also known as Paulus Soncinas.

BARCENA, ALONZO DE (1528–1598), missioner. Born in Baeza, Spain, he became a Jesuit in 1565, went to Peru in 1569, and served in the missions of Bolivia, Argentina, and Paraguay. He wrote grammars and catechisms in nearly a dozen Indian languages before he died in Cuzco, Peru, on Jan. 15.

BARCLAY, ALEXANDER (1475?–1552), poet. Born in Gloucestershire, England, he probably attended both Oxford and Cambridge, and perhaps Paris as well, studied for the priesthood, and after ordination spent five years at the College of St. Mary at Ottery, Devonshire, as chaplain, choirmaster, and librarian. There he wrote *The Shyp of Folys* (1509), a satire on contemporary evils and based on the Latin of Jakob Locher (*Stultifera navis*) and the German of Sebastian Brant (*Das Narrenschiff*); the work introduced him to Thomas More, John Colet, Nicholas Vaux, and the duke of Norfolk. In 1511 he became a Benedictine at Ely, where he remained until 1520. Shortly after this he wrote *The Introductory to Wryte and to Pronounce Frenche* (1521), became a Franciscan Observant at Canterbury, fell in with William Tyndale, and went to Germany and into Lutheranism in 1528. He had translated Sallust's *Jugurthine War* (1520) and Domenicus Mancinus' *Myrrour of Good Maners* (1523), and had published the first *Eclogues* in English (1524), free paraphrases of satirical opinions of Aeneas Silvius and Battista Mantuanus. He returned to the Church through the influence of Cardinal Wolsey, who had been one of the objects of his censures. He held pastorates in Essex and Somersetshire, escaped a prison sentence through the intervention of the duke of Norfolk when he refused to preach against Catholicism, and died as pastor of All Hallows church, London.

BARCLAY, JOHN (1582–1621), author. Born on Jan. 28 in Pont-à-Mousson, France, he went to London with his father in 1603. Although trained by the Jesuits, he threw his fortunes in with King James I against Cardinal Bellarmine, wrote a political narrative on the gunpowder plot, and the four-part *Euphormionis Lusinini Satyricon* (1604–14), dedicated to the king. Poems were published in 1607 and 1615. In 1616 he went to Rome on the invitation of Pope Paul V, was well received by Bellarmine, given a pension, and completed his Latin novel, *Argenis*, the year of his death in Rome in Aug. This, which was later translated into English by Thomas May and by Ben Jonson, also influenced Fénelon's *Télémaque* and Calderon's *Argenis y Poliarco*.

BARCLAY, WILLIAM (1546–1608), jurist. Born in Aberdeenshire, Scotland, he studied at Aberdeen, Paris, and Bourges, became in 1578 dean of the faculty of law at Pont-à-Mousson and a councilor of state under the duke of Lorraine. He went to England in 1603, where he was made lucrative offers by King James I to become his legal adviser, but returned to Europe to protect his faith, and became professor of law at Angers, France, where he died on July 3. In 1609 his *De potestate papae*, which denied the temporal jurisdiction of the pope, was published with a preface by his son John; Bellarmine wrote against it and John Locke later approved it.

BARCO CENTENERA, MARTIN DEL (1535–1602?), poet. Born in Logroño, diocese of Plasencia, Spain, he went to Argentina in 1572 as chaplain to the expedition of Juan Ortiz de Zárate, and became archdeacon of the church in Paraguay. After twenty-four years he returned to Spain and published *La Argentina*, a long poem on the South American missions, with references to volcanoes, life in Peru, and the piratical raids of the English sea captains Drake and Cavendish.

BARD, HENRY (1604–1660), diplomat. Son of the vicar of Staines, England, he went to Eton and Cambridge, toured Europe and the Near East, lost an arm while a cavalier colonel during the English civil war, served as governor of Guernsey and of Worcester, distinguished himself at the battles of York and Naseby, and was created Baron Bard, Viscount Bellamont, in 1646. Imprisoned by the Cromwell forces, he was released, joined the court-in-exile of Charles II at The Hague, and became a convert there. In 1656 he was sent as Charles's ambassador to the shah of Persia; he died in Arabia.

BARDI, DONATO DI NICOLÒ DI BETTO. *See* Donatello.

BARDO, ST. (982?–1053), archbishop. Born in Oppershofen, he was educated at Fulda, became a Benedictine there, then served as abbot of Werden and, in 1031, of Hersfeld; he also became archbishop of Mainz in that year. As chancellor and chief almoner of the empire he was noted both for his charities and his austerities. These last were so extreme that Pope Leo IX ordered more moderation when he met Bardo at two synods in Mainz which were convoked against simony and to defend celibacy. F. D. June 10.

BARDUCCI, LORENZO. See Credi, Lorenzo di.

BARENT VAN BRUSSEL. See Van Orley, Bernaert.

BARHADBESABA, ST. (d. 355), martyr. A deacon in Arbela, he was arrested during the persecution of King Sapor II of Persia, racked, and, when an apostate named Aggai failed to kill him, was beheaded. F. D. July 20.

BARING, MAURICE (1874–1945), author. Born in London on Apr. 27, to Edward and Louisa Bulteel Baring, he studied at Eton and Cambridge, left without a degree, and in 1898 entered the diplomatic service. He was in Paris, Copenhagen, and Rome, resigning in 1904 to become a correspondent for the *Morning Post* during the Russo-Japanese War and later in St. Petersburg and Constantinople, and for the London *Times* in 1912. He wrote verse plays (*The Black Prince*, 1902, and *Gaston de Foix*, 1903), light satire (*Dead Letters*, 1910, and *Diminutive Dramas*, 1913), memoirs (*With the Russians in Manchuria*, 1905), and criticism (*Landmarks in Russian Literature*, 1910). He became a convert in 1909, served with the air force in World War I, and wrote poetry and fiction (*Damozel Blanche; Cat's Cradle; The Lonely Lady of Dulwich*); biography (of Sarah Bernhardt and Mary Stuart, *In My End Is My Beginning*); autobiography (*The Puppet Show of Memory*, 1922); and humor (*Have You Anything to Declare?* 1936). He was a fellow of the Royal Society of Literature, an officer of the Legion of Honor, and decorated by the British government. He died in Beauly, Scotland, on Dec. 14.

BARKER, WILLIAM (d. 1578?), translator. He studied at Cambridge, England, became a fellow in 1539, entered law, was a four-time member of parliament, was in Italy from 1549 to 1553, and served as secretary to the Duke of Norfolk from 1554 to the latter's execution in 1572. He himself was in the Tower from 1571 to 1574, but was exonerated of any part in the Norfolk plot. He translated Xenophon (at the home of the Earl of Surrey), Appian, and Isocrates; rewrote Lodovico Domenicho's *Nobility of Women* for the English scene, mentioning Thomas More's three daughters; and prepared English versions of Giovanbat-

tista Gelli's *Circe* and *The Fearful Fantasies of the Florentine Cooper*.

BARKWORTH, BL. MARK (1572–1601), martyr. Born in Lincolnshire, England, and educated at Oxford, he became a convert at Douai and was ordained at Valladolid in 1599. On his way to England he became a Benedictine, was arrested a few months after landing, having worked as Mr. Lambert, and tried by a jury which included former classmates. He was hanged and brutally butchered at Tyburn, the first Benedictine martyr of Elizabeth's reign. F. D. Feb. 27.

BEDE CAMM, *Nine Martyr Monks* (London, Burns, Oates, and Washbourne, 1932).

BARLAAM, ST. (4th century?), martyr. He was tortured and slain at Antioch (not Caesarea, as in the Roman Martyrology), during the Diocletian persecution. St. Basil wrote a homily in his honor. F. D. Nov. 19.

BARLAAM, ST. (d. 1193), abbot. Born of wealthy parents in Novogorod, Russia, he gave his inheritance to the poor and lived as a hermit at Khutyn on the Volga, where he founded a monastic community. F. D. Nov. 6.

BARLAAM. See Josaphat, St.

BARLETTA, GABRIEL (d. 1480?). A Dominican, born near Naples, Italy, and perhaps a student of St. Antoninus, he was an exceptionally influential preacher whose sermons were published in 1497 and ran into many editions. He is also known as Gabriel de Barolo.

BARLOW, BL. EDWARD AMBROSE (1585–1641), martyr. Born in Barlow, near Manchester, England, baptized Edward but brought up as a Protestant, he was converted and studied at Douai and Valladolid. He became a Benedictine monk in 1615, was sent to Lancashire after ordination, and labored there for twenty-four years. Imprisoned and released four times, he was finally arrested, convicted of being a priest, and hanged, drawn, and quartered at Lancaster. He was beatified in 1929. F. D. Sept. 10.

BARLOW, WILLIAM RUDESIND (d. 1696), theologian. Brother of Bl. Edward Barlow, he was educated at Douai, became a Benedictine at Cella Nueva, Spain, in 1605, and a doctor of divinity at Salamanca in 1611. In 1616 he became professor of theology at St. Vaast's College, Douai, where he remained until his death on Sept. 19. He was general of the English congregation from 1621 to 1629 and is said to have written much, but nothing is extant.

BARNABAS, ST. (1st century), apostle. Born of a Jewish family on Cyprus, and originally called Joseph, he was one of the earliest converts in Jerusalem, where he sold his estate, gave the proceeds to the apostles of Christ (Acts 4:35–37), and introduced St. Paul to them. He preached in Antioch, to which he brought Paul from Tarsus (Acts 11:23–26), then joined the latter and John Mark on the mission to Seleucia, Salamis, Paphos, Perga, and, with Paul alone, to Antioch in Pisidia (13:115; 42–52). The first missionary journey continued through Iconium, Lystra (where they were mistaken for Hermes and Zeus), Derbe, and back to Syria (14:1–27). Paul and Barnabas then went to the council in Jerusalem which defended their position that baptism, but not circumcision, was required of pagan converts (15:1–35). Barnabas followed St. Peter in refusing to eat with Gentiles and finally parted from Paul on the eve of the latter's second mission. Barnabas went with John Mark to Cyprus (Acts 15:36–40). Although he was still alive in 56 or 57 (I Cor. 9:5–6), he is said to have been stoned to death at Salamis about 60. The *Gospel of Barnabas* is Mohammedan; the *Epistle of Barnabas* is apocryphal and not written by the saint; the *Acts of Barnabas* date from the fifth century and were not written by John Mark. That he became bishop of Milan is mere legend. F. D. June 11.

BARNABAS. The name used by the author (not Barnabas, the companion of St. Paul), of a letter written no later than 150 and perhaps as early as 70, possibly at Alexandria. The epistle is a somewhat confused warning against an acceptance of a literal meaning of the Old Testament, particularly with reference to the continuation of the formal practices of the Law.

BARNARD, ST. (777–841), archbishop. Born in the Lyonnais, France, he was brought up in Charlemagne's court, became a Benedictine monk at Ambronay, and later was abbot there. He became bishop of Vienne in 810, founded the abbey of Romans about 837, became its archbishop, and died there. His cult was approved in 1907. F. D. Jan. 23.

BARNES, ARTHUR STAPYLTON (1861–1936), historian. Born in Kussonli, India, on May 31, he studied at Eton, Oxford, and Cambridge, served with the army, was ordained an Anglican minister, and in 1895 became a convert. He was ordained a priest in 1898 and served as chaplain at Cambridge from 1902 to 1916 and at Oxford from 1918 to 1926. He wrote *St. Peter in Rome* (1900), *The Man of the Mask, Bishop Barton and Anglican Orders, The Catholic Schools in England, The Martyrdom of St. Peter and St. Paul*, and *The Holy Shroud of Turin* (1934). He died on Nov. 13.

BARNOCH. *See* Barrog, St.

BAROCCIO, FEDERIGO (1528–1612), painter. Born in Urbino, Italy, son of the sculptor Ambrogio Baroccio and nephew of the architect Bartolomeo Genga, he studied perspective with the latter, made copies of Titian and Correggio, and studied at Rome. With Federigo Zuccaro he decorated the Vatican palace of the Bosco di Belvedere for Pope Pius IV. It is said that those jealous of his success poisoned him; he was ill during the rest of his long life. Several of his canvases on religious subjects are in the London National Gallery, the Louvre, Loretto, Perugia, and Rome. He died in Urbino on Sept. 30.

BAROCCHIO, GIACOMO. *See* Vignola, Giacomo Barocchio da.

BAROLO, GABRIEL DE. *See* Barletta, Gabriel.

BARON, BONAVENTURA (1610–1696), theologian. Born in Clonmel, Ireland, he became a Franciscan there and also studied at Louvain and the College of St. Isidore in Rome, which had been founded by his uncle, Luke Wadding. He taught theology there, wrote philosophy and history, and published a defense of Duns Scotus. About 1651 he went to Schwaz in the Tyrol and to Salzburg, became provincial commissary in Hungary about 1656, taught at Lyons, then returned to Italy. He became bibliographer to Cosimo de' Medici in 1676, wrote a history of the Order of the Holy Trinity for the redemption of captives, and was made a member of the Academy of Florence. He died in Rome on Mar. 18.

BARON, VINCENT (1604–1674), theologian. Born in Martres, France, on May 17, he studied in Toulouse, became a Dominican, and taught at the University of Toulouse, in philosophy and theology. He was prior of several houses and visitor to the foundations in Portugal. He was known for his successful lectures in southern France, later published as *L'Hérésie convaincue* (1668). In his last years he wrote several volumes of theology, including a defense, against Jean de Launoy, of the authenticity of the *Summa Theologica* of St. Thomas Aquinas. He died in Paris on Jan. 21.

BARONIUS, VEN. CESARE (1538–1607), cardinal and historian. Born in Sora, Italy, on Aug. 30, he studied at Veroli, Naples, and Rome. There he met St. Philip Neri, joined his confraternity at the church of San Girolamo, gave up his law studies to devote himself to charity, and was disowned by his angry father. He lived in poverty for six years, teaching and caring for the sick, began priestly studies, and was ordained in 1564. At the direction of St. Philip he began the study of history, putting his findings into his sermons and conferences for three years. For the next twenty years he continued his research, all the while serving in the Oratorian parish, even as servant and cook. When the Oratory was canonically approved in 1575, he moved to Santa Maria at Vallicella, continuing his previous labors. Pope Gregory XIII then asked him to revise the Roman Martyrology, and he issued this in 1586 (and revised it in 1589). In 1588 he published the first of twelve volumes of *Annales ecclesiastici*, to the preparation of which St. Philip Neri had directed him and which was the answer to the equally large, but inaccurate, *Centuries of Magdeburg*, which Lutheran leaders published at Basle from 1559 to 1574. In 1593, Baronius succeeded Philip as superior; in 1595 he became confessor to Pope Clement VIII and was made a cardinal in 1596 and Vatican librarian and director of the new press in 1597. All these tasks slowed up the *Annales*, which he was only able to bring up to the events of the year 1198. The work was standard for three centuries and still is a model of historical devotion and thoroughness. Its extensive quotation of primary documents is invaluable, although a few sources have since been shown to be unauthentic; its weaknesses lie in the inadequate treatment of the Eastern world and in errors of dating which arose from the scheme of a strict year-by-year account of the history of the Church even when chronology was uncertain. The *Annales* was continued to the year 1583 by three Oratorians, Raynaldus, Laderchi, and Theiner; and to 1647 by Bishop Spondé, who also prepared a digest of the whole. Baronius died in Rome on June 30.

BARONTIUS, ST. (d. 695?). A Benedictine at the abbey of Lonray in Berry, France, he retired to set up a hermitage near Pistoia with a monk named Desiderius. F. D. Mar. 25.

BAROZZIO, GIACOMO. *See* Vignola, Giacomo Barocchio da.

BARR. *See* Finbar, St. (d. 633).

BARRADAS, SEBASTIAN (1543–1615), scholar. Born in Lisbon, Portugal, he became a Jesuit in 1558, was professor of scripture at Coimbra and Evora, and wrote a commentary on Exodus and a four-volume study of the gospel. He died in Coimbra, Portugal.

BARRAL, LOUIS MATHIAS DE (1746–1816), archbishop. Born in Grenoble, France, on Apr. 26, he studied at St. Sulpice, Paris, and became coadjutor to his uncle, the bishop of Troyes, whom he succeeded in 1790. He lived in exile in Switzerland and England during the persecution of 1791, returned in 1801, and was appointed archbishop of Tours in 1805. He often served as intermediary in the negotiations between Napoleon and Pope Pius VII, who was under house arrest; he later became Empress Josephine's almoner, a senator, and count of the empire. He fell from political favor at the second restoration of the Bourbons and worked on two studies of church history before his death in Paris on June 7.

BARRANDE, JOACHIM (1799–1883), geologist. Born in Sangues, France, on Aug. 11, he studied at Paris, and became tutor to the young count de Chambord. He accompanied Charles X into exile in 1830, living in England and Bohemia with the royal family, and was administrator for the duke after the king's death. After 1840, Barrande devoted himself to the study and classification of the fossils of Bohemia, published in twenty-two volumes, and to other writing on geology and paleontology. He died at Frohsdorff, Austria, on Oct. 5.

BARRASA, JACINTO (d. 1704), historian. Born in Lima, Peru, he became a Jesuit, published two volumes of sermons and a panegyric on St. Rose of Lima, and prepared a lengthy manuscript chronicle of the work of his Society in Peru. He died in Lima on Nov. 22.

BARRE, ANTOINE LEFEBVRE DE LA (1622–1690), governor. Born in Paris, France, he became a court counselor in 1646, held several government posts, became governor of Guiana, and about 1664 wrote a history of the French settlement there. He was a naval captain in 1671 and replaced Frontenac as governor general of Canada in 1682. His rule was a poor one, marked by private arrangements with trading groups, a disastrous expedition against the Iroquois, and a forced treaty with them which jeopardized the work of La Salle. De la Barre was removed in 1685, and sent back to serve as governor of Guiana. He died in Cayenne.

BARRÉ, BL. JEAN LOUISE (d. 1794), martyr. An Ursuline nun, she took the name Sister Cordulia, and was guillotined at Valenciennes during the French Revolution. She was beatified in 1920. F. D. Oct. 17.

BARREAU DE LA TOUCHE, BL. LOUIS (d. 1792), martyr. He was a Benedictine of the French Congregation of St. Maur, was seized at St. Florent-de-Saumur, and executed at Paris on Sept. 2 during the French Revolution.

BARREIRA, BALTHASAR (1531–1612), missioner. Born in Lisbon, Portugal, he became a Jesuit, and was sent to Angola, Africa, from where he sent back detailed relations of missionary success and ethnic customs. He died in Angola.

BARRETT, JAMES FRANCIS (1888–1934), novelist. Born in Bridgeport, Connecticut, on Sept. 1, he was educated there and in seminaries at Boston and Baltimore. He was ordained in 1914 and for sixteen years served as a curate in Hartford and as principal of Immaculate Conception School. He wrote two novels in popular style, *The Loyalist* and *The Winter of Discontent*, and psychological studies and texts. He became pastor in Farmington, Connecticut, in 1930 and died on May 29.

BARRFOIN, ST. (6th century). Said to have preached in Offaly and Donegal, Ireland, he may have been a bishop. He is also said to have made a journey to America and to have reported descriptive details to St. Brendan. F. D. May 21.

BARRIENTOS, LOPEZ DE (1382–1469), bishop. Born in Medina del Campo, Spain, he graduated from Salamanca, became a Dominican at eighteen, and was appointed to the first chair of theology at his university. He became confessor to King John II of Castile and Leon in 1433 and tutor to his sons, Henry IV and Alphonsus. He also served as inquisitor general and as bishop, successively, of Segovia, Avila, and in 1444 of Cuenca. As royal chancellor he gave wise counsel and also was noted for his charities and patronage of learning. He wrote on the sacraments, doctrine, and moral theology, and died in Cuenca, Spain, on May 21.

BARROG, ST. (7th century). A follower of St. Cadoc of Wales, he lived as a hermit off the coast of Glamorgan on Barry Island, since named for him. He is also known as Barnoch. F. D. Sept. 27.

BARROS, JOÃO DE (1496–1570), historian. He went from his native Portugal to the African colonies in 1522 and became treasurer of the trading company offices at Mina and Ceuta. In 1539 he led an expedition of 900 men to settle in Brazil, but the ten ships were wrecked and nearly all, probably including Barros' two sons, were drowned. Under a grant from the king he thereafter devoted himself to the writing of *Asia*, a three-volume history of Portuguese colonization and missionary efforts in Africa and the Far East. He died in Portugal on Oct. 20.

BARROTTI, BL. ODDINO (1324–1400). Appointed to the parish church of St. John the Baptist in his native town of Fossano, Piedmont, he became so extreme in his charities that the bishop of Turin had to order him to retain sufficient income to support himself. In 1374 he was appointed provost of the chapter of Fossano, but resigned four years later to direct a religious confraternity. He became a Franciscan tertiary and in 1381 made a pilgrimage to the Holy Land. On his return he became governor of the Guild of the Cross, which cared for the sick and sheltered pilgrims, and built a hospital and church. In 1396 he again became provost. He died on July 7 while tending the sick and dying in plague-beset Fossano. His cult was confirmed in 1808. F. D. July 21.

BARROW, JOHN (1735–1811). Born in Westby, Lancashire, England, on May 13, he studied at Rome, and on his return was captured at Portsmouth and impressed into naval service for five years. In 1761 he resumed his studies and was ordained at Douai in 1766. He later served as pastor and town overseer of Claughton, where he died on Feb. 12.

BARROW, BL. WILLIAM (1609?–1679), martyr. Born in Lancashire, England, and also known as Harcourt and as Waring, he became a Jesuit at St. Omer in 1632, and labored in the English mission from about 1643. He was arrested and charged by Titus Oates with providing the headquarters for the "plotters" against the life of King Charles II. He was

hanged and quartered at Tyburn, and beatified in 1929. F. D. June 20.

BARRY, JOHN (1745–1803), naval officer. Born in Tacumshane, Wexford, Ireland, he became a sailor, reached Philadelphia, Pennsylvania, at fifteen, and made it his home. He was engaged in the West Indian trade and had captained several vessels before the outbreak of the revolution. He volunteered for service, received, on Dec. 7, 1775, the first naval commission issued by the new nation, and was assigned as captain of the *Lexington* and then of the *Effingham*. When the British captured Philadelphia, Barry fought in the battles of Trenton and Princeton, was aide to Generals Cadwallader and Washington, and led several naval raids on the Delaware River. In 1778 he returned to sea in command of the *Raleigh*, the *Delaware*, and the *Alliance*. In command of the last, on which he brought Lafayette to the United States, he engaged in a half-dozen major encounters. When the American navy was permanently organized in 1794, Barry's commission as captain, first on the roster, was signed by President Washington. He supervised the building of the frigate *United States* in 1801, then, suffering the effect of battle wounds, retired to Philadelphia, where he died on Sept. 13.

BARRY, JOHN (1799–1859), bishop. Born in Oylegate, Wexford, Ireland, he was ordained in Charleston, South Carolina, in 1825. He labored in Georgia, started the first Catholic school in Savannah, and served as vicar general at Charleston and as superior of the seminary there in 1844. He was consecrated at Baltimore in 1857 to succeed Bishop Gartland of Charleston, who had died of plague three years before. While in Europe in search of health, he died at Paris on Nov. 19.

BARRY, PATRICK (1816–1890). Born near Belfast, Ireland, in May, he came to the United States in 1836, became partner of a nursery business in Rochester, New York, was editor of the *Genesee Farmer* and the *Horticulturalist*, and wrote widely on fruit cultivation. He died in Rochester on June 23.

BARRY, PATRICK JOSEPH (1868–1940), bishop. Born in Ennis, Clare, Ireland, on Nov. 15, he studied at Mungret Apostolic College, Royal University of Ireland, and St. Patrick's seminary, Carlow, and was ordained in Carlow in 1895. He went to the United States, served as curate and pastor in Jacksonville, Florida, was vicar general of St. Augustine from 1917, administered the see in 1921–22, when he was appointed bishop, and reigned until his death on Aug. 13.

BARRY, PAUL DE (1587–1661). Born in Leucate, France, he became a Jesuit, served as rector of three colleges and as provincial of Lyons, and wrote on the Virgin Mary, Joseph, and other saints. He died at Avignon, France, on July 28.

BARRY, WILLIAM FRANCIS (1849–1930), author. Born in London on Apr. 21, he studied at Oscott and the English College and the Gregorian, Rome, where he was ordained in 1873. He taught philosophy and was vice-president of Birmingham diocesan seminary in 1873–77, became professor of theology at Oscott, was made pastor in Dorchester in 1883 and in Leamington in 1908, and became a monsignor in 1923. He wrote regularly for the *Dublin Review*, biographies of Newman and Renan, novels (*The New Antigone, The Place of Dreams, The Two Standards, The Dayspring*), and *The Papal Monarchy from St. Gregory the Great to Boniface* (1902), *The Papacy and Modern Times* (1911), *Memories and Opinions, Roma Sacra*, and *The Catholic Revival* (1929). He died in Oxford on Dec. 15.

BARRY-DOYLE, RICHARD (1878–1933), sociologist. Born in Airdowns, Wexford, Ireland, he studied at St. Peter's there and at St. John's seminary, Waterford, and was ordained in 1905. He was an army chaplain in Egypt and Palestine in World War I, was stationed in Turkey in 1917–20, and on his return worked for the establishment of schools, orphanages, and seminaries in Athens under the direction of the Catholic Near East Welfare Association, of which he was founder and first president and which in 1926 came under the direction of the Vatican. He became a monsignor in 1920 and was named archimandrite of Athens in 1926. He died on Mar. 8 in Leicester, England, where he was pastor of St. Peter's church.

BARSABAS, ST., martyr. An abbot in Persia, tortured and beheaded with his twelve monks at Ishtar during the persecution of Sapor, he probably is identical with the leader of a group slain at Persepolis (*c.* 342) and honored on Oct. 20, or with St. Simon Barsabae (Apr. 21). F. D. Dec. 11.

BARSANUPHIUS, ST. (d. 550?). He lived in a cell at Gaza, Syria, and may have written epistles on the hermit life and on sin. F. D. Apr. 11 (sometimes, Feb. 6).

BARSENORIUS, ST. (7th century). He was abbot of the Benedictine monastery of La Croix-St. Leuffroi, in the diocese of Évreux, France. F. D. Sept. 13.

BARSES, ST. (d. 379?), bishop and martyr. He was banished from his see in Edessa, Syria, to the Egyptian-Libyan border by Emperor Valens during the Arian heresy and died in exile. F. D. Jan. 30.

BARSIMAEUS, ST. Called the third bishop of Edessa in Syria and honored on Jan. 30, he might have lived between 100 and 250; other biographical details match those of St. Abibus, a fourth-century martyr. His independent existence is doubted.

BARTHEL, JOHANN (1679–1771), canonist. Born in Kitzingen, Bavaria, on June 10, he studied there and at the Jesuit college and the seminary in Würzburg, and was ordained in 1721. He studied canon law in Rome under the future Pope Benedict XIV, and became rector of the Würzburg seminary in 1727 and professor of canon law at the university in 1728 and later its vice-chancellor. He sought to distinguish between essentials and non-essentials, stressed the historical approach to ecclesiastical law, was well known as a lecturer, and wrote *Promemoria* (1751), *De pallio*, and on Church-state relations in Germany. He died on Apr. 8.

BARTHÉLEMY, JEAN JACQUES (1716–1795), archaeologist. Born in Cassis, Provence, France, he studied at the Oratorian college in Marseilles and oriental languages at the Lazarist seminary, made a study of numismatics, and became royal keeper of medals at Paris. He was elected to the Academy of Inscriptions and Belles Lettres in 1747, wrote a study of ancient Greece, a novel on classical themes, and his memoirs, and was elected to the French Academy in 1789. He was imprisoned, released, but impoverished by the French Revolution, and died in Paris.

BARTHOLI, FRANCESCO DELLA ROSSA (d. 1272?), historian. Born in Assisi, Italy, he studied at Perugia and Cologne, was a Franciscan, and served as lector in theology at the Portiuncula. He wrote an account of the Passion of Christ and a treatise on the Portiuncula Indulgence, and has been identified by some as the Francesco Rubea who supported Michael de Cesena, and by others as Franciscus de Assisi (who was charged at Florence with heresy).

BARTHOLOMAEUS ANGLICUS (13th century), scholar. An Englishman, he was teaching theology at Paris in 1224 or 1225 when he joined the new order of Franciscans with Haymo of Faversham and others. In 1231 he was sent to Magdeburg, Germany. He compiled *De proprietatibus rerum*, an encyclopedic account of contemporary learning, which drew from Arabic, Greek, Jewish, and Latin scholars; the work remained a popular compilation through the Middle Ages.

BARTHOLOMAEUS PARVUS. See Bartholomew of Armenia.

BARTHOLOMEW, ST. (1st century), apostle. That he was the son of Tolmai and was one of the twelve apostles is certain; some scholars identify him with Nathanael (John I). According to tradition, he preached in India and Greater Armenia, where he is said to have been flayed alive and then beheaded at Albanapolis on the west coast of the Caspian Sea. F. D. Aug. 24.

BARTHOLOMEW, ST. (d. 1065?). Born in Rossano, Italy, he was a disciple of St. Nilus at the Greek abbey of Grottaferrata, in Frascati, near Rome, the construction of which he completed as its third abbot. He wrote a number of hymns in Greek and is said to have persuaded Pope Benedict IX to reform his life and do penance as a simple monk. F. D. Nov. 11.

BARTHOLOMEW, BL. (d. 1067). Benedictine abbot of Marmoutier, he became bishop of Tours, France, in 1052 and tried, unsuccessfully, to bring Berengarius back to Catholicism. F. D. Nov. 11.

BARTHOLOMEW, BL. (1200?–1271), bishop. Born in Vicenza, Italy, he studied at Padua and about 1220 became a follower of St. Dominic, who bestowed the habit on him. He served as prior at several houses and in 1233 in Bologna established, with Fr. John of Vicenza, the Fratres Gaudentes to preserve order in the city. In 1248 he was appointed bishop of Nimesia, Cyprus, visited Palestine where he met and became friendly with St. Louis, served as papal legate to King Henry III of England, and in 1256 was translated by Pope Alexander IV to the see of Vicenza. He became involved in a struggle with Ezzolino da Romano, leader of the Ghibellines, was exiled, but eventually returned to rebuild the spiritual and material bases of his see. He wrote sermons, scriptural commentaries, a study of the *Hierarchy* of Dionysius the Areopagite, and died on July 1. His cult was approved in 1793. F. D. Oct. 23.

BARTHOLOMEW AIUTAMICRISTO (d. 1224). Born in Pisa, Italy, he became a Camaldolese laybrother at the monastery of San Frediano there. He received his surname because the expression "Christ aid me" was his frequent utterance. His cult was approved in 1857. F. D. Jan. 28.

BARTHOLOMEW OF ARMENIA (d. 1333), bishop. Born in Bologna, Italy, he became a Dominican and in 1318–20 worked with Dominican missioners in Armenia at the request of Pope John XXII, who sought to keep that nation loyal to Rome. Consecrated bishop of Maragha, he had a successful mission, converting many schismatics and Mohammedans, among them the learned orthodox scholar, John of Kherna. Bartholomew mastered the Armenian language, translated the psalter, works on the sacraments, and selections from Thomas Aquinas and Augustine into that tongue, and moved his see to Nachidjewan to be at the center of his apostolate. He also is called Bartholomaeus Parvus. He died on Aug. 15.

BARTHOLOMEW OF BRAGA, VEN. (1514–1590), archbishop. Born near Lisbon in May, he became a Dominican in 1527, taught at a Lisbon monastery and other houses for twenty years, and received his master's degree

at Salamanca in 1551. He was tutor to Dom Antonio, son of Infante Dom Luis, for two years, and in 1558, against his wishes, became archbishop of Braga. He attended the Council of Trent in 1561–64, held a provincial synod in 1566, worked to introduce Tridentine reforms in his see, resigned in 1582, and retired to a monastery at Viana, where he died on July 16. He was declared Venerable by Pope Gregory XVI in 1845.

BARTHOLOMEW OF BRAGANÇA, BL. *See* Bartholomew, Bl. (1200?–1271).

BARTHOLOMEW OF BRESCIA (d. 1258), canonist. Born probably in Brescia, Italy, he studied Roman and canon law at Bologna, taught there, and issued revisions of canonical rules prepared earlier by Damascus, Benencasa, Gratian, Tancred, and others. He also wrote *Quaestiones dominicales et veneriales*. He is said to have been murdered by the Ghibilline leader, Ezzolino, during the capture of Brescia.

BARTHOLOMEW OF CEVERE, BL. (1420–1466), martyr. Born in Savigliano, Italy, he taught theology at Turin, became inquisitor for Piedmont, and was slain by heretics at Cevere. His cult was approved by Pope Pius IX. F. D. Apr. 23.

BARTHOLOMEW OF EDESSA (8th century), apologist. Born probably in Edessa, Syria, he became a monk there, and wrote a refutation of Mohammedanism, addressed to Agarenus, which also explained Catholic belief.

BARTHOLOMEW OF LUCCA (1227?–1327), historian. Born in Lucca, Italy, he became a Dominican, won the attention of the founder by his sense of dedication, was in Rome and Naples with him in the early 1270s, and in 1288 was prior in Lucca. In 1301 he became prior of Santa Maria Novella, Florence, was secretary to Cardinal Patrasso at Avignon in 1309–18, then of Cardinal William of Bayonne. He became the friend and confessor of Pope John XXII, who named him bishop of Torcello in 1318. The appointment of an abbess in that see led to conflict with the patriarch of Grado, who excommunicated him in 1323. He was forgiven and returned to Torcello in 1327 and died there. He compiled *Annales* for the period 1061–1303; his *Historia ecclesiastica nova* reports on the Christian world up to 1294, with appendices to 1314. He also wrote *Historia tripartita* and a work on the *Hexaemeron*, and completed the *De regimine principum* of St. Thomas Aquinas.

BARTHOLOMEW OF PISA. *See* Albisi, Bartolommeo; also, Riconico, Bl. Bartolommeo.

BARTHOLOMEW OF SAN CONCORDIO (1260–1347), canonist. Born in San Concordio, near Pisa, Italy, he became a Dominican in 1277, studied at Pisa, Bologna, and Paris, and taught at Lucca, Florence, and Pisa. His alphabetically arranged *Summa de casibus conscientiae*, based on the *Summa confessorum* of a contemporary Dominican, Johann Rumsik (d. 1314), proved to be a valuable digest and was to be printed frequently, initially with a 1444 supplement by Nicholas of Osimo.

BARTHOLOMEW OF SAN GIMIGNANO. *See* Buonpedoni, Bl. Bartolo.

BARTHOLOMEW DE VIR (d. 1157). Bishop of Laon, France, from 1113 to 1151, he helped St. Norbert in establishing Prémontré, and in 1121 built the abbey of Foigny, where he became a Cistercian thirty years later. F. D. June 26.

BARTOLI, DANIELLO (1608–1685), historian. Born in Ferrara, Italy, on Feb. 12, he became a Jesuit in Rome in 1623, and taught and preached throughout Italy. As a result of his observations of the contemporary waste of youth in the cities, he wrote *The Learned Man*. From 1650 on he was directed to dedicate himself to writing, produced some fifty works, chiefly in Italian, one of the most significant of which is his six-volume *History of the Society of Jesus*. He died in Rome on Jan. 12.

BARTOLO, MATTEO DI GIOVANNI DI (1435?–1495), painter. Born in Borgo San Sepolcro, Italy, he became, as Matteo da Siena, a leading painter of the fifteenth-century Sienese school. Among his masterpieces are: *Assumption* in Borgo, *Madonna della Neve*, *St. Barbara*, and *Virgin and Child* in Siena, and *Virgin and Child* in Pienza.

BARTOLOCCI, GIULIO (1613–1687), scholar. Born in Celleno, Naples, Italy, he studied Hebrew under Giovanni Battista, and in 1651 became professor of Hebrew at Collegium Neophytorum, Rome, and attached to the Vatican Library. With Battista he compiled *Bibliotheca magna rabbinica*, the basis of many later studies on Jewish biography, customs, and writings. He died in Rome on Oct. 19 as abbot of the monastery of St. Sebastian.

BARTOLOMMEO, FRA (1475–1517), painter. Born in the Florentine area, Bartolommeo di Pagholo del Fattorino (often called Baccio) studied under Cosimo Rosselli with Mariotto Albertinelli, whose business partner he was from 1490 to 1512. They painted the fresco of the *Last Judgment* for the church of Santa Maria Nuova, Florence; the upper half is Bartolommeo's. Strongly influenced by Savonarola, he threw all his mythological drawings away and after the Dominican's death he joined that order in 1500. He was never ordained, but devoted himself to his studies so attentively that he seems to have done no painting for eight years. About 1508 Raphael visited him; he returned the visit later when he went to Rome. Bartolommeo became aware of the art of Michelangelo there, as he had been of Titian's work during a brief period in

Venice. He returned to Florence and, except for a brief stay at Lucca, was stationed at San Marco's until his death. His figures are graceful; his groupings symmetrical; his religious feeling tender. Among his major works are *Vision of St. Bernard, Marriage of St. Catherine, Mother of Mercy, Ecce Homo, St. Mark, Risen Saviour, St. Stephen, John the Baptist, Descent from the Cross*, and other religious portraits.

BARTOLOMMEO DA MURANO. *See* Vivarini, Bartolommeo.

BARTOLOZZI, FRANCESCO (1727–1815), engraver. Born in Florence, Italy, he studied under his father, a goldsmith, at the Florentine Academy, and with the engraver, Wagner. He worked in Rome and Venice and in 1764 went to London as royal librarian and engraver; he was named a member of the Royal Academy in 1768. While in England he made 2000 engravings in the popular French "red-chalk" style, on which he improved. His work was hailed by Sir Joshua Reynolds and his pupils were many. He went to Lisbon, Portugal, in 1802, where he was knighted, and where he labored until his death.

BARTON, ELIZABETH (1506?–1534). As a servant in Aldington, Kent, England, she claimed at nineteen to have experienced visions during an illness which ended with dramatic suddenness. Fr. Richard Masters, her pastor, vouched for her holiness; a commission of seven, appointed by Archbishop Warham, investigated; and the girl entered a Benedictine convent near Canterbury. There "the Holy Maid of Kent" continued to warn the country of its evil ways, and her censure of Henry VIII for his proposed divorce was so forceful that Thomas Cromwell imprisoned her in 1533. She and Frs. Masters, Hugh Rich and Richard Risby (Franciscans), and Edward Bocking (a Benedictine), who served on the Warham commission, were questioned by Cranmer, declared guilty of treason, and executed at Tyburn. Bishop John Fisher and five others who supported her were imprisoned or fined. Before her execution on April 20 at Tyburn she was forced to sign a confession of fraud and to do public penance, but the order is said to have originated with Henry's paid clerics. Whether she was a fraud or whether the case was built on false documents will probably never be factually established. Letters of St. Thomas More, whose name was linked with her cause, indicate that he did not question her holiness, but that he feared she was being used by the king's enemies to foment dissension.

BARTON, GEORGE (1866–1940), journalist. Born in Philadelphia on Jan. 22, he studied there, began working for the Philadelphia *Inquirer* at nineteen, married Sophie McCauley in 1893, became an editorial writer for the *Bulletin*, then returned to the *Inquirer* in that capacity. He wrote juveniles, 200 detective stories, *Little Journeys around Philadelphia, Walks and Talks about Old Philadelphia, Columbus the Catholic, Angels of the Battlefield* (on the nuns of the Civil War), and *Barry Wynn* (on Congress). He died in Philadelphia on Mar. 16.

BARULA, ST. (d. 304), martyr. *See* Romanus, St.

BARYPSABAS, ST. (1st century), martyr. An Eastern hermit, he was put to death in Dalmatia. F. D. Sept. 10.

BASIL, ST. (d. 335). He was bishop of Bologna, Italy, from 315 until his death. F. D. Mar. 6.

BASIL, ST. (d. 370?). He and St. Emmelia were the parents of SS. Basil, Gregory of Nyssa, Peter of Sebaste, and Macrina the Younger. They were exiled during the persecution of Galerius Maximinus, but later were able to return to Caesarea, Cappadocia, where they died. F. D. May 30.

BASIL, ST. (329–379), Doctor of the Church. Born in Caesarea in Cappadocia, one of ten children of SS. Basil the Elder and Emmelia, he was educated by his father, by St. Macrina, his grandmother, and at Constantinople and Athens, with Gregory Nazianzen and Julian (later the apostate) as classmates. He then taught rhetoric at Caesarea in 355, was baptized, and withdrew to a retreat at Annesi. There, with Gregory, he prepared *Philocalia*, a selection of excerpts from Origen, and drew up some monastic rules. He traveled to investigate ascetic life, then with his youngest brother, Peter, and others he established what probably was the first organized monastery in Asia Minor, on the banks of the Iris River in Cappadocia. He directed this for five years, supervising the studies and farming labor of his followers, and developing a plan of living, eating, and praying in common, in houses of controllable size. St. Benedict leaned heavily on the Basilian rule when formulating his own. In 363, Basil left to be ordained, but returned to the monastery because of the jealousy of Eusebius, archbishop of Caesarea. Two years later they were reconciled, and in 370 Basil succeeded Eusebius and became metropolitan over fifty suffragan bishops, many of whom were openly hostile, as was Emperor Valens. Eventually, he won them over by tact and patience. He preached twice a day to vast crowds, built a large hospital, took care of victims of drought and famine, fought the white-slave market which flourished in the Near East, and worked with great energy to repair the damage caused by the spread of Arianism. He was widely slandered and 'even accused of heresy by his enemies. He wrote on faith, baptism, the cardinal virtues, asceticism, monastic life, the Psalms, the responsibility of the wealthy, the evils of usury, and the acceptance of the penitent, and nearly 400 letters. He died on Jan. 1. F. D. June 14.

SR. MARGARET MURPHY, *St. Basil and Monasticism* (Washington, Catholic University Press, 1930).

BASIL, ST. (4th century), bishop and martyr. *See* Aetherius, St.

BASIL, ST. (d. 521). He came from Arles to Provence, to serve as the second bishop of Aix. F. D. Jan. 1.

BASIL, ST. (d. 750?). He and St. Procopius were staunch in their opposition to the Iconoclast heresy of Emperor Leo the Isaurian. F. D. Feb. 27.

BASIL, ST. (d. 764), martyr. *See* Stephen, St.

BASIL OF ANCYRA, ST. (d. 362), martyr. A Galatian priest, he fought Arianism under Emperors Constantius and Julian the Apostate. Because of the effectiveness of his preaching he was tortured, imprisoned, and executed at Caesarea, Palestine. F. D. Mar. 22.

BASIL THE YOUNGER (852–952), hermit. From his cell in the desert outside Constantinople he was brought in to be tortured as a spy by Emperor Leo VI, but continued to speak out boldly against the evil lives of the aristocracy, including Princesses Anastasia and Irene, even though he was often persecuted for his words. F. D. Mar. 26.

BASILEUS, ST. (1st century), bishop and martyr. He is said to have been the first bishop of Braga (Portugal), where he was killed for his faith. F. D. May 23.

BASILEUS, ST. (d. 258), martyr. He and Jovinus were put to death at Rome during the persecution of Gallienus and Valerian. F. D. Mar. 2.

BASILEUS, ST. (d. 319). Bishop of Amasea, he was put to death by drowning, in Pontus, during the persecution of Licinius. F. D. Apr. 26.

BASILIDES, ST. (d. 202), martyr. *See* Plutarch, St.

BASILIDES, ST. (d. 205), martyr. A soldier in Egypt who defended St. Potamiana from an insulting mob as she was on her way to death, he became a convert and was executed shortly after, during the persecution of Septimius Severus. F. D. June 30.

BASILIDES, ST. (d. 250), martyr. *See* Theodulus, St.

BASILIDES, ST. (d. 270?), martyr. A Roman soldier, he was scourged and beheaded at Rome during the persecution of Aurelian. Tripos, Mandal, and twenty others are said to have died between 270 and 275 and also are commemorated on June 10; the Roman Martyrology, under June 12, repeats some names and adds those of Cyrinus, Nabor, and Nazarius, soldiers executed at Milan at some time during the persecutions of Diocletian and Maximian.

BASILISCUS, ST. (d. 298?), martyr. He, SS. Cleonicus, Eutropius, and more than forty others, probably soldiers, were put to death in Pontus during the Diocletian persecution. F. D. Mar. 3.

BASILISCUS, ST. (d. 312), bishop and martyr. The bishop of Comana, in Pontus, was beheaded near Nicomedia, Armenia, during the persecution of Maximin the Thracian. F. D. May 22.

BASILISSA, ST. (d. 68?), martyr. *See* Anastasia, St.

BASILISSA, ST. (d. 250), martyr. She and St. Callinica were wealthy women in Galatia who used their fortune aiding imprisoned Christians, and were themselves imprisoned and put to death. F. D. Mar. 22.

BASILISSA, ST. (3rd century). Wife of St. Julian, she devoted her life to the care of poor and sick women in Egypt. Although she suffered persecution, she was not killed. Her story may be a pious legend. F. D. Jan. 9.

BASILISSA, ST. (d. 303?), martyr. The Roman Martyrology says she was a nine-year-old girl put to death at Nicomedia during the Diocletian persecution. F. D. Sept. 3.

BASILIUS VALENTINUS. *See* Thölde, Johannes.

BASILLA, ST. (d. 304), martyr. She was put to death at Rome and buried in the catacomb of St. Cyriacus; her remains were discovered in 1654. F. D. May 20 (or Sept. 22).

BASIN, THOMAS (15th century). Bishop of Lisieux, France, he wrote a history of King Charles VII and was associated with those who sought to clear the name of Joan of Arc from the defamation of a predecessor, Bishop Cauchon.

BASINUS, ST. (d. 705?), bishop. He was abbot of the Benedictine monastery of St. Maximin before he became bishop of Trèves. He helped the English missionaries under St. Willibrord and in his old age retired to his former abbey. F. D. Mar. 4.

BASOLUS, ST. (555?–620?). A native of Limoges, he became a monk after a period in the army, was sent to the monastery of Verzy, and spent the remaining forty years of his life as a hermit on a hill overlooking Rheims. F. D. Nov. 26.

BASSA, ST. (d. 304), martyr. Wife of a pagan priest, she was slain at Edessa, Syria, during the Diocletian persecution, after she exhorted her sons, SS. Agapius, Fidelis, and Theogonius, to remain firm under torture. F. D. Aug. 21.

BASSAND, BL. JOHN (1360–1445). Born in Besançon, France, he became a canon regular of St. Paul, then joined the Celestine Benedictines in Paris, worked to establish his order in England and Aragon, and was spiritual director of St. Colette. F. D. Aug. 26.

BASSIAN, ST. (d. 413), bishop. Born in Sicily, he became a friend of St. Ambrose and attended the Council of Aquileia with him in 381 as bishop of Lodi, Lombardy. F. D. Jan. 19.

BASSUS, ST. (d. 257?), martyr. Bishop of Nice, he was crucified during the reign of Decius. F. D. Dec. 5.

BATHILDIS, ST. (d. 680). An English girl brought to France as a slave, she became the wife of King Clovis II in 649 and the mother of Clotaire III, Childeric II, and Thierry III in a brief five years of marriage. She distinguished herself as regent of the nation, was active in redeeming captives, founded the abbey of Corbie, and contributed large gifts to other establishments. In 665 she retired to the convent at Chelles and spent her last years, marked by serious illness, in unusually humble service. F. D. Jan. 30.

BATHORY, STEPHEN. *See* Stephen Báthory.

BATTANDIER, ALBERT (1850–1921), canonist. Born in St. Félicien, France, he studied in Mongré and Viviers, was ordained in 1875, and took his doctorate in canon law at the French seminary in Rome in 1879. He served Cardinal Pitra, bishop of Frascati and Porto, was secretary and vicar general, was named consultor to the Congregation of Bishops and Regulars in 1881, wrote a canonical study of religious vows, edited *Analecta juris canonici* (1891–92), and became a member of the Society of Biblical Studies. With the Bailly brothers he edited *Annuaire pontifical catholique* (1898–1921), an encyclopedia of religious information, became consultor to the Congregation of Latin and Oriental Rites, and returned to France in 1907 and became canon of the cathedral of Viviers. He died in St. Félicien on May 25.

BATTISTA, GIOVANNI GUIDA GIONA (1588–1668), scholar. Born in Safed, Galilee, on Oct. 28, Jehuda Jona ben-Isaac became a Jewish rabbi, went to Poland, became a convert, and taught Hebrew and Aramaic at Pisa and at the Propaganda, Rome. He translated the gospels into Hebrew (1668) and taught Giulio Bartolocci, to whom he gave the plan for the latter's *Bibliotheca magna rabbinica*. He died in Rome on May 26.

BAUBERGER, WILHELM (1809–1883), novelist. Born in Thannhausen, Bavaria, on Mar. 3, he became a physician and published a series of narratives based on history and legend. The most famous, *Die Beatushöle*, was written while he was in medical school. His poetry and dramas were not successful. He died in his native town on Feb. 8.

BAUDELIUS, ST., martyr. Said to have been killed because he objected to a pagan festival, he is known to have been martyred at Nîmes, of which French city he is patron. The date of his death is variously given as 187, 297, and

380, but his shrine was popular as early as the sixth century. He is also known as Baudille.
F. D. May 20.

BAUDILLE. *See* Baudelius, St.

BAUDOIN, MICHAEL (1692–1768?). Born in Quebec, Canada, on Mar. 8, he became a Jesuit in France at twenty-one, returned to serve among the Choctaw Indians, and was superior general of the Louisiana mission from 1749 until the dispersal of his Society in 1763. Because of his age he was not banished, but stayed with a friendly planter until his death about 1768 in New Orleans.

BAUDRILLART, HENRI MARIE ALFRED (1859–1942), cardinal. Born in Paris on Jan. 6, he was educated at L'École Normale Supérieure, taught history at Laval, Caen, and L'Institut Catholique and Collège Stanislas, Paris, went to Spain to study eighteenth-century Franco-Spanish relations, and published a study of Philip V which won the Gobert Prize. He received his doctorate in 1890, became an Oratorian that year, and was ordained in 1893. He was rector of L'Institut Catholique in 1907 and vicar general in 1908, developed its laboratories and faculty, and continued his research. He wrote *Quatre cents ans de concordat, La Vie catholique dans la France contemporaine, L'Église catholique, la renaissance, le protestantisme, Charité aux premiers siècles du christianisme,* biographies of SS. Germain d'Auxerre and Severin, Frederic Ozanam, and Msgr. d'Hulst, was co-founder and became editor of *Revue Pratique d'Apologetique,* and was elected to the French Academy (an honor also attained by his father, grandfather, and great-grandfather) in 1918. He became titular bishop of Himeria in 1921, archbishop of Militene in 1928, and vicar general of Paris; Pope Pius XI made him a cardinal in 1935 and a member of several papal congregations. He died in Paris on May 18.

BAUDRY. *See* Balderic, St.

BAUER, GEORGE. *See* Agricola, George.

BAUMANN, ÉMILE (1868–1942), novelist. Born in Lyons, France, he studied there, became a convert, taught in Roanne and at the universities of Algiers, Sens, and Mans, and published his first work, *Les grandes formes de la musique,* in 1905, dedicated to his friend Saint-Saëns. *St. Paul* and *Trois villes saintes* were followed by essays and philosophical studies; he was best known for a series of seven realistic, almost merciless, novels on the moral lesson of sin, admittedly thesis novels, forceful though harsh. His preoccupation with the dark aspects of life makes him comparable to Mauriac.

BAUMGARTNER, ALEXANDER (1841–1910), poet. Born in St. Gall, Switzerland, on June 27, he became a Jesuit in 1860, studied at Maria-Einsiedeln, Münster, Maria-Laach, and

Ditton, was ordained in 1874, and went to Copenhagen and Stockholm for advanced study in Scandinavian languages. He wrote on Goethe and Schiller, a history of world literature, and translations from the Icelandic, Spanish, and Henry W. Longfellow, and was editor of *Stimmen aus Maria-Laach* from 1874 until his death in Luxembourg on Sept. 5.

BAUMGARTNER, GALLUS JACOB (1797–1869), chancellor. Born in Altstätten, Switzerland, on Oct. 18, he studied law at Fribourg, Switzerland, and Vienna, taught in Hungary, returned to Austria, and was expelled from Vienna in 1819 after the murder of Kotzebue. He entered Swiss politics, became chancellor of the canton of St. Gallen in 1825 and chief magistrate from 1831 to 1846. He was influenced by Josephinism during this period, sought to have the state educate a political clergy, and dissolved monasteries. When a period of looting and chaos followed, he reversed his position and became an active supporter of the Church. His outline of a constitution was the basis of the later unification of the cantons. He died at St. Gallen on July 12, having completed two volumes of a history of the district.

BAUNARD, LOUIS PIERRE ANDRÉ (1828–1919), author. Born in Bellegarde, France, on Aug. 24, he studied in Orléans, was ordained in 1852, took doctorates in letters and theology, served as professor at the Catholic University of Lille (and later, 1888, as its rector) and at St. Joseph's College (1881–88). He became a monsignor in 1908, retired to Gruson (where he died on Nov. 9), and published eight volumes of spiritual writings, twelve biographies of saints, works on education, and a collection of poems.

BAUNY, ÉTIENNE (1564–1649). Born in Mouzon, France, he became a Jesuit in 1593, taught theology for sixteen years, and was spiritual adviser to Cardinal François de la Rochefoucauld. He was called too lenient in some matters of moral theology and was harshly attacked by the Jansenists for his stringency. He died at St. Pol de Léon, France, on Dec. 3.

BAUSSET, LOUIS FRANÇOIS DE (1748–1824), cardinal. Born in Pondichéry, France, he became a priest, served at Aix and Digne, and was made bishop of Alais in 1784. He was a member of the assembly in Languedoc, but refused to take the oath demanded of the clergy at the time of the French Revolution. He went into exile in Switzerland, returned in 1792, was imprisoned, and after release retired to write. Napoleon appointed him a canon of St. Denis; he became a member of the French Academy, a cardinal, and a peer in 1817 and a minister of state in 1819. His historical writings are marred by errors, as is his biography of Fénelon. He died in Paris.

BAUTISTA, JUAN (1555–1610?). Born in

Mexico, he became a Franciscan, headed several houses, and made ten studies of the Nahuatl language which aided mission and education work.

BAVO, ST. (589–655?). A native of Hesbaye, Brabant, he led an irregular life, but after his wife died he was so moved by a sermon of St. Amand that he distributed his wealth and became a Benedictine monk under the latter at Ghent. He founded the abbey of St. Peter, accompanied Amand on missions in Flanders and France, and spent his last years as a hermit. He is also known as Allowin. F. D. Oct. 1.

BAWDEN, WILLIAM (1563–1632), educator. Born in Cornwall, he studied at Oxford, Douai, and Rheims, and was ordained in Rome in 1586. In 1590 he became a Jesuit and taught theology at Louvain. He was arrested in Germany for alleged complicity in the gunpowder plot, imprisoned and tortured over the course of eight years in the Tower of London, and sent into exile. He was rector of Louvain in 1621 and then of St. Omer, where he died on Sept. 28.

BAYA. See Brigid, St. (5th century).

BAYARD, PIERRE DU TERRAIL (1475–1524). Called "le chevalier sans peur et sans reproche," he was born near Grenoble, France, served under Charles VIII and Louis XII, and gained fame in battles against Naples, Spain, and England. While with King Francis I he captured Prosper Colonna, defended Mézières against Charles V in 1522, and died in battle at the Sesia River in northern Italy on Apr. 30. He was heralded in later literature as "the knight without fear or blemish."

BAYER, ADÈLE. See Parmentier, Andrew.

BAYEU Y SUBIAS, FRANCISCO (1734–1795), painter. Born in Saragossa, Spain, on Mar. 9, he studied at Tarragona and Madrid, impressed Raphael Mengs, court painter to Charles III, and was commissioned to work in several palaces and churches. In 1788 he became director of San Fernando Academy in Madrid. His frescoes are in Toledo and Saragossa; major religious canvases are in the Prado. He died in Madrid on Aug. 4.

BAYEU Y SUBIAS, RAMÓN (1746–1793), painter. Younger brother and pupil of Francisco, he worked with him on frescoes in the churches of Saragossa, his birthplace.

BAYLES, CHRISTOPHER. See Bales, Bl. Christopher.

BAYLEY, JAMES ROOSEVELT (1814–1877), bishop. Born on Aug. 23, in Rye, New York, grandson of the surgeon Dr. Richard Bayley and nephew of Mother Seton, he studied at Amherst and Trinity College, Hartford, and was ordained an Episcopal minister in 1835. In 1842 he became a convert, entered St. Sulpice, Paris, and was ordained a Catholic priest in Rome in 1844. He taught at St.

John's College (now Fordham), became its president, chancellor of the New York diocese and secretary to Bishop Hughes in 1846, and in 1853 was consecrated first bishop of the newly created diocese of Newark, New Jersey. He attended the Vatican Council in 1869–70 and was transferred to Baltimore as archbishop in 1872. He wrote a history of the Church in New York and a biography of Bishop Bruté. He died in Newark on Oct. 3.

BAYLON, ST. PASCUAL (1540–1592). Born in Torre Hermosa, Aragon, Spain, he took care of his parents' sheep until he was twenty-four, when he became a Franciscan laybrother with a group which followed the austere reforms of St. Peter of Alcantara. He was known for his exceptional devotion to the Blessed Sacrament and is now the patron of Eucharistic congresses. He was canonized in 1690. F. D. May 17.

BAYMA, JOSEPH (1816–1892), mathematician. Born in Piedmont, Italy, on Nov. 9, he became a Jesuit in 1832, was rector of the seminary at Bertinoro in 1860 when religious were forced out of Italy, taught philosophy at Stonyhurst College, England, for seven years, was rector of St. Ignatius College, San Francisco, California, and died at Santa Clara, where he was professor of mathematics, on Feb. 7. He wrote several textbooks; *Molecular Mechanics* (1866), on the constitution of matter, was widely discussed.

BAYSIO, GUIDO DE (d. 1313), canonist. Born in Italy, possibly at Reggio, he studied law, was a canon at Parma and Sabina, archdeacon at Bologna and chancellor of its university, and then went to Avignon, where he died on Aug. 10. He wrote a *Rosarium* (1300), a commentary on the *Decretum* of Gratian, and a defense of the orthodoxy of Pope Boniface VIII.

BAZIN, JOHN STEPHEN (1796–1848), bishop. Born in Duerne, France, on Oct. 15, he was ordained at Lyons in 1822, went to the United States in 1830, worked in the Mobile, Alabama, area for seventeen years, and became vicar general of that diocese. After a visit to France he brought back Jesuits for Spring Hill College and Brothers of the Christian Schools for an orphanage. In 1847 he was made third bishop of Vincennes, Indiana, and died there on Apr. 23.

BAZIN, RENÉ (1853–1932), novelist. Born in Angers, France, on Dec. 26, he studied law at the Catholic University there, continued his education at Paris, and returned to Angers in 1878 to teach criminal law, a position he held until his death. He married Aline Bricard, published his first novel, *Stephanette*, in 1884, attracted the attention of Ludovic Halévy, and was invited to contribute regularly to *Journal des Debats*. Thereafter he wrote some forty novels, chiefly about village life and about the conflict of good and evil; he was more optimistic and romantic than were many French Catholic contemporary writers. Chief among these tales are *Ma tante Giron, Une tache d'encre, Humble amour, De toute son âme, La Terre qui meurt* (translated as *Autumn Glory*), and *Magnificat* (1931). He also wrote travel books (*Les italiens d'aujourd'hui; Sicile; Terre d'Espagne; Croquis de France et d'orient*) and the autobiographical *Fils de l'église* (1927). He became a member of the French Academy in 1904, a Knight Commander of the Order of St. Gregory the Great, and president of the Corporation des Publicistes Chrétiens. He died in Paris on July 20.

BAZZI, GIOVANNI ANTONIO (1477?–1549), painter. Born in Vercelli, Piedmont, Italy, he was apprenticed in 1490 to a glass painter, but established his own name by completing the frescoes of Signorelli in the convent of Monte Oliveto Maggiore after 1505. Although of low moral character (he was generally called Il Sodoma) and the target of malicious contemporary jests, he drew with accuracy and ease. His art, influenced by Leonardo da Vinci and Raphael, is characterized by rich, sensuous color, charm, and the beauty of the faces of his women and children. Among his outstanding works were *Flagellation of Christ* in San Francisco church and the frescoes in the chapel of St. Catherine in San Domenico's, Siena; *Marriage of Alexander with Roxana* and *Alexander in the Tent of Darius*; the frescoes, especially the *Ecstasy* and the *Swooning*, from St. Catherine's life, in the Villa Farnesina; decorations in the chapel of San Spirito, for which Emperor Charles V made him a count palatine; and decorations commissioned by Pope Julius II in the Camera della Segnatura of the Vatican, most of which were replaced by Raphael's frescoes. He died in Siena.

BEAN, ST. (11th century), bishop. He was the first bishop of Mortlach, Scotland, which later became the diocese of Aberdeen. F. D. Oct. 26.

BEARDSLEY, AUBREY (1872–1898), artist. Born in Brighton, England, on Aug. 21, he was, except for two months in art school, a self-taught illustrator. At twenty-one he completed the decorations for *Morte d'Arthur* (published to counterbalance the success of William Morris' press); he then worked for publishers, drew posters, satirized his era in sharp black-and-white sketches, was praised by Pennell and Whistler, and gained sudden and wide fame. He illustrated editions of Wilde's *Salome*, Jonson's *Volpone*, Pope's *Rape of the Lock*, as well as of *Lysistrata* and some erotica. He was something of a dandy and dabbled in poetry and prose, but was serious as art editor of the *Yellow Book* in 1894 and later, with Arthur Symons, of the *Savoy*. He became a convert in 1895 and, after a severe attack of tuberculosis, from which he long had suffered, died in Menton, France, on Mar. 16.

BEARNE, DAVID (1856–1920), editor. Born in Castle Donington, England, on Feb. 28, he became a convert in 1877, a Jesuit in 1878, and was ordained in 1896. He was stationed at Bournemouth, Roehampton, and Wimbleton, at which last he died on Feb. 25. He edited the *Sacred Heart Messenger*, wrote verse, and published some thirty volumes of popular juvenile fiction.

BEATA, ST. (d. 273), martyr. See Augustine, St.

BEATON, DAVID (1494–1546), cardinal. Born in Fife, Scotland, son of John Beaton of Balfour, he studied at St. Andrews, Glasgow, and Paris, served in the French court in 1519 for King James V of Scotland, and returned to work in two Scots parishes. He became a member of parliament in 1525, became lord privy seal, and arranged the marriages of King James to Magdalen, daughter of Francis I, and, when she died after two months, to Mary of Guise. He then became bishop of Mirepoix, near Toulouse, France, and in 1538 was made cardinal by Pope Paul III. He was coadjutor bishop of St. Andrews, with the right of succession to his uncle, James Beaton, and became primate of Scotland in 1539. As Henry VIII intensified his drive to bring Scotland under subjection, Beaton was vilified, slandered, and finally marked for assassination. Henry invaded in 1542, defeated the Scots at Solway Moss, and King James died shortly after. His daughter Mary, a week old, was left in the hands of Beaton and three nobles, all of whom were to serve as regents. The earl of Arran claimed the throne, imprisoned Beaton, gained custody of the princess, and agreed to Henry's demands for a marriage contract with Prince Edward. When Scotland was placed under papal interdict, the people became so restless that the cardinal had to be released; with his friends he reversed the arrangements made by a subject parliament and even won Arran over to the Church. When Beaton was made chancellor, Henry ordered him killed. His agents worked for three years; one of them, George Wishart, was captured, tried, and executed for heresy. The others forced their way two months later into the cardinal's residence at St. Andrews and hacked him to death on May 29. Henry VIII's historians then began the assassination of his character.

BEATON, JAMES (1473?–1539), bishop. Youngest of six sons of John Beaton of Balfour, Fife, Scotland, he studied at St. Andrews, held several church posts, and in 1505 became royal treasurer. In 1508 he was appointed bishop of Galloway, but before he could assume his post was sent to succeed Robert Blackader as archbishop of Glasgow. In 1515 he became chancellor of Scotland and was one of the regents of the three-year-old King James V. In 1522 he was transferred to St. Andrews and as primate strengthened the alliance with France and the nation against the plots of Henry VIII of England. He founded St. Mary's, the divinity school of St. Andrews University. He died in St. Andrews.

BEATON, JAMES (1517–1603), bishop. Nephew of Cardinal James Beaton, he became archbishop of Glasgow, Scotland, in 1551, before he was ordained a priest, and was consecrated at Rome in 1552. He staunchly defended Mary of Guise, widow of King James V, against a traitorous group of Scots nobles; after her death, when the pillaging of the monasteries and other church property had begun, he went to Paris in 1560. There he served as Mary of Scotland's ambassador to the French court; he was reappointed to this post in 1586 by the young King James VI. He died in Paris on Apr. 24.

BEATRICE, ST. (d. 304?), martyr. Sister of SS. Faustinus and Simplicius, she recovered the bodies of her brothers, who had been tortured and beheaded during the persecution of Diocletian, and buried them at Rome. Denounced by a neighbor, she was strangled on May 11. The Acta of these martyrs are not trustworthy. F. D. July 29.

BEATRICE D'ESTE I, BL. (1206–1226). Orphaned at six, she ran away from relatives when a surviving brother sought to marry her off for political advantage, became a Benedictine at fourteen in a convent near Padua, and then was stationed at Gemmola. Her cult was confirmed in 1763. F. D. May 10.

BEATRICE D'ESTE II, BL. (d. 1262). Niece of Bl. Beatrice I, she was a Benedictine at the convent of St. Antony in Ferrara, Italy, formerly founded by her wealthy family, which she entered with a group of friends after her fiancé had died in battle. Her cult was confirmed in 1774. F. D. Jan. 18.

BEATRICE OF ORNACIEUX, BL. (d. 1309), mystic. A Carthusian nun born at Isère, France, who was firmly devoted to the Eucharist, she is said to have experienced many visions and diabolic attacks during years of extreme austerities at Parménie. She died on Nov. 25. Her cult was confirmed in 1869. F. D. Feb. 13.

BEATUS OF VENDÔME, ST. (3rd century). He evangelized the districts of Garonne, Vendôme, Nantes, and Laon. He is often confused with a legendary Swiss hermit of the late first century, whose story had him ordained at Rome by St. Peter and slaying a dragon near the lake of Thun. F. D. May 9.

BEATUS, ST. (d. 789). Born in Asturias, Spain, he was a priest at Liébana, strongly attacked Archbishop Helipandus of Toledo and other Adoptionists, denounced the heresy at the Council of Frankfort, and was angrily censured by his adversaries. When the heresy was condemned, Beatus retired to the monastery at Valcavado, where he wrote on the Apocalypse. F. D. Feb. 19.

BEAUCHAMP, RICHARD DE (1382–1439), governor. Born in England, he became earl of Warwick in 1401, fought at the battle of Shrewsbury (1403), made a pilgrimage to the Holy Land in 1408, returned to England in 1410, was on the peace commission in France in 1413, and attended the Council of Constance in 1414. He also was in charge of the garrison at Calais in 1414, became tutor and guardian of Henry VI in 1422, and in 1437 was named lieutenant in charge of Normandy, a post he governed until his death in Rouen on Apr. 30.

BEAUFORT, HENRY (1377?–1447), cardinal. Born in Beaufort castle in Anjou, natural son of John of Gaunt and Katherine Swynford, and half-brother of King Henry IV, he was legitimized by Richard II in 1397, and became a priest and dean of Wells. He was appointed bishop of Lincoln in 1398, chancellor of Oxford in 1399, was chancellor of England in 1403–4, 1413–17, 1424–26, and was appointed bishop of Winchester in 1404. He attended the Council of Constance in 1417, convinced Emperor Sigismund of the advisability of electing a pope before Church reforms were inaugurated, helping to end the Western schism. He was guardian of the infant Henry VI when Henry V died in 1422, and was created cardinal-priest in 1426. He served as papal legate in Germany, Hungary, and Bohemia, crowned Henry king of France in Paris in 1431, and returned to England, where he completed building Winchester cathedral. He died on Apr. 11.

BEAUFORT, MARGARET (1441–1509), countess. Daughter of John Beaufort, first duke of Somerset, she married Edmund, earl of Richmond and brother of King Henry VI, who died soon after in 1456; their son became Henry VII. In 1459 she married a cousin, Sir Henry Stafford, who died in 1482. She then married Thomas, Lord Stanley, later earl of Derby. She was an active agent in bringing an end to the War of the Roses, was a generous patron of learning, founded Christ's and St. John's colleges at Cambridge, translated *The Mirror of Gold for the Sinful Soul*, and was widely known for her great charities. Bishop John Fisher served as her confessor and preached her famous funeral sermon.

BEAUNE, RENAUD DE (1527–1606), bishop. Born in Tours, France, he served in parliament and as chancellor to Francis, duke of Touraine. In 1568 he became bishop of Mende and in 1581 archbishop of Bourges. He became almoner and adviser to King Henry IV, who in 1595 appointed him archbishop of Sens. Papal approval was not granted until 1602. His work on the royal commission appointed to reform the University of Paris was published in 1605. He was active in bringing peace to the nation, tried to reform the king, and, without right, granted conditional absolution to Henry while the king was under censure from Rome. His funeral sermon on Mary Queen of Scots and Catherine de' Medici were published, as well as a translation of the Psalms. He died in Paris.

BEAUREGARD, JEAN NICOLAS (1733–1804). Born in Metz, Lorraine, on Dec. 4, he became a Jesuit in 1749, taught at Nancy and other colleges, and preached widely through the country and at court. During the revolution he fled to England, and later returned to Maestricht and Cologne. He died in Gröningen, Germany, on July 27.

BEAUREGARD, PIERRE GUSTAVE TOUTANT (1818–1893), general. Born near New Orleans, Louisiana, on May 28, he was commissioned in 1838 after studies at West Point, served as an engineer at the siege of Vera Cruz and other strongholds during the United States-Mexican War, and was wounded at Mexico City. After the war he directed coastal construction along the Gulf of Mexico and in January 1861 was appointed superintendent of the United States Military Academy. He resigned the next month, joined the Confederacy, and was in charge of the southern forces at the first battle of Bull Run. Sent to Tennessee, he succeeded A. S. Johnson when the latter was killed at the battle of Shiloh; held Charleston, South Carolina, against a year-and-a-half siege; joined Lee in 1864 and defended Petersburg, Virginia; then tried, unsuccessfully with Gen. J. E. Johnson, to stop the advance of Sherman through Georgia. After his surrender in 1865 he became president of a railroad and adjutant general of Louisiana and wrote two military studies. He died in New Orleans on Feb. 20.

BEAUVAIS, GILLES FRANÇOIS DE (1693–1773?). Born in Mans, France, on July 7, he became a Jesuit in 1709, preached at court, and wrote lives of Ignatius Azevedo and John de Britto. He died in Paris.

BEAUVAIS, JEAN BAPTISTE CHARLES MARIE DE (1731–1790), bishop. Born in Cherbourg, France, on Oct. 17, he became a distinguished preacher; his sermons at court resulted in his appointment in 1773 to the see of Senez. In 1783 he resigned as bishop, settled in Paris, and in 1789 became a member of the States-General. He died in Paris on Apr. 4.

BEAUVAU, JEAN DE (14th century). He was seneschal of Anjou, in the service of Louis I of Anjou (d. 1384), king of Sicily, and wrote *Le Roman de Troyle et de Criseida*, a translation of Boccaccio's *Il Filostrato*, and now believed to be a major source of Chaucer's *Troilus and Criseyde*.

BEAVEN, THOMAS DANIEL (1851–1920), bishop. Born in Springfield, Massachusetts, on Mar. 1, he studied at Holy Cross and the Grand seminary, Montreal, where he was ordained in 1875. He did parish work in Massachusetts for the next seventeen years, was appointed bishop of Springfield in 1892, and reigned until his death there on Oct. 25.

BÉBIAN, ROCH AMBOISE AUGUSTE (1789–1839). Born in Pointe-à-Pitre, Guadeloupe, on Aug. 4, he studied at Paris and became interested in the deaf and dumb while working with his godfather, Abbé Sicard, and Abbé Jauffret there. Bébian directed an institution at Paris, worked on ways of bettering the sign language, and published a number of studies on new principles. He founded another institution for the deaf and dumb in Paris, one in Rouen, and one for Negroes in Guadeloupe, where he died on Feb. 24.

BECAN, ST. (6th century). A relative of St. Columba, he founded a monastery at Kill-Beggan, Westmeath, Ireland. Another saint of the same name and time (F. D. May 26) was a hermit near Cork. F. D. Apr. 5.

BECAN, MARTIN (1563–1624), apologist. Born in Hilvarenbeek, Holland, on Jan. 6, he became a Jesuit in 1583, taught theology in Würzburg, Mainz, and Vienna, and was confessor to Emperor Frederick II from 1620 until his death at Vienna. He wrote forty-six works on the Eucharist, free will, and infallibility, and against Calvin, Luther, and the Anabaptists. His *Controversia Anglicana* on the relations of king and pope was placed on the Index in 1613 to prevent interpolations by the University of Paris faculty; statements in it which might have been considered exaggerated were removed, and the volume was soon approved. He died in Vienna on Jan. 24.

BECCARIA, GIOVANNI BATTISTA (1716–1781), physicist. Born in Mondivi, Italy, on Oct. 3, he joined the Clerks Regular of St. Joseph Calasanctius when sixteen, taught in Palermo and Rome, and in 1748 became professor of physics at Turin. He did extensive research on the properties of electricity, experimented with kites and rockets in his studies of atmospheric electricity, was the first to realize that the electrical charge on a conductor is confined to the surface, and wrote *Dell' eletricismo artificiale e naturale* (1753) and other treatises. He was elected a fellow of the Royal Society in 1755. He died in Turin, Italy, on May 27.

BECHE, BL. JOHN (d. 1539), martyr. Of unknown birthplace and parentage, his name may have been Thomas Marshall. He received a doctor's degree in divinity from Oxford in 1515, became abbot of St. Werburgh's, Chester, and in 1533 of St. John's, Colchester. Although a friend of SS. Thomas More and John Fisher and opposed to Henry VIII's new Church policies, he and his monks took the oath of supremacy in 1534. He was arrested in 1539 when he opposed the dissolution of his abbey and was hanged, drawn, and quartered at Colchester. He was beatified in 1895. F. D. Dec. 1.

BECKEDORFF, GEORG PHILIPP LUDOLF VON (1778–1858). Born in Hanover, Germany, on Apr. 14, he studied theology at Jena and medicine at Göttingen, and practiced the latter profession from 1799 to 1810. He then was tutor to the crown prince of Anhalt-Bernburg, member of the high privy council of Prussia, minister of public worship, and supervisor of the school system. As attorney general for the University of Berlin he continued his interest in religious sects and in 1827 became a Catholic and retired from public office. King Frederick William later made him a noble and president of the state agricultural department. He published two volumes in that field, several on Church-state relations, and others on education. He built a church, charity home, and school in the vicinity of his estate at Grünhof, Pomerania, where he died on Feb. 27.

BECKER, THOMAS ANDREW (1832–1899), bishop. Born in Pittsburgh, Pennsylvania, on Dec. 20, he became a convert and was ordained at Rome in 1859. He was in charge of a mission at Martinsburg, West Virginia, professor at Mt. St. Mary's College, Maryland, and secretary to Archbishop Spalding. In 1868 he was consecrated as first bishop of Wilmington, Delaware, and in 1886 was transferred to Savannah, Georgia. He served as secretary at the fourth plenary Council of Baltimore, wrote on the meaning of university education, and was active in the temperance movement. He died in Washington, Georgia, on July 29.

BECKMAN, FRANCIS JOSEPH (1875–1948), archbishop. Born in Cincinnati, Ohio, on Oct. 25, he studied at Mt. St. Mary of the West seminary there, was ordained in 1902, and pursued further studies at Louvain and the Gregorian, Rome, where he received a doctorate in theology in 1908. He taught philosophy at Mt. St. Mary's in 1908–12, was president of its theological seminary from 1912 to 1924, when he also taught theology, and was censor librorum for the Cincinnati archdiocese. He helped to found the Catholic Students Mission Crusade (which was to reach a membership of 1,000,000) in 1918, served as its chairman and director, and in 1920 was made a domestic prelate. In 1923 he was appointed bishop of Lincoln, Nebraska, served as apostolic admin-

istrator of Omaha in 1926–28, and in 1930 became archbishop of Dubuque, Iowa. He founded the Catholic Youth Organization orchestra in 1937, the Dubuque symphony orchestra in 1938, the Columbian Museum in Dubuque, and the National Antiquarian Society. He reigned until 1946, when he resigned and was appointed titular archbishop of Phulla. He died on Oct. 17 in Chicago.

BECKX, PIERRE JEAN (1795–1887). Born in Sichem, Belgium, on Feb. 8, he was ordained in 1819 and within a year decided to join the Jesuits. He served as chaplain to the duke of Anhalt-Köthen, converted many in the area, went to Rome and Vienna, became provincial of Austria in 1852 and in 1853 became the twenty-second general of his Society. Although many new provinces were established through the world, he saw the Society expelled from Italy, Spain, Germany, and France. In 1873 he settled in Fiesole for ten years, then resigned his post and resided in Rome until his death on Mar. 4.

BECQUEREL, ALEXANDRE EDMOND (1820–1891), physicist. Son of Antoine César Becquerel, he was born in Paris on Mar. 24, studied under his father and was his assistant at the Musée d'Histoire Naturelle. He was appointed professor at the Agronomic Institute in 1849, was appointed to the chair of physics at the Conservatoire des Arts et Métiers in 1853, and succeeded his father as professor at the Musée. He specialized in the study of various aspects of light (especially the photochemical effects of solar radiation and electric light), the properties of phosphorescence, developed the phosphoroscope to measure and observe the effects of exposure to light on uranium compounds and sulphides, developed a modification of Faraday's law, and wrote *La Lumière* (two volumes, 1867–68). He died in Paris on May 11.

BECQUEREL, ANTOINE CÉSAR (1788–1878), physicist. Born in Châtillon-sur-Loing, Loiret, France, on Mar. 8, he studied at L'École Polytechnique, served in the engineers corps of the army in 1810–15, and retired as a major to devote himself to the study of electricity. He constructed the first pile with a constant current, refuted Volta's theory of contact, and showed that chemical action had to be present for the generation of electricity, invented a method of electrotyping, and produced several metals by slow electric action, among them aluminum, silicium, and glacium. He studied the magnetic properties of antimony before the discoveries of Faraday; constructed an electric thermometer and with it measured the heat of animal bodies, the soil, and the atmosphere. He became a member of the Academy of Sciences in 1829, professor of physics at the Musee d'Histoite Naturelle in 1837, a position he held until his death, and received the Copley Medal of the Royal Society in 1837 for his studies in electricity. He wrote numerous treatises on his researches, among them *Elements of Electrochemistry* (1843), *Complete Treatise on Magnetism* (1845), and *Elements of Terrestrial Physics and of Meteorology* (1847), with his son Alexandre. He died in Paris on Jan. 18.

BECQUEREL, ANTOINE HENRI (1852–1908), physicist. Son of Alexandre Edmond Becquerel, he was born in Paris, on Dec. 15, studied at L'École Polytechnique, and in 1875 entered government service in the department of bridges and fountains, of which he became head in 1894. He was appointed professor in L'École Polytechnique in 1895, was the discoverer of radioactivity when in 1896 he discovered uranium emits invisible radiation (Becquerel rays), and in 1903 was awarded, with Marie and Pierre Curie, the Nobel Prize for physics. In 1908 he was appointed life secretary of the Academy of Sciences. He also did important research in the fields of light polarization and light absorption in crystals, magnetism and phosphorescence. He died in Croisic, France, on Aug. 25.

BÉDARD, PIERRE (1762–1829), jurist. Born in Charlesbourg, near Quebec, Canada, on Nov. 13, he became a lawyer and from 1792 to 1812 served as a member of the assembly. He spoke strongly on the need for clarifying and defining constitutional government, and stated many of his convictions in *Le Canadien*, a newspaper founded in 1806. As a result he was jailed for the year 1810 by Sir James Craig, the governor. When Sir George Prévost replaced the latter in 1813, Bédard was appointed judge of the superior court at Three Rivers, a post he held until he became seriously ill in 1827. He died two years later on Apr. 26 at Three Rivers.

BEDE, ST. (672?–735), historian and Doctor of the Church. Born near the monastery of SS. Peter and Paul at Wearmouth-Jarrow, Northumberland, England, he was given at seven into the care of St. Benedict Biscop, and later of Abbot Ceolfrid, to be educated. He spent his life in the monastery, was ordained at thirty, and spent much time annotating scripture and the Fathers of the Church; on his deathbed he still was busy dictating a translation of the gospel of St. John. He was the most learned individual of his day and had a major influence on literature in England; it would have been greater if his area had not been devastated by the Danes. His *Historia ecclesiastica* (731), translated into English as *Ecclesiastical History of the English People* at the request of Alfred the Great, is a mine of information about the nation up to 729. Bede was a careful scholar, distinguishing between firsthand information and hearsay, or legend, competent as an interpreter, effective as a storyteller, moving as a stylist. The "father" of English history was also the first to use the convention of dating events *anno Domini* (from the year of our Lord's birth). He also wrote *Historia abbatum*, on those in charge of his twin monasteries; a general history of the world, *De temporibus liber* (705); *De temporum ratione* (725); lives of St. Cuthbert and others; a pastoral letter to Egbert of York; a theory of music; *De natura regum*; and on music, metrics, grammar, rhetoric, and many hymns. He long was referred to as "Venerable" Bede, partly because there were so few priest-monks, especially with his ideal devotion to his abbey, and partly to acknowledge his wisdom and learning. He was the only Englishman signalized in Dante's *Paradiso*. He was declared a Doctor of the Church in 1899 by Pope Leo XIII. F. D. May 27.

BEDE THE YOUNGER, ST. (d. 883). An official in the court of Charles the Bald of France, he became a Benedictine at Gavello, Italy, and refused several times to become a bishop. F. D. Apr. 10.

BEDFORD, GUNNING S. (1806–1870). Born in Baltimore, Maryland, nephew of a framer of the United States Constitution for whom he was named, he graduated from Mt. St. Mary's College, Maryland, in 1825, took his medical degree at Rutgers and additional courses abroad, and in 1833 was appointed professor of obstetrics at the medical college in Charleston, South Carolina. He also taught in Albany, New York, and in New York City; there he established the first obstetrical clinic for charity patients, founded the University Medical College in 1840, wrote two medical textbooks, and died on Sept. 5.

BEDFORD, HENRY (1816–1903). Born in London, England, on Oct. 1, he studied at Cambridge, was ordained an Anglican minister, preached in London, was attracted by the leaders of the Oxford Movement, and became a convert in 1851. He taught science at All Hallows College, near Dublin, Ireland, from 1872 until his death on May 21. He wrote frequently in Irish periodicals.

BEDINGFIELD, FRANCES (1616–1704). Born in Norfolk, England, she and her eleven sisters entered religious life. Frances joined the English Institute of Mary at Munich, became superior there, and in 1669 established a house in London at the request of Catherine of Braganza, wife of King Charles II. She wore ordinary clothing, was known as Mrs. Long, and directed an additional school in York, though under frequent government interference. In 1694, she and her niece, Dorothy Paston Bedingfield, were jailed at York; twice the school was threatened with destruction. In 1699, Mother Frances turned over the superiorship to her niece and returned to Munich, where she died.

BEDINGFIELD, SIR HENRY (1509–1583). He and Sir Henry Jerningham were instrumental in achieving the coronation of Mary Tudor, and proclaimed her queen at Norwich. As lieutenant of the Tower of London, he had Elizabeth as his prisoner, but did not treat her with cruelty, as John Foxe declared. Correspondence exists to show that Elizabeth acknowledged his title and personal worth; as the penal laws became more stringent, Bedingfield was assessed heavy fines, his house was frequently searched, and his travel was restricted.

BEDINI, CAJETAN (1806–1864), cardinal. Born in Sinigaglia, Italy, on May 15, he was commissioner extraordinary for Bologna from 1849 to 1852 and in 1853 was appointed papal nuncio to Brazil. On his way to his post he visited the United States, where his reception by President Franklin Pierce touched off charges that he was seeking diplomatic recognition of the Vatican. The Know-Nothing furor was then at its height; there were riots in New York City, where a group led by the apostate priest and exile Gavazzi sought to assassinate the archbishop; riots against him in Cincinnati cost several lives. As a result, Bedini cut short his visit. He became a cardinal in his last years and bishop of Viterbo, Italy, where he died on Sept. 6.

BEELEN, IAN THEODOR (1807–1884). Born in Amsterdam, Holland, on Jan. 12, and educated at Rome, he was professor of scripture and oriental languages at Louvain from 1836 to 1876. He wrote a great number of biblical studies, of which his commentary on Romans was most important, a translation of the Psalms, a study of Clement of Rome, and was responsible for the revival of oriental studies in Belgium. He died in Louvain on Mar. 31.

BEER, BL. RICHARD (d. 1537), martyr. He and nine other Carthusians were the only ones left after nineteen others bowed to Henry VIII's demand that they take the Oath of Supremacy; their London house was stripped of its library and furnishings. With Fr. Beer (who died on Aug. 31) stood Frs. Thomas Green (June 15) and Thomas Johnson; Thomas Davy (June 6), a deacon; and William Greenwood (June 16), William Horne, Walter Pierson (June 6), Thomas Reding (June 15), Robert Salt (June 6), and Thomas Scryven (June 15), laybrothers. They were thrown into prison, tied up, fed for a while by St. Thomas More's daughter, Margaret Clement, who came in disguise, then, when this ruse was discovered, left to starve to death in chains. Bro. Horne, who outlasted the others, was executed at Tyburn on Aug. 4, 1540. They were beatified in 1886.

L. HENDRICKS, *The London Charterhouse* (London, 1889).

BEESLEY, VEN. GEORGE (d. 1591), mar-

tyr. Born in Lancaster, England, he was ordained at Rheims in 1587 and sent to the English mission in 1588. He was captured in 1590, tortured by Topliffe almost beyond recognition, and executed on July 2 for being a priest in Elizabethan England.

BEETHOVEN, LUDWIG VAN (1770–1827), composer. Born in Bonn, Germany, on Dec. 15 or 16, of Flemish descent, he studied music under his father, a singer in the chapel of the archbishop of Cologne, and the court organist, Christian Neefe, who recognized his genius. He was appointed assistant court organist in 1784 and served as teacher, court organist, pianist, and conductor until 1792, when he went to Vienna. He studied under Richard Haydn, Albrechtsberger, Johann Schenck, and Antonio Salieri, and was patronized by Princes Karl Lichnowsky and Josef Franz Lobkowitz, Count Waldstein, and Archduke Rudolph, who introduced him to Vienna's exclusive social and musical circles. He became noted for his skill on the pianoforte, made his first public appearance in 1795, which also saw his first publications, *Trios Op. 1* and the *Sonatas Op. 2*. About 1800 he began to be bothered by the hardness of hearing which was to develop into total deafness. He attracted attention with the originality of his *Sonata Pathétique*. He produced his *Symphony No. 1* in C major in 1800 and *Symphony No. 2* in D major in 1802. In 1803 he became composer at the Theater an der Wien where he produced his oratorio *Christus am Ölberge* (*Mount of Olives*), left this position when the theater was sold in 1804, and in the next decade produced the remarkable series of symphonies and other musical works, including the piano sonatas from Op. 31 to 81 (including *Waldstein*, the *Appassionata*, and *Les Adieux*), *Fidelio*, the overtures to *Coriolanus* and *Egmont*, the three *Rasumovsky Quartets* and the fourth and fifth piano concertos and the violin concerto. In this same decade he wrote *Symphony No. 3* in E flat major [*Eroica*] in 1803, *Symphony No. 4* in B flat major in 1806, *Symphony No. 5* in C minor in 1805–6. *Symphony No. 6* in F major (*Pastoral*) appeared in 1807–8, *No. 7* in A major and *No. 8* in F major were finished in 1812. By 1807 he was the musical sensation of the century and his musical works, which he turned out at a prodigious pace, were in tremendous demand. In 1808 he was invited by Jerome Bonaparte, king of Westphalia, to become choirmaster at Cassel, but gave up the idea when a group of friends agreed to pay him an annual pension of 4000 florins, giving him for the first time a fixed income which would enable him to concentrate on his work. By 1814 his deafness was total, but despite his affliction he continued to compose. From 1817 to 1823 he was engaged on the *Symphony No. 9* in D minor (*Choral*), produced in 1826, and the *Missa solemnis*, produced in 1823, and spent his last years composing quartets—works considered among his greatest and which foreshadowed the whole development of nineteenth-century music. He wrote other masses, overtures, sonatas (including the *Kreutzer*), minuets, cantatas, songs, and ballet, chamber, and military music. He died in Vienna on Mar. 26.

BEGA, ST. (d. 698?). That she lived in Northumbria and founded a convent on a spit of land in Cumberland seems fact; that she was the daughter of an Irish king, who fled to escape marriage to the son of a Norwegian king and then received the veil from St. Aidan, is probably legend. F. D. Sept. 6.

BEGGA, ST. (d. 698?). Daughter of Bl. Pepin of Landen and Bl. Ida, she married Ansegisilus, son of St. Arnulf of Metz. Their son Pepin of Herstal was the first of the Carolingian dynasty. After her husband's death in 691, she founded a convent at Andenne and became its abbess. F. D. Dec. 17.

BÉGIN, LOUIS NAZAIRE (1840–1925), cardinal. Born in La Point-Lévis, Canada, on Jan. 10, he studied at St. Michel in Quebec, Laval, and the French College and Gregorian in Rome, was ordained in 1865, and spent two years at Innsbruck. He taught theology and history at Laval until 1884, was principal of its normal school for four years, and in 1888 became bishop of Chicoutimi. He was made coadjutor at Quebec in 1891, administrator of the archdiocese in 1894, and succeeded to the see in 1898. He wrote on the papacy and a history of the United States, worked for better social legislation, founded Catholic Social Action, and was named a cardinal in 1914. He died in Quebec on July 18.

BEGNUDELLI-BASSO, FRANCESCO (d. 1713). Born in Trent, he became vicar general there in 1675, was a canon of the cathedral at Freising in 1679, and in 1696 was vicar general of the latter diocese. His work on canon law was authoritative during the eighteenth century. He died in Freising, Germany, on Oct. 9.

BEHAIM, ALBERT VON. *See* Albertus Bohemus.

BEHAIM, MARTIN (1459–1507), cartographer. Born in Nuremberg, Germany, he is said to have studied mathematics and astonomy under Regiomontanus. He became a merchant, worked in Antwerp, and went to Lisbon about 1481. King John II appointed him to a commission to find a better method of determining latitude; Behaim then went with Diego Cam on an exploratory voyage along the west coast of Africa, discovering the mouth of the Congo. In 1492, Behaim prepared, probably with the help of Hartmann Schedel of Nuremberg, the first known globe. It is twenty-one inches in diameter, shows the equator and the tropics, but is without latitude and longitude markings. Only the islands in the region of Greenland show any indication that North America existed; South America is totally lacking; Japan is located where northwestern Mexico is. There is no evidence at all that Columbus and Magellan were aware of Behaim's work. He died in Lisbon on July 29.

BEHN, HERNAND (1880–1933), executive. Born in St. Thomas, Virgin Islands, on Feb. 19, he was educated in Corsica and Paris, and in Puerto Rico in 1904 organized with his brother Sosthenes the banking firm of Behn and Co., of which he was president. He branched into New York City and organized the International Telephone and Telegraph Co., which had subsidiaries in forty-two countries. In 1930 he installed a telephone system in the Vatican, developed its wireless station, and modernized telephone communications in Spain. He was three times honored by papal decorations. He died in St. Jean de Luz, France, on Oct. 7.

BÉLA I (d. 1063), king of Hungary. After defeating his brother Andrew in battle, he succeeded him as king in 1061, suppressed the last pagan uprising, put into effect financial and commercial reforms, and strengthened the royal power, often at the expense of the Church, which was weakened during his reign.

BÉLA III (d. 1196), king of Hungary. Son of King Geza II, he was educated at the Byzantine court in Constantinople, married Agnes of Châtillon, and with the military support of Emperor Manuel was crowned king in 1173. He became a Catholic, married Margaret, sister of Philip Augustus of France, on the death of Agnes, and established close ties between the two countries. During his reign he successfully resisted Venice's attempts to annex Dalmatia in two wars (1181–88 and 1190–91), and aided Greek Emperor Isaac II Angelus against the Bulgarians.

BÉLA IV (1206–1270), king of Hungary. Son of King Andrew II, he succeeded his father as king in 1235, attempted recovery of royal lands his father had dissipated, was opposed by the magnates, who set up rival rulers, and attempted to secure support against them by permitting some 40,000 Cuman families to settle in the Theiss area. Aware of the impending Mongol invasion, he pleaded in vain for help from the emperor, the pope, and the duke of Austria, and in 1241 he was crushed at Mohi on the Sajo River by Mongol invaders, who devastated the country and massacred thousands. He was forced to flee to the Dalmatian Islands, where he lived for a year. When the Mongols withdrew at news of the Great Khan's death, he labored to rebuild the destroyed churches, monasteries, and public and private buildings, attempted to repopulate his land with foreign colonists, and encouraged the building of castles for defensive purposes. In 1246 he defeated and slew the last Babenberg duke of Austria, who had used the Mongol invasion to seize the western part of his dominions, ending the male Babenberg line, warred with Ottocar II of Bohemia, who defeated him, and saw the last years of his reign torn by rebellion headed by his son Stephen V, who succeeded him as king. Béla died on May 3.

BELASYSE, JOHN (1614?–1689). Son of Thomas, first Lord Fauconberg, he served in parliament until the English civil war, raised six regiments of infantry and cavalry, fought on the royalist side in the major battles and was often wounded. He became general of the royal forces in the north, governor of York, and was created baron by King Charles I in 1645. During the Commonwealth he acted as agent for the government of Charles II, then in the Netherlands; at the restoration, he was lord lieutenant in Yorkshire, governor of Hull, and governor of Tangier. He resigned his offices in 1673 when the Test Act removed all those who wished to remain Catholics. He was impeached as a traitor at the time of the Titus Oates Plot, and imprisoned as the designated commander in chief of the alleged army of invasion. He was restored to honor by James II, but his appointment to the treasury department brought public censure and was partly responsible for the religious turmoil which brought about the monarch's self-exile.

BELCHIAM, VEN. THOMAS (d. 1537), martyr. A Franciscan Observant in England, he opposed the divorce of Henry VIII, wrote against the actions of the king and of the bishops who defected to his service, was jailed with thirty members of his order, and starved to death in prison. He died on Aug. 3.

BELGRADO, GIACOPO (1704–1789). Born in Udine, Italy, on Nov. 16, he became a Jesuit in 1723, taught at Venice and Parma, and in 1742 became confessor to Duke Philippo and court mathematician. In 1757 he built the observatory at Parma. He wrote widely on electricity, heat, geometry, and in 1773 became rector of the college at Bologna. He died in Udine on Mar. 26.

BELIN, ALBERT (d. 1677). Born in Besançon, France, he became a Benedictine in 1629, served as prior and abbot at Nevers and Paris, and wrote many spiritual and apologetical works.

BELINA, ST. (d. 1135). She was a French peasant at Troyes who died in defense of her virtue, and was canonized in 1203. F. D. Feb. 19.

BELL, VEN. ARTHUR (1590–1643), martyr. Born near Worcester, England, on Jan. 13, he studied at St. Omer and in Spain, was ordained, and became a Franciscan in 1618. He wrote a life of St. John of the Cross, taught Hebrew to the community of Friars Minor at Douai, was sent to Scotland in 1623 as first provincial of his order there, and was captured and declared a spy in 1643 by Cromwell's troops. He was hanged, drawn, and quartered at London on Dec. 11.

BELL, BL. JAMES (1520?–1584), martyr. Born in Warrington, England, and educated at Oxford, he was ordained in England, apostatized under Elizabeth, then became reconciled, and was arrested while serving as a priest. He was executed at Lancaster, and was beatified in 1929. F. D. Apr. 20.

BELLACI, BL. TOMASSO (1370–1447). A native of Florence whose youth was dissipated, he became a Franciscan laybrother at Fiesole and was appointed master of novices. In 1414 he accompanied John of Stroncone to Naples and spent the next few years in Corsica and southern Italy preaching, opposing the Fraticelli in Tuscany, and establishing new foundations. In 1439 he went to preach in Syria and Ethiopia, was seized and tortured by the Turks, but ransomed by Pope Eugenius IV. He died in Rieti on Oct. 31 while on the way to Rome to ask permission to return to the East. His cult was approved in 1771. F. D. Oct. 25.

BELLAMY, JEROME (d. 1586). Born near London, he was a sympathizer with Mary Queen of Scots and harbored Babington and other supporters of the queen in his house. Seized with them, he was tried and executed, within a week, on Sept. 21.

BELLARINI, JOHN (1552–1630). Born in Castelnuovo, Italy, he became a Barnabite, taught theology at Padua and Rome, twice served as assistant general of his order, wrote commentaries on the Council of Trent and on the catechism, handbooks for confessors, and a study of St. Thomas Aquinas on predetermination. He died in Milan on Aug. 27.

BELLARMINE, ST. ROBERT FRANCIS ROMULUS (1542–1621), cardinal, Doctor of the Church. Born in Montepulciano, Tuscany, Italy, on Oct. 4, he became a Jesuit at Rome in 1560, studied in Florence and Mondovi, and at Padua and Louvain, was ordained at Ghent, and in 1570 became the first Jesuit to become a professor at Louvain. He lectured on the *summa* of St. Thomas Aquinas, counteracted the teachings of Baius, and gained a reputation as a brilliant preacher; he also studied Hebrew and wrote a Hebrew grammar to prepare himself for scriptural interpretation. He was recalled to Rome in 1576, taught at the Roman College, and prepared *Disputationes de controversiis* (1581–93), a study of the Christian faith, written in answer to the Protestant *Centuries of Magdeburg*. He went to Paris on a diplomatic mission in 1589 and was in the eight-month siege of the city. In 1592 he engaged in the preparation of the revision of the Clementine edition of the Vulgate and wrote its preface. He also was named rector of the Roman College in that year, was provincial of Naples in 1594, and in 1597 became theologian to Pope Clementine VIII, preparing two catechisms which are still in vogue. In 1599, Clement created him a cardinal and in 1602, archbishop of Capua; he resigned in 1605 to return to Rome at the request of Pope Paul V. He then became a major voice in Church and international affairs. He carried the brunt of the discussion with the Servite Paolo Sarpi, in defense of the papal interdict laid on Venice. He censured the Archpriest Blackwell of England, who had taken the oath of allegiance to King James I. Bellarmine crushed James, who published two books to support his theory of supremacy; the cardinal's answer, asserting that current interpretations of the divine-right-of-kings theory were false, made France angry as well as England and the French parliament ordered his book burned; his position that the pope had only indirect jurisdiction over civil rulers aroused the hostility of Pope Sixtus V, even though it was written to defend him against the Scots philosopher William Barclay. Bellarmine wrote many other polemical tracts, answering a score of voices raised throughout Europe. He was also entangled in the situation involving Galileo (whose close friend he was) and his 1616 admonition to the astronomer to accept the judgment that he term his findings hypotheses for the time being was accepted with grace. Thereafter, Bellarmine wrote spiritual works, including an *Art of Dying Well* and a commentary on the Psalms. He died on Sept. 17 in Rome, was canonized in 1930, and was declared a Doctor of the Church in 1931. F. D. May 13.

JAMES BRODRICK, *Robert Bellarmine, Saint and Scholar* (Westminster, Md., Newman, 1961).

BELLASIS, EDWARD (1800–1873), lawyer. Born in Basildon, England on Oct. 14, son of an evangelical minister, he became a lawyer, served as counsel to the enlarging railroad companies, and was made a serjeant-at-law (an honor since abolished) in 1844. His first wife died in 1832; in 1835 he married Eliza Garnett, by whom he had ten children. He became a convert in 1850; his family followed. In 1852 he was one of the defense in the libel suit Achilli brought against John Henry Newman; the later cardinal dedicated *The Grammar of Assent* to his friend in 1870. He died in Hyères, France, on Jan. 24.

BELLECIUS, ALOYSIUS (1704–1757). Born in Freiburg im Breisgau, Germany, on Feb. 15, he became a Jesuit, served as a missioner along the Amazon River in South America for four years, returned to direct the seminary of Porrentruy, near Basle, and wrote a number of ascetical treatises. He died in Augsburg, Germany, on Apr. 27.

BELLENDEN, JOHN (d. 1587?), poet. Born in Scotland, he attended St. Andrews and Paris, translated the *Historia Scotorum* of Hector Boece into Scots at the request of King James V, began a translation of Livy, and wrote some original poetry. Appointed archdeacon at Moray, he was forced to flee during the persecution and died at Rome. He is also known as John Ballantyne.

BELLESINI, BL. STEFANO (1774–1840). Born at Trent, on Nov. 25, he became an Augustinian at sixteen, studied at Rome and Bologna, and developed into a vigorous speaker and competent instructor of children. He became inspector of schools for the government and when his order was permitted to return to Italy, master of novices. He died of cholera on Feb. 2 while caring for others at Genazzano, Italy, where he had been appointed parish priest. He was beatified in 1904. F. D. Feb. 3.

BELLINGS, SIR RICHARD (d. 1677), historian. Son of Sir Henry Bellings of Leinster, he was born near Dublin, studied law in London, and became a member of the Irish Confederation in 1642 and secretary of its supreme council. He was active in Ireland with the Royalist forces from 1645 to 1649, went to France when his property was confiscated by Cromwell, and returned in 1660 with King Charles II. He wrote a defense of the Irish Catholics, a history of the war in Ireland (1641–48), and, earlier, a supplementary sixth book to Sir Philip Sidney's *Arcadia*.

BELLINI, GENTILE (1427?–1507), painter. Oldest son of Giacomo, he was born in Venice, studied under his father, and used recognizable figures, formal processions, and elaborate architectural backgrounds. His *Sermon of St. Mark at Alexandria* and designs for the council chamber of the doge's palace, which he completed with his brother Giovanni, mark this early period. A trip to Constantinople resulted in many oriental portraits and the introduction of eastern color and detail in later work.

BELLINI, GIACOMO (1400–1471), painter. Born in Venice, he studied under Gentile da Fabriano in Florence, completed commissions in Padua, and opened a studio in Venice with his two sons, Gentile and Giovanni, who are considered founders of the Venetian school of painting.

BELLINI, GIOVANNI (1428?–1516), painter. Born in Venice, son of Giacomo, he worked with his father and brother, was influenced by Antonello da Messina, and abandoned tempera for oil. His historical work has been lost, but portraits of the doges and religious figures (*pietàs* and madonnas) are realistic and colorful. He attempted landscape as background for his *Baptism of Christ, Death of St. Peter Martyr*, and a St. Jerome.

BELLINUS, ST. (d. 1151), martyr. He was slain while bishop of Padua and canonized in the fifteenth century by Pope Eugene IV. F. D. Nov. 26.

BELLOC, HILAIRE (1870–1953), author. Born in La Celle, St. Cloud, France, on July 27, he was educated at the Oratory, Edgbaston, England, under Cardinal Newman, completed his military service with the French army, and returned to graduate from Oxford in 1895. He married Elodie Hogan of California in 1896, became a British subject in 1903, and served in the House of Commons in 1906–10. He wrote of this last experience in *The Party System*, with Cecil Chesterton as his collaborator. The latter succeeded him as editor of the *Eye-Witness* later called the *New Witness*, in the columns of which Belloc developed his economic theory of distributism. Early poetry in the tradition of Edward Lear, *A Bad Child's Book of Beasts* (1896) and *New Cautionary Tales*, was followed by ballads, drinking songs, satires, and epigrams, gathered in *Collected Poems* (1923). Travel books include *The Path to Rome* (1902) and *The Cruise of the Nona*; criticism, such as *Caliban's Guide to Letters* (1903) was developed into collections of formal and informal essays: *On Nothing* (1903), *On Everything, On Anything,* and *On*. His novels were often illustrated by G. K. Chesterton: *Emmanuel Burden, The Missing Masterpiece, The Postmaster General*. He had taken honors in history at Balliol; his lifelong interest is manifest in his modernization of Lingard's *History of England*, begun in 1927; in his series of biographies of Wolsey, Cranmer, Milton, James II, Richelieu, Danton, Robespierre, and Marie Antoinette; and in his brief *How the Reformation Happened* and *The French Revolution*. He was successful in every form of literature, excepting only the drama. He lectured widely, taught at Fordham and Notre Dame universities on visits to the United States, and wrote for many newspapers and journals. He stopped writing only when incapacitated by a stroke in 1946. He died at his home in Sussex, England, near West Grinstead, on July 24.

J. B. MORTON, *Hilaire Belloc, A Memoir* (New York, Sheed, 1955); ROBERT SPEAIGHT, *The Life of Hilaire Belloc* (New York, Farrar, 1957).

BELLOY, JEAN BAPTISTE DE (1709–1808), cardinal. Born in Morangles, France, on Oct. 9, he was ordained at Paris and received his doctorate in theology there in 1737. He became bishop of Glandèves in 1751, brought peace to the Church by his plea for moderation at the 1755 assembly of the French clergy, and saved the diocese of Marseilles, to which he was transferred, from schism. When the government suppressed his see in 1790, he protested by letter and retired to Chambly. He was the first of the bishops to resign at the request of the pope at the time of the concordat, and was appointed archbishop of Paris by Napoleon. Though ninety, he visited his entire ecclesiastical area and ruled vigorously and well. He became a cardinal in 1805. He died in Paris on June 10; Napoleon erected the monument to him at Notre Dame.

BELLUDI, BL. LUKE (1200–1285). Born in Padua, Italy, of a wealthy family, he joined St. Francis of Assisi in that city when he was twenty. He was one of the two friars present at the death of St. Antony of Padua and was instrumental in erecting the basilica in his honor. His cult was confirmed in 1927. F. D. Feb. 17.

BELMONT, FRANÇOIS VACHON DE (1645–1732). Born in Grenoble, France, he became a Sulpician, was sent to Canada in 1680 as a missioner, and in 1700 became fifth superior at Montreal. He built a seminary, wrote a history of Canada, and preached funeral sermons on Marguerite Bourgeoys and Bishop Laval.

BELSON, VEN. THOMAS (d. 1589), martyr. Born in Oxfordshire, England, he studied at Rheims, and was arrested on his return to England near Oxford with his servant Prichard and two priests, George Nicols and Richard Yaxley. They were tried in London, tortured in the Tower, and sent back to Oxford to be executed on July 5 during the Elizabethan persecution.

BELSUNCE DE CASTELMORON, HENRI FRANÇOIS XAVIER DE (1671–1755), bishop. Born in Périgord, France, he studied at Paris and Clermont, became a Jesuit, but left the Society in 1699 to become vicar general of Agen and, in that year, bishop of Marseilles. He distinguished himself during the plague of 1720–21, when the nobility fled but the clergy remained, losing 250 of their number while serving the populace. He was honored by the French king, by Alexander Pope in his *Essay on Man*, by French poets, and by Pope Clement XII. He wrote on the history of his see, translated selections from St. Augustine and Bellarmine, and was active at the Synod of Embrun (1727) and through his later years against Soanen, Colbert of Pamiers, and other Jansenists. He died in Marseilles.

BELZONI, GIAMBATTISTA (1778–1823), explorer. Born in Padua, Italy, he went to Rome at fifteen, studied hydraulics, traveled to Holland, Great Britain, and Egypt. In the latter country he unearthed a bust of Memnon, explored pyramids, discovered mummies and other archaeological treasures, and penetrated Libya. His drawings, *The Tombs of the Kings,* were published in 1829. He died in Gato, Africa, on Dec. 3.

BEMBO, PIETRO (1470–1547), cardinal. Born in Venice on May 20, he studied at Florence, Messina, and Padua, and took up residence at the court of Ferrara. In 1512 he went to Rome with Giuliano de' Medici, served as secretary to Pope Leo X, fell in love with Morosina, and in 1520 retired in ill health to Padua. There he continued his Renaissance enthusiasm for learning, collected books and medals, and was host to most of the brilliant minds of Italy. In 1529 he became historiographer of the republic of Venice, then librarian of St. Mark's, and in 1539 was given a cardinalate by Pope Paul III. He thereupon abandoned his pagan ways, devoted himself to scriptural study, and served as bishop of Gubbio and later of Bergamo. He was respected as one of the most significant men of letters of his day, writing brilliant correspondence in Latin and Italian; a history of Venice from 1487 to 1513; a dialogue on Platonic love, dedicated to Lucrezia Borgia; a study of the Italian language; and several volumes of poems. He also edited Petrarch's Italian poems and Dante's *terza rima*. He died in Rome on Jan. 18.

BÉNARD, LAURENT (1573–1620), founder. Born in Nevers, he became a Cluniac Benedictine, studied at Paris, and suggested the formation of the Congregation of St. Maur, which was approved in 1618. He wrote on monastic history and discipline.

BENAVENTE Y MARTINEZ, JACINTO (1866–1954), dramatist. Born in Madrid on Aug. 12, son of Mariano Benavente, a physician, he studied law at the university there, and changed his interest to literature when his father died in 1885. He had known José Echegaray, who often visited his house as a patient, and through him became interested in the theater. He traveled with acting troupes and with the circus, published *Versos* in 1893, and in 1894 saw the first of more than 150 plays, *El nido ajeno*, produced. He was more successful with *Gente conocida* (*In Society*; 1896), and became widely known for *The Bonds of Interest* (the first production of the New York Theater Guild, in 1919), *La malquerida* (*Passion Flower*), *La noche del Sábado* (*Saturday Night*), *La Princesa Bébé*, and *La Gobernadora*. John Garrett Underhill has translated sixteen of his plays in four series (1917–24); others in English are *The Smile of Mona Lisa*, *Brute Force*, and *At Close Range*. His range includes humor, satire, subtle allegory, revelations of peasant and court life, all marked by penetrating psychological insight. He also wrote criticism (*Table Talk*, *Marginalia*, and *The Popular Theatre*), edited the journal *La Vida Literaria*, and established a children's theater, for which he wrote many plays such as *El prin-*

cipe que todo lo aprendió en los libros. He was elected to the Spanish Academy in 1913, became a director of the Spanish Theatre in 1920, was awarded the Nobel Prize in 1922, and honored in his own country before and after its civil war. He died in Madrid on July 14.

WALTER STARKIE, *Jacinto Benavente* (Oxford, 1924).

BENAVIDES, ALONZO (17th century), bishop. Born on the island of San Miguel, off the coast of El Salvador, Central America, he became a Franciscan in Mexico in 1603, served at several missions, was custos of New Mexican missions, wrote two valuable ethnological studies on the Indians of New Mexico, returned to Spain in 1630, and was appointed archbishop of Goa, Portuguese India.

BENAVIDES, PEDRERIAS DE (16th century). Born in Toro, Spain, he became a physician, went to Honduras in 1550, and directed the hospital "del Amor de Dios" in Mexico City from about 1553 to about 1561, when he returned to Spain. In 1567 he published *Secretos de chirurgía* at Valladolid on Indian medicinal practices.

BENEDETTO DA ROVEZZANO. See Gratini, Benedetto.

BENEDICT I (d. 579), pope. A Roman, son of Boniface, he was imperially confirmed as pope on June 5, 575, nearly eleven months after the death of John III. The marauding Lombards made communications difficult and kept his reign from being a peaceful one. A famine followed, and Benedict died in Rome on July 30.

BENEDICT II, ST. (d. 685), pope. Born in Rome, he served Pope SS. Agatho and Leo II and succeeded the latter on June 26, 684, after the see was vacant for nearly a year because imperial approval had not been received. Benedict persuaded Emperor Constantine IV to remove the requirement, making the approval of the clergy and people of Rome sufficient for election. F. D. May 8.

BENEDICT III (d. 858), pope. A learned Roman, son of Peter, he was chosen to succeed Leo IV, who died in July 855, but the legates sent to gain the approval of the emperor supported Anastasius, whom they tried to force on the people in Aug. Most of the city remained faithful to Benedict, who was consecrated on Sept. 29 and condemned the antipope at his first synod. He also censured the Frankish bishops for permitting the dissension which was shaking the Frankish Empire; tried to curb the subdeacon Hubert, brother-in-law of Lothaire II, king of Lorraine, who was responsible for much of the trouble; maintained the balance of ecclesiastical power in the East between Bishop Gregory of Syracuse and Patriarch Ignatius of Constantinople; received the English King Ethelwulf and his son Alfred; and restored the English College and other buildings damaged in the Saracen raid on Rome in 846. He died in Rome on Apr. 17.

BENEDICT IV (d. 903), pope. A Roman, son of Mammalus, he became pope in Jan. or Feb. 900, crowned Louis the Blind as emperor, excommunicated the murderer of Archbishop Fulk of Rheims, and aided Fulda and other monasteries and churches and such areas as Amasia which had suffered from Saracen depredations. He died about July.

BENEDICT V (d. 965). A learned Roman, called Grammaticus, and a cardinal-deacon, he was elected pope on May 22, 964, following the death on May 14 of John XII, who had been deposed by Emperor Otto and replaced by Leo VIII. The Romans would not accept Leo and expelled him. Otto thereupon marched on Rome, seized Benedict on June 23, deposed him at a council in the Lateran at which Leo presided, and carried him a prisoner to Germany. Placed in the care of Archbishop Adaldag of Hamburg-Bremen, he was still acknowledged as pope by many of the German clergy. He died in Hamburg on July 4 and was later buried in Rome. Since Benedict did not seize the papal throne he is listed as a legitimate pope, but if Leo's election was more than imperially valid, then Benedict is, technically, an antipope.

BENEDICT VI (d. 974), pope. A Roman, son of Hildebrand, he was cardinal-archdeacon when selected in Sept. 972 as successor to John XIII, did not receive imperial ratification until four months later, and was consecrated on Jan. 19, 973. A year and a half later he was seized by a group led by the patrician Crescentius and the deacon Boniface Franco, who imprisoned him in Castle Sant' Angelo, and after two months gave orders in June that he be strangled. Boniface then seized the papal throne as antipope Boniface VII.

BENEDICT VII (d. 983), pope. A Roman, son of David, and bishop of Sutri, he was elected pope in Oct. 974 by the clergy and people of Rome and with the approval of Sicco, envoy of Emperor Otto II, who arrived in the city too late to prevent the murder of Pope Benedict VI. He was supported in his position by the emperor, and Boniface (who held the throne in June–July 974) was forced into flight. Benedict worked to lessen the evil of simony, developed monasticism, and aided the Church in Northern Africa. He died on July 10.

BENEDICT VIII (d. 1024), pope. Theophylact, son of Count Gregory of Tusculum, and brother of John XIX, was a layman when he was unwillingly thrust into the papacy on May 18, 1012. He removed antipope Gregory, who claimed the papal throne, and worked for peace at home and abroad. He subjugated the Crescenti, defeated the Saracens, and allied himself to the Normans in southern Italy. He crowned Henry II as emperor, from whom he received confirmation of the donations of Charlemagne and Otto, consecrated the cathedral of Bamberg, and visited Fulda. He held a synod at Pavia in 1022 to initiate opposition to clerical immorality and simony, supported the Cluniac reformation, and encouraged the "truce of God." He died on Apr. 9.

BENEDICT IX (11th century), pope. Nephew of Popes Benedict VIII and John XIX, and also named Theophylact, as was Benedict VIII, Count of Tusculum, he was placed on the papal throne in Oct. 1032 at twenty by his father, Alberic. Havoc resulted. He fought with numerous civil and ecclesiastical leaders and excommunicated those hostile to him; his dissolute life led one faction in Rome to rebel and depose him in 1044. Bishop John of Sabina was elected in his place as Sylvester III but driven out after two months, in Feb. 1045. Benedict then sought to arrange his resignation, some say to marry, and gained the approval of his archpriest John Gratian (Hildebrand), who seemingly approved the precedentless action on the grounds that the papal throne would be better off without its current occupant. Gratian then succeeded, as Gregory VI, but Benedict regretted his step, reclaimed the throne, and sought to depose Gregory. King Henry III intervened and the three popes submitted their resignation at the Council of Sutri in Dec. 1046. Clement II was elected in their place, but when he died within ten months, Benedict stepped in for the third time and ruled from Nov. 8, 1047, to July 17, 1048, when he was finally driven from the city. If Benedict's triple stepping down (in 1044, in his arrangement with Gratian, and at the synod of 1046), are to be set aside, then Sylvester III, Gregory VI, and Clement II are to be considered antipopes. Tradition has it that Benedict formally resigned his office and, under the direction of Abbot Bartholomew, died as a penitent at the monastery of Grottaferrata.

BENEDICT X. There was no pope of this number.

BENEDICT X (d. 1059?), antipope. A Roman named Giovanni, he ruled as antipope from Apr. 5, 1058, to Jan. 24, 1059, following the reign of Pope Stephen X; he was displaced by Nicholas II.

BENEDICT XI, BL. (1240–1304), pope. Born Nicholas Boccasini in Treviso, he became a Dominican when seventeen, was appointed professor at Venice and Bologna in 1268, became prior provincial for Lombardy, and in 1296 was elected ninth master general of his order. Two years later he became cardinal-bishop of Ostia. He was one of the two cardinals who supported Pope Boniface VIII in his struggle against the infamous charges of King

Philip of France, and on the death of Boniface he was elected pope on Oct. 22 and consecrated on Oct. 27, 1303. He attempted to heal the breach between Philip and the papacy but died, at Perugia, before he could accomplish much. He was beatified in 1736. F. D. July 7.

BENEDICT XII (d. 1342), pope. Jacques Fournier was born in Saverdun, Toulouse, France, became a Cistercian monk at Boulbonne, was stationed at Fontfroide, received his doctorate in theology at Paris, and succeeded his uncle, Arnold Novelli, as abbot of Fontfroide in 1310. He became bishop of Palmiers in 1317, was transferred to the see of Mirepoix in 1327, and made a cardinal in that year. When Pope John XXII died, the cardinals demanded of the most likely candidate, Cardinal de Comminges, a promise to continue the papal residence at Avignon; when he refused, the conclave chose Fournier, obscure but French, on Dec. 20, 1334. He was consecrated as Benedict XII on Jan. 8, 1335. Although he wished to return to Rome, civil war and famine worked against his return; he restored St. Peter's basilica and the Lateran, sent aid in large quantities to the suffering Roman populace, and set about removing as many abuses as possible. He dismissed many hangers-on at the papal court, revoked the evil custom of naming commendatory abbots and holders of benefices, sought to end pluralities, and modified the ecclesiastical tax system. He was active in the support of monasticism and increased the efforts of the inquisition against heresy, though he was unusually lenient toward heretics. In the spiritual realm he enjoyed a successful reign; in the political world, for which he had little tolerance, he failed. He built the elaborate and costly papal palace at Avignon and too often took political direction from King Philip IV of France, particularly against Emperor Louis of Bavaria, who thereupon allied himself with Edward III of England against Philip and the pope. Nothing was gained, since Philip eventually allied himself with Louis against the pope. Philip refused to live up to his promise to aid the crusade and appropriated money collected for supplying the crusading force. Benedict was violently satirized by his friend Petrarch, chiefly because he failed to return to Rome. He died in Avignon on Apr. 25.

BENEDICT XIII (1649–1730), pope. Pietro Francesco Orsini was born on Feb. 2 to Ferdinando and Giovanna Frangipani Orsini, became a Dominican at sixteen (taking the name Vincenzo Maria), a professor at Venice at twenty-one, and, against his wishes, a cardinal at twenty-three. In 1675 he was named archbishop of Siponto, governed his see well, was active in charities, visited all communities, and left an influential pastoral letter when he was transferred to Cesena in 1680, another poor

diocese. He went to Benevento in 1686, building hospitals and churches, and caring for the victims of two major earthquakes. At four conclaves he had voted with those cardinals who were opposed to all considerations of worldly prudence; on May 29, 1724, he was elected pope, again in spite of efforts to the contrary, and was consecrated on June 4. He was firm in reforming ecclesiastical discipline, formed a commission to consider the reorganization of seminary education, and energetically opposed luxury. In temporal matters he had difficulty with Victor Amadeus of Savoy, King John V of Portugal, and the excommunicated Henry IV of France, but avoided war. He always placed such confidence in those with whom he had dealings that he was often gulled and exploited while an archbishop; he suffered particularly during his papacy from the greed of Cardinal Nicolò Coscia, whom he had appointed his coadjutor at Benevento. Benedict died in Rome on Feb. 21.

BENEDICT XIV (1675–1758), pope. Prospero Lorenzo Lambertini was born in Bologna on Mar. 31 to Marcello and Lucrezia Bulgarini Lambertini, studied in Rome, took his doctorate in civil and canon law at nineteen, became a papal advocate in 1700, promoter of the faith in 1708, canon theologian at the Vatican in 1712, titular bishop of Theodosia in 1725, and bishop of Ancona in 1727. He was named cardinal in 1728 and archbishop of Bologna in 1731. He directed his sees with close attention, devoted himself to scholarship, and was widely admired for his learning. His election to the papacy on Aug. 17, 1740, broke a six-month deadlock; he was consecrated pope on Aug. 22. A new edition of the Roman Martyrology was issued with his approval in 1752, but the notes Fabio Danzetto prepared on proposed changes in the breviary were so full that Benedict made no changes. He wrote the regulations for the process of beatification and canonization; on the mass, feast days, the oriental rite; against superstitious images; a collection of significant pastoral letters, *Institutiones ecclesiasticae*; on diocesan administration, *De synoda diocesana*; a *Thesaurus* of the Roman congregations; collections of bulls, letters, and cases in canon law. He remained in contact with major scholars, writers, and artists through his reign. He founded four academies for the study of Christian and Roman antiquities, the history of the councils and of canon law and the liturgy, established a museum, and commissioned a cataloguing of the manuscripts of the Vatican Library. He maintained good relations with the Eastern churches, recognized the Melchite leader and approved the national council which unified the Maronites, and issued bulls to end the tolerance of Chinese and Malabar heathen customs among the Christians, including missionaries, of those lands. He made great concessions to Portugal, Spain, and Sardinia regarding allotment of benefices and taxes on ecclesiastics; brought an end to the quarrel between Naples and the Knights of Malta; approved the kingship of Prussia for the elector of Brandenburg; and got along well with the Sultan. His encyclical *Ex omnibus christiani orbis* insisted on the authority of the earlier *Unigenitus*, which upset much of Europe, France in particular, but demanded punishment only for those who were loud and notorious in their objections; hitherto, all who could not accept *Unigenitus* were barred from the sacraments. Only the political struggle between Venice and the emperor over Aquileia remained unsettled at the pope's death in Rome on May 3.

BENEDICT XIII (1328–1423), antipope. Pedro de Luna was born in Illueca, Aragon, Spain, studied law at Montpellier, received his doctorate there, and taught canon law. He was created a cardinal in 1375 by Pope Gregory XI, voted for Pope Urban VI in the conclave of 1378, but later in the year, convinced that the threats under which the election had been conducted invalidated it, withdrew his allegiance and joined a group of non-Italian cardinals at Fondi, who on Sept. 20 elected uncanonically Robert of Geneva pope (antipope Clement VII), creating a schism and the Avignon line of popes. He served as legate to Spain and Portugal, securing their support for Clement, and in 1393 was legate to France, Brabant, and the British Isles. When Clement died, de Luna was elected at Avignon on Sept. 28, 1394 (antipope Benedict XIII), was ordained on Oct. 3 and consecrated on Oct. 11, and promised to end the schism by renouncing his papal throne if necessary. But he spent the next two decades scheming to end the schism and to have himself universally recognized as pope. In 1409 cardinals of both obediences (Avignon and Rome) met at Pisa, voted to depose both popes, and elected Alexander V, thus creating a third pope. Pope Gregory XII refused to recognize the legality of the proceedings, and Benedict refused to accept the decision. He took up residence at Perpignan, was formally deposed by the Council of Constance on July 26, 1417, but continued to claim the papal throne until his death at Peñiscola, Spain, on May 23.

BENEDICT XV (1854–1922), pope. Giacomo della Chiesa was born in Genoa on Nov. 21, studied at its university, went to seminaries in Rome, including the Gregorian, was ordained in 1873, and took his doctorate in civil and canon law in 1879. He served Bishop Rampolla as secretary there and at Madrid, was undersecretary of state in 1901-7, became bishop of Bologna in 1907, cardinal in 1914, and later that year, on Sept. 3, was elected pope, being consecrated on Sept. 6. His pontif-

icate was saddened by World War I, reflected in several encyclicals, notably *Ad beatissimi apostolorum principis* (1914) and *Pacem Dei munus pulcherrimum* (1921), which expressed hope for a successful peace conference. He often offered his services to mediate the struggle and worked earnestly on behalf of prisoners, refugees, and the wounded. Many of his tangible proposals for peace made in his message of Aug. 1, 1917, were introduced in the final treaty, but he was personally ignored and his correspondence unacknowledged by the Allied leaders. His reign was also marked by the revision of the canon-law code, support of the teachings of St. Thomas Aquinas, condemnation of modernism, and enlargement of mission areas. He died in Rome on Jan. 22.

BENEDICT, ST. (480?–547?), abbot. Born in the Sabine town of Norcia (Nursia), he was sent to Rome to be educated, but was so repelled by the vice of the schools and streets that he withdrew to Enfide and later to mountainous Subiaco. There he lived three years in a cave, served on occasion by a monk named Romanus. Shepherds and others came to listen to his wisdom. For a while he directed a monastic community at Vicovars, but left when his stern discipline led them to try to poison him. He returned to Subiaco, established twelve monasteries under individual priors, introduced manual work, and then, about 530, retired to Monte Cassino. Disciples flocked to him there, as well, and he carefully organized a large monastic settlement, built guesthouses, and finally wrote a rule, evolving a plan of prayer, reading, work, community life, and moderate asceticism distinct from the extremely austere and basically penitential form of Eastern monasticism. His Rule, which he may have written specifically for those on Monte Cassino or, at the request of Pope St. Hormisdas, for all Europe, stressed humility, obedience, and zeal, and affected Western spiritual life for six centuries. Benedict was active in caring for the sick and poor of the area, and in attempting to alleviate the sufferings resulting from the invasion of the Lombard Totila. Most of the details of his life are from the second book of St. Gregory the Great's *Dialogues*. F. D. Mar. 21 (also, July 11). JUSTIN MC CANN, *St. Benedict* (Garden City, N.Y., Image Books, 1955); CUTHBERT BUTLER, *Benedictine Monachism* (London, 1942).

BENEDICT, ST. (d. 654?), bishop. He is said to have been bishop of Sebaste, Samaria, who escaped the persecution of Julian the Apostate, and built a hermitage near Poitiers, France. F. D. Oct. 23.

BENEDICT, ST. (d. 820?). He was bishop of Angers, France, during the reign of Louis the Pious. F. D. July 15.

BENEDICT, ST. (d. 997), martyr. *See* Adalbert, St.

BENEDICT, ST. (d. 1003?), martyr. A friend of St. Bruno of Querfurt, who wrote an account of his martyrdom, he was sent with four other Italian Benedictines—Christian, Isaac, John, and Matthew—to evangelize the Slavs of Pomerania. They were murdered in Kazimierz, near Gnesen, Poland, on Nov. 11, and are venerated as the Five Polish Brothers. F. D. Nov. 12.

BENEDICT, ST. (d. 1020?), martyr. *See* Andrew, St.

BENEDICT, ST. (d. 1113?), bishop. He was a Benedictine monk in Cagliari, Sardinia, served as bishop of Dolia, from 1107 to 1112, resigned and retired to his abbey. F. D. Feb. 17.

BENEDICT OF ANIANE, ST. (750?–821), abbot. Son of Aigulf of Maguelone, he served in the court and army of King Pepin, became a hermit, then a Benedictine at St. Seine near Bijon, and again a hermit on his estate at Languedoc. Joined by a number of other holy men who had also left their monasteries to live more austere lives, he became their superior and built their monastery for them. In time he became inspector of monasteries throughout the empire and adviser to King Louis the Pious. He was a force at the reforming Council of Aachen (817), drew up statutes and a code of rules which elaborated on the original discipline of St. Benedict of Nursia, wrote many homilies, and compiled a collection (Codex regularum) of existing monastic laws. F. D. Feb. 11.

BENEDICT DELL' ANTELLA, ST. (d. 1268). A merchant in Florence, Italy, he became one of the seven founders of the Servites, taking the name Manettus. He was provincial in Tuscany, then general of his order, attended the Council of Lyons in 1246, introduced the order to France at the request of St. Louis, and retired to Monte Senario, Italy, where he died. F. D. Aug. 20 (also, Feb. 12).

BENEDICT BISCOP, ST. (628–690). A courtier serving King Oswy of Northumbria, he retired at twenty-five to make several pilgrimages to Rome, became a monk at Lérins, and later was sent back to England with SS. Theodore and Adrian. He directed the monastery of SS. Peter and Paul at Canterbury for two years, went again to Rome, returned with a large library and art collection, and in 674 built St. Peter's monastery at Wearmouth. Its church was of stone, with a lead roof, and windows of glass—the work of imported French artisans. In 685 he built at Jarrow, on land given him by King Egfrid, the monastery of St. Paul. On his last trip to Rome he gathered more treasures and also brought back a Vatican abbot and musician named John to introduce Gregorian chant. The library he built up served St. Bede. St. Benedict (whose real name was Biscop Baducing) was crippled by paralysis in his last three years. F. D. Jan. 12 (sometimes, Feb. 13).

BENEDICT THE BRIDGE-BUILDER, ST. (d. 1184). A shepherd near the Rhone River, he announced to the bishop of Avignon that he had been told in a vision to build a bridge. He began the construction of a stone span in 1177, miraculously overcame obstacles before his death, and was buried in a chapel erected upon it when it was completed in 1188. F. D. Apr. 14.

BENEDICT CRISPUS, ST. (d. 725). He was archbishop of Milan for forty-five years and is listed in the Roman Martyrology under Mar. 11.

BENEDICT THE HERMIT, ST. (d. 550?). A recluse in Campagna, Italy, he was placed in an oven and left by the invading Goths, but was rescued, unharmed, a day later. He may be the same as a St. Benedict venerated at Lavello, also on Mar. 23.

BENEDICT THE MOOR, ST. (1526–1589). Born of Negro serfs near Messina, Sicily, he joined a young hermit named Lanzi and settled with other solitaries near Palermo, and was chosen superior. After about sixteen years Pope Pius IV ordered the group to accept some established rule, and they became Franciscans. Benedict became a laybrother cook at the friary of St. Mary. In 1578 he was its superior, though he could neither read nor write; he later served as vicar and as master of novices. In his last years, by his own choice, he again became cook, but his hours were also filled by visits from the sick, disturbed, and poor. He was canonized in 1807 and is patron of the Negroes of North America. F. D. Apr. 5.

BENEDICT OF PETERBOROUGH (d. 1193). Educated at Oxford, he became in 1174 chancellor to Archbishop Richard of Canterbury and in 1175 prior of Christ Church, Cambridge. Abbot of Peterborough from 1177 until his death, he enlarged its library by many manuscripts accessions and transcriptions and wrote a history of Thomas à Becket.

BENEDICT REVELLI, ST. (d. 900), bishop. A Benedictine monk at Santa Maria dei Fonti, and then a hermit on an island off Genoa, he was chosen bishop of Albenga, Liguria, in 870. His cult was approved by Pope Gregory XVI. F. D. Feb. 12.

BENEDICT RICASOLI, BL. (d. 1107?). Born in Coltiboni, Italy, he became a Benedictine at a monastery built by his parents and later was permitted to live nearby as a hermit. His cult was confirmed in 1907. F. D. Jan. 20.

BENEDICTA, ST. (d. 362), martyr. *See* Priscus, St.

BENEDICTI, JEAN (16th century). A Franciscan, he was attached to the province of Tours and Poitiers, France, became secretary of the order, toured Europe and the Holy Land, wrote on penance and exorcism, and was a distinguished linguist.

BENEDICTUS POLONUS (13th century). A Franciscan Friar Minor, he wrote a chronicle of a journey to the Tatars about 1245, which contains a letter from the khan to Pope Innocent IV; the work was first published in 1839 at Paris.

BENEFATTI, BL. JACOPO (d. 1338), bishop. A native of Mantua, Italy, he became a Dominican and the friend and adviser of his master general, Nicholas Boccasini, who became Pope Benedict XI and about 1303 appointed James to the see of Mantua, where he became known for his care of the poor. His cult was confirmed in 1859. F. D. Nov. 26.

BENEN. *See* Benignus, St. (d. 467).

BENETTIS, JEREMIAH (d. 1774). A Capuchin at Piedmont, Italy, he wrote a study of astronomy and ancient religious rites, a biblical commentary, and a defense of the primacy of the pope.

BENGTASSON, JÖNS OXENSTJERNA (1417–1467), bishop. A priest in Upsala, Sweden, he was appointed archbishop of that city in 1448. He reigned during a period of civil strife engendered by bad government under a new Scandinavian union. The archbishop three times led popular opposition to intensive taxation, twice acted as regent, and twice was forced into exile. While he earnestly defended the rights and property of the Church, he also was partisan toward his own noble family, against which one of the kings with whom he fought, Karl Knutsson, had long been at enmity.

BENGY, ANATOLE DE (1824–1871), martyr. Born in Bourges, France, on Sept. 19, he studied at Brugelette and became a Jesuit in 1843. He was a chaplain during the Crimean and Franco-Prussian wars, teaching in the years between. On April 3, 1871, the French Commune sent troops to seize those at the school of Ste. Geneviève; with two Jesuits and forty others he was executed on May 26.

BENIGNUS, ST. (3rd century?), martyr. An actual martyr, venerated particularly at Dijon, France, he has been incorrectly listed as a disciple of St. Polycarp in Smyrna and slain during the reign of Marcus Aurelius. F. D. Nov. 1.

BENIGNUS, ST. (d. 303?), martyr. He was a priest slain at Todi, Italy, during the Diocletian persecution. F. D. Feb. 13.

BENIGNUS, ST. (d. 467), bishop. Son of a chieftain in Meath, Ireland, he became a disciple of St. Patrick (he was called "St. Patrick's Psalmsinger") and succeeded him as chief bishop of Ireland. He evangelized Clare and Kerry and is reputed to have ruled a monastery at Drumlease for twenty years. According to William of Malmesbury, he joined St. Patrick in Glastonbury in 460, but there is no basis for this story. He is also called Benen. F. D. Nov. 9.

BENIGNUS, ST. (d. 477?). He was arch-

bishop of Milan, Italy, during the occupation of the city by Odoacer. F. D. Nov. 20.

BENIGNUS, ST. (6th century). He was a bishop who was permitted to give up his see and live in seclusion at Utrecht. F. D. June 28.

BENIGNUS, ST. (d. 725). A Benedictine monk at Fontenelle, France, he was exiled, lived at Flay, where he became abbot of a group of followers, and later directed both houses. F. D. Mar. 20.

BENIGNUS, ST. (13th century), martyr. He and other Cistercian monks were murdered by the Tatars at an abbey in Breslau. F. D. June 20.

BENIGNUS VISDOMINI, BL. (d. 1236). A priest in Florence, he became a sinner, repented, and joined the Vallombrosans at the abbey of Vallombrosa, Italy. Although he became abbot general, his past so disturbed him that he retired and died as a hermit. F. D. July 17.

BENILDIS, ST. (d. 853), martyr. She was burned to death at Cordova, Spain, by the Moors on the day after St. Athanasius was slain there. F. D. June 15.

BENINCASA, BL. (d. 1194). A Benedictine, he ruled as eighth abbot of La Cava, near Salerno, from 1171 to 1194, and was beatified in 1928. F. D. Jan. 10.

BENINCASA, BL. (1376–1426). A member of an important Florentine family, he became a Servite, then at twenty-five retired as a hermit near Siena. His cult was confirmed in 1829. F. D. May 11.

BENINCASA, CATHERINE. *See* Catherine of Siena, St.

BENJAMIN, ST. (d. 421?), martyr. When Bishop Abdas burned the Temple of Fire and refused to rebuild it, King Yezdigerd of Persia and his successor Varanes carried out a forty-year persecution of the Christians. One who suffered extreme tortures before his death, when he refused to promise not to preach the gospel, was a deacon named Benjamin. F. D. Mar. 31.

BENJAMIN, CLETUS J. (1909–1961), bishop. Born in Old Forge, Pennsylvania, on May 2, he studied at St. Charles Borromeo seminary, Philadelphia, and the North American College in Rome where he was ordained in 1935. After further study at the Gregorian, he served as Cardinal Dougherty's secretary in 1938–43, was chancellor of Philadelphia in 1945–54, and was appointed titular bishop of Binda and auxiliary of Philadelphia in 1960. He died in Philadelphia on May 16.

BENKERT, FRANZ GEORG (1790–1859), apologist. Born in Nordheim, Germany, on Sept. 25, he studied at Würzburg, was ordained in 1816, became assistant rector of the seminary there and, later, dean of its cathedral. To combat Josephinism and to arouse a strong theological sense in the clergy, he founded and edited three pastoral periodicals between 1822 and 1840. While appealing to younger priests, he alienated many of the older clergy, dropped his editorial posts, and devoted his last years to the study of local history. He died in Coburg, Bavaria, on May 20.

BENNETT, JOHN GEORGE (1891–1957), bishop. Born in Dunnington, Indiana, on Jan. 20, he studied at St. Joseph's and St. Meinrad's, Indiana, and was ordained in 1914. He engaged in parish work in Fort Wayne until 1929, when he was appointed pastor of St. Joseph's in Garret. He was appointed first bishop of Lafayette in 1944, where he reigned until his death on Nov. 20.

BENNO, BL. (d. 940), bishop. A canon in Strassburg, he became a recluse at the Swiss hermitage of St. Meinrad, restored the shrine to Mary there, and eventually founded the Benedictine monastery of Einsiedeln at Schwyz, Switzerland. He became bishop of Metz in 927, succeeded in reforming much of the area, but was blinded by a group whom he had censured, and returned to Einsiedeln. F. D. Aug. 3.

BENNO, BL. (d. 1088), archbishop. Born in Löhningen, Swabia, he was educated at Reichenau by Bl. Herman the Cripple, saved the cathedral of Speyer from collapsing, and was made official architect by Emperor Henry III. In 1047 he was put in charge of the cathedral school in Hildesheim, accompanied the emperor on his campaign against the Hungarians, and then became provost of the cathedral of Gozlar. In 1068 he was appointed bishop of Osnabrück. Eight years later he became involved in the struggle between Emperor Henry IV and Pope St. Gregory VII, siding with the former. He was excommunicated, but later absolved when the German bishops went to Canossa to ask forgiveness. He died at the Benedictine monastery he had founded at Iburg, near Osnabrück, Germany. F. D. July 12.

BENNO, ST. (1010–1106), bishop. Born in Hildesheim, Germany, and educated in the abbey of St. Michael, he became a canon at Gozlar in Hanover, chaplain to Emperor Henry III, and, in 1066, bishop of Meissen. He was imprisoned for a year for backing the nobility against Henry IV, supported Pope Gregory VII, was deposed by the bishops who sold out to the emperor, shifted his allegiance to the antipope Guibert, and appears to have been heavily enmeshed in contemporary politics. Sources, however, are untrustworthy. In his last years he was a missioner to the Wends. He was canonized in 1523. F. D. June 16.

BENOÎT, MICHEL (1715–1774), scientist. Born in Autun or Dijon, France, on Oct. 8, he became a Jesuit in 1737, studied astronomy at Paris, and went to Peking, China, about 1744.

Although missioners generally were hunted down, Benoît's scientific skills allowed him to serve Emperor Kien Lung for thirty years. He designed the fountains and copies of European houses for the royal gardens, taught the emperor the use of the telescope, engraved maps of the world and the Chinese Empire, printing the latter from copper plates, translated the *Imitation of Christ* into Chinese, and wrote many observant letters to colleagues in France and elaborate *Mémoires*. He died in Peking on Oct. 23.

BENSON, ROBERT HUGH (1871–1914), novelist. Born at Wellington College, England, on Nov. 18, son of Edward, archbishop of Canterbury, he studied at Eton and Cambridge, took Anglican orders in 1894, and served in several parishes and missions until his conversion in 1903. He was ordained in Rome in 1904, was chaplain at Cambridge to 1908, and was given permission to retire and write. Historical novels include *By What Authority* (1904), *Come Rack, Come Rope* (1912), and *Lord of the World*; he also wrote poetry, plays, sermons, and *The Friendship of Christ* and other devotional works. He died in Salford on Oct. 19.

BENTIVENGHI, MATTEO (1235?–1302), cardinal. Born in Aquasparta, Umbria, Italy, he became a Franciscan, received his master's degree in theology at Paris, and taught at Bologna. In 1280 he was appointed lector in the curia, was elected general of his order in 1287, and created a cardinal in 1288, and then cardinal-bishop of Porto and grand penitentiary. He acted as Pope Boniface VIII's ambassador in 1297 and 1300 to Lombardy, Romagna, and Florence in an unsuccessful attempt to establish peace between the Guelphs and Ghibellines. He died in Rome on Oct. 29. He is also known as Matteo of Aquasparta.

BENTIVOGLIO, CORNELIO (1668–1732), cardinal. Born in Ferrara, Italy, he was made archbishop of Carthage. Sent to Paris in 1712 as papal nuncio, he failed in his dealings with the Jansenists and was recalled in 1715. In 1719 he was made cardinal and, in 1726, Spanish minister plenipotentiary at Rome, which position he held until his death.

BENTIVOGLIO, GUIDO (1579–1644), cardinal. Born in Ferrara, Italy, he studied at Padua, served as papal nuncio to Flanders in 1607 and to France in 1617, was quite successful in smoothing Huguenot-Catholic relations, and was made a cardinal in 1621. King Louis XIII appointed him protector of French interests at Rome, a position he retained until 1641 when he became bishop of Palestrina. He died in Rome.

BENTIVOGLIO DE BONIS, ST. (d. 1232). Born in San Severino, Italy, he was one of the first to follow St. Francis of Assisi, is mentioned in the *Fioretti*, and died on Dec. 25. His cult was confirmed by Pope Pius IX. F. D. Jan. 2.

BENTLEY, JOHN FRANCIS (1839–1902), architect. Born in Doncaster, Yorkshire, England, he became an architect's apprentice at sixteen, and set out for himself in 1858. He was an effective draftsman and stone carver, much interested in mediaeval design. His most important monuments are the church of the Holy Rood, Watford; Beaumont College chapel, Old Windsor; St. Anne's cathedral, Leeds; the Sacred Heart chapel at the Jesuit church on Farm St., London; and, as a climax, Westminster cathedral, London. He died in London on Mar. 2.

BENTNEY, WILLIAM (1609–1692). Born in Cheshire, England, he became a Jesuit in 1630 and was sent on the English mission in 1640, where he worked with success for forty-two years. Arrested for administering the sacraments, he was condemned to death and imprisoned; three years later James II released him, but he was rearrested in 1688 and left in Leicester jail, where he died on Oct. 30.

BENVENUTI, GIOVANNI BATTISTA (1490?–1525?), painter. A student of the work of Raphael and Bagnacavallo at Bologna in 1512–13, he executed paintings for churches in his native Ferrara area. His work is so like that of Garofalo that critics have often confused their paintings. He was known as "L'Ortolano" because his father was a gardener.

BENVENUTO, BL. (d. 1232). Born in Gubbio, Umbria, Italy, he was an unlearned soldier who in 1222 became a Franciscan Friar Minor, devoted his life to the care of lepers, and had many supernatural gifts. His cult was approved for Venice and Amalfi by Pope Gregory IX in 1236. F. D. June 27.

BENVENUTO MARENI, BL. (d. 1289). Born in Recanati, near Loreto, Italy, he became a Franciscan laybrother, known for his humble devotion to kitchen tasks and for his supernatural gifts. His cult was confirmed by Pope Pius VII. F. D. May 21.

BENVENUTO SCOTIVOLI, ST. (d. 1282), bishop. Born in Ancona, Italy, he took his degree in law at Bologna, was named archdeacon of Ancona, and became bishop of Osimo. He became a Franciscan at the time of his consecration. He was canonized by Pope Martin IV. F. D. Mar. 22.

BENZIGER, CHARLES (1799–1873), publisher. Born in Feldkirch, Austria, son of Joseph Benziger, he developed his father's book business, began to issue hand-colored lithographs of religious pictures, founded the *Einsiedelner Kalender* in 1840, published a popular magazine, *The Pilgrim*, and served as president of the canton of Schwyz. A sales branch of the firm was opened in New York City in 1853. His brother Nicholas was the technical half of

the firm of Benziger Brothers, developing new methods of bookbinding and experimenting with the latest printing and engraving processes at the company's plant in Einsiedeln. When the brothers retired in 1860, the firm was continued by Nicholas' sons (Nicholas, Adelrich, and Louis) and Charles's (Charles, Martin, and J. N. Adelrich). They began *Alte und Neue Welt* (1867), the first illustrated popular Catholic magazine in Germany, and began publishing school texts, bible histories, and books of devotional reading. J. N. Adelrich Benziger (d. 1878) and Louis (d. 1896) developed the New York branch as a publishing house and opened offices in Cincinnati and Chicago. The American company later became totally independent.

BENZIGER, JOSEPH CHARLES (1762–1841), publisher. Born in Einsiedeln, Switzerland, he opened a religious-articles store, went to Austria during the French Revolution, returned in 1800 to a pillaged area, became a bookseller and publisher, and in 1833 was succeeded by his sons.

BENZONI, GIROLAMO (b. 1519?). Born in Milan, Italy, he went to Central and South America in 1541, apparently as a trader, and returned to Italy in 1556. His *History of the New World* (1565) abounds in historical errors and is noted only for his uncontrolled hatred of the Spanish in America and an uncritical attack on the treatment of Indians. Because of the force of his diatribe, he had considerable contemporary appeal; his distortion of fact, suppression of evidence, and basic ignorance make the book almost worthless.

BEOADH, ST. (d. 520?), bishop. To the name of the Irishman Aedh was prefixed *bo* (meaning "especially holy"); he became bishop of Ardcarne, Roscommon, and was long venerated on Mar. 8.

BEOCCA, ST. (d. 870?), martyr. Benedictine abbot of Chertsey, England, he was brutally murdered during a Danish raid, together with ninety monks, and a priest named Hethor. Abbot Hedda was slain with his community of eighty-four at Peterborough; Torthred and three hermits died near Thorney. These and other martyred victims of the barbarians are venerated on Apr. 10.

BERACH, ST. (6th century). He was admired for his sanctity by St. Patrick, became a follower of St. Kevin, and was abbot-founder of Clusin-Coirpte, Connaught, Ireland. He is the patron of Kilbarry, near Dublin. F. D. Feb. 15.

BERARD, ST. (d. 888), martyr. *See* Ageranus, St.

BERARD OF CARBIO, ST. (d. 1220), martyr. An Italian Franciscan priest, he sought actively to convert the Moors, first in Spain, then in Morocco, where he and four companions were frightfully tortured and then beheaded by Sultan Abu Jacob. SS. Otto and

Peter were also priests; SS. Accursio and Adjuto were laybrothers; all were canonized in 1481. F. D. Jan. 16.

BERARDI, CARLO SEBASTIANO (1719–1786), canonist. Born in Oneglia, Italy, on Aug. 26, he studied theology at Savona, was ordained, took his law degree at Turin and joined its faculty in 1749. His four-volume edition of Gratian's *Decretum* (1752–57) was standard until Agostino's was issued. He wrote several other treatises on the theory and practice of canon law, not all of which are fully competent.

BERARDO, ST. (12th century), cardinal. Of the noble family of the counts of Marsi, he studied at Monte Cassino, became pontifical governor of the Campagna, and was so firm in his administration of justice there that he was imprisoned by Pietro Colonna. Pope Paschal II made him bishop of Marsi and a cardinal.

BERARIUS, ST. (7th century). He was bishop of Le Mans, France, in 680. F. D. Oct. 17.

BERAULT-BERCASTEL, ANTOINE HENRI DE (1720–1794?), historian. Born in Briey, Lorraine, on Nov. 22, he was ordained a Jesuit, but left the Society to serve as a parish priest at Omerville and Noyon. He wrote a scholarly twenty-four-volume *History of the Church* (up to the year 1721), which is good except for the late years. It was brought up to 1844 by Hevrion; a condensation was edited by Gams (1854–60). He died in Noyon, France.

BERCEO, GONZALO DE (1195?–1265?), poet. He became a Benedictine priest at San Millán, Rioja, Spain, wrote saints' lives, religious poems, hymns, and a collection of narrative poems on the Virgin Mary.

BERCHAN. *See* Berthane, St.

BERCHARIUS, ST. (d. 696). A Benedictine monk at Luxeuil, he became first abbot of Hautvilliers, and founded the monastery of Moutier-en-Der and the convent of Puelle-Moutier. He was stabbed to death by a monk he had censured, and died on Mar. 26. F. D. Oct. 16.

BERCHEURE, PIERRE (1290–1362). Born in St. Pierre du Chemin, France, he became a Benedictine, served at Avignon for twelve years, and in 1354 was made prior of St. Eligius at Paris. He wrote moral commentaries and translated Livy; his principal work, widely popular for centuries, was *Reportorium morale*, an alphabetical list of biblical words with moral commentaries on each.

BERCHMANS, ST. JOHN (1599–1621). The son of a shoemaker, he was born in Diest, Brabant, on Mar. 13, entered the Jesuit college of Malines in 1615, and joined the Society the following year. He was sent to Rome in 1618 for his novitiate and died there on Aug. 13. His holiness impressed all with whom he came in contact, and his stress on perfection in little things anticipated St. Thérèse's "little way." He was canonized in 1888 and is the patron of young altar boys. F. D. Nov. 26.

BERCTUN, ST. (d. 733). A follower of St. John of Beverley, he became first abbot of the Benedictine monastery of Beverley, England. F. D. Sept. 24.

BEREGISUS, ST. (8th century). Confessor to Pepin of Herstal, he founded the Benedictine monastery of St. Hubert, in the Ardennes, France. F. D. Oct. 2.

BERENGARIUS (999?–1088). Born in Tours, France, he was educated there and under Fulbert at Chartres. He was a brilliant and independent student, who, on Fulbert's death in 1029, took charge of the school of St. Martin at Tours. He attracted many brilliant followers. He was appointed archdeacon of Angers in 1039, but remained at Tours. About 1047, Berengarius was censured for his interpretation of the Eucharist as no more than a figure of Christ. When he appealed to the writings of John Scotus Erigena, Lanfranc declared them heretical. The reply of Berengarius was read and condemned at a council at Rome in 1050 which Lanfranc was attending, and he was ordered to appear before a council at Vercelli. Imprisoned by King Henry I, titular abbot of St. Martin's, he was unable to attend that council and his doctrine was officially condemned. At the Council of Tours (1055) and a council at Rome (1059), Berengarius personally signed professions of faith and accepted transubstantiation, but on his return lapsed into heresy. He was condemned at three later councils, again retracted his opinions at Lateran councils (1078–79), attacked the traditional doctrine once more, was condemned at the Council of Bordeaux (1080), and retired to the Island of St. Cosme, where he died at peace with the Church. Although no major theologians followed him until the sixteenth century, Berengarius had considerable influence. His errors on marriage, baptism, and other doctrinal matters also spread; one result was greater clarification of language in the decisions of subsequent councils of the Church.

BERENGARIUS, BL. (d. 1108). In 1094 he became first abbot of the Benedictine monastery of Formbach, Bavaria. F. D. Oct. 29.

BÉRENGER, PIERRE. *See* Peter of Poitiers.

BERENGERIO DA CARPI, JACOPO (1470–1530), anatomist. Born in Carpi, Italy, he became professor of surgery at Pavia and in 1502 at Bologna, where he lectured until 1527, and wrote treatises on his anatomical researches. He was called the restorer of anatomy by Fallopius.

BERENICE, ST. (4th century), martyr. *See* Domnina, St.

BERENSON, BERNARD (1865–1959), critic. Born in Vilno, Lithuania, he was brought to Boston, Massachusetts, by his parents, graduated from Harvard in 1887, and went to Italy to study art. He became a convert in 1891, married Mary Logan, a Quaker, in the chapel of his villa at Settignano, near Florence, in 1900, but soon drifted into philosophical skepticism, violently preferring Walter Pater to Aquinas. He opposed the institutional nature of the Church, but was attracted by its spirit and mysticism. He often wrote as a rationalist and humanist in his historical and autobiographical asides. He became one of the most significant modern art critics, publishing in international journals, editing portfolios of reproductions, and writing on the artists of Florence, Venice, central and northern Italy in a series of major studies. In his last years, spent at Vallombrosa, Italy, his skepticism lessened, and he returned to the Church before his death there on Oct. 7.

BERGIER, NICHOLAS SYLVESTRE (1715–1790), theologian. Born in Darney, Lorraine, on Dec. 31, he studied at Besançon and Paris, was ordained, and in 1769 became canon of the cathedral in Paris. He wrote on philology, paganism, divorce, and the problem of evil; his principal writings were against Voltaire and the deists, notably his eight-volume *Dictionnaire théologique*, written in answer to the Encyclopedists. He died at Versailles on Apr. 9.

BERHTWALD, ST. (d. 731), archbishop. Benedictine abbot of Reculver in Kent, England, he was made archbishop of Canterbury in 692, and worked with SS. Aldhelm and Boniface. F. D. Jan. 9.

BERHTWALD, ST. (d. 1045), bishop. A Benedictine monk at Glastonbury, England, he was a benefactor of that abbey and of Malmesbury, and in 1005 became bishop of Ramsbury, a see later translated to Salisbury. The name is also spelled Brithwald. F. D. Jan. 22.

BERINGTON, CHARLES (1748–1798). Born in Stock, Essex, England, he attended Douai and a Paris seminary, took his doctorate at the Sorbonne in 1776, became a chaplain in England and coadjutor to Bishop Thomas Talbot. In 1788 he joined the Catholic committee which was seeking the repeal of the penal laws, and signed the documents of the extremists, the so-called "blue books," which were condemned by the pope. When Douglass was appointed vicar apostolic, the lay rebels sought to disavow him and to elect Berington in his place; the latter then publicly separated himself from their aims and company, thus contributing to the decline of the group. In 1795, he was selected to succeed Bishop Talbot as vicar apostolic of the Midland district but only if he disavowed the "blue books." However, he refused to retract his signature until Oct. 1797; he died near Wolverhampton on the following June 8 of apoplexy, before papal approval of his succession to Talbot reached England.

BERINGTON, JOSEPH (1743–1827). Born in Winsley, Hertfordshire, England, on Jan. 16, he studied at Douai, where he was ordained and held the chair of philosophy. His tendency toward Liberalism led to his resignation and he returned to England, serving as chaplain and tutor for the family of Thomas Stapleton. With his cousin Charles he soon became involved in the extreme actions of the Catholic committee seeking the repeal of the penal laws, actively supporting the suspended Benedictine, Joseph Wilkes, and becoming more and more anti-episcopal. His unorthodox writings on English Catholicism, a history of Abelard, friendship with Hawkins, an apostate priest, led to two suspensions of his clerical privileges. He wrote a satisfactory statement of his position in 1801, his suspension was lifted, and he spent his last years at Buckland, writing his *Literary History of the Middle Ages* (1811). He died there on Dec. 1.

BERISFORD, HUMPHREY (d. 1588?). A native of Derby, England, he became a convert, studied for two years at Douai, was condemned as a recusant on his return by his own father, jailed for seven years, and died in prison at Derby.

BERISLAVICH, PETER (d. 1520). He was *ban* (political administrator) of Croatia and bishop of the area, led a victorious army against the invading Turks in 1513, and was honored by Pope Leo X; when Emperor Charles V failed to come to his assistance during a later invasion, he was defeated and slain at the battle of Korenica.

BERISTAIN Y MARTIN DE SOUZA, JOSÉ MARIANO (1756–1817). Born in Puebla, Mexico, on May 22, he became an archdeacon in Mexico City and dean of the metropolitan church. His manuscripts on economics have been lost, but his *Biblioteca hispano-americana*, which he began as a revision of an incomplete bibliography by Bishop de Eguira, became an independent work of considerable value (though with some errors in names and dates). He died in Mexico City on Mar. 23.

BERLAGE, ANTON (1805–1881), theologian. Born in Münster, Westphalia, on Dec. 21, he studied there, at Bonn, Tübingen, and Munich, was ordained in 1832 without seminary training, had a long teaching career at the Academy of Münster, and became dean of the faculty there in 1849. His seven-volume *Katholische Dogmatik* was published in 1839–64. He died in Münster on Dec. 6.

BERLAND, PIERRE (1375–1457), bishop. Born in Médoc, France, he studied at Bordeaux and Toulouse, was ordained, became secretary to the archbishop of Bordeaux, and pastor at Soliac. In 1430 he became archbishop of Bordeaux, whose university he founded in 1441. Although the nobility of the area favored the

English, Berland had no sympathy for those who killed Joan of Arc, refused to approve Henry VI, who had himself crowned at Paris, and gave his allegiance to Charles VII. His action swayed the province of Guyenne to the French crown and helped to end the Hundred Years' War. He died in Bordeaux.

BERLIOZ, HECTOR (1803–1869), composer. Born in La Côte St. André, near Grenoble, France, on Dec. 11, he went to medical school in Paris at his doctor father's request, took his bachelor of science but not a medical degree, learned how to play the guitar and flute with slight skill, studied harmony briefly, sang in a theater chorus, composed a mass, and with effort was admitted to the Paris conservatory in 1824. He opposed the classicism of the school's master, Cherubini, developed original and romantic work, and struck out in the direction of program music, related to specific events and elaborated by narrative explanation. His personal life was melodramatic. He pursued a minor English actress, Henrietta Smithson, whom he first saw in 1827, dedicated *Symphonie fantastique* (1828) to her, tried to commit suicide in her scornful presence, and married her in 1833 when her acting career had ended. The marriage failed, although he took care of her into her last invalid years. He married Marie Recio, his mistress, in 1854, a year after his first wife's death, but this marriage also failed. His *Sardanaple* (1830), a cantata, won him the Prix de Rome. There followed: *Lélio*, a symphonic poem; *Harold en Italie* (1834), a symphony; *Waverley, Rob Roy, The Corsair, King Lear*, and *Roman Carnival* overtures; *Roméo et Juliette* (1839), a symphony; and two operas: *Benvenuto Cellini* (1838), a failure, and *Damnation de Faust* (1846), which contained popular individual numbers. His religious music was far from liturgical: an oratorio, *L'Enfance du Christ*, an extravagant *Te Deum*, and *Messe des morts* (1837), written for orchestra, double chorus, and four bands. He was somewhat successful in tours as a conductor on the Continent and in England, and was elected to the Academy in 1856. He wrote controversial criticism in several periodicals, including *Gazette musicale de Paris* and *Journal des débats*; the important *Traité d'instrumentation*, which Richard Strauss brought up to date in 1905; and *Mémoires*, painful self-revelations of defeat and disillusionment. His last operas, *La prise de Troyes* and *Les Troyens à Carthage* (1863), failed to gain the reputation he desired. He died in Paris on Mar. 8.

BERNA, BL. PETER (d. 1583), martyr. Born in Ascona on Lake Locarno, Switzerland, he studied in Rome, became a Jesuit, was sent to India, ordained at Goa, and put to death at Cuncolim with Bl. Rudolph Aquaviva. He was beatified in 1893. F. D. July 27.

BERNADETTE OF LOURDES, ST. (1844–1879). Born at Lourdes, France, on Jan. 7, the oldest of six children of Francis and Louise Casterot Soubirous, Marie Bernarde was a delicate child who suffered from asthma and the results of a cholera epidemic in 1854, from an impoverished home, and from lack of religious education. On Feb. 11, 1858, Bernadette, as she was known, saw the Virgin Mary near a natural cave close to the Gave River. Two other children, who had been sent to gather wood with her, found her rapt in prayer but laughed at her story. Bernadette alone saw the vision on Feb. 14, and daily from Feb. 18 through Mar. 4. Crowds assembled in increasing numbers, but civil and ecclesiastical hostility or skepticism was strong. On Feb. 25 she was directed to originate the spring, which still flows; a month later she heard the words, "I am the Immaculate Conception," and again was asked to plead for the building of a chapel on the site. The area, however, was boarded up and the girl sheltered as much as possible from the stream of curious who made their way to the then-out-of-the-way place. In 1866 she became a Sister of Notre Dame at Nevers, a nursing group, and remained there until her death. The visions were later ecclesiastically approved, and she was canonized in 1933. F. D. Apr. 16.

MICHEL DE SAINT-PIERRE, *Bernadette of Lourdes* (Garden City, N.Y., Image Books, 1955); FRANCIS TROCHU, *Saint Bernadette Soubirous* (New York, Pantheon, 1957).

BERNAL, AGOSTINO (1587–1642). Born in Magallon, Spain, he became a Jesuit in 1603, taught at Saragossa, and published studies of the Incarnation and the sacraments. He died at Saragossa on Sept. 13.

BERNANOS, GEORGES (1888–1948), novelist. Born in Paris on Feb. 20, of Spanish origin, he was brought up in Fressin, studied at Vaugirard, L'Institut Catholique, and the Sorbonne, was wounded and decorated while with the cavalry in World War I, and then became associated with Daudet and others on *L'Action Français*. His first novel, *Sous le soleil du Satan* (*Star of Satan* in its English translation) was published in 1926; within ten years he issued *L'Imposture, La Joie*, and *Le Journal d'un curé de campagne*. The last two received national prizes and international recognition. Bernanos wrote on the effects of the Spanish Revolution on the Balearic Islands, where he was living in 1936, attacked Franco and his supporters in *Diary of My Times*, and took his family to Paraguay and then to Brazil. He returned to France after World War II and became an outspoken supporter of Charles de Gaulle, with whom he had gone to college. He also wrote on St. Joan of Arc; *Nos autres français* and *Scandale de la verité* (both from South America); *Lettre aux anglais*; and *The Open Mind*

(1945). His most popular work, translated as *Diary of a Country Priest*, was, like his other fiction, a psychological study and analysis of the soul's conflict with the power of evil. He died in Neuilly on July 5.

BERNARD, ST. (8th century), bishop. Born in Bagnorea, Tuscany, he became bishop of Vulcia, then transferred the see to Ischia di Castro. He was alive in 800. F. D. Oct. 20.

BERNARD, ST. (778?–842), archbishop. A member of the court of Charlemagne, he founded the monastery of Ambronay in 800 and later became monk and abbot there. He was made archbishop of Vienne in 810 and, later, founded the abbey of Romans. F. D. Jan. 23.

BERNARD, ST. (d. 1109), bishop. Born in Capua, Italy, he served as chaplain to Duke Richard II, became bishop of Forum Claudii in 1087, and transferred the see in 1100 to Caleno (Carinola). F. D. Mar. 12.

BERNARD, ST. (d. 1133), cardinal. Born in Florence of the noble Uberti family, he became a Vallombrosan monk, abbot of San Salvi monastery, then abbot general of his order. In 1097 he was appointed cardinal and papal legate, and in 1106 bishop of Parma, center of support for the antipope. Because of his ardent support of the true pope and the reforms he instituted, he was twice exiled from his see. F. D. Dec. 4.

BERNARD, ST. (1091–1153), Doctor of the Church. Son of Tescelin Sorrel, a noble of Burgundy, and Aleth, daughter of Bernard, lord of Montbard, he was born in the castle of Fontaines, near Dijon, France, and studied at Châtillons-sur-Seine. In 1112, after several years of rather boisterous living following the death of his mother when he was nineteen, he decided to enter the religious life and induced thirty-one of his friends to follow him to Cîteaux (which had been founded in 1098), where they were welcomed by St. Stephen Harding. After three years he was sent with twelve monks to found a new house in Champagne. They settled in the Vallée d'Absinthe, where serious difficulties arose, partly due to the austerities and strict discipline imposed by Bernard as abbot, but soon Clairvaux (as it was now called) became famed and new houses were founded. The rigid asceticism practiced by Bernard during these years undermined his health. His eloquence and his reputation as a miracle worker became widely known. In 1130 he proclaimed the legitimacy of Pope Innocent's election against the claims of the antipope Anacletus II and successfully led the struggle for Innocent. He was the leader in securing the Lombards' acceptance of Lothaire II as emperor, and in 1140 became embroiled in his dispute with Peter Abelard, whose rationalism and extreme exaltation of human reason he condemned. So powerful was Bernard's refutation at the Council of Sens that the council condemned Abelard, who was forced to retire. When a former monk of Clairvaux, Peter Bernard of Pisa, became Pope Eugenius III, St. Bernard wrote a classical work, *De consideratione,* for the pope's guidance. In 1145, at the request of the papal legate, Cardinal Alberic, Bernard preached against the Albigensian heresy in southern France. In 1146 he was also successful in preaching a crusade against the Turks, though the crusade itself was a failure, which he blamed on the wickedness and lack of dedication on the part of the crusaders. In 1147 he was responsible for exposing and denouncing the errors of Gilbert de la Poirée (who taught that the divine nature did not became incarnate). Justly called the second founder of the Cistercians, he saw sixty-eight Cistercian monasteries founded during his lifetime and sent his monks all over Europe. He wrote widely. His mystical works had great influence, contributing more than any other single influence to form the mysticism of the Middle Ages. His sermons, especially on the Canticle of Canticles, his treatises, especially *On the Love of God,* his *Life of St. Malachy,* and many hymns and letters have all survived. He died at Clairvaux. He was canonized in 1174 and declared a Doctor of the Church in 1830. F. D. Aug. 20.

ÉTIENNE GILSON, *Mystical Theology of St. Bernard* (New York, Sheed & Ward, 1940); THOMAS MERTON, *The Last of the Fathers* (New York, Harcourt, 1954).

BERNARD, ST. (d. 1180?), martyr. Son of the Moslem caliph of Lérida, Spain, he became a Christian, changed his name from Achmed, joined the Cistercians at Poblet, and converted his sisters, Zoraida and Zaida, who took Mary and Gracia as their new names. When they tried to convert their brother Almanzor, he denounced them and saw to their execution. They are the patrons of Alcira, Valencia. F. D. June 1.

BERNARD, ST. (12th century). A Benedictine monk who was stationed at Valdeiglesias in Spanish Galicia in 1155, he is the patron of Candelada, Spain. F. D. Aug. 20.

BERNARD, ALEXIS XYSTE (1847–1923), bishop. Born in Beloeil, Quebec, Canada, on Dec. 29, he studied at Montreal, was ordained in 1871, served as president of Sorel College, canon of the cathedral, and vicar general of the diocese. In 1906 he was appointed bishop of St. Hyacinth. He edited the pastoral letters of the bishops of Montreal and organized the Institute of the Sisters of St. Joseph. He died on June 17.

BERNARD, CLAUDE (1588–1641). Born in Dijon, France, on Dec. 23, he studied at Dôle, lived in Paris society until a close friend was killed in a duel, then decided to study for the priesthood. After ordination he gave his wealth to the poor of Belley, whose bishop, Pierre le Camus, had long been his friend, and devoted his life to prisoners and the sick. He founded the seminary of the Trente-Trois in Paris for the training of impoverished candidates for the priesthood, popularized the *Memorare*, and was highly regarded by St. Vincent de Paul. He died in Paris on Mar. 23.

BERNARD, CLAUDE (1813–1878), physiologist. Born in St. Julien, France, on July 12, he studied at the Jesuit college at Villefranche, became a pharmacist's assistant at Lyons, wrote two plays, and set out in 1834 for Paris and the advice of the critic Girardin. The latter suggested medicine as a surer profession. Made assistant to Prof. Magendie of the Collège de France, he began research in the physiology of the pancreas, proved the formation of sugar in the liver, isolating the substance he called glycogen, and discovered the vasomotor system as a result of his studies of the relationship between the nerves and animal heat. He also investigated the physiological effects of curare and carbon monoxide poisoning. In 1855 he succeeded Magendie as professor, was seriously ill from 1862 to 1870, then accepted two laboratories from Napoleon III, continued his research, and revised his lectures for publication in seventeen volumes. In 1868 he was elected to the Academy of Sciences and on his death in Paris on Feb. 10 was given a state funeral.

BERNARD OF ARCE, ST. (9th century). Returning from a pilgrimage to the Holy Land, this Englishman (or Frenchman) settled as a recluse at Arpino, Italy; his relics are honored at Rocca d'Arce. F. D. Oct. 14.

BERNARD OF BADEN, BL. (1428–1458). Son of James I, margrave of Baden, he renounced his right of succession in order to attempt to launch a crusade against the Turks. He died of the plague at the monastery at Moncalieri while on his way to Rome to enlist the support of Pope Callistus III. F. D. July 15.

BERNARD OF BESSE (13th century), chronicler. A native of Aquitaine, he served St. Bonaventure as secretary, gathered legend and fact for his *Liber de laudibus beati Francisci* (1280), compiled a catalogue of the order's ministers general up to 1300, and wrote a life of Bl. Christopher of Cahors.

BERNARD OF BOLOGNA. *See* Toselli, Floviano.

BERNARD OF BOTONE (d. 1266?), canonist. Born in Parma, Italy, he studied and held the chair of canon law at Bologna, became a canon of the cathedral there, and served Popes Innocent IV and Alexander IV as chaplain. He wrote on the Decretals of Gregory IX, his glosses serving later writers for three centuries.

BERNARD CALVO, ST. (d. 1243). Born in Manso Calvo, Catalonia, Spain, he became a Cistercian, was first abbot of Santas Creus, near Tarragona, and in 1233 was named bishop of Vich. F. D. Oct. 24.

BERNARD OF CLUNY. *See* Bernard of Morlaix.

BERNARD OF COMPOSTELLA (13th century). Called "Antiquus," he was born in Compostella, Spain, taught canon law at Bologna, and compiled a collection (1208) of the decrees of Pope Innocent III.

BERNARD OF COMPOSTELLA (13th century). Called "Modernus" to distinguish him from "Antiquus," he was born in Galicia, Spain, served as chaplain to Pope Innocent IV, and wrote commentaries on papal decretals.

BERNARD OF CORLEONE. *See* Latini, Bl. Philip.

BERNARD GUIDONIS (1261–1331), bishop. Born in Royères, France, he became a Dominican, was professed in 1280, and served as prior at Albi, Carcassonne, Castres, and Limoges. He was inquisitor at Toulouse during the Albigensian heresy, and was made bishop of Tuy by Pope John XXII and later transferred to Lodève. He wrote treatises on the mass and the Immaculate Conception, chronicles of kings, emperors, and Dominican establishments, a history of his order, a universal history (to 1331), saints' lives, lists of the bishops of Limoges and of Toulouse, and an explanation of the precise duties of an inquisitor, with detailed instructions for examination and condemnation. He died at Lauroux, France, on Dec. 30.

BERNARD OF LIPPE, BL. (d. 1217), bishop. A Westphalian count, he became a Cistercian at Dünemunde, then its abbot, and later a bishop of Semgallen in Kurland. F. D. Jan. 23.

BERNARD OF LUXEMBOURG (d. 1535). Born in Strassen, Germany, he became a Dominican, studied at Cologne and Louvain, served as inquisitor of the archdioceses of Cologne, Mainz, and Trèves, and published a catalogue of heretics. He died at Cologne on Oct. 5.

BERNARD OF MENTHON, ST. (996?–1081?). Legend calls him son of Count Richard of Menthon in Savoy, Italy, but nothing is known of his parentage and early life. He became vicar general of the diocese of Aosta about 1040, visiting the most distant Alpine areas, converting heathens, aiding travelers, and setting up two hospices which eventually came under Augustinian direction. In 1923, Pope Pius XI made him the patron of mountain climbers; he is the hero of Henri Ghéon's drama, *La merveilleuse histoire du jeune Bernard de Menthon*. F. D. May 28.

BERNARD OF MORLAIX (12th century),

poet. He was a Benedictine monk at Cluny during the time of Peter the Venerable (d. 1156), wrote sermons, a dialogue on the Trinity, and was the probable author of a set of monastic regulations. His most famous work is *De contemptu mundi,* a poem of some 3000 lines, written about 1140. It is a brilliant and virile satire against contemporary immorality, the simony of bishops, insolence and incompetence of papal legates, weaknesses of the popes themselves, and monastic leanings toward luxury. Matching his angry lashing of the enormity of sin is the flowing lyricism of his praise of meditation, virtuous living, and the grandeur of union with God in heaven. The poem apparently was known to Dante; it had a great effect and was widely quoted by apologists of both sides during the Reformation. Several hymns (some, like *Jerusalem the Golden,* still popular) were interspersed. Bernard is the probable author of the *Hymn of St. Casimir,* also attributed to St. Anselm and to St. Bernard; it has been translated by Cardinal Wiseman. He is also known as Bernard of Cluny.

BERNARD OF OFFIDA, BL. (1604–1694). Born in Appignano, Italy, he became a Capuchin laybrother in 1626 at Offida. His zeal, charity, and wisdom were exceptional. In old age he served as doorkeeper of the monastery at Fermo, where he received a stream of visitors who sought his advice. He died on Aug. 22. F. D. Aug. 26.

BERNARD OF PAVIA (d. 1213). He became bishop of Faenza, Italy, in 1190, was transferred to Pavia in 1198, and made several compilations of canon law which were used as introductory textbooks. He died on Sept. 18.

BERNARD PALEARA, ST. (d. 1122), bishop. A Benedictine monk at Monte Cassino, he became bishop of Teramo, Italy, in 1115. F. D. Dec. 19.

BERNARD THE PENITENT, BL. (d. 1182). Born in Provence, he was condemned to seven years of great penance to atone for a crime which may have been participation in a riot killing a civil official. Weighed down by iron chains, he went to the major shrines of Compostella, Rome, and Jerusalem. When he arrived at St. Omer, he was accepted by the Benedictines of the monastery of St. Bertin, and cleaned churches and performed works of charity; he enjoyed several supernatural gifts. F. D. Apr. 19.

BERNARD DE RUTHENIS, BL. (d. 1079), cardinal. Abbot of the Benedictine monastery of St. Victor at Marseilles, France, in 1064, he spread the Cluniac observance, was made a cardinal by Pope St. Gregory VII, and papal legate to Germany in 1077 and to Spain in 1078. F. D. July 19.

BERNARD OF THIRON, ST. (1046–1117). Born near Abbeville, France, he joined the Benedictines at St. Cyprian's, Poitiers, became abbot, went to preach on the missions with Bl. Robert of Arbrissel, then in 1109 founded a monastery at Thiron, Picardy. His disciples spread into England and Scotland. He was canonized in 1861. F. D. Apr. 14.

BERNARD OF TOULOUSE, BL. (d. 1320), martyr. A Dominican friar, he was seized by the Albigensians, and sawed in two. F. D. Dec. 3.

BERNARDINO DA FELTRE, BL. (1439?–1495). Born in Feltre, Italy, Martino Tomitano, eldest of ten children of a noble family, studied at Padua, joined the Franciscans in 1456 and took the name Bernardino, and was ordained in 1463. He soon became a popular and exciting preacher, condemning current evils before huge crowds and placing blame wherever he felt it belonged: on the prince of Mantua, King Ferdinand I of Naples, the powerful Oddi and Baglioni families, local nobles, and the usurers who were charging exorbitant interest. He expanded the *monti di pietà* (money-lending offices to aid the poor), beginning with one in Mantua and eventually opening a score or more. His activity aroused the hostility both of the Lombards who controlled the loan business and of many theologians who contended that even the low rate of interest he charged to make the offices self-sustaining was usury. This controversy raged until 1515, when the fifth General Council, at the Lateran, declared them legal and to be encouraged. He died at Pavia and his cult was approved in 1728. F. D. Sept. 28.

BERNARDINO OF FOSSA. *See* Amici, Bl. Bernardino.

BERNARDINO DE SAHAGÚN (1500?–1590), missioner. Born in Sahagún, León, Spain, he studied at Salamanca, joined the Franciscans, and in 1529 was sent as a missioner to Mexico. He taught at Santa Cruz College in Tlaltelolco for sixty years and became the leading authority on the Aztecs. He wrote a grammar and a dictionary of the Aztec language, *Historia general de las cosas de Nueva España* (unpublished until 1829, although widely circulated in manuscript in Spain on its completion in 1569), and numerous spiritual books in Aztec for the natives. He died in Mexico on Oct. 23.

BERNARDINO OF SIENA, ST. (1380–1444). Born in Massa Maritima, Italy, where his father was governor, Bernardino degli Albizzeschi became an orphan at seven, was brought up by an aunt, worked for the poor and sick, especially through the plague of 1400, and directed a group of friends who also belonged to a confraternity of Mary. He entered the Franciscans on his birthday and was ordained exactly two years later, on Sept. 8, 1404. He lived a life of solitude at Colombaio outside Siena for twelve years, then preached with exceptional brilliance and success throughout Italy, calming strife-torn cities, shaming gamblers, lashing vice, and especially recommending devotion to the Holy Name. He was censured by enemies, who complained to Pope Martin V, but he was cleared of all charges and even offered a bishopric, which he refused. In 1430 he became vicar general, in charge of 300 Friars of the Strict Observance; at his death there were 4000. For them he recommended more scholarship and further study of theology and canon law; the earlier friars had not been so concerned with learning. He returned to preaching during his last two years and died at Aquila, Italy. He was canonized in 1450. F. D. May 20.

M. WARD, *St. Bernardino, The People's Preacher* (St. Louis, Herder, 1914).

BERNARDUS PAPIENSIS (d. 1213), canonist. Born in Pavia, Italy, he studied at Bologna, was provost of the Pavia cathedral, became bishop of Faenza, and, in 1198, of Pavia, where he died on Sept. 18. He wrote philosophical studies and a life of Lanfranc and compiled *Breviarium extravagantium,* a collection of ancient canonical texts not in Gratian's *Decretum.*

BERNIER, ÉTIENNE ALEXANDRE (1762–1806), bishop. Born in Daon, France, on Oct. 31, he taught theology at Angers, became pastor of St. Laud's church there, and roused the people of Anjou and Vendée to revolt when the government sought to impose the Civil Constitution of the Clergy. A clever politician, he was chosen to represent Napoleon in discussions with the papal envoys over the concordat. Soon after its signing, Napoleon appointed him bishop of Orléans, where he died on Oct. 1.

BERNINI, DOMENICO (18th century), historian. Son of the architect, he was a canon of Santa Maria Maggiore, Rome, wrote a four-volume history of heresies (1705–17), an account of papal concern in the wars against the Saracens (1685), and an account of the rota (1717).

BERNINI, GIOVANNI LORENZO (1598–1680), architect. Born in Naples, Italy, on Dec. 7, he went with his father, a sculptor and painter, to Rome in 1608. Giovanni completed his sculpture, *David with a Sling,* at fifteen; thereafter he was patronized by Pope Paul V and his five successors. He became architect of St. Peter's in 1629 and superintendent of public works in Rome. He visited Paris in 1665 and did an equestrian statue of Louis XIV; he also carved busts of King Charles I and Queen Henrietta Maria of England. He was well known for his verse comedies and other writings, and painted over 200 canvases. But he was chiefly active as an architect. As the seventh to work on St. Peter's, he conceived the plan of the colonnade, the giant ellipse of Tuscan columns united to the portico of the basilica. He also worked on the Barberini and Odescalchi palaces, designed the great canopy and the Chair of St. Peter, numerous statues, and the bridge of Sant' Angelo. His decorative style, in keeping with the melodramatic effects once so admired, is most evident in the statues for the façade of St. Peter's and the Lateran. He died in Rome on Nov. 28.

BERNINI, GIUSEPPE MARIA (d. 1753), missioner. Born near Carignan, Piedmont, Italy, he was a Capuchin missioner in the Orient, made detailed studies of Indian beliefs and customs, prepared several historical studies, and made extensive translations. He died in Hindustan.

BERNIS, FRANÇOIS (1715–1794), cardinal. Born in St. Marcel, France, on May 22, he was sent to St. Sulpice, made a name as a wit, and was elected to the French Academy. He met Mme. de Pompadour, who lifted him out of poverty and arranged his appointment as French ambassador to Venice. He settled the differences between the Venetians and Pope Benedict XIV, was recalled to Paris as minister of foreign affairs, but was held responsible thereafter for the alliance with Austria and the French defeat in the Seven Years' War. He lost his position and popularity, as well as the friendship of Pompadour, whose own incompetent appointment of generals had really caused the national debacle. He was banished by Louis XV, and was on his way to exile in 1758 when he learned that he had been made a cardinal by Pope Clement XIII. He was ordained, lived in retirement for six years, then was recalled by the crown and made archbishop of Albi in 1769 and ambassador to Rome in 1769. He published poems and letters, along with his *Mémoires.* He died in poverty in Rome on Nov. 2, serving the needs of victims of the French Revolution who had escaped to Italy.

BERNO, ST. (d. 927), abbot. Born in Burgundy, he became a Benedictine at the monastery of St. Martin, Autun, restored Baume-les-Messieurs, then founded Gigny, Bourg-Dieu, and Massay. At the suggestion of Duke William of Aquitaine he founded Cluny, and was its first abbot from 910 to 926. F. D. Jan. 13.

BERNO (d. 1048). Born near Trèves, France, he studied at St. Gall, became a Benedictine and in 1008 abbot of Reichenau, and introduced wide reforms in liturgical music. His written studies indicate that Gregorian melodies originally had short as well as long notes. He also wrote on musical instruments. He died on June 7.

BERNO (d. 1190?), bishop. A Cistercian

monk at Amelungsborn, Germany, he was chosen as bishop of Mecklenburg by Prince Henry of Saxony in 1155 and consecrated by Pope Adrian IV. Because Germany and Catholicism were equally disliked by the Savic Obotrites (Wends), Berno's episcopal mission was a difficult one; he was forced by Prince Niklot to move his see to Schwerin (in present Germany). By 1171 he had converted much of the area surrounding that city, built its cathedral, and brought in Cistercians for two monasteries, Doberan and Dargun. Berno supported Pope Alexander III against Frederick Barbarossa and the archbishop of Bremen, who backed the antipopes, went to Rome in 1178 after the schism was healed, and attended the Lateran Council. While he was there, the Wends attacked the Germans, destroyed Doberan, and killed seventy-eight Cistercians there; it was rebuilt by 1186.

BERNOCCHI, BL. CONSTANTIUS (d. 1481). Born in Fabriano, Italy, he became a Dominican at Santa Lucia at fifteen, studied under Bl. Conradin and St. Antoninus, and was prior at San Marco, Florence, which he reformed. He was beatified in 1811. F. D. Feb. 25.

BERNOLD OF CONSTANCE (1054?–1100), apologist. Born in Swabia, he studied and in 1084 was ordained at Constance, Switzerland. In 1079 he had attended the synod at Rome which condemned Berengarius; in 1086 he served with Bishop Gebhard as counselor to King Herman; later, he became a Benedictine at the monastery of St. Blasien. He wrote seventeen tracts in defense of the policies of Pope Gregory VII, a treatise on the liturgy, and a chronicle of contemporary events. He died at Schaffhausen, Switzerland, on Sept. 16.

BERNWARD, ST. (d. 1022), bishop. Orphaned at an early age, he was raised by his uncle, bishop of Utrecht, and educated and ordained at Mainz. In 987 he became tutor of Emperor Otto III, then a child, and in 993 was made bishop of Hildesheim, and ruled peacefully except for a jurisdictional dispute with St. Willigis of Mainz which was resolved by the papacy in Bernward's favor. He was famous as an architect, painter, sculptor, and metal worker. He was canonized in 1193. F. D. Nov. 20.

BERRETTINI, PIETRI (1596–1669), painter. Born in Cortona, Tuscany, on Nov. 1, he studied under his uncle, Filippo Berrettini, at Florence under Andrea Commodi, and at Rome with Baccio Ciarpi. Cardinal Sacchetti for whom he painted *Rape of the Sabines*, became his patron; he then decorated a chapel in the church of Santa Bibiana for Pope Urban VIII. He contributed decorations to the Barberini palace, frescoes for the Pitti palace in Florence, and mosaics for St. Peter's dome. As architect, he designed the church of San Martino, Rome, where he was buried after his death there on May 16. He is also known as Pietro da Cortona.

BERRIO-OCHOA, BL. VALENTINE (1827–1861), bishop and martyr. A native of Ellorio, Spain, he became a Dominican, was sent to the Philippines, and in 1858 went to Tonkin, Indochina, as titular bishop and vicar apostolic. He was beheaded with Bl. Jerome Hermosilla and Bl. Pedro Almató and was beatified in 1909. F. D. Nov. 1.

BERRUGUENTE, ALONSO (1480?–1561), painter. Born in Paredes de Nava, Castile, he studied briefly under his father, Pedro Berruguente, then became a successful lawyer at Valladolid. After his father's death he went to Florence, and studied under Michelangelo, went with him to Rome, and worked as an assistant in Vatican projects. At Florence he completed the altarpiece for the convent of San Geronimo begun by Filippo Lippi. In 1520 he returned to Spain, was made court painter by Charles V, and given continuing honors and rewards by Philip II. His work appears in churches in Saragossa, Valladolid, Toledo, and Madrid; his best paintings are in the cathedral at Palencia and the church in Ventosa, of which he was lord. He died in Toledo.

BERRUYER, ISAAC JOSEPH (1681–1758). Born in Rouen, France, he became a Jesuit and wrote an elaborate *History of the People of God*, first published in 1728. It was journalistic, romanticized, seemingly Nestorian, and was condemned by his superiors, by the French bishops, and finally placed on the Index.

BERRY, JOHN (d. 1921). Born in England and educated at Ushaw, he was ordained in 1884 and stationed in Liverpool, where he later became rector of the church of St. Philip Neri, principal of the Catholic Institute, and the organizer of homes for destitute and orphaned boys. He wrote widely on social welfare and died in Measham.

BERRYER, PIERRE ANTOINE (1790–1868), jurist. Born in Paris on July 4, he studied at the Oratorian college of Juilly, became a member of the Paris bar in 1811, and entered political life as an independent monarchist. As a lawyer, he defended Marshal Ney and Generals Debelle, Cambronne, Canuel, and Donnadieu against the new ministry of the Restoration; because of his vigor, he was forced to defend himself against the charge of treason. Later, he defended the duchesse de Berri and Chateaubriand against charges of complicity in insurrection. As a member of parliament he led the defeat in 1834 of the United States claim for reparations for American ships seized by Napoleon. He was counsel for the defense of Louis Napoleon after the attempted Boulogne coup in 1840. In 1855 he was elected to the French Academy. He spoke and wrote widely in defense of the Church, pointing out that the leaders of Gallicanism sought destruction, not separation; pleading for the establishment of religious schools and the restoration of religious orders; opposing divorce; and attacking a proposal for a married clergy in France. He advocated, and made his position clear in a court trial, that workers had the right to combine and to earn a living wage; this became the basis for his campaign for national acknowledgment of liberty of association. He died in Angerville, an estate purchased for him in 1830 by his friends, on Nov. 29.

BERTHA (d. 612?). Daughter of the Frankish Charibert, she married the pagan King Ethelbert of Kent, bringing her chaplain Liudhard to England with her. She restored the church of St. Martin at Canterbury, welcomed St. Augustine and his missionaries, and eventually saw the conversion of her husband.

BERTHA, ST. (d. 685?), martyr. She was put to death while abbess of the convent of Avenay, at Châlons-sur-Marne, France, which she had founded. F. D. May 1.

BERTHA, ST. (d. 725?). Married to a nobleman at twenty, she had five daughters. After her husband's death she with two of them entered the Benedictine convent of Blangy in Artois, France, which she had founded, and became its abbess. F. D. July 4.

BERTILA, ST. (9th century). After the death of her pagan husband, she brought up her young son as a Christian and with him founded a number of hospices for the poor. After distributing all their possessions they became hermits near Bingen, later called Rupertsberg, near Diessenberg, Germany. F. D. May 15.

BERTHA ALBERTI, BL. (d. 1163). Born in Florence, she joined the Vallombrosans at the convent of St. Felicitas there and in 1153 became abbess at Cavriglia. F. D. Mar. 24.

BERTHANE, ST. (d. 840?). A Scot, he is said to have been a monk at Iona, then bishop of Kirkwall in the Orkney Islands, before he died near Galway, Ireland. He is also known as Berchan. F. D. Apr. 6.

BERTHARIUS, ST. (d. 884?), martyr. Of royal descent, he became Benedictine abbot of Monte Cassino in 856, wrote poems and homilies, and was slain with several of his monks by invading Saracens. F. D. Oct. 22.

BERTHELOT, BL. PIERRE (1600–1638), martyr. Born in Honfleur, France, he went to sea at nineteen, became a pilot and cartographer, and in 1635 became a Carmelite, taking the name Dionysius of the Nativity, at Goa. He was ordained in 1638 and that year went as pilot on a mission to Sumatra, accompanied by Bl. Thomas Rodriguez da Cunha (Bro. Redemptus of the Cross). At the arrival

of the expedition in Achin, the Sumatrans seized the ambassador and his group and put the two Carmelites to death. They were beatified in 1900. F. D. Nov. 29.

BERTHIER, GUILLAUME FRANÇOIS (1704–1782). Born in Issoudun, France, he became a Jesuit, taught at Rennes, Rouen, and Paris, edited *Mémoires de Trévoux* from 1745 to 1762 and was bitterly attacked by Voltaire, published part (volumes 13–17) of a history of the Church in France from 1320 to 1559, became tutor to the Dauphin's sons after the Jesuits were suppressed in 1762 in France, resigned, and spent ten years in Germany. He returned to Bourges in 1774 and continued his biblical studies of the Psalms and Isaias, which were published posthumously.

BERTHOALD, ST. (7th century). He was fifth bishop of Cambrai, France. F. D. Oct. 13.

BERTHOLD, BL. (1090–1142). Born in the region of Lake Constance, he became a Benedictine monk at Blasien on the death of his wife about 1120. He served as prior there, at Goettweig, Austria, and at Stayer-Garsten, Styria. F. D. July 27.

BERTHOLD, ST. (d. 1195?). After theological studies at Paris, he went on the crusade and was at the siege of Antioch. After this he joined a group of priests on Mt. Carmel and was for forty-five years their first superior; as a result he is often called the "founder" of the Carmelite order. F. D. Mar. 29.

BERTHOLD OF CHIEMSEE. *See* Pürstinger, Berthold.

BERTHOLD OF HENNEBERG (1441–1504), archbishop. After study at Erfurt, Germany, he became in 1464 a canon of the cathedral in Cologne, was attached to the court of Frederick III in 1467, and consecrated archbishop of Mainz in 1485. As chancellor, he made suggestions for sweeping changes in the imperial structure, which were rejected; his attempts to reform the clergy and to better their education proved more successful. He attacked abuses associated with indulgences and in 1486 set up a censorship of the press. He died in Mainz, Germany, on Dec. 21.

BERTHOLD OF RATISBON, BL. (1210?–1272). Born in Ratisbon, Germany, he became a Franciscan at a mature age, preached with success through Bavaria and Switzerland, and did mission work in Austria, Moravia, Bohemia, and Silesia. In 1263 he was asked by Pope Urban IV to preach the crusade, and worked with Albertus Magnus. He preached in German and reached his huge alien audiences through interpreters; the sermons were later written down in Latin, with German glosses, were discovered and published in 1824, and had considerable influence on preaching, besides being of value to historians of thirteenth-century mid-European culture. He died in Ratisbon on Dec. 14.

BERTHOLD OF REICHENAU (d. 1088?), chronicler. A Benedictine monk at the abbey of Reichenau, Switzerland, he was a disciple of Herman the Cripple, who empowered him to complete and carry on his historical labors and left him his notes. The chronicle is an account of the years before the pontificate of Gregory VII; scholars variously maintain that Berthold's original work extends from 1054 to 1066 or to 1080. He died on Mar. 12.

BERTI, GIOVANNI LORENZO (1696–1766), theologian. Born in Sarravezza, Tuscany, on May 28, he became an Augustinian at fifteen, held various offices, including that of assistant to the general, taught in the major Italian cities, and in 1748 became professor of church history at Pisa. He wrote his *De theologicis disciplinis* (1739–45), an interpretation of St. Augustine, was violently and widely attacked as Jansenistic, but was examined and approved by Pope Benedict XIV. He wrote other treatises on Augustine and a history of the Church. He died at Pisa on Mar. 26.

BERTILIA OF MAREUIL, ST. (d. 705?). After a lifetime of dispensing charity in cooperation with her noble husband, she became a solitary, after his death, at a church and oratory she built in Flanders. F. D. Jan. 3.

BERTILLA, ST. (d. 705?). A native of the Soissons area, she was raised at the monastery of Joarre and became a Benedictine nun there and later its prioress. When the abbey of Chelles was restored by St. Bathildis, she served as its first abbess for forty-six years. F. D. Nov. 5.

BERTILLA. *See* Boscardin, St. Anna Francesca.

BERTILO, BL. (d. 880?), martyr. He and his community in the Benedictine abbey of St. Benignus at Dijon, France, were massacred by invading Norsemen. F. D. Mar. 26.

BERTINUS, ST. (d. 700?). Born in Coutances, France, he became a Benedictine monk at Luxeuil under St. Walbert, and was sent to help St. Omer in evangelizing the Morini. He and his associates, SS. Bertrand and Mummolinus, built two monasteries, and Bertinus became abbot of that at Sithiu about 661. In 663 he established churches and monasteries at St. Omer and Wormhout, near Dunkirk. F. D. Sept. 5.

BERTOARA, ST. (7th century). She was abbess of Notre Dame de Sales in Bourges, France, from 612 to 614. F. D. Dec. 4.

BERTONI, BL. JAMES PHILIP (1444–1483). Given over at nine by his father to be educated by the Servites in their priory in Faenza, Italy, he later became a priest there, holding various offices until his death on May 25. His holiness led to a popular cult, which was approved in 1766. F. D. May 30.

BERTONIO, LUDOVICO (1552–1625), missioner. Born in Rocca Contrada, near Ancona, Italy, he became a Jesuit in 1575, was sent to South America in 1581, and labored among the Indians of Peru and Bolivia. He wrote a number of works on the grammar and customs of the Aymará tribe, published by the press the Jesuits set up at Juli, Peru. He died at Lima, Peru, on Aug. 3.

BERTRAM, ADOLPH (1859–1945), cardinal. Born in Germany, he was ordained, became archbishop of Breslau, and pleaded with the people of his see to resist Nazi attacks on religion. He died in Breslau on Aug. 12.

BERTRAN, ST. LUÍZ (1526–1581). Born in Valencia, Spain, he became a Dominican at eighteen and was ordained in 1547. In 1552 he was a master of novices and about 1557 met St. Teresa, whom he encouraged in her plans to establish a reformed Carmelite group. In 1562 he was sent to Cartagena, Colombia, where his preaching led to thousands of baptisms. He traveled throughout the Caribbean area, preaching, making converts, and trying to secure better treatment for the Indians. In 1569 he was recalled to Spain, where he served as prior of several houses and trained many preachers. He was canonized in 1671. F. D. Oct. 9.

BERTRAN, BL. LUÍZ (d. 1629), martyr. Born in Barcelona, Spain, he became a Dominican, served in the Philippines and Japan, and was burned alive at Omura, Japan, with Bl. Peter of the Holy Mother of God, a native Dominican catechist. He was beatified in 1867. F. D. July 29.

BERTRAND, ST. (d. 623), bishop. Born in Autun, France, he was ordained by St. Germanus, served at the cathedral school in Paris, and was made bishop of Le Mans in 587. A supporter of the Neustrian faction in France, he was more than once expelled from his diocese by the kings of Austrasia, but was settled in power in 605 by King Clotaire II. He was active in charities, building, and agricultural reforms. F. D. June 30.

BERTRAND, ST. (8th century). Trained by St. Bertinus, he aided St. Omer in converting Flanders and northern France, and served as abbot of the Benedictine abbey of St. Quentin. F. D. Jan. 24.

BERTRAND, ST. (d. 1123), bishop. Son of a military lord, he followed in his father's footsteps, then became an archdeacon at Toulouse. In 1075 he became bishop of Comminges and reigned with energy and success for fifty years. He attended the synod at Poitiers which excommunicated King Philip I in 1100. He was canonized sometime before 1309, possibly by Pope Alexander III. F. D. Oct. 16.

BERTRAND, BL. (d. 1149). He was Cistercian abbot of Grandselve for twenty years and died on July 11. F. D. Oct. 23.

BERTRAND, ST. (1260–1350), bishop and martyr. Born near Cahors, France, he became dean of the cathedral of Angoulême and patriarch of Aquileia, Italy, and died while defending his church. His cult was approved by Pope Benedict XIV. F. D. June 6.

BERTRAND, LOUIS (1866–1941), author. Born in Spincourt, France, on Mar. 20, he studied in Bar-le-Duc and L'École Normale, Paris, taught at Aix in 1888 and at Algiers in 1891–1900, became an intense nationalist, modeled his work on that of Cervantes and Flaubert, and worked out of his deep pessimism by discovering the backgrounds of North African tradition. His first biography after his re-acceptance of the Church was of St. Augustine; his second, of Teresa of Avila. He took his doctorate at Algiers in 1897, published *La Fin du classicisme* (1897), *Le Sang des races* (1899), *La Cina, Sanguis martyrum, Mlle. de Jessincourt, Les villes d'or*, a history of Spain, and biographies of Flaubert and Louis IV. He was elected to the French Academy in 1926 and died in Cap d'Antibes, France, on Dec. 6.

BERTRAND, PIERRE (1280–1348?), cardinal. Born in Annonay, France, he studied law and taught at Avignon, Montpellier, Orléans, and Paris, became a member of the French parliament, the king's council, and the queen's chancery. He then studied for the priesthood, was ordained, and became bishop of Nevers and then of Autun. He established scholarships at Autun, built charitable institutions at Annonay, defended the Church against the attempts of the Valois dynasty to limit its strength, and instituted ecclesiastical reforms to remove evils pointed out by the opposition. He was made a cardinal in 1331 by Pope John XXII. He died at Montaud, near Avignon, France.

BERTRAND OF GARRIGUES, BL. (d. 1230?). Born in Garrigues, France, he became a priest, joined the Cistercian mission as a preacher, and soon after 1208 met St. Dominic. In 1215, with five other preachers, he joined Dominic in the formation of the Order of Preachers. In 1217 he was sent to Paris with six companions to found a house near the university, thence to do the same at Bologna. He was a constant companion of St. Dominic and in 1221 was appointed prior general of the Provence province. He spent the rest of his life preaching in southern France and died at the abbey of Bouchet. His cult was confirmed in 1881 by Pope Leo XIII. F. D. Sept. 6.

BERTUIN, ST. (d. 698?), bishop. An Anglo-Saxon monk at the Benedictine abbey of Othelle, he became a missionary bishop and, after two years in Rome, abbot-founder of Malonne in the mission territory of Namur. F. D. Nov. 11.

BERTULF, ST. (d. 640), abbot. Of Frankish origin, he was brought up a pagan, was converted by St. Arnoul of Metz, and in 620 became a monk at Luxeuil under St. Eustace. After several years he went to the monastery at Bobbio, became its abbot on the death of St. Attalas, and ruled rigorously. When Bishop Probus of Tortona claimed jurisdiction over the monastery, Bertulf appealed to Pope Honorius I, who ruled it exempt from episcopal control and subject directly to the papacy, the first such exemption recorded. F. D. Aug. 19.

BERTULF, ST. (d. 705?). Born a pagan in Germany, he was brought up in Flanders, where, after his conversion, he wisely served Count Wambert and his wife Homburga as a steward, even to the point of being slandered, unsuccessfully, because of his honesty. Eventually, he was designated as heir of their estate at Renty. After their death he retired to a monastery he had founded there. F. D. Feb. 5.

BÉRULLE, PIERRE DE (1575–1629), cardinal. Born at Château Cérilly, Champagne, France, on Feb. 4, he became chaplain to King Henry IV, and worked with St. Francis de Sales to convert the Huguenots. He helped Marie Acarie to introduce the reformed Carmelite nuns to France and in 1611 founded a French congregation of the Oratory in imitation of that established in Rome by St. Philip Neri. He became its superior general, continued to work for reforms within the Church, arranged the marriage of Henrietta of France with King Charles I of England, and in 1627 was made a cardinal by Pope Urban VIII. He wrote *Discourse on Inner Abnegation*, other spiritual discourses, and a life of Christ. He died on Oct. 2.

BERVANGER, MARTIN DE (1795–1865). Born in Sarrelouis, France, on May 15, he was ordained, served as pastor in his native city, set up two institutions to give schooling and professional training to poor workers (which were destroyed during the revolution), and another, in 1827, L'Institut de St. Nicolas, which taught religion, morality, and manual training to poor boys. After initial difficulties the school flourished and a branch was set up at Issy. In 1859 he turned his work over to Cardinal Morlot of Paris, who staffed it with Christian Brothers. He died in Paris.

BESANGE, JEROME LAMY (1726–1781). Born in Linz, Austria, he became a Benedictine, taught scripture at Salzburg for twenty-four years, and published a treatise on the Passion and several biblical commentaries.

BESAS, ST. (d. 250), martyr. A soldier who opposed the treatment given by an Alexandrian mob while SS. Gabriel and Eunus were going to death during the persecution of Decius, he was beheaded because of his expressed admiration. F. D. Feb. 27.

BESCHEFER, THEODORE (1630–1711), missioner. Born in Châlons-sur-Marne, France, on May 25, he became a Jesuit in 1647, taught in several French colleges, and went to Canada in 1665. He served at Quebec for three years, was among the Iroquois from 1670 to 1672, and then was superior of the Canadian mission until 1687 and spiritual director of the Ursulines there. He returned to France in 1689 to become procurator of the missions, and died in Rheims, France, on Feb. 4.

BESCHI, COSTANZO GIUSEPPE (1680–1746?), missioner. Born in Castiglione, Italy, he became a Jesuit in 1698 and was sent to Madura, India, in 1710. He mastered Sanskrit, Tamil, and other languages, composed dictionaries and grammars, and wrote a number of spiritual and polemic treatises in Tamil. He wrote long poetic lives of St. Quiteria and St. Joseph, and a satire, *Paramartaguru Kadey*, on the ignorance and vanity of native teachers. He still is considered one of the major figures in Tamil literature. He died at Manapar, where he was serving as rector of the mission in southern India.

BESOLDUS, CHRISTOPHER (1577–1638), jurist. Born in Tübingen, Würtemberg, he received his law degrees and taught at Tübingen, becoming professor in 1610. He mastered nine languages, read widely in scripture and the Fathers of the Church, and in 1635 became a convert. In 1637 he accepted the chair of Roman law at Ingolstadt, Bavaria. He wrote on the beginnings of the Thirty Years' War in three volumes of documents edited from the Stuttgart archives. He died at Ingolstadt on Sept. 15.

BESSARION, ST. (4th century). He was a follower of SS. Antony and Macarius and was highly admired by the desert fathers of Egypt. F. D. June 17 (in the East, June 6).

BESSARION, JOHANNES (1403?–1472), cardinal. A native of Trebizond, Turkey, he began his studies at Constantinople in 1413, entered the order of St. Basil in 1423, studied under the Platonist Pletho, but lectured on the harmony of Plato and Aristotle as he developed disciples of his own. He was made bishop of Nicaea in 1436, but never went there. He went with Emperor John VIII to the Council of Ferrara in 1438 and succeeded by his eloquence in helping to bring the Eastern and Latin bishops into unity; later, he was at Florence with Pope Eugene IV, who made him a cardinal in 1439 or early 1440. Although the act of union was soon disregarded, Bessarion remained with Rome, wrote a defense of the Council of Ferrara, and worked with Christians of the Eastern rite. Pope Nicholas V made him bishop of Ulazzara in 1449 and sent him

as papal delegate to strife-torn Bologna; he established peace and ruled well there for five years, also reforming its courts, rebuilding many churches, and strengthening its university. When Constantinople fell to the Turks, Bessarion pleaded with Venice, Germany, and Hungary to undertake a crusade. Negotiations dragged; Pope Pius II made him patriarch of Constantinople; in 1463, the Republic of Venice signed a treaty with Matthias Corvinus, king of Hungary, but, though the crusade was proclaimed, there was still no success. Another attempt was made in 1470 and also by Pope Sixtus IV. Bessarion died at Ravenna on Nov. 18 on his return from vain discussions with Burgundy and France. In other directions, the cardinal developed the Basilian abbey of Grotta-Ferrata as a learned center, supported the study of Greek, translated parts of Aristotle, Xenophon, and others, and left a great library which became the foundation of the Library of St. Mark, Venice.

BESSE, JEAN MARTIAL LÉON (1861–1920), historian. Born in St. Angel, Corrèze, France, on Oct. 31, he became a Benedictine in 1881, studied in Austria, was master of novices at Ligugé and Fontenelle, taught history at the monastery at Silos, Spain, in 1895–97, returned to Ligugé, and in 1902 was named librarian at Chevetogne, Namur. He founded *Bulletin de St. Martin* (1892), *Revue Mabillon* (1905), *La Vie et les arts liturgiques* (1912), edited the weekly newspaper *L'Univers* through World War I, and wrote many studies of monasticism. He was honored by the French Academy for his *Les moines de l'ancienne France*. He died in Namur on July 26.

BESSEL, JOHANN FRANZ (1672–1749), historian. Born in Buchen, in the duchy of Baden, on Sept. 5, he studied at Würzburg, Bamberg, and Salzburg, joined the Benedictines in 1692, and was ordained in 1696. He became attached to the archiepiscopal court of Mainz in 1699, studied the practice of the rota in Rome for two years, and returned to serve as chief judge of the archdiocese. He also served Archbishop von Schönborn on several diplomatic missions, became imperial theologian, and honorary rector of the University of Vienna. In 1714 he became abbot of Göttweig, enlarging its library holdings and, after its destruction by fire, rebuilding it to greater worth. He wrote much, discovered two letters of St. Augustine to Bishop Optatus, and left the still-valuable *Chronicon Gottwicense*, a collection of early registers and archives, inscriptions and seals, treating of the geography, palace domains, and districts of Germany; it is the basis of study for German diplomatic history. He died at Göttweig, near Krems, Lower Austria, on Jan. 22.

BEST, KENELM DIGBY (1835–1914), poet.

Born in Botleigh Grange, Hampshire, England, he studied in Ampleforth and Ware, became an Oratorian, and was ordained in 1858. His poems include *A May Chaplet* and *Rosa Mystica;* he also published *The Victories of Rome, The Catholic Doctrine of Hell,* and translations of Carthusian works. He died in London on Sept. 14.

BESTE, HENRY DIGBY (1768–1836). Son of a minister at Lincoln cathedral in England, he studied at Oxford, settled the family estates after the death of his parents, became an Anglican deacon, preached at Lincoln, and was converted in 1798. He published a defense of Christianity against the French philosophers, an explanation of absolution, and three biographies. He died at Brighton on May 28.

BETANZOS, DOMINGO (d. 1549), missioner. A native of León, Spain, he studied law at Salamanca, became a Benedictine, lived as a hermit for five years on the Island of Ponza, and then became a Dominican. He served in the missions on Santo Domingo in 1514 and was sent to Mexico in 1526. He established the Dominican provinces of Santiago there and of Guatemala. He was provincial of Mexico in 1535, returned to Spain in 1549, and died at Valladolid.

BETANZOS, JUAN DE (16th century). Born in Spain, he went to Peru when young, mastered the Quichua language, wrote a catechism in that tongue, married an Indian, and served as an official interpreter. In 1551 he completed his *History of the Incas,* gathered less than fifteen years after the landing of Pizarro; only part of the work is extant.

BETANZOS, PEDRO DE (d. 1570), missioner. Born in Spanish Galicia, he was one of the first Franciscans in Guatemala, mastered fourteen Indian languages, wrote the first book to be printed there (no longer extant), on language and beliefs, and was the first to bring the Church to Nicaragua. He died in that country, at Chomez.

BETHELM; BETHLIN. *See* Bettelin, St.

BETTELIN, ST. (8th century). On the death of the hermit St. Guthlac, of whom he was a disciple, he continued to live a monastic life with his companions, Cissa, Egbert and Tatwin, at the Benedictine monastery at Croyland, Lincolnshire, England, where he died. F. D. Sept. 9.

BETTEN, FRANCIS SALESIUS (1861–1942), historian. Born in Wocklum, Germany, on Apr. 16, he studied in Paderborn, became a Jesuit in 1881 in Holland, continued his studies in Austria and England, and went to the United States in 1898. He taught history at Canisius, St. Louis, John Carroll, and Marquette, wrote texts on ancient and modern history, *Historical Terms and Facts* (1924), on

church architecture, the Index, *St. Boniface and St. Virgil,* and a collection of historical essays.

BETTI, GIOVANNI (1485–1549), sculptor. Born probably in San Martino a Mensola, Italy, he went to France with his brothers, Antonio (1479–1519) and Andrea (b. 1483?), where they took up sculpture. Giovanni studied under Michel Colombe in Tours, while Antonio worked at Gaillon. When Colombe died, Giovanni was recognized as the leader of the group (called Juste, after their grandfather Giusto), and was commissioned by Francis I to execute a mausoleum of Louis XII in St. Denis. The brothers worked on it for fifteen years (to 1531); they also completed other memorials, marked by effective realism.

BETTINGER, FRANZ (d. 1917), cardinal. He became archbishop of Munich-Freising in 1909, organized his see well, and helped Michael Buchberger to spread the Catholic Youth Movement and Lewis Müller to develop the Catholic Press Organization. He was field bishop for Bavarian troops during World War I and died on Apr. 12.

BETTO, BERNARDINO DI. *See* Pinturicchio.

BEUGNOT, AUGUSTE ARTHUR (1797–1865), historian. Son of Jacques Claude, he was born in Bar-sur-Aube, France, on Mar. 25, won a prize for history in 1818, published *The Jews of the West* (1822), and *History of the Destruction of Paganism in the West* (1831; placed on the Index), edited *The Assizes of Jerusalem* (1841–43), Beaumanoir's *Customs of Beauvaisis* (1842), and the annual registers of the 1839–48 parliament of Paris. He entered politics in 1841, and spoke often in favor of the rights of bishops and other citizens to petition, and for liberty of teaching and the right of association. He died in Paris on Mar. 15.

BEUNO, ST. (d. 630?). Born in Wales, he founded several monasteries in Wales, including Clynnog Fawr (Carnarvonshire). F. D. Apr. 21.

BEUZEC. *See* Budoc, St.

BEYERLINCK, LAWRENCE (1578–1627). Born in Antwerp, he studied at Louvain, was ordained in 1602, became pastor at Herent, taught in several colleges and seminaries, and in 1614 was made a monsignor. He compiled a biographical dictionary for the years 1572–1611 and a popular seven-volume encyclopedia. He died in Antwerp on June 22.

BEZZOLI, BL. JUSTINA (d. 1319). Born in Arezzo, Italy, she became a Benedictine there at thirteen, lived for years as a hermit near Civitella, and in her last years, when blind, returned to the convent at her birthplace. Her cult was confirmed in 1890. F. D. Mar. 12.

BIANCHI, ST. FRANCIS XAVIER (1743–

1815). Born in Arpino, Italy, he studied for the priesthood, was opposed by his father, but later permitted to enter the Barnabites at the suggestion of St. Alphonsus Liguori, and ordained in 1767. Known for his success in literature and science, he became superior of two colleges for fifteen years but preferred work as a confessor, to which he devoted so many hours that his health declined and he was left alone at the college when his order was exiled from Naples. He was canonized in 1951. F. D. Jan. 31.

BIANCHI, GIOVANNI ANTONIO (1686–1768), theologian. Born in Lucca, Italy, on Oct. 2, he became a Friar Minor at seventeen, provincial at Rome, where he was highly regarded by Popes Clement XII and Benedict XIV, and taught philosophy and theology. He wrote a defense of papal power, against Pietro Giannone, and of the modern theater, against the Dominican, Daniel Concina, as well as poetry and plays. He died in Rome on Jan. 18.

BIANCHINI, FRANCESCO (1662–1729), historian. Born in Verona, Italy, on Dec. 13, he studied science and theology, was ordained deacon (but no higher), and went to Rome to serve as librarian to Cardinal Pietro Ottoboni and to the latter's nephew of the same name. He was secretary to the papal commission on calendar reform, historiographer of the Lateran Council of 1725, and wrote a history of the popes, on the paschal controversy, and on the calendar. He died in Rome on Mar. 2.

BIANCHINI, GIUSEPPE (1704–1764), historian. Born in Verona, Italy, he wrote on scripture, liturgy, church history, and the fourth volume of the history of the popes left incomplete by his uncle, Francesco. He died in Rome.

BIANCONI, CHARLES (1785–1875). Born in Milan, Italy, on Sept. 26, he became a wealthy merchant in Ireland, establishing an inexpensive system of public and mail transportation. He interested himself in the foundation of the Catholic University of Dublin, was known for his philanthropy, and died at Clonmel, Tipperary, on Sept. 22.

BIANCONI, BL. JACOPO (1220–1301), prior. Born in Mevania (now Bevagna), Italy, he joined the Dominicans at Spoleto at sixteen, founded a friary in his native town, helped the area when it was sacked in 1248 by Emperor Frederick II, and combated Manichaeanism vigorously. His cult was approved by Pope Boniface IX in 1400 and by Clement X in 1674. He is also known as James of Bevagna. F. D. Aug. 23.

BIANOR, ST. (4th century), martyr. He and St. Sylvanus were hacked to death in Pisidia, Asia Minor. F. D. July 10.

BIARD, PIERRE (1567–1622), missioner. Born in Grenoble, France, he became a Jesuit, taught theology and Hebrew at Lyons, and in

1611 was sent to the mission at Port Royal, Acadia. The Huguenots, who prevailed in number there, proved so hostile that he and Fr. Edmond Masse were transferred to Bar Harbor, Maine, where they established San Sauveur. There they were captured in 1613 by the English under Samuel Argall, brought to Virginia, and barely rescued from being hanged. The English then took the two Jesuits with them on an expedition which razed Port Royal and San Sauveur and spread the word that Fr. Biard had ordered the destruction. After drifting across the Atlantic to the Azores and Wales in a prison ship, he managed to return to France, where he was violently criticized as a murderer until Champlain cleared his name. Thereafter he taught theology, did mission work in southern France, and served as an army chaplain. He died in Avignon on Nov. 17.

BIBBIENA. See Dovizi, Bernardo.

BIBIANA, ST., martyr. According to mediaeval legend, she was a Roman, daughter of Flavian, an ex-prefect, and was lashed to death by order of Julian the Apostate. Her father was branded and exiled to Acquapendente; her mother, Dafrosa, was beheaded; and her sister Demetria dropped dead when brought before the judge. All that is certain is that she died at Rome for her faith. F. D. Dec. 2.

BIBLIS, ST. (d. 177), martyr. See Pothinus, St.

BICCHIERI, BL. EMILIA (1238–1314). Born in Vercelli, Italy, she induced her father to build a convent there and at twenty became the prioress of the first convent of Dominican regular tertiaries. She died on May 3 and her cult was approved in 1769. F. D. Aug. 19.

BICHIER DES ANGES, ST. ELIZABETH (1773–1838), foundress. Born in the Château des Anges, near Le Blanc, France (her father was lord of the manor), she was sent at ten to a convent at Poitiers. On the death of her father in 1792, she undertook a long-drawn-out but successful struggle to save the family's property from confiscation by the national assembly. In 1797 she met St. Andrew Fournet, who was trying to re-establish his parish church at Maillé, and under his guidance she devoted herself to teaching and caring for the sick and needy. After her mother died in 1804 she joined the Carmelites at Poitiers; eight months later, the Society of Providence; in 1806, with four assistants, who had been formed into a community by Abbé Fournet, she moved into Château de Molante, near Maillé, and the Daughters of the Cross (also called Sisters of St. Andrew) came into being. The congregation received diocesan approval in 1816 and spread rapidly. In Igon, in the Basque country, she met Fr. Michael Garicoits, spiritual adviser of the house there, and encouraged him in founding the Priests of the Sacred Heart of Bétharram. She was canonized in 1947. F. D. Aug. 26.

BICKELL, GUSTAV WILHELM HUGO (1838–1906), theologian. Born in Cassel, Germany, he studied at Marburg and Halle, was ordained in 1867, and taught at Münster. He became professor of archaeology and Semitic languages at Innsbruck in 1874 and of Semitic philology at Vienna in 1891. He wrote theological and philological studies, translated the poems of St. Ephraem, and edited the works of Isaac of Antioch.

BICKERDIKE, VEN. ROBERT (d. 1585), martyr. Born near Knareborough, England, he was arrested for serving ale at York to a priest, acquitted, watched, and retaken for allegedly traitorous remarks. He was put to death at York during the Elizabethan persecution, on either Aug. 5 or Oct. 8.

BICKERSTAFFE-DREW, FRANCIS BROWNING (1858–1928), novelist. Born in Headingly, Leeds, England, on Feb. 11, he studied at Oxford and St. Thomas' seminary, Hammersmith, and was ordained in 1884. He spent the rest of his life as an army chaplain, was twice cited and four times decorated during World War I, when he held the rank of assistant principal chaplain royal. He also was made a monsignor and papal count. He published his memoirs, a book of impressions of America, and twenty novels under the pseudonym John Ayscough, including: *Rosemary, A Roman Tragedy,* and *A Prince in Petto.* He died in Salisbury on July 3.

BICKNOR, ALEXANDER (d. 1349), bishop. He was prebendary of Maynooth, treasurer of Ireland, elected archbishop of Dublin in 1310, but not seated for seven years, and made lord justice in 1318. He served the English king on diplomatic missions, then joined Queen Isabelle in an attempt to remove the royal favorites, the Despensers; the king countered by stating that he had embezzled funds while treasurer. Bicknor supported the queen's faction in declaring Prince Edward guardian of the kingdom; Edward seized the archbishop's diocesan revenues in retaliation. In 1330, Bicknor was made papal collector; his last years were marked by continuing quarrels with Edward II and new ones with the bishop of Ossory and the archbishop of Armagh.

BIDERMAN, JAMES (1578–1639), theologian. Born in Ehingen, Germany, he became a Jesuit in 1594, taught at Munich and Dillingen, and went to Rome in 1624. He wrote poetry, drama, biography, and more than a dozen theological studies on grace, miracles, the sacraments, and the divinity of Christ. He died in Rome on Aug. 20.

BIEL, GABRIEL (1425?–1495), theologian. Born in Speyer, Germany, he became vicar of the cathedral at Mainz, superior of the Brethren of the Common Life at Bützbach, and provost of the church at Urach. He worked with Count Eberhard to found the University of Tübingen, and was its first professor of theology from 1484 until his death there. He wrote on the canon of the mass, a commentary on the *Sentences* of Peter Lombard, a defense of papal authority, and sermons. As a political economist, he defended merchants, defined just price, and attacked the debasing of currency, arbitrary taxation, and encroachment on peasant lands.

BIELSKI, JOACHIM (1540–1599). In 1597 he published *Kronika Polska,* a revision of his father's *Universal Chronicle,* which he brought up to date. He served as secretary to King Sigismund III.

BIELSKI, MARCIN (1495–1575), historian. Born on an estate in Biala, Poland, he was educated at Cracow, fought against the Wallachians and Tatars, and was called the father of Polish prose. His works include *Lives of the Philosophers* (1535), a *Universal Chronicle* of Polish history from 550 to 1564, a treatise on military tactics and the Polish army (1569), and political and satirical poetry.

BIENVILLE, JEAN BAPTISTE LE MOYNE DE (1680–1767), governor. Born in Montreal, Canada, on Feb. 24, he accompanied his brother Iberville on an exploratory mission to the mouth of the Mississippi in 1698–99. They founded Biloxi, where Jean Baptiste became commandant in 1700 and governor in 1706, when his brother died. He was appointed lieutenant governor of Louisiana by Antoine Crozat, served from 1712 to 1715, and became governor on Cadillac's death. In 1716 he fought the Natchez Indians; he introduced slave labor from Guinea in 1719; fought Spain in 1719 and twice attacked Pensacola, Florida; and in 1722 moved his capital to New Orleans. He resigned and went to France for his health in 1726, but the king reappointed him governor in 1734. War against the Chickasaw Indians ended in defeat in 1736 and in victory in 1739. He then returned to France and died in Paris on Mar. 7.

BIEUZY, ST. (7th century), martyr. A Briton, he went to Brittany as a missioner with St. Gildas, and was slain there. F. D. Nov. 24.

BIGGAR, JOSEPH GILLIS (1828–1890). Born in Belfast, Ireland, he studied there, worked in his father's produce store, which he inherited in 1861, and entered local politics in 1869, became town councilor, and was active in the home-rule movement. He became a member of parliament in 1874, was briefly associated with the Fenians, and with Parnell spoke often and at great length to call attention to his country's demands. He became treasurer of the new land league in 1879, fought the Irish land bill proposed by the British government, and went to France in 1881–82 when the land league was suppressed and changed its headquarters to Paris, and when he and other Irish leaders were suspended from parliament. He was allowed to return to parliament in 1888, after he had successfully defended himself in the trial of Parnell supporters. He died in Clapham Common, England, on Feb. 19.

BIGI, FRANCESCO DI CRISTOFANO (1482–1525). Born in Florence, Italy, he studied under Piero di Cosimo and Albertinelli, was influenced by Andrea del Sarto and worked with him on many frescoes (notably *Life of the Virgin* at Santissima Annunziata, Florence). He did a *Life of John the Baptist*, *Virgin with Job and St. John*, *Annunciation*, *Last Supper*, *Temple of Hercules*, and contemporary portraits.

BIGNE, MARGUERIN DE LA (1546?–1595), theologian. Born in Bernières-le-Patry, Normandy, he studied at Caen and the Sorbonne, was ordained, and became dean of the church in Le Mans. After a quarrel with the bishop of Bayeux he retired from parish work and returned to the Sorbonne to prepare a careful, heresy-free edition of the Fathers of the Church. His compilation of the work of 200 figures appeared in 1575–79; he also edited St. Isidore of Seville and the episcopal statutes of Parisian bishops.

BIGORDI, RIDOLFO (1483–1561), painter. Born in Florence on Feb. 5, he studied under Ghirlandaio and was eleven when his father died, then worked with his uncle Davide, and, after 1503, was influenced by Leonardo da Vinci. His closeness to the latter is evident from the former attribution of Ridolfo's *Annunciation*, *Goldsmith*, and *Old Man* to his master. A *Coronation of the Virgin* for the cathedral in Prato, *Virgin Honored by Saints* for San Pietro Maggiore, Pistoia, *Betrothal of St. Catherine*, and an *Old Woman* in the style of Raphael are among his best work. In his last years he delegated too much to poor assistants.

BIGORDO, DOMENICO DI TOMMASO CURRADI DI DOFFO. *See* Ghirlandaio, Domenico.

BILFRID, ST. (d. 758?). A Benedictine monk, he bound and ornamented St. Cuthbert's copy of the gospels at Lindisfarne. The name is also spelled Billfrith. F. D. Mar. 6.

BILHILD, ST. (630?–710?). After the death of her husband, duke of Thuringia, she became abbess-foundress of the Benedictine convent of Altenmünster, Mainz. F. D. Nov. 27.

BILLIART, BL. MARY ROSE JULIE (1751–1816), foundress. Born in Cuvilly, Picardy, she taught catechism to others from the age of seven on, advocated frequent Communion, and,

though an invalid for years, worked to find places of refuge for the clergy during the French Revolution, was hunted from place to place as a traitor, and lost her speech as a result of her exertions. The dumb and crippled woman was completely cured by 1804, by which time she had joined a noblewoman, Frances Blin de Bourdon, in charitable and catechetical work at Amiens and Bettencourt. The beginnings of the Institute of Notre Dame were made at this time, with spiritual direction from Fr. Joseph Varin. Julie and her associates opened convents in Namur, Ghent, and Tournai; in Amiens, a new chaplain interfered with the rule and, as a result of great misunderstanding, the group was banned by the bishop. Most of the community accompanied Mother Julie to Namur in 1809, where the bishop welcomed them and they set up their mother house. She was beatified in 1906.

SR. FRANCES DE CHANTAL, *Julie Billiart and Her Institute* (New York, Longmans, 1939); M. G. CARROLL, *The Charred Wood* (London, Sands, 1951).

BILLICK, EBERHARD (1499?–1557). Born in Cologne, he became a Carmelite in 1513, was ordained in 1525, and served as prior at Cassel and at Cologne and as provincial of Lower Germany. He bettered the Carmelite plan of studies, restored and reformed several monasteries, revealed the heretical position of Archbishop von Wied of Cologne which led to the latter's deposition, argued with Bucer, Luther, and Melancthon, and attended the Council of Trent in 1551. He saved the Cologne diocese for the Church and died there on Jan. 12.

BILLOT, LUDOVICO (1846–1931), cardinal. Born in Sierch, Moselle, France, on Jan. 22, he was ordained a Jesuit, taught dogmatic theology at the Gregorian, Rome, for twenty-five years, and was active in the controversy against modernism. He was named cardinal-deacon in 1911 and resigned this honor in 1927 at the height of the controversy over *L'Action française*. He retired to the Jesuit novitiate at Rocca di Papa and died in Rome on Dec. 18.

BILLUART, CHARLES RENÉ (1685–1757), theologian. Born in Revin, Belgium, on Jan. 28, he studied at Charleville, became a Dominican, and was ordained in 1708. He taught at Louvain, where he held the chair of philosophy from 1710 to 1715, and served as master of studies, as prior at Revin, and three terms as provincial. He prepared a nineteen-volume edition of the *Summa* of St. Thomas Aquinas, a shortened compendium of this, a collection of sermons, an explanation of the Eucharist, and other theological studies. He died in Revin on Jan. 20.

BILLY, JACQUES DE (1535–1581), theologian. Born in Guise, Picardy, France, he studied at Paris, Orléans, and Poitiers, then turned from law to the classics and retired to Avignon. When his older brother Jean decided to become a Carthusian, he turned over his titular control of two abbeys to Jacques, who already had two of his own. Jacques then became a Benedictine, lived a life of austerity, and ruled his establishments well until civil wars destroyed that of St. Michel-en-l'Herme and drove him from city to city. His chief editions are of SS. Gregory Nazianzen, Irenaeus, John of Damascus, John Chrysostom, and Epiphanius. He also wrote spiritual treatises. His forced journeyings undermined his health, and he died at Paris on Dec. 25.

BINCHOIS, GILLES (1400?–1460), composer. He was born in Bins, Hainaut, became a soldier, then a singer in the chapel of Philip the Good of Burgundy. He composed masses and fifty-two secular songs, in rondeau form, with musical settings.

BINET, ÉTIENNE (1569–1639). Born in Dijon, France, he became a Jesuit in 1590, was rector of the colleges at Rouen and Paris, provincial of Paris, Lyons, and Champagne, and author of a large number of saints' lives, books of popular devotions, and spiritual treatises. He died in Paris.

BINET, HENRI CHARLES (1869–1936), cardinal. Born in Juvigny, Aisne, France, on Apr. 8, he studied at St. Sulpice, Paris, where he was ordained in 1893, and then taught. He was a chaplain during World War I, became vicar general of Laon in 1919, bishop of Soissons in 1920, and cardinal-priest and archbishop of Besançon in 1927. He died on July 11.

BINET, JACQUES PHILIPPE MARIE (1786–1865). Born in Rennes, Brittany, France, on Feb. 2, he worked for the government in the department of bridges and roads, taught mathematics, became inspector general of studies, and in 1823 accepted the chair of astronomy at the Collège de France. In 1843 he was elected to the Academy of Sciences and was later its president. He wrote widely on mathematics, physics, and astronomy, and died in Paris on May 12.

BINIUS, SEVERIN (1573–1641), historian. Born in Randerath, Germany, he studied in Cologne, taught at the gymnasium there, was ordained, taught church history at the university, and during 1627–30 was its rector. Canon of the cathedral, he became in 1631 vicar general. He worked with other scholars to produce a four-volume edition of the councils of the Church (1606), adding elaborate notes; a third, larger edition appeared in 1618. He also edited the ecclesiastical histories of Eusebius, Theodoret, and others.

BINTERIM, ANTON JOSEPH (1779–1855), author. Born in Düsseldorf, Germany, on Sept.

19, he became a Franciscan there in 1796, was ordained in 1802, and, after the suppression of the order the next year, served as parish priest and pastor at Bilk for his last forty-eight years. He engaged in theological controversy with Hermes, for which he was imprisoned for six months, and also wrote on Christian archaeology, on matrimony, on the Jesuits, and histories of the German councils and of the diocese of Cologne. He died in Bilk, Ukraine, on May 17.

BIONDO, FLAVIO (1388–1463), historian. Born in Forlì, Italy, he studied at Cremona, became secretary to Pope Eugenius IV at Rome and in exile, and also secretary to Popes Nicholas V, Callistus III, and Pius II. He compiled three encyclopedias, gathering his materials from original sources, which have become the basis for subsequent study of Roman archaeology; he also wrote on the monuments, the topography, and the churches of the city, on the institutions and customs of the ancient Romans, and on the history of Italy from the fall of the empire to 1440.

BIOT, JEAN BAPTISTE (1774–1862), physicist. Born in Paris, France, on Apr. 21, he served with an artillery regiment, entered L'École Polytechnique, taught at Beauvais and Paris, and in 1800 accepted the chair of mathematical physics at Collège de France. In 1804 he made a balloon ascent with Gay-Lussac to a height of 13,000 feet. He worked on the measurement of the quadrant of a meridian, to standardize the meter; verified geodetic operations in England and on the Continent; discovered the laws of rotary polarization of crystalline bodies; and made discoveries in double refraction of light. Elected to the Academy of Sciences in 1803 and to the French Academy in 1856, he fought to keep the meetings closed to the general public and to matters of politics. He published several volumes and over 250 papers to learned journals. A revolutionary at the turn of the century, he mellowed in time and was notably religious in his last years. He died in Paris on Feb. 3.

BIRD, BL. JAMES (1574–1593), martyr. Born in Winchester, England, he became a convert, went to the college at Douai, returned to his home, and, when he refused to take the oath of supremacy, was hanged, drawn, and quartered. He was beatified in 1929. F. D. Mar. 25.

BIRILLUS, ST. (1st century), bishop. He is said to have been consecrated first bishop of Catania, Sicily, by St. Peter, with whom he came from Antioch. F. D. Mar. 21.

BIRINUS, ST. (d. 650?), bishop. A Roman priest, he was sent as a missionary to Britain by Pope Honorius I, was consecrated in Genoa, and arrived in West Saxony in 634. He converted the king, Cynegils, became bishop of

Dorchester, and was so successful in his conversion work he was called the "Apostle of Wessex." F. D. Dec. 3.

BIRKOWSKI, FABIAN (1566–1636). Born in Lwow, Poland, he studied at Cracow, taught philosophy there from 1587 to 1592, then became a Dominican, gained fame for his sermons, and was appointed court preacher by Sigismund II. Fabian also preached crusades against the Turks in 1617–18. He is considered one of the greatest writers of Polish prose in his century.

BIRKS, HENRY (d. 1864). He graduated from Cambridge, became an Anglican minister, was influenced by the Oxford Movement, and was converted in 1845. He was ordained in 1849, after teaching at Oscott under Cardinal Wiseman.

BIRNBAUM, HEINRICH (d. 1439). A learned lawyer, he was provost of St. Kunibert's, Cologne, and is sometimes confused with his nephew, the Carthusian.

BIRNBAUM, HEINRICH (1403–1473). He became a Carthusian at Cologne in 1435, served as prior at Tournai for eleven years, and also at Wesel, Rettel, Trèves, Diest, and Liège. He retired to the monastery at Cologne for his last ten years, because of failing health, and wrote ascetical treatises and an explanation of the Immaculate Conception. He died on Feb. 19.

BIRNDORFER, ST. CONRAD (1818–1894). Born in Parzham, Bavaria, on Dec. 22, youngest of nine children, and baptized John, he became a Capuchin laybrother when his parents died and was stationed at Altötting, where he served as porter at the shrine of Our Lady for forty years. He had the gift of prophecy, and was canonized in 1934. He died in Altoetting, Bavaria. F. D. Apr. 21.

BIRNSTAN, ST. (d. 934?). A Benedictine, he succeeded St. Frithestan as bishop of Winchester, England. He is also called Brynstan. F. D. Nov. 4.

BIRT, HENRY NORBERT (1861–1919), historian. Born in Valparaiso, Chile, son of an English physician, he studied in Ramsgate, became a Benedictine at Downside in 1880, was ordained in 1889, and taught and did parish work in Coventry. He was secretary to Cardinal Gasquet, chaplain during the Boer War and World War I, and died in London on Aug. 21. He edited and wrote pamphlets for the Catholic Truth Society, published an abridgement of Lingard's *History*, and wrote *The Elizabethan Religious Settlement, Benedictine Pioneers in Australia*, and other works on his order.

BISCHOFF, JOSEPH (1828–1911), novelist. Born in Niedergeilbach, Germany, on Aug. 9, he studied at Blieskastel, Speyer, and Munich. He was ordained in 1852, and served as pastor in several parishes. Taking the pen name Conrad von Bolanden, he wrote many historical novels on the periods of Charlemagne, the crusades, Frederick II, and Gustavus Adolphus. Based on original sources, they are effective in plot, but overly popular in style and didactic in tone.

BISCOSSI, BL. SIBYLLINA (1287–1367). Born in Pavia, Italy, and left an orphan, she became a servant at the age of ten and went totally blind at twelve. She was befriended by some Dominican tertiaries and in 1302 became a recluse, living a most austere life, giving counsel to visitors, and showing special devotion to the Holy Spirit. Her cult was confirmed in 1853. F. D. Mar. 23.

BISHOP, EDMUND (1846–1917). Born in Totnes, England, on May 17, he studied in Ashburton, Exeter, and Belgium, was secretary to Thomas Carlyle, and from 1864 to 1884 worked in the education department of the privy council office. He became a convert in 1867, copied and annotated 300 papal letters (fifth–eleventh century) to England, later included in *Monumenta Germaniae*, and in 1885 became a Benedictine postulant. Ill health interfered and he left to work from 1892 to 1901 with Cardinal Gasquet as co-author of *Edward VI and the Book of Common Prayer*. He died in Barnstaple on Feb. 19. His essays were collected as *Liturgica historia* and published posthumously in 1918.

BISHOP, WILLIAM (1553–1624). Born in Brailes, Warwickshire, England, he studied at Oxford and Douai, was ordained in Rome, and returned to England, only to be imprisoned and banished. Back in England, he supported the secular clergy against the religious orders in the so-called archpriest controversy, objected to the superior appointed for the English mission, and carried his case to Rome to seek a reduction in Jesuit power. There he was imprisoned for three months on order of Cardinal Cajetan; four years later, on his return to England in 1603, he and twelve other priests drew up a letter of allegiance to Elizabeth. She died before seeing it; nothing was done for or against the rebellious group. Ten months before he died, Bishop was made vicar apostolic of England, established a chapter of canons who were to have jurisdiction should there be no superior, and reorganized ecclesiastical government under secular direction. He died on April 16.

BITHEUS, ST. (6th century). A British monk, he accompanied St. Finnian of Clonard on the Irish mission. F. D. Apr. 18.

BLACKBURNE, ROBERT (d. 1748). Son of Richard Blackburne of Thistleton, Lancaster, England, he was seized in 1695 for alleged complicity in the Lancashire Plot and left in prison for fifty-three years. Although parliament was often asked to release him, he was allowed to die there.

BLACKWOOD, ADAM (1539–1613). Born in Dunfermline, Scotland, he studied at Paris and Toulouse through the generosity of his great-uncle, Bishop Reid of Orkney, and Queen Mary. He taught philosophy at Paris, wrote on the relation of religion and government, a defense of Mary Stuart, a volume of meditations, and a scriptural commentary. He became judge of the parliament at Poitiers, France, where he died.

BLAIS, ANDRÉ ALBERT (1842–1919), bishop. Born in St. Vallier, Quebec, Canada, he studied at St. Anne de la Pocatière, took his doctor of canon law degree in Rome, where he was ordained, and returned to teach at Laval. He was consecrated titular bishop of Germanicopolis and coadjutor of Rimouski in 1890, succeeded to the see as its second bishop in 1891, founded a normal school, and was interested in laymen's mutual aid societies. He died on Jan. 23.

BLAISE, ST. (d. 316?), bishop and martyr. Bishop of Sebastea in Armenia, he was martyred during the persecution of Licinius. In one of the many legends later associated with his name, he is said to have saved a boy who was choking to death because a fishbone was stuck in his throat. As a result, he became patron of those who suffer from throat ailments and is commemorated in the rite of the blessing of throats on Feb. 3.

BLAITHMAIC, ST. (d. 823?), martyr. An Irish abbot, he was slain on the altar of the church of the abbey of Iona by invading Danes. F. D. Jan. 15.

BLAKELY, PAUL LENDRUM (1880–1943), editor. Born in Covington, Kentucky, on Feb. 29, he studied at Xavier, Cincinnati, St. Louis, and Fordham, and taught English and classics at Detroit and St. Louis. From 1914 until his death in New York City on Feb. 26 he was chief editorial writer for the weekly *America*, writing nearly 7000 such comments and 1200 articles under his own name and under the pseudonyms John Wiltbye and Cricket Wainscott, chiefly on social and political questions, constitutional law, and educational legislation. He also published three volumes of spiritual readings.

BLANC, ANTHONY (1792–1860), bishop. Born in Sury, France, on Oct. 11, he was ordained at Lyons in 1816 by Bishop Dubourg of New Orleans, Louisiana, at whose request he went to the United States in 1817. He served as a missioner in the Mississippi Valley for fifteen years, became administrator of the diocese of Louisiana and Mississippi in 1833–35 and of Texas, as well, in 1838, became bishop of New Orleans in 1835, built a seminary, and introduced Jesuits, Redemptorists, Christian

Brothers, and several orders of sisters to the diocese. He attended the first Plenary Council of Baltimore in 1852, was in Rome for the proclamation of the dogma of the Immaculate Conception in 1854, and became first archbishop of New Orleans in 1851. He died there on June 20.

BLANCA (d. 1442), queen of Navarre. Daughter of Charles III, she became queen in 1425, and married John II of Aragon, son of Ferdinand I, in 1429. On her death, civil war broke out. Blanca had named their son Charles as her successor, but John, goaded by his second wife, Juana Enriquez of Castile, supported their son Ferdinand in 1452. Charles was defeated by his father at Aybar, and never gained the crown.

BLANCA II (d. 1464), queen of Navarre. See Charles of Navarre.

BLANCHARD, JEAN BAPTISTE. *See* Duchesne, Jean Baptiste.

BLANCHET, AUGUSTIN MAGLIORE (1797–1887), bishop. Born near St. Pierre, Quebec, on Aug. 22, he studied at the seminary in Quebec with his brother François, and was ordained in 1821. He served as a curate in St. Gervais, was a missioner on Cape Breton Island and the gulf provinces, and four times a pastor in Montreal. In 1846 he was consecrated first bishop of Walla Walla, Washington, and arrived at The Dalles a year later. In 1850 the see of Nesqually was erected in place of Walla Walla, and the bishop built a log cathedral in Fort Vancouver, opened schools for Indians and new settlers, and established missions. He attended the first Plenary Council of Baltimore in 1852 with his brother, resigned his see in 1879 for reasons of age, and died in Fort Vancouver on Feb. 25.

BLANCHET, FRANÇOIS NORBERT (1795–1883), archbishop. Born in St. Pierre, Quebec, Canada, on Sept. 3, he studied at the Sulpician seminary in Quebec, was ordained in 1819, and after a year at the cathedral was sent as a missionary to the Micmac Indians and Acadians of New Brunswick. He returned to parish work near Montreal in 1827, was sent as a missionary to the Oregon regions about 1833, became embroiled in a dispute with Methodist missionaries, was named vicar general of the Oregon Territory in 1837, first vicar apostolic in 1843, and consecrated titular bishop of Adrasus in 1845. He was appointed first archbishop of the newly created see of Oregon City in 1846, while touring Europe seeking priests for his area. He attended the first and second plenary councils of Baltimore, toured South America in 1855 to raise funds for his missions, moved his see to Portland in 1862, built a cathedral, and in 1871 founded St. Michael's College. His dispute with Secretary of the Interior Delano over the latter's assignment of Indian reservations predominantly Catholic to Protestant missionaries led to the formation of the Catholic Indian Commission in Washington by the hierarchy. He attended the Vatican Council in 1870, resigned in 1880 and was named titular archbishop of Amide, and died in Portland on June 18. He wrote several books, among them *Historical Sketches of the Catholic Church in Oregon.*

BLANCO, ST. FRANCISCO (d. 1597), martyr. Born in Monterey, Spain, he studied at Salamanca, became a Franciscan, and was sent to the missions in Mexico and, in 1594, to the Philippines and Japan. He was crucified at Nagasaki with St. Peter Baptist, and was canonized in 1862. F. D. Feb. 5.

BLANDA, ST. (3rd century), martyr. *See* Calepodius, St.

BLANDINA, ST. (d. 177), martyr. *See* Photinus, St.

BLANE, ST. (d. 590?), bishop. Born in Bute, Scotland, he is said to have spent seven years in Ireland as a monk with SS. Comgall and Canice. When he returned he was ordained by his uncle, St. Cathan, and devoted himself to evangelizing the Scots. F. D. Aug. 11.

BLATH, ST. (d. 523). A holy laywoman, she was cook at St. Bridget's convent in Kildare, Ireland. F. D. Jan. 29.

BLATHMAC. *See* Blaithmaic, St.

BLEMMYDES, NICEPHORUS (1198?–1272?), theologian. Born in Constantinople, he lived and was educated in Asia Minor, and about 1223 he became a monk, built a monastery near Ephesus, and became its abbot. He barred the mistress of Emperor John Ducas from attending church and the ruler accepted the rebuke; he taught a later emperor, Theodore Lascaris; and supported and wrote a defense of the Latin Church. Other writings include a rule for his monks, geography, physics, logic, poems, orations, an autobiography, and biblical commentaries.

BLENK, JAMES HUBERT (1856–1917), archbishop. Born in Neustadt, Bavaria, on July 28, he was brought to the United States as a child, baptized a Catholic at twelve, studied in New Orleans and New York, taught at the Marists' Jefferson College in Louisiana, and joined that order. After study in France and Ireland he was ordained in 1885, taught again at Jefferson, and became its president in 1891. He did parish work in Louisiana and in 1899 was appointed first bishop of Puerto Rico. He was appointed archbishop of New Orleans in 1906, rebuilt the educational structure of the see, and died in that city on Apr. 20.

BLENKINSOP, PETER (1818–1896), educator. Born in Dublin on Apr. 19, he was taken to Baltimore, Maryland, in 1826, by his father, Peter, Sr. (who became a publisher), studied at Georgetown, and became a Jesuit in 1834.

He was ordained in 1846, served as president of Holy Cross College from 1854 to 1857, and taught at Georgetown and St. Joseph's, Philadelphia. He died in the latter city on Nov. 5. His brother William (1819–1892), ordained in 1843, worked on the Mississippi mission and later was a pastor in Boston, Massachusetts. Their sister Catherine became a Sister of Charity at Emmitsburg, Maryland, took the name Euphemia, and directed her order's establishment in the South during the Civil War.

BLESILLA, ST. (363–383). Daughter of St. Paula, she became a student of Hebrew, encouraged St. Jerome in his translation of scripture, and died at Rome after a brief life of holy austerity to which she devoted herself after the death of her husband of seven months. F. D. Jan. 22.

BLESINGTON, BL. JOHN (d. 1679), martyr. Born in Dimples, Lancashire, England, he studied at Valladolid, and returned to Flintshire as a priest. He was arrested, charged with conspiring to kill King Charles II; his defense is one of the few printed, and clearly calls Titus Oates and his conspirators against the Church perjurers. Blesington, also known as William Pleasington and Mr. Scarisbrick, was hanged on Tyburn, and beatified in 1929. F. D. July 19.

BLIDULF, ST. (d. 630). He was a monk in Bobbio, Italy, who strenuously opposed King Ariovald of the Lombards for heresy. F. D. Jan. 2.

BLINLIVET, ST. (9th century). He was twenty-fifth bishop of Vannes, Brittany, who resigned in old age to become a monk at Quimperlé. F. D. Nov. 7.

BLITMUND, ST. (d. 650). He was a monk at the monastery in Bobbio, Italy, who went to France with St. Walaricus, helped to found the abbey of Leucone, and became its second abbot. F. D. Jan. 3.

BLOIS, FRANÇOIS LOUIS DE (1506–1566). Born in Donstienne, near Liège, Flanders, he served as a royal page, then became a Benedictine at fourteen, studied at Louvain, and in 1530 became thirty-fourth abbot of Liessies. When he sought to reform the monastery at the time of the invasion of Francis I in 1537, all but three monks transferred to other settlements; de Blois set up a strict house at Ath, gained new members, returned to Liessies in 1545, and began rebuilding the ruins. He wrote a *Speculum monachorum* (1726; translated by John Coleridge in 1872 as *Mirror for Monks*) and works of spiritual advice. He died at Liessies.

BLOMEVENNA, PETER (1466–1536). Born in Leyden, Holland, he became a Carthusian, was prior at Cologne from 1506, and wrote on the Eucharist, purgatory, the authority of the Church, a book for preachers (*De bonitate* *divina*), and edited the writings of Dionysius the Carthusian. He died on Sept. 30.

BLONDEL, MAURICE (1861–1949), philosopher. Born in Dijon, France, on Nov. 2, he studied there and at the Sorbonne, taught in lower schools and at Collège Stanislas, Paris, and at Lille and, after 1897, at Aix-en-Provence. He retired, almost blind, in 1927. He published *La Pensée, L'Être et les êtres*, a revision of *L'Action* (his controversial doctoral thesis), *Le Procès de l'intelligence, Le Problème de la mystique, Le Problème de la philosophie catholique*, and *Patrie et humanité*. Two volumes of a proposed triology on *La Philosophie et l'esprit chrétien* also appeared. He died in Aix, France, on June 3.

BLOY, LÉON (1846–1917), author. Born in Périgueux, Guyenne, France, on July 11 of French-Spanish parentage, he had lost his faith by the time he arrived in Paris at eighteen. He fought in the Franco-Prussian War, became secretary to Barbey d'Aurevilly, and returned to the Church by the turn of the century. He is known for his critical essays (on Carlyle and others), *Journal*, correspondence (*Lettres à la fiancée, Lettres à Véronique*), pamphlets (such as *Les dernières colonnes de l'église*), the visionary *Le Salut par les Juifs*, and two novels: *La Femme pauvre* (1897; translated in 1939 as *The Woman Who Was Poor*) and *Le Désespéré*. He married Jeanne Molbeck, daughter of a Danish poet. His work, often furious attacks on injustice, bestiality, and neglect, was heavily autobiographical. He was influenced by Huysmans (with whom he quarreled), Baudelaire, and Fr. Tardif de Moidrey. He died in Bourg-la-Reine, France on Nov. 3.

BLUM, PETER JOSEPH (d. 1884), bishop. He became third bishop of Limburg, Germany, in 1842, gained independence from restricting government laws for his diocese, built and staffed new schools, gave public missions, saw a protectory, hospital, normal school, and two colleges built, and after an eight-year struggle won the right to appoint his own clergy and fill vacant parishes. Much was undone by the Kulturkampf of 1872, when Prussia absorbed Nassau, many institutions were closed, and the bishop himself was expelled from office by the government in 1876. He governed from Haid, Bohemia, until 1883, when he returned to Limburg, where he died.

BLUNDELL, WILLIAM (1560–1638), poet. Born in Crosby, near Liverpool, England, and the son of Richard Blundell who was put to death in 1592 for harboring a priest, William was educated at Douai. He was imprisoned with his father, but released. He wrote considerable poetry, including *A Recusant's Prayer*.

BLYSSEN, HEINRICH (1526–1586), apologist. Born in Cologne or Bonn, Germany, he became a Jesuit and was sent to Bohemia by St. Ignatius Loyola to debate with the followers of Luther and Hus. In 1556 he became professor of theology and Hebrew at Prague and published explanations of Church doctrine against various heretical leaders. He died in Graz, Styria, Austria, on Apr. 24.

BLYTH, FRANCIS (1705?–1772). Born in England, he became a convert while young, a Carmelite at Modena in 1723, studied on Malta, and after ordination worked in Wiltshire. From 1742 to 1755 he was vicar provincial of the English Carmelites and in 1756 became chaplain at the Portuguese embassy in London. He wrote biblical commentaries and sermons; his principal work was the revision, with Bishop Challoner, of the Douai version of the Bible. He died in London on Dec. 11.

BLYTON, WILLIAM JOSEPH (1887–1944), journalist. Born in England to Samuel and Catherine Blyton, he married Elsie Hull in 1912, became a convert in 1923, edited the *Ransomer* from 1926 to 1932, was London editor of the Manchester *Daily Dispatch*, and lived on a small Catholic farm colony at Marydown, Sussex, until uprooted by World War II. He wrote novels on the country scene: *Gale Warning, Arrows of Desire*; and such other works as the *Law of Self Sacrifice, The Rolling Years: a Farmer's Log*, and *English Cavalcade*.

BOBADILLA, NICOLÁS (1511–1590). Born in Valencia, he taught philosophy in Spain, went to Paris for classics, met St. Ignatius Loyola, and was one of the original members of the Society of Jesus formed in 1534. He served as chaplain in the army of Charles V, then was sent by Pope Paul III to the diets of Nuremberg, Speyer, and Ratisbon (1543–46). When the Interim of Augsburg was published by Charles, Bobadilla fought it as a measure weakening the Church and was banished from Germany. He wrote biblical commentaries, tracts on the sacraments and predestination, and a defense of the Council of Trent against Melancthon and Calvin. He died in Loreto, Italy, on Sept. 23.

BOBBO. *See* Eligius, St.

BOBINUS, ST. (d. 766?), bishop. Born in Aquitaine, he became a Benedictine monk at Moutier-la-Celle and in 760 primate of the French see of Troyes. F. D. Jan. 31.

BOBOLA, ST. ANDREW (1591–1657), martyr. Born in Sandomir, Poland, he became a Jesuit in 1609 at Vilna, Lithuania, did parish work there after ordination, and was superior at Bobrinsk. He preached widely and successfully for the next twenty years, though he met intense anti-Catholic opposition. Five years after he had established a center at Pinsk in 1652 at the invitation of Prince Radziwill and had called in other Jesuits from swampland huts where they lived in hiding, the Cossacks attacked the city and captured him. Fr. Bobola was burned, flayed, and lacerated to death on May 16. He was canonized in 1938. F. D. May 31.

BOCCACCINO, BOCCACCIO (1460–1525?), painter. Born in Cremona, Italy, he studied at Ferrara with followers of Mantegna. He did a large number of religious frescoes and paintings for the churches of his native city. His work has been compared to that of Perugino.

BOCCACCINO, CAMILLO (1511–1546), painter. Born in Cremona, Italy, son of and student of Boccaccio Boccaccino, he completed several paintings on New Testament subjects; his best work has been compared to that of Correggio.

BOCCACCIO, GIOVANNI (1313–1375), author. Born in Paris, illegitimate son of a French noblewoman named Jeanne, who was deserted by his father, he studied in Florence and law at Naples. He abandoned this to join the literary circle of the Anjou court there, became infatuated with Maria d'Aquino, already married, whom he called Fiammetta in later work, and returned to Florence in 1340. In 1348, at his father's death, he became guardian of his younger brother, served on diplomatic missions to Bologna, Rome, Padua, the Tyrol, and Avignon, and in 1350 began his lifelong friendship with Petrarch. His first work was *Filocolo*, written before 1338, based on the Fleur and Blanchefleur legend; *Ameto* is an allegorical novel which told in part the tragic life of his mother; *Amorosa visione* is an allegory in praise of love; *Corbaccio*, an angry and weary satire against all women. Three other legends were widely popular: *Teseide*, the story of Palemon and Arcite, was annotated by Tasso and imitated by Chaucer in his *Knight's Tale*; *Filostrato*, the story of Troilus and Chriseis, and possibly autobiographical, was developed by Chaucer in *Troilus and Criseyde*; and *Ninfale Fiesolano*, on a nymph of Diana whose child founded Florence. Most popular of his works is the *Decameron* (probably begun before 1348 and published in 1353), a series of 100 narratives told in framework form: by seven ladies and three young men staying at a villa outside Naples to escape a raging plague, each telling a story a day to fill the hours and revealing in detail the world in which Boccaccio lived. The sources are many (history, tradition, contemporary life, European and oriental literature), but the tales are developed with great originality and possess wide variety. Like their contemporary counterparts, some are bawdy and some anti-clerical; others are not so marked. Many of them became the material of later poems and plays, especially in England. He became quite meditative after 1354, and deeply religious after 1362. Boccaccio is also significant for his dictionary of classical mythology, *De genealogiis deorum gentilium* (1356–64),

which contains sound literary criticism; two accounts, also in Latin, of men and women of antiquity; and Latin eclogues. In 1373 he gave a series of lectures in Florence on Dante, which he was recasting as a commentary at the time of his death, in Certaldo, Italy, on Dec. 21. He had published an important life of Dante in 1364.

BOCKEN, PLACIDUS (1690–1752), canonist. Born in Munich, Bavaria, on July 13, he became a Benedictine, was ordained in 1713, and in 1721 was made professor of canon law at Salzburg, where he taught for twenty years. He became vice-chancellor of the university in 1729, and was counselor to four bishops of Salzburg and to the abbot of Fulda. He resigned in 1741, and in 1743 was superior of Maria Plain. He wrote treatises on the decretals and published his important commentary on canon law in 1735–39. He died in Salzburg on Feb. 9.

BOCKING, EDWARD (d. 1534). Born in East Anglia, England, he went to Oxford, became a doctor of divinity there in 1518, and a Benedictine monk in Canterbury in 1526. Sent to investigate the alleged visions of Elizabeth Barton, "the Holy Maid of Kent," he may have been responsible for the political features of her claims. He and six others were arrested and charged with treason against Henry VIII, and were hanged at Tyburn on Apr. 20.

BODAGISIL, ST. (d. 588). He left the Frankish court to become founder-abbot of a monastery on the Meuse, and was praised by St. Gregory of Tours. F. D. Dec. 18.

BODEY, BL. JOHN (1549–1583), martyr. Born in Wells, Somerset, England, he was educated at Winchester and Oxford, was converted, studied law at Douai, and, on his return to England, married. In 1580 he was arrested and imprisoned until 1583, when he was convicted with Bl. John Slade of denying the supremacy of Queen Elizabeth I in spiritual matters and hanged at Andover. He was beatified in 1929. F. D. Nov. 2.

BODO, ST. (d. 670?), bishop. A native of Toul, France, he, with his wife, became a religious at the Benedictine abbey in Laon, which his sister, St. Salaberga, directed. After he became bishop of Toul, he founded abbeys at Estival, Bon Moutier, and Affonville. F. D. Sept. 11.

BOÉ, JACQUES (1798–1864), poet. Born in Agen, France, he studied briefly in its seminary, became a hairdresser, and began to write humorous and lyric poetry under the name Jasmin. He was awarded the cross of the Legion of Honor and in 1852 a cash prize by the French Academy. Called the "barber poet of Agen," he wrote several volumes in his native Provençal patois: *Charivari* (1825), *Soubenis*, *Papillotos*, *Françounnetto*, and *La semaine d'un* *fils* (1849), among others. He died on Oct. 4.

BOECE, HECTOR (1465?-1536), historian. Born in Dundee, Scotland, he studied at Paris and taught at Montaigu, where he met Erasmus. From 1495 on, he worked with William Elphinstone, bishop of Aberdeen, to found a university in that city; they founded a college in 1505, and organized their teaching in accordance with that at Paris and Orléans. Boece, as principal, taught theology and medicine; he also was canon of Aberdeen and rector at Tyrie. He wrote on the bishops of Murthlack and Aberdeen and a history of Scotland which Holinshed used as one of his sources.

BOERI, PETRUS (d. 1388?), bishop. Born in Laredorte, France, he was Benedictine abbot of St. Chinian in Narbonne in 1350. In 1364, Pope Urban V appointed him bishop of Orvieto and transferred him to Vaison in 1370. Boeri returned to Orvieto at the pope's death in 1371 and remained there until 1379, when he was removed by Urban VI for supporting the antipope Clement VII. He then became Emperor Charles V's ambassador to Avignon, but fell out of favor with Clement and was deposed. Among other writings he completed two commentaries on the Rule of St. Benedict.

BOETHARIUS, ST. (6th century). Chaplain to King Clotaire II, he was made bishop of Chartres, France, about 595. F. D. Aug. 2.

BOETHIAN, ST. (7th century), martyr. A follower of St. Furfey, he went from Ireland to Laon, France, where he built the Benedictine monastery of Pierrepont. When he censured a number of persons in the area for their vice-ridden lives, they murdered him. His shrine was long popular. F. D. May 22.

BOETHIUS, ST. ANICIUS MANLIUS SEVERINUS (480?-524), philosopher and martyr. A member of the famous Anicia family of Rome, he was raised as an orphan by Q. Aurelius Symmachus, whose daughter Rusticiana he married. As early as 507 he was well known for his learning, and began to translate many of the works of Plato, Aristotle, Pythagorus, Ptolemy, Nichomachus, Euclid, and Archimedes into Latin. He also wrote treatises on logic, mathematics, geometry, music (his *De musica* profoundly affected the course of music development), and theology (*De Trinitate* and several other of his treatises are extant), and exerted great influence on the terminology, method, and doctrine, especially in logic, of the Middle Ages. Aptly called "the last of the Roman philosophers and the first of the scholastic theologians," he was especially influential through his *De consolatione philosophiae*. In 510, Emperor Theodoric, the Ostrogoth, appointed him consul and, later, master of the offices. When he defended ex-consul Albinus against Theodoric's charge of treason, he was imprisoned for nine months at Ticinum (Pavia) and charged with treason and sacrilege (practicing astrology). While in prison he wrote *The Consolation of Philosophy*. He was executed without a hearing after great tortures and has been considered a martyr, although his death was probably for political rather than religious reasons. His cult was approved in 1883 by Pope Leo XIII. F. D. Oct. 23.

BOETTO, PIETRO (1871-1946), cardinal. Born in Vigone, near Turin, Italy, on May 19, he became a Jesuit at seventeen, was ordained in 1901, was rector of the Jesuit college in Turin in 1903, provincial in Spain, and procurator in Italy in 1922-30. He was created a cardinal-deacon in 1935 and cardinal-priest and archbishop of Genoa in 1938. He served with the Congregation of Eastern Churches and on other papal commissions from 1930 until his death in Genoa, Italy, on Jan. 31.

BOEYNAMS, LIBERT HUBERT (1857-1926), bishop. Born in Antwerp, Belgium, on Aug. 18, he studied in Antwerp and Mechlin and at Louvain. He joined the Picpus Society at Louvain in 1875, was ordained there in 1881, and engaged in missionary work in the Hawaiian Islands for the rest of his life. He was appointed titular bishop of Zeugma and vicar apostolic of the Sandwich Islands in 1903, and died in Honolulu on May 13.

BOGGIANI, TOMMASO PIO (1863-1942), bishop. Born in Bosco Marenga, Italy, on Jan. 19, he was ordained, became bishop of Porto and Santa Ruffina and papal chancellor, and died in Rome on Feb. 26.

BOGUMILUS, ST. (d. 1182), archbishop. Born in Dobrow, Poland, he studied at Paris and returned to his native town to build a church and to become its pastor. In 1167 he succeeded his uncle as archbishop of Gnesen and gave up a number of his estates to found the Cistercian monastery of Coronowa. When his clergy rebelled at his disciplinary rule, he received permission to resign his see and to spend his last ten years as a Camaldolese monk at Uniejow. His cult was approved in 1925. F. D. June 10.

BOHACHEVSKY, CONSTANTINE (1884-1961), archbishop. Born in Manaiw, western Ukraine on June 17, he studied at Lwow, Poland, and Innsbruck, Austria, was ordained in 1909, took his doctorate at Innsbruck, and returned to Lwow to teach theology. He did parish work in that city, served as spiritual director of its seminary in 1915, and became consultor to the consistory there in 1916. He went to the United States in 1924 as titular bishop of Amissus and apostolic exarch of Ukrainian Catholics, developed a parochial school system, and opened a cultural museum and library in Stamford, Connecticut. He was named assistant to the papal throne in 1950, titular archbishop of Beroe in 1954, and first metropolitan of the American Ukrainian see (exclusive of New York and New England) and director of 300,000 Catholics in 1958. He died in Philadelphia on Jan. 6.

BOIARDO, MATTEO (1434?–1494), poet. Born near Scandiano, Italy, son of Giovanni di Feltrino and Lucia Strozzi, he was a polished courtier and humanist, and, as count of Scandiano, was the friend of Borso d'Este, duke of Ferrara, and served as governor of Reggio and of Modena. He wrote poems in the manner of Petrarch, eclogues in Latin, and a comedy; his special fame rests on *Orlando innamorato* (1495), left unfinished and a decided influence on Berni, Ariosto, and Tasso. This long poem of chivalry and love develops a series of episodes in the tradition of the literary romance: Orlando and other knights are suitors of the beautiful Angelica, daughter of the king of Cathay; the latter's capital, Albracca, is besieged by Tatars; finally, the Moors attack Paris and are met by Charlemagne's army. Boiardo died at Reggio, Italy, on Dec. 20.

BOIL, BERNARDO (15th century). A Spaniard, he became a Friar Minor and in 1493 was named by Pope Alexander VI the first vicar apostolic of the New World. It is not certain that he knew of the appointment, inasmuch as, through the efforts of King Ferdinand, the document seems to have been tampered with and Bernardo Boyl, a Benedictine, was given the post and sent to America. The name is also spelled Buil.

BOIL, JUAN MARTINO DE (d. 1534), missioner. Born in Valencia, Spain, he became a Friar Minor at Mayorga, built a monastery, and in 1523 was sent to Mexico with twelve other Franciscan missioners; they were so successful with converts that they were called the "Twelve Apostles" of Mexico. As apostolic delegate he presided at the first synod held in the New World (1524); he also established the Custody of the Holy Spirit, of which he twice was elected custos. He died in Tlalmanalco, Mexico, on Aug. 31. He is also known as Martin of Valencia.

BOILEAU-DESPRÉAUX, NICHOLAS (1636–1711), poet. Born in Paris on Nov. 1, he was educated at Beauvais, studied law to please his father, and from the age of twenty-one, possessed of an independent income, devoted himself to writing poetry. In a series of satiric poems he imitated Juvenal and Horace; in poetical statements of his critical position he followed the latter. Even in these early works he did much to open larger horizons for French poetry and to show the value of an ordered and polished mode of expression. His *Epistles* appeared in 1660; *Le Lutrin* (which influenced Alexander Pope's *Rape of the Lock*) in 1674; *L'Art poétique*, his most ambitious work, stands traditionally between Horace's *Ars poetica* and Pope's *Essay on Criticism* as a monument of the classical literary position. He died in Paris on Mar. 13.

BOILET, NICOLETTE DE. *See* Colette, St.

BOISGELIN, JEAN DE DIEU RAYMOND DE CUCÉ DE (1732–1804), cardinal. Born in Rennes, Brittany, on Feb. 27, he was ordained, served as vicar general of Pontoise, became bishop of Lavaur in 1765, and archbishop of Aix in 1770. He built bridges and canals and other public works, founded schools, and devoted himself to the poor. In 1776 he was elected to the French Academy. He represented his province at the States-General of 1789, made wise suggestions on Church-state relationships, and voted for the abolition of feudal privilege and for the political rights of the individual. He opposed the confiscation of church property and, when the Civil Constitution of the Clergy was drawn up, wrote the *Exposition of Principles*, indicating its viciousness, and found that all but four of the French bishops signed it. Forced out of France, he went to England, where Edmund Burke praised him; he returned in 1801, became archbishop of Tours under the concordat, and was made cardinal. He wrote poems, translations of the Psalms and of Ovid, and pamphlets on government policies. He died on Aug. 22.

BOISIL. *See* Boswell, St.

BOISSARIE, GUSTAVE (1836–1917). Born in Sarlat, France, on Aug. 1, he studied medicine in Paris, took over the practice of his father, Dr. Lucien Boissarie, and in 1891 was named second president of the Bureau des consultations at Lourdes. He demanded strict scientific tests for all reported miracles, publicly disproved the distortions of Zola's *Lourdes*, checked the findings and reports of nearly 8000 physicians, and in 1907 published *Histoire médicale de Lourdes*. He died in Sarlat on June 28.

BOJANI, BL. BENVENUTA (1254–1292). Born in Cividale, Italy, the last of seven daughters, she became a Dominican tertiary at an early age, and lived a life of prayer and penance while caring for her family at home. Her cult was approved in 1765. F. D. Oct. 30.

BOKENHAM, OSBERN (1393–1447?), poet. Born, probably in Norfolk, England, he spent five years in Italy, became an Augustinian at Stoke Clare, Suffolk, and wrote a series of saints' legends (including that of St. Ursula) in *ottava rima* and a genealogical *Dialogue*.

BOLAND, FRANCIS JOSEPH (1896–1960), educator. Born in Everett, Massachusetts, on Jan. 29, he studied at Notre Dame and took his doctorate at Catholic University in 1924, a year after his ordination in the Congregation of Holy Cross. He taught economics and was vice-president at St. Edmund's, Austin, Texas, was professor of politics and dean at the School of Economics at Notre Dame, and from 1949 to 1955 was president of Stonehill College, North Easton, Massachusetts. He wrote *Catholic Principles of Politics* (with John A. Ryan; 1940) and *The Popes and Christian Citizenship* (1941), and served as a navy chaplain during World War II. He died in New York City, where he was chaplain of a veterans' hospital, on Dec. 31.

BOLANDEN, CONRAD VON. *See* Bischoff, Joseph.

BOLCAN, ST. (d. 480?), bishop. Sent to Gaul for study by St. Patrick, he returned to become bishop of Derkan in northern Ireland and to develop a brilliant school in his see. F. D. Feb. 20.

BOLESLAV I CHROBRY (d. 1025), king of Poland. He succeeded his father, Mieszko I, in 992, and ruled over territory ranging from the Baltic past the Carpathians and from the Oder to territories beyond the Vistula. He took the title king, and was crowned by the archbishop of Gnesen in 1024. Boleslav ("the Brave") succeeded in having some of the hierarchy appointed independently of Germany, but foreign missioners still had a difficult time against pagan strongholds.

BOLESLAV II SMIALY (1039–1079), king of Poland. Son of Casimir I, he became king in 1058, revolted from the empire when Emperor Henry IV was fighting Pope Gregory VII, and re-established the independence of his nation. He won, then lost, Ruthenia from Russia. He was disliked by the nobles because of his strongly centralized government; by the people at large because of the constant drain resulting from continuous warfare; by the clergy, because he demanded reforms and insisted on enforcing the papal order imposing celibacy on the clergy. Rebels joined Bishop Stanislav of Cracow against the king; the bishop excommunicated Boleslav, and the latter declared Stanislav guilty of treason and had him put to death. In the civil war which followed, Boleslav ("the Bold") was defeated and fled to Hungary, where he died.

BOLESLAV III (1086–1139), king of Poland. Called "Wry-mouth," the son of Ladislas I became king in 1102 by defeating his illegitimate half-brother to whom half the kingdom had been bequeathed and who was supported by Pomerania, Bohemia, and the German emperor. Boleslav later (1110) soundly defeated Emperor Henry V at Hunsfeld. Emperor Lothair III gave him Pomerania as a fief in 1135, an area into which Boleslav had already introduced Christianity by sending a mission led by Bishop Otto of Bamberg.

BOLESLAV IV (d. 1173), king of Poland. He succeeded Ladislas II in 1146 as king and similarly suffered from attacks by the Germans and Danes. By 1147 the Poles were pushed out of the territory on the Baltic and that west of the Vistula. Emperor Frederick Barbarossa forced his complete submission in 1157.

BOLESLAV V (d. 1279), king of Poland. He became king in 1227 and had a reign marked by increasing feudal anarchy and attacks by surrounding powers. Duke Conrad of Masovia, head of the Teutonic Knights, cut off Poland's access to the sea; Mongol invaders devastated the country after 1241 and carried many into captivity; and German settlers, invited in to colonize the areas about Posen and Silesia, gained great concessions under the Magdeburg Law. Internal and external difficulties continued through the reigns of Leszek the Black, who ruled to 1288, and of Henry Probus, who was king until 1290.

BOLLIG, JOHANN (1821–1895). Born near Düren, Prussia, on Aug. 23, he became a Jesuit in Rome in 1853, taught theology in Syrian seminaries, and on his return in 1863 was professor of Arabic and Sanskrit at the Gregorian and the Sapienza. He was pontifical theologian during the Vatican Council and in 1880 was prefect of the Vatican Library. His writings on oriental philology are unpublished. He died in Rome.

BOLOGNA, GIOVANNI DA. *See* Boulogne, Jean de.

BOLONIA, ST. (d. 362), martyr. A fifteen-year-old girl, she was put to death during the reign of Julian the Apostate. F. D. Oct. 16.

BOLTON, EDMUND (1575?–1633?). Born in Leicestershire, England, he went to Cambridge and studied law in London. He shared the antiquarian interests of William Camden and wrote a life of Henry II which was rejected for publication as too favorable toward St. Thomas à Becket; his poems appeared in *England's Helicon* with those of Sidney, Spenser, and Raleigh. He also wrote a dialogue on heraldry, a history of the reign of Nero, a translation of the *Histories* of Florus, and *Hypercritica*, a useful work in literary criticism, published posthumously. He briefly held a minor court post under James I, lost it under Charles I, and was frequently in prison as a recusant debtor.

BOLTON, MARGARET (1873–1943), educator. Born in Richfield Springs, New York, she went to the Albany Normal School and Columbia, taught in Patchogue and New York City schools from 1892 to 1902, and became a member of the Society of the Cenacle. She taught in its training school from 1906 to 1913 and, although a member of an enclosed community, was given permission to give courses in methods of religious training at Fordham (1928–33), Boston College, Loyola (Chicago), Providence, and St. Johns. She wrote *The Spiritual Way*, religious texts; several other books for children; *Foundation Material for Catholic Action* and *A Way to Achievement*. Mother Bolton died on Feb. 27.

BOLZANO, BERNARD (1781–1848), mathematician. Born in Prague, on Oct. 5, he was ordained and taught at Prague in 1805, was accused of rationalistic tendencies in his lectures, and was dismissed in 1820. He retired to devote himself to study, and soon became famed for his studies in mathematics. Among his most notable contributions were his theory of parallel lines, the theory of functions of one real variable, and his studies in the concept of infinity, the theory of differentiation and the binomial theorem. He wrote numerous treatises, chief of which were the four-volume *Science of Religion* (1834) and the four-volume *Science of Knowledge*. He died on Dec. 8.

BONA, GIOVANNI (1609–1674), cardinal. Born of French ancestry in Mondovi, Piedmont, he became a Cistercian at Pignerola, worked at Turin for fifteen years, and served as prior at Asti and abbot at Mondovi. In 1651 the whole order was under his direction. He wrote ascetical works, including the popular *Manuductio* (comparable to the *Imitation of Christ*), a collection of patristic commentaries on the mass, a study of the use of the psalter, and an encyclopedic study of the liturgy of the mass. He was made a cardinal in 1669 and died in Rome on Oct. 28.

BONACUM, THOMAS (1847–1911), bishop. Born near Thurles, Tipperary, Ireland, on Jan. 29, he was taken as a child to Missouri, studied at St. Vincent's, Cape Girardeau, and Würzburg, Germany, and was ordained in St. Louis in 1870. He became pastor of Holy Name Church there, was Bishop Kenrick's theologian at the third Plenary Council at Baltimore, and was recommended by the council for the new diocese of Belleville. Instead, he was appointed first bishop of Lincoln, Nebraska, in 1887, and reigned until his death there on Feb. 4.

BONAGRATIA OF PERGAMO. See Boncortese.

BONAL, FRANÇOIS DE (1734–1800), bishop. Born near Agen, France, he became vicar general there, director of the Carmelite nuns of the country, and, in 1776, bishop of Clermont. After refusing to accept the Civil Constitution of the Clergy he went to Flanders and Holland, where he was captured by revolutionary troops and sentenced to exile. He escaped into Germany and died in Munich.

BONAL, RAYMOND (1600–1653?), founder. Born in Villefranche, France, on Aug. 15, he studied at Cahors and took degrees in canon law and theology at Toulouse. After ordination, he began in 1632 a community of priests whose life and work was to be modeled on that of St. Francis de Sales. He began with two others, was joined by many others, established a seminary and college at Toulouse, and received papal approval in 1665. His Congregation of the Priests of St. Mary languished and after a century was absorbed by the Lazarists. He died at Agde, France.

BONALD, LOUIS GABRIEL AMBROISE (1754–1840). Born in Monna, France, on Oct. 2, he was educated at Juilly, served in the infantry, became mayor of Millau in 1785, and in 1790–91 served in the departmental assembly. He then left the country, later serving in the army of Condé, living in Germany, and returning to France in 1797. Under the name Saint Severin he wrote on the natural law and against divorce, and joined Chateaubriand in editing *Mercure de France*. He was appointed to the council of the University of Paris in 1810, to the assembly in 1815, and to the French Academy in 1816. He lent his support to the royalists and was staunch in his attacks on Liberalism, was made vicomte in 1823, and worked with Chateaubriand, Lamennais, and Berryer on the *Conservateur* and *Défenseur*. He retired from public life in 1830 and died in Paris on Nov. 23.

BONALD, LOUIS JACQUES MAURICE (1787–1870), cardinal. Born in Rouergue (Aveyron), France, on Oct. 30, fourth son of Vicomte Louis Gabriel, he was ordained at Paris in 1811, was attached to the royal chapel, served Bishop Latin of Chartres as vicar general, and became bishop of Puy in 1823 after the concordat brought peace to the Church in France. In 1839 he was transferred to Lyons; in 1841, Gregory XVI made him a cardinal. He called a provincial synod in 1845 to outline plans to remove the remnants of Gallicanism and Jansenism; in 1840 and again in 1846 he gave great aid to flood victims. His social concern was also evident in the support he gave the victims of the closed silk factories at Lyons, his work with Spanish refugees, and his collected pastoral letters, which touched on education, government, relief, and human dignity. He died at Lyons on Feb. 25.

BONAPARTE, CHARLES JOSEPH (1851–1921), lawyer. Born in Baltimore, Maryland, on June 9, son of Jerome Napoleon, he studied at Harvard, passed the bar, and in 1904 was named legal adviser to the board of Indian commissioners. He was secretary of the navy (1905) and attorney general (1906–9) under President Theodore Roosevelt and was active in reforming the civil service. He died in Bella Vista, Maryland, on June 28.

BONAPARTE, CHARLES LUCIEN (1803–1857), ornithologist. Son of Napoleon's brother Lucien, he was born in Paris on May 24, educated in Italy, married his cousin Zenaide, and went to Philadelphia, Pennsylvania, in 1822. He completed Wilson's *Orni-*

thology (1825–33), listing a hundred or more species of birds he discovered, wrote on that subject for scientific journals, and returned to Italy in 1828 to continue his studies. At his father's death in 1840 he became prince of Canino and Musignano, entered politics, joined the anti-papal faction in Italy and was vice-president of the republican assembly. He fled Italy in 1848, settled in France in 1850, and became director of the Jardin des Plantes in 1854. His *Geographical and Comparative List of Birds of Europe and North America* appeared in 1838; several other major studies were published between 1827 and 1858. He died in Paris on July 29.

BONAVENTURE, ST. (1221–1274), cardinal and Doctor of the Church. Born in Bagnorea, near Viterbo, Italy, son of Giovanni di Fidanza and Maria Ritella, he is said in legend to have changed his name from John to Bonaventure. St. Francis of Assisi is said to have used the term *bona ventura* after he had miraculously cured him of an extreme childhood illness. He became a Franciscan in 1238 or 1243, studied at Paris, and taught theology and scripture there from 1248 to 1255. In 1257 he and St. Thomas Aquinas became doctors of theology. He already was famous both for his lectures and his *Commentary on the Sentences of Peter Lombard*. He also had become known during the bitter attacks on the mendicant friars made by the other professors at the university, a dispute finally resolved by Pope Alexander IV, who denounced the attack and vindicated and reinstated the friars. St. Bonaventure's *The Poverty of Christ* helped answer the attacks. In 1257 he also was chosen minister general of the Friars Minor and served in that capacity for seventeen years. The order was suffering from disputing factions, those demanding stricter observance and those championing a relaxed rule. He followed a policy of moderation, requiring a disciplined observance of the rule but condemning the excesses of both extremes. At a chapter held in Pisa in 1263 he suggested that a bell be rung at nightfall to honor the Annunciation, a practice from which the Angelus seems to have developed. In 1264 he founded one of the earliest confraternities honoring Mary: the Society of the Gonfalone. He refused the archbishopric of York in 1265, but in 1273 Pope Gregory X made him cardinal-bishop of Albano. At Gregory's request he prepared the agenda for the fourteenth Ecumenical Council at Lyons, called to arrange for the reunion of the Greeks with Rome. Although the pope presided, Bonaventure dominated the council, was brilliantly successful, and the reunion was effected. He died while the council was still in session. Known as the "Seraphic Doctor," Bonaventure was one of the greatest minds of the mediaeval

Church and outstanding among its scholastic philosophers and theologians. Besides his *Commentary* he wrote three related theological texts: *Breviloquium, Itinerarium mentis in Deum,* and *De reductione artium ad theologium*. He was a follower of Alexander of Hales, and derived also from Augustine, Aristotle, and some of Plato. Other works include three volumes of spiritual reading: *Perfection of Life, Soliloquy,* and *The Threefold Way;* reflections on the passion of Christ; numerous biblical commentaries, particularly on the gospels of Luke and John; nearly 500 sermons; an explanation of the Franciscan rule; and a carefully worded life of St. Francis. He died on July 15. He was canonized in 1482 by Pope Sixtus IV and declared a Doctor of the Church in 1588 by Pope Sixtus V. F. D. July 14.

BONAVENTURE, BL. (1651–1711). Born in Potenza, Naples, he joined the Franciscans at Nocera, became a missioner in southern Italy, and was novice master at Amalfi. He had particular devotion to the Immaculate Conception and was beatified in 1775. F. D. Oct. 26.

BONAVENTURE OF FORLÌ. See Tornielli, Bl. Bonaventure.

BONCOMPAGNI, BALTHASAR (1821–1894), mathematician. Born in Rome on May 10, he studied and wrote widely on mathematics and physics, became a member and later librarian of the Accademia dei Lincei, and founded and edited a mathematical bulletin from 1868 to 1887. He also edited writings of Pietro Cossalo and Leonardo da Vinci and translated an important Arabic mathematical treatise. He died on Apr. 13.

BONCORTESE (d. 1343). He became a Friar Minor, was the opponent of Ubertino of Casale, carried the interpretation of the poverty of Christ and His apostles from the Franciscan chapter at Perugia in 1322 to the papal court at Avignon, was rebuked and imprisoned for a year. In 1330, he went with Michael of Cesena and William of Occam to the court of Emperor Louis at Munich, where he died. He is also known as Bonagratia of Pergamo.

BONER, BL. ISAIAH (d. 1471). Born in Cracow, Poland, he became a doctor of divinity, joined the Augustinians at Kazimiertz, and taught scripture to the friars there. He was especially devoted to the care of the sick. F. D. Feb. 8.

BONET, JUAN PABLO (17th century), educator. Born in Spain, he was a minor official in Castile and, to educate his deaf-mute brother, invented a set of signs to aid pronunciation, developed a manual alphabet, and explained the principles behind his endeavors in a tract published in 1620.

BONET, NICHOLAS (d. 1360?), theologian. Born in France, he taught at Paris, played an important part in the discussion of the beatific vision, wrote on the Immaculate Conception and on Duns Scotus and was sent to China by Pope Benedict XII with three other Franciscans. They arrived at Peking in 1342 after six years' travel, remained at the court of Kubla Khan until 1346, and returned to Avignon in 1352. Bonet was made titular bishop of Mileve for his missionary work in Mongolia.

BONFADINI, BL. ANTONIO (1400–1482). Born in Ferrara, Italy, he became a Franciscan of the Observance there in 1439, became known for his teaching and preaching, and was sent on missions to the Holy Land. He died at Cotignola, Italy. F. D. Dec. 1.

BONFILIUS, ST. (1040–1125). Born in Osimo, Italy, he became a Benedictine monk, was abbot at Storace, and in 1078 was made bishop of Foligno. After a pilgrimage to the Holy Land in 1096 he resigned and returned to monastic life. F. D. Sept. 27.

BONFRÈRE, JACQUES (1573–1642). Born in Dinant, Belgium, on Apr. 12, he became a Jesuit in 1592, taught scripture and Hebrew at Douai and was rector of the Scots College there, wrote on the Pentateuch and other biblical commentaries, and died in Tournai, Belgium, on May 9.

BONIFACE I, ST. (d. 422), pope. A Roman priest, he was elected pope on Dec. 28 or 29, 418, and was immediately faced with an antipope, Eulalius, who had been proclaimed by a mob which had seized the Lateran. After almost four months of disorders, Emperor Honorius intervened and Boniface was installed on April 10. His pontificate was further disturbed by the claims of the patriarch of Constantinople and the Eastern emperor, which he resisted, emphasizing the rights and primacy of Rome. He also had to face the rise of Pelagianism and strongly supported St. Augustine, who dedicated several of his treatises against the Pelagians to him. F. D. Sept. 4.

BONIFACE II (d. 532), pope. An archdeacon of Pope Felix IV at Rome, apparently of German origin since he was known as son of Sigisbald, he was appointed pope by the dying Felix in the presence of a number of Roman senators and patricians. A group of priests in the city objected to his lack of a formal election, feared German influence on the papacy, and elected Dioscorus of Alexandria as antipope. Both men were consecrated on Sept. 22, 530. Dioscorus died less than a month later, on Oct. 14. Boniface then officially condemned his dead rival, and also announced his own choice as successor, Vigilius. The priests who opposed him, but who had been forgiven, burned his anathema against Dioscorus; Boniface himself was forced to burn the document naming Vigilius. As pope, Boniface approved the stand of the Council of Orange, which brought an end to the semi-Pelagian heresy, helped the

Church in northern Africa after the Vandal invasion, claimed that Rome not Constantinople had jurisdiction over Illyricum, and was extremely charitable to the poor and victims of famine. He died on Oct. 17.

BONIFACE III (d. 607), pope. A Roman, son of John Cataadioce, he had served as papal legate to Constantinople in 603, succeeded Sabinianus after a year in which the papacy was vacant, was consecrated on Feb. 19, 607, and died on Nov. 12. At a council held in Rome he directed the attending bishops to see to it, under pain of excommunication, that no one, during the lifetime of a bishop or pope, was to discuss the appointment of a successor.

BONIFACE IV, ST. (d. 615), pope. A native of Valeria, Italy, where his father was a physician, he is said to have studied under Pope St. Gregory VII in Rome. It was during his reign, which began on Aug. 25, 608, that Emperor Phocas gave to him the pagan Pantheon, which was thereupon consecrated as the church of Our Lady and All Martyrs (familiarly, Santa Maria Rotonda). F. D. May 8.

BONIFACE V (d. 625), pope. A native of Naples, he succeeded Pope Deusdedit more than a year after the latter's death and was consecrated on Dec. 23, 619. He showed great concern for the sanctity and competence of the clergy, wrote to King Edwin of Northumbria in 625, pleading that he embrace Christianity, and to Queen Ethelberga, praising her efforts on behalf of religion. Boniface died on Oct. 25.

BONIFACE VI (9th century), pope. A Roman, he became pope in April 896 and reigned for fifteen days; he may have died of gout or may have been physically removed for the accession of Stephen VI. Boniface had previously been twice silenced, as a subdeacon and as a priest. In 898 a council declared his election null, but his name was not erased from the list of popes.

BONIFACE VII. There is no pope of this number.

BONIFACE VII (d. 985), antipope. Bonifacio Francone, a Roman cardinal, was placed on the papal throne by Crescentius, son of Empress Theodora, after Pope Benedict VI was imprisoned by rebels. Boniface killed Benedict and fled to Constantinople within a month, taking the Vatican treasury with him. In 984 he returned to Rome, threw Pope John XIV into prison (where he died after four months), claimed that there had been no break in his succession, and saw Rome embroiled in civil strife until he died the following July, probably by violence. His body was dragged through the streets by a mob and flung naked under an imperial statue, before it was charitably gathered and given burial.

BONIFACE VIII (1235?–1303), pope. Benedetto Gaetani was born in Anagni, Italy, studied at Todi and Spoleto and perhaps at Paris, and gained his doctorate in civil and canon law. In 1276 he became directly associated with the papal curia. Pope Martin IV made him cardinal-deacon in 1281 and Nicholas IV, cardinal-priest in 1291; he served as papal delegate to France and Sicily in these years. When Celestine V resigned in 1294, Cardinal Gaetani was elected his successor on the third ballot of a conclave held in Naples on Dec. 24, revoked all privileges granted and appointments made by his predecessor, and was crowned in Rome on Jan. 23, 1295. The eighty-year-old Celestine was considered a possible tool in the hands of the Spanish faction, the Fraticelli, and his own Celestines; he was ordered arrested, twice escaped his apprehenders, and was finally placed in custody in Boniface's castle in Anagni, where, at whose direction it is not known, he was treated with great cruelty and died within ten months. Boniface's main aims, of bringing peace to Europe and rescuing the Holy Land, were those of his predecessors; so were the perfectly legal views he held on the position of the papacy. But he was a man who regarded too highly the temporal position of the papal state, who was easily angered, unfortunate in his choice of documentary language, sometimes unaware of major changes in history, and open to serious censure for the extent of his contributions to nepotism. Boniface was not successful in diplomacy: he lost in his attempt to give Sicily to Charles II of Anjou, king of Naples, and in spite of battle and excommunication had to accept Frederick of Aragon as king in 1303; he failed to end the war between Venice and Genoa, whose assistance he needed in a projected crusade; he made Charles of Valois the governor of Tuscany to end its war with Florence, and saw Charles destroy the Bianchi (the old Ghibellines), ruin Dante, and embitter the state against the papacy. As cardinal, Boniface had gained enormous power and wealth—in 1291 he was receiving income from sixteen benefices—and had trodden on many in his rise to the top. Chief among his opponents, though they had voted for him, were Cardinals Jacopo and Pietro Colonna. In 1297, Boniface crushed their forces, razed the city of Palestrina to ruins, and sent the Colonna faction into propertyless exile. He entered Church-state quarrels in Denmark and Hungary and placed both countries under total interdict. He also was embroiled with England and France, who were going bankrupt as a result of their long war with each other. To gain funds, Edward I demanded half of all clerical income, then an additional fifth (which the clergy reduced to a tenth). Church leaders appealed to Rome, and in 1296 Edward outlawed all clerics. Philip the Fair also increased existing taxes, imposed new

ones, and seized funds which had been collected for the crusade. Boniface issued the bull *Clericos laicos* (1296), which condemned the monarchs for their tax policies and denied them the right to levy claims against clerics without the express permission of the papacy; he later had to modify its stand. The Colonnas had been given refuge in Paris. There soon evolved a plan (allegedly written by a Pierre Dubois) for creating a new Byzantium, in which France would rule the world and the pope would be paid a small salary as a spiritual administrator. The papal legate was imprisoned, and ordered tried in a civil court on the charge of treason; the archbishop of Rheims placed an interdict on the diocese which held the legate; Boniface ordered Philip to Rome to explain his conduct, and issued *Ausculti fili*, a confidential letter on pope-king relationships. The document was destroyed at court; a forged one, written by Pierre Flotte, was circulated; and nationalistic spirit ran high. The king had allied himself with the Franciscan rebels and the Albigensians, and was successful because of the passivity of the majority of the French bishops. Flotte announced in Notre Dame that Boniface was the equivalent of antichrist. The laity supported the king; the clergy temporized. In 1300 Boniface proclaimed a holy year; Rome was jammed with pilgrims, and the pope was deeply moved by the show of spiritual vigor of the Church, but not one monarch made a visit. In 1302 the Council of Rome, under the direction of Aegidius Colonnus, archbishop of Bourges, drew up the bull *Unam sanctam*, which, among other general remarks, declared that for men to be saved they must be subject to the pope. In 1303, Boniface sent briefs that Philip had been excommunicated and that the French hierarchy should come to Rome. They refused; the council of state declared Philip the protector of the Church and Boniface a false heretic; Guillaume de Nogaret, Colonna, and other councilors drew up a bill which charged Boniface with idolatry, heresy, murder, magic, perversion (none accurate); twenty-five of twenty-six bishops present at the Louvre approved. When the pope further censured France, Nogaret and Sciarra Colonna invaded Italy, plundered the papal palace at Anagni, and imprisoned Boniface. After three days he was released by the townspeople, but died in Rome of a violent fever within a month, on Oct. 11.

BONIFACE IX (d. 1404), pope. Piero Tomacelli was born in Naples and was elected pope on Nov. 2, 1389, and consecrated a week later. He found himself immediately entangled in political matters. The antipope Clement VII had crowned Louis of Anjou as king of Naples; Boniface supported Ladislaus, heir of King Charles III of Naples, defended the kingdom for ten years, and drove out the Angevin forces. In his attempt to establish a strong Papal States he reduced the power of the citizens of Rome and often had to live at Perugia, Assisi, and other towns, to lessen popular violence, but was eventually successful. When King Wenceslaus of Germany supported the antipope, he was removed by the electors in 1400, and Boniface approved the choice of Rupert of Bavaria as successor. Another antipope, Benedict XIII, also caused trouble; Constantinople was attacked by Bajazet and asked for help; pardoners and others debased the meaning of indulgences as they roamed Europe seeking funds for papal needs. The Church also had difficulties in England, where Wyclif rose in importance and where Boniface's policy of making ecclesiastical appointments had to be surrendered to King Edward III. Boniface also introduced the method of claiming half of the first year's income of new appointments, a valuable aid to his treasury but one which aroused great hostility, especially in Germany, for the next century. Although Boniface, like other pontiffs, introduced members of his family to important posts in government, for the purpose of strengthening his political position, he was not interested in personal power. He was generally prudent, mild, and charitable; extraordinary expenses were entailed by the continuing schism at Avignon, and foreign commitments. He died on Oct. 1 at Rome.

BONIFACE, ST. (3rd century), martyr. He, his wife, Thecla, and their twelve children were put to death at Hadrumetum in northern Africa during the Decian persecution. F. D. Aug. 30.

BONIFACE, ST. (d. 307?), martyr. He was beheaded at Tarsus in Cilicia; his biography is fiction. F. D. May 14.

BONIFACE, ST. (d. 484), martyr. See Liberatus, St.

BONIFACE, ST. (d. 484), martyr. See Dionysia, St.

BONIFACE, ST. (6th century), bishop. He was highly praised by St. Gregory the Great for his piety and his direction of the see of Ferentino, Tuscany. F. D. May 14.

BONIFACE, ST. (680?–754), bishop and martyr. The apostle of Germany was born in Devonshire, England, as Winfred, studied at a monastery near Exeter, and at fourteen entered the Benedictine monastery of Nutshalling. He was made director of the school there, and wrote the first Latin grammar for English students. He was ordained at thirty, preached and wrote homilies, and in 716 went to Friesland as a missioner, but the political situation forced his return to England. In 718 he sought a missionary assignment from Pope St. Gregory II, who sent him to Germany; his name now

was Boniface. He worked in Thuringia with some success, then for three years with St. Willibrord in Friesland. His success here was great, and he was recalled to Rome in 722 to be consecrated regionary bishop. With a letter of protection given by Charles Martel, he labored among the heathens in Hesse, Thuringia, and Franconia. Many English missioners joined him, as he had founded two monasteries and many churches. Pope Gregory III made him metropolitan apostolic legate in 731, and in 738 he went to Bavaria to reform the Church and reorganize its administration. He established numerous bishoprics, founded the great abbey of Fulda in 741 with the help of St. Sturmius, and then turned to reform the Church in France, which Charles Martel had plundered and misdirected. With the help of the latter's sons, Carloman and Pepin, Boniface convoked five synods between 741 and 747. When Carloman entered a monastery, Pepin was crowned king of the united Frankish kingdoms, and Boniface made Mainz the metropolitan see. In 752 he appointed St. Lullus his successor, and returned to Friesland to evangelize the pagans of the northern section. A group of them attacked him and slew him and fifty-two companions, including St. Eoban, at Dokkum (now Netherlands), on the eve of Pentecost. F. D. June 5.

GOTEFROID KURTH, *St. Boniface*, trans. Victor Day (Milwaukee, Bruce, 1935).

BONIFACE, ST. See Bruno, St. (d. 1009).

BONIFACE, ST. (d. 1260), bishop. Born in Brussels and educated at Paris, he taught dogma at the university there for seven years, then transferred to Cologne. He was bishop of Lausanne from about 1230 to 1239, but seems to have been as publicly critical of the clergy there as he had been untactful at Paris. After being set upon and wounded, probably by agents of Emperor Frederick II, he received papal permission to resign, and became chaplain at the Cistercian convent of La Cambre, near Brussels. He was canonized in 1702. F. D. Feb. 19.

BONIFACE. See Kyrin.

BONIFACE OF MONTFERRAT (d. 1207), king. Marquis of Montferrat, Italy, he fought against Saladin, was taken prisoner at Hittin in 1187, joined the fourth crusade in 1201, and succeeded Theobald of Champagne as its leader. In 1204 he was made king of Thessalonica and ruler of Macedonia. He died near Mosynopolis, Thrace, while battling a Bulgarian invasion.

BONIFACE OF SAVOY, BL. (d. 1270), bishop. Son of Thomas, count of Savoy, he became a Carthusian at the Grande Chartreuse when very young and, as a subdeacon, was made bishop of Belley, Burgundy, in 1234. In 1241 he became administrator of Valence, and that same year was appointed archbishop of Canterbury; his niece Eleanor was queen of Henry III of England. He found the see weighed down by a debt of 22,000 marks, abolished a great number of offices, and gained from Pope Innocent IV (who consecrated him at the Council of Lyons in 1245) the privilege of using the revenues of vacant benefices and of levying special taxes. Several prelates objected and were excommunicated; when the sub-prior of St. Bartholomew's in London claimed that Boniface had no jurisdiction, the latter struck him to the ground and was badly beaten in turn. The archbishop then went to Rome, where a compromise was reached and the direct visitations of Boniface limited. In 1269 he set out with Edward I on a crusade but died in Savoy on the way. His cult was confirmed by Pope Gregory XVI in 1838. F. D. July 14.

BONIFACE OF TARSUS. In a number of popular mediaeval legends he appears as the dissolute companion of a wealthy Roman named Aglae, who sent him to the East to bring back some Christian relics. Instead of obeying her whim, he became a Christian, and was tortured and beheaded. His former mistress had changed her way of life, and when the embalmed body of Boniface was brought back to Rome, she built a church for it and was herself buried there.

BONISCAMBI, UGOLINO (1256?–1343?), historian. He became a Friar Minor at Roccabruna, Italy, before 1270, was stationed at Santa Maria at Monte Giorgio, and late in life became provincial of Macerata. He was named bishop of Abruzzi in 1295 by Pope Celestine V, but that pope died before he could be consecrated, and Boniface VIII refused to honor the selection. Ugolino (formerly called Brunforte of Sarnano) knew Brothers John of Penna and James of Massa, and after 1276 began to gather anecdotes which became the *Fioretti*, or *Little Flowers of St. Francis*, in the text compiled before 1328.

BONITUS, ST. (623–706), bishop. Born in Auvergne, he was chancellor of King Sigebert III of Austrasia, then governor of Marseilles in 677, and bishop of Clermont in 689, succeeding his brother, St. Avitus II. Later, with the permission of St. Tillo, he resigned and became a hermit at the Benedictine abbey of Manlieu at Clermont. F. D. Jan. 15.

BONIZO (1045?–1090), bishop. Born in Cremona, Italy, he was a subdeacon at Piacenza, went to Rome in 1074, and was appointed bishop of Sutri by Pope Gregory VII. He attended councils in Rome, was papal legate to Cremona, and was captured in 1082 by Emperor Henry IV and imprisoned for a year by the antipope, Clement III, before he escaped to Tuscany. He wrote on canon law, moral theology, the sacraments, a history of the

Church in his day, a study of judges in the Roman Empire, and a treatise against the schism of Cardinal Hugo Candidus. He was appointed bishop of Piacenza, but was barred from his see and eventually slain by anti-papal forces on July 14.

BONNARD, BL. JEAN LOUIS (1824–1852), martyr. Born in St. Christôt en Jarret, France, on Mar. 1, he studied at St. Jodard and seminaries in Lyons and Paris, and was ordained a member of the Society of Foreign Missions in 1850. He was sent to western Tonkin in 1851, arrested in 1852, and executed on Apr. 30 during a major persecution there. He was beatified in 1900. F. D. Nov. 6.

BONNAUD, BL. JACQUES (d. 1792), martyr. Vicar general of the Jesuit group in Lyons, France, he and thirteen of his Society were hacked to death in the chapel and garden of the Carmelite convent in Paris on Sept. 2, when the mob led by Violette directed the brutal slaughter of 143 other priests and bishops there. They were beatified in 1926. F. D. Sept. 4.

BONNECHOSE, HENRI MARIE GASTON BOISNORMAND DE (1800–1883), cardinal. Born in Paris, he studied law, became attorney general for the district of Besançon in 1830, was ordained at Strassburg, and appointed to the college in Besançon founded by Cardinal de Rohan. After the latter's death, Bonnechose went to Rome; in 1847 he was appointed bishop of Carcassonne, was transferred to Évreux and made archbishop of Rouen in 1854, and created cardinal in 1863. He worked actively to lessen friction between civil and religious authorities over matters of education and law, and went to Versailles on behalf of the citizens of Rouen to seek a reduction in the reparations sum imposed on the city by Wilhelm of Germany after the Franco-Prussian War. The cardinal died in Paris.

BONNER, EDMUND (1500?–1569), bishop. Born in Worcestershire, England, he graduated from Oxford and was ordained about 1519. He received his degree of doctor of civil law in 1525 and entered the service of Cardinal Wolsey. At first he was a time-server, defending Henry's attempts at divorce and acting as his agent at Rome. He was rewarded with numerous benefices, took the Oath of Supremacy, which Fisher and More had refused to do, and was schismatically consecrated bishop of London in 1540. In this post he tried many who were brought up on charges of heresy under the king's Six Articles. After Henry's death in 1547, Bonner proved less subservient, refused to use the new Book of Common Prayer, and as a result of unapproved sermons was imprisoned until the accession of Mary in 1553. Restored to freedom, he obtained absolution from Cardinal Pole and set about restoring the celebration of mass through the diocese of

London. Attacks on the clergy, in and out of church buildings, and destruction and profanation were frequent; offenders were tried in ecclesiastical tribunals, directed by Bonner; 120 heretics were handed over to the civil authorities, a number which moved John Foxe and ex-bishop John Bale to vilify him. When Elizabeth became queen, Bonner was arrested and tried frequently between 1560 and 1568, but successfully defended himself by showing that his questioners did not have valid orders; he died in Marshalsea prison, London, on Sept. 5.

BONNETTY, AUGUSTIN (1798–1879), philosopher. Born in Entrevaux, France, on May 9, he was too young to be ordained when he completed his theological studies, decided not to become a priest, and in 1825 went to Paris. In 1830 he began to issue *Annales de philosophie chrétienne*, and as editor stressed the continuing contribution of science to the truths of Christianity. He also directed *Université catholique* from 1838 to 1846, when he bought it out and ended its publication in favor of the older review. A number of his philosophical articles were later published in book form. He died in Paris on Mar. 26.

BONO, BL. CASPAR DE (1530–1604). Born of poor parents in Valencia, Spain, he was a successful silk merchant, then a soldier, and, after being badly wounded in battle, he became a Minim friar on his recovery. He was ordained in 1561, rose to high office, died at Valencia, and was beatified in 1786. F. D. July 14.

BONOMO, BL. JANE MARY (1606–1670). Born in Asiago, near Vicenza, Italy, she became a Benedictine at Bassano in 1622, served as mistress of novices and as abbess, suffered persecution from a number in her community, and had supernatural gifts. She was beatified in 1783. F. D. Mar. 1.

BONONIUS, ST. (d. 1026). Born in Bologna, Italy, he became a Camaldolese there, was sent by St. Romuald to preach in Africa, and served later as abbot of Locedio in Piedmont. F. D. Aug. 30.

BONOSA, ST. (d. 273?), martyr. He and SS. Eutropius and Zosima were put to death at Porto, near Rome, in the reign of Aurelian. F. D. July 15.

BONOSUS, ST. (d. 363?), martyr. He and another Roman officer stationed at Antioch, Maximian, are listed as having refused to remove Constantine's Christian banner when ordered to by Julian the Apostate. They were scourged and racked, refused to renounce their faith, and were beheaded. F. D. Aug. 21.

BONTEMPS, GAUDENTIUS (1612–1672), theologian. Born in Brescia, Italy, he became a Capuchin, preached and taught theology in Italy, wrote a study of the work of St. Bonaventure, and died in Oriano on Mar. 25.

BONUS, ST. (d. 257), martyr. A priest, he and SS. Faustus, Maurus, and nine others were put to death at Rome during the persecution of Valerian. F. D. Aug. 1.

BONVICINO, ALESSANDRO (1498–1554), painter. Born in Brescia, Italy, he studied under Fioravante Ferramola and was influenced by Lotto and Titian. His early work was done for churches in and near Brescia; in 1544 he completed *Christ in the House of the Pharisee* for Santa Maria della Pietà, Venice. Other work includes *Christ in the Desert*, *Madonna with Doves*, *Elijah*, *Vision of Moses*, and *St. Justina*. His work is often touched by a silvery tone, reveals an effective contrast of light and shade, and introduced secular groups among his religious figures. He taught many artists, including Giambattista Moroni, of Bergamo, and died in Brescia. He is also known as Moretto da Brescia.

BONZANO, GIOVANNI (1867–1927), cardinal. Born in Casteletto, Italy, he was ordained in Rome in 1890, and served as vicar general of Vigevano and rector of the Pontifical Urban College, Rome. He was named apostolic delegate to the United States in 1912 and titular archbishop of Mytilene, a cardinal in 1922, and papal legate to the Eucharistic Congress at Chicago in 1926. He died in Rome on Nov. 26.

BORCHARDT, HERMANN (1888–1951), author. Born in Berlin, Germany, on June 14, he studied at its university and at Greifswald, served in the medical corps in World War I, and taught in Berlin as an active Socialist and then as a Communist. In 1934–36 he taught at Minsk, Russia, escaped when ordered to become a citizen, and was imprisoned by the Nazis on his return. Released after a year, he escaped to New York. He wrote *The Brethren of Halberstadt* (1838), *The Conspiracy of the Carpenters* (1943), and *The Wife of the Police Commissionaire* (1946). He became a convert in 1947, and died on Jan. 23.

BORDONE, PARIS (1500–1570?), painter. Born in Treviso, Italy, he studied under Titian and Giorgione, imitating the former closely, especially in portraiture. He worked in Venice, Vicenza, Treviso; at the French court, where he was knighted (probably by Francis II); in the Fugger palace, Munich, and the chapel of St. Jerome, Milan. His monumental *Fishermen Presenting the Ring of St. Mark to the Doge* was completed for the Venice Academy. Christian and pagan scenes and portraits are in many European galleries. He died in Venice.

BORELLI, GIOVANNI ALFONSO (1608–1679), biologist. Born in Naples, Italy, he became professor of mathematics at Pisa and Messina, was led to an interest in anatomy by Marcello Malpighi, prepared a treatise on the flight of birds, *De motu animalium* (1680), and was the first to point out that comets follow a parabolic path.

BORGESS, CASPAR HENRY (1824–1890), bishop. Born in Kloppenburg, Hanover, Germany, on Aug. 1, he went to the United States as a young man, studied at seminaries in Cincinnati and Philadelphia, was ordained in 1848, served ten years at Columbus, was pastor in Cincinnati in 1859, and appointed titular bishop of Calydon and coadjutor of Detroit in 1870. He became third bishop of that city later in 1870 and saw its Catholic population change from predominantly French and Belgian to English-speaking. He resigned in 1888, was appointed titular bishop of Phacusa, and died at Kalamazoo, Michigan, on May 3.

BORGIA, ST. FRANCIS (1510–1572). Great-grandson of Pope Alexander VI and of King Ferdinand V of Aragon, he was born near Valencia, son of the duke of Gandia of the Spanish branch of the Borgia family. He was educated by his uncle, the archbishop of Saragossa, served as page to the Infanta Caterina, and in 1528 joined the court of Charles V. In 1529 he married Eleanor de Castro, was high in the emperor's regard for ten years, and in 1539 was appointed viceroy of Catalonia. On the death of his father in 1543 he became duke of Gandia and master of the household of Prince Philip of Spain. When the prince's betrothal to the princess of Portugal was broken, Francis retired to private life, built a convent at Lombay, and led an exemplary family life with his wife and eight children. In 1546 his wife died; in 1548 he became a Jesuit and went to Rome in 1550. He returned to Spain the next year, turned over his title and wealth to his son Charles, and was ordained. He traveled widely in Spain and Portugal, preaching and attracting huge crowds. In 1554 he was appointed commissary general of the Jesuits in Spain by St. Ignatius and in 1556 was placed in charge of the Society's missionary activities. He established many houses and colleges in Spain and became the spiritual confidante of dowager Queen Joanna and the abdicated Emperor Charles V. In 1561, Pope Pius IV called him to Rome, and in 1565 he became vicar general of the Jesuits, devoting himself particularly to spreading the missions and combating the reformation. He established novitiates, built Sant' Andrea and began the Gesu, set up a Polish province, built colleges in France, and opened American missions. He published a new edition of the Rule in 1567 and instilled such new vigor in the Society that he is often called its second founder. He died in Rome on Oct. 1 and was canonized in 1671 by Pope Clement X. F. D. Oct. 10.

MARGARET YEO, *Greatest of the Borgias* (Milwaukee, Bruce, 1936).

BORGIA, STEPHANO (1731–1804), cardi-

nal. Born in Velletri, Italy, on Dec. 3, he was educated under the direction of his uncle Alessandro, became a member of the Academy of Cortona, and founded a museum at Velletri for coins and manuscripts, which he opened to scholars. Pope Benedict XIV appointed him governor of Benevento, then secretary of the Congregation of the Propagation of the Faith. He became a cardinal in 1789, was left in charge of Rome during the French invasion, helped Pius VII to reorganize the Papal States, served as rector of the Roman College, and published many antiquarian and historical writings. He died at Lyons, France.

BORGOGNONE, AMBROGIO. *See* Fossano, Ambrogio da.

BORGONGINI DUCA, FRANCESCO (1884–1954), cardinal. Born in Rome on Feb. 26, he was ordained in 1906, became papal secretary for extraordinary affairs, wrote the treaty between Italy and Vatican City in 1929 and became the first envoy to modern Italy. He was then made titular bishop of Heraclea and in 1953 a cardinal. He wrote *The Seven Weeks of Daniel*, which established Apr. 7, 30, as the date of Christ's crucifixion, and popular meditations, *The Word of God*, translated by Francis Cardinal Spellman, who had once been his student. He died in Rome on Oct. 4.

BORIE, PIERRE ROSE URSULE DUMOULIN (1808–1838), bishop and martyr. Born on Feb. 20 in Beynat, France, he studied at Beaulieu, Servières, Tulle, and Paris, was ordained in 1830 as a member of the Society of Foreign Missions, and worked in the missions of Macao, China, and Tonkin. After six years of endeavor during a raging persecution, he was captured and beheaded with two native priests. His appointment as vicar apostolic of western Tonkin and as bishop reached him in prison just before his death on Nov. 24.

BORIS, ST. (d. 1010?), martyr. Son of St. Vladimir of Kiev, duke of Muscovy, and of Anne of Constantinople, he was murdered with his brother Gleb by followers of their oldest brother, Svyatopolk, to prevent them from receiving paternal inheritance. Boris, who is patron of Moscow, is sometimes called Romanus; Gleb is also known as David. Their feast was approved in 1724 by Pope Benedict XIII. F. D. July 24.

BORRAS, FRANCISCO NICOLAS (1530–1610), painter. Born in Cocentaina, Spain, he studied art under Vicente Joanes at Valencia, was ordained, worked on an altarpiece for the seminary of St. Jerome at Gandia, and was professed a Benedictine there in 1576. He completed more than a hundred paintings for churches in Valencia, Madrid, San Miguel, Aldaya, and Ontiente. He died in Gandia, Spain.

BORROMEO, ANDREA (d. 1683). Born near Milan, Italy, son of Count Giulio, he became a Theatine in 1637, served in Russian Georgia as a missionary from 1657 to 1668, became procurator of the missions, and wrote a history of his order's work in this field.

BORROMEO, ST. CHARLES (1538–1584), cardinal. Son of Count Gilbert Borromeo and Margaret de' Medici, sister of Pope Pius IV, he was born in the family castle of Arona, Italy, on Oct. 2. He received the tonsure at twelve when he became a titular abbot. He studied at Milan and Pavia and, when his uncle was chosen pope in 1559, he was appointed secretary of state; cardinal and administrator of the vacant see of Milan, though he was still in minor orders; administrator of the Papal States; legate of Bologna, Romagna, and Ancona; protector of Portugal, the Low Countries, and Switzerland; and had many of the major religious orders under his protection. He was instrumental in causing the Council of Trent to be reassembled in 1562 and was the outstanding figure in its deliberations (he helped produce the catechism embodying the council's teaching and revised the missal and breviary). In 1563 he was ordained and consecrated bishop; in 1565 he called a provincial council in Milan, but it was not until 1566 that Pope St. Pius V allowed him to assume his see. He instituted widespread reforms in the face of severe opposition (in 1567 and in 1569 he had a series of disagreements with the senate and governor over his jurisdiction which were settled in his favor by King Philip II of Spain and the pope); established the Confraternity of Christian Doctrine; originated Sunday schools; instituted, in 1578, the Oblates of St. Ambrose (now, Oblates of St. Charles); and held eleven diocesan synods and six provincial councils. When he instituted the reform of the Humiliati, the opposition caused an attempt on his life in 1569 (the Order of the Humiliati was abolished in 1571 by Pope St. Pius V). In 1570 another jurisdictional dispute with the governor, Luís de Requesens, broke out, resulting in Requesens' excommunication and eventual removal from office by Philip. In 1576 he organized relief for the multitudes stricken by the plague, after the city officials had fled. In 1583 he went to Switzerland as apostolic visitor and worked to combat Protestantism there. The following year the ill health he had suffered for several years, aggravated by his incessant labors, austerities, and traveling, worsened and he died in Milan. St. Charles was one of the towering figures of the counter-Reformation in Italy. An aristocrat by birth and a patron of learning (he founded a literary academy of clergy and laity in the Vatican) and of the arts (he was a member of the commission set up to reform church music which selected Palestrina to compose three masses, one of which was *Missa Papae Marcelli*), he

used his position and power, marked by great personal sanctity and unselfish zeal, to advance from within the much-needed Reformation of the Church, by fearless attacks on the abuses and evil ways of living so prevalent among the clergy and nobility, and by untiring opposition to the multiple new heresies and their teachings. He was canonized by Pope Paul V in 1610. F. D. Nov. 4.

BORROMEO, FEDERIGO (1564–1631), cardinal. Born in Milan, Italy, on Aug. 18, son of Count Giulio and brother of Andrea, he studied at Bologna and Pavia, began ecclesiastical studies at Rome in 1580, became a cardinal in 1587 and archbishop of Milan in 1595. He was a brilliant preacher, zealous in the direction of his priests, and devoted to the poor of his see. During the famine and plague of 1627–28, he daily fed 2000 people and led his associates in direct care which cost the lives of ninety-five priests; his devotion and leadership are recorded by Manzoni in *I Promessi Sposi*. In 1609 he founded the Ambrosian Library, for writers and artists and also open to the public. The range of his own writing was remarkable. He died in Milan on Sept. 22.

BORRUS, CHRISTOPHER (1583–1632). Born in Milan, Italy, he became a Jesuit in 1601, served in Macao and Cochin China from 1618 to 1622, and was sent to teach mathematics at Coimbra. In 1632 he became a Cistercian and died in Rome on May 24. He wrote widely on the missions, on the magnetic variation of the compass, on methods for determining longitude at sea, and was the forerunner of Halley in his magnetic charts of the Atlantic and Indian oceans.

BORSI, GIOSUE (1888–1915), editor. Born in Leghorn, Italy, on June 10, he had published two volumes of verse before he was eighteen, a commentary on Dante at twenty, took his degree in law at Leghorn, and in 1900 succeeded his father, Averado Borsi, as editor of the anti-clerical *Il nuova giornale* in Florence. Association with Franciscans and studies at the Florence observatory led in 1914 to his reacceptance of Catholicism. His autobiographical *Spiritual Soliloquies* are in the tradition of Augustine's *Confessions*. He died in battle at the Isonzo River, Italy, on Nov. 10.

BOSA, ST. (d. 705), bishop. A Benedictine monk at Whitby, England, he was consecrated bishop of York by St. Theodore in 678 when St. Wilfrid was driven from his see by King Egfrid, was replaced by Wilfrid in 686, and was restored in 691. He was highly praised by Bede. F. D. Mar. 9.

BOSCARDIN, ST. ANNA FRANCESCA (1888–1922). Born on Oct. 6 in Brendola, Italy, of a peasant family, she became a Sister of St. Dorothy at Vicenza at sixteen, taking the name Bertilla, and served as kitchen maid at Treviso. She nursed Italian troops during World War I and afterward took charge of the children's ward in the hospital at Treviso. She was noted for her exceptional patience, and died of cancer at Treviso, Italy. She was canonized in 1961 by Pope John XXIII. F. D. Oct. 20.

BOSCO, ST. JOHN (1815–1888), founder. Born of poor parents in Becchi in Piedmont, Italy, on Aug. 16, 1815, he was ordained at Chieri in 1841. He then studied at the theological college in Turin, where he began his famous catechetical and recreational work among neglected boys with the help of his mother and the encouragement of St. Joseph Cafasso. In 1844 he was appointed chaplain at St. Philomena's Hospice, Turin, but continued to house destitute boys, and to open workshops and schools for them. By 1856 he had homes for 150 and oratories for 500 others, with ten priests assisting him. He preached, wrote popular books, and sought charitable donations all through this period. He founded the Society of St. Francis de Sales (Salesians) in 1857, carried on with the support of cabinet minister Urban Rattazzi, who, though anticlerical, was impressed with his work. In 1859 he drew up tentative rules, but did not gain final approbation until 1874. In 1872 he founded the Daughters of Our Lady, Help of Christians (Salesian Sisters), to care for poor and neglected girls. He was canonized in 1934 by Pope Pius XI. F. D. Jan. 31.

LANCELOT C. SHEPPARD, *Portrait of a Parish Priest* (Westminster, Md., Newman, 1958); HENRI GHÉON, *Secret of St. John Bosco* (New York, Sheed & Ward, 1936).

BOSCOVICH, RUGGIERO GIUSEPPE (1711–1787), astronomer. Born in Ragusa, Italy, on May 18, he became a Jesuit at fourteen, studied and taught at Rome, and before his ordination was professor of mathematics in the Roman College. He planned its observatory and that at the College of Brera, Milan, suggested and directed the draining of the Pontine marshes, and recommended the use of iron bands when the dome of St. Peter's cathedral began to crack. He went to Brazil and Ecuador on an expedition planned by King John V of Portugal and obtained data for defining the spherical shape of the earth. In England he made preparations for observations of the 1761 transit of Venus and by his experiments seems to have anticipated Dollond's creation of an achromatic telescope. He returned by way of Poland and Constantinople, where he made archaeological studies, taught at Pavia, then went to Paris as director of marine optics for King Louis XV. He wrote *Theoria philosophiae naturalis*, a three-volume *Elements of Mathematics*, tracts on sunspots, fixed stars, comets, and other phases of astronomy, considerable poetry, and helped to remove the hostility to the Copernican system and to popularize Newton's law of gravitation. He invented many instruments, such as the ring micrometer, was honored by kings and scientific academies throughout Europe, and remained in high repute after his Society was suppressed. He died in Milan on Feb. 13.

BOSGRAVE, BL. THOMAS (d. 1594), martyr. A nephew of Sir John Arundel, he was convicted of aiding a priest, and was hanged with Bl. John Cornelius and his own two servants at Dorchester, England. He was beatified in 1929. F. D. July 4.

BOSIO, ANTONIO (1576?–1629), archaeologist. Born in Malta, he studied in Rome, turned from law to archaeology, and worked in the city's catacombs for thirty-six years. He made elaborate notes from the acts of the martyrs and conciliar records, mapped the area, and explored many new burial locations. His monumental *Roma sotterranea*, detailing his findings, was published three years after his death. In spite of some shortcomings and useless illustrations by poor copyists, his accurate scientific approach laid the foundation for Christian archaeology.

BOSO (d. 970). A Benedictine at Ratisbon, Bavaria, he was sent by Emperor Otto I to evangelize the Wends, mastered their language, gained their respect, and by 968 had established three sees. Adalbert of Magdeburg consecrated him bishop of Merseburg, and his fellow Benedictines, Burchard and Hugo, bishops of Meissen and Zeitz, respectively, on Christmas, 968.

BOSO (d. 1181?), cardinal. A Benedictine monk at St. Alban's abbey, England, and nephew of Pope Adrian IV (whose surname Breakspear he also had), he wrote prose lives of the popes of the eleventh and twelfth centuries and metrical lives of the saints. He was appointed cardinal-deacon in 1155, served as legate to Portugal and as governor of Sant' Angelo in Rome, and apparently led the majority of twenty-three cardinals who elected Pope Alexander III after the small German minority chose Cardinal Octavian as the antipope Victor IV. Boso was made cardinal-priest in 1163 and was present at Venice when Frederick Barbarossa made peace with the pope and brought the schism to an end. He died in Rome.

BOSSU, JACQUES DE (1546–1626), theologian. Born in Paris, he became a Benedictine at St. Denis, prior there, and preceptor to Cardinal de Guise in the struggle with King Henry III. When the cardinal was executed in 1587, de Bossu was without support, and went to Rome in 1591. He worked there with the group established to settle the conflict between the

Jesuits and Dominicans about the definition of grace; he published an attack on the Jesuit Molina and his Scotist position. He died in Rome.

BOSSUET, JACQUES BÉNIGNE (1627–1704), bishop. Born in Dijon, France, on Sept. 27, son of Bénigne, a parliamentary judge, and Madeleine Mochet Bossuet, he was tonsured at eight, made a canon of the cathedral of Metz at thirteen, went to Paris in 1642 to study at the Collège de Navarre and privately under St. Vincent de Paul, and took his doctorate in divinity. He was ordained in 1652, studied scripture and the Fathers of the Church, and preached more than 200 sermons, many against non-Catholics, while at Metz for seven years. His preaching was dogmatic, carefully philosophical, and without artificiality; his funeral sermons were emotionally poetic. He was brought to Paris, became court preacher in 1661, won converts, though he disturbed many by his immoderate language, and published the influential *Exposition of the Doctrine of the Catholic Church*. In 1669 he was appointed bishop of Condom, but resigned in 1671. He was tutor to the dauphin in 1670–81, was elected to the French Academy in 1671, and still served at Metz, where he had been made dean of the chapter in 1664. While instructing Louis XIV's son, he wrote the prince's textbooks *Discourse on Universal History*, *The Art of Governing*, and treatises on *The Knowledge of God and Oneself* and *The Knowledge of God*. Underlying his religious treatises was the idea of Providence: it appears also in his *Free Will* and *Concupiscence*. When the dauphin married, Bossuet was named his almoner, royal councilor, and bishop of Meaux, a diocese to which he gave great care. He played an important role in the assembly of the clergy in 1682 and thereafter, gained freedom for the Gallican faction of the Church, and made energetic attacks on probabilism, quietism, and Jansenism, and on Fénelon, Richard Simon, the mystic, Maria d'Afreda, and others. Much of his position was presented in *History of the Variations of the Protestant Churches* (1688). He died in Paris on April 12.

BOSSUET, JACQUES (d. 1743), bishop. He became bishop of Troyes, France, edited several works by his uncle, Jacques Bénigne Bossuet, and wrote an elaborate series of letters on the position of Fénelon regarding quietism.

BOSTE, BL. JOHN (1544?–1594), martyr. Born in Dufton, Westmoreland, England, he was educated at Oxford, converted in 1576, and ordained at Rheims in 1581. He labored in the English mission for twelve years, was captured near Durham, tortured in the Tower of London, and hanged, drawn, and quartered for being a priest. He was beatified in 1929. F. D. July 24.

BOSWELL, ST. (d. 664). Probably trained under St. Aidan, he succeeded St. Eata as abbot of Melrose, England, was distinguished as a scripture scholar and also as a preacher to the poor, and taught St. Cuthbert. He is praised as St. Boisil by Bede. F. D. Feb. 23 (sometimes, Sept. 9).

BOTTI, BL. VILLANA DE (1332–1360). Daughter of a Florentine merchant, she married and led a dissolute and scandal-giving life, but reformed suddenly, became a Dominican tertiary, and devoted the rest of her days to prayer and the care of the poor. She had numerous supernatural gifts. She was beatified in 1824. F. D. Feb. 23.

BOTTICELLI, SANDRO (1444?–1501), painter. Alessandro di Mariano Filipepi was born in Florence, Italy, to a tanner, was brought up by his brother Giovanni, from whom he received the nickname Botticelli ("small cask")—and much later was apprenticed to a goldsmith of that name. He also studied under Fra Filippo Lippi, was influenced by the Pollaiuoli, and worked at Spoleto in 1467. He sketched the Medici and himself in *Adoration of the Magi*, also using good landscape background, and completed a fresco of St. Augustine for the church of Ognissanti, Florence. He was brought to Rome in 1481 by Pope Sixtus IV to decorate the Sistine Chapel, and completed two somewhat crowded frescoes of the life of Moses, *Temptation of Christ*, and portraits of five popes. He returned to employment by the Medici and other Florentine families; painted *Birth of Venus*, a nude floating on a shell, *Venus and Mars*, *Spring*, and other mythological and secular scenes; became an enthusiastic follower of Savonarola, and painted *Birth of Christ* as a memorial to him. Other major work includes scenes from the life of St. Zenobius; *Pallas and the Centaur* representing Lorenzo's defeat of opposing factions; *Lucretia*; *Allegory of Calumny*; and ninety illustrations in silverpoint of Dante's *Divine Comedy*. He is particularly known, also, for his many madonnas, particularly *Magnificat*, *Madonna of the Pomegranate*, and *Coronation of the Virgin*. His faces are marked by great naturalness and reflect many different moods: dreamy, wistful, eager, grief-stricken. He died in Florence and was buried at Ognissanti on May 17.

BOTULF, ST. (d. 680). He and his brother Adulf were Anglo-Saxons or Irishmen who were educated in Germany or Belgium and became monks on the Continent. Adulf remained and may have become a regionary bishop near Maestricht. Botulf returned to England and built a monastery on land given him by Ethelmund, king of the southern Angles, at Icanhoh (Botulf's Stone, Boston) in Lincolnshire or at Iken in Suffolk. His brother joined him before his death. F. D. June 17.

BOTURINI BENADUCCI, LORENZO (18th century). Born in Milan, Italy, he went to Mexico in 1736, mastered the Nahuatl language, and wrote a history of that country, published ten years later in Madrid.

BOTVID, ST. (d. 1100). A native of Sweden, he was converted while in England and returned to his own country to preach as a layman. He was murdered by a Finnish slave he had freed. F. D. July 28.

BOUCHER, PIERRE (1622–1717). Born in Lagny, France, he went to Canada in 1634, served with Jesuit missioners among the Hurons, as a soldier in Quebec, and as an official interpreter. In 1648 he was commissary general at Three Rivers and as elected captain of the militia repelled an Iroquois attack in 1653. From then until 1667, except for a trip to France to plead for favorable treatment of colonists, he was governor of Three Rivers. Made a seigneur by King Louis XIV, he founded near Montreal the parish of Boucherville, where he died. His history of Canada was published in 1664.

BOUGAUD, LOUIS VICTOR ÉMILE (1823–1888), bishop. Born in Dijon, France, on Feb. 28, he studied at Autun, Dijon, and Paris, was ordained in 1846, taught church history at Dijon until 1851, and served as chaplain of the Visitation convent there for the next ten years. In 1861 he became vicar to Bishop Dupanloup of Orléans and in 1881, bishop of Laval. He wrote saints' lives, a study of the contemporary Church in France, and a five-volume *Le Christianisme et les temps presents.* He died in Laval, France, on Nov. 7.

BOUGEANT, GUILLAUME HYACINTHE (1690–1743). Born in Quimper, Brittany, he became a Jesuit in 1706, taught at Caen and Nevers, and wrote studies of the Thirty Years' War and the Treaty of Westphalia, a catechism, a treatise on the Eucharist, and three satiric comedies against the Jansenists. One of these plays, *La femme docteur,* had many editions. He died in Paris.

BOUHOURS, DOMINIQUE (1632–1702). Born in Paris on May 15, he became a Jesuit at fifteen, taught at Paris, Tours, and Rouen, translated the New Testament into French, and wrote widely against the Jansenists. His lives of SS. Ignatius Loyola and Francis Xavier were influential in France and in England after their translation there. His *Art of Criticism,* translated and published in London in 1705, also was of importance. He died on May 27.

BOUILLART, JACQUES (1669–1726). Born near Chartres, he was professed a Benedictine in 1687 and wrote a history of the abbey of St. Germain-des-Prés from its foundation in 543. He died on Dec. 11.

BOUILLON, EMMANUEL THEODORE DE LA TOUR D'AUVERGNE DE (1643–1715), cardinal. Born in Turenne, France, son of Frederick Maurice, prince of Sedan, he was appointed canon of Liège in 1658, became a cardinal in 1669, and served as chief almoner to King Louis XIV. Sent as ambassador to Rome, he defended Fénelon against Bossuet, tried to prevent condemnation of the former's *Explication,* and refused to return to France when recalled. Threatened with seizure of his property, he returned, but was captured and exiled to the abbey of Tournus. There he entered into negotiations with the British leaders during the War of the Spanish Succession and in 1710 fled a warrant for his arrest. He later regained some revenues and permission to live in Rome; there he died on Mar. 2.

BOUIX, MARCEL (1806–1889). Brother of Marie Dominique, he was born in Bagnères-des-Bigorre, France, on June 25, became a Jesuit at nineteen, taught in Spain and Switzerland, and spent forty years preparing new editions and translations of the great spiritual writers such as SS. Teresa of Avila, Peter of Alcantara, Francis de Sales, and Francis Borgia. He also translated the letters of St. Ignatius Loyola and works by other Jesuit pioneers. He died in Paris on Dec. 28.

BOUIX, MARIE DOMINIQUE (1808–1870), canonist. Born in Bagnères-de-Bigorre, France, on May 15, he became a Jesuit, taught classics and theology, but withdrew from the Society in 1842 because of ill health. Later he became a curate in a Paris parish, chaplain to soldiers garrisoned there, founded the Society of St. Maurice for them, and became editor of *Voix de la Verité.* He served on an educational commission with Montalembert, devoted himself to the victims of the 1849 cholera, and published a study of provincial councils in 1850, which attacked Gallicanism and cost him his position as chaplain. He spent four years in Rome, was made doctor of canon law by Pope Pius IX, and returned to France in 1855 to try to lessen French clerical hostility to discipline. He founded at Arras in 1861 the *Revue des sciences ecclésiastiques,* writing for it for ten years and leading a quiet, philosophical battle against Gallicanism. He attended the Vatican Council as theologian to the bishop of Montauban; on his return, he was working on a history of the Church when he died at Montech, France, on Dec. 26.

BOULAINVILLIERS, HENRI DE (1658–1722), historian. Born in St. Saire, France, on Oct. 11, he served in the army until his father's death in 1697 led him to search back through family titles, which resulted in his interest in history. He wrote several studies of feudalism, in which he sought to show that the nobility had true sovereignty, that the king was no more than a civil servant, and that government in France had declined steadily from the time of the Franks. He died in Paris on Jan. 23.

BOULANGER, ANDRÉ DE (1578–1657). Born in Paris, France, he became an Augustinian and famous as a preacher, continuing the witty style of speech and wordplay to which Boileau and others objected strongly. Fr. Boulanger was several times provincial of his order before his death in Paris on Sept. 27.

BOULAY, CÉSAR EGASSE DU (d. 1678). Born early in the century at St. Ellier, France, he taught at Navarre and Paris, became rector of the latter university, and wrote several volumes on its history. He died on Oct. 16.

BOULOGNE, ÉTIENNE ANTOINE (1747–1825), archbishop. Born in Avignon, France, on Dec. 26, he was educated by the Christian Brothers, was ordained in 1771, and became famous as a preacher in Paris and at the Versailles court. He refused to take the revolutionary oath, was three times arrested, escaped, was recaptured and ordered deported, and again escaped. As editor of *Annales Catholiques*, which he continued to publish, under various names and in various places, until 1807, he continued to attack the Civil Constitution of the Clergy. Napoleon made him his chaplain and, later, bishop of Troyes. In 1811, Bishop Boulogne preached the sermon at the opening of the council called in Paris by Napoleon and attacked the emperor for holding Pope Pius VII captive and for attempting to destroy the papacy; the bishops elected him secretary of the council, but Napoleon imprisoned him until 1814. Under King Louis XVIII he became peer of France and Pope Leo XII made him an archbishop. He died in Troyes on Mar. 13.

BOULOGNE, JEAN DE (1524?–1608), sculptor. Born in Douai, Flanders, he studied in Rome, was adopted by Bernardo Vecchietti of Florence, and became known as Giovanni of Bologna. He lost to Cellini in the competition for a *Neptune*, but left a monumental *Mercury*, a marble *Rape of the Sabines* and a bronze equestrian *Cosimo I*. Typical of his times, he was as equally competent in designing Venus and Bacchus as Samson and a series of crucifixions. He died in Florence.

BOUQUET, MARTIN (1685–1754). Born in Amiens, France, on Aug. 6, he became a Benedictine of the Congregation of St. Maur in 1706, was ordained, and served as librarian of the monastery of St. Germain-des-Prés. He prepared an eight-volume collection of sources for the history of France to the year 987; fifteen other volumes were published by other editors after his death. He died in Paris on Apr. 6.

BOUQUILLON, THOMAS JOSEPH (1840–1902), theologian. Born in Warneton, Belgium, on May 16, he studied at St. Louis College, the Bruges seminary, and the Gregorian, Rome, where he was ordained in 1865. He received his doctorate in divinity and taught moral theology at Bruges in 1867, was appointed to the chair of theology at the Catholic University in Lille in 1877, and remained there until 1899, when he was appointed to the chair of moral theology at the new Catholic University in Washington, D.C., a position he held until his death in Brussels Nov. 5. A leader in restoring Thomism and moral theology to Catholic education, he wrote theological treatises and on education, and translated French and Latin works into English.

BOURASSÉ, JEAN JACQUES (1813–1872). Born in St. Maure, France, on Dec. 22, he was ordained at Paris, taught science at the seminary in Tours, and wrote on church architecture and archaeology. He died at Tours on Oct. 4.

BOURCHIER, THOMAS (1406–1486), cardinal. Son of William Bourchier, earl of Eu, and Lady Anne Plantagenet, he studied at Oxford, held several clerical posts in Coventry and London, and became chancellor of Cambridge in 1433 and bishop of Worcester in 1434. He was enthroned as bishop of Ely in 1446 and as archbishop of Canterbury in 1455. Bourchier presided at the trial of Bishop Reginald Peacock in 1457, forced him to resign his see, and unwarrantedly kept him a prisoner for two years. He became chancellor to King Henry VI and acted for him during his madness, but his official actions were often interrupted by the course of the War of the Roses. In 1461, having since joined the Yorkist cause, he crowned Edward IV as king. His reward was delayed, but he finally became cardinal in 1473. Bourchier delivered the child Edward V and his brother Richard to Richard, duke of Gloucester, pledging their safety. After the children's deaths Richard III was crowned by the archbishop; when York was crushed, he crowned the victorious Henry VII in 1485. Bourchier died at his estate at Knowle on Apr. 6.

BOURDALOUE, LOUIS (1632–1704). Born in Bourges, France, on Aug. 20, he became a Jesuit at fifteen, and had attained wide fame for his preaching by 1665. His sermons, carefully planned, were delivered in Paris over a thirty-four year period and fill a dozen volumes. He died in Paris on May 13.

BOURDEILLES, BL. HÉLIE DE (1423?–1484), cardinal. Born in Périgord, France, he became a Franciscan, and was appointed bishop of Périgueux in 1447, archbishop of Tours in 1468, and cardinal in 1483. He suffered imprisonment by the English and wrote a Latin defense of Joan of Arc. F. D. July 5.

BOURDON, JEAN (1612–1668). Born in Rouen, France, he went to Canada in 1634 as engineer and in 1663 became first attorney general of the chief council of Quebec. He surveyed and laid out the domains and land grants of its territory and mapped the territory and the city. He was the companion of St. Isaac Jogues on a trip to Albany to seek peace with the Iroquois and later led an expedition to Hudson's Bay which was stopped by Indian attacks. He died at Quebec, where a division, St. Jean, is named after him.

BOURGADE, FRANÇOIS (1806–1866). Born in Gaujan, France, on July 7, he was ordained in 1832 and became a missioner in Algeria and Tunisia. He founded hospitals and schools and wrote on the Koran, on linguistics, and a refutation of Renan's life of Christ. He died in Paris on May 21.

BOURGADE, PETER (1845–1908), archbishop. Born in either Clermont or Puy-de-Dôme, France, on Oct. 17, he studied at Billom, and was ordained in Santa Fe, New Mexico, in 1869. He did missionary and pastoral work in Arizona, New Mexico, and Texas the next sixteen years (except for 1872–74, when he returned to France in ill health), and was consecrated titular bishop of Thaumacus and vicar apostolic of Arizona in 1885. He was appointed first bishop of Tucson in 1897, was promoted to archbishop of Santa Fe in 1899, and died there on May 17.

BOURGEOYS, BL. MARGUERITE (1620–1700), foundress. Born at Troyes, France, she tried at twenty to enter religious life but met with many disappointments. In 1652 the governor of Montreal came looking for a teacher, and she went to Canada with his party, to become housekeeper, tutor of the children at the garrison, and helper in its hospital. In 1658 a school building was established, for a dozen students, but Marguerite returned to France to persuade four others to return with her to build for the future; a second trip in 1670 brought six more women and gained the support of King Louis XIV. On her return she set up a religious community, the Congregation of Notre Dame of Montreal, which was officially approved by Bishop Laval in 1676. He and his successor were not too favorable toward the independence of the group, and it was not until 1698 that twenty-four sisters could make their first vows. A boarding school had been opened in 1673, a school for the Iroquois in 1676, and five others as far as Quebec. Today there are over 200 establishments in the United States and Canada. She was beatified in 1950. F. D. Jan. 19.

E. F. BUTLER, *Life of the Ven. Marguerite Bourgeoys* (New York, Kenedy, 1932).

BOURGET, IGNACE (1799–1885), bishop. Born at Point Lévis, Quebec, Canada, on Oct. 30, he was ordained in 1822, became vicar general of Quebec in 1836, coadjutor bishop to Bishop Lartigue in 1837, and bishop of Montreal in 1840. He installed a chapter of canons, built an asylum for deaf-mutes, and intro-

duced a number of religious congregations to his diocese. He was in Rome for the proclamation of the dogma of the Immaculate Conception (1854) and for the Vatican Council (1870). In 1870 he also laid the cornerstone of the new cathedral, fire having destroyed the former building in 1852. He was active in bettering his clergy and his parishioners, and was the first to divide the city into more than one parish. He retired in 1876 to Sault-au-Recollet, near Montreal, and died on June 8.

BOURGET, PAUL (1852–1935), novelist. Born in Amiens, France, he studied in Strassburg and at Collège Louis le Grand, Paris, and Ste. Barbe. He taught briefly, traveled, worked as a free-lance writer, and supported himself by tutoring. He became an agnostic and Liberal, wrote a volume of poems, began to publish short stories and novels, and soon attained great success for his psychological portraits, often on the edge of pessimism. He returned to the Church about 1889 and became a conservative leader. *A Tragic Idyll, The Weight of a Name, Two Sisters, The Night Cometh*, and *Le Démon de midi* are among the best known of his seventy books.

BOURGOGNE, JEAN DE. *See* Mandeville, Jean de.

BOURGOING, FRANÇOIS (1585–1662). Born in Paris, France, he was curé at Clinchy when he was attracted to Cardinal de Bérulle and became one of the ten early Oratorians. In 1631 he was assistant to the superior general, Fr. de Condren, whom he succeeded in 1641. He wrote treatises on asceticism.

BOURNE, FRANCIS ALPHONSUS (1861–1935), cardinal. Born in Clapham, England, on Mar. 23, son of Henry and Ellen Byrne Bourne, he studied at St. Cuthbert's and St. Edmund's, at the seminary in Hammersmith, St. Sulpice, Paris, and Louvain. He was ordained in 1884, held several curacies, and in 1889 was in charge of a minor seminary in Sussex. He was made a monsignor in 1895, coadjutor at Southwark in 1896, succeeding to the see in 1897 when Bishop Butt resigned, and succeeded Cardinal Vaughan as fourth archbishop of Westminster in 1903. He worked for educational reform, held an international Eucharistic Congress in 1908, and consecrated his cathedral in 1910. He became a cardinal in 1911, published *Ecclesiastical Training* in 1926, and served as papal legate at the Joan of Arc celebration at Rouen in 1931. He died in Westminster on Jan. 1.

ERNEST OLDMEADOW, *Francis, Cardinal Bourne* (2 vols. London, Burns, 1940–43).

BOURNE, GILBERT (d. 1569), bishop. Son of Philip Bourne of Worcestershire, England, he attended Oxford, served in London and Essex parishes under appointment from King Henry VIII, barely escaped assassination because of his sermons, and was consecrated bishop of Bath and Wells in 1554. He was president of the Council of Wales under Queen Mary, but lost the post on Elizabeth I's accession. He was deprived of his bishopric in 1559 and jailed in the Tower and other prisons for ten years, three of them in solitary confinement. He died in prison at Silverton, Devonshire, on Sept. 10.

BOUVENS, CHARLES DE (1750–1830). Born in Bourg, France, he was ordained and was vicar general to Archbishop de Conzié of Tours until the revolution forced them into exile in Germany. When de Conzié died, his vicar went to England, where he preached several funeral orations before the French court in exile. When Louis XVIII returned in 1815, de Bouvens served as his chaplain. He resigned in 1828 and was driven out of Paris by the uprising of 1830.

BOUVET, JOACHIM (d. 1732), missioner. Born in Le Mans, France, he became a Jesuit, studied astronomy and geography, and was sent by King Louis XIV with five others of his Society to China to collect scientific data. Arriving at the Chinese court of Khang-hi in 1688, he and Fr. Gerbillon served the emperor by writing mathematical works in Tatar, later translated into Chinese. Bouvet returned to France with a gift of books for the king and returned with engravings and other gifts in 1699. He brought ten missioners with him, was again well received, became interpreter for the emperor's son, and from 1708 to 1715 directed a survey of the empire and mapped several provinces. He wrote a life of the emperor, who allowed him to seek converts, had great missionary success, and contributed much to the scientific development of China. He died in Peking on June 28.

BOUVIER, JEAN BAPTISTE (1783–1854), bishop. Born in St. Charles-la-Forêt, France, on Jan. 16, he was ordained in 1808, and taught philosophy and theology in several colleges and seminaries. From 1819 to 1834 he was vicar general of Le Mans and superior of its seminary, becoming bishop of the diocese in the latter year. His *Institutiones theologicae* (which had some traces of Gallicanism through its first seven editions) appeared in a revised version in 1853 and was widely used as a textbook. He was a strong opponent of Jansenism and a friend of Pope Pius IX, who brought him to Rome for the proclamation of the dogma of the Immaculate Conception; Bouvier died there on Dec. 28.

BOVA, ST. (d. 680?). Sister of St. Baldericus, she became first abbess of the convent of Our Lady of Rheims, which he founded, and was succeeded by her sister, St. Doda. F. D. Apr. 24.

BOWDEN, HENRY SEBASTIAN (1836–1920). Born in London on Feb. 16, he studied

at Eton, left when his father was converted, became a Catholic in 1852, and studied under Newman at the Catholic University of Dublin. He served in the army from 1855 to 1867, became a captain, and resigned to become an Oratorian. He was ordained in 1870, served in a parish near Brompton, was superior of the English Oratorians three times, taught, and published saints' lives and controversial and devotional writings. He died in London on Sept. 26.

BOWES, EDWARD E. (1874–1946), executive. Born in San Francisco, California, on June 14, he had little schooling, as he was eight when his father died, lost a real-estate fortune in the 1906 earthquake, but gained another as the city was rebuilt, and was active in political and police reform. He became a theater manager, an executive in Metro-Goldwyn-Mayer motion pictures, opened the Capitol and other theaters in New York City and Boston. As Major Bowes (he was an intelligence officer in World War I and a major in the reserve army) he became popular as a radio entertainer, developer of amateur theatrical talent, and in 1934 director of a large merger of radio stations. In his last years he became a convert and was well known for his philanthropies. He died in Rumson, New Jersey, on June 13.

BOWES, VEN. MARMADUKE (d. 1585), martyr. See Taylor, Ven. Hugh.

BOWYER, SIR GEORGE (1811–1883), judge. Born in Berkshire, England, on Oct. 8, he studied law in London and was called to the bar in 1839. After his *The English Constitution* (1841) and *Commentaries on the Civil Law* (1844), Oxford gave him an honorary degree. He became a convert in 1850, explained the appointment of Catholic bishops in England by writing pamphlets and letters, and published *Commentaries on Universal Public Law* in 1854 and *Introduction to the Study and Use of the Civil Law* in 1874. From 1852 to 1868 he was a member of parliament from Dundalk; after a six-year absence he served as member for Wexford from 1874 to 1880. He had succeeded his father to the baronetcy in 1860. The hospital of St. John of Jerusalem in London was built from his charities. He died in London on June 7.

BOYCE, JOHN (1810–1864), novelist. Born in Donegal, Ireland, he studied at Navan and Maynooth, was ordained in 1837, and went to Eastport, Maine, as a missioner in 1845. He was transferred to Worcester, Massachusetts, in 1847, where he died on Jan. 2. He wrote popular fiction, such as *Shandy Maguire or Tricks upon Travellers* (1848), *The Spaewife or the Queen's Secret* (1853), and *Mary Lee or the Yankee in Ireland* (1859). He also was a contributor to the Boston *Pilot* and to magazines.

BOYL, BERNARDO. *See* Boil, Bernardo.

BOYLAN, JOHN J. (1889?–1953), bishop. Born in New York City, on Oct. 7, he studied in Emmitsburg and Rochester seminaries, at Catholic University and the Pontifical Athenaeum, Rome, and was ordained in 1915. He did parish work in Council Bluffs, Iowa, taught at Dowling College, Des Moines, from 1918 to 1923, and was its president to 1942. He was vicar general of the diocese of Des Moines from 1934 to 1942 and was consecrated bishop of Rockford, Illinois, in 1943. He died near Narragansett, Rhode Island, on July 19.

BOYLAN, WILLIAM A. (1869–1940), educator. Born in New York City on Jan. 6, he studied at St. Francis Xavier, taught in the public schools of the city, was associate superintendent of schools in 1927–30, and from 1930 until 1938 served as first president of Brooklyn College. He died in New York City on July 8.

BOYLE, HUGH CHARLES (1873–1950), bishop. Born in Cambria City, Pennsylvania, on Oct. 8, he studied at St. Vincent's College and seminary, and was ordained in 1898. He did parish work (except in 1909–16 when he was superintendent of Catholic schools in the Pittsburgh diocese) until 1921, when he was appointed bishop of Pittsburgh, where he reigned until his death on Dec. 22.

BOZON, NICHOLAS (14th century), poet. Scholars believe he was of a Norfolk, England, family, who became a Franciscan, was stationed in Nottingham, wrote *Contes moralisés* after 1320, and possibly died a victim of the plague of 1349. Many of his Anglo-Norman poems were written in the late thirteenth century; he is best known for metrical prayers and lives of SS. Agatha, Agnes, Christine, Edmund, Elizabeth of Hungary, Juliana, Lucy, Margaret, Martha, Mary Magdalen, and the Virgin Mary. These biographies drew heavily from the *Golden Legend* of Jacobus de Voragine; an incomplete life of St. Thomas Canterbury is also extant.

BRACCATONI, IL. *See* Ricciarelli, Daniele da.

BRACKEN, THOMAS (1843–1898), journalist. Born in Ireland on Dec. 21, he went as an orphan to Australia in 1855, moved to New Zealand in 1869, was on the staff of three newspapers, and founded and was part owner of the *Saturday Advertiser* of Dunedin. He twice served in parliament and wrote four volumes of popular verse, including *Musings in Maoriland* (1890). He died in Dunedin, New Zealand, on Feb. 16.

BRACTON, HENRY DE. *See* Henry of Bracton.

BRADLEY, BERNARD JAMES (1867–1936), educator. Born in East Braintree, Massachusetts, on Feb. 19, he studied at Mt. St. Mary's, Maryland, was ordained in 1892, and after a brief parish appointment in Brooklyn returned to his college as teacher of classics and philosophy (1892–97), treasurer, vice-president, and, after 1911, president. He doubled enrollment and introduced many educational reforms. He was made a monsignor in 1913. He died in Washington, D.C., on Sept. 21.

BRADLEY, DENIS MARY (1846–1903), bishop. Born at Castle Island, Kerry, Ireland, on Feb. 25, he was brought when he was eight to the United States by his mother, who settled her family of five in Manchester, New Hampshire. Denis graduated from Holy Cross College in 1867, was ordained at Troy, New York, in 1871, and served at Portland, Maine, where he became chancellor of the diocese, and at Manchester. When the latter city was raised to diocesan status in 1884, he became its first bishop. He directed the care of the widely scattered Catholics in the state and held a synod for further organization in 1886. He died in Manchester on Dec. 13.

BRADSHAIGH, EDWARD (d. 1652). Born near Wigan, Lancashire, England, he became a Carmelite in Belgium in 1619, taking the name Elias à Jesu. He was sent to the English mission in 1626, was soon arrested and charged with being a priest, but was freed at the request of the king of Spain and exiled to France. He served in Paris until 1632, when he returned to his father's house, Haigh Hall, and served the Catholics of that area. He wrote two studies on English archaeology, both lost, and is called the author of *Virginalia* (1632), a volume of sonnets on the Virgin Mary. He died in Benfold on Sept. 25.

BRADSHAW, HENRY (d. 1513). Born in Chester, England, he became a Benedictine, studied at St. Werburga's monastery and at Oxford, and wrote a history of Chester and a popular biography of St. Werburga in verse.

BRADY, JOHN J. (1884–1950), admiral. Born in New York City on Jan. 8, he was ordained, became a monsignor, entered naval service as a chaplain, and was the first Catholic chaplain to attain the rank of rear admiral in the United States Navy. He received several decorations from this country and France. He died in New York City on Aug. 16.

BRADY, MATTHEW FRANCIS (1893–1959), bishop. Born in Waterbury, Connecticut, on Jan. 15, he studied at St. Thomas seminary, Hartford, Louvain, and St. Bernard's seminary, Rochester, New York, and was ordained in 1916. He served as chaplain in World War I, engaged in pastoral work, taught at St. Thomas in 1922–32, and in 1938 became bishop of Burlington, Vermont. He was appointed bishop of Manchester, Vermont, in 1944, was episcopal chairman of the education department of the National Catholic Welfare Conference in 1950–56, chairman of the United States Bishops' Committee for the Confraternity of Christian Doctrine in 1956, a position he held until his death, and president general of the National Catholic Educational Association in 1957–58. He died on Sept. 20 in Burlington.

BRADY, WILLIAM MAZIERE (1825–1894). Born in Dublin, Ireland, on Jan. 8, son of Nicholas W. Brady, lord mayor of the city, he graduated from Trinity College there, held Anglican posts in Maynooth, Kilkeedy, and Dublin, served as chaplain to the viceroy, and was vicar of Farrahy and Clonfert, Cork, and of Kilbery, Meath. He edited a collection of records of parishes in Cork, Cloyne, and Ross, and wrote several volumes on the church in Ireland during the reign of Elizabeth I and on the contemporary English Church in Ireland. After a trip to Rome to study further documents on the actions of Irish bishops during the Elizabethan period, he returned, resigned his posts, and became a convert in 1873. His Vatican research was published as *Episcopal Succession in England, Scotland, and Ireland, 1400–1875.* This was followed by *Annals of the Catholic Hierarchy in England and Scotland, 1585–1876.* He was a correspondent for the London *Tablet*, engaged in the political controversy of the day, corresponded with Gladstone, and died in Rome on Mar. 19.

BRAILLE, LOUIS (1809–1852), educator. Born in Coupvray, France, on Jan. 4, he became blind at three, was educated at the Institute for the Blind in Paris, showed aptitude in music, and was retained as a member of the staff of the school. Braille developed the methods of printing raised letters and sounds invented by Valentin Hauy and Charles Barbier, using combinations of six dots for letters, numerals, punctuation, and musical notes. His explanation of his system was published in 1892. His work has since been modified by others, but remains the basis of methods for the education of the blind. Braille died in Paris on Jan. 6.

BRALION, NICHOLAS DE (1600?–1672). Born in Chars-en-Vexin, France, he became an Oratorian in 1619, and from 1625 to 1640 was in Rome, working on translations of Cardinal de Bérulle's *Élévation* and Ribadeneira's biographies. For the rest of his life he was attached to the church of St. Honoré, where he wrote on the bishop's pallium, on liturgical ceremony, a life of St. Nicholas, and historical works. He died in Paris on May 11.

BRAMANTE, DONATO (1444?–1514), architect. Born in Monte Asdrualdo, Italy, he at first was a painter, studied at Milan, and in 1476 became court architect to Lodovico Sforza. He completed the choir and sacristy in the church of Santa Maria presso S. Satiro and the transept and choir in that of Santa Maria delle Grazie and remodeled the court of the Ospedale Maggiore, all in Milan. His early work also is found in Pavia, Legnano, Como, Crema, and Lodi. He had worked at Rome as early as 1492, but went there permanently in 1499 after the fall of the Sforzas. He worked on the Palazzo Giraud Torlonia, the circular and domed temple in the courtyard of San Pietro in Montorio. After the accession of Pope Julius II, Bramante was chosen to direct the rebuilding of St. Peter's; at least three sets of plans were made and the work was begun as early as 1506. Raphael, who worked on St. Peter's after Bramante's death in Rome on Mar. 11, made changes. Michelangelo (with whom Bramante apparently had been at odds while alive) returned to the original plan, making slight modifications in the dome. He died in Rome on Mar. 11.

BRAMANTINO, IL. *See* Suardi, Bartolommeo.

BRANCACCINI, DOMENICO (d. 1689). A Servite in Italy, he was a scholar in canon law and wrote *De jure doctoratus.*

BRANCACCIO, FRANCESCO MARIA (1591?–1675), cardinal. Born in Naples, Italy, he served as bishop of Capacio, Viterbo, and Porto, and was in 1634 made cardinal by Pope Urban VIII.

BRANCACCIO, LANDOLFO (d. 1312). Born in Naples, Italy, he was made a cardinal in 1294 by Pope Celestine V, was legate for Boniface VIII and Clement V, and attended the General Council of Vienne in 1311–12. He died in Avignon, France.

BRANCACCIO, LUIGI (d. 1411). Born in Naples, Italy, he became known as a canonist, was appointed papal nuncio to that kingdom by Innocent IV, became archbishop of Taranto, and was made cardinal by Pope Gregory XII.

BRANCACCIO, RINALDO (d. 1427). Born in Naples, Italy, he was made a cardinal in 1384 by Pope Urban VI, served on several diplomatic missions, attended the Council of Constance (1414–18), and died in Rome.

BRANCACCIO, STEFANO (1618–1682). Born in Naples, Italy, nephew of Francesco, he served as papal nuncio to Florence and Venice, became bishop of Viterbo in 1670, and was made cardinal in 1681.

BRANCASINO, BL. SANTES (d. 1490). Born in Monte Fabri, Urbino, Italy, he became a Franciscan laybrother at Scotameto. His cult was approved by Pope Clement XIV. F. D. Aug. 14.

BRANCATI, FRANCESCO (1607–1671). Born in Sicily, he became a Jesuit in 1634 and was sent to China in 1637. He had great missionary success, building some ninety churches, and writing in Chinese a catechism, sermons, homilies, and instructions on the sacraments. He was exiled from Peking in 1665 and died in Canton, China.

BRANCATI DI LAURIA, FRANCESCO LORENZO (1612–1693), cardinal. Born in Lauria, Italy, on Apr. 10, he became a Minor Conventual in 1630, taught philosophy, held the chair of dogmatic theology at the Roman University, was made consultor to the Congregation of the Holy Office by Pope Alexander VII and Vatican librarian by Clement X. He was a man of great learning and charity, and followed his order's vows even after he was appointed cardinal by Innocent XI in 1681. He published a commentary on Books 3–4 of the *Sentences* of Duns Scotus, wrote on predestination, and prepared an elaborate epitome of canons from the councils, decretals, and papal documents up to Gregory IX. He died in Rome on Nov. 30.

BRAND, JACOB (1776–1835), bishop. Born in Mespellbrunn, Franconia, on Jan. 29, he was ordained, served in a Wicskirchen parish, and in 1827 became first bishop of Limburg, in the duchy of Nassau. He had to direct 133 parishes and the city of Frankfort in a run-down area and with a small government allotment, suffering from restricting laws to which he himself had previously agreed. He opened a seminary in 1829.

BRANDAN, ST. (5th century). An Irishman who preached in Britain and suffered there under Pelagian opposition, he went to a monastery in Gaul and died there as its abbot. F. D. Jan. 11.

BRANLY, EDOUARD (1846–1940), physicist. Born in Amiens, France, on Oct. 23, he was educated at St. Quentin and Paris, receiving degrees in mathematics and natural science. He taught three years at the Sorbonne, where he attained his doctor's degree, served as professor of physics at the Catholic University of Paris from 1876 and at the same time studied for a medical degree, which he received in 1882. He wrote texts on physics, experimented with electrical waves, made studies of the effects of ultraviolet rays and of the electrical conductivity of gases. He discovered the principle of wireless telegraphy, developed by Marconi, by inventing a coherer (a glass tube containing metallic filings, with wire terminals) which could be made part of a battery circuit, and was extended to serve as a receiver. Other experiments evolved the predecessor of receiving antennae.

BRANN, HENRY A. (1837–1921). Born in Parkstown, West Meath, Ireland, on Aug. 15, he went to the United States in 1849, studied in Wilmington, Delaware, New York City, and St. Sulpice, Paris, and was ordained in Rome in 1862 with the first class from the North American College. He was professor of theology and vice-president of Seton Hall College, South Orange, New Jersey, in 1862–64, was stationed in several parishes, and in 1867 became a Paulist. He directed the seminary in Wheeling, West Virginia, and was pastor in New York City (at St. Elizabeth, 1870–1889, and then at St. Agnes) until his death on Dec. 28. He was made a monsignor in 1910. He wrote on the papacy, purgatory, immortality, and education, a history of the American College, a biography of Archbishop Hughes, and several replies (including his *Age of Unreason*, 1880) to Robert Ingersoll.

BRANT, SEBASTIAN (1458?–1521), poet. Born in Strassburg, he studied philosophy and law at Basle, began teaching there in 1484, married Elisabeth Burg in 1485, took his doctorate in 1489, and became interested in the work of the printers in the Swiss city. He soon was advising, editing, reading proof, and writing prefaces and publicity for them. He had praised in verse the election of Maximilian as emperor in 1486; in 1494 he issued *Das Narrenschiff* (*Ship of Fools*) in German, and in 1498, *Varia carmina* in Latin. In his *Narrenschiff* he gathered a set of 110 sinners (fools), inventing witty, popular, or rustic names for some of his characters, whom he satirized with biting scorn. The language is simple, the moral point clear, and the effect of six editions in Brant's lifetime, each with accompanying woodcuts, was wide. In 1501 he became syndic of Strassburg, then city clerk and chancellor. He was active in the city's literary society and was host to Erasmus. His last years were marked by the expression of increasing concern over the decline of morality and the attacks on Church dogma. He died in Strassburg, Alsace, on May 10.

BRANWALLADER, ST. (6th century?). He is said to have been a bishop on the Isle of Jersey. F. D. Jan. 19.

BRASSEUR DE BOURBOURG, CHARLES ÉTIENNE (1814–1874). Born in Bourbourg, France, he went to Canada in 1845, taught ecclesiastical history at Quebec, served as vicar general of the Boston diocese in 1846, then went to Rome to find documents relating to South America. He served as chaplain of the French legation in Mexico City and, with several interruptions for visits to France, toured Central America from 1854 to 1865. He served briefly as ecclesiastical administrator in Guatemala and as a member of the French scientific mission in Mexico. During his years in the field he was active both as a missioner and archaeologist, learned much about Indian language and ethnology, and wrote a dozen major works on pre-Columbian and later history. He died in Nice in Jan.

BRASSICANUS, JOHANN (d. 1514). Father of Johann Alexander and Johann Ludwig, he taught Latin at Urach and Tübingen, Germany, wrote a widely used grammar, *Institutiones grammaticae,* was a leading humanist, and died in Wildaad. The family name, Köl, was Latinized to Brassicanus.

BRASSICANUS, JOHANN ALEXANDER (1500–1539). Born in Cannstatt, Germany, he studied at Tübingen, took his master's degree at seventeen, and at eighteen was made laureate by Emperor Maximilian. He edited the eclogues of Calpurnius and Nemesianus, lectured on the Latin poets, served on the staff of the diplomat, Maximilian von Bergen, and took the degree of doctor of laws at Ingolstadt, where he was given the chair of philosophy in 1522. He showed some sympathy for Luther, but did not join the reformers. He went to Vienna in 1524 and became in succession professor of rhetoric, law, and Greek literature. Although his career was interrupted by the Turkish invasion, he devoted his last ten years to studies and editions of the Fathers of the Church. He died in Vienna on Nov. 25.

BRASSICANUS, JOHANN LUDWIG (1509–1549). Born in Tübingen, Germany, he went to Vienna in 1524 with his brother Johann Alexander, became court historiographer, studied law at Heidelberg, was professor of Greek at Padua and Vienna, and later professor of canon law, dean, and twice rector of the University of Vienna. He died there on June 3.

BRAULIO, ST. (d. 651), bishop. A monk at St. Engratia's, Saragossa, he was sent to study at Seville under St. Isidore and was ordained by his own brother John, whom he succeeded as bishop of his native city, Saragossa. With St. Isidore he worked to restore order in ecclesiastical affairs; he also fought Arianism, devoted himself to the poor, gained a reputation as preacher, poet, and writer of saints' lives, and attended three councils at Toledo. He died in Saragossa, Spain. F. D. Mar. 26.

BRAUN, PLACIDUS (1756–1829), historian. Born in Peitung, Bavaria, on Feb. 11, he became a Benedictine in 1775, was ordained in 1779, and as librarian of the monastery of SS. Ulrich and Afra at Augsburg published an annotated catalogue of its holdings. When the abbey was made a military barracks in 1806, he moved with his fellows to a house nearby and wrote histories of the monastery and diocese. He died in Augsburg, Bavaria, on Oct. 23.

BRAVER, THEODOR (1880–1942), economist. Born in Cleve, Germany, on Jan. 16, he studied in France, became a businessman in Cleve, and was a leader in social action. He served on the staff of the Catholic Volksverein in 1907, of the Christian Trade Unions at Cologne in 1908, and as editor of the monthly *Deutsche Arbeit.* Late in life he completed his college course and took a doctorate

in labor legislation at Bonn. He was on the executive staff of the Kolping Society in Cologne, taught economics in Karlsruhe, and, in 1928, sociology at Cologne. He directed the Christian Trades Union College at Königswinter, was jailed by the Nazis, released, and managed to flee to St. Paul, Minnesota, where he became professor of economics at St. Thomas University. He wrote *The Catholic Social Movement in Germany, Economy and Society,* and other studies. He died in St. Paul on Mar. 19.

BRAVO, FRANCISCO (16th century). Born in Ossuna, Spain, he began the practice of medicine in Seville in 1533, later went to Mexico, and in 1570 published *Opera medicinalia,* the first book of medicine printed in the new world.

BREACA, ST. (5th century). She is said to have been a follower of St. Brigid, who went from Ireland to Cornwall about 460. She is also known as Banka, Branca, and Breague. F. D. June 4.

BRÉBEUF, ST. JEAN DE (1593–1649), martyr. Born in Condé-sur-Vire, Normandy, on Mar. 25, he probably attended the university in nearby Caen, managed his family's farm for three years, then became a Jesuit at Rouen in 1617. He was ordained in 1622 when hope for his recovery from tuberculosis was almost lost. In 1625 he was sent, at his own request, to Canada, where he labored for twenty-four years, against opposition from Huguenots, trading-company officials at home and abroad, and renegade Indians. There was one brief interruption. When the English captured Quebec in 1629 and expelled the Jesuits, Brébeuf returned to France, served as treasurer at the college in Eu, and was able to get back to his missions in 1633. In 1637 a smallpox epidemic struck the Huron area, thousands died, and the medicine men blamed the missioners. Brébeuf remained among the Indians until 1640, was in Quebec for four years, then rejoined them. He composed a dictionary and catechisms in Huron, and before his death saw 7000 converted and baptized. His journal and the relations of others reveal his sanctity and courage. Captured by the Iroquois, he died after four hours of the most extreme torture, on Mar. 16, at Ste. Marie, near Georgian Bay, Canada. He was canonized in 1930. F. D. Sept. 26.

FRANCIS X. TALBOT, *Saint among the Hurons* (Garden City, N.Y., Image Books, 1956).

BREGWYN, ST. (d. 765). A Benedictine, he became twelfth archbishop of Canterbury in 761; his biography was written by Eadmer. F. D. Aug. 26.

BRÉHAL, JAN (d. 1479?), theologian. A Dominican, he received his doctorate in theology at Caen, France, in 1443, served as prior of the monastery of St. Jacques, Paris, and from

1452 to 1474 was inquisitor general of France. His chief work was the review of the trial of St. Joan of Arc and an official reversal of the original condemnation. He later retired to Évreux, where he devoted himself to study and writing, and where he died.

BRÉMOND, HENRI (1865–1933), author. Born in Aix-en-Provence, France, on July 31, he studied there and in England, was influenced by Cardinal Newman, became a Jesuit in 1882, and was ordained in 1892. On his return to France in 1899 he taught philosophy and classics, wrote for *Études religieuses*, where he met Abbé Ernest Dimnet, and published much literary criticism. His books include *Ames religieuses* (1902), *La Provence mystique au XVII siècle*, *Le Roman et l'histoire d'un conversion*, and *Prière et poésie* (1926). Most significant of his titles is the six-volume *L'Histoire littéraire du sentiment religieux en France*. This and *Prayer and Poetry* were translated widely; also appearing in English were *Thomas More*, *The Mystery of Newman*, and *Thundering Abbot* (on Armand de Rancé). His *Ste. Chantal* was placed on the Index. He left the Jesuits in 1904, lived in many areas of France as a secular priest, and during his last ten years shared quarters in Paris with Abbé Dimnet. He became a member of the French Academy in 1933. He died in Pau, France, on Aug. 17.

BRENAN, MICHAEL JOHN (1780–1847). Born in Kilkenny, Ireland, he was ordained, became famous as a preacher, was later suspended for his pride, joined the Protestant Priest's Protection Society, publicly renounced his defection, and became a Franciscan at Wexford. In his last years he wrote an ecclesiastical history of Ireland. He died in Dublin in Feb.

BRENDAN, ST. (d. 562?). Friend of St. Columba and contemporary of St. Brendan the Navigator, he was abbot of Birr in Offaly. F. D. Nov. 29.

BRENDAN, ST. (d. 583?). Born, possibly in Tralee, Ireland, and educated by St. Ita and ordained by Bishop Erc, he became a monk and founded a large monastery at Clonfert. Many fantastic details have been added to this brief knowledge, usually based on the fictional *Navigatio* in which he is described as searching for the Isles of the Blessed, touching the Canaries, and even discovering America. It is possible that he actually made visits to Scotland and Wales. F. D. May 16.

BRENNAN, ANDREW JAMES (1877–1956), bishop. Born in Towanda, Pennsylvania, on Dec. 14, he studied at Holy Cross, St. Bernard's seminary, Rochester, and the North American College, Rome, where he was ordained in 1904. He taught at St. Thomas College, Scranton, was chancellor of the Scranton diocese in 1908–23, also serving as rector of St.

Peter's church there in 1914–24, and was consecrated titular bishop of Thapsus and auxiliary of Scranton in 1923. He was appointed bishop of Richmond, Virginia, in 1926, founded the diocesan paper, the *Catholic Virginian* in 1931, and held a diocesan synod in 1933. He resigned in 1945 and was appointed titular bishop of Telmessus, and died on May 23.

BRENNAN, THOMAS FRANCIS (1853–1916), bishop. Born in Tipperary, Ireland, on Oct. 6 or 10, he studied at Innsbruck, and was ordained in Brixen, Austria, in 1880. He then went to the United States, did pastoral work in Erie, Pennsylvania, was made a papal chamberlain in 1888, and in 1891 was appointed first bishop of Dallas, Texas. He resigned in 1892, transferred to St. John's, Newfoundland, and was called to Rome in 1904. He was made titular bishop of Caesarea in 1905, and died on Mar. 20 at Grotta Ferrata, Italy.

BRENTANO, KLEMENS MARIA (1778–1842), poet. Born in Thal-Ehrenbreitstein, Germany, on Sept. 8, he studied at Jena, married Sophie Mereau, the divorced wife of one of his professors, and moved to Heidelberg. With Achim von Arnim he published the three-volume collection of folk songs, *Des Knaben Wunderhorn* (1805–8), which established him as one of the leaders of romanticism. He married again, but his wife's temper caused him to leave her and he drifted across Europe until he reached Berlin in 1818. He then became interested in Catholicism, into which he had been born, rejoined the Church, made a six-year record of the stigmatic Anne Catherine Emmerich, wrote *Romances of the Rosary*, and in 1833 joined the group of Catholic scholars at Munich under Joseph Görres. He died at Aschaffenburg, Switzerland, on July 28, while visiting his brother Christian, who published his collected works in 1851–55.

BRERELEY, JOHN. *See* Anderton, Lawrence.

BRESSANI, FRANCESCO GIUSEPPE (1612–1672), missioner. Born in Rome on May 6, he became a Jesuit in 1626, studied at Rome and Clermont, taught in Italy and France, and was sent to Canada. In 1644 he was captured by the Iroquois Indians and tortured for two months, ransomed by the Dutch, and returned to France. He went back to Quebec in 1645 and worked with the scattered Hurons until 1650, when ill health forced his return to Italy. There he preached widely and died at Florence on Sept. 9.

BRETANNION, ST. (d. 380?), bishop. Emperor Valens exiled him from his see in Tomi, Scythia, because of his attacks on Arianism, but was forced to recall him when the people of the area rose up and demanded his return. F. D. Jan. 25.

BRETON, RAYMOND (1609–1679), missioner. Born in Baune, France, on Sept. 3, he became a Dominican at seventeen, studied at Paris, and was sent to the French West Indies in 1635. He spent twelve years on San Domingo and eight more on other islands in the Antilles, learning many Carib languages. He returned to France in 1654, wrote a catechism, dictionary, and grammar in Carib, as well as a history of his missions, and instructed missionaries departing for the Caribbean. He died in Caen, France, on Jan. 8.

BREWER, HEINRICH (1640–1713?), historian. Born in Puffendorf, Germany, on Sept. 6, he studied at Cologne, became curate at Bonn, was rector of a Cologne convent from 1669 to 1682 and from then until 1712 was pastor of the church of St. Jacob in Aachen. While rector he was able to complete the eight-volume *Historia universalis Brachelio-Thuldenana*, adding primary documents, maps, and drawings. He wrote a life of Thomas à Kempis, other histories, and received the title of imperial historiographer. He resigned his pastorate a year before his death in Puffendorf.

BRIACH, ST. (d. 627?). An Irishman, he became a monk in Wales, serving St. Tudwall, with whom he went to Brittany, becoming founder-abbot of a monastery at Guingamp. F. D. Dec. 17.

BRIAND, JOSEPH OLIVIER (1715–1794), bishop. Born in Plérin, Brittany, he was ordained in 1739 and went to Canada to serve under Bishop Pontbriand. He distinguished himself during the siege of Quebec in 1759, became administrator of the diocese on the bishop's death, and was successful in gaining leniency for his people from the British victors. He was consecrated seventh bishop of Quebec at Paris in 1766. Partly through his efforts, the Habeas Corpus Act granted Catholics in Quebec the rights and privileges of other British subjects, the Quebec Act extended religious freedom to Catholics, and the Test Act was rewritten to be acceptable by the pope. He also arranged with the papacy for two assistant bishops, with right of succession. Because of his fiery preaching, Canada remained loyal to the British crown during the American invasion. His catechism, published in 1765, was the first book printed in Canada. Briand died in Quebec on June 25.

BRIANT, BL. ALEXANDER (1556–1581), martyr. Born in Somerset, England, he attended Oxford, was reconciled to Catholicism, and was ordained at Douai. In 1579 he was sent back to England, was captured in 1581 in London, tortured in the Tower to force him to reveal the whereabouts of Fr. Persons, and hanged, drawn, and quartered at Tyburn with Bl. Edmund Campion and Ralph Sherwin. He became a Jesuit during his imprisonment. He was beatified in 1886. F. D. Dec. 1.

BRICE, ST. (d. 444), bishop. Educated by St.

Martin of Tours at Marmoutier, he was a vain, overly ambitious cleric, quite jealous of his teacher. On Martin's death he became bishop of Tours in 397 and served with indifference until 430, when he was driven from his see. During a seven-year exile at Rome he completely reformed, returned to his see, and led a life of such remarkable holiness that he was acclaimed a saint on his death. F. D. Nov. 13.

BRIÇONNET, GUILLAUME (d. 1514), cardinal. Born in Tours, France, son of Jean Briçonnet, Lord of Varennes, he served King Louis XI as a superintendent of finances and Charles VIII as secretary of the treasury and as chief adviser on the council of state. After the death of his wife, Briçonnet studied for the Church and became bishop of St. Malo. His chief interests remained political. He swayed the king to support the claim of Ludovico Sforza of Milan to the kingdom of Naples and went with a French force into Italy; the result was disastrous to French finances, only a sixth of the army returned alive, and Pisa was sacrificed to Florence. Briçonnet had been promised a cardinalate by the Sforza group; he now was promised one by Pope Alexander VI if he would take Charles out of Italy. When he reconciled king and pope in 1495, he received his reward. He also arranged that he become bishop of Nîmes, though that see did not fall to him until litigation ended in 1507; meanwhile, he became bishop of Toulon and archbishop of Rheims, both in 1497. In 1498 he crowned Louis XII and furthered the monarch's plan to limit the powers of Pope Julius II. Briçonnet took a group of cardinals out of Rome and opened an anti-papal council at Pisa, fleeing to Milan and Lyons when pursued. The pope excommunicated him; the king gave him the rich abbey of St. Germain-des-Prés and made him governor of Languedoc. Pope Leo X later restored him to the sacred college and he became archbishop of Narbonne, France, where he died on Dec. 14.

BRIÇONNET, GUILLAUME (1472–1534), bishop. Born in Tours, France, son of Cardinal Briçonnet, he became a priest, was made bishop of Lodève, chaplain to the queen, and successor to his father as abbot of St. Germain-des-Prés. He went to Rome as ambassador and defended King Louis XI before Pope Leo X and the college of cardinals. King Francis I also used him as an ambassador and appointed him bishop of Meaux. Briçonnet was a serious churchman, regularized his monastery, corrected abuses in many quarters, defended the parish clergy against encroachments by religious, held a number of synods at Meaux to check immorality and strengthen discipline, promoted learning among the clergy, enlarged the monastic library, and, like his father and uncle, was a patron of letters. He died near Montereau, France, on Jan. 24.

BRIÇONNET, ROBERT (d. 1497), bishop. Son of Jean Briçonnet, lord of Varennes, he rose from canon at Orléans to abbot of St. Vaast at Arras through the influence of his cardinal brother, Guillaume, and became archbishop of Rheims in 1493. King Charles VIII placed him in charge of finances and made him chancellor. He died in Moulins, France, on June 3.

BRICTIUS, ST. (d. 312?), bishop. He was seized in his diocese of Martola, near Spoleto, Italy, and imprisoned during the persecution of Diocletian, but lived to serve under Constantine. F. D. July 9.

BRIDAINE, JACQUES (1701–1767). Born in Chusclan, France, on Mar. 21, he studied at Avignon, was ordained, and preached missions throughout France. His methods were sometimes sensational, but always stirring, and he commanded large audiences and made many converts. Five volumes of sermons were published and his *Cantiques spirituels* ran through forty-seven editions. He died in Roquemaure, France, on Dec. 22.

BRIDE. *See* Brigid of Ireland, St.

BRIDGET, ST. (1303–1373), foundress. Daughter of the governor of Upland, Sweden, she was born on June 14 and brought up by an aunt after her mother's death. At fourteen she married Ulf Gudmarsson; they had eight children, including St. Catherine of Sweden. In 1335 she became lady in waiting to Blanche of Namur, wife of King Magnus II. When her husband died at the Cistercian monastery of Alvastra, she stayed there for four years during which visions she had experienced since childhood became more frequent. She denounced King Magnus and his court for their sinful lives; partly as a result he endowed the monastery of Vadstena on Lake Vättern, where she founded the Order of the Most Holy Saviour, the Bridgettines, in 1344. She wrote Pope Clement VI, urging him to return to Rome from Avignon and to end the war between England and France. In 1349 she went to Rome and remained there, except for pilgrimages, the rest of her life. She prophesied many events of her time, never hesitated to denounce high or low, pope or friar, if she knew he acted wrongly, and devoted her time to the sick and poor. She herself lived in great austerity. In 1370, Pope Urban V confirmed the Rule of her congregation. In 1371 she went to the Holy Land with St. Catherine, and her sons Birger and Charles (who died on the way). She returned to Rome in 1373 and died there on July 23. She related many of the revelations and visions she had experienced to Peter of Alvastra, who recorded them in Latin. Cardinal Torquemada examined them and, despite opposition, declared them

doctrinally sound. She was canonized in 1391 by Pope Boniface IX and is the patron saint of Sweden. F. D. Oct. 8.

JOHANNES JÖRGENSEN, *Bridget of Sweden* (New York, Longmans, 1956).

BRIDGETT, THOMAS EDWARD (1829–1899). Born in Derby, England, on Jan. 20, he attended Oxford, but refused to take the Oath of Royal Supremacy required to graduate. In 1850 he became a convert and joined the Benedictines at St. Trond, Belgium. He was ordained in 1856, served in London for five years and in Limerick, Ireland, for nine; in 1868 he founded the Confraternity of the Holy Family. From 1871 until his death on Feb. 17 he was rector of St. Mary's church, Clapham. He wrote two volumes of verse, biographies of John Fisher and Thomas More, and studies on the devotion to the Virgin Mary in mediaeval England, on the Eucharist in Great Britain, and on the deposition of the Catholic hierarchy by Queen Elizabeth I.

BRIDGEWATER, JOHN (1532?–1596?), apologist. Born in Yorkshire, England, he studied at Oxford, was ordained after 1556, became rector of Lincoln College, Oxford, in 1563, but resigned in 1574 and went to Douai with a group of students when pressures to change religious dogma became intense. He had, while in England, voted against the Six Articles of the Church of England, and later wrote an account of the action; in 1588 he published a record of the attempts of the Church to preserve its purity under Elizabeth I and an account of over 100 martyrs; this *Concertatio ecclesiae catholicae in Anglia* was of great value to later historians. He died abroad, probably at Trèves, France.

BRIEUC, ST. (420?–510?). Born in Cardiganshire, Wales, he was educated at Auxerre by St. Germanus, returned to convert his parents, and is said to have built and become abbot of a monastery near Tréguier, Brittany, and another on the site of the present French town of St. Brieuc. The name is also spelled Brioc and Briomaglus. F. D. May 1.

BRIGGS, JOHN (d. 1861), bishop. Born in England, he was ordained, served as president of St. Cuthbert's College, Durham, in 1832–36, became titular bishop of Trachis and coadjutor vicar apostolic of the northern district of England in 1833, and vicar in 1836. He was transferred to Yorkshire in 1840, was made titular bishop of Beverley in 1850, and resigned in 1860. He built many chapels and schools, particularly for the influx of Irish immigrants, and died in York on Jan. 4.

BRIGID, ST. (5th century?). According to legend, she and her sister Maura were daughters of a Scottish chieftain and were murdered by outlaws in Picardy while on a pilgrimage to Rome. St. Gregory of Tours calls her St. Britta.

She is also identified as the abbess St. Baya, honored on Nov. 2. F. D. July 13.

BRIGID, ST. (450?–525?), Irish abbess. Called "the Mary of the Gael" and also known as St. Bride, the patroness of Ireland, was born near Dundalk, and founded a double settlement at Kildare for men and women, over which she probably presided. Other biographical details are legendary. F. D. Feb. 1.

ALICE CURTAYNE, *St. Brigid of Ireland* (Dublin, Browne & Nolan, 1935).

BRIGNON, JOHN (1629–1712). Born in St. Malo, France, he became a Jesuit and translated into French the *Imitation of Christ*, some treatises of Robert Bellarmine, Edmund Campion's *Decem rationes*, and several works of devotion; he also published an edition of *Introduction to the Devout Life* by St. Francis de Sales. He died in Paris on June 12.

BRIL, PAUL (1556–1626), painter. Born in Antwerp, Holland, he studied there, followed his brother Matthys (1548?–1584) to Rome, imitated the landscapes of Titian and in turn influenced the landscapes of Rubens, Carracci, and Lorraine. He worked in the Vatican with his brother, whose pension Pope Gregory XIII transferred to him. His heroic fresco is in the Sala Clementina; compositions are also in the Sistine Chapel, the Scala Sancta of the Lateran, and the church of Santa Maria Maggiore. He died in Rome on Oct. 7.

BRILLMACHER, PETER MICHAEL (1542–1595). Born in Cologne, Germany, he became a Jesuit in 1558, studied in Paris, and became a major apologist during the spread of the new heresies in Germany and a valuable adviser on questions of state to several German princes. He wrote a catechism, a commentary on Aristotle's logic, and several explanations of the Eucharist (in opposition to John of Münster and Stephen Isaac). His preaching and writing were so powerful that he was invited to a conference with Protestant leaders at Mainz, Germany, where he died of poison on Aug. 25.

BRINDHOLM, BL. EDMUND (d. 1540), martyr. An Englishman ordained on the Continent, he was a parish priest at Calais when accused of conspiracy to turn the city over to the French. He, Bl. Clement Philpott and William Horne, and several others were returned to England and slain at Tyburn on Aug. 4.

BRINKLEY, BL. STEPHEN (d. 1550?), printer. He was a wealthy member of the group organized in England by George Gilbert for the purpose of raising funds for the support of the underground clergy and the faithful in danger of arrest during the Elizabethan persecution. Bl. Robert Persons set up a printing press at Eastham and later at Henley, which Brinkley and seven assistants ran. They bought paper secretly, used a Douai imprint, and issued a great number of tracts by Edmund Campion and others. Brinkley and an assistant, William Carter, were captured in 1581; the latter was executed at Tyburn. Although tortured during imprisonment in the Tower, Brinkley was released in 1583, went to Rome with Fr. Persons, helped George Flinton at Rouen in printing Catholic books, and succeeded to the latter's business in 1585. Nothing is known of him after this date.

BRIOC. *See* Brieuc, St.

BRISACIER, JACQUES CHARLES DE (1641–1736). Born in Bourges, France, he became a member of the Paris Society of Foreign Missions at twenty-five, was elected superior in 1681, held that office for eight terms, and prepared its Rule in 1698. He served as chaplain to Marie Thérèse, wife of King Louis XIV, and together with Bourdaloue and Fénelon compiled the regulations for St. Cyr, founded by Mme. de Maintenon, and actively engaged in the controversy over Chinese ceremonies and superstitions. He died in Paris on Mar. 23.

BRISACIER, JEAN DE (1592–1668). Born in Blois, France, on June 9, he became a Jesuit in 1619, was rector of colleges at Aix, Blois, and Rouen, and superior at Paris. He was an opponent of Jansenism; the tone of some of his attacks on personalities at Port Royal brought censure from Archbishop di Gondi of Paris. He died in Blois on Sept. 10.

BRISCHAR, JOHANN NEPOMUCENE (1819–1897), historian. Born in Horb, Würtemberg, he studied at Tübingen, and from 1853 until his death there was parish priest at Bühl. He wrote on Pope Innocent III, edited *Catholic Pulpit Orators of Germany*, and completed volumes 45–54 of Leopold Stolberg's *History of the Religion of Jesus Christ*.

BRISTOW, RICHARD (1538–1581), apologist. Born in Worcester, England, he completed studies at Oxford in 1562, held a public disputation with Edmund Campion before Queen Elizabeth, was made fellow of Exeter College, began to object to prevailing views of the divinity faculty, and left the country. At Douai, William Allen made him prefect of studies; he served as acting rector in Allen's absences. He worked on the Douai translation of the Bible, published annotations on the Rheims New Testament translation, a commentary on the *Summa* of St. Thomas Aquinas, and many tracts on current heresies. He returned to England in ill health in 1581 and died at Harrow on Oct. 18.

BRITHWALD. *See* Berhtwald.

BRITIUS, ST. (d. 711), martyr. *See* Albertus.

BRITIUS, FRANCIS (17th century). He became a Capuchin, was stationed at Rennes, Brittany, studied oriental languages while in the Levant, and, called to Rome, translated the Bible into Arabic (1671), as well as an abridgment of Baronius' *Annales ecclésiastiques* (1653–71).

BRITO, ST. (d. 386). He was bishop of Trèves, France, and an opponent of Priscillianism. F. D. May 5.

BRITTAIN, THOMAS LEWIS (1744–1827). Born near Chester, England, he became a Catholic at sixteen, went to the Continent, and was professed a Dominican at Bornheim in 1767. He taught at Bornheim and Brussels and in 1790 became director of the exiled English Dominican nuns, a post he held until his death. In 1794 he moved the group from Brussels back to England, to Hartpury Court, near Gloucester, in order to escape attack by the French. He was provincial of his order from 1814 to 1818 and wrote an English grammar, poems, and works of apologetics. He died in Hartpury Court.

BRITTON, VEN. JOHN (d. 1598), martyr. Born near Barnsley, Yorkshire, England, he suffered persecution for many years, was falsely accused of making speeches against Queen Elizabeth I, and was executed at York on Apr. 1 when he refused to renounce his faith.

BRITWIN, ST. (d. 733?). He was Benedictine abbot of Beverly, England. F. D. May 15.

BROCADELLI, BL. LUCIA (1476–1544). Born in Narni, Italy, eldest of eleven children, she in 1491 married a Count Peter. He respected her vow of virginity and in 1494 allowed her to become a Dominican regular tertiary. She retired to Viterbo, received the stigmata, and in 1499 was prioress of a convent which Duke Ercole of Ferrara founded for her. She was not suited to administration, was deposed in 1505, forced into seclusion by her successor, and for thirty-nine years suffered humbly and patiently the indignities and slights of her associates. She died on Nov. 15; her cult was confirmed in 1710. F. D. Nov. 16.

BROCARD, ST. (d. 1231?). Successor to St. Berthold about 1195 as superior of the Frankish hermits on Mt. Carmel, he secured a rule for his monks from St. Albert, papal legate in Palestine (which was confirmed by Pope Honorius III about 1226), under which the Order of Mt. Carmel developed in the West. F. D. Sept. 2.

BROCK, DOMINICUS (15th century). *See* Tobias.

BROGAN, ST. (7th century?). Abbot of Ross Tuirc, Ossory, Ireland, he is called the author of a hymn to St. Brigid. F. D. Sept. 17. Others of the name (Broccan, Bracan, Brogan) and of the sixth or seventh century are venerated on Jan. 1, Apr. 9, June 27, July 8, and Aug. 25. Clearly distinguishing details are missing.

BROGLIE, AUGUSTE THEODORE PAUL DE (1834–1895). Born in Anteuil, France, on May 18, son of Achille Victor, duc de Broglie, and the daughter of Mme. de Staël, he became

a naval officer, then began religious studies and was ordained in 1870. He wrote on the history of religions, on biblical studies, and on the state of the Church in France. He died on May 11, when attacked by an insane person to whom he was ministering.

BROGLIE, JACQUES VICTOR ALBERT DE (1821–1901), historian. Born in Paris, France, on June 13, he was briefly in diplomatic service, then devoted himself to writing. His *L'Eglise et l'empire romain au IVe siècle* (1856) won him a seat in the French Academy; he also edited memoirs of his father and of Talleyrand and the letters of Duchesse Albertine de Broglie, and published a series on the diplomacy of King Louis XV. The duc de Broglie was ambassador to England in 1871, was recalled the next year, and entered the assembly as an opponent of Thiers and the republic. He was president of the council in 1873 and 1877, but retired to private life after political defeat. He died in Paris on Jan. 19.

BROGLIE, MAURICE JEAN DE (1766–1821). Born in Paris on Sept. 5, son of Field Marshal Victor François, duc de Broglie, he studied at St. Sulpice, was ordained, left France during the reign of terror, and became a canon at Posen. He returned in 1803, became Napoleon's almoner, and was made bishop of Acqui, Italy, in 1805 and of Ghent, Belgium, in 1807. By 1809, however, he had fallen from favor and had even censured the emperor for some of his anti-Catholic actions. In 1811, when he voted against the emperor's demand that the pope accept Napoleonic appointments, de Broglie was imprisoned for four months and then exiled. Napoleon also deposed him as bishop of Ghent, but the pope disregarded this and on the emperor's death de Broglie returned to his see. He now faced the encroachments of William of Nassau, whose 1815 constitution deprived Catholics of all rights. After a long battle on behalf of his people and the Church at large, he was deported and died in Paris on June 20.

BROGNY, JEAN ALLARMET DE (1342–1426), cardinal. Born in Brogny, Savoy, he was a swineherd whose wisdom impressed two passing monks, who saw to it that he had opportunity for study at Geneva and Avignon. He supported Robert of Geneva, the antipope Clement VII, who made him bishop of Viviers in 1380, cardinal in 1385, and chancellor. Clement's successor, antipope Benedict XIII, promoted the bishop from Viviers to Ostia-Velletri, but the Avignon court began to appall him and he left in protest. At the Council of Pisa he led the neutral party which elected antipope Alexander V; when the latter died a year later, the cardinal presided over the conclave which elected antipope John XXIII. The latter appointed him archbishop of Arles. With the schism widening as the result of three papal claimants and with heresy spreading because of John Huss, de Brogny as chancellor presided at the Council of Constance and by effective diplomacy brought about the deposition of Clement, Benedict, and John; Martin V was then elected. The cardinal founded Dominican convents at Tivoli and Annecy, a leprosarium at Brogny, and the College of St. Nicholas at the University of Avignon. He died in Rome and was buried in Geneva.

BROMYARD, JOHN (d. 1390?), theologian. Born in Herefordshire, England, he became a Dominican, studied theology and law at Oxford, and taught there and at Cambridge. He was a leader in the struggle against Wyclif and aided in the composition of the decree of condemnation approved by the synod at London in 1382. His *Summa praedicantium* ran into several editions and his *Opus trivium* long was of service to preachers.

BRON, ST. (d. 511?). He was consecrated bishop of Cassel-Irra, Sligo, Ireland, by St. Patrick. F. D. June 8.

BRONDEL, JOHN B. (1842–1903), bishop. Born in Bruges, Belgium, on Feb. 23, he studied there and at Louvain, was ordained in 1864, and served in the Indian missions from Walla Walla, Washington, north into Alaska for fifteen years. He was consecrated third bishop of Vancouver Island, British Columbia, in 1879, was named administrator of the vicariate of Montana in 1883, and first bishop of Helena in 1884. He traveled more than 9000 miles a year serving the missions of his diocese and caring for the Blackfeet, Crows, Flatheads, and Nez Percés, who looked up to him and relied on him as mediator with the American government. He built sixty-five churches (including the first in Olympia and Tacoma), 100 chapels, schools, asylums, and other social-welfare homes. He died in Helena, Montana, on Nov. 3.

BRONISLAVA, ST. (d. 1259). Cousin of St. Hyacinth, she joined the Premonstratensians near Cracow when twenty-five, and was allowed to live the life of a recluse in a cave near the monastery until her death. Her cult was confirmed in 1839. F. D. Aug. 30.

BRONZINO, IL. *See* Allori, Angiolo.

BROOKBY, ANTHONY (d. 1537), martyr. A classical scholar and lecturer in divinity at Oxford, he was a Friar Minor, and an influential preacher. When he censured Henry VIII's way of living during a sermon, he was seized and tortured to the point of reducing him to a skeleton. Released, he was strangled two weeks later, on July 19, on orders from the king. The name is also spelled Brorbey.

BROOKES, JAMES (1512–1560). Born in Hampshire, England, he studied at Oxford, became master of Balliol College in 1547, gained a reputation as a preacher, and was consecrated bishop of Gloucester in 1554. He was appointed a papal sub-delegate on the royal commission appointed to try Cranmer, Latimer, and Ridley, and refused on legal grounds to degrade the last two. He was imprisoned when Elizabeth became queen and died in prison.

BROOKS, PETER ANTHONY (1893–1948), educator. Born in Watertown, Wisconsin, on June 14, he studied in Chicago, served as an artillery lieutenant in World War I, completed his studies at Marquette, and became a Jesuit in 1921. He taught at Loyola (Chicago) and St. Louis, was provincial of the Missouri province in 1937–43, became president of Marquette in 1944, and died in Milwaukee on May 16.

BRORBEY, ANTHONY. *See* Brookby, Anthony.

BROSSART, FERDINAND (1849–1930), bishop. Born in Buechelberg, Bavaria, Germany, on Oct. 14, he studied at Louvain, went to the United States, and was ordained in 1892 in Covington, Kentucky. He was appointed bishop of that see in 1915, and reigned there until his death in Melbourne, Kentucky, on Aug. 6.

BROSSE, JEAN BAPTISTE DE LA (1724–1782), missioner. Born in Magnac, France, he became a Jesuit at Bordeaux in 1740, was ordained in 1753, and sent to Canada in 1754. He worked on the Abenaki mission, taught in Quebec, and then set up a mission center at Tadousac for the Montagnais and French traders. He ranged to Labrador and Prince Edward Island, taught reading and writing to the Montagnais, wrote a dictionary of their language, printed their alphabet and a catechism and prayer book (1767) for them, and was among the first to gain converts among the savage Naskapi tribe. He died in Tadousac, Quebec, Canada.

BROSSE, JOSEPH DE LA (1636–1697), missioner. Born in Toulouse, France, he became a Discalced Carmelite under the name Ange de St. Joseph, studied Arabic at Rome, and was sent to Smyrna, Turkey, in 1664. He spent ten years in Persia, mastering that language and serving as prior at Ispahan, and later was superior in Holland, England, and Ireland. He wrote widely on oriental pharmacology.

BROUGHTON, RICHARD (1558?–1634). Born in Great Stukely, Huntingdonshire, England, he was ordained at Rheims in 1593, returned to England, was successful in making converts, and established a reputation as an antiquarian. He wrote *Ecclesiastical History of Great Britain* (1633), a life of the martyr Nicholas Garlick, and many apologetical works. He died in England on Jan. 18.

BROUN, HEYWOOD CAMPBELL (1888–1939), author. Born in Brooklyn, New York, on Dec. 7, he graduated from Harvard in 1910, when he joined the staff of the New York *Morning Telegraph,* went to the *Tribune* in 1912 as feature writer, sports writer, drama critic, and was war correspondent in France during World War I. On his return he became literary editor and wrote a daily book column. He transferred to the New York *World* in 1921 and soon became widely known for his column, "It Seems to Me." He was discharged in 1928 when he refused to discontinue his bitter columns on the Sacco-Vanzetti case, joined the staff of the New York *Telegram* (which absorbed the *World* in 1931), and became one of the most widely syndicated columnists in the United States. He ran unsuccessfully as a Socialist for Congress in 1930, founded the American Newspaper Guild in 1933, and became its first president. He became a convert in 1939. He lectured at Columbia and elsewhere, edited the *Connecticut Nutmeg,* a weekly, and was an amateur painter. His books include: *Seeing Things at Night* (1922), *Sitting on the World* (1924), *Gandle Follows His Nose* (1926), *Anthony Comstock* (with Margaret Leech, 1927), *Christians Only* (with George Britt, 1931), and the autobiographical *The Boy Grows Older* (1922). He died in New York City on Dec. 19.

BROUWER, CHRISTOPH (1559–1617), historian. Born in Arnheim, Holland, on Mar. 12, he became a Jesuit in 1580 and taught philosophy at Trèves, France, where he served as rector and a history of whose bishops he wrote. The work was not published until 1626, because Brouwer's honesty would not permit him to make flattering references to the current archbishop; the work was completed by Fr. Jacob Masenius in 1670. Another large work on ecclesiastical buildings in the archdiocese was not printed until 1855. Other writings include a history of the diocese of Fulda, an edition of Venantius Fortunatus, of the poems of Rhabanus Maurus, and a life of St. Martin. He died in Trèves.

BROWN, GEORGE HILARY (1786–1856), bishop. Born in England on Jan. 13, he was ordained, was pastor of St. Peter's, Lancaster, for twenty-one years, and in 1840 became titular bishop of Bugia (later of Tloa) and vicar apostolic of the Lancashire district. The district was divided into three sees in 1850, with Bishop Brown in charge of Liverpool. He died there on Jan. 25.

BROWN, WILLIAM (1777–1857), admiral. Born in County Mayo, Ireland, he was brought to the United States in 1786, shipped out from Philadelphia as a cabin boy, was captured by the French, and escaped to England, where in 1809 he married. He entered the merchant trade but lost his only ship on the coast of South America. He then established a packet service between Buenos Aires and Montevideo.

In 1814, when Argentina revolted against Spain, Brown led a few vessels to victory over a fleet of nine Spanish warships and was made an admiral. In 1826, during the war with Brazil, Brown broke the blockade of Buenos Aires and, with a fleet of seven, defeated seventeen Brazilian warships. He was commissioner for Argentina at the 1827 conference at Montevideo, which ended hostilities. He died in Buenos Aires on May 3.

BROWNE, CHARLES FARRAR (1834–1867), humorist. Born in Waterford, Maine, on Apr. 26, he became at fourteen an apprentice on the Skowhegan *Clarion* and then on the *Carpet Bag* in Boston. He became a journeyman printer, touring the eastern states, and settling for a while in Toledo, Ohio, where he contributed to the *Commercial.* In 1858 he became a regular reporter for the Cleveland *Plain Dealer,* using the name Artemus Ward, and writing satiric accounts of sporting events, séances, and politics. In 1860 he went to New York to join the staff of the comic magazine *Vanity Fair* and soon became its editor. Collections of his writings appeared in 1865 and 1867; long before that, his rustic humor, deliberate misspellings, and extravagant narratives made him the favorite of thousands, including Abraham Lincoln, who quoted him often. Browne gave up journalism when a lecture appearance brought instant success and he gained an international reputation as a speaker. Ill for two years with consumption, he seemingly recovered, went to London for a music-hall engagement, but died seven weeks later at Southampton, England, on Mar. 6. He was buried in Waterford.

BROWNE, HENRY J. (1853–1941). Born in Birkenhead, England, he studied in Birmingham and at Oxford and St. Bueno's, Wales, became a Jesuit in 1877, and was ordained in the Irish province of the Society. He was a founder of the Classical Association of Ireland and its president in 1913, worked on government commissions for archaeology and museum development, and was professor of Greek at University College, Dublin. He wrote on the revival of classical studies, on Homer, and methods of teaching the classics, Greek and Latin textbooks, and *The Road to Rome,* and edited *City of Peace.*

BROWNE, BL. WILLIAM (d. 1605), martyr. A layman from Northamptonshire, England, he was hanged, drawn, and quartered at Ripon on Sept. 5, and was beatified in 1929. F. D. Aug. 1.

BROWNLOW, WILLIAM (1836–1901), bishop. An archaeologist, and author with James S. Northcote of an authoritative work on the catacombs, he became fourth bishop of Clifton, England, in 1893. He died on Nov. 1.

BROWNRIGG, ABRAHAM (1836–1928),

bishop. Born in Kildavin, Carlow, Ireland, on Dec. 23, he studied at St. Peter's (Wexford) and Maynooth and was ordained in 1861. He taught at St. Peter's to 1865, and served the missionary community at Enniscorthy until 1884, when he became bishop of Ossory. He died in Kilkenny on Oct. 1.

BROWNSON, ORESTES AUGUSTUS (1803–1876), philosopher. Born in Stockbridge, Vermont, on Sept. 16, he was a Congregationalist, Presbyterian, Universalist, and Owenite in turn. He then joined Robert Dale Owen in his Auburn, New York, utopian colony (Albigensian in essence), writing from New York City for the cult's *Free Enquirer*. He became interested in the Workingmen's party, but in 1831 returned to preaching, edited the Universalist *Gospel Advocate* and then his own *Philanthropist*, in which he preached a religion of "humanity." For the next twelve years he was a Unitarian, serving in New Hampshire and Massachusetts parishes, and forming a new religious group in Boston. In 1838 he founded the Boston *Quarterly Review*, with contributions from Bronson Alcott, George Bancroft, and Sarah Fuller, and began attacking democracy, inheritance and property rights, industrialism, wage labor, as well as Christianity. The socialist position frightened some of his associates, but the skill of his argument won new supporters. He merged the *Review* with the *U. S. Democratic Review* in 1842, then astounded all his followers by becoming a convert to Catholicism in 1844. His magazine essays on government were later published as *The American Republic*. He changed his journal's title to *Brownson's Quarterly Review* in 1844–75 (published regularly except for a suspension in 1865–72). He lived in Elizabeth, New Jersey, from 1857 to 1875, wrote strongly on the rights of workers, and was commended for his stand by the American bishops at Baltimore in 1849 and by Pope Pius IX in 1854. He published *The Convert* in 1857, *Conversations on Liberalism and the Church* in 1869; his complete works were published posthumously in 1883–87. He died in Detroit, Michigan, on Apr. 17.

THEODORE MAYNARD, *Orestes Brownson* (New York, Macmillan, 1943).

BRUCE, EDWARD (d. 1318), king. Brother of Robert I of Scotland, he aided his brother, defeated the English at Bannockburn, invaded Ulster (to which he had a justifiable claim), and became king of Ireland in 1316. He failed to unite Ireland or protect his gains, and died there in battle at Dundalk on Oct. 5.

BRUCE, ROBERT (d. 1602). A Scot in the service of Archbishop James Beaton of Glasgow, he studied at the Scots College in France, became envoy of the prince of Parma to King James VI of Scotland in 1587, and tried to win

him back to the Catholicism in which he had been baptized. He was later captured at Brussels and charged with misappropriating funds and being a secret agent. Released, he died in Paris.

BRUCHÉSI, LOUIS JOSEPH PAUL (1855–1939), archbishop. Born and educated in Montreal, Canada, he studied also in France and Rome, where he was ordained in 1878. He did parish work in Montreal, taught apologetics at Laval in 1887, became its vice-rector, was supervisor of Catholic schools in the province of Quebec and in 1897 became archbishop of Montreal. He was interested in the temperance movement, forestry, and hospitals, and introduced several nursing orders in his see. He retired in 1919, and died in Montreal on Sept. 20.

BRÜCK, HEINRICH (1831–1903), bishop. Born in Bingen, Germany, on Oct. 25, he studied in the seminary at Mainz, was ordained in 1855, did further study at Munich and Rome, and in 1857 taught ecclesiastical history at Mainz. The seminary was closed by the government from 1878 to 1887; Brück returned to teaching in that year, became a canon of the cathedral in 1889 and in 1899 bishop of Mainz. He wrote a manual of church history, a five-volume account of the Church in Germany in the nineteenth century, and a study of rationalism in Germany. He died in Mainz, Germany, on Nov. 4.

BRUCKNER, ANTON (1824–1896), composer. Born in Ansfelden, Austria, on Sept. 4, he became organist of the Linz cathedral in 1855, of the Hofkapelle in Vienna in 1867, professor of harmony and counterpoint in the Vienna conservatory, and in 1875 lecturer at the University of Vienna. He gave organ concerts in Paris and London, and composed church music and symphonies, most notable of which were his *Te Deum, Mass in F Minor*, and seventh and ninth symphonies. He died in Vienna on Oct. 11, 1896.

BRUEL, JOACHIM (d. 1653), historian. Born in Vorst, Belgium, he became an Augustinian, studied at Bourges, and served as prior in Cologne and prior provincial of his order in that area in 1640 and 1649. He wrote a Latin version of the history of the Augustinians in Peru by Antonio de la Lamancha and translated Mendoza's history of China. He died on June 29.

BRUEYS, DAVID AUGUSTIN DE (1640–1723), theologian. Born in Aix, France, he studied law and theology, became a member of the consistory at Montpellier, wrote against Bossuet, and was converted by the latter in 1682. After his wife's death he became a priest, wrote on the mass, the liturgy, the Eucharist, the temporal power of the popes, reason and faith, and a philosophical history of his times.

With Palaprat, he wrote comedies and tragedies, published in 1712. He died in Montpellier, France, on Nov. 25.

BRUGÈRE, LOUIS FRÉDÉRIC (1823–1888), historian. Born in Orléans, France, on Oct. 8, he studied there and in Paris, received his doctorate, and was ordained. He taught in Orléans in 1846–61, except for two years as a parish priest, and in 1862 became a Sulpician. He taught apologetics and church history in Paris until his death in Issy on Apr. 11. He wrote *De vera religione, De ecclesia*, and an outline of the history and literature of the Church.

BRUGMAN, JOHN (d. 1473). Born in Kempen, near Cologne, before 1400, he became a Friar Minor, taught theology, and was viceprovincial at Cologne. He was widely known as a preacher, wrote—to support the work of the Brethren of the Common Life—two lives of Bl. Lydwina (one later summarized by Thomas à Kempis), a life of Christ, and poems. He is honored by the Franciscans on Sept. 19, the date of his death at Nijmegen, Holland.

BRUMIDI, CONSTANTINO (1805–1880), painter. Born in Rome, he decorated the palace of Prince Torlonia there, worked three years at the Vatican under Pope Gregory XVI, and went to New York City when the French seized Rome in 1849. He became an American citizen, decorated several churches, and painted an allegory of the Trinity for the cathedral in Mexico City (1864), allegorical and historical frescoes in the Capitol in Washington, particularly in the rotunda, and SS. Peter and Paul in the Philadelphia cathedral. He died in Washington on Feb. 19.

BRUMOY, PIERRE (1688–1742). Born in Rouen, France, he became a Jesuit in 1704, led the humanistic movement voiced in part in *Journal de Trévoux* (1722–39), of which he was editor for a while, wrote volumes 11–12 of the *History of the Gallican Church*, tragedies, translations from the Latin, and a Latin poem on the emotions, *De motibus animi*. His three-volume study of Greek tragedy, *Le Théâtre des Grecs*, was translated into English (1759) by Charlotte Lennox, Samuel Johnson, and others. Fr. Brumoy died in Paris.

BRUNELLESCO, FILIPPO (1377–1446), architect. Born in Florence, he was a goldsmith, sculptor, and student of mathematics, scripture, and the works of Dante. As a sculptor he worked in silver and in wood, outshone his friend Donatello in his early years, and then turned to architecture. He studied the classic structures in Rome and in 1419 undertook the completion of the cathedral of Santa Maria del Fiore in Florence by means of a dome within a dome. He also designed domes for the sacristy of San Lorenzo and the church of Santa Maria degli Angeli, both in Florence, designed the Pazzi chapel and Santo Spirito church, the foundling hospital, many homes, and part of the Pitti palace. He died in Florence on Apr. 16.

BRUNETIÈRE, FERDINAND (1849–1906), critic. Born in Toulon, France, on July 19, he studied in Paris, fought during the Franco-Prussian War, taught in private schools, began to write for *Revue des Deux Mondes* in 1874, strongly opposing the naturalists, and became its editor in 1893. He taught at L'École Normale from 1886 to 1905, was elected to the French Academy in 1893, and lectured at Johns Hopkins University in Baltimore, the Sorbonne, and elsewhere. His critical articles were published as *Études critiques sur l'histoire de la littérature française, Questions de critique, Essais sur la littérature contemporaine, Manuel de littérature française*, and *L'Évolution de la poésie lyrique au XIXᵉ siècle*. After his conversion he wrote *Le Besoin de croire* and *L'Action catholique*. He died in Paris on Dec. 9.

BRUNFORTE OF SARNANO, UGOLINO. *See* Boniscambi, Ugolino.

BRUNI, LEONARDO (1369–1444). Born in Arezzo, Italy, he studied classics and law, and from 1405 to 1415 was papal secretary to Innocent VII, Gregory XII, Alexander V, and antipope John XXIII. For a few months in 1410 he was chancellor of the republic of Florence, returned to the city after the deposition of John XXIII in 1415, wrote a *History of Florence*, and was made an honorary citizen. He was chancellor from 1427 until his death on Mar. 9, contributed to the renewed enthusiasm for the classics, translated Aeschines, Aristotle, Demosthenes, Plato, and Plutarch from Greek to Latin, and was a widely hailed humanist leader. He also wrote commentaries on contemporary history, on the origin of Rome, and on the wars with the Goths; the ten-volume *Epistolae familiares*, valuable for the history of his times; and biographies, in Latin, of Aristotle and Cicero and, in Italian, of Dante and Petrarch. He is sometimes called Aretino, from his birthplace.

BRUNNER, NICOLAUS JOSEPH (1795–1859), founder. Born in Mümliswil, Switzerland, on Jan. 10, he became a Benedictine at Maria Stein in 1812, was ordained in 1819, transferred to the Trappists at Oehlemberg until their house was suppressed by the government, founded a school for boys at Löwenberg, and in 1838 joined the Congregation of the Most Precious Blood. After training at Albano, Italy, he returned to develop a German province, met continuing government hostility, and moved with eight priests to Norwalk, Ohio, where he established their first American house. He died in Lichtenstein on Dec. 29 while in Europe seeking funds for his missions.

BRUNNER, SEBASTIAN (1814–1893),

author. Born in Vienna on Dec. 10, he studied at the university there, was ordained in 1838, took his doctorate at Freiburg, Germany, and taught philosophy at Vienna. He edited the anti-Josephinist journal *Wiener Kirchenzeitung* from 1848 to 1865, and wrote a biography of Clemens Hofbauer, books of ascetics and travel, sermons, and a history of the Church in Austria. He wrote considerable humor and satire in prose and verse, published (1864) in eighteen volumes. He died in Vienna on Nov. 27.

BRUNO, ST. (974?–1009), bishop and martyr. Born in Querfurt of Saxon nobility, he served as court chaplain to Otto III, went to Rome with the emperor, and became a Camaldolese monk there about 1000, taking the name Boniface. He worked near Ravenna, then in Germany, where he became a missionary archbishop, Poland, and finally reached Kiev. During an attempt to evangelize the Prussians he was slain with eighteen others on Mar. 14 on the Russian border, near Braunsberg, Poland (later named for him). F. D. June 19.

BRUNO, ST. (d. 1045), bishop. Son of Duke Conrad of Carinthia, he became bishop of Würzburg, Germany, in 1033, built the cathedral of St. Kilian, served as counselor to Conrad II and Emperor Henry III, and wrote several commentaries on scripture, prayer, and the creed. F. D. May 17.

BRUNO, ST. (1030?–1101), founder. Born at Cologne, of the prominent Hartenfaust family, he studied at the cathedral school in Rheims, and was ordained about 1055 at Cologne and became a canon there. In 1056 he returned to Rheims to teach; in 1057 he became head of the school and remained there eighteen years. In 1074 he became chancellor of the archdiocese, became embroiled in a dispute with the archbishop, Manasses de Gournai, whom he accused of being unfit for his office at a council in Autun in 1076, and returned to Cologne in 1080 when the clergy of Rheims wanted to elect him archbishop. In 1084 he retired with several friends to a hermitage near Molesmes under St. Robert. Not satisfied, they offered their services to Bishop St. Hugh of Grenoble. Given property in La Grande Chartreuse, an Alpine area, they established a monastery of hermit monks, following roughly the Rule of St. Benedict. This later developed into the Carthusian Institute. In 1090, St. Bruno was summoned to Rome by Urban II (whom he had taught at Rheims) as papal adviser. When the pope was forced to leave Rome, Bruno went with him, was offered and refused the see of Reggio, and at his earnest request was allowed to found St. Mary's hermitage at La Torre in Calabria. He became a close friend of Count Robert of Sicily and remained at St. Mary's until his death. St.

Bruno wrote commentaries on the Psalms and on the epistles of St. Paul. He has never been formally canonized, as the Carthusians are opposed to public honors, but in 1674 Pope Clement X extended to the entire Western Church the feast which Leo X approved for the order in 1514. F. D. Oct. 6.

BRUNO, ST. (1049–1123), bishop. Born in Solero, Piedmont, Italy, he became a canon at Siena. At a 1079 synod in Rome he defended the Church's doctrine of the Eucharist against Berengarius of Tours, who retracted. In 1080, Pope St. Gregory VII appointed him bishop of Segni. He staunchly supported the pope's reform movement and was imprisoned by Count Inulf, a follower of Emperor Henry IV. He accompanied Pope Urban II to the Council of Clermont in 1095. In 1102, against the wishes of his people, he became a Benedictine monk at Monte Cassino. The abbot persuaded the pope to allow Bruno to remain, without resigning his see. In 1107 he was elected abbot. He wrote a number of significant scriptural commentaries; he also wrote zealously in support of ecclesiastical discipline and against simony and lay investiture. He even rebuked Pope Paschal II, who had made concessions to Emperor-elect Henry V in ecclesiastical matters, and as a result was ordered to resign his abbacy and return to his see, which he did. He was canonized in 1183 by Pope Lucius III. F. D. July 18.

BRUNO, GIUSEPPE (1875–1954), cardinal. Born in Sezzadio, Italy, on June 30, he was ordained at twenty-two, and entered an administrative career. He was prefect of the Congregation of the Council and of the supreme tribunal of the Apostolic Signatura, the highest papal court of appeals, a member of other congregations, and chamberlain of the sacred college. He was named a cardinal in 1946. He died in Rome on Nov. 10.

BRUNO THE GREAT, ST. (925?–965), archbishop. Youngest son of Emperor Henry the Fowler and St. Matilda, he was educated at Utrecht, became confidential secretary to his brother, Emperor Otto I, in 940, and abbot of Lorsch and Corvey, and was ordained in 950. He became Otto's chancellor and in 953 was appointed archbishop of Cologne. He was noted for his activity in reforming clergy and monasteries, the high caliber of his cathedral school and of the men he appointed to office. He was active in the temporal affairs of the empire, and, when Otto went to Rome in 961 to be crowned emperor, Bruno was appointed co-regent. His cult was confirmed in 1870. F. D. Oct. 11.

BRUNO SAXONICUS (11th century), historian. A Saxon monk attached to the court of Archbishop Werner of Magdeburg, he wrote *Historia de bello saxonico* on the revolt, of which Werner was a leader, against Emperor Henry IV up to 1081. After 1078, when the archbishop died, Bruno was in the service of Bishop Werner of Merseburg.

BRUS, ANTON (1518–1580), archbishop. Born in Müglitz, Moravia, on Feb. 13, he joined the religious order of the Knights of the Cross with the Red Star, was ordained, served as chaplain in the Austrian army in the war with Turkey (1542–45), and was elected grand master general of his order at thirty-four. He became bishop of Vienna in 1559 and archbishop of Prague in 1561. He was Bohemian legate to the Council of Trent in 1562, tried, without success, to end the Utraquist schism, and refused to ordain its candidates in spite of the interference of well-meaning Emperor Maximilian. Brus died on Aug. 28.

BRUSASORCI. *See* Riccio, Domenico.

BRUSO, BL. CHRISTINA (1242–1312). Born in Stommeln, near Cologne. In 1267 the young Dominican, Peter of Dacia, began to record her mystical experiences; when he left Cologne in 1277, the parish priest, John, and later a young schoolmaster of Stommeln, Master John, continued his record until 1288. Although many of the extraordinary phenomena associated with her life have been seriously questioned, she was widely venerated and Pope St. Pius X confirmed her cult in 1908. F. D. Nov. 6.

BRUTÉ DE RÉMUR, SIMON GUILLAUME GABRIEL (1779–1839), bishop. Born in Rennes, France, on Mar. 20 to a royal official of the same name, he went to school there until the revolution, became a compositor in the printing house of his mother, Jeanne de Vauhelle Vatar, and received his medical degree in 1803, but never practiced. He went to St. Sulpice, was ordained in 1808 as a Sulpician, taught theology for two years in Paris, and then in Baltimore and Emmitsburg, Maryland, where he became spiritual director of Mother Elizabeth Seton. In 1815–18 he was president of St. Mary's College, Baltimore, returned to Mt. St. Mary's in Emmitsburg until 1834, then was consecrated first bishop of Vincennes, Indiana. He served this diocese, including the entire state and part of Illinois, for five years and died in Vincennes on June 26.

BRUYAS, JACQUES (1635–1712), missioner. Born in Lyons, France, on July 13, he became a Jesuit in 1651, went to Canada in 1666, and worked for forty-six years among the Iroquois. He was superior general in 1693–98, wrote a catechism and prayers, and prepared the oldest known Iroquois grammar. He died in Sault St. Louis, Canada, on June 15.

BRYANT, JOHN DELAVAU (1811–1877), author. Born in Philadelphia, he studied at the University of Pennsylvania and the Episcopal seminary in New York City, went to Europe in 1840, and became a convert in 1842. He took his degree in medicine at Pennsylvania, became prominent in Philadelphia medical circles, worked at Norfolk, Virginia, during the yellow-fever epidemic of 1855, and was editor of the *Catholic Herald* in Philadelphia for two years. He published poetry, a novel, *Pauline Seward*, and an explanation of the dogma of the Immaculate Conception.

BRYCHAN (5th century), king. A Welsh monarch, he probably was succeeded by his son St. Cledwyn; his oldest son, St. Pabiali, is said to have gone to Spain. The sons are honored on Nov. 1.

BRYNOTH, ST. (d. 1317), bishop. Of Swedish descent, he became bishop of Scara in West Gothland, died on Feb. 6, and was canonized in 1498. F. D. May 9.

BRYNSTAN. *See* Birnstan.

BUCELIN, GABRIEL (1599–1681), historian. Born in Diessenhofen, Germany, on Dec. 29, he became a Benedictine at Weingarten at thirteen, studied at Dillingen, and was ordained in 1624. He was master of novices at St. Trudpert and Weingarten, taught humanities in Feldkirch in 1635–46, and was prior of St. John's, Feldkirch, in 1651. He wrote more than fifty studies of phases of German history, including the valuable *Germania sacra*, and works dealing with his order. He died in Weingarten, Germany, on June 9.

BUCHE, HENRI MICHAEL (d. 1666). A shoemaker in Arlon, Luxembourg, he formed a religious guild for his fellow craftsmen, developed it, with the assistance of Baron de Renty, as the Frères Cordonniers when he went to Paris in 1645, and saw it branch to other cities. The workers followed a strict rule, visited prisoners and the sick, and inspired the formation of a similar group among tailors. He is known as Henry the Good and often called saint, though never canonized.

BUCK, VICTOR DE (1817–1876), scholar. Born in Oudenarde, Flanders, on Apr. 21, he studied at Soignes and Rouler, became a Jesuit in 1835, and completed his studies at Namur. He was assistant to the Bollandist group in Brussels in 1840–45, studied theology at Louvain, was ordained in 1848, and returned to work with the Bollandists from 1850 until his death on June 28. He contributed much to volumes 7 and 9–13 of *Acta sanctorum;* he also wrote lives of the saints, church history, archaeology, and, with Antoine Tinnebroeck, a defense of the rights of the regular clergy. Other work included an explanation of the religious vow of poverty, a treatise on religious life in nineteenth-century Belgium, and a controversial pamphlet on the proper identification of martyrs buried in the catacombs. He also served as official theologian at the Vatican Council.

BUCKLEY, PATRICK ALPHONSUS (1841–

1896), jurist. Born near Castletownsend, Cork, Ireland, he studied at St. Colman's, Fermoy, the Irish College in Paris, and at Louvain. He led the Irish recruits of the Papal Brigade from Ostend to Vienna, served with them in defense of Pius IX, and was captured at Ancona. He returned to Ireland, studied law, and went to Wellington, New Zealand. He became a member of the provincial council and, when it was abolished in 1875, of the legislative council in 1878. He was colonial secretary in 1884–87, attorney general, and acted as leader of the house and of the opposition in his long term of legislative service, to 1895, when he was named judge of the supreme court. He was knighted in 1892 and died in Lower Hutt, New Zealand, on May 18.

BUDÉ, GUILLAUME (1467–1540), scholar. Born in Paris, he studied there and at Orléans, mastered Greek, philosophy, theology, medicine, and law, and served the French king on missions to Popes Julius II and Leo X. He served King Louis XII as secretary, accompanied Francis I on his travels, recommended the establishment of the Collège de France (1530), prevailed on Francis not to ban the establishment of a printing press (1533), and founded the Bibliothèque de Fontainebleau (later the Bibliothèque Nationale). He wrote much in defense of the study of Greek; pleas for humanistic study, *De contemptu rerum fortuitarum* and *De studio litterarum*; on Roman coins and weights; annotations on the Pandects, which revolutionized the study of Roman law; a translation of Plutarch's *Lives*; and historically important letters to Erasmus, More, and Rabelais. He died in Paris on Aug. 22.

BUDEAUX. *See* Budoc, St.

BUDOC, ST. (6th century?). According to unreliable sources, he was the son of King Goello in Brittany and Azenor, daughter of the king of Brest, raised in a monastery near Waterford, Ireland, of which he became bishop, migrated to Brittany, and succeeded St. Maglorius in the see of Dol. Another tradition calls him an Irish hermit who came to Britain and settled at Budock near Falmouth. Possibly there are several Budocs. The name is sometimes spelled Budeaux and Beuzec. F. D. Dec. 9.

BUFALARI, BL. GIOVANNI (d. 1350?). Brother of Bl. Lucia of Amelia, John of Rieti was born at Castel Porziano, near Rome, and became an Augustinian friar hermit at Rieti. His cult was confirmed in 1832. F. D. Aug. 9.

BUFALARI, BL. LUCIA (d. 1350). Born in Castel Ponziano, near Rome, and a sister of Bl. Giovanni, she was an Augustinian nun in Amelia, where she became prioress. Her cult was confirmed in 1832. F. D. July 27.

BUFFALO BILL. *See* Cody, William Frederick.

BUFFIER, CLAUDE (1661–1737), philosopher. Born in Poland of French parents on May 25, he studied in Rouen, became a Jesuit in 1679, taught in Paris and Rouen, and from 1701 to 1731 was associated with *Journal de Trévoux*. He wrote a life of Louis de Sales, St. Francis de Sales's brother, a French grammar, a method of memorization, and works in history, ascetics, and philosophy. He died in Paris on May 17.

BUGIARDINI, GIULIANO (1475–1554), painter. Born in Florence, Italy, he studied with Ghirlandaio and Bertoldo, was influenced by Bartolommeo and Raphael, and in 1508 was invited by Michelangelo to join him in Rome in working on the Sistine Chapel. He painted *Marriage of St. Catherine, John the Baptist,* many madonnas, and a portrait of Michelangelo.

BUGLIO, LOUIS (1606–1682). Born in Mineo, Sicily, on Jan. 26, he became a Jesuit in 1622, studied at the Roman College, and went to China where he preached so effectively that he was imprisoned during a persecution. Freed at Peking in 1648, he worked with other Jesuits in reforming the Chinese calendar; he also wrote eighty works in explanation of Christianity, translating the missal and breviary into Chinese. He died in Peking on Oct. 7.

BUIL, BERNARDO. *See* Boil, Bernardo.

BUITHE, ST. (d. 521). A Scot, he returned from the Continent to evangelize the Picts. F. D. Dec. 7.

BULHOES, FERNANDO DE. *See* Anthony of Padua, St.

BULLAKER, VEN. THOMAS (1604?–1642), martyr. Born in Chichester, England, son of a physician, he studied at St. Omer, France, and Valladolid, Spain, became a Franciscan, and was ordained in 1628. He was sent to the English mission, was arrested at Plymouth on landing, released, and worked for twelve years among the London poor. He was seized while saying mass, condemned as a priest, and hanged, drawn, and quartered at Tyburn on Oct. 12.

BULLION, ANGÉLIQUE (17th century). Born in Paris to Guichard and Madeleine Brulart de Sillery Favre, she married Claude de Bullion, keeper of the royal seals. Left a fortune by her father, she anonymously endowed the foundation of Ville Marie (to become the city of Montreal), the Hôtel Dieu under the direction of the Sisters of St. Joseph, and the defense fund which kept the city safe from attacks by Iroquois.

BULSTRODE, RICHARD (1610–1711), biographer. Born in England, he studied at Cambridge and law in the Inner Temple, and served as an adjutant general of cavalry and as quartermaster general during the civil war. Directed to arrange the funeral of Lord Strafford, he faced unexpected expenses, fled to Bruges, Flanders, was imprisoned, but released when Charles II paid the debt. He later became auditor of a Scots regiment in the Netherlands, agent at the court in Brussels, was knighted in 1675, and made envoy to Brussels in 1685. He went into exile with King James II, wrote the latter's life, memoirs on the reigns of Charles I and Charles II, and poems, and died in Paris.

BUNDERIUS, JOANNES. *See* Van den Bundere, Johannes.

BUONACCORSI, BL. BONAVENTURA (1240?–1315). A native of Pistoia, Tuscany, Italy, he was a leader of the Ghibellines there until 1276, when he was converted by St. Philip Benizi and joined the Servites. He accompanied St. Philip through Italy, became prior at Orvieto in 1282, and later at Montepulciano, was made preacher apostolic for all Italy, helped St. Agnes found her community in Montepulciano, and became renowned for his efforts to restore peace. He died at Orvieto, Italy, and his cult was approved in 1822. F. D. Dec. 14.

BUONAGIUNTA, ST. JOHN (13th century). *See* Monaldo, St. Buonfiglio.

BUONCOMPAGNI, BALDASSARE (1821–1894), scholar. Born in Rome, the prince of Piombino became in 1847 a member of the pontifical Accademia de' Nuovi Lincei, and later served as its secretary and librarian. He wrote on the astronomer, Guidone Bonatti, on Leonardo Pisano, and other studies, and from 1868 to 1887 edited *Bolletino delle scienze matematiche e fische*.

BUONPEDONI, BL. BARTOLO (d. 1300). Born in Mucchio, Tuscany, Italy, he became a servant in a Benedictine monastery at Pisa and then a Franciscan tertiary. He was ordained at thirty, served a parish in Peccioli, was stricken with leprosy in 1280, and thereafter was chaplain of the leper house in Celloli. His cult was confirmed in 1910. He was also known as Bartholomew of San Gimignano. F. D. Dec. 14.

BURCHARD, ST. (d. 754), bishop. An English priest from Wessex, he joined St. Boniface about 732 in his missionary labors in Germany. Boniface consecrated him first bishop of Würzburg, and in 749 he went to Rome as Pepin's envoy and secured the approval of Pope St. Zachary to Pepin's claim to the Frankish throne. He founded several Benedictine abbeys and in 753 resigned his see and spent the rest of his life in monastic retirement in Homburg. He died on Feb. 2. F. D. Oct. 14.

BURCHARD, BL. (965?–1025), bishop. Born in Hesse, Germany, he was educated in Cologne, became a Benedictine monk at Lobbes, entered the service of Archbishop Willigis of Mainz after 975, rose rapidly, and in 1000 was named by Emperor Otto III bishop of Worms. He was ordained, took office, and prepared a series of laws for the better handling of justice, wiped out a criminal stronghold near the city, and built monasteries and churches, including the cathedral of St. Peter. He sponsored synods, took direct care of ecclesiastical students, and was deeply interested in education. He prepared a manual of ecclesiastical law and moral theology, often called *Brocardus*, used for more than a century, until the similar *Decretum* of Gratian appeared. F. D. Aug. 20.

BURCHARD (d. 1107), bishop. Of the family of the counts of Neuenburg, he was attached to the court of King Henry IV, who made him bishop of Basle, Switzerland, in 1072. He fought many of Henry's wars, laid waste to civil and ecclesiastical property, and was heavily rewarded by land grands from the monarch. He condemned Pope Gregory VII—at Worms in 1076, for which he was excommunicated and in 1077 absolved, and probably at Brixen in 1080—marched into Rome with Henry, and attended the installation of antipope Clement II in 1084. Burchard remained faithful to the king in the quarrel between Henry and his son Henry V. After the death of Gregory and the election of Pope Urban II, Burchard sought a reconciliation with the papacy, restored and founded many monastic settlements, and died on Apr. 12, no longer in rebellion.

BURCHARD, BL. (d. 1122). He was the first abbot of the Benedictine monastery of Mallersdorf, Bavaria, to which he had come from the abbey of St. Michael, Bamberg. F. D. June 25.

BURCHARD (d. 1131). He became bishop of Cambrai, France, in 1115 and sent St. Norbert and his Premonstratensians to Antwerp to combat the heresy of Tanquelin and his followers regarding the Eucharist.

BURCKMAIR, HANS (1473–1531), painter. Born in Augsburg, he studied under his father Toman and in Alsace under Schongauer, went on to Italy, and, on his return, painted with Hans Holbein the Elder three of the major churches of Rome for the monastery of St. Catherine, Augsburg, Bavaria. He also completed a *Coronation of the Virgin* for its cloister, a *Madonna with Grapes* at Nuremburg, *St. George*, and other religious scenes. The Renaissance influence appears in his use of color and reliance on landscape or contemporary architecture as background. He decorated a prayer book for Emperor Maximilian and designed nearly 500 woodcuts as book illustrations.

BURGESS, THOMAS (1791–1854). He became second bishop of Clifton, England, in 1851, established a cathedral chapter in 1852, and inherited the archives of Wales and southwestern England, covering the years since 1780; earlier records were burned during the Gordon Riots. The bishop died on Nov. 27.

BURGIS, EDWARD AMBROSE (1673?–1747), historian. Born in England, son of an Anglican minister, he became a convert as a young man, joined the Dominicans in Rome, and studied there and at Naples and Louvain. He taught philosophy, theology, and scripture for thirty years at the College of St. Thomas at Louvain and twice served as its rector. He became provincial in 1730, was prior of the English Dominican house at Bornhem in 1741, and vice-general of his order in Belgium in 1746. He published *Annals of the Church* (to 300) in 1712 and revised it in 1738, and other work in theology and scripture. He died in Brussels on Apr. 27.

BURGOA, FRANCISCO (1600?–1681), historian. Born in Oaxaca, Mexico, he became a Dominican in 1629, was curate in several parishes, knew the Zapotec and Mixteco languages well, was provincial of San Hipólito de Oaxaca in 1649 and in 1662, vicar general, inquisitor, and inspector of libraries after a trip to a chapter at Rome in 1656. He published widely on the history and geography of his province and died in Teopozotlan, Mexico.

BURGUNDOFARA, ST. (d. 657). Sister of SS. Cagnoald and Faro, she was opposed by her father, a French court official, but eventually allowed to enter religious life, becoming abbess of Brie for thirty-seven years. The convent later became the Benedictine abbey of Faremoutiers. She is also called Fare. F. D. Apr. 3.

BURIANA, ST. (6th century). An Irishwoman, she became a hermit in Cornwall; the place-name Buryan perpetuates her memory. F. D. June 4.

BURIDAN, JEAN (14th century), philosopher. Born in Béthune, France, at the end of the thirteenth century, he studied at Paris under William of Occam, taught there and directed the Picardy group, and was rector in 1327. In 1345 he was sent by the university as ambassador to the papal court in Avignon. He wrote commentaries on Aristotle, particularly the *Politics*, and a logic. His philosophical position, which identified intellect and will, and which adhered to a skepticism regarding the power of reason, was consistently condemned.

BURIGNY, JEAN LÉVESQUE DE (1692–1785), historian. Born in Rheims, France, he worked with his brothers on a dictionary of universal knowledge, was co-author with St. Hyacinthe of the twelve-volume *L'Europe savante* (1718), wrote histories of Sicily and Constantinople, biographies of Bossuet, Erasmus, Grotius, and Plotinus, and a study of papal authority, which he termed merely honorary. He died in Paris.

BURKARD, FRANZ (d. 1539), jurist. Born in Germany, he taught canon law at Ingolstadt in 1519, fought to stem Lutheranism, and with his brother Peter was prosecutor at the trial of Andreas Seehofer for teaching heretical doctrines. Seehofer retired to a monastery, but the Burkards were violently attacked; they defended themselves, with John Eck, before the university. Franz died at Rain, Bavaria, on Dec. 9.

BURKARD, FRANZ (d. 1584), jurist. Born in Germany, he was legal adviser to the Bavarian chancellor, August Loesch, chancellor to Ernest of Bavaria, elector of Cologne, and praised by St. Peter Canisius. He died in Bonn, Germany, on Aug. 6. *De autonomia*, published in Munich in 1586 under his name, was actually written by Andreas Erstenberger, private secretary to King William V of Bavaria.

BURKE, EDMUND (1753–1820), bishop. Born in Maryborough, Kildare, Ireland, he studied and was ordained in Paris, returned briefly to his native parish, and in 1786 went to Quebec. He taught philosophy and mathematics at its seminary, became its rector, and worked on Indian missions from 1794 to 1801. He correctly diagnosed the loss of faith among the Indians to race prejudice and stirred up a storm of opposition. He was at Halifax, Nova Scotia, as vicar general of Quebec in 1801, became vicar general of Nova Scotia in 1815, and was consecrated titular bishop of Zion and first vicar apostolic of Nova Scotia in 1818. He died in Halifax on Nov. 29.

BURKE, JOHN JOSEPH (1875–1936). Born in New York City on June 6, he studied at St. Francis Xavier and Catholic University, was ordained as a Paulist in 1899, edited the *Catholic World* from 1904 to 1922, and helped found the Catholic Press Association in 1911. In 1917 he founded the National Catholic War Council to co-ordinate Catholic war activities, successfully fought for a single unified war-work fund rather than separate denominational funds, and received the Distinguished Service Medal in 1919. He received the hierarchy's support in 1919 to continue his organization as the National Catholic Welfare Council (now National Catholic Welfare Conference) to co-ordinate Catholic activities in the United States, and served as its general secretary until his death in Washington, D.C., on Oct. 30. He was active in presenting the bishops' Program of Social Reconstruction, drawn up in 1919, and applying it to the Depression of the thirties, worked with the state department and Mexican President Callas to restore religious freedom in Mexico in 1928, and was made a monsignor in 1936.

BURKE, JOSEPH HENRY (1876–1940). Born in Richwood, Wisconsin, on Apr. 10, he studied at Notre Dame, and Catholic University, was ordained in 1909, and was on the faculty of Notre Dame from 1909 to 1925, serving as dean from 1915. He was president of

St. Edward's University, Austin, Texas, from 1925 to 1931, then on the staff of a military school, back at Notre Dame, and from 1937 pastor in Watertown, Wisconsin, where he died on Dec. 30.

BURKE, MAURICE FRANCIS (1845–1923), bishop. Born in Ireland on May 5, he went to the United States, studied at St. Mary's of the Lake, Notre Dame, and the North American College, Rome, and was ordained in 1875. He served in Chicago parishes in 1875–78, as pastor in Joliet in 1878–87, became bishop of Cheyenne, Wyoming, in 1887, and was transferred to St. Joseph, Missouri, in 1893. Because of ill health, he retired in favor of an administrator in 1921. He died in St. Joseph on Mar. 17.

BURKE, THOMAS (1709?–1776), bishop. Born in Dublin, he studied in Rome, became a Dominican at fourteen by special permission, was highly praised by Pope Benedict XIII for his learning, was regent of studies for six years, and was given the degree of master of theology in 1742. He returned to Dublin in 1743, was definitor twice and historian of his province, and in 1759 was made bishop of Ossory. He published *Hibernia dominicana* in 1762 (at Cologne on the title page, but really at Kilkenny) and a *Supplementum* in 1772. Since the work treated of Irish relations with England and defended Rinuccini, nuncio of Pope Innocent X, seven Irish bishops declared their allegiance to King George III and condemned both volumes by Bishop Burke. He died in Kilkenny, Ireland, on Sept. 25.

BURKE, THOMAS MARTIN ALOYSIUS (1840–1915), bishop. Born in Ireland on Jan. 10, he went to Utica, New York, studied at St. Michael's in Toronto, and St. Mary's and St. Charles, Maryland, and was ordained in 1864. He served in Albany, New York, parishes from 1864 to 1894, was appointed vicar general in 1887, and was consecrated fourth bishop of that see in 1894. He consecrated its cathedral in 1902, built schools and asylums, and died there on Jan. 20.

BURKE, THOMAS NICHOLAS (1830–1882). Born in Galway, Ireland, on Sept. 8, he became a Dominican in Perugia, Italy, in 1847, studied in Rome, was named master of novices at Woodchester, England, and was subsequently ordained, in 1853. He founded the novitiate in Tallaght, Ireland, in 1855, was prior there in 1863, served as rector of San Clemente, Rome, in 1864–67, returned to Ireland, was Bishop Leahy's theologian at the Vatican Council in 1870, and was sent as visitor to the United States in 1871. Already known throughout Europe as a preacher, he gave 400 lectures and uncounted sermons during his eighteen months in America. He died in Tallaght on July 2.

BURLEIGH, WALTER (1275–1337), philosopher. Born in England, he became a Franciscan or Augustinian (he is claimed by both orders), was classmate at Oxford with William of Occam under Duns Scotus, and was appointed tutor to Edward III as a prince. He taught at Paris, opposed Occam's nominalism and the exaggerated realism of the followers of Duns Scotus, and wrote on philosophy and theology.

BURNAND, FRANCIS COWLEY (1836–1917), dramatist. Born in London on Nov. 29, of Huguenot descent, he studied at Eton and Cambridge, and was preparing for the Anglican ministry when he was influenced by the Oxford Movement. He became a convert in 1857, studied law and was admitted to the bar in 1860, then turned to the theater. He wrote 120 farces, burlesque librettos, and translations from the French, including *Black-Eyed Susan, Cox and Box*, and *Dido*. He wrote a column for *Punch* beginning in 1862, was its editor from 1880 to 1906, and published *Happy Thought* (1868) from his papers and two autobiographical works. He became editor of the English *Catholic Who's Who*, was knighted in 1902, and died in Ramsgate, England, on Apr. 21.

BURNETT, PETER HARDEMAN (1807–1895), governor. Born in Nashville, Tennessee, on Nov. 15, he was taken to Missouri as a child, returned to Tennessee at nineteen, married Harriet Rogers, was a businessman, and passed the bar in 1839. He edited the *Far West*, a weekly newspaper, in Liberty, Missouri, became a Campbellite, moved to Oregon in 1843, and served in the territorial legislature in 1844–48. He became a convert in 1846, moved to California in 1848, served in the legislature, and was a superior-court judge in 1849. He helped to frame the state constitution, became chief justice, and was governor in 1850–51. He resumed his law practice until 1857, was supreme-court justice in 1857–58, and president of the Pacific Bank from 1863 to 1880, when he retired. He wrote the story of his conversion and *The American Theory of Government* and *Recollections and Opinions of an Old Pioneer*. He died in San Francisco on May 16.

BURNS, JAMES (1808–1871), publisher. Born near Montrose, Scotland, son of a Presbyterian minister, he left the University of Glasgow in 1832 to work in London with a publishing house, set up his own firm, specializing in Church of England books, became attracted by the Oxford Movement, and was converted in 1847. He published Cardinal Wiseman's *Fabiola* and Newman's *Callista*, devotional works, musical compositions, and his own writings on church music. His firm became Burns & Oates and later Burns, Oates, and Washbourne. He died of cancer in London on Apr. 11.

BURNS, JAMES ALOYSIUS (1867–1940), educator. Born in Michigan City, Indiana, on Feb. 13, he studied at Notre Dame, was ordained in 1893, was president of Holy Cross College in 1900 and of Notre Dame in 1919–22, and in 1904 was a founder of the Catholic Education Association. He became provincial superior of the Congregation of Holy Cross in 1927 and assistant superior general in 1938. He died in South Bend, Indiana, on Sept. 9.

BURROWS, ERIC (1882–1938), scholar. Born in Ramsgate, England, on Mar. 26, he became a convert in 1904, soon after graduation from Oxford, studied as a Jesuit at Stonyhurst, Beirut, and St. Beuno's, and was ordained in 1917. He did biblical research in Rome and the Holy Land, was the official cuneiform expert with the Chaldean expedition at Uri (1925–29), and by his work on the language records of Babylon and Assyria contributed much to history and made specific new information available about the Deluge and the times of Abraham. His *Oracles of Jacob and Balaam* (1939) and *Gospel of the Informer* (1941) were published after his sudden death in an auto accident near Eynsha, England, in late June.

BURTSELL, RICHARD LALOR (1840–1912). Born in New York on Apr. 14, he studied at the Propaganda in Rome, was ordained in 1862, was a curate in New York City, and in 1868 became pastor of Epiphany parish. He supported Fr. McGlynn in his rebellion against the archdiocesan authorities and in 1889 was ordered to retire to a small parish in Roundout, New York. He twice appealed to Rome for reinstatement and was refused; in 1905, however, he was made a monsignor by Pope Pius X and named pastor of St. Mary's, Kingston, New York, where he died.

BUS, VEN. CÉSAR DE (1544–1607), founder. Born in Cavaillon, France, he fought with the king against the Huguenots at eighteen, became a poet, painter, and adventurer, sought the benefice of his dead brother at Salon for personal wealth, reformed his ways, began serious studies, and was ordained in 1582. He was noted for his charities and in 1592 organized the Seculars of Christian Doctrine, priests devoted to catechetical instruction. The congregation was approved in 1597 by Pope Clement VIII. He also founded an order of women, Filles de la Doctrine Chrétienne, later absorbed by the Ursulines. He died in Avignon, France, on Apr. 15, and was declared Venerable in 1821.

BUSCH, JOSEPH FRANCIS (1866–1953), bishop. Born in Red Wing, Minnesota, on Apr. 18, he studied at Canisius College, Sacred Heart (Prairie du Chien, Wisconsin), Innsbruck, and Catholic University, and was ordained in Austria in 1889. He was Archbishop Ireland's secretary in 1890–92, did parish work for the next decade, was director of the St. Paul diocesan mission band in 1902–10, and was appointed bishop of Lead (later Rapid City), South Dakota, in 1910. He was translated to St. Cloud in 1915, and held three diocesan synods. He died on May 19.

BUSÉE, PIERRE (1540–1587), theologian. Born in Nijmegen, Holland, he became a Jesuit at twenty-one, was master of novices at twenty-seven, and taught at the college in Cologne. He completed, with scriptural references, the large catechism of St. Peter Canisius (1569–70) with the latter's approval. In 1571 he taught scripture at Vienna and in 1584 was called to Rome to prepare a new course of studies for his Society. He was rector of the College of Nobles in Vienna at the time of his death. The name is also spelled Buys.

BUSEMBAUM, HERMANN (1600–1668), theologian. Born in Notteln, Westphalia, he became a Jesuit at nineteen, taught widely, was rector of colleges in Hildesheim and Münster, and adviser to Prince-bishop Christoph von Galen of Cologne. He wrote the influential *Medulla theologiae moralis*, based in part on notes by Hermann Nünning and Friedrich Spe, which ran through forty editions in his lifetime. His explanations of the moral problems involved in regicide were often misrepresented; his book was condemned in Paris and burned in Toulouse in the eighteenth century. He died in Münster, Germany, on Jan. 31.

BUSS, FRANZ JOSEPH VON (1803–1878), jurist. Born in Zell, Baden, on Mar. 23, he studied at Freiburg, Bonn, and Göttingen, became attorney for the city of Freiburg and taught jurisprudence at its university. He met great anti-Catholic pressure while a member of the lower house, *Landtag*, of Baden in 1837 and again in 1846; he resigned during his first term, but was so powerful during his second that the government dissolved the *Landtag*. He wrote *Methodology of Canon Law, The Influence of Christianity on Law and the State, The German Union and the Love for Prussia*, a life of St. Thomas of Canterbury, and many polemical works. He made his house into an ecclesiastical college; organized more than 400 separate German Catholic societies into a workable union; fed thousands during the famine of 1846 and cared for German prisoners in the Austro-Italian War; was leader of the greater Germany party, favoring Austria over Prussia, in the *Landtag* in Frankfort. He did not favor the new Germany, although he rejoiced at the defeat of France in 1870, served for a fourth time in the Baden lower house as a member of the Centre party in 1874–77, and retired from public life after the death of his youngest son. He died in Freiburg im Breisgau, Germany, on Jan. 31.

BUSTAMENTE, CARLOS MARÍA (1774–1848), historian. Born in Oaxaca, Mexico, on Nov. 4, he studied law in 1796, commanded a regiment in the war for independence from Spain in 1812, was imprisoned in Vera Cruz, joined Santa Anna, and marched to capture the capital in 1821. He alternately held high positions in the new government and was banished by Itúrbide and those who sought to restore native tyranny, particularly over his remarks in his weekly newspaper, *La avispa de Chilpancingo*. He edited early historical chronicles by Bernardino de Sahagún, Gomara, Veytia, and others; the work sometimes is careless and the anti-Spanish tone is always present. More significant are his autobiography (1833) and his history of the war with the United States, which is a detailed study of the Mexican side of the conflict and a strong condemnation of his nation's decay. He died in Mexico City on Sept. 29.

BUSTON, THOMAS STEPHEN (1549–1619), missioner. Born in Salisbury, England, he became a Jesuit in 1576, and was sent to Portuguese India in 1578. From 1584 until his death he was superior at Goa. He wrote a grammar of the Canara tongue, instructional works, a catechism, one of the first works printed in Hindustani, and *Purana*, poems on the chief tenets of Christianity.

BUTEUX, JACQUES (1600–1652), missioner. Born in Abbeville, Picardy, France, on Apr. 11, he became a Jesuit in 1620, studied at La Flèche, taught at Caen, and was prefect at Clermont. In 1634 he was sent to Three Rivers, Canada, and worked among the Montagnais and Algonquin Indians for eighteen years. He wrote an account of the captivity of St. Isaac Jogues and was himself ambushed and tomahawked to death by Iroquois along the upper St. Maurice River, Quebec, on May 10.

BUTLER, ALBAN (1710–1773), historian. Born in Appletree, Northamptonshire, England, on Oct. 10, he studied at Douai, was ordained in 1735, and taught philosophy and theology there. He helped Richard Challoner in the preparation of the latter's *Memoirs of Missionary Priests*; toured Europe in 1745 with the earl of Shrewsbury; served as mission priest in the Midlands and as chaplain to the duke of Norfolk; and tutored the latter's nephew, Edward Howard, in Paris. There he completed his *Lives of the Fathers, Martyrs, and Other Principal Saints*, containing 1600 biographies, on which he had been working for thirty years; it was published in London in 1756–59. He became president of the English College at St. Omer in 1766 and served as vicar general of four surrounding dioceses. He also wrote *Travels, Meditations*, and a life of Sir Tobie Matthews, all published posthumously. He died in St. Omer, France, on May 15.

BUTLER, CHARLES (1750–1832). Nephew of Alban Butler, he was born in London, studied in Hammersmith and at Douai, studied law, but was prevented by his religion from becoming a barrister and became a conveyancer instead. He practiced for forty years, became secretary of a committee of laymen formed to seek repeal of the penal laws against Catholics, published their views, and had some success when parliament voted partial relief in 1791. Butler was invited to the bar in that year, and continued to work for Catholic Emancipation. He and his committee frequently clashed with Bishop Milner and others, who seemed to resent the lead taken by the laity. Butler collaborated with Hargrave on a significant study of Coke-Littleton, published other legal works, and wrote *On Impressing Seamen, The Coronation Oath, Historical Memoirs of English, Scottish, and Irish Catholics* (1819), to which Milner also replied, biographies of Alban Butler, Bossuet, Fénelon, Erasmus, Grotius, and Thomas à Kempis, *The French Church, Church Music*, and *Reminiscences* (1822). He died in London on June 2.

BUTLER, CUTHBERT. *See* Butler, Edward Joseph.

BUTLER, EDMUND (d. 1550). Natural son of Pierce, earl of Ormond, he became prior of Athassal abbey and in 1523 was named archbishop of Cashel, Ireland. Although he was a strong supporter of Henry VIII in the king's struggle with the papacy, Butler appeared not to have left the Church.

BUTLER, EDWARD JOSEPH (1858–1934), historian. Born in Dublin on May 6, he studied at Downside, and became a Benedictine in 1876, taking the name Cuthbert. He was ordained in 1884, taught and was prefect at Downside, and by 1900 had achieved recognition of the center as an abbey conforming to Benedictine tradition. He edited the *Lausiac History* by Palladius in 1898–1904, while serving as superior of Benet House, Cambridge. He returned to Downside in 1904, was abbot in 1906 and in 1914, and president of the English Benedictines from 1914 to 1921. He edited the *Rule* of St. Benedict and wrote *Benedictine Monachism* (1919), *Western Mysticism* (1922), *Life and Times of Bishop Ullathorne* (1926), and *The Vatican Council* (1930). He died in Clapham, England, on Apr. 1.

BUTLER, ELIZABETH SOUTHERDEN (1846–1933), painter. Born in Lausanne, Switzerland, daughter of Thomas and Christiana Weller Thompson, and sister of Alice Meynell, she was educated by her father. In 1866 she studied at the South Kensington Museum and in 1869 in Italy. She became a

189

convert in 1873, exhibited *The Roll Call*, the first of many military oils, at the Royal Academy in 1874, and was suddenly successful. John Ruskin praised her *Quatre Bras*; her sketches of horses and the quiet scenery of her water colors were in striking contrast to the detail and movement of her army and historical canvases. She married General Sir William Francis Butler in 1877; after his death in 1910 she lived in Tipperary and Meath, Ireland. She died in Gormanston castle on Oct. 2.

BUTLER, MARY JOSEPH (1641-1723). Born in Callan, Kilkenny, Ireland, she was sent at twelve to be educated in the Benedictine convent at Ghent, where her aunt, Lady Knatchbull, was abbess. She was professed at the convent in Boulogne at sixteen, went to the Irish Benedictine abbey at Ypres, Belgium, in 1683, and in 1686 became abbess. She established a convent and school in Dublin in 1688 at the request of King James II, but it was sacked during the Battle of the Boyne in 1690, and Dame Butler returned to Ypres. She faced years of poverty and hardship, but reestablished a successful settlement before her death there on Dec. 22.

BUTLER, MARY JOSEPH (1860-1940), educator. Born in Kilkenny, Ireland, on July 22, she became a member of the Religious of the Sacred Heart, and was founder and president from 1918 to 1926 of Marymount College, Tarrytown, New York. She then served as superior general of her congregation until her death in Tarrytown on Apr. 23.

BUTLER, PIERCE (1866-1939), jurist. Born near Northfield, Minnesota, on Mar. 17, he studied at Carleton, was admitted to the bar in St. Paul in 1888, and was elected county attorney in 1893 and 1895. He began his law practice in 1897, became widely known for his cases, especially those involving railroad rates, and in 1922 was appointed justice of the United States Supreme Court despite the opposition of Senators Norris and La Follette. He consistently opposed increased centralization of power in the government, and when the New Deal came into control in 1933 produced one dissenting opinion after another, seventy-three during his last three years in office. He died in Washington, D.C., on Nov. 16.

BUTLER, THADDEUS (d. 1897), bishop. Appointed bishop of Concordia (the see was transferred to Salina in 1944) in northwestern Kansas, he died in Rome on July 17 before he could occupy his see.

BUTLER, WILLIAM FRANCIS (1838-1910), general. Born in Suirville, Tipperary, Ireland, on Oct. 31, he studied in Tullabeg and Dublin, joined the British army in 1858, served in Burma and India until 1864, and wrote a history of the 69th Infantry Regiment. He was stationed in Canada in 1858, traveled through Saskatchewan and Manitoba, and wrote *The Great Stone Land* in 1872 and *The Wild North Land* in 1873. He went to West Africa to fight the Ashanti in 1873-74, was councilor in Natal, directed the base at Natal in the Zulu war, then went to Egypt. He directed the Nile flotilla which rescued Charles George Gordon and evolved the plans for the English victory at Kirbekan in 1885. He was made a brigadier general in that year, was knighted in 1886, wrote *The Campaign of the Cataracts* in 1887, then served at Cape Town as a major general. He directed an army district in England in 1899-1905 as lieutenant general, then retired. He was interested in the Gaelic League and in Irish education, wrote biographies of Gordon and of Red Cloud, and an autobiography (1911). He died at Bansha castle, Tipperary, on June 7.

BUXTON, BL. CHRISTOPHER (d. 1588), martyr. Born in Tideswell, Derbyshire, England, he studied there under the martyr, Nicholas Garlick, and then went to Rheims and Rome, where he was ordained in 1586. Sent on the English mission, he was captured, imprisoned in Marshalsea, and hanged, drawn, and quartered on Oaten Hill, outside Canterbury, for being a priest. He was beatified in 1929. F. D. Oct. 1.

BUYS, PIERRE. *See* Busée, Pierre.

BYRD, WILLIAM (1543-1623), composer. Born in London, he studied music under Thomas Tallis, was organist at Lincoln cathedral in 1563, chorister in the Chapel Royal in 1570, and its organist in 1575. He was the first Englishman to write madrigals, an older Italian form of dance-song; he published graduals for the church year in 1607; his *Psalms, Songs, and Sonnets Fit for Voyces of Viols* appeared in 1611, as did *Parthenia*, music for virginals, in which he collaborated with Bull and Gibbons. He also wrote the canon, *Non Nobis, Domine*, and many masses and motets. His name is also spelled Byrde, Byred, Bird, or Birde. He died on July 4.

BYRNE, ALFRED (1882-1956), mayor. Born in Dublin, he was a member of the dail from 1923, was active in social reform, and served ten terms as lord mayor of Dublin, where he died on Mar. 15.

BYRNE, EDWARD (1802-1862), bishop. Born in Navan, Meath, Ireland, on Dec. 5, he studied at the diocesan seminary there, went to the United States under Bishop John England's patronage, and was ordained in Charleston in 1827. He acted as the bishop's assistant and vicar general, was his theologian at the second Provincial Council in Baltimore, moved to New York in 1836 and served as pastor of several churches, and in 1843 was appointed first bishop of Little Rock, where he developed missionaries for the Indians, brought in priests and sisters from Ireland, and encouraged immigration to the Southwest. He died in Helena, Arkansas, on June 10.

BYRNE, CHRISTOPHER E. (1867–1950), bishop. Born in Byrnesville, Missouri, on Apr. 21, he studied at St. Mary's College, Kansas, and St. Mary's seminary, Baltimore, and was ordained in 1891 in St. Louis. He did parish work in Missouri until 1918, when he was appointed bishop of Galveston, Texas. He convened a diocesan synod in 1930, and died on Apr. 1.

BYRNE, EDMUND (d. 1724), archbishop. A parish priest at St. Nicholas, Dublin, he became archbishop of that see in 1707, erected three new parishes, went into hiding in 1710 during an anti-Stuart uprising, and ruled with increasing difficulty until his death in Jan.

BYRNE, EDWARD L. (1872–1940), archbishop. Born in Dublin on May 10, he was ordained, and became archbishop of Dublin in 1921 and primate of Ireland in 1927. He died in Dublin on Feb. 9.

BYRNE, JULIA CLARA (1819–1894), author. Born in England, daughter of Hans Busk, who taught her classics and French at home, she married William Pitt Byrne in 1842, and wrote an anonymous account of the secrets of the cloister in 1855. After meeting Cardinal Manning she became a convert. Her *Undercurrents Overlooked* (1860) seriously discussed abuses in English workhouses; *Cheel, the City of the Simple* (1869) explained the Belgian treatment of the insane; *The Beggynhof*, the French method of caring for the unmarried. She also wrote light travel accounts of trips to Spain and Hungary, *Flemish Interiors and Feudal Castles in France*, and the popular *Gossip of the Century* (1892). She died in London on Mar. 29.

BYRNE, RICHARD (1832–1864), general. Born in Cavan County, Ireland, he went to the United States in 1844, joined the army in 1849, fought with the 2nd Cavalry against Indians in Florida and Oregon, and was commissioned a lieutenant at the outbreak of the Civil War. In 1862 he became colonel of the 28th Massachusetts Volunteers, fought with the Army of the Potomac at Fredericksburg, Chancellorsville, and Gettysburg, recruited replacements, and was given command of the Irish Brigade in 1864. He was mortally wounded at Cold Harbor, Virginia, and died in Washington, D.C., on June 10.

BYRNE, THOMAS SEBASTIAN (1841–1923), bishop. Born in Hamilton, Ohio, on July 29, he studied at St. Thomas, Bardstown, Kentucky, and Mt. St. Mary of the West, Cincinnati, seminaries, and the North American College, Rome, and was ordained in Cincinnati in 1869. He taught at Mt. St. Mary's in 1869–75, did parish work in Cincinnati until 1887, when he became rector of the seminary, and in 1894 was consecrated bishop of Nashville, Tennessee. He died there on Sept. 4.

BYRNE, WILLIAM (1780–1833), missioner. Born in Wicklow County, Ireland, he went to the United States at twenty-five, studied at Georgetown and Mt. St. Mary's, Emmitsburg, Maryland, and went to St. Thomas' seminary, Bardstown, Kentucky, where he was ordained in 1819. He was in charge of missions near Louisville, opened St. Mary's College near Bardstown in 1821, rebuilt it when it twice was destroyed by fire, and taught 1200 boys before he turned the school over to the Jesuits. He died in Bardstown on June 5 while serving during a cholera epidemic.

C

CABALLERO, FERNAN. *See* Faber, Cecilia Böhl von.

CABALLERO, RAIMUNDO DIOSDADO (1740–1829?). Born at Palma, Majorca, on June 19, he became a Jesuit in 1752, taught literature at Madrid, and was deported to Italy when his Society was suppressed in 1767. He wrote biblical commentaries, on the use of Syriac by Christ and the Apostles, on the Church in America, and a supplement to Jesuit bibliography. He died in Rome in 1829 or 1830.

CABALLERO Y OCIO, JUAN (1644–1707). Born in Querétaro, Mexico, on May 4, he became its mayor, was ordained, and later refused the governorship of California which the king of Spain offered him. His charities were large: a Jesuit college in his native city, Dominican and Franciscan churches there, in Mexico City, and Guadalajara. He gave his family jewels to build a Capuchin convent and a hospital and presented $150,000 to the new missions in California. He died in Querétaro on Apr. 11.

CABASSUT, JEAN (1604–1685). Born in Aix, France, he became an Oratorian at twenty-one, taught canon law at Avignon, and, returning to Aix after a stay in Rome as companion to Cardinal Grimaldi, wrote a history of Church councils (1680) and a text on canon law (1660).

CABELLO DE BALBOA, MIGUEL (17th century). Born in Archidona, Spain, he was ordained, went to Peru in 1566, and then to Quito, Ecuador. By 1586 he had finished *Miscelánea antártica*, published only in part, containing detailed studies of Indian origins, first white missioners, and Inca legends. He was alive as late as 1603.

CABEZA DE VACA, ALVAR NUÑEZ (16th century), explorer. Born in Jerez, Andalusia, Spain, he went to Florida in 1526 as treasurer of the expedition led by Pámfilo de Narvaez. With three other survivors he toured the coast of Louisiana and Texas, was frequently captured by Indians, and was spared only because of his knowledge of medicine; nine years later they reached Sonora, Mexico, and Mexico City in 1536. He was the first European to travel across North America and the first to describe the buffalo. He returned to Spain in 1537, was made governor of La Plata, Argentina, in 1541, but was not a good ruler and was ousted by rebellion in 1543. Sent back to Spain, he was a prisoner for eight years. *Naufragios*, his account of his first venture, was published in 1542; *Comentarios*, on his South American mission, appeared in 1555; both are important historical sources.

CABOT, JOHN (1450–1498). Born in Genoa, Italy, as Giovanni Cabota, he lived in Venice from 1461 to 1476 and became a citizen there, made commercial journeys to Arabia, and about 1490 went to England. He probably led an exploratory voyage from Bristol into the Atlantic in 1491, only to be recalled because his ships were needed by the navy. He persuaded King Henry VII to support an expedition and set sail from Bristol in May 1497 with eighteen men. After fifty days they reached the American mainland near Cape Breton Island, or Labrador, on June 24. In July 1498 he sailed west again, with five ships and 300 men, and sailed the American coast from Newfoundland south to Cape Hatteras. Nothing is known of him after this voyage. The claims of England to North America were based on his explorations and discoveries.

CABOT, SEBASTIAN (1474?–1557?), explorer. Son of John Cabot, and born in Venice, Italy, he may have accompanied his father on the 1498 voyage to North America. He sought a Northwest Passage in 1508–9, and entered Hudson Bay, served King Henry VIII as cartographer in 1512, and went to Spain, where Ferdinand V made him a captain. He made an unsuccessful voyage for the Spanish crown to Argentina and Paraguay in 1526, where he put ashore several companions, an act for which he was banished to Oran, Africa, in 1532. Pardoned in 1533, he returned to Spain and became pilot major in 1547, then went to England, where he was given the title of great pilot. His accounts of his trips have been lost; his map of the landing on the American mainland near

Cape Breton has been questioned; only his 1544 map of the world remains.

CABOTA, GIOVANNI. *See* Cabot, John.

CABRAL, FRANCESCO (1529–1609), missioner. Born in Govillou, Portugal, he became a Jesuit in 1554, was sent to Japan, and enjoyed great missionary success. He was superior there for twelve years, visitor to India, and rector of four colleges. He died at Goa, Portuguese India.

CABRAL, PEDRO ALVAREZ (b. 1460?), explorer. Born in Portugal, son of Fernão Cabral, governor of Beira, he became a seafarer and in 1500 was appointed by King Emmanuel to continue the work of Vasco da Gama and set sail for the Indies. He left Lisbon in March, discovered Brazil a month later, circled the Cape of Good Hope, and reached Mozambique by July and Calcutta, India, by Sept. He made successful trading treaties in Cochin and Kanahur, sailed for home in Jan. 1501, and arrived six months later.

CABRIÈRES, FRANÇOIS MARIE ANATOLE DE ROVÉRIÉ DE (1830–1921), cardinal. Born in Beaucaire, Gard, France, on Aug. 30, he studied in Nîmes and at St. Sulpice, Paris, was ordained in 1853, became director of the College of the Assumption, Nîmes, vicar general, and in 1875 was consecrated bishop of Montpellier. He was made cardinal-priest in 1911 and served the Congregation of Religious. He attacked the anti-Christian attitudes of the Third Republic, the educational laws of Jules Ferry, and the theory that politically assailed clergy had no right to defend themselves. He was active in relief work during World War I, was given the Cross of the Legion of Honor in 1921, and died in Montpellier, France, on Dec. 23.

CABRILLO, ESTÉVAN (d. 1543), explorer. Also known as Juan Rodríguez, he was a Portuguese who went to Mexico with Narváez in 1520, entered the Spanish naval service and in 1540 commanded two vessels which were the first to explore the Pacific Coast from Navidad, Mexico, north the full length of California, discovering in 1542 what were to be called San Diego, Santa Catalina, Santa Monica, and Monterey. His treatment of Indians encountered on the voyage was exceptionally kind. He died on the Island of San Miguel off the coast of California on Jan. 3.

CABRINI, ST. FRANCES XAVIER (1850–1917), foundress. The youngest of thirteen children, she was born near Sant' Angelo Lodigiano, Lombardy, Italy, on July 15, and studied to be a teacher. Orphaned in 1870, she tried to become a religious, but was twice refused because of health. She directed an orphanage at Codogno, which later became the mother house of the community she founded, the Missionary Sisters of the Sacred Heart. Devoted to the education of Christian girls, her institute received the approval of the bishop of Lodi in 1880 and papal approval in 1887. In 1889, at the request of Archbishop Corrigan and with approval of Pope Leo XIII, she came to New York to work among Italian immigrants. During the next twenty-seven years she traveled through the United States (of which she became a citizen in 1909), Italy, France, England, South and Central America, opening convents, hospitals, orphanages, and schools. She died in Chicago, and her body is enshrined in New York City. She was canonized in 1946, the first American citizen to be so honored. F. D. Dec. 22.

PIETRO DI DONATO, *Immigrant Saint* (New York, McGraw, 1960); THEODORE MAYNARD, *Too Small a World* (Milwaukee, Bruce, 1945). **CABROL, FERNAND** (1855–1937), scholar. Born in Marseilles, France, he studied there and at Solesmes, where he became a Benedictine and was ordained in 1882. He was prior there in 1890–96, then became first prior of St. Michael's, Farnborough, England, founded by the exiled Empress Eugénie. He was named its first abbot in 1903, became interested in liturgical scholarship, published *La Paléographie musicale* and, with Dom Henri Le Clerc, *Dictionnaire d'archéologie chrétienne et de liturgie*, as well as studies of the mass, the Western rite, St. Benedict, and popular prayer books. He was several times honored by the British and French governments.

CADALUS. *See* Honorius II, antipope.

CADFAN, ST. (6th century). A native of Letavia (usually considered as in Brittany but possibly a section of southeast Wales), he preached in Wales, founded monasteries in Towyn, Merioneth, and Llangadfan, Montgomeryshire, and is reputedly the founder of the monastic center on Bardsey Island (Ynys Enlli), of which he was abbot and which developed into a great center of monasticism. F. D. Nov. 1.

CADFARCH, ST. (6th century). A follower of St. Illtyd, he founded churches at Aberech and Penegoss, Wales. F. D. Oct. 24.

CADILLAC, ANTOINE DE LA MOTHE DE (1656?–1730), governor. Born in Toulouse, France, he entered the army at sixteen, was given property off Maine, which an English military expedition destroyed, moved to Quebec, married well, and in 1691 joined the staff of Frontenac, the governor of New France. Cadillac rose swiftly in the military ranks, was commandant at Michillimakinac, and saw to it that the western Indians joined neither the Iroquois nor the English. Greed marred much of his life: though his wife was wealthy, he seemed always poor; he supplied brandy to the Iroquois at great profit; even when he established the settlement at Detroit in 1701 he managed to gain a trading monopoly within four years. He was at odds with the government at Quebec, the Jesuit missioners, and the merchants of Montreal. Sieur de Cadillac was recalled to France in 1710 and sent in 1711 to Louisiana as governor, where he engaged in mining and trade. He was deposed in 1716, imprisoned in the Bastille, restored to favor, and finally made governor of Castelsarrasin, France, where he died on Oct. 16.

CADOC, ST. (d. 575?), bishop. A Welshman, he was the son of SS. Gundleus and Gwladys and was educated at Caerwent by St. Tatheus. He became a monk, founded a monastery at Llancarfan near Cardiff (which became one of the great monasteries of the age), spent three years in Ireland, went to Brecknock for further study, and then returned to Llancarfan as abbot. He founded a monastery at Cambuslang, attended the synod of Llandewi Frefi, and went on pilgrimage to Rome and Jerusalem. Some say he died in Benevento, Italy, while another story has him martyred while with the Britons in their struggle against the invading Saxons at Weedon. He is also known as Cadog and Docus. F. D. Sept. 25.

CADROE, ST. (d. 976). A Scots prince, he was educated at Armagh, Ireland, returned to Scotland to inspire vocations, became a pilgrim to England and a monk at a French monastery in Péronne, entered the Benedictines at Cluny, and later served as abbot of Waulsort and of St. Clement at Metz. F. D. Mar. 6.

CADWALLADOR, ST. (d. 682?). He was a Welsh king. F. D. Nov. 12 (also, Oct. 9).

CADWALLADOR, VEN. ROGER (1568–1610), martyr. Born in Stretton Sugwas, near Hereford, England, he studied at Rheims and the English College, Valladolid, was ordained in 1594, and was sent on the English mission. He labored among the poor for sixteen years, was captured near Hereford, imprisoned, and hanged, drawn, and quartered with exceptional brutality on Aug. 27 at Leominster.

CAECILIAN, ST. (d. 304), martyr. *See* Apodemius, St.

CAECILIUS, ST. (1st century). He is said to have been one of the first group sent by the apostles to evangelize Spain, preaching from headquarters at Granada. St. Ctesiphon worked at Verga; St. Euphrasius, at Andujar; St. Hesychius, at Gibraltar; St. Indaletius, near Almeria; St. Secundus, at Avila; and St. Torquatus, at Guadix. Most of them were martyred; they are honored on May 15.

CAECILIUS, ST. (3rd century). He was a Christian in Carthage whose teachings and way of life converted St. Cyprian, and at whose home the latter spent many years. F. D. June 3.

CAEDMON (d. 680?), poet. An unschooled shepherd who served as a brother at Whitby, and who turned scriptural passages and commentary into English poetry and sang the results to the monks and nuns at St. Hilda's double monastery, he is recorded in Bede's *Ecclesiastical History*. He was commemorated as St. Caedmon at Whitby on Feb. 11.

CAEDWALLA (d. 689), king. After a long military campaign to consolidate his kingdom in England, the ruler of West Saxony went to Rome, where he was baptized by Pope St. Sergius I and died soon after.

CAEREALIS, ST. (d. 251), martyr. A soldier, converted by Pope St. Cornelius, he was put to death with his wife Sallustia in Rome during the Decian persecution. F. D. Sept. 14.

CAESAR OF SPEYER (d. 1239). He studied in Paris, went to the Holy Land in 1217, and became a Friar Minor there at the hands of Bro. Elias of Cortona. He was sent to Germany in 1221 and became minister provincial; he returned to Italy in 1223 and probably wrote the Rule at the dictation of St. Francis for the general chapter at Assisi. His life was marked by contemplative zeal and poverty; because of his opposition to the Relaxati he was imprisoned by Bro. Elias. He was murdered by a lay-brother left to guard him.

CAESARIA, ST. (d. 529?). Sister of St. Caesarius, bishop of Arles, Gaul, she directed a convent of 200 cloistered nuns there, who devoted themselves to the care of children and of the poor and sick. The community supported itself by weaving, needlework, laundering, and the transcription of manuscripts. F. D. Jan. 12.

CAESARIUS, ST. (d. 250), martyr. He and SS. Germanus, Theophilus, and Vitalis were put to death at Caesarea, Cappadocia, during the Decian persecution. F. D. Nov. 3.

CAESARIUS, ST. (d. 309), martyr. Father of the Arian Eudoxius, he was burned to death at Arabissus, Armenia, during the persecution of Maximian. F. D. Dec. 28.

CAESARIUS, ST. (7th century). He was bishop of Clermont, France, in 627 and either the nineteenth or twenty-second to rule that see. F. D. Nov. 1.

CAESARIUS, ST., martyr. His legendary story is that he was a deacon from Africa who, while passing through Terracina, Italy, protested the practice of sacrificing a young man to Apollo, was imprisoned for two years, and then drowned with a priest named Julian. F. D. Nov. 1.

CAESARIUS OF ARLES, ST. (470–543), bishop. A native of Châlons, Burgundy, he became a monk at eighteen at Lérins. Sent to Arles for his health, he attracted the attention of the bishop, Eonus, his uncle, who had him transferred from Lérins, ordained him, and made him head of a neighboring monastery. On the death of Eonus, Caesarius was, against his wishes, chosen his successor in 503. He labored to improve the Christianity of his recently converted diocese, strenuously opposed Arianism, and became known for his down-to-earth sermons and homilies, many still extant. He was one of the first of the popular preachers. He founded a convent at Arles (called St. John's, but later St. Caesarius') with his sister, St. Caesaria, as abbess, and drew up its rule, which was relied upon by many other monasteries and convents. He presided over several church synods in his position of metropolitan, most important of which was that of Orange (529), which condemned semi-Pelagianism. He published the adaptation of Roman law, *Breviarium Alarici*, which was to become the civil code of Gaul. In 505, King Alaric II of the Visigoths banished him to Bordeaux for supposedly aiding the king of Burgundy, though Alaric later found him innocent. When the Burgundians attacked Arles in 508, Caesarius sold the church treasure to help relieve the distress of the inhabitants. When Theodore the Ostrogoth seized Alaric's domain on the latter's death, he caused the arrest of Caesarius, but on meeting him at Ravenna in 513 freed him at once. From there Caesarius went to Rome, where he received the pallium from Pope St. Symmachus, the first western European bishop to receive it. In 536, when Arles was captured by the Franks, he went into semi-retirement, and spent much of the remainder of his life at the convent he had founded. F. D. Aug. 27.

CAESARIUS OF HEISTERBACH (1170?–1240). Born near Cologne, he studied there, became a Cistercian at Heisterbach, near Bonn, Germany, in 1199, served as master of novices, taught theology, and was prior from 1228 to 1240. His best-known work is *Dialogues of Visions and Miracles* (1238?), a collection of fantastic stories which served as popular entertainment and as illustrative analogues in sermons. As a serious historian, he wrote a biography of the murdered St. Engelbert, archbishop of Cologne (1227–37), and a study of the archbishops of that diocese from 94 to 1238. He also wrote a life of St. Elizabeth of Hungary and left a collection of sermons.

CAESARIUS NAZIANZEN, ST. (d. 369). Brother of St. Gregory Nazianzen (who preached his funeral oration), he studied philosophy and medicine at Alexandria and at Constantinople, later returned to serve as physician to Julian the Apostate and then as treasurer to Valens. Although he resisted court attempts to win him to paganism, he remained a catechumen, but was not baptized until 368. He spent his last year as a poor penitent. F. D. Feb. 25.

CAESARIUS OF PRÜM (13th century), historian. Born in Milendonk, Germany, he became a Benedictine monk at Prüm and in 1212 its abbot. At the time this was a wealthy and undisciplined monastery and Caesarius left in 1217 to join the Cistercians at Heisterbach. In 1222 he wrote a historically valuable commentary on the Register of the Estates of Prüm, written by an unknown monk in 893. He probably is the author of a study of the abbots of Prüm.

CAESIDIUS, ST. (3rd cent.), martyr. Said to have been the son of the martyred St. Rufinus and himself a priest, he was slain with other Christians at Lake Fucino, near Rome. F. D. Aug. 31.

CAFASSO, ST. JOSEPH (1811–1860). Born in Castelnuovo d'Asti, Italy, third of four children of John Cafasso and Ursula Beltramo, he was educated there and at Chieri, and ordained at Turin in 1833. In spite of a deformed spine he became a brilliant lecturer in moral theology at the Institute of St. Francis, succeeding Fr. Luigi Guala as rector in 1848. He was active against Jansenism, noted for his work with penitents, and effective in forming priests who would remain strong in the Church-state quarrels ahead. He directed retreats at the Jesuit house at Lanzo after the suppression of the Society, became famous for his kindness to convicts, and aided in the development of many charitable institutions. Indebted to him for spiritual advice and direct aid were Don Bosco, whose concern was the education of boys; Fr. John Cocchi, who established a college for craftsmen; Peter Merla, who took care of delinquent children; and Frs. Francis Bono, Clement Marchisio, and Dominic Sartoris, who were active in the establishment of religious orders for women. Fr. Cafasso died in Turin, Italy, on June 23, of pneumonia. He was canonized in 1947. F. D. June 23.

CAGIANO DE AZEVEDO, OCTAVIUS (1845–1927), cardinal. Born in Spain, he was ordained, became major-domo of the Vatican in 1901 and a cardinal in 1905, and died in Anzio, Italy, on July 11.

CAGLIARI, PAOLO. See Veronese, Paolo.

CAGNOALD. See Chainoaldus, St.

CAGNOLI, BL. GERARD (1270?–1345). Born of a noble Italian family, he was orphaned as a youngster and led the life of a wanderer and hermit in Sicily until about 1310, when he became a Franciscan laybrother, vested with supernatural gifts, until his death on Dec. 30. His cult was confirmed in 1908. F. D. Dec. 1.

CAHIER, CHARLES (1807–1882), antiquarian. Born in Paris, France, on Feb. 26, he became a Jesuit in 1824, taught in France, Switzerland, and Belgium, and devoted himself to collecting, classifying, and commenting on mediaeval art. With Fr. Arthur Martin, a draftsman, he published a monograph on the stained glass of Bourges cathedral (1841); eight volumes followed on Carlovingian and

Romanesque Plate, ivories, tapestries, and paintings. He also wrote on everyday customs in relation to liturgy and on the popular and artistic view of the saints. He died in Paris on Feb. 26.

CAHILL, DANIEL WILLIAM (1796–1864). Born in Ashfield, Ireland, on Nov. 28, he studied at Carlow and Maynooth, was ordained, taught science at Carlow for about ten years, and from 1835 to 1841 directed a school which he founded at Seapoint. He edited the Dublin *Telegraph* and became well known as a polemic lecturer against the British government and the established church in Ireland. He died in Boston, Massachusetts, on Oct. 28 while on a scientific lecture tour.

CAIDOC, ST. (7th century). He and St. Fricor (or Adrian), another Irishman, served as missioners in the country of the Morini, near Amiens, France. F. D. Apr. 1.

CAILLAU, ARMAND BENJAMIN (1794–1850). Born in Paris on Oct. 22, he was ordained in 1818 as a member of the Missions de France, became rector of Ste. Geneviève, and in 1824 joined the reorganized Fathers of Mercy. He wrote many devotional works, *Thesaurus patrum* (a digest of patristic writings), a history of lives of the saints, an edition of St. Gregory Nazianzen, and a translation of Tertullian's *De spectaculis*. His *Collectio selecta patrum* in 133 volumes (1829–42) was abandoned when Migne's *Patrology* was announced. He died in Paris.

CAIMIN, ST. (d. 653). His reputation for holiness attracted so many followers to his island refuge in Lough Derg, Ireland, that he built a monastery and church for them and made a copy of a psalter. F. D. Mar. 24.

CAIRLON, ST. (6th century). He was an abbot before he became archbishop of Cashel, Ireland. F. D. Mar. 24.

CAIUS, ST. (d. 296), pope and martyr. Believed to have been born in Dalmatia and related to Emperor Diocletian, he became pope on Dec. 17, 283, officially approved the minor orders below the priesthood, and was forced to direct the Church from a hiding place in the catacombs, where he lived for the eight years before his death. F. D. Apr. 22.

CAIUS, ST. (1st century). He is said to have succeeded St. Barnabas the apostle as bishop of Milan, Italy, where he ruled for twenty-four years and baptized SS. Vitalis, Gervase, and Protase. His relics are enshrined in the church of St. Francis there. F. D. Sept. 27.

CAIUS, ST. (1st century), bishop. He was baptized at Corinth by St. Paul (I Cor. 1:14), probably was Paul's host (Rom. 16:23) and the person to whom St. John addressed his third epistle, and is traditionally called bishop of Thessalonica, where he is said to have been martyred. F. D. Oct. 4.

CAIUS, ST. (d. 172?), martyr. *See* Alexander, St.

CAIUS, ST. (d. 254?), martyr. An officer of the imperial palace, he was put to death by drowning with some thirty other Christians; the place is not listed. F. D. Mar. 4.

CAIUS (3rd century). A cleric, he held a disputation with Proclus, a Montanist leader, in Rome during the papacy of Zephyrinus, fragments of which are quoted by Eusebius; the latter historian quotes an important reference to the veneration of the bodies of SS. Peter and Paul in Rome about the year 200.

CAIUS, ST. (d. 300?), martyr. *See* Aggaeus, St.

CAIUS, ST. (d. 302?), martyr. *See* Ampelius, St.

CAIUS, ST. (d. 303), martyr. *See* Anthes, St.

CAIUS, ST. (d. 303?), martyr. He, SS. Dasius and Zoticus, and twelve other Roman soldiers were executed for their faith at Nicomedia during the Diocletian persecution. F. D. Oct. 21.

CAIUS, ST. (d. 304), martyr. He was slain for his faith, with St. Crementius, at Saragossa, Spain, during the Diocletian persecution. F. D. Apr. 16.

CAIUS, ST. (d. 304), martyr. *See* Apodemius, St.

CAIUS, JOHN (1510–1573), physician. Born in Norwich, England, on Oct. 6, he studied at Cambridge and took his medical degree at Padua in 1541. After a tour of the Continent he lectured in London for twenty years on anatomy. He wrote on the "sweating sickness," a history of Cambridge University, and translations of Galen and Hippocrates. He was president of the College of Physicians for nine terms and left a manuscript record of its history from 1520 to 1565; refounded, in 1558, the college at Cambridge now called Gonville and Caius; and served as royal physician to King Edward VI and Queen Elizabeth I until he was dismissed because of his Catholicism. He died in London on July 29.

CAJETAN, ST. (1480–1547), founder. Born in Vincenza, Italy, in Oct., he received his doctorate in civil and canon law from Padua in 1504. He became a senator of Vicenza, a prothonotary of Pope Julius II in 1506, and later was the co-founder of a confraternity of devout priests in Rome. He was ordained in 1516, entered the Oratory of St. Jerome at Venice, and for the next few years devoted himself to the care of the sick and the poor. In 1523, distressed by the condition of the Church and laxity of the clergy, with John Peter Caraffa, bishop of Chieti (later Pope Paul IV), as its first superior, and Paul Consiglieri and Boniface da Colle, he founded the Theatines, an order of regular clergy living in community and bound by vows. They engaged in pastoral work and dedicated themselves to the sick and the restoration of a proper religious feeling among the people and the clergy. He was elected superior in 1530 and devoted the rest of his life to laboring for religious reforms and combatting heretical teaching. Later in his life, with Bl. John Marinoni, he popularized the *montes pietatis*, pawnshops authorized by the fifth Lateran Council to eliminate usury among the poor. He was one of the great Catholic reformers and anticipated and put into effect many of the reforms of the Council of Trent. Also known as Gaetano, he died in Naples, and was canonized in 1671. F. D. Aug. 7.

CAJETAN, CONSTANTINO (1560–1650). Born in Syracuse, Sicily, he became a Benedictine in 1586 and because of his learning was called to Rome by Pope Clement VIII. He edited the works of St. Peter Damien, wrote biographies of SS. Isidore of Seville and Ildephonso of Toledo, studies of papal primacy, and a history of Benedictine writers. On occasion, his enthusiasm carried him to such extremes that he claimed for his order SS. Columban, Thomas Aquinas, and Francis of Assisi. He also supported Jean Gerson as author of the *Imitation of Christ*; his denial that St. Ignatius Loyola wrote the *Exercises* placed his treatise on the Index. Cajetan was, however, in other directions a very careful scholar and was of great help to Cardinal Baronius in the preparation of *Annales ecclesiastici*. Cajetan was custodian of the Vatican Library under four popes and was active in founding a college for training Benedictines for foreign missions, which Pope Gregory XV modified and developed into the College of Propaganda. Cajetan became its first consultor and left to it and to the Sapienza the great library he had amassed. He died in Rome on Sept. 17.

CAJETAN, ST. GIACOMO TOMMASO DE VIO GAETANI (1469–1534), cardinal. Born in Gaeta, Italy, on Feb. 20, he became a Dominican at sixteen, studied at Naples, Bologna, and Padua, and taught metaphysics at Padua. He engaged in controversy with Scotists and Averroists, wrote *De ente et essentia*, presented a brilliant defense of varied theses at the general chapter in Ferrara in 1494, and was made master of sacred theology. He then taught at Brescia, Pavia, and Milan, was called to Rome in 1500, and in 1501 became procurator general of his order and held the chairs of philosophy and exegesis at the Sapienza. He became vicar general of the Dominicans in 1507 and general in 1508. He attacked as disobedient the cardinals and bishops who attended the illegal Council of Pisa in 1511, defended the monarchical power of the pope, and prevented a potential schism led by Louis XII. Cajetan then persuaded Pope Julius II to call the fifth Lateran Council, sent Dominican missioners to the New World, was named a cardinal in 1517, apostolic delegate to Germany, and in 1518 bishop of Gaeta. He played a part in the election of Charles V as emperor, met Luther and tried to stem his complete rebellion in many conferences, went to Hungary to encourage that nation in its battles with the Turks, and returned to become Clement VII's adviser. He was captured and ransomed during the sack of Rome by the imperialist army in 1527, was one of the nineteen cardinals who supported the validity of the marriage of Henry VIII and Catherine of Aragon, and continued through his career to be a leading exponent of Thomism. His commentaries on the *Summa theologiae* (1507–22) were of such significance that in 1879 Pope Leo XIII ordered them included in the official Leonine edition of St. Thomas. He prepared a literal translation of the Bible from the Greek, including the New Testament and all of the Old Testament through part of Isaias, following St. Jerome and the annotations of Erasmus, and wrote over a hundred titles in theology, philosophy, and biblical commentary. He died in Rome on Aug. 9. He was canonized by Pope Clement X. F. D. Aug. 7.

CALAIS. *See* Carilefus, St.

CALANCHA, ANTONIO DE LA (1584–1654), historian. Born in Sucre, Bolivia, he studied at Lima, where he became an Augustinian when fourteen, held a number of posts, and was rector of the College of San Ildefonso. He wrote a two-volume study of his order in South America and on the antiquities and Indian customs of Peru and Bolivia. He relied, somewhat uncritically, on previous Jesuit and Augustinian chronicles, but contributed much of historical value. He died on Mar. 1.

CALANICUS, ST. (d. 637?), martyr. He and St. Florian were among sixty Christians slain by Mohammedan invaders at Eleutheropoli, Palestine. F. D. Dec. 17.

CALASANCTIUS, ST. JOSEPH (1556–1648), founder. Last of five children, he was born on Sept. 11 in his father's castle near Peralta, Aragon, Spain. He studied at Lérida, where he received his doctorate in law, Valencia, and Alcalá. He was ordained in 1583, engaged in pastoral work under the bishop of Urgel until 1592, then went to Rome for five years under the patronage of Cardinal Colonna. While working with the Confraternity of Christian Doctrine to educate needy children, he decided to devote himself to this work and in 1597 he opened his first free school, with three priests. The institute (called Clerks Regular of the Religious Schools, or, more familiarly, Scolopi or Piarists) was so successful it acquired powerful enemies, but Popes Clement VIII and Paul V took it under their protection; it was recognized as a religious order in 1621, with Joseph as superior general. Internal revolt made

his last years unhappy, but he bore deposition and false charges with great courage. He was restored to power before his death on Aug. 25 in Rome, and was canonized in 1767. F. D. Aug. 27.

CALASIO, MARIO DI (1550?–1620). Born in Calasio, Italy, he became a Friar Minor and a Hebrew scholar. He compiled a biblical concordance and a Hebrew dictionary, was confessor to Pope Paul V, and died in Rome on Feb. 1.

CALDANI, LEOPOLD MARCO ANTONIO (1725–1813), anatomist. Born in Bologna, Italy, on Nov. 21, he took his medical degree there in 1750, became professor of practical medicine in 1755, studied under Morgagni at Padua, was made professor of theoretical medicine, and, after Morgagni's death in 1771, professor of anatomy. His findings on the function of the spinal cord, the effect of electricity on the nerves, the anatomical atlas he completed with his nephew Floriano, and a dozen volumes on anatomy and physiology established his reputation. He died in Padua, Italy, on Dec. 20.

CALDARA, POLIDORO (1492?–1543), painter. Born in Caravaggio, Italy, he went to Rome at eighteen, worked as a laborer, began to imitate Raphael, and was a pupil of Maturino and Udine. He was particularly successful in the use of chiaroscuro, and decorated the façades of many Roman buildings in *sgraffito*, a design scratched on a light layer imposed on a darker one, often of stucco. After the sack of Rome in 1527 he began a school in Naples which emphasized the naturalistic style of painting, completed many frescoes, then went to Messina, Sicily. His masterpiece in oil is *Christ Bearing the Cross*; he also did *Passage of the Red Sea* and several Magdalens. He was murdered at Messina by a servant trying to rob him. He is sometimes surnamed Caravaggio, after his birthplace.

CALDAS-BARBOSA, DOMINGOS (1740–1800), poet. Son of a white father and Negro mother, he was born in Rio de Janeiro, Brazil, studied at the Jesuit college there, and wrote such effective lampoons against the Portuguese whites that he was seized and forced into army life for several years. He then went to Portugal, was sponsored by two nobles, took minor orders, and obtained a chaplaincy. Although he enjoyed some literary success, he was socially rebuffed as no more than a mulatto entertainer. All but one contemporary poet, however, accepted him, and he composed a number of popular cantigas. He died in Lisbon on Nov. 9.

CALDERÓN DE LA BARCA, PEDRO (1600–1681), dramatist. Born in Madrid, Spain, on Jan. 17, he studied for six years at the Jesuit college there, and at Alcalá and Salamanca, fought in Italy and Holland in 1623–24, and returned to Madrid to manage a theater. In 1637 he became a member of the Order of Santiago, fought with them against the rebellious Catalans in 1640–41, and in 1651 was ordained. He became honorary chaplain to the crown in 1663 and superior of the Congregation of St. Peter in 1666. He was admired by the monarchy from the beginning, and Philip IV gave him encouragement, an expense account, and a pension. Calderón wrote a score of short interludes and farces; some eighty *autos sacramentales*, explaining the Eucharist by means of allegorical figures and striking lyricism, and produced in celebration of the feast of Corpus Christi; and at least 120 comedies. His secular work is characterized by intense poetry, considerable bombast, an exaggerated respect for the rules of honor, and some monotony of plot, particularly as his vein ran out and he began paraphrasing, sometimes closely, the work of others. Typical plays are *Purgatorio de San Patricio*, *Los escantos de la culpa* (*The Sorceries of Sin*), *El mágico prodigioso* (on St. Cyprian of Antioch, and comparable to the Faust legend), *El principe constante*, praising Fernando of Portugal as an ideal ruler. Among his best tragedies is *El alcalde de Zalamea* (1642), based on his experiences in the Catalan war; *La dama duende* and *Casa con dos puertas mala es de guardar* (both 1629) are comedies of love and intrigue in the manner of Lope de Vega, whose style he continued; his most frequently read play is *La vida es sueno* (*Life Is a Dream*; 1635), a philosophical study, marked by fancy, of destiny and will, the mundane and the spiritual, in relation to man. He died in Madrid on May 25.

CALEPINO, AMBROGIO (1440?–1511?). Born in Calepio, Italy, he became an Augustinian in 1458 and compiled a Latin dictionary (1502), enlarged in later editions to include eleven languages. The work was still popular and useful in 1718, and the name *calepinus* was often used as a synonym for dictionary.

CALEPODIUS, ST. (d. 222), martyr. He is said to have been a priest who was beheaded at Rome during the persecution of Alexander Severus. With him, in a brutal decade of terror, died a married couple, Felix and Blanda; the consul Palmatius and forty-two of his household; and Simplicius, a senator, with more than sixty from his estate. F. D. May 10.

CALETRICUS, ST. (529–580?). Born in Chartres, France, he served as its bishop from about 557 until his death. F. D. Sept. 4.

CALIARI, PAOLO. *See* Veronese, Paolo.

CALIMERIUS, ST. (d. 190?), bishop and martyr. A Greek, he was educated at Rome by Pope St. Telesphorus, became bishop of Milan, Italy, and was put to death by drowning during the reign of Commodus. F. D. July 31.

CALLAGHAN, DANIEL H. (1890–1942), admiral. He was naval aide to President Frank-

lin D. Roosevelt in 1938–41, chief of staff of the naval forces in the South Pacific during World War II, and was rear admiral in command of the force attacking Guadalcanal when wounded; he died on shipboard near Savo Island on Nov. 13.

CALLAHAN, PATRICK HENRY (1865–1940), executive. Born in Cleveland, Ohio, on Oct. 15, he studied at Spencerian College and became Mark Hanna's secretary in 1886. After working for several firms, he joined the Louisville Varnish Co. in 1892 and spent the rest of his life there, as president in his last thirty years. He inaugurated a profit-sharing plan for employees, based on suggestions by Msgr. John A. Ryan, and became widely known for employees'-welfare plans. He founded the Catholic Layman's League of Georgia in 1916, headed the Knights of Columbus Committee on War Activities during World War I, helped found the Catholic Association for International Peace in 1926–27, and was active on numerous state and national boards of President Franklin D. Roosevelt's New Deal. He died in Louisville, Kentucky, on Feb. 4.

CALLIÈRES BONNEVUE, LOUIS HECTOR DE (1646–1703), governor. Born in Cherbourg, France, he entered the army, became a captain, was sent to Canada in 1684, and made governor of Montreal the same year at the request of the Sulpicians there. He marched to relieve the siege of Quebec by the British in 1690, succeeded Frontenac as thirteenth governor of New France in 1699, sent Cadillac to found Detroit, and crowned an honorable career by the 1701 Treaty of Montreal which was agreed to by representatives of all Indian tribes in the colony. He died in Quebec on May 26.

CALLINICA, ST. (d. 250), martyr. *See* Basilissa, St.

CALLINICUS, ST. (d. 251), martyr. *See* Thyrsus, St.

CALLINICUS, ST. (3rd century?), martyr. Born in Gangra, Paphlagonia, he was burned to death during a persecution in Asia Minor. F. D. July 29.

CALLIOPIUS, ST. (d. 303?), martyr. He was crucified at Pompsiopolis in Cilicia during the Diocletian persecution. F. D. Apr. 7.

CALLISTHENE, ST. (4th century). *See* Adauctus, St.

CALLISTRATUS, ST. (d. 300?), martyr. He and fifty soldiers from Africa were sewn in sacks and thrown into the sea at Constantinople during the Diocletian persecution. F. D. Sept. 26.

CALLISTUS I, ST. (d. 222?), pope and martyr. The Roman slave of a member of the emperor's household who handled and lost some of his master's funds, he fled, was captured in Porto, and imprisoned. Freed at the importunings of his master and creditors, he was again arrested for causing a disturbance in a synagogue, presumably trying to recover his lost funds, and sentenced to the mines of Sardinia. When released with the other Christians, he returned to Rome and was made overseer of the Christian cemetery by Pope Zephyrinus, who ordained him deacon. In 217 he was elected pope and was faced with an antipope, Hippolytus, who had been elected by a dissident group and who, with Tertullian and Novatian, denounced Callistus for his leniency to sinners and in matters of discipline—criticism entirely unjustified. Callistus condemned Sabellianism and other heresies and probably suffered martyrdom, though how and why are not known. F. D. Oct. 14.

CALLISTUS II (d. 1124), pope. Guy of Burgundy, son of Count William, was related to the royal houses of Europe, became archbishop of Vienne in 1088, and was appointed papal legate to France by Pope Paschal II. When Emperor Henry V extorted the Privilegium from Paschal in 1111, regaining investiture privileges which had been outlawed, the archbishop violently opposed the emperor, convened an assembly of French and Burgundian bishops at Vienne in 1112, and excommunicated Henry. The pope approved their action, though not with enthusiasm, and made Guy a cardinal. Gelasius II was elected pope at Paschal's death in 1118, but was immediately driven out of Rome by Henry's forces and died at Cluny a year later. Although the emperor had set up Archbishop Burdinus of Braga as antipope Gregory VIII, Guy was lawfully elected pope on Feb. 2, 1119, and consecrated at Vienne on Feb. 9. Callistus held reforming synods at Toulouse and Rheims, then went to Rome; Gregory fled and was imprisoned in 1121; with the military backing of the princes of southern Italy, Callistus was now enabled to deal with Henry. A truce was arranged and in 1122 the Concordat of Worms was signed, which compromised the investiture quarrel by leaving the controlling influence within Germany in the emperor's hands and regaining papal supremacy for Italy and Burgundy. Callistus spent his remaining years in restoring and improving the city of Rome, bettering Church conditions in Italy, France, and Spain, seeking to end the quarrel between King Henry I of England and his brother Robert of Normandy, supervising the passage of laws against simony and forgery of ecclesiastical documents, and working on behalf of the crusaders. He died on Dec. 13.

CALLISTUS III (1378–1458), pope. Alfonso de Borja (Borgia) was born in Valencia, Spain, on Dec. 31, completed his ecclesiastical studies, and was appointed a canon by antipope Benedict XIII. When King Alfonso V of Aragon decided to abandon the schism and support the true pope, Martin V, Borja acted as mediator. Pope Martin made him bishop of Valencia in 1429 and Pope Eugene IV made him a cardinal in 1444. He was elected pope on Apr. 8, 1455, and consecrated on Apr. 20. Although Constantinople had just fallen to the Turks and Europe was ripe for invasion, none of the powers, many of whom were already at war with one another, heeded the pope's call for a crusade. Genoa sent a fleet, and an army led by Hunyady won a major victory over Mohammed II at Belgrade. Hunyady died of fever, Scanderbeg of Albania continued the war, but the rest of Europe would not even raise imposed papal taxes. Aragon, which had attacked Genoa during the absence of its fleet, now claimed Naples and Sicily; the pope objected and unfortunately appeared ready to give his own claim to the territories to a worthless nephew. Other nephews, one of them to become Pope Alexander VI, were made cardinals and the charge of nepotism proved hurtful. During his reign he reopened the trial of Joan of Arc which resulted in clearing her name. Callistus died in Rome on Aug. 6.

CALLISTUS, ST. (d. 528). Bishop of Todi, Italy, and active against Arianism, he was slain by the servants of a group of nobles whose lives he had condemned. F. D. Aug. 14.

CALLISTUS, ST. (d. 1003). Born in Huesca, Aragon, Spain, he went to France and died with St. Mercurialis in battle against the Saracens. They are especially honored at Tarbes. F. D. Oct. 15.

CALLOT, JACQUES (1592–1635), engraver. Born in Nancy, France, son of a noble, he studied under the court painter and royal engraver, ran away to Italy in 1604 to learn engraving at Florence, returned home, and was sent as envoy of Duke Henry II of Lorraine to the Vatican. He developed there as an engraver and etcher, became a master of macabre, grotesque, and sometimes humorous realism, toured the courts of Europe, and left portraits and series of plates on beggars and on the miseries of war. He died in Nancy on Mar. 28.

CALLY, PIERRE (d. 1709), philosopher. Born in Mesnil-Hubert, France, he taught philosophy at Caen, was rector of the Collège des Arts there in 1675, and in 1684 was pastor of St. Martin's church. He wrote a philosophical text defending Descartes, biblical homilies, an edition of Beothius' *De consolatione philosophiae*, and an explanation of the Holy Eucharist. He died in Caen, France, on Dec. 31.

CALMET, AUGUSTIN (1672–1757). Born near Commercy, Lorraine, he was ordained a Benedictine in 1696, taught philosophy and theology at Moyen-Moutier, and began to gather material for scriptural exegesis. He published a *Literal Commentary on the Old and*

New Testaments (1707–16), with prefaces to each book and studies of special problems, but without satisfying explanation of difficult passages. Other scriptural studies, a biblical dictionary, a history of Lorraine, and a study of the Rule of St. Benedict appeared between 1718 and 1751. He also taught at Münster, was abbot of St. Léopold and of Senones, and twice served as superior general. He died at Senones, near St. Dié, France, on Oct. 25.

CALMETTE, BL. CHARLES DE LA (d. 1792), martyr. *See* Du Lau, Bl. John.

CALMINIUS, ST. (d. 690?). A hermit, he founded monasteries at Villars and Mauzac, in Gaul. F. D. Aug. 19.

CALOCERUS, ST. (d. 130?). He succeeded St. Apollinaris as bishop of Ravenna, Italy. F. D. Feb. 11.

CALOCERUS, ST. (2nd century?), martyr. Called an official in the court of Emperor Hadrian, he is said to have been converted when he witnessed the torture of SS. Faustinus and Jovita in Lombardy, and to have been beheaded at Albenga. He possibly is identical with a later bishop of Ravenna. F. D. Apr. 18.

CALOCERUS, ST. (3rd century), martyr. He and his brother Parthenius are said to have been Armenians in the service of Tryphonia, wife of Emperor Decius, who became Christians and were beaten to death at Rome. F. D. May 19.

CALOGERUS, ST. (d. 486?). A monk in Rome, he became a successful missioner on Lipari, then lived as a recluse at Girgenti, Sicily, for thirty-five years. F. D. June 18.

CALOGERUS, ST. (5th century). *See* Gregory, St.

CALOSIRTO, ST. CARLO GAETANO (1654–1734). St. John Joseph of the Cross was born on the Island of Ischia near Naples, Italy, of a large family which was most devoted to the poor, and became a Franciscan friar at sixteen. He was superior of the Alcantarines at Naples three years before he was ordained in 1677. He was master of novices and superior at several houses, helped to settle the serious breach between Spanish and Italian factions, and gave evidence of possessing unusual supernatural gifts. He died in Naples, and was canonized in 1839. F. D. Mar. 5.

CALVAERT, DENIS (1540?–1619), painter. Born in Antwerp, Holland, he studied under Christiaen van Queecborne, then went to Bologna to work under Prospero Fontana in 1570 and Lorenzo Sabbatini, with whom he went to Rome to work from 1572 to 1574 in the Vatican. He returned to Bologna and founded a school which taught Albani, Guido Reni, and Domenichino. Outstanding are his *Assumption* and *Madonna and Child with St. Anthony*. He is also called Dionysio Fiammingo.

CALVERT, CECIL (1606–1675). Eldest son of George Calvert, he was educated at Oxford, married Anne Arundel about 1623, and inherited the charter of Maryland and became lord of Maryland and Avalon and second Lord Baltimore on his father's death in 1632. A group of twenty colonists and 300 laborers set sail for Maryland in 1633 under the leadership of his brother Leonard and established a settlement at St. Mary's. Leonard became governor, but was unable to enact lasting laws, inasmuch as Cecil was kept in England by enemies who tried throughout his lifetime to break the royal grant, gain the plantation for Virginia, and destroy its religion.

CALVERT, CHARLES (1637–1715), governor. Born in London, England, on Aug. 27, son of Cecil Calvert, he became third Lord Baltimore and served as governor of Maryland from 1661 to 1675 and lord proprietor from 1675, on his father's death, to 1691. He defeated Protestant efforts, directed from Virginia and England, to make the Church of England the only permitted religion, introduced new laws to take care of the steady increase of population, and with his uncle Philip met William Penn and settled the boundary dispute with Pennsylvania. They also amicably settled boundary issues with Virginia and Delaware. He returned to England in 1684 to take care of colonial interests, but anti-Catholic feeling was strong. In 1691, William and Mary seized the charter for the crown and Charles also lost his Irish estate on the charge that he was a Catholic outlaw; King William had the wording changed so that the taint of treason was removed. He failed to regain his property and died in Epsom, Surrey, on Feb. 20.

CALVERT, GEORGE (1580?–1632). The first Lord Baltimore was born in Kipling, Yorkshire, England, he graduated from Oxford in 1597 and lived on the Continent for a while, where he met Lord Cecil, whose private secretary he became on his return in 1606. He held political posts in Ireland, was in parliament in 1609, and in 1613, on Cecil's death, became clerk of the privy council. He served King James I on several missions, was knighted in 1617, became a secretary of state in 1619, served in parliament in 1621 and 1624, and favored the proposed Spanish marriage of Prince Charles. He became a Catholic in 1624 and resigned his secretaryship, but James kept him as a member of his council and made him Baron Baltimore of Baltimore, Longford, Ireland. In 1620 he had purchased a plantation in Newfoundland which he called Avalon and which he visited in 1627. It suffered during the war with France, and the next year Lord Baltimore asked for a grant in a warmer area. He visited Virginia to look over possible sites, was badly treated because of his religion, and returned to ask from King Charles I a grant of land northeast of the Potomac River. He died in London on Apr. 15, before the details were completed, but it was issued to his son Cecil later that year.

CALVERT, LEONARD (1606–1647), governor. Born in England, second son of George Calvert, he went to Avalon, Newfoundland, to protect his family's holdings against attacks by the French fleet. In 1633, at the direction of his older brother Cecil, he sailed for Maryland with the *Ark* and the *Dove*, landing at Port Comfort, Virginia, on Feb. 24, 1634, and the following month founded St. Mary's. As governor, he had difficulties from the beginning. Virginia, which once held trading posts in the new grant, continually interfered; in time, the enemies of the Calverts drove the governor out in 1644, sent the Jesuit missioners to England, and attempted to impose an oath of allegiance to Protestantism, which none of the colonists would take. After two years Calvert returned and restored to the settlers the right of self-government. The area became a haven for victims of religious persecution, particularly for the Puritans of Massachusetts, and was the first to put tolerance into actual practice. Leonard died in Maryland on June 9.

CALVINUS, JUSTUS BARONIUS (1570?–1606?). Born of Calvinist parents in Xanthen, Germany, he was educated at Heidelberg, became a convert in 1601, and wrote an *Apologia* and a defense of the Church based on the writings of the Fathers.

CAMACHO, AVILA (1898–1955), president. Born in Teziutlán, Mexico, on Apr. 24, he joined the revolt against Victoriano Huerta in 1914, and in the next fifteen years rose in the army to the rank of general. He entered politics, became minister of defense in 1937 under Cárdenas, and was president in 1940–46. He astounded many by winning in spite of his admission that he was both a conservative and a Catholic. He sought to establish better economic and social conditions and better relations with the United States during his presidency. He died near Mexico City on Oct. 13.

CAMARA Y CASTRO, TOMÁS (1847–1904), bishop. Born in Logrono, Spain, on Sept. 19, he studied at Burgos and became an Augustinian at Valladolid. He taught at the latter university, became bishop of Salamanca, founded the College of Calatrava and built several churches there, and wrote lives of St. Juan de Sahagún, Alonso de Orozco, and Vizcondesa de Jorbalán, a collection of sermons, and a study of the alleged conflict between science and religion. He died in Villaharta on May 17.

CAMARGO, DIEGO MUÑOZ (b. 1522?), historian. Born in Mexico of a Spanish father and Indian mother, he was educated by the Franciscans, made detailed studies of the Nahuatl Indians, served as official interpreter for the government, and wrote a valuable *Historia de Tlaxcala* on tribal customs and antiquities.

CAMBIANI, BL. PIETRO (d. 1365), martyr. A native of Piedmont, he joined the Dominicans, was appointed inquisitor general for Piedmont, Upper Lombardy, and Liguria in 1351 and for fourteen years labored among the dissident sects in northern Italy, particularly the Waldensians, who murdered him in Susa. His cult was confirmed in 1856. F. D. Nov. 7.

CAMBIASO, LUCA (1527–1585), painter. Born in Moneglia, near Genoa, Italy, he studied under his father, Giovanni (said to be the originator of the practice of dividing the human body into squares to establish anatomical proportion), and later in Florence and Rome. He painted swiftly and often, was graceful in composition, and effective in the use of architectural background. He went to Spain in 1583 with his son Orazio, completed several commissions for King Philip II, and died in Madrid. He is also known as Luchetto da Genova.

CAMEL, GEORGE JOSEPH (1661–1706), botanist. Born in Brunn, Moravia, on Apr. 21, he became a Jesuit laybrother in 1682 and went to the Philippines in 1688. His detailed studies of plants and natural history were published in the *Philosophical Transactions* of the Royal Society of London; he issued a volume on *Medicinal Plants* of the islands and opened a pharmacy in Manila for the poor. Linnaeus named the flowering evergreen shrub after him, as the camellia. Bro. Camel died in Manila on May 2.

CAMELIAN, ST. (d. 525). He was bishop of Troyes, Gaul, from 478 until his death. F. D. July 28.

CAMERINUS, ST. (d. 303?), martyr. *See* Luxorius, St.

CAMILLUS DE LELLIS. *See* Lellis, Camillus de.

CAMÕES, LUIZ VAZ DE (1524?–1580), poet. Born in Portugal at Lisbon or Coimbra, of a sea captain who died when Luiz was young, he may have been educated at Coimbra, where his uncle Bento was a canon in 1539. At court he fell in love with Caterina de Athaide (the Natercia of his lyric poems), but marriage was forbidden and he was banished. Between 1546 and 1549 he fought in Africa, where he lost an eye in a naval battle, returned to Lisbon, wounded an officer, was imprisoned, and in 1553 released on condition he go to India. There he was an army private, the lover of a native girl, an incompetent administrator at Macao, imprisoned and charged with malfeasance. Ill and impoverished, he set out for Portugal in 1567 and arrived in 1570. In 1572 he published his epic, *Os Lusiadas*, written in the octave stanza used by Ariosto and in the style of Vergil. Its hero is Vasco da Gama, to whose family Camões was related and with whom his grandfather, Antão Vaz, had sailed. The poem has da Gama recount the grandeur of his nation's history and describe his homeland and his voyage to India and return. Striking passages are those on the tragedy of Inés de Castro, the giant Adamastor, and the storm at the Cape of Good Hope. Realistic details came from observations made on his own wanderings; the poetry developed from his earlier successes in shorter forms. He also wrote three verse comedies, received a stingy pension from King Sebastian, to whom he had dedicated the epic, and died forgotten in a Lisbon hospital on June 10.

CAMPAGNA, GIROLAMO (1552–1626?), sculptor. Born in Verona, Italy, he studied there under Sansoveno and Cattaneo, going with the latter to Venice, where he completed many of his master's works. After Cattaneo's death, Campagna completed reliefs for the chapel of St. Anthony, Padua. At Venice he did statues of SS. Francis, Clare, Giustina, Sebastian, Gabriel, Rose, and Thomas Aquinas. Christ on a globe supported by the evangelists was completed in bronze for the church of San Giorgio Maggiore there. Verona has a *Madonna* and *Annunciation*.

CAMPAGNOLA, DOMENICO (1490?–1564?), painter. Born in Padua or Venice, Italy, he completed engravings, frescoes, etchings, and pen-and-ink drawings in both cities. He spent most of his life in Padua, where he studied with his brother Giulio and may have assisted Titian, than whom he was bolder in the treatment of the nude. His *Adam and Eve* was completed for the Pitti palace, Florence; other pictures include *Birth of Christ, Holy Family, Four Prophets*, as well as madonnas and landscapes.

CAMPAN, JEANNE LOUISE HENRIETTE (1752–1822). Born Jeanne Genest at Paris on Nov. 6, she tutored the daughter of King Louis XV, was given an annual pension by the crown when she married a secretary to the queen, and served Marie Antoinette as first lady of the bedchamber from 1770 to 1792. When the queen was murdered, Mme. Campan retired to Coubertin, established a school for girls at St. Germain, and had as pupil Napoleon's daughter Hortense. In 1807, Napoleon appointed her superintendent of the Imperial Academy of Ecouen, which was closed in 1814. She published *Mémoires sur la vie de Marie-Antoinette, L'Education des femmes, Journal anecdotique*, letters, and school texts. She died in Mantes, France, on Nov. 6.

CAMPAÑA, PEDRO. See Kempeneer, Pieter de.

CAMPANELLA, GIOVANNI DOMENICO

(1568–1659), philosopher. Best known as Tommaso, he was born in Stilo, Calabria, Italy, on Sept. 5, became a Dominican at fourteen, and wrote his first philosophical study at twenty-two. At Rome and Padua he proposed philosophical and theological arguments, later included in about eighty books, which attacked Aristotle and made many enemies among the leaders of both old and new schools of thought. He had an encyclopedic mind, but did not organize well. He was in difficulty most of his life, often before the Inquisition, and several times in prison, either for alleged heresy or alleged conspiracy against Spanish power. He was highly regarded by Popes Clement VIII, Paul V, and Urban VIII, the last two arranging his release from imprisonment. In 1634 he was sent to France, where Richelieu gave him a pension and where he lived at the Dominican St. Honoré in Paris until his death on May 21. He was vocal in his attacks on skepticism and atheism, defended the astronomical theories of Galileo, and preceded Francis Bacon in insisting on the value of direct observation and experiment in science. He is best known today for his *Civitas solis* (*City of the Sun*), on a fictional commonwealth somewhat comparable to the Utopia of Thomas More.

CAMPANELLA, TOMMASO. See Campanella, Giovanni Domenico.

CAMPANI, GIUSEPPE (17th century), astronomer. He lived in Rome, became an expert in grinding lenses, built powerful telescopes, observed the spots on Jupiter, and wrote on Saturn. He also built the lenses which King Louis XIV ordered for the astronomer Cassini. Giuseppe worked with his brother, Matteo Campani-Alimensis, a pastor in Rome, who was also noted for his work with timepieces.

CAMPBELL, IGNATIUS ROY DUNNACHIE (1902–1957), poet. Born in Durban, Natal, on Oct. 2, he went to sea, served in the South African infantry at fifteen, briefly attended Oxford, and worked as a fisherman out of Mediterranean ports. He married Mary Gorman before he was twenty, lived in Wales, published his first poems as *The Flaming Terrapin*, then returned to Africa, edited a magazine for a short time, and published the satire *Wayzgoose*. Stays in England, Provence, Portugal, and Spain followed; he became noted for his life of violent action: bullfighting, water jousting, horsebreaking. He fought with the nationalist forces during the Spanish Civil War, was roundly attacked by the then Communist-dominated literary circles of London for doing so, and faced almost complete ostracism in later reviews. He wrote war correspondence for the London *Tablet*, saved the Carmelite archives during the siege of Toledo, and twice was ordered executed. *The Flowering Rifle* was the immediate result of his experiences; his translations of the poems of St. John of the Cross came later. He served with the British intelligence during World War II. Other volumes include: *The Gum Trees, Mithraic Emblems, Pomegranates, The Georgiad* (a scathing attack on corrupt aestheticism in contemporary literature), *Flowering Reeds, Adamastor*, the prose *Taurine Province*, an autobiography marred by uncontrolled prejudices, and three volumes of collected poems. He was killed in an auto accident in Setubal, Portugal, on Apr. 22.

CAMPBELL, JAMES (1812–1893). Born in Philadelphia, Pennsylvania, on Sept. 1, he became a lawyer in 1833, was a city commissioner and member of the board of education, and initiated the foundation of Girls' High School. He had several state judgeships between 1840 and 1851, was appointed attorney general of Pennsylvania in 1852, and in 1853 became postmaster general in President Pierce's cabinet. He was defeated for the United States Senate in 1861. He served as president of the trustees of Jefferson Medical College and as vice-president of St. Joseph's orphan asylum for twenty-five years, and in 1869 was appointed to the Philadelphia County board of city trusts, supervising forty-two institutions, including Girard College. He died in Philadelphia on Jan. 27.

CAMPBELL, JOSEPH (1879–1944), poet. Born in Belfast, Ireland, he studied at St. Malachy's, taught in country schools, wrote for the *United Irishman* and other journals under the name Seosamh MacCathmhaoil, and published many volumes of poetry on the countryside, folklore, religious spirit, and people of the fields and hills. These include *The Garden of the Bees* (1905), *The Rushlight, The Man-Child, The Gilly of Christ, The Mountainy Singer*, and *Irishry* (1913). Two plays were produced by the Ulster Literary Theatre and the Abbey in Dublin. *The Earth of Cualaan* (1917) contains some of his best poetry. In the early years of the twentieth century he was associated with Padraic Colum, Yeats, and others; in London, he served as secretary of the Irish Literary Society; returning to Ireland in 1916, he worked with the revolutionary underground, and was captured and imprisoned for a year and a half. He then went to the United States, lectured and taught, and in 1925 founded the School of Irish Studies, affiliated with Fordham in 1928–37. He then directed the Irish Foundation, returned to Ireland, published more poems and stories in Irish journals, and died in Wicklow on June 9.

CAMPBELL, ROY. *See* Campbell, Ignatius Roy Dunnachie.

CAMPBELL, THOMAS JOSEPH (1848–1925), editor. Born in New York City on Apr. 29, he studied at St. Francis Xavier, became a Jesuit, was ordained in Belgium in 1880, and served as provincial of the New York-Maryland province in 1889–95. He was president of Fordham in 1885–89 and 1896–99, and from 1910 was editor of *America*. He died in Monroe, New York, on Dec. 14.

CAMPEGGIO, LORENZO (1472–1539), cardinal. Born in Bologna, Italy, he studied civil law under his father, Giovanni, there and at Padua and, after the death of his wife in 1509, began ecclesiastical life. In 1512 he was named bishop of Feltre by Pope Julius II and a member of the supreme rota; Leo X sent him as papal legate to Emperor Maximilian I to organize a quarreling Christian world in a crusade. He was made a cardinal in 1517 while in Germany, then sent to England as legate. He impressed King Henry VIII, who made him bishop of Salisbury (until 1534), but irritated Cardinal Wolsey, who demanded precedence and who arranged a treaty between France and England instead of the alliance against the Turks the pope asked for. Campeggio returned to Rome in 1519 and under Pope Adrian VI begged for reform of the curia, the curbing of indulgences, and the compromises in current concordats. Pope Clement VII named him bishop of Bologna and sent him as legate to Germany in 1524. Lutheran advances were too great for him to have any success; Campeggio gained a promise from Emperor Charles V to carry out the Edict of Worms, but met with insults from the populace, saw the beginning of the Peasants' War, and was forced to return to Rome. He held the city of Rome during the pope's absence, when the city was attacked by imperial troops in 1527, then was sent to England to work with Wolsey in forming a court to try Henry's divorce case. Despite bribery, he was a careful judge and in July 1529 adjourned the court and saw to it that the case was reserved to papal decision. He returned to Bologna for the papal coronation of Charles V, went to Augsburg as legate, and advocated harsh measures against heretics. He was named bishop of Palestrina by Pope Paul III. He died in Rome on July 25.

CAMPI, ANTONIO (d. 1591?), painter. The second son of Galeazzo and born before 1536, he assisted his father at Cremona, Mantua, Milan, Brescia, Lodi, and Piacenza, and studied under his brother Giulio. He was called to Madrid by King Philip II, and also was an architect.

CAMPI, BERNARDINO (1522–1590?), painter. Born in Cremona, Italy, he studied under his father Pietro, a goldsmith, and under Giulio Campi at Cremona and Ippolito Corta at Mantua. He was an imitator of Titian and Correggio, successful in portraits, did frescoes at Cremona and Reggio, was author of a text on painting and master of many pupils. His most important work is the series of frescoes in the cupola of San Sigismondo, Cremona. He died in Reggio, Italy.

CAMPI, GALEAZZO (1475?–1536), painter. Born in Cremona, Italy, he was an imitator of Perugino, and completed a *Raising of Lazarus* and *Virgin and Child*. His three sons, Antonio, Giulio, and Vincenzo, became painters.

CAMPI, GIULIO (1500?–1572?), painter. Eldest son of Galeazzo, he was born in Cremona, Italy, studied under his father and, at Mantua, under Giulio Romano. He was influenced by Pordenone, Romanino, Raphael, and Correggio, and developed a composite style. His frescoes are in churches at Cremona, Mantua, and Milan, particularly in St. Margaret's, Cremona, in which city he died.

CAMPI, VINCENZO (1532–1591), artist. Brother of Giulio, under whom he studied, he completed portraits and still life, but was the least competent of the family.

CAMPIN, ROBERT (1375–1444). Possibly "Le Maitre de Flémalle" whose altarpiece was found in the Flemish abbey of that name (although the identification is also applied to his pupil, Jacques Daret), he worked at Tournay and was considered the greatest painter of his day after the Van Eycks. He decorated many panels and triptychs with religious scenes and portraits (*Descent from the Cross*; *St. Barbara*; *Adoration of Shepherds*) with strong simplicity. *Virgin and Child in a Room*, the *Virgin*, and *Virgin and Child with Angels* are among his best work. Rogier Van der Weyden was his pupil.

CAMPION, BL. EDMUND (1540?–1581), martyr. Born in London, the son of a bookseller, he studied at Oxford, where he was a brilliant student and orator (he spoke before Elizabeth on her visit to the university in 1566), took the oath of supremacy and became a deacon in the Anglican Church in 1564, and in 1569 or 1570 went to Ireland where he wrote his *History of Ireland*. There he became reconciled to the Catholic Church, returned to England in 1571, and then fled to Douai. In 1573 he became a Jesuit at Rome and was sent to Bohemia, where, after his novitiate in Brno and ordination in 1578, he taught at Prague. In 1580 he was sent on the English mission with Fr. Robert Persons. He worked in Berkshire, Oxfordshire, and Northamptonshire, and was so successful that he became one of the most hunted men in English history. In 1581 the distribution of his *Decem rationes* on the benches of the university church in Oxford caused a sensation and the premature publication of his famous "Brag" (written to insure a presentation of his case if he was captured) led

to redoubled efforts to capture him. He was betrayed at Lyford, Berkshire, imprisoned in the Tower, offered freedom and honors if he would apostatize, tortured, and condemned for allegedly preaching rebellion but actually for his priesthood. He was hanged, drawn, and quartered at Tyburn with Bl. Alexander Briant and Ralph Sherwin. They were beatified by Pope Leo XIII in 1886. F. D. Dec. 1.
EVELYN WAUGH, *Edmund Campion* (Garden City, N.Y., Image Books, 1956).

CAMUS, JEAN PIERRE (1584–1652), bishop. Born in Paris on Nov. 3, he was ordained, and at twenty-six was consecrated bishop of Belley by St. Francis de Sales, with papal permission. He represented the French clergy in 1614 as a delegate to the States-General, retired to the abbey of Aulnay at Francis' death, but was recalled to episcopal life to serve as auxiliary bishop of Rouen until 1651. He wrote nearly 200 books of fiction, sermons, spiritual and controversial work. His best is *L'Esprit de St. François de Sales*, his worst a series of violent tracts against the mendicant orders. Work which Voltaire ascribed to him was written by Claude Pitous, an apostate monk. His treatise on the love of God was condemned in Spain for its alleged Jansenism. He died in Paris on Apr. 25, while serving at the Hospice des Incurables.

CAÑAL, JOSÉ DE LA (1768–1845), historian. Born in Ucieda, Santander, Spain, on Jan. 11, he studied at Burgos, where he became an Augustinian in 1785. He taught philosophy at Salamanca, Burgos, and Madrid, was librarian at Salamanca from 1789 to 1800, director of the Royal Academy of History, author of biographies, and translator of French historical and theological works. He is particularly known for his work on the monumental *España sagrada*, a collection of annotated documents on ecclesiastical history; he completed volumes 43–44 with Fr. Merino and volumes 45–46 alone. He died in Madrid on Apr. 17.

CANCER DE BARBASTRO, LUIS (d. 1549). Born in Aragon, Spain, he became a Dominican, and went to Guatemala with Las Casas, whom he defended before the convocation in Mexico City in 1546. He wrote a catechism in verse, now lost, in Zapotecan and in 1549 was sent to convert the Indians of Florida. He and two fellow Dominicans were betrayed by an apostate interpreter and killed near Tampa, Florida.

CANCIANI, PAOLO (d. 1795?). A Servite in Italy, he was a scholar in canon law and wrote *Barbarorum leges antiquae*.

CANDIDA, ST. (d. 302), martyr. *See* Artemius, St.

CANDIDA, ST. (d. 798?), hermit. *See* Emerius, St.

CANDIDA OF CARTHAGE, ST. (4th century?). She was slain at Carthage, North Africa, probably during the reign of Maximian. F. D. Sept. 20.

CANDIDA THE ELDER, ST. (d. 78?). She is said to have been welcomed at Naples by St. Peter, who miraculously cured her of illness, and to have converted St. Aspren. F. D. Sept. 4.

CANDIDA THE YOUNGER, ST. (d. 586?). She gained a reputation for holiness during her married life at Naples, Italy. F. D. Sept. 10.

CANDIDUS, ST. (d. 254?), martyr. He, St. Piperion, and some twenty other Christians were put to death in northern Africa during the persecution of Valerian and Gallienus. F. D. Mar. 11.

CANDIDUS, ST. (d. 287?), martyr. *See* Maurice, St.

CANDIDUS BRUUN (9th century). A Benedictine, he was taught by Abbot Eigil of Fulda and by Einhard at the court of Charlemagne, where he became skilled in art. In 822, Candidus was made head of the monastic school at Fulda. He wrote lives of Eigil and Abbot Baugulf, a commentary on the Passion, and (though his authorship has been questioned) *Dicta de imagine mundi*, aphorisms on ontology, drawn in part from St. Augustine and using the syllogistic method.

CANDRES, ST. (5th century). A missionary bishop who worked in the area about Maastricht, he is honored in the diocese of Rouen, France. F. D. Dec. 1.

CANES, VINCENT (d. 1672). Born in England, he was a convert at twenty, went to Douai and became a Friar Minor, and taught philosophy and theology abroad before being sent on the English mission. He wrote several controversial works, including *The Reclaimed Papist* (1655), *Fiat Lux* (1662), and an answer to Edward Stillingfleet, who was the leading Anglican spokesman in England.

CAÑETE, MANUEL (1822–1891), critic, Born in Seville, Spain, he wrote poems and plays, but established his reputation as a dramatic critic on *Illustración Española y Americana* from 1833 until his death. He published anthologies of Spanish dramatists and of Spanish-American writers, served on government commissions, and was secretary to the Infanta Isabel.

CANETULI, BL. ARCHANGELO (d. 1513). Born in Bologna, Italy, he became an Augustinian canon regular after his father and brothers were killed during a riot, and was attached to houses at Gubbio and Castiglione. He was elected archbishop of Florence, but never served in that post. F. D. Apr. 16.

CANEVIN, JOHN FRANCIS REGIS (1852–1927), bishop. Born in Westmoreland County, Pennsylvania, on June 5, he studied at St. Vincent's seminary and was ordained in 1879. He was on the staff of the Pittsburgh cathedral in 1881–86, was chancellor of the diocese in 1888–93, and held several pastorates. He was titular bishop of Sabrata and consecrated coadjutor of Pittsburgh in 1903 and succeeded to the see in 1904. He resigned in 1920, was made titular archbishop of Pelusium, and died in Pittsburgh on Mar. 22.

CANICE, ST. (515?–599). Born in Glengiven, Derry, Ireland, he became a monk at Llancarfan, Wales, where he was ordained. After study at Clonard under St. Finian, he founded monasteries at Aghaboe and Kilkenny and accompanied St. Columba to Scotland, where he built a church at St. Andrews. The name is sometimes spelled Kenneth. F. D. Oct. 11.

CANION, ST. (5th century), bishop. *See* Priscus, St.

CANISIUS, HENRICUS (d. 1610). Born in Nijmegen, Holland, nephew of St. Peter Canisius, he studied at Louvain, became professor of canon law at Ingolstadt, and wrote on that subject, on marriage, and antiquities. He died on Sept. 2 at Ingolstadt, Germany.

CANISIUS, ST. PETER (1521–1597), Doctor of the Church. Born in Nijmegen, Holland, on May 8, oldest son of Jacob Kanis, the burgomaster, he studied at Cologne and Paris, met St. Peter Faber, became a Jesuit in 1543, edited the works of SS. Cyril of Alexandria and Leo the Great, was ordained in 1546, and attended two sessions of the Council of Trent. He was called to Rome by St. Ignatius, taught at Messina, and in 1549 was sent by St. Ignatius to Ingolstadt at the urgent request of Duke William IV of Bavaria. He reformed the university, of which he became rector, and had great influence in the heretical world outside the campus. In 1552 he went to Vienna on a similar mission and won over a very hostile city by his work with criminals and victims of the plague and finally by his university lectures and cathedral sermons. There he also prepared three versions of his *Catechism* (1555), which were translated into fifteen languages during his lifetime. In Prague he founded a college and in 1556 was named provincial of southern Germany, Austria, and Bohemia. Within thirty years he was to cover 20,000 miles, lecturing, preaching, working with converts, and founding six colleges. He worked at Augsburg from 1559 to 1565, persuading the *Reichstag* to reopen public schools destroyed by Protestants, and publishing a *Manual for Catholics*, a martyrology, a revision of the breviary, and an edition of St. Jerome's letters. The amazing strength and diplomacy he had shown at the interfaith conference at Worms in 1556 continued; he prevented a spiritual breach in Poland in 1558, healed a quarrel between the emperor and Pope Pius IV, and was selected to promulgate in Germany the decrees of the Council of Trent. At Dillingen until 1580, he began a series of corrective volumes answering the propaganda of the Centuriators of Magdeburg. He then went to Fribourg, where he founded the college which is now the Swiss university. In 1591 he suffered a paralytic stroke, but was able to dictate his writings until his death on Dec. 21 in Fribourg, Switzerland. He was canonized and declared a Doctor of the Church in 1925. F. D. Apr. 27.

JAMES BRODRICK, *St. Peter Canisius* (London, Burns, Oates, 1935).

CANISIUS, THEODORICH (1532–1606). Half-brother of St. Peter Canisius, he was born in Nijmegen, Holland, studied at Louvain, and became a Jesuit at Rome. He taught theology in Vienna, was rector of the Jesuit colleges at Munich and, for twenty years, at Dillingen, and Ingolstadt. He helped to introduce reforms in the teaching of philosophy and to test the revised *Ratio studiorum*. He died in Ingolstadt, Germany, on Sept. 27.

CANNATUS, ST. (5th century). He succeeded St. Honoratus as bishop of Marseilles, Gaul. F. D. Oct. 15.

CANO, ALONSO (1601–1667), sculptor. Born in Granada, Spain, on Mar. 19, he studied architecture under his father, Miguel, and, at Seville, sculpture under Juan Montanes and painting under Juan del Castillo and Pacheco. He completed three colored statues for altarpieces which gained him a reputation, then fled to Madrid in 1637 after a duel. Through the influence of Velásquez he was made royal painter, designed palaces, and was architect of the cathedrals of Granada and Toledo. Charged in 1644 with the alleged murder of his wife, he fled to Valencia, then to the Carthusian house of Porta Coeli, where he completed early paintings. He returned to Madrid to prove his innocence, studied for the priesthood, and in 1652 was made a canon of the Granada cathedral. His best painting, *The Seven Joys of the Virgin*, is at Granada; he completed many pen-and-ink drawings; but he is best known for his realistic statues, simple poses, with intensity of expression. He died in Granada on Oct. 3 or 5.

CANO, JUAN SEBASTIAN DEL (d. 1526), explorer. Born in Guetaria, Spain, he was in command of a ship trading in Africa and the Levant, commanded the *Victoria* on Magellan's expedition and became its chief after Magellan's death in 1521, and returned a year later, becoming the first officer to circumnavigate the earth. He was second in command to Loaisa on another expedition of five ships which cruised along the Pacific coast of North America.

CANO, MELCHIOR (1509–1560), theologian. Born in Tarancón, Cuenca, Spain, on Jan. 1, son of Ferdinand, a judge, he studied at Salamanca, became a Dominican in 1524, and was professor of theology at Valladolid from 1546 to 1552. He attended the Council of Trent, served as rector of St. Gregory's College, Valladolid, in 1553–57, and held other offices in the order. He engaged in scholastic controversy with Carranza, was a strenuous opponent of the Jesuits, and the author of *De logis theologicis* (1563), based on wide reading, which began a new era in the history of theology, and of treatises on penitence and the sacraments. He died in Toledo, Spain, on Sept. 30.

CANOG, ST. (d. 492?), martyr. Son of King Brychan of Wales, he was slain during a barbarian invasion. F. D. Oct. 7.

CANOSSA, BL. MAGDALENA DI (1774–1835), foundress. Born in Verona, Italy, of Marquis Ottavio Canossa and Teresa Szlukhe, she and three other children were sent to live with a relative when her father died and her mother remarried and moved to Mantua. At thirty-four she took over a Verona convent which she asked Napoleon to give her during the French occupation, teaching there and caring for poor girls. With others to help her, she set up similar establishments in Venice, Milan, Bergamo, and Trent. Her group, known as the Canossian Daughters of Charity, also opened high schools, colleges, schools for the deaf and dumb, and retreat houses. In 1831 she helped to form a group of religious men in Venice to carry on similar work for boys. She died in Verona, Italy, on Apr. 10, and was beatified in 1941 by Pope Pius XII. F. D. May 14.

CANOVA, ANTONIO (1757–1822), sculptor. Born in Possagno, Treviso, Italy, on Nov. 1, he was taught stonecutting by his grandfather, Pasino Canova, gained Senator Giovanni Falieri as a patron, studied sculpture with Torretto at Bassano, and went to Venice, where he completed a baroque *Daedalus and Icarus* at twenty-two and the classical *Theseus and the Minotaur* by 1782. He was in Rome from 1790 to 1798, where he did a monument to Pope Clement XIV, the tomb of Clement XIII, with carved lions, *Cupid and Psyche, Kneeling Magdalen, Hebe Pouring Nectar, Venus and Adonis, Hercules,* and two boxers. In all of these he revealed great anatomical accuracy and vigor. He traveled in Austria and Germany for two years, then completed *Perseus* and *Medicean Venus* for the Vatican. Napoleon brought him to Paris in 1802, 1805, and 1810, and he did statues of the emperor and of members of his family. He completed an elaborate tomb for the Archduchess Maria Christina in Vienna and for the poet Alfieri, the Stuart princes, and Pope Pius VI in Rome. In 1815 he was sent to Paris as papal envoy, negotiated successfully with Napoleon for the return of many art objects stolen from Italy, and was created marquis of Ischia as a reward. He was noted for his generosity, his willing patronage of new artists, and his development of sculpture from the low state into which it had fallen. He died in Venice on Oct. 13 and was buried in Possagno in a church which he had built.

CANTIANELLA, ST. (d. 304?), martyr. *See* Cantius, St.

CANTIANUS, ST. (d. 304?), martyr. *See* Cantius, St.

CANTIUS, ST. (d. 304?), martyr. He, his brother Cantianus, and sister Cantianella were orphans brought up in Rome by a Christian tutor, Protus, who gave up their property to the poor, freed their slaves, and left the city when the persecution of Diocletian came near. Seized, the four were ordered to sacrifice to the pagan gods, and beheaded when they refused. F. D. May 31.

CANTÙ, CESARE (1804–1895), historian. Born in Brivio, near Milan, Italy, on Dec. 5, he studied theology, then taught literature at Sondrio, Como, and Milan. He wrote a poetic romance, *Algiso* (1828), a study of the diocese of Como, and a history of seventeenth-century Lombardy (1832), the liberal sentiments of which resulted in thirteen months' imprisonment. This experience led to the writing of the popular novel, *Margherita Pusterla* (1838). He published poetry and juvenile fiction, but is best known for his historical work, begun in 1837, particularly the thirty-five volume *Storia universale*, a somewhat romantic account of the modern world to the time of Pope Pius IX, based on German and French secondary works, and histories of the Italians, of Italy from 1750 to 1850, of Italian literature, of the independence movement, and of the city of Milan. He was a friend of Manzoni, whose biography he wrote. His clerical support made him suspect by the government, and he left the country during the revolution of 1848. On his return he served in parliament from 1859 to 1861, was made director of archives of Lombardy in 1874, and died in Milan on Mar. 11.

CANTWELL, JOHN JOSEPH (1874–1947), archbishop. Born in Limerick, Ireland, on Dec. 1, he studied at Sacred Heart College there and St. Patrick's, Thurles, and was ordained in 1899. He went to the United States in that year, became a curate in San Francisco, secretary to the archbishop in 1904–14, and was vicar general from 1914 to 1917, when he was appointed bishop of Monterey-Los Angeles. He was transferred to Los Angeles-San Diego in 1922 and became an archbishop when Los Angeles was made an archdiocese in 1936. He founded the Los Angeles minor seminary in 1926 and its major seminary in 1939. He died in that city on Oct. 30.

CANUTE (994?–1035), king of England and Denmark. Son of Sweyn, king of Denmark, and Sigrid of Sweden, he was declared king of England by the leaders of the Danish fleet in 1014 after his father was slain during a raid on England. When he returned with larger forces, Ethelred was slain, Wessex conquered, and London besieged and conquered. Canute made peace with Eadmund Ironside, Ethelred's successor, received Mercia and Northumbria to rule, and the right to levy the danegeld (tax) for the expenses of his navy. When Eadmund died, Canute removed other opposition by murder, and controlled England at the age of twenty-three. In 1018 he succeeded to the throne of Denmark on the death of his brother Harold. He brought eighteen years of peace and order to England, practiced the Christianity which he had disregarded since his baptism as an infant, established the abbey of Bury St. Edmunds, introduced missionaries to Denmark, was a patron of poets, and made a pilgrimage to Rome in 1026. He conquered Norway and Denmark about 1028 and added Scotland to his triumphs when he subdued Malcolm Clanmore. He died in Shaftesbury, England, on Nov. 12.

CANUTE IV, ST. (d. 1086), king of Denmark. He became king of Denmark in 1081, after he had led an unsuccessful attempt to take England six years before. He built many churches in Denmark, helped missioners in northern Europe, and gave such wide privileges to clerics that some became too powerful feudal lords and neglected their spiritual duties. With Olaf of Norway and his father-in-law Robert of Flanders, he again sought to capture England, but the people rebelled over taxes in 1085, and Canute fled to the sanctuary of a church on the island of Fünen. He was struck by a stone thrown by a mob led by his brother Olaf and died on July 10. Because he was kneeling at the altar after confession and Communion, he was termed a martyr and canonized by Pope Paschal II in 1101 at the request of King Eric III. F. D. Jan. 19.

CANUTE LAVARD, ST. (d. 1131), king. The second son of King Eric the Good of Denmark, he became duke of Jutland during a period of Viking raids. He brought peace to the area and gave support to the missionary endeavors of St. Vicelin, but when he became king of the western Wends in 1129, this angered his uncle and led to his murder. He was canonized in 1169 at the request of his son Valdemar. F. D. Jan. 7.

CAPECELATRO, ALFONSO (1824–1912), cardinal. Born in Marseilles, France, on Feb. 5, where his father, the duke of Castel Pagano, was in exile, he was brought to Italy in 1826. He became an Oratorian in 1847, wrote biographies of SS. Alphonsus Liguori, Catherine of Siena, Peter Damian, Philip Neri, and others, and a life of Christ based on modern research, as well as a refutation of Renan's *Life of Jesus*. Pope Leo XIII made him assistant librarian at the Vatican, archbishop of Capua in

1880, and a cardinal in 1885. He died on Nov. 14.

CAPEFIGUE, BAPTISTE HONORÉ RAYMOND (1802–1872), historian. Born in Marseilles, France, he studied law at Paris, became editor of *Messager des chambres* in 1827, and served in the ministry of foreign affairs, but was ousted during the revolution of 1848. He was an ardent royalist, wrote on the Bourbons and Napoleon, several ambitious histories of Europe, and popular biographies. His most serious works, the least marred by speed in the writing, were studies of Henry IV and of Philippe-Auguste. He died in Paris on Dec. 22.

CAPEL, THOMAS JOHN (1836–1911), educator. Born in England on Oct. 28, he founded, with others, a training college for teachers in London, and after three years became its principal at twenty. He was ordained by Cardinal Wiseman, and while in France for his health he founded at Pau a mission for English-speaking Catholics and was made a domestic prelate in 1873 as a result. Returning to England, he established and was rector of the Catholic University of Kensington in 1874, made a number of converts, engaged in controversy with Gladstone, is pictured as Catesby in Disraeli's novel *Lothair*, and in 1883 went to California, where he died on Oct. 21.

CAPEROLO, PIETRO (d. 1480). A Franciscan, he preached in northern Italy, and obtained from Pope Sixtus IV permission to separate several houses of his order from direction by the Observants. The new group, under obedience to the Conventuals, had a right to elect their own superior and became known as the Caperolani. After the death of their founder at Velletri, Italy, they returned to the obedience of the Observants.

CAPGRAVE, JOHN (1393–1464), historian. Born in Lynn, Norfolk, England, on Apr. 21, he attended either Oxford or Cambridge, was ordained an Augustinian about 1418, became provincial of his order, and wrote biblical commentaries, sermons, biographies of SS. Augustine, Catherine (a poem), and Gilbert of Sempringham, of famous Augustinians and of Humphrey of Gloucester, a chronicle of English history to 1417, and *De illustribus Henricis*. The last two works, in modern editions, are historically valuable. He died in Lynn on Aug. 12.

CAPILLAS, BL. FRANCISCO FERDINANDO DE (1606–1648), martyr. Born in Vacherim, Valladolid, Spain, he became a Dominican at seventeen, was ordained at Manila in 1631, and served in Luzon for ten years. After learning Chinese, he went with Fr. Francisco Diaz to Fokien. Their work was successful until, at the fall of the Ming dynasty, civil war broke out and the Manchu Tatars who took the area captured Fr. de Capillas, who was attempting to enter Fogan, Fokien, China, to serve his converts, and tortured and beheaded him. He was beatified in 1909. F. D. Jan. 15.

CAPITANO, ST. BARTHOLOMEA (1807–1833), foundress. Born in Lovere, near Brescia, Italy, she took a vow of chastity and devoted herself to teaching when her parents refused to let her become a nun. With Catherine Gerosa (St. Vincenza), she founded the Congregation of the Italian Sisters of Charity. Her spiritual notes were published, as were some 300 letters from a wide correspondence. F. D. July 26.

CAPITOLINA, ST. (d. 304), martyr. She and her maid Erotheis were put to death in Cappadocia during the Diocletian persecution. F. D. Oct. 27.

CAPITON, ST. (4th century), bishop and martyr. *See* Aetherius, St.

CAPOCCI, FILIPO (1840–1911), composer. Born in Rome, he studied under his father, Gaetano (1811–1898), and in the Accademia di Santa Cecilia, became organist at St. John Lateran in 1875, and in 1898 succeeded his father as choirmaster. He wrote five sonatas and an oratorio, *Sant' Anastasio*, among other compositions, and served as a member of the pontifical commission on sacred chant. He died in Rome on July 24.

CAPOCCI, GAETANO (1811–1898), composer. Born in Rome, Italy, on Oct. 16, he studied organ and composition there and in 1839 was appointed organist of the church of Santa Maria Maggiore. From 1855 he was director of the Cappella Pia of the Lateran, wrote masses and motets, two oratorios (*Battista* and *Assalone*), and a *Responsori* for Holy Week. He died in Rome on Jan. 11.

CAPOCCI, BL. GIACOMO (d. 1308), bishop. Born in Viterbo, Italy, he became an Augustinian, studied at Paris under Aegidius Romanus, was an ardent and learned Thomist, became archbishop of Benevento in 1302, and was transferred the next year to Naples by Pope Boniface VIII. His cult was approved in 1911. F. D. Mar. 14.

CAPOTOSI, LUIGI (1863–1938), cardinal. Born in Montegiberto, Italy, on Feb. 9, he was ordained, was created cardinal-priest in 1926, and served as head of the apostolic datary from 1933 until his death in Vatican City on Feb. 16.

CAPPONI, GINO (1792–1876), historian. Born in Florence, Italy, on Sept. 13, he traveled widely, helped to found a number of historical, agricultural, educational, and critical journals, became blind in 1840, directed Tuscany during the revolution of 1848, and later became a senator. His valuable *History of Florence* appeared in 1875 (covering the years to 1530 and based on primary sources); he also issued a collection of Tuscan folklore, an edition, with others, of

Dante's *Divina Commedia*, and works on education, economics, sociology, and literature. He died in Florence on Feb. 3.

CAPPONI, SERAFINA (1536–1614), theologian. Born in Porrecta, Italy, he became known later as Serafino Porrecta. He joined the Dominicans in 1552 in Bologna and taught there for the rest of his life, except when he taught at a Carthusian monastery in 1606–8. He became famed as one of the outstanding authorities on St. Thomas Aquinas' writings. The edition of the *Summa*, with Porrecta-Cajetan commentaries, was the most highly regarded edition for centuries. He died in Bologna, Italy, on Jan. 2.

CAPPUCI, BL. PIETRO (1390–1445). Born in Tiferno (now Città di Castello), Italy, he became a Dominican at fifteen, was ordained and spent most of his life at the friary in Cortona. He was called "the preacher of death" because he preached with a skull in his hands. His cult was confirmed by Pope Pius VII. F. D. Oct. 21.

CAPRANICA, DOMENICO (1400–1458), cardinal. Born in Capranica, near Palestrina, Italy, he studied at Padua and Bologna, became doctor of canon and civil law at twenty-one, secretary to Pope Martin V, and bishop of Fermo. About 1426 he was made a cardinal, but was never formally raised to the rank and was denied the honor by the cardinals and by Pope Eugene IV for political reasons. He lost all his honors, served Aeneas Sylvius as secretary, and was restored to favor and given his cardinalate in 1434. He was papal legate to the Council of Ferrara, which dealt with Greek reunion, and served on a dozen other embassies. Fearless and stern, fervent for reform and charitable toward the poor, he drew up a plan for the Reformation of the Church which he submitted to Pope Nicholas V in 1449. He attacked Callistus III for his nepotism, was an outspoken critic of the worldly hierarchy in Rome, remained in Rome during the plague of 1456 when others fled, preached a crusade, and founded the Collegio Capranica for poor scholars. His *Art of Dying Well* was published in 1487. He died in Rome on July 14.

CAPRARA, GIOVANNI BATTISTA (1733–1810), cardinal. Born in Bologna, Italy, on May 29, he was papal nuncio at Cologne in 1767, at Lucerne in 1775, and at Vienna in 1785, and was made cardinal-priest in 1792 and bishop of Jesi in 1800. Caprara did not oppose Emperor Joseph II strongly enough while at Vienna and, when sent to Paris as papal legate in 1801, he was easily influenced by Napoleon. He failed to condemn the constitutional bishops, as directed by Pius VII, and was censured by that pope as he had been by Paul VI; however, he did object strongly to the organic articles added to the concordat. Napoleon made him archbishop of

Milan in 1802, but he remained as papal legate in France until the imprisonment of Pius VII. He died in Paris on July 27.

CAPRASIUS, ST. (4th century?), martyr. According to legend he was the first bishop of Agen, France, and fled, with his flock, during Diocletian's persecution of the Christians. He later surrendered to the prefect Dacian and was tortured and beheaded with Alberta, sister of St. Faith, and two brothers, Primus and Felician, when they refused to sacrifice to the gods. F. D. Oct. 20.

CAPRASIUS, ST. (d. 430). The learned teacher of St. Honoratus and his brother Venantius accompanied them to the Near East, returned to Gaul after the latter died in Greece, and assisted Honoratus in establishing the monastery of Lérins, off the coast of France. F. D. June 1.

CAPREOLUS, JOHN (1380?–1444), theologian. Born in Rodez, France, he became a Dominican and lectured at Paris on Thomas Aquinas, on whom he wrote an elaborate commentary (1409–33), with elaborate refutations of Averroës, Duns Scotus, William of Ockham, and the nominalists. He died in Rodez on Apr. 6.

CAPTIER, LOUIS RAPHAEL (d. 1871), martyr. Superior of the College of Arcueil, near Paris, he, his fellow Dominicans, and the lay faculty of the college were seized by revolutionaries during the last days of the siege of Paris by the German army, led from prison to prison for a week, and on May 25 shot to death in the street by scattered snipers. Several, left in the gutters, did not die until the following day; they included Frs. Bourard, Chatagneret, Cottrault, and Delhorme, and eight laymen.

CARABANTES, JOSÉ DE (1628–1694). Born in Aragon, Spain, he became a Capuchin, was a missionary in South America, and wrote dictionaries of Indian languages for use by missioners.

CARACCIOLO, ST. ASCANIO (1563–1608), founder. Born in Villa Santa Maria in the Abruzzi, Italy, on Oct. 13, he was ordained, and joined a group caring for prisoners, especially those facing execution. In 1588 a letter from John Augustine Adorno, a Genoese priest, outlined plans for an order which would combine the active and contemplative life; their joint proposal was approved that year by Pope Sixtus V. The Minor Clerks Regular took a fourth vow, to refuse all positions of dignity; made themselves aware of the value of penance by extreme austerities; and were particularly devoted to the Eucharist. They worked outside in hospitals, prisons, and retreat houses. When Fr. Adorno died at forty, Ascanio (who took the name Francis) became general, begged in the streets for humility, set up foundations in Spain, and finally directed Santa Maria Maggiore in Naples as prior and master of novices. He died at Agnone, Abruzzi, Italy, while establishing a novitiate on property given to his order by St. Philip Neri. He was canonized in 1807. F. D. June 4.

CARADOC, ST. (d. 1124). Harper in the court of King Rhys of South Wales, he left courtly life to become a monk at Llandaff and then a hermit. F. D. Apr. 14.

CARADOSSO. *See* Foppa, Ambrogio.

CARAFFA, VINCENT (1585–1649). Born in Naples, Italy, on May 5, a relative of Pope Paul IV, he became a Jesuit in 1604, taught, served as provincial of Naples, and in 1645 became seventh general of the Society. Writing under the name Aloysius Siderius, he published *Idea christiani hominis, Fascetto di mirra* (*Bundle of Myrrh*), and other ascetical works. At his suggestion, the Confraternity of Bona Mors was instituted. He died in Rome on June 8.

CARAMUEL Y LOBKOWITZ, JUAN (1606–1682). Born in Madrid, Spain, on May 23, he became a Cistercian, preached in Spain and Flanders, was royal envoy to Emperor Ferdinand III, abbot of Melrose, Scotland, abbot superior of the Benedictines in Vienna, and vicar to the archbishop of Prague. He helped to defend that city when it was attacked by Sweden in 1648, became bishop of Königratz, archbishop of Otranto, and bishop of Vigevano. He wrote over 200 volumes of poetry, grammar, philosophy, canon law, politics, and science. Because of his fondness for argumentation for its own sake and his dabbling in the solution of theological problems by mathematical rules, St. Alphonsus Liguori called him "Prince of the Laxists." He died in Vigevano, Italy, on Sept. 8.

CARANTOC, ST. (6th century). He founded a church in Cardiganshire, Wales, visited Britain and Brittany, and died at a monastery in Cernach (variously identified as in Ireland, as Crantock in Cornwall, and as Carhampton in Somerset). He is sometimes identified with a fifth-century Welshman who worked in Ireland with St. Patrick. F. D. May 16.

CARAUNUS, ST. (5th century), martyr. He went from Rome to preach in Gaul and was set upon and slain by outlaws near Chartres. He is also known as Cheron. F. D. May 28.

CARAVAGGIO, MICHELANGELO (1569–1609), painter. Michelangelo Amerighi (or Morigi or Merighi) was born in Caravaggio, Italy, worked as a plasterer for Milanese fresco artists as a youth, took the name of his birthplace, went to Venice where he studied under an unknown artist, and then to Rome, where he worked for Cesare d'Arpino, filling out the ornamental portions of his portraits, and acquired tremendous success as the founder of the naturalist school. Forced to flee

because of a murder he committed, he worked in Naples and Malta, where he was imprisoned for a time, and escaped to Syracuse and then to Naples, where he was pardoned for his crime in Rome. He was mistakenly taken captive by a group of Spaniards on his way to Rome, but fell ill when liberated and died at Port Ercole, Italy. His paintings are characterized by their vigor, daring, almost brutal emphasis, careless detail and unusually bold use of light and shadow. Outstanding are *The Entombment, The Supper at Emmaus, Death of a Virgin,* portrait of the Grand Master of the Knights of Malta, and *The Card Players.*

CARAVAGGIO, POLIDORO CALDARA DA. *See* Caldara, Polidoro.

CARAYON, AUGUSTE (1813–1874), historian. Born in Saumur, France, on Mar. 31, he became a Jesuit in 1848, compiled a bibliography of Jesuit history, edited documents of his Society, wrote on its labors in Canada and Louisiana and other historical studies and works of asceticism. He died in Poitiers, France, on May 15.

CARBERY, JAMES JOSEPH (1823–1887). Born in Westmeath, Ireland, on May 1, he became a Dominican, studied at Navan, Viterbo, and Rome, held several major posts in his order, and in 1883 was appointed third bishop of Hamilton, Ontario, Canada. He died in Cork on Dec. 17 while on a visit to Ireland.

CARBONARA, MICHELE DA (1836–1910). Born in Carbonara, Italy, on Oct. 10, he became a Capuchin, was sent to East Africa as mission superior, and became prefect apostolic of Erythrea, where he died on June 24.

CARBONELLE, IGNATIUS (1829–1889), editor. Born in Tournai, Belgium, on Feb. 1, he became a Jesuit in 1844, and taught in Calcutta, India, from 1861 to 1867, where he edited *Indo-European Correspondence* for two years. He taught mathematics and astronomy at Louvain, was assigned to the staff of *Études,* founded the Scientific Society of Brussels in 1875, and from 1877 until his death there on Mar. 4 was editor of its *Annales* and of *Revue des questions scientifiques.*

CARDANO, GIROLAMO (1501–1576), mathematician. Born in Pavia, Italy, on Sept. 24, the illegitimate son of Facio Cardano, a jurist, he took his degree in medicine at Pavia, held the chair of mathematics at Milan in 1534–52, and the chair of medicine at Pavia in 1559–62, and at Bologna in 1562–70. He obtained this last post at the urging of St. Charles Borromeo. He apparently ran through his wife's fortune and was imprisoned for debt in Bologna, went to Rome in 1571, was given a pension by Pope Gregory XIII, and died there on Sept. 21. His philosophical work was totally erroneous; he was a master of astrology and an eccentric; but his contributions to mathematics were significant. In *Ars magna* (1545) he contributed to the solution of biquadratic equations (with his student Ferrari) and presented the solution of the cubic equation, now named after him, but discovered in 1541 by Tartaglia. Although Cardano acknowledged his indebtedness to Tartaglia and Ferrari, and developed their contributions to mathematical research, a long controversy over originality resulted.

CARDENAS, JUAN (1613–1684), theologian. Born in Seville, Spain, he became a Jesuit at fourteen, held several posts in the Society, wrote ascetical treatises and pious biographies, and a controversial study of theology in which he evaluated the extreme views of the laxists and rigorists (1670); a corrected compendium was published in 1704. He died on June 6.

CARDUCCI, BARTOLOMMEO (1560–1608), painter. Born in Florence, Italy, he executed pictures for the Jesuit church there, then went with Zuccaro to Spain and joined him in decorating the Escorial. He completed the library walls and several frescoes, did some work as architect and sculptor, and drew a *Descent from the Cross* for the church of San Felipe, Madrid.

CARDUCCI, VINCENZO (d. 1638), painter. Younger brother of Bartolommeo, by whom he was brought to Spain in 1585 when quite young, he was appointed court painter by King Philip III, completed work for churches and palaces in Madrid, and fifty-four pictures of the life of St. Bruno for the Carthusians at Paular. He wrote a book on painting and in 1637 was successful in having the tax on works of art abolished. He became insane early in 1638.

CAREW, THOMAS (1590–1672?), historian. Born in Tipperary, Ireland, he became a priest, served as chaplain to an Irish regiment in Austria, and witnessed much action during the Thirty Years' War, which he used in his *Itinerarium*. He died in Vienna as choral vicar of St. Stephen's cathedral.

CAREY, BL. JOHN (d. 1594), martyr. An Irish servant of Bl. Thomas Bosgrave, he was martyred with his master at Dorchester, England, and beatified in 1929. F. D. July 4.

CAREY, MATTHEW (1760–1839), publisher. Born in Dublin, Ireland, on Jan. 28, he became a bookseller and printer at fifteen, published in 1779 an anonymous pamphlet demanding the repeal of the penal laws against Catholics, and fled to France with a price on his head. He worked in the Paris office of Benjamin Franklin, returned to Dublin to publish the *Freeman's Journal* and then the *Volunteers Journal* (1783), was arrested, imprisoned, and on his release went to Philadelphia. There he established the *Pennsylvania Herald* with money given him by Lafayette, whom he had

met in France; in it he published detailed accounts of the debates of the state assembly. He became the political opponent of Eleazer Oswald, editor of the *Independent Gazetteer*, who opposed immigration. In a subsequent duel, Oswald seriously wounded him. He was one of the founders of the *Columbia Magazine* (1786), but a year later began the *American Museum*, which he ran until 1792. He was engaged in bookselling and publishing until 1821. His publishing house was very active, and in 1790 he published the first American edition of the Douai Bible. During the yellow-fever epidemic of 1793 he was a member of the department of health, was active in checking the spread of the plague, and published a report on it. He also founded the Hibernian Society that year and in 1786 founded the Sunday School Society, with Bishop White. He wrote *The Porcupiniad* (1799), an attack on the English historian and publisher, William Cobbett; newspaper articles favoring the rechartering of the U. S. Bank (1810); *The Olive Branch* (1814), in an attempt to end the War of 1812; *Vindiciae Hibernicae* (1818), an answer to the lies on which the English novelist William Godwin based his *Mandeville*; and a series of pamphlets favoring a protective tariff. In 1819–22 he unfortunately supported Fr. William Hogan in the schism which shattered St. Mary's parish. Carey's autobiography was published in the *New England Magazine* in 1833–34. He died in Philadelphia on Sept. 15.

CARHEIL, ÉTIENNE DE (1633–1726), missioner. Born in Carentoir, France, he became a Jesuit in 1652, taught in Rouen and Tours, and labored for thirty years among the Indians of Canada. Because of his vocal opposition to Cadillac's illicit brandy trade, he was recalled to Quebec in 1703, and limited to parish work in and around Montreal. He died in Quebec on July 27.

CARILEFUS, ST. (d. 540?). Born in Auvergne, France, he was ordained with his friend St. Avitus at Miey near Orléans. He became a hermit, but so many sought his guidance that he founded a monastery, Anisole, to which to retire. He also is known as Calais. F. D. July 1.

CARINA, ST. (d. 360), martyr. *See* Melasippus, St.

CARISSIMI, GIACOMO (1604–1674), composer. Born in Marino in the Papal States, he studied music at Rome and became choirmaster at Assisi in 1624 and of the church of St. Apollinaris, Rome, in 1628. He wrote masses, motets, cantatas, and oratorios, and taught Buononcini, Cesti, Charpentier, and Alessandro Scarlatti, among others. He added a lyric quality and vibrant variety to the orchestral accompaniment of the oratorio, which had already been somewhat developed from the simple works originally composed for St. Philip Neri's prayer meetings. *Jephthah, Judicium Solomonis, Baltazar,* and *Jonas* have been published; other oratorios, generally on biblical subjects, have been lost; he died in Rome on Jan. 12.

CARISSIMUS, ST. (d. 90?). *See* Romulus, St.

CARLETTI, BL. ANGELO (1411?–1495). Born in Chivasso, near Turin, Italy, he became doctor of canon law at Bologna, senator in Piedmont, and, on the death of his mother, a Franciscan at Genoa. He served the poor and sick, helped to establish pawnshops to crush usury, became confessor to Duke Charles I of Savoy, and was elected vicar general three times. He preached among the Saracens for Pope Sixtus IV and at eighty won back many Waldensian heretics for Innocent VIII. He retired to the convent at Cuneo, Piedmont, Italy, in 1493, and died there. His cult was approved by Pope Benedict XIII. F. D. Apr. 12.

CARLI, DIONIGI (17th century). A Capuchin missioner, he left Genoa, Italy, in 1666 for Lisbon, Brazil, and the Congo. The expedition was spiritually successful, but most of the friars died of disease. In 1672, Carli published at Bologna the manuscript record kept by Fr. Michele Angelo Guattini, to which he added his own observations on travel and mission difficulties.

CARLIN, FRANCIS. *See* MacDonnell, James.

CARLIN, JAMES JOSEPH (1872–1930), educator. Born in Peabody, Massachusetts, on Apr. 14, he graduated from Boston College and became a Jesuit in 1892. After ordination he taught theology and canon law at Woodstock in 1904–10 and philosophy at Holy Cross. He was assistant to the Maryland provincial, and from 1918 to 1925 was president of Holy Cross. He then became president of the Ateneo de Manila and in 1927 superior of the Jesuit mission in the Philippines. He died in Los Angeles on Oct. 1.

CARLOMAN, BL. (705–755), king. Eldest son of Charles Martel, he succeeded his father as king of Austrasia, helped to found the abbeys of Fulda, Lobbes, and Stavelot, and aided St. Boniface in his mission in Germany. Later he gave over the crown to his brother, Pepin the Short, and became a Benedictine monk on Mt. Soracte, at Monte Cassino, and in Vienne, Gaul, where he died. F. D. Aug. 17.

CARLOMAN (751–771), king. Son of King Pepin the Short, he became joint ruler of the Franks, with his brother Charlemagne, on the death of their father in 768. His territory was Neustria, Burgundy, and part of Aquitaine. He differed with his brother on the conduct of military operations in Aquitania, but died shortly after at Samoussy on Dec. 4. Though he had two sons, Charlemagne took over his territory.

CARLOMAN (d. 884), king. Son of King Louis II, the Stammerer, he became joint ruler, with his brother Louis III, of France on the death of his father in 879, and received Burgundy and southern France as his share of the kingdom. Though there were some doubts as to their legitimacy, they enforced their claims to the kingdom. Carloman put down revolts in Provence and Burgundy, and in 881 he and Louis defeated the Normans at Abbeville. On the death of his brother in 882 he became sole ruler, defeated the invading Normans again at Aisne, and had secured their agreement to withdraw when he died hunting on Dec. 12.

CARLYLE, BENJAMIN FEARNLEY (1874–1955). Born on Feb. 7 in Sheffield, England, he was raised in Argentina, studied medicine in London, and at twenty-two formed an Anglican brotherhood there, which became the order of St. Benedict on Caldey Island. He called himself Aelred; in 1913 he and twenty-two of his monks became converts. He was ordained in 1914, left Caldey in 1921, spent a short period in a Carthusian monastery in Spain, then served as a parish priest in Vancouver, British Columbia, until 1951. He spent his last years at Prinknash abbey in Gloucester, England, where he died on Oct. 14.

CARMICHAEL, MONTGOMERY (1857–1936), author. Born in Birkenhead, England, he studied at Bonn and Munich, became a convert in 1881, married Maud Parker in 1887, and entered the diplomatic service. He was vice-consul and consul at Leghorn, Italy, in 1892–1922, and consul general to San Marino and for Tuscany in 1912–22. *Sketches and Stories* appeared in 1896; *Tuscany* in 1901; they were followed by *The Major General, John William Walshe,* and *Christopher and Cressida,* novels. He also wrote travel books and edited *Lady Poverty* from a mediaeval original. He remained in Italy after his retirement and died there.

CARMODY, MARTIN H. (1872–1950). Born in Grand Rapids Township, Michigan, he studied at Valparaiso Normal College and Michigan Law School, practiced law, and was head of the Knights of Columbus from 1927 to 1939. He directed the expenditure of flood-relief funds, led boys' conferences, initiated camp and guidance projects, and was active in war relief. He received honorary degrees from Notre Dame and Michigan, was decorated by the papacy and many foreign governments, and died in Grand Rapids on Dec. 9.

CARNEIRO, MELCHIOR (d. 1583), bishop. Born in Coimbra, Portugal, he became a Jesuit in 1543, and served as rector of colleges at Evora and Lisbon. In 1555, at Rome, he was consecrated coadjutor to John Nugnez, patriarch of Ethiopia, the first Jesuit to become a bishop. He was unable to enter Ethiopia, and continued to India, serving at Goa and along the Malabar coast until 1567. From 1567 to 1569 he was first bishop of China and Japan. He died at Macao on Apr. 25.

CARNOT, JOHN RUDOLPH (1865–1935), author. Born in Sammann, Switzerland, on Jan. 26, he studied at Schwyz and Innsbruck, became a Benedictine in 1885, taking the name Maurice, and was ordained in 1888. He taught at the monastery of Disentis, Switzerland, for nearly fifty years, lectured on history and language, and was successful in gaining national approval of Raeto-romansch as the fourth language of his country. He wrote poetry, fiction, and more than a dozen plays. He died at his monastery.

CARNOY, JEAN BAPTISTE (1836–1899), biologist. Born in Hainaut, Belgium, on Jan. 22, he was ordained, devoted himself to natural science, received his doctorate and a government grant, and worked at Leipzig, Berlin, Bonn, Vienna, and, in Rome, with Francesco Castracane, the naturalist. On his return he became vicar at Celles, near Tournai, and published on anatomy. He taught microscopy at Louvain, became the founder of the school of cytology there, equipping a laboratory at his own expense, and founded the journal *La cellule* in 1884. His researches on the nucleus, cell segmentation, and the albuminoid membrane were significant. He died in Schuls, Switzerland, on Sept. 6.

CARO, FRANCISCO (1627–1667), artist. Son of Francisco Lopez-Caro, he was born in Seville, studied in the studio of Alonzo Cano in Madrid, and completed scenes from the life of the Virgin Mary for a chapel in St. Andrew's, Madrid, and a *Portiuncula Indulgence* for the Franciscan convent, Segovia. He also did portraits. He died in Madrid.

CARO RODRIGUEZ, JOSÉ MARÍA (1866–1958), cardinal. Born in Pichelemu, Chile, on June 23, he studied at the Santiago seminary and the South American College in Rome, was ordained in 1890, and received his doctorate in theology the following year. He taught theology, Greek, and Hebrew at the Santiago seminary for the next twenty years, was appointed bishop of Iquique, Chile, in 1911, and there earned the title of "bishop of the salt mines" for his devotion to the needy and his interest in the social and economic problems of the inhabitants of an area rich in salt and nitrate mines. He was transferred to La Serena in 1925, was made a Roman count by Pope Pius XI in 1937, and in 1939 became an archbishop when La Serena was raised to an archdiocese. He was transferred to Santiago after three months, was created a cardinal in 1946, and died in Santiago, Chile, on Dec. 4. He wrote *Foundations of the Faith, Christian Marriage,*

and The Historical Personality of Our Lord.

CAROCHI, HORACIO (1586?–1666), missioner. Born in Florence, Italy, he became a Jesuit and was sent to Mexico. He mastered the Nahuatl and Othomí languages and wrote on both, compiled a grammar and a dictionary, and published *Arte de la lengua mexicana* in 1645.

CARON, RAYMOND (1605–1666). Born in Athlone, Ireland, he became a Franciscan there, studied at Drogheda, Salzburg, and Louvain, and became professor of theology at the latter university. He published a defense of Catholic doctrine in 1635; in 1648 he was sent to Ireland as visitator, lived at Kilkenny, tried to end factionalism there, but by extreme means (imprisoning all the members of his order who opposed Ormond). His actions and publications brought him under ecclesiastical censure for a brief period. He died in Dublin.

CARON, RENÉ EDOUARD (1800–1876), jurist. Born in St. Anne de Beaupré, Quebec, on Oct. 13, he passed the Canadian bar in 1826, served as mayor of Quebec for ten years, was elected to the legislative assembly, served as speaker of the upper house and as a member of the cabinet. He was widely respected for his labors in Quebec during the plague of 1834 and the fire of 1845, and on behalf of responsible government and equal rights for non-Tory Canada. In 1853 he was appointed judge of the superior court, became judge of the court of the queen's bench in 1855, and served on the commission to codify the civil laws of Lower Canada. He was lieutenant governor of his province from 1872 until his death, in Quebec, on Dec. 13.

CARPACCIO, VITTORE (1455?–1525?), painter. Vittore Scarpazza was born in Venice, studied under Lazzaro Bastiani, worked with Bellini, and produced many large pageant paintings, notably nine depicting the life of St. Ursula, nine others on the career of St. George, and six on the life of the Virgin Mary. Individual works include *Lion of St. Mark. Dismissal of the Ambassadors, St. Jerome in His Study, Call of St. Matthew, Presentation in the Temple, Holy Family,* a panorama of Jerusalem, and a number of views of Venice. He is noted for effective portraiture and use of light. He lived for a time in Capo d'Istria, but returned to Venice, where he died.

CARPENTER, ALEXANDER (15th century). A scholar at Oxford University, he wrote the didactic *Destructorium viciorum* about 1420 against the vices of his day.

CARPENTER, JOHN (d. 1786). He became archbishop of Dublin in 1770, compiled careful records of his diocesan history, and died in his see city on Oct. 29.

CARPI, UGO DI (1480?–1523?), painter. An Italian artist and engraver, he claimed in a letter he sent to the Venetian Academy in 1516 that he was the inventor of chiaroscuro engraving, but Lucas Cranach and others predated him. Only twelve of his engravings remain.

CARPINI, GIOVANNI DE PIANO. *See* Piano Carpine, Giovanni da.

CARPONIUS, ST. (d. 304?), martyr. He and his brothers Evaristus and Priscian and sister Fortunata were put to death at Caesarea, Palestine, during the Diocletian persecution. F. D. Oct. 14.

CARPOPHORUS, ST. (d. 295), martyr. He and St. Rufus were slain at Capua during the Diocletian persecution. F. D. Aug. 27.

CARPOPHORUS, ST. (d. 295?), martyr. He and SS. Cassius, Exanthus, Licinus, Secundus, and Severinus were soldiers executed at Como, Italy, during the reign of Maximian. F. D. Aug. 7.

CARPOPHORUS, ST. (d. 300?), martyr. A priest, he was put to death with his deacon, Abundius, at either Rome, Seville, or Spoleto. F. D. Dec. 10.

CARPOPHORUS, ST. (d. 303?), martyr. *See* Fidelis, St.

CARPOPHORUS, ST. (d. 305?), martyr. He and SS. Severus, Severian, and Victorinus, called "the four crowned martyrs," died at Albano, Italy. There is considerable confusion between their names and martyrdom and those of the group associated with St. Castorius. F. D. Nov. 8.

CARPUS, ST. (1st century). He was the resident of Troas on the Hellespont with whom St. Paul left his cloak (II Tim. 4:13); some Greek writers list him as a bishop. F. D. Oct. 13.

CARPUS, ST. (2nd or 3rd century), bishop and martyr. He refused to sacrifice to idols at his see of Thyateira, Lydia, and was tortured and burned to death at Pergamos during the persecution of Marcus Aurelius or of Decius. Papylus, a deacon, his sister Agathonice, their servant Agathadorus, and others were put to death with him. F. D. Apr. 13.

CARR, JAMES (1826–1913), educator. Born in Preston, England, he studied at Ushaw, was ordained in 1850, established schools in Liverpool and on the Isle of Man, and labored there and in small parishes. In 1880 he became diocesan inspector for training schools in England and Scotland, wrote several texts, and was made a monsignor. He was president of St. Edward's College, Liverpool, from 1885 to 1895 and vicar general of the diocese. He died in Formby, England, on Nov. 9.

CARRACCI, AGOSTINO (1557–1602), painter. Born in Bologna, Italy, on Aug. 16, son of a tailor, he became a goldsmith, then studied painting under Fontana and Passerotti. He was influenced by Correggio, went with his brother

Annibale to Parma and Venice, became friendly with Tintoretto, studied engraving under Cort, then returned to Bologna with Annibale and joined his uncle Lodovico in working and teaching art there. In their joint labors, the design and composition were Agostino's; the execution, the others'. He completed *Last Communion of St. Jerome*, *Adulteress before Christ*, *Hercules and Atlas*, portraits of Duke Ranuccio, and, for the Farnese palace, *Triumph of Galatea* and *Rape of Cephalus*. He also did numerous frescoes and was a poet of some note. He died at the Capuchin monastery in Parma, Italy, Mar. 22, after a fit of apoplexy.

CARRACCI, ANNIBALE (1560–1609), painter. Born in Bologna on Nov. 3, he studied under his uncle Lodovico and at Parma and Venice. In 1589 he returned to Bologna and helped to found the Academy of the Desiderosi with his brother and Lodovico. In 1600 he went to Rome with Agostino to decorate the palace of Cardinal Farnese; their work was highly praised by Nicholas Poussin and Sir Joshua Reynolds. After a quarrel a year later, Agostino left Rome. Outstanding paintings are *The Three Maries*, *Holy Family*, *Christ and the Woman of Samaria*, *Resurrection*, *Assumption*, *Pietà*, and a self-portrait. Annibale died in Rome on July 15.

CARRACCI, ANTONIO MARZIALE (1583–1618), painter. Son of Agostino, he was born in Venice, Italy, studied under his father and uncle, went to Rome with Annibale, to whom he was devoted, and decorated the chapel of Cardinal Tonti and that of St. Charles Borromeo. He died in Rome.

CARRACCI, FRANCESCO (1595–1622), painter. Son of Giovanni Antonio Carracci, he was born in Bologna, Italy, studied under Lodovico at the latter's school there, and broke away to found what he called the "True School of the Carracci." When this proved a failure, he went to Rome, tried again, but died in poverty.

CARRACCI, LODOVICO (1555–1622), painter. Born in Bologna, Italy, he was a tailor who slowly developed competence in art, traveled to study great paintings, and returned to Bologna to found in 1589 an academy with his two nephews. Among their pupils were Albani, Bonzi, Domenichino, Guido Reni, and Spada. His works include *Ecce Homo*, *Miracle of the Loaves and Fishes*, *Sermon of John the Baptist*, *Conversion of St. Paul*, *Burial of Mary*, and *Hercules Encouraged by Virtue*. He was the founder of the eclectic school of Italian art, which sought to blend the best features of Correggio, Michelangelo, Raphael, and Titian, but his nephew Agostino developed the theory. Gradually, they admitted the need of being more individual in their work. Lodovico's paintings have more virility and pathos, but less power and coloring, than those of his nephews. He died in Bologna on Nov. 13.

CARRANZA, BARTOLOMÉ (1503–1576) bishop. Born in Miranda de Arge, Navarre, Spain, he became a Dominican in 1520, studied at Salamanca, and taught there and at Valladolid. He was appointed censor by the Inquisition, held posts within his order, and went to the Council of Trent (1545–47) as imperial theologian. He was active in discussions on the sacraments, proposed reforms, and twice refused bishoprics which Charles V offered him. He became provincial on his return to Spain, attended the council reconvened in Trent (1550–52), served as royal almoner, and was in England from 1554 to 1557, in advance of the marriage of Prince Philip and Queen Mary. Returning, he was made archbishop of Toledo and consecrated in 1558 at Brussels. A rumor arose that he had led the late king of Spain into heresy; his catechetical commentary and other documents were declared suspect, fellow Dominicans censured him, and in 1558 King Philip II imprisoned him for a hearing before the Inquisition. The investigation dragged on for nine years; in 1567 the trial was transferred to Rome, where, after another nine years, he was condemned for Lutheran leanings. He abjured the suspect statements, but maintained that he had always been faithful and had not knowingly promulgated heresy. He was sentenced to five years of penance in Rome, but died a month later, on May 2. Pope Gregory XIII allowed a monument with an honorary inscription to be erected over his grave.

CARRANZA, DIEGO (b. 1559), missioner. Born in Mexico, he became a Dominican in 1577, worked with the Chontal Indians, living with them in their villages and preparing several works in their language. He died at Tehuantepec, of leprosy, when quite young.

CARREL, ALEXIS (1873–1944), physician. Born in Ste. Foy les Lyon, France, on June 28, he took his medical degree at Lyon, served in hospitals there, and taught at its university. He experimented almost from the beginning of his career: discovering new ways of sewing the ends of arteries while at the Hull laboratory in Chicago, Illinois, for suturing blood vessels and transplanting organs, for which he won the Nobel Prize in 1912. He did cancer research, and created an antiseptic which saved many with infected wounds in World War I. He had served on the staff of the Rockefeller Institute for Research in New York from 1905, served with the French army in 1914–19 (his wife, Anne de la Motte drove an ambulance), and was decorated. He developed the beginnings of an artificial heart pump with Charles Lindbergh in 1934, wrote *Man the Unknown* in 1935, retired from his Rockefeller post in 1939, and went to Europe to study the effects of malnutrition on children, went to Spain, and became a convert two weeks before his death on Nov. 5 in Paris.

CARRELL, GEORGE ALOYSIUS (1803–1868), bishop. Born in Philadelphia, on June 13, he studied at Mt. St. Mary's, Maryland, and Georgetown, was ordained in 1827, engaged in pastoral work in Philadelphia, joined the Jesuits in 1835, and became rector of St. Francis Xavier church in St. Louis. He was appointed first bishop of Covington, Kentucky, in 1853, and during his fifteen years' bishopric tripled the Catholic populace in his see. He died there on Sept. 25.

CARRENO DE MIRANDA, JUAN (1614–1685), painter. Born in Avilés, Asturia, Spain, he set up his own studio at twenty, was approved by Velásquez, and in 1660 was appointed court painter. He painted numerous portraits, imitated Velásquez closely, and with Francisco Ricci completed *Magdalen in the Desert*. He died in Madrid.

CARRERI, BL. GIOVANNI FRANCESCO (d. 1470). Born in Mantua, Italy, he became a successful Dominican preacher, widely known as Matthew of Mantua. He was an advocate of strict observance in his order and was devoted to the Passion. He died in Vigevana on Oct. 5; Pope Sixtus IV allowed his cult a few years later. F. D. Oct. 7.

CARRIÈRE, JOSEPH (1795–1864), theologian. Born in Le Panouze de Cernon, France, he was ordained a Sulpician in 1817, taught theology, and while visiting the United States took part in the first Provincial Council at Baltimore, Maryland, in 1829. He wrote on marriage, law, and theology in relation to the Napoleonic Code, and was an opponent of Lamennais. From 1850 until his death in Lyons, France, on Apr. 23 he was thirteenth superior of the Society of St. Sulpice.

CARRIÉRES, LOUIS DE (1622–1717). Born in Avrillé, Angers, France, on Sept. 1, he became an Oratorian and wrote an elaborate biblical commentary in twenty-four volumes. Highly praised by Bossuet, it contains a number of errors and since-abandoned opinions, but appeared in later and corrected versions.

CARRILLO, ALONSO (15th century). Archbishop of Toledo, he was given papal approval in 1459 for establishing professorships in the proposed University of Alcalá in Spain.

CARROLL, CHARLES (1703–1783). Son of Charles Carroll, who left Ireland in 1688 to escape persecution of Catholics and became attorney general under the third Lord Baltimore, Charles Carroll of Annapolis held important posts in Maryland, actively opposed the laws against Catholics in the royal colony, became a wealthy landowner, and married Elizabeth Brooke. Their son was Charles Carroll of Carrollton, the statesman.

CARROLL, CHARLES (1737–1832), senator. Born in Annapolis, Maryland, on Sept. 19, he studied in Maryland, went abroad with his cousin John to St. Omer's for six years, and then to Rheims, Paris, and Bourgos. He resided in London for several years and studied law, then returned to America in 1765 to take over an estate at Carrollton, Maryland. In 1770 he wrote in the *Maryland Gazette* against royal taxation without representation; four years later he was elected to the provincial convention, although Catholics had been disenfranchised. In 1775 he served on the committee which formed the Association of the Freeman of the colony; later, on committees to arm the state, manufacture gunpowder, and seek aid from Canada. By his efforts he swung a hostile Maryland government to approve the move toward independence supported by the Continental Congress. He was elected to that Congress in 1776 and signed the Declaration of Independence. At that time he was one of the wealthiest men in America, and thus risked much. He was a member of the war board, was one of seven delegates appointed to draw up the state constitution, and in 1778 resigned from Congress to become a member of the state senate. He served twice as its president, and in 1789 was elected United States senator from Maryland, favoring the tariff, Hamilton's financial measures, the strengthening of the national government, and helped to revise the senate journal. In 1792, when law made it impossible to hold two posts at the same time, Carroll resigned from the senate to serve his state, remaining in its senate until 1801. His last years were spent in political retirement, though he continued to comment on public events, opposing the second war with Britain in 1815. He died near Baltimore on Nov. 14.

CARROLL, DANIEL (1733–1829), congressman. Born in Upper Marlboro, Maryland, brother of Archbishop John Carroll, he was a quiet country gentleman until he became active in the revolution. He served as a member of the Continental Congress from 1780 to 1784, was a delegate to the Constitutional Convention in Philadelphia in 1789, and fought the anti-Federalist Samuel Chase, who opposed Maryland's adoption of the Constitution. He was a member of the national Congress from 1789 to 1791 and one of three commissioners appointed to lay out the site of the capital in Washington; Carroll himself donated a quarter of the land for the capital, where he died.

CARROLL, HOWARD JOSEPH (1902–1960), bishop. Born in Pittsburgh, Pennsylvania on Aug. 5, he studied at Duquesne and St. Vincent's, Pennsylvania, and at Fribourg, Switzerland, where he was ordained in 1927.

He was stationed in Pittsburgh from 1928 to 1938, and taught philosophy at Mt. Mercy College there in 1930–38. He went to Washington as assistant general secretary of the National Catholic Welfare Conference, of which he became general secretary in 1944; he also was secretary to the board of trustees of the National Catholic Community Service. He became a papal chamberlain in 1942, a domestic prelate in 1945, and was named bishop of Altoona, Pennsylvania, in 1957. He built the cathedral of the Blessed Sacrament there and died in Washington, D.C., on Mar. 21.

CARROLL, JOHN (1735–1815), archbishop. Born in Upper Marlboro, Maryland, on Jan. 8, he studied at St. Omer, France, became a Jesuit in 1753, studied at Liège, Belgium, and was ordained in 1769. He taught in Flanders for four years, was chaplain to Lord Arundel in England, and returned to Maryland when the Jesuits were papally suppressed in 1773. He built a mission church at his mother's house in Rock Creek, served the Catholic population of the area and of nearby Virginia, and in 1776 went to Canada with Benjamin Franklin on a futile mission to secure Canadian neutrality. In 1783 he and several other priests banded together and appealed to Rome for permission to continue their mission work in the state and to work under some sort of superior chosen from among them. This led to Carroll's appointment as superior of the missions of the thirteen states, with power to confirm. In 1784 he wrote *An Address to the Roman Catholics of the United States of North America* in reply to the anti-Catholic attacks of Charles Wharton, a distant relative and ex-Jesuit; his pamphlet, published in Annapolis, was the first work published by an American Catholic in the United States. In 1786, Fr. Carroll took up residence in Baltimore, became a popular figure, head of the Library Company and of the trustees of Baltimore College, a trustee of St. John's College, Annapolis, and a co-founder of Georgetown College (1791) and the Maryland Historical Society. He made frequent recommendations to the federal Congress on the question of religious liberty. In 1789 he was appointed the first American bishop, and the first see was established in Baltimore. He held a synod in 1791, invited the Sulpicians to the city to open a seminary, and recommended to Washington bills for the religious training of Indians and the appointment of Catholic chaplains among them. In 1808 he was raised to archbishop and held the first Provincial Council in 1810. He died in Baltimore on Dec. 3.

PETER GUILDAY, *The Life and Times of John Carroll* (Westminster, Md., Newman, 1954).

CARROLL, JOHN PATRICK (1864–1925), bishop. Born in Dubuque, Iowa, on Feb. 22, he studied at St. Joseph's there and Grand seminary, Montreal, and was ordained in 1886. He became a professor at St. Joseph's, was appointed its president in 1894, was named a domestic prelate in 1902, and in 1904 bishop of Helena, Montana. He died in Fribourg, Switzerland, on Nov. 1.

CARSON, CHRISTOPHER (1809–1868), general. Kit Carson was born in Madison County, Kentucky, on Dec. 24, was taken to Missouri when young, and was a saddler's apprentice, hunter, and trapper. He made two trips to California and Idaho before he became scout on Frémont's expeditions of 1842, 1843–44, and 1845–46. In 1853 he led a herd of 6500 sheep to California; in the next year he became Indian agent among the Utes at Taos, New Mexico. He was illiterate until his last few years and dictated his autobiography (1858) to Lt. Col. De Witt C. Peters. During the Civil War he served in the southwest area, particularly against the Apaches and Navahos, and was breveted a brigadier general in 1865. He died on May 23 in Boggsville, Colorado.

CARTER, WILLIAM (d. 1581), martyr. He was an assistant to Bl. Stephen Brinkley in running the underground printing plant at Eastham and Henley, England, during the Elizabethan persecution, and was captured shortly after the seizure of Edmund Campion and beheaded at Tyburn.

CARTERIUS, ST. (d. 304). A priest at Caesarea in Cappadocia, he was put to death during the Diocletian persecution. F. D. Jan. 8.

CARTERIUS, ST. (d. 315?), martyr. *See* Agapius, St.

CARTHACH, ST. (d. 637?), bishop. A young follower of St. Carthach the Elder, and presumably named Cuda, he was born in Castlemaine in Kerry, Ireland, was ordained, became a hermit, and about 595 the abbot of Rahan, directing some 800 monks. For them he drew up a rule, in rhyme, a later version of which has survived. After forty years, during which he also was bishop of Fircall, he and his community were ousted by a local chieftain. In his last two years he established what was to be the monastic school of Lismore and founded its diocese. He is also known as Carthage and Mochuda. His cult was confirmed in 1903. F. D. May 14.

CARTHAGE, ST. (d. 540?), bishop. Known as Carthage or Carthach the Elder, he succeeded St. Kieran as bishop of Ossory, Ireland. F. D. Mar. 5.

CARTIER, GEORGES ÉTIENNE (1814–1873), premier. Born in St. Antoine, Quebec, Canada, on Sept. 16, he studied at Montreal, fought during the Canadian rebellion of 1837–38, fled to the United States, and returned to practice law in Montreal. In 1848 he was elected a member of the assembly on the Con-

servative ticket; in 1856, provincial secretary; premier of Canada in 1858 and 1864; and four times attorney general. After the confederation of Upper and Lower Canada in 1867 he was minister of militia. He was active in supporting railroad building, establishing normal schools, abolishing seignorial tenure, codifying the laws, safeguarding minority rights, framing a constitution for Manitoba, acquiring the Northwest Territory, and bringing British Columbia into the union. He was made a baronet in 1868, went to England in poor health, and died in London on May 20.

CARTIER, JACQUES (1491–1557), explorer. Born in St. Malo, Brittany, he may have accompanied expeditions to Brazil and Newfoundland before he offered his services to Admiral Philippe de Chabot to investigate a northern route to China. Cartier sailed from Brittany in 1634 with two small ships, explored Newfoundland, Labrador, Prince Edward Island, and the Gaspé basin where he landed and claimed the country for France. A year later he returned with three ships, sailed up the St. Lawrence to Montreal, wintered at Quebec, and reported to the French king in May 1636. In 1641, Cartier went back, founded Charlesbourg, failed to meet Sieur de Roberval, the newly appointed governor, who waited off Newfoundland, and was allowed, after a delayed meeting, to return to France. Of a fourth voyage, in 1643 to rescue Roberval, no details are known. The king gave Cartier a manor at Limoilou, near St. Malo, France, to which he retired and where he died on Sept. 1. Cartier's explorations were of major geographical importance and formed the basis for France's claims to North America.

CARTON DE WIART, HENRI (1869–1951), premier. Born in Belgium, he entered government service, was elected to the chamber of deputies in 1895, was minister of justice in 1911–18, and prime minister in 1920–21. He served as permanent Belgian representative to the League of Nations, was chairman of the Inter-Parliamentary Union, and is said to have influenced King Leopold not to abdicate in 1946. He became a member of the cabinet in 1946, was minister of justice in 1950, arranged the transfer of the crown to Prince Baudouin, and was a leader of the Catholic party. He died in Brussels on May 6.

CARUCCI, JACOPO (1494–1557), painter. Born in Pontormo, Italy, he was a pupil of Leonardo da Vinci, Albertinelli, Piero di Cosmo, and Andrea del Sarto, and became heavily influenced by Dürer and Michelangelo. He did a *Visitation* for the Annunciation, and *Deposition* for Santa Felicità, both in Florence; a decorative lunette at Poggio a Caiano; and portraits of *Cosimo de' Medici, Lady with Dog,* and other figures. He is also known as Jacopo da Pontormo.

CARUSO, ENRICO (1873–1921). Born in Naples, Italy, on Feb. 25, he studied under Guglielmo Vergine, made his debut at Caserte in 1895 in *L'Amico Francesco*, and achieved his first great success at the Fondo Theater in Naples in 1896 in *La Traviata, La Favorita*, and *La Gioconda*. His voice, outstanding for its power and his control of it, and his dramatic skill brought him world renown. He appeared in operas throughout Europe and North and South America, and was the leading tenor of the Metropolitan Opera in New York in 1903–21. His extensive repertoire was in French and Italian operas exclusively and his appearance in *Aïda, Pagliacci, Rigoletto, Samson and Delilah*, and *La Bohème* highlighted the opera season. He died in Naples on Aug. 2.

CARVAJAL, BERNARDINO LOPEZ DE (1455–1523), cardinal. Born in Plasencia, Estremadura, Spain, he went to Rome and advanced rapidly in Church positions. Pope Innocent VIII made him bishop of Astorga in 1488, of Badajoz in 1489, of Cartagena, and papal nuncio. Spain made him ambassador to Pope Alexander VI, and he became a cardinal in 1493. He twice served as papal legate to the imperial court, was governor of Campagna, Italy, became bishop of Siguenza in 1503, and from 1507 to 1509 was cardinal-bishop of Albano, Frascati, Palestrina, and Santa Sabina in turn. Although a good theologian and effective speaker, he loved splendor, power, and wealth; his ambition led to rebellious support of the excommunicated Louis XII of France and his leadership at the schismatical Council of Pisa in 1511. Some claim that he became antipope Martin VI when that council was transferred to Milan, but he is not so listed in current catalogues. Pope Julius II excommunicated him, but he formally renounced his errors in 1513 and was restored to office by Pope Leo X. He then was made cardinal-bishop of Ostia. He lived in Rome under eight popes and died there on Dec. 16.

CARVAJAL, GASPAR DE (1500?–1584), missioner. Born in Estremadura, Spain, he became a Dominican, went to Peru in 1533, and worked with the Indians. In 1540 he accompanied the expedition of Gonzalo Pizzaro up the Amazon River, of which only eighty out of 400 returned, served on the Tucaman mission, and became provincial in 1557. He died in Lima, Peru.

CARVAJAL, JUAN (1400?–1469), cardinal. Born in Truxillo, Estremadura, Spain, he took his degree in canon and civil law and rose to high position in Rome, where he became auditor of the rota and governor of the city. He served as papal legate on more than twenty occasions, was successful in working with Cardinal Nicholas of Cusa in ending the quarrel of the German princes with Pope Eugene IV and ar-

ranging concordats in 1447 and 1448. He was made a cardinal in 1446. Although he was unsuccessful with the Hussites in Bohemia, he preached a crusade in Hungary in 1455 and was in that country for six years as it withstood Turkish attacks from Constantinople. With St. John of Capistrano, he raised an army of 40,000 men, joined forces with John Hunyady, and raised the siege of Belgrade in 1456. He also made peace between King Ladislaus and Emperor Frederick III, and among quarreling Magyar nobles. He returned to Rome in 1461 in poor health and was made cardinal-bishop of Porto and Santa Rufina. He helped to plan in 1464 a forthcoming crusade and was appointed to serve as papal legate to Venice in 1466. He long had been bishop of Plasencia, Spain, built a college at Salamanca, brought Basle and Constance back into friendship with Rome, and was internationally respected as a churchman unspoiled by the pride of the Renaissance world. He died in Rome on Dec. 6.

CARVAJAL, LUIS DE (b. 1500?), theologian. Born in Baetica, Spain, he was ordained a Franciscan and taught at Paris, and, sent to the Council of Trent as legate of Cardinal Angelus, discussed original sin and defended the doctrine of the Immaculate Conception, on which he later wrote. Other works include a defense of the religious orders against Erasmus and a study of theology.

CARVAJAL, LUISA DE (1568–1614). Born in Jaraizejo, Spain, on Jan. 2, she was orphaned at six, brought up by an uncle and aunt at Pampluna, and on their death about 1592 joined a group of young women devoted to a life of prayer, but not under spiritual rule. In 1604 their Jesuit adviser allowed them to go to England, where they set up a similar home, ministered to imprisoned Catholics, and guided converts. She was twice in prison, released through the Spanish embassy, and about to be banished when she died in London on Jan. 2.

CARVALHO, BL. DIEGO (1578–1624), martyr. Born in Coimbra, Portugal, he became a Jesuit in 1594, went to the Orient in 1600, was ordained on Macao, and served in the missions near Kyoto, Japan, from 1609 to 1614, when persecution began. He seems to have been transferred to Cochin China for three years, but returned and was the first to say mass on Hokkaido. He and his group of Christians were captured there the winter of 1623, stripped of their clothes, and driven across the island to Sendai. Those who faltered were beheaded; the survivors were tied to stakes, in pits of freezing water. Most died quickly, but eight survived from Feb. 18 through Feb. 22. Fr. Carvalho was the last to die. He was beatified in 1867. F. D. Feb. 22.

CARVALHO, BL. VINCENZO (d. 1632),

martyr. Born in Alfama, near Lisbon, Portugal, he became an Augustinian, went to Mexico in 1621, and in 1623 was sent to Japan, where he was burned alive at Nagasaki. He was beatified in 1867. F. D. Sept. 3.

CARYLL, JOHN (1625–1711), poet. Born in West Harting, Sussex, England, son of John Caryll and the daughter of William, second Baron Petre, he studied at St. Omer and the English College in Rome. He wrote poems, translations of Ovid and Vergil, a tragedy (*The English Princess*, 1666), and a comedy (*Sir Solomon Single*, 1671). He was arrested, but released, during the Titus Oates Plot, was sent to Rome as King James II's representative to Pope Innocent XI, served as secretary to Queen Mary of Modena, and accompanied the English royal family from London to St. Germain after the revolution of 1688. His property was confiscated because of his allegiance to the Stuarts; he served King James III, the "Pretender," as secretary; wrote a prose translation of the Psalms in 1700; died on Sept. 4, and was buried in Paris. His nephew John Caryll redeemed his West Harting estate and is mentioned in Alexander Pope's *Rape of the Lock*.

CASAL, MANUEL AYRES DE (1754–1840), geographer. Born and ordained in Portugal, he settled in Goyaz, Brazil, traveling and compiling data for a two-volume geographical study of the area, sponsored by King John VI and published in 1817.

CASALI, GIOVANNI BATTISTA (1715–1792). Born in Rome, he was choirmaster of the church of St. John Lateran in Rome from 1759 until his death there. He wrote masses, motets, and opera, and was one of the last to compose for *a capella* voices.

CASANATA, GIROLAMO (1620–1700), cardinal. Born in Naples on July 13, he studied law there, entered orders, was made private chamberlain by Pope Innocent X, and governor of Sabina, Febriano, Ancona, and Camerino in turn. Pope Alexander VI sent him to Malta in 1658 as inquisitor; thereafter he held a series of important judicial and other posts at the Vatican. He was made cardinal-deacon in 1673 and cardinal-priest in 1686. Pope Innocent XII made him librarian of the Vatican in 1693. Although the curial labors on which he was engaged directly or indirectly fill 1125 manuscript volumes, the cardinal found time to maintain an interest in the arts and sciences, to be active as literary patron, and to amass a library of 25,000 which he left to the Dominican library at Santa Maria sopra Minerva, later called the Biblioteca Casanatatense and secularized in 1884. He died in Rome on Mar. 3.

CASANOVA, ST. PAOLO GERONIMO (1676–1751). Born in Porto Maurizio, Italy, son of a mariner, he attended the Roman College, became a Franciscan of the Strict Observ-

ance, taking the name Leonard, at Ponticelli in 1697, and was ordained in 1703. In 1709 he was sent to Florence and from there began to preach the Tuscan missions with exceptional success. He was particularly active in spreading devotion to the Blessed Sacrament, Sacred Heart, Immaculate Conception, and the Stations of the Cross. In 1744, Pope Benedict XIV sent him to preach in Corsica, but he was received more as a political enemy than as a missionary. He continued his preaching until his death at Rome. He wrote widely, including thirteen ascetical works. He was canonized in 1867. F. D. Nov. 26.

CASANOVA Y MARZOL, VINCENZO (1854–1930), cardinal. Born in Borja, Spain, he was ordained, made a bishop in 1907, archbishop of Granada in 1921, and a cardinal-priest in 1925. He died in Saragossa on Oct. 23.

CASAS, BARTOLOMÉ DE LAS (1474?–1566), missioner. Born in Seville, Spain, son of Franciscus Casas (who had gone on Columbus' second voyage), he studied law at Salamanca, gained the confidence of the governors of the Antilles, and made a trip to Cuba in 1502. Spain was disturbed, for economic reasons, about the decline of the Indian population in the New World, due to overwork and pestilence; replacement by Negro slave labor had been introduced in Venezuela as early as 1505. Las Casas developed a colony, but after hearing sermons by the Dominican Montesino freed his slaves, became a Dominican himself, and was ordained in 1510. He worked strenuously after 1514 for better human treatment of conquered peoples. He went to Spain to seek imperial aid, but Charles V was in Flanders and the court was hostile. Cardinal Ximines supported him and gave him the title Universal Protector of the Indians. In 1516, to aid colonization, Las Casas compromisingly approved the importation by each colonist of twelve Negro slaves to replace Indians who would be freed by the new laws. The concession was painfully unfortunate, and he sought to undo its results. He established a colony at Cumaná, Venezuela, in 1520, where the natives were experimentally placed under Church direction, but the settlement was destroyed by Indians during his absence and he retired to Cuba for eight years. He worked with natives in Mexico in 1531 and in Nicaragua in 1534, and returned to Spain in 1539 to serve as adviser to the Council of the Indies to 1544. As a result of its discussions the Spanish government promulgated new laws for the Indies in 1542 (amended in 1543–44); radical changes regarding the use of Indian labor were introduced; Las Casas contended that reforms did not go far enough; the settlers claimed that the concessions made brought economic ruin. He continued to speak boldly against the enemies of his plans, but alienated many by his intemperate language and unqualified charges. In 1544 he was named bishop of Chiapa, Mexico, and in 1547 resigned the see and retired to Atocha monastery in Madrid, where he died. He spoke out most angrily in favor of the Indians and against the Spanish in *Brévissima relación de la destruycion de las indias* (1552), often reprinted in Europe as proof of total Spanish guilt in the conquest of America, and in his *Historia de las indias,* publication of which was withheld until 1875.

CASDOE, ST. (d. 368), martyr. *See* Dadas, St.

CASEY, JOHN (1820–1891), mathematician. Born in Kilkenny, Cork, Ireland, on May 12, he was educated there and in Mitchelstown, and became headmaster of the central school in his native town. He was interested in mathematics, solved Poncelet's theorem geometrically, went to Trinity College on a scholarship, and from 1862 to 1873 taught in Kingstown. He was elected to the Royal Irish Academy in 1866, served on its council, and in 1873 was offered a chair in mathematics at Trinity College. Instead, he joined the faculty of the new Catholic University, taught there until 1881, then went to the faculty of University College. He won the Cunningham Medal of the Royal Irish Academy, was elected to scientific societies in England, Belgium, and France, and was honored by the Norwegian government, and received honorary degrees from Dublin and the Royal University of Ireland. He wrote texts on plane geometry and trigonometry and studies of cubic transformations, conic sections, and Euclidian problems. He died in Dublin on Jan. 3.

CASEY, TIMOTHY (1862–1931), archbishop. Born in Charlotte County, New Brunswick, Canada, on Feb. 20, he studied at St. Joseph's and Laval and was ordained in 1886. He did parish work in Fredericton, became titular bishop of Utina in 1899, bishop of St. John in 1901, and archbishop of Vancouver in 1912. He developed schools and charitable institutions, expanded his diocese, and died in Vancouver, on Oct. 5.

CASGRAIN, HENRI RAYMOND (1831–1904), author. Born in Rivière Ouelle, Quebec, on Sept. 16, he studied classics at the College of St. Anne, studied law, then theology, and was ordained in 1856. He taught in Quebec until 1873, gradually lost his sight, was elected president of the Royal Society of Canada in 1889, and died in Quebec on Feb. 2. His early narratives were romantic accounts of early settlers; he then wrote biographies of Chauveau, Crémazie, Garneau, and Gaspé, Marie de l'Incarnation, and Montcalm. His historical work treats of the Hôtel Dieu, the Acadians, and the Sulpicians. He edited the poems of Octave Crémazie and, with Abbé Laverdière, Desbarat's *Oeuvres de Champlain* and *Journal des Jesuites.* His most ambitious project, undertaken at the direction of the government of Quebec, was the collection of primary sources dealing with the English-French wars in Canada, *Documents de Lévis* (1888–95).

CASILDA, ST. (d. 1050?). Of a Moorish family, she was converted, became a hermit in the diocese of Burgos, Spain, and was widely venerated there and at Toledo after her death. F. D. Apr. 9.

CASIMIR I (1015–1058), king of Poland. Son of Mieszko II, he gained control of his rebellion-torn land in 1040 after a six-year interregnum, established law and order, had some success in uprooting idolatry, and was called "the Restorer."

CASIMIR II (d. 1194), king of Poland. Youngest son of Boleslav III, he fought his brother Mieszko for the throne, became king in 1177, and in 1180 gained from the Congress of Leczyka, in return for concessions to the aristocratic and ecclesiastical leaders, hereditary rights for his family.

CASIMIR III (1310–1370), king of Poland. Called "the Great," he succeeded his father, Ladislas III, in 1333. In 1344 he repelled a Tatar invasion and gained part of Russia. He restored internal order; aided agriculture and commerce; built cities, forts, and roads; codified laws (1347) to aid the peasants and established a supreme court; developed education, founding the University of Cracow in 1364; and invited the Jews to seek refuge in the kingdom. Seven religious orders of men built and staffed schools and libraries, hospitals and asylums; the Cistercians made particular contributions to farming and forestry. Five orders of nuns devoted themselves to the education of girls, who proved to be more interested in learning than did the laymen. Casimir strengthened the power of the crown at the expense of the nobles, and quieted the Teutonic Knights by giving them Pomerania. The Piast dynasty ended with his death on Nov. 5.

CASIMIR IV JAGELLON (d. 1492), king of Poland. Son of Ladislas II and brother of Ladislas VI whom he succeeded as king in 1447 after a three-year interregnum, he gained support from the gentry by approving the demand that no laws be passed or wars declared without their consent, and lessened the strength of the higher nobility and the clergy (by assuming the power of investiture). He fought and defeated the Teutonic Knights (1454–66), winning access to the Baltic and much Prussian territory by the Treaty of Thorn, by which the military order became a Polish vassal.

CASIMIR OF POLAND, ST. (1458?–1483?). Third of thirteen children of King Casimir IV of Poland and Elizabeth of Austria, he followed an ascetic regimen in youth, and refused at fifteen to lead an army against Hungary as his father had ordered, which resulted in his imprisonment. His few remaining years were devoted to study and prayer. F. D. Mar. 4.

CASOT, JEAN JACQUES (1728–1800). Born in Liège, Belgium, on Oct. 4, he became a Jesuit laybrother in 1753 at Paris, went to Quebec, Canada, in 1756, was ordained, and was the last Jesuit in Canada when the British suppressed the Society there. On his death in Quebec on Mar. 16, the property of the Society was seized by the British crown.

CASPAR (1st century). *See* Balthasar.

CASSANDER, GEORGE (1513–1566), theologian. Born in Pittheim, Flanders, on Aug. 15, he graduated from Louvain in 1533, taught briefly at Bruges, traveled, and settled permanently at Cologne, where he died on Feb. 3. All his writings—liturgical, biblical, and polemical—are on the Index. In attempts to restore peace between religious factions he offended both sides and was attacked by Luther and by Bishop William Lindanus of Roermonde. He died in Cologne, Germany, on Feb. 3, probably in submission to the Church.

CASSANI, JOSEPH (1673–1750). Born in Madrid on Mar. 26, he became a Jesuit in 1686, was a founder of the Accademia de la Lengua Española in Madrid, compiled a six-volume Castilian dictionary, and wrote on astronomy, fortification, and the missions in Colombia.

CASSERLY, EUGENE (1822–1883), senator. Born in Ireland, son of Patrick S. Casserly (classical scholar and editor of the *Weekly Register* in New York, where he died), he graduated from Georgetown University, became a lawyer in New York, moved to San Francisco in 1850, and served as United States senator from California from 1869 to 1873, when he resigned to practice law. He died in San Francisco on June 14.

CASSIAN, ST. (d. 298?), martyr. A stenographer at the trial of St. Marcellus in Tangier, he denounced the injustice of the court, embraced Christianity, and was put to death. He is praised by Prudentius. F. D. Dec. 3.

CASSIAN, ST. (d. 340?). He was bishop of Benevento, Italy. F. D. Aug. 12.

CASSIAN, ST. (d. 350?). Probably an Egyptian, he went to Gaul, where he succeeded St. Reticius as bishop of Autun. F. D. Aug. 5.

CASSIAN, ST. (4th century), bishop and martyr. He was converted by Bishop St. Pontian of Todi, Italy, whom he succeeded as bishop, and was put to death during the reign of Maximian. F. D. Aug. 13.

CASSIAN. *See* John Cassian.

CASSIDY, JAMES EDWIN (1869–1951), bishop. Born in Woonsocket, Rhode Island, on Aug. 1, he studied at St. Charles College, St. Mary's seminary, and Johns Hopkins, all in Maryland, and was ordained in 1898. He taught at St. Joseph's seminary, Yonkers, New York, in 1896–99, did pastoral work in Massachusetts, was appointed vicar general of Fall River in 1909, and was consecrated titular bishop of Ibora and auxiliary of Fall River in 1930. He was appointed administrator of the see in 1930, and succeeded to the see in 1934, two weeks after he was made coadjutor. He died on May 17.

CASSINI, GIOVANNI DOMENICO (1625–1712), astronomer. Born in Perinaldo, Italy, on June 8, he studied at Vallebone and Genoa, and became interested in astronomy. In 1644 he helped Marquis Malvasia build an observatory at Bologna, accepted the chair of astronomy at the university there in 1650, served on a papal commission to end a dispute between Bologna and Ferrara over navigation and river rights, and became inspector of waterways. In 1669, on loan from the Vatican, Cassini went to Paris, and never returned. An observatory was built under his direction, and he trained many astronomers, including the Jesuit scholars who went to China. He calculated the rotation periods of Jupiter, Venus, and partly of Mars; discovered four satellites of Saturn; developed a theory of the motion of comets; systematically observed zodiacal light; and improved the gnomon and meridian for the purpose of fixing the solstices and reforming the calendar. Besides his astronomical writings, he suggested to the Jesuit Riccioli that the Immaculate Conception should receive more attention and be venerated on a special feast. Cassini became totally blind in 1711 and died in Paris on Sept. 14. Jacques (1677–1756) succeeded his father as director of the Paris Observatory in 1712. The position passed to his son, César François, who began a topographical map of France. This was completed by the latter's son, Jacques Domenique, the fourth Cassini in succession to hold the post of royal astronomer. He completed his father's map in 1789 but was imprisoned during the French Revolution.

CASSIO, PAMENO. *See* Cordara, Giulio.

CASSIODORUS SENATOR, FLAVIUS MAGNUS AURELIUS (490?–583). Born in Squillace, southern Italy, he was a councilor in 501, quaestor before 511, governor of Lucania and Brutium, and consul in 514. He was an adviser to Theodoric and the subsequent regent, Amalaswintha. Soon after the latter was slain by the man he had made king, Theodahadus, Cassiodorus retired from public life to his private estate, where he erected a monastery. During his public career he wrote panegyrics and formal speeches, a composite of historical chronicles, a *History of the Goths*, and a collection of letters, *Variae*, disappointingly avoiding all specific reference to the turbulent events of his day. Before 540 he wrote *De anima,* heavily influenced by St. Augustine; the latter also affected his seven-year study of the Psalms. He made translations and compilations, generally careless, though later popular (particularly the error-filled *Historia tripartita,* based on Theodoret, Sozomen, and Socrates). His most important work is *Institutiones divinarum et saecularium litterarum,* written between 543 and 555. This is an elaborate plan of study, intended for monks, and demanding detailed attention to scripture and the Fathers of the Church, under a liberal-arts program which commented on grammar, rhetoric, dialectic, mathematics, music, astronomy, and other sciences. His *Institutiones musicae* is of value for information on early instruments, the ancient tradition of rhythmic chant, and Greek theories as expounded by the Roman critic Albinus, whose original work is lost. He died in Squillace.

CASSIUS, ST. (d. 260), martyr. He, Maximus, Victorinus, and other Christians were put to death at Clermont in Gaul by the invading Teuton barbarians. F. D. May 15.

CASSIUS, ST. (d. 267?), martyr. *See* Anatolianus, St.

CASSIUS, ST. (d. 295?), martyr. *See* Carpophorus, St.

CASSIUS, ST. (d. 303), martyr. He was put to death with St. Florentius and others at Bonn, Germany, during the persecution of Maximian. F. D. Oct. 10.

CASSIUS, ST. (d. 558), bishop. He was highly praised by St. Gregory the Great for his generosity and devotion to the people of Narni, Italy, which he directed from 537 until his death. F. D. June 29.

CASSON, FRANÇOIS DOLLIER DE (1636–1701). Born near Nantes, France, he served as a captain under Marshal Turenne, entered the seminary of St. Sulpice, Paris, in 1657, and was sent to Canada in 1666. With Fr. Galinée, another Sulpician, he explored Lakes Erie and Ontario; in 1671 he became fourth superior of St. Sulpice, Montreal. He helped to develop the city, laid out its streets, began its canal, and wrote a history of its foundation and progress.

CASSULO, ANDREW (1869–1952), archbishop. Born in Castelletto D'Orba, Italy, he became archbishop and apostolic delegate to Turkey in 1947. He died in Istanbul on Jan. 9.

CASTAGNO, ANDREA DEL (1390–1457), painter. Born near Florence, he tended cattle, somehow became interested in art, completed some commissions by the Medici for their palace, and in 1454 was invited by Pope Nicholas V to decorate Vatican apartments. His most significant works are an equestrian portrait of Niccolò da Tolentino, a *Last Supper,* a *Crucifixion* in the realistic manner of Masaccio, and frescoes for the Villa Carducci, all in Florence; the last were transferred to the National Museum. He died in Florence on Aug. 9. The published story that he murdered Domenico Veneziano to become sole possessor of the art of painting in oil is a myth.

CASTAÑEDA, BL. HYACINTH (d. 1773), martyr. Born in Sétavo, Spain, he was ordained a Dominican and sent to the missions in China and Tonkin, where he was beheaded. He was beatified in 1906. F. D. Nov. 7.

CASTELLANOS, JUAN DE (16th century). Born in Spain, he went to South America as a cavalry officer before 1545, became a priest at Cartagena, Colombia, and wrote *Elegias de Varones,* an epic on the historical and ethnological history of the northern part of South America from the time of Columbus.

CASTELLET, BL. DOMINIC (1592–1628), martyr. Born in Esparraguera, Spain, he joined the Dominicans at Barcelona, was sent to the Japanese mission, where he became vicar provincial, and was burned to death at Nagasaki. Beheaded on the same day were John Tomaki, a Japanese layman and Dominican tertiary; Dominic Tomaki, his sixteen-year-old son, and three other sons; two other mission helpers and Dominican tertiaries, John Inamura and Louis Nifaki; and the latter's sons, Dominic, two, and Francis, five. They were beatified in 1867. F. D. Sept. 8 (also, June 1).

CASTELLI, BENEDETTO (1577–1644), physicist. Born in Perugia, Italy, he became a Benedictine at Monte Cassino, became interested in mathematics and hydraulics, studied under Galileo, and taught Toricelli. In 1623, Urban VII made him papal mathematician and professor at the University of Rome. He wrote on drainage, flood control, currents, and is credited by some with the invention of the helioscope. He died in Rome.

CASTELLI, PIETRO (1574–1662), scientist. Born in Rome, he studied under Andrea Cesalpino, taught at Rome and Messina, laid out the botanical gardens in the latter city in 1635, and also became a distinguished chemist and surgeon. He pleaded for direct observation of the human body through dissection, and wrote more than 150 pamphlets on science, many on the use of medicinal plants. He died in Messina, Sicily.

CASTELLO, GIOVANNI BATTISTA (1509?–1579), painter. Born in Gandino, near Bergamo, Italy, he studied painting under Aurelio Busso of Crema, then in Genoa and Rome. He decorated the Genoa palace of his patron, Tobia Pallavicino, completed the *Martyrdom of St. Sebastian* for the monastery of St. Sebastian there, the ceiling of the Nunziata di Portoria, and ornamented the palace of the Pardo, Spain, with scenes from Ovid. He was made Charles V's royal architect and added decorations to the Escorial and other palaces. He died in Madrid.

CASTIGLIONE, BALDASARE (1478–1529). Born in Casatico, near Mantua, Italy, on Dec. 6, he studied at Milan, was attached to the courts of Ludovico il Moro at Milan, Francesco Gonzaga at Mantua, and Guidobaldo da Montefeltro at Urbino, in which last he spent most of his life after 1504. In 1513 he was made a count, and later an ambassador to the Vatican, by Guidobaldo's successor, Francesco Maria della Rovere. In 1524 he was sent by Pope Clement VII as envoy to Charles V to plead for the integrity of the city of Rome, but the mission failed, Rome was sacked in 1527, and the disaster is said to have hastened Castiglione's death in Toledo, Spain, on Feb. 7. He is particularly known for *Il cortegiano* (*The Courtier*), begun in 1514 and polished and restyled many times before its publication in 1528; it was a portrait of the ideal courtier of the Renaissance, describing his social, intellectual, and moral characteristics.

CASTIGLIONE, CARLO OTTAVIO (1784–1849). Born in Milan, Italy, he made a wide study of Indo-Germanic and Semitic languages, became interested in numismatics, and published studies of coins of the Mediterranean world which revealed much of its history. He edited a translation of fragments of the Gothic Bible of Ulfilas and wrote some unpublished linguistic studies. He died in Genoa on Apr. 10.

CASTIGLIONE, GIOVANNI BENEDETTO (1616–1670), painter. Born in Genoa, Italy, he made studies there of the work of Van Dyck and Rubens, traveled through Italy, and was subsidized by Charles II, duke of Mantua. He painted animals, portraits, historical and biblical subjects (*Nativity, Noah, Adoration of the Shepherds*), and was particularly fond of rural scenes, which he filled with the picturesque pastoralism of the Dutch school. He also was successful as an etcher. He died in Mantua, Italy.

CASTILHO, ANTONIO FELICIANO DE (1800–1875), poet. Born in Lisbon, Portugal, he was blind from the age of six, was educated by his brother, and published a translation of Ovid's *Metamorphoses* in 1841, followed by other classical translations and five volumes of original work. He also wrote a study of Portuguese versification.

CASTILLA, RAMÓN (1796–1867), president. Born in the province of Tarapaca, Peru, he entered military service in 1816 but in 1821 joined the movement for independence, became prefect of his native province, chief of staff of the army, and brigadier general. In 1837 and 1841 he fought against Bolivia. He was elected president of Peru in 1845 and placed the country on a firm economic basis, but his work was undone by his successor, Echenique. In the civil war that followed, in 1854, Castilla defeated Echenique, ruled alone from 1855 to 1858, then was elected president until 1862, when he resigned and became president of the senate. Castilla abolished slavery and the tribute paid to landed proprietors by Indians, reformed government finances, granted universal suffrage, encouraged railroad building, established Catholicism as the national religion, and wrote a new constitution. He died on May 30 near Tarapacá, Peru (now Chile).

CASTILLEJO, CRISTÓBAL DE (1491–1556), poet. Born in Ciudad Rodrigo, Salamanca, Spain, he was at fifteen a courtier with Ferdinand, younger brother of Emperor Charles V, lived in Austria as the latter's secretary, and late in life entered monastic life near Vienna, where he died on June 12. He was an exponent of the older Spanish meters, polish, and exactness of diction, and fought the influence of Italian poetry. He wrote on love, conversation, and religion; was successful as a satirist in his *Transformation of a Drunkard into a Mosquito*; and was censured by the Inquisition for his early *Sermon on Love* and other poems containing phrases construed as anti-clerical.

CASTILLO, BL. JUAN DE (d. 1628), martyr. *See* Gonzalez, Bl. Roque.

CASTLE, EGERTON (1858–1920), novelist. Born in London on Mar. 12, he studied at Cambridge, Paris, and Glasgow, served with the army engineering corps, wrote for the *Saturday Review*, two plays (*Saviolo* for Henry Irving and *Desperate Remedies* for Richard Mansfield), and jointly with his wife, Agnes Sweetman, several popular novels (*The Bath Comedy; Pamela Pounce*). He was captain of English fencing teams in the 1908 Olympic games and later wrote two books on fencing. He became a convert before his death in London on Sept. 16.

CASTNER, CASPAR (1655–1709), missioner. Born in Munich, Bavaria, on Oct. 7, he became a Jesuit in 1681, studied at Ingolstadt, taught at Ratisbon, and in 1696 was sent to China in charge of a missionary group. He brought a second group with him to the East in 1706 after a trip to Rome. He advised the Portuguese government on navigation routes, mapped large areas of the Chinese empire, and was made president of the mathematical tribunal and tutor to the heir to the Chinese throne. He erected a memorial to St. Francis Xavier at his death place, prepared many valuable maps, and wrote elaborate reports with Franciscus Noel on the question of Chinese rites. He died in Peking on Nov. 9.

CASTOR, ST. (d. 425?), bishop. A native of Nîmes, Gaul, he married a wealthy widow from Marseilles. They separated by mutual consent to enter religious life, and he became abbot-founder of the monastery of Mananque. He was later chosen bishop of Apt, but remained deeply interested in his monks and asked St. John Cassian to write *De institutis coenobiorum* for their guidance. F. D. Sept. 2.

CASTORIUS, ST. (d. 305?), martyr. He and SS. Claudius, Nicostratus, and Symphorian, called "the four crowned martyrs," were tortured and slain in Pannonia (Hungary) during the Diocletian persecution. A fifth martyr of the same time and place was later identified as St. Simplicianus. There is considerable confusion between their names and martyrdom and those of the group associated with St. Carpophorus. F. D. Nov. 8 (also, July 7).

CASTRANCE DEGLI ANTELMINELLI, FRANCESCO (1817–1899), naturalist. Born in Fano, Italy, on July 19, he studied and was ordained in Rome, was canon of the cathedral at Fano from 1844 to 1852, and then went to Rome to devote himself to biological studies. As early as 1862 he was successful with his photographs of objects under the microscope, made elaborate studies of the physiology and reproduction of microorganisms and discovered 225 new species. His research and published papers aided biologists, geologists, and hydrographers. He was president of the Accademia dei Nuovi Lincei for many years. He died in Rome on Mar. 27.

CASTRENSIS, ST. (5th century), bishop. *See* Priscus, St.

CASTRITIAN, ST. (d. 137). He was bishop of Milan, Italy, from the year 95 until his death. F. D. Dec. 1.

CASTRO, ALPHONSUS DE (1495–1558), theologian. Born in Zamora, León, Spain, he became a Friar Minor at fifteen, taught theology at Salamanca, and served for forty-three years as confessor and court preacher to Charles V and Philip II. He was active at the Council of Trent (1545) in the discussions on original sin and on the translation of scripture into the vernacular. He wrote against heresy and was named archbishop of Compostella, but died in Brussels on Feb. 11 before he was consecrated.

CASTRO ANDRADE Y PORTUGAL, PEDRO ANTONIO FERNÁNDEZ DE (1634–1672). The tenth count of Lemos and seventh marquis of Sarría, son of the patron of Cervantes, was appointed viceroy of Peru in 1667. He was stern in attempting to stop the lawless rivalry of silver-mine owners and on one occasion ordered the execution of forty-two hired outlaws. Thereafter he devoted himself to performing menial services and to spiritual austerity in expiation of his extreme measures, and died soon after, on Dec. 6.

CASTRO PALAO, FERNANDO (1581–1633), theologian. Born in León, Spain, he became a Jesuit at fifteen, taught at Valladolid, Compostella, and Salamanca, was rector at Medina, and served the Inquisition. St. Al-

phonsus admired him as a major moral theologian; he published a seven-volume work in this field and also a manual of meditation. He died in Medina, Spain, on Dec. 1.

CASTRO Y BELLVÍS, GUILLÉN DE (1569–1631), dramatist. Born in Valencia, Spain, he followed a military career, enjoyed the patronage of the duke of Osuna, but lost friends because of his sour disposition. In his last years he wrote plays for a living, some forty of which were published (1618–25) and two of which, *Las mocedades del Cid*, and *Las hazañas del Cid*, directly influenced Corneille. Castro was heavily influenced by Lope de Vega, used historical, chivalric, and mythological themes, and dramatized ballad and epic material and parts of *Don Quixote*. His output was quite uneven. He died in poverty at Madrid.

CASTULUS, ST. (d. 273), martyr. *See* Craton, St.

CASTULUS, ST. (d. 286), martyr. Chamberlain of Emperor Diocletian, he sheltered Christians in his own house and arranged for religious services inside the imperial palace. Because of his activity in bringing converts to Pope St. Caius to be baptized, he was captured, tortured, and put to death. F. D. Mar. 26.

CASTUS, ST. (d. 250), martyr. *See* Aemilius, St.

CASWALL, EDWARD (1814–1878), poet. Born in Yately, Hampshire, England, on July 15, where his father was vicar, he studied at Oxford, was ordained an Anglican minister in 1839, and was appointed curate at Stratford. He was attracted by the Oxford Movement, went to Rome, and was converted there by Cardinal Acton in 1847. After the death of his wife in 1849, he became an Oratorian, was ordained in 1852, and wrote several manuals of devotion, a translation of hymns from the breviary and missal, called *Lyra Catholica*, and a collection of original religious verse, *The Masque of Mary*, admired by Cardinal Newman. Caswell died in Birmingham, England on Jan. 2.

CATALANO, GIUSEPPE (18th century). A member of the Oratory of San Girolamo della Carità, he wrote a number of scholarly commentaries on the history and rubrics of the Roman liturgy, on the reading of gospels at mass, and on curial offices, and edited (1736–49) an important history of the ecumenical councils. In 1753 he published at Rome a new edition of Cardinal d'Aguirre's collection of Mexican and South American conciliar documents.

CATALDO, JOSEPH MARIA (1837–1928), missioner. Born in Terracina, Spain, on Mar. 17, he became a Jesuit in 1852, studied at Louvain, was ordained in 1862, and continued his studies at a Jesuit seminary in Massachusetts. He taught at Santa Clara in 1863–64, and in 1865 was sent as a missioner to the Indians of the Rocky Mountain region. He directed the Jesuit missions in the Pacific Northwest from 1877 to 1893, opened missions in Alaska in 1885, and in 1887 founded Gonzaga College in Spokane, Washington. He spent his last thirteen years with the Nez Percé Indians at St. Joseph's mission near Lewiston, Idaho. He died near Pendleton, Oregon, on Apr. 9.

CATALDUS. *See* Cathal, St.

CATELLUS, ST. (9th century). He was bishop of Castellammare, near Naples, and became its chief patron. F. D. Jan. 19.

CATENA, VINCENZO DI BIAGIO (1470?–1531?), painter. A pupil of Giovanni Bellini and influenced later by Giorgione, he was a highly regarded member of the Venetian school; his best works include *Knight Adoring the Christ Child, Christ Giving the Keys to St. Peter,* and *Martyrdom of St. Christina.*

CATHAL, ST. (d. 685?), bishop. Born in Munster, Ireland, this monk taught at Lismore, and on his return from a pilgrimage to Jerusalem was chosen to direct the see of Taranto, Italy, of which he is patron. He is also called Cataldus. F. D. May 10.

CATHARINE OF BRAGANZA (1638–1705), queen. Daughter of John IV of Portugal and Luisa de Guzman, she became an international pawn after her father's death and in 1662 Luisa married her to King Charles II of England. Spain tried to prevent the marriage; Portugal gave Tangier, Bombay, trade concessions, and £300,000, and merely gained a weak ally in England. Charles gave her slight attention, since he had a succession of mistresses, but protected her against anti-Catholic abuse at court. She lived in seclusion after his death in 1685, returned to Portugal in 1692, acted as regent for her brother, Don Pedro, and died suddenly on Dec. 31.

CATHARINE OF VALOIS (1401–1437), queen. Daughter of King Charles VI of France, she was married in 1420 to the conquering Henry V of England at Troyes, was crowned queen in 1421, and gave birth to the later Henry VI. Her husband died after two years of marriage, and she later married Owen Tudor, a Welsh tutor to her son. She died at Bermondsey abbey. Henry VII was her grandson in this line.

CATHERICK, BL. EDMUND (1605?–1642), martyr. Born in Lancashire or Yorkshire, England, he studied at Douai, was ordained, and was sent to the English mission about 1635. He served under the name Huddleston (possibly his mother's maiden name), was captured near Watlas, and hanged, drawn, and quartered in York with Fr. John Lockwood. He was beatified in 1929. F. D. Apr. 13.

CATHERINE (15th century), queen of Navarre. Daughter of Francis Phoebus (king from 1479 to 1483) and Madeleine of France, she was sought as a bride for Ferdinand II of Aragon, but married Jean d'Albret in 1494. When Navarre refused to join the Holy League against France, Ferdinand invaded in 1512, d'Albret fled, and Navarre came to an end as an independent nation as the Navarrese accepted the rule of Spain.

CATHERINE, ST. (4th century), martyr. Unreliable sources say she was born in Alexandria, Egypt, of a patrician family, was converted by a vision, rebuked Maxentius for his persecution of Christians, converted his wife and 200 of his soldiers, was sentenced to death on a spiked wheel, and beheaded when it broke down. Since she is reputed to have bested fifty philosophers during her trial, she is considered a patron of philosophers. F. D. Nov. 25.

CATHERINE OF ARAGON (1485–1536), queen. Daughter of Ferdinand and Isabella of Aragon and Castile, she was born in Spain on Dec. 15 and married by royal agreement to Arthur, son of King Henry VII of England, in Nov. 1501. When Arthur died in Apr. 1502, a betrothal was arranged with his twelve-year-old brother, Henry; papal dispensation was granted in 1504, and they were married in 1509 after he took the throne as Henry VIII. Popular hostility toward a Spanish queen during a period of English alliance with France and considerable disappointment that no male heir survived created some difficulties; they became serious when Henry took Anne Boleyn as his mistress. Attempts were made before 1527 to have the marriage declared null on the alleged grounds of marriage to a brother's widow; Cardinal Wolsey considered a collusive suit; the case went to Rome as a plea for divorce. Pope Clement VII did not act with speed; Henry put Catherine aside with the approval of his bishops and married Anne early in 1533; the king's new archbishop, Cranmer, later that year declared the marriage to Catherine void; the pope declared it valid in Mar. 1534. Queen Catherine lived under guard in Bedfordshire and Huntingdonshire until her death on Jan. 8 in Kimbolton castle, Huntingdonshire, England. She was a well-educated woman, a Latin scholar, directed her own daughter Mary's education, and remained steadfast and successful in parrying every effort of the king to induce her to sign away her name, reputation, and right of succession for Mary.

GARRETT MATTINGLY, *Catherine of Aragon* (Boston, Little, Brown, 1941).

CATHERINE OF CARDONA, BL. (1519–1577). Born in Naples, Italy, of a noble Spanish family, she left the court of King Philip II to become a recluse at Roda for twenty years, and then a Carmelite. F. D. May 21.

CATHERINE OF GENOA, ST. (1447–1510). Born in Genoa, Italy, to James Fieschi and Francesca di Negro, she was married at sixteen to Giuliano Adorno. For ten years, due to his profligacy and extravagances, the marriage was a failure; bankruptcy forced them into utter poverty and him into reform. Thereafter they devoted themselves to caring for the sick. In 1490, Catherine became matron of the hospital at Pommatone and served heroically through the violent plague of 1493. She continued to work with the sick and unfortunate. After Giuliano's death in 1497 she had many mystical experiences and wrote a treatise on purgatory and a *Dialogue between the Soul and the Body*. She died in Genoa, and was canonized in 1737 by Pope Benedict XIV. F. D. Sept. 15.

CATHERINE LABOURÉ, ST. (1806–1876). Daughter of a farmer, Zoé Labouré was born in Fain-les-Moutiers, France, on May 2. When her mother died, she became at eight the housekeeper of the family and was unable to attend school. She joined the Sisters of Charity of St. Vincent de Paul in 1830 and was sent to their convent in Paris. There in 1830–31 she experienced a series of visions of the Virgin Mary, in which Catherine was asked to have a medal made, honoring the Immaculate Conception. In 1832, with the permission of her confessor, Fr. Aladel, and Archbishop de Quelen of Paris, 1500 miraculous medals (as they are now known) were struck off. Catherine lived quietly at the Hospice d'Enghien, Paris, until her death there forty-five years later on Dec. 31. She was canonized in 1947. F. D. Nov. 28.

JOSEPH I. DIRVIN, *St. Catherine Labouré of the Miraculous Medal* (New York, Farrar, 1958).

CATHERINE OF PALLANZA, BL. (1437?–1478). Born in the diocese of Novara, Italy, she was orphaned by a plague when fourteen and became a recluse near Varese. There she lived a life of fasting and austerity for fifteen years, was joined by a number of other holy women, and became their prioress under the Augustinian rule. She was beatified in 1769. F. D. Apr. 6.

CATHERINE OF PARC-AUX-DAMES, BL. (13th century). Daughter of Jewish parents in Louvain, she was converted at seven by the chaplain of the duke of Brabant, and ran away from home to the nearby Cistercian abbey, where she later joined the community, changing her name from Rachel to Catherine. F. D. May 4.

CATHERINE DEI RICCI, ST. (1522–1590). Alexandrina dei Ricci was born in Florence, on Apr. 23, became a Dominican at the convent of St. Vincent in Prato when she was thirteen, taking the name Catherine, and filled various offices before she became mistress of novices and, at thirty, prioress. She possessed a number of supernatural gifts, including the stigmata and visions of the passion of Christ. She devoted herself to many hours of prayer and self-denial, was a most competent administrator, gave counsel to the many who came to her convent, and labored actively for the poor and sick of the area. She died in Prato, Italy, on Feb. 2, and was canonized in 1747. F. D. Feb. 13.

CATHERINE OF SIENA, ST. (1347–1380). Born in Siena on Mar. 25, youngest of twenty-five children of a dyer, she became a Dominican tertiary at sixteen, and three years later began to work in hospitals and with lepers. As a result of her spiritual insight and personal gaiety, a large group of young men became her followers. Scandalous charges against her were cleared by a Dominican chapter general at Florence and Bl. Raymund of Capua was appointed her chaplain. On her return she worked through a plague, continued to experience visions, and in 1375 received the stigmata. She served as peacemaker between Florence and Pope Gregory XI, going to Avignon for the purpose and suggesting that the pope return to Rome. On Gregory's death in 1378, Urban VI was chosen at Rome, but the French faction set up a rival at Avignon. She spent her remaining time trying to end the great Western schism, which was to last for seventy years, and was invited to Rome to advise Urban. Her writings include some 400 letters and the mystical *Dialogue*. She died in Rome on Apr. 29, was canonized in 1461, and made the patron of Italy in 1939. F. D. Apr. 30.

ALICE CURTAYNE, *Saint Catherine of Siena* (New York, Sheed, 1934); JOHANNES JORGENSEN, *St. Catherine of Siena* (New York, Longmans, 1938).

CATHERINE OF SWEDEN, ST. (1331–1381). The fourth of St. Bridget's eight children, she was born at Ulfasa, Sweden, in 1331 or 1332 and married Eggert von Kyren, with whom she lived in virginity. In 1350, a year before he died, she went to join her mother in Rome and shared her work there for twenty-five years. She then returned to Sweden, and built up the Bridgettine order at the convent in Vadstena, though she returned to Rome from 1375 to 1380 seeking papal approval of the rule and her mother's canonization. She died in Vadstena. F. D. Mar. 24.

CATHERINE DE VIGRI, ST. (1413–1463). Daughter of a lawyer in Bologna, she became at eleven a maid of honor to Margaret d'Este, with whom she was educated. At fourteen she became a Franciscan tertiary, then mistress of novices and later abbess of a community of Poor Clares. She kept a diary of her religious difficulties and supernatural experiences, wrote a verse reflection on the mysteries of the rosary, several hymns, and a treatise on spiritual strength, and drew a number of pictures, two of which are museum pieces. She was canonized in 1712. F. D. Mar. 9.

CATROU, FRANÇOIS (1659–1737), historian. Born in Paris, France, on Dec. 28, son of Mathurin Catrou, secretary to King Louis XIV, he became a Jesuit at eighteen, was a noted preacher for ten years after ordination, and in 1701 founded the *Journal de Trévoux*, on whose staff he served for twelve years. He wrote a history of the Mogul Empire, based on that of Domenico Occhi; a study of the Anabaptists and Quakers; a twenty-one-volume history of Rome, annotated by Fr. Rouillé; and a life of Vergil and somewhat free translation of the *Aeneid*. He died in Paris on Oct. 12.

CATTANI-AMADORI, FEDERICO (1856–1943), cardinal. Born in Marradi, Italy, on Apr. 17, he was ordained at twenty-three, served in his native province as vicar general, and was brought to Rome in 1906 for work with the poor at Opera Pia Amadori (hence his second surname). He was auditor of the rota in 1909–24, was named cardinal-deacon in 1935, served as secretary of the supreme tribunal of the Signatura, and died in Rome on Apr. 12.

CATUS, ST. (2nd century), martyr. He was put to death in Numidia, Africa, with SS. Germana, Gerontius, Januarius, Julius, Paul, Pia, Saturninus, and Successus. F. D. Jan. 19.

CAUCHY, AUGUSTIN LOUIS (1789–1857), mathematician. Born in Paris on Aug. 21, he studied there, served as an engineer in the elaborate public-works program sponsored by Napoleon, and was elected to the Academy of Sciences. From 1811 to 1830 he was professor of mathematics at L'École Polytechnique, which he had attended. He then joined Charles X in exile, held the chair of mathematical physics at Turin, was tutor to the king's grandson at Prague, for which service he was made a baron, and returned to France in 1838. His religion kept him out of academic office until 1848, when he was made a professor at the Sorbonne. He wrote several hundred articles and books; established rules for investigating the convergency of series; demonstrated the number of real and imaginary roots of equations; invented the calculus of residues; placed integral calculus on a logical basis; formulated the refractive index in terms of wave length; and was a pioneer in molecular mechanics and optics. He died in Sceaux, France, on May 23. His *Works* were published by the French government.

CAULET, FRANÇOIS ÉTIENNE (1610–1680), bishop. Born in Toulouse, France, he studied at La Flèche, helped M. Olier to found Vaurigard seminary and the Company of St. Sulpice, and succeeded him as rector in 1642. He was made bishop of Pamiers in 1644, developed schools, tried to reform the chapters at Foix and Pamiers, and encountered hostility which was crushed only by papal intervention on the bishop's behalf. He was one of the few bishops who in 1673 staunchly opposed attempts by King Louis XIV to appropriate church revenue and to fill empty sees. In 1668 he had difficulty with the Jesuits in his diocese over approbation for hearing confessions; he was attacked later, and charged with Jansenism, because of seeming reservations about the formulary of Alexander VII. Popes Clement IX and Innocent XI praised him, however. He died in Pamiers, France.

CAUN, BL. VINCENT (d. 1626), martyr. Born in Seoul, Korea, he was taken to Japan in 1591 as a prisoner of war, was converted, and became a Jesuit at the seminary of Arima. He served for thirty years as a catechist in China and Japan before he was burned alive at Nagasaki with Bl. Francis Pacheco. He was beatified in 1867. F. D. June 20.

CAUSSIN, NICHOLAS (1583–1651). Son of a physician, he was born in Troyes, France, became a Jesuit in 1609, and was invited by Richelieu to serve as spiritual adviser to young King Louis XIII. When Caussin advised the monarch to recall the queen mother, Marie de' Medici, and others of her faction from exile, the cardinal accused him of treason and had him banished to Brittany. He wrote *La Cour sainte*, five volumes of moral reflections; a life of St. Isabelle of France; a study of eloquence; and a thesaurus of Greek poetry. These were published when he returned to Paris after Richelieu's death in 1643; he himself died there on July 2.

CAVAGNIS, FELICE (1841–1906), cardinal. Born in Bordogna, Italy, on Jan. 13, he studied at the Pontifical seminary in Rome, was its professor of ecclesiastical law from 1880 to 1895, held a number of Vatican offices, served on several commissions, including that for codifying canon law, and was made a cardinal in 1901. Of his works, *Elements of Public Ecclesiastical Law* is most significant. He died in Rome on Dec. 29.

CAVALIERI, BONAVENTURA (1598–1647), mathematician. Born in Milan, Italy, he joined the Congregation of Hieronymites at fifteen, studied at Pisa, and worked under Castelli and Galileo. He was professor of mathematics at Bologna from 1629 until his death in that city on Dec. 3. In 1635 he published his method of the determination of areas and volumes which was a forerunner of integral calculus. He demonstrated the theorem of Pappus, popularized the use of logarithms, and wrote on geometry and trigonometry.

CAVANAGH, JAMES (1831–1901), general.

Born in Tipperary, Ireland, he went to New York at sixteen, became a carpenter, served with the 69th Regiment during the Civil War, rose from private to major, and was wounded at Fredericksburg. After his recovery he rejoined the regiment, reorganized in peacetime as the National Guard, and rose from lieutenant colonel to brigadier general. He retired from service in 1894 and became a customs inspector in New York City, where he died on Jan. 7.

CAVANILLES, ANTONIO (1805–1864), historian. Born in Corunna, Spain, he studied at Alcalá, became a jurist, was elected to the Royal Academy of History and the Royal Academy of Moral and Political Sciences, and wrote a *History of Spain* (1861–63) to the reign of Philip II.

CAVAZZI, GIOVANNI ANTONIO (d. 1692), missioner. Born in Montecucolo, Italy, he became a Capuchin friar at Bologna, was sent to the Congo in 1654, served there for a long period, and, on his recall, prepared an account of his experiences. This was edited and published by Fortunato da Bologna in 1687. Cavazzi died in Genoa, Italy.

CAVEDONI, CELESTINO (1795–1865), archaeologist. Born in Levizzano-Rangone, Italy, on May 18, he studied in the seminary at Modena and at the University of Bologna and was appointed custodian of the Numismatical Museum, Modena, and then city librarian there. He taught at its university, helped to edit the works of Bartolommeo Borghesi, and wrote on numismatics and archaeology and a refutation of Renan's life of Christ. He died in Modena, Italy, on Nov. 26.

CAVO, ANDRES (b. 1729), historian. Born in Guadalajara, Mexico, on Jan. 21, he became a Jesuit in 1758, served as a missioner in the northwestern area, and went to Italy when the Jesuits were expelled in 1767. He wrote a chronicle of Mexican history from 1521 to 1767, edited and continued to 1836 by Bustamente.

CAXTON, WILLIAM (1422?–1491), publisher. Born in Kent, England, he was well educated, and because of the presence of Flemish weavers in his native area was apprenticed to a London cloth merchant in 1438–41. He went to the Continent, by 1446 settled in Bruges with a good reputation for business, was admitted to the English mercers' guild in 1453, and in 1463–69 was governor of the merchant adventurers, an organization of English merchants in Bruges. In 1469 he gave up the cloth business to enter the service of Margaret, duchess of Burgundy, sister of King Edward IV, who commissioned him to translate Raoul le Fevre's *Recuyell of the Historyes of Troye* in 1471. He studied printing, probably in Cologne in 1471–72, hired Colard Mansion, an illuminator, as assistant at the press he set up in Bruges in 1474, and his translation became his first production and the first book printed in English. His *Game and Playe of the Chesse*, a blended translation of two French works, followed. Caxton then moved to Westminster, where he set up his press in 1476. He issued Lydgate's *Temple of Glass*, Chaucer's *Anelida* and *Arcite*, Burgh's *Cato*, and a *Book of Courtesy*, among other titles. The first dated book printed in England was from his press, *Dictes and Sayings of the Philosophers* (1477), translated from Guillaume de Tignoville by Anthony Wodville, Earl Rivers; a second translation by the latter was *The Moral Proverbs* of Christine de Pisan. Some ninety volumes came from his press, many of them with elaborate prefaces or epilogues by Caxton himself, which reveal him to be an astute, and often amusing, critic. Major titles include Chaucer's *Canterbury Tales*, and his *Troilus and Criseyde* and *House of Fame*, *The Chronicles of England*, Higden's *Polychronicon*, Lydgate's *Life of Our Lady*, Gower's *Confessio Amantis*, *The Golden Legend* of Jacobus de Voragine, Ovid's *Metamorphoses*, Thomas Malory's *Morte d'Arthur*, and many mediaeval romances. Caxton printed many translations of his own which had great influence on the development of English prose, as did all the work from his press; these include: *The Mirror of the World*, *Reynard the Fox*, *The History of Godfrey of Bologne*, *The Book of the Knight of the Tower*, *Aesop's Fables*, *The Order of Chivalry*, and Jerome's *Lives of the Fathers*. He also issued four editions of a *Book of Hours*, a psalter, and other liturgical books for the use of Westminster cathedral. He took great pains with all his work and was particularly satisfied to realize that he was greatly responsible for contemporary taste in literature. He died in Westminster, England.

CAYLUS, ANNE CLAUDE PHILIPPE DE (1692–1765), archaeologist. Born in Paris, France, he became a soldier at seventeen, fought in Spain and Germany, traveled through Europe and the Near East after 1714, and became a member of the Academy of Painting in 1731 and of the Academy of Inscriptions in 1742. He published a seven-volume study of Egyptian, Greek, Roman, Etruscan, and French antiquities; worked with others in an edition of old paintings found at Rome; completed paintings and engravings of his and found a new method for inlaid colors in marble; and wrote short novels and fantasies, published in English as *Oriental Tales*.

CAYLUS, MARIE MARGUERITE LE VALOIS DE VILLETTE DE MURCAY DE (1673–1729). Mother of Anne Claude and member of a prominent French Protestant family, the marquise was converted by Mme.

de Maintenon, was the subject of Racine's prologue to his *Esther*, and left informative and witty *Souvenirs* regarding the court of King Louis XIV.

CAZALÈS, EDMOND DE (1804–1876). Born in Grenade-sur-Garonne, France, he was the son of Jacques Antoine (1758–1805), royalist politician who fought a duel with Barnave and fled to England during the revolution. Edmond studied law, tried to reconcile the Church with the principles of the revolution, and in 1843 was ordained. He taught history at Louvain, became rector of seminaries in Nîmes and Montauban, was involved in the revolution of 1848 and a deputy to the national assembly, and wrote historical studies on contemporary Germany (1853).

CAZEAU, CHARLES FÉLIX (1807–1881). Born in Quebec, Canada, on Dec. 24, he was ordained there, served as secretary to six bishops through a fifty-six-year period, was four times administrator of the diocese, and chaplain of the Good Shepherd orphanage from 1856 until his death on Feb. 26.

CEALLACH, ST. (6th century), bishop. A disciple of St. Kieran, he served as bishop of Killala and then retired as a hermit. F. D. May 1.

CEALLACH MAC AEDH, ST. (1079?–1129), archbishop. A layman, he was consecrated bishop of Armagh, Ireland, at twenty-six, restored ecclesiastical discipline and introduced liturgical reforms with the help of St. Malachy, probably rebuilt the cathedral, and acted as peacemaker between Irish chiefs. He died on Apr. 1. F. D. Apr. 6.

CECIL, ALGERNON (1879–1953), author. A descendant of Queen Elizabeth I's treasurer, Lord Burghleigh, and James I's secretary of state, Robert Cecil, he was born in England on Jan. 31, to Lord Eustace and Gertrude Scott Cecil. He attended Eton and Oxford, become a barrister in 1905, served in the intelligence division and the foreign office during World War I, became a convert in 1915, and in 1923 married Lady Guendolen Godolphin-Osborne. He wrote *Six Oxford Thinkers* (1909), *Essays in Imitation, Life of Robert Cecil, The World We Live in, British Foreign Secretaries, Metternich, Portrait of Thomas More,* and the autobiographical *The House on Bryanston Square* (1944). He died on Apr. 13.

CECILIA, ST., martyr. Legend calls her a Roman patrician, raised as a Christian, who had dedicated her virginity to God. Against her will, she was forced to marry a young patrician, Valerian, whom she converted and who agreed to live a life of celibacy with her. His brother Tiburtius also became a convert, but both brothers were arrested for burying the bodies of martyrs, tortured, and beheaded near Rome for refusing to sacrifice to the gods. Cecilia was arrested when she recovered the bodies and was tortured and beheaded. Hundreds who had come to plead with her to save her life by apostatizing were converted at the time. All that is known is that she, Valerian, and Tiburtius were buried in the cemetery of St. Praetextatus in Rome, probably having been martyred at different times in the second or third century. St. Cecilia is the patron of music and musicians; early art portrayed her playing the organ—a mistranslation of the legend, which had pipes playing for her wedding day. F. D. Nov. 22.

CECILIA, ST. (d. 1290). Born in Rome of the Cesarini family, she was a nun in the convent at Trastevere when the group was reformed by St. Dominic. She is said to have been the first woman to receive the Dominican habit, and served as abbess there and at the convent of St. Agnes in Bologna. There, Bl. Jordan of Saxony was her spiritual adviser and Bl. Diana one of her followers. She was beatified in 1891. F. D. June 9.

CEDD, ST. (d. 664), bishop. A native of Northumbria, England, and brother of St. Chad of Lichfield, he was a monk at Lindisfarne and was sent in 653 with three other priests to evangelize the Middle Angles, later was sent to Essex, and was consecrated bishop of the East Saxons by St. Finan. He founded the monasteries of Bradwell, Tilbury, and Lastingham, attended the Synod of Whitby, where he accepted the Roman observances, and spent the last years of his life at Lastingham, Yorkshire, where he died during a plague. F. D. Jan. 7 (also, Oct. 26).

CEILLIER, REMI (1688–1763), patrologist. Born in Bar-le-Duc, France, on May 14, he became a Benedictine at Moyen Moutier in 1705, taught and became dean there, and was prior of two monasteries. In 1718 he published a reply to Jean Barbeyrac, professor at Lausanne, who had attacked patristic tradition. His research led him to devote himself to a twenty-three-volume study (1729–63) of the lives and thought of, and critical commentaries on, supported by illustrative excerpts, the work of the Fathers of the Church. He was assisted by other Benedictines in the project. He died at Flavigny monastery, near Dijon, France, on May 26.

CELE-CHRIST, ST. (728?), bishop. A hermit known as Christicole (devotee of Christ), he was chosen a bishop in Leinster, Ireland, against his will. F. D. Mar. 3.

CELERINUS, ST. (3rd century), martyr. *See* Ignatius, St.

CELESTINE I, ST. (d. 432), pope. Born in Campania, he became pope on Sept. 10, 422, and strenuously opposed the twin errors of Pelagianism and Nestorianism, particularly through the Councils of Rome (430) and Ephesus (431). He supported St. Germanus of Auxerre against Pelagius, sent Palladius to work in Ireland before the mission of St. Patrick, whom he later sent to Ireland, and carried on correspondence with St. Augustine. F. D. July 27 (in Ireland, Apr. 6).

CELESTINE II (d. 1144), pope. Born in Castello, Tuscany, Guido del Castello was a disciple of Peter Abelard and was made a cardinal in 1128. In 1140 he became legate to France, but displeased St. Bernard because he protected Arnold of Brescia. He succeeded Innocent II as pope on Sept. 26, 1143, was consecrated on Oct. 3, lifted the interdict imposed on France because of King Louis VII's interference in episcopal appointments, and died six months later, on Mar. 8.

CELESTINE III (1106?–1198), pope. Giacinto Bobone, a Roman of the Orsini family, was made a cardinal in 1151 and was elected pope on Mar. 30, 1191, to succeed Clement III. Although eighty-five, he was only a deacon; he was ordained a priest on Apr. 13 and consecrated bishop and pope the next day. His reign was marred politically by the destruction of Tusculum, which the populace demanded before they would permit Celestine to crown the invading King Henry VI of Germany as emperor; and by his tolerance of Henry's attack on Sicily and the latter's oppression of churches in Germany and support of Leopold of Austria's imprisonment of Richard I of England. Celestine in 1191 confirmed the new Order of Teutonic Knights, worked vainly for a crusade, and was firm in reminding several European kings of the sanctity of marriage. He died in Rome on Jan. 8.

CELESTINE IV (d. 1241), pope. Gofredo Castiglioni, a nephew of Pope Urban III, was born in Milan, Italy, was probably a Cistercian, and succeeded Gregory IX as pope on Oct. 25, 1241. He was consecrated on Oct. 28 and died two weeks later on Nov. 10.

CELESTINE V, ST. (1210–1296), pope. Pietro del Murone, eleventh of twelve children born to a family of peasants in Isernia, in the Abruzzi, Italy, retired to a hermitage at twenty, left his cell to study for the priesthood at Rome, became a Benedictine at Faizola in 1246, and was permitted to take up life as a solitary. When disciples surrounded him at Monte Morone, he set up a monastery for them, gave them a strict rule, and in 1274 received approval for an order later known as Celestines. Two years of political quarreling followed the death of Pope Nicholas IV; the cardinals assembled at Perugia, chose Peter on July 5, and he was consecrated unwillingly on Aug. 29, 1294. He was eighty-four at the time, was dominated by Charles of Naples, thirteen of whose appointees he made cardinal, and resigned, after five months, on Dec. 13, 1294. His successor, Boniface VIII, brought him back

to Rome and imprisoned him, but his holiness weighed more than his administrative ineptness and he was canonized in 1313. F. D. May 19.

CELLACH, ST. (9th century?), archbishop. He is said to have served as abbot of Iona and to have founded the monastery of Kells before he was raised to the Irish see of Armagh. F. D. Apr. 1.

CELLI, BL. GREGORIO DEI (1225?–1343). Born in Verucchio, Italy, he became an Augustinian at fifteen at a monastery he and his widowed mother had built. When she died, ten years later, he was driven out, apparently because of his strictness, joined the Franciscans near Reati, and lived there to a great age. His cult was confirmed in 1769. F. D. May 4.

CELLIER, ELIZABETH (17th century). Married to Pierre Cellier, a Frenchman, and a convert from Anglicanism, she visited the Catholic prisoners in London during the Titus Oates Plot hysteria in 1680. She was charged with high treason that year, freed, and published *Malice Defeated*, a pamphlet against the informer Thomas Dangerfield. She was then retried, heavily fined, and punished in the pillory. During the reign of King James II she worked to establish a corporation of midwives (she herself was skilled as one) and to build an orphanage. She disappeared from view after 1688.

CELLINI, BENVENUTO (1500–1571), sculptor. Born in Florence, Italy, on Nov. 3, son of Giovanni Cellini, an architect and musician, and Elizabeth Granacci, he became a musician and goldsmith. He was devoted and generous to his family, but was also hot-tempered; he killed a man in a street brawl, was banished from Florence, and later pardoned by the pope. He studied the goldsmith's art in Florence and Rome, wrote treatises on it, and produced fine rings, coins, seals, armor and vestment decorations, and a famous salt-cellar. At forty Cellini turned to sculpture and made statues of Mars and Jupiter for King Francis I at Paris. In 1545 (he returned to Florence in that year) he completed his bronze Perseus holding the head of Medusa for Cosimo de' Medici. Armor for Charles IX of Sweden, a hand bell for Pope Clement VII, and a white marble Christ on a black cross for Philip II of Spain are also outstanding. He was a soldier in Rome in 1527; was imprisoned from 1537 to 1539 on the charge of stealing church funds, and treated with excessive cruelty; his complicity was open to doubt and he received a papal pardon in 1540. In 1554 Florence made him a noble; at sixty-four he married Piera Parigi, by whom he had son and daughter. Other details of his life, colored by more boastfulness than wit, puff out the highly adventurous material of a somewhat plodding *Autobiography*. He died in Florence on Feb. 13.

CELSUS, ST. (d. 68?), martyr. *See* Nazarius, St.

CÉNEAU, ROBERT (1453–1560), bishop. He was born and died in Paris, France, and studied at the Sorbonne. In 1515 he became bishop of Vence, in 1530 of Riez, and in 1532 was transferred to Avranches. He wrote a number of polemical works on marriage, celibacy, and other topics treated by Calvin and other heretics, an edition of the synodal statutes of Riez, and an insignificant *Historia Galliae*.

CENNINI, BL. AGOSTINO (d. 1420), martyr. He and three other Servite friars—Lorenzo Nerucci, Giovanni Batista Petrucci, and Bartolommeo Sonati—were sent to Bohemia by Pope Martin V. With sixty other Servites they were burned to death in their church in Prague by the Hussites. Their cult was approved in 1918. F. D. Aug. 11.

CENNINI, BERNARDO (15th century), printer. A Florentine goldsmith, he printed *Commentary on Vergil*, by Servius, in 1471, and is said to have introduced printing to his city.

CENNINI, CENNINO (1365?–1440), painter. Born in Celle, Tuscany, Italy, he is said to have completed illustrations of the life of Christ for a church in Volterra. His *Treatise on Painting* was a technical study.

CENSURIUS, ST. (d. 486). He was bishop of Auxerre, France, from 448 until his death. F. D. June 10.

CENTURIONI, ALOYSIUS (1685–1757). Born in Genoa, Italy, he was ordained a Jesuit, was elected seventeenth general of his Society, in 1755, and inherited the opposition to the Society which disturbed the generalate of Fr. Visconti, his predecessor. He died on Oct. 2 at Castel Gandolfo, near Rome.

CEOCO, FRANCIS, ST. (d. 1530). A Franciscan tertiary, he lived with other tertiaries in a community at Pesaro, Italy. His cult was confirmed in 1859. F. D. Aug. 13.

CEOLFRID, ST. (642–716). Born in Northumbria, he became a monk at eighteen at Gilling, Yorkshire, and was ordained at the Benedictine monastery at Ripon. He became prior of St. Peter's, Wearmouth, where his strictness caused such hostility that he returned to Ripon in 672. About 678 he accompanied St. Benedict Biscop to Rome, and in 685 was appointed deputy abbot of the newly founded St. Paul's monastery at Jarrow. Shortly after, a plague wiped out the entire community except Ceolfrid and one other. Benedict nominated Ceolfrid as his successor as abbot; Ceolfrid developed the twin monasteries of St. Paul and St. Peter as great centers of learning. He built up their libraries and became a scripture scholar. In 716 he resigned because of age and

ill health and set out for Rome, but died at Langres, France, on the way. One of the first extant Vulgate texts, the Codex Amiatinus, long attributed to southern Italy, has been shown to have originated in his monasteries and may have been in his possession when he died. F. D. Sept. 25.

CEOLLACH, ST. (7th century?). A priest in Ireland, he went to England as bishop of the Mercians or Middle Angles, retired to Iona, and died in Ireland. F. D. Oct. 6.

CEOLWULF, ST. (d. 764). A Northumbrian king, to whom Bede dedicated his *Ecclesiastical History*, he spent his last years as a monk at Lindisfarne. F. D. Jan. 15.

CEPEDA, FRANCISCO (1532–1602). Born in La Mancha, Spain, he became a Dominican, was sent to Mexico, simplified and reorganized the Indian grammars in use there, published a study of four native languages, with a Spanish counterpart, in 1560 (the first such multilingual book printed in America), and in 1593 became provincial of his order in Guatemala, where he died.

CERA, ST. (7th century). Born in Tipperary, Ireland, she governed convents at Kilkeary and at Tehelly. F. D. Jan. 5.

CERATIUS, ST. (d. 455?), bishop of Grenoble, France, he attended the Council of Orange (441) and was highly regarded more than a century after his death. His cult was confirmed in 1903. F. D. June 6.

CERAUNUS, ST. (7th century). He was bishop of Paris and lived past 614. F. D. Sept. 27.

CERBONIUS, ST. (d. 400?). He was bishop of Verona, Italy. F. D. Oct. 10.

CERBONIUS, ST. (d. 575?), bishop. He accompanied St. Regulus to Populonia (now Piombino), Tuscany, Italy, when the latter was driven from Africa by the Vandals, and succeeded him as bishop. According to St. Gregory's *Dialogues*, he was thrown to the wild beasts by the invading King Totila of the Ostrogoths for sheltering Roman soldiers and freed when they did not attack him. He accompanied the Lombards in their exile on Elba and lived there his remaining thirty years. F. D. Oct. 10.

CERCHI, BL. HUMILIANA DE' (1220–1246). Born in Florence, she married at sixteen, soon became a widow, and was the first cloistered Franciscan tertiary in her native city. Her cult was approved by Pope Innocent XII. F. D. May 19.

CEREALIS, ST. (d. 120?), martyr. *See* Getulius, St.

CERIOLI BUZECCHI, BL. PAULA (1816–1865), foundress. Born in Soncino, Italy, last of sixteen children, she was married in 1834 and had three children. In 1854, her husband, Gaetano Buzecchi, died and she determined to devote her wealth to caring for and raising orphans. She attracted several disciples and in 1857 the Institute of the Holy Family was founded at her estate, Comonte, near Seriate, Lombardy, to be followed in 1862 by a brothers' branch at Villa Compagna, near Soncino. She died at Comonte, and was beatified in 1950. F. D. Dec. 24.

CERNEUF. *See* Serenus the Gardener.

CERRETTI, BONAVENTURE (1872–1933), cardinal. Born in Orvieto, Italy, on June 17, he attended the Pontifical seminary in Rome and was ordained in 1895. He was secretary of the apostolic delegation to Mexico in 1904–6, auditor of that at Washington to 1914, made titular archbishop of Corinth and apostolic delegate to Australasia in 1914–17. He then directed papal relief of war prisoners and was papal envoy on behalf of missions at the Paris peace conference of 1917. He was papal nuncio to France in 1921 to 1926, was made a cardinal in 1925, and served as papal legate to the Eucharistic Congress in Sydney, Australia, in 1928. He died in Orvieto on May 8.

CERVANTES SAAVEDRA, MIGUEL DE (1547–1616), novelist. Born in Alcalá de Henares, Spain, on Oct. 9, he studied in Madrid and perhaps in Seville, but attended no university, went to Rome in 1569 in the entourage of Cardinal Acquaviva, joined the Spanish forces fighting the Turks, and lost the use of his left hand in the battle of Lepanto (1571). He also fought in North Africa, was imprisoned in Algiers for five years, and after being ransomed in 1580 returned to Spain. His interest in Catalina de Salazar y Palacios, whom he married in 1584, is reflected in the pastoral romance, *Galatea* (1582). He wrote several unsuccessful plays, including *Trato de Argel*, which reflects his prison sufferings, and the posthumously published tragedy *Numancia*. Poverty led him to become collector of taxes in Granada, but the irregularities of a subordinate caused him to be jailed in 1597. There, allegedly, he conceived the idea of *Il ingenioso hidalgo Don Quijote de la Mancha*, published in 1605. A so-called continuation (1614) under the signature Alfonso Fernandez de Avellaneda led Cervantes to write a "second part" in 1615. His *Novelas ejemplares* (1613) are twelve tales, picaresque but not cynical, which had a great influence on seventeenth-century English drama and eighteenth-century English fiction, as did *Don Quijote*. Cervantes also wrote *Entremeses*, dramatic interludes; *Viaje del Parnaso* (1614), an account of contemporary poetry in *terza rima*; and *Los trabajos de Persiles y Sigismunda*, a novel of adventure. He died in Madrid on Apr. 23. In his major work, which he himself called a satire on the countless tales of artificial and attitudinized knightly daring and adventure which lowered the reading taste of con-

temporary Europe, Cervantes was not attacking chivalry or idealism, or tradition; but misdirected zeal. The chief value of the work lies in the author's success in the humorous double contrast: of Don Quijote and his squire, Sancho Panzo (mental and physical), and of the real and conjured-up worlds in which they meet their adventures.

J. FITZMAURICE-KELLY, *Miguel de Cervantes Saavedra* (New York, Oxford, 1913); M. J. BERNADETTE and A. FLORES, eds., *Cervantes across the Centuries* (New York, Dryden, 1947).

CERVANTES DE SALAZAR, FRANCISCO (1513–1575). Born in Toledo, Spain, he went to Mexico in 1550 and was professor of rhetoric on the first faculty of its university, opened in 1553, until his death in the capital. He published *Dialogos Latinos* (1554), an archaeological, historical, and topographical history of Mexico City; several theological works; a lost history of Mexico; and an elaborate account of the memorial services for the death of Charles V.

CESALPINO, ANDREA (1519–1603), botanist. Born in Arezzo, Tuscany, Italy, on June 6, he studied medicine and botany at Pisa under Colombo and Ghini, taught those subjects and philosophy there, and in 1554 succeeded Ghini as second director of the Pisan botanical gardens. He may later have been director of the gardens in Rome, where he was called as professor of medicine at the Sapienza and physician to Pope Clement VIII. As a philosopher he was influenced by Aristotle and Averroës; in medicine he made important contributions to the study of the circulation of the blood; his *De plantis* (1583) is one of the most important botanical studies before Linnaeus and is marked by original observations and by the first careful classification of flowering plants. The herbarium he prepared about 1550 for Bishop Tornabono is also one of the first such volumes; his *De metallicis* (1596) reveals him as a forerunner of Lavoisier and also indicates his knowledge of fossils. He died in Rome on Feb. 23.

CESARE DA SESTO (1477?–1523?), painter. Born in Sesto Calende, Italy, he studied under Leonardo da Vinci, was later influenced by Raphael, and became known for his skillful technique in *St. Jerome, Adoration of the Magi, Virgin with Scales, Salome*, and numerous madonnas.

CESARI, GIUSEPPE (1568?–1640), painter. Born in Rome, he was hired at seventeen by Pope Gregory XIII to work with others, including Roncalli, on the decoration of the Vatican. His work was sometimes rough and careless, at other times called too daring. He had commissions from four other popes. Roman and Neapolitan nobility, and Cardinal Richelieu. His best work includes the *Ascension* in St.

John Lateran and the frescoes of the Olgiati chapel in Santa Prassede, and the Borghese chapel, Santa Maria Maggiore.

CESARINI, GIULIANO (1398–1444), cardinal. Born in Rome, he studied at Perugia, where he later taught Roman law (Nicholas of Cusa was a pupil). He was sent to Germany and Bohemia in 1419, was appointed cardinal-bishop of Frascati by Pope Martin V in 1426, led an unsuccessful mission to the Hussites in 1431, and presided at the Council of Basle. Pope Eugene IV sought to dissolve the council, and Cesarini opposed the move until he realized that the group was becoming anti-papal. The cardinal then headed a commission appointed by the council, which was papally transferred to Ferrara, to seek peace with the Hussites. When the council moved again, to Florence, he was the leader in the negotiations with the Eastern churches. In 1443 he was sent as papal legate to Hungary to preach a crusade against the Turks; instead, he had King Ladislaus break the peace treaty with Sultan Amurath III. The cardinal was slain in the disastrous defeat of the Christian army at Varna, Bulgaria, on Nov. 10.

CESI, FEDERIGO (1585–1630), scholar. A Roman prince, he gathered a great library and museum, built a botanical garden, and in 1603 established at his palace the Accademia dei Lincei (using the lynx as a symbol for the study of natural philosophy). Co-founders were Fabio Colonna, author of a study of rare plants, *Fitobasano*, and Francesco Stelluti, author of *Legno fossile minerale*. The society fell into oblivion after 1651, but was revived as Accademia dei Nuovi Lincei by Pope Pius IX in 1847. Cesi wrote *Theatre of Nature* and *Explanation of Natural Phenomena*.

CESLAUS, BL. (d. 1242). A native of Silesia, Poland, he became a Dominican with his brother, St. Hyacinth, in Rome at the hands of St. Dominic. He preached in Silesia, Pomerania, and Bohemia, became spiritual adviser to St. Hedwig, and served as provincial of the Dominicans in Poland. His cult was confirmed in 1713. F. D. July 17.

CÉSPEDES, PABLO DE (1538–1608), painter. A native of Cordova, Spain, he studied art at Rome, became associated there with Federigo Zuccaro, and in 1577 became canon at the cathedral in Cordova, which he decorated with a *Last Supper* and other work. He wrote several art studies and a poem on the art of painting. He died in Cordova.

CETHEUS, ST. (d. 600?), bishop and martyr. Also known as Peregrinus, he was put to death by drowning at Amiternum (Aquila), Italy, when he pleaded for a prisoner of the Arian Lombards. F. D. June 13.

CETINA, GUTIERREZ DE (1518?–1557?), poet. Born in Seville, Spain, he served with the

army in Italy, North Africa, and Flanders, retired about 1547 and went to Mexico, revisiting Seville briefly before his death at Los Angeles. He wrote in the Italianate school and was a master of sonnets, anacreontics, and madrigals.

CETTIN, ST. (5th century), bishop. He was a follower of St. Patrick in Ireland, by whom he was consecrated missionary bishop. F. D. June 16.

CEVA, TOMMASO (1648–1737), mathematician. Born in Milan, Italy, on Dec. 21, he became a Jesuit in 1663, wrote on poetry and mathematics, worked on equipment for the trisection of an angle, evolved in 1678 the theorem in geometry which bears his name, and wrote Latin poetry, including *Philosophia novo-antiqua*. He died in Milan on Feb. 23.

CÉZANNE, PAUL (1839–1906), painter. Born in Aix, Provence, France, on Jan. 19, he studied at Collège Bourbon there, was unsuccessful in his father's banking business, studied law briefly, and in 1861 went to Paris to study art. He joined the group of young revolutionary artists opposing Ingres and the conservative school and fell under the influence of Gustave Courbet's and Eugene Delacroix's work. The paintings of this period are somber and heavy-handed, executed in a thick medium, often with a palette knife, with few of the distinctive features of his later style. In 1872, he came into Pissarro's orbit, studied under him at Auvers-sur-Oise, Provence, changed his style, and began turning out works characteristic of the impressionist school, which, however, were derided. He then abandoned the impressionists' preoccupation with superficial lighting effects and developed an original style, with vivid color, distorted forms, and emphasis on geometrical constructions and thinly laid on elongated parallel brush strokes. The full effect of his influence was not felt until after his death, when he was recognized as the forerunner of modern abstract design. Ill the last seven years of his life, he died at Aix, France, where he had lived in virtual retirement, on Oct. 23.
GERSTLE MACK, *Paul Cézanne* (New York, Knopf, 1935).

CHABANEL, ST. NOEL (1613–1649), martyr. Born near Mende, France, on Feb. 2, he became a Jesuit in 1630 and in 1643 was sent to New France as a missioner to the Hurons. In 1649 he became assistant to Fr. Charles Garnier at the Indian village of Etarita. On his return, two days before the martyrdom of Fr. Garnier, from a visit to neighboring Ste. Marie, he was murdered on Dec. 8 by an apostate Indian. He was canonized in 1930 by Pope Pius XI. F. D. Sept. 26 (also, Mar. 16).
JOHN A. O'BRIEN, *The American Martyrs* (New York, Appleton, 1953).

CHABRAT, GUY IGNATIUS (1787–1868),

bishop. Born in Chambres, Cantal, France, on Dec. 28, he studied at St. Fleur seminary, went to the United States in 1809, studied at St. Thomas' seminary, Kentucky, joined the Sulpicians, and was ordained in 1811. He did missionary work in Kentucky, became superior of the Congregation of the Sisters of Loretto on the death of Fr. Nerinckx in 1824, retaining this office until 1846, and was consecrated titular bishop of Bolina and coadjutor of Bardstown in 1834. He administered the see in 1835–39, but blindness caused him to resign in 1847, when he returned to France, where he died at Mauriac on Nov. 21.

CHACIM, FRANCISCO (d. 1828), bishop. A Franciscan, he became bishop of Macao in 1805, founded charitable institutions, reformed the diocesan statutes, and collected its ecclesiastical documents.

CHAD, ST. (d. 672), bishop. Born in Northumbria, he studied with his brother St. Cedd at Lindisfarne under St. Aidan. After working in Ireland with St. Egbert, he returned to become abbot of Lastingham, Yorkshire, and, a year later, bishop of York. St. Theodore of Canterbury transferred him to Mercia, the see was changed from Repton to Lichfield, and he lived there in quiet simplicity until his death. F. D. Mar. 2.

CHADWICK, JAMES (1813–1882), bishop. Born in Drogheda, Ireland, on Apr. 24, he studied at Ushaw College, was ordained in 1836, and served on the college staff until 1849. He was relieved as vice-president when his health broke down, directed retreats until 1856, then returned to Ushaw as professor of philosophy. He was made second bishop of Hexham and Newcastle in 1866. He served briefly as president of Ushaw, wrote on meditation, and died in Newcastle, England, on May 14.

CHAEREMON, ST. (d. 250), martyr. An aged bishop of Nilopolis, Egypt, he took refuge from Decius' persecution in the Arabian mountains with many of his flock; they were never heard of again. F. D. Dec. 22.

CHAEREMON, ST. (3rd century). He suffered in the persecution at Alexandria, Egypt, which took the life of St. Dionysius (Oct. 3); he was subsequently exiled. F. D. Oct. 4.

CHAIGON, PIERRE (1791–1883). Born in St. Pierre, Mayenne, France, he became a Jesuit in 1819, spent thirty years after ordination in giving retreats to the French clergy, wrote on prayer, meditation, and peace of soul, and founded a Union of Prayer for Deceased Priests. He died in Angers, France, on Aug. 14.

CHAINOALDUS, ST. (d. 633?), bishop. Brother of SS. Faro and Burgundofara, he became a monk at Luxeuil, France, under St. Columban. He accompanied the latter in exile to Bobbio, became sixth bishop of Laon, and

attended the Council of Rheims in 630. He is also called Cagnoald. F. D. Sept. 6.

CHALIFOUR, ONÉSIME (1899–1956), editor. Born in Canada on May 1, he became owner of a lumber business, president of the Quebec Building Exchange, and president of L'Action Sociale. He was editor of *L'Action Catholique*, leading French daily in Quebec, where he died on July 13.

CHALLONER, RICHARD (1691–1781), bishop. Born in Sussex, England, on Sept. 29, of a Presbyterian wine cooper, he was a convert at thirteen, sent to Douai in 1705, and ordained there in 1716. He taught literature and philosophy for nine years, became vice-president and professor of theology in 1719, and took his doctorate in divinity in 1727. He published *Think Well on't* (a series of meditations) in 1728. He went on the English mission in 1730, and published apologetical works, some in opposition to the powerful Anglican, Conyers Middleton, which led to prudent but brief exile. In 1741 he was consecrated coadjutor bishop to Dr. Peter, vicar apostolic of London; Challoner succeeded him in 1758. Though forced to work underground after 1765 because of the penal laws, he founded schools for boys and for girls and helped to establish a society for aiding the old and infirm poor. He is best known for his revision of the New Testament (1749) and Old Testament (1750) which eliminated obscure Latinisms; there were more than 2000 emendations in the third edition of 1752, which became the basis of much subsequent English translations. Other works include catechisms, an edition of the *Imitation*, a translation of St. Augustine's *Confessions*, a prayer book called *Garden of the Soul*, saints' lives, and many works of meditation and instruction. Most significant were his *Memoirs of Missionary Priests* for the years 1577–1681, *British Martyrology* (1761), and several biblical studies. He died in London on Jan. 12, having suffered a paralytic shock after the Gordon Riots, when hostile mobs burned Catholic chapels, destroyed the homes of his parishioners, and demanded that he be found and dragged through the streets.

CHAMBRUN, CHARLES DE (1875–1952), diplomat. Born in France on Feb. 10, a descendant of Lafayette, he entered the diplomatic service, was minister to Vienna and Athens, chargé d'affaires in Washington, D.C., from 1921 to 1923, and ambassador to Rome from 1933 to 1936. He died in Paris on Nov. 6.

CHAMOND. *See* Annemund, St.

CHAMPLAIN, SAMUEL DE (1567–1635), explorer. Born in Brouage, Saintonge, France, son of Antoine, a sailor, he went on several voyages with his father, served in the army of d'Aumont against the Huguenots, and in 1598 was placed in charge of a naval expedition sailing against the British who had attacked Puerto Rico. He wrote an account of his voyage to the Gulf of Mexico, suggested a canal across Panama, was made royal geographer, and in 1603 went to Canada with Pontgravé. He opposed Tadousac as a permanent settlement and proposed Quebec. From there he explored the St. Lawrence River, collected information from the Indians about the Great Lakes, returned to France the same year, published *Des sauvages*, and returned in 1604. In July 1608 he began the settlement of Quebec, became lieutenant governor, and in 1609 led an attack on the Iroquois and Mohawks and discovered the lake named after him. He journeyed widely in all directions from the city and published six volumes on his findings, the geography of the area, its prospects as a colony, and the lack of cooperation on the part of the mercantile element. Champlain gave the name *La place royale* to the island area discovered earlier by Cartier and named the island opposite Montreal, Ste. Hélène, for Hélène Boullé, to whom he was married in 1610. She joined him in Canada in 1620 when she became twenty. In 1629 he surrendered Quebec to an English fleet, was taken prisoner to England for four years, and returned to Quebec (again French territory) in 1633. He died there on Dec. 25.

CHAMPNEY, ANTHONY (1569?–1643?). Born in England, he studied at Rheims and Rome, was ordained, was imprisoned at Wisbech, engaged in controversy with the Jesuits, became president of the English College at Arras, and was vice-president of Douai from 1619 to 1625. He returned to England in 1628, published many controversial pamphlets between 1601 and 1624, and disappeared after the outbreak of the civil war.

CHAMPOLLION, JEAN FRANÇOIS (1790–1832), orientalist. Born in Figeaci, Lot, France, on Dec. 23, he studied Hebrew and half a dozen oriental languages, and published two volumes on the geography of Egypt (1814). Working with the Rosetta Stone, he succeeded in finding the key to the mystery of the hieroglyphics (on which he had worked since 1808) and announced his findings in 1822–23. He catalogued their Egyptian holdings for Naples, Florence, and Rome; gathered a rich hoard of antiquities for the Louvre; explored Egypt with Rossellini (his daily letters were published in 1833); held the new chair of archaeology at the Collège de France; and retired to Quercy to complete an Egyptian grammar and dictionary, published after his death at Paris on Mar. 4, by his brother, Jean Jacques (1778–1867).

CHAMPS, ÉTIENNE AGARD DE (1613–1701), theologian. Born in Bourges, France, on Sept. 2, he became a Jesuit in 1630, taught at Paris, served as rector at Rennes and at Paris,

was provincial of Lyons and twice of all France. He wrote widely against Jansenism under the name Richard Antonius and died at Paris or La Flèche on July 31.

CHANCA, DIEGO ALVAREZ (15th century). Court physician to Ferdinand and Isabella of Spain, he went to America on the second expedition of Columbus in 1493, saved the life of the commander and others attacked by malaria, selected the site for the first permanent settlement of Isabella, Haiti, and wrote a detailed and accurate account of the New World as he saw it during a three-month stay. After his return to Spain he published in 1506 a study of the treatment of pleurisy.

CHANCHE, JOHN MARY JOSEPH (1795–1852), bishop. Born in Baltimore, Maryland, on Oct. 4, he studied at St. Mary's there, where he joined the Sulpicians and was ordained in 1819. He taught at St. Mary's, became its president in 1835, and in 1840 was appointed first bishop of Natchez, Mississippi. He dedicated his cathedral in 1842, was active in building up his diocese and in missionary work among Negroes, and attended the first Plenary Council in Baltimore. He died in Frederick City, Maryland, on July 22.

CHANDLER, JOSEPH RIPLEY (1792–1880). Born on Aug. 25, in Kingston, Massachusetts, he studied at the University of Pennsylvania, taught, and in 1815 opened a school for young ladies in Philadelphia. He became editorial writer of the *Gazette of the United States* in 1822, with two friends purchased it in 1826, and edited it until 1847 when forced to resign because of ill health. He edited *Graham's American Monthly Magazine of Literature* in 1843–49, became Grand Master of the Masons in Pennsylvania, and in 1849 became a Catholic. He served three terms in the House of Representatives beginning in 1849, was a vigorous defender of the rights of the Church, and in 1858–61 was ambassador to the Two Sicilies. In the latter part of his life he became interested in improving prison conditions and wrote several essays on the subject. He died on July 10.

CHANEL, ST. PIERRE LOUIS (1803–1889), martyr. Born in Cluet, France, he became a priest in 1827, did parish work, joined the Marists in 1831 and taught for five years in their Belley seminary. He was sent as superior of their first Oceania mission, gained considerable success on Fortuna Island, mastered the language, cured the ill, and won friends among the natives. When the chieftain's son asked to be baptized, Fr. Chanel was murdered, but the mission continued to flourish. He was canonized in 1954 by Pope Pius XII. F. D. Apr. 28.

CHANTAL, ST. JANE FRANCES DE (1572–1641), foundress. Daughter of Bénigne

Frémyot, president of the Burgundy parliament, she was born on Jan. 28 in Dijon, France. At twenty she married Christopher de Rabutin, baron de Chantal, had seven children (three of whom died), and was widowed at twenty-eight when her husband died as the result of a hunting accident. Greatly influenced by St. Francis de Sales, who became her spiritual adviser and with whom she had an extended correspondence, she devoted her life to the care of her children and the poor. She wanted to become a Carmelite, but in 1610 he persuaded her instead to form with him a new congregation, of the Visitation of the Virgin Mary, at Lake Annecy, whose purpose was to provide the aged and the ill with a refuge. It was for her and her nuns that St. Francis de Sales wrote his treatise, *On the Love of God.* Despite initial opposition, the congregation flourished and five more convents were established including one at Paris. In 1622 the death of St. Francis, and in 1627 the death of her son, followed by the death of others close to her brought periods of desolation. But her work gave her strength and by 1636 she had some sixty-five convents, all of which she visited. She died in Moulins, France, on Dec. 13 and was canonized in 1767. F. D. Aug. 21.

HAROLD J. HEAGNEY, *Madame de Chantal* (N.Y., Kenedy, 1950).

CHANTELOU, CLAUDE (1617–1664). Born in Vion, France, he became a member of the Order of Fontrevault, then joined the Benedictines of St. Maur and was professed in 1640, edited the sermons of St. Bernard, a selection of patristic comments on the spiritual life, and writings of St. Basil on monasticism. A history of the abbey of Montmajor and other historical material on the Benedictines in France were published posthumously. He died in Paris on Nov. 28.

CHAPDELAINE, BL. AUGUSTE (1814–1856), martyr. The ninth child of a French peasant family, he was ordained, did parish work, joined the Society of Foreign Missions, and was sent to China. He was put to death in Kwang-si, after frightful tortures, and was beatified in 1900. F. D. Feb. 27.

CHAPEAUVILLE, JEAN (1551–1617), theologian. Born in Liège, Belgium, on Jan. 5, he studied at Cologne and Louvain, was ordained, and stationed in parishes in Liège from 1578 to 1600, when he was appointed archdeacon of Famenne. He had become inquisitor in 1582, taught theology in the seminaries of Liège, and served Bishops Ernest of Bavaria and Ferdinand of Bavaria as vicar general. He wrote a history of the sixteenth-century bishops of Liège, commentaries on the catechism, and numerous theological works. He died in Liège on May 11.

CHAPELLE, PLACIDE LOUIS (1842–

1905), bishop. Born in Runes, Lozère, France, on Aug. 28, he studied at Enghien, Belgium, was ordained in Baltimore, Maryland, in 1865, served in parishes there and in Washington, D.C., and was Archbishop Spalding's theologian at the Vatican Council in 1870. In 1891 he was consecrated coadjutor bishop of Santa Fe, New Mexico, succeeded to the see in 1894, and in 1897 was transferred to New Orleans, Louisiana. In 1898 he was apostolic delegate to Cuba and Puerto Rico and in 1899 to the Philippines. He assured the protection of church property in former Spanish territory while in Paris at the peace conference after the Spanish-American War, and while in Manila secured the release of priests and religious who had been taken prisoner by Aguinaldo. He returned to New Orleans in 1905, began a visitation of his parishes, and became a victim of the yellow-fever epidemic on Aug. 9.

CHAPLEAU, JOSEPH ADOLPHE (1840–1898), governor. Born in Ste. Thérèse de Blainville, Quebec, Canada, he studied at St. Hyacinthe, and began a law career. He entered politics in 1859, passed the bar in 1861, and practiced in Montreal. He bought the newspaper *Le Colonisateur* in 1862, was its editor for two years, and was elected to parliament in 1867. He retained his government post until 1892, when he was named lieutenant governor. He married Marie King in 1874, continued his law work, specialized in criminal procedure, taught criminal jurisprudence at Laval, and was solicitor general in 1873–74. He was provincial secretary in 1876–78, leader of the conservative opposition in 1878–79, and minister of agriculture and public works. He achieved good relations with France, helped to establish a steamship line between Le Havre and Montreal, and produced a balanced budget. In 1882 he became secretary of state and a member of the privy council, led a commission investigating Chinese immigration, and in 1892 was minister of customs. He was knighted by Great Britain and the pope, honored by France, and presented an honorary degree by Laval. He died in Montreal on June 13.

CHAPTAL, EMMANUEL ANATOLE (1861–1943), archbishop. Born in Paris on Dec. 25, he entered the diplomatic service, was secretary in the embassies at St. Petersburg, Stockholm, Constantinople, and Munich, studied at St. Sulpice, and was ordained in 1897. He became titular bishop of Issouda and assistant to the cardinal-archbishop of Paris in 1922. As archbishop in World War II he led other priests in wearing a Star of David in protest against anti-Jewish terrorism by the German army. He died in Paris about May 28.

CHAPTAL, JEAN ANTOINE (1756–1832), chemist. Born in Nogaret, Lozère, France, on June 4, he took his doctorate in medicine at

Montpellier in 1777 and accepted the chair of chemistry there in 1781. During the French Revolution he was professor of organic chemistry at the Polytechnic Institute in Paris, returned to Montpellier after the fall of Robespierre, and reorganized the university. Napoleon made him minister of the interior and he established commercial exchanges, reorganized loan offices, introduced productive labor for prisoners, and directed the Sisters of Charity into hospital work. He also built roads in the Alpine region, recommended more careful attention to the vineyards of Luxembourg, set up industrial exhibits, and later had full control of manufacture and commerce. The emperor made him a senator, treasurer of the senate, and comte de Chanteloup. Chaptal was a member of the French Institute and of the Academy of Sciences, and in 1819 served in the chamber of peers. He improved the manufacture of sulphuric acid, of saltpeter for gunpowder, of beet-root sugar, dyes, and other items; as a technical chemist he supplemented many of the investigations initiated by Lavoisier. He died in Paris on July 30.

CHARALAMPIAS, ST. (d. 203). He was a priest who died at Magnesia in Asia Minor with five other Christians during the persecution of Septimius Severus. F. D. Feb. 18.

CHARBONNEAU, JOSEPH (d. 1959), archbishop. Born in Lefaivre, Ontario, Canada, he studied at St. Theresa and Grand seminary, Montreal, and was ordained in 1916. He also studied at Catholic University and the Canadian College, Rome, became superior of Ottawa's major seminary, vicar general of Ottawa, and in 1939 was consecrated first bishop of Hearst, Ontario. He was appointed coadjutor archbishop of Montreal in 1940, succeeded to the see later in the same year, and became known for his work in welfare, education, and immigration. Ill health caused him to resign in 1950, whereupon Pope Pius XII appointed him titular archbishop of Bosphorus. He died in Victoria, British Columbia, on Nov. 19.

CHARBONNEL, ARMAND FRANÇOIS MARIE DE (1802–1891), bishop. Born in Monistrol-sur-Loire, France, on Dec. 1, he became a Sulpician, went to Canada in 1850 as second bishop of Toronto, Ontario, developed the see out of his personal wealth (he was a count), enlarged educational opportunities, and attended the first and second provincial councils of Quebec. He resigned in 1860 to become a Capuchin, was named titular bishop (later archbishop) of Sozopolis, and died on Mar. 29.

CHARDIN, TEILHARD DE. See Teilhard de Chardin, Pierre.

CHARDON, JEAN BAPTISTE (1672–1743), missioner. Born in Bordeaux, France, on Apr. 27, he became a Jesuit in 1687, and was sent to Canada in 1699, labored near Ottawa for two years, and for the rest of his days served the missions centered about Green Bay, Wisconsin. He died in Quebec on Apr. 11.

CHARDON, MATHIAS (1695–1771). Born in Yvoi-Varignan, Ardennes, France, on Sept. 22, he became a Benedictine at St. Vannes in 1712, was forced to resign as professor of theology because he objected to the bull *Unigenitus,* wrote a six-volume history of the sacraments, and died at the monastery of St. Arnold in Metz, France, on Oct. 21.

CHARETTE DE LA CONTRIE, ATHANASE CHARLES MARIE (1832–1911). Born in Nantes, France, he studied at the military academy in Turin, served as a lieutenant with an Austrian regiment at Modena from 1852 to 1859, and offered his services to Pope Pius IX in 1860. He became captain of the pontifical zouaves and was wounded at Castelfidardo. He later fought in the Franco-Prussian War and was wounded and captured. Though made a general in 1871 and elected to the assembly, he refused honors and retired to private life. He died in Basse Motte, France, on Oct. 9.

CHARETTE DE LA CONTRIE, FRANÇOIS ATHANASE (1763–1796), general. A French royalist officer, he served with Cathelineau and La Rochejaquelein and led the republican army in the Vendée. He was captured and shot by the revolutionaries.

CHARISIUS, ST. (d. 257), martyr. See Athanasius, St.

CHARITA, ST. (d. 165?), martyr. See Justin Martyr, St.

CHARITINA, ST. (d. 304?), martyr. She was tortured to death, probably at Amisus on the Black Sea during the Diocletian persecution. F. D. Oct. 5.

CHARITON, ST. (d. 165?), martyr. See Justin Martyr, St.

CHARITON, ST. (d. 303?), martyr. He and St. Zeno were put to death at Nicomedia during the Diocletian persecution. F. D. Sept. 3.

CHARITY, ST. See Faith, St.

CHARLEMAGNE (742–814), emperor. Charles the Great was born in Aachen or Liège on Apr. 2, son of Pepin the Short, mayor of the palace of Childeric III of the Franks, and Bertha, daughter of Count Charibert of Laon. In 753, Pepin, Charles, and his younger brother Carloman were anointed with the oil of kingship at Quierzy by Pope Stephen III and the so-called Carlovingian dynasty established. In Sept. 768, Pepin divided the kingdom between his sons, somewhat on racial lines; Charles received Austrasia (the original land of the Franks), Neustria (including Paris), and most of Aquitaine. When Carloman died in 771, Charles accepted the allegiance of most of the leaders in Thuringia, Alamannia, Burgundy, and Bavaria. Charles was apparently married to Himiltrude, a Frank; in 767, his mother arranged his marriage with Desiderata, daughter of the powerful king of the Lombards, Desiderius, and a papal opponent; in 770, Charles set her aside and married Hildegarde of Swabia. Wars with the Frisians to the north followed; when Stephen III died in 772, Desiderius marched on Rome, and Pope Adrian I called on Charles, who had inherited the title "Patricius Romanorum" from his father, for aid. Charles crossed the Alps, routed the Lombard army, partly to help the pope and partly to prevent his own nephew Pepin from being made king, and entered Rome. Charles was consecrated as champion of the Church in 774, Pavia was captured, Desiderius banished, and Lombardy added to the Frankish Empire. During the next twenty-four years he fought some fifty separate campaigns, a dozen in defense of the Church. He subdued the Saxons, who were nibbling at his borders; crushed a Lombard uprising fomented by Adalghis, son of Desiderius, in 776; invaded Spain in 778, at the request of one group of Moors who were opposed to the reigning Moorish king of Cordova; and returned to Saxony in 778-85 to crush Widukind and his devil-worshiping army, whom he obliged (illicitly) to choose between baptism or death. Rebellions in Bavaria, Thuringia, Lombardy and three more in Saxony were crushed. In 783, Hildegarde died and Charles married Fastrada of Austrasia. A revolt by Pepin the Hunchback, son of Charles and Hildegarde, was put down and Pepin placed in a monastery; another son, Carloman, was renamed Pepin and made king of Lombardy, and aided his father in defeating the powerful Avars in Hungary. When Fastrada died in 794, Charles married Liutgarde. Adrian I died in 795 and was succeeded by Leo III; when the latter was beaten and left unconscious in the streets of Rome by his enemies in 799, he was rescued by Charles's emissaries. The emperor crossed into Italy with his army a year later, saw that a synod was held which cleared Leo's name, and on Dec. 25, 800, was crowned Carolus Augustus in St. Peter's. This was the beginning of the custom of anointing emperors in Rome through the Middle Ages. The honor and responsibilities were twofold: the emperor became the highest temporal leader and protector of Christianity in the West. When clearly understood, as it was by his advisers, Agobard of Lyons and Jonas of Orléans, the arrangement meant that the emperor worked with the pope in developing mission areas, extending culture, organizing sees, enforcing conformity to canon law. When not clearly understood, double coinage and conflicting jurisdiction resulted. Constantinople was not pleased; it still claimed sovereignty over all Italy except

the papally owned duchy of Rome and exarchate of Ravenna, but Empress Irene approved the territorial lines in 802, as did Emperor Michael in 812. The rest of Italy—ruled by King Pepin, Charles's son, since 780—did not revert to the papacy, as Adrian and his successors hoped. In moments of peace, Charles organized and codified the laws of the Franks and of countries he conquered; divided the country into counties and hundreds for purposes of government, with a parliament in which counts and bishops were expected to work side by side; instituted an appeal system; created royal envoys who toured the entire empire; and gave considerable attention to agricultural and manorial economy. He was interested in clerical administrative reforms, divided the empire into twenty-one provinces, each with a bishop; had a deep interest in church music and brought leaders from Rome for singing schools in France; duly collected tithes for the support of church affairs; spread the Vulgate through the realm with the help of Alcuin; conserved existing schools, gave teachers and students greater opportunities, and gave recognition and aid to those who showed intellectual competence. His own philosophical ignorance resulted in unfortunate interference; he rightly opposed adoptionism, but erred regarding the Iconoclast heresy and directed the Synod of Frankfort to condemn the second Council of Nicaea. He exceeded his authority with disastrous effects when he convened a council at Aachen in 809 to recommend that the Credo of the mass include the phrase "Filioque" usually included in the Western liturgy, and recently added by some Greek monks. The monks were accused of heresy, but were supported by Charles; their letter to Pope Leo III did not gain approval. Leo favored the doctrine of the procession of the Holy Spirit, but did not wish to antagonize the Greek Church at that time, and could not accept Charles's action, however right its decision. Charles died in Aachen on Jan. 28. To please Frederick Barbarossa, he was canonized in 1165 by antipope Paschal III; this was never officially approved.

CHARLES II (823–877), emperor. Surnamed "the Bald," he was born on June 13 at Frankfort-on-Main, son of Emperor Louis I, became king of the Franks west of the Rhone on the death of his father in 840, while the rest of the empire was divided between his brothers: Lothair, who became emperor, and Louis the German. He united with Louis against Lothair, defeated him at Fontenoy-en-Puisaye in 841, and forced him to accept the Treaty of Verdun in 843 which gave Charles the kingdom of the western Franks (practically present-day France). During the next three decades Charles defeated an invasion of Louis the German in 858, unsuccessfully tried to seize the territory of his nephew Charles of Provence in 860, and fought frequent rebellions in Provence and against the invading Bretons and Normans. When Emperor Louis II died in 875, Charles invaded Italy and was crowned emperor by Pope John VIII in Rome. Louis the German invaded Charles's dominions in 875, and, when he died in 876, Charles attempted to seize his kingdom and was defeated at Andernach. Charles died near Mont Cenis in the Alps on Oct. 6 while returning from an Italian campaign against the Saracens undertaken at the request of Pope John VIII.

CHARLES III (839–888), emperor. Son of Louis the German, and surnamed "the Fat," he became king of Swabia when the empire was divided between him and his two brothers, Carloman and Louis, on the death of their father in 876. When Carloman (d. 880) and Louis (d. 882) died without lawful heirs, Pope John VIII crowned Charles emperor in 881 in Rome. He undertook several expeditions to Italy in unsuccessful attempts to drive out the Saracens, was plagued by Norman invasions, and in 886 his treaty with the Normans, by which he paid them a ransom to withdraw and gave them permission to ravage Burgundy on their return to Friesland, caused such discontent that he was deposed as emperor by his nephew Arnulf in 887. He died at Neidingen, Swabia, on Jan. 18.

CHARLES IV (1316–1378), emperor, German king. Son of John of Luxembourg, king of Bohemia, and Elizabeth, sister of Wenceslaus III, he was born in Prague on May 14, was raised at the court of his uncle, Charles IV of France, married Blanche, sister of King Philip VI, and in 1333 was made margrave of Moravia. In 1346 he was elected emperor through the influence of Pope Clement VI, who had excommunicated Emperor Louis IV in 1346 and declared him deposed. Charles fought for the French at Crécy (1346) where his father was killed, making Charles king of Bohemia, and when Louis died in 1347 was recognized as emperor, and was crowned in Rome in 1355. In 1356 he promulgated the "golden bull," which set up the system of electing the emperor by seven electors: four secular princes, and three ecclesiastics. He constantly strove to add to his possessions, took over Brandenburg in 1373, abandoned any imperial claims to Italy, supported Pope Urban V's return to Rome and accompanied him there in 1375, and in 1376 secured the election of his son Wenceslaus as king of the Romans, a move finally approved by Pope Urban VI. The election caused a revolt in the Swabian cities, which Charles ended by liberal concessions. He encouraged trade and agriculture, particularly the extension of vineyards, founded the University of Prague in 1348, drew up a code of law in 1350, *Maiestas carolina*, which the nobles rejected, and aided the growth of the Church. He died in Prague on Nov. 29.

CHARLES V (1500–1558), emperor. Born in Ghent on Feb. 24 to Duke Philip I of Burgundy and Joanna, daughter of Ferdinand and Isabella of Aragon and Castile, he became ruler over Burgundy at his father's death in 1506. He was taught the humanities by the theologian Adrian of Utrecht and politics by his father's counselor, William of Chièvres. When Ferdinand died in 1516, Charles entered Spain and became king of Castile, placed Spaniards in positions of power, and quieted his opposition. He was elected emperor in 1519, outmaneuvering Francis I of France and Henry VIII of England, and was crowned in 1520, though opposed by the Papal States. As king of Aragon, Charles controlled the kingdom of Naples, a papal fief; as emperor, he also controlled Milan. Pope Leo X and King Francis I were frightened by the extent of power in the hands of one man. The papal delegate to the imperial court was ready to surrender before rising Lutheranism; Charles was not, called Luther before him in 1521, and, when no retraction of heresy was voiced, issued a ban against him which was supported by the imperial diet. Charles returned to Spain in 1522 to make it his center of action against increasing insurrection; he gave his Austrian possessions to his brother Ferdinand that year and made him king of Rome in 1530. His aunt, Margaret of Austria, was appointed regent of the Netherlands from 1522 to 1530, and his sister Maria of Hungary served from then until 1555. Charles arranged for better laws, taxation, and agricultural, commercial, and industrial activity. Clothmaking, especially of linen, flourished, more in Flanders than in Spain. Charles also strengthened his colonial policy and outlined plans for bettering overseas areas; his viceroys often disregarded his directives. Francis and Leo went to war against Charles to lessen his power in Italy, but the emperor defeated and imprisoned the French king and, when Pope Clement VII continued the war, marched on Rome. His soldiers sacked the city, lesser princes accepted Charles, and the papacy signed a peace treaty at Cambrai in 1529. The emperor then went to the pope to discuss the Turkish and Lutheran problems. The edict against Luther had not been enforced, a new state church had been set up, and Catholic worship was forbidden in various parts of his empire; the Turks controlled the Mediterranean, all of Hungary, and had occupied Vienna. Pope Clement VII accepted Charles as emperor in 1530 and approved his proposal for action. On land, Charles recovered much of Hungary; with Andrea Doria he defeated Barbarossa and his pirates and won victories in Tunisia and

Algeria. The religious difficulties were to be brought up in a general council, which Charles long had asked for and which Clement's successor, Paul III, finally convened. Meanwhile, Francis I had been active in lining up alliances against the emperor; he joined forces with Protestant princes in Germany and Scandinavia, offered to lend the French fleet to support the Turks in the Mediterranean, and invaded the Netherlands in 1542. The next year Charles defeated Cleves and Guelders, strengthened the entire German border, invaded France in 1544, and forced Francis to accept peace at Crespy. Charles then, after the opening of the Council of Trent in 1546, pushed on against the rebellious German princes who had supported Luther, occupied southern Germany and Saxony, defeated the elector of Mühlberg and Philip of Hesse, and proposed a reorganization which would have aided the general welfare and lessened religious hostility on all sides. The princes delayed acceptance until they recouped their power; in 1551, Maurice of Saxony attacked the emperor from one direction and Henry II of France from another. More setbacks followed; Ferdinand was directed to conclude the treaty of Passau with the rebel princes in 1552; in 1555 Lutheranism and Catholicism were given equality. Charles abdicated in 1558 and asked the electors to accept Ferdinand in his place; the Netherlands and Spain were given over to the emperor's son Philip. Charles then retired to a monastery in Yuste, Spain, where he died on Sept. 21.

GERTRUDE VON SCHWARZENFELD, *Charles V, Father of Europe* (Chicago, Regnery, 1957).

CHARLES VI (1685–1740), emperor. Second son of Leopold I by his third marriage to Eleanor, daughter of Philip William of Neuburg, he was born in Vienna on Oct. 1, and claimed the Spanish throne in 1700 on the death of Charles II. When the Bourbon French duke of Anjou (Philip V), supported by Louis XIV of France and most Spaniards, mounted the throne, Austria, England, and Portugal united behind Charles, whom they proclaimed Charles III of Spain, and the War of the Spanish Succession resulted. The French victory at Almanza in 1707 secured the throne for Philip. Charles married Elizabeth Christina of Brunswick-Wolfenbüttel in 1708, succeeded his brother Emperor Joseph I as emperor and king of Hungary in 1711, lost England's support by the Treaty of Utrecht in 1713, and by the Peace of Rastatt in 1714 surrendered his claims to the Spanish crown in return for the Spanish Netherlands and Spanish territories in Italy. He fought against the Turks, achieved territorial concessions from them in Austria by the Treaty of Passarowitz in 1718, strove to extend and perpetuate Hapsburg rule, and in 1713 issued the pragmatic sanction, providing that the succession would pass to the daughter of the reigning monarch (in his case Maria Theresa) if there were no direct male heirs. To secure assent of the European nations to this sanction, he was obliged to make numerous concessions. The Treaty of Vienna (1735), ending the War of the Polish Succession, gave him Parma and other territories and recognized his pragmatic sanction, but cost him many of his Italian possessions. In 1739 the Peace of Belgrade with the Turks lost him most of the gains of the Treaty of Passarowitz. He died in Vienna on Oct. 20.

CHARLES VII (1697–1745), emperor. Son of Maximilian Emmanuel, elector of Bavaria, and his second wife, Theresa Cunigunda, daughter of King John Sobieski of Poland, he was born in Brussels on Aug. 6, was imprisoned with his father and brothers when Joseph I took Bavaria. He married Joseph's daughter Maria Amelia in 1722, succeeded his father as elector in 1726, opposed the pragmatic sanction of Emperor Charles VI, and when Charles died in 1740 claimed the empire and secured the backing of France, Prussia, and several German princes, thus launching the War of the Austrian Succession. He was at first successful and was elected emperor in 1742 in opposition to Maria Theresa's husband Francis I, but his armies were defeated by the Austrians and he became a pawn in the struggle. He died in Munich, Germany, on Jan. 20.

CHARLES I THE GREAT, king of France. *See* Charlemagne.

CHARLES II, king of France. *See* Charles II, emperor.

CHARLES III (879–929), king of France. Charles the Simple, son of Louis II of France, was kept from succeeding Emperor Charles III (the Fat), but was elected by a segment of the nobility in 893 and became ruler in 898 on the death of Eudes. He added Lorraine and ceded Normandy to the Norse invaders in 911. He met a rebellious army under Robert I, brother of Eudes, at Soissons in 923; although Robert was killed, Charles was defeated, and died a prisoner of Raoul of Burgundy.

CHARLES IV (1294–1328), king of France. Charles the Fair, youngest son of Philip IV of France, he succeeded his brother, Philip V, in 1322. He strengthened the royal power, partly by coinage manipulation, was offered the crown as Holy Roman emperor in 1324 by Pope John XXII (though nothing resulted), invaded Guienne, then an English possession, and took the Agen and Bazas areas from England. He was the last of the Capetian line.

CHARLES V (1337–1380), king of France. Surnamed "the Wise," he was born in Vincennes, near Paris, on Jan. 21, son of John II. He acted as regent while his father was captive of the Black Prince in England in 1356–60, put down a revolt of the Jacquerie, a peasant group, in 1358, and ascended the throne on his father's death in 1364. His reign was spent mainly in war with the English, from whom he eventually recovered most French territory, except Calais and Bordeaux, which the English had gained under Edward III. He strengthened the position of the crown, established an army and navy, ending feudal military service, encouraged the arts, and established the Royal Library, which was the basis of the present Bibliothèque Nationale. He died in Vincennes on Sept. 16.

CHARLES VI (1368–1422), king of France. Surnamed "the Mad" and "the Well-beloved," he was born in Paris on Dec. 3, son of King Charles V of France and Jeanne of Bourbon, and succeeded his father as king in 1380. The government was ruled by a regency of his uncles—the dukes of Anjou, Burgundy, and Berry—during his youth, but he led military expeditions in Flanders in 1382 and 1385, and in 1388 assumed the government. After 1392 he was forced to retire from active ruling because of fits of insanity, and the royal dukes took over again as rulers. In the struggle which broke out between the duke of Burgundy and Charles's brother Louis, duke of Orléans, whom Charles selected as his counselor, Burgundy was successful and ran the country until his death in 1404. His son Jean inherited his title and ambitions, and his murder of the duke of Orléans in 1407 set off the war of the Burgundians and Armagnacs. In 1413 the dauphin Louis attempted to seize the throne, and the ensuing confusion led to the invasion of France by Henry V of England and the French defeat at Agincourt in 1415. In 1420 the Burgundians negotiated the Treaty of Troyes by which Henry recognized Charles as king and the Burgundians accepted Henry as king of France on Charles's death. Charles died in Paris on Oct. 21. It was during his reign that the custom of addressing the kings of France as *Rex Christianissimus* (Most Christian King) began.

CHARLES VII (1403–1461), king of France. Surnamed "the Victorious," and "the Well-served," the son of King Charles VI was born in Paris on Feb. 22, became dauphin in 1416, but was barred from the throne by the Treaty of Troyes (1420), which recognized Henry V of England as successor of Charles VI as king of France. He claimed the throne in 1422 on Henry's death, but his weakness and vacillations prevented his claim from becoming a reality until the efforts of his followers (particularly Joan of Arc, Duke Arthur III of Brittany, Dunois, and La Hire) freed much of the country from the English and led to his crowning at Rheims in 1429. In 1423 he sent an embassy to Pope Martin V to arrange a concordat, thus establishing the principle of direct negotiation between the French king, over the heads of the French hierarchy, and the pope. He made peace with Burgundy by the Treaty of Arras in 1435, put down the Praguerie in 1440, and in 1444 signed a peace with England. England was expelled from Normandy by the battle of Formigny in 1450 and from Guienne by the battle of Castillon in 1453. He issued the Pragmatic Sanction of Bourges in 1438, proclaiming for France the principles of the Council of Basle which Pope Eugene IV had condemned. Eugene declared the sanction was not the king's doing and began a discussion of a concordat with him. The last years of his reign were disturbed by the continued revolts of the dauphin, later Louis XI. Charles died in Mehun-sur-Yèvre, near Bourges, France, on July 22.

CHARLES VIII (1470–1498), king of France. Surnamed "the Affable," he was born in Amboise in June, son of Louis XI and Charlotte of Savoy, and became king in 1483. He was at first under the regency and influence of his sister Anne de Beaujeu, but assumed full power on his marriage to Duchess Anne of Brittany in 1491. In 1494 he invaded Italy to fulfill his dream of conquering Naples (his father had claimed Naples as sole surviving descendant of Louis II of Naples), made an alliance with Ludovico Sforza, and captured Naples in 1495. Ferdinand of Spain, Emperor Maximilian I, Venice, Pope Alexander VI, and the Sforzas formed an alliance against him, and he was forced to retreat though he defeated their combined armies at Fornovo in July 1495. His army of occupation in Naples was ousted by the Spaniards soon after, and Charles died at Amboise on Apr. 7 while preparing for a new invasion of Italy.

CHARLES IX (1550–1574), king of France. Son of King Henry II and Catherine de' Medici, he was born at St. Germain-en-Laye, near Paris, on June 27, and succeeded his brother Francis II as king in 1560. His mother ruled in his minority and in 1562 war broke out between Catholics and Protestants. Charles married Emperor Maximilian II's daughter, Elizabeth, in 1570, made a peace treaty with the Huguenots, and arranged a marriage between his sister Margaret and Henry of Navarre in 1572. On the night of the wedding festivities (St. Bartholomew's Day, Aug. 24), Protestants in Paris and many other parts of France were rounded up and thousands were slain. He died in Vincennes near Paris on May 30.

CHARLES X (1757–1836), king of France. Son of the youngest brother of King Louis XVIII, dauphin Louis (son of Louis XV) and Marie Josephe of Saxony, Charles Philippe, count of Artois, was born in Versailles on Oct. 9, married Maria Theresa of Savoy, daughter of the king of Sardinia, in 1773, opposed every concession to the rising revolutionary movement, was forced to flee from France in 1789, and became leader of the emigrés. He went from court to court seeking aid for the restoration of the monarchy in France, led an expedition in 1795 which ended in disgrace at Quiberon, La Vendée, when he feared to land, and returned to England. After the Napoleonic regime he returned to France on the restoration of the Bourbons in 1814, was active in ultra-royalist affairs, opposed any liberal concessions, and in 1824 succeeded Louis XVIII as king. He attempted to restore the ancient regime, but encountered increasing resistance to his policies from the chamber of deputies as he attempted to restore all the former rights and privileges of king and nobles. When the chamber opposed his ministry headed by Prince de Polignac, it was dissolved in 1830; an election led to a majority opposed to Charles. When he again attempted to dissolve the chamber, revolution broke out and he was forced to abdicate. He retired to England and died at Görz, Austria (now Gorizla, Italy), on Nov. 6.

CHARLES I (1288–1342), king of Hungary. Son of Charles Martel of Naples, who had fought King Andrew III for the throne of Hungary, and Clemencia, daughter of Emperor Rudolf, he was supported by Pope Boniface VIII for the throne of Hungary, as the grandson of Stephen V, on the death of Andrew III in 1301, but war broke out between three claimants for the throne, Wenceslaus, Duke Otto of Bavaria, and Charles. The latter was elected by the diet in 1308 and crowned in 1309. He encouraged trade and mining, reformed the currency on a sound basis, reorganized the army on a feudal basis and imposed direct land taxes to pay for it, and granted the cities numerous privileges. He labored to increase his dominions and establish his line, married the daughter of King Ladislas of Poland, and secured the succession to the Polish throne for his son Louis in 1339. He frequently violated Church rights by filling vacant sees and other Church offices, claiming the revenue of vacant benefices for himself, and demanding payment of newly elected or appointed Church officials. Despite the objections of some of the Hungarian hierarchy, he remained on good terms with the papacy. He died on July 16, and is also known as Charles Robert of Anjou.

CHARLES II (1345–1386), king of Hungary and Naples. Charles of Durazzo, count of Anjou, became king of Naples in 1381 after he had captured and put to death Joanna I of Naples, who had been deposed and excommunicated by Pope Urban VI in 1380. He was elected king of Hungary in 1385, and was assassinated in Buda.

CHARLES III, king of Hungary. See Charles VI, emperor.

CHARLES II (d. 1387), king of Navarre. He succeeded his mother, Joanna, in 1349, and was known as "the Wicked" because of his cruelty and intrigues.

CHARLES III (d. 1425), king of Navarre. Son of Charles II and surnamed "the Noble," he became king in 1387, introduced much-needed government reforms, and developed the country in several ways, notably by building canals aiding transportation on the Ebro River.

CHARLES I, king of Spain. See Charles V, emperor.

CHARLES II (1661–1700), king of Spain. Son of Philip IV and Marie Anne of Austria, he became king in 1665 at the age of four, was controlled until 1676 by a regency headed by his mother, and was ill and imbecilic through most of his life. He inherited a government torn by dissension. The opposition was led by the younger son, John Joseph of Austria, who had the king under his control until his death in 1679, when Maria Anne again took over. Louis XIV of France attacked the Spanish Netherlands in 1667–68, seized more territory in 1674, and in 1697 Spain gave up Haiti. Charles II died on Nov. 1 as England, Holland, and France were engaged in dividing Spanish colonies abroad; he had selected Philip of Anjou as his successor.

CHARLES III (1716–1788), king of Spain. Son of Philip V and Elisabetta Farnese, he became in 1734 king of the Two Sicilies, which he gave to his son Ferdinand when he became king of Spain in 1759. He recaptured Minorca from England (1756) at the end of the Seven Years' War; then joined France against England and lost Cuba and the Philippines. They were restored by the Treaty of Versailles (1763) in exchange for Minorca and Florida; France also gave up Louisiana to Spain. Charles introduced effective administrative and economic reforms. He also expelled the Jesuits in 1767, exporting 10,000 of them to the Papal States.

CHARLES IV (1748–1819), king of Spain. Son of Charles III, he became king in 1788, fought the inroads of the French Encyclopedists and revolutionaries with the help of his ministers, Floridablanca and Aranda, and tried to save the life of Louis XVI of France. Charles's wife fought him and succeeded in replacing Aranda by her lover, Godoy. In 1793–97, Spain joined England to fight France (and lost Santo Domingo and part of Catalonia), then joined France to fight England (and lost Trinidad and Louisiana). War with Portugal followed in 1801; the Franco-Spanish fleet was defeated at Trafalgar in 1805; the Treaty of Fontainebleau (1807) divided Portugal between Charles and Godoy. The French then invaded, captured Lisbon, and a popular uprising overthrew Godoy. Ferdinand, Charles's son, forced his father to abdicate in 1807; Ferdinand was himself removed by Joseph Napoleon within three months.

CHARLES OF BLOIS, BL. (1320?–1364). Son of Guy de Châtillon, count of Blois, and Margaret, sister of King Philip VI of France, he married Joan of Brittany in 1337, claimed the dukedom of Brittany, and was opposed by John de Montfort; the resultant war filled his lifetime. Edward III of England allied himself with de Montfort and in 1346 defeated France at Crécy. Charles was captured and was imprisoned in the Tower of London until 1356. Released, he took up arms again and was slain at Auray, France. His cult was confirmed by Pope St. Pius X in 1904. F. D. Sept. 29.

CHARLES THE GOOD, BL. (1081–1127), martyr. Son of King Canute of Denmark, Charles, count of Flanders, accompanied his uncle Robert II on the second crusade and then into battle against the English. He succeeded Robert's son Baldwin and ruled Flanders with exemplary benevolence, defending the poor, educating the people, and introducing agricultural reforms. When he crushed the profiteers of Bruges, he was set upon by assassins during mass, which he attended daily, and was cut in two in the cathedral. He was beatified in 1883. F. D. Mar. 2.

CHARLES MARTEL (689?–741), king of France. Illegitimate son of Pepin of Heristal, he was imprisoned in 714, when Pepin died, and the succession was established for the latter's grandson, six-year-old Theodoald. Rebellions broke out everywhere in the empire, and Charles escaped from prison and, after setbacks, declared himself mayor of the palace in about 717; by 730 he had by brilliant military strategy re-established the earlier borders of the Frankish world. Later uprisings were suppressed and his associates were rewarded by the seizure of ecclesiastical, and often of civil, property. Later bright spots in his career were: he gave great support to St. Boniface, who said that he would not have been able to defend his priests, prevent idolatry, or advance his missions if he had not received this help from 723 on; and he crushed the invasion of the Moors between Tours and Poitiers in Oct. 732, a major battle on which the cultural future of Europe depended. His conduct in this battle won him the name Martel, "the Hammer." He died in Quierzy, France, on Oct. 21.

CHARLES OF NAVARRE (d. 1461). Son of John II of Aragon and Blanca I of Navarre, he was named by his mother (through whom the succession came) as king of Navarre at her death in 1442. Ferdinand, John's son by his second wife, was declared king in 1452 and civil war ensued. John defeated Charles at Aybar in 1451 and imprisoned him for two years (during which time he wrote the *Chronicle of Navarre*). Charles sought the help of France, was again imprisoned, and became governor of Catalonia. He left the throne of Navarre, to which he never was allowed to succeed, to his sister Blanca II, who was imprisoned by John II and died in 1464.

CHARLES ROBERT OF ANJOU. *See* Charles I, king of Hungary.

CHARLES OF SAYN, BL. (d. 1212). He became a Cistercian at Hemmerode in 1185, prior of Heisterbach in 1189, and abbot of Villers, Brabant, in 1197. He resigned in 1209 and returned to Hemmerode. F. D. Jan. 29.

CHARLES OF SEZZE, ST. (1613–1670). John Charles Marchionne (or Melchiori) was born in Sezze, Italy, on Oct. 22, had a simple education, worked as a shepherd, and became a Franciscan Brother at Nazzaro, taking his vows in 1636 and working thereafter as cook, gardener, and porter at various monasteries near Rome. He wrote several mystical works, served heroically during the plague of 1656, and lived a life of extreme mortification. He died in Rome on Jan. 6, and was canonized in 1959 by Pope John XXIII. F. D. Jan. 19.

CHARLEVOIX, PIERRE FRANÇOIS XAVIER DE (1682–1761), historian. Born in St. Quentin, France, on Oct. 29, he studied at Collège Louis le Grand, Paris, became a Jesuit, taught in Quebec, Canada, in 1705–9, and returned to the Parisian college and served as its rector. He returned to Canada in 1720 and visited the Jesuit missions along the St. Lawrence and Great Lakes, descending the Illinois and Mississippi rivers to New Orleans, and was shipwrecked in the Gulf of Mexico in 1622. His six-volume *Histoire de la Nouvelle France* (1744) is a full account of his travels and a detailed description of mid-America. He also wrote histories of Japan, Santo Domingo, and Paraguay. He resumed teaching in France, and died in La Flèche on Feb. 1.

CHAROST, ALEXIS ARMAND (1860–1930), cardinal. Born in Le Mans, France, on Nov. 14, he studied at its seminary and in Rome and Angers and was ordained in 1883. He taught at Holy Cross College, Le Mans, and was vicar general of Rennes, titular bishop of Miletopolis, and auxiliary at Cambrai. He became first bishop of Lille in 1913, was imprisoned by the Germans, and after World War I became chancellor of the University of Lille. In 1920 he was made coadjutor of Rennes and titular archbishop of Chersonese. He rose to archbishop in 1922 and was made a cardinal by Pope Benedict XV. He died in Paris on Nov. 7.

CHARPENTIER, FRANÇOIS PHILIPPE (1734–1817), inventor. Born in Blois, France, he studied engraving at Paris, developed a machine for engraving in aquatint and in color and, set up by King Louis XVI as royal mechanician, invented a machine for drilling metal, a fire engine, a new kind of lighthouse, an instrument for boring six gun barrels at the same time, and another for copying elaborate lace designs in a matter of hours, a task which formerly took more than six months. He sold many of his labor-saving devices outright or was duped by schemers, and died in poverty at Blois on July 22.

CHARRON, PIERRE (1541–1603), philosopher. Born in Paris, he studied law at Bourges, was ordained, and was a much-sought-after preacher for thirty years. He was chaplain to Marguerite, wife of Henry IV, and in 1594 became vicar general of Cahors. He was the friend and literary disciple of Montaigne, and made the latter's sister his heir. Two solid works, *Traité des trois verités* (1594) and *Les discours chrétiens* (1600), were followed by the internationally influential *Traité de la sagesse* (1601), which Charron intended as an introduction to the others. *Sagesse*, however, reveals the philosophical uncertainty, almost the skeptical surrender, of Montaigne, even though it probably was not written in opposition to revelation. Corrections were necessary before the second edition was approved; while editing it, Charron died of apoplexy in Paris on Nov. 6.

CHARTIER, ALAIN (1390?–1440?), poet. Born in Bayeux, France, he probably attended the University of Paris, wrote much love poetry during the period of the English occupation after Agincourt, a code of knighthood (*Bréviare des nobles*), and *La belle dame sans merci* (a title later used by John Keats). In prose he wrote *Quadrilogue invectif* (1422), begging all factions to join lest France be swallowed up in civil war following the defeat at Agincourt; homilies on hope and virtue; and *Curial*, on the dangers of life at court. He was private secretary to King Charles VII and served on diplomatic missions to Germany and Scotland in 1424 and 1428. He died between 1430 and 1440.

CHARTRAND, JOSEPH (1870–1933), bishop. Born in St. Louis, on May 11, he studied at the university there and St. Meinrad's, Indiana, and was ordained in Indianapolis in 1892. He did parish work in the Indianapolis diocese, became vicar general in 1910, and later that year was appointed titular bishop of Flavias and coadjutor of Indianapolis. He succeeded to the see in 1918, was promoted to Cincinnati in 1925 but asked to remain in Indianapolis, and died there on Dec. 8.

CHASTAN, BL. JACQUES (d. 1839), martyr. *See* Imbert, Bl. Laurence.

CHASTELLAIN, GEORGES (1405?–1475), historian. Born in Alost, Flanders, he studied at Louvain, was a soldier in the service of Philip the Good of Burgundy to 1435, was secretary to Pierre de Brézé of Poitou in 1436, worked to better Franco-Burgundian relations, in 1446 entered Philip's service, served as legate, and in 1455 became Burgundian historiographer. He wrote *Chronique des ducs de Bourgogne*, covering the events of 1419–74, several political works, poems (including *Temple de Bocace* for Margaret of Anjou), and didactic allegories. He died in Valenciennes, France.

CHASTELLAIN, PIERRE (1606–1684), missioner. Born in Senlis, France, he became a Jesuit in 1624 and at thirty went to Canada with Frs. Isaac Jogues and Charles Garnier. He served at many Huron missions, wrote *Affectus amantis Christum* (1647), and died in Quebec on Aug. 14.

CHATARD, FRANCIS SILAS (1834–1918), bishop. Born in Baltimore on Dec. 13, he graduated from Mt. St. Mary's in 1853, received a medical degree from the University of Maryland, and began his medical practice, but abandoned it to study for the priesthood at the Urban College in Rome. He was ordained there in 1862, received his doctorate in divinity in 1863, was appointed rector of the North American College in Rome in 1868, was named a monsignor in 1875, and made bishop of Vincennes, Indiana, in 1878. He moved the see to Indianapolis in 1898, built a new cathedral, and died there on Sept. 7.

CHATEAUBRIAND, FRANÇOIS AUGUST RENÉ DE (1768–1848). Born in St. Malo, Brittany, on Sept. 4, he studied at Dol, Rennes, and Dinan, became an army officer in Paris, was sent to America in 1791, and returned to fight for the royalists. He escaped to England in 1793, returned to France in 1800 under an assumed name, held diplomatic posts at Rome and Valais, Switzerland, for Napoleon, served as ambassador to Berlin and London under King Louis XVII, and was a staunch liberal from 1824 to 1830, when he retired from politics. His writings include *Essai historique, politique et moral sur les révolutions anciennes et modernes* (1797), heavily influenced by the Encyclopedists; *Atala* (1801) and *René* (1802), novels drawing their color from his journeys in America from the Great Lakes to Florida and having a decided influence on romanticism; *Les martyrs* (1809), on the superiority of Christian themes over pagan as sources for poetry; an account of a trip to Jerusalem; numerous political volumes; a twelve-volume autobiography, *Les mémoires d'outre-tombe*, published after his death; and *Le Génie du Christianisme* (1802), a florid description of the "beauties" of Christianity, with an aesthetic appeal which had great influence in an age and place which had derided faith as ridiculous and uncultured. He wrote it in 1802, after the death of his mother in 1798 helped to bring about his return to the Church, and as a public apology for his anti-Catholic *Essai*. He died in Paris on July 4.

CHAUCER, GEOFFREY (1340?–1400), poet. Born in London where his father was a wealthy wine importer, he was a page in the service of Elizabeth, wife of Lionel, duke of Clarence, fought in France with Edward III, and was captured in 1359 and ransomed. He apparently entered the royal service, and in 1367 was given a small pension, probably on the occasion of his marriage to Philippa de Rost. In 1368 he was a royal esquire, wrote the *Book of the Duchess* as an elegy on the death in 1369 of Blanche, wife of John of Gaunt, his patron, and was several times abroad on royal business, going as far as Italy, where he may have met Petrarch. He served in the customs department in 1372–78, received wardships, continued on royal missions (perhaps serving at the 1377 peace negotiations in France). King Richard I made him comptroller of the port of London and later of hides and wool; he became justice of the peace for Kent and knight of the shire in 1386. After a brief period of poverty (when his patron Gaunt was out of the country), he was restored to his commissionerships, particularly of public works. On Henry IV's accession his positions were again royally confirmed, but no pension seems to have been paid him. His *Romaunt of the Rose* was a translation of the allegorical dream-vision of the *Roman de la Rose* (by Guillaume de Lorris and Jean de Meung). His *A. B. C.* on the Virgin Mary was developed from Guillaume de Deguilleville. He then became interested in the achievement of the Italian Renaissance, and is said to have read widely in Latin and Italian literature. In the decade of Italian influence (1375–85), he produced *The House of Fame*, on earthly reputation, drawn in part from Vergil and Dante; *The Parliament of Fowls*, a fable of the mating of birds on St. Valentine's day; and the monumental love story of *Troilus and Criseyde*, built from narrative details in Boccaccio's *Il Filostrato*, and, it is now believed, from a French translation of the latter by Jean de Beauvau. Chaucer's *Canterbury Tales*, in their amazing variety of characterization and plot, and presented in the framework of stories told by pilgrims going to the shrine of St. Thomas à Becket, established the dialect of the London area as the basis of what has become modern English. Begun about 1387, it mirrors courtly, diplomatic, military, religious, and business types he met during his career, and sketches them with humor and deep psychological insight. Some 17,000 lines in length, the poem was never completed. Other works include *The Legend of Good Women*, with a striking prologue; *Boece*, a translation of Boethius, prob-

ably with the assistance of Jean de Meung's *Li Livres de confort de philosophie;* the prose *Astrolabe*, written for his son Lewis, and short lyrics like *Complaint to His Purse*. His favorite writers seem to have been Boccaccio, Boethius, Jerome, Petrarch, Ovid, and Vergil, though he refers to many others in his poems. Chaucer died in London, probably on Oct. 25, and is buried in what became the Poets' Corner of Westminster abbey.

MARCHETTE CHUTE, *Geoffrey Chaucer of England* (New York, Dutton, 1946); G. K. CHESTERTON, *Chaucer* (New York, Farrar, 1932); ROBERT K. ROOT, *The Poetry of Chaucer* (Boston, Houghton Mifflin, 1934).

CHAULIAC, GUY DE (1300?–1380?). Born in France, he practiced medicine in Lyons, served as papal physician at Avignon, and in 1363 wrote in the vernacular the long-valuable medical manual, *Chirurgia magna.*

CHAUMONOT, PIERRE JOSEPH (1611–1693), missioner. Born in Châtillon-sur-Seine, France, he became a Jesuit in Rome at twenty-one (and is often listed as Calmonotti), was sent to Canada in 1639, and, except for three years among the Onandagas in New York, devoted his life to work with the Huron tribe. He wrote a Huron grammar and dictionary of dialects, a valuable autobiography, established Lorette on the St. Charles River, and founded the Congregation of the Holy Family. He died in Quebec on Feb. 21.

CHAUNCY, MAURICE (d. 1581), historian. Son of John Chauncy of Ardeley, Hertfordshire, England, he studied at Oxford, took his law degree in London, became a Carthusian, and in 1535 accepted the oath of supremacy demanded by King Henry VIII. He went in exile to Bruges in 1537, returned under Queen Mary and became prior of Sheen, went to Bruges in 1558, to Louvain in 1578, and died in Bruges on July 2. He wrote two accounts of the English martyrs and has been called the author of the manuscript *Divine Cloud of Unknowing.*

CHAUVEAU, PIERRE JOSEPH OLIVIER (1820–1890), premier. Born in Quebec, Canada, on May 30, he studied law and was admitted to the bar in 1841. He had written for *Le Canadien* and *Le Courrier des États-Unis* before this, and later published a novel, a biography, and poems. He was elected to the assembly in 1844, became solicitor general and provincial secretary, and retired from politics in 1855. He had been particularly interested in education, and for the next twelve years served as superintendent of education in Quebec, setting up the first teachers' colleges and editing and contributing much to *Journal de l'instruction publique*. In 1867–73 he became first premier of Quebec, a senator in 1873 and president of that body, president of the harbor commission, and in 1877 sheriff of Montreal.

He taught law at Laval, served as dean of its law school, wrote on education and politics, published poetry, biography, and a novel, *Charles Guérin* (1852), and died in Montreal on Apr. 4.

CHEF. *See* Theuderius, St.

CHELIDONIUS, ST. (d. 304), martyr. *See* Emeterius, St.

CHELIDONIUS, BENEDICTUS. *See* Schwalbe, Benedict.

CHEMINAIS DE MONTAIGU, TIMO-LÉON (1652–1689). Born in Paris on Jan. 3, he became a Jesuit at fifteen, taught at Orléans, became famous as a preacher, and became attached to the court. His published sermons were widely translated; he also wrote *Sentiments de piété* and a selection of the remarks of King James II of England. He died on Sept. 15.

CHERON. *See* Caraunus, St.

CHERUBINI, MARIA LUIGI CARLO ZENOBIO SALVATORE (1760–1842), composer. Born in Florence, Italy, on Sept. 14, he studied music under his father and then under Giuseppe Sarti in Bologna. His first opera, *Quinto Fabio*, was produced in 1780, and in the next half century he produced thirty-two operas, twenty-nine church works, cantatas, motets, and instrumental pieces. He settled in Paris in 1786, and also produced operas in London and Vienna. He was named inspector of the Paris Conservatoire in 1795, was made a chevalier of the Legion of Honor by Napoleon in 1815, professor of composition in 1816, with Leseur was appointed composer and conductor to the Royal chapel by King Louis XVIII, and in 1822 became permanent director of the Conservatoire. Among Cherubini's outstanding operas are *Armida* (1782), *Adriano in Siria* (1782), *La Finta Principessa* (1785), *Ifigenia in Aulide* (1787), *Demophon* (1788), *Lodoiska* (1791), *Médée* (1797), *Las deux journées* (1801), *Faniska* (1805), and *Ali Baba* (1833). Of his church music, outstanding are *Mass in F* (1809), *Requiem in C* (1817), *Requiem in D Minor* (1836), a *Te Deum* and a *Credo*. His *Symphony in D* (1815) and his chamber music are still popular. He also wrote the widely used *Treatise on Counterpoint and Fugue*. He died in Paris on Mar. 15.

CHESTERTON, GILBERT KEITH (1874–1936), author. Born in London on May 29, he studied at St. Paul's (where he founded *The Debater*, a school magazine) and briefly at the Slade School of Art, worked for two publishing houses, and in 1899 joined the staff of *The Speaker*. Two volumes of verse, *The Wild Knight* and the self-illustrated *Greybeards at Play*, appeared in 1900; he married Frances Blogg in 1901; and then threw himself into the world of politics and journalism. He violently opposed imperialism, the Boer War, Kipling,

Shaw, and Wells, and put his views into *Napoleon of Notting Hill* (1904) and *Heretics* (1905). Biographies of G. F. Watts, Robert Browning, Dickens, and Shaw followed; *Orthodoxy* (1908) was an attempt at self-analysis; by 1910 he had finished twenty books. In 1911 he published the first of his detective stories, *The Innocence of Father Brown*. *What's Wrong with the World* (1910) was one of a series of sociological studies which continued through *Outline of Sanity* (1926). The variety of his talent was shown in the appearance of *The Ballad of the White Horse* (1911), a poem; *Manalive* (1912), a prose fantasy; *The Victorian Age*, still effective as criticism, and *Magic*, a play (both 1913). Serious illness and the war interrupted him; from 1916 to 1923 he edited the *New Witness*, founded by his brother Cecil (d. 1918), and revived it as *G. K.'s Weekly* in 1925. After his conversion in 1922 he wrote *The Everlasting Man*, biographies of St. Francis, St. Thomas Aquinas, Stevenson, Cobbett, and Chaucer, a play, *The Judgment of Dr. Johnson*, and collections of essays and poems. He lectured at the University of Notre Dame in 1930–31 and in Canada, talked for the British Broadcasting Corporation, and continued to sketch (he earlier had illustrated many novels by his friend, Hilaire Belloc). He died in Beaconfield, England, on June 14.

G. K. CHESTERTON, *Autobiography* (New York, Sheed, 1936); MAISIE WARD, *Gilbert Keith Chesterton* (New York, Sheed, 1944).

CHEVERUS, JEAN LOUIS LEFEBVRE DE (1768–1836), cardinal. Born in Mayenne, France, on Jan. 28, he was ordained, with special permission, in 1790 and succeeded his uncle as pastor and vicar general of Mayenne. He escaped to London during the French Revolution, learned English, and went to Boston, Massachusetts, in 1796. He served the New England missions for twenty-seven years, learning many Indian dialects, working heroically in two yellow-fever epidemics, and successfully lessened Puritan hostility to the Church. He was named first bishop of Boston in 1808, though not consecrated until 1810. For reasons of health he was recalled to France, and made bishop of Montauban in 1823, archbishop of Bordeaux in 1826, a cardinal in 1835, and ennobled by King Charles X. He died in Bordeaux on July 7.

ANNABELLE M. MELVILLE, *Jean Lefebvre de Cheverus* (Milwaukee, Bruce, 1958).

CHEVREAUX, BL. AUGUSTINE AMBROISE (d. 1792), martyr. He was superior general of the Benedictine Congregation of St. Maur and was imprisoned and put to death in the massacre at the Carmelite monastery in Paris during the French Revolution. He was beatified in 1931. F. D. Sept. 2.

CHEVREUL, MICHEL EUGÈNE (1786–1889), chemist. Born in Angers, France, on Aug. 31, he studied there and went to Paris at seventeen to work for a chemical manufacturer, becoming director of the laboratory there in three years and author of several scientific journals. He taught at the Lycée Charlemagne, was made a member of the Academy of Sciences, and was appointed by King Louis XVIII the director of the Gobelins' dyeing department. His published study of animal fats (1823) demonstrated that they can be separated into acids and glycerin and led to the manufacture of stearin candles and commercial glycerin. In physics, his *Law of Simultaneous Contrast of Colors* (1839) led to elaborate study of dye-stuffs and the use of benzol. His was a powerful voice against materialism and skepticism. He was honored by France and England and on his 100th birthday was given an honorary doctorate by Harvard. He died in Paris on Apr. 9.

CHÉZY, ANTOINE LÉONARD DE (1773–1832), orientalist. Born in Neuilly, France, on Jan. 12, son of Antoine de Chézy (1718–98), an engineer, he studied Arabic and Persian at Paris, became a librarian at the Bibliothèque Nationale, began the study of Indian manuscripts, and was the first in Europe to hold a professorship in Sanskrit, at the Collège de France. He edited and translated many oriental works, particularly Kalidāsa's drama, *Sŭkuntalā*, and wrote a study of Sanskrit meter. He died in Paris on Aug. 31.

CHIABRERA, GABRIELLO (1552–1638), poet. Born in Savona, Italy, on June 8, he was brought up by an uncle in Rome, educated there, was devoted to ancient Greek literature and an opponent of the Petrarchan vogue in Italian poetry, and opened the way to Italian classicism. He lived in Florence and Genoa, was patronized by several nobles, he wrote five heroic poems, a dozen poetic dramas, and Anacreontic and Pindaric odes. He himself was influenced by Ronsard and influenced Parini and Carducci. He died in Savona in Oct.

CHICHELE, HENRY (1362–1443), bishop. Born in Higham Ferrers, Northamptonshire, England, he studied at Winchester and Oxford, obtained his doctorate in law in 1396, and held a number of parish posts in Wales, Salisbury, and Winchester. He served on several diplomatic missions for the king and was at Lucca, Italy, in 1408 when Pope Gregory XII consecrated him bishop of St. David. He attended the Council of Pisa in 1409 and briefly assumed his see in 1411. He was ambassador to France in 1413, became archbishop of Canterbury and royal adviser in 1414, approved war with France and went there with the army of King Henry V in 1419 and 1420.

He endowed a seminary in his birthplace and scholarships at Oxford, and built the Cistercian College of St. Bernard there (now St. John's), to which he retired in his last years. As archbishop he was active against the Lollards, but so firm a supporter of the king against the pope that he was looked on as one who sought the establishment of a national church. His position twice cost him a cardinalate and resulted in a lesser bishop being made papal legate. In 1428 he took a firmer stand and tried to lessen anti-papal feeling in the House of Commons. He died in Oxford on Apr. 12.

CHIEREGATI, FRANCESCO (1479–1539), bishop. Born in Vicenza, Italy, he was sent by Leo X as papal nuncio to England in 1515, to Portugal, and in 1519 to Spain. Pope Adrian VI made him bishop of Teramo, Naples, and sent him to the Diet of Nuremberg in 1522. There the bishop was unsuccessful in his attempt to persuade the German princes to take a more active interest in the eviction of the Turks from Europe and in the details of the Edict of Worms against Luther. He died in Bologna, Italy, on Dec. 6.

CHIGI, FLAVIO (1810–1885), cardinal. Born in Rome on May 31, he was an officer in the papal guard before he was ordained and made bishop of Mira. He was papal representative at the coronation of Czar Alexander II, and nuncio to Bavaria and at Paris from 1861 to 1873, when he was made a cardinal and returned to the Vatican. He died in Rome on Feb. 15.

CHIHWATENHWA, JOSEPH (d. 1640). Son of a Huron chief, he was one of the first Canadian Indians to be converted, in 1637, by Jean de Brébeuf; he was found slain three years later, on Aug 2, apparently by tribesmen who objected to his firmness of faith.

CHILD, RICHARD WASHBURN (1881–1935), ambassador. Born in Worcester, Massachusetts, on Aug. 5, he studied at Harvard, took his law degree there in 1906, worked as a journalist, and opened a law office in New York in 1915. He was a war correspondent in World War I, was an editor of *Collier's* magazine in 1919–21, and was appointed ambassador to Italy in 1921 by President Harding. He became an enthusiastic supporter of Mussolini, whom he helped write his autobiography in 1928, and was an adviser to Cordell Hull at the London Economic Conference in 1934. He became a convert the day before his death in New York City on Jan. 31.

CHIMALPAIN, DOMINGO (17th century). An Indian, born in the mid-sixteenth century, he was educated at the University of Mexico City, and is called the author of *Historia mexicana antigua* (1597) and several other chronicles of his country from 1068 through the conquest by the Spaniards.

CHINCHÓN, LUIS DE CABRERA BOBA-DILLA CERDA Y MENDOZA DE (d. 1647), viceroy. He served as viceroy of Peru in 1629–39, sent Christóbal de Acuña on an Amazon expedition, and popularized quinine, an Indian remedy, which was used to treat Countess Chinchón. Linnaeus called the quina-quina tree *Cinchona* after her.

CHIONIA, ST. (d. 304), martyr. *See* Agape, St.

CHIROLI, AMIDEO (d. 1700?). An Italian Servite, he wrote theological treatises, including *Lumina fidei divinae.*

CHISOLM, AENEAS (1836–1918), bishop. Born in Inverness, Scotland, he studied at Blairs College, Aberdeen, and at the Gregorian, Rome, was ordained in 1860, did parish work, and in 1890 became rector of Blairs. He was consecrated fourth bishop of Aberdeen in 1899 and died there on Jan. 13.

CHOLONEC, PIERRE (1641–1723), missioner. Born in Finistère, France, on June 29, he became a Jesuit in 1659, taught at Moulins and Eu, studied further at Paris, and was sent to Canada in 1674. He was stationed at St. François Xavier du Sault, where Catherine Tekakwitha lived, wrote her biography, was superior of the Jesuit house in Montreal, and died in Quebec on Oct. 30.

CHORON, ALEXANDRE ÉTIENNE (1772–1834), musician. Born in Caen, France, on Oct. 21, he studied the musical theories of Rameau and of Nicolò Sala and published a study of the Italian school. As a result he was chosen to reorganize the church choirs of Paris and other cities, became director of the Opéra, and in 1817 founded a royal institute of music, which he directed until 1830, producing the choral work of Palestrina, Bach, and Handel. He translated many theoretical works from the German, a dictionary of musicians (with François Fayolle), studies of plain chant and choral singing, and a musical encyclopedia. A small grant by the crown allowed Louis Niedermeyer to keep L'Institut de Musique Classique et Religieuse and Choron's methods and interest in reform alive. Choron died in Paris on June 29.

CHRESTIEN DE TROYES (1140?–1195?), poet. Born probably in Troyes, France, and attached to the court of Champagne, then of Flanders, and possibly of England, to which he traveled, he wrote romances of love and chivalry, developed the Arthurian legend, and added the story of the Holy Grail to his *Perceval le Gallois.* His other principal works are *Erec et Enide, Yvain, Le Chevalier à la charrette,* and *Cligès.*

CHRETIEN, BL. ROSE (1741–1794), martyr. Born in Évreux, France, she married and was widowed while quite young, became a Carmelite at Compiègne as Sister Julie-Louise,

and was guillotined at Paris during the French Revolution. F. D. July 17.

CHRISTIAN, BL. (d. 873?). He was the thirty-seventh bishop of Auxerre, France. F. D. Nov. 22.

CHRISTIAN, ST. (d. 1003?), martyr. *See* Benedict, St.

CHRISTIAN, ST. (d. 1138), bishop. Croistan O'Morgair, brother of St. Malachy of Armagh, Ireland, became bishop of Clogher in 1126. F. D. June 12.

CHRISTIAN, BL. (d. 1186). Giolla Chriost O'Conarchy is said to have become a Cistercian at Clairvaux at the hands of St. Bernard, to have returned to set up the order's first foundation in Ireland about 1142, and to have become papal legate and bishop of Lismore. F. D. Mar. 18.

CHRISTIAN (d. 1245), bishop. A Cistercian monk in Poland, he was in 1209 placed in charge of the Prussian area between the Vistula and Memel rivers by Pope Innocent III, made a bishop in 1212, and consecrated first bishop of Prussia in 1215. A pagan revolt caused his withdrawal, and he removed the see to Culm; inroads led to his contract in 1228 with the Teutonic Order, whereby in return for military aid he gave over all his property in Culmerland and one third of his possessions in Prussia, but retained ecclesiastical jurisdiction. The knights disregarded the latter part of the agreement, gained Dominican support, and, when Christian was imprisoned by Prussian pagans from 1233 to 1239, arranged with Pope Gregory IX to make three dioceses of the area. Christian was released when hostages took his place (whom he redeemed at great cost), but William of Modena, the papal legate, succeeded in barring him from his see. William then influenced Pope Innocent IV to divide the area into four dioceses and, though Cistercian abbots wrote on his behalf, Christian died without resuming office.

CHRISTIANA. *See* Oringa, St.

CHRISTIE, ALEXANDER (1848–1925), bishop. Born in Highgate, Vermont, he studied at St. John's College, Minnesota, and in Montreal. He was ordained in 1877, served as pastor in Waseca and Minneapolis, was consecrated bishop of Vancouver Island in 1898, and in 1899 became fourth archbishop of Oregon City, Oregon. He increased the number of parishes and built an orphanage for girls at Marylhurst in 1908 and the Levi Anderson Industrial School in 1924. He was active in defense of parochial-school education, arguing against groups, generally from outside the state, which helped to put through a law demanding that all children under sixteen had to attend public schools under penalty of fine and imprisonment. In 1925 the United States Supreme Court, by a unanimous decision, declared the law unconstitutional. The archbishop had died two months earlier, on Apr. 6, in Portland, Oregon.

CHRISTINA, ST. (3rd century?), martyr. She is said to have been a convert, put to death after most extreme tortures during the Diocletian persecution, but her story is unsubstantiated. F. D. July 24.

CHRISTINA ALEXANDRA (1626–1689), queen of Sweden. Daughter of Gustavus Adolphus II of Sweden, she was born in Stockholm on Dec. 8, brought up as a tomboy by her mother and as a lady of culture by her aunt. She was crowned queen in 1646 (thirteen years after the death of her father), and began her reign free of regency control with a show of wisdom, prudent management, and patronage of men of learning from other parts of Europe. She then tired of culture, endangered the economy by costly excitement, saw her health suffer, and expressed the wish to retire to private life, especially since she had not married and the people wished her to supply an heir. In 1654 she resigned in favor of her cousin, Charles Augustus, went to Brussels, and became a convert. Except for trips to France, a return to Stockholm on the death of Charles, and a brief stay at Hamburg, she resided in Rome until her death there on Apr. 19, and devoted herself to charity, patronage of painters and sculptors, and the social world attracted to her residence at the Palazzo Farnese and Palazzo Riario.

CHRISTINA OF AQUILA. See Ciccarelli, Bl. Matthia.

CHRISTINA THE ASTONISHING (1150–1224). Born near Liège, Belgium, she was orphaned at fifteen. She suffered from epilepsy, experienced a series of spiritual adventures according to a contemporary biography, and was held in such great local repute in her last years that she long was honored at Trond on July 24.

CHRISTINA OF SPOLETO, BL. (1436?–1458). A girl whose extravagant austerities apparently brought about her early death, she has been falsely identified as Christina Visconti; she probably was Augustina Comozzo, a doctor's daughter who sought to make up for a dissolute earlier life. Her cult was confirmed in 1834. F. D. Feb. 13.

CHRISTINA OF STOMMELN, BL. See Bruso, Bl. Christina.

CHRISTINE DE PISAN (1364–1430?), poet. Born in Venice, Italy, she was taken to Paris at five by her father, Thomas de Pisan, secretary to King Charles V. She was educated at court, married Étienne du Castel at fourteen, was widowed at twenty-five, and decided to earn a living for her three children by writing. Her prose includes homilies, a treatise on the education of princes, and a defense of Isabel de Bavière, whom she considered defamed in the *Roman de la Rose*. She wrote many short and graceful lyrics and ballades, and such long romances as *Le Livre des mutations de fortune*, *Le Chemin de longue étude*, and *Le Livre des cent histoires de Troie*.

CHRISTOPHER (d. 904), antipope. A Roman, he became a cardinal-priest and was considered a legitimate pope by several of his successors and numerous church historians. He assumed office by seizing and imprisoning his predecessor, Pope Leo V, in July or September 903. Leo died in the latter month and Christopher was deposed and spent his last days as a monk. Sergius III became pope the following January.

CHRISTOPHER, ST. (d. 251?), martyr. He died in Lycia during the persecution of Decius. Legend makes him an ugly giant in Canaan who sought to find one who could master him; he finally decided that this was Christ, inasmuch as the latter was feared by the devil himself. The most popular story, that generally portrayed in art, is of a huge hermit, devoted to carrying pilgrims across a turbulent river. One day, a small child on his back grew so heavy that Christopher feared they both would be drowned; the child then revealed Himself as Christ, who was carrying the weight of the world in His hand. The name Christopher means Christ-bearer. Because of the legend he has been adopted as patron of travelers. F. D. July 25.

CHRISTOPHER, ST. (d. 852), martyr. A monk at the monastery of St. Martin de la Rojana, near Cordova, Spain, he was beheaded there during a Moorish persecution, with St. Leovigild, a local pastor. F. D. Aug. 20.

CHRISTOPHER, BL. (1172?–1272). A parish priest at Romagnola, Italy, he became a disciple of St. Francis of Assisi at forty, was sent as a missioner against the Albigensians, and established the order at Cahors, France, where he died. His cult was approved in 1905. F. D. Oct. 25.

CHRISTOPHER, ST. (d. 1490?), martyr. A three-year-old boy, he was crucified at Guardia, Spain, by enemies of the Church who had kidnaped him. His cult was confirmed in 1805 by Pope Pius VII. F. D. Sept. 25.

CHRISTOPHER, BL. (d. 1500?), martyr. A Portuguese Knight of the Order of Christ (Cistercian), he was beheaded by a Mohammedan ruler in Ceylon. F. D. Nov. 12.

CHRISTOPHER OF MILAN, BL. (d. 1484). Ordained a Dominican early in the century, he preached successfully in Milan and throughout Liguria, and became prior of a monastery a grateful populace built for him at Taggia, Italy. He was beatified in 1875. F. D. Mar. 1.

CHRODEGANG, ST. (d. 766), bishop. Born near Liège, he became secretary of Charles Martel, was made bishop of Metz in 742 (though a layman), served as ambassador of King Pepin to Pope Stephen III, and arranged territorial grants to the papacy. He then returned to Metz, sought to reform the clergy, wrote a code of rules for the canons who were to meet daily in chapter, saw the changes made widespread by Charlemagne, introduced Roman liturgy and Gregorian chant, and built many establishments, including the abbey of Gorze, Italy. F. D. Mar. 6.

CHROMATIUS, ST. (3rd century). He is said to have been a prefect of Rome and the father of St. Tiburtius. F. D. Aug. 11.

CHROMATIUS, ST. (d. 407?), bishop. Probably a native of Aquileia, Italy, he was ordained, took part in the synod which denounced Arianism in Aquileia in 381, and succeeded St. Valerian as bishop there about 388. He was a friend of St. Jerome and Rufinus, whom he had baptized, and vainly tried to reconcile them. He was an outstanding scholar and prelate, vigorously defended St. John Chrysostom, helped finance Jerome's translation of the Bible, and wrote biblical commentaries. F. D. Dec. 2.

CHRONIDAS, ST. (d. 121?), martyr. He was slain in Illyria during the reign of Hadrian. F. D. Mar. 27.

CHRYSANTHUS, ST., martyr. Son of a patrician from Alexandria, Egypt, he was baptized in Rome and married Daria, a priestess of Minerva, whom he converted to Christianity. They were so successful in converting Romans that they were denounced to the tribune Claudius, who ordered them tortured and demeaned. Their constancy so impressed Claudius that he, his wife, Hilaria, his two sons, and several soldiers became Christians and were slain. Chrysanthus and Daria were stoned and buried alive. When some of their followers, among them St. Diodorus, a priest, and Marianus, a deacon, prayed for them in their crypt, they also were entombed alive. That they actually lived and suffered martyrdom is known, but the rest of their story is based on legend. F. D. Oct. 25.

CHRYSOGONUS, ST. (d. 304?), martyr. He was beheaded at Aquileia, Italy, during the Diocletian persecution. F. D. Nov. 24.

CHRYSOLIUS, ST. (4th century), martyr. An Armenian, he went to Flanders during the Diocletian persecution, where he is said to have become a bishop and been slain. F. D. Feb. 7.

CHRYSOTELUS, ST. (d. 250), martyr. *See* Parmenius, St.

CHU, SIMON (1868–1960), bishop. Born in Shanghai, on Oct. 30, he became a Jesuit at twenty and was ordained in 1898. He was named first bishop of the Haimen vicariate in 1926, and was consecrated in Rome with five fellow Chinese bishops, the first natives of China to become bishops in modern times. He

was appointed bishop of Haimen in 1946 when the vicariate was made a diocese, opposed the Communists when they began to take over China, and in 1955 was placed under house arrest and repeatedly denounced by the Communist press when he refused to endorse the schismatic Patriotic Association of Chinese Catholics. In 1959 the Communists illegally deposed him and replaced him with an illicitly consecrated bishop. He remained under arrest until his death on Feb. 27 in Haimen, China.

CHUNIALD, ST. (7th century). He and St. Gislar were Celtic missioners who preached in Germany and Austria under the direction of St. Rupert of Salzburg. F. D. Sept. 24.

CIAMPINI, GIOVANNI GIUSTINO (1633–1698), archaeologist. Born in Rome, he studied law there, became interested in coins, statuary, and archaeology, and in 1679 founded an academy of science under the patronage of Queen Christina of Sweden. His chief works include a history of the churches built by Constantine the Great and a study of the art of mosaic. He died in Rome.

CIASCA, PASQUALE (1835–1902), cardinal. Born in Polignano a Mare, Bari, Italy, on May 7, he became an Augustinian in 1856, was ordained in 1858, studied at Rome, became an oriental scholar, and held several high posts in his order, including that of assistant general. In 1866 he held the chair of Hebrew in the College of Propaganda, was a theologian at the Vatican Council, professor of oriental languages and later dean at the Roman seminary, papal consultant, and in 1891 archbishop of Larissa and prefect of the Vatican archives. He presided at the Ruthenian synod held at Lemberg, was made a cardinal in 1899, and edited Coptic fragments of scripture, a harmony of the gospels by Tatian, and other biblical studies. He died in Rome on Feb. 6.

CIBOT, PIERRE MARTIAL (1727–1780), missioner. Born in Limoges, France, on Feb. 14, he became a Jesuit in 1743, was sent to Macao and China, and reached the imperial court at Peking in 1760. He wrote widely on history, antiquities, botany, and natural science. He died in Peking, China, on Nov. 7.

CIBOULE, ROBERT (d. 1458), theologian. Born in Eure, France, he was chancellor of Notre Dame, Paris, dean at Évreux, and chamberlain to Pope Nicholas V. He was consulted on the wisdom of reconsidering the trial of St. Joan of Arc, which he approved, went to the Council of Basle in 1437, and was French ambassador to Pope Eugene IV at Florence in 1439.

CICCARELLI, BL. MATTHIA (d. 1543). Born in Luco, in the Abruzzi, Italy, she became an Augustinian hermit under the name of Sr. Christina, living a life of remarkable humility and devotion. She died as prioress at

Aquila. Her cult was confirmed in 1841. F. D. Jan. 19.

CICCIONE, ANDREA (d. 1440?), sculptor. Born in Naples, Italy, he studied under the younger Masuccio, and is said to have built the cloister of San Severino and the monastery of Monte Oliveto. For Joanna II he completed the tomb of King Ladislaus as well as the tomb for her lover, Gian Garacciolo, with colored allegorical figures, both in the church of San Giovanni a Carbonara, Naples.

CICCO, BL. (d. 1350). Born in Pesaro, Italy, he became a Franciscan tertiary and lived as a hermit. His cult was confirmed by Pope Pius IX. F. D. Aug. 4.

CICOGNARA, LEOPOLDO (1767–1834), archaeologist. Born in Ferrara, Italy, on Nov. 26, he was a member of the legislature in Milan in 1798, minister to Turin in 1799, deputy to the Council of Lyons in 1801, and councilor of state. He retired after eight years of public life, marked by the French occupation of his country, charges of plots, and exile, and from thirty-eight years devoted himself to the arts. He wrote *Del bello ragionamenti* in 1808, served as director of the Academy of Fine Arts at Venice in 1818–27, established its museum, published a three-volume history of sculpture (1813–18) and a study of the monuments of Venice, popularized enamel (*niello*), and collected early engravings. He died in Venice on Mar. 5.

CIEPLAK, JOHN (1857–1926), archbishop. Born in Dombrova, Russia (later Poland), he was administrator and head of the Russian hierarchy after Archbishop Edward de Ropp of Mohilev, whose auxiliary he was, was driven from Russia by the communists. He and Monsignor Butkevitch were tried in 1923 for protecting church treasures from seizure by the state; the latter was executed, but, after a storm of protests, Cieplak's death penalty was commuted. He was imprisoned in Butrika prison for a year, then expelled to Poland. He was named archbishop of Vilna, Poland, in 1926, while visiting the United States, but died in Passaic, New Jersey, on Feb. 17 before he was able to occupy his see.

CIGNANI, CARLO (1628–1719), painter. Born in Bologna, Italy, he studied painting under Francesco Albani, was influenced by the Carracci, Correggio, and Guido Reni, decorated the palace of Cardinal Farnese in Bologna, did historical murals for the church of San Michele in Bosco, and painted the fresco of *The Assumption of the Virgin* for the cathedral at Forlì from 1681 to 1706, on the completion of which Pope Clement XI appointed him president of the Academy of Bologna. Other work includes *Joseph and Potiphar's Wife, Pera and Cimon,* and *Entry of Paul III into Bologna.* He died in Forlì, Italy.

CIGNANI, FELICE (1660–1724), painter. Son of Carlo, he succeeded to his father's fortune, dabbled in art, and completed decorations for two churches in Bologna, Italy.

CIGNANI, PAOLO (1709–1764), painter. Nephew of Carlo, under whom he studied art, he worked at Bologna, Italy, in the refined manner of the later baroque; few of his paintings are known.

CILINIA, ST. (5th century). She was the mother of SS. Principius of Soissons and Remigius of Rheims, and died at Laon, France, sometime after 458. F. D. Oct. 21.

CILLENE, ST. (d. 752?). He was elected abbot of Iona in 726. F. D. July 3.

CIMA DA CONEGLIANO, GIOVANNI BATTISTA (1459?–1517?), painter. Born in Conegliano, Treviso, Italy, he studied at Vicenza, was established in Venice by 1492, and returned to his birthplace in 1516. He may have studied with Vivarini or Bellini, and was early influenced by Montagna in executing scenes from the Old and New Testament. His *Baptism of Christ* reveals the importance of local background in the new art of Italy; *The Baptist with Four Saints, Tobias and the Angels,* and *Glorification of St. Peter* reveal the influence of Giorgione and the Venetian style. His *Incredulity of St. Thomas, SS. Anthony, Roche, and Lucy,* and many madonnas reveal his simplicity and freshness.

CIMABUE, CENNI DI PEPO (1240?–1302?), painter. Born probably in Florence, Italy, and often called Giovanni, he was living in Rome in 1272, completed a mosaic of St. John the Baptist for the apse of the cathedral in Pisa in 1301, and contracted for an altar screen of the Madonna for Santa Chiara. Other stories concerning him, calling him the founder of Italian painting and the master of Giotto, are false legend; references to alleged paintings refer to the actual work of Duccio de Buoninsegna of Siena. Cimabue does seem to have been a painter of some significance, and is referred to by Dante in *Purgatorio.*

CINDEUS, ST. (d. 300?), martyr. A priest, he was burned to death in Pamphylia, Asia Minor, during the Diocletian persecution. F. D. July 11.

CINI, BL. JOHN (d. 1433). A soldier at Pisa, Italy, he became a Franciscan in 1396, developed several charitable institutions, and organized a group of flagellants. His cult was approved in 1856. F. D. Nov. 14.

CINNIA, ST. (5th century). She was a princess in Ulster, Ireland, converted by St. Patrick. F. D. Feb. 1.

CINO DA PISTOJA. See Sinibaldi, Guittoncino.

CINTHIO. See Giraldi, Giovanni Battista.

CIONE, ANDREA DE'. See Verrocchio, Andrea del.

CIONE, ANDREA DI (1308?–1368), painter. Son of a goldsmith, Andrea (also known as Arcagnuolo, Arcangia, and Orcagna) was born in Florence, studied his father's trade, sculpture under Andrea Pisano, and in 1343 was a member of the painters' guild in Florence. He was a follower of Giotto, was in 1358 appointed chief architect of the Orvieto cathedral, and executed mosaics for its façade and the marble tabernacle at Orsan Michele which has been called the most perfect in Italian Gothic. Chief among his paintings are the frescoes of the choir of Santa Maria Novella, Florence, and the altarpiece in the Strozzi chapel, both painted with his brother Nardo; *St. Matthew*, completed with his brother Jacopo; *Coronation of the Virgin* and *Vision of St. Bernard*.

CIRIACO D'ANCONA. *See* Pizzicolli, Ciriaco.

CISELLUS, ST. (d. 303?), martyr. *See* Luxorius, St.

CITTINUS, ST. (d. 180), martyr. *See* Speratus, St.

CIVITALI, MATTEO (1436–1501), sculptor. Born in Lucca, Italy, on June 5, he studied at Florence, probably under Rossellini, lived at Lucca until he moved to Carrara in 1495, and died at Lucca on Oct. 12. The cathedral there contains several busts, angels, tombs, the pulpit, and the altar of St. Regulus; other work includes madonnas, a marble relief of *Faith* at Florence, a terra-cotta *Angel of the Annunciation*, and statues for the chapel of St. John the Baptist in the cathedral in Genoa. He also built a bridge and the fortifications of his native city.

CIVITALI, NICCOLAO (1482–1560?). Son and pupil of Matteo, he achieved fame as a sculptor and architect in Lucca, Italy, as did his son, Vincenzo (1523–1597).

CIWA, ST. (7th century). A Welsh saint from Monmouthshire, she may have lived in the sixth century. Her name is variously spelled: Cigw, Cwick, Kewe, Kigwe, Kigwoe. F. D. Feb. 8.

CIXILA (d. 783?). He became archbishop of Toledo, Spain, about 774 and wrote a life of his predecessor, St. Ildephonsus.

CLAMENGES, MATHIEU. *See* Clémanges, Mathieu.

CLANCY, WILLIAM (1802–1847), bishop. Born in Feb. in Cork, Ireland, he studied at St. Patrick's College, Carlow, and St. Patrick's seminary, Maynooth, where he was ordained in 1823. He taught at that college from 1823 until he was appointed titular bishop of Oreus and coadjutor bishop of Charleston, South Carolina, in 1834. He was translated to the vicariate apostolic of British Guiana in 1837, and died in Cork on June 19.

CLARE, ST. (1194–1253), foundress. One of five children born in Assisi, Italy, on July 16, she refused at fifteen to marry, and after listening to St. Francis preach in 1212 she ran away from home. Francis accepted her vows and placed her in the Benedictine convent of St. Paul, near Bastia. When her relatives attempted to remove her forcibly, he moved her to the convent of Sant' Angelo di Panzo, where her younger sister Agnes joined her. Finally established at San Damiano, she founded the order now known as the Poor Clares. She practiced great austerities, despite the fact that she was ill for her last twenty-eight years, and required her community to do likewise and to follow St. Francis' admonition never to possess property but to subsist on day-to-day contributions. Appointed abbess by St. Francis in 1215, she governed the convent of San Damiano for forty years. Her influence became widespread, and popes, cardinals, and bishops frequently came to consult her. She died on August 11; two years later she was canonized by Pope Alexander IV. She was named patroness of television in 1958. F. D. Aug. 12.

CLARE OF MONTEFALCO, ST. (1268?–1308). Born in Montefalco, near Spoleto, Italy, she joined a convent of Franciscan tertiaries under her sister Joan's direction. In 1290 the group became Augustinians and erected a new convent of which she became abbess. Also called Clare of the Cross, she was canonized in 1881. F. D. Aug. 17.

CLARE OF PISA. *See* Gambocorta, Theodora.

CLARE OF RIMINI, BL. (d. 1346). A wealthy wastrel, she sought to make up for the folly of her earlier years by the most extreme austerities. At thirty-four she became a Franciscan tertiary and, on the death of her second husband, replaced her jewelry with iron chains, often slept out of doors, and begged for the support of the Poor Clares who had been displaced by war. The extent of her mortifications, not approved by her religious associates, eventually resulted in loss of sight and speech. The example of her reform, however, did much good. She died in her native Rimini, Italy. F. D. Feb. 10.

CLARENO DA CINGOLE, ANGELO (1247?–1337). Born in Fossombrone, Italy, he became a Franciscan about 1262 and, convinced that the order was not following the spirit of its founder, retired with a small group to found the Clareni. They were influenced by the plea for strictness uttered by Joachim of Floris, an abbot in Calabria. Because of his independent step toward reform, Angelo wandered through Italy and the Near East, and finally was called to Avignon in 1311 to face charges of heresy. Cleared, he retired to a hermitage near Marsico, where he died.

CLARENTIUS, ST. (d. 620?). He succeeded

St. Etherius as bishop of Vienne, France. F. D. Apr. 26.

CLARET, ST. ANTONIO (1807–1870), founder. Born in Sallent, Catalonia, Spain, he followed his father's trade of weaving until 1829, when he entered the Vich seminary. He was ordained in 1835, was pastor of Sallent in 1837, did missionary work in Catalonia, and in 1848 went to the Canary Islands with Bishop Codina for fifteen months. He returned to Vich to found a missionary congregation, the Missionary Sons of the Immaculate Heart of Mary (Claretians), was appointed archbishop of Santiago, Cuba, was consecrated in 1850 and took possession of his see in 1851. For the next six years he labored to reform his see, incurring bitter enmities which caused several attempts on his life (he was seriously wounded in 1856 in Holguín). In 1857 he was recalled to Spain to be Queen Isabella II's confessor, resigned his see in 1858 (his resignation was not accepted by the pope until 1860, when he was named titular archbishop of Trajanopolis), and was appointed director of the Escorial. In 1865 he broke with the queen over her recognition of the new Italian nation, but in 1868, when revolution swept Spain, accompanied her in exile to France. He served at the Vatican Council and then retired to Prades, but was forced to flee (to avoid the Spanish ambassador's demand that he be arrested) to a Cistercian monastery near Narbonne, France, where he died. He revealed an unusual sense of foreknowledge and prophecy, wrote prolifically (publishing some 144 works, the proceeds of which he used to promote Catholic reading), and is reputed to have preached more than 25,000 sermons. F. D. Oct. 23 (formerly, Oct. 24).

FRANCHON ROYER, *St. Anthony Claret* (New York, Farrar, 1957).

CLARK, ELEANOR GRACE (1895–1952), educator. Born in Neenah, Wisconsin, on July 6, she studied at Oberlin, Bryn Mawr, Oxford, and Edinburgh, taught in Portland, Oregon, and Moorestown, New York, and was on the faculty of Bryn Mawr in 1923–30 and of Hunter College, New York City, from 1930 until her death there on Apr. 24. She became a convert in 1925 and was the author of *Pembroke Plays* (1928), *Elizabethan Fustian* (1938), *Raleigh and Marlowe* (1941), and other work on the Tudor-Stuart world.

CLARK, WILLIAM (d. 1603), martyr. Born in England, he was educated at Douai and Rome, was ordained in 1589, and sent on the English mission in 1592. He was active in the quarrel between the secular clergy and the Jesuits, supporting the former in the appeal made against Blackwell's appointment as archpriest. Fr. Persons criticized him and he published a reply. He was imprisoned in the Tower

for aiding Catholicism and executed on Nov. 29.

CLARKE, EGERTON (1899–1944), poet. Born in Dinard, Brittany, son of Percy Clarke, Anglican chaplain there, he attended Canterbury and Oxford, served in World War I, and became a convert in 1922. He married Teresa Kelly in 1926 and held positions with English publishing firms. He was vice-president of the Catholic Poetry Society of London and published six volumes of poetry, including *The Death of Glass* (1923), *The Seven Niches* (1932), and *Alcazar* (1937).

CLARUS, ST., bishop and martyr. A regionary bishop sent from Rome to Aquitaine, he died there at an unknown date. F. D. June 1.

CLARUS, ST. (d. 397). Born in Tours, Gaul, he became a monk under St. Martin at Marmoutier, was ordained, and lived as a hermit near the abbey. St. Paulinus wrote his epitaph. F. D. Nov. 8.

CLARUS, ST. (d. 660?). A monk in the abbey of St. Ferreol, he became chaplain at St. Blandina, a convent for widows where his own mother was stationed, and then of the monastery of St. Marcellus in Vienne, France. His cult was approved in 1907. F. D. Jan. 1.

CLARUS, ST. (d. 875?), martyr. A priest at Rochester, England, he crossed to Normandy, where he became a Benedictine monk, then a hermit at Vexin, near Rouen. He was murdered when he repulsed the advances of a noblewoman. F. D. Nov. 4.

CLARUS, LUDWIG. *See* Volk, Wilhelm.

CLATEUS, ST. (d. 64?), bishop and martyr. He was one of the first bishops of Brescia, Italy, and died for his faith during the persecution of Nero. F. D. June 4.

CLAU, CHRISTOPH (1538–1612), mathematician. Born in Bamberg, Bavaria, he became a Jesuit in 1555, studied at Coimbra and Rome, and published widely (under the name Clavius) on geometry, algebra, the astrolabe, the construction of sundials, and in defense of the Gregorian calendar reform. He wrote a treatise on the *Spheric* of Theodosius and on the *Sphaera* of Johannes de Sacro Bosco, and devised a method of dividing the scale into divisions of any wished-for smallness, which predated Vernier's measure. An astronomer and close friend of Galileo, he died in Rome on Feb. 12.

CLAUDE, ST. (d. 699?), bishop. Born in Franche-Comté, France, he became a canon at Besançon after ordination, and twelve years later a monk at Condat abbey, where, as abbot, he introduced the Benedictine rule. He is said to have served as bishop of Besançon from 685 to 692, when he returned to the monastery. This center, called St. Claude after his death, became a popular shrine. F. D. June 6.

CLAUDE II DE LORRAINE (1525–1573).

Son of Claude I, duc d'Aumale, he was governor of Burgundy, was at the capture of Calais in 1558, fought during the civil war, was a major opponent of Coligny and the Huguenots, and died at the siege of La Rochelle.

CLAUDE LORRAINE (1600–1682), painter. Born in Champagne, France, Claude Gelée was orphaned at twelve, studied wood carving under an older brother in Freiberg, painting under Gottfried Wals in Naples, and in 1615 joined Agostino Tassi's household in Rome as assistant and student. He made a pilgrimage to the Holy Land in 1625, painted the ceiling of the Carmelite church in Nancy, and in 1627 returned to Rome, where Pope Urban VIII became his patron. He became famed for his classical landscapes and etchings, and exercised an influence on European landscape painting which was to endure down to the time of the impressionists. His works were widely copied and forged. Outstanding pictures are: *Seaport at Sunset, Embarkation of St. Ursula, Esther and Ahasuerus, Morning, Noon, Evening, Night,* and *Nuptials of Isaac and Rebecca.* He died in Rome on Nov. 21.

CLAUDEL, PAUL (1868–1955), author. Born in Villeneuve-sur-Fère, France, on Aug. 6, he studied there and at Collège Louis le Grand, Paris, and later pursued law and political science. He had been indifferent to his religion, but returned to the Church in 1890. He entered the diplomatic service in 1890 and worked in consulates in New York, Boston, and China. He married Reine Marie Perrin in 1906 at the time of his second appointment to China. He was ambassador to Japan in 1921–25, to the United States in 1927–33, and to Belgium until his retirement in 1936. Many of his experiences were recorded in *The East I Know.* He wrote more than a dozen plays, from *Tête d'or* to *The Tidings Brought to Mary* (produced in New York in 1923) and *The Satin Slipper* (1929; produced in Paris in 1944). He wrote considerable poetry (influenced to some extent by Arthur Rimbaud and demanding the reader's closest attention), translations of three plays by Aeschylus, libretti for operas, ballets for the music of Darius Milhaud, biographies, and fiction. He was elected to the French Academy in 1946. He died in Paris on Feb. 26.

CLAUDIA, ST. (1st century). She is mentioned by St. Paul (II Tim. 4:21); legends call her the daughter of a British king, the wife of Aulus Pudens, a Roman senator, and the mother of St. Linus, the second pope. F. D. Aug. 7.

CLAUDIA, ST. (d. 300), martyr. *See* Alexandra, St.

CLAUDIAN, ST. (d. 250?), martyr. He is one of a group of shepherds, including SS. Conon, Diodorus, and Papias, who were tortured and executed at Pamphylia in Asia Minor during the persecution of Decius. F. D. Feb. 26.

CLAUDIAN, ST. (d. 284), martyr. A citizen of Corinth, tortured there and banished to Egypt, he was hacked to pieces in Diospolis on orders of the tyrant Sabinus. Six others suffered with him: Dioscorus was burned alive; Papias was drowned; Serapion was hanged and then beheaded; Nicephorus, Victor, and Victorinus were beaten to death. F. D. Feb. 25 (also, Jan. 21).

CLAUDIANUS MAMERTUS (d. 473?), theologian. He became a monk, assisted his brother, the bishop of Vienne, Gaul, and directed the chanting of psalms by alternate groups during mass. He wrote a collection of scriptural readings for use through the liturgical year; a prose treatise, *On the State of the Soul,* against Faustus of Riez and the semi-Pelagians; and letters. He was not the author of *Pange, lingua,* as once believed, nor did he write poetry.

CLAUDIUS, ST. (d. 273?), martyr. *See* Julia, St.

CLAUDIUS, ST. (d. 273), martyr. *See* Lucillian, St.

CLAUDIUS, ST. (3rd century), martyr. According to legend, he was a tribune at Rome who was converted by the example of SS. Chrysanthus and Daria in martyrdom. He was drowned by order of Emperor Numerian, and his sons Jason and Maurus were slain along with several soldiers. Hilaria, his wife, died later in prison. F. D. Dec. 3.

CLAUDIUS, ST. (d. 300?), martyr. He and his brothers Lupercus and Victorius, sons of St. Marcellus, were slain at León, Spain, during the persecution of Diocletian. F. D. Oct. 30.

CLAUDIUS, ST. (d. 303?), martyr. *See* Asterius, St.

CLAUDIUS, ST. (d. 304), martyr. *See* Antoninus, St.

CLAUDIUS, ST. (d. 305?), martyr. *See* Castorius, St.

CLAVER, ST. PETER (1581–1654). Born in Verdú, near Barcelona, Spain, he studied at the University of Barcelona and at twenty became a Jesuit at Majorca, where he came under the guidance of St. Alphonsus Rodriguez. In 1610 he was sent to Cartagena, Colombia, where he was ordained in 1615 and devoted himself to helping better the indescribable conditions of the Negro slaves who poured into that center of the slave trade. He tended prisoners, the sick, and other unfortunates, preached missions with great success, and is said to have baptized 300,000. He died on Sept. 8. Canonized in 1888, he was in 1896 made the patron of all Catholic missionary activities among Negroes. F. D. Sept. 10.

ARNOLD LUNN, *A Saint in the Slave Trade* (New York, Sheed, 1935); ANGEL VALTIERRA,

Peter Claver (Westminster, Md., Newman, 1960).

CLAVIJERO, FRANCISCO JAVIER (1731–1787), historian. Born in Vera Cruz, Mexico, on Sept. 9, he became a Jesuit at seventeen, wrote several historical works and made a study of the documents left by Siguenza y Gongora, and, when the Jesuits were expelled in 1767, went to Bologna, Italy, where he began detailed study of Mexican antiquities. His *Historia antica del Messico* appeared in 1780, paying strict attention to sources and containing a catalogue of Indian authors; a history of the conquest of Mexico followed; *Storia della California* was published after his death on Apr. 2 in Bologna.

CLAVIJO, RUY GONZALEZ DE (d. 1412). Born in Madrid, Spain, he was sent to the Orient by King Henry III of Castile as ambassador to Tamerlane. He traveled to Samarkand by way of Armenia and Persia, arriving in 1404, and on his return two years later published an account of his journey, a valuable literary and historical document.

CLAVIUS, CHRISTOPHER. See Clau, Christoph.

CLAVUS, CLAUDIUS. See Swart, Claudius.

CLAXTON, BL. JAMES (d. 1588), martyr. A native of Yorkshire, England, he was educated and ordained at Rheims in 1582 and sent on the English mission. Banished in 1585, he returned and was hanged at Isleworth for being a priest. He was beatified in 1929. F. D. Aug. 28.

CLAYTON, JAMES (d. 1588). Born in Sheffield, England, he was apprenticed to a shoemaker, educated himself, studied at Rheims, and was ordained in 1585. He served in the English underground mission for three years, was arrested while bringing solace to prisoners in the Derby jail, imprisoned, and condemned to death. He died of illness on July 22 before the sentence could be carried out.

CLAYTON, JOSEPH (1868–1943), author. Born in London on Apr. 28, he studied at Worcester and Oxford, taught in Leeds in 1912–14, became active in labor movements, secretary of the Labor party in Leeds, a lecturer for the Fabian Society, and, with his wife Margaret Souter Clayton (whom he married in 1898), active in the suffragette movement. He edited *Labor Chronicles* (1896–98) and *New Age* (1906–7), wrote novels (*Grace Marlow* and *The Under Man*) and biographies of Anglican leaders, and became a convert in 1910. He served in the army in India, Burma, and France in 1914–19, became a fellow of the Royal Historical Society in 1920, and lectured and wrote thereafter. He continued his social interests in the publication of *The Rise of Democracy, Economics for Christians, Rise and Decline of Socialism, Cooperation and Trade*

Unions. His historical interests produced *St. Anselm, The Protestant Reformation in Great Britain, Luther and His Work, Robert Kett and the Norfolk Rising of 1549, St. Hugh of Lincoln, Sir Thomas More*, and *Pope Innocent III and His Times*. He died in Chipping, England.

CLEARY, WILLIAM D. (1882–1949), general. Born in Ireland on July 11, he studied at St. Flannan's College, was ordained in Paris in 1908, served in Brooklyn, New York, parishes, and became an army chaplain in 1918. He organized the chaplain school in 1942, trained 7300 men, and became deputy chief of army chaplains and a brigadier general. He died in Washington, D.C., on Aug. 6.

CLEDWYN, ST. (5th century), king of Wales. See Brychan.

CLÉMANGES, MATHIEU NICOLAS POILLEVILLAIN DE (1360?–1440?), theologian. Born in Champagne, France, he studied at Paris, began to lecture there in 1391, and was rector from 1393 to 1395, resigning when his letter to Avignon pleading for a council to bring an end to the Western schism was spurned. He became canon and dean at St. Clodoald, then canon and treasurer at Langres. He was secretary to the antipope Benedict XIII at Avignon from 1397 to 1408, resigned when a conflict arose with King Charles VI, and retired briefly to Carthusian monasteries, where he wrote several theological studies and an objection to the scholastic method in philosophy. He later was attached to churches in Langres and Bayeux and attended the councils of Constance in 1414 and Chartres in 1421, defending Church unity and attacking clerical corruption at the first, and speaking for the liberty of the Gallican church at the second. He returned to teach theology and rhetoric at Paris from 1425 until his death.

CLÉMENCET, CHARLES (1702–1778), historian. Born in Painblan, Côte d'Or, France, he became a Benedictine of St. Maur, taught at Pont-le-Voy, and was transferred to Paris for historical research. He produced an elaborate study on verifying historical dates, in which, however, his opinions were touched by Jansenism and strongly attacked by the Jesuits, who also attacked two books he wrote on Port Royal. He wrote a life of St. Bernard and volumes 10–11 of *Histoire littéraire de France*, and edited the first volume of the works of Gregory of Nazianzus. He died in Paris on Aug. 5.

CLEMENS, FRANZ JACOB (1815–1862), philosopher. Born in Coblenz, Germany, on Oct. 4, he studied at Fribourg, Coblenz, and Bonn, received his doctorate in philosophy at Berlin, and taught at Bonn from 1843 to 1856. He was elected a member of the Frankfort parliament in 1848, attended the first Congress of German Catholics at Mainz, and suggested the formation of the St. Vincent de Paul Society in Germany. In 1856 he was appointed professor of philosophy at the Academy of Münster, to which a large number of students followed him from Bonn. He wrote on Giordano Bruno and Nicholas of Cusa, on the subordination of philosophy to theology, and on the works of A. Günther, with whose views he engaged in pamphlet controversy. Clemens died in Rome, to which he had retired for his health, on Feb. 24.

CLEMENT I, ST. (d. 97), pope and martyr. The fourth pope's life is quite obscure, but he was probably a freedman, possibly of Jewish descent; was not connected, as sometimes stated, with the Flavian family; and probably knew Peter and Paul. According to tradition he was banished by Trajan, for his conversion activities, to the quarries in Crimea. He became pope in 88 and was faced in 96 with a bitter dispute among members of the Church in Corinth. To settle it, he dispatched a letter to the Corinthians which became one of the outstanding documents of the early Church. It is a model of a pastoral letter, and in it he emphasized the necessity for men to follow Christian teaching, the need of a hierarchy and its consequent discipline, and the pre-eminence of the bishop of Rome. He was early venerated as a martyr, but how, when, or where he suffered martyrdom is not known. F. D. Nov. 23.
Epistles of St. Clement of Rome, trans. by James A. Kleist (Westminster, Md., Newman, 1946).

CLEMENT II (d. 1047), pope. Born in Saxony, Suitger, lord of Morsleben and Hornburg and bishop of Bamberg, accompanied Henry III on his trip to Italy to gain the imperial crown, and was selected as pope by Henry at the request of the nobles of the city, who were weary of a situation which saw three claimants (Sylvester III, Benedict IX, and Gregory VI) expecting allegiance. A synod declared the papal throne vacant and Clement II was elected on Dec. 24 and consecrated on Dec. 25, 1046. He then crowned Henry and Agnes of Aquitaine, his wife, and gave the new emperor the title *patricius*; he and his successors misinterpreted the title and the office to mean that the emperor had the right to name papal successors and to make all other ecclesiastical appointments—a difficulty which remained until the time of Hildebrand. Clement made simony a matter of excommunication, settled disputes between Italian bishoprics, and went to Germany with Henry, having retained his see at Bamberg. On his return he died at Pesaro, Italy, on Oct. 9; poisoned, it was claimed, by adherents of Benedict IX.

CLEMENT III (1025?–1100), antipope. Born in Parma, Italy, Guibert was imperial chancellor of Italy in 1057–63, was instrumental in electing Cadalus of Parma as antipope Honorius II in 1061, and in 1072 he was appointed archbishop of Ravenna by Emperor Henry IV and reluctantly confirmed by Pope Alexander II. He opposed Pope Gregory VII and his reforms, participated in a synod of German bishops at Worms in 1076 which declared Gregory deposed, and was excommunicated by the pope in 1078. In 1080, Henry called a synod of German and Lombard bishops at Brixen which declared Gregory deposed, and Guibert was elected his successor as Clement III on June 25. Henry at once recognized him as pope and, when Henry captured Rome in 1084, enthroned him at St. John Lateran and in turn was crowned emperor by Guibert at St. Peter's. The struggle continued through the reigns of the next three popes, though Guibert had fewer and fewer followers as Henry's power declined. He withdrew to Ravenna when Henry was forced out of Italy, but in 1100 led a force against Paschal II and died in Città Castellana, Italy, on Sept. 8.

CLEMENT III (d. 1191), pope. Paolo Scolari was born in Rome, where he became well liked by the populace, served as cardinal-bishop of Palestrina, and was elected pope on Dec. 19, 1187, and consecrated on the next day. He organized the third crusade in which Frederick Barbarossa lost his life, dispatched legates to the courts of Europe to seek international amity, and ended diocesan quarrels in Germany and Scotland. When William II of Sicily died and the pope approved the succession by the illegitimate Tancred of Lecce, Emperor Henry IV invaded from Germany and demanded the kingdom. Pope Clement died on Mar. 27, before the imperial army could reach Rome.

CLEMENT IV (d. 1268), pope. Guido Fulcodi (Guy le Gros Foulques) was born in St. Gilles, France, served as a soldier, lawyer, and judge, was a counselor to St. Louis, and, when his wife died, studied for the priesthood. He rose quickly: bishop of Puy in 1256; archbishop of Narbonne in 1259; cardinal-bishop of Sabina in 1261. He had returned to France from a diplomatic mission to England when the cardinals meeting in Perugia asked him to report there; they informed him he had been chosen pope (on Feb. 5) and he was consecrated on Feb. 15, 1265. Italy had been torn by interference from the Hohenstaufen emperors; Manfred, illegitimate son of Frederick II, had laid waste to the peninsula and claimed Sicily for two-year-old Conradin, son of Emperor Conrad IV. The new pope threw his support to Charles of Anjou, brother of St. Louis; the Angevin invaded by sea, captured the southern peninsula, restored Rome to the papacy, and was crowned king of Sicily in Jan. 1266. He then defeated the German army at

Benevento; Manfred was slain by Charles in Naples. Charles, cruel in his victories, was constantly rebuked by the pope; he totally disregarded the pope's plea for the young prince's life. Clement died in Viterbo, Italy, on Nov. 29; the papal throne was vacant for three years thereafter.

CLEMENT V (1264–1314), pope. Bertrand de Got was born in Villandraut, Gascony, France, educated at Toulouse, Orléans, and Bologna, and was successively canon at Bordeaux, vicar general to his brother, the archbishop of Lyons, papal chaplain, bishop of Comminges, and archbishop of Bordeaux. On June 5, 1305, fifteen cardinals meeting in Perugia elected him pope and asked him to come to Italy to be consecrated; he ordered them, instead, to Lyons, where he was crowned on Nov. 14. As bishop, Bertrand had been a vassal of the king of England, but had a strong friendship with Philip the Fair of France. As pope, he remained in France, settling at Avignon in 1309 and beginning the exile which was to last for seventy years. Italy was in a state of confusion and anarchy, even under the papally appointed commission of three, headed by the pope's brother Arnaud. The Colonna and Orsini families tore Rome itself to shreds, though the city was under the rule of a senator. Venice had seized Ferrara, a papal fief; the kingdom was outlawed, an army under Cardinal Pélagrue defeated the Venetians in Aug. 1309, and Robert of Sicily was made papal vicar. Politically, Clement was a weak ruler. When King Edward I of England demanded it, the pope removed Robert of Winchelsea as archbishop of Canterbury; Robert was restored only when Edward II became king and asked for his return. Because of a Scots rebellion against England the pope excommunicated two bishops and, for his part in the murder of Red Comyn, the national hero, Robert Bruce. Archbishop Robert's crime had been support of Pope Boniface VIII, whom Edward I and Philip the Fair hated. The French monarch now demanded that Clement declare Boniface a heretic, blasphemer, and immoralist, that his name be stricken from the list of popes, and that his body be disinterred and burned. The pressure continued through much of Clement's reign, to the point in 1311 where the French king began calling witnesses and taking depositions to defame Boniface's name. The king had previously spread the word that a posthumous trial was to take place at Avignon, presided over by the pope, but was forced to publicly retract the story. The story was also spread that, if the new pope did not follow the king's every wish, Clement would be declared as evil a figure as Boniface and might even be put to death. Boniface was finally defended at the Council of Vienne in 1311. In the meantime,

Philip and his advocate general, William Nogaret, struck at the Knights Templars. This ecclesiastico-military body had acquired great wealth and greater power as a result of the crusades, and was the object of great envy. King Philip wanted their property and sought to have the order suppressed. A campaign of such calumny was launched that the pope came to believe the charges brought forward. Clement temporized, then bowed to Philip's will and ordered the group dissolved. Although the pope seemed to be trying to prevent the king from gaining control of the papacy or from creating another disastrous schism, his surrender to Philip on the issue resulted in the deaths of the grand master of the order, Jacques de Molay, and a great number of knights. The only time Clement stood strongly against the will of France was in suggesting that the new king of Germany should be Henry of Lützelberg rather than Charles of Valois, Philip's brother. As a scholar, Clement compiled the decretals of Popes Boniface VIII, Benedict XI, and himself and was a learned canonist. Because of Clement's weakness, the corruption of his court at Avignon, and his nepotism—the pope made cardinals of five relatives and bishops of others in a preponderantly French hierarchy—Dante censured him in *Inferno* 19 as a bad shepherd. He died in Roquemaure, France, on Apr. 20.

CLEMENT VI (1291–1352), pope. Pierre Roger was born in Maumont castle, Corrèze, France, became a Benedictine at Chaise Dieu at ten, studied and taught at Paris, and served as prior and as abbot at various monasteries. In 1328 he became bishop of Arras and chancellor of France; in 1329, archbishop of Sens; in 1330, of Rouen. He held a provincial council there in 1335, was made a cardinal in 1338 by Pope Benedict XII, and was elected pope on May 7, 1342, and crowned at Avignon on May 19. He was a staunch supporter of France in the war against England; twenty-five cardinals he appointed were French, and, of these, twelve were his relatives. He purchased the sovereignty of Avignon from Joanna of Naples, and declared her innocent of the murder of her husband. He loved expensive feasts and colorful receptions, depleted the papal treasury, made many direct appointments of bishops and priests responsible to him and taxable by him, and imposed increasingly high taxation. He was violently opposed by King Edward III on the question of benefices; launched a crusade in 1344, which was unsuccessful; made great demands of Emperor Louis the Bavarian and eventually saw that Charles of Luxembourg replaced him, which would have resulted in civil war if Louis had not suddenly died; but showed better judgment in condemning the arrogant Cola di Rienzi, tribune of Rome. In Clement's favor are his great charities during the time of the Black Death (1348–49), his protection of large numbers of Jews threatened with massacre, his condemnation of the Flagellants and defense of the mendicant friars against the secular clergy, and his acceptance of the submission of the group led by the schismatic William of Occam. He reformed the calendar in 1345, was the patron of the artist Simone Martini, endowed the poet Petrarch, and created the first chair in Greek for Barlaam at Rome. Clement died in Avignon on Dec. 6 and was buried at Chaise Dieu in Haute Loire, where his remains were dug up and burned in 1562 by Huguenots.

CLEMENT VII (1478–1534), pope. Giulio de' Medici was born in Florence, Italy, was educated by his uncle, Lorenzo the Magnificent, became a cardinal in 1513, and succeeded Adrian VI as pope on Nov. 19, 1523. He was consecrated on Nov. 26, was wildly greeted by the Roman populace, but began a political career marked by Medicean tradition and personal irresoluteness. Under Pope Leo X, whose adviser he had been, he had favored Emperor Charles V; when Francis I of France took Milan, he shifted allegiance; when the latter was defeated by Spain in 1525, he inclined toward the emperor but made a secret treaty with France. Cardinal Colonna, with Charles's support, then attacked Rome and imprisoned the pope; German mercenaries in the north of Italy became disaffected, marched on Rome, and, joined by Spaniards, violated property and populace with murderous, lecherous, and sacrilegious violence. Peace came to Italy when Clement abandoned Francis and was released by Charles in 1527. He crowned the latter emperor in 1530 after Genoa and Naples helped to defeat France. In England, meantime, Henry VIII had sought to divorce Catherine of Aragon. Her marriage to his brother Arthur had not been consummated, but the lack of impediment was now questioned and had to be established. Further, Henry, who sought to marry Anne Boleyn, had already included her sister Mary among his mistresses, and this question of incest also had to be considered. Pope Clement withstood pressure from Wolsey, Gardiner, and Foxe to try the divorce case, sent Cardinal Campeggio as his legate to set up court in London, and supported the latter's findings regarding the authenticity of a dispensation granted Henry at the time of his marriage to Catherine by Pope Julius. Henry then rebelled against Rome, though he made a last apparent gesture of friendship by asking the pope to appoint Cranmer as archbishop of Canterbury. Clement approved this appointment, when the French king begged him to, whereupon Cranmer immediately declared Henry's marriage to Catherine to be invalid. In the meantime, Henry had secretly married himself to Anne; Cranmer then publicly validated this union in 1533. Diplomatic relations between England and the papacy were broken off. Not until 1594 did the papacy itself declare the original marriage valid beyond question. Clement supported Franciscan and Capuchin reforms in Italy, was a protector of the Jews, sought to arouse interest in a crusade against the Turks, and returned from almost complete poverty in 1530 to become an eager patron of the arts, aiding Raphael and Michelangelo, Aretino and Machiavelli, and helping to start Cellini on his career. Clement died in Rome on Sept. 25.

CLEMENT VIII (1536–1605), pope. Ippolito Aldobrandini was born in Fano, Italy, studied law under his father, held a post in the rota, was made cardinal-priest in 1585, was widely admired for his sanctity, and was reliant for thirty years on St. Philip Neri as his confessor. He was elected pope on Jan. 30, 1592, and crowned on Feb. 9, and made a personal visit to all ecclesiastical foundations in Rome. He founded Collegio Clementino for the education of the wealthy and Collegio Scozzese for training missioners to Scotland, instituted the Forty Hours' Devotion, issued revisions of the breviary and missal, spoke out firmly against dueling, and sought to restore discipline everywhere, both among churchmen and among the lawless Roman nobility. He absolved King Henry IV of France when that king abjured Calvinism in 1593 and convinced Spain that the conversion was genuine and not political. The pope arranged peace treaties between France and Spain and between France and Savoy; gave support to the emperor for war against the Turks in Hungary; sought to lessen the controversy between the Jesuits and Dominicans over grace; and welcomed the Ruthenian clergy and people who returned to the Church after the Synod of Brest in 1600. He wrote the hymn *Pater superni luminis*, was the patron of the poet Tasso, and appointed Cesare Baronius librarian of the Vatican. Beatrice Cenci and Giordano Bruno were executed during his reign; his appointment of two nephews as cardinals was criticized, as was the separation granted to Henry IV and Margaret of Valois. Clement died in Rome on Mar. 3.

CLEMENT IX (1600–1669), pope. Giulio Rospigliosi was born in Pistoia, Italy, on Jan. 28, studied in Rome and Pisa, and after receiving his doctorate at twenty-three became professor of philosophy at Pisa. Rospigliosi wrote several operas: *Sant' Alessio* (with music by Stefano Landi), *Santa Teodora, San Bonifazio,* and *San Eustachio*; the English poet, John Milton, attended a performance of his *Chi soffre, speri* (with music by Mazzochi and Marazzoli) in 1639; his *La comica del cielo* (music by Abbatini) was produced at Rome in 1688.

Pope Urban VIII made him titular archbishop of Tarsus and in 1644 nuncio to the Spanish court; he served Pope Alexander VII as secretary of state, being made cardinal-priest in 1657. Learned, cheerful, charitable, and with good administrative skill, he was admired by the Romans, was unanimous choice for pope on June 20, 1667, and was consecrated on June 26. He continued to hear confessions, visited hospitals, and avoided nepotism. He reorganized the Church in Portugal when that nation became independent of Spain, gained a peace between Spain and France, condemned the aggressive actions of King Louis XIV, and gained a temporary armistice in the quarrel with the French Jansenists. Although he gave aid to Venice, which attempted to relieve the siege of Crete, the pope could not make the rest of Europe see the seriousness of the Mediterranean situation; Louis XIV was actually in alliance with the Turks; Crete fell in 1669 and 30,000 Christians were slain. The loss hastened Clement's death at Rome on Dec. 9.

CLEMENT X (1590–1676), pope. Emilio Altieri was born of a noble family in Rome on July 13, became a lawyer, then was ordained and became bishop of Camerino. He held office under four previous popes: in charge of flood control in Ravenna, as nuncio to Naples, as secretary of the Congregation of Bishops and Regulars, and as superintendent of the treasury. He was created a cardinal by Pope Clement IX, just before the latter's death in 1669, and was a compromise candidate at a long conclave in 1670; he was elected on Apr. 29 and crowned on May 11 at the age of eighty. He sought to preserve peace in Europe; continued the attempt to limit the growing ambition of Louis XIV of France; supported Poland in its war against the invading Turks, which resulted in the victory of John Sobieski at Chocim in 1673; and presided at the canonization of many saints. Much administrative work was turned over to an adopted relative, Cardinal Paoluzzi-Altieri, which embittered the Romans. Clement died in Rome on July 22.

CLEMENT XI (1649–1721), pope. Giovanni Francesco Albani was born in Urbino, Italy, on July 23, studied at Rome, and published translations from the classics at eighteen which gained him Queen Christina of Sweden as a patron. He became a doctor of canon law, served in parishes at Rieti, Sabina, and Orvieto, was vicar of St. Peter's, secretary of papal briefs, and in 1690 was made cardinal-deacon and later cardinal-priest. He was elected pope on Nov. 23, 1700, objected for three days to the decision, and was crowned on Nov. 30. He avoided nepotism, prohibited the exportation of Italian art masterpieces, was a capable administrator, and directly served the poor, sick, and imprisoned, distributing a million dollars

from his own fortune. He was active in missionary work, continued to build up the Vatican Library, wrote against the Jansenists, and decided in favor of the Dominicans over the Jesuits in the question of permitting certain rites in China. In the political world he had little success. The elector of Brandenburg in 1701 assumed the title of king of Prussia; the office should have been chosen by the pope at the suggestion of the Order of Teutonic Knights. Charles II, the last Spanish Hapsburg, died childless in 1700, and left the crown to Philip of Anjou, grandson of Louis XIV. Charles's nearest relative was Emperor Leopold I, who wanted the Spanish throne for his own son, Charles. When Philip assumed power, France was the greatest power in Europe. Louis attacked the Dutch before they could attack him or the Spanish Netherlands (Belgium), and faced the alliance of England, Holland, Austria, parts of Germany, and finally Portugal. The War of the Spanish Succession lasted from 1702 to 1713. The French were defeated at Blenheim and driven out of Italy by Prince Eugene of Savoy; England seized Gibraltar and captured the Netherlands. In 1711 young Charles inherited the Austrian and imperial thrones, which frightened the anti-French forces. The peace treaty gave Naples, Milan, and Sardinia to Austria. Sicily was given to Victor of Savoy. The latter, long an enemy of the pope, drove out 3000 of the clergy, and the island was placed under interdict for five years. Cardinal Alberoni also fought him, giving papal Parma and Piacenza over to a Spanish infante and sending the Spanish fleet, which had been raised to attack the Turks, to capture Sardinia instead. The Turks were defeated by Prince Eugene at Temesvár; Augustus of Saxony, king of Poland, returned to the Church; but the great powers continued to act in petty fashion. Clement died in Rome on Mar. 19.

CLEMENT XII (1652–1740), pope. Lorenzo Corsini was born in Florence, Italy, on Apr. 7, studied at Rome and Pisa, practiced law in Rome under the direction of his uncle, Cardinal Neri Corsini, and when the latter died in 1685 began to study for the priesthood. In 1691 he became titular archbishop of Nicomedia; in 1696, governor of Castel Sant' Angelo and papal treasurer; in 1706, cardinal-deacon. He held judicial posts under Pope Benedict XIII, and became cardinal-priest, then cardinal-bishop of Frascati. On July 12, 1730, when he was seventy-eight, he was elected pope after a conclave of four months; he was crowned on July 16, and became blind two years later. He directed papal affairs from a sickbed, appointed good administrators, punished malicious churchmen, and revived a public lottery (from the profits of which he built or restored many Roman structures, paved the city, and bought sculpture for the Capitoline Museum). He built the port of Ancona, drained the marshes of Chiana, restored San Marino to independence, was outspoken against Jansenists and Freemasons, labored diligently for the end of the Eastern rebellion, and received 10,000 Copts in reunion with Rome. Politically, the local picture was disastrous. Sardinia captured Lombardy; Spain invaded Italy and set up the child Don Carlos as Charles III of Sicily and Naples; and papal Parma and Piacenza went to Emperor Charles VI, who gained more than he had lost in earlier battles on Italian soil. Clement died in Rome on Feb. 6.

CLEMENT XIII (1693–1769), pope. Carlo della Torre Rezzonico was born in Venice on Mar. 7, educated at Bologna and Padua, and appointed to a legal post at Rome in 1716, when he also became governor of Rieti. He was governor of Fano in 1721, auditor of the rota at Venice in 1725, was made cardinal-deacon in 1737 by Clement XII, and bishop of Padua in 1743 by Benedict XIV. In 1747 he became cardinal-priest and on July 6, 1758, was elected pope, being crowned on July 16. During his pontificate the widespread attack on the Jesuits, as a prelude to the destruction of the Catholic Church hoped for by Voltaire and the Encyclopedists, was begun. In Portugal, Marquis de Pombal, chancellor of the weak and licentious Joseph I, imprisoned a hundred superiors and drove the rest of the society to Italy. In 1760, Portugal broke off diplomatic relations with the papacy. In France, the Jansenist parliament attacked in many ways: slanderous documents were circulated and King Louis XV was easily swayed by his mistress, Mme. de Pompadour, and his Voltairian counselors. Parliament suppressed the Society in 1762 and the king, in spite of letters from Clement, added his approval in 1764. In Spain the council, also secret adherents of the French philosophers, persuaded King Charles III to suppress the Society in 1767; all its members were shipped to Rome. Clement already had the Portuguese Jesuits in Rome and had no room for the Spaniards, who were ordered to Corsica, where they were joined by those expelled from Mexico and Central and South America. The kingdoms of Naples and Parma, also controlled by the Voltaire group, then barred the Society. The pope's enemies were strong. Besides Voltaire, they included Helvétius, Mésenguy, D'Alembert, Diderot, Febronius (formerly Nicholas Houtheim, a bishop in Trèves), and the ex-Jesuit Berruyer; their works were officially condemned. When the ambassadors of France, Spain, and Naples presented an ultimatum to him demanding the suppression of the Jesuits throughout the world, Clement suffered a stroke and died two weeks later on Feb. 2, in Rome.

CLEMENT XIV (1705–1774), pope. Giovanni Vincenzo Antonio Ganganelli, a surgeon's son, was born in Sant' Angelo, near Rimini, Italy, on Oct. 31, was educated in Rimini and Urbino, and became a Friar Minor at nineteen, taking the name Lorenzo. He became definator general of his order in 1741, papal consultor, and cardinal in 1759. He was elected pope on May 19, 1769, and consecrated on June 4, after a bitter three-month conclave which suffered from secular interference and during which France and Spain, through their cardinals, vetoed the names of more than half of the forty-seven members of the sacred college. Although he sought peace with Europe's rulers, Clement was unable to arrange reconciliation for long. Even before his election he had agreed to consider demands to suppress the Jesuits, which he did in June 1773, under special pressure from Naples, Charles III of Spain, and to a lesser degree from Louis XV of France. The order was dispersed and Fr. Lorenzo Ricci, its general, and his assistants imprisoned. Ricci died in prison; the others were released by Pope Pius VI when the order was found not guilty of any charges raised. Catholic Poland and Austria delayed their attacks, but King Stanislaus favored the Freemasons and Maria Theresa bowed to pressure from her son, Emperor Joseph II. The non-Catholic Frederick the Great of Prussia gave asylum to the order and established a church in Berlin; and Catherine II allowed them to settle in White Russia. However, anti-Catholic education spread throughout Germany (though the pope was able to found the University of Münster in 1773) and Catherine dealt a major blow by appointing a schismatic bishop over the Ruthenians and by other hostile acts. In the Near East seven Nestorian bishops rejoined Rome, but this was small comfort in the face of increasing defection and rebellion. The Roman nobility, many of the cardinals, and a large part of the populace were bitter, and unhappiness overwhelmed his own last years. He died in Rome on Sept. 22.

CLEMENT, ST. (1st century), martyr. He and SS. Apelles and Lucius were among the first disciples of Christ. F. D. Sept. 10.

CLEMENT, ST. (d. 298), martyr. He, St. Zoilus, and seventeen others were slain in Cordova, Spain, during the Diocletian persecution. F. D. June 17.

CLEMENT, ST. (d. 303?). Said to have been bishop of Ancyra (now Ankara, Turkey), at twenty, he was tortured for a number of years before he was beheaded there during the Diocletian persecution. F. D. Jan. 23.

CLEMENT, ST. (d. 800). He was abbot of Santa Lucia, the first Benedictine monastery in Sicily. F. D. Mar. 5.

CLEMENT, CAESAR (d. 1626). He studied at Douai, Rheims, and Rome, was ordained in

1585, served as dean at Brussels and as vicar general of the Spanish army in Flanders, and was a benefactor of fellow English exiles who settled in the Douai region. He died in Brussels on Aug. 28.

CLÉMENT, FRANÇOIS (1714–1793), historian. Born in Bèze, Côte d'Or, France, he studied at Dijon, became a Benedictine of St. Maur, and was sent to Paris to work on scholarly projects. He prepared volumes 11–12 of *Histoire littéraire de France*, covering the years 1141–67, edited by Clémencet; and volumes 12–13 of *Receuil des historiens des Gaules et de la France* (1786), on the introductions and notes to some 400 original documents of which he spent ten years; a fourth edition of this was completed from Clément's notes by Viton de St. Allais in 1818; the latter also edited his work on the verification of historical dates. Clément died in Paris on Mar. 29.

CLEMENT HOFBAUER, ST. (1751–1820). John Dvorak, the ninth of twelve children of a butcher who changed his Moravian name to a German equivalent, was born in Tasswitz, Moravia, on Dec. 26. Benefactors sent him and Thaddeus Hübl, who had the desire but not the means, into theological studies. They became Redemptorists in Rome (John taking the name Clement Mary), were ordained in 1785, and went to Warsaw because Emperor Joseph II had banned religious orders in Austria. They were joined by Emmanuel Kunzmann, who had been a hermit with Clement and who now became a laybrother; in twenty years they gained great numbers of converts, established orphanages and schools, and spread the order to Switzerland and Germany. Their social achievements were ended by Napoleon's exile of the Redemptorists. After Fr. Hübl's death, St. Clement went to Vienna, where he became chaplain of the Ursulines, a popular confessor, welcome visitor in the hospices, founder of a Catholic college, and with Prince Ludwig of Bavaria a force which prevented the establishment of a nationalized German church. The nationalists at the Congress of Vienna fought him, but he had gained the admiration of Emperor Francis I. In his last years he saw great progress for his order throughout Europe. He died in Vienna, and was canonized in 1909. F. D. Mar. 15.

CLEMENT, JACQUES (d. 1558?), composer. Born in Flanders, he was choirmaster at the court of Emperor Charles V, wrote elaborate contrapuntal forms, and was the predecessor of Palestrina and Lassus. Numerous masses, motets, and psalms set to familiar Dutch melodies were published. His fame was such that he was known as "Clemens non Papa," to distinguish him from Pope Clement VII.

CLEMENT, JOHN (1500?–1572). Born in Yorkshire, England, he studied at Oxford, became tutor to the children of St. Thomas More, taught rhetoric and Greek at Oxford, studied medicine, and became a fellow of the College of Physicians in 1528 and its president in 1544. He went to Louvain when Edward VI took the throne and was one of the few exiles not pardoned by the king. He practiced in Essex during the reign of Mary and went into exile at the accession of Elizabeth. He wrote poems and epigrams, and translated into Latin the letters of St. Gregory Nazianzus and Pope Celestine I and the homilies of Nicephorus Callistus. He died in Mechlin, Germany, on July 1.

CLEMENT OF ALEXANDRIA (150?–215?), philosopher. Titus Flavius Clemens was born of pagan parents, probably in Athens, studied in Greece and Syria, settled in Alexandria, Egypt, about 180, and succeeded Pantaeus as head of the catechetical school there. Origen was one of his pupils. He wrote an *Exhortation to the Greeks*, asking them to heed "the minstrel," Christ; scriptural exegesis; and *Paidagogos* (*The Teacher*), on moral conduct. Some of his philosophy is tinged with gnosticism, and his moralizing (proper in tone for the day and circumstances of a collapsing civilization, today sounds extravagantly narrow. These were written about 189–90; *Stromateis*, further suggestions for a perfect life, was completed by about 202, the last books after he fled from Alexandria during the persecution of Septimus Severus. He is believed to have died in Antioch.

CLEMENT OF LLANTHONY (d. 1190?), theologian. Perhaps a brother of Miles de Gloucester, earl of Hereford, he was educated at the monastery of Llanthony, Gloucestershire, Wales, where he became canon and later its prior. He wrote a harmony of the four gospels (said to have been translated by Wycliffites), a commentary (relying heavily on quotations from the Fathers of the Church), on the gospels, and others on the Acts of the Apostles, the canonical epistles, and the Psalms. He died in Llanthony of a paralytic stroke.

CLEMENT OF OKHRIDA, ST. (d. 916), bishop. Probably a native of southern Macedonia, he was the first Slav to become a bishop, at Velitsa. His efforts as a missionary in Bulgaria were so successful that he is known as one of the seven apostles of Bulgaria, ranking with SS. Cyril and Methodius. He died at the monastery at Okhrida (Yugoslavia), which he had founded. F. D. July 17.

CLEMENT OF OSIMO, BL. (d. 1291). Born in St. Elpido, Italy, he became prior general of the Augustinian Hermits in 1270 and again in 1284, and either composed or revised their constitutions. For this reason he has been called the order's second founder. He died at Orvieto, Italy. His cult was approved in 1572. F. D. Apr. 8.

CLEMENT SCOTUS, ST. (9th century). Born in Ireland, he went to France in 772 with Albinus, another learned monk, and became a teacher at the request of Charlemagne. Clement was regent of the school at Paris until his death, sometime after 818. He is said to have died at Auxerre, France, on Mar. 20.

CLEMENT OF UTRECHT. *See* Willibrord, St.

CLEMENTI, JACOPO DI (1554–1640), painter. Born in Florence, Italy, he studied art under Tomasso di San Friano, was influenced by Andrea del Sarto, and moved toward the baroque mood in his *Christ in Gethsemane, St. Ives, Sacrifice of Isaac, San Borromeo*, and numerous portraits.

CLENOCK, MAURICE (d. 1580?). Born in Wales and educated at Oxford, he was almoner and secretary of Cardinal Pole, served in several parishes, and was chancellor of an ecclesiastical court at Canterbury. In 1558 he was named bishop of St. Asaph, but was never consecrated, going to Rome at the accession of Queen Elizabeth. Pope Gregory XIII turned the English hospital there into a college and Clenock became its first rector, but favored the Welsh over the English, which caused such dissension that he was forced to resign after a year. He went to Rouen and died at sea while sailing for Spain. He is called Clynog and Dr. Morrice in contemporary documents.

CLEOMENES, ST. (d. 250), martyr. *See* Theodulus, St.

CLEONICUS, ST. (d. 298?), martyr. *See* Basiliscus, St.

CLEOPAS. *See* Joachim, St.

CLEOPATRA, ST. (d. 319?). She is said to have been a Christian widow in Palestine, who recovered the body of St. Varus, and brought it to Adraha, where she built a basilica for it. F. D. Oct. 19.

CLEOPHAS, ST. (1st century). He was one of the two disciples met by Christ on the road to Emmaus after the Resurrection (Luke 24). Stories call him the Clopas who was the father of St. James the Less; the brother of St. Joseph; and also a martyr in the house in which he was host to Christ. F. D. Sept. 25.

CLERICATO, GIOVANNI (1633–1717). Born in Padua, Italy, of English descent (his family name may have been Clark), he was ordained, wrote widely and well on civil and canon law, a biography of Cardinal Barbarigo, and *Decisiones sacramentales* (1727). He was vicar general at Padua at the time of his death.

CLERKE, AGNES MARY (1842–1907), astronomer. Born in Skibbereen, Cork, Ireland, on Feb. 10, she wrote a history of astronomy before she was fifteen, moved to Dublin and Queenstown, worked in Italy in the 1870s, and settled in London in 1877. She wrote articles for the *Edinburgh Review, Dictionary of National Biography*, and *Encyclopaedia Britannica*, won the Actonian Prize in 1892, became an honorary member of the Royal Astronomical Society in 1903, and published *Popular History of Astronomy in the 19th Century, The System of the Stars, Problems in Astrophysics*, and *Modern Cosmogonies*. She died in London on Jan. 20.

CLERKE, ELLEN MARY (1840–1906). Born in Skibbereen, Cork, Ireland, sister of Agnes, she lived in Italy and London, contributed to Italian and English periodicals, published a collection of essays, translations of Italian poetry, *Flowers of Fire* (a novel), and was an editorial writer for the London *Tablet*. She died in London on Mar. 2.

CLERUS, ST. (d. 300?), martyr. A Syrian deacon, he was put to death at Antioch during the Diocletian persecution. F. D. Jan. 7.

CLET, BL. FRANÇOIS REGIS (1748–1820), martyr. Born in Grenoble, France, where his father was a merchant, he studied there and at the diocesan seminary, became a Lazarist at Lyons in 1769, was ordained in 1773, and taught at Annecy for sixteen years. When his group was scattered by the revolution he asked to be sent to China, and labored in Hou-Kouang for twenty-seven years, often escaping death during furious persecutions. He was betrayed for a large reward, imprisoned and mistreated for eight months, and strangled on Feb. 18 near Hankow. He was beatified in 1900. F. D. Feb. 17 .

CLETHER, ST. (d. 520?), martyr. A member of the clan of King Brychan of Brecknock, Wales, he is said to have been slain in Herefordshire. Churches (St. Cleer, Clydog) are dedicated to him, although another St. Clether (or Cledog) is honored on Aug. 19. F. D. Oct. 23.

CLETUS, ST. (d. 88), pope and martyr. Now considered identical with Anacletus (or Anencletus), this Roman apparently was the third in the succession of popes. He assumed the chair in 76, and was put to death during the persecution of Domitian. F. D. Apr. 26.

CLICERIUS, ST. (d. 438?). He was bishop of Milan, Italy. F. D. Sept. 20.

CLICHTOVE, JOSSE (1472–1543), theologian. Born in Nieuport, Flanders, he studied at Louvain and Paris, received his degree in theology in 1506, became professor at the Sorbonne, and also taught at Tournai and Chartres. He spoke out for Church reform, attacked the doctrines of Luther, was active at the Council of Sens, and wrote Aristotelian commentaries, biblical and patristic studies, a defense of the Eucharist, spiritual readings, and a collection of sermons. He died in Chartres, France.

CLIFFORD, CORNELIUS CYPRIAN (1859–1938). Born in New York City on Aug. 24, he studied at City College and at

Fordham, became a Jesuit in 1879, and studied further at Woodstock, Louvain, and Innsbruck. He left the Society with permission in 1899, a year after his ordination, and taught at Wimbleton and Roehampton, England, and St. Beuno's, Wales. He returned to the United States, was editor of the Providence *Visitor* in 1900–3, and was stationed in Morristown and Whippany, New Jersey, parishes from 1907 until his death in the latter town on Dec. 4. He wrote *Introibo* and *The Burden of Time*, studies of the breviary and missal, and lectured at Columbia for twenty-six years.

CLIFFORD, WILLIAM (d. 1670). Son of Henry Clifford, baron of Cumberland, and Elizabeth Thimelby (d. 1642, who became an Augustinian nun at Louvain after the death of her husband), he studied and was ordained at Douai. He was vice-president of the English College in Lisbon, superior of Tournai College, Paris, declined a bishopric, and died in Paris on Apr. 30. He published *Observations upon kings reigns since the conquest* and several devotional and controversial pamphlets.

CLIMENT, JOSÉ (1706–1781), bishop. Born in Castellón de la Plana, Spain, he studied at Valencia, taught in that city, and became bishop of Barcelona in 1766. He founded hospitals and schools, quelled a riot in his see against military conscription, was denounced by the royal court for praising the Church of Utrecht and cleared by an ecclesiastical court, and was widely known for his pastoral instructions and charities. When offered a transfer to the diocese of Málaga he refused, resigned his post in 1775, and retired to his birthplace, where he died on Nov. 25.

CLITHEROW, BL. MARGARET (1555?–1586), martyr. Born Margaret Middleton in York, England, she married a well-to-do butcher in 1571 and became a convert two or three years later. She was fined repeatedly for not attending Anglican services and once was imprisoned for two years; it was while in prison that she began her practice of fasting four days a week. On her release she arranged to have mass said secretly either in her own house or in one she rented nearby; her home became one of the important stations in the underground mission. This led to her martyrdom, when a visiting child was forced to disclose the closet in which a missal and secret vessels were hidden. She was pressed under a weight of 800 pounds for six hours and died in York. Two sons and a daughter later entered religious life on the Continent. She was beatified in 1929. F. D. Mar. 25.

MARGARET T. MONRO, *Bl. Margaret Clitherow* (New York, Longmans, 1947).

CLODOALD, ST. (524?–560?). Grandson of King Clovis of the Franks and son of Clodomir, he and his two brothers were raised by his grandmother, St. Clotilde, when his father was killed in battle. His uncle Childebert plotted to take over the kingdom; Clodoald's two brothers were slain, but the eight-year-old prince was taken safely to Provence. When he came of age he became a hermit, went to Paris where he lived as a recluse under St. Severinus, then founded a hermitage at Nogent, near Versailles, now called St. Cloud, where he died. F. D. Sept. 7.

CLODULF, ST. (605–696), bishop. Son of SS. Arnulf and Doda, he succeeded his father in 656 as bishop of Metz, wrote a biography of Arnulf, and enjoyed a reign of forty years marked by great charities. He is also called Clou. F. D. June 8.

CLOTILDA, ST. (474?–545), queen. Born in Lyons, daughter of King Chilperic of Burgundy, she married Clovis, king of the Salian Franks, in 493 and by her prayers and example converted him in 496. After his death in 511 she suffered much from the civil strife which embroiled three of their sons. Early stories which long portrayed her as fanning the fires which kept civil war aflame have since been discredited as mere legend. F. D. June 3.

CLOTSINDIS, ST. (635?–714). Daughter of SS. Adalbald and Rictrudis, she was educated at the Benedictine convent of Marchiennes, Flanders, where she succeeded her mother as second abbess in 688. F. D. June 30.

CLOU. *See* Clodulf, St.

CLOUD. *See* Clodoald, St.

CLOUET, FRANÇOIS (1510?–1580?), painter. Born in Tours, France, before 1520, son of Jean the Younger, he succeeded his father as court painter at thirty-five, and also held the position under King Charles IX. His work is delicate yet realistic, sharp, and without sentimentality. He did miniatures, detailed drawings of court functions, and striking portraits of Francis II, Henry II, Charles IX, and Elizabeth of Austria. The genuine picture of Mary of Scotland, listed as by "Jennet the Frenchman," was by this artist, often called François Janet. He died in Paris during the decade after 1570.

CLOUET, JEAN (1485?–1541?), painter. Born in Tours, France, son of Jean the Elder, a Flemish painter who went from Brussels to Paris in 1460, Jean the Younger was court painter to King Francis I, did many portraits, including an equestrian one of the monarch, of his wife Eleanor, and of Margaret of Valois. His work is sharp and uncluttered, and in the manner of Van Eyck. He died in Paris.

CLOVIO, GIORGIO (1498–1578), painter. Also known as Giulio and as Il Macedone, he was born in Grizani, Croatia (perhaps as Glović), went to Italy at eighteen, engraved medals and seals for Cardinal Grimani, painted *The Judgment of Paris* and *Lucretia* at Buda for King Louis II, returned to Italy, decorated manuscripts, a missal and other books, and filled commissions for various nobles. A pictorial life of Charles V for King Philip II and a prayer book for Cardinal Farnese were among his masterpieces. In the elaborate decoration and pagan ornamentation of much of his miniature work he popularized the de luxe, but somewhat decadent, taste of some Renaissance art. He died in Rome.

CLOVIS I (466?–511), king of the Franks. He succeeded his father Childeric as king of the Franks in 481, conquered part of northern Gaul and was called king of Soissons, conquered Cambrai and Tongres, and ruled most of modern Belgium and France to the Rhine River. Much of his early career is from legend and romance, poetical exaggerations appearing even in the biographical treatment by Gregory of Tours. About 492, Clovis married Clotilda of Burgundy, a Christian; the king became a convert, with 3000 of his soldiers, on Christmas in 496 after the victory against the Alemanni at Tolbiac. In 500 he attempted to settle a struggle between his wife's uncles, King Gondebad of Vienne and Godesigil of Geneva. Though defeated at Dijon by a Genevan army aided by Clovis, Gondebad later reconquered his territory and put his brother to death. Clovis also warred against Alaric II, Visigoth king of Aquitaine, routed his army, and killed him at Vouillé in 507. This campaign rescued the great majority of the populace, suffering under Arian oppression, as far as the Rhone and the Pyrenees. After the death of King Sigebert of Cologne and his son Chloderic, Clovis inherited the territory of the Rhenish Franks. He directed the various areas of his now large nation by the appointment of counts, reduced the Salic Law to written form, settled many Church-state problems, introduced wide social reforms, and brought unity to an area which rose from the collapse of the Roman Empire. He died in Paris on Nov. 27.

CLYNN, JOHN (1300?–1349?), historian. A Franciscan, he was guardian of his order's house at Carrick, Ireland, in 1336, and later at Kilkenny. He wrote a chronicle of world history, which is important for the annals of 1315–49, particularly the mistreatment of the poor by the government at Dublin and of the great plague of 1348–49, of which he apparently was a victim at Kilkenny.

COBO, BARNABÉ (1582–1657), historian. Born in Lopera, Spain, he went to Venezuela in 1596, to Lima, Peru, in 1599, became a Jesuit in 1601, and served in the mission fields and as college president in northern South America until 1630. He then worked in Mexico for twenty years, returning to Peru in 1650. His ten-volume work on botany has not been found; his name has been given, however, to a genus

of plants in Mexico. His published *History of the New World* is of primary importance regarding the inhabitants, natural history, and cultural antiquity of South America. He died in Lima on Oct. 9.

COCCAIO, MERLIN. *See* Folengo, Teofilo.
COCCALEO, VIATORA (d. 1793). So named because of his birthplace, Coccaglio, Italy, he became a Capuchin friar, taught theology, wrote several theological studies, a defense of papal supremacy, an explanation of the devotion to the Sacred Heart, attacks on Jansenism, and studies of the epigrams of Prosper of Aquitaine and of the latter's poem, *Contra ingratos*.

COCHIN, JACQUES DENIS (1726–1783). Born in Paris, France, on Jan. 1, he studied theology at the Sorbonne, was ordained in 1755, and attached to the parish of St. Jacques. He published spiritual works and sermons and built a hospital for the Sisters of Charity, the endowment of which was one of his many philanthropic gifts. He died in Paris on June 3.
COCHIN, PIERRE S. A. (1823–1872), sociologist. Born in Paris, France, on Dec. 12, he wrote economic articles for several journals, published on the Christian view of industry, the educational methods of Pestalozzi, the condition of French workers, poverty in England, and attacked Renan's life of Christ. In 1853 he became mayor of the tenth district in Paris; he later was associated with the Liberal group surrounding Montalembert and Lacordaire. He died in Versailles on Mar. 13.
COCHLAEUS, JOHANN. *See* Dobeneck, Johann.
CODRATUS, ST. (d. 258?), martyr. Born in the wastes near Corinth, Greece, where his mother had hidden during the Decian persecution, he became a student of medicine and an ascetic, and was scourged and beheaded with five companions during the Valerian persecution. F. D. Mar. 10.
CODRATUS, ST. (d. 302?), martyr. *See* Apollo, St.
CODRINGTON, THOMAS (d. 1691?). Born in England, he was educated and ordained at Douai, taught briefly there, served Cardinal Howard in Rome as secretary and chaplain, became a member of the Institute of Secular Priests Living in Community, and on his return to England in 1684 introduced the group there. He was royal chaplain to King James II from 1685 in London and in exile at St. Germain. The plan for community life proved unworkable in England and was dropped after a few years.
CODY, WILLIAM FREDERICK (1846–1917). Born on a farm in Scott County, Iowa, on Feb. 26, he became famed as an Indian scout in the West, earning the nickname Buffalo Bill for his feats in killing buffaloes for

the laborers on the Kansas Pacific Railroad. He was chief of scouts for the 5th Kansas Cavalry in 1868–72 and 1876, was on the stage in 1872–83, and organized a "Wild West Show" in 1883 which played in the United States and Europe. He died in Denver, Colorado, on Jan. 10.

COEFFETEAU, NICOLAS (1574–1623), bishop. Born in Château du Loir, Maine, France, he became a Dominican in 1588 at Sens, taught at Paris from 1595 to 1612, served as prior and as vicar general during that time, was almoner to Queen Margaret of Valois, and in 1608 was made court preacher to King Henry IV. In 1617, Pope Paul V made him bishop of Dardania and administrator of Metz, where he restored abbeys and monasteries as well as discipline and order. In 1621 he was appointed to Marseilles, but ill health forced the selection of a coadjutor. He retired to Paris, where he died on Apr. 21. He was noted as a preacher and polemicist; he wrote five treatises on the Eucharist against the Calvinist Pierre du Moulin; a refutation of the apostate Archbishop de Dominis of Spalato; and a series on papal power and authority, marked by moderate Gallicanism.

COELCHU. *See* Colgan, St.

COELDE, THEODORE (1435–1515). Known as Theodore of Münster, from his birthplace, he studied at Cologne, became an Augustinian, and in 1454 became a Friar Minor in the Netherlands. During the plague of 1489 he is said to have given the last rites to more than 32,000 persons. His *Kerstenspiegel* (1470), mirror of the Christian faith, went through dozens of editions; also popular was his series of meditations on the sufferings of Christ. He died in Louvain on Dec. 11.

COELHO DE ALBUQUERQUE, DUARTE (1537–1579?), governor. Born in Olinda, Pernambuco, son of Duarte Coelho Pereira, captain general of Pernambuco, whom he succeeded in 1554, he finished his studies in Europe, took possession of his new post in 1560, and ruled until 1572. Returning to Portugal, he went on a military expedition to Africa, was captured by Moors, and died in prison at Fez, Morocco.

COELHO, GONÇALO (d. 1506), explorer. A Portuguese navigator, he was commander of a ship at Senegambia in 1488, led an expedition to the Brazilian coast in 1501, was in command of the fleet of six vessels sent to sail past Brazil to the Orient, was shipwrecked, explored the Rio de Janeiro, and returned to Lisbon in 1506.

COELLO, ALONZO SÁNCHEZ. *See* Sánchez, Alonzo Coello.

COELLO, CLAUDIO (1621?–1693), painter. Born in Madrid, Spain, he studied under Francisco Rizi, Carreño de Mirando, and José Donoso, decorated many churches, including the ceiling of the cathedral in Toledo, and did frescoes for several palaces. He became court painter to King Charles II, completed the altarpiece for the sacristy of the Escorial, with fifty portraits, and was known as the last painter of the Madrid school. His later work was imitative of that of Rubens and Titian.

COENRED (8th century). Also called Kenred and Chrenred, he was the son of King Wulfhere, who died in 675. He became king of the Southumbrians in 702 and succeeded his uncle Ethelred as king of Mercia when the latter entered a monastery in 704. Coenred gave up his throne to Ethelred's son Coelred in 709, went to Rome with King Offa of the East Saxons, and became a monk.

COFFEY, PATRICK J. (1846–1921), educator. Born in Tipperary, Ireland, he went to the United States in 1864, became a Christian Brother, taking the name Alpheus, and served as director of an academy in Albany, New York, and of De La Salle Institute, Clason Point Academy, and the Catholic Protectory, all in New York City. He died in New York City on Feb. 20.

COFFIN, EDWARD (1570–1626). Born in Exeter, England, he studied at Rheims and Ingolstadt, was ordained at Rome, and became a Jesuit in 1598 while in Flanders. Captured by the Dutch, he was sent to England, where he was a prisoner for five years before his banishment in 1603. He was confessor at the English College in Rome for twenty years, wrote or edited many apologetical tracts, and died at St. Omer on Apr. 17.

COFFIN, ROBERT ASTON (1819–1885), bishop. Born in Brighton, England, on July 19, he studied at Harrow and Oxford, received Anglican orders, was appointed vicar at Oxford, became a follower of John Henry Newman, and was converted in 1845. He was ordained at Rome in 1847, returned to England to serve at Newman's oratory, then studied and was professed as a Redemptorist in Belgium. He was rector of St. Mary's church, Clapham, from 1855 to 1865, provincial of the English Redemptorists until 1882, then became second bishop of Southwark. He translated most of the Italian works of St. Alphonsus as well as *The Oratory of the Faithful Soul* by Blosius, and published verse of his own. He died in Teignmouth, England, on Apr. 6.

COGITOSUS, ST. (9th century?). A monk of Kildare, Ireland, he wrote in Latin an exuberant life of St. Brigid and of the pilgrimages to her shrine at Kildare before it was plundered by the Danes in 835. F. D. Apr. 18.

COGOLLUDO, DIEGO LÓPEZ DE (16th century). Born in Alcalá de Henares, Spain, he became a Franciscan in 1629, was sent to

Yucatán, Mexico, taught there, served as provincial, and in 1688 published a *History of Yucatán* based in part on the writings of Bishop Diego de Landa, on oral tradition, and on personal research.

COHEN, HERMANN (1820–1871). Born in Hamburg, Germany, on Nov. 10, son of a Jewish merchant, he led a bohemian life at Paris, where he studied music under Liszt, became a convert in 1847, with de la Bouillerie began the practice of nocturnal adoration, and in 1851 was ordained a Carmelite priest. He preached in England and on the Continent, founded several houses for his order, and was in charge of a leprosarium at Spandau, Germany, at the time of his death on Jan. 20. He wrote five collections of sacred songs, a mass, and published a history of Catholicism in England.

COINTHA, ST. (d. 249), martyr. She was dragged to death through the streets of Alexandria, Egypt, during the Decian persecution. She is also known as Quinta. F. D. Feb. 8.

COIRPRE, ST. (7th century), bishop. *See* Eoghan, St.

COLBERT, JACQUES NICOLAS (1655–1707). Brother of Charles Joachim Colbert (1667–1738), bishop of Montpellier, he became archbishop of Rouen, France. Critics are divided as to his orthodoxy; some praise his interest in seminary training; others call him as militant a Jansenist as his brother Charles, who rebelled against the Church during the papacy of Innocent XI.

COLBERT, JEAN BAPTISTE (1619–1683), economist. Born in Rheims, France, on Aug. 29, the later marquis de Seignelay worked in the office of the war secretary, Le Tellier, and became minister of finance to King Louis XIV on the death of Mazarin, who had sponsored him. He gained a conviction of fraud against his predecessor, Fouquet, recovered funds from those with whom Fouquet had dealt, reduced public debt, and set up a strong financial system. He failed to continue reductions in taxes because of Louis' extravagances and military demands, and gradually became an unpopular figure. He sought to develop agriculture and manufacturing, developed shipbuilding, the navy, and fortifications at Brest and Rochefort, and was a patron of the arts and contributor to the French Academy and founded the Academy of Inscriptions in 1663 and the Academy of Sciences in 1666. His nationalism appears in his support of Gallicanism at the assembly of the clergy called in 1682 at Colbert's suggestion. In his reliance on De Bourseys he contributed heavily to the advance of Jansenism, which he failed to recognize as a danger. He died in Paris in Sept.

COLE, HENRY (1500?–1579). Born in Godshill, Isle of Wight, he studied at Winchester and Oxford, became a fellow of the latter school in 1523, was in Italy from 1525 to 1532, held several parish posts in England, apparently defected to Protestantism, but returned to Catholicism in 1547. He was vicar general of Cardinal Pole in 1557, served on the commission which restored Bishops Tunstal and Bonner, on that which investigated Cranmer, Ridley, and Latimer, and on one sent to suppress heresy in Ireland. Under Elizabeth he was heavily fined, stripped of his offices and wardenships, and in 1560 imprisoned for nearly twenty years in the Tower and then in the Fleet prison, London, where he died.

COLEMAN, BL. EDWARD (d. 1678), martyr. Born in Suffolk, England, son of an Anglican cleric, he studied at Cambridge, became a convert, and served as secretary to the duchess of York. He was arrested during the Titus Oates Plot, and letters he had written to the chaplain of the French king, asking for money for Catholic labors in England, were offered at his trial as proof that he sought to overthrow Charles II. He was hanged, drawn, and quartered at Tyburn as the first victim of the new persecution. He was beatified in 1929. F. D. Dec. 3.

COLERIDGE, HENRY JAMES (1822–1893), editor. Born in Devonshire, England, on Sept. 20, son of Sir John Taylor Coleridge, a judge, and grandnephew of Samuel, the poet, he attended Eton and Oxford, took honors in classics, and became a fellow of Oriel. He became an Anglican minister in 1848, edited the *Guardian*, the newspaper of the high-church party, became a supporter of Newman, and in 1852 a convert. He was ordained in Rome in 1856, returned to England to begin studies as a Jesuit, and from 1865 to 1881 was editor of the *Month*. He wrote biographies of SS. Francis Xavier and Teresa, a harmony of the gospels and other biblical studies, and a *Public Life of Our Lord*. He died in Roehampton, England, on Apr. 13.

COLET, JOHN (1467–1519), educator. Born in London, son of Sir Henry Colet, the lord mayor, he was educated at Oxford, appointed to numerous benefices concurrently, toured Italy and became attracted to the Renaissance spirit, returned to England, and was ordained in 1498. He lectured at Oxford on the personality of St. Paul and on the New Testament, became associated with Erasmus, was in 1504 appointed dean of St. Paul's, London, and served as spiritual adviser to Thomas More. He inherited a fortune at his father's death in 1505, and in 1509 established the famous cathedral school whose curriculum was based on the classics, whose running he directed personally, and some of whose texts he wrote. He wrote biblical commentaries, a study of the sacraments, statutes for St. Paul's School, a much-reprinted Latin grammar, and spiritual readings. He died in London on Sept. 18.

COLETI, NICOLA (1680–1765), historian. Born in Venice, he studied at Padua, was ordained, served in a parish in Venice, and began to publish a revised edition of Ughelli's *Italia sacra* (1717–22). He then issued a twenty-three volume history of Church councils, based on previous work by Labbe, Baluze, and Hardouin, and of great value. He also wrote studies of the church history of Venice and of Cremona and edited a manuscript of Scipio Maffei. He died in Venice.

COLETTE, ST. (1381–1447). Daughter of a carpenter in Corbie, France, Nicolette de Boilet was born on Jan. 13, became an orphan at seventeen, then lived for a while as a recluse under the spiritual direction of Fr. Henri de Balme. When she sought to restore the rule of the Poor Clares to its original strictness she met with some opposition, but was approved by the Avignon Pope Benedict XIII, who made her superior of the order. St. Colette's reforms spread across Europe. She founded seventeen new convents, had unusual supernatural gifts, exerted great influence on the nobility, and helped St. Vincent Ferrer in undoing the damage of the Western schism. She died in Ghent, Flanders, and was canonized in 1807. F. D. Mar. 6.

COLGAN, ST. (d. 796?). A friend of Alcuin, he became abbot of Clonmacnoise, in Offaly, Ireland, and was known as the "chief scribe" of the Scots. He also is called Coelchu. F. D. Feb. 20.

COLGAN, JOHN (1592–1657?), historian. Born in Donegal, or Derry, Ireland, he became a Franciscan, studied and taught at St. Anthony of Padua in Louvain, was ordained in 1618, and was relieved of teaching to work on a history of Irish saints, based on manuscript materials gathered by Fr. Hugh Ward (d. 1635). Colgan's biographies of saints whose feast days are in Jan.–Mar. appeared as *Acta sanctorum hiberniae* in 1645. The second volume, *Trias thaumaturga* (1647), contained lives of SS. Patrick, Brigid, and Columba, with supplementary material on Irish ecclesiastical antiquities. Though Colgan had a knowledge of Irish, he did not know the older forms of the language and made some errors in dating and, at times, in translation. He also published a life of Duns Scotus in 1655.

COLIN, king. *See* Culen.

COLIN, FRÉDÉRIC LOUIS (1835–1902). Born in Bourges, France, he was ordained at St. Sulpice, Paris, in 1859, was sent to Canada in 1862, taught at and became rector of the seminary in Montreal, and from 1881 until his death was superior of Sulpicians in Canada. He founded the Canadian College in Rome in 1885, a minor seminary in Montreal in 1892, and Laval University, to which he brought a brilliant French and Belgian faculty. He died in Montreal on Nov. 27.

COLIN, JEAN CLAUDE (1790–1875), founder. Born in St. Bonnet le Troncy, France, on Aug. 7, he was ordained at Lyons in 1816, was appointed assistant pastor at Cerdon, and with a group of former associates at the seminary of St. Irénée outlined a religious society dedicated to Mary. His provisional rules were canonically approved by Pope Gregory XVI in 1836, over the opposition of the bishop of Belley, who tried to make the society a diocesan one. Fr. Colin was superior of the Marists from 1836 to 1854, establishing houses and colleges in France and sending missionaries to Oceanea. During his last twenty years, spent at Notre Dame de la Neylière, France, where he died on Feb. 28, he devoted himself to revising the constitutions of the order and organizing it firmly in relation to its announced aims.

COLLADO, DIEGO (d. 1638), missioner. Born in Miajadas, Estremadura, Spain, he became a Dominican at Salamanca about 1600. In 1619 he was sent to Japan, served three years during heavy persecution, returned to Rome and Spain, then went back to the Orient in 1635. He attempted to establish a house in the Philippines for the missions of the Asiatic continent, but was opposed by Spanish authorities on the islands. He wrote a Japanese grammar and dictionary, a Chinese dictionary, a history of the missions, and several spiritual works. He died in a shipwreck while returning to the Philippines from Spain.

COLLERT. *See* Gerard Sagreda, St.

COLLINS, JOHN (1889–1961), bishop. Born in Cork, Ireland, he joined the Society of the African Missions, was ordained in 1913, and served as a missionary in Liberia for fifty years. He was appointed titular bishop of Thala and vicar apostolic of Liberia in 1934, and in 1951 was named internuncio to Liberia and vicar apostolic to Monrovia. He resigned his vicariate in 1960 because of ill health, was named apostolic administrator of the vicariate, and died in Monrovia, Liberia, on March 3.

COLLINS, MICHAEL (1890–1922). Born in Woodfield, Cork, Ireland, on Oct. 16, he studied in the local school, went to London at sixteen, working as a clerk and educating himself until 1915. He was active in the London group of the Irish Republican army, returned to Ireland before the Easter 1916 outbreak, and was captured and imprisoned for the rest of that year. He became the organizer of the underground Sinn Fein movement, was imprisoned in 1918, and early the next year was elected to parliament and named minister of home affairs and then of finance. He arranged the escape of De Valera, and went underground when the British closed down the parliament. Guerrilla warfare continued; the Irish and British leaders met in 1921 to sign a treaty establishing the Irish Free State. Collins became chairman of the government and minister of finance. Civil war broke out in June 1922; Collins, commander in chief of the Free State army, was shot to death at Macroon in an ambush by irregulars on Aug. 22.

COLM. *See* Columba, St.

COLMAN, ST. (d. 595?). Confused with several other Colmans, he seems to have labored as a missioner in Wexford, Ireland, and to have lived near Mt. Leinster at the monastery called Temple Sean Bothe (Senboth-Fola). He has been associated with St. Maidoc, bishop of Ferns, and with St. Aidan. F. D. Oct. 27.

COLMAN, ST. (522–600?), bishop. Born in Munster, Ireland, he was almost fifty when converted by St. Brendan. Later ordained, he became first bishop of Cloyne and is reputed to have taught the young St. Columba. He was renowned as a poet and was royal bard at the court of Cashel. F. D. Nov. 24.

COLMAN, ST. (6th century), bishop. Born in Argyll, Scotland, he became the first abbot-bishop of Druim Mór (Dromore), which he founded in County Down, Ireland, about 514. He had been a student of SS. Coelan and Ailbhe; he himself taught St. Finan. His cult was approved in 1903. F. D. June 7.

COLMAN, ST. (d. 659). He was abbot of Glendalough, Ireland. F. D. Dec. 12.

COLMAN, ST. (605?–676), bishop. Born in Connacht, Ireland, he became a monk at Iona, was third bishop of Lindisfarne after SS. Aidan and Finan, and represented the Irish monastic view at the Synod of Whitby (663). There he objected to the almost universally accepted date of Easter and solutions to other differences on discipline, and gave up his post to withdraw to Ireland. In 668 he established separate monasteries at Inisboffin, Mayo, for English and Irish monks, rulings over both groups as abbot. He died there on Aug. 8. He is highly praised by Bede. F. D. Feb. 18.

COLMAN, ST. (d. 689), martyr. *See* Kilian, St.

COLMAN, ST. (d. 702?), bishop. He became abbot-bishop of his monastery in Lismore, Ireland, in 698 and brought it to great fame. F. D. Jan. 23.

COLMAN, ST. (d. 1012). A pilgrim from Ireland or Scotland, he was on his way to the Holy Land when he was mistaken for a spy, and tortured and killed at Stockerau, near Vienna. He was subsequently honored as one of the patron saints of Austria. F. D. Oct. 13.

COLMAN ELO, ST. (555?–611). Born in Glenelly, Tyrone, Ireland, he studied under St. Columba, his uncle, built the monastery of Lynally (Lann Elo), in Offaly, about 590, then founded and became first abbot of Muckamore,

and later bishop of Connor. He was the author of the *Alphabet of Devotion*, and is also called Colman Macusailni. He died at Lynally, Ireland, on Sept. 26.

COLMAN OF KILMACDUAGH (d. 632?), bishop. Son of a chieftain, he was born in Corker, Ireland, lived as a recluse in Clare, and founded the monastery of Kilmacduagh, of which he became abbot-bishop. His cult was approved in 1903. F. D. Oct. 29.

COLMAN MACCATHBAD, ST. (6th century). A follower of St. Ailbe of Emly, he became abbot-bishop of Kilroot, near Carrickfergus, Connor, Ireland. F. D. Oct. 16.

COLMAN MAC ROI, ST. (6th century). A follower of St. Columba, he was abbot-founder of the monastery at Reachrain, near Dublin. F. D. June 16.

COLMAN, MACUALA OIGHSE, ST. (6th century). He was a follower of SS. Columba and Finan, and was abbot-founder of a monastery at Oughaval, Ireland. F. D. May 15.

COLMAN, WALTER (d. 1645), martyr. Born of a noble English family, he went to Douai when young, became a Franciscan there in 1625 under the name Christopher of St. Clare, was sent on the English mission, captured, and imprisoned when he refused to take the Oath of Allegiance. Later released, he labored in the capital, published a poem, *The Duel of Death*, then returned to the Continent. Back in England in 1641, he was seized with two Benedictines and four diocesan priests and condemned to death; the sentence was delayed by the intervention of the French ambassador, but Colman died in Newgate prison, London, four years later, of starvation.

COLMAR, JOSEPH LUDWIG (1760–1818), bishop. Born in Strassburg, on June 22, he was ordained in 1783, taught history and Greek, served as curate in Strassburg, and remained in the city during the French reign of terror to continue his priestly labors. Because of his success with the underground clergy, Napoleon appointed him bishop of Mainz in 1802; Colmar rebuilt and refurnished its desecrated cathedral, restored religious fervor, saved the cathedral of Speyer from destruction, taught catechism at the lowest level, and battled the rationalist intellectuals at the highest. He was honored for his intensive labors during the plague of 1813–14, edited a collection of old church hymns and several prayer books, and published seven volumes of sermons. He died in Mainz, Prussia, on Dec. 15.

COLMCILLE. *See* Columba, St.

COLMENARIO, BL. FRANCISCO (d. 1590). He was a Spanish missioner who had considerable success in the West Indies and Guatemala. F. D. Apr. 24.

COLOMAN (1070–1114), king of Hungary. Illegitimate son of King Géza I, he fled to

Poland to escape his father's plan to make him a monk, returned to Hungary on the death of St. Ladislaus in 1095, and seized the throne. He added most of Dalmatia to his realms by overcoming King Peter of Dalmatia in 1097, and expanded his territories while seeking a Hungarian sea line despite the opposition of the emperor, Venice, and the pope. His legitimate brother Almos secured the support of Emperor Henry V, who unsuccessfully invaded Hungary in 1108. The brothers were reconciled, but in 1113 Coloman seized Almos and his son Béla, blinded both, and imprisoned them in a monastery. Coloman (or Koloman) died on Feb. 3.

COLOMBIÈRE, BL. CLAUD LA (1641–1682). Born near Lyons, France, became a Jesuit in 1659, studied at Avignon and Paris, and became a well-known preacher. He was directly aware of the inroads made by Calvinism and Jansenism, consecrated himself to the Sacred Heart, was solemnly professed in 1675, and became rector of the college at Paray-le-Monial that same year. There he became the confessor of St. Margaret Mary Alacoque, inspiring in her the same devotion to the Sacred Heart as an antidote to heresy. He was then sent to England as preacher for Mary of Modena, wife of the duke of York (later, King James II), and was charged with conspiracy in the Titus Oates Plot to kill Charles II, imprisoned, and then banished. In France he served his last three years, his health ruined by prison, as spiritual adviser to St. Margaret Mary. He died in Paray-le-Monial, France, and was beatified in 1929. F. D. Feb. 15.

MARGARET YEO, *These Three Hearts* (Milwaukee, Bruce, 1940).

COLOMBINI, BL. GIOVANNI (1304?–1367), founder. Born in Siena, he became a successful businessman and chief magistrate, married Biagia Cerretani, and had two children. He was known for his avarice and temper, but reformed and devoted himself to penance and works of charity. After his son had died and his daughter had become a nun, with his wife's consent and after leaving her means to live, he gave his wealth to charity and began caring for the sick. In this work he was joined by Francisco Mini and others; they were banished from Siena, visited other cities, and in 1367, at Viterbo, gained the approval of Pope Urban V for their institute, known as the Apostolic Clerics of St. Jerome, or Gesuati. He died on the road to Acquapendente, Italy, and was beatified by Pope Gregory XIII. The congregation grew smaller and in 1668 was suppressed by Pope Clement IX. F. D. July 31.

COLOMBO, MATTEO REALDO (1516–1559), anatomist. Born in Cremona, Italy, he studied medicine at Padua under Vesalius, became his assistant and successor, was first professor of anatomy at Pisa from 1545 to 1548, then moved to Rome to occupy the chair of anatomy at the papal university until his death. In his *De re anatomica* (1559) he completely described the circulation of the blood, a discovery which Harvey acknowledged in his own later work. Colombo was the first to use living animals in laboratory experiments and demonstrations, especially to illustrate the function of heart and lungs. He died in Rome.

COLONNA, ASCANIO (1560?–1608), cardinal. A relative of Cardinal Marcantonio, he was made cardinal in 1586 by Pope Sixtus V at the request of King Philip II. He refused to support the Spanish choice for pope at the conclave of 1592, fell out of royal favor, and left his wealth to the Lateran. He wrote a Latin treatise on the Sicilian monarchy.

COLONNA, EGIDIO (1247–1316), theologian. Born in Rome, Aegidius Romanus became an Augustinian there, was sent to Paris, studied under Thomas Aquinas, and became the first of the Order of Hermits to serve on the university's faculty. At the Council of Paris in 1281 he sided with the bishops in supporting the mendicants against the canons regular. He served as tutor to the French prince who became King Philip IV in 1285. That same year Pope Honorius IV asked him to retract certain theological opinions (denying that Adam possessed grace before the fall) to which Archbishop Tempier of Paris had objected; the chapter general of his order supported him against French opposition and he was elected superior general in 1292. Pope Boniface VIII made him archbishop of Bourges in 1295 (although Pope Celestine V had already selected Jean de Savigny for the post) and the king supported Boniface's choice. He attended the Council of Vienne (1311) at which the Knights Templars were suppressed. He wrote many biblical commentaries and theological studies, often favoring Augustine over Aquinas. In philosophy he wrote glosses on Peter Lombard's *Sentences* and on Aristotle. His important *De regimine principum* (first printed in 1473), discusses the virtues and duties of a king, family life in general, and the position of the state in peace and war. Equally important is his *De potestate ecclesiastica*, in which he defended papal rights and which is so similar in tone to the bull *Unam sanctam* of Boniface VIII that it is believed Colonna was its author as well. Colonna also defended the papacy in his study of the legitimacy of the resignation of Celestine. He died in Avignon, France, on Dec. 22.

COLONNA, GIACOMO (d. 1318), cardinal. He was created cardinal-deacon in 1278 by Pope Nicholas III, after a period of twenty-three years in which his noble family, allied to the Ghibellines, were actively opposed to the papacy. He quarreled violently with Pope Gregory VIII, was deposed in 1297, reinstated by Clement V, and died at Avignon, France.

COLONNA, GIOVANNI (d. 1209), cardinal. Born in Italy, he was made cardinal-priest in 1192 by Pope Celestine III, bishop of Sabina by Innocent III, and papal legate to Germany, Spain, Sicily, and France. He was a friend of St. Francis of Assisi, helped to gain papal approval for the Franciscan Rule, and built a hospital at Amalfi. He died in Rome.

COLONNA, GIOVANNI (d. 1245), cardinal. Giovanni the Younger was born in Italy, was nephew of Egidio, became cardinal-priest in 1212, served in the Near East from 1217 to 1222 as papal legate, built two hostels near the Lateran, and erected a church in Rome for the "pillar of the scourging," which he brought back with him from Jerusalem. His political career was particularly stormy, and in 1240, with other Ghibellines, he and his family threw their support to Emperor Frederick II against Pope Gregory IX.

COLONNA, GIOVANNI (d. 1348), cardinal. Nephew of Cardinal Pietro Colonna, he was in 1327 made a cardinal by Pope John XXII. He wrote *Lives of the Roman Pontiffs*, was honored in an elegiac sonnet by Petrarch, and was a distinguished member of a loyal faction led by his father, Count Stefano, against the schismatic Sciarra.

COLONNA, GIOVANNI (d. 1508), cardinal. Nephew of Cardinal Prospero Colonna, he was made a cardinal-deacon at twenty-four by Pope Sixtus IV, imprisoned two years later, freed a year later, a runaway exile during the war between Pope Alexander VI and the Roman barons, and the recipient of restored favors under Julius II.

COLONNA, GIOVANNI PAOLA (1637–1695), composer. Born in Bologna, Italy (where he died on Nov. 28), he studied music there and at Rome, where he became organist of the church of St. Apollinaris. In 1659 he became choirmaster at St. Petronio's, Bologna, a charter member of the Accademica Filarmonica, and founder of a school which produced such distinguished musicians as Buononcini. He composed a great deal of church music, for choir, organ, and orchestra, most of it with exacting and elaborate apparatus.

COLONNA, MARCANTONIO (d. 1597), cardinal. Trained by the Franciscan Felice Peretti (later Pope Sixtus V), he was made cardinal-priest in 1565, established seminaries, became librarian of the Vatican, and devoted himself to the spread of education and the alleviation of poverty in Rome.

COLONNA, PIETRO (d. 1326), cardinal. Nephew of Cardinal Giacomo Colonna, he was made cardinal-deacon by Pope Honorius IV about 1288. With his uncle he built and endowed the hospital of St. Giacomo for incur-

ables, the Franciscan convent in Capite, hired Turrita to do the mosaics in Santa Maria Maggiore, Rome, and was a munificent patron of the arts. Also like his uncle, he was the bitter opponent of Pope Boniface VIII, was deposed in 1297, restored to office in 1305, and died at Avignon, France.

COLONNA, POMPEO (d. 1532), cardinal. Nephew of Cardinal Prospero Colonna, he was made a cardinal in 1517 by Pope Leo X, vice-chancellor by Clement VII, then joined the army which desecrated St. Peter's and the Vatican in 1526. He became somewhat shocked by the massacre of the citizens which followed and tried to hide some of them. Clement mildly forgave him in 1529 and appointed him viceroy of Naples, where he died.

COLONNA, PROSPERO (d. 1463), cardinal. He was raised to princedom in 1430, while still a youth, by his uncle, Pope Martin V. He was a patron of the arts, led a revolt against Pope Eugene IV, was deprived of office, and was reinstated by Nicholas V.

COLONNA, VITTORIA (1490–1547), poet. Born in Marino, Italy, daughter of Fabrizio Colonna, grand constable of Naples, she married Ferrante d'Avalos, a general under Charles V. He died in 1525 when his plot to gain the crown of Naples failed. His widow lived in various convents thereafter, was a close and inspiring friend of Michelangelo, was admired by Cardinal Bembo, and worked with Cardinal Pole of England and others to hasten the reform of the Church from within. She wrote a prose meditation on the life of Christ, elegies on the death of her husband, religious sonnets, and the long *Trionfo di Cristo*, which shows the influence of Dante and Petrarch. She died in Rome on Feb. 25.

COLTON, CHARLES HENRY (1848–1915), bishop. Born in New York City on Oct. 15, he studied at St. Francis Xavier College, and St. Joseph's seminary, Troy, where he was ordained in 1876. He did parish work in New York until 1897, was appointed chancellor, and held this position until 1903, when he was appointed bishop of Buffalo. He died there on May 9.

COLUM. *See* Columba, St.

COLUM, MARY MAGUIRE (1887–1957), critic. Born in Ireland, she was educated in Vaals, Netherlands, and in the Dominican College and National University in Dublin. She was associated with the literary circle which included Yeats and Synge, wrote for the *Irish Review, United Irishman,* and *Irish Statesman.* She married Padraic Colum in 1912 and came to the United States in 1914. She wrote for numerous magazines, including *Dial, Scribner's, Saturday Review, Nation,* and *Forum* (in which she had a column from 1933 to 1940); held Guggenheim fellowships in criticism in 1930 and 1938; received the John Ryder Randall medal from Georgetown University in 1934; was elected to the National Institute of Arts and Letters in 1953; and taught at Columbia from 1952 to 1956. She wrote a critical study, *From These Roots*, in 1937 and her autobiography, *Life and the Dream*, in 1947. She died in New York City on Oct. 22.

COLUMBA, ST. (d. 548). Born in Leinster, Ireland, he served St. Finnian and became abbot of Tyrdaglas, Munster. F. D. Dec. 12.

COLUMBA, ST. (521?–597). Born, probably in Donegal, Ireland, of royal descent, he studied at Moville under St. Finnian, then in Leinster, and at the monastery of Clonard under another St. Finnian. He was ordained before he was twenty-five, and spent the next fifteen years preaching and setting up foundations at Derry, Durrow, and Kells. Possibly because of a family feud which resulted in the death of 3000 and for which he considered himself partly responsible (it had begun when a clansman was taken from sanctuary in Columba's monastery and killed by King Diarmaid's soldiers), he left Ireland at forty-two and landed on the island of Iona, off the coast of Scotland. There he built the monastery which was to become world-famous. With SS. Canice and Comgall he spread the gospel to the Picts; he also developed a monastic rule which many followed until the introduction of St. Benedict's. He died on Iona, and is also known as Colm, Colum, and Columcille. F. D. June 9.

ADAMNAN, *Life of St. Columba*, ed., J. T. Fowler (New York, Oxford U., 1921).

COLUMBA, ST. (d. 853), martyr. A native of Cordova, Spain, she became a nun, despite her mother's wish that she marry, at the double monastery of Tabanos of which her brother Martin was an abbot. During a Moorish persecution the nuns were forced to flee in 852. She took refuge at Cordova, where she publicly denounced Mohammedanism and was beheaded. F. D. Sept. 17.

COLUMBA OF RIETI, BL. *See* Guardagnoli, Bl. Angelella.

COLUMBA OF SENS, ST. (d. 273), martyr. According to tradition, she was a Spaniard, of noble, pagan parents, who migrated to Gaul when sixteen and settled at Sens, where she was beheaded near Meaux during the reign of Aurelian. F. D. Dec. 31.

COLUMBAN, ST. (543?–615). Born in West Leinster, Ireland, he early decided, despite his mother's opposition, to become a man of God, spent some time at Lough Erne with Abbot Sinell, and then went to the monastery of Bangor, where he lived until he was about forty-five. At that time, with twelve other monks, he was sent to Gaul as a missioner, arriving probably in 585. About 590 he built a monastery in Annegray, which was so successful he built two

more: at Luxeuil and Fontes (now Fontaines). From these centers his followers spread throughout Europe, building monasteries which became spiritual—and cultural—oases in France, Germany, Switzerland, and Italy. In 602 he became embroiled in a dispute with the Frankish bishops because of the Celtic usages he installed in his monasteries and his refusal to accept the bishops' authority over his monasteries. In 610 he and all the Irish monks were ordered deported by King Theodoric II of Burgundy, whom he had denounced for his concubines and refusal to marry. When his ship was wrecked, he resumed his missionary activities, first from the court of King Clotaire of Neustria, who urged him to remain, and in 611 under the aegis of Theodebert II of Austrasia in the Lake Constance area. Both missions were unsuccessful, and when Burgundy defeated Austrasia in war Columban decided to go to Italy. He was welcomed at Milan by Arian King Agilulf of the Lombards. He established a monastery at Bobbio, between Milan and Genoa, which became one of the great monastic centers of northern Italy, and there he died. He was the author of treatises on penance and against Arianism, sermons, poetry, and his monastic rule. F. D. Nov. 23.

COLUMBINUS, ST. (d. 680?). He succeeded St. Deicolus as abbot of Lure, France. F. D. Sept. 13.

COLUMBUS, BARTOLOMMEO (1445–1515). Elder brother of Christopher Columbus, he was born probably in Genoa, became a sailor, shared Christopher's fortunes in the West Indies, and was governor during the admiral's absence. He introduced bloodhounds to the West Indies in order to track down and kill those natives who failed to report with their gold assessments. The slave policy was such that by 1508 there were only about 60,000 natives on Santo Domingo of the quarter of a million there in 1492; by mid-century the number would be reduced to 500. He died in Santo Domingo in May.

COLUMBUS, CHRISTOPHER (1446?–1506), explorer. Born probably in Genoa, Italy, to Domenico and Suzanna Colombo, he claimed that he went to sea at fourteen. He was engaged in the weaving trade at Genoa in 1470–73, probably made voyages to Iceland and England, and in 1478 married Felipa de Perestrello e Moñiz in Portugal. He visited Porto Santos, where her brother was governor, in 1479. He corresponded with mapmakers and presented his plans to sail for the Orient before both the Spanish and Portuguese courts, but without immediate success. By 1486 he had gained Queen Isabella's serious attention, and gradually interested such men as Alonso de Quintanilla, Fray Hernando de Talavera, the queen's confessor, Cardinal Pedro Gonzalez de

Mendoza, and Fray Juan Pérez, guardian of the monastery of La Rábida. He paused in his plan to go to France and when Granada was taken from the Moors saw the court's interest become definite. Pérez, Luís de Santangel, and others found money and crews; the expedition was fitted out, and on Aug. 3 set sail from Palos, Spain, with about ninety men. Columbus was on the *Santa Maria*; Martín Alonso and Vicente Yañez Pinzón, brothers, commanded the *Pinta* and *Niña*. The three left Tenerife, Canary Islands, on Sept. 6; there was some grumbling by Sept. 17; birds were sighted on Oct. 7; on Friday Oct. 12 the crew sighted what is believed to have been Watling's Island in the Bahamas, which Columbus called San Salvador. Cuba, Santo Domingo, Haiti, and three other islands were also discovered. Columbus left forty-four men on Santo Domingo after the *Santa Maria* ran aground and Martín Pinzón and the *Pinta* deserted him, sailed for Europe on the *Niña*, and reached the court at Barcelona in Mar. 1493. His second expedition (seventeen ships, 1500 men, twelve missioners) sailed from Cadiz in Sept.; it discovered Montserrat, Antigua, Guadeloupe, Puerto Rico, and the Virgin Islands. Columbus later found Jamaica, built new settlements, and in June 1495 sent five shiploads of Indian slaves to Seville. Indian attacks, civil rebellion, and charges of mismanagement drove Columbus back to Spain in June 1496. Gold was not forthcoming in the quantity dreamed of by the Spaniards at home, and the queen was rightly displeased by the slave trade. Columbus' third voyage (May–Aug. 1498) took him to Trinidad, revealed the coast of South America and the mouth of the Amazon, opened up the possibility of wealth in pearls, and unveiled many new Carib islands before he returned to face a bad situation in Santo Domingo. Mounting hostility had echoed to Spain, charges were believed without investigation, and in May 1499, Francisco Bobadilla was named governor. In the meantime Columbus had seen some progress toward the conversion of Indians, gold production had been stepped up (at the expense of native farming), and he had restored order. But Bobadilla sent the admiral and his two brothers to Spain in chains. When he arrived, the court changed its attitude and proved friendly, gave Columbus compensation for his losses, a new fleet of ships, and orders to remove Bobadilla. In April 1502, with four ships, Columbus set out once more for what he thought was Asia, discovered St. Lucia, sailed the coast of Central America, established a colony in Honduras, went down the South American coast, stayed at Panama (only twelve miles from the Pacific, which he never sighted), went to Jamaica, became ill, and sailed for Spain in Sept. 1504. He died in Valladolid on May 20.

SAMUEL ELIOT MORISON, *Admiral of the Ocean Sea* (2 vols., Boston, Little, Brown, 1942).

COLUMBUS, DIEGO (d. 1510?). Younger brother of Christopher Columbus, he went on the second voyage to America, was sent back to Spain in chains in 1500 with Christopher and Bartolommeo, became a priest, and returned to the West Indies in 1509.

COLUMBUS, DIEGO (1476–1526). Oldest son and heir of Christopher Columbus, he was born in Lisbon, Portugal, brought up in Porto Santo in the Madeiras, became a page to Queen Isabella in 1492, remained in the Spanish court until 1508, and in 1509 went to Santo Domingo as admiral of the Indies and governor of Cuba. He met opposition there and in Spain and spent much of his later life attempting to clear up the financial claims of his family against the crown. He died in Montalvan, near Toledo, Spain, on Feb. 23.

COLUMBUS, FERNANDO COLÓN (1488–1539). Illegitimate son of Christopher Columbus by an affair with Beatriz Enríquez de Hrana, he was born in Cordova, Spain, on Aug. 15, became his father's favorite, and accompanied him on his last voyage to America. He was a page to Queen Isabella in 1498. He wrote a travel description of Spain, and a life of his father (sometimes partial, sometimes censorious). He established the Biblioteca Columbina in Seville, where he died on July 12.

COLUMCILLE. *See* Columba, St.

COMBEFIS, FRANÇOIS (1605–1679). Born in Marmande, Guyenne, France, in Nov., he studied at Bordeaux, became a Dominican in 1624, taught in several schools, was sent to Paris in 1640, and began a lifetime of the study of patristic texts. He edited works by Amphilochus of Iconium, Methodius of Patara, Andreas of Crete, and St. John Chrysostom. His *Novum auctarium graeco-latinae bibliothecae patrum* (1648) gained him an annual grant from the assembly of French bishops; as a result he issued acts of the martyrs in 1660, *Preachers' Library of the Fathers* in 1662; prepared three volumes of the work of Maximus Confessor, two of St. Basil, and other editions, and polemical writings of his own. He died in Paris on Mar. 23.

COMBONI, DANIEL (1831–1881), bishop. Born in Limone San Giovanni, near Brescia, Italy, on Mar. 15, he studied at Verona, was ordained in 1854, served briefly in the African missions, then taught three years at Mazza's Institute in Verona. He toured Europe seeking funds for the missions, founded one institute to educate priests and brothers for work among the Africans and another for feminine helpers, and opened similar institutes in Cairo, Egypt. In 1872 he was appointed pro-vicar apostolic of Central Africa and added three large missions to the two already existing. In 1877 he was made vicar apostolic of Central Africa. He was successful in lessening the slave trade, crushing it in the Sudan with the help of the khedive. He wrote much on native languages, geography, science, and mission history. He died at Khartoum, Sudan, on Oct. 10.

COMELLAS Y CLUET, ANTONIO (1832–1884). Born in Berga, Spain, he studied at Vich and Solsona, was ordained in 1856, and taught Latin and philosophy at Solsona. In 1880 he wrote a refutation of William Draper's *Conflict between Science and Religion*, an introduction to philosophy (1883), and an explanation of the Trinity. He died in Berga on June 3.

COMGALL, ST. (516?–601). Born in Ulster, Ireland, he became founder and abbot of Bangor, where he taught St. Columban, and from which he directed some 3000 monks. He seems to have preached later in Wales and Scotland with St. Columba. F. D. May 10.

COMGAN, ST. (8th century). Son of the prince of Leinster, Ireland, whom he succeeded, he fled to Scotland with his sister and her children when he was defeated in battle, and founded a monastery at Lochalsh, where he died. F. D. Oct. 13.

COMMENDONE, GIOVANNI FRANCESCO (1523–1584), cardinal. Born in Venice, Italy, on Mar. 17, he studied at Padua, went to Rome in 1550, became secretary to Pope Julius III, and served on many diplomatic missions, including important conferences with Queen Mary of England in 1553. Commendone was also secretary under Paul IV, who made him bishop of Zante in 1555 and also employed him on diplomatic missions. He spent the year 1561 touring Germany, Scandinavia, and the Netherlands, seeking, without much success, leaders from the Catholic and Protestant Estates to attend the proposed reopening of the Council of Trent; his letters to St. Charles Borromeo on religious conditions in Germany were later published. In 1563 he met with Emperor Ferdinand at Innsbruck, then went to Poland as legate of Pope Pius IV, and succeeded in gaining King Sigismund's support of the Tridentine decrees and the promise to allow the Jesuits to return. In 1565 Commendone was made a cardinal; in 1566 he attended the Diet of Augsburg as legate of Pope Paul V; in 1568 he persuaded Maximilian II not to make further concessions to the Protestant Estates. He made an apostolic visitation of the church establishments in Germany (his reports on Benedictine and Cistercian monasteries were published), went back to Poland and after the death of Sigismund helped to arrange the succession of Duke Henry of Anjou as king, then returned to Italy. Pope Gregory XIII made him a member of the Congregatio Germanica in 1573, and he devoted his remaining years to the interests of the Church in Germany. He died in Padua, Italy, on Dec. 26.

COMMER, FRANZ (1813–1887), composer. Born in Cologne, Alsace, on Jan. 23, he studied music there and became organist at its Carmelite church. In 1832 he went to Berlin for further study, became choirmaster at St. Hedwig's church, taught singing at a number of schools, and with Küster and Kullack founded the Berlin Tonkünstlerlerverein in 1844. He was a senator of the Berlin Akademie, founded the Gesselschaft für Musikforschung in 1868 with Robert Eitner, and composed masses, cantatas, and choral works. He died on Aug. 17.

COMMINES, PHILIPPE DE (1445–1509), historian. Born near Hasebrouck, Flanders, son of Colard van der Clyte, chief bailiff of the duke of Burgundy, he was raised as a knight in the latter's court at Lille. From 1464 to 1472 he served as squire to the duke's son, later King Charles the Bold, was with him in several battles, and represented him on diplomatic missions. He then abandoned Charles, supported Louis XI, and was rewarded with great estates and with a marriage to a wealthy heiress, Hélène de Chambes of Poitou. In 1478, on a mission to Italy, he protected the position of the Medici, allies of France, against the dukes of Milan and the papacy, and then made firm the French hold on Savoy. When King Louis died, Commines supported the duke of Orléans against the regent, Anne of Beaujeu, was imprisoned in an iron cage, and later banished to his estate. In 1491 he was brought back to court, went to Italy to try to stem opposition to Charles VIII, but failed to break up the league against the French king. He again lost favor at the accession of Louis XII in 1498. His manuscript *Mémoires*, an analytical survey of the political history of Europe from 1464 to 1498 and an incisive series of portraits of those who made it, was for the use of Archbishop Angelo Cato of Vienne, who was writing a life of Louis XI, but was published in 1524. He died at Château d'Argenton, France, on Oct. 18.

COMMODIANUS (5th century), poet. Perhaps from Palestine and probably a convert from paganism, he wrote a collection of eighty acrostic poems, *Instructiones per litteras versuum primas*, on the levels of Christian belief, often satirical in tone, and influenced by St. Cyprian's *Testimonia*. His larger *Carmen apologeticum* treats of Christ, faith, and salvation, contains a vivid description of the impending end of the world, and is in error about the Trinity.

COMNATAN. *See* Connat, St.

CONALL, ST. (7th century). He was abbot of Inniscoel, Donegal, Ireland, named after him, as was a holy well in the area. F. D. May 22.

CONAN, ST. (d. 648?), bishop. He seems to

have gone from Scotland to serve in the Isle of Man and in the Hebrides; he may have been the tutor of St. Fiacre during the latter's childhood. F. D. Jan. 26.

CONATY, THOMAS JAMES (1847–1915), bishop. Born in Kilnalec, Ireland, on Aug. 1, he was brought to the United States when three, and was educated at Holy Cross and the Sulpician seminary, Montreal, where he was ordained in 1872. He was pastor of Sacred Heart church in Worcester, Massachusetts, in 1880–97, president of the Catholic Total Abstinence Union in 1888–90, helped to found the National Catholic Education Association, of which he was president in 1899–1903, and founded the *Catholic Home and School Magazine* in 1892, serving as editor until 1897. He was appointed rector of Catholic University in 1897, monsignor in 1898, and titular bishop of Samos in 1901. He became bishop of Monterey and Los Angeles, California, in 1903, and remained there until his death on Sept. 18.

CONCANEN, RICHARD LUKE (1747–1810), bishop. Born in Kilbegnet, Roscommon, Ireland, on Dec. 27, he studied at Louvain, San Clemente and the Minerva, Rome, joined the Dominicans in 1764, and was ordained in Rome in 1770. He was stationed at San Sisto e San Clemente in Rome for the next forty years, serving as prior in 1781–83, was librarian of the Minerva, and agent of the Irish bishops and Bishop John Carroll of Baltimore. After declining two Irish sees, he was appointed first bishop of New York in 1808, but never reached his see. He died of fever in Naples on June 19 when his second effort to take ship for New York was prevented by his detention by the French military authorities as a British subject.

CONCHA, JOSÉ VICENTE (1867–1929), president. Born in Bogotá, Colombia, on Apr. 21, he studied law at the National University, and rose high in political and diplomatic circles. He founded a newspaper, *El Dia*, and wrote legal textbooks, served as attorney general, minister of war, of government, and of foreign relations, and was minister to the United States and to France. He was president of Colombia from 1914 to 1918 and from 1919 until his death in Rome on Dec. 8 was ambassador to the Vatican.

CONCINA, DANIELLO (1687–1756), theologian. Born in the province of Friuli, Italy, on Oct. 2, he studied in Austria, was professed a Dominican in 1708, studied theology at Venice, and in 1717 taught philosophy and theology at Forlì. He attained fame as a preacher, both in northern Italy and Rome, refuted the early Bollandist claim that St. Dominic was heavily influenced by St. Francis, then wrote against the Jesuits in a study of probabilism and rigorism. He supported Pope

Benedict XIV's definition of the Roman fast, became consultant to several congregations, and attacked laxism wherever he found it. His major work, *Theologia christiana*, was published in 1749, attacked by the Jesuits as erroneous, and reissued in 1752 with an explanatory preface approved by the pope. He died in Venice on Feb. 21.

CONCORDIUS, ST. (d. 302), martyr. See Zeno, St.

CONCORDIUS, ST. (d. 305?), martyr. See Valentine, St.

CONCORDUS, ST. (d. 178?), martyr. A subdeacon, he was tortured and beheaded in Umbria, Italy, when he refused to sacrifice to idols. F. D. Jan. 1.

CONDAMINE, CHARLES MARIE DE LA (1701–1774), physicist. Born in Paris, on Jan. 28, he served in the army, then as a scientist explored the coasts of northern Africa, Asia Minor, and equatorial South America. During his eight years in Ecuador he made a better determination of the shape of the earth by measuring a meridian and defining the flattening of the globe at the poles; discovered the effect of mountains in deflecting the pendulum; and made many observations on the interior of the country, particularly its topography. On his return to France he was made a member of the Academy of Sciences and the French Academy. He was instrumental in introducing inoculation against smallpox into France. He died in Paris on Feb. 4.

CONDEDUS, ST. (d. 685?). An Englishman seeking solitude, he settled at Fontaine de St. Valéry, France, lived as a Benedictine monk at Fontenelle, then became a hermit on the Island of Belcinac in the Seine near Caudebec, where he built two chapels and was befriended by King Thierry III. F. D. Oct. 21.

CONDILLAC, ÉTIENNE BONNOT DE (1715–1780), philosopher. Born in Grenoble, France, on Sept. 30, he became abbé of Mureaux, but retired to solitary study. While tutor of the duke of Parma, grandson of Louis XV, he wrote *Cours d'études*, later placed on the Index. He was elected to the French Academy in 1768. Condillac popularized the philosophy of John Locke, went beyond the Englishman in defining the ego as no more than a bundle of sensations, evolved confused definitions of science, logic, and communication, and produced a contradictory corpus of writing which adds up only to nominalism and agnosticism. He died near Beaugency on Aug. 3.

CONECTE, THOMAS (d. 1433). Born in Rennes, France, he became a Carmelite, preached with extreme fervor against gambling, feminine fashions, and the worldliness of the clergy, had to flee France because of his public remarks, and while in exile in Italy introduced the strict observance at the Carmelite house near Florence which developed as the Congregation of Mantua. He was equally outspoken there and at Venice and Rome. When he attacked the manners of the papal curia he was labeled a conspirator, condemned as a heretic, and publicly burned on orders of Pope Eugene IV, who later repented of the harsh sentence. He died in Rome.

CONGOREGGI, BL. RAYNALD (d. 1321), bishop. Born in Milan, Italy, he was ordained, served as canon at Lodi, and in 1296 was made bishop of Vicenza. He held various papal offices, befriended the Knights Templar, and in 1303 became archbishop of Ravenna, Italy. His cult was confirmed in 1852. F. D. Aug. 18.

CONINCK, GILES DE (1571–1633), theologian. Born in Bailleul, French Flanders, on Dec. 20, he became a Jesuit at twenty-one, studied at Louvain under Lessius, and succeeded him in the chair of theology for eighteen years. He wrote widely on morals and was highly praised by St. Alphonsus. He died at Louvain on May 31.

CONINDRUS, ST. (d. 450?). He and St. Romulus were among the first missionary bishops on the Isle of Man. F. D. Dec. 28.

CONLETH, ST. (d. 519?), bishop. An Irish metal craftsman and hermit along the Liffey River, he was called by St. Brigid to serve as spiritual director of her convent at Kildare. There he became bishop. F. D. May 10.

CONNAT, ST. (d. 590?). She directed the convent which St. Brigid established in Kildare, Ireland. She is also called Comnatan. F. D. Jan. 1.

CONNELLY, CORNELIA PEACOCK (1809–1879), foundress. She was born in Philadelphia, Pennsylvania, the youngest of six children by her mother's second marriage. In 1831 she married Pierce Connelly, an Episcopalian minister, and became the mother of five children. In 1835 she became a convert, as, three months later in Rome, her husband also did. In 1843, Pope Gregory XVI granted them permission to separate so that Pierce could become a priest, with the proviso that Cornelia become a nun. She became a postulant at the Sacred Heart convent in Rome and took her final vows in 1847; Pierce was ordained in 1845. At Cardinal Wiseman's request, the Pope ordered Cornelia to England to help found a religious order, which became the Society of the Holy Child Jesus. In 1849, Pierce attempted to gain control of the Society and, on failing, renounced his allegiance to the Church. He sued Cornelia for the return of his conjugal rights, gained a verdict in the lower courts, but dropped action when a new trial was ordered by the privy council. In 1853 he returned to Rome as an Episcopalian minister, remaining there until his death in 1883. Meanwhile, Cornelia's group flourished and became famed for its edu-

cational theories. She died in St. Leonards, England, on Apr. 18.
JULIANA WADHAM, *The Case of Cornelia Connelly* (Garden City, N.Y., Image Books, 1960).

CONNOLLY, JAMES BRENDAN (1868–1957), author. Born in South Boston, Massachusetts, on Oct. 28, he worked with the army engineering corps in South Atlantic waters, took a program in engineering at Harvard, left to compete in the Olympic games in Athens in 1896 (and won the hop, step, and jump championship for the United States), worked on two Boston papers, and fought in the 1898 war with Spain. He worked on fishing vessels, crossed the Atlantic, and began to write stories about his adventures and friends. *Out of Gloucester* (1902) was a collection of short stories which established his reputation and gained him a steady income by free-lance writing for magazines. *The Seiners, Deep Sea Toll,* and *Head Winds* followed; then a novel about the Olympic games of 1906; syndicated articles about the war in Mexico in 1914; *The U-Boat Hunters* on the navy's part in World War I; and nearly twenty volumes on Gloucester and its activities. His autobiography, *Sea Borne,* appeared in 1944. He died in Boston on Jan. 20.

CONNOLLY, JOHN (1750–1825), bishop. Born in Slane, Meath, Ireland, he became a Dominican, was ordained in Rome, taught theology at St. Clement's, was prior there, and was instrumental in saving the English, Irish, and Scotch colleges and his own church and library from being looted when the French army invaded Rome. He was consecrated second bishop of New York City in 1814, reached his diocese (comprised of New York and New Jersey and served by four priests) late the next year, built several churches and charitable institutions, and brought in the Sisters of Charity. He died in New York on Feb. 6.

CONNOLLY, TERENCE L. (1888–1961), author, educator. Born in North Attleboro, Massachusetts, on Sept. 26, he became a Jesuit in 1908, studied at Woodstock and Georgetown, and was ordained in 1922. He taught English at Fordham in 1915–30, and at Boston College in 1926–45, where he was head of the graduate English department, and from 1945 until his death was librarian. He was an authority on the writings of Francis Thompson, edited the definitive collection of his poems (revised edition, 1941), and *The Man Has Wings* (1957) a collection of Thompson's poems and plays, and other works on Thompson, Patmore, the Meynells, and other literary figures. He died in Newton, Massachusetts, on March 24.

CONNOLLY, THOMAS LOUIS (d. 1876), bishop. Born in Cork, Ireland, he studied there and in Rome, was ordained a Capuchin at

Lyons in 1838, and served in the Capuchin church, Dublin, until 1842. He then went to Canada and in 1852 was consecrated bishop of New Brunswick. He built a cathedral and, after a cholera epidemic in 1854, built an orphanage and founded a group of Sisters of Charity to care for it. He was transferred to Halifax in 1859 and built St. Mary's Cathedral. He died in Halifax, Nova Scotia, Canada.

CONNOR, JOSEPH P. (1896-1952), composer. Born in Kingston, New York, he studied music at the Wyoming, Pennsylvania, conservatory under Ergildo Martinelli, was ordained, and wrote sacred music, popular songs, and the musical scores for several motion pictures and Broadway plays. These included *Love Sends a Little Gift of Roses, By a Waterfall, When I Take My Sugar to Tea* (many under pseudonyms); a *Pater Noster, Ave Maria, Prayer of St. Francis*, and a *Mass of Our Lady of Victory*. He became pastor of St. Joseph's, West New York, New Jersey, in 1947, and died in Teaneck, New Jersey, on Mar. 31.

CONOGAN, ST. (d. 460). He succeeded St. Corentin as bishop of Quimper, Brittany, and is also known as Albinus and Gwen. F. D. Oct. 16.

CONON (d. 687), pope. Said to have been son of an officer stationed in Thrace, educated there and ordained in Rome, he was consecrated pope on Oct. 21, 686, apparently after his election had been confirmed by the exarch of Ravenna. He sent St. Kilian into Franconia as a missionary bishop and was accepted by the savage Emperor Justinian II. He died in Rome on Nov. 21.

CONON, ST. (d. 250), martyr. A gardener in Mandona, Pamphylia, he was put to death during the reign of Decius. F. D. Mar. 6.

CONON, ST. (d. 250?), martyr. *See* Claudian, St.

CONON, ST. (d. 275), martyr. He and his twelve-year-old son were burned and racked to death at Iconium in Asia Minor during the persecution of Aurelian. F. D. May 28.

CONON, ST. (d. 1236). He was abbot of the Basilian monastery of Nesi, Sicily. F. D. Mar. 28.

CONRAD IV (1228-1254), emperor. Born in Andria, Apulia, Italy, on Apr. 26, son of Emperor Frederick II and Isabella of Brienne, he was elected king of the Romans in Vienna in 1237 after his half-brother Henry had been deposed. In 1240 he called a meeting at Eger and, when many of the princes opposed the pope, warred against Archbishop Siegfried of Mainz and the papal supporters. In 1246, the election of Henry Raspe as antiking to Conrad at the demand of Pope Innocent IV, who had deposed Frederick at the Council of Lyons in 1245, plunged Germany into civil war; when William of Holland, supported by the pope and

the Guelphs, succeeded as antiking in 1247, the war became more violent. Frederick died while invading Italy in 1250, and Conrad claimed the imperial crown. He went to Italy in 1251, added Capua and Naples to his kingdom of Sicily, and reigned as king of Naples and Sicily. The pope offered the throne to various princes, and had it accepted by Edmund, earl of Cornwall. Innocent excommunicated Conrad in 1254, and, as war broke out, Conrad died of fever at Lavallo, Italy, on May 21.

CONRAD I (d. 918), German king. At the death of Louis the Child in 911, Conrad, duke of Franconia and a distant relative of Arnulf, succeeded to the Carolingian throne. From 912 until his death on Dec. 23 he was at war with Duke Henry of Saxony. Conrad favored the Church and supported it, but could not control the powerful and independent dukes. He lost Lorraine, fought unsuccessfully against Bavaria and Swabia, and suffered continuing Hungarian incursions.

CONRAD II (990?-1039), king. He became king of the Germans in 1024 after the extinction of the Saxon line and founded the Franconian dynasty. He supported the canons against the monastic clergy, invaded Italy in 1026, crushed the rebellious Italians, whose king he became at Milan, and in 1027 he was made Holy Roman Emperor by the pope. Recalled to Germany by civil war, he added Burgundy to his kingdom in 1034, returned to Italy to end some but not all opposition there in 1036, added Arles to his kingdom, crushed Stephen of Hungary, and ceded Schleswig to Canute. He died in Utrecht, Netherlands, on June 4.

CONRAD III (1093?-1152), German king. Son of Frederick of Swabia and nephew of Emperor Henry V, he joined his brother Frederick, who had been defeated in his bid for the kingship in the election of 1125, in rebellion against Emperor Lothair II. He was elected antiking in 1127 and was crowned in Milan in 1128, but was excommunicated by Pope Honorius II. He submitted to the Holy See in 1135, succeeded Lothair as king in 1138, and gave the possessions of Henry the Proud (Lothair's son-in-law) to Albert the Bear (Saxony) and to Leopold of Austria (Bavaria). Henry went to war against his usurpers, drove Albert from Saxony and was preparing to invade Bavaria when he died in 1139; his son Henry the Lion continued the war until a truce was declared in 1142. In 1146, St. Bernard persuaded Conrad to join the second crusade; he fought at the unsuccessful siege of Damascus, returned to Germany in 1149, and died on Feb. 15. Conrad founded the Hohenstaufen dynasty of rulers.

CONRAD IV, German king. *See* Conrad IV, emperor.

CONRAD, ST. (d. 975), bishop. Son of Henry, count of Altdorf, and a member of the Guelph family, he studied at the cathedral school at Constance, Switzerland, was ordained, and made provost. In 934 he became bishop of Constance. Though he accompanied Emperor Otto I to Italy in 962, his forty-year reign was remarkable for his devotion to ecclesiastical affairs, avoidance of political disputes, and great charities. He was canonized in 1123. F. D. Nov. 26.

CONRAD, ST. (d. 1066). Of a noble Swabian family, he was appointed bishop of Trèves by his uncle, St. Anno of Cologne, but his opponents objected to the selection as illegal and threw him from a castle tower to his death. F. D. June 1.

CONRAD, BL. (12th century). One of the first followers of St. Francis of Assisi, he was sent from Italy to Germany and established the order at Hildesheim. F. D. Apr. 14.

CONRAD, BL. (1241?–1306). A native of Offida, Italy, he became a Franciscan at fourteen, served at Forano and Alvernia, was ordained, and became a famed preacher. He favored the spiritual group of Friars Minor, and is mentioned in the *Fioretti* with his companion, Bl. Peter of Treja. He died while preaching at Bastia, Corsica, and was buried there. His cult was confirmed in 1817. F. D. Dec. 14.

CONRAD OF ASCOLI, BL. (1234–1289). Conrad Miliani was born in Ascoli Piceno, Italy, became a Franciscan with the later Pope Nicholas IV, and served as a missioner in northern Africa. He served the pope-to-be on diplomatic missions to France, taught in Paris, and died in Ascoli on his way to Rome to become a cardinal. His cult was approved by Pope Pius VI. F. D. Apr. 19.

CONRAD OF BAVARIA, BL. (1105–1154). Son of Duke Henry the Black of Bavaria, he studied at Cologne, became a Cistercian at Clairvaux under St. Bernard, and died on Mar. 15, possibly at Molfetta, Italy, while returning from a pilgrimage to the Holy Land. His cult was approved in 1832. F. D. Feb. 14.

CONRAD OF BRESLAU (d. 1447). Duke of Oels, he became bishop of Breslau, Silesia, in 1417, headed the Silesian Confederation, succeeded in barring Poles from diocesan offices, and saw his see suffer from debt and the Hussite wars.

CONRAD OF GELHAUSEN (1320–1390), theologian. Professor of theology at Paris, he became chancellor of Heidelberg and suggested several plans for ending the great Western schism; these were gathered together as *Epistolae concordiae*.

CONRAD OF HIRSAU (12th century). As a monk in Germany he wrote an *Epithalamium virginum*; his *Dialogus super auctores* is a valuable compendium of references to the classical authors studied in his day.

CONRAD OF HOCHSTADT (d. 1261), archbishop. Son of Count Lothar of Hochstadt and Mathilde of Vianden, he received as a benefice a parish near Düsseldorf, was canon and later provost of the cathedral in Cologne, and in 1238 was elected archbishop of that city. He was ordained a priest and consecrated as bishop in 1239. His career is particularly political. He supported Emperor Frederick II against Pope Gregory IX, but shifted his allegiance in 1239. He fought the neighboring princes who refused to acknowledge his temporal control of Cologne. He helped to engineer the election in 1245 of Henry Raspe, landgrave of Thuringia, as successor to the deposed Frederick; when Henry died, Conrad influenced the acceptance of William of Holland. As a reward, Pope Innocent IV made him apostolic legate in Germany, but when the pope refused to add the archbishopric of Mainz, Conrad ended their friendship. He also became cool toward King William, then sought to dethrone him; only William's premature death saved the king from military defeat. Conrad then sold his vote as imperial elector to Richard of Cornwall, and crowned him at Aachen in 1257. Conrad died on Sept. 28.

CONRAD HOLYINGER (d. 1279). Also called Conrad of Saxony and Conrad of Brunswick, he became a Friar Minor, was minister of the Saxon province in 1245, wrote sermons and *Speculum Beatae Mariae Virginis*, and died at Bologna while on his way to a general chapter of his order. He sometimes is confused with a Conrad of Saxony, also a Friar Minor, who was martyred in 1284.

CONRAD OF LEONBERG (1460–1521?). Born in Leonberg, Swabia, he became a Cistercian and in 1490 was secretary to the general of the order. He sought to spread the use of classical instead of scholastic Latin, encouraged the study of Greek and Hebrew, and was active in the printing office of Amerbach in Basle. He studied Hebrew under Reuchlin and became one of the great scholars of his time. He published Latin poems and orations, a Bible, and edited works by Paul of Burgos and Mathias Thoring. He died in Engenthal, near Basle, Switzerland, after 1520.

CONRAD OF MARBURG (d. 1233). A diocesan priest, born in Marburg, Germany, he was an earnest preacher of the crusade proclaimed in 1213 by Pope Innocent III, papal mediator in Saxony, and official reformer of monastic centers as directed by the Synod of Mainz in 1225. From that year until her death in 1231 he was spiritual adviser to St. Elizabeth, wife of Ludwig, landgrave of Thuringia, and made all ecclesiastical appointments in the area. He wrote a biography for her process of canonization. He was most active against the Catharist, Waldensian, and Luciferian heresies and in 1231 he was appointed the first papal inquisitor in Germany. Released by the pope of the necessity of following strict canonical procedure, Conrad, who was advised to proceed with caution and wisdom, proved intensely severe, relied on too many simple testimonies or frightened confessions, worked only with a lay-brother and a lay assistant, and delivered an inordinate number to death. He was censured by a synod convened at Mainz in 1233, but persisted in his extreme ways, began what he called a crusade against heretic nobles, and was waylaid and slain near Marburg on July 30 with his companion, the Franciscan Gerhard Lutzelkolb.

CONRAD OF MONTERRAT (d. 1192). The marquess of Montferrat defended Tyre against Saracen attack and became its lord in 1187. He joined Guy of Lusignan at the siege of Acre in 1189, then opposed Guy's claim to the crown of Jerusalem, and married Isabella, daughter of Almaric I, to secure his own claims. He was acknowledged as king by Richard I of England, but was assassinated a month later.

CONRAD NANTWIN, BL. (d. 1268), martyr. He was burned at the stake at Wolfrathshausen, near Munich, Germany. His cult was approved by Pope Boniface VIII. F. D. Aug. 10.

CONRAD OF PARZHAM, ST. See Birndorfer, St. Conrad.

CONRAD OF PIANCENZA, ST. (1290–1351). A nobleman who became so interested in the condition of the poor that he gave away what was left of his fortune after a damage suit, and lived as a recluse in Sicily, then at the hermitage of William Bocherio, and finally in a cave near Noto, Sicily. He was canonized by Pope Paul III. F. D. Feb. 19.

CONRAD OF SAXONY. See Conrad Holyinger.

CONRAD OF SELDENBÜREN, BL. (d. 1126). Of a noble family, he gave half of his fortune to establish a convent and the remainder to build the Benedictine abbey of Engelburg in Unterwalden, where he became a lay-brother. He was slain at Zürich, Switzerland, where he had gone to clear up a lawsuit involving the property he had ceded. F. D. May 2.

CONRAD OF URACH (1180?–1227), cardinal. A canon of the church of St. Lambert in Liège, he became a Cistercian in 1199, then prior of the monastery in Villers, Belgium. He became abbot there in 1209, of Clairvaux in 1217, and of Cîteau in 1217; he also was made general in that year. He was created cardinal in 1219 by Pope Honorius III and sent to France to crush the Albigenses and then to Germany to arrange the crusade which Emperor Frederick II had promised to undertake.

CONRAD OF UTRECHT (d. 1099), bishop. Chamberlain of Archbishop Anno II of Cologne and tutor to the later Henry IV, he in 1706 succeeded the excommunicated William of Utrecht as bishop. Conrad supported Emperor Henry against Pope Gregory VII and condemned the pope as a heretic at the Synod of Brizen in 1080. Conrad was defeated in battle by Count Robert of Flanders and lost his episcopal territory; the emperor gave him three districts in Friesland in compensation. He founded the church of Notre Dame in Utrecht, Netherlands, and was slain there on Apr. 14 by the architect whom he had dismissed. Some contemporary historians call him a schismatic bishop.

CONRAD OF ZÄHRINGEN, BL. (d. 1227), cardinal. Born in Seyne, Flanders, he became a canon of St. Lambert's, Liège, joined the Cistercians, and became successively abbot of Villiers, Clairvaux, and Cîteaux between 1209 and 1217. He was named cardinal-bishop of Porto and Santa Rufina in 1219, served as papal legate in Languedoc in 1224–26, and died in Bari, Italy. F. D. Sept. 30.

CONRADIN OF BORNADA (d. 1429). He had a brilliant career in law at Padua, became a Dominican in 1419, served as prior at Brescia and Bologna, and gained great reputation as preacher and for his service to the city when it was stricken by the black plague and his successful labors as mediator between a riotous populace in Bologna under the Bentivogli and the supporters of papal authority. Pope Martin V sought to make him a cardinal, but he refused. He became a victim of the recurring plague and died in Bologna, Italy, on Nov. 1 while serving the sick.

CONRAN. Said to have been a bishop in the Orkney Islands in the sixth or seventh century, and long listed as a saint, he is probably the creation of a scribal error for Colum or Colm.

CONROY, JOHN JOSEPH (1819–1895), bishop. Born in Clonaslee, Leix, Ireland, on July 25, he studied at the Sulpician College, Montreal, Mt. St. Mary's College, Maryland, and St. Joseph's seminary, Troy, New York, and was ordained in 1842. He was vice-president and then president of St. John's College, Fordham, in 1842–44, did parish work in the New York archdiocese the next twenty-one years, was a theologian at the first Plenary Council of Baltimore in 1852, and in 1864–65 served as administrator of the New York archdiocese. He was appointed bishop of Albany in 1865, attended the second Plenary Council of Baltimore in 1866 and the Vatican Council in 1870. He resigned his see in 1877, was appointed titular bishop of Curium in 1878, and died in New York City on Nov. 20.

CONROY, JOSEPH HENRY (1858–1939), bishop. Born in Watertown, New York, on

Nov. 8, he studied at Montreal College and the Grand seminary, Montreal, and St. Joseph's seminary, Troy, and was ordained in Troy in 1881. He served as curate and pastor in upper New York, became rector of St. Mary's in Ogdensburg, New York, in 1883, its vicar general in 1901, and domestic prelate in 1905. He was appointed titular bishop of Arindela and auxiliary of Ogdensburg in 1912, succeeded to the see in 1921, founded a preparatory seminary in 1924, and died in Ogdensburg on Mar. 20.

CONRY, FLORENCE (1560–1629), bishop. Born in Galway, Ireland, he studied in the Netherlands and Spain, became a Franciscan at Salamanca, and in 1588 provincial of the order in Ireland. He sailed with the Spanish Armada, escaped death, re-entered Ireland and then returned to Spain with Hugh Roe O'Donnell, prince of Tyrconnell. After the latter's death, Fr. Conry helped his brother, Rory O'Donnell, and arranged for his exile in Rome. There Conry was consecrated archbishop of Tuam in 1609. He had in the meantime worked for the Irish College in Salamanca; in 1616 he founded at Louvain the College of St. Anthony of Padua, later taught there, and aided the success of its printing press. He was unable to occupy his see, but kept aware of Irish affairs, and wrote a strong condemnation of the parliament in Dublin which ceded the six counties of Ulster to the English crown. He wrote on grace, free will, original sin, unbaptized children, and the Immaculate Conception, and was noted as an Augustine scholar. He died in Madrid on Nov. 18.

CONSALVI, ERCOLE (1757–1824), cardinal. Born in Rome on June 8, he studied at Urbino, Frascati, and Rome, and was appointed private chamberlain to Pope Pius VI in 1783. He served on many committees and held several judgeships until 1796. He then was made assessor of a military commission created to prevent disturbances which might lead to French intervention in the Papal States; when Gen. Duphot was killed in Rome at the end of 1797, the city was occupied, the pope stripped of temporal power, and Consalvi taken prisoner. Condemned to French Guiana, he finally was allowed to stay quietly in Naples. When he asked to be allowed to join Pius VI, he was sent to prison in Florence. Late in 1798 he was able to go to Venice, attended the consistory which elected Pius VII, and became secretary of state and a cardinal in 1800. In Rome he reformed the currency, introduced free trade, restored old monuments, and added to museum holdings. Consalvi engaged in the long negotiations with Napoleon which preceded the signing of the Concordat with France, but condemned the "Organic Articles" which the government added. When the pope refused to accept the overlordship of Napoleon, Consalvi was blamed and put in such a position that he resigned in 1806. After the deportation of the pope, Consalvi went with other exiled cardinals to Paris, but, when he refused to acknowledge the validity of Napoleon's second marriage, the emperor ordered him shot, then changed his mind and ordered the twelve Italian cardinals stripped of their titles and distinguishing clothing. Consalvi, sent off to Rheims, wrote his *Memoirs* there; four years later, when Napoleon abdicated and Pius returned to Italy, the cardinal was renamed secretary of state. In subsequent negotiations in Paris and London and at the Congress of Vienna he regained most of the papal territory which the French had seized. He then abolished former aristocratic privileges in the Italian cities, clarified civil and criminal law, reorganized education, and attended the cares of the needy. Before his death in Rome on Jan. 24, he concluded six new concordats with European monarchs and was widely commended for his statesmanship.

CONSCIENCE, HENDRIK (1812–1883), novelist. Born in Antwerp on Dec. 3, of French and Flemish descent, he received a limited formal education because of a crippled condition, served six years in the army, then was a minor official at Antwerp and at Courtrui. He tutored the sons of King Leopold I, in 1868 became commissioner of the royal museums, and in 1869 a member of the Royal Academy of Belgium. From 1837 until his death in Brussels on Sept. 10 he wrote more than 100 narratives in Flemish, romantic, highly descriptive, and inspirational. The best known are *The Lion of Flanders* (1838), *Jacob van Artevelde, The Conscript*, and *The Year of Miracles*.

CONSORTIA, ST. (d. 570?). She is said to have founded a convent which was supported by King Clotaire of France after she had cured his daughter. F. D. June 22.

CONSTABILIS, ST. (1060–1124). Born in Lucania, Italy, he became a Benedictine at Cava, near Salerno, was chosen abbot in 1122, and built the town of Castel Abbate. He was canonized in 1893. F. D. Feb. 17.

CONSTABLE, CUTHBERT (d. 1746). Son of Francis Tunstall of Wycliffe Hall, Yorkshire, England, he succeeded to the estates of Burton Constable, a maternal relative, in 1718 and changed his name to Constable. He studied at Douai, received a medical degree at Montpellier, became a patron of letters, and supplied information and manuscripts to Bishop Challoner for his *Memoirs of Missionary Priests* and to the antiquarian Thomas Hearne. By his first marriage, to Amy Clifford, he had three children: William, Cicely, and Winifred; by his second, to Elizabeth Heneage, he had a son,

Marmaduke, who resumed the name Tunstall. Cuthbert died on Mar. 27.

CONSTABLE, JOHN (1676?–1743), apologist. Born in Lincolnshire, England, on Nov. 10, he became a Jesuit in 1695, and served as chaplain to the Fitzherbert family in Swinnerton, where he died on Mar. 28. Under the names John Lacey and Clerophilus Alethes he wrote replies to anti-Catholic works by Abbé Courayer, Hugh Tootel, Joseph Trapp, and others.

CONSTANT, ST. (d. 777), martyr. A priest who lived as a hermit at Lough Erne, Ireland, he long was venerated as a martyr. F. D. Nov. 18.

CONSTANT, GUSTAVE LÉON MARIE (1869–1940), historian. Born in St. Laurent-sur-Sèvre, Vendée, France, on Jan. 28, he studied in France and Rome, was ordained in 1893, served on scientific missions to Austria and Spain, and taught ecclesiastical history at the University of Liverpool. He was professor of church history at L'Institut Catholique, Paris, from 1908 until his death at Cannes, France, on Apr. 19. He wrote widely on the Council of Trent, the counter-Reformation in Germany, and the rise of Anglicanism. Major studies include *Histoire de l'église de France*, *La Reforme en Angleterre* (later translated into English, with a preface by Hilaire Belloc), *Marie Tudor*, and *Elizabeth*.

CONSTANT DE LA MOLETTE, PHILIPPE DU (1737–1793), theologian. Born in Côte St. André, France, on Aug. 29, he studied at the Sorbonne, became vicar general of Vienne, and established a reputation as a student of the early books of the Old Testament. His treatment of Genesis was written to refute Voltaire; other works of explanation are misleading in places. He was guillotined in Paris during the Reign of Terror.

CONSTANTI, CELSO (1876–1958), cardinal. Born in Castion di Zoppola, near Venice, Italy, on Apr. 3, he was ordained in 1899, did parish work in Concordia, and during World War I saved many art treasures in northern Italy. He became rector of the Aquileia basilica and director of the art museum there, was administrator of Fiume in 1920, and in 1921 was made an archbishop. In 1921 he became apostolic delegate to China, headed the first Plenary Council at Peiping, established fourteen seminaries for native priests, returned to Rome for the ordination of six Chinese bishops in 1926, and was recalled in 1935 to become secretary of the Congregation of Propaganda. He became a cardinal in 1953. He wrote *Aspects of the Missionary Problem*, *Christian Art in the Missions*, and other works on sacred art. He died in Rome on Oct. 17.

CONSTANTIA, ST. (1st century), martyr. *See* Felix, St.

CONSTANTIAN, ST. (d. 570). Born in Auvergne, he became a monk at Micy and was abbot-founder of Javron. F. D. Dec. 1.

CONSTANTINE (d. 715), pope. A Syrian, he was consecrated pope on Mar. 25, 708, accepted two pilgrim English kings, Coenred of Mercia and Offa of East Saxony, as monks, and weathered a great famine in Rome. Because of the effect of the Trullan Council called in 692 by Emperor Justinian II, which wrote several new canons, including one which declared the patriarch of Constantinople independent of Rome, the pope went to the East in 709. Justinian acknowledged papal supremacy and Constantine seems to have approved those canons not opposed to faith and morals. In 711, Justinian was overthrown by Philippicus Bardanes, who began to revive Monothelism, burned the Acts of the sixth General Council, and sent an angry delegation to Rome. Before action could be taken against the pope, Philippicus was deposed in 713 by Anastasius, who professed his allegiance, as did John, patriarch of Constantinople. Constantine died in Rome on Apr. 9.

CONSTANTINE, ST. (d. 589?), king. After the death of his wife, the king of Cornwall entered an Irish monastery, later became ordained, and went to Scotland as a missioner. There he was killed by pirates, and later venerated as the nation's first martyr, on Mar. 11, but details are confusing.

CONSTANTINE I (d. 879), king of Scotland. Son of Kenneth Mac Alpine, he became king in 863, and was attacked by Northmen from Ireland from 865 through 879, when he was killed in battle on Apr. 2 and buried on Iona.

CONSTANTINE II (d. 952), king of Scotland. Son of Aedh, whom he succeeded in 900, he suffered from Norse raids in 903, was victorious over them in 904, and called a council at Scone in 906 to bring the churches of the Scots and Picts closer together. He made his brother Donald king of Strathclyde in 908, fought Regnwald of Denmark from 908 to 918, then lost to his piratical invaders and was driven out of Northumbria. He was also attacked by Athelstan of Wessex, who claimed Northumberland, in 933–34, and was defeated at Brunanburh, Yorkshire, in 937. He resigned in 943 and became a monk at St. Andrews, Scotland, where he died.

CONSTANTINE III (d. 997), king of Scotland. Son of Culen, he became king in 995, and was murdered two years later.

CONSTANTINE, ST. (d. 529). He was the first bishop of Gap, France. F. D. Apr. 12.

CONSTANTINE, ST. (d. 560?). He succeeded St. Benedict at the abbey of Monte Cassino. F. D. July 21.

CONSTANTINE, ST. (d. 706?), bishop. He is said to have been a monk at Jumièges before he succeeded to the see of Beauvais, France. F. D. June 15.

CONSTANTINE (1020?–1087?). Born in Carthage and often called "Africanus," he studied medicine and oriental languages, served both Emperor Constantine Monomachus and Duke Robert of Salerno as secretary, taught medicine at Salerno, and spent his last twenty years as a Benedictine at Monte Cassino. He translated many influential Greek and Arabic medical works; his *Liber Pantegni* is a translation of *Khitaab el Maleki* of Ali Ben el Abbas.

CONSTANTINE THE GREAT (275?–337), emperor. C. Flavius Valerius Constantinus was born in Naissus (Serbia) on Feb. 27 to an officer who became Emperor Constantius of Rome and St. Helena between the years 275 and 288. He was brought up in the court of Diocletian, fought for Galerius in Austria and his father in Britain, and waited out the quarrel of the claimants to the throne after the death of Constantius in 306. Striking with a small but efficient army, he crushed Maxentius at Turin, Verona, and at the Milvian Bridge outside Rome (where Constantine's pagan soldiers carried a monogram of Christ's name on their shields). As a result of this victory in 312, Constantine, with Licinius, by the Edict of Milan (313) permitted Christians to practice their religion throughout the empire and released all religious prisoners. Licinius, to whom the emperor gave his sister in marriage, proved hostile; the two men met in battle four times between 314 and 324; after his surrender Licinius was forgiven, but again began to plot against Constantine, and was ordered executed by the senate in 325. In that same year he convened the Council of Nicaea. Constantine then moved the capital to Constantinople, reorganized the empire from there, and was baptized shortly before his death in Ancyrona, Nicomedia, on May 22. Although he brought up his sons as Christians, Constantine II leaned toward paganism, and Constantius, though an opponent of paganism, became an Arian.

CONSTANTIUS, ST. (d. 161), martyr. *See* Simplicius, St.

CONSTANTIUS, ST. (d. 170), bishop. He and a number of others in his diocese of Perugia, Italy, were put to death during the reign of Marcus Aurelius. F. D. Jan. 29.

CONSTANTIUS, ST. (d. 287?), martyr. He and SS. Crescentius, Justin, Maxentius, and others were put to death at Trèves during the Diocletian persecution. F. D. Dec. 12.

CONSTANTIUS, ST. (5th century). A priest in Rome, he suffered greatly from persecution by the Pelagians. F. D. Nov. 30.

CONSTANTIUS, ST. (d. 520?). Bishop of Aquino, Italy, he is honored by Pope St. Gregory the Great in his *Dialogues*. F. D. Sept. 1.

CONSTANTIUS, ST. (6th century). He was sacristan of the church of St. Stephen at Ancona, Italy. F. D. Sept. 23.

CONTARINI, GASPARO (1483–1542), cardinal. Born in Venice, Italy, on Oct. 16, he studied at Padua, held several offices in the Republic of Venice, and in 1520 was appointed to an ambassadorial post to the court of Emperor Charles V, to defend the alliance between Venice and France. In 1527 he represented his state at the Congress of Ferrara, where the league against the emperor was formed. He was sent as ambassador to Pope Clement VII in 1528 to defend the seizure of Ravenna and Cervia and to invite the papacy to join France against Spain, but failed in both missions. Contarini later arranged the peace with Charles V in 1530 and was present at his coronation. He became a senator; Pope Paul III made him a cardinal in 1535 and gave him the diocese of Cividale di Belluno in 1536. Contarini led the commission which recommended reforms in the curia, helped to gain papal approval of the new Society of Jesus, went to Germany as papal legate to seal the breach in the Church, and then was sent as legate to Bologna, Italy, where he died on Aug. 24. Many of his writings, particularly on faith, are colored by the opinions of the day, though he clearly professed his orthodoxy and allegiance.

CONTARINI, GIOVANNI (1549?–1605), painter. Born in Venice, Italy, he imitated Titian and Tintoretto, decorated ceilings of churches in Venice, completed a somewhat romantic *Virgin and Child with SS. Mark and Sebastian*, numerous canvases on mythological subjects, and became court painter to Emperor Rudolph II.

CONTENSON, VINCENT (1641–1674), theologian. Born in Altivallare, France, he became a Dominican at seventeen, taught at Albi and Toulouse, wrote *Theologia mentis et cordis* (published posthumously), which relied heavily on patristic citation, and became active as a preacher of missions. He died at Creil-sur-Oise, France, on Dec. 26.

CONTESTUS, ST. (d. 510?). He became bishop of Bayeux, France, in 480. F. D. Jan. 19.

CONTI, ANDREW. *See* Andrew of Anagni.

CONTI, GREGORY. *See* Victor IV, antipope.

CONTI, NICCOLÒ DEI (15th century). Born in Milan, Italy, he mastered oriental languages, traveled in Egypt, Arabia, Persia, and India, between 1419 and 1444, and reported his findings to Poggio Bracciolini, secretary to Pope Eugenius IV, at Venice. His account of his travels was first published in 1723.

CONTUCCI, ANDREA (1460–1529), sculptor. Born in Monte San Sovino, Italy, he studied in Florence with Bertoldo and Pollaiuolo, did the tombs of Cardinals Basso and Sforza in Santa Maria del Popolo church, Rome, reliefs in Santo Spirito, Florence, and Casa Santa, Loreto, and a *Madonna and Child* and *St. John the Baptist* for the Genoa cathedral. He is often referred to as Andrea del Sansovino. .

CONTZEN, ADAM (1573–1635). Born in Montjoie, Prussia, he became a Jesuit in 1595, taught philosophy at Würzburg for four years and scripture at Mainz from 1610 to 1621, and was chancellor of the University of Molsheim, Alsace, in 1622–23. He defended the view of Bellarmine against Pareus of Heidelberg, wrote on ways of restoring religious peace in Germany, wrote a model of statecraft, *Politicorum,* considered by many to be an effective answer to Machiavelli. In it he recommended state ownership of some industries, state aid, a luxury tax, and a combination of free trade and a protective tariff. While confessor to Elector Maximilian of Bavaria after 1623 he wrote commentaries on the gospels and epistles and *Methodus doctrinae civilis, seu Abissini regis historia,* a novel expounding his political and economic views. He died in Munich, Germany, on June 19.

CONUS, ST. (d. 1200?). Born in Diano, Italy, he became a Benedictine monk at Cardossa, Lucania. F. D. June 3.

CONVOYON, ST. (d. 868). Deacon at Vannes and later a hermit, he served at the monastery of Glanfeuil, then founded that of St. Saviour at Redon in Brittany with six Benedictine companions, where he was abbot until the Norsemen overran the area. His cult was approved in 1866. F. D. Jan. 5.

CONWALL, ST. (d. 630?). An Irish follower of St. Kentigern, he preached in Scotland, where he died. F. D. Sept. 28.

CONWAY, BERTRAND (1872–1959). Born in New York City on May 5, he studied at St. Charles, Maryland, and Catholic University, and was ordained a Paulist in 1896. He became famed as a convert-maker, founded the Catholic Unity League in 1917 to distribute books to non-Catholics, and was treasurer of his order in 1931. He wrote many pamphlets, nearly 100 reviews a year for the *Catholic World,* translated Vacandard's *Inquisition* and D'Hulst's *The Christian Family,* and is best known for his *The Question Box* (1903), which sold more than four million copies. He died in New York on Dec. 9.

CONWELL, HENRY (1745–1842), bishop. Born in Moneymore, Derry, Ireland, he studied at the Irish College in Paris, served as parish priest at Dungannon and vicar general of Armagh, and, in 1820 at seventy-four, accepted papal appointment as second bishop of Philadelphia, Pennsylvania. The see had been vacant from 1814 until Conwell's arrival in Dec. 1820;

during that time it had been administered by a board of trustees led by the eccentric individualist, Fr. William Hogan. When the new bishop, unaware of all the ramifications and of the problems of six years, revoked Hogan's faculties, a schism developed; matters became worse when Conwell acknowledged the trustees' right of veto as to salaries and appointments. The bishop was called to Rome, censured, permitted to return to Philadelphia with no administrative power, and replaced in 1830 by Francis P. Kenrick. Conwell spent his last years in prayerful seclusion before his death in Philadelphia on Apr. 22.

COOK, BL. HUGH (d. 1539), martyr. Usually surnamed Faringdon after the town in Berkshire, England, where he was born, he became a monk at Reading abbey and in 1520 its abbot. He was a close friend of Henry VIII (signing the petition to Pope Clement VII which sought nullification of the king's marriage). In 1539 he refused to surrender his abbey, was arrested, probably for denying royal supremacy, and hanged on Nov. 15, with Bl. John Eynon, parish priest of St. Giles, Reading, and Bl. John Rugg, a retired prebendary of Chichester, both living at the abbey. All were beatified in 1895. F. D. Dec. 1.

COOMBES, WILLIAM HENRY (1767–1850). Brought up in Meadowgate, Somersetshire, England, where his uncle, Fr. William Coombes (d. 1822) lived, he studied at Douai, was ordained in 1791, escaped to England during the French Revolution, and acted as vice-president of Old Hall seminary. He wrote spiritual readings, biographies of SS. Francis de Sales and Jane Frances de Chantal, and edited selections from SS. Basil and John Chrysostom. He died at Downside abbey, England.

COPERNICUS, NICOLAUS (1473–1543), astronomer. Born in Thorn, Prussia, on Feb. 19, of a Polish family which emigrated from Cracow, he was brought up after the age of ten by his uncle, Bishop Watzelrode Lucas, when his merchant father died. Nicolaus was sent to Cracow, where he studied classics and mathematics, and to Bologna, where he also studied canon law. He knew the astronomers Blar and Novara at these schools. He and his brother Andreas became canons of Frauenburg in 1497. In 1500 he lectured at Rome on astronomy, gained a leave of absence from his canonry, and studied medicine and law at Padua and Ferrara, taking his doctorate in canon law at the latter school. He practiced medicine at Heilsberg from 1506 to 1512, was administrator of the diocesan castle of Allenstein until 1520, then returned to Frauenburg, and became its administrator. Whether he ever rose to the priesthood is uncertain. In 1522 he issued a treatise on monetary reform which so impressed the king of Poland that Copernicus was named deputy counselor for finance in Prussia until 1529. He had, at various locations, been making detailed observations of the heavens; as early as 1514 he was asked by Bishop Paul of Fossombrone for suggestions as to reforming the calendar; but said he had not yet learned enough. By 1531 he had developed his theory of a sun-centered universe to the point where he could present it in the form of seven axioms. George Joachim Rheticus left his chair of mathematics at Wittenberg in 1539 to work with Copernicus and to prepare his manuscripts for publication. Parts (chiefly on trigonometry) were issued, but there was great hostility from Protestant theologians; Rheticus was barred from returning to his university; Copernicus himself became partially paralyzed. Neither man authorized the printing of the first edition of *Six Books on the Revolutions of the Celestial Orbits*, which Copernicus saw at Frauenburg on May 24, the day of his death, and which the reformer Osiander had printed with his own preface, and with a title page indicating that the findings were merely a hypothesis. Copernicus had long been requested by Cardinal Schönberg of Capua, Bishop Giese of Culm, and Pope Paul III to issue his findings. The corrected edition by Rheticus was published in 1566; in 1616, a few Catholics during the era of Galileo had the work placed on the Index; it was removed in 1758 by Pope Benedict XIV. Copernicus' concepts gained universal acceptance and resulted in a revolutionary approach to the world of science.

COPLEY, ANTHONY (1567–1607?), poet. Son of Thomas Copley, a distant relative of Queen Elizabeth I, he was born in England, joined his parents in 1582 at Rouen (where they had fled after conversion to Catholicism), and studied at the English College, Rome. He was in the service of the king of Spain in 1586–90, returned to England, was captured, imprisoned, and released. His long poem of 335 stanzas, *A Fig for Fortune*, states his religious and political position and was written as part answer to Spenser's *Faerie Queene*, Book One. In 1603, on the death of Elizabeth, he joined the conspiracy to place Arabella Stuart on the throne, was captured and condemned to death, but again released. He then went to the English College, Rome; nothing is known of him after 1607.

COPLEY, THOMAS (1595–1652). Born in Madrid, Spain, to an English family which went into exile during the Elizabethan persecution, he became a Jesuit, went to Maryland in 1637, taking the name Fr. Philip Fisher, and was arrested and sent to England in chains in 1645 with Fr. Andrew White. He was released after three years and returned to the American mission, where he died.

COPPÉE, FRANÇOIS EDOUARD JO-

ACHIM (1842–1908), novelist. Born in Paris, France, on Jan. 26, he had something of a high-school education, supplemented in later years by private study, but had to leave school, supporting his family as a government clerk. In 1863 he joined the group of poets called the Parnassians, and published *Le reliquaire* (1866), followed by four other volumes of poems and seven poetic dramas, chief among which are *Severo Torelli* (1883), *Les Jacobites* (1885), and *Le Pater*, which attacked the Commune and was banned until 1890. Several romantic novels and three collections of short stories on simple themes and scenes, often of the humbler side of Paris, gained him great popularity and election in 1884 to the French Academy. He was dramatic critic of *La Patrie* from 1880 to 1884, and in the years before his last and long illness turned to themes in poetry (poverty, the worker, the shame of national defeat) more serious than those of his early thin lyricism. He returned to the Church in 1897, and recorded this in the novel *La bonne souffrance*; other novels include *Fille de tristesse*, *Le coucher du soleil*, and the psychological *Le coupable*. He died in Paris on May 23.

COPPINGER, JOHN JOSEPH (1834–1909), general. Born in Queenstown, Ireland, on Oct. 11, he fought in the papal army against the Italian unionists, then went to the United States, was a captain with the 14th Infantry, served in Indian wars in 1866–68, became a colonel, and in 1895 a brigadier general. He was major general of volunteers at Camp Wheeler, Alabama, during the Spanish-American War and retired from service in 1898.

COQUART, CLAUDE GODEFROI (1706–1765), missioner. Born in Pays de Caux, France, on Feb. 20, he became a Jesuit in 1726, studied in Paris and taught at Arras and Hesdin, and in 1740 was sent to Canada. He went to the Northwest with the explorer Verendrye, served on the Saguenay mission from Quebec and briefly in Acadia from 1746 until his death on July 4 at Chicoutimi, and wrote an Abenaki grammar and dictionary and an economic report on eastern Canada.

CORBETT, TIMOTHY (1861–1939), bishop. Born in Mendota, Minnesota, on July 10, he was educated in France, Canada, and Boston, was ordained in 1886, served as curate in St. Paul, Minnesota, to 1889 and pastor of the Duluth cathedral to 1910, when he was appointed first bishop of Crookston, Minnesota. He died on July 20.

CORBICAN, ST. (8th century). An Irishman, he became a recluse in the Low Countries and devoted himself to giving religious training to peasants. F. D. June 26.

CORBIE, AMBROSE (1604–1649). Born near Durham, England, he studied at St.

Omer's and the English College in Rome, became a Jesuit in 1627, taught at St. Omer's, and was a confessor in Rome, where he died on Apr. 11. He wrote on his family, a manuscript life of Bro. Thomas Stillington, and a printed account of the martyrdom of Thomas Holland and Henry Morse.

CORBIE, GERARD (d. 1637). After living near Dublin and Durham, the family became exiles because of their religion and settled in the Low Countries. After his sons Ambrose, Ralph, and Richard became Jesuits (a fourth, Richard, died while a student at St. Omer's) and his daughters Mary and Catherine became Benedictine nuns at Brussels, he and his wife, Isabella (Richardson), entered religious life. Gerard became a Jesuit laybrother at Watten in 1628 and Isabella (d. 1652) a Benedictine at Brussels.

CORBINGTON, BL. RALPH (1598–1644), martyr. Born of English parents living in exile in Maynooth, Ireland, on Mar. 25, he was five when they returned to England. He studied at St. Òmer, Seville, and Valladolid, and in 1631 joined the Jesuits and was ordained at Watten, Flanders. In 1632 he was sent on the English mission, labored around Durham for twelve years as Mr. Corby, and was captured near Newcastle while saying mass. He was convicted with Bl. John Duckett of being a priest, and hanged, drawn, and quartered at London. He was beatified in 1929. F. D. Sept. 7.

CORBINIAN, ST. (670–725). Born in Chartres, France, he lived as a hermit for fourteen years and, on a visit to Rome, met Pope Gregory II, who sent him to evangelize Germany. He settled at Freising in Upper Bavaria, denounced the marriage of Duke Grimoald to his brother's widow, and suffered persecution from her until the duke's death. It is not certain whether he was bishop of Cornouaille, Brittany. F. D. Sept. 8.

CORBMAC, ST. (6th century). He was a follower of St. Columba, whom the latter placed in charge of the monastery at Durrow, Ireland. F. D. June 21.

CORBY, RALPH. *See* Corbington, Bl. Ralph.

CORCORAN, FRANCIS VINCENT (1879–1939), educator. Born in Pittsburgh, Pennsylvania, on May 6, he became a member of the Congregation of the Missions in 1894, and was ordained in 1902. He taught theology (1907–30) and was vice-president (1926–30) at Kenrick seminary, St. Louis; was president of De Paul University, Chicago, in 1930–35; and rector at Los Angeles from 1936 until his death there on Jan. 28.

CORCORAN, JAMES ANDREW (1820–1889), theologian. Born in Charleston, South Carolina, on Mar. 30, he was ordained at Rome in 1842, mastered oriental languages, particularly Syriac, and received his doctorate in theol-

ogy. He taught in the Charleston seminary, became co-editor of the *U. S. Catholic Miscellany*, the first such literary journal in America, and pastor in Wilmington, North Carolina. He was a secretary of the provincial councils at Baltimore in 1855 and 1858 and at the second Plenary Council of 1866. He was selected as theologian to represent the American hierarchy at the Vatican Council, supported papal infallibility, and returned to the chair of theology at Overbrook seminary, Philadephia, and to the editorship of the *American Catholic Quarterly Review*. He went to Rome in 1883 to make preparations for the third Plenary Council of Baltimore, serving the bishops as secretary then and when the council opened. He was made a monsignor in 1884 and died in Philadelphia on July 16.

CORCORAN, MICHAEL (1827–1863), general. Born in Carrowkeel, Sligo, Ireland, on Sept. 21, he served in the Royal Irish Constabulary from 1846 to 1849, when he resigned and emigrated to New York. He rose through the ranks of the state's 69th Regiment of militia, became colonel in 1859, and was up for trial when he refused to permit his men to parade in honor of the Prince of Wales in 1860. The court-martial was dropped when the Civil War began. Col. Corcoran was captured at Bull Run and imprisoned for thirteen months. Released, he raised four regiments in New York, called the Irish Legion, which he led in Virginia engagements for a year as brigadier general. He was thrown from his horse at Fairfax Court House, Virginia, on Dec. 22 and died on that same day.

CORDARA, GIULIO CESARE (1704–1785), historian. Born in Alessandria, Piedmont, Italy, on Dec. 14, he became a Jesuit at fourteen, taught at several colleges, wrote poetry (his satire on the Cabalists won him membership in the Academy of the Arcadians), a play (*La morte di Nice*, in honor of Prince James III of England), and a Latin history of the Scots expedition of Charles Edward Stuart. His *Literary History of the Times* (1737) is effective satire; two volumes on the history of his Society from 1616 to 1633 followed. He also wrote a history of the German College in Rome and some fifty other items, even in old age while living at Alessandria after the suppression of the Society. He died there on Mar. 6. His pseudonym was Pameno Cassio.

CORDELL, CHARLES (1720–1791). Born in Kent, England, on Oct. 5, he studied at Douai, and after ordination was sent in 1748 to the English mission, serving at Arundel, Yorkshire, the Isle of Man, and Newcastle. He prepared two catechisms and translated a life of Pope Clement XIV and several other works from the French, including Bergier's

Deism Self-refuted. He died at Newcastle-on-Tyne, England, on Jan. 26.

CORDIER, BALTHASAR (1592–1650), scholar. Born in Antwerp on June 7, he became a Jesuit in 1612, taught in several schools, then devoted himself to translating and editing the Greek Fathers of the Church, particularly SS. Cyril and Dionysius the Areopagite. He also published an original commentary on Job. He died in Rome on June 24.

COREBUS. Although claimed to be a Roman prefect in Messina, Sicily, and converted by St. Eleutherius, martyred in 138 during the reign of Hadrian, and honored on Apr. 18, he seems to be merely the hero of a pious legend.

CORELLI, ARCANGELO (1653–1713), composer. Born in Fusignano, Italy, on Feb. 12 or 13, and considered the greatest violinist of his times, he gave weekly concerts at the palace of his patron, Cardinal Ottoboni. In his rich *Opus* 6 he laid the foundation for the later *concerto grosso*, giving it definite form; in *Opus 5* (twelve sonatas for violin and bass accompaniment) he helped to set a more definite form for the sonata. Henry Purcell, François Couperin, and George Teleman were indebted to him. He died in Rome, on Jan. 10.

CORENTIN, ST. According to legend, he was a hermit in Cornouaille (Quimper), Brittany, who became its first bishop. His dates are variously listed as fourth and sixth century. F. D. Dec. 12.

CORIOLIS, GASPARD GUSTAVE DE (1792–1843), physicist. Born in Paris, where he studied engineering, he taught mathematics and physics at L'École Polytechnique, and became its director of studies in 1838, having been made a member of the Academy of Sciences in 1836. He published two volumes on mechanics, worked with Gen. Poncelet to reform the teaching of that subject, and evolved a theorem of relative motion. He died in Paris.

CORKER, JAMES (1636–1715). Born in Yorkshire, England, he became a Benedictine at the abbey of Lamspringe, near Hildesheim, Germany, taking the name Maurus, and entered England as a missioner in 1665. He was imprisoned at the time of the Titus Oates Plot, acquitted in 1679 of treason, but sentenced to death as a priest. Friends gained a delay, and Fr. Corker gained a number of converts while in Newgate prison and prepared Archbishop Oliver Plunkett for martyrdom. At the accession of King James II, Corker was released, served at court as ambassador of Ferdinand of Bavaria, and lived at Clerkenwell until his chapel was destroyed by a mob and he was forced to flee to the Continent. In 1691 he was abbot of Cismar, in 1693 of Lamspringe, and from 1696 until his death lived in England as a missioner. He published several pamphlets in defense of those implicated in the Oates Plot, and died in Paddington, England, on Dec. 22.

CORMAC, ST. (6th century). A friend of St. Columba, he became an abbot in Ireland. F. D. Dec. 12.

CORMAC, ST. (d. 908). King of Munster, Ireland, and compiler of the Psalter of Cashel, he probably was first bishop of Cashel, and was slain in battle. F. D. Sept. 14.

CORMAC MAC CUILENAN (836–908), bishop. He studied in southern Ireland, was ordained, and was made bishop of Cashel. In 900, because of his descent from the race of Eoghanact, he became king of Cashel. King Flann and King Ceorbhall of Leinster invaded in 906 and were defeated at Tollamore; they returned in 908, defeated the Munstermen at Ballymoon, and slew Cormac in battle. Cormac left a glossary of 1400 Irish words which throw light on ancient customs, the *Sanas Chormaic*.

CORMONT, THOMAS (12th century), architect. With his son Reynaud he was active in the first stages of the building of the cathedral of Amiens, France.

CORNARO, CATERINA (1454–1510), queen. Born in Venice, Italy, she married King James II of Cyprus in 1472 and succeeded him when he died a few months later. In 1489, Venice forced her to abdicate, fearing that a marriage with Prince Alfonso of Naples would upset the balance of power. Her remaining years were spent at Asolo, near Venice. Her cousin, Cardinal Pietro Bembo, described her in *Coli Asolani* and she was the heroine of several later novels and operas.

CORNARO-PISCOPIA, ELENA LUCREZIA (1646–1684). Born in Venice, Italy on June 5, daughter of Giovanni, procurator of St. Mark's, she mastered classical and European languages, as well as Hebrew, Arabic, mathematics, theology, taking her doctorate in philosophy at Padua in 1678. She was a member of numerous academies, wrote treatises, translations, and, in her last years, devotional tracts. She became a Benedictine Oblate in 1665, but was not a nun. She died in Padua, Italy, on July 26.

CORNEILLE, JEAN BAPTISTE (1646?–1695), painter. Born in Paris, France, youngest son of Michel, he studied under his father and briefly at Rome, worked with Jacques Vouet in decorating the Tuileries, and in 1692 became professor at the Royal Academy. Major paintings include *Punishment of Busiris by Hercules* (Louvre) and *Deliverance of St. Peter from Prison* (Notre Dame). He also attained fame as an etcher, working in the style of Agostino Carracci. He died in Paris on Apr. 12.

CORNEILLE, MICHEL (1601?–1664), painter. Born in Orléans, France, he studied with Simon Vouet, whom he imitated closely in his early work; his later art shows the influence of the Carracci and the "post-Raphaelite school." He was one of the twelve men who founded the Royal Academy in 1648 and was its rector in 1656. His *St. Paul and St. Barnabas at Lystra* was completed for Notre Dame cathedral. Like his children, he also was an etcher. He died in Paris.

CORNEILLE, MICHEL (1642–1708), painter. Born in Paris, France, son of Michel, and often called the elder Corneille (to distinguish him from his brother Jean Baptiste, the younger), he studied under his father, Mognard, and Lebrun, won academy prizes and went on to Rome, as his brother did, also was influenced by the Carraccis, returned to Paris in 1663, and in 1690 became a professor at the Royal Academy. He completed paintings for the king's palaces and for several Paris churches. Outstanding among his religious work are *Repòs en Egypte*, *Baptism of Constantine*, and *Apparition of Christ to St. Peter*; his strong sense of color is lost because of later fading. He, too, was an etcher. In his last years he resided at the Gobelins' factory at Paris, where he died on Aug. 16.

CORNEILLE, PIERRE (1606–1684), dramatist. Born in Rouen, France, on June 6, he became a lawyer in 1624 and held minor legal positions until 1650. *Mélite* (1629) and *La Veuve* (1633) were among his first comedies, but his early work was constricted by contemporary convention and the trivialities of the comedy of manners. He was for a time in the literary service of Richelieu, after 1634, but fell out of favor when he objected to some of the plots offered him for dramatization and uttered other hostile criticism. His first original tragedy was *Médée* (1635). *Le Cid*, based on the Spanish account by de Castro, followed in 1636 and, though it became the center of a literary controversy, it proved immensely popular and influential on subsequent French and English drama. *Horace, Cinna*, and *Polyeucte*, all effective tragedies, followed; *Nicomède* (1651) and the earlier *Le Menteur*, a comedy, belong with his best. He was elected to the French Academy, wrote additional work, which did not attain popularity, and in 1652, after the failure of *Pertharite*, retired to Rouen until 1659. During those years he put the *Imitation of Christ* into verse, wrote other devotional poetry, and issued defensive criticism. The rival popularity of Molière and Racine brought him back into the theater, but he was able only to write eleven uneven and generally mediocre plays before 1674. He was effective in his presentation of honor, love, and duty conflicts, but often allowed discussion to replace action; he was at times too interested in the mental attitudes of his characters toward their problems. His reliance on the narrowest interpretation of the dramatic unities began a century-long debate about the stage, Aristotle, and literary criticism. His lengthy, poetry-charged speeches were at their best effectively stirring; at other times they became declamatory and bombastic. Corneille died in poverty on Oct. 1 in Paris.

CORNELISZ, JACOB (1471?–1567), painter. Also called Jacob van Amsterdam and Jacob van Oostzann, he worked in the Flemish style, relied on realistic (sometimes harsh) backgrounds, and avoided Italian influences. He completed several altarpieces, including an elaborate St. Jerome for the Belvedere palace, Vienna; *Adoration of the Trinity* (Cassel); *Crucifixion* (Cologne); *Nativity* (Naples); and *Adoration of the Magi* (Antwerp).

CORNELIUS, ST. (d. 253), pope and martyr. A Roman priest, he was elected pope in March, 251, fourteen months after Pope St. Fabian was martyred. A few weeks later, he was confronted by the first antipope, Novatian, who taught that the Church had no power to forgive those who committed certain sins and, particularly, those who had apostatized. A synod of Western bishops at Rome supported the pope and excommunicated Novatian and his followers. During the persecution of Gallus, Cornelius was banished to Centumcellae (Civita Vecchia), Italy, and died there in June from his sufferings. F. D. Sept. 16.

CORNELIUS, ST. (1st century). He was the centurion baptized by St. Peter at Caesarea in Palestine (Acts 10); traditionally, he is called the first bishop of Caesarea. F. D. Feb. 2.

CORNELIUS, ST. (1120?–1176), archbishop. Cornelius Mac Conchailleadh became an Augustinian canon regular in Armagh, Ireland, in 1140, abbot in 1151, and archbishop of Armagh in 1174. He died in Chambéry, Savoy, while returning from a pilgrimage to Rome. F. D. June 4.

CORNELIUS CORNELII A LAPIDE. *See* Steen, Cornelis van den.

CORNELIUS, BL. JOHN (1557–1594), martyr. Born of Irish parents at Bodmin, England, he studied at Oxford, Rheims, and Rome, and was ordained in 1583. He worked for ten years on the English missions and was arrested in 1594, the year he joined the Jesuits. Convicted as a priest, he was hanged, drawn, and quartered in Dorchester, England. He was beatified in 1929. F. D. July 4.

CORNELIUS MALACHY, BRO. *See* Hession, Martin J.

CORNELIUS, PETER VON (1783–1867), painter. Born in Düsseldorf, Germany, on Sept. 23, he studied at Rome from 1811 to 1819, then returned to serve as director of the Academy of Fine Arts and to complete several large paintings for the prince of Bavaria, later Louis I. In 1825 he was named director of the Academy of Munich, but detractors made life unpleasant and he became director of the Academy of Fine Arts in Berlin under the protection of Frederick IV of Prussia. In his first years he illustrated editions of Goethe's *Faust*, Shakespeare's *Romeo and Juliet*, and the *Nibelungenlied*. While in Rome he worked with a group called the Nazarenes which sought to establish a new German-Christian school of art; with them he completed frescoes in a number of residences, including that of the Prussian ambassador, Bartholdy. Once he had independent means, he was able to develop by himself. His greatest works were the fresco of the *Last Judgment* in the Ludwigskirche, Munich, and apocalyptic wall paintings for the royal mausoleum in Berlin. He died in Berlin on Mar. 6.

CORNELIUS OF WYCK, BL. (d. 1572), martyr. Born in Dorestat, near Utrecht, Holland, he became a Franciscan laybrother, and was seized with the community at Gorkum by a mob of Calvinists, and tortured and hanged at Briel, Holland. He was beatified in 1867. F. D. July 9.

CORNELY, KARL JOSEF RUDOLF (1830–1908), scholar. Born in Breyell, Germany, on Apr. 19, he studied at Münster, Paderborn, and Bonn, became a Jesuit in 1852, was ordained in 1860, studied scriptural languages for five years in Syria, Egypt, and France, and in 1868 became professor of scripture and oriental languages at Maria-Laach. The Jesuits were expelled from Germany in 1872; Fr. Cornely went to Tervueren, near Brussels, from which he edited *Stimmen aus Maria-Laach* until 1879. He had been a contributor before 1872; he began to add supplements containing elaborate scholarship in all fields of learning. In 1873 he founded *Die katholischen Missionen*, which reported on German missionary priests and the areas of the world in which they labored. In 1879 he became professor of scripture at the Gregorian in Rome, where he outlined the plan and wrote the first volumes of *Cursus scripturae sacrae*, a biblical encyclopedia. To this he devoted all his time after 1889, publishing the general and special introductions to all scriptural units. He died in Trier, Germany, on Mar. 3.

CORNET, NICOLAS (1572–1663), theologian. Born in Amiens, France, he studied there, took his doctorate in theology at Paris, and became president of the College of Navarre and syndic of the Sorbonne. He engaged in strong controversy with the Jansenists, who appealed to parliament against him; was successful in having the assembly of the clergy condemn the propositions in Jansenius' *Augustinus*; and possibly collaborated with Richelieu in the writing of *Méthodes de controverse*. He died in Paris, where Bossuet preached at his funeral.

CORNEY, BL. JOHN CHARLES (1809–1837), martyr. Born in Loudon, France, he entered the Society of Foreign Missions at Paris,

was sent to Annam, seized at Tonkin, caged, displayed, beaten, and finally beheaded on Sept. 20. He was beatified in 1900. F. D. Feb. 8.

CORNOLDI, GIOVANNI MARIA (1822–1892). Born in Venice, Italy, on Sept. 29, he became a Jesuit in 1840, taught at Bressanone and Padua, and from 1880 until his death was an editor of *Civiltà Cattolica*. He wrote much on philosophy, and commentaries on Dante's *Divina Commedia* and St. Thomas Aquinas. He founded the Academy of St. Thomas at Bologna and established its journal and also *La Scienza Italiana*. He died on Jan. 18.

CORNTHWAITE, ROBERT (d. 1890), bishop. Born in England, he was ordained, was canon of Hexham and Newcastle, served as rector of the English College, Rome, in 1851–57, and became bishop of Beverley in 1861. His diocese was divided into that of Leeds and of Middlesborough in 1879. He died on June 16.

CORONA, ST. (d. 176?), martyr. *See* Victor, St.

CORONADO, FRANCISCO VASQUEZ DE (1510?–1554), explorer. Born in Salamanca, Spain, he was in Mexico in 1535, was appointed governor of Nueva Galicia in 1538 by Antonio de Mendoza, the viceroy, and in 1539 led a colonizing expedition into New Mexico with 300 Spaniards and 1000 Indians. They established headquarters at Zuñi and Santa Fe, and Coronado explored Arizona as far as the Colorado River. In 1541, acting on reports of rich metal regions, he led part of his force through Arkansas up to Nebraska, but found only nomadic tribes or settlements where corn was grown. His report was of great geographical and ethnological value, but the settlers in New Mexico were unhappy and moved south, leaving the Franciscan missioners. The viceroy was displeased and Coronado fell out of favor, lost his governorship, and died in comparative obscurity in Mexico City.

CORONEL, GREGORIO NUÑEZ (1548?–1620?), theologian. Born in Portugal, he became an Augustinian and after ordination gained wide reputation as a theologian and preacher. He was for a time chaplain to the duke of Savoy, then took his doctorate in theology at Rome, and taught in that city for years. He was appointed by Popes Clement VIII and Paul V to act as secretary to the judiciary body seeking to settle the controversy between the Jesuits and Dominicans over grace and free will. He was offered a bishopric as reward, but declined the honor. He wrote on good government, the apostolic tradition, and the marks of the true Church.

CORONEL, JUAN (1569–1651), missioner. Born in Spain, he studied at Alcalá, became a Franciscan of the Strict Observance, and was sent to Yucatán, Mexico, in 1590. He served in the Indian missions there until his death, wrote a Mayan grammar and catechism, and taught the language to the historian Cogolludo. He died in Meridá, Mexico.

CORONELLI, MARCO VINCENZO (1650–1718), geographer. Born in Venice, Italy, he became a monk, constructed two large globes at Paris for King Louis XIV, returned to Venice in 1685 and was made geographer of the republic in 1702, and published maps, histories, and a study of Rhodes.

COROT, JEAN BAPTISTE CAMILLE (1796–1875), artist. Born in Paris on July 16, he studied at Rouen, was apprenticed to a draper, but at twenty-six began studying art under Victor Bertin and exhibited at the salon in 1827. After his third visit to Italy in 1843 he came under the influence of the Barbizon school and became a leading exponent of their style, famed for his landscapes, though he did some figure pictures, and a few etchings and pencil sketches. He was made a member of the Legion of Honor in 1846, and died in Paris on Feb. 22. Among his outstanding paintings are *La Dance des nymphs, Souvenir des environs de Florence, Pastorale, Biblis, Le Lac, Vue d'Italie, Orphée, Le Repòs de Christ au Jardin des Oliviers, Matin,* and *Soirée.*

CORREGGIO, ANTONIO ALLEGRI DA (1494–1534), artist. Antonio Allegri was born of a merchant family in Correggio, near Mantua, Italy, lived in Parma from 1518 to 1530, then returned to his birthplace, where he died on Mar. 5. At the start of his career as a painter he showed the influence of the Ferrara school, then that of Mantegna and da Vinci; later, he attained individuality, and became a master of chiaroscuro. He did a number of nativity scenes, (such as *La Notte*), *Marriage of St. Catherine, Madonna of St. Francis, Assumption,* and *Vierge au Panier.*

CORRIGAN, DOMINIC (1802–1880). Son of a Dublin shopkeeper, he studied medicine at Dublin and Edinburgh, and returned to his native city to the staff of the Jervis Street Hospital. He made detailed studies of heart conditions, particularly diseases of the aortic valves, on which he published; and out of his devoted labors during famine and plague came *Lectures on Fevers* (1853). He was made baronet for his long services as commissioner of education; was a Liberal member of parliament from 1869 to 1874; was five times elected president of the Dublin College of Physicians; and directed other professional groups as well. Corrigan's pulse is named in his honor. He died in Dublin on Feb. 1.

CORRIGAN, MICHAEL AUGUSTINE (1839–1902), archbishop. Born in Newark, New Jersey, on Aug. 13, he studied at St. Mary's College in Wilmington, graduated from Mt. St. Mary's, Maryland, in 1859, was one of the first twelve seminarians at the North American College in Rome, and was ordained in Rome in 1863. He received his doctorate in 1864 from the Propaganda, taught at Seton Hall seminary in New Jersey, became its president in 1868, and vicar general of the Newark diocese, which he administered in 1869–70 and 1872–73, and in 1873 was appointed bishop of Newark. He fought for Catholic chaplains in the state reform schools, and when unsuccessful built several Catholic protectories, ably administered the diocese, encouraged the building of educational institutions, and in 1880 was made titular archbishop of Petra and coadjutor of the New York archdiocese, to which he succeeded in 1885. He was soon involved in a controversy with Fr. McGlynn over the latter's economic and political views and removed him from his pastorate of St. Stephen's, an action which caused resentment among McGlynn's numerous followers (the priest was excommunicated in 1887, but restored in 1892). He also engaged in a sharp difference of opinion with Archbishop Ireland over the Church's attitude toward public-school education, which was sharpened by the latter's support of Sylvester L. Malone for a vacancy on the board of regents of the State University of New York against his choice of Bishop McQuaid. He was noted for his conservatism, his vigorous sponsorship of the parochial school, his administrative ability, and as a great builder. He died in New York City on May 5.

CORSINI, ST. ANDREW (1302–1373), bishop. Born in Florence and wasting his adolescence in dissipation, he suddenly reformed after many prayerful rebukes from his mother, and was ordained a Carmelite in 1328. He also studied at Paris and Avignon and then became prior at Florence. He became bishop of Fiesole in 1349, working hard for the poor, continuing to lead a life of extreme mortification, and acting as peacemaker with such success that Urban V sent him to Bologna to bring leaders and people together, which he achieved. He died in Fiesole, Italy, on Jan. 6, and was canonized in 1629. F. D. Feb. 4.

CORSINI, BL. TOMMASSO (d. 1345). Born in Orvieto, Italy, he became a Servite laybrother, refused in humility to become ordained, and devoted his years to begging for his order. He was beatified in 1768. F. D. June 23.

CORTE-REAL, GASPAR (1450?–1501?), explorer. Born in Portugal, he was sent to search for the Northwest Passage by King Manuel I and is believed to have discovered Greenland in 1500 and perhaps the North American mainland as well. In 1501 he made a second voyage with his brother Miguel and probably reached Newfoundland; the two men were separated and both perished, Miguel in 1502 while still searching for Gaspar.

CORTÉS, HERNANDO (1485?–1547), explorer. Born in Medellin, Spain, he studied briefly at Salamanca, left home for the New World, lived in the Antilles from 1504 to 1519, and established a reputation of military ingenuity and daring and personal quarrelsomeness and immorality. He went twice to Yucatán and in 1519 was appointed commander of an expedition of eleven ships by Velásquez, governor of Cuba. Cortés made additions out of his own fortune, Velásquez tried to stop the venture, but Cortés sailed on his own. He marched up the coast of Mexico, winning two outstanding battles: one with 260 soldiers in a quick thrust against the 900 led by Narváez and sent by the viceroy to capture him and bring him back for trial for treason; the second against the 20,000 Indians who had seized the garrison of 140 Spaniards under Alvarado whom Cortés had left inland. He had no understanding of Mexican tribal government and his seizure of Montezuma, an elected chieftain, did not have the importance he attached to it. His execution of Cuauhtemotzin as he moved toward Honduras was another mistake. Cortés generally was kind toward the natives and did what he could to introduce missionaries. His sense of power, however, went to his head. He maintained that he alone had captured Mexico for the Spanish crown and became bitter when the king did not give him the rewards he sought and particularly when Spain did not invest in the care he thought necessary for the new colony. Cortés limited the travels of the first royal investigator in 1522; the second commissioner apparently was murdered shortly after his arrival in Mexico. He never gained the power he craved, and saw his reputation fail when Spanish court circles, fearing that Cortés was about to head a rebellion, charged that Cortés had murdered his first wife. Although evidence indicated that he had strangled her, the court's decision was officially kept secret. Cortés was allowed to join the expedition against Algiers in 1541, but the attack proved disastrous, and he died, embittered by failure, in Castilleja de la Cuesta, near Seville, Spain, on Dec. 2.

CORTESE, GIOVANNI ANDREA (1483–1548), cardinal. Born in Modena, Italy, he studied there and at Bologna and Padua, and became a doctor of laws at seventeen. He was legal auditor of the papal curia, but resigned in 1507 to become a Benedictine. By his zeal the Benedictine reform begun by the Monte Cassino congregation was spread throughout Italy. In 1516 he went to the French island of Lérins to introduce the reform, established an academy, and helped to spread the intellectual aspects of the Italian Renaissance to France. He was abbot of Lérins from 1524 to 1527, returned to Italy, and served as abbot at Modena, Perugia, and Venice. At San Giorgio Maggiore in the latter city he was the focus of the humanist movement which included Pietro Bembo, Gasparo Contarini, and Reginald Pole. In 1536 he was appointed by Pope Paul III to the committee of twelve to define ecclesiastical abuses and recommend reforms. He then was apostolic visitor for all Italy; after a period of illness he served as abbot at Polirone and as visitor general of his order. He was made cardinal-priest in 1542, a member of the committee chosen to prepare for the Council of Trent, and bishop of Urbino. Among his many writings are poems, epistles, a treatise on the presence of St. Peter in Rome, a history of the destruction of Genoa, and a Latin translation of the Greek New Testament. He died in Modena on Sept. 21.

CORTIE, ALOYSIUS LAURENCE (1859–1925), astronomer. Born in London on Apr. 22, he studied at Stonyhurst and St. Beuno, became a Jesuit in 1878, and was ordained in 1892. He became director of the Stonyhurst observatory in 1881, a fellow of the British Astronomical Society in 1891, director of its solar section in 1900–10, and president of the Manchester Astronomical Society. He reported on the eclipses of 1905, 1911, and 1914, taught physics and mathematics at Stonyhurst for twenty-seven years, and was director of music there for nineteen years. He died on May 17.

CORY, HERBERT ELLSWORTH (1883–1947), critic. Born in Providence, Rhode Island, on Oct. 8, he studied at Brown and Harvard, taught at California from 1910 to 1918 and edited its *Chronicle* in 1912–14, served on the War Labor Policies Board at Washington, D.C., and returned to teaching in 1923, at the University of Washington, where he remained until his death on Feb. 1. He became a convert in 1933, wrote of his experiences in *The Emancipation of a Freethinker*, and in 1940 received the De Smet Medal. His other writings include *The Critics of Edmund Spenser* (1911), *Spenser, the School of Fletcher, and Milton* (1912), *Edmund Spenser, a Critical Study* (1917), *The Intellectuals and the Wage-Workers* (1919), *Progress*, and *The Significance of Beauty*.

COSA, JUAN DE LA (1460–1510), navigator. Born in Santa Maria del Puerto, Spain, he had explored much of South Africa before Columbus hired him and his ship, the *Santa Maria*, for his first voyage and his services as cartographer for his second expedition to America. In 1499 he was chief pilot on the voyage of Alonso de Ojeda and Vespucci to South America. From 1501 on he made several important maps of the New World; in that of 1500 he drew Cuba as an island, a fact which Columbus had denied. In 1503, de la Cosa represented Queen Isabella in a deputation to the Portuguese court which objected to Portugal's incursions upon Spanish settlements. He made five other voyages to South America, Haiti, Jamaica, and Panama. On the last he piloted 300 colonists from Cuba to Panama, landed at Cartagena, Colombia, on orders of Pizarro but against his own unheeded advice, and was slain there in a massacre by natives on Feb. 28.

COSGROVE, HENRY (1834–1906), bishop. Born in Williamsport, Pennsylvania, on Dec. 19, he moved to Davenport, Iowa, was ordained in 1857, was appointed to St. Marguerite's church there, became vicar general of the diocese, and in 1884 its second bishop. He helped to build Sacred Heart cathedral and St. Vincent's orphanage, became ill in 1904, and died on Dec. 22 in Davenport.

COSIE, BL. CATHERINE (1493–1565). Born in Montenegro, where she was a shepherd and the daughter of Orthodox parents, she went to work for a Catholic woman, then became a Dominican tertiary and recluse. Known as Osanna of Cattaro, she possessed many supernatural gifts, and great crowds sought her counsel. Her cult was approved in 1928. F. D. Apr. 27.

COSIN, EDMUND (16th century). Born in Bedfordshire, England, he studied at Cambridge, was ordained, served as fellow in several colleges and as master of St. Catherine's, and was in charge of Norfolk parishes during the reign of Queen Mary. He also served as rector of Trinity College and chaplain to Bishop Bonner, was elected vice-chancellor of Cambridge in 1558, but refused to acknowledge Queen Elizabeth's religious supremacy, lost all his offices, lived in retirement at Caius College until 1568, when he went into exile on the Continent. He was alive in 1576.

COSMAS, ST. (d. 303?), martyr. He was probably an Arabian who studied medicine in Syria and became a physician with his twin brother, Damian. They lived at Aegeae, Cilicia, and dispensed their services so generously that they are called "Anargyroi" ("the Penniless Ones"), because they refused payment. They were beheaded during the Diocletian persecution. Their three brothers—Anthimus, Euprepius, and Leontius—died with them according to legend. F. D. Sept. 27.

COSMAS (6th century), geographer. Called Indicopleustes ("the Indian Voyager"), he was a merchant born in Alexandria, Egypt, who traveled through the Mediterranean and Red seas and the Persian Gulf, and in later life entered the monastery of Raithu on Sinai. There he wrote his *Christian Topography*, an imaginative description of a flat universe, below a sky in which the stars were carried by angels. Cartographically it is worthless; its value lies in his reports on Zanzibar, Ceylon, the Indian Ocean, Abyssinia, Egypt, and inner Africa, and

on the spread of Christianity in those regions.

COSMAS (8th century), bishop. Called Cosmas Hagiopolites, he was foster brother of St. John of Damascus, with whom he went to Jerusalem to become a monk at St. Sabas. Cosmas left there in 743, was appointed bishop of Maiuma (Gaza), wrote a prose commentary on the poems of Gregory Nazianzen and a great number of hymns, whose use became universal in the Orthodox church. His feast day among the Greeks is Oct. 14.

COSMAS (1045?–1125), historian. Born in Prague, Bohemia, he studied there and at Liège, was ordained in Hungary in 1099, stationed at St. Vitus, Prague, and became dean of its chapter. His *Chronica Bohemorum* is a three-volume history of his country to 1125; the first book relies heavily on popular tradition, but the last is firmly established on contemporary documents and eyewitness accounts. The author carefully distinguished between hearsay and evidence and had good power of characterization. He died in Prague on Oct. 21.

COSMAS, ST. (d. 1160), bishop and martyr. Born in Palermo, Italy, he was consecrated bishop of Aphrodisias by Pope Eugene III, captured by Saracens who invaded his see, and so maltreated that he died. His cult was approved by Pope Leo XIII. F. D. Sept. 10.

COSSA, BALDASSARE. *See* John XXIII, antipope.

COSSA, FRANCESCO (1438?–1485), painter. Born in Ferrara, Italy, son of Cristofano del Cossa, he was his father's assistant in decorating the bishop's palace at Ferrara, and also created frescoes there with Cosimo Tura. He went to Bologna in 1470, where he did two *Virgin and Child* frescoes, with contemporary portraits. His work also includes an altarpiece on the life of St. Vincent Ferrer, an *Allegory of Autumn*, an *Annunciation*, a portrait of Duke Ercole I of Ferrara, and a window in the church of San Giovanni, Monti.

COSTA, LORENZO (1460–1535), painter. Born in Ferrara, Italy, he was a pupil of either Francesco Cossa or Cosimo Tura, went to Bologna in 1483, completed a fresco in the church of San Giacomo Maggiore, an altarpiece for that of San Giovanni, Monti, and other work under the patronage of the Bentivoglio family, and often in association with Francia. Later work was done as court painter in Mantua, Italy, where he died.

COSTADONI, GIOVANNI DOMENICO (1714–1785), historian. Born in Venice, Italy, on Oct. 6, he chose not to enter his father's profitable mercantile business and became a Camaldolese monk at St. Michael's on the island of Murano. With Mittarelli he worked for eighteen years in preparing *Annales Camaldulenses* (1755–73), and also wrote several articles on archaeology and treatises on theology. He died in Venice on Jan. 23.

COSTANZO, BL. CAMILLO (1572–1622), martyr. An Italian Jesuit from Calabria, he arrived in Japan as a missionary in 1602, was exiled in 1611, went to Macao where he wrote several articles in Japanese defending Christianity, and returned to Japan in 1621 disguised as a soldier. He was captured the next year and burned to death on Sept. 15 at Firando. During the next few days Bl. Augustine Ota and Caspar Cotenda, Japanese catechists, and two children, Bl. Francis Taquea, twelve, and Peter Kikiemon, were executed there. They were beatified in 1867. F. D. Oct. 12.

COSTER, FRANCIS (1532–1619), theologian. Born in Mechlin, Belgium, on June 16, he was accepted into the Society of Jesus in 1552 by St. Ignatius Loyola, taught scripture and astronomy at Cologne, was twice provincial of Belgium and once of the Rhine province, and wrote some forty titles. These include ascetical works, meditations on Mary, sermons on the Sunday gospels, and the significant *Enchiridion* of contemporary religious controversy, which ran through seven editions in his lifetime, evoked major attacks, and led to published replies by Coster. He died in Brussels on Dec. 16.

COSTIGAN, JOHN (1835–1916), jurist. Born in St. Nicholas, Quebec, Canada, he was educated at St. Anne's, passed the bar, became a common-pleas judge, and served in the New Brunswick legislature in 1861–66. After the confederation of Canada he served in the national house of commons from 1867 to 1896. He played an important role in lessening restrictions on Roman Catholics in education and worked for fiscal reform and fisheries control. In 1892–96 he was active on behalf of Ireland's attempts at independence. From 1907 until his death he was a senator and supporter of the Laurier government.

COSWAY, MARIA (1759–1838), painter. Born in Florence, Italy, Maria Hadfield studied there and achieved fame as a painter before she was nineteen, when she was elected a member of its Academy of Fine Arts. She went to England in 1778 after her father's death and married the miniaturist Richard Cosway in 1781. Her paintings were exhibited annually until 1801, she made effective copies of her husband's miniatures, and her salon was praised by Horace Walpole and other recorders of London society. She established a school for girls in Lyons, which was closed in 1811; after her husband's death she built up a teaching community in Lodi, Italy, later merged with the Dames Inglesi, and left an endowment for its upkeep. She died in Lodi on Jan. 5.

COTELIER, JEAN BAPTISTE (1629–1686), theologian. Born in Nîmes, France, in Dec., he was educated by his father, a minister in the reformed church and later a convert, then studied at Paris and the Sorbonne, where he received his bachelor of theology degree in 1647, though he was never ordained. In 1654–59 he was counselor to Archbishop d'Aubusson at Embrun; in 1667, Colbert commissioned him to catalogue the Greek manuscripts in the Royal Library; in 1676 he became professor of Greek at the Collège Royal, Paris. He edited the writings of the Apostolic Fathers (and is responsible for that title as applied to SS. Barnabas, Polycarp, and their contemporaries) and left several manuscripts on Christian antiquity. He died in Paris on Aug. 19.

COTON, PIERRE (1564–1626). Born in Néronde, Forez, France, on Mar. 7, he studied law at Paris and Bourges, became a Jesuit at twenty-five, studied theology at Rome, and preached in many French cities. Because of his friendship with King Henry IV he was violently attacked when the exiled Jesuits were recalled to France, and further libeled after the king was assassinated, particularly in pamphlets by the Calvinist Pierre Dumoulin. Fr. Coton remained as confessor to King Louis XIII until 1617, when he went on pilgrimage to Italy, returning to France as provincial. He wrote several controversial works, including *Genève plagiaire* and *Sacrifice de la messe*, before his death in Paris on Mar. 19.

COTTAM, BL. THOMAS (1549–1582), martyr. Born in Dilworth, Lancashire, England, he graduated from Oxford, became a convert, studied at Douai and Rome, was ordained a Jesuit at Rheims, and entered the English underground mission in 1580. He was tortured to extremes in the Tower, then forced to watch three of his fellow priests hanged, drawn, and quartered before he met like treatment. He was beatified in 1886. F. D. May 30.

COTTER, JOSEPH B. (1844–1909), bishop. Born in Liverpool, England, on Nov. 19, he went to the United States, studied at St. Vincent's College, Beatty, Pennsylvania, and St. John's, Collegeville, Minnesota, and was ordained in 1871. He became pastor of St. Thomas in Winona, and in 1889 was consecrated bishop of that see, where he died on June 28.

COTTOLENGO, ST. JOSEPH BENEDICT (1786–1842), founder. Born in Bra, near Turin, Italy, he served as parish priest there and in 1827 opened a small home for the sick poor. The Little House (*piccola casa*) of Divine Providence was set up in Valdocco after an 1831 cholera epidemic, and to its hospital unit were added shelters for the deaf, dumb, blind, crippled, and epileptic, for the orphans and aged, for the abandoned and the insane. The members of his permanent staff were called the Brothers of St. Vincent and the Daughters of St. Vincent de Paul (Vincentian Sisters). The huge establishment, caring at times for thousands of patients a day, subsisted on alms alone. To his original helpers he added Daughters of Compassion, whose concern was for the dying; Daughters of the Good Shepherd, whose care extended to those in spiritual danger; Hermits of the Holy Rosary, and Priests of the Holy Trinity. He died of typhoid, and of exhaustion, at Chieri, Italy, and was canonized in 1934. F. D. Apr. 30.

COTTON, FRANCIS R. (1895–1960), bishop. Born in Bardstown, Kentucky on Sept. 19, he studied at Valley Stream seminary, Canada, St. Meinrad's, Indiana, St. Mary's, Baltimore, and the Sulpician College, Washington, D.C., and was ordained in 1920. He engaged in pastoral activities in Kentucky, served as chancellor in Louisville, and in 1937 was appointed first bishop of Owensboro, Kentucky, where he reigned until his death there on Sept. 25.

COTTUS, ST. (d. 272?), martyr. See Priscus, St.

COUCY, ROBERT DE (d. 1311). He succeeded his father, also Robert, as chief builder of the cathedral of Rheims; in 1263 he succeeded Hugues Libergier as director of the building of the church of St. Nicaise there, destroyed during the French Revolution.

COUDERC, BL. MARIE THÉRÈSE (1805–1885), foundress. Born in Sablières, France, she joined a community founded by Fr. Jean Terme in Aps to teach school. When he was sent on missionary work to La Louvesc, he recommended that she and two other nuns run a hostel for women at the shrine of St. John Francis Regis in 1827 and made her superior the next year of the Daughters of St. Regis. In 1829 he had the community begin retreats for women, a work which was continued and expanded after Fr. Terme's death in 1834 when the Jesuits took over the shrine. She later built a new foundation at Lyons and also served at Paris. With Fr. Terme she was declared by Bishop Guibert of Viviers the co-foundress of the Congregation of Our Lady of the Retreat in the Cenacle. She was beatified in 1951. F. D. Sept. 26.

MOTHER EILEEN SURLES, *Surrender to the Spirit* (New York, Kenedy, 1951).

COUDERT, FRÉDÉRIC RENÉ (1832–1903), lawyer. Born in New York City on Mar. 1, he studied at Columbia, was admitted to the bar, and acted as legal adviser to the government during the Bering Sea seal-fishing dispute with Great Britain and in the boundary dispute between Venezuela and British Columbia. Though active in politics, he refused several political offices, agreeing to serve, unsalaried, as a member of the board of education of New York. He died in Washington, D.C., on Dec. 20.

COULOMB, CHARLES AUGUSTIN (1736–1806), physicist. Born in Angoulême, France, on June 14, he was an engineer in the West Indies, won the Academy of Sciences award for his *Theory of Simple Machines* in 1779, and became intendant of the waters and fountains of France in 1784. He retired from public service at the outbreak of the revolution, devoted himself to scientific research, and made numerous important discoveries in the fields of friction, electricity, and magnetism. He was the inventor of the torsion balance, which measured the magnetic and electrostatic forces between two charges, and also discovered the principle, now called Coulomb's law, that such force is inversely proportionate to the square of the distance between the forces and directly proportional to their product. The coulomb, a unit quantity of electrical energy, is named in his honor. He was elected to the French Academy in 1781.

COUNNOUT, JEAN DE (14th century), astronomer. A disciple of Jean de Linières, Jean de Counnout wrote several astronomical works, notably *Canones super tabulas Alfonsii regis Castellae* (1327). He is often confused with Johannes Danko (also an astronomer and follower of de Linières) who wrote *Notulae super compontum* (1297), since both men were identified as de Saxonia or de Saxe.

COUPERIN, FRANÇOIS (1668–1733), composer. Born in Paris on Nov. 10, he studied under his father, was appointed organist of the royal chapel in 1693, and *ordinarie* of the king's chamber music in 1717. He is noted for his clavecin works and chamber music. His *Pièces de clavecin,* a collection of his programmatic dance suites (four volumes, 1713, 1716, 1722, 1730), was highly regarded by Bach. He also wrote church music, including two organ masses. He died in Paris on Sept. 12.

COURTENAY, WILLIAM (1342?–1396), archbishop. Born in Exeter, England, son of Hugh, earl of Devon, and Margaret, daughter of Humphrey Bohun, earl of Hereford, he received his doctor of canon law from Oxford and became chancellor of the university in 1367. He was consecrated bishop of Hereford in 1370 and supported the prince of Wales and Bishop Wykeham of Winchester against the anti-clerical faction of John of Gaunt and against the Lollards. He became bishop of London in 1375, archbishop of Canterbury in 1381, and, for three months in 1382, chancellor of the realm. He resigned to continue his labors against Wyclif and the Lollards, eventually won over Oxford and Leicester, but had little success in Exeter and Salisbury. He founded the College of St. Mary and All Saints at Maidstone, attacked King Richard II for his extravagance, and was mediator between king and parliament when civil war seemed imminent. He died at Maidstone, England, on July 31.

COUSIN, ST. GERMAINE (1579–1601). Born in Pibrac, near Toulouse, France, daughter of Laurent Cousin, a farmhand, she had a deformed arm, suffered from scrofula, and was neglected by her father and mistreated by her stepmother. She worked as a shepherdess, taught religion to younger children, fed the poor from her own scraps of food, and accepted the scorn of villagers for years until they and even her family came to acknowledge her sanctity. She died in Pibrac, and was canonized by Pope Pius IX in 1867. F. D. June 15.

COUSIN, JEAN (1500?–1560?), painter. Born in Soucy, near Sens, France, he studied glass painting there, and while a student published on mathematics and geometry. In 1530 he probably did the *Legend of St. Eutropius* windows for the Sens cathedral, went to Paris, and then designed the windows for Ste. Chapelle. Vincennes, regarded as the finest in France. He also worked in oil, his *Last Judgment* and *Descent from the Cross* being considered his finest work in that medium. He designed woodcuts for a Bible and for editions of Ovid, did miniatures for a prayer book for Henry II, etched, and sculpted two tombs. He published a treatise on perspective in 1560.

COUSIN, JEAN (1522?–1594), painter. Called "the Younger," he was born in Sens, France, son of Jean Cousin, under whom he studied. He designed windows in the castle of Fleurigny there and probably in the church of St. Gervais, Paris, painted portraits in oil, did illustrations for editions of Aesop and Ovid, and wrote a study of portrait painting and perhaps the illustrated *Book of Fortune*.

COUSSEMAKER, CHARLES EDMOND HENRI DE (1805–1876), historian. Born in Bailleul, France, on Apr. 19, he studied law in Paris, as well as singing and harmony. He wrote a history of mediaeval harmony and edited early harmonists and troubadours. His theory of the origin of neums in Latin accents has since been disproved. He died in Lille, France, on Jan. 10.

COUSTANT, PIERRE (1654–1721), scholar. Born in Compiègne, France, on Apr. 30, he became a Benedictine of St. Maur in Rheims at seventeen, studied there and at Soissons, and in 1681 was sent to St. Germain-des-Prés, Paris, to work on an edition of St. Augustine. His labors in separating the spurious from the genuine led to his selection as editor of St. Hilary of Poitiers. After a term as prior of Nogent-sous-Coucy, he worked on a new edition of the Maurist breviary, then on an index to the works of Augustine, and for twenty years in compiling the letters of the popes. Before his death he published the first volume, covering the years 67 to 440, with an elaborate preface on papal supremacy; a second volume, containing letters from 461 to 521, and based on Coustant's man-

uscripts, did not appear until 1867. He died at St. Germain on Oct. 18.

COUSTOU, GUILLAUME (1716–1777), sculptor. He studied under his father, Guillaume Coustou (1677–1746), an academician, won the Prix de Rome in 1735, and produced *Apotheosis of St. Francis Xavier* for St. Paul's, Bordeaux, and a tomb for the father of Louis XVI in the cathedral at Sens, France.

COUSTOU, NICOLAS (1658–1733), sculptor. Born in Lyons, France, on Jan. 9, he studied wood carving under his father, François, went to Paris at eighteen, and worked with his uncle, the sculptor Antoine Coysevox. Receiving the Colbert prize, he went to Rome from 1683 to 1686, returned to Paris, and worked on independent and royally granted commissions with his brother Guillaume. From 1720 until his death in Paris on May 1 he was rector of the Academy of Painting and Sculpture. *Daphne Pursued by Apollo*, a *Descent from the Cross* in Notre Dame, statues of Julius Caesar and Louis XIV outlasted the destruction of the revolution. Guillaume did a terracotta statue of him (Louvre).

COUTURIER, LOUIS CHARLES (1817–1890). Born on May 17 at Chémille sur Dôme, Tours, France, he studied at Anjou and Angers, was ordained in 1842, and taught history at Coimbrée from 1836 to 1854, when he became a Benedictine at Solesmes. He was prior in 1861, succeeded Guéranger as abbot in 1875, became consultor for the Index, and was twice driven out of his monastery, with his community, by the hostile French government. As president of the French Congregation of Benedictines he opened or reopened several monasteries in France and Spain before his death at Solesmes, France, on Oct. 29.

COVARRUBIAS Y LEYVA, DIEGO (1512–1577), bishop. Born in Toledo, Spain, on July 25, he studied law under Martin Aspelcueta, became professor of canon law at Salamanca at twenty-one, directed the reform of that university, and at twenty-six became professor at Oviedo. In 1560 he was made bishop of Ciudad Rodrigo, attended the Council of Trent, and formulated the decrees *De reformatione*. In 1565 he became bishop of Segovia; in 1572, a member of the council of Castile, and, in 1574, its president. He wrote widely on canon law, wills, oaths, excommunication, punishment, and even on coins. He died in Madrid on Sept. 27.

COVENTRY, FRANCIS. *See* Davenport, Christopher.

COXCIE, MICHIEL (1499–1592), painter. Born in Mechlin, Flanders (where he also died), he studied under his father and Barend van Orley, went to Rome in 1532, returned to Mechlin, and became a member of its academy in 1539. He was court painter to King Philip

II, executed a tapestry with designs from Raphael, and also did large paintings for Emperor Charles V. By his marriage to Ida van Hasselt in Italy he had three children: William and Ralphael, painters, and Anne, a sculptor; at seventy he married Jeanne van Schelle, and had two sons: Michiel, a painter, and Conrad.

COYSEVOX, CHARLES ANTOINE (1640–1720), sculptor. Born in Lyons, France, on Sept. 29, he worked at Versailles and Marly for King Louis XIV, of whom he made two bronzes, became a member of the French Academy in 1676, and directed a school attended by his nephew-sculptors Nicolas and Guillaume Coustou. He sculpted many contemporary figures; his most ambitious work was *La Renommée* at the Tuileries, winged horses carrying Mercury and Fame, much admired by Napoleon. He died in Paris on Oct. 10.

COZZA, LORENZO (1654–1729), cardinal. Born near Bolsena, Italy, on Mar. 31, he became a Friar Minor, held posts at Naples and Viterbo, became confessor to Cardinal Sacchetti, and superior of the Franciscan monastery in Jerusalem. As papal legate there he reconciled the Maronites and Patriarch Jacobus Petrus of Antioch. In 1723 he was elected minister general; in 1726 Pope Benedict XIII made him a cardinal. He died in Rome on Jan. 18.

COZZA-LUZI, GIUSEPPE (1837–1905), scholar. Born in Bolsena, Italy, on Dec. 24, he became a Basilian at the monastery of Grottaferrata, near Rome, of which he became abbot in 1882. In 1898 he was relieved of all duties and began editing several Vatican manuscripts. With Carlo Vercellone he supervised the printing of the Greek text of the Codex Vaticanus; he also edited other scriptural material, published fragments of the *Geography* of Strabo, volumes 8–9 of Cardinal Mai's *Nova bibliotheca patrum*, and the cardinal's letters, and wrote on the antiquities of Bolsena, Orvieto, and Assyria. He died in Bolsena on June 1.

CRABITES, PIERRE (1877–1943), jurist. Born in New Orleans, on Feb. 17, he studied at Immaculate Conception College and Tulane, passed the bar in 1900, practiced in Louisiana, and went to Egypt to master Arabic. He was chosen by President Taft in 1911 to represent the United States at the Mixed Tribunals in Egypt, which had jurisdiction over civil suits involving at least one non-native. He remained in Cairo for twenty-five years and wrote seven studies on that country and the Sudan, including *Ismail, the Maligned Khedive* (1933), *Gordon, the Sudan, and Slavery*, and *The Spoliation of Suez* (1940). He also wrote on Beneš of Czechoslovakia, the Spanish Civil War, and Pope Clement VIII. He was a special lecturer at Louisiana State University law school on trips home during those years. At the outbreak of World War II he was sent to Cairo on special diplomatic service; in 1942 he was appointed special aide to the American minister in Iraq, where he died on Oct. 9.

CRAIGIE, PEARL MARY TERESA (1867–1906), novelist. Born in Boston, Massachusetts, on Nov. 3, daughter of John Richards, a Calvinist merchant, she was taken to England as an infant, studied at University College, London, married Reginald Walpole Craigie of England in 1887, was legally separated, and in 1892 became a convert. She wrote some moralistic novels under the pseudonym John Oliver Hobbes; most popular were *The School for Saints* (1897), *A Serious Wooing, Robert Orange,* and *The Sinner's Comedy*. She also wrote many plays, including the one-acter, *Journeys End in Lovers' Meetings,* for Ellen Terry (1895). She died on Aug. 13.

CRANE, MARTIN (d. 1901), bishop. An Irish Augustinian, he was consecrated bishop of Sandhurst, Victoria, Australia, in 1874, and arrived in his see in 1875 with two priests, including Stephen Reville, also an Augustinian, who became his coadjutor in 1885.

CRANE, MICHAEL JOSEPH (1863–1928), bishop. Born in Ashland, Pennsylvania, on Sept. 8, he studied at St. Charles Borromeo seminary, Philadelphia, and Catholic University, and was ordained in 1889. He did parish work in Downington, Reading, and Philadelphia, was made a domestic prelate in 1914, became vicar general of Philadelphia in 1920, and titular bishop of Curium and auxiliary of that see in 1921. He died in Philadelphia on Dec. 26.

CRASHAW, RICHARD (1612?–1649), poet. Born in London, son of a Puritan preacher, he studied at Charterhouse and Cambridge, became a classical scholar, friend of Nicholas Ferrer and Abraham Cowley, and published *Epigrammatum sacrorum liber* at twenty-one. He became an Anglican cleric at Cambridge in 1639. *Steps to the Temple* appeared in 1646. He served King Charles I at Oxford in 1643, went into exile, became a convert, probably in France, and was found in poverty in Paris by Cowley, who introduced him to Queen Henrietta Maria. The latter gained a post for him in the household of Cardinal Palotta, but he disliked the ecclesiastical world of Rome; the cardinal soon found him a minor benefice at Loreto, Italy. He published sacred songs as *Carmen Deo nostro;* others, as *Delights of the Muses*. His poetry is highly figurative, affected by the Italian and Spanish baroque; in its religious quietness it is comparable to that of George Herbert; when it is fiery and lavish in conceits, it is that of Marino or the mystics; on occasion, it leans toward the philosophical contortions of John Donne. Crashaw died at Loreto, Italy, on Apr. 24.

CRASSET, JEAN (1618–1692). Born in Dieppe, France, on Jan. 3, he became a Jesuit in 1638, was stationed in Paris, where he became famous as a preacher and as director of a sodality for men, and wrote many ascetical works. He died in Paris on Jan. 4.

CRATON, ST. (d. 273), martyr. Philosopher and teacher of rhetoric, he became a follower of Bishop Valentine and was slain at Rome with his wife, children, and servants. SS. Castulus, Lucius, Magnus, Saturninus, and others from the diocese of Terni, Italy, were also put to death. F. D. Feb. 15.

CRATZ, BL. JOHN GASPARD (d. 1737), martyr. *See* Alvarez, Bartholomew.

CRAVEN, PAULINE (1808–1891), novelist. Pauline Marie de la Ferronnays was born in London, England, on Apr. 12, of a family impoverished by exile during the French Revolution. Her father, Comte Auguste-Marie, became French ambassador to Russia and then to Rome, where she met Augustus Craven, attaché to the British legation at Naples. They were married in 1834. Her husband, who soon became a convert, held diplomatic posts in Lisbon, Brussels, and Stuttgart; in 1853 they moved to Naples and became a center of social life. After 1870 she lived, for the most part, in Paris, even after her husband's death in 1884. Her writings, reflecting the world of society and the legation, include: *Le Mot de l'énigme*, *Le Récit d'une soeur* (1866), *Anne Severin*, *Fleurange* (crowned by the French Academy), biographies of Nathalie Narishkin and Lady Georgiana Fullerton (her English translator), and replies to Prime Minister William Gladstone's attacks on the Church. Much of her work was published in the United States by Fr. Hecker's *Catholic World*. She died in Paris on Apr. 1.

CRAWFORD, FRANCIS MARION (1854–1909), novelist. Born in Bagni di Lucca, Italy, on Aug. 2, son of Thomas Crawford, a sculptor, and Louise Ward, sister of Julia Ward Howe, he became a convert as a young man. He studied at Cambridge, Karlsruhe, Heidelberg, and Rome, edited the *Indian Herald* in Allahabad, and spent five years in the East Indies and the United States as a journalist. In 1884 he settled with his wife at Sorrento, where he died on Apr. 9. He wrote some forty novels, including *Mr. Isaacs* (1882), *Dr. Claudius* (1883), *Saracinesca* (1887), and *A Cigarette Maker's Romance* (1890). The last was dramatized; another play, *Francesca da Rimini*, was produced in Paris for Sarah Bernhardt. He also wrote biography, history, travel, and a study of the novel. His colorful stories popularized the cosmopolitan scene and satisfied a large demand, though many of his historical sources were secondary and unauthoritative.

CRAWLEY-BOEVEY, MATEO (1876?–1960). Known as Father Mateo, he was a Peruvian ordained in Chile who devoted his life to preaching the Sacred Heart and spent 1914–35 touring in Europe, 1935–40 in Asia, and 1940–56 in the United States and Canada, advocating the enthronement of the Sacred Heart in the home, a devotion he had founded. He died in Valparaiso, Chile.

CRAYER, GASPARD (1584–1669), painter. Born in Antwerp, Flanders, he studied under Raphael van Coxcie, became painter to the governor, and decorated many churches and public buildings in Brussels and Ghent. His works include *Centurion and Christ*, admired by his friend Rubens, *Death of the Virgin*, and portraits in the manner of Van Dyck. He died in Ghent.

CREAGH, PETER (d. 1705), archbishop. Grandnephew of Archbishop Richard Creagh, he was made bishop of Cork, Ireland, in 1676, and imprisoned for two years at the time of the Titus Oates Plot, but acquitted in 1682. He became archbishop of Tuam in 1686, went into exile in France with King James II, and, though appointed archbishop of Dublin in 1693, was unable to take possession of that see. He died as coadjutor bishop of Strassburg, Alsace.

CREAGH, RICHARD (d. 1585), archbishop. Born in Limerick, Ireland, he entered his father's mercantile business, studied and was ordained on the Continent, and returned to teach in Limerick. In 1564 he was made archbishop of Armagh and ran into major difficulty with Shane O'Neill, the Ulster leader. When Creagh declared for loyalty to England, O'Neill burned the cathedral; inasmuch as a priest had been killed during the fire, Creagh excommunicated the fiery leader. In spite of his political loyalty, his popularity in Ireland and the staunchness of his religious position made him appear a danger to Elizabeth and he was imprisoned in the Tower of London from 1567 until his death there.

CREDAN, ST. (d. 780?). He was eighth abbot of the Benedictine monastery of Evesham, England. F. D. Aug. 19.

CREDI, LORENZO DI (1459–1537), painter. Born in Florence, Italy, son of the goldsmith Andrea di Credi (though some authorities believe he was surnamed Barducci and adopted the name of Credi, who made him his heir), he studied under Andrea Verrocchio, with Perugino and Leonardo da Vinci. He is known for his remarkably accurate copies of da Vinci's works, and in his own right for his many portraits and religious scenes, particularly the altarpiece of the Pistoia cathedral, *Madonna and Child with SS. Julian and Nicholas*, a *Nativity* at Florence, and *Madonna and Child* now in the Louvre.

He donated a large farm to the hospital of Santa Maria Nuova at Casciano, and died in Florence on Jan. 12.

CREIGHTON, EDWARD (1820–1874). Born near Barnesville, Ohio, on Aug. 31, he made a fortune with his brother John (Oct. 15, 1831–Feb. 7, 1907) building roads and telegraph lines in the West and South. The fortune he left was the basis for the founding of The Creighton University, the first free Catholic college in the United States. Edward died on Nov. 5. John, who received the Laetare Medal from Notre Dame in 1900, also left large bequests to Creighton which helped finish the college buildings.

CREIGHTON, JOHN A. *See* Creighton, Edward.

CRELIER, HENRI JOSEPH (1816–1889), scholar. Born in Bure, Switzerland, on Oct. 16, he taught at the College of Porrentruy from 1845 to 1855, then became chaplain of the Religious of the Sacred Heart at Besançon, France, wrote scriptural commentaries, the articles on Genesis, Exodus, Leviticus, and the Acts for Lethielleux' *Commentaries on the Bible*, attacked Renan, and held parish posts at Rebeuvelier and Bressancourt, where he died on Apr. 22.

CREMENTIUS, ST. (d. 304), martyr. *See* Caius, St.

CREMONESI, CARLO (1866–1943), cardinal. Born in Rome, he studied at the seminary there, taught at the College of the Propagation of the Faith for twenty years, served Pope Leo XIII as chamberlain, became secretary of the administration of religious works in 1909 under Pius X, and was made apostolic delegate of Pompeii Sanctuary in 1922. He was in charge of the distribution of papal charities for fourteen years before being made a cardinal in 1935. He died in Rome on Nov. 25.

CRÉPIEUL, FRANÇOIS DE (1638–1702), missioner. Born in Arras, France, on Mar. 16, he studied there and at Douai, became a Jesuit in 1659, taught at Lille and Cambrai, and was sent to Canada in 1670. He labored on the Montagnais and Algonquin missions for twenty-eight years, wrote a series of instructions for missionaries, became vicar apostolic for the Montagnais in 1696 or 1697, went to Quebec when the mission was closed at the end of the century, and died there.

CRESCENS, ST. (2nd century), bishop and martyr. A follower of St. Paul (II Tim. 4:10), he was a bishop among the Galatians. The story that he was the first bishop of Mainz, in Gaul, is historically untenable. The Roman Martyrology says that he was slain in the Near East during the reign of Trajan. F. D. June 27 (also, Dec. 29).

CRESCENS, ST. (d. 244?), martyr. He and SS. Dioscorides and Paul were burned at the stake during a Roman persecution. F. D. May 28.

CRESCENS, ST. (d. 258?), martyr. He was slain with St. Anectus and others at Corinth during the reign of Valerian. F. D. Mar. 10.

CRESCENS, ST. (5th century), bishop. He and African bishops Crescentian, Cresconius, Eustace, Felix, Florentian, Hortulanus, and Urban died on their way into exile imposed by the Arian King Genseric. F. D. Nov. 28.

CRESCENTIA, ST. (d. 300?), martyr. *See* Vitus, St.

CRESCENTIAN, ST. (d. 130?), martyr. He was put to death at Sassari, on Sardinia, during the reign of Hadrian. F. D. May 31.

CRESCENTIAN, ST. (d. 258?), martyr. He and SS. Generalis, Rosula, and Victor are said to have been slain in North Africa at the time of Cyprian's martyrdom. F. D. Sept. 14.

CRESCENTIAN, ST. (d. 285?), martyr. *See* Ariston, St.

CRESCENTIAN, ST. (d. 309), martyr. He was racked to death in Rome during the persecution of Maxentius. F. D. Nov. 24.

CRESCENTIAN, ST. (5th century), bishop. *See* Crescens, St.

CRESCENTIO, ST. (d. 260?), martyr. He and St. Narcissus were slain in Rome; in the *Acta* of St. Lawrence, Narcissus cured Crescentio of blindness. F. D. Sept. 17.

CRESCENTIUS, ST. (d. 90?). *See* Romulus, St.

CRESCENTIUS, ST. (d. 287?), martyr. *See* Constantius, St.

CRESCENTIUS, ST. (d. 300?), martyr. Son of St. Euthymius, he was tortured and beheaded at eleven, during the Diocletian persecution in Rome. F. D. Sept. 14.

CRESCENTIUS, ST. (d. 396?). He served as a subdeacon in Florence, Italy, under St. Ambrose. F. D. Apr. 19.

CRESCENTIUS (d. 984). Leader of the aristocratic families of Rome, almost with the power of consul, and brother of Pope John XIII, he led the Roman opposition to the imperial designation of popes, which rebelled against, dethroned, and strangled Benedict VI, and appointed Boniface VII in 974. When the latter was forced out by Emperor Otto II, Crescentius worked for his restoration, achieved in 984. Crescentius became a monk in his last years and died at the monastery of St. Alexius in Rome on July 7. His son Crescentius (executed in 998) and grandson John Crescentius continued their quarrel both with Emperor Otto III and various popes and antipopes; the family died out with the death of the latter in 1012.

CRESCENTIUS (10th century). The first known bishop of Cività Castellana, Italy, he discovered the relics of SS. Martianus and Johannes there in 998.

CRESCIMBENI, GIOVANNI MARIO (1663–1728), critic. Born in Macerata, Italy, on Oct. 9, he studied law at Rome, took his doctorate in 1679, was made a canon of Cosmedin in 1705, and was ordained in 1719. His chief interest was literature: he wrote poems and tragedies, and founded the Accademia degli Arcadi, of which he was president from 1690 until his death. Its purpose was to maintain a simple and natural literary language in opposition to the bombastic and euphuistic style then prevailing. The pastoral tone the academy members adopted often went to equal extremes, but the aims of the group saw fruit in excellent analysis of Dante and other Italian writers. Crescimbeni wrote a six-volume history of Italian poetry (1698); its supplementary five volumes (1702) are of distinct critical value. He died in Rome.

CRESCITELLI, BL. ALBERIC (1863–1900), martyr. Born near Naples, he spent twelve years preaching and establishing schools along the Han River in China. When the Boxer Rebellion broke out, he was seized, tortured, and hacked to death on July 22. He was beatified in 1951. F. D. July 9.

CRESCONIUS, ST. (5th century), bishop. *See* Crescens, St.

CRESCONIUS (7th century?), canonist. Possibly an African bishop, he compiled *Concordia canonum*, a collection of apostolic canons, canons of councils of the fourth and fifth centuries, and papal decretals of the latter period. Based on the work of Dionysius Exiguus and Fulgentius Ferrandus, it is valuable for the history of the Church in northern Africa and southern Gaul. He has been identified with a poet who lived around 697 and also with the Latin poet, Flavius Cresconius Corippus, who lived in 550.

CRESPI, JUAN (1721–1782), explorer. Born in Spain, he became a Franciscan, went to Mexico in 1749, and in 1767 was placed in charge of the Mission Purísima Concepción in Lower California. In 1769 he went on the Portola expedition to San Diego and Monterey and in 1770 founded San Carlos Borromeo Mission at Carmel. He was chaplain of the Pérez expedition to the North Pacific in 1774, and left diaries of his journeys.

CRESSY, HUGH PAULINUS SERENUS DE (1605?–1674), theologian. Born in Thorpe-Salvin, Yorkshire, England, he studied at Wakefield and Oxford, became a fellow of Merton College, took Anglican orders, and accompanied Lucius Cary, Lord Falkland, to Ireland in 1638. When the latter was killed during the English civil war in 1643, Cressy went to Europe and became a convert in Rome in 1646. He was professed as Benedictine in 1649 and

in 1660 was sent to London as a chaplain to the English queen, Catherine of Braganza. He wrote an account of his conversion (*Exomologesis*), several controversial pamphlets, a *Church History of Brittany and England* (1668), and edited the mystical writings of Walter Hilton, Augustine Baker, Juliana of Norwich, and Maurice Chauncey. He died at East Grinstead, Sussex, England, on Aug. 10.

CRESTI, DOMENICO (1558–1638), painter. Born in Passignano, Italy, and known as Il Passignano, he lived in Florence, Pisa, and Venice, and became an imitator of Tintoretto. His chief work, completed rapidly and marred by thin use of colors, is the fresco in San Andrea in Rome. He was honored by Popes Clement VIII and Urban VIII and became a member of the Academy of Florence, in which city he died.

CRESWELL, ARTHUR (1557–1623?). Born in Yorkshire, England, he studied at Rheims, became a Jesuit at Rome in 1583, and in 1589 succeeded Fr. Robert Persons as rector of the English College there and as vice-prefect in Spain, where he was embroiled in controversy with the Benedictines. In 1614 he was transferred to Belgium and became rector at Ghent in 1621. He wrote under various names (Joseph Creswell, John Perne, Peter Manrique), and published *De vita beata*, meditations on the rosary, translations of Salvian, a brief history of the Society for King Philip III of Spain, and pamphlets in reply to actions of Elizabeth and James I of England.

CRÉTENET, JACQUES (1606–1667), founder. A surgeon, he became a priest after the death of his wife, and founded at Belley, France, the congregation called the Joséphistes.

CRÉTIN, JOSEPH (1799–1857), bishop. Born in Montluel, Ain, France, on Dec. 19, he studied at Alix and Paris, was ordained in 1823, became pastor at Ferney, built a new church and a college for boys, and in 1838 volunteered to work for Bishop Loras in the United States. He was appointed vicar general of Dubuque, Iowa, in 1839, and also served the Winnebago Indian missions; in 1851 he was consecrated first bishop of St. Paul, Minnesota. He built a cathedral and hospital, and introduced several teaching communities. He was active also in welcoming Catholic immigrants from Europe, and frequently visited the entire extent of the new see, so large that he often was the only priest in the city itself. He died there on Feb. 22.

CRÉTINEAU-JOLY, JACQUES (1803–1875), historian. Born in Fontenay-le-Comte, Vendée, France, on Sept. 23, he studied theology briefly at St. Sulpice, Paris, taught philosophy in his native town, and in 1823 became secretary to the French ambassador to Rome. He published a number of irreligious poems there, then returned to France to edit Liberal and Bourbonist newspapers. He wrote a four-volume military history of Vendée, a six-volume history of the Jesuits, prepared under their auspices, and *L'église romaine en face de la révolution* in two volumes. He died at Vincennes, France, on Jan. 1.

CRÈVECOEUR, HECTOR ST. JOHN DE (1735–1813). Born in Caen, France, on Jan. 31, he went to England at sixteen, served with Montcalm in Canada, and later traveled through the midwestern United States as a surveyor. He settled in New York State in 1769, returned to France on business in 1780, and introduced the potato to Norman farmers, and on his return was arrested in New York City as a spy, but released. In 1782 he published *Letters of an American Farmer;* other letters were published in 1925 under the modern title, *Sketches of Eighteenth-Century America.* Many of his French friends came to America and settled in Pennsylvania, but their community was later destroyed in an Indian raid. After the American Revolution, Crèvecoeur acted as consul for French interests in the port of New York. He was one of the founders of St. Peter's church in that city, and served as a trustee. He wrote on the Pennsylvania community, and under the pseudonym Agricola contributed columns on farming to American journals. He also introduced European crops, notably alfalfa, to America. He died at Sarcelles, near Paris, on Nov. 12.

CREWENNA, ST. (5th century). He was one of the associates of St. Breaca on a mission from Ireland to Cornwall. F. D. Feb. 1.

CRIADO, BL. MARK (1522–1569), martyr. Born in Andujar, Spain, he became a Trinitarian in 1536, and was tortured and put to death in Almeria, Spain, by the Moors. His cult was approved by Pope Leo XIII. F. D. Sept. 25.

CRICHTON-STUART, JOHN PATRICK (1847–1900), author. Born in Montstuart, Bute, England, on Sept. 12, son of the second marquess of Bute and Lady Sophia Hastings, he studied at Harrow and Oxford, became a convert in 1868, married Gwendolen Howard in 1872, and settled on his estates in Scotland and Wales. He was mayor of Cardiff and provost of Rothesay Island, a lavish patron of Catholic missions in England and scholarly publications, and rector of St. Andrews University. He published *The Altus of St. Columba, Early Days of Sir William Wallace,* antiquarian works, and a translation of the breviary into English. He died in Ayrshire, Scotland, on Oct. 9.

CRIMONT, JOSEPH RAPHAEL JOHN (1858–1945), bishop. Born in Ferrières, France, on Feb. 2, he studied at Collège de la Providence, Amiens, where he joined the Jesuits in 1875, and College of St. Louis, Jersey Island,

went to the United States in 1886, continued his studies at Woodstock, and was ordained in 1888. He did missionary work among the Crow Indians in Montana until 1894, when he went to Alaska as superior of the Holy Cross mission on the Yukon in 1897. He was president of Gonzaga College, Washington, in 1901–4, and was appointed prefect apostolic of Alaska in 1904. He was named titular bishop of Ammaedera in 1917 and vicar apostolic of Alaska, where he remained until his death on May 20.

CRIQUE, PIERRE ALBERT (1857–1925), theologian. Born in Ardennes, France, he became a Sulpician and taught philosophy in the Boston and Baltimore seminaries. After 1918 he was rector of the Grand seminary in Montreal and dean of its faculty of theology. He died in Montreal on Nov. 23.

CRISPIN, ST. (d. 287?), martyr. According to legend, he and his brother Crispinian came to Gaul from Rome to preach Christianity, settled at Soissons, and became shoemakers. They were so successful with pagans that they were denounced and beheaded. A local English tradition says they fled the persecution and settled in Faversham, Kent. They were quite popular through the Middle Ages, are mentioned in Shakespeare's *Henry V,* and are patrons of leatherworkers. F. D. Oct. 25.

CRISPIN, ST. (d. 302), martyr. See Felix, St.

CRISPIN, ST. (4th century), martyr. He was bishop of Ecija, Andalusia, under Maximian. F. D. Nov. 19.

CRISPIN, ST. (5th century), bishop. He represented his see of Pavia, Lombardy, at the Council of Milan (451), called by Pope St. Leo the Great. Another St. Crispin was bishop of Pavia for thirty-five years early in the third century. F. D. Jan. 7.

CRISPIN OF VITERBO, BL. (1668–1750). Born in Viterbo, Italy, he became a Capuchin laybrother at twenty-five, taking the name Crispin and serving as gardener, cook, infirmarian, and alms gatherer. He was stationed at Tolfa, Albano, Orvieto, and elsewhere, was widely respected, and beatified in 1806. F. D. May 21.

CRISPINA, ST. (d. 304), martyr. A wealthy matron of Thebeste in Numidia and mother of several children, she was subjected to great indignities and put to the sword in her native city for refusing to sacrifice to the gods. St. Augustine preached a panegyric in her honor. F. D. Dec. 5.

CRISPINIAN, ST. (d. 287?), martyr. See Crispin, St.

CRISPULUS, ST. (1st century), martyr. He and St. Restitutus may have been slain in Rome during the persecution of Nero, or in Spain. F. D. June 10.

CRISPULUS, ST. (d. 130?), martyr. He and St. Gabinus were put to death for preaching the gospel at Torres, on Sardinia, during the reign of Hadrian. F. D. May 30.

CRISPUS, ST. (1st century). He was baptized at Corinth by St. Paul (I Cor. 1:14), where he was ruler of the synagogue (Acts 18:1), and is traditionally known as bishop of Aeginia, where he was martyred. F. D. Oct. 4.

CRISPUS, ST. (d. 303?), martyr. He and St. John were priests who gave proper burial at Rome to victims of the Diocletian persecution, for which they also were slain. F. D. Aug. 18.

CRISTIOLUS, ST. (7th century). Brother of St. Sulian, he founded churches in Pembroke-shire and Anglesey, Wales. F. D. Nov. 3.

CRIVELLI, CARLO (1430?–1493?), painter. Perhaps a student of the Muranos, he worked for twenty-two years near Ancona, Italy. He completed an altarpiece for San Silvestro, Massa, as early as 1468, several madonnas, *pietàs*, a portrait of St. Francis of Assisi, and a notable *Coronation of the Virgin*. He was knighted in 1490 by Ferdinand II of Naples.

CROCE, GIOVANNI (1557–1609), com-poser. Born in Chioggia, near Venice, Italy, he studied music under Zarlino, was ordained, be-came vice-director of the choir boys of St. Mark's, and choirmaster in 1603 on the death of Baltazzaro Donati. He wrote madrigals, motets, canzonetti, and much church music. He died in Venice on May 15.

CROCKETT, BL. RALPH (d. 1588), martyr. Born in Barton, Cheshire, he was educated at Cambridge and Oxford, and taught in Norfolk and Suffolk. He was ordained at Rheims in 1586. Arrested with Bl. Edward James on his arrival in England, and imprisoned in London, they were hanged, drawn, and quartered in Chi-chester during the Elizabethan persecution. He was beatified in 1929. F. D. Oct. 1.

CROESE, BL. GIOVANNI (1804–1866). Born near Ventimiglia, Italy, he became a Capuchin laybrother at the friary of the Im-maculate Conception, Genoa, taking the name Francis of Camporosso, worked there for forty years, and died while aiding cholera victims. He was beatified in 1929. F. D. Sept. 16.

CROISET, JEAN (1656–1738). Born in Mar-seilles, France, he became a Jesuit in 1677, and rector of the novitiate in Avignon, and wrote ascetical and moralistic works, including popu-lar lives of the saints, a well-known *Devotion to the Sacred Heart*, four volumes of *Medita-tions* and the eighteen-volume *Christian Year*. He died in Avignon on Jan. 31.

CROISSY, BL. FRANCES DE (1745–1794), martyr. Born in Paris, she became a Carmelite nun at Compiègne in 1764, served as prioress from 1779 to 1787, and was mistress of novices when the convent was attacked and the com-munity taken to Paris to be guillotined. She was beatified in 1906. F. D. July 17.

CROKE, THOMAS WILLIAM (1824–1902), archbishop. Born near Mallow, Cork, Ireland, on May 24, he studied in Paris and Rome, taught at St. Patrick's College, Carlow, and did mission work in the Cork diocese from 1849 to 1858. He then served as president of St. Colman's College, Fermoy, until 1865, was pastor at Doneraile for five years, and bishop of Auckland, Australia, until 1874. In that year he became archbishop of Cashel, Ireland, and strongly supported the home-rule movement led by Isaac Butt and the reforms demanded by Parnell. He tried to enlist the support of the Vatican in the cause of Irish independence, but failed; he withdrew from active politics at the death of Parnell. He himself died at Thurles, Ireland, on July 22.

CROLLY, WILLIAM (1780–1849), arch-bishop. Born in Ballykilbeg, near Downpatrick, Ireland, on June 8, he studied at Maynooth, was ordained in 1806, taught there for six years, was pastor of Belfast until 1825, and then made bishop of Down and Connor. He per-suaded the Vatican to change the diocesan cen-ter to Belfast, which was done, founded St. Malachy's seminary, and in 1835 became arch-bishop of Armagh. He founded St. Patrick's seminary there, began its cathedral, and worked actively during the plague years. He died in Drogheda, Ireland, on Apr. 6.

CROMER, MARTIN (1512–1589), bishop. Born in Biecz, Poland, he studied in Cracow, served as secretary to the son of Sigismund I and on diplomatic missions to Pope Paul V and Emperors Charles V and Ferdinand I. His history of Poland to 1505 and *Polonia*, on geography and statistics, were significant pub-lications. He was named bishop of Ermland in 1578.

CRONAN, ST. (d. 626?). Born in Offaly, Ire-land, he established a great many monasteries and a school at Roscrea, and died as a recluse in extreme old age. F. D. Apr. 28.

CRONAN, ST. (8th century). He contrib-uted much to the systematization of canon law in Ireland and probably is the same per-son as St. Ronan, bishop of Lismore. F. D. Feb. 9.

CRONAN, ST. *See* Cuaran, St.

CRONAN BEG, ST. (7th century). He was a bishop in Aendrum, Down, Ireland. F. D. Jan. 7.

CRONIAN. *See* Eunus, St.

CROS, PIERRE DE (d. 1304). He became bishop of Clermont, France, in 1301 and was named by St. Thomas Aquinas to complete his *Summa theologica*.

CROTATES. *See* Codratus, St.

CROTUS, JOHANN. *See* Jäger, Johannes.

CROWLEY, PATRICK EDWARD (1864–1953), executive. Born in Cattaraugus, New York, on Aug. 25, he became a messenger boy for the Erie Railroad, for which his father worked, and rose through the ranks of the New York Central from dispatcher in 1889 to vice-president in 1916 and president in 1924. He married Carrie Nichols in 1891, moved to the line's advisory board from 1931 until his retirement in 1940, and died in Mount Vernon, New York, on Oct. 1.

CRUMMINE, ST. (5th century), bishop. He was a follower of St. Patrick, who placed him in charge of a bishopric in Westmeath, Ireland. F. D. June 28.

CRUZ CANO Y OLMEDILLA, RAMÓN DE LA (1731–1795), dramatist. Born in Madrid, Spain, he held minor government posts, was a protégé of the duchess of Benaventa, and became a member of the Royal Academy of Seville and the Academy of the Arcadians of Rome. He published ten volumes of plays between 1786 and 1791, translated and adapted Molière, Racine, Goldoni, Metastasio, and Ducis (*Hamleto*), and turned out nearly 500 works for the theater. His greatest success was in the *sainete*, a short, satiric sketch of middle and lower class types and customs, often composed on the spot and produced within a day or two. The realistic characters spoke dialect; the humor was colorful and exuberant; the satire, of court gallants and dandies, or would-be actors, and even of leaders in public life sharp and witty. He died in Madrid on Nov. 4.

CRUZ, JUAN DE LA. *See* John of the Cross, St.

CRUZ, JUANA DE LA. *See* Santillana, Juana Inés de.

CSAHOLY, FRANZ (d. 1526). He became bishop of Csanád, Hungary, in 1514 and was killed with most of his subjects when the diocese was overrun by Zápolya, an ally of the Turks.

CSAKY, BL. MAURICE (1281–1336). Son of a Hungarian count, he was married at twenty, but by mutual consent he and his wife entered lives of religion, Maurice as a Dominican on the island of St. Margaret. He was never formally beatified, but long was venerated in Hungary on Mar. 20.

CSAKY, NICHOLAS (d. 1514?). Bishop of Csanád, Hungary, he was seized and put to death by impaling during a peasant uprising.

CSERNOCH, JOHANN (1852–1927), cardinal. Born in Kalocsa, Hungary, he studied at Graz and Vienna, was ordained in 1874, taught theology at Graz, and became secretary of the chancery and in 1893 canon of the cathedral there. He was a founder of the Catholic party and was elected to parliament. He became bishop of Temesvar in 1908, of Kalocsa in 1911, archbishop of Graz in 1913, and a cardinal in 1914. He was expelled from his see when Bela Kun took over the government, but was later restored, and died in Budapest, Hungary, on July 25.

CTESIPHON, ST. (1st century). *See* Caecilius, St.

CUAN, ST. (6th century). Also known as Mochua, he founded a number of churches and monasteries in Ireland and lived to be nearly 100. F. D. Jan. 1.

CUARAN, ST. (7th century). He was an Irish bishop who, incognito, became a monk at Iona under St. Columba, but was identified because of his wisdom. F. D. Feb. 9.

CUCUPHAS, ST. (d. 304), martyr. Born in Scillis, Africa, and of aristocratic Carthaginian descent, he went to Spain and was slain near Barcelona; his death is memorialized by Prudentius. F. D. July 25.

CUDAHY, EDWARD ALOYSIUS (1860–1941), executive. Born in Milwaukee, Wisconsin, on Feb. 1, he was in the meat-supply business from 1875, was a founder of Cudahy Packing Co., its president in 1910, and chairman of the board from 1926. He died in Chicago on Oct. 18.

CUDAHY, MICHAEL (1841–1910), executive. Born in Callan, Kilkenny, Ireland, on Dec. 7, he was taken to Milwaukee, Wisconsin, in 1849, worked in the meat-packing business after 1856, and introduced the refrigeration process in 1870, which revolutionized the industry. He became a partner with Armour and Co., in 1875, and in 1887 established the Armour-Cudahy Packing Co. with his brother, Edward, and Philip Armour in South Omaha, Nebraska. He set up his own company in 1890 and served as its president until his death in Chicago on Nov. 27.

CUDDIHY, HERBERT LESTER (1896–1953), publisher. Born in New York City on Oct. 12, he studied at Lawrenceville and Princeton, and became associated with the publishing firm of Funk & Wagnalls Co. in 1918. He was general manager and president in 1940–46 and chairman of the board from 1946 until his death at Southampton, New York, on July 4.

CUDDIHY, ROBERT JOSEPH (1862–1952), publisher. Born in New York City on Dec. 31, he was publisher of the *Literary Digest* from 1890 to 1937, head of Funk & Wagnalls Co., from 1914 to 1948, developed the plan for the *Standard Encyclopedia* (1912), and issued sermons and religious reference works for various faiths. He died in New York City on Dec. 22.

CUÉNOT, BL. STEPHEN THEODORE (1802–1861), bishop and martyr. A native of Beaulieu, France, he studied at the Society of Foreign Missions seminary in Paris, and was sent to Annam in 1829. When a persecution of Christians broke out in 1833 he was ordered to Siam. In 1835 he was made vicar apostolic of East Cochin China, consecrated in Singapore, and slipped back into Annam, where in the next fifteen years he established three separate vicariates. He suffered through continuous persecutions, was captured in the province of Binh-Dinn, and was apparently poisoned in his cell on Nov. 14. He was beatified in 1909. F. D. Feb. 8.

CUEVA, JUAN DE LA (1550?–1610?), poet. Born in Seville, Spain, he wrote fourteen poetic dramas after 1579, avoiding classical conventions, reducing the length from five to four acts, and experimenting with meter. He defended his position in *Ejemplar poético* (1606). There is not too much distinction between his characters, because of the author's highly romantic language, on one emotional plane; the plays also suffer from implausibility, sensationalism, and the fantastic. His subject matter was the nationalistic glories of Spain's past (*Bernardo de Carpio*), ancient legend (*La muerte de Ajax*), and contemporary events such as the Italian campaign of Charles V (*El saco de Roma*). His *El infamador* (1581) is a predecessor of Molina's Don Juan. He also published collections of poems and of a hundred romances, and an epic, *La conquistade la Bética*, on the conquest of Seville by St. Ferdinand. He later lived in Portugal and is said to have visited the West Indies or Mexico.

CUFITELLA, BL. GUILELMO (1316?–1411). A Franciscan tertiary, he lived in Sicily seventy years as a solitary, working for the sick poor and joining Bl. Conrad of Piacenza in an annual Lenten fast. He was beatified in 1537. F. D. Apr. 7.

CULEN (d. 971?), king of Scotland. Also called Colin, he became king in 967 when he defeated Dubh, who had seized the crown, and was himself defeated and slain by the Britons about 971.

CULIOYE, BL. FRANCIS (d. 1627), martyr. A Franciscan tertiary, he was burned to death at Nagasaki for having sheltered missioners. With him died Francis Curobioye, also a native and a Dominican tertiary, and Francis of St. Mary, a Franciscan priest, born in Mancha, Spain, who had arrived in the East in 1605 and had been sent to Japan in 1622. They were beatified in 1867. F. D. Aug. 17.

CULLEN, BERNARD A. (1903–1960). Born in New York City on Aug. 3, he studied at Cathedral College and St. Joseph's seminary, and was ordained in 1930. He did pastoral work in the New York archdiocese, became interested in the welfare of Indians, and served as director general of the Marquette League for American Indian missions. He was made a papal chamberlain in 1954, and died in Miami, Florida, on Sept. 3.

CULLEN, PAUL (1803–1878), cardinal. Born in Prospect, Kildare, Ireland, on Apr. 29, he studied at Carlow and the Propaganda, Rome, was ordained about 1828, taught scripture and Hebrew at the Propaganda, and served

as rector of the Irish College in Rome from 1832 to 1850, and, for a while, was concurrently rector of the Propaganda. He was named archbishop of Armagh in 1850, was transferred to Dublin in 1852, and became the first Irish cardinal-priest in 1857. He held a synod at Thurles in 1850 and convened a national synod at Maynooth in 1875, and between those dates worked to restore ecclesiastical discipline. He labored to gain educational opportunities for Catholics and gave direct support to the Catholic University of Ireland, which failed for reasons beyond his control. He opposed the Young Ireland and Fenian movements as agents of useless dissent, but backed other political efforts to introduce industrial schools, amend land-tenure acts, and better the condition of those in poorhouses. His petition to the crown saved the Fenian leader Thomas F. Burke from the gallows. He founded the seminary of the Holy Cross at Clonliffe, went to Rome in 1854 for the definition of the dogma of the Immaculate Conception, and at the later Vatican Council worded the definition of papal infallibility finally accepted by the cardinals. He edited the *Lexicon* of Hedericus and the *Acta* of the Congregation of Propaganda, and died in Dublin on Oct. 24.

CULMATIUS, ST. (d. 364), martyr. *See* Gaudentius, St.

CUMIAN, ST. (590?–665?). Son of Fiachna, king of West Munster, he became a monk in charge of the school at Clonfert. He later founded a monastery at Kilcummin, of which he became abbot, and in a learned reply (the *Paschal Epistle*) to a rebuke from the abbot of Iona vigorously defended the Roman observance of Easter. He is often surnamed Fota, or Fada, "the tall." F. D. Nov. 12.

CUMINE, ST. (d. 669). Called "the White," he was an Irish monk who became abbot of Iona and wrote a life of St. Columba. F. D. Feb. 24 (sometimes, Oct. 6).

CUMMIAN, ST. (8th century). An Irish bishop, he traveled to Italy and became a Benedictine monk at the abbey in Bobbio. F. D. June 9.

CUMMINGS, JEREMIAH WILLIAMS (1814–1866). Born in Washington, D.C., he was ordained in Rome, appointed an assistant in St. Patrick's cathedral in New York City, and in 1848 made pastor of St. Stephen's, which he built and which became popular because of his sermons and musical taste. Fr. Cummings was a friend of Orestes Brownson, brought him from Boston to New York, contributed to his *Review*, and was the center of a group of clergy and laymen which roused wide hostility. They objected orally and in print to the European grasp on seminary teaching in the United States, demanded better colleges and universities than the "incompetent" ones then in existence, and suggested a more ecumenical approach to those outside the Church in distinction to the prevailing one of hostility. Archbishop Hughes wrote a reply to the group in his *Reflections on the American Press*. Fr. Cummings died in New York City on Jan. 4.

CUNEGUND, ST. (d. 1033?). Daughter of Siegfried and Hedwig of Luxembourg, she married St. Henry II, duke of Bavaria, who became Holy Roman emperor in 1013. He built the cathedral of Bamberg and she, the Benedictine convent at Kaufungen, Hesse, which she entered in 1024 after her husband's death. She was canonized in 1200. F. D. Mar. 3.

CUNEGUNDA, ST. (1224–1292). Daughter of King Bela IV and niece of St. Elizabeth of Hungary, she married King Boleslaus V of Poland at sixteen. On his death in 1279 she became a Poor Clare at the convent of Sandeck, which she had founded. She also built churches and hospitals, ransomed Christians captured by the Turks, and served the poor and ill. She is also known as St. Kinga. Her cult was confirmed in 1690. F. D. July 24.

CUNGAR, ST. (6th century?). Possibly a native of Devon, he may have been the founder of monasteries in Somerset and Glamorgan and of a church in Cardiff, later going with St. Sybi to Ireland, and returning to die at Congresbury. He is probably identical with St. Docco (Docuinus, Doguinus). F. D. Nov. 27.

CUNHA, TRISTÃO DA (1460?–1540?), explorer. Born in Portugal, he led an expedition to the Indies in 1506 with d'Albuquerque, fought in Madagascar, served as ambassador extraordinary from Portugal to Pope Leo X on colonial matters, and later became a royal councilor. He discovered three volcanic islands in the Atlantic Ocean, one of which is named for him.

CUNHA, VINCENT DA (d. 1737), martyr. *See* Alvarez, Bartholomew.

CUNIBERT ST. (d. 663?), bishop. Said to have been a courtier at the French court of Clotaire II, he was ordained and became archdeacon at Trier. In 625 he was made bishop of Cologne, remained a counselor of the court, and was appointed one of the guardians of Sigebert when Dagobert I appointed his son king of Austrasia. He built many churches and monasteries, and aided the evangelization of the Frisians. F. D. Nov. 12.

CUNIBERT, ST. (d. 680?). He succeeded St. Humbert as Benedictine abbot of Maroilles, in the diocese of Cambrai, France. F. D. Sept. 16.

CUNNINGHAM, JOHN F. (1842–1919), bishop. Born in Kerry, Ireland, he studied at St. Benedict's College, Atchison, Kansas, was ordained in 1865, was appointed vicar general of the diocese of Leavenworth, and in 1898 became bishop of Concordia, Kansas. Fr. T. J. Butler of Chicago, Illinois, had been appointed

second bishop, but died in Rome before he was consecrated. Bishop Cunningham built many schools and charitable institutions. He died on June 23.

CUOQ, ANDRÉ JEAN (1821–1808), philologist. Born in Le Puy, France, he became a Sulpician in 1844, was sent to Canada in 1846, mastered the Algonquin and Iroquois tongues while working in mission territory, and published an Algonquin dictionary and grammar, and several other philological and historical studies. He died at Oka, near Montreal.

CURCODOMUS, ST. (3rd century). A deacon in Rome, he was sent to Gaul with St. Peregrinus, and served him in the see of Auxerre. F. D. May 4.

CURIG, ST. (6th century). He is said to have been bishop of Llanbadarn, Wales; there are several saints of this name. F. D. June 16.

CURLE, GILBERT (16th century). He, his sister, Elizabeth (who attended Queen Mary Stuart), and his wife, Barbara Mowbray, made their home in Antwerp, Flanders, a shelter for other Catholic exiles from Great Britain. Gilbert left a large endowment to the Scots College at Douai.

CURLEY, DANIEL JOSEPH (1869–1932), bishop. Born in New York City, on June 16, he studied at St. Francis Xavier, St. Joseph's seminary, Troy, and North American College, Rome, where he was ordained in 1894. He engaged in parish work in New York, was Archbishop Corrigan's secretary in 1901–2, was pastor of Our Lady of Solace in New York from 1902 to 1923, and in 1923 was appointed bishop of Syracuse. He died there on Aug. 3.

CURLEY, JAMES (1796–1889), astronomer. Born in Athleague, Roscommon, Ireland, on Dec. 26, he went to the United States in 1817, worked as a bookkeeper in Philadelphia, Pennsylvania, taught mathematics in Frederick, Maryland, and became a Jesuit in 1827. He was ordained in 1833, taught philosophy and mathematics at Georgetown and also served as chaplain at the Visitation convent in Washington, D.C., for nearly fifty years. He planned the Georgetown observatory and was its first director and historian. He died at Georgetown on July 24.

CURLEY, JAMES MICHAEL (1874–1958), governor. Born in Boston, on Nov. 20, he entered politics on his graduation from high school, was elected to the city council at twenty-five, and was elected mayor of Boston in 1913, 1921, 1929, and 1945. This last term was interrupted in 1947 when he spent five months in jail for mail fraud in connection with war contracts; when his sentence was commuted by President Truman, he returned to continue the legend of the political boss. He became governor of Massachusetts in 1934 and was elected to the national House of Representatives in 1942. His autobiography, *I'd Do It Again*, was published in 1957. He died in Boston on Nov. 13.

CURLEY, MICHAEL JOSEPH (1879–1947), archbishop. Born in Athlone, Westmeath, Ireland, on Oct. 12, he studied at Mungret College, Limerick, the Royal University, Dublin, and the Propaganda, Rome, and was ordained in 1904. He went to the United States that year and served as a missioner in Florida until 1914, when he was appointed bishop of St. Augustine. He succeeded Cardinal Gibbons as archbishop of Baltimore in 1921, and in 1939 became the first archbishop of Washington, D.C. He died on May 16.

CUROBIOYE, BL. FRANCIS (d. 1627), martyr. *See* Culioye, Bl. Francis.

CURONOTUS, ST. (d. 258?), martyr. Bishop of Iconium in Asia Minor, he was put to death there during the reign of Valerian. F. D. Sept. 12.

CURR, JOSEPH (d. 1847). Born in Sheffield, England, he studied at Ushaw College, was ordained, and stationed in Manchester, Callaly, St. Albans, Whitby, and Sheffield. He wrote a manual for catechetical schools, *Spiritual Retreat*, explanations of Catholicism during a controversy with the Protestant Bible Association, and a translation from St. Francis Liguori. He died in Leeds, England, on June 29, where he had gone to offer his services during a typhus epidemic.

CURRAN, JOHN JOSEPH (1859–1936). Born in Hawley, Pennsylvania, on June 20, he began work in the coal mines at seven, studied at Wyoming seminary, Kingston, and St. Vincent College, Latrobe, Pennsylvania, and Montreal's Grand seminary, and was ordained in Scranton in 1887. He spent the rest of his life as curate and pastor in the coal-mining area of Pennsylvania and became famed for his support of miners and their unions, in particular the United Mine Workers and John Mitchell, its president. He achieved national fame for his prominent role in the bitter strike of 1902, was thanked by President Theodore Roosevelt for his aid, and helped settle several subsequent strikes. He was made a papal chamberlain in 1930 and died in Wilkes-Barre, Pennsylvania, on Nov. 7.

CURRY, JOHN (d. 1780). Born in Dublin, Ireland, he studied medicine at Paris and Rheims, practiced in Dublin, wrote two studies of fevers, and engaged in controversy with the Protestant pamphleteer Walter Harris. A result was *An Historical and Critical Review of the Civil Wars in Ireland* (1775). He also worked for the repeal of the penal laws and was a founder of the Catholic Committee for political relief.

CURTIS, ALFRED A. (1831–1908), bishop. Born in Somerset County, Maryland, on July 4, he became an Episcopalian minister; in 1872, while in England, he was converted by Cardinal Newman. He returned to study at St. Mary's seminary, Baltimore, and was ordained in 1874. He did pastoral work in Baltimore, was Archbishop Bayley's secretary and chancellor of the archdiocese in 1874–86, and in 1886 was consecrated second bishop of Wilmington, Delaware. He spent the next decade laboring to pay off the heavy debt of the see, built the Visitation monastery, and established a mission for Negroes. He resigned in 1896, was named titular bishop of Echinus, was administrator of Wilmington in 1896–97, served as vicar general of Washington in 1897–1908, and died in Baltimore on July 11.

CUSACK, MARY FRANCES (1820–1899), foundress. Born near Dublin, she became an Anglican sister in England, became a convert, and on her return to Ireland joined the Poor Clares in their work with friendless girls. She established their convent at Kenmare in 1861, became interested in a similar, independent group, and in 1884 received papal approval from Leo XIII for her Sisters of Peace. She wrote on SS. Bridget, Columba, and Patrick, on the Virgin of Knock, on women in modern society, and an autobiography, *The Nun of Kenmare*.

CUSACK, THOMAS FRANCIS (1862–1918), bishop. Born in New York City on Feb. 22, he studied at St. Francis Xavier, was ordained in 1885, served as superior of the New York diocesan missionaries in 1897–1904, then became auxiliary bishop of New York, and was transferred to Albany as fifth to direct that see. He died on July 12.

CUSICK, PETER (1876–1939), educator. Born in Scranton, Pennsylvania, he became a Jesuit, was ordained in 1895, was president of Canisius in 1923–29, director of the shrine of the North American martyrs at Auriesville in 1931–38, and died in New York on Feb. 7.

CUSPINIAN, JOHANNES (1473–1529), diplomat. Born in Schweinfurt, Franconia, he studied at Leipzig, took his degree in medicine at Vienna, and in 1500 became rector of that university. He had gained the attention of Emperor Frederick III and the patronage of Maximilian for his edition of *Liber hymnorum* by Prudentius, his panegyric on St. Leopold, and his lectures on classical Roman authors. He became councilor to Maximilian, chief librarian, and custodian of the imperial archives. He was prefect of Vienna in 1515 and served Maximilian and Charles V on diplomatic missions to Hungary, Bohemia, and Poland. He collected and edited a great variety of manuscripts, published a *History of the Roman Emperors*, wrote on Turkey and Austria, and left a detailed political diary covering the years 1502–27. He died in Vienna on Apr. 19.

CUTHBERT, ST. (d. 687), bishop. A Briton, he was a shepherd in Northumbria before he became a monk at Melrose. He served briefly at Ripon under St. Eata in 661, then returned to Melrose, where he aided the countryside during a plague, preached in the remotest hamlets, and became prior. After the Council of Whitby he went to the Benedictine monastery of Lindisfarne, where he was prior and Eata bishop after the departure of St. Colman. He saw that reforms were carried out, again preached widely, but preferred solitary asceticism and retired to one of the Farne islands in 676. He was recalled in 685 and became abbot-bishop of Lindisfarne, England, and devoted himself to preaching, teaching, and caring for plague-stricken and war-torn poor. His shrine, which was established in Durham cathedral in 975, was a favorite pilgrimage site before it was pillaged and destroyed by Henry VIII. F. D. Mar. 20 (sometimes, Sept. 4).
B. COLGRAVE, *Two Lives of St. Cuthbert* (New York, Macmillan, 1940).

CUTHBERT (d. 758), archbishop. Abbot of Liminge, Kent, England, he became bishop of Hereford in 736 and was transferred to Canterbury in 740. He defined the duties of monks and priests at two councils held at Cloveshoe in 742 and 747, and gained some ecclesiastical privileges from King Ethelbald of Mercia. His report of the second council was sent to Germany, where his friend St. Boniface made good use of it; Cuthbert also wrote poems, two of which were saved by William of Malmesbury. Cuthbert died in Canterbury on Oct. 25.

CUTHBURGA, ST. (d. 725?). Sister of King Ine of Wessex, she married King Aldfrid of Northumbria in 688, who allowed her to retire to the convent at Barking. With her sister, St. Queenburga, early in the 8th century, she founded the abbey of Wimborne, in Dorset, of which she became abbess. F. D. Sept. 3.

CUTHMAN, ST. (d. 900?). A devout shepherd, he built a cottage at Steyning in Sussex, England, for his aged mother, and began to raise a church nearby with his own hands, his example moving the villagers to join in its completion. He is featured in Christopher Fry's play, *The Boy with a Cart* (1939). F. D. Feb. 8.

CUYPERS, PETER J. H. (1827–1921), architect. Born in Roermond, Holland, he studied at the Academy of Antwerp, became interested in mediaeval traditionalism, built sixty-four churches, including Haarlem cathedral, and restored 570 others, including Mainz cathedral. He also designed the national museum, Amsterdam, served on the advisory board of historical and artistic monuments, was an officer of the French Legion of Honor, and several times president of the International Congress of Architects. He died on Mar. 3.

CYBY, ST. (6th century). Said to have been born in Cornwall, a cousin of St. David of Wales, and to have settled in Monmouthshire to avoid becoming king, he became a bishop when he settled near Tregony, and may have spent some time in Ireland before he returned to found a monastery near Holyhead, Wales. F. D. Nov. 8.

CYNFRAN, ST. (5th century). Son of a Welsh chieftain, he built a church in Carnarvonshire; his name was given to a holy well. F. D. Nov. 11.

CYNEWULF (8th century?), poet. His identity is unknown; he has been identified as bishop of Lindisfarne, England, and also as Cynwulf, a priest in the diocese of Dunwich early in the ninth century. He seems to have been a converted minstrel, and signed his name to a number of poems in the Northern dialect. These are: *Juliana*, the biography of a martyr; *Elene*, a narrative of the finding of the true cross by St. Helena; the short *Fates of the Apostles*; and *Christ*, based on a homily on the Ascension by Gregory the Great. Some critics have attributed *The Dream of the Rood* to him. His descriptions are vivid, his action scenes well handled, and his lyric passages a genuine advance over the older heroic poetic tradition.

CYPRIAN, ST. (200?–258), bishop and martyr. Probably born in Carthage, Africa, Thascius Caecilius Cyprianus was a lawyer, orator, and teacher, was converted to Christianity by an old priest, Caecilius, and became an expert on the Bible and the great religious authors. He was ordained and in 248 became bishop. When Emperor Decius launched a persecution in 249, many Christians apostatized; Cyprian fled into hiding, for which he was criticized. From his hiding place he wrote letters to his flock, many of which letters are still extant. While there, Novatus, a priest who had opposed Cyprian's election, went into schism; on Cyprian's return, he excommunicated Novatus and his followers at a council at Carthage. It was also at this council that Cyprian read *De unitate* on the oneness of the Church and the supremacy of the pope. It was decided those who had apostatized and sacrificed to the gods could receive Communion only at death, whereas those who had bought official statements that they had sacrificed were allowed to receive only after considerable time and penances. This practice was repealed in the following year when new persecutions broke out. He also vigorously supported Pope St. Cornelius against the claims of Novatian (with whom Novatus had allied himself) and it was at this time he wrote his treatise on the *lapsi*, the controversy which was then seriously disturbing the Church and one aspect of which led to Novatianism. During the plague in Carthage (252–54) Cyprian was the leader in organizing relief and wrote *De mortalite* to comfort his stricken flock. Shortly thereafter he led the African bishops, in opposition to Pope St. Stephen I, in refusing to recognize the validity of baptism administered by heretics and schismatics—an impossible position. In 257, Emperor Valerian ordered all priests to participate in the official state religion. Cyprian refused, was tried, and exiled to Curubis by the proconsul Paternus; in 258, Galerius Maximus succeeded Paternus, brought Cyprian back to Carthage, ordered him to sacrifice and, when he refused, had him beheaded. F. D. Sept. 16.

CYPRIAN, ST. (d. 301?), martyr. See Straton, St.

CYPRIAN, ST. (d. 484?), bishop and martyr. See Felix, St.

CYPRIAN, ST. (d. 582). He was bishop of Brescia, Italy. F. D. Apr. 21.

CYPRIAN, ST. (d. 586). A monk at Périgueux, France, he became a hermit and was memorialized by St. Gregory of Tours. F. D. Dec. 9.

CYPRIAN, ST. (6th century), bishop. A monk at St. Victor's, Marseilles, France, he became bishop of Toulon in 516, wrote a life of St. Caesarius of Arles, and opposed the Semi-Pelagians. F. D. Oct. 3.

CYPRIAN. A pious legend dating from the fourth century, with no foundation in fact, calls Cyprian an evil magician from Antioch who tried to seduce Justina, a Christian. Her goodness so changed him that he became a priest and bishop. Both were said to have been beheaded at Nicomedia during the persecution of Diocletian and were commemorated as saints on Sept. 26.

CYRA, ST. (5th century). She and St. Marana became hermits near Beroea, Syria. F. D. Aug. 3.

CYRAN. See Sigiramnus, St.

CYRENIA, ST. (d. 306), martyr. She and St. Juliana were burned to death at Tarsus during the Diocletian persecution. F. D. Nov. 1.

CYRIACA, ST. (d. 249), martyr. A Roman widow of wealth, she harbored the persecuted Christians in her home, which was also the center for the distribution of alms by St. Laurene and others. She was scourged to death. She is also called Dominica. F. D. Aug. 31.

CYRIACA, ST. (d. 307), martyr. She and five other Christian girls were burned to death at Nicomedia during the persecution of Maximian. F. D. May 19.

CYRIACUS, ST. (d. 140), martyr. He and SS. Theodulus and their parents, Exuperius and Zoe, all slaves, were put to death at Attalia, Pamphylia. F. D. May 2.

CYRIACUS, ST. (d. 250), martyr. He and SS. Faustinus, Florentius, Julian and Marcellinus were beheaded for their faith at Perugia during the persecution of Decius. F. D. June 5.

CYRIACUS, ST. (3rd century), martyr. See Antiochus, St.

CYRIACUS, ST. (d. 303), martyr. See Anastasius, St.

CYRIACUS, ST. (d. 304?). He and his six brothers, SS. Firminus, Firmus, Heros, Longinus, Orentius, and Pharnacius are said to have been Roman soldiers who were expelled from the army under Maximian and slain in exile. F. D. June 24.

CYRIACUS, ST. (d. 304?), martyr. He is said to have been a deacon, who with SS. Largus, Smaragdus, and twenty others, was tortured and beheaded at Rome during the persecution of Maximian. F. D. Aug. 8 (also, Mar. 16).

CYRIACUS, ST. (d. 305), martyr. He and St. Paula were stoned to death at Málaga, Spain, during the persecution of Diocletian. F. D. June 18.

CYRIACUS, ST. (d. 556). A hermit in Palestine, he became abbot and died at the laura of St. Sabas. St. Cyril of Scythopolis wrote his biography. F. D. Sept. 29.

CYRIACUS, ST. (d. 606), patriarch. He was administrator, then patriarch of Constantinople, and highly honored in the East. F. D. Oct. 27.

CYRIACUS. See Judas Quiriacus, St.

CYRICUS, ST. (d. 304?), martyr. See Julitta, St.

CYRIL, ST. (d. 250), bishop. He was tortured and beheaded at Gortyna, Crete, during the persecution of Decius. F. D. July 9.

CYRIL, ST. (d. 251?), martyr. A boy in Caesarea in Cappadocia, he became a Christian without his father's knowledge. The governor threatened him with death by fire, had him brought back to the court, and, when he complained that he had been tricked by this approach to martyrdom, was beheaded on the spot. F. D. May 29.

CYRIL, ST. (d. 271?), martyr. See Restituta, St.

CYRIL, ST. (3rd century), martyr. See Anastasia, St.

CYRIL, ST. (d. 300?), bishop. He succeeded Timaeus as patriarch of Antioch in 280, and suffered during the Diocletian persecution, though he was not slain. F. D. July 22.

CYRIL, ST. (d. 365?), martyr. A deacon at Heliopolis, Lebanon, he was set upon by pagans during the reign of Julian the Apostate, and beaten and torn to death because he had destroyed their temples. F. D. Mar. 29.

CYRIL, ST. (5th century). He was bishop of Trèves, Gaul. F. D. May 19.

CYRIL, ST. (d. 869). Born in Thessalonica, he was baptized Constantine (he took the name Cyril shortly before his death) and at an early age was sent to Constantinople to study at the imperial university under Photius, eventually taking over the latter's chair and earning the appellation "the philosopher." In 861 he was sent by the emperor, with his brother

Methodius, to convert the Khazars in the region between Dnieper and the Volga. At the request of the emperor of Moravia they were sent by Photius in 863 to evangelize Moravia. Because of their knowledge of the Slavonic tongue they were extremely successful, but incurred the enmity of the German clergy. They were particularly handicapped when the German bishop of Passau would not ordain their candidates for the priesthood. They went to Rome to secure papal support, bringing the alleged relics of Pope St. Clement, and were warmly received by Pope Adrian II, who approved their use of the liturgy in Slavonic and decreed they were to receive episcopal consecration and that their neophytes were to be ordained. It is not certain whether Cyril was consecrated bishop, as he died while still in Rome on Feb. 14. He and Methodius are called the Apostles of the Slavs and to this day the liturgical language of the Russians, Serbs, Ukranians and Bulgars is that of the two brothers who also reputedly designed the characters of the languages from the Greek. The feast of SS. Cyril and Methodius was extended to the whole Western Church in 1880 by Pope Leo XIII. F. D. July 7.

CYRIL, ST. (d. 1182), bishop. A monk, then a hermit, he was called to become bishop of Turov, near Kiev, Russia, where he developed the allegorical interpretation of scripture, wrote prayers strongly marked by the theme of the Redemption, preached widely, and maintained strict discipline in monastic life. F. D. Apr. 28.

CYRIL OF ALEXANDRIA, ST. (376?-444), Doctor of the Church. When he succeeded his uncle, Theophilus, as archbishop of Alexandria in 412, he began a brief period of impulsive, often violent, actions: he closed the churches of the Novatians, drove all Jews (many of whom had been charged with sedition and other crimes) from the city; wrote strongly against Juilan the Apostate, but continued his family's hostility toward the name of St. John Chrysostom. By 428, however, he had settled down as a widely respected spiritual leader and when Nestorius became archbishop of Constantinople in that year and began denying the Incarnation of Christ, Cyril protested. The case was brought to Pope Celestine I, who condemned Nestorius as a heretic and directed Cyril to depose him. Cyril presided over the 200 bishops who attended the third General Council at Ephesus (431) which considered and condemned all the doctrines which had stemmed from Nestorius or his followers. When Archbishop John of Antioch arrived late with forty-two bishops, they insisted that Nestorius was innocent of the charges, met in private conclave, and declared Cyril deposed. The emperor arrested both Cyril and Nestorius, but released Cyril after papal legates arrived and investigated the entire situation. In 433, Archbishop John's group joined in the condemnation of the heresy, and Nestorius went into exile. In his remaining years Cyril so clarified the doctrine of the Incarnation that Nestorianism and Pelagianism never were able to take deep root; he also increased popular devotion to the Eucharist. He was declared a Doctor of the Church in 1882 and was particularly honored by Pope Pius XII in his 1944 encyclical, *Orientalis ecclesiae*. F. D. Feb. 9.

CYRIL OF JERUSALEM, ST. (315?-386), Doctor of the Church. Apparently brought up in Jerusalem by Christian parents and well educated, he was ordained by St. Maximus, who set him to instructing catechumens. He was a careful student of scripture, a clear expositor of early ritual and of formal theology, and quite successful in his sermons. Although he instructed candidates for baptism for several years, only nineteen of his discourses, delivered in 348, are extant. He succeeded Maximus as archbishop of Jerusalem, being duly consecrated, but ran into difficulty when Acacius, metropolitan of Caesarea, sought to assume jurisdiction over the see, called a synod of his Arian supporters, and charged Cyril with selling church property to aid victims of famine. Deposed, Cyril went to Tarsus, but was reinstated after two years. Acacius persuaded Emperor Constantius that additional charges were true and Cyril was again exiled; in 361, on the emperor's death, he was recalled by Julian. In 367, Emperor Valens exiled all the churchmen who had returned in the Apostate's reign, and Cyril was banished until about 378. When he returned, he found his see torn by crime, factionalism, and the Arian heresy. He and his associate, St. Gregory of Nyssa, attended the second Ecumenical Council at Constantinople in 381 and completely accepted the amended Nicene Creed. The church historians Socrates and Sozomen claim that Cyril had not always done so, and St. Jerome was hostile toward him; the bishops at the council, however, indicated that, although he had been friendly with many semi-Arian leaders, he was known as a firm opponent of the heresy. He was proclaimed a Doctor of the Church in 1822. F. D. Mar. 18.

CYRIL OF JERUSALEM (d. 1235?). It is known only that he became prior general of the Carmelites in Palestine in 1232. He appears on a list of saints because of a confusion of names.

CYRILLA, ST. (d. 270?), martyr. Daughter of St. Tryphonia, she was noted for her charities in Rome and was put to death there in the reign of Claudius II. F. D. Oct. 28.

CYRILLA, ST. (d. 300?), martyr. An aged widow, she was slain with other Christians at Cyrene, Lybia, during the Diocletian persecution; she died under torture. F. D. July 5.

CYRINUS, ST. (d. 251), martyr. *See* Alphius, St.

CYRINUS, ST. (3rd century), martyr. He was slain during the Diocletian persecution, and praised by Pope St. Marcellinus. F. D. Oct. 25.

CYRINUS, ST. (d. 304), martyr. *See* Antoninus, St.

CYRINUS, ST. (d. 320), martyr. He and SS. Primus and Theogenes were soldiers who were put to death at Cyzicus on the Hellespont when their faith was discovered during the persecution of Licinius. F. D. Jan. 3.

CYRUS, ST. (d. 303?), martyr. An Alexandrian physician, he sought to inspire the Christian Athanasia and her three daughters to remain firm in spite of what they had suffered, but was captured with his companion John. All six were tortured and beheaded at Canopus, Egypt. He is memorialized by St. Cyril of Alexandria and by the names Abukir, where a shrine was built, and St. Passera, a church near Rome. F. D. Jan. 31.

CZAPLICKA, MARIE ANTOINETTE (d. 1921), anthropologist. Born near Warsaw, Poland, she went to England in 1910, studied at Oxford, went to Siberia and central Asia on archaeological expeditions, and published widely in English, Russian, and Polish. Her books include *Aboriginal Siberia* (1912), *My Siberian Year* (1916), and *Turks of Central Asia* (1919).

D

DABIUS, ST. He is probably identical with St. Movean.

DABLON, CLAUDE (1618–1697), missioner. Born in Dieppe, France, he became a Jesuit at twenty-one, went to Canada in 1655, worked on Iroquois missions, went in 1661 with Druillettes on an exploration of Hudson Bay, and in 1668 crossed the Great Lakes, founded Sault Ste. Marie, and sent Marquette to the upper Mississippi. He was superior general of the Canadian missions from 1670 to 1680 and from 1686 to 1693. His contributions to the Jesuit *Relations* are significant, and it was he who preserved Marquette's letters and charts for publication. He died in Quebec on May 3.

DABROWSKI, JOSEPH (d. 1903). Born in Zoltance, Poland, he studied at Lublin and Warsaw, fought in the rebellion against Russia in 1863, fled to Germany, studied theology in Rome, and was ordained in 1869. He went to the United States, where he worked with Polish-Americans and became pastor at Polonia, Wisconsin, from 1870 to 1882. Ill health forced his retirement, but in 1884 he began building the seminary of SS. Cyril and Methodius in Detroit, Michigan, of which he was rector until his death on Feb. 15.

DACIER, ANDRÉ (1651–1722), translator. Born in Castres, France, on Apr. 6, he was a Huguenot, married Anne Lefèvre, daughter of Ranneguy Lefèvre who first hired him to translate for the Delphine series of the classics, and two years later, in 1685, became a convert. His translations (often with now-outdated commentaries) include Aristotle's *Poetics*, Epictetus, Hierocles, Hippocrates, Horace, Plutarch, Pythagoras, and Sophocles. He was a member of the Academy of Inscriptions and of the French Academy, of which he was secretary, and royal librarian. He died on Sept. 18.

DACIER, ANNE LEFÈVRE (1651–1720), translator. Born in Saumur, France, of a Huguenot family, Anne Lefèvre married André Dacier in 1683, became a convert with him in 1685, and published translations of Anacreon, Aristophanes, Callimachus, Homer, Plautus, Sappho, and Terence. Her 1699 edition of the *Iliad* had a preface important to the international quarrel between the "ancients and moderns"; she later published a censure of Houdart de la Motte for his short and modernized poetic revision of that epic. She was joined in the literary battle by Fénelon and opposed by the Jesuit Hardouin, to whom she replied in a critical tract. She died in Paris on Apr. 17.

DA CUNHA, BL. THOMAS RODRIGUEZ (d. 1638), martyr. *See* Berthelot, Bl. Peter.

DADAS, ST. (d. 303), martyr. He and his brothers, Maximus and Quintilian, were beheaded at Ozobia (Bulgaria) during the persecution of Diocletian. F. D. Apr. 13.

DADAS, ST. (319?–368), martyr. A Persian noble, he was put to death with Casdoe, his wife, and Gabdelas, probably their son, and others during the persecution of King Sapor II. F. D. Sept. 29.

DAEGER, ANTHONY THOMAS (1872–1932), bishop. Born in North Vernon, Indiana, on Mar. 5, he studied at St. Francis, Cincinnati, became a Friar Minor, taking the name Albert, continued his studies, and was ordained in 1896. After pastoral work in Ohio, Missouri, and Nebraska, he worked with the Indians at Peña Blanca, New Mexico, from 1902 to 1919, when he was appointed bishop of Santa Fe, New Mexico. He died there on Dec. 2.

DAFROSA, ST., martyr. *See* Bibiana, St.

DAGAEUS, ST. (d. 560?). He was bishop of Iniskin, near Dundalk, Ireland. F. D. Aug. 18.

DAGOBERT II (d. 679), king. Son of King

Sigebert III, he succeeded in 656 to the Austrasian throne while still a child. He was exiled by his guardian, Grimoald, spent some time in Ireland, and recovered his crown in 675 on the murder of Childeric II. He himself was murdered while on a hunting trip, reputedly at the instigation of Ebroin, mayor of the palace. Although the murder was a political one, it was traditional to speak of him as a martyr and he was honored locally on Dec. 23.

DAGUESSEAU, HENRI FRANÇOIS (1668–1751), chancellor. Born in Limoges, France, on Nov. 27, he studied law under his father, became advocate general of the parliament of Paris at twenty-two, and after ten years became attorney general. He re-established judicial order, reformed the management of hospitals, and served with fame during a period of war and famine. He opposed the bull *Ungenitus* as a firm Gallican, was chancellor for a short time in 1717, and again from 1720 to 1722. He then agreed to the registration of the papal bull. His political opponent, Cardinal Dubois, forced him out of office and he retired to his estate at Fresnes for five years. He served again as chancellor from 1727 to 1750, worked to make uniform the laws of the various provinces of France, and died in Paris on Feb. 5.

DALBERG, ADOLPHUS VON (1678–1737). Born on May 29, he was provost of Zelle, Hanover, and was elected prince-abbot of Fulda in 1724. Interested in restoring the educational reputation of that center, he founded a university, called Alma Adolphina, which took its philosophy and theology faculties from the Jesuit and Benedictine staffs already there, and built law and medicine by bringing in scholars from abroad. The school was opened in 1733, passed to the Benedictines when the Jesuits were suppressed in 1773, and closed in 1805 after their monastery was secularized. He died in Hammelburg, Franconia, on Nov. 3.

DALBY, BL. ROBERT (d. 1589), martyr. Born in Hemingborough, England, he became a convert while a minister, went to Douai, where he was ordained, re-entered England in 1588, and was hanged, drawn, and quartered at York for his priesthood. F. D. Mar. 16.

DALGAIRNS, JOHN DOBREE (1818–1876). Born on the Island of Guernsey on Oct. 21, he graduated from Oxford in 1839, joined John Henry Newman at Littlemore in 1842, wrote a series of lives of early English saints for Newman, and became a convert in 1845. He was ordained in 1846, became an Oratorian in 1847, and worked in London and Birmingham until he succeeded Fr. Frederick Faber as superior in 1863. In 1869 he began an intensive series of debates with Thomas Huxley, John Morley, Leslie Stephen, and James Martineau, which drained his health. Other members of the Metaphysical Society to which he belonged were Manning and Ward. He died near Brighton, England, on Apr. 6.

DALLAN FORGAILL, ST. (d. 598). Born in Connaught, Ireland, he was a scholar and poet (*Ambra Choluim Kille* was written in praise of St. Columba), became blind, and was killed by pirates. He was honored locally as a martyr. F. D. Jan. 29.

DALLEY, WILLIAM BEDE (1831–1888). Born in Sydney, Australia, he was educated at St. Mary's College there, became a lawyer in 1856, and was a representative in the first parliament in 1857, solicitor general in 1858–69, and attorney general in 1875–77 and again in 1883–85. He was acting premier in the latter year and sent troops to the Sudan after the fall of Khartoum. In 1887 he became the first Australian to be named to the imperial privy council. He died in Sydney on Oct. 28.

DALLYN, VIOLA MEYNELL (1888?–1956), author. Daughter of Wilfrid and Alice Meynell, she was educated chiefly in their English home in Kensington, where she was born. She married John Dallyn, a Sussex farmer, in 1922, and wrote *Girl Adoring* (1928), *Alice Meynell: A Memoir* (1929), *The Frozen Ocean* (poems; 1931), *The Poets Walk* (1936), *Kissing the Rod* (short stories; 1937), *Friends of a Lifetime* (1940), and *Louise* (more stories; 1954). She died in Greatham, near Pulsborough, England, on Oct. 27.

DALMATIUS, ST. (d. 304), bishop and martyr. Born a pagan in Monza, he preached in Italy and Gaul, became bishop of Pavia, Italy, in 303, and was slain during the reign of Maximian. F. D. Dec. 5.

DALMATIUS, ST. (d. 580). He became bishop of Rodez, France, in 524 and suffered from the inroads of the Visigoth King Amalric. F. D. Nov. 13.

DALTON, JOHN (1814–1874), translator. Born in Ireland, he was brought up in Coventry, England, went to Oscott College, was ordained in 1837, and served in parishes in Northampton, Norwich, and Lynn. He translated the autobiography of St. Teresa and several of her other writings and a life of Cardinal Ximenes. He died in Maddermarket, Norwich, England, on Feb. 15.

DALY, JAMES J. (1872–1953), editor. Born in Chicago, Illinois, on Feb. 1, he studied at St. Ignatius College there and at St. Louis, and was ordained in 1905. He was literary editor of *America* in 1909–11, taught in several schools and colleges, including Detroit, and served as assistant editor of *Queen's Work* from 1920 to 1924 and as literary editor of *Thought* from then until 1939. He wrote *Life of St. John Berchmans*, *The Jesuit in Focus*, two collections of essays (*A Cheerful Ascetic* and *The Road to Peace*), and *Boscobel*, a collection of poems. His reviews were penetrating and of great assistance to younger writers. He died in Detroit on Aug. 17.

DALY, THOMAS A. (1864–1941). Born in Kerry, Ireland, he was ordained in 1900, engaged in mission activities, established the Good Shepherd parish in New York City in 1912, and from 1934 until his death there on Jan. 8 was first consultor of the Paulists.

DALY, THOMAS AUGUSTINE (1871–1948), journalist. Born in Philadelphia on May 28, he studied at Villanova and Fordham, but did not graduate, and received an honorary doctorate from the latter in 1910; he also was honored by Notre Dame and Boston College. He was a reporter on the Philadelphia *Record,* editor of the *Catholic Standard and Times* there (1898–1915), then on the staff of the *Evening Ledger* and the *Record,* and from 1929 until his death a columnist on the *Evening Bulletin.* He married Nannie Barrett in 1896 and published *Songs of Wedlock* (1916); a humorous series in Italian dialect — *Canzoni* (1906), *Carmina* (1909), *Madrigali* (1912), *McAroni Ballads* (1919); *Selected Poems* in 1936; an amusing prose narrative of family life, *Herself and the Houseful;* and, with Christopher Morley, *The House of Dooner.* Much of his work is autobiographical; it all reveals a sympathetic and light touch. He died in Philadelphia on Oct. 4.

DAMASUS I, ST. (306?–384), pope. Of Spanish descent, he was probably born in Rome, the son of a priest, and became a deacon in his father's church. He succeeded Pope Liberius to the papacy on Oct. 1, 366, after a minority of the clergy had elected another deacon, Ursinus, who accepted their vote, became an antipope, and was expelled from Rome by Felix Valerian. In 374, Damasus called a council at Rome which listed the authentic books of the Bible. He successfully opposed Arianism and practically eliminated it from the empire. During his pontificate, in 380, Theodosius in the East and Gratian in the West declared Christianity the religion of the Roman Empire. In 382 he convoked a council to denounce Apollinarianism. St. Jerome came to Rome to participate, remained as Damasus' secretary, and at the pope's request and encouragement began his biblical commentaries and studies which were to lead to the Vulgate. Damasus did much to enhance the prestige of the papacy and to consolidate its supremacy (he proclaimed Rome superior to the patriarchates of Alexandria and Antioch). A patron of the arts, he restored many shrines, buildings, and tombs of the martyrs (many of the inscriptions and epigrams he composed for them are extant), and developed the Latin liturgy. F. D. Dec. 11.

DAMASUS II (d. 1048), pope. Poppo of Bavaria was the third German to be raised to the papacy. News of the death of Clement II reached Emperor Henry III late; Benedict IX was still supported by Tuscany; Henry appointed Poppo, who was bishop of Brixen, in Jan. 1048. He was enthroned at the Lateran palace in Rome on July 17, but died of malaria at Palestrina, Italy, in less than a month, on Aug. 9.

DAMBERGER, JOSEPH FERDINAND (1795–1859), historian. Born in Passau, Bavaria, on Mar. 1, he studied law at Landshut, and theology at Salzburg and Munich, and was ordained in 1818. He preached at Landshut and Munich and in 1837 became a Jesuit, spending ten years at Brieg, Switzerland. He taught church history at Lucerne, published his missionary sermons, and went to Innsbruck and then to Ratisbon when the Jesuits were expelled in 1847. He died in Schäftlarn, Bavaria, on Apr. 1. He wrote several historical studies, including the fifteen-volume history of the Church in the Middle Ages to the year 1378.

DAMIAN, ST. (d. 303?), martyr. *See* Cosmas, St.

DAMIAN, ST. (d. 710). Appointed bishop of Pavia, Italy, in 680, he firmly opposed the Monothelite heresy and served as peacemaker between Byzantium and Lombardy. F. D. Apr. 12.

DAMIAN, ST. Two martyrs of unknown dates are honored on Feb. 12: one was put to death in northern Africa, the other in Rome.

DAMIEN, FATHER. *See* Veuster, Joseph de.

DANDOLO, ENRICO (1105?–1205). Of a leading Venetian family, he went to Constantinople in 1171 to ask for peace terms from Emperor Manuel Comnenus for the plague-stricken Venetian army; he was tortured by the emperor and almost lost his sight. He held several other diplomatic posts, was one of the electors of the doge in 1178, and became doge of Venice in 1192. He ended the commercial quarrel with Verona, fought Zara and Pisa, and continued to meet difficulty in his relations with the Eastern emperor, now Alexis III. In 1201 he joined the fourth crusade, attacked Zara in 1202, suggested the occupation of Greece, and led the Venetian fleet in its assault on the sea wall of Constantinople and entered that city in 1203. The eastern empire was then partitioned between Venice and the crusaders. He died in Constantinople on June 14, soon after a disastrous attack on Bulgaria.

DANEHY, THOMAS JOSEPH (1914–1959), bishop. Born in Fort Wayne, Indiana, on May 19, he studied at seminaries in Detroit, Collegeville, and Cincinnati, and in 1934 entered Maryknoll. He was ordained in Rome in 1939, taught in Clarks Summit, Pennsylvania, and in 1942 was among the first Maryknoll priests assigned to mission work in Bolivia. He spent the rest of his life among the Aymara Indians at the headwaters of the Amazon River and was called the "jungle bishop." In 1949 he was appointed apostolic administrator of the Pando vicariate and titular bishop of Bita in 1953. He died in Lima, Peru, on Oct. 9.

DANEI, PAOLO FRANCESCO. See Paul of the Cross, St.

DANIEL, ST. (d. 168), martyr. A deacon assisting St. Prosdocimus in evangelizing northern Italy, he was put to death near Padua. F. D. Jan. 3.

DANIEL, ST. (d. 309). See Elias, St.

DANIEL, ST. (d. 329?). He, SS. Leontius, Maurice, and forty-two others were put to death at Nicopolis in Armenia during the last years of the persecution of Licinius. F. D. July 10.

DANIEL, ST. (d. 344), martyr. He was put to death, with St. Verda, during the persecution of King Sapor II of Persia. F. D. Feb. 21.

DANIEL, ST. (d. 545). St. Dyfrig consecrated him the first bishop of Bangor, Wales. F. D. Sept. 11.

DANIEL (d. 745), bishop. Educated under the Irish scholar Maildubh at Malmesbury, England, he was a scholar, friend and informant of SS. Aldhelm and Bede, and one of the chief forces inspiring the mission of St. Boniface in Germany. He was named bishop of the West Saxons, a see including seven large shires, of which he retained only Hampshire and Surrey as time passed; he also ruled the diocese of Winchester from 705 until 744. He was blind in his last years.

DANIEL, ST. (d. 1227), martyr. Franciscan provincial of Calabria, Italy, he was sent with six other friars (Angelo, Domnus, Hugolino, Leo, Nicholas and Samuel) by St. Francis to evangelize the Mohammedans. When they arrived in Ceuta, Morocco, they were thought to be madmen; when they were found to be missioners they were beheaded. They were canonized in 1516. F. D. Oct. 10.

DANIEL, ANTOINE (1601–1648), martyr. Born in Dieppe, France, on May 27, he studied law but entered the Jesuit novitiate in Rouen in 1621. After teaching at Rouen for four years, he studied theology at Clermont, was ordained in 1630, and assigned to the College of Eu. In 1632, with three other priests, he was sent as a missionary to Cape Breton Island in Acadia, New France. After a year he was assigned to Quebec, from which mission headquarters he became most successful with young Hurons. In 1636 he founded a school for Indian boys at Quebec. He continued to travel and preach until he was slain on July 4 by an Iroquois war party at Teanaustaye near Hillsdale, Ontario. He was canonized by Pope Pius XI in 1930. F. D. Sept. 26 (also, Mar. 16).

JOHN A. O'BRIEN, The American Martyrs (New York, Appleton, 1935).

DANIEL, CHARLES (1818–1893). Born in Beauvais, France, on Dec. 31, he became a Jesuit in 1841, taught at St. Acheul, and in 1857, with Fr. Gagarin, founded Études de théologie et d'histoire, which he edited until 1870. For it he wrote short biographies, an account of the Vatican Council, and studies of optimism and positivism; his published books include biographies of St. Margaret Mary Alacoque and of earlier Jesuit teachers. He died in Paris on Jan. 1.

DANIEL, GABRIEL (1649–1728), historian. Born in Rouen, France, on Feb. 8, he became a Jesuit in 1667, was appointed historiographer to King Louis XIV, wrote against Descartes' Voyage du monde and Provincial Letters, against the Jansenists, and against the Dominican Natalis Alexander on probabilism and grace. His seventeen-volume History of France, completed in 1713, was his most important work. He died in Paris on June 23.

DANIEL, JOHN (1745–1823). Born in Lancashire, England, he studied and was ordained at Douai, taught philosophy and theology there, and became president of the college in 1792. He was imprisoned for two years at the start of the French Revolution, and released and sent to England in 1795, where he lived in Lancashire until 1802. From that date until 1815 he was in France seeking restitution of damage to church property at Douai amounting to half a million pounds; this was paid by the French government, but immediately seized by the British government and never returned. Daniel wrote an Ecclesiastical History of the Britons and Saxons (1815). He died in Paris on Oct. 3.

DANIEL THE STYLITE, ST. (409?–493). A native of Maratha, on the upper Euphrates, he entered a nearby monastery at twelve and became a monk there. While on a journey to Antioch with his abbot, he saw St. Simeon on his pillar and was so impressed that, after a pilgrimage to the Holy Land and nine years as a hermit outside Constantinople, he decided to imitate the life of Simeon. Emperor Leo I built him a series of pillars, on which he lived thirty-three years of his life. He became widely known, preaching to, advising, and comforting great crowds. Counselor to Emperors Leo I and Zeno, he came down from his pillar only once, to denounce Basilicus for supporting the Eutychians and for usurping the throne of the exiled Zeno. F. D. Dec. 11.

DANTE ALIGHIERI (1265–1321), poet. Born in Florence, Italy, in May or June, son of Alighiero Alighieri, a Guelph notary, and Bella Abati (said to have been the daughter of a Ghibelline noble), he was writing poetry by the age of eighteen, influenced by Guido Cavalcanti, Guido Guinicelli, and Brunetto Latini, and probably lived in Bologna in 1287. He fought with Guelph cavalry at the battle of

Campaldino in 1289, which crushed Ghibelline power; after the rewriting of the Florentine constitution he joined the guild of physicians and apothecaries, and spoke frequently before the general council on the need of judicial and other reforms. His *Vita nuova*, part poetry, part prose, had been completed by 1294, and recounts his love for Beatrice (probably daughter of Folco Portinari and wife of Simone de' Bardi), whom he had known from the time they both were nine, and who died in 1290. Dante married Gemma Donati in 1292. He held conciliar posts in Florence from 1295 on, was one of six priors in charge of the magistracy in 1300, approved existing anti-papal measures, faced increasing factionalism, and so strongly opposed the papal legate, Cardinal Matthew d'Asquasparta, that Florence was placed under interdict. Dante voted in 1301 to refuse to supply 100 horsemen for the papal army of Boniface VIII and went to Rome to present the Florentine position. When the pro-papal French faction triumphed and Charles of Valois entered Florence, Dante (who probably was in Siena at the time) and other leaders were heavily fined, barred permanently from holding office, and later in 1302 condemned to be burned to death. He worked with other Guelph exiles in Arazzo, Forlì, and Siena, then seems to have avoided politics for a while. He wrote of his exile in *Canzone of the Three Ladies*; other lyrical poems, amatory and allegorical, and the unfinished *De vulgari eloquentia* (a Latin treatise on the use of the vernacular for lyric poetry) were written before 1306, probably at Verona, where Lord Bartolommeo della Scala (d. 1304) gave him refuge. Dante probably began at Lunigiana his prose *Convivio*, a reflection on philosophy and poetry, also unfinished, written between 1304 and 1308. About 1309 (and dating continues to be conjectural) he wrote *De monarchia*, supporting the need of a single emperor for Christendom, who would direct man in earthly felicity while the pope called man's attention to revelation and led him toward eternal life. The inspiration was Henry of Luxembourg, who became Emperor Henry VII in 1308. Although Henry came to the edge of Florence, he failed to take the city, and died in 1313; Dante's letter to the cardinals after the death of Pope Clement V in 1314, pleading with them to return the papacy to Rome from France, also met with no success and further crushed his hopes. He settled in Ravenna about 1317, still under sentence of death at Florence, and looked up to twenty-five-year-old Can Grande della Scala, imperial vicar in Lombardy, as the new ideal leader of Italy and Christendom. He was now at work on the *Divine Comedy*. He completed *Inferno* and *Purgatorio*, and in 1319–21 sent installments of *Paradiso* to Can Grande as they were finished. The *Commedia*

(Dante's complete title), a poem of 100 cantos, written in *terza rima* which he developed to formal perfection, is an allegory of human life. It is pointedly didactic, aimed to rebuke, redeem, and restore a corrupt world which had turned from moral and intellectual goodness to avoid reason, and embrace the seven deadly sins. Evil, temporizing, uncontrolled emotion mislead man; the poet-narrator-hero learns this as he passes from the tragedy of hell, inhabited by those who turn their back on truth or help injustice to triumph, to purgatory, amid the beauties of nature, where love is set in order and man is led past the highest of seven terraces to the earthly paradise. Beatrice, who represents philosophy illumined by revelation, leads the pilgrim through the nine preparatory heavens to a place of full understanding at the edge of the beatific vision; there she is replaced by the contemplative St. Bernard, who commends the narrator to the Virgin Mary; the poem and the quest end when the understanding and will become one with the divine. Into the poem Dante threw the breadth of his knowledge of theology (chiefly that of Thomas Aquinas) and philosophy, mediaeval mysticism and contemporary history, scientific speculation and ordinary daily living. An encyclopedic number of persons is described along the way, from Vergil of the pagan classical world to kings, princes, popes, and the lesser estates, to Lucy and other saints, including Beatrice, at hand to inspire in all three parts of the narrative. The artistic fusion makes his work a unique literary and philosophical achievement. Dante died in Ravenna, Italy, on Sept. 14.

MICHELE BARBI, *Life of Dante*, trans. Paul Ruggiers (Berkeley, U. of California, 1954); CHARLES H. GRANDGENT, *Discourses on Dante* (Cambridge, Harvard, 1924); GERALD G. WALSH, *Dante Alighieri, Citizen of Christendom* (Milwaukee, Bruce, 1946).

DANTI, PELLEGRINO (1537–1586), mathematician. Born in Perugia, Italy, he learned painting and architecture from his family, became a Dominican in 1555 and took the name Ignazio, devoted himself to the study of science, and in 1567 was invited to Florence by Duke Cosmo I of Tuscany. For Pope Sixtus V he drew the plans for a Dominican church at Bosco; for the duke's court he furthered mathematical and astronomical studies which prepared the way for Galileo. He directed the building of canals in the Florentine area, mapped the Perugian republic, taught mathematics at Bologna, and was brought to Rome by Pope Gregory XIII to serve on the commission to reform the calendar. Danti made the plans used by the architect Fontana in repairing the Claudian harbor, was in charge of the painters completing the work in the Vatican begun by Raphael, translated and annotated part of Euclid, and wrote a life of the architect Vignola. In 1583, Gregory made him bishop of Alatri; there he held a reform synod and was highly regarded by the grateful poor. He died in Alatri, Italy, on Oct. 10.

DANTI, VINCENZO (1530–1576), sculptor. Brother of Pellegrino, he was born in Perugia, Italy, and was a goldsmith, architect, and poet. A statue of Pope Julius III in Perugia, the *Decapitation of St. John the Baptist* and the completion of Sansovino's *Baptism of Christ*, both for the baptistry at Florence, and other marbles there are his best works. He died on May 24.

DANTINE, MAURUS (1688–1746). Born in Gourieux, Belgium, on Apr. 1, he became a Benedictine, prepared the chronological charts for the Maurist *Art of Verifying Dates*, translated the Psalms, with a commentary, and worked with Dom Carpentier on a new edition of the DuCange *Lexicon*. He died in Paris on Nov. 3.

DA PONTE, LORENZO. *See* Ponte, Lorenzo da.

DARBOY, GEORGES (1813–1871), archbishop. Born in Fayl-Billot, France, he was ordained in 1836, was curate at St. Dizier, taught in Langres, and became a canon of Notre Dame, Paris, and a monsignor. In 1859 he was named bishop of Nancy, where he built a school, enlarged the seminary, and published on education. Other writings include lives of SS. Thomas à Becket and Denis the Areopagite. He became archbishop of Paris in 1863, consecrated the restored basilica of Notre Dame and brought discipline to the see, but was a Gallican in political outlook. He opposed papal infallibility and left the Vatican Council before the question was brought to a vote; he later subscribed to it, however. During the siege of Paris by the Commune, he was a model pastor; he was seized in April 1871 by that anti-religious body and executed at La Roquette on May 24. With him died Frs. Deguerry, pastor of La Madeleine; Allard, who had served with the medical corps during the battle; two Jesuits, Frs. Ducoudray, rector of the army preparatory school of Ste. Geneviève, and Clerc, a distinguished naval officer; and Senator Bonjean, a judge.

DARDEL, JEAN (14th century), bishop. Born in Estampes, France, he became a Friar Minor and about 1375 went to Jerusalem and then to Cairo. He became adviser to the imprisoned King Leo of Armenia, traveled through Europe seeking ransom, and eventually persuaded the king of Aragon to intercede. Leo was released in 1382, paid homage to the antipope Clement VII and settled in Spain. As a reward Clement made Dardel bishop of Tortiboli, Italy, where he wrote *Chronique d'Arménie*.

DARESTE DE LA CHAVANNE, ANTOINE (1820–1882), historian. Born in Paris on Oct.

25, he taught in Versailles, Rennes, and Paris, then at Grenoble. He held the chair of history at Lyons for twenty years, was dean of the faculty of letters, and wrote several histories of France honored by the French Academy, including an account of the period from St. Louis to Louis XVI. He was active in the founding of the Catholic University of Lyons. He died in Lucenay-les-Aix, France, on Aug. 6.

DARET, JACQUES (15th century), painter. Possibly "Le Maitre de Flémalle" (although the identification is also applied to Robert Campin), whose work was found in the Flemish abbey of that name, he studied under Campin at Tournay, where he became a member of the painters' guild in 1432. He was also active in Lille, Bruges, and Arras, in which last place he painted the altarpiece for the abbey of St. Vaast. He was alive as late as 1468.

DARIA, ST., martyr. *See* Chrysanthus, St.

DARLUGDACH, ST. (d. 524?). She succeeded St. Brigid as abbess of Kildare, Ireland. F. D. Feb. 1.

DARRAS, JOSEPH EPIPHANE (1825–1878), historian. Born in Troyes, France, he studied and was ordained there, but was forced out of his teaching position at its seminary by Napoleon because of his defense of the bishops in 1811. He continued to oppose Gallicanism, served as tutor to Prince Eugène de Bauffremont, and wrote a history of the Church, a life of Christ, a biography of St. Denis, and worked with Collin on a twenty-five-volume series of lives of the saints. His work was often marred by a lack of knowledge of historical research, particularly into the background of ecclesiastical history. He died in Paris on Nov. 8.

DARRELL, WILLIAM (1651–1721), theologian. Born in Buckinghamshire, England, he became a Jesuit in 1671, wrote controversial and apologetical works, of which *A Gentleman Instructed in the Conduct of a Virtuous and Happy Life* was most frequently reprinted, and died at St. Omer, France, on Feb. 28.

DASIUS, ST. (d. 303?), martyr. A Roman soldier stationed at Durostorum, Bulgaria, he was beheaded, according to legend, when he refused to sacrifice to the gods. F. D. Nov. 20.

DASIUS, ST. (d. 303?), martyr. *See* Caius, St.

DATHUS, ST. (d. 190). He was bishop of Ravenna, Italy, during the reign of Emperor Commodus. F. D. July 3.

DATIUS, ST. (d. 552), bishop. His storm-beset career included an attempt to save Milan, of which he became bishop in 530, from the Goths. It is believed that he was captured and later liberated through the help of Cassiodorus. Traveling to Constantinople, he worked in support of Pope Vigilius against Emperor Justinian. F. D. Jan. 14.

DATIVA, ST. (d. 484), martyr. *See* Dionysia, St.

DAUBLAIN, BONAVENTURE (18th century). The forty-sixth and last Norbertine abbot of Bonne-Ésperance, near Binche, France, he saw his abbey attacked by revolutionary forces in 1792 and again in 1794, when he and sixty-seven associates were driven out.

DAUBRÉE, GABRIEL AUGUSTE (1814–1896), geologist. Born in Metz, Lorraine, on June 14, he studied engineering in Paris, was in charge of the mines in Alsace at twenty, served on commissions to foreign countries, wrote on ore deposits in Scandinavia and the geology of the Rhine basin, and was appointed professor of geology at Strassburg. He became famous for studies in producing artificial minerals, the formation of crystalline rocks, the physics of mountain making, the chemistry of hot springs, and the classification of meteorites. In 1861 he was elected a member of the Academy of Sciences and became professor of geology at the Paris Museum of Natural History. The meteorite mineral daubréelite is named for him. He died in Paris on May 29.

DAUMER, GEORG FRIEDRICH (1800–1875), poet. Born in Nuremberg, Germany, on Mar. 5, he studied there under Hegel and at Leipzig and Erlangen, and taught at the gymnasium of Nuremberg until 1832, when ill health forced his retirement. He was guardian and tutor of Kaspar Hauser, writing several books on that controversial figure. His first philosophical works were bitterly anti-Christian, a position he reached after leaning toward pietism, skepticism, and pantheism. He went to Frankfort in 1850, was converted in 1858, and wrote four philosophical works, one against the writings of David Strauss. Two volumes of imitations of Persian poetry (some of them later set to music by Brahms) and four of original poetry appeared between 1852 and 1862. He died in Würzburg, Bavaria, on Dec. 14.

D'AURIOL, PIERRE. *See* Petrus Aureoli.

D'AVENANT, WILLIAM (1606–1668), dramatist. Born in Oxford, England, in Feb., son of an innkeeper and possibly the godson of Shakespeare, he was educated in the grammar school there and entered the service first of the duchess of Richmond and then of Fulke Greville, Lord Brooke. He succeeded Ben Jonson as poet laureate, became manager of the Cockpit Theatre in 1638, fought for the king in the civil war, was knighted in 1643, went into exile to France, and became a convert there about 1644. He was imprisoned for two years on his return. In 1658 he reopened the Cockpit and directed plays during the reign of Charles II. He himself wrote some thirty dramas, as well as *Gondibert*, a long fragment of an unfinished epic poem. He revised Shakespeare's *Measure for Measure* and, with Dryden, *The Tempest*. He introduced opera to the English stage and was the first to use women for female roles. He died in London on Apr. 7.

DAVENPORT, CHRISTOPHER (1598–1680), theologian. Born in Coventry, England, son of John Davenport, a local alderman, he studied there and at Dublin and Oxford, became a convert, and went to Douai in 1615. There he became a Franciscan, taking the name Franciscus à Sancta Clara, took his degree in theology at Salamanca, and returned as professor at St. Bonaventure's College in Douai. He served in England as chaplain to Queen Henrietta Maria, published a treatise on the Thirty-nine Articles hoping to bring about reunion, and was condemned by the Spanish Index but not by Rome. In 1637 he was appointed provincial of the English Recollects, a position he held three times. He later was chaplain to Queen Catharine of Braganza, converted Anne, duchess of York, shuttled between Flanders and England, and wrote nearly a score of books on his order, the Church in England, the belief of Catholics, and contemporary controversy. He died on May 31. He is also known as Francis Hunt and Francis Coventry.

DAVID I (1084–1153), king of Scotland. Son of Malcolm III and St. Margaret, he married Countess Matilda of Northampton and became an English baron thereby, was prince of Cambria, and succeeded his brother Alexander I as king of Scotland in 1124. He fought for Queen Matilda, his niece, against King Stephen, but was defeated in 1138, joined her again in 1140, and failed in an attempt to invade England in 1149. He founded sees, introduced monastic settlements, particularly of the Cistercians, including Melrose, and Augustinian Holyrood, founded many boroughs, established Norman law as the law of the land, began the feudal court, and set up the office of chancellor. He was noted for his justice and charities, died in Carlisle, Scotland, on May 24, and is listed as a saint in both Catholic and Protestant calendars, with a feast day of May 24. Though never canonized, he had a popular cult and his shrine was a place of honor until the Reformation.

DAVID II BRUCE (1324–1371), king of Scotland. Son of Robert I Bruce and Elizabeth de Burgh, he was born in Dunfermline, Scotland, on Mar. 5, succeeded his father in 1329, and was crowned in 1331. His army, led by Archibald Douglas, the regent, was defeated by English-supported Edward Baliol at Halidon Hill in 1333 and the young prince fled to France, where he remained until 1341. He took over the reins of government in 1342, invaded England at the urging of Philip of France, and was captured in 1346 and held prisoner for eleven years. He paid a huge ransom to England for his final release. He was married to Joanna, sister of Edward III, in 1328 and a year after her death in 1362 married Margaret Drummond, a widow, from whom he separated in 1369. Church and state both suffered from wide neglect during his reign. He died in Edinburgh on Feb. 22.

DAVID, ST. (520?–589?), bishop. Born in Cardigan, Wales, and ordained, he studied with St. Paulinus, founding a great many monasteries before he settled at Mynyw. His asceticism was intense and he directed the spiritual career of many who sought him out. A legend-packed biography by Rhygyfach was adapted by Giraldus Cambrensis. He is the patron of Wales. F. D. Mar. 1.

DAVID, BL. (d. 1179). Born in Florence, Italy, he became a Cistercian at Clairvaux in 1131, and was sent to Himmerode, Germany, as abbot-founder. F. D. Dec. 11.

DAVID. *See* Gleb; also, Pathy.

DAVID, ARMAND (1826–1900), zoologist. Born in Esplette, France, he became a member of the Congregation of the Mission in 1848 and was ordained in 1862 and sent to Peking, China. There he developed a large scientific museum and was able to send rare specimens of animals and plants back to France. He helped the development of systematic zoology, identifying some 200 species of wild animals in China (sixty-three hitherto unknown) and 800 species of birds (sixty-five unknown). He also made large collections of reptiles, fish, and insects, and located fifty-two new species of rhododendron and an equal number of gentian. In the midst of this scientific activity he served as a devoted missionary priest in China and Tibet.

DAVID, GERARD (1450?–1523), painter. Born in Oudewater, Holland, son of the painter and illustrator John David, he became a master painter in 1484 and dean of the Guild of St. Luke in 1501, probably traveled to Italy, and on his return in 1496 married Cornelia Cnoop, daughter of the dean of the goldsmiths' guild. His best religious work, influenced by Van Eyck and Hans Memling, was done before 1515. His Child Jesus, a figure in many paintings, was an influence on subsequent painters; he drew portraits with detailed costuming, interesting landscapes, and many miniatures. His wife also was a miniaturist. He died in Bruges, Flanders, on Aug. 13.

DAVID, JOHANNES BAPTISTA (1801–1866), philologist. Born in Lier, Flanders, he held the chair of Belgian history and Flemish literature at Louvain for thirty years. Besides work in philology he published a ten-volume history of Belgium, interrupted by his death.

DAVID, JOHN BAPTIST MARY (1761–1841), bishop. Born in Couëron, Brittany, France, on June 4, he studied at Nantes College and the seminary there, joined the Sul-

picians in 1783, and was ordained in 1785. He became a lecturer at the minor seminary at Angers under Fr. Flaget, and accompanied him with Stephen Badin and Guy Chabrat to the United States in 1791. He worked at various missions in Maryland until 1804, when he taught philosophy at Georgetown, then at the Sulpician seminary in Baltimore, became adviser of Mother Seton's Sisters of Charity, and in 1811 accompanied the new Bishop Flaget to his Bardstown, Kentucky, see. He became famed for his missionary activities, founded a seminary there, St. Joseph's College, helped found St. Mary's College and in 1812, the Sisters of Charity of Nazareth. He was named titular bishop of Mauricastro and co-adjutor of Bardstown in 1817, not consecrated until 1819, and succeeded to the see in 1832. He resigned in the following year, attended the second Provincial Council of Baltimore in 1833, and died in Nazareth, Kentucky, on July 12. He wrote such titles as *Compilation of Church Music* (1815), *True Piety* (1814), and *Catechism of Christian Doctrine* (1825), and translated treatises by Bellarmine and St. Alphonsus Liguori.

DAVID OF AUGSBURG (d. 1272), mystic. Born probably in Augsburg, Bavaria, he became a Franciscan at Ratisbon, was master of novices, and with Berthold of Ratisbon inspected Franciscan houses, made missionary tours after 1250, preached widely, and served on the inquisitional body investigating the Waldenses. His *Formula novitiorum, Expositio regulae*, and other Latin works were often attributed to St. Bonaventure and others; in German, David wrote *Der Spiegel der Tugend, Christi Leben unser Vorbild, Von der Anschauung Gottes* and other treatises which made their impress on early German mysticism. He died in Augsburg on Nov. 19.

DAVID OF MUNKTORP, ST. (d. 1080?), bishop. An English monk, he was sent to Västmanland, Sweden, as a missioner and established a monastery at Munktorp. He is reputed to have become the first bishop of Vasteras. F. D. July 15.

DAVID SCOTUS (d. 1139?), historian. An Irishman or Welshman, he became a chaplain at the court of Emperor Henry V at Würzburg, went with the latter to Italy in 1100, and served as royal historiographer. Malmesbury says he was consecrated bishop of Bangor, Wales, in 1120, and attended several English synods. Other annalists say he became a monk under St. Macarius in Würzburg, at the monastery of St. James, founded in 1140.

DAVIES, VEN. WILLIAM (d. 1593), martyr. Born probably in Crois in Yris, Denbighshire, Wales, he studied at Rheims, was ordained in 1585, and returned to the Welsh area for underground service to Catholics there. He was arrested at Holyhead in 1592, managed to continue to say mass in the Beaumaris castle prison through the kindness of an indulgent jailor, but was condemned to death at Ludlow on the charge of being a priest. He was hanged, drawn, and quartered at Beaumaris, Wales, on July 27.

DAVILA Y PADILLA, AUGUSTIN (1562–1604), historian. Born in Mexico City, he received his master's degree from its university at sixteen, became a Dominican in 1579, and taught philosophy and theology in Tlascala and Mexico City. He held high posts in his order, was sent to Rome and Madrid, and wrote an important chronicle of the American mission. He died in Santo Domingo, where he had been made bishop in 1601.

DA VINCI, LEONARDO. See Leonardo da Vinci.

DAVIS, JAMES J. (1852–1926), bishop. Born in Tinvawn, Killarney, Ireland, probably on Nov. 7, he studied at the Carmelite college, Doncmagin, and St. Patrick's, Carlow, and was ordained in 1878. He went to Dubuque, Iowa, in 1878 and did pastoral and missionary work, became chancellor of Davenport, Iowa, and in 1904 was appointed titular bishop of Milopotamus and coadjutor of Davenport. He succeeded to the see in 1906, and died there on Dec. 2.

DAVITUS, ST. (d. 257), bishop and martyr. See Nemesian, St.

DAVITUS, ST. (d. 304), martyr. See Saturninus, St.

DAVY, BL. THOMAS (d. 1537), martyr. See Beer, Bl. Richard.

DAWSON, AENEAS McDONNELL (1810–1894), apologist. Born in Scotland on July 30, he studied at the seminary in Paris, was ordained in 1835, served in the Scots mission until 1855, went to Canada, and was pastor of St. Andrew's, Ottawa. He wrote on the temporal power of the pope, biographies of St. Vincent de Paul and Pius IX, studies of the Northwest Territory, translations from the French, and some poetry. He was a member of the Royal Society of Canada and died in Ottawa on Dec. 29.

DAY, GEORGE (1501?–1556), bishop. Born in Shropshire, England, he graduated from Cambridge, became vice-chancellor of the university, provost of King's College, and in 1543 was consecrated bishop of Chichester by Cranmer. He appears to have accepted Henry VIII's ecclesiastical leadership, but balked at Edward VI's, and voted in parliament against bills approving the Eucharist under two kinds and introducing the Book of Common Prayer. His preaching was declared seditious; he was imprisoned in the Fleet and deprived of office in 1551, being transferred to the custody of the bishop of Ely in 1552. Oddly, he preached both at the funeral of Edward and at the accession

of Mary, whose almoner he became. Cardinal Pole confirmed his bishopric in Jan. 1555; he died on Aug. 2.

DAY, JOHN CHARLES (1826–1908), judge. Born near Bath, England, he studied at Rome and Fribourg, graduated from London, and rose through the legal profession to serve on the Queen's High Court of Justice from 1882 to 1901. He was knighted in 1882, published *Common Law Procedure Acts*, edited Roscoe's *Evidence at Nisi Prius*, was made privy councilor in 1902, and died in Newbury on June 13. Because of the severity of his legal decisions he was called "Day of Reckoning" and "Judgment Day" in contemporary writings.

DEAN, BL. WILLIAM (d. 1588), martyr. Born in Linton, Yorkshire, England, he became a minister, was converted, and was ordained at Rheims in 1581. He returned to England, was captured, and hanged in London for being a priest. He was beatified in 1929. Ven. Henry Webley, accused of aiding him, was put to death with him. F. D. Aug. 28.

DEASE, THOMAS (1568–1651), bishop. Born in Ireland, he studied in Paris, was ordained, was rector of the Irish College there, and in 1662 was consecrated bishop of Meath, Ireland. He returned to Ireland, preached loyalty to England, was accused by the papal nuncio of having caused the break in the friendship of Preston and O'Neill, the nationalist generals, and died in Galway.

DECHAMPS, ADOLPHE (1807–1875), statesman. Born in Melle, Belgium, on June 17, he attracted political attention by his writings in Catholic newspapers, and was cofounder of *Revue de Bruxelles*. In 1834 he was elected to the chamber of representatives and played an active part in supporting bills for reorganizing the communes and establishing religious instruction in the schools. He became governor of Luxembourg in 1842 and later was minister of public works and of foreign affairs (1843–45). From 1847 to 1864 he was leader of the Catholic minority in the chamber, resigned, wrote several historical studies, and died at Manage, near Brussels, Belgium, on July 19.

DECHAMPS, VICTOR AUGUSTIN (1810–1883), cardinal. Brother of Adolphe, he was born in Melle, Belgium, on Dec. 6, studied in Tournai and Louvain, was ordained in 1834, and in 1835 became a member of the Congregation of the Most Holy Redeemer. He taught theology at Witten, was rector at Liège, gained a reputation as a preacher, and helped to found the Confraternity of the Holy Family. In 1849 he became consultor general of his congregation, served at Naples and Rome, and in 1865 was named bishop of Namur and in 1875 archbishop of Mechlin and primate of Belgium. He published seventeen volumes of sermons, was active in the defense of Catholic schools, labored at the Vatican Council for the approval of papal infallibility, and died in Mechlin, Belgium, on Sept. 29.

DECKER, HANS (15th century), sculptor. Living in Nuremberg, Germany, he established a reputation between 1432 and 1446 for realistic stone carvings; two works in local churches were particularly influential: a St. *Christopher* and a *Burial of Christ*. He strove for anatomical accuracy as well as vivid portrayal of emotion.

DECLAN, ST. (6th century?), bishop. Born in Decies, Waterford, Ireland, and a disciple of St. Colman, he visited Rome twice, met St. David in Wales, and was consecrated bishop of Ardmore, Ireland. F. D. July 24.

DECOROSUS, ST. (d. 695). He became bishop of Capua, Italy, about 665, and attended the Council of Rome in 680. F. D. Feb. 15.

DECUMAN, ST. (d. 716). A Welshman, he lived as a recluse in Somersetshire, England, where he was murdered. F. D. Aug. 27. (qd)

DEDEROTH, JOHN (d. 1439). A Benedictine at Münden or Nordheim, he effected great reforms at the monastery of Clus while abbot in 1430–33, and was asked by Duke Otto of Brunswick to reform Bursfield abbey. He was successful there and at Reinhausen before his death on Feb. 6. His reforms resulted in the formation of his three abbeys and three others into the Bursfield Union, secured by John of Hagen in 1446.

DEGER, ERNST (1809–1885), painter. Born in Bockenem, Hanover, on Apr. 15, he studied under Wach in Berlin and Schadow at Düsseldorf, went to Italy in 1837 to study frescoes, was influenced by Overbeck, and returned to Remagen in 1843. In the church of St. Apollinaris there he worked eight years on frescoes depicting the life of Christ; in 1851 he began twelve frescoes on the redemption of man for Frederick William IV of Prussia's chapel near Coblenz. In his later years he painted madonnas and other religious figures in oil, and helped to bring an end to the enthusiasm for the baroque which prevailed. He taught in the academies of art in Munich and Düsseldorf and was a member of the Berlin Academy. He died in Düsseldorf, Germany, on Jan. 27.

DEHAN, RICHARD. *See* Graves, Clotilde.

DEHARBE, JOSEPH (1800–1871), theologian. Born in Strassburg, Alsace, on Apr. 11, he became a Jesuit in 1817, taught in Brieg, Switzerland, served as a missioner, was cofounder of the Academy of St. Charles Borromeo at Lucerne in 1845, and two years later was forced into exile when his order was suppressed. He worked on missions in Germany and prepared a long-popular series of cate-

chisms. He died at Maria-Laach near Andernach, Germany, on Nov. 8.

DEICOLUS, ST. (d. 625?). A Welsh monk, he traveled to France as a companion of St. Columbinus, established the monastery of Lure, and died there as a hermit. F. D. Jan. 13.

DEIFER, ST. (6th century). He was the founder and abbot of the monastery of Bodfari, Flintshire, Wales. F. D. Mar. 7.

DEJARDIN, BL. MARIE MAGDALEN (d. 1794), martyr. An Ursuline sister, under the name Marie Augustin, she was guillotined with others of her community at Valenciennes during the French Revolution. She was beatified in 1920. F. D. Oct. 17.

DE LA CROIX, CHARLES (1792–1869), missioner. Born in Hoorbeke St. Corneille, Belgium, on Oct. 28, he studied in Ghent, was imprisoned when the seminary students refused to acknowledge the bishop Napoleon imposed on them (his brother Joseph died while they were prisoners), and after release and ordination went to the United States to serve Bishop Dubourg of Louisiana. He worked at Barrens, Missouri (where he built a seminary), at Florissant, among the Osage Indians, and helped to prepare the mission area for Fr. De Smet and other Jesuits. He labored in parishes in lower Louisiana before his health broke, returned to Ghent, Belgium, and served as canon of its cathedral until his death on Aug. 20.

DELACROIX, FERDINAND VICTOR EUGÈNE (1798–1863), painter. Born in Carenton St. Maurice, France, on Apr. 26, he studied there under Guérin, engaged in hack work to keep himself alive through great poverty, and began to make a name for himself about 1818 with the first of a number of romantic narrative canvases. The classicists condemned him harshly, but the quarrel over his worth aided him; he visited England in 1825 and studied the colorists there; after 1830 he was a success and was made a chevalier of the Legion of Honor and a member of the Institute of France. His many major works (his total output was more than 9000) reveal his knowledge of history, his poetic instinct, and his command of color. The subjects ranged from the lively *Roman Matrons Sacrificing Their Jewelry* and *Capture of Constantinople by the Crusaders* to the pictorial *Richelieu Saying Mass*, the violently realistic *Murder of the Bishop of Liège*, the deeply tragic *Christ in the Garden of Gethsemane*. The color and excitement of most of his work, particularly those on Spanish and Moorish themes, made him the founder of the French romantic school. His theories were clearly expressed in published essays and letters. He had little business sense and government commissions helped to sustain him. He decorated the interior of the chamber of deputies in the Bourbon palace, the ceiling of the gallery of Apollo in the Louvre, and the library in the Luxembourg (with illustrations from the *Divina Commedia*). He also illustrated editions of Goethe, Scott, and Shakespeare. He died in Paris on Aug. 13.

DELANOUE, BL. JOAN (1666–1736), foundress. Born in Saumur, Anjou, France, she was the youngest of twelve children. On the death of her mother she took over the family shop and developed into an avaricious and selfish woman. Shortly before she was thirty she reformed, and thereafter devoted herself to the care of the sick and poor. In 1704, with two companions, she founded the Sisters of St. Anne and, despite great obstacles, opened the first of many homes for orphans and the destitute. She was beatified in 1947. F. D. Aug. 17.

DELANY, JOHN BERNARD (1864–1906), bishop. Born in Lowell, Massachusetts, on Aug. 9, he studied at Holy Cross, Boston College, and St. Sulpice, Paris, and was ordained in 1891. He served in parishes in Manchester and Portsmouth, New Hampshire, was appointed chancellor of Manchester in 1898, served as the bishop's secretary, and in 1904 was appointed second bishop of Manchester. He died in Manchester on June 11. He was the founder of the diocesan magazine, *Guidon*, and edited it until 1904.

DELANY, SELDEN PEABODY (1874–1935). Born in Fond du Lac, Wisconsin, on Jan. 24, he studied at Harvard and Western Theological seminary, Chicago, and became an episcopal minister in 1899. He was stationed at churches in Massachusetts, Wisconsin, and New York City, edited the *American Church Monthly*, and became a convert in 1930. He was ordained in Rome in 1934. He wrote *Why Rome?* and *Rome from Within*, and *Married Saints*. He was a chaplain in Highland Mills, New York, at his death on July 5.

DELAROCHE, HIPPOLYTE PAUL (1797–1856), artist. Born in Paris on July 17, and better known as Paul, he studied under Watelet and Baron Gros, attracted attention with *Joash Saved from Death by Jehoshabeth* which he exhibited at the Salon in 1822, and became famed for his historical paintings most of which became popular engravings. He became a knight of the Legion of Honor in 1828, a member of the French Institute in 1832, and a professor at the French Academy in 1833. Among his most popular subjects were *Death of Queen Elizabeth*, *Execution of Lady Jane Grey*, *Napoleon at Fontainebleau*, and *The Young Martyr*. Although realistic in scene setting he was overly sentimental in works such as *The Last Prayer of the Children of Edward IV*, and hasty and casual in others. His most spectacular work was the twenty-seven-meter-long hemicycle of the great artists, architects,

and sculptures of the modern period for the École des Beaux-Arts. He died in Paris on Nov. 4.

DE LA SALLE, ST. JEAN BAPTISTE (1651–1719), founder. The eldest of ten children of Louis and Nicolle Moet de la Salle, he was born in Rheims, France, on Apr. 30, tonsured at eleven, educated at St. Sulpice, Paris, and ordained in 1678. He was sent to Rheims, received his doctorate in 1681, and became so interested in education that he gave up his canonry and devoted himself to developing a faculty for four free schools under his direction. At this period, teachers were strikingly ignorant, the profession was not respected, and juvenile delinquency flourished. Twelve men joined St. Jean in a new community, the Brothers of the Christian Schools (papally approved in 1725); others studied at the first teachers' colleges, which he originated at Rheims (1684), Paris (1699), and St. Denis (1709); younger men were placed in a junior seminary which he established. In Paris he began to draft his Rule and completed *The Management of Christian Schools*, outlining group rather than tutorial instruction and stressing the use of the vernacular rather than Latin. He taught the poor at the primary level, as well as establishing a college for the Irish exiles who had followed King James II of England to France. His schools on all levels were later closed because of opposition by Jansenists and by those who wanted manual training as the chief subject taught. The tide turned, however, and the order enjoyed great success. In 1705 he established a reformatory for boys and in 1715 a school for adult criminals. He died on Apr. 7 in St. Yon, Rouen, France, was canonized in 1900, and in 1950 was made patron of teachers by Pope Pius XII. F. D. May 15.

DE LA TAILLE, MAURICE (1872–1933). Born in Semblancay, France, on Nov. 30, he studied in England, became a Jesuit in 1890, did further study at the Sorbonne, and was ordained in 1902. He taught at Angers in 1905–16, was a chaplain during World War I, and after 1919 taught theology at the Gregorian, Rome. He wrote a study of grace and an elaborate presentation of human existence, *Mysterium fidei* (1921). He died in Paris.

DEL BUFALO, ST. CASPAR (1786–1837), founder. Born in Rome, a son of a chef, he was ordained in 1808, only to face exile when Napoleon's army took the city. In 1815, while at Giano, and with the help of Cardinal Cristaldi and Pope Pius VII, he founded the Congregation of the Missioners of the Precious Blood. Italy needed spiritual attention, and new houses were established at Albano and throughout the Kingdom of Naples. At Rome he established many charitable centers, as well as a night oratory. His own missionary endeavors were rigorous and exhausting, and he fell a victim of cholera while preaching in Rome during the plague of 1836. He was canonized in 1954. F. D. Jan. 2.

DELEHAYE, HIPPOLYTE (1859–1941), scholar. Born in Antwerp, Belgium, he studied there and at Louvain and Innsbruck, became a Jesuit in 1876, and was ordained in 1890. He taught at St. Michael's College in Belgium, wrote on Henry of Ghent, was attached to the staff of *Analecta Bollandiana* in 1888, and devoted the rest of his life to hagiographical research, editing the Bollandists' *Acta sanctorum*, except for a period of imprisonment by the Germans in World War I, until his death on Apr. 1. He wrote on the methods and problems of Bollandist research, on the Greek martyrs in Persia, on the pillar-sitting saints, and a biography of St. John Berchmans. He also edited the *Synaxarium ecclesiae Constantinopolitanae*, was honored by Belgium, France, and Britain, and served for more than twenty years as president of the Society of Bollandists. He died in Antwerp.

DELFAU, FRANÇOIS (1637–1676), theologian. Born in Montel, France, he became a Benedictine at seventeen, and an authority on conciliar and patristic matters. He, Robert Guérard, and five others of his order were commissioned by the Congregation of St. Maur to prepare a critical edition of St. Augustine; two volumes were completed after four years of work, but Delfau and Guérard were banished from Paris when the king became offended by Delfau's outspoken attack in *L'abbé commendataire* (1673) against royal appointments of churchmen. He also published an edition of the *Imitation of Christ* with an essay on its authorship. He died in Landevenec, Normandy, on Oct. 13.

DELFINO, DANIEL (18th century), cardinal. He was coadjutor in 1714 to Patriarch Dionigio of Aquileia, Italy, then its 109th and last patriarch. He became a cardinal in 1747.

DELFINO, PIETRO (1444–1525), theologian. Born in Venice, Italy, he became a Camaldolese at Murano, was abbot there in 1479, and general of his order from 1480 to 1513. His more than 4000 letters form a significant account of contemporary Church life, including the difficulties over Savonarola. Delfino refused a cardinalate and died in Venice on Jan. 16.

DELGADO Y CEBRIAN, BL. IGNATIUS (d. 1838), bishop and martyr. He left Spain as a Dominican missioner and served in Tonkin for fifty years, becoming vicar apostolic and bishop. He died of hunger and mistreatment when he was caged for public exhibition at Annam, Indochina. He was beatified in 1900. F. D. July 11.

DELILLE, JACQUES (1738–1813), poet.

Born in Aigueperse, France, on June 22, he studied in Paris, taught at the Collège de la Marche there, and translated Vergil's *Georgics* (1769), which won him membership in the French Academy and the chair of poetry at the Collège de France. He took minor orders but was not ordained, traveled to the Near East, and went into exile from 1794 to 1802, translating *Paradise Lost* while in England. He returned to teaching in France until he went blind, and issued several volumes of descriptive verse. He achieved popularity by his *Les jardins* (1782), *L'Homme des champs* (1800), and *La Pitié* (1803). He died in Paris on May 1.

DE LISLE, AMBROSE. *See* Philips, Ambrose.

DELISLE, CLAUDE (1644–1720), cartographer. A lawyer, he settled in Paris, where he tutored in geography and history, served as royal censor, and designed a map of the world in 1696. He assisted his son Guillaume in the latter's new methodology.

DELISLE, GUILLAUME (1675–1726), cartographer. Born on Feb. 28 in Paris, he worked with his father, Claude, on a *Map of the World* and a *Map of the Continents*, published in 1700, working from new astronomical information and all known existing maps, and producing work of careful and correct topography and scale. He was a member of the Academy of Sciences, taught geography at court, and was the first to hold the office of royal geographer. He died in Paris on Jan. 25.

DELLA CHIESA, BL. ANTONIO (1395–1459). Born in San Germano, near Vercelli, Italy, he became a Dominican at twenty-two despite parental opposition. He was a preaching companion of St. Bernardino of Siena and was prior at Como, Savona, Florence, and Bologna. He died in Como, Italy, on Jan. 22. His cult was approved in 1819. F. D. July 28.

DELORME, PHILIBERT (1515?–1570), architect. Son of Jean de L'Orme, master builder in Lyons, France, who taught him, he also studied in Rome, returned to Lyons about 1536, served as military controller until 1545, then was appointed royal architect. He prevented an English attack on Brest, became a royal almoner, and was given several benefices and made canon of Notre Dame in Paris. It is uncertain whether he remained a layman or took minor orders. From 1541 to 1559 he served Kings Francis I and Henry II as royal architect and restored several châteaux, including Fontainebleau and Vincennes. His fortunes faded at Henry's death; he began a few buildings subsequently, wrote a treatise on architecture which is highly autobiographical, and died in Paris on Jan. 8.

DELPHINA, BL. (1283–1358). Born at Château Puy Michel, Languedoc, France, she married St. Elzear, directed their Neapolitan estates with model kindness, and served Queen Sanchia of Naples as companion. When the latter died, Delphina returned to Provence and became a recluse at Cabrières and then at Apt, where she died on Nov. 26. She and her husband, whom she outlived by thirty-seven years, are reported to have been Franciscan tertiaries. Her cult was approved by Pope Urban VIII. F. D. Dec. 9.

DELPHINUS, ST. (d. 403?). The second bishop of Bordeaux, Gaul, he was known for his part in the conversion of St. Paulinus of Nola. He held a synod in 385–86 to curb Priscillianist errors. F. D. Dec. 24.

DELRIO, MARTIN ANTON (1551–1608), theologian. Born in Antwerp, Belgium, on May 17, he studied at Paris, Douai, Louvain, and Salamanca, became senator, vice-chancellor, and procurator general. He became a Jesuit in 1580 and taught philosophy, theology, and scripture at Douai, Liège, Louvain, Graz, and Salamanca. He wrote studies of Ennius, Seneca, and Polyhistor; a history of Belgium; treatises on the Virgin Mary, magic, civil law, and the poetry of SS. Orientius and Aldhelm; biblical commentaries; and controversial pamphlets against Joseph Scaliger. He died in Louvain, Belgium, on Oct. 19.

DELUIL-MARTIGNY, MARY (1841–1884), foundress. Born in Marseilles, France, on May 28, she was educated there and in Lyons, and in 1872 received the approval of the archbishop of Malines to found the Congregation of the Daughters of the Sacred Heart of Jesus. She established houses at Berchem, near Antwerp, Aix-en-Provence, and at La Servianne, near Marseilles, where she was assassinated by a gardener on Feb. 27. The constitutions of her order were papally approved in 1902.

DEMERS, MODESTE (1809–1871), bishop. Born in St. Nicholas, Quebec, Canada, on Oct. 11, he was ordained at Quebec in 1836 and volunteered for the missions in Oregon. He and Fr. F. N. Blanchet reached Walla Walla, Washington, in Nov. 1838, from where he devoted himself to the care of the Indian tribes south and north of the Columbia River, making converts even as far as at Stuart Lake in British Columbia. In 1847 he was consecrated bishop of Vancouver Island. He brought in the Sisters of St. Anne for the lower schools and the Oblate Fathers for missionary work and for a college in Victoria. The bishop attended the second Plenary Council at Baltimore in 1866 and the Vatican Council, and died in Victoria, British Columbia, on July 21.

DEMETRIA, ST. (d. 363), martyr. She is said to have been daughter of SS. Flavian and Dafrosa and sister of St. Bibiana. F. D. June 21.

DEMETRIAN, ST. (d. 912?), bishop. A native of Cyprus, he became a monk at St. An-

tony's monastery there after his wife's early death. He was later ordained, became abbot, and despite his objections was appointed to the see of Khytri about 887. Late in his life Cyprus was raided by Saracens, and through his intercession many enslaved Cypriot Christians were freed. F. D. Nov. 6.

DEMETRIUS, ST. (126–231), bishop. Patriarch of Alexandria, Egypt, for forty-two years, he made the catechetical school there famous. He appointed Origen its director, but objected to his preaching as a layman in Caesarea, and expelled him from the diocese fifteen years later when Origen was ordained later without his permission. F. D. Oct. 9.

DEMETRIUS, ST. (4th century?), martyr. Probably a deacon in Sirmium, Dalmatia, and a native of Salonica, he is said to have been speared to death for preaching the gospel. He became a patron of the Crusaders. F. D. Oct. 8 (in the East, Oct. 26).

DEMETRIUS, ST. (5th century). See Gregory, St.

DEMETRIUS, ST., martyr. He and SS. Florus and Honoratus (or Honorius) were put to death at the mouth of the Tiber near Rome and are listed in the Roman Martyrology on Nov. 21 and on Dec. 22.

DEMETRIUS, ST., martyr. A bishop, he, his deacon Ananias, Eustosius, and twenty others were slain at Antioch, Syria, early in the Christian era. F. D. Nov. 10.

DEMETRIUS OF TIFLIS, BL. (d. 1321), martyr. See Thomas of Tolentino, Bl.

DÉMIA, CHARLES (1636–1680), founder. Born in Bourg, he founded at Belley, France, the teaching order of the Sisters of St. Charles.

DEMPSEY, JAMES (d. 1667). After the death of Bishop Thomas Fleming, his vicar apostolic was to succeed to the archbishopric of Dublin, but he was imprisoned and exiled. Dr. Dempsey, vicar capitular of Leighlin, was appointed in his place, tried to gather the few Catholics who remained alive (hardly enough for three parishes), and suffered from the intrigues of the Franciscan Peter Walsh.

DEMPSTER, THOMAS (1579–1625), writer. Born in Cliftbog, Scotland, on Aug. 23, he drifted from school to school, taught at several colleges in France, served briefly as historian to King James I in London, taught law in Florence and humanities in Bologna, was charged with unorthodoxy, and defended himself successfully before the Inquisition. His autobiography is quite belligerent and egotistical and his work in hagiography has been severely censured by Irish ecclesiastical scholars. He also edited Claudian and some historical works and wrote poems and plays. He died in Bologna, Italy, on Sept. 6.

DENAUT, PIERRE (1743–1806), bishop. Born in Montreal, Canada, on July 20, he studied there and in Quebec, was ordained in 1767, and appointed pastor of Soulanges at twenty-four. He was transferred to Longueuil in 1787, where he remained even after his consecration as coadjutor bishop of Quebec in 1795. He became tenth bishop of Quebec in 1797, visited his entire diocese, founded Nicolet College in 1803 and enlarged Montreal College in 1804, and was a firm and respected defender of Church rights who smoothed the way for later civil recognition. He died on Jan. 17 in Longueuil, Quebec.

DENIFLE, JOSEPH HEINRICH SEUSE (1844–1905), historian. Born in Imst, Austria, on Jan. 16, he studied at the seminary in Brixen, became a Dominican in 1861, taking the name Heinrich, and was ordained in 1866. He studied in Graz, Marseilles, and Rome, and taught at Graz from 1870 to 1880. He began his long career of writing with an article on Gregorian chant (1872), then engaged in research on the theological soundness of fourteenth-century German mysticism which resulted in *Das geistliche Leben* (1873), an edition of Henry Suso (1880), and studies of Tauler and Eckhart. In 1880 he was appointed assistant to the general of his order, called to Rome, directed by Pope Leo XIII to gather manuscripts for an edition of St. Thomas Aquinas, and in 1883 was made assistant archivist of the Vatican. In the course of his work he made a detailed study of the mediaeval university system, publishing a first and only volume in 1885 and showing that the universities did not originate from cathedral schools and that, except at Paris, theology was not taught at the beginning. With Émile Chatelain, librarian of the Sorbonne, he then was selected by the University of Paris to edit four volumes of its records covering the years 1200–1452. This *Chartularium* was followed by the publication of the two-volume *Auctorium*. For this work Denifle examined 200,000 letters and devoted the years 1887–97. In the meantime he also was writing regularly (on religious orders, the papacy, Abelard, mediaeval scholarship) for *Archiv für Litteratur und Kirchengeschichte des Mittelalters* which he had founded in 1885 with Fr. Ehrle, S.J., of the Vatican; was in frequent consultation with paleographers; and combed 300 volumes of registers of petitions sent to Clement VI and Urban V from 1342 to 1393. The result was the publication of two volumes on the effect of the Hundred Years' War on churches, monasteries, and charitable institutions. Published in 1897, they led to his research into the causes of the low state of ecclesiastical life from the thirteenth to the sixteenth century, both in France and Germany. This prepared him for his monumental study of *Luther and Lutheranism* (1904), in which he devastatingly exploded

many myths about Luther and monastic vows, justification by faith, and autobiographical errors. Notes for a second volume were prepared by Fr. A. Weiss, O.P., in 1908, following Denifle's death in Munich, Germany, on June 10.

DENIS (d. 258?). *See* Dionysius, St.

DENIS, JOHANN NEPOMUK COASMAS MICHAEL (1729–1800), poet. Born in Schärding, Bavaria, on Sept. 27, he studied in Passau, Lower Bavaria, became a Jesuit in 1747, taught at Graz and Klagenfurt, Austria, and was ordained in 1757. He taught in Vienna until the suppression of the Jesuits in 1773, then served as court librarian and privy councilor, and published important bibliographies. As a poet he was heavily influenced by James Macpherson and translated the latter's *Ossian* in 1768; with others he was part of a bardic school (calling himself Sined) which romantically confused Germanic and Celtic antiquities. Other poems dealt with the Seven Years' War, or were based on court activities or religious themes. He was instrumental in popularizing Klopstock and Gellert in Austria. He died in Vienna on Sept. 29.

DENMAN, WILLIAM (1784–1870), publisher. Born in Edinburgh, Scotland, on Mar. 17, of German descent, he was an associate of William Andrews of London, a publisher, emigrated to New York in 1824, and in 1825 founded the weekly newspaper, *The Truth Teller*, with George Pardow. Although it lasted thirty years, it lost favor steadily because of its support of lay trusteeship of the churches. Denman died in Brooklyn on Sept. 12. His youngest son, also named William, became editor of the Brooklyn *Tablet*.

DENNING, JOSEPH M. (1866–1927). Born in Cincinnati, Ohio, on Apr. 19, he studied at Xavier and St. Mary's seminary, was ordained in 1891, and served as pastor in Ohio parishes. In 1922 he was named consul general at Tangiers by President Harding, the first priest to hold office in the American consular service. He remained during the Morocco crisis, returned in 1924 to Cincinnati, and died there on July 26.

DENONVILLE, JACQUES RENÉ DE BRISAY DE (1638–1710), governor. Born in France, he was an army colonel and was sent to Canada as governor in 1685. The Quebec area was heavily attacked by Iroquois and other Indian tribes acting in concert with the aims of Governors Andros of New England and Dongan of New York, and Denonville was recalled after a 1689 massacre at Montreal. He became tutor to the royal household on his return to France.

DENS, PIERRE (1690–1775), theologian. Born in Boom, Belgium, on Sept. 12, he studied at Mechlin and Louvain, taught theology in the Mechlin seminary from 1723 to 1729, was pastor there until 1737, and president of the seminary from 1735 to 1775. He published treatises on penance and the virtue of religion, tracts against Thomson, a Recollect, and Maugis, an Augustinian, and reformed theological instruction in the diocese and greatly aided its poor. His *Theology*, in catechetical form, was long popular. He died in Mechlin, Belgium, on Feb. 15.

DENYS THE CARTHUSIAN. *See* Van Leeuwen, Denys.

DENZA, FRANCESCO (1834–1894), astronomer. Born in Naples, Italy, on June 7, he became a Barnabite at sixteen and studied theology, meteorology, and astronomy in Rome. He was on the faculty of the order's college at Moncalieri from 1856 to 1890, built an observatory there, and in 1859 founded the *Bolletino mensile di meteorologia*. In 1872 he began elaborate research on terrestrial magnetism; in 1881 founded the Italian Meteorological Society; in 1883 was director and chairman of awards of the scientific section of the national exposition at Turin. He represented the pope at international scientific congresses abroad, began work on an elaborate eighteen-observatory mapping of the heavens, became president of the Accademia dei Nuovi Lincei, and in 1890 was named director of the Vatican observatory. He published many scientific studies and died in Rome on Dec. 14.

DENZIGER, HEINRICH JOSEPH DOMINICUS (1819–1883), theologian. Born in Liège, Belgium, on Oct. 10, he studied at Würzburg, where he took his doctorate in philosophy, attended the seminary there and the German College, Rome, and was ordained in 1844. He served as a curate in Hassfurt, taught at Würzburg from 1848, and became professor of theology in 1854. He continued the historical development of theology begun by Johann Möhler and Döllinger, and published on oriental rites, Philo Judaeus, the Immaculate Conception, and papal infallibility, and editions of mediaeval theology. His most important work is his *Enchiridion symbolorum et definitionum* (1854), a handbook of decrees, conciliar definitions, condemned doctrines, and other information, often re-edited and brought up to date since his death, and still of great value. He died in Würzburg, Germany, on June 19.

DEOCHAR, ST. (d. 837). A hermit in Franconia, he became first abbot of the Benedictine monastery of Herriedon, which Charlemagne had founded, and an imperial legate. He is also known as Theutger. F. D. June 7.

DEODATUS, ST. (d. 473), bishop. He was deacon under and then successor to St. Paulinus as bishop of Nola, Italy. F. D. June 27.

DEODATUS, ST. (d. 525?). The later town of St. Dié grew up around the monastery which

this holy recluse supervised near Blois, France. F. D. Apr. 24.

DEODATUS, ST. (d. 679?), bishop. He became bishop of Nevers, France, in 655 and resigned his office after a few years, became a recluse in the Vosges, then in a community on an island near Strassburg from which the abbey of Ebersheim was to develop, and finally at the monastery he founded about 660 at the junction of the Rothbach and Meurthe rivers. F. D. June 19.

DEOGRATIAS, ST. (d. 457), bishop. After fourteen years without a Church leader, Carthage was permitted by the Vandal King Genseric to have a bishop. Two years later, when the king brought back thousands of captives after the sack of Rome, Deogratias sold everything he could find to ransom them, and housed and fed them in church buildings. He escaped Arian plots to kill him, but died of exhaustion after a year. F. D. Mar. 22.

DEPRÈS, JOAQUIN (1450?–1521), composer. Born in Condé, Hainault, Belgium, he was a choirboy there, studied counterpoint under Okeghem, was in the Sforza court at Milan from 1471 to 1480 and in that of Lorenzo the Magnificent at Florence until 1486. He was in the choir of Pope Innocent VIII in 1486–94 (except for a year at Ferrara) and then went to the court of Louis XII of France. He wrote thirty-two masses and numerous shorter works, marked by freedom from contemporary convention but suffering temporary neglect because of their composition during a transitional period in musical taste and because he was overshadowed by his successors, Lassus and Palestrina. He died in Condé, Belgium, on Aug. 27.

DERFEL GADARN, ST. (6th century). A Welsh soldier, he became a recluse at Merioneth; the church there became a shrine until Thomas Cromwell ordered it destroyed in 1538. Part of his equestrian statue made the pyre for the martyr, Bl. John Forest. F. D. Apr. 5.

DERMOT. *See* Diarmis, St.

DE ROALDES, ARTHUR WASHINGTON (1849–1918). Born in Opelousas, Louisiana, on Jan. 25, he studied at the University of France and took degrees in medicine in Louisiana (1869) and Paris (1870). He was a surgeon in the French army during the Franco-Prussian War, was decorated for bravery, and returned to New Orleans in 1872. He directed the charity hospital in 1880–83, founded that for eye, ear, nose, and throat diseases in 1889, and taught at Tulane. He was honored by Pope Pius V, the city, and by five foreign governments. Long interested in the blind, he lost his own sight some years before his death in New Orleans on June 12.

DÉROULÈDE, PAUL (1846–1914), poet. Born in Paris on Sept. 2, he studied there, passed the bar, was captured at Sedan during the Franco-Prussian War, and founded the anti-German League of Patriots, of which he was president in 1886–1908. He was a member of the chamber of deputies from 1890 to 1900, was banished for ten years for action against the constitution, but pardoned in 1905. He wrote a number of plays, four volumes of poetry on military themes, many demanding revenge against Germany, and *Writings by the Way*. He was a convert in his last years and died in Mont-Boron, near Nice, France, on Jan. 30.

DERPHUTA, ST. (d. 300), martyr. *See* Alexandra, St.

DERRY, GEORGE HERMANN (1878–1949), educator. Born in Portland, Maine, on May 27, he studied at Holy Cross, Paris, and Marquette, taught at Holy Cross, Bryn Mawr, Kansas, Union, and Marquette, and became president of Marygrove College in 1927. He later was president of St. Joseph's, Portland, and international director of social education for the Knights of Columbus. He died in Gloucester, Massachusetts, on Jan. 18.

DESA, JOSEPH. *See* Joseph of Cupertino, St.

DESAINS, PAUL QUENTIN (1817–1885). Born in St. Quentin, France, on July 12, he studied there and in Paris, and taught science in Caen and Paris. From 1853 until his death in Paris on May 3, he held the chair of physics at the Sorbonne. His experiments with terrestrial magnetism and the law of cooling were significant; his most important contribution was proof, with La Provostaye, that radiant heat is a disturbance in the air, spreading by waves. He also reorganized methods of teaching physics and built a modern physical laboratory.

DESAULT, PIERRE JOSEPH (1744–1795), anatomist. Born in Magny Vernois, France, on Feb. 6, he became assistant to the barber-surgeon there and worked in the military hospital at Belfort, since poverty prevented attendance at a medical school. In 1766 he established a school of anatomy in Paris, with 300 pupils, applying mathematical principles to medical research with great success. In 1782 he was chief surgeon at the Charity Hospital. He wrote a three-volume treatise on operations; was imprisoned in 1793; but released when his patients prevailed upon the revolutionary powers to release him; and died of pneumonia on June 1 in Paris.

DESCARTES, RENÉ (1596–1650), philosopher. Born in La Haye, France, on Mar. 31, he studied at La Flèche and Poitiers, became a soldier, became interested in the advance of human knowledge, and concluded from a dream that he was directed to dedicate himself to this end. He traveled through Europe, was encouraged by Cardinal Bérulle in his devotion to science, left Paris after a four-year stay, and settled in Holland in 1629. He wrote an essay on algebra and *Compendium of Music* before 1628 and *Le Monde* in 1633, but did not publish this lest he meet with the reception given Galileo; then completed *Discours de la méthode* (1637), *Meditations* (1641), *Principes* (1644), and *Passions* (1649). He sought to reach truth by avoiding reliance on authority; the intelligent mind was to avoid the mere experience of the senses and the syllogistic method of argument; instead, it was to seek mathematical evidence by intuition and deduction, the latter process aided by memory. He experimented widely himself and was aware of contemporary findings of scientists; eventually, he expected that intelligence and experience would unite. In his plan God is the Creator, immutable, undeceiving, and knowable. Late in life Descartes attempted to evolve a system of ethics, touching upon the need of subjecting the emotions to reason in the *Passions*, but he never completed this project. His influence in mathematical logic, analytical geometry, and speculative philosophy was lasting. He died in Stockholm, Sweden, where he had gone in 1649 at the invitation of Queen Christina, on Feb. 11.

DESCHAMPS, EUSTACHE (1340?–1410?), poet. Born in Vertus, Champagne, France, he studied in Rheims and at Orléans; was a royal messenger to the Near East, and is said to have been enslaved in Egypt; and served Charles V and Charles VI in several high posts, though he later lost his offices and his pension. He had studied under Guillaume de Machault, and wrote much poetry in the conventional forms, as well as that with moral and political commentary. One ballade is addressed to Chaucer; his long *Miroir de mariage* has 13,000 lines. It is likely that his condemnation of the evils of court life led to his fall from royal favor.

DESCHAMPS, NICOLAS (1797–1872). Born in Villefranche, Rhône, France, he became a Jesuit in 1826, taught literature in several colleges, and wrote polemical studies of the state control of theological education, communism, contemporary paganism, and the relationship between freemasonry and Manichaeanism. He died in Aix-en-Provence, France.

DESCLÉE, JULES (1828–1911), publisher. Born in Belgium, he and his brother Henri, interested in Catholic art, education, music, and liturgy, founded the Benedictine monastery of Maredsous, Namur, to which a college and technical school were added in 1882 and 1902. In 1882 they also began a publishing firm at Tournai, which issued the first new collections of plain chant and later expanded to distribute books in all fields.

DESCLOT, BERNAT (13th century). His *Libre del rey* is the oldest work of significance in the Catalan language, retaining value both as an historical account and as a linguistic document.

DESFONTAINES, PIERRE FRANÇOIS GUYOT (1685–1745). Born in Rouen, France, he became a Jesuit and taught rhetoric at Bourges, then left the order to serve as editor of *Journal des Savants* from 1724 to 1727. He engaged in a critical battle with Voltaire in several published volumes.

DESGRANGES, MICHAEL (1736–1822). Born in Lyons, France, he became a Capuchin in 1751 as Archange de Lyon, was exiled but secretly returned to France during the revolution, and reopened the Valence house of his order in 1822. He wrote on Catholic education, usury, theology, and the state of the Church in France.

DESHON, GEORGE (1823–1903). Born in New London, Connecticut, on Jan. 30, he graduated from West Point in 1843, finishing second in his class, taught mathematics and ethics at the Military Academy, resigned a captaincy in 1851, and became a convert and Redemptorist. He was ordained in 1855, worked with Frs. Hecker and Hewit, was released from his order in 1858, and helped to form the new Paulist Institute in New York City in 1859. He served as novice-master, superior, and minister, helped in planning the church of St. Paul, founded a Paulist house in Chicago, and did much mission work. He died in New York City on Dec. 30.

DESIDERATUS, ST. (d. 550?), bishop. Brother of SS. Desiderius and Deodatus, whose parents ran a charity hospital in Soissons, he became a courtier and diplomat under King Clotaire. He succeeded St. Arcadius as bishop of Bourges in 541, and was active as a peacemaker and opponent of Nestorianism at the fifth Council of Orléans and the second Council of Auvergne. F. D. May 8.

DESIDERATUS, ST. (6th century), bishop. He succeeded St. Avitus to the see of Clermont, Auvergne, France. F. D. Feb. 10.

DESIDERI, HIPPOLITO (18th century). A Jesuit missioner in Tibet, he wrote, in Tibetan, against eclecticism in religion (1716) and against transmigration of souls (1721).

DESIDERIO DA SETTIGNANO (1428–1464), sculptor. Born in Settignano, Tuscany, Italy, son of a stonecutter, he studied under Donatello, and became famed for the appealing delicacy of his marble carving, which was often confused with Donatello's. Among his outstanding works are the tomb of Carlo Marsuppini in Santa Croce church, a tabernacle at San Lorenzo, and a bust of Marietta Strozzi. He died in Florence.

DESIDERIUS, ST. (d. 305?), martyr. *See* Januarius, St.

DESIDERIUS, ST. (d. 607), bishop and martyr. Born in Autun, Gaul, he became bishop of Vienne, and was so forceful in his attacks on simony and clerical and courtly corruption that Queen Brunhildis brought charges of paganism against him (which were laughed at by Pope St. Gregory the Great, since they were founded on nothing more than information that Desiderius read the classics). Nevertheless, he was forced out of his diocese by a packed council she called. After his return four years later, he was slain by three assassins after he had censured King Theodoric of Burgundy. F. D. May 23.

DESIDERIUS, ST. (d. 625?). He succeeded St. Aunacharius as bishop of Auxerre, France; he sometimes has been confused with St. Desiderius of Vienne. F. D. Oct. 27.

DESIDERIUS, ST. (d. 655), bishop. Born near Albi, France, he served at the court of King Clotaire II of Neustria, and, though a layman, succeeded his brother, Rusticus, who had been murdered, as bishop of Cahors. He restored strict clergy discipline and encouraged the building of churches and monasteries. He is also known as Céry. F. D. Nov. 15.

DESIDERIUS, ST., bishop and martyr. He is believed to have gone from Genoa, Italy, to preach in France, where he became bishop of Langres; he was killed there during an undated barbarian invasion from the north. F. D. May 23.

DESIDERIUS, BL. (d. 1194), bishop. A Belgian Cistercian at the abbey at Cambron, he founded the monastery of Blandecques ("Blandyke") near St. Omer. Also called Didier, he is said to have become thirty-third bishop of Thérouanne in 1169. F. D. Jan. 20.

DESJARDINS, ALPHONSE (1841–1912), mayor. Born in Terrebonne, Quebec, Canada, he studied at Masson College and Nicolet seminary, was active in law from 1862 to 1868, then joined the staff of *L'Ordre* and became chief editor of *Le Nouveau Monde*. He helped to form the Canadian Zouaves sent to aid the pope in 1868, was a framer of the Programme Catholique, and was rewarded with the Order of Pius IX in 1872. He was a Conservative member of parliament from 1872 to 1892, held several ministerial posts, and was mayor of Montreal for a term. He retired from politics in 1896.

DESMAISIÈRES, ST. MARY MICAELA (1809–1865), foundress. Born in Madrid, the viscountess of Sorbalán was educated by the Ursulines and in 1848 founded the Institute of Handmaids, Adorers of the Blessed Sacrament and of Charity, devoted to aiding fallen women, which received papal approval in 1859. She was stricken while administering to cholera victims in Valencia, Spain, and died on Aug. 24. She was canonized in 1934. F. D. Aug. 25.

DESMARETS DE SAINT SORLIN, JEAN (1595–1676), dramatist. Born in Paris, France, he held several court posts, was royal counselor and secretary of the navy in the Near East, and became first chancellor of the French Academy. At the suggestion of Richelieu he wrote for the theater; *Scipion, Roxane,* and *L'Europe,* the last a picture of the cardinal's political outlook, had some success. His conversion in 1645 resulted in a series of religious poems: a metrical version of the Office of the Blessed Virgin and the Imitation of Christ (both bitterly satirized at later dates); *Clovis ou la France chrétienne,* a narrative on the divine origin of monarchy (strongly criticized by Boileau); and works condemning the Jansenists of Port Royal. His *Clovis* became one of the immediate causes of the violent critical battle between the "ancients and moderns," when its author wrote a tract to show that the French language, especially that of contemporary literature, was greater than that of classical Greece and Rome. He died in Paris on Oct. 28.

DE SMET, PIERRE JEAN (1801–1873), missioner. Born in Termonde, Belgium, on Jan. 30, he went to the United States in 1821, became a Jesuit in Maryland, and in 1923 became one of the founders of the Jesuit province in the West, centered at Florissant, Missouri. He did missionary work among the Indians, arranged a peace between the Sioux and Potawatamis, and in 1840 began the first of several long journeys overland to the Northwest. He worked among the Flatheads, Nez Percés, and Crows, twice went to Europe for recruits and funds, explored the new territory as far as Fort Vancouver, British Columbia, and established missions in Washington and Montana, and among the Blackfeet, to whom he made a successful plea for peace in 1846. He left other missioners among the tribes and in the settlements he visited, was recalled to St. Louis, and devoted his next years to pleading for the cause of the Indians both in Europe and before the American Congress. In 1851, 1858, 1862, and 1868 he effected peace treaties with dangerously rebellious Indians at the request of the government, climaxed by the treaty agreed to by the Sioux under Sitting Bull. He traveled 180,000 miles on his missions and was highly respected by all leaders in every conference. He published *Letters and Sketches* (1843), *Oregon Missions and Travels* (1847), *Western Missions and Missionaries* (1863), and *New Indian Sketches* (1865). He died in St. Louis on May 23.

HELÈNE MAGARET, *Father de Smet, Pioneer Priest of the Rockies* (New York, Farrar, 1940).

DESMOND, DANIEL FRANCIS (1884–1945), bishop. Born in Haverhill, Massachusetts, on Apr. 4, he graduated from Holy Cross in 1904, studied at Duquesne and St. John's seminary, Brighton, Massachusetts, and was ordained in 1911. He did parish work, was pastor in Somerville from 1917 to 1932 (except for a year as army chaplain) and then was appointed bishop of Alexandria, Louisiana. He died there on Sept. 11.

DESMOND, THOMAS (d. 1468). The eighth earl of Desmond founded the wardenship of Youghal in the diocese of Cloyne, Ireland, in 1464 and was hanged on Feb. 15 by the viceroy during the War of the Roses.

DE SOTO, HERNANDO (1500?–1542), explorer. Born in Barcarrota, Spain, he became a soldier, served Governor Davilá of Darien as a captain of calvary, took part in the conquest of Honduras and Nicaragua, and in 1532 was second in command to Pizarro of the expedition which set out from Panama to conquer Peru. He was ambassador to the chieftain Atahualpa, visited him often in prison after the fall of Cizco and the capture of the area around the capital, broke with Pizarro after the murder of the Incan noble, and returned to Spain in 1536. A year later he sold his estate to outfit an expedition to Florida and obtained the title of marquis and governor of Cuba from Charles V. He established his rule in Cuba, naming Gonzalo de Guzmán lieutenant governor at Santiago and his wife, Inés de Bobadilla, daughter of Davilá director of affairs of state. In May 1539 he sailed with 1000 soldiers, landed in Tampa Bay, and spent three years in northwestern Florida, at war with Indians who deceived them constantly and whom they treated with extreme cruelty. De Soto, lured by rumors of great riches, pushed on through Alabama, suffered military defeat and the loss of supplies near Mobile, set out for Mexico, but was harassed on a twisted overland course through Mississippi and Arkansas, probably reaching as far west as Oklahoma, succumbed to fever, and was buried in the Mississippi River on May 21. Reports of the disastrous expedition are significant for the early history of the territory and of Cherokee, Creek, Seminole, and other Indian tribes.

DESPORTES, PHILIPPE (1546–1606), poet. Born in Chartres, France, he served as secretary to the bishop of Puy, went to Italy, was influenced by Ariosto and Petrarch, and became a court poet on his return. A canon of Ste. Chapelle, he also wrote some religious poems.

DESPRETZ, CÉSAR MANSUÈTE (1798–1863), physicist. Born in Lessines, Belgium, on May 11, he taught in Bruges, went to Paris to study, and attracted the attention of Gay-Lussac, who gained him a post at L'École Polytechnique. He then taught physics at the Collège Henri IV and in 1837 was given a chair at the Sorbonne. He was naturalized in 1838, elected to the French Academy in 1841, and published widely. Major research included work on latent heat, the elasticity of vapors, heat conductivity, steam, animal heat, density of gases under pressure, limits of sound, the mercurial thermometer, volatization of solids, and a carbon product used for polishing gems. He died in Paris on May 11.

DESURMONT, ACHILLE (1828–1898). Born in Tourcoing, France, on Dec. 23, he studied in Brugelette and Cambrai, became a member of the Congregation of the Most Holy Redeemer in 1850, and was ordained in 1853. He taught theology until 1865, when he became superior of the French province. He founded the review, *La Sainte Famille*, in 1875; other ascetical writings fill nearly twenty volumes. Much of his life was spent in giving retreats to priests and religious, as well as in arranging foundations of his order in Holland and South America. He died on July 23.

DETRE, WILLIAM (b. 1668), missioner. Born in France, he became a Jesuit, was sent to South America in 1706, became superior of the Amazon mission in 1713, translated the catechism into eighteen Indian languages, and prepared a map of the region published in 1707 by Fr. Samuel Fritz, S.J. He became president of the college at Cuenca in 1727; a study of race was dated 1731.

DEUSDEDIT, ST. (d. 618), pope. Beyond the fact that he was a Roman, that he worked unceasingly to help the victims of a plague in Rome, and that he became pope on Oct. 19, 615, nothing is known of his life. Although often called a Benedictine, there is no proof. He is also known as Adeodatus I. F. D. Nov. 8.

DEUSDEDIT (d. 676), pope. See Adeodatus, Pope.

DEUSDEDIT, ST. (6th century). A poor shoemaker in Rome, he gave to those poorer than himself what he earned from his trade during the week. He was honored by Pope St. Gregory the Great. F. D. Aug. 10.

DEUSDEDIT, ST. (d. 664), archbishop. The first Anglo-Saxon to direct the see of Canterbury, he was consecrated by St. Ithamar, first English bishop of Rochester, and died on Oct. 28 during a plague. F. D. July 14.

DEUSDEDIT, ST. (d. 700?). As bishop of Brescia, Italy, he spoke at several councils against the Monothelite heresy. F. D. Dec. 10.

DEUSDEDIT, ST. (d. 836), martyr. A Benedictine monk at Monte Cassino, he was chosen abbot about 830. His gifts to the poor aroused the greed of the tyrannical Sicard of Benevento, who imprisoned him and so mistreated him that he died of hunger. F. D. Oct. 9.

DEUSDEDIT (d. 1100?), cardinal. Born in Todi, Italy, he became a Benedictine, was a friend of Pope St. Gregory VII, defended his reforms, and perhaps after a trip to Germany was named a cardinal. In 1078 he attended a synod in Rome, at which he presented the opinions of Berengarius of Tours. He compiled by 1087, from Burchard of Worms and from original Lateran documents, canons on the power of the Church, clerical immunities, and the clergy at large. Another work, completed in 1099 for Pope Urban II, discussed simony and ecclesiastical investiture. He may have written, or edited, the *Dictatus papae*, on papal privileges, long assigned to Gregory VII.

DEUTINGER, MARTIN (1815–1864), philosopher. Born in Langenpreising, Bavaria, on Mar. 24, he was ordained in 1837, taught philosophy at Freising, Munich, and Dillingen, and attempted to create a system which would harmonize Catholicism and contemporary idealism. His work is highly colored by subjectivism and comparable to that of Hegel. He died in Päfers, Switzerland, on Sept. 9.

DEVAS, CHARLES STANTON (1848–1906), economist. Born in Woodside, England, on Aug. 26, he became a convert, studied at Eton and Oxford, took honors in law and history, and devoted himself to the study of political economy in relation to history and ethics. He wrote many pamphlets and articles; three major studies, which also were translated into German: *The Groundwork of Economics* (1883), *Manual of Political Economy* (1892), and *Studies in Family Life* (1886); and the popular *Key to the World's Progress* (1906), an apologetical refutation of nineteenth-century historical errors. He married Eliza Mary Ward in 1874, had nine children, and was active increasing higher educational opportunities for Catholics. He died on Nov. 6.

DE VERE, AUBREY THOMAS HUNT (1814–1902), poet. Born in Curragh Chase, Limerick, Ireland, on Jan. 10, he studied at Trinity College, Dublin, visited England and began lifelong friendships with Wordsworth, Coleridge, Newman, and Sir Henry Taylor. In 1848 he published a strong condemnation of English misrule in Ireland. He became a convert at Avignon in 1857. His poetry includes *May Carols and Legends of Saxon Saints* (1857); *The Legend of St. Patrick* (1872), and *Mediaeval Records and Sonnets* (1898). *The Search after Proserpine* and *St. Thomas of Canterbury* are plays in the tradition of Robert Browning; two volumes of critical essays appeared in 1887–89. His *Recollections* (1897) contain important comments on major literary figures and on his interest in the Celtic renaissance. He died in Curragh Chase, Ireland, on Jan. 21.

DE VERE, STEPHEN EDWARD (1812–1904), poet. Born in Curragh Chase, Ireland, on July 12, second son of Sir Aubrey de Vere, he long was active in working to better the social and political conditions of his countrymen. He became a baronet on the death of Sir Vere de Vere, his oldest brother, and became a convert as a result of the charitable work he did for Irish peasants. He went to Canada by steerage in 1847 to dramatize the plight of emigrants; a revised Passenger Act was passed which somewhat changed shipboard conditions. He served as a member of parliament from 1854 to 1859, wrote translations from Horace, and built a Gothic church on Foynes Island in the Shannon River, where he died on Nov. 10.

DEVEREUX, JOHN C. (1774–1848), mayor. Born on Aug. 5, near Enniscorthy, Wexford, Ireland, he went to New York in 1797, opened a store in Utica in 1802, became mayor of that city in 1840, and with his brother Nicholas founded a savings bank there. He died in Utica on Dec. 11.

DEVEREUX, NICHOLAS (1791–1855), executive. Born near Enniscorthy, Ireland, on June 7, he went to New York in 1806, established an Irish colony upstate, and became a wealthy merchant and banker in Utica. His charities helped the foundation of St. Bonaventure's College, the North American College, Rome, churches, and an orphanage. He died in Utica on Dec. 29.

DEVINE, ARTHUR (1849–1919), theologian. Born in Kilmactiege, Sligo, Ireland, on Dec. 1, he became a Passionist in 1865, was ordained in 1872, and taught theology at St. Joseph's, London, for about thirty years; his last twelve years he taught theology and scripture at St. Paul's Retreat, Mt. Argus, Dublin, where he died on Apr. 20. He was active in the Gaelic revival, and published sermons and a dozen devotional works.

DEVINICUS, ST. (6th century). A Scot, he worked in evangelizing Caithness, Scotland, probably as a bishop. F. D. Nov. 13.

DEVLIN, JOSEPH (1871–1934). Born in Belfast, Ireland, on Feb. 13, he studied there as a boy, wrote for the *Irish News* and *Freeman's Journal*, and became secretary of the Young Ireland Society and later of the United Irish League. He served in parliament in 1902–21 and 1929–34, refounded the Ancient Order of Hibernians (and was its president from 1905 to 1934), vigorously advocated union with the Irish Free State, and served in the Irish Convention in 1917–18. He made trips to the United States and Australia to raise funds for Irish freedom, was in the North Ireland parliament from 1921 to 1929, gained educational rights for Catholics, and founded a home for working women. He died in Belfast on Jan. 18.

DEVOTA, ST. (d. 303), martyr. The patron of Monaco and of Corsica (where she was born) was put to death on the rack during the Diocletian persecution. F. D. Jan. 27.

DEVOTI, GIOVANNI (1744–1820), canonist. Born in Rome, Italy, on July 11, he taught canon law at the Sapienza from 1764 to 1789, was bishop of Anagi until 1804, and resigned to serve actively in the papal court as titular archbishop of Carthage. He joined Pope Pius

VII in exile in France. He wrote several works on the practice of canon law which have historical value; one, *Institutionum canonicarum,* published in 1785, was long attributed to Cardinal Castiglione. He died in Rome on Sept. 18.

DE WOHL, LOUIS (1903–1961), author. Born in Berlin, son of Lajos Wohl, a Hungarian cavalry officer, and Austrian Baroness Victoria von Dreifus, on Jan. 24, he studied at Prinz Heinrich's gymnasium in Berlin, worked briefly in a bank and doing publicity work for a film company, and at twenty-one had his first novel, *Der grosse Kampf,* published. He then devoted himself exclusively to writing, mainly light novels of action and adventure, many of which became films in Germany. In 1935 he fled to England to escape Hitler's rule, served in British Army Intelligence as an astrologer in World War II, and became a British subject. After the war he resumed his writing but turned to historical novels, most of them with a religious theme, which were extremely successful and led to his being honored by the pope. Among his sixty books were *The Living Wood* (1947), *The Quiet Light* (1950), *The Restless Flame* (1951), *The Golden Thread* (1952), *The Spear* (1955), *The Last Crusader* (1956), and *The Glorious Folly* (1957). He was made a member of The International Institute of Arts and Sciences shortly before his death in Lucerne, Switzerland, on June 2.

DE WULF, MAURICE (1867–1947), philosopher. Born in Poperinghe, near Ypres, Belgium, on Apr. 6, he studied at Alost, Louvain, Berlin, and Paris, obtained three doctorates, and in 1893 was named to the chair of Thomistic philosophy at Louvain. In 1894, with Désiré (later Cardinal) Mercier, he founded *Revue Néo-Scholastique,* of which he was director in 1907–47. He wrote *Histoire de la philosophie médiéval* (1900; which he revised in its sixth edition, 1947), *Introduction à la philosophie néo-scholastique, Philosophy and Civilization in the Middle Ages* (1922), and *Medieval Philosophy Illustrated from the System of St. Thomas* (1929), and founded *Les philosophes belges,* a series of scholarly texts. He taught at Poitiers in 1914–18, lectured at Cornell, Toronto, Princeton, and Chicago, and in 1920–27 held the new chair of mediaeval philosophy at Harvard. He also taught in major European universities. He died in Popcringhe on Dec. 23.

DEYMANN, CLEMENTINE (1844–1896). Born in Klein-Stavern, Oldenburg, Germany, on June 24, he was brought to the United States in 1863, studied in Teutopolis, Illinois, where he became a Franciscan, was ordained in 1872, and taught until 1879. He was pastor of German churches in Joliet and Chillicothe, became definitor of the province, superior of an orphanage in Watsonville, California, and commissary of the Pacific province shortly before his death at Santa Barbara, California, on Dec. 4. He published a number of ascetic treatises.

DEYNIOLEN, ST. (d. 621). He was abbot of Bangor when his Welsh monastery was destroyed in 616 and his monks slain by King Ethelfrid of Northumbria. He himself seems not to have died at that time. F. D. Nov. 22.

DEZA, DIEGO (1444–1523), bishop. Born in Toro, Spain, he became a Dominican, taught theology at Salamanca, tutored Prince John, was bishop of Zamora, Salamanca, Jaén, and Palencia, and in 1505 became archbishop of Seville. He was an encouraging patron of Christopher Columbus.

DHARMAPALA, JUAN (d. 1597). Converted in Lisbon in 1541, he succeeded his grandfather, Buwenekabahu VII, as king of Ceylon in 1542, helped the spread of Catholicism, and introduced Dominicans, Augustinians, and Jesuits to the island to aid in the work begun by Franciscan missionaries. When the Dutch ousted the Portuguese, the former religion was barred from 1642 until 1796, when the English took control and restored religious liberty.

DHUODA (9th century). Wife of Bernard, duke of Septimania, whom she married in 824, she lived at court until he was condemned in 844 for rebellion. She left a *Liber manualis* for the instruction of her son William (born in 826), which she completed in 843. It is a valuable treatise on virtue, revealing something of the history of the times of Louis the Pious and Charles the Bald and the ways of education of her time. She is also known as Dodana.

DIADOCHUS (5th century). He was bishop of Photike, Epirus, and wrote a sermon on the ascension and 100 *Chapters on Spiritual Perfection*. He is sometimes confused with Marcus Diadochus.

DIANA, BL. *See* Andalo, Bl. Diana d'.

DIANA, ANTONIO (1586–1663), theologian. Born in Palermo, Sicily, he became a Theatine in 1630, was renowned as a consultant in difficult cases of conscience, was highly regarded by Popes Urban VIII, Innocent X, and Alexander VII, and was made an examiner of bishops in Sicily. His *Resolutiones morales* was widely consulted. He died in Rome on July 20.

DIARMAID, ST. (d. 851?), archbishop. Born in Ireland, he became archbishop of Armagh in 834, was driven out in 835 by the usurper Foraunan, and saw the churches of his diocese leveled by Norse invaders in 841. He ruled from Connacht and had a reputation for great learning. F. D. Apr. 24.

DIARMIS, ST. (6th century). He taught St. Kieran of Clonmacnoise and later founded and directed a monastery on the island of Inisclo-

tran, Ireland. He is also known as Dermot. F. D. Jan. 18.

DÍAS DE NOVAES, BARTOLOMEU (d. 1500), explorer. A Portuguese navigator, he went to the Gold Coast in 1481 with Diogo d'Azambuja, served as master of the royal warehouses, and led an expedition ordered by King John II to sail around Africa in search of Prester John. He sailed in 1487, made several discoveries in western Africa, and discovered the land he named Cape Tormentoso (but which King John is said to have changed to Good Hope) in 1488. He captained ships engaged in African trade from 1490 on, went with Vasco da Gama to the Cape Verde Islands in 1497, and was lost at sea on May 29, on his return from Pedro Cabral's expedition which discovered Brazil.

DIAZ, BL. FRANCISCO (d. 1648). *See* Serrano, Bl. Francisco.

DIAZ, BL. FRANCISCO (d. 1747), martyr. *See* Sanz, Bl. Peter.

DIAZ, PEDRO (1546–1618), missioner. Born in Lupia, Spain, he became a Jesuit at twenty, and in 1572 was sent to Mexico by St. Francis Borgia. He served in the missions, was rector of colleges in Guadalajara and Mexico City, founded colleges at Oaxaca and Merida, and held several posts in his society. He often is confused with a Portuguese Jesuit, Pedro Dias, of the same century.

DIAZ Y BARRETO, PASCUAL (1876–1936), archbishop. Born in Zapopani, Jalisco, Mexico, on June 22, he went to the Guadalajara seminary, was ordained in 1896, and became a Jesuit in 1903. He studied in France and Belgium, received his doctorate at Anguien, and on his return to Mexico became vicar of San Pedro Analco, taught philosophy at Guadalajara, was secretary to Archbishop Ortiz, and held several posts in his Society. In 1922 he became bishop of Tobasco, was exiled by government persecution in 1924, returned briefly in 1926 and permanently in 1929. He was named archbishop, led the fight for Church rights, was fined and attacked, but continued to represent his persecuted followers until his death in Mexico on May 19.

DÍAZ DE SOLÍS, JUAN (1470?–1516), explorer. Born in Spain, he explored Central America in 1506, Brazil in 1508, and in 1512 succeeded Vespucci as pilot-major, by royal appointment. In 1515 he sailed south from Lepe to the mouth of the Rio de la Plata, explored the region as far inland as the junction of the Uruguay and Paraná rivers, landed there to claim the territory for Spain, and was slain by natives. Other Spanish historians have said that two explorers before him had discovered the same region.

DIBDALE, VEN. ROBERT (d. 1586), martyr. *See* Adams, Ven. John.

DICCONSON, EDWARD (1670–1752), bishop. Born in Lancashire, England, on Nov. 30, he studied and was ordained at Douai in 1701, taught theology there, and became its vice-president in 1713. He frequently met the exiled Stuarts and admired the man called James III by many, and went to England in 1720, where he served as a private chaplain, then as vicar general to Bishop Stoner, and finally as vicar apostolic of the English Northern District. He was consecrated in Ghent in 1741, ordained several priests at Douai, opposed Jansenism, gathered a valuable library of controversial works, and died in Finch Mill, England, on May 5. Francis Petre became his coadjutor in 1750 when he sought assistance because of age.

DICHU, ST. (5th century). An Irish chieftain, he is said to have led a pagan attack against St. Patrick's landing in 432, and to have become the latter's first convert. Patrick often visited him at Saul (Sabhall), capital of the small kingdom of Lecale, in Down, Ireland. F. D. Apr. 29.

DICKENSON, BL. FRANCIS (d. 1590), martyr. Born in Yorkshire, England, he was ordained at Rheims in 1589, entered England as a missioner, and was hanged, drawn, and quartered at Rochester for his priesthood. He was beatified in 1929. F. D. Apr. 30.

DICKENSON, BL. ROGER (d. 1591), martyr. Born in Lincoln, England, he was educated at Rheims, where he was ordained in 1583. Helped by a Ralph Milner, he pursued his priestly work in the Winchester area in England until he was captured, tried, and executed as a priest. He was beatified in 1929. F. D. July 7.

DICTINUS, ST. (d. 420), bishop. He was converted from the Priscillianist heresy by St. Ambrose and became bishop of Astorga, Spain, shortly after 400. F. D. July 24.

DICUIL (8th century), geographer. An Irish monk at a Frankish monastery, he wrote a prose and verse treatise on astronomy about 815 and a more famous geographical study, *De mensura orbis terrae*, in 825. The latter was based on a *Mensauratio orbis* prepared for Theodosius II, on Pliny and Orosius and other authors, and on his own observations during his travels. It has considerable value as a compilation of the accounts of contemporary travelers incorporated in his work.

DIDACUS, BL. (1743–1801). Born in Cadiz, Spain, on Mar. 29, he became a Capuchin in Seville in 1759, and after ordination preached with great success, particularly on the Trinity, throughout Andalusia. He was beloved as a confessor and spent whatever time he could in visiting hospitals and prisons. He is also known as Diego of Cadiz. His cult was confirmed in 1894. F. D. Mar. 24.

DIDIER. *See* Desiderius, Bl.

DIDIUS, ST. (d. 311?), martyr. *See* Hesychius, St.

DIDON, JEAN HENRI (1840–1900). Born in Touvet, France, on Mar. 17, he studied in Grenoble, became a Dominican at Flavigny in 1858, completed his course in Rome, and in 1868 began a great preaching career in Paris. He was so violently attacked for his sermons on contemporary social problems, even by those within the Church, that he was sent into retirement for twelve years by his superiors. Before that, he had published a series of conferences on the indissolubility of marriage (1879); on his return he issued his *Life of Christ* (1890) and began preaching again in Paris in 1892. Conferences on the divinity of Christ, an examination of educational theories (*Les Allemands*), and several spiritual writings also were published. He died in Toulouse, France, on Mar. 13.

DIDOT, AMBROISE FIRMIN (1790–1876), publisher. Born in Paris on Dec. 7, he was in the diplomatic service, was attaché at Constantinople, traveled through the Near East, and located the site of Pergamacum. When his father, Firmin, retired in 1827, he joined his brother Hyacinthe in the direction of the family publishing house; they published long series of classical and French authors. He died in Paris on Feb. 22.

DIDOT, FIRMIN (1764–1836), publisher. Second son of François Ambroise, he was born in Paris on Apr. 14, invented stereotypography, prepared engravings of handwriting types, printed books in imitation of fifteenth-century editions, wrote plays and critical essays, and became a member of the chamber of deputies. He died on Apr. 24.

DIDOT, FRANÇOIS (1689–1757), publisher. Born in Paris, France, he opened a bookstore there (La bible d'or) in 1713, became syndic of the Booksellers' Corporation in 1735, received a royal charter in 1754 which permitted him to publish, and issued the Abbé Prévost's *Histoire des voyages*, among other titles. He died on Nov. 2.

DIDOT, FRANÇOIS AMBROISE (1730–1804), publisher. One of eleven sons of François, whom he succeeded, he was born in Paris on Jan. 7, was appointed printer to the clergy in 1788, published a Bible, editions of the classics, fiction, invented a new printing press, and was the first modern printer to use vellum paper. He died on July 10.

DIDOT, PIERRE (1760–1853), publisher. Eldest son of François Ambroise, he was born on Jan. 25, published an edition of Vergil, and the Louvre editions of Racine, La Fontaine, and Horace. He also was an original poet and made translations of Vergil and Horace. He died on Dec. 31. His son Jules (1794–1871) designed type and established the royal printing house at Brussels in 1825. There he printed a translation of Johnson's *Lives of the Poets* made by Edouard (1797–1825), son of St. Léger Didot.

DIDOT, PIERRE FRANÇOIS (1732–1795), publisher. Brother of François Ambroise, he was born in Paris on July 9, founded a paper factory, made improvements in type founding, and published an *Imitation of Christ* and other volumes. His son Henri (1765–1852) was a type founder and engraver; he made the paper money used in the French Revolution. A younger son, St. Léger (1767–1829), developed the father's paper mill at Essone and invented a machine to make paper in "endless" rolls. He died on Dec. 7.

DIDRON, ADOLPHE NAPOLÉON (1806–1867), archaeologist. Born in Hautvillers, France, on Mar. 13, he studied in Meaux and Rheims, and taught history in Paris. Guizot named him in 1835 secretary of the commission to publish unedited documents relating to the history of France, four volumes of which Didron published. He taught iconography at the Royal Library, founded *Annales archeologiques*, published many articles on that science, and founded a glass factory and goldsmith's shop in which he dabbled with design. He died in Paris on Nov. 13.

DIDYMUS THE BLIND (309–394), philosopher. Born in Alexandria, Egypt, he lost his sight at four, became a brilliant student of culture, mastered scripture, and headed the catechetical school in his native city for fifty years, living as an extreme ascetic. Rufinus studied under him, and Palladius and St. Jerome consulted him. Jerome called him "the seer" until the time Didymus began to lean toward Origen. His writings, which began to show the effects of heresy—but not the man himself—were condemned by the sixth and seventh Councils of Constantinople. He opposed Arianism and Manichaeanism; wrote commentaries on the Psalms, the Catholic Epistles (translated by Epiphanius), an important *De Trinitate* (379), and a study of the Holy Spirit which St. Jerome translated into Latin.

DIEGO, ST. (1400?–1463). Born in San Nicolas del Puerto, Seville, Spain, he lived as a hermit, then joined the Franciscans at Arrizfa as a laybrother. Sent to the Canary Islands for convert work, he was appointed guardian of Fuerteventura there in 1445. Recalled to Spain, he spent the rest of his life in various friaries, notably at Salcedo and Alcalá, and was especially devoted to the Eucharist. He was canonized in 1588. F. D. Nov. 13.

DIEGO OF CADIZ. *See* Didacus, Bl.

DIEGO Y MORENO, FRANCISCO GARCIA (1785–1845), bishop. Born in Lagos, Jalisco, Mexico, on Sept. 17 (possibly in 1786),

he studied at Tridentino seminary, Guadalajara, and the Apostolic College, Guadalupe, became a Franciscan at seventeen, and was ordained in 1808. He taught in Guadalupe, was vicar in Zacatecas and rector of the Apostolic College, Zapopan, did missionary work, and in 1830 was appointed prefect of the Indian missions of California. He settled in Santa Clara, restored many missions, but in 1834 saw his work undone when the Mexican congress passed a decree of secularization. He returned to Mexico to fight the decree and in 1836 secured its repeal and the restoration of the missions to the Church. In 1840 he was appointed first bishop of the newly established diocese of the Two Californias. He struggled to restore the missions, which were practically in ruins, opened a seminary in Santa Ynez in 1844, and died in Santa Barbara, California, on Apr. 30.

DIEKAMP, WILHELM (1854–1885), historian. Born in Geldern, Germany, on May 13, he studied at Münster and Würzburg, took his doctor's degree in philology, and taught in schools in Münster, Arnsberg, and Aachen. He published a life of St. Ludger, edited documents of the papal chancery of Westphalia, and went to Rome to do further research in the Vatican archives on diplomatics. He died there of typhoid fever on Dec. 25.

DIEMOTH (1060?–1130?). A recluse at the Benedictine monastery of Wessobrunn, Bavaria, she was enclosed in a cell near the church and spent her life in prayer and in copying some forty-five major manuscripts. She was a friend of Bl. Herlucka, with whom she corresponded. She sometimes is listed as blessed and given the F. D. Mar. 30.

DIEPENBEECK, ABRAHAM VAN (1599?–1675), painter. Born in Bois le Duc, Netherlands, he became pupil and then assistant to Rubens, and painted mythological and historical subjects. He studied glassmaking at Antwerp and about 1629 created the "Mercy" windows for its cathedral and scenes from the life of St. Paul for windows in the Dominican church. He was admitted to the painters' guild in 1638, became its director in 1641, traveled to Italy, and returned to work in oil. He visited England, painted portraits in the court of Charles I, and completed a *Virgin in the Clouds* for the Carmelite church in Antwerp, a *St. Norbert* for the church in Deurne and a *Martyrdom of St. Julia*. His religious and classical works are in many European museums. He also did engravings for the Plantin printing house. He died in Antwerp.

DIEPENBROCK, MELCHIOR VON (1798–1854), cardinal. Born in Bocholt, Westphalia, on Jan. 6, he served as an officer of militia in 1815 against France, studied finance at Landshut and theology at Ratisbon, and was ordained in 1823. He was made dean of the cathedral and vicar general of Ratisbon in 1835, and became prince-bishop of Breslau in 1845. He aided victims of famine and of the revolution of 1848, bettered the training of the clergy and reintroduced retreats for priests, and protected his diocese against the inroads of secularism. He became apostolic delegate for the Prussian army in 1849, was named cardinal in 1850, published sermons and pastoral letters, a life of Henry Suso, and an anthology of poetry, and left his estate to the diocese on his death in Johannisberg, Upper Silesia, on Jan. 20.

DIERINGER, FRANZ XAVER (1811-1876), theologian. Born in Rangeningen, Germany, on Aug. 22, he studied in Tübingen, was ordained at Freiburg in 1835, and taught at the seminary there and at Speier, and also in the lyceum in the latter city. He became professor of dogma at Bonn; helped to establish a seminary there, where he taught homiletics; and founded *Katholische Zeitschrift für Wissenschaft und Kunst* to combat Hermesianism. He helped to found the Society of St. Charles Borromeo in 1845, was its president from 1846 to 1871, served in parliament at Frankfort in 1848, and in 1853, though he remained at Bonn, was made canon of Cologne and ecclesiastical counselor. He opposed the doctrine of papal infallibility, but submitted to the decision of the Vatican Council; to lessen factionalism over the doctrine he resigned from the university and took up parish work. He was three times proposed for bishoprics, but was opposed by the government. He published many theological studies before his death at Veringendorf, Germany, on Sept. 19.

DIETENBERGER, JOHANN (1475?-1537), theologian. Born in Frankfort on the Main, Germany, he was educated there, became a Dominican, studied at Cologne, Heidelberg, and Mainz, where he received his doctor's degree, and from 1516 to 1526 was prior at Frankfort. He then was prior at Coblenz, attended the Diet of Augsburg in 1530, and was one of the twenty Catholic theologians chosen to refute the Protestant Confession. He was inquisitor for the dioceses of Cologne and Mainz, taught theology at the latter's academy, and wrote several polemical tracts, a catechism, and an influential translation of the Bible. He died in Mainz, Germany, on Sept. 4.

DIETRICH OF MINDEN (d. 880), bishop and martyr. He was killed by the pagan Norsemen, who trapped the army of Duke Bruno, brother-in-law of King Louis III, near Ebsdorf in Saxony and put the royal entourage to death. F. D. Feb. 2.

DIGAIN, ST. (5th century). Son of the chieftain Constantine of Cornwall, his name is perpetuated in Llangernw, Denbighshire, Wales. F. D. Nov. 21.

DIGBY, EVERARD (1578-1606). Born on May 16, at fourteen he inherited his father's estates in Leicester, Lincoln, and Rutland counties, England, married Mary Mulsho in 1596, and became a convert with her about 1599 after their meeting with Fr. John Gerard, S.J. He was knighted by King James I in 1603. In Oct. 1605 he was approached by Catesby, ringleader of the Gunpowder Plot, told of the venture, and joined the rebellion by agreeing to lead a military force into London once the initial blow had been struck. When the plot was uncovered, Digby joined Catesby and others in a hastily arranged troop, was captured, and was hanged, drawn, and quartered in St. Paul's churchyard in London on Jan. 30.

DIGBY, KENELM (1603-1665), diplomat. Born in Gayhurst, Buckinghamshire, England, on July 11, son of Everard Digby, whose estates he inherited, he studied at Oxford, left without a degree, and after service in Spain was knighted by King James I. He married Venitia Stanley in 1625, commanded two ships and defeated French and Venetian galleys at Alexandretta, lost his wife in 1633 and, apparently earlier, his faith. He was reconciled with the Church while in France in 1636, was imprisoned for a year for his religion in 1641, lost his property by confiscation, and went to Paris. There he published the *Nature of Bodies* and *Immortality of Reasonable Souls*. He twice went to Rome on diplomatic missions for the English Catholic Committee, was also sent to England and promptly banished, returned in 1654 and did diplomatic work for Cromwell on the Continent, and came back to London with the English court in 1660. He became a member of the Royal Society in 1663, and died in Westminster, England, on June 11.

DIGBY, KENELM HENRY (1800-1880), historian. Born in Clonfert, Ireland, youngest son of William, Anglican dean there, he attended Cambridge, published *The Broad Stone of Honour*, a study of chivalry, in 1822, and rewrote the work in four volumes (1826-27) after he became a convert. He wrote other prose, some verse, and gained his greatest reputation from an encyclopedic eleven-volume study of the outlook of the mediaeval world: *Mores Catholici, or Ages of Faith*. He died in Kensington, England, on Mar. 22.

DIGBY, MABEL (1835-1911). Born near Staines, Middlesex, England, on Apr. 7, she became a convert in 1854, entered the Society of the Sacred Heart in 1857, worked in Tours for thirteen years, eight as superior, and at Roehampton for twenty-two years as superior vicar. She went to Paris in 1894, was elected superior general the following year, and moved to Brussels, Belgium, in 1909, where she died on May 21.

DI GIROLAMO, ST. FRANCIS JEROME (1642-1716). Born in Grottaglie, Italy, on

Dec. 17, oldest of eleven children, he studied with some priests in the area, then at Naples, and was ordained in 1666. He taught for five years in the Jesuit college there, and entered the Society of Jesus at twenty-eight. He trained mission priests, visited prisons and hospitals, and preached inspiringly in the kingdom of the Two Sicilies. He died in Naples, and was canonized in 1839. F. D. May 11.

DIGNA, ST. (d. 254), martyr. She and St. Emerita (d. 259) died at Rome while praying before anti-Christian courts during the reign of Valerian. F. D. Sept. 22.

DIGNA, ST. (4th century). She was a recluse in the mountains near Todi, Umbria, during the Diocletian persecution. F. D. Aug. 11.

DIGNA, ST. (d. 853), martyr. *See* Anastasius, St.

DIMAN, ST. (d. 658), bishop. He was a monk with St. Columba before he became abbot-bishop of Connor, Ireland, and was one of the Irish leaders to whom Pope Honorius wrote in 640 on Pelagianism and the dating of Easter. F. D. Jan. 6.

DIMNET, ERNEST (1866–1954), author. Born in Trélon, France, on July 9, he studied in Cambrai, Lille, and the Sorbonne, was ordained in 1893, and taught at Douai, Lille, and Collège Stanislas, Paris. He taught English literature at the latter from 1902 to 1923, was correspondent to several English journals, and frequently visited the United States as a lecturer. While in Paris he was associated with George Tyrrell in the modernist movement, and his study of contemporary English Catholicism (1907) was placed on the Index after the papal condemnation of the movement as heretical. He wrote a critical study of the Brontë sisters in 1910, the popular *Art of Thinking* (1928), and the autobiographical *My Old World* (1935) and *My New World* (1937). He died in Paris on Dec. 8.

DINGAD, ST. (5th century). Son of the chieftain Brychan of Brecknock, he became a recluse in Llandingad, Monmouthshire, Wales. F. D. Nov. 1.

DINGLEY, VEN. THOMAS (d. 1539), martyr. Prior of the Knights of St. John of Jerusalem, he was without trial declared guilty of treason when that organization was suppressed, and was beheaded on Tower Hill, London, on July 9.

DINIZ (1261–1325), king of Portugal. Son of Alfonso III and known as "the Cultivator," he was born in Lisbon, became king in 1279, and brought peace to a nation torn by internal dissension for nearly a century, once he had established himself by crushing a civil war led by his brother. He restored property seized by his predecessors, respected the ecclesiastical position, confirmed the laws of the nation and saw them carried out, and developed agriculture, commerce, and the navy. In 1290 he established the University of Lisbon (which later moved to Coimbra), and gave property of the Templars (after their international suppression) to the new Order of Christ. Also known as Denis, he was himself a poet and the center of troubadour creativity; his wife, St. Isabel, helped him to govern with justice. He died in Santarem, Portugal, on Jan. 7.

DINNIS, ENID (1873–1942), novelist. Born in London, daughter of an Anglican cleric, she became a convert in 1897, studied in Belgium, and returned to write poetry and humor for *Punch* in 1898–1908. She then published historical novels: *Mr. Coleman, Gent.* (1914), on the Titus Oates Plot; *The Three Roses*, on King Henry VI; and *Bess of Cob's Hill*. She also wrote sketches, *Mystics All*, *Once upon Eternity*, and *More Mystics*; the Middle Ages inspired *The Anchorhold* and *The Shepherd of Weepingwold*. Her striking lyrics were collected in *Meadowsweet and Thyme*. She died near Richmond-on-the-Thames, England, in November, having served as a librarian there in her last years.

DIOCLETIUS, ST. (d. 304), martyr. He and SS. Florentius and Sisinius were slain in Osimo, Italy, during the Diocletian persecution. F. D. May 11.

DIOCLETIUS, ST. (d. 397), martyr. *See* Alexander, St.

DIODORUS, ST. (d. 250?), martyr. *See* Claudian, St.

DIODORUS, ST. (d. 283), martyr. He, Marianus, and a number of others were apparently surprised at prayer in the Roman catacombs and suffocated by being walled up during the Numerian persecution. F. D. Dec. 1.

DIODORUS (d. 392), bishop. A student of Bishop Silvanus of Tarsus, he studied at Athens before he became a monk, headed a monastery near Antioch, and had St. John Chrysostom as a disciple. Diodorus was partly responsible for the practice of singing Psalms by alternate choirs. He was ordained about 361, worked with Flavian in preaching to Christians during the persecution of Valens (364–78), and was several times banished. In 372 he met St. Basil in Armenia, who named him bishop of Tarsus and metropolitan of Cilicia. He attended the Council of Antioch in 379 and that of Constantinople in 381. He wrote against pagan philosophy, on fate, and a number of literalist interpretations of scripture. Some of his comments on the humanity of Christ were not accurately worded and St. Cyril declared him a heretic; St. John Chrysostom and others defended him. Nestorianism came into heretical popularity through a disciple of Diodorus, Theodore of Mopsuestia.

DIODORUS, ST. (4th century), martyr. He and another deacon, St. Rhodopianus, were put to death at Caria, in Asia Minor, during the Diocletian persecution. F. D. May 3.

DIODORUS, ST., martyr. *See* Chrysanthus, St.

DIOGENES, ST. (d. 345?), martyr. He and St. Timothy were slain at Philippi in Macedonia, probably by Arians. F. D. Apr. 6.

DIOMEDES, ST. (d. 300), martyr. Born in Tarsus, Cilicia, he became a physician, was active in spreading Christianity, and put to death at Nicaea, Bithynia, during the Diocletian persecution. F. D. Aug. 16.

DIOMMA, ST. (5th century). Said to have instructed St. Declan of Ardmore and others, he became the patron of Kildimo, in Limerick, Ireland. F. D. May 12.

DIONYSIA, ST. (d. 250), martyr. *See* Epimachus, St.

DIONYSIA, ST. (d. 251), martyr. *See* Peter, St.

DIONYSIA, ST. (d. 484), martyr. She was tortured and burned to death in Africa during Arian King Huneric's persecution. With her were martyred her son Majorica and her sister Dativa. Her cousin Emilian, a physician, and Leontia, Tertius, and Boniface were flayed alive. F. D. Dec. 6.

DIONYSIO FIAMMINGO. *See* Calvaert, Denis.

DIONYSIUS, ST. (d. 268), pope. Probably a Greek, he was a priest in Rome when elected to the papacy on July 22, 259, after the Holy See had been vacant almost a year. He vigorously opposed Sabellianism, was active in aiding ravaged churches in other lands, and was most successful in rebuilding the Church when Emperor Gallinus proclaimed his edict of tolerance. He is the first pope who is not honored liturgically as a martyr. F. D. Dec. 26.

DIONYSIUS, ST. (d. 180?), bishop. The writer of numerous episcopal letters to the Christians of Greece, Crete, and Rome, informing and exhorting them during a period of heresy and persecution, the bishop of Corinth is praised and quoted in Eusebius' *Ecclesiastical History.* F. D. Apr. 8.

DIONYSIUS, ST. (2nd century), bishop. Said to have been one of the missioners sent by Pope Sixtus I to Gaul with St. Peregrinus, he succeeded St. Justus as bishop of Vienne, Gaul, and was alive in 193. F. D. May 8.

DIONYSIUS, ST. (d. 220), martyr. A pagan priest, he was converted, and was crucified with Socrates and Theodore, soldiers, and Philippa, the latter's mother, at Perge, Pamphilia, during the persecution of Heliogabulus. F. D. Sept. 20.

DIONYSIUS, ST. (d. 257), martyr. He and others at Alexandria, Egypt, were banished to Libya under Decius and brought to trial and slain during the reign of Valerian. F. D. Oct. 3.

DIONYSIUS, ST. (d. 258?), bishop and martyr. According to St. Gregory of Tours, he was born in Italy and about 250 was sent to Gaul

with six other missionary bishops and became the first bishop of Paris. They settled on an island in the Seine and evangelized the surrounding areas so successfully that he, a priest, Rusticus, and deacon, Eleutherius, were beheaded at Paris and their bodies thrown into the Seine during Decius' persecution. Their bodies were buried by a Christian lady named Catulla and around their tomb arose the Benedictine abbey of St. Denis, founded by King Dagobert I about 638. He was often confused with Dionysius the Areopagite. He is popularly known as St. Denis and regarded as the patron saint of France. F. D. Oct. 9.

DIONYSIUS, ST. (d. 273), martyr. *See* Lucillian, St.

DIONYSIUS, ST. (d. 275), martyr. He was stabbed to death at Pamphylia with another Christian, St. Socrates, during the Aurelian persecution. F. D. Apr. 19.

DIONYSIUS, ST. (d. 290?), martyr. *See* Paul of Narbonne, St.

DIONYSIUS, ST. (d. 303), martyr. *See* Agapius, St.

DIONYSIUS, ST. (d. 303?), bishop and martyr. A convert, he became first bishop of Augsburg, Germany, and was slain during the Diocletian persecution. F. D. Feb. 26.

DIONYSIUS, ST. (d. 304), martyr. Uncle and guardian of St. Pancras, he is said to have come to Rome from the East, and, after their conversion, died in prison during the Diocletian persecution. F. D. May 12.

DIONYSIUS, ST. (d. 360?), bishop. Appointed to the see of Milan in 351, he attended the synod convoked by the Arian Emperor Constantius, and, when he joined Eusebius of Vercelli and Lucifer of Cagliari in defending St. Athanasius, he was exiled with them. St. Dionysius died in Cappadocia. F. D. May 25.

DIONYSIUS OF ALEXANDRIA, ST. (d. 265), bishop. Born in Alexandria, Egypt, he became a convert, studied in Origen's catechetical school, and succeeded him as master in 232. In 247 he became bishop of Alexandria, but was exiled in 249 during the persecution of Decius and ruled his see from Libya. On his return he denounced the followers of Novatian, became involved in the controversy over the validity of baptism by heretics, and outspoken against Sabellianism. In 257, Valerian's persecution drove him again to Libya, from which he returned in 260. He was a tireless and powerful defender of the faith and an outstanding theologian, and was called the "Teacher of the Catholic Church" by St. Athanasius. F. D. Nov. 17.

DIONYSIUS THE AREOPAGITE, ST. (1st century). When St. Paul was in Athens he preached on the Hill of Mars (Areopagus) his famous sermon on "the unknown God," converting Dionysius of Corinth (Acts 17:15–34).

Eusebius says he became first bishop of Athens and other early writers add that he was martyred about 95. Great confusion has grown up between him and St. Dionysius of Paris (the Roman Martyrology incorrectly attributed the writings of Dionysius of Paris to him) and an ecclesiastical writer of the fifth century. F. D. Oct. 9.

DIONYSIUS THE CARTHUSIAN. *See* Van Leeuwen, Denys.

DIONYSIUS EXIGUUS (6th century), canonist. Born in Scythia, he was abbot of a monastery near Rome, and translated a life of St. Pachomius and the *De opificio hominis* of St. Gregory of Nyssa from Greek into Latin. He began the systematic collection of canon law; his *Collectio Dionysiana* includes decrees in Latin and Greek of Eastern synods and four ecumenical councils (325–451)—another version adds canons of the Council of Carthage held in 419—and papal constitutions for the years 384 to 498. In writing on the dating of Easter he introduced a system of chronology called the Era of the Incarnation (dating that event as Mar. 25 of the year 754 from the founding of Rome). The system, also called the Dionysian Era, was widely used in Italy and Spain, officially approved by Charlemagne, adopted in England during the eighth and ninth centuries, and employed in the papal chancery during the tenth century. Dionysius died sometime before 544.

DIONYSIUS OF THE NATIVITY, BL. (d. 1653). *See* Berthelot, Bl. Pierre.

DIONYSIUS THE PSEUDO-AREOPAGITE. He probably was a pagan in Syria, who lived in the later fourth (or fifth) century and became a convert to Christianity, but no biographical details have been agreed upon. His work reveals his knowledge of Plotinus, Proclus, and other Neoplatonists and great familiarity with scripture and the apocrypha. He wrote on the Trinity (and in such highly figurative language drawn from the world of nature that he has been called pantheistic), on the hierarchy of angels, the sacraments, and on mystical theology. He also wrote ten letters to contemporary monks, priests, and deacons on the points raised in his treatises. He was for years quoted by Catholic writers and by Monophysites to support even contrary views; he long was popular as a source for mediaeval scholastics and writers of the Greek Orthodox Church; he later was to be termed completely false and completely genuine. Close comparison of his writings with those of the Neoplatonists is now held to establish genuineness and a single and actual author.

DIOSCORIDES, ST. (d. 244?), martyr. *See* Crescens, St.

DIOSCORUS, ST. (d. 250), martyr. *See* Arsenius, St.

DIOSCORUS, ST. (d. 284), martyr. *See* Claudian, St.

DIOSCORUS, ST. (d. 305?), martyr. A lector at Kynopolis, Egypt, he was burned to death there during the Diocletian persecution. F. D. May 18.

DIOSCORUS (d. 530), antipope. Born in Alexandria, Egypt, he was a deacon, served as papal legate to Theodoric the Goth at Ravenna and to Justinian at Constantinople under Popes Symmachus and Hosmisdas, and during the reign of Pope Felix IV was leader of the Byzantine faction which opposed the papal preference for the Gothic powers. Felix designated Boniface, an archdeacon, as his successor and died in Sept. 530. But sixty of sixty-seven Roman priests refused to acknowledge the designation and elected Dioscorus. Both were consecrated on Sept. 22. The schism ended when Dioscorus died three weeks later on Oct. 14, and those who had elected him submitted to Boniface. Boniface II anathematized him, but the document was burned by Pope Agapetus I in 535 and the condemnation officially lifted.

DI ROSA, ST. PAULA (1813–1855), foundress. Born in Brescia, Italy, of a well-to-do family, she refused the marriage arranged by her father, but stayed at home to manage his household. In 1836 she labored in the local hospital during the cholera epidemic that ravaged Italy, and in the next few years devoted herself to helping abandoned girls, and founding a school for deaf and dumb girls. In 1840 she founded (with Gabriela Bornati) the Handmaids of Charity to look after the sick in hospitals, which despite some opposition was immediately successful. In 1850, Pope Pius IX approved their constitutions and in 1852 the first twenty-five sisters took their vows with Paula, who took the name of Maria Crocifissa. The congregation spread through Italy where most of its houses are located. She died in Brescia. F. D. Dec. 15.

DISIBOD, ST. (674?). Supposedly an Irishman and a bishop, he was unsuccessful in reforming his own people and migrated with several companions to Bingen, Germany, where he founded a Benedictine monastery in the Nahe Valley which became Disibodenberg. St. Hildegarde wrote a life of him in 1170. F. D. Sept. 8.

DISMAS, ST. This is the name most often given to the good thief who was pardoned as he died on the Cross next to Christ. He also is called Titus and Zoathan in various legends, one of which had him preventing a companion from attacking the Holy Family during the flight to Egypt. F. D. Mar. 25.

DISSEN, HEINRICH VON (1415–1484). Born in Osnabrück, Westphalia, on Oct. 18, he studied in Cologne, became a Carthusian there, and was superior from 1457 until his death on

Nov. 26. While in the monastery he was copyist in the library and wrote commentaries on scripture, the Lord's Prayer, and the Athanasian Creed, as well as sermons and homilies.

DITHMAR (975–1018), bishop. Born on July 25, son of Count Siegfried of Walbeck, he studied at the Quedlinburg, Bergen, and Magdeburg monasteries, was ordained in 1003, and in 1009 became fourth bishop of Merseburg, Germany. He defended canonical liberty against the secular princes, reformed spiritual life, and wrote *Chronicon Thietmari* on the reigns of the Saxon Emperors Otto I, II, and III, and Henry I and II. He was counselor to Henry II and brought his court experience to bear on this revealing commentary of the imperial world and that of the Poles and Hungarians. He died on Dec. 1.

DIVINI, ST. CHARLES ANTONY (1653–1721). Born in San Severino, Italy, on Mar. 1, he was orphaned at five, raised with great severity by an uncle, became a Friar Minor of the Observance at seventeen, and was ordained at twenty-five, taking the name Pacifico. He taught for two years and was an effective preacher. In 1688 he was stricken by blindness and deafness and became crippled. In 1705 he was transferred to San Severino, where he spent the rest of his life, marked by many supernatural experiences. He died there, and was canonized in 1839. F. D. Sept. 24.

DIVISCH, WENCESLAUS (1698–1765). Born in Senftenberg, Bohemia, on Mar. 26, he studied in Znaym and Bruck, became a Premonstratensian, taking the name Procopius, was ordained in 1726, took his doctorate in theology at Salzburg in 1733, and continued his interest in science while pastor of a small church in Prenditz. He was one of the first to employ electricity in the treatment of disease, discovered the property of lightning rods and erected some in 1754 before Franklin's experiments were known or put into practice, and developed a musical device which imitated string and wind instruments. He died at Prenditz, Moravia, on Dec. 21.

DIXON, JOSEPH (1806–1866), archbishop. Born in Coalisland, Tyrone, Ireland, he studied at Maynooth, was ordained in 1829, and was professor of scripture and Hebrew at the seminary from 1834 to 1852, in which latter year he published *Introduction to the Sacred Scriptures*. He then became archbishop of Armagh, held a synod in 1854, developed the diocesan chapter, introduced many religious orders, and nearly completed the cathedral. He died in Armagh, Ireland, on Apr. 29.

DLUGOSZ, JAN (1415–1480), historian. Born in Brzeznica, Poland, he studied at Cracow, was ordained in 1440, and became secretary to Cardinal Oleśnicki. He was stationed at the cathedral, served as tutor to the children

of King Casimir IV, as ambassador to Bohemia and Hungary, and as delegate to the Council of Basle. He carefully examined Polish, Bohemian, Hungarian, Ruthenian, and German documents for his twelve-volume *Historia Polonica;* he also wrote biographies of SS. Kinga and Stanislaus and of many Polish bishops and lesser histories. He founded several churches and monasteries, established scholarships for poor students, and shortly before his death in Cracow, Poland, on May 19 was named archbishop of Lemberg.

DOBENECK, JOHANN (1479–1552). Born in Wendelstein, Germany, he studied at Nuremberg, Cologne, and Bologna, and was ordained at Rome. Between 1520 and 1523 he wrote several works on the priesthood, grace, baptism, all against the rising tide of Lutheranism. Some 200 more polemical writings followed, as well as his valuable *History of the Hussites,* and because of the vigor of his attacks against the reformers he was forced to move from city to city. He was a canon in Mayence, Breslau, and Eichstätt, and attended diets at Nuremberg, Ratisbon, and Speyer to seek an end to growing rebellion. His most important work against Luther was *Commentaria de actis et scriptis M. Luther* and against Melanchthon, *Philippicae.* His humanistic writings often appeared under the name Cochlaeus. He died in Breslau, Germany, on Jan. 11.

DOBMAYER, MARIAN (1753–1805), theologian. Born in Schwandorf, Bavaria, he became a Jesuit in 1773 and, after the Society's suppression, a Benedictine, being ordained in Bamberg in 1778. He taught philosophy and theology in Neuburg, Amberg, Ingolstadt, and Weissenohe. He published two studies in theology and died in Amberg, Bavaria, on Dec. 21.

DOBRIZHOFFER, MARTIN (1717–1791), missioner. Born in Graz, Styria, on Sept. 7, he became a Jesuit in 1736, and in 1748 was sent to South America for eighteen years. When the Jesuits were expelled in 1767 he returned to Austria, was frequently consulted by Empress Maria Theresa, and was named court preacher in 1773. He published a three-volume *Historia de Abiponibus* (1783–84) on four Indian colonies in Paraguay, later translated by Sara Coleridge. He died in Vienna on July 17.

DOCCO. *See* Cungar, St.

DOCUS. *See* Cadoc, St.

DODA, ST. (7th century). *See* Bova, St.

DODANA. *See* Dhuoda.

DODO, ST. (d. 750?). Born in Laon, France, he became a Dominican monk at Lobbes and abbot of Wallers-en-Faigne. F. D. Oct. 1.

DODO, BL. (d. 1231). A Premonstratensian, he received permission to become a hermit in Friesland, and possessed unusual healing powers. F. D. Mar. 30.

DODOLINUS ST. (7th century). He was bishop of Vienne, France. F. D. Apr. 1.

DOGFAN, ST. (5th century), Welsh martyr. Son of a chieftain, he was slain in Pembrokeshire, Wales, by pagan invaders. F. D. July 13.

DOGMAEL, ST. (6th century?). A Welshman, he labored for the faith in Pembrokeshire, Wales, and later in Brittany. F. D. June 14.

DOLAN, FRANCIS JAMES (1893–1939), educator. Born in Jamaica Plain, Massachusetts, on July 14, he became a Jesuit in 1912, was ordained in 1926, and was president of Holy Cross College from 1933 until his death in Worcester, Massachusetts, on Sept. 6.

DOLBEAU, JEAN (1586–1652), missioner. Born in Anjou, France, on Mar. 12, he became a Recollect friar at nineteen, went to Quebec, Canada, with three others of his order, and said the first mass there in May 1615. He built the first Recollect monastery in Quebec in 1620, returned to France in 1625, and held numerous posts in his order until his death in Orléans, France, on June 9.

DOLCI, ANGELO MARIA (1867–1939), cardinal. Born in Civitella d'Agliano, Italy, on July 12, he was ordained in 1890, and made bishop of Gubbio in 1900, and archbishop of Amalfi in 1911. He was apostolic delegate to Constantinople in 1914, nuncio to Belgium in 1922, and to Rumania in 1923–33. He was created a cardinal in 1933 and attached to the administrative staff of the curia. He died in his birthplace on Sept. 14.

DOLCI, CARLO (1616–1686), painter. Born in Florence, Italy, on May 25, he studied under Vignali, precociously completed exciting work when eleven, and worked in the prevailing gentle method of the late Florentine school. He generally limited himself to heads or upper bodies, though his *St. Andrew Praying before His Execution* is life-size. Heads of Christ and madonnas exist in great number; most famous is his *Madonna del Dito* (Madonna of the Thumb). He died in Florence on Jan. 17. Agnese Dolci (d. 1686), his daughter, copied many of her father's works and was herself an effective painter of religious subjects; notably, *Consecration of the Bread and Wine*.

DOLLARD, WILLIAM (d. 1851), bishop. Born in Ballytarina, Kilkenny, Ireland, he studied in the Quebec seminary, and after ordination served as a missioner at Cape Breton and Miramichi. He became vicar general of Charlottetown and in 1843 became bishop of New Brunswick. He died on Aug. 29.

DOLLFUSS, ENGELBERT (1892–1934), chancellor. Born in Texing, Lower Austria, on Oct. 4, he studied law at Vienna, served as a lieutenant during World War I, and took his doctorate in political economy at Berlin. He became secretary of the local Peasants' Union and helped to found the Lower Austrian Chamber of Agriculture, which he served as director in 1927, and the Agricultural Laborers' Insur-

ance Institute. He was a representative of the Christian Socialist party, minister of agriculture and forestry in the cabinets of Otto Ender and Karl Buresch, and became chancellor in the government of President Miklas in 1932 and also minister of foreign affairs as well as of agriculture and forestry. He floated an international loan to prevent economic collapse, but promised those nations who subscribed to it that he would keep Austria independent and economically neutral. To prevent seizure by Germany, Dollfuss dissolved parliament in 1933, forbade the wearing of Nazi uniforms, and set up controls on all media of information. German leaders were jailed, but Hitler's schemes went forward. An attempt was made on the chancellor's life late in 1933; Dollfuss proclaimed martial law and crushed several Nazi revolts. He was shot and left to bleed to death in the Vienna chancellory on July 25 by a group of 144 Germans who seized the building and invaded his office during a cabinet meeting.

DOLMAN, CHARLES (1807–1863), publisher. Born in Monmouth, England, on Sept. 20, son of Charles Dolman, a surgeon, he was educated at the Benedictine college of St. Benedict, Downside, studied architecture in Preston, and became interested in the publishing and bookselling firm of his grandfather, Thomas Booker, in London. In 1840 the firm became Booker & Dolman; later, his name alone was used. He published *The Catholic Magazine* from 1838 to 1844, *Dolman's Magazine* from 1845 to 1849, and other short lived periodicals. His publishing ventures failed when he issued books which were worth while but for which there was little popular demand; disillusioned, he retired to Paris and died there on Dec. 31.

DOMENEC, MICHAEL (1816–1878), bishop. Born in Ruez, Tarragona, Spain, he studied at Madrid and the Lazarist seminary in Paris, where he joined the Lazarists in 1832, and in 1838 went to the United States. He finished his theological studies at St. Mary's seminary, Missouri, where he was ordained in 1839, worked as a missionary in Missouri and taught at the seminary, and in 1845 was sent with a group of Lazarists to oversee St. Vincent's seminary, Germantown, Pennsylvania. He also engaged in pastoral work, became pastor of St. Vincent de Paul church in Germantown, and in 1860 was appointed bishop of Pittsburgh. In 1876 the see was divided, at his request, with the formation of the new diocese of Allegheny City, of which he became first bishop. Ill health caused his resignation the following year and he retired to Spain, where he died in Tarragona on Jan. 5.

DOMENECH, EMMANUEL HENRI DIEUDONNÉ (1826–1886), missioner. Born in Lyons, France, on Nov. 4, he studied in the seminary there, completed his theology in St. Louis, Missouri, was ordained, and labored in the German settlement in Castroville, Texas, in 1848, being later transferred to Brownsville. His years there were marked by the lawlessness of the postwar years, Indian attacks, and an epidemic of cholera. In 1852, in poor health, he returned to France, accompanied Emperor Maximilian as chaplain during the 1861 invasion of Mexico, and returned to France where he died in June. He wrote on the American missions, a history of Mexico, an account of Jansenism, and theological works.

DOMENICHINO. *See* Zampieri, Domenico.

DOMINATOR, ST. (d. 495?), martyr. He was fourteenth bishop of Brescia, Italy. F. D. Nov. 5.

DOMINIC, ST. (d. 612?). Succeeded St. Anastasius as bishop of Brescia, Italy. F. D. Dec. 20.

DOMINIC, BL. (9th century). Legend calls him a Benedictine monk, stationed at Comacchio, Italy, who went to the Holy Land in 820 and brought the relics of St. Mark to Venice from Alexandria. F. D. June 21.

DOMINIC, ST. (1170–1221), founder. Born in Calaruega, Old Castile, Spain, son of Felix Guzman and Bl. Joanna of Aza, he studied at the University of Palencia in 1184–94, apparently was ordained before he finished, and was appointed canon of the cathedral at Osma and became prior-superior of the chapter he reformed. In 1203 he was sent with Bishop Diego of Osma to Italy to make arrangements for the marriage of the daughter of the lord of the Marches to Prince Ferdinand, and again in 1204 to escort her to Castile. The princess died on the way, and the two clerics went to Rome to ask permission, which was denied, to found a new order to combat heresy and spread truth. They had seen the spiritual devastation caused by the Albigensians, who denied the value of marriage, as they passed through Toulouse on their journeys. Pope Innocent III directed them, instead, to go to Languedoc and to strengthen the Cistercians there. They induced the Cistercians to adopt an austere life, since the worldliness of many of them had proved a painful contrast to the asceticism of the highest order among the Albigensians, the *perfecti*. They also preached widely in the area, easily refuting their opponents because of their university training. Converts increased; Dominic then established a convent at Prouille in 1206 with the approval of Bishop Fouques of Toulouse, to give spiritual purpose to the many women who had given up the wayward life approved by the heresy. His new enthusiasts thus began the foundation of the sisters of the second order of St. Dominic. The work was now chiefly his alone. Many Cistercian houses closed up or had their communities recalled; Diego died in Spain while seeking replacements; and one of the two Cistercian legates

also died. When the second legate, Pierre de Castelnau, was assassinated in 1208 by the Albigensians, the crusade against them, led by Simon de Montfort, began. Dominic accompanied the army, preaching the restoration of morality and pleading for safe treatment of civilians as city after city fell. After the climactic victory at Muret in 1213, de Montfort built the chapel of Our Lady of the Rosary, which indicates that this devotion, traditionally believed to have been revealed to St. Dominic, had been adopted before this. The civil strife ended in 1215. Dominic was for a time associated with the Inquisition as a theological authority (but was neither its director or founder; it had been set up as early as 1198). He continued preaching, attracted a group of six devoted followers, and in 1215 their foundation at Toulouse was canonically approved by Bishop Fouques, who gave him a chaplaincy to guarantee some income. The group's horizons were still limited to a single diocese; they widened when Dominic accompanied Fouques to the Ecumenical Council in Rome in 1215. One of the topics discussed was the failure of contemporary preaching, but the council members were suspicious of Dominic's request that his group be established as an order of preachers, and denied it. He returned to Toulouse, the group adopted the older Rule of St. Augustine (the council had forbidden new rules), requested confirmation from Honorius III, and received papal approval in 1216, and the Order of Preachers (Dominicans) was founded. Dominic preached in Rome, became papal theologian, reformed the orders of women in the city, received the church of St. Sixtus as his first Roman center, and sent two of his followers to the University of Paris and fourteen others to preach through Europe. New members continued to join in increasing numbers; houses were established in Italy, Spain, and France, many of them by Dominic himself. He and his associates preached so successfully in Lombardy in 1220 against rising heresy that 100,000 were reclaimed; at this time he instituted his third order (or Militia of Christ) for the laity. He held two general councils at Bologna; as a result, Dominicans were sent to England, Hungary, and Greece, a center was formed at Oxford, and a firm and effective balance was established between the intellectual life and popular needs. Dominic died in Bologna, Italy, on Aug. 6. He was canonized by Pope Gregory IX in 1234. F. D. Aug. 4.

BEDE JARRETT, *Life of St. Dominic* (New York, Benziger, 1924).

DOMINIC, BL. (d. 1300). A Dominican friar, he was preaching in the southern Pyrenees with Bl. Gregory when they were killed by a landslide near Perarua. Their cult was confirmed by Pope Pius IX in 1854. F. D. Apr. 26.

DOMINIC DE LA CALZADA, ST. (d. 1109?). A Basque from Vittoria, he became a hermit at Rioja, served St. Gregory of Ostia in his travels until the latter's death, then settled in the forest of Bureba, at La Calzada, Spain, through which he built a highway for those traveling to the shrine of St. James of Compostela. F. D. May 12.

DOMINIC LORICATUS, ST. (995–1060). Born in Umbria, he became a priest and, when he learned that his father had bribed the bishop to ordain him, began a lifetime of penance and mortification. He became a hermit under John of Montefeltro in the Apennines, and about 1042 a Benedictine under St. Peter Damian. His surname *loricatus* ("the mailed") came when it was learned he wore a coat of rough iron mail next to his skin. F. D. Oct. 14.

DOMINIC OF PRUSSIA (1382–1461). Born in Poland, he went to the University of Cracow, was a vagabond until twenty-five, reformed under the influence of Adolf of Essen, and became a Carthusian at St. Alban, near Trèves, in 1409. His life was marked by heavy discipline and spiritual gifts. He wrote an autobiography, *De contemptu mundi, De vera obedientia,* and fourteen other treatises. He and Adolf were influential in spreading the devotion of the rosary and recommended patterns of reflection. Dominic died at St. Alban, France.

DOMINIC OF SILOS, ST. (1000?–1073). Born in Canas, Spanish Navarre, he was a shepherd in his youth and then a Benedictine monk at the monastery of San Millán de la Cogolla and its prior. When he refused to surrender some of the monastery land, he was exiled by King García III of Navarre, but was appointed abbot of St. Sebastian monastery in Silos by King Ferdinand I of Old Castile. Under Dominic's rule Silos became one of the outstanding monasteries in Spain; its scriptorium produced some of the greatest Spanish Christian art. He also was active in rescuing Christian slaves from the Moors. F. D. Dec. 20.

DOMINIC OF SORA, ST. (951?–1031). Born at Foligno, Italy, he founded numerous Benedictine establishments in Italy, moving from one to another as abbot, engaging actively as converter of souls, with intervals for solitary contemplation. F. D. Jan. 22.

DOMINICA, ST. (d. 303?), martyr. A legendary figure who is supposed to have been beheaded in Campania during the Diocletian persecution, she may be the St. Cyriaca (the Greek can be translated as Dominica) martyred at Nicomedia and venerated in the East. F. D. July 6.

DOMINICA, ST. (d. 710?). *See* Indractus, St.

DOMINICA. *See* Cyriaca.

DOMINICI, BL. JOHN (1376–1419), cardinal. Born in Florence, Italy, he joined the Dominicans at eighteen, studied in Paris, and became famous as a preacher and theologian. He founded houses in Venice and Fiesole, served as prior in Florence, and led in restoring strict discipline in the order. He wrote scriptural commentaries; a number of hymns in the vernacular; two important treatises on education, *Lucula noctis* and *Regola del governo di cura familiare;* and an ascetical tract on charity. In 1406 he was appointed archbishop of Ragusa and cardinal by Pope Gregory XII, as whose confessor he served. He was active in attempting to lessen the pagan extremes of the Renaissance, was successful in arranging the resignation of Pope Gregory XII, which brought the Western schism to an end, converted many Hussites while Martin V's papal legate to Bohemia, and died at Buda, Hungary. His cult was confirmed in 1832. F. D. June 10.

DOMITIAN, ST. (347?–440?). Born in Rome, he became a monk and was ordained at Lérins, later founding the monastery of Bebron in Gaul; biographical sources are unreliable. F. D. July 1.

DOMITIAN, ST. (d. 560?), bishop. Born in France, he was elected bishop of Tongres, a see later transferred to Maastricht, Holland. He fought heresy at the Synod of Orléans (549) and a later famine, and evangelized the Meuse Valley. He is patron of Huy. F. D. May 7.

DOMITIUS, ST. (d. 361), martyr. A Phrygian, he was beheaded, probably at Caesarea, Palestine, for attacking the paganism rampant under Julian the Apostate. With him died SS. Aquila, Eparchius, Pelagia, and Theodosia. A St. Domitius listed in the Roman Martyrology for July 5 is probably the same person. Their feast day is Mar. 23.

DOMITIUS, ST. (d. 362?), martyr. A Persian convert, he became a monk at Nisbis, Mesopotamia, lived in a cave as a deacon, denounced Julian the Apostate, and was ordered stoned to death. F. D. Aug. 7. He probably is identical with the Phrygian Domitius who was beheaded at Caesarea on Julian's orders and is honored on Mar. 23 and on July 5.

DOMITIUS, ST. (8th century). A deacon, possibly a priest, of the diocese of Amiens, France, he lived as a hermit. F. D. Oct. 23.

DOMNA, ST. (d. 303), martyr. *See* Agapes, St.

DOMNINA, ST. (d. 303), martyr. She was tortured with extremity and died in prison at Anazarbus. F. D. Oct. 12.

DOMNINA, ST. (d. 303?), martyr. *See* Asterius, St.

DOMNINA, ST. (d. 4th century), martyr. She and her daughters, SS. Berenice and Prosdoce, were slain in Syria during the Diocletian persecution at the start of the century. F. D. Oct. 4.

DOMNINUS, ST. (d. 304), martyr. Leaving Parma, Italy, during an outbreak of persecution, he was captured and beheaded a few miles away. F. D. Oct. 9.

DOMNINUS, ST. (d. 374?). *See* Marcellinus, St.

DOMNINUS, ST. (4th century). He is said to have been first bishop of Grenoble, France. F. D. Nov. 5.

DOMNINUS, ST., martyr. A physician, sent to the mines as a slave, he was burned alive in Palestine sometime before the reign of Maximian. F. D. Nov. 5.

DOMNINUS, ST. (4th century), martyr. He and SS. Achaicus, Palotinus, and Philocalus were put to death in Thessalonica, Greece, during the persecution of Maximian. The Domninus listed in the Roman Martyrology for Oct. 1 is the same person. The St. Victor, slain with ten associates, and honored jointly on Mar. 30, died elsewhere.

DOMNIO, ST. (d. 295?), martyr. He was put to death at Bergamo, Italy, during the Diocletian persecution. F. D. July 16.

DOMNIO, ST. (d. 300?), martyr. He probably was slain during the Diocletian persecution; legend has him appointed first bishop of Salona, Dalmatia, by St. Peter the apostle. F. D. Apr. 11.

DOMNIO, ST. (4th century). He was a priest at Rome, highly praised by SS. Augustine and Jerome. F. D. Dec. 28.

DOMNOLUS, ST. (d. 581), bishop. He is said to have been abbot of a monastery in Paris when King Clotaire I bestowed on him the see of Le Mans, which he ruled for twenty-one years. He built a monastery, church, hospice, and is listed as attending the Council of Tours (566). St. Gregory of Tours praised him highly. F. D. May 16.

DOMNUS, ST. (d. 527). He succeeded St. Desiderius as bishop of Vienne, Gaul, and devoted himself to ransoming captives. F. D. Nov. 3.

DOMNUS, ST. (d. 1227), martyr. *See* Daniel, St.

DONAHOE, PATRICK (1811–1901), publisher. Born in Munnery, Cavan, Ireland, on Mar. 17, he went to Boston, Massachusetts, in 1821 and became a printer's apprentice. He worked on the staff of the *Jesuit* in 1832, renamed it the *Literary and Catholic Sentinel* when he and H. L. Devereaux became its editors, and in 1836 began publishing the *Pilot* (later the official newspaper of the archdiocese of Boston). Donahoe also engaged in publishing and bookselling, founded a bank, and, when two fires destroyed his printing house, sold the *Pilot* in 1876 to Archbishop Williams. Donahoe then directed a tourist agency, published the monthly *Donahoe's Magazine*, and in 1881 was able to repurchase the *Pilot*. He received the Laetare Medal in 1893 and died in Boston on Mar. 18.

DONAHUE, JOSEPH P. (1870–1959), bishop. Born in New York City on Nov. 6, he studied at City College, then at Manhattan (which gave him an honorary doctorate in 1940). He studied at St. Joseph's seminary, Troy, was ordained in 1895, and was a curate in New York City and Mamaroneck. In 1937, Cardinal Hayes made him a member of the diocesan board of consultors; he was made a monsignor that year and auxiliary bishop of New York in 1945. He also served as chairman of the archdiocesan school board (its present office building is named after him), and worked with Catholic Charities, the orphan asylum, and the Eucharistic League. He died in New York City on Apr. 26.

DONAHUE, PATRICK JAMES (1849–1922), bishop. Born in Malvern, Worcestershire, England, on Apr. 15, he graduated from the University of London in 1869, went to the United States in 1873, studied law at Columbian (now George Washington) University, Washington, was admitted to the bar, and practiced law from 1876 to 1882 in Washington, D.C. He then studied for the priesthood at St. Mary's, Baltimore, was ordained in Baltimore in 1885, became chancellor of the Baltimore archdiocese in 1886, was appointed rector of the cathedral in 1891, and in 1894 was appointed bishop of Wheeling, West Virginia. He died there on Oct. 4.

DONALD, ST. (8th century). He lived at Oglivy in Forfarshire, Scotland, had nine daughters, also known for their saintliness, and on his wife's death formed a religious community. F. D. July 15.

DONAT O'HAINGLY (d. 1095), bishop. An Irish Benedictine monk at Canterbury, he was consecrated there in 1085 by Lanfranc as third bishop of Dublin, where he died of plague.

DONATA, ST. (d. 180), martyr. *See* Speratus, St.

DONATELLO (1386?–1466), sculptor. Donato di Nicolò di Betto Bardi was born in Florence, Italy, son of a wool comber, and may have gone to Rome at seventeen with Brunellesco. Up to 1425 his work, completed chiefly in Florence, shows Gothic tendencies and the emergence of the classical. He executed *St. John the Evangelist, Moses, David,* and other figures for the cathedral; *St. George* and others for the exterior of Or San Michele; bronze doors and an *Annunciation* for San Lorenzo; and a great sandstone lion. His second period (to 1443) was marked by his association with the architect Michelozzi; work in bronze; the tomb of antipope John XXIII in Florence; statuettes for the baptismal font in San Giovanni, Prato; and the first modern bronze relief, a *Salome,* for the baptistery of the cathedral of Siena. In 1433 he went to Rome again, completed decorations for the coronation of

Emperor Sigismund, and designed a ciborium for St. Peter's. He returned to Florence in 1423 and did eight medallions and a nude *David* for the Medici palace. In his last period he designed a series of bronze statues for the altar in the cathedral in Padua (completed by his pupils); the first modern equestrian statue, of Erasmo da Narni, Padua; *Judith and Holofernes*; and busts of contemporary persons. His faces are highly realistic, dramatic, and powerful, revealing great attention to character. He returned to Florence from Padua and a brief tour of northern cities in 1457. Bedridden during his last years, he was supported by the work of his pupils, whom Piero de' Medici paid. His influence dominated sculpture in the cities of northern Italy for the rest of the century. He died in Florence on Dec. 13.

DONATI, BL. BARTHOLOMEW (d. 1420), martyr. *See* Nerucci, Bl. Laurence.

DONATIAN, ST. (3rd century), martyr. A native of Nantes in western Gaul, he was put to death with his brother Rogatian about 300 during the Diocletian persecution for refusing to sacrifice to pagan gods. F. D. May 24.

DONATIAN, ST. (d. 390). A Roman, he became bishop of Rheims in 360 and is venerated as the patron saint of Bruges. F. D. Oct. 14.

DONATIAN, ST. (d. 484?), bishop and martyr. During the persecution by Huneric, Arian king of the Vandals, Catholic churches were closed and thousands driven into exile. Among them were Donatian, who with four other bishops of Byzacene, Fusculus, Germanus, Mansuetus, and Praesidius, was scourged and sent into the desert to die. Laetus, bishop of Leptis Minor, was burned alive on this occasion. F. D. Sept. 6.

DONATILLA, ST. (d. 304), martyr. She and SS. Maxima and Secunda, a twelve-year-old, were slain at Tebourba, Africa, during the Diocletian persecution. F. D. July 30.

DONATUS, ST. (3rd century), martyr. He and SS. Herena and Justus are named in a group of fifty Christians who were put to death in northern Africa during the Decian persecution. F. D. Feb. 25.

DONATUS, ST. (3rd century), martyr. *See* Aquilinus, St.

DONATUS, ST. (d. 303?), martyr. *See* Honoratus, St.

DONATUS, ST. (d. 304), martyr. He and SS. Romulus and Secundian are named in a group of eighty-nine Christians who were put to death at Porto Gruaro, near Venice, Italy, during the Diocletian persecution. F. D. Feb. 17.

DONATUS, ST. (d. 305?), martyr. He and SS. Fructuosa, Restitutus, Valerian, and twelve other Syrians were put to death at Antioch. F. D. Aug. 23.

DONATUS, ST. (d. 362), martyr. He and St. Primus were deacons who were slain when Donatists attempted to seize the Catholic church in Lavallum in northern Africa. F. D. Feb. 9.

DONATUS, ST. (d. 362), bishop. The Roman Martyrology refers to the bishop of Arezzo as a martyr, in Tuscany, but there is no evidence. He is often confused with the bishop of Euroea. F. D. Aug. 7.

DONATUS, ST. (4th century), bishop. He was praised by Sozomen and others for the holiness of his direction of the see of Euroea, Albania. F. D. Apr. 30.

DONATUS, ST. (d. 483?), martyr. *See* Appian, St.

DONATUS, ST. (d. 535?). Born in Orléans, France, he lived as a hermit on Mt. Jura, near Sisteron, Provence. F. D. Aug. 19.

DONATUS, ST. (d. 660?). A Benedictine monk at Luxeuil, he became bishop of Besançon, France, in 624 and founded the abbey of St. Paul there. F. D. Aug. 7.

DONATUS, ST. (d. 876?), bishop. Born in Ireland, he made a pilgrimage to Rome in 816, served Lothair and Louis, princes of Italy, and while on his way back to Ireland in 829 was chosen bishop of Fiesole, Italy, by popular acclaim. He ruled that see until about 876. He wrote several poems, and taught grammar and poetry. F. D. Oct. 22.

DONATUS, ST. (1179–1198). Born in Ripacandida, Rapallo, Italy, he became a Benedictine monk at Petina in 1194 and died before he was twenty. F. D. Aug. 17.

DONCHAD O'DALY (d. 1250). Cistercian abbot of Boyle abbey, Elphin, Roscommon, Ireland, he was widely hailed as a poet.

DONDERS, PETER (1807–1887), missioner. Born in Tilburg, Holland, on Oct. 27, he studied in Herlaar, was ordained in 1840, and labored with the Negro plantation workers in Dutch Guiana from 1842 until stricken by plague in 1851. He converted more than 1200 and after his convalescence worked with the Indians of Saramaca. In 1855 he added the leper colony in Batavia to his labors and served there until his death on Jan. 14. When the area was transferred to the Redemptorists in 1865, Fr. Donders joined that order.

DONGAN, THOMAS (1634–1715), governor. Born in Castletown Kildrought (Celbridge), Kildare, Ireland, son of Sir John Dongan, a member of the Irish parliament, he went into exile in France after the death of King Charles I in 1649. He served as colonel of an Irish regiment, returned to England in 1678, was appointed lieutenant governor of Tangiers in that year, and in 1682 was sent to the bankrupt colony of New York, the first Catholic governor of the American colonies. He set the boundaries of the state as a result of conferences with Connecticut, Pennsylvania, and Canadian authorities; outlined an Indian policy which kept the Five Nations on the side of England; established a post office in 1685, and granted charters to New York City and Albany in 1686, which remained in use for 135 and 184 years respectively. His most important contribution to government was his Charter of Liberties, signed on Oct. 30, 1683, after its acceptance by the assembly. It made the assembly the equal of the British parliament, established courts, assured religious liberty, no taxation without representation, or quartering of troops, protected realty holdings, defined the right to vote and election by a majority. The document was a model for colonial resistance later in the century, and after the revolution became the framework of England's own colonial policy in Canada and Australia. The duke of York approved the charter and returned a signed copy to New York; but it apparently was not given to King Charles II. When York became King James II in 1685, he approved the action of the Board of Trade and Plantations in vetoing the charter; in 1687, James dissolved the provincial assembly and sent Andros as governor in 1688. Dongan retired to Staten Island, was driven out in 1691 by religious persecution, and returned to England. On the death of his brother William, governor of Munster, in 1698, Thomas became earl of Limerick. He died in London on Dec. 14.

DONLEVY, ANDREW (b. 1694?). Born in Sligo, Ireland, he went into exile when the penal laws became stringent, studied in the Irish College in Paris, was ordained there, and served as its prefect from 1728 to 1746. He took degrees in theology and law at Paris, wrote a new code of laws for the Irish College, and published an Irish-English catechism (1742).

DONNAN, ST. (6th century). Son of Beoadh and brother of St. Ciaran, he was a monk at the monastery of Clonmacnoise, Ireland.

DONNAN, ST. (6th century). Son of Liath and nephew of St. Senan, who trained him, he succeeded St. Ciaran of Clonmacnoise as abbot of Aingin, a monastery on Hare Island in the Shannon River, Ireland.

DONNAN, ST. (d. 618), martyr. An Irish monk at Iona under St. Columba, he became the founder and abbot of a monastery on Eigg Island in the Inner Hebrides, where he and fifty-two companions were murdered or burned to death on Easter Sunday by raiding outlaws. F. D. Apr. 17.

DONNE, HENRY (d. 1593), martyr. Brother of the English poet John Donne, he remained a Catholic, was captured and imprisoned for harboring Bl. William Harrington, a missionary priest martyred the following year, and died of jail fever.

DONNELLY, FRANCIS P. (1869–1959), educator. Born in Pittston, Pennsylvania, on Dec. 10, he studied at Villanova and Fordham,

became a Jesuit in 1888, and was ordained in 1903. He taught classics and rhetoric for fifty years, at Boston College, Holy Cross, and Fordham. He received three honorary degrees in recognition of his texts on education, writing, criticism, and analysis of Latin authors, as well as twenty devotional works. He died in Poughkeepsie, New York, on Apr. 18.

DONNELLY, GEORGE J. (1889–1950), bishop. Born in St. Louis, Missouri, on Apr. 23, he studied at Kenrick seminary there and was ordained in 1921. He was appointed titular bishop of Coela and auxiliary of St. Louis in 1940, and in 1946 was named bishop of Leavenworth, Kansas, where he died on Dec. 13.

DONNER, GEORG RAPHAEL (1692–1741), sculptor. Born in Essling, Austria, on May 25, he studied in Vienna, entered the imperial service and, in 1729, that of Prince Esterházy, and completed classical and religious figures in bronze and marble for the archbishop's palace in Salzburg and the Pressburg cathedral. An equestrian statue of St. Martin, Pressburg, and a fountain in the Neu Markt in Vienna, were outstanding. He died in Vienna on Feb. 15. His brother Matthäus (1704–56) taught and became rector of the Vienna Academy and is known for his medals and relief carvings.

DONNET, FERDINAND FRANÇOIS AUGUSTE (1795–1882), cardinal. Born in Bourg-Argental, France, he studied in Lyons, taught in Belley, was ordained in 1819, was pastor at Irigny and Villefranche, and became coadjutor bishop of Nancy in 1835. As bishop of Bordeaux from 1837 until his death, he convened provincial councils, restored shrines, and battled for freedom of religious education and publication. He became a cardinal in 1852, attended the Vatican Council in 1870, and died in Bordeaux, France.

DONO, PAOLO DI. *See* Uccello, Paolo.

DONOGH MÓR O'DALY (d. 1244), poet. An Irishman, he wrote considerable religious poetry, of which thirty examples are extant. He is buried at Boyle, Ireland, where he may have been abbot.

DONOSO CORTÉS, JUAN FRANCISCO MARÍA DE LA SALUDAD (1800–1853), diplomat. Born in Valle de la Serena, Estremadura, Spain, on May 6, he studied at Salamanca and Seville, became professor of literature at Caceres, a follower of Rousseau, a leading Liberal, and minister of justice. The revolution of 1834 turned him against political liberalism and made him a supporter of the crown. He became secretary of the council, lectured in Madrid on political rights, became a deputy in the Cortes, and after the revolution of 1840 went to Paris with Queen Maria Cristina as her secretary. He tutored Princess Isabella, was named marqués of Valdegamus, became a senator, and led the attack in the Cortes on philosophical liberalism. His brother's death had made him a firm defender of Catholicism from 1849 until his death on May 3 in Paris. He was minister plenipotentiary to the court at Berlin and then at Paris. His study of *Catholicism, Socialism, and Liberalism,* condemned by Bishop Gaudel of Orléans, was supported by Louis Veuillot and later by the papacy. His correspondence (1849–53) with Count Raczyski, Prussian ambassador to Madrid, later published, reveals astute awareness of the forthcoming rise of Germany and political decline of France.

DONOSO, JUSTO (1800–1868), bishop. Born in Santiago, Chile, he became rector of the Seminario Conciliar there, professor of theology and secretary of the theological faculty of the university, and judge of the ecclesiastical court. He was one of the founders of *Revista Católica,* became bishop of Ancud in 1844, and was transferred to La Serena, Chile, in 1855. He published a study of canon law in South America and a theological dictionary. He died in La Serena on Feb. 22.

DONUS (d. 678), pope. Born in Rome, son of Mauricius, he was consecrated pope on Nov. 2, 676, restored and repaired church structures, accepted the submission of Reparatus, archbishop of Ravenna, which ended the schism begun by Archbishop Maurus, and died in Rome on Apr. 11.

DOOLEY, THOMAS ANTHONY (1927–1961), physician. Born in St. Louis, Missouri, on Jan. 17, he studied at Notre Dame, but had his career interrupted by service as a hospital corpsman in World War II, then took his medical degree at St. Louis in 1953. He re-enlisted in the navy, was sent to Vietnam as a medical officer, and for his heroic work as the only doctor serving 600,000 refugees from communism was awarded the Legion of Merit. From the proceeds of *Deliver Us from Evil,* an eyewitness account of the nation's collapse, he worked with three other navy veterans to establish a hospital in Laos and to start a nursing school. Out of the navy, he worked as a civilian, published *The Edge of Tomorrow,* another report, and teamed with Dr. Peter Comanduras to found Medico (Medical International Co-operation Organization) which sought to provide health services in underdeveloped areas of the world. By 1960 they were active in ten countries. Dr. Dooley spent as much time as possible in Laos with his native patients, was stricken with cancer in 1959, published a third account of the Far East in *The Night They Burned the Mountain,* and campaigned for funds for Medico. He died in New York City on Jan. 18.

DORAN, THOMAS FRANCIS (1856–1916), bishop. Born in Berrington, Rhode Island, on Oct. 4, he studied at Mt. St. Mary's, Maryland, and was ordained in 1880. He did parish work in the Providence diocese, was appointed chancellor in 1884, vicar general in 1894, and was made a domestic prelate in 1895. He was appointed titular bishop of Halicarnassus and auxiliary of Providence in 1915, and died there on Jan. 3.

DORBHENE, ST. (d. 713). A descendant of St. Columba's brother, he served as abbot of Iona. F. D. Oct. 28.

DORÉ, PIERRE (1500?–1559), author. Born in Orléans, France, he became a Dominican in 1514, preached widely, was prior at Blois in 1545, reformed the Carthusian monastery of Val des Choux, wrote Latin poems, made translations of hymns by Thomas Aquinas, and completed some thirty-five ascetical and theological works. He was active against the Calvinists and Huguenots, was satirized for his descriptive style by Rabelais, and died in Paris on May 19. He is remembered particularly for his defense of the Eucharist and the mass and for an office for a feast of St. Joseph, written at the request of Pope Paul III.

DORIA, ANDREA (1468–1560), admiral. Born in Oneglia, Italy, on Nov. 30, he served as a papal guard, in the Neapolitan army, and as a Knight of St. John of Jerusalem. In 1503 he returned to a peaceful Genoa, directed the subjection of the rebellious Corsicans, and outfitted eight galleys with his own money and set up an independent naval arm. He cleared the Mediterranean of Barbary pirates from 1507 to 1519. When civil strife broke out again in Genoa, he served Francis I as governor general of the galleys of France and raised the blockade of Marseilles by defeating the navy of Charles V. In 1525 he was commander of the navy of Pope Clement VII, went back to France in 1527, compelled Genoa to acknowledge the supremacy of Francis I, then broke with the monarch when he was not paid. With his nephew Filippo he entered the service of Charles V, established order in Genoa, which now accepted the emperor, and drew up a constitution for the city-state which lasted until 1798. He continued to scour the Mediterranean with the combined fleets, under the Austrian flag, besieged Tunis, defeated the Turks in Greece, and with ships from Venice, the papacy, and the Knights of Malta defeated Barbarossa in the Gulf of Arta in 1536. Retiring with great honors, he lived thereafter in his palace at Fassolo. In 1547 he cruelly suppressed a revolt by Genoese nobles who had slain his nephew Gianettino. He died in Genoa on Nov. 25.

DÖRING, MATTHIAS (1390?–1460), historian. Born in Kyritz, Brandenburg, between 1390 and 1400, he became a Friar Minor there, studied at Oxford and Erfurt, taught theology and scripture, and from 1443 to 1449 was minister general of the Conventuals. He was active in the Council of Basle which declared that a general council had supremacy over a pope, voted to elect Felix V as antipope, and was excommunicated. He resigned all offices in 1461 and retired to Kyritz, where he wrote a continuation of the *Chronicle* of Dietrich Engelhus, covering the years 1420–64, and where he died on July 24. Other works, chiefly controversial, have been assigned to him.

DORMAN, THOMAS (d. 1572?), theologian. Born in Berkhampstead, Hertfordshire, England, he was educated there, at Winchester, and at Oxford, became fellow of All Souls during the reign of Queen Mary, and went to Antwerp after Elizabeth's accession. In 1565 he took his doctorate in theology at Louvain, joined the faculty of the new college in Douai, and wrote controversial pamphlets. He died in Tournai, Flanders, before 1577.

DORNIN, BERNARD (1761–1836), publisher. Born in Ireland, he went to New York in 1803, began a bookselling and publishing firm, printed a New Testament (Brooklyn, 1805), set up his business in Baltimore in 1809 and in Philadelphia in 1817, and shortly before his death retired to Ohio.

DOROTHEUS, ST. (d. 303?), martyr. *See* Gorgonius, St.

DOROTHEUS, ST. (d. 362?), martyr. He is said to have been bishop of Tyre, exiled during the persecutions of Diocletian and of Julian the Apostate. He may have been the author of some popularly current scriptural biographies and may have died at the age of 107 at Varna (Bulgaria) of the effects of scourgings. F. D. June 5.

DOROTHEUS THE ARCHIMANDRITE, ST. (d. 640?). A monk in Gaza, he directed a large monastery somewhere in the Near East, at which St. Dositheus was one of his holiest followers. He wrote a series of twenty-four discourses on monastic life, which the Abbot de Rancé later had translated for his Cistercian monks. F. D. June 5.

DOROTHEUS OF KHILIOKOMOS (11th century). Born at Trebizond on the Black Sea, and sometimes called "the younger," he fled at twelve to avoid an arranged marriage, entered the monastery of Genna in Pontus, and was ordained. Later, he built a monastery near Amisos (now Samsun, Turkey), in honor of the Trinity. F. D. June 5.

DOROTHY, ST. (1st century?), martyr. She and SS. Erasma, Euphemia, and Thecla were put to death at Aquileia, Italy. F. D. Sept. 3.

DOROTHY, ST. (d. 303?), martyr. She was killed probably in Cappadocia during the persecution of Diocletian. Legends tell of the attempts of the governor of Caesarea to make her sacrifice to idols, and of the laughter of a

lawyer named Theophilus who jeered at her as she went to her death, defying her to send him flowers from "the garden" to which she had joyously announced she was going. In mediaeval art an angel appears before him after her death with a basket of apples and roses, and stories tell of his subsequent conversion and martyrdom. F. D. Feb. 6.

DOROTHY OF MONTAU (1347–1394). Born in Montau, Prussia, on Feb. 6, she married a wealthy swordsmith, Albrecht of Danzig, when seventeen, had nine children, and suffered from her husband's surliness until her patient acceptance changed him. When he died in 1390 she lived as a recluse at Marienwerder, where she is said to have had many visions, and where she died on June 25. Although never canonized, she is often regarded as patroness of Prussia and honored in many localities on Oct. 30.

DORSEY, ANNA HANSON (1815–1896), novelist. Born in Washington, D.C., on Dec. 12, daughter of William McKenney, a navy chaplain, she married Lorenzo Dorsey in 1837 and became a convert in 1840. She wrote more than a score of novels, with such titles as *Tears of the Diadem, Conscience or the Trials of May Brooke, Nora Brady's Vow,* and *The Old Gray Rosary.* In 1889 she received the Laetare Medal. She died in Washington on Dec. 25.

DORYMEDON, ST. (d. 277?), martyr. He and SS. Sabbatius and Trophimus were put to death, probably at Antioch, Syria, during the persecution of Probus. F. D. Sept. 19.

DOSITHEUS (d. 530?). A pagan, converted at Jerusalem, he became an ascetic under the direction of Dorotheus at the monastery of Abbot Seridos in Gaza. He was recorded as a very willing and prayerful follower of their rule, and later honored on Feb. 23, but has never formally been recognized as a saint.

DOSQUET, PIERRE HERMAN (1691–1777), bishop. Born in Liège, Flanders, he became a Sulpician in Paris, served in Canada (1721–23), as superior of the seminary in Liseux, France, as procurator general for oriental missions, and was named titular bishop of Samos by Pope Benedict XIII in 1725. In 1729 he went to Quebec as coadjutor to Bishop Mornay, succeeded to the see in 1733, contributed to educational advancement and to the mission areas of the Atlantic coast, resigned in ill health in 1739, and went to Rome. He died in Paris on Mar. 4.

DOSSO DOSSI. *See* Lutero, Giovanni Nicolo di.

DOTTI, BL. ANDREA (1256–1315). Born in Borgo San Sepolcro, Tuscany, he became a Servite tertiary at seventeen, and on hearing St. Philip Benizi preach became a Servite friar. He accompanied St. Philip on several of his missionary journeys through Italy and was a noted speaker. In 1310 he retired to live as a hermit. His cult was approved in 1806. F. D. Sept. 3.

DOUGHERTY, DENNIS (1865–1951), cardinal. Born in Ashland, Pennsylvania, on Aug. 16, he worked in the mines, went to St. Mary's, Montreal, at sixteen, and St. Charles's seminary, Philadelphia, at eighteen, and was ordained in 1890 after further studies at the North American College, Rome. He taught at St. Charles until 1903, when he was consecrated first American bishop of Nueva Segovia in the Philippines in 1903. He ended a major schism there, was transferred to Jaro, Philippine Islands, in 1908, returned to serve as bishop of Buffalo in 1916, and was made archbishop of Philadelphia in 1918. In 1921 he became the fifth American to be named a cardinal. He was active in temperance movements and against communism, sought to raise the moral tone of motion pictures, and established seventy-two new parishes, ninety schools (including three high schools and a seminary), and forty-eight churches during the time he was archbishop. He died in Philadelphia on May 31.

DOUGLAS, ALFRED BRUCE (1870–1945), poet. Born in Ham Hill, near Worcester, England, on Oct. 22, son of John Douglas, marquess of Queensberry, and Sybil Montgomery, he attended Winchester and Oxford, where he edited student magazines. He met Oscar Wilde in 1891, was cut off by his father, lived off gifts from his divorced mother, and remained close to Wilde until the latter's death in 1900. Douglas married Olive Custance in 1902, was unsuccessful as editor of the *Academy* in 1907–10, and became a convert in 1911. He was involved in many libel suits over his relations with Wilde, and jailed in 1923 for questioning Winston Churchill's accuracy as an historian. He wrote sonnets and humorous poems, two contradictory volumes on Wilde, *Collected Satire* (1927), *Complete Poems* (1928), *Autobiography* (1929), and *Without Apology* (1938). He died in Lancing, Sussex, England, on Mar. 20.

DOUGLAS, ARCHIBALD (1449?–1514?). He became fifth earl of Angus when his father, George, died in 1462. He plotted with Edward IV of England and Alexander Stuart, duke of Albany, against King James III of Scotland, and, when James invaded England in 1482, Douglas headed a group of Scots nobles who plotted against him, captured the king's favorite, the earl of Mars, and hanged him. He acquired his name of "Bell-the-Cat" for planning this feat because he offered to bell the cat (Mars) for the conspirators; he is also called the "Great Earl." He later left the rebels, served as lord chancellor of Scotland in 1493–98 during King James IV's reign, and when he opposed James lost most of his holdings, but

received in return the lordship of Bothwell. He lived his last years in the priory of Whithorn, Galloway, where he died. His grandson Archibald married Margaret, sister of King Henry VIII of England and widow of James IV of Scotland.

DOUGLAS, GAVIN (1474?–1522), poet. Son of Archibald, fifth earl of Angus, he was educated at St. Andrews and Paris, returned to Scotland for parish duty, and in 1501 became provost of the church of St. Giles, Edinburgh. Named bishop of Dunkeld in 1515 through the influence of Queen Margaret, who had married his nephew, Archibald, he failed to obtain the office; the queen was deprived of her regency for making an ecclesiastical appointment without the consent of parliament and Douglas was jailed for a year for conspiracy. Released, he took office with papal approval, but was driven out in 1520. He went to London in 1521 to seek support from King Henry VIII and died there in Sept. of the plague. While a parson in East Lothian he wrote the allegorical poem, *The Palice of Honour*, and other poems in the Chaucerian manner (*King Hart* and *Conscience*), translated Ovid's *De remedio amoris*, and made an adaptation (1513) of Vergil's *Aeneid*, with an original verse prologue to each book marked by lyric enthusiasm for Scots landscape.

DOUGLAS, MARGARET (1515–1578). Daughter of Archibald Douglas, sixth earl of Angus, and Margaret Tudor, she was born in Harbottle castle, Northumberland, served Princess Mary of England at Beaulieu in 1531, was imprisoned by Henry VIII when she became engaged to Thomas Howard, changed her intentions, married Matthew Stewart, and was barred from the line of succession to the English throne because of her Catholicism. She arranged the marriage between her son, Lord Darnley, and Mary Queen of Scots, was arrested in 1562 for this by Elizabeth I, who called the action treasonable, and was imprisoned in the Tower. Although she attacked Mary for the latter's alleged part in the murder of Darnley, she reversed herself and supported her. She died on Mar. 7.

DOUGLAS, WILLIAM (d. 1611). Greatgrandson of William Douglas of Glenbervie, second son of Archibald "Bell-the-Cat," he succeeded his father William in 1591 as earl of Angus, became a convert, and died in Paris.

DOUGLAS-IRVINE, HELEN (d. 1947), author. Born in Pittenweem, Fife, Scotland, she traveled with her parents, was educated in England and at St. Andrews, and wrote *Royal Palaces of Scotland*, *History of London*, and *Mediaeval Markets and Fairs*. She served in a Serbian hospital during World War I, worked for the International Labor Office after that war, became a convert in 1917, edited the

Catholic Citizen (London), published *The Making of Rural Europe*, and went to South America in 1922, making her home in Chile after 1931. There she wrote novels (*Magdalena; Fray Mario; Mirror of a Dead Lady*), short stories (*Angelic Romance*), and travel accounts for newspapers there and in England. She returned to London to work in the censorship office during World War II and published *Torchlight Procession* in 1945. She died in Chile.

DOUTRELEAU, STEPHEN (b. 1693), missioner. Born in France on Oct. 11, he became a Jesuit, went to Louisiana in 1727, was at Vincennes in 1728, and set out for New Orleans in 1730, unaware that the Natchez Indians had been slaughtering settlers. His party was attacked during the celebration of mass, and Fr. Doutreleau was wounded and a companion killed. He reached a friendly area, was chaplain of French troops and of a hospital in New Orleans, returned to his mission among the Illinois Indians, and went back to France in 1747. The date of his death is unknown.

DOVIZI, BERNARDO (1470–1520), cardinal. Born on Aug. 4 in Bibbiena, Italy, which he used as a pen name, he became a scholar, wit, and friend of Giovanni de' Medici, whom he followed into banishment in 1494. When Giovanni became Pope Leo X in 1513, Bibbiena became treasurer and, in 1518, papal legate to France. His sympathy for France cost him Leo's favor. He was a patron of artists, including Raphael, who did his portrait, and wrote *La Calandra*, a play based on Plautus and influencing Ariosto and Machiavelli. He died in Rome on Nov. 9.

DOWDALL, GEORGE (1487–1558), archbishop. Born in Drogheda, Louth, Ireland, he became a member of the Order of Crutched Friars, was prior of their monastery at Ardee when it was seized by Henry VIII, received a small royal pension, acknowledged the king as head of the Church, and was royally named archbishop of Armagh. Nevertheless, he fought the advance of Protestantism in Ireland during Henry's reign and that of Edward VI, retired to the Continent, renounced his schism, and in 1553 was papally appointed archbishop of Armagh. He held a synod at Drogheda in 1554 and died in London on Aug. 15.

DOWDALL, BL. JAMES (d. 1600), martyr. A merchant in Drogheda, Ireland, trading with England and the continent, he was shipwrecked in Devonshire when returning from a trip to France, arrested by William Bourchier, and imprisoned in Exeter. He refused to acknowledge the ecclesiastical supremacy of Queen Elizabeth I, was frequently tortured in prison, and on Sept. 20 was hanged, drawn, and quartered in Exeter, England.

DOWLING, AUSTIN (1868–1930), arch-

bishop. Born in New York City on Apr. 6, he graduated from Manhattan in 1887, studied at St. John's seminary, Boston, and Catholic University, and was ordained in 1891. He taught at St. John's in 1894–96, edited the Providence *Visitor* the next two years, and after several years of pastoral work was appointed rector of SS. Peter and Paul cathedral in Providence in 1905. He became first bishop of Des Moines, Iowa, in 1912, founded Des Moines Catholic (now Dowling) College in 1918, and in 1919 was appointed second archbishop of St. Paul, Minnesota. He served as episcopal chairman of the educational department of the National Catholic Welfare Conference and died in St. Paul on Nov. 29.

DOWLING, JOHN P. (1860–1940), archbishop. Born in Freshford, Ireland, on June 23, he became a Dominican in 1881, was ordained in 1887, was superior in Trinidad in 1905, and in 1909 became archbishop and metropolitan of Port of Spain, Trinidad, where he died on June 5.

DOWNES, THOMAS (1617–1678). Born in Norfolk, England, he studied at St. Omer and Vallodolid, became a Jesuit in 1639, continued his studies in Liège and Pont-à-Mousson, and in 1671 was named chaplain to the duke of York, later King James II. He served with distinction on the royal flagship in battles against the Dutch. He was known as Fr. Bedingfeld (his mother's maiden name) and James called him Fr. Mumford. In 1678 he was sent forged letters, which tied his name to the Titus Oates conspiracy; King Charles II spoke openly of the priest's innocence, but he was imprisoned in Gatehouse, where he died on Dec. 21.

DOWNEY, RICHARD (1881–1953), bishop. Born in Kilkenny, Ireland, he became bishop of Liverpool, England, in 1928, was interested in education and agrarian movements, was strenuous in his attacks on communism and bureaucracy, twice went to the United States for lecture tours, and died in Liverpool on June 16.

DOYLE, HENRY. Son of John Doyle, he was born in England, became commissioner for the Papal States and the international exposition at London in 1862, was secretary of the National Portrait Gallery in 1865–69, then became director of the National Gallery of Ireland. He married Jane Ball in 1866, dabbled in art, completed some portraits (of his brother Richard and his patron, Cardinal Wiseman), and drew political cartoons for *Fun*. He became a justice of the peace for Wicklow in 1884 and died in Ireland on Feb. 17.

DOYLE, JAMES WARREN (1786–1834), bishop. Born near New Ross, Wexford, Ireland, he studied at the Augustinian college there, joined that order, went to Coimbra, Portugal, returned to Ireland in 1808, and was ordained in 1809. He taught logic at New Ross for eight years, at Carlow from 1817 to 1819, and then was named bishop of Kildare and Leighlin. He defied the penal laws by publishing on religious and civil liberty and the injustice of courts and landlords, was called before two parliamentary committees in London, where he proceeded to lecture his inquisitors, joined the Catholic Association, supported Daniel O'Connell, and led the battle against tithes. As bishop he conducted retreats, built churches and schools, established libraries, and actively attacked intemperance and secret societies. He died in Carlow, Ireland.

DOYLE, JAMES WILLIAM EDMUND (1822–1892). Eldest son of John Doyle and brother of Henry, he was born in London on Oct. 22, studied painting, produced a popular portrait of *Samuel Johnson Reading the Vicar of Wakefield*, then abandoned art for history. He published *Chronicle of England* (from Caesar to 1485), then began to issue a list of English aristocrats from the Conquest to 1668. His *Official Baronage of England* was later brought down to 1885, and described the succession, titles, and heraldic bearings of the nobility; it was not the success he hoped, inasmuch as his sources were not always accurate, and the total effect is uneven. He died in London on Dec. 3.

DOYLE, JEREMIAH JOSEPH (d. 1909), bishop. One of the first priests to serve the Lismore area of Australia, he was consecrated first bishop of Grafton in 1887, lived at Lismore and had its name adopted for the new see, built the cathedral between 1892 and 1908, and died on the following June 4.

DOYLE, JOHN (1797–1868), painter. Born in Dublin, Ireland, he studied under Gabrielli and Comerford, went to London in 1821 as a portrait painter, and from 1827 to 1851 produced caricatures of political life under the initials H. B. Some 600, preserved in the British Museum, are valuable commentaries on the century and some contain the only known sketches of prominent figures. He died in London on Jan. 2.

DOYLE, MICHAEL FRANCIS (1877–1960), jurist. Born in Philadelphia, he took his law degree at the University of Pennsylvania in 1897, practiced in his native city, and became an authority on international law. He represented the state department in Europe during World War I, caring for Americans there and acting as special counselor in the Swiss legation and Austrian embassy. In 1916 he was defense counsel for Sir Roger Casement, condemned for high treason and hanged by the British; he also defended Eamon de Valera, whose death sentence was commuted to life imprisonment. He was counsel for other Irish revolutionary leaders in 1922 and helped to draft the constitution of the Irish Free State. He was special assistant to the American chief of ordnance in 1917–18, counsel for Haiti and Santo Domingo before the state department in 1922, chairman of the American commission at the League of Nations in Geneva from 1923 on, and United States delegate to the Inter-American Conference for Peace which met at Buenos Aires in 1936. He was a member of the permanent court of arbitration at The Hague from 1938 to 1951, president of the electoral college of the United States in 1937, 1941, 1945, and 1949, and special counsel to the Philippine Republic. He was honored by France, Bulgaria, and the Philippines, many Latin-American and European countries, and by his native state, and received two honorary degrees. He was a founder of the National Conference of Catholic Charities and of the National Near East Association, for which he also was counsel, was instrumental in gaining permission from Russia for American missioners to serve in Moscow, and six times was honored by the Vatican, which named him a papal chamberlain in 1959. He died in Philadelphia on Mar. 25.

DOYLE, RICHARD (1824–1883), artist. Son of John Doyle, he was born in London, inherited his father's powers as caricaturist, and from 1843 to 1850 was on the staff of *Punch*, designing its cover and writing and illustrating a regular column. When the magazine began anti-Catholic attacks in 1850, Doyle resigned and became a water-colorist and book illustrator, decorating in Ruskin's *King of the Golden River* and Thackeray's *The Newcomes*. He died in London on Dec. 11.

DRACH, DAVID PAUL (1791–1868). Born in Strassburg, Alsace, on Mar. 6, son of a Talmudic scholar, he served as rabbi in Colmar, Alsace, joined the Central Jewish Consistory in Paris, and tutored children of prominent Jewish and Christian families. He began the study of patristic literature and of the Septuagint, and became a convert in 1823, with three of his children. In 1827 he became librarian of the College of Propaganda, Rome. He advised Franz Libermann in founding the Congregation of the Immaculate Heart of Mary, published an autobiography, an annotated Bible, a Hebrew-Chaldaic dictionary of the Old Testament, and several scholarly studies. He died in Rome in Jan.

DRACH, PAUL AUGUSTIN (1817–1895). Born on Aug. 12, son of David Paul Drach, he studied in Rome, where he was ordained in 1846, became canon of Notre Dame, and edited a biblical commentary, for which he wrote the sections on the epistles and the Apocalypse. He died on Oct. 29.

DRACONTIUS, BLOSSIUS AEMILIUS (5th century), poet. Born in Carthage, North Africa, he studied grammar under Felician, and became wealthy through his law practice and the favor of the proconsul until support of Roman policy led to a quarrel with King Gunthamund and a long imprisonment. In prison he wrote *De laudibus Dei* and *Satisfactio* (480), on providence, the creation, Incarnation, and redemption. He also wrote secular poems on mythological subjects and *Romulea*, a series of prose rhetorical debates. He died sometime after 496.

DRANE, AUGUSTA THEODOSIA (1823–1894). Born in Bromley, near London, she was taken to Devonshire, became interested in the Oxford Movement, and was converted in 1850. She entered the third order of St. Dominic as Mother Frances Raphael in 1852, was stationed at Stone as mistress of studies, and became prioress in 1872 and provincial in 1881. She wrote biographies of SS. Dominic and Catherine of Siena, and edited those of Mother Margaret Hallahan, foundress of her order, and Archbishop Ullathorne, its patron. She also wrote historical narratives, educational treatises, and some poetry. She died in Stone, England, on Apr. 29.

DRAUSIUS, ST. (d. 674?), bishop. Educated by St. Anseric, he became archdeacon to Bishop Bettoein, and succeeded them as bishop of Soissons, France, where he built a double monastery. He is also known as Drusio. F. D. Mar. 7.

DRESCHEL, JEREMIAS (1581–1638). Born in Augsburg, Germany, on Aug. 15, he became a Jesuit in 1598, taught at Augsburg and Dillingen, and was court preacher to the elector of Bavaria for twenty-three years. He wrote nearly forty books on ascetics, including the popular *Considerationes de aeternitate* (1620), *Zodiacus christianus*, *The Guardian Angel's Clock*, and *Gymnasium of Patience*. He died in Munich, Germany, on Apr. 19.

DREVES, LEBRECHT BLÜCHER (1816–1870), poet. Born in Hamburg, Germany, on Sept. 12, he wrote poems in German and Latin before he was fifteen, completed two volumes of lyrics before he finished his law degree in 1838, and became a convert in 1846. Two more volumes of songs appeared, and a comedy (*Der Lebensretter*), a collection of church hymns, and an edition of historical sources on the history of Hamburg. He issued his collected poems after careful advice from his poet-friend, Joseph von Eichendorff. His interest in church music and poetry was carried on by his son, who edited *Analecta hymnica medii aevi*. Dreves died in Feldkirch, Voralberg, Austria, on Dec. 19.

DREVET, CLAUDE (1705–1782), engraver. Born in Lyons, France, nephew of Pierre the Elder, he followed the style of the latter and of his cousin, and succeeded to the family's business and fortune.

DREVET, PIERRE (1663–1738), engraver. Born in Loire, France, he studied in Lyons and Paris, became court engraver in 1696, and in 1707 was made a member of the Académie des Beaux-Arts. His early work was in the style of Nanteuil. He was a careful draftsman, created effective reproductions of originals, and is known for his portraits and religious scenes. He engraved most of the paintings of Hyacinthe Rigaud, received so many commissions that he could not fill them all, and worked with his son, Pierre the Younger, in his later years. He died in Paris.

DREVET, PIERRE IMBERT (1697–1739), engraver. Born in Paris, he was a successful engraver at thirteen, worked in the style of Lebrun and of his father, and produced many portraits and historical and religious scenes. On occasion he himself drew the original which he reproduced. He was a member of the Académie de Peinture, suffered from insanity over his last thirteen years, although he continued his art, and died in Paris.

DREXEL, FRANCIS ANTHONY (1824–1885), banker. Born in Philadelphia, Pennsylvania, on June 20, son of Francis Martin Drexel, a Tyrolese artist and musician turned banker, he entered his father's business at thirteen and at the latter's death in 1863 became senior member of a firm which had offices in Paris and an association with J. P. Morgan in New York City. Of his daughters by his first wife, Hannah Langstroth, Elizabeth (Mrs. Walter George Smith) died in 1890, and Katharine founded the Sisters of the Blessed Sacrament. Louise (Mrs. Edward Morrell) was his only child by his second marriage, to Emma Bouvier. Mrs. Smith and Mrs. Morrell founded the St. Francis Industrial School at Eddington, Pennsylvania, and established the Drexel chair in moral theology at Catholic University out of the fortune left them; other large bequests to charity appeared in his own will. He died in Philadelphia on Feb. 15.

DREXEL, MARY KATHARINE (1858–1955), foundress. Born in Philadelphia, on Nov. 26, to Francis and Hannah Langstroth Drexel, she inherited her father's fortune on his death in 1885 and devoted it to the foundation and development of the Sisters of the Blessed Sacrament, who worked among Negroes and Indians, and had forty-nine houses at the time of her death. She was extremely active in missionary endeavors, developed teachers and catechists for many Indian centers in this country, and built sixty-three schools, including Xavier University, New Orleans. She died in Cornwells Heights, Pennsylvania, on Mar. 3.

DREY, JOHANN SEBASTIAN (1777–1853), theologian. Born in Killingen, Germany, on Oct. 16, he studied in Ellwangen, supported himself by tutoring, went to Augsburg for theology, and was ordained at Pfaffenhausen in 1801. He taught religion, mathematics, and physics in the academy in Rottwell from 1806 to 1812, then was appointed to teach dogma and theology at the new University of Ellwangen. In 1817 this was incorporated in the University of Tübingen, where Drey remained until 1838 and where he was a co-founder of *Theologische Quartalschrift*. A book on confession was not well received, but studies of the teachings of the apostles and on the history of theology had great influence. He died in Tübingen, Germany, on Feb. 19.

DRITHELM (d. 700?). A native of Northumbria, England, he was stricken in 693, reportedly died, but arose saying he had had a terrifying vision. He was admitted to the abbey of Melrose as a monk at the request of King Aldfrid, and lived a life of great austerities in a cell nearby. Though referred to as a saint by Alcuin, there is no known cult of him.

DROCTONIUS. *See* Drotté, St.

DROGO, ST. (1105?–1189). Orphaned at birth, he became a penitential pilgrim, settled for six years as a shepherd near Valenciennes, France, then after nine more journeys to Rome became a hermit at Sebourg, for forty years. He is the patron of shepherds. The name is also spelled Druon. F. D. Apr. 16.

DROSSAERTS, ARTHUR JEROME (1862–1940), archbishop. Born in Breda, Holland, on Sept. 11, he studied at the Haaren seminary, was ordained in 1889, and went to the United States in 1890. He did parish work in the New Orleans diocese, and was appointed bishop of San Antonio in 1918. He founded St. John's seminary, San Antonio, in 1920, convened diocesan synods in 1921 and 1930, became the see's first archbishop in 1926, was appointed assistant at the pontifical throne in 1934, and died on Sept. 8.

DROSTAN, ST. (d. 610?). A member of the royal Irish family of Cosgrach, he was a monk under St. Columba and the first abbot of the monastery of Deer in Aberdeenshire. He is said to have lived the life of a hermit and is venerated as one of the apostles of Scotland. F. D. July 11.

DROSTE-HÜLSHOFF, ANNETTE ELISABETH VON (1797–1848), poet. Born on Jan. 10 near Münster, Westphalia, and sickly all her life, she had a keen mind and vivid imagination. She early became interested in writing poetry and became famous for her lyrics, pastorales, and ballads. A collection of her letters also was published, as well as stories. She died at Meersburg on Lake Constance on May 24.

DROSTE-VISCHERING, CLEMENS AUGUST VON (1773–1845), archbishop. Born in Münster, Germany, on Jan. 21, he studied at its university, joined the learned circle led by Baron von Fürstenberg and Princess Amelia von Gallitzin, and was ordained in 1798 by his brother, Caspar Maximilian, then auxiliary bishop of Münster. He was named coadjutor by Bishop von Fürstenberg in 1807 and, when the latter resigned within the year, succeeded as administrator. He lost his post in 1813 when Napoleon selected his own bishop, had difficulty with the Prussian government over mixed marriages and the teaching of theology, and finally retired to direct charities. In 1835 the government unexpectedly called him to Cologne, where he was elected archbishop and consecrated in 1836. He worked to undo the errors of Hermes, whose teaching had been condemned by the Holy See in 1835, but again met difficulties over government policy on mixed marriages. Frederick William III of Prussia imprisoned him for two years; Joseph Görres wrote his defense; and the government released him in 1839. It forced him to accept a coadjutor to run the diocese. The archbishop wrote a clear statement on Church-state relations and ascetical works. He died in Münster on Oct. 19.

DROTTÉ, ST. (d. 580?). Born in Auxerre, he studied under St. Germanus at the abbey of St. Symphorien, succeeded him as abbot, then served at the monastery of St. Vincent and of the Holy Cross which King Childebert built at Paris. He is also known as Droctonius and Droctoveus. F. D. Mar. 10.

DRUILLETTES, GABRIEL (1610–1681), missioner. Born in France on Sept. 29, he became a Jesuit in 1629, was sent to Canada in 1643, and worked among the Montagnais and Abenakis. He traveled as far south as Augusta, Maine, established missions along the Kennebec in 1646, and in 1650 and 1651 was sent to Boston and New Haven to negotiate commercial treaties with the English and military protection against the Iroquois. Although well received, he could not obtain the desired pacts. He worked in Canadian missions from Ottawa to the Saguenay, explored possible river routes to the North Sea, and after 1670 labored in Michigan and Wisconsin. He died in Quebec on July 28.

DRUM, HUGH ALOYSIUS (1879–1951), general. Born in Fort Brady, Michigan, on Sept. 19, son of Capt. John Drum, he was attending Boston College when he received a chance for an army commission awarded by President McKinley to sons of five veterans killed in the Spanish-American War. He was a second lieutenant in 1898, served in the Philippines, captured Guerro and was cited for bravery, and was with the force which occupied Vera Cruz, Mexico, in 1914. He married Mary Reaume in 1903, was brigadier general and chief of staff of the American First Army in World War I, and deputy chief of staff under Gen. Douglas MacArthur until the outbreak of World War II. He commanded the First Army in its initial training period and became head of the Eastern Defense Command. He retired as a lieutenant general in 1943, was commander of the New York State Guard to 1948, and became president of the Empire State Building Corporation in 1944. He died in New York City on Oct. 3.

DRUMM, THOMAS W. (1871–1933), bishop. Born in Fore, Westmeath, Ireland, on July 12, he went to the United States in 1888, studied at St. Joseph's, Dubuque, the Grand seminary, Montreal, and Catholic University in Washington, D.C. He was ordained in Montreal in 1901, engaged in pastoral work in Iowa, and in 1919 was consecrated bishop of Des Moines, Iowa. He reigned until his death there on Oct. 24.

DRUMGOOLE, JOHN C. (1816–1888). Born in Granard, Longford, Ireland, on Aug. 15, he was taken to New York City in 1824, supported his mother by working as a cobbler, sexton, and bookseller, studied at St. John's and St. Francis Xavier colleges, and was ordained in 1869. After parish work at St. Mary's, where he had been sexton, he engaged in care of orphans, built a large mission in Manhattan, founded St. Joseph's Union for their relief, and built a million-dollar foundation at Mt. Loretto, Staten Island, to care for 2000 homeless boys. The home, complete with vocational school buildings, is still flourishing. He died in New York on Mar. 28.

DRUMMOND, LISTER MAURICE (1856–1916), judge. Born in England, he became a convert in 1875, studied law, passed the bar in 1879, was secretary of the Irish Evicted Tenants' Commission in 1892, became a police magistrate in 1913, and chairman of the Central Council of the Catholic Confederation. In 1887 he had founded with Fr. Philip Fletcher the Guild of Our Lady of Ransom and spoke for its aims (the conversion of England) at Hyde Park outdoor assemblies. He died in London on Feb. 27.

DRUON. *See* Drogo, St.

DRURY, VEN. ROBERT (1567–1607), martyr. Born in Buckinghamshire, England, he studied in Rheims, France, and Valladolid, Spain, was ordained, and was sent to the English mission in 1593. Imprisoned at Wisbech, he signed the letter of allegiance to the queen prepared by Bishop William Bishop and twelve other priests in 1600, but firmly defended his religious rights. He was again arrested in 1606, refused to acknowledge the supremacy of James I, and was executed at Tyburn on Feb. 26.

DRUSUS, ST., martyr. He and SS. Theodore and Zosimus were slain in Syria and honored in a memorial homily by St. John Chrysostom. F. D. Dec. 14.

DRUTHMAR, ST. (d. 1046). A Benedictine at the monastery of Lorch, he was in 1014 appointed abbot of New Corbie, Saxony, by Emperor Henry II. F. D. Feb. 15.

DRUYS, JEAN (d. 1635). Born in Cumptich, near Tirelemont, Brabant, he studied at Liège, Namur, and Louvain, became a Norbertine in 1587, taught and was abbot at Parc, vicar general of Prémontré, and was appointed to the private council of Archduke Albert. He spent several years reforming the University of Louvain, was named visitor of Douai and elsewhere, and in 1628–30 undertook a revision of the statutes of his order in conformity to the recommendations of the Council of Trent. He died on Mar. 25.

DRUZBICKI, GASPAR (1589–1662). Born in Sierady, Poland, he became a Jesuit in 1609, taught and held several positions in his Society, was rector of colleges at Kalisz, Ostrog, and Posen, and twice served as provincial. He wrote ascetical works in Latin and Polish, which were widely translated into French and English, a defense of the Jesuits, and instructions for novices. He died in Posen, Poland, on Apr. 2.

DRYDEN, CHARLES (1665?–1704). Eldest son of John Dryden, he was born in Charlton, Wiltshire, England, educated at Westminster, wrote poems and translations from Juvenal, served Pope Innocent XII as chamberlain for about five years, and returned to England about 1697. He was drowned in the Thames on Aug. 20.

DRYDEN, JOHN (1631–1700), author. Born in Aldwinkle, Northamptonshire, England, on Apr. 30, he studied at Westminster and Cambridge, where he took his degree at Trinity in 1654, lived on a small paternal pension, then moved to London. He wrote poetry in college, gained attention by his *Heroic Stanzas* on the death of Cromwell (1658), then turned to hail the restoration of the Stuarts in *Astraea Redux* (1660) and *Panegyric on the Restoration* (1661). He became a member of the Royal Society and married Lady Elizabeth Howard in 1662. He wrote for the stage, producing comedies, in which his humor is sometimes as forced as his immoralities, which matched the taste of the times: *The Wild Gallant* (1663), *The Rival Ladies, The Assignation, An Evening Love* (from Corneille), *Ladies à la Mode*, and *Marriage à la Mode* (the last a success). With Sir Robert Howard he wrote *The Indian Queen;* another tragedy, *The Indian Emperor* followed. He then issued the significant *Essay on Dramatick Poesie* (1668) and was made poet laureate in 1670. Other adaptations from the French (*Secret Love and Sir Martin Mar-All*) or from Shakespeare (he and Davenant completed a *Tempest*) preceded his more serious *Almanzor and Almahide, Amboyna, Aurengzebe,* and *All for Love* (1678; on the Antony-

Cleopatra story). He put *Troilus and Cressida* into dramatic form and wrote such operas as *The State of Innocence* (1674; based on Milton) and *King Arthur*. Later plays include *Oedipus*, *The Spanish Friar*, *The Duke of Guise*, *Amphitryon*, *Don Sebastian*, and *Love Triumphant*. His poetic satire, *Absalom and Achitophel* (1681–82), had nine editions within a year; *The Medal* (also on Shaftesbury's trial for treason) and *MacFlecknoe* (on the incompetence of Thomas Shadwell as poet) were also popular. *Religio Laici* (on Roman Catholics and other non-conformists to Anglicanism) appeared in 1681. Dryden became a convert in 1685, explained his reasons in *The Hind and the Panther* (1687), wrote *Britannia rediviva* (in honor of Prince James Stuart), and translated the life of St. Francis Xavier by Fr. Dominic Bouhours. He retained his faith after the revolution of 1688, although he lost his posts as laureate and royal historiographer and had to earn his living by such hack work as translations of Ovid, other classical writers in *Miscellanies* (anthologies which he edited), and a translation of Vergil (1697). His *Veni, Creator Spiritus* appeared in 1696 and his *Songs for St. Cecelia's Day* in 1687–97. *Fables, Ancient and Modern* (paraphrases of Ovid, Boccaccio, and Chaucer, with an important preface) appeared shortly before his death of gout in London on May 1.

MARK VAN DOREN, *John Dryden* (New York, Harcourt, 1920); LOUIS BREDVOLD, *The Intellectual Milieu of John Dryden* (Ann Arbor, U. of Mich., 1934).

DUBOIS, GUILLAUME (1656–1723), cardinal. Born in Brive, Limousin, France, he was educated there and at the Collège St. Michel, Paris, was a tutor for many years, and in 1700 became secretary of the duke of Orléans. He was state councilor in 1716, secretary of foreign affairs in 1717, archbishop of Cambrai in 1720, cardinal in 1721, and minister of state in 1722, all during the regency of Philippe d'Orléans. His plan of education for the young duke was published and admired; diplomatically he arranged the triple alliance of England, Holland, and France against Spain; as a churchman he too often made his appointments serve his political purposes, and he was not ordained until old age. He was widely attacked by Jansenists and the nobility, was vilified by Saint-Simon, and suffered charges of bribery, impiety, and extreme immorality both from libels circulated during his lifetime and from the apocryphal *Mémoires du cardinal Dubois*. He died in Versailles, France.

DUBOIS, JEAN ANTOINE (1765–1848). Born in St. Remèze, France, he was ordained, became director of the seminary of the Foreign Missions Society, a member of the Royal Society of England and of France, and at the begin-

ning of the French Revolution went as a missioner to India. He wrote *Description of the Character, Manners, and Customs of the People of India*, which the East India Company published in 1816 and which he issued in a better edited French version in 1825; he also wrote on Brahmin theology, on the *Pantchatantra*, and contributions to the *Bulletin universel des sciences*. His thirty-two years in the mission field, ending in 1823, were recorded in *Letters on the State of Christianity in India*, in which he stated his doubts about the possibility of converting the Hindus. He died in Paris on Feb. 17.

DUBOIS, JOHN (1764–1842), bishop. Born in Paris on Aug. 24, he studied with Robespierre at the Collège Louis-le-Grand, was ordained at the Oratorian seminary of St. Magloire in 1787, became an assistant at St. Sulpice, and escaped to Norfolk, Virginia, at the outbreak of the French Revolution. He did missionary work there and in Richmond, was pastor in Frederick, Maryland, and in 1808, becoming a Sulpician, he founded Mt. St. Mary's, Emmitsburg, Maryland. His plans did not materialize, and he decided to continue the institution as a college. He was of great assistance to Mother Seton, whose Sisters of Charity community was nearby. In 1825 he was named third bishop of New York, and was consecrated eighteen months later; the see then included all of that state and half of New Jersey. His eighteen priests cared for 150,000 souls; he brought others from Europe, fought the growing problem of lay trusteeism, and in 1837 passed over most of his duties to John Hughes, named his coadjutor. He died in New York City on Dec. 20.

DUBOIS, LOUIS ERNEST (1856–1929), cardinal. Born in St. Calais, Sarthe, France, he studied at Le Mans, was ordained in 1879, served in French parishes, and became bishop of Verdun in 1901. He was made archbishop of Bourges in 1909 and transferred to Rouen in 1916, when he was also named a cardinal, and to Paris in 1920. He died in Paris on Sept. 23.

DU BOS, CHARLES (1882–1940), critic. Born in Paris, he studied there and at Oxford, returned to France in 1902, lectured and wrote widely, mixed with various intellectual groups, was associated with André Gide during World War I in directing a canteen for soldiers, and became a convert in 1927. He published seven volumes of literary criticism called *Approximations*, served with Maritain, Claudel, and Mauriac on the staff of the Catholic periodical *Vigile* in 1930, and in 1937 he became visiting professor at Notre Dame, Indiana. He also wrote *Reflections on Mérimée, François Mauriac and the Problem of the Catholic Novelist*, and *What Is Literature?* He died in Aug. on a trip to France.

DUBOURG, LOUIS GUILLAUME VAL-

ENTIN (1766–1833), bishop. Born in Cap Français, Santo Domingo on Feb. 14, he studied in Paris, was ordained a Sulpician in 1788, and was superior of the seminary at Issy in 1788–92 until the French Revolution forced him to flee to Spain, and in 1794 he went to Maryland. He served as president of Georgetown in 1796–99, then as superior of St. Mary's College, Baltimore, was superior of the Sisters of Charity in 1809–10, and in 1812 was named apostolic administrator of Louisiana and Florida. He was consecrated bishop of Louisiana, Upper and Lower, in Rome in 1815, founded in St. Louis (Upper Louisiana) a seminary and an academy, the latter of which later became a university, continued his struggle with lay trustees (which had plagued his predecessor and often kept the bishop out of New Orleans), and eventually resigned his see in 1825. He was appointed to the see of Montauban, France, in 1826, was transferred to Besançon, France, as archbishop in 1833, and died there on Dec. 12.

DUBRICIUS. See Dyfrig, St.

DUBTACH, ST. (d. 513?). He became archbishop of Armagh, Ireland, in 497. F. D. Oct. 7.

DUBUIS, CLAUDE MARY (1817–1895), bishop. Born in Iche, Loire, France, on Mar. 10, he was ordained in Lyons in 1844 as a member of the Congregation of Holy Cross. He went to the United States, where he did missionary work in Texas, and in 1862 was consecrated, in Lyons, France, bishop of Galveston, Texas. He reigned until 1881, when he resigned, though he retained the title of bishop of Galveston until 1892, when he was appointed titular bishop of Arca, and retired to Vernaison, France, where he died on May 22.

DU CANGE, CHARLES DUFRESNE (1610–1688), historian. Born in Amiens, France, on Dec. 18, he was educated there and at Orléans, was admitted to the bar in Paris in 1631, became treasurer of France in 1645, and moved to Paris in 1668. He made elaborate studies of Byzantine Greek and Low Latin, which he published, and which permitted him to complete research for his *History of the Byzantine Empire under French Monarchs, Chronicon Paschale*, a biography of St. Louis, and miscellaneous treatises published two centuries later. He died in Paris.

DUCCIO DI BUONINSENGA (1260?–1319?), painter. A native of Siena, Italy, he began work at Florence, choosing to follow the original Byzantine tradition rather than the Gothic. He did the *Madonna de' Ruccellai* (once attributed to Cimabue) and, in 1311, the reredos for the main altar of the cathedral in Siena, consisting of many scenes from the life of Christ and symbolic representation of the two testaments. His work had a decided effect on the later Sienese school. He died on Aug. 3. Other works attributed to him are *Madonna and Child with Saints* and *Crucifixion*.

DUCHESNE, JEAN BAPTISTE (1731–1797). Born in Tourteron, France, he became a Jesuit in 1746, taught at Metz, Verdun, and Ponte-à-Mousson, and left the Society in 1762. After its suppression he changed his name to Abbé Blanchard. Under this name he wrote widely on physical and moral education, a corrective of Rousseau's negative principles, and a program of instruction for women, who were to have no independence. He died on June 15.

DUCHESNE, LOUIS MARIE OLIVIER (1843–1922), scholar. Born in St. Servan, France, on Sept. 13, he studied at St. Brieuc seminary, was ordained in 1867, and taught at St. Charles College in St. Brieuc. He pursued his studies further at Paris and Rome, went on several scientific trips to Greece, and in 1877 became a professor at L'Institut Catholique in Paris. He went to L'École des Hautes Études in 1884, became director of studies in 1892, and a leader in the use of scientific and critical methods in the teaching of history. He became a member of the Academy of Inscriptions in 1888, director of the French School in Rome in 1895, and was elected to the French Academy. He was made a prothonotary apostolic in 1900, wrote numerous historical treaties, and had *Histoire ancienne de l'Église* placed on the Index in 1912, though a revised edition in 1925 was approved. He died in St. Servan on Apr. 21.

DUCHESNE, BL. ROSE PHILIPPINE (1769–1852). Born in Grenoble, France, on Aug. 29, she studied with the Visitation nuns, joined that order when seventeen, but returned home when they were expelled from France. When her attempt to rebuild the convent after the revolution proved unsuccessful, she offered it to St. Madeleine Sophie Barat in 1804 and became a member of her recently founded Society of the Sacred Heart. In 1818 she was sent with four companions to St. Charles, Missouri, moved to Florissant, near St. Louis, in 1819, founded a novitiate and school, and six houses. In 1840 she resigned as superior and went to work among the Potawatomi Indians at Sugar Creek, Kansas. After a year, ill health caused her to return to St. Charles, where she died on Oct. 18. She was beatified in 1940. F. D. Nov. 17.

DUCKETT, BL. JAMES (d. 1602), martyr. Born in Gilfortrigs, Westmoreland, he became a printer's apprentice in London, was converted, and devoted himself to the secret printing and distribution of Catholic books. He spent nine of his twelve years of married life in prisons, but was released for lack of evidence. Finally, a binder named Peter Bullock testified against him. Duckett was executed at Tyburn, London, exhorting his informer, whom he forgave and who was being hanged with him, to be firm in his faith. He was beatified in 1929. F. D. Apr. 19.

DUCKETT, BL. JOHN (1613–1644), martyr. Related to Bl. James Duckett, he was born in Underwinter, Yorkshire, England, and was ordained at Douai in 1639. He was hanged, drawn, and quartered at Tyburn with Bl. Ralph Corbington, and beatified in 1929. F. D. Sept. 7.

DU COUDRAY, PHILIPPE CHARLES JEAN TRONSON (1738–1777), general. Born in Rheims, France, on Sept. 8, he became an army engineer and was adjutant general of artillery when he volunteered for service in the American Revolution. Benjamin Franklin had promised him the rank of major general, but, when he arrived with twenty-nine officers, some of the colonial leaders became jealous. Du Coudray was named inspector general as a compromise, was placed in charge of fortifications along the Delaware River, and was drowned near Philadelphia on Sept. 11, after four months of service.

DUCRUE, FRANCIS BENNON (1721–1779), missioner. Born in Munich, Bavaria, on June 10, he became a Jesuit in 1738, and from 1748 to 1767 worked in the California missions, where he was superior at the time of his Society's expulsion. He wrote an account of his journey through California to Mexico, which the historian Bancroft praised, and a report on the expulsion. He died in Munich on Mar. 30.

DUDIK, BEDA FRANCISCUS (1815–1890), historian. Born in Kojetein, Moravia, on Jan. 29, he studied in Brünn and at Olmütz, became a Benedictine in 1836, and was ordained in 1840. He taught classics and history in the academy in Brünn until 1854 and at the University of Vienna until 1859, when he was named historiographer of Moravia. He traveled to major European libraries and through Russia, collected a library on the Teutonic Order, and wrote some fifteen studies on Middle European history. His twelve-volume *Mährens allgemeine Geschichte*, a history of Moravia to 1350, is the most significant. He was abbot and titular bishop of the monastery of Raigern, near Brünn, Moravia, at his death on Jan. 18.

DU DUC, FRONTON (1558–1624), theologian. Born in Bordeaux, France, he became a Jesuit, taught in several colleges, including Clermont, where he also was librarian, wrote a play on Joan of Arc, acted before Charles III, and engaged in published debate with Du Plessis-Mornay on the Eucharist. He was selected to prepare revised editions of the Greek Fathers, edited John Chrysostom and Nicephorus Callistus, and a collection of Greek texts with Latin translations, *Bibliotheca veterum patrum*. He died in Paris on Sept. 25.

DUEÑAS, BL. PEDRO DE (1378–1397), martyr. Born in Palencia, Spain, he became a Franciscan and went to Granada in 1396 with Bl. Juan de Cetina to preach to the Moors. They were seized and beheaded a year later. F. D. May 19.

DUFAL, PETER (1822–1898), bishop. Born in La Mure, Puy-de-Dôme, France, on Nov. 8, he studied in Le Mans, joined the Congregation of the Holy Cross in 1852, and was ordained later that year in Blois. He engaged in missionary work in India, was made titular bishop of Dercos, and vicar apostolic of eastern Bengal in 1860, and served as superior general of the congregation in 1860–68. He was appointed coadjutor bishop of Galveston, Texas, in 1878, but because of ill health retired in 1880 to his congregation's foundation in Neuilly, France. He died in Paris on Mar. 15.

DUFF, EDWARD ALOYSIUS (1883–1953). Born in Philadelphia on May 30, he studied at St. Charles seminary there, was ordained in 1911, served as a curate in Charleston, South Carolina, and became a navy chaplain in 1916. He was the first Catholic priest to become chief of chaplains, an office he held in 1937–39. He died in Philadelphia on Feb. 11.

DUFFY, CHARLES GAVAN (1816–1903). Born in Monaghan, Ireland, on Apr. 12, he was on the staff of the newspapers *Northern Herald* and Dublin *Morning Register*, and from 1839 to 1842 edited the Belfast *Vindicator*. He then went to Dublin and, with the assistance of Thomas David and John Dillon, edited the *Nation*, supported the repeal movement, and was imprisoned with O'Connell in 1844 as a result of the vigor of his stand. He later broke with O'Connell, supported the Irish Confederation, and in 1848 called for drastic action in face of the plague and British oppression. The *Nation* was suppressed and he was tried four times for treason, but released; in 1849 the revived paper again took up the fight for constitutional reforms and helped to establish the Tenant League, which placed forty members in parliament in 1852, including Duffy. Inner dissension broke up the party and in 1856 Duffy went to Australia, where he was a member of the Victorian parliament, minister of public works, public lands, and prime minister. He was named speaker, worked earnestly for the rights of labor and the farming class, and was knighted. He left Australia in 1880 and wrote *Young Ireland* (1884), *Four Years of Irish History*, and *My Life in Two Hemispheres*. He died in Nice, France, on Feb. 9.

DUFFY, FRANCIS PATRICK (1871–1932). Born in Cobourg, Ontario, Canada, on May 2, he studied at St. Michael's, Toronto, St. Francis Xavier, New York, and St. Joseph's seminary, Troy, and was ordained in 1896. He continued his studies at Catholic University, became an American citizen in 1902, taught at St. Joseph's seminary, Yonkers, New York, to 1912, then engaged in pastoral work. He was chaplain of the "Fighting 69th" Regiment during World War I and was decorated for heroism by the American, Canadian, and French governments. He was pastor of Holy Cross church, New York City, from 1920 until his death on June 26. His life was featured in several books, a motion picture, and his autobiography, *Father Duffy's Story* (1919).

DUFFY, JOHN ALOYSIUS (1884–1944), bishop. Born in Jersey City, New Jersey, on Oct. 29, he studied at Seton Hall and the North American College, Rome, and was ordained in Rome in 1908. He taught at Seton Hall and Immaculate Conception seminary until 1915, when he was appointed chancellor of the diocese, was vicar general in 1924–33, and then was appointed bishop of Syracuse, New York. He was transferred to Buffalo in 1937, and reigned there until his death on Sept. 27.

DUFOUR, BL. MARIE (d. 1794), martyr. *See* Lidoin, Bl. Marie.

DUFRESSE, BL. GABRIEL JOHN TAUTIN (1751–1815), bishop and martyr. Born in Ville-de-Lezoux, Clermont, France, he joined the Society for Foreign Missions in 1774, was sent to China in 1777, worked for seven years in Szechwan, and was captured and exiled to Manila. In 1800 he became titular bishop of Tabraca, and returned to China as vicar apostolic over 40,000 converts. After fifteen years of mission success he was betrayed by a renegade Christian and beheaded by his persecutors on Feb. 17. He was beatified in 1900. F. D. Sept. 14.

DUGGAN, JAMES (1825–1899), bishop. Born in Maynooth, Kildare, Ireland, on May 22, he studied there, went to the United States in 1842, studied at St. Vincent's and St. Louis, Missouri, and was ordained in 1847. He was superior of St. Louis seminary, Carondelet, Missouri, in 1847–50, did parish work in the St. Louis diocese, and was appointed vicar general in 1854 and titular bishop of Gabala and auxiliary of St. Louis in 1857. He was transferred to the vacant see of Chicago as administrator in 1858, and was appointed its fourth bishop in 1859. He built up the parochial-school system, attended the second Plenary Council in Baltimore in 1866, became mentally ill, and in 1869 was placed in a St. Louis asylum, where he remained until his death on Mar. 27.

DUGLIOLI, BL. HELENA (1472–1520). Born in Bologna, Italy, she married against her will at seventeen, but lived happily for thirty years. On her husband's death she devoted herself to charitable work and died shortly after. She was revered while alive, and at her death a spontaneous cult sprang up which was confirmed in 1828. F. D. Sept. 23.

DUHAMEL, JEAN BAPTISTE (1624–1706), scholar. Born in Vire, Normandy, France, on June 11, he studied at Caen and Paris, became an Oratorian in 1643, left ten years later to take up diocesan parish work at Neuilly, was chancellor at Bayeux, and from 1666 to 1697 was chosen by Colbert as secretary of the newly founded Académie des Sciences. At eighteen he wrote on the *Spherics* of Theodosius; later work includes studies of astronomical physics, meteors and fossils, the mind, the emotions, texts on philosophy and theology, an edition of the Bible, a scriptural commentary, and a comparison of the Greek philosophers and Descartes. He died in Paris on Aug. 6.

DUHEM, PIERRE MAURICE MARIE (1861–1916), physicist. Born in Paris on June 10, he studied in Paris, taught at Lille, Rennes, Bordeaux, and Louvain, and wrote on physics and religion. He died in Cabrespine, France, on Sept. 14.

DU LAU, BL. JEAN (d. 1792), bishop and martyr. During the French Revolution mob violence crushed those Catholics who would not take the oath upholding the civil constitution of the clergy, an anti-religious act passed by the new assembly but denounced by the French hierarchy and by Pope Pius VI. One bloodthirsty mob attacked a monastery in Paris, L'Abbaye, where a group of priests were imprisoned, demanded that they take the oath, and murdered them when they refused. The first to die was the king's confessor, Bl. Alexandre Lenfant. The mob then went to the Carmelite church on the rue de Rennes, where 150 priests and a layman, Charles de la Calmette, comte de Valfons, were imprisoned. Bl. François Joseph de la Rochefoucauld, bishop of Beauvais; his brother, Bl. Pierre Louis de la Rochefoucauld, bishop of Saintes; Bl. Ambroise Chevreux, superior general of the Maurist Benedictines; and Bl. François Hébert, another confessor of King Louis XVI, were put to death with Bl. Jean du Lau, archbishop of Arles. They are known as the "martyrs des Carmes" and were beatified in 1926. F. D. Sept. 2.

DULCARDUS, ST. (d. 584). A monk at Orléans, France, he became a hermit near Bourges; St. Doulchard is named for him. F. D. Oct. 25.

DULCIDIUS, ST. (d. 450?). He succeeded Phoebadius as bishop of Agen, Gaul. F. D. Oct. 16.

DULCISSIMUS, ST. (d. 90?). *See* Romulus, St.

DU LHUT, DANIEL GREYSOLON (1640?–1710). Born in St. Germain-en-Laye, France, he was a lieutenant in the royal army, fought in Flanders, and in 1674 went to Montreal, Canada. In 1678 he moved west with a small force, took possession of Sioux territory, explored

Lake Superior and the sources of the St. Lawrence and Mississippi, built several forts, saved Fr. Hennepin from captivity, and was admired by the Indians, whom he kept loyal to France. In 1686 he began the post at Detroit; in 1696, as a captain, he was given command of Fort Frontenac. The city of Duluth, Michigan, is named in his honor. He died in Montreal on Feb. 26.

DUMAS, JEAN BAPTISTE (1800–1884), chemist. Born in Alais, France, on July 14, he was a pharmacist in Geneva, Switzerland, wrote on the physiology of the nervous system, studied chemistry in Paris, and taught at the Athénée there. He published on the vapor intensity of the elements, on alcohols and ethers, hydrogen and amide compounds, physiological and medical chemistry, and the relationship of science and the arts. He made advances in replacing hydrogen by chlorine in organic bodies; and published important research on the atomic weight of carbon; with Boussingault, on the composition of water and the atmosphere; and with Stas, on the composition of carbon monoxide. In 1829 he was a co-founder of L'École Central des Arts et Manufactures. He became professor at the École Polytechnique, at the Sorbonne (where he became dean of the faculty of sciences), and at L'École de Médecin. In 1849, to the disappointment of the scientific world, he entered politics; he was elected deputy from Nord, was named minister of agriculture and commerce, and became a senator. He became a member of the Academy of Sciences in 1832, its perpetual secretary in 1868, and a member of the French Academy in 1878. He died in Cannes, France, on Apr. 10.

DUMETZ, FRANCISCO (d. 1811). Born in Majorca, Spain, he became a Franciscan, was sent to Mexico City in 1770 and to California in 1771, and labored at Monterey and other missions until 1797. He then founded San Fernando mission, continued his work with the Indians, and died at San Gabriel, California, on Jan. 14.

DUMONT, HUBERT ANDRÉ (1809–1857), geologist. Born in Liège, Belgium, on Feb. 15, he took his doctorate in mathematics and physical science and in 1835 was named to the faculty of Liège, a position he held until his death there on Feb. 28. He issued a geological map of Belgium in 1849, wrote other geological studies, and served as rector of the university.

DUMOULIN-BORIE, BL. PIERRE (1808–1838), martyr. Born in Cors, France, he joined the Society for Foreign Missions in 1829, was ordained, worked in Tonkin from 1832 to 1836, and was in prison when he learned he had been appointed bishop. He was beheaded at Annam, Indochina. He was beatified in 1900. F. D. Nov. 24.

DUNBAR, WILLIAM (1460?–1520?), poet.

Born in Salton, Scotland, he studied at St. Andrews, became a Franciscan novice, lived in Picardy, returned to Scotland about 1490, and entered the service of King James IV, who sent him on diplomatic missions and gave him a small pension. He was ordained about 1500, wrote *The Thrissil and the Rois* (*The Thistle and the Rose*) to celebrate James's marriage to Margaret of England, *The Golden Targe* (on the triumph of love), *The Dance* (on the seven deadly sins), and some humorous and religious poetry. Dunbar, of noble lineage, wrote as a courtier; his style is facile and artificial, somewhat indebted to Chaucer and the French in manner but not in outlook; on occasion he is boisterous, coarsely realistic, and abusively satiric.

DUNCAN (d. 1040), king of Scotland. He became king about 1018, fought Eadulf of Northumbria, who raided his Cambrian holdings in 1038, tried to control the nation by visiting its castles in turn, and was defeated (and some say assassinated) by his general, Macbeth.

DUNCHADH, ST. (d. 717). Of the house of Conall Gulban, he became abbot of Killochuir (perhaps in County Down), Ireland, and possibly was coadjutor to the abbot of Iona after 707. He was listed as an abbot when the paschal controversy was settled there and the monastery adopted Roman practice. He is also called Dunchaid. F. D. May 25.

DUNCHAID O'BRAOIN, ST. (d. 988). He was a hermit at Clonmacnoise, Ireland, until 969, when he became abbot of the monastery there. F. D. Jan. 16.

DUNGAL (9th century). An Irish priest, perhaps educated at Bangor, Wales, he was at the monastery of St. Denis, near Paris, in 811, when he wrote a letter to Charlemagne regarding an eclipse of the sun. In 825 he was appointed master of a school in Pavia. A number of poems have been attributed to him, together with a reply to Bishop Claudius of Turin on the veneration of images. He left his library to the monastery of St. Columbanus at Bobbio, and may have been stationed at the Irish center on the Trebbia.

DUNIN, MARTIN VON (1774–1842), archbishop. Born in Wat, Poland, on Nov. 11, he studied in Rome, was ordained in 1797, served in Cracow, Gnesen, Posen, and elsewhere, became adviser to the government on matters of education, was named administrator of the archdiocese of Gnesen and Posen, Prussia, in 1829, and succeeded to the see in 1831. He reconstructed the seminaries, built or repaired churches, and ran into difficulty with the Prussian government over the question of mixed marriage. By 1838 the matter came to a head; the archbishop was tried in Posen, and imprisoned in Berlin and Colberg. Difficulties lessened when Frederick IV took the throne in 1740; the archbishop was released, and a compromise was achieved. Von Dunin died in Posen on Dec. 26.

DUNN, JAMES PHILLIP (1884–1936), composer. Born in New York City on Jan. 10, he studied at City College and music at Columbia under Edward MacDowell, and became organist in New York and New Jersey churches. He was an associate editor of *Singing*, wrote *The Galleon*, an opera, three symphonic poems (*Annabelle Lee, Lovesight,* and *We*), songs, an overture on Negro themes, and works for violin and piano. He died in Jersey City on July 24.

DUNNE, EDWARD JOSEPH (1848–1910), bishop. Born in Gortnahoe, Tipperary, Ireland, on Apr. 23, he was brought to the United States when a boy, studied at St. Francis, Milwaukee, and St. Mary's, Baltimore, and was ordained in 1871 in Baltimore. He did pastoral work in the Chicago archdiocese, and was consecrated second bishop of Dallas, Texas, in 1893. The cathedral school, an industrial school for Negroes, and colleges and sanatoriums were built during his reign. He died on Aug. 5 in Green Bay, Wisconsin.

DUNNE, EDMUND MICHAEL (1864–1929), bishop. Born in Chicago, on Feb. 2, he studied at St. Ignatius College there, Niagara University, New York, Seminaire de Fioreffe, Louvain, and the Gregorian in Rome, and was ordained in Louvain in 1887. He served in several Chicago churches, was appointed chancellor of the archdiocese in 1905, and in 1909 was appointed bishop of Peoria, Illinois, a position he held until his death there on Oct. 17.

DUNNE, PETER FINLEY (1867–1936), journalist. Born in Chicago, Illinois, on July 10, he worked on local newspaper staffs after his graduation from high school, and created the character of "Mr. Dooley" in 1893 for a series of weekly articles in dialect for the *Evening Post*. Chief editorial writer there, he transferred to the *Journal* as managing editor in 1897, and his column was soon syndicated. He published eight volumes of his humorous observations between 1898 and 1919. He married Margaret Abbott in 1903. In 1907–13 he was an editor of *American Magazine*, and later worked on *Collier's* and *Liberty*. He died in New York City on Apr. 14.

DU NOUY, PIERRE LECOMTE (1883–1947), scientist. Born in Paris on Dec. 20, he studied at the Sorbonne, took degrees in philosophy, science, and law, wrote fiction and drama, and during World War I served with a medical unit under Dr. Alexis Carrel. After research at the Rockefeller Institute in New York City (1920–27) he went to the Pasteur Institute in Paris, where he developed a laboratory of molecular biophysics. His opposition to materialism cost him his position in 1936. He

published *L'Homme devant la science* (1939), *L'Avenir de l'esprit* (1941), *Le Temps et la vie* (translated in 1937 as *Biological Time*), and *La Dignité humaine*. He was noted for his observations on the cicatrization of wounds, the absorption phenomenon of surface tension, the molecular properties of serum in relation to immunity, and the changing characteristics of plasma. He returned to the Church shortly before his death in New York City on Sept. 22.

DUNS SCOTUS, JOHN (1270?–1308), theologian. Born apparently in the British Isles, he became a Friar Minor, about 1290, was ordained, and taught at Oxford as a member of the English province. He probably took his doctorate at Paris about 1304 and later taught at Cologne, where he died. He wrote commentaries on scripture and on Aristotle, and became famous for his *Opus Oxoniense*, his commentary on the *Sentences* of Peter Lombard, and his shorter theological supplement, *Reportata Parisiensia*. He was particularly interested, in philosophy, in the concept of being, reality, ideality, matter, and form. His psychology is basically that of St. Thomas; he discussed sense perception as an active process, and discussed intellectual knowledge, habit formation, and freedom of will at length. In theology he discussed the proofs of the existence of God, the humanity of Christ and the significance of redemption, the Immaculate Conception of Mary, the nature of angels, original sin, grace, morality, and the sacraments. He argued from authority and from reason, stressed the value of mathematics and science, defended revelation and faith, and often departed, but not erroneously, from Aristotle, St. Thomas, and his scholastic predecessors in original strikings-out toward tenable explanations of debatable truths. His language is sometimes awkward, but many misconceptions of his work are due to subsequent Scotists rather than to his own notes.

DUNSTAN, ST. (910?–988), archbishop. Born near Glastonbury, England, he was educated by Irish monks, and in service at the court of King Athelstan. He became a Benedictine at Glastonbury, living nearby as a recluse. Here he worked with metals, illuminated manuscripts, and, a skilled harpist, composed music; one chant, *Kyrie Rex splendens*, is extant. In 943 he became abbot, enforcing strict discipline, developing other monasteries, and making Glastonbury an important center of learning. He then went to court as counselor to King Edred, but offended many by censuring the immorality of the Saxon nobility and demanding peace with the Danes. Nearly seven years later, in 955, the sixteen-year-old Edwy became king; his scandalous conduct brought strong censure from Dunstan, who was exiled to Ghent. Edwy's brother Edgar led a rebellion, recalled Dunstan, and made him bishop of Worcester (957). When the civil war ended, he became archbishop of Canterbury in 961, and also papal legate representing John XII. With SS. Ethelwold of Winchester and Oswald of York he set about reforming the clergy, replacing canons by monks, rebuilding destroyed monastic centers, and censuring the nobility, including the new king. He remained as counselor under Kings Edward the Martyr and Ethelred, whom he consecrated in 970. Shortly after this he retired to Canterbury to teach in the cathedral school, and died there. F. D. May 19.

DUPANLOUP, FÉLIX ANTOINE PHILIBERT (1802–1878), bishop. Born in St. Félix, France, on Jan. 3, illegitimate child of Anne Dechosal, who educated him at home and sent him to Collège Ste. Barbe, he studied at Issy and St. Sulpice, and was ordained in 1825. He founded the Académie de St. Hyacinthe, tutored the royal children, and introduced new methods of catechetical instruction while stationed at the Madeleine in Paris. He was director of St. Roch, superior of the seminary of St. Nicholas from 1837 to 1845, and worked with Montalembert and against Thiers in the matter of education laws, writing many tracts while canon at Notre Dame in 1845–49. Under Louis Napoleon, Falloux became minister of education and drew up a school bill, with the help of a commission on which Dupanloup served, which was moderately acceptable. In 1849 he was named bishop of Orléans, held several synods, founded minor seminaries, developed his catechetical methods, and completed the cathedral of Ste. Croix. In 1854 he was elected to the French Academy; he introduced the cause of Joan of Arc's beatification, raised funds for the victims of famine in Ireland, and pleaded with the United States to end the slave trade. He strongly opposed the dogma of papal infallibility, but accepted it once it was defined at the Vatican Council. He lessened the conditions imposed on his see city by the Germans after the war of 1870; was aided by gifts from Ireland sent in memory of former charities to that country; served in the national assembly and gained passage of bills to approve military chaplains and authorize Catholic institutes; and became a senator in 1875. Besides biographies and pastoral letters he published *L'éducation en général*, *La haute éducation intellectuelle*, and *Lettres sur l'éducation des filles*. He died in Lacombe, France, on Oct. 11.

DUPERRON, JACQUES DAVY (1556–1618), theologian. Born in St. Lô, Normandy, France, on Nov. 25, he was brought up in Switzerland, where his Calvinist parents sought refuge from persecution, became a convert about 1577, helped to bring Henry IV back to the Church, and in 1591 was appointed bishop

of Évreux, although not in orders. He caused the Fontainebleau conference, which investigated and sustained his charges that Du Plessis-Mornay had distorted patristic texts in his work on the Eucharist. He became a cardinal in 1604, advised Pope Paul V not to condemn Molina, defended the writings of Bellarmine and condemned those of Edmond Richer, and became archbishop of Sens in 1611. Besides his work on the Eucharist and moral and spiritual treatises, he wrote poetry and an important controversial answer to King James I of England on the essence of Catholicism. He died in Battignolles, near Paris, on Sept. 5.

DUPIN, LOUIS ELLIES (1657–1719), editor. Born in Normandy on June 17, he studied at the Sorbonne, and took his doctorate in theology there in 1684. In 1686 he began to issue *Nouvelle bibliothèque des auteurs ecclésiastiques*, on the dogma, criticism, and biography of the early Fathers. He worked with great speed, allowed errors to creep into his comments, and was violently attacked by Petit-Didier and Bossuet. Critical warfare ensued, pamphlets were published on both sides, and, although Dupin submitted to the censure forced from the archbishop of Paris, he was publicly condemned and after his death the *Bibliothèque* was placed on the Index. Although somewhat Gallican in leaning, Dupin was not a Jansenist or heretic. His dealings with Archbishop Wake of England were for the purpose of attempting to reconcile the separated Anglicans; his association with Jansenists was the result of his family relationship with Jean Racine and the playwright's friends. Dupin also edited Gerson, Optatus of Mileve, and the Psalms, and wrote theological tracts and historical abridgments. He died in Paris on June 6.

DUPIN, PIERRE CHARLES FRANÇOIS (1784–1873), mathematician. Born in Varzy, France, on Oct. 6, he studied at the École Polytechnique, became a naval engineer, inspector general of the navy, and in 1818 was elected to the Academy of Sciences. He wrote on geometry, commerce, education, and economics, and taught at the Conservatory. His *Voyages en Grande Bretagne de 1816 à 1819* was a six-volume estimate of the commerce and industry of England. He was made baron in 1824, served in the assembly for forty years, and became a senator under Napoleon III. He died in Paris on Jan. 18.

DUPLESSIS, MAURICE (1890–1959), premier. Born in Three Rivers, Quebec, Canada, on Apr. 20, he studied in Montreal and St. Joseph seminary in Three Rivers, received his law degree at Laval, and practiced law in Three Rivers. He was elected to the provincial legislature in 1927, was re-elected each election until his death, and became leader of the Conservative opposition in 1933. In 1936 his group, known as the Union Nationale, swept the Liberal administration out of power for the first time in thirty-nine years and Duplessis became premier of Quebec. He immediately launched an unrelenting attack on communism, opposed participation in World War II, a stand which brought the Liberals back to power in 1939, but returned party to victory in 1944. He built up a powerful political machine (which was severely criticized for its corruption by two Laval University priests in 1956) and became a vocal and vigorous defender of French culture, ruling the province of Quebec practically as his principality. He served as premier five times. He died in Schefferville, Quebec, on Sept. 7.

DUPONCEAU, PETER STEPHEN (1760–1844), philologian. Born in St. Martin de Ré, France, on June 3, he studied at the Benedictine college, went to the United States in 1777 as secretary to Baron Steuben, and held the rank of captain with the American forces until 1781. He settled in Philadelphia, studied law, was admitted to the Pennsylvania bar, and wrote and translated legal and historical tracts. He had long been interested in language, and his reputation rests on an elaborate study of the grammatical system of Indian languages. He wrote much for the American Philosophical Society, of which he became a member in 1791 and was president from 1827 until his death in Philadelphia on Apr. 1.

DUPONG, PIERRE (1885–1953), premier. Born in Heisdorf, Luxembourg, on Nov. 1, he studied at Paris, Berlin, and Freiburg, practiced law, and married Sophie Schroeder and entered parliament in 1915. He was minister of finance in Luxembourg, then minister of agriculture, and in 1937–45 was premier, holding that position with the government-in-exile in Canada and England. He was an active proponent of a united Europe and introduced a model social-security plan in his nation. He died in Luxembourg on Dec. 22.

DUPRAT, ANTOINE (1463–1535), cardinal. Born in Issoire, France, on Jan. 17, he studied law and in 1507 became first president of the parliament of Paris, and in 1515 was appointed chancellor of France by Francis I. After his wife's death, he studied theology, was ordained in 1517, was bishop of several dioceses, and became archbishop of Sens, France, in 1525, cardinal in 1527, and papal legate in 1530. He arranged the concordat of 1516 with Pope Leo X, though this kept alive the power of royal appointments. He directed an elaborate financial system, was active against religious innovators, helped to compile *Coutumes d'Auverge*, and was a patron of letters. He died near Meaux, France, on July 9.

DUPRAT, GUILLAUME (1507–1560), bishop. Son of Cardinal Antoine Duprat, he was born at Issoire, France, was named bishop

of Clermont in 1529, attended the last sessions of the Council of Trent, and helped the Jesuits to found Collège de Clermont in Paris. He died in Beauregard, near the Grande Chartreuse, France.

DUPRÉ, GIOVANNI (1817–1882), sculptor. Born in Siena, Italy, on Mar. 1, he was a wood carver who taught himself sculpture, won a prize at Florence, and completed statues of Cain, Abel, St. Antony, and a *Triumph of the Cross* while in that city, a prize *Pietà* while in Siena, and the Cavour monument in Turin. His *St. Francis*, for the cathedral of San Rufino, Assisi, was completed by his daughter Amalia. His *Memoirs* were published in Florence (1884–1906), where he died on Jan. 10.

DUPUYTREN, GUILLAUME (1777–1835), anatomist. Born in Pierre-Buffière, Limousin, France, on Oct. 6, he was a charity student at the Collège de la Marche, won a post at eighteen at the new École de Médecin, Paris, by competitive examination, and in 1803 became assistant surgeon at the Hôtel Dieu. He taught operative and clinical surgery at the school and was head surgeon at the hospital by 1815. He became quite wealthy and endowed a chair of anatomy at the École de Médecin and founded a home for needy doctors. He died in Paris on Feb. 8.

DUQUESNOY, FRANÇOIS (1594–1646), sculptor. Born in Brussels, Belgium, son of a Dutch sculptor under whom he studied, he went to Rome in 1619. There he did the baldachinum over the high altar and the statue of St. Andrew, both in St. Peter's. In Brussels he did a figure of justice; in Ghent, the tomb of Bishop Triest; he also is known for his ivory drinking cups and marble-and-bronze playful children. He is sometimes called Flamand. He died in Leghorn, Italy, on July 12.

DURAN, NARCISCO (1776–1846). Born in Castellon de Ampurias, Spain, on Dec. 16, he became a Franciscan in 1792, and from 1806 to 1844 worked at the mission of San José, California. He was three times president of the missions, sought unsuccessfully to stem the despoliation and seizure of church property, and was so active in his legal moves to slow the pillaging process that Governor Figueroa sought to have him exiled. He was protected by the government at Mexico City. For a brief period he was administrator of the diocese of California. He died at Santa Barbara, California, on June 1.

DURAND, URSIN (1682–1771), editor. Born in Tours, France, on May 20, he became a Benedictine at Marmoutier at nineteen. In 1709–13, with Edmond Martène, he searched the archives of nearly a thousand abbeys and churches for material for a new edition of *Gallia Christiana*; they continued to tour Europe for historical materials which were used in several major publications, including their nine-volume anthology of ancient writers. With Dantine and Clémencet, Durand published a handbook for verifying dates, and worked with others on Maurist publications. He was banished from St. Germain-des-Prés in 1734 on the unproved charge of Jansenism, and went to the monastery of St. Eloi and later to Paris, where he died on Aug. 31.

DURANDUS (1012?–1089). Born in Le Neubourg, France, he became a Benedictine, was stationed at Mont Ste. Catherine and St. Vandrille, and was abbot of the newly founded St. Martin of Troarn. He wrote poetry, music, and an elaborate defense of the Eucharist against Berengarius. He died at Troarn, near Caen, France.

DURANDUS (d. 1332), bishop. Born in St. Pourcain, Auvergne, France, he became a Dominican at Clermont, took his doctorate at Paris in 1313, and lectured on scripture at Avignon at the invitation of Pope John XXII. He was made bishop of Le Puy-en-Velay in 1318 and transferred to Meaux in 1326. He wrote a commentary on the *Sentences* and many philosophical works heavily marked by nominalism. His *De statu animarum* was censured for its errors; theological works also are open to correction. He died in Meaux, France, on Sept. 13.

DURANDUS, WILLIAM (1237–1296), canonist. Born in Puimisson, Béziers, Provence, he studied law at Bologna, taught at Modena, and was called to Rome by Pope Clement IV, made a subdeacon, and given two titular canonics. He served the papal court, was Gregory X's secretary at the second Council of Lyons (1274), and in 1279 became dean of Chartres, but remained non-resident. He was papal governor in Romagna, was elected bishop of Mende, France, in 1286, but did not appear until 1291. He served Boniface VIII as governor of Romagna and Ancona. He wrote *Rationale divinorum officiorum* (1286) on the ceremonies and customs of the Roman rite, together with a mystical interpretation and symbolic and allegorical comment on vestments and ritual; *Speculum judiciale*, on the canonical rights of legates; commentaries on the decretals; and a semi-official explanation of the canons of the second Council of Lyons. He died in Rome on Nov. 1.

DURANDUS, WILLIAM (d. 1328), canonist. Called the Younger, to distinguish him from his uncle of the same name, he was an archdeacon at Mende, France, administrator of the diocese in 1286–91, and bishop there after his uncle's death. He attended the Council of Vienne (1311–12), went to Syria on a papal mission, wrote a study of the canonical process of calling councils for Pope Clement V, and died in Cyprus.

DURÃO, JOSÉ DA DANTA RITA (1737–1783), poet. Born in Infecçaoado, Brazil, he became a Jesuit in the diocese of Mariana, and wrote several novels and the poem, *Caramurú*.

DURBIN, ELISHA JOHN (1800–1887). Born in Madison County, Kentucky, on Feb. 1, he studied at the seminary of St. Thomas and at Bardstown, and was ordained in 1822. In 1824 he was given a parish of one third of his state; he covered the 11,000-mile region on horseback for the next sixty years. He then directed a small mission at Princeton, Kentucky, and was chaplain at an academy in Shelbyville, Kentucky, where he died.

DÜRER, ALBRECHT (1471–1528), painter. Born in Nuremberg, Germany, on May 21, he studied under his father, a goldsmith, and the engraver Michel Wohlgemut. He visited Switzerland in his early years, married Agnes Frey, and sketched madonnas, coats of arms, and landscapes. He also executed woodcuts and copper engravings, altarpieces, and a self-portrait. His most memorable work up to 1505 includes his fifteen woodcuts of the *Apocalypse*, seven of the *Larger Passion*, and sixteen of the *Life of the Virgin*. He was in Venice in 1505–7, completing the *Festival of the Rosary* in color and *Christ on the Cross* in oil. Before 1520 he had completed a monumental *Adoration of the Trinity* and such familiar works as *Virgin with the Pear*, the engravings of *Knight with Death and the Devil* and *St. Jerome*, and woodcuts for the *Little Passion*. Varied portraits and the marginal decorations for Maximilian's prayer book also belong to his second period. After 1520 he did *St. Jerome with a Skull*, portraits of Erasmus, Willibald Pirkheimer (his humanistic adviser), the four evangelists, and Christ. In his final years Dürer wrote on anatomical proportion, fortification, and geometry. He died in Nuremberg on Apr. 6.

DURIER, ANTHONY (1833–1904), bishop. Born on Jan. 3, at St. Bonnet-des-Quarts, France (though Aug. 8, 1832, and Rouen are also suggested), he studied at the Lyons seminary, went to the United States, and continued his studies at Mt. St. Mary of the West seminary, Cincinnati, and was ordained in 1856. He served in New Orleans parishes from 1857 to 1884, when he was appointed bishop of Natchitoches (later, the see of Alexandria). He died there on Feb. 28.

DURKIN, MARTIN PATRICK (1897–1955), executive. Born in Chicago, Illinois, on Mar. 18, he had no formal education, became a steam fitter's assistant at seventeen, and served in the army during World War I. He was head of the Illinois state labor department for eight years, bettering the unemployment-compensation benefits and conciliation service. In 1941 he left to become secretary-treasurer of the United Association of Plumbers and Steam

Fitters and was its president in 1943, by which time there were 225,000 union members. Though a Democrat, he served as secretary of labor in President Eisenhower's cabinet from Jan. to Sept. 1953, when he resigned after proposed changes in the Taft-Hartley Act were not introduced. He died in Washington, D.C., on Nov. 13.

DUTHLAC, ST. (d. 1065), bishop. Educated in Ireland, he labored as bishop of Ross, Scotland; his shrine was a place of veneration until the Reformation. F. D. Mar. 8.

DUTTON, IRA BARNES (1843–1931). Born in Stowe, Vermont, on Apr. 27, he moved to Wisconsin, served as a lieutenant during the Civil War, and was with the war claims department for ten years. He became a convert, entered the Trappist monastery at Gethsemane, Kentucky, as a laybrother, taking the name Joseph, and in 1886 went to Hawaii to join Fr. Damien in his work with lepers on Molokai. After Damien's death, Bro. Joseph became administrative assistant of the colony, founded Baldwin Home for 1300 men and boys, and was honored by the Hawaiian government. He died in Honolulu on Mar. 26.

DUVERNAY, LUDGER (1799–1852), journalist. Born in Verchères, Quebec, Canada, on Jan. 22, he was a writer, then edited at Three Rivers *La Gazette* (1817), *Le Constitutionnel* (1832), and *L'Argus* (1826), and at Montreal *La Minerve*, which he founded with N. Morin in 1827. He founded the Society of St. John the Baptist in 1834, chose the maple leaf as Canada's national emblem, and was extremely active in the cause of French Canada. He served briefly in the legislature, but was forced to flee the country after the rebellion in 1837–38, settled in Burlington, Vermont, and founded *Le Patriote Canadien* in 1849. He returned to Montreal after the union of Canada, again edited *La Minerve*, continued to battle all attempts to absorb Lower Canada, and died on Nov. 28.

DWENGER, JOSEPH GREGORY (1837–1893), bishop. Born in Stattotown (now Minster), Ohio, on Sept. 7, he was orphaned at twelve, studied at Mt. St. Mary's of the West, Cincinnati, joined the Congregation of the Precious Blood, and was ordained in 1859. He became secretary of the congregation in 1867, engaged in missionary work, attended the second Plenary Council of Baltimore as Bishop Purcell's theologian, and in 1872 was appointed second bishop of Fort Wayne, Indiana. He founded the congregation's seminary at Carthagena, Ohio, and served as its first president, built a model parochial-school system in his diocese, was known as the "orphan's friend" (he built orphanages in Lafayette and Fort Wayne), and led the first official American pilgrimage to Lourdes in 1874. He was one of the three prelates designated to bring the decrees of the third Plenary Council of Baltimore in 1884 to Rome, and died in Fort Wayne on Jan. 22.

DWIGHT, THOMAS (1843–1911), anatomist. Born in Boston, Massachusetts, on Oct. 13, he became a convert in 1856, took his undergraduate and medical degrees from Harvard, studied abroad, taught at Harvard and Bowdoin, and in 1883 succeeded Oliver Wendell Holmes as professor of anatomy at Harvard. He published several studies on bone structure, arranged the osteology section of the Warren Museum, and wrote *Thoughts of a Catholic Anatomist* (1911). He died in Nahant, Massachusetts, on Sept. 8.

DYFAN, ST. (2nd century). He is said to have been one of the missioners Pope St. Eleutherius sent to Britain at the request of King St. Lucius, and according to an ancient and widely held tradition, he died a martyr. F. D. May 26.

DYFRIG, ST. (d. 545?), bishop. A Welsh monk, born probably in Madley, he founded monasteries at Henllan and Moccas which became centers from which developed many churches and monasteries in Herefordshire and Monmouthshire. Called the first bishop of Llandaff (which is unlikely) and the archbishop of Caerleon-on-Usk who crowned King Arthur at Colchester (he is the "high saint" of Tennyson's *Idylls of the King*), he did appoint St. Samson abbot of the monastery of Caldey Island. He died and was buried on Bardsey Island, off the coast of Wales. He is also known as Dubricius. F. D. Nov. 14.

DYMOKE, ROBERT (d. 1580), martyr. Son of Sir Edward Dymoke of Lincolnshire, England, he harbored Bl. Richard Kirkman in his estate at Scrivelsby, where that martyr tutored his children, and was himself reconciled to the Church in 1580. He was seized with his wife Bridget while attending mass and, although a paralytic, was imprisoned in Lincoln, where he died on Sept. 11.

DYMPNA, ST. (d. 650?), martyr. Her relics were found at Gheel, near Antwerp, in the thirteenth century, where a sanatorium now exists. She is invoked as the patron of epileptics and the insane. Legend calls her the daughter of a British (or Celtic) king, who fled her father's incestuous desire, was pursued, and slain with her chaplain, St. Gerebernus. He is the patron of Sonsbeck, near Münster, Germany, where he is buried. F. D. May 15.

E

EADBERT. *See* Edbert.

EADMER (1064?–1124), historian. Brought up at Christ Church, Canterbury, England, he became a Benedictine, was St. Anselm's companion from 1079 to 1109, and after the latter's death devoted himself to writing a life of his patron; verse biographies of SS. Dunstan, Wilfred, Odo, and Oswald, *Historiae novarum*, and an important treatise on the Immaculate Conception. He was elected bishop of St. Andrews in 1121, but remained precentor of Canterbury when he was unable to occupy his see.

EADNOT (d. 1016). A Benedictine monk at Worcester, England, he became abbot of Ramsey and in 1006 was named bishop of Dorchester, where he aided St. Oswald of York. He died in battle against the Danes and is sometimes listed as a martyr, honored on Oct. 19.

EANBALD (d. 796), archbishop. A monk at York, England, he worked with Alcuin in rebuilding the monastery there, developed its library, and became archbishop of York in 778 or 782. He crowned Eardulf king of Northumbria in June 796.

EANBALD II (d. 810), archbishop. A student of Alcuin at York, he succeeded his namesake as archbishop of that see and was consecrated in 797. He called a synod in 798 to consider ecclesiastical courts, probably introduced the Roman ritual after the acceptance of the Roman dating of Easter, and may have compiled a volume of decrees.

EANFLEDA, ST. (d. 700?). Daughter of St. Edwin, king of Northumbria, and St. Ethelburga, she became a Benedictine nun at Whitby after the death of her husband. F. D. Nov. 24.

EANSWIDA, ST. (d. 640?). Daughter of King Edbald of Kent, she refused an arranged marriage with a pagan prince, founded a monastery near Folkestone, England, in 630, and was its abbess until her death on Aug. 31. F. D. Sept. 12.

EARLS, MICHAEL (1875–1937), author. Born in Southbridge, Massachusetts, on Oct. 2, he studied at Holy Cross and Georgetown, began seminary work at Montreal in 1898, but became a Jesuit in 1899 and was ordained in 1912. He taught at Boston College and Holy Cross, directed the literary publications of both schools, did parish work, and published two volumes of essays, two novels and two collections of short stories, and five volumes of poetry. Among his best-known titles are *Under College Towers*, *Manuscripts and Memories*, *From Bersabee to Dan*, and *The Hosting of the King*. Because of his long career at Holy Cross (1913–31) he was named director of the alumni association in 1931. He died in New York City on Jan. 31.

EASDIN (d. 1050). Archbishop of Canterbury, he anointed Edward the Confessor as king of Anglo-Saxon England, and resigned his see a few years before his death.

EASTON, ADAM (d. 1397), cardinal. Born in Easton, Norfolk, England, he became a Benedictine at Norwich, went to Rome, probably in the company of Archbishop Langham, was attached to the papal court, and in 1381 was made a cardinal-priest by Urban VI. In 1385 he was imprisoned with five other cardinals on the charge of conspiring against the pope, was released in 1389 by Boniface IX, and later served at Salisbury cathedral. He died in Rome, probably on Sept. 15.

EATA, ST. (d. 686), bishop. A native of Northumbria, England, he was trained by St. Aidan at Ripon, became Benedictine abbot of Melrose, and after the Synod of Whitby accepted the Roman observance and succeeded St. Colman at Lindisfarne. In 678 he was appointed bishop of Lindisfarne, but later exchanged sees with St. Cuthbert, bishop of Hexham. F. D. Oct. 26.

EBBA, ST. (d. 870?), martyr. Benedictine abbess of Coldingham, on the Scots border, she died with her community when Danish marauders set fire to their convent. F. D. Aug. 23.

EBBA THE ELDER, ST. (d. 683). Sister of Oswy of Northumbria, she was told to marry the king of the Scots, refused, and entered a convent at Lindisfarne. Later, she founded a double monastery at Coldingham. F. D. Aug. 25.

EBBO, ST. (d. 740). Born in Tonnerre, France, he was a Benedictine monk at St. Pierre-le-Vif, in Sens, of which diocese he became bishop in 709. He saved the city when it was besieged by Moors in 725. F. D. Aug. 27.

EBBO (d. 851), archbishop. A French serf, he was freed and educated by Charlemagne, ordained, and made librarian and counselor by Louis the Debonair. He was royally appointed archbishop of Rheims in 816, became papal legate for the north in 822, and with Bishops Halitgar and Willerich preached with some success to the Danes, though the country was not converted. In 833 he joined the rebellion of Lothair against his father and forced the emperor to do public penance at Soissons for sins he had not committed. In 835, Ebbo publicly recanted in the cathedral of Metz and was deposed. When Lothair became emperor,

Ebbo was reinstated, but unlawfully; he lived off the incomes of several abbeys which were his reward, pleaded with Pope Sergius II for reinstatement, and was eventually turned out even by Lothair. Louis the German appointed him bishop of Hildesheim after 845. He died on Mar. 20.

EBENDORFER, THOMAS (1385–1464), historian. Born in Haselbach, Austria, on Aug. 12, he received his degree at Vienna, taught philosophy there until 1427, then served as dean and professor of philosophy until his death on Jan. 8. He was three times rector of the university, was a canon of St. Stephen's, and a missionary preacher as well. He attended the Council of Basle (1432–34) until it attacked pope and emperor, served Emperor Frederick III as ambassador, but fell out of favor with the latter when he defended the rights of the university against the crown. He also failed to mediate the quarrel between Frederick and Albert of Brandenburg. Ebendorfer's *Chronicon Austriae* is a valuable historical record for the years 1400–63; he also wrote a chronicle of Roman emperors, biblical commentaries, a history of the popes, and an account of the Council of Basle. He died in Vienna on Jan. 8.

EBERHARD, BL. (d. 958). Born of Swabian nobility, he was provost of the cathedral of Strassburg when he decided in 934 to join Bl. Benno at the hermitage of Einsiedeln, Switzerland. Eberhard built the Benedictine monastery and church there and became first abbot. F. D. Aug. 14.

EBERHARD, BL. (d. 1150?). Count of Mons, Flanders, he went on pilgrimages as penance for the violence of his military career, and became a swineherd and then a monk at the Cistercian abbey of Morimond. He founded both Einberg and Mont St. George. F. D. Mar. 20.

EBERHARD, ST. (1085?–1164), archbishop. Born in Nuremberg, Germany, and educated at Bamberg, where he was ordained and became a canon, he went to Paris for advanced study, and in 1125 became a Benedictine at Prüfening. In 1133 he became abbot of Biburg, which had been founded by his brothers and sister and which he developed in size and learning. He was chosen archbishop of Salzburg in 1147, spent much time as a mediator and reformer, and staunchly supported Pope Alexander III against antipope Victor IV, the choice of Emperor Frederick Barbarossa. Eberhard died on June 11 at the Cistercian monastery of Rein, Styria. F. D. June 22.

EBERHARD (13th century), historian. An Augustinian canon in Ratisbon or Salzburg, he flourished from 1294 to 1305; his *Annales* cover the history of Bavaria and surrounding areas from the time of the election of Rudolf of Bavaria to the latter date, and record many contemporary documents.

EBERHARD, MATTHIAS (1815–1876), bishop. Born in Trier, Germany, on Nov. 15, he studied there, was ordained in 1839, did parish work in Cologne, and in 1842 taught moral theology at the seminary in Trier. He was its rector from 1849 to 1862, was a representative in the Prussian lower chamber from 1852 to 1856, became auxiliary bishop in 1862, and bishop of Trier in 1867. He bettered seminary education and catechetical instruction in his diocese, attended the Vatican Council and opposed the definition of infallibility as badly timed, then approved it. He was a leader in the struggle against the government's attempts to crush the Church, and was imprisoned in 1874. He died in his see city, which had been stripped of priests, on May 30. His sermons were collected and published after his death.

EBNER, CHRISTINA (1277–1355). Born in Nuremburg, Germany, she became a Dominican at thirteen, suffered from a strange illness for ten years, underwent mystical experiences which caused her to be misunderstood by many, and wrote a spiritual diary of her life from 1317 to 1353 at the direction of Fr. Konrad of Füssen, her confessor. She died in Engelthal convent, near Nuremberg, on Dec. 27.

EBNER, MARGARETHA (1291–1351). Born in Donauwörth, Germany, she became a Dominican nun near Dillingen, was professed in 1306, suffered from serious illness for ten years, had numerous mystical experiences, and recorded them in a lengthy correspondence with Henry of Nördlingen, who became her spiritual director in 1332. She died on June 20.

EBONTIUS (d. 1104), bishop. Born in Comminges, France, he became a Benedictine at Ste. Foi, Tomières, abbot of St. Victorien, near Ainsa, Aragon, Spain, and bishop of Barbastro, Spain, after its release from Moorish occupation.

EBRULF, ST. (517–596). Born in Bayeux, Normandy, he was raised at the court of King Childebert I. Soon after marriage he and his wife separated, she to enter a convent and he to become a monk. He later became abbot-founder of Ouche and other monastic centers. F. D. Dec. 29.

ECCLESIUS, ST. (d. 532). He became bishop of Ravenna, Italy, in 521. F. D. July 27.

ECCLESTON, SAMUEL (1801–1851), archbishop. Born near Chestertown, Maryland, on June 27, he studied at St. Mary's College, Baltimore, became a convert, studied in that city and in France, was ordained a Sulpician in 1825, and became president of St. Mary's in 1829. In 1834 he was made coadjutor bishop of Baltimore and a month later succeeded to the see as its fifth archbishop. He was active in developing educational opportunities and held five provincial councils. He died in Washington, D.C., on Apr. 22.

ECHARD, JACQUES (1644–1724), historian. Born in Rouen, France, on Sept. 22, son of a royal official, he became a Dominican in Paris, and, at the death of Jacques Quétef in 1698, took over the one-quarter-completed history of the writers of his order. This annotated list of editions, spurious writings, and locations of material was published in 1721. He died in Paris on Mar. 15.

ECHAVE, BALTASAR DE (17th century), painter. Born in Zuyama, Spain, he went to Mexico late in the sixteenth century, where he completed many religious paintings, especially for churches near the capital. A *San Sebastian* in the cathedral is probably the work of his wife, who may also have been his instructor.

ECHTER VON MESPELBRUNN, JULIUS (1545–1617), bishop. Born in Spessart, Bavaria, on Mar. 18, he was educated at Louvain, Douai, Paris, Angers, Pavia, and Rome, returning in 1567 as canon of Würzburg. He became dean of the chapter in 1570, and in 1573, before his ordination, was appointed prince-bishop of Würzburg. He was very active as a reformer, founded the University of Würzburg in 1582, restored churches and monasteries, endowed the Julius Hospital, reduced taxes, and limited clerical offices to Jesuits and to seculars who were beyond suspicion. As a result of his efforts, sometimes extreme, he brought back 100,000 persons to the Church in three years. The Catholic League which he founded had a strong influence on other parts of Germany then and later. He died in Würzburg, Bavaria, on Sept. 13.

ECIJA, JUAN DE (1510–1591), missioner. Born in Fuenteovejuna, Spain, he went to Mexico and became a Dominican about 1531, taking the name Domingo de la Anunciación. He had great success in teaching Indians, worked zealously during the plague of 1545, was shipwrecked off Florida in 1559, and held several offices for his order before he became blind in 1585.

ECK, JOHANN MAIER VON (1486–1543), theologian. Born in Eck, Swabia, on Nov. 15, he studied theology, law, science, classics, and Hebrew at Heidelberg, Tübingen, Cologne, and Freiburg-im-Breisgau. He was ordained in 1508 (the age limit was waived) and took his doctor's degree at Freiburg im Breisgau in 1510. He taught theology at Ingolstadt, was chancellor and rector there, and pastor and canon in Eichstätt. From 1519 on he was Luther's principal opponent, writing, debating, and serving on diplomatic commissions. He had published *Obelisci* (1518) in reply to Luther's theses of rebellion, and in 1520 was appointed papal legate and directed, with Alexander and Caracciolo, to promulgate the bull which excommunicated Luther. He also strengthened the Bavarian dukes to support the old rebellion, helped to organize the Catholic Federation in 1524, wrote against Zwingli, and combated the Augsburg Confession. When he drew up a list of 404 heretical tenets and called for discussion, no one accepted his challenge. He attended the convocations at Worms in 1540 and at Regensburg in 1543. His writings were voluminous, as were replies to him. Many of the latter, however, were merely personal lampoons; the unpublished debates were of a higher tone. He died in Ingolstadt, Germany, on Feb. 10.

ECKART, ANSELM (1721–1809), missioner. Born in Bingen, Germany, on Aug. 4, he became a Jesuit at nineteen, was sent to the missions in Brazil, and was imprisoned for eighteen years with his associates when the Portuguese king ordered the Society suppressed. He wrote a chronicle of their sufferings, went to Russia on his release in 1777, and taught in the College of Polstok, where he died on June 29.

ECKHART, JOHANN (1260?–1307), theologian. Born in Hochheim, near Gotha, Germany, Meister Eckhart became a Dominican, taught, and served as prior in Erfurt and vicar provincial of Thuringia in 1298. In 1300 he began to lecture at Paris, was made master of sacred theology by his order in 1301, and became provincial of Saxony in 1303 and in 1307 and vicar general of Bohemia in 1307–11. He then returned to teach at Paris, Strassburg, and Cologne. In his catechetical sermons, which had a decided influence on German prose, he followed Albertus Magnus and Thomas Aquinas, and discussed the essence of God, relations between God and man, and the traits of the human soul. Eckhart is chiefly known as a mystic, following Hugh of St. Victor, and influencing Tauler and Suso in ideas and style. Some of his statements were challenged, but their orthodoxy was approved after investigation; when the archbishop of Cologne persisted in condemning him, he appealed to Rome. Pope John XXII termed some propositions heretical and others injudicious in their wording; Eckhart made a full profession of faith. He died in Cologne.

ECKHART, JOHANN GEORG VON (1664–1730), historian. Born in Duingen, Germany, on Sept. 7, he studied theology and history at Leipzig, served as secretary to Count Flemming of Saxony, then was assistant to the historian Leibnitz at Hanover. He became professor of history at Helmstedt in 1706, councilor at Hanover in 1714, librarian and royal historian to the house of Hanover, was ennobled by Emperor Charles VI, and changed his name from Eccard. He gave up his positions in 1723, went to Corbie and Cologne, and became a convert. He died in Würzburg,

Bavaria, on Feb. 9. His writings, which had great influence on the critical trend in historical writing, include *Origines Austriacae, Corpus historicorum medii aevi,* and a study of Teutonic languages.

ECKHEL, JOSEPH HILARIUS (1737–1798). Born in Enzersfeld, Austria, on Jan. 13, he studied in Vienna, became a Jesuit in 1751, and was ordained in 1764. He taught in several schools and colleges, wrote Latin and German poetry, and became interested in coins. He made a scientific study of numismatics and archaeology and when his Society was suppressed was given charge of the national collection in Vienna. He lectured at the Jesuit college there and wrote widely in German, French, and Latin on numismatics before his death on May 16.

EDANA, ST. Patroness of a number of parishes in western Ireland, she may be identical with St. Modwenna.

EDBERT (d. 768), king. Son of Eata and brother of Egbert, archbishop of York, he succeeded St. Ceolwulf as king of Northumbria in 738. He allied himself with the Picts and Franks, and when his army was destroyed in battle in 756 entered the Benedictine abbey at York and spent the last ten years of his life there. His name is also spelled Eadbert.

EDBURGA, ST. (d. 751). Of the royal family of Kent, she was a disciple of St. Mildred and succeeded her as abbess of Minster-in-Thanet. She met St. Boniface while on pilgrimage to Rome, corresponded with him, though none of her letters are extant, and supplied him with books and vestments. F. D. Dec. 12.

EDBURGA, ST. (d. 960). Daughter of King Edward the Elder, she became abbess of the royally founded Benedictine monastery at Winchester, England. Her shrine at Pershore, Worcestershire, long was popular with pilgrims. F. D. June 15.

EDDOGWY, ST. (d. 600?). Son of Budic, prince of Brittany, he was educated in Wales by his uncle, St. Teilo, whom he may have succeeded as abbot. He has been incorrectly listed as bishop of Llandaff. He is also known as Oudacius. F. D. July 2.

EDELINCK, GÉRARD (1640?–1707), engraver. Born in Antwerp, Belgium, on Oct. 20, he studied under Huybrecht there and at Paris under de Poilly, attracted royal attention, and was given a pension and made professor in the Gobelins Academy. He was naturalized in 1675, made a member of the Royal Academy in 1677, and produced some 400 engravings in a masterly style, with a new technique of line which revolutionized the art. He depicted the leaders of his day, left fourteen portraits of Louis XIV, and engraved Raphael's *Holy Family* and other popular paintings. He died in Paris on Apr. 2. His brothers, Jean (1643?–

1680) and Gaspard François (1652–1722), studied under him and also became engravers.

EDELINCK, NICOLAS (1680–1730), engraver. Son of Gerard, under whom he studied and whose portrait he drew, he was born in Antwerp and died there. He lived for some years in Venice, and made engravings of work by Correggio, Raphael, and Kneller, including the latter's portait of John Dryden.

EDEYRN (13th century), poet. Called David Aur, "the Golden-tongued," he wrote Welsh poetry, a study of prosody, and a grammar about 1270.

EDFRITH (d. 721). Bishop of Lindisfarne, England, he directed his abbey in a compromise Roman-Celtic liturgy, promoted the manuscript preparation of St. Cuthbert's works, and initiated the copying project of the Lindisfarne gospels.

EDGAR (944?–975), king. Son of Edward or Edmund the Magnificent, he became ruler of Northumbria and Mercia in 957 when the north of England rebelled against his brother Edwyn, and in 959, when Edwyn died, became king of West Saxony as well. With the advice of Archbishop Dunstan, his counselor, he consolidated the English nation, improved the courts, supported the reform of clerical life, and built a fleet to protect the nation against Norse raids. He was called "the Peaceful," and died on July 8.

EDGAR (1072–1107), king of Scotland. Younger son of Malcolm III, he fled to England when Donald Bane took over in 1094, and was made king of Scotland in 1097 by William II of England, whom he acknowledged as his feudal overlord. He surrendered all western islands off his coast to King Magnus Barefoot of Norway in 1098. He aided the development of the Church in Scotland.

EDGAR ATHELING (d. 1120?). Grandson of Edmund Ironside, he was probably born in Hungary, was proclaimed king in London to succeed Harold II of England after the latter's defeat and death at the battle of Hastings (1066), but quickly acknowledged William the Conqueror as king. He joined rebellions in the north in 1068 and in 1069, took refuge with Malcolm III of Scotland, who married Edgar's sister, St. Margaret, supported William II of England, and in 1097 put his nephew Edgar on the Scots throne by a military coup. He went on the crusade in 1099, joined Robert of Normandy against Henry I of England on his return, and was taken prisoner at Tinchebray in 1106, but was soon released.

EDGEWORTH DE FIRMONT, HENRY ESSEX (1745–1807). Born in Edgeworthstown, Longford, Ireland, son of Robert Edgeworth, its Protestant rector, who became a convert, he was taken into exile by his parents at the age of four and was brought up in Toulouse. Henry studied at the Sorbonne, was ordained in Paris, and served there. He was made vicar general of Paris when its archbishop was forced to flee in 1792. He prepared King Louis XVI for death and accompanied him to the guillotine, was himself listed for death, resided secretly in Bayeux and other cities, and went to England in 1796 after the death of his mother and of the king's sister Elizabeth, whom he had sworn to protect. He later went to the court of the exiled Louis XVIII at Mittau, Russia, where he remained until his death on May 22, of fever contracted from French prisoners whom he was tending after the defeat of the Napoleonic army.

EDISTIUS, ST. (d. 303?), martyr. He was put to death at Ravenna, Italy, during the Diocletian persecution. F. D. Oct. 12.

EDITH OF POLESWORTH, ST. (d. 925?). Probably the sister of King Athelstan, she married Sihtric, the Viking king of York, in 925. After his death, she became a Benedictine nun at Polesworth in Warwickshire, where she may have been abbess. F. D. July 15.

EDITH OF WILTON, ST. (961?–984). Daughter of Edgar, king of the English, and Wulfrida, she was taken, shortly after her birth in Kemsing, to Wilton abbey. At fifteen she became a nun, refused the abbacy of three monasteries offered by her father, and remained a nun at Wilton where her mother had become abbess. On the murder of her half-brother Edward the Martyr, who had succeeded Edgar, she was offered the throne but refused it. F. D. Sept. 16.

EDMUND, ST. (841–870), king and martyr. At fourteen he was proclaimed king of the East Angles, and ruled wisely until 870, when the Danes under Ingvar, who had begun an invasion of England in 866, defeated and captured him at Hoxne, Suffolk. When the king refused the victor's terms, he was tortured and beheaded. The great Benedictine settlement of Bury St. Edmund's was named after him. F. D. Nov. 20.

EDMUND (921–946), king. He succeeded his half-brother Athelstan as king of Wessex in 940, fought at Brunanburh, was pushed back by an invasion of Irish Vikings, and regained the lost Northumbrian area when the Vikings quarreled among themselves in 944. He made an alliance with King Malcolm of Scotland. He was killed when defending one of his officials against an outlawed criminal.

EDMUND (13th century), founder. Son of Richard, earl of Cornwall, he founded a monastery at Ashridge, Hertfordshire, about 1283, became rector in 1285, and directed the community of twenty canons, known as Boni Homines (or Bonshommes). It became a college and existed until seized in 1529 by King Henry VIII.

EDMUND OF ABINGDON, ST. (1180–1240), archbishop. Born in Abingdon, near Oxford, England, he studied at Oxford and Paris, took his doctorate, was ordained, and taught theology at Oxford for eight years. In 1222 he became canon at Salisbury cathedral and in 1227, at Pope Gregory IX's request, preached the sixth crusade in England. In 1233 he was elected archbishop of Canterbury and consecrated in spite of his objections. He acted as mediator for King Henry III with the Welsh and with several of the king's ex-ministers and fearlessly defended the rights of the Church against the monarch's continued infringements. In 1237 he visited Rome to plead his cause against the king and a group of rebellious monks of Canterbury and Rochester. On his return he excommunicated seventeen of them. Cardinal Otto, whom Henry had had appointed as papal legate, rescinded the penalty. Edmund then became embroiled with Otto over the king's practice of leaving benefices unoccupied so that the crown could collect the revenues. When the pope failed to support him (Rome had given him authority to fill offices left vacant for six months, but withdrew it), Edmund decided his office was meaningless, and in 1240 left England for the Cistercian abbey at Pontigny. He died a few months later at Soissons, France, and was canonized in 1247. F. D. Nov. 16.

EDMUND IRONSIDE (d. 1016), king of England. Son of Ethelred the Unready, he fought against Canute in 1015, whose close friend he then became. He became king of England in 1016, lost the battle of Assandun to the Danes, and died in London six months later.

EDRED (d. 955), king of England. Son of Edward the Elder, he succeeded his brother Edmund in 946 as king of England and fought off invasions of Irish Vikings and Norwegians in Northumbria. He re-established peace in his nation in 954, and relied for advice on St. Dunstan, who arranged a workable pattern by which English and Danes could live side by side.

EDWARD I (1239–1307), king of England. Son of Henry III and Eleanor of Provence, he was born in Westminster on June 17 or 18, married Eleanor of Castile in 1254, fought in Wales, went on the crusade of 1270, and returned to England in 1274, two years after his father's death. On his accession in 1274 he faced wars with Wales, Scotland, and France. He selected John de Baliol over Robert Bruce as king of the Scots in 1290. Edward forced Baliol to resign after defeating the Scots at Dunbar in 1296, saw his choice defeated at Stirling Bridge by the patriot William Wallace in 1297, and then defeated the Scots at Falkirk in 1298. In 1303 he made peace with

France, and then invaded Scotland, received Bruce's submission, and ordered Wallace's execution in 1305. In spite of constant military activity he developed English law. In 1297 his statute of mortmain forbade extension of church property without the king's permission; other laws forbade subinfeudation, developed courts, and defined police powers. Because of his wars the barons were able to gain many concessions in return for extra taxes; parliament became especially powerful after 1295, and in 1297 forced the king to confirm its right to give consent to all tax levies. He died at Burgh-on-the-Sands, near Carlisle, England on July 7.

EDWARD II (1284–1327), king of England. Son of Edward I and Eleanor of Castile, he was born at Carnarvon Castle, on Apr. 25, became prince of Wales in 1301, and because of his fondness for a school companion, Piers Gaveston, lost the support of the barons and the trust of his father. Robert Bruce led a successful attack in Scotland and regained the nation from England; court dissension increased after Edward became king in 1307. Gaveston was sent to Ireland as lord lieutenant in 1309, but Edward recalled him to favor in 1309 and married him to his niece. In 1310 a group of nobles took over the reins of government, while Edward was in the north, forced him to accept their direction, and sent Gaveston into exile. Edward brought him back in 1312, but the barons then killed him to end his influence. The Scots victory at Bannockburn in 1314 and Edward's intrusion of new favorites, especially the younger Henry Despenser, led to greater unpopularity. After a disastrous Welsh invasion, Despenser and his father were exiled in 1321, but Edward recalled them, brought the Mortimers under his control, and marched against the rebellious north. Edward's wife, Isabella, sister of Charles IV of France, went to Aquitaine with her son (Edward III to be), began an affair with Roger Mortimer, and invaded England in 1326. Edward II, abandoned by all his nobles, was captured and deposed; the Despensers were executed. He was forced to abdicate in Jan. 1327, and then put to death on orders of Isabella and Mortimer at Berkeley castle, near Gloucester, England, on Sept. 21.

EDWARD III (1312–1377), king of England. Son of Edward II and Isabella of France, he was born in Windsor, England, on Nov. 13, was made guardian of England in 1326, and, when his father was deposed in 1327, became king. He married Philippa of Hainault in 1328, fought unsuccessfully against Scotland, and was forced to agree to its independence in 1329. He seized the reins of government from his mother and her lover, Roger Mortimer, defeated the Scots at Halidon Hill in 1333, but failed to retake Scotland; in 1337 the Hundred Years' War with France began. Edward fought in many land and sea battles; his son, Edward the Black Prince (so-called from his armor), won the battle of Poitiers in 1356. Victories at home were inconclusive and costly; parliament gained more control as new taxes were demanded. The Black Death (1348–49) cut heavily into the population, upset the Church by decimating the clergy, and created grave social and economic upheaval; religious unrest increased as John Wycliffe proved a popular preacher. Edward was embroiled with the Church when he sought to seize additional sources of income. Factionalism increased when the nobles sided with John of Gaunt or Edmund Mortimer and the Black Prince; each side triumphed at times as Edward heeded the whims of his mistress, Alice Perrers. John of Gaunt was exiled, but, when the Black Prince died in 1376, John returned and led parliament into a position of supremacy over the king which he was able to maintain. Edward died at Shene (Richmond), England, on June 21.

EDWARD IV (1442–1483), king of England. Born in Rouen, France, on Apr. 28, he led the Yorkist faction after the death of his father, Richard, in 1460, defeated the Lancastrians at Mortimer's Cross in 1461, and was proclaimed king in London. He defeated the Lancastrians again at Towton in 1461, secretly married Elizabeth Woodville, and when he filled the court with her relatives was faced by rebellion led by the earl of Warwick, his cousin. Edward was defeated and went to Holland in 1470, returned with his brother Richard in 1471, and defeated Warwick at Barnet and the Lancastrian forces at Tewksbury. His brother, the duke of Clarence, was murdered in 1478, presumably for plotting against the crown; the earl of Gloucester (later Richard III) rose to power and easily undermined the selfishly preoccupied monarch. Edward was autocratic, disregarded parliament, acted with ruthless disdain, and lived a dissolute life (Jane Shore was one mistress). He died on Apr. 9.

EDWARD V (1470–1483), king of England. Son of Edward IV and Elizabeth Woodville, he was born in Westminster on Nov. 2 or 3, was a pawn in the power politics involving his father's brother, the earl of Gloucester (later Richard III), and Earl Rivers, an uncle on his mother's side. Rivers was arrested and sent to the Tower, as were young Edward, who succeeded his father in 1483, and his younger brother, Richard, duke of York. The children died there, smothered on orders of Richard III according to Lancastrian propaganda and ordered put to death by Henry VII according to Yorkist counter-propaganda. Since the Lancastrians triumphed at the defeat and death of Richard III, the imputation of the crime to the latter became the prevailing view and was accepted by Thomas More for his biography of Richard.

EDWARD (d. 1438), king of Portugal. Son of John I, whom he succeeded in 1433, he was more interested in philosophy than government, and undertook a disastrous invasion of Tangier, which resulted in the capture of Prince Ferdinand. He also is known as Duarte.

EDWARD THE CONFESSOR, ST. (1004–1066), king of England. Son of King Ethelred the Unready of England and his Norman wife Emma, he was born in Islip and in 1014 was forced to flee with his mother to Normandy when the Danes under Sweyn and his son Canute invaded England. The year after Ethelred's death in 1016, Emma married Canute, who became king of England. Edward remained in Normandy until 1042, when, on the death of his half-brother Hardicanute, he became king. In 1044 he married Edith, daughter of the powerful Earl Godwin (who had tortured Edward's brother Alfred, which had caused his death in 1036). Despite the marriage, trouble arose between Edward and Godwin, partly as a result of Edward's partiality to the Normans, and in 1051 the king exiled Godwin and his family who took refuge in Flanders. The earl raised a fleet and sailed up the Thames to London, but armed rebellion was averted when the two settled their differences. In 1053, the earl died, but the difficulties continued between his sons: Harold, who aspired to the royal succession, since Edward was childless; and Tostig, earl of Northumbria. In 1065, Tostig was driven from Northumbria by a revolt and was banished to the continent by Edward, who named Harold his successor. Edward died on Jan. 5, the week after the consecration of Westminster abbey (where he is buried), which he rebuilt in place of a vow he had made while in exile to go on pilgrimage to Rome. He was canonized in 1161. F. D. Oct. 13.

EDWARD THE ELDER (d. 924), king of England. Son of Alfred the Great, he served his father in wars against the Danes, apparently was joint king of England with him, and became king of Wessex in 899 (although the claim was disputed by his cousin Ethelwold, who declared war on him). Ethelwold died about 905; Edward then had to face increasing attacks from the Danes on land and sea. He became ruler of England south of the Humber River, absorbed Mercia, was accepted by Welsh chieftains, and may have gained the fealty of Scotland through the alleged submission of Constantine II (on which action later English kings based their claim to the Scots crown).

EDWARD THE MARTYR (d. 979), king of England. Son of Edgar the Peaceful by his first wife, Ethelfled, he succeeded his father as king of England in 975, faced civil war, and was slain at Corfe, allegedly by servants of his stepmother, Elfrida, and his half-brother, Ethelred the Unready. He was honored at Shaftesbury as a saint and martyr on Mar. 18.

EDWEN, ST. (7th century). Said to have been daughter of King Edwin of Northumberland, she is the patron of Llanedwen, Wales. F. D. Nov. 6.

EDWIN, ST. (585?–633), king. Son of Aella, king of Deira, he was three when his father died. Deprived of his throne by King Ethelfrith of Bernicia, his brother-in-law, Edwin of Deira became king of Northumbria when Ethelfrith was defeated and slain in 617 in a battle at the Idle River by King Raedwald of the East Angles, with whom Edwin had taken refuge. Edwin married Ethelburga, daughter of King Ethelbert of Kent, in 625, and allowed St. Paulinus to come to his kingdom with her and to preach. In 627, Paulinus baptized him and this began the Christianization of Northumbria. He established law and order in his kingdom and became the most powerful monarch in England. He died at Hatfield Chase in battle against the invading pagan Mercians under Penda and the Welsh under Cadwallon. Since he died resisting the pagans, he is venerated as a martyr in England. F. D. Oct. 12.

EDWOLD, ST. (9th century). Brother of St. Edmund, king of East Anglia, he became a hermit at Carne, Dorsetshire. F. D. Nov. 27.

EDWY (910?–959), king of England. Son of Edmund I and St. Elgiva, he became king at fifteen when Edred, his uncle, died. His reign was an unfortunate one: he estranged himself from his subjects by frequent interference in their lives and by exiling his pious grandmother, Eadgive; fought and was defeated at Gloucester by his younger brother, Edgar; accepted the southern part of the English nation when the thanes met to end the civil strife; and became the enemy of St. Dunstan, who opposed his marriage, and whose abbey he plundered and whom he drove into exile. In his last year or two he governed with more moderation. He died on Oct. 1.

EFFLAM, ST. (d. 700?). Son of a British prince, he became abbot-founder of a monastery in Brittany. F. D. Nov. 6.

EGAN, BOETIUS (1734–1798), archbishop. Born near Tuam, Ireland, he studied at the Irish College in Bordeaux, France, returned to Ireland, and became bishop of Achonry in 1785, and archbishop of Tuam in 1787. He died there soon after enjoying the benefits of the Catholic Relief Act of 1793.

EGAN, MICHAEL (1761–1814), bishop. Born in Ireland, probably in Galway, he became a Franciscan, was director of the Irish house in Rome for three years, worked as a missioner in Ireland, and went to Pennsylvania at the turn of the century. He was a pastor in Philadelphia in 1803, was named first bishop of Philadelphia in 1808, and consecrated in Baltimore in 1810. His episcopate was marked by a violent quarrel with lay trustees of St. Mary's church, who insisted on the right to appoint and remove pastors; the rebellion was increased by two Irish priests, the brothers James and William Harold. Bishop Egan died in Philadelphia on July 22.

EGBERT (d. 839), king. Son of Ealhmund, a king in Kent, he was banished by Offa and Beorhtric and lived at the court of Charlemagne until 802, when he returned to England and became king of the West Saxons. He defeated a Cornish force in 825, regained Kent and Mercia by 828, and was overlord of Northumbria by 829. He was defeated by Norsemen at Charmouth in 835, but defeated them and an army of Cornishmen in 837.

EGBERT, ST. (639?–729). An English monk from Lindisfarne, he lived and taught in Connaught before he went to Iona and spent his last thirteen years convincing the monks there to accept the Roman date of Easter. He died on the day they first so celebrated the paschal feast in common with the rest of Europe. F. D. Apr. 24.

EGBERT (d. 766), archbishop. Son of Eata and nephew of King Eadbert of Northumbria, he studied in an English monastery, was ordained a deacon at Rome, and was appointed bishop of York in 732 by King Ceolwulf. He became second archbishop of the diocese in 735, with power over the northern bishops, and carried out many reforms at the direction of St. Bede. He developed musical services, decorated his cathedral with gold, enlarged his parish system, and founded the school of York and its famous library. Alcuin was one of his pupils. He made a collection of canonical regulations; and wrote *Pontificale*, an important liturgical text, as well as a treatise on the foundation of the Church. He died in York, England, on Nov. 19.

EGBERT (d. 993), archbishop. Son of Count Theodoric I and Countess Hildegarde of Holland, he was educated at Egmont, was imperial chancellor at Mainz in 976, and in 977 became archbishop of Trier. He restored churches destroyed by the Norsemen, built new abbeys and other centers, and accompanied Otto II to Italy in 983. A highly decorated book of gospels and a psalter, both named after him, resulted from the religious renaissance he inspired in his diocese. He died in Trier on Dec. 8.

EGBERT (d. 1184). Born in the region of the Middle Rhine, he was a canon at Bonn, became a Benedictine at Trier, and in 1166 was named second abbot of Schönau. He was active against the heretical Cathari, wrote ser-

mons and meditations, and also published a life of his sister, the mystic Elizabeth of Schönau. He died at his monastery near Bonn, Germany, on Mar. 28.

EGDRED, ST. (d. 870), martyr. See Theodore, St.

EGDUNUS, ST. (d. 303), martyr. He and seven other Christians in Nicomedia were suffocated to death over a fire during the Diocletian persecution. F. D. Mar. 12.

EGELNOTH. See Ethelnoth, St.

EGELRED, ST. (d. 870?), martyr. A Benedictine monk at Croyland, England, he died when the monastic community was massacred by invading Danes. F. D. Sept. 25.

EGFRID (650–685), king. He succeeded to the throne of Northumbria on the death of Oswy, defeated the Picts and the Mercians, had dreams of conquest, extended his borders into Cumberland and Lancashire, and in 684 sent an expedition into Ireland. He was ambushed and slain by the Picts.

EGILHARD, ST. (d. 881). He was abbot of the Benedictine monastery of Cornelimünster, near Aix-la-Chapelle, and was killed by the invading Norsemen. F. D. May 25.

EGILO, ST. (d. 871). A Benedictine monk at Prüm, Germany, he served as abbot there, then restored the abbeys of Flavigny and Corbigny, France. F. D. June 28.

EGINHARD. See Einhard.

EGINO, ST. (d. 1122). Born in Augsburg, Bavaria, he became a Benedictine at the abbey of SS. Ulric and Afra, was expelled because he chose to support the pope over the emperor, transferred to the abbey of St. Blaise, became abbot at Augsburg in 1109, but suffered from Bishop Herimann, whose simony was condemned, and in 1120 fled to Italy, where he died in the Camoldolese monastery in Pisa. F. D. July 15.

EGINO (12th century). Bishop of Chur, Switzerland, he sided with Pope Alexander III during the quarrel with Frederick Barbarossa, and was in 1170 awarded the title of prince of the empire.

EGLOFFSTEIN, FREDERICK W. VON (1824–1885). Born in Aldorf, Bavaria, on May 18, he served in the army, emigrated to New York, and engaged Samuel Sartain, an engraver, to work with him on a new engraving process involving photography and glass screens covered with an opaque varnish. He served as a colonel with New York volunteers during the Civil War, was wounded in North Carolina, and retired from military service as a brigadier general. He died in New York City.

EGMONT, LAMORAL OF (1522–1568). Born in Hainault on Nov. 18, he went to Spain and Algeria with his brother Charles and, when his brother died of wounds in 1541, inherited the family estates in Holland, the principality of Gâvre, and several baronies. In 1544 the count married Duchess Sabina of Bavaria, by whom he had eleven children. He served in the army and diplomatic corps of Emperor Charles V, defeated the French at St. Quentin and Gravelines as a cavalry officer under Philip II, and was in 1559 named stadtholder of the province of Flanders and councilor for the Low Countries. His jealousy of Cardinal Granvella, the king's confidant, led Egmont to tolerate the nationalistic rise of William of Orange. The advance of sectarian groups he was actually powerless to crush. William went into exile and Egmont, who did not consider himself a member of any plot against the Spanish government and who firmly protested his allegiance to the Church, was condemned as a traitor to Spain and executed at Brussels on June 5 with the count of Hoorn. Goethe made him the hero of a tragedy, *Egmont* (1788).

EGUIARA Y EGUREN, JUAN JOSÉ (d. 1763), bishop. Born in Mexico in the late sixteenth century, he studied at the College of San Ildefonso, mastered many fields of learning, and became rector of the University of Mexico. He became bishop of Yucatán, but resigned to continue work on a monumental *Bibliotheca Mexicana*, a Latin survey of American biography. He also wrote fourteen volumes of sermons, and other treatises. He died in Mexico on Jan. 29.

EGWIN, ST. (d. 717), bishop. Succeeding to the see of Worcester, England, as third bishop in 692, he ruled with such vigor that he had to go to Rome to defend himself against accusations of overseverity. On his return, he founded the Benedictine abbey at Evesham, and about 709 again went on pilgrimage to Rome with Kings Cenred and Offa. He was buried at Evesham. F. D. Dec. 30.

EHRLE, FRANZ (1845-1934), cardinal. Born in Isny, Württemberg, Germany, on Oct. 17, he studied at Münster, became a Jesuit in 1861, continued his studies at Maria-Laach and in England, and was ordained. He was engaged in historical study at Rome in 1880-90, was on the council of the Vatican Library, and served as its prefect from 1895 to 1915. He returned to Germany during World War I, but was recalled to the Vatican in 1922, and made a cardinal-deacon, Vatican librarian and archivist, and a member of several congregations. He wrote on the frescoes of Pinturicchio, illuminated manuscripts, the library itself, and from 1885 on edited, with Denifle, *Archiv für Litteratur und Kirchengeschichte*. Münster, Louvain, Cambridge, and Oxford gave him honorary degrees. He died in Rome on Mar. 30.

EICHENDORFF, JOSEF KARL BENEDIKT VON (1788-1857), poet. Born in Lubowitz, Upper Silesia, on Mar. 10, he studied in Breslau and at Halle and Heidelberg, and began to write for several romantic journals. His first novel was *Ahnung und Gegenwart* (1811). He joined the army at Breslau during the War of Liberation and served until the occupation of Paris in 1815. He then entered the Prussian civil service, served on the Catholic board of education in Danzig, became interested in Marienburg, house of the Teutonic Knights, and wrote its history in 1844, as well as a tragedy, *Der letzte Held von Marienburg*. In 1831 he went to Berlin as councilor in the ministry of public worship and education, from which he resigned in 1845 when he was unable to defend the anti-Catholic policy of the government. He continued to write romantic lyrics, many of which had great popularity as songs set to music by leading composers. His short stories and novels are somewhat marred by lengthy expository and reflective digressions; his epic *Lucius* and his plays move with more success, particularly *Ezelin von Romano* and *Die Freier*. He also wrote a history of German poetry, valuable for the firsthand account of the romantic movement, and a study of the eighteenth-century novel in Germany, and made major translations from the Spanish. He died in Neisse, Germany, on Nov. 26.

EIGIL, ST. (d. 822). Born in Norica, he was sent to Fulda, Germany, to be educated by St. Sturm, whose biography he later wrote. He remained there for twenty years, succeeding Ratgar, whom Charlemagne removed as abbot about 1817, and ending the factionalism there. F. D. Dec. 17.

EIGRAD, ST. (6th century). Brother of St. Sampson of York, he preached and founded a church in Anglesey. F. D. June 6.

EILHARD VON OBERGE (12th century), poet. He wrote the first German version of Tristran and Isolde, basing his romance on French sources.

EILUNED. See Almedha, St.

EINHARD (770?-840), historian. Born in the Frankish Empire, he studied at Fulda, was sent to the court of Charlemagne to be taught by Alcuin and others at the palace school, and became the emperor's adviser and director of public building. He directed the construction of the cathedral and palace in Aachen, arranged negotiations for the return of Saxon captives in 802, and went to Rome in 806 to gain papal approval for the partition of the empire. He also was a trusted councilor under Louis the Pious and Lothair. In 830, when unable to end the imperial struggle begun by Empress Judith, he retired to his estate at Mühlheim, with his wife Emma, sister of Bishop Bernhar of Worms, established a Benedictine abbey, and, though not a priest, served as its abbot until his death on Mar. 14. His most important work is *Vita Caroli magni*, written in imitation of Suetonius, and a full biography of his patron and king. He also wrote on SS. Marcellinus and Peter, whose relics he had translated to Mühlheim, and some seventy letters which cast revealing light on the reign of Louis the Pious. His name appears also as Eginhard.

EINHILDIS, BL. (8th century). She served as Benedictine abbess of Niedermünster, Germany; with her was St. Roswinda, sister of St. Ottilia. F. D. Dec. 13.

EIS, FREDERICK (1843–1926), bishop. Born in Arbach, Germany, on Jan. 20, he was taken to the United States by his parents in 1855, studied at St. Francis seminary, Milwaukee, and Joliette seminary, Canada, and was ordained in 1870. He did parish work in Sault Ste. Marie and Marquette, Michigan, until 1899, when he administered the see for a short period and then was appointed bishop later that same year. He resigned in 1922, was appointed titular bishop of Bita, and died in Marquette on May 5.

EITHENE, ST. (6th century). She and her sister St. Sodelbia, daughters of Aidhe, son of King Caibre of Leinster, Ireland, lived as holy women near Dublin and are said to have experienced visions. F. D. Mar. 20.

EITHNE, ST. (5th century). Daughter of Leogrhaire, high sovereign of Ireland in 433, she is said to have asked to be baptized with her younger sister by St. Patrick in Connaught and to have died the same day, immediately after he gave them their first Communion. F. D. Jan. 11.

EKBERT, BL. (d. 1075). A Benedictine monk at Gorze, he became abbot of Münsterschwarzach, Bavaria. F. D. Nov. 25.

EKHARD, BL. (d. 1084). A canon at the cathedral of Magdeburg, Germany, he became the first abbot of the Benedictine monastery of Huysburg. F. D. June 28.

EKKEHARD I (d. 973). Born a noble in Toggenburg, Switzerland, he became a Benedictine at St. Gall, where he had been educated and where he became director of the inner school and dean of the monastery. He built a hospice; wrote a Latin narrative poem, *Waltharius*, on the elopement of Walter of Aquitaine with Princess Hildegunde of Burgundy and the war which followed; and composed several hymns and sequences on the Trinity and SS. Benedict and John the Baptist. Ekkehard is the hero of a novel by Joseph Viktor von Scheffel. He died on Jan. 14.

EKKEHARD II (d. 990). A nephew of Ekkehard I, under whom he studied at St. Gall, Switzerland, where he became a Benedictine, he taught there, tutored the Duchess Hadwig of Swabia, negotiated peace between St. Gall and Reichenau, was an adviser to Emperor Otto I, and was provost of the cathedral of Mainz, Germany, where he died on Apr. 23.

He wrote a number of hymns, including a sequence on St. Desiderius.

EKKEHARD III (10th century). Another nephew of Ekkehard I, he also studied and became a Benedictine at the monastery of St. Gall, directed the studies of the clergy in Hohentweil, and for thirty years was dean of that Swiss abbey. He died early in the eleventh century.

EKKEHARD IV (b. 980?). Born possibly in Alsace, he studied under Notker Labeo at St. Gall, Switzerland, became a Benedictine there, mastered Greek, Latin, mathematics, and astronomy, and from 1022 to 1031 directed the cathedral school in Mainz, Germany. Back at St. Gall he carried on the abbey chronicle, brought up to date (972) by Notker, issued *Liber Benedictionum*, metrical inscriptions and liturgical and festal poems written by himself at Notker, and wrote some music. He died between 1036 and 1060.

EKKEHARD V (d. 1220?). He became a Benedictine at the abbey of St. Gall, Switzerland, was dean there during the papacy of Innocent III, was a master of ecclesiastical music, and wrote a life of St. Notker Balbulus.

EKKEHARD OF AURA (1050?–1125?), historian. A Benedictine monk at the monastery of St. Michael, Bamberg, he made a pilgrimage to the Holy Land, and became abbot of Aura about 1108. The *Chronicon universale* named after him is a compilation of comments on history since the creation, with a valuable fifth section on the history of Germany from 1080 to 1125. This probably was edited by Ekkehard, whose original contribution seems to have been only the account of the reign of Emperor Henry V.

ELAETH, ST. (6th century). A king in North Britain, he was driven out by the Picts, became a monk in Wales, and wrote poetry which is extant. F. D. Nov. 10.

ELAPHIUS, ST. (d. 580). He was bishop of Châlons-sur-Marne, France. F. D. Aug. 19.

ELBÉE, MAURICE LOUIS JOSEPH GIGOT D' (1752–1794). Born in Dresden, Germany, he was a member of the constituent assembly in France at the outbreak of the revolution, emigrated in 1791, but returned the next year as commander in chief of the "Catholic and Royalist" army. After a series of brilliant victories he was defeated and captured at the battle of Chollet in Oct., court-martialed, and executed in Jan.

ELBEL, BENJAMIN (1690–1756), theologian. Born in Friedberg, Bavaria, he became a Franciscan, and published a three-volume work on moral theologians which influenced St. Alphonsus. He died in Söflingen.

ELDER, BENEDICT (1882–1961), editor. Born in Taylorsville, Kentucky, on June 19, he studied at the Trappist college, Gethsemani, and law at Western Reserve, Cleveland, practiced law in Oklahoma and Kentucky, was managing editor of the Louisville *Record* in 1919–46, and president of the Catholic Press Association in 1930–32. He died in Louisville, Kentucky, on Jan. 12.

ELDER, GEORGE (1793–1838). Born in Hardin's Creek, Kentucky, on Aug. 11, he studied at Mt. St. Mary's College in Maryland and at St. Mary's seminary, Baltimore, was ordained in 1819, and became an assistant at the cathedral in Bardstown, Kentucky. He founded a college there in 1820 and served as its president from 1830 until his death on Sept. 28. As one of the editors of the Louisville *Catholic Advocate* (1836), he wrote the satirical columns, "Letters to Brother Jonathan," on contemporary education and controversy.

ELDER, WILLIAM HENRY (1819–1904), bishop. Born in Baltimore, Maryland, on Mar. 22, he studied at Mt. St. Mary's College, Maryland, and at the Propaganda, Rome, where he was ordained in 1846. He taught and was president at Mt. St. Mary's until 1857, when he was consecrated third bishop of Natchez, Mississippi. He was tried and convicted in 1864 when he refused to order prayers for President Lincoln at the direction of the occupying federal troops; the decision was later reversed. He was heroically active during the yellow-fever epidemic of 1878, was named coadjutor bishop of Cincinnati, Ohio, in 1880, succeeded to the see as second archbishop in 1883, and built two seminaries and enlarged St. Joseph's orphanage. He died in Cincinnati on Oct. 31.

ELEAZAR, ST. (3rd century), martyr. She and Minervus, and eight children, who may have been theirs, were put to death at Lyons, France. F. D. Aug. 23.

ELED. *See* Almedha, St.

ELESBAAN (d. 555?), king. Christian king of the Aksumite Ethiopians, he waged a victorious campaign against and executed Dhu Nowas, who had perpetrated the massacre of the Christians at Najram. His own campaign was marked by great cruelty, but he is reputed to have resigned his throne and become a hermit in Jerusalem toward the end of his life. Though listed in the Roman Martyrology on Oct. 27, he may have been a Monophysite.

ELEUCHADIUS, ST. (d. 112), bishop. A Greek convert, he was bishop of Ravenna, Italy, about 100, during the absence of St. Apollinaris. F. D. Feb. 14.

ELEUSIPPUS. One of triplets, he and Meleusippus and Speusippus are said to have been martyred in France about 155, during the reign of Marcus Aurelius, but there is no evidence of their existence outside pious legends.

ELEUTHERIUS, ST. (d. 189), pope. Born in Nicopolis, Epirus, Greece, he was a deacon under Popes Anicetus and Soter, and was elected to the papacy in 175. His reign was marked by difficulties with the heretical Gnostics and Marcionites, as well as with the rising Montanist movement, toward whom Bishop Irenaeus of Lyons advised moderation. Pope Eleutherius is often credited with receiving and accepting as a Christian King Lucius of Britain; the story, though repeated by Bede, is a legend. The pope died on May 24 and was buried on Vatican Hill. F. D. May 26.

ELEUTHERIUS, ST. (d. 258?), martyr. *See* Dionysius, St.

ELEUTHERIUS, ST. (d. 310?), martyr. Chamberlain to Emperor Maximian Galerius at Constantinople, he became a Christian and was beheaded in Bithynia. F. D. Aug. 4. He probably is the bishop of the same name honored on Feb. 20.

ELEUTHERIUS, ST. (d. 532), bishop. Said to have been born in Tournai, Gaul, he was an effective preacher and convert-maker, and was named bishop of Tournai in 486. Because of the success of his labors against Arianism he was attacked outside his church by a group of heretics and never recovered from the beating. F. D. Feb. 20.

ELEUTHERIUS, ST. (d. 561). He became bishop of Auxerre, Gaul, in 532. F. D. Aug. 16.

ELEUTHERIUS, ST. (d. 590?). Abbot of the Benedictine monastery of St. Mark, near Spoleto, Italy, he went to that of St. Gregory the Great at Rome, where he lived as a simple monk. F. D. Sept. 6.

ELEUTHERIUS, ST. (7th century?). An English pilgrim, said to have been the brother of St. Fulk, he died at Rocca d'Arce, near Aquino, Italy, where he was to be venerated as patron. F. D. May 29.

ELEUTHERIUS, ST., martyr. A soldier, he was martyred (in legend, because he was falsely accused with others of burning Diocletian's palace) at Nicomedia. F. D. Oct. 2.

ELEUTHERIUS. Said to have been bishop of Illyria and to have been the victim of a series of extravagant tortures before he was put to death with his mother Anthia and eleven companions during the persecution of Hadrian, he is now known to have been merely a pious legend.

ELEVETHA. *See* Almedha, St.

ELFGETE, ST. (d. 870), martyr. *See* Theodore, St.

ELFLEDA, ST. (d. 714). Daughter of King Oswy of Northumbria, she was entered in the convent at Hartlepool as a child, followed St. Hilda to Whitby, and succeeded the latter as co-abbess with her mother, Queen Eanfleda. Elfleda arranged peace between Theodore of Canterbury and Wilfred of York, was a friend of St. Cuthbert, and famed in Irish annals and the histories of Bede and William of Malmesbury. F. D. Feb. 8.

ELFLEDA, ST. (d. 936?). An Anglo-Saxon princess, she became a recluse under the discipline of the Benedictine monastery at Glastonbury, England, and was highly regarded by St. Dunstan. F. D. Oct. 23.

ELFLEDA, ST. (d. 1000?). Daughter of Earl Ethelwold, who founded the Benedictine convent in Ramsey, England, she became a nun there and later its abbess. F. D. Oct. 29.

ELGAR, EDWARD WILLIAM (1857–1934), composer. Born in Broadheath, England, on June 2, he studied music under his father and succeeded him as organist of St. George's, Worcester (1885–89). He also studied violin and played in and directed the orchestra of the Worcester glee club. His schooling had ended at fifteen, and he taught himself from the analysis of scores. *Intermezzo*, performed at Birmingham in 1883, was his first brief success. After his marriage in 1889 to Caroline Alice Roberts he moved to London, then to Malvern. Between 1890 and 1899 he wrote *Froissart*, an overture, *The Black Knight*, a cantata, *The Light of Life*, an oratorio, and *Scenes from the Saga of King Olaf* for chorus. He produced his successful *Orchestral* (*"Enigma"*) *Variations* and the oratorio, *The Dream of Gerontius*, based on Cardinal Newman's poem, and Oxford gave him an honorary doctorate of music in 1900. Oratorios (*The Apostles* and *The Kingdom*), marches (*Pomp and Circumstance*), overtures (*Cockaigne*), and *Introduction and Allegro* for strings were completed before 1905. *Falstaff*, two symphonies, a violin concerto, and chamber music followed. He wrote the music for the coronation of King Edward VII, was knighted in 1904, taught at Birmingham in 1905–8, was made master of the king's music in 1924, and a baronet in 1931. His work was highly influenced by that of Wagner, Brahms, and Delibes. After his wife's death in 1920 he produced no major work, and died in Worcester, England, on Feb. 23.

ELGIVA, ST. (d. 971). Wife of King Edmund of England and mother of Edwy and Edgar, she retired to the Benedictine convent at Shaftesbury on her husband's death. F. D. May 18.

ELHUYAR Y SUVISA, FAUSTO DE (1755–1833), chemist. Born in Logroño, Castile, Spain, he was professor in the School of Mines in Vergara from 1781 to 1785. With his brother Juan José he isolated tungsten in 1783, and named it wolfram. He then went to Mexico, founded the Royal School of Mines in 1792, and was superintendent of mining until the revolution, when he returned to Spain as general director of mines. He wrote on a method of silver ore reduction, on the minting of coins, and on the relationship of mineralogy to agriculture and chemistry.

ELIACIM. *See* Joachim, St.

ELIAN, ST. (6th century). Perhaps a Breton, he was related to Ismael and labored in the missions of Cornwall, England. F. D. Jan. 13.

ELIAS, ST. (d. 309), martyr. Captured while on his way to visit Christian prisoners in the mines of Cilicia, he was tortured and beheaded at Caesarea, with SS. Daniel, Isaias, Jeremy, and Samuel, during the persecution of Maximian and Maximus. F. D. Feb. 16.

ELIAS, ST. (d. 310?), martyr. *See* Peleus, St.

ELIAS, ST. (d. 518), bishop. An Arab, he was educated in an Egyptian monastery, was driven out of Egypt in 457 because of his Catholicism during the Monophysite heresy, and went to Palestine and founded a monastery in Jericho. He was ordained by Bishop Anastasius of Jerusalem, and became bishop of Jerusalem in 494. Although he accepted Emperor Zeno's *Henotikon* of 482, which, attempting to settle Catholic-Monophysite differences, favored the latter group and was condemned by Rome, he remained loyal to the Church and fought the incursion of Monophysitism. The Synod of Sidon in 512 summoned by the government to condemn the Council of Chalcedon (451) and depose Elias and Bishop Flavian of Antioch instead supported them and refused to denounce Chalcedon. Emperor Anastasius I, however, deposed Flavian. Elias was then ordered to sign a Monophysite formula or suffer exile; he refused and was banished to Aila, on the Red Sea, in 513, where he died. F. D. July 20 (in the East, Feb. 18).

ELIAS, ST. (d. 660). A Benedictine monk, he became bishop of Syracuse, Sicily. F. D. Aug. 26.

ELIAS, ST. (d. 856), martyr. A priest at Cordova, Spain, he and two young men he had been instructing, Paul and Isidore, were put to death by the Moors. St. Eulogius was an eyewitness. F. D. Apr. 17.

ELIAS, BL. (d. 1042). An Irishman, he became a monk and later abbot of the Benedictine abbey of St. Martin the Great at Cologne, Lorraine. F. D. Apr. 16.

ELIAS OF BOURDEILLES (1407–1484), cardinal. Born in Périgord, France, he became a Franciscan, was made bishop of Périgueux in 1437, archbishop of Tours in 1468, and a cardinal in 1483. He was confessor to King Louis XI and wrote a defense of St. Joan of Arc. He died on July 5.

ELIAS OF CORTONA (1180?–1253). Born, probably at Vevila, Italy, to a family known as Bonusbaro or Bonibarone, he was a mattress maker and catechist in Assisi, then a notary, and became about 1211 one of the first followers of St. Francis. In 1217 he went from Tuscany to Palestine with a group of missioners, became first provincial of the province of Syria, received Caesar of Speyer into the order, and from 1221 to 1226 was vicar general. He wrote of the death of St. Francis and of the stigmata in a letter to the order and began plans for the erection of a memorial basilica. He obtained papal permission to collect money, but was removed from office by Franciscan leaders who wished to live by the strictest rule of poverty and who objected to his intellectual pursuits and preference for learning. He saw the cornerstone of the basilica laid the day after Francis was canonized and secretly translated the body to the consecrated building in 1230. When he failed in an attempt to depose Giovanni Parenti, who had succeeded him in 1227 as general, he retired to a hermitage. But he replaced Parenti at the chapter of 1232 and thereafter split the order by disregarding its original membership and purpose and by sending incompetent inferiors to exact tax money for the upkeep of the basilica and of his own now wealthy household. Aymon of Faversham and a group of northern provincials sought to depose him, but he excommunicated them; he was ordered to explain his action to Gregory IX, refused to accept censure or to resign, and was removed as general by the pope in 1239. When Elias threw in his fortunes with the excommunicated Emperor Frederick II he was himself excommunicated. He lived at Cortona with a few loyal followers, built a church there, and became reconciled with the Church before his death there on Apr. 22.

ÉLIE DE BEAUMONT, JEAN BAPTISTE (1798–1874), geologist. Born in Canon, near Caen, France, on Sept. 25, he studied in Paris, toured the mines of England, on which he wrote a book, and with Dufrénoy spent eighteen years preparing a geological map of France. He became professor of geology at L'École des Mines in 1827 and Collège de France in 1832; he then was chief engineer of mines, inspector general, a member of the Academy of Sciences, its permanent secretary, and president of the Geological Society. He became a senator in 1852 and a grand officer of the Legion of Honor. His books include other descriptive studies of geology in France and of the age and origin of mountain ranges. He died in Canon on Sept. 21.

ELIGIUS, ST. (588?–660), bishop. Born of Romano-Gallo parents in Chaptelat, near Limoges, France, he followed his father's trade of metalsmith. He studied under Abbo, master of the mint there, worked under Babo, the royal treasurer, and was appointed master of the mint at Paris by Clotaire II and called Bobbo. In 629, Dagobert I appointed Eligius his chief counselor. In 632 he founded Solignac abbey and a convent at Paris. In 636, as ambassador, he induced the Breton king, Judicael, to submit to the authority of the Frankish

king. As a result of his increased influence Eligius was able to make extensive gifts to the poor, to ransom captives, and to build churches, monasteries, and convents. In 640 he became a priest and in 641 was made bishop of Noyon. He evangelized the area around Antwerp, Courtrai, and Ghent, aided the sick and needy, served as adviser to the queen regent, St. Bathildis, and became one of the best known and loved figures of his time. His reputation remained strong through the Middle Ages, particularly as patron of metalworkers. He died in Noyon, France. F. D. Dec. 1.

ELIPHIUS, ST. (d. 362), martyr. An Irishman or Scot, he was slain at Toul, France, during the reign of Julian the Apostate. F. D. Oct. 16.

ELISHÉ (d. 480), historian. Born in Armenia, he is said to have been a companion of Gen. Vartan in the war of religious independence against Persia in 449–51, who later became a recluse near Lake Van, where he died. He wrote a history of the struggle which is regarded as a classic in Armenian literature and a valuable philological influence in that it employed no Greek words. He also wrote a commentary on Josue and on Judges and an explanation of the *Pater Noster*. He sometimes is identified with Elishé, bishop of Amaduni, who attended the Synod of Artashat in 449.

ELIZABETH, ST. (1st century). She was mother of St. John the Baptist, whose visit by the Virgin Mary is narrated in Luke 1. F. D. Nov. 5.

ELIZABETH OF HUNGARY, ST. (1207–1231), queen. Born in Pressburg, Hungary, daughter of King Andrew II and niece of St. Hedwig, she was betrothed to Louis IV of Thuringia at the age of four, when she was brought to Landgrave Herman's court at Wartburg. In 1221 she and Louis were married, had four children, and led an ideal married life until 1227, when Louis died of the plague at Otranto while on crusade with Emperor Otto II. Her charity to the poor was so great that her husband's family charged her with mismanagement of the estate. She left Wartburg (probably forced out by her brother-in-law) and found refuge with her uncle, the bishop of Bamberg. In 1228 she became a Franciscan tertiary, with Conrad of Hamburg as her spiritual adviser (some authorities condemn his severity with her), and led a life of exceptional poverty and humility. She returned to her castle less than four years before her death when the usurper relented and recognized the right of succession of her son. She died at Marburg, Hesse, on Nov. 17. She was canonized in 1235 by Pope Gregory IX. F. D. Nov. 19.

ELIZABETH, PHILIPPINE MARIE HÉLÈNE (1764–1794). Sister of King Louis XVI of France, she was known as Mme. Elizabeth, was praised for her charities, but when she chose to come to Paris to be near the imprisoned monarch was declared a traitor and executed on May 10.

ELIZABETH OF PORTUGAL, ST. (1271–1336), queen. Daughter of King Peter III of Aragon and Constantia, she was married at twelve to King Denis of Portugal, who allowed her to pursue a life of piety and charity. When their son Alfonso took arms against his father, Elizabeth the peacemaker stopped the clash, but Denis banished her from the court, believing she had favored her son. She also was peacemaker between Ferdinand IV of Castile and his cousin, and the king and her brother James II of Aragon. She nursed Denis assiduously in his last illness and was rewarded by his expression of sorrow for his dissolute life. On his death in 1325, she wished to enter the Poor Clares convent at Coimbra which she had founded, was dissuaded, and instead was professed as a Franciscan tertiary. She died on July 4 in Estremoz, Portugal, and was canonized in 1626. F. D. July 8.

ELIZABETH ROSE, ST. (d. 1130). A Benedictine nun at Chelles, France, she founded Ste. Marie du Rozoy, near Courtenay, and was its abbess. F. D. Dec. 13.

ELIZABETH OF SCHÖNAU (1126–1164). At twelve she entered the double monastery of Schönau, near Bonn, where she was professed as a Benedictine in 1147, and became abbess in 1157. She recorded a great number of visions, supernatural experiences, and demoniac persecutions in a simple published report. Her *Book of the Ways of God* castigated the spiritual carelessness of the day, begged for more show of penance, but lapsed into political support of the antipope Victor IV, a friend of her brother Egbert, who was a canon at Bonn. A third book elaborated on the already fantastic legend of St. Ursula and her fellow martyrs. Although honored locally on June 18, she was never canonized.

ELLIOTT, WALTER (1842–1928). Born in Detroit, Michigan, on Jan. 6, he studied at Notre Dame, served through the Civil War with the 5th Ohio Volunteers, and in 1872 was ordained as a Paulist. He worked in New York, directed missions for fifty years, published a life of Christ, and a collection of sermons. The publication of his life of Isaac Hecker, with a preface by Abbé Félix Klein, in France in 1897 caused a furore in European religious circles, erupted into a major controversy over Americanism, and led to the writing of Pope Leo's apostolic letter, *Testem benevolentiae*, in 1898. In 1903, with Fr. Alexander Doyle, Fr. Elliott founded the Apostolic Mission House in Washington, D.C., where he died on Apr. 18.

ELLIS, PHILIP MICHAEL (1652–1726), bishop. Born in Waddeston, Buckinghamshire,

England, son of its Anglican vicar, he became a convert while at Westminster School, went to Douai at eighteen and became a Benedictine, and after ordination returned to England in 1685, as chaplain to King James II. In 1688 he was named vicar apostolic of the Western District, was imprisoned during the brief revolution, and went to France and then to Rome. His knowledge of English made him valuable in the papal court; he became bishop of Segni, Italy, in 1708 and rebuilt the monastery of St. Chiara as a seminary. He died on Nov. 16.

ELMO, ST. *See* Erasmus, St.; Peter Gonzalez, Bl.

ELOQUIUS, ST. (7th century). He succeeded St. Fursey as Benedictine abbot of Lagny, France. F. D. Dec. 3.

ELPHEGE, ST. (d. 951). Bishop of Winchester, England, and a Benedictine, he inspired St. Dunstan, a relative, to become a monk, and later ordained him and St. Ethelwold. He is also known as Alphege. F. D. March 12.

ELPHEGE, ST. (954–1012), bishop and martyr. He became a Benedictine at Deerhurst abbey, Gloucestershire, then a hermit, abbot at Bath, bishop of Winchester in 984, and, after 22 years, succeeded Archbishop Elfric of Canterbury. He had removed poverty from his first see and was making headway in the new area when he was seized by invading Danes and imprisoned for his censure of their massacres. He was slain at Greenwich, England, when he refused to permit the collection of an enormous ransom for his life. F. D. Apr. 19.

ELPIDEPHORUS, ST. (d. 345), martyr. *See* Acindynus, St.

ELPIDIUS, ST. (d. 362), martyr. An official in the court of Emperor Constantius, he, SS. Eustachius, Marcellus, and others were tortured and burned to death by Julian the Apostate. F. D. Nov. 16.

ELPIDIUS, ST. (4th century). He lived for twenty-five years in a cave in Cappadocia, surrounded by many disciples; his relics were taken to a village in Italy, now named after him. F. D. Sept. 2.

ELPIDIUS, ST. (4th century), bishop and martyr. *See* Aetherius, St.

ELPIDIUS, ST. (d. 422). He succeeded St. Antiochus as bishop of Lyons, France. F. D. Sept. 2.

ELPIDIUS, ST. (5th century), bishop. *See* Priscus, St.

ELSTAN, ST. (d. 981), bishop. A Benedictine monk at Abingdon, England, he succeeded St. Ethelwold as abbot there and as bishop of Winchester. F. D. Apr. 6.

ELWIN, ST. (6th century). He is said to have gone from Ireland to Cornwall with St. Breaca. F. D. Feb. 22.

ELZEAR, ST. (1285–1323). Born in Ansouis,

Provence, he was educated at St. Victor's monastery at Marseilles and at sixteen married Delphina of Glandèves. At twenty-three, on his father's death, he became baron of Ansouis and lord of Ariano. He restored his Neapolitan estates by his firmness and prudence and with Delphina became greatly beloved as an ideal married couple. In 1317 he became tutor of Charles, son of King Robert of Naples, and served on diplomatic missions. He died in Paris and was canonized in 1369 by Pope Urban V; his wife, who outlived him by thirty-seven years, attended the ceremony. F. D. Sept. 27.

EMANUEL (1469–1521), king of Portugal. Called Manoel the Fortunate, he became king in 1495, succeeding his cousin, John II, and saw great exploratory advances in the East, which led to a trade monopoly. He sent an embassy to Rome in 1514 with tribute from India, a suggestion to form a league against the Turks, and a plea for the reform of the Church. The Church in Ethiopia submitted to the pope through Portuguese efforts; at home, the bishops began again to visit their sees (a practice long neglected) and monasteries became more strict. In his attempt to gain control of Castile he married the daughter of Ferdinand and Isabella; one condition was that he rid his country of Jews, who up to this time had enjoyed the protection of the monarchs. They were given the choice of exile or conversion; many were converted; others reaccepted Judaism and suffered heavily when the Inquisition was introduced by Emanuel's son, John III.

EMARD, JOSEPH MEDARD (1853–1927), archbishop. Born in Canada, he was ordained in 1876, was a canon of the Montreal cathedral, served as first bishop of Valleyfield in 1892–1922 and as bishop of the Canadian army during World War I. In 1922 he became archbishop of Ottawa, where he died on Mar. 28.

EMEBERT, ST. (d. 710?). Bishop of Cambrai, France, he is said to have been the brother of SS. Gudula and Rainaldes. He is also known as Ablebert. F. D. January 15.

EMERENTIANA, ST. (d. 304?), martyr. Said to have been the foster sister of St. Agnes, she was put to death and buried in Rome not far from the latter's grave. F. D. Jan. 23 (formerly, Sept. 16).

EMERIC (d. 1204), king of Hungary. Brother of Andrew II, he warred with his brother over the throne of Hungary on the death of Béla III in 1196 when he claimed the crown. The dispute was not finally resolved until his death, when Andrew became sole ruler.

EMERIC, ST. (1007–1031). The only son of St. Stephen, first Christian king of Hungary, he was educated by St. Gerard Sagredo and groomed by his father to succeed to the crown, but was killed in a hunting accident. He was canonized in 1083. F. D. Nov. 4.

EMERIC, ST. (d. 1318). He became bishop of Aosta, Italy, in 1301. His cult was approved in 1881. F. D. Aug. 1.

EMERITA, ST. (d. 259), martyr. See Digna, St.

EMERITUS, ST. (d. 304), martyr. See Saturninus, St.

EMERIUS, ST. (8th century). A French Benedictine, he founded and became first abbot at St. Stephen of Bañoles in Gerona, Spain. His mother, St. Candida, became a recluse nearby. Both are honored on Jan. 27.

EMERY, JACQUES ANDRÉ (1732–1811). Born in Gex, France, on Aug. 26, he studied in Lyons, and at St. Sulpice, Paris, where he joined the Sulpicians and was ordained in 1758. He taught in Orléans and Lyons, was superior of the seminary in Angers, and in 1782 was selected superior general of his order. He had some success in ecclesiastical reform before the start of the revolution and remained in Paris as administrator of the diocese after its outbreak. He advised the acceptance of several oaths demanded of the clergy by the government; as the revolutionary temper increased, he opposed its outlook, refused to accept the civil constitution of the clergy, and was imprisoned. He was freed and reopened St. Sulpice when Napoleon came to power, but defended the pope in his quarrel with the emperor, and was ordered expelled. He successfully defended his rights before Napoleon. Fr. Emery died in Paris on Apr. 28.

EMETERIUS, ST. (d. 304), martyr. Said to have been the son of St. Marcellus, he was executed with his brother St. Chelidonius at Calahorra, Spain, during the Diocletian persecution. They are mentioned in several poems by Prudentius, are the patrons of Santander, and are honored on Mar. 3.

EMIDIUS. See Emygdius, St.

EMILAS, ST. (d. 852), martyr. A young Spanish deacon, he and a companion Jeremias were beheaded at Cordova during the Moorish persecution. F. D. Sept. 15.

EMILIAN, ST. (d. 259), martyr. See Agapius, St.

EMILIAN, ST. (d. 362), martyr. He was put to death at Silistria, Bulgaria, during the persecution of Julian the Apostate. F. D. July 18.

EMILIAN, ST. (d. 484), martyr. See Dionysia, St.

EMILIAN, ST. (420?–520). After forty years as a hermit, he became bishop of Vercelli, Italy. F. D. Sept. 11.

EMILIAN, ST. (d. 574). A Spanish shepherd, he became a hermit in the mountains above Burgos, where, according to tradition, he lived for forty years. He then was ordained and became a parish priest at Berceo. When this life proved unsuitable, he returned to his ways of solitude, became surrounded by a group of followers, acted as their abbot, and founded what was to become the Benedictine monastery of La Cogolla. Because of this last, he is also known as Millán de la Cogolla and is sometimes listed as the first Spanish Benedictine. F. D. Nov. 12.

EMILIAN, ST. (d. 675). An Irishman, he became a Benedictine monk and, later, abbot of the monastery of Lagny, France. F. D. Mar. 10.

EMILIAN, ST. (d. 767). Born in Vannes, France, he became a Benedictine at the abbey of Saujon, and then a hermit in the forest of Combes, near Bordeaux. F. D. Jan. 7.

EMILIAN, ST. (d. 820?). Bishop of Cyzicus, Asia Minor, he died in exile because of his opposition to the Iconoclast heresy. F. D. Aug. 8.

EMILIAN. Formerly honored on Oct. 11, as a hermit in Rennes, Brittany, France, he is probably identical with St. Melanius, bishop of Rennes (d. 530?).

EMILIANA, ST. (d. 550?). See Tharsilla, St.

EMILIANA, ST. (6th century). An aunt of St. Gregory the Great, she lived in Rome and was praised for her exemplary life by that pope. F. D. Jan. 5.

EMILIANI, ST. JEROME (1481–1537), founder. Born in Venice, Italy, he served in the army, was captured, and escaped. He became mayor of Treviso, but returned to Venice, where he was ordained in 1518. He then devoted himself to relieving the victims of plague and famine, particularly orphans. About 1532 he and two other priests established a congregation of men, the Clerks Regular of Somasca, with its chief work the care of orphans. He is said to have been the first to use a regular catechism for the education of the young. He died on Feb. 8 in Somasca, Italy, of a disease caught while he was tending the sick. His congregation was approved by Pope Paul III in 1540. He was canonized in 1767, and in 1928 Pope Pius XI named him patron of orphans and abandoned children. F. D. July 20.

EMILY DE RODAT, ST. (1787–1852), foundress. Born near Rodez, France, she became a nun at Maison St. Cyr when eighteen. In 1815, after much dissatisfaction, she decided that her vocation was in teaching poor children. With the approval of Abbé Marty, her spiritual adviser, and the aid of three young assistants, she began this work in her room at St. Cyr. This was the start of the Congregation of the Holy Family of Villefranche. It grew rapidly, establishing its own mother house and branches. In time, St. Emily extended its activities to caring for unfortunate women, orphans, and the aged. She saw thirty-eight institutions established before she died. She was canonized in 1950. F. D. Sept. 19.

EMMA, BL. (d. 1045?). After the death of her husband, Count William, about 1035, Emma founded the abbey of Gurk in Carinthia, Aus-

tria. Her cult was confirmed in 1938. F. D. June 29.

EMMANUEL, ST. (d. 304?), martyr. See Quadratus, St.

EMMANUEL, BL. (d. 1198). Bishop of Cremona, Italy, from 1190 to 1195, he retired to the Cistercian monastery of Adwerth. F. D. Feb. 27.

EMMERAMUS, ST. (d. 690?), bishop. A native of Poitiers, France, of which he may have been bishop, he went to Regensburg, Bavaria, to preach at the request of Duke Theodo. He is said to have become abbot of a Benedictine monastery in Ratisbon and bishop there. He was waylaid and murdered on a trip to Rome. F. D. Sept. 22.

EMMERICH, ALEXANDER LEOPOLD FRANZ (1794–1849), bishop. The prince of Hohenlohe-Waldenburg-Schillingsfürst was born on Aug. 17 in Kupferzell, Austria. He studied at Vienna, Berne, Tyrnau, and Ellwangen, was ordained in 1815, and was assigned to pastoral work in Stuttgart and Munich. He was made ecclesiastical councilor in 1817 and canon of Bamberg in 1821. He became canon (1824), provost (1829), and vicar general of Grosswardein, and in 1844 titular bishop of Sardica. From 1821 he became famed for several apparently miraculous cures, notably of the paralytic Princess Mathilda. He died in Vöslau, on Nov. 14.

EMMERICH, BL. ANNE CATHERINE (1774–1824), mystic. Born in Flamsche, Westphalia, Germany, on Sept. 8, she was a servant and seamstress, and at twenty-eight became an Augustinian nun at Dülmen. The convent was closed in 1812, and she soon became bedridden in her refuge in a widow's home. Because she received the stigmata and showed other signs of the supernatural, she was subjected to many inquiries; visitors were all too frequent, but she won many friends by her patience and genuine simplicity. The poet Klemens Brentano took down her dictated writings, which she carefully edited. They were published after her death at Dülmen, Germany: *The Dolorous Passion of Our Lord Jesus Christ* (1833), *Life of the Blessed Virgin Mary* (1852), and the two-volume *Life of Our Lord*, prepared from Brentano's notes by Fr. Schmoeger and issued in 1858–80. F. D. Feb. 9.

EMMERICH, GUSTAV ADOLF (1823–1896), cardinal. The prince of Hohenlohe-Schillingsfürst was born in Rottenburg on Feb. 26, studied at Erfurt, Bonn, Breslau, Munich, and Rome, and was ordained in 1849. Pope Pius IX named him almoner and bishop of Edessa. In 1866 he was made a cardinal-priest and in 1879 cardinal-bishop. He resigned his bishopric in 1884 and retired to Germany, but returned to Rome, where he died on Oct. 30.

EMMET, THOMAS ADDIS (1828–1919).

Born in Charlotte, Virginia, on May 29, he was educated in New York, took his medical degree at Virginia, practiced obstetrics in New York City, was president of several medical societies and of the Irish Federation of America, became a convert, and died in New York City on Mar. 1.

EMSER, HIERONYMUS (1477–1527), apologist. Born in Ulm, Germany, on Mar. 20, he studied classics at Tübingen and law and theology at Basle, became secretary to Cardinal Peraudi, and in 1504 gave a series of lectures at Erfurt, where Luther heard him. He then studied canon law, was secretary to George of Saxony, and was ordained about 1512. After 1519 he engaged in violent controversy with Luther, with whom he had been friendly. He translated the New Testament into German in 1527, with annotations in opposition to Luther's interpretations, and died in Dresden, Germany, on Nov. 8.

EMYGDIUS, ST. (d. 304), bishop and martyr. Legend calls him a Teuton, who went to Rome after his conversion, was consecrated bishop by the pope, and sent to convert the people of the Marches of Ancona. He was beheaded at Ascoli, Italy, with three companions during the Diocletian persecution. F. D. Aug. 9.

ENAMBUC, PIERRE BÉLAIN D' (1570?–1636), governor. Born in Allouville, France, he sailed from Dieppe in 1625, took possession of St. Christopher, one of the Leeward Islands, formed the Company of the American Islands with the approval of Richelieu, and recruited colonists for the settlements. In 1635 he brought 150 colonists to Martinique, founded the city of St. Pierre, and returned to his post on St. Christopher as governor of the French colonies. The name is also spelled Esnambuc.

ENCINA, JUAN DEL (1469–1534?), dramatist. Born in Encina, near Salamanca, Spain, on Aug. 7, he studied at Salamanca and Madrid, served on the staff of the first duke of Alva, was ordained in Rome, made a pilgrimage to the Holy Land which he recorded in verse, and was named prior of León. He wrote 170 lyrics and songs (*Cancionero*), but is best known for fourteen dramatic eclogues, called *representaciones*, which are the origin of secular drama in Spain. Though slight in plot, they were acted as early as 1492. His critical *Arte de poesía castellana* appeared in 1497.

ENCISO, DIEGO XIMINEZ DE (b. 1585?), dramatist. Born in Andalusia, Spain, he wrote a dozen comedies and historical plays (including *Los Médicis de Florencia*), only three of which were printed. The plays are in poetic form, formal in tone, imaginative in treatment, varied in versification. He disappeared from critical view about 1632.

ENCISO, MARTÍN FERNÁNDEZ DE (1470?–1528?), geographer. Born in Seville,

Spain, he went to the New World and took up residence on Santo Domingo, where by 1508 he had become wealthy in the practice of law. He outfitted the 1509 expedition to Panama led by Alonzo de Ojeda, followed with another ship in 1510, and, when he learned that Ojeda had returned, founded the settlement of Santa María la Antigua del Darien. Balboa, who had secretly joined Enciso's party, led a rebellion and exiled Enciso to Spain. The latter returned in 1514 and ruled his city as mayor until 1517. He returned to Spain and published *Suma de geografía*, an accurate account of Spanish discoveries (1519). He died in Seville.

ENCRATIS, ST. (4th century), martyr. A Christian woman whose vehement defense of her faith goaded her persecutors to the extremest tortures, which she withstood, living on in a prison at Saragossa, Spain, she is honored with St. Apodemius and his companions on Apr. 16, but probably suffered during or close to the lifetime of Prudentius, who wrote of her.

ENDA, ST. (6th century). He was an Irish warrior-raider until his sister, St. Fanchea, persuaded him to change his ways. He may have been ordained in Rome, returning to build churches on the Boyne River and several religious houses on Aran. F. D. Mar. 21.

ENDLICHER, STEPHAN LADISLAUS (1804–1849), botanist. Born in Pressburg, Hungary, on June 24, he studied in Pest and Vienna, became interested in botany in 1826 at the suggestion of his physician father, and pursued that science while in charge of manuscripts at the Imperial Museum in Vienna. In 1836 he became curator of the botanical department of the Royal Natural History Museum and in 1840 director of the botanical garden and professor of botany at the university. He made a systematic arrangement of herbs, publishing a classified study, founded the *Annalen* of the museum, was joint author of studies of South American plants, and issued a study of Chinese grammar and an atlas based on reports of Jesuit missionaries. He died in Vienna on Mar. 28.

ENGEL, LUDWIG (d. 1674), canonist. Born at Castle Wagrein, Austria, he became a Benedictine at Melk in 1654, studied law at Salzburg, and was ordained in 1658. He became professor of law at the University of Salzburg, published four important canonical studies, and served as vice-chancellor from 1669 to 1674, when he was brought back to Melk to prepare to succeed as abbot. He died in Grillenberg on Apr. 22.

ENGELBERT (1186–1225), archbishop. Son of the count of Berg, he was presented as a boy with several church benefices, lived a lusty life as a youth, and was excommunicated for fighting against Emperor Otto IV. After joining a crusade against the Albigensians, he had the excommunication lifted and in 1217 he became archbishop of Cologne. He inaugurated many reforms, restored clerical discipline, encouraged monastic life, and administered his diocese with justice. When Frederick II went to Sicily in 1220, he appointed Engelbert regent during the minority of his son Henry; in 1222, Engelbert crowned his twelve-year-old charge as king of the Romans. In 1225, Engelbert denounced his cousin Count Frederick of Isenberg for his thefts from the nuns of Essen, for whom the count was administrator. On the way to Schwelm, Engelbert was attacked by the count and his men at Gevelsberg, Germany, and murdered on Nov. 7. Engelbert was never canonized though he is listed in the Roman Martyrology as a martyr.

ENGELBERT (1250?–1331). Born in Völkersdorf, Styria, he became a Benedictine in 1267, studied at Prague and Padua, and in 1297 was elected abbot of Admont, a post he held until his resignation at eighty. He wrote some thirty-eight books in all major fields of learning; works on free will, providence, music were most important, as were *De regimine principum* and *De ortu Romani imperii*, on politics and education. He died on May 12.

ENGELBRECHTSZ, CORNELIS (1468–1533), painter. Born in Leyden, Holland, he studied under Jan van Eyck and is said to have been the first Dutch painter to work in oils. Several *pietàs* and crucifixion scenes survive, but most of his work was destroyed by Iconoclasts in the sixteenth century. His sons, Cornelis (1493–1544) and Luke (b. 1495), also were painters. The father died in Leyden.

ENGELHARDT, CHARLES ANTHONY (1851–1934), historian. Born in Bilshausen, Hanover, on Nov. 13, he was brought to the United States as an infant, studied at St. Francis, Cincinnati, became a Franciscan, taking the name Zephyrin, and was ordained in 1878. After teaching at St. Joseph's, Cleveland, he was assigned to the Menominee Indian mission at Keshena, Wisconsin. In 1885 he went to the Franciscan monastery at Superior. He edited *Pilgrim of Palestine* and *Messenger of St. Francis*, was vice-commissary of the Holy Land in 1887, spent the next thirteen years at Indian missions in California, Michigan, and New Mexico, and in 1900 was sent to Santa Barbara, California. There he remained, except for a five-year period at an orphanage near Watsonville, until his death on Apr. 27. He was a leading scholar of the history of the missions of the Southwest and wrote *Missions and Missionaries of California* (1908–16), *The Franciscans in California* (1897), *The Franciscans in Arizona*, and a life of Catherine Tekakwitha.

ENGELMUND, ST. (d. 739?), abbot. Educated as a Benedictine in England and active as priest and abbot, he became a missioner to the Netherlands under St. Willibrord, working out of Velsen, near modern Haarlem. Because his own family had come from that region he was most successful with converts. F. D. June 21.

ENGHENEDL, ST. (7th century). He was a Welshman, to whom a church in Anglesey has been dedicated. F. D. Sept. 30.

ENGLEFIELD, FELIX (d. 1767). Born in Reading, England, and baptized either Charles or Francis, he became a Franciscan, taking the name Felix, at Douai, where he was ordained about 1732 and taught theology from 1734 to 1746. He held several positions in his order there and in England, where he may have been stationed from 1749 until his death. He was provincial from 1755 to 1758, living at Horton.

ENGLEFIELD, HENRY CHARLES (1752–1822). Nephew of Felix Englefield, he succeeded his father Henry, sixth baronet, in 1780, and was a fellow of the Royal Society and of the Society of Antiquaries. He was president of the latter, contributed studies of Durham, Exeter, and Gloucester to its series of engravings of English cathedrals, and was replaced in office by the earl of Aberdeen when objection was raised to his Catholicism. He wrote many antiquarian studies (on London Bridge, the Isle of Wight), published papers on comets, translated Terence's *Andria*, and wrote on science for *Archaeologia*, the Linnaean Society, and numerous journals. He was a member of the Dilettanti Society and its secretary for fourteen years; was a member of the Catholic Committee of the laity, which helped to modify the relief bill of 1791; and was active in public affairs until his sight failed. His portrait was painted by Sir Thomas Lawrence. Sir Henry died in London on Mar. 21.

ENGLAND, JOHN (1786–1842), bishop. Born in Cork, Ireland, one of ten children, on Sept. 23, he studied at St. Patrick's, Carlow, and was ordained in 1808. He became noted for his forceful preaching in the Cork cathedral, was instrumental in securing better conditions for prisoners transported to Australia, was rector of the Cork diocesan seminary in 1812–17, became inspector of poor schools, founded *The Religious Repository*, and was one of the leaders in the fight for Catholic emancipation and opposed allowing the government a voice in the selection of Irish and English bishops. He gained episcopal displeasure by his outspokenness in the conflict (several bishops had supported the proposal) and was transferred to the small village of Bandon in 1817. In 1820 he was appointed bishop of Charleston, South Carolina. He incurred the wrath of Bishop Conwell in 1822 for his intervention in the Hogan schism in Conwell's see in Philadelphia, as well as that of the bishops in New York and Baltimore who felt he was interfering in matters outside his province. He established a diocesan board of clerical and lay advisers to help govern his see, a plan looked on unfavorably by his fellow bishops, abolished the pew system and trusteeism, founded the Philosophical and Classical seminary of Charleston in 1822, opened a school for free Negroes in 1835, which he was forced to close soon after, and defended the fact of slavery, declaring the Church had accepted it. He was a popular lecturer, was the first Catholic priest to deliver an address to Congress, in 1826, and founded the *United States Catholic Miscellany* in 1822, the first fully Catholic paper in the United States. He vigorously espoused the cause of Irish freedom, was constantly at odds with the French clergy, especially the Sulpicians, in the United States, whom he accused of monarchical tendencies as opposed to his own concept of democracy, and was a prolific and often controversial writer (his works were published in five volumes in 1849). He was a vigorous proponent of a native clergy, turned down an offer of an Irish see to remain in debt-ridden Charleston, and was apostolic delegate to Haiti in 1833-37 to draft a concordat which Pope Gregory XVI refused because of the concessions he had made. He died in Charleston on Apr. 11.

PETER GUILDAY, *Life and Times of John England* (2 vols., New York, America Press, 1927).

ENGLATIUS, ST. (d. 966). He is said to have been a bishop at Tarves, Aberdeenshire, Scotland. F. D. Nov. 3.

ENGRATIA, ST. (d. 715?), martyr. She and her brother Valentine were slain by Moors at Sepúlveda, Castile; their brother Frutos, also captured, escaped, and lived as a hermit. They are patrons of Segovia. F. D. Oct. 25.

ENGUERRAMMUS (d. 1045). Educated at the Benedictine abbey of St. Riquier, he became its abbot in 1022, wrote considerable Latin verse, and was called "the Wise." He is also known as Angilram.

ENNATHA, ST. (d. 297), martyr. *See* Antoninus, St.

ENNODIUS, ST. (473-521), bishop. Magnus Felix Ennodius was born in Arles, southern Gaul, of a prominent family and was educated at Milan. After marriage (or engagement, according to some writers), he decided to become a priest and his wife, a nun. He was ordained deacon before 500 by St. Epiphanius of Pavia, was secretary to the papal claimant Laurentius of Milan, and became bishop of Ticinum (now Pavia), Italy, about 514. He twice was sent to Constantinople by Pope St. Hormisdas to remonstrate with Emperor Anastasius II for his leniency with the heretical Monophysites, but

both missions failed. He wrote biographies of St. Epiphanius and of Antonius of Lérins, an autobiography, letters of historical value, a great deal of occasional and epigrammatic poetry, and a handbook of rhetoric, in which he revealed strong respect for the classic tradition. He died in Ticinum. F. D. July 17.

ENODOCH, ST. (d. 520?). Conflicting stories identify this Welsh name (also spelled Wenedoc) with that of a man, St. Enoder, and of a woman, St. Qwendydd of Brychan.

ENOGATUS, ST. (d. 631). He was bishop of Aleth, Brittany. F. D. Feb. 13.

ENSINGEN, MATTHÄUS (15th century), architect. Son of Ulrich, he worked on the Strassburg cathedral with his father, on that at Berne from 1421 to 1449, was architect at Esslingen from 1419 to 1463, and was master builder in charge of construction at Ulm in 1451. His son Vincenz worked at Berne, Constance, and Basle.

ENSINGEN, ULRICH (d. 1419), architect. Perhaps a pupil of Heinrich the Younger at Ulm, Germany, he worked on the cathedral of Ulm from 1391 until his death on Feb. 10, completing the choir and beginning the nave. He became a master architect in 1397, shortly after a brief stay in Milan, where disagreement with the duke brought his work on the cathedral of that city to an end. He was master builder of the cathedral in Strassburg from 1399, working on the north tower, and completed the nave and part of the tower of the church of Our Lady in Esslingen. His three sons, Caspar, Matthias, and Matthäus, worked with him. He died in Strassburg, Alsace, on Feb. 10.

EOBAN, ST. (d. 755), martyr. A Benedictine priest of Irish descent, he worked on missions with SS. Willibrord and Boniface and was put to death with the latter at Dokkum, Holland. F. D. June 5.

EOCHOD, ST. (d. 597). An apostle to the Picts, he was one of the twelve associates of St. Columcille in the evangelization of northern Britain. F. D. Jan. 25.

EOGHAN, ST. (d. 618?), bishop. According to unreliable sources, he was born in Leinster, Ireland, was carried into slavery to Britain and then to Brittany with two other boys, Tigernach and Coirpre. They were released and returned to Ireland, Coirpre to became a bishop at Coleraine while Eoghan became a monk at Kilnamanach, Wicklow. He remained there with St. Kevin for fifteen years, then helped Tigernach found a monastery at Clones about 576 and later settled at Ardstraw in Tyrone, of which he became first bishop about 581. He is also known as Eugene and Owen. F. D. Aug. 23.

EOGHAN, ST. (6th century). Son of Saran of Cloncullen, Tipperary, Ireland, he is venerated in Tallaght and Donegal. F. D. Mar. 15. Another Eoghan, a bishop, is also venerated in Tallaght on Apr. 18. The name is also spelled Eugene and Owen.

EOGHAN MAC GILLAWEER (d. 1216). He was appointed bishop of Armagh, Ireland, in 1203, but was caught in the struggle between King John of England and the papacy over the privilege of selecting Church leaders. He attended the Lateran Council in 1215 at Rome, and died there.

EOSTERWINI (650–686). A Northumbrian aristocrat, he served in the army of King Egfrid until he was twenty-four, when he entered the monastery at Wearmouth, England, ruled by his uncle, St. Benedict Biscop. He was ordained in 679, became abbot of Wearmouth in 682, and died there of the plague on Mar. 7.

EPAPHRAS, ST. (1st century). Mentioned several times by St. Paul, he is said to have been bishop of Colossae and a martyr there. F. D. July 19.

EPAPHRODITUS, ST. (1st century), bishop. He is said to have been one of the original seventy-two disciples of Christ, mentioned by St. Paul (Phil. 2:35), and is traditionally listed as first bishop of Philippi, Macedonia. Andriacia in Lycia and Terracina in Italy also list the name as first bishop in their areas; the three men named Epaphroditus are probably identical. F. D. Mar. 22.

EPARCHIUS, ST. (d. 361), martyr. *See* Domitius, St.

EPARCHIUS, ST. (504–581). Duke of Périgord, he entered a monastery over parental opposition, then lived in solitude near Angoulême, France. Persuaded to accept ordination, he directed a community which followed him there to devote itself to a life of prayer. He is also known as Cybar. F. D. July 1.

EPÉE, CHARLES MICHEL DE L' (1712–1789). Born in Versailles, France, on Nov. 25, he studied theology, was denied ordination when he refused to condemn Jansenism, studied law, and was then ordained by the bishop of Troyes. In Paris he founded with his own money a school for the education of the deaf and dumb and developed a successful sign alphabet for their instruction, completed by Abbé Sicard. He died in Paris on Dec. 23.

EPHRAEM, ST. (306?–373?), Doctor of the Church. Born in Nisibis in Roman-occupied Mesopotamia, probably of pagan parents, he was put out of the house when converted as a boy. After his baptism at eighteen he served St. James, bishop of Nisibis, accompanied the latter to the Council of Nicaea (325), and probably was head of the catechetical school there until his city was handed over to the Persians in 363. Ephraem then took up residence in a cave near Edessa, living austerely, but often preaching to the Christians there,

though he seems to have been no higher than a deacon. To offset the success of the Gnostics in propagating heresy by way of popular songs, he wrote poems of superior merit, used their tunes, and had them sung by choirs of women. His hymns on Mary were particularly effective. The Gnostics and Arians were defeated by his stronger propaganda. He visited St. Basil at Caesarea in 370, then returned to exhaust himself in distributing food and money to the poor during the famine of 372 and in organizing relief for the sick. He wrote widely in Syriac and his doctrinal and scriptural commentaries and hymns and poems were translated into Greek, Latin, and Armenian. He died in Edessa, Mesopotamia. He was highly praised by SS. Basil and Jerome; the Eastern Church termed him "the harp of the Holy Spirit"; Pope Benedict XV declared him a Doctor of the universal Church in 1920. F. D. June 18 (in the East, Jan. 28).

EPHRAIM (d. 545). Born in Amida, Mesopotamia, he attended the Council of Chalcedon in 451, was count of the East under Emperor Justinian I, succeeded Euphrasius as patriarch of Antioch in 527, and opposed Severus and the Monophysites. Writings against their heresy, sermons, and letters are no longer extant.

EPHREM, ST. (4th century), bishop and martyr. *See* Aetherius, St.

EPHYSIUS, ST. (d. 303), martyr. He is said to have been put to death on Sardinia during the Diocletian persecution. F. D. Jan. 15.

EPICHARIS, ST. (d. 300?), martyr. She is said to have been the wife of a Roman senator and put to death at Byzantium during the Diocletian persecution. F. D. Sept. 27.

EPICTETUS, ST. (d. 250?), martyr. He, SS. Felix, Jucundus, Secundus, Vitalis, and seven others were put to death in northern Africa, probably during the persecution of Decius. F. D. Jan. 9.

EPICTETUS, ST. (d. 300?), martyr. He and SS. Felix, Maprilis, Martial, Saturninus, and others on a pilgrimage to the shrines of the apostles were thrown into the sea at Porto Romano. F. D. Aug. 22.

EPIGMENIUS, ST. (d. 300?), martyr. A priest, he was put to death in Rome during the Diocletian persecution. F. D. Mar. 25.

EPIMACHUS, ST. (d. 250), martyr. A native of Alexandria, Egypt, he was tortured and burned at the stake with St. Alexander during Decius' persecution. Their sufferings were described by St. Dionysius, an eyewitness, who described also the martyrdom of four women, Ammonaria, Mercuria, an aged woman, Dionysia, the mother of several children, and another Ammonaria who were beheaded at the same time. F. D. May 10 (also, Dec. 12).

EPIPHANIUS, ST. (438?–497), bishop. Outstanding as a peacemaker and profuse in his charities, he wore himself out by his efforts as bishop of Pavia, Italy. He took care of great numbers of those who suffered from famine and war, gained freedom for captives, tamed and converted barbarians, achieved reduction in taxes, and traveled widely to try to quiet the leaders, in a crumbling world, of such diverse interests and personalities as Emperor Anthemius, the Visigothic King Euric, the Ostrogothic King Theodoric, the Burgundian Gundobad, and King Odoacher (who had sacked Pavia). Epiphanius died of fever at Pavia, while returning from Burgundy, where he had gone to redeem many taken into slavery. His biography was written by Ennodius. F. D. Jan. 21.

EPIPHANIUS (d. 535), bishop. He succeeded John II as patriarch of Constantinople in 520 and was given authority by Pope Hormisdas to reconcile all those who abandoned their Monophysite errors. Epiphanius announced his own orthodoxy, accepted the *Tome* of Pope Leo I, and continued his correspondence with Hormisdas.

EPIPHANIUS (6th century), translator. Called Scholasticus, he prepared for Cassiodorus a compilation of the works of Socrates, Sozomen, and Theodoret, known as *Historia tripartita*, and translated the commentary of Didymus on the Catholic Epistles and on Proverbs, of Epiphanius of Salamis on the Canticle of Canticles, and of Codex encyclicus, listing expressions of episcopal approval of the decrees of the Council of Chalcedon (451).

EPIPHANIUS OF SALAMIS, ST. (315?-403), bishop. Born in Palestine, he became a monk in Egypt as a youth, founded a monastery at Besanduk when he returned to Judaea, was ordained after 333, and became known for his scholarship and asceticism. He was made bishop of Constantia (Salamis) and metropolitan of Cyprus in 367, a position he filled for the rest of his life, and became active in combating heresies, particularly Origenism and Arianism. He supported Bishop Paulinus in 376 in Antioch against the claims of Meletius and the Eastern bishops, and in 382 participated in the Council of Rome for the same purpose. He went to Jerusalem about 394 to combat the Origenism of Bishop John, to Constantinople in 402 during the controversy involving St. John Chrysostom, whom he believed guilty of Origenism, and became involved in controversy with Chrysostom and John of Jerusalem, and in so doing trespassed on their jurisdiction. He died on his return to Cyprus. He was an authority on devotion to the Virgin Mary and explicitly taught the primacy of St. Peter among the apostles. Among his theological treatises are: *Ancoratus* (374), treating particularly of the Trinity and the Resurrection; *Panarion* (374-77), treating of eighty heresies and refutations of them, valuable for its information about fourth-century religious passages from authors whose works are otherwise lost; *De mensuribus et ponderibus*, an introduction to the Bible, and a treatise on the ornaments of the high priest's breastplate. F. D. May 12.

EPIPODIUS, ST. (d. 178), martyr. Captured with St. Alexander after the martyrdom of St. Pothinus, he was tortured and beheaded at Lyons, France, in the reign of Marcus Aurelius. F. D. Apr. 22.

EPISTEME. *See* Galation, St.

EPITACIUS, ST. (1st century), bishop and martyr. He is said to have been the first bishop of Tuy in Spanish Galicia, where he was killed for his faith. F. D. May 23.

EPOLONIUS, ST. (d. 250?), martyr. *See* Babylas, St.

EPPING, JOSEPH (1835-1894), astronomer. Born in Neuenkirchen, Westphalia, he studied in Rheine and Münster, became a Jesuit in 1859, taught mathematics and astronomy at Maria-Laach, and was ordained in 1870. In 1872 he went to Ecuador, taught mathematics at the University of Quito, wrote a geometry text in Spanish, and went to Holland in 1876 after political upheavals in South America. He taught until his death at Exaeten, Holland, on Aug. 22. He attacked the materialism of the Kent-Laplace nebular hypothesis, evolved a key for the study of Babylonian astronomy, and wrote on Assyrian chronology and science.

EPPO, BL. (d. 1143). In 1122 he became the second abbot of the Benedictine monastery of Mallersdorf, Bavaria. F. D. June 27.

EPVRE. *See* Aprus, St.

EQUITIUS, ST. (d. 540?). He founded monasteries in the province of Valeria, Italy, and was praised by Pope St. Gregory the Great. F. D. Aug. 11.

EQUITIUS, ST. (d. 560?). He lived as a hermit in Valeria, east of Rome, then traveled through Italy preaching and founding monasteries. Since he was not a priest, some clerics demanded that he be silenced, but the pope approved of his work. He died on Mar. 7. F. D. Aug. 11.

ERASMA, ST. (1st century?), marytr. *See* Dorothy, St.

ERASMUS, ST. (d. 303?), bishop and martyr. Bishop of Formiae, Campania, Italy, he probably was put to death during the Diocletian persecution. He is sometimes confused with a Syrian of the same name who was bishop of Antioch and is honored on Nov. 25; it is possible that they are one and the same. St. Erasmus later became the patron of Gaeta. The mariners of Naples referred to the strange lights which appeared on the masts of ships toward the end of storms as St. Elmo's fire (Erasmus was corrupted to Elmo), but the

Portuguese associate this phenomenon with their patron of mariners, Bl. Peter Gonzalez. F. D. June 2.

ERASMUS, DESIDERIUS (1467–1536), scholar. Born in Rotterdam, Holland, on Oct. 28, illegitimate son of Gerard of Gouda, he was an orphan by fourteen and was placed by his guardians and against his wishes in a monastery at Emaus. In 1491 the bishop of Cambrai removed him from the monastic life he disliked, ordained him in 1492, made him his secretary, and opened up a life of scholarship to him. He completed his studies at Paris, where he disliked the corrupt scholasticism that he observed, was stationed in Orléans, where he worked on his *Adagia*, tutored, and went to England in 1498–99, where he met Thomas More and John Colet. The latter suggested that he study Greek and devote himself to scriptural commentary. On his return to the Continent he published his collection of proverbs, *Adagia* (1500), *Enchiridion militis christiani* (1502), a plea for a truer display of piety, and an edition of Lorenzo Valla's *Annotationes* to the New Testament (1505). He went to Italy in 1506, took his doctorate in divinity at Turin, became a friend of the printer, Aldus Manutius, and was well received at the court of Cardinal Giovanni de' Medici (later Pope Leo X) and others. He left Italy in 1509 and began writing *Laus stultitiae* (*Praise of Folly*), influenced in part by Lucian, in part by his conversations with More, and in part by the popularity of "fool" literature in Europe (notably that by Brant and Barclay). The objects of his attacks in *Praise of Folly* appeared in his other work as well: the contemporary tolerance of the seven deadly sins, the triumph of emotionalism over reason, the waste of war, the shortcomings of philosophers, the venality of merchants, the vanity of ecclesiastical leaders who failed to be leaders, misuse of church funds, and appeals to superstition in the limitless devotions, prayers, pilgrimages, and shrines. He returned to England, lectured briefly at Cambridge as professor of Greek, realized that he would not obtain a permanent appointment in a court which had become anti-intellectual under Henry VIII's change of mind, and returned to Brabant. He served Archduke (later Emperor) Charles as councilor, wrote *Institutio principis christiani* on the ideal ruler, and in 1518 *Colloquia familiara*, on the study of the Latin language, with many asides on contemporary ecclesiastical shortcomings. His Greek New Testament followed, with annotations which ran counter to many existing views, which struck out in injudicious language, and which made many authorities conclude that his insistence on a rational interpretation (as against any allegory) put him in the forefront of humanists who sought to destroy the Church. In his attempt to restore religious life to its earliest simple form, Erasmus may have been intemperate in stating that too much time and energy were spent on theological quarrels of no concern to the average Christian; similarly, the language of his seemingly rationalistic approach to the Eucharist and confession, his uncertainty as to papal infallibility, and his ecumenical broadness placed him in a position where he was considered more and more with suspicion and hostility. When the reformers quoted from his works, he became widely referred to as one of the first Protestants. By 1517, Luther had become convinced that Erasmus was not in agreement with him except in their mutual dislike of contemporary evils; Erasmus, as late as 1519, hoped that good would come shortly out of the current battles. The Louvain theologians joined in the attacks on Erasmus and he moved to Basle in 1521, where for eight years he was editor for the Froben press, preparing an edition of Aristotle and other works. When no compromise seemed possible to heal the growing religious breach, he abandoned his deliberate neutralism and wrote a series of major treatises against Luther between 1524 and 1533. After 1529, when he took up residence in the Catholic city of Freiburg, he devoted himself more and more to humanistic learning, which he felt was also a major victim of the religious wars. He was upheld throughout his career by the popes, none of whom censured him, although many of his writings were condemned in local areas. Erasmus died in Basle, Switzerland, on July 12.

LOUIS BOUYER, *Erasmus and His Times*, trans. F. X. Murphy (Westminster, Md., Newman, 1960); JOHN J. MANGAN, *Life, Character, and Influence of Desiderius Erasmus of Rotterdam* (2 vols., New York, Macmillan, 1927).

ERASTUS, ST. (1st century). He was treasurer of the city of Corinth when converted by St. Paul and worked as a missioner in and near that city. Tradition calls him a bishop at Philippi Paneas (Palestine) or Philippi (Macedonia) and a martyr. F. D. July 26.

ERBERMANN, VEIT (1597–1675), theologian. Born in Rendweisdorff, Bavaria, on May 25, he became a convert while young and a Jesuit in 1620, and studied in Mainz and Würzburg. He served as rector of the seminary at Fulda, was active as an opponent of the reformers, and published critical works in theology. He died on Apr. 8.

ERBLON. *See* Hermenland, St.

ERBO, BL. (d. 1162). A Benedictine at the monastery of St. George in the Black Forest, he was appointed abbot of Prüfening, near Ratisbon, Germany, which he ruled for forty years. F. D. Aug. 27.

ERCILLA Y ZÚÑIGA, ALONSO DE

(1533–1594), poet. Born in Madrid, Spain, on Aug. 7, he became a page in the royal court, was well educated, and traveled through Europe with Prince Philip. He accompanied Jerónimo de Alderete to Panama in 1555, and, after the latter's death a year later, pushed on to Peru and Chile, served under Governor Mendoza, gained honors as a soldier, and returned to Spain in 1562. In *La Araucana*, an epical poem, he recounted the Chilean insurrection which he had suppressed; published in 1569–90, it is still of value to historians. He died in Madrid on Nov. 29, in poverty and neglect.

ERCONGOTA, ST. (d. 660?). Daughter of King Ercombert of Kent and St. Sexburga, she became a Benedictine nun at the abbey of Faremoutiers under her aunt, St. Ethelburga. F. D. July 7.

ERCONWALD, ST. (d. 686), bishop. He built and was abbot of Chertsey in Surrey, and set up the convent of Barking in Essex, where his sister St. Ethelburga became abbess, before he became bishop of London in 675. F. D. Apr. 30.

ERDESWICKE, SAMPSON (d. 1603), antiquarian. Born in Sandon, Staffordshire, England, son of Hugh (harassed for his religion during the reign of Elizabeth), he studied at Oxford and wrote a *Survey of Staffordshire*, not published for more than a century after his death.

EREMBERT, ST. (d. 672?), bishop. Born in Waucourt, France, he became a Benedictine at Fontenelle at the hands of St. Wandrille about 640, and was appointed bishop of Toulouse about 656 by King Clotaire III, a post he resigned after twelve years because of ill health. F. D. May 14.

EREMBERT, BL. (11th century). A Benedictine, he was elected abbot of Kremsmünster, Austria, in 1050. F. D. June 24.

ERENTRUDIS, ST. (d. 718?). The niece, or perhaps sister, of St. Rupert of Bavaria directed a community of Benedictine nuns at Salzburg, who took care of the lepers in the diocese of Worms. F. D. June 30.

EREPTIOLUS, ST. (4th century). He is listed as one of the earliest bishops of Coutances, France.

ERHARD, ST. (d. 686?). Auxiliary bishop of Ratisbon, Germany, he baptized St. Odilia, and may have been abbot of Ebersheimmünster. F. D. Jan. 8.

ERIC IX, ST. (d. 1160), king of Sweden. He began his reign in 1150, had Sweden's laws collected as the Code of Uppland, invaded and defeated Finland, which long had been raiding his country, and left St. Henry to evangelize the Finns. Several of his nobles, objecting to the new faith, plotted with the Danes, and killed the king near Uppsala, Sweden. Never

officially canonized, he was considered the patron of Sweden until the Reformation and honored on May 18.

ERIGENA. *See* John Scotus Eriugena.

ERIZZO, BL. (d. 1094). Born in Florence, Italy, he was the first follower of St. John Gualbert and later became general of the Vallombrosans. His cult was confirmed in 1600. F. D. Feb. 9.

ERKEMBODEN, ST. (d. 714), bishop. A Benedictine monk at Sithen, France, he succeeded St. Bertinus as abbot, then served also as bishop of Thérouanne for twenty-six years. F. D. Apr. 12.

ERLAFRID, ST. (9th century). Count of Calw, he founded Hirschau abbey in Swabia, where he later became a Benedictine monk. F. D. Nov. 6.

ERLUPH, ST. (d. 830), bishop and martyr. A Scot, he became a missioner in Germany and was bishop of Werden when he was killed by pagans. F. D. Feb. 10.

ERMENBURGA, ST. (d. 650?). A Kentish princess married to the king of Mercia, she was the mother of SS. Mildred, Milburga, and Mildgith, and founded the convent of Minster in Thanet. F. D. Nov. 19.

ERMENFRIDUS, ST. (d. 670?). A courtier, he became a Benedictine at Luxeuil, France, and was abbot-founder of Cusance. F. D. Sept. 25.

ERMENGARD, BL. (832?–866). The daughter of Charlemagne's grandson, King Louis the German, she was abbess of the Benedictine convent at Buchau and, later, of Chiemsee, Bavaria. Her cult was confirmed in 1928. Her name is also spelled Irmengard. F. D. July 16.

ERMENGILD, ST. (d. 703). Daughter of Ercombert, king of Kent, and St. Sexburga, she married Wulfhere, king of Mercia, and helped to spread Christianity in her husband's realm until his death in 675. She then became a religious, serving under her mother at the English abbeys of Minster and of Ely, succeeding her as abbess at both places. Her daughter St. Werburga also entered Ely. F. D. Feb. 13.

ERMINOLD, ST. (d. 1121). Entering the cloister at Hirschau, Germany, he later became abbot of Lorsch, then of Prüfening, in 1114, and died when struck during a riot by his subjects over the strictness of his administration. F. D. Jan. 6.

ERMINUS, ST. (d. 737), bishop. Born in Laon, France, he became a priest, entered the Benedictines at Lobbes, and was appointed abbot and regionary bishop there by St. Ursmarus. F. D. Apr. 25.

ERNAN, ST. (6th century?). He was a monk at Cluvain-Deoghra, Meath, Ireland. F. D. Jan. 11.

ERNAN, ST. (6th century). Uncle of St. Columba, he was one of the twelve who went with him from Ireland to Iona. He became abbot of a monastery on the island of Hinba, which became a favorite refuge for Columba. **ERNAN, ST.** (d. 640?). Nephew of St. Columba, he was abbot of the monastery of Druim-Tomma, Donegal, Ireland, and may have visited Scotland. A St. Ethernanus (F. D. Dec. 21) is patron of Killernan, Ross-shire. They may be identical. F. D. Jan. 1.

ERNAN, ST. (d. 650?). Son of Colman and a follower of St. Columba, he became abbot of the monastery on the island of Torach, Donegal, Ireland, and died on Aug. 17.

ERNEST, ST. (d. 1148), martyr. He was Benedictine abbot of the German monastery of Zwiefalten, who was captured in Arabia while preaching during the crusade, and tortured to death at Mecca. F. D. Nov. 7.

ERNST OF HESSE-RHEINFELS (1623–1693), landgrave. Born on Dec. 9 at Cassel, he was an officer in the Hessian unit which served with Sweden during the Thirty Years' War. Captured, he became interested in Catholicism as a prisoner and was converted in Vienna in 1650 after his release. He wrote a defense of his action, which began a violent controversy, published his autobiography in 1669, and died in Cologne, Germany, on May 12.

ERNULF (1040–1124), architect. Born in Beauvais, France, he studied under Lanfranc at Bec, became a Benedictine, and after 1070 went to Christ Church, Canterbury, where he was prior. He was abbot of Peterborough in 1107 and in 1114 became bishop of Rochester. He rebuilt the eastern part of the church at Canterbury, erected the chapel of St. Andrew, and built new structures at Peterborough and Rochester. He edited documents on the history of his see and wrote treatises on theology and canon law.

EROTHEIS, ST. (d. 304), martyr. *See* Capitolina, St.

ERRÁZURIZ, CRESCENTE (1839–1931), archbishop. Born in Santiago, Chile, on Nov. 28, he was ordained in 1863 and edited *Revista Católica* in 1863–74 and *Estandarte Católico* in 1874–84. He then became a Dominican, taking the name Raimundo, and served as librarian and prior at several monasteries. He became papal prothonotary in 1916 and archbishop of Santiago in 1918. He taught canon law at the national university and in 1915 became director of the Chilean Academy, of which he had been a member since 1879. He wrote *Los origines de la iglesia chilean* (1873), a biography of García de Mendoza, and several histories of Chile. He died in Santiago on June 5.

ERRINGTON, VEN. GEORGE (d. 1596), martyr. *See* Knight, William.

ERRINGTON, WILLIAM (1716–1768),

educator. Born in Wiltshire, England, on July 17, he went to Douai in 1737, was ordained in 1747, and went to London the next year to serve under Bishop Challoner. Errington made four attempts to found a school for middle-class boys, being successful only at Sedgley Park, Wolverhampton. Established in 1763, it lasted for over a century. In his last years, Fr. Errington was archdeacon and treasurer of the chapter in London, where he died on Sept. 28.

ERSKINE, CHARLES (1739–1811), cardinal. Born in Rome, Italy, on Feb. 13, son of Colin Erskine, earl of Kellie and Mar, he was educated at the Scots College there and became a doctor of laws in 1770. He held papal offices under Pius VI, went to England in 1793 as papal envoy, and was made a cardinal in 1803. He served as protector of Scotland, was imprisoned with the pope when Rome fell to the French in 1808, stripped of his property, and forced to live on an allowance from Protestant relatives. In 1810, Napoleon called him to Paris, where he died on Mar. 20 after a year of illness.

ERTH, ST. He was the brother of SS. Ia and Unvy and went from Ireland to the missions of Wales. F. D. Oct. 31.

ERTHAL, FRANZ LUDWIG VON (1730–1795), bishop. Born in Lohr on the Main, Germany, on Sept. 16, he studied theology at Mainz, Würzburg, Rome, and law in Vienna, and became president of the secular government at Würzburg in 1762. He became privy councilor and inspector of the supreme court under Emperor Joseph II and was imperial commissioner at the Diet of Ratisbon in 1776. He became prince-bishop of Würzburg in 1779 and of Bamberg in 1780. He enlarged the hospital of St. Julius, bettered educational, economic, and agricultural conditions, fought Febronianism and rationalism, and was noted for his personal charities. He died in Würzburg, Bavaria, on Feb. 16.

ERVERTO, BL. (12th century). He was archbishop of Conza, Avellino, Italy, in 1169.

ERWIN (d. 1318), architect. He and his sons Erwin and Johannes were heads of the stonemason guild of Strassburg, Alsace, and supervising architects of the cathedral there. The elder Erwin began the façade about 1277, added the ornamental decoration, and repaired part of the nave which had been damaged by fire in 1298. The chapel of the Virgin and the monument to Conrad of Lichtenberg in the chapel of St. John also came from his workshop. He died in Strassburg on Jan. 17.

ERZBERGER, MATTHIAS (1875–1921), diplomat. Born in Buttenhausen, Würtemberg, on Sept. 20, he studied at Fribourg, was a teacher, edited *Deutschen Volksblatt* from 1896 to 1903, became a representative from Würtemberg as a member of the Centre party, and moved to Berlin to edit its publications and gain a reputation in the *Reichstag*. His political and anti-military activities failed, as did his attempt to bring about peace in 1917. He was chairman of a commission appointed to deal with the Allies, and was its only member to sign the terms of the treaty of Versailles in 1919. He had often been journalistically condemned as a traitor, favored a league of nations, and suffered several attempts to kill him. After the war he was minister of finance, bitterly attacked the war profiteers and imposed heavy taxes on capitalists, and was assassinated at Griesbach, Germany, on Sept. 20.

ESCH, NICOLAUS VAN (1507–1578), theologian. Born in Oisterwijk, Holland, he studied at Louvain, was ordained in 1530, and settled in Cologne, where he tutored St. Peter Canisius and other university students and became friendly with Carthusian leaders. He became pastor at Diest, founded several diocesan seminaries according to the Tridentine Rule, and wrote studies of mystical theology. He died on July 19.

ESCOBAR, VEN. MARINA DE (1554–1633), foundress. Born in Vallodolid, Spain, on Feb. 8, daughter of Iago de Escobar, lawyer and governor of Osuna, she attained distinction for learning and for charitable concern for others as well as for extreme bodily afflictions which made her a complete invalid from the age of fifty. She established a branch of the Order of the Holy Saviour (Brigittines), with modified rules, which gained success after her death. Her spiritual autobiography was prepared at the direction of her confessor, Luis de Ponte, who also published her life. She died in Vallodolid on Feb. 8.

ESCOBAR Y MENDOZA, ANTONIO (1589–1669). Born in Valladolid, Spain, he became a Jesuit at sixteen, was noted as a preacher, and wrote six studies in theology. Although sometimes obscure or unsharp in logic, they do not merit Pascal's charges that they were marked by laxism and hypocrisy. He died in Valladolid on July 4.

ESGLIS, LOUIS PHILIPPE MARIAUCHAU D' (1710–1788), bishop. Born in Quebec, Canada, on Apr. 24, he studied there, was ordained in 1734, served as pastor of St. Pierre d'Orléans, and was made coadjutor bishop of Quebec in 1772. He succeeded to the see in 1784 and suffered great interference from the British government, which objected to the importation of priests from France. Because of the scarcity of assistants, the bishop authorized a layman to administer baptism and witness marriage contracts; in his pastoral letters he pleaded with the Catholics of the provinces to remain steadfast. He died in Quebec on June 4.

ESKIL, ST. (d. 1080?), bishop and martyr. He went from his native England to Sweden with St. Sigfrid, was consecrated at Strängnäs as a regionary bishop, and reclaimed for the faith many who had lapsed since the time of St. Anskar. King Inge, who approved the mission, was murdered, and paganism flourished under his successor. Eskil was stoned to death at Strängnäs, Sweden, when he pleaded with the audience at a heathen festival to return to Christianity. F. D. June 12.

ESKIL (1100?–1181), archbishop. Born of a noble Jutish family, he went to the cathedral school at Hildesheim, became provost of the cathedral of Lund in 1131, bishop of Roskilde in 1134, and in 1137 succeeded his uncle Asser as archbishop of Lund, Sweden. He completed the romanesque cathedral, which he dedicated in 1145, and bettered its chapter. He waged an unsuccessful crusade against the Wends, but his spiritual efforts effected their conversion before his death. In 1152 he was made primate of Sweden and papal legate for northern Europe. He was a major patron of the Benedictines, Augustinians, Premonstratensians, and Cistercians; he especially admired St. Bernard, whom he visited in 1152 and to whose grave he made a pilgrimage in 1153. On his return from Rome he was imprisoned for four years, apparently at the instigation of the archbishop of Bremen; soon after his release he learned that King Waldemar was supporting the antipope Victor. Archbishop Eskil then went into voluntary exile, living in Clairvaux near Pope Alexander III. When the king was reconciled with the pope, Eskil returned in 1168. With papal permission, he resigned his offices in 1177, named Bishop Absalom of Roskilde as his successor, and retired to Clairvaux, France, to live as a monk. He died there on Sept. 6 or 7.

ESNAMBUC, PIERRE DE. *See* Énambuc, Pierre.

ESPEJO, ANTONIO DE (16th century), explorer. Born in Cordova, Spain, he became a wealthy mine owner in Mexico. When he learned of the murder of three Franciscan missioners at Bernalillo, New Mexico, he led an expedition of his own to investigate when government authorities refused to act. He found several Christian Indians left behind by Coronado in 1540, pressed on as far as the northern Arizona line, located a number of silver-ore areas, and prepared a report and map of the expedition, which toured from Nov. 1582 to Sept. 1583.

ESPENCE, CLAUDE D' (1511–1571), theologian. Born at Châlons-sur-Marne, France, he studied at Navarre, became rector at Paris in 1540 (two years before he received his doctorate there), and later became attached to the court of Cardinal de Lorraine. He attended consultations at Mélun (1544) and Orléans (1560) and at the Conference of Poissy (1561) firmly opposed Beza. He wrote on the primitive Church, the validity of marriage, predestination, and the epistles of St. Paul, as well as sermons and poems. He died in Paris on Oct. 5.

ESPINEL, VICENTE MARTÍNEZ (1551–1634), poet. Born in Ronda, Malaga, Spain, he studied at Salamanca, became a soldier, was ordained, and was chaplain of the hospital in his birthplace. He was the friend and teacher of Lope de Vega in Madrid, where he was to die in poverty. His novel, *Relaciones de la vida y hechos del escudero Marcos de Obregón* (1618), was a popular account of a picaresque hero (often called autobiographical); Le Sage seems to have relied on it heavily for *Gil Blas*. Espinel translated Horace's *Art of Poetry*; his own poems, *Diversas rimas*, appeared in 1591 and popularized a ten-octosyllabic-line stanza known as the *décima* (sometimes as the *espinel*, erroneously making him its originator). Espinel also was a musician and is said to have added the fifth string to the guitar.

ESPINOSA, ALONSO DE (16th century), historian. A Dominican missioner, sent from Spain to Guatemala, he wrote an elaborate study of the conquest of the Canary Islands by Spain, *Guanches of Tenerife* (1594). The work describes the customs of the tribe, the early history of the island, and the devotion to Our Lady of Caldelaria.

ESTAING, CHARLES HECTOR D' (1729–1794), admiral. Born at the Château de Ravel, Auvergne, France, on Nov. 28, he was colonel of infantry, later a brigadier general, fell prisoner at the siege of Madras (1759), served the French East India Company, and led a naval expedition which destroyed British holdings in Sumatra. Again captured by the British and released, he was named lieutenant admiral in 1763, vice-admiral in 1777, and was in charge of a fleet sent to aid the American colonies. A storm prevented a planned battle near Newport, Rhode Island; d'Estaing then captured Grenada and St. Vincent, W. Indies, and damaged Admiral Byron's fleet in 1779. On his return to France in 1780 he was out of favor with the court, regained his honors in 1783, was commandant of the national guard in 1789, and was made an admiral in 1792. Although he favored the revolution at the start, he was loyal to the king, spoke in defense of Marie Antoinette at her trial, and was executed on Apr. 28 in Paris. He wrote a tragedy, *Les Thermopyles* (1755), a book on America, and poems.

ESTERWINE, ST. (d. 686). A courtier in Northumbria, he entered the Benedictine abbey of Wearmouth, founded by his relative,

St. Benedict Biscop, whom he succeeded as abbot in 682. F. D. Mar. 7.

ESTIENNOT DE LA SERRE, CLAUDE (1639–1699). Born in Varennes, France, he became a Benedictine at Vendôme, taught briefly, and was sent to St. Germain-des-Prés, Paris, to work with Mabillon on research in Flemish libraries. In 1670 he was sub-prior of St. Martin's, Pontoise, the history of which he wrote; he then compiled *Antiquités bénédictines* (1673–82) on the work of his order in French dioceses. In 1684 he was named Benedictine procurator in the Curia Romana; on his way to Rome and during his lifelong position there he collected vast quantities of monastic material, which he sent back to Mabillon for use in the compilation of *Gallia Christiana* and *Annales O.S.B.* He died in Rome.

ETERNUS, ST. (7th century), bishop. He was the ninth to direct the French see of Evreux, living past 660. F. D. July 15.

ETHBIN, ST. (6th century). He probably was a Briton educated by St. Samson and a monk in Brittany under St. Winwaloe. When the abbey of Taurac was destroyed by the Franks in 556, he went to Ireland, where he lived as a recluse and then as abbot of Kildare. F. D. Oct. 19.

ETHELBALD (d. 640), king. Son of Ethelbert, whom he succeeded as king of Kent, England, he married his father's widow, broke off the incestuous relationship when he was converted to Christianity, and built churches at Canterbury and Folkstone.

ETHELBALD (d. 757), king. He became king of Mercia in 716 and ruled over England as far north as the Humber River. He was well disposed toward the Church, invaded Wessex in 733, was defeated by Cuthred in 752, and was killed at Seccandune.

ETHELBALD (d. 860), king. He succeeded his father Ethelwulf as king of the West Saxons in 856, and married Judith, his father's widow, in 858, but separated from her at the insistence of St. Swithin.

ETHELBERT, ST. (d. 616), king. He became king of Kent in England about 560, was defeated by the West Saxons in 568, built up his kingdom, and became a strong ruler. His Frankish wife, Bertha, was a Christian. Ethelbert welcomed St. Augustine, permitted him to preach widely, and was himself baptized between 597 and 601, leading thousands of his followers into the Church, including King Sabert of the East Saxons, though he correctly opposed conversion by anything less than conviction. He made Canterbury the political and religious center of his realm, and codified his laws, the first extant collection in the German tradition. His name is also spelled Aedilberct. F. D. Feb. 25.

ETHELBERT, ST. (d. 794). Son of Ethelred, king of East Anglia, he succeeded his father as king. While on a mission to the court of King Offa of Mercia at Sutton Walls, Herefordshire, to seek marriage with Offa's daughter Alfreda, Ethelbert was murdered at the instigation of Offa's wife, Cynethryth. Although the murder was probably politically motivated, Ethelbert has since been honored as a martyr on May 20.

ETHELBERT, ST. (d. 670). He and his brother Ethelred, great-grandsons of St. Ethelbert of Kent, England, were put to death at Estry, near Sandwich. They were revered at a shrine at Ramsey abbey, Huntingdonshire, on Oct. 17.

ETHELBERT (d. 781?), archbishop. A relative of Archbishop Egbert, he studied at the school the latter founded at York, England, was ordained, became master of the school, and taught Alcuin, whose close friend he became. A man of wide learning, he was particularly interested in the Old Testament. He became archbishop of York in 766. His influence on education was great, and he made personal tours of the continent in search of books for the York library. He held a council in Northumbria on missionary needs, and sent Willehad to the Frisians and Alubert and Liudger to northern Germany. In 780 he named Eanbald, who had helped Alcuin in the restoration of York minster, his coadjutor, and placed Alcuin in charge of the library and school. Ethelbert then retired to a cell for private devotions until his death in York on Nov. 8, 781 or 782.

ETHELBURGA, ST. (d. 647?). Daughter of St. Ethelbert, king of Kent, she married Edwin, king of Northumbria, whom she helped to convert. When pagans overran the region after Edwin's death, she founded a convent at Lyminge and became its abbess. F. D. Apr. 5.

ETHELBURGA, ST. (d. 664?). One of the children of Anna, king of the East Angles, she, with her half-sister Sethrida, became a Benedictine nun at the abbey of Faremoutier in France. Known there as St. Aubierge, she succeeded Sethrida as abbess. F. D. July 7.

ETHELBURGA, ST. (d. 678?). Born in Stallington, Lindsey, England, she was the sister of St. Erconwald, who founded a double monastery at Barking, Essex, and made her its abbess. F. D. Oct. 12.

ETHELRED I (d. 871), king of England. He became king of Wessex and Kent, and in 866 of all England. He defeated the Danes in 868, but was routed by them at Ashdown and fatally wounded in the battle of Merton on their return.

ETHELRED THE UNREADY (968?–1016), king of England. Son of Edgar, he became king in 878 when his brother Edward

was slain. He was known as the Unready (meaning "resourceless") and remained in the power of his favorites. At the advice of one, Ethelsine, he attacked the see of Rochester in 986. He allied himself with Olaf Tryggvason in 991, defeated the latter's fleet in 992, and bought him off by a huge payment in 994. He massacred the Danes living in England in 1002 and was attacked by Malcolm of Scotland in 1006. Because of the unpopularity of his new favorite, Eadric, and the latter's support of the Danes, Ethelred lost national support. He was forced to buy off the Danes in 1012 and to flee to France in 1013 after Swend of Denmark was named king by the nobles. After Swend's death in 1014 he returned, expelled King Cnut, and murdered Sigeferth and Morker, Danish thanes, in 1015.

ETHELDREDA, ST. (d. 679). Born in Exning, Suffolk, daughter of King Anna of the East Angles, she was married to Tonbert, who respected her vow of virginity and who died three years later. She lived for five years on the island of Ely, then was married to Egfrid, merely a boy, son of Oswy, king of Northumbria. In later years Egfrid demanded that she disregard her vow and sought to bribe St. Wilfrid of York and his ecclesiastical court as the case came to trial. Etheldreda, who won, entered religious life, at Coldingham, and later founded a double monastery at Ely, which she directed. Her shrine long was a place of pilgrimage; the word "tawdry" (a corruption of St. Audrey, which she was often called) comes from references to the "artistic junk" sold at Ely's annual fair. F. D. June 23.

ETHELGITHA, ST. (d. 720?). She was abbess of a Benedictine convent in Northumbria, England. F. D. Aug. 22.

ETHELGIVA, ST. (d. 896). Daughter of King Alfred the Great of England, she became abbess of Shaftesbury. F. D. Dec. 9.

ETHELHARD (d. 805), archbishop. Possibly a student at a monastery in Lincolnshire, England, and later its abbot, he was named archbishop of Canterbury in 791 through the influence of King Offa of Mercia. He was embroiled in several jurisdictional disputes as the king sought to centralize ecclesiastical power, defended the integrity of his own see, and condemned the cleric Eadbert Praen who led Kentish rebels against Offa. Ethelhard fled his see, but returned after the death of Eadbert in 798; Alcuin, who had censured him for his flight, pleaded with him to do penance for it, and remained his friend. In 801, Ethelhard went to Rome, where Pope Leo III deposed the archbishop of Lichfield (created by Offa) and restored lost privileges to Canterbury. Ethelhard died in Canterbury on May 12.

ETHELNOTH, ST. (d. 1038), archbishop.

Surnamed "the Good," this Benedictine monk was archbishop of Canterbury, England, from 1020 until his death. He was held in high regard by King Canute, whom he persuaded to rebuild Chartres. F. D. Oct. 30.

ETHELRED, ST. (d. 716), king. He gave up the throne of Mercia, England, to become a Benedictine monk at Bardney, where he later was abbot. F. D. May 4.

ETHELRED, ST. (d. 670). See Ethelbert, St.

ETHELRED. See Aelred.

ETHELWALD, ST. (d. 699). A Benedictine monk from Ripon, England, he took over St. Cuthbert's hermitage on Farne Island and lived a life of solitary prayer for twelve years. F. D. Mar. 23.

ETHELWALD, ST. (d. 740?), bishop. Assistant to St. Cuthbert, he became prior of Old Melrose abbey in Scotland and, in 721, succeeded Eadfrith to the see of Lindisfarne. F. D. Feb. 12.

ETHELWIN, ST. (8th century), bishop. He went with St. Egbert to Ireland and became the second to hold the see of Lindsey. F. D. May 3.

ETHELWOLD, ST. (d. 984), bishop. Born in Winchester, England, he was ordained by St. Alphege the Bald and in 944 became a Benedictine at Glastonbury. In 955 he was abbot of Abingdon. With SS. Dunstan and Oswald he began the restoration of monasticism, which had almost been wiped out by the Danes. He became bishop of Winchester in 963 and his systematic policy of reforming abbeys, installing Benedictines in place of weak canons, and restoring such monasteries as Ely, Newminster, and Peterborough, earned him the title "Father of Monks." F. D. Aug. 1.

ETHELWULF (d. 858), king. Son of Egbert, he ruled Kent, England, before his father's death in 839, then became king of Wessex, fought the Danish invaders, and with his brother Ethelbald defeated them at Aclea in 851. He made a pilgrimage to Rome in 855 and, when he learned that his son Ethelbald would resist his return to power, ceded Wessex to him and returned to rule only over Kent.

ETHELWULF (d. 1156), bishop. He was prior of the Augustinian canons whom King Henry I of England established at Carlisle in 1102, royal confessor, prior at Nostell, Yorkshire, and in 1133 became first bishop of Carlisle. He built a Norman cathedral there.

ETHERIANUS, HUGH (12th century). A scholarly theologian at the court of Emperor Comnenus at Constantinople, he wrote an elaborate defense in Latin and Greek of the *Filioque* and the disputes between Catholic and Orthodox leaders, and sent copies to Pope Alexander III and Patriarch Aimerikos of An-

tioch. The work relied heavily on the early Church Fathers as well as on the writings of his opponents; it was later used by Thomas Aquinas and Cardinal Bessarion. His brother Leo was an official court interpreter of Latin correspondence.

ETHERIUS, ST. (d. 303?), martyr. He was slain in Nicomedia during the Diocletian persecution. F. D. June 18.

ETHERIUS, ST. (d. 573). He became bishop of Auxerre, Gaul, in 563. F. D. July 27.

ETHERIUS, ST. (d. 602). He was bishop of Lyons, France, whom St. Augustine was to visit on his way to evangelize Britain. F. D. Aug. 27.

ETHERIUS, ST. (d. 675?). He was bishop of Vienne, in Gaul. F. D. June 14.

ETHOR, ST. (9th century), martyr. See Beocca, St.

ETTO, ST. (d. 670?), bishop. Said to have crossed from Ireland to Belgium, he became a missionary bishop with headquarters at the Benedictine abbey of St. Peter at Fescan, where he also served as abbot. F. D. July 10.

EUBULUS, ST. (d. 309), martyr. When he refused to sacrifice to pagan gods, during the Diocletian persecution, he was beheaded at Caesarea in Palestine after scourging and torture on Mar. 7. F. D. Mar. 5.

EUCARPIUS, ST. (d. 304?), martyr. He and St. Trophimus were soldiers who, when sent to round up Christians, became converted and were burned to death at Nicomedia during the persecution of Diocletian. F. D. Mar. 18.

EUCHARIUS, ST. (1st century). He is said to have been the first bishop of Trèves in Gaul. F. D. Dec. 8.

EUCHERIUS, ST. (d. 449), bishop. A Gallo-Roman, he married Galla (their sons, Salonius and Veranus, became bishops), and in 422 became a monk at Lérins; Galla became a nun. He left to live as a hermit on a nearby island, wrote many ascetical works, and about 434 was made bishop of Lyons, Gaul. F. D. Nov. 16.

EUCHERIUS, ST. (d. 743), bishop. Born in Orléans, France, he became a Benedictine at Jumièges in 714 and was consecrated bishop of Orléans, against his wishes, seven years later. He opposed Charles Martel's practice of seizing Church revenues for use as war expenditures, and for this was exiled to Cologne and then to Liège. Because he proved very popular in both places he was released and allowed to retire to a monastery near Maastricht, Flanders. F. D. Feb. 20.

EUDES (860?–898), king of France. Son of Robert the Strong, he became count of Paris, was a leader of the defense of Paris against the Normans in 885–87, and, when Emperor Charles III was deposed in 887 and died in 888, he was elected king of the Franks by the nobles in 888. He continued to fight the Normans, faced an increasing tide of opinion in favor of the legitimate Carolingian heir to the throne, Charles the Simple, who contested his claim to the throne, and in 894 had Emperor Arnulf, who had recognized his kingship, withdraw his support in favor of Charles. He made peace with Charles in 897, giving him Laon, and the country between the Seine and the Rhine, and ransomed Paris from the Normans.

EUDES, ST. JOHN (1601–1680), founder. Born in Ri, France, on Nov. 14, of a farming family, he was sent at fourteen to the Jesuit college at Caen. He became an Oratorian at Paris in 1623, was ordained in 1625, twice volunteered to care for victims of plagues in Normandy, and became famous for preaching missions and his opposition to Jansenism. In 1641, with Madeleine Lamy, he founded the Sisters of Our Lady of Charity of the Refuge to care for penitent women of ill repute. This was papally approved in 1666. In 1643 he left the Oratorians to found the Congregation of Jesus and Mary (Eudists), whose secular priests, bound by vows, were to conduct seminaries. He founded seminaries at Lisieux (1653) and at Rouen (1659) but failed to gain papal approval. In 1670, by his book *The Devotion to the Adorable Heart of Jesus,* he originated the liturgical cult of the Sacred Heart and Confraternities of the Hearts of Jesus and Mary in the Eudist seminaries. He composed the mass for the feast of the Sacred Heart in 1668. He died in Caen, France. He was canonized in 1925. F. D. Aug. 19.

EUDES DE MONTREUIL (d. 1289), architect. A relative of Pierre de Montreuil, he went to the Holy Land with St. Louis the Crusader, built fortifications at Jaffa, returned to Paris in 1254, and built churches and an asylum for the blind. He became royal architect in 1254.

EUDO, ST. (d. 760?). He was abbot-founder of the Benedictine monastery of Cormèry-en-Velay (later St. Chaffre, France), having previously studied at Lérins. F. D. Nov. 20.

EUDOCIA (d. 460?), empress. Athenais, daughter of Leontius, a rhetorician at Athens, was converted and baptized at Constantinople, taking the name Eudocia, and married Emperor Theodosius II in 421. She was educated by her husband's sister, Pulcheria, although there later was rivalry between them. From a pilgrimage to Jerusalem in 438 she brought back St. Peter's chains, half of which she sent to her daughter Eudoxia in Rome, who gave them to the pope. In 441 the empress was unjustly charged with adultery with Paulinos, an imperial official; he was murdered and she banished. She lived in Jerusalem until her death. She was briefly a supporter of the Monophysite heresy, but was reconverted by Pope St. Leo I, on whose behalf she was active in persuading Palestinian leaders to support the Catholic

faith at the Council of Chalcedon (451). She wrote much religious poetry: biblical paraphrases, lives of SS. Cyprian and Justina (comparable in part to the Faust legend), and a life of Christ in Homeric hexameters.

EUDOCIA, ST. (2nd century), martyr. A Samaritan in Heliopolis who was converted from an evil life, she was put to death during the reign of Trajan (98–117). F. D. Mar. 1.

EUDOXIUS, ST. (2nd century), martyr. He, Macarius, Zeno, and hundreds of other Christian soldiers were put to death in Armenia during the reign of Trajan. F. D. Sept. 5.

EUDOXIUS, ST. (d. 315?), martyr. *See* Agapius, St.

EUELPISTUS, ST. (d. 165?), martyr. *See* Justin Martyr, St.

EUGENDUS, ST. (d. 510?). A classical and scriptural scholar, he became abbot of the monastery of St. Oyend, at Condat, France, which he rebuilt. F. D. Jan. 1.

EUGENE I, ST. (d. 657), pope. A Roman, he served in place of Pope St. Martin I, who was captured and taken to Constantinople by Emperor Constans II; he assumed his regency, with Martin's approval, on Aug. 10, 654, and succeeded to full power at Martin's death in Sept. 655. He allegedly was approved by Constans, but he refused to accede to a demand that the Monothelite heretics be tolerated and that he acknowledge the patriarch of Constantinople. F. D. June 2.

EUGENE II (d. 827), pope. On the death of Pope Paschal I in Feb. 824, the Roman nobles (though constrained by recent legislation from taking part in the election of a pope) joined with Frankish elements and pushed through the choice of Eugene, a humble archpriest of St. Sabina, Rome, who was consecrated in May. Lothair, son of Emperor Louis the Pious, was sent to Rome to arrange a concordat and strengthen the Frankish position. Eugene's short reign was also marked by difficulties with Emperor Michael II, who broke his promise to end the Iconoclast heresy. A meeting of bishops at Paris in 825, arranged by Louis, made ignorant and worthless findings as to the question of images. In 826 the pope convened a council of eighty-six bishops in Rome, at which it was recommended that all ignorant clergy were to be suspended until they learned enough to properly perform their duties. He died in Aug.

EUGENE III, BL. (d. 1153), pope. Pietro Paganelli was born at Montemagno, near Pisa, became a Cistercian at Clairvaux under St. Bernard, whose name he took in religion, and was sent to Rome as abbot of Tre Montane. On Feb. 15, 1145, he was the unexpected choice for pope, but had to flee the city immediately with the cardinals because a faction led by Arnold of Brescia sought to seize the temporal power. He was consecrated secretly at the abbey of Farfa on Feb. 18, then lived briefly at Viterbo. Arnold arranged a dishonest truce, the pope returned, but the rebels began to pillage churches, burned the palaces of the cardinals, took over St. Peter's as an armory, and drove the pontiff out of Rome. In 1147 he went to France at the invitation of Louis VII and initiated the second crusade; this was a failure, in spite of the efforts of St. Bernard who preached it, and of the pope who inspired the formation of two large armies. In 1148 he returned to Italy, excommunicated Arnold, and threatened to use force against the Romans. They came to terms when they found him serious in his new tactics, but in 1150 political power prevailed, and the pope withdrew to Campania; he died at Tivoli. In spite of the turmoil, his courage and simplicity (he continued to wear the Cistercian habit) endeared him to many. He convoked several synods to correct clerical conduct, removed unworthy churchmen, fought the recurrence of Manichaeism, continued to work for unity with the East, and gave earnest support to the intellectual interests of Peter Lombard and Gratian. His cult was approved in 1872 by Pope Pius IX. F. D. July 8.

EUGENE IV (1383–1447), pope. Gabriello Condulmerio, nephew of Gregory XII, was born in Venice of a wealthy family. He gave his fortune to the poor, became an Augustinian, and at twenty-four was named bishop of Siena, resigned when the city objected to him as an outsider, and in 1408 was created cardinal-priest. He served as papal legate under Martin V, ended the seditious conflict of Bologna, and was elected pope on Mar. 3, 1431, and consecrated on Mar. 11. His simple way of living alienated Roman society and his opposition to nepotism led to an immediate conflict with the Colonna family, who were defeated only when Florence, Naples, and Venice came to the pope's aid. In July 1431 the Council of Basle (convoked by Martin V) met in a mood which Eugene distrusted and, while only a few cardinals and bishops had convened and no action was taken, the pope dissolved it and announced a new meeting for Bologna. Those at Basle refused to leave and early the next year announced the Gallican doctrine that a general council was superior to a pope and commanded Eugene and his court to appear before them. Sigismund, who came to Rome to receive the imperial crown, succeeded in having the pope withdraw the bull for a new council, but Eugene's enemies began a civil war in the city which drove him to exile in Florence. While Eugene's lack of tact had caused trouble up to this date, the council, led by Cardinal d'Allemand, now exceeded all authority; to crush Eugene it cut off sources of papal revenue and

limited his power. The tide turned when the Greeks sought to discuss union and insisted on Italy as the seat of discussion; the council publicly condemned the pope, but Eugene convoked a council at Ferrara in Jan. 1438. The meeting was a success, and the Greeks, Armenians, Jacobites, and Nestorians were reunited before 1445 (though the union was not a lasting one). Initial military and naval victories against the Turks (before the crushing defeat at Varna in 1444) also aided papal prestige. The group at Basle then fell into schism and in 1439 declared Eugene deposed and in 1439 the group (of one cardinal and eleven bishops) elected Felix V, duke of Savoy, as antipope. Eugene was able to return to Rome in 1443, set about restoring the condition of the city, and signed the Frankfort Concordat with Germany, but was unable to end French hostility. He died in Rome on Feb. 23.

EUGENE, ST. (3rd century?), martyr. A disciple of St. Dionysius, he is reputed to have been martyred near Paris. The Roman Martyrology mistakenly listed him as archbishop of Toledo. F. D. Nov. 15.

EUGENE, ST. (d. 305?), martyr. He and SS. Mardonius, Metellus, and Musonius were put to death in northern Africa during the Diocletian persecution. F. D. Jan. 24.

EUGENE, ST. (d. 362), martyr. He and St. Macarius were priests who were exiled to Arabia, then beheaded on orders of Julian the Apostate. F. D. Dec. 20.

EUGENE, ST. (4th century), bishop and martyr. See Aetherius, St.

EUGENE, ST. (d. 422). A disciple of St. Ambrose in Milan, he became a deacon at Florence under St. Zenobius. F. D. Nov. 17.

EUGENE, ST. (d. 484?), martyr. See Aquilinus, St.

EUGENE, ST. (d. 485?), bishop and martyr. He and two other North African bishops, SS. Longinus and Vindemialis, were tortured extremely and put to death by the Vandal King Hunneric. F. D. May. 2.

EUGENE, ST. (d. 657), archbishop. A Goth, born in Toledo, Spain, he became a monk at Saragossa, archdeacon of St. Braulio there, and, against his wish, was appointed archbishop of Toledo in 646. He wrote considerable poetry and prose, and was a gifted musician. F. D. Nov. 13.

EUGENE. See Eoghan, St.

EUGENIA, ST. (d. 257?), martyr. She was slain at Rome during the persecution of Valerian and buried on the Via Latina; other biographical details are mere legend. F. D. Dec. 25.

EUGENIA, ST. (d. 735). Daughter of Duke Adalbert of Alsace, she succeeded St. Odilia as abbess of Hohenburg. F. D. Sept. 16.

EUGENIAN, ST. (4th century), bishop and martyr. A defender of the faith as bishop of

Autun, France, he is said to have died a victim of Arian persecution. F. D. Jan. 8.

EUGÉNIE (1826–1920), empress. Eugénie Marie de Montijo de Guzman y de Porto-Carrero was born in Granada, Spain, on May 5, of Spanish-Scots descent, married to Emperor Napoleon III of France in 1853, and acted as regent of the empire in 1870. She went to England during the communist revolution and after Napoleon's death in 1873 retired to seclusion in Madrid. Their son died in battle in Africa in 1879. She died in Madrid on July 11.

EUGENIUS, ST. (d. 505), bishop. At the end of the fifth century, because of the invasions of the Vandals, the see of Carthage had been vacant for half a century. In 481, Huneric, their king, permitted the Catholics to choose a bishop, but there were so many restrictions on the one hand and, on the other, Eugenius was so influential because of his charity and learning, that the Vandal leader closed the churches to his people. After the meaningless Council of Carthage (484), several Catholic bishops, including Eugenius, were exiled to Tripoli, and tortured there by Antony, an Arian bishop. Eugenius returned briefly to Carthage in 488, again met Vandal opposition, was condemned to death by King Thrasimund, but banished to Languedoc, France, instead. He died in exile there at a monastery near Albi. Because of their sufferings, the bishop and a group of young lectors (Muritta, Salutaris, and others) were called martyrs. F. D. July 13.

EUGENIUS I (d. 647), archbishop. Trained in the monastery of Agli, Spain, he gained fame as an astronomer and mathematician, became archbishop of Toledo, and presided at the fifth Council of Toledo, which, a kind of parliament, was convoked by the crown and attended by civil as well as Church leaders. He also attended the sixth council, which banished the Jews, and the seventh, which required the bishops of Toledo to reside in the city at least one month a year.

EUGENIUS II (d. 657), archbishop. A Goth, he was attached to the cathedral of Toledo and succeeded Eugenius I as archbishop in 647. He wrote a treatise on the Trinity against the Arian Visigoths, poems on religious and contemporary themes, and a recension of the *Hexaemeron* of Draconius, to which he added a "Seventh Day," a reflection on creation; he also edited the *Satisfactio* of Draconius, heavily revising both its poetical form and theological expression. He died in Toledo, Spain, on Nov. 13.

EUGENIUS, ST., martyr. See Eustratius, St.

EUGRAPHUS, ST., martyr. See Mennas, St.

EULALIA OF MÉRIDA, ST. (d. 304?), martyr. A Christian girl of twelve, she was tortured and burned at the stake in Mérida, Spain, during Diocletian's persecution. Pru-

dentius wrote a hymn in her honor and St. Augustine mentions her. F. D. Dec. 10. She is believed to be identical with the St. Eulalia of Barcelona honored on Feb. 12.

EULAMPIA, ST. (d. 310?), martyr. See Eulampius, St.

EULAMPIUS, ST. (d. 310?), martyr. It is said that he was a child in Nicomedia who took refuge in caves to escape the persecution of Galerius. Captured by a soldier when he was trying to buy food, he was subjected to torture; his sister Eulampia ran from the crowd to embrace him and both were beheaded. F. D. Oct. 10.

EULOGIUS, ST. (d. 259), martyr. See Fructuosus, St.

EULOGIUS, ST. (d. 364?), martyr. He and many other Christians were put to death at Constantinople during the persecution of the Arian Emperor Valens. F. D. July 3.

EULOGIUS, ST. (4th century), bishop. Because of his firmness against Arianism he was banished to Egypt from his parish in Edessa, Mesopotamia, but returned on the death of Emperor Valens in 375 and was chosen bishop of Edessa. F. D. May 5.

EULOGIUS, ST. (d. 607?), bishop. Born in Syria, he became a monk and then abbot of Mother of God monastery at Antioch. In 579 he was made patriarch of Alexandria, Egypt. On a journey to Constantinople he met St. Gregory the Great; some of their correspondence is extant, notably one letter referring to Augustine's work in England. Eulogius was most active in combating Monophysitism and other heresies. F. D. Sept. 13.

EULOGIUS, ST. (d. 859), martyr. Brought up in Cordova, Spain, under the restrictions of the Moorish occupation, he studied under Abbot Sperandes, and became a learned priest. During the 850 persecution he wrote an *Exhortation to Martyrdom* to encourage two girls to remain firm in their faith in spite of threatened dishonor, was himself imprisoned, and wrote a long *Memorial of the Saints* about those already put to death. When he tried to hide St. Leocritia, a Moorish convert, he was captured and beheaded. F. D. Mar. 11.

EUMENES, ST. (3rd century). He was bishop of Gortyna, Crete. F. D. Sept. 18.

EUNAN, ST. (8th century). Once honored on Sept. 23, he is now believed to be identical with St. Adamnan of Iona.

EUNICIAN, ST. (d. 250), martyr. See Theodulus, St.

EUNUS, ST. (d. 250), martyr. See Gabriel, St.

EUPHEMIA, ST. (1st century?), martyr. See Dorothy, St.

EUPHEMIA, ST. (d. 300), martyr. See Alexandra, St.

EUPHEMIA, ST. (d. 303?), martyr. She is

said to have refused to attend festivities at Chalcedon in honor of Ares, and to have been seized, tortured, and thrown to wild animals; in another record, she was burned at the stake. F. D. Sept. 16.

EUPHEMIANUS, ST. (d. 820). Born in Constantinople, Anne was married unwillingly, and on the death of her husband adopted male attire and became a recluse in a monastery on Mt. Olympus, taking the name Euphemianus. F. D. Oct. 29.

EUPHRASIA, ST. (d. 300), martyr. See Alexandra, St.

EUPHRASIA, ST. (d. 420?). Daughter of a relative of Emperor Theodius I, she went with her widowed mother to an Egyptian hermitage. At twelve she was an orphan, and wrote to Constantinople that the family wealth be given to the poor, that her slaves be freed, and that she be released from a marriage contract arranged by the emperor. When he acceded, she remained in the desert as an ascetic. F. D. Mar. 13.

EUPHRASIUS, ST. (1st century), martyr. He and SS. Faustian, Inischolus, Januarius, Mannonius, Massalius, and Saturninus, known as "the Seven Holy Thieves," were said to have been converted to Christianity by St. Jason; they later were martyred on Corfu. F. D. Apr. 29.

EUPHRASIUS, ST. (1st century). See Caecilius, St.

EUPHRONIUS (4th century). Bishop of Colonia, Armenia, and later of Nicopolis, he was a friend and correspondent of St. Basil the Great.

EUPHRONIUS, ST. (5th century). He was bishop of Autun, France, in 475 and a friend of St. Lupus of Troyes. F. D. Aug. 3.

EUPHRONIUS, ST. (530–573). He became bishop of Tours, France, in 554. F. D. Aug. 4.

EUPHROSYNE. This daughter of a wealthy citizen of Alexandria, Egypt, turned her back on wordliness and fled into the desert in boy's clothes to spend her life in prayer there. Typical of the heroines of many similar stories, she is probably a pious fiction.

EUPHROSYNE OF POLOTSK, ST. (d. 1173). Daughter of Prince Svyatoslav of Polotsk, Russia, she entered a sisterhood there at twelve, became a recluse, but worked as a copyist of manuscripts, traveled to serve the sick and poor, founded a convent at Seltse, and died while on a pilgrimage to the Holy Land. F. D. May 23.

EUPLIUS, ST. (d. 304), martyr. A deacon at Catania, Sicily, he was racked and beheaded during the Diocletian persecution because he owned a copy of the gospels and refused to sacrifice to the pagan gods. F. D. Aug. 12.

EUPORUS, ST. (d. 250), martyr. See Theodulus, St.

EUPREPIUS, ST. (1st century). He was first bishop of Verona, Italy, sent there, according to tradition, by St. Peter. F. D. Aug. 21.

EUPREPIUS, ST. (d. 303?), martyr. See Cosmas, St.

EUPSYCHIUS, ST. (d. 130?), martyr. He was put to death at Caesarea, Cappadocia, during the reign of Hadrian. F. D. Sept. 7.

EUPSYCHIUS, ST. (d. 362), martyr. He was put to death at Caesarea in Cappadocia on the charge of having destroyed the Temple of Fortune during the days of Julian the Apostate. F. D. Apr. 9.

EUROSIA, ST. (8th century?). Legend calls her a native of Bayonne, France, hunted down and slain at Jaca in the Pyrenees of Aragon, near the French border, by Saracens after she had refused to marry a Moorish officer. F. D. June 25.

EUSEBIA, ST. (3rd century), martyr. Niece of St. Domnio, she was slain near Bergamo, Italy, during the reign of Maximian. F. D. Oct. 29.

EUSEBIA, ST. (d. 680?). Daughter of SS. Adalbald and Rictrudis, she was sent to her grandfather at Hamage after her father was murdered. She became abbess at Hamage, near Doudi, France, was transferred with her community to Marchiennes, of which her mother had charge, and later returned to her own convent. F. D. Mar. 16.

EUSEBIA, ST. (d. 731?), martyr. Abbess of a Benedictine convent at Marseilles, she and forty of her community were put to death at St. Cyr, Gaul, by Mohammedans. F. D. Sept. 20.

EUSEBIUS, ST. (d. 309?), pope. Son of a Greek physician, he was elected pope on Apr. 18, 309 (or 310). He was exiled to Sicily, where he died five months later, by Emperor Maxentius, probably because of the disturbances caused by the *lapsi* under Heraclius, who had opposed both Eusebius and his predecessor, St. Marcellus. F. D. Aug. 17.

EUSEBIUS, ST. (d. 192), martyr. He and SS. Peregrinus, Pontian, and Vincent were slain at Rome during the persecution of Commodus. F. D. Aug. 25.

EUSEBIUS, ST. (d. 254), martyr. During the persecution of Valerian, this Roman priest and Marcellus, his deacon, were beheaded with Mary and Neon. During the same decade, Adria and Hippolytus were beaten to death; Paulina died of torture; Maximus was drowned and Aurelia and Martana were slain. F. D. Dec. 2.

EUSEBIUS, ST. (d. 269), bishop. He was a deacon when he suffered in the persecution at Alexandria, Egypt, which took the life of St. Dionysius (Oct. 3), was ordained, and became bishop of Laodicea. F. D. Oct. 4.

EUSEBIUS, ST. (3rd century), martyr. He

was put to death in Palestine by Maximian. F. D. Aug. 14.

EUSEBIUS, ST. (d. 304), martyr. See Philip, St.

EUSEBIUS, ST. (d. 357?). That he founded a parish in Rome is known, but that he opposed Pope Liberius and was forbidden to say mass is unsubstantiated historically. F. D. Aug. 14.

EUSEBIUS, ST. (d. 362?), martyr. With his brothers, Nestabus and Zeno, he helped destroy a pagan temple at Gaza, Palestine. Imprisoned and scourged, they were carried off by a mob and torn to pieces. Another Christian, Nestor, was scourged, escaped, but died soon after from his wounds. F. D. Sept. 8.

EUSEBIUS, ST. (283?-371), bishop. Born on Sardinia, he was raised in Rome by his mother (his father is reputed to have suffered martyrdom), became lector there, and went to Vercelli, Piedmont. In 340 he was elected its first recorded bishop; according to St. Ambrose, he was the first Western bishop to unite monastic and clerical life. In 355 he attended the Council of Milan called by Emperor Constantius to resolve the difficulties between Catholics and Arians, though he had not intended to appear, as he was convinced the emperor-supported Arians would refuse to accept the decrees of the Nicene Council. He refused to sign the council's decree condemning Athanasius, and demanded that all the delegates sign the Nicene Creed before even considering Athanasius' case. The emperor threatened him, St. Dionysius of Milan, and Lucifer of Cagliari with death if they did not sign the condemnation. They refused and deplored the use of temporal power to enforce ecclesiastical decisions, whereupon the emperor exiled them to the East. Eusebius was sent to Scythopolis in Palestine, under an Arian bishop, Patrophilus, and was subjected to great persecutions by the Arians, then was moved to Cappadocia, and then to Upper Thebaid in Egypt, where he continued his uncompromising resistance to Arianism. On Constantius' death in 361, Emperor Julian permitted the exiled bishops to return to their sees. Eusebius remained in the East to help restore peace to the Church and in 362 attended a council in Alexandria which agreed to deal mildly with repentant apostate bishops. He then went to Antioch to reconcile the Eustathians (adherents of bishop St. Eustathius, exiled by the Arians in 331) and the Meletians (adherents of Bishop Meletius, who had been elected mainly by Arian bishops in 361). He found that Lucifer of Cagliari, a brother legate, had consecrated Paulinus, leader of the Eustathians, bishop, whereas the Alexandrian council had decreed that St. Meletius be recognized as bishop. Lucifer refused to recognize the council's decree and thus began the Luciferian schism. Unable to do anything further in Antioch, Eusebius continued his travels in the East and Illyria, and returned to Vercelli in 363. For the rest of his life he joined with St. Hilary of Poitiers in fighting Arianism in the Western Church and with him was the chief opponent of Arian Bishop Auxentius of Milan. Eusebius was one of the authors of the Athanasian Creed and is generally believed to be the author of the Codex Vercellensis, the oldest manuscript of the Latin gospels in existence. He is called a martyr in the Roman Martyrology because of his sufferings; his death on Aug. 1 at Vercelli, Italy, was peaceful. F. D. Dec. 16.

EUSEBIUS, ST. (d. 379?), bishop. Struggles with the Arians, including Emperor Constantius, marked the reign of this forceful bishop of Samosata, Syria, who first appears in history at the synod in 361 which chose St. Meletius as successor to Eudoxus as patriarch of Antioch. For two years Eusebius tried to bring about unity, but failed. In 372 he went to Caesarea to smooth the way for the appointment of St. Basil as bishop; he then toured the Near East, strengthening the Church against the attack of Emperor Valens, and being exiled to Thrace as a result. He returned to his see in 378, but died soon after when he was felled by a tile thrown by an Arian woman from a roof top as he was installing a bishop at Dolikha, near Samosata. F. D. June 21.

EUSEBIUS, ST. (d. 400?). He became bishop of Bologna, Italy, about 370, was a friend of St. Ambrose and an active opponent of Arianism. F. D. Sept. 26.

EUSEBIUS, ST. (d. 465). Probably of Greek birth, he succeeded St. Lazarus as bishop of Milan in 449, and helped Pope St. Leo I to stifle the Eutychian heresy. F. D. Aug. 12.

EUSEBIUS, ST. (d. 884), martyr. An Irishman who became a monk at St. Gall in Switzerland, he later became a recluse near Röttris, Austria, where he was cut down by a scythe when he denounced the paganism of the peasantry. F. D. Jan. 31.

EUSEBIUS OF ALEXANDRIA (5th century?). He may have been bishop of Alexandria, Egypt, shortly after the death of St. Cyril; he wrote a number of sermons and homilies popular in the sixth and seventh centuries, one of them a valuable commentary on the phrase, "He descended into hell," of the Creed. After ruling his see for seven or twenty years (he is not on any list of bishops, however), he is said to have retired to the desert. Other accounts make him a fifth-century monk; others, a chaplain of Justinian I.

EUSEBIUS BRUNO (11th century), bishop. He studied at Tours under Berengarius, became bishop of Angers in 1049, attended the synod of Rheims that year, and wrote to Rome in defense of Berengarius when the latter was condemned for his false teachings on the Eucharist. At the Council of Tours (1054) he induced Berengarius to admit the real presence of Christ in the Eucharist and seems to have been correct in his later writings. He died in Angers, France, on Aug. 29.

EUSEBIUS OF CREMONA, ST. (d. 423?). Having met St. Jerome in Rome, he became the latter's friend, contributed to his support, and vigorously supported the attack on Origen. Other biographical details and attribution of writings are suspect or baseless. F. D. Mar. 5.

EUSEBIUS OF DORYLAEUM (5th century), bishop. A lawyer at Constantinople, he became known after 423 when as a layman he began to protest strongly against the heretical views proclaimed by Anastasius and Nestorius. Sometime after 430, Eusebius became bishop of Dorylaeum in Asia Minor and found it necessary to condemn his former friend, Eutyches. In 448, Eusebius presented formal charges of heresy against Eutyches before a snyod at Constantinople presided over by Flavian. Eutyches was deposed, but wrote the pope, and another hearing was held in Constantinople in 449. A council was then unlawfully convened at Ephesus by Dioscurus of Alexandria, which deposed and exiled Eusebius and Flavian; Flavian died of mistreatment three days after the verdict. Their names were later cleared by the pope and by Emperor Marcian in 451. Eusebius then attended the Council of Chalcedon, which condemned Dioscurus.

EUSEBIUS OF LAODICEA (d. 268?), bishop. A deacon at Alexandria, Egypt, he, Bishop Dionysius, and five others were tried as Christians and banished at mid-century. Eusebius remained in the city, serving the persecuted Christians; he was still active there during the plague of 260. In 264, Dionysius sent him as legate to Syria to discuss the troubles brewed by Paul of Samosata; there he was made bishop of Laodicea, succeeding Socrates.

EUSEBIUS PAMPHILI (260?–340?), bishop. Born in Palestine, he studied under a learned priest and biblical scholar named Pamphilus, and escaped the persecutions of Diocletian which martyred his master, whose biography he wrote. He also write a life of Constantine and a defense of Origen, became bishop about 313, and was involved in the theological and ecclesiastical battles over Arianism. In spite of some writing to the contrary, including the expressed hostility of St. Jerome, he remained firm and played an important part at the Council of Nicaea. He produced more than fifty works, many of them scriptural commentaries; his most significant are the *Epitome of Universal History* and the *Ecclesiastical History*, from which much information is obtained about early popes, bishops and martyrs.

R. J. DEFERRARI, intro., *Ecclesiastical History* (2 vols. New York, Fathers of the Church, 1953–55).

EUSIGNIUS, ST. (d. 362), martyr. A soldier, he refused to sacrifice to idols on the command of Julian the Apostate and was tortured and beheaded at Antioch, reputedly at the age of 110. F. D. Aug. 5.

EUSTACE, ST. (d. 118?), martyr. Supposedly a Roman officer under Trajan, he became a Christian with his wife Theopistis and two sons, Agapitus and Theopistus; when they refused to sacrifice to the gods they were roasted alive. The story is probably a pious legend. F. D. Sept. 20.

EUSTACE, ST. (d. 235), martyr. *See* Anatolius, St.

EUSTACE, ST (d. 335?), bishop. Born in Side, Pamphylia, he was made bishop of Beroea, Syria, and later was transferred to Antioch. He vigorously opposed Arianism and attended the Council of Nicaea. He spent his last years in exile, after the Arians deposed him from his patriarchate. F. D. July 16.

EUSTACE, ST. (5th century), bishop. *See* Crescens, St.

EUSTACE, ST. (d. 625), abbot. He succeeded St. Columban as the second abbot of Luxeuil, France. F. D. Mar. 29.

EUSTACE, ST. (d. 1211). Born near Beauvais, France, he became a priest there, then joined the Cistercian order and became abbot of Flay (St. Germer). Pope Innocent III appointed him apostolic legate to England and later in southern France to combat Albigensianism. F. D. Sept. 7.

EUSTACE, ST. (d. 1342), martyr. *See* Antony, St.

EUSTACE, BARTHOLOMEW JOSEPH (1887–1956), bishop. Born in New York City, on Oct. 9, he studied at St. Francis Xavier, St. Joseph's seminary, Yonkers, and the North American College, Rome, and was ordained in Rome in 1914. He did parish work in the New York archdiocese, taught at St. Joseph's from 1916 to 1937, then was appointed first bishop of Camden, New Jersey. He died on Nov. 11.

EUSTACE, JOHN CHETWODE (1762?–1815). Born in Ireland of English parents, he was educated at Douai, taught and was ordained at Maynooth, went to England as a private chaplain, and became a tutor at Cambridge. He made several trips to the Continent, attained fame with his *Classical Tour* (1813), became friendly with the literary circle of Edmund Burke, and published a *Political Catechism* (1810), *Letter from Paris* (1814) and *The Proofs of Christianity* (1814). His work was not above error, and he was censured for indifferentism by his vicar apostolic. He died of malaria in Naples on Aug. 1.

EUSTACE, MAURICE (d. 1581), martyr.

Born in Castle-Martin, Kildare, Ireland, he was educated at Bruges, Flanders, wished to become a priest, but was recalled to Ireland by his father, Sir John Eustace, and put into military service as a cavalry captain. A servant and a younger brother reported his secret ordination to his father, who had him imprisoned. When he refused to give up his faith he was publicly hanged in Dublin in Nov.

EUSTACHIO BARTOLOMMEO (d. 1574), anatomist. Born in San Severino, Italy, he was well educated in the classics and Arabic, took his degree in medicine, and became physician to St. Charles Borromeo and Cardinal della Rovere. He went to Rome with the latter, became professor of medicine at Sapienza in Rome in 1562, and published widely on the kidneys, blood vessels, the teeth of children, mastoid muscles, cranial nerves, fetal circulation, and anatomical structure. His name has been given to the canal linking the ear and the mouth, and also to the valve carrying blood from mother to child during pregnancy. His experiments and reports were recorded in a series of annotated illustrations, *Tabulae anatomicae* (1552), which were scattered when he died suddenly in Rome in Aug.; they were not edited and published until 1714.

EUSTATHIUS, ST. (270?–340?), bishop. Born in Side, Pamphylia, he was made bishop of Beroea in Syria and transferred to Antioch about 323. He participated in the Council of Nicaea (325) and was a leader in the struggle against the Arians. When they gained control, they deposed him in 330 and exiled him to Trajanopolis in Thrace. The people of the area had such high regard for him that they refused not only to accept his Arian successor but also Bishop Meletius, the compromise choice of the Arians and the Christians. Unfortunately, this independence resulted in the Meletian schism, which lasted nearly a century. Eustathius wrote much, but little is extant beyond a homily on Lazarus and his sisters and a criticism of Origen for extremes in the allegorical interpretation of scripture. F. D. July 16.

EUSTATHIUS (d. 1194?), archbishop. Born in Constantinople, he studied there, became a monk at St. Florus, served as deacon of St. Sophia, teacher of rhetoric, and imperial secretary, tutor to the children of Manuel Comnenus I, and in 1174 became archbishop of Myra. Before his installation the emperor moved him to Thessalonica, where he sought to introduce monastic reforms and protected his flock against excessive taxation and during the Norman invasion of 1185. He wrote a history of this event, *Considerations on the Monastic Life*, festal sermons, a tract on hypocrisy, commentaries on Homer, Pindar, and other authors, and theological studies. Because of his outspoken criticism of those in high places,

monastic and civil, he was removed from his see, but appears to have died in office in Thessalonica.

EUSTERIUS, ST. (5th century). He is listed as fourth bishop of Salerno, Italy. F. D. Oct. 19.

EUSTOCHIUM, ST. (d. 362), martyr. She was tortured and died in prison at Tarsus, Cilicia, during the persecution of Julian the Apostate. F. D. Nov. 2.

EUSTOCHIUM, ST. (d. 419?). Daughter of Toxotius (who died when she was twelve), she went to Jerusalem with her mother, St. Paula, to accept the spiritual direction of St. Jerome. She was the first noble Roman girl to take the vow of perpetual virginity, which was the occasion of Jerome's *Concerning the Keeping of Virginity* (384). The two women helped Jerome in his translation of the Bible when his sight failed, and he dedicated several of his commentaries to them. On the death of Paula in 404, Eustochium became superior of the community at Bethlehem, whose monastery was burned down in 417, an action protested by Pope St. Innocent I in a letter to John of Jerusalem. She died in Bethlehem. F. D. Sept. 28.

EUSTOCHIUM OF MESSINA, BL. (1432–1468). Daughter of the count of Calafato, and called Smaragda, she became a Franciscan Conventual at Basico, Italy, after her father's death, and devoted herself to the care of the poor and plague-stricken. After eleven years she was allowed to found a convent under a stricter rule, at Monte Vergine, where she was joined by her sister and niece, and where she became abbess at thirty. Her cult was approved in 1782. F. D. Feb. 15.

EUSTOCHIUM OF PADUA (1443–1469). Daughter of a seduced nun, she herself became a sister at San Prosdosimo in Padua, the convent in which she had been born. Her actions for long periods of time were called evidence of diabolical possession; she was kept prisoner as a madwoman, denounced as a witch after the abbess became mysteriously ill, and completely shunned by the community for four years. Her confessor insisted on her innocence and she was allowed to take her vows; later, through patience and devotion, she gained the great respect of her associates. She was called Blessed in the locality and commemorated on Feb. 13.

EUSTOCHIUS, ST. (d. 362), martyr. *See* Elpidius, St.

EUSTOCHIUS, ST. (d. 461). He succeeded St. Brice in 444 as bishop of Tours, France. F. D. Sept. 19.

EUSTORGE DE MONTAIGU (d. 1250). He became archbishop of Nicosia, Cyprus, in 1217, was an effective administrator, established schools, built the cathedral of St. Sophia, and died at the siege of Damietta, Egypt.

EUSTORGIUS, ST. (d. 300?), martyr. A

priest in Nicomedia, he was put to death there, probably during the Diocletian persecution. F. D. Apr. 11.

EUSTORGIUS, ST. (4th century). A Greek, he was bishop of Milan, Italy, from 315 to past 331, and was active against Arianism. F. D. Sept. 18.

EUSTORGIUS II, ST. (d. 518). He became bishop of Milan in 512, having lived in Rome before that time. He was widely respected for his piety and competence, even by Theodoric the Great, and exhausted his fortune in ransoming parishioners who were captured by barbarian hordes. F. D. June 6.

EUSTOSIUS, ST., martyr. See Demetrius, St.

EUSTRATIUS, ST. (4th century), martyr. According to the Roman Martyrology, he was an Armenian who was tortured in Sebastea, Armenia, during Diocletian's persecution and then burned to death in a furnace. With him suffered Orestes, a soldier, who was roasted to death on a gridiron; the latter's servant, Eugenius; and Mardarius and Auxentius, friends of Eugenius, who were martyred when they pleaded for his life. There is no definite proof of their existence. F. D. Dec. 13.

EUTHALIUS (5th century), bishop. A deacon at Alexandria, Egypt, he developed earlier schemes for marking off scriptural divisions into chapters and verses. Ammonius had done this for the gospels; Euthalius completed the divisions, except for the Apocalypse. He also made a systematic arrangement of passages from the epistles to be read on each Sunday of the year and on four major feasts. Scholars are able to date writings which quote according to his arrangement, though it no longer is used. He also prepared a catalogue of quotations from the Old Testament and a life of St. Paul and was bishop of Sulca (perhaps Psilka, near Syene, in the Thebaid).

EUTHEMIUS, ST. (4th century). A Roman, he escaped with his wife and child, St. Crescentius, to Perugia, Italy, during the Diocletian persecution. F. D. Aug. 29.

EUTHYMIUS, ST. (d. 303), martyr. He was slain at Nicomedia, Bithynia, after encouraging others martyred during the Diocletian persecution. F. D. Dec. 24.

EUTHYMIUS, ST. (d. 840), bishop and martyr. As bishop of Sardis in Lydia he opposed the Iconoclast heresy and was banished by Emperor Nicephorus. He was in exile for twenty-nine years before he was scourged to death. F. D. Mar. 11.

EUTHYMIUS, ST. (824?–898). Born at Opso, near Ancyra, Galatia, and baptized Nicetas, he married early, had a daughter, and left in 842 to become a monk on Mt. Olympus in Bithynia and later a hermit on Mt. Athos. In 863 he went to Salonika, lived on a tower, was ordained deacon, and then restored the nearby

monastery of St. Andrew, which he ruled for fourteen years. He spent the remainder of his life in solitude at Athos and is known as "the New," "the Younger," and "the Thessalonian." F. D. Oct. 15.

EUTHYMIUS, ST. (d. 1028). Son of St. John the Iberian, he followed his father into seclusion on Mt. Athos and in building the monastery of Iviron, where in 1002 he succeeded his father as abbot. He translated biblical commentaries, the *Institutes* of Cassian, the *Dialogues* of Gregory the Great, and the work of other Church Fathers into Georgian. After fourteen years as abbot he gave up his post to devote all his time to translating. He died in Constantinople. F. D. May 13.

EUTHYMIUS THE GREAT, ST. (378–473). Born of wealthy Armenian parents, he retired from the world at twenty-nine, and, after a pilgrimage to Jerusalem, became a hermit outside that city. About 411 he joined an even more remote group, becoming their spiritual director and enjoining them to earn their living by manual labor and to avoid extremes in fasting. His charity and cures attracted so many Arab converts that he was consecrated a bishop by Patriarch Juvenal. He attended the Council of Ephesus in 431, won back the heretical Empress Eudoxia in 459, taught the young St. Sabas, and died at ninety-five after sixty-eight years of the strictest solitude that these and many similar interruptions permitted. F. D. Jan. 20.

EUTICIUS, ST. (d. 305?), martyr. See Januarius, St.

EUTROPIA, ST. (d. 253?), martyr. She was put to death in Africa, probably during the Valerian persecution. F. D. Oct. 30.

EUTROPIA, ST. (d. 303?). A girl of twelve, she was ordered shot to death by arrows during the persecution of Diocletian. Two sisters, Leonis and Lybe, were burned to death at the same time, in Palmyra, Syria. F. D. June 15.

EUTROPIA, ST. (d. 451?), martyr. See Nicasius, St.

EUTROPIS. See Basiliscus, St.

EUTROPIUS, ST. (d. 273?), martyr. See Bonosa, St.

EUTROPIUS, ST. (d. 298?), martyr. See Basiliscus, St.

EUTROPIUS, ST. (3rd century), bishop and martyr. Sent from Rome to evangelize Saintes, France, he became its first bishop, was barred from his see, but preached just outside it, converted the governor's daughter, Eustella, and was chopped to death when this was discovered. F. D. Apr. 30.

EUTROPIUS, ST. (d. 404), martyr. A reader at Constantinople, he, with St. Tigrius, a priest, was tortured by torches after the senate building was destroyed by fire following the banishment of St. John Chrysostom. Although he disclosed no information, he died under the severity of the punishment. F. D. Jan. 12.

EUTROPIUS, ST. (d. 476?), bishop. Born in Marseilles, France, he became a priest after the death of his wife, became bishop of Orange, and raised his diocese out of the spirit of defeat into which it fell after the Visigoth invasion. F. D. May 27.

EUTROPIUS (d. 610?), bishop. A monk in Valencia, Spain, he wrote three letters, referred to by St. Isidore, on baptism, monastic discipline, and the eight deadly sins (pride, vanity, covetousness, gluttony, lust, anger, sadness, and faintheartedness), in his discussion of which he follows Cassian. These were written before 589, when he became bishop of Valencia. He is sometimes called saint, though there is no evidence of a cult.

EUTYCHES, ST. (d. 99?), martyr. He and SS. Maro and Victorinus went into exile on Ponza with St. Flavia Domitilla, returned to Rome, and were put to death there during the reign of Trajan. F. D. Apr. 15.

EUTYCHIAN, ST. (d. 283), pope. A native of Luni, Italy, he succeeded St. Felix I as pope on Jan. 4, 275. It is unlikely that he was a martyr, although he is so listed in the Roman Martyrology. F. D. Dec. 7.

EUTYCHIAN, ST. (d. 285?), martyr. See Ariston, St.

EUTYCHIAN, ST. (d. 301?), martyr. See Straton, St.

EUTYCHIAN, ST. (d. 437), martyr. See Arcadius, St.

EUTYCHIUS, ST. (1st century). A Phrygian, he was a disciple of St. Paul, is said to have served St. John at Patmos and to have been martyred; he sometimes is identified with the young man raised from the dead by Paul (Acts 20). F. D. Aug. 24.

EUTYCHIUS, ST. (3rd century), martyr. He and SS. Polius and Timothy were deacons in Mauretania, and put to death there during the Diocletian persecution. F. D. May 21.

EUTYCHIUS, ST. (d. 300?), martyr. He and SS. Honorius and Stephen were slain at Asta, Spain, during the Diocletian persecution. F. D. Nov. 21.

EUTYCHIUS, ST. (d. 356), martyr. A subdeacon in Alexandria, he was sentenced by the Arians to life in the mines, but died while being driven there as a slave; many others also were put to death at the time for their loyalty to the Church and to St. Athanasius. F. D. Mar. 26.

EUTYCHIUS, ST. (4th century), martyr. He was starved in a Roman prison for twelve days and then put to death by drowning. F. D. Feb. 4.

EUTYCHIUS, ST. (4th century), martyr. He was put to death either at Cadiz or Mérida, Spain. F. D. Dec. 11.

EUTYCHIUS (512?–582), patriarch. Born in Phrygia, he became a monk in Pontus, and while on a diplomatic mission to Constantinople in 552 was selected by Emperor Justinian I to succeed Mennas as patriarch. He presided at the fifth General Council of Constantinople in 553, to the convening of which Pope Vigilius had given and then refused approval; the council condemned Origen and others, but did not stem the advance of Monophysitism, as Justinian hoped. When the emperor approved heretical teaching as to the nature of Christ's human body, Eutychius objected and in 565 was deposed and exiled. In 577 he returned from Amasea at the request of Emperor Justin II, but fell into heresy himself, denying the immortality of the body. He returned to the Church after correction by St. Gregory the Great, then papal legate at Constantinople, before his death on Apr. 6.

EUTYCHIUS, ST. (6th century). He was abbot of a monastery at Valcastoria, Italy, and was highly praised by St. Gregory the Great for his holiness. F. D. May 23.

EUTYCHIUS, ST. (d. 741), martyr. A patrician who refused to give up his faith, he was mercilessly tortured and burned to death with many other Christians at Carrhae in Mesopotamia during an Arab persecution. F. D. Mar. 14.

EVA OF LIÈGE, BL. (d. 1265?). She was a recluse near the church of St. Martin, Liège, Flanders, to which Bl. Juliana went when driven from Cornillon; she shared Juliana's interest in the celebration of Corpus Christi and lived to see the feast liturgically instituted. F. D. May 26.

EVAGRIUS, ST. (d. 380?). He was chosen bishop of Constantinople in 370, but was banished for life after a few months by the Arian Emperor Valens. F. D. Mar. 6.

EVAGRIUS PONTICUS (345–399). Born in Ibora on the Black Sea, he was taught by St. Gregory of Nazianzus, was given lower orders by St. Basil the Great, and went as deacon with St. Gregory of Nyssa to the second Council of Constantinople (381). He left the city because he condemned its way of life, became a hermit in Jerusalem and Egypt, and was famous for his ascetical writings. They were criticized by St. Jerome and condemned as Origenistic by the sixth, seventh, and eighth ecumenical councils.

EVAGRIUS SCHOLASTICUS (536–594?), historian. Born in Epiphania, Syria, he was an advocate at Antioch, defended Patriarch Gregory before the Council of Constantinople (588), held several imperial posts, and wrote an *Ecclesiastical History* (a sequel to Eusebius, Socrates, Sozomen, and Theodoret), covering the period from the Council of Ephesus (431) to the end of the reign of Emperor Maurice

(594). It contains personal sketches and references to art, as well as detailed political and religious history. He quotes judiciously from other writers, recounts many legends, is moderate toward heretics, but overly kind toward Constantine.

EVAL, ST. (6th century). He was a bishop in Cornwall. F. D. Nov. 20.

EVANGELIST, BL. (d. 1250?). A school companion in Verona, Italy, of Bl. Peregrine, he entered the Augustinians there at the same time; they devoted themselves to prayer and the healing of the sick, and died on the same day. Their cult was approved in 1837. F. D. Mar. 20.

EVANS, BL. PHILIP (1645–1679), martyr. Born in Monmouthshire, Wales, he was educated at St. Omer and became a Jesuit at twenty. After ordination at Liège in 1675 he was sent to southern Wales. Arrested in 1678, he was charged with association in the Titus Oates Plot and hanged in Cardiff, Wales, with Bl. John Lloyd. He was beatified in 1929. F. D. July 22.

EVARISTUS, ST. (d. 105), pope. He succeeded St. Clement in 97. According to *Liber pontificalis* (written in the sixth century), he was born in Jerusalem of a Jewish father, but is later listed as a Greek. There is no evidence of his martyrdom. F. D. Oct. 26.

EVARISTUS, ST. (d. 250), martyr. See Theodulus, St.

EVARISTUS, ST. (d. 304?), martyr. See Carponius, St.

EVASIUS, ST. (d. 362?), martyr. He is said to have been the first bishop of Asti, Italy, put to death at Casale Monferrato during the persecution of Julian the Apostate. F. D. Dec. 1.

EVELLIUS, ST. (d. 66?), martyr. He is said to have been a counselor to Nero, who was converted by observing the patience of Christians, and who was thereupon put to death in Pisa, Italy. F. D. May 11.

EVENTIUS, ST. (d. 113?), martyr. See Alexander, St.

EVENTIUS, ST. (d. 304), martyr. See Apodemius, St.

EVERAERTS, JAN NICOLAI (1511–1536), poet. Born at The Hague, he studied law at Bourges, traveled in Italy and Spain, was secretary to Cardinal Tavera of Toledo, and went with Charles V on his expedition to Tunis. He wrote much graceful Latin poetry; *Basia* appeared in 1539 and his *Opera poetica* was compiled by his brothers in 1541. He is also known as Joannes Secundus.

EVERGISLUS, ST. (d. 600?), bishop. According to the Roman Martyrology, he was raised and educated by St. Severinus of Cologne, became his archdeacon, succeeded him as bishop, and was murdered by robbers in Tongres. The facts of his life are confused, but

he probably lived later and died peacefully. F. D. Oct. 24.

EVERILDIS, ST. (d. 700?). Daughter of a noble family, she went to York, England, with two companions, founded a convent there after she was professed by St. Wilfrid, and became the first abbess of its large community. F. D. July 9.

EVERMOD, ST. (d. 1178), bishop. He entered religious life after hearing St. Norbert preach, then worked for the spread of the Premonstratensians in Flanders, succeeded his master as superior at Gottesgnaden, in 1138 became abbot at Magdeburg, and in 1154 the first bishop of Ratzeburg. He is called the apostle to the Wends. F. D. Feb. 17.

EVERMUND, ST. (d. 730?). Born in Bayeux, France, he was a married courtier, founded several religious centers, and, when his wife agreed to become a nun, became abbot-founder of the Benedictine monastery of Fontenay-Louvet, in the diocese of Séez, France. F. D. June 10.

EVILASIUS, ST. (d. 303), martyr. See Fausta, St.

EVODIUS, ST. (d. 64?), bishop. Traditionally called one of the seventy disciples of Christ, he is said to have been the predecessor of St. Ignatius as bishop of Antioch. The historian Malabas says that St. Peter consecrated the latter after he had visited the deathbed of Evodius. F. D. May 6.

EVODIUS, ST. (5th century). He was bishop of Rouen, France. F. D. Oct. 8.

EVODIUS, ST. (6th century). He was bishop of Le Puy, France, as late as 560. F. D. Nov. 12.

EVORTIUS, ST. (d. 340?). He came from Rome to serve as bishop of Orléans, Gaul. F. D. Sept. 7.

EWALD THE DARK, ST. (d. 695?), martyr. See Ewald the Fair, St.

EWALD THE FAIR, ST. (d. 695?), martyr. With his brother Ewald, who was called "the Dark," he was a priest from Northumbria who, after a period of study in Ireland, preached the gospel to the Old Saxons in Westphalia. In 694 they followed St. Willibrord to Germany to preach and were slain at Aplerbeke, near Dortmund. F. D. Oct. 3.

EWEN. See Hywyn.

EWING, CHARLES (1835–1883), general. Born in Lancaster, Ohio, on Mar. 6, fifth son of Thomas and Maria Ewing, he studied in the nearby Dominican college, at Gonzaga College, Washington, and at Virginia, and in 1860 began law practice in St. Louis, Missouri. He served as a captain with the 13th Infantry Regulars at the start of the Civil War, was in the Arkansas and Mississippi campaigns, wounded three times at Vicksburg, made a lieutenant colonel, and joined his brother-in-law Gen. Sherman on the march through Georgia.

He became a brigadier general, was cited for gallantry at Vicksburg and Atlanta, and in 1867 returned to his law practice. In 1873 he became Indian commissioner. He died in Washington, D.C., on June 20.

EWING, HUGH BOYLE (1826–1905), general. Born in Lancaster, Ohio, on Oct. 31, third son of Thomas and Maria Ewing, he graduated from West Point, studied law, and practiced in St. Louis, Missouri, from 1854 to 1856 and at Leavenworth, Kansas, from 1856 to 1858 with his brother Thomas. He was colonel of the 30th Ohio Volunteers at the start of the Civil War, became a brigadier general in 1862, led the assault on Vicksburg in May 1863, and led the 4th Division of the 15th Corps in the Chattanooga and Missionary Ridge campaigns. He left the army as a major general and was appointed by President Johnson to serve as minister to The Hague from 1866 to 1870. He wrote a number of popular narratives, including *The Grand Ladron, a Tale of Early California,* based on a visit he made in 1849. He died in Lancaster on June 30.

EWING, PHILEMON (1820–1896), judge. Born in Lancaster, Ohio, he graduated from Miami University, was admitted to the bar in 1841, and went into partnership with his father, Thomas. He was active as a Whig and Republican, became judge of the court of common pleas in 1862 and of the state supreme court in 1873, and, like his father, was a strong opponent of reconstructionist policies. He died in Lancaster on Apr. 15.

EWING, THOMAS (1789–1871), lawyer. Born in West Liberty, in what is now West Virginia, on Dec. 28, he was brought up in Ohio, studied at home, then entered Ohio University, where in 1815 he received the first degree granted in the western area. He was admitted to the bar in 1816, practiced in Lancaster, was elected United States senator in 1830, defended Clay's tariff, opposed slavery, and resisted President Jackson. He returned to law in 1837, was named secretary of the treasury by President Harrison in 1841, and resigned late that year when his bill for the recharter of the Bank of the United States was vetoed. He was secretary of the interior in 1849–50 under Taylor, filled an unexpired senatorial term until March 1851, and returned to his law work. He was an adviser to President Lincoln during the Civil War, secured the freeing of the English envoys, Mason and Slidell, and opposed the extremists of the reconstruction period. In 1820 he had married an Irish Catholic girl, Maria Wills Boyle, and he became a convert in 1869. Although they had a large family of their own, they adopted William Tecumseh Sherman at nine, when his father died in 1829. Ewing died in Lancaster, Ohio, on Oct. 26.

EXANTHUS, ST. (d. 295?), martyr. *See* Carpophorus, St.

EXANTHUS, ST. (d. 303?), martyr. *See* Fidelis, St.

EXMEW, BL. WILLIAM (d. 1535), martyr. *See* Middlemore, Bl. Humphrey.

EXUPERANTIUS, ST. (d. 303?), martyr. *See* Sabinus, St.

EXUPERANTIUS, ST. (d. 418). He became bishop of Ravenna, Italy, in 398, saved part of the city from the raiding army of Stilicho, and built the town of Argenta. F. D. May 30.

EXUPERANTIUS, ST. (5th century). Believed to be of African origin, he became bishop of Cingoli, near Ancona, Italy. F. D. Jan. 24.

EXUPERATUS, ST. (4th century). He is listed as one of the earliest bishops of Coutances, France.

EXUPERIUS, ST. (d. 140), martyr. *See* Cyriacus, St.

EXUPERIUS, ST. (d. 170), martyr. He and SS. Felician and Severinus were slain at Vienne, Gaul, during the reign of Marcus Aurelius. F. D. Nov. 19.

EXUPERIUS, ST. (d. 287?), martyr. *See* Maurice, St.

EXUPERIUS, ST. (d. 412?), bishop. Probably born in Arreau, Gaul, he became bishop of Toulouse about 405. St. Jerome dedicated his commentary on Zacharias to him and wrote of his gifts to the poor of Palestine. Pope St. Innocent I also wrote him, answering a request for a list of authentic books of the Bible. F. D. Sept. 28.

EYB, ALBRECHT VON (1420?–1475). Born near Ansbach, Franconia, he studied at Erfurt, Pavia, and Bologna, was a canon at Eichstätt and Bamberg, returned to Bologna from 1452 to 1459 for his law degree, and was appointed chamberlain by Pope Pius II. He wrote *Ehebüchlein* (1472), a popular work on marriage which quickly ran through numerous editions; *Spiegel der Sitten,* a commentary on morals; *Margarita poetica,* a humanistic rhetoric; and translations of two plays by Plautus. He was at Eichstätt and Würzburg during his last years.

EYMARD, BL. PETER JULIAN (1811–1868), founder. Born in La Mure, France, he worked at his father's trade as cutler until eighteen, when he went to the seminary at Grenoble and was ordained in 1834. He served as a parish priest for several years, then joined the Marists and in 1845 became their provincial at Lyons. He outlined to his superiors his plan for a religious congregation devoted to the Blessed Sacrament and in 1857 received approval and a residence from the archbishop of Paris. In 1858 he established the Servants of the Blessed Sacrament, whose nuns devoted themselves to perpetual adoration; in 1859,

Pope Pius IX approved his Priests of the Sacred Heart. Bl. Peter also founded the Priests' Eucharistic league, organized the Archconfraternity of the Blessed Sacrament, and wrote several books on the Eucharist. He died on Aug. 1 at La Mure and was beatified in 1929. F. D. Aug. 4.

EYMERIC, NICOLAS (1320?–1399), theologian. Born in Gerona, Spain, he became a Dominican in 1334, wrote on philosophy, and was appointed grand inquisitor of Aragon after 1357. His zeal aroused hostility and he was removed after three years, turning to teaching and writing theology. He was again inquisitor by 1366, vigorously opposed the writings of Ramón Lull, and supported antipope Clement VII. Although banished by King John I at the instance of Lull's friends, Eymeric remained inquisitor; he resided at Avignon and wrote in support of Clement and of Benedict XIII, as well as *Directorium inquisitorum*. He returned to his monastery in Gerona in 1397, and died there on Jan. 4.

EYNON, BL. JOHN (d. 1539), martyr. *See* Cook, Bl. Hugh.

EYRE, CHARLES (1817–1902), archbishop. He was consecrated titular archbishop of Anazarba and became administrator apostolic of the vicariate of Scotland, residing in Glasgow, in 1869. When the Scots hierarchy was restored in 1878 by Pope Leo XIII, Eyre became archbishop of Glasgow, reorganized the diocese, established a cathedral chapter, and instituted educational reforms. He also built a seminary at his own expense. He died on Mar. 27.

EYRE, THOMAS (1748–1810), educator. Born in Glossop, Derbyshire, England, he was educated at Douai, ordained there, and sent back to Newcastle in 1775. He taught in several localities, added to his charges the exiled students who had been studying under the historian Lingard, and set up what was to be called Ushaw College. He served as its first president from 1794 to 1808 (though the school was known as St. Cuthbert's until 1803). He gathered materials for a church history which he left to the college, together with a small fortune. He died in Ushaw on May 8.

EYSTEIN ERLANDSSON (d. 1188), archbishop. Chaplain of King Inge of Norway in 1157, he was consecrated bishop of Nidaros (now Trondhjem) at Rome by Pope Alexander III, and returned as papal legate. He crowned the eight-year-old Magnus as king in 1164 at Bergen, established communities of Augustinian canons regular in the hope of recommending celibacy to the native clergy, and introduced helpful civil laws. When Sverre claimed the throne in 1181, Eystein went to England, from where he excommunicated the rebel. In England he wrote *The Passion* and *Miracles of St. Olaf* and became devoted to St. Thomas à Becket, devotion to whom he brought back to Norway. He sought to return in 1183, but was shunted to Denmark when he ran into a naval engagement. When Magnus died in battle, Eystein was apparently reconciled with the new king and restored to his see. He was called saint at the thirteenth-century Norwegian synod and honored on Jan. 26, but the decree was never confirmed by the papacy.

EYSTON, CHARLES (1667–1721). Born in East Hendred, England, he succeeded to the family estates on the death of his father, George, in 1691, married Winifred Fitzherbert, and wrote a history of English abbeys (unpublished) and an account of Glastonbury published by Thomas Hearne, the antiquarian. He died on Nov. 5.

EYZAGUIRRE, IGNATIUS VICTOR (19th century). Born in Chile, he was ordained and worked there for many years. He went to Rome in 1857 and proposed the establishment of a South American College for seminarians from the Spanish and Portuguese areas of the New World. Pope Pius IX, who had served in Chile as apostolic delegate, favored the plan, found quarters, and contributed the start of a library. Fr. Eyzaguirre, who had been made a monsignor, returned to South America to collect funds. The college was formally opened in Nov. 1858.

EZNIK (5th century). Born in Golp, northern Armenia, he studied under Katholikos Isaac and in Edessa and Constantinople, and probably was the bishop of Bagrevand who attended the Synod of Artashat in 449. He wrote biblical studies, a collection of moral epigrams, and *Against the Sects* (after 441), a study of Greek heresies and that of Marcion.

EZZO (11th century), poet. A priest in Bamberg, Germany, he wrote *Cantilena de miraculis Christi* on the creation, fall, and redemption of man, at the request of Bishop Gunther; the poem, in the East Franconian dialect, was widely popular.

F

FAA DI BRUNO (1825–1888), mathematician. Born in Alessandria, Italy, on Mar. 7, he was a captain in the Sardinian army, studied at Paris and Turin, was ordained, and taught mathematics at Turin until his death there on Mar. 26. He wrote on the theory of elliptic functions and of binary forms, numerous other mathematical papers, ascetical works, and some musical compositions.

FABER, CECILIA BÖHL VON (1796–1877), novelist. Born in Morges, Switzerland, on Dec. 25, she was brought to Cadiz, Spain, in 1813 after her family had been to Germany and Italy. She married and lost three husbands, the last being Antonio Arrón de Ayala, Spanish consul in Australia. At his death in 1863 she settled in Seville. She had written for newspapers and journals under the pen name Fernán Caballero and her first novel *La Gaviota* (*The Sea Gull*) appeared serially in 1849; others were *Clemencia, La Familia de Albareda,* and *Elía,* which dealt with Andalusian customs and family life. Her complete works were published in thirteen volumes (1860–61). She died in Seville, Spain, on Apr. 7.

FABER, FELIX (1441?–1502). Born in Zurich, Switzerland, he studied in Basle and Ulm, became a Dominican, was provincial in Germany in 1486, following a pilgrimage to Palestine and Syria in 1483–84, of which he published an account. His *Historia Suevorum* details the history of the Swiss to 1489; he also translated a life of Henry Suso. He died in Ulm, Germany.

FABER, FREDERICK WILLIAM (1814–1863). Born in Calverley, Yorkshire, England, on June 28, he studied at Harrow and Oxford, began to translate the Fathers of the Church, was ordained an Anglican minister in 1839, and became rector at Elton in 1843. In 1844 he preached in favor of the Oxford Movement and the next year became a convert. In 1846 he formed in Staffordshire a religious community called the Wilfridians, after St. Wilfrid, whose life he had written; he was ordained in 1847, and in 1848 transferred himself and many of his followers to Newman's oratory in Birmingham. He founded and was first superior of the oratory in London in 1849, opened a school for the poor, was widely admired as a confessor and counselor, and began writing hymns for evening services he directed. In the next ten years he published forty-nine devotional lives of the saints, eight ascetical volumes, two volumes of sermon notes, and a collection of poetry. His last nine years were spent at South Kensington, England, where the oratory moved in 1854, and where he died on Sept. 26.

FABER, JOHANN (1478–1541), theologian. Born in Leutkirch, Swabia, he studied at Tübingen and Freiburg, was minister of Lindau, in 1518 vicar general of Constance, in 1524 chaplain to King Ferdinand I of Austria, and in 1530 bishop of Vienna. He was a student of the Fathers of the Church and an active reformer who at first was sympathetic toward Melanchthon and Zwingli, but who later opposed them and Luther in debate and published work. He wrote on faith and good works, the mass, consolation, the religion of Russians, and polemical tracts, one of which, *Malleus haereticorum* (1524) gave him the name "Hammer of Heretics." He died in Vienna on May 21.

FABER, JOHANN AUGUSTANUS (1470?–1531?), theologian. Born in Fribourg, Switzerland, he became a Dominican in Augsburg, taking the name Augustanus, took his doctorate in theology, and in 1511 became vicar general for Upper Germany. He was court preacher and counselor under Emperor Maximilian I and again under Charles V, to whom he was recommended by Erasmus. He was a classical humanist, but failed in a proposed plan to make peace with Luther and the reformers.

FABER, JOHANN (1504–1558). Born in Heilbronn, Wittenberg, he became a Dominican at sixteen, preached briefly at Augsburg in 1534 until Catholic speech was banned, and returned to Cologne to study and edit works by Richard Rolle. He worked at Wimpfen and Colmar, preached in Augsburg from 1545 to 1552, took his doctorate in theology at Ingolstadt under Peter Canisius, and returned to Augsburg, Bavaria, where he died on Feb. 27. He wrote on St. Peter, the gospels, and other biblical studies and doctrinal expositions.

FABER, PHILIP (1564–1630), theologian. Born in Spinata di Brisighella, Italy, he became a Conventual Franciscan at Cremona in 1582. He taught in several schools before being named professor of theology at Padua in 1606. He became provincial in 1625 and wrote numerous commentaries on Duns Scotus, as well as studies of the primacy of Peter and the *Metaphysics of Aristotle*. He died in Padua, Italy, on Aug. 28.

FABIAN, ST. (d. 250), pope and martyr. A Roman layman, he came into the city from his farm and was unanimously chosen to succeed St. Anterus on Jan. 10, 236, fought the African heresy of Privatus, was an effective administrator, and died during the persecution of Decius. He was praised by SS. Cyprian and Jerome and by Eusebius. F. D. Jan. 20.

FABINYI, TIHAMER I. DE (1891–1953), economist. Born in Hungary he studied at Budapest, Paris, Cambridge, Berlin, and Leipzig, practiced before the League of Nations as an international lawyer, served as minister of commerce in 1932–35 and of industry and finance in 1935–38, then took over the direction of the largest bank in his country. He fled to Switzerland in 1944, went to the United States in 1945, and became professor of international economics and finance at the

Boston College graduate school. He died in Boston, Massachusetts, on June 10.

FABIOLA, ST. (d. 399). A noble Roman lady of the Fabia family, she married, then divorced her husband for his dissolute life, and married again. On her second husband's death she did public penance, returned to the Church, and devoted her wealth to charity, founding at Rome the first recorded Christian hospital in the West. In 395 she visited her friend St. Jerome in Palestine, decided against entering St. Paula's convent, and returned to Rome where she founded a hostel for pilgrims. F. D. Dec. 27.

FABIUS, ST. (d. 300), martyr. A soldier, he was beheaded at Caesarea in Mauritania, when he refused to carry a standard topped by pagan symbols. F. D. July 31.

FABIUS, ST. (d. 304), martyr. He and SS. Bassus and Maximus were slain during the Diocletian persecution. F. D. May 11.

FABRE, JEAN HENRI CASIMIR (1823–1915), entomologist. Born in St. Léons, France, on Dec. 21, he studied in Rodez and Vaucluse, and taught mathematics and physics in Carpentras and Ajaccio. He had long been interested in plants and animals, made some expeditions to Corsica, but became interested in insects after reading Léon Dufour. He took his doctor's degree in Paris, taught in Avignon in 1852, in Orange in 1870–79, then retired to Sérignan, France, where he died on Oct. 11. His publications were admired by Dufour and Darwin; after 1879 he published a long series of volumes based on direct observations of the spider, fly, mason and bramble bee, hunting and mason wasp, caterpillar, grasshopper, beetles, and weevils. He was honored in 1910 by the French Academy and the Royal Academy of Sweden.

FABRE, JOSEPH (1824–1892). Born in Cuges, France, on Nov. 14, he studied in the Marseilles seminary, became an Oblate of Mary Immaculate in 1845, and was ordained in 1847. He was director of the Marseilles seminary, procurator of his order, and in 1861 was chosen its second superior general. His mission activities were extensive, and he doubled the membership of the Oblates during his thirty-year rule. He also served as director general of the Association of the Holy Family, an institute of nuns founded at Bordeaux. He died near Paris on Oct. 26.

FABRI, HONORÉ (1607?–1688), theologian. Born in Ain, France, he became a Jesuit at Avignon in 1626, taught philosophy and mathematics (in which fields he wrote thirty books), and for thirty years was theologian of the court of the papal penitentiary in Rome. He died in Rome on Mar. 8.

FABRICIAN, BRO. See Pelerin, Felix.

FABRICIUS, HIERONYMUS (1537–1619),

anatomist. Born in Acquapendente, Italy, he studied classics and philosophy at Padua, learned medicine from Fallopius, and succeeded the latter at twenty-five, holding the chairs of anatomy and surgery from 1562 to 1609. Padua built him a laboratory, gave him an annual pension which allowed him to be independent of patients' fees, and encouraged the studies on the speech of animals, the formation of the fetus, and the relationship of blood valves (described, but not fully understood before his time), which William Harvey, who studied under him at Padua, acknowledged in his discovery of circulation. Fabricius also published an elaborate study of anatomy, with sixty-one detailed plates, and a work on surgery. He died in Padua, Italy, on May 21.

FABYAN, ROBERT (d. 1513), historian. A clothier and alderman in London, he resigned his political post in 1502 and wrote a *Concordance of Histories,* an unsuccessful attempt at blending previous historians up to the reign of King Richard III. A second edition (1533) has a good summary of municipal life under Henry VII.

FACCIOLATI, JACOPO (1682–1769), philologist. Born in Torreglia, near Italy, on Jan. 4, he studied in the seminary in Padua, taught logic, and served as regent of the university for forty-five years. In 1719 he revised the Latin dictionary of Ambrogio Calepino, *Lexicon septem linguarum,* then spent forty years in collaboration with Forcellini reading Latin literature, inscriptions, and coins in preparation for the four-volume *Totius latinatus lexicon* (1771). He died in Padua, Italy, on Aug. 26.

FACHANAN, ST. (6th century), bishop. Born in Tulachteann, Ireland, he was a pupil of St. Ita and founded the monastery of Molana and the influential monastic school at Ross (now Rosscarbery). He is patron of his diocese of Ross, Cork. F. D. Aug. 14.

FACTOR, ST. NICOLÒ (1520–1583). Born in Valencia, Spain, son of a Sicilian tailor, he joined the Observant Friars Minor in 1537, and became known as an itinerant preacher and for his austerities and supernatural gifts. He died in Valencia on Dec. 23 and was beatified in 1786. F. D. Dec. 14.

FACUNDINUS, ST. (d. 620?). He was bishop of Taino, Umbria, Italy. F. D. Aug. 28.

FACUNDUS, ST. (d. 300?), martyr. Born in León, Spain, he and St. Primitivus were beheaded near the present town of Sahagun. F. D. Nov. 27.

FAGAN. See Fugatius, St.

FAGILDUS, ST. (d. 1086). He was abbot of the Benedictine monastery of St. Martin, at Compostella, Spain. F. D. July 25.

FAGNANI, PROSPERO (d. 1678), canonist. Born in Italy between 1587 and 1598, he studied at Perugia, was a doctor of civil and canon law at twenty and a conciliar secretary at twenty-two. He wrote against probabilism, was termed "prince of the rigorists" by St. Alphonsus, and, though blind at forty-four, wrote an elaborate and long-valuable commentary on the decretals of Pope Gregory IX.

FAGNANO, GIULIO CARLO DE TOSCHI DI (1682–1766). Born in Sinigaglia, Italy, he became interested in mathematics long after he had completed his schooling in Rome, and wrote especially on the length and division of arcs. He died in Sinigaglia on May 18.

FAGUET, ÉMILE (1847–1916), critic. Born in La Roche-sur-Yon, France, on Dec. 17, he studied at L'École Normal, taught in Bordeaux and La Rochelle, became professor at Paris in 1890, drama critic of *Journal des Débats* in 1896, and a member of the French Academy in 1900. He wrote on the history of French literature, particularly of the seventeenth century and on contemporary drama, and died in Paris on June 7.

FAHY, FRANCIS PATRICK (1880–1953), lawyer. Born in Galway, Ireland, he studied at Mungret College and the Royal and National universities, taught at St. Vincent's, Castelnock, and in 1908 married Anna Barton. He took part in the 1916 uprising, was sentenced to ten years' imprisonment but released after serving one, and elected to parliament in 1918. He did not take his seat until 1927, worked with the Fianna Fail party of de Valera, and served as speaker of the dail from 1932 until his retirement in 1951. He died in Dublin on July 12.

FAILBHE, ST. (d. 680?). Brother of St. Finan of Rath, he preceded St. Adamnan as abbot of Iona. There are some twenty Celtic saints of this name. F. D. Mar. 22.

FAILBHE THE LITTLE, ST. (674?–754). He died at Iona, where he had served as abbot for seven years. F. D. Mar. 10.

FAILE. *See* Foila, St.

FAILLON, ÉTIENNE MICHEL (1800–1870), historian. Born in Tarascon, France, on Jan. 3, he studied in Avignon, became a Sulpician in 1821, was ordained in 1824, and wrote ascetical works and biographies of Marguerite Bourgeoys, Jeanne Mance, Mother d'Youville, and others who influenced the development of Canada. After a visit to Montreal, he completed three volumes (on the years 1534–1675) of an elaborately conceived account of the French colonization of the area. He died in Paris on Oct. 25.

FAIRMAN, VIRGIL. *See* Klarmann, Andrew.

FAITH, ST. Pious legend makes her, with two sisters, Hope and Charity, the daughter of St. Wisdom; they are said to have been beheaded in Rome during the second century. F. D. Aug. 1.

FAITH. A legendary figure, she was reputedly tortured and burned to death by Dacian, the procurator at Agen, France, during the third century. Her shrine at Conques was popular during the Middle Ages, when she was honored on Oct. 6.

FALBOURG. *See* Walburga, St.

FALCO, ST. (d. 512). He served as bishop of Maastricht, Flanders, from 495. F. D. Feb. 20.

FALCO, BL. (d. 1146). He became a Benedictine at the abbey of Cava, Italy, abbot of St. Mary at Cirzosimo, and then of Cava. His cult was confirmed in 1928. F. D. June 6.

FALCO, BL. (d. 1440). Born in Calabria, Italy, he became a hermit in the Abruzzi. His cult was approved in 1893. F. D. Aug. 9.

FALCO, JUAN CONCHILLOS (1641–1711), painter. Born in Valencia, Spain, he studied under Esteban March, and opened a school of design for younger artists, whom he taught to sketch in charcoal. His own sketches of roadside scenes and incidents possess considerable humor. He completed large commissions for the church of San Salvador, Valencia, and the church of St. John and altarpieces for the Cistercian monastery in Valdigna before he became totally crippled and blind. He died on May 14.

FALCONIERI, ST. ALEXIS (d. 1310), founder. *See* Monaldo, St. Buonfiglio.

FALCONIERI, ST. JULIANA (1270–1341), foundress. Daughter of Chiarissimo and Riguardata Falconieri, she was born in Florence, Italy, was instructed after her father's death by her uncle St. Alexis, and became a Servite tertiary at sixteen. After her mother's death in 1304, Juliana left her home to live with a group of women devoted to prayer and charity, unwillingly became their superior, and drew up a rule which was approved 120 years later for Servite nuns by Pope Martin V. She is called foundress because she prepared their rule, although she was not the first in the order, and was canonized in 1737. F. D. June 19.

FALKNER, THOMAS (1707–1784). Born in Manchester, England, on Oct. 6, he studied medicine under Richard Mead, became a surgeon in Manchester, and sailed to Buenos Aires for his health in 1731 as a ship's surgeon. He remained in Argentina, became a Jesuit in 1732, and labored in the missions of Paraguay and Patagonia until the Society was expelled from South America in 1768. Returning to England, he held a series of chaplaincies until his death in Shropshire on Jan. 30. His account of Patagonia and Falkland Island, with a grammar and vocabulary, was edited and published by William Combe in 1774.

FALLON, MICHAEL M. F. (1867–1931), bishop. Born in Kingston, Ontario, Canada, on May 17, he studied at Ottawa, became a member of the Oblates of Mary Immaculate, pursued further studies in Rome, taught in Ottawa, did parish work there and in Buffalo, New York, became provincial of the American province in 1903, and in 1910 was consecrated bishop of London, Ontario. He died on Feb. 22.

FALLOPIO, GABRIELLO (1523–1562), anatomist. Born in Modena, Italy, he studied at Ferrara, taught in several medical schools, and returned to Ferrara in 1548 as professor of anatomy. He went to Pisa in 1549 and to Padua in 1551, where he succeeded Vesalius as professor of anatomy, surgery, and botany, and was in charge of the botanical gardens. His particular interest was the head; he added much knowledge to what was known about the ear, described the tympanum in detail, as well as the tear ducts, and was the first to indicate the connection between the middle ear and the mastoid cells and the first to use an aural speculum in diagnosing diseases of the ear. The canal through which the facial nerve passes after leaving the auditory has been named for him. So has the tube which leads from the ovary to the uterus, the function of which he was the first to recognize. He published on surgery, the generative organs, syphilis, ulcers, tumors, thermal baths, and the composition of drugs. He died in Padua, Italy, on Oct. 9.

FALLOUX DE COUDRAY, FRÉDÉRIC ALFRED PIERRE DE (1811–1885), statesman. Born in Angers, France, on Mar. 7, he became a controversial figure in French political life. He published the pro-monarchist *Histoire de Louis XVI* in 1840 and an attack on heresy, *Histoire de St. Pie V*, in 1844, and served as deputy for Segré in 1846 and as member of the constituent assembly for Maine et Loire in 1848. He was chairman of the committee which ended the national workshops, an act which resulted in bloodshed and rebellion. He served as minister of education in 1848–49 and drew up the bill for freedom of education, opposed by Victor Hugo, which was passed in 1850 when he was no longer a member of the ministry. It was praised and condemned by leading Catholics. De Falloux was elected to the French Academy in 1856, retired from public life during the Second Empire, and sought for political compromise and peace during the Third Empire. He died in Angers on Jan. 6. The publication of his *Mémoires* (1888) resulted in further controversy, led by Eugène Veuillot.

FANCHEA, ST. (6th century). Sister of St. Enda, she entered religious life and may have built a convent at Rossory, Ireland. F. D. Jan. 1.

FANDILAS, ST. (d. 853), martyr. Born in Andalusia, Spain, he was ordained and was abbot of the monastery of Peñamelaria, Cor-

dova, when the Moorish emir ordered him beheaded. F. D. June 13.

FANGI, BL. AGOSTINO (1430–1493). Born in Biella, Piedmont, Italy, and called Augustine of Biella, he became a Dominican there, served as prior, and achieved great success as a preacher and miracle-worker. He died at Venice on July 22. His cult was approved in 1872. F. D. July 24.

FANTI, BL. BARTOLOMMEO (1443–1495). Born in Mantua, Italy, he became a Carmelite when seventeen, a noted preacher, and founded the Confraternity of Our Lady of Mt. Carmel. His cult was confirmed in 1909. F. D. Dec. 5.

FANTINUS, ST. (10th century). Said to have been a Basilian monk in Calabria, abbot of the Greek monastery of St. Mercury, he went with two companions to Salonika, Greece, after a Saracen invasion destroyed his abbey. F. D. Aug. 30.

FANTOU, BL. THÉRÈSE (1747–1794), martyr. See Fontaine, Bl. Madeleine.

FANTUCCI, BL. MARCO (1405–1479). Born in Bologna, Italy, he became a Franciscan in 1430 and succeeded St. John Capistran as vicar general. He raised funds for the ransom of his friars after the fall of Constantinople, directed the foundation of a convent of Poor Claires by St. Catherine of Bologna, visited his missioners in Middle Europe and the Near East, was one of several who set up pawnshops for the poor in order to free them from the usurers, and persuaded Pope Sixtus IV not to merge the Friars of the Observance with the Conventuals. He died in Piacenza, Italy. His cult was confirmed in 1868. F. D. Apr. 10.

FARAUD, HENRI (1823–1890), bishop. Born in Gigondas, France, on Mar. 17, he became an Oblate of Mary Immaculate, was sent to the Canadian mission, and ordained at St. Boniface, Manitoba, in 1847. He labored with the Indians of the north for nearly forty years, was in 1862 named first vicar apostolic of Athabasca-Mackenzie, returned briefly to France in 1885 for the general chapter of his order, and on his return was located at St. Boniface, where he died on Sept. 26.

FARE. See Burgundofara, St.

FARIBAULT, GEORGE BARTHÉLEMY (1789–1866). Born in Quebec, Canada, on Dec. 3, he studied law, was admitted to the bar in 1811, and served in the militia during the American invasion of 1812. He was in the Canadian civil service from 1822 to 1855, and assistant clerk of the legislative assembly for twenty-three years until he retired because of ill health. He edited historical and bibliographical works, left his library to Laval University, and led the movement to erect a monument to Montcalm. He died in Quebec on Dec. 22.

FARIBAULT, JEAN BAPTISTE (1774–1860). Born in Berthier, Canada, on Oct. 19, he was the son of Barthélemy Faribault, a French lawyer who served as military secretary to the army in Canada. Jean Baptiste held several positions, joined the Northwest Fur Co., and in 1798 went to the Michigan-Minnesota region where he traded with the Indians until 1809. He then settled in Prairie du Chien, Wisconsin, began his own trading business, lost his property during the War of 1812, and in 1815 became an American citizen. His relations with Indians and missionaries were exemplary. His last years were spent in Faribault, Minnesota, named after his eldest son; he died there on Aug. 20.

FARINATO, PAOLO (1525?–1606), painter. Born in Verona, Italy, he studied under Giolfino in the tradition of Liberale, completed colorful frescoes, decorated façades in Piazza dell' Erbe, then went to Mantua, where he was influenced by Giulio Romano. He completed a *St. Martin, Christ Walking on the Waves, Massacre of the Innocents, Miracle of the Loaves and Fishes*, and other biblical studies. *The Council of Trent* assigned to Titian has also been claimed for Farinato. He also executed a few highly regarded engravings. He died in Verona.

FARINGDON, HUGH. See Cook, Bl. Hugh.

FARLATI, DANIELE (1690–1773), historian. Born in San Daniele del Friuli, Udine, Italy, on Feb. 22, he studied in Görz, became a Jesuit in 1707, taught in Padua and Rome, and was ordained in 1722. He worked for twenty years with Fr. Filippo Riceputi on a church history of Illyria; when the latter died, Farlati continued with Fr. Jacopo Coleti. Four volumes appeared before his death on Apr. 25; three others were completed by 1818.

FARLEY, JOHN MURPHY (1842–1918), cardinal. Born in Newton Hamilton, Armagh, Ireland, on Apr. 20, he studied at St. McCartan's College, Monaghan, went to New York, studied at Fordham and St. Joseph's seminary, Troy, and at the North American College, Rome, and was ordained in 1870. He served as pastor on Staten Island, New York, was secretary to Cardinal McCloskey in 1872–84, was made a monsignor in 1884, vicar general of New York in 1891, and titular bishop of Zeugma and auxiliary in 1895. He became fourth archbishop of New York in 1902, greatly expanded the educational facilities of the see, held diocesan synods every three years, and gave particular attention to immigrants. He founded Cathedral College in 1903, consecrated St. Patrick's cathedral in 1910, and was created a cardinal in 1911. He wrote a biography of Cardinal McCloskey and a history of his cathedral, and died in New York City on Sept. 17.

FARNABY, THOMAS (1575?–1647), scholar. Born in London, and educated at Oxford, he became a convert, was educated further in Spain, accompanied Sir Francis Drake and John Hawkins on their last voyage, fought in the Low Countries, and returned to Somersetshire, where he set up a school at Martock. It later was transferred to London and, after the plague of 1636, to Oxford. Farnaby published annotated editions of Juvenal, Lucan, Martial, Ovid, Persius, the tragedies of Seneca, Terence, and Vergil, and issued a popular Latin grammar for schools.

FARNESE, ALESSANDRO (1520–1589), cardinal. Eldest son of Pietro Luigi Farnese, duke of Parma, he was born on Oct. 7, became administrator of the diocese of Parma, Italy, in 1534, while still a student at its university, and later that year cardinal-deacon. He was given several other honors and posts before 1536, when he became bishop of Monreale, Sicily. He founded its Jesuit college in 1552 and held a synod in 1559. In 1538 he was also bishop of Massa; in 1553, archbishop of Tours, transferring to Cahors, and leaving to accept the bishopric of Benevento in 1556 and of Montefiascone in 1557. He was active in poor relief, was a patron of the arts, built the church of the Gesù in Rome and the Farnese palace at Caprarola, and several times was papal legate to Charles V. He was named cardinal-bishop of Ostia and Velletri in 1580 and was active in promoting Tridentine reforms. He died in Rome in Feb.

FARO, ST. (d. 672?), bishop. Brother of SS. Chainoaldus and Burgondofara, he was raised in the court of King Theodebert of Austrasia, married, and served at the court of Clotaire II. When he was thirty-five he and his wife decided to enter religious life; he became a monk at Meaux, was ordained, and became bishop there about 628. He became chancellor of Dagobert I, helped St. Fiacre found a monastery at Breuil, and founded Holy Cross monastery. F. D. Oct. 28.

FARRELL, WALTER (1902–1951), theologian. Born in Chicago on July 21, he studied at its Quigley seminary, became a Dominican in 1920, was ordained in Washington in 1927, and took his doctorate at Fribourg in 1930. He taught theology at the Dominican house of studies in Washington from 1930, became regent of studies for the eastern province in 1939, was a navy chaplain in 1942–46, returned to Washington, lectured widely, and founded the *Thomist*. He wrote *Natural Moral Law according to St. Thomas and Suarez*, the four-volume *Companion to the Summa* (1938–42), and *Only Son*, a life of Christ which was incomplete at the time of his death in River Forest, Illinois, on Nov. 23.

FARRELLY, JOHN PATRICK (1856–1921),

bishop. Born in Memphis, Tennessee, on Mar. 15, he studied at Georgetown, Notre Dame de la Paix (Namur, Belgium), and the Propaganda, Rome, and was ordained in 1880. He did parish work in the Nashville diocese until he was appointed spiritual director of the North American College in Rome in 1904-9. In 1909 he was appointed bishop of Cleveland, Ohio, where he remained until his death on Feb. 12.

FASANI, BL. DONATO ANTONIO (1681-1742). Born in Lucera, Italy, he became a Conventual Friar Minor at fifteen, was ordained at Assisi in 1705, and sent to teach at the Franciscan college at Lucera. He served as minister provincial of the Sant' Angelo province and devoted himself to the poor and prisoners. He was beatified in 1951 by Pope Pius XII. F. D. Nov. 29.

FASTRED DE CAVÁMIEZ, BL. (d. 1163). Born in Hainault, he became a Cistercian under St. Bernard at Clairvaux, founded Cambron in 1148, and served also at Cîteaux. F. D. Apr. 21.

FATATI, BL. ANTONIO (1410?-1484), bishop. He served as a priest in Ancona, Italy, and in Siena, as canon of the Vatican, and as bishop of Teramo before he was transferred to the see of Ancona. He died on Jan. 9. His cult was approved by Pope Pius VI. F. D. Jan. 19.

FAULHAUBER, MICHAEL VON (1869-1952), cardinal. Born in Kloster-Heidenfeld, Germany, on Mar. 5, he studied at Würzburg, and was ordained in 1892. He served as a parish priest, studied in Rome, Oxford and Spain, taught at Würzburg (1899-1903) and Strassburg (1903-11), and in 1911 was appointed bishop of Speyer. He was chaplain general of the Bavarian army in World War I, was appointed archbishop of Munich in 1917, and was ennobled by the king of Bavaria. He arranged the Bavarian concordat after the war, was created a cardinal in 1921, worked unceasingly to alleviate the suffering and starvation in Germany after the war, and in 1923 helped defeat Hitler's bid for power. He fiercely opposed Nazism, attracted huge crowds with his speeches against the Nazis, and in 1938 had his house attacked by Storm Troopers. After World War II he devoted his efforts to rebuilding the churches of his see and combatting the rising materialism of the times. He died in Munich, Germany, on June 12.

FAUNT, LAWRENCE ARTHUR (1554-1591), theologian. Born in England, he studied at Oxford, Louvain, and Munich, became a Jesuit in 1570 or 1575, taught theology in the English College, Rome, and in 1581 was named rector of the new Jesuit college in Posen by Pope Gregory XIII. He taught Greek there for three years and theology for nine, writing

on the veneration of the saints, the Eucharist, and contemporary controversy with Lutheranism and Calvinism. He died in Wilna, Poland, on Feb. 28.

FAURE, FRANÇOIS FELIX (1841-1899), president. Born in Paris on Jan. 30, he became wealthy from his tanning business and as a merchant in Havre. He fought against the commune during the Franco-Prussian War, became a republican deputy of the national assembly in 1881, was undersecretary for the colonies in 1882-85 and 1888, and became minister of marine in 1894. The following Jan. he was elected president of France. He died in Paris on Feb. 16.

FAURIE, URBAIN (1847-1915), botanist. Born in Dunières, France, on Jan. 1, he studied in Monistozol, became a member of the Society of Foreign Missions in 1869, was ordained in 1873, and went to Japan. He taught in Tokyo and Niigata, became interested in botany, discovered *Fauria japonica*, and sent specimens to American and European museums, as well as building up his own herbarium, which he later transferred to the Imperial University. He did mission work in the northern islands of Japan from 1882 to 1894, returned to France for his health in 1895-96 (during which time he arranged 25,000 botanical specimens), and returned to the missions for seventeen more years of labor. He died on Formosa on July 4.

FAURIEL, CLAUDE CHARLES (1772-1844), historian. Born in St. Étienne, France, on Oct. 27, he studied in Tournon, Lyons, served in the army, joined the cabinet of Fouché, an ex-Oratorian, as secretary, and supported the revolutionary movement. He soon abandoned the new philosophy and turned to the study of foreign languages. He helped to popularize Shakespeare and German literature in France, spread the enthusiasm for romanticism, including acceptance of the *Ossian* of James Macpherson, and edited Basque and Celtic texts. He published translations of a Danish epic poem, a play by Manzoni, and songs of the Greek struggle for independence. In 1830 he was given the new chair of foreign literature at the University of Paris, compiled a three-volume history of Provençal poetry, contributed to the Benedictine edition of *Histoire littéraire de la France*, and served as assistant curator of manuscripts in the Royal Library. He was named to the Academy of Inscriptions and Belles-Lettres in 1836, and died in Paris on July 15.

FAUSTA, ST. (d. 303), martyr. A thirteen-year-old girl, she remained steadfast under cruel treatment by the magistrate Evilasius at Cyzicum, Pontus, during the Diocletian persecution; her constancy won over the judge, who also was put to death. F. D. Sept. 20.

FAUSTIAN, ST. (1st century), martyr. *See* Euphrasius, St.

FAUSTINIAN, ST. (d. 303?). As bishop of Bologna, Italy, he kept his diocese together during the Diocletian persecution and against Arianism. F. D. Feb. 26.

FAUSTINUS, ST. (d. 121?), martyr. Born in Brescia, Italy, he and his brother Jovita are said to have been great convert-makers, and to have been tortured and beheaded on orders of Emperor Hadrian, but information is sketchy and suspect. F. D. Feb. 15.

FAUSTINUS, ST. (d. 250), martyr. *See* Cyriacus, St.

FAUSTINUS, ST. (d. 304?), martyr. *See* Beatrice, St.

FAUSTINUS, ST. (d. 362?), martyr. He and SS. Timothy and Venustus were put to death during the reign of Julian the Apostate. F. D. May 22.

FAUSTINUS, ST. (d. 381), bishop. He succeeded St. Ursicinus as bishop of Brescia, Italy, in 360 and wrote the Acts of SS. Faustinus and Jovita, from whom he claimed descent. F. D. Feb. 16.

FAUSTINUS, ST. (4th century). An associate of St. Felix, bishop of Spello, Italy, and present at his martyrdom, he died in Todi, Italy. F. D. July 29.

FAUSTUS, ST. (d. 190?), martyr. A soldier, he was put to death in Milan, Italy, during the reign of Commodus. F. D. Aug. 7.

FAUSTUS, ST. (d. 250), martyr. He was crucified, shot with arrows, and left to die five days later during the Decian persecution. F. D. July 16.

FAUSTUS, ST. (d. 250), martyr. He, St. Macarius, and ten others were beheaded at Alexandria, Egypt, during the Decian persecution. F. D. Sept. 6.

FAUSTUS, ST. (d. 257), martyr. *See* Bonus, St.

FAUSTUS, ST. (d. 304?), martyr. With SS. Januarius and Martial, he was burned alive at Cordova, Spain, during the Diocletian persecution for refusing to sacrifice to the gods. They are called "the Three Crowns of Cordova" by Prudentius. F. D. Oct. 13.

FAUSTUS, ST. (d. 311?), martyr. He and SS. Ammonius, Didius, and bishops Hesychius, Pachomius, Phileas, and Theodore were among the hundreds slain in Egypt during the persecution of Maximian. F. D. Nov. 26.

FAUSTUS, ST. (4th century), martyr. He was a deacon who accompanied St. Dionysius of Alexandria into exile, and who was executed as a very old man during the Diocletian persecution. He is probably identical with a St. Faustus venerated on Oct. 3 and Oct. 4. F. D. Nov. 19.

FAUSTUS, ST. (403?–493?), bishop. Born probably in Brittany, he may have been a law-yer before he became a monk at Lérins, where he was ordained; he became abbot there in 433 and bishop of Riez, France, in 452. He opened many monasteries, fought Arianism and Pelagianism, but has been condemned for his semi-Pelagianism which appeared in two treatises he prepared on free will and grace at the request of the synods of Arles and Lyons in 475. The treatises were attacked on their appearance, but were not formally condemned until the Council of Orange in 529. About 478, Arian King Euric of the Visigoths exiled him from his see for his attacks on Arianism. He returned on Euric's death. F. D. Sept. 28.

FAUSTUS, ST. (d. 607?). As abbot of the monastery of Santa Lucia, Syracuse, Sicily, he taught Zosimus, future bishop of that see. F. D. Sept. 6.

FAVRE, BL. PETER (1506–1546). A farm boy born in Vilardet, Savoy, as Lefèvre, he went to the College of St. Barbe in Paris in 1525, where he met Ignatius Loyola and roomed with Francis Xavier. He was ordained in 1534 and celebrated the mass at Montmartre which marked the beginning of the Society of Jesus, when the seven pioneers took their first vows. In 1538 he went to Rome with Ignatius and Laynez, and served as professor in the university there. Pope Paul III sent him to the diets of Worms (1540) and Ratisbon (1541) called by Emperor Charles V to settle religious differences. Appalled at the indifference of Catholics to their religious duties, he preached widely and effectively, traveling through Germany, France, Portugal, and Spain and giving retreats based on the *Spiritual Exercises*. He felt that formal conferences were not the way to overcome current evils or the excesses of the Reformation and maintained that men had to be won over through their hearts. SS. Peter Canisius and Francis Borgia were among those he attracted to the Jesuits by his persuasive power. He died in Rome while preparing to leave for the Council of Trent. His cult was confirmed in 1872. F. D. Aug. 11.

FAYE, HERVÉ AUGUSTE ÉTIENNE ALBANS (1814–1902), astronomer. Born in St. Benoît-du-Sault, France, on Oct. 1, he studied at L'École Polytechnique, at Paris, and in Holland, and in 1836 in the Paris observatory. In 1843 he discovered the comet which bears his name, was elected to the Academy of Sciences in 1847, taught in L'École Polytechnique from 1848 to 1854, was rector and professor of astronomy at Nancy until 1873, and back at Paris until 1893. He held numerous education posts, including that of minister of public instruction and inspector general of higher education, and attained the rank of commander in the Legion of Honor. He wrote several astronomical studies, contributed 400 notes to scientific journals, invented the zenithal collimator, used photography and electricity in his studies, reformed methods of astronomical measurement, and added to the knowledge of comets, meteors, and sunspots. He died in Paris on July 4.

FAZZIO, ST. (1190–1272). A goldsmith in Verona, Italy, he established at Cremona the Order of the Holy Spirit, which was developed at Rome by Pope Innocent III for the care of pilgrims and the sick. F. D. Jan. 18.

FEATHERSTONE, RICHARD. *See* Fetherston, Bl. Richard.

FEBRONIA. Probably the heroine of a pious fiction, though honored in the Ethiopian Church and in parts of Italy on June 25, she is said to have been a beautiful nun at Nisibis, Mesopotamia, who was extravagantly tortured and beheaded there in 304 during the persecution of Diocletian.

FEBRONIUS, JUSTINUS. *See* Hontheim, Johannes Nicolaus von.

FECHIN, ST. (d. 665?), abbot. Born in Connaught, Ireland, and probably trained at St. Nathy, he founded a monastic settlement at Fore in Westmeath, and died during a plague. His name is sometimes corrupted to Vigean. F. D. Jan. 20.

FECKENHAM, JOHN DE (1515?–1585). Born in Feckenham Forest, Worcestershire, England, he became a Benedictine at Evesham, took his degree at Oxford in 1539, taught briefly in the juniorate at Evesham, served Bishop Bell of Worcester and Bishop Bonner of London as domestic chaplain (1543–49), and was rector at Solihull between 1544 and 1554. He twice was imprisoned in the Tower by Cranmer, was released by Queen Mary in 1553, and was named her chaplain, and dean of St. Paul's, London, in 1554. He visited prisoners, prepared Sir John Cheke for death, and pleaded successfully for the release and pardon of Elizabeth after Wyatt's rebellion. In 1556 he became abbot of Westminster, directing a community of twenty-eight Benedictines gathered from seized abbeys, but was expelled in 1559 by Elizabeth, who had offered him the archbishopric of Canterbury if he would become an Anglican. He twice more was a prisoner in the Tower, committed to the custody of pseudo-bishops, who failed to weaken his faith, released to live in Holborn and Bath, where he built a hospital, rearrested, and confined in Wisbech castle prison, where he died on Oct. 16. He was confined for twenty-three years in all during Elizabeth's reign.

FEDER, JOHANN MICHAEL (1753–1824), theologian. Born in Oellingen, Bavaria, on May 25, he studied in the Würzburg seminary, was ordained in 1777, served as chaplain in the Julius Hospital, as professor of theology and oriental languages at the university, and in 1791 as director of its library. He made several translations of the Fathers of the Church, revised Heinrich Braun's German Bible, translated lives of Bossuet and Fénelon, and edited a magazine. Some of his writing is heavily marred by philosophical Liberalism. He was removed as librarian in 1811, suffered a stroke of apoplexy in that year, from which he never fully recovered, and died in Würzburg, Bavaria, on July 26.

FEEHAN, DANIEL FRANCIS (1855–1934), bishop. Born in Athol, Massachusetts, he studied at St. Mary's College, Montreal, and St. Joseph's, Troy, New York, and was ordained in 1879. He was pastor in Fitchburg and West Boylston, Massachusetts, was named second bishop of Fall River in 1907, and died there on July 19.

FEEHAN, PATRICK AUGUSTINE (1829–1902), archbishop. Born in Killenaule, Tipperary, Ireland, on Aug. 28, he studied at Castle Knock College, Maynooth, went to the United States, and was ordained after further study at the Carondelet seminary in St. Louis in 1852. He taught at the seminary, of which he became rector, was a pastor in St. Louis, where he became well known for his help to the poor and his ministrations to wounded soldiers during the Civil War, and in 1865 was appointed bishop of Nashville after declining the honor the previous year because of ill health. He rebuilt his war-ravaged diocese, attended the Vatican Council in 1870, won the affection of his fellow citizens by his unselfish labors during the cholera epidemic of 1878, and was appointed first archbishop of Chicago in 1880. He built some 150 schools and more than 100 churches, encouraged Catholic education, was noted for his charitable works, and was a leader in the Catholic social movement. He was one of the founders of the Catholic Knights of America in 1877, defended the Ancient Order of Hibernians at the third Council of Baltimore where secret societies were attacked by several of the bishops, established the diocesan paper, *The New World*, in 1892, and labored to integrate the vast numbers of immigrants in his diocese into the American way of life. He died in Chicago on July 12.

FEENEY, THOMAS JOHN (1894–1955), bishop. Born in Boston on Sept. 4, he studied at Boston College, joined the Jesuits in 1915, continued his studies at Woodstock and Weston, taught in Buffalo, and served as a missionary to the Philippine Islands in 1921–24. He was ordained at Weston in 1927, taught at the Jesuit juniorate in Massachusetts, and was associate editor of *Jesuit Missions* from 1931 to 1939. He was superior of the Jesuit missions in Jamaica, British West Indies, from 1939 to 1945, when he became procurator of the New England province, and in 1947–51 was superior of the Marshall Islands missions. He was appointed titular bishop of Agno and vicar apostolic of the Caroline-Marshall Islands in 1951, and died on Sept. 9. He wrote *Padre of the Press* (1931).

FEILDING, RUDOLPH WILLIAM BASIL (1823–1892). The eighth earl of Denbigh and ninth earl of Desmond studied at Eton and Cambridge, became a convert in 1850, assisted Cardinal Wiseman in the direction of many charitable works, and built a Franciscan monastery at Pentasaph, Wales.

FELBIGER, JOHANN IGNAZ VON (1724–1788), educator. Born in Gross Glogau, Silesia, he studied at Breslau, became an Augustinian Canon Regular in 1746, was ordained in 1748, and became abbot of the monastery at Sagan, Silesia, in 1758. He established a teachers' college, introduced a Silesian catechism, and issued new methods of teaching on all school levels. In 1774 he was called to Vienna by Empress Maria Theresa and named commissioner general of education. He published his influential *Methodenbuch* in 1775. His religious outlook displeased Emperor Joseph II, who removed him from office, but sent him to Presburg, Hungary, as provost and in 1782 made him an inspector. He sought to increase the qualifications of teachers as well as social respect for the profession, and stressed class rather than individual instruction. He died in Presburg on May 17.

FELICE, ETTORE (1881–1951), archbishop. Born in Segni, Italy, on Mar. 12, he was ordained in 1903, appointed to the Vatican department of state in 1916, and served as auditor of the nuntiature in Belgrade, Yugoslavia, in 1920. He also was sent to Lisbon, was papal nuncio to Chile (1927–37), to Yugoslavia (1937–45), and to Ireland. He was made titular archbishop of Corinth in 1937, and died in Dublin on May 9.

FELICIAN, ST. (d. 170), martyr. *See* Exuperius, St.

FELICIAN, ST. (160?–254?), bishop and martyr. Consecrated bshop of Foligno, Italy, probably by Victor I, he served in that office for fifty years, successfully converting many in Umbria. During the persecution of Decius, he was tortured so excessively that, when he was being transferred to Rome for execution, he died on the road. F. D. Jan. 24.

FELICIAN, ST. (d. 297?), martyr. He and his brother Primus were Roman patricians who were converted to Christianity, spent a number of years aiding the poor and visiting prisoners, and were captured in old age, scourged, and beheaded at Nomentum, near Rome, during the persecution of Diocletian and Maximian. F. D. June 9.

FELICIAN, ST. (d. 304), martyr. *See* Victor, St.

FELICIAN, ST. (d. 305?), martyr. *See* Valentine, St.

FELICISSIMA, ST. (d. 304?), martyr. *See* Gracilian, St.

FELICISSIMUS, ST. (d. 256), martyr. *See* Rogatian, St.

FELICISSIMUS, ST. (d. 258), martyr. *See* Sixtus II, St.

FELICISSIMUS, ST. (d. 285?), martyr. *See* Ariston, St.

FELICISSIMUS, ST. (d. 303), martyr. She and SS. Heraclius and Paulinus were put to death, probably at Todi, Italy, during the persecution of Diocletian. F. D. May 26.

FELICISSIMUS, ST. (d. 303?), martyr. He was slain at Perugia, Italy, probably during the Diocletian persecution. F. D. Nov. 24.

FELICITAS, ST. (d. 165?), martyr. She is believed to have been a Christian widow in Rome who converted many before she was arrested, ordered to sacrifice to the pagan gods, and beheaded during the persecution of Marcus Aurelius. The story of her alleged sons, the so-called Seven Brothers, is a pious legend. F. D. Nov. 23.

FELICITY, ST. (d. 203), martyr. A young Carthaginian slave, who gave birth to a daughter while imprisoned during the persecution of Severus, she was exposed with St. Perpetua to wild beasts in the arena and finally stabbed by gladiators. F. D. Mar. 5.

FELICULA, ST. (d. 90?), martyr. Said to have been the foster sister of the martyred St. Petronilla, she was dungeoned when she refused to sacrifice to the gods, forced to join the Vestal virgins, whose food she would not touch, and, after two weeks of starvation, racked and thrown into a Roman sewer. Her body was recovered by St. Nicomedes. F. D. June 13.

FELIM, ST. (6th century), bishop. Son of Dediva and follower of St. Columba, he is traditionally venerated as the first bishop of Kilmore, Ireland, where a village grew up around his cell. His name also appears as Fidelminus. F. D. Aug. 9.

FELINUS, ST. (d. 250), martyr. He and Gratianus, soldiers in the Roman army, were put to death in Perugia, Italy, during the persecution of Decius. F. D. June 1.

FELIX I, ST. (d. 274), pope. A Roman, he became pope on Jan. 5, 269, and died five years later on Dec. 30. Confusion with another St. Felix, who was martyred in Rome, led to incorrect identification. Other biographical details are either errors or probable forgeries. Even his feast day, May 30, is the result of a scribal error.

FELIX II (d. 365), antipope. Archdeacon of the Church in Rome, he was invited to Milan in 355 by Emperor Constantius, who had exiled Pope Liberius. Felix was declared pope by Acacius of Caesarea and two other Arian bishops, but the populace did not accept him as pope. In 357 the people demanded the recall of Liberius; the bishops, meeting at Sirmium, wrote to Felix suggesting joint governorship; when Liberius returned, the people drove Felix from Rome. He was officially banished by the senate and retired to Porto, where he died on Nov. 22. An earlier Roman martyr named Felix was buried on the Via Aurelia, where the antipope may have built a church. An erroneous tradition arose that the antipope and the martyr were identical and led to his earlier inclusion in the Roman Martyrology for July 29.

FELIX III [II], ST. (d. 492), pope. Consecrated on Mar. 13, 483, he was called Felix III to distinguish him from the antipope who called himself Felix II. He was occupied in his pontificate with the Monophysite heresy, which continued at Constantinople with his excommunication of Acacius, and eventually led to the Byzantine schism. He restored the Church in Africa after it had been crushed by the Arian Vandals. F. D. Mar. 1.

FELIX IV [III], ST. (d. 530), pope. A native of Samnium and a priest, he was nominated for the papacy by Emperor Theodoric and elected on July 12, 526. He was greatly loved by the Romans for his simplicity and aid to the poor. He built the basilica of SS. Cosmas and Damian, condemned semi-Pelagianism at the Synod of Orange (529), and strengthened clerical immunity from civil jurisdiction. F. D. Sept. 22.

FELIX V (1383–1451), antipope. Duke Amadeus VIII of Savoy was born on Dec. 4 and became a wealthy and powerful prince who ruled his territory wisely and was zealous in support of the Church. Emperor Sigismund raised the county to the status of a duchy in 1416 and in 1422 added to it the county of Geneva. When his wife died, Amadeus named his son Ludwig regent and retired to Ripaille, on Lake Geneva, where with five others he formed the Order of St. Maurice and drew up its rule. He was named pope by the schismatic Council of Basle on Nov. 5, 1439, promptly excommunicated by Pope Eugene IV, was consecrated by a German cardinal on July 24, 1440, and proceeded to rule over Savoy, Switzerland, and several Austrian and German duchies and universities. The Basle assembly closed in 1443. Felix retained his title for six more years, finally submitting on Apr. 7, 1449, to Pope Nicholas V, who named him cardinal and vicar general of Savoy, Basle, and Strassburg. His was the last papal schism. Felix died in Ripaille, on Lake Geneva, on Jan. 7.

FELIX, ST. (1st century), martyr. He and St. Constantia were put to death at Nocera, Italy, near Naples, during the Neronian persecution. F. D. Sept. 19.

FELIX, ST. (d. 150?), martyr. He and SS. Januarius and Philip were beaten to death at Rome during the persecution of Antoninus when they refused to sacrifice to the pagan gods. Legend has incorrectly made them and four others the sons of St. Felicitas and blossomed into the story of the Seven Brothers. F. D. July 10.

FELIX, ST. (d. 180), martyr. See Speratus, St.

FELIX, ST. (2nd century). He is said to have been the third bishop of Metz and to have ruled the Gallic see for forty years. F. D. Feb. 21.

FELIX, ST. (2nd century), martyr. See Andochius, St.

FELIX, ST. (d. 212), martyr. Sent to Valence, France, with two deacons, Fortunatus and Achilleus, he converted many pagans before he and his companions were tortured and beheaded. F. D. Apr. 23.

FELIX, ST. (d. 235), martyr. He and St. Florentius were among the eighty soldiers put to death at Furcona, near Aquileia, Italy, during the reign of Maximian. F. D. June 25.

FELIX, ST. (d. 250?), martyr. See Epictetus, St.

FELIX, ST. (d. 257), martyr. A priest at Sutri, Tuscany, he was scourged to death during the persecution of Valerian. F. D. June 23.

FELIX, ST. (d. 257), bishop and martyr. See Nemesian, St.

FELIX, ST. (d. 284?), martyr. See Hilary, St.

FELIX, ST. (d. 285?), martyr. See Ariston, St.

FELIX, ST. (296?), martyr. He and his brother Fortunatus were born in Vicenza, Italy, and tortured and beheaded at Aquileia during the persecution of Diocletian and Maximian. F. D. June 11.

FELIX, ST. (3rd century), martyr. He was put to death with his sister Regula near Zurich, Switzerland, during the persecution of Maximian. F. D. Sept. 11.

FELIX, ST. (3rd century), martyr. See Calepodius, St.

FELIX, ST. (d. 300?), martyr. See Epictetus, St.

FELIX, ST. (d. 302), martyr. He, SS. Crispin, Gratus, Julius, Potamia, and seven others were slain at Thagura, Numidia, during the Diocletian persecution. F. D. Dec. 5.

FELIX, ST. (d. 303), martyr. He was put to death at Gerona, Spain, during the Diocletian persecution, and honored later by Prudentius. F. D. Aug. 1.

FELIX, ST. (d. 303), bishop and martyr. When the bishop of Thibiuca, Africa, refused to surrender sacred books during the persecution of Diocletian he was tortured and beheaded at Carthage, probably on July 15. F. D. Oct. 24.

FELIX, ST. (d. 303?), martyr. Legend makes him and St. Nabor Moorish soldiers stationed in Milan, who were beheaded for their faith in Lodi, Italy, during the persecution of Diocletian. F. D. July 12.

FELIX, ST. (d. 303?), martyr. *See* Honoratus, St.

FELIX, ST. (d. 304), martyr. *See* Apodemius, St.; also, Saturninus, St.

FELIX, ST. (d. 304?), bishop and martyr. Bishop of Spoleto, or of Spello nearby in Umbria, Italy, he was put to death during the persecution of Diocletian. F. D. May 18.

FELIX, ST. (d. 304?), martyr. A priest at Rome, he was tortured and condemned to death during the Diocletian persecution. As he traveled to his execution, an unknown was heard to murmur his belief in Christianity, whereupon he was seized and beheaded with St. Felix. Since the stranger's name was not known he was called Adauctus, the one added (to the martyrdom). F. D. Aug. 30.

FELIX, ST. (d. 307?), martyr. *See* Narcissus, St.

FELIX, ST. (d. 390?), bishop. A friend of St. Ambrose, he is said to have been the first bishop of Como, Italy. F. D. July 14.

FELIX, ST. (d. 400?). Consecrated bishop of Trèves, Gaul, in 386 by St. Martin of Tours, he was questioned about this appointment by both Pope Siricius and St. Ambrose, because his electors were said to have caused the death of Priscillian. He retired in 398 to a monastery he had built. F. D. Mar. 26.

FELIX, ST. (d. 429). A deacon who served St. Ambrose at Milan, Italy, he became fifth bishop of Bologna. F. D. Dec. 4.

FELIX, ST. (d. 434?), martyr. He and SS. Fortunatus, Saturninus, Secundinus, Servulus, Siricius, Verulus, and other Catholics were put to death in northern Africa by the Arian Vandals. F. D. Feb. 21.

FELIX, ST. (d. 484?), bishop and martyr. The Arian King Huneric unleashed a persecution in Africa and drove 4966 Christians into the desert to die. Felix, aged bishop of Abbir, and paralyzed, was among the victims. He ministered to them, as did Bishop Cyprian; both died in the Libyan desert. Victor of Utica, a contemporary, records their sufferings. F. D. Oct. 12.

FELIX, ST. (5th century). He is listed as a bishop of Lyons in Gaul. F. D. Feb. 3.

FELIX, ST. (5th century), martyr. He and more than twenty Christians were put to death in northern Africa by the Arian Vandal, King Huneric. F. D. Mar. 23.

FELIX, ST. (5th century), bishop. *See* Crescens, St.

FELIX, ST. (d. 580?), bishop. He attended the Council of Paris in 573 as bishop of Bourges, France, and was highly praised for his charity by Gregory of Tours. F. D. Jan. 1.

FELIX, ST. (513?–582), bishop. A married nobleman of Aquitaine, he separated from his wife upon his appointment as bishop of Nantes in 549, and she retired to a convent. He ruled his see judiciously for almost thirty-three years,

built a cathedral, and died on Jan. 6. F. D. July 7.

FELIX, ST. (6th century). He was a Benedictine monk at the monastery at Fondi, Italy, and honored by St. Gregory the Great. F. D. Nov. 6.

FELIX, ST. (d. 650?), bishop. During the forty years he ruled the see of Brescia, Italy, he was active against the Lombard Arians. F. D. Feb. 23.

FELIX, ST. (7th century), martyr. He was an English slave, sold in France and ransomed by St. Gregory the Great, ordained, and slain in Champagne with Augebert, a deacon, as they were preparing to return to England as missioners. F. D. Sept. 6.

FELIX, ST. (d. 750?). *See* John of Atarés, St.

FELIX, ST. (d. 790?), martyr. A Benedictine monk at Fritzlar, Germany, he is said to have been slain by pagan Saxons. F. D. June 5.

FELIX, ST. (d. 852?), martyr. *See* Aurelius, St.

FELIX, ST. (d. 853), Spanish martyr. *See* Anastasius, St.

FELIX, ST. (d. 1038). Born in Brittany, he lived as a hermit, then became a Benedictine at St. Benoit, Fleury, and was sent to restore the monastery of Rhuys, founded by St. Gildas and destroyed by the Norsemen, where he ruled as abbot. F. D. Mar. 4.

FELIX, ST., martyr. He died in prison at Thynissa in North Africa while awaiting execution and was later memorialized in a festal sermon by St. Augustine. F. D. Nov. 6.

FELIX, CÉLESTIN JOSEPH (1810–1891). Born in Neuville-sur-l'Escaut, France, on June 28, he studied in Cambrai, became a Jesuit in 1837, was ordained at Louvain in 1842, and taught in Brugelettes and Amiens. He was sent to Paris in 1851, where his preaching won him the post of orator at Notre Dame from 1853 to 1870. His Lenten conferences were published in the fifteen-volume *Progrès par le Christianisme*. He was stationed at Nancy from 1867 to 1883. Besides preaching in most cathedrals of France and Belgium, and in Copenhagen, he published notes for retreats and founded the Society of St. Michael for the distribution of literature. He went to Lille, France, in 1883, and died there on July 7.

FELIX OF CANTALICE, ST. (1513–1587). Born in Cantalice, Apulia, Italy, he was a shepherd and farm laborer, then joined the Capuchins at Anticoli as a laybrother. He was sent to Rome in 1549 and for the rest of his life begged alms, cared for the sick, and practiced the extremest austerities. SS. Philip Neri and Charles Borromeo profited from his advice. He was canonized in 1709. F. D. May 18.

FELIX OF DUNWICH, ST. (d. 648), bishop. A Burgundian, he became bishop of the East Angles at the request of King Sigebert, preached with great success in Norfolk, Suffolk, and Cambridgeshire, England, and established a flourishing school. F. D. Mar. 8.

FELIX OF NICOSIA, BL. (1715–1787). Born in Sicily, the son of a poor cobbler, he was accepted as a Capuchin laybrother at twenty-seven. He took care of the poor, healed the sick, consoled prisoners, and reformed many sinners. He was beatified in 1888. F. D. June 1.

FELIX OF NOLA, ST. (d. 260?). Born near Naples, he was ordained by St. Maximus, whom he was asked to succeed as bishop, because of the reputation for holiness he established during the persecution of Decius. He refused, however, and worked with the poor of the area as a simple priest. St. Paulinus of Nola, who followed him by a century, was particularly devoted to him; the devotions at the shrine which he set up inspired St. Augustine's *Care for the Dead.* F. D. Jan. 14.

FELIX O'DULLANY (d. 1202), bishop. He was a Cistercian monk in Kilkenny, Ireland, before he was appointed bishop of Ossory and took up residence at Aghahoe, Ireland.

FELIX OF VALOIS, ST. (1127–1212), founder. A hermit near Meaux, France, when he was seventy he founded, with his disciple, St. John of Matha, the Order of the Most Holy Trinity (Trinitarians) to ransom captives from the Moors. He received papal approval in 1198 and extended the order through Italy and France. When St. John returned from the Barbary slave markets, Felix guided the French province from its house at Cerfroid, where he died on Nov. 4. His cult was confirmed in 1666 by Pope Alexander VII, and he is believed to have been canonized in 1262 by Pope Urban IV. Some later writers, however, have contended that his existence is fictional. F. D. Nov. 20.

FELLER, FRANÇOIS XAVIER DE (1735–1802). Born in Brussels, Belgium, on Aug. 18, he studied in Luxembourg and Rheims, became a Jesuit (1754), and after the suppression of the Society went to Paderborn and then to the court of Prince-Bishop Joseph von Schroffenburg of Bavaria. He wrote controversial works, as well as collections of articles on politics, philosophy, and literature which he originally published in *Journal historique et littéraire.* He was its sole contributor from 1773 to 1794; he had written for it when it was titled *La Clef du cabinet* from 1760 on. It was suppressed in Austria by Emperor Joseph II and forced to move to Maastricht. Fr. Feller died in Ratisbon, Bavaria, on May 22.

FELTON, BL. JOHN (d. 1570), martyr. Born in Bermondsey, England, he affixed a copy of Pope St. Pius V's bull, *Regnans in excelsis,* excommunicating Queen Elizabeth, to the door of the Anglican bishop of London's house. For this he was racked, then hanged, drawn, and quartered in St. Paul's churchyard. He was beatified in 1886. F. D. Aug. 8.

FELTON, BL. THOMAS (1568–1588), martyr. Son of Bl. John Felton, he was born at Bermondsey, England, was educated at Rheims, and became a Minim friar. He returned to England, and when he attempted to return to his monastery was imprisoned for two years and finally hanged at Isleworth during the Elizabethan persecution. He was beatified in 1929. F. D. Aug. 28.

FENEBERG, JOHANN MICHAEL NATHANAEL (1751–1812). Born in Oberdorf, Bavaria, on Feb. 9, he became a Jesuit in 1770, was ordained in 1775 after the suppression of the Jesuits, taught in several schools, and became pastor of Seeg. When a relative, Martin Boos, took refuge with him and sought to popularize his new group of Awakened Brethren, Feneberg was called before an ecclesiastical tribunal at Augsburg in 1797 and abjured the group's false mysticism and other errors. In 1805 he was transferred to Vöhringen, Germany, as pastor, where he died on Oct. 12.

FÉNELON, FRANÇOIS DE SALIGNAC DE LA MOTHE (1651–1715), bishop. Born in Périgord, France, on Aug. 6, to Count Pons de Salignac and his second wife, Louise de la Cropte, he studied at Cahors, Collège du Plessis, Paris, and the seminary of St. Sulpice, where he was ordained in 1675. He became a Sulpician and in 1678 was by Archbishop de Champvallon of Paris given charge of the Nouvelles Catholiques center for converts or those interested in the Church. After the revocation of the Edict of Nantes, in 1685, Fénelon went to Saintonge and elsewhere to preach a return to Catholicism; he succeeded in getting the king to agree not to send troops to areas in which he was preaching, but was often charged with sometimes relying on force or legal punishment rather than persuasion in reclaiming Huguenots and others. Inspired by his friend Bossuet he wrote *Réfutation du système de Malebranche sur la nature et sur la grâce* (unpublished until 1820); for the duke and duchess of Beauvilliers and their eight daughters he wrote *Traité de l'education des filles.* When the duke became governor of the royal grandchildren in 1689 he named Fénelon tutor of the duke of Burgundy. To mold his character, the prelate wrote *Fables, Dialogues des morts,* and the fictional *Télémaque.* Louis XIV rewarded Fénelon with the abbey of St. Válery. He was elected to the French Academy, became spiritual director of Mme. de Maintenon and adviser to her school of St. Cyr, and in 1695 was appointed bishop of Cambrai. He soon met and was impressed by the piety and mystical writings of Mme. Guyon. When her works were charged with verging on quietism, they were submitted to a board of inquiry, on which Fénelon sat, and mildly condemned; she herself submitted, having had no intention of spreading quietism, but her works had great influence on English religious thought and on the poetry of William Cowper. To make his position on the examining commission clear, Fénelon published *Explication des maximes des saints*, on true and false mysticism. King Louis XIV objected to the book, as did Bossuet; it was submitted to Rome in 1695 after a widespread conflict had broken out as to its orthodoxy; it was papally condemned in 1697, and Fénelon accepted the censure. The king, however, remained hostile and forbade the bishop to leave his diocese. Fénelon spent his remaining years in giving careful attention to the needs of his see, which was seriously disturbed during the War of the Spanish Succession, and in preaching, wide visitation, and directing the education of the clergy. He was active in the battle against a suddenly revived Jansenism, writing much against the anonymous *Cas de conscience* and Quesnel's *Réflexions morales sur le nouveau testament*; the latter was condemned by the papal bull *Unigenitus*, and Fénelon again wrote earnestly to gain support for the papal position. The bishop's mind appears most revealingly in ten volumes of his letters; his views on politics are clear from his memoirs of the War of the Spanish Succession, *Essai sur le gouvernement civil*, and a study of the rights of royalty. He also wrote comments on literature and a widely translated *Traité de l'existence du Dieu*. He died in Cambrai, France, on Jan. 7.

FÉNELON, FRANÇOIS DE SALIGNAC DE LA MOTHE (1641–1679), missioner. Half-brother of his namesake, he was born in France, became a Sulpician in 1664, and went to Quebec in 1666. He worked with the Cayugas on the shores of Lake Ontario. A waterfall north of Lindsay, Ontario, is named for him. He questioned the devotion of Frontenac to the ideal of a great leader in a sermon he delivered in Montreal in 1674, was haled before the Quebec council, and recalled to France. He was refused permission to return to mission work, and died in France.

FENLON, JOHN F. (1875–1943). Born in Bedford, Indiana, on Oct. 8, he became a Sulpician and was provincial of his Society and president of St. Mary's seminary, Baltimore, Maryland, from 1925 until his death in Lisbon, Portugal, on July 21.

FENN, BL. JAMES (1540?–1584), martyr. Born in Montacute, England, and a graduate of Oxford, he taught in Somersetshire after he lost his fellowship for religious reasons, and at forty, after the death of his wife, studied and was ordained a priest at Rheims. On his return to the English mission, he was captured, charged with plotting to kill Elizabeth, and hanged at Tyburn. He was beatified in 1929. F. D. Feb. 12.

FENN, JOHN (d. 1615). Born in Montacute, Somersetshire, England, eldest brother of the martyred James Fenn, he went to Winchester and Oxford, was headmaster of Bury St. Edmund's School, and lost his position when he refused to accept Queen Elizabeth I as head of the Church. He went to Rome, was ordained there about 1566, served as chaplain with an English regiment in Flanders, and spent forty years at Louvain. He contributed to the histories of the Church in England compiled by Fr. John Gibbons (1583) and Bridgewater (1588), collected spiritual treatises for the use of the Brigettine nuns at Syon, and in 1609 became chaplain of the English Augustinian Canonesses at Louvain. He made several valuable translations, including Bishop John Fisher's *Treatise on the Penitential Psalms* into Latin and the Tridentine catechism into English. He became blind in 1611 and died in Louvain, Belgium, on Dec. 27.

FENWICK, BENEDICT JOSEPH (1782–1846), bishop. Born near Leonardstown, Maryland, on Sept. 3, he studied at Georgetown and the Sulpician seminary in Baltimore, joined the Jesuits in 1806 when the Society was reestablished in the United States, and was ordained in 1808. He was sent to New York in 1809, administered the see in 1815–17, returned to Georgetown in 1817 as president, and in 1818 was sent to Charleston to act as vicar general, receiving the actual appointment in 1820. He successfully ended several local schisms, returned to Georgetown as procurator of the Jesuits in the United States and minister of the college in 1822, and was again its president in 1822–25. He was appointed bishop of Boston (the see then included all of New England) in 1825, labored to overcome anti-Catholic hostility, which in 1834 caused a mob to burn the Carmelite convent in Charlestown, Massachusetts, founded the journal, *The Jesuit, or Catholic Sentinel*, (later *The Pilot*) in 1829, established Holy Cross College in 1852, and died on Aug. 11 in Boston after a long illness.

FENWICK, EDWARD DOMINIC (1768–1832), bishop. Born in St. Mary's County, Maryland, on Aug. 19, he was orphaned at six, studied at Holy Cross College in Bornhem, Belgium, and Liège, joined the Dominicans, and was ordained in Ghent in 1793. He was imprisoned by the invading French, but was freed because he was an American, taught at Carshalton College, Surrey, England, and in 1804 returned to the United States to found a Dominican province. He settled in Kentucky in 1805, established the American mother house near Springfield, and in 1807 founded the College of St. Thomas Aquinas. He engaged in missionary activity in Kentucky and Ohio, and in 1821 was appointed first bishop of the newly created see of Cincinnati. He toured Europe in 1827 seeking priests for his diocese, was appointed Dominican provincial for life in 1828, founded the Athenaeum (now St. Francis Xavier College) and the *Catholic Telegraph* in 1831, and died of cholera in Wooster, Ohio, on Sept. 26.

FENWICK, BL. JOHN (1629–1679), martyr. A native of Durham, England, he became a convert, studied at St. Omer, and joined the Jesuits in 1656. He was sent to the English mission in 1675, was known as Mr. Caldwell, and was arrested and charged with plotting to kill King Charles II. He was hanged and quartered at Tyburn, and beatified in 1929. F. D. June 20.

FEOLOGELD (d. 832), archbishop. He was abbot of a monastery in Kent, England, in 803 and succeeded Wulfred as archbishop of Canterbury in 832. He is sometimes called Swithred. He died on Aug. 30.

FERBER, NICOLAUS (1485–1534). Born in Herborn, Germany, he became a Friar Minor, was provincial of the Franciscan province of Cologne, and papally appointed vicar general of the Cismontane Observance. He wrote against contemporary heresy, scriptural commentaries, and was sent to Copenhagen to counteract Danish Lutheranism. He died in Toulouse, France, on Apr. 15.

FERDINAND I (1503–1564), emperor. Son of Philip the Handsome, son of Emperor Maximilian I, and Joanna, daughter of Ferdinand and Isabella of Spain, he was born at Alcalá de Henares, Spain, on March 10. He was invested with the Austrian duchies of the Hapsburgs by his brother Emperor Charles V, married Anna, sister of Louis II of Hungary and Bohemia, in 1521, and claimed the crown and was crowned king of Bohemia on Louis' death at the battle of Mohacs in 1526. He was opposed by John Zapolya for the crown of Hungary and, though acknowledged king of Hungary by one faction in 1527, was opposed by a coalition of Zapolya and the Turks which prevented his occupying the kingdom. At the Treaty of Grosswardein in 1538, Hungary was divided between them, Ferdinand recognized John Zapolya as king of Hungary, and he in turn was recognized as John's successor. When John died in 1540, the Turks advanced his son John Sigismund for the throne and the ensuing war lasted intermittently until a truce was reached in 1562. Ferdinand often acted as regent in Germany for Emperor Charles V, who had appointed him governor of Württemberg about 1521, was elected king of the Romans in 1531, and opposed the Reformation, though he hoped to reconcile the Catholics and Protestants. He put down a revolt in Bohemia after fighting in the war of the League of the Schmalkalden in 1546–47, arranged the Peace of Passau in 1552, ending Philip's war with Maurice of Saxony, and in 1555 was chiefly responsible for the Peace of Augsburg, which allowed each prince to decide the religion of his subjects. After 1556, when Emperor Charles V retired to a monastery, Ferdinand practically ran the government; when Charles formally abdicated in 1558, Ferdinand was elected emperor. He sought in vain for the reunion of Protestants to Rome at the Council of Trent, where he favored clerical marriage, had his son Maximilian crowned king of Bohemia in 1562, of Hungary in 1563, and of the Romans in 1562, and died in Vienna on July 25.

FERDINAND II (1578–1637), emperor. Eldest son of Charles, duke of Styria, and Maria of Bavaria, he was born in Graz, Styria, on July 9, studied at Graz and Ingolstadt, ruled three Adriatic duchies under a regent when his father died in 1590, and pledged himself to the destruction of heresy. The childless Emperor Matthias made him king of Bohemia in 1617 and of Hungary in 1618, but died in 1619 before he could assure the Austrian throne for Ferdinand. Unable to accept the Bohemian nobles because of his Catholicism, he was faced with rebellion when they began the "Demonstration of Prague." When they chose the Protestant Frederick V as their leader in 1619, the Thirty Years' War began. Ferdinand, who had been elected emperor in 1619 by all the electors (except those of Bohemia and the Palatinate), allied himself with Maximilian I of Bavaria; they soon broke the siege of Vienna and defeated Frederick at the battle of White Mountain, near Prague, in 1620. Protestantism was crushed in Bohemia, Moravia, and southern Austria; the Silesians were treated more mildly. From 1625 on, the Protestant Union of Frederick, Christian IV of Denmark, and Saxon and other German rulers fought against the forces of the Catholic League, whose armies were led by Ferdinand, Wallenstein, and Tilly. Each side had success and defeat; the Austrian peasantry rebelled against the emperor; Ferdinand demanded restoration of church property under his Edict of Restitution; countries changed hands in the long struggle. After initial hesitancy, Gustavus Adolphus of Sweden threw himself into battle in 1630 and overwhelmed and occupied Germany and its southern neighbors. Gustavus was killed at the battle of Lutzen in 1632, but Wallenstein failed to pursue this advantage. Ferdinand's fortunes took a turn for the better when he crushed the Swedish army at Nördlingen in 1634. His position might have been secured if France had not heeded the appeals of the Protestants in southwestern Germany and treacherously thrown itself against him. Ferdinand saw his son crowned king of Bohemia and Hungary and elected emperor, but died in Vienna on Feb. 15, before the end of the Thirty Years' War.

FERDINAND III (1608–1657), emperor. Son of Emperor Ferdinand II, he was born at Gratz, Styria, Austria, on July 13, became king of Hungary in 1625, of Bohemia in 1627, and nominal commander of imperial forces in the Thirty Years' War after Wallenstein was deposed in 1634. He was crowned king of the Romans in 1636, succeeded his father as emperor in 1637, and in the next decade suffered numerous reverses in a war which became increasingly ruinous for all of Europe. In 1648 he agreed to the Peace of Westphalia, which granted religious freedom to Protestants, though he kept his own dominions Catholic. He spent the rest of his reign striving to close up the breaches and dislocations caused by the war. In 1656 he dispatched an army to Italy to aid Spain against the French, and joined Poland in an alliance against Charles X Gustavus of Sweden in 1657, but died, before it could take effect, in Vienna on April 2.

FERDINAND (1793–1875), emperor of Austria. He succeeded Francis I as emperor in 1835, was ill most of his reign and finally insane, and had to leave the reins of government in the hands of Metternich. He abdicated in 1848 when revolution brought in Francis Joseph I.

FERDINAND I (1379?–1416), king of Aragon and Sicily. Second son of John I of Castile, he refused that crown when his brother Henry III died, and served as regent for his nephew, John II. He captured Antequera from the Moors, claimed the vacant throne of Aragon and Sicily, and was elected king in 1412, restored order in his territory, and worked with Emperor Sigismund to remove antipope Benedict XIII.

FERDINAND II (1452–1516), king of Aragon and Castile. Son of John II of Aragon and Sicily, he was born in Sos, Aragon, on Mar. 10, and was married to Isabella, stepsister of Henry IV of Castile, in 1469. In 1475 the Cortes of Segovia recognized the two as joint rulers (Isabella had assumed the throne in 1474, though opposed by Portugal and others); Ferdinand defeated the Portuguese in 1476 at Toro and inherited the crown of Aragon in 1479. They restored the power of royalty, revised and strengthened town charters, deprived the larger feudal leaders of much property and power, and codified Spanish law (*Libro de Montalvo*, 1485). The concordat of 1482 established Ferdinand as grand master of the powerful orders of knights. Granada, the last major Moorish stronghold, was retaken in 1492. The Inquisition, increasingly powerful since 1478, expelled 200,000 Jews (many of whom had publicly accepted Christianity and then returned to their former faith) and thousands of Moors. After the Moorish threat was removed, the monarchs became interested in the exploration of the New World and its economic and spiritual possibilities, and supported the expeditions of Columbus to the East. Ferdinand's interest in Italy caused conflict. Ferdinand joined the pope against Charles VIII of France, retained Naples by the Treaty of Blois, and after Isabella's death in 1504 married the niece of Louis XII of France, Germaine de Foix, on whom French claims to Naples rested. His daughter Joanna, who married Archduke Philip of Austria, succeeded to the throne of Castile in 1506; by treaty, Ferdinand agreed that Philip would become regent, but Philip died in that year and Joanna was insane until her death in 1555. As a result, the union of Aragon and Castile continued, and under Ferdinand's sole direction. Spanish armies invaded North Africa and took Oran and Tripoli in 1509–11, seized Navarre in 1512, then joined Venice and the Papal States against France and the empire and won the battle of Novara in 1513 (after many about-faces on the part of Ferdinand, and broken treaties). He is listed as Ferdinand V of Castile, is known as "the Catholic," and died in Estremadura, Spain, on Jan. (or Feb.) 23.

FERDINAND I (d. 1065), king of Castile and León. Called "the Great," he became first king of Castile in 1035, conquered León by 1037, and ruled the two kingdoms, adding parts of Navarre after the death of his brother García. He made the Moorish strongholds of Saragossa, Seville, and Toledo capitulate and become his vassals, recommended reforms at the Council of Coyanza (1050), assumed the title of "emperor," but divided his lands among his children at his death on Dec. 27.

FERDINAND III, ST. (1199?–1252), king of Castile and León. Son of Alfonso IX of León and Berenguela, daughter of King Alfonso III of Castile, he was born near Salamanca, ascended the throne of Castile at eighteen when his mother waived the succession for herself, and in 1230 succeeded his father and ruled León as well. He inaugurated a period of internal peace for the two kingdoms, ruled wisely and justly, was an excellent administrator, and chose Archbishop Ximenes as his chancellor. He founded the university of Salamanca in 1243. For twenty-seven years he fought to drive the Moors from Spain, capturing Cordova (1236), Cadiz, and Seville (1248), among other cities. However, when the Moorish emperor met difficulties in Africa, Ferdinand sent him aid, in return for permission to establish a Christian mission there; he later gave the emir Granada as a capital, but gained the Moorish leader as his vassal. Ferdinand died in Seville, and was canonized in 1671 by Pope Clement X. F. D. May 30.

FERDINAND II (d. 1188), king of León. Second son of Alfonso VII and brother of Sancho III of Castile, he became king in 1157, fought against Portugal and the Moors, and invaded Castile when his brother abdicated in 1158.

FERDINAND I (1423-1494), king of Naples. Illegitimate son of Alfonso V of Aragon, he claimed the throne of Naples, was passed over in favor of John of Anjou by Pope Callistus III, but was recognized by Pope Pius II. With the help of the latter, the duke of Milan, and Scanderbeg of Albania, Ferdinand defeated John at Troja in 1462. He introduced printing, developed commerce and industry, and drove out the Turks in 1481.

FERDINAND I (1345-1383), king of Portugal. *See* Pedro I.

FERDINAND VI (1713?-1759), king of Spain. Son of Philip V and Marie Louise of Savoy, he became king in 1746 and saw the end of the War of the Austrian Succession, which by the Treaty of Aix-la-Chapelle (1748) assured Parma, Piacenza, and Guastalla to his brother Philip and Naples and Sicily to his brother Charles. A concordat with the Vatican (1754) gave the government the right to make Church appointments. He lived in retirement after the death in 1758 of his queen, Maria Barbara de Braganza, who had been a major influence on his career.

FERDINAND, ST. (13th century). He became the fifth bishop of Cajazzo, Spain. F. D. June 27.

FERDINAND OF BAVARIA (1577-1650), bishop. Son of William V, whom he succeeded as duke, he was born in Arnsberg, Bavaria, educated at Ingolstadt, served as coadjutor to his uncle Ernst in 1595, and on the latter's death in 1612 succeeded him as elector of Cologne and bishop of Liège, Münster, Hildesheim, and also after 1618, Paderborn.

FERDINAND THE CONSTANT, BL. (1402-1443). Born in Santarem, Portugal, on Sept. 29, to King John I and Philippe, daughter of John of Gaunt, he led an unusually pious life as a prince. After his father's death he was papally appointed grand master of the Knights of Aviz, and later refused the offer of a cardinalate. A poorly planned and undermanned attack on Tangier, approved by King Edward, his brother, resulted in defeat; another brother, Henry the Navigator, escaped, but Ferdinand was held as a hostage, chained, mistreated, and dungeoned for nearly six years. The Portuguese court refused to surrender the stronghold of Ceuta in exchange for his freedom, and he died in prison on June 5; his body was then hung from the walls of Fez. His secretary, Juan Alvarez, wrote the prince's biography after his own release; on it Calderón based one of his most popular tragedies, *El príncipe constante*. Ferdinand's cult was approved in 1470. F. D. June 5.

FERGUS, ST. (d. 583), bishop. He was sixth in descent from King Coelbad, built a monastery at Killmbian, and became first bishop of Down, Ireland. F. D. Mar. 30.

FERGUS, ST. (d. 778). He was bishop of Duleek, Ireland, and is mentioned in the *Annals of the Four Masters*.

FERGUS, ST. (8th century?), bishop. Reputedly an Irish bishop of Downpatrick, he came to Scotland, built several churches, and devoted himself to missionary activities. He may be the Fergustus, bishop of the Scots, who attended a synod in Rome in 721. F. D. Nov. 27.

FERLAND, JEAN BAPTISTE ANTOINE (1805-1865), historian. Born in Montreal on Dec. 25, he studied at Nicolet, was ordained in 1828, served in country parishes to 1841, and returned to Nicolet as director of studies. He became its superior in 1848, served as chaplain to the English garrison at Quebec and as a member of the bishop's council, and in 1855 was named professor of Canadian history at Laval University. He had previously published several historical studies and now went to France to collect original source material. His public lectures in Quebec from 1858 to 1862 became the basis of his *Cours d'histoire du Canada*, which covered the period to 1759. He was named dean of Laval in 1864. He died in Quebec on Jan. 11.

FERNÁNDEZ, BL. AMBROSE (1551-1620), martyr. Born in Sisto, Portugal, he sailed to Japan as an adventurer, became a Jesuit lay-brother there in 1577, and died in prison at Omura, Japan. He was beatified in 1867. F. D. Mar. 14.

FERNÁNDEZ, ANTONIO (1569-1642), missioner. Born in Lisbon, Portugal, he became a Jesuit and went to India in 1602 and to Ethiopia in 1604. King Melek Seghed, who was converted in 1622, was favorable to Catholicism and the faith flourished until a schism was supported by the crown prince. Fr. Fernández was held for ransom after capture by a minor chieftain, but a younger missioner volunteered to take his place. Although eighty, he then returned to India, where he died in Goa on Nov. 12. He translated liturgical works into Ethiopian.

FERNANDEZ, BL. ISABEL (d. 1622). *See* Spinola, Bl. Charles.

FERNÁNDEZ, BL. JOSEPH (1774-1838), martyr. A Spaniard, he was sent to Tonkin as a Dominican in 1805, became provincial vicar, and was beheaded. He was beatified in 1900. F. D. July 24.

FERNÁNDEZ, JUAN (d. 1567), missioner. Born in Cordova, Spain, he became a Jesuit laybrother and went with St. Francis Xavier to Japan, where he had success as a catechist and compiled the first Japanese grammar and dictionary for mission work. He died in Japan on June 20.

FERNÁNDEZ DE PALENCIA, DIEGO (16th century), historian. Born in Palencia, Spain, he became a soldier, went to Peru shortly after 1545, and fought under Alonso de Alvarado against Francisco Hernández de Giron. He began to write an account of the rebellion for the viceroy, but on his return to Spain enlarged his plan, at the suggestion of the president of the Council of the Indies, and published *Historia del Peru* in 1571.

FERONA, ST. (d. 637). He succeeded St. Columba as abbot of Iona. F. D. Mar. 2.

FÉROTIN, MARIUS (d. 1915). A Benedictine monk at Farmborough, England, from 1875, he wrote authoritative studies of the mozarabic rite in Spain, a history of the abbey of Silos, and an edition of its cartularies. He died on Sept. 16.

FERRARA, DOMENICO (1847–1914), cardinal. Born in Gradoli, Italy, he studied in Orvieto, was named titular bishop of Thessalonica in 1885, and served as nuncio to Belgium and France. Pope Leo XIII made him a cardinal in 1896. He served on four congregations at the Vatican and was named papal secretary of state in 1914.

FERRARESE, IL. *See* Mazzolini, Lodovico.

FERRARI, ANDREA CARLO (1850–1921), cardinal. Born in Lalatta, Italy, on Aug. 13, he was ordained at the seminary in Parma, served as its vice-rector and rector, and was canon of the cathedral there. He became bishop of Guastalla in 1890, was transferred to Como in 1891, and was made metropolitan of Milan and cardinal in 1894. He held three diocesan synods, aided the populace and military during World War I, for which he was decorated by the government in 1919, and in 1920 gave a memorial purse he received to help found Casa del Populo in Milan. He also helped to establish the Catholic University there, wrote on theology and a book of meditations, and died of cancer of the throat in Milan, Italy, on Feb. 2.

FERRARI, GAUDENZIO (1480?–1546), painter. Born in Valduggia, Italy, he studied the art of Bramante, Bramantino, and Mantegna, and was heavily influenced by the older Milanese school and by the Germans. He is one of the few painters of the Italian Renaissance who was deeply religious, who worked exclusively for religious institutions, and who painted sectional episodes of saints' lives. Several of his figures were made to stand out in relief, as though sculptured. His major work includes *Carrying of the Cross*, at Cannabio; *Calvary*, at Vercelli; *Descent from the Cross*, at Turin; and an elaborate series of scenes from the life of Christ for the Pietist center on Sacro Monte de Varallo. In his later years his work shows the influence of Correggio: *Assumption*, at Vercelli; *Glory of the Angels*, at Saronno; and *Flight into Egypt*, at Como. He was still active as a painter at the age of seventy. He died in Milan, Italy, on Jan. 31.

FERRARI, LUDOVICO (1522–1565), mathematician. Born in Bologna, Italy, he studied under Cardan, became a noted mathematician, and discovered the method of resolving equations of the fourth degree named after him.

FERRARIS, LUCIUS (18th century), canonist. Born in Solero, Italy, he became a Franciscan, served as provincial and as consultor of the Holy Office, and wrote an encyclopedic *Prompta bibliotheca* of ecclesiastical information, published before 1763 (a date by which he seems to have died) and still in existence, with supplementary volumes.

FERRATA, DOMENICO (1847–1914), cardinal. Born in Gradoli, Italy, on Mar. 4, he studied at Orvieto, the seminary in Montefiascone, and the Gregorian in Rome. He taught canon law at the Gregorian in 1876, was named consultor to the Congregation of Extraordinary Ecclesiastical Affairs in 1877, and served as papal nuncio to Paris in 1879 and to Belgium in 1885, when he was consecrated titular archbishop of Thessalonica; after four years in Brussels he returned to Paris. He became a cardinal in 1896. His long service was climaxed by his appointment by Benedict XV as secretary of state in 1914. He died a month later, on Oct. 10.

FERRE, VINCENT (d. 1682), theologian. Born in Valencia, Spain, he became a Dominican in Salamanca, taught in several houses, including that at Burgos, and served as regent of the Dominican College of St. Thomas in Rome for eighteen years. On his return he became regent and prior at Salamanca. He wrote commentaries on the *Summa theologica* of St. Thomas.

FERREIRA, ANTONIO (1528–1569), dramatist. Born in Lisbon, Portugal, he studied law at Coimbra, became judge of the supreme court, and enjoyed the patronage of the circle of John III. He wrote poetry in Portuguese (rather than the prevailing Spanish), imitated the classical and Italian Renaissance poets, and then turned to the theater. *Bristo*, a comedy in the tradition of Terence, *O Cioso*, a character study of a jealous husband, and the blank-verse *Inés de Castro* (based on a theme treated by Camões and others) are his chief works. He died in Lisbon of the plague in Nov.

FERRELO, BARTOLOME (16th century), explorer. He was pilot of the expedition (1542–43) under Cabrillo sent by Coronado to seek a strait along the Pacific Coast of North America.

When Cabrillo died, Ferrelo sailed to the shores of Oregon and returned to Mexico.

FERRER, RAFAEL (1570–1611), missioner. Born in Valencia, Spain, he became a Jesuit and in 1593 was sent to Ecuador. From Quito he explored the territory of the hostile Cofanis, whom he pacified, then traveled 3600 miles among the savage Indians of the Napo River region. On his return he was named governor and judge of the Cofanis, with whom he remained, except for some further explorations, until his death at San José, Peru, at the hands of a chief who would not abandon polygamy. He wrote on the language of his colony and translated the catechism and the gospels into their tongue.

FERRINI, BL. CONTARDO (1859–1902). Born in Milan, Italy, on Apr. 4, the son of a schoolteacher, he studied law at Pavia and Berlin, and acquired fluency in many languages. He became professor of Roman law at Pavia and at Medina, was associated with the Ambrosian Library, and wrote some 200 monographs in his field. He died of typhoid at Suna, Italy, on Oct. 17, and was beatified in 1947.

FERREOLUS, ST. (d. 212?), martyr. He was ordained by St. Irenaeus of Lyons and went with St. Ferrutio, a deacon, to preach in Besançon and surrounding Gaul. They had thirty years of success before they were captured and beheaded. F. D. June 16.

FERREOLUS, ST. (d. 304), martyr. An officer in the imperial army in Vienne, Gaul, he was censured by the governor for not having revealed the religion of St. Julian of Brioude, who resided with him. Ferreolus declared his own Christianity and was tortured and beheaded. F. D. Sept. 18.

FERREOLUS, ST. (d. 581), bishop. Born in Narbonne, France, he founded a monastery, wrote its rule, became bishop of Uzès, and was particularly active in converting the Jews of his diocese. F. D. Jan. 4.

FERREOLUS, ST. (d. 591?). The fifth bishop of Limoges, France, he was highly praised by St. Gregory of Tours. F. D. Sept. 18.

FERREOLUS, BL. (d. 670?). Bishop of Grenoble, France, he is said to have resisted a tyrant and to have been driven into exile as a result. His cult was confirmed in 1907. F. D. Jan. 16.

FERRER, ST. VINCENT. See Vincent Ferrer, St.

FERRETTI, BL. GABRIEL (1385–1456). A native of Ancona, Italy, he joined the Friars Minor at eighteen, was engaged in missionary work in the Marches, served as provincial of Piceno there, and became superior of the Observants of Ancona where he died. His cult was confirmed in 1753. F. D. Nov. 12.

FERRETTI, PAOLO MARIA (1866–1938). Born in Subiaco, Italy, on Dec. 3, he became

abbot of Palma, was brought to the Vatican to revise the antiphonary, served as president of the Pontifical Institute of Music from 1911, and wrote on Gregorian chant. He died in Bologna, Italy, on May 5.

FERRON, MARIE ROSE (1902–1936). Born on May 24, 1902, at St. Germaine de Grantham, Quebec, she was the tenth of fifteen children. The family moved to the United States and in 1925 to Woonsocket, Rhode Island. There she was reputed to have been given the stigmata, and died after great suffering on May 11. The claims made by her adherents have never been accepted by the Church.

FERRONIUS, JUSTINIUS. See Hontheim, Johannes Nicolaus von.

FERRUTIO, ST. (d. 212?), martyr. See Ferreolus, St.

FERSTEL, HEINRICH VON (1828–1883), architect. Born in Vienna, Austria, on July 7, he studied architecture, worked for his uncle Stache in restoring churches and castles, traveled across Europe, and in Italy came to admire Bramante and the late Renaissance style. To its simplicity he added polychrome effect through the use of graffiti and terra cotta, as in his Austrian Museum. A bank, burgomaster's house, stock exchange, insurance headquarters, university, and other buildings began to transform the Vienna scene, with his Votivkirche an outstanding design. He also designed churches in Brünn and Schönau and many palaces. He taught at the Polytechnic school in 1866, was chief inspector of public works in 1871, and was made *Freiherr* in 1879. He died in Grinzing, Austria, on July 14.

FESCH, JOSEPH (1763–1839), cardinal. Born in Ajaccio, Corsica, on Jan. 3, he studied at Aix, became provost of the chapter in Ajaccio, went to France after the British occupation of the island, and was commissary of war under Napoleon, his nephew, from 1795 to 1799. He helped to negotiate the concordat of 1801, and was named archbishop of Lyons in 1802 and cardinal in 1803 by Pope Pius VII. That year he was ambassador to Rome, where he persuaded the pope to go to Paris to crown the French emperor. He became royal almoner, director of St. Lazare and St. Sulpice, and in 1806 coadjutor to Dalberg, prince-primate at Ratisbon. Fesch refused the see of Paris in 1808, quarreled with Napoleon in 1811 while president of the national ecclesiastical council, tried to communicate his position to Pope Pius VII but had his letters intercepted, and retire dto Lyons. He was briefly restored to his diocese in 1814 and named a senator by Napoleon, but was banished by the Bourbons in 1815 and died in Rome on May 13. He was active in the reform of his archdiocese (up to the time of his per-

manent banishment) and in the education of
the clergy; he avoided schism in directing the
acts of the ecclesiastical commissions of 1810–
11 in nominating bishops; in domestic and
international diplomacy he found himself
often under great political pressure and sometimes was overly kind to the emperor, though
he as often sought to check his misdirected
energy.

FESSLER, JOSEF (1813–1872), bishop.
Born in Lochau, Austria, on Dec. 2, he studied
at Innsbruck and Brixen, was ordained in 1837,
and in 1841–52 taught history and canon law
at the Brixen seminary. He was elected to the
Frankfort parliament in 1848, held the chair
of church history at Vienna in 1852 and of
canon law in 1856–61, was a member of the
Congregation of Rites in 1862, and in 1864
was named bishop of St. Pölten. He had published studies of provincial councils and diocesan synods and an elaborate analysis of the
Fathers of the Church; his appointment in
1869 as secretary of the Vatican Council was
not surprising. After the council he published
The True and False Infallibility of the Popes,
based on the discussions of 1870 and intended
especially to answer Professor Shulte of Prague.
The work was highly praised by Pope Pius IX.
Fessler died on Apr. 25.

FESTA, COSTANZO (1490?–1545), composer. Born probably in Rome, he was a member of the Vatican choir in 1517, and soon
after this began his lifelong career as its
maestro. Honored as the forerunner of Palestrina, he composed masses, motets, litanies,
and madrigals; outstanding is a *Te Deum*, featured in Corpus Christi services at the Vatican.

FESTUS, ST. (d. 305?), martyr. *See* Januarius, St.

FETHERSTON, BL. RICHARD (d. 1540),
martyr. A secular priest and a doctor of theology from Cambridge, he was one of Catherine
of Aragon's chaplains and a tutor of Princess
Mary. Because he supported the validity of the
queen's marriage he was hanged, drawn, and
quartered at Tyburn, in London. He was
beatified in 1886. F. D. July 30.

FETI, DOMENICO (1589–1624), painter.
He was born in Rome, where he was influenced by the work of Ludovico Cardi and
Caravaggio. After his apprenticeship he became
court painter to Ferdinand Gonzaga, cardinal-
duke of Mantua, completed a few altarpieces,
and specialized in themes illustrative of the
parables and dramatic Old Testament narratives. His mob figures are realistic, his coloring crude and violent, his use of baroque picturesqueness extreme. *Guardian Angel* and
Melancholy are among his best works. He died
in Venice at thirty-four.

FEUARDENT, FRANÇOIS (1539–1610),
theologian. Born in Coutances, Normandy, he

studied at Bayeux, became a Friar Minor, took
his doctorate in theology at Paris in 1576, and
taught there. He was a leading preacher for the
Catholic League, worked actively for religious
peace, and wrote biblical commentaries, refutations of Calvinism, and other controversial
works, and edited Nicholas of Lyra and SS.
Ildephonso and Irenaeus. He died in Paris on
Jan. 1.

FEUCHTERSLEBEN, ERNST VON (1806–
1849), educator. Born in Vienna, Austria, on
Apr. 29, he took his degree in medicine there
in 1833, began to lecture on psychiatry at the
university in 1844, was named dean of the
medical faculty in 1845, and vice-director of
medical studies in 1847. He served briefly in
the state department, wrote several popular
works on medical psychology, critical essays,
and philosophical poems, one of which was set
to music by Mendelssohn, and died in Vienna
on Sept. 3.

FEUILLET, LOUIS (1660–1732), botanist.
Born in Mane, Provence, France, he became a
Franciscan, mastered mathematics and astronomy, and in 1699 was sent with Cassini to the
Near East on a royal expedition to locate port
cities; subsequent trips to Martinique, the
Antilles, and South America won national
honors and the rank of royal mathematician.
He made a second trip to South America
(1707–11), returned with many botanical
specimens, was given an observatory at Marseilles by the crown, and published his scientific observations. He died in Marseilles on
Apr. 18.

FÉVAL, PAUL HENRI CORENTIN (1817–
1887), novelist. Born in Rennes, France, on
Sept. 27, he studied law there, was admitted
to the bar at nineteen, went to Paris when he
lost his first case, worked in advertising and
journalism, and published short stories with
growing success. Under the pseudonym of
Francis Trolopp he published *Les mystères de
Londres* in eleven volumes (gaining the success Eugène Sue did with *Mystères de Paris*).
He wrote in the romantic tradition of the
elder Dumas, and with great haste, sometimes
issuing four novels a year, some of which were
also recast for stage production. He had left
the Church but returned around 1877, published a revised edition of his works which removed many philosophical errors, served as
president of the Société des Gens des Lettres,
and died of paralysis on Mar. 8 at the hospital
of the Brothers of St. John of God in Paris.

FEY, CLARA (1815–1894), foundress. Born
in Aachen, Germany, on Apr. 11, she later
made her house a meeting place for the clergy
and discussions of religious and social problems. In 1837, with three companions, she
rented a house and established a school where
they taught, fed, and clothed poor pupils. They

bought and staffed other buildings, became a religious community as the Sisters of the Poor Child Jesus in 1844, soon had fifty orphans and 150 others under their care, and received approval of their rule from Cardinal Geissel of Cologne and the pope. They branched into establishing high schools for girls, training servants, erecting residences for businesswomen, and preparing embroidered church linen. The order spread into Belgium, Holland, and Austria under the superiorship of Mother Clara, who was assisted by her own brother, Andreas, as spiritual director. She died on May 8.

FEYJÓO Y MONTENEGRO, BENITO JERÓNIMO (1676–1764), critic. Born in Casdemiro, Galicia, Spain, on Oct. 8, he became a Benedictine in 1688, and was stationed at a monastery in Oviedo, where he died on Sept. 26. He wrote widely on all major subjects, contributed to the educational reform of schools and universities, and sought to arouse the country to a realization of its backwardness in science, medicine, and mathematics. His *Teatro crítico universal*, published from 1726 to 1739, was a series of essays on scientific discovery, clerical life, popular customs, folk superstition, the position of women, human ignorance in general, and has been compared in its influence to Addison's *Spectator* papers in England. The approach was continued in his *Cartas eruditas y curiosas* (1742–60).

FFAGER. *See* Fugatius, St.

FIACE, ST. (5th century). An Irish bishop, he wrote a hymn to St. Patrick, with whom he had labored. F. D. Oct. 12.

FIACHAN, ST. (7th century). Born in Munster, Ireland, he became a monk at Lismore and was associated with St. Carthage the Younger. F. D. Apr. 29.

FIACRE, ST. (d. 670?). Reportedly a hermit at Kilfiachra, Ireland, he went to Gaul where St. Faro, bishop of Meaux, gave him land for a hospice. His piety attracted many disciples, for whom he built the abbey of Breuil, and his shrine in Seine-et-Marne attracts pilgrims today. He is the patron of gardeners and of the cab drivers of Paris. F. D. Sept. 1.

FIBITIUS, ST. (d. 500?). Abbot of a monastery at Trèves, he became twenty-first bishop of that see. F. D. Nov. 5.

FICHET, GUILLAUME (14th century). He was rector of the University of Paris in 1467, established the first printing press in France at the Sorbonne with the help of three printers brought from Mainz in 1470, and published *Lettres de Gasparino* in 1470, followed by his own study of rhetoric and his correspondence.

FICINO, MARSILIO (1433–1499), philosopher. Born in Florence, Italy, on Oct. 19, he studied at Florence and Bologna, and began to translate the works of Plato under the spon-

sorship of the Medici, to whom his father had been physician. He became president of the Platonic Academy, recommended the reading of Plato in the churches, and kept a lamp burning before the philosopher's bust. As a result of Savonarola's influence, Ficino became more orthodox, was ordained in 1477, and served as a canon of the cathedral of Florence. He translated widely from the Latin and Greek and devoted himself to making Plato, whom he placed higher than Aristotle, known throughout Europe. He died in Correggio, Italy, on Oct. 1.

FICKER, JULIUS VON (1826–1902), historian. Born in Paderborn, Germany, on Apr. 30, he studied at Bonn, Münster, and Berlin, and taught political and legal history at Innsbruck, Austria, from 1852 to 1879, when he was ennobled by the emperor and retired. He published widely, contributed to the study of diplomatics, supported the theory that Austria was the logical successor of the old German Empire, edited *Acta imperii selecta* and *Regesta imperii* (left unfinished by his friend and patron, the historian Böhmer), and was elected to the Academy of Sciences. Ficker died in Innsbruck, Austria, on June 10.

FIDATI, BL. SIMON (1295?–1348). Born in Cascia, Italy, he was preaching as an Augustinian by 1318, writing a great number of letters every day to encourage penitents, and founding refuges for unmarried mothers. His biography was written by John of Salerno. F.D. Feb. 3.

FIDELIS, ST. (d. 303?), martyr. According to unreliable sources, he was an officer in the Roman army who helped five Christian prisoners in Milan to escape, but was captured near Como. Two soldiers who aided him, Carpophorus and Exanthus, were also tortured and beheaded. F. D. Oct. 28.

FIDELIS, ST. (d. 304), martyr. *See* Bassa, St.

FIDELIS, ST. (d. 570?). He came from the Near East and succeeded St. Paul as bishop of Mérida, Spain. F. D. Feb. 7.

FIDELIS OF SIGMARINGEN, ST. (1577–1622), martyr. Mark Rey was born in Sigmaringen, Prussia, studied at Freiburg im Breisgau, and took up law. He practiced in Alsace, devoting himself to the poor, but became disgusted by the crudities of his legal colleagues and in 1612 became a Capuchin. He was appointed guardian of several of their houses, preached with such success that his conversions were many, and was sent with eight others into the Zwinglian stronghold of the Grisons, Switzerland. His continuing success enraged the Protestant faction, who beat him to death after a sermon at Sewis in the diocese of Chue, Switzerland. He was canonized by Pope Benedict XIV. F. D. Apr. 24.

FIDELMINUS. *See* Felim, St.

FIDENTIUS, ST. He may have been bishop of Padua, Italy, in the second century. F. D. Nov. 16.

FIDHARLEUS, ST. (d. 762). An Irishman, he restored the abbey of Rathin. F. D. Oct. 1.

FIDOLUS, ST. (d. 540?). Son of a Roman official in Gaul, he was captured by the army of King Clovis and ransomed from slavery by Aventinus, abbot of Aumont, near Troyes, whom he later succeeded. He is also known as Phal. F. D. May 16.

FIELD, MICHAEL. *See* Bradley, Katherine, and Edith Emma Cooper.

FIETTA, GIUSEPPE (1883–1960), cardinal. Born in Ivrea, Piedmont, Italy, on Nov. 6, he was ordained in 1905, engaged in diocesan work in Sicily, was sent to Central America as secretary to the apostolic internunciature there in 1923, and was appointed titular archbishop of Serdica, and internuncio in 1926. He was nuncio to Haiti and the Dominican Republic in 1930–36, to Argentina in 1936–53, and in 1953 to Italy. He was created a cardinal in 1958, and died in Ivrea on Oct. 1.

FIGLIUCCI, FELICIO (1525?–1590?), theologian. Born in Siena, Italy, he studied at Padua, was in the service of Cardinal del Monte, was known as a poet and classical scholar, became a Dominican in 1551, taking the name Alexus, and was stationed at Florence. He wrote on Aristotle, Demosthenes, Ficino, and others, and translated the Italian catechism approved by the Council of Trent, which he had attended.

FIGUEROA, FRANCISCO DE (1540?–1620), poet. Born in Alcalá de Henares, Spain, he studied at its university, was a soldier in Italy and Flanders, wrote pastoral poems, sonnets, and *canzoni* in the Italian manner, and followed the blank-verse tradition of Boscán and Garcilaso, whom he is said to have surpassed. His eclogue *Tirsi* was praised by Cervantes in *Galatea*. Most of Figueroa's poetry was burned, at his own direction, shortly before his death at Alcalá de Henares.

FIGUEROA, FRANCISCO GARCÍA DE LA ROSA (18th century). Born in Toluca, Mexico, he became a Franciscan, and for forty years held major offices in his order, including that of provincial and of prefect of studies at Tlaltelulco. He is best known for the thirty-two volumes (of 1000 pages each), which he prepared between 1791 and 1794 at royal direction, of documents copied from monastic and private archives on the history of the Mexican provinces, missions of Texas and California, Indian nations, and major cities of Mexico.

FILBY, BL. WILLIAM (1555–1582), martyr. Born in Oxfordshire, England, and a graduate of Oxford, he became a convert, was ordained at Rheims in 1581, was arrested in England that year with Bl. Edmund Campion, and hanged, drawn, and quartered at Tyburn. He was beatified in 1886. F. D. May 30.

FILCOCK, VEN. ROGER (d. 1601), martyr. He was a priest who was hanged, drawn, and quartered at Tyburn with Bl. Mark Barkworth during the Elizabethan persecution.

FILELFO, FRANCESCO (1398–1481). Born in Tolentino, Italy, on July 25, he studied at Padua, began to teach there at eighteen, and transferred to Florence in 1417, where he became a citizen. In 1419 he became secretary to the Venetian consul general at Constantinople, studied Greek there and served Emperor John Palaeologus on diplomatic missions. He returned to teach at Venice in 1427, and then at Bologna, Florence, Siena, Milan, and Rome. He brought many Greek books to Italy, published his speeches, satires, and correspondence, made many translations, completed a 12,800-line epic, the *Sforziad*, on Duke Francesco Sforza, and died in Florence on July 31 after a life marked by humanistic energy, great arrogance, and country-wide quarrels.

FILICAJA, VINCENZIO DA (1642–1707), poet. Born in Florence, Italy, on Dec. 30, he studied law at Pisa, was a member of the Accademia della Crusca and of the Arcadia in Florence, and enjoyed the patronage of Christina, former queen of Sweden. He became a senator and served as governor of Volterra in 1696 and of Pisa in 1700. He wrote a series of odes on the victory of John Sobieski at Vienna, sonnets on the inroads of foreign power in Italy, and many religious lyrics in Italian and Latin. He died in Florence on Sept. 24.

FILIPEPI, ALESSANDRO DE MARIANO. *See* Botticelli, Sandro.

FILIPPINI, ST. LUCIA (1672–1732), foundress. Born in Tarquinia, Italy, on Jan. 13, she was orphaned when a child, studied at Montefiascone monastery under the direction of a religious group which had been started by Cardinal Barbarigo, and was put in charge of a school for young girls the cardinal had founded at the monastery with Bl. Rose Venerini. Her work soon expanded into the training of teachers and the founding of a congregation to carry on this work, Maestre Pie Filippini, in 1692. In 1707 at the request of Pope Clement XI she opened a school at Rome; her schools soon spread all over Italy, and are now found throughout the world. Ill with cancer the last years of her life, she died in Montefiascone, Italy, and was canonized in 1930 by Pope Pius XI. F. D. Mar. 25.

FILIPPO DI CAMPELLO (13th century), architect. An Italian Franciscan, he designed several churches, chief of which was Santa Chiara in Assisi.

FILLAN, ST. (8th century). Son of St. Kentigerna, he went from Ireland to Scotland with his mother, became a solitary attached to a monastery near St. Andrews, was its abbot, and then was allowed to resign and return to his hermitage. Also called Foelan and Foilan, he is the hero of many extravagant legends. Robert Bruce was devoted to him and carried his relic into the battle of Bannockburn. F. D. Jan. 19.

FILLASTRE, GUILLAUME (1348–1428), cardinal. Born in La Suze, France, he studied and taught law at Rheims, became dean of its chapter, worked to end the Western schism, and in 1411 was made cardinal by antipope John XXIII. He was archbishop of Aix, France, in 1413, attended the Council of Constance and sought to have all rival claimants to the papacy abdicate, was named legate to France by Pope Martin V in 1418, and was transferred to the see of St. Pons-de-Thomières in 1422. He kept a diary of the Council of Constance which details the nationalist problems behind the scenes, the method of voting, the work of the chief figures, and the confirmation of Sigismund as Holy Roman emperor. While at Florence, Fillastre made translations of Plato, and copied maps and Ptolemy's geography, which he sent back to Rheims. He died in Rome on Nov. 6.

FILLIUCCI, VINCENZO (1566–1622). Born in Siena, Italy, he became a Jesuit at eighteen, taught and became rector of the Jesuit college in Siena, taught moral theology in the Roman College for ten years, and then was named penitentiary of St. Peter's by Pope Paul V. He published on moral theology and confessional problems, and was violently censured by the Jansenists and mocked by Pascal in garbled quotations taken from his writings. He died in Rome on Apr. 5.

FINA. See Seraphina, St.

FINAN, ST. (6th century). A native of Munster, Ireland, and follower of St. Brendan, he founded a monastery at Kinnitty in Offaly. F. D. Apr. 7.

FINAN, ST. (d. 661), bishop. An Irish monk at Iona, he succeeded St. Aidan as bishop of Lindisfarne and governed Northumberland, Durham, and York through ten peaceful years, during which he converted Prince Penda and King Sigebert. At their request for missionaries, he sent Bishop Diuma to the Middle English and St. Cedd to the East Saxons. F. D. Feb. 17.

FINBAR, ST. (6th century). He was abbot of the monastery at Innis-Doimhle, Wexford, Ireland. F. D. July 4.

FINBAR, ST. (d. 633), bishop. Said to have been an illegitimate child and a native of Connaught, Ireland, he was educated in Kilkenny. He is reputed to have made two trips to Rome and to have met St. David in Wales. He

preached through southern Ireland and, probably, Scotland, and founded a monastery on the river Lee, around which grew the city of Cork. He probably died at Cloyne. He is also known as Bairre or Barr. F. D. Sept. 25.

FINCH, BL. JOHN (d. 1584), martyr. A native of Lancashire, England, he was a married farmer who harbored priests on the English mission and served as a catechist. He was condemned for his activities and executed at Lancaster, and was beatified in 1929. F. D. Apr. 20.

FINGAR, ST. (5th century), martyr. He and his sister, St. Phiala, were slain with their entourage by a pagan chieftain in Cornwall on their arrival from Ireland. F. D. Dec. 14.

FINGLOW, VEN. JOHN (d. 1586), martyr. Born in Barnby, Yorkshire, England, he was ordained at Rheims in 1581, sent to the English mission, where he labored in the northern area, captured at York, and hanged, drawn, and quartered on Aug. 8.

FINI, TOMMASO DI CRISTOFORO DI FINI. See Masolino da Panicale.

FINIAN, ST. (d. 579), bishop. Born near Strangford Lough, Ireland, he became a monk at the monastery at Whitern, Scotland, was ordained at Rome, established a monastery at Moville in County Down of which he became abbot-bishop and which became one of the great centers of Irish learning, another at Dromin, and a church at Llanfinnan. F. D. Sept. 10.

FINIAN OF CLONARD, ST. (470?–552?). Born in Myshall, Carlow, Ireland, he became a monk in Wales and when he returned to Ireland founded many churches, schools, and monasteries, most famous of which was Clonard in Meath. He became famed as the "teacher of Irish saints" and was reputed to have taught 3000 disciples, including the so-called Twelve Apostles of Ireland, among whom was St. Columba. He was an outstanding biblical scholar. F. D. Dec. 12.

FINIAN LOBHAR, ST. (d. 560?). Born in Leinster, Ireland, he was ordained, and because of an extreme skin affliction came to be called "the leper." It is probable that he spent his last thirty years as abbot of Clonmore. F. D. Mar. 16.

FINK, MICHAEL LOUIS MARY (1834–1904), bishop. Born in Triftersburg, Bavaria, Germany, on July (or June) 12, he studied at St. Vincent's, Beatty, Pennsylvania, became a Benedictine in 1854, and was ordained in 1857. He did pastoral work in New York, New Jersey, Illinois, Kentucky, and Kansas, was appointed prior of St. Benedict monastery, Atchison, Kansas, in 1868, and in 1871 was appointed titular bishop of Eucarpia and coadjutor of the vicariate of Kansas and the Indian Territory. He succeeded as vicar in 1874, became first bishop of Leavenworth in 1877, was transferred to Kansas City in 1891 when Leavenworth was suppressed, and in 1897 returned to Leavenworth when it was restored. He died in Kansas City, Kansas, on Mar. 17.

FINLUGH, ST. (6th century). Brother of St. Fintan of Doon, he became a disciple of St. Columba in Scotland, then became abbot of a monastery in Derry, Ireland. F. D. Jan. 3.

FINN, WILLIAM JOSEPH (1881-1961), musician. Born in Boston, Massachusetts, on Sept. 7, he studied at St. Charles, Maryland, New England Conservatory of Music, St. Paul's College, and Catholic University, became a Paulist in 1900, was ordained in 1906, and traveled in Europe to study music. He founded the Paulist Choristers, which he was to head the next thirty-six years, at St. Mary's church, Chicago, in 1904, was transferred to St. Paul the Apostle church in New York in 1918, and built the Choristers into a world-famed organization which often toured the United States and Canada. He was forced by ill health to retire in 1940, and died in Bronxville, New York, on Mar. 20. He wrote several musical textbooks and his autobiography, *Sharps and Flats in Five Decades*.

FINNEGAN, HUGH (d. 1929), educator. He was ordained a Jesuit, served as a missioner in Montana and Oregon for thirteen years, was chaplain at Marquette for twenty years, taught science at St. Ignatius (later called Loyola), Chicago, and was the second president of Creighton University. He died in Milwaukee, Wisconsin, on Nov. 26.

FINNIGAN, GEORGE JOSEPH (1885-1932), bishop. Born in Potsdam, New York, on Feb. 22, he studied at Notre Dame, the Gregorian, Rome, and Laval, Quebec, joined the Congregation of Holy Cross in 1902, and was ordained in Rome in 1915. He did mission work, was an army chaplain, and served as rector of Holy Cross seminary (1920-24), vice-president of Notre Dame (1924-26), and provincial superior of his order (1926-27). In 1927 he was consecrated bishop of Helena, Montana, and died there on Aug. 14.

FINOTTI, JOSEPH M. (1817-1879). Born in Ferrara, Italy, on Sept. 21, he became a Jesuit at Rome in 1833, taught in various colleges, went to Maryland, was ordained, and was given a parish in Alexandria, Virginia. He left the Society in 1852, served as literary editor of the Boston *Pilot*, held pastorates in Brookline and Arlington, Massachusetts, and Central City, Colorado. He wrote, edited, and translated a dozen works of asceticism and fiction. His most important work was *Bibliographia Catholica Americana* (1872), listing books published in the United States by Catholic authors down to the year 1820. Fr. Finotti died in Central City, Colorado, on Jan. 10.

FINTAN, ST. (6th century). A follower of St. Comgall, he became the patron of Doon, County Limerick, Ireland, where a holy well bearing his name attracted pilgrims. F. D. Jan. 3.

FINTAN, ST. (d. 603). Trained as a monk by St. Columba, he became abbot of the monastery at Cloneenagh, introducing an extreme asceticism to which the monks there and elsewhere in Ireland objected, and which he modified, though not for himself. F. D. Feb. 17.

FINTAN, ST. (d. 635?). After serving as a monk for eighteen years under St. Senell at Cluain Inis, Ireland, he went to Iona but returned about 597 to Ireland and founded the monastery of Taghmon in Wexford in 599, which became a famous center of learning. He was a strong supporter of the Celtic Easter date and customs at the Synod of Magh Lene in 630. F. D. Oct. 21.

FINTAN, ST. (d. 879). A native of Leinster, Ireland, he was carried to the Orkney Islands by Norse raiders, but escaped to Scotland. After two years there he made a pilgrimage to Rome, became a Benedictine at Farfa, and settled at the abbey of Rheinau, Switzerland, where he lived as a recluse for his last twenty-two years. F. D. Nov. 15.

FIORE D'URBINO. *See* Baroccio, Federigo.

FIRAIAMA-DIAZ, BL. JOACHIM d. (1622), martyr. *See* Zuñiga, Bl. Pedro.

FIRMIAN, ST. (d. 1020?). He was abbot of the Benedictine monastery of San Sabino Piceno, in the Marches of Ancona, Italy. He is apparently listed erroneously in the Roman Martyrology as Firminus, an abbot at Amiens. F. D. Mar. 11.

FIRMICUS MATERNUS, JULIUS (4th century). He wrote *De errore profanarum religionum* about 347, gathering data on early pagan religions and contributing original commentary on the mysteries of Eleusis, Isis, and Mithra. The work begs Emperors Constantius II and Constans I to stamp out superstition, and makes reference to the Persian wars. Before his conversion he wrote on astrology in *Matheseo* about 336.

FIRMILIAN (d. 269?), bishop. A Cappadocian, he was a friend of Gregory Thaumaturgos; together, they were disciples of Origen, whom Firmilian invited to his country about 232. At this time Firmilian apparently was bishop of Caesarea and was attacking the heresy of Novatian. Later he was to become a strong supporter of the necessity of rebaptizing the lapsed Christians, using the arguments of St. Cyprian and the African bishops, in opposition to the papal position. Firmilian attended the councils at Antioch in 264-65 which deposed Paul of Samosata, and was on his way to a third council there when he died at Tarsus. Though he was excommunicated by Pope Stephen, subsequent pontiffs did not consider him in total error. He is honored in the Greek Church on Oct. 28.

FIRMINA, ST. (d. 303?), martyr. She was tortured to death at Amelia, Umbria, during the Diocletian persecution. F. D. Nov. 23.

FIRMINUS, ST. (d. 304?), martyr. *See* Cyriac, St.

FIRMINUS, ST. (4th century?), bishop and martyr. He is said to have been a native of Pampeluna, Spanish Navarre, and martyred in Amiens, as whose first bishop he is sometimes listed, though the first known bishop of Amiens was Eulogius. He may have been a missionary bishop at Toulouse, Gaul. F. D. Sept. 25.

FIRMINUS, ST. (d. 496). Born in Italy or Greece, he went to Metz, Gaul, where he became bishop about 488. F. D. Aug. 18.

FIRMINUS, ST. (516–553). Born in Narbonne, Gaul, he was educated by his uncle, whom he succeeded as bishop of Uzès in about 538. F. D. Oct. 11.

FIRMINUS, ST. (6th century). He was bishop of Viviers, France, F. D. Mar. 29.

FIRMINUS, ST. (6th century). He was seventh bishop of Verdun, France. F. D. Dec. 5.

FIRMINUS, ST. Called the third bishop of Amiens, Gaul, and said to have been son of a convert of an earlier St. Firminus, he may be identical with that bishop. F. D. Sept. 1.

FIRMUS, ST. (d. 290?), martyr. He was put to death in the Near East during the persecution of Maximian. F. D. June 1.

FIRMUS, ST. (d. 290?), martyr. A leading citizen of Bergamo, Italy, he was put to death at Verona with a relative, St. Rusticus, during the reign of Maximian. F. D. Aug. 9.

FIRMUS, ST. (d. 304?), martyr. *See* Cyriac, St.

FISCHER, ANTONIUS (1840–1912), cardinal. Born in Jülich, Germany, on May 30, he was educated at Cologne, Bonn, Münster, and Tübingen, was ordained in 1863, and taught religion for twenty-five years at the gymnasium in Essen. He became in 1889 assistant to the auxiliary bishop of Cologne, its archbishop in 1902, and a cardinal in 1903. He was especially active in gaining government support for labor legislation, advised miners, worked on ecumenical committees, and consecrated hundreds of churches. He died in Neuenahr, Germany, on July 30.

FISHER, ST. JOHN (1469–1535), cardinal and martyr. Born at Beverley, Yorkshire, he went to Cambridge at fourteen, distinguished himself in scholarship, and was ordained at twenty-one. He continued to serve the university as fellow, master, and vice-chancellor, founded St. John's College, established a number of readerships, and brought Erasmus and other scholars to the faculty. In 1504 he became chancellor of the university as well as

bishop of Rochester. Despite the dual work load, he continued his studies and wrote much, including sermons on the penitential Psalms; tracts on prayer, the sacraments, and consolation; a discourse on the identity of Mary Magdalen; and confutations of the heretical positions of Luther and Escolampadius. His contributions to the intellectual world were internationally recognized. Henry VIII's attempt to divorce Catherine of Aragon found him, in 1529, as one of the queen's councilors, emphasizing the validity and indissolubility of the marriage, a stand which roused Henry's enmity. He then turned his full energies to the defense of the Church and of the supremacy of the pope. He was twice imprisoned and two attempts were made on his life. When he refused to agree to the bill of succession because the oath accompanying it became an oath of royal supremacy over the Church, he was stripped of his offices and sent to the Tower for ten months. On May 21, 1535, Pope Paul III made him a cardinal; in fury, Henry immediately ordered Fisher tried. He was declared guilty of high treason, at a farcical hearing, and beheaded at Tyburn on June 22. He was canonized in 1935 by Pope Pius XI. F. D. July 9.

E. E. REYNOLDS, *St. John Fisher* (New York, Kenedy, 1956); PHILIP HUGHES, ed., *St. John Fisher: the Earliest English Life* (London, Burns, Oates, 1935).

FISHER, JOHN (1569–1641), theologian. Born in Holmside, Durham, England, he was educated in Rheims and Rome, was ordained in 1593, became a Jesuit in 1594, suffered persecution in Holland and England, was arrested in 1610 and banished, and became professor of theology at Louvain. Returning to England, he was imprisoned for three years and again banished; once more he returned, converted the countess of Buckingham, and was banished for the third time. He engaged in written controversy with Archbishop Laud.

FISHER, JOHN. *See* Percy, John.

FITTER, DANIEL (1628–1700). Born in Worcestershire, England, he studied at Lisbon, was ordained in 1651, and about 1653 became chaplain to William Fowler of Staffordshire. He opened and directed a school in Stafford from 1685 to 1688, but it was closed by the new penal laws. He was named first provincial in mid-England of the institute of clergy founded in Germany by Fr. Bartolomaus Holzhauser; the group was dissolved in 1702. He died at St. Thomas priory, near Stafford, England, on Feb. 6.

FITTON, JAMES (1805–1881). Born in Boston, Massachusetts, on Apr. 10, he studied there and in New Hampshire, was trained and ordained by Bishop Fenwick in 1827, and traveled through all of New England as a missioner, suffering hostility and insult during a violently anti-Catholic period of history. In 1840 he was a pastor in Worcester, Massachusetts, and purchased land and erected a building for the education of young men, which he turned over to the bishop in 1842 and which became Holy Cross College. From 1855, he was pastor of the church of the Most Holy Redeemer, East Boston, where he died on Sept. 15.

FITZALAN, HENRY (1511?–1580). Son of William, eleventh earl of Arundel, and Lady Anne Percy, he was Henry VIII's godson, educated in the royal palace, and served as governor of Calais from 1540 to 1543. He inherited his father's title that year, led the capture of Boulogne in 1544, and was appointed lord chamberlain. He was attacked by Warwick during the reign of Edward VI, and supported Lady Jane Grey, but gave his allegiance to Queen Mary on her accession and served as a royal steward. He held offices in the reign of Elizabeth I, though in disgrace from 1564 to 1568. Powerful leader of the Catholic party, he favored the marriage of Mary Queen of Scots and the duke of Norfolk; after the discovery of the Ridolfi plot in 1571 he was arrested and remained in retirement until his death in London on Feb. 24.

FITZALAN, HENRY GRANVILLE (1815–1860). Son of Henry Charles Howard and Charlotte, daughter of the duke of Sutherland, he studied at Cambridge, entered the army but resigned when he became captain, and married the daughter of Lord Lyons in 1839. He served in the House of Commons in 1837–42, became fourteenth duke of Norfolk in 1856, was converted after a meeting with Montalembert in 1839, and was active in charitable and philanthropic work.

FITZGERALD, EDWARD (1833–1907), bishop. Born in Limerick, Ireland, on Oct. 26, he was brought to the United States by his parents in 1849, studied at the Lazarist seminary in Barrens, Missouri, Mt. St. Mary of the West, Cincinnati, and Mt. St. Mary's, Maryland, and was ordained in Cincinnati in 1857. He spent the next nine years as pastor of St. Patrick's in Columbus where he overcame a trustee situation which had the parish under an interdict when he arrived, and was preconized bishop of Little Rock, Arkansas, in 1866. He voted against the doctrine of papal infallibility at the Vatican Council in 1870, though he immediately submitted; attended the third Plenary Council of Baltimore in 1884, where he advocated prudence in establishing compulsory attendance at parochial schools, though he actively encouraged Catholic education in his see; resigned and retired to Hot Springs, Arkansas, because of ill health in 1906, and died there on Feb. 21.

FITZGERALD, JOHN FRANCIS (1863–1950), mayor. Born in Boston, Massachusetts, on Feb. 14, he studied at Harvard, became a member of the Boston city council in 1892, a state senator in 1893–94, served in Congress in 1895–1901, and was mayor of Boston in 1906–7 and in 1910–16. He was a member of the Boston port authority at the time of his death in Boston on Oct. 2. His daughter's husband, Joseph P. Kennedy, became ambassador to Great Britain and his grandson John Fitzgerald Kennedy became the thirty-fifth President of the United States.

FITZGERALD, JOHN M. (1888–1952), engineer. Born in New York City, he took his degree in engineering at Manhattan in 1907, then worked for the city board of water supply, except for two years in the army during World War I, until his death in New York on Apr. 1. He worked on the Shandaken tunnel of the Catskill water-supply system and was engineer in charge of the Delaware aqueduct of the Kensico system. He became chief engineer of the board in 1948.

FITZGERALD, WALTER JAMES (1883–1947), bishop. Born in Peola, Washington, on Nov. 17, he studied at Gonzaga, Immaculate Conception College, Montreal, and Los Gatos, California, became a Jesuit in 1902, and was ordained in 1918. He taught at Gonzaga, was president there in 1921–27, of Manresa Hall seminary, Washington, in 1927–29, and of Seattle College in 1929–30. He was provincial of the Oregon province in 1932–38, and in 1938 was appointed titular bishop of Tymbrias and coadjutor vicar apostolic of Alaska. He succeeded as vicar apostolic in 1945, and died on July 19.

FITZGIBBON, CATHERINE (1823–1896). Born in London on May 12, she was brought to Brooklyn, New York, at nine and became a Sister of Charity at Mt. St. Vincent, taking the name Irene, in 1850. In 1869 she founded a home for abandoned children, which became the New York Foundling Hospital; St. Ann's Maternity Hospital for homeless mothers in 1880; a children's hospital in 1881; and Seton Hospital for incurable consumptives in 1896 at Spuyten Duyvil. She died in New York City on Aug. 14.

FITZGIBBON, MAURICE (d. 1578), martyr. A Cistercian abbot, he was appointed bishop of Cashel, Ireland, in 1567, was deprived of his see by Queen Elizabeth, lived for a time in France and Spain, returned secretly, was captured and tortured, and died at Cork after great suffering.

FITZHERBERT, ANTHONY (1470–1538), jurist. Born in Norbury, Derbyshire, England, he succeeded his father as lord of the manor, may have studied at Oxford, became a lawyer in London, and published in 1514 *La Graunde*

Abridgement, a digest of yearbooks of English law. He edited the Magna Charta and other statutes in 1519 and was knighted and made a judge of common pleas in 1522. He held several royal commissions and acted as vice-chancellor for the fallen Wolsey in 1529. Though he made his objections clear, he was one of the judges at the trial of SS. Thomas More and John Fisher; he also strongly opposed the suppression of the monasteries. In 1534 he published *La nouvelle natura brevium,* long a classic law study, and later issued works on the duties of justices of the peace, bailiffs, constables, and other legal officers. He died on May 27.

FITZHERBERT, MARIA ANNE (1756–1837). Daughter of Walter Smythe of Brambridge, Hampshire, England, where she was born on July 26, she married Edward Weld in 1775, who died that same year, and in 1778 married Thomas Fitzherbert, who died in 1781. She met George, prince of Wales (later King George IV), and six years her junior, about 1784 and was married to him by an Anglican cleric and two witnesses on December 15, 1785, though the Royal Marriage Act of 1772 forbade the marriage of a member of the royal family to a Catholic. In 1794, George was forced into a state marriage to his cousin Princess Caroline of Brunswick and put Mrs. Fitzherbert aside with a pension. The latter returned to the prince in 1800, with the approval of Church authorities in Rome, but finally ended the relationship in 1811 when she felt she had been slighted at a public affair by George. She retired from public life and died in Brighton, England, on March 29.

FITZHERBERT, THOMAS (1552–1640). Born in Swynnerton Staffs, England, he went to Oxford, apparently left because of his religion and went into hiding, was imprisoned in 1572, helped the Catholic underground movement on his release, aided Fr. Campion in the writing of *Decem rationes,* and was forced to flee to France in 1582. From the death of his wife in 1588 until 1607 he was in the service of the duke of Feria, traveling through Europe; he frequently was cited in diplomatic letters to England as an alleged conspirator in plots to kill Elizabeth and as a leading Catholic agent; in Spain, he was looked upon as an agent in the pay of the English queen. In 1602 he was ordained in Rome, became a Jesuit in 1613, and was superior in Flanders from 1616 to 1618 and rector of the English College in Rome until 1639. He wrote several apologetical works, particularly about the oath of allegiance to King James I of England, translated an Italian life of St. Francis Xavier, and died in Rome on Aug. 17.

FITZMAURICE, JOHN EDMUND (1839–1920), bishop. Born in Newton Sandes, Kerry, Ireland, on Jan. 8, he went to the United States and was ordained in Philadelphia in 1862. He did parish work, was appointed rector of St. Charles Borromeo seminary, Philadelphia, in 1866, and in 1897 was appointed titular bishop of Amisus and coadjutor of Erie, Pennsylvania. He succeeded to the see in 1899, and died there on June 18.

FITZPATRICK, CHARLES (1853–1942), jurist. Born in Quebec, Canada, he was educated in its seminary and at Laval and admitted to the bar in 1876. He was named crown prosecutor for the city, became famous as a criminal lawyer, served as a member of the Quebec legislature from 1890 to 1896 and as a Liberal member of the House of Commons from 1896 to 1906. During this term he was solicitor general for six years and minister of justice for four; in 1906 he was appointed chief justice of the supreme court; in 1908, a member of The Hague peace tribunal. He served on the commission which revised the public statutes, was a delegate to the Irish nationalist convention in 1896, and a lay delegate to the first missionary congress of 1908. He was knighted in 1907, became a member of the privy council in 1908, and received an honorary degree from Harvard in 1914. He died on June 17 in Quebec.

FITZPATRICK, JOHN BERNARD (1812–1866), bishop. Born in Boston, on Nov. 15, he studied at Collège de Montreal and St. Sulpice in Paris, and was ordained in Paris in 1840. He was assigned to Boston, was consecrated titular bishop of Callipolis and coadjutor in 1844, and succeeded to the see in 1846 as its third bishop. His episcopacy was marked by his aid to the Irish immigrants who poured into Boston, his battle against the foes of Catholic schools and colleges, and his interest in literature. In 1861, Harvard College granted him an honorary degree in sacred theology, the first Catholic bishop to be so honored. He died in Boston on Feb. 13.

FITZPATRICK, JOHN CLEMENT (1876–1940). Born in Washington, D.C., on Aug. 10, he joined the staff of the *U. S. Government Advertiser* in 1894, and became a member of the manuscripts division of the Library of Congress in 1897. He wrote several brochures on manuscript collecting and cataloguing, and edited Martin Van Buren's *Autobiography,* George Washington's *Diaries,* and four volumes of the Continental Congress journals. He was appointed acting chief of the manuscripts division in 1927, resigned the following year when he was passed over for the position of chief, became editor of the thirty-nine-volume George Washington Bicentennial Commission edition of the collected works of Washington (1931–44), and was president of the American Catholic Historical Association in 1928–29. He died in Washington on Feb. 10.

FITZ PATRICK, WILLIAM JOHN (1830–1895), historian. Born in Dublin, Ireland, on Aug. 31, he studied at Clongowes Wood, wrote a number of popular biographies, carefully detailed but poor in style, and carried on a fruitless controversy to claim that Sir Walter Scott plagiarized his novels from his brother Thomas Scott. He taught history at the Hibernian Academy of Arts after 1876, published a history of Ireland before the union, lives of Fr. Thomas Burke and Charles Lever, then issued two solid works: *The Correspondence of Daniel O'Connell, with His Life and Times* (1888) and *Secret Service under Pitt* (1892). He received a papal decoration and an honorary degree from the Royal University of Ireland. He served as high sheriff for Longford County for two terms and died in Dublin on Dec. 24.

FITZRALPH, RICHARD (1295?–1360), archbishop. Born in Dundalk, Louth, Ireland, he studied at Oxford, taught at Balliol, and became chancellor of the university in 1333, chancellor of Lincoln cathedral in 1334, and dean of Lichfield in 1337. He was consecrated archbishop of Armagh in 1346. He sought to better the educational opportunities of the clergy. Probably while at Avignon in 1350 he took part in the discussions between the pope and the Armenian delegates which resulted in his study of Greek and Armenian heresies. He also argued for many years against the privileges granted the mendicant friars and wrote several works in defense of the position of parish clergy; the most important is *De pauperie salvatoris*, which was quoted at length by Wyclif. The archbishop died in Avignon, France, on Dec. 16.

FITZ SIMON, HENRY (1566–1644). Born in Dublin, Ireland, he was educated at Oxford and Paris, became a leading Protestant controversialist, and when beaten in debate with Fr. Thomas Derbyshire became a Catholic and, in 1592, a Jesuit. He taught at Douai, was sent to the Irish mission, where he worked with success for four years near Waterford, was imprisoned for five years, banished in 1604, labored on the Continent, and in 1620 became a chaplain with an Irish force in Flanders and Bohemia. He returned to Ireland in 1630, had a price on his head, lived in the Wicklow mountains, and continued his labors from hiding during the civil war. He wrote controversial tracts, a catalogue of Irish saints, and a rhymed explanation of the mass. He died on Nov. 29, probably in Kilkenny.

FITZSIMON, LAURENCE (1895–1958), bishop. Born in San Antonio, Texas, on Jan. 31, he studied at St. Anthony's College there, the North American College in Rome and St. Meinrad's seminary, Indiana, and was ordained in 1921. He taught at St. John's seminary in San Antonio until 1925, was a pastor at Runge and Seguin, Texas, for the following sixteen years, and became chancellor of the San Antonio archdiocese in 1941. He was consecrated bishop of Amarillo, Texas, later in the year, and remained there until his death on July 2.

FITZ SIMONS, THOMAS (1741–1811), merchant. Born in Ireland, he went to the United States sometime before 1758, married Catherine Meade in Philadelphia in 1763, and was a business partner of her brother George until 1784. He was a deputy to the Carpenter's Hall conference and to the first Continental Congress, was elected provincial delegate in 1774, organized a company of militia, and fought at the battle of Trenton. He then joined other merchants in the Philadelphia area in supplying the Continental army. He was a member of Congress in 1782, served in the Constitutional Convention in 1787 (he and Daniel Carroll were the only Catholic delegates), signed the Constitution he had helped draw up, and was elected to the first, second, and third Congresses of the United States. He was a staunch Federalist, a leader in economic society, and one of the founders of Georgetown University. He died in Philadelphia on Aug. 26.

FITZWALTER, ROBERT (d. 1235). Keeper of Hertford Castle, England, he opposed King John, whom he accused of trying to seduce his daughter, and brought the monarch to terms (after his estates had been seized and he had been banished) when he led an army of barons and helped to force the signing of Magna Charta. He was in danger of losing his life for his part in this action, served with the crusading army in 1219–20, and returned to England to find favor in the court of King Henry III.

FIXMILLNER, PLACIDUS (1721–1791), astronomer. Born in Achleuthen, Austria, he studied at Salzburg, became a Benedictine at sixteen, continued his interest in mathematics, became director of the observatory of the abbey Kremsmünster, Upper Austria, and taught canon law and directed its college. After Herschel discovered Uranus, Fixmillner was the first to compute its orbit; he made observations of Mercury which Lalande used, and published several works in his field. He died at the abbey on Aug. 27.

FIZEAU, ARMAND HIPPOLYTE LOUIS (1819–1896), physicist. Born in Paris on Sept. 23, he attended Stanislas College, studied medicine but gave it up because of poor health, then studied at the observatory and at the Collège de France. With Foucault he made many experiments in optics, identifying radiant heat and light, the regularity of light vibrations, and, after they parted to work separately, the velocity of light, determined in 1849. He studied the expansion of crystals, developed the effectiveness of the induction coil, and was awarded the grand prize of the Academy of Sciences in 1856. He became a member in 1860; he had been honored by the Legion of Honor in 1849, and became an officer in 1875. He won the Rumford Medal of the English Royal Society in 1866. He published on photography, light, heat, and crystallization, and died in Nanteuil, France, on Sept. 18.

FLACCILLA. *See* Aelia Flaccilla.

FLAGET, BENEDICT JOSEPH (1763–1850), bishop. Born in Contournat, France, on Nov. 7, he studied at Clermont, attended the Sulpician seminary there and at Issy, joined the Sulpicians in 1783, and was ordained in 1788. He taught theology at Nantes and Angers until the French Revolution, sailing to Baltimore, Maryland, in 1792. He did missionary work in Indiana, taught at Georgetown in 1795–98, and helped establish the Sulpician college while stationed in Havana, Cuba, in 1798–1801. He was at St. Mary's, Baltimore, from 1801 until 1808, when he was named first bishop of Bardstown, Kentucky, refused the honor but was ordered to accept, and was consecrated in 1810. He built a seminary, worked with the Indians, and visited the settlements in his huge territory, from the Alleghenies to the Mississippi. He consecrated his cathedral in 1819, consecrated J. B. M. David (with whom he had first sailed from France) as his coadjutor that year, attended the first Council of Baltimore in 1829, and consecrated Bishop Richard Kenrick in 1830. He continued to oversee his sprawling diocese, directed missions among the Indians, resigned his office in 1832 but was reinstated the next year by popular demand, and built colleges, asylums, seminaries, and churches. By 1834, with Bishop Chabrat as coadjutor, he had only Kentucky and Tennessee to supervise; the latter became a separate diocese in 1838. He was in Europe from 1835 to 1839, seeking aid for his parishes, returned and transferred his see to Louisville in 1841, consecrated Martin Spalding as his third coadjutor, and died in Louisville, Kentucky, on Nov. 11.

FLAMAND, FRANÇOIS. *See* Duquesnoy, François.

FLANAGAN, EDWARD JOSEPH (1886–1948), sociologist. Born in Roscommon, Ireland, on July 13, he went to the United States in 1904 after study at Sligo, continued his education at Mt. St. Mary's, Maryland, the Gregorian, Rome, and Innsbruck, and was ordained in 1912. He worked in Omaha, Nebraska, parishes from 1912 to 1917, established a workingmen's hotel there, and in the latter year began an orphanage for two newsboys and three juvenile delinquents whom the court paroled in his custody. From this developed Boys Town, Nebraska, which was world-famous by 1938, when its story became the basis of a motion picture; the city was incorporated in 1939, when its population was 500; in his lifetime, Fr. Flanagan cared for 5000 youths. His plan was widely imitated in other parts of the world, and its founder was making an inspection tour of youth facilities supported by army personnel when he died in Berlin, Germany, on May 15.

FLANAGAN, THOMAS (1814–1865), historian. Born in England, he studied at Sedgley Park and Oscott, was ordained in 1842, taught and served as prefect of studies until 1850, then was rector of Sedgley Park and a canon of the cathedral in Birmingham. He returned to Oscott in 1853. He wrote a manual of English and Irish history and a history of the Church in England. In his last years he was an assistant at St. Chad's, Birmingham, and died in Kidderminster, England, on July 21.

FLANDRIN, AUGUST (1804–1842), painter. Elder brother of Hippolyte, he studied at L'École des Beaux Arts in Lyons, became a lithographer, joined his brothers in Paris in 1832, went to Italy, and on his return opened a studio in Lyons, where he popularized the work of Ingres.

FLANDRIN, JEAN HIPPOLYTE (1809–1864), painter. Born in Lyons, France, on Mar. 23, he studied sculpture under Legendre and Revoil, went to Paris with his brother Jean Paul, and became a pupil of Ingres. In 1832 he attained success by his *Recognition of Theseus*, which won the Grand Prix de Rome. He followed Ingres to Rome, where he remained from 1834 to 1838, and completed *Dante and Vergil*, *Euripides*, *St. Clare*, and religious scenes. Back in Paris he led the revolt against the decorative art of the eighteenth century, showed the influence of the Italian Nazarenes in his church murals, and led a group of artists devoted to instructive art. He decorated the sanctuary, choir, and nave of St. Germain-des-Prés, completed a frieze at St. Vincent de Paul portraying fifteen centuries of the Church, both in Paris, and worked on the apse of the church of Ainay, near Lyons. The basic concept of these works is brilliant, the sense of balance and command of allegory effective, but the result somewhat cold. Naturalness and charm are revealed in his portraits, particularly *Young Girl with a Pink*, *Young Girl Reading*, and *Napoleon III*. He died of smallpox in Rome on Mar. 21.

FLANDRIN, JEAN PAUL (1811–1902), painter. Younger brother of Hippolyte, he studied at L'École des Beaux Arts in Lyons, went to Paris to work under Ingres, went to

Rome in 1834, and became his brother's assistant. He completed the decorations in St. Germain-des-Près after the latter's death, worked by himself in St. Séverin and the Palais de la Chancellerie, and also painted landscapes.

FLANNAN, ST. (7th century?), bishop. Son of an Irish chieftain, Turlough, he made a pilgrimage to Rome where Pope John IV consecrated him. On his return he became first bishop of Killaloe, and also preached in the Hebrides. F. D. Dec. 18.

FLASCH, KILIAN CASPER (1831–1891), bishop. Born in Retzstadt, Bavaria, on July 16 (or 9), he was brought to the United States in 1847, studied at Notre Dame and St. Francis seminary, Milwaukee, and was ordained in La Crosse, Wisconsin, in 1859. He taught at St. Francis, became its rector in 1879, and in 1881 was consecrated bishop of La Crosse. He died there on Aug. 3.

FLATHERS, VEN. MATTHEW (1580?–1607), martyr. Born in Weston, Yorkshire, England, he studied at Douai, was ordained at Arras in 1606, sent to the English mission, and captured almost immediately. Charged with being ordained abroad, he was condemned to death, but the sentence was commuted to banishment. He then returned to England, was again captured, and was hanged, drawn, and quartered at York on Mar. 25.

FLAVIA, DOMITILLA (2nd century). Niece of Emperors Domitian and Titus, she married the consul, Flavius Clemens, became a convert, and after his martyrdom was banished to the island of Bandataria in the Tyrrhenian Sea. Her mother, wife of Emperor Vespasian, and grandmother, had the same name. Another account has her put to death with her foster-sisters, Euphrosyne and Theodora, in Terracina, Italy, and honored on May 7.

FLAVIAN, ST. (d. 259), martyr. See Victoricus, St.

FLAVIAN, ST. (d. 304?), martyr. A deputy prefect in Rome, he was put to death during the Diocletian persecution when his Christianity was discovered. F. D. Jan. 28.

FLAVIAN, ST. (d. 362), martyr. He is said to have been a prefect of Rome, who was exiled as a branded slave to Acquapendente, Tuscany, by Julian the Apostate. F. D. Dec. 22.

FLAVIAN, ST. (d. 449), patriarch and martyr. Succeeding St. Proclus in 447 as patriarch of Constantinople, he offended the imperial chamberlain, Chrysaphius, by condemning bribery. Flavian also condemned the abbot Eutyches, who began the Monophysite heresy, which denied that Christ had two natures after the Incarnation. Eutyches appealed to Pope Leo I, but was censured in the famous *Tome*; he then worked with Chrysaphius and

Bishop Dioscorus to set up a rump court at Ephesus (which the pope called the Robber Council) to remove Flavian. All but the papal legates were cowed into submission, the session broke up in violence, and Flavian was so badly beaten that he died soon after near Sardis, Lydia. The legates brought a full explanation to Pope Leo, who deposed and excommunicated Dioscorus; on his accession, Emperor Martian executed Chrysaphius, and the heresy lessened. F. D. Feb. 18.

FLAVIAN, ST. (d. 512), bishop. A Syrian monk, he was appointed patriarch of Antioch in 498. He supported Emperor Zeno's *Henotikon* (482), which, in attempting to settle the dispute between Catholics and Monophysites, favored the heretics and was condemned by Rome. Flavian was loyal to the Church and was exiled for refusing to support the pro-Monophysite Emperor Anastasius. He died at Petra, Arabia. F. D. July 20.

FLAVIAN, ST. (7th century). He is listed as twenty-first bishop of Autun, France. F. D. Aug. 23.

FLAVIAN, ST. See Bibiana, St.

FLAVIO, BIONDO (1388–1463), historian. Born in Forlì, Italy, he was its ambassador to Milan in 1388, lived in Venice from 1423 to 1432 as secretary to Barbaro and Barbarigo, and then became secretary to Pope Eugene IV. He was among the first to analyze the changing intellectual climate and the transition from the mediaeval world, and he set a new standard for research and objectivity in his *Decades*, modeled on the historical method of Livy. He died in Rome.

FLAVIUS, ST. (d. 300?), bishop and martyr. The bishop of Nicomedia was put to death with his brothers, Augustine and Augustus, in his see city during the Diocletian persecution. F. D. May 7.

FLAVIUS CLEMENS, ST. (d. 96?), martyr. Brother of Emperor Vespasian and husband of Flavia Domitilla, he was consul in 95 with his uncle, Domitian, who ordered him beheaded when he learned of his Christianity. F. D. June 22.

FLÉCHIER, VALENTIN ESPRIT (1632–1710), bishop. Born in Pernes, France, on June 10, he studied in Tarascon, was ordained a member of the Congregation of Christian Doctrine, left that order, and went to Paris in 1660. A Latin poem won the favor of King Louis XIV, and he became tutor in the household of Caumartin, councilor of state, and helped to educate the dauphin. He became a member of the French Academy in 1673, with Racine; was appointed bishop of Lavaux in 1685, and transferred to Nîmes in 1687; and was known for his charities to Calvinists and Catholics, his success in making converts, and his sacred oratory, which was compared to that of Bossuet. His sermons were published, as well as *Mémoires* and biographies of Cardinal Ximenes and Theodosius the Great. He died in Montpellier, France, in Feb.

FLEMAEL, BERTHOLET (1614–1675), painter. Born in Liège, Flanders, on May 23, son of a glass painter, he studied under Trippez and Douffet, worked in Rome, Florence, and Paris, and did several church paintings in Liège. He returned to Paris in 1670, painted the ceiling of an audience room in the Tuileries, became professor at the Royal Academy, and was admired by Louis XIV. In his last years he returned to Liège, where he designed churches, became a lay canon of the church of St. Paul, lapsed into mild insanity, and died.

FLEMING, CHRISTOPHER (1599–1631), martyr. Born in Lagan, Louth, Ireland, on Apr. 17, he studied in Douai and Louvain, became a Franciscan in 1617, taking the name Patrick, and was ordained in Rome in 1623. He taught philosophy at Louvain, became first superior of the house of the Strict Observance in Prague, and taught theology until driven out by the Thirty Years' War. He and Matthew Hoar were slain by a Calvinist peasant mob on Nov. 7 during their flight from Prague. He wrote biographies of St. Columba and Archbishop Hugh MacCaghwell of Armagh, and a chronicle of St. Peter's monastery in Ratisbon.

FLEMING, RICHARD (1360?–1431), bishop. Born in Yorkshire, England, he studied at Oxford, served as one of twelve commissioners appointed to examine the work of Wyclif, became rector in Boston after 1415, and was elected bishop of Lincoln in 1419. He headed an embassy to Germany in 1422, was English representative at the Council of Pavia in 1423, where he supported the pope against the council, and was named archbishop of York in 1424. On his return he found that the king had already given the see to another, and he gave up his claim. He founded Lincoln College, Oxford, in 1427. He died in Sleaford, England, on Jan. 25.

FLEMING, THOMAS (1593–1655), archbishop. Son of the baron of Slane, Ireland, he studied in Louvain, became a Franciscan and taught there, and in 1623 was named archbishop of Dublin by Pope Urban VIII. He presided at a diocesan synod in 1640, attended the Synod of Kilkenny during the civil war, sought peace, and tried to negotiate with Ormond. He lost his see in 1649 during the Cromwellian persecution, and went to Galway, Ireland, where he died.

FLETCHER, JOHN (d. 1848), theologian. Born in Ormskirk, England, he studied in Douai and Paris, was ordained, taught at St. Omer, was captured at the outbreak of the revolution, and not released until 1795. Re-

turning to England, he held several parish posts and chaplaincies, and was in Northampton from 1844 to 1848. He wrote sermons, a prayer book, on Church and state and transubstantiation, contemporary controversy, and translated Edmund Campion, Fénelon, and others.

FLETE, WILLIAM (14th century). Born in England and educated at Cambridge, he became an Augustinian Hermit, sought a stricter life than that of the friars in England, and began a contemplative and solitary life in caves near Siena, Italy. He studied and prayed there by day and returned to a monastery at night, became known as the "Bachelor of the Wood," and met St. Catherine, at whose death he wrote a panegyric. He reformed the monastery in Lecceto and may have returned to England in 1383. He wrote a number of unpublished epistles and treatises.

FLEURIOT, ZÉNAIDE MARIE ANNE (1829–1890), novelist. Born in St. Brieuc, France, on Sept. 12, she wrote *Les souvenirs d'une douairière* in 1859, and followed this with a series of popular novels in the simplest style, under her own name or that of Anna Edianez de St.-B., including *La Clef d'or* and *Sans beauté*. She died in Paris on Dec. 18.

FLEURY, ANDRÉ HERCULE DE (1653–1743), cardinal. Born in Lodève, France, on June 26, he became chaplain to Empress Maria Theresa in 1679 and to King Louis XIV in 1683. He was bishop of Fréjus from 1698 to 1715, when he directed the abbey of Tournus and was appointed tutor to young Louis XV. He became the latter's prime minister in 1723 and was named a cardinal in 1726. His economic policy was austere; he sought acceptable relations with Austria, though he foresaw lasting enmity with the Hapsburgs, severely opposed the rise of Jansenism and the Jansenist faction in parliament, was active in supporting the scientific expeditions proposed by the Academy, and completed the Bibliothèque Nationale. He died in Paris on Jan. 29.

FLEURY, CLAUDE (1640–1725), historian. Born in Paris on Dec. 6, he studied at Clermont, passed the bar at eighteen, established a reputation in that profession for the next nine years, as well as in literature, history, and archaeology, moved with the cultural elite of the capital, then entered the seminary, and was ordained sometime before 1672. He published his study of French law in 1674 and of ecclesiastical law in 1677, became a follower of Bossuet, and wrote a book in support of Gallicanism in 1690. From 1672 to 1680 he had been tutor to the princes de Conti, then tutored the comte de Vermandois, legitimized son of Louis XIV, and in 1684 was named abbot of Loc Dieu. He traveled with Fénelon, returned to the court, tutored the royal grandchildren from 1689 to 1705, and continued his studies and writing. He was elected to the Academy in 1696, supported Fénelon during the quietist controversy of 1697 with Bossuet, but was protected by the latter although Fénelon lost favor, and in 1706 became prior of Notre Dame d'Argenteuil. At the death of Louis XIV he was brought back to Paris as confessor and adviser to King Louis XV, a position he held until he asked for retirement in 1722. His chief publication is his *Histoire ecclesiastique*, twenty volumes of which he issued between 1691 and 1720. It is an edifying presentation of the chief events to the year 1414, tinged with Gallicanism when he treats of the papacy. The 1766 abridgment, violently anti-Christian, is not his work. Fleury also wrote sermons and a treatise on law. He died in Paris on July 14.

FLICK, LAWRENCE FRANCIS (1856–1938), physician. Born in Carroll Township, Pennsylvania, on Aug. 10, he studied at St. Vincent's, Latrobe, and medicine at Jefferson Medical College, Philadelphia. He moved to California in 1881 in an attempt to find a cure for his tuberculosis, evolved a method for its control, and returned to Philadelphia in 1883, where he specialized in the study of tuberculosis. He became convinced of its contagious nature and advocated isolation in special hospitals—a step which resulted in great controversy with his fellow doctors. He founded the Pennsylvania Society for the Prevention of Tuberculosis in 1892, hospitals and societies for the treatment of the disease, and in 1929 helped found the Philadelphia Institute for the Study and Prevention of Nervous and Mental Diseases, of which he was president until 1935. He also helped found the Philadelphia branch of the American Catholic Historical Society in 1884, serving as its president in 1893–96 and 1913–14, received the Laetare Medal in 1920, and was the recipient of several honorary degrees. He died in Philadelphia on July 7.

FLOCELLUS, ST. (2nd century), martyr. He was tortured and thrown to beasts in the amphitheater in Autun, Gaul, during the reign of Marcus Aurelius. F. D. Sept. 17.

FLODOARD (894–996), historian. Born in Epernay, France, he studied in Rheims, became canon of the cathedral and archivist there, went to Rome about 937, and wrote a Latin narrative poem on the history of Christ, the early Church, and the popes. He later was counselor to his patron, Archbishop Artold of Rheims, and became abbot (probably of St. Basil's monastery) in 952, holding this position until he was seventy. His chief works are a history of the Church in Rheims and a detailed and valuable *Annales* covering life in France, Lorraine, and East Franconia from 919 to 966.

FLOOD, JOHN. *See* Griffith, Michael.

FLORA, ST. (d. 851), martyr. Daughter of a Mohammedan father, she was raised as a Christian in Cordova, Spain, by her mother. Denounced as a Christian by her brother, she was scourged, escaped, but surrendered herself to the authorities with a friend, Mary. Both were beheaded. F. D. Nov. 24.

FLORA OF BEAULIEU, BL. (1310–1347). Born in Auvergne, France, she entered the Hospitallers of St. John of Jerusalem at Beaulieu in 1324 despite her parents' attempts to have her married. She encountered unusual ridicule because of her many supernatural experiences. F. D. Oct. 5.

FLORENCE, ST. (d. 303). He was a martyr at Agde, France, with SS. Modestus and Tiberius during the Diocletian persecution. F. D. Nov. 10.

FLORENCE OF WORCESTER (d. 1118), historian. A monk in Worcester, England, he compiled *Chronicon ex chronicis*, a universal history based on the work of Marianus Scotus, Bede, a no-longer extant version of the *Anglo-Saxon Chronicle*, and independent information of particular interest for the years 1030–1117. His work was continued to 1141 by John, another monk at Worcester, and by others to 1295.

FLORENTIAN, ST. (5th century), bishop. *See* Crescens, St.

FLORENTIN (13th century). As archbishop of Arles, France, he presided at a council held there in 1260, which attacked the errors of Joachim of Flora and which protected the position of the diocesan clergy against encroachments by the religious orders.

FLORENTINA, ST. (d. 636?). Born in Cartagena, Spain, sister of SS. Fulgentius, Isidore, and Leander, she was brought up by the latter after the death of their parents and later entered and ruled a convent for which Leander wrote the rule. F. D. June 20.

FLORENTINI, THEODOSIUS (d. 1865). Famous as a missioner, he served as vicar general of Chur, Switzerland, from 1860 until his death. He built the Hospital of the Cross there in 1852 and brought in two religious congregations to care for the sick and to educate children.

FLORENTINUS, ST. (d. 304), martyr. *See* Alexander, St.

FLORENTINUS, ST. (4th century). He succeeded St. Severianus as bishop of Trèves, Gaul. F. D. Oct. 16.

FLORENTINUS, ST. (6th century). He succeeded St. Eutychius as abbot of a monastery at Valcastoria, Italy, and was praised by St. Gregory the Great. F. D. May 23.

FLORENTIUS, ST. (d. 235), martyr. *See* Felix, St.

FLORENTIUS, ST. (d. 250), martyr. *See* Cyriacus, St.

FLORENTIUS, ST. (3rd century), martyr. He was put to death at Trois Châteaux, Burgundy. F. D. Oct. 27.

FLORENTIUS, ST. (d. 303), martyr. *See* Cassius, St.

FLORENTIUS, ST. (d. 304), martyr. *See* Alexander, St.

FLORENTIUS, ST. (d. 304). *See* Diocletius, St.

FLORENTIUS, ST. (d. 312), martyr. He was burned at the stake in Thessalonica during the reign of Maximinus Daza. F. D. Oct. 13.

FLORENTIUS, ST. (4th century), bishop and martyr. The bishop of Vienne, France, was put to death at some date after 374. Another Bishop Florentius of Vienne is listed as having been martyred about 275. F. D. Jan. 3.

FLORENTIUS, ST. (d. 451?), martyr. *See* Nicasius, St.

FLORENTIUS, ST. (d. 485?). He was widely respected in the area of Seville, Spain, where he labored. F. D. Feb. 23.

FLORENTIUS, ST. (5th century). Born in Bavaria, he was ordained by St. Martin of Tours, sent to Poitou, France, as a missioner, retired to Mt. Glonne, Anjou, as a hermit, attracted many followers, and built for them the monastery later known as St. Florent le Vieux, where he died. F. D. Sept. 22.

FLORENTIUS, ST. (d. 526?). He was eighth bishop of Orange, France. F. D. Oct. 17.

FLORENTIUS, ST. (d. 693?), bishop. Probably an Irishman who migrated to Alsace, he lived as a hermit and founded a monastery at Haslach. About 678 he became bishop of Strassburg and founded the monastery of St. Thomas outside the city. F. D. Nov. 7.

FLORENTIUS, ST. (7th century). He was abbot of Bangor, Ireland. F. D. Dec. 15.

FLORENTIUS, ST. (d. 1156). He was abbot of the Benedictine monastery in Carracedo, León, Spain. F. D. Dec. 10.

FLORES, ISABELLA DE SANTA MARIA DE. *See* Rose of Lima, St.

FLORES, BL. LUÍZ (1570–1622), martyr. Born in Antwerp, Belgium, of Spanish parents, he went with his family to Mexico, became a Dominican, served as master of novices, and in 1602 was sent to the Philippines. In 1620 he was captured at sea by the Dutch, given over to the Japanese, and tortured, imprisoned for two years, and burned to death at Nagasaki. He was beatified as one of the martyrs of Nagasaki in 1867. F. D. Aug. 19.

FLÓREZ, ENRIQUE (1701–1774), historian. Born in Valladolid, Spain, on Feb. 14, he became an Augustinian at fourteen, and wrote on the genealogy of the Spanish kings, coins, and the Roman occupation of Spain. His greatest achievement is *La España sagrada,* an elaborate history of the Church in his country, based on original sources, which he issued in twenty-nine volumes from 1747 until his death in Madrid on Aug. 20. Later, twenty-two volumes were added. He also wrote the five-volume *Cursus theologiae.*

FLORIAN, ST. (d. 304), martyr. A Roman military authority stationed in Austria, he was scourged and put to death at Lorch by drowning during the Diocletian persecution when he became a Christian in emulation of those who had been arrested by the soldiers of the governor, Aquilinus. He is a patron of Upper Austria and of Poland. F. D. May 4.

FLORIAN, ST. (d. 637?), martyr. *See* Calanicus, St.

FLORIAN, JEAN PIERRE CLARIS DE (1755–1794), novelist. Born in Gard, France, on Mar. 6, he studied at St. Hippolyte, served as a page and in the army, and was elected to the Academy in 1788. He was arrested in 1793 and died in a revolutionary prison at Sceaux, France, on Sept. 13. He wrote pastoral and picturesque novels (*Estelle, Galatée,* and *Numa et Pompilius*), comedies (*Le bon père* and *Jeannot et Colin*), fables, short stories, and religious poems.

FLORIBERT, ST. (d. 660?). He was abbot of the Benedictine abbeys of Mont Blandin and St. Bavon, near Ghent, Flanders. F. D. Nov. 1.

FLORIBERT, ST. (d. 746), bishop. Son of Floribert and St. Hubert, he succeeded his father as bishop of Liège and ruled for eighteen years. He is often confused with St. Floribert, abbot of St. Peter in Ghent, Flanders. F. D. Apr. 27.

FLORIUS, ST. (d. 250?), martyr. *See* Lucian, St.

FLORUS, ST. (2nd century?), martyr. Greek legend says he and his brother Laurus were stonemasons building a pagan temple in Illyria. After it was finished they and the owners, Proculus and Maximus, were converted, and destroyed the idols and made the structure into a church. For this they were put to death by drowning. F. D. Aug. 18.

FLORUS, ST. (d. 389). He was first bishop of Lodève, Languedoc, France. F. D. Nov. 3.

FLORUS (d. 860?). Born probably in France, he was a deacon at Lyons about 827, and wrote poems and on canon law, liturgy, and theology. His knowledge of theology made him much sought after in the Frankish world. Important writings are a defense of Archbishop Agobard of Lyons; treatises against Amalarius of Metz; commentaries on predestination, in which he took issue with Gottschalk and John Scotus Erigena; treatises on the election of bishops, the mass, and the empire (commenting on the conflict between Louis the Pious and Lothair); a commentary on St. Paul; and a martyrology of Bede.

FLORUS, ST., martyr. *See* Demetrius, St.

FLOSCULUS, ST. (5th century). He was bishop of Orléans, Gaul, about 480, and is also called Flou. F. D. Feb. 2.

FLOWER, VEN. RICHARD (d. 1588), martyr. *See* Shelley, Bl. Edward.

FLOWER, BL. ROBERT (1160?–1218?). Born in York, England, he became a postulant at the Cistercian abbey of Newminster in Morpeth, but after a few months gave it up and became a hermit near Knaresborough. He moved to escape curious crowds and eventually went back to St. Giles' chapel, where his fame spread as "the Holy Hermit of Knaresborough." He was noted for his aid to the poor and oppressed and for his holiness; his cult was never confirmed. He may have died as late as 1235. F. D. Sept. 24.

FLOXEL, ST. (4th century), martyr. Born in the district of Cotentin, France, he was put to death near Avranches.

FLOYD, JOHN (1572–1649). Born in Cambridgeshire, England, he studied at Eu, Rheims, and Rome, became a Jesuit in 1592, and in 1606 was back in England as a priest. He was arrested and banished after a year, taught at St. Omer until 1609, then returned to the English mission, and, though often apprehended, managed to avoid death. He engaged in controversy under a variety of pen names, translated Molina on the mass and Augustine's meditations, attacked the apostate Marc Antonio de Dominis, former archbishop of Spalato who became dean of Windsor, and engaged so violently in the controversy between the Jesuits and seculars over the wisdom of appointing a resident bishop in England that his works were condemned and the quarrel closed by the pope. Fr. Floyd spent his last years teaching at St. Omer, France, where he died on Sept. 16.

FLYNN, EDMUND JAMES (1847–1927), premier. Born in Percé County, Quebec, on Nov. 16, he studied at the Quebec seminary and Laval, was admitted to the bar in 1873, and served in the legislature from 1878 to 1905. He was commissioner of crown lands, minister of railroads, and solicitor general, and in 1896–97 was prime minister. He was professor of law at Laval from 1874 to 1914, served as dean, and held various judgeships from 1914 until his death in Quebec on June 7.

FLYNN, WILLIAM J. (1889–1936). Born in Rochester, New York, on May 27, he studied at Mt. St. Mary's, Maryland, was ordained in 1915, and did parish work in Pittsburgh to 1924. He lectured at the Catholic Indian Bureau, Washington, in 1924–25, became director in New York City of the Marquette League for Indian Missions, and was made a monsignor in 1931. He died in Brooklyn, New York, on Dec. 29.

FOCH, FERDINAND (1851–1921), general. Born in Tarbes, France, on Oct. 2, he studied at St. Clement's, Metz, and L'École Polytechnique, was commissioned as an artillery officer in 1873, and in 1896 taught at the war college, later becoming its director. In World War I he was in charge of the 20th Corps at Nancy, then the Ninth Army at the Marne, and in 1917 became chief of staff and president of the Allied board of strategy. In 1918 he became generalissimo of the Allied armies in France, maréchal de France, and a field marshal in the British and Polish armies. He was many times decorated, pleaded at the peace conference for the Rhine as a French boundary, and wrote *Les principes de la guerre*, *De la conduite de guerre*, and *Eloge de Napoleon*. He died in Paris on Mar. 20.

FOGAZZARO, ANTONIO (1842–1911), novelist. Born in Vicenza, Italy, on Mar. 25, he wrote poetry and fiction; his novel *Il Santo* was placed on the Index for its modernism and condemned by Pope Pius X. He submitted to censure, and castigated his former friends, who refused to change their philosophical position, in his last novel, *Leila*. He died on Mar. 7 at Vicenza.

FOGLIETTA, UBERTO (1518–1581), historian. Born in Genoa, Italy, of a noble family, he studied at Padua and Rome, and was banished from his native city when his study of its condition was published in 1559. Stripped of his estate, he went to Rome, where he gained Church support. He published *Clarorum ligurum elogia* (historical essays) and *Historiae Genuensium* there in 1579 and 1585.

FOGOLLA, BL. FRANCIS (1839–1900), bishop and martyr. Born in Tuscany, Italy, he was a Franciscan and coadjutor bishop of Bishop Grassi, vicar apostolic to northern Shansi, when the Boxer Rebellion broke out. He was beheaded with Bishop Grassi, and beatified in 1946. F. D. July 9.

FOIK, PAUL JOSEPH (1880–1941). Born in Stratford, Ontario, Canada, on Aug. 14, he studied there and at Notre Dame, became a member of the Congregation of Holy Cross, was ordained in 1911, and took his doctorate at Catholic University. He developed the new library at Notre Dame and established that at St. Edward's University, Austin, Texas, where he taught literature and served as dean. As founder and president of the Texas Catholic Historical Society he collected some 70,-000 documents of significance. He died on Mar. 1.

FOILA, ST. (6th century). She is said to have been the sister of St. Colgan; her shrine at Kil-

Faile, Galway, Ireland, was long a place of pilgrimage. The name is also spelled Faile. F. D. June 1.

FOILLAN, ST. (d. 655?). Brother of SS. Fursey and Ultan, he left Ireland to accompany them to England about 630. They established a monastery at Burgh Castle near Yarmouth and labored among the East Angles until the monastery was destroyed by the Mercians; Foillan and Ultan then followed Fursey, who had gone to Gaul. Foillan established a monastery at Fosses, Belgium, worked among the Brabanters, and was murdered by robbers. He is venerated as a martyr in Belgium and is sometimes incorrectly called a bishop. F. D. Oct. 31.

FOIX, PAUL DE (1529–1584), bishop. He studied at Paris and Toulouse, taught law, became councilor of the Parliament of Paris at nineteen, and rose rapidly under the sponsorship of Catherine de' Medici. He served as ambassador to England, minister to Venice, Florence, and Rome, was named archbishop of Toulouse in 1577, and was ambassador to Rome from 1579 until his death in that city.

FOLENGO, TEOFILO (1496–1544), poet. Born near Mantua, Italy, on Nov. 8, he studied at Bologna, became a Benedictine, left the order in 1524, returned in 1534, and served as prior in Sicily in 1537–43. As Merlin Coccaio he published *Baldus* in 1517 (enlarged in 1521), a satiric poem grossly parodying Vergil, Ariosto, Dante, the clergy, and the contemporary world; Rabelais used it as a source for *Gargantua*. Other satires include *Zanitonella*, against the Vergilian pastoral; *Orlandino*, on the extravagant romances; and *Moschaea*, a forerunner of the seventeenth-century mock-heroic poem. After his readmission to the Benedictines, Folengo wrote *Janus* (an apology for his former work) and religious poems. He died at Santa Croce di Campese, Italy, on Dec. 9.

FOLEY, HENRY (1811–1891), historian. Born in Astley, Worcestershire, England, on Aug. 9, son of a Protestant cleric, he became a lawyer, was attracted by the Oxford Movement, and became a convert in 1846. When his wife died in 1851, he became a Jesuit lay-brother and devoted thirty years to the compilation of the eight-volume *Records of the English Province of the Society of Jesus*. He died in Roehampton, England, on Nov. 19.

FOLEY, JAMES A. (1882–1946), jurist. Born in New York City, he studied at City College and New York Law School, was admitted to the bar in 1903, became active in Democratic politics, and served in the state assembly in 1907–12 and senate in 1912–19. He married Mabel Murphy in 1919, when he was elected surrogate of New York City, a post

he held for twenty-six years. He introduced many legal reforms and helped to revise inheritance laws; his decisions were widely cited as precedents. He also served on the state reconstruction commission. He died in New York City on Feb. 11.

FOLEY, JOHN SAMUEL (1833–1918), bishop. Born in Baltimore, Maryland, on Nov. 3, he studied at St. Mary's, Baltimore, and the Apollinaris, Rome, was ordained in 1856, served as curate and pastor in the Baltimore archdiocese, and in 1888 was named fourth bishop of Detroit, Michigan. He established a special seminary for students of Polish descent and was successful in ending a schism caused by nationalistic elements of that ethnic group. He died in Detroit on Jan. 5.

FOLEY, THOMAS PATRICK ROGER (1822–1879), bishop. Born in Baltimore on Mar. 6, he studied at St. Mary's College and seminary there, and was ordained in Baltimore in 1846. He worked as a missionary and in parish work in the surrounding area and Washington, D.C., was appointed rector of the Baltimore cathedral, and in 1851 became chancellor of the diocese. He was secretary of the first Plenary Council of Baltimore in 1852 and notary of that of 1866, and in 1870 was consecrated titular bishop of Pergamum and coadjutor and administrator of the diocese of Chicago, whose bishop was mentally ill. He was forced to rebuild many of the institutions of the diocese, including the cathedral, destroyed in the Chicago fire, and greatly expanded the facilities of the see during his regime. He died in Chicago on Feb. 19.

FOLQUET (1155–1231), poet. Born in Marseilles, France, of a wealthy family, he became a troubadour and wrote a considerable body of poetry, of which thirty examples are extant. When almost forty he abandoned his roving life, was ordained, and in 1203 was named bishop of Toulouse. His last years were marked by great personal asceticism and strenuous opposition to heresy.

FONSECA, JOSÉ RIBEIRO DA (1690–1752), bishop. Born in Evora, Portugal, he became a Franciscan in Rome in 1712, held several posts in his order, founded the library of Ara Coeli, was patron of Luke Wadding's *Annales Minorum*, and in 1741 was named bishop of Oporto, Portugal, where he died on June 16.

FONSECA, PEDRO DA (1528–1599), theologian. Born in Cortizada, Portugal, he became a Jesuit at Coimbra in 1548, studied there and at Evora, and was a brilliant lecturer on philosophy and an effective administrator. He proposed a solution to the problem of reconciling grace and free will later developed by Molina, helped to draw up the Jesuit *Ratio studiorum*, aided the foundation of the Irish

College in Lisbon, advised Pope Gregory XIII and King Philip II, published significant studies on Aristotle, and initiated the publication of *Coimbricenses* while he was provincial at Coimbra. He died in Lisbon on Nov. 4.

FONSECA SOARES, ANTONIO DA (1631–1682). Born in Vidigueira, Portugal, on June 25, he was a soldier, fled to Brazil after a fatal duel, and returned and lived a dissolute life until 1662. He then became a Franciscan, taking the name Antonio das Chagas, and wrote a great number of influential ascetical works. He died in Torres Vedras, Portugal, on Oct. 20.

FONTAINE, BL. MADELEINE (1723–1794), martyr. Born in Etépagny, France, she became a Sister of Charity of St. Vincent de Paul in 1748, and was superior at Arras from 1767 until her arrest by revolutionary forces. When ordered to subscribe to the new antireligious oath, she refused and was guillotined. With her died three other sisters of her order: Bl. Thérèse Fantou, forty-seven, from Brittany; Bl. Françoise Lanel, forty-nine, a native of Eu, near Rouen; and Bl. Joan Gérard, forty-two. They were beatified in 1920. F. D. June 27.

FONTANA, CARLO (1634–1714), architect. Born in Bruciato, near Como, Italy, he studied under Bernini in Rome, and restored and decorated a large number of churches in that city, fountains, Grimazzi and Bolognetti palaces, and the tomb of Queen Christina of Sweden in St. Peter's. With Pope Innocent XI as his patron he built San Michele at Ripa and the baptismal chapel in St. Peter's, and restored the Minerva Library. He wrote on the Templum Vaticanum, the Flavian amphitheater, the aqueducts, and made suggestions for city planning. His nephews, Francesco and Girolamo, worked with him. He died in Rome.

FONTANA, DOMENICO (1543–1607), architect. Born in Mili, Italy, he studied architecture in Rome and for Cardinal Montalto built the chapel of the manger in Santa Maria Maggiore and completed the nearby Palazzo Montalto at his own expense when the cardinal's fortunes failed. When the latter became Pope Sixtus V, Fontana added the lantern to the dome of St. Peter's and the arcade to the loggia of St. John Lateran and designed fountains with his brother Giovanni. He began building the Lateran palace in 1586, made additions to the Quirinal palace, and erected the obelisk in St. Peter's Square and three others elsewhere. After the death of Sixtus, Fontana went to Naples in 1592, where he built the Palazzo Reale, designed canals, and died. His son Giuglio Cesare succeeded him as royal architect.

FONTANA, FELICE (1730–1805), naturalist. Born in Pomarolo, in the Tyrol, on Apr. 15, he studied at Padua and Bologna, taught philosophy at Pisa, and was made court physiologist by Duke Peter Leopold at Florence. He developed and organized its museum, adding wax anatomical models, which he duplicated for Vienna at the request of Emperor Joseph II. In his last years he was curator of the museum in Florence, where he died on Jan. 11. He wrote on the eye, poisons, gases, and established that the sheep disease called staggers was caused by hydatids in the brain.

FONTANA, GIOVANNI (1540–1614), architect. Born in Mili, Italy, brother of Domenico, he designed the Giustiniani palace, Rome, the fountains of the Vatican garden and the Villa Mondragone, Frascati, supervised the draining of the Tiber, restored the Cloaca Maxima, and built aqueducts. He was papal architect under Clement VIII.

FONTANA, LAVINIA (1552–1614?), painter. Born in Bologna, Italy, daughter of Prospero, she studied under him and in Rome, and completed many popular historical and religious paintings and was successful as a portrait painter (*Pope Gregory XIII*). Her husband, Paolo Zappi, an amateur, assisted her at Rome, where she was made a member of the Academy of St. Luke.

FONTANA, MICHELE. *See* Tartaglia, Nicolò.

FONTANA, PROSPERO (1512–1597), painter. Born in Bologna, Italy, he studied there under Innocenzio da Imola, was influenced by Vasari, was recommended to Pope Julius III by Michelangelo, and assisted Primaticcio on decorations for Fontainebleau. His portraits received more praise than his historical work. He spent his last years at Bologna, Italy, where the Caracci worked with him for a short while but abandoned his leadership. He died in Rome.

FONTANELLA, BL. MARIA (1661–1717). The ninth of eleven children of Count Fontanella, she was born in Baldinero near Turin, Italy, and joined the Cistercians in Saluzza when twelve, but on the death of her father returned home. In 1676 she became a Carmelite in Turin, was appointed novice-mistress in 1691, prioress three years later, and in 1703 founded the Carmel of Moncaglieri, although she remained as prioress of Santa Cristina in Turin until her death. She was noted for her extreme austerities and mortifications. Also known as Bl. Mary of the Angels, she was beatified in 1865. F. D. Dec. 16.

FONTBONNE, JEANNE (1759–1843). Born in Basen-Basset, Velay, France, on Mar. 3, she became a Sister of St. Joseph at Monistrol in 1778, and as Mother St. John served as superior of her community from 1785 until the outbreak of the revolution. Her community was scattered and she was driven out of her property by a mob; though she escaped to her family home, she was followed and made a prisoner in St. Didier. In 1807, at St. Étienne, she was superior of a group of women from various dispersed groups; she later restored the convent and asylum in Monistrol, and in 1816 became superior general of her order. She founded a mother house and novitiate at Lyons, affiliated the scattered houses of the order by 1828, sent a mission to the United States, and saw the establishment of 200 new communities. She died in Lyons, France, on Nov. 22.

FONTEIUS (6th century). Bishop of Feltre, Italy, he attended a council in Aquileia in 579 and was living in 591 when he dedicated a book to Emperor Mauritius.

FOPPA, AMBROGIO (1445–1527?), sculptor. Born in Mondonico or Pavia, Italy, he served Duke Ludovico of Milan, struck numerous medals, designed reliquaries and crosiers for many churches, jewelry, a tiara for Pope Julius II, and terra-cotta reliefs in the sacristy of San Satiro, Rome. He was known as Caradosso and is mentioned by Cellini as the designer of a medal honoring Bramante for his design of St. Peter's.

FOPPA, VINCENZO (1527?–1515), painter. Born in Brescia, Italy, he probably studied at Verona, or under Squarcione in Padua, and later was influenced by Bramante. After 1456 he did frescoes for the Sforzas at Pavia and Milan and religious scenes in churches at Bergamo and Savona. Grand in style, with effective use of silver-gray, his work influenced that of all northern Italy until the time of Leonardo. He died in Brescia.

FORANNAN, ST. (d. 982). With twelve associates, this Irish bishop left to found the Benedictine monastery at Waulsort on the Meuse River, Belgium, where he became abbot in 962. F. D. Apr. 30.

FORBES, JOHN (1570–1606). Son of John, eighth Lord Forbes, he became a convert in 1587 as a result of letters from his brother, a Capuchin at Brussels. After fleeing Scotland to avoid an arranged marriage, he was impressed into the British army in Flanders, was captured and released by the Spaniards, and became a Capuchin at Tournai, Flanders, in 1593. Ordained, and known as Fr. Archangel, he served as chaplain of the Spanish forces at Dixmude, and died of plague at Ghent, Flanders, before he could fill his appointment as missionary apostolic to Scotland. A biography by Faustinus Cranius was published in 1620.

FORBES, JOSEPH G. (1865–1940), archbishop. Born in Ile Perrot, Canada, on Aug. 10, he was ordained in 1888, became archbishop of Ottawa in 1928, and died there on May 22.

FORBES-LEITH, WILLIAM (1833–1921), historian. Born in Aberdeen, Scotland, he became a Jesuit in Alsace in 1851, studied in France and England, and was ordained in Wales. He taught philosophy and literature in Paris from 1865 to 1880, except for brief service as an army chaplain in 1870, and wrote on the history of Scotland of the pre-Reformation period and of the seventeenth and eighteenth centuries. He died in Roehampton, England, on Apr. 30.

FORBIN-JANSON, CHARLES AUGUSTE MARIE JOSEPH DE (1785–1844), bishop. Born in Paris on Nov. 3, he served in the army, was auditor of Napoleon's council of state in 1805, studied at St. Sulpice in 1808, and was ordained in 1811. He was named vicar general of Chambéry, founded the Missionaires de France with Abbé de Rauzan, and worked to reaffirm faith shaken by the revolution. In 1823 he was appointed bishop of Jancy and Toul. He helped Pauline Jaricot to establish the Society for the Propagation of the Faith. Because he never had signed the Gallican Declaration he was driven from France in 1830. He was sent to the United States in 1839, contributed one third of the purchase price of Spring Hill College, Mobile, Alabama, visited Canada, attended the fourth Provincial Council at Baltimore, returned to France in 1841, and was made a papal count in 1842. In 1843 he founded the Society of the Holy Childhood, spreading its work through France, Belgium, and Great Britain. He died at his family's castle near Marseilles, France, on July 12.

FORCELLINI, EGIDIO (1688–1768), lexicographer. Born in Fener, near Treviso, Italy, on Aug. 26, he entered the seminary in Padua in 1704, worked with his teacher, Facciolati, in revising the seven-language dictionary of Ambrosius Calepinus, and began forty years of study for a dictionary of his own. He directed the seminary at Cenada from 1724 to 1731, but all his other years were given to the study of Latin and Greek literature, history, and inscriptions. His four-volume *Totius latinitatis lexicon* (with Italian and Greek equivalents) was published three years after his death in Padua, Italy, on Apr. 4.

FORD, FRANCIS X. (1892–1952), martyr. Born in Brooklyn, New York, on Jan. 11, he studied at Cathedral College in New York and was the first student to enter Maryknoll seminary in 1912. He was ordained in 1917, was sent to China the following year, and developed Maryknoll missions in the Kaying section of southern China. In 1935 he was appointed bishop of Kaying. He was active in relief work during World War II as chairman of the Chinese Catholic Welfare Conference for southern China, returned for a brief visit to the United States after the war, and on his return found Kaying overrun by communists. He was arrested in 1950, subjected to tortures during the next fourteen months as the Reds vilified him at a series of public trials, and is reported to have died in prison on Feb. 21 as a result of his mistreatment.

FORD, JEREMIAH DENIS MATHIAS (1873–1958), scholar. Born in Cambridge, Massachusetts, on July 2, he studied at Cork when his parents returned to Ireland. He graduated from Harvard in 1894, received his doctorate in 1897, and taught there for forty-eight years, retiring in 1943. He married Winifred Fearns in 1902. He became internationally known as an authority on Spanish and Portuguese literature, wrote widely on linguistics and belles-lettres, *Main Currents of Spanish Literature* standing out among his books, and received many honorary degrees and national awards. He was given the Laetare Medal in 1937 and was elected to the French Academy in 1945. He held office in many major scholarly societies and was editor of *Speculum* from 1927 to 1936. He died in Cambridge on Nov. 13.

FORD, BL. THOMAS (d. 1582), martyr. Born in Devonshire, England, he graduated from Oxford, where he became a convert, went to Douai, was ordained in 1573 and sent to the England mission in 1576. He worked with success in Oxfordshire and Berkshire, was arrested with Bl. Edmund Campion, and hanged, drawn, and quartered at Tyburn. He was beatified in 1886. F. D. May 28.

FORDNEY, JOSEPH WARREN (1853–1932), executive. Born in Hartford City, Indiana, on Nov. 5, he had no formal education, worked in a lumber camp in Michigan when he was 15, and in the next three decades became one of the leading lumbermen in the United States, with holdings in the Midwest, on the Pacific coast, and in Louisiana and Mississippi. He entered politics in 1895 as an alderman in Saginaw, Michigan, was elected to Congress in 1898, and served for twelve consecutive terms. He was an ardent protectionist and co-author of the Fordney-McCumber Tariff of 1922, became a convert in 1925, and died on Jan. 8.

FOREMAN, ANDREW (d. 1522), bishop. Born in Hatton, Scotland, he became an influential cleric, served on diplomatic missions for King James IV, arranged the king's marriage with Margaret, daughter of Henry VII, in 1501, and became bishop of Moray in 1502 and commendatory abbot of several monasteries. He served as ambassador to Henry VIII in 1509, was sent to France to arrange a crusade for universal peace, and was named archbishop of Bourges by King Louis. Pope Leo X made him archbishop of St. Andrews in 1514, where he held a synod in an attempt to reform abuses and develop learning. He died at Dunfermline, Scotland, one of his many abbeys.

FORER, LAURENZ (1580–1659). Born in Lucerne, Switzerland, he became a Jesuit at twenty, taught philosophy at Ingolstadt and Dillingen from 1615 to 1621, became chancellor at the latter university, and was in the Tyrol from 1632 to 1643. In 1650 he became rector at Lucerne. He wrote many controversial works against contemporary apostates and heretics, a defense of his order, and a life of Christ. He died in Ratisbon, Bavaria, on Jan. 7.

FOREST, BL. JOHN (d. 1538), martyr. A Franciscan of the Strict Observance at seventeen in Greenwich, England, he studied theology at Oxford, returned to Greenwich, and then became confessor to Queen Catherine of Aragon. He attempted to prevent Henry VIII's suppression of his order, but failed and was imprisoned in 1534. He reappears, under house arrest, in a 1538 document; then, when he refused to subscribe to the Act of Supremacy which declared Henry to be head of the Church, was burned to death at Smithfield, England. He was beatified in 1886. F. D. May 22.

FOREST, JOHN ANTHONY (1838–1911), bishop. Born in St. Martin-la-Sauveté, Loire, France, on Dec. 25, he went to the United States and was ordained in New Orleans in 1863. He served in the South until 1895, when he was consecrated bishop of San Antonio, Texas, and died there on Mar. 11.

FORMBY, HENRY (1816–1884). Born in Lancashire, England, he studied in London and at Oxford, became vicar in Ruardean, was influenced by the Newman group, and was a convert in 1846. He studied at Oscott and was ordained in 1847, was stationed at St. Chad's cathedral, developed its choir, and published several studies of plain chant, collections of hymns, pictorial scripture studies, saints' lives, and devotional works. He was in charge of the mission at Wednesbury from 1857 to 1864, then went to the Dominican priory at Hinckley, where he trained novices and continued his apologetical writings. He died in Leicester, England, on Mar. 12.

FORMOSUS (816?–896), pope. Born probably in Rome, he was named cardinal-bishop of Porto in 864, had success as papal legate to Bulgaria in 866, and was sent to France in 869, and to Trent in 872 to consider the question of a successor for Emperor Louis II, who was without heir. When Louis died in 875, Pope John VIII sent Formosus and others to France to offer the imperial crown to Charles the Bald. The latter was duly crowned in Rome, but anti-French opposition arose and many bishops left Rome to escape the pope's anger toward the imperial faction. When Formosus failed to return after a direct command he was condemned as a person plotting for the papal throne and excommunicated at a synod called in Rome. The censure was repeated at Troyes in 878, when the pope went to France and Formosus appeared to face the charge; it was lifted when he promised not to visit Rome or exercise his priestly functions. Formosus lived in Sens until 882 when the new pope, Marinus, released him from the promise and restored him to his diocese. Formosus was unanimously elected pope on Oct. 6, 891, by the clergy and people. His pontificate was marked by great strife. He confirmed the position of his predecessors regarding Photius of Constantinople, who had been ejected from his see; the pope declared that Photius had never been a bishop and that his ordinations were void. He supported Archbishop Adalgar of Hamburg against Archbishop Hermann of Cologne in the claim to the suffragan of Bremen, and supported Charles the Simple against Odo of Paris in the struggle for the French crown. Political problems multiplied when the pope asked King Arnulf of Germany to protect Italy against Guido, former duke of Spoleto. Arnulf rewon the area north of the Po River by Dec. 894, when Guido died, leaving the crown to his son Lambert, whom Formosus had already crowned. Arnulf then moved south, attacked Queen Agiltrude, the regent, in Rome itself, entered the city early in 896, was crowned emperor, and marched on Spoleto. He died of paralysis before he reached the city and Formosus himself died on Apr. 4. After his death, and at the insistence of Lambert and Agiltrude, the corpse of Formosus was placed on a throne before the new pope, Stephen VI, farcically tried, declared no pope, mutilated, and thrown into the Tiber. Later popes honored and dishonored Formosus and declared all the measures taken during his pontificate valid or invalid, depending on their politics. History has established the validity of his position and of his actions.

FORREST, WILLIAM (fl. 1530–1581), poet. He probably was born and educated at Oxford, England, since he reported in one poem on the anger of the city over the treatment of Catherine of Aragon, and was a Cistercian by 1540. He then seems to have been secularized as a scribe in London, during which time his writing was tinged by the world of Edward VI; in 1546 he was a canon of Oxford cathedral. However, as chaplain of Queen Mary, he wrote a number of ballads and religious poems and, possibly, eighteen six-part masses.

FÖRSTER, ARNOLD (1810–1884), entomologist. Born in Aachen, Germany, on Jan. 20, he completed his lower education slowly because of his father's death, studied medicine at Bonn, and gave it up for natural science. From 1836 until his death there on Aug. 12, he taught in the *Realgymnasium* of his native city. As a youth he studied entomology under Meigen, became an authority as a result of his

observations and published work, and received an honorary degree from Bonn in 1853.

FORSTER, FROBENIUS (1709–1791). Born in Königsfeld, Bavaria, on Aug. 30, he studied at Freising and Ingolstadt, became a Benedictine in 1728, and was ordained in 1733. He taught philosophy and theology at St. Emmeran, Ratisbon, in 1734–45 and 1747–50, and philosophy and physics at Salzburg in the years between. He then was named librarian and prior there, appointed to the new Bavarian Academy of Sciences in 1759, and in 1762 became prince-abbot of St. Emmeran. He developed the study of science and of philosophy there, sought to reconcile scholasticism with the schools of Descartes and Leibniz-Wolff, built up museum displays, published a commentary on the Vulgate, philosophical treatises, and an edition of Alcuin. He died at the monastery on Oct. 11.

FORSTER, THOMAS IGNATIUS MARIA (1789–1860), astronomer. Born in London on Nov. 9, he had no formal education in youth, but mastered several languages and made a detailed study of science. In 1805 he published *Liber rerum naturalium*, turned to phrenology, then to astronomy, and in 1819 discovered a new comet. He began the study of law, but changed to medicine, and took his degree in 1819. Around 1824 he became a convert in Europe, published his *Perpetual Calendar* that year, and returned to England to pursue studies in the effect of atmosphere on disease, particularly cholera. He edited the letters of Locke, Shaftesbury, and Sydney in 1830, and went abroad in 1833. He continued his wide interests, published a variety of work (including poems and music for the violin), and was in correspondence with most of the scientists of his day. He died in Brussels on Feb. 2.

FORT, ST. (1st century). He is venerated as the first bishop of Bordeaux, Gaul, and as a martyr. F. D. May 16.

FORTCHERN, ST. He may have been either a sixth-century bishop of Trim, Ireland, or a fifth-century follower of St. Patrick. F. D. Feb. 17.

FORTESCUE, BL. ADRIAN (1476–1539), martyr. A cousin of Anne Boleyn, he was born at Punsbourne, England, of an old Devonshire family, and in 1499 married Anne Stonor (by whom he had two daughters) and after her death Anne Rede (by whom he had three sons). He spent his early years at court, became a Dominican tertiary at Oxford, and a Knight of Malta. He was imprisoned in 1534 (on unknown charges), but released in 1535, arrested again in 1539, refused to take the Oath of Supremacy, which Henry VIII claimed made him head of the English Church, was declared a traitor by parliament, and beheaded, with Ven. Thomas Dingley, on July 8 or 9 on Tower

Hill, London. He was beatified in 1895. F. D. July 11.

FORTESCUE, JOHN (1394?–1476), judge. Born in Devonshire, England, he took his degree at Oxford, was appointed to the king's courts, and in 1442 became chief justice of the king's bench. He lost popularity when he supported the Lancastrian faction against Richard of York and King Edward IV. When it was defeated in 1471 he went to France, and wrote *De laudibus legum Angliae* for Prince Edward and the influential study of monarchy, *The Governance of England* (not published until 1885). He was captured at Tewkesbury by Edward IV, but granted a pardon.

FORTIS GABRIELI, BL. (d. 1040). Born in Gubbio, Italy, he became a hermit near Scheggia, then a Benedictine at the monastery of Fontavellana, with permission to continue a life of solitude. His cult was approved in 1756. F. D. May 13.

FORTIS, GIOVANNI BATTISTA (1741–1803), naturalist. Born in Padua, Italy, he became an Augustinian, and published an account of his travels to Dalmatia and of the natural history of Italy.

FORTUN GARCIA (9th century), king of Navarre. Son of García Eneco, he became king in 882, was captured by the Moors and kept a prisoner for fifteen years, and in 904 became a monk at Leyra, Navarre, Spain.

FORTUNATA, ST. (d. 304?), martyr. *See* Carponius, St.

FORTUNATO OF BRESCIA (1701–1754), biologist. Born in Brescia, Italy, he became a Friar Minor of the Reform in 1718, secretary general of his order, and as a philosopher tried to blend scholasticism and the physical sciences. He made a serious study of microscopic anatomy, studied the histology and embryology of human organs, and was particularly interested in the central nervous system. He was the first to distinguish between organs and 'tissues, developed a systematic microscope technique, and completed his morphological classification before Bichat's work of 1800. He died in Madrid.

FORTUNATUS (1st century). *See* Achaicus, St.; also, Hermagoras, St.

FORTUNATUS, ST. (d. 212), martyr. *See* Felix, St.

FORTUNATUS, ST. (d. 296?), martyr. *See* Felix, St.

FORTUNATUS, ST. (d. 303), martyr. *See* Anthes, St.; also, Honoratus, St.

FORTUNATUS, ST. (d. 400?). A priest, he was noted for his charitable work in a parish near Spoleto, Italy. F. D. June 1.

FORTUNATUS, ST. (d. 434?), martyr. *See* Felix, St.

FORTUNATUS, ST. (d. 537). Bishop of Todi, Italy, he saved his city from being pil-

laged by King Totila the Goth. F. D. Oct. 14.

FORTUNATUS, ST. (d. 569), bishop. Driven from his see in Lombardy to France, he taught at Paris, and was called "the Philosopher" to distinguish him from his contemporary, Venantius Fortunatus. F. D. June 18.

FORTUNATUS (6th century). Bishop of Catania, Sicily, he was sent with Ennodius by Pope Hormisdas to Constantinople in 1514 and again in 1516 to seek reunion of the Eastern Church with Rome.

FORZATEI, BL. GIORDANO (1158–1248). Born in Padua, Italy, he became a Benedictine monk, was abbot of St. Justina, was placed in charge of Padua by Frederick II, but was captured by Count Ezzelino and imprisoned for three years. He died in Venice, Italy. F. D. Aug. 7.

FOSSANO, AMBROGIO STEFANI DA (1455?–1523), painter. Perhaps of Flemish descent, he was born in Milan, Italy, and came to be known as Borgognone. His early work, in tempera and oils, was completed in Certosa and Milan; later he came under the influence of Leonardo da Vinci. He executed some portraits, but most of his work is on New Testament themes; he also was an architect. He died in Milan.

FOSTER, JOHN GRAY (1823–1874), general. Born in Whitfield, New Hampshire, on May 27, he graduated from West Point, served with an engineers corps in the Mexican War, served with the coastal survey in 1852–54, and taught engineering at West Point in 1855–57. He built Fort Sumter, and was repairing Fort Moultrie in Charleston, South Carolina, harbor, when the Civil War erupted. He transferred his forces to Sumter, and was raised to major for the gallantry of his defense. He served Burnside as a brigadier general in the North Carolina campaign of 1861, was converted to Catholicism before the end of that year, and commanded the department of North Carolina to July 1863, of Virginia and North Carolina to Nov., and the army and department of Ohio until Feb. 1864, when he relinquished his command because of injury. He was with Sherman at Savannah, commanded the department of Florida in 1865–66, improved the harbors of Boston and Portsmouth, New Hampshire, and engaged in and wrote on submarine operations. He died in Nashua, New Hampshire, on Sept. 2.

FOTHAD, ST. (8th century). A monk at Faham-Mura, Donegal, Ireland, he became counselor and bard to King Aedh Oirnidh after 794, accompanied him on his expedition against Leinster in 804, and is said to have gained exemption from military service for the clergy as a reward. His plea for this favor, the *Remonstrance*, was known thereafter as a canon and its author was called Fothad na Canoine.

FOUARD, CONSTANT (1837–1903). Born in Elbeuf, France, on Aug. 6, he studied in Boisguillaume, Issy, and St. Sulpice, was ordained in 1861, did not join the Sulpicians because of ill health, and taught at Boisguillaume, the College of St. Barbara, Paris, and at Rouen. At Paris, his teacher was Abbé Le Hir, who also taught Renan; Fouard wrote five elaborate and critical studies of Christ, Peter, Paul, John, and the early years of Christianity, gathered as *Les origines de l'église,* and written in answer to Renan. He became a canon of the cathedral of Rouen in 1884, a member of the biblical commission in 1903, and died in Elbeuf, France, on Dec. 3.

FOUCAULT, JEAN BERTRAND LÉON (1819–1868), physicist. Born in Paris, on Sept. 18, he studied medicine, abandoned it for medical microscopy, worked with Donné, and in 1845 succeeded him as editor of *Journal des débats.* He is particularly known for his research on the speed of light, and in 1850 he was awarded the Copley Medal by the Royal Society of London for work on energy and magnetism, and proved that the velocity of light is greater in air than in water. In 1851 he invented a pendulum which clearly demonstrated the rotation of the earth; in 1852 he invented the gyroscope, for which he received the cross of the Legion of Honor. The currents named after him, Foucault or eddy currents, were discovered when electricity was generated in a metal plate rotating between the poles of a magnet. He improved telescopic lenses while physicist of the Paris observatory, invented the mercury interrupter used with induction coils, an engine governor which modified Watts's work, an automatic regulator for the electric arc lamp, and wrote on scientific education, binocular vision, and many aspects of physical research. He died in Paris, after a paralytic stroke, on Feb. 11.

FOULQUES, BL. (d. 1202). After a wastrel life, he decided to study at Paris, was ordained, and served as a curé in Neuilly-sur-Marne. He preached to great crowds in France, Burgundy, and Flanders, was particularly hostile toward usurers and the dissolute, and noted for his own rigorous asceticism. In 1198 he preached the fourth crusade with the permission of Pope Innocent III; he claims to have enlisted 200,000. He attended the chapter at Cîteaux in 1201, gave money to the Cistercians with which the fortifications at Acre and Tyre were repaired, and died in Neuilly, France, before the campaign of 1204 began. The name is also spelled Fulk. F. D. Mar. 2.

FOULQUES II (938–958). Known as "the Good," he was count of Anjou and an active patron of learning, comparing ignorant rulers to "crowned asses."

FOULQUES III (972–1040). He became count of Anjou in 987, was a successful warrior, was called "the Black" for his crimes, and made many penitential pilgrimages to the Holy Land.

FOULQUES V (1092–1143), king. He became count of Anjou in 1109, went to Jerusalem in 1129, married Mélisande, daughter of King Baldwin II, and succeeded his father-in-law as king of Jerusalem in 1131. He was successful against the Saracens.

FOUQUET, JEHAN (1415?–1480?), painter. Born in Tours, France, son of Huguet, who worked for the dukes of Orléans, he was influenced by the art of Burgundy and Flanders, particularly of the Van Eycks. He seemingly went to Italy, was influenced by Fra Angelico, and many others of Rome and Florence, and painted a portrait of Pope Eugene IV (now lost). On his return he was made court painter to King Charles VII (whose portrait he painted) and then to Louis XI. A few other portraits (Guillaume Juvenal des Ursins, Agnes Sorel, and himself) and 100 miniatures survive. The best of these last are in a published paraphrase of Boccaccio, the book of hours of Étienne Chavalier, Josephus' *Antiquities of the Jews,* and *Les grandes chroniques de France.* His use of gold is strikingly effective, his faces appealing, his detail deftly crowded, touched with gaiety, humor, love of luxuriant digressions, and a firm sense of the narrative and dramatic basis of illustration. His backgrounds and figures are contemporary and are a treasure house of information on life in his time.

FOURIER, ST. PETER (1565–1640), founder. Born in Mirecourt, Lorraine, on Nov. 30, he studied at the Jesuit university at Pont à Mousson, opened a school in his home town, and when twenty joined the Augustinian canons regular. He was ordained in 1589, took his doctorate, became procurator of the abbey parish of Chamousey and, in 1597, curé of Mattaincourt, a run-down and neglected parish. He worked there for thirty years, attempted unsuccessfully to provide free education for boys, but was successful, with Alix Le Clercq, in organizing a group of women into the Canonesses Regular of St. Augustine of the Congregation of Our Lady (which received papal approval in 1616). In 1622 the Bishop of Toul assigned him the task of uniting the houses of his order into one congregation, which was completed in 1629 when the canons regular of Lorraine were united into the Congregation of Our Savior and elected Peter superior general in 1632. The last four years of his life were spent in exile, when he refused to take the Oath of Allegiance to King Louis XIII. He died at Gray, Haute-Saône, France. He was canonized in 1897. F. D. Dec. 9.

FOURNET, ST. ANDRÉ HUBERT (1752–1834), founder. Born in Maillé, France, on Dec. 6, he went to school at Poitiers; much later he was ordained and appointed parish priest in his native town. During the French Revolution he served his people from a forest hiding place, went to Spain on the orders of his bishop, but returned in 1797 to work once again with the underground clergy. In 1807 he and St. Elizabeth des Anges guided a group of women who nursed the sick and poor and taught children; they became the Congregation of the Daughters of the Cross. He died in La Puye, France, and was canonized in 1933. F. D. May 13.

FOWLER, GENE (1891–1960), journalist. Born in Denver, Colorado, he began his newspaper career on the Denver *Republican* and then moved to New York, where he became a sports writer and then sports editor of the *Daily Mirror*, managing editor of the *American* in 1925, and editor of the *Morning Telegraph*. In 1931 he went to Hollywood as one of the highest-paid scenario writers. He became a convert in 1950, and died in West Los Angeles, California, on July 2. He wrote several novels and biographies, most popular of which are *Good Night, Sweet Prince*, on John Barrymore; *The Great Mouthpiece*, on the criminal lawyer William J. Fallon; and *Beau James*, on James J. Walker, mayor of New York.

FOWLER, JOHN (1537–1579), publisher. Born in Bristol, England, he was educated at Winchester and Oxford and remained at the university until 1559, when he was dismissed because he refused to accept Elizabeth as head of the Church. He went to Louvain, married Alice, daughter of John Harris (once Thomas More's secretary), and became a printer. He apparently had presses at Antwerp and Louvain, perhaps even at Douai, and published most of the English books issued on the Continent from 1565 to 1578. He wrote poetry and epigrams, edited the *Dialogue of Comfort against Tribulation* of More, and published translations and a compendium of the *Summa* of St. Thomas, as well as the contemporary controversial works of others. He died in Namur, Flanders, on Feb. 13.

FOX, JOHN M. (1880–1940), educator. Born in Dorchester, Massachusetts, he became a Jesuit, was ordained in 1913, served as president of Holy Cross College in 1929–33, and died in Pomfret, Connecticut, on Feb. 15.

FOX, JOSEPH JOHN (1855–1915), bishop. Born in Green Bay, Wisconsin, on Aug. 2, he studied at St. Francis seminary, Milwaukee, and Louvain, and was ordained in Mechlin in 1879. He engaged in pastoral work in Wisconsin, became secretary to Bishop Krautbauer, and served as vicar general of Green Bay from 1894 to 1904. He was made a domestic prelate in 1898 and in 1904 was appointed bishop of Green Bay. He resigned in 1914, was appointed titular bishop of Jonopolis, and died three months later in Green Bay on Mar. 14.

FRACASTORO, GIROLAMO (1483–1553).

Born in Verona, Italy, he taught logic at Padua, attained a reputation as a physician, and wrote medical studies on the treatment of contagious disease, and was appointed physician to the Council of Trent. He also wrote considerable poetry.

FRAGAN, ST. (5th century). He and St. Gwen, parents of SS. Wenwaloe, Jacut, and Guithern, fled from Britain to Brittany with other exiles after the Roman occupation came to an end. F. D. July 5.

FRAKNOI, VILMOS (1843–1924), bishop. Born in Urmény, Hungary, on Feb. 23, he studied at Pest, was ordained, and became professor at Gran in 1865, and librarian of the National Museum in 1875. He became titular bishop of Arbe in 1892, and in 1900 inspector of the Hungarian Historical Institute, Rome, which he had founded. He was chief supervisor of Hungary's museums and libraries, general secretary of the Hungarian Academy, and wrote a popular history of Hungary, scholarly studies of the relations of the nation with the papacy, and on events and figures of the fifteenth and sixteenth centuries. He died in Budapest on Nov. 20.

FRANC, MARTIN LE (1410–1461), poet. Born in Normandy, he served as secretary to the duke of Savoy (later Pope Felix V) and then to Nicholas V, and held other papal positions. His poem, *Le Champion de dames* (1530) is significant for its contemporary color; he also wrote the prose *L'Estrif de fortune et de vertu* (1519).

FRANCA VISALTA, ST. (1170–1218). Born in Piacenza, Italy, she was sent to the Benedictine convent there at seven, was professed at fourteen and soon made abbess. Her rule was so strict that she objected to cooking vegetables in wine, and was rebelliously replaced by the bishop's sister and vilely calumniated. A friend, Carentia, tried to comfort her, persuaded her own parents to build a convent at Pittoli, and invited Franca to become abbess there. She introduced the Cistercian rule, with added austerities. She was canonized by Pope Gregory X, a relative of Carentia, and venerated at least locally on Apr. 26.

FRANCES OF ROME, ST. (1384–1440). Born in Rome of a wealthy and aristocratic couple, Paul and Jacobella Busso, she married Lorenzo Ponziano at thirteen. With her sister-in-law Vannozza she made frequent visits to the poor and distressed, cared for the most extreme hospital cases, worked with intensity through a plague, and lived as simple a life as possible, devoted to her husband and children. Tragedy struck when the anti-papal army of Ladislaus of Naples invaded the city in 1408, attacked all supporters of the legitimate pope, captured her brother-in-law Paluzzo, and wounded her husband. A second attack came in 1410; Lorenzo escaped, but the women could not, turned their ruined home into a hospital, and worked with the victims of war. A son and daughter died of the plague; her oldest son, captured twice, escaped to his father; Frances herself was ill almost beyond hope. When peace came she nursed her husband back to health, continued her charities, and organized the Oblates of Tor de' Specchi, affiliated with the Benedictines. She entered their house in 1436, after her husband died, and against her wishes was made superior. Her last years were marked by extreme austerities, and many supernatural gifts were added to her earlier power of healing. She died in Rome, and was canonized in 1608. F. D. Mar. 9.

FRANCESCHI, PIERO DE' (1420?–1492), painter. Born in Borgo San Sepolcro, Tuscany, Italy, he was probably an assistant to Domenico Veneziano (who, with Paolo Uccello, greatly influenced him) in 1438, worked with the former at Loreto and Rimini in 1451, and in 1445 painted his first work as an independent artist, an altarpiece in his native town. He is widely regarded as the connecting link between the art of Masaccio and of Raphael, and the founder of the realist school of painters. He is noted for his innovations in perspective and decorative designs, his depiction of architectural backgrounds, his finished details, and the way he combined geometry and art. Among his masterpieces are *Story of the True Cross*, a series of frescoes in San Francesco at Arezzo, *Flagellation of Christ* in the Urbino cathedral, *Resurrection* in the Borgo San Sepolcro town hall, *Magdalen* in the Arezzo cathedral, *Hercules, Triumph of Chivalry, Nativity* and *Baptism of Christ*. He wrote two art treatises, *De prospectiva pingendi* and *Libellus de quinque corporibus regularibus*. He is reputed to have become blind in his later years, and died in Borgo San Sepolcro on July 5. He is also known as Piero di San Sepolcro, from his birthplace, and Piero della Francesca.

FRANCESCHINI, BALDASSARE (1611–1689), painter. Born in Volterra, Italy, he studied under Matteo Rosselli and Giovanni di San Giovanni at Florence, then in Rome, and followed the Mannerist group in style. He painted for the ducal palace and completed frescoes for several churches in Florence, particularly Santissima Annunziata, and for a convent in Volterra.

FRANCESCHINI, MARCANTONIO (1648–1729), painter. Born in Bologna, Italy, he studied under Galli and Carlo Cignani, worked with the latter in Bologna, Modena, and Reggio, and also was influenced by the Carracci. He completed the ceiling of the Ranazzi palace in Bologna, frescoes in the Pallavicini and Durazzo palaces, Genoa, cartoons for mosaics in St. Peter's (at the request of Pope Clement

XI), and frescoes for the Lichtenstein palace, Vienna. He also decorated a church at Crema, a convent in Bologna with a history of the Servite founders, and a *Thomas of Villanova* at Rimini. He was active up to his death in Bologna.

FRANCHI BOCCAGNI, BL. ANDREW DEI (1335–1401), bishop. A Dominican who served as prior of three houses of the order in Italy, he became bishop of Pistoia, in 1378, resigning a year before his death. He died on May 26; his cult was confirmed in 1921. F. D. May 30.

FRANCIA. *See* Raibolini, Francesco.

FRANCIABIGIO. *See* Bigi, Francesco di Cristofano.

FRANCICA-NAVA, GUISEPPE (1846–1928), cardinal. Born in Catania, Italy, on July 23, he was created a cardinal in 1899, and died in Rome on Dec. 7.

FRANCIS I (1708–1765), emperor. Son of Duke Leopold of Lorraine and Elizabeth Charlotte of Orléans, he was born on Dec. 8 in Nancy, France, succeeded to his father's duchy in 1729 but surrendered it for Tuscany in 1735, and married Maria Theresa of Austria in 1736. He became her co-regent on her accession to the throne in 1740, though he had little to do with the running of the government, was elected emperor in 1745 to succeed Charles VI, headed Austria's armies against France until peace was negotiated in 1748, and died in Innsbruck, Austria, on Aug. 18.

FRANCIS I, emperor of Austria. *See* Francis II, emperor.

FRANCIS II (1768–1835), emperor. Son of Emperor Leopold II and Maria Louisa of Spain, he was born in Florence, Italy, on Feb. 12, married Elizabeth of Württemberg in 1788, and on her death in 1790 married Maria Theresa of Naples. He succeeded his father as emperor in 1792, was immediately involved in a war with France, which was ended by the Treaty of Campo Formio in 1797, and then joined a coalition with Russia and England against the French, which was ended by the peace of Lunéville in 1801. In both cases Austria was forced to surrender territory to the victorious French. In 1804 he became hereditary emperor of Austria as Francis I of Austria, and joined England and Russia against Napoleon, who annihilated Austrian forces at Austerlitz in 1805 and forced Austria to accept the treaty of Pressburg, ceding Tyrol and Venice to France. Napoleon's formation of the Confederation of the Rhine and the consequent end of his influence in the Germanic states caused Francis to renounce the title of Holy Roman emperor, thus ending that "empire" in 1806. Again defeated by Napoleon in 1809, he married his daughter Marie Louise to the French emperor in 1810, again joined a coalition against Napoleon in 1813, and was finally successful when Napoleon was defeated. The Congress of Vienna, held in his capital, returned Venice and Lombardy to Austria. Francis left most of the management of foreign affairs in the hands of Metternich, who was foreign minister in 1809–49. Francis died in Vienna on Mar. 2.

FRANCIS I (1494–1547), king of France. Born in Cognac, France, son of Charles of Orléans and Louise of Savoy, on Sept. 12, he succeeded his cousin (and father-in-law) Louis XII in 1515, and set out to make France a major power directed by the crown. He destroyed the independence of nobles and bishops, fought four wars against Emperor Charles V between 1520 and 1546, used Protestants and Mohammedans in his attacks on the Holy Roman Empire, employed Barbarossa against Genoa, and succeeded in destroying the concept of Christendom in Europe. He was a patron of the arts, brought Italian painters to his great châteaux, was patron of the poets Marot and du Bellay, founded Collège de France, and was at times tolerant of and hostile toward the spread of contemporary heresy. He died in Rambouillet, France, on Mar. 31.

FRANCIS II (1544–1560), king. Eldest son of Henry II of France and Catherine de' Medici, he was born in Fontainebleau, France, on Jan. 19, and succeeded to the French throne in 1559, a year after he married Mary Stuart of Scotland. The duke of Guise and cardinal of Lorraine directed the country for the sixteen-year-old monarch, whose brief reign was marred by civil wars. He died in Paris on Dec. 5.

FRANCIS, BL. (d. 1350?). Born in Pesaro, Italy, of well-to-do parents, he became a Franciscan tertiary in 1300, lived in a hermitage he built there, and attracted a group of disciples whom he supported by begging. He helped Bl. Michelina Metelli found the Confraternity of Mercy in Pesaro and built a hospice for pilgrims at Almetero. His cult was confirmed by Pope Pius IX in 1859. He is commonly called Bl. Cecco. F. D. Oct. 1.

FRANCIS, BL. (d. 1507). Born in Calderola, Italy, he became a Friar Minor of the Observance, an outstanding missioner and confessor, and worked with Bl. Bernardino of Feltre. He died in Colfano, Italy, on Sept. 12, and his cult was approved by Pope Gregory XVI. F. D. Sept. 28.

FRANCIS ANTONY OF LUCERA. *See* Fasani, Bl. Donato.

FRANCIS OF ASSISI, ST. (1181?–1226), founder. Born in Assisi, Umbria, Italy, of a well-to-do merchant, Francis Bernadone was an extravagant and pleasure-seeking youth. In 1202 he was a prisoner of war, reverted to his old ways on his release, and was stricken with a serious illness. On his recovery in 1205 he

again set out for the wars, but returned and decided to change his life after a vision he had at Spoleto. After a pilgrimage to Rome in 1206, he devoted himself to the poor and sick, began to repair a ruined church, and was denounced and disinherited by his father as a madman. He then spent 1207–8 at Gubbio, returned to Assisi, finished repairing the churches of St. Damian and St. Peter, and retired to a little chapel called the Portiuncula, where he began his career of poverty and preaching. He was never ordained. Among the first of the followers he attracted were Bernard da Quintavalle, a rich merchant, and Peter of Cattaneo, a canon of the cathedral. These he robed on Apr. 16, 1209, the date of the founding of the Friars Minor (Franciscans). He drew up a rule which was approved verbally by Pope Innocent III in 1210. In 1212 the Benedictines gave him the Portiuncula chapel on Monte Subasio. The new order quickly attracted many disciples and in 1212, St. Clare, after hearing Francis preach and despite the violent objections of her family, became one of his followers. In the fall of the same year he set out for Syria to preach to the Mohammedans. He was shipwrecked on the way and returned to Italy where he preached the next year, having been given Mt. Alverna as a retreat. In the winter of 1213–14 he again attempted to go to the Mohammedans, set out for Morocco, but was taken ill in Spain and forced to return to Italy. In 1216 he secured the Portiuncula indulgence from Pope Honorius III and probably met St. Dominic in Rome in 1217. By this time the order had so enlarged that it was necessary to organize provinces and in 1217 the first general chapter was held at the Portiuncula. In 1219 some 5000 friars were reported to have attended the general chapter from which he sent his first missionaries to the infidels in Tunis and Morocco; he himself set out with twelve friars to evangelize the Mohammedans in Palestine and Egypt. Despite a talk with Sultan Malek al-Kamil, at Damietta, Egypt, which the crusaders were besieging, his mission was a failure and after visiting the Holy Land he hastened back to Italy. Two of his friars, Matthew of Narni and Gregory of Naples, had led a movement away from Francis' original rule of simplicity, humility, and poverty. He resigned as head of the order in 1220, secured the appointment of Cardinal Ugolino as protector, revised the rule, and at a general chapter at the Portiuncula in 1221 presented his new rule, which was finally approved by Pope Honorius III in 1223. In 1223, while spending Christmas in Grecchio, he fashioned a crib at the hermitage, a custom which has endured in churches to the present day. In 1224 he retired to a cell on Mt. Alverna and there on Sept. 14 received the stigmata. He earlier had experienced numerous supernatural powers and had influenced thousands by his devotion to poverty, his gentleness, his compassion to the poor and the sick, and his delight in the works of God as revealed in nature. He died in Assisi, and was canonized in 1228. F. D. Oct. 3.

JOHANNES JÖRGENSEN, *St. Francis of Assisi* (Garden City, N.Y., Image Books, 1955); G. K. CHESTERTON, *St. Francis of Assisi* (Garden City, N.Y., Image Books, 1957).

FRANCIS OF CAMPOROSSO. *See* Croese, Giovanni.

FRANCIS CARACCIOLO. *See* Caracciolo, St. Ascanio.

FRANCIS OF FABRIANO, BL. (1251–1322?). Son of Compagno and Margaret Venimbeni, he became a Franciscan at sixteen, studied at Assisi under Brother Leo, wrote a defense of the Portiuncula indulgence, and was the first of the order to gather a library. His cult was approved in 1775. F. D. Apr. 22.

FRANCIS JOSEPH (1830–1916), emperor of Austria, king of Hungary and Bohemia. Son of Archduke Francis Charles Joseph and Sophia, daughter of the king of Bavaria, he was born on Aug. 18, and succeeded to the Austrian throne when his uncle, Ferdinand, was forced to abdicate in the revolution of 1848. With the aid of Russia he put down a rebellion in Hungary in 1849; his army also defeated Charles Albert of Sardinia to end disturbances in Lombardy. He married Amelia Eugenia, daughter of the duke of Bavaria, in 1854. In 1859 he was forced to free Lombardy when French and Sardinian forces defeated him at Solferino. He joined Prussia in the conquest of Schleswig-Holstein in 1864, but in 1866 was decisively beaten by Prussia in the Seven Weeks' War which ended Austria's leadership of the German states. In 1867 he was forced to restore Hungary's constitutional autonomy. His attempts to expand eastward among the Slavs caused resistance by Russia and Italy, and his annexation of Bosnia and Herzegovina in 1908 was one of the events leading to World War I. Committed to a policy of conservatism, he was constantly threatened by dissident elements throughout his none-too-firm empire, had to make great concessions to the Liberals, and was shaken during his last years by the mysterious murder of his son Rudolf in 1889, the assassination of his wife in 1898, and that of the heir apparent, his nephew Francis Ferdinand, at Serajevo in 1914. This last was the direct cause of World War I, which followed Austria's attack on Serbia. During his reign the Church's liberties and prerogatives were constantly attacked and constrained by the Liberals, who controlled the government and in 1870 abrogated the concordat of 1854. The emperor died in Vienna on Nov. 21.

FRANCIS OF PAOLA, ST. (1416–1507),

founder. Born in Paola, Calabria, Italy, he studied with the Franciscans at San Marco, and became a hermit at fifteen. By 1452 a number of followers joined him at Paola, a church was built, and a rule established which introduced a fourth vow of perpetual fasting. The order was approved by Pope Sixtus IV in 1474 as the Hermits of St. Francis of Assisi; in 1492 they were named Minim Friars (from *minimi*, least). In 1482, Francis went to France to comfort the dying King Louis XI, and remained at the monastery of Plessis, France, which Charles VIII built for him, until his death. He was canonized in 1519. F. D. Apr. 2.

FRANCIS PATRIZZI, BL. (d. 1328). Born in Siena, Italy, he was accepted by St. Philip Benizi as a Servite at twenty-two after the death of his blind mother, and became widely known as a preacher and confessor. His cult was approved in 1743. F. D. May 12.

FRANCIS OF ST. BONAVENTURE, BL. (d. 1622). *See* Franco, Bl. Apollinaris.

FRANCIS OF ST. MARY, BL. (d. 1627), martyr. *See* Culioye, Bl. Francis.

FRANCIS OF ST. MICHAEL, ST. (d. 1597), martyr. Born in Parilla, near Valladolid, Spain, he became a Franciscan laybrother, and went from the Philippines to Japan in 1593 with St. Peter Baptist. He was captured at Verela and crucified after a year of prison indignities. He was canonized in 1862. F. D. Feb. 5.

FRANCIS PHOEBUS (d. 1483), king of Navarre. *See* Catherine, queen of Navarre.

FRANCIS DE SALES, ST. (1567–1622), bishop, Doctor of the Church. Born in Thorens, Savoy, on Aug. 21, he studied at Annecy and the Jesuit College of Clermont, Paris, and became a doctor of law at Padua at twenty-four. In spite of paternal opposition, he refused marriage and the offer of a senatorship, and was ordained in 1593 and stationed in Geneva. He and his cousin Louis worked as missioners among the Chablais, and were attacked by wolves, by assassins, and by crowds of angered Calvinists. Years of preaching, visitation, and pamphlet writing won a great number of lapsed Catholics as well as new converts. Hostility had been intense because of the attempts of the duke of Savoy's army to force Catholicism upon the region. He served three years as coadjutor to Bishop Claud de Granier during his illness and succeeded to the see of Geneva in 1602. That year he also was sent to Paris, where he was for a time the confessor of Bl. Marie Acarie. In 1604 he met St. Jeanne de Chantal and with her, in 1610, founded the Order of the Visitation. His *Introduction to the Devout Life* (1609), developed from notes written for a cousin for marriage, was widely translated, as was his *Treatise on the Love of God* (1616). He founded schools, taught catechism, and organized his diocese well. Possessed of a great intellect and of theological wisdom which astonished the papal court itself, he wrote and spoke in basically simple terms, with grace and earnestness, reaching out to many people and problems, and stressing that sanctity was possible in everyday life. He died in Lyons, France, on Dec. 28 while returning from Avignon, was beatified the same year (the first solemn beatification to take place in St. Peter's), and canonized in 1625. He was declared a Doctor of the Church in 1877, and Pope Pius XI designated him in 1923 as patron of journalists. F. D. Jan. 29.

ABBÉ HAMON, *Life of St. François de Sales*, adapted by W. G. Trochu (2 vols., London, 1941).

FRANCIS OF VITTORIA (1480?–1546), theologian. Born in Vittoria, Navarre, Spain, he studied at Burgos, Valladolid, and Paris, became a Dominican, and taught at St. James, Paris in 1516–22, St. Gregory College, Valladolid in 1522–24, and Salamanca, where he held the chair of theology in 1524–44. He wrote on what was to become international law, maintaining that non-combatants should be spared, that slavery was not a justifiable consequence of conquest, that looting was wrong, and that hostages could not be put to death, and that pagans had basic rights to life, liberty, and possessions. His publications include *De jure belli, De indis insulis, Summa sacramentorum ecclesias, Instruccion y refugio del alma*, and a commentary on St. Thomas Aquinas. He died on Aug. 12.

FRANCIS XAVIER, ST. (1506–1552). Born in the family castle of Xavier, near Pamplona in the Basque area of Spanish Navarre on Apr. 7, he was sent to the University of Paris in 1525, secured his licentiate in 1528, met Ignatius Loyola and became one of the seven who in 1534, at Montmartre, founded the Society of Jesus. In 1536 he left Paris to join Ignatius in Venice, from whence they all intended to go as missionaries to Palestine (a trip which never materialized), was ordained there in 1537, went to Rome in 1538, and in 1540, when the pope formally recognized the Society, was ordered, with Fr. Simon Rodriguez, to the Far East as the first Jesuit missionaries. King John III kept Fr. Simon in Lisbon, but Francis, after a year's voyage, six months of which were spent at Mozambique where he preached and gave aid to the sick, eventually arrived in Goa, India, in 1542 with Fr. Paul of Camerino, an Italian, and Francis Mansilhas, a Portuguese. There he began preaching to the natives and attempted to reform his fellow Europeans, living among the natives and adopting their customs on his travels. During the next decade he converted tens of thousands to Christianity. He visited the Paravas at the tip of India, near Cape Comorin, Tuticorin (1542), Malacca

(1545), the Moluccas near New Guinea and Morotai near the Philippines (1546–47), and Japan (1549–51). In 1551, India and the East were set up as a separate province and Ignatius made Francis its first provincial. In 1552 he set out for China, landed on the island of Sancian within sight of his goal, but died before he reached the mainland. Working against great difficulties, language problems (contrary to legend, he had no proficiency in foreign tongues), inadequate funds, and lack of cooperation, often actual resistance, from European officials, he left the mark of his missionary zeal and energy on areas which clung to Christianity for centuries. He was canonized in 1622 and proclaimed patron of all foreign missions by Pope Pius X. F. D. Dec. 3.

JAMES BRODRICK, *Saint Francis Xavier* (Garden City, N.Y., Image Books, 1955).

FRANCISCO, BL. ANTONIO (d. 1583), martyr. A Jesuit priest from Italy, he joined Bl. Rudolph Aquaviva and others in attempting to establish a church at Cuncolim, India, and was killed by natives. He was beatified in 1893. F. D. July 27.

FRANCISCO DE JÉSUS-MARIA (d. 1677), theologian. Born in Spain, he became a Discalced Carmelite, made studies of the sacraments at Salamanca, and established the moral theology of his group with Antonio del SS. Sagramento, Sebastian de San Joaquin (d. 1714), and Andrés de la Madre de Dios (d. 1674). The entire plan of study was completed by Alonso de los Angeles; it was highly praised by St. Alphonsus Liguori.

FRANCK, CÉSAR AUGUSTE JEAN GUILLAUME HUBERT (1822–1890), composer. Born in Liège, Belgium, on Dec. 10, he studied there and at the Paris conservatory, under Benoist and others, succeeding Benoist on the faculty in 1872. His early music was played at Liszt's private concerts in Weimar, but later work was not accepted: oratorios (including *Ruth* and *Les béatitudes*), operas (*Hulda* and *Ghisèle*), symphonic poems, many "pieces" for organ, and *Symphony in D* (1889). Only his *String Quartet* (1890) was acclaimed during his lifetime; though he was made a chevalier of the Legion of Honor in 1885, this distinction noted only his work as organist (he was at Ste. Clotilde for his last thirty-two years) and as teacher (of private pupils and at the Jesuit school of Vaugirard). He developed themes cyclically from briefly announced suggestions, repeating earlier material to achieve a strong unity. The logic of form was Germanic and classical; his reliance on mood, tense chords, and expressive dissonance were from French romanticism. The apparent clash sometimes offended directors and audience alike; at a major performance only two persons attended. After the Franco-German War he was one of the founders of the Societé Nationale de Musique, which sought to restore pride by supporting work by French composers. Ernest Chaussan, Henri, Duparc, Vincent d'Indy, and Gabriel Pierné were devoted to and influenced by him; Debussy also was an admirer. Franck died in Paris on Nov. 8.

FRANCK, KASPAR (1543–1584), theologian. Born in Ortrand, Saxony, on Nov. 2, he became a successful Lutheran minister, but when Duke Albert restored Catholicism, Franck debated with Martin Eisengrein and after studies at Ingolstadt became a convert in 1568. He was ordained, did parish work in Haag and Krailburg, and in 1573 became rector of Ingolstadt, an office he filled also at later dates. He took his doctorate in theology at Siena, was honored by Pope Gregory XIII, and wrote works in theology which reveal deep knowledge of the Fathers of the Church. He died in Ingolstadt, Bavaria, on Mar. 12.

FRANCO (d. 1135). The second abbot of the Benedictine monastery of Afflighem, near Alost, Brabant, he succeeded Fulgentius in 1122 and was the author of a treatise on grace.

FRANCO, BL. APOLLINARIS (d. 1622), martyr. Born at Aguilar del Campo Castile, Spain, he received his doctor's degree in law at Salamanca, became a Franciscan of the Observance, was sent to the Philippines in 1600, and became commissary general of Franciscan missions in Japan in 1614. In 1617 he went to Omura province, was imprisoned for five years, then burned to death at Nagasaki on Sept. 12 with seven others, including Bl. Lucy de Freitas, the eighty-year old Japanese widow of a Portuguese merchant, in whose home a priest had been apprehended, Richard of St. Anne, Francis of St. Bonaventure, and Paul of St. Clare, the last two whom he had received into the Franciscans in prison. He was among the 205 beatified by Pope Pius IX in 1867 as the martyrs of Japan. F. D. Sept. 10.

FRANCO, GIOVANNI BATTISTA (1510–1580), painter. Born in Udine, Italy, he studied in Rome, worked with Vasari on a Medici palace, completed portraits of the Medici, and made more than 100 etchings, half on original designs and half representations of the work of Raphael, Titian, and others. He died in Venice and is often called Il Semolei.

FRANCO LIPPI, BL. (1211–1291). He was born in Grotti, Italy, became leader of a band of bandits, and led a life of crime and violence until he was fifty, when he became blind. He recovered his sight after a pilgrimage to Compostella, did public penance in Siena, became a Carmelite laybrother at seventy, and spent his last ten years in fervent penance. His cult was confirmed in 1670. F. D. Dec. 11.

FRANCO, RAMÓN (1806–1939), general. Born in Spain, he entered the army, was one of three who made the first flight across the southern Atlantic (from Cadiz to Buenos Aires), directed the aviation branch of the ministry of war after 1931, and became chief of the air force during the Spanish Civil War of 1936, led by his brother Francisco. He died in an airplane crash near Palma, Majorca, on Oct. 28.

FRANCUCCI, INNOCENZO DI PIETRO (1494?–1550?), painter. Born in Imola, Italy, he went to Bologna about 1506 to study under Francesco Francia, and probably for a time at Florence with Mariotto Albertinelli, then settled in Bologna (where he died) under the patronage of Count Giovanni Bentivoglio. He painted in the tradition of Raphael, though he never met him, and became known for his altarpieces: *Marriage of St. Catherine, Archangel Michael and Satan, St. Michael with Saints, Death and Assumption of the Virgin*, and *Madonna with Kneeling Donors*. He is also known as Innocenzo da Imola.

FRANK, MICHAEL SIGISMUND (1770–1847), artist. Born in Nuremberg, Germany, on June 1, he studied drawing, painted wooden boxes for numerous manufacturers, married the daughter of an innkeeper, and when she died five years later sold the hotel and bought a porcelain factory. He lost most of his income while trying to recapture the secret of staining molten glass, succeeded in 1804, sold many samples of his art, and after 1808 was patronized by King Maximilian I of Bavaria, for whom he designed many religious scenes after originals by Raphael, Rubens, van Leyden, and others. In 1818 he was appointed to the royal porcelain factory in Munich, and in 1827 became director and chief instructor at the royal institute for stained glass. He died in Munich, Bavaria, on Jan. 16.

FRANKENBERG, JOHANN HEINRICH (1726–1804), cardinal. Born in Gross Glogau, Silesia, on Sept. 18, he attended the Jesuit college there, went to Breslau and the German College in Rome, and was ordained in 1749. He was coadjutor to the bishop of Görz in 1750–54, dean in Prague and in Alt Bunzlau, and named archbishop of Mechlin, Belgium, and primate of the Low Countries in 1759. He proved unpopular at the court of Maria Theresa when he opposed the standards of living of the nobility, became a cardinal in 1778, and clashed with Emperor Joseph II when the latter introduced heretical teaching in the seminaries and declared the state supreme in all matters. Back in Belgium, the cardinal opposed the establishment of Joseph's general seminary in a *Declaration* which had widespread effect in Europe and was blamed by the emperor for resultant insurrections. He was ordered arrested, but this step was not taken. After the revolution of 1789 had freed Belgium of Austrian control, Joseph's successor, Leopold II, became king and relaxed Joseph's measures. Frankenberg served as a member of the States-General, suffered again when the French entered the scene and demanded an oath of clerical allegiance, and was banished to Prussia in 1797. To ease political tension, he resigned his see in 1801 so the concordat between France and the Holy See could be signed. French hostility later drove him from Emmerich to Borken to Breda, Netherlands, where he died on June 11.

FRANZELIN, JOHANN BAPTIST (1816-1886), cardinal. Born in Aldein, Tyrol, on Apr. 15, he studied at Bolzano, became a Jesuit in 1843, taught in Poland and in Rome, left during the revolution of 1848, and was ordained in France in 1849. In 1850 he returned to teach dogma at the Roman College; from 1853 to 1857 he was prefect of studies at the German College; until 1876 he taught dogmatic theology at the Roman College. He was a consultor to several congregations, served on the planning board of the Vatican Council, and against his wishes was named cardinal in 1876 by Pope Pius IX. He distributed his income to the poor, lived and worked without secretarial help in the Jesuit novitiate in Rome, wrote on scriptural tradition, the Eucharist and the other sacraments, the Trinity, and the significant *De ecclesia Christi*. He died in Rome on Dec. 11.

FRASER, SIMON (1667?-1747). Son of Thomas Fraser, Lord Lovat, and Sybilla Macleod, the twelfth baron Lovat studied at Aberdeen, gained control of large areas in Inverness through a forced marriage with the widow of the clan leader, and was entangled in many broils as a result. He fled to the Continent in 1702 at the accession of Queen Anne, became a convert, and, though outlawed, returned to Scotland in 1713. He supported the 1715 insurrection against England, reversed his position and regained his estates, but was active on behalf of Charles Stuart in 1745, was captured, taken to London, and beheaded.

FRASER, SIMON JOSEPH (1871-1933). Born in Beauly, Inverness-shire, Scotland, on Nov. 25, son of the thirteenth Baron Lovat and Alice Weld-Blundell Fraser, he studied in Edgbaston and at Oxford, and succeeded to his father's title in 1887. He served in the army in 1894-97, was with a zoological expedition to the Nile region, and commanded the Lovat Scouts during the Boer War. In 1910 he married Laura Lister. He worked on defense needs, helped to formulate the plan for the officers' training corps, and during World War I commanded a regiment at Gallipoli in 1915. Invalided, he became first chairman of the royal commission on forestry, undersecretary of state for the dominions, and chairman of the overseas settlement committee. He was interested in agriculture, introduced cotton planting in the Sudan, promoted fisheries, and originated the

Empire Forestry Conference, first held in Canada in 1923. He died in Little Tew, England, on Feb. 18.

FRASER, WILLIAM (d. 1851), bishop. He studied at the Scots College, Vallodolid, Spain, and succeeded Fr. Edmund Burke as vicar apostolic of Nova Scotia in 1827; he was named bishop of the newly created see of Halifax (which included all of Nova Scotia) in 1842, and was transferred to Arichat in 1844 when the larger see was divided. He died on Oct. 4.

FRASINETTI, BL. PAULA (1809-1882), foundress. Born in Genoa, Italy, on Mar. 3, she served her brother in his rectory in Quinto, teaching poor children there. Others joined her in this work and she founded the Sisters of St. Dorothy; her institute was formally approved in 1863 and spread to Portugal and Brazil. She was beatified in 1930. F. D. June 11.

FRASSEN, CLAUDE (1620-1711), theologian. Born near Péronne, France, he became a Franciscan there at seventeen, studied at Paris, and served there for thirty years as professor of philosophy and theology. He received his doctorate from the Sorbonne in 1662, became definitor general in 1682, and attended general chapters in Toledo and Rome. He was an adviser to King Louis XIV, wrote biblical commentaries, and is best known for his *Scotus academicus*, a detailed analysis of the work of Duns Scotus. He died in Paris on Feb. 26.

FRATERNUS, ST. (d. 450?). He was bishop of Auxerre, France, and is traditionally listed as a martyr. F. D. Sept. 29.

FRAUNHOFER, JOSEPH VON (1787-1826), physicist. Born in Straubing, Bavaria, on Mar. 6, tenth son of a glass grinder, he was orphaned at twelve and apprenticed to a lens grinder for six years. Councilor von Utzschneider became interested in him, bought his release, gave him books, and persuaded the king to make a small grant, with which the boy bought a machine. His craftsmanship in glass and metal engraving led to partnership in the councilor's firm at Benediktbeuern; they entered a new partnership in 1814, and in 1819 moved the firm to Munich. He gained honors quickly, from several nations and scientific societies. Although self-taught, he had great success in optics, developing measuring devices for telescopes, making measurements of the wave lengths of light, establishing the chromatic refraction of glass, and designing the lens for the great telescope at Dorpat. He discovered and wrote on spectrum analysis and was the first to note the dark lines, now named after him, in the solar spectrum. He died in Munich, Bavaria, on June 7.

FRAYSSINOUS, DENIS ANTOINE LUC DE (1765-1841), bishop. Born in Curières, France, he preached in Paris through the first years of the nineteenth century (except from

1809 to 1814 when Napoleon forbade it) and did much to lessen the effects of the French Revolution. He was in 1817 named court preacher and almoner to Louis XVIII, was elected to the French Academy in 1822, was minister of public worship from 1824 to 1828, titular bishop of Hermopolis, a peer, and after the revolution of 1830 went to Rome and Prague. His conferences at Notre Dame were published as *Défense du christianisme;* other writing was touched with Gallicanism. He died in St. Geniez, Provence, to which he had retired in 1838.

FRÉCHETTE, LOUIS HONORÉ (1839–1908), author. Born in Point Lévis, Quebec, Canada, on Nov. 16, he studied at the seminary of Nicolet and Laval, followed the law, and was admitted to the bar in 1864. He had no success, went to Chicago, Illinois, for seven years to work as a journalist and secretary, and on his return to Canada he served briefly in parliament and in 1879 began writing for half a dozen newspapers. He published seven volumes of French-Canadian poetry, several plays, and prose sketches, and translated William Dean Howells and George Washington Cable into French. He was honored by the French Academy in 1879, was an original member and later president of the Royal Society of Canada, and received honorary degrees from three Canadian universities. From 1889 until his death in Quebec on Nov. 16 he was clerk of the legislative council.

FRECULUS (d. 850). A student at the palace school founded by Charlemagne, he became bishop of Lisieux, France, and wrote a world history.

FREDEGAND, ST. (d. 740?). Also known as Fregaut, he was trained in Ireland, directed the Benedictine monastery of Kerkelodor, near Antwerp, and possibly was a fellow missioner with St. Willibrord. St. Turninus, an Irish priest, went to the Netherlands at about the same time. F. D. July 17.

FREDEGIS OF TOURS (d. 834). Born in England, he studied under Alcuin at York and at the court of Charlemagne, succeeded his teacher in 804 as abbot of Tours, wrote poems, and prepared a treatise on pre-creation chaos (*De nihilo et tenebris*) in which he employed the dialectical method so popular with later scholastics. He is also called Fridugisus.

FREDERICK I BARBAROSSA (1123?–1190), emperor. Son of Frederick of Swabia and Judith, daughter of Henry the Black, and thus related on his mother's side to the Guelphs, he defeated Duke Conrad of Zähringen in 1146 and in 1152 succeeded Conrad III as king of Germany. He believed in the strongest power for the monarch, visited all quarters of his realm to cement his relations with the nobles, and depended on his chancellor, Arch-

bishop Rainald von Dassel, and the uncanonically promoted Archbishop Wichmann of Magdeburg, to lead the nationalistic hierarchy in their hostility toward and dissatisfaction with papal policy. The king's own interpretation of the rule of Charlemagne, and of the emperor's supremacy over the pope in matters of appointments and government, led to a long quarrel with the papacy. A major and early struggle was over Italy; if Frederick conquered it, he would have been supreme over the papal states. The pope was harried by the Normans and could not even expel the rebel Arnold of Brescia from Rome; Frederick agreed to the terms of the Treaty of Constance and marched to the pope's aid, in return for the promise of being crowned emperor. Two years later he arrived, to meet the new pope, Adrian IV, and after some legal haggling was crowned in June 1155. Frederick strengthened his position at home and re-established his position in Burgundy by marrying Beatrice, heiress of the country, after he had received curial permission to give up his wife, Adela von Vohburg. The emperor returned to Italy to support his claims of superiority; Adrian was now friendly with the Normans; the emperor took Milan. When Adrian died, Pope Alexander III refused to accept the German translation of *beneficium* as a feudal concession, and clung to the interpretation of the gifts to Frederick as personal benefits. The quarrel over supremacy continued, with popes and antipopes engaged in the conflict; after the battle of Lepanto, which indicated the power of the papal forces, without Frederick's help, the Treaty of Venice (1177) assured the pope of his position and ended Frederick's political aspirations. He once more became a major threat when he defeated Henry the Lion, who sought to lead the Guelphs in northern Italy, which Frederick now occupied (1183), and when his son Henry, married to Constance of Sicily, closed the circle to the south and shook the position of Urban III. Chiefly through the efforts of Philipp von Heinsberg, prince-archbishop of Cologne, pressure was brought to bear at home and Frederick ceased to imperil the Papal States. At the election of Gregory VIII the world realized the increasing danger from the East and some moves toward Western unity were made. Frederick himself became a crusader in 1188 and died in Asia Minor on June 10 during a crossing of the Saleph River.

FREDERICK II (1194–1250), emperor. Son of Henry VI and Constance of Sicily, he was born on Dec. 26, sought peace in Germany, making such concessions to nobles and hierarchical leaders that they gained great independence, and preferred to consider Italy the center of his political world. When Pope Innocent III selected Frederick to destroy the Guelph leader, Otto IV, Frederick agreed on his part to end the usurpation of power in church matters (1215). Although he had promised to go on the crusade, troubles at home kept him close to the German scene. In 1227, after many delays irritated Gregory IX, the pope excommunicated Frederick for not fulfilling his crusader's promise. Two years later, against papal orders, Frederick left for the Holy Land, declared himself king of Jerusalem in 1229, landed at Brindisi on his return, and frightened the pope into lifting the excommunication. Frederick sought to organize northern Italy, but was called home by the rebellion of his son Henry, whom he defeated in 1235. Between 1231 and 1235 he had secured his position in southern Italy, published his imperial constitutions, and continued his interest in the University of Naples, which he had founded. He then attacked the Lombards, opposed the pope's leanings toward being considered a world ruler, and sought to become king of the Romans. Pope Gregory excommunicated him again in 1239 and Innocent IV did the same at the Council of Lyons in 1245. Frederick granted great concessions to the secular aristocracy, at the expense of the bishops and abbots, and in gaining military allies in this way split the loyalties of Germany. His conflict with the papacy continued until his death in Fiorentina, Apulia, on Dec. 13.

FREDERICK III (1415–1493), emperor. Son of Ernest of Hapsburg, he was born at Innsbruck, Austria, on Sept. 21, was raised at the court of his uncle, Count Frederick IV of Tyrol, after his father's death in 1424, and in 1435 became co-ruler with his brother Albert of Styria and Carinthia. He was selected as head of the Hapsburg family at the death of Emperor Albert II in 1439, was elected German king, as Frederick IV, and emperor in 1440, and crowned in 1442. He ignored the diet's decision to remain neutral in the struggle between Pope Eugene IV and the Council of Basle and followed the advice of his adviser Aeneas Silvius Piccolomini (later Pope Pius II) in reaching an agreement with Eugene in 1446 by which he agreed to support the pope in return for papal crowning in Rome and concessions over church lands and revenues. He signed the concordat of Vienna in 1448 with Pope Nicholas V and the council was soon dissolved, ending the schism. He failed in his attempt to conquer the Swiss, was faced with revolts in Austria and Hungary, and in 1451 went to Rome, where he married Leonora of Portugal in 1452 and was crowned emperor by Pope Nicholas, last emperor to be crowned in Rome. On his return to Germany he found growing unrest. He failed in his attempt to secure the crown of Hungary and Bohemia after the death of Ladislaus in 1457, but united Upper and Lower Austria when he succeeded to Lower

Austria on the death of his brother Albert in 1463. In 1477 he married his son Maximilian to Mary, daughter of Charles the Bold, duke of Burgundy; Maximilian was elected king of the Romans in 1486. His possessions were under incessant attacks from the Bohemians and Hungarians, the Turks were beginning to raid, and he was driven from Austria by Matthias Corvinus of Hungary in 1485. He turned the running of the country over to Maximilian, and returned to Linz, Austria, where he spent the rest of his life in gardening and study until his death on Aug. 19.

FREDERICK IV, German king. *See* Frederick III, emperor.

FREDERICK, ST. (d. 838), bishop. Grandson of Radbod, king of the Frisians, he was most successful with converts while a priest. Chosen bishop of Utrecht, Flanders, after 820, he sent priests to the north of his diocese to drive out paganism. According to tradition, he incurred the enmity of Emperor Louis the Debonair and his family, particularly Empress Judith, whom he reproached for her immorality, and of the inhabitants of Walcherin, who resented his corrections. He is said to have been stabbed to death at Maastricht, Flanders, by two assassins hired either by Judith, or the Walcherins, though probably the latter. F. D. July 18.

FREDERICK, BL. (d. 1020). Son of Count Geoffrey of Verdun, he gave up his wealth and became a Benedictine at St. Vannes, then served at the abbey of St. Vedast in Arras, France, where he became prior. F. D. Jan. 6.

FREDERICK, BL. (d. 1070?), abbot. Born in Swabia, he became a Benedictine monk at Einsiedeln, Switzerland, was sent to reform the abbey of Hirschau in 1066, met with great opposition, was removed by a local count, and retired to Ebersberg. F. D. May 7.

FREDERICK, ST. (d. 1121), bishop. He replaced Alexander as bishop of Liège, Flanders, when the latter was deposed for simony in 1119, suffered from those who were strengthened by this move, and was, perhaps, poisoned by the count of Louvain, an associate of Alexander. F. D. May 27.

FREDERICK, BL. (d. 1175). He was abbot-founder of the Premonstratensian monastery of Mariengarten. F. D. Mar. 3.

FREDERICK, BL. (d. 1329). Born in Ratisbon, Bavaria, he became an Augustinian laybrother there, served as a carpenter, and died on Nov. 30. His cult was approved in 1909. F. D. Nov. 29.

FREDIANO, ST. (d. 588?), bishop. Said to have been son of a king of Ireland, and educated there, he made a pilgrimage to Italy, became a hermit on Monte Pisano, and against his will was made bishop of Lucca by Pope John II. His cathedral was burned by the

Lombards, but he restored it, converted many of the invaders, and formed a group of canons regular who were merged, in 1507, with the Congregation of St. John Lateran. He is known in Ireland as St. Frigidian. F. D. Mar. 18.

FREDOLI, BERENGER (1250?–1323), cardinal. Born in Vérune, France, he held several canonries, was secular abbot of St. Aphrodise in Béziers, held the chair of canon law at Bologna, and was chaplain to Pope Celestine V. He was consecrated bishop of Béziers in 1294, drew up the *Decretals* for Boniface VIII, sought to bring pope and Philip the Fair together, attended the Council of Rome in 1302, and was named cardinal by Clement V in 1305 and cardinal-bishop of Frascati in 1309. He investigated charges made against the Knights Templar and against some Franciscans, deposed those who had plotted against the life of John XXII, and wrote on canon law. He died in Avignon, France, on June 11.

FREDOLI, BERENGER (d. 1323), cardinal. Nephew of Berenger (d. 1323), he succeeded his uncle as bishop of Béziers, France, in 1309 and was named cardinal-bishop of Porto, Portugal, in 1317.

FREEMAN, BL. WILLIAM (1558?–1595), martyr. Born in Yorkshire, England, he was educated at Oxford. Moved by the death of Bl. Edward Stransham in 1586, he went to Rheims, was ordained in 1587, and worked in the English mission for six years. Convicted of being a priest during the Elizabethan persecution, he was hanged, drawn, and quartered at Warwick, England. He was beatified in 1929. F. D. Aug. 13.

FREGAUT. *See* Fredegand, St.

FREGOSO, FEDERIGO (1480?–1541), cardinal. Son of Agostino Fregoso, governor of Genoa, and nephew of Duke Giobaldo of Urbino, he grew up in the latter's court, was ordained, and in 1507 was named archbishop of Salerno. Spain refused to recognize the appointment. Fregoso was more active as a humanist than as a churchman, associated himself with Bembo and Castiglione, and advanced classical studies. In 1513 his brother Ottaviano became doge of Genoa; Federigo became chief counselor, and led the army against civil insurrection and the navy against the Barbary pirates. He led the defense of Genoa when it was attacked by Charles V in 1522, was wounded, and fled to France. There King Francis I gave him the abbey of St. Benignus at Dijon, where he studied Greek and Hebrew but offended the monks by his severity. He returned to Italy, resigned his see in 1529, was named titular bishop of Gubbio, and in 1539 cardinal-priest. He died in Gubbio, Italy, on July 22.

FREITAS, BL. LUCY de (d. 1622). *See* Franco, Bl. Apollinaris.

FREJES, FRANCISCO (d. 1845), historian. Born in Guadalajara, Mexico, he became a Franciscan, preached widely, and when he sought to pursue historical studies was appointed to Guadelupe in Zacatecas, where he became superior in 1838. He wrote two important studies of the conquest of Mexico.

FREMIN, JACQUES (1628–1691), missioner. Born in Rheims, France, on Mar. 12, he became a Jesuit in 1646, and in 1655 was sent to the Indian missions in Canada. He worked among the Onondagas, Cayugas, and Mohawks, established the first Catholic settlement in Vermont, on Isle La Motte, and brought what comfort he could to captured Hurons everywhere. He made 10,000 converts in his lifetime and after 1670 was in charge of the Christian Indian settlement at La Prairie, near Montreal. Except for journeys to France seeking aid for the missions, he served in Canada until his death at Quebec on July 2.

FRENCH, NICHOLAS (1604–1678), bishop. Born in Ballytory, Wexford, Ireland, he studied at Louvain, was president of a college there, and returned in 1640 to a Wexford parish. He supported the Confederation faction, was a member of the assembly of Kilkenny, and in 1645 was consecrated bishop of Ferns. He opposed Preston and Ormond, went to France to offer the duke of Lorraine the protectorship of Ireland in return for war against Cromwell, and had to remain on the Continent until his death in Ghent, Flanders, to whose bishop he was assistant, on Aug. 23. He wrote important pamphlets while abroad, covering the events of the years 1645–75.

FREPPEL, CHARLES ÉMILE (1827–1891), bishop. Born in Ober-Ehnheim, Alsace, on June 1, he studied there, was ordained in Strassburg in 1849, took his doctorate at the Sorbonne, and became chaplain at St. Geneviève, Paris. He preached there and at other Paris churches and later published these discourses. He was named to the chair of sacred eloquence at the Sorbonne, lectured on the Fathers of the Church (his ten-volume study was published in 1885), gave a Lenten series at the Tuileries for Napoleon III (published as *La Vie chrétienne*), and in 1863 published a strong refutation of Renan. He was named to the committee preparing the Vatican Council, defended papal infallibility at the council, was consecrated bishop of Angers, France, in 1870, and founded its Catholic university in 1875. In 1880 he was elected to the chamber of deputies from Finistère, a post he held for eleven years, during which he spoke boldly on political and social problems, and frequently attacked Bismarck. His polemical writings, a study of the French Revolution, and works on Bossuet, St. Irenaeus, Origen, and Tertullian have also been published. He died in Paris on Dec. 22.

FRESNEL, AUGUSTIN JEAN (1788–1827), physicist. Born in Broglie, Normandy, on May 10, he studied at Caen, served with the engineering corps, except for five years when out of Napoleon's favor, and became a member of the lighthouse commission in 1819 and its secretary in 1824. His work with lenses universally changed lighthouse illumination. He was named a member of the Academy of Sciences in 1823 and received the Rumford Medal of the Royal Society of London shortly before his death at Ville d'Avray, near Paris, on July 14. His particular contributions were in applied optics, the phenomena of diffraction and interference, double refraction, and transverse waves, and, with Arago, polarized light.

FRICOR, ST. (7th century). *See* Caidoc, St.

FRIDESWIDE, ST. (d. 735?). Daughter of Didan, king of a region around the upper Thames, England, she was supposed to have fled marriage to a neighboring king, Algar, and founded the Benedictine convent of St. Mary's on the site of what is now Oxford, of which she is patron. F. D. Oct. 19.

FRIDOLIN, ST. (d. 650?). Possibly an Irish missioner, he wandered through France and Switzerland as a missioner, preaching, building churches, monasteries, and schools, and finally founding Säckingen, on the Rhine, where he served as abbot. F. D. Mar. 6.

FRIDUGISUS. *See* Fredegis of Tours.

FRIEDEL, XAVER EHRENBERT (1673–1743), missioner. Born in Linz, Austria, on Mar. 11, he became a Jesuit in 1688 and in 1705 was sent to China, where he served for ten years (1708–18) on the elaborate cartological survey of the empire. He later was rector of a church in southern Peking, where he died on June 4.

FRIEDRICH VON HAUSEN (d. 1190), poet. Born in the Rhenish territory, he was in Italy in 1175 and again in 1186, when he accompanied Henry VI; he was at Worms in 1188 with Count Baldwin V; later he served Emperor Frederick, with whom he went on the crusade, and died at the battle of Philomelium (now Arsehir, Turkey) on May 6. He was one of the first of the minnesingers who imitated the French and Provençal styles; his romantic lyrics are artificial in style and somewhat rough in form.

FRIGIDIAN. *See* Frediano, St.

FRITHBERT, ST. (d. 766), bishop. He succeeded St. Acca as bishop of Hexham, England, where he presided for thirty-four years. F. D. Dec. 23.

FRITHESTAN, ST. (d. 933). A Benedictine monk and disciple of St. Brimbald, he became bishop of Winchester, England, about 910. F. D. Sept. 10.

FRITZ, SAMUEL (1654?–1728), missioner. Born in Trautenau, Bohemia, he became a Jesuit in 1673 and was sent to Quito, Ecuador, in 1684. He served the Indians in that area for forty-two years, converted many, mapped the upper Marañon between Quito and Peru, explored the Amazon River to Pará, and was honored by the Spanish crown for his geographical work. He died on Mar. 20.

FRODOBERT, ST. (d. 673?). A Benedictine at Luxeuil, he became founder and abbot of Moutier-la-Celle, near Troyes, Gaul, where he was admired for his austerities and devotion to prayer. F. D. Jan. 8.

FROILAN, ST. (d. 1006), bishop. A native of Lugo, Galicia, he became a hermit at eighteen and with the fifteen-year-old Attilanus organized a Benedictine community at Moruela, Old Castile, of which Froilan became first abbot. In 990 he was made bishop of León and Attilanus was made bishop of Zamora. They were responsible for the restoration of Benedictine monasticism in western Spain as it was reclaimed from the Moors. F. D. Oct. 3.

FROISSART, JEAN (1337?–1410?), historian. Born in Valenciennes, France, he was tonsured as a cleric, but took to travel through Europe, went to England in 1361 to offer Queen Philippa a poem on the war between France and England, remained as a royal secretary until 1366, went to France with the Black Prince and to Italy with the duke of Clarence, and returned to Valenciennes when Philippa died. He then entered the service of Duke Wenceslas of Luxembourg, composing poems, and of Count Guy de Blois, who made him curé at Lestinnes and in 1384 canon of Chimay. He spent some years at the court of Gaston Phebus, comte de Foix, gathering additional material for the history of France in the fourteenth century; he wrote the four books of his *Chroniques* in 1390–91 at Valenciennes. He was in Paris in 1392, went to London later and offered his poems to King Richard II, returned to the Continent, and entered the service of Duke Philip the Bold of Burgundy, after a quarrel with Guy de Blois. Although favoring the French, his chronicle is a vivid and detailed account of life and warfare from 1328 to 1400 (in a later revision); he gained much of his information at first hand. He also wrote love poems; the autobiographical *Dit du florin*; and *Méliador*, a long romance on the Round Table.

FROMENTIN, EUGÈNE (1820–1876), painter. Born in La Rochelle, France, on Oct. 24, he studied law at Paris, practiced as a lawyer, became interested in literature and art, studied landscape painting under Cabat, and after a trip to Africa in 1846 began painting seriously. He held his first exhibition in 1847, won the medal of the Legion of Honor, and produced many picturesque and influential studies of Arab scenes, customs, and horsemen in Algeria. He also wrote a novel, *Dominique*

(1862), a critical history of Dutch and Flemish painting, *Maîtres d'autrefois* (1876), and two accounts of his stays in Algeria. He died suddenly at St. Maurice, France, on Aug. 27.

FRONTENAC, LOUIS DE BUADE DE (1620–1698), governor. Born in Paris, son of a captain in the royal service, he entered the army, was a colonel at twenty-three and a brigadier general at twenty-six, and saw service in Holland, Italy, Germany, and Crete. He served as governor of Canada from 1672 to 1682, and again from 1689 until his death in Quebec on Nov. 28. During his first term he built forts to contain the Iroquois, sent La Salle to explore the Mississippi, but proved contentious and vain. He clashed with many leaders when he sought to absorb more power than permitted by his office, tried to overrule the missionaries' objections to liquor trade (particularly with the Indians), quarreled with Governor Perrot of Montreal, and created such factionalism that he was removed. When he returned after disastrous defeats of French forces, he sent three armies into New York, New Hampshire, and Maine, defeated the English and the Iroquois, defeated an English fleet under Admiral Phipps, razed strongholds in Acadia, and captured St. John's, Newfoundland. As a result, he brought peace and unity to the colony. He had little sympathy for churchmen, particularly Jesuits and Sulpicians, but supported the Recollects. The French government honored him for his final successful thrust against the Mohawks in 1696.

FRONTO, ST. (1st century), bishop. According to legend, he was born in Lycaonia and became a follower of Christ, was baptized by Peter, and became one of the seventy-two disciples. He is said to have accompanied St. Peter to Antioch and Rome, from where he was sent with a priest, George, to convert the Gauls. He is supposed to have become the first bishop of Périgueux, and George the first bishop of Le Puy, both in France. F. D. Oct. 25.

FRONTO, ST. (d. 304), martyr. *See* Apodemius, St.

FROWIN OF ENGELBERG, BL. (d. 1178). A Benedictine at St. Blasien, he became abbot of Engelberg, Switzerland, in 1143, founded its school and library, and wrote its history and several tracts on asceticism. F. D. Mar. 7.

FRUCTUOSA, ST. (d. 305?), martyr. *See* Donatus, St.

FRUCTUOSUS, ST. (d. 259), bishop and martyr. Highly respected by pagans and Christians alike, the bishop of Tarragona, Spain, was nevertheless ordered by the Roman governor to sacrifice to the gods during the Valerian persecution. When he refused, he and his deacons, Augurius and Eulogius, were burned to death in the arena. St. Augustine later wrote a memorial. F. D. Jan. 21.

FRUCTUOSUS, ST. (d. 665), archbishop. On the death of his father, a Visigoth general, he freed his slaves, distributed his wealth, retired as a hermit, and established a number of monasteries and convents under a modified Benedictine rule when his life attracted imitation by hundreds. Against his wishes he was made bishop of Dumnium and, in 656, archbishop of Braga, Portugal. F. D. Apr. 16.

FRUGENTIUS, ST. (d. 675), martyr. A Benedictine from Fleury, he was at Lérins, France, when a rebellious group of monks seized St. Aigulphus and others, took them to Corsica, and murdered them there. F. D. Sept. 3.

FRUMENTIUS, ST. (d. 380?), bishop. A native of Tyre, he was taken on a voyage by a philosopher, Meropius, and a companion, Aedisius (who may have been his brother). In Ethiopia the natives murdered the crew and many passengers of their ship. They became prisoners of the king at Aksum, who eventually made Frumentius his secretary and Aedisius his cupbearer. On the king's death they were freed, but at the queen's request remained to assist her in her regency. They introduced Christianity to the country and brought in traders from the West. When the king came of age, Aedisius returned to Tyre, where he became a priest, but Frumentius went to Alexandria and asked St. Athanasius to send missionaries to Ethiopia. Athanasius consecrated him bishop about the middle of the fourth century and sent him back as bishop of the Ethiopians. He was most successful in evangelization and converted the royal brothers, Abreha and Asbeha. F. D. Oct. 27.

FRUMENTIUS, ST. (d. 484), martyr. *See* Victorian, St.

FRUTOS, ST. (8th century). *See* Engratia, St.

FUCHS, JOHANN NEPOMUK VON (1774–1856), chemist. Born in Mattenzell, Bavaria, on May 15, he studied at Freiburg, Berlin, and Paris, and taught chemistry and mineralogy at Landshut in 1805 and at Munich in 1826. He was named to the Academy of Sciences in 1823, and was ennobled by the king of Bavaria and made conservator of the museum of mineralogy in Munich in 1854. He wrote several volumes in his two scientific fields, particularly on dyes, sugar manufacture, and crystals. He developed a process of making a soluble glass used in fresco painting and also valuable in the surgical application of bandages. Fuchsite, a variety of muscovite, has been named after him. He died in Munich, Bavaria, on Mar. 5.

FUGATIUS, ST. (2nd century). Also known as Fagan and Ffager, he is said to have been sent by Pope Eleutherius to Britain as a missioner with St. Dyfan. F. D. May 26 (sometimes, Jan. 3).

FÜHRICH, JOSEPH VON (1800–1876), painter. Born in Kratzau, Bohemia, on Feb. 9, son of a poor painter, he studied under Bergler at Prague at sixteen, was influenced by Dürer and by the literary romantics, illustrated Tieck's *Genoveva* with fifteen etchings, and went to Rome in 1827, where he joined the Nazarene group. He added three scenes from Tasso to the Villa Massimi, returned to Prague in 1829, then went to Vienna in 1834, was appointed professor at the academy there in 1841, and lived in that city until his death on Mar. 12. His chief works are the frescoes in the church of St. John Nepomuk (1844–46) and that of Altlerchenfeld (1854–61), Vienna, for which last he was knighted. His historical paintings, on biblical subjects, are strong in landscape, effective in draftsmanship, and pleasantly inspiring rather than deeply realistic. His idyllic touch is particularly evident in his *Way to Bethlehem* and *He Is Risen* sequences. He also designed woodcuts for a *Legend of St. Gwendolen,* a *Life of Mary,* and a psalter; copper engravings for *The Prodigal Son* and *Ruth;* and etchings for the *Imitation of Christ.*

FULBERT OF CHARTRES, ST. (952?–1028?), bishop. Born before 962 either in Italy, perhaps Rome, or France, perhaps Laudun, he studied under Gerbert at Rheims, and in 990 opened a school at Chartres, where he also served as chancellor and as treasurer of St. Hilary's, Poitiers. He opposed the growing rationalism, pleaded for careful scripture readings, and built his school into one of the most famous in Europe. In 1007, at the suggestion of King Robert of France, a former classmate, he was named bishop of Chartres, but continued to teach. He instituted clerical reform, condemned the appointment of laymen to ecclesiastical posts, and censured bishops who engaged in war. He wrote two scriptural homilies, twenty-seven hymns, many letters still of historical value, and a series of five sermons on the Virgin Mary. When his cathedral burned in 1020 he began its reconstruction with aid furnished by many European kings and nobles. F. D. Apr. 10.

FULCHERI, BL. DAMIAN DEI FINARIO (d. 1484). Born in Perti, near Finario, Italy, he became a Dominican at Savona, had great renown as a preacher, and died in Reggio, Italy. His cult was confirmed in 1848. F. D. Oct. 26.

FULCO OF NEUILLY (d. 1201). A missionary priest in the north of France, he attacked usurers and those of lax morals with such vigor that he was often imprisoned. He censured King Richard I of England to his face for his evil life, and preached the fourth crusade with such success that he is said to have raised 200,000 volunteers for Pope Innocent III. He died before he himself could leave on the expedition.

Honored on Mar. 2, he was never formally beatified.

FULCRAN, ST. (d. 1006). He was bishop of Lodève, France, for more than fifty years. F. D. Feb. 13.

FULGENTIUS, ST. (468–533), bishop. Fabius Claudius Gordianus Fulgentius, born to a noble Carthaginian family, became a monk at twenty-two, served as superior in various abbeys, was tortured by the Arians in 499, and suffered exile a number of times at their hands. In 508 he became bishop of Ruspe, but King Thrasimund soon banished sixty bishops to Sardinia. There, Fulgentius built a monastery, engaged in written controversy with the king, and at the latter's death in 523 went back to clear his see of Arian abuses. F. D. Jan. 1 (sometimes, May 16).

FULGENTIUS PERRANDUS (6th century), theologian. A deacon at Carthage, he probably went with his master, Fulgentius of Ruspe, into exile in Sardinia, returning to Africa in 523. He was a major figure in the struggle against Arianism, defending the Trinity, the two natures of Christ, speaking on the meaning of the sacraments, writing a handbook of Christian conduct for soldiers, and compiling a summary of 232 canons of the teachings of the early councils. When Justinian condemned the writings of Theodore of Mopsuestia and others, Fulgentius stood against the emperor, and attended the Council of Carthage, presided over by Archbishop Rusticus, which condemned Pope Vigilius for his position on the Three Chapters.

FULGENTIUS, ST. (d. 633?), bishop. Brother of SS. Isidore of Seville, Leander, and Florentina, he was active in preaching in Andalusia, and became bishop of Ecija, Spain. F. D. Jan. 16.

FULK, ST. (d. 600?). While on a pilgrimage to Rome, he stopped to serve the plague-stricken village of Castrofutli, near Arpino, Italy, died there of the pestilence, and was venerated as patron of the area. F. D. May 22.

FULK, ST. (1164–1229), bishop. Born in Piacenza, Italy, of Scots descent, he became a canon there, studied in Paris, was named bishop of Piacenza about 1210, and was transferred to Pavia about 1216. F. D. Oct. 26.

FULK, BL. (1155?–1231), bishop. A minstrel in Genoa, Italy, he became a Cistercian at Thoronet and abbot there in 1200. He was made bishop of Toulouse, France, in 1206 and helped St. Dominic in establishing his order. F. D. Dec. 25.

FULK. *See* Foulques; also, Fulco.

FULK NERRA (972–1040), king of Aragon. He became count of Anjou in 1040, fought the counts of Blois and Rennes, captured Nantes and Tours, and made three pilgrimages to the Holy Land.

FULLERTON, GEORGIANA CHARLOTTE (1812–1855), novelist. Born in Staffordshire, England, on Sept. 23, daughter of Lord Granville Gower and Lady Harriet Cavendish, she was educated in Paris, where her father was ambassador. In 1833 she married Alexander George Fullerton, an embassy attaché; he became a convert in 1843, while traveling in Italy, and his wife followed in 1846. *Ellen Middleton* (1846), *Grantley Manor* (1847), *Lady Bird* (1852), *La Comtesse de Bonneval* (1857, in French), *Too Strange Not to Be True* (1864), and *Constance Sherwood* (1865) were among her novels; others appeared posthumously. She also wrote poetry, biography, and translations from the French and Italian. She died in Bournemouth, England, on Jan. 19.

FULRAD, ST. (d. 784). Born in Alsace, he became a Benedictine and in 750 abbot of St. Denis, near Paris. He was a trusted adviser of the Frankish emperors, including Pepin and Charlemagne, chaplain, councilor, and, as ambassador to the papacy, played a prominent role in bringing about papal reliance on the Frankish rulers rather than on Byzantium for temporal support. F. D. July 16.

FULTHERING, VEN. JOHN (d. 1605), martyr. Born in Yorkshire, England, he was arrested for attempting to convert his neighbors, and hanged, drawn, and quartered. F. D. Aug. 1.

FULTHROP, BL. EDWARD (d. 1597), martyr. A Yorkshire gentleman who was condemned for having returned to Catholicism, he was hanged, drawn, and quartered with others at York, and beatified in 1929. F. D. July 4.

FUMASONI-BIONDI, PIETRO (1872–1960), cardinal. Born in Rome on Sept. 4, he served in the Italian army, studied at the Roman seminary, was ordained in 1897, and received doctorates in theology and law. He did parish work in Cosmedin, became a secretary to Cardinal Ciasa in 1901, and then to Cardinal Martinelli. He taught Latin at the Propaganda, served with the Congregation of the Propagation of the Faith for twelve years, and in 1916 was named titular archbishop of Doclea and apostolic delegate to India. In 1919 he became first apostolic delegate to Japan, returned to serve as secretary of his congregation, and in 1922 was made apostolic delegate to the United States, acting also for Mexico during the civil wars there. He was recalled to Rome in 1933, made a cardinal and prefect of the Congregation of the Propagation of the Faith and a member of several other congregations. He established a record number of missions and raised funds for areas stricken by the 1930 depression and the subsequent wars. His health and eyesight failed in 1958 and he died in Rome on July 12.

FUMO, BARTOLOMMEO (d. 1545), theologian. Born in Villon, Italy, he became a Dominican, an authority on canon law, inquisitor at Piacenza, and wrote a valuable compendium of cases of conscience, condemning probabilism. He also wrote on the immortality of the soul and a commentary on St. Paul.

FUÑES, GREGORIO (1749–1830), historian. Famous as a preacher and influential as rector of the University of Córdoba, Argentina, he became dean of the cathedral there, and published a study plan for the university, a history of Paraguay, and an examination of Church-state relations.

FUNK, FRANZ XAVER VON (1840–1907), historian. Born in Abtsgemünd, Württemberg, on Oct. 12, he studied in Ellwagen and at Tübingen, where he won a prize for a political-economy essay in 1862. He took his doctorate in theology in 1863, was ordained in 1864, and studied economics at Paris in 1865–66. He was appointed professor of church history at Tübingen in 1868, adding patrology and archaeology in 1875. He wrote on early Christian figures, penitential discipline, clerical celibacy, the ecumenical councils, and the Eucharist. In 1870 he became editor of *Theologische Quartalschrift* and wrote many articles for it and other journals and encyclopedias. His most famous titles are his *Opera patrum apostolicorum* and *Die apostolischen Konstitutionen*; much of his shorter work was revised for the three-volume *Kirchengeschichtliche Abhandlungen und Untersuchungen* (1897–99). He died in Tübingen, Germany, on Feb. 24.

FURNISS, JOHN (1809–1865). Born near Sheffield, England, on June 19, he studied at Oscott and Ushaw, was ordained in 1834, and served in a Doncaster parish for five years. When his health broke down he traveled in Europe for eight years, and on his return worked in London with waifs and strays. In 1851 he became a member of the Congregation of the Most Holy Redeemer. From 1855 until his death in London on Sept. 16, he gave missions to children, setting prayers to simple tunes, dramatizing illustrative stories, and later publishing *The Sunday School Teacher* and *God and His Creatures* for children; the works were attacked by the historian Lecky and by atheist journals as lurid and sensational, but his methods had great success.

FURSA. See Fursey, St.

FURSEY, ST. (d. 648?). Abbot-founder of a monastery in Rathmat, Ireland, he went to Britain after 630 with his brothers, SS. Foillan and Ultan, established another monastery near Yarmouth, and after 640 crossed to Neustria in Gaul, where he set up still another at Lagny. He is often called Fursa. F. D. Jan. 16.

FÜRSTENBERG, FRANZ FRIEDRICH WILHELM VON (1729–1810), educator. Born in Herdingen, Westphalia, on Aug. 7, he studied at Cologne, Salzburg, and the Sapienza in Rome, became canon of the cathedral of Münster in 1748 and later of Paderborn, and became a subdeacon. In 1761 the bishop of Münster named him minister and privy councilor; in 1770 he became curator of educational institutions. He introduced economic and agricultural reforms in the prince-bishopric which helped to raise it from the state in which the Seven Years' War had left it, imposed an income tax, organized the seminary, completed the university, and put into practice educational reforms which restored respect for Christianity. Although he lost his ministerial post when Emperor Joseph II's brother became coadjutor bishop in 1780, he continued to direct education and supervised the reform of elementary schools through 1801. He resigned his post in 1805 after the Prussian government interfered with his work, and died in Münster, Prussia, on Sept. 16.

FUSCA, ST. (d. 250?), martyr. A young girl, she was put to death with her nurse, St. Maura, at Ravenna, Italy, during the persecution of Decius. F. D. Feb. 13.

FUSCHI, MICHAEL. See Michael of Cesena.

FUSCIAN, ST., martyr. According to legend, Fuscian and Victoricus were third-century Roman missioners in Gaul. On the way to visit St. Quintinus, who had been martyred, they stopped at the home of Gentian, near Amiens.

All three were captured, tortured, and beheaded. F. D. Dec. 11.

FUSCULUS, ST. (d. 484?), martyr. See Donatian, St.

FUST, JOHANN (d. 1466?), printer. A wealthy citizen of Mainz, Germany, he became partner with Gutenberg in a printing venture there in 1450 and issued the first printed book, the forty-two-line-to-the-page Bible. In 1455 he sued his partner for the money advanced and seized the equipment he had supplied, when Gutenberg was unable to satisfy his demands. Fust then worked with Peter Schöffer, his son-in-law, until 1462, when the city was sacked, the printers scattered, and the secrets of the trade made common knowledge. With Schöffer he printed a psalter (1457) and Cicero's De officiis (1465). Fust is believed to have gone to Paris in 1466 and to have died there of the plague.

FYTCH, WILLIAM BENEDICT (1563–1610). Born in Canfield, Essex, England, he was a Calvinist until he went to London for higher studies. After his conversion he went to Paris, became a Capuchin, was sent to the English mission in 1599, imprisoned shortly after his arrival for three years, and released at the request of the French ambassador. Back in France, he became master of novices, wrote *The Will of God*, and was highly thought of by the French court.

G

GABDELAS, ST. (d. 368), martyr. See Dadas, St.

GABINUS, ST. (d. 130), martyr. See Crispulus, St.

GABINUS, ST. (d. 295?), martyr. Born in Rome, and father of St. Susanna, he was ordained late in life, and is said to have died in prison about the same time as his brother, Pope St. Caius. F. D. Feb. 19.

GABRA, BL. MICHAEL (1791–1855), martyr. A monk of the Orthodox Church of Ethiopia, known for his scholarship, he was a member of the group sent to Egypt in 1841 to ask the Coptic patriarch of Alexandria to appoint a primate. He went from Egypt to Rome with Bl. Justin de Jacobis (who had accompanied the group) and on his return, in 1844, became a convert. They established a native college, with Michael at its head, provided a catechism for the natives, and were so successful they were banished to the island of Massawa, where Bl. Justin was consecrated bishop. On their secret return he ordained Michael in 1851, and they resumed their missionary activities most successfully until Theodore II seized the crown

in 1855. Michael and four companions were then thrown into jail, tortured for months, and condemned to death. At the request of the British consul, Walter Plowden, a reprieve was granted, but Michael was so ill-treated that he died on Aug. 28. He was beatified in 1926. F. D. Sept. 1.

GABRIEL, ST. (d. 250), martyr. A native of Alexandria, Egypt, he was scourged and burned alive during the persecution of Decius. Unable to stand or walk because of the gout, he was carried to martyrdom by two slaves, one of whom, St. Eunus, joined him in death. F. D. Feb. 27.

GABRIEL MARY, BL. See Nicolas, Gilbert.

GABRIEL OF OUR LADY OF SORROWS, ST. See Possenti, Francis.

GABRIELS, HENRY (1838–1921), bishop. Born in Wannegem, Belgium, on Oct. 6, he studied at Audenarde, St. Nicholas, Ghent, and Louvain, and was ordained in Ghent in 1861. After his ordination he taught at St. Joseph's seminary, Troy, New York, for twenty-eight years from 1864, serving as its president from 1871. He was appointed bishop of Ogdensburg,

New York, in 1891 and reigned until his death there on Apr. 23. He wrote a book on rubrics and translated *Rudiments of Hebrew Grammar*.

GADDI, AGNOLO (1333?–1396), painter. Son of Taddeo, he was born in Florence, Italy, studied under Jacopo del Casentino and Giovanni di Milano, and completed thirteen frescoes in the cathedral at Prato, eight panels, the *History of the Holy Cross*, in the Florence church of that name, and a *Raising of Lazarus*.

GADDI, GADDO (1260?–1333?), painter. Born in Florence, Italy, he was the first of a line of painters, and is said to have completed the mosaics in the portico of Santa Maria Maggiore, Rome, those of the portal of the upper church at Assisi, and *Coronation of the Virgin* over the portal in the Florence cathedral.

GADDI, GIOVANNI (1335?–1383), painter. Son of Taddeo, he was born in Florence, Italy, studied under his older brother Agnolo, and completed work for the church of San Spirito, Florence. Most of the paintings of the members of this family are no longer in existence.

GADDI, TADDEO (1300?–1366?), painter. Born in Florence, Italy, son of Gaddo, and godson of Giotto, whose assistant he was for twenty-four years, he followed his master in style and coloring, though without the same depth and animation. He did the frescoes, *History of Christ, History of St. Francis*, and *History of the Virgin*, for the Baroncelli chapel in Santa Croce, Florence, others at Arezzo, Megognano, and Pisa, a *Last Supper*, and a *St. Laurence*. He is said to have designed the Ponte Vecchio, Florence, and to have completed work on Giotto's campanile.

GAGARIN, IVAN SERGEYEVITCH (1814–1882), apologist. Born in Moscow, Russia, on Aug. 1, son of Prince Sergius Gagarin and Barbara Pushkin, he served in the state department, was attaché to his uncle, Prince Gregory, at Munich, became secretary to the legations in Vienna and Paris. His conversion in 1842 ended his inheritance and his career. He became a Jesuit in 1843, taught in Brugelettes, Vaugirard, and Ste. Geneviève, and in 1856 founded, with Fr. Daniel, *Études de théologie*, which in 1862 became *Études religieuses, historiques et littéraires*. He wrote for many journals on the Slavonic schism; spent some time in Constantinople, where he founded the Society of St. Dionysius, which worked for reunion; and published several books on the oriental churches, collections of Russian hymns, studies of Russian culture, the clergy, Church and state, and his Society. He died in Paris on July 19.

GAGELIN, BL. FRANÇOIS ISIDORE (1799–1833), martyr. Born in Montperreux, France, he went to Cochin China in 1822 as a priest of the Society of Foreign Missions of China, was strangled during a persecution, and beatified in 1900. F. D. Oct. 17.

GAGERN, MAX VON (1810–1889). Born in Weilburg, Nassau, Germany, on Mar. 25, son of the Nassau minister of state, he studied in Kreuznach, Mannheim, and Weilburg, and law at Heidelberg, Utrecht, and Göttingen. He became a member of King William I of the Netherlands' cabinet, joined the Dutch army in 1830 against the Belgian revolutionaries, retired from government service in 1833 and taught at Bonn. He entered the duke of Nassau's service in 1840, became a convert in 1843, was appointed the duke's envoy to the Netherlands and Belgium in 1844, and in 1848 worked for the unification of German states, excluding Austria. He became undersecretary for foreign affairs, and a prominent Liberal member of the Frankfort parliament. He returned to the duke of Nassau's service in 1850, but was forced to leave in 1854 for his German activities, entered government service in Austria in 1855 and served in a variety of positions to 1873. In 1881 he was made a life member of the upper house of the Austrian parliament by the emperor. He died in Vienna on Oct. 17.

GAGLIARDI, ACHILLE (1537–1607). Born in Padua, Italy, he studied at its university, became a Jesuit in 1559, taught at the Roman College and at Padua and Milan, and directed several houses of his Society. He published a popular catechism in 1584, a commentary on the *Spiritual Exercises*, an exhortation to Christian perfection, and works on asceticism and mysticism. He died in Modena, Italy, on July 6.

GAGUIN, ROBERT (1425?–1501), historian. Born in Calonne-sur-la-Lys, France, he studied at Paris, became professor of canon law there in 1463 and dean of the faculty, and taught Erasmus and Reuchlin. He served Kings Louis XI and Charles VIII on diplomatic missions across Europe and also as court librarian. His principal publication (1495) was *Compendium de origine et gestis Francorum* to the year 1491.

GAHAN, WILLIAM (1732–1804). Born in Dublin, Ireland, on June 5, he became an Augustinian in 1748, studied at Louvain, and was ordained in 1755. After taking his doctorate in divinity he returned to Dublin, working in several parishes, and publishing sermons and ascetical works. He served as prior in 1770–78 and 1803–4. He was the center of an important trial involving the seal of the confessional, in which he refused six times to declare whether Lord Dunboyne, whom he had attended in his last illness, had died "a relapsed papist." He was briefly jailed for his refusal, and also saw Dunboyne's will, which left property to Maynooth College, set aside by the court as a result of his silence. Fr. Gahan died in Dublin on Dec. 6.

GAIANA, ST. (d. 312?), martyr. *See* Rhipsime, St.

GAILLARD, CLAUDE FERDINAND (1834–1887), painter. Born in Paris on Jan. 7, he began studies under the engraver Léon Cogniet in 1850, entered L'École des Beaux Arts that year, and won the Prix de Rome in 1856. On his return to Paris he studied under Sellier, began reproducing Renaissance masters, and achieved a soft style with effective relief, delicate touch, and blending lines. He completed original portraits of Popes Pius IX and Leo XIII and the comte de Chamborde, and copies of Ingres, Donatello, Michelangelo, Botticelli, and Rembrandt. The latter's *Pilgrims of Emmaus*, Raphael's *St. George*, and Bellini's *Virgin* are considered among his best. He became an officer of the Legion of Honor in 1886, president of the Société des Graveurs au Burin in 1886, and died in Paris on Jan. 27.

GAIUS (1st century). This name (also written Caius) occurs five times in the New Testament: one such figure was a Corinthian baptized by St. Paul and his host (I Cor. 1:14; Rom. 16:23); a Gaius, a Macedonian companion of Paul (Acts 19:29), may be the native of Derbe (Acts 20:4) and even the Gaius to whom 3 John is addressed. All may be identical or separate.

GALANTINI, BL. HIPPOLYTO (1565–1619). Born in Florence, Italy, on Oct. 12, he joined his father as a silk weaver, became a catechist at twelve, began a life of asceticism in his own home, and organized a group of catechists to instruct children and others ignorant of their faith. This group received a formal rule in 1602, was called the Institute of Christian Doctrine, and was a model for similar groups in Italy, approved by Pope Leo XI. He collected alms for its support, spread his work to Volterra, Lucca, Modena, and other communities, and introduced the custom of nocturnal adoration to counteract contemporary amusements. He was violently persecuted, condemned of heresy, and charged with excessive cruelty, but all opposition was removed after papal investigation brought official approval. He was beatified in 1824. F. D. Mar. 20.

GALATINO, PIETRO COLONNA (d. 1539?), theologian. Born in Galatia (Cajazzo), Italy, he became a Friar Minor in 1480, studied in Rome, became provincial of Bari, and was penitentiary under Leo X. At the request of the pope he completed in a year and a half a dialogue between Capnio (representing Jacob Reuchlin) and a Dominican inquisitor on the historicity of the early years of Christianity. The work, *De arcanis catholicae veritatis* (1516), was undertaken to answer the increas-

ing number of Jewish writings against Christ; it was based to a great extent on *Pugio fidei* of Raymond Martini and reveals the haste of its writing as well as the breadth of Galatino's readings in the Cabbala and other Jewish works. His *De vera theologia*, completed shortly before his death in Rome, contains a defense of the Immaculate Conception.

GALATION. He and his wife Epistemis, a former pagan, were said to have been martyred at Emessa, Phoenicia, in 252 during the persecution of Decius; they are so described in the Roman Martyrology for Nov. 5. Modern scholars hold that they never existed and that their story is a Christianization of the romance of Clitophon and Leucippe.

GALBERRY, THOMAS (1833–1878), bishop. Born in Naas, Kildare, Ireland, he came to the United States when three, graduated from Villanova in 1851, entered the Augustinians in 1852, and was ordained in 1856. After teaching at Villanova and filling various pastoral posts, he was appointed superior of Augustinian missions in the United States in 1866, and in 1872 was appointed president of Villanova. He was named provincial of St. Thomas province in 1874, and, in 1875, fourth bishop of Hartford, Connecticut. He founded the diocesan newspaper, the *Connecticut Catholic*, in 1876 (now the *Catholic Transcript*). He died in New York City on Oct. 10.

GALDINUS DELLA SCALA, ST. (1100–1176), cardinal. Born in Milan, Italy, he became chancellor and archdeacon to Archbishop Hubert, with whom he went into exile to escape the invasion of Frederick Barbarossa against Pope Alexander III. Galdinus became archbishop of Milan in 1165 and cardinal in 1166 and preached widely through Lombardy. On his return he helped to rebuild Milan, which the emperor had razed, and gave great assistance to war victims and the poor. F. D. Apr. 18.

GALGANI, ST. GEMMA (1878–1903). Born in Camigliano, Tuscany, she suffered from tuberculosis and, even more, from the scorn with which her relatives and the townspeople treated her when she apparently became subject to supernatural phenomena, including the stigmata. She was staunchly supported by her Passionist confessor and canonized in 1940 in respect of her exceptional patience. F. D. Apr. 11.

GALGANUS, ST. (d. 1181). After a worldly life he retired to live in prayerful solitude at Monte Siepe, Tuscany, and was canonized by Pope Alexander III. F. D. Dec. 3.

GALIANI, FERDINANDO (1728–1787), economist. An Italian priest, he had a reputation for wit as a result of eulogies he wrote on the public executioner at Naples; later, he wrote in favor of low tariff protection, against the superfluity of precious metals in Italy as a cause of high prices, and other treatises.

GALIEN, JOSEPH (1699–1762?), theologian. Born in St. Paulien, France, he studied at Avignon, became a Dominican, taught philosophy in Bordeaux in 1726, and held the chair of theology at Avignon from 1745 to 1751. He then devoted himself to the study of physics and meteorology, published a book on the effects of electricity, and prepared an "entertainment" on air travel in which he imagined a spaceship larger in size than the city of Avignon, which could transport an entire army through a lighter-than-air stratum. He died in the Dominican monastery in Le Puy, France, in 1762 or at Avignon in 1782.

GALILEI, ALESSANDRO (1691–1737), architect. Born in Florence, Italy, he was appointed architect to Grand Dukes Cosimo III and Giovanni Gastone, was invited to Rome by Pope Clement XII, and designed the façade of San Giovanni de' Fiorentini and that of San Giovanni in the Lateran, as well as the latter's Corsini chapel.

GALILEI, GALILEO (1564–1642), astronomer. Born in Pisa, Italy, on Feb. 18, he was intended by his parents for the medical profession, but chose natural philosophy instead. He began as a physicist, developed the science of mechanics, and almost created that of dynamics. By twenty he had discovered the isochronism of the pendulum (as a result of observing a swinging lamp in the cathedral of Pisa) and this he developed fifty years later when he built an astronomical clock. His treatise on the center of gravity in solids (1588) won him a lectureship at Pisa. He corrected an Aristotelian error that the speed of falling bodies is proportionate to their weight in his famous demonstration from the Leaning Tower of Pisa and roused such a storm of protest that he transferred to the chair of mathematics at Padua in 1592. After eighteen years he became mathematician to the duke of Tuscany. In these years he illustrated the law of projectiles and the properties of the cycloid. He also demonstrated the laws of equilibrium, established the principles of virtual velocities and of flotation, and invented a thermometer. He is chiefly remembered in the popular world as an astronomer. He had abandoned respect for the inherited Ptolemaic system long before 1597; when the Dutch optician, Lippershey, developed a magnifying glass in 1609, Galileo made a study of refraction and built a series of telescopes, which brought the moon, sun, Jupiter, Venus, and other planets within descriptive range. Although he drew upon his observations to support Copernicus, he failed to consider the work of his contemporary, Kepler (who went farther and whose findings led to Newton's achievements), and failed, because of the tenuousness of his

arguments, to convince either Tycho Brahé or Francis Bacon. Many scientists and leading churchmen interested in intellectual pursuits supported both Copernicus and Galileo; the latter was triumphantly received in Rome in 1611, when he set up a telescope in the Quirinal Garden to lecture on sunspots. By 1615, a number of literal-minded Church leaders, concluding that the new astronomy undermined the accuracy of scriptural language (which was read to make the earth and not the sun the center of the universe), forced a trial of the new views before the Inquisition. An organization of skeptics, seeking to overthrow religion, was active at the time and widely supported their own interpretation of Galileo's findings; further, one of Galileo's friends, the Carmelite friar Foscarini, had published astronomical commentaries in the vernacular which were confusing the ignorant. As a result of its considerations, the Inquisition told Galileo in Dec. 1615 that his system was scientifically false and anti-scriptural and that he must not teach it; he agreed to accept their order. In Mar. 1616 the inquisitorial body (with no reference to Galileo) condemned all advocacy of the Copernican system. Cardinal Barberini (later Pope Urban VIII) opposed the condemnation. It was finally agreed that, provided the phrase "hypothetical" was added to readings and interpretations of the Copernican system, the latter might be further pursued. Galileo himself accepted this limitation. However, he persisted in his attacks on the Ptolemaic system, broke his promise to refrain from sponsoring the Copernican system, and engaged in violent and reckless invectives against his enemies. In 1624 he received a pension from Pope Urban, though the latter refused to lift the inquisitorial judgment. In 1632, Galileo published a dialogue in which a Ptolemist was logically destroyed by two Copernicans. He was haled before the Inquisition again, condemned as a heretic, and remained under this sentence until his death on Jan. 8 in his villa at Arcetri, near Florence. The famous phrase, "E pur si muove," which he is said to have spoken as a gesture of conviction, is sheer myth. Other myths include the story of his imprisonment (he was not imprisoned), of his blinding by the inquisitors (he became blind from ordinary causes five years before he died), and of his being barred Christian burial. Pope Urban refused to permit the erection of a monument over his tomb, but sent him a blessing on his deathbed, and directed that he be buried within the church of Santa Croce in Florence. Finally, the condemnation of Galileo by the Inquisition had nothing to do with the question of papal infallibility, since no question of faith or morals was papally condemned ex cathedra.

GALILEO. *See* Galilei, Galileo.

GALITZEN, ELIZABETH (1797–1843). Born in St. Petersburg, Russia, on Feb. 22, daughter of Prince Alexis Andrevitch and Countess Protasof, she became a convert four years after her mother entered the Church, and became a member of the Society of the Sacred Heart at Metz, Lorraine, in 1826. She was professed in Rome in 1832, served as secretary general to St. Madeleine Sophie Barat in 1834, and became assistant general and visitor to the convents of the order in the United States. She died while nursing victims of yellow fever in Louisiana on Dec. 8.

GALL, ST. (486?–551), bishop. Despite paternal opposition he became a priest and was ordained by Bishop Quintain, as whose representative he served and whom he succeeded as bishop of Clermont, France. His nephew was St. Gregory of Tours. F. D. July 1.

GALL, ST. (d. 640?). Born in Ireland, he studied at the monastery at Bangor, where he was probably ordained, under St. Columban, whom he accompanied to France, where they founded Annegray and Luxeuil and lived for twenty years. In 610, Columban was banished and Gall accompanied him to Switzerland, where their missionary activities met with indifferent success. When Columban went to Italy in 612, Gall, because of illness, remained behind and became a hermit at Steinach and attracted disciples in large numbers. A monastery developed and eventually around it the town of St. Gall, which became a great center of learning. He is supposed to have refused two offers of bishoprics as well as the abbacy of Luxeuil and is considered the apostle of Switzerland. He died sometime between 627 and 645, at Arbon, Switzerland. F. D. Oct. 16.

GALLA, ST. (d. 550?). Daughter of a Roman consul, Quintus Aurelius Symmachus, and sister-in-law of Boethius, she was widowed a year after her marriage, joined a community of women on Vatican Hill, and devoted herself to prayer and the care of the needy. She is referred to by St. Gregory in his *Dialogues* and St. Fulgentius' letter *Concerning the State of Widowhood* was probably addressed to her. F. D. Oct. 5.

GALLA PLACIDIA (393–450), empress. Daughter of Theodosius the Great and his second wife, Galla, Placidia was raised in the Lombardy home of her stepbrother, Honorius. When Rome fell to Alaric, he kept her as hostage among the Visigoths; when he died, Ataulf became king, married Placidia in 414, and at her plea made peace with Honorius. After the murder of Ataulf in 415, his brother Sigeric succeeded to the throne and drove her from the palace. In 416 she was returned to Honorius and in 417 married his chief general, Constantius. She became empress when he was made Emperor Constantius III in 421. When

he died, she took refuge at the court of Theodosius II at Constantinople and on Honorius' death in 423 became regent for her son Valentinian III. She exercised great influence over Valentinian until her death in Rome on Nov. 27, built and restored many churches, and supported Pope Leo I's pleas to Theodosius to end the Eutychian heresy. She died on Nov. 27.

GALLAGHER, HUGH PATRICK (1815–1882). Born in Donegal, Ireland, he was ordained in 1840, went to the United States, did parish work in Pennsylvania, and in 1852 became assistant to Archbishop Alemany in California. There he built churches, established schools, paid close attention to the need of immigrants, and was highly respected as a civic leader.

GALLAGHER, MICHAEL JAMES (1866–1937), bishop. Born in Auburn, Michigan, on Nov. 18, he studied at Assumption College, Sandwich, Ontario, Mungret College, Limerick, Ireland, and at Innsbruck. He was ordained in Innsbruck in 1893, engaged in parish work in Michigan, became pastor of St. Andrew's cathedral in Grand Rapids, the bishop's secretary in 1896, and was chancellor of the diocese from 1900 to 1912. He was vicar general in 1912–16, was consecrated titular bishop of Tipasa and coadjutor of Grand Rapids in 1915, and succeeded to the see in 1916. He became bishop of Detroit when the see was moved there in 1918, and died there on Jan. 20.

GALLAGHER, NICHOLAS ALOYSIUS (1846–1918), bishop. Born in Temperanceville, Ohio, on Feb. 19, he studied at Mt. St. Mary's seminary, Cincinnati, and was ordained in Columbus in 1868. He engaged in parish work in Columbus, was president of St. Aloysius seminary there in 1871–76, became pastor of St. Patrick's in 1876, and served as administrator of the diocese in 1878–80. He was vicar general from 1880 to 1882, when he was consecrated titular bishop of Canopus and administrator of Galveston, Texas. He succeeded to the see in 1892, and ruled until his death there on Jan. 21.

GALLAIT, LOUIS (1810–1887), painter. Born in Tournai, Belgium, on May 10, he won a prize for a painting made when he was ten, went to Paris after study at Antwerp, became a member of the Institute of France, worked in oil and water color, and produced historical scenes, sometimes melodramatic and sentimental, such as *Christ Healing the Blind*, *Abdication of Charles V*, *Death of Egmont*, and *The Minstrel Boy*. He died in Brussels on Nov. 20.

GALLAND, ANTOINE (1646–1715). Born in Rollot, Picardy, France, he studied at Noyon and Paris, went to the Near East in 1670 and twice later with de Nointel, French ambassador to Constantinople, and learned oriental lan-

457

guages and modern Greek. In 1701 he became a member of the Academy of Inscriptions and in 1709 held the chair of Arabic in the Collège de France. He did many translations of fables and history from the Turkish and Persian, particularly the first European version of *The Arabian Nights* (1704–17), wrote on coins and Greek and Roman epigraphy, and collaborated on Herbelot's *Bibliothèque orientale*, which he completed after its author's death. He himself died in Paris.

GALLANDI, ANDREA (1709–1779?). Born in Venice, Italy, on Dec. 7, he became an Oratorian, published a collection of commentaries on the origin of canon law, and compiled the fourteen-volume collection of writings by 380 figures during the first seven centuries of the Church, publishing Greek originals and translating into Latin many previously rare works. He died in Venice on Jan. 12.

GALLEGO, JUAN NICASIO (1777–1853), poet. Born in Zamora, Spain, on Dec. 14, he studied at Salamanca, became court chaplain in 1805, was associated with the literary group about Quintana, whose technique he imitated, and achieved fame with *El dos de mayo*, a patriotic ode on the Spanish opposition to French attack. He became a deputy to the Cortes for Cadiz, was imprisoned from 1814 to 1820 by Ferdinand VII for his political views, and when freed was appointed archdeacon of Valencia. He became a member in 1830 and permanent secretary in 1839 of the Royal Spanish Academy. Other poems were on patriotic and lyric themes. He died in Madrid on Jan. 9.

GALLERY, J. EUGENE (1898–1960), educator. Born in Baltimore on Sept. 29, he studied at Georgetown and Fordham, and was ordained a Jesuit in 1939. He taught sociology at Scranton until 1947, when he was appointed its president, served until 1953, then became treasurer of St. Joseph's College, Philadelphia. He died in Washington, D.C., on July 28.

GALLETTI, PIETRO LUIGI (1724–1790), historian. Born in Rome, he became a Benedictine there, discovered a number of inscriptions while he was stationed at the abbey of St. Paul without the Walls, built up a museum, became keeper of archives for his order at Florence, and was named titular bishop of Cyrene. He wrote on the antiquity of Rome, the early curia, the papacy, the bishops of Viterbo, and studies on inscriptions and Christian archaeology. He died in Rome on Dec. 13.

GALLGO, ST. (6th century). He founded the monastery of Llanallgo, Anglesey, Wales. F. D. Nov. 27.

GALLICANUS, ST. (d. 352?). A patrician, he was joint consul with Symmachus in 330, and a benefactor of the Church in Rome, who made gifts of land as well as of precious arti-

facts. Stories of his exile and martyrdom under Julian are fabrications. F. D. June 25.

GALLICANUS, ST. (6th century). Bishop of Embrun, France, he attended the Council of Carpentras in 527, and probably appeared at the second Council of Orange and the third Council of Vaison in 529. Another Gallicanus, listed as ruling the see two terms later, may be the same person; he attended the fourth Council of Orléans (541) and may have been bishop from 518 to 554. F. D. June 25.

GALLIFET, JOSEPH DE (1663–1749). Born near Aix, France, on May 2, he became a Jesuit at fifteen, studied under Fr. de la Columbière, served as rector at Grenoble and elsewhere, was provincial at Lyons, wrote on the Virgin Mary, and marked a lifetime of devotion (establishing over 700 confraternities) with his *De cultu sacrosancti cordis*. He died in Lyons on Sept. 1.

GALLITZEN, ADELE AMALIE (1748–1806). Born in Berlin on Aug. 28, daughter of Count von Schmettau, she married Prince Dimitri Gallitzen in 1768 and lived in Paris, Turin, and The Hague while he was Russian ambassador there. Later, in Münster, she became interested in the educational work of Fürstenberg, Overberg, and a group including the philosopher Hamann and the poets Claudius and Goethe. She returned in 1786 to the Church, which she had left in adolescence, became the center of Catholic life in the Westphalian capital, helped to bring Count Stolberg and others back to the faith, and directed many charities. Her diaries and correspondence have been published. She died in Angelmodde, Westphalia, on Apr. 27.

GALLITZEN, DEMETRIUS AUGUSTINE (1770–1840), missioner. Born in The Hague, Holland, on Dec. 22, son of Prince Demetrius Gallitzen, Russian ambassador to Holland, he was baptized in the Greek Orthodox Church but became a convert when seventeen. After serving as aide-de-camp to Austrian Gen. von Lillien, he went to the United States in 1792, often using the name Augustine Schmet or Smith as a pseudonym, and entered St. Mary's seminary, Baltimore. He was ordained in 1795, did missionary work in Maryland, Pennsylvania, and Virginia, and in 1799 founded a settlement in western Pennsylvania for Catholics which became the town of Loretto. He spent the rest of his life ministering to the settlers, and encouraged migration by purchasing land and offering it to settlers at low cost, a practice which cost him his fortune and plunged him into debt which plagued him until his death. He suffered from the intrigues and calumnies of his enemies, frequently engaged in controversy in defense of the Church, was appointed vicar general of western Pennsylvania in 1827 and declined the bishoprics of Cincinnati and Detroit. He died at Loretto on May 6.

GALLO, ST. ANNA MARIA (1715–1791). Born in Naples, she became a Franciscan tertiary in 1731, took the name Mary Frances, and is known as Mary Frances of Naples. She lived a life of piety and austerity at home, despite ill-treatment and the scorn of her family; later, she served as a priest's housekeeper for thirty-eight years. She experienced many supernatural phenomena, and was canonized in 1867. F. D. Oct. 6.

GALLUPPI, PASQUALE (1770–1846), philosopher. Born in Tropea, Italy, on Apr. 2, he studied at Naples, held a position in the finance department, and at sixty became professor of philosophy at the University of Naples. He wrote on will, transcendentalism, and Cartesianism, and was heavily influenced by Kant and Leibniz. He died in Naples on Dec. 13.

GALLUS. *See* Handl, Jacob.

GALMIER. *See* Baldomerus, St.

GALSWINTHA (d. 567). A Frankish princess, sister of Brunhilda, she was the wife of Chilperic I of Neustria, by whom she was murdered.

GALURA, BERNHARD (1764–1856), prince-bishop. Born in Herbolzheim, Breisgau, on Aug. 21, he studied there and the seminary in Freiburg, was ordained in 1788 in Vienna, and returned for parish work in Germany. In 1805 he was named spiritual referee at Günzberg and in 1815 at Innsbruck; he became vicar general at Vorarlberg in 1819, auxiliary bishop of Brixen, Italy, in 1820, and its bishop in 1829. He restored religious life, brought back the Jesuits and introduced the Sisters of Mercy in his schools, and proved an effective administrator. He wrote on church history and ascetical, homiletical, and theological works. He died on May 17.

GALVANI, LUIGI (1737–1798), physician. Born in Bologna, Italy, on Sept. 9, he studied medicine, married Lucia, daughter of Galeazzi, and succeeded his father-in-law as professor of anatomy at Bologna in 1762. He also taught at the Institute of Sciences. His wife died in 1790; he resigned his post in 1798 when he refused to take the civil oath demanded by the republic. He wrote studies on the kidneys of birds and on their hearing organs. More important was his published study on electricity in animal muscles, which resulted from his wife's observation that the legs of a frog, touched by chance with a magnetized scalpel during dissection, began to twitch. Years of experimentation followed, at the end of which Galvani proposed the now-discarded theory that there was an electric fluid within the bodily nerves; however, his studies led to discussions with Volta and the latter's advances in electricity. Galvanism is still used as a term for the manifestations of electric current. He died in poverty in Bologna, Italy, to which he had returned on the promise that he would be appointed professor emeritus, on Dec. 4.

GÁLVEZ, BL. FRANCISCO (1567–1623). Born in Utiel, Spain, he became a Franciscan at Valencia in 1591, went to Manila in 1609 and then to Japan. He preached widely, was hunted down, and burned to death at Yeddo, Japan. He was beatified in 1867. F. D. Dec. 4.

GÁLVEZ, BL. PEDRO (d. 1623), martyr. *See* Angelis, Bl. Jerome de.

GAMA, JOSÉ BASILIO DA (1740–1795), poet. A Jesuit in the diocese of Mariana, Brazil, he wrote the epic *Uruguay*.

GAMA, VASCO DA (1460?–1524), explorer. Born in Simes, Portugal, son of a court officer, he defended the Portuguese colonies in Guinea against the French in 1490, and was chosen by King Emmanuel to take command of an expedition to the Orient in 1497. He, and his brother Paolo (who died at Angra in the Azores), and Nicoláo Coelho sailed from Lisbon in July, reached Mozambique in March and Calcutta, India, in May 1498; after six months dedicated to strengthening the colony, he returned, arriving in Lisbon in Sept. 1499, the first European to sail around Africa and reach India by sea. As a reward, da Gama was made admiral of the Indian Ocean. He was sent back to Calcutta in 1502 with twenty ships, besieged the city, which had been taken over by Arab leaders, destroyed a fleet of twenty-nine vessels, and treated the Arabs with extreme cruelty. He wrote profitable commercial treaties and returned with merchandise worth a million dollars. He then was named Count Vidiguera and given feudal overlordship of two cities. He returned to India in 1524 as viceroy of King John III, re-established order, and died in Cochin on the Malabar coast of Madras, India, on Dec. 24. His successes were the subject of Camoes' *Lusiad.*

GAMALIEL, ST. (1st century). He was the Jewish doctor of the law whom St. Paul consulted (Acts 22:3) and whose advice saved Peter and John (5:34–39). He is traditionally called a convert; his feast day (Aug. 3) celebrated the finding of his body and those of St. Stephen and others.

GAMANS, JEAN (1606–1684). Born in Ahrweiler, Germany, he became a Jesuit in 1623, studied at Trier and Cologne, taught at Würzburg, was ordained in 1633, served as a military chaplain in 1634, did missionary work in Baden, and died at the College of Aschaffenburg, near Frankfort, Germany, on Nov. 25. He worked for thirty years on Bollandist research and wrote a manuscript history of the house of Baden.

GAMBA, GIUSEPPE (1857–1929), cardinal. He was appointed bishop of Biella, Italy, in 1901, archbishop of Turin in 1923, and a cardinal in 1926. He died in Rome on Dec. 26.

459

GAMBACORTA, BL. PIETRO (1355–1435), founder. Brother of Bl. Clare Gambacorta and son of the ruler of the republic of Pisa, he retired from court at twenty-five after a wasted youth to become a begging solitary at Monte Bello in Umbria. By 1380 several companions had surrounded his oratory and he outlined a plan of heavy fasting and penitential rule for the group, which was called the Hermits, or Poor Brothers, of St. Jerome. Their rule was approved in 1421 by Pope Martin V. They spread through Italy and in 1668 the community of St. Jerome of Fiesole was united with them, but lack of members brought an end to the order in 1933. When his father and brothers were assassinated in 1393, Pietro forgave the murderers, as did his sister. He was beatified in 1693. F. D. June 17.

GAMBACORTA, BL. THEODORA (1362–1419). Known also as Clare, she was born in Pisa, Italy, was married at twelve, and widowed at fifteen, whereupon she entered the Poor Clares. Her father demanded her release for another arranged marriage, and she was returned and kept captive for several months before he relented. She then joined the Dominicans at a convent the family built and became its prioress. In her last years she accepted there the widow and daughters of Giacomo Appiano, who had killed her father and three brothers during civil turmoil. Her cult was approved in 1830. F. D. Apr. 18.

GAMBARA-COSTA, BL. PAULA (1473–1515). Born near Brescia, Italy, and married at twelve to the aristocratic Ludovico Antonio Costa, she lived a life of great religious devotion under the direction of Bl. Angelo Carletti, and gave away so much of her husband's stores in periods of drought that he turned against her and brought his mistress into their home. When the girl died, after Paula had obtained the last sacraments for her, the noblewoman was charged with poisoning her rival. She was cleared, however, and proceeded to win back her husband and to devote herself again to prayerful austerity and widespread charity. F. D. Jan. 31.

GAMBARELLI, ANTONIO DI MATTEO (1427–1478), sculptor. Born in Florence, Italy, youngest of five brothers, all sculptors (known under the name of Rosselino), he studied under Donatello, and completed work for churches in Florence, Naples, and Bargello. Outstanding are monuments for the duchess of Amalfi and Francesco Neri and reliefs of the Assumption and the martyrdom of St. Stephen at Prato.

GAMBARELLI, BERNARDO DI MATTEO (1409–1464), architect. Born in Florence, Italy, one of the Rosselino sculptors, he built the Rucellai palace, Florence; a cathedral and palaces in Castel Corsignano; the Palazzo Nerucci and Palazzo Piccolomini, Siena; and

several tombs in Florence, notably those of Leonardi Bruni and Beata Villana, and in Pistoia. While in the service of Popes Nicholas V and Pius II he worked on plans for the new St. Peter's (his choir was later developed by Bramante) and the Vatican.

GAMS, PIUS BONIFACIUS (1816–1892), historian. Born in Muttelbuch, Württemberg, on Jan. 23, he studied at Tübingen and the seminary in Rottenburg, was ordained in 1839, and held parish posts and taught philosophy at Hildesheim after 1847. He took his vows as a Benedictine in 1856 at Munich, served as prior of the abbey of St. Boniface there, and wrote a history of the early Church in Spain and compiled a list of bishops in early times, including those of the Eastern Church. He died in Munich, Germany, on May 11.

GANDOLPHI, PETER (1779–1821). Born in London on July 26, he studied at Liège and Stonyhurst, was ordained in 1804, and was stationed on the Isle of Wight and in London. His *Book of Common Prayer* and a number of sermons seemed too inexact to Bishop Poynter, who denounced them and suspended him; Fr. Gandolphi was cleared in Rome after a personal defense, made apologies to the bishop on his return, but could not heal the personal breach. He resigned his post in 1818 and retired to Surrey, England, where he died on July 9.

GANDULF OF BINASCO, BL. (d. 1260). Born near Milan, Italy, he became a Franciscan and spent all of his religious life preaching in Sicily. F. D. Apr. 3.

GANGALA, ST. JAMES (1394–1476). Born in Montebrandone, Ancona, Italy, he studied law, became a Franciscan in Assisi in 1416, studied under St. Bernardino of Siena at Fiesole, and was ordained in 1423. He became a famous preacher and fellow missionary of St. John Capistran in Italy, Bohemia, Germany, Hungary, and Poland. In 1426, with St. John, he was named by Pope Martin V as inquisitor against the Fraticelli, a mission which resulted in great violence and caused many protests. He participated in the Council of Basle and helped reconcile the Hussites, attempted unsuccessfully to end a quarrel between the Franciscan Conventuals and Observants, and in 1456 was sent to Austria and Hungary to preach. He died at Naples, and was canonized in 1726 as St. James of the Marches. F. D. Nov. 28.

GANSS, HENRY GEORGE (1855–1912), composer. Born in Darmstadt, Germany, he was brought to Lancaster, Pennsylvania, was ordained in 1878, built a church at Milton, and worked at the Indian school in Carlisle. He organized bands and musical groups, and wrote hymns and masses.

GARAKONTHIE, DANIEL (1600?–1676). Chief of the Onondaga Indians, he was held hostage by the French during negotiations with the Mohawks and Iroquois, and kept his tribe at peace while the French and Indians battled. He became friendly toward the French governors, welcomed Jesuit missioners, and in 1670 was baptized at Montreal by Bishop Laval. He was a major force in continuing negotiations with the French, English, and his own people.

GARAVITO, PEDRO. *See* Peter of Alcantara, St.

GARBHAN, ST. (7th century). An Irish saint, his name remains in the place name Dungarvan. F. D. Mar. 26.

GARCÍA (d. 914), king of León. He became king in 910 when he helped his mother and brothers dethrone their father, Alfonso III, and made the city of León his capital.

GARCÍA SEMEN (d. 860), king of Navarre. Eldest son of the count of Alvaris, he succeeded Eneco Arista (839–52) as king.

GARCÍA II ENECO (d. 882), king of Navarre. Son of Eneco Arista, he became king of Pamplona and Navarre in 860, defended his country against the Moors, and was killed at the battle of Aybar.

GARCÍA III (d. 1054), king of Navarre. Eldest son of Sanchez the Great, he became king in 1035 and also inherited Guipuzcoa and Vizcaya.

GARCÍA, ST. (d. 1073?). Born in Quintabilla, Castile, he became a Benedictine monk, was made abbot at Artanza in 1039, and was counselor to King Ferdinand I. F. D. Sept. 29.

GARCÍA, BL. ANNE (1549–1626). A shepherdess in Almendral, Spain, she entered the Carmelite convent of St. Joseph in Avila at twenty, and served as a laysister, taking the name Anne of St. Bartholomew. She was a companion of St. Teresa, whose secretary she became. She was also advanced to choir sister and became prioress at Pontoise, Tours, and Mons. She established a convent in Antwerp, particularly for refugees from England. She wrote considerable religious verse, and was beatified in 1917. F. D. June 7.

GARCÍA, ST. GONSALO (d. 1597), martyr. *See* Peter Baptist, St.

GARCÍA MORENO, GABRIEL (1821–1875), president. Born in Guayaquil, Ecuador, son of a Spanish businessman, Gabriel García Gomez, on Dec. 24, he was brought up by his widowed mother, Mercedes Moreno, and Fray José Betancourt, and received his degree in law at Quito in 1844. He joined the revolutionary movement which replaced Flores with Roca in 1846, wrote political satire in *El Zurriago*, and served on the municipal council of Quito. He was admitted to the bar in 1848, went into exile in 1849 when Roca fell, and on his return from Panama brought in a number of Jesuits exiled from New Granada. He was violently attacked by the Liberals for this action,

was publisher of *La Nación* in 1853, for which he was again exiled, and studied chemistry and physics in France. On his return in 1856 he became rector of the University of Quito and a member of the senate (to which he had previously been elected but barred from taking office), and was vilified by the Liberals. He published another paper, *La Union Nacional*, became the acknowledged leader of the popular classes and the chief target of the anti-Catholic factions. When civil war broke out, intensified by danger of Peruvian attack, García Moreno took the field as military leader, defeated the rival government force under General Franco, established peace, and declared amnesty for political opponents. He was elected president in 1861 and established political and fiscal reforms. The Urbina faction, which had attacked him from the beginning of his law career, continued to do so from self-exile in Peru, and General Mosquera worked from the north to create an empire centered about Colombia and planned to absorb Ecuador. When García Morena signed a concordat with Pope Pius IX in 1862, Mosquera struck. The president was again victor, and ruled in peace until the end of his term in 1865. His successor, Carrión, sent him to Peru (where an attempt on his life failed) and to Chile during their war with Spain. On his return he found that the Conservatives had overthown Carrión, who was supporting the Urbina faction, and had named him head of the provisional government. He was elected president in 1869 and again in 1875, but was assassinated at Quito, Ecuador, on Aug. 6 before he was inaugurated.

GARCÍA RAMIREZ (d. 1150), king of Navarre. Grandson of Sancho the Great, he became king in 1134 and succeeded Alfonso I of Aragon when Navarre was once again separated from Aragon. He lost Rioja to Castile and Tarragona to Aragon, proved an incompetent leader, and finally declared himself a vassal of Alfonso VII of Castile.

GARCÍA SANCHEZ (d. 970), king of Navarre. Son of Sancho García I and Teuda, and called "the Trembler," he suffered from Moorish incursions and relied on the strong diplomatic policy of his mother.

GARCILASSO DE LA VEGA (1503–1536), poet. Born in Toledo, Spain, on Feb. 6, he served as a soldier in the army of Charles V during his Italian campaign, was imprisoned for a year when he aided his nephew in marrying a royal ward, regained Charles's favor, was in the Spanish expedition against Tunis in 1535, and died at Nice on Oct. 14 of wounds received while attacking a castle in southern France. He wrote pastoral poetry influenced by Horace, Sannazzaro, and Bernardo Tasso, and with Boscán introduced the Italian sonnet and other forms into Spanish poetry.

GARCILASSO DE LA VEGA (1539–1617). *See* Vega y Vargas, Garcia Laso de la.

GARDELLINI, ALOISIO (1759–1829). Born in Rome on Aug. 4, he collected the decrees of the Congregation of Rites relating to the mass and the sacraments, published them with a prefatory study on liturgy and a commentary on the Forty Hours' Devotion, in six volumes (1807–19), and issued a carefully revised edition in 1827. He died in Rome on Oct. 8.

GARDINER, BL. JERMYN (d. 1544), martyr. Educated at Cambridge and secretary to Stephen Gardiner, bishop of Winchester, he was one of the victims of Henry VIII and executed at Tyburn, London, for his faith. He was beatified in 1886. F. D. Mar. 11.

GARDINER, STEPHEN (1483–1555), bishop. Born in Bury St. Edmund's, England, he studied at Cambridge, took doctorates in civil and canon law, and became fellow and lecturer there, tutor to the duke of Norfolk, and secretary to Cardinal Wolsey. He was master of Trinity Hall from 1525 to 1549, went to France with Wolsey in 1527, and twice was sent to Rome to discuss the question of Henry's divorce. Henry made him archdeacon of Norwich in 1529 and of Leicester in 1531; later that year he was elected bishop of Winchester. He was in France as ambassador for two years, approved the nullification of Henry's marriage to Catherine, and participated in the coronation of Anne Boleyn. Although he resigned from the court in 1534, he was still loyal to the king, and wrote *De vera obedientia* (1535) in favor of royal supremacy, without doctrinal change. He served on later diplomatic missions to France and Germany, returned to write the Six Articles supporting Henry's ecclesiastical position, and celebrated the monarch's funeral mass in 1547. He was then imprisoned by Cromwell and others as an enemy of the new religion, released briefly, and sent to the Tower until the accession of Queen Mary. He was restored to his see and made lord chancellor in 1553, opposed foreign alliance and marriages (though he gave his blessing to Mary and Philip at Winchester), gained from the pope approval of a plan to leave property seized during the reigns of Henry VIII and Edward VI in the hands of present owners, and strongly opposed trials for heresy. He died in London on Nov. 12.

GARESCHÉ, EDWARD (1876–1960), founder. Born in St. Louis, Missouri, on Dec. 27, he studied at St. Louis University, took his master's and law degrees there, practiced law for three years, and became a Jesuit in 1900. He studied at St. Mary's, Kansas, was ordained in 1912, served on the staff of *America* in 1913, and from 1914 to 1922 was editor of the *Queen's Work*. He reorganized the American sodality organization, was stationed at Marquette, and edited *Hospital Progress* for

the Catholic Hospital Association. From 1929 until his death he was president of the Catholic Medical Mission Board. He established the International Guild of Catholic Nurses, with a membership of 320,000 and founded two religious communities, the Daughters of Mary, Health of the Sick, in 1935, and the Sons of Mary, Health of the Sick, in 1952, of which he became superior general. He also was a founder of the International Marian Academy of Rome. He wrote more than sixty books, including collections of his poetry, spiritual readings, and prayer books. He died in Framingham, Massachusetts, on Oct. 2.

GARIBALDUS, ST. (d. 762), bishop. Consecrated by St. Boniface about 740, he assisted the latter in evangelizing Bavaria. F. D. Jan. 8.

GARICOITS, ST. MICHAEL (1797–1863), founder. Born near Bayonne, France, this poor shepherd was sent by a parish priest to study at the college in St. Palais, then at Aire and Dax. He was ordained in 1823, became an assistant at Cambo, where his popular devotions to the Sacred Heart helped to lessen the inroads of Jansenism, professor of philosophy and rector of the seminary at Bétharram, and organizer of a group of priests to do mission work in the area. In 1838 they were ready for their labors, received a rule based on that of St. Ignatius, but failed to gain more than local tolerance. In 1877 the Society of Priests of the Sacred Heart of Bétharram was papally approved. He was canonized in 1947. F. D. May 14.

GARLICK, VEN. NICHOLAS (1555?–1588), martyr. Born in Dinting, Derbyshire, England, he studied at Oxford but did not take his degree, taught in Tideswell, was ordained in Rheims, France, in 1582, was sent to England, arrested and exiled, returned, and was seized and put to death in Derby on July 24.

GARNEAU, ALFRED (1836–1904), poet. Born in Quebec, and educated in its seminary, he studied law, passed the bar in 1860, entered the civil service and in 1873 became French translator to the senate. He wrote *Les seigneurs de Frontenac* (1866), edited his father's history of Canada, and died in Montreal. His poems were published in 1906 by his son Hector, a lawyer and journalist.

GARNEAU, FRANÇOIS XAVIER (1809–1866), historian. Born in Quebec on June 15, he studied law, and was city clerk from 1844 to 1864. He worked from colonial correspondence and completed a three-volume *Histoire de Canada*. A number of doctrinal errors were corrected in the revised edition (1852) of this work, to the writing of which he devoted twenty-five years. He died in Quebec on June 15.

GARNET, BL. THOMAS (d. 1608), martyr. Born in Southwark, England, nephew of Bl. Henry Garnet, he was educated at Horsham and St. Omer's, returned briefly to England, where he was imprisoned in 1595, then went to Spain and was ordained at Valladolid. He served the English mission for six years, became a Jesuit, was arrested and tortured at the time of the Gunpowder Plot, and deported to Flanders. On his return he was betrayed, ordered to take the Oath of Supremacy, and at his refusal hanged at Tyburn. He was beatified in 1929. F. D. June 23.

GARNIER, ST. CHARLES (1605?–1649), martyr. Born in Paris, France, son of the treasurer of Normandy, he was educated at Louis-le-Grand, entered the Jesuit novitiate in Paris in 1624, studied at Clermont College, taught three years at Eu, and was ordained in 1635. In 1636 he was sent to Quebec with Fr. Chastellain and two other missionaries, and assigned to missionary work among the Hurons. On Dec. 7, 1649, the Indian village of Etarita, where he was stationed, was attacked and destroyed by the Iroquois and he was killed. He was canonized in 1930 by Pope Pius XI. F. D. Sept. 26 (also, Mar. 16).

GARNIER, JEAN (1612–1681), theologian. Born in Paris on Nov. 11, he became a Jesuit at sixteen and taught at Clermond-Ferrand and Bourges. He edited the works of Marius Mercator against the Pelagians and wrote studies of the papacy, grace, confession, and of Nestorianism and Theodoret of Cyprus. He died in Bologna, Italy, on Nov. 26 while on his way to Rome.

GARNIER, JULIEN (1643–1730), missioner. Born in Connerai, France, on Jan. 6, he became a Jesuit in 1660, was sent to Canada, was the first of his Society to be ordained there, in 1668, and worked with the Oneida, Onondaga, and Seneca tribes. He had particular success with the latter Indians, in spite of intense mistreatment of them by the government, and left valuable historical accounts. In his late years he worked in missions along the St. Lawrence River and died in Quebec.

GAROFALO, IL. *See* Tisio, Benvenuto.

GARRAGHAN, GILBERT JOSEPH (1871–1942), historian. Born in Chicago, he studied at Loyola there, became a Jesuit in 1890, was ordained in 1904, taught at Xavier (Cincinnati), Creighton, and St. Louis universities, took his doctorate at the latter, and published on Cardinal Newman. He issued studies of the Church in Kansas City (1920) and in Chicago (1921), was editor of *Mid-America* in 1929–34, issued *Chapters in Frontier History* in 1934, then published on the Church in Maryland, La Salle, Marquette, and an edition of the latter's letters. Significant later work includes the monumental *Jesuits of the Middle United States* (1938), covering the years 1823–1923, and the scholarly *Guide to Historical Method*. He died in Chicago on June 6.

GARRIGAN, PHILIP JOSEPH (1840–1919), bishop. Born in Whitegate, Cavan, Ireland, on Sept. 8, he was brought to the United States by his parents in 1844, graduated from St. Charles's College, Maryland, in 1862, studied at St. Joseph's seminary, Troy, New York, and was ordained in 1870. He became director of the seminary in 1872, a pastor in Fitchburg, Massachusetts, in 1875, was appointed vice-rector of the Catholic University in Washington, D.C., in 1888, and helped found the neighboring Trinity College. He was appointed first bishop of Sioux City, Iowa, in 1902, and died there on Oct. 14.

GARROLD, RICHARD PHILIP (1874–1920), novelist. Born in Hereford, England, on Feb. 2, he studied at Oxford, became a convert in 1896, a Jesuit, served as an army chaplain in World War I, wrote a number of popular novels for boys, and died on July 7.

GARRUCCI, RAFFAELE (1812–1885), critic. Born in Naples on Jan. 23, he became a Jesuit at fifteen, was interested in the Fathers of the Church, toured Europe in search of archaeological materials, and wrote on the catacombs, early glass, and other antiquities. His six-volume *Storia dell' arte cristiana* was an erudite study of decorative and industrial arts in the first eight centuries of the Christian era; its critical judgments have been supplemented or displaced by many later scholars. He died in Rome on May 5.

GARTLAND, FRANCIS XAVIER (1805?–1854), bishop. Born in Dublin, Ireland, on Jan. 19, he studied at Mt. St. Mary's, Maryland, and was ordained in Philadelphia in 1832. He did work there, served as vicar general in 1845–50, and in 1850 was consecrated first bishop of Savannah, Georgia. He died on Sept. 20 in Savannah.

GARVEY, EUGENE AUGUSTINE (1845–1920), bishop. Born in Carbondale, Pennsylvania, on Oct. 5, he studied at St. Charles, Maryland, and St. Charles Borromeo seminary, Philadelphia, and was ordained in Scranton in 1869. He served as pastor in several Pennsylvania towns, among them Williamsport, where he was pastor from 1871 to 1899, and was consecrated bishop of Altoona, Pennsylvania, in 1901. He died in Altoona on Oct. 22.

GASCA, PEDRO DE LA (1485?–1567?), governor. Born in Spain, he became a lawyer, was ordained, went to Peru, and in 1546 became president of the council in Lima. He worked to have the legal changes brought about by Las Casas revoked, crushed the rebellion of Pizarro in 1548, and brought peace of a sort to a disordered nation. He returned to Spain in 1550 and died as bishop of Siguenza and Palencia.

GASCOIGNE, WILLIAM (1350?–1419), jurist. Born in England, he studied law in London, entered the king's judicial system in 1397, and was attorney for the duke of Hereford (later Henry IV) when the latter was banished. Sir William became chief justice in 1400 and established a reputation for honor and impartiality. Details added by Shakespeare in *Henry IV, Part 1*, that Gascoigne sent Prince Henry to prison, are fictional.

GASPARRI, PIETRO (1852–1934), cardinal. Born in Usita, Macerata, Italy, on May 5, he studied at the Pontifical seminary, Rome, was ordained in 1877, and taught there. From 1880 to 1890 he held the chair of canon law at L'Institut Catholique, Paris, urged the French clergy to support the republic, and acted on behalf of the Associations Law of 1901 which approved supervision of religious schools. He was made a bishop in 1898 and titular archbishop of Caesaria later that year, and sent as apostolic delegate to Ecuador, Bolivia, and Peru. He returned to Rome in 1901, was secretary of the Congregation for Extraordinary Ecclesiastical Affairs, and in 1904 was appointed by Pius X to the commission codifying canon law. He was created a cardinal-priest in 1907 and served as chairman of that commission until the promulgation of the new canon-law code in 1917. Pope Benedict XV made him secretary of state in 1914; he drafted the peace proposals Benedict made to the heads of state in 1917, and was chamberlain in 1916. He continued as secretary of state under Pius XI, who was elected pope in 1922, bettered Vatican relations with several European and South American countries, and in 1929 signed the Lateran Treaty (on the details of which he had worked for three years) ending the quarrel with Italy and establishing Vatican City. Although he resigned in 1930, he returned to the state department in 1931 to prevent Catholic Action clubs from becoming political tools of the nationalist movement of Mussolini. Gasparri was codifying oriental canon law at the time of his death in Rome on Nov. 18.

GASPÉ, PHILIPPE AUBERT DE (1786–1871), novelist. Born in Quebec on Oct. 31, he studied at its seminary, became a lawyer and sheriff, and at forty-five retired to study and write. At seventy-five he published a historical novel, *Les anciens Canadiens,* and in 1866 issued his *Mémoires.* He died in St. Jean Port Joli, Quebec, Canada, on Jan. 29.

GASPERI, ALCIDE DE (1881–1953), premier. Born in Pieve Tesimo, Tyrol, Austria, on Apr. 3, he studied at Vienna, became a crusading editor of *Voce Catolica,* served as a member of the Austrian parliament in 1911, but spent more time in Italy. He met Don Luigi Sturzo on one trip, with him founded the Popular party after World War I, directed *Il Nuovo Trentino,* opposed the rising Mussolini, and, after his newspaper was suppressed, was imprisoned. He was released through Vatican intervention and given a job in the Vatican Library, where he lived in practical exile from 1928 to 1943. After World War II he founded and led the Christian Democratic party, became foreign secretary in the cabinet of Premier Bonomi, became premier himself in 1945, spoke for Italy at the Paris peace conference in 1946, and was almost assassinated in 1947. He was forced by communist pressure directed by Palmiro Togliatti to reorganize the government three times before 1951, but weathered the storms, and kept Italy comparatively unified in tense elections. A weakened heart forced him to resign in 1953, and he died of a heart attack in Sella Val Sugana, Italy, on Aug. 19.

GASQUET, FRANCIS NEIL AIDAN (1846–1929), cardinal. Born in London on Oct. 5, he studied at Downside, and became a Benedictine in 1866, taking the name Aidan. He was ordained in 1874 and taught, was headmaster, and in 1878 became prior at Downside, which he enlarged. He resigned as prior in ill health in 1885 and devoted himself to study. He published *Henry VIII and the English Monasteries* (1888–89) and other mediaeval and Tudor studies, was appointed chairman of the papal commission to reform the English Benedictines, served on a commission to consider the validity of Anglican orders in 1896 and was instrumental in the issuance of the papal bull *Apostolicae Curae* denying their validity, and was abbot-president of the English Benedictines from 1900 to 1914. In 1907, Pope Pius X asked him to direct the preparation of a translation of the Vulgate; he set up headquarters in Rome, was made cardinal-deacon in 1914, served as adviser to several congregations, and became Vatican librarian in 1917 and archivist of the Church in 1920. He was made cardinal-priest in 1924 and died in Rome on Apr. 5.

GASSENDI, PIERRE (1592–1655), philosopher. Born in Champtercier, France, on Jan. 22, he studied at Digne and Aix, taught at both places, and became doctor of theology at Aix. He was ordained in 1617 and became canon and in 1623 provost of the cathedral in Digne. In 1645 he was appointed professor of mathematics at the Collège Royal, Paris. As a scientist he was particularly interested in astronomy, engaged in correspondence with leading thinkers, and, though he defended the Copernican system, he accepted it only as a theory. In philosophy he opposed Aristotle and professed Epicurus, attempting unsuccessfully to temper the latter's views by strong insistence on providence. Staunchly Catholic, he nevertheless attempted to separate current philosophical thought from its reliance on scholasticism and was opposed by Descartes, who remained his friend. He died in Paris on Oct. 24.

GASSER VON VALHORN, JOSEPH (1816–1900), sculptor. Born in Prägraten, Austria, on Nov. 22, he studied with his father, and in Vienna and Rome, settled in Vienna in 1852, and designed the figures for the portal of the Speyer cathedral, seven reliefs for the Kaiserhalle there, statues of the seven liberal arts for the Vienna opera house, twenty-four designs for the cathedral of St. Stephen, and busts of historical and contemporary figures for the university, court theater, museum, and several churches. He taught at the academy from 1865 to 1873 and was ennobled in 1879. He died in Vienna on Oct. 28.

GASSNER, JOHANN JOSEPH (1727–1779). Born in Braz, Austria, on Aug. 22, he was ordained in 1750, served various missions, went to Klösterle, Switzerland, in 1758, and was dean at Pondorf in 1776. He established a great reputation as an exorcist and was the center of violent controversy over his achievements and his genuineness; Mesmer led the attack against him and he received the support of Bishop Fugger of Ratisbon and the Calvinist leader Lavater. He died in Pondorf, near Ratisbon, Bavaria, on Apr. 4.

GASSON, THOMAS IGNATIUS (1859–1930), educator. Born in Sevenoaks, Kent, England, on Sept. 23, he studied at St. Stephen's, London, Woodstock, Maryland, and Innsbruck. He was ordained a Jesuit in 1891, taught at Boston College, and, while its president in 1907–14, purchased its Chestnut Hill site. He was dean of the graduate school at Georgetown until 1924 and dean of studies at Loyola, Montreal, until his death there on Feb. 27.

GASTON OF DAUPHINÉ (11th century), founder. He and his son, in gratitude for good health after an epidemic, built a hospital at St. Didier de la Mothe, France, about 1095 and directed a group of laymen who cared for the sick. Pope Honorius III required the group to take religious vows in 1218 and in 1297 they became Augustinian canons regular. The order, Disciples of St. Anthony, or Antonians, was suppressed during the French Revolution.

GASTON, WILLIAM (1778–1844), jurist. Born in New Bern, North Carolina, on Sept. 19, son of an Irish Presbyterian surgeon killed during the revolution, he was brought up by his Catholic mother, studied at Georgetown and Princeton, and was admitted to the bar in 1798. He was elected to the state senate in 1800, 1812–13, and 1818–20, to the state assembly in 1808–10, and to the national Congress in 1813–17. He then returned to his law practice, returned to the assembly in 1827–29 and 1831–32, was named to the state supreme court in 1833, and was active at the convention of 1835 which succeeded in repealing the laws limiting the franchise and other privileges of Catholics. He died in Raleigh, North Carolina, on Jan. 23.

GATARD, AUGUSTINE (1852–1920). Born in St. Brevin, France, on May 18, he studied at St. Sulpice and the Institut Catholique, Paris, was ordained a Benedictine in Nantes in 1886, taught there, and in 1895 founded St. Michael's abbey, Farnborough, England. He introduced Solesmes plain song to Westminster cathedral, directed the Gregorian Congress held in New York City in 1920, and wrote on Gregorian chant and plain song. He died in London on Nov. 22.

GATIAN, ST. (3rd century), bishop. About the middle of the third century he came from Rome to Gaul with St. Dionysius of Paris and five other missionary bishops, and worked around Tours, of which he became bishop, for almost fifty years. A worthless legend has him one of the seventy-two disciples, and sent to Gaul by St. Peter. F. D. Dec. 18.

GATTERER, CHRISTIAN (1839–1900), theologian. Born in Sexten, in the Tyrol, he studied at Brixen, became a Capuchin in 1858, and was ordained in 1862 as Fr. Hilarius. After pastoral work he taught theology at Meran in 1872, was examiner of confessors for Trent in 1882, and served as lector, guardian definitor, and minister provincial of his order. He published a compendium of theology and a treatise on the sacraments. He died on Oct. 30.

GAU, FRANZ CHRISTIAN (1790–1854), architect. Born in Cologne on June 15, he studied in Paris and Italy, made archaeological findings in Nubia in 1817, on which he published in 1822, completed Mazois' work on the ruins of Pompeii, and became a French citizen in 1825. He directed the restoration of the churches of St. Julien le Pauvre and St. Séverin, built La Roquette prison, all in Paris, and began the revival of Gothic architecture in France with his plans for the church of Ste. Clotilde in Paris, where he died.

GAUBIL, ANTOINE (1689–1759), missioner. Born in Gaillac, France, on July 14, he became a Jesuit in 1704, went to China in 1722, taught Latin to the Manchus, served as head of the imperial colleges, and was a leading astronomer and historian. He wrote on astronomy and mathematics, translated the history of Ghengis Khan from the Chinese, part of the annals of the T'ang dynasty, and the *Book of History*, wrote a treatise on chronology, and left manuscripts on Japan and Korea. He was a member of the Academy of Sciences at Paris, to which he sent reports, and of the Academy of St. Petersburg. He died in Peking on July 24.

GAUCHERIUS, ST. (1060–1140). Born in Melan-sur-Seine, France, he built a hermitage in the forests of Limoges, which attracted others and led to the foundation of the double monastery of Aureil, under the Augustinian rule. Among his followers were SS. Lambert, Faucherius, and Stephen of Grandmont. He was canonized in 1194. F. D. Apr. 9.

GAUDENTIUS, ST. (d. 359?), bishop. He came from the East to Rome in 332 and in 346 became first bishop of Rimini, Italy. He was probably martyred by the Arians, whom he opposed at the Council of Rimini in 357. F. D. Oct. 14.

GAUDENTIUS, ST. (d. 364), bishop and martyr. He, his deacon Culmatius, a layman named Andrew, and more than fifty-five others were put to death at Arezzo, Tuscany, during the reign of Valentinian I. F. D. June 19.

GAUDENTIUS, ST. (d. 410?), bishop. A pupil of St. Philastrius, he went on a pilgrimage to Jerusalem, where he became a monk at Caesarea in Cappadocia, but was recalled to suceed Philastrius and made bishop of Brescia, Italy, by St. Ambrose about 387. In 405, Pope St. Innocent I sent him to the East to defend St. John Chrysostom. He was cast into prison in Thrace, but refused to desert St. John's cause and eventually made his way back to Italy where he died. F. D. Oct. 25.

GAUDENTIUS, ST. (d. 418?), bishop. Serving as priest at Ivrea, near Turin, Italy, he was a friend of SS. Eusebius of Vercelli and Laurence, and succeeded the latter as bishop of Novara, Italy, ruling his see for twenty years. F. D. Jan. 22.

GAUDENTIUS, ST. (d. 465?). He was bishop of Verona, Italy. F. D. Feb. 12.

GAUDENTIUS, ST. (d. 997), martyr. *See* Adalbert, St.

GAUDENTIUS, ST. (d. 1004?), archbishop. Brother of St. Albert of Prague and a Benedictine with him at the monastery of St. Alessio, Rome, he went to Prussia, escaped the massacre which took his brother's life, and was appointed to the see of Gnesen, Poland, in 1000 by Emperor Otto III. F. D. Jan. 5.

GAUDENTIUS, ST. (d. 1044). He became bishop of Ossero in Istria in 1030, but resigned his see in 1042 to become a Benedictine. F. D. June 1.

GAUDIOSUS, ST. (d. 445?). He was bishop of Brescia, Italy. F. D. Mar. 7.

GAUDIOSUS, ST. (d. 455?). Bishop of Abitina, North Africa, he was exiled in 440 by the Vandal King Genseric, and founded a monastery at Naples. F. D. Oct. 27.

GAUDIOSUS, ST. (d. 585?), bishop. Son of Guntha, a military official at the Visigothic court of King Theodoric, he was educated at Asan, near Burgos, Spain, where St. Victorianus was abbot, and about 565 was named bishop of Tarazona, Aragon, Spain. He died on Oct. 29. F. D. Nov. 3.

GAUDIOSUS, ST. (7th century). He was bishop of Salerno, Italy. F. D. Oct. 26.

GAUFRIDUS, BL. (d. 1139). He succeeded St. Vitalis in 1122 as abbot of the Benedictine monastery of Savigny, France, and saw the establishment of twenty-nine houses in Normandy, England, and Ireland. F. D. Sept. 9.

GAUGERICUS, ST. (d. 625?), bishop. Born in Yvoi, in the Ardennes, France, he was ordained by St. Magnericus and devoted thirty-nine years to eradicating paganism from the see of Cambrai and Arras. He is called founder of the city of Brussels, since a settlement grew up around the chapel he built on an island in the Senne. He also is called Géry. F. D. Aug. 11.

GAULLI, GIOVANNI BATTISTA (1639–1709), painter. Born in Genoa, Italy, he studied there under Borzone, and in Rome under Bernini and da Fiori, and became a well-known portrait and historical painter, known as Il Baciccio. His figures of children and representations of seven popes and many cardinals through the pontificate of Clement XI are successful, as is his *Assumption of St. Francis Xavier* in the church of the Gesù, Rome; ceilings and altarpieces in other churches show signs of haste and superficiality. He died in Rome.

GAULTIER, ALOISIUS EDOUARD CAMILLE (1745?–1818), educator. Born in Asti, Italy, of French parents, he was ordained in Rome, taught in France from 1780 to 1786, directed a school in Paris until he was forced to flee to England during the revolution, returned in 1801, and directed and wrote on elementary school methods. He served on the commission for the reorganization of public instruction and published a great number of texts for the primary grades. He died in Paris on Sept. 18.

GAUME, JEAN JOSEPH (1802–1879), theologian. Born in Fuans, France, he was ordained in 1825, taught theology, directed the seminary, and was vicar general in the diocese of Nevers, went to Rome in 1841, received his doctorate in theology at Prague, and in 1854 was named a monsignor by Pope Pius IX. He became the center of a violent controversy over the teaching of the classics, which he condemned as dangerously pagan, and which developed into a condemnation of contemporary journalism for criticizing his strictures. He was supported by Louis Veuillot and attacked by Bishop Dupanloup. The quarrel was finally quieted from Rome. Abbé Gaume published *Bibliothèque des classiques chrétiens* in thirty volumes, and works on his teaching theories.

GAUTHIER, JOSEPH ALEXANDRE GEORGES (1871–1940), archbishop. Born in Montreal, Canada, on Oct. 9, he graduated from Montreal College, was ordained in 1894, taught at the Grand seminary in 1896, and in 1912 was named titular bishop of Philippopolis and auxiliary of Montreal. He became titular archbishop of Tarona and coadjutor in 1923, succeeded to the see in 1939, and died there on Aug. 31.

GAVAN, BL. JOHN (1640?–1679), martyr. Born in London, he became a Jesuit at twenty, studied at St. Omer, Liège, and Rome, and was sent on the English mission about 1670. He was hanged and quartered at Tyburn for alleged conspiracy in the Titus Oates Plot, and was beatified in 1929. F. D. June 20.

GAVANTO, BARTOLOMMEO (1569–1638). Born in Monza, Italy, he became a Barnabite, general of his order, and in 1623 was named consultor to the Congregation of Rites by Pope Urban VIII. He was famed as a liturgist and in 1628 published a study of the origin and significance of sacred rites, with commentary on the rubrics, and a discussion of pertinent decrees. He died in Milan, Italy, on Aug. 14.

GAVARDI, FEDERICO NICOLÒ (d. 1715). He is the most important of the modern exponents of the theological "school" of Egidio Colonna. His six-volume *Theologia exantiqua* was published at Naples in 1683–86.

GAVIN, MICHAEL (1845–1919). Born in Kilpeacon, Limerick, Ireland, on Jan. 5, he studied at Astleknock and Stonyhurst, became a Jesuit in Rome in 1864, and taught theology at St. Beuno's, Wales, from 1878 to 1881. His last thirty-five years were spent in London, where he published sermons and a study of the mass. He died in Roehampton, England, on June 28.

GAYARRÉ, CHARLES ETIENNE ARTHUR (1805–1895), historian. Born in New Orleans, Louisiana, he studied there and in Philadelphia, was admitted to the Pennsylvania bar in 1828 and that of Louisiana in 1829, was elected to the state legislature that year, deputy attorney general, judge of the city court, and United States senator in 1835. Ill health kept him from Washington, and he spent eight years in France, working in archive collections. He published *Histoire de la Louisiana* in 1846–47 (enlarged to four volumes in its revised and translated edition of 1903). It is a highly personal, though valuable, account of early history, filled with acknowledged legend and citing many poems. Two historical romances, *Fernando de Lemos* (1872) and *Aubert Dubayet* (1882), also recreate the color of the territory. He served in the state legislature for two terms and was secretary of state from 1846 to 1853, developing the state library and historical holdings. He advocated both emancipation of slaves and secession. He died in New Orleans on Feb. 11.

GAY-LUSSAC, JOSEPH LOUIS (1778–1850), chemist. Born in St. Léonard, Haute Vienne, France on Dec. 6, he studied at the school which became L'École Polytechnique and under Berthollet, whose assistant he became. In 1804, he and Biot ascended 13,000 feet in a balloon to study the intensity of magnetic force; in subsequent ascents he proved magnetic force was little affected by elevation and that the composition of air was the same at the height of his ascent as on earth. He was elected to the Academy of Sciences in 1806 after he discovered the law that air and gases are uniformly expanded by increased temperatures. He became professor of chemistry at L'École Polytechnique in 1809, taught at the Sorbonne in 1808–32, wrote on his and Thénard's experiments with a voltaic pile, *Recherches physico-chimiques* (1811), on his experiments with boric, potassium, and prussic acids, and, with J. Dalton and A. Avogado, *Foundations of the Molecular Theory*. He discovered cyanogen in 1815, invented a hydrometer and an alcoholometer, and postulated Gay-Lussac's law (or the law of combining volumes) that the volumes of gases involved in a chemical reaction are in the ratio of small whole numbers to each other, and each to the volume of the new gas produced by the reaction. He also did important research on the manufacture of bleaching chlorides and on the assaying of silver. He became superintendent of the government gunpowder factory in 1818, chief assayer to the mint in 1829, was elected to the chamber of deputies in 1831, became professor of chemistry at the Jardin des Plantes in 1832, and was made a peer of France in 1839. He died in Paris on May 9.

GAZOTICII, BL. AGOSTINO (1262–1323), bishop. Born in Trau, Dalmatia, he became a Dominican, studied at Paris, and became renowned as a missioner in Italy and Bosnia. He was sent to Hungary and in 1303 was chosen bishop of Zagreb. He reformed the Croatian diocese, attended the Council of Vienna in 1311–12, and returned to suffer persecution under Miladin, governor of Dalmatia, whose tyranny he had opposed. In 1317 he was papally transferred to the see of Lucera (Nocera), Italy. His cult was confirmed in 1702 by Pope Clement XI. F. D. Aug. 3.

GAZZÁNIGA, PIETRO MARIA (1722–1799), theologian. Born in Bergamo, Italy, on Mar. 3, he became a Dominican, taught philosophy and ecclesiastical history at several centers of his order and at Bologna, taking the chair of dogmatic theology at Vienna in 1760. He was a leader of the Thomists, ran counter to the Molinists, effectively opposed Jansenism in Austria, and succeeded in establishing Thomism as the basis of theological teaching. After twenty years at Vienna he returned to Italy, and died in Vicenza on Dec. 11.

GEBHARD, ST. (d. 995). He became bishop of Constance, Switzerland, in 979 and founded the Benedictine abbey of Petershausen in 983. F. D. Aug. 27.

GEBHARD III (1040?–1110), bishop. Son of Duke Bertold I of Zähringen, he was provost at Xanten, became a Benedictine at Hirschau, and in 1084 was consecrated bishop of Constance, Switzerland. He was unable to occupy his see until 1086 because of his support of Pope Gregory VII, who had excommunicated Bishop Otto I, the see's occupant, who supported Emperor Henry IV. Otto died in 1086. Gebhard consecrated the new cathedral in 1089, reformed the Benedictine monastery of Petershausen, defended the papacy against the emperor, was apostolic vicar to Germany in 1089, and held a synod in Constance in 1094 and attended that in Piacenza in 1095. He was driven from his see in 1094–95 by the imperial usurper Arnold, and on his restoration attended a synod at Nordhausen, the diet at Mainz, went to Rome in 1106 as imperial legate, and attended the Council of Guastalla. He sided with Emperor Henry V against Pope Paschal II, was reprimanded, retired from public life and devoted himself to his diocese. He died in Constance on Nov. 12.

GEBHART, ÉMILE (1839–1908), historian. Born in Nancy, France, on July 19, he studied there and at Athens and Nice, and taught foreign literature at Nancy. He held the chair of southern European literature at the Sorbonne from 1880 to 1906, was elected to the French Academy in 1905, and wrote widely on the antiquities of Greece, the Italian Renaissance, and mysticism, and published biographies of SS. Francis of Assisi and Catherine of Siena. He died in Paris on Apr. 22.

GEBIZO, ST. (d. 1087?). Born in Cologne, he became a Benedictine monk at Monte Cassino in 1076. He went to Croatia to crown King Zwoinimir at the request of Pope St. Gregory VII. F. D. Oct. 21.

GEBUINUS, ST. (d. 1080). He was archbishop of Lyons, France. F. D. Apr. 18.

GEDEON, ST. (d. 796). He became bishop of Besançon, France, in 790. F. D. Aug. 8.

GÉDOYN, NICOLAS (1667–1744), critic. Born in Orléans, France, on June 17, he taught at Blois, was named canon of Ste. Chapelle in Paris and given two abbeys, was elected to the Academy of Belles-Lettres in 1711, and worked to modernize educational methods. He translated Quintilian and Pausanias, wrote on the ancients-and-moderns controversy, and essays on a variety of urbane topics. He died at Port Pertuis, France, on Aug. 10.

GEDROYE, BL. MICHAEL (d. 1485). Born near Vilna, Lithuania, dwarfed and crippled in body, he joined the Augustinians, but was allowed to become a recluse near their church in Cracow. There he spent a life marked by great austerities and numerous supernatural gifts. F. D. May 4.

GEGENBAUER, JOSEF ANTON VON

(1800–1876), painter. Born in Wangen, Württemberg, on Mar. 6, he studied in Munich under Robert von Langer, was in Rome from 1823 to 1826, was named court painter on his return, and decorated the royal villa of Rosenstein. He did frescoes in Rome in 1829, and from 1836 to 1854 decorated the royal palace at Stuttgart. His output was both biblical and mythological, ranging from *St. Sebastian* to *Neptune and Thetis, Moses Striking the Rock* to *Hercules and Omphale*. He died in Rome on Jan. 31.

GEILER VON KAYSERSBERG, JOHANN (1445–1510). Born in Schaffhausen, Switzerland, on Mar. 16, he studied at Kaysersberg, Freiburg im Breisgau, and Basle, and was ordained. At Basle, where he took his doctorate in theology, he was the friend of Sebastian Brant, and, like him, became a leading voice in demanding widespread ecclesiastical reform. In 1476 he became rector at Freiburg, preached in Würzburg, then settled in Strassburg, Alsace, in 1478, where he preached for thirty years, until his death there on Mar. 10. His sermons were widely popular, written in simple language, often vernacular and realistically coarse, yet fully aware of contemporary events and literature; one series was based on Brant's *Ship of Fools*. He also served as counselor to Emperor Maximilian and had direct influence on Schott and Wimpheling.

GEISSEL, JOHANNES VON (1796–1864), cardinal. Born in Gimmeldingen, Germany, on Feb. 5, he studied in Neustadt, Edeshem, and Mainz, was ordained in 1818, served in a Hambach parish, taught in Speyer, became canon and dean of its cathedral chapter, and was consecrated bishop of Speyer in 1838. In 1841 he was papally named coadjutor to the archbishop of Cologne and succeeded to that see in 1846. He was named cardinal in 1850 by Pope Pius IX. He served in the Prussian assembly after the revolution of 1848 and gained protection for the Church in the new national constitution, ended difficulties at the university of Bonn by suspending the philosophers who supported Hermesianism, established seminaries at Neuss and Münstereifel, and developed missions and popular devotions. He held a convocation at Würzburg in 1848 and a council in Cologne in 1860, and completed the cathedral (except the towers) in his see city in 1863. Among his writings are poems and satirical essays published in the periodical *Katholik* (1821–37), and historical studies of Speyer and of Bavaria. He died in Cologne, Germany, on Sept. 8.

GELASIUS I, ST. (d. 496), pope. Born in Rome, son of an African named Valerius (and probably, though not certainly, a Negro), he succeeded Pope St. Felix II on Mar. 1, 492. He was noted for his personal learning and holiness, active concern for the poor who were crowding into the city from the war-torn provinces, and serious difficulties with Euphemius, patriarch of Constantinople, over the Acacian heresy, and with Anastasius, the Eastern emperor, over papal supremacy. He is said to have directed Christians to receive the Eucharist in two forms, a move opposing the Manichaeans, who preached that wine was unlawful and therefore abstained from Communion. Although reputed to have written widely, little remains; it has been definitely established that he was not the author of *Decretum de libris recipiendis et non recipiendis*, identifying the canonical books of the Bible, or of the Gelasian *Sacramentary*. F. D. Nov. 21.

GELASIUS II (d. 1119), pope. Born in Gaeta, Italy, he became a Benedictine at Monte Cassino, was chancellor of the Holy See, adviser to Paschal II, and at an advanced age was secretly elected pope on Jan. 24, 1119, at a monastery on the Palatine Hill, Rome. The secrecy was due to the known plan of Emperor Henry V to approve the selection of a subservient candidate. When the news was released, Cenzio Frangipani of the imperial faction attacked the new pope, dragged him through the streets to a dungeon, and only released him when the Romans rose against him. Frangipani then begged and received absolution, but Henry invaded Italy, and the pope was forced to flee to Gaeta, where he was ordained (he had only been a deacon) and consecrated a bishop. When Henry raised Maurice Burdinus of Braga as antipope Gregory VIII, Gelasius excommunicated the Portuguese opportunist, fled to France, returned briefly to Italy to consecrate the cathedral in Pisa, laid plans for the Council of Rheims, and died in Cluny, France, on Jan. 28.

GELASIUS, ST. (d. 250), martyr. *See* Theodulus, St.

GELASIUS, ST. (3rd century), martyr. *See* Aquilinus, St.

GELASIUS (5th century). Son of a priest at Cyzicus, he was living in Bithynia in 475, where he wrote against Monophysitism. He also wrote *Syntagma*, a report on the actions taken at the Council of Nicaea, with a biographical account of Constantine to the year 323. His principal sources are Eusebius, Rufinus, Socrates, and Theodoret; the inclusion of long speeches and letters makes the work of considerable value.

GELASIUS, ST. (d. 1174), archbishop. He was abbot of a monastery in Derry, Ireland, and became archbishop of Armagh in 1137. F. D. Mar. 27.

GELEÉ, CLAUDE. *See* Claude Lorraine.

GEMELLI, EDOARDO AGOSTINO (1878–1959), psychologist. Born in Milan, Italy, on Jan. 18, he was an anti-clerical and Marxist Socialist as a youth, took his degree in medicine at Pavia, served as a doctor in the Italian army, and became a convert. He joined the Franciscans, taking the name Agostino, and was ordained in 1908. He received degrees in histology and philosophy from Louvain, did research in psychology, and in 1914 founded the monthly, *Vita e Pensiero*. He served in the Italian army in World War I as priest and doctor, founded Sacred Heart University in Milan in 1921, serving as its president until his death, was appointed to the Pontifical Academy of Sciences in 1951, and later became its president. He died in Milan on July 15. He was internationally honored for his studies in experimental psychology, especially in the field of criminology and of the military world.

GEMELLUS, ST. (d. 362), martyr. He was crucified at Ancyra, Galatia, during the persecution of Julian the Apostate. F. D. Dec. 10.

GEMINIAN, ST. (d. 300?), martyr. *See* Lucy, St.

GEMINIAN, ST. (d. 348), bishop. He was an opponent of Jovinianism and gave refuge to St. Athanasius in his see city of Modena, Italy, when the latter was on his way to exile in Gaul. F. D. Jan. 31.

GEMINUS, ST. (3rd century), martyr. *See* Aquilinus, St.

GEMINUS, ST. (d. 484?), martyr. *See* Aquilinus, St.

GEMINUS, ST. (d. 815?). A monk at Sanpaterniano, Umbria, Italy, he is claimed to have been a Basilian and a Benedictine, and is the patron of San Gemini. F. D. Oct. 9.

GEMMA, ST. (d. 1429). Born of a peasant family in Solmona in the Abruzzi, Italy, she is said to have been kidnaped at twelve by a local noble, and, when she refused to marry him, to have entered a hermitage which he built at her request and where she lived for forty-two years. Her cult was approved in 1890. F. D. May 12.

GEMMA. *See* Galgani, St. Gemma.

GENEBALD, ST. (d. 555?). A relative of St. Remigius, he was bishop of Laon, France. F. D. Sept. 5.

GÉNEBRARD, GILBERT (1535–1597). Born in Riom, France, on Dec. 12, he became a Benedictine, and studied in Mausiac and St. Allyre and at the Collège de Navarre, Paris, where he took his doctorate in theology in 1562. He taught Hebrew at the Collège Royal, was prior of St. Denis, was in Rome from 1578 to 1588, became a supporter of the Holy League on his return, and in 1592 was consecrated archbishop of Aix. Although he lessened his activity in the league and submitted to King Henry IV in 1593, he was briefly banished to Avignon in 1596. He wrote on the Trinity, biblical commentaries on the Psalms and Joel, and edited the works of Origen. He died at the monastery of Semur, Côte-d'Or, France, on Feb. 16.

GENERALIS, ST. (d. 258?), martyr. *See* Crescentian, St.

GENEROSA, ST. (d. 180), martyr. *See* Speratus, St.

GENEROSUS, ST. (d. 682?), abbot. He directed the Benedictine abbey of St. Jouin-de-Marnes, Poitou, France. F. D. July 16.

GENESIUS, ST. (d. 660?), bishop. He was elected bishop of his native Clermont, France, at the death of St. Proculus, maintained a reputation for learning and charity, built a church, a hospice, and the monastery of Manlieu. One of his chief advisers was St. Praejectus. The name is also spelled Genet. F. D. June 3.

GENESIUS, ST. (d. 679), bishop. Prior of Fontenelle, France, he became a chaplain of Queen Bathildis and in 658 bishop of Lyons. F. D. Nov. 1.

GENESIUS, ST. (d. 725). Count of Clermont, he was a friend of SS. Bonitus and Meneleus, endowed many churches and religious foundations, and was buried in Combronde, France. F. D. June 5.

GENESIUS, ST. (d. 888), martyr. *See* Ageranus, St.

GENESIUS OF ARLES, ST. (d. 303?), martyr. A court notary at Arles, France, of which he is patron, he refused to record the anti-Christian edicts of the emperors, proclaimed his Christianity, and was beheaded. F. D. Aug. 25.

GENESIUS THE COMEDIAN, ST., martyr. Legend says that while acting at Rome in a farce mocking Christianity he was convinced of the truth of what he was burlesquing, announced his conversion, and was put to death by Emperor Diocletian. The same story is told of SS. Gelasinus, Ardalio, and Porphyrius. He may also be identified with St. Genesius of Arles, in whose honor a church was built in Rome. F. D. Aug. 25.

GENET. *See* Genesius, St.

GENEVIÈVE, ST. (422–500). Born at Nanterre, near Paris, she became a nun at fifteen. She suffered hostility because of her prophecies, but praise from St. Germanus changed public opinion, as did her prediction that Atilla's Huns would skirt the city on their way south, which actually happened after Geneviève had led the citizens in a crusade of prayer. Previously, she broke the siege of the city by the Franks under Childeric and brought in boatloads of food. Childeric and Clovis both listened to her pleas for captive prisoners. She was particularly devoted to St. Martin of Tours and led pilgrimages to his shrine, built a church in honor of St. Dionysius, and persuaded Clovis to erect the church of SS. Peter and Paul. Her remains were destroyed during the French Revolution when the church in which she was buried was secularized as the Pantheon. F. D. Jan. 3.

GENGA, GIROLAMO (1476–1551), painter.

Born in Urbino, Italy, he studied under Luigi Signorelli and Perugino, worked in Orvieto, Florence, and Siena, was aided by Guidobaldo II in Urbino, and painted the *Resurrection* altarpiece for the church of St. Catherine of Siena, Rome. He joined Duke Francesco Maria in Urbino, went into exile with him at Cesena, and is known for a *Holy Family* and *Four Fathers of the Church*. He also was a sculptor and architect, worked in clay and terra cotta, designed vestments and musical instruments, and was something of a musician. He died in Urbino.

GENGULF, ST. (d. 760). A Burgundian knight, he left part of his wealth to his unfaithful wife, gave the rest to the poor, and became a hermit near Auxerre; he was murdered by his wife's lover. Hroswitha wrote an elegy on his career, details of which became highly colored by time. F. D. May 11.

GÉNICOT, EDOUARD (1856–1900), theologian. Born in Antwerp, Belgium, on June 18, he became a Jesuit in 1872, taught in Ghent and Antwerp, was ordained, and was professor of canon law and moral theology at Louvain from 1889 until his death there on Feb. 21. He published *Casus conscientiae* and theological texts and studies.

GENINGS, BL. EDMUND (1567–1591), martyr. Born in Lichfield, England, he became a convert about 1583, and was ordained at Rheims in 1590. He was sent on the English mission the same year and was captured while saying mass at the home of Bl. Swithin Wells, along with Bl. Polydore Plasden, a priest, and two laymen: John Mason, a native of Kendal, Westmorland, and Sidney Hodgson. Fr. Genings was hanged, drawn, and quartered at Gray's Inn Fields, London; the others, at Tyburn. They were beatified in 1929. F. D. Dec. 10.

GENINGS, JOHN (1570?–1660). Born in Lichfield, England, he reformed his life after the martyrdom of his brother Edmund, became a convert, went to Douai, and was ordained in 1607. He was sent to England, where he became a Franciscan about 1610, returned to Flanders, gathered a group of Englishmen around him to found a new English Franciscan province. He established headquarters of the province at Douai in 1618, became vicar and then custos, director of the English Poor Clares and, in 1629, provincial. He died in Douai, France, on Nov. 12.

GENNADIUS (5th century). Called Scholasticus, he was a priest at Marseilles who wrote against the heresies of Nestorius, Eutyches, and Pelagius, was himself marked by semi-Pelagianism, wrote belittlingly of St. Augustine, and about 491 completed a continuation of *De viris illustribus* of St. Jerome.

GENNADIUS, ST. (d. 936), bishop. A monk

in Argeo, Spain, he restored and became abbot of the Benedictine abbey of San Pedro des Montes at Peñalba, was bishop of Astorga from about 895 to 931, and spent his last five years at his monastery. F. D. May 25.

GENNARD, ST. (d. 720). Educated at the court of King Clotaire III of France, he became a Benedictine monk at Fontenelle, abbot of Flay, near Beauvais, and spent his last years at Fontenelle, France. F. D. Apr. 6.

GENNARI, CASIMIRO (1839–1914), cardinal. Born in Maratea, Italy, on Dec. 20, he was ordained in 1863 and stationed in the diocese of Conversano. In 1875 he founded *Il monitore ecclesiastico*, a monthly review of theology and canon law. He became bishop of Conversano in 1888, was brought to Rome in 1897, made a cardinal in 1900, and appointed prefect of the Congregation of the Council in 1908. He died in Rome on Jan. 31.

GENNARO. *See* Januarius, St.

GENOCUS, ST. (6th century). A British monk, he accompanied St. Finnian of Clonard on the Irish mission. F. D. Apr. 18.

GENOUDE, ANTOINE EUGÈNE (1792–1849). Born in Montélimar, France, he was an encyclopedist, was converted to Catholicism, worked for universal suffrage and the Bourbon cause, and entered journalism. He edited *Le Défenseur* (1820), *L'Étoile* (1821), and *Gazette de France* (1825), in which he attacked the Martignac ministry and the new party which followed the revolution of 1830. When his wife died in 1835 he became a priest. He wrote *La Raison du chistianisme*, a translation of the Church Fathers, and a sixteen-volume history of France.

GENTIAN, ST. (d. 287?), martyr. *See* Fuscian, St.

GENTILE DA FABRIANO. *See* Massi, Gentile.

GENTILI, ALOYSIUS (1801–1848). Born in Rome on July 14, he studied at the Irish College there, was ordained in 1830 as a member of the Institute of Charity, and went to England in 1835 with a mission which settled in Prior Park, of which he was president for two years. He was interested in the Oxford Movement and converted William Lockhart; others followed in increasing numbers as a result of retreats he directed at Grace Dieu, Manchester, Newcastle, and Dublin. He died in Dublin on Sept. 26.

GENTILI, BL. CAMILLA (d. 1486). She was noted for her piety and is venerated in the region of San Severino, Italy. Her cult was approved in 1841. F. D. May 18.

GENTILIS, BL. (d. 1340), martyr. Born in Matelica, Italy, he became a Friar Minor, was ordained, went as a missioner to Egypt, and accompanied the Venetian ambassador to Persia, where he was put to death at Toringa

for preaching Christianity. His cult was approved by Pope St. Pius V. F. D. Sept. 5.

GENUINUS, ST. (7th century). He was bishop of Sabion, no longer in existence, in the Tyrol. F. D. Feb. 5.

GENULF. He supposedly is a German missioner sent from Rome to Gaul in the third century, and sometimes listed as first Bishop of Cahors, honored on Jan. 17. There is no evidence of his existence.

GEOFFREY OF CLAIRVAUX (1115?–1189?). Born in Auxerre, France, before 1120, he studied under Peter Abelard, followed St. Bernard to the monastery of Clairvaux, became the latter's secretary, and traveled with him through France and Germany in 1145–47. He attended the Council of Rheims in 1148, became abbot of Igny in 1159, and in 1162 the fourth abbot of Clairvaux. He resigned in 1165, became abbot of Fossa Nuova, Italy, in 1170, and of Haute Combe, Savoy, in 1176, and sought to bring the quarreling kings of Europe to peace. He collected more than 300 letters of St. Bernard, wrote the latter's life and accounts of his travels, an objection to the errors of Gilbert de la Porrée, sermons, and scriptural commentaries. He died at Haute Combe after 1188.

GEOFFREY OF DUNSTABLE (d. 1146). A scholar from Normandy, he was invited to England by Richard, abbot of St. Alban's, founded a school at Dunstable, became a monk, and succeeded Richard as abbot at St. Alban's in 1119. He built a convent at Markyate, opened a leprosarium, and died at St. Alban's on Feb. 26. He also was known as Geoffrey of Gorham.

GEOFFREY OF MONMOUTH (1100?–1154), historian. Born in Monmouth, son of a priest named Arthur, he was educated in Wales and Oxford, became archdeacon at St. Teilo's, Llandaff, where he founded schools, and wrote *Historia regum Britanniae* before 1139, completing a revised version in 1147. He was consecrated bishop of St. Asaph in 1152, having been ordained a week before, but died in Llandaff before he could occupy his see. His history, based in part on Kymric tradition and in part on the eighth-century *Historia Britonum* of Nennius, had great influence on English literature (on Layamon's *Brut*, Shakespeare's *King Lear* and *Cymbeline*, and Tennyson's *Idylls of the King* in particular); he told the legend of the founding of Britain by Brut, great-grandson of Aeneas, and that of King Arthur. He also wrote a life of Merlin and a Latin version of the *Prophecies of Merlin*; it and the *History* were of value to Sir Thomas Malory in his account of Arthurian legend.

GEOFFREY OF VENDÔME (d. 1132), cardinal. Born in Angers, France, he became a Benedictine and in 1103 abbot of the monastery of the Blessed Trinity at Vendôme. In 1094 he went to Rome to bring about the surrender of antipope Clement III, led Pope Urban II to take repossession of the Lateran, and was made a cardinal-priest. He visited Rome twelve times on behalf of the popes and was thrice imprisoned by Clement's followers. He welcomed Urban and Pope Paschal II to his monastery, and attended the Councils of Clermont (1095), Saintes (1096), and Rheims (1131). He wrote on the investiture problem, on the sacraments, ascetical treatises, sermons, and hymns to the Virgin and to St. Mary Magdelene. He died in Angers on Mar. 26.

GEOFFREY DE VILLEHARDOUIN (1160?–1212), historian. Probably born in Villehardouin, near Aube, France, he was maréchal de Champagne in 1191, joined the fourth crusade in 1199, was one of Count Thibaud III of Champagne's ambassadors to solicit Venetian aid for the crusaders in 1201, was influential in diverting the crusade to Constantinople, participated in its siege in 1204, and served on numerous embassies. He became maréchal of Romanie in 1204 when the Latin Empire was established, campaigned against the Bulgars in 1205, and received the fief of Messinople from Henry II for his role in the naval battle against Theodore Lascaris. He died in Messinople. His description of the siege of Constantinople and the events of the fourth crusade, from 1198 to 1207, *Conquête de Constantinople*, is a major Western source, though strongly pro-occidental.

GEOFFREY DE VINSAUF (13th century), poet. He lived in England about 1200, wrote a poem in Latin hexameter variously called *Ars poetica*, *Nova poetica*, and *Poetria novella*, and was called the author of a poem on vine culture, which gave him his name, *de vino salvo*.

GEOFFROY, JULIEN LOUIS (1743–1814), critic. Born in Rennes, France, he edited *Année littéraire* and the royalist *Journal de monsieur* and *L'ami du roi*, fled at the outbreak of the French Revolution, and returned to serve as dramatic critic on *Journal des débats* in 1806. He strenuously opposed the work of Voltaire and the Encyclopedists; wrote *Discours sur la critique* in 1779; his essays were later published as *Cours de littérature dramatique*.

GEOFFROY DE MONTBRAY, BL. (d. 1093). A friend of William the Conqueror, he became bishop of Coutances, France, in 1049, built its cathedral, and aided in establishing the Benedictine abbeys of Lessay, Montebourg, and St. Saveur le Vicomte.

GEORGE, ST. (1st century), bishop. *See* Fronto, St.

GEORGE, ST. (d. 300?), martyr. The patron of England, Portugal, Germany, Aragon, Genoa, and Venice was said to have been put to death at Diospolis, Palestine. Revered in England before the eleventh century, he was a favorite

saint of crusaders, as he had been of soldiers in the East before that. His adventures are recounted early in the poetry of Aelfric, and later in William Caxton's translation of *Legenda Aurea*. The story of his rescue of a king's daughter, the slaying of a dragon, and the conversion of Libya is a twelfth-century Italian fable. F. D. Apr. 23.

GEORGE, ST. (d. 699?). Bishop of Vienne, France, he may have lived into the eighth century. He was canonized in 1251. F. D. Nov. 2.

GEORGE, ST. (d. 814), bishop. He came to the second Council of Nicaea from his see at Antioch and, because of the action he and his associates took against the Iconoclast, Emperor Leo the Armenian, was banished and died in exile. F. D. Apr. 19.

GEORGE, ST. (d. 816?). Called "the Younger," he was bishop of Mitylene, Lesbos, to distinguish him from two other St. Georges who held the see shortly before him. F. D. Apr. 7.

GEORGE, ST. (d. 825?), bishop. Born in Cromna on the Black Sea, he became a priest, hermit, and later monk at the monastery of Bonyssa. Chosen bishop of Amastris against his will, he served his people well and arranged their successful defense of the city against the Saracens. F. D. Feb. 21.

GEORGE, ST. (d. 852?), martyr. *See* Aurelius, St.

GEORGE, ST. (d. 884?), bishop. Born near Rodez, France, he was a Benedictine at St. Foi in Rouergue when the Norsemen overran the area in 862; he became bishop of Lodève, France, at an advanced age. F. D. Feb. 19.

GEORGE, ST. (1014–1066). Surnamed Mtasmindeli ("of the Black Mountain," in Armenia), he lived as a hermit in Syria, was abbot of a monastery on Mt. Athos, revised the scriptural translations of St. Euthymius, wrote much in the Iberian language, and was a doctor of the Georgian Church. F. D. June 27.

GEORGE HAMARTOLUS (9th century). A monk at Constantinople, he wrote a universal chronicle, in which his comments on the recent Iconoclast persecution and the years before the schism of Photius are of importance; he ended his work at 842; later continuations carried it to 948.

GEORGE LIMNIOTES, ST. (d. 730?), martyr. A hermit on Mt. Olympus, he was put to death at ninety-five for defending icons during the persecution of Emperor Leo the Isaurian. F. D. Aug. 24.

GEORGE PISIDES (7th century), poet. Born in Pisidia, Asia Minor, he was deacon, archivist, and official in other posts at St. Sophia's, Constantinople, a friend of Emperor Heraclius and his companion against the Persians in 622, and the author of some 5000 lines of poetry on historical and theological subjects. It is significant for his eyewitness account of the Persian campaign, comments on the emperor, and his attack on the Monophysite heresy.

GEORGE OF SAXONY (1471–1539). Called "the Rich" and "the Bearded," he was born in Dresden on Aug. 27, son of Albert the Brave of Saxony and Sidonia, daughter of the king of Bohemia. In 1496 he married Barbara, daughter of King Casimir IV of Poland, became governor of Friesland in 1498, and assumed the dukedom of Saxony on his father's death in 1500. Trouble in Friesland caused him to sell it to Burgundy; he sought to suppress the robber barons in Saxony and to better justice, supported the humanistic program at Leipzig, administered his court well, and sought to stem the advance of Lutheranism. He originated the Disputation of Leipzig in 1519, attacked the abuse of indulgences at the Diet of Worms in 1521, and pleaded for Church reform from within. He also was an active figure in the formation of the League of Dessau and the League of Halle, which in 1538 became the League of Nuremberg. His treatment of Lutherans became more hostile during these last years, and he decreed expulsion from the duchy for those who held anti-Catholic ideas. All his children died before he did, and the duchy passed to George's Lutheran brother Heinrich. George died in Dresden, Saxony, on Apr. 17.

GEORGE OF TREBIZOND (1396?–1486). Born in Crete, he went to Italy about 1420, studied Latin under Vittorino da Feltre, taught Greek in Mantua, Venice, and Florence, and became a professor at the University of Rome in 1431. He translated works by Eusebius and Ptolemy from Greek into Latin, was secretary to Popes Eugene IV (who appointed him papal abbreviator in 1464) and Nicholas V, engaged in numerous academic quarrels, and defended Aristotle against Plato, which lost him the friendship of Cardinal Bessarion and Gemistus Plethon. He died in obscurity in Rome.

GEORGIUS SYNCELLUS (9th century), historian. A monk in Palestine, he became secretary (*syncellus*) to Patriarch Tarasius of Constantinople (appointed in 784), possibly as a bishop, and retired to a monastery in 806 to write *Extract of Chronography*, a universal history to the year 316. He relied on the Septuagint, Eusebius, Annianus, and the Greek Fathers of the Church, and made an important contribution to Byzantine literature.

GERALD, ST. (d. 732). Born in Northumbria, England, he went from Lindisfarne to an island off the coast of Mayo, Ireland, where he became abbot of the English monks who had followed St. Colman. F. D. Mar. 13.

GERALD, ST. (855–909). The count of Aurillac, France, after a long illness as a youth, devoted much of his wealth to the poor, practiced great austerities, and built a church and

Benedictine monastery on his estate. St. Odo of Cluny wrote his biography, praising him as an exceptional noble. F. D. Oct. 13.

GERALD, ST. (d. 927), bishop. A Benedictine monk at Brou, he became bishop of Mâcon, France, served for forty years, then resigned to return to his former abbey. F. D. May 29.

GERALD, ST. (d. 1077), bishop. He was Benedictine prior at Cluny, France, before Pope Alexander II called him to Rome to succeed St. Peter Damian as bishop of Ostia, Italy. He served as papal legate to France, Spain, and Germany. F. D. Feb. 6.

GERALD, ST. (d. 1123). He was bishop of Beziers, France. F. D. Nov. 5.

GERALD, BL. (d. 1177). Born in Lombardy, he became a Cistercian at the monastery in Fossanuova, Italy, and later its abbot. He was abbot of Cîteaux in 1170 and was killed by an unruly monk while making a canonical visit at Igny. F. D. Oct. 16.

GERALD DE BARRI. *See* Giraldus Cambrensis.

GERALD OF SAUVE-MAJEURE, ST. (d. 1095). Born in Corbie, Picardy, he joined the monks there, was ordained in Rome after a severe illness, became abbot of St. Vincent in Laon, which he failed to restore to the strictest discipline, and moved on to found an abbey near Bordeaux. Here he instituted the practice of offering mass for a month after the death of any of the Benedictine community. He was canonized in 1197. F. D. Apr. 5.

GERALDINI, ALESSANDRO (1455–1525), bishop. Born in Amelia, Italy, he was a soldier, fought in the Spanish campaign against Portugal in 1475–76, studied in a Spanish seminary, was ordained, and was attached to the court at Castile. He is said to have helped to gain an audience for Columbus, served Ferdinand and Isabella, as well as the papacy, on diplomatic missions, and was bishop of several Italian sees. In 1520 he was named first bishop of Santo Domingo; wrote an account of his voyage there, a description of the place, and religious treatises. He died on the island.

GÉRAMB, FERDINAND DE (1772–1848). Of Hungarian descent, he was born in Lyons, France, on Jan. 14, was a lieutenant general in the monarchist army which fought the French Revolution, and was imprisoned by Napoleon at Vincennes from 1808 to 1814. His wife had died in 1808, and he placed his four living children in the care of his brother and on his release became a Trappist. He took his vows in 1817 as Brother Mary Joseph, was at the monastery of Mt. Olivet, Alsace, from 1827 to 1833, then became procurator general of La Trappe, with offices in Rome. Pope Gregory XVI made him a titular abbot. He wrote ascetical works and died in Rome on Mar. 15.

GÉRANDO, JOSEPH MARIE DE (1772–1842), educator. Born in Lyons, France, on Feb. 29, he defended the city against invading revolutionists, was wounded, imprisoned, and escaped to Switzerland, won a prize offered by the French Institute while he was in the army at Colmar, and founded at Paris in 1815 the Société pour l'instruction élémentaire, introducing the English Lancastrian system of education of the poor. He was a member of the council of state under Napoleon and Louis XVIII, the Academy of Belles-Lettres and also of Sciences, and in 1837 of the Chambre de Paris. He worked in school and hospital administration, wrote on the philosophy of thought, and published several works on the education of the deaf and public welfare. He died in Paris on Nov. 10.

GERARD, ST. (935–994), bishop. Born and educated in Cologne, he was a canon of its cathedral, and in 963 became bishop of Toul, Lorraine. Although weighed down with civil and judicial tasks as well as ecclesiastical ones, he built widely, introduced Greek and Irish monks to make his see a scholarly center, and dispensed great charities during famine and plague. He was canonized by Pope St. Leo IX. F. D. Apr. 23.

GERARD (d. 1051), bishop. Chaplain to Emperor Henry II of Germany, he was his aide in negotiations with Robert the Pious of France. He converted the Gondulphians, heretics who denied the Eucharist, and became bishop of Cambrai, France, in 1013.

GERARD (d. 1108), archbishop. Nephew of Bishop Walkelin of Winchester, England, he was a precentor in Rouen cathedral, and a clerk in the chapel of William II of England, in whose diplomatic service he went to Rome in 1095. He was consecrated bishop of Hereford in 1096, having been ordained a day before, and in 1100 became archbishop of York. He quarreled with St. Anselm over investitures, refused to accept the primacy of Canterbury, seems to have misrepresented the pope's position to the king, and was excommunicated. He acknowledged Anselm in time, though he maintained that York, where he was successful with many reforms, was still independent. His opposition to Anselm, even after their reconciliation, was so strong that popular ill-feeling ran high, particularly after his sudden death at Southwell on May 21, while he was on the way to a council in London, when the canons refused to bury him in the cathedral.

GERARD, ST. (d. 1109). He was prior of La Charité-sur-Loire, a Benedictine abbey near Namur, Belgium, abbot at Soigny, and founder of several Cluniac houses in France. He died at La Charité. F. D. Dec. 6.

GERARD, ST. (d. 1119). Born in Piacenza, Italy, he became bishop of Potenza in 1099 and was canonized by Pope Callistus II. F. D. Oct. 30.

GERARD DE BROGNE, ST. (d. 959). Born in Staves, Namur, of the family of the dukes of Lower Austrasia, he trained for the army, but was attracted to a life of piety. About 917 he was sent by the count of Namur on a mission to the French court and stayed at the abbey of St. Denis. He was so attracted to the life that he returned after his mission was finished, became a monk, and was ordained eleven years later. In 919 he founded an abbey on his estate at Brogne, Belgium, and became a recluse. The archbishop of Cambrai sent him to reform the Benedictine abbey of St. Ghislain in Hainault. So successful was he that Arnulf, count of Flanders, put him in charge of all abbeys and monasteries in Flanders, Lorraine, and Champagne. His next twenty years were devoted to reforming and restoring strict monastic rule through the area. He died in Brogne. F. D. Oct. 3.

GERARD OF CLAIRVAUX, BL. (d. 1138). While a prisoner after he had been severely wounded in battle, he determined to join his brother, St. Bernard, as a monk. He instructed the laboring monks at Clairvaux, France, and lived a fervent life of prayer. F. D. June 13.

GERARD OF CREMONA (1114–1187). Born in Cremona, Italy, he studied Arabic at Toledo, Spain, and translated the complete works of Avicenna into Latin, together with seventy-five other titles in philosophy, geometry, and physics. He was one of the leaders of the group of scholars inspired by Bishop Raymond of Toledo and did much to make Arabic culture available for the thirteenth-century writers of scholasticism. He died in Cremona. Some of the works ascribed to him were by Gerard of Sabionetta, who lived two centuries later.

GERARD OF GALLINARO, ST. According to local Italian legend, he and SS. Arduin, Bernard, and Fulk were English pilgrims to the Holy Land in the seventh or twelfth century who visited the shrine of St. Michael at Monte Gargano and died in the Abruzzi. F. D. Aug. 11.

GÉRARD, BL. JOAN (1752–1794), martyr. See Fontaine, Bl. Madeleine.

GERARD DE LUNEL, ST. (1275–1298). A Frenchman and Franciscan tertiary, he died at Monte Santo, Italy, while returning from a pilgrimage to Jerusalem. His cult was approved by Popes Benedict XIV and Pius VI. F. D. May 24.

GERARD, JOHN (1564–1637). Born in England on Oct. 4, he was brought up in recusant circles; his father, Sir Thomas Gerard, had been imprisoned, though released, for allegedly plotting to free Mary of Scotland. John was at Oxford in 1575–77, entered Douai in 1577, and went to Rheims when the college was transferred there in 1578. He was at Clermont,

Paris, in 1580–82. On his return to England he was captured and imprisoned in Marshalsea prison in 1583–84, then went to Paris, was at the English College, Rome, in 1586, was ordained in 1588, became a Jesuit that year, and was sent immediately on the English mission. He labored successfully for six years, although anti-Catholic feeling ran high because of the Spanish Armada excitement; he was captured in 1594, tortured frequently, and escaped in 1597. He served underground until 1605, when he was forced into exile by the Gunpowder Plot (of which he wrote an account), leaving with the Spanish ambassador. He was on the faculty of several colleges in Europe, helped Mary Ward to found her religious community, and during his last ten years was spiritual director at the English College, Rome, where he died on July 27. He is best known for his Latin autobiography, well written, vivid, detailed, and of considerable historical significance for its comments on Sir Robert Cecil, Sir Edward Coke, Sir Everard Digby, Henry Garnet, Edward Oldcorne, Richard Southwell, Lord Vaux, Henry Walpole, William Wiseman, and others of the Elizabethan and Jacobean period.

JOHN GERARD, *Autobiography of a Hunted Priest*, trans. Philip Caraman (Garden City, N.Y., Image Books, 1955).

GERARD, JOHN (1840–1912), editor. Born in Edinburgh, Scotland, on May 30, he studied at Stonyhurst and London, was ordained a Jesuit in 1873, and was editor of *The Month* from 1894 to 1897 and from 1900 to 1912. He was superior of the English province in the years between, wrote a reply to the evolutionist Ernst Haeckel, *The Old Riddle and the Newest Answer*, and died in London on Dec. 13.

GERARD, BL. MILES (d. 1590), martyr. Born near Wigan, England, he taught, then went to Rheims, where he was ordained in 1583. Entering the English underground mission as a William Richardson, he was captured and hanged at Rochester. He was beatified in 1929. F. D. Apr. 30.

GERARD, RICHARD (1635?–1680), martyr. Of the same family as Fr. John Gerard, he was born in Hilderstone, Staffordshire, England, was falsely charged with complicity in the Titus Oates Plot, and imprisoned in Newgate for ten months without trial. He died in prison on Mar. 11. His son Philip (d. 1733) became a Jesuit; he was at St. Omer's College with two of his brothers at the time of the plot, and tuition fees sent abroad may have been read by Stephen Dugdale, the informer, as his "proof" that Gerard was helping to finance a Jesuit-inspired invasion from abroad.

GERARD MAJELLA, ST. (1725–1755). Born in Muro, Italy, in Apr., he was obliged to leave school when his father died, was apprenticed to a tailor, and in 1745 opened his own shop. In 1748 he became a Redemptorist laybrother and attracted the attention of the founder, St. Alphonsus. He was professed in 1752 and became tailor for the community. He experienced extraordinary supernatural manifestations, became spiritual adviser to several communities of nuns, and was widely known. He died at Naples of consumption, was canonized in 1904, and is a patron of childbirth. F. D. Oct. 16.

GERARD SAGREDA, ST. (d. 1046), bishop and martyr. A native of Venice, Italy, he became a Benedictine at San Giorgio Maggiore, and its abbot. On a pilgrimage to Jerusalem he met King St. Stephen of Hungary, who persuaded him to return and become tutor to his son, Bl. Emeric. He preached widely and successfully and became first bishop of Csanad in 1035. When Stephen died in 1038, a pagan reaction set in, anarchy prevailed, and a group of rebel soldiers attacked Gerard at Buda, murdered him, and threw his body in the Danube. He is called the Apostle of Hungary, where he is known as St. Collert. F. D. Sept. 24.

GERARD TINTORIO, BL. (d. 1207). Born in Monza, Lombardy, Italy, he devoted his wealth to the building and upkeep of a hospital for the poor, and himself to the care of lepers and beggars. His cult was confirmed in 1582. F. D. June 6.

GERARD OF VILLAMAGNA, BL. (1174–1245). Orphaned at twelve, he entered the service of a Florentine noble, served with him on the third crusade, was captured and ransomed, and became a Franciscan tertiary at a hermitage in Tuscany, practicing severe austerities for twenty years. His cult was confirmed in 1833. F. D. May 23.

GERARDESCA, BL. (d. 1260?). Born and married in Pisa, Italy, she agreed with her husband to enter the religious life; he became a Camaldolese monk, and she lived as a solitary near the monastery of San Salvio. Her cult was confirmed in 1856. F. D. May 29.

GERARDUS ODONIS (d. 1348), theologian. Born probably in Châteauroux, France, he became a Franciscan, and was elected minister general in 1329 to succeed Michael of Casena, who had opposed the rule of poverty and was deposed by Pope John XXII. Gerardus took the same position at the chapter of 1331 and was opposed by the pope and by King Robert and Queen Sanzia of Naples and Sicily. Gerardus drew up new statutes for the order which were confirmed by Pope Benedict XII, but only retained through the latter's lifetime. As general, Gerardus increased the number of Franciscan missions, was sent to Hungary to crush the Patarene heresy, discussed the beatific vision at Paris and Avignon in 1334, and served on diplomatic missions for both popes. He was named patriarch of Antioch in 1342 and wrote commentaries on scripture, the *Sentences*, and Aristotle's *Ethics*, a natural philosophy (marked by atomism), and sermons. He died in Catania, Sicily.

GERASIMUS, ST. (d. 475). Born in Lycia, he became a recluse first in his homeland, then in Egypt, and finally in Palestine, where some seventy followers joined him in ascetic seclusion. F. D. Mar. 5.

GERBERON, GABRIEL (1628–1711). Born in St. Calais, Sarthe, France, on Aug. 12, he studied in Vendôme, and became a Benedictine at St. Mélaine, Rennes, in 1649. He was stationed at a number of monasteries, wrote the second volume of *L'abbé commendataire*, for which he was ordered arrested by Louis XIV (1682), and fled to Holland. In Brussels in 1690 he was arrested by the archbishop of Mechlin for writing Jansenist pamphlets and turned over to Louis XIV. After imprisonment from 1703 to 1710 he retracted his errors, retired to Paris, and died at the monastery of St. Denis on Mar. 29. He wrote at least sixty volumes, most of which are marked by Jansenism, which had caused his superiors to stop his teaching career as early as 1663.

GERBERT, MARTIN VON (1720–1793). Born in Horb in the Black Forest, Germany, as baron von Hornau, he studied at Ehingen, Freiburg im Breisgau, and Klingenau. He completed his philosophy and theology at St. Blaise, was ordained a Benedictine in 1744, and taught and was librarian there. From 1759 to 1762 he toured Europe for musical collections. He became prince-abbot of St. Blaise abbey in 1764, but managed to continue his interest in music and liturgy, writing much in both fields, particularly the valuable *De cantu et musica sacra* and *Scriptores ecclesiastici de musica sacra*. He died in St. Blaise in the Black Forest on May 13.

GERBERT DE MONTREUIL (13th century), poet. He flourished about 1250, writing several romances, including *Roman de la violette* and a sequel to the *Perceval* of Chrestien de Troyes.

GERBET, OLYMPE PHILIPPE (1798–1864), bishop. Born in Poligny, France, he studied in the seminary of Besançon and at St. Sulpice and the Sorbonne, and was ordained in 1822. He was closely associated with Lamennais, but accepted the papal encyclicals of 1832–34 which condemned Lamennais' teaching and tried to win him back to the Church. He was in Rome from 1839 to 1849, writing *Esquisse de Rome chrétienne*. He also had written on penance, the Eucharist, certitude, human knowledge, and the history of philosophy, but all his work was influenced by the view of Lamennais. Returning to France, he was named professor of sacred eloquence at the Sorbonne, vicar general of Amiens, and in 1854

bishop of Perpignan. In 1860 he issued a pastoral letter on contemporary errors, which served Pope Pius IX as a model for his *Syllabus*. Gerbet died in Perpignan, France.

GERBILLON, JEAN FRANÇOIS (1654–1707), missioner. Born in Verdun, France, on June 4, he became a Jesuit in 1670, taught for seven years, and in 1685 was sent to China. Stationed at Peking, he learned the language of the court, served as ambassador to settle boundary disputes with Russia, was in charge of the French college in Peking, and later superior general of the Chinese mission. In 1692 he gained from the emperor the right to pursue his mission work actively; he wrote on mathematics, on the geography and customs of Tatary, and may have been the author of a Tatar grammar; and died in Peking on Mar. 27.

GERBOLD, ST. (d. 690?). A Benedictine monk at Ebriciacum, he became abbot-founder of Livray and bishop of Bayeux, Normandy. F. D. Dec. 5.

GERBRAND, BL. (d. 1218). He was second abbot of the Cistercian monastery of Klaarkamp, Frisia, and in 1191 founded Bloemkamp. F. D. Oct. 13.

GERDIL, HYACINTHE SIGISMOND (1718–1802), cardinal. Born in Samoëns, Savoy, on June 20, he became a Barnabite at Annecy, studied at Bologna, taught philosophy in Macerata and Turin, and became provincial of his order. He was tutor to the prince of Piedmont, was in 1773 named cardinal *in petto* by Pope Clement XIV and publicly advanced to that honor in 1777 by Pius VI, and made a consultor and prefect of the Propaganda. He wrote *Anti Emile* against the educational theories of Rousseau, a study of the immortality of the soul against Locke and in defense of Malebranche, opposition to deism and Febronianism, and volumes on canon law, history, and science. He died in Rome on Aug. 12.

GEREBALD, ST. (d. 885). He was bishop of Châlons-sur-Seine, France, from 864 until his death. F. D. June 12.

GEREBERNUS, ST. (d. 650?), martyr. See Dympna, St.

GERECHT, JOHN (1489–1539). Born in Landsberg, Bavaria, he studied at Cologne, became a Carthusian in 1509, and was novice-master in Cologne and prior at Contave. He was sub-prior of St. Barbara's, Cologne, from 1534 until his death there on Aug. 11. He wrote biblical paraphrases, homilies, sermons, such ascetical treatises as *Alloquia Jesu Christi ad animam fidelem* and *Pharetra divini amoris*, and a Latin edition of the *Revelations* of St. Gertrude. He is known also as Lanspergius and John Justus.

GEREMARUS, ST. (d. 658?), abbot. Born in Beauvais, France, he served in the court of Dagobert I. With the consent of his wife he became a monk at Pentale, near Brionne, and later its abbot. He was so strict that several monks were reported to have attempted his murder, whereupon he resigned and became a hermit. Five years later, in 655, he founded a monastery (later called St. Germer) and became its first abbot at Flay. F. D. Sept. 24.

GEREMIA, BL. PIETRO DE (1381–1452). Born in Palermo, Italy, he studied law at Bologna, became a professor there, then joined the Dominicans. Ordained, he became a famous preacher, shone at the Council of Florence, was sent by Pope Eugenius IV as apostolic visitor to Sicily, and died at Palermo. His cult was approved in 1784. F. D. Mar. 10.

GEREON, ST. (d. 287?), martyr. See Maurice, St.

GERHARD OF ZÜTPHEN (1367–1398). Born in Zütphen, Holland, he was one of the first of the Brothers of the Common Life founded at Deventer, Netherlands, by Gerhard Groote and others, was well schooled in theology and canon law, served as their librarian, wrote *Homo quidam* and *Beatus vir*, and was the probable author of works on vernacular prayer and scripture translation. He died in Windesheim, Netherlands.

GERHOH (1093–1169), theologian. Born in Polling, Bavaria, he studied in Freising, Mosburg, and Hildesheim, was associated with the cathedral school in Augsburg, where he was also a canon, went to the Lateran Council of 1123 with Bishop Hermann, and resigned his canonicate in 1124 and with his father became an Augustinian at Raitenbuch. He was ordained in 1126 and in 1132 was named provost of Reichersberg monastery near Linz, Austria. He went to Rome several times for Archbishop Conrad I of Salburg, and also to Bohemia and Moravia. He was an extremely zealous reformer, writing on the need for reform, against simony, and on the corruption of the clergy during the reign of Pope Eugene III. These views also appear in his *De investigatione antichristi*, which treats of the second crusade. He also wrote a commentary on the Psalms. When he supported the election of Alexander III against antipope Victor IV, he was banished in 1166 and his monastery sacked. He died in Reichersberg on June 27, soon after his return.

GERING, ULRICH (1440?–1510). A printer in Switzerland, he was called to Paris in 1470 by Guillaume Fichet, rector of the Sorbonne, to set up the first French printing press, which he completed with the assistance of Martin Crantz and Michel Friburger.

GERINUS, ST. (d. 676). Brother of St. Leodegarius, he was persecuted by Ebroin, mayor of the palace, and stoned to death near Arras, France. He is also called Werinus. F. D. Oct. 2.

GERKEN, RUDOLPH ALOYSIUS (1887–1943), archbishop. Born in Dyersville, Iowa, on Mar. 7, he studied at the University of Dallas, Texas, and St. Joseph's, Indiana, and taught in public schools in Texas from 1910 to 1912 when he became an instructor at the University of Dallas. He entered Kenrick seminary in St. Louis, was ordained in Dallas in 1917, and engaged in pastoral work in Texas for the next decade. He was consecrated first bishop of Amarillo, Texas, in 1927, founded Price Memorial College in Amarillo in 1928, and in 1933 was made archbishop of Santa Fe. He died on Mar. 2.

GERLAC (d. 1170?). A worldly soldier until the death of his wife, he then determined to lead a life of austerity, and cared for the sick in Rome for seven years. On his return to Valkenburg, Holland, he built a home in a tree, leaving only to attend church. He was never canonized, but was honored locally on Jan. 5.

GERLAND, ST. (d. 1104?), bishop. Born in Besançon, France, he accompanied two Norman relatives on the conquest of Sicily, where he later accepted office, was consecrated bishop of Girgenti by Pope Urban II, and worked successfully to convert many Moslems. F. D. Feb. 25.

GERMAIN. See Germanus, St. (d. 448).

GERMAINE. See Cousin, St. Germaine.

GERMANA, ST. (2nd century), martyr. See Catus, St.

GERMANICUS, ST. (d. 155?), martyr. A Christian who encouraged those who suffered in Smyrna during the persecution of Marcus Aurelius, which also took the life of St. Polycarp, he was torn to death by wild beasts. F. D. Jan. 19.

GERMANUS, ST. (d. 120?), martyr. See Astius, St.

GERMANUS, ST. (d. 250), martyr. See Caesarius, St.

GERMANUS, ST. (d. 297), martyr. See Antoninus, St.

GERMANUS, ST. (d. 305?), martyr. He and his brother Servandus, sons of St. Marcellus of León, were put to death at Cadiz, Spain. F. D. Oct. 23.

GERMANUS, ST. (d. 390?), martyr. He succeeded St. Desideratus as bishop of Besançon, Gaul, and is said to have been killed by Arians. F. D. Oct. 11.

GERMANUS, ST. (378?–448), bishop. A native of Auxerre, France, he studied in Gallic schools, went to Rome, and became a successful lawyer. With his wife, Eustochia, he went back to Gaul as governor of several border provinces and in 418 was named bishop of Auxerre. At the request of Pope St. Celestine he went to England in 429 with St. Lupus to combat Pelagianism and was most successful. While there he led the Britons to a great victory against the Picts and the Saxons. As related by Constantius, his biographer, he placed the outnumbered Britons in a valley between high mountains and when the enemy approached had them shout "Alleluia" three times. The echoing shouts frightened away the Saxons, who thought from the magnified volume of sound that a mighty army was encamped. In 440 he returned to Britain to fight Pelagianism and wiped out the heresy. After his return to Gaul, he attempted to prevent the barbarian chief Goar, sent to crush a revolt in Amorica by the Roman general Aetius, from pillaging the province. Goar agreed to hold off his men while Germanus went to secure a pardon from Emperor Valentinian III at Ravenna. He is also known as Germain. F. D. July 31.

GERMANUS, ST. (d. 460?), martyr. Of Celtic origin, he crossed to the Continent, was converted by St. Germanus of Auxerre, whose name he took, and was put to death in Normandy. F. D. May 2.

GERMANUS, ST. (d. 474?), bishop. He is said to have been a nephew of St. Patrick and to have served as a missionary bishop in Ireland, Wales, Brittany, and the Isle of Man. F. D. July 3.

GERMANUS, ST. (d. 484?), martyr. *See* Donatian, St.

GERMANUS, ST. (d. 540?), bishop. A close friend of St. Benedict, he was bishop of Capua, Italy, and was one of the delegation sent by Pope Hormisdas to Emperor Justin at Constantinople in 519 which ended the Acacian schism. F. D. Oct. 30.

GERMANUS, ST. (496?–576), bishop. Born near Autun, France, he was ordained, became abbot of St. Symphorian, and was named bishop of Paris in 554 by King Childebert I, whose wasteful way of life he changed, as well as that of many licentious courtiers. He was not as successful with King Charibert, who disregarded the bishop's example and exhortations, and whom he excommunicated. He founded many religious establishments and was beloved by the poor before his last years were disturbed by his ineffectual attempts to be a peacemaker in the warring quarrels of Childebert's nephews. F. D. May 28.

GERMANUS, ST. (d. 732), bishop. Son of a senator, he was born in Constantinople, became a priest then bishop of Cyzicus, Asia Minor, and patriarch when the see was transferred in 715 to Constantinople. In 727, Emperor Leo the Isaurian supported the Iconoclast heresy; Germanus, nearly ninety, opposed him so strenuously by sermon, letter, and tract that the emperor practically forced him out of office; he died in Constantinople in monastic seclusion. F. D. May 12.

GERMANUS, ST. (906?–1000?). Born in Montfort, France, he studied at Paris, was ordained, became Benedictine prior at Talloires and a recluse in his last years. F. D. Nov. 1.

GERMANUS, ST. (14th century?). *See* Sergius, St.

GERMANUS OF GRANFEL, ST. (d. 677?), martyr. Born in Trèves, Gaul, he became a Benedictine at Remiremont monastery, served at Luxeuil under St. Walbert, and was made abbot of Granfel and two other foundations in the Moutier Valley. When Germanus pleaded for the poor of the district, who were being robbed on orders of Duke Cathic, he and a companion, Randcald, were slain by soldiers. F. D. Feb. 21.

GERMERIUS, ST. (480?–560?), bishop. Born in Angoulême, Gaul, and educated at Toulouse, he received a grant of land from King Clovis, on which he built a church. He also built a monastery at Dux, where he died after a charity-marked reign of fifty years as bishop of Toulouse, Gaul. He is also known as Germier. F. D. May 16.

GEROLD, ST. (d. 806), bishop. He was in turn a courtier with Charlemagne, a Benedictine at the abbey of Fontenelle, and, in 787, bishop of Évreux, France. He later resigned and died at the monastery. F. D. June 14.

GEROLD, ST. (d. 978). Born of a noble Rhaetian family, he gave his land to the Benedictine abbey of Einsiedeln, Switzerland, where his sons Cuno and Ulrich were monks, and became a hermit in a forest near Mitternach. F. D. Apr. 19.

GERONTIUS, ST. (2nd century), martyr. *See* Catus, St.

GERONTIUS, ST. (d. 501?). Bishop of Cervia, Italy, he was waylaid and slain near Ancona, on his return from a synod at Rome, and was honored as a martyr. F. D. May 9.

GERONTIUS, ST. (d. 508?), king. Son of Erbin and king of Devon, he died in battle against the pagan Saxons. Another St. Gerontius, king of Cornwall, died in 596. The name persists in the poetic legend of Geraint and Enid. F. D. Aug. 10.

GEROSA, ST. CATHERINE (1784–1847), foundress. Born in Lovere, Italy, she worked there for forty years, bringing up a family which became her responsibility after the death of her parents. About 1823 she worked with St. Bartholomea Capitanio in helping to train young children, whose education was neglected during the Austrian occupation. Together they founded the institute of the Sisters of Charity of Lovere, which followed the rule of the group formed in France by St. Vincent de Paul. Though her associate died in 1833 at twenty-six, Sr. Vincenza (Catherine's name in religion) carried on the work with great success. She was canonized in 1950 by Pope Pius XII. F. D. June 4.

GERSON, JEAN CHARLIER DE (1363–

1429). Eldest of twelve children of Arnauld and Elizabeth, he was born in Gerson, France, on Dec. 14, studied at Collège de Navarre, Paris, and received his doctorate in theology in 1394. In 1395 he was named to succeed his teacher, Pierre d'Ailly, as chancellor of the university and of Notre Dame. From 1397 to 1401 he was dean of St. Donatien, Bruges, returned to Paris as a curé (retaining his chancellorship), attended the Council of Rheims in 1408, and publicly attacked Duke John of Burgundy from 1407 to 1415 for the murder of the duke of Orléans and his counsel, Jean Petit, for defending tyrannicide as moral. At the Council of Constance in 1415 Gerson took part in the condemnation of John Hus and of the Flagellants, and opposed Matthew Grabon's hostility to religious orders. Duke John had previously sacked his house and had tried to kill him; Gerson was unable to return to Paris and went into exile at the Benedictine monastery of Mölk, Germany. When John was slain in 1419, Gerson went to Lyons, France, to remain until his death there on July 12. While he pleaded for years with all three claimants to the papal throne to step down and thus end the Western schism, he held the position of Willian of Occam and maintained at Constance that the pope was not a universal bishop, not infallible, and was subject to the superiority of a council; eventually these errors became fundamental to Gallicanism. As a mystic and as the author of *De parvulis ad Christum trahendis* he had great influence; he defended the spirituality of St. Joan of Arc, increased devotion to the Virgin Mary and St. Joseph, demanded the reform of the Church from within, and was a powerful preacher, with no set style: sometimes cold and analytical, sometimes highly emotional and allegorical. He wrote more than 400 treatises.

GERTRUDE, ST. (d. 649). She founded and was the first abbess of the Benedictine convent of Hamaye, Flanders, near Douai. F. D. Dec. 6.

GERTRUDE, ST. (626–659). Daughter of Bl. Pepin of Landen and St. Itta, she joined her mother at the double monastery which they built at Nivelles, France, after Pepin's death, and became its first abbess. Later, she turned its administration over to her niece and devoted herself to the study of scripture and to extreme penitential disciplines. F. D. Mar. 17.

GERTRUDE, ST. (d. 675?). She was third abbess of the Benedictine convent at Remiremont, France. Her cult was approved in 1091 by Pope Leo IX. F. D. Nov. 7.

GERTRUDE, ST. (d. 690?). Sister of St. Adolphus, she became a Benedictine nun at the convent of St. Mont, near Remiremont, France, and about 654 succeeded her aunt, St. Clare, as abbess. Her cult was approved in 1051. F. D. Nov. 7.

GERTRUDE OF ALTENBERG, BL. (1225?–1297). Daughter of St. Elizabeth of Hungary and Louis IV of Thuringia (he died, while away on a crusade, two weeks before his child's birth), she became a Premonstratensian at the convent of Altenberg, Thuringia, and was abbess from 1247 until her death. Her cult was authorized by Pope Clement VI. F. D. Aug. 13.

GERTRUDE OF DELFT, BL. (d. 1358). Born in Voorburch, Netherlands, she became a servant, and followed a life of contemplation, but outside any formal community. When it appeared that she was given the stigmata, she was unable to continue in prayerful privacy because of the crowds who were attracted by her reputation for holiness. She is also known as Gertrud van Oosten. F. D. Jan. 6.

GERTRUDE THE GREAT, ST. (1256?–1302?), mystic. Of unknown parentage, she was born in Eisleben, Germany, and at five was left at the Benedictine monastery in Helfta, Saxony, where she came under the care of St. Mechtildis and became a nun. In 1281 she experienced the first of the many visions which she recorded in her *Book of Extraordinary Grace*. Her writings helped spread devotion to the Sacred Heart. She also recorded much of St. Mechtildis' teaching. Although she never was formally canonized, celebration of her feast was ordered extended through the Church by Pope Clement XII in 1677. She is a patroness of the West Indies. F. D. Nov. 17.

GERTRUDE OF HACKEBORN (1232–1292). Born near Halberstadt, Thuringia, sister of St. Mechtildis, she became a Benedictine nun at Rodersdorf, was its abbess at nineteen, and in 1243 founded with her brothers Albert and Louis the convent of Hedersleben. She transferred her own community to Helfta, Halberstadt, in 1258, and made it a center of mysticism, liberal-arts education, and scriptural studies. St. Gertrude the Great was a nun there under her namesake. She died at Helfta.

GERUNTIUS, ST. (d. 100?), martyr. He is said to have been a missionary bishop, slain near Talco (Italica), Spain. F. D. Aug. 25.

GERUNTIUS, ST. (5th century). He was bishop of Milan, Italy, from about 465 to 470, succeeding St. Eusebius. F. D. May 5.

GERVAISE, FRANÇOIS ARMAND (1660–1716?). Born in Paris, he became a Discalced Carmelite, was prior, sought a more austere life, and became a Trappist in 1695. He was abbot of La Trappe in 1696–98, but was so exacting that he resigned in the face of rebellion. He wandered from monastery to monastery for the rest of his life. He wrote biographies of Abelard, Suger, Abbé de Rance (whom he had succeeded at La Trappe), and several Church Fathers; his history of the Cîteaux reform was hostile to his superiors and he was banished to Reclus, near Troyes, France, where he died.

GERVASE, ST., martyr. His body and that of St. Protase were unearthed in a Milan cemetery shortly after St. Ambrose had completed the great basilica there; the relics were brought to the new building in great honor. SS. Ambrose and Augustine record the event. He is also known as Jervis. F. D. June 19.

GERVASE OF CANTERBURY (1141?–1210?), historian. Born in England, probably in Kent, he was professed a monk of Christ Church, Canterbury, by Thomas à Becket in 1163 and buried that saint seven years later. He defended the monks in deputations before Archbishop Baldwin and before King Richard I, was in 1193 in the service of Archbishop Walter, and is significant for his writings. These include: *Chronicles*, for 1100–99; *Gesta regum*, a summary of earlier reigns, important for its firsthand account of King John; a history of the archbishops of Canterbury; and *Mappa mundi*, which located ecclesiastical foundations in Britain.

GERVASE, GEORGE (1569–1608), martyr. Born in Bosham, Sussex, England, he sailed, apparently unwillingly, on Sir Francis Drake's last expedition to the Indies, then served with the Spanish army in Flanders for two years. In 1599 he began study at Douai, was ordained in 1603, and worked for two years in England before being captured and exiled. He went to Rome, became a Benedictine in 1607, re-entered England, was captured after two months, and hanged at Tyburn. He was beatified in 1929. F. D. Apr. 11.

GERVASE OF TILBURY (1150?–1220?), historian. Born probably in Tilbury, England, he studied and taught canon law at Bologna, was in the English court in 1183, served in the court of William II of Sicily until 1189, was appointed marshal of Arles, France, by Otto IV in 1198, and served him at least until his defeat and banishment in 1214. For him Gervase wrote *Otia imperialia* (also called *De mirabilibus mundi*) on concepts of geography, physics, and history, including comments on Church-state relations. He died in Arlington, England.

GERVINUS, ST. (d. 1075). Born near Rheims, France, he was educated there, became a canon, entered the Benedictine abbey of St. Vannes in Verdun, and in time became abbot of St. Riquier, whose library and buildings he enlarged. He had a reputation as preacher and confessor throughout northern France and in England, where he became friendly with St. Edward the Confessor. In his last four years he suffered from leprosy. F. D. Mar. 3.

GERVINUS, BL. (d. 1117). A monk at St. Winnoc, then a hermit at Münster, Germany, he became abbot of the Benedictine monastery of Oudenburg, Flanders, in 1095. F. D. Apr. 17.

GÉRY. *See* Desiderius, St.; also, Gaugericus, St.

GETULIUS, ST. (d. 120?), martyr. The husband of St. Symphorosa was living in a Christian colony near Tivoli, Italy, as a retired officer, when he converted Cerealis, an imperial legate who had been sent to arrest him. Cerealis, Getulius, the latter's brother Amantius, who was a Roman tribune, and another Christian named Primitivus were tortured and executed. F. D. June 10.

GÉZA II (d. 1161), king of Hungary. When he assumed the throne in 1141 the Byzantines were attempting to extend their dominion over Hungary, and in 1156 Géza recognized the suzerainty of the Byzantine emperor. During Géza's reign large numbers of Saxon colonists were allowed to settle in Upper Hungary and Transylvania about 1150 to defend the country against Eastern aggression and the Polish threat.

GÉZA (d. 997). Duke of the Magyar tribe, he became ruler of Hungary in 970, married Adelaide, sister of Polish Duke Miezko, and through her became aware of Catholicism. In 985, St. Adalbert, archbishop of Prague, who had come to Hungary at Adelaide's request, baptized Géza and his son Vaik (St. Stephen). Géza led large numbers of his followers into the Church with him.

GFRÖRER, AUGUST FRIEDRICH (1803–1861), historian. Born in Calw, Württemberg, on Mar. 5, he studied at the evangelical seminary in Tübingen, and in 1859 was named vicar in Stuttgart. He lost his faith soon after, resigned his post, became librarian in Stuttgart, and devoted himself to reading and writing. He wrote on Philo Judaeus, a rationalist life of Christ, a history of the Thirty Years' War, and a biography of Gustavus Adolphus between 1831 and 1835. He then wrote on the Church in Germany before 1305 and was appointed professor of history at the Catholic University in Freiburg im Breisgau, Germany. He was elected to parliament in 1848, actively opposing Prussia, and in 1853 became a Catholic. Thereafter he wrote on tradition, Pope Gregory VII, a history of the eighteenth century, a study of Byzantium, and a church history. He died in Karlsbad (now Karlovy Vary, Czechoslovakia), on July 6.

GHÈBRE, MICHAEL. *See* Gabra, Michael.

GHÉON, HENRI. *See* Vangeon, Henri.

GHIBERTI, LORENZO DI CIONE (1378–1455), sculptor. Born in Florence, Italy, son of Cione di Ser Buonaccorso, he was adopted by his stepfather, was originally a goldsmith, began to work in bronze relief, and used the details familiar to painting in his panels for the bronze doors of the north and east sides of the baptistery of San Giovanni in his native city. The illustrations are from the Old and New Testaments, with effective surrounding decorations; he worked on them from 1401 to 1452. He also completed three statues for Or San Michele, the best being that of St. Stephen; reliquaries of SS. Zenobius and Giacinto; a baptistery in Siena; elaborate grave slabs; and papal miters. In gracefulness he stood between Donatello and Lucca della Robbia. He also wrote *Commentaries* on contemporary art and a treatise on architecture. He died in Florence on Dec. 1.

GHIRLANDAIO, DOMENICO (1449–1494), painter. Domenico di Tommaso Curradi di Doffo Bigordo, nicknamed Ghirlandaio ("the Garland Maker"), was born in Florence, began work as a goldsmith, studied fresco under Alessio Baldovinetti, and made his first attempts in that form before 1472. His now lost work in the Vespucci chapel and the church of Ognissanti, Florence, was followed by crowd-filled scenes from the life of St. Fina for the church of San Gimignano. He worked in Rome on the *Resurrection* and *The Calling of the Apostles* in the Sistine Chapel and on six papal portraits. From 1482 until his death on Jan. 11 he remained in Florence. There he completed figures of Roman statesmen for the Palazzo della Signoria, six frescoes on the life of St. Francis for the Sassetti chapel in Santa Trinità, and fifteen on the life of St. John the Baptist and of the Virgin Mary for the Tornabuoni chapel in Santa Maria Novella. He used contemporary persons for his faces, dressed his figures in Florentine costumes, and arranged them in rooms which reveal in full detail the structural and decorative taste of his times. Palaces, towers, churches, and squares form his exterior backgrounds, and copies of paintings and sculpture by other artists adorn his sets. *Old Man and Child* and other contemporary portraits reveal his skill in this form; he also completed several altarpieces. He taught his brothers Davide (1452–1525) and Benedetto (1458–1497), his brother-in-law Bastiano Mainardi, Francesco Granacci, and Michelangelo.

GIAMBERTI, GIULIANO. See San Gallo, Giuliano da.

GIANELLI, ST. ANTONIO (1789–1846), bishop and founder. Born in Cerreto, near Genoa, Italy, he completed his seminary course with distinction and was ordained in 1812. While active as a parish priest he organized a group of priests as the Missioners of St. Alphonsus Liguori, and also the Sisters of St. Mary dell' Orto, to teach and nurse the poor. He became bishop of Bobbio in 1838, and was canonized in 1951 by Pope Pius XII. F. D. June 8.

GIANFRANCHESI, GIUSEPPE (1875–1934), scientist. Born in Arcevia Marche, Italy,

on Feb. 21, he studied engineering at Rome, became a Jesuit, and was ordained in 1907. He taught science at the Instituto Massimo and the Gregorian, at both of which he served as rector. In 1921 he became president of the Pontifical Academy of Sciences, was chaplain of Umberto Nobile's dirigible expedition to the North Pole in 1928, and in 1930 left the Gregorian to become director of the Vatican radio station. He represented the Vatican at scientific conferences at Toronto, Madrid, and within the League of Nations. He died in Vatican City on July 9.

GIANNI, LAPO DEI RICEVUTI (13th century), poet. Born in Florence, Italy, where he became a notary, he was a friend of Dante and Guido Cavalcanti, and wrote a number of *ballate* and lyrics in the emotional and idealistic manner of love poetry then prevalent.

GIANNUZZI, GIULIO DEI. *See* Giulio Romano.

GIBARDUS, ST. (d. 888?). He and his monks at the Benedictine abbey of Luxeuil, France, were captured and put to death by invading Huns. F. D. Apr. 7.

GIBAULT, PIERRE (1737–1804?), missioner. Born in Montreal, Canada, he studied in Quebec, was ordained in 1768, and sent to missions in Illinois and Indiana, where, for a while, he was the only priest. He recommended that the inhabitants of Kaskaskia swear allegiance to Virginia when George Rogers Clark captured the settlement in 1778, went with the American army to Vincennes, and helped to win the allegiance of the settlers in that post and of many surrounding Indian tribes. In 1791 he retired to the Spanish area beyond the Mississippi where he probably died.

GIBBONS, JAMES (1834–1921), cardinal. Born in Baltimore on July 23, he was brought back to Ireland by his parents when three years old, returned to the United States in 1853, and entered the grocery business in New Orleans. He studied at St. Charles College, and St. Mary's seminary, Baltimore, and was ordained in Baltimore in 1861. He served in several parishes in the Baltimore area and as chaplain at nearby Fort McHenry, and in 1865 became secretary to Archbishop Spalding. He was assistant chancellor at the second Plenary Council of Baltimore in 1866, was appointed vicar apostolic of North Carolina and titular bishop of Adramyttium in 1868, and was the youngest bishop at the Vatican Council in 1870. He was appointed bishop of Richmond in 1872, titular bishop of Jonopolis and coadjutor of Baltimore in 1877, and succeeded to that see later the same year. He took an active interest in matters of public concern, was a friend of Presidents Cleveland, Theodore Roosevelt, and Taft, and throughout his career tirelessly preached the compatibility of Catholicism and American democracy, of which he was a vigorous proponent. He helped organize and presided as apostolic delegate at the third Plenary Council of Baltimore in 1884, the decrees of which did so much to shape the Catholic Church in the United States. He was an active supporter of an American Catholic University and served as chairman of its board of trustees until his death. In 1886 he was created the second American cardinal, and while in Rome was instrumental in dissuading the pope from condemning the Knights of Labor in the United States (after the Canadian hierarchy had done so in Canada) and later had the Canadian ban lifted. He voiced a belief in the efficacy of free discussion of labor and economic problems, particularly when he prevented ecclesiastical denunciation of Henry George's *Progress and Poverty*, supported Archbishop Ireland's educational experiments, and was the prime mover in defeating the plan to appoint bishops and establish parishes on the basis of national groups, declaring that the flood of immigrants should be assimilated into the American society as rapidly as possible. He helped settle the question of compensation for "friar lands" in the Philippines by the United States, which had annexed the islands after the Spanish-American War, fought socialism, and was president of the National Catholic War Council to co-ordinate Catholic activities during World War I. He wrote *Faith of Our Fathers* (1876), *Our Christian Heritage* (1889), *Ambassador of Christ* (1896), and *Retrospect of Fifty Years* (1916), among other books. He died in Baltimore on Mar. 24.

JOHN TRACY ELLIS, *The Life of James Cardinal Gibbons* (2 vols., Milwaukee, Bruce, 1952).

GIBBONS, JOHN (1544–1589), theologian. Born near Wells, Somersetshire, England, he studied at Oxford, took doctorates in philosophy and theology in Rome, became a canon of Bonn, and in 1578 a Jesuit at Trier. He taught and was rector at the college there, engaged in controversy with Lutherans and Calvinists, and wrote controversial works. He died on Aug. 16 at Himmelbrode monastery near Trier, Germany.

GIBBONS, FLOYD PHILLIPS (1887–1939), journalist. Born in Washington, D.C., on July 16, he studied at Gonzaga and Georgetown, then worked from 1907 to 1912 on newspapers in Milwaukee, Minneapolis, and Chicago, and established his name by reporting the 1914 war with Mexico for the *Tribune*. He was blinded in the left eye while serving as a war correspondent at Belleau Wood, France, and was head of the *Tribune's* foreign bureau from 1919 to 1927. He covered rebellions in Ireland, Germany, Russia, North Africa, and Spain, the Italian invasion of Ethiopia, and the beginnings of World War II in the Far

East; some of his accounts appeared in book form. He also was a radio commentator for the National Broadcasting Co. He died near Stroudsburg, Pennsylvania, on Sept. 24.

GIBBONS, RICHARD (1549?–1632), editor. Born in Winchester, England, brother of John, he studied in Louvain and Rome, became a Jesuit in 1572, taught mathematics and philosophy for twenty-three years in various countries, and held several offices. From 1610 until his death in Douai, France, on June 23 he translated, edited, and printed theological and scriptural studies, meditations on prayer, a history of the Church in England by Nicholas Harpsfield, and Bellarmine's *Christian Doctrine*.

GIBERT, JEAN PIERRE (1660–1736), canonist. Born in Aix, Provence, he became a cleric (but was not ordained), took his doctorate in theology at Aix, taught in the seminary there and in Toulouse, settled in Paris in 1703, and wrote significant works, sometimes marked by Gallicanism, on marriage, the sacraments, and the whole body of canon law. He died in Paris.

GIBERTI, GIAN MATTEO (1495–1543), cardinal. Natural son of Francesco Giberti, a naval officer, he was born in Palermo, Italy, served in the household of Cardinal Giulio de' Medici, and became a member of the Accademia Romana and the cardinal's secretary. He was an adviser to Pope Leo X, to whose attention he directed many literary figures. After his ordination he served on diplomatic missions, accompanied Pope Adrian VI to Rome, and was appointed datary by Clement VII and in 1524 bishop of Verona. He failed to establish peace between Francis I and Charles V, gained Clement's support for the French monarch, and fled Rome when the imperialist forces sacked it in 1527. Always a notably religious person, he now abandoned politics, completely reformed his see, gained the admiration of St. Charles Borromeo for his pre-Trent reforms, developed the choir school, set up a printing press which issued the Greek Fathers of the Church, and gathered a group of brilliant scholars in the city. He died in Verona, Italy, on Dec. 30.

GIBSON, HUGH S. (1883–1954), diplomat. Born in Los Angeles, California, on Aug. 16, he graduated from the École Libre des Science Politique, Paris, in 1907, entered the diplomatic service in 1908, and was secretary of the legation in Honduras, London, Havana, Brussels, and Paris until 1918. He was the first United States minister to Poland in 1919–24, minister to Switzerland in 1924–27, ambassador to Belgium in 1927–33 and 1937–38, to Brazil in 1933–37, and served as United States representative to numerous international conferences. He was European director of the Commissions for Polish Relief and for Belgium Relief in 1940–41. He wrote several books, among them *Rio* (1937), *Belgium* (1939), *The Road to Foreign Policy* (1944), and, with Herbert Hoover, *Problems of Lasting Peace*. He died in Geneva, Switzerland, on Dec. 12.

GIBSON, VEN. WILLIAM (d. 1596), martyr. *See* Knight, William.

GIESE, TIEDEMANN (d. 1549). A friend of Copernicus, he succeeded Johann von Höfer as bishop of Culm, Poland, in 1538, and continued the difficult task of saving the remnants of his flock from the inroads of Lutheranism.

GIFFARD, BONAVENTURE (1642–1734), bishop. Born in Wolverhampton, England, he studied in Douai and Paris, was ordained, took his doctorate at the Sorbonne, and became court preacher to King James II of England. Pope Innocent XI named him vicar of the Midlands and he was consecrated bishop in 1688. The king named him president of Magdalen College, Oxford, that year, in spite of the college electors' choice of John Hough, a Protestant. Early in 1689 he was removed, was imprisoned in Newgate for two years, then spent twenty-four years (often in hiding) serving his vicariate and that of the Western District as well. His brother Andrew (d. 1714) served as his vicar general. Bonaventure died in Hammersmith, England, on Mar. 12.

GIFFARD, GODFREY (1235?–1301), bishop. Born in Wiltshire, England, he served under his brother Walter, bishop of Bath and Wells, as canon and chancellor of the exchequer. When Walter became archbishop of York, Godfrey became chancellor of England; he also held numerous benefices, though only in minor orders, which his brother gave him, and in 1268 was elected bishop of Worcester. He remained chancellor until 1269 and bishop until his death in Worcester on Jan. 26. His reign was marked by several jurisdictional disputes; he built a church at Hartlebury, ornamented his cathedral, served as a respected justice, and bettered civil and criminal procedure in the courts.

GIFFORD, WILLIAM (1554–1629), bishop. Born in Hampshire, England, he studied at Oxford, Louvain, where he studied theology under Bellarmine, Paris, Rheims, and the English College in Rome. He was ordained in 1582, taught theology at Rheims for about twelve years, was chaplain to Cardinal Allen in Rome, dean of Lille from 1597 to about 1606, and rector of Rheims University in 1606–8. He then became a Benedictine as Fr. Gabriel of St. Mary, founded a community at St. Malo, was president of the English province in 1617, and coadjutor to Cardinal Louis de Lorraine of Rheims, whom he succeeded as archbishop, duke of Rheims, and first peer of the realm. He

wrote sermons, published controversial tracts and translations, and worked with Anthony Champney on *Protestant Ordinations* (1616). He died in Rheims, France, on Apr. 11.

GIGLIO, ALOISI (16th century). A native of Cirò, Calabria, Italy, he was professor of medicine at Perugia in 1552 and was the principal author of the Gregorian calendar. His manuscript on calendar reform was posthumously presented to the Roman curia by his brother in 1576; the new calendar received papal approval in 1581. His name is also written as Aloysius Lilius.

GIL DE ABORNOZ. *See* Abornoz, Gil de.

GIL, BL. FRANCISCO (1702–1744), martyr. Born in Tortosa, Spain, he became a Dominican in Barcelona, went to the Philippine missions and then to China, where he was captured, imprisoned for several years, and beheaded at Checo. He was beatified in 1906. F. D. Jan. 22.

GILBERT, ST. (d. 1152). He was abbot-founder of the Premonstratensian monastery of Neufontaines. F. D. June 6.

GILBERT, BL. (d. 1167). An Englishman, he became a Cistercian, probably at Ourscamp, France, where he was made abbot in 1147. He was transferred to Cîteaux in 1163 and became a noted theologian. F. D. Oct. 17.

GILBERT, BL. (d. 1185). A Benedictine monk at St. Crespin, Soissons, France, and second abbot of the monastery of Jean Baptiste, Valenciennes, he was persecuted by the count of Hainault. F. D. Aug. 21.

GILBERT, ST. (d. 1245), bishop. Born in Moray, Scotland, he became bishop of Caithness in 1223, and built asylums for the poor and a cathedral at Dornoch. F. D. Apr. 1.

GILBERT FOLIOT (d. 1186), bishop. Born of an Anglo-Norman family, he became a monk at Cluny, France, was prior there, and abbot in Abbeville and in Gloucester, England. In 1147 he became bishop of Hereford, was adviser to Archbishop Theobald of Canterbury, and in 1163 was transferred to the see of London. When the quarrel broke out between Thomas à Becket and Henry II, he sided with the king and was loud in his opposition to the renewal of the royal excommunication in 1170.

GILBERT, JOHN THOMAS (1829–1898), historian. Born in Dublin on Jan. 23, he studied there and in Prior Park, England, and from 1846 until his death on May 23 resided at Blackrock, a Dublin suburb. He was elected to the council of the Celtic Society at nineteen, published *Historical Literature of Ireland* in 1851, was a member of the Royal Irish Academy, and secretary of the Irish Archaeological Society. He published histories of Dublin, of the national public records, the Irish viceroys, the British campaign of 1641–49, and a seven-volume *Calendar of the Ancient Rec-*

ords of Dublin. He was librarian of the Royal Irish Academy for twenty-four years, and was knighted in 1894. He also published *History of the Viceroys of Ireland* (to 1500), *Calendar of the Ancient Records of Dublin 1641–49,* and a dozen other studies, editions, and compilations of records. He died in Dublin on May 23.

GILBERT DE LA PORRÉE (1076–1154), philosopher. Born in Poitiers, France, he studied under Hilary there, Bernard at Chartres, and Anselm at Laon, taught philosophy and the arts at Chartres for fifteen years, while serving as canon and at times as chancellor, taught at Paris in 1141, and became bishop of Chartres in 1142. His *Liber sex principiorum* on the six categories of Aristotle was a mediaeval textbook for three centuries; in other work he followed the rationalism of Abelard, and his commentary on Boethius and his *De Trinitate* he fell into difficulties which marked much writing at the beginnings of scholasticism. He carried his failure in distinguishing mental distinctions from real into theology; when reported for the novelty of his interpretation of the Trinity he debated the question with St. Bernard before Pope Eugene III at the councils of Paris (1147) and Rheims (1148), a dispute which ended amicably and without definite conclusion.

GILBERT, NICOLAS JOSEPH LAURENT (1751–1780), poet. Born in Fontenoy-le-Château, France, he studied in Dôle, went to Nancy and Paris, gained the patronage of the archbishop of Paris, and lived off the income of three pensions. He wrote a novel in the oriental style; a prose satire, *Le Carnaval des auteurs* (1773); several strong satires against the philosophers of his age, including *Mon apologie* (1778); and *Ode imitée de plusiers psaumes* (1788), which revealed traces of the forthcoming triumph of melancholy romanticism. He died in Paris on Nov. 12.

GILBERT, ROSA MULHOLLAND (d. 1921). Born in Belfast, Ireland, she wrote stories, a collection of poems, *Spirit and Dust,* and a life of her husband, Sir John Gilbert.

GILBERT OF SEMPRINGHAM, ST. (1083–1189), founder. Born in Sempringham, Lincolnshire, England, son of a Norman knight, he studied in France, became a priest, returned to receive several benefices from his father, and then became a clerk in the service of Bishop Robert Bloet of Lincoln and his successor, Alexander, who ordained Gilbert. He succeeded his father as lord of Sempringham in 1131. He served as adviser to a group of young women who lived as recluses in his parish, and soon had so many followers, laymen and laywomen, that he went to Cîteaux to offer the foundation to the Cistercians. They were unable to absorb it, and in 1147 Pope Eugenius III sug-

gested that St. Gilbert be a director. He added a group of canons regular, and the order flourished as the Gilbertines, which had twenty-six monasteries in England which were taken over at the time of Henry VIII. The order was strict, the nuns following the Rule of St. Benedict and the canons that of St. Augustine. In 1165 Gilbert was falsely imprisoned on the charge of supporting St. Thomas à Becket (then in exile), was cleared by King Henry VII, and in 1170 successfully overcame a revolt of lay-brothers. He continued to direct the order as master general until he lost his sight and named Roger of Manto to succeed him. His life was written by John Capgrave. He died in Sempringham, and was canonized in 1202 by Pope Innocent III. F. D. Feb. 16 (sometimes, Feb. 4).

GILDARD, ST. (d. 514?). He became bishop of Rouen, France, about 500. He is also called Godard. F. D. June 8.

GILDAS, ST. (500?–570?). Born in Scotland, and then an ascetic in Wales, he served in Britain for many years, writing his *De excidio Britanniae* (c. 540) on the moral degradation which he felt had despoiled that country, and trying for widespread reform. He later visited Ireland and finally settled as a hermit on an island off the coast of Brittany. F. D. Jan. 29.

GILES, ST. (d. 712?). He probably was a hermit from Provence who lived in a cave on the Rhône, around which grew up a monastery and of which he was abbot. Legend calls him an Athenian who, to avoid praise after he cured a cripple, went to Gaul as a hermit and impressed the Gothic king Flavius, who built him a monastery. He is one of the Fourteen Holy Helpers, and his shrine became one of the great popular pilgrimage centers of mediaeval Europe. He is a patron of cripples, beggars, and blacksmiths. F. D. Sept. 1.

GILES, BL. (d. 1203?). He was abbot of the Cistercian monastery of Castañeda, Spain, and noted as a confessor. F. D. Sept. 1.

GILES OF ASSISI, BL. (d. 1262). He followed Bernard and Peter as the third associate of St. Francis of Assisi, went on pilgrimages to Spain and the Holy Land and on an unsuccessful mission to Tunis, then lived at Fabriano, Rieti, and Perugia as a spiritual counselor to hundreds who sought his advice. He had numerous supernatural gifts and is spoken of at length in the *Fioretti*. F. D. Apr. 23.

GILES OF LORENZANA, BL. (1443?–1518). At first a hermit, he later became a Franciscan laybrother in Lorenzana, in the Kingdom of Naples. He received many supernatural gifts, and his cult was approved in 1880. F. D. Jan. 14.

GILES MARY OF ST. JOSEPH, BL. (1729–1812). Born near Taranto, Italy, he became at twenty-five a member of a Discalced Friars

Minor of St. Peter of Alcantara in Naples, and devoted himself to the care of the leprous poor of that city. He was beatified in 1888. F. D. Feb. 7.

GILES OF PORTUGAL, BL. (1185–1265). Born in Vaozela, Portugal, son of Rodrigues de Vagliaditos, governor of Coimbra, he became a necromancer in Toledo and for seven years lived a most dissolute life. He then went to Paris, became a physician, continued to practice sorcery, but reformed and became a Dominican friar at Valencia. A prayerful and penitential life was spent for the most part at Santarem, Portugal. F. D. May 14.

GILES OF ROME. *See* Colonna, Egidio.

GILES OF SAUMUR, BL. (d. 1266), archbishop. Chaplain of St. Louis, he accompanied the French king on his crusade, and became bishop of Damietta, Egypt, in 1243 and archbishop of Tyre, Syria, two years later. He died in Belgium. F. D. Apr. 23.

GILL, ARTHUR ERIC (1882–1940), sculptor. Born in Brighton, England, on Feb. 22, he studied there, at an art school in Chichester, and in 1899 under the architect, William Caröe, in London. He became interested in masonry, lettering, and engraving. He married Mary Moore in 1904, lived in London until 1907, then settled in Ditchling, Sussex. His first exhibition of sculpture, praised by Augustus John, was held in 1911. He became a convert in 1913, carved the stations of the cross for Westminster cathedral, war memorials, and the relief *Driving the Money Changers from the Temple* for Leeds University. He began illustrating the publications of St. Dominic's Press, Ditchling, and wrote essays for its magazine, *The Game.* He lived at Capel-y-ffin in 1924–28, carved a wooden altarpiece for Rossall School chapel, several marbles, and made engravings for the Golden Cockerel Press. He designed ten type faces, including Perpetua and Gill sans-serif. He published *Art-Nonsense* (1929) *Typography* (1931), and completed illustrations for the *Canterbury Tales,* his well-known *Four Gospels,* and sculpture for Broadcast House. Between 1936 and 1938 he visited Jerusalem, carved ten panels for the Palestine Museum, did the relief *Creation of Adam* for the League of Nations council hall in Geneva, and published *The Necessity of Belief.* He became a member of the Royal Academy and received an honorary degree from Edinburgh. In his writings he defended responsibility and craftsmanship, and attacked puritanism, emotionalism, and commercialism. He died of a lung ailment in Harefield, England, on Nov. 17.

ERIC GILL, *Autobiography* (New York, Devin-Adair, 1940).

GILLEBERT (d. 1140), bishop. Educated at Bangor, Ireland, he traveled through Europe, met St. Anselm at Rouen, and perhaps through the influence of the latter became bishop of Limerick and apostolic delegate to Ireland. He introduced liturgical reforms in interest of unity, presided at the Synod of Rathbreasail in 1118, and resigned as legate in 1139.

GILLESPIE, ELIZA MARIA (1824–1887), educator. Born in Washington County, Pennsylvania, on Feb. 21, she was brought up in Lancaster, Ohio, studied in Washington, D.C., was active in the society of the Ohio and national capitals, and in 1853 became a Sister of Holy Cross, as Sr. Mary of St. Angela. She studied in France, was made superior of St. Mary's Academy, Bertrand, Michigan (later transferred to Notre Dame, Indiana), organized a corps of nursing sisters during the Civil War, and set up a hospital in Cairo, Illinois. In 1869 the Sisters of Holy Cross became independent of the French congregation and Mother Angela was named first superior. She compiled two series of readers for elementary schools, established thirty-five communities of her order, and helped to found *Ave Maria* in 1865. She died in St. Mary's, Indiana, on Mar. 4.

GILLESPIE, NEAL HENRY (1831–1874), educator. Brother of Eliza, he was born in Pennsylvania, on Jan. 19, graduated in 1849 with the first class from Notre Dame University, became a member of the Congregation of Holy Cross in 1853, and was ordained in Rome in 1856. He was vice-president of Notre Dame in 1856–59, then president of the College of St. Mary of the Lake, Chicago, until 1863, and was stationed at Le Mans, France, to 1866. On his return he served as editor of *Ave Maria* until his death in Notre Dame, Indiana, on Nov. 12.

GILLET, STANISLAUS (1875–1951), theologian. Born in Louppy-sur-Loison, Meuse, France, on Dec. 14, he became a Dominican, taking the name Martin, and was ordained in 1902. He took his doctorate at Fribourg, taught moral theology at Louvain and Saulchoir, and after service in World War I became professor of philosophy at L'Institut Catholique, Paris. During his stay from 1921 to 1927 he translated the *Summa* into French, helped edit *Revue des jeunes,* then became provincial, and was master general of his order from 1929 to 1946. He found a new home in Rome for the Pontifical Institute of the Angelicum, restored the basilica of St. Sabina, and established the Dominican Historical and Liturgical Institute, a new training school, and the commission for the Leonine edition of St. Thomas Aquinas. He was named titular archbishop of Nicaea and consultor of the Congregation of the Holy Office and of Studies in 1946. He wrote on education, social justice, moral theology, SS. Dominic and Catherine of Siena, and on Paul Valéry. Translated volumes are *Education and Character, Innocence and Ignorance,* and *St. Thomas Aquinas.* He died in Rome on Sept. 4.

GILLIS, JAMES (1802–1864), bishop. Born in Montreal, Canada, on Apr. 7, he studied in Montreal, went to Scotland in 1816, studied in seminaries there and in France, and was ordained in 1827. He was stationed in Edinburgh, collected funds in France for the establishment of an Ursuline convent, the first religious house begun in Scotland since the sixteenth century, and in 1838 was consecrated as titular bishop of Limyra. In 1852 he became vicar apostolic of the Eastern District, introduced many religious orders to Edinburgh, preached frequently in France, and died in Edinburgh on Feb. 24.

GILLIS, JAMES MARTIN (1876–1957). Born in Boston, Massachusetts, on Nov. 12, he studied at St. Charles College, Maryland, St. John's seminary, Boston, and after he joined the Paulists in 1898 at St. Thomas College and Catholic University. He was ordained in 1901, and taught at St. Paul's until 1910, when he was appointed to the mission band. He spent the next dozen years in missionary work and in 1922 became editor of the *Catholic World.* He was popular as a preacher and his editorials in the *Catholic World,* a widely syndicated newspaper column, his books, and radio programs on the "Catholic Hour" made him highly influential. Ill the last years of his life, he resigned as editor of the *Catholic World* in 1948, and died in New York City on Mar. 14.

GILLOW, JOSEPH (1850–1921), historian. Born in Hale, England, he studied at Ushaw and wrote a series of studies of post-Reformation Catholicism, including the five-volume *Biographical Dictionary of English Catholics* (1885–1902), *Lancashire Recusants,* catalogues of martyrs, and studies of missions. He helped to found the Catholic Record Society and served as a member of the Manchester school board. He died in Hale on Mar. 17.

GILMORE, PATRICK SARSFIELD (1829–1892), musician. Born in Ballygar, Galway, Ireland, on Dec. 25, he went to Boston, Massachusetts, in 1848, organized bands in that city and Salem, and served during the Civil War with Gen. Burnside in South Carolina. In 1869 and 1872 he organized the national and international peace jubilees in Boston, directing 2000 musicians and 10,000 singers. In 1873 he became director of the 22nd Regiment band in New York City, where he played at Gilmore's Garden (later called Madison Square Garden); toured Europe in 1878 with a band under his own name; and in 1892 toured the United States. He was the first to balance brass with reeds, and composed many marches and popular songs. He died in St. Louis on Sept. 24.

GILMOUR, RICHARD (1824–1891), bishop.

Born in Glasgow, Scotland, on Sept. 28, he was brought to America by his parents when a child, became a convert in 1842, studied at St. Michael's seminary, Pittsburgh, and Mt. St. Mary's, Maryland, and was ordained in Cincinnati in 1852. He engaged in pastoral and missionary work in Ohio, taught at Mt. St. Mary's of the West, Cincinnati, in 1868, and after a pastorate at St. Joseph's church, Dayton, was appointed bishop of Cleveland in 1872. He fought anti-Catholicism in his diocese, was a vigorous proponent of Catholic education, and successfully fought attempts to tax school property, founded the weekly diocesan paper, the *Catholic Universe,* in 1874, was embroiled with several religious communities over his demands their property be held by the bishop and with some of his clergy over his strict discipline, and was a firm adherent of the independence of the American hierarchy. He wrote a successful series, *Catholic National Readers* (1874–89) and *Bible History* (1869). He died in St. Augustine, Florida, on Apr. 13.

GIMARRA, BL. MATTEO (d. 1450), bishop. Born in Girgenti, Sicily, he joined the Franciscan Conventuals but, attracted by St. Bernardino of Siena, whose close friend he became, moved over to the Observants. With St. Bernardino he traveled over Italy and became famed for his preaching and denunciation of simony, religious indifference, and other evils of the day. Despite his unwillingness, Pope Eugenius IV appointed him bishop of Girgenti (he is also known as Matteo of Girgenti); his reforms led to bitter denunciations, but the pope supported him. Eventually, opposition led him to resign his see. He died in the Conventual house at Palermo, Sicily. His cult was confirmed in 1767. F. D. Oct. 21 (also, Feb. 3).

GINOULHIAC, JACQUES MARIE ACHILLE (1806–1875), bishop. Born in Montpellier, Hérault, France, he was ordained there in 1830, taught in its seminary, was named vicar general of Aix in 1839, and in 1853 was consecrated bishop of Grenoble. He opposed the dogma of papal infallibility at the Vatican Council and left Rome before the session which defined it. In 1870 his see was transferred to Lyons, where he began the shrine of the Virgin Mary at Fourvières. He wrote against Renan's life of Christ and the contemporary journalistic attacks on the papacy and the *Syllabus,* a history of dogma up to the Council of Nicaea, on the Pauline epistles, the sermon on the mount, and *Le concile oecuménique,* and *Les origines du christianisme.* He died in Montpellier on Nov. 17.

GIOCONDO, GIOVANNI (1435?–1525?), architect. Born in Verona, Italy, he became a Dominican at eighteen, and later a Franciscan. He was ordained, taught classics in Verona, with Scaliger as a pupil, wrote on the antiquities of Rome, and sketched its ancient manuscripts as an early leader of Renaissance culture. Returning to Treviso from Rome, he built bridges and planned defenses, designed the Palazzo del Consiglio in Verona in 1476, and at Venice planned methods of protecting the canals from the sea. In 1496–99 he was architect to the king of France, designed bridges, decorated interiors, and built the château de Gaillon, Normandy. He edited a manuscript of Pliny the Younger which he discovered, returned to Venice to write on its waterways, built the Fondaco dei Tedeschi in 1508, replanned the Rialto after it was burned in 1513, went to Rome, and after Bramante's death helped to supervise the building of St. Peter's. He also edited Caesar's *Commentaries*, Cato's *De re rustica*, Vitruvius, and others. He died in Rome on July 1.

GIORDANO, LUCA (1632–1705), painter. Born in Naples, Italy, he studied under Ribera at thirteen and Pietro da Cortona, in Rome, copied the works of earlier masters, completed work in churches in Naples and Florence, covered the ceiling and stair well of the Escorial in Madrid, working there and in Toledo from 1692 to 1702, then returned to Naples, where he died on Jan. 12. He worked in pastel-made etchings, and turned out so many paintings and at such a pace that he was called Luca Fa Presto ("make haste"). He completed a *St. Francis Xavier Baptizing Indians* in less than two days and his *Story of Judith* for the Tesoro di San Martino, Naples, in forty-eight hours. Others are on biblical and mythological themes.

GIORDANO DI SAN STEFANO. *See* Ansaloni, Giordano.

GIORDANO, TOMASSO (1738–1806), composer. Born in Naples, Italy, he went to London in 1752 and to Dublin in 1754, and was a leading musician in the latter city from 1764 until his death, except for two years (1781–83) in London. He ran a music shop, wrote several operas, an oratorio, *Isaac* (1767), overtures, sonatas, concertos, and songs. He was organist in the cathedral from 1784 to 1798.

GIORGIONE (1478?–1510), painter. Born in Castelfranco, Italy, he probably was the child of Treviso peasants. He and Titian studied together in Venice under Giovanni Bellini; he became a successful lutist and singer, mixed in Venetian society, and painted portraits of the great. He was one of the first to paint landscapes with figures, used color intensely, avoided the instructive scene, and maintained that the painter's primary purpose is decorative effect. He painted in tempera, glazed the result in oil, and achieved striking and lasting effects in this manner. He painted altarpieces, decorated furniture, covered the fronts of houses, including the Fondaco dei Tedeschi, with fresco, and produced many works whose authenticity has

not been established. He himself has often been taken for Titian, and a flood of imitations by the "school of Giorgione" has added to the confusion. Among his pupils were del Piombo, Pordenone, and Palma Vecchio. His *Madonna and Child, with SS. Liberale and Francis* was hailed by John Ruskin; *The Chaldean Sages, Judgment of Solomon, Trial of Moses, Christ Bearing the Cross, Madonna and Child, Knight of Malta, The Concert,* and *Fête Champêtre* are among his most admired works. He died in Venice, probably during the Sept.–Nov. plague.

GIOTTINO (1324?–1357), painter. He did work in the church of Santa Chiara, Assisi, and completed a life of St. Nicholas in the lower church in that town. He also is very likely the Giottino who did an *Adoration, Crucifixion,* and *Deposition,* and the legend of Pope Sylvester and Constantine in Santa Croce, Florence. He is probably the same as Giottodi Maestro Stefano (or Tommaso di Stefano) listed in the Florentine guild register and the Masodi Banco whom Vasari lists as a pupil of Ciotto.

GIOTTO (1266?–1337), painter. Giotto di Bondone was born in Vespignano, near Florence, Italy, and grew up in the world of Jacopo Torriti, Duccio, and the Pisanos, but nothing is known of his career until he went to Assisi in 1294, possibly as a follower of Cimabue. He was commissioned by Giovanni de Mura, general of the Franciscans, to do twenty-eight scenes from the life of St. Francis for the upper church at Assisi. Giotto completed twenty-one (the others were finished by his pupils) and introduced detailed realism in the figures and backgrounds, contemporary events, customs, scenery, dress, interiors, and figures. Biographical details were carefully followed from St. Bonaventure's life. In 1298, Giotto went to Rome and executed mosaics of the life of Christ for the vestibule and choir of St. Peter's and of the baptism of Constantine for the Lateran basilica, which have since been destroyed. He probably went to Florence in 1301, painted a *Last Judgment* for the Podestà chapel in which he portrayed Dante and other Florentines in a hierarchy of recent society. He did scenes from the life of the Virgin and of Christ at Padua and more frescoes for the lower church at Assisi, notably the *Triumph of St. Francis* in the roof groin over the altar. He settled in Florence in 1320, decorated many chapels and churches, became master of municipal construction, and drew the designs for the campanile in 1334. He had a lasting influence on the art of the North, had many followers and imitators, and also was known as a poet and satirist. He died in Milan, Italy, on Jan. 8.

GIOVANELLI, RUGGIERO (1560–1625), composer. Born in Velletri, Italy, he became choirmaster of San Luigi de Francesi, Rome, in 1584, then of the Chiesa dell' Anima. He published six books of madrigals and one of canzonets and villanelles between 1585 and 1606. He succeeded Palestrina in 1594 and wrote numerous masses. He died on Jan. 7.

GIOVANNA OF ORVIETO, ST. (d. 1306). Orphaned at five and adopted by an Italian family, she ran away from Orvieto, Italy, to avoid an arranged marriage and became a Dominican tertiary. She devoted herself to the poor and experienced a number of supernatural manifestations. Her cult was approved in 1754. F. D. July 23.

GIOVIO, PAOLO (1483–1552), bishop. Born in Como, Italy, on Apr. 8, he studied medicine at Padua and practiced in Rome. He became interested in history and so favorably impressed Pope Leo X, to whom he read part of his *Historiarum sui temporis* (1494–1544), that he was appointed professor at the Roman College. In 1528, Clement VII named him bishop of Nocera, but he returned to Como in 1543, where he built a palatial villa and became an avid art collector, then went to Florence, where he died on Dec. 11. He also wrote *Vitae virorum bellica virtute illustrium*. He is also known as Paulus Jovius.

GIRALD, ST. (d. 1031). A Benedictine monk at Lagny, France, he became abbot of St. Arnoul and later of Fontenelle, where he was murdered by a rebellious monk. He is also called Giraud. F. D. Dec. 29.

GIRALDI, GIOVANNI BATTISTA (1504–1573). Born in Ferrara, Italy, he studied philosophy and medicine there, served as secretary of state to the dukes of Ferrara, then taught at Mondovi, Turin, and Pavia. When he became a member of the Accademia delle Affidati he took the name Cintio or Cinthio (under which he is best known) and wrote *Gli hecatommiti* (1565), a hundred tales, two of which became sources of Shakespeare's *Othello* and *Measure for Measure*. He wrote a pastoral drama, *Egle*, an epic, *Ercole*, a comedy, *Eudemoni*, nine tragedies, including *Didone*, *Cleopatra*, *Selene*, and *Orbecche*, and a critical study of epic, romance, and drama. He died in Ferrara, Italy.

GIRALDI, UBALDO (1692–1775), canonist. Born in Italy, he became a Piarist, twice served as general counselor, was provincial at Rome, and rector of his congregation's college there. He published an edition of canon law by Remy Maschat; texts of the decretals and findings at the Council of Trent, with a brief commentary; and a new edition of Barbosa's work on parish clergy.

GIRALDUS CAMBRENSIS (1147?–1220?), historian. Gerald de Barri was born in Manorbeer, Pembrokeshire, England, of a Norman family, educated by his uncle, bishop of St. David's, Wales, and studied in Paris. He was or-

dained, probably in 1172, became archdeacon of Brecknock and a strict disciplinarian, was named to succeed his uncle, but passed over for a royal favorite, and retired to Paris from 1176 to 1180. He went with Prince John to Ireland in 1184; wrote *Topographia Hibernica* and *Expugnatio Hibernica*, partly accurate in description and narrative, but heavily marked by legend; then toured Wales in 1188 with Archbishop Baldwin of Canterbury to preach the crusade; out of this came *Itinerarium Cambriae*. He several times attempted to gain the see of St. David's, twice taking his case to Rome, but failed, and eventually resigned his archdiaconate to study. Although of slight historical and social value, his chronicles had an effect on English literature; Gerald also wrote saints' lives, *Speculum ecclesiae*, and a catalogue of his library.

GIRARD, JEAN BAPTISTE (1765–1850), educator. Born in Fribourg, Switzerland, on Dec. 17, he became a Franciscan in Lucerne at sixteen, studied and was ordained at Würzburg, did missionary work and taught in Fribourg from 1789 to 1799, and outlined a plan for Swiss education for the ministry of arts and sciences at Berne. He returned to Fribourg in 1804, was director of its schools from 1807 to 1823, introduced compulsory education, discarding memorization as a method, and became an admirer of Pestalozzi, whom he met. The Church and civil authorities objected to Girard's monitorial system, and he left to teach philosophy in Lucerne. He returned to Fribourg in 1834 and wrote on history, language teaching, and recommendations for the use of the concrete example. He died in Fribourg on Mar. 6.

GIRARDON, FRANÇOIS (1628–1715), sculptor. Born in Troyes, France, he studied under François Anguier, then in Rome, and returned to serve Louis XIV, working under Lebrun. He became professor of the academy of sculpture and later its chancellor, followed the style of Bernini, carved an equestrian statue of the king for the Place Vendôme, a sarcophagus of Richelieu in the Sorbonne church, a bust of Boileau, several monuments of contemporary figures, allegorical designs, and mythological groupings. He died in Paris.

GIRAUD DE BORNEIL (1160?–1219?), poet. Born in Limoges, France, he became a troubadour, studied under the great teachers of the period each winter, and with two singers toured the courts of his royal patrons during the summer. He was influenced by Arnaud Daniel, wrote a number of dawn songs, some political satires, and pastorals; Dante called him one of the three greatest troubadours.

GIRAUD. See Girald, St.

GIRLANI, BL. ELEANORA (1460–1494). Born in Trino, Italy, she became a Carmelite at Parma, as Sr. Archangela, when seventeen.

She served as prioress there and founded a new convent at Mantua. Her cult was confirmed in 1864. F. D. Feb. 13.

GISBERT, BLAISE (1657–1731), critic. Born in Cahors, France, on Feb. 21, he became a Jesuit in 1672, was famous as a preacher, and spent ten years in writing *Le bon goût de l'éloquence chrétienne* (1702), which was widely translated. He also wrote comments on the preachers in France in the century before Bossuet. He died in Montpellier, France, on Feb. 21.

GISLAR, ST. (7th century). *See* Chuniald, St.

GISLENUS, ST. (d. 680?). A French hermit, he founded a Benedictine monastery (now St. Ghislain) about 650 in Hainault, near Mons, where he directed many followers for thirty years. According to legend, he came from Attica. F. D. Oct. 9.

GIULIANI, ST. URSULA (1660–1727). Born in Mercatello, Italy, she showed signs of unusual piety while quite young and vowed to become a nun, which she did in 1677 at the Capuchin convent of Città di Castello, in Umbria, taking the name Veronica. She experienced visions, the stigmata, and many other supernatural gifts, all attested by eyewitnesses. She served as mistress of novices for thirty-four years, was elected abbess in 1716, and was canonized in 1839. F. D. July 9.

GIULIO ROMANO (1492–1546), painter. Giulio del Giannuzzi (also known as Giulio Pippi) was born in Rome, studied under Raphael at nineteen, and in 1519 assisted his master in excavating the ancient city and other undertakings. He is said to have had little originality or insight, and filled in or enlarged many of the sketches Raphael made for his work between 1513 to 1521; his violent speed, poor coloring, and imperfect workmanship are said to have spoiled the *Transfiguration* and made the *Battle of Constantine* and *Coronation of the Virgin* almost unrecognizable as Raphael's design. From 1522 to 1546 he directed artistic creation in Mantua at the invitation of Duke Federigo Gonzaga and introduced his dilettantism, commonplace pagan fables, and poor imitations of Michelangelo's grandeur in decorations for the ducal palace. As an architect he refashioned the cathedral, the church of San Benedetto to the south, and the Palazzo del Tè, outside the city walls. He decorated his residence with the *Story of Psyche* and the *Fall of the Giants*, called realistic, brassy, and antiquarian by critics. He did an *Adoration of the Magi, Madonna del Catina*, and frescoes for Sant' Andrea in his later years. Before he could accept an appointment as chief architect of St. Peter's, he died on Nov. 1, of plague contracted while draining the Mantuan marshes.

GIUNTA PISANO (1202?–1258), painter.

He worked at Pisa, Italy, before Cimabue, designed a crucifix and a *Crucifixion*, produced work marked by dramatic, though exaggerated, action, and may have done the frescoes in the right transept of the upper church in Assisi sometimes attributed to Cimabue.

GIUSTI, GIUSEPPE (1809–1850), poet. Born in Monsumano, near Pescia, Italy, he studied in Florence and at Pisa, took his degree in law in 1834, traveled through Italy for his health, wrote some poetry, and became a member of the Accademia della Crusca. He served as a deputy in the first and second Tuscan assemblies, opposing Austrian encroachment. He published love lyrics in the Petrarchan tradition; strong political satires; *Fiducia in Dio*, in which he set down his religious beliefs; and an edition of Tuscan proverbs. He died in Florence, Italy, of tuberculosis, on Mar. 31.

GIUSTIANI, BL. PAOLO (1476–1528). Born in Venice, Italy, he became a Camaldolese Benedictine, established the new congregation of Monte Corona, and wrote extensively. F. D. June 28.

GIUSTINI, FILIPPO (1852–1920), cardinal. Born in Cinete Romano, Italy, on May 8, he taught canon law at the Roman seminary in 1878, was auditor of the rota in 1897, was secretary of the Holy Office and other Vatican commissions, and from 1904 to 1917 of the Commission of Canon Law. He was named cardinal-deacon in 1914 and died in Rome on Mar. 17.

GIUSTINIANI, ST. LORENZO (1381–1455), patriarch. Born of a noble Venetian family, he early practiced severe mortifications and penances. At nineteen he joined the canons regular of St. George in Alga, was ordained in 1406, and soon after was made provost and devoted himself to teaching religion and to preaching. In 1433 he was appointed bishop of Castello and gained a reputation for humility and generosity to the poor, sick, and needy. In 1451, Pope Nicholas V named him patriarch of Venice. He wrote treatises on mystical contemplation, among them *The Degree of Perfection*, finished shortly before his death on Sept. 8. He was canonized in 1690. F. D. Sept. 5.

GLADYS, ST. (6th century). Wife of St. Gundleus, a rough Welsh chieftain, she became the mother of St. Cadoc, who reformed his parents and persuaded them to live in spiritual retirement during their last years. F. D. Mar. 29.

GLAIRE, JEAN BAPTISTE (1798–1879). Born in Bordeaux, France, on Apr. 1, he studied there and at St. Sulpice, Paris, was ordained in 1822, and taught Hebrew at this seminary, and then at the Sorbonne. He was dean of the faculty from 1841 to his retirement in 1851. He wrote a Hebrew and Chaldaic lexicon and grammar, biblical studies, and a translation of the New Testament. He died in Issy, France, on Feb. 25.

GLAPHYRA, ST. (d. 324?), martyr. A slave of Constantia, wife of Emperor Licinius, she fled to protect her chastity and sought refuge with St. Basil, bishop of Caesarea, but was recaptured, condemned to death, and died on the way to her execution. F. D. Jan. 13.

GLAREAN, HENRY. *See* Loriti, Heinrich.

GLASS, JOSEPH SARSFIELD (1874–1926), bishop. Born in Bushnell, Illinois, on Mar. 13, he graduated from St. Vincent's College, Los Angeles, in 1869, joined the Congregation of the Mission of St. Vincent de Paul (Vincentians) in 1891, continued his studies at St. Mary's seminary, Missouri, and the Minerva, Rome, and was ordained in Los Angeles in 1897. He taught theology at St. Mary's and was president of St. Vincent's College, Los Angeles, from 1901 to 1911 and pastor of St. Vincent's church there from 1901 to 1915, when he was consecrated bishop of Salt Lake City, Utah. He was one of the four bishop directors of the National Catholic War Council during World War I, and died in Los Angeles on Jan. 26.

GLASTIAN, ST. (d. 830), bishop. He was able to lessen the suffering of the Picts after their subjugation by the Scots, and is honored as patron of Kinglassie in Fife, Scotland, on Jan. 28.

GLEB. *See* Boris, St.

GLENNON, JOHN JOSEPH (1862–1946), cardinal. Born in Kinnegad, Westmeath, Ireland, on June 14, son of a naturalized American citizen, he studied at St. Mary's, Mullingar, and All Hallows, Dublin, went to the United States in 1883, and was ordained in Kansas City, Missouri, in 1884. After pastoral work there, he continued his studies at Bonn, was stationed at the Kansas City cathedral on his return in 1888, became vicar general in 1892, and administered the diocese in 1894–96. He was appointed titular bishop of Pinara and coadjutor of Kansas City in 1896, was transferred to St. Louis as coadjutor in 1903, and succeeded to that see as archbishop later the same year. He laid the cornerstone for his cathedral (it was consecrated three months after his death) in 1908, built Kenrick seminary in 1913–15, erected forty-seven new parishes during his forty-three-year episcopate, and directed the expansion of secondary-school education. He encouraged a colonization program and encouraged the National Catholic Rural Life Movement, was one of the founders of the National Catholic War Council (which later was transformed into the National Catholic Welfare Conference), and labored to integrate the various nationalities in his see into the American way of life. He was appointed assistant at the pontifical throne in 1921, and was created a cardinal in 1946, but died in Dublin nineteen days later, on Mar. 9, while returning from Rome.

GLODESINDIS, ST. (d. 608?). When her courtier husband was arrested and slain on their wedding day, she became a nun at a convent at Metz, France, and later served as abbess. F. D. July 25.

GLORIEUX, ALPHONSUS JOSEPH (1844–1917), bishop. Born in Dottignies, Belgium, on Feb. 1, he studied there and at Courtrai College and Louvain, and was ordained in 1867, did missionary work in Oregon, was head of St. Michael's College, Portland, from 1871 to 1885, and was consecrated second vicar apostolic of Idaho and titular bishop of Apollonia in 1885. He became first bishop of Boise, Idaho, in 1893, and reigned there until his death in Portland, Oregon, on Aug. 25.

GLUCK, CHRISTOPH WILLIBALD VON (1714–1787), composer. Born in Neumarkt, Upper Palatinate, on July 2, he studied in Kommontav, Bohemia, and in Prague, sang in church choirs, and earned a living with his violin. In 1736 he was asked to join the private orchestra of Prince Melzi, who shortly sent him to Milan to study under Sammartini. His first opera was *Artaserse* (1741); seven others produced in northern Italy were also successful. He was a failure in a brief excursion to London in 1745–46, came to know Rameau's work during a stay in Paris in 1747, then developed as a serious student of music and language. He married Marianna Pergin in Vienna in 1750 and in five years wrote eight operas and a cantata. For his *Antigono* (1756) he was ennobled as a chevalier. His next works were comparative failures, but he changed the usual course of musical history by becoming successful at the close of his career. *Orfeo ed Euridice* (1762), *Alceste* (1767), and *Paride ed Elena* (1770), all with libretti by Calzabigi, were followed by *Iphigénie en Aulide*, which he wrote in French in 1772 and produced in Vienna. It was produced in Paris in 1774, gained the support of and a pension from Marie Antoinette, but became the center of a quarrel over the values of operas of various national origins. Gluck returned to Vienna in 1775 and died there on Nov. 15. He also composed overtures, a concerto, several hymns, music for songs by Klopstock and others, and an uncompleted cantata, *Le Jugement dernier*.

GLYCERIA, ST. (d. 177?), martyr. She was put to death at Heraclea, in Greece, where a church was later built in her honor and was a popular seventh-century shrine. F. D. May 13.

GLYCERIUS, ST. (d. 303), martyr. A priest, he was burned to death at Nicomedia during the Diocletian persecution. F. D. Dec. 21.

GLYCERIUS, ST. (d. 438?). He was archbishop of Milan, Italy. F. D. Sept. 20.

GLYNN, MARTIN H. (1871–1924), governor. Born in Kinderhook, New York, he studied at Fordham, became managing editor of the Albany *Times-Union* in 1895, was admitted to the bar in 1897, was a representative at Washington (1899–1901), controller of the state (1906–8), and was elected lieutenant governor in 1912. He was acting governor during the impeachment proceedings against William Sulzer and completed the latter's term when the governor was convicted in 1913. Glynn was defeated in the campaign of 1914, was temporary chairman of the Democratic National Convention in 1916, served on the Federal Industrial Committee in 1919–20, and acted as liaison between Prime Minister Lloyd George of England and Eamon de Valera in helping to settle the Irish rebellion. He died in Albany, New York, on Dec. 14.

GNOFFI, BL. GUILERMO (d. 1317?). A native of Polizzi, Italy, he became a hermit, beggar, and then a solitary dedicated to great austerity. F. D. Apr. 16.

GOAR, ST. (d. 575?). Born in Aquitaine, he worked for years as a parish priest, then decided to become a hermit near Oberwesel, on the Rhine River. Other details are legendary. F. D. July 6.

GOAR, JACQUES (1601–1653), scholar. Born in Paris, he became a Dominican there in 1619, was sent to the East to study Greek theology and documents, was prior of St. Sebastian, Chios, from 1631 to 1639, and worked closely with Orthodox scholars. He returned to Rome with valuable manuscripts in 1640 and to Paris in 1643. He wrote widely on Greek liturgy and prepared editions of Theophanes and others. He was vicar provincial at Paris when he died on Sept. 23.

GOBAN, ST. (d. 670?), martyr. He became a Benedictine under St. Fursey in Suffolk, England, went to France, built a church and hermitage near Prémontré, and was slain by German marauders at what is now St. Gobain, France. F. D. June 20.

GOBAT, GEORGE (1600–1679), theologian. Born in Charmoilles, France, on July 1, he became a Jesuit in 1618, taught in Fribourg, Halle, Munich, Ratisbon, and Constance from 1631 to 1660, and was rector at both Halle and Fribourg. He wrote on indulgences, the sacraments, and *Disputationes in Aristotelem*. His leniency was papally condemned in 1679 and his *Opera moralia* (1701) was censured by the bishop of Arras. He died in Constance, Switzerland, where he was penitentiary of the cathedral, on Mar. 23.

GOBBAN SAER (560?–645?), architect. Born in Turvey, Dublin, Ireland, he built churches and bell towers in many parts of Ireland, in wood and stone, and was the center of much legendary comment.

GOBELINUS, PERSONA (1358–1421), historian. Born in Westphalia, he studied at Paderborn and Italy, became a minor official in the papal court under Urban VI, was ordained in 1386, returned to Paderborn, and studied science at Erfurt. He was chaplain to Bishop Wilhelm von Berg, reformed monasteries against some opposition, and was made dean of Bielefeld, where he labored for at least twelve years. He wrote a life of St. Meinolf of Paderborn and *Cosmidromius*, a universal chronicle, of particular value for firsthand reports on the years 1347–1418. He retired in that year to the monastery of Böddeken, near Paderborn, Westphalia, where he died on Nov. 17.

GOBERT, BL. (d. 1263). Count of Apremont, he fought in Palestine as a crusader, then became a Cistercian at Villiers, Brabant. F. D. Aug. 20.

GOBNATA, ST. (6th century). She is said to have ruled a convent at Ballyvourney, Cork, Ireland; a holy well there remained a place of pilgrimage. F. D. Feb. 11.

GOBRIAN, ST. (725). A monk in Brittany, he became bishop of Vannes, Gaul, and retired at eighty-seven to become a recluse. F. D. Nov. 16.

GODARD. *See* Gildard, St.; also, Gothard, St.

GODDEN, THOMAS. *See* Tylden, Thomas.

GODEAU, ANTOINE (1605–1672), bishop. Born in Dreux, France, he early established a reputation as a poet, was one of the first members of the French Academy, moved to Paris, and became a literary dictator at the Hôtel Rambouillet. He published a critical study of Malherbe (1629), metrical paraphrases of the Psalms, religious poems, and a verse history of the Church in 15,000 lines. His poetry was hostilely criticized by Boileau. His prose history of the Church was marked by frequent errors; he also wrote saints' lives, prayers, meditations, on the Eucharist, an important philosophical attack on the casuists, and valuable prose paraphrases of the New Testament. In 1636 he was appointed bishop of Grasse by Richelieu, became a model prelate, and transferred to Vence, France, where he died on Apr. 21. He played an important part in the general assembly of the clergy in 1645 and in 1655.

GODEBERTA, ST. (640?–700?). Born in Amiens, France, she accepted a residence at Noyon from King Clotaire III, and presided over twelve girls who entered religious life with her. St. Eligius wrote their rule. F. D. Apr. 11.

GODEFRIDUS DE FONTIBUS. *See* Godfrey of Fontaines.

GODEHARD. *See* Gothard, St.

GODET DES MARAIS, PAUL (1647–1709), bishop. Born in Talcy, near Blois, France, he studied in St. Sulpice, Paris, took his doctorate at the Sorbonne, was ordained, served as superior of the Séminaire des Trente-trois, and became bishop of Chartres in 1692. He was spiritual director to Mme. de Maintenon, for whom he wrote *Lettres de direction*, and opposed quietism, Jansenism, and the pseudo-mysticism of Fénelon and Mme. Guyon in books and pastoral letters. He died in Chartres, France.

GODFREY, ST. (1065–1115), bishop. Born in the province of Soissons, France, he was sent at five to the abbey of Mont St. Quentin, where he became a Benedictine monk and was ordained. He was sent to Nogent, Champagne, in 1096 as abbot, rebuilt it as a flourishing monastery, refused the abbacy of St. Remi, and in 1104 was appointed bishop of Amiens. He restored strict discipline to his diocese, fought simony and incontinence among the clergy, and led a life of great austerity. F. D. Nov. 8.

GODFREY OF BOUILLON (1060–1100), king. Born probably in Boulogne-sur-mer, France, he was the son of Count Eustache II of Boulogne and Ida, daughter of Duke Godfrey the Bearded of Lower Lorraine. He succeeded his uncle, Godfrey the Hunchback, as duke of Lower Lorraine in 1076, lost the territory to Henry IV, but had it returned to him in 1089 after he had served the French king in the war over investitures and had invaded Italy against Pope Gregory VII. In 1096 he answered the call of Pope Urban II for a crusade, and led an army of 40,000 Flemings and Walloons under amazingly strict discipline as far as Constantinople. Emperor Alexius sought to keep Godfrey from meeting the Norman-Italian force of Bohemond, cut off the crusaders' supplies, apparently defeated Godfrey in battle, and forced him to pay homage. Later, the crusading forces were united and Godfrey fought at Nicaea and Dorylaeum. In 1098 he reconciled Bohemond and Raymond de St. Gilles, count of Toulouse, joined Count Robert of Flanders in a four-month march on Jerusalem, and took the city in July. Elected king, he used the title "duke and advocate of the Holy Sepulcher," firmly protected the Church, defeated the Turks at Ascalon in 1099, and rebuilt the port city of Jaffa. He died of plague in Jerusalem on July 18. Many legendary feats became attached to his name in later mediaeval romances.

GODFREY OF DUYNEN, ST. (d. 1572), martyr. A parish priest who had been rector of a school at Paris, he was seized by Calvinists and hanged at Briel, Holland. He was canonized in 1867 as one of the martyrs of Gorkum. F. D. July 9.

GODFREY OF FONTAINES (13th century), theologian. Born near Liège, Belgium, before 1250, he was a canon there and also of Paris and Cologne, taught theology at Paris from about 1275 to 1300, and was a member of the Sorbonne. Also known as Godefridus de Fontibus, he engaged in many contemporary disputes, and supported Thomism, though he differed from St. Thomas on the value of the mendicant orders and on the difference between being and essence. His manuscript XIV *Quodlibeta* were widely used in mediaeval classes.

GODFREY OF KAPPENBERG, BL. (1097–1127). Count of Kappenberg, he came under the influence of St. Norbert, to whom he turned over his castle and his wealth. He built a convent nearby (where his wife and two of his sisters became nuns), established hospitals, and served as a canonical novice with the Premonstratensians. F. D. Jan. 13 (also, Jan. 16).

GODFREY DE LA HAYE (15th century). Physician to Margaret of Burgundy, the wife of William VI, count of Holland, he was called Godfrey "Zonderdank" because he used this phrase when he refused payment of fees from the poor. He attested to the unusual nature of the maladies of Bl. Lydwina of Schiedam, on the site of whose home his son built a hospital.

GODFREY OF MERVILLE, ST. (d. 1572), martyr. A painter, he was custos at the Franciscan house at Gorkum, Holland, when he was seized and hanged by Calvinists at Briel, Holland, with a group known as the martyrs of Gorkum. They were canonized in 1867. F. D. July 9.

GODFREY OF VITERBO (12th century), historian. Born in Germany, he was brought to Bamberg in 1133 by Lothair, studied there, and became a cleric in the courts of Conrad III and Frederick I, serving the latter through forty years on diplomatic missions and as chaplain. He was rewarded by a grant of land at Viterbo, Italy, probably in 1169. He wrote *Speculum regum*, a universal history, about 1183; another, *Memoria saeculorum*, in prose and verse, was finished in 1185; that year he began a third, *Pantheon*. All contain much folklore. He also wrote *Gesta Friderici*, a verse account of the career of the king, completed in 1181.

GODLEVA, ST. (1049?–1070). Born of noble parentage in Landefort-lez-Boulogne, she married Bertulf of Ghistelles, a Flemish lord, when eighteen. She was ill treated by him and his mother, escaped to her parents, and took the case to the count of Flanders and the bishop of Tournai, who ordered her back to Bertulf on his promise to treat her properly. Instead, he had her strangled. Although venerated locally as a martyr, she did not die for her faith. F. D. July 6.

GODO, ST. (d. 690?). Born in Verdun, France, the nephew of St. Wandrille, he became a Benedictine at Fontenelle and was the abbot-founder of Oye. F. D. July 24.

GODOY Y ALCAYAGA, LUCILLA. See Mistrál, Gabriela.

GODRIC I (870–941). When Abbot Theodore of Croyland, England, was slain by the Danes he was succeeded by Godric, unanimous choice of the remaining monks. King Boerred of Mercia seized all the monasteries in his realm; on his death in 874, a servant, Ceolwulf, succeeded him, and almost taxed the monasteries out of existence. At Godric's death only five associates were left.

GODRIC II (1005–1081). Abbot of the monastery of Croyland, England, he was harassed by excessive taxation on the part of King Ethelred the Redeless and by frequent attacks by Danes and demands for ransom made by King Sweyn of Denmark. When a flood isolated the monastery, it became the refuge of hundreds, which further drained the resources of the community. The monastery gained some relief when Cnut became king of England in 1017.

GODRIC, ST. (d. 1170). Born in Walpole, Norfolk, England, he was a peddler, sailor, merchant, steward to a noble, and finally retired to a hermitage in Finchdale for sixty years; his austerities were extreme and his spiritual gifts many. Four rhymed hymns were copied by his biographer, Reginald. F. D. May 21.

GODWIN, ST. (d. 690?). He directed the Benedictine monastery of Stavelot-Malmédy, Belgium. F. D. Oct. 28.

GOERIC, ST. (d. 647), bishop. Born in Aquitaine of the Ansbertina family, he became an officer in King Dagobert I's court, lost and regained his sight, and succeeded St. Arnulf as bishop of Metz, Lorraine, on the latter's resignation in 629. Goeric founded a convent at Epinal, of which his daughter Precia became first abbess. He is also known as Abbo. F. D. Sept. 19.

GOES, BENITO DE (1562–1606). Born on San Miguel in the Azores, he became a Jesuit in 1588, and in 1603 was sent to China. He traveled extensively through Asia, announced in 1605 that Cathay and China were identical countries (not so indicated on earlier maps), and made geographical notes later published by Matteo Ricci, the Jesuit missionary.

GOES, DAMIÃO DE (1501–1573), historian. Born in Alemquer, Portugal, he served King John III on diplomatic missions to Flanders, Poland, Denmark, and Sweden (1523–33), studied philosophy and history in Italy, fought during the siege of Louvain by the French, and was a prisoner in 1542–45. On his release he became national archivist, was later charged with Lutheranism, and condemned by the Inquisition to confinement at the monastery of Batalha, where he died.

GOES, PEDRO DE (1503–1554). Born in Lisbon, Portugal, he went to Brazil in 1530 with de Sousa, received a grant of coastal territory, and introduced the raising of sugar. After his plantation was destroyed, he returned to Portugal for royal assistance, was one of the first to bring tobacco to Europe, and returned to Brazil to organize the government with de Sousa and make peace with the Indians.

GOESBRIAND, LOUIS DE (1816–1899), bishop. Born in St. Urbain, France, on Aug. 4, he studied at Quimper seminary and St. Sulpice, Paris, and was ordained in 1840. He did parish work in Cincinnati and Cleveland, Ohio, was vicar general of Cleveland in 1847–53, and was consecrated first bishop of Burlington, Vermont, in 1853. He had five priests for a Catholic population of 20,000, went to France seeking volunteers, held a synod in 1855, attended the Vatican Council in 1869, built parishes and schools, and retired in 1892. He wrote *Catholic Memoirs of Vermont and New Hampshire* (1886), among other books, and died in Burlington on Nov. 3.

GOETHALS, PAUL (1841–1901), archbishop. A Jesuit, he was sent to India, became vicar apostolic of western Bengal in 1877, and in 1866 became first bishop of Calcutta. He held his first provincial council in 1894 and died at Calcutta in July.

GOETZ, MARIE JOSEPHINE (1817–1874). Born in Strassburg, Alsace, on Mar. 7 and orphaned at an early age, she was educated by an aunt, and became a member of the Society of the Sacred Heart in Montet at seventeen. She directed their school in Besançon in 1842, was mistress of novices at Conflans in 1847, superior there, and in 1864 became vicar general. She became the close associate of St. Madeleine Sophie Barat and succeeded the foundress as second superior general of her Society in 1865, consolidating its work, establishing a normal school, and developing educational curricula. She died on Jan. 4.

GOEZNOVEUS, ST. (d. 675), bishop. Born in Cornwall, England, brother of St. Maughan, he went to Brittany and became bishop of Léon. F. D. Oct. 25.

GOFFE, STEPHEN (1605–1681). Son of a Protestant rector of the same name, he was born in Stanmer, Sussex, England, educated at Oxford, took Anglican orders, served as an army chaplain in the Low Countries and also at the court of Charles I, and was named doctor of divinity in 1636. He was imprisoned during the civil war on the charge of trying to rescue the king. After the execution of Charles, Goffe was released, went to France, became a convert and in 1651 an Oratorian. He became superior of Notre Dame des Vertues near Paris in 1655, helped English refugees, was tutor to the duke of Monmouth, and suffered from much published vilification. He died in Paris on Dec. 25.

GOFFINE, LEONARD (1648–1719). Born in Cologne (or Broich), Germany, on Dec. 6, he became a Norbertine at nineteen, studied in Cologne, and was ordained in 1676. He worked at Dunwald and Ellen for eight years, became novice-master at Steinfeld in 1680, and was pastor in six towns, serving at Oberstein, Germany, from 1696 until his death on Aug. 11. He wrote the widely translated *Handpostille* on the epistles and gospels of the mass in 1687 and also published sermons, catechetical texts, and liturgical studies.

GOGARTY, OLIVER ST. JOHN (1878–1957), writer. Born in Dublin on Aug. 17 and educated at Trinity College there and at Stonyhurst and Oxford, he married Martha Duane and set up medical practice in his native city. He was widely known as a throat specialist, a Fellow of the Royal College of Surgeons, and an associate of the literary group which included William Butler Yeats, George Russell, Lady Gregory, and James Joyce (although the latter satirized his former friend in *Ulysses*). His own writings include several volumes of poetry: *Wild Apples* (1929) and a collected edition in 1933; plays produced by the Abbey Theatre; novels; travel sketches; and the witty, semi-autobiographical *As I Was Going Down Sackville Street* (1937) and *It Isn't This Time of Year* (1954). He also was associated with the heroes of the Irish revolution and once saved the life of Michael Collins by hiding him in his medical office and pretending to operate. Gogarty served as a member of the parliament of Ireland from 1922 to 1936 and came to the United States in 1939. He died in New York City on Sept. 22 and is buried in Galway.

GOHARD, ST. (d. 843), bishop. He and his assistants were slain during high mass by raiding Norsemen who then burned the church and slew the monks of a nearby monastery. He was bishop of Nantes, France. F. D. June 25.

GOJDIC, PETER PAVEL (1888–1960), bishop. Born in Slovakia on July 17, he joined the Basilians of St. Josaphat (a Byzantine rite order), and was ordained in 1911. He was made a bishop and head of the only Eastern rite Catholic see in Czechoslovakia in 1927, and in 1940 was appointed bishop of Presnov. He was arrested in 1950 by the communists, who determined to liquidate his see and its priests, tried at Bratislava in 1951, and sentenced to life imprisonment. He is reported to have received the stigmata while in prison, and died in Ilava prison, western Slovakia, sometime in July.

GOLDONI, CARLO (1707–1793), dramatist. Born in Venice on Feb. 25, he ran away from home to join a group of strolling players and soon began writing plays. He studied law in Venice, was a clerk in the criminal court in Chioggia, held jobs in the diplomatic service, and practiced law in northern Italian cities. He was named dramatic poet of the San Angelo theater, Venice, in 1746 and transferred to the San Luca theater in 1752. In 1761 he went to the Théâtre Italien in Paris, when the literary warfare between those supporting the artificial *commedia dell' arte* and those preferring character plays (such as those by Molière), as Goldoni did, became too intense. After his contract expired he remained as tutor to the daughters of Louis XV, received a royal pension, and died in Paris on Jan. 6. He wrote 150 plays; some in Venetian dialect, in whole or in part; a large group, particularly comedies, in Italian; and two in French. He also published letters and *Mémoires* which are valuable for study of the literary world and dramatic repertoire of the time.

GOLDWELL, THOMAS (1510?–1585), bishop. Born near Ashford, Kent, England, between 1501 and 1515, he studied science at Oxford, took his degree in divinity, served as chaplain to Cardinal Pole, with whom he went into exile, and shortly after 1538 became a Theatine in Rome. He returned to London with Pole at Queen Mary's accession, was named bishop of St. Asaph, Wales, in 1555, went to Rome to report on the state of religion in England, was consecrated there, and returned to his see. He was to be transferred to Oxford in 1558, but Elizabeth's succession made this impossible; he was tried as an enemy of the state and exiled. He was superior of the Theatine house in Naples in 1561, served at the English Hospital in Rome, was the only English bishop present at the Council of Trent, became vicar general to St. Charles Borromeo at Milan in 1563, and in 1574 vice-regent of Rome. At Trent he had worked on the revision of the missal and breviary; before he died in Rome on Apr. 3 he was engaged in revising the Roman Martyrology.

GOLLEN, ST. (7th century). His name appears in Welsh legend and in the place name, Llangollen, Denbighshire. F. D. May 21.

GOLVINUS, ST. (7th century?), bishop. An Englishman, he became bishop of St. Pol de Léon, Brittany, and died at Rennes. F. D. July 9.

GOMA Y TOMÁS, ISIDRO (d. 1940), cardinal. Born in La Riba, Tarragona, Spain, on Aug. 19, he was ordained, and in 1927 became bishop of Tarazora. He was named archbishop of Toledo and primate of Spain in 1933 and a cardinal in 1935. During the civil war he was provisional representative of the Vatican at Burgos, denounced civil interference in ecclesiastical affairs, threw his support to Gen. Franco, and escaped from Toledo to Pamplona just before government forces stripped his cathedral and residence and executed his chancery priests. He died in Pamplona, Spain, on Aug. 22.

GÓMARA, FRANCISCO LOPEZ DE (1510–1559?). Born in Seville, Spain, he studied at Alcalá and was secretary and chaplain to Cortés on an Algerian expedition. From Cortés and other witnesses he gathered materials for *Hispania victrix*, a history of the

Indies and the conquest of Mexico (1552). It contained so many errors and was so partisan toward Cortés that it was officially banned in 1553 by Philip II (then a prince).

GOMES DE AMORIM, FRANCISCO (1827–1891), poet. Born in Avelomar, Portugal, on Aug. 13, he left school at ten because of his family's poverty, went to Brazil to work, returned at twenty, and wrote with romantic enthusiasm about the revolutionary movements of 1848. Influenced by Almeida Garrett, whose biography he wrote, he abandoned poetry for drama, and wrote eight plays between 1851 and 1859 on national themes. Several novels reflect his stay in Brazil. His poetic fame rests on *Cantos matutinos* and *Ephemeros* (both 1858). He died on Nov. 4.

GONET, JEAN BAPTISTE (1616?–1681), theologian. Born in Béziers, France, he studied there, became a Dominican at seventeen, took his doctorate at Bordeaux, and taught theology there. He became provincial in 1671, retired to Béziers in ill health in 1678, and died there on Jan. 24. He wrote on predestination, the morality of human acts, and attacked the laxists, rigorists, and probalists. His elaborate sixteen-volume study of Thomistic philosophy (1659–69) also appeared in abridged form.

GONNELIEU, JÉROME DE (1640–1715), theologian. Born in Soissons, France, on Sept. 8, he became a Jesuit in 1657, taught and preached widely, and wrote a number of ascetical works on methods of prayer, the spiritual life, and devotion to the Eucharist. He probably is the author of an annotated translation of the *Imitation of Christ* (1712), sometimes attributed to the printer, Jean Baptiste Cusson. He died in Paris on Feb. 28.

GONSALO OF AMARANTE, BL. (d. 1259?). He was a Portuguese Dominican who seems to have lived as a hermit, though his career has been filled in by extravagant legendary material. His cult was confirmed in 1560. F. D. Jan. 16.

GONZAGA, ST. ALOYSIUS (1568–1591). Born in Lombardy on Mar. 9, eldest son of Ferrante, marquis of Castiglione, and Marta Tana Santena, both of whom were in the service of Philip II of Spain, he was brought up in court and in army camps. At nine he was taken to Florence to be educated; at eleven he was teaching catechism to the poor children of Castiglione, fasting three days a week, and practicing extreme austerities and long devotions. After four years of opposition from his father, Aloysius was allowed to transfer his right of succession to his brother and to join the Jesuits in 1585. He died at Rome, the victim of a plague which struck him down while attending the overflow of patients in the Jesuit hospital there. He was canonized in 1726; Benedict XIII declared him protector of young students and

Pope Pius XI, the patron of Christian youth. F. D. June 21.

C. C. MARTINDALE, *The Vocation of Aloysius Gonzaga* (London, 1927).

GONZAGA, ERCOLE (1505–1563), cardinal. Born in Mantua, Italy, on Nov. 23, he studied at Bologna, was given the see of Mantua in 1520 or 1525 by his uncle, Cardinal Sigismondo Gonzaga, and made a cardinal in 1527. He built the diocesan seminary, worked zealously for reform, established scholarships for young priests, and wrote *Vitae christianae instituto*. He served on many diplomatic missions for the papacy, was regent of the duchy of Mantua and guardian of the sons of Federico II from 1540 to 1556, and in 1561 was named legate to the Council of Trent by Pope Pius IV. He died of fever at Trent, Italy, on Mar. 2.

GONZAGA, SCIPIONE (1542–1593), cardinal. Born in Mantua, Italy, on Nov. 11, he was brought up by Cardinal Ercole Gonzaga, studied at Bologna and Padua, founded the Accademia degli Eterei, and was liberal as a patron of letters, supporting both Tasso and Guarino. He was ordained in Rome, became bishop of Mende, France, was named patriarch of Jerusalem by Pope Sixtus V, and, in 1587, cardinal. He served on many diplomatic missions, was the friend of SS. Charles Borromeo, Philip Neri, and his cousin Aloysius Gonzaga, and wrote of his own career in *Commentarii*. He died in San Martino on Jan. 11.

GONZALEZ DE CASTRILLO, ST. JUAN (1419–1479). Born in Sahagún, Spain, he was educated there at the Benedictine monastery of San Fagondez, became a canon at the cathedral of Burgos at twenty, and also was given four other benefices. He fought against the evil of such pluralities, and remained as a priest at St. Agatha's, Burgos. He went to Salamanca for higher studies, served as a parish priest and chaplain there, and in 1464 became an Augustinian. He was well known as a peacemaker and confessor, and became master of novices and prior. His sermons against contemporary vice were so strong that he not only won over notorious sinners, but also angered several in high places. He suffered several attacks and died of probable poisoning. Also known as John of Sahagún, he was canonized in 1690. F. D. June 12.

GONZALEZ DAVILA, GIL (1578–1658). Born in Avila, Spain, he served in minor orders at Salamanca and was named royal chronicler of Castile in 1612 and of the Indies in 1641. He wrote histories of the Church in Spain, the Indies, and New Spain, and on Spanish cathedrals.

GONZALEZ, BL. ROQUE (1576–1628), martyr. Son of a Spanish noble, he was born in Asunción, Paraguay, where he was educated and ordained in 1599. He served among the

Indians until 1609, became a Jesuit, and labored in that Society's "reductions" at St. Ignatius and then in six settlements he founded deep in the South American jungles. He was bitterly opposed by civil authorities because of his championship of Indian rights, but was axed to death on Nov. 15 by a raiding party of Indians at Caaró (southern Brazil) with Bl. Alonso Rodriguez. Bl. Juan de Castillo, a companion, was murdered two days later at Ijuhi mission. Known as the martyrs of Paraguay, they were beatified in 1934. F. D. Nov. 17.

GONZÁLEZ DE SANTALLA, THYRSUS (1624–1705), theologian. Born in Arganda, Spain, on Jan. 18, he became a Jesuit in 1643, taught at Salamanca, preached from 1655 to 1687, and became general of the Jesuits that year. He wrote an attack on probabilism which appeared in approved form in 1695; St. Alphonsus Liguori claimed that it exaggerated rigorism. He also wrote treatises on the Immaculate Conception, infallibility, and against Jansenism. He died in Rome on Oct. 27.

GONZÁLEZ, ZEFERINO (1831–1894), cardinal. Born in Villoria, Oviedo, Spain, on Jan. 28, he became a Dominican in 1844, was sent to the Philippines, ordained in 1854, and taught in the University of Manila until 1867. Returning to Spain, he became rector of Ocania College, bishop of Cordova in 1865, and archbishop of Seville in 1883. In 1884, Pope Leo XIII made him a cardinal; the next year he became primate of Spain, patriarch of the Indies, and royal chaplain. He wrote on philosophy and sociology, was made a member of the Royal Academy, chancellor of Castile, and adviser to the crown before he retired in 1889. He died in Madrid on Nov. 29.

GONZALO DE BERCEO (1180?–1247?), poet. Born in Berceo, Castile, Spain, he lived in or near the monastery of San Millan de la Cogolla, was ordained in 1237, and wrote rhymed lives of several saints, poems in praise of the Virgin Mary, and hymns. He strove to make the vernacular respected, and adopted many of the mannerisms of the Castilian minstrels.

GOODIER, ALBAN (1869–1939), archbishop. Born in Great Harwood, Lancashire, England, he studied at Stonyhurst, became a Jesuit in 1887, completed his studies at the University of London, and taught at Stonyhurst. He was ordained in 1903, held chaplaincies, edited eighteen titles in the Catholic Library series, and in 1915–19 was rector of St. Xavier's College, Bombay, whose German Jesuit faculty had been interned because of World War I. He was archbishop of Bombay from 1919 to 1926, then returned to England as titular archbishop of Hierapolis. For two years (1930–32) he was auxiliary bishop of Westminster, but most of his last years were devoted

to writing. He published *St. Ignatius and Prayer, The Meaning of Life*, and spiritual readings; he is best known for his *Public Life of Our Lord Jesus Christ* and *Passion and Death of Our Lord Jesus Christ*. He died in Teignmouth, England, on Mar. 13.

GOODMAN, GODFREY (1583–1656). Born in Ruthin, Denbighshire, Wales, on Feb. 28, he went to Westminster School and Cambridge, entered the Anglican ministry, held several rectorships and deanships, and in 1625 was named bishop of Gloucester. He was chaplain to Mary, wife of King James I, but was severely criticized for his use of the crucifix and other "Roman trappings," frequently disagreed with Archbishop Laud, and was impeached by parliament and stripped of office in 1640. He became a convert around 1643 and lived in London until his death on Jan. 19.

GOODMAN, VEN. JOHN (1590–1642), martyr. Born in Bangor, Wales, he studied at Oxford, became a minister, was converted in Paris, studied at Douai from 1621 to 1624, was ordained, and sent on the English mission. He was captured and imprisoned three times, and died in Newgate prison, London, after a year during which he was so violently attacked by parliament and defended by Charles I that he begged the king to permit his ordered execution lest his case split the country by further dissension.

GOOSSENS, PIERRE LAMBERT (1827–1906), cardinal. Born in Perck, Belgium, on July 18, he taught at Bruel, was on the cathedral staff in Mechlin, secretary to the archbishop, vicar general, coadjutor in 1883, and bishop of Namur in 1884. Later that year he became archbishop of Mechlin, and was made cardinal-priest in 1889. He opened several hundred elementary schools in a diocese where education was now permitted for Catholics, and built numerous high schools and ten colleges. He was active in other social work, co-operative with labor groups, and the author of collections of sermons, discourses on sociology, and religious conferences. He died in Mechlin, Belgium, on Jan. 25.

GORAN, ST. (6th century). A friend of St. Patrick, he apparently served in Cornwall, England, where several churches are dedicated to him. F. D. Apr. 7.

GORAZD, ST. (9th century), archbishop. A missionary to Bulgaria, he was designated by St. Methodius as his successor as archbishop of Moravia and Pannomia. He is one of the major apostles of Bulgaria. F. D. July 17.

GORDIAN, ST. (d. 362), martyr. A boy, he was put to death in Rome for his faith; his epitaph was written by Pope Damasus. F. D. May 10.

GORDIUS, ST. (d. 304), martyr. A soldier at Caesarea in Cappadocia, he was dismissed for his religion, became a desert recluse, declared his faith during the Diocletian persecution, and was beheaded. F. D. Jan. 3.

GORDON, ANDREW (1712–1751), physicist. Born in Cofforach, Forfarshire, Scotland, he became a Benedictine in 1737, taught natural philosophy at Erfurt, and wrote on electricity, friction, and the lightning rod. He developed the metallic apparatus known as the electrical whirl, the earliest known electrostatic reaction motor. He (not Benjamin Franklin) was the first to develop electric chimes, the earliest application of electric convection. He died in Erfurt, Saxony, on Aug. 22.

GORETTI, MARIA. See Maria Goretti, St.

GORGONIA, ST. (d. 372?). The eldest child of St. Gregory Nazianzen the Elder and St. Nonna, she married and led an exemplary married life. Her brother, St. Gregory Nazianzen, preached a panegyric on her death. F. D. Dec. 9.

GORGONIUS (d. 303), martyr. He and Dorotheus were officials at the court of Emperor Diocletian in Nicodemia. When they objected to the tortures imposed on Peter, a Christian, they were subjected to great tortures and hanged either in Nicaea, Bithynia, or Antioch, Syria. He is honored on Mar. 12, and is often confused with another Gorgonius buried in Rome who is honored on Sept. 9; one who died in Nice, France, and one who died in Sebaste (now Sivas, Turkey), both on Mar. 10.

GORMAN, ST. (d. 965). A Benedictine at Reichenau, Germany, he was a missioner along the Baltic and became bishop of Schleswig. F. D. Aug. 28.

GORMAN, DANIEL MARY (1861–1927), bishop. Born in Wyoming, Iowa, on Apr. 12, he studied at St. Joseph's, Dubuque, and St. Francis, Milwaukee, and was ordained in 1893. He taught at St. Joseph's from 1894, was its president (its name was changed to Dubuque University) from 1904 to 1918, and in that year was consecrated second bishop of Boise, Idaho. He died at Lewiston, Idaho, on June 9.

GORMCAL, ST. (d. 1016). He was abbot of the monastery of Ardoilen, Galway, Ireland. F. D. Aug. 5.

GÖRRES, GUIDO (1805–1852), poet. Born in Coblenz, Germany, on May 28, son of Johann Joseph, he studied there and at Strassburg, Bonn, and Munich. He published studies of Nicholas of Flüe (1831) and Joan of Arc (1834), founded, with Count Franz Pocci, the first illustrated juvenile journal in German, *Festkalender* (1834–39), and after 1838 edited *Historisch-politische Blätter*. He also published, with Pocci, the short-lived *Deutsches Hausbuch* (1846–47), translated the *Imitation of Christ*, edited the *Märchen* of Klemens Brentano, and issued a collection of *Marienlieder* (1838) and six volumes of poetry of his own. He died in Munich, Germany, on July 14.

GÖRRES, JOHANN JOSEPH (1776–1848), apologist. Born in Coblenz, Germany, on Jan. 25, son of Morits, a timber merchant, he studied there, became a rationalist and supporter of the French Revolution, went to Paris in 1799 as a delegate from the Rhine and Moselle provinces, and lost his enthusiasm for the revolution as a result of firsthand observation. On his return he taught physics in Coblenz, published scientific studies and translations, wrote for the new magazines, and in 1806 became docent at Heidelberg. With Johann Eichendorff's help he published *Teutschen Volksbücher* (1807) and *Alteutschen Volksund Meisterlieder* (1817) as a leader in the German romantic movement. He returned to Coblenz in 1808, published a study of the origin of myths (1810), and in 1814–16 edited *Der reinische Merkur*, a weekly paper opposed to Napoleon and advocating German imperialism. On its suppression he also lost his teaching position, engaged in relief work, and continued to write influential pamphlets. The Prussian government seized his papers and ordered his arrest in 1819, but he escaped to Strassburg. He published the significant *Europa und die Revolution* in 1822, returned to scientific studies, and became increasingly interested in matters of religion. He published on St. Francis of Assisi, a preface to an edition of Henry Suso, and a study of Swedenborg. In 1827 he was appointed to the faculty of Munich by King Ludwig I of Bavaria and became the center of Catholic intellectual life in Europe. He wrote on a wide range of topics: the Christian interpretation of history, church architecture, Church and state, scientific agnosticism, and Christian mysticism. Outstanding were *Athanasius* (1834), a defense of Archbishop Clement August of Cologne for performing his pastoral duties; *Die Triarier* (1838), against Bruno and other liberals in scientific philosophizing; and the four-volume *Die christliche Mystik* (1836–42) on mediaeval mystics, modern cases of ecstasy, and rationalist opposition. He also wrote regularly through twenty years for *Historisch-politische Blätter*, which he had helped to found. He died in Munich, Germany, on Jan. 29.

GOSBERT, ST. (d. 859?), bishop. He is listed as the fourth to hold the see of Osnabrück, Germany, and a follower of St. Anskar. F. D. Feb. 13.

GOSCELIN (d. 1099?), biographer. Born in France, he became a Benedictine monk at St. Bertin in Omer, went to Rome in 1049 with Bishop Hermann of Salisbury, and probably went with the latter to England in 1053. He collected materials for the lives of English saints, particularly those associated with Canterbury, where he lived for many years; he wrote on SS. Augustine, Etheldreda, Ives, and

Swithin, among others. He died on May 15.

GOSLIN. *See* Gozzelinus, St.

GOSS, ALEXANDER (1814–1872), bishop. Born in Ormskirk, Lancashire, England, on July 5, he studied at Ushaw and the English College in Rome, was ordained in 1841, did parish work in Manchester, and in 1842 became vice-president of the College of St. Edward, near Liverpool. After ten years he was named coadjutor bishop of Liverpool, and succeeded to that see in 1856. He edited several texts for the Chetham and Manx societies, notably *Abbott's Journal* and *Chronica regum Manniae*. He was active in social reform and educational advancement, and died in Liverpool, England, on Oct. 3.

GOSSAERT, JAN (1470?–1541?), painter. Born in Mabuse, Hainault, Flanders, he went to Rome in 1508 with Bishop Philip of Burgundy, remained in the latter's service when he was transferred to Utrecht, and at his death in 1524 went to the court of Adolphus of Burgundy. He married Marguerite de Molenaer: their son Pierre became a painter; their daughter Gertrude married the painter Henri van der Heyden. His early work was rough, but his year in Rome brought him into contact with architectural beauty, details of which he copied carefully. Thereafter, in his decorative backgrounds he relied heavily on structural settings, of a style which helped to bring an end to the Gothic. Renaissance breadth marks his heroic-sized *St. Luke Painting the Virgin Mary* and *Adoration of the Magi* and also his sketches for tapestries. His portraits (*Children of Christian of Denmark*; *Madonna*; *Monk*) are also effective in their skin tone, grace, and realism. Other work, particularly on mythological figures, is thin-colored, affected, and seemingly without inspiration. He died in Middelburg, Flanders. He is known as Jan de Mabuse, from his birthplace.

GOSSELIN, JEAN EDMÉ AUGUSTE (1787–1858). Born in Rouen, France, on Sept. 28, he studied at St. Sulpice, Paris, was ordained in 1812, became a Sulpician in 1814, and was vice-president of the seminary at Issy from 1814 to 1830 and superior from 1831 to 1844, when ill health forced his resignation. His high regard for Fénelon appears in his edition of Fénelon's *Works* (twenty-two volumes) and *Correspondence* (eleven volumes); the archbishop's influence is evident in Gosselin's *Power of the Pope in the Middle Ages*, which proved that the pope exerted temporal power, but maintained that sovereignty came from contemporary law and not from divine authority. He died in Paris on Nov. 27.

GOSWIN, ST. (d. 1165). Born in Douai, France, he studied at Paris, taught theology as a canon at Douai, became a Benedictine at Anchin, near Douai, in 1113, and abbot there in 1130. F. D. Oct. 9.

GOTHARD, ST. (d. 1038), bishop. Born in Reichersdorf, Bavaria, he was educated by several bishops and given an ecclesiastical post by Archbishop Frederick of Salzburg. After ordination he entered the monastery of Nieder-Altaich, where he became abbot; in addition, he was asked to reform three other German houses, and aid six more. At sixty, Emperor Henry nominated him as bishop of Hildesheim; though unwilling to accept, he acceded, repaired churches, tightened canonical discipline, built asylums, and developed the cathedral school. He was canonized in 1131. He is also known as Godard and Godehard. F. D. May 4.

GOTHER, JOHN (d. 1704), apologist. Born in Southampton, England, he became a convert, studied at the English College in Lisbon, and was ordained in 1682. He returned to England and wrote *A Papist Misrepresented and Represented*, a digest of current misconceptions; it was attacked by Stillingfleet, and praised for its style by Dryden. A dozen works, on current controversy, or explaining the sacraments, scripture, and early Christianity, followed. He became a chaplain in Northamptonshire, where he converted the later Bishop Richard Challoner, and was on his way to Lisbon when he died at sea, on Oct. 2.

GOTTESCHALK (d. 1066). A prince of the Wends, he gave up Christianity when his father was slain, served in the army of Canute of Denmark and with the force which followed Sweyn into England, where he became a Christian again. At home once more, he was active in introducing missioners. Because he was slain in an anti-Christian revolt he has been listed as a saint and martyr, with a feast day on June 7.

GOTTFRIED VON STRASSBURG (13th century), poet. A learned German, who knew Latin and French and was familiar with court life, he may have been a noble. Using a poetic version by Thomas of Brittany, Gottfried developed a story of *Tristran und Isolt* which was widely read and imitated. His version includes the episodes of the love potion drunk in mistake by the two principals, their subsequent affair after Isolt's marriage to King Mark of Cornwall, and Tristran's flight and meeting with another Isolt. Never completed, it is believed to have been written about 1210, and was continued by Ulrich von Türheim and Heinrich von Freiburg later in the century.

GOTTI, GIROLAMO MARIA (1834–1916), cardinal. Born in Genoa, Italy, on Mar. 29, he became a Carmelite in 1854, was ordained, taught mathematics and science at the Genoa Naval Academy, attended the Vatican Council as theologian of his order, and was elected general in 1881 and again in 1889. He was appointed archbishop of Petra in 1892, sent to Brazil as nuncio, and made a cardinal in 1895. He was prefect of several congregations, settled a controversy between the sees of Annecy and Bourges, and in his last years was prefect of the Propaganda. He died in Rome on Mar. 19.

GOTTI, VINCENT LOUIS (1664–1742), cardinal. Born in Bologna, Italy, on Sept. 5, he became a Dominican at sixteen, studied at Salamanca and Mantua, taught in Rome and Bologna, and in 1716 was elected superior of the Bologna province. He was inquisitor at Milan from 1715 to 1717, when he asked to be relieved to teach theology again at Bologna. Pope Benedict XIII made him a cardinal-priest and patriarch of Jerusalem in 1728. He served with distinction on several commissions and wrote a number of major theological studies. He died in Rome on Sept. 18.

GOTTIFREDI, ALOYSIUS (d. 1652). Born in Rome, he became a Jesuit, taught theology at and was rector of the Roman College, was secretary to Fr. Mutius Vitelleschi (sixth general), and became ninth general of his Society two months before his death in Rome on Mar. 12.

GOUGAUD, LOUIS (1877–1941), historian. Born in Malestroit, France, he studied at St. Vincent's College and Rennes, became a Benedictine on the Isle of Wight in 1902, and was ordained in 1909. For the rest of his life, except for service in the French army in World War I, he was stationed at St. Michael's abbey, Farnsborough, England. He established a wide reputation for his scholarship on Celtic and monastic history and was given an honorary degree by the National University of Ireland. His major titles are: *Les chrétientés celtiques* (1911), *Gaelic Pioneers of Christianity, Devotions et pratiques ascetiques de moyen âge, Ermites et reclus, Christianity in Celtic Lands, Anciennes coutumes claustrales,* and *Les saints irlandais.* He died on Mar. 24.

GOUNOD, CHARLES FRANÇOIS (1818–1893), composer. Born in Paris on June 17, son of a painter and architect who died when his son was young, he was educated by his mother, a pianist, and at the Lycée St. Louis. He studied music at the conservatory, and in 1839 won the Grand Prix de Rome for his cantata *Fernand;* this included a travel grant of three years in Rome and one in Germany. He wrote two masses in Vienna, which were performed there, returned to Paris in 1842, was choirmaster at the Society of Foreign Missions church for nearly five years, studied at St. Sulpice for a year, then devoted himself completely to the writing of operas. He worked with the librettists Émile Augier, Jules Barbier, and Michel Carré on the romantic and lyrical *Faust, Polyeucte, Roméo et Juliette,*

Sapho, La Reine de Saba, and others. He went to London from 1870 to 1875, and wrote the oratorio *Redemption; Mors et Vita* followed; several masses (*St. Cecilia, Sacred Heart, Joan of Arc*); and other religious music, more sentimental than spiritual. He died in Paris on Oct. 17.

GOUPIL, ST. RENÉ (1606–1642), martyr. A native of Anjou, France, he studied at the Jesuit notiviate but was forced to leave because of ill health. He then became a successful surgeon, but, still attracted to the Jesuits missions, went to Quebec in 1638. He worked in the hospital there and became a *donné* for the Huron mission in 1640. He joined St. Isaac Jogues in 1642 and, while on a journey with him, both were captured by the Iroquois. After almost two months of terrible tortures and mutilations, St. René was tomahawked on Sept. 29, in St. Isaac's presence, at Osserneon, near Albany, New York, the first of the American group of martyrs to die. He was canonized by Pope Pius XI in 1930. F. D. Sept. 26 (also, Mar. 16).

JOHN A. O'BRIEN, *The American Martyrs* (New York, Appleton, 1953).

GOUSSET, THOMAS MARIE JOSEPH (1792–1866), cardinal. Born in Montigny-les-Charlieu, France, he was ordained in 1817, taught moral theology in the seminary at Besançon until 1830, was vicar general there until 1835, then became bishop of Périgueux, archbishop of Rheims in 1844, and cardinal in 1850. He edited and annotated the twenty-six-volume *Conférences d'Angers* and Bergier's *Dictionnaire théologique,* wrote on canon and civil law, moral and dogmatic theology, and the temporal sovereignty of the pope. He died in Rheims, France, on Dec. 24.

GOVEN, ST. (5th century), queen. Wife of King Tewdrig of Glamorgan, she is remembered in the Welsh parish name of Llangoven. She is also called Gowan. F. D. Dec. 28.

GOWAN. See Goven, St.

GOWER, JOHN (1330?–1408), poet. Born, probably in Kent, England, after 1327, he may have been a wealthy merchant, and was well known in the court of King Richard II. He later supported Henry IV, was a generous benefactor to Church charities, and died at the priory of St. Mary Overy, Southwark, where he was living after he became blind in 1400. He wrote three major poems in three languages. His *Mirour de l'omme,* an allegory of nearly 30,000 lines on the war between the soul and sin, social rank, contrition and sorrow, and biographical accounts of Christ and the Virgin Mary, probably was written about 1376–79. His *Cinkante* (actually fifty-four) *Balades,* written at various times and gathered in 1399, and *Traitié,* a defense of marriage vows, also were written in French. His *Vox Clamantis,* of more than 10,000 lines in Latin, recounted the Peasants' Revolt of 1381, advised on the selection of royal counselors and the duties of a king, condemned the vices of the contemporary clergy and other professional leaders, and pleaded for strong religious faith. It was written between 1382 and 1399. Richard and Henry IV appear in *Cronica Tripertita,* and a number of minor political poems also were written in Latin. In English he wrote *In Praise of Peace,* dedicated to Henry, and *Confessio Amantis,* nearly 34,000 lines in length (exclusive of Latin sections), begun about 1383, completed in 1393, and issued in two revisions. This shows great narrative skill and polished workmanship. It begins as a dialogue between a lover and Venus; the lover becomes old, distinguishes between emotion and reason, is handed over by Venus to Genius, who hears his confession, and spends his last days praying for the regeneration of mankind. Many familiar stories and exampla are included: morality-play versions of the seven deadly sins; Chaucer's Man of Law's tale and that of the Wife of Bath; the romance of Apollonius of Tyre; the narrative of Shakespeare's *Pericles;* material from Ovid, scripture, and mediaeval fiction.

GOYA Y LUCIENTES, FRANCISCO JOSÉ DE (1746–1828), painter. Born in Fuendetodos, Aragon, Spain, on Mar. 31, he studied art with the monks of Santa Fe, and under José Martínez at Saragossa, and at Madrid. At twenty he went to Rome, earning his way by acting as a bullfighter. He won a prize at Parma, did a portrait of Pope Benedict XIV, returned to Spain in 1775, and was commissioned to sketch the designs for Prado and Escorial tapestries. Thereafter he lived at court, in the circle of the king's brother Luis. He married Josefa, daughter of the painter Francesco Bayeu, who bore him twenty children. He painted more than 200 portraits, generally with great speed; his *Christ Crucified* and *St. Francis on the Mountain* won him election to the Fernando Academy; in 1789 he became court painter to Charles IV and in 1795 a director of the Madrid Academy. He painted frescoes in many churches across Spain, revealing great vitality and much of the history and life of the day. He then turned to etching; his *Capriccioso* (1792–96) is a series attacking contemporary vices and follies with great sharpness; equally famous is the series, *The Miseries of War.* In his last years he studied lithography, made the first important lithograph at seventy-three, and completed his series on bullfighting when eighty, deaf, and almost blind. He is equally famous for his two portraits of La Maja, Charles IV, and the duke of Wellington, and for many aquatints. He died in Bordeaux, France, on Apr. 16.

GOYAU, GEORGES PIERRE LOUIS THÉ-

OPHILE (1869–1939), historian. Born in Orléans, France, he studied there and in Paris, taught at L'École Français, Rome, wrote for *Journal des Débats, Revue des Deux Mondes,* and *Figaro,* and became a leader of the Conservatives. He taught in Paris, international law at The Hague after 1925, and history at L'Institut Catholique, Paris, after 1927. He began his writing career with *Le pape, les catholiques et la question social* (1893); was sent to Germany by Brunetière to report on the religious situation, and produced *L'Allemagne religieuse: le protestantisme, L'Allemagne religieuse: le catholicisme,* and *Bismarck et l'église.* The first won for him the Bordin Prize of the French Academy (1898); he won the Prix Vitet in 1908, was elected to the Academy in 1922, and became its permanent secretary in 1938. Other books include: *Le Vatican papauté et chrétienté sous Benoit XV, Missions et missionaires, Histoire religieuse de la nation française, Le Visage de Rome chrétienne, Le Christ* (1940), biographies of St. Louis, Joan of Arc, Frédéric Ozanam, Mère Marie de la Passion, Joseph Le Maistre, and Cardinals Mercier and Lavigerie, and studies of French Canada. He died in Bernay, France, on Oct. 25.

GOYAU, LUCIE FÉLIX FAURE (1866–1913), author. Born in Amboise, Touraine, daughter of Félix Faure (later president of France), she lived in Paris while he was in the state department, was educated there and by foreign travel, and wrote on Mediterranean culture, a study of Cardinal Newman, lives of SS. Gertrude and Mechtilde, poems, and *Journal intime.* She married Georges Goyau in 1903, and was politically active in the feminist movement.

GOZZELINUS, ST. (d. 1153). He was the second abbot of the Benedictine monastery of San Solutore, near Milan, Italy. He is also called Goslin. F. D. Feb. 12.

GOZZI, CARLO (1720–1806). Born in Venice, Italy, he served in the army, dabbled in literature, was a member of the conservative Accademia dei Granelleschi, and engaged in dramatic criticism against the bombast of Chiari and the opposition of Goldoni to the *commedia dell' arte.* He began to write a series of *Fiabe,* dramas based on oriental and Spanish sources, highly improbable, and using the dialect of Venice to ridicule Goldoni. Among them were *The Love of Three Oranges* (set to music later by Prokofiév), *Turandot* (adapted for Puccini's opera), *The Green Bird,* and *The Monster.* Their popularity, though short-lived, drove Goldoni to France. Goethe, Schiller, and Wagner read them with pleasure; the latter said they were basically operatic in plot. He also wrote a comedy, some mock-heroic poetry, and an autobiography. He died on Apr. 14.

GOZZOLI, BENOZZO DI LESE DI SAN-

DRO (1420–1498), painter. Benozzo di Lese was born in Florence, Italy, worked in Rome and Orvieto as a pupil of Fra Angelico and, after 1450, independently. He did frescoes in the church of St. Francis, Montefalco, and in that of San Fortunato nearby. He completed the elaborately costumed *Procession of the Magi* for the Riccardi palace chapel in Florence, including portraits of the Medici; a *Martyrdom of St. Sebastian* and seventeen frescoes on the life of St. Augustine for churches in San Gimignano; and biblical illustrations and a portrait of St. Thomas Aquinas while in Pisa. His command of landscape, success in suggesting a narrative, and lively imagination outweigh the sometimes obvious ineptness in arranging groups of figures. He died in Pisa, Italy, on Oct. 4 and was buried in the Campo Santo, whose northern wall he had decorated with Old Testament scenes.

GRABMANN, MARTIN (1875–1949), scholar. Born in Winterzhofen, Germany, on Jan. 5, he became professor of theology and philosophy at Munich in 1918, was editor of *Beiträge zur Geschichte der Philosophie des Mittelalters*, and wrote on St. Thomas Aquinas, Aristotle, and Catholic thought. He died in Eichstätt, Germany, on Jan. 9.

GRACE, JOSEPH P. (1872–1950), executive. Born in Great Neck, New York, on June 9, he graduated from Columbia in 1894, went into the shipping business, and by 1909 had developed William R. Grace & Co. to world-wide success. He became president of that firm in that year, president of its board of trustees in 1929, and retired in 1949. He merged other interests to establish Pan American-Grace Airways in 1929. He was trustee of many charitable institutions and was well known for his philanthropies. He died in Great Neck on July 15.

GRACE, THOMAS (1841–1921), bishop. Born in Wexford County, Ireland, on Aug. 2, he studied at St. Peter's there and All Hallows, Dublin, and was ordained in 1876. He went to the United States and engaged in parish and missionary work in Nevada and surrounding areas. He was rector of the Marysville cathedral for eight years, served as pastor of the Sacramento cathedral from 1881 to 1896, was administrator of the diocese in 1895–96, and in 1896 was preconized bishop of Sacramento. He died in Sacramento, California, on Dec. 27.

GRACE, THOMAS LANGDON (1814–1897), archbishop. Born in Charleston, South Carolina, on Nov. 16, he studied at the Cincinnati seminary and St. Rose's priory, Kentucky, where he became a Dominican in 1830. He continued his studies at the Minerva in Rome, was ordained in 1839, and returned in 1844 to parish and missionary work in Kentucky and Tennessee. He was appointed bishop of St. Paul in 1859, encouraged immigration, the extension of Catholic educational facilities, and charitable works. He resigned in 1884 and was appointed titular bishop of Menith, and in 1889 was made titular archbishop of Siunia. He died in St. Paul, Minnesota, on Feb. 22.

GRACE, WILLIAM RUSSELL (1832–1904), merchant. Born in Queenstown, Cork, Ireland, on May 10, he was taken to Peru in 1850, and remained there when his father returned to Ireland. He became a partner in a business firm in Callao, which eventually became Grace Brothers & Co. and W. R. Grace & Co. He opened offices in other cities in South America and in New York and San Francisco, enlarged his financial interests, and founded the New York and Pacific Steamship Co. He went to New York in 1864, lived in Brooklyn and Manhattan, contributed heavily to Irish family relief in 1878–79, and in 1880 was elected the first Catholic mayor of New York City. He was re-elected in 1884, refused a third term, and in 1897 established the Grace Institute for the education of dressmakers, domestic servants, and office girls; other grants aided workers' families and the poor. He died in New York City on Mar. 21.

GRACIA, ST. (d. 1180?), martyr. *See* Bernard, St.

GRACIÁN Y MORALES, BALTASAR (1601–1658). Born in Belmonte, Aragon, Spain, on Jan. 8, he was brought up by his uncle Antonio at Toledo, became a Jesuit in 1619, taught at several colleges, and was rector of Tarragona. He wrote on Eucharistic devotion, literary criticism, and Ferdinand the Catholic. His *Oráculo manual ó arte de prudencia* (*The Art of Worldly Wisdom*; 1647) was his most popular work and influenced the English essayists in their discussion of taste and manners and La Bruyère and La Rochefoucauld. His philosophical novel *El Criticón* (1651–57) was an allegory of man in nature and civilization and was admired by Schopenhauer. His style is marked by subtlety, compression, and refined and epigrammatic wit of the style known as *conceptismo*. Gracian died in Tarragona, Spain, on Dec. 6.

GRACILIAN, ST. (d. 304?), martyr. While in prison in Faleria she restored the sight of a blind girl named Felicissima, converted her, and was beheaded with her. F. D. Aug. 12.

GRADENIGO, BL. JOHN (d. 1025). A Venetian nobleman, he became a Benedictine at Cuxa, in the Pyrenees, with St. Peter Urseolo, and later a hermit near Monte Cassino. F. D. Dec. 5.

GRADWELL, ROBERT (1777–1833), bishop. Born in Clifton, Lancashire, England, on Jan. 26, he went to Douai in 1791, was a prisoner of French revolutionists until 1795, returned to Durham, and completed his education and was ordained there in 1802. He taught at Crook Hall and Ushaw College, became rector of the English College in Rome in 1818, and coadjutor to Bishop Bramston of London in 1828. He published two apologetical works and died in London on Mar. 15.

GRAHAM, PATRICK (d. 1478), archbishop. Grandson of Robert III of Scotland, he studied at St. Andrews, became dean of its arts faculty in 1457, and was named bishop of Brechin in 1463 and of St. Andrews in 1466, both in Scotland. He was consecrated in Rome, and was the center of stormy opposition when on his return his see was raised to an archdiocese, of which he was first archbishop, in 1472, and was given control of twelve lesser sees, including some in England and Norway. Ecclesiastical quarrels led to outlandish charges; King James III was bribed by opposing bishops to bring charges against his cousin to Rome; a papal nuncio was appointed to investigate; and Graham was deposed and imprisoned, probably the victim of political pressure. He died at the castle of Lochleven, Scotland.

GRAMONT, CHARLES DE (d. 1544). He became archbishop of Bordeaux, France, in 1530, aided the foundation of the College of Guyenne (1533), and was a patron of art.

GRAMONT, EUGÉNIE DE (1788–1846). Born in Versailles, France, on Sept. 17, daughter of Count de Gramont d'Aster of the royal court, she was taken to England during the French Revolution, lived at Richmond, and on her return to France became a religious of the Sacred Heart at Amiens in 1806. She taught in Paris schools until the revolution of 1830, was superior there as soon as peace returned, twice differed strongly with St. Madeleine Sophie Barat, foundress of her order, but remained in the latter's affection and in her post until her death in Paris on Nov. 19.

GRANCOLAS, JEAN (1660?–1732), theologian. Born near Chateaudun, France, he took his doctorate in theology at Paris in 1685, was chaplain to the brother of Louis XIV until his patron's death, made detailed studies of liturgical ceremonies, and wrote more than twenty volumes on the sacraments, particularly confession and the Eucharist, a history of the Church, a commentary on the breviary, an edition of the *Imitation,* and a refutation of the quietism of Molinos. He died in Paris on Aug. 1.

GRANDE, BL. JUAN (1546–1600). Born in Carmona, Andalusia, Spain, he was in the linen trade, then gave up his possessions at twenty-two and became a hermit. In humility he called himself Juan "Grande Pecador" (the great sinner), and cared for prisoners and the sick in the poorly run hospital in Xeres. Its directors persecuted him because his earnestness was a rebuke, but a wealthy family built a new hospital and placed him in charge. He af-

filiated this with the Order of Hospitallers, which he joined at Granada. He also took charge of orphans, raised dowries for poor girls, and had several supernatural gifts. He died in Xeres, Spain, during a great plague and was beatified in 1853. F. D. June 3.

GRANDERATH, THEODOR (1839–1902), historian. Born in Giesenkirchen, Rhine Province, Germany, on June 19, he studied in Neuss and at Tübingen, became a Jesuit at Münster in 1860, was ordained in 1874, and from then until 1887 taught canon law and dogma at Ditton Hall in England. In 1887 he worked at Exaeten, Holland, and from 1893 to 1901 in Rome, preparing a history of the Vatican Council. He edited its *Acta et decreta* in 1890 and *Constitutiones dogmaticae* from 1892; the first two volumes of his *Geschichte des vaticanischen Koncils* were completed at Valkenburg, Holland, where he died on Mar. 19; a third volume was completed by Fr. Konrad Kirch.

GRANDIDIER, PHILIPPE ANDRÉ (1752–1787), historian. Born in Strassburg, Alsace, on Nov. 9, he was archivist of that diocese at eighteen, was made a canon of its cathedral, and royal historiographer for Alsace. He wrote a history of the Church there to 965, an account of its cathedral, a history of the province, and left five volumes of correspondence, chiefly with savants in the twenty-five learned societies of France and Germany of which he was a member. He died in Luntzel Abbey, Sundgau, Alsace, on Oct. 11.

GRANDIN, VITAL J. (d. 1902), bishop. He became a member of the Oblates of Mary Immaculate, did missionary work in Canada for five years after his ordination, became titular bishop of Satala and coadjutor to the bishop of St. Boniface, Manitoba, in 1859, and in 1871 became first bishop of St. Albert, Alberta, Canada. He died on June 3.

GRANJON, HENRY (1863?–1922), bishop. Born in St. Étienne, Loire, France, on June 15 (possibly April 15, 1859), he studied at St. Chamond College, St. Sulpice, Paris, and the Apollinaris and the Minerva, Rome, and was ordained in Lyons in 1887. He went to the United States, where he engaged in missionary work in Arizona, headed the Society of the Propagation of the Faith in 1897–1900, and was consecrated bishop of Tucson, Arizona, in 1900. He died in Brignais, France, on Nov. 9.

GRANT, THOMAS (1816–1870), bishop. Born in Ligny-les-Aires, France, on Nov. 25, son of Bernard Grant, an Irish army sergeant, he studied at Ushaw and the English College, Rome, was ordained in 1841, served Cardinal Acton as secretary for three years, and was rector of the English College from 1844 to 1850. He gathered documents and prepared material for the restoration of the hierarchy in England and in 1851 was consecrated first bishop of

Southwark. He was the mediator between the government and Cardinal Wiseman, gained the appointment of military and prison chaplains, and was a valuable participant at English synods and administrative meetings. He was sent to the Vatican Council, but died in Rome of cancer on June 1.

GRANVELLE, ANTOINE PERRENOT DE (1517–1586), cardinal. Born in Besançon, France, on Aug. 20, son of Charles V's prime minister, Nicolas Perrenot, he studied at Padua, Paris, and Louvain, received many ecclesiastical benefices, became archdeacon of Besançon and of Cambrai, and about 1538 was made bishop of Arras. He lived at Brussels instead of in his diocese, took an active part in imperial politics, attended the Council of Trent in 1545, succeeded his father in 1550 as secretary of state, and was named archbishop of Mechlin in 1559 and cardinal in 1561. He was a member of the council of state in the Low Countries, counselor to Margaret of Parma, the regent, and so powerful that a coalition of nobles had him removed to France. He went to Rome in 1565 and helped to form the Holy League, was viceroy of Naples in 1571–75, and in 1579 became a royal counselor at Madrid. He resigned his see at Mechlin and in 1584 was named archbishop of Besançon. He was a patron of the arts, worldly and vain, brilliant as a statesman, inept as a Renaissance churchman. He died in Madrid on Sept. 21.

GRASSE-TILLY, FRANÇOIS JOSEPH PAUL DE (1723–1788), admiral. Born near Toulon, France, he fought against Turkey and Morocco at the age of fifteen with the Knights of Malta, and in the French navy from 1739 to 1747, when he became a prisoner in England for two years. On his return he rose steadily in rank, served in the Seven Years' War and in the East Indies, was a rear admiral in the West Indies campaign during the American Revolution, was made admiral in 1781, and with a fleet of twenty-three ships defeated Admiral Hood off Martinique. De Grasse then captured Tobago and, seeking to join the French fleet stationed at Newport, engaged the English off Chesapeake Bay and prevented the reinforcement of their army at Yorktown. He captured St. Kitts in 1782 but later that year was defeated and captured by Admiral Rodney and imprisoned in Jamaica and London. After his return to France he blamed his subordinates for the naval disaster, was exonerated but not given an active post, and retired in 1784. He died in Paris on Jan. 11.

GRASSI, BL. ANTONIO (1592–1671). Born in Fermo, in the Italian Marches, he joined the Oratorians there at seventeen, was ordained, and became famous as a confessor. He was elected superior of the Fermo Oratory in 1635, an office to which he was re-elected every three

years until his death. He was beatified in 1900. F. D. Dec. 13.

GRASSI, BL. GREGORIO (1833–1900), bishop and martyr. A native of Piedmont, Italy, he had served as a Franciscan missioner in China for forty years and was vicar apostolic to northern Shansi when the Boxer Rebellion broke out. He was beheaded by Yu Hsien, governor of Taiyuanfu, notorious for his hatred of Christians. He was beatified in 1946. F. D. July 9.

GRASSIS, PARIS DE (1470?–1528). Born in Bologna, Italy, brother of Achille, he became master of ceremonies to Popes Julius II and Leo X. His *Diarium*, official record of curial activity and procedure, is of historical significance for the Julian campaign in Romagna and court anecdotes. He died in Rome on June 10.

GRATIA, ST. (d. 1180?), martyr. See Bernard, St.

GRATIA OF CATTARO, BL. (1438–1508?). Born in Cattaro, Dalmatia, he was a sailor until 1468, when he became an Augustinian lay-brother in Padua, Italy. He died on Nov. 9 and his cult was approved in 1889. F. D. Nov. 16.

GRATIAN, JEROME (1545–1614). Born in Valladolid, Spain, on June 6, he was educated at Madrid and Alcalá, was ordained in 1569, and became a Discalced Carmelite in 1572, taking the name Jerome of the Mother of God. He was pro-vicar apostolic of the Calced Carmelites in Andalusia, who objected to his orders, and established a foundation for his own group at Seville. He was given wide powers of reform by the papal nuncio, but was censured by rebels and restricted to Alcalá. He served St. Teresa of Avila as spiritual director from 1575 until her death, and became superior of the Discalced Carmelites when they were canonically approved in 1580. Although supported by St. John of the Cross, he was strongly opposed by a faction led by Nicholas Doria and in 1592 was expelled from his order. On his way to Rome to appeal the verdict he was captured by pirates, worked among Christian slaves in North Africa, and nearly two years later was cleared of charges by Pope Clement VIII. To avoid a revival of dissension he was affiliated with the Calced Carmelites, preached in Ceuta and Tetuan, and after 1606 lived in Brussels, in the service of Archduke Albers. He died there on Sept. 21.

GRATIAN, JOHANNES (12th century), canonist. Born in Italy, perhaps at Chiusi, he was a Camaldolese or Benedictine monk, taught at Bologna, and founded the science of canon law by compiling *Concordantia discordantium canonum* (generally called *Decretum Gratiani*) between 1140 and 1151.

GRATIANUS, ST. (d. 250), martyr. See Felinus, St.

GRATINI, BENEDETTO (1490–1530),

sculptor. Born in Rovezzano (or Canapale), Italy, he became noted for his sculptures, especially of tombs, and in 1524 went to England, where Cardinal Wolsey engaged him to execute a tomb which eventually was used for Admiral Nelson. He spent the last years of his life, blind, in Florence, where he died. His name is also spelled Grazini, but he is better known as Benedetto da Rovezzano, from his birthplace.

GRATIUS, ORTWIN (1475–1542). Born in Holtwick, Westphalia, he was educated by his uncle in Deventer, took his doctorate at Cologne, and became adviser to the Quentell press there. A leading humanist, he defended the Dominicans against Reuchlin, and was widely lampooned by younger intellectuals. He was ordained in 1520 and compiled a series of sixty-six treatises on Church history and canon law, with a preface asking for widespread reform; because of the extremity of some of the passages cited, the work was placed on the Index as anti-clerical. He died in Cologne, Germany, on May 22.

GRATRY, AUGUSTE JOSEPH ALPHONSE (1805–1872). Born in Lille, France, on Mar. 30, he studied in Paris and Strassburg, was ordained in the latter city in 1832, and in 1841 transferred to Paris as director of Collège Stanislas. He was chaplain of L'Écols Normale in 1846–51, restored the Oratory in France with Fr. Pététot in 1852, was vicar general of Orléans in 1861, professor of moral theology at the Sorbonne in 1863, and in 1867 was elected to the French Academy. He was condemned for living outside his community, and obliged to leave the Oratorians, and censured again in 1870 for violently attacking the dogma of papal infallibility. After its promulgation he made a public retraction. He died in Montreux, Switzerland, on Feb. 7.

GRATUS, ST. (d. 302), martyr. *See* Felix, St.
GRATUS, ST. (d. 470?). Bishop of Aosta, Italy, he is its patron saint. F. D. Sept. 7.
GRATUS, ST. (d. 506?). He was first bishop of Oloron, in southern Gaul. F. D. Oct. 11.
GRATUS, ST. (d. 652?). He was bishop of Châlons-sur-Saône, Gaul. F. D. Oct. 8.
GRAU, BL. BONAVENTURA (1620–1684). A shepherd at Riudoms, near Barcelona, Spain, he married at seventeen, was widowed at nineteen, and became a Franciscan laybrother. He experienced visions, served at a friary in Rome where he was consulted by the pope and his advisers, and established several retreat houses. His cult was approved in 1906. F. D. Sept. 11.
GRAVES, CLOTILDE (1863–1932), novelist. Born in Barracks, Cork, Ireland, on June 3, she was educated at a convent in Lourdes, France, returned to play minor roles in the theater and publish cartoons, and became a convert in 1896. Her literary career was at first associated with

the stage: sixteen plays were produced in London and New York between 1887 and 1913, including A *Matchmaker*, A *Maker of Comedies*, *The Bond of Ninon*, and A *Tenement Tragedy*. She then turned to the novel and published a score between 1912 and her death in Middlesex, England, on Dec. 3. *Between Two Thieves* dealt with the Crimean War; *The Doctor*, with the Boer conflict; *The Lovers of the Market Place* and *The Pipers of the Market Place* are on English small-town life. Other titles are: *The Villa of the Peacock*, *The Just Steward*, and *The Man in the Mask*. She wrote under the name Richard Dehan.

GRAVIER, JACQUES (1651–1708), missioner. Born in Moulins, France, he became a Jesuit in 1670, was sent to Canada in 1685 after ordination, and for ten years developed the Illinois mission, working with Kaskaskia and Peoria Indians near Fort St. Louis. In 1696 he became superior at Michilimackinac (now Mackinac, Michigan), returning to the Indians in 1700. He was wounded by the Peorias in 1706 and died of the effects of a still-imbedded arrow two years later, while in Louisiana.

GRAVINA, DOMINIC (1573?–1643), theologian. Born in Sicily, he became a Dominican in Naples, taught there and at the Minerva and other schools, became dean of the theological college at Naples, and preached through Italy. He served as prior and provincial, was made a master of the sacred palace by Pope Urban VIII, and wrote widely on theology and mysticism. He died in Rome on Aug. 26.

GRAVINA, GIOVANNI VINCENZO (1664–1718), jurist. Born in Rogliano, Italy, on Jan. 21, he studied classics in Naples and law in Rome, was co-founder in 1690 of Accademia degli Arcadi for the support of poetry, and, after a literary quarrel, founded a rival group. He wrote five tragedies and a study of that dramatic form, several works on civil and canon law, and had just been invited to the chair of law at Turin when he died in Rome on Jan. 6.

GRAY, JOHN (1817–1872), bishop. He was third vicar apostolic of Scotland, residing at Glasgow, and was consecrated titular bishop of Hyposopolis. He resigned in 1869.

GREBÁC-ORLOV, IGNAC (1888?–1957), poet. Born in Namestov, Slovakia, he became well known for his poetry, won a number of national prizes, and apparently was a fellow prisoner with the primate of Slovakia, Bishop Jan Vojtassak, at the time of his death.

GRECO, EL (1548?–1614), painter. Domenico Theotocopuli was born in Phodele, near Candia, Crete, studied in Titian's workshop in Venice under Tintoretto and the Bassani, who greatly influenced his work, and in 1570 went to Rome, where he was patronized by

Cardinal Alessandro Farnese and studied the works of Michelangelo. In the spring of 1576 he went to Spain and became famed for the design and the altarpiece of Santo Domingo el Antiguo church in Toledo (his *Assumption of the Virgin* was the center panel). Among his other great works are *Assumption of the Virgin, Resurrection of Christ, Adoration of the Shepherds, Dream of Philip II, Burial of Count Orgaz, St. Louis, Holy Family, Portrait of an Unknown Man, Madonna on Throne of Clouds, St. Martin, St. Jerome as Cardinal, Golgotha, Toledo, Vision of St. Dominic, St. Ildefonso, Christ Despoiled of His Garments, The Healing of the Blind,* and *Christ Driving the Money Changers from the Temple,* and *The Trinity.* His early works are characterized by their glowing color, religious fervor, and pronounced Italian influence, but his Spanish works, for which he is more famous, are characteristically somber, produced by his use of gray and pale tones, with emotional intensity and dramatic power which are overwhelming. He died in Toledo, Spain, on Apr. 7.

GREDIFAEL, ST. (7th century). He went with St. Padarin from Brittany to Wales and probably became abbot of Whitland, Pembrokeshire. F. D. Nov. 13.

GREEN, BL. HUGH (1584?–1642), martyr. Born in London and educated at Cambridge, he became a convert, was ordained at Douai in 1612, and returned to serve English Catholics in Dorset. He was hanged, drawn, and quartered at Dorchester on the charge of priesthood, and beatified in 1929. F. D. Aug. 19.

GREEN, BL. THOMAS (d. 1537), martyr. *See* Beer, Bl. Richard.

GREEN, BL. THOMAS (1560?–1642), English martyr. Often called Thomas Reynolds, he was born in Oxford, educated in France and Spain, and ordained at thirty. He served in the English mission for fifty years; though he was exiled in 1606, he returned, was captured in 1628, and left in prison until he was hanged at Tyburn. He was beatified in 1929. F. D. Jan. 21.

GREEN, THOMAS LOUIS (1799–1883). Born in Stourbridge, Worcestershire, England, he studied at Sedgley Park and Oscott, was ordained in 1825, and engaged in formal controversy while serving at Norwich, Tixall, and various Shropshire parishes and chaplaincies. Many of these were published, as well as apologetical works. He died in Newport, England, on Feb. 27.

GREENE, EDWARD LEE (1843–1915), botanist. Born in Hopkinton, Rhode Island, he went with his family to Wisconsin, studied under the Swedish botanist, Knure Kumlein, fought during the Civil War, and took degrees at Albion and Jarvis. He became a convert in 1885, taught at the University of California, published *Manual of Botany for San Francisco Bay, Pittonia, Some West American Oaks,* established that Cesalpino (not Linnaeus) was the founder of scientific botany, and discovered and named 5000 new specimens. He taught at Catholic University from 1895 to 1904, then became an associate of the Smithsonian Institution, and died in Washington, D.C., on Nov. 10.

GREENWOOD, BL. WILLIAM (d. 1537), martyr. *See* Beer, Bl. Richard.

GREGORY I THE GREAT, ST. (540?–604), pope and Doctor of the Church. Born in Rome of a patrician family which had supplied two earlier popes (Agapitus I and Felix III), and well educated by his father Gordianus and mother St. Silvia, he entered public life and was prefect of the city before he was thirty. Five years later he resigned, founded six monasteries on his Sicilian estate, distributed his great wealth, and became a Benedictine monk at his own home on the Caelian Hill, which he renamed St. Andrew's. After five years of seclusion he was ordained, made one of the seven papal deacons, and from 579 to 585 served Pope Pelagius II as nuncio at Constantinople. There he met St. Leander of Seville, who recommended that he prepare a commentary on the Book of Job; this, the *Moralia,* was completed at Rome. In 586 he was recalled by Pope Pelagius, became abbot of St. Andrew's, and on Sept. 3, 590, was elected pope by the people and clergy of Rome. During his pontificate he wrote *Cura pastoralis,* on the duties of bishops as preaching shepherds and establishers of discipline, an influential book spread through England by St. Augustine, through France by Charlemagne, and translated by King Alfred. Gregory was a firm disciplinarian himself, removed unworthy clerics from office, forbade the exaction of fees for many services, preached frequently, directly oversaw the welfare of tenants on papal property, and emptied the treasury to ransom captives of the Lombards, victims of plagues and famine, and the persecuted Jews. In 593 he wrote his widely popular *Dialogues* on the lives and miracles (sometimes extravagant in the telling) of Italian saints and on the immortality of the soul, intended to encourage his countrymen in an age of disheartening turmoil when invaders again reached the gates of Rome. He was most earnest in regard to the conversion of England, sending forty monks from his own St. Andrew's, but was unsuccessful in dealing with the arrogance, incompetence, and financial extortions of Byzantium. He is particularly remembered for popularizing the work of St. Augustine; for making some changes in the liturgy; for strengthening respect for doctrine; and for introducing the Lenten custom of papal masses at various churches (stations) in Rome. The custom of saying thirty successive masses for the dead began in his time and bears his name. Whether he revised and rearranged the system of church music, founded a music school, and composed several hymns is disputed. He died in Rome. F. D. Mar. 12 (also, Sept. 3).

F. H. DUDDEN, *Gregory the Great* (New York, Longmans, 1905); WILLIAM THOMAS WALSH, *Saints in Action* (Garden City, N.Y., Hanover House, 1961).

GREGORY II, ST. (d. 731), pope. Born in Rome, he served four popes as treasurer and librarian, and succeeded Pope Constantine on May 19, 715. He fought strenuously against heretics, particularly the Iconoclasts under Emperor Leo III, worked zealously to inspire more discipline and morality in religious life, built a hospital and several monasteries, helped to rebuild Monte Cassino and other establishments destroyed by the Lombards, and consecrated SS. Boniface and Corbinian to lead the mission to Germany. F. D. Feb. 11.

GREGORY III, ST. (d. 741), pope. A Syrian by birth and a priest, he succeeded Gregory II to the papacy on Mar. 18, 731, elected by popular acclamation. He became embroiled with Emperor Leo III the Isaurian, who supported the Iconoclasts, and called a synod in Rome which condemned the heresy and approved excommunication of those who supported it. He encouraged missionary activities, made Boniface a bishop, and sent St. Willibald to Germany to aid him. Breaking with tradition, when the Lombards threatened Rome he appealed to Charles Martel and the Franks rather than to the Eastern emperor, but the appeal was fruitless. He died in Nov. F. D. Dec. 10.

GREGORY IV (d. 844), pope. Son of John, and a Roman, he was ordained by Paschal I, made cardinal-priest of the basilica of St. Mark, and was elected pope late in 827. Because of interference by the Frankish representatives of Emperor Louis the Pious, he was unable to take office until March, 828. His reign was disturbed by the long quarrels between Louis and his sons, and between Lothair, the eldest, and his two brothers and half-brother. The Frankish Empire came to an end in 841 at the battle of Fontenay. The Saracens took advantage of the warfare to occupy Sicily and move into southern Italy. Gregory fortified Ostia, repaired some churches, and aided St. Anschar in his mission efforts in Sweden. The pope died in Jan. and was buried in St. Peter's.

GREGORY V (970?–999), pope. Bruno, Saxon son of Duke Otto of Carinthia, was nominated by Otto III, his cousin, when the Romans asked his choice after the death of Pope John XV. He left his imperial chaplaincy and was consecrated in Rome on May 3, 996, the first German to become pope. He crowned Otto as emperor later that month; when Otto left Rome, Crescentius Numentanus captured the city. Gregory fled to the north and John Filagato of Rossano was made antipope, reigning as John XVI until captured by Otto and blinded, mutilated, and deported. Crescentius was hanged. Gregory held a number of punitive synods and aided Aelfric in developing Canterbury and encouraging monasteries in Germany; he died on Feb. 4.

GREGORY VI (d. 1048?), pope. When Pope Benedict IX sought to marry, he consulted his godfather, John Gratian, who advised him that he was correct in thinking he had been thrust unwillingly into the papacy. Gratian, eager to rid Rome of the libertine, according to a now discredited legend accepted a sum of money and the papal crown and on May 5, 1045, was recognized as Pope Gregory VI. Sylvester III, who had been chosen pope when Benedict was expelled from Rome in 1045, continued to rule until Oct.; Benedict, when his marriage plans failed, also reclaimed the office. Gregory called on King Henry III to invade Italy to settle the matter; at a synod held in Sutri on Dec. 20, 1046, Benedict's claim was disallowed, Sylvester's election was declared invalid, and Gregory abdicated. Gregory went to Germany in May 1047 with his chaplain Hildebrand and died, sometime after 1047, probably in Cologne.

GREGORY VII, ST. (1020?–1085), pope. Born in Ravacum, Tuscany, Italy, and baptized Hildebrand, he was brought up by an uncle, studied at the Lateran school under John Gratian, became the latter's secretary while he was Gregory VI, then retired to a monastery, probably in Rome. He returned to Rome in 1049 with Bishop Bruno of Toul when the latter became Pope Leo IX, and remained as counselor to the next four pontiffs. He was made a cardinal-deacon, directed papal finances, and was legate to France during the controversy over the Eucharist. He presided at the Council of Sens which in 1054 condemned Berengarius, but accepted that theologian's profession of faith in 1079. Gregory also presided at councils held in Lyons and Châlons, and was legate to the imperial court and to Milan. By the reign of Alexander II he was one of the best known and most influential men in Rome. On Apr. 22, 1073, he was elected pope by acclamation and was consecrated on June 30. That the times were bad is attested to by the writings of St. Peter Damien: leaders of Church and state were corrupt and dissolute, simony was universal, celibacy was disregarded, monasteries employed waitresses, church property was passed on to pastors' children. At his first synod (1074) Gregory attacked simony and the married clergy; at his second (1075) he ordered an end to the practice of lay investiture (distribution of ecclesiastical offices by nobles and other laymen). The problem was a particularly difficult one, since the people and their feudal rulers did not yet distinguish between the conferring of a church office and the temporal powers which accompanied it. Since Gregory could not trust the bishops to carry out his orders, he appointed monks as legates. William I of England crushed simony and enforced all papal decrees except that on investiture; progress was very slow in France; opposition was almost complete in Germany, northern Italy, and Rome itself. Gregory tried to win Emperor Henry IV's support, achieved a degree of peace in 1074, but had greater success when he tried to reform the sees of Augsburg, Cologne, Hamburg, and Mainz. The emperor would not abandon the profits of simony, and twenty-seven bishops, opposed to simony but fearing loss of independence under the direction of a firm pope, met at Worms in 1076, denounced Gregory, and called for his expulsion. The emperor took the position that he was absolute master of his people and of the pope as well. Gregory then excommunicated Henry and the archbishops of Cologne and Mainz. It was the first deposition of a king by the papacy and had lasting effects. In 1077, Henry presented himself to the pope at a castle in Canossa, claimed that he was contrite, and, though Gregory had reason to remain suspicious, had the ban lifted. When Rudolf of Swabia was elected emperor by opposition forces in Germany, the pope took a neutral stand. Henry broke all his promises almost immediately, began making ecclesiastical appointments, and was again censured and deposed. He was supported by nobles and bishops and in 1080, after Rudolf was slain in battle, arranged the election of Archbishop Guibert of Ravenna as antipope Clement III. Henry invaded Italy in 1081 and attacked Rome four times, keeping the pope a virtual prisoner. When the city fell in 1084, Gregory was besieged in Sant' Angelo until the Normans came to his rescue; however, they sacked the city in the flush of victory, the Romans turned on Gregory, and he fled to Monte Cassino and later to Salerno. Before his death in Salerno on May 25 he lifted all excommunications except those against Henry and Guibert. Gregory had worked to rescue Spain from the Moors, sought reform there, and had hopes for a crusade against the Saracens, but these plans never matured because of imperial interference. He also instituted systematic research in libraries for decretals and gathered materials later to be used by Alselm of Lucca and others in codifying canon law. Gregory was canonized in 1606 by Pope Paul V; Benedict XIII made his feast day (May 25) universal in 1728, although France objected and its celebration was forbidden in Austria.

GREGORY VIII (d. 1137?), antipope.

Mauritius Bourdin (also called Bordhino and Burdinus) was born in France, probably in Limoges, studied and became a Benedictine at Cluny, and went to Toledo, Spain, with Archbishop Bernard. He was named bishop of Coimbra in 1098 and moved to Braga in 1111. After he quarreled with Bernard he was suspended by Pope Paschal II in 1114. When he went to Rome, Bourdin was well liked and became an important member of the papal court. When Henry V invaded, Paschal fled to Benevento and sent Bourdin to negotiate with Henry. He sold out to the invader, crowned him emperor on Easter Sunday, 1117, and was promptly excommunicated. Henry made him "pope" on Mar. 8, 1118, on Paschal's death, but the college of cardinals had already licitly elected Gelasius. Henry announced that the latter's election was null and void and bribed the Romans to accept Bourdin. He was captured in time and handed over to Pope Callistus II, who ordered him to live in a series of monasteries.

GREGORY VIII (d. 1187), pope. Alberto de Morra was born early in the century in Benevento, Italy, became a Cistercian or Benedictine, and was made cardinal-deacon in 1155 and cardinal-priest in 1158. In 1172 he became chancellor to Pope Alexander III and was sent to England to investigate the murder of St. Thomas à Becket; he also crowned Alfonso II of Portugal. He was elected pope on Oct. 21, 1187, and consecrated on Oct. 25. Because Saladin had captured Palestine and occupied Jerusalem, the new pope planned a new crusade, made peace overtures to Barbarossa, and went to Pisa to end hostilities with Genoa. He died in Pisa, Italy, on Dec. 17, less than two months after his election.

GREGORY IX (1145?–1241), pope. Ugolino, count of Segni, was born in Anagni, Italy, educated at Paris and Bologna, and was appointed papal chaplain and cardinal-deacon in 1198 by his uncle, Innocent III. In 1206 he was named cardinal-bishop of Ostia and Velletri, went to Germany in 1207 as papal legate (and lifted the excommunication of Philip of Swabia), and again in 1209 to ask the princes to accept Otto of Brunswick as king. In 1216 he and Cardinal Guido of Preneste were empowered to appoint a new pope, in order to save time, and chose Honorius III. Ugolino preached the crusade in northern Italy and effected peace between warring city-states. In 1227 he was one of three cardinals empowered to select a new pope; when they could not agree, the other two selected Ugolino on Mar. 19, and he was consecrated on Mar. 21. When Emperor Frederick II failed to keep his promise to lead the crusade, Gregory excommunicated him. The Frangipani faction in Rome then rose in rebellion; the Ghibelline mob threatened the pope, and he fled to Viterbo and Perugia in 1228. Frederick went to the Holy Land, but the pope reaffirmed the excommunication and released the crusaders from their oath of allegiance to the emperor; Frederick then defeated the papal army in Sicily and arranged a temporary peace. Excommunication was lifted in 1230 but restored in 1239 when the emperor continued to march through Italy with the admitted intention of seizing the entire area. Many bishops refused to support the papacy; others were forbidden to travel to papally convened synods or were captured while en route. Frederick was besieging Rome when the pope died there on Aug. 22. Gregory was especially active against heretics; up to his time the duty of identifying them rested with bishops; he created the monastic inquisition in 1233. He directed William of Auvergne and others to correct the error-filled Latin translations of Aristotle and thus helped to begin the restoration of Aristotelianism as the basis of scholastic philosophy. Canon law was also codified in five books and published in 1234.

GREGORY X, BL. (1210–1276), pope. Teobaldo Visconti was born in Piacenza, Italy, studied canon law at Paris, became an archdeacon at Liège, served Cardinal Ottoboni on a mission to England, and went with Prince Edward on a pilgrimage to the Holy Land. He was not a priest when he was selected as pope on Sept. 1, 1271, by six cardinals designated to find a successor to Clement IV after a three-year vacancy. Recalled to Rome from Palestine, he was ordained on Mar. 19 and consecrated pope on Mar. 27, 1272. In the political sphere he worked to bring an end to the Guelph-Ghibilline warfare; placed Florence under interdict when it refused to be reconciled with its neighbors; approved Rudolph of Hapsburg as German emperor; and arranged the renunciation of claims by Alfonso of Castile. He opened the Council of Lyons in 1274, at which the Greek delegates returned Byzantium to communion with Rome (a short-lived political move by the emperor), arranged a tax for the support of a crusade, and worked for reform. He was exceptionally charitable, above faction, and admirably simple. He died in Arezzo, Italy, on Jan. 10. His cult was approved in 1713 and he is venerated as a saint in several Italian dioceses. F. D. Jan. 10.

GREGORY XI (1331–1378), pope. Pierre Roger de Beaufort was born in the castle of Maumont, Limoges, France, received many benefices and the cardinalate (at nineteen) from his uncle, Pope Clement VI, studied law at Perugia, and was unanimously elected pope at Avignon on Dec. 30, 1370. He was consecrated on Jan. 5, 1371, the day after his ordination. He condemned the heresy of John Wyclif, brought peace to Sicily, Naples, and

Spain, but failed to control fiefs in northern Italy. Duke Bernabò Visconti fought against him, forced him to accept dictated peace terms, and continued the struggle when the pope brought in French advisers and legates. The wars pushed the Papal States deeply into debt, and were fought in spite of direct pleas and warnings from SS. Bridget of Sweden and Catherine of Siena. Gregory returned to Rome from Avignon, against opposition from all his cardinals but one, and from his own father, early in 1377, but met rioting mobs and had to retire to Anagni within four months. He died in Rome on Mar. 27.

GREGORY XII (1327?–1417), pope. Angelo Correr was born in Venice of a noble family and became bishop of Castello in 1380 and titular patriarch of Constantinople in 1390. Pope Innocent VII appointed him apostolic secretary, legate of Ancona, and, in 1405, cardinal. He was unanimously elected pope on Nov. 30, 1406 (when he was eighty), but when he failed to meet with the antipope Benedict XIII of Avignon to settle the western schism, a group of cardinals assembled at Pisa in 1409, illegally disposed of both, and elected Cardinal Peter Philarges as Alexander V and on his death in 1410, elected Baldassare Cossa as John XXIII. The dispute continued until 1415, when a council was convoked at Constance. Gregory resigned as pope on July 4 and was then appointed bishop of Porto and perpetual legate at Ancona, and died two years later at Recanati, Italy, on Sept. 18.

GREGORY XIII (1502–1585), pope. Born in Bologna, Italy, on Jan. 7, Ugo Buoncompagni led a dissolute life as a youth (he had an illegitimate son, Giacomo), studied at Bologna, taught there after receiving his doctorate in law, and in 1539 went to Rome, where Pope Paul III appointed him a judge and in 1545 sent him to the Council of Trent. He served on other diplomatic missions and in 1558 was appointed bishop of Viesti. In 1559, Pope Pius IV returned him to Trent as his confidential deputy and he remained there until 1563. He was named cardinal-priest in 1564, sent as legate to Spain, and in 1566 was secretary of papal bulls. He was elected pope on May 13, 1572, and consecrated on May 25. He showed great interest in the education of the clergy (founding some twenty-three seminaries, including major national colleges in Rome, and spending millions on behalf of poor seminarians) and the laity (opening colleges across Europe and three in Japan). His attempt to conquer the Saracens failed because Spain and Venice signed treaties with Turkey; he was successful in his efforts to restore Catholicism in defecting countries. In 1578 he reformed the Julian calendar by establishing that called after him and still in use; he also emended the Roman Martyrology in 1580–84 and provided an official Roman edition of the *Corpus juris canonici* (1582) on which a committee had worked since 1566. His education and mission endeavors cost so much and he sought revenues so vigorously that he met great opposition from the aristocracy. He died in Rome on Apr. 10.

GREGORY XIV (1535–1591), pope. Niccolò Sfondrati was born in Somma, Italy, on Feb. 11, son of a senator, studied at Perugia and Padua, was ordained, and in 1560 became bishop of Cremona. He took part in the Council of Trent in 1561–63 and was created cardinal-priest in 1583. He was elected pope on Dec. 5, 1590, supported the French League, and renewed the excommunication of Henry IV when the latter failed to keep his promises. Gregory was a friend of SS. Charles Borromeo and Philip Neri, ordered the release of all Indian slaves in the Philippines, and appointed a commission to revise the Sixtine Bible and the breviary. He died in Rome on Oct. 15.

GREGORY XV (1554–1623), pope. Alessandro Ludovici was born in Bologna, Italy, on Jan. 9 or 15, studied there and in Rome, and was appointed a judge by Gregory XIII. In 1612 he was named by Paul V as archbishop of Bologna and nuncio to Savoy, and in 1616 became cardinal-priest. He was elected pope on Feb. 9, 1621, laid down rules for secret papal elections which are still in effect, established the Congregation of the Propagation of the Faith in 1622, approved new religious congregations, regained Moravia and Bohemia for the Church, and in 1623 effected the transfer of the Palatinate from a Protestant to a Catholic. In gratitude for this service to the empire, Duke Maximilian of Bavaria presented a collection of 35,000 manuscripts to the pope, which became the basis of the Gregoriana Library. Gregory canonized SS. Albertus Magnus, Bruno, Francis Xavier, Ignatius Loyola, Peter of Alcantara, Philip Neri, and Teresa of Avila, among others. He died in Rome on July 8.

GREGORY XVI (1765–1846), pope. Bartolomeo Alberto Cappellari was born in Belluno, Italy, on Sept. 8, became a Camaldolese, taking the name Mauro, in 1783 at Venice, and was ordained in 1787. He was sent to Rome in 1795, and wrote *Il trinofo della santa sede* on papal infallibility. In 1805 he was appointed abbot of San Gregorio, became procurator general in 1807, and in 1808 went to Venice and then to Padua to teach. When political tension lessened he returned to Rome in 1813, served as consultor, and in 1826 was publicly named cardinal and prefect of the Congregation for the Propagation of the Faith. He arranged concordats for Holland in 1827 and Armenia in 1829. He was elected pope on Feb. 2, 1831, and consecrated on Feb. 6. He

put down long-smoldering rebellion with the assistance of Austria, but use of foreign troops did not help the situation; unrest and sporadic revolts continued; but he eventually agreed to wide reforms in the government of the Papal States and accepted civil courts. In 1832 he issued the encyclical *Mirari vos*, condemning modernism and Lamennais, Lacordaire, Montalembert, and their followers in France. This quarrel continued when he issued *Singulare nos* in 1834 in reply to Lamennais' answer. He fought the rising tide of libertarianism, anticlericalism, and secret societies in Germany, Portugal, Spain, and Poland. He encouraged the arts, established museums in Rome, and repaired or built several churches, hospitals, and orphanages. He died in Rome on June 9.

GREGORY, ST. (5th century), bishop. He, and St. Demetrius, an archdeacon, and St. Calogerus, an abbot, were driven from Africa by the Arians and settled near Fragalata, Sicily, which became a center for their preaching activity. F. D. June 18.

GREGORY, ST. (d. 539), bishop. Count of the district of Autun, France, he had an excellent reputation for justice; after the death of his wife he devoted himself exclusively to religious life, was elected bishop of Langres, and worked actively for captives and those who ran afoul of the law. He was the father of St. Tetricus and the great-grandfather of St. Gregory the Great. F. D. Jan. 4.

GREGORY, ST. (455?–540?). He was twelfth bishop of Auxerre, France, a see he ruled for thirteen years. F. D. Dec. 19.

GREGORY, ST. (d. 603?), bishop. The unreliable story of his life is that he was born near Girgenti, Sicily, spent four years in Byzantine monasteries in Palestine where he was ordained deacon in Jerusalem, and after some time spent in Antioch, Constantinople (where he acquired a reputation as a scholar), and Rome was made bishop of Girgenti by Pope St. Gregory the Great. He wrote a commentary on Ecclesiastes. He may have died as late as 638. F. D. Nov. 23.

GREGORY, ST. (9th century). A native of Decapolis in Asia Minor, he suffered much while opposing the Iconoclast heresy. F. D. Nov. 20.

GREGORY, BL. (d. 933). He was abbot of the Benedictine abbey of Nonantula, near Modena, Italy. F. D. Aug. 3.

GREGORY, ST. (d. 996). An Anglo-Saxon, he became a Benedictine at Rome and served as abbot of Einsiedeln, Switzerland. F. D. Nov. 8.

GREGORY, ST. (d. 999). A Basilian monk at Cerchiara, Calabria, he fled the Saracens to Rome, where he met Emperor Otto III, who built the abbey of Burtscheid near Aix-la-Chapelle, France. F. D. Nov. 4.

GREGORY, ST. (d. 1044?), cardinal. A Benedictine, he was bishop of Ostia, Italy, papal legate to Navarre and Castile, and died in Logroño, Spain. F. D. May 9.

GREGORY (d. 1161), archbishop. He became fifth bishop of Dublin, was consecrated at Lambeth by Archbishop Ralph of Canterbury in 1121, and was learned in his command of languages. The see, which was generally disregarded by the other ecclesiastics on the island, was sometimes claimed by Glendalough, but was created an archdiocese in 1152 by Cardinal Pararo at the request of Pope Eugene III. Thereafter the diocese was free of its dependence on Canterbury.

GREGORY, BL. (d. 1300). *See* Dominic, Bl.

GREGORY BAETICUS (d. 392?). Bishop of Elvira, Baetica, Spain, he was noted for his defense of the Nicaean creed and enmity to Arianism. He is reputed by St. Jerome to have written many theological treatises. He is venerated as a saint in Spain on Apr. 24.

GREGORY OF HEIMBURG (d. 1472). Born in Würzburg, he studied at Padua, taking his doctorate in law in 1430, was syndic of Nuremberg from 1433 to 1461, supported Eugene IV at the Council of Basle, and served on many diplomatic missions. He entered the service of Albert II of Austria in 1458 and was largely responsible for defeating Pius II's attempt to begin a crusade against the Turks. He was excommunicated in 1460 for his support of Sigismund of Austria, who had captured Bishop Nicholas of Cusa. Gregory appealed to a general council to overrule the pope, but the excommunication was renewed. In 1460 he served the king of Bohemia, whose anti-Roman policies he influenced, violently attacked Pope Paul II, and was again excommunicated. He fled to Saxony in 1471 and applied to the Council of Würzburg and then to Pope Sixtus IV for absolution, which was granted. He died in Tharandt, near Dresden, Saxony.

GREGORY THE ILLUMINATOR, ST. (d. 330?), bishop. He is traditionally called son of Anak, a Parthian who murdered King Khosrov I of Armenia. Hidden in Caesarea, Cappadocia, to escape the dying king's order to massacre Anak's family, he was baptized and raised, marrying there and bringing up two sons, SS. Aristakes and Vardanes. When Khosrov's son Tiridates returned to the Armenian throne, Gregory was permitted to return but, because of his success in Christianizing the populace, was persecuted by the king. When Gregory converted Tiridates, the monarch proclaimed Christianity the official religion of Armenia. Gregory was consecrated bishop of Ashtishat and began to organize the Church. He was represented by St. Aristakes at the first Council of Nicaea, consecrated him as his successor, and retired to a hermitage in Taron, where he died. He is called the "Apostle of Armenia." F. D. Sept. 30.

GREGORY MAKAR, ST. (d. 1010?), bishop. An Armenian, he served as a monk and later as bishop of Nicopolis in his own country, but left his see to spend his last seven years as a preacher and ascetic in Pithiviers, France. F. D. Mar. 16.

GREGORY NAZIANZEN THE ELDER, ST. (276?–374), bishop. A pagan official in Cappadocia, he was converted in 325 by his wife, St. Nonna; three years later he was elected bishop, fell into heresy, but was reconverted by his son, St. Gregory the Younger in 361. His other children, Caesarius and Gorgonia, also were saints. F. D. Jan. 1.

GREGORY NAZIANZEN, ST. (329?–390), bishop and Doctor of the Church. Born in Arianzus, Cappadocia, son of SS. Gregory and Nonna, he studied at nearby Caesarea, with his brother St. Caesarius and St. Basil as classmates. Gregory went on to study rhetoric and law at Caesarea in Palestine, then at Alexandria, and for ten years at Athens. Now thirty, he began a life of pious austerity, probably as a result of his belated baptism, and joined Basil as a desert recluse for two years. His father's advanced age made it necessary for young Gregory to return to manage the family estate; once at home, however, he was ordained a priest suddenly, and by force, and fled in confusion to the desert. He returned within three months, having written a tract on the glory of the priesthood, worked to reconcile dissident opinion during the semi-Arian confusion, preached funeral orations on the death of his brother and of his sister Gorgonia, and acted as assistant to his bishop-father. In 370, Basil was elected metropolitan of Caesarea and made Gregory bishop of Sasima in Arian territory which was torn by civil strife. When Gregory refused to accept and Basil charged him with neglect of duty, mutual coldness resulted. However, Gregory preached a memorial panegyric after Basil's death. Gregory became coadjutor at Nazianzus, suffered five years from ill health, but after the death of Emperor Valens was asked to revitalize the Church in the East. He worked unostentatiously at Constantinople, preaching on the articles of faith, notably a famous series on the Trinity. He suffered from slander and physical mistreatment, failed to regain many churches from the Arian forces, even saw a pretender attempt to usurp his place during illness. In 380, Emperor Theodosius was baptized and ordered the Arians to give up their beliefs or leave the city; when the leaders went, Gregory was installed as archbishop. His stay was brief; the validity of his election at the Council of Constantinople in 381, at which he served as presiding officer, was questioned, and he retired in favor of Nectarius. He returned to serve the area about Nazianzus, practicing extreme austerities, and writing a number of religious and autobiographical poems, the longest being *De vita sua*. F. D. May 9.

GREGORY OF NYSSA, ST. (330?–395?), bishop. Son of SS. Basil and Emmelia, he was born in Caesaria, Cappadocia, and brought up by his brother St. Basil the Great and sister Macrina. He became a teacher of rhetoric, married Theosebeia, studied for the priesthood, and served at Iris in Pontus. When his brother, now bishop of Caesarea, was beset by opposition from their uncle, Bishop Gregory of Pontus, the young Gregory tried to end the quarrel by writing a series of letters which pretended to be offers of peace from Basil. Bishop Basil censured his brother lightly, and decided to put his well-intentioned energies to better use. In 372, Gregory, against his own wishes, was made bishop of Nyssa and sent to fight heresy in Lower Armenia. When he called a local synod of bishops, the meeting proved a failure; soon after, he was arrested by Arians on a false charge of stealing church property. He escaped his jailers, wrote a letter proving by witnesses that there had been no financial irregularity, but was deposed. He regained his see from a usurper in 378. Thereafter his career was more successful. He attended the Council of Antioch which considered the Meletian heresy and the General Council of Constantinople in 381 which attacked Arianism. He also traveled to Palestine and Arabia to investigate heresies and pilgrimage abuses. His chief writings include a *Catechetical Discourse*, *On Virginity*, expositions on the heresies of Apollinaris and Eunomius, commentaries on scripture, several orations, and letters. He was highly influenced by Plato and Origen. F. D. Mar. 9.

GREGORY OF RIMINI (d. 1358), theologian. A native of Rimini, Italy, he became a professor, and then rector, of the Augustinian seminary there and taught theology at the Sorbonne. He was famous for his support of St. Augustine (except on grace), a leader of the nominalists, and author of treatises on scripture and the *Commentaries*. In 1357 he was elected general of the Augustinian Hermits. He died in Vienna.

GREGORY OF SPOLETO (d. 304?), martyr. Said to have been a priest slain in Italy during the persecution of Maximian, and honored on Dec. 24, it is probable that he is the creation of legend.

GREGORY THAUMATURGUS, ST. (213?–268), bishop. Born in Neo-Caesarea, Pontus, of pagan parents, he went to Caesarea, Palestine, to study law, met Origen, who converted him and his brother Athenodorus, and became one of his disciples. About 238 he returned to his native city and shortly after became its bishop.

During the next thirty years he was highly successful with his preaching and became known as the "wonder-worker." He also wrote several treatises on Church matters. F. D. Nov. 17.

GREGORY OF TOURS, ST. (538?–594), bishop. Born in Clermont-Ferrand, Gaul, Georgius Florentius was of a distinguished Gallo-Roman family, was raised by his uncle, Gallus, bishop of Clermont, after his father's death, studied under St. Avitus I in Clermont, and in 573 became bishop of Tours. In 576, Chilperic, king of Neustria, took over Tours and became Gregory's enemy when the latter supported the king's son, Meroveus, against him. He was accused of treason to the king, exonerated on Chilperic's death in 584, and had no difficulties with his successors, Guntram, king of Burgundy, and Childebert II. He filled his office with great ability and justice, rebuilt the cathedral, built several churches, and administered his see wisely. He wrote widely, and is best known for his historical and hagiographical writings. His *History of the Franks* is one of the best sources of Merovingian history and his biographies of the saints and martyrs, though less trustworthy, were very popular. F. D. Nov. 17.

GREGORY OF TRAGURIO, BL. (d. 1369), martyr. *See* Antony of Saxony, Bl.

GREGORY OF UTRECHT, ST. (707?–775). Born in Trèves, Gaul, he was so impressed by an exposition by St. Boniface at the convent of Pfalzel, of which his grandmother was abbess, that he became the constant companion and disciple of the saint, who made him abbot of St. Martin's, Utrecht, Flanders, which became a great missionary center. On the death of St. Eoban he administered the see for twenty years, though he never was more than a priest. F. D. Aug. 25.

GREGORY OF VALENCIA (1550?–1603), theologian. Born in Medina, Spain, he studied at Salamanca, became a Jesuit in 1565, was called to Rome by St. Francis Borgia to teach philosophy, and was ordained there. He was appointed to the chair of theology at Dillingen in 1573 and at Ingolstadt from 1575 to 1592, when he resigned to complete his *Commentatorium theologicorum*, which covered all scholastic theology. He also published on contemporary religious quarrels and on witchcraft, infallibility, usury, and *Analysis fidei catholicae* (1585). In 1598 he taught theology in Rome and in 1602 was chosen to defend the Jesuit teaching on grace in public debate before Pope Clement VIII against the formal Dominican denunciation of Molina. His health broke during the debates; he went to Naples to recover, but died there on Apr. 25.

GREISINGER, BL. JAMES (1407–1491). Born in Ulm, Germany, he joined the army in Italy in 1432, left it to become a lawyer's secretary in Capua, and in 1441 a Dominican lay-brother at Bologna. The rest of his life was devoted to his paintings on glass for which he became famous. He was beatified in 1825. F. D. Oct. 11.

GREITH, KARL JOHANN (1807–1882), bishop. Born in Rapperswyl, Switzerland, on May 25, he studied at St. Gall and Munich, went to Paris in 1829, entered the Sulpician seminary there, and was ordained in 1831. After teaching at St. Gall he went to Rome because of the unsettled Swiss political situation; on his return in 1847 he was made dean of the cathedral, professor of philosophy in 1853, and bishop of St. Gall in 1862. He opposed the declaration of the dogma of papal infallibility at the Vatican Council, but on its proclamation did his utmost to induce Döllinger, whose close friend he was, to accept it. He wrote on early church history, the early Irish Church, and apologetics. He died in St. Gall, Switzerland, on May 17.

GRESEMUND, DIETRICH (1477–1512). Born in Speyer, Germany, son of the physician to the elector of Mainz, he studied at Mainz, Padua, Bologna, Ferrara, and Heidelberg. After a period in Rome he returned to Mainz and became canon of St. Stephen's in 1505, vicar general in 1506, and a judge in 1508. He wrote on archaeology, poems, and dialogues on teaching grammar, the liberal arts, and carnival life. He died in Mainz, Germany.

GRESLON, ADRIEN (1618–1697), missioner. Born in Périgueux, France, he became a Jesuit at Bordeaux in 1635, taught for twenty years, was sent to China in 1655, and returned to France in 1670. He wrote on the Old Testament patriarchs and a history of China.

GRESSET, JEAN BAPTISTE LOUIS (1709–1777), dramatist. Born in Amiens, France, on Aug. 29, he became a Jesuit at sixteen and taught at several schools and the Collège Louis le Grand, Paris. In 1734 he published a poem, *Vert vert*, on a convent parrot, which attracted wide attention; his epicurean *La Chartreuse* caused his dismissal from the Society. He then wrote plays: *Edouard III* (1740), *Sydney* (1745), and the successful *Le méchant* (1747). He was elected to the French Academy in 1748, declined the offer of King Frederick of Prussia to join his court, and in 1759 retired to live in Amiens in secluded austerity, for which Voltaire mocked him. He died on June 16 at Amiens, France.

GRETSER, JACOB (1562–1625). Born in Markdorf, near Constance, Switzerland, he became a Jesuit in 1578, taught at Ingolstadt for twenty-four years, and wrote more than 200 works on archaeology, philosophy, theology, apologetics, and contemporary religious controversy. He died at Ingolstadt, Germany.

GREUZE, JEAN BAPTISTE (1725–1805), painter. Born in Tournus, Ardeche, France, he studied in Lyons, went to Paris in 1755, achieved immediate success, and became an associate of the French Academy. He traveled in Italy for two years and on his return devoted himself to painting scenes praising the bourgeois life, such as *L'Accordée de village*. His moralistic and sentimental canvases, such as *Mort du bon père de famille*, and their engraved copies brought him a fortune. Interest in antiquity and the revolutionary ideals changed public taste; Greuze separated from his wife, lost his following, and died, forgotten and in poverty, in Paris on Mar. 21.

GRIFFIN, GERALD (1803–1840), novelist. Born in Limerick, Ireland, on Dec. 12, he lived with his brother when his parents went to the United States, and moved to London in 1822. He wrote unsuccessful plays, worked for a publishing house, translated for magazines, and completed a series of popular short stories called *Holland-Tide*. He wrote *The Collegians*, a novel of Irish life, in 1828, studied law briefly in London, and published *The Invasion* in 1832. In 1838 he became an Irish Christian Brother, taking the name Joseph. He died of typhus at a monastery near Cork, Ireland, on June 12.

GRIFFIN, JAMES ALOYSIUS (1883–1948), bishop. Born in Chicago on Feb. 27, he studied at St. Ignatius College there and the North American College, Rome, and was ordained in Rome in 1909. He did parish work in Chicago, was pastor in Coal City and Joliet from 1917 to 1924, and in 1924 was consecrated bishop of Springfield, Illinois. He participated in civic affairs, successfully completed several building campaigns, and dedicated the cathedral in 1928. He died in Springfield on Aug. 5.

GRIFFIN, MARTIN IGNATIUS JOSEPH (1842–1911), journalist. Born in Philadelphia on Oct. 23, he wrote for the Philadelphia *Catholic Herald*, became part owner of the *Guardian Angel* in 1867, was an editor on the Philadelphia *Catholic Standard* from 1870 to 1873, founded and edited from 1873 to 1894 the *Journal* of the Irish Catholic Benevolent Union (of which he was secretary for twenty-two years), and published *Griffin's Journal* from 1894 to 1900. He became owner of *American Catholic Historical Researches* in 1886, and edited it until his death, and was noted for his objective and conscientious historical researches. He wrote several biographies and historical works, among them *Commodore John Barry* (1903) and the three-volume *Catholics and the American Revolution*. He died in Philadelphia on Nov. 10.

GRIFFIN, ROBERT STANISLAUS (1857–1933), admiral. Born in Fredericksburg, Virginia, he graduated from the United States Naval Academy in 1878, served on various ships and naval bureaus, and became engineer of the North Atlantic Fleet in 1901–5. He spent the rest of his life in the Bureau of Steam Engineering, becoming a rear admiral in 1913 as its chief. He became first editor of the *Journal of the Society of Naval Engineers* and served as president of the society in 1908, 1912, and 1913. He was in charge of the extensive naval construction and repair program during World War I, retired in 1921, and died in Washington, D.C., on Feb. 21.

GRIFFIN, WILLIAM A. (1885–1950), bishop. Born in Newark, New Jersey, on Nov. 20, he studied at Seton Hall and Immaculate Conception seminary, and was ordained in 1910. He taught at Seton Hall until 1915, when he was assigned to parish work, was made a papal chamberlain in 1929, and served as national treasurer of the Society for the Propagation of the Faith in 1935. He was appointed titular bishop of Sanavus and auxiliary of Newark in 1938, became bishop of Trenton, New Jersey, in 1940, and died there on Jan. 1.

GRIFFITH, MICHAEL (1587–1652). Born in London, England, he became a Jesuit at Louvain in 1607, studied at Seville, served at Naples and Rome, and in 1620 was rector of the college at Ghent. In 1628 he was sent to the English mission, arrested on his arrival but released, and active in the underground for the next thirty-three years. He wrote *Annales ecclesiastici et civiles britannorum, saxonum, et anglorum* and *Britannia illustrata* and died at St. Omer, Flanders. He is often known under his aliases, Michael Alford and John Flood.

GRIFFITHS, THOMAS (1791–1847), bishop. Born in London on June 2, he studied at St. Edmund's College, was ordained in 1814, and was president there from 1818 to 1833, when he was appointed coadjutor of the London District and consecrated titular bishop of Olena. In 1836 he succeeded to the vicariate and opened many missions for Irish immigrants. He died in London on Aug. 12.

GRIGNION, LOUIS MARIE. *See* Louis of Montfort, St.

GRIJALVA, JUAN DE (1489?–1527), explorer. Born in Cuellar, Spain, he was sent by his uncle, Governor Diego Velásquez of Cuba, to explore Mexico, where he discovered the river now given his name. He claimed the Yucatán and surrounding Mexican territory for Charles V, called it New Spain, but was dismissed from the governor's service on his return because he had not set up permanent establishments. He was slain later in Nicaragua.

GRILLET, JEAN (1630?–1676?), explorer. Born in France, he became superior of the Jesuit house in British Guiana after 1666 and penetrated the region of the Acoqua Indians, 570 miles southwest of Cayenne, with Fr. François Béchamel in 1674. They wrote a detailed account of the geography and customs of the region, later published, and died a few years after their return and from the hardships of their journey.

GRILLPARZER, FRANZ (1791–1872), dramatist. Born in Vienna on Jan. 15, he studied law, and worked in the customs service from 1813 to 1856. Influenced by Schiller, he produced the successful *Die Ahnfrau* in 1817, followed by his trilogy, *Das goldene Vleiss* (1821). Subsequent plays were based on Bohemian and Hungarian history and on classical mythology; *Der Traum ein Leben* (1834) was based on a story by Voltaire; his comedy, *Weh dem, der lügt* (1838), was a failure and caused him to retire from the theater. He also wrote lyric poetry, dramatic criticism, and an autobiography (1836). His private life, like his public career, was filled with disappointment. His mother was a suicide in 1819; a poem on the Campo Vaccino ruins of Rome brought wide censure; he failed to gain promotion and was denied a library post he sought; a succession of love affairs added to his bitterness. He died in Vienna on Jan. 21.

GRIMALD, ST. (d. 903). Born at St. Omer in Flanders, he was a Benedictine monk and then prior at St. Bertin. He went to England in 885 at the invitation of King Alfred, who wanted him as archbishop of Canterbury. He refused, retired to Westminster, and later became abbot of a monastery at Winchester. F. D. July 8.

GRIMALD, NICHOLAS (1519?–1559), poet. Born in Huntingdonshire, England, and educated at both Cambridge and Oxford, he lectured at the latter university from 1547 to 1552. He wrote a number of Latin plays; *Archipropheta* (on St. John the Baptist; 1548), was one of the first classical plays produced in England. The tone of his literary work was anti-papal and he served for a while as a spy against Catholics. He became a preacher and was chaplain to Bishop Ridley, but became suspect as a possible heretic and jailed. He was converted to Catholicism, apparently while in prison in 1555; after his release he joined Bishop Thomas Thirlby at Ely. A translation of Cicero appeared in 1556, but his greatest contribution to literature was the editing of *Tottel's Miscellany* of English poetry (1557), in which between ten and fifty pieces of his own appeared.

GRIMALDI, DOMENICO (16th century), cardinal. He came of a long line of Italian seafarers, distinguished himself at the battle of Lepanto in 1571, became a cardinal and vicelegate at Avignon, and was active against heresy.

GRIMALDI, FRANCESCO MARIA (1613–1663), physicist. Born in Bologna, Italy, on Apr. 2, he became a Jesuit in 1632 and after his ordination in 1638 taught in Jesuit colleges for the next twenty-five years. He devoted himself to research in physics and astronomy and made important discoveries in optics (diffraction, interference, the dispersion of the sun's rays passing through a prism). He also was noted for studies of the moon's surface. He died in Bologna on Dec. 28.

GRIMALDI, GERONIMO (1576–1658), cardinal. Of the Genoese family of the Grimaldi, he founded a refuge for the poor and other charitable institutions and was active in clerical reform.

GRIMALDI, GIOVANNI FRANCESCO (1606–1680), painter. Born in Bologna, he studied under the Carracci, went to Rome where he completed some fresco decorations for Pope Innocent X, and was invited to Paris to decorate rooms in the Louvre. On his return he was in the service of Popes Alexander VI and Clement IX, president of the Academy of St. Luke, and produced landscapes and etchings. He died in Rome.

GRIMES, JOHN (1852–1922), bishop. Born in Brooklawn, Limerick, Ireland, on Dec. 18, he studied at the Jesuit college there, at St. Hyacinthe, Quebec, and the Grand seminary, Montreal, and was ordained in Albany in 1882. He served as pastor in several parishes, last of which was St. Mary's in Syracuse, New York, was made a domestic prelate in 1904, was consecrated titular bishop of Hemeria and coadjutor of Syracuse in 1909, succeeded to the see in 1912, and died there on July 26.

GRIMKELD, ST. (d. 870), martyr. See Theodore, St.

GRIMMELSHAUSEN, HANS JAKOB CHRISTOPHEL VON (1625?–1676), novelist. Born near Gelnhausen, Hesse, he fought in the Thirty Years' War and in 1667 wrote his first novel, *Der keusche Joseph*. After his conversion he entered the service of the bishop of Strassburg as bailiff of Renchen, Baden, a position he held until his death there on Aug. 17. His most famous work is *Der abenteuerliche Simplicissimus* (1669), a picaresque and probably autobiographical novel. Many humorous and romantic works appeared under pseudonyms; he acknowledged *Dietwald und Amelinde* (1670) and *Proximus und Lympide* (1672).

GRIMONIA, ST., martyr. Legend has her the daughter of a fourth-century pagan Irish king, converted at twelve. When her father tried to force her to marry, she fled to France, became a hermit in Picardy, and was beheaded by envoys who followed her. The same story is told of others. F. D. Sept. 7.

GRISAR, HARTMANN (1845–1932), historian. Born in Coblenz, Germany on Sept. 22, son of a baker, he studied at Münster and Innsbruck, was ordained in 1868 at Rome, and became a Jesuit in Austria. He taught at Innsbruck, was a co-founder in 1877 of *Zeitschrift für katholische Theologie*, wrote on Galileo,

the Council of Trent, the work of James Laynez, and *History of Rome and the Popes in the Middle Ages* and *Martin Luther, His Life and Work*.

GRISWOLD, VEN. ROBERT (d. 1604), martyr. Born in Rowington, Warwickshire, England, he became the assistant of Fr. John Sugar, was captured with the latter, was offered his life if he would abandon his religion, and hanged at Warwick on July 16.

GRIVOT, BL. MARY HERMINA (1866–1900), martyr. Born in Baune, Burgundy, she had been in China fifteen months when the Boxer Rebellion broke out. Her courage spurred on the nuns under her to meet the martyrdom which they suffered. F. D. July 9.

GROCYN, WILLIAM (1446?–1519), scholar. Born in Wiltshire, England, he studied at Oxford in 1465, was appointed divinity reader at Magdalen College in 1481, went to Italy, where he became enthusiastic about the new humanism, and returned to England to be ordained in 1491 and to teach Greek at Oxford in 1492. Thomas More was one of his pupils, as was Erasmus, who was aided financially by his teacher. He lectured on the ecclesiastical hierarchy in St. Paul's, London, in 1503, and was appointed to the church of All Hallows, Maidstone, in 1506. He remained there until his death. Although he was one of the most learned men of his day and wrote much, nothing is extant except a letter to Aldus Manutius, the printer, and his will.

GRODECZ, BL. MELCHIOR (d. 1619), martyr. See Körösy, Bl. Mark.

GRONBERGER, SVEN MAGNUS (1864–1916), anthropologist. Born in Soderköping, Sweden, on Aug. 19, he went to the United States when he was about twenty, served on the library staff of the Smithsonian Institution, Washington, became a convert, and wrote on the frogs of the capital district, the birds of Greenland, and *The Origin of the Goths*. He died in Washington, D.C., on Apr. 24.

GRÖNE, VALENTIN (1817–1882), theologian. Born in Paderborn, Germany, on Dec. 7, he was ordained in 1844, received his doctorate in theology at Munich in 1848, was a chaplain until 1857, then was appointed rector of high schools in Fredeburg and Schmallenberg. In 1868 he became pastor at Irmgarteichen, Westphalia, where he remained until his death on Mar. 18. He wrote studies of the papacy, the sacraments, church history, and on Luther and Tetzel.

GROOTE, GERARD (1340–1384), founder. Born in Deventer, Netherlands, he studied at Aachen and the Sorbonne, and taught in Deventer and Cologne, where in 1366 he was appointed professor of philosophy and theology. He held prebends in Aachen and Utrecht, served on a mission to Pope Urban V in Avignon, and was famed for his learning. About 1370 he gave up his honors to pursue an ascetic life and in 1377 withdrew to the Carthusian monastery of Munnikhuizen, near Arnheim, where he came under the influence of Bl. John Ruysbroek. He then began preaching and attracted widespread attention by the vigor of his sermons and unsparing attacks on vice at all levels. Enemies had his license to preach withdrawn in 1383. He appealed to the pope, retired to the monastery of Woudrichem, near Deventer, but died on Aug. 20 before his appeal could be considered. When he began preaching in 1379, he attracted a group of followers who became the Brethren of the Common Life, a voluntary monastic organization devoted to learning and preaching, which spread through Germany and the Netherlands. Thomas à Kempis wrote his biography.

GROPPER, JOHN (1503–1559), cardinal. Born in Soest, Westphalia, he was canon in Xanten in 1522 and received his doctorate in civil law at Cologne in 1525. He became pastor and dean in Soest, helped to reorganize ecclesiastical law in the province of Archbishop Hermann V of Wied, and prepared the decrees for the provincial council held in Cologne in 1536. In his eagerness to effect reunion with the reformers he seemingly sacrificed principles and his *Enchiridion* was placed on the Index. He submitted to correction as soon as the Council of Trent (which he attended in 1551 and where he was most active) defined the Catholic doctrine of justification. He appealed to Pope Paul III against the archbishop of Cologne, who almost abandoned his province to the reformers and helped to restore Catholicism there. He was named provost of Bonn and, in 1556, a cardinal. He died in Rome on Mar. 13.

GROSS, WILLIAM HICKLEY (1837–1898), bishop. Born in Baltimore, Maryland, on June 12, he studied at St. Charles College, became a Redemptorist in 1857, and was ordained in 1863. He was interested in the condition of Negroes, became superior of his order in 1871, and in 1873 was appointed bishop of Savannah, Georgia. He was transferred to Oregon City as archbishop in 1885, and died in Baltimore on Nov. 14.

GROSSETESTE, ROBERT (1175?–1253), bishop. Born in Stradbroke, England, he probably studied at Oxford and Paris, served for a time as head of Oxford, with which he maintained close relations, and received many benefices, which he relinquished before he was elected bishop of Lincoln in 1235. His interests were most varied. He wrote on mathematics, meteorology, physics, and optics, more than sixty theological treatises, and hundreds of sermons and discourses. His biblical commentaries, studies in Christian antiquities, and

translations from Greek and Hebrew attest his demand that scholars rely on authorities and original sources. His annotated translations of Aristotle's *Logic, Physics, Eudemian Ethics,* and *Nichomachean Ethics* were particularly significant. He encouraged the Franciscans when they first came to Oxford in 1224 and made them an important part of his diocese. In 1239 he became embroiled in a dispute, as a result of his visitations, over the rights of dean and chapter in the churches of his dioceses who claimed they were exempt from such visitations. The dispute was not resolved until 1245 when Pope Innocent IV ruled in his favor while he was attending the General Council in Lyons. His disputes with the monasteries and his insistence that they provide worthy parish clergy and churches continued throughout his entire episcopate. In 1250 he went to Lyons to see the pope in an attempt to end the exemption of the Cistercian houses from his visitations. His disagreements with the papacy have been misrepresented; he fully acknowledged the pope's authority, but his condemnation of contemporary abuses, at all levels, was outspoken. He died on Oct. 9.

GROSSI, LUDOVICO (1564–1645), composer. Born in Viadana, Italy, he became a monk, was organist and choirmaster at Mantua, Venice, and other cities, and published much, particularly *Cento concerti* and *Sinfonie musicali.* He is also known as Ludovico Viadana. He died in Gualtieri, Italy, on May 2.

CROUARD, EMILE JEAN BAPTISTE (1840–1931), archbishop. Born in Brulon, France, on Feb. 2, he attended the seminary in Le Mans, and in 1860 was sent to the missions in Canada. He labored in western Canada, was named titular bishop of Egine in 1890 and vicar apostolic of Grouard, Alberta, in 1891. He resigned his office in 1929 and died in that city on Mar. 7.

GROVE, BL. JOHN (d. 1679), martyr. *See* Iremonger, Bl. William.

GRUEBER, JOHANN (1623–1665), missioner. Born in Linz, Germany, on Oct. 28, he became a Jesuit in 1641 and was sent to China in 1656. In 1661 he returned to Rome, going overland because a Dutch blockade of Macao made it impossible to journey by sea. His 214-day trip was a sensation and provided material for the first authentic account of Tibet and Nepal. He left his notes and charts for use by Fr. Athanasius Kirscher. While on his return to Peking he died, either in Florence, Italy, or Patak, Hungary.

GRÜN, ANASTASIUS. *See* Auersperg, Anton Alexander von.

GRUSCHA, ANTON JOSEPH (1820–1911), cardinal. Born in Vienna, he was ordained in 1843, taught at the Theresianum and the University of Vienna, and became monsignor in 1858, canon of St. Stephen's in 1871, bishop of Karrhä in 1878, archbishop of Vienna in 1890, and cardinal in 1891.

GSELL, FRANCIS XAVIER (1872–1960), bishop. Born in Benfeld, France, on Oct. 30, he was ordained in 1896, worked as a Missionary of the Sacred Heart in Papua and the Gilbert Islands, and in 1906 went to Australia, founding a mission station in Bathrust Island in 1911, and working among the natives for the next twenty-seven years. He was appointed the first bishop of Darwin in 1938, and became known as the "bishop with 150 wives" for his custom of buying and caring for aboriginal girls promised in marriage to polygamous old men. He retired in 1948, was decorated by the French and British governments for his championship of the Australian aboriginals, and died in Sydney.

GUALA, BL. (1177?–1244), bishop. At forty, Guala Romanoni, with his brother Roger, became a disciple of St. Dominic at Bergamo. He established houses at Bologna and Brescia, became bishop of Brescia about 1230, but in 1241 was exiled from his see during a civil uprising and retired to the Vallombrosan monastery at d'Astino where he died. His cult was confirmed in 1868. F. D. Sept. 3.

GUALFARDUS, ST. (d. 1127). A German leatherworker, he settled in Verona, Italy, in 1096, to which he had come with a group of merchants, gave most of his earnings to the poor, and, to avoid praise, fled into solitude. He spent his last ten years in the city as a Camaldolese monk. He is also called Wolfhard. F. D. Apr. 30.

GUARDAGNOLI, BL. ANGELELLA (1467–1501). Born in Rieti, Italy, she became a Dominican tertiary at Perugia in 1490 with a number of others, set up a convent there, followed an austere life, led penitential processions, advised the governors, and overcame a charge of sorcery. Her cult was confirmed in 1627. She is also known as Columba of Rieti. F. D. May 20.

GUARINI, GIAMBATTISTA (1538–1612), poet. Born in Ferrara, Italy, on Dec. 10, he studied in Padua, joined the court of Duke Alfonso II of Ferrara in 1567, and also served the dukes of Savoy, Mantua, Tuscany, and Urbino. In 1589 he published *Il Pastor Fido*, an artificial and pastoral play, popularized in English by John Fletcher in *The Faithful Shepherdess*. He also wrote a comedy, a political treatise on the control of Florence by the Medici, lyric poems, and letters. His private life was confused: his daughter Anna was murdered by her brother and Ercole Trotti, her husband; he engaged in many bitter quarrels; and was often embroiled in lawsuits. He died in Venice, Italy, on Oct. 7.

GUARINO DA VERONA (1370–1460).

Born in Verona, Italy, he studied Greek in Constantinople, brought back more than fifty Greek manuscripts to Venice in 1408, and devoted his life to teaching in Florence, Verona, and other cities. In 1436 he was appointed professor of rhetoric at Ferrara, where he stayed until his death. He translated and wrote commentaries on Latin and Greek classics, issued a Latin grammar and catechism, and served as interpreter at meetings of Roman and Greek Church leaders. He died in Ferrara, Italy, on Dec. 14.

GUARINUS, ST. (d. 1150), bishop. A monk at Molesmes, he became abbot of St. John of Aulps near Geneva. A commendatory letter exists, written to the community by St. Bernard, expressing regret that Guarinus (also called Guérin) was to be taken from them and made bishop of Sion, Switzerland. F. D. Jan. 6.

GUARINUS, ST. (d. 1159), cardinal. Born in Bologna, Italy, he became a priest, then, because he wished a more austere life, joined the Augustinians at Mortaria. After forty years, and against his wishes, he was sought out by Pope Lucius II and consecrated bishop of Praeneste (Palestrina), Italy, and cardinal. He distributed the wealth of the see to its poor. F. D. Feb. 6.

GUARNERIUS. *See* Irnerius.

GUASACHT, ST. (4th century), bishop. Son of the man under whom St. Patrick was a slave in Ireland, he was converted and served as a missionary bishop of Granard, Ireland. F. D. Jan. 24.

GUDELIA, ST. (d. 340), martyr. She was slain in Persia during the persecution of Sapor II. F. D. Sept. 29.

GUDENUS, MORITZ (1596–1680). Born in Cassel, Germany, on Apr. 11, he studied at Marburg, where he became deacon of the reformed church, lost his post when he refused to accept Lutheranism, and became pastor of Abterode in 1625. In 1630 he and his family became converts. He wrote on the Eucharist, served as bailiff of Treffurt, near Erfurt, Saxony, and died there in Feb. Of his sons, John Daniel became auxiliary bishop of Mainz; John Maurice was imperial counselor and historian of Erfurt; John Christopher was diplomatic representative at Vienna of the archdiocese of Mainz; Urban Ferdinand became a university professor.

GUDULA, ST. (d. 712?). Daughter of Count Witger and St. Amalburga, she devoted her life to prayer and charities. Charlemagne was particularly devoted to her memory. She is also known as Goule, Ergoule, and Goelen, and is the patron of Brussels, Belgium. F. D. Jan. 8.

GUENHAEL, ST. (d. 550?). Born in Brittany and educated by St. Winwaloe, he became abbot of Landevenec. F. D. Nov. 3.

GUENNINUS, ST. (7th century). He was bishop of Vannes, Brittany. F. D. Aug. 19.

GUÉNOT, BL. THEODORE (1802–1861), bishop and martyr. Born in Bessieux, France, he joined the Society of Foreign Missions, became vicar apostolic of Cochin China, and died in prison of ill treatment. F. D. Nov. 4.

GUÉRANGER, PROSPER LOUIS PASCAL (1805–1875), abbot. Born in Sablé-sur-Sarthe, France, on Apr. 4, he was ordained in 1827, did parish work, wrote history, and in 1832 bought a priory in Solesmes, where he was joined by five other priests who sought to reestablish the Benedictine rule. In 1837, Pope Gregory raised the priory to an abbey and named him abbot and superior general in France. He fought Gallicanism, naturalism, and Liberalism, supported the definition of papal infallibility, and attracted many associates and followers. He established monasteries in Ligugé and Marseilles, as well as a Benedictine convent near Solesmes, France, where he died on Jan. 30. His most important writing was *L'année liturgique*, containing a commentary on and explanation of prayer.

GUÉRARD, ROBERT (1641–1715). Born in Rouen, France, he collaborated on the Maurist edition of St. Augustine's works, was ordered to leave St. Denis by the king, who erroneously suspected him as one of the authors of *L'abbé commendataire*, went to Abronay, discovered at Portes a manuscript of Augustine's *Opus imperfectum* against Julian of Eclanum, and wrote an abridgment of the Bible. He later served at Fécamp and St. Ouen, where he died on Jan. 2.

GUERCINO, IL. *See* Barbieri, Giovanni.

GUÉRIN, EUGÉNIE DE (1805–1848). Born in Languedoc, France, on Jan. 15, she lived her whole life at the family château, where she took care of her youngest brother, Maurice, always in delicate health. After he left she wrote him letters and kept a private journal; they were published in 1862. She died on June 8.

GUÉRIN, GEORGES MAURICE DE (1810–1839), poet. Born in Languedoc, France, brother of Eugénie, he studied at the Collège Stanislas, Paris, and La Chênaie, went to Paris after a year, and lost his faith. He taught at Collège Stanislas, married an Indian girl in 1838, returned to the family château where Eugénie brought him back to his religion, and died on July 19. His poem *Le Centaure*, published the year after his death, was enthusiastically received; twenty years later, his *Journal*, day-by-day accounts of his life written to Eugénie, was published with his letters and poems.

GUÉRIN. *See* Guarinus, St.

GUERRA, BL. ELENA (1813–1914), foundress. Born in Italy, she taught herself from the books of her brother who was training for the priesthood, founded a school at the suggestion of Don Bosco, began the Institute of the Oblates of the Holy Ghost (also called Sisters of St. Zita) in 1873, became its superior, and received diocesan approval in 1881. She wrote several works on devotion to the Holy Spirit and suggested to Pope Leo XIII that he issue the encyclical *Divinum illud munus*. She died on Apr. 11, and was beatified in 1959 by Pope John XXIII.

GUERRICUS, BL. (d. 1157?). Born in Tournai, Belgium, he studied there, became canon and director of the cathedral school, went to Clairvaux, and in 1138 was sent by St. Bernard to be first abbot of the Benedictine monastery of Igny, in the see of Rheims, France. He wrote many ascetical treatises. F. D. Aug. 19.

GUERTIN, GEORGE ALBERT (1869–1931), bishop. Born in Nashua, New Hampshire, on Feb. 17, he studied at St. Charles Borromeo and St. Hyacinthe in Canada and St. John's seminary, Brighton, Massachusetts, and was ordained in Manchester, New Hampshire, in 1892. He served in New Hampshire parishes, was pastor of St. Anthony's, Manchester, from 1900, and in 1907 was consecrated bishop of Manchester. He died in Morristown, New Jersey, on Aug. 6.

GUESNOVEUS, ST. (d. 675). Bishop of Quimper, Brittany, he founded a monastery near Brest, where he died. F. D. Oct. 25.

GUEVARA, JUAN GUALBERTO (1882–1954), cardinal. Born in Arequipa, Peru, on July 11, he studied there at St. Vincent de Paul and St. Augustine colleges, was ordained in 1906, served in Africa for four years, and on his return was rector of the seminary in Arequipa. He began writing for *El Deber*, daily newspaper of his native place, went to Rome for advanced study at the Latin American College and the Gregorian, and returned in 1928 to become director of the newspaper. He was named bishop of Trujillo in 1940, made archbishop in 1943, transferred to Lima in 1945, and raised to the cardinalate in 1946. He died in Lima, Peru, on Nov. 26.

GUEVARA, BL. MARIANA NAVARRA DE (1565–1624). Born in Madrid, Spain, she joined a discalced community of Mercedarians there as Sr. Mariana of Jesus and lived a life of penance. F. D. Apr. 27.

GUEVROCK, ST. (6th century). A Briton, he worked in the missions of Brittany with SS. Tugdual and Paul of Léon. F. D. Feb. 17.

GÜGLER, JOSEPH HEINRICH ALOYSIUS (1782–1827). Born in Udligerschwyl, Switzerland, on Aug. 25, he studied at Einsiedeln, Petershausen, Solothurn, and Lucerne, was appointed professor of exegesis at the lyceum in Lucerne, was ordained in 1805, and became a canon at St. Leodegar there. His teaching of scripture and theology attracted widespread attention and opposition. He had disputes over teaching methods with Thaddaeus Müller, a pastor of Lucerne, which led to his dismissal in 1810 as professor and touched off a storm of protest which caused his reinstatement six weeks later; with Marcus Lutz, pastor at Leufelfigen; and with the philosopher, Ignaz Troxler. He wrote a philosophical exposition of revelation in the Old Testament, other biblical studies, and a treatise on Augustine's *Christian Doctrine*, and in 1823 founded the journal, *Zeichen der Zeit im Guten und Bösen*. He died at Lucerne, Switzerland, on Feb. 28.

GUGLIELMINI, GIOVANNI BATTISTA (1763–1817), astronomer. Born in Bologna, Italy, on Aug. 16, he published his first treatise in 1789 on the earth's rotation and in 1791–92 experimented with falling objects from the tower in Bologna. From 1794 to 1817 he taught mathematics at its university, holding the chair of astronomy from 1801; in 1814–15 he was rector. From 1802 to 1810 he directed Bologna's waterworks. He died there on Dec. 15.

GUIBERT, ST. (d. 962). A Lotharingian noble and military hero, he became a hermit, then established a monastery on his estate at Gembloux, Brabant, with Herluin as abbot; he himself entered the Benedictine abbey at Gorze. Several claims to the other property were made by relatives and courtiers, and he was forced to return several times to Gembloux before he made its title clear. He was a successful missioner among Slavic and Hungarian soldiers who remained in the region after an invasion. He was canonized by Pope Innocent III in 1211. F. D. May 23.

GUIBERT, JOSEPH HIPPOLYTE (1802–1886), cardinal. Born in Aix-en-Provence, France, on Dec. 13, he joined the Oblates of Mary Immaculate, became bishop of Viviers in 1842, archbishop of Tours in 1857, was translated to Paris in 1871, and was created a cardinal in 1873.

GUIBERT DE NOGENT (1053?–1124?). Born in Clermont, France, he became a monk at St. Germer de Fly, was abbot of Nogent-sous-Coucy in 1104, and wrote a history of the first crusade, which boasted of the Franks as the most important people in Christendom and the greatest defenders of the West. His *Gesta Dei per Francos* was based in part on the anonymous *Gesta Francorum*, was written between 1108 and 1112, and mixed epic legend and contemporary history, but is not an eyewitness account.

GUICCIARDINI, FRANCESCO (1483–1540), historian. Born in Florence, Italy, he studied law, became a lawyer, and in 1511 was appointed Florentine ambassador to Spain.

He served the Medici family in 1514; as governor of Moderno and Reggio for Pope Leo X, defending Parma in 1521; influenced Clement VII to form the League of Cognac in 1526; and led the papal forces for the next five years. In 1531–34 he was papal vice-legate to Bologna, then returned to Florence to support the Medici, Alessandro and Cosimo. His influence waned when he tried to curtail their growing power, and he spent his last years at Arcetri writing *Storia d'Italia*, covering the years 1492–1534, a history of Florence, and the sternly practical, almost Machiavellian, *Ricordi politici e civili* (1530). He died in Florence on May 23.

GUIDI, JACOPO. *See* James of Certaldo.

GUIDI, TOMMASO DI SER GIOVANNI DI SIMONE DEI. *See* Massaccio, Tommaso.

GUIDO, ST. (11th century). He was abbot of the Benedictine monastery of Cassoria (Casauria), in the Abruzzi, Italy. F. D. Nov. 25.

GUIDO OF AREZZO (995?–1050?), musician. Born near Paris, he became a Benedictine monk at St. Maur des Fossés. When he tried to improve the teaching and performance of liturgical music there, he was moved to a monastery in Pomposa, Italy, and about 1034 to Arezzo. He soon perfected his system of notation, was invited to Rome by Pope John XIX but was unable to stand the climate, and returned to die in Arezzo (or near Avellano). He added two lines to the then-used red (for F) and yellow (for C) lines and made use of the spaces between, thus establishing rhythm as well as melodic interval. Before his time liturgical melodies were spread by oral transmission and, in the eighth century, by fifteen Greek letters and spacing of notes close to or far from related syllables. Guido wrote several musical treatises and affected music for several centuries.

GUIDO RENI (1575–1642), painter. Born in Calvenzano, Italy, on Nov. 4, he studied under Denis Calvaert and about 1595 under the Carracci. In 1598, his frescoes of the Palazzo Pubblico in honor of Pope Clement VIII's visit to Bologna attracted wide attention. He went to Rome in 1600 and became Caravaggio's rival. He painted in Vienna, St. Petersburg, Dresden, and Italian cities, and was noted for his coloring, vigor, and skillful composition. He was also an outstanding engraver and etcher. Among his masterpieces are the frescoes in the church San Gregorio Magno in Rome (includes *God the Father above a Concert of Angels*), the *Aurora* fresco in the Rospigliosi palace, the frescoes in the Ravenna cathedral (which include *Israelites Gathering Manna*), *Ecce Homo*, *Mater Dolorosa*, and the *Crucifixion of St. Peter* in the Vatican. He died in Bologna, Italy, on Aug. 18.

GUIDONI, BL. PHILIPPA (d. 1335). A follower of Bl. Santuccia of Gubbio, she founded and was first abbess of the Benedictine convent of Santa Maria di Valverde, Arezzo, Italy. F. D. Aug. 29.

GUIGUES DU CHASTEL (1083?–1137?). Born in St. Romain, Dauphiné, France, he became a Carthusian monk in 1107 and was elected fifth prior of the Grande Chartreuse in 1110. In twenty-seven years of his priorship he reinvigorated the Carthusian order, added nine charterhouses to the two in existence, put in writing (in 1127 or 1128) the basic rules of the order, *Consuetudines,* and rebuilt the Grande Chartreuse after its destruction by an avalanche in 1132. He wrote a life of St. Hugh of Grenoble and edited the letters of St. Jerome. He died on July 27 and is sometimes honored as blessed on that date, although there is no evidence of any cult.

GUIJENO, JUAN MARTÍNEZ (d. 1557), cardinal. Born in Spain, he was ordained, was known for his nationalism and charity toward the poor, and became archbishop of Toledo in 1546. He founded the Colegio de Doncellas Nobles, Colegio des Infantes (for cathedral choirboys), and the Monasterio de Recodigas. He is often called Silicius.

GUIJON, ANDRÉ (1548–1631), bishop. Born in Autun, France, son of Jean, a physician, he became vicar general to Cardinal de Joyeuse and in 1586 was consecrated bishop of Autun. He wrote several treatises which were published in 1658 with the prose works and poems of his brothers Jacques, Jean, and Hugues, all of whom were lawyers.

GUILDAY, PETER (1884–1947), historian. Born in Chester, Pennsylvania, on Mar. 25, he studied at St. Charles Borromeo seminary, Philadelphia, and Louvain, Belgium, was ordained in 1909, and taught history at the Catholic University, Washington, from 1914 until his death. He was editor of *Catholic Historical Review* which he founded in 1915, served as president of the American Catholic Historical Association which he founded in 1918, and wrote numerous historical works among them *Life and Times of John Carroll* (1922), *Life of John Gilmary Shea* (1927), *Life and Times of John England* (1927), *An Introduction to Church History* (1925), *History of the Councils of Baltimore* (1932), and *Catholic Philosophy of History* (1936). He was made a domestic prelate in 1935, received honorary degrees from Notre Dame, St. Mary's, Loyola, Marquette, Georgetown, and Fordham, and was honored by the Belgian government for his aid in the restoration of Louvain's library. He died in Washington, D.C., on July 31.

GUILFOYLE, RICHARD THOMAS (1892–1957), bishop. Born in Adrian, Pennsylvania, on Dec. 22, he studied at St. Bonaventure, New York, and was ordained in Buffalo in 1917. After parish work in Oil City, Pennsylvania, he was appointed secretary to Bishop Gannon of Erie in 1921, pastor of the cathedral in 1923, became a papal chamberlain in 1924, and chancellor of the diocese in 1936. He was appointed bishop of Altoona, Pennsylvania, in 1936, and remained there until his death on June 10.

GUINEY, LOUISE IMOGEN (1861–1920), poet. Born in Boston, Massachusetts, on Jan. 7, daughter of Gen. Patrick Robert Guiney, she studied there and in Providence, Rhode Island, obtained a post-office appointment in spite of strong religious opposition, wrote for newspapers and magazines (including *Scribner's* and *Atlantic Monthly*), and after 1904 resided in Oxford. She published *Patrins* and other volumes of poetry, biographies, and editions of Matthew Arnold, James Clarence Mangan, and Henry Vaughan. Her study of the recusant poets of England appeared after her death at Chipping-Campden, England, on Nov. 2.

GUINEY, PATRICK ROBERT (1835–1877), general. Born in Parkstown, Ireland, on Jan. 15, he was taken to Portland, Maine, at six, studied at Holy Cross College, was admitted to the bar in 1856, married Janet Doyle, and moved to Boston. He served with the 9th Massachusetts Regiment during the Civil War (rising from private to brigadier general), was in thirty engagements, was decorated, and partially blinded at the battle of the Wilderness. He was assistant district attorney, founder of the Catholic Union, and member of civic organizations in Boston, where he died on Mar. 21.

GUINOC, ST. (d. 838?). He was a bishop in the vicinity of Aberdeen, Scotland. F. D. Apr. 13.

GUISASOLA Y MENÉNDEZ, VICTORIANO (1852–1920), cardinal. Born in Oviedo, Spain, on Apr. 21, he became a lawyer, was ordained, served as secretary to the bishop of Orihuela and head of its cathedral school, and became canon of Compostella in 1884 and bishop of Osma in 1893. He was transferred to Madrid in Valencia, was archbishop of Toledo, patriarch of the East Indies, cardinal in 1914, national chaplain of the Spanish army, and founder of guilds for the spiritual and social welfare of factory workers and farmers. He died in Madrid on Sept. 2.

GUISE, CHARLES DE LORRAINE DE (1524–1574), cardinal. Born in Joinville, France, on Feb. 17, brother of François de Guise, he was appointed archbishop of Rheims in 1538 and cardinal in 1547, being known as cardinal of Guise and, later, of Lorraine. He defended Rabelais and Ronsard against their critical enemies and was a major benefactor of the University of Rheims. His compromises with German Lutheran princes led to charges that he put his personal policies above those of France. At the Colloquy of Poissy (1561) he was the defender of Catholicism against Theodore de Beza; at the Council of Trent (1562–63) he defended Gallicanism, demanded major Church reforms, condemned the pope when Pius IV showed his displeasure, then modified his nationalism and attempted to have the council's decrees proclaimed through France (but was opposed by Catherine de' Medici). He tried to marry Catherine's nephew Henri to Margaret of Valois, and when this failed prevented Margaret from marrying the king of Portugal. He was in and out of favor with the kings of France (as archbishop of Rheims he crowned Henry II, Francis II, and Charles IX), who regarded him with suspicion as a threat to the throne. He died in Avignon, France, on Dec. 26.

GUISE, CHARLES DE LORRAINE DE (1554–1611). Son of François and brother of Henri de Guise, he fought with his brother in the Huguenot wars, and against the Turks, and served under the duke of Anjou beginning in 1573, though he did not trust the latter when the duke became Henry III. When Henri was assassinated, Charles (the Duke of Mayenne) escaped the king's men, raised an army, and marched on Paris. Meanwhile, three-part civil war had burst over France, with Henry III desultorily fighting Henry of Navarre and both of them fighting Charles and the Holy League. In 1589 Henry III was poisoned, Henry of Navarre assumed the crown as Henry IV and laid siege to Paris, Mayenne's stronghold, but was unable to capture it. The war dragged on, dissension broke out in the league between the moderates and the radicals, and in 1593 Navarre signed a truce with Mayenne by which the former abjured Protestantism and Navarre was generally recognized as king. In 1596, Mayenne dissolved the league, made a final agreement with Henry IV, and retired to his estates. He died at Soissons, France, on Oct. 3.

GUISE, CHARLES DE LORRAINE DE (1571–1640). Son of Henri, third duc de Guise, he was born on Aug. 20. When his father was murdered in 1588, he was seized and imprisoned at Tours until 1591. He was considered as a possible successor to the crown and for marriage with the daughter of Philip II of Spain, but his uncle, the duke of Mayenne, opposed him. In 1594, Charles pledged allegiance to Henry IV and fought for him against the Holy League, ending the Guise family tradition. He fought against the Protestant forces, but after siding with Marie de'

Medici, went to Italy, where he died in Siena on Sept. 30.

GUISE, CLAUDE DE LORRAINE DE (1496–1550). Born in Château de Condé, France, on Oct. 20, son of Duke René II of Lorraine, he was granted the countship of Guise and Aumale, the barony of Joinville, and two seignories by his father, joined the court of King Francis I, and married the pious and charitable Antoinette de Bourbon in 1513. He fought in Italy (where he was wounded at Marignano in 1515) and against Charles V. He was created first duc de Guise and a chamberlain by the French monarch. In 1525 he crushed an Anabaptist invasion of Lorraine, checked the imperial forces thrusting toward Paris from Luxembourg in 1542, and became governor of Burgundy. His ambition and wealth caused Francis to withdraw his favor. Claude died in Joinville, France, on Apr. 12, of poison, according to his son François.

GUISE, FRANÇOIS DE LORRAINE DE (1519–1563). Son of Claude de Guise, the second duke was born on Feb. 17 at Château de Bar and was early attracted to the military. He married Anne d'Este, granddaughter of King Louis XII; they had six sons and one daughter. He won renown by his successful defense of Metz in 1552 against Charles V, and was a leader of the group favoring war against Philip II. In 1557 he led an army into Italian territory, but was recalled to France by Henry II, made lieutenant general of the kingdom, and early in 1558 wrested Calais from the English, and won further victories until peace (which he opposed) was signed in 1559. When Francis II and Mary Stuart, niece of François, ascended the throne in 1559, the latter became the most powerful man in the kingdom. He violently suppressed a plot led against him in 1560 by the princes of Bourbon and Condé. When Francis II died on Dec. 5, 1560, François retired, but soon emerged to form, in April 1561, a triumvirate with Montmorency and St. André which opposed the pro-Protestant policy of the regent, Catherine de' Medici. War broke out between Catholics and Protestants in 1562; Guise took the field, may have been responsible for the massacre of the Protestants at Vassy, captured Rouen, and won the battle of Dreux. He was besieging Huguenot Orléans when he was assassinated by Jean Poltrot de Méré, reportedly at the instigation of Coligny, and died six days later on Feb. 24.

GUISE, HENRI I DE LORRAINE DE (1550–1588). Son of François de Guise and Anne d'Este, the third duc de Guise was born on Dec. 31, went to Hungary in 1566 to fight the Turks, and returned to fight in the Huguenot wars in France. He proposed marriage to Charles IX's sister, Margaret of Valois, which displeased the monarch, but in 1570 married Catherine de Cleves, by whom he had fourteen children. With Catherine de' Medici he precipitated the St. Bartholomew's Day massacre in 1572 to restrain the Huguenots, and his men slew Coligny (whom he held responsible for his father's murder) in the course of it. He became so popular with many factions in the kingdom that Henry III began to fear for his throne. In 1576, Henri formed (with the king as nominal head) the Holy League, ostensibly to defend Catholicism in France. This soon wielded such influence that it annulled in 1577 the Peace of Beaulieu, which Henry had signed with the Protestant princes, and started new religious wars. The death of the heir presumptive to the throne, François of Valois, in 1584 made Henry of Navarre heir apparent and resulted in civil war when Henri de Guise and the league refused to recognize his succession. Henry of Navarre was papally excommunicated and Henri de Guise won victories across France. He entered Paris in 1588 against the orders of Henry III; the States-General acknowledged him as their political leader and the king moved to put him to death. On Dec. 25 the king summoned de Guise to the court, where he was murdered by guards; the next day Henri's brother Louis (b. 1555), cardinal of Lorraine, was also slain.

GUISE, HENRI DE LORRAINE DE (1614–1664), archbishop. Son of Charles, fourth duc de Guise, he was archbishop of Rheims, opposed Richelieu in 1641, and was forced into exile in Flanders. He was a leader in the revolt of the Masaniello of Naples against Spain in 1647 in an attempt to secure the throne of Naples, was captured and imprisoned by the Spaniards until 1652, attempted again unsuccessfully in 1654 and then returned to France, joined the court, and became a grand chamberlain.

GUISE, JEAN DE LORRAINE DE (1498–1550), cardinal. Brother of Claude, he was made coadjutor of Metz when three, the first cardinal of Lorraine at twenty, bishop of Toul, Metz, Verdun, and other sees, and archbishop of Lyons, Rheims, and Narbonne. He became a member of the royal council in 1530 and acted as Francis I's ambassador to Charles V in 1536. He supported his brothers' activities, but in 1542 fell into the king's disfavor because of the enormous power which resulted from his plural benefices. He went to Rome, returned later to France, and died on May 18 in Nogent-sur-Yonne.

GUISE, LOUIS I DE LORRAINE DE (1527–1578), cardinal. Brother of François, second duc de Guise, he was born on Oct. 21, was named bishop of Troyes in 1545, of Albi in 1550, cardinal in 1553, and archbishop of Sens in 1561, a see he resigned in 1562. He was variously praised for his luxurious banquets and his political sagacity, and died in Paris on Mar. 24.

GUISE, MARIE DE (1515–1560), queen. Daughter of Claude, first duc de Guise, she was born at Bar-le-Duc on Nov. 22, married Louis II d'Orléans in 1534, was widowed in 1537, refused to marry Henry VIII of England, and in 1538 married James V of Scotland. Their daughter was Mary Stuart, born in 1542, the week before James died. Henry VIII attempted to gain control of Scotland and forced Marie to approve her infant daughter's marriage to his son Edward. Marie repudiated the forced agreement when she sent Mary to France; there the princess married Francis, son of King Henry II of France. Marie's brothers then sought to have Francis and Mary Stuart proclaimed king and queen of England and Ireland (since Elizabeth was held to be illegitimate) and prevailed upon Marie to try all non-Catholics for heresy. John Knox led the revolt in 1559; churches and monasteries were pillaged, and Marie was deposed as regent. French troops regained Edinburgh for her, but during the city's siege by Elizabeth's troops; Mary died on June 10. She is also known as Mary of Lorraine.

GUITART, JUSTINO (1874–1940), bishop. Born in Spain, he was ordained, became bishop of Urgell, as a prince was co-ruler of Andorra, and died in Barcelona on Jan. 31.

GUITMARUS, ST. (d. 765?). He was fourth abbot of the Benedictine monastery of St. Riquier, France. F. D. Dec. 10.

GUITMOND (d. 1095?), bishop. Born in Normandy, he became a Benedictine at Évreux, studied at Bec about 1060, denounced the Norman invasion of England, and about 1073–77 wrote a treatise on the Eucharist against the attacks of Berengarius of Tours. He lived in a monastery at Rome, was appointed bishop of Aversa, Italy, by Pope Urban II in 1088, and died there after 1090.

GUMESINDUS, ST. (d. 850), martyr. A parish priest, he was put to death at Cordova, Spain, with St. Servusdei, a monk, during the Moorish persecutions. F. D. Jan. 13.

GUMILLA, JOSÉ (1690–1758). Born in Barcelona, Spain, he became a Jesuit, went to South America in 1714, and in 1728 was superior of the missions along the Orinoco River. On his return to Spain he published a botanical and ethnological study of the mission area and became rector of the college at Cartagena, and in 1738 of the University of Madrid.

GUMMARUS, ST. (717–774?). Son of the lord of Emblem, Brabant, he became a courtier of King Pepin and married Guinimaria on the king's recommendation, but she became an extravagant shrew and he obtained a separation after eight years. He then lived as a recluse, and with St. Rumold founded the Benedictine abbey of Lierre, Flanders. F. D. Oct. 11.

GUMMERMANN, JOHN (1876–1960). Born in Kirmsees, Bavaria, on July 27, he became a Capuchin in 1895, taking the name Basil, and was ordained in 1902. He served in parishes in Wisconsin, Minnesota, Michigan, Brooklyn and Yonkers, New York. He taught at St. Lawrence seminary in Mt. Calvary, Wisconsin, and for his last twenty-four years was professor of theology at St. Anthony's friary in Marathon, Wisconsin. He also was director and later commissary provincial of the third Order of St. Francis. He died in Wausau, Wisconsin, on Feb. 13.

GUNDEBERT, ST. (d. 676?), bishop. He retired from the see of Sens, France, about 660 to found the Benedictine abbey of Senones. F. D. Feb. 21.

GUNDEBERT, ST. (8th century), martyr. He is believed to have been a Frankish monk, killed in Ireland by pagan raiders. F. D. Apr. 29.

GUNDECHAR, ST. (d. 754), martyr. A German, he became a Benedictine monk, worked with St. Boniface, and was put to death with him in Dokkum, Frisia. F. D. June 5.

GUNDELINDIS, ST. (d. 750?). Daughter of the duke of Alsace, she succeeded her aunt, St. Ottilia, as abbess of the Benedictine convent at Niedermünster, Alsace. She is also called Gwendoline. F. D. Mar. 28.

GUNDENIS, ST. (d. 203), martyr. She was put to death at Carthage during the reign of Septimus Severus. F. D. July 18.

GUNDISALVUS, ST. (d. 1135?). He was first abbot, or prior, of the Cistercian abbey of Las Junias, Portugal. F. D. Oct. 10.

GUNDISALVUS, ST. (d. 1422). Born in Lagos, Portugal, he became famous as an Augustinian preacher. His cult was approved in 1778. F. D. Oct. 21.

GUNDLEUS, ST. (6th century). A Welsh chieftain, whose marriage to St. Gladys produced St. Cadoc; the latter convinced his parents to give up a life of brigandage and to spend their last years as hermits. A legend recounts how Gundleus stole his bride and with King Arthur's help defeated her pursuing father. F. D. Mar. 29.

GUNDULF, ST. (6th century). A Gallic bishop, he is said to have died at Bourges. F. D. June 17.

GUNDULPHUS, ST. (d. 607?), bishop. He became bishop of Maastricht, Flanders, about 600, succeeding Monulphus. He may have lived until 614, if he is identical with the Betulphus who attended the Council of Paris in that year. F. D. July 16.

GUNDULPHUS, ST. (d. 823), bishop. He

followed Anilgram as bishop of Metz, France, in 891, after a twenty-five-year vacancy in the see. He died probably in Gorze. F. D. Sept. 6.

GUNN, JOHN EDWARD (1863–1924), bishop. Born in Five Mile Town, Tyrone, Ireland, on Mar. 15, he studied at St. Mary's, Ireland, the Marist college in Paignton, England, the Catholic University of Ireland, Dublin, and the Gregorian in Rome. He was professed in the Society of Mary in 1884, ordained in Rome in 1890, and taught at the Marist House of Studies at Catholic University, Washington, D.C., in 1892–98. He was a pastor in Savannah, Georgia, in 1898–1911, then was preconized bishop of Natchez, Mississippi. He died in New Orleans on Feb. 19.

GUNNER (1152–1251). Educated at Paris, he became a Cistercian in 1208, abbot of Öm in 1216, and bishop of Viborg, Denmark, in 1222. He devoted himself to training his clergy, probably wrote the Law of Jutland (*Jydske Lov*), and died at Asmild on Aug. 25.

GUNTER, BL. WILLIAM (d. 1588), martyr. A native of Raglan, Monmouthshire, England, he was educated at Rheims and ordained there in 1587. He was captured and hanged at Shoreditch, England, for being a priest, during the Elizabethan persecution, and was beatified in 1929. F. D. Aug. 28.

GUNTHER, BL. (955–1045). A cousin of St. Stephen of Hungary and a nobleman, he led a worldly life until he met St. Gothard of Hildesheim in his fiftieth year. He then gave his property to the monasteries of Hersfeld and Göllingen (of which he retained ownership), went on pilgrimage to Rome, and on his return became a monk at Niederaltaich, Bavaria. At his insistence he was made abbot of Göllingen, which caused great friction. He finally resigned, returned to Niederaltaich, and in 1008 became a hermit in Lalling. With a number of disciples he founded a monastery at Rinchnach, Bavaria, from which he made numerous preaching trips until his death in Bohemia. F. D. Oct. 9.

GÜNTHER, ANTON (1783–1863), philosopher. Born in Lindenau, Bohemia, on Nov. 17, he studied at Prague and became a tutor in Prince Bretzenheim's household. He lost faith but regained it after meeting St. Clement Hofbauer, and, after study at Vienna and Raab, was ordained in 1820. In 1828 he began to publish a series of eight works seeking to demonstrate the truth of positive Christianity in the light of reason alone, confuting pantheism but also rejecting scholasticism. They were widely hailed and condemned, had great influence on the Old Catholic group, and in 1857 were placed on the Index. He submitted to the decree, published nothing more, and died in Vienna on Feb. 24.

GÜNTHER OF COLOGNE (d. 873), archbishop. Of a noble Frankish family, he was consecrated archbishop of Cologne in 850 and became embroiled in a jurisdictional dispute with St. Anskar over Hamburg (resolved in Anskar's favor by Pope Nicholas I about 860). In 860 he presided at synods in Aachen which freed King Lothair II from his lawful wife Thietberga and in 862 approved the king's marriage to his concubine, Waldrada, an action approved by a bribed synod at Metz in 863. Later that year the synods were condemned by the pope and Günther was excommunicated. He persisted in calumnious attacks on the papacy and supported the invasion of Italy by Emperor Louis II. The ban was finally lifted in 869 when Günther made public retraction. He had his brother Hilduin of Cambrai rule for him during his excommunication; when Lothair II died, Günther recognized the new archbishop of Cologne, gave up his claim, and retired in 870. He died on July 8.

GUNTHILDIS, ST. (d. 748?). A Benedictine nun, she went from Wimborne, England, to Germany at the request of St. Boniface, directed a convent in Thuringia, and was inspector of the English schools in Germany. F. D. Dec. 8.

GUNTHRAMMUS, ST. (d. 592), king. He ruled Burgundy with a strong hand, divorced his wife, ordered the execution of his doctor, reformed, condemned his own actions, and was penitent over them through his last years. F. D. Mar. 28.

GURIAN, WALDEMAR (1902–1954), author. Born in St. Petersburg, Russia, on Feb. 13, he studied at Bonn, Munich, Breslau, and Cologne, became a convert, was editor of a Cologne newspaper in 1923–24, observed the rise of European dictatorships, and went to the United States in 1931. He became professor of political science at Notre Dame, editor of *Review of Politics* in 1939, and wrote *Bolshevism* (1932), *Hitler and the Christians*, *The Rise and Decline of Marxism*, studies of French Catholicism and socialism and of Charles Maurras, and was co-editor of *The Catholic Church in World Affairs*. He died in South Haven, Michigan, on May 26.

GURIAS, ST. (d. 306), martyr. With St. Samonas, he was tortured and then beheaded in Edessa, Syria, during Diocletian's persecution. F. D. Nov. 15.

GURLOES, ST. (d. 1057). A Benedictine monk, he served as prior at Redon, England, and in 1029 became abbot of St. Croix at Quimper, Brittany. F. D. Aug. 25.

GURVAL, ST. (6th century?). Possibly a Briton or Welshman, he made several monastic settlements in Brittany, perhaps as a missionary bishop. F. D. June 6.

GURY, JEAN PIERRE (1801–1866), theologian. Born in Mailleroncourt, France, on Jan.

23, he became a Jesuit in 1824 and taught moral theology at the seminary in Vals from 1834 until his death in Mercoeur, France, on Apr. 18. His *Compendium theologiae moralis* (1850) and *Casus conscientiae* (1852) are his most important works.

GUSMÃO, BARTHOLOMEU LOURENÇO DE (1685–1724). Born in Santos, São Paulo, Brazil, he studied in Bahia and at Coimbra, where he took his doctorate in canon law, and in 1709 secured the support of King John V of Portugal for his plans for an airship. He became a charter member of the Academia Real da Historia in 1720, court chaplain in 1722, and professor at Coimbra. He died of fever in Toledo, Spain, on Nov. 18.

GUTENBERG, JOHANN (1397?–1468?), printer. Born probably in Mainz, Germany, son of Friele Gänsfleisch, of a noted family, and Else Wyrich, he took the name of Gutenberg from the name of his mother's birthplace. He spent some time in Strassburg, probably for political reasons, beginning in 1434 and joined the goldsmiths' guild there. In 1437 he was sued for breaking his engagement to a local girl and about 1444 left Strassburg. It was during this period he began working on his printing press and in 1448 printed his first work, a poem and a calendar. He was the first European to print with movable type. In 1450 he entered into a partnership with Johann Fust, finished his forty-two-line Bible in 1455, and later that year lost his machinery and type to Fust when the latter sued him for a loan Fust had made to him. Gutenberg produced new printer's equipment when Conrad Humery backed him in Mainz, and printed several books. In 1465 he was in the service of Archbishop Adolf of Nassau, and probably died in Mainz, Prussia, late in 1467 or early 1468.

GUTHLAC, ST. (667–714). A soldier in the service of King Ethelred of Mercia, he entered the Benedictine abbey at Repton at twenty-four, and lived as a hermit in Lincolnshire, England, for some twenty years. His refuge was a shrine for many years and the site of the Norman abbey of Croyland. F. D. Apr. 11.

GUTIERREZ, BL. BARTHOLOMEW (1580?–1632). Born in Mexico, he became an Augustinian Friar in 1596, was ordained, went to the Philippines in 1606, and in 1612 was prior at Ukusi, Japan. He was seized in 1629, imprisoned for three years, and burned alive at Nagasaki. He was beatified in 1867. F. D. Sept. 28.

GUY, ST. (10th century). He directed the Benedictine abbey of Baume, France, until he resigned about 940 to spend his last years in a hermitage. F. D. June 18.

GUY, ST. (d. 1012?). Surnamed "the poor man of Anderlecht," he was born near Brussels, became sacristan of Our Lady of Laeken church in Brabant, lost his money in a business venture, went on a seven-year pilgrimage to the Holy Land, and died penniless at Anderlecht. F. D. Sept. 12.

GUY, BL. (d. 1045). He was Benedictine abbot of the monastery of Casauria, near Chieti, Italy. F. D. Nov. 23.

GUY, BL. (d. 1070). He was bishop of Acqui in Monferrato, Italy, from 1034 until his death. His cult was confirmed in 1853. F. D. June 2.

GUY OF DURNES, BL. (d. 1157?). A trusted follower of St. Bernard of Clairvaux, he became abbot-founder of the Cistercian monastery of Our Lady at Cherlieu. He revised his order's liturgical chant. F. D. Sept. 23.

GUY OF POMPOSA, ST. (d. 1046). Born near Ravenna, Italy, he renounced his wealth, studied at Rome under a hermit named Martin, and became a monk at the abbey of Pomposa, near Ferrara, and then at the Benedictine monastery of St. Stephens in Ravenna. In time he became abbot of each house, built a third for his father, brother, and the many others who were attracted by his sanctity and wisdom. He died near Parma, Italy. F. D. Mar. 31.

GUY OF VICOGNE, BL. (d. 1147). After founding the Premonstratensian abbey at Vicogne, in Arras, France, he retired there to become a member of the order. F. D. Mar. 31.

GUY VIGNOTELLI, BL. (1185?–1245?). A young man already known for his charities, he joined St. Francis of Assisi at Cortona, Italy, in 1211, was ordained, and gained a reputation as a preacher. F. D. June 16.

GUYON, JEANNE MARIE BOUVIER DE LA MOTTE (1648–1717), mystic. Born in Montargis, France, on April 13, daughter of Claude Bouvier, a governmental official, she married Jacques Guyon in 1664, had five children, and in 1676 lost her elderly husband and two children. When Père Lacombe became her spiritual director, her mystical experiences, which she described in her autobiography, began. In 1681 she left her children, joined Fr. Lacombe in Annecy, and placed herself under his guidance. She was denounced and they were expelled by the bishops of Geneva and of Grenoble. In 1686 she and Père Lacombe went to Paris, where she aroused the opposition of King Louis XIV, who was fighting the quietism of Molinos, which Mme. Guyon's teaching resembled. Late in 1688 she met Fénelon,

who accepted her views and influenced Mme. de Maintenon and the ladies of St. Cyr. Her published works were placed on the Index in that year and in 1694 were condemned by the archbishop of Paris. Though she signed a retraction of her theories and a submission to thirty-four articles of faith before Bishop Bossuet at Issy, she was imprisoned in the Bastille from 1695 to 1703. On her release, she retired to a village near Blois, where she remained in seclusion until her death there fifteen years later on June 9. She died declaring her allegiance to the Church and Catholic doctrine, but her influence had lasting and damaging effects.

GUZMAN, ALONSO PEREZ DE. *See* Medina Sidonia, Alonso de.

GUZMAN, FERNANDO PERÉZ DE (1376–1458), poet. He wrote considerable poetry, including the didactic *Proverbios* and *Diversas virtudes; Loores de los claros varones de España,* biographical sketches of thirty-six figures in the courts of Henry III and John II; and the prose *Generaciones e semblenzanas.*

GWEN, ST. (d. 492?), martyr. She is said to have been daughter of Brychan of Brecknock and murdered by Saxons at Talgarth, Wales, F. D. Oct. 18.

GWEN, ST. (5th century). *See* Fragan, St.

GWEN, ST. (6th century). She is said to have been sister of St. Nonna and mother of SS. Cadfan and Cyby. F. D. Oct. 18.

GWENAFWY, ST. (6th century). Daughter of Caw, a chieftain in North Britain, and sister of St. Samson of York, she settled in Cornwall after an attack on her home by the Picts. The town of St. Veep, Wales, is named after her. F. D. July 1.

GWENDOLINE. *See* Gundelindis, St.

GWINOC, ST. (6th century). He and his father, Aneurin (or Gildas), were Welsh monks; the son wrote a number of Celtic poems. F. D. Oct. 26.

GWYN, BL. RICHARD (1537–1584), martyr. Born in Llanidloes, Wales, he was educated at Cambridge, became a convert, opened a school at Overton, Flintshire, moved to Erbistock with his family, was arrested in 1579, escaped, and was captured in 1580 at Wrexham. After four years of imprisonment and torture (while in jail he wrote religious poetry in Welsh), he was put death with great brutality at Wrexham, Wales, on Oct. 15. He was beatified in 1929. F. D. Oct. 25.

H

HAAKON THE GOOD (920?-961), king of Norway. Son of Harold Fair Hair, he was raised in the court of King Athelstan of England. At his father's death in 932, Eric Blodoexe became king of Norway, but aroused such hatred that the nobles turned to his brother Haakon, who forced Eric into exile and took the crown in 935 or 936. After a successful war against Denmark, Haakon reformed the government, promoted commerce, and aided the spread of Christianity. When Eric's sons became of age they tried to regain the throne; Haakon sought the aid of powerful pagan groups in his kingdom and even had to participate in pagan rites. When the pagans increased their attacks on the Christians, war ensued. In 960 or 961, three of Eric's sons attacked Haakon's outnumbered forces at Fitje, Norway, and fatally wounded the king.

HAAS, FRANCIS JOSEPH (1889-1953), bishop. Born in Racine, Wisconsin, on Mar. 18, he studied at St. Francis seminary, Milwaukee, was ordained in 1913, taught literature at the seminary, and took his doctorate at Catholic University. He taught sociology at Marquette, edited the *Salesianum*, a quarterly, and lectured at the Milwaukee School of Social Work in 1922-31. He served on state and municipal social committees, and also became a member of the advisory council of the American Association for Social Security and of the League of Nations Association, and a member of the Committee on Cultural Relations with Latin America. From 1931 to 1935 he was in Washington as director of the National Catholic School of Social Service, and taught economics at Catholic University, became a member of President Roosevelt's Labor Advisory Board in 1933, worked under Harry Hopkins in the Works Progress Administration in 1935-39, and as a member of the Wisconsin Labor Relations Board in 1937-39. He was appointed in 1940 to the National Resources Planning Board, went to Puerto Rico to investigate wage problems in 1941, founded the Catholic Conference on Industrial Relations, and served on the conciliation board of the Department of Labor from 1935 until his death. He was made dean of the School of Social Science at Catholic University and a monsignor in 1937, became chairman of the Council against Intolerance, the Catholic Association for International Peace, and the American Association for Labor Legislation, and founded the Catholic Conference on Industrial Problems. He wrote *Shop Collective Bargaining* (1922), *Man and Society* (1930), and pamphlets for the numerous governmental organizations with which he was associated. He was consecrated bishop of Grand Rapids, Michigan, in 1943, where he died on Aug. 28.

HABENTIUS, ST. (d. 851), martyr. *See* Peter, St.

HABERL, FRANZ XAVER (1840-1910). Born in Ober Ellenbach, Bavaria, Germany, on Apr. 12, he studied in Passau, where he was ordained in 1862, became choirmaster of the Passau cathedral, and was director of music in the major and minor seminaries there. In 1867-70 he was choirmaster at Santa Maria dell' Anima, Rome, at the cathedral in Ratisbon in 1871-88, founded the School of Ecclesiastical Music in Ratisbon in 1874, and was named honorary canon of Palestrina by Pope Pius IX in 1879. He founded the Palestrina Society in that year to continue the publication of Palestrina's works, and was joint editor of the thirty-three-volume edition of Palestrina's works completed in 1894. He wrote *Magister choralis* (1865), was editor of *Musica Sacra* after 1868, and published editions of Lassus, Bertalotti, Frescobaldi, the Psalms, and a catalogue of the archives of the Sistine choir. He was named a member of the papal commission for the revision of hymnals, was president of the St. Cecilia Society from 1899 to 1910, and became a monsignor in 1907. He died in Ratisbon, Germany, on Sept. 5.

HABERMANN, FRANZ WENZEL (1706-1783), composer. Born in Lázne Kynzvart, Bohemia, on Sept. 20, he studied at Klatovy and in Prague, traveled through Europe, and about 1731 became conductor of the orchestra of Prince Louis de Conde. He returned to Prague in 1740, served as choirmaster of various churches until 1773 and of the cathedral of Cheb (Eger), West Bohemia, until his death there on June 7. He wrote masses and other ecclesiastical music, two oratorios, and a drama for the Jesuit school in Prague.

HABET-DEUS, ST. (d. 500?), bishop and martyr. While bishop of Luna in Tuscany, he was put to death by Arians. F. D. Feb. 17.

HABETS, JEAN GUILLAUME, co-founder. *See* Haze, Jeanne.

HABINGTON, THOMAS (1560-1647), historian. Son of Queen Elizabeth's treasurer, he was born in Thorpe, Surrey, England, on Aug. 23, educated at Oxford, Paris, and Rheims, where he became a convert, and on his return was imprisoned with his brother Edward on the charge of aiding the Babington plot to free

Mary Stuart. Released after six years, he gave asylum to Frs. Garnet and Oldcorne at Hindlip castle, near Worcester, was condemned to death at the time of the Gunpowder Plot, then exiled. He wrote a translation of Gildas (1637), a *History of Edward IV* (1640), and two antiquarian studies of Worcester. He died in Hindlip, England, on Oct. 8.

HABINGTON, WILLIAM (1605–1654), author. Son of Thomas Habington, an antiquarian, he was born in Hindlip, Worcestershire, educated at St. Omer and Paris, married Lucy Herbert about 1632, and in 1634 published *Castara*, a series of poems to his wife, which was very successful. He published *Queene of Arragon*, a play acted at court; *Historie of Edward IV*, supposedly written (1640) at the request of King Charles I; and *Observations upon History* (1641). He died on Nov. 30.

HACKSHOT, VEN. THOMAS (d. 1601), martyr. *See* Tichborne, Ven. Nicholas.

HADELIN, ST. (d. 690?). Born in Gascony, he was a Benedictine in the monasteries of Solignac, Maastricht, and Stavelot, founded that of Celles, near Liège, Belgium, and lived as a hermit in his last years. F. D. Feb. 3.

HADELIN, ST. (d. 700?). He was appointed abbot of the Benedictine monastery of Crespin in Hainault, Gaul, by St. Landelinus. F. D. June 27.

HADELIN, ST. (d. 910?). He was abbot of the Benedictine monastery of St. Calais, France, and about 884 became bishop of Séez. He is also known as Adelheim. F. D. Nov. 10.

HADULPH, ST. (d. 728?). The Benedictine abbot of the monastery of St. Vaast was concurrently bishop of Arras-Cambrai, France. F. D. May 19.

HADULPH, ST. (d. 754), martyr. This Benedictine associate of St. Boniface was put to death with him at Dokkum, Flanders. F. D. June 5.

HAEFTEN, BENEDICT VAN (1588–1648), founder. Born in Utrecht, Holland, he studied at Louvain, became a Benedictine, and was ordained in 1613. He became prior of Afflighem abbey in 1616 and provost in 1618. In 1628 he and eight of his monks transferred to the stricter Congregation of St. Vannes in Lorraine and founded the Congregation of the Presentation of the Blessed Virgin (dissolved in 1654). He wrote on the life and rule of St. Benedict as well as several treatises on asceticism. He died in Spa, Belgium, on July 31.

HAFEY, WILLIAM JOSEPH (1888–1954), bishop. Born in Springfield, Massachusetts, on Mar. 19, he studied at Holy Cross, law at Georgetown, and theology at Mt. St. Mary's, Maryland, and was ordained in Baltimore in 1914. He engaged in pastoral work in Baltimore, and served as chancellor from 1924–25, when he was appointed first bishop of Raleigh,

North Carolina. He was transferred to Scranton, Pennsylvania, as coadjutor and administrator in 1937, and succeeded to that see in 1938. He died on May 12.

HAGEN, GOTTFRIED (d. 1299). A native of Cologne, Germany, and town clerk there, he wrote the *Book of the City of Cologne*, a rhymed chronicle, about 1270; it is an exaggeratedly nationalistic and somewhat unreliable picture of mediaeval city life in Germany, though with some value.

HAGEN, JOHANN GEORG (1847–1930), astronomer. Born in Bregenz, Austria, on Mar. 6, he studied at Münster and Bonn, was ordained a Jesuit, and taught mathematics at Prairie du Chien, Wisconsin, in 1880. He was director of the observatory at Georgetown in 1888–1906 and then of the Vatican observatory. He wrote widely on astronomy, and prepared an index of the works of Leonard Euler and an atlas of variable stars. He died in Vatican City on Sept. 6.

HAGSPIEL, BRUNO M. (1885–1961). Born in Germany on Mar. 14, he joined the Society of the Divine Word in Silesia, and was ordained in Vienna in 1910, after which he went to the United States to teach at St. Mary's seminary in Illinois. He founded the *Little Missionary* in 1914, *Our Missions* in 1921, and became rector of St. Mary's in 1925, provincial of his order in the United States in 1928, and rector of St. Francis' seminary, Duxbury, Massachusetts, in 1942–48. He spent his last decade at the Divine Word seminary in Girard, Pennsylvania, and died in nearby Erie on Feb. 14.

HAHN-HAHN, IDA (1805–1880), novelist. Daughter of Count Karl Friedrich von Hahn, she was born in Tressow, Mecklenburg, on June 22, married her cousin, Adolf von Hahn, in 1826, divorced him in 1829, and traveled through Europe for twenty years, leaving a wake of scandal. In 1850 she became a convert and took up residence in a convent of the Sisters of the Good Shepherd which she founded in Mainz, Germany; she died there on Jan. 12. She wrote Byronic poetry, travel books, devotional works, and novels. *Gräfin Faustine* and *Maria Regina* are her best-known fiction; *Sibylle* and *Von Babylon nach Jerusalem* are autobiographical.

HAID, HERENAUS (1784–1873). Born in Ratisbon, Germany, on Feb. 16, he was a shepherd, studied in Neuberg and Landshut, where he was ordained in 1807, and at Munich, where he received his doctorate in divinity. From 1813 to 1818 he taught exegesis at St. Gall; he also was curate and pastor in Munich parishes. In 1824 he was moved by government pressure to Unsere liebe Frau, where he developed a catechism course, translated the *Summa* of St. Peter Canisius, and wrote the latter's biography. He died on Jan. 7.

HAID, LEO MICHAEL (1849–1924), bishop. Born near Latrobe, Pennsylvania, on July 15, he studied at St. Vincent's, Beatty, joined the Benedictines in 1869, and was ordained in Beatty in 1872. He taught at St. Vincent's abbey until 1885 when he was elected abbot of the newly founded Belmont abbey in North Carolina. He was appointed vicar apostolic of North Carolina and titular bishop of Messene in 1888, the first abbot-bishop in the United States, and in 1910 was appointed abbot-ordinary when Belmont was made a cathedral abbey by Pope Pius X. He helped to develop Belmont Abbey College. He died at Belmont abbey on July 24.

HAILANDIÈRE, CELESTINE RENÉ LAURENT GUYNEMER DE LA (1798–1882), bishop. Born in Combourg, Brittany, France, on May 2, he studied at the Rennes seminary, was ordained in Paris in 1825, and went to the United States as a missionary in 1836 under Bishop Bruté of Vincennes. He became vicar general of that see, went to France to seek priests and financial aid, and while there was appointed titular bishop of Axierne and coadjutor of Vincennes in 1839. When Bishop Bruté died, the new coadjutor immediately assumed the Indiana see. He brought in the Congregation of Holy Cross in 1841, and the following year presented to the group headed by Fr. Edward Sorin a tract of land on which the first building of Notre Dame was erected in 1843, resigned in 1847 because of differences and difficulties with his clergy, and returned to France and died in Triandin on May 1.

HAILE, BL. JOHN (d. 1535), martyr. A parish priest stationed at Islesworth, Middlesex, England, he was seized early in the Henrican persecution, and brutally put to death at Tyburn with Bl. John Houghton. He was beatified in 1886. F. D. May 5.

HAIMHAUSEN, KARL VON (1692–1767). Born in Munich, Bavaria, on May 28, he became a Jesuit in 1709, and was sent to Chile as a missioner in 1724, where he taught theology and became rector of the Collegium Maximum in Santiago. He held other offices in the province of Chile and built churches, retreat houses, and a prospering crafts school. He died on Apr. 7.

HAITO (763–836), bishop. Born of a noble Swabian family, he studied at the abbey of Reichenau, became head of its monastic school and library, abbot in 806, and bishop of Basle. In 811 he was sent to Constantinople by Charlemagne. On his return he rebuilt his cathedral, but in 823 he resigned his abbacy and bishopric and retired as a monk to Reichenau, South Baden, Germany, where he died on March 17. He wrote *Visio Wettini*, a biography of the head of the monastic school at Reichenau, which contains a vivid and poetical description of heaven, hell, and purgatory.

HALDEMAN, SAMUEL STEMAN (1812–1880), scientist. Born in Locust Grove, Pennsylvania, on Aug. 12, he studied in Harrisburg and at Dickinson, managed his father's sawmill, and devoted his spare time to the study of natural history. He later experimented with the use of anthracite in the ore-smelting plants owned by his brothers, married Mary Hough in 1835, and became a convert in 1846. He helped in the geological survey of New Jersey, wrote on fresh-water mollusks, insect sounds, orthography, etymology, Indian languages, and variations within the vernaculars of Europe. He taught zoology at the Franklin Institute, Philadelphia, natural history at the University of Pennsylvania and Delaware College, geology at Pennsylvania Agricultural College, and from 1868 until his death was the first professor of comparative philology at the University of Pennsylvania. He was a founder of the National Academy of Sciences, and died in Chickies, Pennsylvania, on Sept. 10.

HALITGARIUS (d. 831). He became bishop of Cambrai, France, in 817, wrote on the Church, and was an apostle to the Danes.

HALLAHAN, CORNELIUS (18th century). An Irish immigrant, he settled at Mill Creek, New Castle County, Delaware, in 1730, established an estate at what is now Mt. Cuba, and was probably the first to arrange Catholic services in the state.

HALLAHAN, MARGARET (1803–1868), foundress. Born in London of Irish parents who died when she was nine, she was sent to an orphanage and from 1814 to 1834 was a servant. In 1842 she became a Dominican tertiary, worked under the direction of Bishop Ullathorne with factory girls in Coventry, and formed the Dominican Congregation of St. Catherine of Siena, which received papal approbation in 1851. She died in London on May 10.

HALLER, KARL LUDWIG VON (1768–1854), jurist. Born in Berne, Switzerland, on Aug. 1, he entered government service at fifteen, became secretary of the Swiss diet, and traveled through Europe as legate. When France invaded Berne in 1798 and dissolved the Swiss republic, he was forced to flee. From 1801 to 1806 he was secretary of the council of war in Vienna; recalled to Berne, he became professor of political law, member of the great council, and privy councilor of the republic. In 1821 he announced his return to the Church, which caused his dismissal. He moved to Paris, then returned to Solothurn, and in 1833 was elected to the great council. He wrote widely for political journals and a six-volume study of political theory, explaining the natural law and in refutation of Rousseau. He died in Solothurn, Switzerland, on Mar. 21.

HALLOY, JEAN BAPTISTE JULIEN D'OMALIUS (1783–1875), geologist. Born in Liège, Belgium, on Feb. 16, he studied in Paris, became interested in natural history, and was commissioned to prepare a geological map of France, which he completed in 1813. He then entered politics and became superintendent of Dinant, secretary of Liège, and in 1815 governor of Namur. He was made a member of the Academy of Brussels and in 1850 its president; he was a member of the Belgian senate in 1848 and its vice-president in 1851. He continued his scientific interests and was a pioneer in modern geology. He died in Brussels on Jan. 15.

HALLVARD, ST. (d. 1043), martyr. A Norwegian trader in the Baltic, he was asked to give refuge on his ship to a woman pursued by three men who said that she was a thief. Although he offered to make up any loss they may have suffered, they shot her and Hallvard. The latter was looked on as a martyr because of his action and is the patron of Oslo. F. D. May 15.

HALM, FRIEDRICH. *See* Münich-Bellinghausen, Eligius Franz Joseph von.

HALMA, NICHOLAS (1755–1826), mathematician. Born in Sedan, France, on Dec. 31, he studied at Plessis in Paris, was ordained, became rector at Sedan in 1791, and was a surgeon in the army in 1793. He held the chair of mathematics at Prytanée and of geography at Fontainebleau, was curator of St. Geneviève Library, and wrote several translations and a history of France. He died in Paris on June 4.

HAMAL, HENRI (1744–1820), composer. Born in Liège, Belgium, nephew of Jean Noel Hamal, he studied under his uncle and in Italy, returned to Liège in 1772, wrote two cantatas, and succeeded Jean as canon and as choirmaster of St. Giles in 1778. He lost his position when the cathedral was destroyed in 1792 and spent his last years writing on culture in Liège, and symphonies, cantatas, hymns, and other ecclesiastical music. He died in Liège on Sept. 17.

HAMAL, JEAN NOEL (1709–1778), composer. Born in Liège, Belgium, on Dec. 23, son of Henri Guillaume Hamal (1685–1752), he sang in his father's choir at the cathedral of St. Lambert, studied in the Jesuit college there and in Rome, and returned to Liège in 1731. He was attached to the cathedral staff, became choirmaster in 1738, and became imperial chaplain in 1745, and canon of St. Giles in 1759. He wrote fifty-six masses, fifteen symphonies, oratorios, motets, cantatas, and overtures; some of this vast output probably was the work of his father (since it is signed with only the surname, Hamal). He died in Liège on Nov. 26.

HAMILTON, JOHN (1511–1571), arch-

bishop. Natural son of the first earl of Arran, he studied with the Benedictines of Kilwinning, Scotland, and at Glasgow and Paris, where he was ordained in 1543. On his return to Scotland, he occupied several offices of state, was appointed bishop of Dunkeld in 1544, and in 1546 succeeded the murdered Cardinal Beaton as archbishop of St. Andrews and primate of Scotland. He became a leader of the Catholic party, instituted widespread clerical reforms, and opposed the parliament of 1560 which adopted Protestantism as the state religion. He was imprisoned in 1563 for saying mass, was released at the request of Mary Queen of Scots, and became one of her staunchest defenders. When her forces were defeated at Langside in 1568, she fled to England and Hamilton took refuge in Dumbarton castle. When it was reduced in 1571, he was captured and hanged in Stirling, Scotland, on April 6.

HAMMER-PURGSTALL, JOSEPH BARON VON (1774–1856), orientalist. Born in Graz, Austria, on June 9, he studied there and at Vienna, entered the Oriental Academy in Vienna in 1788, and devoted the rest of his life to the study of oriental languages. In 1796 he entered the Austrian diplomatic service and served in Egypt and Constantinople until 1807 when he returned to Vienna. In 1847 he was elected president of the Academy of Science. He translated Turkish, Persian, and Arabic works, wrote histories of Persian and Turkish poetry, and founded the periodical *Fundgruben des Orients*. He died in Vienna on Nov. 23.

HAMPTON, JOHN (15th century), composer. He may have been organist of Worcester cathedral, England; he wrote a *Salve Regina* during the reign of Henry VII, and may have been the author of ballads for which that king rewarded a composer named Hampton in 1495.

HANARD, MARTIN (15th century), composer. Born in Flanders, he may have been a canon at Cambrai, was frequently in Rome, wrote a motet, *Le Serviteur*, and, probably, the *Lamentation* for the death of his master, Dufay, in 1474.

HAND, JOHN (d. 1846). A priest in Dublin, he began in 1840 to develop a college for the education of priests who would serve in Irish areas of English-speaking countries. He gained the approval of Pope Gregory XVI and the support of Daniel O'Connell and Archbishop Murray and opened All Hallows College, Dublin, in 1842. The college has been under the direction of the Vincentians since 1892.

HANDL, JACOB (1550–1591), composer. Born in Rybnica, Carniola, on July 31, and called Gallus (probably the Latinized form of his Slovenian name, Petelin), he became a Cistercian and was stationed at Zwelle and Melk in Austria. He was attached to the court chapel in 1574–79, worked near Brno, Moravia, was choirmaster of Bishop Pavlovsky of Olomouc from 1579 to 1585, and then of the church of St. John in Prague. He wrote masses, motets, dirges, and hymns. His *Passion* (1587), *Ecce quomodo moritur justus*, and *Mirabile mysterium* are particularly effective. He died in Prague, Bohemia, on July 18.

HANEBURG, DANIEL BONIFACIUS VON (1816–1876), bishop. Born in Tanne, Bavaria, on June 17, he studied at Kempten and Munich, and was ordained in 1839. He lectured at Munich, on scripture from 1840 to 1872, became professor of Hebrew and scripture in 1844, wrote widely in both fields, and served as tutor to the court of Bavaria. In 1850 he became a Benedictine, was named abbot of St. Boniface, Munich, in 1854, and attended the Vatican Council, where he at first opposed, then accepted, the dogma of papal infallibility. He became bishop of Speyer, Bavaria, in 1872, and died there on May 31.

HANISET, BL. MARIE (d. 1794), martyr. *See* Lidoin, Bl. Marie.

HANNA, EDWARD JOSEPH (1860–1944), archbishop. Born in Rochester, New York, on July 21, he studied at the Propaganda and North American colleges in Rome, at Munich and Cambridge, and was ordained in Rome in 1885. He taught theology at the Propaganda in 1886–87 and at St. Andrew's and at St. Bernard's seminaries, Rochester, in 1887–1912. He was appointed titular bishop of Tiliopolis and auxiliary of San Francisco in 1912. He succeeded to that see as archbishop in 1915, served as chairman of the National Catholic Welfare Conference administration committee in 1919–35, and in 1934 was appointed chairman of the longshoremen's board of arbitration by President Roosevelt. In 1932 he received a medal for his efforts to achieve good will between Christians and Jews, resigned his see in 1935 and was appointed titular archbishop of Gortyna, and died in Rome on July 15.

HANNEGAN, ROBERT EMMET (1903–1949). Born in St. Louis, Missouri, on June 30, he studied at St. Louis University, became a lawyer, and rose through the political ranks to Democratic city chairman. He married Irma Protzmann, was named district collector of internal revenue in 1942, and became chairman of the Democratic National Committee in 1944–47. Through his strategy Harry S. Truman became senator in 1940 and vice-president in 1944. Hannegan was postmaster general of the United States in 1943–47 and was joint owner of the St. Louis Cardinals baseball team in 1947–48. He died in St. Louis on Oct. 6.

HANSE, BL. EVERARD (d. 1581), martyr. Born in Northamptonshire, England, he studied at Cambridge and became a popular Protestant minister. After his conversion he went to

Rheims and was ordained in 1581. He returned to England in that year, using the name Evans Duckett, was arrested while visiting Catholic prisoners in Marshalsea prison, and was hanged, drawn, and quartered in Newgate prison, London. He was beatified in 1886. F. D. July 31.

HANSIZ, MARKUS (1683–1766), historian. Born in Volkermarkt, Austria, he became a Jesuit in 1698, was ordained in 1708, taught at Vienna and Graz, and wrote histories of several German sees, including Ratisbon.

HANSJACOB, HEINRICH (1837–1916), author. Born in Haslach, Baden, Germany, on Aug. 19, he was ordained at twenty-six, pastor at Hagnau for fifteen years, and transferred to Freiburg in 1884. He twice was a member of the legislature of the duchy, was imprisoned during the Kulturkampf, and wrote thirty volumes of character sketches and fiction, humorous, idealized, but with realistic dialogue, description, and identifiably country people. His *Black Forest Stories* were widely serialized in America. He died on June 23.

HANTHALER, CHRYSOSTOMUS (1690–1754), historian. Born in Marenbach, Austria, he joined the Cistercians, became librarian of Lilienfeld monastery in lower Austria, wrote a history of the monastery, *Fasti Campililienses*, and of the Babenberg dukes of Austria and Steyer, and books on numismatics and other subjects.

HANXLEDEN, JOHANN ERNST (1681–1732). Born in Osteroappeln, Hanover, he became a Jesuit, went to the East Indies, and labored on the mission in Malabar. He was one of the first Europeans to study Sanskrit, wrote a Sanskrit grammar and lexicon, religious poems, songs, and a life of Christ.

HARAHAN, WILLIAM JOHNSON (1867–1937). Born in Nashville, Tennessee, on Dec. 22, he graduated from St. John's, New Orleans, in 1885, began working on the Louisville and Nashville Railroad, and spent the rest of his life in railroading, eventually becoming president of the Chesapeake and Ohio in 1920. He retired in ill health from 1929 to 1935, then resumed his presidency and also that of the Nickel Plate and Père Marquette. He died in Clifton Forge, Virginia, on Dec. 4.

HARCOURT, WILLIAM. *See* Barrow, William.

HARDECANUTE (1019?–1042), king of England. Younger son of Canute and Emma of Normandy, he succeeded his father as king of Denmark in 1037, planned to invade England with Emma in 1039, and was chosen king of England in 1040. He disinterred and debased the body of his half-brother, King Harold; invited another half-brother, Edward the Confessor, to court; and died suddenly at a banquet.

HARDEE, WILLIAM J. (1817–1873), general. Born in Savannah, Georgia, he graduated from West Point in 1838, served against the Florida Indians, in the West, and in the Mexican war with distinction, prepared a manual of tactics, and in 1856 was appointed commandant of cadets at the Military Academy. He fought for the Confederacy during the Civil War and became a lieutenant general. At the war's end he retired to his Alabama plantation. He died in Wythesville, Virginia, on Nov. 6.

HARDESTY, VEN. ROBERT (d. 1589), martyr. *See* Spenser, Ven. William.

HARDEY, MARY ALOYSIA (1809–1886). Born in Piscataway, Maryland, on Dec. 8, she went with her family to Louisiana in 1822, where she entered the Society of the Sacred Heart in 1825. In 1835 she was appointed assistant superior and in 1836 superior of St. Michael's convent, opened the first Sacred Heart school in New York in 1841, went to Rome and Paris in 1842, and on her return was appointed superior of the New York convent. In 1844 she was appointed provincial of the houses in the eastern United States and Canada and founded many convents and schools. From 1847 to 1872 she worked from the new center called Manhattanville (later to become a college), then was named assistant general of her congregation, residing in Paris (making visits to the United States in 1874, 1878, and 1882). She died in Paris; her remains were brought to the general novitiate of the order, Albany, New York, in 1905.

MARGARET WILLIAMS, *Second Sowing* (New York, Sheed, 1942).

HARDING, ST. STEPHEN. *See* Stephen Harding, St.

HARDING, THOMAS (1516–1572). Born in Combe Martin, Devon, England, he studied at Barnstaple, Winchester, and Oxford, taught Hebrew, and was ordained. He became a Protestant, but when Mary became queen declared his Catholicism. In 1554 he became doctor of divinity, and secured several preferments, which he lost on his imprisonment when Elizabeth ascended the throne. On his release he fled to Louvain, and from there carried on his controversy with the Anglican Bishop Jewel of Salisbury in books, sermons, and pamphlets from 1564 to 1568. In 1566 he and Dr. Sander were appointed apostolic delegates to England by Pope Pius V, and he was instrumental in founding the English college at Douai. He died on Sept. 13 in Louvain, Flanders.

HARDOIN, ST. (7th century). Also known as Ouardon, he was bishop of St. Pol de Léon, Brittany. F. D. Nov. 29.

HARDOUIN, HENRI (1724?–1808), composer. Born in Grandpré, Ardennes, France, he was a chorister in Rheims, was ordained, became canon of its cathedral, and choirmaster

there. He wrote masses and published *Methode nouvelle pour apprendre le plain-chant* in 1762.

HARDOUIN, JEAN (1646–1729), historian. Son of a bookseller, he was born on Dec. 23 in Quimper, Brittany, became a Jesuit in 1660, and taught rhetoric and theology. On his appointment as librarian of Louis le Grand College in Paris, he wrote on ancient numismatics, aroused controversy by his aspersions on the validity of the authorship of the writings of many of the Greek, Latin and early Christian writers, and declared that the Alexandrian version and Hebrew text of the Old Testament were not authentic. He also wrote on the chronology of the life of Christ, interpretations of the Old and New Testaments, and a critical edition of the texts of the councils. He died in Paris on Sept. 3.

HARDOUIN, JULES (1646–1708), architect. Born in Paris, he studied construction under his granduncle, François Mansard, whose surname he took, and enjoyed success under the patronage of King Louis XIV, who made him a count and superintendent of buildings in 1699. Combining the classical with the style of François and of LeBrun, he developed a baroque manner of his own, which is most evident in the church of the Invalides. He also did the Grand Trianon, the Colonnades, and, with Leveau, finished the Château of Versailles. He designed Place des Victoires and Place Vêndome before his death at Marly, France.

HARDUIN, ST. (d. 662?). Bishop of Le Mans, France, he founded the monastery of Notre Dame d'Evron. F. D. Aug. 20.

HARÉAU, JEAN BARTHÉLMY (1812–1896), historian. A native of Paris, he studied at Louis le Grand and Bourbon colleges there, became a contributor to several newspapers, editor of *Courrier de la Sarthe* in 1838, and librarian of the city of Le Mans until 1845, when he was dismissed. On his return to Paris he resumed his newspaper career, served in the constituent assembly of 1848, as keeper of manuscripts at the Bibliothèque Nationale (which he resigned in 1851 in protest against Louis Napoléon's coup), as librarian of the Association of Advocates (1861), and in 1871–82 as director of the Imprimerie Nationale. He wrote voluminously: translations (Lucan's *Pharsale* and Seneca's *Facetie sur la mort de Claude*); history (*Literary History of Maine, Francis I and His Court*); philosophy (*Histoire de la philosophie scolastique*); and volumes 14–15 of *Gallia christiana*. He returned to the Church before his death in Paris.

HARKINS, MATTHEW (1845–1921), bishop. Born in Boston, on Nov. 17, he studied at Holy Cross, Douai, and St. Sulpice, Paris, and was ordained in 1869. He did parish work in Arlington and Boston until 1887, when he was appointed bishop of Providence, Rhode

Island. He labored to provide for the needs of large French-Canadian and Italian groups in his see. He died in Providence on May 25.

HARKS, ANNA (1868–1943), educator. She studied in Germany, taught in Toledo, Ohio, became a School Sister of Notre Dame, as Sister Mary Evarista, and was superior of her order in Covington, Kentucky. She directed the establishment in 1922 of Notre Dame College, South Euclid, Ohio, and served as its president and also as superior of the Cleveland province until her death in the latter city on Aug. 1.

HARLAND, HENRY (1861–1905); novelist. Born in St. Petersburg, Russia, son of Thomas Harland, a Connecticut lawyer, he went to the College of the City of New York and to Harvard. While with the surrogate's court in New York, he wrote a trilogy on Jewish life and seven other novels under the pen name Sidney Luska. He went to Paris and London in 1887, where he settled, wrote a drama (*The Light Sovereign*) and short stories, and joined Aubrey Beardsley in the publication of the quarterly *Yellow Book* (1894–97). Harland became a convert in 1897 and published *The Cardinal's Snuff Box* (1898), *The Lady Paramount* (1902), and *My Friend Prospero* (1904), his most popular fiction. He died in San Remo, Italy, on Dec. 20 and was buried in Norwich, Connecticut.

HARLAY, ACHILLE DE (1536–1619), diplomat. Born in Paris on Mar. 7, he became councilor of the Parliament of Paris in 1558, president in 1572, and *premier président* in 1582. He opposed the Holy League when it backed Henri of Guise and supported the cause of Henry IV, for which he was imprisoned by the league until Henry III's death. He died in Paris on Oct. 21.

HARLAY, ACHILLE DE (1581–1646). A member of the clergy and bishop-elect of Lavaur, France, he decided in 1601 to give up his ecclesiastical state and become a soldier. He was sent as ambassador to Constantinople in 1611 by Marie de' Medici, the queen regent, and in 1617 was imprisoned by the Turkish government for allegedly aiding a Polish prisoner to escape. He was recalled to Paris and the Turkish government apologized. In 1619 he joined the Oratorians, and supported many oratories in France. In 1625 he accompanied Henrietta of France to London, and in 1631 was appointed bishop of St. Malo. A firm supporter of Cardinal Richelieu, whose *Mémoires* he edited, he was interested in rare manuscripts several of which he had brought to France from Constantinople. He died on Nov. 20.

HARLAY, FRANÇOIS DE (1585–1653), archbishop. Born in Paris, he became abbot of St. Victor and in 1616 archbishop of Rouen. He encouraged religious orders, instituted widespread clerical reforms, encouraged scholarship, and established a famous center of scriptural studies. He resigned his see in 1651 in favor of his nephew, and died on Mar. 22.

HARLAY-CHANVALLON, FRANÇOIS DE (1625–1695), archbishop. Born in Paris on Aug. 14, he became abbot of Jumièges and in 1651 succeeded his uncle to the see of Rouen, despite the opposition of St. Vincent de Paul. In 1671 he was appointed archbishop of Paris. He became an adviser of King Louis XIV, a bitter enemy of Jansenism and Protestantism, was most influential in the assemblies of the clergy, and became a member of the French Academy. He died in Conflans, France, on Aug. 6.

HARLEZ DE DEULIN, CHARLES JOSEPH DE (1832–1899), orientalist. Born in Liège, Belgium, on Aug. 21, he studied law at Liège. Ordained in 1858, he was appointed director of St. Quirin College in Huy, in 1861 head of the art school in Louvain, and in 1871 was appointed professor of oriental languages there, and translated the Zoroastrian Bible. He became interested in Chinese literature, founded the journal *Muséon* in 1881, published a Sanskrit manual, and in 1884 a handbook of the Manchu language. He developed the school of oriental studies at Louvain into an outstanding center, received a domestic prelateship, and became a member of the Académie Royale of Belgium. He died on July 14 in Louvain, Belgium.

HARMEL, LÉON (1829–1915), executive. Born in Val des Bois, France, on Feb. 17, he studied at Senlis College and took over the management of the family spinning factory. He built it into a large and successful business, and after his wife's death in 1870 devoted himself to improving working conditions, providing housing, forming co-operatives, inviting his workers to participate in the management of the business, and instituting widespread benefits. His factory was regarded as a model institution, and, when Leo XIII's *Rerum novarum* was issued, Harmel used it as a guide for his business dealings. He died in his native town on Nov. 25.

HAROLD I (d. 1040), king of England. Called "the Harefoot," the supposed son of King Cnut and Elfgithu was in 1035 elected king with Danish support, and held the territory north of the Thames River. He is said to have killed Alfred in 1037, whereby he became king of all England. He was buried in St. Clement Danes after his body had been disinterred by Hardicanute.

HAROLD II (1022?–1066), king of England. Second son of Godwin and Gytha, he became earl of East Anglia in 1045, raised an army in Ireland and attacked England in 1052, and succeeded his father in Wessex in 1053. He became earl of Hereford in 1058, subdued Welsh leaders in 1062–63, and swore allegiance to

William of Normandy in 1064. He was chosen king of England in 1066 and was recognized by Northumbria; lacking national support, he was easily defeated by the invading Normans at Hastings, and died in the battle on Oct. 14.

HARRINGTON, BL. WILLIAM (1566–1594), martyr. Born at Mt. St. John, Yorkshire, England, he met Edmund Campion when he was fifteen, and in admiration went to Rheims and Tournai, to become ordained in 1592. Re-entering his own country as an underground missioner, he was captured after a year, imprisoned, and hanged, drawn, and quartered at Tyburn on the charge of priesthood. The poet John Donne's brother Henry, who retained his faith, died in prison in 1593, charged with having hidden Fr. Harrington. F. D. Feb. 18.

HARRIS, JOEL CHANDLER (1848–1908), author. Born in Eatonton, Georgia, on Dec. 9, he became a printer, and worked on various newspapers until 1876, when he joined the Atlanta *Constitution*, of which he became editor in 1890. He became famous for his stories in Negro dialect and his "Uncle Remus" character became known all over the world. His "Bre'r Rabbit" animal stories, and his novels, *Mingo* (1884), *Free Joe* (1887), *Balaam and His Master* (1891), and *Aaron* (1893) also were popular. He became a convert two weeks before his death on July 3 in Atlanta, Georgia.

HARRISON, JAMES (d. 1602), martyr. Born in Lichfield, England, he studied at Rheims where he was ordained in 1583. Sent on the English mission in 1584, he worked in Yorkshire, where he was captured, charged with being a priest, and hanged, drawn, and quartered on Mar. 22.

HARRISON, MARY ST. LEGER (1852–1931), novelist. Born in Eversley, Hampshire, England, on June 4, daughter of the novelist Charles Kingsley and Frances Grenfell, she studied at the Slade School of Fine Art, married William Harrison, a minister, in 1876, and lived in North Devon. Under the pen name Lucas Malet she wrote *Colonel Enderby's Wife* (1885), *The Wages of Sin* (1891), and *The History of Sir Richard Calmady* (1901), romantic accounts of village life and London society. She became the friend of Henry James and, during a long stay in France, of the literary circle surrounding Romain Rolland. She became a convert in 1902 (her husband had died in 1897), was given a government pension, and died in Tenby, Wales, on Oct. 27.

HARRISON, WILLIAM (1553–1621). Born in Derbyshire, England, he went to Douai in 1575, was ordained in Rome in 1579, and was in England from 1581 to 1587, when he returned to study at Paris. After two years as director of a school in Eu, he became procurator of the English college at Rheims and taught

theology there until 1603. After five years in Rome he returned to England, and in 1615 was appointed archpriest of England by Pope Paul V. He died on May 11.

HART, BL. WILLIAM (d. 1583), martyr. Born in Wells, England, he studied at Oxford, became a convert, trained at Rheims, was ordained in Rome, and came back secretly to work in Yorkshire. Betrayed, he was captured in the home of Bl. Margaret Clitherow, and hanged for his priesthood. He was beatified in 1886. F. D. Mar. 15.

HARTLEY, JAMES JOSEPH (1858–1944), bishop. Born in Columbus, Ohio, on June 5, he studied at Mt. St. Mary of the West, Cincinnati, and Holy Angels seminary, Niagara Falls, and was ordained in Columbus in 1882. He served in Steubensville, Ohio, parishes until 1904, when he was consecrated bishop of Columbus. He founded the Catholic Press Association in 1911 and served as its honorary president until his death, was named an assistant at the pontifical throne in 1929, and died on Jan. 12.

HARTLEY, BL. WILLIAM (d. 1588), martyr. Born in Wilne, Derbyshire, he was educated at Oxford, became an Anglican minister, was converted, and was ordained at Rheims in 1580. Sent on the English mission, he aided Bl. Edmund Campion and Robert Persons in their secret publishing projects, was captured in 1582, imprisoned, and deported in 1585. On his return, he was captured at Holborn, England, in 1588 and hanged at Shoreditch. He was beatified in 1929. F. D. Oct. 5.

HARTMANN, BL. (d. 1164), bishop. Born in Polling, Austria, he studied at the Augustinian monastery at Passau, became dean of the cathedral of Salzburg in 1122, instituted wide reforms, and in 1140 was made bishop of Brixen (Bressanone), Italy. His cult was confirmed in 1784. F. D. Dec. 23.

HARTMANN, FELIX VON (1851–1919), cardinal. Born in Westphalia on Dec. 15, he was ordained in 1874, served as a chaplain in Rome, vicar at Havizbech, and vicar general and dean at Emmerich. He was consecrated bishop of Münster in 1911, transferred to Cologne in 1913, and became cardinal-priest in 1914, and a member of the Prussian house of lords in 1916. He died in Cologne, Germany, on Nov. 11.

HARTMANN, GEORG (1489–1564), physicist. Born in Eckoltsheim, Bavaria, he concentrated his studies in theology and mathematics, and became vicar of St. Sebaldus' church in Nuremberg, Germany, where he died on Apr. 9. In 1544 he discovered the inclination of the magnetic needle.

HARTMANN VON AUE (1170?–1215), poet. Born in Swabia, he was well educated, served the lords of Aue as a knight, went on the crusade (in 1189 or 1197), and wrote lengthy epical romances: *Erec*, which introduced the Arthurian story to Germany; *Iwein*, on the devotion of woman; *Gregorius*, a happy-ending variant of the Oedipus story; and *Der arme Heinrich*, on a German hero. He also wrote lyric poetry.

HARTWIG, BL. (d. 1023). Archbishop of Salzburg, Austria, he is listed as the twenty-first to hold the see, which he ruled from 991 until his death. F. D. June 14.

HARTY, JEREMIAH J. (1853–1927), archbishop. Born in St. Louis, Missouri, on Nov. 7, he studied at the university there and at St. Vincent's College, was ordained in 1878, held parish posts in his native city, and in 1903 was appointed archbishop of Manila, the Philippines. He arrived in Jan. 1904; the first provincial council of the islands was convoked by the apostolic delegate in 1907. Archbishop Harty was transferred to Omaha, Nebraska, in 1916 and died on Oct. 29.

HARUCH, ST. (d. 830?), bishop. A Benedictine abbot, he served as missionary bishop in the region of Werden. F. D. July 15.

HASCHKA, LORENZ LEOPOLD (1749–1827), poet. Born in Vienna on Sept. 1, he became a Jesuit, but when the Society was suppressed in 1773 became a poet, a freemason, wrote against the pope and religious orders, but returned to Catholicism when the death of the emperor brought an end to Josephinism. He composed the Austrian national anthem, became assistant librarian at the University of Vienna, and died there on Aug. 3.

HASPINGER, JOHANN SIMON (1776–1856), general. Born in Gries, Tyrol, on Oct. 28, he fought in 1796 against the invading French. He became a Capuchin in 1802, taking the name Joachim, was ordained in 1805, and served as an army chaplain. When Tyrol was ceded to Bavaria by the Treaty of Pressburg, the Tyrolese rose in rebellion in 1807, and Haspinger became one of their leaders. At first a successful general, he was routed with his rebel force by Napoleon's troops in 1809 and was forced to flee to Switzerland and then to Klagenfurt. Assigned to a parish in Lower Austria, he again supported a rebellion in 1816, then became pastor in Frauenfeld, and in 1836 retired to Heitzing. In 1848 he became chaplain of a Tyrolese company in the successful uprising against Piedmont. He died in Salzburg, Austria, on Oct. 28.

HATEBRAND, ST. (d. 1198). He became a Benedictine at the monastery of St. Paul at Utrecht, Netherlands, was abbot at Olden-Klooster in his native Frisia, and active in the spread of monasticism. F. D. July 30.

HATTO (850?–913), archbishop. Of a noble Swabian family, he was educated at Ellswangen monastery, joined the Benedictines, and became abbot of Reichenau in 888 and of Ellswangen in 889. In 891 he was appointed archbishop of Mainz, and presided over a synod in Frankfort in 892 and a political-clerical council in Tribur in 895. He accompanied King Arnulf on expeditions to protect Pope Formosus in 894–896. He was active in German politics, striving to build a strong central government, served as regent for King Louis the Child, whom he had elected king on the death of Arnulf in 899, and on Louis' death in 911 secured the election of Duke Conrad II of Franconia, whom he served as adviser until his death on May 15.

HATTO, BL. (d. 985). Son of a Swabian noble, he gave his wealth to the Benedictine monastery of Ottobeuren, where he became a monk, then an extern directing his former property, and once again a member of the monastic community. F. D. July 4.

HATTON, EDWARD ANTHONY (1701–1783?). Son of a recusant family, he was educated and professed at the Dominican college in Bornhem, Holland, ordained in 1730, and spent the rest of his life in mission work in England, twice serving as English provincial, in 1754–58 and 1770–74. He died on Oct. 23 (possibly in 1781) near Leeds. He wrote several volumes of apologetics, sermons, and a history of the Reformation in England.

HAUGHERY, MARGARET GAFFNEY (1813?–1882). Born in Cavan, Ireland, she was brought to Baltimore, Maryland, in 1818, was orphaned in 1822, and in 1835 married Charles Haughery and moved to New Orleans. On the death of her husband and child the following year, she devoted the rest of her life to charitable works with the proceeds from a dairy and bakery she established. She died in New Orleans on Feb. 9. She is the heroine of Fr. Edward Murphy's novel, *Angel of the Delta*.

HAUTEFEUILLE, JEAN DE (1647–1724), physicist. Born in Orléans, France, on Mar. 20, he was patronized by the duchess of Bouillon, was ordained, experimented with watch mechanisms (he invented the spiral spring which moderates the movements of a watch), acoustics, optics, and tidal phenomena, and wrote treatises on each of his interests. He died in Orléans on Oct. 18.

HAUTESERRE, ANTOINE DADIN D' (1602–1682), historian. Born in the diocese of Cahors, France, he became professor of law at Toulouse University in 1644, then dean, and was known for his knowledge of the Fathers and the councils of the Church. He wrote on Roman and feudal law, the early ecclesiastical and monastic history of France, and the works of Gregory of Tours.

HAUY, RENÉ JUST (1743–1822), mineralogist. Born in St. Just, Picardy, France, on Feb. 28, son of a poor weaver, he studied at Navarre College in Paris and taught Latin there. He later was ordained, and began to teach at Cardinal Lemoine College. His accidental dropping and breaking of a prism of calcareous spar led him to the exhaustive studies which revealed that crystals of the same composition possessed the same internal nucleus, though their external forms might vary. He established the law of symmetry and showed that forms of crystals are definite and based on fixed laws, discoveries which caused a sensation when announced to the Academy of Sciences and led to his being chosen as a member in 1783. He was imprisoned during the revolution in 1792 when he refused to take the oath required of priests, but was soon released, and in 1794 was appointed director of the School of Mines and professor of physics at the Normal School. In 1802 he became professor of mineralogy in the Museum of Natural History in Paris and was granted a pension by Napoleon, who named him canon of Notre Dame and one of the first members of the Legion of Honor. He also pioneered in the development of pyroelectricity. He wrote studies and texts in his field, and died in Paris on June 3.

HAUY, VALÉNTIN (1745–1822). Born in St. Just, Picardy, France, on Nov. 13, brother of René, he was educated there and in Paris. After teaching, he secured a position as interpreter in the ministry of foreign affairs, became interested in aiding the blind, and in 1784 opened the first school for the blind. In 1786 he discovered a method of printing in relief for the blind and printed the first book by this method. His success attracted the attention of the king, who put the school under his patronage. It struggled through the revolution and in 1801 was put under state control by Napoleon, who retired him on a pension. He began a private school in 1802, and in 1808 at the invitation of the czar founded a school for the blind in St. Petersburg, neither of which prospered. He died in Paris on Mar. 19.

HAUZEUR, MATTHIAS (1589–1676), theologian. Born in Verviers, Belgium, he joined the Franciscans and attained fame as a theologian and controversialist, particularly in a series of debates in 1633 with Gabriel Hotton, a Calvinist preacher. He wrote in defense of the Church, and on St. Augustine, and translated several of the latter's works into French and Flemish. He died in Liège, Belgium, on Nov. 12.

HAVESTADT, BERNHARDT (1714–1779?). Born in Cologne, Germany, on Feb. 27, he joined the Jesuits in 1732 and in 1746 was sent as a missioner to Chile. When the Jesuits were expelled from the Spanish colonies, he returned to Germany where he published a work on Chilidugu, the Chilean Indian language. He died in Münster, Germany.

HAWARDEN, EDWARD (1662–1735), theologian. Born in Lancashire, England, on Apr.

9, he studied at Douai, was ordained in 1686, taught at Oxford in 1688, but was forced to return to Douai at the outbreak of the revolution which drove King James II from England. In 1707, Hawarden returned to England, serving at various missions until 1717, when he was sent to London. The rest of his life until his death in London on Apr. 19 was devoted to writing sermons and controversial treatises.

HAWES, STEPHEN (1474?–1523?), poet. A native of Suffolk, England, he studied at Oxford, traveled and studied abroad, and became groom of the chamber of King Henry VII. He became famed for his wit and as a poet. His best-known works are *The Passetyme of Pleasure* (about 1506), *The Example of Virtue,* and *The Conversion of Swearers.* He admired Lydgate, praised Chaucer, and wrote traditional (and strongly didactic) allegory.

HAWKER, ROBERT STEPHEN (1803–1875), poet. Born in Plymouth, England, on Dec. 3, son of a vicar, he studied at Oxford, married Charlotte L'ans while there in 1823, and in 1827 won the Newdigate Prize for a poem on Pompeii. In 1831 he became a Church of England minister, filled a curacy in Cornwall, and in 1834 was appointed vicar of Morwenstow, where he spent the remainder of his life, restoring his church and school, aiding indigent sailors, and studying the folklore of Cornwall. He wrote essays and poetry, including *Records of the Western Shore* (1836), *Ecclesia* (1840), *Echoes from Old Cornwall* (1845), *The Quest of the San Greal* (1864), *Cornish Ballads* (1869), and *Ballad of Trelawney.* He married Pauline Kucynski a year after the death of his first wife in 1863, and had three daughters. He became a convert shortly before his death in Plymouth on Aug. 15.

HAWKINS, HENRY (1817–1907), jurist. Son of a lawyer, he was born in Hitchin, Hertfordshire, England, on Sept. 14, studied in Bedford and at the Middle Temple in London, was admitted to the bar in 1843, practiced successfully, and in 1858 became a queen's counsel. One of his more famous was the Tichborne case, in which he exposed and prosecuted a fraudulent claimant; he was appointed a judge of the queen's bench and knighted in 1876. He married Jane Louisa Reynolds in 1877, served with distinction as a judge until his retirement in 1898, and was raised to the peerage as Lord Brampton in 1899. In 1898 he became a convert. He died in London on Oct. 2.

HAWTHORNE, JULIAN (1846–1934), author. Son of Nathaniel Hawthorne, he was born in Boston, Massachusetts, on June 22, studied at Harvard, worked as a hydrographic engineer in the New York City dock department in 1870–72, then went to Europe for ten years to write. He issued a dozen novels between 1873 and 1899, including *Bressant, Idolatry, John*

Parmlee's Curse, The Professor's Sister, and *A Fool of Nature.* He also wrote *Confessions and Criticisms* (1886), *American Literature,* a *History of the United States,* and his autobiography, *Shapes That Pass* (1928). *The Subterranean Brotherhood* (1914) was a narrative of his term in the federal prison in Atlanta, to which he was sent for writing publicity for a gold-mining company which turned out to be a fraud. He also edited his father's unfinished *Dr. Grimshawe's Secret* and wrote *Nathaniel Hawthorne and His Wife* (1903) and *Hawthorne and His Circle* (1928). He died in San Francisco on July 14.

HAWTHORNE, ROSE. *See* Lathrop, Rose Hawthorne.

HAY, EDMUND (1540?–1591). Son of Peter Hay of Megginch, baillie of Errol, he studied at Paris. In 1562 he accompanied Fr. Nicolas de Gouda on a mission from Pope Pius IV to Mary Queen of Scots. On his return to Rome he joined the Jesuits, was sent to Innsbruck, where he became confessor to the archduchess of Austria, and then was made rector of Clermont College near Paris. In 1566–67 he was again sent on a mission to Mary. On his return to the Continent he was appointed provincial of France (1567–74), then rector of Pont-à-Mousson College until 1581, when he returned to Paris as consultor of the province. In 1585 he was again sent to Scotland, until 1587 or 1588, when he was appointed assistant of the Society for Germany and France at Rome, where he died on Nov. 4.

HAY, GEORGE (1729–1811), bishop. Born in Edinburgh, Scotland, on Aug. 24, he studied medicine there, and in 1749 became a convert. He went to the Scots College in Rome, was ordained in 1758, returned to Scotland as Bishop Grant's assistant in Banffshire, and was consecrated in 1769 as his coadjutor when the bishop was appointed Lowland vicar apostolic. He labored to have the discriminatory Scots laws against Catholics repealed, published the first English Catholic Bible printed in Scotland, and wrote *The Sincere, Devout and Pious Catholic.* He died at Aquhorties, Aberdeenshire, Scotland, on Oct. 18.

HAYASAKA, JANUARIUS (1883–1959), bishop. Born in Japan on Sept. 17, he studied and was ordained in Rome in 1917, and in 1927 was consecrated there as the first native Japanese to become a bishop. He was the fifth to preside over the see of Nagasaki, and resigned in 1937 because of ill health. He served as chaplain to a convent in Nagasaki after World War II and died at Sendai, Japan, on Oct. 26.

HAYDN, JOHANN MICHAEL (1737–1806), composer. The younger brother of Joseph Haydn was born in Rohrau, Austria, on Sept. 14, followed his brother in 1745 into the choir of St. Stephen's cathedral in Vienna, and succeeded him as soloist. In 1757 he was appointed choirmaster in Grosswardein, and in 1762 conductor of the orchestra in Salzburg, organist of St. Peter's there and later of the cathedral, positions which he filled in such a manner as to arouse the criticism of Leopold and Wolfgang Mozart. He composed profusely, wrote twenty-four masses, symphonies, marches, minuettes, serenades, preludes for the organ—practically every form of composition—none of which, however, made any great impress on the musical world. He died in Salzburg, Austria, on Aug. 10.

HAYDN, JOSEPH (1732–1809), composer. Born in Rohrau, Austria, on April 1, he early displayed great aptitude for music. In 1740 he became a chorister at the choir school of St. Stephen's, Vienna, and for nine years was soloist. He studied under Emmanuel Bach, Dittersdorf, and Porpora and soon achieved prominence. In 1759 he joined the orchestra of Count Morzin as assistant choirmaster, a position he occupied in 1761 in Eisenstadt and in 1766 with Prince Nicholaus at Esterházy. Meanwhile he contracted a loveless marriage with Maria Anna Keller and in 1785 joined the freemasons, seeing no problem in joining them and continuing to practice his religion. He went to London in 1791 and 1794, where his brilliant conducting of his own compositions brought tremendous success and caused Oxford to bestow a doctorate of music on him. He died in Vienna on May 31. Haydn has been called "the father of instrumentation," the "inventor of the symphony," and "creator of modern chamber music." The founder of the Viennese school of composition, he broke with convention and employed such daring liberties that he is one of the men from whom modern composition dates. Hundreds of compositions flowed from his pen: 125 symphonies, thirty-one concerti, twenty operas, seventy-seven quartets, trios, masses, offertories, and anthems, *Te Deums,* and more than 300 wood-and-string instrument compositions. His masses were particularly popular in Europe, though they cannot be played in liturgical services.

HAYDOCK, VEN. GEORGE (d. 1584), martyr. Brought to trial with Bl. John Fenn (whom he had never seen before) and charged with plotting jointly to kill Queen Elizabeth I, this English priest was hanged with four others at Tyburn. F. D. Feb. 12.

HAYDOCK, GEORGE LEO (1774–1849). Born in Cottam, Lancashire, England, he studied at Douai in 1785 (but fled in 1793 to escape the revolution) and at Croon Hall College, Durham, in 1796, and was ordained in 1798. After five years as general prefect, he served at missions in Yorkshire and Lancaster until 1831. After 1839 he was stationed at

Penrith, England, where he died on Nov. 29. He published five books on the Church and also a new English translation of the Vulgate (1812–14).

HAYES, MAURICE RICHARD JOSEPH (d. 1930), physician. He studied at Sacred Heart and Mungret colleges, Limerick, and the Catholic University, Dublin, and became radiologist on the staff of Mater Misericordia Hospital in Dublin in 1907. He was a captain with the medical corps in World War I and in 1922 was major general with the Irish Free State army medical service. He also was professor of medicine at University College, Dublin, and wrote widely on radiology. He died in Dublin on Mar. 2.

HAYES, PATRICK JOSEPH (1867–1938), cardinal. Born on Nov. 20 in New York City, he studied at Manhattan, and St. Joseph's seminary, Troy, and was ordained in 1892. After two years of graduate study at Catholic University, he served in New York as a parish priest, and in 1895 became secretary to Bishop John M. Farley. When the latter became archbishop of New York, Fr. Hayes became chancellor and was commissioned to establish Cathedral College, of which he became first president in 1903. He became chancellor, was made domestic prelate in 1907 by Pope Pius X and, in 1914, was appointed titular bishop of Tagaste and auxiliary bishop to Cardinal Farley. Pope Benedict XV named him ordinary of the armed forces in 1917; on the death of Cardinal Farley, he was named archbishop of New York and installed in 1919. He established Catholic Charities in New York and was one of the founders of the National Catholic Welfare Conference. In 1924, Pope Pius XI elevated him to the cardinalate. He died on Sept. 4, 1938, at St. Joseph's Villa, Sullivan County, New York, and was buried in St. Patrick's Cathedral, New York City.

HAYM, GILLES. *See* Hayne, Gilles.

HAYMO (d. 853), bishop. He joined the Benedictines at Fulda, studied under Alcuin in Tours, became chancellor of the monastery of Fulda, and may have taught theology there. In 840 he went to the monastery at Hersfeld and later that year was appointed bishop of Halberstadt. His episcopate was devoted almost entirely to ecclesiastical matters, and his attendance at the Council of Mainz in 847 was to protect his ecclesiastical rights and privileges. He wrote profusely, mainly commentaries on the Bible, and it was for him that his friend Rabanus Maurus wrote *De universo* on the duties of the episcopal office. He died on Mar. 26.

HAYMO OF FAVERSHAM (d. 1243?). Born in Faversham, Kent, England, he studied at Paris, where he became a well-known lecturer. In about 1224 he joined the Franciscans, was

appointed custos in Paris, and attended the general chapter at Assisi in 1230 when he was sent as one of the delegates to Pope Gregory IX, seeking clarification of the Rule. He lectured at Oxford in 1232, participated in a mission in 1233 to Constantinople for the return of the Greek Church to Rome, lectured at Tours, Bologna, and Padua, and was the chief reviser of the breviary of the Roman curia (published in 1241). In 1239, at the general chapter of the Franciscans in Rome, he was one of the main leaders in the successful opposition to Brother Elias, who was deposed as general. He served as English provincial, was elected general of the order in 1240, and devoted the rest of his life until his death in Anagni, Italy, to the reform of the order.

HAYNALD, LAJOS (1816–1891), cardinal. Born in Szécsény, Hungary, on Oct. 3, he was educated at Pozsony, Hagyszombat, and Vienna, was ordained in 1839, received his doctorate in theology (1841), and taught at the seminary in Gran in 1842. Appointed secretary to Archbishop Kopácsy in 1846, he spent the next two years abroad studying ecclesiastical training and administration, and on his return in 1848 was appointed chancellor, a position he lost when he refused to publish the Hungarian parliament's declaration of independence. After a year as coadjutor to the bishop of Transylvania, he succeeded him in 1852, and soon became embroiled in a dispute with the Viennese government when he championed the union of Transylvania and Hungary. When he resigned in 1864, Pope Pius IX called him to Rome and appointed him titular archbishop of Carthage. In 1867 he was appointed archbishop of Kalocsa-Bács, attended the Vatican Council in 1870, opposed but submitted to the dogma of papal infallibility, and was appointed cardinal by Pope Leo XIII in 1879. He died in Kalocsa, Hungary, on July 3.

HAYNE, GILLES (d. 1650), composer. Born in Flanders, he studied in Italy, was precentor of St. John the Baptist church in Liège, Belgium, from 1631 until his death there in May, and also served as choirmaster to Duke Wolfgang of Neubyrg. He became a canon of St. Lambert's chapter in 1643, and wrote a requiem for the funeral of Marie de' Medici, other masses, and motets. He also is known as Hennius, Heyne, and Haym.

HAZART, CORNELIUS (1617–1690). Born in Oudenarde, Netherlands, he was educated at Louvain, joined the Jesuits in 1635, and was ordained in 1647. His life was spent preaching throughout Holland and Belgium in defense of the Church and against the Calvinists. He also wrote profusely, some ninety works in all, mainly apologetic and polemical, though his *Kerkelijke Historie van de gleheele wereldt*, a history of the Church, was one of his best known. He died in Antwerp, Belgium, on Oct. 25.

HAZE, JEANNE (1782–1876), foundress. Born in Liège, Belgium, she was assisted by Fr. Jean Guillaume Habets in organizing the Daughters of the Cross there in 1833. She became its superior, taking the name Mother Marie Thérèse. The order based its rule on that of St. Ignatius and received final papal approval in 1851. Its members are devoted to the education of poor girls, to nursing, and to the direction of orphanages and homes for the poor.

HEAGEN, MATTHEW LEO (1871–1951). Born in New York City, he studied in Kentucky and Ohio, was ordained a Dominican at Louvain in 1895, taught in California, was superior of his order in Columbus and Washington, and became provincial in 1909. He died in New York City on Sept. 21.

HEALY, GEORGE PETER ALEXANDER (1808–1894), painter. Born in Boston, Massachusetts, he began to draw at sixteen and to paint at eighteen. In 1834 he went to Europe to study, and in his sixteen years there earned a reputation as an outstanding portrait painter. On his return he lived in Chicago until 1869, when he went to Paris and Rome. He returned to Chicago in 1892 and died there on June 14. He painted many of the prominent men of his day: Pius IX, Lincoln, Grant, Webster, Calhoun, Hawthorne, Longfellow, Liszt; and historical scenes such as *Webster's Reply to Hayne* and *Franklin Urging the Claims of the Colonists before Louis XVI*. He was an honorary member of the National Academy of Design and author of *Reminiscences of a Portrait Painter*.

HEALY, JAMES (1824–1894). Born in Dublin on Dec. 15, one of twenty-three children of John and Mary Meyler Healy, he studied at St. Vincent's College and Maynooth, was ordained in 1850, served in Dublin parishes, and in 1858 went to Bray. He was administrator of Little Bray from 1867 to 1893, when he went to a Ballybrack parish. He was well known as a wit (some stories are collected in *Memories*), visited the United States in 1886, and died in Ballybrack, Ireland, on Oct. 28.

HEALY, JAMES AUGUSTINE (1830–1900), bishop. Born in Macon, Georgia, on Apr. 6, son of an Irish immigrant plantation owner and a Negro slave, he was sent north in 1837, graduated from Holy Cross in 1849, studied at the Sulpician seminary, Montreal, and St. Sulpice, Paris, and was ordained in 1854. He became secretary to Bishop Fitzpatrick of Boston, was appointed chancellor of that see in 1855 and vicar general in 1857, was pastor of St. James there from 1866, and in 1875 was appointed second bishop of Portland, Maine. His reign of a quarter of a century was featured by the extension of Catholic churches and missions in the small towns of his see, his concern for the French-Canadians in his see, and his interest in schools and orphanages. He died in Portland on Aug. 5.

ALBERT S. FOLEY, *Bishop Healy: Beloved Outcast* (New York, Farrar, 1954).

HEALY, JOHN (1841–1918), archbishop. Born in Ballinafad, Sligo, Ireland, on Nov. 14, he studied in Athlone and at Maynooth, was ordained in 1867, and taught and did parish work until 1879, when he was given the chairs of classics and theology at Maynooth. In 1883 he went to Dunboyne as prefect, became coadjutor bishop of Clonfert, succeeded to that see in 1896, and in 1903 was transferred to Tuam. He founded the Catholic Truth Society of Ireland, wrote nationalistic poetry, and published *Life and Writings of St. Patrick, Ireland's Ancient Schools and Scholars*, and *Irish Essays*. He served on the Irish university commission created by parliament, and helped to arrange a solution satisfactory to Catholics; he also revived the pilgrimage to Croaghpatrick. He died in Tuam, Ireland, on Mar. 16.

HEALY, TIMOTHY MICHAEL (1855–1931), governor. Born in Bantry, Cork, Ireland, on May 17, he studied in Fermoy, but went to work at thirteen and was mainly self-educated. He went to Newcastle, England, in 1871, became secretary of the Home Rule Association, moved to London, and contributed to the *Nation*, a political paper which supported Parnell, and was the latter's secretary and associate from 1880 until he broke with the leader in 1890. He also was elected to parliament in 1880, helped the passage of the Land Act which benefited Irish tenant farmers, married Erina Sullivan in 1882, was imprisoned in 1883 for agrarian agitation, and was called to the Irish bar in 1884. He fought the Parnell group, particularly John Dillon and T. P. O'Connor, from 1892 on, was expelled from the National League in 1895, and from the national party in 1902. He was co-founder of the All for Ireland League in 1910, and after his defeat for a parliamentary seat devoted himself to defending suffragettes and Irish fishermen, and continued to work for a solution of the home-rule question. From 1916 on he supported the political aims of, but not the use of force by, the Sinn Fein. In 1922 he became governor general of the new Irish Free State, retired in 1928, and died near Dublin on Mar. 26.

HEATH, NICHOLAS (1501?–1578), archbishop. Born in London, he was educated at Oxford and Cambridge, where he became a fellow in 1521. He was ordained and became vicar of Hever, Surrey, in 1531, archdeacon of Stafford in 1534, was elected bishop of Rochester schismatically in 1539, and translated to Worcester in 1543. Although he seems to have accepted the new religious decrees, he was imprisoned in 1550 and deprived of his see when he refused to accept the new form of ordination promulgated by Cranmer. He was restored to his see by Queen Mary, absolved of his schism by the pope in 1555, and elected archbishop of York and given the pallium the same year. The next year he became lord chancellor of England, proclaimed Elizabeth queen in 1558 and then resigned, refusing to crown her when she inaugurated her religious changes. He continued to resist her in parliament, was deprived of his see and was imprisoned in the Tower from 1560, except for occasional periods, until 1571. About 1574 he was again imprisoned and died in the Tower about Dec. 12.

HÉBERT, BL. FRANÇOIS (d. 1792), martyr. *See* Du Lau, Bl. Jean.

HECKER, ISAAC THOMAS (1819–1888), founder. Born in New York City on Dec. 18, he worked in a foundry and bakery, and during 1842–43 joined the Brook Farm and then the Fruitlands community. In 1844 he became a convert, joined the Redemptorists the next year, was ordained in 1849 in London, served as a parish priest, and in 1851 was sent back to the United States. During the next six years he worked among immigrants, but became convinced of the need for ministering to native Americans and sought to establish a headquarters for the English-speaking members of the Redemptorists to work among native Americans. In 1857 he went to Rome and through a misunderstanding was dismissed from the order by the general. On his appeal to Pope Pius IX he was dispensed from his vows as a Redemptorist and authorized to form a new congregation devoted to the conversion of the United States. On his return in 1858 the Congregation of the Missionary Priests of St. Paul the Apostle (Paulist Fathers) was founded, with Fr. Hecker as superior in New York. During the next thirty years he devoted himself to building up the congregation, founded the *Catholic World* in 1865, the Catholic Publication Society (which became the Paulist Press) to distribute Catholic books and pamphlets, in 1866, a juvenile journal, the *Young Catholic*, in 1870, and became a leading exponent of the apostolate of the press. He attended the Vatican Council in 1870, and in 1887 published a collection of essays, *The Church and the Age*. Beginning in 1871 he suffered a series of nervous breakdowns which left him in ill health the rest of his life, and practically an invalid for his last five years. He died in New York City on Dec. 22.

HEDDA, ST. (d. 705), bishop. Monk and abbot at Whitby, England, he was made bishop in 676 of the divided diocese of Wessex, residing first at Dorchester and later removing his see to Winchester. He was one of King Ina's advisers in drawing up the latter's legal code and one of the chief benefactors of Malmesbury. F. D. July 7.

HEDDA, ST. (d. 870), martyr. *See* Theodore, St.

HEDDE, FELIX (1879–1960), bishop. Born in Brest, France, on Mar. 31, he became a Dominican in 1898, was ordained in 1902, was sent to Cuba as a missionary, and remained there until 1914, when he became a chaplain in the French army. He was sent to Langson, Vietnam, in 1925, was appointed apostolic prefect in 1928, and in 1939 vicar apostolic of Langson and Caobang. He was ordered expelled from North Vietnam in 1958 after the Communists successfully split the country, but remained in his vicariate until his death on May 5.

HÉDELIN, FRANÇOIS. *See* Aubignac, François Hédelin de.

HEDLEY, JOHN CUTHBERT (1837–1915), bishop. Born in Morpeth, England, on Apr. 15, he graduated from Ampleforth, became a Benedictine, was ordained in 1862, and taught at Belmont. In 1873 he was consecrated auxiliary bishop of Newport and Menevia, succeeding to the see in 1881. He approved the attendance of Catholics at English universities, was an editor of the *Dublin Review*, published three volumes of sermons, a commentary on the Rule of St. Gregory the Great, and spiritual readings. He died in Llanishen, Wales, on Nov. 11.

HEDWIG, ST. (1174?–1243). Daughter of Count Berthold of Andechs, Bavaria, where she was born, she was raised in a monastery until she was married at twelve to Henry of Silesia. When her husband became duke of Silesia in 1202, she persuaded him to found the Cistercian convent in Trebnitz, near Breslau, Germany, the first of many such houses they were to build. They had seven children. When her husband died, Duchess Hedwig moved into Trebnitz, but never became a nun. She was canonized in 1267. F. D. Oct. 16.

HEDWIG OF POLAND, BL. (1371?–1399). Daughter of King Casimir II of Poland, she was married in 1386 against her will to Jagello, duke of Lithuania, who abandoned paganism, brought many of his people with him into Christianity, and began an alliance of 400 years between the nations. She was a sympathetic and well-loved queen, who did much to help the poor of her country. She is sometimes called Jadwiga. F. D. Feb. 28.

HEELAN, EDMOND (1868–1948), bishop. Born in Elton, Limerick, Ireland, on Feb. 5, he studied at All Hallows, Dublin, and was ordained there in 1890. He went to the United States in that year, was assistant rector at St. Raphael's cathedral, Dubuque, in 1890–93, serving also as chancellor of the see in 1891–93, pastor in 1893–97, and pastor of Sacred Heart in Fort Dodge from 1897 until his consecration as titular bishop of Gerasa and auxiliary of Sioux City, Iowa, in 1919. He became bishop of Sioux City in 1920, and died on Sept. 20.

HEENEY, CORNELIUS (1754–1848). A native of Dublin, Ireland, he migrated to the United States in 1784, was a partner of John Jacob Astor in a New York store, and became a wealthy merchant notable for his charitable works. He served five terms in the New York State assembly, 1818–22, retired in 1837, and put his fortune into an estate to aid the poor and orphans. He died in Brooklyn, New York, on May 3.

HEEREMANN VON ZUYDWYK, CLEMENS VON (1832–1903), statesman. Born in Surenburg, Westphalia, he studied law at Bonn, Heidelberg, and Berlin, became a member of the *Landtag* (1870), Reichstag (1871), and the council of Münster in 1874. A member of the Centre party, he fought against the restrictive religious laws of the Kulturkampf, served as second vice-president of the Prussian *Landtag* from 1879–82 and as first vice-president until his death in Berlin on Mar. 23. He was interested in art, wrote *Die älteste Tafelmalerei Westfalens* in 1882, founded *Zeitschrift für christliche Kunst* in 1887, and had a lively interest in history and archaeology.

HEFELE, KARL JOSEPH VON (1809–1893), bishop. Born in Unterkochen, Württemberg, on Mar. 15, he studied at Tübingen. Ordained in 1833, he served as vicar, tutor, and instructor of church history in Tübingen, becoming professor in 1840. His lectures were famous; he wrote hundreds of articles for the *Kirchenlexikon* and periodicals, and many books, most important of which was his seven-volume *Conciliengeschichte* (1855–74). He sat in parliament from 1842 to 1845, headed the diocesan society for Christian art from 1854 to 1862, was made rector of the university in 1852, knighted in 1853, spent 1868 in Rome as consultor of the Vatican Council, and in 1869 was appointed bishop of Rottenburg. He attended the Vatican Council, where he opposed the dogma of papal infallibility, and did not proclaim it in his diocese until a year after the council, a course of action which caused great criticism. He died in Rottenburg, Germany, on June 5.

HEFFRON, PATRICK RICHARD (1860–1927), bishop. Born in New York on June 1, he studied business at St. John's, Collegeville, Minnesota, entered the Grand seminary, Montreal, in 1878, studied further at the Sapienza and Apollinaris, Rome, and was ordained in Montreal in 1884. He became pastor of the cathedral in St. Paul in 1886, rector of the St. Paul seminary in 1898–1910, and in 1910

bishop of Winona, Minnesota. He founded St. Mary's College, Winona, in 1921, established the diocesan *Courier*, and died in Winona on May 23.

HEGESIPPUS, ST. (d. 180?). A Jewish convert in Jerusalem, he lived in Rome for twenty years and wrote a history of the Church from the Passion to the pontificate of St. Eleutherius. Only a few chapters remain, but Eusebius drew heavily on the original for his *Ecclesiastical History*. A translation of Josephus once attributed to him was written by Iosippus. F. D. Apr. 7.

HEGIUS, ALEXANDER (1433–1498), humanist. Born probably in Heeck, Westphalia, he was a pupil of Rudolph Agricola and a priest. In 1469 he was made rector of a school in Wesel, then in Emmerich, and in 1474 head of Deventer, Netherlands, where he became known as a teacher and humanist, numbering among his pupils Erasmus, Murmellius, and Mutianus, and where he died on Dec. 7.

HEIM, FRANÇOIS JOSEPH (1787–1865), painter. Born near Belfort, France, he evinced an early aptitude for painting, studied under Vincent in Paris and won an academy prize and scholarship in 1807. He became a member of the Academy of Arts in 1829, a professor in 1831, and was appointed painter to the Institute of France. His best paintings are of historical and religious subjects and portraits. He died in Paris.

HEINRICH VON AHAUS (1371–1439), founder. Illegitimate son of Ludolf, lord of Ahaus, he joined the Brethren of the Common Life in Deventer, Netherlands, about 1396. About 1400 he founded the German branch of the Brethren, devoted to the training and reform of the clergy, education, and the spiritual life of the Germans in Münster. He established houses in Cologne (1416), on his family estate of Springbrunnen (1429), Wesel (1435), and Osnabruck, as well as five communities of sisters. The Brethren were opposed by many of the clergy and laity and Heinrich was obliged, successfully, to defend them at the Council of Constance against attacks by Matthäus Grabow, a Dominican. He died at Münster, Germany.

HEINRICH DER GLÎCHEZÂRE (12th century). Probably a pseudonym, this is the name of a German poet reputed to have written about 1180 a narrative poem, *Reinhart Fuchs* (*Reynard the Fox*), the first known German beast-epic.

HEINRICH VON LAUFENBERG (d. 1460), poet. A priest, and dean of the cathedral in Freiburg, Germany, he wrote prose, sermons and religious poems on Christ and the Virgin Mary. He entered the cloister of the Knights of St. John in Strassburg, Alsace, in 1445 and spent the rest of his life there.

HEINRICH VON MEISSEN (1250?-1318), poet. A native of Meissen, Germany, he spent most of his life traveling through Germany until 1311, when he settled in Mainz. He composed many lyric poems, particularly in honor of women. He is reputed to have founded the first school of Meistersingers, for whom he became the model. He died in Mainz, Germany.

HEINRICH VON MELK (12th century), poet. A member of the knightly class, he became a laybrother in the convent of Melk, Styria, where he wrote, about 1160, his most famous satirical poems, *Von des tödes gehugede* and (probably) *Priesterleben.*

HEINRICH VON VELDEKE (12th century), poet. A German knight, patronized by the landgrave of Thuringia, he lived near Maastricht on the lower Rhine, and wrote in his native dialect and in more polished courtly Middle High German. He wrote *Eneide*, an imitation of a French poem by Benoît de Ste. More; *Von Salomo und der Minne*; the biographical *Servarius*; and many rhymed lyrics.

HEINZ, JOSEPH (1564-1609), painter. Born in Basle, Switzerland, on June 11, he studied painting under Hans Bock and Hans von Aachen, became court painter to Rudolf II of Bohemia in 1591, and in 1593 was sent to Rome by the emperor to make copies of ancient works of art. He enjoyed great fame for his portraits and landscapes, among them *Rape of Proserpine, Lot and His Daughters*, and *Ecce Homo.* He died near Prague, Bohemia, in Oct.

HEIS, EDUARD (1806-1877), astronomer. Born in Cologne, Germany, on Feb. 18, he graduated from Bonn in 1827, and, after teaching mathematics and science in Cologne (1829-37) and Aachen (1837-52), was appointed to the chair of mathematics and astronomy at Münster in 1852, which he occupied until his death. He was made rector in 1869, foreign associate of the Royal Astronomical Society in 1874, and honorary member of Leopoldine Academy and Scientific Society of Brussels in 1877. He devoted his astronomical studies to zodiacal light, shooting stars, the Milky Way, variable stars, and sunspots. He published scientific treatises and mathematical textbooks, including *Atlas coelestis.*

HEISS, MICHAEL (1818-1890), archbishop. Born in Pfahldorf, Bavaria, on Apr. 12, he studied at the University of Munich and the Eichstätt seminary, and was ordained in 1840. He engaged in pastoral and missionary activity in and near Raitenbuch until 1842, when he accepted Bishop Purcell's invitation to go to the United States. He became Bishop John Henni's secretary in 1844, accompanied him to Milwaukee, Wisconsin, where he became pastor of St. Mary's, and was first rector of St. Francis seminary from 1856 to 1868, when he was appointed first bishop of La Crosse, Wisconsin. He attended the Vatican Council in 1870, was appointed titular archbishop of Hadrianople and coadjutor of Milwaukee in 1880, and succeeded to that see in 1881. In 1883 he was called to Rome to advise the pope on American church matters, and was active in establishing Catholic University in Washington, D.C. Widely regarded as a theologian, he wrote *De Matrimonio* and *The Four Gospels.* He died in La Crosse on Mar. 26.

HELDRAD, ST. (d. 842?). Son of a Provençal noble, he sought to lessen the godlessness of the local fair by building a church and hostel, then gave away his fortune to the poor, became a pilgrim, and, at a Benedictine monastery on Mont Cenis, a priest, master of novices, and vineyard keeper. When Hugh, Charlemagne's son, died, Heldrad succeeded him as abbot and built up the library as well as a rescue service. His cult was approved in 1904. F. D. Mar. 13.

HELEN OF SKÖVDE, ST. (d. 1160?). She was a Swedish lady born in Västergötland who, on the death of her husband, a noble, devoted herself to the poor. On her return from a pilgrimage to Rome she was killed by relatives of her son-in-law, who falsely claimed she had murdered her husband. Her cult was recognized by Pope Alexander III in 1164. F. D. July 31.

HELENA, ST. (250?-330?). Probably the daughter of an innkeeper and born in Drepanum, Bithynia, she married Constantius Chlorus, a Roman general, about 270. When he became emperor he divorced Helena to marry Theodora, stepdaughter of Emperor Maximian. On the death of Constantius in 306, Helena's son Constantine became emperor and by the Edict of Milan (313) allowed Christianity in the empire. Helena soon became a Christian and devoted her last years to building churches and aiding prisoners and the poor. After Constantine's victory over Licinius in 324 made him emperor of the East, she visited the Holy Land. When eighty she returned to Jerusalem and was responsible for the discovery of the relics of the cross on which Christ was crucified. F. D. Aug. 18.

HELENA ENSELMINI, BL. (1208?-1242). Born in Padua, Italy, she became a Poor Clare at Arcella when twelve, experienced visions, and is said to have lived for months on no food but the Eucharist. She died on Nov. 4 and her cult was approved in 1695. F. D. Nov. 7.

HELENA OF POLAND. *See* Jolenta of Hungary.

HELIAE, PAUL (1480?-1534?). Born in Warberg, Denmark, he joined the Carmelites, became provincial in 1519 and professor at Copenhagen University. His warm defense of Catholicism against the encroaching Protestantism and his criticism of King Christian II's morals resulted in his forced exile from Denmark until Frederick I ascended the throne. On his return he was suspected of Protestantism when he translated Luther's *Betbüchlein*, earned the name of *Vendekaabe* ("Weathercock"), but fought a losing though valiant battle for Catholicism. Some authorities believe he suffered martyrdom during the siege of Roskilde in 1536; others, that he died in a convent in Holland.

HELICONIS, ST. (d. 250?), martyr. A native of Thessalonica, she was beheaded at Corinth during the Decian persecution. F. D. May 28.

HELIER, ST. (6th century). Supposedly from Tongres, Limburg, he was raised as a Christian by a priest, Cunibert, who was murdered by Helier's father. Helier then retired to life in a cave on the isle of Jersey and was himself murdered by robbers whom he was trying to convert. F. D. July 16.

HELIMENAS, ST. (d. 250), martyr. *See* Parmenius, St.

HÉLINANDE (1150?–1227?), author. Born in Pronleroi, France, he led a dissipated youth, but about 1190 he became a Cistercian in Froidmont, near Beauvais. After ordination he devoted his life to preaching and writing sermons, ascetic treatises, a *passio*, and a chronicle of world history to 1204. He died in 1223, 1227, or 1237. Beauvais honors him as a saint on Feb. 3.

HELIODORUS, ST. (d. 270?), martyr. He and other Christians were put to death in Pamphylia during the reign of Aurelian. F. D. Nov. 21.

HELIODORUS, ST. (3rd century), martyr. With St. Venustus and six others he was put to death during the persecution of Diocletian, probably in Africa; St. Ambrose claims that seventy others who were said to have died at the same place and time were slain in Milan, Italy, instead. F. D. May 6.

HELIODORUS, ST. (d. 303?), martyr. *See* Mark, St.

HELIODORUS, ST. (332?–390?), bishop. A Dalmatian, he became the disciple of St. Jerome in 372 and helped him in the translation of the Bible. When he failed to stay in the Palestinian desert, Jerome rebuked him. He became bishop of Altino, near Venice, Italy, and was known as an outstanding opponent of Arianism. F. D. July 3.

HELLADIUS, ST. (d. 387). He was bishop of Auxerre, France, from about 357, and converted St. Amator, who succeeded him. F. D. May 8.

HELLADIUS, ST. (d. 633), archbishop. A member of the Visigothic court, he represented the king at the Council of Toledo in 589, showed interest in religious life, and entered the monastery of Agali, Spain, where he became abbot in 605. Ten years later he succeeded Archbishop Aurasius as archbishop of Toledo. F. D. Feb. 18.

HELLO, ERNEST (1828–1885), philosopher. Born in Lorient, Brittany, he studied in Rennes and Paris, married Zoe Berthier, a writer, in 1857, and that year founded with Georges Seigneur a Catholic daily newspaper, *Le Croisé*. The editors quarreled and the venture ended after two years; Hello then wrote for many journals in France and abroad. His published work includes a translation of Angela of Foligno; *L'Homme*, on life, science, art, and the Catholic; and *Renan* (1858), later issued as *Philosophie et athéisme*. He died near Lorient on July 14.

HELMOD (d. 1177?), historian. Probably a native of Holstein, Germany, he studied under Gerold, bishop of Oldenburg and St. Vicelinus, became a parish priest in Bosow, and wrote *Chronica Slavorum*, a chronicle of the Wends which is an important source of the history of his times, based as much of it is on information he received from Gerold and Vicelinus.

HELMONT, JAN BAPTISTA (1577–1644), scientist. Born in Brussels, Belgium, he was raised by his uncle, studied at Louvain, received his medical degree in 1599, and was appointed to the chair of surgery. He traveled through Europe studying medical practice in various countries. After his marriage to the wealthy Margarert van Ranst, he settled in Vilvorde, Belgium, where his fame as a physician became widespread and where he died on Dec. 30. He was the first to make scientific use of the term "gas." The role of acid in gastric juices was one of his discoveries, as was the discovery of sulphuric and nitric acids and nitrogen oxide.

HÉLYOT, PIERRE (1660–1716), historian. Born in Paris of a noble family, he became a Franciscan tertiary in 1683 and devoted the rest of his life to traveling through Europe and collecting material for a monumental history of the religious orders, published in 1714–19. He died in Paris on Jan. 5 while the fifth volume was on the press; it was finished by Maximilian Bullot. He is also called Hippolyté.

HEMERFORD, BL. THOMAS (d. 1584), martyr. Born in Dorsetshire, England, he studied at Oxford and Rheims, was ordained at Rome in 1583, was captured on the English mission, and hanged at Tyburn with Bl. James Fenn and two other priests. He was beatified in 1929. F. D. Feb. 12.

HEMMERLIN, FELIX (1388?–1460?). Born in Zurich, Switzerland, he studied at Erfurt, and law at Bologna, became a canon in the collegiate church in Zurich in 1412, and then at Zofingen, received his bachelor's degree in canon law in 1413, and attended the Council of Constance, where he became associated with the reform group. In 1421 he became provost at Solothurn and devoted himself to the reform of the collegiate church and clergy there. In 1424 he received his doctorate in canon law at Bologna and in 1430 was ordained in Solothurn. He attended the Council of Basle, participated in the debates against the Hussites, and supported antipope Felix. After a successful reform of the collegiate church in Zofingen, he attempted the same in Zurich in 1439, but was vigorously opposed and wounded in an attempt on his life. His attacks on the Swiss, who were opposed by the populace of Zurich, resulted in a life-imprisonment sentence in 1456 when Zurich and Switzerland settled their differences. He spent the last years of his life confined to a Franciscan monastery in Lucerne. He was the author of some thirty polemical treatises, some of them highly critical of the Roman curia and pope. Though called by some writers a forerunner of the Protestant Reformation, he was interested in the reform of clerical abuses from within the Church.

HEMPTINNE, HILDEBRANDE DE (1849–1913). Born in Ghent, Belgium, on June 10, he served in the papal army, became a Benedictine, and was ordained in 1872. In 1890 he became abbot of Maredsous, and in 1896 was named by Pope Leo XIII as abbot of St. Anselmo de Urbe and primate of his order. He was consultor of several congregations and representative at Rome of the Greek Melchite patriarch of Antioch. He died in Beuron, Germany, on Aug. 13.

HENARES, BL. DOMINIC (d. 1838), bishop and martyr. A Dominican friar, he went from Spain to the Tonkin mission, where in 1803 he became coadjutor bishop to Bl. Ignatius Delgado. He and a native catechist, Bl. Francis Chien, were beheaded. They were beatified in 1900. F. D. June 25.

HENDERSON, ISAAC AUSTIN (1850–1909), author. Born in Brooklyn, New York, he studied in private schools and at Williams College, where he also took a doctorate in civil law. In 1872 he joined the New York *Evening Post,* of which his father was part owner, and became assistant publisher in 1875, and publisher in 1877. In 1881 he sold his interest in the *Post,* went to Europe, and began writing novels (*The Prelate,* 1886; *Agatha Page,* 1888) and dramas. In 1896 he became a convert. He died in Rome in Mar.

HENDREN, JOSEPH WILLIAM (1791–1866), bishop. A Franciscan, he was consecrated vicar apostolic of the Western District of Wales and southwestern England in 1848 and in 1850 was appointed by Pope Pius IX the first bishop of Clifton, England. He was transferred to Nottingham the next year, and died on Nov. 14.

HENDRICK, THOMAS AUGUSTINE (1849–1909), bishop. Born in Penn Yan, New York, on Oct. 29, he studied at Fordham,

Seton Hall, and St. Joseph's seminary, Troy, was ordained in 1873, and labored in parish work in the Rochester diocese until 1903, when he was appointed twenty-second bishop of Cebu, Philippine Islands, the first American to occupy the see. He spent the rest of his life restoring order to his diocese, which had been disorganized by the American occupation of the Philippines following the Spanish-American War. He died in Manila on Nov. 29.

HENDRICKSEN, THOMAS FRANCIS (1827–1886), bishop. Born in Kilkenny, Ireland, on May 5, he studied at St. Kieran's there, Maynooth, and All Hallows, Dublin, where he was ordained in 1851. He did parish work in the Hartford diocese, and in 1872 was consecrated first bishop of Providence, Rhode Island. He began building a new cathedral (which was finished in 1886), was faced with a great influx of French Canadians into his see and resultant nationalistic problems, and died in Providence on June 11.

HENEDINA, ST. (d. 130?), martyr. She and SS. Justa and Justina were put to death on Sardinia for their faith during the persecution of Hadrian. F. D. May 14.

HENGLER, LAWRENCE (1806–1858). Born in Reichenhofen, Württemberg, he studied in Leutkirch, Ehingen, Tübingen, and mathematics and astronomy at Munich, where he invented the horizontal pendulum which became the basis for the seismograph. He was ordained in Rottenburg in 1835. He died in Tigerfeld, Belgium, where he was pastor.

HENNEPIN, LOUIS (1640–1701?), explorer. Born in Ath, Hainaut, Belgium, on Apr. 7, he was baptized Johannes and probably took the name Louis when he joined the Recollects in Bethune, Artois, preached and begged throughout Italy and Germany, spent a year as preacher at the Halles convent, and ministered to the ill in Maastricht in 1673 and the wounded at the battle of Seneffe in 1674. In 1675 he went to Canada on the same ship as Robert de la Salle, who obtained his services as chaplain for his Fort Frontenac seigniory on Lake Ontario in 1678. He accompanied La Salle on the latter's expedition to the Illinois country in 1679, and in 1680 accompanied the group under Michael Aco sent by La Salle to explore the upper Mississippi. He was captured by the Sioux Indians, rescued by Duluth, and returned to France in 1682, where he published *Description de la Louisiane* (1683), one of the most important descriptions of early American exploration. He was expelled from France about 1690 for reasons not known, returned to Belgium, and published *Nouveau voyage* (1696) and *Nouvelle decouverte* (1697), in which he claims to have sailed to the mouth of the Mississippi, an evident falsehood. He was refused permission to return to Canada by King

Louis XIV, was in Rome in 1701, and then disappears from history. His works are valuable descriptions of the country he saw but marred by his penchant for exaggeration and unscrupulous use of other writers' material.

HENNESSY, JOHN (1825–1900), archbishop. Born in Bulgaden, Limerick, Ireland, on Aug. 20, he studied at All Hallows, Dublin, and when twenty-two went to the United States, studied at the seminary in Carondelet, Missouri, and was ordained in St. Louis in 1850. After several years of pastoral work he returned to Carondelet in 1854 to teach, was appointed president in 1857, was the archbishop of St. Louis' representative in Rome in 1858–59, served as pastor in St. Joseph on his return, and in 1866 was appointed bishop of Dubuque, Iowa. He founded Columbia College in Dubuque in 1873 and was one of the leading proponents of a Catholic parochial-school system at the third Plenary Council in Baltimore in 1884. He was made archbishop when his see was raised to an archdiocese in 1893, and died in Dubuque on Mar. 4.

HENNESSY, JOHN JOSEPH (1847–1920), bishop. Born near Cloyne, Cork, Ireland, on July 19, he was brought to the United States as a child, studied at the Christian Brothers' college, St. Louis, St. Francis seminary, Milwaukee, St. Vincent's, Missouri, and was ordained at twenty-two with special permission. He did mission work in Missouri, was procurator of the St. Louis Protectory in 1878–86, edited *Youth's Magazine* in 1880–86, and was rector of St. John's parish in St. Louis until 1888. He then was appointed bishop of Wichita, Kansas, where he served until his death there on July 13.

HENNI, JOHN MARTIN (1805–1881), bishop. Born in Misanenga, Grisons, Switzerland, on June 15, he studied in Lucerne and at the Propaganda in Rome, and in 1828 went to the United States, where he completed his studies at the Bardstown, Kentucky, seminary and was ordained in 1829. He taught at the Athenaeum, Cincinnati, was vicar general of Cincinnati in 1829–34, founded the first German Catholic newspaper, *Wahrheitsfreund*, in the United States in 1837 and edited it for six years, and in 1843 was appointed first bishop of Milwaukee, Wisconsin. He founded St. Francis seminary, was raised to archbishop in 1875, when Milwaukee was made a metropolitan see, and died there on Sept. 7.

HENNINGS, VINCENT (d. 1520). Bishop of Skara, Sweden, he was beheaded by King Christian II at the massacre in Stockholm on Nov. 8.

HENNIUS, GILLES. *See* Hayne, Gilles.

HENRIETTA ANNE (1644–1670). Daughter of King Charles I of England and Henrietta Maria of France, she was born in Exeter on June 16, taken to France in 1646, and brought up as a Catholic by her mother. She married Philippe, duc d'Orléans, in 1661, and was a patron of Molière, Corneille, and Racine. She was an adviser to her brother-in-law, Louis XIV, and acted as his intermediary with Charles II of England, at whose court she often lived. She went to England to negotiate the Treaty of Dover in 1670, and died suddenly on her return, by poison, it has been alleged, on June 30.

HENRIETTA MARIA (1609–1669), queen. Youngest daughter of Henry IV of France and Marie de' Medici, she was born in the Louvre palace, Paris on Nov. 25, was married to King Charles I of England by proxy, arrived in England in 1625, and began to engage in political affairs about 1635. She tried to have the penal laws against Catholics lifted, allegedly directed funds to Scotland in 1639 for war against England, and left England for Holland in 1642. She returned, was impeached by parliament in 1643, joined her husband's army at Oxford, and returned to France in 1644. She gained promises of aid from France and Ireland, but nothing tangible, lived in poverty at the Louvre, tried to enlist sympathy and aid in England for her daughter Henrietta Anne, and attempted to break off the marriage of King James II and Anne Hyde in 1660. She left England in 1665 and died in Colombes, France, on Aug. 31.

HENRION, MATHIEU RICHARD AUGUSTE (1805–1862), jurist and historian. Born in Metz, Lorraine, on June 19, he became a member of the Paris bar, and was appointed counselor at the court of appeals of La Guadeloupe and later of Aix by Napoleon III, where he remained until his death on June 19. The baron became editor of *L'Ami de la Religion* in 1840 and wrote many historical works, principally *Histoire des ordres religieux* (1831), *Histoire de la papauté* (1832), and *Histoire générale de l'église* (1843).

HENRÍQUEZ, CRISÓSTOMO (1594–1632), historian. Born in Madrid, Spain, he became a Cistercian at thirteen, was professed in 1612, and studied in Spain. In 1619, at the request of his parents who were at the court of Archduke Albert, governor of Flanders, he was sent to the Netherlands and assigned the task of writing the history of the Cistercians. This started him on a writing career, which in the next thirteen years resulted in biographies of the saints and great Catholic figures, and his most famous work, the history of the Cistercian order, *Menologium Cisterciense*. Before his death in Louvain on Dec. 23 he served as historian and vicar general of the Spanish Cistercian congregation.

HENRÍQUEZ, ENRIQUE (1536–1608), theologian. Born in Oporto, Portugal, he became

543

a Jesuit in 1552, became a noted theologian and philosopher, and taught at Cordova and Salamanca, where Francisco Suarez and Gregory of Valencia were his students. He left the Jesuits for the Dominicans in 1593, but returned to the Jesuits on the advice of Gregory. Among his theological works are *Theologiae moralis summa* (1591–93), which was forbidden by decree in 1603, and *De pontificis romani clave* (1593), which was burned by the apostolic nuncio on the ground that it allowed sovereigns too great authority in ecclesiastical matters. He died in Tivoli, Italy, on Jan. 28.

HENRY II, ST. (972–1024), emperor. Son of Duke Henry II of Bavaria and Gisela of Burgundy, he was born in Bavaria on May 6, and on the death of his cousin Emperor Otto III in 1002 had himself crowned emperor at Mentz. He conquered Arduin of Ivrea, leader of the opposition in Italy, who had had himself crowned king of Milan in 1002, and was crowned king of Italy by the archbishop of Milan in 1004. In 1005 he drove Boleslav I of Poland from Bohemia, but peace with the Poles was not finally achieved until 1018. He was crowned Holy Roman emperor in 1014 by Pope Benedict VIII. During his reign he restored many episcopal sees, founded that of Bamberg, built several monasteries, supported the Cluniac reform, and worked strenuously for the welfare of the Church with his wife, St. Cunegundis. In 1021 he returned to Italy a third time, to combat the Greeks in Apulia, an expedition which was not too successful. He died on July 13 at Göttingen, Germany, was canonized in 1146, and declared the patron saint of Benedictine Oblates by Pope St. Pius X. F. D. July 15.

HENRY III (1017–1056), emperor. Son of Emperor Conrad II and Gisela, widow of Duke Ernest I of Swabia, he was born in Bodfeld, Germany, on Oct. 28, became duke of Bavaria and Swabia in 1027 and joint king in 1028, married Gunhild of Denmark (d. 1038) in 1036, and succeeded his father as emperor in 1039. He was unsuccessful in an expedition against the Bohemians in 1040, but a second campaign in 1041 caused the Bohemian leader, Bratislaus, to become his vassal. He married Agnes, daughter of Duke William V of Guienne, in 1043; invaded Hungary in 1043, saw his candidate for the throne, Peter, crowned, deposed, reinstated by Henry in 1044, and again deposed in 1046; in 1043 he and the Hungarians agreed on the Leitha and March rivers as the boundary between Hungary and Austria—a boundary which endured until 1919. In 1044 his division of Lorraine into two parts caused Godfrey, duke of Upper Lorraine, to rebel. Imprisoned in 1045, the duke on his release in 1046 again revolted, and, when the barons of the Low

Countries joined him, war raged from 1047 to 1050. Always interested in religious matters, Henry led an austere life, very conscious of his role as a Christian ruler. He urged Church reforms, opposed simony and clerical marriages, preached the love of God at a synod in Constance in 1043, and in 1046 presided at the Synod of Sutri, which denounced the three popes vying with each other for the papacy (Benedict IX, Sylvester III and Gregory VI), declared them deposed, and elected Clement II pope. Henry was crowned emperor by Clement in Rome in 1046. He was obliged to return to Italy in 1055 to quell a disturbance caused by Godfrey of Lorraine, who now ruled Tuscany by his marriage to Beatrice, widow of Margrave III of Tuscany, and who fled, on Henry's approach to Flanders, where he caused new disorders. Henry died in Bodfeld on Oct. 5.

HENRY IV (1050–1108), emperor. Son of Emperor Henry III and Agnes of Poitou, he was born at Goslar, Prussia, on Nov. 11, was elected German king in 1053, made duke of Bavaria in 1055, and succeeded his father as emperor in 1056 when not yet six. During his minority the power of the nobles and ecclesiastics was increased at royal expense. In 1062 he was kidnaped by Archbishop Anno of Cologne, who with Archbishop Adalbert of Bremen plundered the royal possessions. Henry was declared of age in 1065, was forced by his nobles to banish Adalbert from the court in 1066, married Bertha, daughter of Count Otto of Savoy, and began at once to restore royal power. He put down revolts in Saxony in 1071 and 1073–75, and in 1075 became involved in a dispute over lay investitures with Pope Gregory VII (who had denounced this practice) when he appointed bishops to Fermo, Spoleto, and Milan. When he was reproved by Gregory, the emperor summoned a council at Worms in 1076 and declared Gregory deposed, whereupon the pope excommunicated Henry and deposed him as emperor. Later in the year a group of nobles agreed not to recognize him as king until he had obtained papal pardon. Henry made a penitential journey to Canossa and was absolved; despite the pope's absolution, the nobles elected Rudolf of Swabia king in 1077 and civil war broke out. Gregory renewed the excommunication and deposition in 1080, which caused a group of German and Italian bishops to join Henry in declaring Gregory deposed; they elected Archbishop Guibert of Ravenna as antipope Clement III at Brixen in 1080. When Rudolf died in Oct. 1080, the revolt in Germany ended and Henry invaded Italy in 1081, captured Rome in 1084, was crowned by Clement, but was forced to retire from Rome when Robert Guiscard, duke of Apulia, came to Gregory's aid. He found Germany again in rebellion, headed by a new antiking, Count Hermann of Würzburg; Henry was defeated near Würzburg in 1088, but, when Hermann retired from the fray in 1090, Henry again became supreme. He returned Clement to Rome in 1090, but in 1093 saw his son Conrad join the papal forces and crowned king of Italy at Monza. In 1098 the diet at Mainz declared Conrad deposed as German king (he had been crowned in 1087) and elected Henry's second son, Henry (later Henry V), in his place. In 1104 his son rebelled, tricked Henry into a meeting promising reconciliation, and imprisoned and forced him to abdicate in 1105. Henry escaped in 1106, but died at Liège, Belgium, on Aug. 7 before he was able to co-ordinate the strong support which materialized in his favor.

HENRY V (1081–1125), emperor. Son of Emperor Henry IV, he was born on Jan. 8, was crowned co-king with his father on the deposition of his brother Conrad in 1098, joined those seeking reconciliation with the pope, and in 1104 led a rebellion against his father. He imprisoned his father in 1105 and forced him to abdicate, and in 1106 was recognized as emperor by the pope. He at once began the practice of lay investiture which had caused the difficulties between his father and Pope Gregory VII, invited Pope Paschal II to come to Germany to settle the issue, but in 1107, after meeting Henry's bishops, Paschal issued a new decree at Troyes against lay investiture. After campaigns against the Bohemians (1107), Hungarians (1108), and Poles (1109), Henry invaded Italy in 1110. Paschal proposed a pact by which the Church would surrender its temporal possessions in Germany to Henry, who would waive the right of investiture. Henry at first accepted, then demurred when followers of both sides violently objected. When Paschal refused to crown the emperor, Henry imprisoned the pope until Paschal submitted, agreed to permit Henry to appoint and invest bishops, and crowned him (1111). After Henry's return to Germany, Paschal repudiated his concessions as having been extorted by force (1112), and revolution broke out in Henry's dominions. He defeated Duke Lothair of Saxony, whom he pardoned in 1113; married Matilda, daughter of Henry I of England, in 1114; and, when he was unsuccessful in an attempt to take Cologne, faced another revolt by Lothair, who defeated Henry at Welfesholz in 1115. Henry then went to Italy to occupy Matilda's fiefs, which Matilda had donated to the papacy on her death in 1115, and to offset his excommunication by Pope Paschal proclaimed Archbishop Burdinas of Braga (antipope Gregory VIII) as successor of Pope Paschal II on the latter's death in 1118, and was again excommunicated by Paschal's successor, Gelasius II. He returned to Germany in 1118,

attempted unsuccessfully to settle his differences with Gelasius' successor, Pope Callistus II, in 1119, and at the Diet of Würzburg put his domestic affairs in order and promised to solve his difficulties with the pope; in 1122 he signed the Concordat of Worms with Callistus, by which he surrendered his claims to investiture and agreed to free election of the clergy and the restoration of church property, and was received back into the Church. He was again opposed by Lothair, planned a campaign against Louis VI of France with his father-in-law, Henry I of England, and died in Utrecht, Netherlands, on May 23.

HENRY VI (1165–1197), emperor. Son of Emperor Frederick Barbarossa and Beatrice of Burgundy, he was born in Nijmegen, Netherlands, was crowned king of the Romans at Aachen in 1169, and of Italy at Milan in 1186 when he married Constance of Sicily, an act which united Germany and Sicily. He succeeded his father as emperor in 1190; Pope Celestine III confirmed his coronation in 1191 when he conquered Tusculum for the Romans, but Henry was unsuccessful in an attempt to take Naples. The murder of Albert, papal candidate for the see of Liège in 1192, set off a rebellion of the Guelphs and lower Rhine nobles. Henry secured custody of Richard I of England in 1194, a stroke which he used to establish peace; he extorted a huge ransom from Richard and also his fealty, and then came to terms with Henry the Lion, Richard's nephew. In 1194, he embarked on a second campaign in Italy, captured Palermo, was crowned king of Sicily on Christmas Day, thus completing his conquest of all Italy except Rome. In 1195 he decided to launch a crusade against the Saracens, preached it in Germany and Italy, savagely suppressed a revolt in Sicily in 1196, and then sent the main body of his army to the Holy Land. He died of a fever on Sept. 28 at Messina, Sicily, but is believed by some authorities to have been poisoned.

HENRY II (1333?–1379), king of Castile. Illegitimate son of Alfonso XI, and his mistress, Leonora de Guzman, Henry of Trastamara fought his half-brother, Pedro the Cruel (who was king from 1350 to 1369). He defeated Pedro and Edward the Black Prince of England at Nájera in 1367 and with Bertrand of Guescelin drove him from the throne. Henry later defeated and killed Pedro. Henry made an alliance with France when he became king in 1369, cleared the channel for France by defeating an English fleet at La Rochelle in 1372, and made peace with Aragon and Portugal in 1374.

HENRY I (1068–1135), king of England. Younger son of William the Conqueror and Matilda of Flanders, he was born in Selby, England, inherited his mother's territories, was attacked by his brothers, William II of England and Robert of Normandy, in 1091, and in 1100 became king of England. He invited Archbishop Anselm to return, reached a compromise with him in 1107 over investitures, married Edith, daughter of Malcolm III of Scotland, and conquered all of Normandy by the battle of Tinchebrai in 1106. He developed a good judicial system, sent out itinerant judges, organized the exchequer, and issued a charter at his coronation which became the foundation of Magna Charta. In 1109 he went to war against Louis VI of France to crush Robert's son, William the Clito, whom Louis supported, imposed fealty, and in 1114 invaded Wales for the same feudal purpose. Henry made peace with Louis at Gisors in 1120 through the mediation of Pope Callistus II. He supported Canterbury against York in a diocesan dispute, tried to enforce clerical celibacy, and supported Pope Innocent II against antipope Anacletus. He married his daughter Matilda to Emperor Henry V and tried to force the English nobility to accept her as his successor; this led to civil war during the subsequent reign of King Stephen. Henry I died in Angers, France, on Dec. 1, and was buried in Reading, England.

HENRY II (1133–1189), king of England. Born in Le Mans, France, on Mar. 25, son of Matilda, daughter of Henry I, and her second husband Geoffrey Plantagenet, count of Anjou, he was brought to England by his mother in 1142 during her conflict with King Stephen of Blois over the succession to the English throne, educated by a tutor in Bristol, and returned to Normandy in 1146. He unsuccessfully sought the aid of the English barons against King Stephen in 1149, was invested with Normandy in 1150 by his father, whose death the following year made him count of Anjou, and married Eleanor of Aquitaine in 1152, whose dowry was Poitou and Guienne, thus making him ruler of half of France. He was recognized as successor to the English throne when he invaded England, and on Stephen's death in 1154 became king of England, establishing the Angevin Plantagenet dynasty. He set about restoring peace in civil-war-ravaged England, subdued the barons, and imposed royal authority and widespread legal and administrative reforms. He appointed Thomas à Becket chancellor in 1155, planned but abandoned the idea of invading Ireland in 1155, invaded Wales in 1157, and recovered the northern counties from Malcolm of Scotland. He was unable to annex Toulouse in 1159 because of the intervention of King Louis VII, with whom he came to terms in 1160 by the betrothal of Louis' daughter to Henry's son. He became embroiled in bitter quarrels with the Church, which intensified after his appointment of Thomas à Becket as archbishop of Canterbury

in 1162. Thomas soon became the leader of the Church forces, and was forced to flee to France when he defied the king in 1164 over the Constitutions of Clarendon, which sharply curtailed ecclesiastical jurisdiction. Henry impounded the revenues of Canterbury and banished many of Thomas' close friends, but, threatened with a papal interdict, reached an uneasy peace with Thomas in 1170. When the archbishop was murdered later that year (though in a fit of anger he had suggested it, it is certain that Henry did not plan the murder nor did he really mean his suggestion), the Christian world was shocked, and he did public penance at Thomas' tomb in 1174. He invaded Ireland in 1171–72, and after 1173 was embroiled in a series of wars with his sons, incited by their mother, Eleanor, Louis VII, and Philip II. In 1173 he quelled a revolt in England led by Henry, Richard, and the king of Scotland. His heir apparent, Henry, was killed during a war against him and his son, Richard the Lion-Hearted, in 1183; he gave approval to the war Geoffrey of Brittany and John waged on Richard in 1184; and when Geoffrey died in 1186 Richard allied with Philip II of France against John (who was secretly allied with them) and Henry who was defeated by the alliance in 1188. He signed a treaty of peace in 1189, and died at Chinon, France, on July 6. In spite of the military aspect of his career, he ruled over a brilliant court, which made major advances in literature, law, philosophy, and history.

HENRY III (1207–1272), king of England. Son of King John, he was born in Winchester, England, on Oct. 1, was crowned king at Gloucester in 1216, received homage from Alexander II of Scotland, faced civil war and continuous wars with the Welsh and French, and in 1223 agreed to confirm the Magna Charta. He married Eleanor of Provence in 1236. In 1229 he had secretly agreed to give the pope a tenth of all property income; about 1240 he raised this to a fifth of the clergy's property and income from benefices. He made some concessions to the barons, but remained restricted by them. In the "mad parliament" of 1258 he attempted to seize a third of all property; this resulted in the appointment of a commission of twenty-four to direct the government. Henry fought de Montfort, whom he had appointed governor of Gascony, marched against the barons, and was defeated at Lewes in 1264. He won and lost to the barons and to parliament in continuing quarrels, forfeited the lands of those who rebelled against him, maintained a strong anti-Jewish policy, and was particularly interested in European association. He died in Westminster on Nov. 16.

HENRY IV (1367–1413), king of England. Son of John of Gaunt, Henry of Bolingbroke was born in Bolingbroke, Lincolnshire, on Apr. 3, and married Mary de Bohun in 1380. Richard II to heed some popular demands, later in 1387 he joined the forces of his uncle, the duke of Gloucester, against Richard II, later gained Richard's favor, went with the Teutonic Knights against Lithuania in 1390, made a pilgrimage to the Holy Land in 1392–93, and on his return to England fell out of royal favor. He was banished for life, but landed in England with Arundel and others in 1399, routed the royal army at Bristol, captured Richard at Flint, and was popularly elected king when Richard was forced to resign. Richard was allowed to die in prison; Henry then turned against the Scots and Welsh, and faced frequent rebellion. He worked with Archbishop Arundel to heal the papal schism, prevented the seizure of church property by confiscation, was interested in literature, and was a patron of John Gower. He died in Westminster on Mar. 20.

HENRY V (1387–1422), king of England. Eldest son of Henry IV and Mary de Bohun, he was born in Monmouth, England, on Aug. 9, studied at Oxford, represented his father against Wales in 1400–3, eventually crushed the Welsh in battle, invaded Scotland in 1407, aided Burgundy against Armagnac in 1412, and succeeded to the English throne in 1413. He made Henry Beaufort, his uncle, chancellor, suppressed the Lollards, invaded France in 1415 to support the English claim to Norman and Angevin territories, routed the French at Agincourt, and made Calais an English base. He made an alliance with Sigismund, king of the Romans, which hastened the end of the Western schism, and developed the navy and maritime and international law. He captured Caen in 1417, Rouen in 1419, gained Normandy by treaty in 1420, married Catherine of France, and captured Paris. He reformed the Benedictine monasteries, took Chartres in 1421 and Meaux in 1422, and was on his way to aid Burgundy when he died in Vincennes, France, on Aug. 31. He was a patron of Hoccleve and Lydgate and was interested in the literary achievement of England.

HENRY VI (1421–1470), king of England. Son of Henry V, he was born in Windsor, on Dec. 6, became king in 1422, was ruled by Gloucester and Warwick in his minority, and was crowned in 1429. He received setbacks in France, due to the leadership of Joan of Arc, and lost Maine, Normandy, and Guienne between 1448 and 1451. He crushed a popular rebellion, led by Jack Cade, in 1450, became insane in 1453–54 (York ruled as protector), then regained his mind. In the civil war which resulted, Henry was captured and York became supreme. He suffered from mental derangement during the next few years, defeated and exiled York and Nevilles in 1459. He was forced to acknowledge Richard, duke of York, as his successor, rather than his own son Edward (born to Margaret of Anjou in 1453). Queen Margaret headed an army in the north, marched against York and killed him at Wakefield in 1460, but the Yorkists set Edward IV on the throne in 1461. Henry VI fled to Scotland, was captured in 1464 and imprisoned in the Tower. He became king again in 1470, but was recaptured and imprisoned in the Tower in 1471. He was murdered there, allegedly by Richard, duke of Gloucester (later Richard III), on May 21.

HENRY VII (1457–1509), king of England. Son of Edmund Tudor, earl of Richmond, and Margaret Beaufort, he was born in Pembroke castle on Jan. 28, was brought up in Wales and Brittany, escaped to France at the time of Buckingham's rebellion against Richard III, and invaded England with the earl of Oxford and others in 1485. He was joined by the Welsh and Sir William Stanley, defeated and killed Richard at Bosworth Field, and was crowned king. He married Elizabeth, daughter of Edward IV, thus uniting York and Lancaster. He had difficulties with France, suppressed rebellions at home, contained the last Yorkist factions and crushed the Scots pretender, Perkin Warbeck, in his attempt to take Ireland, and astutely arranged treaties with Scotland, Burgundy, and Emperor Maximilian. He became belatedly interested in exploration in the New World, promoted commerce, was concerned about education, and sent men to Italy to bring back manuscripts and the learning of the Renaissance. He died in Richmond on Apr. 21.

HENRY I (1008?–1060), king of France. Grandson of Hugh Capet, and son of Robert II and Constance of Aquitaine, he was anointed king in Rheims in 1027 and succeeded to the throne in 1031 on his father's death. He became embroiled in a civil war with his brother Robert, made territorial concessions to Robert I of Normandy and Geoffrey Martel of Anjou for their aid, and came to terms with his brother, ceding him Burgundy. He married Anne, daughter of Grand Duke Yaroslav I of Kiev in 1051, and spent most of his reign in constant warfare with his vassals and neighbors, notably with the son of Robert of Normandy, William the Conqueror, who twice successfully resisted invasions by Henry (1055 and 1058). Henry died on Aug. 4.

HENRY II (1519–1559), king of France. Born in St. Germain-en-Laye, near Paris on Mar. 31, son of Francis I and Claude, he married Catherine de' Medici, in 1533, became dauphin in 1536 when his brother Francis died, and succeeded to the throne in 1547. He negotiated a truce with England in 1550 which returned Boulogne to France. In 1552 he joined an alliance of Protestant princes against Emperor Charles V, was successful at first, adding Metz, Toul, and Verdun to his dominions, but when deserted by his allies signed a five-year truce with Charles in 1556. He issued a series of edicts against the Protestants, and labored to establish absolute royal power. War broke out the following year with Charles's son Philip II, who decisively defeated the French at St. Quentin. In 1558 the French recovered Calais, which had been occupied for two centuries by the English. In 1559, Henry signed the Treaty of Cateau-Cambrésis with Philip giving up Savoy and ending his hopes in Italy, but retaining Calais, Metz, and Verdun, and providing for the marriage of Philip and Henry's daughter, Elizabeth. Henry was accidentally wounded on June 30 at the tournament held to celebrate the marriage, and died of the wound, on July 10 in Paris.

HENRY III (1551–1589), king of France. Son of Henry II and Catherine de' Medici, he was born in Fontainebleau on Sept. 19, was made duke of Anjou, became leader of the Catholic party, and defeated the Huguenots at Jarnac and Moncontour in 1569. He refused to consider marriage with Elizabeth of England in 1571 for religious reasons, was a leader in the St. Bartholomew's Day massacre in 1572, and in 1573 was elected king of Poland. He left Poland to ascend the French throne on the death of his brother Charles IX in 1574 and found France torn by war between the Catholics under Henry, duke of Guise, and the Huguenots under Henry of Navarre. When he made concessions to the Protestants by the Treaty of Beaulieu in 1576, which brought about an uneasy peace, the Catholics formed a Holy League, headed by Henry, duke of Guise, which he felt it expedient to head. When King Henry's brother, Duke François d'Alençon, died in 1584, the question of succession became of paramount importance. Henry of Navarre, leader of the Huguenots, was heir presumptive, whereupon the Holy League proclaimed Cardinal Charles de Bourbon heir presumptive, and war again broke out in 1585. In 1587, Henry of Navarre was victorious at Contras; when King Henry recognized him as heir apparent the following year, the war of the three Henrys erupted. The Parisians revolted and forced King Henry to flee to Rouen. When Guise was murdered in 1588, King Henry was held responsible and excommunicated by Pope Sixtus V. He then joined Henry of Navarre against the league, and was mortally stabbed by a monk, Jacques Clément, on Aug. 1 at Navarre's camp at St. Cloud. He was the last of the Valois line of kings.

HENRY IV (1553–1610), king of France. Born in Pau, France, on Dec. 14, son of Antoine de Bourbon, duke of Vendôme, and Jeanne d'Albret, daughter of Henri d'Albret, king of Navarre, he was reared a Protestant by his mother, and in 1569 was recognized as chief of the Protestant party when he joined the Protestant army headed by his uncle, Gaspard de Coligny, prince of Condé. In 1572, he became king of Navarre when his mother died a few days before his marriage to Margaret of Valois, sister of King Charles IX, the result of an agreement between his mother and Catherine de' Medici. He was saved from death in the St. Bartholomew's Day massacre by abjuring Protestantism, but was kept under close surveillance at the court until 1576, when he escaped, rejoined the Protestant army and returned to Protestantism. When Francis of Anjou, brother of King Henry III, died in 1584, he became heir presumptive to King Henry III. The Catholics refused to recognize his succession, forced King Henry to exclude him from the succession, and named Cardinal Charles de Bourbon as heir apparent. The war of the three Henrys then broke out and in 1587 Henry of Navarre won a decisive battle at Coutras and King Henry III joined him in a siege of Paris, the populace of which had driven the king out. When the monarch was assassinated in 1589, he named Navarre his successor and Navarre claimed the throne. He defeated the forces of the Catholic League under the duke of Mayenne at Arques in 1589 and Ivry in 1590, but was unable to capture Paris. In 1593 he abjured Protestantism and professed his Catholicism to the French bishops, made liberal concessions to both factions, and in 1594 entered Paris. In 1595, Pope Clement VIII absolved Henry and the breach between the monarchy and the papacy was closed. He made peace with Spain in 1598, issued the Edict of Nantes, which granted freedom of religion to all, and gained the full support of his countrymen. He opposed the Hapsburgs and followed a policy of opposition to their rule by diplomacy and alliances directed against them, subsidized the Dutch against Spain, made alliances with many of the German Protestant princes, Swiss cantons, and Sweden, and made alliances with Italian powers, among them Tuscany, Mantua, Venice, Savoy, and Pope Paul V. He encouraged agriculture, manufacture, and commerce, introduced the silk industry, reformed and strengthened the country's finances, built roads and canals, signed commercial treaties with England, Holland, Spain, and Turkey, and made the royal authority all-powerful. On the death of his mistress, Gabrielle d' Estrées, in 1599, he married Marie de' Medici in 1600. The first Bourbon king of France, Henry was assassinated in Paris by François Ravaillac on May 14, on the eve of his declaration of war against Emperor Rudolph II over the succession of the duchy of Cleves.

HENRY I (1210?–1274), king of Navarre. Son of Theobald I, he took over the rule of the country during the absence of his brother, Theobald II, on the crusade, and died a year after the latter.

HENRY (d. 1580), king of Portugal. He was grand inquisitor, succeeded Sebastian after the latter's death in battle, but died two years later. The nation then passed into the control of Spain.

HENRY, BL. (d. 880?). Headmaster of the Benedictine monastic school at St. Germaine d'Auxerre, France, he wrote several saints' lives. F. D. June 24.

HENRY, ST. (d. 1156?), bishop. An Englishman, he accompanied Adrian IV, then a cardinal, on a mission to Scandinavia in 1151, and was consecrated bishop of Uppsala, Sweden, by the legate. Henry went with St. Eric, king of Sweden, on a punitive attack against Finnish pirates, and remained in the invaded country to gain numerous converts. He may have been assassinated by a malcontent, but stories of possible martyrdom differ. He became patron of Finland and was honored on Jan. 20. F. D. (elsewhere) Jan. 19.

HENRY, BL. (d. 1188), cardinal. A French Cistercian called Henricus Gallus, he was appointed cardinal-bishop of Albano, Italy, in 1179. F. D. July 4.

HEYNE, GILLES. *See* Hayne, Gilles.

HENRY, HUGH THOMAS (1862–1946), author. Born in Philadelphia, he studied at La Salle, the University of Pennsylvania, and St. Charles seminary, and was ordained in 1889. He taught English and Latin at St. Charles, Overbrook, in 1889–94, and music and literature in 1889–1917. He also served as principal of the Philadelphia Catholic High School from 1902 to 1919, when he went to Catholic University as professor of homiletics. He became a monsignor in 1915. He edited *Church Music*, wrote an annual section of the *Records* of the Philadelphia Catholic Historical Society, and published *Eucharistica, Hints to Preachers, Customs and Symbols*, and poems. He died in Jessup, Pennsylvania, on Mar. 12.

HENRY OF BRACTON (d. 1268), jurist. Born probably in Devon, England, he may have received his doctorate in civil and canon law at Oxford before he entered the service of King Henry III. He held various judgeships between 1245 and 1267, pleading before the king on occasion. He also held parish posts and from 1264 until his death was chancellor of Exeter cathedral. His most famous contribution was *De legibus et consuetudinibus angliae*, written before 1259, based on 450 cases, and revealing the influence of Roman law as well as English innovations.

HENRY OF BURGUNDY (d. 1112). A descendant of King Robert of France, he went to Spain to fight against the Moors, was made count of Portugal by King Alfonso VI of Castile in 1093, and married the latter's illegitimate daughter, Teresa. He established himself as a reckless military leader; their son, Alfonso, became the first king of Portugal.

HENRY OF COCKET, ST. (d. 1127). A Dane, he settled on the Island of Cocket, off Northumberland, where he lived a life of austerity. F. D. Jan. 16.

HENRY OF FRIEMAR (d. 1355), theologian. Born in Friemar, Thuringia, he became a Hermit of St. Augustine, studied at Paris, where he taught, after he became master of sacred theology, until 1318. He then became regent of studies of St. Thomas monastery in Prague and provincial of Thuringia and Saxony. He was a well-known theologian and produced half a dozen treatises before his death in Erfurt, Germany.

HENRY OF GHENT (1218?–1293), theologian. He was born near Ghent, Belgium, of an unknown family (the name van Goethals attributed to him was fictitious). By 1267 he was a secular priest at Tournai and subsequently became archdeacon of Bruges and later of Tournai. He taught at Paris, received his doctorate in theology there, and in 1282 was one of the three selected by Pope Martin IV to arbitrate the dispute over mendicant friars hearing confessions. He was an active scholastic, a worthy contemporary of St. Thomas Aquinas, Duns Scotus, and St. Bonaventure, with whom he often disputed, and the author of several treatises, best known of which are his *Quodlibeta* and *Summa theologica*. He died in Paris or in Tournai, Flanders.

HENRY THE GOOD. *See* Buche, St. Henri Michael.

HENRY OF HERFORD (d. 1370), historian. A native of Herworden, Westphalia, he joined the Dominicans in Minden, where he wrote *Liber de rebus memorabilioribus*, a chronicle summarized from earlier historians and then continuing to 1355, a valuable source for the fourteenth century. He also wrote a summary of theology and a treatise on the Immaculate Conception before his death in Minden, Westphalia, on Oct. 9.

HENRY OF HUNTINGDON (1080?–1155), historian. Born probably near Ramsey, Huntingdonshire, England, he studied under Albinus of Angers while a member of the household of Robert Bloet, bishop of Lincoln, was ordained, and about 1109 was made archdeacon of Huntingdon. About 1139 he began work on a general history of England, *Epistola de contemptu mundi*, which he brought down to 1154. The period from 1127 to 1154 was an eyewitness account and is a valuable source book of the period. He also wrote *De miraculis* and other treatises, as well as epigrams.

HENRY OF KALKAR (1328–1408), theologian. Born in Kalkar, Cleves, he studied at Cologne and Paris, taught theology, obtained canonries in two collegiate churches, returned to Cleves in 1362, and in 1365 joined the Carthusians. He served as prior in charterhouses at Arnheim (1368–72), where he converted Gerard Groote, Ruremonde (1372–77), which he built, Cologne (1377–88), and Strassburg (1384–96), and as visitor of his province for twenty of these years. He was known for his piety, was reputed to have experienced several visions, and exerted great influence for the reform of the Church in the Netherlands. He wrote widely on diverse subjects: music, theology, spiritual treatises, and sermons. His *Exercitatorium monachale* appeared in several manuscripts as part of the *Imitation of Christ* (which was sometimes attributed to his authorship) and as part of several other mystical works. He retired to the charterhouse of Cologne, Germany, in 1396, where he died on Dec. 20.

HENRY OF LANGENSTEIN (1325?–1397), theologian. Born near Langenstein, Hesse, he studied at Paris, became a professor of philosophy there in 1363, of theology in 1375, and wrote several treatises debunking astrology as a science. In 1378 he supported Pope Urban VI against antipope Clement VII, wrote treatises denouncing the Western schism, in support of Urban, and pleading for reform in the Church. In 1382 he was forced to leave the university when he refused to acknowledge Clement, and after a period of time at a monastery was invited to found a theological faculty at Vienna in 1384 and spent the rest of his life until his death on Feb. 11 teaching there. He also wrote in defense of the Immaculate Conception, polemics, sermons, and political and historical works.

HENRY DE LOUNDRES (d. 1228), archbishop. He was archdeacon of Stafford when he was named archbishop of Dublin, added the see of Glendalough when its Bishop William Piro died, and saw the beginnings of friction which resulted from the existence of two cathedrals and two chapters, one monastic and the other secular.

HENRY THE NAVIGATOR (1394–1460), prince. Born in Oporto, Portugal, on Mar. 4, son of King John I, founder of the Aviz dynasty in Portugal, and Philippa, daughter of John of Gaunt, he was knighted for valor at the capture of Ceuta in 1415 and made duke of Viseu. In 1416 he founded a naval arsenal at Sangres as a base for his operations; he successfully defended Ceuta in 1418 from an attack by the Mohammedans, was created governor of Algarve, the southernmost province of Portugal, in 1419, and became interested in exploration. He established an observatory and a school for the study of geography and navigation at Sangres, sent out numerous navigators on exploratory trips, one of whom, Zarco, rediscovered the Madeiras in 1420, began colonizing the Madeiras in 1424–25, commissioned Diogo de Seville in 1427 and Gonçalo Velho Cabral in 1431 to explore the Azores, and gradually had the west coast of Africa explored. Cape Bajador was reached in 1434, Cape Blanco in 1440, and in 1442 a slave-trading post was established on the Bay of Arquim. His disastrous expedition against Tangier in 1437 and the confused political situation in Portugal after the death of King Edward (Duarte) in 1438 brought a temporary halt to his exploring activities. In 1441 he resumed and in the next few years ships he sent out reached Senegal, rounded Cape Verde, and almost reached Sierra Leone. In 1441 the first slaves from Guinea were brought to Portugal, and the ensuing evils caused Henry to forbid the kidnaping of Negroes in 1446. Vigorous opposition from Castile and lack of support from the Portuguese government defeated his plan to take over the Canary Islands in 1445–46. In 1447 his brother Pedro revolted against the king and was crushed when Henry supported the monarch. Henry became grand master of the Order of Christ (successor of the Templars in Portugal), under whose banner most of his expeditions sailed, encouraged knowledge of navigation, cartography, and mathematics by inviting experts in these fields to his service, and made his court a center of geographical knowledge and activity. In 1455–60 his expeditions sailed down the coast as far as Sierra Leone, and discovered Cape Verde Islands. He died on Nov. 13 at Villa do Iffante, a town he had founded in 1438 and developed.

HENRY OF NORDLINGEN (14th century). He was a Bavarian priest, extremely active in the mystical movement which swept Germany in the fourteenth century, was spiritual adviser of Margaretha Ebner, influential among the *Gottefreunde*, many of whom he encouraged to write of their mystical experiences, traveled through northern Europe, and was popular as a preacher and confessor. In addition to his letters he translated Mechtilde into High German.

HENRY PROBUS (d. 1290), king of Poland. *See* Boleslav V.

HENRY OF REBDORF. He is the alleged author of the middle-fourteenth-century *Chronica*, a sequel to the *Flores temporum*, a chronicle of world history, covering the period 1294–1362. It is now believed no such person ever lived.

HENRY DE ST. IGNACE (1630–1719?), theologian. Born in Ath, Hainaut, Belgium, he joined the Carmelites, and became a professor of moral theology, noted for his leaning toward Jansenism and his enmity to the Jesuits. He produced several theological tracts, the best known of which is *Ethica amoris*, the third volume of which was condemned by Rome and censured by his fellow Carmelite theologians. He died near Liège, Belgium.

HENRY OF TREVISO, BL. (d. 1315). Born in Bolzano, Italy, he was an uneducated laborer who spent much time in prayer and all his income in charity. In his last years he lived on alms, even sharing these gifts with those poorer than himself. He is also known as San Rigo. His cult was approved by Pope Benedict XIV. F. D. June 10.

HENRY VON THANN (d. 1248). He became bishop of Constance, Switzerland, in 1233, and shifted his allegiance from the emperor to the papacy in 1246, ending a century and a half of separation of the see from papal allegiance.

HENRYSON, ROBERT (1420?–1500?), poet. He may have studied at Paris or Louvain, probably was master of a Benedictine school in Dunfermline, Scotland, and in 1462 was on the faculty at Glasgow. He produced two long poems, *Testament of Cresseid* and *Orpheus and Eurydice*, a collection of Aesop's fables, and several shorter poems, best known of which is *Robene and Makyne*.

HENSCHEN, GODFREY (1601–1681), scholar. Born in Venray, Limburg, Netherlands, on June 21, he became a Jesuit in 1619, was ordained in 1634, and was assigned in 1635 to Fr. John von Bolland in the preparation of the *Acta sanctorum*. He considerably modified his former teacher's method, forcing a revision of the first volume, which was already in type; toured Europe in search of new primary sources, and, by the time of his death, had seen twenty-four volumes through the press. He made himself particularly responsible for the lives of Greek and oriental saints and those of France and Italy; Fr. Bolland worked on those of Germany, Spain, Brittany, and Ireland. He died in Antwerp, Belgium, on Sept. 11.

HENSEL, LUISE (1798–1876), poet. Born in Linum, Brandenburg, Prussia, on Mar. 30, daughter of a Lutheran parson, she studied in Berlin where she began writing religious poetry. She became a convert in 1818, tutored several children of the aristocracy, and then became head teacher of a girls' school in Aachen for six years. After teaching at Neuburg, Cologne, and Wiedenbrück, she entered the convent of the Daughters of Christian Love in Paderborn, Germany, where she died on Dec. 18, although she never joined the congregation.

HENTEN, JOHN (1499–1566). Born in Nalinnes, Belgium, he joined the Hieronymites, but left to become a Dominican about 1548. He taught in Louvain, became prior, and in 1556 was made defender of the faith and inquisitor. He joined the theological faculty at Louvain, wrote scriptural commentary, and died there on Oct. 10.

HERACLAS, ST. (d. 247), bishop. Brother of St. Plutarch, he was a student of Origen, whom he succeeded as head of the catechetical school at Alexandria, Egypt; he became bishop there in 231. F. D. July 14.

HERACLIDES, ST. (d. 202), martyr. *See* Plutarch, St.

HERACLIUS, ST. (d. 263?), martyr. He and St. Zosimus were put to death at Carthage during the persecution of Valerian and Gallienus. F. D. Mar. 11.

HERACLIUS, ST. (d. 303), martyr. *See* Felicissimus, St.

HERACLIUS, ST. (d. 305?), martyr. She and SS. Januaria, Paul, and Secundilla were put to death near Rome during the Diocletian persecution. F. D. Mar. 2.

HERACLIUS, ST. (5th century), bishop. *See* Priscus, St.

HERACLIUS, ST. (d. 515?). Bishop of Sens, Gaul, he was present at the baptism of Clovis and built the abbey of St. John. F. D. June 8.

HERADIUS, ST. (d. 303), martyr. *See* Aquilinus, St.

HERAIS, ST. (d. 202), martyr. *See* Plutarch, St.

HERBERMANN, CHARLES GEORGE (1840–1916), editor. Born in Saarbeck, Westphalia, Germany, on Dec. 8, he was taken to New York City in 1850, and studied at St. Francis Xavier College. He taught there from 1858 to 1869, obtaining his doctorate after a master's degree from St. John's. In 1869 he began teaching Latin at City College, and was made librarian in addition in 1873. He helped to found the Catholic Club in New York, reorganized and became president of the Catholic Historical Society, was editor of nine volumes of *Historical Records and Studies*, and from 1905 to 1914 was editor in chief of the Catholic Encyclopedia. He received honorary degrees from St. Francis Xavier, Holy Cross, and Catholic University, was twice honored by the papacy, and was awarded the Laetare Medal in 1913. He was made professor emeritus in 1915 and died in New York City on Aug. 24.

HERBERT, ST. (d. 687). A priest who became a recluse on Lake Derwentwater, an island now named after him in England, he was a close friend of St. Cuthbert of Lindisfarne and died on the same day. F. D. Mar. 20.

HERBERT OF BOSHAM (12th century). Probably a native of Sussex, England, he became a member of Thomas à Becket's household shortly after 1160, remained with the archbishop until the latter's murder, and then probably fled to the Continent. He is known for a biography of Thomas, the accuracy of which is challenged by most scholars.

HERBERT, ELIZABETH (1822–1911). Daughter of General Charles A'Court, she married Sidney Herbert at twenty-four, assisted Florence Nightingale in the Crimean hospitals, and in 1866 became a convert, five years after her husband's death. She wrote travel sketches, short stories, saints' lives, and translations from the French. She died in London on Oct. 30.

HERBERT HOSCAM, ST. (d. 1180). An Englishman, he became archbishop of Conza, Italy, and its patron saint. F. D. Aug. 20.

HERBERT, JOHN ROGERS (1810–1890), painter. Born in Malden, Essex, England, on Jan. 23, he studied at the Royal Academy, where his first painting was exhibited in 1830. He became a convert in 1840, an associate of the Royal Academy in 1841 and a full member in 1846. His subsequent paintings were predominantly religious scenes, including a *Virgin Mary* for Queen Victoria. He died in London on Mar. 17.

HERBLAND. *See* Hermenland, St.

HERBST, JOHANN GEORG (1787–1836). Born in Rottweil, Württemberg, he studied oriental languages, and was ordained in 1812. He was sent to the seminary in Ellwangen, taught Hebrew and Arabic at the university there, and in 1814 became professor of oriental languages and Old Testament exegesis. In 1817 he transferred to Tübingen where he also taught biblical archaeology and church history. He was appointed head librarian of the Royal University in 1832. He died on July 31, five years before his introduction to the Old Testament was published.

HERCULÁNO DE CARVALHU E ARAUJO, ALEJANDRO (1810–1877), author. A native of Lisbon, Portugal, he was educated in Paris, forced to live in exile in Paris and England from 1828 to 1831 because of his liberal political views, and returned to his native land in 1832. He became prominent in politics, attracted attention by his political works, among them *Paroles d'un croyant* and *Voz do propheta*, and in 1837 founded the magazine *O Panorama*. In 1844 his first historical novel, *Eurico o Presbytero*, was published, followed by a succession of others. He also wrote *Historia de Portugal*, a history of the Inquisition in Portugal, and a collection of essays and treatises. He died near Santarem, Portugal, on Mar. 28.

HERCULANUS, ST. (d. 180?), martyr. He was slain at Porto, near Rome, probably in the reign of Marcus Aurelius. F. D. Sept. 5.

HERCULANUS, ST. (2nd century), martyr. He is said to have been a soldier converted by Pope St. Alexander I, who was slain soon after. F. D. Sept. 25.

HERCULANUS, ST. (d. 547?), bishop and martyr. He was tortured and beheaded by or-der of King Totila of the Ostrogoths when they captured his see city of Perugia, Italy. He probably was a Syrian sent from Rome to evangelize Perugia. F. D. Nov. 7.

HERCULANUS, ST. (d. 550?). He was bishop of Brescia, Lombardy. F. D. Aug. 12.

HERCULANUS OF PIEGARO, BL. (d. 1451). Born in Emilia, Italy, he became a Franciscan of the Strict Observance, was sent out to preach, with great success, particularly in Lucca, founded a house at Castronovo, Tuscany, and lived a life of great austerity. He was beatified in 1860. F. D. June 1.

HERDER, BARTHOLOMAUS (1774–1839), publisher. Born in Rottweil on the Neckar, Swabia, he founded in 1801 the publishing house bearing his name, later moving it from Meersburg to Freiburg im Breisgau. In 1813 he was appointed publisher of the official war bulletins and in 1815 accompanied Metternich to Paris as press liaison agent. He founded an institute for lithography and engraving which produced highly acclaimed atlases, and expanded his list of scholarly publications. He died in Freiburg, Germany, on Mar. 11.

HERDER, BENJAMIN (1818–1888), publisher. Son of Bartholomaus, he was trained in the publishing business by his father, traveled through Europe in his youth and with his brother Karl, and took over the management of the firm on the death of their father in 1839. He took charge of the publishing end of the business and issued works in theology, hagiography, biography, and other fields. His greatest contributions to Catholic publishing was the *Kirchenlexikon*, a monumental encyclopedia covering every aspect of theology, which he published in 1856, *Theologische Bibliothek*, a theological library in the making for thirty years, and a popular general encyclopedia, *Konversations-Lexikon*. By his far-flung and varied publishing programs Benjamin was a major influence in the Catholic revival in nineteenth-century Germany. In 1873 he opened branches in St. Louis, Missouri, and Munich, and in 1886 in Vienna. He died on Nov. 10.

HERDER, KARL RAPHAEL (1816–1865), publisher. Elder son of Bartholomaus, he took over the management of the publishing firm with his brother Benjamin on the death of their father. His entire career was devoted to the commercial side of the house until his retirement in 1856.

HERDTRICH, CHRISTIAN WOLFGANG (1625–1684), missioner. Born in Graz, Styria, Austria, he joined the Jesuits in 1641 and in 1656 was sent to China. In 1671 he was called to the court in Peking by Emperor Kang-he as mathematician. He became an authority on Chinese language and literature, translated

Confucius into Latin, and was the author of what probably was the first Chinese-Latin dictionary. In 1675 he was appointed superior of the mission of Kiangtcheon, Shan-si, where he died in July.

HERENA, ST. (3rd century), martyr. *See* Donatus, St.

HERESWITHA, ST. (d. 690?). Princess of Northumbria, England, sister of St. Hilda and mother of SS. Ethelburga, Sexburga, and Withburga, she became a Benedictine nun at Chelles, France. F. D. Sept. 3.

HERGENRÖTHER, JOSEPH (1824–1890), cardinal. Born in Würzburg, Germany, on Sept. 15, he studied at the university there and the German College in Rome, and was ordained in 1848. He received his doctorate in theology from Munich in 1850, taught there and at Würzburg in 1852, and was noted as a leading church historian. He early became opposed to Döllinger and his followers, and wrote several treatises critical of their teaching and theories. In 1868 he was appointed a consultor to prepare for the Vatican Council, was made a domestic prelate in 1877, a cardinal-deacon in 1879, and the first cardinal-prefect of the Vatican Archives. He also served in the Congregations of the Index, Studies, and Extraordinary Ecclesiastical Affairs. He died at Mehrerau Cistercian abbey on the Bodensee on Oct. 3. He wrote *Photius Patriarch von Constantinopel* (1867–70), *Anti-Janus* (1870), *Katholische Kirche und christlicher* (1872), *Handbuch der allgemeinen Kirchengeschichte* (1876), and volumes 8–9 of the continuation of Hefele's *History of the Church Councils* (1887–90).

HERIBALD, ST. (d. 857?), bishop. A Benedictine monk at St. Germanus, where he served as abbot, he was called to become bishop of Auxerre, France. F. D. Apr. 25.

HERIBERT, ST. (d. 1021), archbishop. A native of Worms, Germany, he studied at Gorze, was ordained, and approved as archbishop of Cologne in 998. He served as chancellor to Emperor Otto III and, in spite of some political misunderstandings, to his successor, St. Henry II. He was active as a peacemaker, in maintaining a disciplined clergy, in caring personally for the sick and the poor, and founded the monastery of Deutz, near Cologne. F. D. Mar. 16.

HERIBERT (d. 1045), archbishop. Elected archbishop of Milan in 1018, he helped King Conrad II of Germany to secure the crown of Lombardy, crowned him in Milan in 1026, and was present when Pope John XIX crowned Conrad emperor in 1027. His ruthlessness in his attempts to secure supreme spiritual dominion over northern Italy led to a revolt. He called on Conrad to suppress it and, when the emperor insisted he explain his actions, denied an explanation on the grounds he was the emperor's equal. When the emperor ousted him, the Milanese rallied to his support, even when Pope Benedict IX excommunicated him in 1038. He subsequently made peace with Conrad's successor, Henry III, in 1040. He died in Monza, Italy, on Jan. 16.

HERIGER OF LOBBES (925–1007). He studied at the cathedral school in Liège, Belgium, joined the Benedictines in Lobbes, and taught in the monastery school. In 989 he went to Rome with Notger of Liège and was elected abbot of Lobbes in 990. He was noted for his learning and wrote a history of the twenty-seven bishops of Liège, lives of SS. Berlendis, Landoald, and Ursmar, and a treatise on Christ.

HERINCX, WILLIAM (1621–1678), bishop. A native of Helmond, North Brabant, he received his doctorate in philosophy at Louvain, and shortly after joined the Franciscans. In 1653 he became lecturer of theology at Louvain, published *Summa theologica scholastica et moralis* (1660–63) and *De conscientiae*. He served successively as minister provincial, definitor general, and commissary general for northern Europe. He was consecrated bishop of Ypres, Belgium, in 1677, and died on Aug. 17 while making his first visitation.

HERLUIN, BL. (994–1078). A native of Normandy, he gave up his career as a knight at the court of Brionne to become a Benedictine monk, founded a monastery on his own estate at Bonneville, and became its abbot. In 1040 the community moved to a site on the river Bec in Normandy, and welcomed Bl. Lanfranc and St. Anselm soon after. Under the guidance of these three men Bec became one of the greatest intellectual centers of the Middle Ages. F. D. Aug. 26.

HERMAGORAS, ST. (1st century), bishop and martyr. According to legend, St. Mark chose him as pastor of his converts at Aquileia, Italy, where he was made bishop after consecration by St. Peter. Hermagoras and his deacon, St. Fortunatus, were then tortured and beheaded during the persecution of Nero. F. D. July 12.

HERMAN, BL. (d. 1200?). A Jewish convert, he became first abbot of the Premonstratensian abbey of Scheda, near Cologne, Germany. F. D. Dec. 23.

HERMAN THE CRIPPLE, BL. (1013–1054), historian. Born a cripple on Feb. 18 in Altshausen, Swabia, Germany, he was sent to the monastery on Reichenau in Constance, Switzerland, in 1020, became a monk in 1033, and spent the rest of his life there until his death on Sept. 21. He had a keen mind and attracted students from all over Europe. He was the author of the first mediaeval universal chronicle still extant, a history of his era,

Geschichte der Mathematik, poetry, and hymns, including *Alma Redemptoris Mater* and, probably, *Salve Regina* (which last, however, is attributed to many poets). He is usually called Blessed and honored on Sept. 25; he also is known as Hermann Contractus.

HERMAN JOSEPH, BL. (1150?–1241). A native of Cologne, he became a Premonstratensian at Steinfeld, and was later ordained. He wrote hymns and prayers, sponsored the cult of St. Ursula, and was so devoted to the Virgin Mary that he was called an earthly Joseph, whence his nickname and the picture by Van Dyck showing him espoused to Our Lady. He possessed a number of supernatural gifts from childhood. F. D. Apr. 7.

HERMANN I (d. 1217), landgrave. Nephew of Emperor Frederick I, he joined his brother Ludwig in war against Duke Henry and was defeated and imprisoned in 1180. His brother transferred the title of Count Palatine of Saxony to him on his release in 1181, and in 1190 he succeeded Ludwig as landgrave of Thuringia. He became a patron of poets, and participated in a crusade in 1197, but on his return his vacillation between the waning Philip of Swabia and Otto of Brunswick almost ruined his domain as the contending armies repeatedly overran his territory. He supported the election of Frederick of Hohenstanfen in 1211 when Pope Innocent III excommunicated Otto. The latter at once invaded Thuringia, but Hermann was saved by Frederick, to whom he remained loyal until his death on Apr. 25 in Gotha, Germany.

HERMANN OF ALTACH (1200?–1275), historian. He was educated at the Benedictine monastery of Niederaltaich, Bavaria, took his vows, and made several trips on monastery business to the emperor and twice to the Roman curia. In 1242 he was elected abbot, a position he retained until his retirement because of ill health in 1273. He wrote a chronicle which is an important source of information about the period, *Annales Hermann*, and several treatises. He died on July 31 in Niederaltaich.

HERMANN CONTRACTUS. *See* Herman the Cripple, Bl.

HERMANN OF FRITZLAR (14th century). He was a layman who traveled widely over Europe and to whom was attributed the authorship of *Das Heiligenleben*, a collection of considerations on the lives of the saints, which is now definitely assigned to Gisiler of Slatheim, and *Blume der Schauung*, a collection of spiritual reflections.

HERMANN OF MINDEN (d. 1294?). Born near Minden, Germany, of the noble Scynne family, he joined the Dominicans, became papal penitentiary and chaplain, provincial of Germany in 1286–90, and vicar of the provincial

1293–94. He was successful in expanding the order in Germany despite vigorous opposition from the secular clergy and several cathedral chapters, and wrote *Tractabus de interdicto* and *De criminum inquisitionibus*.

HERMANN OF SALZA (1180–1239). Born in Langensalza, Thuringia, of the noble Salza family, he became in 1210 grand master of the Teutonic Order, which he revitalized as one of the greatest powers in Europe. In 1211 he sent a group of knights to aid Hungarian King Andrew II to repulse the pagan Cumanes. In 1219 he went on crusade and in 1226 effected a peace between Frederick II and the Lombard cities. In 1228–29 he went to Jerusalem with the excommunicated Frederick and in 1230 had the excommunication lifted by the Treaty of San Germano. He died on Mar. 19 in Barletta, Italy.

HERMANSSÖN, BL. NICHOLAS (1331–1391), bishop. Born in Skeninge, Sweden, he was educated at Paris and Orléans, ordained, and became tutor to the sons of St. Brigid of Sweden. Appointed bishop of Linköping, Sweden, he brought many reforms to his diocese, devoting his wealth to its improvement and its poor. He also was well known as a poet and liturgist. He died on May 2 and was reportedly canonized in 1414. F. D. July 24.

HERMAS, ST. (1st century). Referred to by St. Paul (Rom. 16:14), he is traditionally said to have been put to death while bishop of Philippi, Macedonia. F. D. May 9.

HERMAS (2nd century). A Christian writer who lived in Italy and wrote in Greek, he was the author of a book called *The Shepherd*, which was held in the highest regard by the early Church Fathers, some of whom considered it scripture, though most of them rightly held it to be worthy of respect but not divinely inspired. Origen believed the author was the Hermas mentioned in Rom. 16:14, but modern scholars believe he was the brother of Pope Pius I (140–155).

HERMAS, ST., martyr. *See* Nicander, St. (date unknown).

HERMENEGILD (d. 585). Son of the Arian king of Spain, Leovigild, he became a Catholic on his marriage to Indegundis, daughter of King Sigebert of Austrasia, was disinherited, revolted against his father, was betrayed by his allies and put to death. Contrary opinions make him the converter of Visigothic Spain by his action, a saint and a martyr with a F. D. of Apr. 13; and a mere rebel with no right to any honors.

HERMENEGILD, ST. (d. 953). He was a Benedictine at Salcedo, Spanish Galicia, who worked with St. Rudesind in spreading the order through northwest Spain. F. D. Nov. 5.

HERMENGAUDIUS, ST. (d. 1035). He became bishop of Urgell, Spain, in 1010, built its cathedral, and placed his canons under Augustinian rule. He is also known as Armengol. F. D. Nov. 3.

HERMENLAND, ST. (d. 720?). Born in Noyon, France, he became a courtier at the court of Clotaire III, studied under St. Lambert at the abbey of Fontenelle, became a monk, and was sent with eleven monks to evangelize the region around Nantes. He became abbot-founder of an abbey on Aindrei, an island at the mouth of the Loire, and also built a school. He is also called Erblon. F. D. Mar. 25.

HERMES, ST. (d. 120?), martyr. He was one of a group ordered slain by the judge Aurelian at Rome. Another of the name died under Aurelian about 270 (F. D. Dec. 31) and another, with SS. Aggaeus and Caius, on Jan. 4. F. D. Aug. 28.

HERMES, ST. (d. 290?), martyr. See Adrian, St.

HERMES, ST. (d. 304), martyr. See Philip, St.

HERMES, GEORGE (1775–1831), philosopher. Born in Dreierwalde, Westphalia, Germany, on Apr. 22, he studied at Münster and was ordained in 1799. His *Untersuchung über die innere Wahrheit des Christentums* was so well received on its publication (1805) that in 1807 he was appointed professor of theology at Münster, where his rationalistic methods attracted a great following but aroused opposition among more conservative churchmen. In 1820 he accepted the chair of dogmatic theology at Bonn. His lectures attracted a huge following and his students soon filled many of the most important chairs in German universities, creating a Hermesian party which aroused bitter opposition. Many of his theories and opinions were attacked as heretical although Baron von Spiegel, archbishop of Cologne, defended him until his death in Bonn, Germany, on May 26. In 1835 Gregory XVI condemned the Hermesian system of philosophy and theology and placed his principal works, *Die philosophische Einleitung* (1819), *Positive Einleitung* (1829), and *Christkatholische Dogmatik*, on the Index.

HERMIAS, ST. (d. 170), martyr. A Roman soldier, he was put to death for his faith at Comana in Cappadocia. F. D. May 31.

HERMIONE, ST. (d. 117?), martyr. One of the daughters of Philip the deacon, she is mentioned in Acts 21:9 as a prophetess, and is said to have been slain in Ephesus. F. D. Sept. 4.

HERMIPPUS, ST. (d. 300?), martyr. See Hermolaus, St.

HERMITE, CHARLES (1822–1901), mathematician. Born in Dieuze, Lorraine, France, on Dec. 24, he was educated at Collèges de Nancy, Henri IV, and Louis le Grand in Paris, early evincing an aptitude for mathematics. He published his first original mathematical thesis in 1842, when he entered L'École Polytechnique for a year's study, and soon after left the Church

(but was reconciled in 1856). He was to return in 1848 to teach, became professor of mathematics in 1869, lectured at L'École Normale Supérieure from 1862 to 1873, and in 1876 became professor at Paris, where he remained until his death on Jan. 14. In 1892 he was made grand officer of the Legion of Honor. During his lifetime he made many important contributions to mathematics, especially with Abelian and elliptic functions and the theory of numbers.

HERMOGENES, ST. (d. 300?), martyr. See Hermolaus, St.

HERMOGENES, ST., martyr. See Mennas, St. (4th century).

HERMOGIUS, ST. (d. 942?), bishop. Born in Tuy, Spain, he founded the Benedictine monastery of Labrugia in Galicia in 915, was captured by the Moors and imprisoned at Cordova, and released when his nephew, St. Pelagius, offered himself as hostage. Hermogius spent his last years at Ribas del Sil. F. D. June 26.

HERMOLAUS, ST. (d. 300?), martyr. A priest who converted St. Pantaleon, he was put to death at Nicomedia during the persecution of Diocletian; with him died two brothers, Hermippus and Hermogenes. F. D. July 27.

HERMOSILLA, BL. JEROME (d. 1861), bishop and martyr. A native of La Calzada, Spain, he became a Dominican and was sent to Manila, where he was ordained. Sent to East Tonkin in 1828, he succeeded Bl. Ignatius Delgado as vicar apostolic, was consecrated bishop, and was beheaded with Bl. Valentine Berrio-Ochoa and Bl. Pedro Almató. He was beatified in 1908. F. D. Nov. 1.

HERMYLUS, ST. (d. 315), martyr. A deacon at what is now Belgrade, Yugoslavia, he and his servant Stratonicus were seized and put to death by drowning in the Danube during the persecution of Licinius. F. D. Jan. 13.

HERO, ST. (d. 202), martyr. See Plutarch, St.

HERODION, ST. (1st century), bishop and martyr. A relative of St. Paul (Rom. 16:11), he became bishop of Patras, Achaia, and was put to death by Jewish opposition. F. D. Apr. 8.

HERON, ST. (d. 136?), martyr. He succeeded St. Ignatius as bishop of Antioch about 116, and was put to death there. F. D. Oct. 17.

HERON, ST. (d. 250), martyr. See Arsenius, St.

HEROS, ST. (d. 304?), martyr. See Cyriac, St.

HÉROUET, ANTOINE (16th century). Bishop of Digne, France, from 1552 to 1568, he was a poet and translator of Plato.

HERRAD OF LANDSBERG (1130?–1195). Born of a noble family in the castle of Landsberg, Alsace, she entered the convent of Hohenburg, near Strassburg, Alsace, where she was abbess from 1167 until her death. She wrote of *Hortus deliciarum*, a profusely illustrated compendium of the sciences she prepared for her novices, which is one of the major documents of the twelfth century.

HERRERA BARNUEVO, SEBASTIANO DE (1619–1671), painter. Born in Madrid, son of a sculptor, he studied with his father and with Alonzo Cano, entered the service of Philip IV, became director of the Escorial, and gained fame as a painter, architect, and sculptor. His best work includes *St. Barnabas, Beatification of St. Augustine,* and *Nativity,* all in Madrid, where he died.

HERRERA, FRANCISCO (1576–1656), painter. Surnamed El Viejo (The Elder), he was born in Seville, Spain, studied painting under Luis Fernandez, but left him to become the founder of the Spanish school of bold, vigorous, natural style, and was noted for his design, coloring, and rapidity of execution. He also did some engraving, painted in fresco, and etched. In 1650 he moved to Madrid, where he died. In addition to his great religious work, *Last Judgment, St. Peter, Moses Smiting the Rock,* he also executed many paintings depicting Spanish life. One of his pupils was Diego Velásquez, who studied under him for a year.

HERRERA, FRANCISCO (1622–1685), painter. Surnamed El Mozo (The Younger), this second son of Francisco el Viejo was born in Seville, studied under his father, but fled to Rome to escape his violent temper and there studied architecture. In 1656 he returned to Seville, founded the Seville Academy, and in about 1661 went to Madrid (reportedly in resentment that Murillo was his superior in the Academy). His magnificent fresco work attracted the attention of Philip IV, who appointed him royal painter and superintendent of royal buildings; Charles VI appointed him master of the royal works. He is famous for his still lifes, *St. Francis, St. Hermengild,* and *Triumph of St. Hermengild,* and his fresco, *Assumption of the Virgin.* He died in Madrid.

HERRERA, FERNANDO DE (1534–1597), poet. Born in Seville, Spain, he took minor orders and, though never ordained, was attached to the church of San Andrés in that city. He wrote sonnets, love lyrics (platonically dedicated to Leonor de Millán), and patriotic odes (on the victory at Lepanto and on the death of King Sebastian of Portugal). His *Algunas obras* appeared in 1582; he also wrote a prose history of the Lepanto battle, a life of Tomás Moro, and annotations on the work of Garcilasso de la Vega. He died in Seville.

HERRERA Y PIÑA, JOSÉ (1868–1927), archbishop. Born in Mexico City, he studied at the Latin American College, Rome, was ordained in 1890, and returned to his own country. He became a bishop in 1907 and archbishop of Monterrey, Mexico, in 1920, and wrote earnest pastorals in an attempt to pro-

tect his people during the anti-Catholic attacks which reached a climax in 1926. He died in Monterrey on June 17.

HERRERA Y TORDESILLAS, ANTONIO DE (1559–1625), historian. Born in Cuellar, Spain, he became secretary to Vespasiano Gonzaga, brother of the duke of Mantua. Philip II appointed him grand historiographer of America and Castile, a position he held under Philip III and IV. He wrote *Historia general de los Castellanos en las islas y tierra firme del mar oceáno* (1601), covering the years 1492–1554, and relying heavily on Bartolomé de las Casas. He also wrote histories of Portugal, Scotland, and England. He died in Madrid on Mar. 27.

HERREGOUTS, DAVID (b. 1603), painter. Born in Mechlin, Netherlands, he studied painting, was admitted to the painters' guild there in 1624, and the Guild of St. Luke of Ruremonde, where he had moved, in 1647. He was noted for his religious pictures.

HERREGOUTS, HENDRIK (1633–1724), painter. Son of David Herregouts, he was born in Mechlin, Netherlands, went to Rome, was in Cologne in 1660, and married in 1661. He became a member of the Guild of St. Luke in Antwerp in 1664 and in 1666 returned to Mechlin, where he was admitted to the local guild. By the time he returned to Antwerp in 1680, where he remained until his death, he was famed for the design, coloring, and expressiveness of his figures. Among his best paintings are *Last Judgment, Martyrdom of St. Matthew,* and *St. Jerome in the Desert.*

HERREGOUTS, JAN (d. 1721), painter. Son of Hendrik Herregouts, he was admitted in 1677 to the Guild of St. Luke in Antwerp, later moved to Bruges, became a member of its guild, and helped found its academy. In addition to his painting he did some engraving and etching. He died in Bruges, Belgium.

HERRGOTT, MARQUARD (1694–1762), historian. Born in Freiburg im Breisgau, Germany, he studied there and at Strassburg, was a tutor, and in 1715 became a Benedictine at St. Blasien. Ordained in 1718, he wrote on monastic customs, represented the estates of Breisgau at Vienna for twenty years, and wrote a history of the Austrian imperial family, for which he was appointed imperial historiographer in 1737. He had to resign in 1749 when he defended the rights of the Church against the crown, returned to Germany, became provost of Krozingen, and governor of Staufen and Kirchofen. He died in Krozingen, Germany, on Oct. 9.

HERROUET, JOHN M. (1884–1961), educator. Born in Baulon, France, he studied at Laval, Vermont, and Montreal universities, became a member of the Society of St. Edmund, and spent fifty-three years of his life at St.

Michael's College, Winooski, Vermont, which he helped to found in 1904. He served as librarian, choirmaster, professor of classics, dean of studies, and trustee of the college. He also was a curate in Swanton, Vermont, pastor there in 1913–14, and became procurator general of his order. He died in Winooski in Jan.

HERST, BL. RICHARD (d. 1628), martyr. Born near Preston, Lancashire, England, he was a farmer who was arrested for his religion. On that occasion a scuffle took place and, in fleeing, one of the summons servers broke a leg and died from gangrene several days later, after testifying that his fall had been accidental. Herst (also called Hurst and Hayhurst), was charged with murder, offered his freedom if he gave up his faith, and hanged at Lancaster, England. He was beatified in 1929. F. D. Aug. 29.

HERTLING, GEORG VON (1843–1919), philosopher. Born in Darmstadt, Germany, on Aug. 31, he studied at Münster, Munich, and Berlin, and taught philosophy at Bonn and Munich. He was a member of the *Reichstag* from 1875 to 1890 and in 1896, was leader of the Centre party in 1909–11, and in 1912 became president of the Bavarian ministry. During World War I he replaced Michaelis as chancellor, resigning in late 1918. He founded and was president of the Görres Gesellschaft and the German Society of Christian Art, was co-founder of *Beiträge zur Geschichte der Philosophie des Mittel-Alters*, and wrote on Aristotle and the soul, Darwin, Locke, Descartes, Augustine, and Albertus Magnus. He died in Ruhpolding, Bavaria, Germany, on Jan. 4.

HERULF, ST. (d. 785), bishop. Son of the count of Ellwangen, he became a Benedictine at St. Gall, founded Ellwangen in 764, and became bishop of Langres, France. F. D. Aug. 13.

HERUNDA, ST. (6th century). She and SS. Redempta and Romula were praised by St. Gregory the Great for their outstanding humility and piety. Herunda had raised Redempta near Palestrina; they later joined Romula in prayerful retirement near the church of St. Mary Major, Rome, about 575. F. D. July 23.

HERVÁS Y PANDURO, LORENZO (1735–1809), philologist. Born in Horjaco, Spain, on May 1, he became a Jesuit in Madrid, studied at Alcalá de Henares, and taught at Murcia. After years in America as a missioner, he went to Italy in 1767 when his Society was suppressed in the Spanish world, was in Spain in 1799–1803, then returned to Rome, where Pope Pius VII made him prefect of the Quirinal Library and where he died on Aug. 24. His chief work was the twenty-one-volume *Idea dell' universo* (1778–87), in which he explored the origins and ethnological relationship of nations from a study of their languages. He also

wrote on paleography, the American colonies, and educational work for deaf mutes.

HERVÉ, ST. (6th century). No facts are known, but his feast of June 17 was long popular and once was a holy day of obligation. Legend has him a blind orphan, brought up by his uncle, who had founded a monastery in Plouvien, Brittany, which Hervé later directed, before he left to establish a monastery at Lanhouarneau, Wales. Ballads tell of a wolf devouring the donkey with which Hervé was plowing as a child, and which was ordered to take its place in the empty harness and finish the field; the wolf also appears with the saint in mediaeval art.

HERVETUS, GENTIAN (1499–1584), theologian. Born in Olivet, France, he studied in Orléans, tutored for several years in France and England, then joined Cardinal Pole's household in Rome, where he translated several of the Greek Fathers into Latin. After teaching at France, he returned to Rome as secretary to Cardinal Cervini (the future Pope Marcellus II), accompanied him to the Council of Trent, and in 1556 was ordained. He became vicar general of Noyons, a canon at Rheims, and wrote several pamphlets against the Calvinists. He died in Rheims, France, on Sept. 12.

HERWEGEN, ILDEFONS (1874–1946). Born in Junkersdorf, near Cologne, Germany, on Nov. 27, he studied there, at the abbeys of Seckau, Maria-Laach, and Beuron, and at San Anselmo, Rome, and became a Benedictine monk in 1895. He had studied archaeology in Rome, developed his interest in monastic history while stationed at Maredsous, Belgium, and went to Bonn for work in law. He became abbot of Maria-Laach in 1913, strengthened the educational policy of the abbey, and developed his interest in liturgy. In 1930 he founded the Benedictine Academy for Monastic and Liturgical Studies, wrote widely in explanation of his aims, served as mentor of Katholischer Akademikerverband, and was given honorary degrees by Tübingen and Bonn and decorations by Popes Pius XI and XII. He published *St. Benedict: A Character Study* and an account of the Rule of St. Benedict, initiated a series of monographs on Benedictine monasticism, and issued nineteen volumes on the liturgy, entitled *Ecclesia orans*.

HESLIN, THOMAS (1845–1911), bishop. Born in Longford County, Ireland, on Apr. 17 (or Dec. 21), he was brought to the United States by Bishop Odin of New Orleans after he had finished his classical studies, studied at St. Vincent de Paul seminary, New Orleans, and was ordained in Mobile in 1869. He did parish work in the New Orleans diocese, became pastor of St. Michael's there, and in 1889 was consecrated bishop of Natchez, Mississippi. He died in Natchez on Feb. 22.

HESPERUS, ST. (d. 135?), martyr. He and his wife Zoe, and their sons Cyriacus and Theodulus, slaves in Pamphylia in Asia Minor, were burned to death during the persecution of Hadrian when they refused to eat food sacrificed to the gods. The story is open to serious question. F. D. May 2.

HESS, BEDE (1885–1953). Born in Rome, New York, on Nov. 16, he studied at St. Francis College, Trenton, New Jersey, and Innsbruck, became a Franciscan, and was ordained in 1908. He taught in Trenton and in Rensselaer, New York, from 1909 to 1914, held several positions in his order, was provincial at Syracuse in 1932–36, and was the second American to be elected as minister general of the Friars Minor Conventual. He died in Assisi, Italy, on Aug. 7.

HESS, LAWRENCE ANTHONY (1866–1939). Born in Brighton, England, on Oct. 27, he became a Capuchin in 1881, and was ordained in 1889, as Fr. Cuthbert. He was principal of the Franciscan house of studies at Oxford from 1911 to 1930 and president of the College of St. Lawrence at Assisi, Italy, from that date until his death there on Mar. 22. He also did mission work, was minister provincial of his order in England in 1922–25, and after 1930 was president of the Capuchin Commission for Franciscan Research Studies. He wrote a biography (1912) and other studies of St. Francis Assisi, a history of the Capuchins, *Catholic Ideals in Social Life, God and the Supernatural,* and *The Mystery of the Redemption.*

HESSELS, JEAN (1522–1566), theologian. Born in Louvain, Belgium, he taught at the Dominican house in Parc and theology at Louvain, and took an active part in the Council of Trent. He was attacked for his Augustinian preferences, but avoided scholastic controversy to devote his energies to writings on the Eucharist, the Immaculate Conception, papal infallibility, and biblical commentaries and a catechism.

HESSION, MARTIN J. (1892–1936), educator. Born in Waltham, Massachusetts, on Jan. 28, he became a Christian Brother in 1905, taking the name Cornelius Malachy, and taught in New York and New Jersey schools until 1922. For five years he was director of studies at Pocantico Hills and in 1927–32 was president of Manhattan College, where he increased the curriculum range, faculty, and student body. He was New York provincial in 1932–35. He died in New York City on Apr. 29.

HESSLAN, EDMOND (1868–1948), bishop. Born in Elton, Limerick, Ireland, on Feb. 5, he studied at All Hallows College, Dublin, and was ordained in 1890. He went to the United States, served in Dubuque, Iowa, parishes until

1897, and in Fort Dodge until 1919, when he became auxiliary bishop of Sioux City, Iowa. He was named bishop of that see in 1920 and died there on Sept. 20.

HESSO, BL. (d. 1133). He came from Hirschau in 1085 as the first abbot of the Benedictine monastery of Beinwil, Switzerland. F. D. Dec. 27.

HESSOUN, JOSEPH (1830–1906). Born in Vrcovic, Bohemia, he was ordained in 1854, went to the United States in 1865, worked strenuously in the interest of his fellow Bohemians, found clergy for their scattered parishes, wrote editorials for the semi-weekly *Hlas,* was made a monsignor, and was pastor of St. John Nepomuk parish in St. Louis, Missouri, at the time of his death on July 4.

HESYCHIUS, ST. (1st century). *See* Caecilius, St.

HESYCHIUS, ST. (d. 120?), martyr. *See* Astius, St.

HESYCHIUS, ST. (d. 300?), martyr. He, SS. Hieron, Nicander, and thirty others died at Mitilene, Armenia, during the Diocletian persecution. F. D. Nov. 7.

HESYCHIUS, ST. (d. 302?), martyr. He was a Roman soldier put to death at Silistria, Bulgaria, during the Diocletian persecution. F. D. June 15.

HESYCHIUS, ST. (d. 302?), martyr. *See* Julius, St.

HESYCHIUS, ST. (d. 303?), martyr. A Roman soldier who embraced Christianity, he was put to death by drowning in the Orontes River. F. D. Nov. 18.

HESYCHIUS, ST. (d. 311?), martyr. *See* Faustus, St.

HESYCHIUS, ST. (d. 380?). He became a monk under St. Hilarion at Majuma, near Gaza, Palestine. He accompanied Hilarion to Egypt and, when the latter fled to find greater solitude than that of the desert, sought him for three years until he finally found him in Sicily. They then lived as recluses in Dalmatia and Cyprus. F. D. Oct. 3.

HESYCHIUS OF JERUSALEM (d. 433?). He was a presbyter (not a bishop) and wrote biblical exegesis and commentary. Some of the material once attributed to him is now said to be the work of Hesychius of Sinai, a Basilian monk who lived in a monastery on Mt. Sinai at an unknown date and who wrote some 200 ascetical maxims.

HETHOR, ST. (d. 870?), martyr. *See* Beocca, St.

HETTINGER, FRANZ (1819–1890), theologian. Born in Aschaffenburg, Germany, on Jan. 13, he studied there and at the German College in Rome, where he was ordained in 1843 and received his doctorate in 1845. He was at the seminary in Würzburg from 1847 to 1856 and then taught patrology at the university there until his death on Jan. 26. He served as rector in 1862–63 and 1867–68, went to Rome to help prepare for the Vatican Council, and in 1879 was made a monsignor. He wrote on Dante, socialism, the priesthood, travel sketches, theological and historical studies, and *Apologie des Christenthums*.

HEUDE, PIERRE (1836–1902), zoologist. Born in Fougères, France, on June 25, he became a Jesuit in 1856 and was ordained in 1867. The following year he was sent as a missionary to China. There he devoted himself to a study of botany and zoology and produced a series of studies of eastern Asiatic mammals based on wide travel in China, the Philippines, Japan, Indochina, and New Guinea which attracted world-wide attention. He founded a museum in Zi-ka-wei, near Shanghai, and died there on Jan. 3.

HEWETT, BL. JOHN (d. 1588), martyr. He was born in Yorkshire, England, educated at Cambridge, and ordained at Rheims in 1586. Sent on the English mission, where he used the names Savell and Weldon, he was arrested in 1587, banished, seized in the Netherlands, and returned to England. He was hanged at Mile End Green for being a priest, and beatified in 1929. F. D. Oct. 5.

HEWINS, WILLIAM ALBERT SAMUEL (1865–1931), economist. Born near Wolverhampton, England, on May 11, he took honors at Oxford, lectured to workers, and organized the London School of Economics at the request of Sidney Webb. He married Margaret Slater in 1892, was a director there from 1895 to 1903, taught economics at King's College, London, in 1897–1903, was a member of the senate of London University in 1900–3, and held the chair of economic history there in 1902–3. He then became secretary of the tariff commission (1903–22). He became a convert in 1914, served in parliament from 1912 to 1918, and wrote on imperialism and commerce, as well as an autobiography, *The Apologia of an Imperialist* (1920). He died in Chelsea, England, on Nov. 17.

HEWIT, AUGUSTINE FRANCIS (1820–1897). Born in Fairfield, Connecticut, on Nov. 27, he studied at Exeter and Amherst, tried the Congregational ministry, was an Anglican deacon in 1844, and was converted in 1846. Ordained in 1847, he taught in Charleston, began editing the works of Bishop England, and in 1849 became a Redemptorist. His mission work with Frs. Isaac Hecker and Francis Baker led him to follow them as the Institute of St. Paul the Apostle (Paulists) was founded in 1858. Fr. Hewit drafted the first constitution, helped to found the *Catholic World*, and became a leading apologist. He wrote *Problems of the Age*, *The King's Highway*, and a life of Fr. Baker. In 1888 he was chosen second su-perior general of the Paulists, and held that office until his death on July 3 in New York City.

HEYNLIN OF STEIN, JOHANN (1425?–1496), theologian. Of Swabian descent, he probably studied at Leipzig, Freiburg, and Paris. He joined the faculty at Basle in 1464, was dean of arts in 1465, took his doctorate in theology at Paris in 1466, was elected rector of that university in 1469, and taught theology at the Sorbonne. He was a major opponent of nominalism and an associate of the leaders of the realist school at Paris. In 1470 he established the first printing plant in Paris, with Fichet, went to Tübingen in 1478 and became rector, and later served at Baden-Baden and Berne. In 1487 he entered a Carthusian monastery and died in Basle, Switzerland, on Mar. 12.

HEYWOOD, ELLIS (d. 1578), novelist. The eldest son of Thomas More's friend, John Heywood, he fled from England to Flanders with his father during the Elizabethan persecution. He later was attached to the Jesuit college in Antwerp and died at Louvain. A romance in the form of a dialogue was published in Florence in 1556.

HEYWOOD, JASPER (1535–1598), translator. Son of John Heywood, he was born in London, was a page to Queen Elizabeth, and studied at Oxford. He became fellow of Merton College (1554) and of All Souls (1558), but resigned when he would not acknowledge the spiritual supremacy of Elizabeth. He was ordained on the Continent, became a Jesuit in Rome, and taught moral theology at Dillingen, Bavaria, until 1581. He then was sent to the English mission, succeeding Fr. Persons as superior. He was on his way to report to Rome when captured, imprisoned for seventeen months, and exiled. He taught at Dole, Burgundy, was sent to Rome in 1589 and then to Naples, and died there of insanity, believed brought on by ill treatment in prison. He made the first English translations of three tragedies by Seneca (*Troas*, *Thyestes*, and *Hercules Furens*) and wrote several poems, which appeared in *The Paradise of Dainty Devices*.

HEYWOOD, JOHN (1497?–1580?), dramatist. A friend of St. Thomas More, whose niece, Eliza Rastell, he married, he served as a choirboy in the royal chapel, was probably a member of Pembroke College, Oxford, and frequently performed for the royal court. He was a favorite of Queen Mary, for whom he wrote many poems, and after her death left England for religious reasons and settled in Mechlin, Brabant. He wrote several satiric comedies, among them *The Four P's*, *The Play of Love*, and *An Allegory of the Spider and the Fly*, some of which may have been produced at the theater at Thomas More's house in London.

HIBERNON, BL. ANDREW (1534–1602). Born in Alcantarilla, Spain, he became a Franciscan laybrother at Elche. His humility was exemplary, he converted many Moors, and enjoyed several supernatural gifts, and was beatified in 1791. F. D. Apr. 18.

HICKEY, ANTONY (1586–1641), theologian. Born in County Clare, Ireland, he studied at Louvain, became a Franciscan in 1607, and after his ordination taught theology at Louvain and Cologne. In 1619 he went to Rome, where he worked with Luke Wadding on a history of his order, prepared an edition of Duns Scotus, wrote treatises on the Immaculate Conception and St. Catherine of Siena, and served on papal committees to revise the breviary and to study the Eastern Church. He was elected definitor general of the Franciscans in 1639 and died in Rome on June 26.

HICKEY, THOMAS FRANCIS (1861–1940), archbishop. Born in Rochester, New York, on Feb. 4, he studied at St. Andrew's seminary there, St. John's, Fordham, and St. Joseph's in Troy, and was ordained in Rochester in 1884. He was a parish priest in Geneva and Moravia, was appointed chaplain of the state industrial school in 1895, rector of the Rochester cathedral in 1898, and became vicar general of that diocese in 1900. He was consecrated titular bishop of Berenice and coadjutor of Rochester in 1905, succeeded to the see in 1909, and was appointed assistant at the pontifical throne in 1925. He resigned his see in 1928, was appointed titular archbishop of Viminacium, and died on Dec. 10.

HICKEY, WILLIAM AUGUSTINE (1869–1933), bishop. Born in Worcester, Massachusetts, on May 13, he studied at Holy Cross, St. Sulpice, Paris, and St. John's seminary, Brighton, Massachusetts, and was ordained in Boston in 1893. He did parish work, was pastor of St. Aloysius, Gilbertville in 1903–17 and of St. John's, Clinton, in 1917–19, and was consecrated titular bishop of Claudiopolis and coadjutor of Providence, Rhode Island, in 1919. He succeeded to that see in 1921, and died in Providence on Oct. 4.

HIDULPHUS, ST. (d. 707?). Count of Hainault, he parted from his wife, St. Aye, by mutual consent and became a Benedictine monk at Lobbes, Belgium. F. D. June 23.

HIERAX, ST. (d. 165?), martyr. See Justin Martyr, St.

HIERO, ST. (d. 885), martyr. An Irish missioner, he was put to death in Holland. F. D. Aug. 17.

HIERON, ST. (d. 300?), martyr. See Hesychius, St.

HIERONIDES, ST. (d. 300?), martyr. An aged deacon, he and SS. Leontius and Serapion (brothers), Seleucus, Straton, and Valerian were thrown into the sea at Alexandria, Egypt, during the Diocletian persecution. F. D. Sept. 12.

HIERONYMUS OF WEERT, BL. (d. 1572), martyr. He was vicar of the Franciscan house in Gorkum, Holland, was seized with eight others of his community, and tortured, mutilated, and hanged by a Calvinist mob at Briel, Holland. He was beatified in 1867. F. D. July 9.

HIGDEN, RANULF (d. 1364). Born in Wessex, England, he became a Benedictine monk at St. Werburga's, Chester, in 1299. He wrote *Polychronicon*, a universal history, about 1350. It describes the geography of known countries, repeats most of the popular mediaeval legends, and was translated into English from Latin by John Trevisa in 1387; its later printings by William Caxton and Wynken de Worde continued its popularity. He may also have written biblical commentaries and didactic treatises.

HILARIA, ST., martyr. See Chrysanthus, St.; also, Claudius, St.

HILARINUS, ST. (d. 731), martyr. See Altigianus, St.

HILARION, ST. (d. 115), martyr. He and St. Proclus were put to death for their faith at Ancyra in Galatia during the reign of Trajan. F. D. July 12.

HILARION, ST. (291?–371?). Born in Gaza, Palestine, of pagan parents, he studied at Alexandria, where he was baptized at fifteen. He began a life of solitude near Majuma, Palestine, attracted great numbers of disciples, and founded several monasteries. At sixty-nine, to find greater solitude, he fled to Sicily, Dalmatia, and Cyprus. His biography was written by St. Jerome. F. D. Oct. 21.

HILARION, ST. (d. 304), martyr. See Saturninus, St.

HILARIUS OF SEXTEN. See Gatterer, Christian.

HILARY, ST. (d. 468), pope. Born in Sardinia, he became legate of Pope St. Leo the Great to the "Robber Council" of Ephesus in 449, but was unable to perform his duties because of the interference of Dioscorus, and barely escaped with his life. He succeeded Leo to the papacy on Nov. 19, 461, strengthened the Church in Spain and Gaul, warred on the doctrine of the Nestorians, and built a library. He died on Feb. 29. F. D. Feb. 28.

HILARY, ST. (d. 284?), martyr. He was bishop of Aquileia, Italy, and was slain during the persecution of Numerian. F. D. Mar. 16.

HILARY, ST. (d. 304?), martyr. See Valentine, St.

HILARY, ST. (d. 361), martyr. A monk, also known as Hilarinus, he was scourged to death in Arezzo, Tuscany, with St. Donatus, during the reign of Julian the Apostate. F. D. Aug. 7.

HILARY, ST. (d. 376). As bishop of Pavia he was active against the spread of Arianism in northern Italy. F. D. May 16.

HILARY, ST. (4th century). He was bishop of Toulouse, France. F. D. May 20.

HILARY, ST. (4th century). He was bishop of Carcassone, France. F. D. June 3.

HILARY, ST. (d. 535), bishop. Born in Mende, France, he was baptized as an adult, became a hermit on the banks of the Tarn, a monk at Lérins, and finally was made bishop of Mende. F. D. Oct. 25.

HILARY, ST. (d. 1045). A native of Matera, Italy, he became abbot of the Benedictine monastery of San Vincenzo, at Volturno in 1011. F. D. Nov. 21.

HILARY OF ARLES, ST. (d. 449), bishop. A relative of St. Honoratus, founder of Lérins, he gave up his wealth to join the monks of that abbey. He followed the elderly Honoratus to Arles when he became its bishop in 426 and was chosen to succeed him at twenty-nine. He became a great preacher, cared for the poor, redeemed captives, maintained high discipline, built monasteries, and attended several councils. It was because of his actions in deposing two Gallic bishops, Chelidonius and Projectus, that Pope St. Leo the Great wrote his careful definition of the duties and limitations of bishops; although Hilary was censured, he and the pope were reconciled. F. D. May 5.

HILARY OF GALEATA, ST. (476?–558). A native of Tuscany, he became a hermit at an early age, found himself surrounded by followers, and built a monastery on land given him by a grateful noble. His holiness was recognized even by Theodoric the Goth, who spared the settlement during his invasion. F. D. May 15.

HILARY OF POITIERS, ST. (315?–368), bishop and Doctor of the Church. Born at Poitiers, France, and probably a convert from paganism, he was not baptized until he was an adult. He studied scripture assiduously, led a virtuous married life, and sincerely sought to reject the bishopric of his native city, but finally accepted. His brilliant leadership edified Gaul, but he ran afoul of Emperor Constantius II, who sided with the Arians and demanded that the Western bishops come to Milan in 355 and repudiate St. Athanasius and his definition of faith. Many bishops bowed to the emperor's demands, but Hilary, who did not go to the meeting, was ordered banished to Phrygia. He studied the heresy at first hand, encouraged the clergy in the East to strong resistance, and so disturbed the emperor and his advisers by his activity that his banishment was ended in 360. In exile he wrote many Latin hymns and prose works, including his elaborate explanation of the Trinity, in which he was particularly clear in showing the divine nature of Christ to be consubstantial with that of the Father, and reality of three divine Persons, anticipating the conclusions of later councils of Chalcedon and Ephesus. He was admired in the writings of SS. Augustine, Jerome, Leo the Great, and Thomas Aquinas, was edited by Erasmus and Dom Coustant, and declared a Doctor of the Church by Pope Pius IX in 1851. He died in Poitiers, probably on Nov. 1. F. D. Jan. 14.

STEPHEN MC KENNA, intro., *The Trinity* (New York, Fathers of the Church, 1954).

HILDA, ST. (617–680). A native of Northumbria, England, she was baptized when thirteen by St. Paulinus with King Edwin of Northumbria, her father's uncle. When thirty-three, she entered a convent on the Wear River and shortly after became abbess of the double monastery at Hartlepool. She then transferred as abbess to Whitby and under her administration it became famous (it was the site of the Synod of 664). Though she defended the Celtic customs, she accepted the Roman usage for Whitby when the synod so decided. During the last seven years of her life she suffered from serious illness but continued her rule with such wisdom that her cult was recognized at once after her death. F. D. Nov. 17.

HILDEBERT, ST. (d. 752). He directed the Benedictine abbey of St. Peter in Ghent, Flanders, was slain by those who opposed his defense of statues, and was venerated locally as a martyr. F. D. Apr. 4.

HILDEBERT OF LAVARDIN (1056?–1133?), archbishop. Born near Montoir, France, he was at Le Mans cathedral school about 1085, archdeacon in 1091, and bishop of Le Mans in 1096. In 1099 he was accused of resisting King William II and taken to England, but released. In 1101 he went to Rome, exiled Henry of Lausanne for preaching heresy while substituting at Le Mans, and was imprisoned in 1111–13 when England and France again were at war. He attended the Lateran synod (1116) and that at Rheims (1119), the first Lateran Council (1123), and presided at a synod in Nantes (1128). After rebuilding his cathedral he was transferred to Tours as archbishop in 1125. He opposed King Louis VI over ecclesiastical rights, supported antipope Anacletus II at first, but was soon convinced by St. Bernard of the validity of the election of Innocent II. He wrote lives of Queen Radegundis and St. Hugh of Cluny, ascetical treatises, and poems (*De mysterio missae* and *De operibus sex dierum*), and was one of the major mediaeval hymn writers. He died on Dec. 8, 1133 (or 1134).

HILDEBOLD (d. 819). He became archbishop of Cologne, in 785, metropolitan over six other sees, and also was chancellor to Charlemagne.

HILDEBRAND, BL. (d. 1209), martyr. *See* Stephen, Bl.

HILDEBRAND, ST. (1119–1219), bishop. Born in Sorrivoli, Italy, he became provost of Rimini, spoke courageously against the evils in the district and almost lost his life as a result. He is the patron of Fossombrone, Italy, which was his see. He is also known as Aldebrandus. F. D. May 1.

HILDEBRAND. *See* Gregory VII, St., pope.

HILDEGARD, BL. (754?–783), empress. Believed to have been a daughter of a Swabian duke, she was seventeen when Charlemagne married her after he repudiated Queen Hermengard. One of their many children was Louis the Debonair. She died at Thionville, France, after a simple and charitable life. F. D. Apr. 30.

HILDEGARD, ST. (1098–1179), mystic. Born in Böckelheim, Germany, she was brought up by Bl. Jutta, who was living as a hermit at Diessenberg. The community which had grown up around Jutta came under Benedictine direction and when Hildegard was fifteen she became a nun there and in 1136 succeeded Jutta as prioress. She experienced visions and other supernatural manifestations, which she recorded on order of her confessor and the archbishop of Mainz. Dictated to a secretary during a ten-year period, they grew into her principal work, *Scivias*. In 1147, Pope Eugenius III examined the writings, discussed them with St. Bernard of Clairvaux, who believed them authentic, and authorized her to publish them. About 1147 she moved her community to Rupertsberg, near Bingen, where she built a large convent and wrote hymns and music for her nuns. Her correspondence was great, directed to popes, kings, clergy, and laity; she rebuked and warned regardless of rank. She was hailed as a saint and denounced as a sorceress, and Rupertsberg became a magnet for crowds. She traveled through the Rhineland, founded a house at Eibingen, addressed gatherings of clergy, and wrote considerable poetry and two scientific studies, on the human body and on natural history. In her own day she was called the "Sibyl of the Rhine." She died at Rupertsberg, Germany. F. D. Sept. 17.

HILDEGRIN, ST. (d. 827?), bishop. He worked with his younger brother, St. Ludger, in the Saxon mission field, became bishop of Châlons-sur-Marne about 802, and is said to have become a Benedictine monk, and later abbot, of Werden. F. D. June 21.

HILDEGUND, ST. (d. 1183). Daughter of Countess Hedwig of Lidtberg, she joined her mother and sister Gertrude in the Premonstratensian convent at Dunwald after the death of her husband. Eventually she was able to make over her estate near Cologne, Germany,

into a convent of prayer, of which she became prioress. Her daughter Hedwig and son Herman were both beatified. F. D. Feb. 6.

HILDEGUND (d. 1188). Orphaned at twelve while returning with her father from a pilgrimage to the Holy Land, she remained disguised as a page named Joseph, worked as a servant in Verona and Cologne, and died as a Cistercian novice at Schönau, Germany. Although such stories were usually mere fiction, hers is accepted as genuine. She has a popular cult and is honored on Apr. 20.

HILDELID, ST. *See* Hildelitha, St.

HILDELITHA, ST. (d. 717?). An Anglo-Saxon princess, she went to France and was veiled at either Faremoutier or Chelles. She returned to England at St. Erconwald's request to train his sister Ethelburga as abbess of a convent at Barking, Essex, which he had built for her. She succeeded Ethelburga as abbess, which office she held for the balance of her long life. She is also known as Hildelid. F. D. Sept. 3 (also, Mar. 24).

HILDEMAR, ST. (9th century). A Benedictine monk at Corbie, France, he was bishop of Beauvais from 821 until past 844. F. D. Dec. 10.

HILDEMAR, BL. (d. 1097?). A hermit at Arrouaise, France, he had so many followers that he established a monastery there, adopting the rule of the Augustinian canons regular. He was killed by an enemy who posed as a novice. F. D. Jan. 13.

HILDEMARCA, ST. (d. 670?). She was the first abbess of the convent attached to the church of the Holy Trinity in the Fécamp valley, France, which had been established by SS. Wandrille and Ouen. With 360 nuns under her direction, she was able to have the divine office sung perpetually by ordered relays. F. D. Oct. 25.

HILDUARD, ST. (d. 750?). A Benedictine and missionary bishop, he founded St. Peter's abbey at Dickelvenne, Flanders. F. D. Sept. 7.

HILDUIN, (d. 840). Of a well-known Frankish family, he was in 815 appointed abbot of St. Denis near Paris, where Hincmar was one of his pupils, and later of St. Germain-des-Prés, St. Médard, and St. Ouen. About 822, Emperor Louis the Pious appointed him chaplain and he went with Lothair to Rome in 824. He supported Louis' sons in their revolt against the emperor in 830 and at their defeat lost his abbeys and was banished, but regained the imperial favor and the abbacy of St. Denis in 831. He wrote a life of St. Dionysius and also helped complete the imperial *Annales*. He died on Nov. 22.

HILDULF, ST. (d. 707?), bishop. Born at Regensburg, Bavaria, he became a monk at the abbey of Maximinus at Trier, Germany, became a regionary bishop, retired to the Vosges mountains in 676, and founded the Benedictine monastery of Moyenmoutier. He was abbot there and, conjointly, of Bonmoutier. F. D. July 11.

HILGARD, EUGENE WOLDEMAR (1833–1916). Born in Zweibrücken, Bavaria, on Jan. 5, he was taken to Belleville, Illinois, at three, studied under his father, a judge, at Heidelberg, where he received his doctorate, and at Zurich and Freiberg. He became assistant state geologist of Mississippi in 1856, went to the Smithsonian Institution in Washington as chemist in 1858, and became a convert. He served the Confederacy and after the Civil War taught at the universities of Mississippi, Michigan, and California. His *Soils of Arid and Humid Regions* helped to end the "desert region" of mid-America; he introduced scientific methods of cotton culture; and his postwar work as geologist of Mississippi opened the way to later studies of the Gulf Coast plain. Columbia and the three universities where he taught gave him honorary degrees; he also was honored by Munich and Paris. He died on Jan. 8.

HILGERS, JOSEPH (1858–1918), theologian. Born in Kückshoven, Germany, on Sept. 9, he studied at the German College in Rome, was ordained in 1882, became a Jesuit in 1883, and taught for ten years. He wrote on the Index, indulgences, and the Virgin Mary as co-mediatrix. He died in Rome.

HILL, LAWRENCE (d. 1679) Servant of Thomas Tylden, chaplain to Queen Catherine, he was seized with his master during the time of the Titus Oates Plot and, though his alibi could not be broken, was convicted of alleged conspiracy in the murder of Sir Edmund Godfrey. He was executed at Tyburn, London, on Feb. 21.

HILLONIUS. *See* Tillo, St.

HILTON, WALTER (d. 1396), mystic. He was an Augustinian, head of the canons at their house in Thurgarton, Nottinghamshire, England, and wrote mystical treatises which drew on the outlook and expression of Richard of St. Victor, Richard Rolle, Dionysius the Areopagite, and SS. Bernard and Bonaventure. His priory was an active center which prepared many works in the vernacular, was especially interested in writings on scripture, and sent out many preachers through England to combat the Wyclifites. Hilton wrote *To a Devout Man in Temporal Estate, Treatise on Mixed Life,* and *Song of Angels;* his most popular work (its popularity was intensified when it was printed in 1494 by Wynkin de Worde) was *The Scale of Perfection* (sometimes called *Ladder of Perfection*), which offered suggestions on following a life of sanctity in the world. Hilton was later stationed at Beauvale

and may have become a Carthusian in his last years in London. He died on Mar. 24.

HILTRUDE, ST. (d. 790?). She lived as an anchorite in a cell near the Benedictine abbey of Liessies, near Cambrai, France, where her brother Gundrad was abbot. F. D. Sept. 27.

HIMERIUS (4th century). He was archbishop of Tarragona, Spain, and the recipient in 385 of the first known papal decretal, sent by Siricius and treating of baptism, the Lenten fast, apostasy, minor orders, and the celibacy of the clergy.

HIMERIUS, ST. (d. 560?), bishop. Born in Calabria, Italy, he established a reputation for austerity, and became bishop of Amelia. F. D. June 17.

HIMERIUS, ST. (d. 610?). He was a missionary monk in the Jura Mountains of Switzerland, in an area now named after him: Val St. Imier. F. D. Nov. 12.

HINCMAR (d. 879), bishop. Nephew of Hincmar of Rheims, he was appointed to the see of Laon in 858. He soon quarreled violently with his uncle and King Charles the Bald. Settled at the Diet of Pistres in 869, the dispute broke out anew and he was imprisoned. He placed his diocese under an interdict, which was set aside by his uncle, and in 871 he was deposed, imprisoned, and blinded (by the king's brother-in-law). His deposition was not confirmed until 875 by Pope John VIII, who in 878 restored some of his privileges and revenues.

HINCMAR OF RHEIMS (806–882), archbishop. Of a distinguished Frankish family, he studied at St. Denis under Hilduin and accompanied that abbot to the court of Louis the Pious in 822 as chaplain, into exile with him at Corbie, and back to St. Denis. In 840 he became counselor to King Charles the Bald and in 845 was appointed to the see of Rheims as successor to the deposed Ebbo. Emperor Lothair I supported Ebbo and for the next two decades the struggle between Hincmar and Ebbo persisted, centering around a group of priests ordained by Ebbo after 840 whom Hincmar forbade to exercise their priestly functions. When King Charles the Bald conferred the see of Bourges upon one of these priests, Wulfad, the conflict broke out anew, to be resolved at the Synod of Soissons in 866 when the clerics in question were restored. He also became embroiled with his fellow bishops over predestination during the controversy over the teaching of Gottschalk of Orbais on the subject. The synods of Quierzy (853), Valence (855), Savonières (859), and Toucy (860) opposed Hincmar's canons on predestination. In 858 he organized the successful resistance against the invasion of Louis the German, thus saving the crown of Charles the Bold, whom he supported. He also became embroiled in controversies with his suffragan, Rothadius of Soissons, whom he deposed in 862, but who was restored to his see by Pope Nicholas I in 865. He denounced Lothair II for putting aside his wife, Theutberga, and marrying Waldrade. He supported Charles as Lothair's successor when the latter died in 869, crowned him despite the opposition of Pope Adrian II, but broke with him when Charles went to Rome in 875 to be crowned emperor. At the synod in Ponthion (876) he refused to recognize Archbishop Ansegis of Sens as vicar apostolic of Gaul and Germany. He attended the synods of Troyes (878) and Fismes (881), and in 882 was forced to retreat to Epernay, France, where he died on Dec. 21, when his domain was invaded by the Norsemen. He published annals of the years 861–82 and on predestination.

HINDERER, ROMAN (1668–1744), missioner. Born in Reiningen, Alsace, on Sept. 21, he became a Jesuit in 1688 and in 1707 was sent to China, where he labored until his death at Shang-ho on Aug. 24. He worked with other Jesuits in preparing maps and charts of Chinese provinces for Emperor K'ang-hi.

HINGSTON, WILLIAM HALES (1829–1907), physician. Born in Hinchingbrook, Quebec, Canada, on June 29, he studied at the Sulpician college, Montreal, and at McGill and Edinburgh, and began medical practice in Montreal in 1853. In 1860 he became surgeon at the Hôtel Dieu, was twice elected mayor of Montreal, became professor of clinical surgery at Victoria University in 1882, held that chair when it became Laval University, was knighted in 1895 and twice decorated by the papacy, and served in the Canadian senate in 1896. He introduced new surgical techniques of continuing value, performed heroically during a cholera epidemic, and published a study of the climate of Canada. He died in Montreal on Feb. 19.

HINKSON, KATHARINE TYNAN (1861–1931), poet. Born in Clondalkin, Dublin, Ireland on Jan. 23 to Andrew and Elizabeth O'Reilly Tynan, farmers, she had a convent education and published her first book of poems, *Louise de la Vallière*, at her father's expense in 1885. She came to know Yeats, George Russell, and the Meynells as a result, and began a writing career which produced more than 100 popular novels. She married Henry Albert Hinkson (d. 1919), a Dublin lawyer and also a novelist, in 1893, and lived in England until their return to Ireland in 1916. She wrote a five-volume autobiography (1913–24), and her *Collected Poems* appeared in 1930. She died in Wimbledon, England, on Apr. 2.

HINSLEY, ARTHUR (1865–1943), cardinal. Born in Carlton, Yorkshire, England, on Aug.

25, he studied at Ushaw and London, and at the English College and Gregorian in Rome, and was ordained in 1893. He was a curate in Yorkshire until 1899, headmaster of a grammar school he set up at Bradford until 1904, and pastor at Sutton Park and Sydenham until 1917. He also taught at the seminary in Wonersh, was adviser to the bishop of Southwark, and aided Belgian refugees in World War I. He was named rector of the English College and a monsignor in 1917, reorganized the school, and became titular bishop of Sebastopolis in 1926. He was vicar apostolic to Africa in 1927, archbishop of Sardis from 1930 to 1934, returned to Rome in poor health, but in 1935 was made archbishop of Westminster. He made financial and educational changes in his archdiocese, inaugurated the Sword of the Spirit Movement for moral international order, was named cardinal-priest in 1937, and given honorary degrees by London and Oxford. He died in Buntingford, England, on Mar. 17.

HIPPARCHUS, ST. (d. 297), martyr. With Philotheus, he was a magistrate of Samosata on the Euphrates who had become a Christian. When Galerius, returning from a campaign against the Persians, ordered sacrifices made to the gods, he discovered the magistrates missing. He had them brought before him—together with five young men they had converted: Abibus, James, Lollian, Paregrus, and Romanus—and ordered them tortured over a two-month period and then crucified. The time of their martyrdom may have been about 308 in Syria. They are known as the Martyrs of Samosata. F. D. Dec. 9.

HIPPOLYTE. See Hélyot, Pierre.

HIPPOLYTUS, ST. (d. 235), martyr. A Roman priest, he was a major theological writer of the early Church, his chief work being *A Refutation of All the Heresies*. He denounced Pope St. Zepherinus for being overlenient with a Montanist named Praxeas, who also began Monarchianism in Rome. In 217 he attacked Pope St. Callistus I and allowed himself to be set up as an antipope. In 235 he was banished with Pope St. Pontian to Sardinia, during the persecution of Maximinus, and was brought back into the Church by Pontian. This ended the schism. Both died as martyrs on Sardinia. He is often confused with the Hippolytus of St. Laurence's Acts, which, completely unreliable, make him an officer converted by Laurence, martyred by being torn apart by wild horses. F. D. Aug. 13.

HIPPOLYTUS, ST. (d. 250?), martyr. A Syrian priest, converted from the Novatian heresy, he was put to death at Antioch. F. D. Jan. 30.

HIPPOLYTUS, ST. (d. 254?), martyr. *See* Eusebius, St.

HIPPOLYTUS, ST. (d. 775?). He was abbot of the Benedictine monastery of St. Claude, France, and bishop there. F. D. Nov. 28.

HIPPOLYTUS, ST., bishop and martyr. A bishop of Porto, who was drowned there for his faith at the time of Emperor Alexander, and honored on Aug. 22, he is not to be confused with the St. Hippolytus whose feast day is Aug. 13.

HIRENARCHUS, ST. (d. 305?), martyr. See Acacius, St.

HIRSCHER, JOHANN BAPTIST VON (1788–1865), theologian. Born on Jan. 20 in Alt-Ergarten, Germany, he studied in Weissenau and at Freiburg im Breisgau, was ordained in 1810, did parish work, and in 1814 taught philosophy in Ellwangen. From 1817 to 1837 he held the chair of moral and pastoral theology at Tübingen, then taught theology and catechetics at Freiburg until his retirement in 1862. He wrote widely on moral theology, homiletics, and catechetics, was bitterly attacked as unorthodox and as working for the establishment of a national church. He fought for Church liberties, played an important role in the religious revival of his country, was personally pious, but was not too well grounded in history and made too many printed errors. He died on Sept. 4.

HITTORP, MELCHIOR (1525?–1584), theologian. Born in Cologne, Germany, he studied theology there, was appointed canon, elected dean of St. Cunibert's in 1593, and published a collection of such earlier Christian authors as Alcuin, Isidore of Seville, and Rhabanus Maurus.

HLADNIK, FRANZ VON PAULA (1773–1844), botanist. Born in Idria, Austria, on Mar. 29, he was ordained in 1796, was a librarian, and became director of the normal school in Laibach in 1803 and prefect of the gymnasium there in 1807. He taught botany and natural history in the central school in Laibach, became noted for his research on the flora of Cariola, and developed a botanical garden of 600 local specimens. He died in Laibach, Carniola, Austria, on Nov. 25.

HLINKA, ANDREAS (1864–1938), diplomat. Born in Černova, Austria-Hungary, on Sept. 27, he studied at the local seminary and was ordained in 1889. He worked in Trich Slacich and Rosenberg parishes, which he made into model communities, was active in the movement toward Slovak independence, and was imprisoned in 1907–10 for his expressions of nationalism and of the value of Slovak culture. He translated the Old Testament into Slovak while in prison, served with the Red Cross during World War I, and in 1918 became editor of *Ludove Noviny* and leader of the People's party in the new Czechoslovak republic, serving as its chairman at Prague,

and working with it for twenty years in its attempt to gain complete autonomy for Slovakia. He became a monsignor, was director of the daily *Slovak* and weekly *Slovak Tyzsdennik*, president of Ludova Banka, and an active force in co-operative movements and welfare groups. He died in Buzomberck, Czechoslovakia, on Aug. 16.

HLOND, AUGUST (1881–1948), cardinal. Born in Breckowicz, Poland, on July 5, he studied at Don Bosco, Turin, and the Gregorian, Rome, became a Salesian, and was ordained in 1905. He directed institutes of his order in Poland, Austria, Hungary, and Germany, and became bishop of Silesia in 1922, archbishop of Gniezno and primate of Poland in 1926, and a cardinal in 1927. He worked with selected sociologists in changing farming and industrial conditions, ended forced ecclesiastical taxation and requested voluntary contributions in its place, and sought to prevent war between Germany and Poland. In 1939 he went into exile, first in Italy, then in France, where he was made a prisoner by the occupying Germans. On his return to Poland in 1945 he ran into communist opposition, particularly in 1945 after the government renounced the concordat with the Vatican. He also objected bitterly to his country's new borders. His nine-year struggle with totalitarianism ended with his death in Warsaw on Oct. 22.

HOBAN, MICHAEL JOHN (1853–1926), bishop. Born in Waterloo, New Jersey, on June 6, he studied at St. Francis Xavier, Holy Cross, St. Charles Borromeo seminary, Philadelphia, and the North American College, Rome, and was ordained in Rome in 1880. He did parish work in Scranton, Pennsylvania, and in 1896 was consecrated titular bishop of Halius and coadjutor of Scranton, and succeeded to that see in 1899. He died there on Nov. 13.

HOBBES, JOHN OLIVER. See Craigie, Pearl.

HOCCLEVE, THOMAS (1368?–1450?), poet. A clerk in the English privy seal office for twenty-four years, he seems from autobiographical references in his works to have been a wastrel in youth, to have reformed after his marriage in 1411, and to have been the recipient of a small pension. He probably knew Geoffrey Chaucer, whose work he imitated but in no way matched; he is more diffuse and without his master's poetic power. His long *De regimine principium* offers political and religious advice in the conventional manner; his *La male règle* has some lively passages; he is most sincere in *Ars sciendi mori*. His name is also spelled Occleve.

HOCK, JOHAN (1859–1936). Born in Hungary, he was ordained, was known for his preaching skill, entered politics, was a deputy of the Kossuth party for twenty years, and became president of the first national council after the revolution of 1918. He lived in Vienna, Paris, and the United States after the communist uprising of 1919, returned to Hungary in 1933, and was imprisoned for a year on the charge of having slandered Admiral Horthy. He died on Oct. 10.

HODGSON, BL. SIDNEY (d. 1591), martyr. *See* Genings, Bl. Edmund.

HOFBAUER, CLEMENT. *See* Clement Hofbauer, St.

HÖFEN, JOHANN VON (d. 1538). Also called Dantiscus, he became bishop of Culm, Poland, in 1530, succeeding Johannes Konopacki (given the see in 1508), who was incompetent and inactive in the face of rising Lutheranism. Bishop von Höfen, with the Dominicans, helped to preserve the faith there.

HOFER, ANDREAS (1767–1810). Born in St. Leonhard, the Tyrol, on Nov. 22, son of an innkeeper, he joined in the revolt against Bavaria and France in 1806. He soon became leader in the Tyrolese struggle, captured Innsbruck, and in 1809 drove out the French. Late that year he lost the last of three battles on Mt. Isel; his hiding place was betrayed to the French, and he was executed on Napoleon's orders in Mantua, Italy, on Feb. 20.

HÖFLER, KARL ADOLF KONSTANTIN VON (1811–1898), historian. Born in Memmingen, Bavaria, on Mar. 26, he studied at Munich and Göttingen and in Italy. On his return he became editor of the *Münchener Zeitung* and in 1838 professor of history at Munich. In 1847 he was removed from this position because of his published criticism of King Ludwig I's affair with Lola Montez. After serving as keeper of archives in Bamberg, he was in 1851 appointed professor of history at Prague, a position he held until his retirement in 1882. He became a member of the Bohemian diet in 1865 and a life member of the Austrian house of lords in 1872, when he was raised to the nobility. He wrote on the papacy, the historical relationship between Germans and Czechs, studies calling John Hus more anti-German than anti-papal, biographies of Boniface, Charles V, and Adrian VI, and poetical drama. He died in Prague, Bohemia, on Dec. 29.

HOGAN, ALOYSIUS J. (1891–1943), educator. Born in Philadelphia, on Aug. 5, he studied at St. Joseph's College there, became a Jesuit in 1908, and went to Woodstock, the Gregorian, and Cambridge, where he took his doctorate in literature in 1927. He taught at Boston College High School in 1915–20 and at St. Andrew's in 1927–30. He was president of Fordham University from 1930 to 1936, and

reorganized its graduate school and general faculty, and was dean of the Georgetown graduate school from then until his death in Washington, D. C., on Dec. 17.

HOGAN, EDMUND IGNATIUS (1831–1917), historian. Born near Cobh, Ireland, on Jan. 23, he became a Jesuit at sixteen and was ordained in 1856. He was associated with Eugene O'Curry and John O'Donovan in working for the revival of Gaelic, taught at Sacred Heart College, Limerick, from 1859 to 1865, and for twenty years held the chair of Irish at the Royal University of Ireland. He served on the council of the Royal Irish Academy, was a governor of the School of Irish Learning, and wrote dictionaries of Gaelic place names and plants, a history of the Jesuits in Ireland under the penal laws, an Irish grammar and a handbook of idioms, *The Irish People*, and an edition of *Vita Sancti Patricii*. He died in Dublin on Nov. 26.

HOGAN, JOHN BAPTIST (1829–1901). Born near Ennis, Clare, Ireland, on June 24, he went to France in 1844, studied in Bordeaux and at St. Sulpice, became a Sulpician in 1851, and was ordained in 1852. He taught dogmatic theology at St. Sulpice from 1853 to 1884, when he went to the United States as first president of St. John's seminary, Boston. In 1889 he became president of the graduate seminary at Catholic University, returning to St. John's in 1894. He died at St. Sulpice, on a trip to France, on Sept. 29.

HOGAN, JOHN JOSEPH (1829–1913), bishop. Born in Bruff, Limerick, Ireland, on May 10, he went to the United States, studied at the diocesan seminary in St. Louis, and was ordained there in 1852. He did missionary and pastoral work in northwestern Missouri until 1868, when he was consecrated bishop of St. Joseph, Missouri. He was transferred to Kansas City, Missouri, in 1880 as its first bishop, though he remained as administrator of St. Joseph as well until 1893, and reigned until his death in Kansas City on Feb. 21.

HOGARDE, MYLES (1505?–1556?), poet. Probably a small merchant in London, he was one of the more active opponents of the religious revolution in England. He appears to have gained a court appointment under Queen Mary. Numerous poems on religious and social themes exist.

HOGUET, JOSEPH PETER (1882–1946), physician. Born in Long Branch, New Jersey, on Aug. 16, he graduated from Harvard in 1904, studied medicine at Columbia, married Helen Gourd in 1912, served as an army surgeon in World War I, and returned to practice in New York City. He taught at Cornell Medical College, and was chief surgeon at the French Hospital until 1930, when he lost a hand in an automobile accident. He became president of the Medical Guild Foundation in 1940, supplied ambulances and equipment during World War II, was decorated by the French government, and was known for his philanthropy. He died in New York City on June 17.

HOHENBAUM VAN DER MEER, MORITZ (1718–1795), historian. Born in Spörl, near Belgrade, Serbia, he studied at Rheinau, Switzerland, became a Benedictine, and was ordained in 1741. He served as prior from 1758 to 1774, was keeper of the archives for the last thirty-six years of his life, and secretary of the Swiss Benedictines from 1776 to his death. He wrote profusely, but few of his treatises have been published. He died at Rheinau on Dec. 18.

HOHENHEIM, THEOPHRASTUS BOMBASTUS VON. *See* Paracelsus, Philippus Aureolus.

HOLBEIN, HANS (1460?–1524), painter. Born in Augsburg, Bavaria, he may have studied under Martin Schongauer. He lived in Ulm in 1499, Frankfort in 1501, and in Basle and Alsace. He displayed talent early and patterned his work on that of Memling, Van der Weyden, and the Van Eycks. Italian Renaissance influences are apparent in later work and he became leader of a new movement in German art, developed further by his son, Hans the Younger. His paintings are characterized by naturalness of figure, splendor of coloring, dramatic power, and the use of architectural backgrounds. Among his most famous are the altarpieces of St. Sebastian in Munich and St. Paul in Augsburg, *Madonna Enthroned* and *Madonna and Child* in Nuremberg, *Conception* in Augsburg, and many portraits. He died in Isenheim monastery in Alsace.

HOLDEN, HENRY (1596–1662). Born in Lancashire, England, he studied at Douai and Paris, taught at the Sorbonne after ordination, and was a grand vicar of the archbishop of Paris. In 1631 he became embroiled on the side of the seculars in their dispute with the order priests, who thought it inadvisable to have a bishop in England, and defended his position in Rome. In 1655 he defended the writings of his friend Thomas White, alias Blackloe, but persuaded him to retract his teachings when they were condemned by Rome. In 1661 he became superior of the Blue Nuns in Paris. He wrote many treatises on religious controversy.

HOLFORD, BL. THOMAS (d. 1588), martyr. Son of a Protestant minister, he was born in Aston, Cheshire, England, and became a teacher in Herefordshire. After his conversion he went to Rheims, was ordained in 1583, returned to Cheshire, where he served under the names of Acton and Bude, was seized, and hanged for being a priest at Clerkenwell dur-

ing the Elizabethan persecution. He was beatified in 1929. F. D. Aug. 28.

HOLLAND, HUGH (1563?–1633), poet. Born in Denbigh, Wales, and educated at Westminster and Cambridge, he became a convert while traveling in Europe; in England he was frequently fined for recusancy during the last years of Elizabeth I's reign. Under James I he fared better, acknowledged Lady Coke, wife of Sir Edward, as his patron, and published poems in numerous miscellanies as well as completing an unpublished history of the previous reign.

HOLLAND, JOHN PHILIP (1840–1914), inventor. Born in Liscanor, Clare, Ireland, on Feb. 29, he studied at Ennistymon and Limerick, taught in Ireland from 1858 to 1872, then went to the United States, where he taught in a Paterson, New Jersey, parochial school and married Margaret Foley. While in Ireland he had developed plans for a submarine, which many hoped would end the supremacy of the British fleet and aid Irish independence, but he gave up active experimentation in 1870 for lack of funds. In Paterson, with money given by the Fenians, he built a fourteen-foot undersea craft, operated by a steam engine and a crew of one, tested it in the Passaic River in 1878, but it ran aground. A thirty-one-foot model of nineteen tons, with a combustion engine and a crew of three, was launched in 1881, also built with Irish republican funds. This, the *Fenian Ram*, was frequently tested in New York harbor, dived to sixty feet, and illustrated the major principles of the modern submarine. Holland had offered his plans to the United States navy in 1875 but was rebuffed; with the help of Admiral Kimball he gained some attention after 1888, but funds were not made available until 1895. He then began work on the $150,000 *Plunger*, but had his construction ideas vetoed by Adm. Melville, and the craft was a failure. With his own money he then built the *Holland*, launched in 1898, fifty-three feet long and of seventy-five tons. The government ordered six more in 1900 and others were purchased by Great Britain, Russia, and Japan. In 1904 he designed a successful device to allow crew members to escape from under water. Holland died in Newark, New Jersey, on Aug. 12.

HOLLAND, ROBERT EMMET (1892–1946), editor. Born in Olympia, Washington, on Feb. 21, he studied in Washington, D.C., became a Jesuit in 1908, and was ordained in 1923. He taught English and classical literature at high schools in Boston, Buffalo, and Philadelphia, served in the Philippine missions, and in 1928–32 was principal of Canisius High School, Buffalo, New York. He then became director of the Fordham University Press, producing books of distinctive design. His own work includes several juveniles, a biography of St. John Francis Regis, *The Song of Tekakwitha* (a poem on the saintly Indian Mohawk maiden, written in the meter of Longfellow's *Hiawatha*), and an account of the formal presentation of her case for possible canonization. He died in New York City on Aug. 2.

HOLLAND, BL. THOMAS (1600–1642), martyr. Born in Sutton, Lancashire, England, he was educated at St. Omer and Valladolid, joined the Jesuits in 1624, and was sent on the English mission (where he used the names Sanderson and Hammond as aliases) in 1635. He served, despite ill health, for seven years before he was arrested in London, convicted of being a priest, and hanged, drawn, and quartered at Tyburn. He was beatified in 1929. F. D. Dec. 12.

HOLSTE, LUCAS (1596–1661), scholar. Born in Hamburg, Germany, he studied there and in Leyden, traveled in Italy and England, and in 1624 became a librarian in Paris. In 1626 he became a convert, went to Rome in 1627 and joined the household of Cardinal Barberini, and in 1636 was his librarian. He served on diplomatic missions for several popes, and Pope Innocent X appointed him librarian of the Vatican. Among his publications were editions of Arrian, Democritus, Demophilus, and Porphyry, biographies of martyrs, and *Codex regularum monasticarum* (1661). He died in Rome on Feb. 2.

HOLTEI, KARL VON (1798–1880), author. Born in Breslau, Germany, he was a farmer and lawyer, fell in love with the theater, married Luise Rogée, an actress, and moved to Berlin. After her death in 1825 he married another actress, Julie Holzbecher, gave dramatic readings, introduced vaudeville, and in 1837 was director of the German theater in Riga. Among his best-known works are the plays *Der alte Feldherr* and *Lenore* (1829); the novels *Christian Lammfell* (1853) and *Der letzte Komödiant* (1863); *Schlesische Gedicht* (1830), poems in Silesian dialect; and his autobiography, *Vierzig Jahre*. He died in Breslau on Feb. 12.

HOLYMAN, JOHN (d. 1558). He was the first and only bishop of Bristol, England, recognized by the papacy, and was appointed by Cardinal Pole sometime after 1554 to replace Paul Bush, who had been appointed in 1542 by Cranmer, married, and fallen into error during Queen Mary's reign.

HOLYWOOD, CHRISTOPHER (1559–1626). Born in Artane, Dublin, Ireland, he studied at Padua, became a Jesuit in 1579, and taught theology and scripture in France and Italy. Sent to Ireland in 1598, he was arrested, imprisoned, and deported. He returned to Ireland in 1604, became superior of the Jesuits there, established five active centers, and helped to keep Catholicism alive during a period of plots and persecution. He died on Sept. 4.

HOLYWOOD, JOHN (d. 1256), astronomer. Born in the British Isles, he studied at Oxford, moved to France, and taught mathematics and astronomy. He wrote *De sphaera mundi*, which became a standard university text until the Copernican theory was accepted in the seventeenth century, and mathematical texts, and is often referred to under the Latinized version of his name, Joannes de Sacrobosco.

HOLZHAUSER, BARTHOLOMEW (1613–1658), founder. Born in Laugna, Bavaria, on Aug. 24, he studied at Neuberg and Ingolstadt and was ordained in 1639. While pastor at Tittmoning he founded the Bartholomites (United Brethren), a congregation of secular priests who were to lead an apostolic life in community, devoted to undoing the damages of the Thirty Years' War. The group was encouraged by Pope Innocent X, though not formally approved until 1680, by Innocent XI. In 1642 he became pastor in Leoggenthal, in the Tyrol, founded seminaries for his order, went to Bingen in 1655, and was named dean of the Angesheim district in 1657. He wrote instructions for his congregation, on humility, a commentary on the Apocalypse, and ten visions. He died on May 20.

HOMAN, HELEN WALKER (1893–1961), author. Born in Helena, Montana, on Oct. 17, she studied at Notre Dame of Maryland and Pensionat Cyrano in Switzerland, and law at New York University Law School, engaged in journalism, and was managing editor of the *Forum* in 1920–22 and assistant editor of the *Commonweal* in 1924–27. She married Dominique A. Homan in 1927, was admitted to the New York bar in 1940, served as correspondent for the National Catholic Welfare Conference News Service during World War II, and then devoted herself to teaching and writing. Among her books are *By Post to the Apostles* (1933), *Letters to the Martyrs* (1951), *Star of Jacob* (1953), *Knights of Christ* (1957), and several juveniles. She died in New York City on Apr. 7.

HOMBELINA, BL. *See* Humbeline, Bl.

HOMOBONUS, ST. (d. 1197). Son of a merchant in Cremona, Lombardy, he followed in his father's footsteps and became a merchant known for his integrity and charity. He is patron of tailors and clothworkers and was canonized two years after his death by Pope Innocent II. F. D. Nov. 13.

HONESTUS, ST. (d. 270), martyr. Born in Nîmes, Gaul, he was sent to Spain by St. Saturninus as a missionary priest, and was put to death for his faith at Pampeluna, Navarre. F. D. Feb. 16.

HONORATA, ST. (d. 500?). She was a nun at a convent in Pavia, Italy, was kidnaped by King Odoacer of the Heruli, and ransomed by her brother St. Epiphanius, bishop of the city. F. D. Jan. 11.

HONORATUS, ST. (3rd century). Born in Navarre, Spain, he succeeded St. Saturninus as bishop of Toulouse, Gaul. F. D. Dec. 21.

HONORATUS, ST. (d. 303?), martyr. He is one of the so-called "twelve brothers" who, though probably not related, were natives of Hadrumetum, Africa, where they were arrested during the reign of Maximian. After being tortured at Carthage they were sent to Italy. Arontius, Honoratus, Fortunatus, and Savinian were beheaded at Potenza on Aug. 27; Felix, Januarius, and Septimus, at Venosa on Aug. 28; Repositus, Sator, and Vitalis, at Velleiano on Aug. 29; Donatus and another Felix, at Sentiano on Sept. 1. F. D. Sept. 1.

HONORATUS, ST. (330?–415). Born in Vercelli, Italy, he was a disciple of St. Eusebius, went with the latter into exile at Scythopolis in 355, and roamed with him through northern Africa and Italy. He was elected bishop in 396 and gave the last rites to St. Ambrose. F. D. Oct. 28.

HONORATUS, ST. (d. 429), bishop. A convert from Roman paganism while being brought up in Gaul, he fled from his consular father's anger and eventually founded the monastery of Lérins about 400. Some three years before his death he was appointed bishop of Arles, Gaul, but exhausted himself by his numerous duties. His life has been recorded by St. Hilary. F. D. Jan. 16.

HONORATUS, ST. (d. 570). He was appointed bishop of Milan, Italy, in 567, suffered much from Arianism and Lombard invaders, and died in exile. F. D. Feb. 8.

HONORATUS, ST. (6th century), abbot. He was founder and first abbot of the monastery of Fondi, Italy. F. D. Jan. 16.

HONORATUS, ST. (d. 600?). Bishop of Amiens, France, he was born in Port-le-Grand, and is the patron of bakers and confectioners. F. D. May 16.

HONORATUS, ST., martyr. *See* Demetrius, St.

HONORATUS A SANCTA MARIA. *See* Vauxelles, Blaise.

HONORIUS I (d. 638), pope. A native of Campania, Italy, he became pope on Oct. 27 (or Nov. 3), 625. He restored churches and other buildings in Rome, repaired the aqueduct of Trajan, aided the Church in Spain, sent St. Birinus to West Saxony, helped King Edwin of Northumbria, and worked closely with Irish leaders so that southern Ireland willingly accepted the Roman liturgy in 633. He is particu-

larly remembered for his part in the Monothelite heresy. In reply to a letter from Sergius, patriarch of Constantinople, he agreed to the latter's suggestion for reuniting dissident elements by accepting the formula that Christ, while having both a divine and a human nature, had but one "activity" or "operation," and seemingly dismissing the quarrel over terms as no more than a question of semantics. When Emperor Heraclius issued Sergius' *Ecthesis* (Exposition) in 638, seeds of a long-lasting struggle were sown. Honorius had died on Oct. 12, but the quarrel was carried on by SS. Sophronius (who had raised objections earlier to Sergius) and Maximus of Constantinople. The language of Honorius' private letter had not denied Christ's human and divine wills, but the papal language was not precise and was easily misunderstood by the Monophysites and others. Honorius was condemned in 680 by the sixth General Council as confirming the heresy and the situation was also discussed at great length during the nineteenth-century attacks on papal infallibility.

HONORIUS II (d. 1130), pope. Born at an unknown date in Fiagnano, Italy, of poor parents, Lamberto Scannabecchi was successively archdeacon of Bologna, canon at the Lateran, cardinal-priest of Santa Prassede, and in 1117 cardinal-bishop of Ostia and Velletri. He accompanied Pope Gelasius II in the latter's flight to France, was sent as legate to Germany in 1119, and in 1122 was successful in reconciling Emperor Henry V, whom Pope Callistus II had excommunicated in 1120. He was elected pope on Dec. 15, 1124, and consecrated on Dec. 21, and was faced by an antipope Celestine II, Cardinal Teobaldo Boccadipecora, who had been elected by the Leoni faction but who resigned a few days later. Honorius was instrumental in having Lothair elected to succeed Henry V of Germany; in return, Lothair acknowledged the supremacy of the pope, finally ending the investiture dispute. Honorius successfully ended Henry I's objections to papal legates in England, restored order in Cluny, Monte Cassino, and Denmark, and approved the formation of the Premonstratensian order. He took up arms against Roger of Sicily, but was obliged to settle the matter in Roger's favor in 1128 and to cede Apulia to him. He died in Rome on Feb. 13.

HONORIUS II (d. 1072), antipope. Cadalus, born of a noble Veronese family, became bishop of Parma, Italy, and on Oct. 28, 1061, was elected as pope by a rebellious body of bishops convened at Basle by Empress Agnes, acting as regent for her son Henry IV. In the spring of 1062, Cadalus marched on Rome, defeated the forces of Pope Alexander II, but was himself defeated by Duke Godfrey of Tuscany and forced to retire to Parma. Archbishop Anno of Cologne replaced Agnes as regent and investigated and approved the election of Pope Alexander. Although Cadalus was excommunicated, he again marched on Rome and occupied Sant' Angelo, and refused to accept the fact of his deposition. He died in Parma.

HONORIUS III (d. 1227), pope. Cencio Savelli was born in Rome, became canon of Santa Maria Maggiore, papal chamberlain in 1188 (in which position he compiled *Liber censuum romanae ecclesiae*, a list of papal revenues), cardinal-deacon in 1193, cardinal-priest, and tutor of the future Emperor Frederick II in 1196. He was elected pope on July 18, 1216, crowned in Rome on Aug. 24, and turned his energies to launching the crusade which had been voted at the Lateran Council of 1215. He urged Frederick to fulfill his oath to go on crusade, agreed to the election of the latter's son Henry as king of the Romans, though this imperiled the papal dominions, and crowned Frederick emperor in 1220. The crusade, gathering excessive numbers of persons unfit to bear arms, captured Damietta in Egypt, but proved a dismal failure. Honorius convinced Louis VIII to launch a crusade against the Albigensians in France in 1226 and undertook a crusade against the Moors in 1218–19. Throughout his pontificate he labored to establish peace in Europe and settled many disputes between Italian cities: Pisa and Genoa in 1217; Milan and Cremona, in 1218; Bologna and Pistoia, in 1219, among others. In England he forced the barons to break off negotiations with Louis, son of King Philip of France, and return their allegiance to young Henry III. He ended the rebellion of Béla IV against his father, King Andrew II of Hungary, and also settled disputes in Spain, Portugal, and Scandinavia. He approved the rule of St. Dominic in 1216 and in 1223 that of St. Francis (to whom, according to many authorities, he had granted the Portiuncula indulgence in 1216), and that of the Carmelites in 1226. He wrote biographies of Celestine III, Gregory VII, sermons, historically important letters, and a collection of decretals. He died in Rome on Mar. 18.

HONORIUS IV (1210?–1287), pope. Giacomo Savelli, grandnephew of Pope Honorius III, was born in Rome, of a wealthy family, studied at Paris, was created cardinal-deacon in 1261, papal prefect in Tuscany, and was one of the six cardinals who elected Gregory X pope by compromise in 1271 and accompanied him to the fourteenth General Council at Lyons in 1276. On Apr. 2, 1285, he was unanimously elected pope on the first ballot, ordained on May 19, and crowned pope the next day. His pontificate was plagued by the political difficulties in Sicily he had inherited from Pope Martin IV; these were still unsettled at his death, though he was successful in securing recognition of his authority in the rest of the papal domain. His relations with Rudolf of Hapsburg were good, and Edward I of England helped to lessen papal hostility toward Alfonso of Spain. Honorius approved the Williamites, aided the Carmelites and Augustinian Hermits, endowed chairs of oriental languages at Paris, and condemned the Apostolici, followers of Gerard Segarelli of Parma. He died in Rome on Apr. 3.

HONORIUS, ST. (d. 300?), martyr. *See* Eutychius, St.

HONORIUS, ST. (d. 483?), martyr. *See* Appian, St.

HONORIUS, ST. (d. 586?). He was called from his seclusion as a hermit and chosen bishop of Brescia, Italy, in 577. F. D. Apr. 24.

HONORIUS, ST. (d. 653), archbishop. A Roman who became a Benedictine monk, he was sent by St. Gregory the Great to convert the English and succeeded St. Justus as archbishop of Canterbury in 627. He sent St. Felix, whom he consecrated, to convert the East Angles, and appointed the first English-born bishop, St. Ithamar of Kent, as successor to St. Paulinus at Rochester. F.D. Sept. 30.

HONORIUS, ST. (d. 1250). A wealthy French cattle dealer, he was robbed by his servants during an absence, who slew him on his return to Parthenay, Poitou. He was canonized in 1444. F. D. Jan. 9.

HONORIUS, ST., martyr. *See* Demetrius, St.

HONORIUS OF AUTUN (12th century), theologian. He is believed to have been a native of Autun, Burgundy, and a priest (though he is sometimes associated with Augst, near Basle, or Augsburg, Swabia, or listed as an Augustinian). Of his thirty-eight known works, most important are: *Imago mundi, De philosophia mundi, Clavis physicae* (a compilation from John Scotus Eriugena), treatises on the soul, the Eucharist, clerical celibacy, and biblical commentary.

HONTHEIM, JOHANN NIKOLAUS VON (1701–1790), bishop. Born in Trier, Germany, on Jan. 27, he studied at Louvain and Leyden, and was ordained in Rome in 1728. He became a canon in Trier, taught at its university, and in 1738–47 was president of the seminary at Coblenz. In 1748 he was appointed dean of St. Simeon, auxiliary bishop, vicar general, and vice-chancellor of the university of Trier. In 1763, under the pseudonym of Justinus Febronius, he published *De statu ecclesiae et legitima potestate romani pontifiis*, which aroused great controversy. In it he held that the supremacy of the Church resided in the whole body of the faithful, that general councils are superior to the pope, that all bishops have equal rights with the pope and are supreme in their dioceses, and that secular authority should be appealed to in the settling of ecclesiastical disputes. The book was condemned in 1764 by Pope Clement XIII, who required the German episcopacy to suppress it. The elector of Trier was one of those who complied, but no action was taken against Hontheim until 1778, nor did he recant completely until 1788. Febronianism provided the basis and impetus for the movement toward establishing national churches and did immeasurable damage to the Church, especially in Germanic areas, in the eighteenth and nineteenth centuries, and led to Josephinism. Hontheim also wrote histories of Trier. He died in Montquintin, Luxembourg, on Sept. 2.

HOOGSTRATEN, JAKOB VAN (1460?–1527), theologian. Born in Hoogstraten, Belgium, he studied at Louvain, became a Dominican, and was ordained in 1496. He taught theology in the Dominican college in Cologne in 1498, was prior in Antwerp in 1500, and became regent of studies and professor of theology at Cologne in 1507. He published a defense of the mendicant orders and theological studies, was named prior in Cologne, inquisitor general of that city, Mainz, and Trier, and condemned the visiting Italian jurist, Pietro Tomasi. He also became involved in a controversy with Jacob Reuchlin, condemned him severely, burned his *Augenspiegel*, and became violently anti-Jewish. Overruled by the bishop of Speyer in 1514, he was deprived of his positions, but was reinstated by Pope Leo X in 1520. He died in Cologne, Germany, on Jan. 24.

HOOKE, LUKE JOSEPH (1716–1796), theologian. Born in Dublin, he studied in Paris, graduated from the Sorbonne, and was given the chair of theology in 1742. He was forced out in 1742 after he signed the error-filled thesis of Abbé Jean Martin de Prades. He was pardoned by Pope Benedict XIV in 1754 when he applied for reappointment, but opposed by Archbishop de Beaumont. Louis XV gave him a pension and in 1763 he was appointed to the chair of Hebrew. He was one of the censors who condemned Rousseau's *Émile*, became curator of the Mazarin Library, and was dismissed in 1791 when he refused to take the oath demanded of clerics, and retired to St. Cloud, France, where he died on Apr. 16. He wrote many treatises, including *Religionis naturalis et revelatae principia* (1752), important as a pioneering approach to modern apologetics.

HOPE, ST. *See* Faith, St.

HOPE, JAMES FITZALAN (1870–1949). Born in London on Dec. 11 to James Hope-Scott and Lady Victoria FitzAlan-Howard, he was educated at the Oratory, Birmingham, though he did not take his degree, and at Oxford. His father died in 1873 and he took the name Hope and became secretary to his uncle, the fifteenth duke of Norfolk. He was a Conservative in parliament in 1900–6 and 1908–29. He held a minor treasury position (1916–19), was secretary to the ministry of munitions (1919–21), and chairman of ways and means and deputy speaker (except for a year when the Labor party was in the majority) until 1929. In 1932 he was made first Baron Rankeillour of Buxted, served on a committee to aid Indian reform, and spoke in the House of Lords on the Indian question and in behalf of Catholic schools. He married Mabel Riddell in 1892; she died in 1938 and in 1941 he married Lady Beatrice Kerr-Clark. He died in London on Feb. 14. His eldest son, Arthur (1897–1958), succeeded to the title.

HOPE-SCOTT, JAMES ROBERT (1812–1873), jurist. Born in Great Marlow, Berkshire, England, on July 15, son of Sir Alexander Hope, commandant at Sandhurst, he studied at Eton and Oxford, and was called to the bar in 1838. After some time in Italy he became associated with Newman's Oxford Movement in publishing tracts in 1841. He married Charlotte Lockhart, granddaughter of Sir Walter Scott, in 1847 and became a convert in 1851. He defended Newman in 1852 in the libel suit Achilli brought against him and helped Newman gain the rectorship of the Catholic University of Dublin. He became quite wealthy from his law practice and contributed to many charities. His wife died in 1858; three years later he married Lady Victoria Howard, who died in 1870. He then retired, a victim of melancholia, and died in London on Apr. 29.

HÔPITAL, GUILLAUME FRANÇOIS ANTOINE DE L' (1661–1704), mathematician. Marquis de Ste. Masme and Count d' Entremont, he was born in Paris, served in the army until forced to resign because of poor eyesight, turned to the study of mathematics, wrote several studies, and became an expert on methods of differential calculus. He died in Paris on Feb. 2.

HOPKINS, GERARD MANLEY (1844–1889), poet. Born in Stratford, England, on July 28, he attended Highgate and Oxford, where he was a student of Walter Pater, became a convert in 1866, studied briefly at Birmingham oratory with John Henry Newman, and in 1868 became a Jesuit. After his ordination in 1877 he worked in the Liverpool slums, preached in London, was stationed at St. Aloysius, Oxford, and in 1884 went to Dublin as fellow of the Royal University and examiner in classics. He had won school prizes for his poems, wrote nothing from his entrance into the Jesuits until 1875, when he produced *The Wreck of the Deutschland*, and then composed a thin volume of deeply religious, sometimes mystical, and always nature-touched poems. Letters to the English poet laureate, Robert Bridges, and others, and prose notebooks were published posthumously, as were the poems which Bridges prepared with an introduction. Hopkins' work avoided ordinary metrical laws and poetic diction, took short cuts in grammar, and reveals a complex, highly patterned, individual style. He returned to the Anglo-Saxon meter for what he called "sprung rhythm," a set series of accented syllables per line and a varying number of unaccented ones. His influence on modern poetry has been widespread. He died in Dublin on June 8.

NORMAN WEYAND, ed., *Immortal Diamond* (New York, Sheed, 1949).

HORMISDAS, ST. (d. 523), pope. Born in Frosinone, Latium, a widower and deacon, he was made pope on July 20, 514, and devoted himself to successfully ending the Monophysite schism of Acacius. He drew up a *Formula* in 519 which was accepted by Emperor Justin and signed by most bishops of the Eastern Church; it has ever since been a rule of faith and was cited by the Vatican Council as evidence of early acceptance of papal primacy. F. D. Aug. 6.

HORMISDAS, ST. (d. 420), martyr. Son of the governor of a Persian province, he refused to renounce Christianity and was deprived of his possessions by King Varannes (also called Bahram), who reduced him to camel tender. How and where he was martyred is unknown. F. D. Aug. 8.

HORNE, BL. WILLIAM (d. 1540), martyr. *See* Beer, Bl. Richard.

HORNER, NICHOLAS (d. 1590), martyr. Born in Grantley, Yorkshire, England, he became a tailor in London, was arrested for harboring priests, imprisoned so long that he lost a leg through blood poisoning, was released, then rearrested and for refusing to acknowledge the queen's supremacy in matters of religion was hanged, drawn, and quartered at Smithfield on Mar. 4.

HORNYOLD, JOHN JOSEPH (1706–1778), bishop. Born in Worcestershire, England, on Feb. 19, he went to Douai in 1728, was ordained and sent back to England, and worked near Grantham. In 1739 he was appointed chaplain in Longbirch, Staffordshire, where he wrote *The Decalogue Explained* (1744). He also wrote *The Sacraments Explained* and a commentary on the Creed. In 1751 he was named coadjutor to Bishop Stoner, whom he succeeded as vicar apostolic of the Midland district from 1756 to 1767. He helped to direct Sedgley Park School after 1768 and died in Longbirch, Staffordshire, England, on Dec. 26.

HORSTMANN, JOHN FREDERICK IGNATIUS (1840–1908), bishop. Born in Philadelphia on Dec. 16, he studied at St. Joseph's College and St. Charles Borromeo seminary there, and the North American College, Rome, where he was ordained in 1865 and received his doctorate in divinity in 1866. He taught at St. Charles for the next eleven years, was appointed rector of St. Mary's in Philadelphia, and in 1885 became chancellor of that diocese. He was consecrated bishop of Cleveland in 1892, founded St. John's College in Cleveland in 1898, established the first diocesan missionary band in the United States, and died in Canton, Ohio, on May 13.

HORTULANUS, ST. (5th century), bishop. *See* Crescens, St.

HOSANNA OF MANTUA. *See* Andreasi, Bl. Hosanna.

HOSIUS OF CORDOVA (256?–358?). Named bishop of Cordova, Spain, in 295, he was a leader in the struggle against Arianism and a warm defender of Athanasius. He was Constantine's adviser in his dealings with the Donatists in 313–24 and acted for him on a mission to Arius and Alexander. He presided at the Council of Nicaea, perhaps as the pope's representative, in 325 and at the Council of Sardica in 343. About 353 he was summoned from Spain to Rome by Constantius II, who tried unsuccessfully to get him to support the Arians. Later in that year he was summoned to Sirmium and under pressure signed the second and heterodox Sirmian formula. It is believed that he recanted on his deathbed.

HOSIUS, STANISLAUS (1504–1579), cardinal. Born of German parents in Cracow, Poland, on May 5, he studied at its university and became secretary to Bishop Peter Tomicki, who paid for his further studies at Padua and Bologna. He returned in 1534 as secretary to the chancery, became secretary to King Sigismund I in 1538, was ordained in 1543, and in 1549 was named bishop of Culm. In 1550, Pope Julius III made him inquisitor of Pomerania; in 1551 he was transferred as bishop to Ermland; in 1558 he went to Rome as a member of the curia. He was sent to Vienna in 1559 to arrange for the reopening of the Council of Trent by Emperor Ferdinand I and also helped to bring the latter's son Maximilian back into the Church. Hosius was made a cardinal in 1561, was one of the five papal legates who presided at the council's start in 1562, then returned to Ermland to repair religious and educational damage in a wide area which had suffered as the result of the religious laxness of Sigismund II. In 1566 the cardinal was named papal legate for Poland; he spent his last ten years in Rome as adviser to the popes and as the voice of Poland in the curia. He wrote the widely translated *Confessio fidei catholicae christianae* (1533–

57), *De expresso verbo Dei*, and *De oppresso verbo Dei*, a treatise on St. John Chrysostom, a biography of his patron, Bishop Tomicki, and studies of the Eucharist and of papal authority. He died in Capranica, near Rome, on Aug. 5.

HOSKOLDSSÖN, HOSKOLD (d. 1537). He became bishop of Stavenger, Norway, in 1513, was its last Catholic leader, and died in prison at Bergen.

HÖSS, BL. CRESCENTIA (1682–1744). Born to a family of weavers in Kaufbeuren, Bavaria, she became a Franciscan at twenty-one when her dowry was supplied by the Protestant burgomaster. The other nuns taunted her because of her poverty and even refused to give her a cell. Eventually, a new superior noted her sanctity; she was accepted, and in time became mistress of novices and superior. She experienced ecstasy and suffered many supernatural torments before her last years were taken up with hours of counseling. She was beatified in 1900 by Pope Leo XIII. F. D. Apr. 5.

HOSSCHE, SIDRON DE (1596–1653), poet. Born in Mercken, Flanders, he became a Jesuit in 1616. He was tutor of Governor General Leopold William's children for two years, but left the court about 1637 to remain in Tongres, Belgium, until his death. Of his poems, which include allegories and ceremonial verse, his elegies (*De Christo patiente*, *De cursu vitae humanae*, and *De lachrymae S. Petri*) are best known.

HOST, JOHANN (1480?–1532?). Born on a farm in Romberg, Westphalia, he became a Dominican at sixteen, studied at Bologna, was appointed to the theological faculty of Cologne in 1520, and was one of the seven Dominicans who opposed Luther there. He edited and wrote theological and controversial treatises and published *Enchiridion sacerdotum* in 1532.

HOUBIGANT, CHARLES FRANÇOIS (1686–1783). Born in Paris, he became an Oratorian in 1704, taught in Juilly, Marseilles, and Soissons, and in 1722 was made head of the conference of church antiquities and discipline at St. Magliore. After losing his hearing he devoted himself to a study of oriental languages and became a biblical scholar. His most important works were the annotated *Biblia hebraica* in four volumes (1753–54) and a Latin translation of the Old Testament (1753). He also wrote scriptural studies and works on philology. He founded a school for girls and a printing press at Avilly, was blind in his last years, and died in Paris on Oct. 31.

HOUDON, JEAN ANTOINE (1741–1828), sculptor. Born in Versailles, France, on Mar. 20, he won the Prix de Rome in 1761 and spent the next ten years studying in Italy. In 1771 he was admitted to the Royal Academy of Painting and Sculpture for his *Morpheus*. He made busts of most of the important European personages of his age (Voltaire, Rousseau, Lafayette, Napoleon), as well as of Americans (Franklin, Jefferson, and a full-length military figure of Washington). Other important works are his *Ecorché*, a human figure, with the skin removed to show muscles and tendons, and used in medical schools since his time; a statue of St. Bruno, in Rome; and one of St. Scholastica, which he renamed "Philosophy" to protect it from destruction by French revolutionary leaders. He died in Paris on July 16 after a period of insanity.

HOUDRY, VINCENT (1631–1729). Born in Tours, France, on Jan. 22, he became a Jesuit in 1647, was ordained, taught for eleven years, then began a preaching career of a quarter century. He then prepared for publication his twenty-two-volume *Sermons sur tous les sujets de la morale chrétienne* (1696–1702) and a twenty-three-volume collection of material for sermons, *La bibliothèque des prédicateurs* (1712–25). He died in Paris on Mar. 21.

HOUGHTON, BL. JOHN (1487–1535), martyr. Born in Essex, England, he graduated from Cambridge, was a parish priest for four years, then became a Carthusian, prior of Beauvale in Northamptonshire and later of the Charterhouse in London. He was arrested in 1534 for refusing to approve the legitimacy of Anne Boleyn's children, released, but sent to the Tower a year later when he refused to subscribe to the Act of Supremacy which Henry VIII said placed him in charge of the Church. Bl. John, two other Carthusian priors, Robert Lawrence and Augustine Wexler, and two priests were then dragged through the streets in their priestly robes, an insult shown few others, and treated with the utmost savagery before and after their hanging at Tyburn. Bl. John's body was chopped to pieces and hung in different parts of the city, one arm over the doorway of Charterhouse. He was beatified in 1886. F. D. May 4.

HOUGHTON, WILLIAM (d. 1298), archbishop. Born in England, where he became a Dominican, he studied at St. James, Paris, where he lectured and became known for his poetry and learning. He twice was provincial of England, and lectured in Paris between his terms. He was ambassador to Rome for King Edward I in 1289 and became archbishop of Dublin in 1297. He persuaded Edward and Philip IV of France to end hostilities and died on Aug. 28 at Dijon, France, on his journey home. He wrote a commentary on the *Sentences*, a speech on the rights of the English king, and philosophical and theological studies.

HOUSELANDER, FRANCES CARYLL (1901–1954), author. Born in Bath, England, she was educated in convent schools in Warwickshire and Sussex, worked in an advertising office in 1945, illustrated books, and enjoyed sculpture and occupational therapy for child victims of World War II. She wrote *This War Is the Passion* (1943), *The Reed of God, The Flowering Tree,* and *Guilt* (1952), poems, and, with Maisie Ward, *This Burning Heat* (1941). She died in London on Oct. 12.

HOWARD, EDMUND BERNARD FITZ-ALAN (1855–1947), viceroy. Born in London on June 1, to Henry FitzAlan-Howard, earl of Arundel, he studied at the Oratory, Birmingham, and married Mary Bertie in 1879. From 1876 to 1921 he was known as Lord Edmund Talbot, was an army officer, was decorated during the Boer War, and from 1894 to 1921 was a conservative in parliament. He served in a minor treasury post, was joint parliamentary secretary in 1915, and chief party whip from 1913 to 1921. In 1921 he was raised to the peerage as Viscount FitzAlan of Derwent and named viceroy of Ireland. He was head of the occupying military force, negotiated with the Sinn Fein leaders, and retired when the Free State was established in 1922. Thereafter he was active in the House of Lords, and as president of the Catholic Union and adviser to Cardinals Bourne and Hinsley. He was several times honored by the government before his death at Cumberland Lodge, England, on May 18.

HOWARD, EDWARD HENRY (1829–1892), cardinal. Born in Nottingham, England, on Feb. 13, he studied at Oscott and Edinburgh, served as an army officer, went to the English College, Rome, and was ordained in 1854. He entered the papal diplomatic service, learned oriental languages, and was sent to India to attempt a solution of difficulties which arose in Portuguese Goa. He was made a titular archbishop in 1872, cardinal-priest in 1877, protector of the English College and archpriest of St. Peter's. In 1884 he was named cardinal-bishop and given the see of Frascati. He died near Brighton, on a visit to England, on Sept. 16.

HOWARD, ESME WILLIAM (1863–1939), ambassador. Born in Greystoke castle, Cumberland, England, on Sept. 15, he studied at Harrow and on the Continent. He entered the diplomatic service in 1885, and went to Ireland on the staff of Lord Lieutenant Carnavon, his brother-in-law, was in Rome (1886–88) and Berlin (to 1890), and retired in 1892. He was secretary to Lord Kimberley in the ministry of state, fought in the Boer War, worked on rubber plantations in the West Indies, became a convert in 1898, and later that year married Lady Maria Gioachina. He rejoined the diplomatic service in 1903. For his work as consul general for Crete he was decorated; he was minister at Berne (1911–13), Stockholm (1913–18), Madrid (1919–24), and Washington (1924–30). On his return he was made first Baron Howard of Penrith, published his memoirs, *Theatre of Life* (1935–36), and died in Hindhead, England, on Aug. 1.

HOWARD, FRANCIS WILLIAM (1867–1944), bishop. Born in Columbus, Ohio, on June 21, he studied at Mt. St. Mary of the West seminary, Cincinnati, and was ordained in Columbus in 1891. He became general secretary of the National Catholic Educational Association and was made a domestic prelate in 1920, and bishop of Covington, Kentucky, in 1923. He died on Jan. 18.

HOWARD, HENRY (1517?–1547), poet. The earl of Surrey's father, third earl of Norfolk, was descended from Edward the Confessor; his mother, the daughter of Elinor Percy, from Edward III. He was privately tutored by the Catholic scholar John Clerk, lived in a home which patronized letters, and soon entered the service of the crown. He served at Windsor and abroad as a companion to Henry Fitzroy, duke of Richmond, an illegitimate son of Henry VIII. Later, he became governor of Boulogne and lieutenant-general of the English possessions abroad. In 1546 he was sent to the Tower on charges of plotting to restore monasticism and other aspects of Catholic life to England, and was executed after three months. His was the first English translation of Vergil, in blank verse; other poetic achievements, in the sonnet and other continental forms, had considerable influence on the literature of the next two generations.

HOWARD, MARY (1653–1735). Born on Dec. 28, daughter of Sir Robert Howard, she was sent in 1671 to study at a Benedictine convent in Paris to escape the unwanted attentions of King Charles II. She became a convert, a Poor Clare at Rouen against her family's wishes and under an assumed name (Parnel), and in 1702 was named abbess. She wrote devotional tracts and died in Rouen, France, on Mar. 21.

HOWARD, BL. PHILIP (1557–1595), martyr. The eldest son of Thomas, fourth duke of Norfolk, and grandson of the poet Surrey, had Philip II of Spain as his godfather. He studied at Cambridge, and lived somewhat wildly as a courtier, almost forgetting the existence of his wife, Anne Dacres, to whom he was married at 12. In 1580, when he became earl of Arundel, he was a convert, having been impressed by Edmund Campion and having studied under William Weston. He was imprisoned in 1586 on the unsustained charge of working treasonably for Mary Queen of Scots and also of plotting (though he was in the Tower at the time) the attack by the Spanish Armada; he finally was attacked for refusing to abjure his faith. He remained in prison until his death, believed to have been from poisoning. He was beatified in 1929. F. D. Oct. 19.

HOWARD, PHILIP THOMAS (1629–1694), cardinal. Born in London on Sept. 21, son of the earl of Arundel and head of the house of Norfolk, and of Elizabeth, daughter of the duke of Lennox, he joined the Dominicans in Italy in 1645, studied at Naples, and was ordained in 1652. Devoted to the ideal of converting England, he was founding prior of Bornhem in Flanders, with a college for young Englishmen and a convent for nuns at Vilvorde. During Charles II's reign he lived in London as Queen Catherine of Braganza's grand almoner, but was forced to return to France. In 1675 Pope Clement X created him a cardinal; he moved to Rome and in 1679 was made protector of England and Scotland. He rebuilt the English College and died in Rome on June 17.

HOWARD, BL. WILLIAM (1616?–1680), martyr. Grandson of Bl. Philip Howard and fifth son of Thomas, earl of Arundel, who became an apostate, William, brought up as a Catholic, married Mary Stafford in 1637 and was made Baron Stafford in 1640. He performed several commissions for King Charles I on the Continent, was interested in America (Stafford County, Virginia, is named after him), and established a large art collection. At the time of the Titus Oates Plot the baron was charged with being on a list of officers who were to lead the "invading army." He was condemned in the House of Lords by a 55–31 vote and seats at his execution at Tyburn brought an extra high price. Jack Ketch, the hangman, was not used to the ax and bungled the execution. Bl. William was beatified in 1929. F. D. Dec. 29.

HOYNES, WILLIAM (1846–1933), jurist. Born near Callan, Kilkenny, Ireland, on Nov. 8, he was brought to the United States as a child, served with Wisconsin infantry and cavalry units during the Civil War, graduated from Notre Dame, and took his law degree at Michigan in 1872. He was editor of daily papers in New Brunswick, New Jersey, and Peoria, Illinois, until 1882, practiced law in Chicago, then taught law at Notre Dame. He was dean of the law school there until his retirement in 1918, was honored by Pope Pius X in 1912, and died in South Bend, Indiana, on Mar. 28.

HRODBERT. See Rupert.

HROSWITHA (935?–1002?), dramatist. She probably was of aristocratic birth (the name Helena von Rossow appears on an early engraving) and born in Lower Saxony. She became a Benedictine nun in her early twenties,

was already a cultured woman, and studied under Riccardis and Geberga, the abbess, niece of Emperor Otto I. Her six plays were discovered at Ratisbon by Conrad Celtes and published in 1501. They were written, she says in a preface, to counteract the influence of Terence, their source. The result was psychologically realistic and piously didactic. *Gallicanus* treats of Constantine's general, who sought a consecrated virgin in marriage and became a martyr; *Dulcitius* portrays an official's lust and is marked by slapstick humor; *Abraham* and *Paphnutius* retell stories of magdalens; *Calimachus* is ugly passion, with a touch of the resurrection theme; *Sapientia* is on the death of Faith, Hope, and Charity. The existence of the plays helps to refute charges of intellectual barrenness in the tenth century. Hroswitha also wrote poems: on the Virgin Mary, a narrative of a recent martyr, St. Pelagius of Cordova, and *Theophilus*, on the Faust theme; two longer poems are on the career of Otto I and a history of her monastery.

HROZNATA, BL. (1160–1217), martyr. A nobleman at the court of Ottokar I of Bohemia, he lost his wife and son when he was thirty, built the Premonstratensian abbey of Tepl and two other houses, and is supposed to have been murdered near Eger for defending ecclesiastical immunity. His cult was approved in 1897. F. D. July 14.

HUBBELL, JOHN LORENZO (1853–1930). Born in Pajarito, New Mexico, on Nov. 27, he settled in Ganado, Arizona, in 1876 as a trader to the Navajo Indians. He became the friend and adviser of the Hopi and Navajo Indians and over the years built up their handcrafts to world-wide fame. He became wealthy from his trading, was twice sheriff of Apache County during its most lawless years, served two terms in the territorial legislature, and died in Ganado on Nov. 12.

HUBER, ALPHONS (1834–1898), historian. Born in Fügen, Tyrol, on Oct. 14, he studied at Halle, Innsbruck, and Vienna, taught history at Innsbruck in 1859, became a member of the Academy of Sciences in 1872, and went to Vienna as professor in 1887. He wrote on Rudolph IV, on the union of Austria and the Tyrol, the five-volume *Geschichte Oesterreichs* (1885–96), the fourth volume of *Fontes rerum germanicarum*, dealing with the fourteenth century, and edited the *Regesta* of Charles IV. He died in Vienna on Nov. 23.

HUBERT, ST. (d. 727), bishop. A married courtier serving Pepin of Heristal, he entered religious life after his wife's death. (According to a late mediaeval legend, a stag he was hunting turned to him with a crucifix in its antlers and this led to his vocation.) After ordination he succeeded St. Lambert as bishop about 705, transferring the see from Maastricht, Flanders, to Liège, and was active in converting pagans. He died on May 30 near Brussels. F. D. Nov. 3.

HUBERT, JEAN FRANÇOIS (1739–1799), bishop. Born in Quebec, Canada, on Feb. 23, he studied at the seminary there, was ordained in 1767, tended to the wounded when the Americans attacked the city in 1775, and was sent on the Huron mission at Detroit in 1781. He was appointed ninth bishop of Quebec in 1785 and devoted the rest of his life to building up the clergy of his diocese (larger than all Europe), despite great opposition from the British. He died on Feb. 23 in Quebec.

HUBERT WALTER (d. 1205), archbishop. Son of Hervey Walter and nephew of Ranulf de Glanville, whose clerk and chaplain he became, he was appointed dean of York in 1184, was baron of the exchequer in 1184–85 and bishop of Salisbury in 1189. He accompanied King Richard I on the third crusade, in 1190, became his chief chaplain, and was active in negotiating a peace with Saladin when Richard fell ill. He returned to England in 1193, repulsed Prince John's attempt to seize the crown, and raised ransom for Richard, who, on his return from Palestine, was captured by Leopold of Austria and imprisoned by Emperor Henry VI. Richard secured Hubert's election to the see of Canterbury in 1193. He was made justiciar in 1193, crowned Richard the next year, and when the king left England was virtual ruler in his stead. He put down the insurrection of William Fitz Osbert in 1196 by methods which alienated the people and clergy, convened a council in 1197 to raise money for Richard's wars, dissolving it when opposition developed to raising money for a foreign war, and arranged a truce between Richard and Philip II of France in Normandy. He remained with Richard until his death in 1199, when he returned to England, crowned John, and resumed his chancellorship. John sent him on several diplomatic missions to the Continent, and he helped to dissuade the king from invading Normandy in 1205. He died on July 10 at Teynham, England, while on the way to arbitrate a dispute between the Rochester monks and their bishop.

HÜBNER, ALEXANDER (1811–1892). Born on Nov. 26 in Vienna, he was educated at its university and began his diplomatic career in the chancery under Metternich, whose close friend he became and who named him to the Austrian legations at Paris in 1837 and Lisbon in 1841 and made him consul general for Saxony at Leipzig. He was sent on a diplomatic mission to Milan in 1848 and to Paris in 1849 to discuss Italian affairs with Louis Napoleon. He served as ambassador to France in 1851–59, was named baron in 1854, and was ambassador at Rome in 1865–67. He wrote a biography of Sixtus V and narratives of his

diplomatic activities and travels, including *A Journey around the World* (1873). He became a member of the Austrian upper house in 1879 and a count in 1888. He died on July 30.

HUC, EVARISTE RÉGIS (1813–1860), missioner. Born in Caylus, France, on June 1, he joined the Lazarists in 1836, was sent to China in 1839, and stayed until 1844 at a mission some 300 miles north of Peking. With a fellow missioner, Joseph Gabet, on the orders of his bishop, he set out on an exploratory journey which took them through Mongolia to Lhasa, Tibet. At first well received (they set up a chapel and residence), they were expelled in 1846 because of the enmity of the Chinese imperial resident, Ki-shan. He returned to France in 1852, left his congregation in ill health in 1853, and published *Souvenirs d'un voyage dans la Tartarie et le Tibet*, *L'Empire chinois*, and *Le Christianisme en Chine*. He died in Paris on Mar. 26.

HUCBALD (840?–930?). A Fleming, he became a Benedictine monk at St. Amand, near Tournai, Belgium, studied at St. Germain d'Auxerre, taught in 883 at St. Bertin, and in 892 helped to re-establish the choral school at Rheims. He was a musical theorist and wrote *Harmonica institutio*. The use of one melody paralleled by another at every fourth or fifth interval, long attributed to him, is outlined in *Musica enchiriadis*, now believed to be by an unknown late tenth-century author.

HUCHOWN. *See* Hugh of Eglinton.

HUDDLESTON, JOHN (1608–1698). Born in Lancashire, England, on Apr. 15, he studied at St. Omer and the English College, Rome, where he was ordained in 1637. He was sent to England in 1639, served as a chaplain, and in 1651 helped to conceal Charles (later king) in flight from defeat by Cromwell at Worcester. Huddleston became a Benedictine before 1661, lived in London under Queen Henrietta Maria's protection, served as secretary of the Benedictine chapter at Douai in 1666, and as chaplain to Queen Catherine in 1669. He reconciled Charles II to the Church on his deathbed in 1685. Fr. Huddleston was buried in London on Sept. 13.

HUDSON, DANIEL ELDRED (1849–1934), editor. Born in Nahant, Massachusetts, on Dec. 18, he worked in a bookstore and for a publisher in Boston, studied at Holy Cross, Worcester, and in 1870 joined the Congregation of Holy Cross at Notre Dame. He was ordained in 1875, became editor of the magazine, *Ave Maria*, a position he held until illness forced his retirement in 1929, and died at Notre Dame, Indiana, on Jan. 12.

HUEBER, FORTUNATUS (d. 1706), author. Born in Neustadt, Germany, he became a Franciscan in 1654, theologian to the elector of Cologne, cathedral preacher in Freising in

1670–76, provincial of Bavaria in 1677, definitor general in 1679, and provincial in Hungary in 1695. He wrote histories of his order, lives of the saints, and spiritual and theological discourses. He died in Munich, Bavaria, on Feb. 12.

HUET, PIERRE DANIEL (1630–1721), bishop. Born in Caen, France, on Feb. 8, he was orphaned early, educated in Paris, became a pupil of Samuel Bochart, the Protestant biblical scholar, and went with him to Sweden in 1652. There he conceived the plan of publishing Origen's exegetical works, soon returned to Caen, and devoted himself to that project for fifteen years. At Caen he founded an academy of science, studied oriental languages, and engaged in critical controversy with Bochart. In 1670, King Louis XIV appointed him assistant to Bossuet in educating the dauphin. He was a chief editor of the Delphin series of the classics, and published Origen's *Commentaria in sacram scripturam* in 1668 and his own *Demonstratio evangelica* in 1679. In 1674 he was ordained, received the abbey of Aulnay from the king, and became a member of the French Academy. In 1680 he retired to Aulnay and in 1692 became bishop of Avranches, a see he directed with close care until his health made him resign in 1699. He then retired to a Jesuit house in Paris until his death on Jan. 26. He wrote so vigorously against Descartes that Bossuet took issue with him; he also issued studies on the origins of French poetry, the city of Caen, commerce and navigation in antiquity, the travels of Solomon, and the ancients-moderns critical controversy. In his *Traité philosophique de la faiblesse de l'esprit humain* (1723) he proved to be a fideist and was strongly censured by Jesuit philosophers.

HÜFFER, HERMANN (1830–1905), jurist. Born in Münster, Westphalia, on Mar. 24, he studied at Bonn and law at Breslau, and taught canon and civil law at Bonn. He served in the Prussian chamber of deputies in 1865–70 and in the North German *Reichstag* in 1867–70. He wrote on the early years of the French Revolution, notably *Diplomatische Verhandlungen aus der Zeit der französischen Revolution*. He died in Bonn, Germany, on Mar. 15.

HUG, JOHANN LEONHARD (1765–1846), scholar. Born in Constance, Switzerland, on June 1, he studied at Freiburg, was ordained in 1789, and taught oriental languages and scripture at his university from 1791. He was invited to set up biblical studies at Breslau, Bonn, and Tübingen at various times between 1811 and 1831. He led the opposition to Johann Semler and the rationalists, stressed the historical basis of the New Testament, and wrote widely and with increasing influence. He died in Freiburg, Germany, on Mar. 11.

HÜGEL, FRIEDRICH JOHN (1852–1925),

theologian. Born in Florence, Italy, on May 8, son of Baron Karl von Hügel, Austrian minister to Tuscany, he studied under the historian Alfred von Reumont. In 1873 he married Mary Herbert and lived in England (often wintering in Rome) from 1876 until his death in Kensington on Jan. 27. He worked with such scholars as Charles Briggs, Loisy, and Ernst Troeltsch, was a member of the Synthetic Society, and in 1905 founded the London Society for the Study of Religion. His interest in mysticism appears in his study of St. Catherine of Genoa. His support of modernism remained strong after papal condemnation of the heresy. He became an English citizen in 1914 and in 1916 wrote *The German Soul* for war propaganda.

HUGH, ST. (d. 730), bishop. Son of Drogo, duke of Burgundy, he became bishop of Rouen in 722, was given the additional sees of Paris and Bayeux, and made abbot of Fontenelle and of Jumièges. He proved an exception to the evil practice of pluralism, governed all areas well, exhausted his wealth in charities, and retired to die as a monk at Jumièges. F. D. Apr. 9.

HUGH OF ANZY, BL. (d. 930?). Born in Poitiers, France, he became a Benedictine at St. Savin in Poitou, served at other monasteries, joined St. Berno in establishing Cluny, where he built a hospital, and died as prior of Anzy-le-Duc, France. F. D. Apr. 20.

HUGH OF BONNEVAUX, ST. (d. 1194). A nephew of Hugh of Grenoble, he became a Cistercian at Mézières, France, and subjected himself to such severe austerities that St. Bernard interfered and forbade them. In 1163 he became abbot of Léoncel, and in 1169 of Bonnevaux. He was the successful mediator at Venice in 1177 between Pope Alexander III and Frederick Barbarossa. F. D. Apr. 1.

HUGH CAPET (938?–996), king. Son of Hugh the Great, count of Paris, and Hedwig, sister of German Emperor Otto I, he succeeded his father as count of Paris in 956. About 970 he married Adelaide of Aquitaine and in 987, on the death of Louis V, last of the Carlovingians, was elected king by the nobles and established the Capetian dynasty of France over the claims of Charles of Lorraine, who contested his claim. In 989, Adalberon, archbishop of the important and influential see of Rheims, died, and his successor, Arnoul, supported Charles. Hugh defeated Charles in 991, and imprisoned him (until his death in 993) and the archbishop. Arnoul was deposed by the Council of St. Basle in 991 and Gerbert, favorable to Hugh, was elected archbishop. Pope John XVI refused to recognize Gerbert's election and the dispute over Rheims never was resolved during Hugh's lifetime. After Charles's defeat, Hugh consolidated and extended his power by a policy of moderation, moved the capital to Paris, supported monastic settlements and freedom, and made every effort to remove the Saxon influence from French life. He died probably on Oct. 24.

HUGH OF DIGNE (d. 1285?). Born in Digne, France, he was a Friar Minor renowned for his preaching and prophecies, was active in the Spirituals, and wrote ascetical treatises, notably *Tractatus de triplici via in sapientiam perveniendi*, and a set of rules for his sister, Bl. Douceline, and her community, the Dames de Roubans. He died in Marseilles.

HUGH OF EGLINTON (14th century), poet. The Huchown who wrote such romances as *The Gret Gest of Arthure*, *The Awntyre of Gawane*, and *The Pystyll of Swete Susan* has been identified as a Sir Hugh who married Egidia, half-sister of King Robert II of Scotland. He also was auditor of the royal accounts, and flourished between 1348 and 1375.

HUGH OF FLAVIGNY (1064?-1150?), historian. Born probably in Verdun, France, he was educated at St. Vannes, became a Benedictine, and followed his abbot, who supported Pope Gregory VII against the emperor, into exile at St. Bénigne in Dijon. He was appointed abbot of Flavigny in 1096 and was twice forced to flee because of differences with the bishop of Autun and his own monks. He then sided with the emperor and in 1111 accepted the abbacy of Verdun from Bishop Richard after the illegal removal of Abbot Laurentius. Deposed himself in 1114, he lived the rest of his life as a monk at Verdun. He wrote a *Chronicle* of world history (to 1102).

HUGH OF FLEURY (d. 1125?). A Benedictine monk, he wrote an ecclesiastical history to 814, a chronicle of the Frankish kings from 842 to 1108, of the French monarchs from Pharamond (the legendary first king of France) to 1108, and other historical works of continuing value. He also is known as Hugh a Sancta Maria (from the name of the church in his native village) and sometimes is confused with another Hugh of Fleury, abbot of Canterbury, who died in 1124.

HUGH OF FOSSES, BL. (1093?-1164). Born near Namur, Belgium, he was educated as a Benedictine priest and was in the service of Bishop Burchard of Cambrai when he met St. Norbert, whom he joined in 1119 as a missioner in the Low Countries. Bishop Bartholomew of Laon suggested that they reform a community of canons regular and the result was the monastery of Prémonstré. In 1128, Hugh became abbot and superior of the new Order of Premonstratensians, which he directed for thirty-five years. His cult was confirmed in 1927. F. D. Feb. 10.

HUGH THE GREAT, ST. (1024-1109). Son of the count of Samur, he entered the monastery of Cluny, France, at fifteen, was ordained at twenty, became prior and then for sixty years developed the great Benedictine establishment as abbot. During this time he was consulted by the nine popes from Leo IX through Pascal II, by the sovereigns of Europe, and by the superiors of some 200 affiliated monasteries. His career began at the Council of Rheims, where he spoke out against simony and clerical marriage; he fought Berengarius of Tours; was peacemaker between Andrew of Hungary and the Holy Roman emperor; and built a hospital at Marcigny where he tended the lepers himself. When Pope St. Gregory VII, who had been a monk at Cluny, became pope in 1073, the two men worked strenuously for Church reforms and a revival of spiritual life. He was universally admired for his intellectual and spiritual attainments and as a man of prudence, simplicity, and justice. He died at Cluny, and was canonized in 1120. F. D. Apr. 29.

HUGH OF GRENOBLE, ST. (1052?-1132), bishop. Born in Châteauneuf, France, he became a canon in the nearby cathedral of Valence, worked against the prevalence of simony, as aide to Bishop Hugh of Dié, and was ordained by the papal legate at Avignon in 1080. He was consecrated bishop of Grenoble by Pope Gregory VII and worked for two years to bring order into a diocese which had fallen into spiritual ruin; then, deciding he was a failure at the task, retired to become a Benedictine at Chaise-Dieu. The pope soon ordered his return, and he spent forty years, marked by painful illness, clearing up evils, giving the monks under St. Bruno the Grande Chartreuse area in which to build, and preaching and dispensing charities widely. He was canonized in 1134 by Pope Innocent II. F. D. Apr. 1.

HUGH OF LINCOLN, ST. (1140-1200), bishop. Born in Avalon castle, Burgundy, son of William, lord of Avalon, he was taken by his father to the monastery of Villard-Benoit at the age of eight when his mother died. Hugh became a monk at fifteen, deacon at nineteen, and prior of St. Maximin. In 1153 he became a Carthusian at Chartreuse, was ordained at thirty, and became procurator ten years later. In 1175, at the invitation of King Henry II of England, he founded the first English Charterhouse at Witham, Somerset, and soon built it into a center of holiness, from which its director's reputation for sanctity and goodness spread throughout the kingdom. In 1181, against his wishes, he was made bishop of Lincoln, which had been without a head for eighteen years. He reformed the see, built his cathedral, cared for the poor, and defended the Jews of his diocese from a wave of bigotry sweeping England. He zealously defended the rights of the Church against Henry (he excommunicated Henry's chief forester and refused to install the king's candidate for a prebendary of Lincoln) and constantly strove to mete out justice to his subjects. He was on a mission to the French king in 1188 when Henry died, attended King Richard I's coronation in 1189, and in 1197 came into conflict with him when he refused to contribute funds for the king's war abroad, the first time in English history that a direct levy by the crown had been so refused. He was sent to France as an envoy by Richard's successor, King John, in 1199, visited Grande Chartreuse the next summer, and on his return fell ill and died on Nov. 16 at the Old Temple in London. He was canonized in 1220 by Pope Honorius III. F. D. Nov. 17.

HUGH OF LINCOLN, ST. (d. 1255). A nine-year-old boy, he was said to have been scourged and crucified by a group of Jews in Lincoln, England. An investigation ordered by King Henry III resulted in the arrest, trial, and execution of a man named Koppin and eighteen other Jews. When the body of the boy was recovered from the well into which it had been thrown, miracles were immediately reported by those who touched it. Many such stories were in vogue during the later Middle Ages (one became the source of Chaucer's *Prioress' Tale*), but their authenticity has been questioned by modern historians. This child, called St. Hugh the Little, was honored on Aug. 13.

HUGH OF MONTAIGU, BL. (d. 1136), bishop. Nephew of St. Hugh of Cluny, under whom he studied and became a Benedictine monk, he became bishop of Auxerre, France, in 1096. F. D. Aug. 10.

HUGH OF PISA. *See* Huguccio.

HUGH DE PUISET (1125-1195), bishop. Born in France, nephew of King Stephen, he went to England before he was twenty, became archdeacon to another uncle, Henry of Blois, and in 1143 was named treasurer of York. He engaged in national and ecclesiastical politics, was aided by his mistress, Adelaide de Percy, succeeded in becoming bishop of Durham in 1153 and later purchased the earldom of Northumbria, joined the rebellion against Henry II, fought Richard I's appointment of the archbishop of York, opposed the selection of Longchamps as chief justiciar, and eventually fell out of favor with Richard and gave up his earldom.

HUGH OF REMIREMONT (d. 1098?), cardinal. Of a noble Lorraine family, he joined the Benedictines at Remiremont, was made cardinal by Pope Leo IX in 1049, supported antipope Cadalus in 1061, but submitted to Alexander II in 1067. He was sent as legate to Spain in 1068, where he enforced celibacy on the clergy and introduced the Roman liturgy. Accused of simony, he was recalled to Rome, sent as legate to France in 1072, again

was accused of simony, and cleared himself in both cases. In 1073, while legate to France and Spain, he was again accused and was deposed by Pope Gregory VII. He attended the anti-Gregorian synods of Worms (1076) and Brixen (1080), and was excommunicated. Nothing is known of his last years.

HUGH OF ST. CHER (1200?-1263), cardinal. Born in St. Cher, France, he studied at Paris, where he taught law, and in 1225 became a Dominican. He was provincial, prior in Paris in 1230, and papal envoy to Constantinople in 1233. Made cardinal by Pope Innocent IV in 1244, he served as legate to Germany after the death of Emperor Frederick II in 1250. He wrote theological treatises, a biblical *Correctorium*, and the first biblical concordance. He died in Orvieto, Italy, on Mar. 19.

HUGH OF ST. VICTOR (1096-1141), philosopher. Oldest son of Count Conrad of Blankenburg, he was born in Hartingham, Saxony (or in Flanders), studied at St. Pancras, Hamerleve, and became an Augustinian Canon Regular. About 1115 he went to the monastery of St. Victor in Paris, where he spent the rest of his life. In 1133 he became head of the school there, which flourished under his direction. He early was the chief opponent of Abelard's school and through his efforts the dialectic method of Catholic theology prevailed. His systematizing of the dogmatic works of the patristic age into a coherent body of doctrine was one of the great accomplishments of mediaeval thought. His treatise on dogmatic theology, *De sacramentis christianae fidei*, had great influence and *Eruditionis didascaliae* propounded a new division of philosophy as theoretical, practical, mechanical, and logical. Knowledge, he maintained, was only a prelude to the mystical life, achieved through thought, meditation, contemplation; his *De vanitate mundi*, *De arca Noe*, and *De amore sponsi ad sponsam* gained a wide audience. His scriptural commentaries also were important milestones.

HUGH OF SASSOFERRATO, BL. (d. 1290?). Born in Serra San Quirico, Italy, he studied at Bologna, became a disciple of St. Silvester, whose order he joined, and died at Sassoferrato. His cult was approved in 1747. F. D. Sept. 19.

HUGH OF VERMANDOIS (1057-1101). Son of Henry I of France, he went on the first crusade in 1096 and after the capture of Antioch in 1098 was sent on an embassy to Constantinople. He returned to France, became a crusader again in 1101, and died near Tarsus, Asia Minor. He is called Hugh the Great, a mistranslation of *maines* ("the Younger").

HUGHES, JOHN JOSEPH (1797-1864), archbishop. Born in Annaloghan, Tyrone, Ireland, on June 24, he followed his father to the United States in 1817. He studied at Mt. St. Mary's, Maryland, and was ordained in 1826. He did parish work in Philadelphia, was a theologian at the first Provincial Council in Baltimore in 1829, founded the *Catholic Herald* in 1833, and in 1837 was named coadjutor bishop of New York. He succeeded Bishop Dubois to the see in 1842, and became its first archbishop in 1850. His episcopate was marked by his abolition of the trustee system; his attempt to secure public funds for Catholic schools and, when this failed, his establishment of a Catholic school system; and his vigorous opposition to such anti-Catholic factions as the Native Americans and Know-Nothings and, within the Church, to those who sought to continue national parishes instead of becoming part of their new country. He was strong in his support of the Union during the Civil War, was sent by Secretary Seward on a mission to Napoleon III which prevented French recognition of the Confederacy, and publicly pleaded for an end to the draft riots of 1863. During his term his flock doubled, even though four dioceses (Albany and Buffalo in 1847 and Brooklyn and Newark in 1853) were created from his original area. He laid the cornerstone of St. Patrick's cathedral in 1858, opened Fordham University (as St. John's College) in 1841, transferred its seminary students to St. Joseph's, Troy, which he built in 1862, and supported the founding of the North American College in Rome. He died in New York City on Jan. 3.

HUGHES, JOHN J. (1856–1919). Born in New York City on Dec. 6, he studied there and in Maryland, was ordained a Paulist in 1884, was assistant superior and, in 1909 and 1914, superior general. He was one of the founders of the Catholic Converts League of New York. He died in New York City on May 6.

HUGO, CHARLES HYACINTHE (1667–1739). Born in St. Mihiel, France, he became a Norbertine, with the name Louis, in 1685, studied at Jovillier abbey, and received his doctorate in theology at Bourges. After teaching at Janneures and Etival he became abbot of St. Joseph's, Nancy, in 1700, coadjutor of Flabémont abbey in 1708, of Etival in 1710, abbot of Fontaine André, Switzerland, in 1712, and of Etival in 1722. A jurisdictional dispute with the bishop of Toul caused him to appeal to Rome, where his right to the abbey of Etival was sustained and he was named bishop of Ptolemais in 1728. He wrote histories of his order and of Lorraine, a biography of St. Norbert, a defense of the Trinity, a treatise on coins, and *Sacrae antiquitatis monumenta*. He died on Aug. 2.

HUGOLINO, ST. (d. 1227), martyr. *See* Daniel, St.

HUGOLINO OF GUALDO, BL. (d. 1260). An Augustinian, he took charge of a monastery in Umbria, Italy, in 1258. His name was honored in the diocese of Spoleto after his death. He was beatified in 1919. F. D. Jan. 1.

HUGUCCIO (d. 1210), canonist. Born in Pisa, Italy, and also called Hugh, he studied and taught canon law at Bologna. He became bishop of Ferrara in 1190, was adviser to his former pupil, Pope Innocent III, and wrote *Liber derivationum* and a *Summa* on Gratian's *Decretum*.

HULST, MAURICE LE SAGE D'HAUTE-ROCHE D' (1841–1896), educator. Born in Paris on Oct. 10, he studied at Stanislas College, St. Sulpice seminary, and in Rome, where he received his doctorate in divinity. After pastoral work, he joined the French army in 1870 as chaplain. In 1873 he became Cardinal Guibert's administrator, helped found the Catholic University in Paris, and became its rector in 1880, a position he held until his death on Nov. 6 in Paris. In 1891 he became preacher of Notre Dame and the next year was elected deputy for Finistère. Always interested in higher education, he helped organize the International Scientific Congresses of Catholics, and wrote *L'Education supérieure*, as well as biographies of Mère Marie Thérèse and Just of Bretenières.

HUMBELINE, BL. (1092–1135?). Sister of St. Bernard, she was born in Dijon, France, married Guy de Marcy, and lived a worldly life until a visit to her brother at Clairvaux changed her spiritual outlook. Several years later, with her husband's consent, she entered the Benedictine monastery of Jully-les-Nonnais near Troyes, later became its abbess, and died there after practicing the severest mortifications in the later years of her life. Her cult was approved in 1703. She is also called Hombelina. F. D. Aug. 21.

HUMBERT, ST. (d. 680?). A follower of St. Amandus, he founded the Benedictine monastery of Marolles, Flanders. F. D. Mar. 25.

HUMBERT III, BL. (1136–1188), king. Born in Avigliana, he was educated by Bishop Amadeus of Lausanne, ruled Savoy with competence, and retired in his last years to the Cistercian abbey of Hautecombe, Savoy. He was beatified in 1838. F. D. Mar. 4.

HUMBERT OF ROMANS (1194?–1277?). Born in Romans, near Valence, France, he studied at Paris, became a Dominican in 1224, taught at the Dominican school in Lyons in 1226, and was its prior in 1236–39. He was elected provincial of the Roman province in 1240, of the French province in 1244, and in 1254 became fifth master general of his order, a position he held until 1263. He resigned to retire to the monastery of Valence, where he died on July 14 (or Jan. 15, 1274). His term was marked by his encouragement of studies, final revision of the Dominican liturgy, insistence on clerical reform, and keen interest in missions to the East. He has a popular cult and is honored on July 14.

HUMILIANA DE' CERCHI, BL. (1220–1246). Born in Florence, Italy, she married at sixteen, was soon widowed, and became the first cloistered Franciscan tertiary, at Florence. Her cult was approved by Pope Innocent XII. F. D. May 19.

HUMILIS OF BISIGNANO, BL. (1582–1637). Born in Bisignano, Italy, this farmhand named Luke became a Franciscan laybrother in 1609, taking the name Humilis. He often was called to Rome as consultant by Popes Gregory XV and Urban VIII, and was beatified in 1882. F. D. Nov. 27.

HUMILITAS, ST. (1226–1310). Born in Faenza, Italy, and named Rosana, she was married at fifteen to a local noble, lost both of her children, and at twenty-four entered the double monastery of St. Perpetua, where her husband became a laybrother. She was briefly a Poor Clare, then for twelve years retired to an extremely austere life in a narrow refuge, under the direction of the Vallombrosan abbey of St. Crispin. The abbot general suggested that she emerge to direct the first Vallombrosan convent, at Malta, near Faenza; she also set up their second convent, in Florence, Italy, where she died. F. D. May 22.

HUMMELAUER, FRANZ VON (1842–1914). Born in Vienna on Aug. 14, he was ordained a Jesuit, wrote commentaries on eight books of the Old Testament for *Cursus scripturae sacrae* (1897–1905), other scriptural studies, and on the priesthood in Israel, and served as a member of the Pontifical Commission for Biblical Studies. He died in Heerenberg, Holland, on Apr. 12.

HUMPHREY, ST. (d. 871), bishop. A Benedictine at Prüm, with SS. Ansbald and Egilon, he became bishop of Thérouanne, in an area which was devastated by the Norsemen. He also repaired the monastery of St. Bertin, which had been set afire by the invaders, and became its abbot. F. D. Mar. 8.

HUMPHREY, BL. LAURENCE (1572–1591), martyr. A native of Hampshire, England, he was converted by Fr. Stanney, S.J., arrested and found guilty of Catholicism, and hanged, drawn, and quartered at Winchester. He was beatified in 1929. F. D. July 7.

HUNGER, ST. (d. 866), bishop. He was driven by a Norman invasion from the see of Utrecht, Flanders, to which he had been raised in 856, to Prüm, Germany, where he died. F. D. Dec. 22.

HUNNA, ST. (d. 679). Daughter of an Alsatian duke, she married Huno of Hunnawayer, and took care of the poor of Strassburg, even

doing their washing. Her son Deodatus was baptized by St. Deodatus, bishop of Nevers, and entered the monastery of Ebersheim, near Strassburg, Alsace, where she joined him. She was canonized in 1520 by Pope Leo X. F. D. Apr. 15.

HUNT, FRANCIS. *See* Davenport, Christopher.

HUNT, VEN. THOMAS (d. 1600), martyr. Born in Norfolk, England, he studied and was ordained at the English College, Seville, returned to England, was imprisoned at Wisbech, but escaped with five others, was captured at Lincoln with Ven. Thomas Sprott, and executed at Lincoln on July 11.

HUNTER, SYLVESTER JOSEPH (1829–1896). Born in Bath, England, on Sept. 13, son of a Protestant minister, he studied at St. Paul's, London, Cambridge, and law at Lincoln's Inn. In 1857 he became a convert, issued two law textbooks, and in 1861 became a Jesuit. Ordained in 1870, he taught at Stonyhurst for ten years, then was appointed rector of St. Beuno's. He published *Outlines of Dogmatic Theology* and died in Stonyhurst, England, on June 20.

HUNTER-BLAIR, DAVID OSWALD (1853–1939). Born at Dunskey castle, Wigtownshire, Scotland, he studied at Malvern, Eton, and Oxford. He became a convert in 1875, took his master's degree at Oxford, served as an army captain, and contributed heavily from his great wealth to churches and monasteries. In 1878 he became a Benedictine, was ordained in 1886 as Fr. Oswald, and served in Brazil. In 1899–1908 he was Catholic chaplain at Oxford, served as abbot of Fort Augustus in 1912–18, went back to Brazil, and returned to Scotland when his health failed. He wrote on the Rule of St. Benedict, translated Bellesheim's *History of the Catholic Church in Scotland*, and wrote the autobiographical *In Victorian Days*, collections of *Memoirs*, and antiquarian notes. He died at Fort Augustus, Scotland, on Sept. 12.

HUNTINGTON, JEDEDIAH VINCENT (1815–1862), novelist. Born on June 20 in New York City, he was educated at Yale, in New York, and in medicine at Pennsylvania, although he never practiced. After teaching psychology for three years he became an Episcopalian minister in 1841, preached in Middlebury, Vermont, resigned in 1846, and in 1849 became a convert with his wife. He edited the short-lived *Metropolitan Magazine* in Baltimore and the *Leader* in St. Louis, and published *Poems* (1843) and popular novels: *Lady Alice* (1849), *The Forest, Rosemary*, and the partly autobiographical *Alban, or the History of a Young Puritan*. He died in Pau, France, on Mar. 10.

HUNYADY, JÁNOS (1400–1456), governor.

Of a noble Hungarian family, he was born in Hunyady, Transylvania, entered the service of the Ujlaky family in 1410–14, of Stefan Lazarevics, a Serbian ruler, in 1414–27, and in 1428–39 was in the military service of King Sigismund, who made him a counselor. In 1438, King Albert made him ban of Szörény and count of Temes and in 1439 gave him the castle of Hunyad, his family seat. Hunyady helped to secure the election of Ladislas VI of Poland as Hungary's king in 1442 after Albert's death, and in turn was made voivode of Transylvania and commander of the fortress of Belgrade. In 1441 he began a war with the Turks, captured Wallachia, invaded Bulgaria, took Sofia, and forced the sultan to make peace in 1444. Later in that year the Hungarians were badly defeated at Varna; the king was killed, but Hunyady, though captured, was soon released. He was elected one of the five governors of Hungary in 1445 and given charge of Transylvania. In 1446 he was elected governor of Hungary and a regent of Ladislaus V. In the next few years he fought against Emperor Frederick III, the Turks, who defeated him at Amselfelde, Serbia, in 1448, and the Hussites under John Žiska. In 1453, Ladislaus came to the throne, and Hunyady resigned as governor and was named captain general. The Turks captured Constantinople in that year and in 1454 reinvaded Hungary. Hunyady defeated them at Szendrö, then retired to private life. In 1456 the Osmanli again threatened under Mohammed II. Hunyady defeated him at Belgrade on July 21–22, but died in Zemun (now Yugoslavia) on Aug. 11 of the plague.

HURLEY, EDWARD NASH (1864–1933), executive. Born in Galesburg, Illinois, he worked at various jobs until 1896 when he founded the Standard Pneumatic Tool Co., retired from it in 1902, then organized the Hurley Machine Co. in 1908, which he developed into a successful producer of electrical labor-saving instruments for the home. He was chairman of the Federal Trade Commission in 1915–17, of the United States Shipping Board, and president of the Emergency Fleet Corporation, directing the building of the merchant fleet required for World War I. He retired to private business in 1919, was decorated by the American, French, Italian, and Chinese governments, and wrote *The New Merchant Marine* (1920) and *The Bridge to France* (1927). He served three presidents—Wilson, Coolidge, and Hoover—in government posts, was given the Laetare Medal in 1926, and died in Chicago on Nov. 14.

HURLEY, MARY (d. 1940), educator. Born in Susquehanna, Pennsylvania, she became a Sister of the Immaculate Heart of Mary, taking the name Mary Josepha, served as president of Marywood College, Scranton, and from 1931 until her death there on Dec. 4 was mother superior of her order.

HURTADO, CASPAR (1574–1647), theologian. Born in Mondejar, New Castile, Spain, he studied and taught at Alcalá de Henares, and resigned in 1607 to become a Jesuit. He lectured at Murcia, Madrid, and Alcalá, where he became dean of the faculty and court preacher. He wrote on the sacraments, beatitudes, and the Incarnation, and died in Alcalá, Spain, on Aug. 5.

HURTER, FRIEDRICH EMMANUEL VON (1787–1865), historian. Born in Schaffhausen, Switzerland, on Mar. 19, he studied in Göttingen, served as a minister in a country parish, and became a clerical leader in Schaffhausen and head of its school board. The publication of the first volumes of his study of Pope Innocent III caused hostility and forced his resignation in 1841. He became a convert in Rome in 1844, imperial counselor and historiographer of the Viennese court in 1848, and was widely honored for his studies of Emperors Ferdinand II and Rudolf II and of Wallenstein. He wrote an autobiography, *Geburt und Wiedergeburt*, and died in Graz, Austria, on Aug. 27.

HUSENBETH, FREDERICK CHARLES (1796–1872). Born in Bristol, England, on May 30, he studied at Sedgeley Park and Oscott, was ordained in 1820, and became chaplain to Baron Stafford in Cossey, Norfolk, in 1821. He became assistant in 1828 to the vicar apostolic of the Midland District and vicar general of the diocese about 1840. He wrote *Life of Bishop Milner, Emblems of the Cross*, more than 1300 contributions to *Notes and Queries*, and edited a Bible and missal. He died in Cossey on Oct. 31.

HUSSEY, THOMAS (1746–1803), bishop. Born in Ballybogan, Meath, Ireland, he studied at the Irish College in Salamanca, joined the Trappists, and was ordained and assigned to the Spanish court. About 1767 he became chaplain to the Spanish embassy in London, where he became known in English society, an acquaintance of Dr. Johnson and Edmund Burke, and was made a fellow of the Royal Society in 1792. When Spain joined France in aiding the United States in its revolution, he handled the Spanish embassy's affairs and was sent by George III to Madrid to persuade Spain to desist. Sent later to Ireland to investigate military unrest, he became first president of Maynooth College in 1795 and bishop of Waterford and Lismore shortly afterward. He died in Tramore, Ireland, on July 11.

HUTTON, PETER (1811–1880). Born in Leeds, Yorkshire, England, on June 29, he went to Ampleforth in 1824, where he began his novitiate in 1829, taught at Prior Park, was sent to Louvain in 1836, and was recalled in 1839 to become president of St. Peter's College, and was ordained. In 1841 he resigned to join the Order of Charity, was ordered back to Prior Park by his bishop, complied, but in 1842 went to Italy and joined the Order of Charity. He was appointed rector of its college in Leicestershire, did parish work in that area, served as vice-president and in 1851 as president of the college at Ratcliffe, England, and was rector of its religious community in 1857. He died there on Sept. 2.

HUYSMANN, RUDOLPH. *See* Agricola, Rudolph.

HUYSMANS, JORIS KARL (1848–1907), novelist. Born in Paris on Feb. 5, he studied at Lycée St. Louis and in 1868 joined the ministry of the interior, where he was to work for the next twenty-nine years. His early writing reflected his materialism, skepticism, and extreme realism, as in *Marthe* (1876), a study of prostitution. He was a founder of the Goncourt Academy, of which he was elected president in 1900. In 1895 he was so impressed by a week he spent at a Trappist monastery that he became a convert; *En route* and *L'Oblat* record the experience. He retired to live near a Benedictine monastery in Ligugé and, when the monks were expelled by anti-religious laws, returned to Paris, where he died on May 12. Other late works include A *Rebours, Là-bas,* and *Les foules de Lourdes* (1905), a reply to Zola.

HYACINTH, ST. (d. 110?), martyr. He is believed to have been put to death during the reign of Trajan. F. D. July 26.

HYACINTH, ST. (d. 120), martyr. *See* Amantius, St.

HYACINTH, ST. (d. 120?), martyr. He had been chamberlain of Emperor Trajan at Caesarea in Cappadocia, and was starved to death in prison when he refused to eat food consecrated as a sacrifice to idols. F. D. July 3.

HYACINTH, ST. (d. 257?), martyr. *See* Protus, St.

HYACINTH, ST. (1185–1257). Born near Cracow, Poland, he became a Dominican in 1217 or 1218 in Rome under St. Dominic, then returned to Silesia. He preached extensively in Scandinavia, Russia, Tibet, and China, although biographical details of this career are somewhat extravagant. He died on Aug. 15 and was canonized in 1594. F. D. Aug. 17.

HYACINTHA, ST. *See* Mariscotti, St. Clarice.

HYDATIUS (d. 468?), bishop. Born in Lemica (Ginzo de Limia), Spain, he met St. Jerome in the Holy Land as a boy, and became a priest about 417. In 427 he was made bishop of Aquae Flaviae (Chaves), Portugal, and in 431 went to Gaul to secure Aetius' help against the Suevi. He wrote a *Chronicle* covering the years 379–468, of value as a contemporary report on events after 427.

HYDE, ANNE (1637–1671). Daughter of the duke of Clarendon, she was taken to Holland at twelve, became maid of honor to the princess of Orange, visited Paris with the latter in 1656, and fell in love with James, duke of York. In 1660, in spite of opposition from both families, she secretly married the future James II of England. She was not recognized by the royal family and slanders against her character were carefully prepared and published; they increased after she became a convert in 1667. Her daughters, Anne and Mary, later queens of England, were brought up as Protestants by government direction. Anne was responsible for the conversion of her husband.

HYGINUS, ST. (d. 140), pope. A Greek, he served as pope from 136 to 140, at a time when the Gnostic heretics were disturbing the papacy and the Church. F.D. Jan. 11.

HYLAN, JOHN FRANCIS (1868–1936), mayor. Born in Hunter, New York, he went to Brooklyn at nineteen, studied at New York Law School, practiced law in Brooklyn, and entered politics. He was appointed justice of the municipal court in 1906 and judge of the Kings County court in 1914, and was elected mayor of New York City in 1917 and in 1921. He was defeated in the Democratic primary in 1925, became justice of the children's court in Jamaica in 1930, and died in Forest Hills, New York, on Jan. 12.

HYPATIUS, ST. (d. 135?), martyr. He and two other Greeks, SS. Leontius and Theodulus, were put to death at Tripoli in Phoenicia. F. D. June 18.

HYPATIUS, ST. (d. 273), martyr. *See* Lucillian, St.

HYPATIUS, ST. (d. 325?), martyr. Bishop of Gangra, Paphlagonia, he was stoned to death by heretics as he was returning from the Council of Nicaea. F. D. Nov. 14.

HYPATIUS, ST. (366?–446?). Said to have been a well-educated Phrygian, he settled with two ascetics named Moschion and Timotheus in the ruins of the monastery of SS. Peter and Paul in Bithynia, rebuilt it, and attracted many followers to the solitary life. F. D. June 17.

HYPATIUS, ST. (d. 735), martyr. *See* Andrew, St.

HYRTL, JOSEPH (1810–1894), anatomist. Born in Eisenstadt, Hungary, on Dec. 7, he studied at Vienna, became curator of the university museum, and in 1837 professor of anatomy at Prague. He returned to Vienna in 1845 and was its rector in 1865. He wrote texts and studies of anatomy and died near Vienna on July 17.

HYWYN, ST. (6th century). A Breton, he is said to have gone with St. Caftan from Brittany to Cornwall in 516 and to have founded Aberdaron, Carnarvonshire. He is also known as Ewen and Owen. F. D. Jan. 6.

I

IA, ST. (d. 360?), martyr. She is said to have been a Greek slave in Persia, who was tortured and executed during the persecution of King Sapor II. F. D. Aug. 4.

IA, ST. (6th century). Possibly from Ireland, she established a hermitage for herself in Cornwall, England, once called Port Ia and now known as St. Ives, and spent her life there in prayer. F. D. Feb. 3.

IBAR, ST. (5th century), bishop. Probably a follower of St. Patrick, though some say he predated him, he preached in Leinster and Meath and founded a monastic school on the island of Beg-Eire, Ireland, where he was bishop. F. D. Apr. 23.

IBAS (d. 457), bishop. A Syrian priest, he was elected bishop of Edessa in 439, was deposed at the Synod of Ephesus (449), but was restored by the Council of Chalcedon (451), where he anathematized Nestorius. His letter criticizing St. Cyril for the methods employed in securing the condemnation of Nestorius at the Council of Ephesus was condemned at the fifth Ecumenical Council (553), but he himself was not.

IBERVILLE, PIERRE LE MOYNE D' (1661–1706), explorer. Son of Charles le Moyne, sieur de Longueuil, he was born in Montreal, Canada, on July 16. In 1686–97 he participated in or led successful expeditions against British posts on Hudson Bay and in 1696 captured all English settlements in Newfoundland. From Brest, France, he was sent in 1698 to discover the mouth of the Mississippi, which he did in Mar. 1699. He built forts in Old Biloxi and Natchez, Mississippi, and establishments in Louisiana. In 1706 he captured the island of Nevis and was about to attack the American colonies of the Carolinas when stricken with yellow fever at Havana, where he died on July 9.

IDA, BL. (1156–1226). Legend says she married Count Henry of Toggenburg, fled to escape his jealousy and maltreatment, lived in a cave for seventeen years, and then gained his permission to become a Benedictine nun at Fischingen, Switzerland. She is also known as Mida. F. D. Nov. 3.

IDA OF BOULOGNE, BL. (1040–1113). Daughter of Duke Godfrey IV of Lorraine, she was married at seventeen to Count Eustace II of Boulogne and became mother of Baldwin and of Godfrey of Bouillon, the latter the conqueror of Jerusalem in the first crusade. She founded and developed numerous religious establishments, distributed charities widely, and in her last years was a Benedictine Oblate at St. Vaast, Arras, France. F. D. Apr. 13.

IDA OF HERZFELD, ST. (d. 825). Born in Alsace, the great-granddaughter of Charles Martel, she was brought up in the court of Charlemagne. After her husband died and her son became a monk at Corvey, she founded a convent at Herzfeld, Westphalia, where she died. F. D. Sept. 4.

IDA OF LOUVAIN, BL. (d. 1300?). Born in Louvain, Belgium, she became a Cistercian at Rossendael, near Malines, possessed numerous supernatural gifts, and is said to have been given the stigmata. F. D. Apr. 13.

IDA OF NIVELLES, BL. (d. 652). After the death of her husband, Pepin of Nanden, she became a Benedictine at the convent of Nivelles, Belgium, where her daughter, St. Gertrude, was prioress. She is also known as Itta. F. D. May 8.

IDESBALD, BL. (1100–1167). A Flemish courtier, he became a canon at St. Walburga's, Furnes, then a Cistercian at Our Lady of the Dunes, near Dunkirk, France, and in 1155 its abbot. His cult was approved in 1894. F. D. Apr. 18.

IDIOTA. *See* Raymundus Jordanus.

IDUS, ST. (5th century), bishop. He was appointed to the see of Alt-Fadha, Leinster, Ireland, by St. Patrick, who had converted him. F. D. July 14.

IGLESIAS DE LA CASA, JOSÉ (1748–1791), poet. Born in Salamanca, Spain, on Oct. 31, he studied there, was ordained in Madrid in 1783, and lived the rest of his life in Salamanca. He became associated with the literary Escuala de Salamanca, was interested in neoclassicism and pastoralism, and was known as Arcadio. His satirical and epigrammatical poems, published posthumously in 1798, attacked contemporary immorality, and, because of their barbs, were condemned by the Inquisition. He died on Aug. 26.

IGNATIUS, ST. (3rd century), martyr. He and his brother and sister, SS. Laurentius and Celerina, were put to death near Carthage during the reign of Decius. Their nephew, Celerinus, suffered so extremely that he also is termed a martyr, though he lived to be ordained a deacon by St. Cyprian. F. D. Feb. 3.

IGNATIUS, ST. (799?–877), bishop. Son of Byzantine Emperor Michael Rangabee, he was mutilated and exiled to a monastery in 813 when Leo the Armenian deposed his father. Ignatius became a monk, was ordained and chosen abbot, and in 846 became patriarch of

Constantinople. He vigorously condemned evil in high places and in 857 refused Communion to Bardas because of his incestuous life; he was then exiled to Terebinthos by Bardas' nephew, Emperor Michael III. Bardas nominated his own secretary, Photius, a layman, as bishop of the see he declared vacant, and a long factional struggle ensued. When Michael was murdered and succeeded by Basil the Macedonian in 867, the latter restored Ignatius; Photius was excommunicated and his followers condemned at the Council of Constantinople (869), called by Pope Adrian II at Ignatius' request. During his last years, Ignatius was at odds with the papacy; John VIII sent legates threatening him with excommunication, but Ignatius was dead before they arrived. F. D. Oct. 23.

IGNATIUS, ST. (d. 1288), bishop. Called from his position as archimandrite of the monastery of the Theophany in Rostov, Russia, he became bishop there in 1262, and defended his see against the depradations of Tatars and of quarreling nobles. F. D. May 28.

IGNATIUS OF ANTIOCH, ST. (d. 107?), bishop and martyr. Said to have been appointed third bishop of Antioch by St. Peter himself, who had been succeeded by Evodius, he was taken prisoner during the persecution of Trajan, and carried to Rome along the coast of Asia Minor and across Greece, suffering violent treatment from his guards, but comforted by the Christians who gathered in great throngs to receive his blessing as he passed through the principal cities of their areas. On his arrival he was rushed to an arena, where he was devoured by lions. Since he had been accompanied by scribes, he was able to write seven major letters of instruction on the traits of the Church and its government, marriage, the Trinity, Incarnation, Redemption, and the Eucharist. F. D. Feb. 1.

IGNATIUS OF LACONI. *See* Peis, St. Francis Ignatius Vincent.

IGNATIUS LOYOLA, ST. (1491–1556), founder. Ignatius de Recalde de Loyola, son of Don Beltran and Marina Saenz de Licona y Balda, was born at the family castle of Loyola in the Basque province of Gúipuzcoa, Spain, youngest of thirteen children, and was christened Iñigo. He joined the army and suffered a shattered leg at the siege of Pampeluna in 1521. On his recovery he went on pilgrimage to Montserrat and spent a year in retreat at Manresa, where he sketched out the main points of what became his *Spiritual Exercises,* finally published in Rome in 1549. In 1524 he began his studies at Barcelona, Alcalá, and Salamanca. He was accused, and exonerated, by the Inquisition there for his preaching. In 1534, at forty-three, he received his master of arts degree. That same year he and six fellow students (Francis Xavier, Peter Favre, Diego Laynez,

Alfonso Salmeron, Simon Rodriguez, and Nicholas Bobadilla) took their first vows in Paris as members of the Society of Jesus. The name was not adopted until Jan. 1537, when the group met in Venice after Ignatius arrived after a year's pilgrimage through Spain. Ignatius was ordained in 1537. In 1539 he and his companions presented their plans for a new order before Pope Paul III; the Society was approved on Sept. 27, 1540, and the group took final vows in 1541. Ignatius was chosen first superior general, despite his vigorous objections, but even before the election he had begun to send his companions to the mission fields. Soon, Jesuit schools, colleges, seminaries spread through Europe. From 1548 to 1551, Ignatius wrote the Jesuit Constitutions, which were tested in various countries, but not adopted until two years after his death in Rome. He was canonized in 1622; Pope Pius XI proclaimed him patron of retreats and spiritual exercises. F. D. July 31.

JAMES BRODRICK, *The Origin of the Jesuits* (Garden City, N.Y., Image Books, 1960); JAMES BRODRICK, *St. Ignatius Loyola: The Pilgrim Years* (New York, Farrar, 1956).

ILDEPHONSUS, ST. (607–667), archbishop. Honored in Spain as a Doctor of the Church, he studied under St. Isidore at Seville and succeeded his uncle, St. Eugenius, to the see of Toledo in 657. Previously, he had been monk and abbot at the monastery of Agli, had established a community of nuns, and had attended the 653 and 655 councils of Toledo. He is known also for his influential tract, *De virginitate perpetua sanctae Mariae.* F. D. Jan. 23.

A. BRAEGELMANN, *Life and Writings of St. Ildephonsus* (London, 1942).

ILLIDIUS, ST. (d. 385). He was the fourth bishop of Clermont, France, and also known as Allyre. F. D. July 7.

ILLTYD, ST. (425?–505). A married courtier, he became a monk under St. Cadoc, founded the monastery of Llan Illtud, Wales, possibly located on Caldey Island, and may have died in Brittany after greatly influencing monastic life in southern Wales. In legend he is made a cousin of King Arthur and is sometimes identified with Galahad. F. D. July 7.

ILLUMINATA, ST. (d. 320). She is honored in the diocese of Todi, Italy. F. D. Nov. 29.

ILLUMINATUS, ST. (d. 1000?). Born in San Severino, Italy, he became a monk at the Benedictine monastery of San Mariano there. F. D. May 11.

ILSLEY, EDWARD (1838–1926), archbishop. Born in Stafford, England, on May 11, he studied at Sedgley Park and Oscott, was ordained in 1861, served as a curate at Longton for twelve years, and in 1873–83 was rector of Olton seminary. He was bishop of Fesse in 1879–88, and archbishop of Birmingham from

1911 until his retirement in 1921. He died in Birmingham, England, on Dec. 1.

IMBERT, BL. LAURENCE (d. 1839), martyr. A native of Aix-en-Provence, France, and a member of the Paris Society of Missions, he was sent to China as a missioner, worked there for twelve years, was made titular bishop of Capsa, and in 1837 followed Bl. Peter Maubant and James Chastan of his order to Korea. In 1839 a violent persecution of Christians broke out. Among the victims were Bl. Agatha Kim, who was tortured and beheaded, and Bl. John Ri, who was bastinadoed and martyred. Bishop Imbert, in an attempt to save the native Christians, gave himself up, as did Frs. Maubant and Chastan. All were beaten and beheaded. In all, eighty-one Catholics were martyred between 1839 and 1847; they were beatified in 1925. F. D. Sept. 22.

IMBONATI, CARLO GIUSEPPE (17th century), scholar. Born in Milan, Italy, he was a Cistercian of the Reform of St. Bernard, a professor of theology and Hebrew in Rome, was appointed an abbot, became assistant to Giulio Bartolocci in preparing *Bibliotheca magna rabbinica*, and completed volumes 4–6 after Bartolocci's death. He included a scriptural chronology and also wrote the didactic *Chronicon tragicum*. He died after 1696.

IMHOF, MAXIMUS VON (1758–1817), physicist. Born in Rissbach, Bavaria, on July 26, he studied at Landshut and became an Augustinian in 1780. He taught in the Munich monastery in 1786–91, became professor of physics and mathematics at the Electoral Lyceum in 1790, was prior in 1798, and director of the Munich Academy of Sciences in 1800. He left his order in 1802 and became a canon in Munich, Bavaria, where he died on Apr. 11. He wrote much in physics.

IMHOFFER, GUSTAV MELCHIOR (1593–1651), explorer. Born near Graz, Styria, he became a Jesuit, went to Peru as a missioner in 1624, explored the Amazon to its source in 1636, and was the first European to publish (1640) an account of his findings. He also wrote on the language and customs of Peru and served as rector of the college at Bahía, Brazil.

IMPERIAL, FRANCISCO (15th century), poet. Son of a Genoese jeweler who lived in Seville, Spain, he knew many European languages as well as Arabic, wrote much poetry, and introduced Italian meters into Spanish poetry, particularly that used in the *decir*. One of his better allegorical poems is *Decir a las siete virtudes*, heavily influenced (as was much of his work) by Dante. He died in the first half of the century.

INA (d. 727). King of the West Saxons from 688 to 726, he founded the church of SS. Peter and Paul at Glastonbury, endowed its monastery, and gave it a vitality which it retained until the ninth-century Danish invasions. He resigned his crown and went to Rome with his wife, Ethelburga, to spend his last year in penitential prayer.

INCHBALD, ELIZABETH SIMPSON (1753–1821), author. Born in Stanningfield, England, on Oct. 15, she married Joseph Inchbald, an actor, in 1772 and joined him on the stage (and became well known as a character actress, a friend of Mrs. Siddons and John Kemble), from which she retired in 1789. She began writing plays in 1782, wrote her first novel in 1791, *A Simple Story* and achieved popularity with the subsequent *Nature and Art* (1796). She died in London on Aug. 1.

INDALETIUS, ST. (1st century). *See* Caecilius, St.

INDES, ST. (d. 303), martyr. *See* Agapes, St.

INDRACTUS, ST. (d. 710?). An Irish noble, he was slain while on a pilgrimage with his sister Dominica and several companions in a Saxon ambush, perhaps near Glastonbury, England. The story seems legendary, though they were listed as martyrs, commemorated on Feb. 5.

INGEBORG (1176?–1237), queen. Born in Denmark, sister of King Canute IV, she was married to King Philip Augustus of France in 1193 and was set aside after three months. When the king married Agnes of Meran in 1196 he was excommunicated and France placed under interdict by Pope Innocent III, who defended Ingeborg. In spite of Philip's promises to restore her, she was held a prisoner until 1213, when he restored her rights to her and recalled her, inasmuch as he needed her political aid.

INGEGNERI, MARCO ANTONIO (1545?–1592), composer. Born in Verona, Italy, he studied under Vincenzo Ruffo, became choirmaster of the Cremona cathedral in 1575, and in 1588 published *Responsoria hebdomadae sanctae*, later erroneously ascribed to Palestrina. He also issued a book of madrigals and two collections of masses for several voices and was the teacher of Monteverdi.

INGEN, ST. (d. 249), martyr. *See* Ammon, St.

INGEN-HOUSZ, JAN (1730–1799), scientist. Born in Breda, Brabant, on Dec. 8, he studied there and at Louvain and Leyden, and practiced medicine at Breda from 1757 to 1765. He then went to England, supported the theory of inoculation against smallpox, inoculated the royal family in Vienna, met Benjamin Franklin in Paris, and returned to London. He discovered the exhalation of oxygen and absorption of carbonic acids by plants (a theory adopted, without credit, by Joseph Priestley), the vegetable nature of algae, and carried on Franklin's experiments with lightning rods and conduction of heat by metals, and invented the plate electrical machine and an air pistol. He proposed the inhalation of oxygen by lung patients, made developments in nautical compasses, and introduced the use of cover glasses in microscopy. He wrote regularly for the *Philosophical Transactions* of the Royal Society and published volumes on plants, electricity, magnetism, and physics. He died in London on Sept. 7.

INGENES, ST. (d. 250), martyr. *See* Ammon, St.

INGHIRAMI, FRANCESCO (1772–1846), archaeologist. Born in Volterra, Italy, he was director of its library and was known for his research in ancient art. His ten-volume *Monumenti Etruschi* is one of the most complete descriptions of Etruscan antiquities; he also wrote *Letters on Etruscan Erudition*.

INGHIRAMI, GIOVANNI (1779–1851), astronomer. Born in Volterra, Italy, on Apr. 16, brother of Francesco, he studied at St. Michael College there, became a Piarist in 1796, and taught mathematics and philosophy in Volterra and Florence, where he was also director of the observatory. He became provincial of his order, went to Rome as general, returned to Florence, where he taught until his death there on Aug. 15, and wrote on physics, hydraulics, astronomy, and mathematics, a topographical atlas of Tuscany, and a section of an astronomical atlas for the Berlin Academy of Sciences.

INGHIRAMI, TOMMASO (1470–1516). Born in Volterra, Italy, he went to Rome and became famed as an orator, called by Erasmus the Cicero of his age. He was appointed director of the Vatican Library by Pope Julius II.

INGLEBY, VEN. FRANCIS (1551?–1586), martyr. Son of Sir William and Anne Mallory Ingleby, he was born in Ripley, England, studied at Oxford and the Inner Temple, and went to the English College, Rheims, in 1582. He was ordained there in 1583 and sent on the English mission in 1584. He labored in the York area, was captured, sentenced as a priest, and executed at York on June 3.

INGRAM, BL. JOHN (1565–1594), martyr. Born in Stoke Edith, Herefordshire, England, and educated at Oxford and Rheims, he became a convert and was ordained at Rome in 1589. In 1592 he was sent to Scotland, was captured, convicted of being a priest, and imprisoned in the Tower of London. He was hanged, drawn, and quartered in Newcastle on July 26. He was beatified in 1929. F. D. July 24.

INGRES, JEAN AUGUSTE DOMINIQUE (1780–1867), painter. Born in Montauban, France, on Aug. 29, son of a sculptor, he studied in Toulouse, was a violinist in a theater orchestra in 1794–96, then went to Paris to study art with Jacques Louis David. He won the Prix de Rome in 1801, lived there in 1806–20, then moved to Florence. During this period he produced pencil portraits (known as the Ingres crayons), classical nudes, and minor historical works. He was influenced by the classical tradition, especially that of Raphael, and when he returned to Paris in 1824 the success of his *Vow of Louis XIII* established him as the leader of Davidian classicism. He was elected to the Academy of Beaux Arts in 1825 and was professor there in 1827; he later became president both of the academy and its school. In 1835–41 he was in Rome as director of the Académie de France. Among his best-known works are: *Bather, Odalisque, Jupiter and Thetis, Source*, and portraits of Countess d'Haussonville and Cherubini. He died in Paris on Jan. 14.

WALTER PACH, *Ingres* (New York, Harper, 1939); GEORGES WILDENSTEIN, *Ingres* (London, Phaidon, 1954).

INGULF (1030?–1109). In 1051 he was secretary to William of Normandy on a visit to England, later made a pilgrimage to the Holy Land, entered the monastery of Fontenelle, Normandy, on his return and became its prior, and served as abbot of Croyland, Lincolnshire, England, from 1087 until his death there on Dec. 17. A history of the abbey once attributed to him is of fifteenth-century authorship.

IÑIGO, ST. (d. 1057). Born in Calatayud, Spain, he became a Benedictine monk at St. Juan de la Peña, in Aragon. At the request of King Sancho the Great, he agreed to serve as abbot of Oña in Old Castile, and to introduce the Cluniac reform there. F. D. June 1.

INISCHOLUS, ST. (1st century), martyr. *See* Euphrasius, St.

INNITZER, THEODOR (1875–1955), cardinal. Born in Weipert, Bohemia, on Dec. 25, he was ordained, became a cardinal in 1933, and was archbishop of Vienna at the time of the seizure of Austria by Germany in 1938. He recommended quiet acceptance of the invasion, tried to achieve peace with the Nazis, and was brought to Rome for censure by Pope Pius XI for politically recommending the union of Germany and Austria. On his return to Vienna he found that the Church was being destroyed by the conquerors and actively opposed them through the war. His palace and cathedral were looted by mobs, and attacks were made on him then and by the Russian occupying forces. The latter accused him in 1949 of acting with Cardinal Mindszenty as an enemy of freedom. In 1950 the Vatican named Franz Jachym as coadjutor of the see. The cardinal died in Vienna on Oct. 9.

INNOCENT I, ST. (d. 417), pope. A native of Albano, near Rome, he became pope on December 22, 401. His pontificate was marked by his emphasis on papal supremacy, as when he commended the African bishops who had condemned Pelagianism at the councils of

Carthage and Milevis in 416 and then referred their decision to the pope for confirmation. He also fought the unjust removal of St. John Chrysostom from his see, and for the celibacy of the clergy. In 410, Rome was captured and sacked by the Goths under Alaric, although Innocent was in Ravenna at the time, seeking aid from Emperor Honorius to resist the Goths. He died in Rome on Mar. 12. Conditions after the fall of the city were so grave that there was a widespread hostility toward Christians, who were even blamed for the national disaster. These charges by the pagans led St. Augustine to write the *City of God*. F. D. July 28.

INNOCENT II (d. 1143), pope. Gregory Papareschi was born in Rome, became a canon of the Lateran, abbot of SS. Nicholas and Primitivus, and was created a cardinal by Pope Paschal II. He accompanied Pope Gelasius II into exile in 1118, was sent as papal legate to Germany in 1119, where he helped draw up the Concordat of Worms (1122), to France in 1123, and on Feb. 14, 1130, was elected pope by a group of eight cardinals appointed by Pope Honorius II to select his successor. A group of rival cardinals then met and elected Peter Pierleone antipope Anacletus II. Both were consecrated on Feb. 23. Supported by Roger of Sicily, Anacletus drove Innocent from Rome. The pope went to France where he received vigorous support from St. Bernard, and at a series of councils, notably at Etampes, and Rheims in 1131, England, France, Germany, Castile, and Aragon pledged their support to Innocent. In 1133, King Lothair of Germany led an army to Rome and reinstated Innocent, who crowned him emperor. As soon as Lothair returned to Germany, Innocent was again forced to flee. He held a council in Pisa in 1135 at which he excommunicated Anacletus and Roger of Sicily, and in 1136 Lothair again invaded Italy and regained Rome for Innocent. Anacletus died in 1138 and the new antipope, Victor IV, soon submitted at St. Bernard's demand. In 1139 Innocent convoked the tenth General Council (the second Lateran Council). It voided Anacletus' acts, silenced Arnold of Brescia, and instigated widespread reforms. In that year, Innocent's forces were defeated by those of Roger of Sicily, and in the resultant Treaty of Garigliano Innocent lifted Rogers' excommunication and recognized him as king of Italy and Roger took an oath of fealty to the pope. In 1141, Innocent placed France under an interdict when Louis refused to accept Pierre de la Chartre as archbishop of Bourges; he also acted as mediator between Alfonso of Spain and Alfonso Henríquez, leader of the revolting Portuguese. Innocent died in Rome on Sept. 24.

INNOCENT III (1160?–1216), pope. Born in Anagni, Italy, perhaps in 1161, son of Count Trasimund of Segni and nephew of Pope Clement III, Lotario de' Conti de' Segni studied at Rome and Paris and law at Bologna, and held offices in Rome under Popes Lucius III, Urban III, Gregory VIII, and Clement III, who created him cardinal-deacon in 1190. He was elected pope on Jan. 8, 1198, and was consecrated on Feb. 22. He at once began to put into effect the theory he had evidently formulated that, since the spiritual was always to take precedence over the material, the Church was superior to any human institution; hence, earthly rulers were subject to the Church in all things. The pope as head of the Church was not only an ecclesiastical ruler, but all monarchs were subject to him; there was no area of human activity in which the Church should not be active. He first restored papal authority in Rome and then in Italy, bringing back Romagna, Ancona, Spoleto, Assisi, and Stora to papal domination. He moved to restore peace between the warring Philip Augustus of France and Richard I of England and, after a threatened interdict, a five-year truce was signed by both kings in 1198. He put France under an interdict in 1199 when Philip refused to leave Agnes, daughter of the duke of Meran, and return to his lawful wife, Ingeborg of Denmark. Philip submitted in 1200, though he was not reconciled to Ingeborg until 1213. He recognized Henry IV's four-year-old son, Frederick II, as king of Sicily in 1198. On the death of the boy's mother, Constance, Innocent became regent and faithfully protected Frederick's rights; he arranged Frederick's marriage to Constance of Hungary in 1209. When Philip of Swabia (Ghibelline) and Otto IV (Guelph) were elected emperor in 1198, war broke out between their adherents, and in 1201 Innocent recognized Otto as king of Germany and emperor. In his decretal *Venerabilem* (1202) Innocent declared the Holy See was the final authority in the selection of emperor—a theory which definitely placed the pope over temporal rulers. By 1207, Otto's actions had alienated so many of the princes that Innocent attempted to persuade Otto to abdicate in favor of Philip. However, when Philip was murdered by Otto of Wittelsbach in 1208, Otto IV was universally accepted and was crowned by the pope in St. Peter's in 1209 after he had agreed to respect the rights of the Church and the integrity of papal possessions, to aid in wiping out heresy, and to forego the revenue of vacant sees. Otto soon betrayed his pledges, seized Ancona, Spoleto, and other papal possessions, and invaded Sicily, whereupon Innocent excommunicated him in 1210. In 1211 at Nuremberg a group of German princes deposed Otto and elected seventeen-year-old Frederick II of Sicily, Innocent's ward, as emperor, and Innocent crowned him at Aachen in 1215. Otto joined John of England in war against King Philip Augustus of France, who had supported Frederick's election, but his defeat at Bouvines in 1214 ended his influence and he died in 1218. Innocent also intervened in England in 1205 when a group of monks of Christ Church elected Hubert of Canterbury archbishop without the knowledge or approval of the English bishops who elected John de Grey, King John's candidate. The pope declared both elections illegal, though he recognized the monks' right to elect the archbishop of Canterbury and approved their new choice of Stephen Langton, whom he had suggested. When John refused to accept Stephen and took possession of the monks' property, Innocent put England under an interdict in 1208, excommunicated John in 1209, and declared him deposed in 1212. John submitted when King Philip of France threatened to invade England and enforce the pope's demands, and in 1213 turned England and Ireland over to the pope and received it back as a fief. When the barons revolted against John and drew up the Magna Charta, Innocent declared it void, since it had been secured by violence. During his pontificate Innocent was also active in the rest of Europe in his role of international mediator. He excommunicated Alfonso X of León for marrying a close relative and caused their separation in 1204; he annulled the marriage of Alfonso of Portugal with Urraca in 1208 for the same reason. He crowned Pedro II of Aragon king in 1204 in Rome after receiving Aragon in vassalage; he encouraged a crusade against the Moors in Spain which led to their defeat at Tolosa in 1212; he decided the successor of King Sverri of Norway; arbitrated disputes in Hungary, Poland, Sweden; and sent his legate to crown Johannitius king of Bulgaria in 1204. He actively campaigned for a crusade against the Turks and saw it launched in 1202; but when the crusaders attacked Christian Zara and Constantinople, he excommunicated the leaders who had agreed to the attack on Constantinople. Innocent labored to reunite the Greek Church with Rome and had some success, though the reunion ended after his death; and to bring the Albigensians back to the Church; and when the papal delegate Castelnau was assassinated in 1208, believed at the instigation of Raymond of Toulouse, whom he had excommunicated, he called for a crusade against the Albigensians. The resultant crusade by Simon of Montfort was notable for its cruelty and soon devolved into a war of conquest by Simon, against which the pope fruitlessly protested. In 1215, Innocent convoked the fourth Lateran Council, which declared for a crusade against the Saracens, denounced Albigensianism, made the reception of Communion mandatory during the Easter season, and canonized the term *transubstantiation*

in defining the Church's doctrine of the Eucharist. During his reign, Innocent approved the founding of the Franciscans and the Dominicans, as well as the Trinitarians (1198) and the Humiliati (1201), supported the Teutonic Knights in the Baltic area and encouraged missionaries to Prussia, and built Santo Spirito hospital in Rome. He died at Perugia on June 16 while traveling through Italy preaching the crusade urged by the fourth Lateran Council. Among his writing are *De contemptu mundi*, an ascetical treatise, *De quadri partita specie nuptiarum*, on marriage, and *De sacro altaris mysterio*.

INNOCENT IV (d. 1254), pope. Born in Genoa, Italy, Sinibaldo de' Fieschi, count of Lavagna, studied at Parma and Bologna, taught at the latter, and in 1224 was auditor of the Roman curia. He was created a cardinal-priest in 1227, was vice-chancellor in Rome in 1228, and became cardinal-bishop of Alberga and legate to northern Italy in 1235. He was elected pope at Anagni on June 25, 1243, in an election delayed a year and a half by Emperor Frederick II's intrigues, and was consecrated on June 28. He announced his intention to free the Church from the emperor. Because of the emperor's unfriendly actions he left Rome the next year and settled in Lyons, France, for six years. He convoked the General Council of Lyons in 1245, which ordered a crusade and declared Frederick deposed. Innocent produced a rival king and even ordered a crusade against Frederick in 1249; the struggle against the German emperors continued against Conrad IV and Manfred after Frederick's death in 1250. Innocent returned to Rome in 1253, became involved in a dispute with Conrad and Manfred over Sicily, which the Holy See claimed, and in 1254 Innocent's army was defeated at Foggia by Manfred. The pope acted as mediator between Henry III and his nobles in England, between Duke Ottocer of Austria and King Béla of Hungary in 1252, and appointed Alfonso III as administrator of Portugal in 1254. He encouraged missionary activities, but devoted most of his pontificate to political matters, especially against the Hohenstaufens. He died in Naples, Italy, on Dec. 7.

INNOCENT V, BL. (1245–1277), pope. Born probably in Champagne, Tarentaise, France, Peter of Tarentaise became a Dominican under Bl. Jordan of Saxony, held a chair at the University of Paris, and became famous as a theologian and preacher. In 1259, with SS. Thomas Aquinas, Albertus Magnus, and others, he drew up the plan of study which is still the foundation of Dominican education. He also wrote commentaries on the epistles of St. Paul and the *Sentences* of Peter Lombard. He was made prior provincial for France at thirty-seven, going on foot to visit all Dominican establishments, succeeded St. Thomas at the university, and was made archbishop of Lyons in 1272 and cardinal in 1273 by Pope Gregory X, a former student. He played a prominent part at the Council of Lyons (1274) which sought to heal the Greek schism, preached at the funeral of St. Bonaventure, and accompanied the pope back to Italy in 1276. When Gregory died, Innocent was unanimously elected his successor on Jan. 21, and crowned on Feb. 22, 1276. He died four months later in Rome as he was proceeding with efforts to unite the Greek Church with Rome and to establish peace between Italian states. His cult was confirmed in 1898. F. D. June 22.

INNOCENT VI (d. 1362), pope. Born in Mont, Limousin, France, Étienne Aubert taught civil law at Toulouse, became an ecclesiastic, was appointed bishop of Noyon in 1338, of Clermont in 1340, and was created a cardinal in 1342 and cardinal-bishop of Ostia and grand penitentiary in 1352. He was elected pope at Avignon on Dec. 18, consecrated on Dec. 30, and inaugurated an era of reform and austerity at the papal court. He dispatched Cardinal Aegidius Albornoz and Cola di Rienzo to Italy to recover papal territory, in which mission they were most successful, though Cola was murdered in 1354. Albornoz restored order and as papal legate crowned Charles IV emperor in 1355. Innocent was successful in ending war between France and England in 1360, clashed with Emperor Charles IV when the emperor attempted to reform the Church in Germany independently of the Holy See, fruitlessly attempted to launch a crusade, and failed in his efforts to reunite the Eastern churches to Rome and establish peace between Castile and Aragon. He died in Avignon, France, on Sept. 12.

INNOCENT VII (1336?–1406), pope. Born in Sulmona, Abruzzi, Italy, Cosmato de' Migliorati studied at Perugia and Padua, and under Lignano at Bologna. He taught at Perugia and Padua, became a member of the curia in Rome, and spent ten years in England as papal collector. He was appointed bishop of Bologna in 1386, was archbishop of Ravenna in 1387–1400, and was created a cardinal-priest in 1389. He was papal legate to Lombardy and Tuscany in 1390, and on Oct. 17, 1404, was elected pope and consecrated on Nov. 11. He was faced by antipope Benedict XIII (1394–1423) and by a revolution in Rome, which King Ladislaus of Naples suppressed, but was forced to flee to Viterbo in 1405, where the populace rose at the news the pope's nephew, Cardinal Ludovico Migliorati, had murdered several papal enemies. Innocent returned in 1406, and excommunicated Ladislaus for raiding papal territory, who thereupon desisted. Though pledged to end the papal schism, Innocent was so preoccupied

in attempting to keep order in Rome he did little toward this end. He died on Nov. 6.

INNOCENT VIII (1432–1492), pope. Born in Genoa, Italy, Giovanni Battista Cibò, son of a Roman senator, led a profligate youth, fathered two illegitimate children, reformed, became an ecclesiastic, and entered the service of Cardinal Calandrini. He was appointed bishop of Savona in 1467, exchanged it for Molfetta in 1472, and was created a cardinal in 1473. He was heavily supported by Cardinal della Rovere at the conclave of 1484, was elected pope on Aug. 29, and was consecrated on Sept. 12. He devoted himself to restoring peace in Christendom, though he was at once involved in war in Naples, where the nobles had revolted against King Ferrante I, and launching a crusade which never took place, despite a meeting of Christian leaders in 1490. He denounced the Hussite heresy in Bohemia, called for a crusade against the Waldensians, forbade the reading of Pico della Mirandola's 900 theses, and was severely criticized for creating and selling posts to refill the papal treasury. He died in Rome on July 25.

INNOCENT IX (1519–1591), pope. Giovanni Antonio Facchinetti was born in Bologna, Italy, on July 22, studied and received his doctorate in law there in 1544, and became Cardinal Nicolò Ardinghelli's secretary in Rome. He then entered the service of Cardinal Farnese, for whom he administered Avignon and Parma, was named bishop of Nicastro in 1560, attended the Council of Trent in 1562, and was papal nuncio to Venice in 1566. He resigned the see of Nicastro in 1572 and went to Rome, became patriarch of Jerusalem in 1575, and was created a cardinal-priest in 1583. He was prominent in the administration of Pope Gregory XIV's reign, and was elected his successor on Oct. 29, 1591, and consecrated on Nov. 3. He reigned only two months, and died in Rome on Dec. 30.

INNOCENT X (1574–1655), pope. Born in Rome on May 6, Giambattista Pamfili studied law at the Roman College, receiving his degree when twenty, became an auditor of the rota, accompanied Cardinal Barberini as datary to France and Spain in the pontificate of Pope Urban VIII, who appointed him titular Latin patriarch of Antioch and nuncio at Madrid, and in 1626 was created cardinal-priest. He attended the Council of Trent where he served on several congregations, and on Sept. 15, 1644, was elected pope and consecrated on Oct. 4. He was involved in a dispute with Cardinal Mazarin, the French prime minister, when he confiscated the properties of the Barberini, nephews of Pope Urban VIII, in 1646 and again in 1652 when he protested Mazarin's arrest of Cardinal Retz. He also quarreled with Duke Ranuccio II of Parma, whom the pope forced to resign his administration, but had friendly relations with Venice, whose leaders he aided against the Turks in their struggle for Candia. He also refused to recognize Juan IV of Braganza as king of an independent Portugal after its secession from Spain in 1640. In 1648 he issued the bull *Zelus domus meae,* declaring that all articles of the peace of Westphalia inimical to the Church were voided, and in 1653 he intervened in the Jansenist controversy in France with his *Cum occasione,* declaring that five propositions extracted by Nicholas Cornet from *Augustinus* were heretical. Innocent inaugurated many projects to beautify Rome, was influenced by his sister-in-law, Donna Olympia Maldalchini, and was severely criticized for the lucrative positions he granted her relatives. He died in Rome on Jan. 7.

INNOCENT XI (1611–1689), pope. Benedetto Odescalchi was born in Como, Italy, on May 16, studied under the Jesuits there and law at Rome and Naples, held numerous posts under Pope Urban VIII, including those of administrator of Macerata and governor of Picena, and was created a cardinal in 1645 by Pope Innocent X. He served as legate to Ferrara, was appointed bishop of Novara in 1650, resigned in his brother's favor in 1656, and returned to Rome. He was unanimously elected pope on Sept. 21, 1676, and consecrated on Oct. 4. He was occupied throughout his reign with the encroachments of Louis XIV on papal rights and territories. In 1682 he annulled the *Déclaration du clergé français,* which an assembly of French bishops called by Louis had drawn up, and which declared the pope subject to a general council, the king subject to the pope in spiritual matters only, and refused to confirm any episcopal nominations of men who had attended the convention. He unenthusiastically accepted the Revocation of the Edict of Nantes in 1685, and sought milder treatment of the French Protestants. In 1687 a French force occupied the papal palace in Rome after Innocent had abolished diplomatic immunity to persons sought by papal courts sheltered in foreign consulates in Rome. When Innocent appointed Joseph Clement archbishop of Cologne against Louis' will in 1688, the king imprisoned the papal nuncio, occupied papal Avignon, and threatened to sever the French Church's ties with Rome. He was lukewarm in his support of James II in England, whom he considered imprudent, encouraged Christian resistance to the Turks in Austria and Hungary, put ecclesiastical reforms into effect, and condemned quietism in his *Coelestis pastor* in 1687. He died in Rome on Aug. 12.

INNOCENT XII (1615–1700), pope. Born in Spinazzola, Italy, on Mar. 13, Antonio Pignatelli was a member of the Roman curia in 1635,

served as legate to Urbino, inquisitor at Malta, and governor of Perugia, was Innocent X's nuncio to Tuscany and Alexander VII's to Poland, where he brought the Armenians back to Rome, and was nuncio to Vienna in 1668. He was created cardinal-priest and bishop of Faenza in 1682, archbishop of Naples in 1687, and on July 12, 1691, was elected pope and consecrated on July 15. He issued decrees curbing nepotism, convinced Louis XIV of France to withdraw the 1682 *Déclaration du clergé français* in 1693, reiterated Innocent XI's condemnation of Jansenism in 1696, and in 1699 condemned twenty-three semi-quietistic propositions in Fénelon's *Maximes,* to which Fénelon at once submitted. The naming of the duke of Anjou by Charles II of Spain as his successor, suggested by Innocent, led to the War of the Spanish Succession. Innocent died in Rome on Sept. 27.

INNOCENT XIII (1655–1724), pope. Michael Angelo dei Conti, son of Duke Carlo II of Poli, was born in Rome on May 13, studied at the Roman College, became a member of the curia, and in 1695 was appointed titular archbishop of Tarsus. He was nuncio at Lucerne and Lisbon, and was created a cardinal-priest in 1706, archbishop of Osimo in 1709, and of Viterbo in 1712, which he resigned in 1719 because of illness. He was elected pope on May 8, 1721, and consecrated on May 18. He decided against the Jesuits in the matter of native usages in the liturgy among Chinese converts and missionaries, condemned seven French bishops who petitioned him to suppress Clement XI's constitution *Unigenitus* condemning Quesnel's errors, and insisted on their submission to the constitution, aided Venice and Malta against the Turks, and in 1723 issued a bull instituting ecclesiastical reforms in Spain. He died in Rome on Mar. 7.

INNOCENT, ST. (d. 287?), martyr. *See* Maurice, St.

INNOCENT, ST. (d. 350?), bishop. Born in Tortona, Italy, he was tortured and imprisoned during the Diocletian persecution, escaped to Rome, became a deacon, and was sent back to his birthplace as bishop about 326 by Pope St. Sylvester. F. D. Apr. 17.

INNOCENT, ST. (4th century). He was bishop of Adrumetum in northern Africa, and went to Italy late in life, where he died at Gaeta. F. D. May 7.

INNOCENT, ST. (d. 559). He was bishop of Le Mans, France, from about 519 until his death. F. D. June 19.

INNOCENZO DA IMOLA. *See* Francucci, Innocenzo.

IPHIGENIA, ST. (1st century). She is said to have been an Ethiopian converted by St. Matthew the apostle. F. D. Sept. 21.

IPOLYI, ARNOLD (1823–1886), bishop.

Born in Ipoly-Keszi, Hungary, on Oct. 20, he studied in Vienna and the seminary at Gran and was ordained in 1847. After years as a tutor he did parish work. He won a prize offered by the Hungarian Academy of Science in 1854 with his *Ungarische Mythologie*. He became canon of Eger in 1863, director of the seminary in Pest in 1869, bishop of Neusohl in 1871, and, in 1886, of Grosswardein, Hungary, where he died on Dec. 2. He was founder and later president of the Hungarian Historical Society, built a fine art collection, and wrote biographical and historical studies.

IRAIS, ST. (d. 300?), martyr. She was slain at Alexandria or Antinoe, Egypt, during the Diocletian persecution. F. D. Sept. 22.

IRCHARD, ST. (7th century). Born in Kincardineshire, Scotland, he was a disciple of St. Ternan, a missioner to the Picts, and may have been consecrated a bishop at Rome by St. Gregory the Great. F. D. Aug. 24.

IRELAND, BL. JOHN (d. 1544), martyr. Pastor of Eltham, Kent, England, he refused to acknowledge Henry VIII as spiritual head of the Church and was executed at Tyburn. He was beatified in 1929. F. D. Mar. 11.

IRELAND, JOHN (1838–1918), archbishop. Born in Burnchurch, Kilkenny, Ireland, on Sept. 11, he was brought to the United States in 1849 by his parents, who lived in Boston and Chicago before settling in St. Paul, Minnesota, in 1853. He studied at Meximieux seminary and the Marist scholasticate in France, was ordained in St. Paul in 1861, served as a chaplain for Union troops in the Civil War, but was forced to resign because of ill health in 1863. He became pastor of the St. Paul cathedral in 1867, was a fiery leader of temperance forces in the Midwest and an untiring opponent of corrupt politicians, and soon became nationally known for his oratorical prowess. He represented his bishop at the Vatican Council, and was named titular bishop of Maronea and coadjutor of St. Paul in 1875. He succeeded to the see in 1884 and became involved in the civic activities of his community and the nation. He encouraged immigration to the West by making land purchase easy through the Catholic Colonization Bureau, which was responsible for founding many towns and villages. His address, "The Catholic Church and Civil Society," at the third Plenary Council of Baltimore in 1884 in which he fervently declaimed on the patriotism of Catholics, a theme which he unceasingly proclaimed throughout his life, attracted nationwide attention. He was made first archbishop of St. Paul in 1888 when his see became an archdiocese, was a leading proponent, with Bishop Keane, of a national Catholic University, which he helped found in 1889, fought the establishment of national churches, and in 1891 was a leader in the successful fight

to defeat Peter Cahensly's petition to the pope requesting the appointment of bishops in the United States on a racial basis proportionate to the population of each national group in the United States. He fought to have English used exclusively in Catholic parochial schools, joined with Cardinal Gibbons and Bishops O'Connell and Keane in the successful fight to prevent papal condemnation of the Knights of Labor which the Canadian bishops had denounced in Canada in 1887, and was a consistent friend of labor, though he repeatedly denounced the use of violence in labor disputes. He favored public schools, but declared a Catholic parochial-school system essential in view of anti-Catholic bias in public schools, and proposed state aid for parochial schools, actually putting such a plan into effect in Faribault, Minnesota, and Stillwater where the parochial schools were turned over to the school boards which paid for their upkeep and teachers' salaries while religious instruction was continued in them as before. This Faribault plan aroused such opposition, even among Catholics, that it was abandoned in 1892, whereupon he devoted his energies to expanding his parochial-school system. He established St. Thomas seminary (now a college) in 1885, St. Paul seminary in 1894, and helped establish the College of St. Catherine in 1905. He became embroiled in a bitter dispute with Bishop McQuaid, who denounced him from his pulpit, and Archbishop Corrigan when he supported Sylvester Malone for regent of the University of New York against Bishop McQuaid. He was a leader in the fight against the anti-Catholic political parties, William Jennings Bryan, bimetallism, and the Spanish-American War (though he announced his full support of the United States when war broke out). He was a friend of Presidents McKinley and Roosevelt. In 1892 he went to France as Pope Leo XIII's unofficial representative to urge Catholic support of the republic. He laid the cornerstone of St. Paul's cathedral in 1907, pleaded for a policy of preparedness before World War I, and was an active supporter of the Allies during that conflict. He died in St. Paul, Minnesota, on Sept. 25.

JAMES HUMPHREY MOYNIHAN, *The Life of Archbishop John Ireland* (New York, Harper, 1953).

IREMONGER, BL. WILLIAM (d. 1679), martyr. Born in Lincolnshire, England, he studied at St. Omer, became a Jesuit there in 1655, was sent to the English mission, where he was also known as William Ireland, was arrested for alleged complicity in the Titus Oates Plot, and executed at Tyburn with his servant, John Grove. They were beatified in 1929. F. D. Jan. 24.

IRENAEUS, ST. (d. 120), martyr. *See* Amantius, St.

IRENAEUS, ST. (125?–203?), bishop. Born in Asia Minor, and educated there by St. Polycarp and others in the earliest apostolic tradition, he went as a missionary bishop to Gaul. He was on a mission to Rome when St. Pothinus was martyred in 177 and returned to succeed him as bishop of Lyons. In his last twenty years he sent many missioners through southern Gaul, checked the spread of Gnosticism, and served successfully as a mediator in a dispute between the pope and groups in the Near East over the date of Easter. He wrote widely against heresy, clarifying the questions of providence and salvation; his Greek was translated into both Latin and Armenian. F. D. June 28 (in East, Aug. 23).

IRENAEUS, ST. (d. 258?), martyr. *See* Abundius, St.; also, Antony, St.

IRENAEUS, ST. (d. 273), martyr. A deacon, he was imprisoned in Chiusi, Italy, for burying the body of the martyred St. Felix. With other Christians, Irenaeus was tended in prison by Mustiola, whose beauty attracted the lust of Turcius, their jailer. When she spurned him, he tortured Irenaeus to death. F. D. July 3.

IRENAEUS, ST. (d. 300?), martyr. He was burned to death at Thessalonica, with SS. Irene and Peregrinus, during the persecution of Diocletian. F. D. May 5.

IRENAEUS, ST. (d. 304), bishop and martyr. Tortured and beheaded during the Diocletian persecution, he had served as bishop of Sirmium (Mitrovica), about forty miles west of Belgrade. F. D. Mar. 24.

IRENAEUS, ST. (d. 310), martyr. *See* Theodore, St.

IRENE, ST. (d. 200?), martyr. She was beheaded at Alexandria, Egypt, with St. Sophia. F. D. Sept. 18.

IRENE, ST. (d. 300?), martyr. *See* Irenaeus, St.

IRENE, ST. (d. 304?), martyr. Sister of SS. Agape and Chionia, she was captured in Thessalonica during the persecution of Diocletian, and ordered to be exposed naked and chained in a brothel. The punishment, for possessing copies of scripture and refusing to eat food sacrificed to the gods, proved ineffective when none would molest her, and she was shot to death with arrows. F. D. Apr. 3.

IRENE, ST. (d. 653?), martyr. She was a Portuguese nun who died in defense of her honor; a shrine was established at Santarem. F. D. Oct. 20.

IRENE, SR. *See* FitzGibbon, Catherine.

IRENION, ST. (d. 389). He was bishop of Gaza, Palestine. F. D. Dec. 16.

IRETON, PETER L. (1882–1958), bishop. Born in Baltimore, on Sept. 21, he studied at St. Charles's College and St. Mary's seminary there and was ordained in Baltimore in 1906. He engaged in parish work in Washington and Baltimore, was named a domestic prelate in 1929, and was appointed titular bishop of Cime and coadjutor and apostolic administrator of Richmond, Virginia, in 1935. He succeeded to that see in 1945, was appointed an assistant at the pontifical throne in 1956, and died in Washington, D.C. on Apr. 27.

IRIARTE, IGNACIO DE (1620–1685), painter. Born in Azcoitia, Guipuzcoa, Spain, he went to Seville in 1642 to study painting under Francisco de Herrera the elder. Never too proficient at painting figures, he became outstanding for his colorful and rugged landscapes, often working with his close friend, Murillo, who painted the figures while he did the landscapes. He was one of the first members of the Academy of Seville and served several times as its secretary. He died in Seville.

IRIARTE, TOMÁS DE (1750–1791), poet. Born in Orotave, Teneriffe Island, on Sept. 18, he studied in Madrid, held several minor government offices, translated plays from the French, and became a dramatist in his own right. He also translated Horace's *Art of Poetry*; wrote *La musica* on the elements of music, praised by Metastasio; and gained lasting fame by his *Fábulas literarias*, ingenious and satiric animal fables in verse. He was brought before the Inquisition in 1786 on the charge of preaching the views of the French Encyclopedists, but cleared himself. He died in Madrid on Sept. 17.

IRMINA, ST. (d. 710?). According to tradition, she was the daughter of King St. Dagobert II of the Franks, became a nun when her fiancé was killed on their wedding day, and persuaded her father to rebuild a Benedictine convent near Trèves. In 698 she gave St. Willibrord the manor which became Echternach, Luxembourg. She died at Weissenburg monastery, Alsace, which her father also had founded. F. D. Dec. 24.

IRNERIUS (1050?–1130?), jurist. He was born in Bologna, Italy, where he taught rhetoric and dialectics before (at the urging of Countess Matilda of Tuscany) he took up the study of law. After studying and teaching in Rome, he founded in 1084 the school of law in Bologna which became the outstanding center of jurisprudence in Europe. He was responsible for a revival of Roman law which had been neglected, and his interlineal and marginal glosses to the Corpus Juris became famous. He became the first of the great glossators. His *Summa codicis* is the first mediaeval system of Roman jurisprudence. Also known as Guarnerius and Warnerius, he defended Henry V and upheld the legality of the election of antipope Gregory VIII. He died in Bologna.

ISAAC, ST. (825?–852), martyr. Born in Cordova, Spain, he mastered Arabic, became a notary under the Moorish government, then withdrew to the nearby monastery at Tabanos.

When he returned to Cordova to engage in a religious debate with the chief magistrate, his remarks on Mohammed led to torture, execution, and public desecration of his corpse. F. D. June 3.

ISAAC, ST. (d. 1003), martyr. See Benedict, St.

ISAAC OF CONSTANTINOPLE, ST. (d. 410?). A hermit who repeatedly condemned Emperor Valens for his support of Arianism and anti-Catholic actions, he was imprisoned, but released and highly respected by Theodosius, who became emperor when Valens was slain in battle. Isaac founded a monastery and attended the first Council of Constantinople. F. D. May 30.

ISAAC THE GREAT, ST. (347?–439). Son of St. Nerses I, he studied at Constantinople, was married there, and became a monk on the death of his wife. He had himself declared primate of the Armenian Church by Constantinople in 390, and began to reform the Armenian Church. He strictly enforced canon law, forbade bishops to marry, encouraged monasticism, and built churches, schools, and hospitals. He had the Bible translated, after St. Mesrop invented an Armenian alphabet, and also works of Greek and Syrian writers. When the Persians conquered part of his territory in 428, he was driven into exile, but returned later to his see at Ashtishat, Armenia, where he died. F. D. Sept. 9.

ISAAC OF SELEUCIA (d. 410), patriarch. After the persecutions of the Christians in Persia by Sapor II, Isaac, who had great influence with King Yazdgerd I, reorganized and revitalized the Persian Church. He was instrumental in organizing the Council of Seleucia at which the grand vizier, in the king's name, authorized the Christians to practice their religion. The council also recognized Isaac, who had been appointed catholicos of Seleucia, as sole head of the Persian Church.

ISAAC OF SPOLETO, ST. (d. 550?). He left Syria during the Monophysite heresy to settle as a hermit in a cave on Monte Luco in Umbria, Italy, and soon had a number of disciples. F. D. Apr. 11.

ISABEL, BL. (d. 1270). Daughter of Louis VIII and Blanche of Castile, and sister of St. Louis, she so devoted herself to study, fasting, and the care of others that she almost died. She refused many royal suitors and, after the death of her mother, founded a house under the rule of the Poor Clares at Longchamps, Paris, which she supported but over which she refused to become abbess. She was beatified in 1521. F. D. Feb. 26.

ISABELLA (1451–1504), queen. Born in Madrigal de las Altas Torres, Spain, on Apr. 22, daughter of Isabella of Portugal and King John II of Castile, she was educated at Santa Ana convent in Avila until she was thirteen, when she was brought to the court of Henry IV, her brother. She refused the crown offered by the rebelling nobles in 1468 (though Henry was forced to acknowledge her as successor to the crown in the same year), married Prince Ferdinand of Aragon in 1469, and on the death of Henry in 1474 became queen of Castile and León. Immediately, war broke out with Portugal, which supported the claims of Henry's presumptive daughter, Joan, who was engaged to Alfonso V of Portugal. Ferdinand defeated the Portuguese at Toro in 1479 and succeeded to the throne of Aragon. In 1480, Joan retired to a convent and Isabella was unquestioned queen. Under the two sovereigns Spain was united and became the most powerful nation in the West. They put into effect administrative reforms, curbed the power of the nobles, established the Inquisition, completed the conquest of Granada in 1492, and in 1493 expelled the Jews. Isabella provided funds for the expedition of Columbus to the New World, encouraged learning, supported monastic reform, and was an example of personal piety, learning, and political wisdom. She died on Nov. 26 at Medina del Campo, Valladolid, Spain.

WILLIAM T. WALSH, *Isabella of Spain* (New York, Sheed, 1933).

ISACIUS, ST. (d. 302?), martyr. See Apollo, St.

ISAIAS, ST. (d. 309). See Elias, St.

ISAIAS, ST. (d. 309), martyr. He, St. Sabas, and thirty-six other monks on Mt. Sinai were attacked and slain by pagan Arabs in one of a series of massacres in the Red Sea area. F. D. Jan. 14.

ISAIAS, ST. (d. 1090), bishop. Born in Kiev, Russia, he became a monk at Caves, abbot of the monastery of St. Demetrius for fifteen years, and bishop of Rostov in 1077. He was a tireless preacher and missioner. F. D. May 15.

ISAURI. See Ansurius, St.

ISCHYRION, ST. (d. 250), martyr. Procurator of a magistrate in Alexandria, Egypt, he was tortured and impaled by his master when he refused to sacrifice to the gods. F. D. Dec. 22 (also, June 1).

ISENBURG, DIETHER VON (1412?–1482), archbishop. He studied at Erfurt, Saxony, was a canon of the cathedral of Mainz at sixteen, held cathedral posts elsewhere, became rector of Erfurt at twenty-two, added other Church posts, worked to become bishop of Trèves and lost, then succeeded in obtaining the see of Mainz, Prussia, in 1459. He appears to have obtained the post by bribery and gained papal approval by lying; he refused to contribute to the papacy, convened a diet at Nuremberg which demanded a general council, was deposed, raised a military force to attack his successor, was defeated, and excommunicated. After an apology to Adolf of Nassau, the new archbishop, and to the pope, he was absolved of the sentence. He was elected archbishop of Mainz in 1475, received papal approbation, and in his earnest efforts to restore discipline, root out simony, and better education indicated that his own reform was genuine. He died at Aschaffenburg, Germany, on May 7.

ISIDORE, ST. (d. 250), martyr. *See* Arsenius, St.

ISIDORE, ST. (4th century), bishop and martyr. He was a bishop in the Near East who was put to death at Antioch by the Arians. Another Bishop Isidore, of Nitria, welcomed St. Jerome on his visit to Egypt; the latter may be the same as St. Isidore of Pelusium. Both fourth-century bishops are honored on Jan. 2.

ISIDORE, ST. (d. 856), martyr. *See* Elias, St.

ISIDORE OF ALEXANDRIA, ST. (d. 404). Giving up his wealth, he became a hermit in the Nitrian desert, then went to Rome in 341 with St. Athanasius to be ordained there, and returned to direct a hospital at Alexandria. After his eightieth year he was condemned by St. Jerome for alleged leanings toward Origen, was excommunicated by Bishop Theophilus, fled to his former desert retreat, and finally to Constantinople. There he was befriended by St. John Chrysostom and died at eighty-five. F. D. Jan. 15.

ISIDORE OF CHIOS, ST. (d. 251?), martyr. Born in Alexandria and an army officer, he was identified as a Christian and beheaded on Chios. His head, thrown in a well, was recovered and buried by a soldier named Ammianus, later put to death at Cyzicus, and St. Myrope. F. D. May 15.

ISIDORE THE FARMER, ST. (d. 1130). Born in Madrid, Spain, of which he is the patron, he worked the fields of an estate outside the city and was married to St. Maria de la Cabeza. He was canonized in 1622. F. D. May 15.

ISIDORE OF PELUSIUM, ST. (d. 450?). A Greek priest who served as superior of the monastery at Pelusium, he was so devoted in his religious duties that he served as a model of conduct for St. Cyril. Some 2000 letters of pious exhortation and theological instruction are extant. F. D. Feb. 4.

ISIDORE OF SEVILLE, ST. (560?-636), bishop and Doctor of the Church. Born in Cartagena, Spain, brother of SS. Leander, Fulgentius, and Florentina, he was educated by his elder brother and succeeded him as bishop of Seville about 600. He continued the conversion of the Arian Visigoths, reorganized the discipline of the Church at several councils, saw to it that seminaries were built in each diocese, and completed the Mozarabic liturgy. An exceptionally well-read scholar, he organized schools which taught the arts (including Hebrew and Greek) as well as medicine and law. His encyclopedic *Etymologies* was a textbook until the sixteenth century; he also wrote histories, including a significant account of the Goths, biographies, treatises on astronomy and geography, rules for monastic life, and theological studies. He was declared a Doctor of the Church in 1722 by Pope Benedict XIV. F. D. Apr. 4.

ISIDORE OF THESSALONICA (d. 1463), cardinal. Of either Greek or Bulgar descent, he became a monk in Constantinople and abbot of St. Demetrius' monastery, where he became known for his scholarship and oratorical ability. Always eager for reunion with Rome, he served as legate of Emperor John VIII to the Council of Basle in 1434 to negotiate reunion. In 1437 he was appointed metropolitan of Moscow, where he took up residence (some scholars believe his see was Kiev). In 1438, despite some opposition from Czar Vasili II, he attended the Council of Ferrara (later moved to Florence) to promote the cause of union. Pope Eugene IV appointed him legate to Russia and cardinal-priest. When he returned to Moscow in 1441 he proclaimed reunion, whereupon the czar called a synod of six bishops who deposed and imprisoned him. He fled to Rome and was sent by Pope Nicholas V as legate to Constantinople in 1452. There he brought 300 Byzantine priests into union with Rome, but in the following year the Turks captured Constantinople and he barely escaped with his life to Rome. There he was appointed bishop of Sabina and died on Apr. 27.

ISLA, JOSÉ FRANCISCO DE (1703-1781), author. Born in Villavidanes, León, Spain, on Mar. 24, he became a Jesuit at sixteen, studied at Salamanca, and taught exegesis and philosophy in several colleges from 1725 to 1747. He preached in Valladolid and Galicia, wrote satirical poetry, and in 1767, when his Society was expelled from Spain, went to Corsica and then to Italy, where he died in Bologna on Nov. 2. Assigned to literary work, he produced *Historia del famoso predicador Fray Gerundio de Campazas* (1758), a satire on contemporary pulpit oratory, which, though condemned by the Inquisition, is an excellent picture of Spanish manners in the eighteenth century; *Triunfo del amor y de la lealtad*, an ironic eulogy on the accession of King Ferdinand VI, who became his patron; and an adaptation of Le Sage's *Gil Blas*.

ISLIP, SIMON (d. 1366), archbishop. Born probably in Islip, England, he took his doctorate in civil and canon law at nearby Oxford, served Bishop Burgersh of London and Archbishop Stratford of Canterbury, and received an increasing number of benefices, becoming in 1337 vicar general of Lincoln. He was chaplain, secretary, and keeper of the seal for King Edward III, went to France in 1342 to arrange peace terms, and was elected archbishop of Canterbury in 1349 at the height of the Black Plague. He was strenuous in his attempts at reform and ecclesiastical discipline, wrote against Edward's demands for church fees in *Speculum regis Edwardi*, and founded a college for monks at Oxford to which he contributed generously. He was stricken with a paralysis in 1363, and died in Mayfield, Sussex, on Apr. 26.

ISMAEL, ST. (d. 362), martyr. He and SS. Manuel and Sabel were Persian legates sent to Chalcedon to sue for peace with Julian the Apostate, who beheaded them because of their faith. F. D. June 17.

ISMAEL, ST. (6th century). A follower of St. Teilo, who consecrated him bishop in Wales, he was widely venerated there. F. D. June 16.

ISNARDO, BL. (d. 1244). Born in Chiampo, Italy, he became a Dominican in 1219 at the hands of St. Dominic, was active as a preacher, and founded and became prior of the friary at Pavia. His cult was confirmed in 1919. F. D. Mar. 22.

ISRAEL, BL. (d. 1014). An Augustinian canon regular in Dorat, Limousin, he became preceptor, served at the French court with the bishop of Limoges, became provost of St. Junian, Haute-Vienne, which he restored, and then returned to Dorat, where he died. F. D. Dec. 31.

ISSERNINUS, ST. (5th century), bishop. *See* Auxilius, St.

ITA, ST. (d. 570?). Second to St. Brigid in popularity among holy Irish women, Ita (also called Ida, Mida, and Deirdre) is said to have been born in Waterford, Ireland, of royal lineage. She established a refuge, with several other maidens, at Killeedy in Limerick and set up a school for young boys, among them St. Brendan. F. D. Jan. 15.

ITHAMAR, ST. (d. 656?), bishop. A native of Kent, England, he was the first Anglo-Saxon to be a bishop, being consecrated by St. Honorius to succeed St. Paulinus at Rochester. His learning was praised by Bede. F. D. June 10.

ITTA. *See* Ida of Nivelles, St.

ITTENBACH, FRANZ (1813–1879), painter. Born in Königswinter, Germany, he studied at the academy in Düsseldorf, became famed for his religious paintings, especially altarpieces, in Bonn, Breslau, and Remagen, and died in Düsseldorf, Germany, on Dec. 1.

IVES. *See* Ia, St. (6th century).

IVES, LEVI SILLIMAN (1797–1867). Born in Meriden, Connecticut, on Sept. 16, he fought in the War of 1812, studied at Hamilton College, and in 1823 became an Episcopalian minister. He was elected bishop of North Carolina in 1831, helped educate and improve

the position of Negroes, and founded the Brotherhood of the Holy Cross, which was dissolved when he was arraigned for his interest in the Oxford Movement. The charges were dismissed, but in 1852 he went to Rome and became a convert with his wife. On his return he taught at St. Joseph's seminary and was founder and president of the Catholic Protectory in New York City, where he died on Oct. 13.

IVO. When a skeleton was unearthed in 1001 near the abbey of Ramsey, a legend grew up which said the body was that of a Persian bishop who had come to England with three companions to live as recluses; he is called St. Ivo in the narrative.

IVO OF CHARTRES (1040?–1116), bishop. An Augustinian, he studied at Paris and under Lanfranc at Bec, about 1078, became provost of the canons regular of St. Quentin, at Beauvais, France, and in 1091 became bishop of Chartres. He was a counselor to King Philip, attacked the greed of contemporary churchmen, was imprisoned for a time for opposing Philip's plan in 1092 to desert his wife Bertha and marry Bertrade of Anjou. Ivo played a prominent role in the investiture dispute, advocating a policy of moderation for both sides, and wrote widely on canon law. His *Decretum* had great influence, and his letters are a valuable reflection of his era. F. D. May 23.

IVO HÉLORY, ST. (1253–1303). Born in Kermartin, Brittany, he studied canon and civil law at Paris and Orléans, returned to his home and served as judge of ecclesiastical cases in the diocese of Rennes and then in Tréguier. He worked especially for the poor, at his own expense, refused fees, and settled as many cases out of court as possible. He became a priest in 1284, gave up his legal post, and devoted his last fifteen years to his parishioners in Trédrez and Lovannec. He was canonized in 1347 and is the patron of lawyers. F. D. May 19.

IXIDA, BL. ANTONY (d. 1632), martyr. A learned Japanese Jesuit, he was tortured in scalding water for thirty-three days with five Franciscans and Augustinians in the attempt to make them deny their faith; they were burned to death at Nagasaki, Japan, and beatified in 1867. F. D. Sept. 3.

IXTLILXOCHITL, FERNANDO DE ALVA (1568–1648), historian. Born in Texcoco, Mexico, a descendant of the Aztec emperors, he was educated at Santa Cruz College in Tlaltelolco and lived most of his life in dire poverty. He wrote many books on the Indian civilization of Mexico and the Spanish conquest, all characterized by a native bias, but of great importance for any study of Mexican history. His best works are his unfinished *Historia de la nación Chichemeca* and *La Entrada de los Españoles en Texcoco*.

J

JACCARD, BL. FRANCIS (1799–1838), martyr. Born in Onnion, Savoy, he became a priest in the Society of Foreign Missions of Paris, went to Cochin China in 1826, and was captured and strangled at Annam. He was beatified in 1900. F. D. Sept. 21.

JACKSON, HENRY MOORE (1849–1908), governor. Born in Grenada, British West Indies, son of an Anglican bishop, he studied at the Royal Military Academy in England, joined an artillery unit in 1870, and retired as captain in 1885. He entered the colonial service in 1880 as commandant of the Sierra Leone police, served as commissioner of Turks and Caicos Islands (1885–90), colonial secretary of the Bahama Islands (1890–93), and of Gibraltar (1894–1901). He was knighted in 1899. He was governor of the Leeward Islands (1901), of the Fiji Islands, high commissioner of the Western Pacific (1902), and governor of Trinidad (1904). He was honored by King Edward VII and died in London on Aug. 29.

JACOB, LUDOVICUS (1608–1670), author. He was born in Châlons-sur-Marne (or Chalon-sur-Saône), France, on Aug. 20, joined the Carmelites there, took the name Ludovicus a S. Carolo, and was professed in 1626. After spending some time in Italy, he returned to France, became Cardinal de Retz' librarian, royal councilor and almoner, and Achille de Harlay's librarian in Paris, where he died on Mar. 10. He finished Gabriel Naudé's *Bibliotheca pontificia* while in Rome, was the author of numerous scholarly works, and the originator of the practice of compiling annual lists of printed books.

JACOB VAN AMSTERDAM. *See* Cornelisz, Jacob.

JACOB OF JÜTERBOCK. *See* Stolzenhagen, Benedict.

JACOBINI, LUDOVICI (1832–1887), cardinal. Born in Genzano, Italy, on Jan. 6, he was ordained and rose rapidly in administrative positions. He became a domestic prelate in 1862, papal undersecretary of state in 1870, archbishop of Thessalonica in 1874, and was sent to Vienna as nuncio in that year. After 1879 he worked in Germany and succeeded in gaining from Bismarck the revocation of the anti-Catholic Falk Laws of 1873. He was made a cardinal in 1879 and papal secretary of state in 1880. He died on Feb. 28.

JACOBIS, BL. JUSTIN DE (1800–1860), bishop. Born in San Fele, Italy, he entered the Congregation of the Missions (Vincentians) at eighteen, was ordained, and became superior of their house at Lecce. In 1839 he was sent as first prefect apostolic to Ethiopia, where his efforts met great opposition. In 1845 he founded a college and seminary at Guala, near Adigrat. Disturbed by Catholic progress, Salama, a monk who had been illegally appointed primate of the Ethiopian Church in a plot directed by the Coptic patriarch of Alexandria, launched a persecution, closed the college, and had Catholicism proscribed in the nation. In 1848, Bishop William Massaia secretly consecrated Fr. de Jacobis as bishop at Massawa, with authority to administer the sacraments according to the Ethiopian rite. By 1853 he had twenty Ethiopian priests serving 5000 Catholics and reopened the college, at Alitiena. Political disorders which followed Kedaref Kassa's ascension to the throne again resulted in a setback to Catholicism and an order of banishment. Bishop de Jacobis escaped arrest and went to Eritrea. He continued his missionary activities on the Red Sea coast, was stricken with fever, and died in the valley of Alghedien. He was beatified in 1939. F. D. July 31.

JACOBUS DE TERAMO (1349–1417), bishop. Of the Palladini family, he was born in Teramo, Italy, studied at Padua, was archdeacon at Aversa in 1384, and later was secretary of papal briefs in Rome. He became bishop of Monopoli in 1391, Tarentum in 1400, Florence in 1401, and Spoleto (where he also was governor of the duchy) in 1410. Pope Martin V sent him in 1417 as legate to Poland, where he died. He wrote a commentary on the *Sentences* of Peter Lombard and *Consolatio peccatorum*.

JACOBUS DE VORAGINE. *See* James of Voragine.

JACOPINO OF CANEPACI, BL. (1438–1508). Born in Piasca, Italy, he was active in begging alms and offering spiritual consolation during his seventy years as a Carmelite laybrother, and was beatified in 1845. F. D. Mar. 3.

JACOPO DE VORAGINE. *See* James of Voragine, Bl.

JACOPONE DA TODI, BL. (1230?–1306), poet. Jacopo Benedetti was born in Todi, Italy, studied law at Bologna, practiced in his native town after he received his doctorate, married Vanna di Guidone in 1267, and lived a life of luxury and ease. After the death of his wife he wandered aimlessly for ten years, then in 1278 became a Franciscan laybrother. For twelve years he wrote poetry, hymns, and songs, chiefly in the Umbrian dialect, which established him as one of the more important poets of the Middle Ages. He also came into increasing conflict with the Conventual friars of his house and with other Franciscans in 1294 asked Pope Celestine V's permission to live apart with other Franciscan Spirituals. In 1297, with Cardinals Jacopo and Pietro Colonna, he issued a manifesto assailing the validity of the election of Pope Boniface VIII and was imprisoned in 1298 when papal forces captured Palestrina, the stronghold of the Colonnas. While in prison he wrote many of his best-known poems. He was released on Boniface's death in 1303, lived for a time at a hermitage near Orvieto, and then at a Poor Clare convent in Collazzone, Italy, where he died on Dec. 25. He is reputed to have written *Stabat Mater dolorosa*, and *Stabat Mater speciosa*, though his authorship is questioned by some. His cult has never been confirmed. Helen White's novel *Watch in the Night*, is based on his life.

JACOTOT, JEAN JOSEPH (1770–1840), educator. Born in Dijon, France, in Mar., he studied at the college there and was appointed professor of classical literature in 1789, later occupying the chairs of science, ancient languages, mathematics, and Roman law. He served in the chamber during the Hundred Days, but was forced to leave France at the second restoration because of his opposition to the Bourbons. He taught in Mons and Brussels, and in 1818 at Louvain, where he originated his "universal method" of education. He returned to France in 1830 and attempted to spread his new theory by a series of books, under the general title *Enseignement universel*, and periodical articles. He died in Paris on July 30.

JACQUES DE VITRY (1160–1240), cardinal. Born in Vitry-sur-Seine, France, he studied at Paris, was ordained, and preached the crusade against the Albigensians in 1210–13. He lived for a while in Oignies, Belgium, where he became an Augustinian. He was elected bishop of St. John of Acre by the Latin clergy, freed captive slaves by payments to the Turks, joined the crusade against the Saracens in 1218, and was present at the capture of Damietta. He returned to Rome in 1227, launched an attack on the heretics of Liège, and in 1229 resigned the see of Acre and was created cardinal and bishop of Tusculum by Pope Gregory IX. He served as legate to France and Germany. He wrote *Historia orientalis seu Hierosolymitana*, a valuable account of the Holy Land in the thirteenth century; a series of letters to Pope Honorius describing the crusade; and *Liber de mulieribus Leodiensibus*, which contains descriptions of the visions of Marie d'Oignies, the mystic. He died in Rome.

JACQUIER, FRANÇOIS (1711–1788), physicist. Born in Vitry-le-François, France, on June 7, he became a Friar Minor in 1717 and studied in Rome. He taught scripture at the Propaganda, physics at Turin (1745), experimental physics at the Roman College, and in 1773 mathematics there. He published on calculus, the relations of philosophy and science, and, with Leseur, a study of the theories of Isaac Newton. He died in Rome on July 3.

JADER, ST. (d. 257), bishop and martyr. *See* Nemesian, St.

JADWIGA. *See* Hedwig of Poland, Bl.

JAEGLE, CHARLES J. (1853–1926), journalist. Born in Freiburg, Germany he went to Pittsburgh, Pennsylvania, in 1868, where he founded and edited (1880–98) the Pittsburgh *Beobachter*, a Catholic newspaper. He then established and edited until his retirement in 1916 the *Catholic Observer*. He was a founder of the Catholic Press Association and died in Pittsburgh on Nov. 6.

JAENBERT (d. 791?), archbishop. He was elected abbot of St. Augustine's, Canterbury, England, in 760 and became its archbishop in 766, minting special coins for the see. He was obliged to accept the division of the diocese in 787 when Offa of Mercia defeated Kent and established the new archdiocese of Lichfield. He held a synod in Chelsea in 787, and died at his old monastery in Canterbury on Aug. 11 or 12. He is also known as Lambert.

JAGELLO, king of Poland. *See* Ladislas II, king of Poland.

JÄGER, JOHANNES (1480?–1539?). Born in Dornheim, Thuringia, and also known as Johann Crotus (or Venator) and Crotus Rubianus, he studied at Erfurt and with Ulrich von Hutten became an active opponent of scholasticism and monasticism. He held several teaching posts, was ordained in 1514, became interested in Luther's reform movement and wrote several anonymous tracts for him, and in 1520 became rector of the University of Erfurt. In 1524 he entered the service of Duke Albrecht of Prussia and wrote a pamphlet in defense of his master's withdrawal from Catholicism. The so-called Reformation did not please him and about 1531 he became councilor to Cardinal Albrecht of Brandenburg, a canon of the cathedral at Halle, and published his *Apologia*, charging that the reformers had not lived up to their ideals but had created civil and moral chaos. He had strong influence on the writings of George Witzel and was violently attacked as "Dr. Kröte" (the Toad) by Luther.

JAMAY, DENIS (d. 1625), missioner. Chosen as provincial commissary of the Recollects in 1615, he accompanied Champlain as head of a missionary group to Canada in that year. He went to France in 1616 on behalf of the colony, returned in 1620, and built a house for his order in Quebec. He went back to France in 1621, where he remained until his death.

JAMBERT, ST. (d. 790), bishop. A Benedictine, he became abbot of St. Augustine's monastery, Canterbury, England, and in 766 succeeded St. Bregwin as archbishop. F. D. Aug. 12.

JAMES I (1208-1276), king of Aragon. Son of Pedro II, he was born in Montpellier, France, on Feb. 2, faced national anarchy after his father's death, rose above the weakness displayed during his minority, and came to be called "the Conqueror." He captured Valencia by 1245, the kingdom of Murcia for Castile in 1266, and cleared his borders of the Moorish threat. He sought a base in Tunis and in 1229-35 captured the Balearic Islands. He died in Valencia, Spain, on July 27.

JAMES II (1260?-1327), king of Aragon and Sicily. Son of Pedro III and brother of Alfonso III, he became king of Sicily in 1282 and of Aragon in 1291, gave up Sicily to his brother Frederick in 1295 in return for Sardinia and Corsica, and began the expulsion of Genoese and Pisans from Sardinia in 1323-24. He founded the University of Lérida in 1300.

JAMES II (1633-1701), king of England. Son of Charles I of England and Henrietta Maria of France, he was born in London on Oct. 14, created duke of York and Albany as an infant, captured with his father during the Civil War, and escaped to Holland in 1648. He served in the French army until Louis XIV signed a treaty with Cromwell, transferred to the Spanish forces, and on the restoration of the Stuarts in 1660 became high admiral of the English fleet in its battles with Holland. He had married Anne Hyde and at her death became a convert, which caused his resignation. His second wife, Mary Beatrice of Modena, brought him politically close to Louis XIV; hostility toward Catholicism in England increased following the Titus Oates Plot, and James sought refuge in Holland. The English House of Commons sought to exclude him from the crown, but the lords defended him. James was in Scotland when his brother, Charles II, died; he succeeded as King James II of England and VII of Scotland in 1685. Like the other Stuarts, he tried to act independently of the growing power of parliament, made legal appointments which were not universally approved, sought to protect his position by maintaining a standing army, and ran afoul of strong religious tensions. In 1687 he issued the Declaration of Indulgence, which protected the religious rights of all dissenters from the established Church of England. Another was issued in 1688, which he ordered read in all churches; seven Anglican bishops refused, were brought to trial, and acquitted.

But when his son James (later hostilely called "the Pretender") was born on June 10, the Protestant leaders, fearing a Catholic succession, spread libels calling the child illegitimate, then secretly invited William, Prince of Orange, to invade the country and protect the established religion. When William landed at Torbay, James, to avoid a second civil war in his own lifetime, retired to France. With a small force begrudgingly supplied by Louis XIV he invaded Ireland in 1689, but did not gain sufficient adherents and was badly defeated at the Battle of the Boyne. He remained in St. Germain, France, until his death on Sept. 6, a noted ascetic in his last years. HILAIRE BELLOC, *James The Second* (Philadelphia, Lippincott, 1928).

JAMES I (1394-1437), king of Scotland. Son of Robert III, he was born in Dunfermline, Scotland, was taken prisoner in 1404, while on his way to France, and kept under guard in England until 1424 on orders of the regent, the duke of Albany. He then returned to Scotland, assumed the throne, condemned Albany to death, curbed the power of the nobles, and confiscated powerful earldoms, crushed Lollardry, and supported the Inquisition. He helped to develop trade, and pleaded for strict obedience to religious rules. He was assassinated by a group of nobles led by the Earl of Athlone on Feb. 20 at Perth, Scotland.

JAMES II (1430-1460), king of Scotland. Born on Oct. 16, he succeeded his father, James I, in 1437 and ruled under the control of Sir William Crichton and Sir Alexander Livingstone. The former executed William, earl of Douglas, and the latter's brother, which created violent civil strife. In 1449, James assumed control, married Mary of Gelderland, and checked the power of the remaining Douglases by murder and exile. He sought to regain Roxburgh from the English by besieging the castle and was killed by cannon shot on Aug. 3.

JAMES III (1451-1488), king of Scotland. Born on July 10, he succeeded his father, James II, in 1460. During his minority the country was ruled by a regency of his mother, Archbishop Kennedy of St. Andrews, and the earl of Angus; after the death of the archbishop in 1466 the rule passed to the Boyd family (Lord Boyd's son, the earl of Arran married James' sister Margaret in 1467). Discontented nobles forced Boyd and Arran to flee in 1469. After James's marriage to Margaret of Denmark the same year he came under the influence of a group of favorites, headed by Cochrane. When the nobles supported the king's brothers, the duke of Albany and the earl of Mar, James turned on them, imprisoned Mar (who died in prison), and caused Albany to flee to France. In 1482, James invaded England, which was supporting Albany's claim to the throne of Scotland. At the height of the campaign a group of dissident nobles, led by Archibald Douglas, fifth earl of Angus, seized the king's favorites, hanged them, and took James back to Edinburgh a prisoner. In 1488, civil war broke out; the lowland barons supported James's son (James IV) against the king and the northern barons. James's forces were defeated at Sauchieburn, near Bannockburn, Scotland, on June 11, and James was murdered as he fled the field of battle.

JAMES IV (1473–1513), king of Scotland. Son of James III and Margaret of Denmark, and grandson of James II, he was born on Mar. 17, and became king in 1488 when his father was murdered. James IV crushed a rebellion led by the earl of Lennox, built up commerce and naval power, concluded a seven-year truce with England in 1497, and aided the peasantry. In 1503 he married Margaret, daughter of Henry VII of England, and the two countries enjoyed a brief period of peace. James introduced judicial and social reforms, worked harmoniously with the council at Edinburgh, and maintained good relations with the Continent. In 1513, however, England declared war. James, an incompetent general, led a large Scots force against an English force under Surrey and lost nearly 10,000 men and his own life in the battle of Flodden Field on Sept. 9.

JAMES V (1512–1542), king of Scotland. Son of James IV of Scotland and Margaret Tudor, daughter of Henry VII of England, he was born in Linlithgow, Scotland, on Apr. 10, and succeeded his father, who was slain in battle, in 1513. The country was torn by factionalism: the regent, duke of Albany, represented French interests; his enemy, the earl of Angus, supported by the queen mother, who married Angus and gave up her Catholic religion, favored the English. At seventeen, James declared the regency at an end, banished Angus and many of his supporters, and in 1536 married Madeleine, daughter of Francis I. She died after a few weeks, and he then married Mary of Lorraine, daughter of the duke of Guise. James refused to support the new religious views of his brother-in-law, Henry VIII, and the two nations were soon at war. Henry twice sent armies into Scotland after 1542, which met defeat; the Scots nobles, however, refused to follow their king into England. Civil strife increased when James clung to Catholicism, yet offended in all directions by his licentious life. When his army of 10,000 men was defeated by a small body of Englishmen at Solway Moss, he retired to Falkland castle, near Edinburgh, and died there on Dec. 14, a week after the birth of his daughter, Mary Queen of Scots.

JAMES VII, king of Scotland. *See* James II, king of England.

JAMES, ST. (d. 259), martyr. A deacon at Cirta, Algeria, he was beheaded with St. Marian, a lector, in a crowd-packed arena at Lambesia, Numidia; hundreds of other Christians were slain with them in the spectacle arranged during the persecution of Valerian. F. D. Apr. 30.

JAMES, ST. (d. 297), martyr. *See* Hipparchus, St.

JAMES, ST. (d. 338), bishop. A Syrian, he was a monk before he became the first bishop of Nisibis, Mesopotamia, about 308. He built a basilica, probably started the theological school in Nisibis, and attended the Council of Nicaea in 325. F. D. July 15.

JAMES, ST. (d. 344?), martyr. *See* John, St.

JAMES, ST. (d. 429?), bishop. He trained at the monastery of Lérins, an island off the coast of France, under St. Honoratus of Arles and became a missioner in Savoy before he was named bishop of Tarentaise, Italy. F. D. Jan. 16.

JAMES, ST. (7th century). An Italian Benedictine and deacon, he went to England with St. Paulinus and labored in Northumbria through the revival of paganism which followed the death of King Edwin. F. D. Aug. 17.

JAMES, ST. (d. 769), bishop. Probably born in Bertigny, Haute Marne, he is believed to have been a monk at Hornbach, near Metz, Gaul, before he became bishop of Toul, in Gaul, in 756. He aided monastic groups, and died at Dijon. F. D. June 23.

JAMES, ST. (d. 865?). An army officer from Constantinople, he was ordained in Gaul, became a Benedictine near Bourges, and later a hermit at Sasseau. F. D. Nov. 19.

JAMES, BL. ROGER (d. 1539), martyr. *See* Whiting, Bl. Richard.

JAMES THE ALMSGIVER, BL. (d. 1304). Born in Città delle Pieve, Lombardy, he studied law, was ordained, and restored an abandoned hospital and chapel where he served as spiritual, medical, and legal adviser to the poor who filled the rooms to overflowing. When he sought to claim past revenues from the diocese of Chiusi, which had seized the land revenues of the rebuilt establishment, the incumbent bishop had him ambushed and slain. He is claimed as a tertiary by both the Franciscans and the Servites. F. D. Jan. 28.

JAMES OF BEVAGNA. *See* Bianconi, Bl. Jacopo.

JAMES OF BITETTO, BL. (d. 1485?). Born in Sebenico, Dalmatia, and called the Slav, he became a Franciscan laybrother at Bitetto near Bari, Italy, served at Conversano, and had supernatural gifts. He was beatified by Pope Innocent XII. F. D. Apr. 27.

JAMES OF BRESCIA (15th century), theologian. A native of Brescia, where he became a

Dominican, he was named inquisitor there in 1450 and was an aide of Bernard da Bosco, papal auditor, in suppressing heresy in Bergamo. About 1462 he was one of three Dominican theologians who debated with Franciscans before a papal court over a theological question involving the blood of Christ.

JAMES OF CERQUETO, BL. (d. 1367). Born in Cerqueto, Italy, he became an Augustinian at Perugia and spent a very long life in prayer. His cult was approved in 1895. F. D. Apr. 17.

JAMES OF CERTALDO, ST. (d. 1392). Born in Certaldo, near Florence, Italy, Jacopo Guidi became a Camaldolese in 1230, directing the parish at Volterra, serving as abbot while a brother and their father were lay-brothers. F. D. Apr. 13.

JAMES, BL. EDWARD (d. 1588), martyr. Born in Breaston, Derbyshire, England, he studied at Oxford, was converted, went to Rheims and was ordained at Rome in 1583. Sent on the English mission in 1586, he was captured on his arrival, imprisoned in London, and hanged, drawn, and quartered at Chichester during the Elizabethan persecution. He was beatified in 1929. F.D. Oct. 1.

JAMES THE GREATER, ST. (d. 44), apostle and martyr. Son of Zebedee and Salome and brother of St. John the Evangelist, he was a native of Galilee and a fisherman by trade, probably at Bethsaida. Christ termed him and his brother "sons of thunder" and called him to be one of His apostles at Lake Genesareth after He had called Peter and Andrew. James was present at the cure of Peter's mother-in-law and at the raising of Jairus' daughter from the dead. He, Peter, and John were the only apostles present at the Transfiguration and were the three taken into Christ's confidence in the Garden of Gethsemane. He was put to death, the first apostle to be martyred, in Jerusalem during the persecution of Herod Agrippa I. Legend says that he visited Spain, and his remains are said to have been brought to Compostela in the ninth century. During the Middle Ages this shrine of Santiago was one of the greatest in Christendom. He is the patron saint of Spain. F. D. July 25.

JAMES INTERCISUS, ST. (d. 421?), martyr. A Persian officer at the court of King Yezdigerd I, he apostatized when the king began to persecute the Christians. After Yezdigerd's death, he repented, openly avowed his Christianity, and was ordered cut to pieces (hence his surname meaning "cut to pieces"), and finally beheaded. F. D. Nov. 27.

JAMES THE LESS, ST. (d. 62?), apostle and martyr. Also called "the Younger" and "the Just," he probably was the son of Alpheus (Matt. 10:3) and thus the cousin of Christ. He became first bishop of Jerusalem and was highly praised by Josephus for his activity. Most scriptural scholars accept his authorship of the canonical epistle which bears his name. According to Hegesippus, he was thrown from the pinnacle of the Temple by the Pharisees and then stoned to death. F. D. May 1.

JAMES OF LODI, BL. (d. 1404). After a plague at Lodi, Italy, carried off their two children, Jacopo Oldi and his wife Catherine became Franciscan tertiaries, made their house over into a church, and devoted themselves to works of charity. James was later ordained, and died of disease contracted from a patient whom he was attending. F. D. Apr. 18.

JAMES OF THE MARCHES. *See* Gangala, St. James.

JAMES OF PADUA, BL. (d. 1322), martyr. Born in Padua, Italy, he became a Franciscan, went to the East Indies with St. Thomas of Tolentino, and was put to death there. His cult was approved in 1809. F. D. Apr. 9.

JAMES OF STREPAR, BL. (1392–1411), archbishop. A Pole, he became a Franciscan, served as vicar general of his order in western Russia, and was raised to the see of Halicz, Galatia, in 1392. His cult was approved in 1791. F. D. June 1.

JAMES THE SYRIAN, ST. (6th century). Born in Syria, he became a recluse outside Amida, Mesopotamia. F. D. Aug. 6.

JAMES OF VORAGINE, BL. (1230?–1298), archbishop. Born at Viraggio, Italy, Jacopo de Voragine became a Dominican at fourteen, taught theology and preached widely after ordination, and from 1267 to 1286 was prior provincial in Lombardy. In 1292, despite objections which he had voiced for six years, he was consecrated archbishop of Genoa. His attempts to heal the feud between the Guelphs and Ghibellines were fruitless. He is better known as the author of *Legenda sanctorum*, popularly called *Legenda aurea* (*The Golden Legend*), the most famous mediaeval collection of saints' lives, which had over 100 editions in all languages by 1500; William Caxton's English translation appeared in 1483. His narratives were not intended as formal biographies, but as examples of devotion, reliance on providence, and admiration for goodness. Many such tales began simply as illustrative material in sermons, not to be confused with fact. They had tremendous influence on literature, from the time of the early drama to H. W. Longfellow's narrative poems. The high regard for the archbishop led to a popular cult, which was approved in 1816. F. D. July 13.

JAMMES, FRANÇOIS (1868–1938), author. Born in Tournay, France, on Dec. 2, he traveled from city to city with his father, a government official, until, at the latter's death in

1888, the family settled in Orthez where he practiced law. *Vers* appeared in 1893, followed by *De l'angelus* and *Quatre prières*, both in 1898. *Clara d'Ellebeuse* and *Almaide d'Estremont,* two novels, followed. In 1905, after a visit from Paul Claudel, who had written him from China in praise of *Clara,* he returned to the Church after years of indifferentism. His characters, in prose and poetry, were chiefly those of the countryside, and his poems stressed a natural simplicity and intense love of animals and the outdoors. *Pensées des jardins* reflects the Franciscan outlook; *La Poete et sa femme* and *Ma fille Bernadette* reveal his domestic contentment. *Les georgiques chrétiennes* (1912) deals with the Church year in an agricultural community; *La Vierge et les sonnets* (1919), three volumes of *Mémoires* (1921), and a selection of all his works (1921) complete his output. He died in Hasparran, France, on Nov. 1.

JANAUSCHEK, LEOPOLD (1827–1898), author. Born in Brünn, Moravia, on Oct. 13, he became a Cistercian in 1846 and studied in Heiligenkreuz, where he was ordained and taught history and canon law until 1877, except for a year at Vienna. He published *Originum Cisterciensum* and *Bibliographia Bernardina,* part of *Xenia Bernardina,* in preparing the first three volumes of which he assisted. He died in Baden, Austria, on July 23.

JANDEL, ALEXANDRE VINCENT (1810–1872). Born in Gerbevilliers, Lorraine, on July 18, he studied in Nancy, was ordained in 1834, became professor of scripture, rector of the seminary at Pont-à-Mousson, and in 1841 a Dominican in Rome. In 1843, with Jean Baptiste Lacordaire, he began re-establishing the Dominicans in France. Pope Pius IX appointed him vicar general in 1850 and general in 1855. In 1862 he was elected sixty-third general of his order. He re-established provinces, opened new houses, and gave new vigor to the order. He died in Rome on Dec. 11.

JANE, BL. (d. 1383). Abbess of the Cistercian convent of St. Benedict at Castro, near Cáceres, Spain, she was the victim of soldiers during a raid. F. D. Dec. 8.

JANE FRANCES DE CHANTAL. *See* Chantal, St. Jane Frances.

JANNER, FERDINAND (1836–1895), theologian. Born on Feb. 1 in Hirschau, Bavaria, he studied in Amberg and at Würzburg and Ratisbon, and was ordained in 1858. He did pastoral work, received his doctorate in theology from Würzburg, was chaplain at Weiden, prefect of the Ratisbon seminary, and taught in Speyer and Ratisbon. He published theological and historical works and a translation of the breviary. He died on Nov. 1.

JANSEN, CORNELIS (1585–1638), bishop. Born in Accoi, Holland, on Oct. 28, he studied at Utrecht, Louvain, and Collège du Pape Adrien VI, where he was influenced by Jacques Janson, who had embraced the teaching of Michael Baius. He went to Paris to tutor in 1604 and about 1606 was appointed director of an episcopal college in Bayonne. In 1617 he was appointed president of the College of St. Pulchérie at Louvain, received his doctorate in theology in 1619, and became professor of exegesis at Louvain in 1630. At Louvain he joined the party opposing the Jesuits, who had just established their own theological school, and in 1624 and 1626 went to Madrid to defend the university in its conflict with the Society. In 1636 he was appointed bishop of Ypres, Flanders, where he died on May 6 during an epidemic. He wrote biblical commentaries, polemical works, and a series of letters to his friend Jean du Verger de Hauranne, abbé of St. Cyran, but the work which has had greatest impact is *Augustinus,* which was published after his death in 1640. It is a treatise on the theology of St. Augustine. Jansen, heavily influenced by Baius, failed to make clear the place of the will in relation to concupiscence and grace. His doctrine spread rapidly over Europe, was condemned in 1641, and in 1653 was prohibited as heretical. Despite this, de Hauranne, the Arnaulds, and others followed the five proscribed theses; in time, the heresy became the movement known as Jansenism.

JANSEN, CORNELIUS, THE ELDER (1510–1576), bishop. Born in Hulst, Flanders, he studied under the Brethren of the Common Life at Ghent, and at Louvain. He lectured at Tongerloo abbey until 1542 and was pastor in Courtrai until 1562, when he received his doctorate in theology and became a professor at Louvain. Appointed dean of the seminary of St. James (which he represented at the Council of Trent) in 1563, he was appointed first bishop of Ghent, Flanders, a position he did not accept until 1568. He founded a seminary there in 1569, held two diocesan synods (1571, 1574), and devoted his episcopate to combating Protestantism. He published exegetical works, most important of which was *Concordia evangelica,* and died in Ghent on Apr. 11.

JANSSEN, BL. ADRIANUS (d. 1572), martyr. Born in Hilvarenbeek, Holland, he was a Premonstratensian who later became a diocesan curate in Monster, Holland. He was seized by a Calvinist mob, taken to Briel, Holland, and tortured and hanged there. He was beatified in 1867. F. D. July 9.

JANSSEN, ARNOLD (1837–1909), founder. Born in Goch, Germany, on Nov. 5, he studied at Gaesdonck, Münster, and Bonn, and was ordained in 1861. He engaged in parish work, was chaplain of an Ursuline convent at Kempen in 1873, and in 1875 established the mission house of St. Michael at Steyl, Holland. Out of this grew the Society of the Divine Word, which was formally approved in 1901. In 1889 he also founded the Servant Sisters of the Holy Ghost, also devoted to foreign missions. He died at Steyl on Jan. 15.

JANSSEN, JOHANN (1829–1891), historian. Born in Xanten, Germany, on Apr. 10, he was a coppersmith's apprentice in 1842–44 and studied in Recklinghausen and at Münster, Louvain, Berlin, and Bonn, where he received his doctorate in philosophy in 1853. He was ordained in 1860, taught history at Frankfort-on-Main gymnasium from 1854 to 1860, served as deputy to the Prussian diet in 1875–76, was made a monsignor by Pope Leo XIII in 1880, and wrote a biography of Abbot Wibald of Stablo and studies of the diocese of Münster, Franco-German boundaries, Schiller as a historian, the partition of Poland, and *History of the German People in the Middle Ages*. He died in Frankfort, Germany, on Dec. 24.

JANSSEN, JOHN (1835–1913), bishop. Born in Keppeln, Prussia, on Mar. 3, he studied at the Münster seminary, went to the United States in 1858 at the request of the bishop of Alton, Illinois, finished his theological studies there, and was ordained in Alton later the same year. He engaged in missionary work in Illinois, became secretary to Bishop Juncker of Alton, was vicar of that diocese from 1870 to 1886 (except for 1877–79 when he was pastor of St. Boniface in Quincy), and administered the diocese in 1886–88. He was consecrated first bishop of Belleville, Illinois, in 1888 and died there on July 2.

JANSSEN, BL. NICASIUS (1522?–1572), martyr. Born in Heeze, Brabant, he took his degree in theology, became a Franciscan, engaged in published controversy with Protestants, and was seized in Gorkum by a group of Calvinists, and tortured and hanged at Briel, Holland. He was beatified in 1867. F. D. July 9.

JANSSENS, ABRAHAM (1575–1632), painter. Born in Antwerp, he studied painting under Jan Snellinck, was admitted to the guild of St. Luke as teaching master in 1601, and became dean in 1606. He was noted for his sense of composition and coloring, particularly for torchlight scenes, where he achieved effective contrasts. Among his best-known paintings are: *The Entombment, Madonna with Saints, Descent from the Cross, Ecce Homo, Adoration of the Magi*, and *Venus* and *Adonis*. Some work is signed Janssens van Nuyssen. He died in Antwerp, Flanders.

JANSSENS, FRANCIS AUGUST ANTHONY JOSEPH (1843–1897), archbishop.

Born in Tilburg, North Brabant, on Oct. 17, he studied at Bois-le-duc seminary and Louvain, was ordained in Ghent in 1867, and in 1868 went to the United States, where he became vicar general of the Richmond, Virginia, diocese in 1872. In 1881 he was consecrated bishop of Natchez, Mississippi, where he built up the diocese and became known for his work among the Choctaw Indians, and in 1888 was appointed archbishop of New Orleans. He founded a seminary at Pontchatoula, was active in missionary work among the Negroes and immigrant Italians, and died at sea on June 10 while on his way to New York.

JANUARIA, ST. (d. 180), martyr. *See* Speratus, St.

JANUARIA, ST. (d. 305?), martyr. *See* Heraclius, St.

JANUARIUS, ST. (1st century), martyr. *See* Euphrasius, St.

JANUARIUS, ST. (d. 150?), martyr. *See* Felix, St.

JANUARIUS, ST. (2nd century), martyr. *See* Catus, St.

JANUARIUS, ST. (d. 258), martyr. *See* Sixtus II, St.

JANUARIUS, ST. (d. 303), martyr. *See* Protus, St.

JANUARIUS, ST. (d. 303?), martyr. *See* Honoratus, St.

JANUARIUS, ST. (d. 304?), martyr. *See* Faustus, St.

JANUARIUS, ST. (d. 305?), bishop and martyr. A native of Naples or Benevento, Italy, he was bishop of Benevento at the start of Diocletian's persecution. Hearing that Sosius, a friend of his and deacon of Miseno, had been imprisoned with another deacon, Proculus, and two laymen, Euticius and Acutius, he visited them and was arrested, along with his deacon, Festus, and a lector, Desiderius. The entire group was thrown to wild beasts, then beheaded at Pozzuoli, Campania, Italy. For the past 400 years, on a number of occasions each year, a sealed vial with a solid red substance reputed to be his blood is exposed in the cathedral church at Naples; after a time, which varies considerably, the substance turns liquid and often bubbles and boils. F. D. Sept. 19.

JANUARIUS, ST. (d. 320), martyr. He and St. Pelagia were beheaded at Nicopolis, Armenia, during the persecution of Licinius. F. D. July 11.

JANUARIUS, ST. (d. 450?), martyr. He was put to death by the Vandals in Africa with SS. Securus, Severus, and Victorinus. F. D. Dec. 2.

JARAVA, ANTONIO MARTÍNEZ DE (1444–1522), scholar. Also known as Antonio de Nebrija, from his birthplace in Spain, he was a leader of the revival of learning was tutor to Queen Isabella, and assisted Cardinal

Ximines in preparing his polyglot bible. He wrote works in philology, history, and theology, poetry, and on medicine and law, and is particularly known for *Dictionarium latino-hispanicum et hispanico-latinum* and *Gramática sobre la lengua castellana*, both published in 1492. He taught for many years at Alcalá.

JARCKE, KARL ERNST (1801–1852), jurist. Born in Danzig, Prussia, on Dec. 27, he was a lawyer in Bonn and Berlin, and wrote a law digest. In 1824 he became a convert and in 1831–37 edited *Politisches Wochenblatt*, a conservative weekly newspaper. He served in Metternich's chancery in Vienna in 1832–38, founded *Historisch-politische Blätter* in 1838 to defend the Catholic position in Germany, and died in Vienna on Dec. 27.

JARICOT, PAULINE MARIE (1799–1862). Born in Lyons, France, on July 22, she founded in 1816 a society of serving girls, Réparatrices du Sacré Coeur de Jésus Christ. She collected funds for foreign missions and in 1822 founded the Society for the Propagation of the Faith. In 1826 she founded the Association of the Living Rosary, to recite the rosary and spread pious books and articles. She died in Lyons on Jan. 9.

JARLATH, ST. (d. 480?). A follower of St. Patrick, he succeeded St. Benignus as bishop of Armagh, Ireland. F. D. Feb. 11.

JARLATH, ST. (d. 550?), bishop. Born of the union of two noble Irish families, he became a priest, first abbot-bishop of the monastery of Tuam, Ireland, and taught SS. Brendan of Clonfert and Colman of Cloyne in the school he founded there. F. D. June 6.

JARRETT, BEDE (1881–1934), historian. Born in England, he studied at Stonyhurst, became a Dominican at seventeen, was ordained at Stafford in 1904, and did further study at Louvain and Oxford. He became prior of Haverstock Hill, London, in 1914, was provincial of the English Dominicans in 1916–32 (for an exceptional four terms), re-established his order at Oxford, and opened a friary at Edinburgh to serve the university there. He was prior of Blackfriars, Oxford, in 1932–34, traveled and lectured widely, and several times visited the United States. He wrote a biography of St. Dominic, *Medieval Socialism, Social Theories of the Middle Ages, The English Dominicans, Emperor Charles IV, A History of Europe*, and collections of his sermons: *House of Gold, Salve Regine*, and *No Abiding City.*

JARRIC, PIERRE DU (1566–1617). Born in Toulouse, France, he became a Jesuit in 1582 and taught at Bordeaux. He wrote a monumental history of Jesuit mission activities, *Historie des choses plus memorables advenues tant ez indes orientales*, based on Portuguese and Spanish sources and intended

to arouse the French king's interest and support. He died in Saintes, France, on Mar. 2.

JASMIN, JACQUES. *See* Boé, Jacques.

JASON, ST. (1st century). It was at Jason's home at Thessalonica that St. Paul stayed on his second missionary journey (Acts 17:6–9). He is also referred to as the kinsman of St. Paul, with Lucius and Sosipater (Rom. 16:21). According to Greek legend, he was bishop of Tarsus in Cilicia and evangelized Corfu, where he died. F. D. July 12.

JASON, ST., (3rd century), martyr. *See* Claudius, St.

JAUREGUI Y AGUILAR, JUAN DE (1583–1640?), poet. Born in Seville or Toledo, Spain, he went to Rome in 1607 and became a portrait painter. A disciple of Fernando de Herrera, the poet, he translated Tasso's *Aminta* in blank verse (1607) and Lucan's *Pharsalia*, and published *Rimas* (1618) and *Orfeo* (1624). He also wrote discourses on painting and poetry. He died in Madrid (perhaps as late as 1650).

JAVOUHEY, BL. ANNE MARY (1779–1851), foundress. Born at Jallanges, France, on Nov. 10, she determined to devote herself to the care of the poor and the education of children. She joined several religious communities but found herself unsuitable to their way of life. Finally, Dom Augustine Lestrange, a Cistercian, advised her to found a new congregation. In 1807, she, her three sisters, and five others were clothed by the bishop of Autun; in 1812 she bought a former Franciscan friary at Cluny, and the Congregation of St. Joseph of Cluny was founded. She opened a school in Paris and in 1817 a missionary school for native children on the island of Réunion. During the next few years her activities extended to Africa and French Guiana in South America. In 1828, the French government asked her to supervise the colonization of Mana in Guiana, on which she worked for four years successfully, and in 1834 to direct the education of 600 Negro slaves about to be freed. She taught them how to live as free men, a task which excited world-wide interest. She left Guiana in 1843 to establish houses for her expanding congregation. She died in Paris, and was canonized in 1950. F. D. July 15.

JAY, MARIE RAOUL (1856–1921), sociologist. Born in Paris on June 1, he taught law at the University of Paris, was a founder of the Union of Social Catholics, secretary of the Association for the Legal Protection of Workingmen, member of the Supreme Council of Labor, was consulted on most of the social legislation proposed in twentieth-century France, and wrote widely. He died in Paris.

JEAN, AUGUSTE (1833–1921), educator. Born in France, on Oct. 15, he became a Jesuit, studied in Lyons and Rome, and in

1875 was sent to India, where he was rector of St. Joseph's College at Negapatan, which in 1883 he transferred to Trichinoply. He was a member of the first Indian educational commission, examiner in French and classics at Madras, instructor of novices in Tamil, and wrote a Latin grammar. He died near Kodaikanal, India, on Sept. 16.

JEAN BAUSSAN (13th century). As archbishop of Arles, France, he presided at a council convened there in 1236 to suppress Albigensianism and to promulgate the decrees of the Lateran and Toulouse councils. He also held a council near Avignon in 1251.

JEAN DE CHELLES (d. 1270?). A French architect and sculptor, he built the portal of the south transept of the cathedral of Notre Dame de Paris and, probably, the chapels of the nave, and worked on the original Louvre.

JEAN CLOPINEL DE MEUNG (1260?–1305?), poet. Born in Meung-sur-Loire, France, he was a Paris burgess in 1300, and became a prolific poet, famed especially for his completion of Guillaume de Lorris' *Roman de la Rose* with some 18,000 narrative, allegorical, and satiric lines, which are a virtual encyclopedia of thirteenth-century knowledge, including quotations, imitations, and translations of authors then known. The work had great influence on Chaucer. Jean de Meung also wrote a sarcastic *Testament* and translated Boethius' *Consolatio philosophiae*. He died in Paris between 1305 and 1320.

JEAN DE SAXE. *See* Johannes Danko.

JEANMARD, JULES BENJAMIN (1879–1957), bishop. Born in Breaux Bridge, Louisiana, on Aug. 15, he studied in St. Joseph's and Holy Cross seminaries, Louisiana, and Kenrick seminary, St. Louis, and was ordained in New Orleans in 1903. He was assigned to the New Orleans cathedral, was the archbishop's secretary in 1906–14, chancellor in 1914–17, and administered the archdiocese in 1917–18. He was appointed administrator of the new diocese of Lafayette in 1918 and appointed its bishop in July. He resigned in 1956 in ill health, and died at Lake Charles, Louisiana, on Feb. 23.

JEANNE D'ARC. *See* Joan of Arc, St.

JEANNELIN OF FÉCAMP. *See* John of Fécamp.

JEAURAT, EDMOND (1688–1738), engraver. Born in Vermenton, France, he was apprenticed to Bernard Picart in Paris as a boy, spent several years in Holland, and returned to Paris, where he was recognized as a master engraver after he had engraved several of his brother Étienne's paintings, and pictures for the de Crozat collection. He died in Paris.

JEHAN PETIT (1360?–1411), theologian. Born in the diocese of Rouen, France, he came under the patronage of the duke of Burgundy, who provided funds for his education, and taught theology at Paris, where he received his doctorate in 1403. He wrote several poems, including *Livre du champ d'or, Complainte de l'Église* and a defense of the Immaculate Conception. In 1407 he served on a mission sent by King Charles VI to urge Benedict XIII and Gregory XII to abdicate in the interests of a united Church. In 1408 he delivered a specious address before the royal court on behalf of the invading Duke John of Burgundy (who had had Charles's brother, the duke of Orléans, assassinated in 1407), based on the proposition that a tyrant deserves to be put to death since his tyranny is treason; hence, Burgundy's act, rather than to be condemned, was meritorious. The king was forced to pardon Burgundy, but Jehan Petit decided it was wise to retire to the duke's estate at Hesdin, Artois, where he died on July 15. The struggle continued after his death. Gerson and the inquisitor of France and the bishop of Paris condemned Jehan's propositions in 1413–14. In 1418, King Charles (after having had Jehan condemned in 1416) reversed himself and annulled the sentence against him on the ground that the censured propositions had not been in the original address. He is also called John Parvus.

JENINGEN, VEN. PHILIPP (1642–1704). Born in Eichstätt, Bavaria, on Jan. 5, he became a Jesuit and a popular missioner at the shrine of Our Lady of Schönenberg in Swabia. He died in Ellwangen, Germany, on Jan. 19.

JENKS, SILVESTER (1656?–1714), theologian. Born in Shropshire, England, he studied at Douai, France, where he was ordained in 1684 and taught philosophy until 1686, when he became preacher in ordinary to James II. When William of Orange invaded England in 1688 he returned to Flanders, then returned to work near London. He was appointed archdeacon of Surrey and Kent, and in 1711 named vicar apostolic of the Northern District, but died in Dec. before he was able to take office. He wrote A *Contrite and Humble Heart,* The *Whole Duty of a Christian,* and on Jansenism.

JENNINGS, PATRICK ALFRED (1831–1897), premier. Born in Newry, Ireland, on Mar. 17, he studied in Exeter, worked for a merchant, went to the gold fields of Australia in 1852, and in three years owned three quartz-crushing mills. He was made a judge in 1857, rose in municipal politics in St. Arnaud, and married Mary Shanahan in 1864. In 1867–69 he served on a special legislative council in New South Wales, was a member of the assembly in 1869–72 and in 1880–87, served on the executive council, was colonial treasurer, and in 1886–87 was premier. His financial policies met great opposition and he retired from politics. He was a patron of music, fellow of St. John's College, was knighted in 1879, papally decorated in 1887, and given an honorary degree by Dublin University. He retired in 1891, and died in Brisbane, Australia, on July 11.

JEREMIAS, ST. (d. 851), martyr. *See* Peter, St.

JEREMIAS, ST. (d. 852), martyr. *See* Emilas, St.

JEREMY, ST. (d. 309). *See* Elias, St.

JEROME, ST. (342?–420), Doctor of the Church. Born in Stridon, Dalmatia, near Aquileia, Eusebius Hieronymus Sophronius studied in Rome under Donatus, acquired skill in Latin and Greek, became familiar with the great classical authors, and was baptized by Pope Liberius in 360. After studying at Trèves, in 370, he settled at Aquileia and joined the group of scholars around Bishop Valerian, among them Rufinus, who became his close friend and was later to be his mortal enemy. After several years a quarrel broke up the group. He traveled widely in the East and in 374 went to Antioch. After a dangerous illness he retired to the desert of Chalcis southwest of Antioch, where he lived as a hermit for four years, fasting, praying, studying Hebrew, and writing a life of St. Paul of Thebes. Meanwhile, the Meletian schism broke out in Antioch and he supported Paulinus' claim to the see, wrote two letters to Pope Damasus (one proclaiming the supremacy of Rome), and his treatise denouncing Meletianism, *Altercatio luciferiani et orthodoxi*. He was ordained by Paulinus (who had been declared bishop) and in 380 went to Constantinople to study scriptures under St. Gregory Nazianzen. In 382 he accompanied Paulinus to a council in Rome and remained there as Pope Damasus' secretary. At the pope's suggestion, he revised the Latin version of the four gospels, the epistles of St. Paul and the Psalms (the Roman psalter). His denunciation, *Adversus Helvidium*, of Helvidius' book (which declared that Mary had many children), was written at this time. He also actively encouraged a group of noble Roman ladies to study the scriptures, and preached so powerfully to them of the virtues of celibacy that he created powerful enemies; they were further enraged by his bitter, satirical attacks on pagan life and influential Romans. When Pope Damasus' death, in 384, deprived Jerome of his patron and supporter, his enemies and vicious rumors (including scandalous talk about him and St. Paula) forced him to return to Antioch, where SS. Paula, Eustochium, and others of the Roman community joined him. After a tour of the Holy Land they settled in 386 in Bethlehem, where Paula built three convents and a monastery for men, and there he lived a life of asceticism and study, the peace of which was frequently interrupted by his violent quarrels. In 393 he wrote *Adversus Jovinianum*, replying to Jovinian, who had proclaimed that Mary had other children besides Jesus and who had decried the desirability of virginity. Between 403 and 406 he wrote *Contra Vigilantium*, a denunciation of Vigilantius' treatise condemning celibacy and the veneration of relics. In 395 his loud and bitter dispute with Rufinus broke out when he violently attacked the heresies in the writings of Origen (in *Apologetici adversus Rufinum*), many of which had been translated into Latin by Rufinus, who supported Origen. Shortly after, St. Augustine felt his wrath when he questioned Jerome's exegesis of a biblical passage. Between 390 and 405 he produced his translation of the Old Testament from the Hebrew and the revision of the Latin version of the New Testament. This version is the Vulgate, declared the official Latin text of the Bible for the Catholic Church by the Council of Trent. Most English versions of the Bible are from the Vulgate. From 405 to his death he wrote his series of commentaries and his denunciation of Pelagianism, *Dialogi contra Pelagianos* (415). So bitter was this attack that he had to flee for his life from his opponents. He remained in hiding until 418, when he returned to Jerusalem; there, after a lingering illness, he died. Jerome corresponded widely (about 120 of his letters still exist, covering a wide variety of subject matter) and his prolific pen produced many other works. F. D. Sept. 30.

JEROME, ST. (d. 787). He was bishop of Pavia, Italy, from 778 until his death. F. D. July 19.

JEROME, BL. (d. 1135). A Vallombrosan monk, he retired to a hermitage to spend his last thirty-five years in austere fasting. F. D. June 18.

JEROME EMILIANI. *See* Emiliani, St. Jerome.

JEROME OF WERDEN, ST. (1522–1572), martyr. Born in Werden, Holland, he became a Franciscan, labored as a missioner in Jerusalem, returned to preach strongly against Calvinism, and became vicar of the friary at Gorkum. He was slain there by Calvinists. He was canonized in 1867. F. D. July 9.

JERVIS. *See* Gervase, St.

JIMÉNEZ DE RADA, RODRIGO (1170?–1247), cardinal. Born probably in Navarre, Spain, he studied at Paris, became a Franciscan, and was named archbishop of Toledo in 1208 and later a cardinal. At the request of St. Ferdinand of Castile he wrote *Historia Gothica* (often called *Chronica rerum gestarum in Hispania*), which he translated into Castilian about 1241. It had considerable influence on literature.

JOACHIM, ST. (1st century). This is the name traditionally given to the father of the Virgin Mary. According to such apocryphal works as the *Protoevangelium of St. James*, which must be regarded as no more than a pious legend, he was born in Nazareth and wed St. Anne at a youthful age. His childlessness brought public reproach, whereupon he went into the desert and prayed and fasted for forty days. An angel appeared, comforted him, and promised a child to the couple. Joachim (elsewhere called Cleopas, Eliacim, Heli, Jonachir, or Sadoc) witnessed the presentation of the infant Jesus in the Temple and died shortly after. F. D. Aug. 16.

JOACHIM OF FLORA (1132?-1202). Born in Celico, Italy, son of a notary, he was raised at the royal court, went to the Holy Land on pilgrimage, and on his return about 1159 entered the Cistercian abbey at Sambucina. He was ordained about 1168, served as abbot to 1182, and then with papal approval retired to the abbey of Casmari to devote himself to scriptural study. He retired to a hermitage at Pietralata in 1187 and founded the abbey of Fiore (Flora) for a more austere branch of the Cistercians, approved by Pope Clementine in 1196. He finished his biblical studies and submitted them to Innocent III in 1200, but died at Fiore, Calabria, Italy, on Mar. 30 before judgment was passed. His three chief works were *Liber concordiae novi ac veteris testamenti, Expositio in Apocalipsim* and *Psalterium decem cordarum.* In them he predicted that a new era, the Age of the Holy Spirit, was about to dawn in which universal love would rule. His teachings on the Trinity were condemned by the Lateran Council in 1215, but when his prophecies were adopted as a new gospel by Franciscan extremists, the so-called Joachists, all his works were condemned by Pope Alexander IV in 1256. His teachings were confuted by St. Thomas Aquinas and its exponents repressed by St. Bonaventure. The movement collapsed when 1260, the year Joachim had predicted would usher in the new era with some great cataclysm, passed uneventfully.

JOAN OF ARC, ST. (1412-1431). Born in Domrémy, near the Lorraine border, on Jan. 6, one of five children of Jacques d'Arc, a farmer, she, and her family, felt the effects of Burgundian raids, the invasion of France by Henry V of England, and the civil war between the dukes of Burgundy and Orléans. The insane Charles VI of France died in 1422; his son, Charles, the idle and frivolous dauphin, did nothing to save the country. At fourteen, and for the next two years, Joan heard voices which insisted that she begin to restore order to a nation which had lost all sense of justice and decency. The French commander laughed her away at their first meeting; at a second, it appeared obvious that she had a gift of prophecy, and he sent her to the dauphin. She identified him, though he was disguised, and asked for troops to raise the siege of Orléans. She saved the city, defeated the English under Sir

John Fastolf at Patay, and opened the way to Rheims, in whose cathedral the dauphin could now be presented for formal coronation. He became King Charles VII in 1429. In an unsuccessful attack on Paris, Joan was wounded; she was captured at Compiègne, handed over to the Burgundians, and completely abandoned by the French. To make an example of a woman who had beaten them in battle, the English bought her for some $50,000, called her a witch, and had her tried by Peter Cauchon, bishop of Beauvais, who sold his honor for the hope of a promised archbishopric. She was examined for fifteen sessions as to her voices, her protective male costume, her attitude toward Church authority. As an uneducated person, she made a number of unsatisfactory replies; as a simple and holy one, she made others which astonished as well as embarrassed the questioners. She apparently was tricked into a false retraction and into resuming male garb under frightful jail conditions, and on these charges was ordered burned to death in Rouen. In 1454, Joan's mother and brothers had the case reopened and two years later the verdict of the earlier servile court was reversed. She was canonized on May 16, 1920. F. D. May 30.

JOHN BEEVERS, *Joan of Arc* (Garden City, N.Y., Hanover, 1959); HILAIRE BELLOC, *Joan of Arc* (N.Y., McMullen, 1949).

JOAN OF AZA, BL. (d. 1190?). Born near Aranda in Old Castile, Spain, she was probably married while quite young to Felix de Guzman, warden of Calarugga, Burgos. They had four children: Antony, Bl. Mannes, a daughter, and St. Dominic. Her cult was confirmed in 1828. F. D. Aug. 8.

JOAN OF FRANCE. *See* Joan of Valois, St.

JOAN OF KENT (1328-1385). Daughter of Edmund, earl of Kent, and granddaughter of King Edward I of England, she married Sir Thomas Holland when the pope supported Holland over another suitor, the earl of Salisbury. She married Edward the Black Prince in 1361 (Holland had died in 1360) and became the mother of future King Richard II, whose quarrel with John of Gaunt she ended. She is known in English legend as "the Fair Maid of Kent."

JOAN OF PORTUGAL, BL. (1452-1490). Born in Lisbon, daughter of King Alfonso V and Elizabeth of Coimbra, she practiced extreme austerities from her early years and entered the Dominican convent at Aveiro in 1472. She had served as regent when her father and brother fought the Moors, and was still looked on as a possible successor to the throne; she was unable to take her vows until 1485, when the succession was established and suggestions for marriage (to Richard III of England, among others) came to an end.

Her cult was approved in 1693. She died in Aveiro, Spain. F. D. May 12.

JOAN OF SIGNA, BL. (1245–1307). Born in Signa, near Florence, Italy, she spent her youth as a shepherd. When twenty-three, she became a recluse near her home on the banks of the Arno until her death forty years later on Nov. 9. Her cult was approved in 1798. F. D. Nov. 17.

JOAN OF TOULOUSE, BL. (14th century). A hermit at Toulouse, France, she is said by the Carmelites to have been, instead, a thirteenth-century tertiary, invested by St. Simon Stock. F. D. Mar. 31.

JOAN OF VALOIS, ST. (1464–1505), foundress. Deformed daughter of King Louis XI and Charlotte of Savoy, she was hated by her father and by his cousin, the duke of Orléans, to whom she was married. When the duke became Louis XII he appealed to Pope Alexander VI to annul his former marriage, principally because he wished to marry Anne of Brittany. The castoff queen submitted without opposition in 1498 and established a group of nuns at Bourges, under the spiritual direction of Bl. Gabriel Mary, her Franciscan confessor, who drew up their rule. The Annonciades of Bourges, a contemplative order, was papally approved and is still in existence. She is also called Joan of France, and was canonized in 1950. F. D. Feb. 4 (sometimes Feb. 14).

JOANNA, ST. (1st century). She is mentioned by St. Luke (8:3; 24:10) as the wife of Chuza, steward of Herod Antipas, and one of the holy women who ministered to Christ. F. D. May 24.

JOANNES DE SACROBOSCO. *See* Holywood, John.

JOANNICUS, ST. (754?–846). A native of Bithynia, he was a swineherd, became a soldier at nineteen, led a licentious life, and was an Iconoclast before his conversion by a monk. At forty, he left the army, became a monk and hermit on Mt. Olympus and then at Eraste. He was a vigorous opponent of Iconoclasm and of Emperor Theophilus, who supported the heresy, and was a close friend of SS. Theodore Studites and Methodius of Constantinople, whom he counseled on the validity of orders received from Iconoclastic bishops. F. D. Nov. 4.

JOÃO DE S. THOMÉ (d. 1585?), martyr. A Portuguese Dominican, he was one of the first missioners to the island of Madagascar, where he was poisoned by natives.

JOAQUINA DEMAS, BL. *See* Vedruna, Joaquina de Mas y de.

JOAVAN, ST. (d. 576?). He went from Ireland to Léon in Brittany, where he succeeded his uncle, St. Paul, as bishop. F. D. Mar. 2.

JOCELIN (d. 1199), bishop. A Cistercian monk, he became prior of Melrose, abbot in 1170, and bishop of Glasgow in 1174. In 1175 he opposed the jurisdiction of York over Glasgow at a council in Northampton, visited Rome in 1182 and secured papal absolution for King William the Lion, and died at Melrose, Scotland.

JOCELIN OF BRAKELOND (12th century), historian. An Englishman at the abbey of Bury St. Edmund's, he served as chaplain to Abbot Samson from 1182 to 1188, and became almoner in 1212. He wrote a chronicle of the abbey for the years 1173–1202 which gives a vivid picture of monastic life in England and was used by Thomas Carlyle as the basis for part of *Past and Present*. He was still living in 1215.

JOCELIN OF WELLS. *See* Troteman, Jocelin.

JODOCUS, ST. (d. 668). Son of King Juthael of Brittany, he occupied the throne for several months when his brother Judicael abdicated, but about 636 became a priest at Ponthieu. On his return from a pilgrimage to Rome he settled at Runiacum (now St. Josse), France, as a hermit. He is also known as Josse. F. D. Dec. 13.

JODOCUS ASCENSIANUS. *See* Badius, Jodocus.

JODOCUS OF ROSENBURG (d. 1467). A Bohemian nobleman and grand prior of the Knights of St. John, he became bishop of Breslau, Silesia, in 1456, and found the area torn by dissension between the Hussite king of Bohemia, George of Podiebrad, and the Catholic German faction in his diocese.

JOEL, BL. (d. 1185). Trained by St. John of Matera, who founded the Benedictine Congregation of Pulsano, Italy, Joel became its third general. F. D. Jan. 25.

JOEST, JAN (1460?–1519), painter. Born probably in Calcker, Holland, he painted scenes from the life of Christ for St. Nicholas church in 1505–8 and for the Hackeneg family in Cologne in 1518. His work is characterized by the delicacy of his faces and the transparency of his coloring. He is also known as Jan Joost van Calcker. He died in Haarlem, Netherlands.

JOGUES, ST. ISAAC (1607–1646), martyr. Born of well-to-do parents in Orléans, France, he studied at the Jesuit school there, joined the Jesuits in 1624, and was ordained in 1636. At his request he was sent as missioner to Quebec. A group of Jesuits under the superiorship of Fr. de Brébeuf ranged as far west as Sault Ste. Marie, successfully converting many Huron Indians. In 1642 a war party of Iroquois attacked and captured them. St. René Goupil was slain, but Fr. Jogues was frightfully tortured, mutilated, and humiliated through a year of imprisonment. Aided by the Dutch at Albany, he escaped to New York and thence to France. In 1644 he returned at his own request to Quebec and in 1646 he and St. Jean de Lalande set out for Iroquois country in the belief a recently signed peace treaty would be observed. They were captured by a Mohawk war party and on Oct. 18 Fr. Jogues was tomahawked and beheaded (Fr. de Lalande was slain the next day) at Ossernenon, near Albany, New York. He was canonized in 1930 by Pope Pius XI. F. D. Sept. 26 (also, Mar. 16).

FRANCIS TALBOT, *Saint among Savages* (Garden City, N.Y., Image Books, 1961).

JOHANN VON SPEYER (d. 1470), printer. Born in Speyer, Bavaria, he was a goldsmith in Mainz, Prussia, in 1460 and there, with his brother Wendelin, learned printing. In 1468 the two brothers established the first press in Venice, received a five-year monopoly in book printing from the senate, and published works of Cicero, Pliny, and Livy. On Johann's death, Wendelin took over the direction of the firm with the aid of Johann von Köln, a German printer, who joined him about 1472. The press was noted for its fine printing of the classics and Church Fathers, and for its innovation of numbering the pages with Arabic numerals and the introduction of the colon and question mark. Wendelin died in 1477.

JOHANNES ANGLICUS. See Bacon, John.

JOHANNES DE BACONTHORPE. See Bacon, John.

JOHANNES DANKO (14th century). Also known as Jean de Saxe, he wrote *Notulae super compotum* in 1297; he also made a copy (1323) of the canons of Jean de Linières.

JOHANNES, FRANCIS (1874–1937), bishop. Born in Mittelstren, Bavaria, on Feb. 17, he was brought to the United States by his parents in 1882, studied at St. Benedict's College, Kansas, and St. Francis seminary, Milwaukee, and was ordained in 1897. He served in St. Joseph, Missouri, from 1897 to 1928, as pastor from 1918, and in 1927 was titular bishop of Thasus and appointed coadjutor of Leavenworth, Kansas. He succeeded to the see in 1929 and died in Denver, Colorado, on Mar. 13.

JOHANNES DE SACROBOSCO (d. 1256?), mathematician. Born probably in Halifax, Yorkshire, England, he studied at Oxford, went to Paris about 1230, and taught mathematics and astronomy there, relying heavily on the findings of Arabian scientists. His *Tractatus de sphaera* (first published in 1472) is a paraphrase of Ptolemy's *Almagest*; equally influential was his study of arithmetic, *Algorismus* (first printed in 1488). He also wrote *De anni ratione*. He is known also as John of Holywood and John of Halifax.

JOHANNES SECUNDUS. See Everaerts, Jan Nicolai.

JOHANNES DE SOARDIS. See John of Paris.

JOHN I, ST. (d. 526), pope. This Tuscan priest succeeded Pope St. Hormisdas on Aug. 13, 523, and was sent against his will on a mission from Emperor Theodoric in the West to Justin at Constantinople, apparently with an order to lessen the persecution of Arians in the East in return for a promise of peace under the Gothic occupation of Italy. On his return he was thrown into prison at Ravenna by Theodoric, who had been active against the Church during the pope's long absence, and died on May 18 from mistreatment. Because of this he generally has been listed as a martyr, but the claim has been seriously contested. F. D. May 27.

JOHN II (d. 535), pope. A Roman by birth, named Mercurius, he was a priest at St. Clement's basilica and was elected pope on Jan. 2, 533, after a two-month vacancy of the see. He seems to have been the first pope to take a name other than his own (obviously because of the pagan connotation of Mercurius). He maintained good relations with the Gothic King Athalric and Justinian, opposed simony, and had a quiet reign. He died on May 8.

JOHN III (d. 574), pope. Of a distinguished Roman family and named Catelinus, he was consecrated pope on July 17, 561. Little is known of his pontificate because the records of his reign perished during the Lombard invasions. He is known to have reversed the decision of a synod in Lyons about 567 and at the request of King Guntram of Burgundy restored their sees to the unworthy Salonius of Embrun and Sagittarius of Gap. In 571, John tried unsuccessfully to persuade Emperor Justinian's general, Narses, who had been recalled to Constantinople, to remain in Italy and drive off the Lombards. When Narses left, John lived in the catacombs, which he repaired, returned to the Lateran in 572, and died on July 13.

JOHN IV (d. 642), pope. Son of a lawyer, Venantius, he was born in Dalmatia and was an archdeacon when elected pope on Dec. 24, 640. His renewal of Pope Severinus' denunciation of the Monothelite *Ecthesis* at a synod in Rome in 640 caused Emperor Heraclius to disown it; John also sent a defense of Pope Honorius to Constantius III, clearing him of the charge of Monothelism. He was active in aiding Dalmatia, which had been invaded by the Slavs, whom he tried to convert, redeemed captives there, and cautioned the Irish about the date for Easter and the dangers of Pelagianism. He died on Oct. 12.

JOHN V (d. 686), pope. Born in Antioch, Syria, he was educated in Rome, served while a deacon as papal legate at the sixth Ecumenical Council at Constantinople in 680, and was elected to the papacy in 685 and consecrated on July 23. He was noted for his scholarship, charity, and justice. He died on Aug. 2.

JOHN VI (d. 705), pope. A native of Greece, he became pope on Oct. 30, 701, and shortly after was obliged to act as peacemaker between the exarch of Italy, Theophylactus, and the residents of Rome. His pontificate was further disturbed by a new invasion by the Lombards under Gisulf, whom he persuaded to retire to his own territory, and whose captives he redeemed. He upheld St. Wilfrid's claim to the see of York and sent letters to the kings of Mercia and Northumbria ordering the archbishop of Canterbury, St. Berhtwald, to restore Wilfrid's see to him. He died on Jan. 11.

JOHN VII (d. 707), pope. Of a distinguished Greek family, he was rector of a palace on the Appian Way and was elected pope on Mar. 1, 705. He restored many churches, received back the papal possessions in the Cottian Alps (which the Lombards had seized) from King Aripert II, restored the monastery of Subiaco which had been sacked by Saracens, but failed to condemn Emperor Justinian II when the latter presented the decrees of the Quinisext Council which contained many articles inimical to the Holy See. He died on Oct. 18.

JOHN VIII (d. 882), pope. Born in Rome, son of Gundus, he was an archdeacon as early as 853, and was elected pope on Dec. 14, 872. On taking office, he was faced with a lack of ecclesiastical discipline and lax morals in high office, which he immediately attacked. On the death in 875 of Emperor Louis II, whom he had supported, though many of the malingerers were on friendly terms with the emperor, he drove the wrongdoers from Rome and excommunicated them (among them Formosus, bishop of Porto, who was later restored and who became pope in 891). He helped secure the election of Charles the Bald to succeed Louis, and crowned him in 875. In 873 he confirmed Methodius' orthodoxy against the charges of the German clergy and princes who had imprisoned the saint, allowed him to use the Slavonic language in the liturgy of the Church, and labored unavailingly to restore the Bulgarians to closer ties with Rome. In 881 he condemned Photius, who had succeeded Ignatius as patriarch of Constantinople. In 878, Lambert, duke of Spoleto, who had been encroaching on papal territories for years, captured Rome. John fled to France, where later the same year he crowned Louis II king. On Charles's death in 877, John attempted to have Boso of Provence elected, but eventually supported Charles the Fat, whom he crowned as Emperor Charles III in 881. John's entire pontificate was disturbed by Saracen incursions, and he several times took the field against them as general and admiral (in 876 he defeated a Saracen fleet) and constantly sought to win over rulers in the south of Italy from Saracen alliances. He died on Dec. 16.

JOHN IX (d. 900), pope. Born in Tivoli, Italy, he became a Benedictine and was ordained by Pope Formosus. He was elected pope in Jan. 898 over Sergius, who was excommunicated and driven from Rome. He confirmed Pope Theodore II's rehabilitation of Formosus and condemned the synod of Stephen VI [VII] which had condemned Formosus and annulled his ordinations. He supported Emperor Lambert over Berengarius and decreed that an imperial envoy must be present at future papal elections. He also established a Moravian hierarchy, despite opposition from the German clergy. He died early in Jan.

JOHN X (d. 928), pope. Born in Tossignano, Romagna, he became a deacon in Bologna and about 905 archbishop of Ravenna. He was elected pope in Mar. 914. In 915 he crowned Berengarius emperor and the following year led a coalition of Italian princes against the Saracens and defeated them. He was active in Germany (where he sent a legate to a synod and was friendly with King Conrad), France (where he appointed the five-year-old son of Count Heribert of Aquitaine archbishop of Rheims in return for the count's release of King Charles), and Italy (where his support of Hugh of Burgundy for king earned the enmity of Marozia and the dominant Roman group she headed). In May 928, Marozia's forces murdered John's brother Peter, prefect of Rome, and imprisoned the pope. John died in prison before the month was out.

JOHN XI (d. 935), pope. Son of Marozia and Alberic, he was born in Rome and through the influence of his mother, who was then the city's ruler, was elected pope in Feb. or Mar. 931. When his younger brother, Alberic II, led a successful revolt against Marozia and King Hugh of Provence, whom she had married, John became ruler of Rome in 933. He and the papacy became completely subordinate to Alberic in the political realm. One of John's few free acts was the granting of privileges to Cluny, which was later to lead ecclesiastical reform. He died in Rome in Dec.

JOHN XII (937?–964), pope. Son of Alberic II, Octavius, count of Tusculum, was born in Rome and at eighteen was elected pope on Dec. 16, 955, as a result of an agreement between his father and the Roman nobles. This inaugurated one of the most scandalous and immoral pontificates in history. He was defeated in a war with Duke Pandulf of Capua and when King Berengarius of Italy occupied the papal domains, John appealed for aid to German King Otto I. The latter forced Berengarius to withdraw and was crowned emperor in Rome in 962. Otto at this time issued his *Diploma*, confirming the Church's territorial possessions, prescribing the canonical form for future papal elections, and requiring the emperor's consent for a pope's election. When Otto left Rome, John began to negotiate with Adalbert, son of Berengarius, and also with Constantinople against the emperor, who, on discovering the plot, returned to Rome in 963.

When his adherents revolted against him, John fled to Tivoli and a synod convened at St. Peter's on Nov. 6 condemned him for various crimes (whereupon John excommunicated all participants) and on Dec. 4, 963, declared him deposed. They chose a layman as Pope Leo VIII in an invalid election. Early in 964, John's followers in Rome rose in revolt and were bloodily suppressed, but a second revolt was successful. Leo fled and John returned to wreak bloody vengeance on his opponents. He called a synod which repealed the decrees of the Nov. 6 group and excommunicated Leo. Meanwhile, Otto had defeated Berengarius and was about to enter Rome when John died on May 14.

JOHN XIII (d. 972), pope. Nephew of Marozia and son of Theodora and John, a consul who later became a bishop, he was born in Rome, where he was ordained, and became bishop of Narni. The choice of Emperor Otto I, he was crowned pope on Oct. 1, 965, was imprisoned by opponents of Otto in Dec., but escaped to the protection of Prince Pandulf of Capua. When the emperor retook Rome in 966, John returned with him. In 967 he crowned Otto's son, Otto II, joint emperor with his father and officiated at his marriage to Byzantine Princess Theophano in 972. He established a Slavic hierarchy in 968 with the consecration of Abbot Adalbert as first archbishop of Magdeburg, established new sees and raised older ones, encouraged and confirmed the decrees of synods in England and France, and was active in carrying out a series of ecclesiastical reforms and in encouraging churches, monasteries, and convents in their work. He died on Sept. 6.

JOHN XIV (d. 984), pope. Born in Pavia, Italy, Peter Campanora became imperial chancellor under Otto II, then bishop of Pavia, and in Dec. 983 was crowned pope. When Otto, who had supported his election, died later in 983, antipope Boniface VII (elected in 974 by the supporters of Crescentius) returned to Rome from Constantinople in Apr. 984, and imprisoned John in the dungeon of the Castle of Sant' Angelo, where he died on Aug. 20 of starvation or of murder at Boniface's orders.

JOHN XV [XVI] (d. 996), pope. After the murder of John XIV, antipope Boniface VII reigned in Rome until his death in July 985, whereupon John, a native Roman and cardinal-priest, was elected pope and crowned in Aug. He was forced to flee Rome to Tuscany because of the treatment of the patrician John Crescentius, but returned on that patrician's promise of a more favorable attitude. The pope acted as mediator between King Ethelred of England and Richard of Normandy, who agreed to peace at Rouen in 991, and was obliged to intervene in France when King Hugh Capet deposed Arnulf as archbishop of

Rheims and appointed Gerbert (later Pope Sylvester II) as his successor at a synod in Rheims in 991. The matter dragged on until 995, when Arnulf's deposition was declared illegal and Gerbert censured at a synod in Mousson. Arnulf was completely restored in 997 after Hugh Capet's death in Oct. 996. In 993, Bishop Ulrich of Augsburg was canonized in the Lateran, the first time a saint was canonized by a pope. John died in Mar. There is some confusion in the number attributed to John because some historians listed another John who is reputed to have reigned for four months as successor to antipope Boniface VII. Actually, this John never existed, but, since he was listed as John XV, the enumeration of subsequent popes named John was upset.

JOHN XVI, pope. There was no pope named John XVI. When John Sicco was named pope in 1003, he was elected through the influence of the patrician, Crescentius III. This Crescentius was the son of the Crescentius who, in 997, had proclaimed John Piligato as Pope (antipope) John XVI though a legitimate pope, Benedict V, occupied the papal throne. Rather than antagonize his sponsor, John Sicco continued the numbering as if John Piligato (Philagathus), antipope John XVI, had really been pope and took the next numeral for the line of Johns, XVII.

JOHN XVI [XVII] (d. 1013), antipope. A native of Rossano, Calabria, John Piligato (Philagathus) became a monk and confidant of Empress Theophano, widow of Otto II. In 988 he was made archbishop of Piacenza and in 995 acted as Otto III's ambassador to Constantinople to arrange a royal marriage. In Apr. 997, despite the pleas of St. Milus of Rossano, he allowed Crescentius, who had driven Pope Benedict V from Rome and opposed Otto, to proclaim him pope. Otto led an army into Rome and reinstated Benedict in Feb. 998. John was captured, mutilated, and formally deposed, but Pope Gregory V spared his life and pardoned him at St. Nilus' request. He spent the rest of his life, except for one later public appearance in Rome in formal robes which were torn off by a mob, in a monastery. He died on Apr. 2.

JOHN XVII [XVIII] (d. 1003), pope. A native of Rome named Siccone, married and the father of three children, he was elected pope through the influence of John Crescentius (III) in June 1003, but died in Dec. Nothing is known of his pontificate.

JOHN XVIII [XIX] (d. 1009), pope. Son of a Roman priest named Leo, Fasano (Phasianus) was elected pope in Jan. 1004 and devoted the energies of his pontificate solely to ecclesiastical matters. There was evidently some kind of reunion with the Eastern Church since his name appeared on the diptychs of the church in Constantinople. He was an enthusiastic supporter of monastic institutions, founded the see of Bamberg, Germany, at the request of Emperor Henry II, and was noted for his piety. He is reported to have abdicated and entered the abbey of St. Paul near Rome, where he died in July as a monk.

JOHN XIX [XX] (d. 1032), pope. Romanus, count of Tusculum, consul, senator, and ruler of Rome when his brother, Pope Benedict VIII, died, had himself, a layman, elected pope in Apr. or May 1024 and inaugurated a pontificate of lavish hospitality and material splendor. When Byzantine Emperor Basil II sent valuable presents and suggested that John recognize the supremacy of the patriarch of Constantinople over all Eastern churches, with the same jurisdiction in the East as Rome in the West, he considered the suggestion, but turned it down after protests by prelates in Italy and France (whereupon the patriarch erased the pope's name from the diptychs of his church). In 1027 he crowned Conrad the Salian as emperor. At the request of King Canute of Denmark and England he abolished Italian customs duties on English and Danish pilgrims to Rome. He called several synods to resolve differences between prelates over precedence, renewed the privileges granted to the abbey of Cluny, and probably was the first pope to grant indulgences in return for alms. He died in Nov. or Dec.

JOHN XX. This numbering was omitted, by error, in the succession of popes.

JOHN XXI [XX] (1210?–1277), pope. Born in Lisbon, Portugal, sometime between 1210 and 1220, Pedro Juliani (also known as Peter of Spain) was educated at the cathedral school of Lisbon and at Paris, where he studied medicine and took courses under Albertus Magnus and John of Parma. In 1247 he became professor of medicine at Siena and there wrote *Summulae logicales* which was widely used as a text on logic for three centuries. He joined Cardinal Ottoboni Fieschi's household about 1261, became deacon in Lisbon, and in 1272 physician of Pope Gregory X, whom he accompanied to the Council of Lyons. During the next year he wrote his widely used *Thesaurus pauperum* (*The Poor Man's Treasury*), a collection of remedies for disease. In 1273 he was elected archbishop of Braga and in 1275 cardinal-bishop of Tusculum. He was elected pope on Sept. 8, 1276, the only Portuguese pope, consecrated on Sept. 20, and took the name John XXI, though numerically he was John XX. During his short pontificate he twice prevailed upon Philip III of France and Alfonso of Castile and León not to go to war over Navarre; acted as peacemaker between Charles of Anjou (to whom he had given Sicily) and Rudolf of Hapsburg; demanded that King Edward

I of England pay papal taxes fifty years in arrears and release Countess Eleanor of Montfort and her brother; and approved a synod at Constantinople, as one result of which Emperor Michael and his son Andronicus acknowledged the supremacy of the pope. John was seriously injured on May 14 when the roof of his scientific laboratory in the papal palace at Viterbo collapsed; he died on May 20.

JOHN XXII (1249–1334), pope. Jacques Duèse (D'Euse; James of Ossa) was born in Cahors, France, studied under the Dominicans there, at Montpellier and Paris, and taught law at Toulouse and Cahors. He was appointed bishop of Fréjus in 1300, became chancellor of Charles II of Naples in 1309, was transferred to Avignon in 1310, and in 1312 was created cardinal-bishop of Porto by Pope Clement V. The bitter enmity between the French and Italians prevented the election of a new pope for more than two years after the death of Clement V, but Duèse was elected pope at Lyons on Aug. 7, 1316, consecrated there on Sept. 5, and took up residence at Avignon. Early in his pontificate he was obliged to intervene in the bitter quarrels among the Franciscans. In 1318 he denounced the Fraticelli and declared many of their doctrines heretical; in 1323 he denounced as heretical the theory of evangelical poverty supported by William of Occam and Michael of Cesena and issued a bull in 1324 declaring those opposing his decision heretics, causing William and Michael to flee to Bavaria, where they were welcomed by Louis of Bavaria, who also supported the Fraticelli. In 1314 the election of Louis of Bavaria at Aachen and Frederick of Austria at Bonn as king of Germany caused John to offer himself as mediator in the dispute. Both refused, and in 1322 Louis' victory at Mühldorf insured his claim to the throne. Louis' actions in supporting opponents of John led to remonstrances from the pope, and in 1324 Louis was excommunicated—a step which led to the strengthening of Louis' position in Germany when the dissident elements there flocked to his support, and to the publication of *Defensor pacis* by Marsilius of Padua and John of Janduno, lauding state supremacy over the Church and denying papal supremacy. The rift deepened into schism when John declared Louis deposed in 1327, and appointed bishops to vacant sees in Louis' realms which Louis had already filled. In 1328 the excommunicated Louis received the imperial crown in Rome from Sciarra Colonna, declared John deposed, and on May 22 proclaimed Pietro Rainalducci of Corbario, one of the Fraticelli, pope with the name Nicholas V. The antipope was driven from Rome three months later. A strong wave in favor of the pope now set in. Louis was forced to return to Germany in 1330, sued for a reconciliation with the pope, and later in that year Nicholas submitted to John. Several other controversies disturbed his pontificate, particularly the conflict over the beatific vision. He had stated that the souls of the faithful dead did not see God until after the last judgment, a statement which was denounced by many theologians who held the traditional belief the souls of the faithful enjoyed the beatific vision at once. John later withdrew his statement. He was also criticized for the large number of French cardinals he appointed, for his continuance of the Holy See at Avignon, for his fiscal policies, which caused many benefices to come to the papal see rather than to the bishops and abbots in whose area they were located, and for the bureaucratic nature of his administration. He was praised for his patronage of the arts, expansion of missionary activities in Africa, and encouragement of higher learning. He died in Avignon, France, on Dec. 4.

JOHN XXIII (1370?–1419), antipope. Born in Naples, of a poor, noble family, Baldassare Cossa served in the military as a youth, studied law at Bologna where he received his doctorate, and entered the employ of the papal curia. In 1402 he was created cardinal-deacon, and served as legate of Romandiola, where he became known for his worldliness and lack of scruples, in 1403–8. In 1408 he deserted Pope Gregory XII to bring about the Council of Pisa to end the schism between Roman (Gregory XIII) and Avignon (Benedict XII) popes, presided over the Council of Pisa in 1409 which illegally deposed these two popes, and was instrumental in electing Pietro Philarghi "pope" as Alexander V. On Philarghi's death in 1410, the seven schismatic cardinals of the Pisan obedience, supported by Louis II of Anjou, elected Cossa "pope" as John XXIII on May 17. He was ordained on May 24 and consecrated on the following day. He at once sought the support of Sigismund of Hungary, allied himself with Louis II against Ladislas of Naples, Gregory XII's ally, accompanied Louis on an expedition to Italy which captured Rome and defeated Ladislas, with whom he later reached an agreement, appointed several new cardinals, and convoked a council in Rome in 1413 which condemned the writings of Hus and Wyclif. He was forced to flee to Florence in 1413 when Ladislas recovered and invaded Rome, and later that year, at the instigation of Sigismund, now king of Germany, issued a call for a general council at Constance. He opened the Council of Constance on Nov. 5, 1414, had a strong following at first, finally agreed to abdicate, but attempted to avoid his promise by flight to his ally, Frederick of Austria, and then to Burgundy in Mar. 1415, was formally deposed on May 29, and was imprisoned by the Palatine Louis. On July 4, 1415, Pope Gregory XII

abdicated; antipope Benedict XIII was deposed on July 26, 1417; and on Nov. 11, 1417, Martin V was elected pope, ending the schism. Cossa was released from prison in 1418, submitted to Pope Martin V, who made him cardinal-bishop of Tusculum, and died in Florence a few months later, on Nov. 22.

JOHN I (1350–1395), king of Aragon. He became king in 1387 and was known as a patron of learning.

JOHN II (1397–1479), king of Aragon. Brother of Alfonso V, he became king in 1458, and was forced to fight his son, Charles of Viana, from 1442 to 1461, and against Catalonia until 1472. He attempted to regain from Louis XI some territories ceded to France.

JOHN I (1358–1390), king of Castile and León. He became king in 1379, defended his position against the English led by John of Gaunt, invaded Portugal, and was defeated by John the Great of Portugal at the battle of Aljubarrota, which cost Castile its long possession of Portuguese territory.

JOHN II (1405–1454), king of Castile. He became king in 1406, but the government was left in the hands of Alvaro de Luna, while John devoted himself to letters and military sports.

JOHN (1167?–1216), king of England. Known as John Lackland because, as the youngest son of Henry II and Eleanor of Aquitaine, he inherited little territory, he was born in Oxford, England, on Dec. 24. He was named king of Ireland and went there in 1185, and returned to join his mother and brothers against his father. John obtained property and titles from his brother, Richard I, against whom he plotted when the king was absent on the third crusade; he was forgiven when Richard returned in 1194. John became king in 1199, faced a revolt by supporters of Arthur of Brittany, his nephew, and from others who objected to his divorce from Isabel of Gloucester and marriage to Isabel of Angoulême (already engaged to Hugh de Lusignan). Arthur was captured and murdered in 1203 (probably on John's orders); Philip II of France continued the war and gained Normandy, Anjou, Brittany, and other continental areas by John's 1204 surrender. John also fought Pope Innocent III by refusing to accept Stephen Langton as archbishop of Canterbury, saw England placed under an interdict in 1108, and was excommunicated and deposed. Fearing a papally supported invasion by Philip, John surrendered to the pope, gave up his feudal control of England to the papacy, then had it lent to him to rule as a fief. He fought Philip in Poitou and was defeated in 1214. Seeking new revenue, he was checked by his barons, who forced him to make concessions in 1215 and to sign the Magna Charta. John was supported against the barons by the pope (because of the explanations of the English clergy), but died in Newark, Nottingham, on Oct. 19 before the situation was clarified.

JOHN I (d. 1316), king of France, Posthumous son of King Louis X and Clemence, daughter of Charles Martel, he was born on Nov. 15 and died a week later on Nov. 22. Philip, brother of Louis, acted as regent and on John's death ascended the throne as Philip V.

JOHN II (1319-1364), king of France. Surnamed "the Good," the son of Philip VI and Jeanne of Burgundy succeeded to the throne in 1350. He paid little heed to the needs of his country and devoted himself to a life of pleasure. He raised a force of nobles to oppose Edward the Black Prince, who had been pillaging Languedoc, was defeated by Edward at Poitiers in 1356, and imprisoned in England until he agreed in the Treaty of Bretigny (1360) to pay a ransom of three million francs. Despite the imposition of heavy taxes, he was unable to raise the ransom, and when his son, whom he had left as hostage, escaped in 1363, John went to England, where he died in London on Apr. 8.

JOHN I, king of Poland. *See* John Albert, king of Poland.

JOHN II CASIMIR (1609-1672), king of Poland. Youngest son of Sigismund III, he became king in 1648 and through twenty years suffered attacks by combined Cossack-Tatar forces to the south and by a Swedish army under Charles Gustavus. The Swedes conquered Poland proper, Lithuania fell to the czar, and Brandenburg occupied Prussia. The nation had almost disappeared when some Paulite monks routed 2000 Swedes near Czestochowa (site of a subsequent Marian shrine); John Casimir then placed the nation under the protection of Mary as Queen of the Crown of Poland in 1656, and rising popular spirit crystallized as a religious war against the Swedes, Russians, and Mohammedan Tatars on three fronts. Worn out by the struggle, John abdicated in 1668 and retired to France.

JOHN III SOBIESKI (1624-1696), king of Poland. Born in Olesko, Galicia, on June 2, son of James Sobieski, castellan of Cracow, he was educated at Cracow, traveled through Europe with his brother Mark, and returned to Poland in 1648. He served in the Cossack rebellion of 1648 (in which Mark was captured and murdered by the Tatars at Batoy in 1652), and the wars against Charles X of Sweden and the Muscovites under George Lubomirski. When the latter revolted, John remained loyal to King John Casimir, became successively field hetman, grand marshal, and grand hetman (in 1668). His victory over Mahomet IV and the Turks at Khotin in 1673 made him a candidate for the throne and, on the death of King Michael Wisniowiecki, he was elected king of Poland in 1674. His reign was constantly occupied by wars with the Turks, whom he repeatedly defeated, and in 1676 he recovered the greater part of the Ukraine for Poland by the Treaty of Zaravno, though he was obliged to surrender Kiev to Russia in 1686. In 1683, he achieved his greatest victory when he raised the siege of Vienna and routed the Turks, saving Europe for Christendom. After this victory his star declined and the last twelve years of his life were marred by treason, mutiny, the deceit of ungrateful allies, and, climactically, the intrigues of his wife, Marya Kazimiera d'Arquien. He died at his castle of Wilanow, Poland, on June 17.

JOHN I (1357?-1433), king of Portugal. Illegitimate son of Pedro I, he became grand master of the Knights of Avis in 1364, and became known as "the Great." He led a rebellion in 1383 against his brother Ferdinand's widow and her lover, who allied themselves with Castile. Illness swept through the Spanish army attacking Lisbon, the siege was lifted, and John was elected king in 1385. After John's victory at Aljubarrota, Portugal's independence was assured. He made an alliance with England, married his daughter Philippa to John of Gaunt, introduced administrative reforms, developed colonial expansion, captured Ceuta in North Africa from the Moors, and saw the beginning of a flourishing literature.

JOHN II (1455-1495), king of Portugal. Called "the Perfect," and son of Alfonso V, he became king in 1481, reduced the power of the nobility, was a patron of the arts, and continued the alliance with England and explorations in Ethiopia and the East. Portuguese Congo was discovered during his reign; Bartholomew Diaz passed the Cape of Good Hope and Vasco da Gama reached India. Internally, John established his grip on the throne by the execution of the duke of Braganza, by his murder of the duke of Viseu, and the execution of the bishop of Evora and others. He maintained good relations with Castile, and agreed to a north-south line through the Atlantic which was to result in Spain's gain of all South America except Brazil.

JOHN III (1502-1557), king of Portugal. Called "the Fortunate" and son of Emanuel, he became king in 1521, saw the spread of his empire in the Far East and had success in a flourishing Brazil. All too soon, agriculture began to decline at home, slavery flourished in his colonies, and, though he was not corrupt, his court was. He introduced the Inquisition in 1531. Capital fled the country and there was a gradual falling off of intellectual achievement.

JOHN IV (d. 1656), king of Portugal. He became duke of Braganza in 1630 and was chosen king during the revolution of 1640 against

Philip IV of Spain. He partially secured his position by an alliance with France, but failed to establish an independent Portugal. He was personally more interested in music and the arts than in the military. Because of the continuing war with Spain, which claimed his nation, he did not gain papal recognition; as a result, sees fell vacant and ecclesiastical discipline was disastrously relaxed.

JOHN V (1689–1750), king of Portugal. Son of Pedro II, he became king in 1706, inherited a country physically split by the War of the Spanish Succession, made peace with France in 1713 and with Spain in 1715, maintained relations with England, and supported Venice by sending a fleet against the Turks and helping to win the naval battle of Matapan (1717). He was interested in administrative reform, but was notoriously licentious, and wasted much of the wealth sent from Brazil on his own pleasures and on expensive and florid buildings in Lisbon and elsewhere.

JOHN VI (1769–1826), king of Portugal. When Joseph (king from 1750) died in 1777, his son Pedro III succeeded him, married Maria I, but died in 1786. When Maria became insane in 1792, their son John replaced her, was formally named regent in 1799, opposed the French Revolution, and aided England against Napoleon. He was defeated by French and Spanish forces in 1801 and his country was split by the treaty of Fontainebleau. When Lisbon was occupied by French troops in 1807, John fled to Brazil with the royal family, became king in 1816 after his mother's death, and was brought back to Portugal by England in 1820. He had to accept a radical constitution, modified it slightly, faced a revolt, and returned to Brazil in 1824.

JOHN, ST. (d. 303?), martyr. An Arabian physician, he sought to inspire the Christian Athanasia and her three daughters to remain firm in spite of what they had suffered but was captured with his companion Cyrus. All six were tortured and beheaded at Canopus, Egypt. He is memorialized by St. Cyril of Alexandria. A shrine was later built at Abukir. F. D. Jan. 31.

JOHN, ST. (d. 303?), martyr. See Crispus, St.

JOHN, ST. (d. 304?), martyr. See Abundius, St.

JOHN, ST. (d. 344?), martyr. Probably a bishop, he died with St. James during the persecution of Sapor II of Persia. F. D. Nov. 1.

JOHN, ST. (d. 362), martyr. A priest, he was slain in Rome during the reign of Julian the Apostate. F. D. June 23.

JOHN, ST. (d. 362?). He and a brother, Paul, are said to have been army officers who were put to death by Julian the Apostate. Though widely honored on June 26, they probably were fictional figures; confusion may have arisen because the basilica raised over their "graves"

probably had been dedicated to the apostles John and Paul.

JOHN, ST. (4th century). He succeeded St. Maurus to the see of Verona, Italy. F. D. June 6.

JOHN, ST. (d. 494). Made bishop of Ravenna, Italy, in 452, he saved its citizens from extreme ravages when it was overrun by Attila the Hun and later by Theodoric the Ostrogoth. F. D. Jan. 12.

JOHN I, ST. (5th century), bishop. He established the shrine of St. Januarius in his see city of Naples. F. D. June 22.

JOHN III, ST. (d. 577), patriarch. Born near Antioch, he gave up his law practice to be ordained, went to Constantinople as patriarchal legate, and became famous for his learning. He was made patriarch there in 565 and enlarged and revised his collection of canons, which became the *Nomokanon*, the compendium of Church law for the East. F. D. Aug. 28.

JOHN, ST. (6th century). Born in Brittany, he became a hermit near Chinon in Touraine, who gave spiritual advice to Queen Radegund of Neustria. F. D. June 27.

JOHN, ST. (6th century). A Syrian, he was a monk at Edessa and an associate of St. Simeon Stylites. F. D. July 21.

JOHN, ST. (6th century). See Antony, St.

JOHN, ST. (d. 609?). He was bishop of Syracuse, Sicily, from 595 to about 609. F. D. Oct. 23.

JOHN, ST. (d. 690?), bishop. Known for his holiness and learning, he was also most active against the Arians in the diocese of Bergamo, Italy, to which he was appointed about 656. F. D. July 11.

JOHN, ST. (8th century). As bishop of Polybotum, Phrygia, he strenuously opposed the Iconoclasm of Emperor Leo, and was widely known as "the Wonder-Worker." F. D. Dec. 5.

JOHN, ST. (d. 800?), bishop. Born in the Crimea, of Armenian ancestry, he became bishop of the Goths in 761, wrote a defense of icons against Emperor Constantine Copronymus, and attended the second Council of Nicaea (787) which defined Catholic doctrine on the veneration of saints and relics. He was driven from his see by a Khazar invasion and died four years later at Amastris, in Asia Minor. F. D. June 26.

JOHN, ST. (d. 813). He became bishop of Pavia, Lombardy, Italy, in 801. F. D. Aug. 27.

JOHN IV, ST. (d. 835), bishop. One of the chief patrons of his see city of Naples, Italy, he was known as "the Peacemaker" during his lifetime. F. D. June 22.

JOHN, ST. (d. 850?), martyr. See Adolphus, St.

JOHN, ST. (d. 900?), martyr. See Andrew, St.

JOHN, ST. (d. 1003?), martyr. See Benedict, St.

JOHN, ST. (d. 1066), bishop and martyr. Born in Scotland, he became a missioner to Germany, bishop of Ratzeburg, and preached in the Baltic area, where he was slain. F. D. Nov. 10.

JOHN, ST. (d. 1094), bishop. A Benedictine monk, probably at Monte Cassino, Italy, he was in 1074 appointed bishop of Monte Marano by the exiled Pope Gregory VII. His cult was approved in 1906. F. D. Aug. 17.

JOHN I, BL. (d. 1146), bishop. A native of Lyons, France, he was a cathedral canon there, made a pilgrimage to Compostela, and joined the Benedictines. In 1117 he founded the abbey of Bonnevaux, then in 1141 was sent to replace the excommunicated Eustace as bishop of Valence, France. His cult was approved in 1901. F. D. Apr. 26.

JOHN, BL. (1123–1160). Born in Almanza, Spain, he studied in France, became a Carthusian at Montrieu, where he was prior after only six years, then went to the Grande Chartreuse. He founded and became prior of the charterhouse at Reposoir in 1151 and wrote a constitution for Carthusian nuns. His cult was approved in 1864. F. D. June 25.

JOHN, BL. (12th century). He was a Cistercian laybrother at the abbey of Sagramenia, Spain, whose life of fasting on bread and water won him the name Juan Pan y Agua. F. D. Dec. 14.

JOHN (13th century). An Italian prelate, he was sent from Rome in 1266 to serve as bishop of Clonfert, Ireland, was consecrated at Athenry, England, and made papal nuncio, and in 1276 collected taxes for the crusade. The sculptures in the Irish Romanesque cathedral in Clonfert may be due to his influence. He was made archbishop of Benevento, Italy, in 1296.

JOHN, ST. (d. 1342), martyr. See Antony, St.

JOHN VIII (d. 1571), archbishop. When Antivari, Albania, fell into the hands of the Turks in 1571, through the treason of its governor, half the population fled to the hills and preserved their faith; the rest accepted Mohammedanism. John VIII, archbishop of the city, was theatrically exhibited by the admiral, Ali-Pasha, and executed after the battle of Lepanto.

JOHN ACHAIUS (d. 1147). He was first bishop of the see of Glasgow after its restoration by St. David in 1115, rebuilt its cathedral, and was suspended by Archbishop Thurstan of York in 1122. He served as suffragan to the patriarch of Jerusalem, was censured by Pope Honorius in 1125, withdrew to Picardy, and in 1129 became chancellor to King David of Scotland.

JOHN ALBERT (d. 1501), king of Poland. Son of Casimir IV and Elizabeth of Austria, he became king in 1492, continued to support the lesser nobility against the greater lords, and by the Statute of Piotrkow (1496) gave the former great concessions at the expense of burghers and peasantry. An invasion of Moldavia (1497–98) resulted in a counter-invasion by the Turks.

JOHN THE ALMSGIVER, ST. (d. 619?), patriarch. Noted for his charity in Cyprus, this widower became patriarch of Jerusalem when he was past fifty. He distributed gold he found in the treasury of his see, the wealthiest in the East, took care of the refugees who fled there after the Persian conquest of Syria and Palestine, argued the governor out of increased taxes, spent days at a time serving as a judge, and lived in a mansion distinguished by lack not only of all luxuries but of most of the necessities. He died on Nov. 11, 619 or 620, while on his way to Constantinople. F. D. Jan. 23.

JOHN THE ALMSGIVER. See Rainuzzi, Bl. Giovanni.

JOHN OF ALVERNIA, BL. (1259–1322). Born in Fermo, Italy, he joined the Friars Minor in 1272 and became a solitary in a cave on Mt. Alvernia, where he received numerous supernatural gifts. He later preached through central and northern Italy and became famous as a convert-maker. He died on Aug. 10 and his cult was approved in 1880. F. D. Aug. 13.

JOHN ANGELOPTES, ST. (d. 433). He became bishop of Ravenna, Italy, in 430 and was metropolitan of Aemilia and Flaminia. F. D. Nov. 27.

JOHN OF ANTIOCH (d. 441), patriarch. A friend of Nestorius, patriarch of Constantinople, he became patriarch of Antioch in 428 and, though at first he opposed Nestorius' views, was convinced by the patriarch of Constantinople that Nestorius' position was valid and defended him against Cyril, patriarch of Alexandria. When the Council of Ephesus convened in 431, John arrived late, refused to participate, and set up his own synod, which condemned Cyril (who had anathemized Nestorius at a synod in Alexandria the previous year), declared Nestorius' deposition unjustified, and refused to recognize Maximian as the new bishop of Constantinople. After affirming his stand at a synod in Antioch, he was reconciled by Emperor Theodosius II and in 433 professed his orthodoxy and signed a condemnation of Nestorius prepared by Cyril. He labored to bring the Nestorians back to the Church and fought Nestorianism for the rest of his life.

JOHN OF ANTIOCH (d. 577). See John Scholasticus.

JOHN OF ATARÉS, ST. (d. 750?). He lived in solitude in a rocky area in the diocese of Vaca, Aragon, Spain, where the Benedictine abbey of St. Juan de la Peña was to be built. He was joined by two brothers from Saragossa, SS. Felix and Votus. F. D. May 29.

JOHN OF AUSTRIA (1547–1578). Illegitimate son of Emperor Charles V and Barbara Blomberg, Don John of Austria was born in Regensburg, Germany, on Feb. 24, he was raised at first by a peasant and then by Luis Quixada, a Spanish nobleman, under the name of Geronimo. He was acknowledged as his son by Charles in his will, and in 1559 was named a member of the Spanish court by Philip II as Don Juan de Austria. In 1568 he commanded a fleet against the Algerian corsairs, subdued the rebellious Moors in Granada in 1569–70, and in 1571 headed the allied armada which ended Turkish ambitions to conquer Europe by annihilating the Turkish fleet at Lepanto. The action is recounted in a poem by G. K. Chesterton. He failed in an attempt to establish a kingdom in Tunis and in 1576 was appointed governor general of the Netherlands. Faced by a revolt led by William of Orange against Spanish rule, he attempted to settle the matter peaceably; when his efforts failed he took to the field and defeated the revolutionists at Gembloux. Handicapped by lack of financial support, he engaged in desultory military activities until he died at Namur, Belgium, on Oct. 1, possibly poisoned.

JOHN OF AUSTRIA (1629–1679), general. Illegitimate son of Philip IV of Spain, he entered military service, joined the viceroy of Naples against Masaniello in 1647, put down a revolt in Catalonia, served as governor of the Netherlands in 1656, fought the regency which took over the direction of Spain on behalf of Charles II in 1665, and drove the dowager queen out of the court in 1677 and established himself as a popular chief minister of state.

JOHN OF AVILA, BL. (d. 1569). Born in Almodovar, New Castile, Spain, he studied at Salamanca, left the university for a life of austerity for three years, then was ordained at Alcalá and with the greatest success preached for nine years through Andalusia. His attacks on vice created enemies and they had him brought before the inquisitorial court on the charge of harshness, but he was cleared and became an even more popular figure thereafter. Among those who sought his advice were Louis of Granada, his later biographer, and SS. Francis Borgia, John of God, Peter of Alcantara and Teresa of Avila. He was beatified in 1894. F. D. May 10.

JOHN DE BALBI. See John of Genoa.

JOHN THE BAPTIST, ST. (1st century). Son of the priest Zachary and Elizabeth, a first cousin of the Virgin Mary, he was born in Juda (probably at Ain-Karim, southwest of Jerusalem), late in his parents' life. Like Christ, he did not begin his public life until he was about thirty (having lived as a desert hermit until that time). He then preached against the materialistic way of life and hypocrisy of the world about him, pleading that men do penance and live up to the duties of their way of life, and baptizing with water. John baptized Christ Himself in the Jordan River, acknowledged His supremacy, and apparently came to know, on that occasion, that Christ was the Messias. When Christ went on to teach in Galilee, John remained preaching in the Jordan valley; it is believed that St. Andrew came to know Christ as a result of hearing John. Herod Antipas, tetrarch of Perea and Galilee, feared John's popularity and power and, when John censured his passion for his niece Herodias, imprisoned him in the fortress of Machaerus. John affected the lives of his many followers even while in prison, and inspired many of them to follow Christ. John was beheaded at the request of Herodias, cleverly voiced as the whim of her daughter Salome, a dancer. He was buried by his disciples and, perhaps at a later date, was entombed at Sebaste, Samaria. This shrine was desecrated during the reign of Julian the Apostate and the saint's charred remains were carried to Alexandria, Egypt. Feasts were instituted for his conception (Sept. 24), execution (Aug. 29), and birth (June 24); the last is the chief liturgical celebration.

JOHN BAPTIST OF THE CONCEPTION, BL. (1561–1613). Born in Almodovar del Campo, Spain, and educated at Baeza and Toledo, he became a Trinitarian and sought to restore the order to its former strictness at the suggestion of King Philip II. The fervor of his labors, begun in 1597, split the order and resulted in the formation of a discalced group. Fr. John was beaten almost to death by his opponents, but he had reformed thirty-four monasteries before he died in Cordova, Spain. He was beatified in 1819. F. D. Feb. 14.

JOHN BECCHETTI, BL. (13th century). Born in Fabriano, Italy, in descent from the family of St. Thomas à Becket, he and his brother Peter became Augustinian Hermits. John may have taught at Oxford. Their cult was confirmed in 1835. F. D. Aug. 11.

JOHN OF BEVERLEY, ST. (d. 721), bishop. Born in Harpham, England, he studied under Adrian in Kent, then under St. Hilda at Whitby. He became bishop of Hexham and succeeded St. Bosa at York. During his notable direction of his see, he frequently retired to solitude so that he might heed his Benedictine rule. He spent his last four years at the abbey of Beverley, which he had built. Bede (whom he ordained) and Juliana wrote highly of him; Alcuin praised him in verse; Henry V claimed to have won Agincourt through his intercession. His shrine was very popular until it was destroyed in the sixteenth century. F. D. May 7 (sometimes, Oct. 25).

JOHN OF BRIDLINGTON. See Thwing, John.

JOHN OF BICLARO (7th century), bishop. Born in Portugal about the middle of the sixth century, he studied at Constantinople and on his return to his native land was exiled to Barcelona by King Leovigild when he refused to embrace Arianism. Sometime after 586 he became the founder of Biclaro, a Benedictine monastery, of which he was abbot until he was appointed bishop of Gerona. He participated in the synods of Sargossa, Barcelona, and Egara in 614 and wrote the continuation of the chronicle of Victor of Tunnuna, covering the years 567–90. He died sometime after 621.

JOHN OF BRIENNE (1148?–1237), king. He was king of Jerusalem from 1210 to 1225, fought in the fifth crusade, captured Damietta in 1219, sought additional military aid from Europe, and married his daughter Yolanda to Emperor Frederick II. The latter then demanded the crown from John, who joined the papal army fighting Frederick in Italy. John was elected emperor of Constantinople in 1229 and defended the city against attack by John II and a Bulgarian army in 1236.

JOHN DE BRITTO, ST. (1647–1693), martyr. Born in Lisbon, Portugal, he became a Jesuit at fifteen and after ordination sailed for Goa, India, in 1673. As superior of the mission at Madura he adopted the life of the Indians themselves and had unusual success, although he faced superstition at every turn and was frequently waylaid and tortured for days at a time. Recalled to Lisbon, he begged to be allowed to return to missionary work and did so in 1670. In spite of fever and political opposition, he continued his heroic labors until he was captured and decapitated at Oriur, near Ramuad, India. He was canonized in 1947. F. D. Feb. 5.

JOHN BUONI, BL. (1168?–1249), founder. A native of Mantua, Italy, he was a licentious court jester, but in 1208, after a serious illness, became a hermit near Cesena. When disciples gathered, he drew up rules as the occasion required until given formal approval by Pope Innocent IV. After his death the eleven units of his Boniti were united to those of other congregations by Pope Alexander IV to form the order of Hermit Friars of St. Augustine. His cult was approved in 1483. F. D. Oct. 23.

JOHN OF BUXHEIM. See Krämer, John.

JOHN CALYBITES, ST. (d. 450?). Born in Constantinople, he left wealth and family at an early age to live in seclusion along the Bosphorus. After six years he set up a hut next to his former home, but did not reveal his identity to his family until he was dying. The same stories, however, are told about SS. Alexis, Onesimus, and many others. F. D. Jan. 15.

JOHN CANTIUS, ST. (1390?–1473). Born in Kanti, Poland, he studied at the University of Cracow, where he was ordained and taught until forced out by jealous associates. He then became a successful preacher, noted for austerities and kindness to the poor, served as a parish priest at Olkusz, and finally returned to Cracow as professor of scripture. He died on Dec. 24 and was canonized in 1767. F. D. Oct. 20.

JOHN OF CAPISTRANO, ST. (1386–1456). Born in the kingdom of Naples, he studied law at Perugia, became its governor in 1412, was imprisoned during a civil war, then at thirty, apparently as a widower, entered the Franciscans, studied under St. Bernardino of Siena, and was ordained in 1420. He became famous as a preacher and convert-maker, drew up plans approved at the general chapter of 1430 for the union of divergent groups within the order, served as papal legate throughout Europe and the Near East, and was inquisitor in proceedings against the Fraticelli, the Gesuats established by Bl. John Colombini, and the Hussites in Austria. After the Turks captured Constantinople in 1453 they planned the conquest of Europe. John raised an army which he led personally. Janos Hunyady's military genius defeated the Turks at Belgrade, ending their threat. John and Hunyady died in the plague which followed; the saint, at Villach, Austria, on Oct. 23. He was canonized in 1724. F. D. Mar. 28.

JOHN CASSIAN (360?–435?), apologist. Of uncertain origin, possibly from Scytha, or perhaps Provence, he became a monk at Bethlehem with his friend Germanus, with whom he went to Egypt to stay as a hermit under Archebius, and retired to the desert of Skete. About 400, they went to Constantinople, where Cassian became a follower of St. John Chrysostom, who ordained him deacon. When the latter was deposed, Cassian was one of those sent in 405 to defend him before Pope St. Innocent I. He probably was ordained during this visit. His whereabouts for the next ten years are unknown but from 415 until his death he lived in or near Marseilles in Gaul. He built the abbey of St. Victor and a convent at Marseilles. From these monasteries the plan of Egyptian asceticism spread through southern Gaul and had the widest effects. Cassian's personal influence was exerted by his early writings: *Institutes of the Monastic Life*, written between 420 and 429, and based on his and Germanus' experiences in Egypt describes the manner of monastic living and the virtues a monk must seek to attain, as well as the power of the seven deadly sins; and *Conferences on the Egyptian Monks*, which dealt with the inner spiritual life and was highly recommended by St. Benedict, whose rule it influenced. A third work, written at the request of the archdeacon of Rome who became Pope Leo the Great, was a defense of the Incarnation against Nestorius, but the writing was hasty and sometimes unclear. A decree attributed to Pope Gelasius condemned certain passages. His language on will and natural goodness contributed to the rise of semi-Pelagianism, was attacked by SS. Augustine and Prosper of Aquitaine and finally condemned by the Council of Orange in 529. He is venerated as a saint in the Marseilles diocese on July 23 and also in the Greek Church.

JOHN OF CHÂLON, ST. (d. 475?). The third bishop of Châlon-sur-Saone, Gaul, was consecrated by St. Patiens. F. D. May 9.

JOHN CHRYSOSTOM, ST. (d. 407), bishop and Doctor of the Church. Born between 344 and 347 at Antioch, Syria, of Secundus, an imperial military commander, and Anthusa, he was brought up by his mother, who became a widow at twenty. He studied rhetoric at Antioch under the orator Libanius, religion under Diodorus, mastered law, and was baptized about 369 by Bishop Meletius. Diodorus had introduced him to the literal or historical interpretation of scripture, a method John followed when writing his sermons and commentaries. About 374 he joined St. Basil and Theodore of Mopsuestia in an ascetic colony, but returned home after two years of solitary life in a cave had undermined his health. He became a deacon in 381 and a priest in 386, serving as assistant to Bishop Flavian for twelve years. He presumably wrote *The Priesthood* soon after his ordination. He preached regularly in Antioch, a city of 100,000, sometimes more than once a day, with great spiritual and social effect, gaining the epithet Chrysostom ("Golden-mouthed"). About 390 he delivered a series of eighty-eight homilies on the gospel of St. John; later he gave ninety on the gospel of St. Matthew and thirty-two on the epistle to the Romans. On the death of Patriarch Nectarius, John was brought to Constantinople as archbishop in 398 by Emperor Arcadius. John stripped ecclesiastical property of luxurious appointments, made extraordinary donations to the poor, sent many missioners to the East, and introduced wide reforms. By his firm stand against idolatry, superstition, lascivious entertainment, and aristocratic waste he made many friends and many enemies. Empress Eudoxia turned against him when he censured her vanity, dress, and lack of charity; Gainas, leader of the Arian Goths, was angered when John put a curb to his exactions; numerous churchmen whose power he curtailed or whose way of living he changed joined against him. Hostile forces were brought together in 403 under Archbishop Theophilus of Alexandria, who had expected to gain the Constantinople post; thirty-six bishops met and signed articles of impeachment and ordered John deposed. City opinion was so sharply divided that there was danger of civil war; when an earthquake shook the capital, the superstitious empress revoked the order of exile. Within a few months, however, Eudoxia was his enemy again, when the public games celebrating the erection of a silver statue of the empress got out of hand; John condemned the abuses, for which he blamed "Jezebel," whereupon the emperor ordered his soldiers to attack those attending services on Holy Saturday. Arcadius sent the archbishop into exile at Cucusus, Armenia, in 404; from there he wrote at least the 238 letters which are still extant. Emperor Honorius and Pope Innocent I sought to call a synod to clarify the issue and restore John to office, but Arcadius either barred or imprisoned all legates. Three years later John was ordered transferred to the Caucasus, but the pace of his guards so exhausted him that he died on Sept. 14 at Comana, Pontus, before reaching his new prison. He was declared a Doctor of the universal Church at the Council of Chalcedon (451) and patron of preachers by Pope Pius X (1909). A full biography, by Bishop Palladius of Hellenpolis, was completed in 403. F. D. Jan. 27 (in the East, Nov. 13).

CHRYSOSTOMUS BAUR, *John Chrysostom and His Time* (2 vols., Westminster, Md., Newman, 1960–61) DONALD ATTWATER, *St. John Chrysostom* (Milwaukee, Bruce, 1939).

JOHN CIRITA, BL. (d. 1164?). A hermit in Galicia, he became a Benedictine at Toronca, Portugal, transferred the abbey to the Cistercians, and is the probable author of the Rule of the Knights of Avis. F. D. Dec. 23.

JOHN CLIMACUS, ST. (570?–649). Probably a Palestinian, he became a monk on Mt. Sinai at sixteen, and at thirty-five entered the Arabian desert as a hermit. He was a careful student of scripture and the Church Fathers, wrote *The Climax, or Ladder of Perfection* as a guide for ascetics, possessed unusual healing and counseling powers, and at seventy was chosen abbot of Mt. Sinai. F. D. Mar. 30.

JOHN COMYN (d. 1212), archbishop. He was named archbishop of Dublin in 1181 by King Henry II of England. He went to Rome, where he was ordained and consecrated bishop by Pope Lucius III, and took up residence in his see city in 1184. He held a synod in 1186, began building St. Patrick's cathedral in 1190, and endowed a chapter of thirteen canons.

JOHN OF CONSTANTINOPLE, ST. (d. 813). He was a firm opponent of the Iconoclast heresy during the reigns of Leo the Isaurian and Leo the Armenian. F. D. Apr. 27.

JOHN OF CORNWALL (12th century). Probably a native of St. German's, Cornwall, England, he was a student of Peter Lombard at Paris, then taught. At first a follower of Peter's erroneous teaching on Christ's humanity, he later denounced it, and wrote a treatise sometime about 1176 attacking the doctrine of Abelard, *Eulogium ad Alexandrum Papam III, quod Christus sit aliquis homo.*

JOHN OF THE CROSS, ST. (1542–1591), Doctor of the Church. Born in Fontiveros, Old Castile, Spain, on June 24, Juan de Yepes was the youngest son of a silk weaver of Toledo. He attended school in Medina del Campo, was apprenticed to a weaver, and, when this proved unsuccessful, entered the service of the governor of the hospital in Medina. He remained there for seven years, while he also studied at Salamanca. In 1563 he became a Carmelite and was ordained in 1567. He was about to transfer to the Carthusians when he met St. Teresa, who persuaded him to remain in the Carmelites and to help her reform movement and in the founding of convents and monasteries. In Nov. 1568, with two other Carmelites—Antonio de Heredia, prior of the Calced Carmelites at Medina, and José de Cristo—he founded the first house of the reform at Duruelo and took the name John of the Cross; this was the origin of the Discalced Carmelites. In 1571 he became rector of the college of the reform at Alcalá. In 1572, St. Teresa called him to Avila as spiritual director of the Convent of the Incarnation and he spent the next five years there. In 1577 the provincial of Seville ordered him to return to Medina and, when he refused (since his orders were from the apostolic delegate), had him imprisoned in Toledo and subjected to great pressure to abandon the reform. During his imprisonment he experienced visions and wrote *Dark Night of the Soul* and some of his *Spiritual Canticle.* He escaped after nine months, became head of the college at Baeza in 1579, and in 1581 prior at Granada. In 1579 the Discalced Carmelites were recognized and a separate province established. He remained at Granada until 1584 and probably finished *Ascent of Mt. Carmel* and *Living Flame of Love* there, was appointed provincial of Andalusia in 1585, and became prior at Segovia in 1588. During these years he established several new houses. In 1591 the Madrid chapter general deprived him of all offices after he had supported the moderate faction in a bitter nine-year dispute, and sent him as a simple monk to La Banuela. Enemies within the order sought to have him expelled, his health gave way, and he died in Ubeda, Spain, on Dec. 14. The mystical writings of St. John of the Cross are now recognized as among the greatest of all times and as classics of Spanish literature. He was canonized in 1726 and proclaimed a Doctor of the Church in 1926. F. D. Nov. 24.

CRISÓGONO DE JESUS, *The Life of St. John of the Cross* (New York, Harper, 1958); E. ALLI-

SON PEERS, ed., *Complete Works* (Westminster, Md., Newman, 1957).

JOHN OF CUPRAMONTANA, BL. (d. 1303). A Camadolese monk, he lived in seclusion in a cave on Monte Massaccio, Italy. F. D. Apr. 11.

JOHN DAMASCENE, ST. (676?–749?), Doctor of the Church. Born in Damascus, he was educated by Cosmas, a brilliant Greek monk who was a slave. John succeeded his father as the caliph's chief revenue officer, may have become a monk before the outbreak of the Iconoclast heresy, and soon afterward went with Cosmas to the desert settlement of St. Sabas near the Dead Sea. He wrote against Emperor Leo and the heretics, and in the desert was so busy composing hymns and poems that he is said to have been banished for not devoting more time to contemplative prayer. John V, patriarch of Jerusalem, made Cosmas bishop of Majuma and John a priest. He later returned to the monastery and was allowed to continue writing. His best-known work is *The True Faith,* relied on by the Greek Church as was the *Summa* of St. Thomas Aquinas in the West. He was made a Doctor of the Church in 1890. F. D. Mar. 27.

JOHN THE DEACON (9th century). A deacon in Naples, he wrote a history of Naples from 762 to 872, a life of St. Januarius, and a history of the translation of the remains of St. Severinus to Naples in the fifth century, which contains an important description of the Saracen devastation of Taormina in Sicily. He died sometime after 910.

JOHN THE DEACON (10th century). A deacon in Venice and probably a relative of Doge Peter II Urseolus, whom he served on missions to Emperors Otto III and Henry II, he wrote *Chronicon Sagornini* on the history of the republic to 1008, and died after that date.

JOHN THE DEACON (12th century). A deacon in Rome, he was canon of the Lateran, about which he wrote a treatise in 1181, supporting that church against claims of precedence made by the canons of St. Peter's.

JOHN OF DUKLA, BL. (1414–1484). Born in Dukla, Polish Galicia, he became a Franciscan at Lemberg, superior of the friary there, and was successful in reclaiming Ruthenian schismatics. He died on Sept. 29 and his cult was approved by Pope Clement XII in 1739. F. D. Sept. 28.

JOHN THE DWARF, ST. (5th century). A native of Basta in Lower Egypt, he became a hermit in the Skete desert and a disciple of St. Poemen. He left the area when it was attacked by the Berbers and settled on Mt. Quolzum, where he died. F. D. Oct. 17.

JOHN OF EGYPT, ST. (304–394). Born in Lycopolis, Lower Thebaid, Egypt, he gave up his work as a carpenter at twenty-five, trained

a number of years for life as a solitary, then walled himself in a cave. Crowds sought him out or filled the area with retreats of a similar nature, and he became internationally known for his counsel, cures, and prophecies. F. D. Mar. 27.

JOHN THE EVANGELIST, ST. (6?–104?), apostle. The author of the fourth gospel, surnamed "the Divine" because of his theological brilliance, was born in Galilee, son of Zebedee and Salome, and younger brother of St. James the Greater. Like his brother and father, he was a fisherman on Lake Genesareth. He probably was a disciple of St. John the Baptist until, with James, he was called by Christ and became the youngest of the apostles. At the Last Supper it was John who asked who the traitor would be, and was called by Christ, with James, "Son of Thunder." James and John were witnesses to many of the significant events in Christ's public life: the raising of Jairus' daughter, the transfiguration, and the agony in the garden. John was the only apostle at the crucifixion and it was to him that Christ assigned the care of Mary. After the ascension he accompanied St. Peter to Samaria, attended the Council of Jerusalem in 49, and probably was present at the passing of Mary. Tradition says he went to Rome during Domitian's reign, miraculously escaped death (Tertullian says he was immersed in a caldron of boiling oil, but escaped unscathed), and was exiled to the island of Patmos (F. D. May 6). There he wrote the Apocalypse. When Domitian died in 96 he returned to Ephesus. Early writers mention his hostility toward the heretic Cerinthus, his reclamation of the outlaw Clement of Alexandria, and his insistent repetition of the precepts, "My little children, love one another" and "God is love." He is represented in art as an eagle because of the soaring majesty of his gospel. This, and his three epistles, were written at Ephesus about the year 100, half a century after his early apostolate. In the fourth gospel, John presupposes the reader's knowledge of many details in the other accounts, stresses the necessity of faith in Christ, and reveals something of his own distinct personality. Manuscript versions date from the beginning of the second century, and John's version was well known at an early date to Ignatius of Antioch, Justin Martyr, and Tatian of Syria. He died in Ephesus. F. D. Dec. 27.

JOHN OF FALKENBERG (d. 1418?), author. Born in Falkenberg, Pomerania, Prussia, he joined the Dominicans and became a master of sacred theology, which he taught. He supported Pope Gregory XII against the antipopes and publicly opposed Bernard de Datis, general of the Dominicans, who supported antipopes Alexander V and John XXIII. He wrote a book defending the Teutonic Order of Knights against King Ladislas of Poland, which declared it lawful to assassinate the Polish king, and a second book, *Tres tractatuli*, declaring Jehan Petit's advocacy of tyrannicide justifiable, which led to his imprisonment by Archbishop Nicolaus of Gnesen when he declared no bishop had the right to condemn his book. A committee appointed to study the work and a chapter of his order recommended its burning, though he was not condemned as demanded by the Poles. Pope Martin V brought John to Rome, where he remained in confinement, probably until his death.

JOHN THE FASTER (d. 595), patriarch. Born and raised in Constantinople, he became a deacon and so known for his ascetic way of life that he was surnamed "the Faster." He succeeded Eutychius as Patriarch John IV of Constantinople in 582, and is principally remembered for the dispute with Rome over his use of the title, ecumenical patriarch, which Pope Pelagius II protested in 588 and which St. Gregory I bitterly denounced in 593, and which the Church had steadfastly contended can never be used by any bishop.

JOHN OF FÉCAMP (d. 1079), author. Born near Ravenna, Italy, he studied at Dijon under Abbot William of St. Benignus, and became skilled in medicine. He accompanied his teacher to Fécamp abbey, France, where he was prior and succeeded William as abbot in 1028. In 1052 he was appointed abbot of Dijon, but resigned from the second post in 1056. He was imprisoned by the Turks while on a pilgrimage to the Holy Land and returned to Fécamp in 1076, where he died on Feb. 22. He wrote ascetical treatises for Agnes of Poitiers, whose spiritual director he became after the death of her husband, Emperor Henry II, in 1056, best known of which are *De divina contemplatione*, *Liber precum variarum*, and *De institutione viduae*. He is also known as Jeannelin.

JOHN OF GENOA (d. 1298?), grammarian. Born in Genoa, John de Balbi gave his belongings to the poor, became a Dominican when well on in years, and wrote *Summa grammaticalis* (popularly called the *Catholicon*), a grammar extensively used in the next century, and theological works. He died in Genoa, Italy.

JOHN OF GOD, ST. (1495–1550), founder. John Ciudad was born in Montemoro Novo, Portugal, on Mar. 8, he lived a dissolute life as a soldier, was overseer of slaves in Morocco, and a shepherd in Spain. At forty he became penitent, and peddled books and pictures in Granada, from the profits of which he aided the poor. A sermon by Bl. John of Avila disturbed him to the point of madness, but the preacher helped him while he was in an asylum, and he found his health and a firm purpose in life at the same time. From 1539 on he built hostels for the relief of the poor, sick, and neglected. The archbishop of Granada and others contributed large sums and the bishop of Tuy suggested a habit and organization for the Brothers Hospitallers, although their rule was not drawn up until after John's death. He died in Granada, Spain, and was canonized in 1690, and made patron of hospitals and the sick in 1886 and of nurses in 1930. F. D. Mar. 8. NORBERT MCMAHON, *St. John of God* (New York, McMullen, 1952).

JOHN THE GOOD, ST. (d. 660), bishop. John Camillus defended the faith against the Monothelite heretics, attended the Lateran Council, and arranged the reorganization of the see of Liguria in its restoration to Milan after eighty years of separation because of the Lombard invasions. F. D. Jan. 10.

JOHN OF GORZE, ST. (d. 974). Born in Vandières, Lorraine, he was educated at Metz and St. Mihiel, and entered the Benedictine monastery of Gorze in 933, where he became prior and, in 960, abbot. He represented Emperor Otto I as ambassador to the Moslems at Cordova; for his order, he introduced many austere reforms, in which he himself led. F. D. Feb. 27.

JOHN OF THE GRATING, ST. (d. 1170), bishop. A Breton of poor parents, he became a Cistercian under St. Bernard and established four abbeys. Against his wishes he was chosen bishop of Aleth, and then transferred his see to St. Malo, Brittany. He was able, before his death, to return to the austerities of monastic life, which he preferred. F. D. Feb. 1.

JOHN GUALBERT, ST. (d. 1073), founder. A member of the powerful Visdomini family in Florence, Italy, he sought to avenge the murder of his brother Hugh, but, meeting the killer, he forgave him. John then became a Benedictine at San Miniato del Monte. Fearing he would be made abbot, he left and took up solitary life at Vallombrosa, near Fiesole. Here, at a new monastery set up for his followers, he stressed charity, poverty, admitted laybrothers, and was visited by great crowds which sought his advice, and saw the spread of the Vallombrosans through Italy. He had many supernatural gifts, died at Passignano, Italy, when he was past eighty, and was canonized by Pope Celestine III in 1193. F. D. July 12.

JOHN OF HALIFAX. *See* Johannes de Sacrobosco.

JOHN DE HAUTEVILLE (12th century), poet. He wrote *Archithrenius* (*The Prince of Lamentations*), a satirical Latin poem which was widely popular. It imitates the usual handling of the vices, attacks those clerics living on the Mount of Presumption, describes the poverty of students in Paris, borrows from Geoffrey of Monmouth for English history, and ends with high praise of nature. It was written, probably in France, about 1184.

JOHN OF HOLYWOOD. *See* Johannes de Sacrobosco.

JOHN HYMONIDES (9th century). A monk at Monte Cassino, surnamed Hymonides, he became a deacon in Rome, where he became a close friend of Anastasius, the Church librarian. He wrote a life of Gregory the Great and began a revision of a life of Clement I, *Gesta Clementis*, but died sometime before 882 before finishing.

JOHN THE IBERIAN, ST. (d. 1002). Born of a noble Georgian family, he occupied an important military post until middle age, when, with his wife's consent, he became a monk on Mt. Olympus in Bithynia. After getting his son St. Euthymius back from the emperor who had been holding him and other Georgian youths as hostages, he was obliged, because of the great crowds attracted by his sanctity, to seek greater seclusion in the monastery of St. Athansius on Mt. Athos in Macedonia. When his brother-in-law, John Thornikios, a general who had become a monk, joined him, they decided in 980 to establish a monastery, Ibiron, for Iberians (Georgians). When Thornikios died, John decided to go to Spain to seek greater solitude, but Constantine VIII persuaded him to return to Mt. Athos, where he became consultant and his son, abbot. F. D. July 12.

JOHN JOSEPH OF THE CROSS, ST. *See* Calosirto, St. Carlo.

JOHN OF KHERNA (14th century). He was abbot of a group of orthodox monks near Alenja, Armenia, and a student of theology under the scholar Isaias. When the Dominican Bartholomew of Armenia arrived, John sought him out for discussion, suggested conversation on the possibility of uniting the Eastern and Roman Churches, and after a year and a half became a convert with a number of his followers. He founded the Uniats of St. Gregory the Illuminator, later incorporated into the Dominican order.

JOHN OF LODI, ST. (d. 1106), bishop. Born in Lodi Vecchio, Italy, he lived as a hermit, became a Benedictine at Fontavellana under St. Peter Damian, whose biography he wrote, was prior there in 1072, and in 1105 was named bishop of Gubbio, Italy. F. D. Sept. 7.

JOHN OF LUXEMBOURG (1296-1346), king of Bohemia. Son of Emperor Henry VII, he became king in 1310, served in the crusades, and, though blind, went to the aid of Philip VI of France against the English invasion, and was killed in the battle of Crécy.

JOHN OF MATERA. *See* John of Pulsano, St.

JOHN OF MATHA, ST. (1160-1213), founder. Born in Faucon, France, he studied theology and was ordained at Paris. He then sought out St. Felix of Valois, a hermit, and outlined to him his plan to devote his life to the rescue of Christians who had been captured by the Moslems. St. Felix, who had been directing his spiritual life, became enthusiastic about the project and the two men set out in 1197 for Rome, where they gained the approval of Pope Innocent III. The Order of the Most Holy Trinity was approved the next year, with John as superior. The order flourished in France, Spain, and Italy, but not in England as once was thought, and sent many of its members, including St. John, into North Africa on successful redemption missions. He died on Dec. 17. He was canonized in 1666. F. D. Feb. 8.

JOHN OF MATHA, ST. (1578–1618). Born in Prados, Spain, he became a Franciscan, was ordained in 1606, and went to Japan. He mastered the language, had considerable missionary success, was captured at Maeco in 1615, imprisoned for three years, and beheaded there. He was beatified in 1867. F. D. Aug. 16.

JOHN OF MEDA, ST. (d. 1159?). Born in Comolar Meda, Italy, he became a hermit at Rodenario, and then a secular priest. In 1134 he joined the Humiliati in Milan and on his advice they adopted the rule of St. Benedict and lived in community, though they still called themselves canons. He was canonized by Pope Alexander III. F. D. Sept. 26.

JOHN OF MONTECORVINO (1246–1328), missionary. Born in Montecorvino, Italy, he joined the Franciscans and in 1289 was sent to Persia with Nicholas of Pistoia. He went from there to India (1291) and China (1294), where he became a friend of the ruler, Timurleng, built churches and a school, translated the New Testament and the Psalms into Chinese, and converted thousands. In 1308 he was consecrated archbishop of Peking, where he spent the rest of his life.

JOHN OF MONTESONO (14th century), theologian. Born in Monzón, Spain, he joined the Dominicans and in 1383 was a lecturer at the cathedral in Valencia. He then taught in St. James in Paris, became master of theology there in 1387, became embroiled with the faculty of Paris when he declared that belief in the Immaculate Conception was heretical, and was condemned by Bishop Orgement of Paris. When Pope Clement VIII, to whom he appealed, referred the case to Avignon, he fled to Sicily, supported Urban VI against Clement, and later returned to Spain.

JOHN OF MONTFORT, BL. (d. 1177). A Knight Templar, this crusader was wounded in Jerusalem and died when taken to Nicosia, Cyprus, where he long was honored on May 24.

JOHN MOROSINI, BL. (d. 1012). Born in Venice, Italy, he became a Benedictine at Cuxá, Spain, returned to his native city, and about 982 founded the monastery of San Giorgio Maggiore, of which he was the first abbot. F. D. Feb. 5.

JOHN NEPOMUCEN, ST. (1340?–1393), martyr. The patron of Bohemia was born in Nepomuk, Bohemia, as John Welflin or Wöfflein, studied at the University of Prague, and became vicar general to Archbishop John of Genzenstein there. The dissolute Wenceslaus IV, after fifteen years of interference with Church affairs, sought in 1393 to take over the Benedictine abbey at Kladrau and make it into an episcopal center for a bishop of his choice; St. John opposed the confiscation, was tortured, bound and thrown into the Moldau River at Prague, Bohemia, on Mar. 20. Many accounts of his death, attributed to a variety of reasons, exist. F. D. May 16.

JOHN OF NICOMEDIA, ST. (d. 303), martyr. A leading Christian in Nicomedia, he was tortured and burned to death on Feb. 24 for tearing down the anti-Christian edict of Diocletian. F. D. Sept. 7.

JOHN OF NIKIU (7th century), historian. An Egyptian, he became administrator of the monasteries in Egypt and Coptic bishop of Nikiû until the severe disciplinary measures he applied to a recalcitrant monk caused the latter's death, whereupon Patriarch Simeon deprived him of his offices and made him a simple monk. He wrote a *Chronicle* from Adam to the conquest of Egypt by the Arabs, which, although in part based upon other chronicles, contained new material on certain periods of Egyptian history.

JOHN OF ORTECA, ST. (d. 1150?). A priest at Burgos, Spain, he went on pilgrimages to the Holy Land, Rome, and Compostela, became a hermit, then joined St. Dominic de la Calzada in his work of building roads and refuges. He is honored locally on June 2.

JOHN OF PARIS (d. 1306), theologian. Born in Paris, he studied at its university, became a Dominican, taught at St. James, and became a master of theology. Known also as Johannes de Soardis, he wrote several treatises which caused him difficulty, particularly *De potestate regia et papali*, directed against Pope Boniface VIII in favor of Philip the Fair, and *De modo existendi corporis Christi in sacramento altaris*, in which he raised tentative questions about transubstantiation. William of Banfet, bishop of Paris, forbade him to defend his interpretation and deprived him of his offices; John appealed to the pope, but died in Bordeaux, France, on Sept. 22 before his case was heard.

JOHN OF PARMA (d. 982?). Born in Parma, Italy, he became a canon of the cathedral there, went on a pilgrimage to Jerusalem, where he joined the Benedictines, then returned to serve as abbot of St. John's from 973 until his death. He is a patron of Parma. F. D. May 22.

JOHN OF PARMA, BL. (1209–1289). Born in Parma, Italy, he joined the Franciscans at twenty-five, studied and was ordained at Paris, lectured there and in Rome and Bologna, and in 1247 became the seventh minister general of his order. He visited all Franciscan establishments and did much to counteract the laxness permitted by Bro. Elias. He served as papal legate to the Eastern emperor, went to Paris to defend the mendicant orders from the attacks of William of St. Amour, resigned his post, and saw St. Bonaventure installed as his successor in 1257. He spent his last thirty years in seclusion at Greccio, Italy. His cult was approved in 1777. F. D. Mar. 20.

JOHN PARVUS. *See* Jehan Petit.

JOHN OF PENNA, BL. (d. 1271). Born in the diocese of Fermo, Italy, he became a Franciscan priest at the monastery of Recanati, and founded several houses during his twenty-five years in Provence. His work with St. Francis of Assisi is recorded in the *Fioretti*. F. D. Apr. 3.

JOHN OF PERUGIA, BL. (d. 1231), martyr. A Franciscan priest in Perugia, Italy, he was sent in 1216 by St. Francis of Assisi with Peter, a Franciscan laybrother from Sassoferrato, to preach to the Moors in Spain. They went to Teruel, Aragon, and then to Valencia, were arrested because of their zealous spiritual activities, and beheaded on Aug. 29. They were beatified in 1783. F. D. Sept. 1.

JOHN OF PINNA, ST. (6th century). A Syrian, he was sent into exile during the Monophysite heresy and established a refuge near Spoleto, Italy, where he served as superior for forty-four years. F. D. Mar. 19.

JOHN OF PRADO, ST. (d. 1631), martyr. Born in Morgobejo, in León, Spain, he graduated from Salamanca, and became a Franciscan of the Strict Observance in 1584. He was master of novices and superior at several houses, preached widely, and was provincial of San Diego in 1610–13. He went to Morocco to serve the Christian slaves there, was arrested, and within the year was burned and stoned to death at Marakesh. He was canonized in 1728. F. D. May 24.

JOHN OF PULSANO, ST. (d. 1139). Born in Matera, near Naples, he became a recluse, rebuilt the church of St. Peter at Ginosa—so well that he was accused of using a hidden treasure and jailed for his devotion. He escaped, joined the group under St. William of Vercelli at Monte Laceno, left to go to Bari, preached effectively, was falsely accused of heresy, returned to Ginosa, then established a community, which came to number sixty monks, at Pulsano. Other religious houses became affiliated with his, under the Benedictine rule, but the Congregation of Monte Pulsano no longer exists. He is also known as John of Matera. F. D. June 20.

JOHN OF RAGUSA (1380?–1443?), bishop. Born in Ragusa, Sicily, he joined the Dominicans and received his doctorate at Paris about 1400. In 1426 he was appointed procurator general of the Dominicans, was chosen papal theologian of the Council of Basle (1431) of which he acted as president at its opening session (for Cardinal Giuliano Caesarini), served as council legate to Constantinople to seek reunion of the Eastern Church with Rome, studied at Constantinople where he produced an etymological treatise on the Greek Bible, and later served as Pope Eugene IV's representative in seeking Emperor John Palaeologus' attendance at a council in Italy. He was appointed bishop of Argos, Greece, where he died.

JOHN OF REOMAY, ST. (425–544?). Born in France, he became a monk at Lérins, returning to the mainland to become one of the leaders of monasticism in Gaul. F. D. Jan. 28.

JOHN OF ROQUETAILLADE (d. 1362?). A native of France, he studied at Toulouse and then became a Franciscan in Orléans. He conducted a series of experiments which produced an elixir which he believed was a cure-all for any disease, and wrote several treatises on the subject, among them *De consideratione quintae essentiae* and *De extractione quintae essentiae*. He also issued prophecies and wrote a series of denunciations of ecclesiastical abuses so violent that they caused his imprisonment in 1345 and 1356. While in prison he wrote on visions and on his tribulations. He probably died in Avignon.

JOHN OF RUPELLA (d. 1271?), theologian. Born in La Rochelle, France, he became a Franciscan, studied at Paris under Alexander of Hales, and was the first of his order to receive a bachelor's degree in theology there. By 1238 he was a master, opposed pluralism, and became an outstanding preacher. He opposed Brother Elias' leadership of the Franciscans and was one of the authors of the explanation of St. Francis' Rule adopted at the 1242 chapter in Bologna. He wrote biblical commentary, psychology, sermons, the widely used *Summa de anima*, and the widely translated *Exposition of the Four Masters*.

JOHN OF SAHAGÚN. *See* Gonzalez de Castrillo, St. Juan.

JOHN OF SALERNO, BL. (1190?–1242). Born in Salerno, Italy, he met St. Dominic while studying at Bologna and became a Dominican. With twelve other friars he was sent in 1219 to Etruria; they concentrated on preaching in Florence, where he established the friary of Santa Maria Novella in 1221. At Pope Gregory IX's request, he labored with the heretical Patarines, bringing many of them back to the Church. His cult was approved in 1783. F. D. Aug. 9.

JOHN OF SALISBURY (1115?-1180), bishop. Born near Salisbury, England, he studied at Paris and Chartres, taught at the abbey of Moutier La Celle, and attended the Council of Rheims in 1148, where St. Bernard introduced him to Archbishop Theobald of Canterbury. After service at the court of Pope Eugene III, he went to England as Theobald's secretary, went on ten missions to Rome for him, and on Theobald's death became Thomas à Becket's secretary. He incurred the enmity of King Henry II because of his defense of the rights of the Church and in 1163 was obliged to flee from England, staying until 1169 with Abbot Peter of LaCelle at St. Remigius' abbey in Rheims. When Thomas à Becket was exiled, John labored to effect a reconciliation with the king, followed Thomas back to England in 1170, and was present at his murder in Canterbury cathedral. He was appointed treasurer of Exeter cathedral in 1174 and bishop of Chartres in 1176. Shortly after attending the third Lateran Council he died, and was buried near Chartres. His writings are valuable sources of information about the intellectual, philosophical, and literary activities of his times. Besides letters, they include: *Polycraticus*, on diplomacy, learning, and philosophy; *Enthelicus*, a summary in Latin poetry of the *Polycraticus*; *Metalogicus*, a defense of the study of philosophy and logic; *Historia pontificalis*, a continuation of Sigebert for the years 1148–52; and a life of Thomas à Becket. His death at Chartres, France, was on Oct. 25.

JOHN THE SAXON, BL. (d. 895). A monk from Saxony, he was appointed abbot of Athelingay in England by King Alfred and designated to restore learning and zeal after the Danish wars. He was slain by two French monks. F. D. Feb. 22.

JOHN SCHOLASTICUS (d. 577), patriarch. Born in Sirimis, Syria, he became a lawyer, was ordained, and in 540–60 compiled the first important, systematic collection of ecclesiastical laws, *Concordia canonum*. In 565 he succeeded the deposed Eutychius I as Patriarch John III of Constantinople and enlarged his compilation by further work of his own and by adding sections from the *Novellae* of Justinian. He is also known as John of Antioch.

JOHN SCOTUS ERIUGENA (9th century), theologian. A native of Ireland, he was in France as a member of the court of Charles the Bald in 847, directed the palace school at Paris, and translated the works of Dionysius the Pseudo-Areopagite into Latin. He remained in Paris, later lived at Laon, where there was a colony of Irish scholars, and died in France. He probably was a cleric and may have been a monk. He wrote commentaries on the gospel of St. John, glosses on works by Martianus Capella and Boethius (whose life he also wrote), a study of predestination, the philosophical *De divisione naturae*, and Latin and Greek poems. His *Liber de praedestinatione*, written after his translation of Dionysius, errs in its attempt to maintain that man is not inclined to sin and punishment but only to grace and heaven. He pushed his argument so far that he showed evil to be non-existent, for which he was attacked by Florus of Lyons and Prudentius of Troyes and condemned at the councils of Valencia (855) and Langres (859). A lost work on the Eucharist erred in calling Communion no more than a figure. His study of nature was posthumously condemned as pantheistic at Vercelli (1050), Paris (1225), and elsewhere. His work had considerable influence on the Albigensians and on Meister Eckhart and other mystics. He is known as Erigena as well as Eriugena.

JOHN OF SEGOVIA (d. 1458?), bishop. Born in Segovia, Spain, he was archdeacon at Villaviciosa, canon of Toledo, professor at Salamanca, and in 1432 was sent to the Council of Basle as representative of the university and of John II of Castile. He became a leading adherent of the supremacy of councils over the popes, declared Pope Eugene IV a heretic, and in 1439 helped elect antipope Felix V, who created him a cardinal in 1440. He represented Felix at various courts, but resigned his cardinalate when the schism ended in 1449, and was appointed bishop of Caesarea by Eugene. He then retired to a Spanish monastery, where he died. He wrote a history of the Council of Basle, treatises on the Immaculate Conception and the procession of the Holy Spirit, a biblical concordance, and a refutation of the Koran.

JOHN THE SILENT, ST. (454–558), bishop. Born in Nicopolis, Armenia, he became a recluse at eighteen when his parents died, and was consecrated bishop of Colonia ten years later. In 491 he set aside his office and settled at the monastery directed by St. Sabas in Jerusalem. There he became guest-master and steward, but spent his last forty years in solitary contemplation. F. D. May 13.

JOHN THE SINNER. *See* Grande, Bl. Juan.

JOHN SORDI, BL. (d. 1183), bishop and martyr. Born in Cremona, Italy, he became a Benedictine at sixteen at the abbey of St. Laurence and, in 1155, its abbot. Because he supported Pope Alexander III against the claims of the antipope Victor, he was exiled by Emperor Frederick Barbarossa, lived at Mantua as a recluse, and was asked in 1174 to become bishop there. When his deposed predecessor was restored by the pope at John's request, the latter was put in charge of the see of Vicenza, Italy. He was waylaid and slain at Vicenza by a man who had withheld payment for land rented from the diocese. F. D. Mar. 16.

JOHN OF ST. THOMAS. *See* Poinsot, John.

JOHN TALAIA (5th century), patriarch. A monk who became administrator of the diocese of Alexandria under Patriarch Timothy Salofaciolus, he served as legate to Emperor Zeno and incurred the enmity of Patriarch Acacius of Constantinople. In 481 he was elected to succeed Timothy as patriarch by the Catholics in Alexandria but was refused recognition by Zeno, who was turned against John by Acacius and appointed Peter Mongus, a Monophysite. In 482, Zeno published the *Henoticon* prepared by Acacius and, when John rejected it, after Mongus' acceptance (whereupon Acacius proclaimed him patriarch), John was forced to flee to Rome. The pope accepted his explanation of the dispute and wrote to Acacius denouncing Mongus, whereupon the Acacian schism broke out. John never regained his see but remained in Rome until his death, though possibly he became bishop of Nolana in the Campagna.

JOHN TOLOMEI. *See* Tolomei, Giovanni.

JOHN DE TROKELOWE (14th century), historian. A Benedictine monk in St. Albans, England, he was in the Tynemouth priory in 1294, joined other monks in attempting to secure their independence from St. Albans, was imprisoned in St. Albans for his efforts, and while in prison wrote his *Annales* for 1259–96 and a valuable account of King Edward II's reign from 1307 to 1332, continued by Henry of Blaneford.

JOHN OF TYNEMOUTH (d. 1290?). A Benedictine in England, he wrote a collection of saints' lives, *Nova legenda angliae*, later edited by John Capgrave.

JOHN OF VALLOMBROSA, BL. (d. 1380?). A monk at the monastery of the Holy Trinity in Florence, Italy, he became a depraved practitioner of black magic and was condemned and given a long prison term. In jail he became a penitent, and when his time was up he gained permission to remain a recluse, devoting himself to prayer and writing through a long life, during which he became a friend of St. Catherine of Siena. F. D. Mar. 10.

JOHN OF VERCELLI, BL. (1205?–1283). Born in Mosso Santa Maria, Italy, he studied at Paris and taught law there and at Vercelli, where he joined the Dominicans and about 1245 became prior. In 1264 he was elected master general, which office he held for the rest of his life, and in 1267 he prepared the plan for the second Ecumenical Council of Lyons. He acted as peacemaker in quarrels involving several Italian states, and with Jerome of Ascoli mediated between Philip III of France and Alfonso X of Castile. He actively maintained rigid standards for the Dominicans and spread

the devotion to the Holy Name. He died in Montpellier, France, on Nov. 30 and his cult was approved in 1903. F. D. Dec. 1.

JOHN OF VESPIGNANO, BL. (d. 1331). Born in the diocese of Florence, Italy, he devoted himself to the care of refugees who filled that city during civil war. F. D. Apr. 9.

JOHN OF VICTRING (1270?–1347), historian. A Cistercian, he became abbot of Victring, Austria, in 1307, secretary and chaplain to Duke Henry of Carinthia, unsuccessfully represented the claims of the duke's daughter to her father's estates in 1335, and became secretary to the successful claimants, Albert II and Otto of Austria. In 1341 he retired to Victring, where he wrote a chronicle of Austria for the years 1231–1341, based on a rhymed chronicle by Ottocar of Styria and his own findings, which he revised several times before his death there on Nov. 12.

JOHN VINCENT, ST. (d. 1012), bishop. Born in Ravenna, Italy, he became a Benedictine at Chiusa, lived as a recluse on Monte Caprario, and was made bishop of a neighboring diocese. F. D. Dec. 21.

JOHN OF WARNETON, BL. (d. 1130), bishop. After study under St. Ivo, he entered the monastery of Mont St. Eloi, from where he was appointed bishop of Thérouanne. He worked so seriously toward monastic reforms that an attempt was made on his life. He refused to prosecute the charges, and proved successful in maintaining bettered acceptance of discipline, and in founding several monasteries. F. D. Jan. 27.

JOHN OF WINTERTHUR (1300?–1348?), historian. Born in Winterthur, Switzerland, where he was educated, he became a Franciscan, and was stationed at Basle in 1328, at Villingen in 1336, and after 1343 at Landau. He wrote *Chronicon a Friderico II imperatore ad annum 1348*, on the problems of Upper Swabia in the early fourteenth century, the contemporary history of his order, and the relations of Louis of Bavaria with the papacy. He probably died in Zurich, Switzerland.

JOHN ZEDAZNELI, ST. (d. 580?). Leader of a group of thirteen Syrian monks who came to Iberia (Georgia) in the Caucasus in the middle of the sixth century (and who are called Fathers of the Iberian Church), he introduced monasticism to that country. His disciples, SS. Scio Mghvimeli and David Gareweli, founded communities of thousands of monks; St. Antony the Recluse became famous as a stylite; and St. Abibus of Nekressi was stoned to death by the Persians for his opposition to Mazdaism. F. D. Nov. 4.

JOHNSON, BL. LAURENCE (d. 1582), martyr. Born in Great Crosby, Lancashire, England, he graduated from Oxford, became a convert, was ordained at Douai in 1577, and sent to serve the Catholics in his native shire. He was seized in 1581, and was hanged, drawn, and quartered at Tyburn. He is also known as Laurence Richardson. He was beatified in 1886. F. D. May 30.

JOHNSON, LIONEL (1867–1902), author. Born in Broadstairs, Kent, England, on Mar. 15, he studied at Winchester and Oxford, became a convert in 1891, was active in the Irish Literary Society of London, and with Yeats and others an enthusiastic supporter of the Irish literary renaissance. He earned his living, precariously, by free-lance reviewing and writing, published a study of the anti-Catholic Gordon Riots of the eighteenth century, the still-valuable *Art of Thomas Hardy* (1894), *Post Liminium* (1911), *Reviews and Other Papers* (1912), and two volumes of poetry. His Celtic poems are colorful, his religious work serious; most of his output reveals his preference for the language, craftsmanship, and intellectual austerity of the classic spirit. He died in London on Oct. 4.

JOHNSON, BL. ROBERT (d. 1582), martyr. Born in Shropshire, England, he was ordained at Douai in 1576, sent back to the English mission, captured in 1580, tortured, and hanged, drawn, and quartered at Tyburn. He was beatified in 1886. F. D. May 28.

JOHNSON, BL. THOMAS (d. 1537), martyr. A Carthusian in the London charterhouse, he was jailed with others in Newgate when they refused to take the Oath of Supremacy affirming Henry VIII as head of the Church. He was starved to death in that prison, and was beatified in 1886. F. D. Sept. 20.

JOHNSTON, RICHARD MALCOLM (1822–1898), educator. Born in Powellton, Georgia, on Mar. 8, he studied at Mercer College and as a legal apprentice, and practiced law in 1843–57. He then taught literature at Georgia until the Civil War closed the university, began a school for boys near Sparta, and after the war founded the Penn Lucy School near Baltimore. In 1875 he became a convert and retired from teaching to write at the suggestion of Sidney Lanier. *Dukesborough Tales*, *The Primes*, *Widow Guthrie*, and half a dozen other popular narratives, which were quiet sketches of Georgia life. He died in Baltimore on Sept. 23.

JOINVILLE, JEAN DE (1225–1317), historian. Born in Champagne and raised in the literary court of his grandfather, Count Thibaut of Burgundy after his father's death in 1233, he went on the first crusade with King Louis IX in 1248. He distinguished himself at the capture of Damietta in Egypt, was captured with Louis at Mansourah in 1250, returned to France in 1254, and became a prominent figure at court. In 1283 he was named by Philip III governor of Champagne, where in 1314 he joined the league of the nobility. When about eighty, at the request of Jeanne de Navarre, wife of Philip the Fair and mother of Louis X, he wrote *Le livre des saintes paroles et des bonnes actions de St. Louis*, a brilliant biography of the king and history of the crusade and the times. He probably was the author of *Chanson d'Acre* (1250). He died in Joinville, France, on Dec. 24.

JOLENTA OF HUNGARY, BL. (d. 1299). Daughter of King Bela IV of Hungary and niece of St. Elizabeth, she went to Poland at five to live with her sister Cunegund, the queen. She was married in 1256 to Boleslaus V of Poland (and is known also as Helena of Poland), founded several religious houses, and on his death in 1279 retired with her daughter and the widowed Cunegund to a convent of the Poor Clares at Sandeck. She later became superior at Gnesen, Poland, which she had founded. Her cult was approved in 1827. F. D. Mar. 6 (also, June 15).

JOLIET, LOUIS (1645–1700), explorer. Born in Quebec, Canada, on Sept. 21, he took minor orders in the Jesuit college there, went to France in 1667 to study hydrography, and spent the next four years trapping in the Great Lakes area. In 1673, with Fr. Marquette and five *voyageurs*, he was sent by Gov. Frontenac to seek the great river that Indians had reported as flowing into the southern sea. On June 17 they became the first white men to enter the upper reaches of the Mississippi. They paddled south to the Gulf of Mexico and returned to Green Bay, a voyage of 2500 miles, and Joliet went on to Quebec to make his report. He married Claire Bissot and in 1680 was given Anticosti Island in the Gulf of St. Lawrence. The British captured his fortified settlement and made a prisoner of his wife in 1690 while he was on an exploring expedition. He was appointed royal hydrographer in 1693, was granted the seignority of Joliet to the south of Quebec in 1697, and died there in May.

JOLLY, PHILIPP JOHANN GUSTAV VON (1809–1884), physicist. Born in Mannheim, Germany, on Sept. 26, he studied at Heidelberg and Vienna, taught mathematics and physics, and in 1846 became professor of physics at Munich, where he experimented and wrote on osmosis, gravitation, and the composition of the atmosphere, and invented a balance and air thermometer named after him, and other apparatus. He died in Munich, Germany, on Dec. 24.

JONAS, ST. (d. 327), martyr. A monk at Beth-Iasa, Persia, he and St. Barachisius went to Habuhan to comfort the Christians in prison and at their execution by King Sapor II of Persia. They were frightfully tortured for refusing to worship the sun and eventually put to death. F. D. Mar. 29.

JONAS OF BOBBIO (7th century), biographer. Born in Sigusia, Piedmont, Italy, he entered the monastery of Bobbio in 618, accompanied Abbot Bertulf to Rome in 628 and then worked with St. Amandus as a missionary in Belgium and France. He served briefly as abbot of a monastery in 659 and died sometime after that. He is particularly known for his life of St. Columbanus (640–43), and also wrote lives of SS. Vaast and Eustace of Luxeuil, Abbess Burgondofara of Evoriac, and Abbots Attala and Bertulf of Bobbio, all of value for an understanding of the period.

JONAS OF ORLÉANS (d. 843?), bishop. Born in Aquitaine, he was elected bishop of Orléans in 818, attended the councils of Paris in 825 (he was one of those sent to Pope Eugene II with a summary of the meeting) and 829, and the Synod of Thionville in 835. He was the author of *De institutione laicali*, *De institutione regiâ* (written for King Pepin of Aquitaine), *De cultu imaginum*, and a rescension of the *Vita S. Huberti*.

JONATUS, ST. (7th century). He was Benedictine abbot of Marchiennes, France, from about 643 to 652 and then of Elnone until about 659. F. D. Aug. 1.

JONES, ARTHUR EDWARD (1838–1918), ethnologist. Born in Brockville, Canada, on Nov. 17, he studied at St. Mary's, Montreal, became a Jesuit, studied in France and the United States, and taught at Fordham and in Montreal. He was president of Loyola College and archivist at St. Mary's, both in the latter city. His study of Huron settlements was published by the Canadian government; his archaeological exhibit at the 1904 St. Louis Exhibition won first prize; and he was active in the preparation of Thwaites' *Jesuit Relations*. He died in Montreal on June 19.

JONES, BL. EDWARD (d. 1590), martyr. Born in the diocese of St. Asaph, Wales, he was ordained at Douai, and was sent to the English mission in 1588. He was hanged for his priesthood in front of the house in Fleet Street, London, where he was captured. He was beatified in 1929. F. D. May 6.

JONES, INIGO (1573–1652), architect. Born in London on July 15, son of a clothworker, he was apprenticed to a joiner and attracted the attention of the earl of Pembroke by his talent for design. The earl provided the means for a trip to Europe and Jones spent several years in Italy, mainly in Venice, studying the remains of Roman architecture and Palladio's renaissance buildings. He accepted the appointment of King Christian IV of Denmark to the Danish court, but returned to England in 1605 and spent the next nine years designing sets for the elaborate masques produced by King James I. In 1614 he again went to Italy, where he met leading architects. In 1615

he returned to England, was appointed surveyor to the king, and began designing such buildings as the royal banquet house in Whitehall, the first English building embodying Palladian principles, which broke completely with prevailing design and marked the starting point of the classical period in England. He designed the queen's house, Greenwich, part of Somerset House, the garden front of St. John's, Oxford, Lincoln's Inn Square, London, and many country mansions. He died in London on June 21.

JONES, BL. JOHN (d. 1598), martyr. Born at Clynog Fawr, Carnarvon, Wales, he became a Franciscan in Rome (as Fr. Godfrey Maurice) and was sent to the English mission in 1592, sometimes using the name John Buckley. He was arrested in 1597, tortured by order of Richard Topcliffe, and hanged at Southwark for being a priest. He was beatified in 1929. F. D. July 12.

JONES, WILLIAM AMBROSE (1865–1921), bishop. Born in Cambridge, New York, on July 21, he studied at Villanova, became an Augustinian in 1888, and was ordained in Philadelphia in 1890. He did parish work in Philadelphia, was master of novices at the Augustinian scholasticate in 1895–99, was sent to Cuba in 1899 as pastor of the first church there for those speaking English, and was president of St. Augustine College in Havana in 1902–7. He was bishop of Puerto Rico from 1907 until his death on Feb. 17.

JONG, JOHANNES DE (1885–1955), cardinal. Born in Nes, Ameland, Holland, on Sept. 10, he was ordained in 1908, took advanced degrees in Rome, and taught history at the seminary in Utrecht from 1914 to 1932. He was its rector in 1933–35, coadjutor in Utrecht in 1935, and succeeded as archbishop of the see in 1936. He was active against the Nazis, was fined for issuing condemnatory pastorals, forbade his flock to give aid to the enemy, and was quite active in protecting the Jews. He was named a cardinal in 1946 and retired in ill health in 1951. Among other works he published a four-volume *Manual of Church History*. He died in Amersfoort, Holland, on Sept. 8.

JORDAN, EDWARD BENEDICT (1884–1951), educator. Born in Dumore, Pennsylvania, on Dec. 17, he studied at St. Thomas, Scranton, and St. Mary's, Emmitsburg, and was ordained in Rome in 1909. He was secretary and later dean of the Catholic Sisters College in Washington, D.C. (1921–36), and taught education at Trinity College there in that period, became vice-rector of Catholic University (1942), director of ecclesiastical studies there (1950), national director of the International Federation of Catholic College Alumnae (1943), and wrote *Catholicism in Educa-*

tion and other works. He died in Washington, D.C., on July 19.

JORDAN, ELIZABETH (1868–1947), author. Born in Milwaukee, Wisconsin, she entered journalism after high school, was on the editorial staff of the New York *World*, assistant editor of its Sunday edition in 1897–1900, was editor of *Harper's Bazaar* until 1913, an editor at Harper's until 1918, and then a freelance literary adviser. She was dramatic critic for *America* for many years, wrote nearly thirty novels (including *Wings of Youth, Miss Nobody,* and several mystery stories), and the autobiographical *Three Rousing Cheers* (1938).

JORDAN OF PISA, BL. (d. 1311). Probably educated at Paris, he became a Dominican in 1280, served at Florence from 1305 to 1308, taught and preached with astonishing success, founded the Confraternity of the Holy Redeemer at Pisa, and inspired a number of holy successors. He is to be credited with popularizing the Tuscan vernacular in his work, as his contemporaries, Dante and Petrarch, did in literature; together they are thus chiefly responsible for the development of the modern Italian language. He died in Piacenza, Italy. His cult was approved in 1833. F. D. Mar. 6.

JORDAN OF PULSANO, BL. (d. 1152). A Benedictine monk at Pulsano, Italy, he succeeded St. John of Pulsano as abbot general of the Benedictine congregation there in 1139. F. D. Sept. 5.

JORDAN OF SAXONY, BL. (d. 1237). Successor to St. Dominic, whose biography he wrote, as master general of the Dominican order, he was a Saxon named Giordanus and became a Dominican at Paris in 1220. A year later he was provincial in Lombardy and in 1222 became master general. He founded monasteries in Germany and Switzerland, sent missioners into Denmark, and at Oxford became the first university chaplain. His preaching attracted Albertus Magnus and Walter the German to the order. He died in a shipwreck off Syria while on his way to the Holy Land. His cult was confirmed in 1828. F. D. Feb. 15.

JORDAN OF SAXONY (d. 1380?). Also known as Jordanus of Quedlinburg, he was born in Saxony before 1299, became an Augustinian about 1313, studied at Bologna and Paris, and became lector at Erfurt about 1322. There he preached, wrote, and served on the court investigating the heretical Luciferians in 1336. He made a canonical visit to the province of France, to the chapter general in Siena in 1338, and in 1346–51 was provincial of the Saxon-Thuringian province. He prepared *Collectanea Augustiniana* (sermons and rules by Augustine, and legends and lives of SS. Augustine and Monica) and wrote lectures on the Lord's Prayer, sermons on the saints and on

the liturgical year, a treatise on the virtues and vices, meditations on the Passion, and *Vitasfratrum,* a moral, ascetical, and historical account of religious life in general and leading Augustinians in particular. Jordan, who had resided at the Augustinian monastery of Quedlinburg, died in Vienne, France, no earlier than 1370.

JORDANIS (6th century), historian. Of an important Goth or Alanic family in the eastern part of the Roman empire, he served for a time as a notary, and may have become a monk and bishop of Cotrone, Italy. He wrote two historical works, *De origine actibusque Getarum,* a history of the Goths based on Cassiodorus, and *De summa temporum vel origine actibusque gentis Romanorum,* both pleading for a peaceful absorption of the Goths into the empire.

JORDANUS OF GIANO (1195?–1262?). Born in Giano, Italy, he became a Friar Minor in 1220, went as a missioner to Germany with Caesarius of Speyer, was ordained in 1223, and traveled to Italy in 1230 and 1238 as a representative of his order. While at a chapter in Halberstadt in 1262 he wrote a history of the Franciscans in Germany from 1207 to 1238.

JORDANUS DE NEMORE (13th century?), mathematician. He was the author of a group of thirteenth- and fourteenth-century mathematics manuscripts: *Algorismus, Elementa arithmeticae, De numeris datis, De triangulis, Planispherium, De speculis,* and *De ponderibus.* He is often called Jordanus Nemorarius and may have been the Dominican Jordanus Saxo.

JÖRG, JOSEPH EDMUND (1819–1901), historian. Born on Dec. 23 in Immenstadt, Bavaria, he studied at Munich under Johann Döllinger, with whom he collaborated on *Geschichte de Reformation.* In 1852 he became editor of *Historischpolitische Blätter;* he was elected to the Bavarian lower house in 1863–81, became district archivist in Landshut in 1866, and served in the *Reichstag* from 1874 to 1879. He became the leader of the Bavarian *Volksparte,* a confirmed monarchist, opposed Bavaria's alliance with Prussia after the Austro-Prussian War of 1866, advocated neutrality in the Franco-Prussian War, and opposed Bavaria's entrance into the German empire in 1870. He clashed with Bismarck in 1874 and left public life in 1881 when he gave up his seat in the Bavarian lower house. He spent the rest of his life near Landshut, Germany, where he died on Nov. 18. He wrote *Deutschland in der Revolutions-periode,* 1522–1526, collections of essays, memoirs, and on socialism and Protestantism.

JÖRGENSEN, JOHANNES (1866–1956), author. Born in Svendborg, Denmark, on Nov. 6, he studied at Copenhagen, and became a follower of George Brandes and Swedenborg, a Socialist, and a member of a dissipated group of young rebels. He published poetry, wrote for *Bors-Tidende*, a liberal newspaper, in 1889–92, then on *Politiken*, and finally on the *Tower*, his own journal, which failed. He published *The Book of the Journey*, a spiritual autobiography, in 1895, became a convert in 1896, and wrote *Truth and Falsehood, Foes of Hell, Parables*, and a collection of his poems. He wrote for *Tiden* and the *Catholic*, went to Italy in 1899 with his wife and family, and published *Roman Mosaics* and *Pictures of Roman Saints*. On his return he wrote *Our Lady of Denmark*, for which he was bitterly attacked as a renegade by his former associates. After trips to Sweden and Rome, he settled in Charlottenlund, wrote for numerous publications, and issued his lives of St. Francis of Assisi, the Curé d'Ars, St. Bridget of Sweden, and St. Catherine of Siena. He died in Svendborg on May 22.

JORJES, DOMININGO (d. 1619), martyr. Born in Aguilar de Sousa, Portugal, he became a soldier, settled in Japan, and when he hid Bl. Charles Spinola was seized and burned to death at Nagasaki on Nov. 18. F. D. Mar. 14.

JORIO, DOMENICO (1867–1954), cardinal. Born in Villa Santo Stefano, Italy, he was ordained in Palestrina at twenty-four, and spent a lifetime in papal administrative positions. He was apostolic datary at thirty, and became a member of the Congregation of the Sacraments in 1900, its secretary in 1926, and its prefect in 1935. He became a cardinal in that year, was a member of the congregations of the Holy Office, Oriental Churches, and Propagation of the Faith, and also served on the Apostolic Signatura, the highest papal court of appeals, until his retirement in ill health in 1947. He wrote ascetical, canonical, and liturgical studies. He died in Rome on Oct. 21.

JOSAPHAT. Called the son of an Indian king, Abenner, who imprisoned him to forestall a prophecy that the prince would become a Christian, he was converted by an ascetic named Barlaam; Abenner also was won over and the three took up life as hermits. The story is a Buddhist romance, but so popular before the time of St. John Damascene that he used it to illustrate the power of zeal; the imaginary saints were even given a feast day, Nov. 27.

JOSAPHAT, ST. (1580–1623), bishop and martyr. John Kunsevich was born in Vladimir, Poland, was educated there and apprenticed to a merchant at Vilna. He refused an offer of marriage to the latter's daughter and in 1604 became a monk in the Ukrainian Order of St. Basil at Holy Trinity monastery, Vilna, taking the name Josaphat. He was ordained in 1609 and became a leading spokesman for the union of the Ukrainian Church with Rome. He

helped to establish new houses in Poland, was appointed abbot of the monastery at Vilna in 1614, and in 1617 was ordained bishop of Vitebsk with right of succession to Polotsk. He exercised this a few months later when Archbishop Brolnitsky died. By 1620 he had greatly reformed his see, which had fallen into complete religious chaos, and had brought his people to Catholicism. A dissident hierarchy was established in the Brest area and Meletius Smotritsky became archbishop of Polotsk, in 1620. A monk named Silvester won over the inhabitants of Vitebsk, Mogilev, and Orcha to the schismatic leader. In 1622, Chancellor Sapieha of Lithuania unjustly accused Josaphat of fomenting trouble by unreasonable and arbitrary acts; the Polish clergy also were not disposed in his favor because he had insisted on equal treatment for the Byzantine rites and clergy. On Nov. 12, while at Vitebsk, Russia, attempting to win its people back to Catholicism, he was murdered by Smotritsky's adherents. In 1867 he became the first saint of the Eastern Church to be formally canonized. F. D. Nov. 14.

THEODOSIA BORESKY, *Life of St. Josaphat* (New York, Comet, 1955).

JOSEPH I (1678–1711), emperor. Son of Emperor Leopold I and his third wife, Eleanora, he was born in Vienna on July 26, was crowned king of Hungary in 1687, of the Romans in 1690, married Wilhelmina Amalia of Brunswick-Lüneburg in 1699, and succeeded his father as emperor in 1705. He was faced by a reign-long revolt (1703–11) in Hungary led by Franz II Rakoczy, and participated in the War of the Spanish Succession (1701–14) with England and Holland against King Louis XIV of France, Spain, Portugal, Bavaria, and Savoy when he supported the claims of his brother Charles for the Spanish throne. He granted religious freedom to the Protestants of Silesia in 1706 at the demand of Charles XII of Sweden. He died in Vienna on Apr. 17.

JOSEPH II (1741–1790), emperor, Austrian king. Son of Empress Maria Theresa and Francis I, he was born in Vienna on Mar. 13, was influenced by the writings of the Encyclopedists and the career of Frederick the Great, became a member of the council of state in 1761, was crowned king of the Romans in 1764, and on the death of his father in 1765 became emperor and co-regent of the Hapsburg dominions with his mother, who continued as the real ruler. He helped in the first partition of Poland in 1772, commanded Austrian forces in the War of the Bavarian Succession in 1778–79, and became sole ruler on the death of his mother in 1780. He immediately put into effect a series of decrees designed to give him absolute power in the state. He reduced the power of the nobles, emancipated the serfs, effected reforms in taxation and the administration of justice, and inaugurated an ecclesiastical program which considered the Church and her institutions as merely arms of the government. He confiscated Church property and funds into one state-controlled religious fund from which all ecclesiastical expenses were to be paid, closed Church schools and institutions, curtailed the religious orders, secular clergy, and hierarchy, and was so extreme in the extent of domination of the Church by the state that his policy was termed Josephinism. In 1781 he issued the Edict of Tolerance, was visited in 1782 by Pope Pius VI, who was unsuccessful in persuading him to mitigate the severity of his attacks on the Church, and while on a visit to Rome in 1783 threatened to establish a state religion. He failed to open the Scheldt River to his Flemish subjects by repudiating the Berrier Treaty of 1714 when France opposed his project, and entered an alliance with Russia to partition Turkey and Venice. When this failed, he attempted to add Bavaria to his realms in exchange for Belgium, succeeding only in allying Prussia, Saxony, Hanover, and other German states against him in the Fürstenbund in 1785. He joined Russia in an attack on Turkey in 1788–89, which brought him nothing but trouble in Hungary, when the nobles took advantage of his absence with the army in the East to revolt, and an uprising in Belgium in 1789, when he attempted to revoke the Belgian constitution. Uprisings in other parts of the realm caused him to revoke his reforms on Jan. 30, 1790, and three weeks later, on Feb. 20, he died in Vienna.

JOSEPH (d. 1777), king of Portugal. He became king in 1750, but lost all control of the government to his chief minister, Pombal; the latter expelled the Jesuits, broke off relations with the Papal States, gained independence from British direction, made effective administrative reforms, and abolished slavery.

JOSEPH, ST. (1st century), patron of the universal Church. Husband of the Virgin Mary, he was of royal descent, a carpenter by trade, and the foster father of Christ, at whose birth he was present and whom he led into Egypt and back to Nazareth. It seems from the absence of scriptural reference that he had died before the time of Christ's Passion. A great number of apocryphal histories and spurious legends became popular. Veneration began early, particularly in the East, but was not widespread until the fifteenth century. The Franciscans preached on his grace, as did St. Vincent Ferrer; Jean Gerson, chancellor of the University of Paris, asked for an annual feast day (finally established by Pope Sixtus IV in 1481); Joseph was featured in miracle plays and in art; and biographies, sermons, and theological treatises by Giovanni d' Orlania and Francis Suarez appeared. Pope Pius IX proclaimed him Protector of the Universal Church in 1870; Leo XIII offered him as a model for fathers of families; Benedict XV put workers under his protection; Pius XI recommended him as the pattern of social justice; Pius XII established May 1 as a new feast of St. Joseph the Workman. F. D. Mar. 19.

F. L. FILAS, *The Man Nearest to Christ* (Milwaukee, Bruce, 1946); HENRI RONDET, *Saint Joseph* (New York, Kenedy, 1956).

JOSEPH, BL. (d. 764), bishop. A Benedictine, he founded the monastery of St. Zeno at Isen in 752 and became bishop of Friesing, Bavaria, in 764. F. D. Jan. 17.

JOSEPH ABIBOS, ST. (d. 590?). He was abbot at Alaverdi, Georgia, and a Syriac disciple of St. John Zedadzneli. F. D. Sept. 15.

JOSEPH OF ARIMATHEA, ST. (1st century). The counselor in the four gospels who sought truth, he was present at the crucifixion of Christ, claimed His body from Pilate, and supervised His burial. Pious legend had him catch the blood of Christ on the cross, inherit the chalice of the Last Supper, land in England, and found Glastonbury; these are presented as historical facts in a spurious addition to the *Chronicle* written by William of Malmesbury. F. D. Mar. 17.

JOSEPH BARSABAS, ST. (1st century). Surnamed "the Just," he was one of the seventy-two disciples of Christ, and with Matthias, who was chosen, was considered as a possible successor to the traitor Judas as an apostle (Acts 1:23–26). F. D. July 20.

JOSEPH CALASANCTIUS. *See* Calasanctius, St. Joseph.

JOSEPH OF CUPERTINO, ST. (1603–1663). Born on June 17 in Cupertino, Italy, of poor parents, Joseph Desa failed as a shoemaker and was refused or dismissed by religious groups because of low intelligence. When accepted as a Franciscan tertiary at Grottella, he underwent an entire change of character and in 1628 was ordained. His last years were marked by a succession of extraordinary supernatural manifestations. He was examined by the inquisitors of Naples and Rome and by Pope Urban VIII, all of whom declared him honest. In 1639 he was sent to Assisi, where he stayed for thirteen years, and in 1653 to a Capuchin friary at Pietrarossa, then to Fossombrone. Crowds pursued him, converts were many, but normal work could not be done in the friaries. In 1657 his order petitioned for his return and he spent the rest of his life in seclusion at Osimo, Italy, where he died. He is the patron saint of air travelers and fliers, was beatified in 1753 by Pope Benedict XIV (who as "devil's advocate" had sought to discredit him earlier), and canonized in 1767. F. D. Sept. 18.

JOSEPH OF EXETER (d. 1224?), poet. Born in Exeter, England, he went to Gueldres in 1180, wrote *De bello Trojano*, accompanied his friend, Archbishop Baldwin of Canterbury, on a crusade to the Holy Land and returned to England when the archbishop died at the siege of Acre in 1190. He also wrote *Antiocheis*, a poem about the crusade.

JOSEPH, FATHER. *See* Tremblay, François Leclerc du.

JOSEPH THE HYMNOGRAPHER (d. 845?). Brother of St. Theodore Studites, he became bishop of Salonica, was an outspoken critic of Emperor Theophilus on the Iconoclast question, and became a major liturgical poet, widely honored in the Byzantine Church. F. D. June 14.

JOSEPH OF LEONESSA, ST. (1556–1612). Born in Umbria, he became a Capuchin friar at eighteen, and later preached through Italy. While a devoted missioner to the galley slaves at Constantinople, he was imprisoned and tortured because of his zeal and his conversion of Moslems, and eventually sent back to Venice. In his last years he suffered patiently from cancer. He was canonized in 1745. F. D. Feb. 4.

JOSEPH OF PALESTINE, ST. (d. 356?). Assistant to Rabbi Hillel, he was present when the latter was baptized on his deathbed. He was deeply impressed by this act and by several Christian books the rabbi left him. He was head of the synagogue at Tarsus when his people found him reading the New Testament, beat him, and threw him into the river. He then became a Christian, received the rank of *comes* from Constantine, and built churches in Galilee. Moving to Scythopolis, he gave refuge to St. Eusebius of Vercelli, St. Epiphanius, the latter's biographer, and others banished by the Arians. F. D. July 22.

JOSEPHA OF BENIGNAM. *See* Albiniana, Bl. Ines.

JOSEPHA, SISTER M. *See* Hurley, Mary.

JOSSE. *See* Jodocus, St.

JOUBERT, JOSEPH (1754–1824), philosopher. Born in Martignac, France, on May 7, he gave up the study of law at Toulouse to become a Doctrinaire in 1768, but left in 1778 to go to Paris, where he became prominent in literary circles. In 1790–92 he was justice of the peace in Martignac, returned to Paris, but retired to Villaneuve-le-Roi when he witnessed the horrors of the revolution. He became inspector general of the University of France in 1809, encouraged the romantic movement, and established a distinguished literary salon. Chateaubriand collected some of his sayings, ranked with those of La Rochefoucauld, and published them as *Pensées* in 1838. Joubert died in Villaneuve, France, on May 4.

JOUFFROY, CLAUDE FRANÇOIS DOROTHÉE DE (1751–1832), inventor. Born in Abbans, France, on Sept. 30, he studied at Quingey and in 1771, while in the army, studied steam navigation. In 1776 he constructed an experimental steamship which he was able to run, but not satisfactorily. In 1781 he built a 150-ton, 140-foot-long steamship which he ran on the Saône River from July 1783 to Oct. 1784. Unable to secure promised government aid and with his own finances exhausted, he was obliged to discontinue his experiments. In 1816 he launched another steamship on the Seine, secured a patent, but failed to gain the financial backing necessary for further development. Bankrupt and ill, he entered a home for old soldiers at Paris in 1831 and died there the following year on July 18.

JOUFFROY, JEAN DE (1412?–1473), cardinal. Born in Luxeuil, France, he studied at Dôle, Cologne, and Pavia, where he became a Dominican and taught theology and canon law in 1435–38. He served on diplomatic missions for Philip the Good, duke of Burgundy, was appointed abbot of Luxeuil about 1450, and bishop of Arras in 1453. Louis XI of France sent him to Rome to express to Pope Pius II the king's willingness to abolish the pragmatic sanction, which declared councils superior to the pope. Pius appointed Jouffroy cardinal at Louis' request; only after this event did Jouffroy reveal the king's demands for a change of pontifical policy toward Naples and other French demands. Pius condemned his double-dealing and refused Louis' demands; the latter condemned the pope and was supported by Jouffroy, who apparently was rewarded with the see of Albi in 1462 and the abbacy of St. Denis in 1464. He died in Rulli, France, on Nov. 24 while with Louis on an expedition against the duke of Armagnac.

JOUIN, LOUIS (1818–1899), philosopher. Born in Berlin on June 14, he became a convert, joined the Jesuits in 1841, was ordained in 1848 at Reggio, Italy, and went to the United States when revolution broke out. He taught for the rest of his life at Fordham and St. Francis Xavier in New York City and for three years at Guelph, Ontario, and wrote on logic, revelation, and moral theology. He died in New York City on June 10.

JOUVANCY, JOSEPH DE (1643–1719), author. Born in Paris on Sept. 14, he became a Jesuit in 1659, taught at Compiègne, Caen, La Flèche, and Collège de Louis le Grand, Paris. In 1699 he went to Rome to finish Niccolò Orlandini's history of the Jesuits and remained until his death there on May 29. He wrote the section on the years 1591–1616, which was placed on the Index in 1722 because certain passages were at variance with subsequently issued decrees on the Chinese liturgy. He also wrote poems in Latin and Greek, tragedies, did translations, edited many Latin school texts (among them works of Terence, Ovid, Horace, and Cicero), and wrote *Christianis litterarum magistris de ratione discendi et docendi*, which became a standard guide for classical studies in Jesuit schools.

JOUVENET, JEAN (1644–1717), painter. Born in Rouen, France, he was the son of a painter, Laurent Jouvenet (1609–81), under whom he studied. In 1660 he went to Paris, attracted attention with his *Cure of the Paralytic*, worked under Charles Le Brun, who was decorating Versailles, was elected to the Academy of Painting in 1675, and became professor there in 1681. On the death of Le Brun in 1692 he became the leader of the French school, famous for the massiveness and color of his paintings, and was patronized by King Louis XIV. He served as director of the Academy from 1705 to 1708 and was appointed one of its four perpetual rectors in 1707. In 1713 a stroke paralyzed his right arm, whereupon he learned to paint with his left hand and completed *Magnificat* for Notre Dame and the ceiling of the Palais de Justice in Rouen. Among his most famous works are *Miraculous Draught of Fishes, Raising of Lazarus, Descent from the Cross, Driving the Money Changers from the Temple,* and *Descent of the Holy Spirit.* He died in Paris on Apr. 5.

JOVELLANOS, GASPAR MELCHIOR DE (1744–1811), author. Born in Gijón, Asturias, Spain, on Jan. 5, he studied at Oviedo, Avila, and Alcalá, where he took up law. He became a judge in Seville and was interested in agriculture and social work. He wrote a tragedy, *El Pelayo,* and a comedy, *El delincuente honrado,* which were well received, and in 1770 was appointed a member of the Royal Academy of Madrid. In 1778 he was transferred to Madrid as chief justice and remained there until 1790 when the political scene changed. He returned to Asturias, founded the Real Instituto Asturiano, and in 1797–99 served as minister of justice under Manuel de Godoy until the latter fell from power. He returned to Gijón, was arrested in 1801, and imprisoned on Majorca until 1808. He became Asturian representative on the supreme junta, but was forced to flee when the French advanced into Spain. He died in Puerto de Vega, Spain, on Nov. 27.

JOVIANUS, FLAVIUS CLAUDIUS (331–364), emperor. Son of Count Varronianus, he was born in Pannonia, and though a Christian became captain in the imperial bodyguard at thirty-three. He was with Emperor Julian the Apostate on the latter's unsuccessful Persian campaign and, when Julian was killed in battle in 363, Jovianus was elected to succeed him by the soldiers. Since his army was in a precarious position, he signed a thirty-year truce with King Sapor II by which he surrendered Roman conquests east of the Tigris, thus ending Roman influence in the East. He returned to Antioch, annulled the decrees of Julian against Christianity, supported the Nicene Creed against the Arians, and reinstated Athanasius as bishop of Constantinople. He died in Dadastana, Bithynia, on Feb. 17, possibly by assassination.

JOVINIAN, ST. (d. 300), martyr. A missioner who accompanied St. Peregrinus of Auxerre, he is believed to have died as a martyr in Gaul. F. D. May 5.

JOVINUS, ST. (d. 258), martyr. *See* Basileus, St.

JOVITA, ST. (d. 121?), martyr. *See* Faustinus, St.

JOVIUS, PAULUS. *See* Giovio, Paolo.

JOYCE, GEORGE HAYWARD (1864–1943), theologian. Born in England, where his father was vicar of Harrow-on-the-Hill, he studied at Oxford and in Germany, entered the Anglican ministry in 1890, and became a convert in 1893. He became a Jesuit that year and was ordained in Wales in 1903. He taught theology at Heythrop, and wrote *Natural Theology* and *Principles of Logic* (for the Stonyhurst philosophy series), *Christian Marriage, The Question of Miracles,* and *The Catholic Doctrine of Grace.* He died at Heythrop, England, on Nov. 15.

JOYEUSE, ANNE DE (1561?–1587). Son of Maréchal Guillaume de Joyeuse, and brother of Henri, he married Margaret of Lorraine, sister of Henry III's wife, and in 1586 was put in command of the army sent against the Huguenots. At first successful, he was defeated and slain at the battle of Coutras in Oct. by Henry of Navarre.

JOYEUSE, FRANÇOIS DE (1562–1615), cardinal. Brother of Henri de Joyeuse, he became the confidant of Henry III, Henry IV, and Louis XIII. He became a cardinal and in 1614 dean of the cardinals at Avignon, France.

JOYEUSE, HENRI DE (1563–1608). Son of Maréchal Guillaume de Joyeuse and brother of Anne and Cardinal François, he married Catherine de la Valette, fought against the Huguenots, and when his wife died in 1587 became a Capuchin as Fr. Ange. In 1592 he was appointed guardian at Arles, but was released from his vows by the pope in order to assume command of the Languedoc troops against the Huguenots. He worked out a three-year truce with Maréchal de Montmorency and when Henry IV abjured in 1593 and a general peace prevailed, the duc de Joyeuse was made marshal of France and governor of Languedoc. In 1599 he rejoined the Capuchins, incurred Henry's anger by his sermons in Paris in 1600 on the indissolubility of marriage, and became guardian in Toulouse and Paris, provincial of France, and definitor general in 1608. He died in Rivoli, Italy, on Sept. 28.

JUAN (10th century). He became bishop of Cordova, Spain, after 962, when Moorish persecution had eased and the city's culture so flourished that it was termed a new Athens.

JUAN DE LA ANUNCIACIÓN (1514?–1594), missioner. Born in Granada, Spain, he became an Augustinian in Mexico in 1554, held several offices, and was rector of the College of San Pablo. He worked with success among the Nahuatl Indians and published two collections of sermons and a manual of religious instruction.

JUAN DE LA ANUNCIATION (1633–1701), philosopher. Born in Oviedo, Spain, he became a Discalced Carmelite and prepared an elaborate system of philosophy from the work of such previous Carmelites as Diego de Jésus (1570–1621), Miguel de la SS. Trinidad (1588–1661), Antonio de la Madre de Dios (1588–1640), Domingo de Sta. Teresa (1600–54). Juan added *De gratia, De justificatione et merito, De Incarnatione,* and work on the sacraments. The entire project was revised by Antonio de S. Juan Bautista (d. 1699), Alonso de los Angeles (d. 1724), and Francisco de Sta. Ana. Juan was general of his congregation from 1694 to 1700.

JUAN OF AUSTRIA, DON. *See* John of Austria.

JUAN BAUTISTA DE TOLEDO (d. 1567), architect. Born in Madrid, he studied under Michelangelo in Rome in 1547 and became architect to Emperor Charles V, in which capacity he designed many of the buildings of Naples. In 1559 he returned to Madrid, where he was appointed architect in chief of Philip II, designed churches, drew up the plans for the Escorial, on which he worked until his death in Madrid on Apr. 23.

JUAN DE CORDOVA (1503–1595). Born in Cordova, Spain, he was a soldier in Flanders, went to New Mexico with Coronado in 1540–42, and became a Dominican in 1543. He served in the mission at Oaxaca, Mexico, from 1548 to 1568, then was named provincial, but ruled with such severity that he was removed in 1570. His last twenty-five years were devoted to preparation of a Zapotecan dictionary and a study of the Indians' language, rites, superstitions, and method of reckoning time. He died in Oaxaca.

JUAN PAN Y AGUA. *See* John, Bl. (12th century).

JUANA (13th century), queen of Navarre. Daughter of Henry I and Blanca, she was not of age when her father died in 1274, saw her country invaded on all sides, and fled to France with her husband, Philip the Fair, whom she had married in 1284. Navarre was under French domination from 1276, when the marriage negotiations began, until 1328.

JUANA LA BELTRANEJA (1462–1530). Illegitimate daughter of Queen Juana (wife of Henry IV of Castile) and, probably, Beltrán de la Cueva, she was acknowledged by the Cortes as heir to the crown of Castile, but the nobles declared for her brother Alfonso. When the latter died, and Henry's death followed in 1374, Henry's half-sister Isabella was proclaimed queen. A number of nobles then changed their allegiance, supported Juana, and invited Alfonso V of Portugal to invade Spain. The civil war ended with Alfonso's defeat at Toro. Juana then entered the convent of Santa Clara in Coimbra, Portugal, where she died.

JUCUNDINA, ST. (d. 466). She lived a life of prayer in Aemilia, Italy, under the direction of St. Prosper. F. D. Nov. 25.

JUCUNDINUS, ST. (d. 273?), martyr. *See* Julia, St.

JUCUNDUS, ST. (d. 250?), martyr. *See* Epictetus, St.

JUCUNDUS, ST. (d. 451?), martyr. *See* Nicasius, St.

JUCUNDUS, ST. (d. 485). He was bishop of Bologna, Italy. F. D. Nov. 14.

JUDAS QUIRIACUS, ST., bishop. The identity of this figure is uncertain; he could have been a bishop of Ancona, Italy, of which he is the patron, who died in Jerusalem; or the bishop of Jerusalem who was killed in a riot there in 133; or the legendary Jew who is said to have found for St. Helena the hiding place of the true cross, later becoming a bishop of Jerusalem and martyred by Julian the Apostate. The name is sometimes spelled Cyriacus. F. D. May 4.

JUDDE, CLAUDE (1661–1735). Born in Rouen, France, on Dec. 20, he became a Jesuit in 1677, was ordained, and became famous as a preacher. He taught in Rouen in 1704–21 and served as rector there; meditations and exhortations were published after his death in Paris on Mar. 11.

JUDE, ST. (1st century), apostle. Usually considered the brother of St. James the Less, he was one of the original apostles of Christ, though how and when he was chosen is not known. According to tradition, he preached in Mesopotamia and then joined St. Simon in Persia, where they were martyred. He is the author of one of the canonical epistles and is also known as Thaddeus. F. D. Oct. 28.

JUDGE, THOMAS AUGUSTINE (1868–1933), founder. Born in South Boston, Massachusetts, on Aug. 23, he studied at St. Vincent's seminary, Germantown, Pennsylvania, joined the Congregation of the Mission (Vincentians), and was ordained in 1899. He became a noted preacher and director of missions and encouraged lay participation in the apostolate and charity work by founding missionary cenacles in Brooklyn (1910), Baltimore (1913), Bridgeport (1914), and Orange

(1915). He was appointed superior at Opelika, Alabama, in 1915, and in 1920 was given permission to live outside the community to devote himself to the Missionary Servants of the Most Holy Trinity and Missionary Servants of the Most Blessed Trinity, which he had founded. They were recognized by Bishop Allen of Mobile in 1924 and by Rome in 1929, and by the time of his death in Washington, D.C., on Nov. 23, had spread to more than forty dioceses in the United States and Puerto Rico.

JUDICAEL, ST. (d. 658), king. After an auspicious reign in Brittany, he gave up the crown to spend his last twenty years in the monastery of Gael, near Vannes, Gaul. F. D. Dec. 17.

JUGE, GABRIEL (1879–1959). Born in St. Julien Chapteuil, France, he became a Brother of the Sacred Heart in 1893, taking the name Albertinus, taught at Paradis, and when anticlerical legislation closed many Catholic schools went to the United States in 1903. Except for two years (1906–8) in the South, he taught at the Metuchen, New Jersey, novitiate of his order until 1922, when he became provincial of the United States. In 1931 he became an assistant to the superior general, and from 1937 to 1952 held the office of superior general. After four years as novice master in Ecully, France, he returned to teach in Metuchen, where he died on Dec. 7.

JULES BOIS, HENRI ANTOINE (1869–1943), author. Born in Marseilles, France, he studied at St. Ignatius College there and at Montpellier, Collège de France, and the Sorbonne, taking doctorates in philosophy, literature, and psychology. He was influenced by the symbolists, wrote verse drama, and treatises on the emancipation of women, preternaturalism, and Hindu philosophy. He was president of the Society for Psychological Research in Paris, and interested in psychophysiology, occultism, and astronomy. *Hippolytus Crowned, Fury,* and *The Two Helens* proved successful on the stage, as did his French-African opera, *Nail.* He also wrote two novels, *The Modern Prodigy* (on subconscious phenomena), *The Psychology of Saints,* and *Essay on Democracy.* He wrote regularly for *Catholic World* and *Commonweal,* was decorated by many governments, and received an honorary doctorate from Providence College. He died in Paris on July 2.

JULIA, ST. (d. 273?), martyr. Seized at Troyes, Gaul, by the soldiers of Emperor Aurelian, she converted Claudius, the officer in charge, and was beheaded with him. Justus, Jucundinus, and others died with them. F. D. July 21.

JULIA, ST. (d. 300?), martyr. She was put to death in Egypt, or Syria, during the Diocletian persecution. F. D. Oct. 7.

JULIA, ST. (d. 302?), martyr. She and SS. Maxima and Verissimus were slain at Lisbon, Portugal, during the Diocletian persecution. F. D. Oct. 1.

JULIA, ST. (d. 303?), martyr. She was slain at Mérida, Spain, with St. Eulalia during the Diocletian persecution. F. D. Dec. 10.

JULIA, ST. (d. 304), martyr. *See* Apodemius, St.

JULIA, ST., martyr. Said to have been taken from Carthage and sold as a slave in Syria, she may have died by crucifixion on Corsica in the fifth century when she refused to sacrifice to the pagan gods; or, more likely, she was seized one or two centuries later and slain by Saracen raiders. She is patron of Corsica and Leghorn. F. D. May 22.

JULIA OF CERTALDO, BL. (1319–1367). Said to have been a servant named Julia della Rena, she became an Augustinian tertiary in Florence at eighteen, then returned to Certaldo, Italy, her birthplace, to live as a recluse for nearly thirty years. Her cult was confirmed in 1819. F. D. Feb. 15.

JULIAN, ST. (d. 160), martyr. He was put to death at Alexandria, Egypt. F. D. Feb. 12.

JULIAN, ST. (d. 250), martyr. *See* Cyriacus, St.

JULIAN, ST. (d. 259), martyr. *See* Victoricus, St.

JULIAN, ST. (d. 260?), martyr. He, St. Peter, and twenty others were put to death at Rome. F. D. Aug. 7.

JULIAN, ST. (d. 290), martyr. *See* Lucian of Beauvais, St.

JULIAN, ST. (3rd century), bishop. Probably a Roman, he became first bishop of Le Mans, France, and was widely honored in England because King Henry II was said to have been baptized in a church of St. Julian in the French see. F. D. Jan. 27.

JULIAN, ST. (3rd century). As bishop of Apamaea, Syria, he fought the Montanist and Cataphrygian heresies. F. D. Dec. 9.

JULIAN (d. 304?), martyr. Husband of St. Basilissa, he devoted his life to the care of sick and poor men in Egypt. He is sometimes confused with St. John the Hospitaller; more than likely he is part of a pious legend, which tells how he suffered two persecutions, ending in his martyrdom with Anastasius, Marcionilla, her son Celsus, and a priest named Antony. All were commemorated on Jan. 9.

JULIAN, ST. (d. 304?), martyr. A native of Vienne, Gaul, he was an officer in the Roman army and a Christian. He retired to Auvergne, but when he heard that the governor was persecuting Christians he acknowledged his faith and was beheaded at Brioude, France. F. D. Aug. 28.

JULIAN, ST. (d. 309), martyr. A catechumen in Caesarea, he paid public respect to the corpses of St. Elias and his four martyred companions, was seized on the spot, and burned to death. F. D. Feb. 17.

JULIAN, ST. (d. 310?), martyr. *See* Ammianus, St.

JULIAN, ST. (d. 321?), martyr. A priest who was slain in Galatia, he may be identical with the St. Gordion slain in France or Switzerland or Moesia and honored on Sept. 17. Macrobius, a Cappadocian slain at Tomis on the Black Sea during the reign of Licinius, may similarly have been confused with St. Macrinus. A Valerian died at the same time. F. D. Sept. 13.

JULIAN, ST. (d. 370?). A westerner who was sold into slavery in Syria, he entered a monastery in Mesopotamia on his release and served under St. Ephrem. F. D. June 9.

JULIAN, ST. (d. 430?), martyr. He, SS. Lucius, Quintian, and sixteen others were put to death in North Africa during the persecution of the Arian King Hunneric. F. D. May 23.

JULIAN, ST. (d. 690), archbishop. Of Jewish descent, he was baptized at Toledo, Spain, trained by St. Eugene II of Toledo, became abbot of the monastery of Agali, and in 680 archbishop of Toledo with primacy over Spain and Portugal. He revised the Mozarabic liturgy, wrote several books on death and immortality, and a historically valuable biography of the Visigoth King Wamba. F. D. Mar. 8.

JULIAN, ST. (d. 730), martyr. He, Marcian, Mary, and seven others were put to death by Emperor Leo the Isaurian when they attempted to prevent the desecration of the icon of Christ over the Brazen Gate in Constantinople. F. D. Aug. 9.

JULIAN, ST. (1127–1208), bishop. Born in Burgos, Spain, he worked as a laborer, while a bishop, to earn money to relieve the poor of his see of Cuenca, Spain, recently retaken from the Moors. He is the chief patron of Cuenca. F. D. Jan. 28.

JULIAN, ST., martyr. *See* Caesarius, St.

JULIAN OF ANAZARBUS, ST. (d. 302?), martyr. A citizen of Cilicia who, during the Diocletian persecution, was tortured and publicly displayed for a year as an object of scorn, he finally was put to death by drowning. His body was brought to Antioch and St. John Chrysostom preached a eulogy. F. D. Mar. 16.

JULIAN OF CAGLIARI, ST., martyr. He is believed to have been a Sicilian count; his martyred remains were found and enshrined in 1615. F. D. Jan. 7.

JULIAN THE HOSPITALLER. A fictitious hero in the *Golden Legend*, he killed his parents in error, withdrew with his wife to lead a life of penitence, and set up an inn to shelter travelers near a wide river. He also cared for the sick and poor and served as a ferryman. His was a very popular mediaeval tale.

JULIAN SABAS, ST. (d. 377), hermit. He is said to have come briefly out of austere retirement in Mesopotamia to encourage and convert great crowds by his refutation of Arianism at Antioch in 372. F. D. Jan. 17.

JULIAN OF SORA, ST. (d. 150?), martyr. A native of Dalmatia, he was tortured and beheaded in Campania during the persecution of Diocletian. F. D. Jan. 27.

JULIAN OF SPEYER (d. 1250?), composer. Born in Speyer, Germany, he studied at Paris, and served as musical director of the royal chapel from 1179 to 1226. He resigned to join the Franciscans and became choirmaster in their Paris house, where he composed the rhymed offices of SS. Francis of Assisi and Anthony of Padua. Among other poetical works ascribed to him is *Legenda S. Francisci*. He died in Paris. He is often called Julianus Teutonicus.

JULIANA, ST. (d. 270?), martyr. She and her brother Paul were beheaded at Ptolemais, Palestine, during the reign of Aurelian. F. D. Aug. 17.

JULIANA, ST. (d. 300), martyr. *See* Alexandra, St.

JULIANA, ST. (d. 306), martyr. *See* Cyrenia, St.

JULIANA (4th century). Called a saint and martyr in the *Golden Legend*, she is said to have been beheaded at Nicomedia during the persecution of Maximian. While in prison between trials and tortures she is said to have fought with a demon; in mediaeval art she is portrayed as binding a winged devil with chains.

JULIANA, ST. (d. 750?). A servant, she became a Benedictine nun at Pavilly, Normandy, and abbess there. F. D. Oct. 11.

JULIANA OF BOLOGNA, ST. (d. 435). When her husband, with her consent, became a priest, she devoted herself to charitable works and was highly praised by St. Ambrose. F. D. Feb. 7.

JULIANA OF COLLATO, BL. (d. 1262). Born in Treviso, Italy, she became a Benedictine at ten at Salarola, went to Gemmola in 1222 with Bl. Beatrix of Este, and in 1226 became abbess and foundress of SS. Biagio and Cataldo in Venice. Her cult was approved by Pope Gregory XVI. F. D. Sept. 1.

JULIANA OF CORNILLON, BL. (1192–1258). The person who first proposed the feast of Corpus Christi was born near Liège, Flanders, where, orphaned at five, she was cared for by Augustinian nuns at Mt. Cornillon. There she became a nun, devoted to the Eucharist and a student of the Church Fathers, and eventually prioress. She proposed her plan for inaugurating the feast to Bl. Eva and Isabel of Huy; churchmen approved; but she was suddenly condemned as a visionary and, through the lay directors of the double monastery, as an embezzler, and expelled from Liège. Restored by Bishop Robert, who proceeded to introduce the feast, she was again driven out at his death, but found refuge at the abbey of Salzinnes in Namur until that city was burned by Henry II of Luxembourg. She died at an abbey in Fosses. Bl. Eva continued to try to spread the feast and when the papacy came to Urban IV, who had supported the proposal during Juliana's lifetime, he affirmed it in 1264, and St. Thomas Aquinas wrote the office. Juliana was beatified in 1869. F. D. Apr. 5.

JULIANA OF NORWICH (1342?-1416?), mystic. Probably born near Carrow, England, and a Benedictine nun, she lived as an anchorite near St. Julian's Church in Norwich, and attracted many who came to consult her. She wrote *Sixteen Revelations of Divine Love*, influenced by Walter Hilton's *Cloud of Unknowing*, the result of twenty years of meditation on a vision of Christ's Passion and suffering she experienced in 1373. Written after 1393, it contains reflections on the love of God, the Incarnation, the Redemption, sin, penance, and divine consolation, and is one of the most important of English mystical writings. She died sometime after 1416.

JULITTA, ST. (d. 303?), martyr. A wealthy Christian widow of Caesarea in Cappadocia, she was burned at the stake when she refused to sacrifice to Zeus during the Diocletian persecution. F. D. July 30.

JULITTA, ST. (d. 304?), martyr. She is said to have been savagely tortured and put to death at Tarsus during the persecution of Diocletian, after her three-year-old son Cyricus (or Quiricus) was hurled to death by the presiding governor. The story is now considered a pious fiction, although the name Cyricus was widely popular in the Near East and appears as St. Cyr in France.

JULIUS I, ST. (d. 352), pope. A Roman, he succeeded St. Mark to the papacy on Feb. 6, 337. He built a number of churches in Rome, including that now called the Twelve Apostles, but most of his reign was marked by Arian strife. Led by Bishop Eusebius of Nicomedia, these heretics fought the return of St. Athanasius to the see of Alexandria in 338 when the latter was supported by the pope and Emperor Constantine II. The group selected George of Cappadocia instead, but the Arians in Egypt put a third bishop, Pistus, in office. Neither faction sent representatives to Rome when the pope summoned a synod to solve the difficulty. At the synod held in Sardica in 342 or 343, the pope's opinion that a deposed bishop had the right of appeal to Rome was sustained by churchmen of East and West. Athanasius, however, was not restored until the death of George in 346. F. D. Apr. 12.

JULIUS II (1443-1513), pope. Born in Albissola, Italy, on Dec. 5, Giuliano della Rovere was educated in Perugia under the guidance of his uncle Francesco, general of the Franciscans (who became Pope Sixtus IV in 1471), became a Franciscan, was made cardinal-priest in 1471, and received as benefices before 1503 some thirteen sees and several abbeys. He also fathered three daughters, one of whom he married to Giovanni Orsini. In 1474 he headed an army to return Umbria to papal rule, was sent as legate to France to settle ecclesiastical affairs in the Avignon diocese, and to France and the Netherlands in 1480 to settle a quarrel between Maximilian of Austria and Louis XI of France and to gain the release of the latter's prisoner, Cardinal Balue. The legate was instrumental in directing the bribe-stained election of Pope Innocent VIII in 1484. Earlier, he had ended the papal treaty with Venice; now he delayed any peace in the war which broke out between the Papal States and Naples. Because of his domination of the papacy and his hatred of the Borgias, he fled to France in 1492 when Alexander VI became pope, and persuaded Charles VIII to invade Italy to dethrone Alexander. But the pope won Charles to his side and Giuliano spent the rest of that pontificate in France and northern Italy. He was elected pope in a brief and bribe-marked election, during which impossible concessions were made to the voting cardinals, on Oct. 31, 1503. He promptly repudiated all promises after his consecration on Nov. 26. Julius devoted his reign to restoring and extending temporal power and territory. He ordered Cesare Borgia to return papal cities in Romagna (of which Borgia was duke, but which were under Venetian rule) to the papacy, and when he refused had him arrested. When most of the cities were restored, Julius led an army against Perugia, Bologna, and Baglioni, forcing them to surrender and acknowledge his authority in 1506. In 1509 he made an alliance with the League of Cambrai (formed by Emperor Maximilian I and King Louis XII of France), crushed Venice, and gained Rimini and Faenza. Then, fearful of French power in Italy, he made an alliance with Venice and the Swiss in 1510 and declared war against France. Louis, with Maximilian's support, convened a synod at Tours, declared the war illicit, and threatened to call a general council; Julius excommunicated Louis and the cardinals who supported Louis, five of whom set up a schismatic synod at Pisa. In 1511, Julius succeeded in getting Spain and England to join him in the Holy Alliance, which at the battle of Ravenna in 1512 drove the French from Italy. Later in that year he convened the fifth Lateran Council (which continued until 1517) to consider ecclesiastical reforms. His reputation rests on his military skill, his interest in the arts (he was the patron of Bramante, Michelangelo, and Raphael), and his establishment of the Capella

Julia for the study of chant. He died in Rome on Feb. 21.

JULIUS III (1487–1555), pope. Born in Rome on Sept. 10, Giovanni Maria Ciocchi del Monte studied law at Perugia and Siena, became archbishop of Siponto (Manfredonia) in 1512, and in 1520 bishop of Pavia as well. He served as vice-legate to Perugia, was twice prefect of Rome and was one of the hostages given the imperialists after Rome was sacked in 1527. He was legate to Bologna, Romagna, Parma, and Piacenza, was created cardinal-priest in 1536, cardinal-bishop of Palestrina in 1543, and in 1545 was first president of the Council of Trent, which he transferred to Bologna in 1547. He was elected pope on Feb. 7, 1550, after a ten-week conclave and against Emperor Charles V's wishes, and consecrated on Feb. 22. He transferred the Council of Trent from Bologna back to Trent in 1550 and ordered its sessions resumed in 1551, but was again obliged to suspend it in 1552 when the French bishops refused to attend. After a brief alliance with Charles V, which ended disastrously with the defeat of Charles by the French and forced Julius to restore Parma to the Farnese family in 1552, he lost interest in politics, and for the rest of his reign accomplished little, though he did issue the bull of foundation, *Collegium Germanicum,* to the Jesuits in 1552. He was also criticized for his nepotism and lavish style of living at his Villa Giulia at Porta del Popolo. He died in Rome on Mar. 23.

JULIUS, ST. (d. 190?), martyr. A Roman senator, he was scourged to death in the capital during the reign of Emperor Commodus. F. D. Aug. 19.

JULIUS, ST. (2nd century), martyr. *See* Catus, St.

JULIUS, ST. (d. 302?), martyr. A soldier in the Roman army occupying Bulgaria, he was beheaded at Durostorum (now Silistria) after a number of legionaries were discovered to be Christians. One, St. Hesychius, was executed a few days later. F. D. May 27.

JULIUS, ST. (d. 302). martyr. *See* Felix, St.

JULIUS, ST. (d. 304?), martyr. According to tradition, he was a Briton who was executed with St. Aaron and others at Caerleon in Monmouthshire during the persecution of Diocletian. F. D. July 3.

JULIUS, ST. (4th century). A priest, he was sent with his brother Julian, a deacon, by Emperor Theodosius to Piedmont to transform pagan temples into churches. Julius died at Novara, Italy, sometime after 390. F. D. Jan. 31.

JULIUS, ST. (4th century), martyr. *See* Ambicus, St.

JUNCKER, HENRY DAMIAN (1809–1868), bishop. Born in Fenétrange, Lorraine, on Aug.

22, he began his studies for the priesthood in France but emigrated to Cincinnati, Ohio, where he studied at St. Francis Xavier seminary and was ordained there in 1834. He served in several parishes before being consecrated first bishop of Alton, Illinois, in 1857. He was successful on a trip to Europe to gather missionary priests for his enlarging diocese, worked actively himself in his large area, and attended the second Plenary Council at Baltimore. He died in Alton on Oct. 2.

JUNGER, AEGIDIUS (1833–1895), bishop. Born in Burtscheid, Germany, on Apr. 6, he studied at the American College, Louvain, and was ordained in 1862. He did missionary work in the state of Washington for the next two years, was secretary to Bishop Blanchet of Nesqually in 1864–79, and was appointed second bishop of Nesqually (which became the see of Seattle in 1907) in 1879. He built a new cathedral in Vancouver, British Columbia, in 1884, and died there on Dec. 26.

JUNGMANN, BERNARD (1833–1895), theologian. Born in Münster, Westphalia, on Mar. 1, he studied at the German and Gregorian colleges in Rome, received his doctorate in philosophy in 1854 and in theology in 1859, and was ordained in 1857. After parish work in Emmerich, he taught philosophy at the seminary in Roulers in 1861 and in Louvain, Belgium, from 1871 until his death there on Jan. 12. He wrote on church history, grace, the Incarnation, the Trinity, and other theological subjects.

JUNIAS, ST. (1st century). *See* Andronicus, St.

JURMIN, ST. (7th century). Probably the nephew of King Anna of East Anglia, he was revered in England and his relics were enshrined in Bury St. Edmunds. F. D. Feb. 23.

JUSSIEU, ADRIEN HENRI DE (1797–1853), botanist. Son of Antoine Laurent, he was born in Paris on Dec. 23, studied at its university, where he took his medical degree, succeeded his father as professor of botany in the Museum of Natural History in 1826, and became a professor at Paris in 1845. He was president of the French Academy of Sciences, published studies of plants and a textbook, and died in Paris on June 29.

JUSSIEU, ANTOINE DE (1686–1758), botanist. Born in Lyons, France, on July 6, he studied medicine at Montpellier, but early became interested in botany and traveled over Europe in botanical research. He became professor at the Jardin du Roi in Paris in 1708, a member of the Academy of Sciences in 1711, and was one of the first to use quassia bark as a medicine. He wrote widely on anatomy, botany, mineralogy, paleontology, and zoology, and revised important works by Tournefort and Barrelier. He died in Paris on Apr. 22.

JUSSIEU, ANTOINE LAURENT DE (1748–1836), botanist. Born in Lyons, France, on Apr. 12, he went to Paris to study medicine in 1765, was the protégé of his uncle Bernard, the botanist, and in 1770, after he received his medical degree, was appointed professor and demonstrator of the Jardin du Roi and devoted himself exclusively to botany. He was elected to the Academy of Sciences in 1773 and in 1774 published his *Exposition d'un nouvel ordre des plantes*, which expanded the natural system of Bernard (who never published anything about his system) and applied it on a practical basis to the different families. In 1789 his monumental *Genera plantarum secundum ordines naturales disposita*, which is the basis of the modern classification of plants, was published. He helped reorganize the Jardin du Roi as the Museum of Modern History in 1790 and became professor of botany and its director. In 1804 he also became professor of botany at Paris and counselor of the university in 1808. He wrote monographs and articles for the *Annales* of the Museum and in 1824 published *Principes de la methode naturelle des végétaux*. He died in Paris on Sept. 17.

JUSSIEU, BERNARD DE (1699–1777?), botanist. Born in Lyons, France, on Aug. 17, brother of Antoine and Joseph, he studied at the Jesuit college in Lyons, accompanied Antoine on a botanical expedition to Spain in 1716, and received his degree in medicine from Montpellier in 1720. He joined his brother in Paris and in 1722 was appointed professor of the Jardin du Roi in Paris. His revised edition of Tournefort's *Histoires des plantes des environs de Paris* in 1725 brought him membership in the Academy of Sciences. He was honored in 1737 by Linnaeus, who named the *genus Jussieua* after him. In 1758 he was appointed superintendent of the royal garden at Trianon by King Louis XV and catalogued all the plants in the garden in a manner which became famous as the Jussieu system, the first attempt at a natural classification of plants. He died in Paris on Nov. 6.

JUSSIEU, JOSEPH DE (1704–1779), botanist. Brother of Antoine and Bernard, he was born in Lyons, France, on Sept. 3, and served as botanist on an expedition to Peru in 1735, collecting valuable information on natural history until 1771, when he returned to Paris. He introduced the garden heliotrope (*heliotropium peruvianum*) to Europe. He died in Paris on Apr. 11.

JUSTA, ST. (d. 130?), martyr. *See* Henedina, St.

JUSTA, ST. (d. 287?), martyr. With her sister Rufina, she sold earthenware in Seville, Spain. When they refused to sell their products for pagan ceremonies they were denounced during the persecution of Diocletian. Ordered to sacrifice to the gods, they refused. St. Justa was racked to death and St. Rufina was strangled. F. D. July 19.

JUSTAMOND, BL. MAGDALEN FRANÇOISE DE (d. 1794), martyr. *See* Justamond, Bl. Marguerite.

JUSTAMOND, BL. MARGUERITE ELÉANORE DE (d. 1794), martyr. A Cistercian nun, Sr. M. St. Henri, at the convent of St. Catherine in Avignon, France, she was guillotined at Orange when she refused to take the republican oath, with its anti-religious significance, during the French Revolution. With her died her sister Magdalen Françoise (in religion, Sr. Marie Magdalen du St. Sacrement). They were beatified in 1925. F. D. July 16.

JUSTE, GIOVANNI. *See* Betti, Giovanni.

JUSTIN, ST. (d. 287?), martyr. *See* Constantius, St.

JUSTIN, ST. (d. 540?). Possibly a bishop of Chieti, he has long been venerated in that Italian city. F. D. Jan. 1.

JUSTIN MARTYR, ST. (110?–165?). Born in Flavia Neapolis to a wealthy pagan or Graeco-Roman family of Samarians, he studied extensively in literature and various philosophies, and became a Christian about 130. As a layman he debated the merits of Christianity with Trypho the Jew in Ephesus (later published as *Dialogue*), then opened a school of philosophy in Rome, where he debated with Crescens the Cynic, wrote a treatise against Marcion, now lost, several exhortations to the Greek residents of the capital, and two *Apologies* of Christianity. The last explained immortality, the sacraments, fasting, free will, and exposed the weaknesses of paganism; they were addressed to Emperor Marcus Aurelius and the first such documents to be addressed to the enemies of the Church. Ten or fifteen years later, when he refused to sacrifice to the gods, he was put to death with SS. Charita, Chariton, Euelpistus, Hierax, Liberianus, and Paeon. F. D. Apr. 14.

C. C. MARTINDALE, *St. Justin the Martyr* (New York, Kenedy, 1923).

JUSTINA, ST. (d. 130?), martyr. *See* Henedina, St.

JUSTINA, ST., martyr. Despite highly laudatory references by St. Venantius Fortunatus, nothing is known of her except from an apparent forgery of the twelfth century which says she was martyred at Padua after her baptism by St. Prosdocimus, supposed first bishop of Padua and disciple of St. Peter. F. D. Oct. 7.

JUSTINA, ST., martyr. *See* Aureus, St.; also, Cyprian, St.

JUSTINIAN I (483–565), emperor. Flavius Anicius Justinianus, called "the Great," was born in Tauresium, Illyricum, on May 11, probably of Slavonic and barbarian parentage, and was originally called Uprauda. He was adopted by Justin I, studied at Constantinople, served his aged uncle when the latter became emperor in 518, and was co-emperor for a short period before he succeeded Justin in 527 at the age of forty-five. He married Theodora in 523. Previous emperors had attempted to clarify existing laws; Justinian established a commission of ten to collect, collate, and revise the ordinances of recent emperors (known as *jus novum*); their work removed the contradictory, obsolete, and obscure, and was issued in 529 as Codex constitutionum. Justinian then appointed a commission of sixteen to consider the statutes of the republic and early empire, senatorial decrees, and juridical commentary; their extracts were compressed and issued in 533 as *Digesta* or *Pandects*, first in Latin, then in Greek translation. The emperor declared repealed all earlier laws, and forbade commentary. The new work, however, though it compressed the equivalent of 106 volumes in about five, was unscientific and inconvenient. A third commission, under the direction of Tribonian (who had served on the previous two), prepared a revised and single-volume Codex, with a prefatory essay. This had a great effect on later civil and ecclesiastical law, and even helped to synthesize them both. The emperor's military career was uneven. He lost heavily to the invading Persians, who took Antioch in 540 and devastated the Black Sea area. He had some success against the Vandals in Africa, but a campaign against the Visigoths in Italy proved disastrous and their king, Totila, had made great inroads by 550. The Goths were defeated by Narses in 552, but a ravaged Italy suffered for many years. The emperor's Eastern opponents were contained, Spain was partly regained, but before his death he had lost his gains. He was interested in architecture, created many structures in Ravenna, and saw to the building of San Sophia and the church of SS. Sergius and Bacchus at Constantinople. He was excessively vain, vigorous, unscrupulous, and shortsighted. He levied heavy taxes for great public works (often unproductive) and created monopolies. Though not personally cruel, as was his empress, he was represented by dishonest officials such as the widely hated John the Cappadocian. Riots over taxation and cruel treatment by imperial agents were frequent; in 532, more than 30,000 persons were slain in Constantinople alone. Justinian was fascinated by theology, wrote many rescripts which he issued as encyclicals for the entire Church, and adopted a similarly superior position in directing the election of bishops. He defined the leadership of the Church under five patriarchs: Rome, Constantinople, Alexandria, Antioch, and Jerusalem

—in that order. He arranged for the exchange of synodal letters between them and himself. He ordered all pagans to be instructed in Christianity, set the death penalty for recantation, closed the University of Athens, and allowed John the Monophysite to burn the books and order the mistreatment of pagan scholars. Eventually, Justinian persecuted all who were not Monophysites (as Theodora was), but sought to reconcile them with Catholicism. Probably at the direction of Theodora, he ordered Pope Silverius to report to his general, Belisarius, in 537, deposed him, and appointed Vigilius in his place. He imprisoned the latter when Vigilius refused to support Justinian's condemnation of selections from the writings of Theodore of Mopsuestia, Theodoret of Cyr, and Ibas of Edessa—known as the Three Chapters. The Council of Chalcedon had condemned the writings, but not the authors. Vigilius, who refused to attend the Council of Constantinople which the emperor called, remained in prison six months, finally approved the council, and died on his return to Rome, a broken man. Monophysitism, which questioned the Incarnation, and thus denied the value of Redemption, continued to prevail. After Theodora's death in 548, Justinian progressed from this to the phantasist heresy, begun by Julian of Halicarnassus; he declared it orthodox and deposed the patriarch of Constantinople when the latter spoke of wide episcopal condemnation of the strange interpretation of Christ's nature and will. Justinian died on Nov. 14 in Constantinople.

JUSTINIANI, BENEDETTO (1550?–1622), theologian. Born in Genoa, Italy, he became a Jesuit in Rome in 1579 and taught at the Roman College (where he was rector for twenty years), Toulouse, and Messina. He served as regent of the Sacred Penitentiaria, was chief preacher to the pope, and theologian to Cardinal Cajetan on a mission to Poland. He wrote theological treatises and two biblical commentaries and died in Rome on Dec. 19.

JUSTUS, ST. (d. 250?), martyr. *See* Macarius, St.

JUSTUS, ST. (d. 273?), martyr. *See* Julia, St.

JUSTUS, ST. (d. 283), martyr. *See* Abundius, St.

JUSTUS, ST. (d. 285?), martyr. *See* Ariston, St.

JUSTUS, ST. (d. 297), martyr. A nine-year-old native of Auxerre, he is said to have been beheaded near Beauvais, France, during the Diocletian persecution, but all details are questionable. F. D. Oct. 18.

JUSTUS, ST. (3rd century), martyr. *See* Donatus, St.

JUSTUS, ST. (d. 303), martyr. He was put to death by drowning at Trieste, on the Adriatic coast, during the Diocletian persecution. F. D. Nov. 2.

JUSTUS, ST. (d. 304?), martyr. With his brother Pastor, who was eight or nine, he was a schoolboy of thirteen at Alcalá, Spain, when the governor ordered them seized, tortured, and beheaded during the persecution of Diocletian. They are highly praised by Prudentius. F. D. Aug. 6.

JUSTUS, ST. (d. 390?), bishop. Born in the Vivarais, he became deacon at Vienne, and bishop of Lyons in 350. He attended the Council of Aquileia in 381 and left there for a monastery in Egypt where, despite the entreaties of his people, he lived as a hermit until his death. F. D. Oct. 14 (sometimes, Sept 2).

JUSTUS, ST. (d. 550?), bishop. Probably the first bishop of Urgel, Spain, he attended the councils of Toledo (527) and Lerida (546) and was the author of a mystical interpretation of the Canticle of Canticles. F. D. May 28.

JUSTUS, ST. (d. 627), archbishop. A Benedictine, he was sent from Rome in 601 by Pope St. Gregory to help St. Augustine on the English mission. In 604, Augustine consecrated him first bishop of Rochester. When King Ethelbert died in 616 and paganism swept over Britain, he went to Gaul with Bishop Mellitus of London, but returned in 617 when St. Laurence converted King Edbald of Kent. In 624 he became the fourth archbishop of Canterbury. F. D. Nov. 10.

JUTTA, BL. (d. 1136). Sister of Count Meginhard of Spanheim, she lived as a recluse and attracted disciples whom she formed into a Benedictine community near Diessenberg, Germany, which she directed for twenty years and where she educated the young St. Hildegard. F. D. Dec. 22.

JUTTA, ST. (d. 1260). The patron of Prussia was born in Sangerhausen, Thuringia, and married at fifteen to a nobleman. After he had died on a pilgrimage and her children had grown, she entered religious life, gave away her fortune, and took to the road to aid sick travelers by means of alms she begged from others, and settled at Kulmsee, Prussia, as a hermit. She spent her last four years there, devoted to prayer and favored by supernatural gifts. F. D. May 5.

JUTTA OF HUY, BL. (1158–1228). Born at Huy, Holland, she became a widow at eighteen, devoted the next ten years to the care of lepers, and in 1182 retired as a solitary. Her prayerful experiences helped to change the lives of her own spiritually negligent family. She is also known as Ivetta. F. D. Jan. 13.

JUVENAL, ST. (d. 376?), bishop. An Eastern physician and priest, he settled in Narni, Italy, which Pope Damasus made a diocese and over which he ruled as bishop for seven years. Other biographical details, including reference to martyrdom, are confused with those of other saints of the same name. F. D. May 3.

JUVENCUS, GAIUS VETTIUS AQUILINUS (290?–331?), poet. According to St. Jerome, he was a Spaniard by birth, of a good family, who became a priest. He wrote *Evangeliorum libri*, a simple poetical life of Christ based on the bible, about 330, and another Christian poem on the mysteries, which has been lost.

JUVENTINUS, ST. (d. 363), martyr. Officers in the imperial guard of Julian the Apostate, he and St. Maximinus objected to the emperor's laws against Christians, were stripped of their estates, scourged, and beheaded at Antioch after they refused to sacrifice to idols. St. John Chrysostom wrote a panegyric on them. F. D. Jan. 25.

JUVENTIUS, ST. (1st century), bishop. He is said to have been sent from Aquileia with St. Syrus to evangelize northern Italy, where he became bishop of Pavia. F. D. Feb. 8 (also, Sept. 12).

K

KAAS, LUDWIG (1881–1952), archaeologist. Born in Trier, Germany, on May 23, he was ordained, became a monsignor, served as head of the German Centre party, and was a member of the *Reichstag*, where he defended Von Hindenburg against the emerging Adolf Hitler. He resigned in 1933 and went to the Vatican. As an archaeologist, he discovered evidence in 1950 to support the belief that St. Peter was buried beneath a basilica in St. Peter's, Rome, a view accepted by Pope Pius XII. He also unearthed many pagan monuments and Christian tombs during ten years of excavating. He died in Rome on Apr. 25.

KADLUBEK, BL. VINCENT (1150?–1223), bishop. Born in Karnow, Poland, he studied in France and Italy, was appointed to the cathedral at Sandomir, and consecrated as its bishop in 1208. He supported several monasteries in the hope of reforming his country, resigned his see after ten years, and became a Cistercian. He wrote a *Chronicle of the Rulers of Poland,* the latter part of which is historically important, but whose earlier sections are based on legend and folklore. He died at Jedrzejow, Poland; his cult was approved in 1764. F.D. Mar. 8.

KAGER, JOHANN MATTHIAS (1566–1634), painter. Born in Munich, Germany, he studied under Pieter de Witte, lived in Rome, and returned to Munich under the patronage of the Elector Maximilian. He decorated churches and palaces, worked in miniatures, and completed *David and Abigail* and *The Last Judgment* for the senate hall in Augsburg, Bavaria, where he spent his last years.

KAIN, JOHN JOSEPH (1841–1903), archbishop. Born in Martinsburg, West Virginia, on May 31, he studied at St. Charles's College, Maryland, and was ordained in Baltimore in 1866. He was pastor in Harper's Ferry until 1875, when he was consecrated bishop of Wheeling. He was procurator of the third Plenary Council of Baltimore in 1884, was made titular archbishop of Oxyrynchia and co-adjutor of St. Louis in 1893, was administrator in 1893–95, and succeeded to the see in 1895. He held two diocesan synods in which he re-organized the entire diocese, began a new cathedral, and died on Oct. 13 in Baltimore.

KAISER, KAJETAN GEORG VON (1803–1871), chemist. Born in Kelheim, Bavaria, on Jan. 3, he became professor of technology at Munich in 1851, taught applied chemistry at the Munich technical high school in 1878, made important findings in the chemistry of fermentation, and wrote scientific articles. He died in Munich, Bavaria, on Aug. 28.

KAKOWSKI, ALEXANDER (1862–1938), cardinal. Born in Dembiny, Poland, on Feb. 5, he was ordained, became archbishop of Warsaw in 1913, and primate of Poland in 1919. He was one of the 3 regents of the provisional government of Warsaw in 1915–18. He died there on Dec. 30.

KALINKA, VALERIAN (1826–1886), historian. Born in Cracow, Poland, he was forced to flee for his political opinions in 1846, worked on a newspaper, *Czas*, in 1848, and then went to Paris, where he wrote *Galicia und Cracoio*. He edited *Political Polish News*, a weekly magazine devoted to Polish national life, most of which he wrote and which closed after four years. In 1863 he published *The Last Years of Stanislaus Augustus*. He became a Resurrection Father in Rome and was chaplain of a convent in Jaroslaw, Poland, at the time of his death. His most important historical work was *Sejmczteroletni* (*The Four Years Diet*), a commentary on Polish politics and leaders.

KANTEN, ST. (8th century). He was founder of Llanganten Abbey, Brecknock, Wales. The name also appears as Cannen. F. D. Nov. 5.

KARNKOWSKI, STANISLAW (1526?–1603), archbishop. A native of Poland, he was appointed bishop of Wlozlawsk in 1563, established a seminary for priests, encouraged learning by opening several schools, and in 1579 had a collection of synodal laws made. He bitterly opposed the inroads of the Reformation under King Sigismund II Augustus and on his death supported Henry of Valois as his successor. Henry was crowned king of Poland in 1574, but left to receive the French crown the same year, whereupon Stanislaw convinced Prince Stephen Bathory of Transylvania to avow his Catholicism and crowned him king in 1576. Karnkowski was named primate of Poland and archbishop of Gnesen in 1581, ruled Poland after Stephen's death in 1586, and elected and crowned the crown prince of Sweden as King Sigismund III Vasa of Poland in 1587. He sponsored a translation of the Bible into Polish and wrote theological tracts on the Eucharist and *Liber epistolarum familiarium et illustrium virorum*. He died in Lowicz, Poland, on May 25.

KASPAR, KAREL (1870–1941), cardinal. Born in Mirosov, Bohemia, on May 16, he studied in Pilsen and at the universities of Pope Urban and of St. Apollinaire in Rome. After ordination he gained fame as a canonist. He wrote on history, canon law, and on his travels in the Near East. He was made titular bishop of Bethsaida (1920), bishop of Králové Hradec (1921–31), archbishop of Prague (1931), and cardinal (1935). As primate of Czechoslovakia he denounced the Munich agreement of 1938 and warned of the effects of absorption by Germany. He died in Prague, Bohemia, on Apr. 21.

KASPER, CATHERINE (1820–1898), foundress. Born in Dernbach, Germany, on May 26, she joined with two companions to form the Poor Handmaids of Jesus Christ in 1851, cared for the sick, poor, and orphaned, turned to teaching, and established boarding and industrial schools. The constitution of the order was approved in 1870 by Pope Pius IX and Catherine (as Sister Mary) was its first superior. The order spread to Austria, Holland, France, England, and the United States. She died on Feb. 2.

KATONA, STEPHEN (1732–1811), historian. Born in Papa, Hungary, he joined the Jesuits when eighteen, became professor at Buda, and was noted for his historical works, chief of which was his forty-volume history of Hungary, *Historia critica rerum stirpis Austriacae*.

KATZER, FREDERICK FRANCIS XAVIER (1844–1903), archbishop. Born in Ebensee, Upper Austria, on Feb. 7, he graduated from Linz in 1864, went to the United States the same year, studied at St. Francis seminary, Milwaukee, and was ordained in Milwaukee in 1866. He taught at St. Francis until 1875, when he became Bishop Krautbauer's secretary, was administrator of the diocese on the bishop's death in 1885, and in 1886 was appointed bishop of Green Bay, Wisconsin. He successfully led the fight against the law making the use of English in all schools compulsory (there were numerous German language schools in Wisconsin) and was appointed third archbishop of Milwaukee in 1891. He died at Fond du Lac, Wisconsin, on July 20.

KAUFFMANN, ANGELICA (1741–1807), painter. Born in Chur, Switzerland, on Oct. 30, she studied painting under her father and came under the patronage of Francis III of Este. In 1757 she painted twelve life-sized pictures of the apostles while helping her father decorate a church in Schwarzenberg. After a trip to Italy she went to England in 1766 under the patronage of Lady Wentworth, where she became a friend of Joshua Reynolds, who painted her portrait, and one of the original members of the Royal Society in 1769. She is known for her portraits, historical paintings, and *Vestal Virgin* and *Christ and the Woman of Samaria*. Her last years were spent in Italy, after her marriage to Antonio Zucchi, a Venetian painter, and she died in Rome on Nov. 5.

KAUFFMANN, LEOPOLD (1821–1898). Brother of Alexander, he was born in Bonn, Germany, on Mar. 13, studied law there, became a friend of leading German composers, founded the Maikäferbund (a poetical society), and the Bonn male choral society, Concordia, in 1845. He was elected burgomaster of Bonn in 1850 (re-elected in 1862 and in 1874, unanimously), chief burgomaster in 1859, and in 1861 was appointed a life member of the upper house by the king of Prussia. In 1875 the confirmation of his re-election as burgomaster was refused because of his Catholicism, though he had declared he would enforce the laws. He was elected to the lower house in 1876 and became a member of the governing committee of the Centre party. He was founder in 1876 and general secretary for fifteen years of the Görresgesellschaft, to encourage science, and in 1882 vice-president of the Borromeo Society, to distribute good books. He wrote biographies of Albrecht Dürer and Philipp Veit, and *Bilder aus dem Rheinland*. He retired from the *Reichstag* in 1896 and died in Bonn on Feb. 27.

KAUFMANN, ALEXANDER (1817–1893), poet. Born in Bonn, Germany, on May 14, he studied at Bonn and in 1844 became teacher of Prince Karl von Löwenstein-Wertheim-Rosenberg, who appointed him to the position he held the rest of his life, keeper of the Wertheim archives, in 1850. He wrote several volumes of poetry (*Gedichte, Mainsagen*, and *Unten den Reben*) and was noted for his knowledge of the folklore and legends of the Rhine. He died in Wertheim, Germany, on May 1.

KAULEN, FRANZ PHILIP (1827–1907).

Born in Düsseldorf, Germany, on Mar. 20, he studied there and at Bonn and was ordained in 1850. He did parish work until 1859, taught scripture at Bonn after 1863, and became professor of theology in 1882. He was made a monsignor in 1890 and was appointed to the Papal Biblical Commission in 1903. He wrote much exegesis and was editor of the second edition of *Kirchenlexikon*. He died in Bonn, Germany, on July 11.

KAVANAGH, EDWARD (1795–1844). Born in Newcastle, Maine, on Apr. 27, he studied at Georgetown, St. Mary's, Baltimore, and in Europe. When he returned to the United States in 1815 he became a lawyer, was elected to the Maine legislature in 1826, the state senate in 1828, and to Congress, where he served two terms, in 1831. He was chargé d'affaires of the American legation in Lisbon in 1835–41. He was re-elected to the Maine senate in 1841 and was one of the four commissioners who negotiated the Webster–Ashburton Treaty, which settled the northeastern boundary dispute with England in 1842. As president of the Maine senate he succeeded to the governorship when the incumbent resigned to enter the United States Senate (the first Catholic governor of any New England state), but was obliged to resign nine months later because of ill health. He died in Newcastle on Jan. 21.

KAVANAGH, JULIA (1824–1877), author. Daughter of Morgan Kavanagh, a poet, she was born on Jan. 7 in Thurles, Tipperary, Ireland, and moved to England and then to France. She returned to England in 1844 and began writing for magazines, then turned to biographies and popular fiction: *Madeleine* (1848), *Nathalie, Daisy Burns, Rachel Gray*, two volumes of *French and English Women of Letters*, and *Forget-Me-Nots*, a collection of short stories. She died in Nice, France, on Oct. 28.

KAYE-SMITH, SHEILA (1887–1956), novelist. Born in Hastings, England, on Feb. 4, she wrote fiction while in school, became a popular novelist with her first books (on wandering preachers and highwaymen), moved to London, and began her serious career with *Sussex Gorse*; *Joanna Godden* (1921) and *The End of the House of Alard* also were well reviewed. In 1924 she married T. Penrose Fry, an Anglican cleric. *Saints in Sussex, Joanna Godden Married*, and *Shepherds in Sackcloth* followed, all on her favorite English area. She and her husband became converts in 1929, settled in Little Doucegrove, Sussex, and did charitable and religious work there. *Susan Spray*, on evangelism; *Ploughman's Progress*, on economic conditions in Britain; *Superstition Corner*, on England's past; *Quartet in Heaven*, four saintly biographies; *Tambourine, Trumpet and Drum*, on three wars, followed; *The Treasures of the Snow* was the last of nearly forty volumes. With

G. B. Stern she wrote *Speaking of Jane Austen* and *More about Jane Austen; Three Ways Home* is her autobiography, supplemented by her later *Kitchen Fugue*. She died near Rye, Sussex, England, on Jan. 14.

KEANE, JAMES JOHN (1857–1929), archbishop. Born in Joliet, Illinois, on Aug. 26, he studied at St. John's seminary in Collegeville, Minnesota, St. Francis Xavier College in New York, and at the Grand seminary in Montreal, where he was ordained in 1882. After pastoral work in St. Paul he became an instructor at St. Thomas College, its rector in 1888, and after serving as a pastor was appointed third bishop of Cheyenne, Wyoming, in 1902. He was appointed archbishop of Dubuque in 1911, founded the diocesan paper, the *Witness*, in 1921, and encouraged educational and charitable foundations in his see. He died in Dubuque, Iowa, on Aug. 2.

KEANE, JOHN JOSEPH (1839–1918), archbishop. Born in Ballyshannon, Donegal, Ireland, on Sept. 12, he was brought to Canada by his parents in 1846, went with them to Baltimore in 1848, studied at St. Charles's College in Maryland and St. Mary's seminary, Baltimore, and was ordained in Baltimore in 1866. He served as curate in Washington, D.C., until 1878 when he was appointed fifth bishop of Richmond, Virginia, supported the proposal for the establishment of Catholic University at the third Plenary Council in Baltimore in 1884, and was appointed its first rector in 1887 and titular bishop of Jasso in 1888. In 1897 he went to Rome as archbishop of Damascus and a member of the congregations of Propaganda and of Studies, returned to promote endowments for Catholic University in 1899, and was named archbishop of Dubuque in 1900. He resigned in 1911 because of ill health and was appointed titular archbishop of Cios, served as vicar general under his successor, and died on June 22 in Dubuque, Iowa. A collection of his sermons, *Onward and Upward*, was published in 1902, and he wrote *Emmanuel* (1915) and other books.

PATRICK HENRY AHERN, *The Life of John J. Keane* (Milwaukee, Bruce, 1954).

KEANE, PATRICK JOSEPH JAMES (1872–1928), bishop. Born in County Kerry, Ireland, on Jan. 6, he studied at St. Patrick's College, Carlow, and Catholic University, Washington, D.C., and was ordained in 1895. He did parish work in San Francisco for the next quarter of a century, and in 1920 was appointed titular bishop of Samaria and auxiliary of Sacramento, California. He succeeded to the see in 1922, and died there on Sept. 1.

KEARNEY, RAYMOND A. (1902–1956), bishop. Born in Jersey City, New Jersey, on Sept. 25, he grew up in Brooklyn, New York, studied at Holy Cross and the North American

College, Rome, and was ordained in 1927. He received his doctorate in canon law from Catholic University in 1929, was appointed chancellor of the Brooklyn diocese in 1930, a papal chamberlain in 1934, and auxiliary bishop of Brooklyn and titular bishop of Lysinia in 1935. He died in Brooklyn on Oct. 1.

KEATING, GEOFFREY (1569?–1644?). Born in Burgess, Tipperary, Ireland, he studied in Munster and Leinster, was ordained at twenty-four, and sent for further study at the Irish College in Bordeaux, France. He returned to Ireland in 1610, but generally had to work in hiding because of the penal laws. He wrote explanations of the mass and the rosary, reflections on death, and considerable poetry. In his underground travels between 1620 and 1626 in Leinster, Connaught, and Ulster he gathered material for his *History of Ireland*, finished by about 1632, and filled with primary sources such as otherwise neglected ecclesiastical records, as well as with compilations of legends which had a profound effect on later literature. He died in Tubbrid, Ireland.

KEATING, FREDERICK WILLIAM (1859–1928), archbishop. Born in Birmingham, England, he studied at Sedgley Park and Olton and the Benedictine college at Douai and was ordained in 1882. He became administrator of St. Chad's cathedral, Birmingham, in 1898, bishop of Northampton in 1907, and archbishop of Liverpool in 1921. He died there on Feb. 7.

KEHREIN, JOSEPH (1808–1876), author. Born in Heidescheim, Germany, on Oct. 20, he studied in Mainz and at Giessen, taught in Darmstadt and Mainz in 1835–45, in Hadamar to 1855, and was director of the Catholic teachers' seminary at Montabaur in 1855–76 and director of the *Realschule* there in 1855–66. He wrote on education and German language and literature.

KEILEY, BENJAMIN JOSEPH (1847–1925), bishop. Born in Petersburg, Virginia, on Oct. 13, he studied at St. Charles's College, Maryland, and the North American College in Rome and was ordained in 1873. He served as pastor in Delaware, and in Atlanta and Savannah, Georgia, and was vicar general of Savannah from 1887 to 1900, when he was consecrated its bishop. He founded the Catholic Layman's Association of Georgia, ruled until 1922, when he resigned because of blindness, was appointed titular bishop of Scillium, and died in Atlanta on June 17.

KELLER, ÉMILE (1828–1909). Born in Belfort, France, he was elected to the chamber of deputies in 1857 and rose to political prominence as head of the Catholic party. He was out of office from 1863 to 1869, then was re-elected, fought in the Franco-Prussian War, and walked out of parliament with other Alsatians when French territory was ceded to Germany. He was re-elected in 1876 and in 1885. He wrote a history of France and studies of religious orders, the French-papal relations of 1789, and religious liberty.

KELLER, JACOB (1568–1631). Born in Säckingen, Baden, Germany, he became a Jesuit in 1589 and taught at Freiburg and Ingolstadt. He served as rector of the Jesuit colleges in Ratisbon in 1605–7, and Munich in 1607–23, and returned as rector of Ratisbon, Bavaria, until his death on Feb. 23. He was an adviser to Emperor Maximilian I and wrote on tyrannicide and other controversial subjects.

KELLEY, FRANCIS ALPHONSUS (1888–1931). Born in Cohoes, New York, on Apr. 19, he studied at St. Michael's, Toronto, and St. Bernard's seminary, Rochester. He was pastor in Albany, Troy, and Cairo, served as chaplain of the 27th Division during World War I, was decorated by the American and British governments, and in 1919 became first national chaplain of the American Legion. He died in Catskill, New York, on Oct. 15.

KELLEY, FRANCIS CLEMENT (1870–1948), bishop. Born in Vernon River, Prince Edward Island, Canada, on Oct. 23, he studied at Laval, St. Dunstan's College, Charlottetown, and Nicolet seminary, and was ordained in 1893. He went to the United States, where he did parish work in the Detroit diocese, was pastor at Lapeer, Michigan, in 1893–1907, serving as a chaplain in the Spanish-American War. He founded the Catholic Church Extension Society in 1905 and was its president until 1924, founded *Extension Magazine* in 1906, of which he was also editor, was made a monsignor in 1915, and in 1924 was appointed bishop of Oklahoma (changed to Oklahoma City and Tulsa in 1930), where he remained until his death on Feb. 1. He was decorated by the Italian and Austrian governments and received an honorary degree from Louvain in 1927. He wrote numerous books, among them *The Last Battle of the Gods* (1907), *The Forgotten God* (1932), *Problem Island* (1937), and *The Bishop Jots It Down* (1939).

KELLNER, LORENZ (1811–1892), educator. Born in Kalteneber, Eichsfeld, Germany, on Jan. 29, he studied in Hildesheim and the seminary at Magdeburg, taught at the elementary school in Erfurt for two years, and became its rector. In 1836 he became assistant to his father, who was head of a teacher's school in Eichsfeld, and in 1848 was appointed to the government district council of West Prussia, and in 1855 of Trier, where he remained until 1884. He founded several teachers' colleges and wrote widely on teaching and the training of teachers. He died in Trier, Germany, on Aug. 18.

KELLY, DENNIS FRANCIS (1868–1938), merchant. Born in Chicago, Illinois, on Aug. 23, he entered business, was manager of Mandel Bros. department store in Chicago in 1901–23, president of another store, The Fair, there in 1925–28, and president of the National Retail Dry Goods Association in 1931. He was head of the layman's committee of Catholic Charities in Chicago from 1918. He died in Bergen, Norway, on July 23.

KELLY, HUGH (1858–1908), merchant. Born in Chicago, Illinois, on Sept. 24, he graduated from the College of the City of New York, began his business career with three commission merchants and a West Indian trading firm, married Mary E. McCabe in 1883, and was co-founder of a sugar-importing house in 1884. He was school commissioner in 1895–98, president of the maritime exchange in 1896–98, state commerce commissioner in 1898–1900, and served as a director of many economic, religious, social, and cultural organizations. He died in New York City on Oct. 30.

KELLY, EDWARD JOSEPH (1890–1956), bishop. Born in The Dalles, Oregon, on Feb. 26, he studied at Columbia University, Oregon, St. Patrick's seminary, California, and the North American College in Rome, and was ordained in Rome in 1917. After missionary work in Oregon he became secretary of the bishop of Baker City in 1919, and then was chancellor of that diocese until 1928, when he was appointed bishop of Boise, Idaho. He died on Apr. 21.

KELLY, FRANCIS MARTIN (1886–1950), bishop. Born in Houston, Minnesota, on Nov. 15, he studied at St. Thomas College, and St. Paul seminary, St. Paul, Catholic University, and the North American College and the Propaganda in Rome, and was ordained in Rome in 1912. He taught at St. Mary's (of which he was vice-rector in 1918–26) and St. Teresa colleges in Winona, Minnesota, was appointed the bishop's secretary in 1914, served as chancellor of Winona in 1919–22, and in 1926 was consecrated titular bishop of Milasa and auxiliary of Winona. He was appointed bishop of the see in 1928, resigned and was appointed titular bishop of Nasai in 1949, and died on June 24.

KELLY, JOHN BERNARD (1888–1957). Born in New York City on Jan. 12, he studied at Cathedral College and St. Joseph's seminary, and was ordained in 1913. After four years of parish work he became spiritual director of the Catholic Big Brothers and then of the Catholic Writers Guild; out of his thirty-three-year association with the latter originated the annual Golden Book Award. He wrote a biography of Cardinal Patrick Hayes and two volumes of verse. He died in New York City on June 21.

KELLY, MATTHEW (1814–1858), antiquarian. Born in Ireland, he taught at the Irish

College in Paris in 1839–41, and at Maynooth in 1851–58, and became canon of Ossory about 1854. He published a *Calendar of Irish Saints* (1857) and a study of Irish church history (1864), translated Gosselin's *Power of the Popes* (1853), and edited numerous antiquarian writings.

KELLY, MICHAEL (1850–1940), archbishop. Born in Waterford, Ireland, on Feb. 13, he was ordained, became archbishop of Sydney, New South Wales, Australia, in 1911, and died there on Mar. 8.

KELLY, PATRICK (1779–1829), bishop. Born in Kilkenny, Ireland, on Apr. 16, he studied at Maudlin Street College there and St. Patrick's, Lisbon, and was ordained in 1802. He taught at St. Patrick's, Maudlin St. College, and St. John's in Ireland, was president at the latter in 1816–20, and was consecrated first bishop of Richmond, Virginia, in 1820. He requested he be relieved in 1822 because of the difficulties raised by various groups in his see, the establishment of which had been vigorously opposed by the archbishop of Baltimore as premature and unwarranted. He was transferred to the diocese of Waterford and Lismore, Ireland, and died in Waterford on Oct. 8.

KELLY, THOMAS HUGHES (1865–1933), executive. Born in New York City, he studied at Seton Hall and law at Columbia, directed the fortune left by his banker father, Eugene Kelly, supported the Irish rebellion of 1916, and was noted for his philanthropies. He was the donor of the Lady chapel in St. Patrick's cathedral, New York City, and received three papal decorations. He died in Paris on Jan. 22.

KEMBLE, BL. JOHN (1599–1679), martyr. Born in Hertfordshire, England, he was ordained at Douai in 1625 and returned to his native land to serve the Catholic segments of the population for fifty-three years. He was arrested during the hysteria of the Titus Oates Plot, charged with treason, and hanged, drawn, and quartered at Hereford at the age of eighty. He was beatified in 1929. F. D. Aug. 22.

KEMP, JOHN (1380?–1454), cardinal. Born in Wye, Kent, England, he studied at Oxford, became an ecclesiastical lawyer, and in 1415 was vicar general of Canterbury and dean of the Court of Arches. He was appointed bishop of Rochester in 1419 and was transferred to Chichester in 1421 and later the same year to London. He served as chancellor of Normandy, opposed the duke of Gloucester on Henry V's death, and was made royal chancellor and archbishop of York in 1426. He resigned his chancellorship in 1432, headed a delegation to the Congress of Arras in 1435, and was made a cardinal in 1439. He again became chancellor in 1450, and in 1452 was transferred to the see of Canterbury. He died in Lambeth, England, on Mar. 22.

KEMPENEER, PIETER DE (1503–1580), painter. Born in Brussels and known in Flanders as Peter van de Velde and in Spain as Pedro Campaña, he studied art in Venice and worked there for his patron, Cardinal Grimiani, and worked in Rome and Bologna in the style of Raphael. He became an excellent master of color and draftsmanship, lived in Seville from 1537 to 1562, and established a school there with Louis de Vergas. He completed paintings for Carmoña and Triana, a monumental *Descent from the Cross* in Seville, and a *Resurrection* and *Purification*. He returned to Brussels as chief engineer to the duke of Alba, in 1563 became art director of the city's tapestry works, and died there.

KENAN, ST. (d. 500?). A disciple of St. Martin of Tours, he became bishop of Damleag, Meath, Ireland. F. D. Nov. 24.

KENELM (d. 812). Son of King Kenulf of Mercia, he allegedly succeeded his father at seven, whereupon he is said to have been murdered at the direction of his sister. There is no evidence to justify the story.

KENNEDY, JAMES (1406?–1466), bishop. Grandson of King Robert III of Scotland, he studied in Europe, was appointed bishop of Dunkeld in 1438, abbot of Scone, and in 1440 bishop of St. Andrews. He was appointed chancellor in 1444 and inaugurated civil and ecclesiastical reforms which roused the ire of many nobles. He soon resigned as chancellor to devote himself to his Church duties, tried to mediate the Western schism, founded St. Salvator's College in 1450, and in 1460, on the death of James II, served as one of the regents during the minority of King James III. He died on May 10.

KENNETH. *See* Canice, St.

KENNETH I MACALPINE (d. 860), king of Scotland. He succeeded Alpin in Galloway in 834, defeated the Picts and united them with the Scots as one nation in 846, established his capital at Scone instead of Argyll, and established Dunkeld as the primatial see (later transferred to Abernethy). He was succeeded by Grig, who helped the Church to become more independent.

KENNETH II (d. 995), king of Scotland. Son of Malcolm I, he became king of the Picts in 971, succeeding Culen, raided Northumbria, made Edinburgh a stronghold, and is said to have been slain by Fenella.

KENNETH III (d. 1005?), king of Scotland. Nephew of Kenneth II, he succeeded Constantine as king of the Picts in 943, became king of Scotland in 997, and died in battle, possibly against Malcolm II.

KENNY, WILLIAM JOHN (1853–1913), bishop. Born in Delhi, New York, on Jan. 12 (Oct. 9 and 14 are also listed), he studied at St. Bonaventure, New York, and was ordained in St. Augustine, Florida, in 1879. He served as pastor of several Florida parishes, was vicar general of St. Augustine in 1889–1901, administered that see in 1901–2, and was consecrated its third bishop in 1902. He died in Baltimore on Oct. 23.

KENRAGHTY (d. 1585), martyr. A native of Kilmallock, Ireland, he decided to abandon his father's profession of silversmith, studied in Europe where he was ordained, and returned to become chaplain to the earl of Desmond, whom he joined in the fight against Queen Elizabeth. He was captured in 1583 and imprisoned at Clonmel until 1585, when Victor White bribed his jailer to allow him to escape. He surrendered to save White's life, refused a pardon on the condition of renouncing his faith, and was executed on April 30 at Clonmel, Tipperary, Ireland.

KENRICK, FRANCIS PATRICK (1797–1863), archbishop. Born in Dublin on Dec. 3, he studied at the Propaganda, Rome, was ordained in 1821, and taught at the Bardstown seminary in Kentucky for nine years. He was Bishop Flaget's secretary and theologian at the Provincial Council of Baltimore in 1829 and was appointed titular bishop of Arata and coadjutor of Philadelphia in 1830, succeeding to the see in 1842. He abolished the lay trustee system, built a diocesan seminary, founded the *Catholic Herald* in 1833, increased the number of churches from four to ninety-four, and built schools and started a new cathedral. His devoted efforts during the cholera outbreak of 1832 won wide admiration and he helped end the Nativists' anti-Catholic riots in 1844 by prudent leadership. In 1851 he was named archbishop of Baltimore and in 1852 presided over the first Plenary Council there as apostolic delegate. He established the Forty Hours' Devotion in the United States in 1853, collected the American bishops' opinions on the promulgation of the doctrine of the Immaculate Conception, and attended its proclamation in Rome in 1854. He wrote on theology, a commentary on Job, *The Primacy of Peter*, and provided a new translation of the Bible. He died in Baltimore on July 8.

KENRICK, PETER RICHARD (1806–1896), archbishop. Born in Dublin on Aug. 17, brother of Francis Patrick, he worked as clerk in his father's office, studied at Maynooth, and was ordained there in 1832. He joined his brother in Philadelphia in 1833, became president of the seminary, editor of the *Catholic Herald*, rector of the cathedral, and vicar general. In Rome in 1840 he met Bishop Rosati of St. Louis and was persuaded to become his coadjutor. He was consecrated titular bishop of Adrasus in 1841 and succeeded Rosati in 1843. To lift the debt of the diocese he became a real-estate investor, founded the *Catholic Cabi-net* as the diocesan paper, was appointed first archbishop of St. Louis in 1847, and succeeded in having the Drake Act, which required clergymen to take a test oath, declared unconstitutional. He opposed the doctrine of papal infallibility at the Vatican Council in 1869 but submitted when it was promulgated. During his episcopate the archdiocese had great growth, even though sixteen new dioceses were created from its original area of Missouri, Arkansas, and part of Illinois. He resigned and was named titular archbishop of Marcianapolis in 1895 and died in St. Louis on Mar. 4.

KENT, WILLIAM CHARLES MARK (1823–1902), author. Born in London, he studied at Prior Park and Oscott, was editor of the *Sun* from 1845 to 1870 and of the *Catholic Weekly Register* from 1874 to 1881. He also studied law, was called to the bar in 1859, was an associate of Charles Dickens, and contributed to the latter's *Household Words* and *All the Year Round*. He published several volumes of poems, collected in a single volume in 1870, and published *Leigh Hunt as an Essayist*, *The Wit and Wisdom of Lord Lytton*, *The Humour and Pathos of Charles Dickens*, and sketches of Robert Burns, Charles Lamb, Thomas Moore, and other literary figures.

KENTIGERN, ST. (518?–603), bishop. Son of Thenew, a British princess, and an unknown father, he became a religious at a community near Glasgow and, noted both for his austerity and preaching skill, was chosen bishop of Strathclyde about 540. When he tried to end the feuds among the chieftains of the area, he was driven into Wales, but returned about 553 as a successful missioner and peacemaker in an area which eventually developed into the city of Glasgow and where he served as its first bishop. He worked in the region of Hoddam, Dumfriesshire, from 573 to 581, when he returned to Glasgow and where he remained until his death there. The arms of the city of Glasgow perpetuates the story of the saint sending one of his monks to catch a salmon which had swallowed the queen's ring; when threatened by her husband over its loss, she had appealed to Kentigern. F. D. Jan. 14.

KENTIGERNA, ST. (d. 734). Daughter of Cellach, Prince of Leinster, she was the mother of St. Fillan; after her husband's death, she entered religious life on an island retreat in Loch Lomond, Scotland. F. D. Jan. 7.

KEON, MILES GERALD (1821–1875), journalist. Born in Keonbrooke, Leitrim, Ireland, on Feb. 20, he studied at Stonyhurst, served in the French army in Algeria, and studied law at Gray's Inn. He gave up law and began writing articles for magazines, was editor of *Dolman's Magazine* in 1846, and from 1847 to 1859 was with the *Morning Post*. In 1859 he was appointed colonial secretary at Bermuda and remained there until his death on June 3. He wrote a biography of St. Alexis and two novels: *Harding, the Money-Spinner* and *Dion and the Sibyls.*

KERBY, WILLIAM JOSEPH (1870–1936), educator. Born in Lawler, Iowa, on Feb. 20, he studied at St. Joseph's, Dubuque, and St. Francis seminary, Milwaukee, and was ordained in 1889. He continued his studies at Catholic University and Berlin, Bonn, and Louvain, taught at St. Joseph's in 1895–96 and at Catholic University from 1906 to 1917. He was dean of the faculty of philosophy to 1919, secretary of the National Conference of Catholic Charities in 1910–20, and of the District of Columbia Board of Charities in 1920–26, and founded the *Catholic Charities Review* in 1916. He was made a monsignor in 1934, edited the *Ecclesiastical Review* from 1927, and wrote *Le Socialisme aux États-Unis, The Social Message of Charity,* and *Problems of the Better Hope.* He died in Washington, D.C., on July 27.

KERNAN, FRANCIS (1816–1892). Born on Jan. 14 in Steuben County, New York, he studied at Georgetown and became a lawyer in New York. He was school commissioner in Utica and official reporter of the New York court of appeals in 1854–57, and served as a member of the state assembly in 1860–62, and in the federal House of Representatives in 1863–65 and the Senate in 1876–82. He was a delegate to the Constitutional Convention of 1867, ran unsuccessfully for governor of New York in 1872, nominated Samuel J. Tilden for the presidency in 1876, and was active in the 1884 Democratic convention on behalf of Grover Cleveland. He died in Utica, New York, on Sept. 7.

KERR, WALTER TALBOT (1839–1927), admiral. Born at Newbattle abbey, Midlothian, Scotland, on Sept. 28, he was educated at Radley School, joined the naval service, and became a convert. He saw action during the Crimean War and Indian Mutiny of 1857, was wounded, and became a lieutenant in 1859. He rose to captain in 1872, married Lady Annabel Cowper in 1873, was secretary at the admiralty from 1885 to 1889, when he became rear-admiral. He was vice-admiral in 1895, senior naval lord and admiral in 1900. He developed a shipbuilding program and reorganized the training of personnel. He retired in 1909 and died at Melbourne Hall, Derbyshire, England, on May 12.

KERSSENBROCH, HERMANN VON (1520?–1585), educator. Born in Mönchof, Prussia, he studied at Münster and Cologne, taught in Düsseldorf, was rector at Hamm in 1548–50, head of the Pauline Gymnasium in Münster for the next twenty-five years, and a great influence on education in Westphalia. In 1875 he became head of the Düsseldorf Schola

Salentina and in 1578 of a school in Werl. His satires and the extreme hostility of his historical writings against the Anabaptists forced him to flee from Munich to Paderborn and from Werl to Osnabrück, Prussia, where he became rector of the cathedral school and remained until his death there on July 5.

KERVYN DE LETTENHOVE, JOSEPH MARIE BRUNO CONSTANTIN (1817–1891), historian. Born in St. Michel-les-Bruges, Belgium, on Aug. 17, he was elected to the chamber of representatives in 1861 and became minister of the interior in 1870. He wrote *Histoire de Flandre, Études sur les Chroniques de Froissart, Marie Stuart,* and other historical studies. He died in St. Michel on Apr. 3.

KESSELS, MATTHIAS (1784–1836), sculptor. Born in Maastricht, Netherlands, he was a goldsmith's apprentice in Venloo, then worked in Paris, St. Petersburg (1806–14), Paris again, and Rome. He won a contest, sponsored by Antoine Canova for young artists, and completed a large *Deluge, St. Sebastian Pierced with Arrows, Discus Thrower,* and other religious and classical figures. He died in Rome on Mar. 3.

KESSOG, ST. (d. 560?), bishop and martyr. Born in Cashel, Ireland, he went to Scotland as a missioner, became bishop of Boyne and Leven, and settled on an island in Loch Lomond. It is not certain whether he was killed at Bandry or on the Continent. F. D. Mar. 10.

KETCHAM, WILLIAM HENRY (1868–1921). Born in Summer, Iowa, he was a convert while at St. Charles College, Louisiana, was ordained in Cincinnati in 1892, and became a missioner among the Creek and Cherokee Indians. He added the Choctaws in 1897, built schools and new mission centers, and ten years later was named director of Catholic Indian missions at Washington. He regained for Indian parents the right to choose their own schools and to receive religious instruction. He wrote a catechism and hymns in Choctaw, was made a monsignor in 1919, and died in Tucker, Mississippi, on Nov. 14.

KETTELER, WILHELM EMMANUEL VON (1811–1877), bishop. Born in Münster, Westphalia, on Dec. 25, he studied at Munich and the Münster seminary, where he was ordained in 1843. He served as curate in Beckum in 1844 and rector of Hopsten in 1846, was elected to the Frankfort parliament in 1848, and attracted wide attention by his speeches and sermons on freedom and the social needs of the German people. In 1850, Pope Pius IX appointed him bishop of Mainz. He quickly became the leader in the fight against state encroachment of ecclesiastical rights, argued for the establishment of theological seminaries, opposed the anti-Roman attitude of many German clerics, urged social reforms on the government and defended the intervention of the Church to remove economic inequities, supported the workers, denounced liberalism, and was a bitter opponent of political and capitalistic absolutism. He believed the definition of the dogma of papal infallibility in 1869 undesirable but submitted to the Vatican Council, prior to its decision, when it proclaimed the dogma. When the unification of Germany took place in 1870–71, he demanded that Bismarck offer the Catholics of Germany the rights Catholics in Prussia had enjoyed, resigned his seat in the German *Reichstag* in 1872 when it was evident religious persecution was to break out, and led the resistance movement. He wrote *The Labor Question and Christianity* (1864), *Liberty, Authority, and the Church,* and *Catholics in the German Empire* (1873). He died in Burghausen, Germany, on July 13.

KETTLE, THOMAS MICHAEL (1880–1916), poet. Born in Dublin, he studied at Clongowes Wood and graduated with honors from University College, Dublin, was admitted to the bar in 1906, became editor of the *Nationist,* and was elected to parliament, representing Tyrone until 1910. In 1909 he held the chair of economics at the National University, married Mary Sheehy, and was a governor of University College. He made translations from the French and German, published *The Day's Burden* (a collection of essays) and a volume of poetry. He organized the Irish National Volunteers in 1914 against the threatened action of Sir Edward Carson, and when World War I began enlisted in the British army. He was a lieutenant with a Leinster regiment when he was killed in battle at Ginchy, France, on Sept. 9.

KEUMURJIAN, BL. GOMIDAS (1656–1707), martyr. Born in Constantinople, son of a priest of the dissident Armenian church, he married at twenty, became a priest, and in 1696, with his family, renounced his schism and acknowledged Rome. He spent some time at the Armenian monastery of St. James in Jerusalem, but because of his Catholicism he was forced to return to Constantinople in 1702. In 1707 he was arrested and condemned to the galleys, but was ransomed by friends. He continued to preach reunion with Rome, was rearrested at the instigation of Armenian priests, offered his freedom if he would embrace Mohammedanism, and when he refused was beheaded. He was beatified in 1929. F. D. Nov. 5.

KEVENHOERSTER, JOHN BERNARD (1869–1949), bishop. Born in Germany on Nov. 1, he studied in Minnesota at St. John's College and the state university, became a Benedictine in 1892, was ordained in 1896, taught at St. John's to 1907, and was pastor of St. Anselm's church in New York City for twenty-three years. He was appointed prefect

apostolic of the Bahamas in 1931 and was consecrated titular bishop of Camuliana in 1933. He became vicar apostolic of the Bahamas in 1941, and died in Nassau, Bahamas, on Dec. 9.

KEVIN, ST. (d. 618?). Said to have been born in Leinster, Ireland, baptized by St. Cronan, and educated by St. Petroc, he took up a life of solitude, eventually settling at Glendalough, where he founded and became abbot of a monastic settlement for his followers. His shrine became a major attraction for pilgrims. F. D. June 3.

KEYES, ERASMUS DARWIN (1810–1895), soldier. Born in Brimfield, Massachusetts, on May 29, he studied at West Point, served in Indian campaigns, rose to captain in 1837, and taught at West Point in 1854–58. He served with the Union army during the Civil War as a brigadier general, left the army in 1864, went to California, where he became a convert in 1866, and engaged in mining and other businesses. He died in Nice, France, on Oct. 14.

KEYES, MICHAEL JOSEPH (1876–1959), bishop. Born in Dingle, Kerry, Ireland, on Feb. 28, he joined the Society of Mary (Marists), in 1901 and was professed in 1905, studied at the Marist seminary, Washington, D.C., and was ordained there in 1907. He taught at the Marist college until 1922, when he was consecrated bishop of Savannah. He resigned in 1935 and was appointed titular bishop of Aeropolis. He died on July 31.

KEYNA, ST. (5th century). Alleged daughter of Brychan of Brecknock, she lived as a hermit in Somersetshire, and died in Wales. Keynsham is named after her. F. D. Oct. 8.

KIARA, ST. (d. 680). She became a religious under the direction of St. Fintan Munnu, and lived near Nenagh, Tipperary, Ireland, a locality now called Kilkeary after her. F. D. Jan. 5 (also, Oct. 16).

KICKHAM, CHARLES JOSEPH (1828–1882), novelist. He was born in Mullinahone, Tipperary, Ireland, took part in the Young Ireland Movement in 1848, later joined the Fenians, was an editor of *The Irish People,* was arrested in Dublin for treason, sentenced to prison for fourteen years, many of them in solitary confinement, and released in 1869. Previously active as a journalist whose work appeared in half a dozen journals under various pen names, he then turned to short stories, and to such successful novels of village life, absentee landlordism, farming, and emigration as *Sally Kavanagh* (1869), *Knocknagow* (1879), and *For the Old Land* (1886). He died in Blackrock, Ireland, on Aug. 22.

KIERAN, JAMES MICHAEL (1863–1936), educator. Born in New York City on Aug. 23, he studied at City College and St. Francis Xavier, and taught in the public schools from

1883 until 1900, when he became a principal. In 1904 he began teaching philosophy and education at Hunter, reorganized the curriculum, and was dean of the college in 1927–28 and then its president until he retired in 1933. In 1912 he founded the New York Academy of Public Education; while at Hunter he developed the uptown campus in the Bronx, made major contributions to the education of women, and initiated and organized Newman clubs in non-Catholic schools. He received honorary degrees from Fordham and Holy Cross. He died in New York City on Apr. 25.

KIERAN OF SAIGHIR, ST. (d. 530?), bishop. Believed to have been Irish-born, and consecrated by St. Patrick at the beginning of the Irish mission, he is considered the first bishop of Ossory and founder of a monastery at Sier-Ciaran, Ireland. F. D. Mar. 5.

KIERAN THE YOUNGER, ST. (d. 556?). He was born in Connacht, Ireland, son of Beoit, a carpenter. At fifteen he went to Clonnard to study under St. Finian and was one of a group eventually called "the twelve apostles of Ireland." He spent seven years on Aran with St. Enda, then visited monasteries throughout Ireland, and became abbot-founder of Clonmacnois in West Meath. F. D. Sept. 9.

KIGWE. *See* Ciwa, St.

KILEY, MOSES ELIAS (1876–1953), archbishop. Born in Margaree, Inverness, Nova Scotia, on Nov. 13, he studied at St. Laurent College, Montreal, St. Mary's seminary, Baltimore, and the North American college, Rome, and was ordained in Rome in 1911. He did parish work in Chicago, was first diocesan director of Catholic Charities there in 1916–26, was made a domestic prelate in 1924, and was appointed spiritual director of the North American College in Rome in 1926 and a consultor on the Russian Commission in 1929. He was appointed bishop of Trenton, New Jersey, in 1934, was promoted to archbishop of Milwaukee, Wisconsin, in 1940, and died there on Apr. 15.

KILIAN, ST. (d. 689), bishop and martyr. An Irish missioner, he was commissioned by Pope John V in 686 to preach the gospel in Baden and Bavaria. He was most successful, and converted Gosbert, duke of Würzburg, who had married his brother's widow Geilana. According to legend, he convinced Gosbert that such a marriage was forbidden, whereupon Geilana, in Gosbert's absence, had Kilian and two companions, Colman, a monk, and Totnan, a deacon, beheaded. F. D. July 8.

KILIAN, ST. (7th century), abbot. He directed a monastery on the island of Inishcaltra, Ireland, and wrote a biography of St. Brigid. F. D. July 29.

KILIAN, ST. (7th century). An Irishman related to St. Fiacre, he became a missionary in Artois, with headquarters at Aubigny, Gaul, where he built a church. F. D. Nov. 13.

KILMER, ALFRED JOYCE (1886–1918), poet. Born in New Brunswick, New Jersey, on Dec. 6, he studied at Rutgers and Columbia, and held several editorial positions, including literary staff work with the New York *Times* from 1908 to 1917. He married Aline Murray in 1908, became a convert in 1913, and published collections of essays (*The Circus*, 1916, and *Literature in the Making*, 1917), poems (*Trees*, 1915, *Main Street*, 1917), and an anthology of Catholic poetry. By his popular style and enthusiastic lectures, he helped to give an impetus to Catholic letters supplementing that of T. A. Daly, Maurice Egan, Louise Guiney, and Agnes Repplier. Kilmer enlisted in the 69th New York Regiment and was killed in World War I in battle along the Ourcy River in France on July 30.

KILWARDBY, ROBERT (d. 1279), cardinal. After studying at Paris and probably at Oxford he taught at Paris for many years and then became a Dominican. He served as provincial of England from 1261 to 1272, when he was appointed archbishop of Canterbury. He attended the Council of Lyons in 1274, where he supported the papal authority, held provincial synods in 1273 and 1277, and instituted ecclesiastical reforms in the diocese. He was appointed cardinal-bishop of Porto and Santa Rufina in 1278 and on his departure for his new see took the archives of Canterbury with him. They were never returned and disappeared. He wrote on philosophy, theology, and grammar, *De divisione scientiarum*, *De passione Christi*, and *De sacramento altaris* being read for many years. He died in Viterbo, Italy, on Sept. 11.

KIM, BL. ANDREW (d. 1846), martyr. A priest of the Society of Missions of Paris, he was the first of seventy-five native Koreans to die during a decade-long persecution. They were beatified in 1925. F. D. Sept. 22.

KIMURA, BL. ANTONY (1595–1619), martyr. A Japanese, he and others of royal blood, including Thomas Cotenda, John Ivanango, John Montajana, and Leo Nacanixi were beheaded at Nagasaki. They were beatified in 1867. F. D. Nov. 27.

KING, HARRIET HAMILTON (1860?–1920), poet. Daughter of Adm. W. A. Hamilton, she engaged in social-welfare work in London, met Mazzini, wrote *The Disciples* in illustration of his ideals, and married her publisher, Henry Samuel King. She later became a convert, and published *Aspromonte*, *A Book of Dreams*, *Ballads of the North*, and the metaphysical *Hours of the Passion*. She died in London on May 10.

KINO, EUSEBIUS FRANCISCO (1645–1711), missioner. Born in Segno, Italy, prob-

ably on Aug. 10, he studied in Trent and Innsbruck, became a Jesuit in 1665, and after ordination volunteered for the missions and was sent to Mexico. He reached there in 1681, published *Explicación astronómica del cometo*, and in 1683 was appointed royal cartographer for a colonizing expedition to California. When the project was abandoned in 1686, he turned to missionary activities in northern Sonora and southern Arizona. Having pioneered the overland route from Mexico to Lower California, proving it not an island but a peninsula, he established headquarters at Mission Dolores in northern Sonora and used it as a base for founding a score of missions. He traveled all over southwestern North America, exploring hitherto unknown country and making maps. He was so successful with the Indians that he was called the "Apostle of the Pimas," introduced cattle ranching in the Southwest, and pioneered in the planting of wheat, European cereals, and fruit in California. He wrote hundreds of letters, drew maps which brought him recognition as an outstanding cartographer, and wrote his autobiography, *Favores celestiales*, which, undiscovered until 1907, was published in 1919. His name is also spelled Kühn. He died in Magdalena, Mexico, on Mar. 15.
HERBERT E. BOLTON, *Rim of Christendom* (New York, Macmillan, 1936).

KIRBY, BL. LUKE (d. 1582), martyr. An English university graduate, he went to the Continent, studied at Douai and Rome, and was sent to the English mission in 1580, underwent exceptional tortures in the Tower, and was hanged, drawn, and quartered at Tyburn. He was beatified in 1886. F. D. May 30.

KIRCHER, ATHANASIUS (1601–1680), scholar. Born in Geisa, Germany, on May 2, he studied in Fulda, became a Jesuit in 1618, studied at Cologne and Mainz, and was ordained in 1628. Appointed professor of mathematics at Würzburg, he was called to Rome by Pope Urban VIII to fill the chair of mathematics at the Roman College. He made a study of Vesuvius in eruption in 1638 (he had himself lowered into the crater to get data for his investigation of subterranean power). He began a collection of antiquities which led to the founding of the Museum Kircherianum, made outstanding contributions in the field of hieroglyphics and linguistics, became an expert on philology, and invented the "magic lantern." The variety and extent of his knowledge and interests were regarded as astounding by his colleagues. He wrote prolifically: *Mundus subterraneus, Oedipus Egyptiacus, Magnes sive de arte magnetica*, and *Ars magna lucis et umbrae* were outstanding. He died in Rome on Nov. 28.

KIRKMAN, BL. RICHARD (d. 1582), martyr. Born in Addingham, Yorkshire, England,

he studied at Douai, was ordained at Rheims in 1579, became tutor to Robert Dymoke's children at Scrivelsby, Lincolnshire, and served as pastor to neighboring Catholics. Forced to flee when the Dymokes were convicted of not attending Anglican services, he worked secretly in Yorkshire and Northumberland, was arrested near Wakefield, accused of treason for not acknowledging Queen Elizabeth's spiritual supremacy, and hanged, drawn, and quartered at Knavesmire, outside York. He was beatified in 1886. F. D. Aug. 22.

KIRSCH, JOHANN PETER (1861–1941), historian. Born in Dippach, Luxembourg, on Nov. 3, he studied there and in Rome, was ordained in 1884, became head of the Historical Institute of the Görresgesellschaft in 1888, and in 1890 was named professor of history at Fribourg. He became a monsignor, revised Hergenröther's work on church history, wrote on the Avignon residence of the papacy and other studies, and edited several scholarly periodicals. He died in Rome.

KISFALUDY, KAROLY (1788–1830), author. Born in Tét, Hungary, on Feb. 5, brother of Sándor, he studied in Raab, saw army service as an officer in Italy (where he was captured by the French) and Germany, resigned in 1811, and became an artist in Vienna. On his return to Hungary he began writing and in 1819 his play, *The Tartar in Hungary*, brought him immediate success. This was followed by *Ilka, Stiber the Chieftain*, and his popular comedy, *The Student Matthias*. In 1821 he established *Aurora*, a literary annual. He also wrote poetry and fiction, became the center of the Hungarian literary world, and died in Pest, Hungary, on Nov. 21.

KISFALUDY, SANDOR (1772–1844), poet. Born in Sümeg, Hungary, brother of Károly, on Sept. 27, he studied in Raab and law at Presburg, but left in 1792 to enter the army. He was captured at Milan in 1796 by the French, released, left the army in 1799, and married Rosa Szagedy. In 1802 he took part in the uprising of the Hungarian nobles. He was famous for his love songs (1801 and 1807), *John Huniades*, and *Ladislaus the Cumanian*, was elected to the Hungarian Academy in 1830, and died in Sümeg, Hungary, on Oct. 28.

KITSON, SAMUEL Z. (1848–1906), sculptor. Born in Huddersfield, Yorkshire, England, on Jan. 1, he studied anatomy and sculpture at Leeds, was in Rome after 1871, where he won four prizes in two years, received many commissions, and soon settled in the United States. He completed busts of Longfellow, Samuel Tilden, Philip Sheridan, and Cardinal Gibbons, the Civil War Memorial in Hartford, Connecticut, and a *Christ the Light of the World* for St. Joseph's seminary, Yonkers, New York. In 1889 he became a convert in

Boston, where he had opened a studio. He died in New York City on Nov. 9.

KLACZKO, JULIAN (1825–1906), author. Born in Vilna, Poland, on Nov. 6, of Jewish parents, he received his doctorate from Königsberg in 1847, studied at Heidelberg, published *Sonnets*, and became a collaborator on the political journal *Deutsche Zeitung*. In 1850 he went to Paris and by a series of articles in *Revue de Deux Mondes* gained recognition as a brilliant political writer. He became a convert and in 1857 began publishing *Wiadomości polskie*, which was forced to suspend in 1860 when banned in Russian Poland and Prussia. His *Études de diplomatie*, sharply critical of European diplomacy, and *Les préliminaires de Sadowa*, an exposé of how Austria was maneuvered into war with Prussia, caused a sensation when published in 1866. Appointed to the ministry of foreign affairs with a seat in the Austrian *Reichsrat*, he resigned in protest in 1870 against Austria's neutrality in the Franco-Prussian War and returned to Paris. He wrote on Dante (*Causeries florentines*), *Les deux chanceliers*, and was engaged on *La Papauté et la renaissance*, of which he had finished one volume, when he was stricken with a paralysis which endured for eight years until his death in Cracow, Poland, on Nov. 26.

KLARMANN, ANDREW F. (1866–1931), author. Born in Oberhaid, Bavaria, Germany, he went to the United States with his brother Charles in 1881, studied at St. Vincent's, Latrobe, Pennsylvania, and became a diocesan priest in Brooklyn on his ordination in 1892. After work as a curate he became pastor of St. Elizabeth's in 1901 and of St. Thomas the Apostle in 1909. He wrote a matrimonial primer and on pastoral medicine and, using the pseudonym Virgil B. Fairman, such plays as *Felix Aeturnus*, *Lost Ring*, and *Vision*, and such novels as *The Princess of Gan-Sar*, *King's Banner*, and *Nizra*. He died in Queens, New York, on Mar. 24.

KLEE, HEINRICH (1800–1840), theologian. Born in Münstermaifeld, Germany, on Apr. 20, he studied at the Mainz seminary, was ordained in 1823, and taught exegesis and theology there in 1824. He took his doctorate at Würzburg and in 1829 became professor at Bonn, where he clashed with Georg Hermes and his followers. In 1839 he filled the chair of dogmatic theology and exegesis at Munich, Bavaria, where he died on July 28. He wrote scriptural commentaries and theological treatises.

KLESL, MELCHIOR (1552–1630), cardinal. Born in Vienna, on Feb. 19, son of a baker, he studied at the university there, was converted with his parents, received his doctorate in 1579, became chancellor of the university, and was ordained. He became chancellor of the

bishop of Passau and the leader of the counter-Reformation in Lower Austria, where he was most successful. He was appointed imperial chancellor by Emperor Rudolf II in 1585 and in 1588, and court chaplain and administrator of the diocese of Wiener-Neustadt. He was made bishop of Vienna in 1598 (but was not consecrated until 1614), became head of the privy council in 1611, and on the accession of Matthias, whom he dominated, to the throne in 1612 practically ran the government. He was named cardinal in 1616. His indecision about taking action against the rebelling Bohemians in 1618 caused Archdukes Max of Tyrol and Ferdinand of Steiermark to seize him, and he remained a prisoner until released by Emperor Ferdinand II in 1623. He was reinstated in his see in 1628 and died in Wiener-Neustadt, Austria, on Sept. 18.

KLEUTGEN, JOSEF WILHELM KARL (1811–1883), theologian. Born in Dortmund, Westphalia, on Apr. 9, he studied at Munich and the Münster and Paderborn seminaries, became a Jesuit in 1834, and was ordained in 1837. He taught at Fribourg (1837–39), Brig (1840–43), and at the German College, Rome, until 1874. He was secretary to the general of the Jesuits in 1856–62, consultor to the Congregation of the Index, and helped to prepare *De fide catholica* for the Vatican Council. He also prepared the first draft of Pope Leo XIII's encyclical *Aeterni Patris* and became a proponent of St. Thomas Aquinas' teaching and a leader in reviving scholasticism. He wrote theological treatises and died at St. Anton, Tyrol, on Jan. 13.

KLINKOWSTROM, FRIEDRICH AUGUST VON (1778–1835), artist. Born in Ludwigsburg, Pomerania, on Aug. 31, he served with the Swedish army in 1793, but resigned his commission in 1802 to study art in Dresden, Paris, and Rome. He taught in Vienna, rejoined the army in 1813, and became a convert in 1815. He illustrated children's books and from 1818 to 1834 was head of a Viennese school for children of the nobility. He died in Vienna on Apr. 4.

KLOPP, ONNO (1822–1903), historian. Born in Leer, East Friesland, on Oct. 9, he studied at Bonn, Berlin, and Göttingen, took his doctorate at Jena, and taught at the Osnabrück gymnasium from 1846 to 1858. Because he criticized King Frederick II of Prussia in the third volume of a commissioned history of East Friesland he lost his teaching post. In 1865 he was appointed state archivist of Hanover, served as ambassador to Prussia for King George V of Hanover in 1866, and in 1873 moved to Vienna, where he became a convert. He wrote on educational reform; methods of teaching foreign languages; German, Prussian, and Austrian history; a fourteen-volume history of the English Stuarts; and an eleven-volume edition of Gottfried Liebniz. He died in Vienna on Aug. 9.

KNABL, JOSEPH (1819–1881), sculptor. Born in Fliess, Tyrol, he studied wood carving in Imst and Munich, became an instructor in the Meyer Institute in 1859, and four years later professor of ecclesiastical sculpture at the Munich Academy. Outstanding are his *Coronation of the Virgin, Christ and the Apostles,* and *Christ on the Cross,* characterized by skillful technique and delicacy of coloring. He died in Munich, Germany.

KNEIPP, SEBASTIAN (1821–1897). Born in Stephansreid, Bavaria, on May 17, he became a weaver, entered the seminary at Munich, and was ordained in 1852. He was a curate in several towns and was made a monsignor by Pope Leo XIII. He experimented in hydrotherapy, gained a wide following by his many apparent cures, and wrote a book on his method of treatment. He died in Wörishofen, Germany, where he had been stationed since 1855, on June 17.

KNIAZNIN, FRANCISZEK DYONIZY (1750–1807), poet. Born in Vitenbsk, Poland, he became a Jesuit, and, when his Society was suppressed in 1773, secretary to Prince Adam Czartoryski. He wrote many laudatory poems for the latter's family, translated Horace and Macpherson's *Ossian* into Polish, and wrote popular sentimental dramas such as *The Spartan Mother* and *The Gypsies.*

KNIGHT, VEN. WILLIAM (d. 1596), martyr. Son of Leonard Knight of South Duffield, England, he was denounced for his Catholicism by his uncle as he came of age and sought to inherit his father's property, and was imprisoned at York with George Errington of Herst and William Gibson of Ripon. While in prison he explained Catholicism to a fellow prisoner, a Protestant clergyman; the latter reported the action after his release and after he had obtained directions from Henry Abbot of Howden, Yorkshire, as to the location of a priest who might give further instructions. Knight, Abbot, Errington, and Gibson were hanged, drawn, and quartered at York, England, on Nov. 29.

KNIGHTON, HENRY (14th century), historian. A canon of St. Mary's, Leicester, England, he wrote *Historiae Anglicanae scriptores decem,* a chronicle of the years 959–1366, the fourth book of which is of particular value as an eyewitness record.

KNÖBLECHER, IGNATIUS (1819–1855), missioner. Born on July 6 in St. Cantian, Carniola, Austria, he studied in Laibach and the Propaganda, Rome, and was ordained in 1845. He was sent to Africa in 1846, became provicar apostolic of Central Africa in 1848, led an expedition to the source of the White Nile in 1849 (of which he published an account), returned to Austria in 1850 to raise funds, and on his return in 1852 established missions at Gondokoro and Angweyn. He died in Naples, Italy, on Apr. 13.

KNOLL, ALBERT JOSEPH (1796–1863), theologian. Born in Bruneck (Brunico), Tyrol, on July 12, he became a Capuchin, was ordained in 1818, and taught theology in Meran from 1823 to 1847, when he was elected definitor general and went to Rome. He returned to the Tyrol in 1853 and died in Bozen (Bolzano), Italy, on Mar. 30. He was the author of several theological treatises.

KNÖPFLER, ALOIS (1847–1920), historian. Born in Schomburg, Würtemberg, on Aug. 29, he studied at Tübingen, was ordained in 1874, became editor of two scholarly journals of church history, and wrote on Albert V of Bavaria, *Lehrbuch der Kirchengeschichte,* and several related studies.

KNOX, RONALD ARBUTHNOTT (1888–1957), author. Born in Kibworth, Leicestershire, England, on Feb. 17, he studied at Eton and Oxford, became a fellow of Trinity, and in 1912 an Anglican minister, serving as chaplain at Oxford until 1917. He became a convert in 1917 and was ordained in 1919 after additional theological studies at St. Edmund's, Westminster. Early work was characterized by wit and satire: *Barchester Pilgrimage, Reunion All Around,* and *Essays in Satire.* A *Spiritual Aeneid* (1918) was autobiographical; a number of popular mystery stories followed; mellow observations marked his *Let Dons Delight; Enthusiasm* studied various religious movements. In his later years he published many collections of sermons, retreat notes, broadcast talks, and spiritual readings. His final achievement was his translation of the Old and New Testaments, begun in 1943. He died in Melles, England, on Aug. 24.

EVELYN WAUGH, *Msgr. Ronald Knox* (Boston, Little Brown, 1959).

KOBER, FRANZ QUIRIN VON (1821–1897), theologian. Born in Warthausen, Würtemberg, Germany, on Mar. 6, he studied in Ehingen and Tübingen, and was ordained in 1845. He became a tutor at Tübingen in 1846 and professor of canon law and pedagogy in 1857. He wrote such theological works as *Der Kirchenbann, Die Deposition und Degradation,* and articles on ecclesiastical subjects. He died at Tübingen, Germany, on Jan. 25.

KOBERGER, ANTHONY (1445?–1513), publisher. A native of Nuremberg, Germany, he became a goldsmith, but early became interested in printing, and in 1470 established the first press in Nuremberg. He published his first dated volume in 1472, a German bible with woodcuts in 1483 (he was to publish fifteen editions by 1500), in 1484 the first book printed in Hungarian, and in 1493 *Weltchronik* with 2000 woodcuts, which had a great influence on later book illustration. By the end of the century Koberger had published some 200 books. He employed traveling salesmen, established agencies in many cities, made use of advertising brochures, produced scientific treatises, and was the largest publisher of his day. He died in Nuremberg on Oct. 3.

KOBLER, ANDREAS (1816–1892), historian. Born in Mühldorf, Bavaria, on June 22, he studied at Landshut and Munich, and was ordained in 1840. After serving as a curate, he became a Jesuit in 1844 and was sent to New York in 1848. On his return in 1853 he taught at Presburg until 1857 and Innsbruck, where he was professor of history until 1871, serving as rector from 1861 to 1866. He taught mathematics at the college in Linz, where he was rector for two years, then returned to Innsbruck, to write. In 1887 he was appointed superior of the seminary in Klagenfurt, Austria, where he died on Nov. 15. He wrote on his Society, ninth-century education, mediaeval learning, and the English martyrs of 1550–1681.

KOCHANOWSKI, JAN (1530–1584), poet. He was born in Sycyna, Poland, studied at Cracow and Padua, lived in France, and returned to Poland on his mother's death in 1557 to receive his inheritance. After serving as a royal courtier and secretary he retired to his estate and died in Lublin, Poland, on Aug. 22. Kochanowski was the first great Polish poet, wrote Latin elegies, Polish songs and lyrics, political pamphlets, translated the Psalms (for which he was called the "Pindar" of Poland) and in 1579 produced a psalter. Among his works are *Fraski, Dziewoslab, Sobotka, Odprawa posłów grekich*, and *Treny*.

KOCHOWSKI, VESPASIAN (1633–1699), poet. Probably born in Sandomir, Poland, he studied at the Jesuit college there, was a friend of King John III Sobieski, and accompanied him to Vienna in 1684 when the Polish king raised the siege by driving off the Turks (he wrote *Commentarius de bello adversus Turcas* to commemorate the event). He became famous for his historical and patriotic poetry, but also wrote love, religious, and satirical poetry. He died in Cracow, Poland.

KÖGLER, IGNAZ (1680–1746), missioner. Born in Landsberg, Bavaria, on May 11, he entered the Jesuits in 1696, taught at Ingolstadt in 1712–14, was ordained, and sent to China in 1715. He attracted the attention of the emperor in Peking by his learning and became president of the astronomical tribunal (a position he held thirty years), a mandarin, the first foreigner to be a member of the supreme court of equity, and served as pro-

vincial of the Chinese and Japanese province. He died in Peking on Mar. 30.

KOHLMANN, ANTHONY (1771–1836). Born in Kaiserberg, Alsace, on July 13, he studied at Fribourg, where he was ordained. In 1796 he joined the Fathers of the Sacred Heart, served as military chaplain for two years, and then was sent to Dillingen, Bavaria, as director of the seminary. After a period at colleges in Berlin and Amsterdam, he joined the newly recognized Jesuits in Russia and entered their novitiate in Dunébourg in 1803. The following year he was sent to Georgetown in the United States and did missionary work in nearby states. In 1808, Bishop Carroll sent him to administer ecclesiastical affairs in New York (which had no bishop as yet), where he initiated needed reforms and established several schools. He became embroiled in a noted case when he successfully refused to break the seal of the confessional, and a book he wrote to accompany the trial report, *The Catholic Question in America*, aroused great controversy. In 1815 he returned to Georgetown, became president of Gonzaga College in 1817, and in 1821 published *Unitarianism, Theologically and Philosophically Considered*. In 1824 he was appointed to the chair of theology at the Gregorian, Rome, and served there until 1829 when he was assigned to the church of the Gésu. He died in Rome on Apr. 11.

KOL (d. 1220). He became bishop of Linköping, Sweden, about 1160 and was killed in battle with pagans at Rotala, Estonia, on Aug. 8.

KOLLER, MARIAN WOLFGANG (1792–1866). Born in Feistritz, Carniola, Austria, on Oct. 31, he studied at Laibach and Vienna, tutored in Steinback for two years, became a Benedictine in 1816, and was ordained in 1821. After three years of pastoral work he taught natural history and physics at Kremsmünster and in 1830 was appointed director of the astronomical observatory. In 1847 he was called to the university of Vienna and helped reorganize the *Realschulen* for the department of education. He died in Vienna on Oct. 31.

KOLOMAN, king of Hungary. *See* Coloman.

KONARSKI, STANISLAUS (1700–1773), educator. Born in Konary, near Cracow, Poland, he joined the Piarists and after his ordination visited Rome where he decided to devote himself to reforming the political and educational system in Poland. He studied French and German education at first hand and on his return to Poland supported King Stanislaus Leszczynski, but, when the latter was forced to abdicate in 1736, decided education must precede political reforms. He educated a new group of teachers in his methods, and provided new textbooks, opened a college for young noblemen in Warsaw in 1740, secured Benedict XIV's permission to amend his order's rule so that every Piarist would be a teacher, and in 1754 opened a Piarist college in Warsaw, providing a steady supply of teachers. When the effects of these moves began to be felt, he turned his attention to politics and secured the abolition of the one-vote veto in the diet by his *Effective Way of Deliberating*. He wrote *De religione honestorum hominum* (to clear himself of a charge of unorthodoxy), *Epaminondas*, a tragedy, and *Volumina legum*.

KÖNIG, JOSEPH (1819–1900). Born in Hausen, Baden, on Sept. 7, he was ordained in 1845 and taught exegesis at Freiburg from 1847 to 1894. He edited the *Freiburger Diozesan-Archiv* and wrote scriptural commentaries. He died in Freiburg, Germany, on June 22.

KÖNIGSHOFEN, JACOB VON. See Twinger, Jacob.

KONINGS, ANTHONY (1821–1884), theologian. Born in Helmond, Holland, he studied at the diocesan seminary, but in 1842 entered the Redemptorists and was ordained in 1848. After teaching and serving as master of novices, he was appointed rector of Amsterdam and then of the Wittem house of studies in 1860. He was appointed provincial of Holland in 1865, but in 1870 was sent to the United States to teach theology and canon law in the Redemptorist house of studies in Ilchester, Maryland, where he died on July 30.

KONRAD (12th century), poet. A German priest in the service of Duke Henry the Proud of Bavaria, he wrote *Rolandslied*, a version of the French *Chanson de Roland*, which he translated into Latin prose and then into German verse about 1131, probably in Ratisbon, Bavaria.

KONRAD OF HOCHSTADEN (d. 1261), archbishop. He became archbishop of Cologne, Germany, in 1238, and defended the pope against Emperor Frederick II, a stand which resulted in his being beaten and imprisoned. He escaped to crown William of Holland as emperor in 1248 and on William's death consecrated Richard of Cornwall in 1257, both against Frederick, who had been declared deposed by Pope Innocent IV. His quarrel with the Hohenstaufen faction ended in 1259 when he regained control of Cologne.

KONRAD OF LICHTENAU (d. 1240), historian. He left the Swabian court to become a monk, probably in Rome, joined the Premonstratensians, was appointed abbot of their monastery in Ursperg, Bavaria, in 1226 and spent the remainder of his life there. He was one of the authors of *Chronicon Urspergense*, a world history from King Ninus to 1229, and probably wrote only of the period from 1225 to 1229.

KONRAD OF MARBURG (d. 1233). A Dominican, he was confessor to St. Elizabeth, wife of Louis IV of Thuringia, was named chief inquisitor for Germany by Pope Gregory IX, and was so severe that the bishops pleaded with the pope for his removal. He was assassinated near Marburg, Prussia.

KONRAD OF MEGENBERG (1309?–1374?), author. Probably born in Mainberg, Bavaria, on Feb. 2, he studied at Erfurt and Paris, where he taught philosophy for several years, and was appointed head of St. Stephen's school in Vienna in 1337. He became a parish priest at Ratisbon in 1342, a cathedral canon, a noted preacher, a member of the town council, and a prolific author. Among his works are *Das Buch der Natur* (c. 1349), the first natural history written in German and based in part on the Latin of the Dominican Thomas de Cantimpré, *Sphaere, Oeconomica, Tractatus contra mendicentes, Speculum felicitatis humanae*, poems, biographies, and local history. He died in Ratisbon, Germany, on Apr. 11.

KONRAD OF WÜRZBURG (1230?–1287), poet. Probably born in Strassburg, Germany, he lived much of his life in Basle, Switzerland, where he died. He was a follower of Gottfried of Strassburg and was indebted also to Chrestien de Troyes and Benoit de St. More. His epic *Der Schwanritter* (which does not mention the Grail) influenced Wagner's *Lohengrin*; other long poems include *Trojarnerkrieg; Engelhart*, on the theme of friendship; *Partonopier*, a French romance; and the allegorical *Der Welte Lohn* (*The World's Reward*). His shorter *Herzemäre* (*Tale of a Heart*) deals with knightly love; *Die goldene Schmiede* (*The Golden Forge*) honors the Virgin Mary; and *Klage der Kunst* allegorizes art's lament for the decay of poetic taste. He also wrote poetic narratives of legends of St. Alexius, Pope Sylvester, and a number of martyrs.

KONSAG, FERDINAND (1703–1758), missioner. Born in Warasdin, Croatia, on Dec. 2, he became a Jesuit in 1719 and was sent to Mexico in 1730. He served as superior of San Ignacio and as visitator of Lower California, where he spent the rest of his life. He prepared maps of the region and wrote historical accounts of the missions. He died on Sept. 10.

KOPP, GEORG (1837–1915), cardinal. Born in Duderstadt, Germany, on July 25, he studied there and in Hildesheim, was ordained in 1862, made vicar general of Hildesheim in 1871, and bishop of Fulda in 1878. He was strong in opposition to the Kulturkampf, was often in consultation with Bismarck, became a member of the Prussian house of lords in 1886, and in 1888 was made bishop of Breslau. This see included Silesia and parts of Austria; in it he established a seminary, developed social welfare, built industrial centers, and saw 650 Church institutions rise during his reign. He was named a cardinal in 1904 and died in Breslau, Germany, on Mar. 4.

KOROSHETZ, ANTON (1872–1940), premier. Born in Jugoslavia, he was ordained, led the Slovene Catholic party, served as minister to the Vatican, held several cabinet posts, was premier in 1928, and died in Belgrade, Yugoslavia, on Dec. 14.

KÖRÖSY, BL. MARK (d. 1619), martyr. Of a distinguished Croat family, he studied at the Germanicum in Rome and returned to Esztergom, Hungary, where he served as a canon. With Bl. Stephen Pongracz, a Hungarian Jesuit, and Bl. Melchior Grodecz, a Czech Jesuit, he was seized near Kosice, Slovakia, by Calvinist soldiers, tortured and put to death. They were beatified in 1905. F. D. Sept. 7.

KOSCIUSZKO, TADEUSZ ANDRZEJ BONAWENTURA (1746–1817), general. Born near Novogrudek, Lithuania (then Poland), on Feb. 12, he studied at the Jesuit college in Breese, the Royal School in Warsaw, and engineering at Mézières. On his return to Poland in 1774 he became a captain in the army and in 1776 went to the American colonies to volunteer his services. He served through the revolution with distinction, achieving the rank of brigadier general, and returned to Poland in 1786. In 1789 he fought against the Russians as a major general, defeating a force of 18,000 with only 4000 men at Dubienka. When King Stanislaus surrendered in 1792, Kosciuszko retired to Leipzig, but returned to the army in 1794 to head the Polish army. With a force of 4000 peasants armed with scythes and farming tools he defeated a Russian army of 6000 at Raclawice. He formed a provisional government, lost to a Prussian force, then to a Russian pincer attack at Maciejowice, and was imprisoned for two years. He went to the United States in 1797 and received a hero's welcome, returned to his estate in Berville, near Paris, the next year, and remained there until 1816. He died in Solothurn, Switzerland, on Oct. 15.

KOSTKA, STANISLAUS. *See* Stanislaus Kostka, St.

KOUDELKA, JOSEPH MARIA (1852–1921), bishop. Born in Chlistov, Czechoslovakia, on Dec. 8, he studied at Klatau, Austria, went to the United States in 1868, studied at St. Francis seminary, Milwaukee, and was ordained in 1875. He did pastoral work in Cleveland, was intensely interested in the welfare of Bohemian immigrants in the United States, edited a Bohemian weekly, *Hlas*, prepared a series of textbooks for Bohemian Catholic schools, became rector of St. Michael's church in Cleveland, and in 1908 was consecrated titular bishop of Germanicopolis and auxiliary bishop of Cleveland with special

jurisdiction over the Slavs in the diocese—the first special-jurisdiction auxiliary bishop appointed for the United States. He was transferred to Milwaukee as auxiliary in 1911, was made bishop of Superior, Wisconsin, in 1913, and died in Superior on June 24.

KOZMIAN, JOHN (1812–1877), author. He was born in Warsaw but was forced to flee to France for his participation in the abortive revolt of 1831. There he married, but on the death of his wife became a priest, took up residence in Posen, and became editor of the *Posen Review*, to which he contributed numerous articles collected and published in three volumes.

KOZMIAN, STANISLAUS (1811–1885), author. Brother of John and born in Warsaw where he was educated, he was forced to flee the country when he participated in the Polish uprising of 1831 and settled in England. He later returned to Posen, became president of the Society of Friends of Science, and devoted himself to literary pursuits. He translated Shakespeare into Polish as well as many of the English romantic poets, wrote poetry (*To the Masters of the World* was his best known), and a collection of essays, *England and Poland.*

KRAFFT, ADAM (1455?–1509?), sculptor. Born in Nuremberg, Germany, he became a leading exponent of Gothic sculpture. Among his best works are the *Seven Falls of Christ, Entombment of Christ,* and *Christ on Mt. Olivet,* carved from sandstone, and the sixty-foot open-work pyramid of the tabernacle of St. Laurence church, Nuremberg. He died in Jan. in Schwabach, Germany.

KRÄMER, JOHN (d. 1440?), author. A Carthusian monk at the charterhouse of Buxheim, Bavaria, he wrote *Breviloquium animi cujuslibet religiosi reformativum,* which was widely read in the monasteries of the period, and *Tractatus exhortativus ad evitandam malam iram.* He is also known as John of Buxheim.

KRASICKI, IGNACY (1735–1801), archbishop. Born in Dubiecko, Poland, he was ordained, became a friend of King Stanislaus Poniatowski, and was appointed bishop of Ermeland in 1767, and archbishop of Gnesen in 1795. He became a favorite of Frederick II of Prussia and was famed for his witty and satirical poems, many of them attacking monasticism. He wrote *Fables* in the manner of La Rochefoucauld, the mock-heroic *Myszeis,* and two novels: *Pan Podstoli,* a patriotic study, and *Doswiadczynski,* in imitation of Johnson's *Rasselas.* He also translated James Macpherson's *Ossian.* He died in Berlin.

KRASINSKI, ZYGMUNT (1812–1859), poet. Born in Paris on Feb. 19, son of a Polish general, he studied at Warsaw, but was sent to Geneva in 1829 when his father forbade him to engage in political activities. An ardent patriot and a disciple of the romantic movement, he poured out his feelings for his native land in a series of poems which are considered among the greatest Polish writings. *Nieboska Komedya (Undivine Comedy), Irydion, Prozedświt (Dawn),* and *Psalms of the Future* are his best-known works. He suffered a breakdown in 1848 and spent his last years travelling for his health. He died in Paris on Feb. 23.

KRAUS, FRANZ XAVER (1840–1901), historian. Born in Trier, Germany, on Sept. 18, he studied there, was ordained in 1864, and continued his studies at Tübingen, Freiburg, and Bonn. In 1872 he taught archaeology at Strassburg, church history at Freiburg in 1878, and was pro-rector in 1890–91. He was appointed to the Baden Historical Commission in 1883 and was curator of religious antiquities of the duchy in 1890. Some of his writings in favor of Liberalism drew severe censure. He wrote widely on literature, religious art, and cultural history. He died in San Remo, Italy, on Dec. 28.

KRAUTBAUER, FRANZ XAVER (1824–1885), bishop. Born in Bruck, Bavaria, on Jan. 12, he studied at Ratisbon seminary and Munich, and was ordained in 1850. He went to the United States, did parish work in Buffalo, became spiritual director of the American Sisters of Notre Dame in 1859, was consecrated second bishop of Green Bay, Wisconsin, in 1875, and died there on Dec. 17.

KREIL, KARL (1798–1862), astronomer. Born in Ried, Upper Austria, on Nov. 4, he studied at Kremsmünster abbey, where he became interested in astronomy. After studying law, he abandoned it for astronomy in 1823, became assistant director of the Vienna observatory in 1827, adjunct of de LaBrera in Milan in 1831, transferred to the Prague observatory in 1838, and was appointed its director in 1845. He reinvigorated the run-down observatory until it became one of the outstanding in Europe. He founded the science of terrestrial physics and in 1851, when he was appointed professor of physics at Vienna, he was instrumental in establishing a central post in Vienna for meteorological observations, was appointed its first director, and extended these observations to the whole continent. He edited astronomical magazines and wrote several books on astronomy. He died in Vienna on Dec. 21.

KREITEN, WILLIAM (1847–1902), critic. Born in Gangelt, near Aachen, Germany, on June 21, he became a Jesuit at sixteen, was ordained in 1873 in France, after the expulsion of his Society from Germany, and spent his last twenty-three years at Kerkrade, Holland, where he died on June 6. He wrote on Voltaire, Molière, Pascal, and Brentano; edited the poems of Annette von Droste-Hülshoff and of Louis Simon Lambert; published a collection of epigrams and of his own poetry; and was on the staff of *Stimmen aus Maria-Laach,* for which he wrote regularly.

KROMER, MARTIN (1512–1589), bishop. Born in Biecz, Galicia, he studied at Cracow, Bologna, and Rome, was ordained, and on his return to Poland became secretary of Bishop Gamrat of Cracow and then of Prince Sigismund August. He served on diplomatic missions for Sigismund, who inherited the throne in 1548, and was made a noble by the king in 1552 and placed in charge of the national archives. He was appointed coadjutor of Ermland in 1570 and succeeded Cardinal Hosius to the see in 1579. He strenuously fought Protestantism in Poland, wrote a catechism in Polish and produced several popular works of apologetics to oppose its spread. As an author he is best known for his scholarly works, chief of which are *De origine et rebus gestis Polonorum* and *Polonia.* He died in Heilsberg, Ermland, on Mar. 23.

KRZYCKI, ANDREW (d. 1535), archbishop. A popular poet in Poland, he wrote epigrams and Latin verses to celebrate festive events such as King Sigismund I's marriage and his victory at Orsza. He was chancellor of the king's two wives, acquired numerous benefices, and, became a bishop, and eventually primate-archbishop of Gnesen. His verse was witty, often coarse, malicious and biting, but well styled. He defended Sigismund's action in accepting the Grand Master of the Teutonic Knights as vassal after he had turned Lutheran and recognizing him as duke of East Prussia—an action assailed by Rome. His most important works were *Religionis et republicae Quaerimonia* and *De asiana dieta.*

KUCERA, LOUIS BENEDICT (1888–1957), bishop. Born in Wheatland, Minnesota, on Aug. 24, of Bohemian parents, he studied at St. John's and St. Thomas colleges, St. Paul seminary, in Minnesota, and the Catholic University, and was ordained in St. Paul in 1915. He did parish work, taught Latin at Loras College, Dubuque, where he was also prefect of discipline, from 1916 to 1925, was pastor of Holy Trinity in Protivin, Iowa, and in 1930 was appointed bishop of Lincoln, Nebraska. He died on May 9.

KUH, EMIL (1828–1876), poet. Born in Vienna of Jewish parents, he studied in Berlin, where he became a convert in 1857, returned to Vienna to work as a literary critic on newspapers, and in 1864 began to teach German language and literature at the Handelsakademie. He wrote poems of his own, edited an anthology of Austrian poetry, and published a biography of Freidrich Hebbel and a study of Franz Grillparzer. With Julius Glaser he edited Hebbel's works.

KÜHN, EUSEBIUS FRANCISCO. *See* Kino, Eusebius Francisco.

KUHN, JOHANNES VON (1806–1887), theologian. Born in Wäschenbeuren, Würtemberg, on Feb. 19, he studied at Gmünd, Ellwangen, Rottweil, Tübingen, and the seminary in Rottenburg, where he was ordained in 1831. He taught exegesis at Giessen in 1832 and at Tübingen in 1837, and from 1839 until his retirement in 1882 held the chair of dogmatic theology there. He wrote prolifically: *Natur und Übernatur,* the unfinished *Katholische Dogmatik,* on grace and redemption, and against Strauss, Clemens, Hegel, and the Hermesians. He died in Tübingen, Germany, on May 8.

KUNSCHAK, LEOPOLD (1871–1953). Born in Austria-Hungary, he was a leatherworker, founded the Christian Social Workers League in 1892, and was three times arrested for political activity, twice under Hitler. He was a member of parliament for South Austria before World War I, elected to the republic's first parliament from 1919 to 1938, served as deputy mayor of Vienna, and as chairman of the Christian Socialist party, but repudiated the policies of Dollfuss and Schuschnigg. He was one of the founders of the Catholic Conservative Workers party in 1944 and president of the new parliament from 1945 until his death in Vienna on Mar. 13.

KUNSEVICH, JOHN. *See* Josaphat, St.

KURTH, GODEFROID (1847–1916), historian. Born in Arlon, Belgium, on May 11, he graduated from Louvain and contributed much to the development of historical scholarship, both in editing of *Archives belges,* which he founded, and in his books. These include: *The Beginnings of Christianity, The Church at the Turning Points of History, La frontière linguistique en Belge, Notger de Liège, La cité de Liège au moyen age,* and *Histoire poetique des Mérovingiens.* He died in Assche, Belgium, on Jan. 4.

KYNEBURGA, ST. (d. 680?). Daughter of the pagan Penda, king of Mercia, she founded and became abbess of Doncaster in Northamptonshire. She was succeeded by her sister Kyneswide. With them at the abbey was a relative named Tibba. The three women are honored on Mar. 6.

KYNESWIDE, ST. (7th century). *See* Kyneburga, St.

KYRIN, ST. (d. 660). Also called Boniface, he was bishop of Ross, Scotland. f. d. Mar. 14.

L

LABAT, JEAN BAPTISTE (1664–1738), missioner. A native of Paris, he became a Dominican in 1684, taught philosophy in Nancy in 1687, and in 1693 was sent to the West Indies. He served as procurator general in Guadeloupe, developed industry there, founded the city of Basse-Terre, and was diplomatic agent of the governor of the islands. In 1706 he went to Rome to report on the effect of plagues and British military attacks on the area, remained for several years, then returned to Paris, where he died. He wrote *Nouveau voyage aux îles de l'Amérique* and two treatises on Africa.

LABBE, PHILIPPE (1607–1667), author. Born in Bourges, France, on July 10, he entered the Jesuits in 1623, became a professor of theology, and produced some fourscore treatises in the field of history, theology, and philology before his death in Paris on Mar. 17. Among his outstanding works are *Sacrosancta concilia ad regiam editionem exacta* (with Cossart, in sixteen volumes), *Tirocinium linguae Graecae, La Geographie royale,* and *De Byzantinae historiae scriptoribus.*

LABOURÉ, CATHERINE. *See* Catherine Labouré, St.

LABRE, BENEDICT JOSEPH, ST. (1748–1783). Born in Amettes, near Boulogne-sur-Me, France, the oldest of fifteen children, he was educated by a priest uncle, sought unsuccessfully to join the Carthusians and Cistercians, and in 1770 began a series of pilgrimages, during which he frequently was beaten or imprisoned as a pauper. In 1774 he settled in Rome, living in the Colosseum for a while, and spending hours in churches, particularly following the Forty Hours Devotion. He was canonized in 1883. f. d. Apr. 16.

LABRIOLLE, PIERRE DE (1874–1941), scholar. Born in France, he became professor of Roman literature at the Sorbonne in 1926, and was a leading ecclesiastical historian. Among his writings are: *Histoire de la littérature latine chrétienne* (1920–26), *La Crise Montaniste, La Réaction paienne.* He died in Nantes, France, on Jan. 15.

LAC, STANISLAS DU (1835–1909), educator. Born in Paris on Nov. 21, of an ancient noble family, he entered the Jesuits in 1853 and was ordained in 1869. He served as rector of the college of St. Croix in Mans (1870), and École Ste. Geneviève (1872–80), and St. Mary's in Canterbury, England, which he founded (1880–89). He returned to Paris in 1889, became famed for his preaching, founded *Syndicat de l'Aiguille,* a loan society, for women in the needlecraft industry, which spread all over France, and wrote two books, *France* and *Jésuites*. He died in Paris on Aug. 30.

LACEY, BL. BRIAN (d. 1591), martyr. A native of Yorkshire, England, he was betrayed by his brother, convicted of aiding a priest, his cousin Ven. Montford Scott, and hanged at Tyburn during the Elizabethan persecution. F. D. Dec. 10.

LACEY, BL. WILLIAM (d. 1582), martyr. Born in Horton, Yorkshire, he was a wealthy lawyer who became suspect because of the number of visitors to his home, fined repeatedly, and eventually forced to flee. In 1579 his second wife died and the next year he went to Rheims, and later was ordained at Rome. Sent to the English mission in 1581, he was caught saying mass in York prison with Bl. William Hart and Fr. Thomas Bell (both of whom escaped), accused of treason for refusing to acknowledge the spiritual supremacy of Queen Elizabeth I, and hanged, drawn, and quartered at Knavesmire, outside York, England. He was beatified in 1886. F. D. Aug. 22.

LA CHAISE, FRANÇOIS D'AIX DE (1624–1709). Born in Forez, France, on Aug. 25, he became a Jesuit in 1649, taught at the Collège de la Ste. Trinité in Lyons, and became its rector. He became provincial of the Jesuits and in 1675 confessor of King Louis XIV, a post he held for thirty-four years. He exercised great influence, was responsible for Louis' breaking off his affair with Mme. de Montespan, advised the king's marriage to Mme. de Maintenon on the death of Maria Theresa in 1682, and favored the revocation of the Edict of Nantes, though he deplored the excesses which resulted. He died on Jan. 20 in Paris.

LACKAYE, WILLIAM (1862–1932), actor. Born in Loudon County, Virginia, on Sept. 30, he studied in Ottawa and at Georgetown, and, after studying for the priesthood for six years, decided to become an actor. He played many roles under the name Wilton Lackaye, notably that of Svengali in *Trilby*, was one of the founders of the Catholic Actors' Guild and Actors' Equity Association, and died in Long Island City, New York, on Aug. 22.

LACOMBE, ALBERT (1827–1916), missioner. Born in St. Sulpice, Quebec, on Feb. 28, he was ordained in 1850, served in the Cree missions of the northwest, became an Oblate of Mary Immaculate in 1855, and founded the Albert mission among the Blackfeet, a name retained by the entire province of Alberta. He became agent for immigration into Manitoba in 1876, helped railroad construction workers, and often went to Europe for funds and on behalf of Ruthenian Catholics. He wrote a grammar, prayerbook, and translation of the New Testament in Cree and a catechism and

prayerbook in Santeux. He died in Midnapore, Alberta, Canada, on Dec. 12.

LACOP, ST. JAMES (d. 1572), martyr. Born in Oudenarde, Flanders, he became a Norbertine at Middelburg, left the Church in 1566 and preached against it, but repented and returned to his abbey. He was put to death at Gorkum, Holland, by the Calvinists. He was canonized in 1867. F. D. July 9.

LACORDAIRE, JEAN BAPTISTE HENRI DOMINIQUE (1802–1861). Born at Recey-sur-Ource, Côte d'Or, France, on Mar. 12, he early abandoned his Catholicism, studied law in Paris, but in 1824 renounced the legal profession to enter the seminary at Issy, and was ordained in 1827. When the revolution broke out in 1830 he became associated with Lamennais and Montalembert in the publication of *L'Avenir*, devoted to freedom of religion, the press, and speech. The Liberalism of the paper caused its condemnation by the French hierarchy, and his appeal to Rome led to the formal condemnation of its policy in Pope Gregory XVI's encyclical, *Mirari vos*, in 1832. He immediately submitted, broke with Lamennais when the latter refused, and began a series of religious conferences at the Collège Stanislas in Paris in 1834. When he was denounced for his Liberalism he engaged in a series of explanatory correspondence with the archbishop of Paris, who offered him the pulpit of Notre Dame for a series of lectures in 1835, which were enormously successful. At the height of his fame he went to Rome, joined the Dominicans there in 1839, made his vows the following year, and then returned to France where he was instrumental in re-establishing the order in 1843. He resumed his conferences on Catholic doctrine at Notre Dame in 1843 over the objections of King Louis Philippe, and continued them until 1852, becoming established as the greatest preacher of his day and one of the clearest exponents of Catholic doctrine. He began a new paper, *L'Ere Nouvelle*, of which he was editor in 1848 and was elected to the constituent assembly, but resigned both positions later in the year. He opposed Napoleon's empire, discontinued his conferences in 1853 to go into voluntary exile, and became head of the military school at Sorèze, France, where he died on Nov. 21. He was elected to the French Academy in 1861. His conferences were collected and published, as were his letters.

LACORDAIRE, JEAN THÉODORE (1801–1870), entomologist. Brother of Jean Baptiste, he was born in Recey-sur-Ource, France, on Feb. 1, was obliged to follow a business career because of family difficulties, but maintained a lively interest in zoology. He went to South America in 1825 on business and made three more trips there in the next seven years to study insect life. In 1836 he was appointed professor of zoology at Liège, Belgium, a post he occupied until his death thirty-four years later on July 18. He became the world's foremost authority on beetles, and wrote many treatises on natural history, chief of them being *Histoire naturelle des insectes*, a fourteen-volume work on beetles on which he labored eighteen years, and *Introduction à l'entomologie*.

LACTAN, ST. (d. 672). Born near Cork, he studied at Beuchor under St. Comgall, who sent him to found the monastery of Achadh-Ur (Freshford), Kilkenny, Ireland. F. D. Mar. 19.

LACTANTIUS, LUCIUS CAECILIUS FIRMINIANUS (4th century), apologist. A North African pagan and student of Arnobius, he taught rhetoric, perhaps at Cirta, and then, at the request of Emperor Diocletian, at Nicomedia. He became a Christian about 303, lost his position, and was reduced to abject poverty. He began to write, was made tutor in Latin to Constantine's son Crispus, and accompanied him to Trèves about 317. He wrote *De opificio Dei*, a poem; *De ira Dei*, against the stoics and epicureans; *De mortibus persecutorum*, on the martyrs; and *De ave phoenice*, on the phoenix legend and the resurrection. He is best known for *Divinarum institutionum* (written between 304 and 311), in which he contrasted pagan and Christian beliefs; it is effective and graceful in style, but Lactantius was still too close to paganism for it to be the outline of theology he intended it to be. He later prepared an *Epitome* of the *Divine Institutions*.

LADERCHI, JAMES (1678?–1738), author. Born in Faenza, Italy, he joined the Oratorians and became noted for his work in church history. He prepared volumes 35–38 of the *Annales ecclesiastici* of Cesare Baronius and wrote biographies of SS. Peter Damian and Crescus, which resulted in great controversy, and other historical treatises. He died in Rome on Apr. 25.

LADEUZE, PAULIN (1870–1940), educator. Born in Belgium, he was ordained, taught scripture and early Christian literature at Louvain from 1898 to 1940, served as rector in 1909–40, was named titular bishop of Tiberius in 1926, and died in Brussels on Feb. 10.

LADISLAS (d. 1414), king of Naples. Son of Charles III, he became king in 1386 and established order, began a campaign to expand through central Italy, bought papal territory from Gregory XII, but had his hopes dashed by the hostility of Florence and Siena.

LADISLAS I HERMAN (d. 1102), king of Poland. After two years of turmoil in his nation, he assumed the throne in 1081 as successor to Boleslav II, but proved incompetent in a world of baronial and ecclesiastical rebellion.

LADISLAS II (d. 1146), king of Poland. *See* Boleslav IV, king of Poland.

LADISLAS II JAGELLO (1350?–1434), king of Poland. He was the son of Prince Olgerd of Lithuania, and succeeded his father in 1377 as grand duke of Lithuania. When in 1386 he married Bl. Hedwig, widow of Louis the Great of Hungary (d. 1382), nephew and heir of King Casimir III of Poland, in order to join Lithuania and Poland, he promised to embrace Christianity, did so, and brought his Lithuanian subjects with him into the Church. He thus became king of Poland. He founded the University of Cracow and continued to battle the Teutonic Knights, defeating them at Tannenberg in 1410.

LADISLAS III, king of Poland. *See* Mieszko III, king of Poland.

LADISLAS IV (1260–1333), king of Poland. Called Lokietek, "the Short," he was the son of Duke Casimir of Cuiavia and made himself king of Poland in 1296 through an alliance with a coalition of the nobles; they deposed him in 1300 in favor of Wenceslas, who died in 1305. Ladislas, who succeeded, fought against Silesia and Bohemia, took Cracow in 1305, and had united Poland under his rule by 1312. He was crowned king in 1320, with papal approval. From 1327 to 1333 he waged a successful war against the Teutonic Knights for possession of Pomerania. His son Casimir married Anna, daughter of Prince Gedemin of Lithuania, and brought that nation into the union. The name is also spelled Wladislaw.

LADISLAS V. *See* Ladislaus V, king of Hungary and Bohemia.

LADISLAS VI (1424–1444), king of Poland and Hungary. Son of King Jagello of Lithuania and Poland and Queen Hedwig of Hungary, he became king of Poland on the death of Jagello in 1434 and of Hungary in 1442 as Wladislaw I. After his election as king of Hungary he devoted himself to that country, leaving Poland to the magnates, but used the armies of both nations to defeat the Turks in 1443. He made a treaty of peace, which he broke, and in a second campaign against them was defeated and slain in the battle of Varna, Bulgaria.

LADISLAS VII (1595–1648), king of Poland. He was elected king in 1632 and suffered heavily when the Cossacks in the southeastern provinces revolted and joined the Tatars, defeating the Poles and ravaging the nation through several later reigns.

LADISLAS JAGELLO. *See* Ladislas II, king of Poland.

LADISLAUS, ST. (1040–1095), king of Hungary. Ladislaus, or Laszlo, son of King Béla, was born in Neustra on July 29. When he was elected king in 1077, the throne was claimed by a relative, Solomon, whom he met and defeated in battle. Ladislaus also saved his nation from the invasion of the Cumans and other barbarian tribes, extending Christianity to them and permitting religious freedom to all within his enlarging borders. When his sister Helen died without issue in 1091, he added Croatia and Dalmatia to Hungary. He married Adelaide, daughter of Duke Welf of Bavaria, supported Pope Gregory VII against Emperor Henry IV, and was chosen to lead the first crusade. He died at Nitra, Bohemia, before the international force marched. He is the hero of many popular stories and, because of his zeal, piety, and moral life, has always been called a saint. He was canonized in 1192 by Pope Celestine III. F. D. June 27.

LADISLAUS IV (1262–1290), king of Hungary. Son of King Stephen V, he succeeded his father as king in 1272. During his minority his Cuman mother, Elizabeth, fought rebellious vassals who were aided by Ottocar II of Bohemia. He joined Emperor Rudolf II against Ottocar and was mainly responsible for the Bohemian's defeat at the battle of Dürnkrut in 1278. Married to Elizabeth of Anjou, he neglected her for a Cuman mistress and came under the influence of the Cumans. He resisted the attempt of the papal legate, Bishop Philip of Fermo, to reform the Church in Hungary by forcibly dissolving the synod of Buda (Ofen) the legate had convened in 1279, but the accusation of undermining Christianity in favor of the Cumans caused him to war on the latter, whom he defeated at Hodmézö. He soon lapsed into his old ways, even adopting Cuman dress, for which he was surnamed "the Cuman," and in 1288 Pope Nicholas IV proclaimed a crusade against him and declared him dethroned. In the ensuing civil strife, Hungary was torn apart. Ladislaus was murdered in his camp at Korosszeq on July 10 by the Cumans for their defeat in 1282. During his reign the monarchy was at low ebb and the country in a state of anarchy, with the great nobles extending their holdings by forceful conquest and the lesser nobles forming leagues for mutual protection.

LADISLAUS V (1440–1457), king of Hungary and Bohemia. Also known as Ladislaus Posthumous because he was the posthumous son of Emperor Albert II, and Elizabeth, daughter of Emperor Sigismund, he was born at Komárom (now Komárno), Czechoslovakia, on Feb. 22, and was raised at the court of Frederick III. In 1444 the Hungarians elected him king, with John Hunyadi as regent. (While Hunyadi ran the government he made ecclesiastical appointments as he saw fit, allowed the great nobles to gain control, and was faced by an invasion of the Turks after

their capture of Constantinople in 1453. He turned them back at Belgrade in 1456, but died several days later.) Frederick refused to give up his young ward until the Austrians rebelled in 1451 for his release (he was duke of Austria). He was freed in 1452 and crowned king of Bohemia in 1453, though George of Podebrad continued to govern. He was raised by his maternal grandfather with a hatred of the Hunyadis and in 1457 his execution of Laszlo Hunyadi raised such an outcry he was forced to flee to Prague, Bohemia. He was to marry Magdalena, daughter of King Charles VII of France, when he died there of the plaugue on Nov. 23.

LADISLAUS, BL. (1440–1505). Born in Giclniow, Poland, and educated at Warsaw, he became a Franciscan of the Strict Observance, provincial, and missioner to Lithuania, where he converted many. He had a number of supernatural gifts, and it was to his intercession that the dispersal and defeat of the Tatars in 1498 were credited. He died on May 4, is a patron of Poland and Lithuania, and was beatified in 1586. F. D. May 11.

LADISLAUS OF HUNGARY, BL. (d. 1369), martyr. *See* Antony of Saxony, Bl.

LAENNEC, RENÉ THÉOPHILE HYACINTHE (1781–1826), physician. Born in Quimper, Brittany, on Feb. 17, he went to Nantes to study and became interested in medicine through his uncle. At Paris he studied under Corvisart, who interested him in diagnosis of pulmonary ailments by chest percussion. He became chief physician of L'Hôpital Necker in 1816, professor of medicine at the Collège de France in 1822, and was advanced to the chair of clinical medicine there in 1823. His *Traité de l'ascultation* was published in 1819. He invented the stethoscope in 1815, conducted research into diseases of the liver, and was the first to use the term cirrhosis. He contracted tuberculosis while studying that disease and died near Douornenez, Finistère, France, on Aug. 13.

LAETANTIUS, ST. (d. 180), martyr. *See* Speratus, St.

LAETUS, ST. (d. 484?), martyr. *See* Donatian, St.

LAETUS, ST. (5th century), martyr. *See* Vincent, St.

LAETUS, POMPONIUS (1425–1497). Born in Calabria, Italy, he studied in Rome under Lorenzo Valla and became infatuated with ancient times and the way of life of the early Romans. He followed the old Roman way of life, founded an academy accused of pagan learnings, and staged the plays of Plautus each year on the anniversary of Rome's founding. In 1468 he was imprisoned for the extremes of his humanist beliefs by Pope Paul II, but was released by Sixtus IV in 1471, became a lecturer at the Roman University, and was famed for his knowledge of the classical authors. He wrote treatises on ancient Rome and translated Vergil (using the names Julius Sabinus and Pomponius Sabinus), Quintus Curtius, Festus, and Pliny the Younger. He died in Rome.

LA FARGE, CHRISTOPHER GRANT (1862–1938), architect. Born in Newport, Rhode Island, on Jan. 5, son of John La Farge, the painter, he studied at Massachusetts Institute of Technology, worked as his father's assistant, and in 1886 formed an architectural firm with his classmate George Lewis Heins. He soon became noted for his architectural designs, notably his plans for the Cathedral of St. John the Divine in New York City (after the death of Heins in 1907, the trustees discarded the original plans and only the apse is his), the Catholic chapel at West Point, the stations of New York's first subway system, and New York's Zoological Park, which he helped to found. He was a member of architectural societies, serving as vice-president of the American Institute of Architects, and died in Saunderstown, Rhode Island, on Oct. 11.

LA FARGE, JOHN (1835–1910), painter. Born in New York City on Mar. 31, then he studied at Mt. St. Mary's and Fordham, traveled to Europe, and began art experiments on his return to Newport, Rhode Island. He was a pioneer in the study of Japanese art, and was influenced by it; became interested in stained glass (examples of his work are at Harvard and in the Worcester Art Museum); was a book illustrator from 1859 to 1879; and did many water colors. His epic style appears in the murals he completed for Trinity church, Boston, church of the Ascension, New York, the capitol in St. Paul, Minnesota, and the Baltimore supreme court building. He also wrote widely on American and Japanese art. He died in Providence, Rhode Island, on Nov. 14.

ROYAL CORTISSOZ, *John La Farge* (Boston, Houghton, Mifflin, 1911).

LA FAYETTE, MARIE MADELEINE PIOCHE DE LA VERGNE DE (1634–1693), novelist. Born in Paris, and baptized on Mar. 18, she was a leader, with Marquise de Sévigné, of the group of ladies who exerted great influence on Louis XIV and his court, Les Précieuses. She married the Count de la Fayette in 1655 and her home became a literary center. Her chief work is the psychological *La Princess de Clèves*; other novels—*Zayde, La Princesse de Montpensier*, and *La Comtesse de Tende*—accurately reflect French social life. She also wrote a memoir of the French court. She died in Paris on May 25.

LAFITAU, JOSEPH FRANÇOIS (1681–1746), missioner. Born in Bordeaux, France,

on Jan. 1, he became a Jesuit in 1696, was ordained, and in 1711 was sent to Canada. There he discovered ginseng, which for a time was highly valued as a medical panacea. In 1717 he returned to France, where he remained until his death in Bordeaux. He wrote *Moeurs des sauvages américains* and *Histoire des découvertes et des conquetes des Portugais dans le nouveau monde* (1733).

LAFITTE, FERMIN (1888–1959), archbishop. Born in Peyrun, France, he was taken to Argentina when young, was ordained at the Latin American College at Rome in 1911, served in a Buenos Aires parish, and was made bishop of Cordova in 1927 and its archbishop in 1944. In 1956 he became administrator of the archdiocese of Buenos Aires and archbishop in 1959. He led campaigns for social justice, slum clearance, and housing developments; gained government recognition of degrees granted by Catholic colleges; and was long known as an opponent of President Juan Perón. The cardinal was named military vicar of the armed forces by Pope Pius XII in 1957 and ordinary of the Eastern Rite Catholics in Argentina by Pope John XXIII in 1958. He died of a heart attack while saying mass on Aug. 8 at the Rio Santiago naval base.

LAFLÈCHE, LOUIS-FRANÇOIS RICHER (1818–1898), bishop. Born in Ste. Anne de la Pérade, Quebec, Canada, on Sept. 4, he studied at Nicolet College, was ordained in 1844, and was assigned pastoral and missionary work among the Sauteux, Cree, and Montagnais Indians in Manitoba. He returned to Nicolet in 1856 to teach and was appointed its president in 1859. In 1866 he was appointed titular bishop of Anthedam and coadjutor of Three Rivers, succeeded to the see in 1870, and died there on July 14.

LAFON, ANDRÉ (1883–1915), poet. Born in Bordeaux, France, he studied in Blaye, and taught in Bordeaux and Paris lycées and at the Collège de Ste. Croix, Neuilly. He published two volumes of poetry, *Poèmes provinciaux* and *La maison pauvre*, the last after he became associated with Jammes, Mauriac, and others on the quarterly review, *L'Amitié de France*. The French Academy crowned *L'Élève Gilles*, his first novel; he finished a second, *La Maison sur la rive*, before the outbreak of World War I. He died while in military training at Bordeaux.

LA FONTAINE, JEAN DE (1621–1695), author. Born in Chateau Thierry, France, on July 8, he studied at the college there and in 1641 entered the Oratory. He left after a year and a half in the seminary, studied law, and was admitted to the bar. He married Marie Héricart in 1647 to please his father, but they separated in 1658. He accepted the patronage of the duchess de Bouillon, who took him to

Paris, where in 1660 he met Nicolas Fouquet, Louis XIV's minister of finance, and was given a pension. In 1664 he became gentleman in waiting to the duchess of Orléans and in 1672, when his fortune was gone, he accepted the patronage of Mme. de la Sablière, in whose household he lived for the next twenty years. In 1683 he was elected to the French Academy (over Boileau), but the king held up the election for a year because of the sensation caused by La Fontaine's scandalous *Contes*. La Fontaine was the author of the celebrated *Fables choisi mises en vers*, the first six books of which appeared in 1658, satires in verse on the society of the period in the form of animal tales which have been translated into and imitated in many languages. His *Contes et nouvelles en vers* (1665; with additions in 1667 and 1671) were modeled on Boccaccio's *Tales*; he also wrote *L'Élégie aux nymphes de Vaux* (on Fouquet's fall), *Amours de Psyche et de Cupidon*, *Voyage en Limousin*, and madrigals and rondeaus. He returned to the Church in 1693, followed an ascetic regimen thereafter, and died in Paris on Apr. 13.

LAFORÊT, NICOLAS JOSEPH (1823–1872), theologian. Born in Graide, Belgium, on Jan. 23, he studied at Namur seminary and Louvain, and in 1848 was appointed to the chair of moral theology. In 1850 he became president of Collège du Pape and in 1865 rector of Louvain, where he established schools of civil engineering, industry, mines, and education, and the Justus Lipsius Institute. He was a member of the Royal Academy of Belgium and was appointed a monsignor by Pope Leo XIII. He wrote widely in philosophy and theology and died in Louvain on Jan. 26.

LA FOSSE, CHARLES DE (1636–1716), painter. Born in Paris on June 15, he studied under François Chauveau and Charles Lebrun (whose most noted pupil he became) in Rome. In 1669 he was commissioned by Louis XIV to adorn the Tuileries, was elected to the French Academy in 1673, and in 1688 went to London to decorate the duke of Montagu's house. He returned to Paris to execute his masterpiece, the fresco in the dome of the Hôtel des Invalides, *St. Louis Placing His Crown and Sword in the Hands of Christ*. He also executed decorative works at Versailles and the Tuileries. Among his best-known works are *Rape of Proserpine*, *Marriage of the Virgin*, *Finding of Moses*, and *Apollo and Thetis*. He died in Paris on Dec. 13.

LAFUENTE Y ZAMALLOA, MODESTO (1806–1866), historian. Born in Ravanal de los Caballeros, Spain, on May 1, he studied at Santiago, Astorga, and Valladolid, and taught theology at the latter two. He resigned to take up journalism in Madrid, where he published *Fray Gerundio*, which because of his brilliant

articles became one of the leading Spanish newspapers. He was the author of the monumental *Historia general de España*, in thirty volumes, and *Teatro social del sigi XIX*. He died in Madrid on Oct. 25.

LA GORCE, JOHN OLIVER (1879–1959), geographer. Born in Scranton, Pennsylvania, on Sept. 22, he graduated from Georgetown, became a telegrapher, as his mother had been, and in 1905 became a secretary on the staff of the *National Geographic*, with which he remained until his death on Dec. 23. He held editorial and advertising posts, became a trustee in 1920, and from 1954 to 1957 was president of the society and editor in chief of its magazine. He received the Bryant Medal of the Geographical Society of Philadelphia, the Grosvenor Medal of the National Geographic Society, and five honorary degrees. He traveled and wrote widely, was editor of *Book of Fishes*, and befriended many scientists. A mountain and glacier in Alaska, La Gorce Arch in Utah, and La Gorce Mountains in Antarctica bear his name. He died in Washington, D.C., on Dec. 23.

LA GRENÉ, PIERRE (1659–1736), missioner. Born in Paris on Nov. 12, he became a Jesuit in 1677, studied at La Flèche, was ordained, and in 1694 was sent to Canada. He spent the next thirteen years at Lorette and Sault St. Louis with the Iroquois, was transferred to Montreal in 1707, and appointed superior there in 1716. He was director of the Montreal Congrégation des Hommes from 1712 to 1723, when he was made prefect of schools in Quebec.

LA HARPE, JEAN FRANÇOIS (1739–1803), author. Born in Paris on Nov. 20, he studied at Collège d'Harcourt, began his writing career with a group of satirical couplets which caused his arrest, met Voltaire (who became his patron), and turned violently antireligious in his beliefs and writings. He began writing for the periodical *Mercure* in 1768, won several prizes from the French Academy, to which he was admitted in 1776, and in 1787 was appointed professor of literature and began a series of literary lectures at the Paris Lycée which were collected and published in eighteen volumes. His enthusiastic ardor for the revolution was dampened by his imprisonment in 1794, and on his release he ardently returned to Catholicism. He died in Paris in Feb. Among his plays are *Warwick*, (which was tremendously successful), *Mélanie* (forbidden by the censor because of its vitriolic attack on religious vows), *Timoléon*, *Virginie*, and *Philoctète*. He also wrote *La Prophétie de Cazotte* and *Le Triomphe de la religion*.

LA HAYE, JEAN DE (1593–1661). Born in Paris on Mar. 20, he lived as a youth in Spain where he joined the Franciscans and became known for his scholarship and preaching ability. He returned to France in 1620 and devoted the balance of his life to writing. His chief works are the five-volume *Biblia magna* and nineteen-volume *Biblia maxima*, several commentaries, and editions of the writings of SS. Francis, Anthony of Padua, and Bernadine of Siena. He died in Paris on Oct. 15.

LA HIRE, LAURENT (1606–1656), painter. Born in Paris, he early turned to painting, became painter to the king, adorned many of the churches of Paris, and produced decorative works, including tapestries for Gobelin. He was one of the founders of the French Academy of Painting and Sculpture. Among his outstanding works are *Apparition of Christ to the Three Marys, Nicholas V Opening the Tomb of St. Francis of Assisi, St. Peter Healing the Sick,* and *Vision of St. Francis.* He died in Paris.

LA HIRE, PHILIPPE DE (1640–1718). Born in Paris on Mar. 18, son of Laurent, he studied painting in Rome but abandoned it for the study of science and mathematics, becoming a pupil of Gaspard Desarques. He became a member of the Academy of Sciences in 1678, worked for the government as a cartographer, and continued the measure of the meridian begun by Jean Picard. In 1682 he was appointed professor at the Collège de France, taught at the Academy of Architecture, and made important contributions to the study of geometry, particularly on conics. He died in Paris on Apr. 21.

LAI, GAETANO DI (1853–1928), cardinal. Born in Malo, Italy, on July 30, he studied at the seminary in Vincenza and was ordained in 1876. He became undersecretary of the Congress of the Council in 1886 and later its secretary and in 1908 that of the Consistorial Congregation. He was created a cardinal in 1907, became bishop of Sabina and Poggio Mirteto, and died in Italy on Oct. 24.

LAICIN. *See* Molagga, St.

LAINEZ, DIEGO. *See* Laynez, Diego.

LALANDE, ST. JEAN DE (d. 1646), martyr. A native of Dieppe, France, he went to Quebec to offer his services to the Jesuit missioners as a *donné.* In 1646 he joined St. Isaac Jogues and set out on a trip to the Iroquois. They were captured by Mohawks and, the day after Fr. Jogues was slain, Lalande was tomahawked and beheaded on Oct. 19 at Osserneneon, near Albany, New York. He was canonized in 1930 by Pope Pius XI. F. D. Sept. 26 (also, Mar. 16).
JOHN A. O'BRIEN, *The American Martyrs* (New York, Appleton, 1953).

LALEMANT, JEROME (1593–1665), missioner. Born in Paris on Apr. 27, brother of Charles, he became a Jesuit in 1610, was sent on the Canadian missions in 1638, and administered to the Hurons as superior. He reorganized the missions on the basis of an Indian census he had taken, founded the *donnés* (lay assistants to the missionaries), and in 1645 was appointed superior of the Canadian Jesuits at Quebec. He was ordered back to France in 1656, was appointed rector of La Flèche College two years later, and returned to Quebec in 1659 as vicar-general and director of the missions, positions he occupied until his death in Quebec on Nov. 16. He wrote several of the *Relations,* and most of *Journal des Jésuites.*

LALEMANT, CHARLES (1587–1674), missioner. Born in Paris on Nov. 17, brother of Jerome, he became a Jesuit and was sent on the Canadian mission in 1625. The following year a letter to his brother began the famous Jesuit *Relations.* He returned to France to protest the trading company's interference with his missionary work among the Indians; and capture by the English, shipwreck, and war prevented his return to Quebec until 1632. On his return to France in 1638 he was appointed procurator of the Canadian missions, and later vice-provincial and superior of the Jesuit house in Paris, where he died on Nov. 18.

LALEMENT, ST. GABRIEL (1610–1649), martyr. Born in Paris on Oct. 10, nephew of Charles and Jerome, he became a Jesuit in 1630, taught at Moulins for three years, studied at Bourges, and was ordained in 1638. He then taught at La Flèche and Moulins until 1646, when he was sent at his own request to Canada. He worked on the Huron mission and in 1649 became assistant to St. Jean de Brébeuf at St. Ignace. On Mar. 16 the Iroquois destroyed that settlement and massacred all except the two priests. After extreme tortures, St. Jean was tomahawked; St. Gabriel suffered the same fate on the next day, Mar. 17. He was canonized in 1930 by Pope Pius XI. F. D. Sept. 26 (also, Mar. 16).
JOHN A. O'BRIEN, *The American Martyrs* (New York, Appleton, 1953).

LALLEMANT, JACQUES PHILIPPE (1660?–1748), author. Born in St. Valéry-sur-Somme, France, he became a Jesuit, wrote a series of effective pamphlets and books against the Jansenists, and was one of the authors of *Réflexions morales sur le nouveau testament.* He died in Paris.

LALLEMANT, LOUIS (1588–1635). Born in Châlons-sur-Marne, France, he became a Jesuit in 1605, was ordained, taught and was master of novices and spiritual director of priests for seven years. A collection of his instructions was published as *Doctrine spirituelle* after his death in Bourges, Frances, on Apr. 5.

LALOR, TERESA (1769?–1846), foundress. Born in Kilkenny County, Ireland, she accompanied her parents to Philadelphia when they migrated to the United States in 1797. Under the encouragement of Fr. Leonard Neale she devoted herself to charitable works, opened an academy which was closed by the yellow-fever epidemic, and in 1799 followed Fr. Neale to Georgetown, of which he had been appointed president. There she founded Georgetown Academy and with two others founded a community for which Bishop Neale in 1816 secured a papal grant attaching it to the Order of the Visitation. She died in Baltimore on Sept. 9.

LA LUZERNE, CÉSAR GUILLAUME (1738–1821), cardinal. Born in Paris, he studied at Collège de Navarre, was ordained, and in 1770 was appointed bishop of Langres. He participated in the Assemblée des Notables in 1788 and the États géneraux in 1789, from which he resigned in protest against that body's policies. When he refused to take the constitutional oath in 1791 he was forced to flee and lived in Constance and Venice until the end of the revolution. He resigned his see in 1801 when Napoleon's concordat was signed, but was appointed cardinal and returned to his see in 1817. He died in Paris.

LAMARCK, JEAN BAPTISTE PIERRE ANTOINE DE MONET DE (1744–1829), naturalist. Born in Bazentin, Picardy, France, on Aug. 1, he studied for the priesthood at the Amiens Jesuit college, but on the death of his father in 1761 joined the army. Illness caused his discharge in 1768, and he studied medicine (which he never practiced), meteorology, and botany. His publication in 1778 of *Flore française*, in which he originated a new system of plant classification, attracted great attention; in 1779 he was elected to the Academy of Sciences and in 1781 he was appointed royal botanist, publishing the four-volume *Dictionnaire de botanique* in 1783–96. In 1789 he was appointed keeper of the herbarium of the Jardin des Plantes and in 1793, when the Muséum d'Histoire Naturelle was reorganized, professor of zoology there. In 1801 his *Système des animaux sans vertèbres* (in which he developed a classification system of vertebrates, after his preliminary breakdown of the animal system into vertebrates and invertebrates) presented his ideas of the origins of the species and is regarded as the foundation of invertebrate paleontology. He developed a concept of evolution known as the inheritance of acquired characteristics theory which is not now generally accepted, but is considered the forerunner of Darwin's theory of evolution. He was also an outstanding meteorologist, published a series of annual meteorologist reports from 1799 to 1810, and was one of the first to attempt weather predictions. He died in Paris on Dec. 18.

LAMARTINE, ALPHONSE DE (1790–1869), author. Born in Mâcon, Saône-et-Loire, France, on Oct. 21, he studied at the College

of Belley which he left in 1809 to study the writings of great authors at home. After a trip to Italy in 1811–12, he joined the guards of Louis XVIII in 1814, fled to Switzerland on Napoleon's return from Elba, and returned to France after the Hundred Days. In 1820 he published *Les méditations poetiques*, which was a tremendous success, and was appointed legation secretary at Florence, where he met and married Eliza Birch, and later was chargé d'affaires. He was elected to the French Academy in 1830 and in 1832 traveled to Palestine, which resulted in his *Pilgrimage to the Holy Land*. He was elected to the chamber of deputies in 1833 and 1837, opposed Louis Philippe and in 1847 published *History of the Girondists*, which was one of the political causes of the revolution of 1848. He became minister of foreign affairs in the provincial government, worked brilliantly and unceasingly for a moderate government, delivered speeches which gained him a reputation as an orator, but retired from politics after the coup d'état in 1851. His chief volumes of poetry were *Harmonies poétiques et religieuses* (1830), *Jocelyn* (1836), and *La Chute d'un ange* (1838); and of prose, *History of the Revolution of 1848 and History of the Girondists*. He died in Paris on Mar. 1.

LAMB, HUGH L. (1890–1959), bishop. Born in Modena, Pennsylvania, on Oct. 6, he studied at St. Charles seminary, Philadelphia, the North American College and the Propaganda, Rome, and was ordained in 1915. He did parish work in Philadelphia, taught at its seminary in 1918–21, and became Cardinal Dougherty's secretary in 1921. He was appointed assistant superintendent of schools in 1923, chancellor of the Philadelphia archdiocese in 1926, made a monsignor in 1927, and auxiliary bishop of Philadelphia in 1935. He became vicar general in 1936, a position he held until he was appointed first bishop of Greensburg, Pennsylvania, in 1951, and served as administrator of the Philadelphia archdiocese when Cardinal Dougherty died a few days after his appointment until the following Jan., when he was installed in his own diocese. He died in Jeanette, Pennsylvania, on Dec. 8.

LAMBECK, PETER (1628–1680), historian. Born in Hamburg, Germany, on Apr. 13, he studied at Amsterdam and Paris, taught at the Hamburg gymnasium in 1652, and became its rector in 1664. He resigned when accused of atheism and went to Rome, where he became a convert. He moved to Vienna and at the request of Emperor Leopold catalogued the imperial library. He wrote *Prodromus historiae literariae* (1659) and histories of the city of Hamburg and of the Byzantine Empire. He died in Vienna on Apr. 4.

LAMBERT, ST. (d. 680?). He and St. Valerius were missioners in the area of Mons, France, with St. Gislenus. F. D. Oct. 9.

LAMBERT, ST. (d. 688), archbishop. Brought up in the court of King Clotaire III of France, he became a monk and, in 666, abbot at the Benedictine monastery of Fontenelle. He was made archbishop of Lyons in 679. F. D. Apr. 14.

LAMBERT, ST. (635?–705?), bishop and martyr. Born of a noble family, he was educated by St. Theodard and succeeded him in 668 as bishop of Tongres-Maastricht, Flanders. Lambert was driven out in 674 by Ebroin, mayor of the palace, and spent seven years as a Benedictine monk at Stavelot. He was restored when Pepin of Heristal succeeded Ebroin. The bishop devoted himself to converting the inhabitants of Brabant and built a convent in Munsterbilzen. When he denounced Pepin for his incestuous relations with Alpiais, his wife's sister, she allegedly had her brother Dodo murder him. In another account, Dodo, a relative of two men killed by Lambert's relatives, came to avenge their death and murdered the bishop. F. D. Sept. 17.

LAMBERT (d. 791?). *See* Jaenbert.

LAMBERT, ST. (d. 900?), martyr. A servant, he was killed at Saragossa, Spain, by his Moorish master; his cult was approved by Pope Hadrian VI. F. D. Apr. 6.

LAMBERT, BL. (d. 1125). Educated at the Benedictine abbey of St. Bertin, in St. Omer, France, he became its fortieth abbot and introduced Cluniac reforms. F. D. June 22.

LAMBERT, BL. (d. 1151). Brother of St. Peter of Tarentaise, he also became a Cistercian monk at Bonnevaux. He was abbot-founder of Chézery, France. F. D. Aug. 22.

LAMBERT, BL. (d. 1163), abbot. He became a Cistercian at Morimond, France, and its abbot after holding a similar position at Clairfontaine. From 1155 to 1161 he was abbot at Cîteaux. He died in retirement at Morimond. F. D. July 12.

LAMBERT OF HERSFELD (1024–1077?), historian. Born in Franconia (or Thuringia), he became a Benedictine at Hersfeld, Hesse in 1058, was ordained, and made a pilgrimage to Jerusalem. He returned to his monastery in 1059 and remained there until his death. He wrote *Annales Lamberti*, a chronicle of world history from the creation to 1077; the period 1068–77 is written with literary merit but is historically untrustworthy. He also wrote a life of Archbishop Lull of Mainz. Lambert has been called identical with Abbot Hartwig of Hersfeld.

LAMBERT LE BÈGUE (d. 1177). Born of poor parents in Liège, Belgium, and known as "the Stammerer" (*bègue*), he became a priest there, attracted a large following by his denunciations of ecclesiastical abuses, and founded

the Béguines. He was accused of heresy and imprisoned. Before he was tried, he escaped and joined the supporters of antipope Callistus III, whom his bishop had recognized. Though he wrote several letters justifying his conduct, disposition of his case is not known. He probably died in Liège. He was the author of *Antigraphum Petri* and translated a life of the Virgin Mary and several commentaries into the vernacular.

LAMBERT, LOUIS A. (1835–1910), editor. Born in Charleroi, Pennsylvania, on Apr. 13, he studied at St. Vincent's College and at the St. Louis seminary, was ordained in 1859, and did parish work in the Alton, Illinois, diocese. He served as chaplain of the 18th Illinois Infantry early in the Civil War, was pastor at Cairo in 1863–68, then taught philosophy and theology at the Paulist novitiate in New York. He became pastor in Waterloo, New York, in 1869, founded the Buffalo *Catholic Times* in 1877 (later merged with the Rochester *Catholic Times*), engaged in controversy with the popular agnostic, Robert Ingersoll, which attracted wide attention, and founded the Philadelphia *Catholic Times*, which he edited for two years. He became involved in a controversy with his ordinary, Bishop McQuaid, who denounced him to Rome for recalcitrance in 1890. He was ordered to remain in the diocese of Rochester, but was transferred to Scottsville, New York, where he was pastor of Ascension parish until his death. He edited the New York *Freeman's Journal* from 1894 to 1910, published *Notes on Ingersoll* (1883) from his newspaper columns, *Tactics of Infidels* (1887), a biblical thesaurus, and a commentary on the Bible. He died in Newfoundland, New Jersey, and was buried in Scottsville.

LAMBERT PÉLOGUIN, ST. (1080?–1154), bishop. Born in Bauduen, France, he was a Benedictine monk in Lérins, was made bishop of Vence, France, against his will in 1114, and became widely known for his learning and healing powers. F. D. May 26.

LAMBERT OF ST. BERTIN (1060–1125), historian. Born of a distinguished family, he entered the monastery of St. Bertin, studied at French schools, and served as prior and in 1095 as abbot of St. Bertin, in St. Omer, France, which he reformed according to the rule of Cluny. He was noted for his learning and wrote now-lost treatises on scripture, free will, original sin, the soul, and science. He is called identical with the canon of St. Omer who wrote *Liber floridus*, an encyclopedic natural history, between 1090 and 1120. He died in St. Bertin on June 22.

LAMBERTINI, BL. IMELDA (1322–1333). Daughter of Count Egano, she was exceptionally pious as a child, was sent at nine to the Dominican convent of Valdi Pietra, Bologna,

Italy, for training, and died at eleven after miraculously receiving Communion on the feast of the Ascension. F. D. May 13.

LAMBERVILLE, JACQUES DE (1641–1710), missioner. Born in Rouen, France, he became a Jesuit in 1661 and was sent to Canada in 1675 to work among the Iroquois Indians. With his brother Jean he became very popular, wielding such influence that he helped pacify the Indians who had been aroused by Governors de la Barre and Denonville. Among his converts was Ven. Catherine Tekakwitha. He died in Quebec.

LAMBERVILLE, JEAN DE (1633–1714), missioner. Born in Rouen, France, he became a Jesuit in 1656 and in 1669 was sent to Canada, where he worked among the Onondaga Indians for fourteen years. He was responsible for saving Gov. de la Barre's expedition from disaster in 1683 and when Gov. de Denonville in 1685–86 attempted to avenge de la Barre's capitulation, it was the Jesuit who worked unceasingly to restore peace. In 1689, his health shattered, he was sent back to France as procurator of the mission and remained there until his death in Paris.

LAMBILLOTE, LOUIS (1796–1855), composer. Born in La Hamaide, Belgium, on Mar. 27, he became organist at Charleroi in 1811, at Dinan, and in 1820 at the Jesuit college in Amiens. In 1825 he became a Jesuit and spent the rest of his life teaching music. He composed hymns, masses, cantatas, oratorios, and cantiques, and was deeply interested in the theory and history of chant. The publication of his *Antiphonaire de St. Grégoire* (1851) paved the way for the revival of Gregorian chant which ensued. He also completed a new edition of liturgical chant books (published after his death) and *Esthétique*, on the theory and practice of Gregorian music. He died in Paris on Feb. 27.

LAMBIN, DENIS (1520?–1572), philologian. Born in Montreuil-sur-mer, Picardy, France, he studied at Amiens and joined the household of Cardinal de Tournon, with whom he traveled in Italy in 1549–60. In 1561 he began teaching Latin and Greek at Collège de France. He translated Cicero, Demosthenes, Horace, Lucretius, and Cornelius Nepos, as well as Aristotle's *Ethics* and *Politics*, into French. He died in Paris.

LAMBRUSCHINI, LUIGI (1776–1854), cardinal. Born in Sestri Levante, Italy, on Mar. 6, he became a Barnabite and was consultor for several Roman congregations. He acted as Cardinal Consalvi's secretary at the Congress of Vienna, was appointed secretary of the Congregation of Extraordinary Ecclesiastical Affairs in 1815, and helped negotiate concordats with Naples, Bavaria, and other states. Appointed archbishop of Genoa in 1819, he was sent as Pope Leo XII's nuncio to Paris in 1827. On his return in 1831 he was made a cardinal by Pope Gregory XVI, who named him his secretary of state in 1836. He received a majority on the first ballot in the conclave of 1846 (not sufficient for election) and, when Pope Pius IX was named, resigned his secretaryship because of his disagreement with the new pope's constitutional policies. He was named secretary of briefs and later prefect of rites. During the revolution of 1848 he was subjected to great peril by the revolutionists because of his conservative position. He was appointed bishop of Porto and Santa Rufina and founded a seminary at Farfa. He died in Rome on May 12.

LAMBRUSCHINI, RAFFAELLO (1788–1873). Born in Genoa, Italy, on Aug. 14, nephew of Luigi, he was ordained in Rome, interested himself in science on his return to Tuscany, founded *Giornale Agrario Toscano* in 1827, and established a school at San Carboni. He published *La guida dell' educatore* (1836–44) and other works on education, became a member of parliament in 1848, and in 1860 a senator. He died in Figline, Tuscany, on Mar. 8.

LAMBTON, VEN. JOSEPH (1569–1592), martyr. Born in Yorkshire, England, he studied at Rheims and Rome, was ordained at twenty-three, and sent on the English mission in 1592. He was arrested on landing at Newcastle, condemned as a priest, and was hanged and mutilated there, probably on July 24.

LAMENNAIS, JEAN MARIE DE (1780–1860), founder. Born in St. Malo, France, he was ordained in 1804. With his brother Félicité he published *Réflexions sur l'état de l'église en France* (1808); they also taught together at St. Malo. When the college was suppressed in 1828, Jean became vicar general at St. Brieuc, then at Troyes, and at Rennes. He helped to found the Congregation of St. Peter and was its superior general; after his brother's apostasy in 1834 he devoted his life to the Institute of the Brothers of Christian Instruction, which he had established in 1817. He died in Ploërmel, Brittany, on Dec. 26.

LAMLISS, ST. (7th century). Said to have been an Irish hermit who lived on Lamlash Bay in the island of Aran, he is probably to be identified with St. Laserian.

LAMOIGNON, GUILLAUME DE (1617–1677), jurist. Born near Bourges, France, he became in 1658 the first president of the French parliament, having been since 1644 its master of requests. He codified French law, was a noted member of the Society of the Holy Sacrament, which protected the clergy from many of Colbert's attempts of interference, and was a close friend of Rapin. Lamoignon's attempt to settle a dispute over the right to a desk in Ste. Chapelle became the subject of a mock-heroic poem by Boileau, *Le Lutrin*, which influenced Alexander Pope's *Rape of the Lock.*

LAMONT, JOHANN VON (1805–1879), astronomer. Born in Braemar, Scotland, on Dec. 13, he was brought to Germany on his father's death in 1816 by Fr. Gallus Robertson, studied at Ratisbon, was appointed assistant to the director of Bogenhausen observatory in 1827 and director in 1835, and in 1852 became professor of astronomy at Munich. He made many contributions to astronomy (notably his observations of stars from the seventh to the tenth magnitude, recording some 80,000) and to the science of magnetism. He died on Aug. 6 in Bogenhausen, Bavaria.

LA MORICIÈRE, LOUIS CHRISTOPHE LÉON JUCHAULT DE (1806–1865), general. Born in Nantes, France, on Feb. 5, he studied at L'École Polytechnique and L'École d'Application, from which he graduated as sub-lieutenant. He was sent to Algiers in 1830 and advanced to the rank of lieutenant general (1843), serving for a time in 1845 as temporary governor of Algiers. He was elected a member of the constituent assembly and served as secretary of war in 1848, resigning when Louis Napoleon was elected president. He continued his opposition to the government until 1852, when he was imprisoned and expelled from France. He traveled through Europe, regained his faith, which he had neglected, and in 1860 was appointed general in chief of the papal army. He was defeated and captured by the Piedmontese at Castelfidardo. On his release he retired to France, where he spent the rest of his life at the château of Chaillon, occupying himself with religious and charitable works. He died on Sept. 11 at the Château de Prouzel near Amiens, France.

LAMORMAINI, WILHELM (1570–1648). Born in Dochamps, Luxembourg, on Dec. 29, he studied at Prague, where he took his doctorate, became a Jesuit in 1590, and was ordained in 1596. In 1600 he taught philosophy at Graz, was rector of the Jesuit college there in 1614, went to Rome in 1621, and became rector of the Jesuit college in Vienna in 1623 and of the academic college there in 1637. In 1624 he became confessor and adviser to Emperor Ferdinand II. He was honored for his civic services, was provincial of Austria in 1643–45, and founded a seminary. He died in Vienna on Feb. 22.

LAMPRECHT (12th century), poet. Surnamed der Pfaffe (the priest), he wrote *Alexanderlied*, the first German epic, based on the popular account of that hero in a poem by Albéric de Besançon, in itself based on Valerius. He probably lived and wrote it about 1130 in the area of the Middle Rhine.

LAMY, BERNARD (1640–1715). Born in Le Mans, France, in June, he became an Oratorian in 1658, studied at Paris and Saumur, taught at Vendôme and Juilly, and was ordained in 1667. He also taught at Le Mans and Angiers. In 1675 he was removed because of Cartesian leanings, but was asked to teach at the Grenoble seminary and at St. Magliore to 1686. In 1689 he was sent to Rouen, where he remained until his death on Jan. 29. His published scriptural commentaries were widely attacked for their controversial opinions.

LAMY, ÉTIENNE MARIE VICTOR (1845–1919), historian. Born in Cire, Jura, France, on June 2, he studied in Sorèze and Paris, took his doctorate in law, and at twenty-five was nominated to the national assembly. He was defeated after ten years of service because of his opposition to the anti-Catholic educational laws of Jules Ferry, became editor of *Le Correspondant*, wrote for other journals, in 1905 was elected to the French Academy, and later became its secretary. He wrote several historical and social studies, including *Le France du Levant* (1898) and *Le second empire* (1899). He died in Paris on Jan. 9.

LAMY, FRANÇOIS (1636–1711), author. Born in Montireau, France, he became a Benedictine of St. Maur in 1658, served as subprior, taught in 1672–79, and became prior of Rebais in 1687. He resigned in 1689 to devote his time to writing. A pioneer among the Maurists in teaching Cartesian philosophy, he also engaged in controversy with Malebranche, attacked Spinoza and defended Augustine, and wrote *Vérité évidente de la religion chrétienne, De la connaissance de soi-même,* and *De la connaissance et de l'amour de Dieu.*

LAMY, JOHN BAPTIST (1814–1888), archbishop. Born in Lempdes, France, on Oct. 11, he studied at the seminary at Montferrand, was ordained in 1838, and the next year went to the United States, where he served in Ohio and Kentucky. He was appointed vicar apostolic to New Mexico in 1848, when the southwest region was transferred to the United States by Mexico, and was consecrated titular bishop of Agathon in 1850, and first bishop of Santa Fe. He became famed for his difficult journeys to every part of his vicariate, and came to be regarded as the perfect exemplar of the pioneer Catholic missionaries and their activities on the frontier. He went to Europe for financial and priestly aid in 1853, and became first archbishop of Santa Fe in 1875 when it was made a metropolitan see. He resigned in 1885, was appointed titular archbishop of Cyzicus, and died in Santa Fe, New Mexico, on Feb. 13. His career was portrayed in part in Willa Cather's *Death Comes for the Archbishop.*

LAMY, THOMAS JOSEPH (1827–1907), scholar. Born in Ohey, Belgium, on Jan. 27, he studied in Floreffe and Namur, was ordained in 1853, and took his doctorate in theology at Louvain in 1859. He taught oriental languages and scriptural exegesis there in 1858 until his retirement in 1900. He was president of Collège Marie Thérèse for thirty years, was made a domestic prelate in 1885, and appointed to the Vatican Biblical Commission in 1903. He wrote over 100 volumes, including *Introductio in sacram scripturam*, commentaries on Genesis and the Apocalypse, translations of hitherto unpublished Syriac writings, and an edition of the writings of St. Ephraem. He died in Louvain, Belgium, on July 30.

LANA-TERZI, FRANCESCO (1631–1687), scientist. Born in Brescia, Italy, on Dec. 10, he became a Jesuit in 1647, studied at the Roman College, was ordained, and taught at Terni, Ferrari, and Brescia. He wrote three volumes of *Magisterium naturae et artis*; in his *Prodromo overo saggio di alcune inventioni* he described plans for heavier-than-air and lighter-than-air aircraft, and methods for speaking at great distances, writing for the blind, and building a sowing machine. He died in Brescia on Feb. 22.

LANCELOTTI, GIOVANNI PAOLO (1522–1590). Born in Perugia, Italy, he studied and taught at the university there, receiving his doctorate in law in 1546. In 1557, Pope Paul IV entrusted to him the task of preparing an elementary work on canon law, published in 1563 as *Institutiones juris canonici*. He died in Perugia on Sept. 23.

LANDELINUS, ST. (625?–686?). Born in Vaux, France, he was a member of a criminal gang at eighteen, but reformed when one of their number was killed. He became a Benedictine monk and lived as a penitent solitary at Lobbes; surrounded by many followers, he built a monastery there in 654. Seeking further solitude, he lived at Aulne (656), Wallens (657), and Crespin (670), at each of which he set up abbeys. He was superior of the last until his death. F. D. June 15.

LANDERICUS, ST. (d. 660?), bishop. He became bishop of Paris in 650, built the hospital of St. Christopher (later to become Hôtel Dieu), exhausted his personal fortune to relieve victims of a famine, and directed the compilation by Marculf of ecclesiastical formulae. F. D. June 10.

LANDERICUS, ST. (7th century), bishop. Son of SS. Vincent Maldegarus and Wandru, he was bishop of Meaux, France, from 641 to 650, then resigned to succeed his father as abbot of the Benedictine monastery of Soignies. F. D. Apr. 17.

LANDOALD, ST. (d. 668?). A Lombard priest who was sent from Rome with his sister St. Vindiciana and others to assist St. Amand in converting the Netherlands, he settled at Wintershoven, from which he went forth to win many from paganism. F. D. Mar. 19.

LANDRIOT, JEAN FRANÇOIS ANNE (1816–1874), bishop. Born in Couches-les-Mines, France, he was ordained in 1839, was appointed superior of the seminary in Autun in 1842, vicar general in 1850, bishop of La Rochelle in 1856, and archbishop of Rheims in 1867. He attended the Vatican Council, where he opposed the definition of papal infallibility but accepted its promulgation. He published sermons and ascetical treatises, including *La Femme forte, La Prière chrétienne*, and *Le Christ et la tradition*. He died in Rheims, France.

LANDULF VARIGLIA, ST. (1070–1134), bishop. Born in Asti, Piedmont, Italy, he became a Benedictine in Pavia and in 1103 bishop of Asti. F. D. June 7.

LANEL, BL. FRANÇOISE (1745–1794), martyr. *See* Fontaine, Bl. Madeleine.

LANFANT, BL. ALEXANDRE (d. 1792), martyr. A Jesuit preacher, he had been particularly active against the Jansenists, and was slain in the street near the Benedictine abbey of St. Germain-des-Prés, Paris, on Sept. 5 during the massacre of the clergy by Parisian mobs. He was beatified in 1926. F. D. Sept. 4.

LANFRANC (1005?–1089), archbishop. Born in Pavia, Italy, he studied law there, continued his studies at Avranches, Normandy, became a teacher there, and in 1042 joined Abbot Herluin's monks at the monastery of Bec, of which he became prior. He founded a school at Bec which became famous for its scholarship. In 1050 his opposition to Berengarius' heresy led to his expositions on transubstantiation, and to a denunciation of private interpretation of this tenet of faith by the Lateran Council in 1059. He became a close adviser to Duke William of Normandy (despite a dispute with William over his proposed marriage to Matilda of Flanders in 1053, which was resolved when Lanfranc secured papal dispensation for the marriage in 1059), was appointed abbot of St. Stephen's in Caen in 1066, secured the pope's sanction for and accompanied the duke on his conquest of England, and in 1070 was appointed archbishop of Canterbury. He introduced Norman practices and reforms into English ecclesiastical affairs, replacing Saxon bishops and abbots with Normans, built churches, established new sees, and in 1072 forced the archbishop of York to admit Canterbury's primacy. In 1074 he acted as regent for the absent William and put down an uprising against the conqueror. He was scrupulous in insisting on ecclesiastical rights against secular intrusion, particularly in the case of investiture, and at a synod in Winchester in 1076 enforced the principle of clerical celibacy. In 1080 he wrote *De Corpore et Sanguine Domini*, which became the classic statement of the dogma of transubstantiation in the Middle Ages. He persuaded William to name his second son, William Rufus, heir to the throne and on William's death in 1087 crowned him William II, though he was never to exert the influence over him as he had over the conqueror. He died in Canterbury, England, on May 24.

LANFRANC BECCARIA, BL. (d. 1194), bishop. Born in Grupello, Lombardy, Italy, he became bishop of Pavia in 1178. His reign was continuously marked by a struggle to prevent the city from seizing church property and revenue. F. D. June 23.

LANFRANCO, GIOVANNI (1581–1647), painter. Born in Parma, Italy, he became a page in the service of Count Scotti when a boy and studied painting under Agostino Carracci. On the latter's death he went to Rome, became an assistant to Annibale Carracci, and with his execution of the cupola of Sant-Andrea della Valle, his masterpiece, became one of the ranking artists of his time. He executed cupolas in many of the great cities in Italy, France, and Austria, and became the rival of Domenischino. He died in Rome. He is also known as Cavaliere Giovanni di Stefano.

LANG, ANTON (1875–1938), actor. Born in Oberammergau, Germany, he became a potter, and was selected to play the part of Christ in the passion plays presented in his native village in 1900, 1910, and 1922. He died in Munich, Germany, on May 18.

LANG, MATTHEW (1468–1540), cardinal. Born in Augsburg, Bavaria, he was educated at Ingolstadt, Tübingen, and Vienna, and after serving in the chancery of Mainz was appointed secretary to Emperor Maximilian I in 1494, provost of Augsburg and Constance cathedrals in 1500, imperial councilor in 1501, coadjutor of Gurk in 1503, bishop in 1505. Though a layman, he held the see until 1522 and never visited it. He became chancellor in 1508, acted as the emperor's legate in diplomatic negotiations from 1508 to 1515, was appointed cardinal in 1511, and in 1514 coadjutor of Salzburg, to which he succeeded in 1519 when he was ordained just before his consecration. He effected a reconciliation between pope and emperor (though he had supported the schismatic Council of Pisa), was instrumental in the election of Emperor Charles V in 1519, and persuaded the emperor to act against Luther in 1521 and during the Peasants' War in 1525–26. He joined the league of Catholic princes at Ratisbon in 1524, supported Church reform at the Mühldorf synods in 1522 and 1537, and became primate of Germany in 1529. He died in Salzburg, Austria, on Mar. 30.

LANGEN, RUDOLPH VON (1438?–1519). Born in Everswinkel, Westphalia, he studied at Erfurt, was appointed provost of Münster cathedral in 1462, developed its school and library, and became the center of the literary and humanist movement in that city and a patron of scholars. He wrote some poetry and prose before his death in Münster, Westphalia, on Dec. 25.

LANGÉNIEUX, BENOÎT MARIE (1824–1905), cardinal. Born in Villefranche-sur-Saône, France, he studied at Paris and St. Sulpice, where he was ordained in 1850, and was curate at St. Roche and other parishes until 1871, when he became vicar general of Paris and archdeacon of Notre Dame. He was appointed bishop of Tarbes in 1873, archbishop of Rheims in 1874, and cardinal in 1886. He was presiding legate at eucharistic congresses in Jerusalem, Rheims, and Lourdes, sponsored the beatification of Joan of Arc, fought the anti-religious legislation of the late century, and was called the cardinal of the workers. He died in Rheims, France, on Jan. 1.

LANGEVIN, JEAN FRANÇOIS PIERRE LA FORCE (1821–1892), bishop. Born in Quebec, on Sept. 22, he studied at its seminary, was ordained in 1844, taught mathematics at the seminary, and wrote on calculus, education, and a history of Canada. He was rector of the normal school associated with Laval in 1858–69 and was named first bishop of Rimouski, Quebec, in 1867. He developed schools, introduced a cathedral chapter in 1878, resigned in 1891, and was named titular archbishop of Leontopolis, and died on Jan. 26.

LANGHAM, SIMON DE (1310–1376), cardinal. Born in Langham, Rutlandshire, England, he joined the Benedictines sometime before 1346, became prior of Westminster abbey in 1349, treasurer of England in 1360, and bishop of Ely in 1362. He was appointed chancellor of England in 1363 and archbishop of Canterbury in 1366, whereupon he resigned his chancellorship. He was created cardinal in 1368 and resigned the archbishopric later that year when Edward III seized the revenues of the see, claiming the archbishop had forfeited his temporalities when he accepted the cardinalate without his permission. In 1369 the cardinal joined the pope in Avignon, France, where he remained until his death on July 22. He was created cardinal-bishop of Palestrina in 1373 and was re-elected archbishop of Canterbury the following year, but was refused permission to return by the pope.

LANGHORNE, BL. RICHARD (d. 1679), martyr. Born in Bedfordshire, England, he became a lawyer in 1654 and attained considerable distinction. He was arrested in 1667 on the charge of assisting Catholics in burning the city of London, and again in 1678 on the charge of conspiring to kill King Charles II. At his trial he made it clear that Titus Oates, Bedloe, and Dugdale had perjured themselves in inventing the plot, but was hanged at Tyburn. He was beatified in 1929. F. D. July 14.

LANGLEY, BL. RICHARD (d. 1586), martyr. Probably born in Grimthorpe, Yorkshire, England, he inherited extensive estates there and at Ousethorpe, East Riding, which he used as hiding places for priests. When two priests were discovered at Grimthorpe, Langley was seized, convicted of harboring priests, and hanged, drawn, and quartered at York. He was beatified in 1929. F. D. Dec. 1.

LANGTON, STEPHEN (1160?–1228), cardinal. Born probably in England, he studied at Paris, taught theology, and in 1206 was summoned to Rome as a member of the household of Pope Innocent III, who created him a cardinal. In 1207 the pope appointed him archbishop of Canterbury to settle the quarrel between Reginald and John de Gray over the succession to the archbishopric, but he was refused permission to enter England by King John, who supported de Gray. The ensuing struggle between pope and king prevented Langton's return to England until 1213, when John, who had been excommunicated when Innocent placed England under interdict in 1208, surrendered England and Ireland to the pope and received his kingdom back as a fief. When the conflict between king and barons broke out, the archbishop vigorously supported the barons and was influential in the preparation of the Magna Charta (his is the first subscribing name), which John was obliged to accept at Runnymede in 1215. The pope ordered the Magna Charta annulled and excommunicated the barons who refused to accede. They continued their revolt against John and, when Langton refused to publish the excommunications, the pope suspended the archbishop. He was absolved in the spring of 1216, but was required to remain in Rome until after the deaths of Innocent III and John in 1216. He returned to England in 1218 and spent the rest of his life in ecclesiastical affairs. He was widely regarded as a scholar and wrote treatises on scripture, laid the foundation for English canon-law procedure, and is generally considered the author of the Magna Charta and as responsible for the division of the Bible into chapters. He died in Slindon Manor, Sussex, England, on July 9.

LANGTON, THOMAS (d. 1561), poet. One of the last monks professed at the Benedictine house at Canterbury, England, in 1534, he was on the staff of the Benedictine establishment at Westminster which Queen Mary restored in 1556, and was imprisoned in the Tower for saying mass. His poems on the contemporary scene have the tone of satiric regret voiced by Langland and Skelton.

LANIGAN, JOHN (1758–1825), historian. Born in Cashel, Tipperary, Ireland, he studied

and was ordained at the Irish College at Rome, taught Hebrew at Padua, and returned to Ireland in 1796 when the French invaded Italy. He taught briefly at Maynooth seminary and in 1799 became assistant librarian of the Royal Dublin Society. He wrote a four-volume *Ecclesiastical History of Ireland* (1822), correcting the early chroniclers, edited Alban Butler's *Meditations and Discourses*, prepared the first edition of the breviary printed in Ireland, and was a co-founder of the Gaelic Society, which sought to preserve the language. He died at Finglas, Ireland, on July 8.

LANSPERGIUS. *See* Gerecht, John.

LANTFRID, BL. (8th century). He founded the Benedictine abbey of Benediktbeuren in Bavaria, was its first abbot, and was succeeded sometime after 770 by his brothers, Waltram and Elilantus. F. D. July 10.

LANTRUA, BL. JOHN (1760–1816), martyr. Born in Triora, Italy, he became a Franciscan at seventeen, taught theology at Corneto, and sailed for China in 1799. He served the persecuted converts in Hupeh and Hunan as their only priest, was captured, tortured, and slowly strangled to death at Changsha on Feb. 7. He was beatified in 1900. F. D. Feb. 17.

LANVINUS, BL. (d. 1120). A Norman, he went to Calabria with St. Bruno, founder of the Carthusians, and succeeded him on his death there in 1101. He served on several missions for Pope Paschal II, was visitor of all monastic houses in the area, and maintained good discipline. He died on Apr. 11 and his cult was confirmed in 1893. F. D. Apr. 14.

LANZI, LUIGI (1732–1810), archaeologist. Born in Monte dell' Olmo, Italy, on June 13, he became a Jesuit in 1749, was assistant director of the Florentine Museum in 1773 after the Jesuits were suppressed, and in 1776 became its curator. He was president of the Accademia della Crusca and an authority on Graeco-Roman antiquities. He published *Saggio di lingua etrusca* (1789), *Storia pittorica dell'Italia* (1792), an edition of Hesiod, three volumes of *Inscriptiones et carmina* (from Catullus, Theocritus, and others), and ascetical works. He died in Florence on Mar. 31.

LA PELTRIE, MARIE MADELEINE CHAUVIGNY DE (1602–1671), educator. Born in Alençon, France, she was forced into marriage by her father, but was widowed at twenty-two. In 1639 she went to Quebec with three nuns to establish the Ursuline convent there, directed a school for Indian and white girls, moved to Montreal in 1642–46, then returned to Quebec to become an Ursuline.

LAPLACE, PIERRE SIMON (1749–1827), astronomer. Born in Beaumont-en-Auge, France, between Mar. 22 and 28, he studied there, at Caen and Paris, taught mathematics at L'École

Militaire in 1768, became examiner of the royal artillery in 1784, member of the Academy of Sciences in 1785, and a professor at L'École Normale. He was minister of the interior for six weeks in 1799, a member of the senate that year, its chancellor in 1803, received the title of count in 1806, was admitted to the French Academy in 1816 and in 1817 was created marquis. Laplace devoted his researches to solving the mechanical problem of the solar system and demonstrating the laws of astronomy. With Lagrange he proved Newton's hypothesis of gravitation and the stability of the planetary system. Among his great discoveries are the causes of the inequality of the motions of Jupiter and Saturn, the theory of Jupiter's satellites, the acceleration of the moon's mean motion, aberrations in the movement of comets, and the theory of tides. In 1796 his *Exposition du système du monde*, which included a summary of the history of astronomy, was hailed as a masterpiece of lucid exposition of the laws of astronomy, but his greatest work was the five-volume *Mécanique céléste* (1799–1825). Among his other important works were *Théorie des attractions des sphéroides et de la figure des planètes* (1785) and *Théorie analytique des probabilités* (1812). He died in Paris on Mar. 5.

LAPPARENT, ALBERT AUGUSTE DE (1839–1908), geologist. Born in Bourges, France, on Dec. 30, he studied at L'École Polytechnique and the School of Mines, and in 1864 was appointed mining engineer and a member of a group preparing a geological map of France. In 1874 he became secretary of a committee planning a tunnel between France and England and in 1875 held the chair of geology at the Catholic University of Paris. He was elected president of the Geological Society of France in 1880, of the French Society of Mineralogy in 1885, and secretary of the Academy of Science, of which he had been a member for ten years, in 1907. He wrote: *Traité de géologie, Cours de minéralogie*, and *Leçons de géographie physique*. He died in Paris on May 12.

LAPRADE, VICTOR DE (1812–1883), poet. Born in Montbrison, France, he studied medicine and law, but after admission to the bar turned to letters and taught in Lyons. A follower of Lamartine and heavily influenced by Wordsworth's outlook on nature, he published *Les symphonies* (1855), poems which led to his election to the French Academy. *Les idylles héroiques* (1858) and *Les poèmes civiques* (1873) were as intensely lyric, but more mature. His prose includes *Le Sentiment de la nature avant le christianisme*. He died in Lyons, France, on Dec. 14.

LAPUENTE, VEN. LUIS DE (1554–1624). Born in Valladolid, Spain, on Nov. 11, he be-

came a Jesuit, studied under Suarez and at Salamanca, and was ordained in 1580. He served as spiritual director to Marina de Escobar for the rest of his life, worked heroically during the plague of 1599 at Villagarcia, and wrote a commentary on the Canticle of Canticles, a four-volume *Christian Life*, meditations on the mysteries of faith, directions for the reception of the sacraments, and biographies. He died in Valladolid on Feb. 16.

LA PUMA, VINCENZO (1874–1943), cardinal. Born in Palermo, Italy, on Jan. 22, he studied at the seminary there and in Rome, was named cardinal and titular bishop of SS. Cosmas and Damian in 1935, served as prefect of the Congregation of Religious, and died in Rome on Nov. 4.

LARGUS, ST. (d. 284?), martyr. *See* Felix, St.

LARGUS, ST. (d. 304?), martyr. *See* Cyriacus, St.

LA RICHARDIE, ARMAND DE (1686–1758), missioner. Born in Périgueux, France, on June 7, he joined the Jesuits in 1703 in Bordeaux. In 1725 he was sent to Canada, spent two years in Lorette learning the Huron language, and was then sent to the area around the present city of Detroit to begin a mission of twenty-four years among the Hurons. He was recalled to Quebec in 1851 because of illness and remained there until his death on Oct. 4.

LARKE, BL. JOHN (d. 1544), martyr. Pastor of St. Ethelburga's church in Bishopsgate, England, then stationed at Woodford, and finally in Chelsea, to which he had been recommended by St. Thomas More, he was executed at Tyburn during the Henrican persecution. He was beatified in 1886. F. D. Mar. 7.

LARKIN, JOHN (1801–1858), educator. Of Irish descent, he was born in Newcastle-upon-Tyne, England on Feb. 2, studied under John Lingard at Ushaw College, traveled throughout the East, and on his return joined the Sulpicians in Paris. He was sent to St. Mary's seminary, Baltimore, where he was ordained in 1827, then assigned to teach at the Sulpician college in Montreal, where he remained until 1840, when he returned to the United States and joined the Jesuits. He established St. Ignatius' Literary Institution in Louisville, Kentucky, in 1841, became noted for his preaching, and in 1846 was sent to St. John's College (now Fordham) to teach. He was founder and first president of St. Francis Xavier College (1847), was appointed bishop of Toronto, an honor he declined, in 1850, and in 1851 was appointed president of Fordham. He was sent to England in 1854 to preach missions, returned to New York in 1856, and resumed his missionary work until his death on Dec. 11.

LA ROCHE DAILLON, JOSEPH DE (d. 1656), missionary. A member of the Recollects, he was sent on the Canadian mission in 1625 with the first Jesuit missionaries, worked among the Hurons and Neutral Nation tribes for the next four years, and was sent back to France, where he died, when the English captured Quebec in 1629. He published an account of his travels and experiences among the Indians.

LA ROCHEFOUCAULD-LIANCOURT, FRANÇOIS ALEXANDRE FRÉDÉRIC DE (1747–1827). Born in La Roche-Guyon, France, on Jan. 11, he was a member of the group at Louis XV's court urging reforms and a democratic monarchy. He established a model farm, where he experimented with scientific farming, and two factories to help the peasants on his estate at Liancourt, and founded L'École d'Arts at Metiers for the sons of poor soldiers (after 1788, called L'École des Enfants de la Patrie). He was elected to the constituent assembly in 1789, presided over it for several weeks, and voted to abolish titles of nobility. He supported public charity and relief and the eventual abolition of private and religious charitable organizations. He was appointed lieutenant of Normandy and Picardy in 1792, fled to England to escape the revolution later the same year, and was in the United States in 1794–97, when he wrote his eight-volume *Voyage dans les États-Unis d'Amerique* (1800). He returned to France in 1799, had his estate restored by Napoleon, and was appointed inspector general of L'École des Arts at Châlons in 1806, and in 1819 a penal inspector. He actively campaigned for hospitals and asylums, for school improvements, founded the Société d'Encouragement à l'Industrie Nationale, the first French savings bank in 1818 in Paris, and in 1821 the Society of Christian Morals, of which he was president until 1825. He died in Paris on Mar. 27. He also wrote *Les prisons de Philadelphie*, and translated books of educational theories into French, among them *Système anglais d'instruction*.

LA ROCHEJACQUELEIN, HENRI AUGUSTE GEORGES DU VERGIER DE (1805–1867). Born in the Château de Citran, France, on Sept. 28, he studied at St. Cyr and fought in the war in Spain (1823) and in the Russo-Turkish war (1828). He was made a peer in 1825, was elected to the legislature in 1842, and ran for president in 1848. He wrote political tracts, became a senator in 1852, and died on Jan. 7.

LA ROCQUE, CHARLES (d. 1875), bishop. He was born in Canada, was ordained, was pastor of St. John's for twenty-two years, and succeeded his cousin Joseph as third bishop of St. Hyacinthe, Quebec, in 1866. He moved the episcopal residence to Beloeil, where he also served as pastor, introduced the Dominicans to his see, attended the Vatican Council, helped

found the Sherbrooke diocese, and died in Beloeil, Canada, on July 15.

LA ROCQUE, JOSEPH (1808–1887), bishop. Born in Canada, he was ordained, became titular bishop of Cydonia and coadjutor of Montreal in 1852, directed the see of St. Hyacinthe, Quebec, in 1856–57 during the illness of Bishop Prince, and succeeded to that see as its second bishop in 1860. He resigned in ill health in 1865, being made titular bishop of Germanicopolis, and died in St. Hyacinthe on Nov. 18.

LA ROCQUE, PAUL (1846–1926), bishop. Born in Marieville, Quebec, Canada, on Oct. 28, he studied at Sts. Thérèse and Hyacinthe, was ordained in 1869, did parish work, and became rector of the cathedral of St. Hyacinthe in 1884. He was consecrated second bishop of Sherbrooke, Quebec, Canada, in 1893 and died there on Aug. 15.

LARRAMENDI, MANUEL DE (1690?–1750?), philologian. Born in Andoain, Spain, son of Domingo de Garagorri, he took his mother's name, studied at Bilbao, was ordained a Jesuit, and taught theology at Valencia, Valladolid, and Salamanca. He served at court as confessor to Queen Maria Anna, widow of Charles II, and retired in 1733 to Loyola to devote himself to writing. His *Antiguedad y universalidad en España del vascuence* (1728) was an attempt to prove that all Spanish dialects were derived from Basque. He wrote other treatises in support of his theory and prepared *Diccionario trilingue, castellano, vascuence y latino* in 1745.

LARRAZOLA, OCTAVIANO AMBROSIO (1859–1930), governor. Born in Allendale, Chihuahua, Mexico, on Dec. 7, he studied at St. Michael's, Santa Fe, and taught in San Elizario, Texas, in 1878–84. He was a court clerk in 1885–88, passed the bar, and in 1890–94 became district attorney for western Texas. He was governor of New Mexico in 1919–21 and in 1928–29 completed the unexpired term of Andrieus Jones in the United States Senate. He died in Albuquerque, New Mexico, on Apr. 7.

LARREY, DOMINIQUE JEAN (1766–1842), physician. Born in Baudéan, France, in July of poor parents, he studied under his uncle, Dr. Alexis Larrey, in Toulouse, joined the navy in 1787, the army in 1792, and in 1793 established an ambulance corps to tend the wounded on the battlefield itself. He was appointed surgeon in chief, accompanied Napoleon, whose close friend he became, to Egypt, and in 1809 was created a baron at the battle of Wagram for his bravery. He developed new operation techniques, made invaluable contributions toward increasing the health of troops in battle, and wrote several books on his surgical and medical observations. When Napoleon was exiled, he was deprived of his honors and spent the rest of his life in obscurity. He wrote *Clinique chirugicale dans les camps et hôpitaux militaires*, a report on cholera, and his memoirs. He died in Lyons, France, on July 25.

LA RUE, CHARLES DE (1643–1725), author. Born in Paris on Aug. 3, he joined the Jesuits in 1659, became professor of humanities and rhetoric, wrote a poem on Louis XII which was translated by Corneille, several tragedies and poems, edited an edition of Vergil and was an outstanding preacher. He died in Paris on May 27.

LA RUE, CHARLES DE (1685?–1739), editor. Born in Corbie, France, on July 29 (or July 12, 1684), he joined the Benedictines at Meaux and made his religious profession in 1703. In 1712 he was sent to Paris as assistant to Dom Bernard de Montfaucon, who set him to editing the works of Origen. After publishing two volumes in 1733 he suffered a stroke which ended his work. He died on Oct. 5 in St. Germain-des-Prés, Paris.

LA SALLE, RENÉ ROBERT DE (1643–1687), explorer. Born in Rouen, France, in Nov., he studied there, became a Jesuit, and left the Society in 1665. He went to Canada in 1666 when he was granted a tract of land near Montreal and engaged in the fur trade. In 1669, on one of his trips, he met Joliet, and with his maps pushed south to discover the Ohio River. In 1673 he was appointed commander of Fort Frontenac on Lake Ontario, was sent to France in 1674 to arrange further expeditions and was made esquire, and in 1677 was royally commissioned to trade in the Mississippi Valley. In 1679 he built the gunboat *Griffon*, and with Henri de Tonty and Fr. Louis Hennepin in his party sailed across Lake Michigan and overland to the Illinois River, where he built Fort Crèvecoeur and sent a party to the upper Mississippi under Fr. Hennepin. He returned overland to Frontenac for supplies and, when he returned, found the fort abandoned because of Indian attacks. After rebuilding the fort he returned to Montreal, and in 1681 set out for the West, with Tonty and Fr. Zenobe Membre, reached the Mississippi on Feb. 6, 1682, named it Colbert, and descended it to the Gulf of Mexico, which he reached on Apr. 9, taking possession of the entire region for France and naming it Louisiana. He returned to France in 1683 when a new governor, Sieur de la Barre, deprived him of his authority, reported his discoveries, received authority from the king to govern and colonize the area between Lake Michigan and the Gulf of Mexico, and was named viceroy of North America. La Salle returned in 1684 with a fleet of four vessels, was unable to locate the mouth of the river from the gulf, was shipwrecked, set off on foot for Canada, and on Mar. 19 was killed by one of his own men in

a mutiny on the banks of the Brazos River in Texas.

LASANCE, FRANCIS XAVIER (1860–1946). Born in Cincinnati, Ohio, on Jan. 24, he studied at Xavier, and St. Meinrad, Indiana, was ordained in 1883, served in Cincinnati parishes for seven years, and was forced to retire in ill health. For most of the rest of his life he was chaplain to the Sisters of Notre Dame de Namur in that city. He wrote a great number of devotional works on the Eucharist and the mass, books for religious and for children, and compiled a variety of popular missals. One of his best known titles is *My Prayer Book*. He died in Cincinnati on Dec. 11.

LASAULX, ERNST VON (1805–1861), philosopher. Born in Coblenz, Germany, on Mar. 16, son of a noted architect and nephew of Johann Joseph Görres, he studied at Bonn and Munich, traveled through Europe and to Palestine, and on his return in 1835 received his doctorate from Kiel and taught at Würzburg. He was among those protesting the imprisonment of Archbishop August of Cologne by the Prussian government in 1837. He was appointed professor of philology at Munich in 1844, but was dismissed by King Louis in 1847 for his attacks on the minister Abel. He was elected to the national assembly in 1848 and was reinstated at Munich in 1849 when he was elected to the Bavarian chamber of deputies, of which he remained a member until his death in Munich on May 9. He wrote *Studies on Classical Antiquity*; in some of his philosophical studies, placed on the Index after his death, he did not explain carefully enough the meaning of revelation.

LASCARIS, CONSTANTINE (1434–1501). Of Greek parents, he was born in Constantinople, imprisoned by the Turks when they captured the city in 1453, and on his release settled in Milan. He became the teacher of Hippolyta, daughter of Duke Francesco Sforza, and was famed for his ability to teach Greek at a time when the language was enjoying the revival heralding the Renaissance. After a year in Naples he settled in Messina, Sicily, in 1466, and remained there until his death, leaving to the city seventy-six manuscripts he had copied. He wrote *Erotemata*, a grammar, the first book printed in Greek.

LASCARIS, JANUS (1445?–1535), scholar. Surnamed Rhyndacenus, after Rhyndacus in Asia Minor where he probably was born, he was taken to Italy when Constantinople fell in 1453, was sent to Padua by his patron, Bessarion, and on the latter's death came under the patronage of Leonardo de' Medici in Florence. He lectured on Greek classicists and collected several hundred manuscripts on trips to Greece sponsored by Lorenzo. On his patron's death in 1492 he entered the diplomatic service of

France in Italy. He was ambassador to Venice from 1503 to 1508, became a member of the Greek Academy in Rome in 1508, helped Louis XII establish the library of Blois and, like Constantine Lascaris, to whom he probably was related, was noted for his influence in reviving interest in Greek learning. He edited several Greek plays and is also known as Andreas Joannes Lascaris. He died in Rome.

LAS CASAS, BARTOLOMÉ DE LAS. *See* Casas, Bartolomé de las.

LAS CASAS, ST. PHILIP DE (d. 1597), martyr. *See* Peter Baptist, St.

LASERIAN, ST. (d. 639), bishop. A monk from Iona, he supported the papal date for the celebration of Easter while at the monastery of Leighlin in southern Ireland, where his brother St. Goban was abbot. He was consecrated at Rome by Pope Honorius I and made apostolic legate to Ireland. By 637 he had succeeded his brother as bishop of Leighlin. He is also called Molaisse. F. D. Apr. 18.

LASKI, JOHN (1456–1531), archbishop. Born in Lask, Poland, he joined the staff of royal arch-chancellor Kurozwcki in 1482, became royal arch-secretary in 1502, arch-chancellor in 1505, coadjutor to the bishop of Gnesen in 1509, and succeeded to the see the following year, when he also became primate of Poland. He pleaded for help for Poland against Turkish attacks in 1513 at the fifth Lateran Council. He instituted ecclesiastical reforms at synods in 1510, 1512, and 1513, and held seven synods to combat Protestantism. In 1517 he sent his nephew, Jerome Laski, to support the brother-in-law of King Sigismund of Poland, John Zapolya, in his quest to oust King Ferdinand of Hungary. When Jerome Laski entered into an alliance with the Turks, the primate was cited to the Vatican for his continued support of his nephew in 1530, but died at Gnesen, Poland, on May 19 before he was able to go to Rome.

LASSBERG, JOSEPH MARIA CHRISTOPH VON (1770–1855), antiquarian. Born in Donaueschingen, Germany, on Apr. 10, he served in the army, studied law and forestry at Strassburg and Freiburg, became chief forester in Prince von Fürstenberg's service in 1804, and privy councilor in 1806. He resigned the latter position in 1817 when the regency of Princess Margaret ended. The balance of his life was spent in the study of old German literature and the building of an outstanding private library. Baron Von Lassberg edited mediaeval German poems, notably *Liedersaal*, many under the pseudonym of Meister Sepp von Eppishusen. He died on Mar. 15.

LASSUS, ORLANDUS DE. *See* Lattre, Roland de.

LATASTE, MARIE (1822–1847), mystic. Born in Mimbaste, France, on Feb. 21, of a poor family, she early experienced supernatural visions, joined the Society of the Sacred Heart in Paris in 1844, and was sent to their house at Rennes, where she lived the rest of a life noted for her sanctity and holiness. Under command of obedience she began a record of her experiences, which has been published. She died on May 10.

LATERA, FLAMINIUS ANNIBALI DE (1733–1813), historian. Born in Latera, Italy, on Nov. 23, he became a Franciscan in 1750. After ordination he taught, served as definitor general in 1790–91, and as superior of the Roman province in 1794–97. When Napoleon suppressed his order in Italy in 1810 he retired to Viterbo, Italy, where he died on Feb. 27. He wrote prolifically on Franciscan history, worked on the reform of the Franciscan breviary, and edited a hymnbook.

LATHROP, GEORGE PARSONS (1851–1898), author. Born in Honolulu, Hawaii, on Aug. 25, he was educated in New York and in Germany, married Rose Hawthorne (daughter of the American novelist) in London in 1871, served as associate editor of the *Atlantic Monthly* from 1875 to 1877, then worked for various Boston and New York newspapers. In 1883 he founded the American Copyright League, which later secured international protection of copyrights. He and his wife were converted in 1891. He wrote poems (*Rose and Rose-tree*, 1875, and *Dreams and Days*, 1892); novels (*Afterglow*, 1876, and *A Story of Courage* 1894); a history of Visitation Convent, Washington, D.C.; edited the works of Nathaniel Hawthorne (1883); and adapted *The Scarlet Letter* for an opera produced in 1896. He died in New York City on Apr. 19.

LATHROP, ROSE HAWTHORNE (1851–1926). Born in Lenox, Massachusetts, on May 20, daughter of Nathaniel Hawthorne, she was brought up in England and Portugal, studied art in Dresden, and married George Parsons Lathrop in 1871. After his death in 1898 she became a Dominican, as Mother Alphonse, established St. Rose's Free Home for Cancer in New York City, then moved her work to Rosary Hill Hospital, Hawthorne, under the direction of the Servants of Relief for Incurable Cancer which she had organized. She was widely honored for her medical and charitable work, wrote stories and sketches, and published poems (*Along the Shore*, 1888), and, with her husband, *Memories of Hawthorne* (1897). She died on July 9 at Hawthorne, New York.

KATHERINE BURTON, *Sorrow Built a Bridge* (Garden City, N.Y., Image Books, 1956).

LATINI, BRUNETTO (1210?–1294). Born in Florence, Italy, he taught philosophy and grammar (Dante was one of his pupils), became a notary, and in 1250 joined the Guelphs in their successful attempt to overthrow the

Ghibellines in Florence. He acted as ambassador of the commune in 1260 to seek the assistance of King Alfonso X of Castile; on his way back he learned of the Guelph defeat at Montaperti and fled to France, returning to Florence in 1266 when the Guelphs were again successful. He became secretary of the commune, an outstanding orator, and a leading statesmen. He wrote *Il tesoretto*, an allegory which influenced Dante, and other poems, and *Li Livres dou trésor*, a compendium of knowledge, compiled while he was in France. He died in Florence.

LATINI, BL. PHILIP (1605–1667). He was a shoemaker near Palermo, Sicily, and a notorious duelist until, after wounding a police officer in 1632, he took sanctuary in a church. While in refuge he decided to reform, and became a Capuchin laybrother at twenty-seven; he was known thereafter as Bernard of Corleone. He sought to make up for his early career by undergoing the most extreme austerities. He was beatified in 1768. F. D. Jan. 19.

LATINUS, ST. (d. 115), bishop. Captured and tortured during the persecution of Domitian, he lived to succeed St. Flavian as fourth bishop of Brescia, Italy, in 84. F. D. Mar. 24.

LATREILLE, PIERRE ANDRÉ (1762–1833), zoologist. Born in Brives, France, on Nov. 29, he was adopted by Abbé Haüy, the mineralogist, in 1778, studied at Lemoine College in Paris, and was ordained in 1786. After studying entomology in Brives for two years he returned to Paris, where he lived until 1792, when he was imprisoned in Bordeaux by the revolutionists. Bory de St. Vincent, the naturalist, procured his release; he was rearrested in 1797 as an emigré, again released, and in 1799 headed the entomological department of the Muséum d'Histoire Naturelle in Paris. He was elected to the French Institute in 1814 and appointed successor to Lamarck as professor of entomology in 1829. He died in Paris on Feb. 6. Latreille is considered the father of modern entomology, established several insect orders, and arranged the insect collection of the museum. He wrote many studies, including the fourteen-volume *Histoire naturelle générale et particulière des crustacés et insectes, Considérations sur l'ordre naturel des animaux,* and *Familles naturelles du règne animal.*

LATTRE, ROLAND DE (1520?–1594), composer. Known in musical history as Orlandus de Lassus, he was born in Mons, Belgium, sang in St. Nicholas' church there, and became a protégé of Ferdinand de Gonzaga, viceroy of Sicily, who took him to Italy in 1536. He left the viceroy to spend three years at the Naples court, then went to Rome, where he was choirmaster of St. John Lateran for two years. He traveled through Europe, settled in Amster-

dam, and from 1557 to 1591 was choirmaster of Dukes Albert V and William V of Bavaria at Munich. He produced some 2000 musical compositions, including *The Penitential Psalms,* fifty masses, as well as motets, magnificats, and songs, characterized by variety, richness, and depth of expression, and was the forerunner of Palestrina. He was raised to the nobility by Emperor Maximilian in 1570 and was decorated by Pope Gregory XIII and King Charles IX of France. He died in Munich, Bavaria, on June 14.

LAUDOMARUS, ST. (d. 593). A priest, he founded the monastery of Corbion, near Chartres, France, and became its abbot. He also is known as Lomer. F. D. Jan. 19.

LAURA, ST. (d. 864), martyr. Born in Cordova, Spain, she became a nun at Cuteclara after she was widowed, and was scalded to death by her Moorish captors. F. D. Oct. 19.

LAURATI, PIETRO. *See* Lorenzetti, Pietro.

LAUREL, BL. BARTHOLOMEW (d. 1627), martyr. Born in Mexico City, he became a Franciscan laybrother, studied medicine in the Philippines after 1609, was sent to Japan in 1622, and was burned alive at Nagasaki. He was beatified in 1867. F. D. Aug. 17.

LAURENCE, ST. (d. 258), martyr. According to early tradition, he was born in Huesca, Spain, and went with his family to Rome, where he became one of the seven deacons of the city under Pope St. Sixtus II. During the persecution of Valerian, Sixtus was executed in 258 and he told Laurence he would follow three days later. The deacon gave away everything that he could find to the poor before the prefect of Rome demanded the church's property and precious vessels for himself. Laurence said he needed three days to gather all the treasures of the church, then brought the poor, the blind, the crippled, the orphaned, and other unfortunates before him. The infuriated prefect ordered Laurence roasted alive on a gridiron, a fate which the deacon bore without complaint, even suggesting that his body be turned to be broiled on the other side. Although the authenticity of this story may be questioned, Laurence has been venerated from the earliest times as the most celebrated Roman martyr. His death must have impressed the Romans deeply; several senators became Christians immediately, and buried the martyr's body on the Via Tiburtina, where his basilica now stands. Prudentius said that his death signalized the decline of Roman idolatry and the beginning of the conversion of Rome itself. SS. Augustine, Ambrose, Leo the Great, and Gregory of Tours also praised him most highly. F. D. Aug. 10.

LAURENCE (d. 505), antipope. A member of the pro-Byzantine party led by Senator Festus who was attempting to get papal approval of Emperor Zeno's heretical *Henoticon*, and archpriest of Rome, he was elected anti-pope on Nov. 22, 498, by a minority of the Roman clergy opposed to Pope Symmachus. Lawrence submitted to Symmachus when Gothic King Theodoric ruled in favor of the lawful pope and was appointed bishop of Nocera, Campania. In 501, Festus' party brought Lawrence back to Rome, accused Symmachus of mismanagement of Church affairs, and again proclaimed Lawrence pope. The schism was prolonged until 505, when Theodoric again declared Symmachus the lawful pope.

LAURENCE, ST. (d. 576), bishop. A Syrian who left his homeland under persecution and came to Rome, he was ordained there by Pope Hormisdas. He fought the Arian heresy in Umbria, retired to a monastery near Spoleto, was called out to become bishop of that see, suffered hostility because he was an alien, but won over those who opposed him. He became known as "the Enlightener" because of his instructional success in Bologna and elsewhere and because of his cures of the physically blind. He died as abbot of the monastery of Farfa, Italy, which he had founded. F. D. Feb. 3.

LAURENCE, ST. (d. 619), archbishop. A priest who had come to Britain in 597 with St. Augustine, he converted King Edbald from paganism and succeeded Augustine as archbishop of Canterbury in 608. F. D. Feb. 3.

LAURENCE, BL. (d. 1457). Born in Ripafratta, Tuscany, Italy, he became a Dominican at Pisa, master of novices at Cortona (St. Antoninus and Fra Angelico were among his charges), and vicar general of the reformed Dominican priories. He was noted as a preacher and biblical scholar. His cult was approved by Pope Pius IX in 1851. F. D. Sept. 28.

LAURENCE OF BRINDISI, ST. (1559-1619), Doctor of the Church. Cesare de Rossi was born in Brindisi, Italy, on July 22, studied in Venice, and at sixteen became a Capuchin at Verona, taking the name Laurence. He studied at Padua, where he mastered languages and scripture, became an outstanding preacher, and in 1596 was made definitor general of his order, a post he was to hold five times. He was quite successful in making Jewish converts and was sent with Bl. Benedict of Urbino to Germany to establish a Capuchin mission to counter Lutheranism. They founded three friaries which later developed as separate provinces. At the request of Emperor Rudolf III he raised an army with the help of German princes to fight the Turks threatening Hungary. He rode with the soldiers, encouraging them by prayer as well as by astute military advice, and saw the tide turned in the victorious battle of Szekes-Fehervar in 1601. He was elected vicar general in 1602, but refused re-election in 1605.

From Germany he went to Spain to ask Philip III to join the Catholic League; while there, he founded a Capuchin house in Madrid. He then went to Munich as papal legate to the court of Maximilian of Bavaria. He retired in 1618 to the friary at Caserta, but was persuaded by the leaders in Naples to go to Spain to plead with Philip to remove the tyrannical Spanish viceroy, the duke of Osuna, before a revolution broke out. He succeeded in having Osuna recalled, but died a few days later in Lisbon, on July 22, and was buried at Villafranca. He was canonized in 1881 and proclaimed a Doctor of the Church by Pope John XXIII in 1959. F. D. July 21.

LAURENCE LORICATUS, BL. (d. 1243). Born in Fanello, Apulia, Italy, he accidentally killed a man during his army career, made a pilgrimage of penance to Compostela, and on his return joined the Benedictines in 1209 at Subiaco. There he lived as a recluse in a mountain cave for thirty-three years, wearing a coat of mail with sharp points next to his skin (hence the name Loricatus, "the Cuirassier"). His cult was approved in 1778. F. D. Aug. 16.

LAURENCE MAJORANUS, ST. (d. 546?). He was bishop of Siponto, Italy, from 492 until his death. F. D. Feb. 7.

LAURENCE OF NOVARRA, ST. (d. 397?), martyr. He was put to death in Piedmont, Italy, with a group of children whom he was teaching as a catechist. F. D. Apr. 30.

LAURENCE O'TOOLE, ST. (1128-1180), archbishop. Lorcan O'Tuathail, son of an Irish chieftain, was born in Kildare. At ten he was taken as a hostage by Dermot McMurrogh, king of Leinster, and held captive for two years. He then became an Augustinian at the monastery of Glendalough, where he was abbot from 1153 to 1161, when he was elected archbishop of Dublin. In 1170 he acted unsuccessfully as peacemaker between the Irish and the English invaders under Richard de Clare, and in 1172 attended a synod at Cashel called by King Henry II and again acted as negotiator between the English king and the Irish princes. In 1175 he went to Windsor to negotiate a treaty between Henry and King Rory O'Conor, and was attacked by a would-be assassin in Canterbury. In 1179 he attended the third Lateran Council at Rome and was appointed papal legate to Ireland by Pope Alexander. While in England in 1180, again negotiating for Rory O'Conor, he was forbidden by Henry to return to Ireland. Laurence followed the king to Normandy, secured his permission to return, but died at Eu, France, on the way home. He was canonized in 1180. F. D. Nov. 14.

LAURENTI, CAMILLO (1862-1938), cardinal. Born in Monteporzio-Catone, Italy, he was ordained, was created cardinal-deacon in 1921 and cardinal-priest in 1935, served as prefect of the Congregation of Rites, and died in Rome on Sept. 6.

LAURENTIA, ST. (d. 302), martyr. *See* Palatias, St.

LAURENTIE, PIERRE SÉBASTIEN (1793–1876), author. Born in Houga, Gers, France, on Jan. 21 he joined La Congrégation, a Parisian charitable society, in 1817, the editorial staff of *La Quotidienne* in 1818, and was appointed inspector general of schools in 1823, from which he was dismissed in 1826 because of his attacks on the Villèle ministry. In 1828 he opposed the Martignac ministry's decrees against the Jesuits and minor seminaries and purchased the College of Ponlevoy in an attempt to continue its existence. After 1830 he devoted himself to writing in defense of religion, legitimism, and freedom of education. Among his chief works are *Lettres sur l'éducation*, *L'Esprit chrétien dans les études*, *De la révolution en Europe*, *L'Athéisme social et l'église*, a ten-volume *Histoire de France*, *Histoire de l'empire romain*, and, after his death, *Souvenirs*. He died in Paris on Feb. 9.

LAURENTINUS, ST. (3rd century), martyr. *See* Ignatius, St.

LAURIANUS, ST. (d. 544?). He is said to have been a Hungarian, ordained a deacon at Milan, who was sent to Spain as a bishop and later martyred at Bourges, France; all details are questionable. F. D. July 4.

LAURIER, WILFRID (1841–1919), premier. Born in St. Lin, Quebec, Canada, on Nov. 20, he studied at Assumption College and law at McGill, practiced law in Montreal, and became editor of *Le Défricheur*, an extremely nationalistic journal, often attacked by Church leaders. He was a member of the House of Commons from 1874 until his death, was leader of the Liberal party after 1878, and faced considerable difficulty from all factions over the question of religious education. He opposed high tariffs and the building of the Canadian Pacific Railroad, and favored reciprocity with the United States. In 1896 he became the first French Canadian premier, and held that position until 1911. His government helped to develop a second transcontinental railroad and the Western territories, regulated freight and communication rates, and made a trade agreement with the United States. He supported the Allies during World War I, though opposing conscription, and remained the leader of his party after it fell in 1911 until his death in Ottawa on Feb. 17. He was knighted by the British government in 1897.

LAUIR, LORENZO (1864–1941), cardinal. Born in Rome on Oct. 15, he was ordained in 1887, served in Rome, was in 1901 named canon of the basilica of San Lorenzo, Damascus, and then to the papal diplomatic service. He was legate to Peru and Spain, and as nuncio

to Poland in 1921–27 arranged a concordat and reorganized the dioceses of the restored nation. He was named cardinal in 1927 and chamberlain (camerlingo) in 1939. He died in Vatican City on Oct. 8.

LAURUS, ST. (2nd century), martyr. *See* Florus, St.

LAURUS, ST. (7th century). A Welshman, he went to Brittany and was founder-abbot of the monastery on the Doneff River, later called St. Léry after him. F. D. Sept. 30.

LAUTO, ST. (d. 568). He became bishop of Coutances, Normandy, in 528; his family estate became the later village of St. Lô. F. D. Sept. 22.

LAUZON, JEAN DE (1583–1666), governor. Born in Paris, he became councilor of the Paris parliament in 1613, master of petitions in 1623, and was appointed intendant of the Company of New France, recovering Quebec in 1629. He was named fourth governor of Canada in 1651, proved successful in administering finance, the fur trade, and justice, but could not control the Iroquois. Old age made him resign in 1656 during his second term. He returned to Paris, where he died on Feb. 16.

LAUZON, PIERRE DE (1687–1742), missioner. Born in Poitiers, France, on Sept. 26, he joined the Jesuits in 1703 and was ordained and sent on the Canadian mission in 1716. He worked among the Caughnawagas (with whom he became so popular that, when he was recalled to teach at Quebec in 1721–22, they threatened to move to English territory), at Sault St. Louis from 1718 until 1731, and was appointed superior of the Caughnawaga mission in 1723. He was superior of the entire Canadian mission in 1732, and as such was rector of the college of Quebec, returned to missionary work in 1739, but ill health caused him to return to Quebec in 1741. He died there on Sept. 5.

LAVAL, VEN. FRANÇOIS DE MONTMORENCY (1623–1708), bishop. Born in Montigny-sur-Avre, France, on Apr. 30, he studied at La Flèche and Clermont, Paris, where he joined the group which developed into the Society of Foreign Missions. He gave up his family title and estates and was ordained in 1647. He became archdeacon at Évreux, served at Caen in 1655–58, was appointed vicar apostolic of New France and titular bishop of Petra, and arrived in Quebec in 1659. He faced a jurisdictional dispute with the archbishop of Rouen, which was resolved when Quebec was defined in 1674 as a diocese responsible directly to Rome. His episcopate was also marked by a running battle with the civil authorities, who persisted in selling liquor to Indians; he succeeded in bringing about the removal of Gov. d'Avaugour, but the struggle continued with his successors. Laval organized an entire educational system, founded a major seminary, which was in turn to found Laval University in 1663 and a minor seminary in 1668, and built an industrial school at St. Joaquim. He helped govern the colony, working to establish the sovereign council, and developed a well-organized parochial and missionary system. He reached, in person or by representative, a large part of a diocese which included all of Canada and the present United States (exclusive of New England and the Atlantic states). He resigned in 1688 to allow a younger man, his vicar general, St. Vallier, to take over, but he disapproved of the latter's rule and during his absences in 1694–97 and 1700–8 administered the see himself. His last years were devoted to the seminary, which had twice burned down; to its upkeep he donated his private income. He died in Quebec on May 6.

LAVAL, JACQUES DÉSIRÉ (1803–1884), missioner. Born in Croth, France, on Sept. 18, he studied at Evreux and the Collège Stanislas, Paris, and took his degree in medicine in 1830. He soon gave up his practice, entered St. Sulpice, was ordained in 1838, and in 1841 became a member of the Congregation of the Immaculate Heart of Mary. He was sent to Mauritius in 1861, worked with the recently freed Negro slaves, and in twenty-three years made over 67,000 converts. He also introduced effective sanitary and agricultural reforms.

LAVAL, JEAN MARIE (1854–1937), bishop. Born in St. Étienne, Loire, France, on Sept. 21, he studied at the Mont Brison seminary, St. Michael College in his home town, and went to the United States in 1872. After further study at the diocesan seminary in New Orleans, he was ordained there in 1877, served as pastor of churches in Baton Rouge, Iberville, Houma, and New Orleans, and was pastor of St. Louis cathedral at the latter city in 1902–11. He was appointed vicar general in 1898, was made a domestic prelate in 1901, and in 1911 he was appointed titular bishop of Hierocaesarea and auxiliary of New Orleans. He died in San Francisco, California, on June 4.

LAVALDÈNE, BL. IPHIGENIE DE GAILLARD DE (d. 1794), martyr. A nun in the convent of the Perpetual Adorers of the Blessed Sacrament in Bollène, she was guillotined at Orange, France, with twelve others of her institute for refusing to take the anti-religious republican oath during the French Revolution. The martyrs of Orange were beatified in 1925. F. D. July 7.

LA VALETTE, JEAN PARISOT DE (1494–1568). Born in Toulouse, France, he joined the Order of the Knights of St. John of Jerusalem and rose through the ranks. In 1537 he was appointed commander and governor of Tripoli, which the order ruled, and in 1557 grand master. He formed an alliance in 1560 with Adm. de la Cerda of Spain to attack Tripoli, which had fallen in 1556, but the expedition was destroyed by the Moors. He then launched a project by which the commanders of the order built ships, which developed into such an important naval force in the Mediterranean that the Turks under Mustapha determined to wipe out the base on Malta. He helped organize the defenses of Malta against the attack of the Turks and in 1565 beat off a four-month assault though overwhelmingly outnumbered, a feat for which he was offered a cardinalcy, which he refused. He died on Malta on Aug. 21.

LA VALLIÈRE, LOUISE FRANÇOISE DE LA BEAUME LE BLANC DE (1644–1710). Born in Touraine, France, and brought to court by her widowed mother, she became the mistress of King Louis XIV and bore him four children. In 1674, when the monarch abandoned her for Mme. de Montespan, she entered the Carmelite convent in Paris, where she spent thirty-six penitential years. *Réflexions sur la miséricorde de Dieu* was published in 1680; her letters appeared posthumously, in 1767.

LAVELLE, MICHAEL J. (1856–1939). Born in New York City, on May 30, he graduated from Manhattan College, studied at St. Joseph's seminary, Troy, and was ordained in 1879. He was assigned to St. Patrick's cathedral, New York, and was its pastor from 1886 until his death in New York City on Oct. 17. He was named vicar general and consultor in 1902, domestic prelate in 1903, and prothonotary apostolic in 1929. He was active in many cultural and welfare organizations and was president of the Catholic Summer School of America in 1896–1903.

LAVERDIÈRE, CLAUDE HONORÉ (1826–1873), author. Born in Château Richer, Quebec, he was ordained in 1851, taught in the Quebec seminary, until his death there, and became assistant librarian at Laval. He published three volumes of the *Jesuit Relations* (1858), edited *Voyages de Champlain* (1870) and *Journal des Jesuites* (1871), wrote a popular history of Canada, and compiled an anthology of French-Canadian hymns and songs.

LAVÉRENDRYE, PIERRE DE (1685–1749), explorer. Born in Three Rivers, Quebec, on Nov. 17, he served in the French army, was wounded in action, and returned to Canada, where he engaged in the fur trade. He established a series of trading posts in western Canada, including Winnipeg, and into the Rocky Mountains in Montana, which he reached in 1742. He took missionary priests with him on his travels, set up permanent chapels, and sent out scouting parties under his sons, one of whom discovered Lake Manitoba. He died in Montreal on Dec. 6.

LAVERLOCHÈRE, JEAN NICOLAS (1812–

1884), missioner. Born in St. Georges d'Espérance, France, on Dec. 6, he joined the Oblates as a laybrother, but studied for the priesthood, was ordained in 1844 in Canada, and engaged in missionary work among the Indians. He was called the "apostle of Hudson Bay" when his letters were published as *Annales de la propagation de la foi*, but was obliged to give up his work when stricken by palsy in 1851. He died in Temiscaming, Canada, on Oct. 4.

LAVIALLE, PETER JOSEPH (1820–1867), bishop. Born in Lavialle, Auvergne, France, on July 15, he went to the United States in 1841 to join Bishop Chabrat, a relative, in Louisville, studied at St. Thomas seminary, Bardstown, and was ordained there in 1844. He served at the cathedral, taught at St. Thomas' seminary in 1849, and in 1856 was appointed president of St. Mary's College. He was consecrated bishop of Louisville in 1865, attended the second Plenary Council in Baltimore in 1866, and died in Nazareth, Kentucky, on May 11.

LAVIGERIE, CHARLES MARTIAL ALLEMAND (1825–1892), cardinal. Born in Huire, near Bayonne, France, on Oct. 31, son of a customs officer, he studied at Laressore, St. Nicolas du Chardonnet, and St. Sulpice seminaries, and was ordained in 1849. He continued his studies at L'École des Carmes and the Sorbonne, where he received doctorates in church history and theology; he later received doctorates in civil and canon law in Rome. He was appointed chaplain of Ste. Geneviève in 1853, associate professor at the Sorbonne in 1854, and three years later occupied the chair of church history there. He organized the Catholic students into clubs, was active in L'Oeuvre des Écoles d'Orient, a philanthropy devoted to erecting Christian schools in the Middle East, went to Syria in 1860 to supervise the dispersal of funds he had raised for persecuted Christians there, and was appointed French auditor to the Roman rota in 1861 and bishop of Nancy in 1863. He had established several colleges, insisted on higher educational requirements for priests and nuns, and organized an episcopal curia when he was transferred to Algiers as archbishop in 1867. He founded the White Fathers and the White Sisters to convert the Moslems (later expanded to helping all Africans) and built hospitals, orphanages, and schools. He was appointed apostolic delegate of Western Sahara and the French Sudan in 1868 and began to expand his missionary activities throughout Africa. He became administrator of Constantina in 1871, founded a clerical seminary for the oriental missions in 1878, and was made head of the vicariate of Tunis in 1882. He was created cardinal in 1881 and in 1884 first primate of the restored see of Car-

thage with jurisdiction over all French Africa. He was a leader in the anti-slavery movement and in 1890 called the Congrès de Paris to consider means to abolish slavery. He vigorously supported Leo XIII's encyclicals, *Nobillisima Gallorum gens* (1884), and *Sapientiae aeternae* (1890), directing French Catholics to support the republic, and caused a sensation in 1890 when he repudiated royalism. He wrote on the Church in Edessa, Jansenism, the Algerian councils, and his work in Africa. He died in Algiers on Nov. 27.

GLENN D. KITTLER, *The White Fathers* (Garden City, N.Y., Image Books, 1961).

LAVITRANO, LUIGI (1874–1950), cardinal. Born in Forio Ischia, near Naples, Italy, on Mar. 7, he was educated in Rome, was ordained in 1898, taught at the Pontifical seminary, was vice-rector of the Leonine Apostolic College, and became an authority on canon law. He was named bishop of Carva and Sarno in 1914, was transferred to Benevento in 1924, and named archbishop of Palermo in 1928. He was prefect of the Congregation of Religious, directed Catholic Action in Italy, and effected peaceful and prompt co-operation between his people and the American forces under Gen. Mark Clark during the invasion of Italy during World War II. He died in Marino, Italy, on Aug. 2.

LAVOISIER, ANTOINE LAURENT (1743–1794), chemist. Born in Paris on Aug. 26, he studied at Collège Mazarin, took up law, but abandoned it for chemistry and mineralogy, in which he achieved early recognition in 1775 when he read his paper to the Academy of Sciences on combustion. In 1766 he won the academy's prize for his plan for improved street lighting in Paris, was appointed to superintend the manufacture of gunpowder, and two years later was elected an associate of the academy. He served on the commission of weights and measures in 1790 and as commissary of the treasury in 1791. He worked to improve social and economic conditions in France, but his position as tax collector incited the hatred of the revolutionists. He was arrested in 1794, condemned to death on the ridiculous charge of adding water to tobacco, and on May 8 was guillotined in Paris. Lavoisier's great contributions in the field of chemistry have caused him to be called the founder of modern chemistry. Building on the findings of Priestly and Cavendish, he discovered the role of oxygen in plant and animal respiration, introduced effective quantitative methods to the study of chemistry, and proved the relationship between oxygen and a substance undergoing combustion by discovering a new chemical theory of combustion, the anti-phlogistonists' theory. He established, with others, the modern system of chemical nomenclature, the modern division into element and compound by his classification of substances, and explained the formation of acids and salts. He wrote *Opuscules physiques et chimiques, Méthode de nomenclature chimique, Traité elémentaire de chimie,* and *Mémoires de chimie,* and other treatises.

LAWLER, JOHN JEREMIAH (1862–1948), bishop. Born in Rochester, Minnesota, on Aug. 4, he studied at St. Francis seminary, Milwaukee, St. Nicholas College and Louvain, and was ordained in 1885. After further study at Louvain, where he was vice-rector of the American College in 1885–87, he became professor of scripture at St. Thomas College, St. Paul, did parish work, and was pastor of the cathedral when he was consecrated titular bishop of Hermopolis and auxiliary of St. Paul in 1910. He became bishop of Lead, South Dakota, in 1916 and of Rapid City, South Dakota, in 1930, when the see was transferred there. He received an honorary doctorate from Louvain in 1927, and died in Rapid City on Mar. 11.

LAWRENCE, BL. ROBERT (d. 1535), martyr. Prior of the charterhouse at Beauvale, Nottinghamshire, England, he was consulting with the Carthusians in London when, attending Bl. John Houghton on a visit to Thomas Cromwell, he was seized and imprisoned in the Tower. At a later trial he refused to subscribe to Henry VIII's Act of Supremacy and was savagely treated before and after being hanged at Tyburn. He was beatified in 1886. F. D. May 4.

LAYAMON (13th century), poet. A priest living at Arnley-on-Severn, Worcestershire, England, about 1200, he wrote *Brut,* a metrical chronicle of the legendary grandeur of British history from the fall of Troy to the death of Cadwalader, the last Celtic king. The poem mentions the Cymbeline and King Lear stories later used by Shakespeare. Layamon relied heavily on the Anglo-Norman poet Wace's *Roman de Brut* (1155). Layamon used alliteration, assonance, and rhyme; his diction is predominantly English rather than French and his narrative manner simple and direct rather than courtly. He relied on the magic of romance in his retelling of the Arthurian legend, but his king is a national patriot rather than the hero of a romance. To the legend Layamon added the dream foreshadowing the treachery of Guinevere and Modred, the actual construction of the Round Table, and the lengthy details of Arthur's final defeat, death, and passing to Avalon.

LAYMANN, PAUL (1574–1635), theologian. Born in Arzl, Austria, he studied at Ingolstadt, where he joined the Jesuits in 1594 and was ordained in 1603. He taught at Ingolstadt (1603–9), the Jesuit house in Munich (1609–25), and at Dillingen (1625–32). He wrote treatises on moral theology, philosophy, and canon law, among them *Theologia moralis,* used extensively as a seminary text for the next century, and *Jus canonicum,* published after his death of the plague in Constance, Switzerland, on Nov. 13.

LAYNEZ, DIEGO (1512–1565), theologian. Born in Almazan, Castile, Spain, he studied at Alcalá, where he received his licentiate in philosophy in 1532, and then at the university of Paris, where he met Ignatius Loyola. He became the second to join and one of the founding members of the Society of Jesus who took their vows at Montmartre in 1534. He spent the next few years in charitable work mainly in northern Italy and was among those who met with Pope Paul III and was assigned to teach theology at the Sapienza. He was selected by Paul as one of the three papal theologians to the Council of Trent, was outstanding in the discussion of the question of justification, and had his statement unanimously accepted by the council in 1547. He received his doctorate in theology from Bologna in 1549, and then acted as chaplain on an African expedition against Dragut the Corsair. He was papal theologian for Pope Julius III when the Council of Trent was resumed in 1551 and is reputed to have written the decrees and canons of the fourteenth session. He was appointed provincial of Italy in 1552, was elected vicar general of the Jesuits in 1556, their second general in 1558, and acted as Pope Pius IV's theologian, with Cardinal Ippolito d'Este, at the Poissy Conference in 1561. He worked successfully for the adoption of his Society's constitutions, was responsible for the direction it took in higher education, and returned to Trent in 1562 to defend the distribution of Communion under one species. His views were accepted at the twenty-second session; he also worked on the decrees and canons relating to the sacrament of holy orders and on defining the jurisdiction of bishops. His name is often spelled Lainez or Leynez. He died in Rome on Jan. 19.

LAZARUS, ST. (1st century). Brother of Martha and Mary of Bethany, all close friends of Christ, he died and was raised from the dead by Jesus (John 11:1–45). He was also present at the banquet given to Christ by Simon the Leper in Bethania (Matt. 26:6–16; Mark 14:3–11; John 12:1–11), but nothing more is told of him except that the Jews wanted to put him to death because his living presence was attracting believers in Christ. Greek tradition makes him bishop of Lanarka (Kition), Cyprus. Mediaeval fiction says he came, with Mary Magdalene and others, to Gaul to become first bishop of Marseilles and a martyr. F. D. Dec. 17.

LAZARUS, ST. (1st century). He was the poor man at the gate of the wealthy man in the parable told by Christ (Luke 16). The military Order of St. Lazarus was founded during the crusades to care for lepers. He is honored in the Abyssinian rite on June 21.

LAZARUS, ST. (d. 344), martyr. He and SS. Marotas, Narses, and Zanitas were put to death for refusing to worship the sun during the persecution of King Sapor II of Persia. F. D. Mar. 27.

LAZARUS, ST. (d. 450?). He ruled as bishop of Milan, Italy, to which he had been appointed in 439, effectively but under great difficulty, during the conquest of the area by the Goths, and died on March 14. F. D. Feb. 11.

LAZARUS, ST. (d. 867?). Called "the Painter," he was a monk at Constantinople who restored many of the icons which had been defaced by the Iconoclast heretics. F. D. Feb. 23.

LAZIOSI, ST. PELLEGRINO (1260–1345). Born in Forlì, Italy, he was a leader of the antipapal faction in Romagna and one of those who attacked and beat St. Philip Benizi. When the latter turned the other cheek, Pellegrino repented and joined the Servites at Siena. Later he returned to establish a house at Forlì and to become a successful preacher. Because he was miraculously cured of advanced cancer of the foot, he is a patron against that disease. He was canonized in 1726. F. D. May 1.

LEAFWINE. See Lebuin, St.

LEANDER, ST. (d. 596), archbishop. Son of Duke Saverian of Cartagena and of the daughter of King Theodoric, he became a monk in Seville, Spain, at an early age, known for his great eloquence and labors to root out Arianism. In 583 he went to Constantinople as ambassador of King Leovigild, became friendly with St. Gregory the Great, and suggested the latter's study of Job. Soon after his return, he became archbishop of Seville. He and his brother St. Fulgentius were banished by the king, who had killed his son Hermengild (a convert of Leander's from Arianism). They were later recalled and Leander converted a second son, Reccared, and, in time, the entire nation of the Visigoths and of the Spanish Suevi. In 589 he presided over the third Council of Toledo, which discussed the Trinity and matters of discipline and liturgy, adding the Nicene Creed to the mass. He wrote a religious rule for his sister St. Florentina; at his death the see passed to his brother St. Isidore. F. D. Feb. 27.

LE BLANT, EDMOND FRÉDÉRIC (1818–1897), archaeologist. Born in France on Aug. 12, he studied law, was appointed to the customs bureau in 1843, and while on a trip to Italy in 1847 decided to become an archaeologist. He became an authority on the people, customs, buildings, and monuments of early Christian times in France, was elected to the Académie des Inscriptions at Belles Lettres in 1865, became director of the L'École Française

in Rome in 1883, and wrote widely. He died in Paris on July 5.

LEBRUN, CHARLES (1619–1690), painter. Born in Paris, on Feb. 24, he began studying painting under Vouet when eleven and in 1642 went to Italy with Poussin, under whom he studied until 1646, when he returned to France. He was admitted to the Academy of Painting in 1648, became first painter to King Louis XIV, and was appointed director of the Gobelin tapestry works, when the king established it in 1662, and was responsible for most of its early designs. He became famed for a series of paintings of the battles of Alexander the Great and for *The Family of Darius*, considered his masterpiece. He died at the Gobelin works, Paris.

LEBUIN, ST. (d. 773?). He was ordained a Benedictine at Ripon, England, and about 754 went with other missioners to Holland. He worked under St. Gregory of Utrecht, preached to the Frisians, and built a church at Deventer which the Saxons destroyed. When he denounced them at a meeting, his courage so impressed them that he was unhampered thereafter in his missionary work. Another of this name, listed as an Irish bishop martyred at Alost, Brabant, about 650, may be the same man. He is also known as Leafwine. F. D. Nov. 12.

LE CAMUS, ÉMILE PAUL CONSTANT ANGE (1839–1906), bishop. Born in Paraza, France, on Aug. 24, he studied at Carcassone, St. Sulpice seminary in Paris, received his doctorate in Rome in 1861, and was ordained in 1862. He became known for his preaching ability, was appointed assistant director of a Dominican school in Sorez in 1875, and founded a school at Castelnaudary of which he was head. He resigned in 1877 to study the New Testament, went to the Holy Land several times, and in 1901 was appointed bishop of La Rochelle and Saintes. He wrote a life of Christ, studies of the apostles, and on seminary education and biblical exegesis. He died in Malvisade, France, on Sept. 28.

LE CAMUS, ÉTIENNE (1632–1707), cardinal. Born in Paris, he became almoner of the king, received a doctorate in theology from the Sorbonne in 1650, was exiled for a period by Mazarin, and retired to La Trappe in 1665. He was appointed bishop of Grenoble in 1671, served as emissary between the pope and King Louis XIV, and was created a cardinal. He died in Grenoble, France.

LE CARDONNEL, LOUIS (1862–1936), poet. Born in Valence-sur-Rhône, France, on Feb. 15, he began to write in Paris for the symbolist magazines, with Mallarmé and Verlaine. In 1886 he entered the seminary at Issy, studied at Solesmes and Rome, and was ordained in 1896. He was a curé at St. Donat, then tried the Benedictine life at Ligugé and the Franciscan at Amiens and Assisi. He went to Rome, was the core of a group of poets, but retired in 1929 to Avignon for seven years of meditation amid growing blindness. His *Poèmes* appeared in 1904; *Carmina sacra* in 1912; *De l'une à l'autre aurore* in 1924. They are marked by deep spirituality, a lyric note reflecting both calm and darkness, and a strong reliance on the liturgy. He died in Avignon, France, on May 28.

LE CARON, JOSEPH (1586–1632), missioner. Born near Paris, he was ordained and became chaplain to the duke of Orléans. On the duke's death, he joined the Recollects, made his profession in 1611, and in 1615 was sent on the Canadian mission, where he became the first missionary to the Huron Indians. He went back to France several times to protect the interests of the colonists, was appointed provincial commissary in 1617, and was elected superior of his order in Quebec in 1626. When the English captured Quebec in 1629, he was sent back to France, where he died of plague on Mar. 29. He wrote the first dictionary of the Huron language and *Quaerimonia Novae Franciae.*

LECLERC DU TREMBLAY, FRANÇOIS (1577–1638). Born in Paris on Nov. 4, he was given the title baron de Maffliers at eighteen and served at court and in Henry IV's army against Spain. In 1599 he joined the Capuchins, became known as Père Joseph, served as provincial in Touraine in 1613, and participated in the negotiations between Marie de Medici and Prince de Condé in 1616. There he met Richelieu, whose close friend and aide and agent he became, serving on diplomatic missions to Rome in 1625 and to Ratisbon in 1630. He founded the Order of the Christian Militia in 1617 to promote a crusade against the Turks, but the project fell through. He directed successful Capuchin missions in France and in the Near East, but was unsuccessful in Abyssinia and Morocco. He died in Rueil, France, on Dec. 18.

LE CLERCQ, BL. ALIX (1575–1622), foundress. Born in Remiremont, Lorraine, she moved with her family to Hymont when she was about nineteen, and there came under the spiritual direction of Fr. Peter Fourier. In 1598, after considerable local misunderstanding and family objection, she and three other girls, who had joined her at the home of a secular canoness, Mme. Judith d'Apremont, determined to establish a new congregation which would devote itself to the education of children. They met with more misunderstanding, moved to six different convents in Lorraine, and finally, in 1613, to Châlons. Three years later, the papacy approved the foundation of the Augustinian Canonesses Regular of the Congregation of Our Lady, and Fr. Fourier invested thirteen of them

after the Bishop of Toul approved their rule. It was then discovered that the original approval seemed to refer only to the convent at Nancy, under the sponsorship of a different bishop, and Ganthe André, one of the original four, replaced Alix as superior. The latter was even neglected by Fr. Fourier, who seemed to have favored Mother Ganthe and to have defined her as co-foundress. Years of severe illness as well as misunderstanding marred her last years, but she was intensely happy while in class with her young pupils. She died in Nancy, France, on Jan. 9, and was beatified in 1947. F. D. Oct. 22.

LECLERQ, CHRÉTIEN (17th century), missioner. A native Fleming, he joined the Recollects in Artois, France, was ordained, and went to the Canadian mission in 1675. He spent the next twelve years, except for a brief trip to France, ministering to the Micmac Indians. He invented a system of writing for the Micmac language and was the author of *Premier établissement de la foy dans la Nouvelle France,* a valuable source book of the history of the Church in North America, and *Nouvelle relation de la Gaspésie.* He died in France sometime after 1698.

LECOT, VÍCTOR LUCIEN SULPICE (1831–1908), cardinal. Born in Montescourt, France, he studied at seminaries in Compiègne and Beauvais, was ordained, became bishop of Dijon in 1886, archbishop of Bordeaux in 1890, and a cardinal in 1893. He opposed the Church separation law of 1901, but sought to effect compromise with Aristide Briand's government over Church-state affairs.

LECOY DE LA MARCHE, RICHARD ALBERT (1839–1897), historian. Born in Nemours, France, he studied at École des Chartes, was appointed archivist of Haute Savoie in 1861 and of the Archives Nationales in Paris in 1864, and taught French history at the Catholic Institute in Paris. He wrote several historical works, chief of which was *La Chaire française au moyen âge.* He died in Paris.

LE COZ, CLAUDE (1740–1815), archbishop. Born in Plouévez-Parzay, France, he studied at Collège de Quimper, became a professor there and then principal. In 1791 he took the constitutional oath forbidden to Catholics, and was elected bishop of Ille-et-Vilaine, an election declared invalid by the pope. He was elected to the legislative assembly, where his defense of religious matters caused him to be imprisoned for fourteen months. He was one of the constitutional bishops recognized by the papacy when the concordat was signed, and became archbishop of Besançon. Though he claimed he never retracted, he was reconciled after a personal meeting with Pope Pius VII. He died at Villevieux, France.

LEDÓCHOWSKI, MIECISLAS HALKA

(1822–1902), cardinal. Born in Gorki, Poland, on Oct. 29, he studied at Radom, Warsaw, and the Academia dei Nobili Ecclesiastici in Rome, and was ordained in 1845. He was appointed domestic prelate in 1846 and auditor of the Lisbon papal nunciature in 1847, served as apostolic delegate to Colombia and Chile in 1861, and was appointed archbishop of Gnesen-Posen in 1865. He served as Pope Pius IX's ambassador to Prussia in quest of the king's aid in re-establishing the Papal States and as mediator between France and Poland. In 1873 he became embroiled in a dispute with the Prussian government when he refused to order the use of German in teaching religion in Posen, which was overwhelmingly Polish, and was imprisoned. He was created cardinal in 1874 while in prison, was released in 1876, and expelled from Prussia. He ruled his diocese from Rome until 1885, when he resigned and was appointed secretary of papal briefs. He was appointed prefect of the Propaganda in 1892 and held that office until his death in Rome on July 22.

LEDÓCHOWSKI, WLADIMIR HALKA (1866–1942). Born in Loosdorf, Austria, on Oct. 7, he was a page in the household of Empress Elizabeth, studied in Vienna, Tarnow, and the German College, Rome, became a Jesuit in 1889, and was ordained in 1894. He became known as a sociologist and was made vice-provincial of Poland and, in 1902, provincial. He was assistant general in 1906 and was elected general of the Jesuits in 1915. During his rule he saw the Society's personnel surpass in numbers the total at the time of its suppression in 1773, revised legislation, promulgated a new *Ratio studiorum* for higher studies in 1941, created three new assistancies (including the American) and twenty-three provinces and vice-provinces, and encouraged Jesuit participation in the apostolate of the press. He died in Rome on Dec. 13.

LEDVINA, EMMANUEL BOLESLAUS (1868–1952), bishop. Born in Evansville, Indiana, on Oct. 28, he studied at St. Meinrad, Indiana, and was ordained in Indianapolis in 1893. He did parish work in Evansville, Indianapolis, was pastor of St. Joseph's, Princeton, New Jersey, in 1895–1907, and in 1907 became first general secretary and vice-president of the Catholic Church Extension Society of Chicago, with which organization he remained until 1921. He was made a domestic prelate in 1918, and in 1921 was consecrated bishop of Corpus Christi, Texas. He resigned his see in 1949, and died on Dec. 15.

LEEN, EDWARD (1885–1944), author. Born in Abbeyfeale, Limerick, Ireland, he joined the Congregation of the Holy Ghost, studied at Rockwell College, Cashel, and the Gregorian, Rome, and was ordained in 1914. He was secretary to Bishop Shanahan, vicar apostolic of

South Nigeria, Africa, in 1920–22, taught at Blackwell College, became dean of studies in 1922 and was president in 1925–31. He became well known for his lectures, retreats, and books, particularly *Progress through Mental Prayer* (1935), *The Holy Ghost* (1936), *Why the Cross* (1938), and *The Church before Pilate* (1939). He was superior of his congregation's house at Kimmage, Ireland, from 1939, and died in Dublin on Nov. 11.

LEEN, JAMES (1888–1949), archbishop. Born in Abbeyfeale, Ireland, on Jan. 1, he was ordained in 1920, and named coadjutor bishop of Port Louis, Mauritius, in 1925, bishop in 1926, and archbishop in 1933. He died there in Dec.

LEEUWEN, DENYS VAN (1402–1471). Born in Ryckel, Limburg, Belgium, he studied in St. Trond, Zwolle, and at Cologne, and became a Carthusian at Roermond in 1423. He studied canon and civil law, mastered Greek and Arabic, and wrote extensively: commentaries on the complete scripture and on Boethius, Peter Lombard, and Dionysius the Areopagite; philosophical and theological treatises on the Virgin Mary, including a defense of the Immaculate Conception, and on asceticism, meditation, liturgy, and ecclesiastical discipline; sermons and homilies. His *De doctrina et regulis vitae Christianae*, written for the Franciscan John Brugman, pleaded for Church reforms. At the request of Nicholas of Cusa he wrote two treatises against Mohammedanism; he accompanied the cardinal while the latter preached a crusade in Germany during 1451–52. Denys was highly regarded by SS. Francis de Sales and Alphonsus Liguori. He died on Mar. 12.

LEFÈBVRE, CAMILLE (1831–1895), missioner. Born in St. Philippe, Quebec, Canada, he taught, studied at St. Cyprien, and in 1852 joined the Congregation of Holy Cross in Montreal. He was ordained in 1855, served as curate, taught at St. Laurent College, and did missionary work. In 1864 he was assigned to pastoral work in Memramcook, New Brunswick, where he established St. Joseph's College to improve the lot of the Acadians and was so successful he was called the "apostle of the Acadians." He also continued his missionary activities, served as provincial, founded the Little Sisters of the Holy Family, and was named apostolic missionary by Pope Pius IX. He died at St. Joseph's, New Brunswick, in Jan.

LEFÈVRE, PETER PAUL (1804–1869), bishop. Born in Roulers, Belgium, on Apr. 30, he studied in Paris under the Lazarists, joined their congregation in 1828, went to the United States, studied at the St. Mary's seminary, Perryville, Missouri, and was ordained there in 1831. He did missionary work in Missouri, Iowa, and Illinois, and while in Rome in 1841 was appointed titular bishop of Zela, and co-adjutor and administrator of Detroit. After his consecration he built up the educational system in Detroit, sought fruitlessly to secure public funds in 1852–53 for his schools, and with Bishop Spalding of Louisville helped found the American College at Louvain in 1857. He died in Detroit, Michigan, on Mar. 4.

LEFÈVRE, PETER. *See* Favre, Bl. Peter.

LEFÈVRE DE LA BODERIE, GUY (1541–1598), scholar. Born near Falaise, Normandy, France, on Aug. 9, he studied at Collège de France, where he became noted for his knowledge of Eastern languages, and may possibly have become a cleric. In 1560 he published a Latin version of the Syriac New Testament and in 1568 was invited by Arias Montanus to help prepare the polyglot bible of Antwerp. He edited the Syriac New Testament, the fifth volume of the polyglot bible, in 1572, and returned to France as secretary to the duke of Alençon. He wrote other treatises on Syriac, several volumes of poetry, and translated from Latin, Italian, and Spanish. He died in his birthplace.

LEFÈVRE D'ETAPLES, JACQUES (1455?–1536), scholar. Born in Etaples, Picardy, France, he studied at Paris, visited Italy in 1492 to study Aristotle, and on his return taught at Cardinal Lemoine's college. In 1507 he went to St. Germain-des-Prés monastery, near Paris, where he engaged in biblical studies until 1520. He then went to Meaux, became vicar general in 1523, and was forced to flee in 1525 when his gospel commentary was condemned by the Sorbonne. He was recalled by Francis I in 1526 and appointed librarian of Blois castle. In 1528 he published his translation of the Old Testament; he had translated the New Testament in 1523 and the Psalms in 1525. His scriptural interpretations aroused much scholarly controversy. In 1531 he accompanied Queen Marguerite of Navarre to Nérac, France, where he died.

LEGAL ÉMILE J. (d. 1920), bishop. Ordained an Oblate of Mary Immaculate, he became titular bishop of Pogla and coadjutor of St. Albert, Manitoba, Canada, in 1897. He succeeded to the see in 1902. He became first archbishop of Edmonton when the see was transferred there and created an archdiocese in 1912, and died on Mar. 20.

LE GAUDIER, ANTOINE (1572–1622), theologian. Born in Château Thierry, France, on Jan. 7, he became a Jesuit at twenty, was rector at Liège, Belgium, and taught scripture at Pont-à-Mousson and moral theology at La Flèche. He also served in those two centers as spiritual director and master of novices. He wrote on the love of God and the Ignatian tradition; his separate titles were gathered as *De natura et statibus perfectionis* after his death. He died in Paris on Apr. 14.

LEGENDRE, NAPOLÉON (1841–1907), author. Born in Nicolet, Quebec, he studied in Montreal, passed the bar in 1865, and entered the civil service in 1876. He was an original fellow of the Royal Society of Canada in 1872, wrote for its *Transactions*, and published *Echos de Québec* (1876), *À mes enfants, Les Perce-Niege, La Langue française au Canada* (1892), and volumes of verse.

LEGER. *See* Leodegarius, St.

LEGGE, PETER (1883–1951), bishop. Born in Brakel, Germany, he studied at Paderborn and Würzburg, was ordained in 1907, and became dean of Marburg in 1924 and bishop of the province of Saxony, with his see city at Meissen, in 1932. He was arrested by the Nazis in 1935 on the charge of sending currency from the country, and after his release lived at a monastery in Westphalia; he returned to Meissen in 1937. At the time of his death in Bautzen on Mar. 9 he was the only Catholic bishop in East Germany.

LEGIPONT, OLIVER (1698–1758), bibliographer. Born in Soiron, Limburg, Belgium, on Dec. 2, he studied at Verviers and Cologne, joined the Benedictines, was ordained in 1723, and received his licentiate in 1728. He was assigned the task of visiting and organizing his order's libraries all over Europe and wrote several treatises on bibliography. He died in Trier, Germany, on Jan. 16.

LE GOBIEN, CHARLES (1653–1708). Born in St. Malo, Brittany, France, on Nov. 25, he joined the Jesuits in 1671, became a professor of philosophy, and procurator of the French missions in China. As secretary, he published in 1702 *Lettres de quelques missionnaires de la compagnie de Jésus, écrites de la Chine et des Indes orientales* to interest the French in the Eastern missions. This developed into his *Lettres édifiantes et curieuses écrites des missions étrangères par quelques missionnnaires*. He died in Paris on Mar. 5.

LEGRAND, LOUIS (1711–1780), theologian. Born in Lusigny-sur-Ouche, Burgundy, France, on June 12, he studied at St. Sulpice, Paris, taught at Clermont in 1733–36, entered the Sulpicians in 1739, was superior of the seminary at Autun in 1743–45, and received his doctorate in theology from the Sorbonne in 1746. He served as director of studies there, wrote on theology, was engaged in many theological disputations, and wrote censuring refutations of Rousseau's *Émile* and Marmontel's *Bélisaire*, and helped to prevent censure of Buffon's *Époques de la nature*, when the latter made changes. Legrand died in Paris on July 21.

LEHAR, FRANZ (1870–1948), composer. Born in Komáron, Hungary, on Apr. 30, he studied violin in Prague, became a military band leader (as was his father), tried to write operas, and in 1905 turned to lighter theatrical compositions with the highly successful *Merry Widow*. *The Count of Luxembourg* (1909) and *Frederica* (1928) were among his nearly thirty popular operettas. He also wrote marches, sonatas, and a violin concerto. He died in Bad Ischl, Austria, on Oct. 24.

LE HAYE, JEAN DE (1540–1614). Born in Bauffe, Hainault, on Sept. 26, he studied at Chièvres, became a Jesuit in 1565, taught theology and philosophy at Louvain and Douai, wrote biblical commentary and a Bible harmony, *Evangelistarum quaternio* (1607), and died at Douai, France, on Jan. 14.

LE HIR, ARTHUR MARIE (1811–1868), scholar. Born in Morlaix, Quimper, France, on Dec. 5, he entered the seminary of St. Sulpice, Paris, in 1833, became a Sulpician after ordination, and taught theology there. He later became professor of scripture and Hebrew, with Renan as one of his pupils. He wrote exegesis on the Old Testament, published posthumously as *Études bibliques*. He died in Paris on Jan. 13.

LEHMKUHL, AUGUSTINE (1834–1918), theologian. Born in Hagen, Westphalia, on Sept. 23, he became a Jesuit in 1853, was ordained in 1862, and taught theology at Maria Laach and at Ditton Hall in England. He wrote a manual of moral theology (1883), a study of modern moral problems (*Casus conscientiae*, 1902), and on probability and social welfare. He died in Valkenburg, Holland, on July 1.

LEIGH, BL. RICHARD (1561?–1588), martyr. Born in London, he studied at Rheims and Rome, where he was ordained in 1586, and was sent on the English mission, taking the name Barth. Banished, he returned, was captured and hanged with five others at Tyburn during the Elizabethan persecution, for being a priest. He was beatified in 1929. F. D. Aug. 30.

LEJAY, PAUL (1861–1920). Born in Dijon, France, on May 3, he studied in Paris, was ordained in 1890, and taught classics at L'Institut Catholique. He wrote on archaeology, linguistics, and theology, collaborated with Vacant in *Dictionnaire théologique*, and was a fellow of the University of France. He died in July.

LEJEUNE, JEAN (1592–1672). Born in Poligny, France, he studied at Dôle and in 1614 became a member of the Oratory of Jesus. He was named director of the Langres seminary and then engaged in missionary work. Though he became blind in 1627 he continued to preach, gained a great reputation for his oratorical power, and published his sermons in 1667. He died in Limoges, France, on Aug. 19.

LELIA, ST. (6th century?). She seems to have led a life of austerity and to have been superior of a convent in Munster, Ireland. F. D. Aug. 11.

LELLIS, ST. CAMILLUS DE (1550–1614), founder. Born in Bocchianico, Italy, he was a soldier in the war against the Turks, where he contracted an incurable disease in his leg, and a wastrel and gambler afterward. In 1574 he tried to enter the Capuchins at Naples, but was refused because of his injury. He then became an attendant at San Giacomo Hospital in Rome and rose to superintendent. With the approval of his confessor, St. Philip Neri, he left, was ordained by Thomas Goldwell, last of the old English bishops, and with two companions founded the Ministers of the Sick, a congregation devoted to those needing care. This spread and was approved in 1591 by Pope Gregory XIV. In 1595 and 1601 its members accompanied troops fighting in Hungary and Croatia, probably forming the first known field medical unit. Camillus died on July 14, was canonized in 1746, and declared patron saint (with St. John of God) of the sick by Pope Leo XIII, and of nurses and nursing associations by Pope Pius XI. F. D. July 18.

C. C. MARTINDALE, *Life of St. Camillus* (New York, Sheed, 1946).

LELONG, JACQUES (1665–1721), bibliographer. Born in Paris on Apr. 19, he joined the Knights of St. John of Malta when ten, studied in Paris, and joined the Oratory of Jesus in 1686. After teaching at Juilly, where he was ordained in 1689, he became librarian at Notre Dame des Vertus seminary in Aubervilliers and in 1699 of the Oratory of St. Honoré, where he lived until his death on Aug. 13. He published a bibliography of early printed bibles in 1709, a treatise on polyglot bibles, and a bibliography of works in French history.

LE LOUTRE, LOUIS JOSEPH (1690?–1770?), missioner. A native of France, he was sent on the Canadian mission in Nova Scotia in 1740, preached to the Micmac Indians, and became vicar general of Acadia and the uncompromising defender of the Acadians and Indians against the English. He accompanied the Indians on several expeditions against the English, who captured and imprisoned him for several years on the Isle of Jersey. On his release he returned to France, where he died.

LEMAÎTRE, FRANÇOIS ELIE JULES (1853–1914), critic. Born in Vennecy, Loiret, France, on Apr. 27, he studied at seminaries in Orléans and Paris, taught at Le Havre and Algiers, and held the chair of French literature at Besançon and Grenoble. He wrote two volumes of poetry and retired in 1884 from teaching to devote himself to letters. He wrote for a number of magazines, was literary critic of *Journal des débats*, published the six-volume *Les contemporains, Les impressions de théâtre* in ten volumes, and won a chair in the French Academy in 1895. He wrote studies of Chateaubriand, Corneille, Fénelon, Racine, Renan, and Rousseau, several psychological and satiric dramas, and pro-royalist political treatises. He died in Tavers, France, on Aug. 5.

LEMAY, LÉON PAMPHILE (1837–1918), author. Born in Lotbiniere, Quebec, on Jan. 5, he studied at the seminary there and at Ottawa, passed the bar in 1865, and became librarian of the Quebec legislature in 1867, retiring in 1892. He translated Longfellow's *Hiawatha* into French (1870), published several volumes of poetry, novels, *De pelerin de Ste. Anne,* and *Fables canadiennes.* He became a fellow of the Royal Society of Canada and wrote the ode on Champlain for the tercentenary celebration of Quebec. He died on June 11 in St. Jean-Deschairlons, Quebec.

LEMCKE, HENRY (1796–1882), missioner. Born in Rhena, Mecklenburg, on July 27, he became a Protestant minister, a convert in 1824, and was ordained in 1826. He was sent to the United States as a missioner, was stationed in Philadelphia and then sent to Loretto, Pennsylvania, as assistant to Prince Gallitzen, whom he succeeded as pastor in 1840. He founded Carrolltown, Pennsylvania, in 1836, and helped bring the Benedictines to the United States, joining that order in 1852. In 1855 he was sent on missionary work to Kansas, spent 1861 to 1877 in Elizabeth, New Jersey, and returned to Carrolltown, where he died on Nov. 29.

LE MERCIER, FRANÇOIS (1604–1690), missioner. Born in Paris on Oct. 4, he joined the Jesuits in 1620, taught in Paris, was ordained, and was sent on the Canadian mission in 1635. He worked among the Huron Indians until the Iroquois wiped out Huronia and the mission was abandoned in 1650, when he returned to Three Rivers and Quebec. In 1653 he was appointed rector of the Jesuit college in Quebec and superior of the Canadian mission, served the next seven years on missions to the Indians and pastoral work in Quebec and Beaupré. He again served as superior from 1665 to 1671, was appointed visitor of the Society's missions in South America in 1673 and superior of these missions in 1674, a position he held until his death on the island of Martinique on June 12. He wrote two volumes of the *Jesuit Relations* and compiled nine others.

LEMERCIER, JACQUES (1585?–1654), architect. Born in Pontoise, France, he studied art and architecture in Italy from 1607 to 1615, became a royal architect no later than 1618, and in 1639 chief architect. In 1624 he was selected by Richelieu to finish Lescot's design of the Louvre and built the Pavilion de l'Horloge. In 1627 he entered the personal service of Richelieu, and built the Château de Richelieu in Poitou, the Palais Royal in Paris, the college and church at the Sorbonne, the Château de Rueil near Paris (for Richelieu in 1635), and the Hôtels de Liancourt and de la Roche-foucauld. He was working on the church of St. Roch in Paris when he died.

LEME DA SILVEIRA CINTRA, SEBASTI-ANO (1882–1942), cardinal. Born in Espirito Santo do Pinhal, Brazil, on Jan. 20, he was ordained, became archbishop of Rio de Janeiro and cardinal in 1930, and died there on Oct. 17.

LEMIEUX, FRANÇOIS XAVIER (1851–1933), jurist. Born in Levis, Quebec, Canada, he studied there and at Laval, read for the law, was called to the bar in 1872, and became famous as a criminal lawyer. He was a leader in the nationalist movement, represented Levis in the legislature from 1883 to 1894, and was made a judge in 1897. He was acting chief justice of the Quebec superior court in 1911–15 and chief justice from 1915 until his death in that city on July 18. He was knighted in 1915 and also received a papal decoration.

LEMOS, THOMAS DE (1555–1629), theologian. Born in Rivadavia, Spain, he joined the Dominicans there, in 1590 became lector in theology, and in 1594 was appointed to the chair of theology at Valladolid. He became a leading exponent of St. Thomas Aquinas' teaching, represented his province at a general chapter in Naples in 1600, and in 1602 was appointed leading defender of St. Thomas in the controversy between the Dominicans and the Jesuits before a congregation appointed by Pope Clement VIII to settle the dispute. At its conclusion in 1606 he was offered a bishopric, but declined. He remained in Rome, where he died on Aug. 23.

LE MOYNE, CHARLES (1626–1683). Born in Dieppe, France, on Aug. 1, he went to Canada in 1641, spent four years in the country of the Huron Indians, then settled at Ville-Marie (Montreal), where he was of service as an interpreter and soldier. He had great influence with the Indians and negotiated a five-year peace with them in 1653. His marriage to Catherine Primot in 1654 produced fourteen children, and founded a noted Canadian family. He was captured but released by Iroquois in 1655, later fought against the Five Nations, and was ennobled by Louis XIV as sieur de Longueuil and received a huge grant of land. He died in Montreal.

LE MOYNE, CHARLES (1656–1729), governor. Born in Montreal on Dec. 10, eldest son of Charles and Catherine Le Moyne, he served in France with the army, returned to Canada as a lieutenant, and at twenty-seven became major in charge of the Montreal garrison. He won distinction in battle against the Iroquois and at the defense of Quebec in 1690, was made a baron, and was governor of Three Rivers and then of Montreal. He was made a baron in 1700, and in 1711 led the victorious army against the British at Chambly.

LE MOYNE, CHARLES (1687–1755), governor. Born in Canada on Oct. 18, the second baron de Longueil entered the army in France, was appointed major of Montreal in 1733, was decorated by the king in 1734, and became governor of Montreal in 1749. He was a protectress of Bl. Marguerite D'Youville, and saved her hospital from destruction.

LE MOYNE, JOSEPH (1668–1734), governor. Born in Montreal on July 22, he became a naval officer, was in command of the fleet sent from France to Hudson's Bay to support his brother Pierre's army units, and was distinguished for bravery there and in campaigns in Florida and Louisiana. The Le Moyne forces drove the Spaniards from Pensacola. Joseph fortified Mobile, expelled the Spaniards from Ile Dauphin, and was made a captain in 1720. He was governor of Rochefort, France, from 1722 until his death.

LE MOYNE, PAUL (1663–1704). Born in Montreal, he became a soldier, accompanied his brothers Pierre and Joseph on the Hudson's Bay campaign, and with only two canoes captured an English cruiser. He was with his brother Jacques (1659–1690) at the defense of Quebec and with a group of 300 repulsed the attack of 1300 men under the English Major Whalley; Jacques was fatally wounded in this action. Paul acted for Frontenac against the Iroquois, forced them to surrender, but was so admired that they asked him to serve as their mediator at the peace table. He died on Mar. 21.

LE MOYNE, PAUL JOSEPH (1701–1778). Born in Canada, he entered the French army at seventeen, became a lieutenant in Normandy, served as commander of Fort Frontenac, governor of Detroit, and commander of Quebec, fought under Montcalm, was decorated by the king, and after the English victory in Canada went to France, where he died at Port Louis.

LE MOYNE, SIMON (1604–1665), missioner. Born in Beauvais, France, he became a Jesuit in 1622 and after ordination was sent to Canada. He worked among the Hurons (the first European to serve the Onondagas) and the Mohawks, and became so popular that he was ambassador to them in 1661. When the Cayuga Iroquois demanded concessions from Montreal, he was tortured and condemned to death, but saved by the Christian chief Garakontié. He died in Cap de la Madeleine, Canada.

LENARTZ, BL. JOHANNES (d. 1572), martyr. Born in Oisterwijk, Holland, he became an Augustinian at Briel, and was spiritual director of a community of Augustinian nuns at Gorkum, when he was captured, tortured, and hanged at Briel, Holland, by a Calvinist mob. He was beatified in 1867. F. D. July 9.

LENFANT, BL. ALEXANDRE (d. 1792), martyr. *See* Du Lau, Bl. Jean.

L'ENFANT, PIERRE CHARLES (1754–1825), engineer. Born in Paris, France, on Aug. 2, son of a painter, he studied engineering and in 1777 accompanied Lafayette to America to assist the colonists in their revolt against England and rose to the rank of major in the American army. He was an early member of the Society of the Cincinnati, converted the old City Hall in New York for the use of the first Congress in 1789, and in 1791 drew up the plans for the new capital city which became Washington, D.C. President Washington was obliged to dismiss him in 1792 because he failed to get along with his superiors, and he spent the next few years designing private and commercial buildings and petitioning Congress for additional recompense for his plans for the capital. He helped to construct fortifications near Washington during the War of 1812 and died in poverty near Blandensburg, Maryland, on June 14.

LENIHAN, MATTHIAS CLEMENT (1854–1943), bishop. Born in Dubuque, Iowa, on Oct. 6, he studied at St. Joseph's College there, St. John's College, Prairie du Chien, Wisconsin, and the Grand seminary, Montreal, and was ordained in 1879. He did parish work in Dubuque, and in 1904 was appointed first bishop of Great Falls, Montana. He resigned his see in 1930 and was appointed titular archbishop of Preslavus, and died on Aug. 19.

LENIHAN, MAURICE (1811–1895), journalist. Born in Waterford, Ireland, on Feb. 8, he studied there and at Carlow, worked for newspapers in Tipperary, Waterford, Limerick, and Cork, and in 1844 was asked by Daniel O'Connell and Bishop Power of Killaloe to edit a repeal paper. He issued the Tipperary *Vindicator* and in 1849 absorbed the Limerick *Reporter*. He became interested in the past and in 1866 published the scholarly *Limerick: Its History and Antiquities*. He was mayor of Limerick in 1884, a justice of the peace and a member of the Royal Irish Academy, and died there on Dec. 25. He was succeeded as editor by his son James.

LENIHAN, THOMAS MATHIAS (1843–1901), bishop. Born in Mallon, Cork, Ireland, on May 21, he studied at St. Thomas College, Bardstown, Kentucky, St. Vincent's seminary, Cape Girardeau, Missouri, and St. Francis seminary, Milwaukee, and was ordained in 1868. He did parish work in Dubuque, Iowa, until 1897, when he was consecrated bishop of Cheyenne, Wyoming. He died in Dubuque on Dec. 15.

LENNIG, ADAM FRANZ (1803–1866), theologian. Born in Mainz, Germany, on Dec. 3, he studied there and at Paris and Rome, where he was ordained in 1827. He taught for a year at Mainz, engaged in pastoral work, and was appointed pastor at Seligenstadt in 1839 and to the cathedral chapter of Mainz in 1845. He founded the *Mainzer Journal* in 1848, became vicar general in 1852, and dean of the chapter in 1856. He died in Mainz on Nov. 22.

LENORMANT, CHARLES (1802–1859), archaeologist. Born in Paris on June 1 he studied and practiced law, but turned to archaeology on a visit to Italy in 1822. He was appointed sub-inspector of fine arts in 1825, when he married the adopted daughter of Mme. Récamier, traveled through Europe, and accompanied Champollion to Egypt. He was appointed curator of art in royal palaces in 1829, of printed books in the Royal Library in 1836, and of the Cabinet of Medals in 1840. He began lecturing at the Sorbonne in 1835, was elected to the Academy in 1839, served as editor of *Correspondant* (1846–55), and was elected to the chair of archaeology of the Collège de France in 1849. He wrote *Questions historiques, Introduction à l'histoire de l'Asie occidentale* and, with others, *Élite des monuments céramographiques.* He died in Athens, Greece, on Nov. 24 while on an archaeological trip.

LENORMANT, FRANÇOIS (1837–1883), archaeologist. Son of Charles Lenormant, he was born in Paris on Jan. 17, studied under his father, published his first article on archaeology when fourteen, and studied law. He accompanied his father in 1859 (when Charles died) and began his excavations at Eleusis, Greece. He was appointed sub librarian of L'Institut de France in 1862, made several trips to Egypt, participated in the siege of Paris in 1870, and became professor of archaeology at the Bibliothèque Nationale in 1874. He founded the *Gazette archéologique* with de Witte in 1875 and was made a member of the Academy of Inscriptions and Belles Lettres in 1881. He was one of the discoverers of the Sumerian language in the cuneiforms. His writings include *Manuel de l'histoire ancienne de l'orient, Les origines de l'histoire d'après la Bible* (placed on the Index in 1887), *Les premières civilisations,* and *La Révolution en Grèce.* He died in Paris on Dec. 9.

LE NOURRY, DENIS NICOLAS (1647–1724). Born in Dieppe, Normandy, France, on Feb. 18, he became a Benedictine at Jumièges in 1665. After his ordination he was sent to Bonnenouvelle to help prepare an edition of the writings of Cassiodorus, to Rouen to prepare the works of St. Ambrose, and in 1684 to Paris, where he remained at St. Germain abbey for forty years until his death on Mar. 24. In addition to his editing he prepared several patristic treatises.

LEO THE GREAT, ST. (d. 461), pope and Doctor of the Church. Born in Tuscany, Italy, he was a deacon under Celestine I and archdeacon and secretary under Sixtus III. In 440 he was sent to Gaul to heal the dangerous breach between two imperial generals, and was recalled to be made pope on Sept. 29. He took his preaching duties seriously; ninety-six sermons on the need for charity and faith are extant; so are many letters. He strenuously fought the Manichaeans, Nestorians, Pelagians, and Priscillianists; carefully defined the requirements for and responsibilities of priests and bishops; and held annual meetings with the hierarchy of Italy. East-West relationships were a great problem, fouled by the duplicity of Emperor Theodosius II. A major instance was over the excommunication of Eutyches, an abbot of Constantinople, by St. Flavian the patriarch. The emperor called a hand-picked council in 448 (now called the Robber Council of Ephesus), over which Dionysius, patriarch of Alexandria, presided. It refused to hear the pope's letter of condemnation, acquitted Eutyches, and so mistreated Flavian that he died soon after. In 450 a general council was held at Chalcedon, with 600 bishops present, which heard Leo's *Tome,* a major clarification of the doctrine of the Incarnation, vindicated Flavian, and excommunicated Dionysius. In 452 the Huns swept through Italy, but Rome was spared as the result of a conference between Leo and Attila; three years later, however, Genseric the Vandal sacked the city, but agreed not to burn it, though he took many captives. The pope sent missioners to aid and redeem as many as he could. He died on Nov. 10 and was declared a Doctor of the Church in 1754. F. D. Apr. 11.

EDMUND HUNT, intro., *Letters of St. Leo the Great* (New York, Fathers of the Church, 1957).

LEO II, ST. (d. 683), pope. Born in Sicily, he was elected pope on Aug. 17, 682. His pontificate was notable for his confirmation of the sixth Ecumenical Council condemning the Monothelite heresy and censuring Pope Honorius I for not formally denouncing it. F. D. July 3.

LEO III, ST. (d. 816), pope. A native of Rome and cardinal of St. Susanna's there, he was unanimously chosen on Dec. 26, 795, to succeed Pope Adrian I and was consecrated the day following. The political supporters of Adrian's ambitious nephew remained hostile, dragged him from his horse and beat him in 799, and made the situation so untenable that Leo fled to Paderborn to join Charlemagne. A synod, presided over by Charlemagne, who came to Rome, cleared the pope, under oath, of trumped-up charges brought by his enemies. On Christmas day, 800, Leo crowned Charlemagne in St. Peter's, and Leo swore temporal homage to him: thus was born the Holy Roman Empire. At the time the pope gained greater power in his own territory and in foreign relations; the emperor was to have control over the Church's spiritual and doctrinal position. Although Charlemagne wanted the *Filioque* ("and the Son") added to the Creed, Leo objected: on the ground of possible political interference and also because he wished to avoid alienating the Eastern Church. When the emperor died in 814, Leo's enemies rose up but were crushed by the pope; in 815 another uprising in Campagna was put down by the duke of Spoleto. He spent large amounts of the money given him by Charlemagne in decorating churches in Ravenna and Rome, where he died. He was declared a saint in 1673. F. D. June 12.

LEO IV, ST. (d. 855), pope. Born in Rome, he was educated at the Benedictine monastery of St. Martin, made a subdeacon of the Lateran, and later a cardinal. He was elected pope in Jan. and consecrated on Apr. 10, 847, at a time when all Rome faced a Saracen invasion. He built the wall around St. Peter's and the Vatican Hill, still called the Leonine City. After the Moslems were routed at Ostia and peace restored, he was able to summon a synod in 853 to improve the state of the clergy. F. D. July 17.

LEO V (d. 903), pope. A native of Priapi, Ardea, Italy, he was a priest at a church outside the city of Rome when he was elected pope, probably in July 903. He reigned for about a month, when he was deposed and imprisoned by Christopher, a cardinal-priest who claimed the papal throne. He died in prison, in Sept., probably of natural causes, though a legend asserts he was murdered.

LEO VI (d. 928), pope. Born in Rome, son of Christopher, prime minister of Pope John VIII, he was a cardinal-priest at St. Susanna when he was elected pope, probably in May 928. Except that he gave the pallium to Archbishop John of Spalato, settling a dispute in ecclesiastical jurisdiction in Dalmatia, nothing is known of his pontificate. He probably died in Dec.

LEO VII (d. 939), pope. A native Roman, he became a priest at St. Sixtus, probably joined the Benedictines, and was elected pope on Jan. 3, 936, largely through Alberic's influence. He summoned Abbot Odo of Cluny to Rome to effect peace when Alberic's rival for the ascendancy in Rome, Hugo, king of Italy, laid siege to the city, made generous grants to monasteries, and appointed Archbishop Frederick of Mainz his vicar in Germany. He died in Rome on July 13.

LEO VIII (d. 965), pope. A native Roman, he was a prothonotary and a layman when he was elected pope on Dec. 4 and consecrated on Dec. 6, 963, through the influence of Emperor Otto I, who had deposed Pope John XII at a council in St. Peter's, though without John's

consent, on Nov. 6. The Romans attempted to oust Leo the next month, were put down by Otto, but rose again when the emperor left the city in Feb. 964, declared Leo's election null at a council on Feb. 26, and expelled him. John returned to Rome and when he died, possibly murdered, on May 14, the Romans elected Cardinal Benedict pope. The emperor then returned to the city with Leo, who brought Benedict to trial, reduced him to deacon, and banished him to Germany. Leo is usually listed as a true pope on the grounds that no protest was entered by Benedict or his followers, but some authorities consider him an antipope. The legitimacy of his pontificate would seem to depend on whether John's deposition was valid. Leo died on Mar. 1.

LEO IX, ST. (1002–1054), pope. Born in Alsace and baptized Bruno, he studied at Toul and Metz, became canon of St. Stephen's in Toul, and, in 1027, its bishop. His twenty-year rule was marked by disciplinary strictness and by the spread of the Cluniac reform to monastic centers. He was selected as pope by Emperor Henry III, a relative, and took office on Feb. 12, 1049, having brought Hildebrand with him from Cluny to Rome as counselor. As pope he deprived of office those clergy guilty of simony or of breaking the law of celibacy; condemned Berengarius for his denial of transubstantiation, and Michael Cerularius, emperor in the East, for increasing the ritual differences with the Latin Church; frequently toured western Europe; and proposed the election of popes directly by cardinals. He was severely criticized by St. Peter Damian and others for leading an army against the Normans in Lombardy, a campaign which he lost and which resulted in his imprisonment at Benevento. He died at Rome soon after his release. F. D. Apr. 19.

LEO X (1475–1521), pope. Giovanni de' Medici, second son of Lorenzo the Magnificent, was born in Florence on Dec. 11, was tonsured in 1482, received many benefices, among them Monte Cassino, and in 1489, when thirteen, was created a cardinal by Pope Innocent VIII. He studied under the greatest humanists of his time (Poliziano, Pico della Mirandola, Ficino, Dovizi) and in 1492 received the insignia of his office. When the Medici were expelled from Florence in 1494 he traveled through Europe until 1500, when he returned to Rome and on the death of Pietro de' Medici in 1503 became head of the family. He became legate in Bologna and Romagna in 1511, headed the papal army against Florence, was captured by the French when they defeated papal and Italian forces at Ravenna in 1512, escaped, and later in the year witnessed the restoration of the family fortunes in Florence. He was elected pope on Mar. 11, 1513, ordained on Mar. 15, consecrated bishop on Mar. 17, and enthroned on Mar. 19. His pontificate was noted for its frivololity, quest of pleasure, extravagant living, and lavish generosity to the arts, literature, and charity, though Leo was exact in his own religious observance. His largesse exhausted the papal treasury by 1515 and the sale of offices and indulgences was resorted to. He entered into an alliance with Maximilian, Spain, and England, which defeated the French at Novara in 1513, and continued his policy of alliances to resist France. In 1515, when Francis I was victorious at Marignano, Leo sued for peace and signed a concordat in 1516 which brought France into close relations with the papacy, and revoked the pragmatic sanctions of Bourges, but granted the French king sweeping grants of authority in ecclesiastical matters which were to haunt the Church in the centuries to come. He continued to follow a policy of expediency throughout his pontificate, swinging to Maximilian's support when the latter warred on the French in 1516, and then finding himself in an untenable position when Maximilian and Francis formed the alliance of Cambrai in 1517. He appointed thirty-one new cardinals in 1517, many for the money they paid. In the same year a group of cardinals (led by Cardinals Petrucci, who was executed for his role in the affair, Sauli, Riario, Soderini and Castellesi) made an attempt on Leo's life by poisoning. He became embroiled in the struggle for the succession to the imperial crown for which Maximilian favored his grandson, Charles of Spain, against Francis I of France. Leo played both sides, favored Francis, but eventually supported Charles when it became evident he was to be elected. Meanwhile, in 1517, the Reformation burst out in Germany, sparked by the abuses of indulgences authorized to raise funds for a crusade proposed in 1517 and 1518 and for the building of St. Peter's. Leo, deep in his concerns over the imperial crown and immersed in his political machinations, failed to appreciate the depth and seriousness of the revolt and took no adequate steps to stop the movement by directing the reforms which might have halted it. He did condemn the heresy with the bull *Exsurge Domine* in 1520 and excommunicated Martin Luther on Jan. 3, 1521. Ironically, he also gave Henry VIII the title "Defender of the Faith" for the latter's treatise against Luther. The fifth Lateran Council, which had begun in the reign of Pope Julius II in 1512 and was continued by Leo, proposed numerous reforms at its close in 1517, but Leo never put into practical effect its proposals and the Reformation grew. Leo died of malaria in Rome on Dec. 1, leaving a city of beautiful art and music monuments, a debt of 400,000 ducats, and a world of political turmoil, spiritual rebellion, social unrest, and moral confusion.

LEO XI (1535-1605), pope. Alessandro Ottaviano de' Medici was born in Florence, Italy, on June 2, son of Giacomo Salviati and Lucrezia Medici, a niece of Pope Leo X, studied under St. Philip Neri, and was ordained. He was appointed an ambassador from Grand Duke Cosimo de' Medici of Tuscany to the papal court in 1569, bishop of Pistoia in 1573, archbishop of Florence in 1574, and cardinal in 1583. Sent as papal legate to France in 1596, he helped combat the Huguenots at the court of Henry IV, was appointed prefect of the Congregation of Bishops and Regulars on his return to Rome, became bishop of Albano in 1600, and was transferred to Palestrina in 1602. He was elected pope on Apr. 1, was consecrated on Apr. 10, but died in Rome within the month, on Apr. 27.

LEO XII (1760-1829), pope. Annibale Francesco Clemente Melchiore Girolamo Nicola della Genga was born in Castello della Genga, Spoleto, Italy, on Aug. 22. He studied at the Collegio Campagna in Osimo, the Collegio Piceno, and the Accademi dei Nobili Ecclesiastici in Rome, and was ordained in 1783. He became canon of the Vatican church in 1792, titular archbishop of Tyre in 1793, and papal nuncio to Lucerne, to Cologne (1794-1804), and in 1805 to the Diet of Ratisbon. He accompanied Cardinal Caprara to Paris in 1808 in a fruitless attempt to arrange a concordat with Napoleon, and when Pius VII was imprisoned by the French retired to Monticelli abbey. In 1814 he was sent on a diplomatic mission to Paris which displeased Consalvi, papal secretary of state, who caused his recall, and he again retired to Monticelli. He was made cardinal and bishop of Sinigaglia in 1816, resigned the see, which he never entered because of ill health, in 1818, and in 1820 was made vicar of Rome and archpriest of the Liberian Basilica. He was elected pope on Sept. 28, 1823, after a conclave marred by the veto of Cardinal Severoli as a possible papal candidate by the Austrian emperor, and was consecrated on Oct. 5. He adopted a reactionary policy in ruling his realms, discouraged all democratic tendencies, forced the Jews in Rome into a ghetto, and supported the legitimist cause in Spain and France (despite the French suppression of Jesuit schools). He proclaimed a jubilee year in 1825, encouraged the movement toward Catholic Emancipation in England, and was a generous patron of the arts—restoring the Vatican printing press, rebuilding St. Paul's, and building up the Vatican Library. He died in Rome on Feb. 10.

LEO XIII (1810-1903), pope. Born in Carpineto, Italy, on Mar. 2, Gioacchino Vincenzo Raffaele Luigi Pecci studied at the Collegio Romano, where he received his doctorate in theology in 1832, and the Accademia dei Nobili. He was appointed domestic prelate in

1837 (while still in minor orders), was ordained late in the same year, and was sent to brigand-overrun Benevento as governor in the pope's name. He restored law and order to the city, reorganized its finances and government, and was so successful in its revival that he was sent to Perugia in 1841, where he was equally successful. He was appointed papal nuncio to Brussels and titular archbishop of Damiata in 1843, encouraged the founding of the Belgian College in Rome in 1844, and in 1846 was appointed bishop of Perugia, where he was to serve for the next thirty-two years. He was created a cardinal in 1853, became involved with the Piedmontese government, which had seized Perugia from the Papal States in 1860, over its anti-clerical measures in the city, strengthened its educational centers, established the Accademia di S. Tommaso in 1872, and in 1877 was appointed camerlengo by Pope Pius IX and moved to Rome. On Feb. 20, 1878, he was elected pope and was consecrated on Mar. 3. He immediately inaugurated a conciliatory policy in an attempt to re-establish papal relations with the great powers. Diplomatic relations with Germany were re-established in 1884, and in 1885, at Bismarck's suggestion, Leo mediated the dispute between Germany and Spain over the Caroline Islands. The Kulturkampf was ended in 1886, and William II made three visits to the pope in Rome (1888, 1893, and 1903). Relations with the Belgian government were broken off in 1880 over the school question, but were restored in 1885. An agreement was reached with Russia in 1883 and diplomatic relations renewed in 1895. In France the pope encouraged Catholics to loyalty to the republic through his support of Cardinal Lavigerie and his encyclicals, *Sapientiae Christianae* (1890), emphasizing the Church's toleration of various forms of government, and *Au milieu des sollicitudes* (1892), addressed to all Frenchmen, urging their support of the existing constitution. In Italy he reasserted Pius IX's policy toward the Italian government, demanded restoration of papal sovereignty and temporal power in 1886, and continued the policy of barring Catholics from participating in Italian political affairs. The result was an increase of anti-clerical laws and Church persecutions which continued through his pontificate. In England his encyclical, *Apostolicae curae* (1896), denying the validity of Anglican orders, offset much of the popularity gained by his creating John Henry Newman a cardinal in 1879 and the beatification of fifty English martyrs in 1886. He restored the Scotch hierarchy in 1878; established a hierarchy in English India in 1886; settled the Goa schism in the Portuguese colony in India; created Archbishop Gibbons a cardinal in the United States in 1886, decided in his favor the controversial

Knights of Labor question, founded the apostolic delegation in Washington in 1892, and in 1898 issued the encyclical, *Testem benevolentiae*, on Americanism; drew up concordats with several others states—Portugal (1886), Montenegro (1886), and Colombia (1887); and in 1879 ended the schism of the Uniat Armenians. A patron of scholarship, he enlarged the Vatican Library, opened the Vatican archives in 1883, encouraged a revival of scholastic philosophy, with emphasis on St. Thomas Aquinas, in his encyclical, *Aeterni Patris*, in 1880 which led to a world-wide revival of Thomism, founded numerous colleges in Rome, and established the Vatican observatory. He created some 300 episcopal sees and vicariates during his pontificate, encouraged biblical study and archaeological research with the encyclical *Providentissimus Deus* (1893) and the creation of the Biblical Commission in 1902, and warmly endorsed the growth of older religious orders and the formation of new ones. His outstanding contribution was probably in the series of remarkable encyclicals he issued, with particular emphasis on social and political questions. Chief among these are: *Rerum novarum* (1891), on the rights and duties of capital and labor which soon became the classic guide to the problems of labor and capital and their solution; *Inscrutabili* (1878), on the evils affecting modern society; *Quod apostolici muneris* (1878), a condemnation of socialism; *Arcanum divinae sapientiae* (1880), on Christian marriage; *Diuturnum illud* (1881), on the origin and nature of civil government; *Humanum genus* (1884), a denunciation of freemasonry; *Immortale Dei* (1885), on the Christian constitution of the state, in which the relationship of Church and state is discussed; *Libertas praestantissimum* (1888), on the nature of human liberty; *In plurimis* (1888), on slavery; *Sapientiae christianae* (1890), on the duty of a Christian citizen; and *Graves de communi* (1901), on Christian democracy. He died in Rome on July 20.

LEO (3rd century). Said to have been put to death about 260 by Lollian, governor of Licia, for destroying idols, he is the hero of a pious legend.

LEO, ST. (d. 541). He was bishop of Sens, France, for twenty-three years, protecting his see against the strong interferences of King Childebert. F. D. Apr. 22.

LEO, ST. (d. 550?). Born at Mantenay, near Troyes, Gaul, he became a monk at the monastery founded there by St. Romanus and succeeded him as abbot. F. D. May 25.

LEO, ST. (703–787), bishop. A priest at Ravenna, Italy, he became bishop of Catania, Sicily. F. D. Feb. 20.

LEO, ST. (856?–900?), bishop. He was born in Normandy and is said, in questionable sources, to have resigned his office as bishop of Rouen to preach among the Basques and to have been slain by pirates at Bayonne, France. F. D. Mar. 1.

LEO, ST. (d. 1000). He was abbot of the Benedictine abbey at Nonantula, near Modena, Italy. F. D. Nov. 20.

LEO, ST. (d. 1079). Born in Lucca, Italy, he became a Benedictine at La Cava, in Naples, and succeeded its founder St. Alpherius as abbot in 1050. His cult was approved in 1579. F. D. July 12.

LEO, ST. (d. 1227), martyr. *See* Daniel, St.

LEO, BRO. (d. 1271). A native of Assisi, Italy, he joined the Franciscans in 1210, was soon ordained, and became secretary, confessor, and companion of St. Francis. He was present when Francis received the stigmata in 1224, and after Francis' death in 1226 he suffered from a bitter controversy with Elias, who had him whipped and expelled from Assisi. He spent the rest of his life at various hermitages of the order, was with St. Clare when she died in 1253, and died at the Portiuncula on Nov. 15. He wrote his memories of Francis in 1246, with Angelo and Rufino, and also wrote or inspired the *Legenda antiqua* of Perugia, *The Mirror of Perfection*, and lives of Bernard and Blessed Giles.

LEO, BL. (d. 1295). A Benedictine, he became fifteenth abbot of the monastery of La Cava, near Naples, Italy, in 1268. His cult was approved in 1929. F. D. Aug. 19.

LEO THE DEACON (950?–1000?), historian. Born in Kaloe, Ionia, about 950, he studied at Constantinople, where he was ordained deacon, fought against the Bulgars in 986, and about 992 began a history of the empire, but completed only the period between 959 and 973.

LEO OF MELUN, ST. Once honored in the Paris area on Nov. 10, he is now identified with St. Leo the Great.

LEO OF ST. BERTIN, BL. (d. 1163). Born in Furnes, Flanders, and a trusted courtier at twenty, he entered the Benedictine monastery of Anchin and then became abbot of Lobbes. In 1138 he was abbot of St. Bertin, which burned to the ground in 1152 and which he rebuilt, and in 1146 went with Thierry of Alsace on the second crusade. F. D. Feb. 26.

LEOBALD. *See* Lieutbault, St.

LEOBARD, ST. (d. 593). He lived as a recluse for twenty-two years near the monastery of Marmoutiers, France, under the direction of St. Gregory of Tours. F. D. Jan. 18.

LEOBINUS, ST. *See* Lubin, St.

LEOCADIA, ST. (d. 304?), martyr. She is said to have been a noble maiden of Toledo, Spain, who was tortured during the persecution of Diocletian and died in prison. She is the principal patron of Toledo. F. D. Dec. 9.

LEOCRITIA, ST. (d. 859), martyr. Converted to Christianity by Litiosa, a relative, she was driven from her home in Cordova, Spain, by her Moorish parents, captured by the conquerors after a great hue and cry, and scourged and beheaded with St. Eulogius. F. D. Mar. 15.

LEODEGARIUS, ST. (616?–679), bishop. Nephew of Didon, bishop of Poitiers, who educated him after early years spent in the court of King Clotaire II, he was ordained and in 651 made abbot of St. Maxentius, where he introduced the Rule of St. Benedict. When Clotaire died in 656, Leodegarius joined St. Bathildis, queen regent, helped her govern, and educated her children. In 663 he became bishop of Autun and reformed a see torn by Manichaeism. In 673, on the death of Clotaire III, he became adviser to King Childeric II, who had been opposed by Ebroin, mayor of the palace. Leodegarius was exiled when he denounced the king's marriage to his first cousin but was restored to his see by King Theodoric III. The duke of Champagne, stirred up by Ebroin, attacked Autun and captured Leodegarius, whose tongue was torn out and who was blinded by hot irons, on accusation of having plotted Childeric's death. The bishop was deposed and his brother, Gerinus, was stoned to death. Two years later, after a mock trial at Marly, he was beheaded. He is also called St. Leger. F. D. Oct. 2.

LEODOVALDUS, ST. (6th century). He was bishop of Avranches, France, in the second half of the century.

LEOFDAC (10th century). He was first bishop of Ribe, Denmark, consecrated in 948 at Hamburg. He is said to have been slain by heathens in his diocese, but was never formally canonized.

LEÓN, LUIS DE (1528–1591), poet. Born in Belmonte, Aragon, Spain, he studied at Salamanca, where he joined the Augustinians and was appointed to the chair of theology. He was arrested for heresy by the Inquisition in 1572 for questioning the authenticity of the Vulgate (and acquitted with a warning in 1576), and in 1582 for his position on predestination, and again acquitted. He was appointed vicar general of his order, and provincial in 1591, but died a few days later on Aug. 23. He wrote lyric poetry, mystical and theological treatises, commentaries, and translated Vergil and Horace.

LEONARD, ST. (d. 559?). He is said to have been a French courtier converted by St. Remigius, who became a monk at the monastery of Micy, near Orléans, and later a hermit near Limoges. On land given him by Clovis I, his godfather, he built the monastery of Noblac (now the town of St. Léonard), from which he evangelized the surrounding area. F. D. Nov. 6.

LEONARD, ST. (d. 570?), hermit. He

founded the monastery of Vandoeuvre (now
St. Léonard-aux-Bois) near Le Mans, France.
F. D. Oct. 15.

LEONARD, BL. (d. 1255). A Benedictine, he
became eleventh abbot of La Cava, Italy, and
was beatified in 1929. F. D. Aug. 18.

LEONARD OF CHIOS (d. 1482), bishop.
Born on the island of Chios where he joined
the Dominicans, he studied at Padua, where
he was ordained, and taught at Padua and
Genoa. He was appointed bishop of Mytilene,
Lesbos, accompanied Cardinal Isidore of Sabina
to Constantinople in 1452 to work out a reunion agreement between Rome and the Greek
Church, and witnessed the fall of the city in
1453 which he described in an often-quoted letter to the pope. In 1456 he was imprisoned in
Constantinople by the Turks when they captured Lesbos, but was freed the following year.

LEONARD OF PORT MAURICE. *See* Casanova, St. Paul.

LEONARDI, ST. JOHN (1550?–1609),
founder. A native of Diecimo, Italy, he was a
pharmacist's assistant in Lucca, studied for the
priesthood, and was ordained in 1572. With
SS. Philip Neri, Joseph Calasanctius, and others
he formed a congregation of secular priests to
aid prisoners and the sick. The bishop of Lucca
reorganized his group in 1583 as an association of secular priests with simple vows. It was
confirmed by Pope Clement VIII in 1595 and
formally recognized as the Clerks Regular of
the Mother of God until 1621. The congregation never spread beyond Italy. He is considered one of the founders of the College for the
Propagation of the Faith and later served as
commissary apostolic of the Vallombrosans and
Monteverginians. He died while ministering to
plague victims. He was canonized in 1938.
F. D. Oct. 9.

LEONARDO DA VINCI (1452–1519), artist. Leonardo di Ser Piero da Vinci was born at
Vinci, near Florence, Italy, the illegitimate son
of Ser Piero da Vinci, a Florentine notary, and
a peasant girl, Caterina, on Apr. 15, was raised
by his father, and became an apprentice under
Andrea del Verrocchio when fifteen. He assisted Verrocchio (he painted the kneeling
angel in his master's *Baptism of Christ*) and
then collaborated with him on various projects
until 1477, when he was patronized by Lorenzo
de' Medici. He became well versed in anatomy,
astronomy, botany, mathematics, engineering
and music. During this period in Florence he
produced a *Madonna and Child, Adam and
Eve* (unfinished), *Adoration of the Magi*, for
an altarpiece, a miniature *Annunciation*, and a
bust of St. John the Baptist. In 1482, while on
a mission for Lorenzo to Ludovico Sforza (il
Moro), duke of Milan, he entered the duke's
service, and in 1485 became director of an
academy of arts and sciences founded by the

duke. During the years (1482–99) he spent
there he became court painter, chief engineer,
director of public works, and producer of the
pageants and festivities put on in Milan. He
built the Martesana canal and planned irrigat-
ing and other engineering projects for Lombardy, helped design the Milan cathedral, and
became famed for his paintings—among them
Virgin of the Rocks and his masterpiece, *The
Last Supper* (early damaged by dampness, the
method of tempera painting on plaster, vandal-
ism, and clumsy eighteenth-century restorers),
for Santa Maria delle Grazie convent—and for
the model of an equestrian statue of Ludovico il Moro on which he labored for fifteen
years but which was never cast because of lack
of bronze. When Ludovico was expelled from
Milan by King Louis XII of France in 1499,
Leonardo went to Mantua and Venice, did a
chalk portrait of Isabella Gonzaga while in
Mantua, and completed his cartoon for the
never executed altarpiece, *Virgin with the
Christ Child in the Lap of St. Anne*, for the
Annunziata in Florence in 1501. He then returned to Florence in the service of Cesare
Borgia, was his chief military engineer in the
Romagna campaigns, and returned to Florence
when his patron was defeated in 1503. He lived
in Florence (1501–6) and Milan (1506–13),
with trips to Rome, Pavia, and Bologna. He did
a cartoon, *The Battle of Anghiari*, depicting the
victory of the Florentines over Milan near
Anghiari, but finished only the central group,
The Battle of the Standard. Neither the cartoon nor the painting has survived. Between
1503 and 1506 he painted the *Mona Lisa*
(Madonna Lisa del Giocondo), now in the
Louvre, Paris. He was in Rome in the Medici
service in 1512, but left, perhaps because of a
disagreement with Pope Leo X or Michelangelo. In 1516 he accepted the offer of King
Francis I and went to France. Ill, he did no
more work of consequence, and remained at
Castle Cloux, near Amboise, France, until his
death on May 2. Leonardo da Vinci was one
of the greatest and most versatile geniuses of
all times. In painting, his knowledge of anatomy
and human nature, coupled with his mastery of
perspective and unrivaled use of light and
color, marked a new era in Italian painting; his
drawings reveal draftsmanship of the highest
order; his engineering accomplishments are
still studied; his notebooks, unpublished until
modern times, reveal a daring and imaginative
thinker; and his inventions reflect a soaring
imagination which designed even flying machines. He wrote *Trattano della pittura* (published in 1551, a more complete edition based
on a newly discovered manuscript was published in 1817); *Literary Works* (1887; enlarged edition 1939); and *Notebooks* (1939).
KENNETH CLARK, *Leonardo da Vinci* (New

York, Macmillan, 1939); RACHEL A. TAYLOR, *Leonardo the Florentine* (New York, Harper, 1927).

LEONIANUS, ST. (d. 570?). Born in Pannonia and taken to Gaul as a slave, he later became a monk at the abbey of St. Symphorianus at Autun. His cult was approved in 1907. F. D. Nov. 6.

LEONIDAS, ST. (d. 304), martyr. He was put to death at Alexandria, Egypt, during the Diocletian persecution. F. D. Jan. 28.

LEONIDES, ST. (d. 202), martyr. A brilliant philosopher at Alexandria, Egypt, he was the father of seven sons, the eldest being Origen, who was seventeen when his father was beheaded and the family property seized during the persecution of Septimius Severus. F. D. Apr. 22.

LEONIS, ST. (d. 303?), martyr. *See* Eutropia, St.

LEONORIUS, ST. (d. 570?), bishop. Born in Wales and educated by St. Illtyd, he was consecrated bishop at Caerleon and went to Brittany, where he founded the monastery of Pontual. He was the son of King Hoel of Brittany and brother of Hoel II. He is also known as Lunaire. F. D. July 1.

LEONTIA, ST. (d. 484), martyr. *See* Dionysia, St.

LEONTIUS, ST. (d. 135?), martyr. *See* Hypatius, St.

LEONTIUS, ST. (d. 300?), martyr. *See* Alexander, St.; also, Hieronides, St.

LEONTIUS, ST. (d. 303?), martyr. *See* Cosmas, St.

LEONTIUS, ST. (d. 329?), martyr. *See* Daniel, St.

LEONTIUS, ST. (d. 337). Bishop of Caesarea, Cappadocia, he was a participant at the Council of Nicaea in 325, and was highly praised by St. Anthanasius. F. D. Jan. 13.

LEONTIUS, ST. (d. 432?). Born probably in Nîmes, Gaul, he may have been a brother of St. Castor, bishop, and was bishop of Fréjus, Gaul, from about 419 to his death; Cassian dedicated ten conferences to him. F. D. Dec. 1.

LEONTIUS, ST. (d. 541?). Called "the Elder," he was bishop of Bordeaux, France. F. D. Aug. 21.

LEONTIUS (485?–543?), theologian. Born probably in Constantinople of a distinguished family, he was a Nestorian during his youth, but was converted and became a monk in Jerusalem. He went to Constantinople, may have been one of the delegation of Scythian monks to Pope Hormisdas in 519 to authorize the "One of the Trinity suffered" formula, and participated in the disputes between Catholics and Monophysites which Justinian arranged in 531. He is also identified by some authorities with the Origenist Leontius of Byzantium, though this is disputed. He probably died in Constantinople, though some authorities believe he died in Jerusalem after 553. He was an outstanding theologian of his times, but authorship of most of the works attributed to him is disputed. Chief among these are *Against The Monophysites, Against the Nestorians, De sectis, Adversus fraudes Apollinaristarum,* and *Contra Nestorianos et Eutychianos.*

LEONTIUS, ST. (d. 640). He was bishop of Saintes, France. F. D. Mar. 19.

LEONTIUS, ST. (d. 1077), bishop and martyr. A Greek monk at Caves, in Kiev, Russia, where he went from Constantinople, became bishop of Rostov, Russia, in 1051, and was successful in the conversion of pagans. Ill-treatment received from others, however, shortened his life and gave him the title of martyr. F. D. May 23.

LEONTIUS THE YOUNGER, ST. (510?–565?). A soldier, he married and settled at Bordeaux in Gaul, but was acclaimed bishop of that city and its civil governor as well. F. D. July 11.

LEOPARDINUS, ST. (7th century). He was slain by assassins while abbot of the monastery of Symphorianus in Berry, France. F. D. Nov. 24.

LEOPARDUS, ST. (d. 362), martyr. A household servant of Julian the Apostate, he was put to death, probably at Rome. F. D. Sept. 30.

LEOPOLD I (1640–1705), emperor. Son of Emperor Ferdinand III and Maria Anna of Spain, he was born in Vienna, on June 9; he became his father's heir when his brother Ferdinand died in 1654. He became king of Hungary in 1655, of Bohemia in 1656, and in 1658 was elected emperor against Louis XIV of France, against whom he fought throughout his reign. After the Turkish advance was checked by their defeat at St. Gotthard in 1664, Leopold negotiated a twenty-year truce which allowed them to retain Transylvania. He headed the coalition against Louis XIV in the Dutch war (1672–78) ended by the Treaty of Nijmegen, then was faced with an uprising in Hungary in 1678 headed by Tököly, who called on the Turks for aid. The Turks were finally stopped at Vienna in 1683, mainly through the efforts of Charles V of Lorraine and John III Sobieski of Poland. The next year Leopold formed the Holy League with Poland and Venice and in 1697 victory at Zenta over the Turks secured Hungary for Austria. In 1700 he joined England and Holland against France in the War of the Spanish Succession. He died, before its conclusion, in Vienna, on May 5.

LEOPOLD, ST. (1073–1136). Born in Melk, Austria, grandson of Emperor Henry III, he became fourth margrave of Austria on his father's death in 1096. He married Agnes, the daughter of Henry IV, in 1106; they had eighteen children. He encouraged the spread of religious institutions and founded the Cistercian, Augustinian, and Benedictine monasteries of Heiligenkreuz, Klosterneuburg (where he died and was buried), and Mariazell. On the death of his brother-in-law Henry V, in 1125, he was offered the imperial crown but refused, preferring to stay with his people, who gave him the surname "the Good." He was canonized in 1486 by Pope Innocent VIII. F. D. Nov. 15.

LEOPOLD OF GAICHE, BL. (1732–1815). Born in Gaiche, Italy, he joined the Franciscans at Cibotola at eighteen, was ordained in 1757 and became widely known as preacher and confessor, served as a papal missioner from 1768 to 1779, and founded and directed a retreat house near Spoleto until the suppression by Napoleon. He was imprisoned for serving as a parish priest, but later returned to mission work. He died at Monte Luco, Italy, on Apr. 15, and was beatified in 1893. F. D. Apr. 2.

LEOTHADIUS, ST. (d. 718). Member of a noble Frankish family, he became a Benedictine monk, served as abbot of Moissac in southern France, and was named bishop of Auch. F. D. Oct. 23.

LEOVIGILD, ST. (d. 852), martyr. *See* Christopher, St.

LE QUIEN, MICHEL (1661–1733), theologian. Born in Boulogne-sur-mer, France, on Oct. 8, he studied at Plessis, Paris, joined the Dominicans there in 1682, and spent the rest of his life writing on historical and theological subjects. Among his works are *Oriens christianus in quatuor partiarchatus digestus, Défense du texte hébreu et de la version vulgate,* and *Panoplia contra schisma graecorum,* and an edition of the works of John Damascene. He died in Paris on Mar. 12.

LERAY, FRANCIS XAVIER (1825–1887), bishop. Born in Château Giron, Brittany, France, on Apr. 20, he studied at Rennes, went in 1843 to Baltimore, where he studied at St. Mary's seminary, and Spring Hill College, Alabama. He went to Natchez with Bishop Chanche, was ordained there in 1852, engaged in missionary work throughout Mississippi, and became a pastor in Vicksburg. He served as a chaplain in the Confederate army during the Civil War, and in 1877 was consecrated bishop of Natchitoches at Rennes, France. He was appointed titular bishop of Janopolis and coadjutor and apostolic administrator of New Orleans in 1879, and succeeded to that see in 1883. He was instrumental in abolishing the board of trustees of the cathedral, which had been involved in numerous disputes with previous bishops, and reduced the immense debt he had inherited from his predecessor, Bishop Perche. He died in Château Giron on Sept. 23 while visiting France.

LEROUX, BL. MARGARET (1747–1794), martyr. Born in Cambrai, France, she was professed an Ursuline in 1769, took the name Sr. Ann Joseph (or Mother Josephine), and was guillotined at Valenciennes during the French Revolution. She was beatified in 1920. F. D. Oct. 23.

LE ROY, ALEXANDRE (1854–1938), archbishop. Born in St. Sénier-de-Beuvron, France, on Jan. 18, he became a member of the Congregation of the Holy Ghost, was ordained in 1876, served in Zanzibar and Pondicherry, India, and became titular bishop of Alinda in 1893 and was vicar apostolic of Gabon, Africa, in 1893–96. He was superior general of his congregation from 1896 to 1926, and died in Paris on Apr. 22.

LEROY-BEAULIEU, ANATOLE (1842–1912), historian. Born in Liseux, France, he wrote a novel, a study of the Second Empire, and the important three-volume *L'empire des tsars et les Russes* (1883–87). He was active against the French liberals, fought anti-Semitism, and in *La papauté, le socialisme, et la démocritie* was the first to welcome Pope Leo XIII's social writings. He died in Paris on June 15.

LE ROY, EDOUARD (1870–1954), philosopher. Born in France, he took his doctorate in mathematics at Paris in 1898, taught, became interested in philosophy, and published *Dogma and Criticism* in 1906. He wrote a study of Henri Bergson in 1912, and succeeded the latter at the Collège de France, where he became professor of philosophy in 1921. He was elected to the French Academy in 1941. He also wrote *The Problem of God* (1930) and *Introduction to the Study of Religious Problems* (1944). He died in Paris on Nov. 9.

LE SAGE, ALAIN RENÉ (1668–1747), author. Born in Sarzeau, France, on May 8, he studied at the Jesuit college in Vannes, was a tax collector for several years, went to Paris in 1692 to study law, was admitted as advocate of parliament in 1694, but after a brief career as a lawyer turned to literature. After unsuccessfully translating several Spanish plays he wrote *Crispin rival de son maître,* which was a great success when produced in 1707. He wrote several other plays, but in 1715 published the first two volumes of the novel, *Gil Blas de Santillane* (finished in 1735), which was his most popular and successful work. He wrote almost a hundred plays and several novels. Most important of his other satirical works are *Le Diable boîteux, Tuscaret ou le financier,* and *Une journée des parques.* He died on Nov. 17 at Boulogne-sur-mer, France.

LESCARBOT, MARC (1565?–1630). Born in Vervins, France, he went to Acadia, Canada, in 1606 and on his return published, among other studies, *Histoire de la Nouvelle France,* an account of his trip and of French colonizing attempts in America. It had great popularity and is a significant historical source. He published other books of travel and later became secretary of the French embassy in Switzerland.

LESCOT, PIERRE (1510?–1571), architect. Born in Paris, he became the outstanding French architect of the early Renaissance. Appointed by Francis I in 1546 to design a new royal palace in Paris, he, with Jean Goujon (who executed his designs as the sculptor), planned the building which assured his fame and on which he spent most of the rest of his life, the Louvre. He also designed Hôtel Carnavalet and Fontaine des Innocents in Paris, was appointed a commendatory abbot of Clagny, and died in Paris.

LESE, BENOZZO DI. *See* Gozzoli, Benozzo di Lese.

LESEUR, JEAN FRANÇOIS (1760–1837), composer. Born in Drucat-Plessiel, France, on Feb. 15, he was a choirboy at nearby Abbeville, studied at Amiens, and directed choirs at Séez, Dijon, Mans, and Tours. He became music master of Notre Dame de Paris in 1786, introduced a full orchestra, and with it achieved novel and operatic effects; he resigned two years later, to write such operas as *Paul et Virginie* (1794), *Telémaque* (1796), and *Ossian* (1804). He held political positions, wrote a *Te Deum* for Napoleon's coronation, and for that of King Charles X, and from 1814 to 1830 was master of the chapel of Louis XVIII, and a teacher at the Paris Conservatoire. Berlioz, Boulanger, and Gounod studied under him. He wrote masses, oratorios, cantatas, other operas, and several polemical pamphlets defending his position. He died in Paris on Oct. 6.

LESLIE, JOHN (1527–1596), bishop. An illegitimate child of the house of Leslie, he was born in Scotland on Sept. 29, studied at Aberdeen, Poitiers, Toulouse, and Paris, became professor of canon law at Aberdeen, and was ordained by special dispensation in 1558. He was named to dispute with Knox in 1560 and accompanied Mary Queen of Scots from France to Scotland in 1561. She appointed him to her privy council in 1565 and in 1566 bishop of Ross; he helped revise the laws of Scotland. He joined Mary when she escaped from Lochleven in 1568, represented her at the conference with representatives of the regent of Scotland and Elizabeth at York later that year, and was imprisoned by Elizabeth in 1571 and deprived of all income from his see for favoring Mary's marriage to Norfolk. He was freed in 1573, expelled from Britain, and spent the years until Mary's death in 1587 pleading her cause at the papal court and before the thrones of Europe. He was appointed vicar general of Rouen in 1579 and died, in exile, at Guirtenburg, Belgium, on May 30. He was the author of the ten-volume *De origine, moribus, ac rebus gestis Scotiae* which records events to 1571.

LESMES. *See* Adelelmus, St.

LESSIUS, VEN. LEONARD (1554–1623), theologian. Born in Brecht, Belgium, on Oct. 1, he entered the Louvain in 1568, received his doctorate in philosophy in 1571, and joined the Jesuits the following year. He taught at Douai until 1581, when he went to Rome, studied under Suarez, and returned to Louvain as professor of theology in 1585, a position he held until 1600, when he retired to devote himself to writing. He was involved in several theological disputes, most heated of which developed from his *Theses theologicae*, which was quieted in 1588 when the pope imposed silence on both sides because of the extremes to which the discussion of grace, scriptural inspiration, and predestination had been carried. He wrote other theological and ascetical treatises, including *De justicia et jure, Quae fides et religio sit capessenda, De summo bono, De providentia numinis,* and *Quinquagenta nomina Dei.* He died in Louvain on Jan. 15.

LESTONNAC, ST. JOAN DE (1556–1640), foundress. Born in Bordeaux, France, and resisting the efforts of her mother, Montaigne's sister, who had become a Calvinist and wished her daughter to follow, Joan married Gaston de Montferrant at seventeen, and became the mother of four children. At forty-seven, as a widow, she entered a Cistercian convent, but the regimen was too hard and she left in ill-health. She then planned a congregation of her own, gathered a number of followers at her home at La Mothe, directed them as nurses during a plague, and, under the advice of the Jesuit Frs. de Bordes and Raymond, developed plans for a teaching order, the Religious of Notre Dame of Bordeaux. This was approved and in 1610 Mother de Lestonnac became superior. Many schools were established and, in spite of a period of painful internal dissension, which even resulted in her being deposed, the organization flourished. She was canonized in 1949. F. D. Feb. 2.

LESTRANGE, LOUIS HENRI DE (1754–1827). Born in Ardèche, France, he was ordained in 1778. He was appointed vicar general of Vienne in 1780, entered La Trappe monastery later the same year, took the name Dom Augustine, and became master of novices. When religious orders were suppressed in France in 1790, he migrated to Switzerland in 1791 and from there established foundations in Spain, Italy, Switzerland, and England. When France invaded Switzerland in 1798, he was forced to flee, but returned in 1802, sent the first Trappists to the United States in 1803, and established a monastery in Genoa in 1804 under Napoleon's protection. When he ordered his monks to retract an oath of allegiance to the empire they had unwittingly taken, he was imprisoned by Napoleon, who ordered the suppression of all Trappist monasteries. He escaped to Germany, went to England and in 1813 to New York, but returned to La Trappe in 1814 when Napoleon was deposed. When he was accused of harshness to his monks and laxity in the running of the monastery, the bishop of Séez claimed jurisdiction over La Trappe. He left the monastery, appealed to Rome, was completely justified, and returned to La Trappe. He died in Lyons, France, on July 16.

LESUEUR, FRANÇOIS EUSTACHE (1685?–1760?), missioner. Born in Countances, Normandy, France, on July 22, he joined the Jesuits about 1704, was sent on the Canadian mission in 1715 or 1716, and spent most of the rest of his life working among the Abenaki Indians. He compiled an Abenaki dictionary, wrote prayers and sermons in Abenaki, and wrote an account of the Calumet dance. He died in Montreal in Apr. (or in Quebec in 1755).

LESZCZYNSKA, MARIA (1703–1769), queen. Born in Breslau, daughter of King Stanislas of Poland, she accompanied her father after his exile, settled with him in Alsace in 1719, and was married to King Louis XV of France, seven years her junior. She lived in retirement at Versailles, active in charity, and died there.

LESZEK I (d. 1227), king of Poland. Called "the Wise," he became king in 1206 and accorded the clergy the right to elect their own bishops and to control church territory.

LESZEK II (d. 1288), king of Poland. *See* Boleslav V.

LE TELLIER, FRANÇOIS MICHEL (1642–1710), archbishop. Born in Turin, France, son of Michel, he studied at the Sorbonne, where he received his doctorate in theology and was ordained in 1666. He was appointed coadjutor of Langres and then of Rheims, to which see he succeeded in 1669. He acted as secretary of the Petite Assemblée in 1681, suggested the Gallican Assembly of 1682 and served as its co-president, and presided at the assembly of 1710 called to consider Jansenism and laxism. Although he extended popular education, reformed clerical training, fought Protestantism, and administered his diocese efficiently, he consistently favored the crown in disputes with the Church. He died in Rheims.

LE TELLIER, FRANÇOIS MICHEL (1639?–1691), chancellor. Born in Paris on Jan. 18, son of Louis XIV's chancellor, with whom he shared the office of secretary of war from 1654, the marquis de Louvois received the office officially in 1666, and reorganized the French army into a well-equipped, well-disciplined fighting force. He founded Hôtel des Invalides, after 1671, exerted great influence

on Louis, supported the revocation of the Edict of Nantes in 1685, and was responsible to a large degree for the despoliation of the Palatinate in 1689. He died in Paris on July 16.

LE TELLIER, MICHEL (1603–1685), chancellor. Born in France on Apr. 19, he became secretary of war through Cardinal Mazarin's influence in 1642, supported the cardinal during the Fronde, acted as minister for the queen-regent, Anne of Austria, when Mazarin was exiled in 1651–53, and in 1677 was appointed chancellor by King Louis XIV. He signed the revocation of the Edict of Nantes four weeks before his death in Paris on Oct. 30.

LE TELLIER, MICHEL (1643–1719). Born in Vast, France, on Oct. 16, he studied in Caen, became a Jesuit at eighteen, taught at Collège Louis le Grand, Paris, and later was its rector. He became provincial in Paris, a member of the Academy of Inscriptions and Belles Lettres in 1709, and in the same year was appointed confessor of King Louis XIV. A vigorous opponent of Jansenism, he was sympathetic to the destruction of Port Royal, though probably not as influential in this decision as once thought, and was among those responsible for Pope Clement XI's condemnation of Quesnel. He was obliged to leave Paris after Louis XIV's death, went to Amiens, and then to La Flèche, France, where he died on Sept. 2. He wrote treatises against Jansenism, a book on the missionary controversy in China, finished Pétau's *De theologicis dogmatibus*, and was one of the founders of the *Journal de Trévoux*.

LETELLIER, VICTOIRE (1778–1859), foundress. Born in Mortain, Normandy, France, on Oct. 24, she studied in Barenton, served the inmates of the Mortain prison, of which her father was warden, and at twenty-eight became an Augustinian in Saumur, taking the name Mère Ste. Angèle. She was superior at the hospital there, until persecuted by civil authorities, moved to Paris, and in 1827 founded the Augustinians of the Holy Heart of Mary. Her institute received papal approval after her death.

LETTO, BL. ALEXANDRINA DI (1385–1458). Born in Sulmona, Italy, she became a Poor Clare at fifteen, founded a convent at Foligno where she became abbess, and with the encouragement of Pope Martin V began a Franciscan reform. F. D. Apr. 3.

LEUCHTELDIS. See Lufthildis, St.

LEUCIUS, ST. (d. 180?). A missioner from Alexandria, he became the first bishop of Brindisi, Italy. F. D. Jan. 11.

LEUCIUS, ST. (d. 251), martyr. *See* Thyrsus, St.

LEUCIUS, ST. (d. 309), martyr. He and SS. Peter and Severus were put to death at Alexandria, Egypt. F. D. Jan. 11.

LEUDOMER, ST. (d. 585). He was bishop of Chartres, Gaul. F. D. Oct. 2.

LEUPRANDUS. *See* Aliprandus.

LEUTFRID, ST. (d. 738). Born and educated at Évreux, France, he distinguished himself at Chartres, returned home to teach, then became a recluse near the monastery of Cailly. He became a monk at Rouen under St. Sidonius, then in 690 built a church and the monastery of La Croix-St. Ouen at Évreux, where he ruled a growing number of followers until his death. He is also known as Leufroi. F. D. June 21.

LEVADOUX, MICHAEL (1746–1815). Born in Clermont-Ferrand, Auvergne, France, on Apr. 1, he joined the Sulpicians in 1769, and was appointed director of their seminary in Limoges in 1774, where he remained until 1791, when he was sent to the United States with a group of Sulpicians to found St. Mary's seminary in Baltimore. After a year as treasurer he was sent on missionary work as Bishop Carroll's vicar general in the Middle West, and in 1796 began pastoral work in Detroit. He was recalled to Baltimore in 1801 and to France in 1803, when he was appointed superior of the seminary in Auvergne, and in 1814 of Le Puy-en-Velay, France, where he died on Jan. 13.

LE VAU, LOUIS (1612–1670), architect. Born in France, he studied architecture and in 1653 became first royal inspector of buildings. He became Louis XIV's councilor and director of royal buildings, built Hôtel Lambert, completed the Louvre's north and south wing, extended Versailles, and also worked on St. Sulpice. He died in Paris on Oct. 10.

LE VERRIER, URBAIN JEAN JOSEPH (1811–1877), astronomer. Born in St. Lô, France, on May 11, he studied at L'École Polytechnique, was appointed to a governmental post, became professor at Collège Stanislas in Paris and in 1846 professor of celestial mechanics at Paris, the year the planet Neptune was discovered as a result of his calculations. He was appointed to the Academy of Sciences in 1846, was elected to the legislative assembly in 1849, was made a senator in 1852, and became director of the Paris observatory in 1854, a position he held, except for the period 1870–73, until his death in Paris on Sept. 25. By calculations of the variations of planetary orbits for a 200,000-year period he proved the stability of the solar system, constructed tables representing the movements of the sun, moon, and planets, and deduced the existence of a planet between Mercury and the sun. He wrote many theses on celestial subjects, established a meteorological service in France, and founded the International Meteorological Foundation and Association Scientifique de France, of which he was president.

LÉVIGNAC, ABBÉ DE. *See* MacCarthy, Nicholas Tuite.

LEWINA, ST. (5th century?), martyr. She is said to have been martyred in Sussex, England, by invading Saxons. F. D. July 24.

LEWIS, BL. DAVID (1616–1679), martyr. Son of a Protestant father and Catholic mother, he was born in Monmouthshire, Wales, studied law in London, and at nineteen went to Europe as a tutor. He became a convert, probably in Paris, studied at Rome, was ordained in 1642, and became a Jesuit in 1644. Sent to England in 1646, he was recalled to become spiritual director of the English College, but in 1648 went to southern Wales, where he labored for thirty-one years. He was seized during the Titus Oates Plot, found guilty of being a priest, and hanged, drawn, and quartered at Usk, Wales. He was beatified in 1929. F. D. Aug. 27.

LEWIS, FRANK J. (1867–1960), executive. Born in Chicago on Apr. 9, he became president of his own roofing materials and coal-tar products company, retired in 1927, established the Lewis Foundation, and gave millions of dollars to charity. He founded the Lewis Memorial Maternity Hospital in Chicago in 1931; gave Lewis Towers, a skyscraper office building, to Loyola University in 1945, and in 1948 established the Stritch School of Medicine there; established the Illinois Club for Catholic Women; and donated a Chicago office building in 1955 to De Paul University. He received three papal decorations and was a papal count. He died in Chicago on Dec. 21.

LEZANA, JUAN BAUTISTA DE (1586–1659), theologian. Born in Madrid on Nov. 23, he joined the Carmelites of the Old Observance in 1600, was professed in 1602, and studied at Toledo, Salamanca, and Alcalá. He lectured at Toledo and Alcalá, but in 1625 was sent to a general chapter in Rome and stayed there to teach and write theology. In 1645 he was elected assistant general, and was also named procurator general. He occupied the chair of metaphysics at the Sapienza and served as consultant for the congregations of the Index and Rites. He died in Rome on Mar. 29.

LEZINIANA, BL. MATTHEW ALONSO (d. 1745), martyr. Born in Navas del Rey, Spain, he was ordained a Dominican and sent to the Philippine missions. Transferred to Tonkin, Indochina, he was beheaded there. He was beatified in 1906. F. D. Jan. 22.

LIBENTIUS, ST. (d. 1013), bishop. Born in southern Swabia, he became bishop of Hamburg in 988, joined the Benedictines that same year, and went on to become one of the apostles to the Slavs. F. D. Jan. 4.

LIBERALIS, ST. (d. 400?). A priest near Ancona, Italy, he suffered much because of his opposition to the Arians. F. D. Apr. 27.

LIBERATA, ST. (d. 580?). Born in Como,

Italy, she founded the convent there with her sister Faustina. F. D. Jan. 18.

LIBERATORE, MATTEO (1810–1892), theologian. Born in Salerno, Italy, on Aug. 14, he studied at the Jesuit college in Naples and in 1826 joined the Society. After his ordination he taught theology from 1837 to 1848 when he was forced by the revolution to flee to Malta. On his return, he founded *Civiltá Cattolica* in 1850 and embarked on a program of reviving interest in the teachings of St. Thomas Aquinas. He wrote hundreds of articles and scores of books on the social and ecclesiastical world in which he lived. He died in Rome on Oct. 18.

LIBERATORE, NICCOLÒ DI (1430?–1502), painter. Born in Umbria, he studied under Bartolommeo Gozzoli and is said to have taught Andrea di Luigi, Perugino, and Pinturrichio. He decorated the Franciscan church of La Diruta, near Perugia; other work is at Milan, Gualdo, Perugia, and Foligno. He is also called Niccolò d'Alunno and Niccolò da Foligno.

LIBERATUS, ST. (d. 484), martyr. Abbot of a monastery near Capsa, Africa, he was summoned to Carthage with Boniface, a deacon; Servus and Rusticus, subdeacons; Rogatus and Septimus, monks; and a child named Maximus. The Arian Vandal, King Huneric, commanded them to renounce their faith; they refused, were tortured, put in a boat which was set afire, and finally beaten to death by oarsmen. F. D. Aug. 17 (also, Dec. 7).

LIBERATUS OF CARTHAGE (6th century). An African archdeacon, he was sent in 535, as legate of an African synod, to Rome to consult with Pope Agapetus I about several matters, was opposed to Justinian's edict against the Three Chapters in 544, and wrote a history of Nestorianism and Eutychianism, *Breviarium causae Nestorianorum et Eutychianorum*, between 555 and 567.

LIBERATUS OF LORO, BL. (d. 1258?). Born in San Liberato, Italy, of the noble Brumforte family, he joined the Friars Minor and is supposed to have introduced the strict observance in the order with BB. Humilis and Pacificus. Though his cult was forbidden in 1730, it was restored in 1731 and approved by Pope Pius IX in 1868. F. D. Sept. 6.

LIBERIANUS, ST. (d. 165?), martyr. *See* Justin Martyr, St.

LIBERIUS (d. 366), pope. Before his election as pope on May 17, 352, he was a Roman deacon. His entire pontificate was plagued with the attempts of the Arians and semi-Arians to win control of the Church. In 353 he petitioned Emperor Constantius to convoke a council at which he hoped Arianism would be unequivocally denounced. Instead, the council held at Arles condemned Athanasius and induced the papal legates to accede. Liberius con-

demned the decision, became involved in a controversy with the Arian-sympathetic emperor who demanded he denounce Athanasius, and requested the emperor to call another council to propound the decrees of Nicaea. When this council, held at Milan in 355, resulted in the emperor's banishment of the bishops who refused to accede to his demands for a condemnation of Athanasius, Liberius wrote a letter, *Quamuis sub imagine*, to the exiled bishops, addressing them as martyrs, refused the bribe offered by the emperor's legate, Eusebius, to denounce Athanasius, and was himself banished to Beroea in Thrace. Constantius then set up the archdeacon Felix in Rome (antipope Felix II), but the Romans refused to accept him as bishop. Liberius returned to Rome, probably in 357, after allegedly signing the formula of Sirmium, a modified form of Arianism, but under pressure. Felix was then expelled. Liberius disapproved the Council of Rimini in 359 which was controlled by the bishops devoted to the emperor, and at which practically the entire episcopate signed an ambiguous definition of the faith which was substantially heretical, and on Constantius' death in 361 publicly condemned its decisions, and decreed that the bishops who had supported them could be restored only after taking vigorous action against the Arians. The new emperor, Julian the Apostate, attempted to restore paganism and to this end encouraged the Arians and Donatists against the Catholics, but Arianism had spent itself and rapidly weakened. In 365 or 366, Liberius received some sixty Eastern bishops led by Eustathius in Rome, and admitted them to communion with the Church after satisfying himself as to their orthodoxy. He died in Rome on Sept. 24.

LIBERIUS, ST. (d. 200?). He is one of the earliest bishops of Ravenna, Italy. F. D. Dec. 30.

LIBERT, ST. (d. 783), martyr. Born in Malines, France, he was educated by St. Rumold, became a Benedictine, and went to the abbey of St. Troud, where he was slain by invading barbarians. F. D. July 14.

LIBERT, ST. (d. 1076), bishop. Born in Brabant, he was educated by his uncle, Gerard, whom he succeeded as bishop of Cambrai in 1051. When he was unable to reach Jerusalem because of Saracen victories, he returned and built the church and monastery of the Holy Sepulcher in Cambrai. He was noted for his direct pastoral concern for his people, for the spiritual and charitable aid he gave them, and for his defense of them against Lord Hugh (who imprisoned him) and against raiders whom he persuaded to leave the city untouched. F. D. June 23.

LIBORIUS, ST. (d. 390), bishop. He became bishop of Le Mans, Gaul, in 348 and directed the see for fifty years; St. Martin of Tours attended his funeral. He was honored as patron of Paderborn, Germany. F. D. July 23.

LICCIO, BL. JOHN (d. 1511). Raised by his aunt when his mother died giving him birth, he became a Dominican under Bl. Peter Geremia in Palermo, Sicily, when fifteen and gained renown as a preacher. He built an abbey in Caccamo, where he was prior in 1494. His cult was approved in 1753. F. D. Nov. 14.

LICERIUS, ST. (d. 548?). Born probably in Lérida, Spain, he was chosen in 506 as bishop of Conserans, Gaul. F. D. Aug. 27.

LICINIUS, ST. (d. 295?), martyr. See Carpophorus, St.

LICINIUS, ST. (540?–616?), bishop. A courtier serving King Clotaire I, he was made count of Anjou by King Chilperic. When his fiancée contracted leprosy, he entered religious life in 580, was ordained, and in 586 was called to the see which he once had governed as civil ruler. He devoted his years to the care of the poor and of prisoners, becoming known as a most moving preacher and devout ascetic. F. D. Feb. 13.

LIDANUS, ST. (1026–1118). Born in Antina, Italy, he founded as abbot the Benedictine monastery of Sezze, directed the draining of the Pontine marshes, and died at Monte Cassino. F. D. July 2.

LIDOIN, BL. MARIE-MAGDALEN (d. 1794), martyr. A Carmelite, Mother Thérèse de St. Augustin, she was prioress of a group at Compiègne, France, which was seized and guillotined during the Revolution. With her died Marie Dufour (Sr. Ste. Marthe), Marie Hanisset (Sr. Thérèse de Coeur de Marie), Marie Ann Piedcourt (Sr. Thérèse de Jésus Crucifé), and Marie Trésel (Sr. Thérèse de St. Ignace). They were beatified in 1925. F. D. July 17.

LIEBER, ERNST MARIA (1838–1902). Born in Kamberg, Hesse-Nassau, on Nov. 16, son of Moriz Lieber, he studied at Würzburg, Bonn, and Heidelberg, received his doctorate in law in 1861, and spent the next four years in further study. He became interested in politics in Nassau, was elected to the Prussian diet in 1870, helped organize the Centre party the same year, was elected to the German *Reichstag* in 1871, and became recognized as a capable parliamentarian and orator. He was a leader in the movement for social reform, opposed the Kulturkampf, and in 1887 led the opposition to Bismarck's legislative program and plan to reduce the *Reichstag's* power. In 1891, on the death of the Centre party's leader, Winthorst, he became involved in disputes within the party between the northern and southern wings, and was elected head of the party in 1893. The elections of 1893 returned the Centre party as the most important in the *Reichstag*, and Lieber turned it to support of the government in building the German Empire. He reorgan-

ized the party, vigorously supported a new Catholic group formed in 1890 to achieve social reform, Volksverein für das katholische Deutschland, and labored to change the direction of the Catholic group from an ecclesiastical party to one with imperial aims with an organization in each of the German states. He died on Mar. 31.

LIEBER, MORIZ (1790–1860). Born in Blankenheim castle, Germany, on Oct. 1, he translated numerous Catholic works into German, was active in opposing the rationalism of his times, was vociferous in his defense of Archbishop von Droste-Vischering of Cologne when the Prussian government imprisoned the latter, and in 1848 was appointed to draw up a memorial to the government by the bishops' meeting in Cologne. He helped found Der katholische Verein Deutschlands, over whose meeting he presided in 1849 and 1859, was a member of the Nassau upper house, and wrote pamphlets defending the Church against government interference. He died in Kamberg, Hesse-Nassau, on Dec. 29.

LIEBERMANN, BRUNO FRANZ LEOPOLD (1759–1844), theologian. Born in Molsheim, Alsace, on Oct. 12, he studied there, entered the Strassburg seminary in 1776, taught at Molsheim, and was ordained in 1783. He taught at the Strassburg seminary, was pastor in Ernolsheim, and in 1792, when forced to flee the French Revolution, became rector of All Saints abbey across the Rhine in Germany. After his return he was arrested in 1804, accused of communicating with the royal family, and imprisoned for eight months. From his release in 1805 until 1823 he was rector of the Mainz seminary; he then became vicar general of Strassburg, Alsace, where he died on Nov. 11.

LIEPHARD, ST. (d. 640). An English companion, possibly a bishop, with King Cadwalla on a pilgrimage to Rome, he was slain on his return at Cambrai, France. F. D. Feb. 4.

LIEUBALT, ST. (d. 650). A Benedictine monk at St. Aignan, he became abbot-founder of Fleury (later called St. Benoît-sur-Loire), also in the diocese of Orléans, France. He also is known as Leobald. F. D. Aug. 8.

LIGUORI, ST. ALPHONSUS MARY DE'. See Alphonsus Mary de' Liguori, St.

LILIOSA, ST. (d. 852?), martyr. See Aurelius, St.

LILIUS, ALOYSIUS. See Giglio, Aloisi.

LILLIS, THOMAS FRANCIS (1861–1938), bishop. Born in Lexington, Missouri, on Mar. 3, he studied at Niagara, New York, St. Benedict's, Kansas, and St. Meinrad's, Indiana, and was ordained in Kansas City, Missouri, in 1885. He did parish work, was pastor of St. Patrick's in Kansas City, Missouri, in 1887–1904, was appointed vicar general in 1903, and in 1904 was consecrated bishop of Leavenworth. He was transferred to Kansas City, Missouri, in 1910 as titular bishop of Cibyra and coadjutor, succeeded to the see in 1913, was appointed assistant at the pontifical throne in 1935, and died in Kansas City on Dec. 29.

LILLY, WILLIAM SAMUEL (1840–1919). Born in Fifehead, England, he studied at Cambridge, and became undersecretary for India in 1869, a convert and controversialist. His writings include: *Ancient Religion and Modern Thought, A Century of Revolution,* and *New France.* He was for fifty years secretary of the Catholic Union of Great Britain. He died in London on Aug. 29.

LIMA, MANOEL DE OLIVEIRA (1867–1928), diplomat. Born in Pernambuco, Brazil, on Dec. 25, he studied at Lisbon and entered the diplomatic service in 1890. He was first secretary of the Brazilian embassy in Washington in 1896–1900 and held other posts in Europe, South America, and Japan. He taught at Harvard in 1915–16, lectured at other colleges, and from 1923 until his death in Washington, D.C., on Mar. 24 was professor of international law at Catholic University. He was a member of the academies of letters in Brazil, Portugal, and Spain, wrote widely in his field, and left a library of 40,000 volumes to Catholic University.

LIMBANIA, ST. (d. 1294). A Cyprian, she became a Benedictine nun and later a recluse at Genoa, Italy. Her cult was approved by Pope Paul V. F. D. Aug. 15.

LIMBOURG, POL DE (15th century), painter. Probably a native of Burgundy, of the Malouel family, he came to Paris with his two brothers at an early age; they were well known by the end of the fourteenth century for their illuminated manuscript illustrations. They provided the illustrations for the first half of the *Très riches heures,* a famous book of hours executed for the duc de Berry about 1416.

LIMINIUS, ST. (d. 267?), martyr. *See* Anatolianus, St.

LIMNAEUS, ST. (d. 450?). A younger companion of St. Thalassius, at Tillimè, Syria, he then trained under St. Malo, and finally moved to a stone enclosure on a mountaintop, where he lived thirty-eight years. Bishop Theodoret of Cyrrhus recounts his healing powers and care of the blind. F. D. Feb. 22.

LINACRE, THOMAS (1460?–1524), physician. Born in Canterbury, England, he studied at the monastery school there, entered Oxford about 1480, and became a fellow in 1484. He accompanied William Selling, Henry VII's ambassador, to Rome, studied in the household of Lorenzo de' Medici under Politian, and then at Vicenza and Padua, where he received his medical degree. After ten years in Italy he returned to England, taught Greek at Oxford

to Thomas More, among others, became physician to Henry VIII and many of the royal court, and resigned in 1520 to become a priest. He established chairs of medicine at Oxford and Cambridge and founded the Royal College of Physicians, of which he was first president. He translated many of the works of Galen into Latin, among them *Methodius medendi, De sanitate tuenda* and *De pulsuum usu.* He died in London on Oct. 20.

LINDANUS, WILLIAM DAMASUS (1525–1588), bishop. Born in Dordrecht, Netherlands, he studied at Louvain and Paris, was ordained in 1552, taught scripture at Dillengen in 1554, and became vicar general of Utrecht in 1556, and then royal counselor and inquisitor in Friesland. He was appointed bishop of Ruremonde in 1562, but because of opposition was unable to occupy his see until 1569. He began to reform his diocese, was forced to flee several times when he opposed the duke of Alba, and in 1578 went to Rome and Spain to secure papal and royal support, and again to Rome in 1584. He wrote many treatises, among them: *De optimo scripturas interpretandi genere, Missa apostolica, Dubitantius,* and *Ruwardius.* He established the royal seminary at Louvain, and in 1588 was appointed to the see of Ghent, which he ruled only three months until his death there on Nov. 2.

LINDE, JUSTIN TIMOTHEUS BALTHASAR VON (1797–1870), ambassador. Born in Brilon, Westphalia, on Aug. 7, he studied at Münster, Göttingen, and Bonn, where he received his doctorate in 1820 and began teaching in 1821. He went to Giessen in 1823, taught law there, and became ministerial counsel at Darmstadt in 1829, director of the board of education in 1832, and chancellor of Giessen, where he established a theological faculty, in 1833. He was named privy councilor in 1836, was raised to the nobility in 1839, and was a member of the Frankfort parliament in 1848 and that of Erfurt in 1850. He then became Prince Lichtenstein's ambassador to the German diet until its dissolution in 1866, when he retired to his country estate at Dreys. He died in Bonn, Germany, on June 9.

LINDEMANN, WILHELM (1828–1879), historian. Born in Schonnebeck, Prussia, on Dec. 17, he studied at Bonn, was ordained in 1852, served as rector of Heinsberg gymnasium (1833–60), as parish priest in Rheinbreitbach and Venrath, and became pastor of Nieder-Kruechten in 1866, a position he held until his death. He was a member of the Prussian diet in 1870–79. He wrote several biographies and historical works, chief of which was *Geschichte der deutschen literatur,* the first Catholic study of German writing. He died on Dec. 20 at Nieder-Kruechten, Germany.

LINDSAY, COLIN (1819–1892). Born in

Muncaster castle, England, on Dec. 6, to James Lindsay, earl of Crawford, and Maria Pennington, daughter of Baron Muncaster, he went to Cambridge but did not take his degree, married Lady Frances Howard in 1845, and lived near Wigan. He restored All Saints' church there, of which he was warden, founded the Manchester Church Society (which became the English Church Union), and was its president in 1860–67. He moved to Brighton and to London and in 1868, two years after his wife, became a convert. He wrote *Evidence for the Papacy* (1870), *De ecclesia et cathedra* (1877), and *Mary Queen of Scots and Her Marriage with Bothwell* (1883). He died in London on Jan. 28.

LINDSAY, LIONEL ST. GEORGE (1849–1921), editor. Born in Montreal, he studied at Laval and in Rome, was ordained in 1875, and from 1894 until his death in Quebec was successively chaplain, inspector of diocesan schools, secretary, and archivist of that archdiocese. He was editor of *La nouvelle France* from 1902 and the author of *Notre Dame de Lorette*.

LINE, BL. ANNE (d. 1601), martyr. Raised a Calvinist, in Dunmow, Essex, England, she was disowned by her father, William Heigham, when she embraced Catholicism. When her husband, Roger Line, exiled for his faith, died in 1594, she acted as housekeeper for Fr. John Gerard in a house of refuge for priests in London. She left when Fr. Gerard was imprisoned, but was arrested in another refuge she had established, convicted of aiding priests, and hanged at Tyburn. She was beatified in 1929. F. D. Feb. 27.

LINGARD, JOHN (1771–1851), historian. Born in Winchester, England, on Feb. 5, he studied and taught at Douai. Forced to flee by the French Revolution, he helped refugees from Douai to establish a college at Crookhall, near Durham, in 1794, and became a professor of philosophy. He was ordained in 1795, became vice-president when the college was moved to Ushaw in 1808, and in 1811 declined the presidency of Maynooth to retire to Hornby to devote himself to writing history. In 1817, while on a trip to Rome to examine material in the Vatican archives, he arranged for the reopening of the English College. The first three of his eight-volume *History of England* were published in 1819 and praised for their scholarly attention to original sources, accuracy, and temperate tone. He received a doctorate from Pope Pius VII in 1821, was made an associate of the Royal Society of Literature, was given a national pension, and received other honors. He wrote and published widely, revised five editions of his *History* (completed in 1830), and in 1845 issued a completely rewritten *History and Antiquities of the Anglo-Saxon Church*, first issued in 1806. He died in Hornby, England, on July 17.

LINUS, ST. (d. 76), pope. The second pope, a native of Tuscany, he reigned from about 67 to 76. St. Ireneaus says he is the Linus mentioned in Timothy 4:21. Though he is venerated traditionally as a martyr, there is no evidence of his martyrdom. F. D. Sept. 23.

LIOBA, ST. (d. 780). Born in Wessex, England, daughter of Dynne and Ebba, she was sent to the Benedictine abbey of Wimborne in Dorsetshire when quite young and became a nun there. She wrote to St. Boniface, a distant relative, when the latter was preaching in Germany, and in 748 at his request she was sent there with thirty nuns, including SS. Thecla and Walburga, and established the convent of Bischofsheim, which became one of the great centers of Christianity in Germany and from which many daughter houses were established, under Lioba's direction. After twenty-eight years as abbess she resigned and retired to nearby Schönersheim. She was baptized Truthgeba, but was called Liobgetha, of which Lioba ("dear one") is a contraction. F. D. Sept. 28.

LIPHARDUS, ST. (477?–550?). A prominent judge in Orléans, Gaul, he became a recluse with St. Urbicius, found himself with many followers, and was given permission to establish a community by the bishop of Orléans, who ordained him and built him a church. This developed into the monastic center of Meung-sur-Loire. F. D. June 3.

LIPPI, FILIPPINO (1458?–1504), painter. Son of Filippo Lippi, he was born in Prato, Italy, orphaned at ten, and raised by Fra Diamante. He studied under Botticelli, achieved notice with his altarpiece *Vision of St. Bernard*, and in 1480 was commissioned to finish Masaccio's frescoes in the Brancacci chapel, which established him as a foremost artist. From 1487 to 1493 he was engaged in painting the frescoes of the life of St. Thomas Aquinas at the Minerva, Rome. Among his masterpieces are *Madonna with Saints*, *Madonna Enthroned*, *Adoration of the Magi*, *Virgin and Child with St. Joseph and a Child Angel*, and a *Crucifixion*. He also executed the frescoes of episodes in the lives of SS. Philip and John in the Strozzi chapel in St. Maria Novella, Florence, completed in 1502. His paintings are characterized by his mastery of color and line, correctness of design, emphasis on costume and unusual accessories, and insertion of portraits of his contemporaries in his larger works. He died in Florence, Italy, on Apr. 18.

LIPPI, FILIPPO (1406?–1469), painter. Born in Florence, he was orphaned at two, placed in a Carmelite monastery at eight, and was taken into the order at fifteen. He observed Masolino and Masaccio at work on the frescoes of the

Brancacci chapel (which Filippo's son was to finish), decided to pursue art as a career, and in 1432 left the Carmelites. Cosimo de' Medici became his patron and the *Madonna* and *Nativity* he painted for his patron launched his career. In 1441 he painted *Coronation of the Virgin* for the nuns of St. Ambrogio and *Vision of St. Bernard* for the chapel of the Signiory in 1447. He was commissioned to paint the choir of the cathedral of Prato in 1452, and his scenes from the lives of St. John the Baptist and St. Stephen are among his greatest work (*Feast of Herod with the Dance of Salome* and the *Death of St. Stephen*, in particular). Although appointed chaplain of St. Giovannino in Florence and rector of St. Quirico in Legnaia during this period, his private life was such that in 1458 he was released from his vows by Pope Pius II, so he could marry. In 1467 he began a series of frescoes from the life of the Virgin Mary in the cathedral in Spoleto; the *Death and Coronation* was finished, after his death in Spoleto, Italy, on Oct. 9, by Fra Diamente and others. He also taught Botticelli, Benozzo Gozzoli, Francesco di Pesello, and Ghirlandajo. He was a great colorist and master draftsman, excelling in the execution of individual figures, noted for their realism, grace, animation, and sensuousness. Other masterpieces are *Madonna with Saints*, *Virgin Adoring the Christ Child*, *Four Saints*, *Madonna and Child with Angels*, *Annunciation*, and *Vision of St. Bernard*.

LIPPOMANO, LUIGI (1500–1559), cardinal. Born in Venice, he was ordained, joined the Oratorio della Carità, and in 1538 was appointed coadjutor to his uncle Pietro, bishop of Bergamo, and titular bishop of Methone. In 1542 he acted as papal nuncio to Portugal, accompanied his uncle to Verona in 1544, and succeeded him to the see in 1548. He acted as a president of the Council of Trent in 1551–52, served as papal nuncio to Poland in 1556, and was transferred to Bergamo in 1558. He was created a cardinal and remained in Rome until his death on Aug. 15. He wrote scriptural commentaries and *Sanctorum priscorum patrum vitae*, an important collection of hagiography.

LIPSIUS, JUSTUS (1547–1606), philologian. Born in Oberryssche, Netherlands, on Oct. 18, he studied at Ath and the Jesuit college in Cologne, joined the Jesuits in 1562, but was taken from the novitiate by his father, who sent him to Louvain to study law. There he became interested in philology, and in 1569 published a collection of Latin readings, *Variae lectiones*. He was Latin secretary of Cardinal Granvelle in Rome in 1569–70, visited several cities, and became a Lutheran in Jena, where he was a professor of history in 1572–74. He married a Cologne widow in 1573 and, when she refused to move to Jena, settled in Cologne in 1574

and published his edition of Tacitus. He lectured at Louvain in 1576–77, taught at Leyden from 1578 to 1591, and wrote such treatises as *De constantia* (1584). He was caught up in the religious controversies of the time despite himself, moved to Mainz in 1591 to escape them, and was reconciled to the Church. After a trip to Spain he was named professor at the Collegium Trilinge of Louvain in 1592, historiographer of the king of Spain in 1595, and honorary member of the state council in 1605. He wrote *Physiologiae stoicorum* and *Manuductionis ad stoicam philosophiam;* treatises on the Roman military prepared for a general work on Roman antiquities, *Fax historica*, which he never finished; and on politics and ethics. He died in Louvain on Mar. 23.

LISTER, THOMAS (1559?–1628?), author. A native of Yorkshire, England, he entered Douai in 1576, returned to England, where he was imprisoned, and after his release went to the English College in Rome in 1579. He became a Jesuit in 1582, was ordained in 1592, sent on the English mission in 1596, arrested in 1598, and imprisoned for several years. He wrote a treatise *Adversus factiosus in ecclesia*, which condemned those priests who had objected to the rule of Archpriest George Blackwell; when their appeal to Rome was sustained, the tract was condemned by papal brief in 1601. He probably lived the rest of his life in England.

LISZT, FRANZ (1811–1886), composer. Born in Raiding, Hungary, on Oct. 22, he made his public debut at nine at Sopron (Ödenburg), was sent to Vienna by a group of Hungarian nobles who agreed to pay for his further musical education, and studied there under Czerny and Salieri. He gave his first concert in Vienna in 1822, attracted the commendation of Beethoven, went to Paris in 1823 to study at the conservatory, and, when refused admittance because of his foreign birth, remained to study further under Paer and Reicha, and had a one-act operetta, *Don Sanche*, performed by the Académie Royale in 1825. On the death of his father in 1827 he settled in Paris, gave music lessons, became acquainted with the great of the artistic world, particularly Chopin and Berlioz, who greatly influenced him, and for a time flirted with Saint-Simonianism, though he later denied he had ever joined the movement. He was so impressed by Paganini that he resolved to become as great on the piano as Paganini was on the violin, and withdrew from public appearances to concentrate on his studies. After 1832 he became the rage of Europe in piano recitals, and in 1839 received a patent of nobility from the Austrian emperor. In 1833 he met Countess d'Agoult, lived with her in Switzerland and Italy during the next six years, and had three illegitimate children (one of whom, Cosima, was to become Richard Wagner's wife). In 1848 he settled in Weimar with Princess Caroline von Sayn-Wittgenstein, though in the next few years he had affairs with numerous other women, among them George Sand, Lola Montez, and Marie Duplessis. He became conductor of the court theater at Weimar, which he made the greatest musical center of Europe, wrote orchestral and choral pieces, and was an enthusiastic promoter of the works of Wagner, many of which he produced. He resigned this position in 1858, broke off his relationship with Princess Wittgenstein in 1861 when he was unable to secure a dispensation to marry her, went to Rome, and in 1865 received minor orders there. He received numberless degrees and honors, was made a royal Hungarian councilor in 1871, president of the Hungarian National Academy of Music in 1875, and honorary canon of St. Albano in Rome in 1879. The last years of his life were spent in teaching and giving concerts and conducting to great acclaim in the great European capitals. In addition to his unrivaled skills as a piano virtuoso, Liszt is noted for his more than 700 musical compositions. He wrote operas, choral works, orchestral works, pianoforte compositions, chamber pieces and songs, and also a biography of Chopin and several musical monographs. He died at Bayreuth, Germany, on July 31.

LITTA, ALFONSO (1608–1679), cardinal. Born in Milan, Italy, he served as governor of the Marches for Pope Innocent X, was appointed archbishop of Milan in 1652, and was created cardinal in 1660. He died in Rome on Aug. 22.

LITTA, LORENZO (1756–1820), cardinal. Born in Milan, Italy, on Feb. 25, he studied at the Clementine College in Rome, was appointed prothonotary apostolic by Pope Pius VI, titular archbishop of Thebes in 1793, and the following year went to Poland as papal nuncio. He acted as the pope's representative at the crowning of Paul I in Moscow and then served as ambassador to St. Petersburg, where he restored several sees, settled jurisdictional disputes between followers of the Uniat Ruthenian and Latin rites, and had the Basilians restored. He returned to Italy in 1789, was created cardinal in 1801, and appointed prefect of the Congregation of the Index and later of Studies. He was expelled from Rome in 1809, wrote a translation of the *Iliad* while in exile, and returned with Pope Pius VII, who made him prefect of the Propaganda. He was appointed bishop of Sabina in 1814 and cardinal vicar of Rome in 1818. He died at Monte Flavio, Italy, on May 1.

LITTEUS, ST. (d. 257), bishop and martyr. *See* Nemesian, St.

LITTLE, ARTHUR (1897–1949), author.

Born in Dublin, on Mar. 31, he studied at Belvedere, Clongowes Woods, and Trinity colleges, became a Jesuit in 1914, and pursued further study at University College and Milltown Park, both in Dublin. He taught philosophy at Tullabeg from 1932 until ill-health interfered in 1946. He wrote a life of Isaac Jogues, *Philosophy without Tears*, *The Nature of Art*, *The Platonic Heritage of Thomism*, lyrics, and *Christ Unconquered*, an epic poem in the tradition and style of Milton's *Paradise Lost*. He died in Dublin on Dec. 5.

LITTRÉ, PAUL MAXIMILIEN ÉMILE (1801–1881), lexicographer. Born in Paris on Feb. 1, he graduated from Lycée Louis le Grand there, was secretary to Count Daru, taught classics, and contributed political articles to *Le National* from 1831 to 1848. He was co-founder of *L'Expérience*, a medical journal, in 1837, was elected to the Academy of Inscriptions and Belles Lettres in 1839, became a follower of Auguste Comte, and between 1845 and 1876 wrote a series of books on positivism. From 1859 to 1872 he issued his *Dictionnaire de la langue française*. He became professor of history and geography at L'École Polytechnique, was elected to the national assembly in 1871, and was made a senator for life in 1874. Late in life he became a convert. He died in Paris on June 2.

LIUDHARD, ST. (d. 602?). Chaplain of Bertha, daughter of King Charibert of Paris, he accompanied her to England for her marriage to King Ethelbert of Kent, and died at Canterbury. F. D. May 7.

LIUTPRAND OF CREMONA (10th century), bishop. Born in Lombardy, he became a member of the court of King Hugo of Arles at Pavia, was educated in the court school, and became a deacon of the cathedral, chancellor of King Berenger II of Ivrea, and, in 949, ambassador to Emperor Constantine VII Porphyrogenitus. After a disagreement with Berenger, he entered the service of Otto I of Germany. From 958 to 962 he was occupied in writing a history of his times, was appointed bishop of Cremona in 961 when Otto became king of Lombardy, and during the rest of his life served as the emperor's ambassador. Among his missions were those to Pope John XII in 963 to protest John's support of Berenger's son, Adelbert, and in the same year his participation in the synod in Rome which deposed John; to Rome in 965, on the death of Leo VIII, when he acted as Otto's envoy to elect John XIII; and in 968 to Constantinople as the emperor's representative in arranging a marriage between the daughter of the Byzantine emperor and Otto's son. He died sometime after 970.

LIUTWIN, ST. (d. 713?). He founded the Benedictine abbey of Mettlach, Germany, and became bishop of Trier. F. D. Sept. 29.

LLEUDADD, ST. (6th century). He went from the monastery of Bardsey, Wales, to Brittany with St. Cadfan. He may be identical with St. Lauto, bishop of Coutances, Gaul. F. D. Jan. 15.

LLIBIO, ST. (6th century). His name is honored in Llanllibio, on the Isle of Anglesey, of which he is patron. F. D. Feb. 28.

LLOYD, BL. JOHN (d. 1679), martyr. A native of Breconshire, Wales, he was a secular priest, educated at Valladolid and sent to the Welsh mission in 1649. He was seized in 1678 and hanged at Cardiff, Wales, with Bl. Philip Evans for alleged complicity in the Titus Oates Plot. He was beatified in 1929. F. D. July 22.

LO. *See* Lauto, St.

LOAISA CARVAJAL, JERÓNIMO (1489?–1575), archbishop. Born in Trujillo, Spain, he became a Dominican at Cordova, taught at Valladolid, and was prior at Carboneras. He was named bishop of Cartegena in 1537, built a cathedral and school there, was transferred to Lima, Peru, in 1543, and became its first archbishop in 1548. He established the hospital of St. Anne, was mediator in several insurrections, and acted as national and military leader after the death of Viceroy Mendoza.

LOAISA, GARCÍA DE (1479?–1546), cardinal. Born in Talavera, Spain, he studied at Dominican convents in Salamanca, Peñafiel, where he was professed in 1495, Alcalá, Valladolid. After teaching philosophy and theology, he was appointed rector of St. Gregory's College, Valladolid, and in 1518 was elected general of the order. He became King Charles V's confessor about 1524, was appointed bishop of Osma the same year, was transferred to the see of Siguenza and created cardinal in 1530, and made commissary general of the Inquisition and archbishop of Seville in 1531. He died in Madrid on Apr. 21.

LOARN, ST. (5th century). A native of western Ireland, he is listed as a regionary bishop of Downpatrick. F. D. Aug. 30.

LOBB, EMMANUEL (1593–1671). Born in Portsmouth, England, he was sent to Portugal to study when eleven, became a convert, studied at the English College, Rome, and St. Omer's, joined the Jesuits at Liège, taught there and at St. Omer's, and in 1647 became rector at the English College, Rome. While there he wrote two plays, *Zeno* and *Mercia,* and published three more tragedies at Liège in 1656. He became provincial of the Jesuits in England, and in 1669 gave instructions to the duke of York (later James II) for his reconciliation with the Church. He died in London. He is also known by his alias, Joseph Simeon, under which he wrote his plays.

LOBBEDY, ÉMILE LOUIS CORNIL (1856–1916), bishop. Born in Bergues, France, on Feb. 29, he took his doctorate in theology in Rome, did parish work in Cambrai, was vicar general of Hazebrouck, became bishop of Moulins in 1906, and was transferred to Arras in 1911. He remained under fire in his see city for the first nine months of World War I and was decorated for bravery. He died in Boulogne, France, on Dec. 26.

LOBERA, VEN. ANA (1545–1621). Born in Medina del Campo, Old Castile, Spain, on Nov. 25, and a deaf-mute until seven, she joined the Carmelites at Avila in 1570 and made her profession in 1571, taking the name Ana de Jesus. She was appointed first prioress of Béas in 1575 by St. Teresa, who later sent her to establish a convent in Granada, of which she became prioress. After St. Teresa's death in 1582 she collected the saint's manuscripts and sent them to Fray Luis de León, who gathered them in the first edition of 1588; and it was at her request that St. John of the Cross wrote *Spiritual Canticle.* In 1586, with the help of St. John of the Cross, she was founder-prioress of the Discalced Carmelite convent in Madrid, where her disagreement with Nicholas Doria, her superior, when she and Jerome Gratian attempted to put into effect their constitution, drawn up by St. Teresa and approved by papal bull in 1590, resulted in Philip II's forbidding the holding of a chapter to put the constitution into effect. The impasse was relieved by a brief of Gregory XIV in 1591. Doria was restored as superior and had her imprisoned, as penance, for three years. She was prioress in Salamanca in 1596–99; went to France in 1604 and established convents in Paris, Pontoise, and Dijon; and in 1607 went to Belgium and founded houses in Brussels, Louvain, Mons, and Antwerp. In 1610, with papal permission, she and her nuns rendered obedience to the Italian Carmelites when the Spanish Carmelites decided not to spread outside of Spain. She died at a convent in Brussels, Belgium, on Mar. 4. She was declared Venerable in 1876.

LOBO, FRANCISCO RODRIGUES (1575?–1627?), poet. Born in Leira, Portugal, he studied at Coimbra, published ballads in 1596, a novel, *O Primavera,* in 1601 (continued as *O Peregrino* and *O Desenganado;* 1608, 1614), imitations of Camões, and an epic on Nuno Alvares Pereira, *El Condestable de Portugal* (1610). His use of Portuguese, during the years of Spanish rule, exerted a great influence on national literature. He died of drowning in the Tagus River, Portugal.

LOBO, JERÓNIMO (1593–1678), missioner. Born in Lisbon, Portugal, he became a Jesuit in 1609, taught at Coimbra to 1621, and was sent to Portuguese India in 1622. In 1625 he went to Abyssinia, was expelled when the Christian king died, was sent back to Goa in 1640, was provincial there, and returned to Lisbon in

1656, where he died. He wrote a manuscript account of his travels, translated and published in French in 1728 and in an abridged English version by Samuel Johnson in 1735.

LOCHNER, STEPHAN (d. 1452), painter. Born at Meersburg, on Lake Constance, he went to Cologne in 1430 and was the painter of the triptych for the altar of the town hall (which was moved to the cathedral choir chapel in 1810). He also painted *Virgin among the Rosebushes* and *Madonna of the Violets* and died in Cologne, Alsace.

LOCKE, MATTHEW (1629–1677), composer. Born in Exeter, England, he was a chorister in its cathedral in 1638–41, and became a convert in 1654. He wrote the music for James Shirley's *Cupid and Death* (1653), provided some music for Sir William Davenant's *Siege of Rhodes*, and in 1661, after scoring the processional music of King Charles II's coronation, was named composer of the king's band. He wrote the music for the Dryden-Davenant version of *The Tempest* (1667) and Thomas Shadwell's *Psyche* (1673) and was deputy master of the king's music in 1676. He died in London in Aug.

LOCKHART, WILLIAM (1820–1892). Born in Waringham, Surrey, England, he entered Oxford in 1838, studied for the ministry, and in 1842 joined John Henry Newman at Littlemore, studying, writing, and translating. In 1843 he became a convert, joined the Order of Charity, was received into the Rosminian Institute, and made his solemn profession in 1845. He was ordained in 1846, engaged in pastoral work at Shepshed in 1847, and in 1853 was assigned to missionary work. In 1854 he founded a Rosminian church in London, and in 1873 purchased thirteenth-century St. Etheldreda's in London and reopened it as a Catholic church in 1879. He was appointed procurator general of his congregation in 1881. He founded *Catholic Opinion*, a periodical, translated several of Antonio Rosmini's works, and wrote *The Old Religion* and a biography of Cardinal Newman. He died in London on May 15.

LOCKWOOD, BL. JOHN (1555?–1642), martyr. Born in Sowerby, Yorkshire, England, he went to Rheims in 1579, studied at Douai and the English College, Rome, and was ordained in 1597. He was sent on the English mission in 1598, was captured, banished in 1610, but returned, served English Catholics until he was eighty-one, was seized as a priest, and hanged, drawn, and quartered at York. He was beatified in 1929. F. D. Apr. 13.

LOGUE, MICHAEL (1840–1924), cardinal. Born in Carrigart, Donegal, Ireland, on Oct. 1, he studied at Maynooth, and Dunboyne, and was ordained in 1866 and sent to teach dogmatic theology at the Irish College, Paris. In 1874 he returned to do parish work in Glens-

willy, was made dean at Maynooth in 1876, and taught Gaelic and theology there. He became bishop of Raphoe in 1879 and coadjutor at Armagh in 1887, and archbishop of that see in 1888. He was made a cardinal in 1893. He withdrew his support from Parnell and later from T. M. Healy, was a patron of the Gaelic League, worked to preserve the native language, and completed the Armagh cathedral. Although he opposed the partition of Ireland, he condemned the Sinn Fein and the British occupying forces, and helped to establish peace in 1921. He died in Armagh, Ireland, on Nov. 19.

LOHEL, JOHANN (1549–1622), archbishop. Born in Eger, Bohemia, he worked as a servant in the Norbertine abbey at Tepl, attended the abbey school, and in 1573 joined the Norbertines. He studied at Prague, was ordained in 1576, and appointed prior of Mt. Sion abbey in Strahov in 1579 and its abbot in 1586. He was named bishop of Sebaste and auxiliary to Prague in 1604, coadjutor in 1612, and succeeded to the see later the same year. He was forced to flee Protestant persecution in 1609, stayed in Vienna until 1620, returned to Prague, Bohemia, and died there on Nov. 2.

LOISEAUX, JEAN JOSEPH (1815–1904), editor. Born in Belgium on Aug. 5, he was ordained in 1838, studied at Louvain and Rome, and in 1846 became professor of canon law and ecclesiastical history at Louvain. He was co-founder of *Mélanges théologiques* in 1847 and founded *Revue théologique* and *Nouvelle revue théologique*, acting as editor of the latter until 1895. He became a Capuchin in 1871, taking the name Piatus of Mons, and died in the monastery of Ste. Claire, Bruges, Belgium, on Apr. 21.

LOLANUS, ST. (d. 1034?). He was a bishop in Scotland; a reference to him as a fifth-century visitor from Galilee is merely legendary. F. D. Sept. 2.

LOLLIAN, ST. (d. 297), martyr. *See* Hipparchus, St.

LOMAN, ST., bishop. He is variously identified as the son of St. Patrick's sister Tigris, who converted the leaders in the area of Trim, Ireland, and later became bishop there before 450; and as a Bishop Loman who held the see in the seventh century. He is also known as Luman. F. D. Feb. 17.

LOMBARD, PETER (1555?–1625), archbishop. Born in Waterford, Ireland, he studied at Oxford and at Louvain, where he received his doctorate in divinity and was ordained. He was appointed professor of theology at Louvain, provost of the cathedral in Cambrai in 1594, and in 1601 archbishop of Armagh, though he never occupied his see. He was president of the Congregatio de Auxiliis, was appointed to settle the controversy which arose over Molina's work on predestination and grace, and wrote *De* *regno Hiberniae sanctorum insula commentarius.* He died in Rome.

LOMER, ST. *See* Laudomarus, St.

LONGHAYE, GEORGES (1839–1920), critic. Born in Rouen, France, on Sept. 8, he studied in Brugelette and Paris, became a Jesuit, wrote plays, and when anti-religious feeling prevailed went to England. He wrote *Théorie des belles lettres* (1885), a four-volume history of the French literature of the seventeenth century, crowned by the French Academy, and a five-volume history of that of the nineteenth century. He died in Paris on Jan. 17.

LONGINUS. This name (developed from the Greek noun for lance) has become attached in many legends to the centurion who acknowledged the divinity of Christ after the crucifixion (Matt. 27:54; Mark 15:39), and piously identified with the soldier who pierced His side (John 19:34). Said in the Roman Martyrology to have been beheaded in Cappadocia for his faith, he was venerated on Mar. 15.

LONGINUS, ST. (d. 304?), martyr. *See* Alexander, St.; also, Cyriac, St.

LONGINUS, ST. (d. 485?), martyr. *See* Eugene, St.

LONGSTREET, JAMES (1821–1904), general. Born in Edgefield, South Carolina, on Jan. 8, he moved to Albany, New York, in 1831, was appointed to West Point, and graduated in 1842. He served in Indian campaigns and the Mexican War, and was commissioned captain in 1852. He resigned his commission at the outbreak of the Civil War to join the Confederate army as brigadier general and became one of the outstanding military leaders of the Confederacy, serving at Antietam, Gettysburg, the Wilderness, and Petersburg. When the war ended, he joined the Republican party, was appointed successively surveyor of customs, supervisor of internal revenue, and postmaster in New Orleans, and United States marshal in Georgia. In 1877 he became a convert. He served as minister to Turkey in 1880–81 and was appointed federal railway commissioner in 1898. He wrote *Annals of the War, Battles and Leaders of the Civil War*, and *From Manassas to Appomattox*. He died in Gainesville, Georgia, on Jan. 2.

LOOTENS, LOUIS (1827–1898), bishop. Born in Bruges, Belgium, on Mar. 17, he was educated at the seminary there and St. Nicholas seminary in Paris, where he was ordained in 1851. He went to western Canada in 1852, worked as a missioner for nine years on Vancouver Island and for six in California, and became first vicar apostolic of Idaho and Montana in 1868. He settled in Granite Creek, attended the Vatican Council in 1869–70, saw the first church built in Boise in 1870, and resigned in 1878. He died on Jan. 13 in Victoria, Vancouver Island, British Columbia.

LOPE DE VEGA CARPIO, FÉLIX. *See* Vèga Carpio, Lope Félix de.

LOPES, FERNÃO (1380?–1459?), historian. Born in Portugal, he began a chronicle of the early kings at the request of Dom Duarte, in 1434. He previously had written an account of John I; he also completed *Chronica de D. Fernando* and *Chronica de D. Pedro*. His large history, with some reliance on legend and romance, but with the color and sweep of Froissart, covered events to 1415.

LOPEZ, GREGORY (1542–1596). Born in Madrid, Spain, of unknown parents, and a page at the court of King Philip II, he went to Mexico in 1562. There he gave his possessions to the poor and lived as a hermit until 1571, when he entered for a short time the Dominican monastery in Mexico City. He suffered from slander, but was completely cleared and highly praised by the archbishop of Mexico, and spent his remaining years in prayer and scriptural study in a hermitage at Michoacan. His process of beatification was never completed, but he is honored locally on July 20.

LOPEZ-CARO, FRANCISCO (1598–1662), painter. Born in Seville, Spain, he studied under Juan de las Roelas, and developed into a portrait painter of some merit. He worked and died in Madrid.

LÓPEZ DE LEGAZPI, MIGUEL (1510?–1572), explorer. Born in Zumárraga, Spain, he went to Mexico in 1545, served as chief secretary of the government, and in 1564 was named by Viceroy Velasco to head an expedition to conquer the Philippines. With four ships he captured the Ladrone Islands (now Marianas) in 1565, explored Cebu, conquered Luzon in 1571 with little bloodshed (his policy was exceptionally humane), and founded Manila.

LÓPEZ-NETO, BL. CASSIAN VAZ (1607–1638), martyr. Born in Nantes, France, of Portuguese parents, he was ordained a Capuchin and worked in Cairo, Egypt, with Bl. Francis Nouri toward reconciling the Coptic Church with Rome. As they entered Abyssinia they were slandered by Peter Heyling, a German Protestant, and stoned to death on orders of King Fasilidas. He was beatified in 1904. F. D. Aug. 7.

LOPEZ Y VICUÑA, BL. VINCENTIA (1847–1890), foundress. Daughter of a well-to-do lawyer, she was born in Cascante, Navarre, studied at Madrid, took a vow of celibacy when nineteen, refused marriage, and entered a Visitation convent, joining an aunt who had founded an orphanage in Madrid. In 1876 she founded the Daughters of Mary Immaculate there, devoted to helping working girls; the congregation soon spread to other cities. She was beatified by Pope Pius XII in 1950. F. D. Dec. 26.

LORAS, JEAN MATHIAS PIERRE (1792–

1858), bishop. Born in Lyons, France, on Aug. 30, he studied at the seminary in L'Argentière, was ordained in Lyons in 1817, and was appointed president of the minor seminary in Meximieux. In 1824 he was made superior of L'Argentière, and in 1829 went to Alabama, where he taught at Spring Hill College, was vicar general of Mobile in 1830–37, and president at Spring Hill in 1833–37. He was appointed first bishop of Dubuque, Iowa, in 1837, encouraged immigrants to his sparsely settled see, refused an archbishopric in France, founded Mt. St. Bernard's seminary in 1850, and with Bishop Hughes of New York was instrumental in having Catholic chaplains appointed to the army in the Mexican War. He died in Dubuque on Feb. 19.

LORD, DANIEL A. (1888–1955), editor. Born in Chicago on Apr. 23, he studied at Loyola and St. Louis, became a Jesuit in 1909, and from 1913 until his death was associated with the editorial staff of the *Queen's Work*. He was ordained in 1923, became editor of *Queen's Work* in 1926 and organized the Sodality of Our Lady and the Knights and Handmaids of the Blessed Sacrament, both nationwide groups, and directed schools of Catholic Action in many parts of the United States. He wrote hundreds of pamphlets, on social, economic, and religious themes, detective stories, religious songs and twenty pageants, including that for the 1951 Detroit centennial celebration and *Joy to the World* for the Marian Year celebration in Toronto in 1954. He also worked with Martin Quigley in evolving the motion-picture code in 1929. His books include: *Armchair Philosophy* (1918), *Religion and Leadership, My Mother, Our Lady in the Modern World, His Passion Forever*, and an autobiography, *Played by Ear*. He died of cancer in St. Louis, Missouri, on Jan. 15.

LORENZANA, FRANCISCO ANTONIO DE (1722–1804), cardinal. Born in León, Spain, on Sept. 22, he studied at the Jesuit college there and after his ordination became canon in Toledo. He was appointed bishop of Plasencia in 1765 and in 1766 archbishop of Mexico. He held a synod in 1771, was recalled to Spain in 1772, and made archbishop of Toledo, where he built a library, hospitals, and asylums. He was created cardinal in 1789, envoy extraordinary from Spain to the Holy See in 1797, and after the conclave of 1799 remained with Pope Pius VII in Rome, where he died on Apr. 17. He compiled the acts of the first three Mexican provincial councils, and published *Historia de Nueva España, SS. patrum Toletanorum opera, Breviarium Gothicum, Missale Gothicum*, and an edition of the works of St. Isidore of Seville.

LORENZETTI, AMBROGIO (14th century), painter. A native of Siena, Italy, he is considered a greater artist than his younger brother, Pietro, though few of his works survive. Among them are six allegories representing good government and tyranny in the Palazzo Pubblico of Siena, *Life of St. Nicholas* and *Presentation in the Temple* in Florence, *St. Agnes*, and *St. Dorothy*. Nothing is known of him after 1348, and he is believed to have died with his brother in the plague. He is sometimes known as Ambrogio di Lorenzo.

LORENZETTI, PIETRO (14th century), painter. A native of Siena, Italy, he studied under Simone di Martino, and probably Duccio, and was greatly influenced by Giotto, whose realism he introduced to Sienese painting. An altarpiece (about 1320) in S. Maria della Pieve at Arezzo is his first known work and he went on to paint in Siena, Florence, Rome, and Pisa. Among his outstanding works are the frescoes in the St. Francis church in Assisi, *Virgin and Child with SS. Francis and John, Birth of the Virgin, Virgin Enthroned, Life of the Desert Fathers*, a fresco in the Campo Santo in Pisa, and with his brother Ambrogio a fresco for a hospital in Siena which has been destroyed. He is also known as Pietro Laurati. There are no works of his known after 1348 and he is believed to have died in the plague.

LORENZO, DOM. *See* Monaco, Lorenzo.

LORITI, HEINRICH (1488–1563), scholar. Born in Mollis, near Glarus, Switzerland, he studied under Michael Rubellus in Rottweil and at Cologne, taught at Basle from 1514 to 1517 and from 1522 to 1529 and at Paris in the years between. He was the associate of several humanists, including Erasmus and Budaeus, and emigrated with the former to Freiburg im Breisgau when Reformation pressure became too great in Switzerland. He edited, with commentaries, Boethius, Caesar, Dionysius of Halicarnassus, Horace, Livy, Lucan, Ovid, Sallust, Terence, and others. His poetic *Helvetiae descriptio* (1515) and *Liber de geographia unus* (1527), on the principles of mathematical geography, also established him as a leading scholar. His *Dodekachordon* (1547), on which he worked for twenty years, was a study of ancient music; in it he introduced the twelve-tone scale. After 1511 he came to be called Glarean, after the town near his birthplace. He died in Freiburg, Germany, on Mar. 27.

LORRAIN, NARCISSE ZEPHYRIN (1842–1915), bishop. Born in St. Martin, Quebec, Canada, he studied at the St. Thérèse seminary, was ordained in Montreal in 1867, taught at the seminary and held parish posts in Canada and New York, and was appointed vicar general of Montreal in 1879. He became vicar general of Pontiac and titular bishop of Cythera in 1881, and when the vicariate became a diocese in 1898 became first bishop of Pembroke, Ontario, Canada. He traveled widely on Indian missions, established hospitals and schools, and died on Dec. 18.

LORRAINE, CLAUDE DE. *See* Claude Lorraine.

LOSSADA, LUIS DE (1681–1748). Born in Quiroga, Asturias, Spain, he became a Jesuit in 1698, taught at Salamanca, and wrote a ten-volume study of philosophy and related works. He died in Salamanca, Spain.

LOSSEN, KARL AUGUST (1841–1893), geologist. Born in Kreuznach, Germany, on Jan. 5, he studied mining engineering at Berlin and Halle, where he graduated in 1866, and was appointed assistant geologist of the Prussian geological survey. He became an instructor in petrology at the Berlin mining academy and lecturer at Berlin in 1870, a member of the Prussian National Geological Institute in 1873, professor in 1882, and professor at the University of Berlin in 1886. He published treatises on his petrographic studies of the Harz Mountains; the mineral lossenite was named after him. He died in Berlin on Feb. 24.

LOTHAIR I (795?–855), emperor. Eldest son of Louis I, king of the Franks, he was crowned by the pope in 823, rebelled against his father, and helped to depose him in 833. He was given Italy in 835–39 and succeeded his father in 840. He was defeated by his brother Louis at Fontanet in 841, but retained Italy, a strip along the Rhine, and the title of Holy Roman emperor. He took monastic garb in his last years and died on Sept. 28.

LOTHAIR II (1070?–1137), emperor. Son of Count Gebhard of Arnsberg who had opposed Emperor Henry IV in Saxony, he adopted his father's attitude to the emperor against whom he fought in the uprising of 1088, was appointed duke of Saxony by German King Henry V in 1106, rebelled against Henry unsuccessfully in 1112 and 1113, but defeated the emperor at Welfesholz in 1115. In 1125, on Henry's death, he was elected emperor by the nobles and higher clergy, thus asserting the elective principle against the hereditary custom; Henry's nephew Frederick of Hohenstaufen was elected by his faction and with his brother Conrad warred against Lothair. Lothair overcame Frederick in 1134 and Conrad in 1135. In 1131 he invaded Denmark and forced King Niels to pay tribute. Lothair supported the election of Pope Innocent II, disputed by antipope Anacletus II, went to Italy in 1132 to restore Innocent, who had been driven out by Anacletus, and was crowned in Rome in 1133. He encouraged mission activity in his northern realms, generously aiding Archbishops Norbert of Magdeburg and Albert I of Bremen, and supported the efforts of Margrave Albert the Bear of the Saxon North Mark and Margrave Conrad I of Meissen and Lusatia to extend his dominions and the spread of Christianity. He was obliged to return to Italy in 1136 to expel Anacletus again, imposed the imperial rule on all of southern Italy, and died on the way home at Breitenwang, Tyrol, on Dec. 3 or 4. He is sometimes listed as Lothair III.

LOTHAIR III, emperor. *See* Lothair II, emperor.

LOTHAIR (941–986), king of France. Son of Louis d'Outremer, he succeeded his father to the French throne in 954, and spent his entire reign attempting to control his vassals, among them Hugh Capet, and engaging in war with Otto II of Germany. By his lack of success in both he had greatly lessened the royal power by the time of his death.

LOTHAIR II (d. 869), king. Son of Lothair I, he was proclaimed king by the nobles of Lorraine at his father's death in 855. He attempted to divorce his wife, Teutberga, to marry his mistress, Walddrada, but was condemned by Pope Nicholas I, who deposed the archbishops of Trèves and Cologne, who had approved the king's action. Lothair accepted the pope's censure.

LOTHARIUS, ST. (d. 756), bishop. He founded a Benedictine abbey at Argentan and became bishop of Séez, France, about 724. He is also known as Loyer. F. D. June 14.

LOTTI, ANTONIO (1667–1740), composer. Born probably in Venice, he studied music under Legrenzi, produced an opera when he was sixteen, was appointed second organist at St. Mark's in 1692, first organist in 1704, and choirmaster in 1716. He composed operas, masses and motets, and was famous as a teacher. He died in Venice on Jan. 5.

LOTTO, LORENZO (1480?–1556), painter. Born in Venice, he painted in Treviso and Recanati (an altarpiece in 1508), possibly studied under Alvise Vivarini, and did some fresco painting in the Vatican in 1509. He lived in Bergamo from 1513 until 1552, when he went to Loreto. His portraits were characterized by his ability to bring out his subject's personality. Among his paintings are *St. Jerome, Annunciation, Madonna and Saints, Bridal Couple, Christ and the Adulteress,* and *Crucifixion.* He died in Loreto, Italy.

LOUGHLIN, JOHN (1817–1891), bishop. Born in Drumboneff, Down, Ireland, on Dec. 20, he was brought to Albany, New York, at six, studied at Chambly College, Montreal, and Mt. St. Mary's, Maryland, and was ordained in New York in 1840. He was stationed in Utica and New York City, was vicar general under Bishop Hughes in 1849–53, and in 1853 became first bishop of Brooklyn (including all of Long Island), in charge of twelve churches and 15,000 Catholics. Some 125 churches, ninety-three schools, two colleges, a seminary, and many charitable institutions were built during his episcopate. He founded St. John's College in Brooklyn in 1869, and attended the second (1866) and third plenary councils (1884) of Baltimore and the Vatican Council in 1869–70. He died in Brooklyn, New York, on Dec. 29.

LOUIS I (778–840), emperor. Called "the Pious" and "the Débonnaire" (weakhearted), the youngest son of Charlemagne was born in Chasseneuil, France, became king of Aquitaine in 781, co-emperor with his father in 813, and emperor of the Franks in 814 and undid the unity of the empire erected by his father. He divided his holdings in 817 among his sons (Lothair, Pepin, and Louis), but his nephew Bernard, king of Italy, revolted, was blinded by Louis I, and died of the mutilation. In 819 Louis married a second wife, Judith of Bavaria; sought to divide his domain four ways to include their son, Charles the Bald, to which his other heirs objected; and in 833 was deposed by Lothair, Pepin, and Louis. Other divisions were proposed later, and the emperor was slain near Ingelheim (Germany) on June 20 in the midst of war with young Louis and the son of Pepin (the latter had died in 838).

LOUIS II (825?–875), emperor. Son of Emperor Lothair I, and surnamed "the German," he was crowned king of Italy by Pope Sergius II in Rome, joint emperor with his father by Pope Leo IV in 850, and became sole emperor on his father's death in 855. He spent most of his reign fighting the Saracens in southern Italy. His power was circumscribed by the powerful independent dukes of Lombardy. He allied himself with Louis the German in 857 against his brother Lothair, king of Lorraine, and Charles the Bald, but was reconciled with Lothair. He supported Nicholas I for the papacy in 858, quarreled with him in 864 when the pope refused to recognize his brother's divorce, and marched on Rome. He was soon reconciled and in 866 defeated the Saracens and captured their headquarters at Sari in 869. He was crowned again in 872, and died on Aug. 12 in the province of Brescia, Italy, while preparing for a new campaign against the Saracens.

LOUIS III (880?–928), emperor. Son of King Boso of Burgundy and Provence, and Irmengarde, daughter of Louis II, he became king of the Franks (with his mother as regent) in 887, took the crown in 890, and became Holy Roman emperor in 901. Defeated by Berengarius, he was ordered out of Italy, returned in 904, was captured and blinded by Berengarius, and sent back to Burgundy in 905. A relative, Hugh, administered his kingdom during his last twenty years and succeeded him. He died in Provence in Sept.

LOUIS IV OF BAVARIA (1287?–1347), emperor. Son of Duke Louis of Upper Bavaria and Matilda, daughter of Emperor Rudolf I, he was born in Munich, Bavaria, inherited Upper Bavaria and the Palatinate with his brother on his father's death in 1294, went to war with his brother Rudolph in 1310–13 to get his share of the inheritance, and claimed the German throne on the death of Henry VII in 1314 against Frederick of Austria. Civil war broke out, with the Ghibelines supporting Louis and the Guelphs backing Frederick. Louis defeated and captured Frederick at the battle of Mühldorf in 1322; Frederick renounced the throne to secure his freedom; his brother Leopold then continued the war until his death in 1326. Pope John XXII had refused to recognize either candidate and named himself administrator of the vacant empire; in 1324 he excommunicated Louis for refusing to resign the German crown. Louis went to Italy in 1327–30, had himself crowned in Rome by a Roman noble in 1328, declared John deposed and set up Pietro Rainalducci as antipope Nicholas V in that same year. He tried to negotiate a reconciliation with the Church after John's death in 1334, but when Benedict XII insisted that he give up the imperial crown, Louis issued the decree *Licet juris* in 1338, after six electors had stated that the majority vote of the electors decided the emperor and king, who thus did not need papal confirmation. In 1346, Pope Clement VI excommunicated and declared him deposed and tried to transfer the crown to Charles IV, who was elected an antiking, but Louis held on until his death in Fürstenfeld, Bavaria, on Oct. 11, in a hunting accident. During his reign Louis added Lower Bavaria, the Tyrol, by the marriage of his son Louis to Margaret Maultasch, wife of the margrave of Moravia (declaring her marriage to the margrave void) in 1345; he obtained Holland, Zeeland, and Friesland on the death of the brother of his second wife, Margaret.

LOUIS I, king of France. *See* Louis I, emperor.

LOUIS II (846–879), king of France. Surnamed "the Stammerer," son of Charles the Bald, he succeeded his father as king of the West Franks in 877, maintained peace with his nobles by generous distribution of duchies, earldoms, and seignories, and died at Compiègne, France, on Apr. 10.

LOUIS III (863?–882), king of France. Son of King Louis II, he succeeded on his father's death in 879 to the kingship of the West Franks, north of the Loire; his brother Carloman ruled south of the Loire. The brothers repelled a Norman attack at Saucourt in 881, which became the theme of the epic *Chanson du Roi Louis* (*Ludwiglied*, in German). Louis died the following year at St. Denis, France, on Aug. 5; Carloman then took over his brother's domain.

LOUIS IV (921–954), king of France. Son of Charles III, he was brought up by his mother from 923 to 936 at the English court of

King Athelstan, and was called D'Outre-Mer when he returned to France from across the sea to become king. He successfully weathered a revolt by Hugh of Paris, William of Normandy, and the invading Otto the Great in 940; tried to seize Normandy, was captured by Duke Richard, but released after a year; and fought Hugh and Richard until 950, when with Otto's help he crushed Hugh. Louis died in Rheims, France, on Sept. 10.

LOUIS V (967?–987), king of France. Son of Lothair, he was called, unjustifiably, Le Fainéant (the Sluggard), became associated with his father in the kingship in 979, and in 986 became the last Carolingian king of France. He died in May.

LOUIS VI (1080?–1137), king of France. Son of Philip I, and called Le Gros (the Fat), he became associated with his father in the kingship in 1100 and succeeded him as king in 1108. He was active in his support of the Church, attempts to add to his territory, successful efforts toward controlling feudal leaders, and his reign-long war with Henry I of England. He died on Aug. 1.

LOUIS VII (1121?–1180), king of France. Surnamed "the Young," son of King Louis VI, he married Eleanor of Aquitaine, and succeeded his father as king in 1137. He became involved with Pope Innocent II over the selection of the archbishop of Bruges and the validity of his sister-in-law's marriage in 1141. The pope put any place sheltering him under interdict and the count of Champagne declared war against him. The dispute was settled when, at St. Bernard's intervention, Louis submitted to Pope Celestine II on both matters in 1144; during the dispute the count of Anjou conquered Normandy and Louis allowed him to hold it. He became reconciled with the papacy and in 1146 Louis went on the second crusade, was unsuccessful, and returned in 1149. His marriage to Eleanor was annulled in 1152, and she then married Henry Plantagenet, bringing to the marriage her extensive dominions in southern France; when Plantagenet became Henry II of England in 1154, these possessions came under the rule of the English throne. Louis went to war with him when he ascended the throne, gave asylum to Thomas à Becket, and after another war with Henry in 1167–69 intrigued with Henry's sons in their revolt against their father in 1173–74, though he gave them little effective aid. He increased the royal power during his reign, and died in Paris on Sept. 11.

LOUIS VIII (1187–1226), king of France. Surnamed "the Lion" and "Lion-hearted," he was born in Paris on Sept. 5, son of Philip II Augustus, married Blanche of Castile in 1200, and led expeditions against the Albigensians in 1215 and 1219. He invaded England in 1216 when the barons offered him the crown despite a papal excommunication. His supporters among the English nobles fell away after the death of King John in Oct. and, when he suffered defeat at Lincoln in 1217, he agreed to return to France. He ascended the throne in 1223, won back Poitou from the English in 1224, was unsuccessful against Gascony, and in 1226, at the suggestion of Pope Honorius III, launched another crusade against the Albigensians and conquered Languedoc. He died at Montpensier, Auvergne, France, on Nov. 8.

LOUIS IX, ST. (1214–1270), king of France. Born at Poissy, France, on Apr. 25, son of Louis VIII and Blanche, daughter of King Alfonso of Castile and Eleanor of England, he succeeded to the throne at twelve, with his mother as regent. With great skill and wisdom she defended his throne against Thibault of Champagne and other ambitious barons, forcing them to submit by propitious alliances and even on the field of battle. In 1233 he married Margaret, daughter of the count of Provence, by whom he had eleven children. In 1235 he reached his majority and took over the government, though his mother remained his trusted adviser until her death. In 1242–43 he put down revolts in southwestern France, defeating King Henry III of England at Taillebourg in 1242 and forcing Poitou to submit in that year and Raymond VII of Toulouse in 1243. In 1248 he led a crusade to Egypt, but his army was routed by the Saracens at El Mansura in 1250 and he was taken prisoner. When he was ransomed, he sailed to the Holy Land, where he remained until 1254, when he returned to France on the death of his mother. In 1258 he concluded treaties with Henry III of England by which he ceded Limoges, Cahors, and Périgueux to England in return for the latter's renouncing its claims to Normandy, Anjou, Maine, Touraine, and Poitou. The Treaty of Corbeil (also 1258) ended Aragon's claim to Provence and Languedoc. In 1270 he embarked on a new crusade, but, shortly after landing at Tunisia, contracted typhus and died there. Louis reigned for forty-four years and even in his lifetime was regarded as a model ruler. He meted out justice fairly and impartially. A model father, he was also noted for his piety, asceticism, and great charities. He founded and sponsored many religious and educational establishments (it was during his reign in 1257 that Robert de Sorbon founded the Sorbonne). He forbade war among the feudal lords, protected vassals from the oppression of their lords, scrupulously kept his word, and made the lords obey treaties and live up to their obligations. He pursued a policy of peacefulness with his European neighbors and was often called in to arbitrate disputes, acting as arbitrator in several disputes in Flanders, Navarre, and Hainaut, involving succession, and attempted to settle Henry III's quarrel with his barons. He was canonized in 1297. F. D. Aug. 25.

LOUIS X (1289–1316), king of France. Son of Philip IV le Bel and Joan of Navarre, surnamed "the Quarrelsome," he was born in Paris on Oct. 4, inherited Navarre from his mother in 1305, and became king in 1314. He married Clemence, daughter of the king of Hungary, was dominated during his short reign by his uncle Charles of Valois, and led an unsuccessful campaign against Flanders. During his reign the royal power suffered as the nobles reasserted themselves. He died on June 5.

LOUIS XI (1423–1483), king of France. Born in Bourges, France, on July 3, son of Charles VII and Mary of Anjou, he was married to Margaret, daughter of James I of Scotland, in 1436, and early sought power. He joined the revolt of the Praguerie against his father in 1440 and was pardoned, fought against the English, and in 1443 aided his father to suppress the revolt of the count of Armagnac. When he joined a conspiracy against Agnes Sorel, the king's mistress, and Pierre de Brézé in 1446, he was exiled to Dauphiné, where he firmly established his rule. Further plots against Charles forced him to flee for protection to Duke Philip the Good of Burgundy in 1456, where he remained until Charles's death in 1461, when he ascended the throne. He at once disposed of his father's ministers, though he later recalled some of the more able among them, and set himself to curbing the powers of the great nobles and increasing those of the crown. His attempt to curb the power of the nobles caused them to form the League of the Public Welfare in 1465; the lesser nobles and people supported Louis. He defended Paris successfully, but was forced to meet the demands of the nobles at the treaties of Conflans and St. Maurles-Fossés. His violation of the treaties and his conquest of Normandy caused a new alliance against him in 1467, headed by Charles the Bold of Normandy, Edward IV of England, and Duke Francis II of Brittany. He conquered Normandy and forced Francis to sign the peace of Ancenis in 1468, but was tricked into making wide concessions to Charles the Bold when the latter made him prisoner. He unsuccessfully attempted to restore Henry VI in England, signed truces with Francis II and Charles the Bold on the death of his brother Charles in 1472, and paid an indemnity to Edward IV of England to call off his invasion of France in 1475. When Charles the Bold died in the battle of Nancy in 1477 he took over much of his territory, including Burgundy, Picardy, Boulogne, and Franche-Comté, fought Charles's son-in-law, Maximilian of Austria, to retain his seizures, and signed the Treaty of Arras with him in 1482 which allowed

Louis to keep most of the seized territory. He revoked his father's pragmatic sanction, but constantly interfered in church affairs as well as in Italian and Spanish matters. He built up the absolute power of the monarchy and by the end of his reign had decisively broken the feudal power of the great lords. He died at Plessis les Tours, near Tours, France, on Aug. 30.

LOUIS XII (1462–1515), king of France. Born in Blois, France, on June 27, son of Duke Charles of Orléans and Marie of Cleves, he married Louis XI's daughter Jeanne. As duke of Orléans, he rebelled against the regency of Anne de Beaujeu, but was captured and imprisoned in 1488. He was released by his cousin King Charles VIII in 1491, accompanied him on his expedition to Naples in 1495, and in 1498 succeeded him as king. He then had his marriage to Jeanne annulled and married Charles's widow, Anne of Brittany, in 1499 to add Brittany to his dominions, and embarked on a policy of French expansion in Italy. He conquered Milan in 1500, and in 1501 entered an alliance with Ferdinand of Spain to divide the kingdom of Naples between them. When Frederick of Naples retired to France, the allies fell out and the Spanish drove Louis' forces from Naples in 1503. He suppressed a revolt in Genoa in 1506–7, joined the League of Cambrai (of Emperor Maximilian I, Ferdinand the Catholic, and Pope Julius II, ostensibly to crusade against the Turks, but really directed against Venice) in 1507, and defeated the Venetians at Agnadello in 1509. Pope Julius was reconciled with Venice in 1510, and in 1511 formed the Holy League against Louis; it forced him to withdraw from Milan in 1512, and defeated the French forces at Novara in 1513 and drove the French from Italy. Louis' defeat at Guinegate also in 1513 by Emperor Maximilian I and Henry VIII caused him to seek peace which he achieved in 1514 with all his opponents except Maximilian. He married Mary Tudor, sister of Henry VIII, in 1514, and died on Jan. 1.

LOUIS XIII (1601–1643), king of France. Son of Henry IV and Marie de' Medici, he was born in Fontainebleau on Sept. 27, and succeeded to the throne on his father's death in 1610, with his mother as regent. Declared of age in 1614, he married Anne of Austria, daughter of Philip III of Spain, in 1615, and in 1617 drove his mother into exile when he overthrew her minister, Concini. Mother and son were reconciled in 1622. Louis accepted her minister, Cardinal Richelieu, in 1624 and became so attached to him that he refused to dismiss him in 1630 at her urging, and instead sent her into exile. For the rest of his reign he left the government of France in the hands of Richelieu, who devoted himself to centralizing the government and increasing the royal authority, the containment of Austria, and the extension of French dominions and the conquest of the Huguenots. In 1642, an attempt against Louis' life was uncovered and his favorite, Cinq-Mars, was executed. Louis died in Fontainebleau, France, on May 14.

LOUIS XIV (1638–1715), king of France. Son of Louis XIII and Anne of Austria, he was born in St. Germain-en-Laye, near Paris, on Sept. 5. He succeeded to the throne when five with his mother, daughter of Philip III, as regent and Cardinal Mazarin as chief minister. During Mazarin's ministry, the Thirty Years' War was ended by the peace of Westphalia in 1648, the War of the Fronde was waged in 1648–53, and the war with Spain was ended in 1659 by the Treaty of the Pyrenees, which called for Louis' marriage to Maria Theresa, daughter of Philip IV of Spain. When Mazarin died in 1661, France was the greatest European power and Louis decided to become his own prime minister. He adopted as the basic tenet of his rule royal absolutism (*L'état, c'est moi*). At the beginning of this period, capable ministers made possible the glory of his reign: chief among them, Colbert, who as treasurer in 1661–83 promoted commerce and industry and built up the treasury; Lionne in the diplomatic area; and his minister of war, Louvois, who in 1666–91 completely reorganized the army into the most powerful military force in Europe. On the death of Philip IV of Spain, Louis claimed Flanders and Franche-Comté through his wife. The resultant War of Devolution or Queen's War (1667–68) was settled by the Treaty of Aix-la-Chapelle, by which he gained several fortified towns on the Belgian frontier. The ensuing Dutch War (1672–78) was ended by the Treaty of Nijmegen in 1678, by which Louis kept most of his conquests. He annexed Strassburg and cities in the Rhine area in 1681, and in 1685 he revoked the Edict of Nantes. The resultant flight of thousands of Huguenots, who were among the wealthiest French citizens, was a bad blow for the nation's economy, and also alienated many of the Protestant powers which had been diplomatically linked with Louis. His attempt to claim the Palatinate led to the ruinous War of the League of Augsburg (1688–97), in which England, the Netherlands, the Empire, Spain, and Savoy joined against him. Though the Treaty of Ryswick ending the war formally ceded Alsace and Strassburg to France, it left France exhausted. In 1701–14 he fought the War of the Spanish Succession against most of Europe, when he claimed the Spanish throne for his grandson Philip of Anjou. Though ultimately successful in making Philip king of Spain, France was obliged to make territorial concessions. These wars prostrated France finan-

cially and left her armies decimated. His harsh taxing policies further impoverished the country. Louis was a generous patron of the arts and his reign is generally considered one of the great periods of French cultural history; nevertheless, his wars, excesses, and extravagances laid the foundations for the revolt which shook France later in the century. His succession of mistresses, Louise de la Vallière, Mme. de Montespan, Mme. de Maintenon (who reconciled him to his wife, whom he secretly married in 1684, and who did much to reform the morals of the court after that) wielded great influence over him. He died in Versailles on Sept. 1 after the longest reign in European history.

LOUIS XV (1710–1774), king of France. Born in Versailles on Feb. 15, son of the duke of Burgundy and Maria Adelaide of Savoy and great grandson of Louis XIV, he succeeded to the throne in 1715, with the duke of Orléans as regent. He was declared of age in 1723, appointed his tutor Cardinal Fleury prime minister in 1726, and practically allowed the cardinal to run the country until his death in 1743. During his reign France was involved in the War of the Polish Succession, by which it gained Lorraine in 1715, was one of the coalition against Maria Theresa, a costly affair which brought France popular military victories but little else, and the Seven Years' War, which cost France its colonial possessions when the Treaty of Paris in 1763 gave Canada, Louisiana, and India to England. The regency period was characterized by extravagance and corruption; Fleury restored the country to a sound basis; but on his death Louis' disastrous rule brought the country to the edge of destruction and paved the way for the French Revolution. Married to Marie Lesczynska in 1725, Louis soon turned to a series of mistresses, among them Mme. de Chateauroux, Mme. de Pompadour, and Mme. du Barry, whose appointees practically ran the government to which Louis paid little attention, while he pursued a life of luxury, extravagance, and vice. He died on May 10 at Versailles, leaving the kingdom bankrupt, seething with unrest and hostility, led by the rationalist intellectuals, to the monarchy.

LOUIS XVI (1754–1793), king of France. Born in Versailles on Aug. 23, son of Louis, dauphin of France, and Marie Joseph of Saxony, and grandson of Louis XV, he married Marie Antoinette, daughter of Maria Theresa of Austria, in 1770, and ascended the French throne in 1774. He appointed Turgot minister of finances, but Turgot's series of reforms to revive the economy of a country so disastrously run down during the reigns of Louis XIV and XV met with such resistance on all sides that he resigned in 1777 and was succeeded by

Necker. Louis aided the American colonists in their war against England with troops and supplies. Necker's resignation in 1781 led to a series of ministers and crises until 1789 when the States-General, which had not met since 1614, was convened. Growing hatred of Marie Antoinette for her extravagances, coupled with Louis' own lack of interest and chronic dilatoriness, brought matters to a head. Instead of acquiescing to royal plans, the legislature displayed revolutionary tendencies and, when ordered dissolved, established itself as the national assembly and forced a constitution on the king. Louis attempted to flee in 1791, but was arrested and kept under close surveillance. He accepted the constitution drawn up by the assembly, and took the oath as constitutional monarch on Sept. 13. He was forced to declare war against Marie Antoinette's nephew, Frederick II, who had threatened to intervene to save his niece, and, when the war was unsuccessful, hatred of the Austrian Marie also turned against the king. During the summer of 1792 mobs several times attacked the king's residence, and in Sept. the monarchy was abolished and a republic declared. Louis was tried for treason before the national assembly in Dec. and was guillotined in Paris on Jan. 21.

LOUIS XVII (1785–1795), king of France. Son of Louis XVI and Marie Antoinette, he was born in Versailles on Mar. 27, became dauphin in 1789, was imprisoned with his parents in 1792, and was proclaimed king by the emigrés on the execution of his father in 1793. He reportedly died in the Temple prison on June 8. A child was buried in an unmarked grave and many legends grew up of his escape and appearance in various parts of the world, but none of the claimants was ever able to prove his claim.

LOUIS XVIII (1755–1824), king of France. Louis Stanislas Xavier, son of the Dauphin Louis, Louis XV's son, and Maria Josepha of Saxony, was born in Versailles on Nov. 17 and was known as the count of Provence. He married Louise Marie Joséphine of Savoy in 1771, was active in literary and political circles, stayed in Paris during the early stages of the revolution but was successful in his escape attempt in 1791. He became leader of the emigrés and head of the government in exile at Coblenz, and after the execution of Louis XVI took the name of Louis XVIII and wandered from one European country to another, eventually settling in England after 1807. He returned to France as king on Napoleon's fall in 1814, proclaimed a constitution based on that of England's, fled to Ghent when Napoleon returned in 1815, and was restored to the throne on the latter's defeat. He died in Paris on Sept. 16.

LOUIS I (1326–1382), king of Hungary and Poland. Surnamed "the Great," son of King

Charles I of Hungary and Elizabeth, daughter of King Ladislas Lokietek of Poland, he succeeded to the throne on his father's death in 1342, established a brilliant court at Buda, and inaugurated one of Hungary's most prosperous reigns. He encouraged increased commerce by the towns, confirmed Andrew II's "golden bull" in 1351, introduced the system of entail to the nobles' estates, decreed that serfs must pay one ninth of their produce to their overlord, and provided a sound currency for his realms. He led two expeditions (1347–48 and 1350–51) against Naples to avenge the death of his brother Andrew at Queen Joanna II's court, and with Genoa waged war against Venice in 1357–58 and 1378–81, gaining Dalmatia and a 7000-ducat annual tribute by the Treaty of Turin in 1381. He was elected king of Poland in 1370 to succeed his uncle Casimir, and made the rulers of Serbia, Wallachia, Moldavia, and Bulgaria his vassals. A patron of art and learning, he founded the University of Pécs, was an ardent supporter of the Church, encouraged religious orders, founded churches and monasteries, labored to secure competent Church officials, and was active in conversion efforts among the Slavs in southern Hungary, the Serbs, Wallachians, and Bulgarians. He died in Nagyszombat, Hungary, on Sept. 10.

LOUIS II (1506–1526), king of Hungary and Bohemia. Son of King Wladislaw II and Anne of Candale, he was born at Buda on July 1, was crowned king of Hungary in 1508 and of Bohemia in 1509, succeeded his father as king in 1516, and married Maria of Austria in 1522. He led a dissolute life and was a weak monarch. During his reign the royal power was scarcely recognized, law and order were supplanted by force, the great nobles raided church property and revenues, ecclesiastical education and discipline practically disappeared, and the Protestant Reformation made great inroads. Rent by internal strife, Hungary was in no condition to face the invasions of the Turks, who captured Belgrade in 1521. In 1526 the nation desperately gathered together its last resources and Louis led a large army against the Turks. It was annihilated at Mohachs, Hungary, in 1526, Louis was killed, and the Turks slaughtered thousands, and especially in the south wreaked havoc on the Church. After his death Hungary practically disappeared as an independent power in a triple political division: the Turks occupied the central portion (they captured Buda in 1541), Ferdinand of Austria claimed the throne (it was under Hapsburg dominion until 1918) and controlled the western portion, and Transylvania was under the control of the local nobles, beginning with John Zápolya in 1526.

LOUIS, ST. (d. 855), martyr. See Amator, St.

LOUIS, ST. (1247–1297), bishop. Son of Charles II of Anjou, king of Naples, and of

Mary, daughter of King Stephen V of Hungary, he was born in Brignolles, Provence, in Feb., and was in a Barcelona prison in 1288–95 with two of his brothers as hostage for his father, who had been defeated by Aragon in 1284. When freed he refused to marry the sister of King James II of Aragon, surrendered his claim to succession, and, despite family opposition, joined the Friars Minor in 1296. He was ordained and, shortly after and against his wishes, was consecrated bishop of Toulouse, France. He lived simply, practiced great austerities, died in Brignolles within six months of his consecration, and was canonized in 1317. F. D. Aug. 19.

LOUIS OF GRANADA (1505–1588), theologian. Born in Granada, Spain, he became a Dominican there in 1524, studied at St. Gregory's, Valladolid, and there began his famous preaching career. He became provincial of the Dominicans in Portugal in 1557 and was confessor and consultant of the queen regent. He wrote on scripture, dogma, ethics, biography, and history; *Rhetoricae ecclesiasticae* (1576), a handbook of pulpit oratory; and such widely translated ascetical works as *La guia de pecadores* (1555; *The Sinner's Guide*) and *Memorial de la vida christiana*. He died in Lisbon, Portugal, on Dec. 31.

LOUIS OF MONTFORT, ST. (1673–1716), founder. Louis Marie Grignion was born in Montfort, France, on Jan. 31, of poor parents, studied at the Jesuit college in Rennes, was ordained in 1700, and worked as a chaplain in a Poitiers hospital. There he built up a group which became the Daughters of Divine Wisdom, whose rule he wrote. But he reorganized the ill-run hospital so effectively, and brought in so many from his order to run it, that he was removed and even barred from the diocese. Going to Rome, he was made a missionary apostolic by Pope Clement XI, returned to Brittany, and, in spite of continued persecution, won over many by dramatic preaching, by original hymns and prayers, and by his devotion to the rosary. This led to the publication of his *True Devotion to the Blessed Virgin* and to his becoming a Dominican tertiary. He carried his labors into the Huguenot stronghold of La Rochelle and won over many converts there. In 1715 he organized a group of priests as Missionaries of the Company of Mary (the Montfort Fathers). He died while preaching in St. Laurent-sur-Sèvre, France, and was canonized in 1947 by Pope Pius XII. F. D. Apr. 28.

E. C. BOLGER, *Life of St. Louis Marie de Montfort* (Liverpool, 1952).

LOUIS PHILIPPE (1773–1850), king of France. Born in Paris on Oct. 6, oldest son of Duke Louis Philip Joseph of Orléans (Philippe Egalité) and Louis Marie of Bourbon, he entered the army in 1790, favored the French Revolution, and served against the Austrians in 1792. His father was executed in 1793 as a noble and Louis fled to Belgium. He taught at Reichenau in 1794, was in the United States in 1796–97, and England in 1800–8, and married Maria Amelia, daughter of King Ferdinand IV of Naples, in 1809. When the Bourbons were restored to the French throne in 1814, he returned to France and was given back his estates and titles. He served as commander of the army of the north to oppose Napoleon when the emperor escaped from Elba, but resigned and during the next fifteen years had little interest in public affairs, though he was a quiet adherent of the liberals opposed to Kings Louis XVIII and Charles X. When the July revolution of 1830 ended the reign of Charles X, he was offered the crown by the chamber of deputies, in large measure because of Thiers's and Lafayette's influence, organized a constitutional monarchy, and became known as the "citizen king." He labored to keep peace, repelled Louis Napoleon's attempt to restore the empire in 1836, extended France's claims in Algeria, but faced growing opposition from republicans, Bonapartists, and royalists; in reaction, he became more conservative. In 1847, a coalition of these groups agitated so strenuously for electoral reform that the king was forced to abdicate in 1848 when revolution broke out. He escaped to England and died there at Claremont on Aug. 26.

LOUIS OF TECK (15th century). Patriarch of Aquileia (metropolitan of Udine), Italy, from 1412 to 1439, he sided with Hungary in the war with Venice and lost all the lands which had been given by the German Empire to the patriarchate.

LOUIS OF THURINGIA (1200–1227). Son of Landgrave Herman I, he married St. Elizabeth of Hungary when he succeeded his father and was a just ruler who defended his people's rights. In 1226 he supported Emperor Frederick II at the Diet of Cremona and in 1227 accompanied him on his crusade as commander of the forces of central Germany. He contracted malaria and died in Otranto, Italy, on Sept. 11. His cult has never been confirmed, but he is still called St. Ludwig in Reinhardsbrunn, where he is buried.

LOUISA, BL. (1461–1503). Daughter of Bl. Amadeus IX, duke of Savoy, she married Hugh of Châlons in 1479, was widowed at twenty-seven, joined the Poor Clares at Orbe, Switzerland, in 1490, and later became abbess. Her charities were outstanding and her cult was approved in 1839. F. D. Sept. 9.

LOUISE DE MARILLAC, ST. (1591–1660), foundress. Born in Paris and married in 1613 to Antony Le Gras, who was in the queen's service, she devoted herself after his death in 1625 to the work directed by St. Vincent de Paul. She was able to direct the Ladies of Charity who were caring for the sick, the poor, and the neglected. She became most competent in her instructions and in 1633 set up a training center in her own home. Recruits flocked to her, a rule was prepared, but the Sisters of Charity of St. Vincent de Paul were not formally approved until 1655. The co-founder became its first superior. Paris hospitals and other institutions came under their care, and she roamed France with energy and devotion. She was canonized in 1934, and named universal patron of social workers by Pope John XXIII in 1960. F. D. Mar. 15.

EMANUEL, PRINCE DE BROGLIE, *Life of Bl. Louise de Marillac* (New York, Benziger, 1933).

LOUTHIERN, ST. (6th century). An Irishman, he is honored as patron of Ludgran, Cornwall, England; he may be identical with St. Luchtighern, abbot of Ennistymon. F. D. Oct. 17.

LOVAT, LORD. See Fraser, Simon.

LOWE, VEN. JOHN (d. 1586), martyr. See Adams, Ven. John.

LÖWENSTEIN - WERTHEIM - ROSEN-BERG, KARL VON (1834–1921). Born at Haid castle, Bohemia, on May 31, he married Princess Adelheid of Isenburg in 1859, who died in 1863, and Princess Sophie of Liechtenstein in 1863. A leader of the Catholic faction in Germany, he served in the Bavarian parliament and the upper house of Baden, Hesse, and Würtemburg by hereditary right. He founded an anti-duelling society, promoted Catholic congresses, and actively opposed Bismarck. Prince Löwenstein harbored Bishop Blum of Limburg for seven years in his castle at Haid during the height of anti-Catholic legislation. When his second wife died in 1899, the prince became a Dominican in Venloo, Holland, and was ordained in 1908, taking the name Raymundus. He died in Cologne, Germany, on Nov. 16.

LOWNDES, MARIE ADELAIDE BELLOC (1868–1947), author. Sister of Hilaire Belloc, she was born of French-English parents and lived in France until she was fifteen. She began writing fiction at sixteen, published *Life and Letters of Charlotte Elizabeth, Princess Palatine* at twenty-one, married Frederic Lowndes, became interested in the psychology of crime, and wrote a number of mystery stories (*The Lodger*) or crime studies (*Lizzie Borden*). Besides three plays and an autobiography she wrote such fiction as *The Heart of Penelope* (1904), *The Uttermost Farthing, The Chianti Flask, The House by the Sea, The Marriage Broker,* and *What of the Night?*

(1943). She died in Eversley Cross, Hampshire, England, on Nov. 14.

LOWNEY, DENIS MATTHEW (1863–1918), bishop. Born in Castletown-Bar Haven, Ireland, on June 1, he studied at St. Laurent's College, Montreal, Manhattan College, New York, and the Grand seminary, Montreal, and was ordained in 1887. He did parish work in Providence, Rhode Island, for twenty years, was chancellor and then vicar general of the diocese, and in 1917 was appointed titular bishop of Adrianopolis and auxiliary of Providence. He died there on Aug. 13.

LOYE, BL. SUSANNE-AGATHE, DE (1741–1794), martyr. Born in Sérignan, near Orange, France, she was a Benedictine nun named Sr. Mary Rose, who, having refused to take the anti-religious republican oath during the French Revolution, was guillotined. She and her associates were beatified in 1925. F. D. July 6.

LOYER. See Lotharius, St.

LOYOLA, IÑIGO DE RECALDE DE. See Ignatius de Loyola, St.

LOZANO, PEDRO (d. 1759?), missioner. Born in Spain, he became a Jesuit, was sent to South America, and taught at the College of Cordova at Tucumán, Paraguay. He wrote on the Indians and geography of Gran Chaco and a history of the work of his Society in Paraguay, and supplied materials for the histories written by Charlevoix.

LUBIN, ST. (d. 558?), bishop. Born to a peasant family near Poitiers, France, he studied with holy men, became a hermit, and was recalled to serve as abbot of Brou, became bishop of Chartres, France, reformed his see, and represented it at the councils of Orléans and Paris after he succeeded Bishop Aetherius. He is also called Leobinus. F. D. Mar. 14.

LUCA, ANTONINO SAVERIO DE (1805–1884), cardinal. Born in Bronte, Sicily, on Oct. 28, he studied for the priesthood at the Monreale seminary and in Rome. He became a counsultor for the congregations of Propaganda and the Index, was appointed bishop of Aversa in 1845, and in 1853 archbishop of Tarsus, and nuncio to Bavaria and in 1856 to Austria. He was created a cardinal-priest in 1863 and cardinal-bishop of Palestrina in 1878.

LUCA, GIOVANNI BATTISTA DE (1614–1683), cardinal. Born in Venusia, Italy, he studied in Naples and Rome, was ordained, and became auditor of the sacred palace. He was created cardinal by Pope Innocent XI in 1681, wrote widely on jurisprudence, and died in Rome on Feb. 5.

LUCANUS, ST. (5th century), martyr. He is believed to have been put to death at Lagny, near Paris. F. D. Oct. 30.

LUCAS, FREDERICK (1812–1855), jour-

nalist. Born in Westminster, England, on Mar.
30, he went to University College, London,
studied law at Middle Temple and was admitted to the bar in 1835, became a member
of the Oxford group, and in 1839 was converted. In 1840 he founded the London *Tablet*, encountered financial difficulties which
he overcame in 1842, and in 1849 transferred
the weekly Catholic paper to Dublin. He was
elected to parliament in 1852, publicly differed
with the archbishop of Dublin, who had prohibited political activity on the part of his
clergy; appealed to Pope Pius IX, who asked
him to prepare a brief on the dispute; but died
in Staines, England, on Oct. 22 before he had
finished.

LUCERIUS, ST. (d. 739). He succeeded St.
Thomas as abbot of the Benedictine monastery of Farfa, near Rome. F. D. Dec. 10.

LUCHESIO, BL. (d. 1260). Born in Gag-
giano, in Umbria, Italy, he fought so actively
for the Guelphs that he had to move; he continued as a moneylender when he went to
Poggibonsi. After he was thirty, he and his
wife, Bl. Bonadonna, heard St. Francis of
Assisi preach, gave up their wealth, and devoted their days to penance and charity as
Franciscan tertiaries. F. D. Apr. 23.

LUCHETTO DA GENOVA. *See* Cambiaso,
Luca.

LUCIAN, ST. (d. 120?), martyr. *See* Astius,
St.

LUCIAN, ST. (d. 250?), martyr. He and
Marcian were practitioners of magic in Nicomedia when they were converted, publicly
burned their magic books, and devoted themselves to spreading their new faith. During the
persecution of Decius they were tortured and
burned alive. Florius and a number of others
died with them. F. D. Oct. 26.

LUCIAN OF ANTIOCH, ST. (d. 312), martyr. He was born in Samosata, Syria, and his
revision of Scripture, prepared after a check
of versions of the Septuagint against Hebrew
texts, was widely used and influenced St.
Jerome. He served as a priest at Antioch,
where he may have been for a while a follower
of the heretic, Paul of Samosata. He was imprisoned at Nicomedia, Bithynia, for nine years
during the Diocletian persecution, and tortured
and starved to death there. F. D. Jan. 7.

LUCIAN OF BEAUVAIS, ST. (d. 290?),
martyr. Possibly a companion of St. Dionysius
on the third-century mission to Paris, he is
said to have been put to death at Beauvais,
where he may have been bishop. Maximian
(also called Messien) and Julian were put to
death with him during a local persecution. The
entire story is questionable. F. D. Jan. 8.

LUCIANI, SEBASTIANO (1485?–1547),
painter. He was born in Venice and studied
under Bellini and Giorgione. His frescoed

altarpiece in San Giovanni Crisostomos, Venice, caused Agostino Chigi to invite him to
Rome about 1510 to paint a series of lunettes
in the Villa Farnesina. He became a friend
of Michelangelo, who greatly influenced his
work, particularly his masterpiece, *The Raising of Lazarus*, for the cathedral in Narbonne. He was named keeper of the papal
seals (and thus was afterward known as del
Piombo) in 1531. He died in Rome on June
21 while working on the chapel of the Chigi
family. His paintings were noted for their
freshness and vigor of color and his portraits
for their lifelike quality. Among his best
works are: *Martyrdom of St. Agatha*, *Pietà*,
the oil, *Flaggellation*, the fresco, *Transfiguration*, and his portraits of Cardinals Pole
and de' Medici, Aretino, and Columbus. He
also painted on stone, *Ecce Homo*, and on
slate, *Holy Family* and *The Dead Christ Supported by Joseph of Arimethea*.

LUCIC, JOHN (d. 1679), historian. Born in
Trojir, Dalmatia, he studied law at Padua and
at Rome, where he received his law degree. He
returned to Trojir in 1633, became interested
in Croatian history, and spent the rest of his
life on this subject. He returned to Rome in
1654, was appointed president of the Congregatio S. Hieronymi, and died there on Jan. 11.
Among his works are *De regno Dalmatiae et
Croatiae*, *Memorie storiche di Tragurio ora
deto Traù*, and *Inscriptiones Dalmaticae*.

LUCILLA, ST. (d. 260?), martyr. *See* Nemesius, St.

LUCILLIAN, ST. (d. 273), martyr. He is
said to have been a pagan priest at Nicomedia
who became a convert and was put to death
there with four younger Christians—Claudius,
Dionysius, Hypatius, and Paul—during the
persecution of Aurelian. Paula, who tended
them after torture, was also killed. The account was highly colored by later legends. F. D.
June 3.

LUCINA, ST. (1st century). A Roman, she
lived in the apostolic period and is mentioned
in the spurious Acts of SS. Processus and
Martinianus. F. D. June 30. The name is also
given to one who took care of those martyred
in the persecution of Decius in 250 and also
to one associated with St. Sebastian and
others put to death under Diocletian.

LUCIUS I (d. 254), pope. He began his
pontificate on June 25, 253, was exiled briefly
during the persecution of Gallus, and returned
to Rome to rule for a total of eight months.
His reign also was marked by his condemnation of the Novatian heresy. F. D. Mar. 5.

LUCIUS II (d. 1145), pope. Gerardo Cac-
cianemici dal Orso was born in Bologna, Italy,
where he became a canon regular and was
created cardinal-priest of Santa Croce in 1124.
He served as papal legate to Germany in 1125,

1130, 1133, and 1136, was instrumental in the appointment of St. Norbert as bishop of Magdeburg, and influenced Lothair III to come to the aid of Pope Innocent II against antipope Anacletus II. Innocent appointed him papal chancellor and librarian, and on Mar. 12, 1144, he was elected pope. King Roger of Sicily invaded papal territory and, when Lucius was forced to accept his terms for peace, a faction in Rome led by Giordani Pierleoni (brother of antipope Anacletus), who declared himself patrician and head of the republic, demanded that he relinquish all temporal authority. Lucius refused, led an attack on the insurgents in the Capitol where the senators met, was defeated, and died in Rome on Feb. 15, probably of injuries suffered in the battle.

LUCIUS III (d. 1185), pope. Ubaldus Allucingoli was born in Lucca, Italy, was created cardinal-priest by Pope Innocent II in 1141, served as papal legate to France and Sicily, and in 1159 was appointed bishop of Ostri and Velletri. He acted as Pope Alexander III's representative at a council in Venice in 1177 to settle the pope's differences with Emperor Frederick I. He was elected pope at Velletri on Sept. 1, 1181, the first pope to be elected by the cardinals, and crowned there on Sept. 6, and entered Rome in Nov. He was driven out by civil disorders early in 1182 and again in Sept. of the following year, when he attempted to reconcile the different factions. He convened a synod in Verona in 1184, with Frederick's assistance, that denounced the Cathari, Waldenses, and Arnoldists. He differed with Frederick on several matters, particularly in refusing to appoint Volkmar bishop of Trier, to validate those bishops appointed by antipopes during Pope Alexander III's pontificate, and to approve the marriage of Frederick's son Henry VI to Constance of Sicily, while Frederick refused to recognize Countess Matilda's donation to the Holy See. Lucius died in Verona, Italy, on Sept. 25.

LUCIUS, ST. (1st century), bishop. Mentioned as being at Antioch by SS. Paul and Barnabas, he is traditionally spoken of as first bishop of Cyrene, northern Africa. F. D. May 6.

LUCIUS, ST. (d. 165?), martyr. See Ptolemy, St.

LUCIUS, ST. (2nd century). According to pious legend, he was a British chieftain or king who sent ambassadors to Pope St. Eleutherius in Rome about 189 asking the pope to send missionaries to Britain. The request first appeared in the *Liber pontificalis*, collected about 530, and has no other basis in fact. Lucius was later said to have been baptized by St. Timothy, and to have served as bishop-

apostle to the Grisons in Switzerland, where he died at Chaur. F. D. Dec. 3.

LUCIUS, ST. (d. 257), bishop and martyr. See Nemesian, St.

LUCIUS, ST. (d. 259), martyr. See Victoricus, St.

LUCIUS, ST. (d. 269), martyr. He was put to death at Rome with SS. Mark, Peter, Theodosius, and nearly fifty other soldiers during the reign of Claudius II. F. D. Oct. 25.

LUCIUS, ST. (d. 273), martyr. See Craton, St.

LUCIUS, ST. (d. 311), martyr. He died with others at Cyprus during the Diocletian persecution; he has been confused with the first-century St. Lucius of Cyrene. F. D. Aug. 20.

LUCIUS, ST. (d. 350), bishop and martyr. Exiled three times from his see at Adrianople by the Arian group which had been condemned by the Council of Sardica, he died in prison after violent treatment given him and a group of staunch laymen who suffered with him. F. D. Feb. 11.

LUCIUS, ST. (d. 430?), martyr. See Julian, St.

LUÇON, LOUIS HENRI JOSEPH (1842–1930), cardinal. Born in Maulévrier, France, on Oct. 28, he was ordained in 1865, became a chaplain in Rome, a curate in Cholet, and in 1888 bishop of Belley. He became archbishop of Rheims in 1906 and a cardinal in 1907. He tried but failed to protect his cathedral against German bombardment in World War I, but proved that it had not been used as an observation post by the French. He reconsecrated the partly restored building in 1927, was decorated for bravery by his government, and published *La nécessité sociale de la religion* (1917). He died in Rheims, France, on May 28.

LUCRETIA, ST. (d. 306), martyr. She was put to death at Mérida, Spain, during the Diocletian persecution. F. D. Nov. 23.

LUCY, ST. (d. 300?), martyr. An aged Roman matron, she is said to have been slain with Geminian, a neophyte, during the Diocletian persecution. Their *Acta* are not trustworthy. F. D. Sept. 16.

LUCY, ST. (d. 304), martyr. Although veneration for St. Lucy is of great antiquity, little is known for certain beyond the fact that she was a Sicilian, born of wealthy parents in Syracuse, who suffered martyrdom during Diocletian's persecution. According to later legends, she early offered her viginity to God, was affianced to a young pagan by her mother Eutychia and, when she refused to marry her suitor, was denounced as a Christian. The judge ordered her exposed in a brothel and, when the guards could not move her, ordered her burned. When this proved unsuccessful,

she was stabbed through the throat. F. D. Dec.
13.

LUCY, BL. (12th century). Born in Bologna,
Italy, she became a Camaldolese at the convent of St. Christina, Settefonti, and is venerated as the foundress of that order's sisterhoods. F. D. Nov. 7.

LUCY OF AMELIA. *See* Bufalari, Bl. Lucia.

LUCY OF CALTAGIRONE, BL. (d. 1304?).
Born in Sicily in the town she was named
after, she spent her life as a Poor Clare at
Salerno and became mistress of novices in the
convent there. Her cult was approved in 1514.
F. D. Sept. 26.

LUDAN, ST. (d. 1202?). Called the son of
a Celtic prince, he died in Alsace while returning from a pilgrimage to the Holy Land.
His cult prospered at Scheerkirche until the
time of the Thirty Years' War. F. D. Feb.
12.

LUDDEN, PATRICK ANTHONY (1836–
1912), bishop. Born in Breaffy, Mayo, Ireland,
on Feb. 4, he studied at St. Jarlath's College,
Tuam, and the Grand seminary, Montreal,
and was ordained there in 1864. He did parish
work in Albany, New York, became rector of
the cathedral, was vicar general of the diocese
in 1872–87, and rector of St. Peter's, Troy,
and in 1886 was appointed first bishop of
Syracuse. During his twenty-six-year reign he
built a new cathedral, consecrated in 1910. He
died in Syracuse, New York, on Aug. 6.

LUDGER, ST. (d. 809), bishop. Born in
Zuilen, he studied under St. Gregory at Utrecht
and crossed to England to study with Alcuin
at York. He became a deacon there and was
ordained at Cologne in 777, then was a missioner in Friesland until the Saxons overran
the area. In 785 he visited Pope Adrian in
Rome, stayed at Monte Cassino for two years,
from which Charlemagne sent him back to
Friesland; he also was particularly successful
in the mission fields of Heligoland and Westphalia. He built monasteries in Werden and
Münster, and became first bishop of the latter
in about 803. He is also called Liutger. F. D.
Mar. 26.

LUDMILA, ST. (d. 860?–921). Daughter of
a Slavic prince, she married Duke Borivoy of
Bohemia, whom she followed into the Church.
They built a church near Prague and tried
unsuccessfully to force Christianity on their
subjects. On the death of Borivoy, his sons
Spytihinev and Ratislav, who had married
Drahomira, succeeded him, and Ludmila
brought up the latter's son Wenceslaus. On
the death of Ratislav, Drahomira became regent, kept Wenceslaus from Ludmila, and
reportedly caused her to be strangled at Tetin.
F. D. Sept. 16.

LUDOLF, ST. (d. 983). A Benedictine, he
was abbot of New Corbie, Westphalia, in 971–

83 and developed the monastic school there.
F. D. Aug. 13.

LUDOLF, ST. (d. 1250), bishop. A Premonstratensian, he became bishop of Ratzeburg,
Scheswig-Holstein, in 1236, built a Benedictine convent at Rehna, but clashed with Duke
Albert, whose ill treatment was so severe that
it caused his death in exile at Wismar, Mecklenburg, Germany. F. D. Mar. 29.

LUDOLPH OF SAXONY (d. 1378), author.
Although surnamed "of Saxony," he may have
been born in Cologne or Mainz. He became
a Dominican, may have studied under Tauler
and Suso, and about 1340 joined the Carthusians in Strassburg. In 1343 he was appointed
prior of the charterhouse in Coblentz, resigned
in 1348 to become a simple monk at Mainz,
and then at Strassburg, Alsace, where he died
on Apr. 13. He wrote a commentary upon
the Psalms, a *Vita Christi* which was tremendously popular and had widespread influence,
and for a time was considered to be the author
of *The Imitation of Christ*. He is also known
as Ludolph the Carthusian.

LUDOVICUS A S. CAROLO. *See* Jacob,
Ludovicus.

LUDWIN, ST. (d. 713), bishop. Born in
Austrasia, he was educated by St. Basinus;
after his wife died, he founded the abbey of
Mettlach, became a Benedictine monk there,
and later was named bishop of Trèves, Gaul.
F. D. Sept. 29.

LUEGER, KARL (1844–1910), burgomaster.
Born in Vienna on Oct. 24, he studied at the
Theresianum there, received his law degree
from Vienna in 1866, practiced law, and was
elected to the Vienna city council in 1875,
1876, and 1878. He was elected to the *Reichsrat* in 1885, became the leader of the Christian Socialist party and an opponent of Liberalism, and was elected to the *Landtag* in 1890.
He was elected burgomaster of Vienna five
times from 1895 to 1897, but was unable to
occupy the office until the Christian Socialists
controlled the *Reichsrat* in 1897. He was reelected in 1903 and 1909 and held the position until his death in Vienna on Mar. 10.

LUERS, JOHN HENRY (1819–1871),
bishop. Born in Luetten, Germany, on Sept.
29, he was brought to the United States in
1831, studied at St. Francis Xavier seminary,
Ohio, and was ordained in Cincinnati in
1846. He did parish work in Cincinnati for
the next decade, was appointed first bishop of
Fort Wayne, Indiana, in 1857, attended the
second Plenary Council in Bathmore, and died
in Cleveland, Ohio, on June 29.

LUFTHILDIS, ST. (d. 850?). Forced to leave
home because of the extent of her charities,
she became a recluse near Cologne. She is also
known as Leuchteldis, Liuthild, and Lufthold.
F. D. Jan. 23.

LUGO, FRANCISCO DE (1580–1652), theologian. A native of Madrid, and brother of Cardinal Juan de Lugo, he became a Jesuit at Salamanca in 1600, was sent to Mexico as a missioner, and taught theology there. On his return to Spain he served twice as rector of Valladolid, was censor of books and theologian to the Jesuit general in Rome, and wrote several theological treatises. He died in Valladolid, Spain, on Dec. 17.

LUGO, JUAN DE (1583–1660), cardinal. Born in Madrid in Nov., he studied law at Salamanca, became a Jesuit in 1603, was appointed professor of philosophy at Medina del Campo in 1611, and then taught philosophy at Valladolid from 1616 to 1621, when he was called to Rome to teach theology. In 1643 he was created a cardinal and served as a member of the congregations of the Holy Office and Council. He wrote such works as *De Trinitate*, *De visione Dei*, *De Incarnatione Domini*, *De iustitia et iure*, *De virtute fidei divinae*, *De sacramentis in genere*, and *De Deo, de angelis, de actibus humanis et de gratia*. He died in Rome on Aug. 29.

LUINI, BERNARDINO (1470?–1533?), painter. Born in Luino on Lake Maggiore, Italy, sometime between 1470 and 1480, he was quite well known by 1500, worked in Lugano and Saranno before 1525, the Monastero Maggiore (St. Maurice) in Milan in 1522–24 and 1529–30, and probably died there sometime after 1530. He became famous for his frescoes, which are noted for their quiet, simple color, loveliness of form, expression of feminine grace, depth of feeling and beauty. Among his most outstanding works are the frescoes, including the *Martyrdom of St. Catherine*, in the Monastero Maggiore; the frescoes, including *Marriage of the Virgin* and *Adoration of the Magi*, at Santa Maria Miracoli, Saronno; *Crucifixion* at Santa Maria degli Angeli, Lugano; the altarpieces in the cathedral in Como, *Adoration of the Shepherds* and *Adoration of the Magi*; and the *Coronation of Our Lord* painted for the Confraternity of the Holy Crown and now in the Ambrosiana.

LUKE, ST. (1st century), evangelist. Where or when he was born is not known, but he was a Gentile physician, probably Greek and possibly from Antioch, according to Eusebius and St. Jerome. He was the author of the third gospel and of the Acts of the Apostles, both written in the classical Greek literary style, for Gentiles. He accompanied St. Paul on his missionary journey about the year 51, staying at Philippi as a lay leader until 57, when he rejoined Paul. He was with Paul at Rome when the latter was imprisoned (61–63) and was his associate there during the second imprisonment. He escaped persecution and, after Paul's execution in 66, seems to have gone to Greece. He died at eighty-four in Boeotia, though not as a martyr. A sixth-century legend calls him a painter of several portraits of the Blessed Virgin, but this is improbable. It is likely, however, that he visited her in Jerusalem when she was seventy, when he may have learned from her the details of the nativity. His gospel, written no later than 63, probably in Rome, is based on oral tradition preserved by the apostles, which Luke investigated. He was a careful and detailed observer, stressed Christ's mercy, forgiveness, and social concern, and preserved many prayers still used by the Church. The Acts of the Apostles record the life of the Church from about 35 to 63, and the establishment of centers in Palestine, Syria, and through the Roman Empire. Luke reveals a good sense of history, geography, dialogue, and characterization. He is the patron of physicians and painters. F. D. Oct. 18.

LUKE, ST. (d. 250), martyr. *See* Parmenius, St.

LUKE, ST. (d. 312), martyr. *See* Silvanus, St.

LUKE THE YOUNGER, ST. (d. 946). A Greek whose family settled as farmers in Thessaly, he encountered many difficulties before he was able, at eighteen, to begin a life of austere solitude on Mt. Joannitsa near Corinth, Greece. F. D. Feb. 7.

LULL, ST. (d. 786), bishop. A monk from Malmesbury, England, he at twenty joined St. Boniface, to whom he was related, in Germany, served as the latter's assistant, and succeeded him as bishop in 756. He became embroiled in a dispute over the exemption of the monastery of Fulda and, when Pepin ruled against him, founded Hersfeld, Germany, to which he retired. F. D. Oct. 16.

LULL, RAMÓN. *See* Ramón Lull.

LULLY, JEAN BAPTISTE (1633–1687), composer. Born near Florence, Italy, on Nov. 23, he went to France about 1647, studied the violin, and became a violinist in the king's string orchestra. He composed popular songs, and music for the court ballet, was appointed court composer by King Louis XIV in 1653, collaborated with Molière in several ballets, and became director of the Royal Academy of Music in 1672. During the next sixteen years he produced twenty operas, which earned him the sobriquet of "father of French opera." They include *Armide et Renaud, Atys, Isis, Thésée,* and *Les fêtes de l'amour*; his best known work, perhaps, is *Au clair de la lune*. He died in Paris on Mar. 22.

LUMPER, GOTTFRIED (1747–1800?), author. Born in Füssen, Bavaria, on Feb 6, he studied at St. George abbey school in Billingen, joined the Benedictines there, and was ordained in 1771. He became director of the gymnasium, taught theology, served as prior

of the abbey, and died there on Mar. 8. He
wrote several historical works, chief of which
were his thirteen-volume *Historia theologico-
critica de vita, scriptis atque doctrina SS. patrum* and *Der Christ in der Fasten.*

LUNAIRE. *See* Leonorius, St.

LUPERCULUS, ST. (d. 300), martyr. He
was put to death, possibly near Tarbes,
Gaul, during the Diocletian persecution. F. D.
Mar. 1.

LUPERCUS, ST. (d. 300?), martyr. *See*
Claudius, St.

LUPERCUS, ST. (d. 304), martyr. *See* Apodemius, St.

LUPERIUS, ST. He was bishop of Verona,
Italy, in either the sixth or eighth century.
F. D. Nov. 15.

LUPICINUS, ST. (d. 480?). A recluse who
joined his brother St. Romanus in the Jura
Mountains and built the monasteries of Condat and Leuconne, he became abbot of the
latter. F. D. Mar. 21.

LUPICINUS, ST. (d. 486). He is listed as a
bishop of Lyons in Gaul. F. D. Feb. 3.

LUPICINUS, ST. (5th century). He is listed
as bishop of Verona, Italy. F. D. May 31.

LUPUS, ST. (383?–478), bishop. Born in
Toul, Gaul, he married a sister of St. Hilary
of Arles, but after six years they separated by
mutual consent and he became a monk at
Lérins. He was a bishop of Troyes in 426 and
in 429 went to Britain with St. Germanus of
Auxerre to combat Pelagianism there. In 453
he persuaded Attila and his Huns not to sack
Troyes. Forced to accompany Attila as a hostage, he was accused of aiding the Hun leader's
escape after the defeat at Châlons, Gaul, and
spent two years as a hermit. F. D. July 29.

LUPUS, ST. (5th century). He was bishop of
Bayeux, France, in 465. F. D. Oct. 25.

LUPUS, ST. (d. 540?). A nephew of St. Remigius of Rheims, he became bishop of Soissons,
France. F. D. Oct. 19.

LUPUS, ST. (d. 542). A monk at Lyons,
France, he became archbishop there and suffered during the political turbulence following
the death of King Sigismund of Burgundy.
F. D. Sept. 25.

LUPUS, ST. (d. 610?). He was bishop of
Châlons-sur-Saône, France. F. D. May 31.

LUPUS, ST. (d. 623), bishop. A monk at
Lérins, he succeeded St. Artemius as bishop of
Sens, France, in 609. When Clotaire became
king, Lupus was banished from his see as the
result of false accusations, but later restored.
The bishop suffered much from confused Burgundian politics. F. D. Sept. 1.

LUPUS, CHRISTIAN (1612–1681), historian. Born in Ypres, Flanders, on July 23, he
joined the Augustinians in 1627, and was appointed professor of theology at Louvain in
1640. Accused of Jansenism by the papal nun-

cio in Brussels, he was cleared of the charge by
Pope Alexander VII in Rome, spent 1655–60
studying there, and on his return to Louvain
in 1660 was elected provincial of the Belgian
province of his order. In 1667 he secured Pope
Innocent XI's condemnation of a series of false
doctrines, was appointed regius professor on his
return to Louvain, Belgium, and died there on
July 10. He wrote a number of theological treatises, most important of which was *Synodorum
generalium et provincialium statuta et canones,*
collected and published after his death.

LUPUS SERVATUS (805?–862?). Born near
Sens, France, he became a Benedictine, studied
at Ferrières and Fulda, where he was a follower
of Einhard, became a close friend and adviser
of Charles the Bald, and was appointed abbot of Ferrières in 840. He served on diplomatic
missions for Charles, was captured and imprisoned while leading the king's troops in the
latter's war with Pepin of Aquitaine in 844,
attended the councils of Verneuil (844), the
Acts of which he wrote, and of Soissons (853),
and was active in the predestination controversy of his times. He probably died at Ferrières, France. He is known for his letters,
which present an excellent picture of his times,
biographies of SS. Maximin and Wigbert, and
De tribus quaestionibus.

LUSCINIUS, OTTMAR (1487–1537). Born
in Strassburg, Alsace, he studied at Paris, Louvain, Padua, and Vienna, and was ordained.
He returned to Strassburg in 1514, because an
enthusiastic supporter of humanism, was appointed organist of St. Thomas in 1515, and
taught Greek at the cathedral school. He received a doctorate in law in Italy, was ousted
as organist in 1520, and in 1523 went to St.
Ulrich's monastery in Augsburg, where he
taught Greek and the Bible. Suspected of Protestant leanings, he soon became a leading
spokesman for Catholicism when appointed
preacher at St. Moriz church and in 1528 was
arrested for calling the evangelical preachers
heretics. In 1529 he was appointed preacher of
the cathedral in Freiburg im Breisgau and
spent the rest of his life there. He wrote several
treatises on the Bible, a harmony of the gospels,
and a translation of Lucian. He died at the
Carthusian house near Freiburg, Germany.

LUSIGNAN, JEAN BAPTISTE ALPHONSE
(1843–1893), author. Born in St. Denis, Quebec, on Sept. 27, he studied at St. Hyacinthe
College, the Montreal seminary, and law at
Laval. After being admitted to the bar he became interested in politics, was editor of the
nationalist *Le Pays* from 1865 to 1868, and
was elected to the Royal Society of Canada in
1885. He died on Jan. 5.

LUSSY, MELCHIOR (1529–1606). Born in
Stans, Switzerland, he became interested in
politics as a youth, served as high bailiff of the

canton of Unterwalden ten times, and acted as representative of the Swiss Confederacy to France and Spain. He was one of the representatives of the Catholic Swiss cantons at the Council of Trent in 1562–63, was a zealous supporter of the council's decrees in Switzerland, and active in establishing a papal nunciature there. He died in Stans on Nov. 14.

LUTERO, GIOVANNI NICOLÒ DI (1479?–1542), painter. Known as Dosso Dossi, he was born probably in Dosso, Italy, studied under Lorenzo Costa in Mantua, then in Venice and Rome for eleven years with his brother Battista (1480–1548), and enjoyed the patronage of Alfonso I and Ercole II, dukes of Ferrara. He completed frescoes for the ducal palace, sketches for tapestries in the cathedral, altarpieces, and several portraits, including one of Ariosto. His work is characterized by the romantic imagination, artificial pastoralism, and brilliant coloring of the Venetian school.

LUTGARDIS, ST. (1182–1246). Born in Tongres, Brabant, she joined the Benedictines at twenty, after boarding at their convent of St. Catherine for eight years. She experienced a number of visions, had other supernatural gifts, and, after a time, sought the stricter Cistercian rule. She transferred to the convent of Aywières, where she lived for thirty years, the last twelve in blindness. Her early biography by Thomas of Cantimpré is somewhat exaggerated. F. D. June 16.

LÜTOLF, ALOYS (1824–1879). Born in Gettnau, Switzerland, on Apr. 8, he studied at the Jesuit college in Schwyz and in Lucerne. After serving in the Sonderbund army, he studied at Freiburg and Munich, and in 1850 was ordained, served on the missions, and taught at St. Gall school until 1856, when he became a parish priest in Lucerne. He was appointed professor of church history at Solothurn seminary in 1858 and canon of St. Leodegar's in Lucerne, Switzerland. He died there on Apr. 8. He wrote treatises on schools, education, and educators.

LUXORIUS, ST. (d. 303?), martyr. A Roman soldier stationed in Sardinia, he was converted to Christianity and executed during the persecution of Diocletian. Legend says that two young boys, Cisellus and Camerinus, who had just been baptized were encouraged in their faith by his example and were executed with him. F. D. Aug. 21.

LWANGA, BL. CHARLES (d. 1886), martyr. He succeeded the martyred Joseph Mkasa as master of pages in the court of King Mwanga of Uganda. The latter's hatred of Catholicism was intensified because he was censured for debauching the pages; he himself killed the young catechist, Bl. Denis Sebuggawo, with a spear. Andrew Kaggwa, a native chief, was beheaded; Pontain Ngondwe, a soldier, and Noah Mawag-

gali, a chieftain, were slain by lances; Mathias Kalemba, a Membo judge, was tortured to death. The resulting riots took the lives of nearly 100. The king then ordered Lwanga, a thirteen-year-old named Kizito, and fifteen others sent off to Namugango. Three were slain on the way; the others, and two soldiers, were burned to death; the chief executioner's nephew, Mbanga, was struck dead before being thrown on the pyre. The martyrs of Uganda were beatified in 1920. F. D. June 3.

J. P. THOONEN, *Black Martyrs* (New York, Sheed, 1941); GLENN KITTLER, *The White Fathers* (New York, Harper, 1957).

LYBE, ST. (d. 303?), martyr. *See* Eutropia, St.

LYDGATE, JOHN (1370?–1450?), poet. Born in Lydgate, Suffolk, England, he entered the Benedictine abbey of St. Edmund's Bury about 1385, probably studied at Oxford and Cambridge, traveled in Europe, and was ordained in 1397. He opened an abbey school for sons of noble families in Bury, was court poet, served as prior of Hatfield Broadoak from 1423 to 1434, and then returned to Bury, where he probably died. One of the most important of the imitators of Chaucer, he wrote more than 140,000 lines of poetry, half of that amount in *The Troy Book* and *The Falls of Princes*, drawn from Boccaccio. Other titles generally attributed to him are: *The Temple of Glass, The Pilgrimage of the Life of Man, Reason and Sensuality, The Court of Sapience, The Flower of Courtesy,* the unfinished *Secrets of the Philosophers,* the effectively lyrical *Life of Our Lady,* and metrical lives of SS. Augustine of Canterbury, Edmund, Giles, and Margaret. In his treatment of allegory, adventure, and amour, he revealed his knowledge of Chaucer's style and technique, but a lack of the latter's energy, emotion, and sense of compression.

LYDIA, ST. (d. 121?), martyr. *See* Philetus, St.

LYDIA PURPURARIA, ST. (1st century). Born in Thyatira, Asia Minor, she was a seller of purple-dyed cloth and was at Philippi when she became St. Paul's first convert (Acts 16:14–15). F. D. Aug. 3.

LYDWINA, BL. (1380–1433). Born at Scheidam, Holland, one of nine children of a laborer, she was injured in 1396 while skating and became a lifelong invalid, her sufferings increasing in intensity each year. She bore them as reparation for the sins of others and by 1407 was given a great number of supernatural gifts. Eventually, almost totally blind and wasted to a skeleton, she was able to subsist on the Eucharist alone. Biographies were written by Thomas à Kempis, John Brugman, and by her cousin John Gerlac, and her cult was confirmed in 1890. F. D. Apr. 14.

LYNCH, JOHN (1599–1673), historian. Born in Galway, Ireland, son of Alexander Lynch, master of a famous school there, he was educated by his father, studied in France, returned to Galway in 1622, and founded a school. He opposed the rebellion of 1641 and approved the peace of 1646 and 1648, was appointed archdeacon of Tuam, and was expelled from Ireland in 1652 when the Puritans captured Galway. He spent the rest of his life in France, and wrote *Alithonologia* and *Cambrensis Eversus.*

LYNCH, JOHN JOSEPH (1816–1888), archbishop. Born in Clones, Monaghan, Ireland, on Feb. 6, he studied in Dublin and Paris, became a Lazarist, taught and did missionary work in Ireland, Texas, and Missouri (where he was president of a Lazarist college), and served as founder-rector of the seminary of Our Lady of the Angels, Niagara Falls, New York. In 1859 he was appointed titular bishop of Aechinas and coadjutor of Toronto. He became third bishop of the Ontario, Canada, see in 1860, developed education, attended the third and fourth Provincial Councils of Quebec, supported papal infallibility at the Vatican Council of 1859–70, and served on congregations of the Missions and Eastern Rites. He became first archbishop of Toronto in 1870, and died there on May 12.

LYNCH, JOSEPH PATRICK (1872–1954), bishop. Born in St. Joseph, Michigan, on Nov. 16, he studied at St. Charles's, Maryland, St. Mary's seminary, Baltimore, and Kenrick seminary, Missouri, and was ordained in 1900. He was stationed at the Dallas, Texas, cathedral, served as pastor in Weatherford, Hardley, and Dallas from 1900 to 1911, became vicar general of Dallas in 1910 and administrator later in the year, and in 1911 was appointed bishop. He was made an assistant at the pontifical throne in 1936, and died on Aug. 19.

LYNCH, PATRICK NEISEN (1817–1882), bishop. Born in Clones, Monaghan, Ireland, on Mar. 10, he was brought to South Carolina in 1818 by his parents. He studied at St. John the Baptist seminary, Charleston, and the Propaganda, Rome, received his doctorate in divinity, and was ordained there in 1840. On his return he served as a pastor, became rector of the Charleston cathedral in 1847, vicar general in 1850, was administrator of the see in 1855, and was consecrated third bishop of Charleston in 1858. His cathedral, residence, diocesan library, and most of the schools and institutions of the city were destroyed by the bombardment of the city in 1861 and the occupation of the area by Sherman's forces toward the close of the Civil War. Most of his episcopate was spent in the attempt to raise funds in America and abroad to pay the see's great debt, which he had almost erased at the time of his death in Charleston on Feb. 26. He rebuilt the cathedral and many institutions, attended the Vatican Council in 1869–70, where he favored the dogma of papal infallibility, and did much to promote better feelings between North and South by his visits to northern cities to raise funds for his ravaged diocese. He also edited the *United States Catholic Miscellany* for years.

LYNDWOOD, WILLIAM (1375?–1446), bishop. A native Englishman, he was ordained and became a leading authority on canon law. In 1414 he was appointed adviser to the archbishop of Canterbury on ecclesiastical law, dean of the Arches in 1426, and in 1433 was the king's proctor at the Council of Basle. He served on diplomatic missions to Portugal, France, and the Netherlands, was made archdeacon of Stowe in 1434, and was appointed bishop of St. David's in 1442. He was the author of *Provinciale*, the monumental commentary on the decrees of the English councils under the archbishop of Canterbury.

LYONS, CHARLES W. (1868–1939), educator. Born in Boston, Massachusetts, on Jan. 31, he became a Jesuit in 1890, was ordained in 1904, and was president of Gonzaga (1908–9), St. Joseph's (1909–14), and Boston (1914–18) colleges and Georgetown University (1924–28). He died in Dorchester, Massachusetts, on Jan. 31.

LYONS, JOSEPH ALOYSIUS (1879–1939), prime minister. Born in Stanley, Australia, on Sept. 15, of Irish emigrant parents, he became a teacher in a rural school at twenty, attended the university, and served in the Tasmanian parliament from 1909 to 1929. He was treasurer of the labor party in 1914, minister for education, railroads, and mines, leader of the opposition from 1916 to 1923, then premier of Tasmania. He married Enid Burnell in 1915; she was elected to parliament in 1943. In 1929 he was returned to the commonwealth parliament and became postmaster general, treasurer in 1930, and for his opposition to the financial proposals of the pro-Socialist Scullin government was expelled from his party. He formed the United Australian party in 1931, won the next election, and was prime minister and treasurer of Australia from 1932 until his death in Sydney on Apr. 7. He also was minister for health, vice-president of the executive council, and a member of the national delegation to the imperial conferences of 1935 and 1937. He received honorary degrees from Melbourne and Cambridge.

M

MAASSEN, FRIEDRICH BERNARD CHRISTIAN (1823–1900), jurist. Born in Wilten, near Innsbruck, Austria, he studied there and law at Jena, Berlin, Kiel, and Rostock, became a convert, and was active in defense of the representatives of the diet against the grand duke of Mecklenburg-Schwerin in 1848. With Franz von Florencourt he founded *Norddeutscher Korrespondent*. He taught at Bonn, wrote *Der Primat des Bischofs von Rom und die alten Patriarchalkirchen* (1853), and as a result was invited to Pest as professor of Roman law in 1855. He taught thereafter at Innsbruck, Graz, and Vienna, until his retirement in 1894. He became a member of the Vienna Academy of Sciences in 1873, was made a life member of the upper house in 1885, and a member of the supreme court of the empire from 1882 to 1897. He was a follower of Döllinger at the Vatican Council, but in 1882 renounced any allegiance to the Old Catholics. He wrote several treatises on law, and died in Wilten, Saxony, Germany, on Apr. 9.

MABILLON, JEAN (1632–1707), scholar. Born in St. Pierremont, Champagne, France, on Nov. 23, he studied at Collège des Bons Enfants, Rheims, became a Maurist Benedictine, and was ordained in 1660. At St. Germain-des-Prés abbey, Paris, from 1664 to 1684 he was a member of a brilliant group of scholars. His edition of St. Bernard's *Works* (1667) and the three-volume *Acta sanctorum O.S.B.* (1668–72) established him as a major historian. He made trips to Flanders, Burgundy, Switzerland, Germany, and Italy, to examine documents and collect books and manuscripts, and in 1675 published the first of four volumes of *Vetera analecta*. In 1681 his *De re diplomatica* established the principles of documentary criticism and paleography as a science. In 1691 he became embroiled in a dispute with Abbot de Rancé of La Trappe, who declared manual work rather than study was prescribed for monks; in reply, Mabillon wrote his defense of monastic learning, *Traité des études monastiques*. In 1698 his protest, under the name Eusebius Romanus, against veneration of unidentified relics from the catacombs caused such a furore the work was denounced to the Holy Office and he was obliged to revise it. His preface to the Maurist edition of St. Augustine published in 1700 caused a storm by his defense of the methods and conclusions of the editors and he was accused of heresy, but was exonerated by the Holy Office. He was ap-

pointed one of the first members of the Academy of Inscriptions in 1701. He also wrote *Annales* of the Benedictine order, four volumes of which he completed between 1693 and his death in Paris on Dec. 26.

MABUSE, JAN DE. *See* Gossaert, Jan.

MABYN, ST. (6th century). Several Welsh saints of this name were associated with the work of St. Teilo; one, daughter of the chieftain Brychan, is venerated as St. Mabenna; another is perpetuated in the place name Ruabon in Denbighshire. F. D. Sept. 21.

MACAILLE, ST. (d. 489?). Bishop of Croghan, he worked in Ireland with St. Mel, with whom he presided when St. Brigid made her vows. F. D. Apr. 25.

MACCALDUS. *See* Maughold, St.

MACAIRE OF GHENT, ST. (d. 1012). Perhaps archbishop in Pisidia, Asia Minor, he is said to have been captured by Saracens, and to have escaped to Europe and settled at the monastery of St. Bavon in Ghent, Flanders. He died of the plague there and is venerated as a patron against pestilence. F. D. Apr. 10.

MACANSIUS, ST. (d. 514), bishop. Said to have been baptized by St. Patrick, he went on a pilgrimage to the Holy Land and Rome, and became abbot-bishop of a church and monastery at Kells, which became the diocese of Connor, Ireland. He is also known as Aengus McNisse. F. D. Sept. 3.

MACARIUS, ST. (2nd century), martyr. *See* Eudoxius, St.

MACARIUS, ST. (d. 250?). He was one of a group of potters, including SS. Justus, Rufinus, and Theophilus, who were put to death during the persecution of Decius, either at Rome or Alexandria. F. D. Feb. 28.

MACARIUS, ST. (d. 250), martyr. *See* Faustus, St.

MACARIUS, ST. (d. 335?), bishop. He became bishop of Jerusalem in 314, defended the Church against Arianism, and attended the Council of Nicaea. According to popular belief, he was present when St. Helena found the true cross, identified it, and built the basilica which Constantine ordered over the sepulcher of Christ. F. D. Mar. 10.

MACARIUS, ST. (d. 350?). He was bishop of Petra, Palestine, attended the Council of Sardica, and was so active against the Arians that he was banished to Africa, where he died. His name was originally Arius. F. D. June 20.

MACARIUS, ST. (d. 362), martyr. *See* Eugene, St.

MACARIUS, ST. (d. 830?). A scriptural student at Constantinople, he became a monk and later abbot at the monastery of Pelekete. He was ordained by St. Tarasius, tortured and imprisoned by the Iconoclastic Emperor Leo the Armenian, and banished by his successor, Michael the Stammerer. F. D. Apr. 1.

MACARIUS, BL (d. 1153). A Benedictine monk from Ireland or Scotland, he became first abbot of the monastery of St. James, Würzburg, Bavaria. F. D. Dec. 19.

MACARIUS. *See* Macaire, St.

MACAROUS OF ANTIOCH (7th century), patriarch. A resident of Constantinople, whose title of patriarch seems to have been an honorary one, since his patriarchate was in Saracen hands, he was deposed at the Council of Constantinople in 681 for his Monothelitism and probably spent the rest of his life in a Roman monastery. In the course of his defense he presented the first letter of Pope Honorius to Sergius (634), which used the formula "one will" in discussing the two natures of Christ, whereupon the council proceeded to denounce Honorius. Pope Leo II confirmed the findings of the council, except its condemnation of Honorius, though he deplored Honorius' laxity in dealing with the whole matter of the Monothelite heresy at that time.

MACARIUS THE ELDER, ST. (300?–390). He left for the Egyptian desert at thirty and lived there in extreme austerity for sixty years. His patience and prayerful advice were so well known and so influential that he and others were banished to an island in the Nile by the Arian Lucius, but were later allowed to return to the wastes of Skete, where he died. F. D. Jan. 15.

MACARIUS MAGNES (4th century), apologist. Generally considered to be bishop of Magnesia, Greece (he sometimes is called Bl. Magnes or Macarius the Magnesian), he attended the Synod of Chalcedon in 403, where he accused Bishop Heraclides of Origenism. He wrote a scriptural defense in *Apocritica* and homilies on Genesis.

MACARIUS THE YOUNGER, ST. (d. 394?). A confectioner in Alexandria, Egypt, he lived in the desert regions of the Thebaid, Libya, and Nitria for sixty years. His fasting and austerities were exceptional. Numerous rules which he composed influenced St. Jerome and survived in the regimen of the monastery of La Trappe, France. F. D. Jan. 2.

MACARTAN, ST. (d. 505?). Said to have been consecrated bishop of Clogher, Ireland, by St. Patrick, Aedh mac Cairthinn also served as abbot of Dairinis. F. D. Mar. 26.

MACASSOLI, BL. CHRISTOPHER (d. 1485). Born in Milan, Italy, he was a Franciscan priest who converted many by his preaching and the example of his holy life at the

friary he founded at Vigevano. His cult was confirmed in 1890. F. D. Mar. 11.

MACBETH (d. 1057), king of Scotland. He succeeded Duncan, whom he defeated (and may have slain) in 1040, and was himself defeated by Edward of Northumbria at Dunsinane, Perthshire, in 1054 and slain by Malcolm III, Duncan's son, at Lumphanan, Aberdeenshire, Scotland. The account was popular in English historical writing and Macbeth became the central figure in Shakespeare's tragedy.

MAC CAGHWELL, HUGH (1571–1626), archbishop. Born in Saul, Down, Ireland, he studied on the Isle of Man, became tutor of Prince Hugh of Tyrone's sons, and was his ambassador to Spain, where he received his doctorate in divinity at Salamanca and became a noted Franciscan theologian. After teaching at Salamanca, he was appointed superior of the College of St. Anthony's (which his influence with the Spanish crown had helped found) and at Louvain, served on several diplomatic commissions for the pope, and helped found the college for Irish students in Rome. He was appointed archbishop of Armagh and primate of Ireland in 1626, but died six months later on Sept. 22. He wrote commentaries on the works of Duns Scotus and a work on penance.

MACAULAY, GENEVIEVE GARVAN BRADY (1884–1938). Born in Hartford, Connecticut, on Apr. 11, she studied at Manhattanville and in Europe, married Nicholas F. Brady in 1906, founded the Carroll Club for girls in New York City, and in 1928 was chairman of the national board of the Girl Scouts and later of their world committee. She was known for her philanthropy: summer camps, local welfare relief, the Jesuit novitiate at Wernersville, Pennsylvania, and rest house at Manhasset, New York, additions to the holdings of Georgetown's library, and the Curie radium fund. Her first husband died in 1930; she married William J. B. Macaulay in 1937. She received four decorations from the Vatican for her charities, an honorary degree from Georgetown, and the Laetare Medal in 1934. She died in Rome, where her husband was Irish minister to the Vatican, on Nov. 24.

MACCALLIN, ST. (d. 497). He was bishop of Lusk, Ireland. F. D. Sept. 6.

MACCALLIN, ST. (d. 978). An Irishman, he became a Benedictine at the monastery of Gorze after a pilgrimage to France, lived for a time as a recluse, then served as abbot of Thiérache and of Walsort. F. D. Jan. 21.

MAC CARTHY, BARTHOLOMEW (1843–1904). Born in Conna, Cork, Ireland, on Dec. 12, he studied in Waterford and Rome, was ordained in 1869, taught classics at Cork for three years, and did parish work until his death at Inniscarra, Ireland, on Mar. 6. He wrote on early ecclesiastical history, philology, and manuscript tradition, and edited volumes 2–4 of the *Irish Annals* in the Rolls Series, dealing in part with the quarrel over the dating of Easter in the early Church.

MAC CARTHY, DENIS FLORENCE (1817–1882), poet. Born in Dublin, Ireland, on May 26, he studied law, was admitted to the bar in 1846, but never practiced. He became professor of poetry at the Catholic University in Dublin and was a regular contributor to the *Nation* (under the name Desmond). He went to Europe in 1864, settled in London, then returned to Dublin in 1881, where he died on Apr. 7. He published *Ballads, Poems, and Lyrics* (1850), *Under-Glimpses*, and *The Bell Founder*, wrote *Shelley's Early Life*, and translated plays of Calderón.

MAC CARTHY, JUSTIN (1830–1912), historian. Born in Cork, Ireland, on Nov. 22, he worked on newspapers in Cork and Liverpool, became parliamentary reporter on the London *Morning Star* in 1860 and its editor from 1864 to 1868, lectured in the United States and was an editor of the *New York Independent* from 1868 to 1871, and returned to work for the *London Daily News*. He was a member of the British parliament from 1879 to 1896, vice-chairman of the Irish party, and the successor to Parnell as its chairman in 1890. He also was chairman of the National Land and Labour League of Great Britain. He wrote nearly twenty novels (including *Dear Lady Disdain* and *Donna Quixote*), between 1867 and 1893, and biographies of Sir Robert Peel, William Gladstone, and Pope Leo XIII, but is best known for his seven-volume *History of Our Own Times* (1888), *Epoch of Reform* (1874), *Modern England* (1899), *Rome in Ireland* (1904), and the four-volume *History of the Four Georges* (1885–1901), the last two volumes of which he wrote with his son, Justin Huntley MacCarthy. He died in Folkstone, England, on June 24.

MAC CARTHY, NICHOLAS TUITE (1769–1833). Born in Dublin, Ireland, on May 19, he was taken to Toulouse in 1773, studied at Paris, and was taking theology at the Sorbonne when driven out by the French Revolution. He was not ordained until 1814, then worked as a missioner in Toulouse, became a Jesuit in 1818, and was widely known for his preaching. He went to Rome when the revolution of 1830 broke out, then retired to Turin to preach and direct retreats. He also is known as Abbé de Lévignac. He died at Annécy, Savoy, on May 3.

MACCUL. *See* Maughold, St.

MAC DONAGH, THOMAS (1878–1916), poet. Born in Cloughjordan, Tipperary, Ireland, he taught in Kilkenny and Fermoy, studied Gaelic on the Aran Islands and in Munster, and joined the staff of Padraic Pearse's school

in Dublin, St. Edna's. His play *When the Dawn Is Come* followed the appearance of two volumes of poetry: *The Golden Joy* (1906) and *Song of Myself*. He took his master's degree at the National University (his undergraduate work had been completed in a seminary), joined Padraic Colum, James Stephens, and others in editing the *Irish Review*, later edited by MacDonagh and Joseph Plunkett. He taught at the National University and published *Literature in Ireland* (1916). When the volunteer army of independence took shape, MacDonagh commanded a corps; he died in Dublin with Pearse and Plunkett during the Easter rebellion.

MAC DONALD, ALEXANDER (1858–1941), bishop. Born in Mabou, Nova Scotia, Canada, he studied at St. Francis Xavier, Antigonish, and the Propaganda, Rome, and was ordained in 1884. He taught literature and philosophy at St. Francis Xavier until 1903, serving as vicar general of Antigonish from 1900. In 1908 he was named bishop of Victoria, British Columbia, attended the plenary council in Quebec in 1909, and succeeded after much legal effort in gaining tax relief for church property, an action begun when the government threatened to seize his cathedral. He wrote on the Apostles' Creed, sermons and ascetical works, retired from Victoria in 1923 and was appointed titular bishop of Hebron, and returned to Antigonish, Nova Scotia, where he died on Feb. 24.

MAC DONALD, JOHN (1742?–1811). Born in Glenaladale, Scotland, he studied at the Scots College in Ratisbon, Bavaria, returned to Scotland, and in 1771 purchased land in Prince Edward Island, Canada, as a refuge for persecuted Catholics. He followed a group there in 1772 and served with such distinction during the American Revolution that he was offered the governorship of the island by the crown, but was unable to accept because of his prescribed religion.

MAC DONALD, WALTER (1854–1920), theologian. Born in Kilkenny, Ireland, he studied at Maynooth, was ordained in 1876, and became rector of St. Kieran's College, where he had completed his own preparatory schooling. In 1881 he became librarian and professor of theology at Maynooth, founded the *Irish Theological Quarterly* in 1906, and wrote the controversial *Some Ethical Questions of Peace and War*. He died on May 2.

MAC DONELL, ALEXANDER (1760–1840), bishop. Born in Inchlaggan, Glengarry, Scotland, on July 17, he studied at the Scots colleges in Paris and Valladolid, was ordained in 1787, and served five years in Lochaber parish. He led his clansmen to Glasgow when they were evicted in 1792, found work for them, and in 1794, when their livelihood was again threatened, formed them into the Glengarry Fencible Regiment (with himself as the first Catholic chaplain in the British army since the Reformation). It was disbanded in 1802 after service in Guernsey and Ireland. In 1804 he went with persecuted Catholics to Canada and was assigned, as vicar general, to Glengarry, Ontario, where from 1806 to 1816 he was one of only two priests in the province. He reorganized the regiment during the War of 1812 and was with them in battle against the United States. In 1819 he was appointed the first vicar apostolic of Upper Canada and became first bishop of Kingston, Ontario, in 1826. He established Iona seminary in 1826 and Regiopolis College at Kingston in 1833 and was appointed to the legislative council in 1831. He died on Jan. 14 in Dumfries, Scotland, while seeking new emigrants.

MAC DONNELL, ANTONY PATRICK (1844–1925). Born in Shragh, Mayo, Ireland, on Mar. 7, he studied in Athlone and Queen's College, Galway, and entered the civil service. He served in Bengal and Bihar, India, wrote a study of *Food-Grain Supply and Famine Relief* (1876) on those areas, and left in 1878 in ill health. He married Henrietta MacDonell in 1878, returned to India in 1881, had a strong hand in the Tenancy Act of 1885, and was home secretary for three years. He also served as chief commissioner for Burma, then of the Central Provinces, and in 1893 was lieutenant governor of Bengal. Other administrative posts followed, and he did much for agrarian reform and plague and famine relief. In 1902 he went to Dublin as undersecretary for Ireland, helped to shape the Irish Land Purchase Bill of 1903, and with Lord Bryce presented the Irish Council Bill of 1907. He met opposition from north and south, but, though offered the governorship of Bombay, stayed on to try to conciliate warring factions. When unable to do so, he resigned in 1908, and was made a baron by King Edward VII. He served as chairman of a civil-service commission in 1912–14, as a member of the Irish Convention in 1917–18, and in 1923 became vice-president of the national bank. He died in London on June 9.

MAC DONNELL, JAMES FRANCIS CARLIN (1881–1945), poet. Born in Bay Shore, New York, on Apr. 7, son of a coachman who died when his son was small, he went to grammar school in Norwalk, Connecticut, but did not finish, worked in a shoe store, educated himself by reading, made two brief trips to Ireland, and became a salesman in Macy's department store in New York. In 1917 he published *My Ireland* at his own expense; *Cairn of Stars* followed in 1919. His work was highly praised by Christopher Morley and Thomas Augustine Daly; he published a few poems in magazines thereafter; and from 1924 to 1939

dropped out of sight to work on a study of the Bible, living in New York City on meager savings. He died there on Mar. 11.

MAC EACHERN, ANGUS BERNARD (19th century). Born in Scotland, he labored in the mission fields in the St. Lawrence Gulf region of Canada, visiting the Scots-Irish and Acadians in Nova Scotia by open boat. He became titular bishop of Rosen in 1821, first bishop of Charlottetown, Prince Edward Island, in 1829, and reigned until his death on Apr. 23.

MACEDO, ST. (d. 121?), martyr. *See* Philetus, St.

MACEDO, FRANCISCO (1596–1681), theologian. Born in Coimbra, Portugal, he became a Jesuit in 1610, a Discalced Franciscan in 1638, and a Franciscan Observant in 1648. He taught at the Propaganda and the Sapienza in Rome, became a consultor to the Inquisition, and was professor of moral theology at Padua, Italy, where he died on May 1. He published more than 100 books on St. Thomas, Duns Scotus, heresy, grace, and the papacy.

MACEDO, JOSÉ AGOSTINHO DE (1761–1831). Born in Beja, Portugal, he became an Augustinian, quarreled with his superiors and left the order, was unfrocked in 1792, but had his ecclesiastical status restored by papal brief. He edited the official *Gazette* of Lisbon, became a royal preacher in 1802, and from 1824 to 1829 was diocesan censor. He wrote much political poetry (*Gama*, 1811, *O Oriente, Meditacão, Newton*) and a serious *Demonstration of the Existence of God*.

MACEDONE, IL. *See* Clovio, Giorgio.

MACEDONIUS, ST. (d. 304?), martyr. He, his wife Patricia, and daughter Modesta are said to have been put to death at Nicomedia during the Diocletian persecution. F. D. Mar. 13.

MACEDONIUS, ST. (d. 362), martyr. He and SS. Tatian and Theodulus were burned to death at Mevos, Phrygia, for destroying idols during the reign of Julian the Apostate. F. D. Sept. 12.

MACEDONIUS, ST. (d. 430?). Syrian, he lived to be ninety, a recluse during his last forty years. Theodoret's *Ecclesiastical History* records many cures, including that of the writer's mother, to whom Macedonius had long given spiritual direction. F. D. Jan. 24.

MACELWANE, JAMES B. (1883–1956), geophysicist. Born near Port Clinton, Ohio, on Sept. 28, he became a Jesuit in 1903, studied at St. Louis, and was ordained in 1918. He began his scientific writing in 1911, was an authority on seismology, and discovered a system of tracking hurricanes at sea. He wrote widely, received four honorary degrees, was president of the Seismological Society of America (1928–29) and of the American Geophysical Union, and was named to the National Science Foundation by President Roosevelt in 1944. He was dean of the St. Louis University Institute of Technology at the time of his death in that city on Feb. 15.

MAC GEOGHEGAN, JAMES (1702–1763). Born in Uisneach, Westmeath, Ireland, he studied at the Lombard College, Paris, was ordained, a vicar at Poissy for five years, chaplain of the Irish troops in French service, and a curate in Paris, where he died. He wrote a *History of Ireland* in French (1858).

MAC GRATH, JOHN MACRORY (15th century). Born in Munster, Ireland, he wrote *Cathreim Thoirdhealbhaigh,* an exaggerated history of the wars of Thormond from 1194 to 1318, which nevertheless gives a valuable picture of the Anglo-Norman period.

MACHABEO, ST. (1104–1174). An Irishman, he was abbot of the monastery of SS. Peter and Paul at Armagh, Ireland, from 1134 until his death. F. D. Mar. 31.

MACHADO, BL. JOHN BAPTIST (1580–1617), martyr. Born in Terceira, Azores, he became a Jesuit at Coimbra, was sent to Japan in 1609, and beheaded at Nagasaki for his mission activity. He was beatified in 1867. F. D. May 22.

MACHAI, ST. (5th century). One of the followers of St. Patrick, he founded a monastery at Bute, Ireland. F. D. Apr. 11.

MAC HALE, JOHN (1791–1881), archbishop. Born in Tubbernavine, Mayo, Ireland, on Mar. 6, he studied at Maynooth, was ordained in 1814, and was appointed professor of theology there in 1820. He became coadjutor bishop of Killala in 1825 and archbishop of Tuam in 1834. He was a close friend of Daniel O'Connell and a prominent champion of Catholic Emancipation, condemned the poor laws and national schools, and led the opposition to the "No Popery" movement of the early 1850s. He organized the relief during the famine of 1846–47. Although he supported the idea of a Catholic university, he fought the appointment of John Henry Newman as rector and his violent disagreement with the archbishop of Dublin over its management brought the educational venture to an end. MacHale attended the Vatican Council in 1869 and opposed the dogma of papal infallibility, but later accepted it. He translated Homer's *Iliad,* Thomas Moore's *Melodies,* part of scripture, and several hymns into Gaelic, and usually preached in the national language, which he labored to preserve. He died in Tuam, Ireland, on Nov. 4.

MACHAR, ST. (6th century), bishop. An Irish missionary, he became a disciple of St. Columba at Iona, accompanied him to Scotland, and after his own consecration was sent to evangelize the Picts in Aberdeenshire, where he established the see of Aberdeen. He is also called Mochumna. F. D. Nov. 12.

MACHEBOEUF, JOSEPH PROJECTUS (1812–1889), bishop. Born in Riom, France, on Aug. 11, he studied there and in Montferrand, was ordained in Clermont-Ferrand in 1836, and went to the United States in 1839 to serve under Bishop Lamy of Santa Fe. He spent ten years in New Mexico (serving as vicar general) and Arizona and eleven more in northern Ohio before he was sent to Denver, Colorado, in 1860. With Fr. John B. Reverdy he covered the large mission area for seven years and was made titular bishop of Epiphania and vicar apostolic of Colorado and Utah in 1868. In 1887 he was consecrated first bishop of Denver. When he died in Denver on July 10, there were 112 churches and ten schools in the diocese.

MACHIAVELLI, NICCOLÒ DI BERNARDO (1469–1527), author. Born in Florence on May 3, son of a lawyer, he entered public life in 1494, became secretary of the second chancellory of the city-state, and served as first secretary of the Council of Ten in 1498, and on diplomatic missions to Catherine Sforza, Louis XII of France, Emperor Maximilian, Cesare Borgia, and Rome. In 1502 he married Marietta Corsini. He supported Soderini and built a force of militia, but both let him down; he was exiled for a year, was tortured for suspected complicity in the 1513 plot against the Medici and imprisoned, but was freed through Pope Leo X. He was obliged to retire from public life and went to Strada to write. He produced *Istorie fiorentine* and *Discorso sopra il riformare lo state di Firenze,* and from 1521 to 1525 served on papal diplomatic missions. He tried fruitlessly to secure a position under the Medici and returned to Florence when they were driven out in 1527. His best-known work is *Il Principe* (*The Prince;* 1532), a political tract in which he discussed the methods to be employed by a successful ruler, modeled on the career of Cesare Borgia, whose cleverness and audacity he admired. In it Machiavelli placed primary emphasis on absolutism and insisted that the ruler should employ any means to secure his ends; it was placed on the Index in 1559. Other writings are *Discorso sopra la prima deca de Tito Livio; Dell' arte della guerra;* plays, chief of which is *La mandragola;* a novel; and *Dialogo sulle lingue.* He died in Florence, Italy, on June 22.

MACHUTIS. *See* Malo, St.

MACKAY, CLARENCE HUNGERFORD (1874–1938), executive. Born in San Francisco, California, on Apr. 17, he studied at Vaugirard in Paris and Beaumont in Windsor, England, and in 1894 began to learn the telegraphy business. He became a director of the Commercial Cable and Postal Telegraph companies in 1896, vice-president in 1897, and president in 1902, succeeding his father, John Mackay. He completed the laying of the trans-pacific cable in 1904. He became president of the Mackay Radio and Telegraph Company and in 1928 chairman of the board of a new company which merged his father's holdings with those of the International Telephone & Telegraph Co. He established the School of Mines at Nevada, a chair in electrical engineering at California, and the Mackay-Roosevelt Hospital unit during World War I. He received the medal of the National Institute of Social Sciences in 1926, was twice honored by the Vatican, and served as chairman of the board of St. Vincent's Hospital and of the Philharmonic Society, both in New York City, as a trustee of the Metropolitan Museum, and director of the Metropolitan Opera Co. He died in New York City on Nov. 12.

MAC KILLOP, MARY (1832–1909), cofoundress. Born in South Australia, she was the first superior of the Sisters of St. Joseph of the Sacred Heart, as Mother Mary of the Cross, founded at Penola by Fr. Julian Tennison Woods (d. 1886) in 1866, who sent her to Savoy to learn the Rule of the Sisters of St. Joseph at Annecy. She obtained papal approval and returned to work in the Australian missions, acting as a catechist, and founding orphanages, an industrial home, and a reformatory. She died in Sydney, Australia, on Aug. 8.

MAC KINNON, COLIN (d. 1859), bishop. A graduate of the Propaganda, Rome, he became second bishop of Arichat, Nova Scotia, in 1852, but was forced by ill health to resign in 1857. He was made titular bishop of Amida and died on Sept. 26.

MACLOU. *See* Malo, St.

MAC MAHON, BERNARD (d. 1747). Bishop of Clogher, Ireland, he succeeded his uncle Hugh at Armagh in 1737 and, like him, spent much of his time serving his people from underground hide-outs. He was succeeded in 1747 by his brother Ross, also bishop of Clogher, who ruled Armagh for a year.

MAC MAHON, HERBER (1600–1650), bishop. Born in Farney, Monaghan, Ireland, he studied at Douai and Louvain, was ordained in 1625, and returned to work secretly in the devastated diocese of Clogher. In 1642 he was named bishop of Down and Connor, and attended the Synod of Kells that year, but was transferred to Clogher in 1643 and never ruled the other diocese. During the Cromwellian invasion he sided with the papal envoys and with Owen Roe O'Neill and strongly condemned the Supreme Council of the Irish and the duke of Ormonde, who seemed to be sacrificing the nation's identity and religion by accepting inimical peace terms. When O'Neill died in 1649, Bishop MacMahon was chosen to lead the

Irish forces then in Ulster, and met defeat at Omagh, Donegal. The English commander, Sir Charles Coote, had promised quarter to the Irish, but broke his word, executed the bishop on June 23, and impaled his head outside Enniskillen castle.

MAC MAHON, HUGH (d. 1737). Bishop of Clogher, Ireland, he was appointed to Armagh in 1714, the first resident primate in twenty-three years. The penal laws, however, generally drove him into the countryside. Though often on the run, he managed to write a history of the primatial rights of his see at the request of the pope.

MAC MAHON, MARIE EDMÉ PATRICK MAURICE DE (1808–1893), president. Born in Sully, Saône-et-Loire, France, on July 13, he acted as Gen. Achard's aide in Algeria in 1830, served in the army there from 1834 to 1854, fought in the Crimean War, helped to break the siege of Sebastapol in 1855, and was created marshal and duc de Magenta on the battlefield of Solferino, Italy, in 1859. He became governor general of Algeria in 1864, was recalled to France in 1870, wounded in the war with Prussia, and surrendered at Sedan. In 1871 he led troops to victory over forces of the French commune and was elected president of France in 1873. He resigned in 1879 after the defeat of the Conservative party and lived in retirement at Montcresson, Loiret, France, until his death there on Oct. 16.

MAC MANUS, SEUMAS (1861–1960), author. Born in County Donegal, Ireland, he came to the United States in 1899, began writing for magazines and in 1900 had the first of his thirty books, *Through the Turf Smoke*, published. He married the Irish poet, Anna Johnston, in 1901, and on her death in 1911 married Catalina Paez. He received an LL.D. from Notre Dame in 1917, and died in New York City on Oct. 23. Among his books are *Donegal Fairy Stories* (1900), *Top O' the Mornin'* (1920), *The Story of the Irish Race* (1921), *Dark Patrick* (1939), *The Rocky Road to Dublin* (1947), and *Heavy Hangs the Golden Grain* (1950).

MAC NEILL, EOIN (1867–1945), historian. Born in Glenarm, Antrim, Ireland, on May 15, he studied at St. Malachy's, Belfast, and the Royal University, and became a law clerk. He studied Gaelic on the Aran Islands, worked on the origin of the language and with Frs. Edmund Hogan, Eugene O'Growney, Douglas Hyde, and others founded the Gaelic League in 1893 to revive the old language. He was its secretary, edited the *Gaelic Journal*, married Agnes Moore in 1898, taught mediaeval history at University College, Dublin, and turned to politics. He became a member of the Irish Volunteers, worked with nationalist extremists, became a leading officer, edited the weekly

Irish Volunteer, but opposed the Easter-week uprising and was denounced as a traitor. After a year in a British prison he helped to organize the Sinn Fein, was in parliament from 1918 to 1925, speaker of the dail in 1921, minister of education in 1922 and a member of the committee which framed the constitution, and representative of the boundary commission in 1924–25. He was again denounced by his associates, lost his political posts, returned to historical writing, and was chairman of the historical manuscripts commission after 1928. He wrote *Phases of Irish History* (1919) and *Celtic Ireland* (1921), *Place Names of Clare*, and *St. Patrick*. He died in Dublin on Oct. 15.

MAC NEVEN, WILLIAM JAMES (1763–1841). Born in Ballynahowna, Galway, Ireland, on Mar. 21, he studied at Prague and Vienna, practiced medicine in Dublin, was imprisoned in 1798 for political activity, and exiled. He served in the Irish brigade of the French army and in 1805 went to New York. He taught at the College of Physicians and Surgeons until 1826, when he helped found the rival Rutgers Medical School; this failed in 1830. He was co-editor of the *New York Medical and Philosophical Journal and Review* and wrote several books, including *An Exposition of the Atomic Theory*. He died on July 12.

MACRA, ST. (d. 287), martyr. She is said to have been captured in Fismes, France, and brutally tortured and put to death there for her faith. F. D. Jan. 6.

MACRINA THE ELDER, ST. (d. 340?). Grandmother of SS. Basil the Great and Gregory of Nyssa, she suffered with her husband the loss of their home in Neo-Caesarea, Pontus, and possessions and went into exile in a nearby forest, in two separate persecutions by the Roman authorities. F. D. Jan. 14.

MACRINA THE YOUNGER, ST. (330?–379). Born in Caesarea in Cappadocia of SS. Basil the Elder and Emmelia, the eldest of their ten children, she helped educate her younger brothers and sisters, among them SS. Basil the Great, Peter of Sebastea, and Gregory of Nyssa. On the death of her father she and her mother established a convent on the family estate on the River Iris in Pontus. When her mother died she disposed of her wealth to live a life of poverty and prayer. F. D. July 19.

MACROBIUS, ST. (d. 321?), martyr. *See* Julian, St.

MAC SWINEY, TERENCE JAMES (1880–1920), mayor. Born on Mar. 28, he had a stormy political career, was jailed after the uprising of 1916, was exiled, and succeeded the murdered Thomas MacCurtain as lord mayor of Cork. He wrote *Principles of Freedom*, and was the center of ethical controversy when he entered a seventy-four-day hunger strike in protest against English rule, which began in a Cork jail and ended in his death in Brixton prison, London, on Oct. 25.

MADDEN, HENRY (1698–1748), composer. Born in Verdun, France, son of an Irish nobleman who went into exile with King James II of England, he was educated by private tutors until he entered a Jesuit seminary. Ordained in 1730, he served as master of music in the Tours cathedral and composed many masses, motets, cantatas, and short orchestral pieces. He was a friend of François and Nicholas Couperin and of André Campa, court composers to King Louis XV. Fr. Madden (also known as Abbé Madin) became master of the king's chapel in 1737 and in 1742 succeeded Campa as master of the king's music and published a treatise on counterpoint. He died at Versailles, France.

MADDEN, JOHN T. (1882–1948), economist. Born in Worcester, Massachuetts, on Oct. 26, he studied at New York University, became a certified public accountant, taught at his college in 1917, and became dean of its school of commerce in 1925. He wrote widely on inflation, currency stabilization, and international finance, was president of the International Accountants Society from 1929 until his death in New York City on July 2, was a governor of the New York Curb Exchange, and was decorated by Romania and Belgium.

MADELGISILUS, ST. (d. 655?). He is said to have gone with St. Fursey from Ireland to England and to Gaul, to have become a Benedictine monk at St. Riquier, then retired, with St. Vulgan, to become a recluse near Monstrelet, France. He is also called Mauguille. F. D. May 30.

MADEN. *See* Madron, St.

MADERN. *See* Madron, St.

MADERNA, CARLO (1556–1629), architect. Born in Bissone, Lombardy, Italy, he was commissioned in 1605 to extend St. Peter's so that it was changed in form from a Greek to a Latin cross. Among other works are the baroque façades of St. Susanna, the Incurabili, and St. Francesca Romana, and the interior of Sant' Andrea del Valle.

MADERNO, STEFANO (1576–1636), sculptor. Born probably near Como, Italy, he gained attention by his exact reproduction of the body of St. Cecilia for the tomb in her church in Trastevere, Rome. He did other statues there, including bas-reliefs in the Pauline chapel of Santa Maria Maggiore, but gave up art when he was given a position in the excise office, and died in Rome.

MADIN, ABBÉ. *See* Madden, Henry.

MADRON, ST. (d. 545?). He probably passed from Wales to Brittany, since a holy well at Madron's chapel in Cornwall was visited even by Protestants well into the seventeenth century. However, he may be the same as St.

Padarn, St. Medran, or Matronus (Maden, Madern), a follower of St. Tudwal. F. D. May 17.

MADRUZZI, CHRISTOPHER (1512–1578), cardinal. Born in Trent, France, on July 5, he studied at Padua and Bologna, received numerous canonries from 1529 to 1537, and in 1539 was appointed prince-bishop of Trent, whereupon he was ordained and in 1542 consecrated. He served on several diplomatic missions for Kings Charles V and Ferdinand I, fought Protestantism, was the emperor's representative at the Diet of Ratisbon in 1541, and one of the leaders in the reform movement at the Council of Trent. Appointed administrator of Brixen, Italy, in 1543, he was created a cardinal that year, resigned the see in 1567, and spent the rest of his life in Italy as cardinal-bishop of Sabina, Palestrina, and Porto. He died in Tivoli, Italy, on July 5.

MAEDOC. *See* Aidan, St. (d. 626).

MAEDHOG, ST. (6th century). An associate of St. Finan, he was abbot of several Irish monasteries, including one at Clonmore. He is also known as Aedhan. F. D. Apr. 11.

MAEL, ST. (6th century). He went with St. Cadfan to Wales from Brittany, and then became a recluse on the isle of Bardsey. F. D. May 13.

MAELBRIGTE. *See* Marianus Scotus.

MAELMUIRE O'GORMAN, ST. (12th century). He was abbot of Knock, Ireland, wrote a menology in verse, and died after 1167. F. D. July 3.

MAELOR. *See* Maglorius, St.

MAERLANT, JACOB VON (1235?–1300?), poet. A Flemish poet of the Middle Ages, his name is from Maerlant on the island of Voorne where he lived as a sexton. He was town clerk in Damme, near Bruges, and died sometime after 1291. He wrote romantic poems in his youth, based on French and Latin sources, but in later years turned to more serious themes and was so successful he is called the father of Flemish poetry. Among his poems are the unfinished *Spiegel Historiael*, begun in 1283, a chronicle based on Vincent of Beauvais; *Wapene Martijn*, a dialogue; *Heimlicheit der Heimlicheden*, a political treatise; *Rijmbijbel*, a scriptural history; and *Van dem Lande van Oversee*, a call to the crusades.

MAES, CAMILLUS PAUL (1846–1915), bishop. Born in Courtrai, Belgium, on Mar. 13, he studied at St. Amandus, seminaries in Rouler and Bruges, and Louvain. He was ordained in Mechlin in 1868, did pastoral work in Michigan, and became chancellor of the diocese of Detroit in 1880. In 1885 he was consecrated third bishop of Covington, Kentucky. He built a stone Gothic cathedral and the first parish school, was an opponent of Archbishop Ireland's Faribault plan, established some thirty

parishes, and extended mission work into eastern Kentucky. In 1894 he founded the Priests' Eucharistic League and in 1895, its magazine, *Emmanuel* (which he edited until 1903), was chairman of the board of bishops for the American College, Louvain, secretary of the board of trustees of Catholic University (whose founding he had strongly advocated in 1887), and founded the *Christian Year* in 1912. He died in Covington on May 11.

MAFALDA, ST. (1203–1252). She was the daughter of King Sancho I of Portugal, and sister of SS. Sanchia and Teresa. After her marriage at eleven to her close kinsman, King Henry I of Castile, was nullified by the pope, she entered the Cistercian convent at Arouca, Portugal, where she founded a hostel for travelers and a home for widows. Her cult was approved in 1793. F. D. May 2.

MAFFEI, BERNARDINO (1514–1549), cardinal. Born in Bergamo, Italy, on Jan. 27, he studied law at Padua, acted as secretary to Cardinal Alessandro Farnese and Pope Paul III, was appointed bishop of Massa Maritima, archbishop of Chieti in 1547, and cardinal two years later. He died in Rome on Aug. 1. He was the author of a commentary on Cicero's letters.

MAFFEI, FRANCESCO (d. 1660?), painter. A native of Vincenza, Italy, he studied under Peranda and executed paintings noted for their coloring and imitative of Paul Veronese for churches in many of the cities of Lombardy. He died in Padua, Italy.

MAFFEI, FRANCESCO SCIPIONE DI (1675–1755), archaeologist. Born in Verona, Italy, on June 1, the marquess dabbled in poetry, had a brief army career, and helped to edit a newspaper at Padua. In 1710 he settled down, made a study of manuscripts at Turin and arranged the royal library there, toured Europe seeking art objects, and eventually built a museum which he bequeathed to Verona. He published a valuable study of mediaeval documents, *Istoria diplomatica*; a defense of the Jesuit position on grace against the stand taken by the Jansenists; a treatise against dueling; another to show that the orders of knighthood dated from the crusades; studies of the antiquities of Verona and France; editions of SS. Hilary, Jerome, and Zeno; plays (including the popular tragedy, *Merope*); and works in several other fields. He died in Verona on Feb. 11.

MAFFEI, GIOVANNI PIETRO (1535–1603), author. Born in Bergamo, Italy, he became a Jesuit at Rome in 1565, and a noted lecturer at the Roman College. He wrote *Historiae Indicae* and a life of St. Ignatius Loyola.

MAFFEI, MARIO (d. 1537), bishop. A native of Volterra, Italy, and brother of Raffaelo and Antonio (who was involved in the Pazzi plot to assassinate the Medici), he became nuncio to France, prefect of the building of St. Peters' in 1507, and bishop of Aquino and Cavaillon. He died on June 23.

MAFFEI, RAFFAELO (1451–1522), author. Born in Volterra, Italy, on Feb. 17, son of Gherardo Maffei (secretary to Popes Pius II, Paul II, and Sixtus IV), he studied in Rome from 1466 to 1477, and accompanied Cardinal Louis of Aragon to Hungary. On his return he settled in Volterra, where he established an academy and founded a monastery. A leading humanist, he wrote the encyclopedic *Commentariorum rerum urbanarum*, on geography, anthropology, and philology; biographies of popes; volumes of theology and philosophy; and translations of Homer and Xenophon and of SS. John of Damascus and Andrew of Crete. He died in Rome on Jan. 25.

MAFFEO, VEGIO (1406–1458), poet. Born in Lodi, Italy, he went to Rome where he became a secretary of Pope Eugene IV. An outstanding Latin poet, he wrote *Astyanax vellus aureum* and *Aeneidos supplementum* (1471), a continuation of Homer's epic; he also wrote religious works in prose.

MAFFI, PIETRO (1858–1931), cardinal. Born in Italy, he was ordained, became archbishop of Pisa and cardinal-priest in 1907, and died in Pisa, Italy, on Mar. 17.

MAGALHÃES, GABRIEL DE (1609–1677), missioner. Born in Pedrogão, Portugal, he became a Jesuit, was sent to India in 1634 and China in 1640, was honored by the emperor, twice escaped death during persecutions, and wrote *Nouvelle relation de la Chine*.

MAGALOTTI, HUGOLINO, BL. (d. 1373). Born near Camerino, Italy, he became a Franciscan tertiary and lived as a hermit. His cult was confirmed in 1856. F. D. Dec. 11.

MAGALOTTI, BL. NICOLINO (d. 1370). A Franciscan tertiary, he lived for thirty years as a recluse near Camerino, Italy. His cult was confirmed in 1856. F. D. Nov. 29.

MAGAUD, ANTOINE DOMINIQUE (1817–1899), painter. Born in Marseilles, France, he went to Paris, where he studied under Léon Cogniet, and developed into an effective portrait painter and landscapist. He decorated many public and church buildings in his native city; his masterpiece is the gallery of fifteen canvases executed for the Marseilles Religious Association, depicting the benefits of Christian civilization. He was president of the École des Beaux Arts in Marseilles, France, where he died.

MAGDALVEUS, ST. (d. 776?). Born in Verdun, France, he became a Benedictine at St. Vannes, and about 736 was made bishop of Verdun. F. D. Oct. 5.

MAGELLAN, FERDINAND (1480?–1521), explorer. Born in Saborosa, Portugal, son of the mayor, he was raised at the court, where he studied astronomy and navigation. In 1505 he accompanied Francisco d'Almeida on a voyage to the East Indies, participated in the conquest of Malacca in 1511, and was wounded the next year on an expedition to Morocco. He left the Portuguese court when Almeida reported unfavorably on his conduct and went to Spain, where in 1518 King Charles I appointed him commander in chief of a five-ship fleet which sailed in 1519 to seek passages to the Moluccas and the East. Attempts were made to sail up Brazilian and Argentine rivers, and a mutiny in 1520 resulted in the execution of two of his captains, but Magellan persisted, discovered the straits which have been named for him, and entered the Pacific Ocean, which he named. After four months of hardship he reached the Philippines, was well received on Cebu, but was killed by poison arrows on Mactan on Apr. 27. The *Victoria*, under Sebastian del Cano, returned to Spain and was the first ship to circumnavigate the world.

MAGENULF, ST. (d. 857?). Of a noble Westphalian family, he was the godchild of Charlemagne, who sent him to the cathedral school at Paderborn. He was ordained and founded a convent at Böddeken, near Paderborn, Germany. He is also called Méen and Meinulf. F. D. Oct. 5.

MAGGI, BL. SEBASTIAN (d. 1496). Born in Brescia, Italy, he joined the Dominicans when fifteen and became a successful preacher. He was Savonarola's confessor for a time and appointed him master of novices at Bologna. He was elected vicar of the Lombard province twice and died in Genoa, Italy. His cult was confirmed in 1760. F. D. Dec. 16.

MAGIN CATALA (1761–1830), missioner. Born in Montblanch, Catalonia, Spain, on Jan. 29, he became a Franciscan in 1777 and was ordained in 1785. He was sent to Mexico City in 1786, taught at San Fernando College, served as chaplain on a ship sailing as far north as Vancouver, and was assigned to the Santa Clara mission in California from 1794 until his death on Nov. 22.

MAGINN, EDWARD (1802–1849), bishop. Born in Fintona, Ireland, on Dec. 16, he studied at the Irish College in Paris, was ordained in 1825, and did parish work in Ireland. He became coadjutor bishop of Derry in 1846. He attacked the secret agrarian societies and the English government for its mistreatment of the poor, its land policy, and its incompetence during the famine of 1847–49. He worked for Catholic Emancipation, tried to heal the breach between O'Connell and the Young Ireland Movement, and supported plans to establish a Catholic university in Dublin. He died in Derry, Ireland, on Jan. 17.

MAGINNIS, CHARLES DONAGH (1867–1955), architect. Born in Londonderry, Ulster,

Ireland, he was trained in Dublin, became associated with Edmund Wheelwright in Boston, Massachusetts, in 1885 as designer, and founded his own firm in 1898. He three times was a gold-medal winner of the American Institute of Architects (and was its president in 1937–38), received the Laetare Medal in 1924, became a Knight of Malta in 1945, and received honorary degrees from Boston College, Harvard, Holy Cross, and Tufts. Among his outstanding monuments are the National Shrine of the Immaculate Conception and Trinity College chapel, Washington; the cathedral, Baltimore; buildings on the campus of Boston College, Holy Cross, and Notre Dame; the Carmelite convent, Santa Clara; the bronze doors of St. Patrick's cathedral, New York City; and many churches, hospitals, and schools across the country. He died in Boston on Feb. 15.

MAGINUS, ST. (d. 304?), martyr. Born in Tarragona, Spain, he converted the people of his area and was beheaded during the Diocletian persecution. F. D. Aug. 25.

MAGISTRIS, SIMONE DE (1728–1802). An Oratorian at Rome, he was a noted orientalist and antiquarian whom Pope Pius VI appointed titular bishop of Cyrene and provost of the Congregation for revising the oriental liturgy. He also was an authority on scripture, wrote a commentary on Daniel, lives of the Roman martyrs, and an edition of Dionysius of Alexandria. He died on Oct. 6.

MAGLIABECHI, ANTONIO (1633–1714). Born in Florence, Italy, on Oct. 29, he became a goldsmith, an avid book collector, and in 1673 was made librarian by Grand Duke Cosimo III of Tuscany. He accumulated 30,000 volumes, which he left as a public library (later the Biblioteca Nazionale); his personal fortune went to the poor. He died at the monastery of Santa Maria Novella, Florence, on July 4.

MAGLORIUS, ST. (d. 586?), bishop. Born in Glamorgan, Wales, son of St. Umbrafael, he was educated by St. Illtyd and became a monk under St. Samson, whom he accompanied to Brittany. He became abbot of a monastery at Kerfunt and is said to have succeeded Samson as abbot and bishop of Dol, Gaul. In old age he retired to the island of Sark, where he built a monastery. He is also called Maelor. F. D. Oct. 24.

MAGNER, FRANCIS J. (1887–1947), bishop. Born in Wilmington, Illinois, on Mar. 18, he studied at Loyola, Chicago, St. Mary's College, Kansas, and the North American College, Rome, and was ordained in 1913. He did parish work and was pastor of St. Mary's in Evanston from 1927 to 1941, when he was consecrated bishop of Marquette, Michigan. He died there on June 13.

MAGNERICUS, ST. (d. 596), bishop. He was raised in the household of St. Nicetius, bishop of Trèves, Gaul, who ordained him and with whom he went into exile when Clotaire I showed anger over his excommunication. Magnericus became the first Frankish bishop of Trèves about 566, was a close friend of St. Gregory of Tours, gave refuge to the bishop of Marseilles (who was exiled in 585), and impressed his people by his piety and learning. F. D. July 25.

MAGNIEN, ALPHONSE (1837–1902). Born in Bleymard, Mende, France, on June 9, he studied at Chirac and Orléans, was ordained in 1860, and taught at La Chapelle St. Mesmin seminary until 1862, when he joined the Sulpicians. He taught at Nantes and Rodez until 1869, when he became professor of philosophy and scripture at St. Mary's seminary in Baltimore, Maryland. He was appointed superior in 1878, a position he occupied until his death, helped found St. Austin's College at Catholic University, Washington, and served as theologian at the third Plenary Council in Baltimore in 1884. He died in Baltimore, Maryland, on Dec. 2.

MAGNOBODUS, ST. (7th century). A Frankish nobleman, he was appointed bishop of Angers, Gaul, by the populace and lived past 670. He is also called Mainboeuf. F. D. Oct. 16.

MAGNUS, ST. (d. 258), martyr. See Sixtus II, St.

MAGNUS, ST. (d. 273), martyr. See Craton, St.

MAGNUS, ST. (3rd century), martyr. See Aquilinus, St.

MAGNUS, ST. (d. 525). He became archbishop of Milan, Italy, in 520. F. D. Nov. 5.

MAGNUS, ST. (d. 660), bishop. Born in Avignon, France, he became governor of that city. After his wife's death he became a Benedictine at Lérins, where his son, St. Agricola, had been, and in 656 became bishop of Avignon. F. D. Aug. 19.

MAGNUS, ST. (d. 660?). Born in Venice, Italy, he became bishop of Oderzo, Italy, on the Adriatic and, as the Lombards advanced, moved his see to Heraclea (Citta Nuova). F. D. Oct. 6.

MAGNUS, ST. (d. 666?). He worked in the European missions with the Irish SS. Columban and Gall and became abbot-founder of the Benedictine monastery of Füssen, Bavaria. F. D. Sept. 6.

MAGNUS (d. 1116). Son of Erling, governor of Orkney Islands, Earl Magnus of Orkney accompanied King Magnus of Norway on a raid of the Scottish coast, refused to fight against those who were not his enemies, fled inland and took refuge with King Malcolm III. When his cousin seized power in the islands, the earl invaded and became joint ruler, but was later tricked and slain on Apr. 16. He long was called a martyr, but was slain for political reasons only.

MAGNUS LADULOS (d. 1290), king of Sweden. He defeated and deposed his brother Waldemar (king in 1250–75), continued the latter's reforms (serfdom had been abolished and commerce developed), set up a hereditary nobility, strengthened ecclesiastical power, and saw the increase of wealth (from mining and trade) among the burghers.

MAGNUS, OLAUS (1490–1558), geographer. Born in Skeninge, Sweden, he studied in Germany until 1517, when he became cathedral provost at Strengnas. He went to Rome in 1537 as secretary to his brother, Archbishop John Magnus of Upsala, when his property was confiscated as Sweden embraced Protestantism, and was appointed John's successor on the latter's death in 1544 but never took the office. He had early become interested in geography and in 1539 published an important map of the northern world. He attended the Council of Trent from 1545 to 1549 and died at Rome on Aug. 1. He was the author of works on the history, geography, natural resources, and customs of Scandinavia.

MAGNUS, VALERIANUS (1586–1661), theologian. Born in Milan, Italy, probably of the noble de Magni family, he joined the Capuchins in Prague, became provincial, and in 1626 apostolic missionary for Germany, Hungary, and Poland. He served on diplomatic missions for Emperors Ferdinand II and Ferdinand III and Polish King Wladislaw IV. He wrote theological treatises, became embroiled in the controversy between the Jesuits and Capuchins, was ordered to Rome for his *Contra imposturas Jesuitarum* in 1659, and was arrested in Vienna in 1661 when he refused to go. Released at the request of Emperor Ferdinand III, he died at Salzburg, Austria, on July 29, while on the way to Rome.

MAGSAYSAY, RAMÓN (1907–1957), president. Born in Zambales, Luzon, the Philippines, on Aug. 31, son of a blacksmith and teacher, he worked his way through college in Manila, became a mechanic, and was manager of a bus-transportation firm at the outbreak of World War II. He became a guerrilla leader, was in charge of a force of 12,000 men who harried the Japanese, and in 1944 was named governor of his native province. He was elected to congress in 1946 and 1948, and in 1950 was made secretary of national defense. In this post he reformed the army and set about eradicating extensive corruption in public posts and the power of the communist rebels known as Hukbalahaps. He reclaimed many of the latter, often by personal conference, and by virtue of his anti-communist and pro-American position was in 1953 elected third president of the Philippines by an overwhelming majority. He,

several aides, government officials, and Benito Ebuen, commanding general of the air force, died on Mar. 17 when their plane crashed on a flight from Cebu City to Manila.

MAGUIRE, JOHN FRANCIS (1815–1872). Born in Cork, Ireland, he studied law, was called to the bar in 1843, was editor-publisher of the *Catholic Examiner* of Cork, and represented Dungarvan and Cork in parliament from 1852 until his death. He was a supporter of home rule, was several times mayor of Cork, and wrote *The Industrial Movement in Ireland, The Pontificate of Pius IX, Rome and Its Rulers, The Irish American*, and a biography, *Father Mathew*. He died in Cork on Nov. 1.

MAHANES, ST. (d. 339), martyr. *See* Sapor, St.

MAHARSAPOR, ST. (d. 421), martyr. A noble Persian, he was seized with others for destroying a temple, tortured, imprisoned for three years, and thrown into a cistern to die of starvation. F. D. Oct. 10.

MAHER, MICHAEL (1860–1918), philosopher. Born in Leighlinbridge, Ireland, he became a Jesuit in 1880 at Stonyhurst, and taught psychology in 1885–91 and 1897–1903. He also did mission work in Edinburgh, wrote the Stonyhurst edition of *Psychology*, received his doctorate at London, and died in Petworth, England, on Sept. 3.

MAHLER, GUSTAV (1860–1911), composer. Born in Kalist, Bohemia, on July 7, the second of twelve children, he studied at the Vienna conservatory, where he met Anton Bruckner in 1878, became choirmaster at Hall, Austria, in the summer of 1880, and in that year wrote *Das Klagende Lied*. He also was choirmaster at Laibach (1881) and Olomouc (1882), and chorus master of the Italian opera in Vienna (1883), wrote *Lieder eines fahrenden Gesellen*, and moved on to Cassel, Prague, and Leipzig (1883–88). He was director in Budapest for two years, drawing praise from Brahms; at the municipal theater in Hamburg in 1891–97; then of the court opera in Vienna until 1907. He became a convert in 1895. He made several visits to the United States and conducted in New York. His ten symphonies (the last was unfinished) were composed between 1888 and 1910; *Das Lied von der Erde*, with lyrics from *Die chinesische Flöte* of Hans Bethge (1908); and songs to poems by Friedrich Röckert, notably *Kindertotenlieder*, (1902), comprise his major productions. He died in Vienna on May 18.

BRUNO WALTER, *Gustav Mahler*, trans. James Galston (London, 1937).

MAHONEY, BERNARD JOSEPH (1875–1939), bishop. Born in Albany, New York, on July 24, he studied at Mt. St. Mary's, Maryland, and the North American College, Rome, and was ordained in 1904. He did parish work in Troy, New York, was spiritual director of the North American College for thirteen years, beginning in 1909, and was appointed bishop of Sioux Falls, South Dakota, in 1922. He died in Rochester, Minnesota, on Mar. 20.

MAHONY, VEN. CHARLES (d. 1679), martyr. An Irish Franciscan, he was shipwrecked and captured off North Wales, and tortured and executed at Ruthin, Denbighshire, on Aug. 12, when not yet forty, on the charge of being a priest.

MAHONY, FRANCIS SYLVESTER (1804–1866), author. Born in Cork, Ireland, on Dec. 31, he studied at Clongowes Wood College and St. Acheul, France, joined the Jesuits in 1821 and finished his studies in Rome. In 1825 he returned to Clongowes, studied at Freiburg and Florence, left the Jesuits, studied for the priesthood in the Irish College in Rome, and was ordained in 1832 in Lucca. After engaging in pastoral work in Cork, he had a disagreement with his superiors, went to London in 1834, and for the last thirty years of his life did not exercise his priestly functions. He joined the editorial staff of *Fraser's Magazine* and Dickens' *Bentley's Magazine* in 1837, served as Rome correspondent for the *Daily News* from 1846 to 1858, and then went to Paris as correspondent for the *Globe*. He remained there until his death on May 18. He was the author of the *Reliques of Father Prout* and *The Bells of Shandon*, which he wrote under the name of Fr. Prout. His name is sometimes spelled O'Mahony.

MAI, ANGELO (1782–1854), cardinal. Born in Schilpario, Italy, on Mar. 7, he joined the Jesuits, became an authority in palaeography, and in 1811 was appointed to the Ambrosian Library, Milan. He discovered many new texts of classical authors, mainly in palimpsests, among them works of Cicero, Isaeus, Plautus, Philo, Marcus Aurelius, Eusebius. In 1819 he left the Jesuits, was appointed chief librarian of the Vatican Library, and uncovered new treasures there, among them six lost books of Cicero's *De republica*. He published works of more than 350 classicists, early Fathers, Italian humanists, Latin poets of the fourteenth and fifteenth centuries, an important Greek manuscript of the Bible, and several major collections: *Scriptorum veterum, Classici auctores, Spicilegium romanum,* each in ten volumes, and the seven-volume *Nova patrum bibliotheca.* He was made a cardinal in 1838 and an associate of the French Institute in 1842. He died in Albano, Italy, on Sept. 9.

MAIGNAN, EMMANUEL (1601–1676). Born in Toulouse, France, on July 17, he studied at the Jesuit college there and in 1619 joined the Order of Minims. He was in Rome from 1636 to 1650, taught at Trinitá dei Monti,

then was provincial at Toulouse until 1653. He wrote scientific and theological treatises, devoted himself to physics and mathematics, and died in Toulouse on Oct. 29.

MAILDULF, ST. (d. 673). He came to England from Ireland and founded the monastery of Malmesbury, where he taught St. Aldhelm among others. F. D. May 17.

MAILLA, JOSEPH ANNA MARIE DE MOYRIA DE (1669–1748), missioner. Born at Château Maillac, France, on Dec. 16, he became a Jesuit in 1686, was sent to China in 1701, and became a resident of the Chinese court. He was selected by Emperor Khang-hi to make a cartological survey of the empire and was made a mandarin as a reward. In 1730 he completed a French translation of an extract from the Chinese annals prepared by the emperor in Manchurian, which was published in twelve volumes in France as *Histoire générale de la Chine* almost thirty years after his death in Peking on June 28. He also translated into Chinese the lives of saints and meditations on the gospels, and was the author of several of the *Lettres édifiantes.*

MAILLARD, OLIVIER (1430?–1502). Born in Juignac, Brittany, he joined the Franciscans of the Observance, and became known for his preaching. He denounced Louis XI, who threatened to throw him in the river; supported Jeanne de Valois when she was repudiated by her husband, the duke of Orléans; and in 1488 at the request of Pope Innocent VIII attempted, unsuccessfully, to secure Charles VIII's renunciation of the Pragmatic Sanction of Bourges. In 1487 he was elected vicar general of the Observants north of the Alps and re-elected in 1493–96 and 1499–1502. He then retired to a monastery at Toulouse, France, where he died on July 22.

MAILLÉ, BL. JOAN MARIE DE (1331–1414). Daughter of Baron Hardouin VI of Maillé, she was born in Roche-St. Quentin, Touraine, France, and was married to Baron Robert de Sillé. On his death sixteen years later, in 1362, she gave her possessions to the Carthusians of Liget and became a Franciscan tertiary, but was disowned by her family and forced to beg for a living. She lived as a recluse at Planche-de-Vaux, near Cléry, and in 1389 went to Tours, France, where she died on Mar. 28, after years devoted to helping prisoners and the poor. Her cult was approved in 1871. F. D. Nov. 6 (also, Mar. 29).

MAIMBOD, ST. (d. 880?), martyr. An Irishman, also known as Mainboeuf, he became a missioner to Alsace, and is said to have been slain near Kaltenbrunn by the pagans among whom he had been preaching. F. D. Jan. 23.

MAIMBOURG, LOUIS (1610–1686), historian. Born in Nancy, France, on Jan. 10, he became a Jesuit in 1626, and became known for his preaching, his opposition to Jansenism and Protestantism, and as the author of many works on church history. He was so active as a defender of the Gallican Church that Pope Innocent XI ordered him expelled from the Jesuits in 1681. He retired to St. Victor abbey in Paris, on a pension granted by King Louis XIV, and continued his writing until his death there on Aug. 13. He wrote histories of Arianism, Iconoclasm, and the Crusades, but works on Calvinism, Lutheranism, the Church in France, and the pontificate of Leo the Great were placed on the Index. He died in Paris on Aug. 13.

MAINBOEUF. *See* Magnobodus, St.; also, Maimbod, St.

MAINE. *See* Mewan, St.

MAINE DE BIRAN, FRANÇOIS PIERRE GONTHIER (1766–1824), philosopher. Born in Grateloup, Dordogne, France, on Nov. 29, he studied at Périgueux, served in the army, opposed the excesses of the revolution, and became a member of the Council of Five Hundred in 1797. His royalist sympathies forced him to retire to Grateloup, where he devoted himself to philosophical writings and in 1803 won a prize from the Institute for his *De l'influence de l'habitude sur la faculté de penser.* In 1809 he was elected to parliament, and in 1815 and 1820 to the chamber of deputies. He returned to the Church in his last years and died in Paris on July 16.

MAINTENON, FRANÇOISE D'AUBIGNÉ DE (1635–1719). Born on Nov. 27 in a prison in Niort, France (her father, Constant d'Aubigné, son of Henry IV's general, had been imprisoned there), she lived on Martinique until her father's death in 1645, when she returned to France and was raised as a Protestant by an aunt. Transferred to the care of a Catholic relative by court order, she returned to her faith when fourteen. She married the noted wit, Paul Scarron, in 1652, and their salon became a literary and intellectual gathering place. Impoverished on his death in 1660, she became governess in 1669 of the illegitimate children of Louis XIV and his mistress, Mme. de Montespan, and was given a sizable income and a house at Vaugirard to raise them. In 1674 she took up residence at the court when Louis legitimized and brought the children there. She incurred the enmity of Mme. de Montespan when Louis showered her with favors, including raising her estate of Maintenon to a marquisate in 1678, and replaced de Montespan as the king's mistress. She was made first lady in waiting to the dauphiness in 1684, and in 1685 was married secretly to Louis. She exercised great influence over the king, and his ministers usually discussed affairs of state with her before presenting them to Louis. Though probably in favor of the revoca-

tion of the Edict of Nantes, she was not responsible for this action, as was once believed. She was a generous patroness of the arts and literature, fought the spread of quietism, and was noted for her charitable work. She founded a home for girls at St. Cyr in 1686, which was endowed by the king. She retired to St. Cyr on the king's death in 1715, and died there on Apr. 15. Her voluminous correspondence gives a vivid picture of France in the late seventeenth and early eighteenth century; she also wrote essays and letters on education which were widely admired.

MAISONNEUVE, PAUL DE CHOMEDEY DE (d. 1676). Born in Champagne, France, he served in the Dutch War, and was sent to Canada as commandant with orders to make a settlement at Ville-Marie, the island of Montreal. Although opposed by Gov. Montmagny, he landed in 1642 and remained there as chief magistrate until 1665. He encouraged colonization, agriculture, and education, arranged marriages, defeated the Iroquois as they made constant raids and finally gained their confidence, and brought several religious orders to the city from France on later trips. When the Company of Montreal ended with Louis XIV's acquisition of Canada, Maisonneuve returned to Paris, where he died on Sept. 9. He had left his personal wealth and proprietory income from Ville-Marie to the religious foundations there.

MAISTRE, JOSEPH MARIE DE (1753–1821), philosopher. Born in Chambéry, Savoy, son of the president of the senate there and of French origin, he was educated by the Jesuits, became a magistrate in 1774, assistant fiscal advocate general in 1780, and senator in 1788. The French invasion in 1792 caused him to leave Savoy and he acted as ambassador of the king of Sardinia at Lausanne until 1796, when the monarch was deposed. In that year his *Considérations sur la France* appeared and, though it was banned in France, circulated and had great influence. When the king regained his throne, de Maistre became grand chancellor in 1799 and was Sardinian ambassador to Russia from 1802 to 1817. On his return to Turin he was minister of state. He was one of the leading opponents of eighteenth-century rationalism and Gallicanism and believed in the theory of authority in every sphere: in the state, the supremacy of the monarch; in the Church, the infallibility of the pope; in the universe, the power and authority of God. His outstanding works were *Du Pape* (1819), *L'Église gallicane* (1821), *Les soirées de St. Pétersbourg* (1821), and *Correspondance*, a collection of some 600 letters. He died in Turin, Italy, on Feb. 26.

MAISTRE, XAVIER DE (1763–1852), novelist. Younger brother of Joseph de Maistre, he was born in Chambéry, Savoy, served in the Sardinian army until 1792 when the French annexed Savoy and he was forced to flee, and in 1799 joined the Austro-Russian forces in Italy. He went to Russia in 1800, became librarian of the Admiralty Museum in 1805, and a general in the Russian army during the Caucasian War. After his marriage to a lady in waiting of the empress, he considered himself a Russian citizen, and except for a brief visit to Savoy in 1825 and Paris in 1839, he spent the rest of his life in St. Petersburg, Russia, where he died on June 12. His short romances include: *Voyage autour de ma chambre* (1794), *Le Lépreux de la cite d'Aoste* (1811), *Les prisonniers du Caucase*, and *La jeune Sibérienne*.

MAJALI, BL. GULIANO (d. 1470). A Benedictine at San Martino delle Scale, Sicily, he was highly regarded by civil and Church leaders and spent his last six years as a recluse. F. D. Oct. 4.

MAJANO, BENEDETTO DA (1442–1498), sculptor. Born in Majano, Tuscany, he studied wood mosaic as a youth but turned to marble when, reportedly, some of his carvings were destroyed during a trip to King Corvinus of Hungary, who had extended his patronage. He produced pulpits, altarpieces, busts, and statuary, and designed several buildings, notably the Strozzi palace in Florence (1489). Among his masterpieces are the pulpit of Santa Croce, Florence, depicting the life of St. Francis of Assisi; the altarpiece in Monte Oliveto church, Naples; a bust of Giotto; and the tomb of Filippo Strozzi. He died in Florence, Italy, on May 24.

MAJELLA, GERARD. *See* Gerard Majella, St.

MAJOLUS, ST. (906?–994). Born in Avignon, France, he studied at Lyons, was archdeacon in Mâcon, and was appointed bishop of Besançon. To avoid this unwilling honor he entered the Benedictines at Cluny, serving there as librarian and treasurer. In 954 he became coadjutor abbot to St. Aymard, who had gone blind; he became abbot in 965, reformed many monasteries, acted as peacemaker and counselor for several rulers, and fostered the spread of learning. He died at Souvigny, France. He is also called Mayeul. F. D. May 11.

MAJORICA, ST. (d. 484), martyr. *See* Dionysia, St.

MAJORICUS, ST. (d. 490?), martyr. Son of St. Dionysia, he was put to death in North Africa by the Arian King Huneric. F.D. Dec. 6.

MAJUNKE, PAUL (1842–1899), journalist. Born in Gross-Schmograu, Silesia, on July 14, he studied at Breslau and was ordained in 1867. He was editor of *Kölnische Zeitung* in 1869–70, of *Germania* from 1871 to 1878, and of *Korrespondenz der Zentrumsblätter* from 1878 to 1884. He was elected to the *Reichstag* in 1874 (when he was imprisoned for a year

for violating the laws concerning the press) and the Prussian house of deputies in 1878. In 1884 he was appointed parish priest of Hochkirch (now Glogau, Germany), where he remained until his death on May 21.

MALACHY, ST. (1095–1148), archbishop. Malachy O'More was born in Armagh, Ireland, the son of a schoolteacher. On the death of his parents, he lived with a hermit, Eimar, and at twenty-five was ordained by St. Celsus. After further study under St. Malchus, he was given the abbey of Bangor to reconstruct as abbot, and in 1125 became bishop of Connor, whose people had lapsed from the faith. In 1127 an invasion drove him to Iveragh, Kerry, where he resumed his monastic life. In 1129 he was named by St. Celsus to succeed him in the see of Armagh. Eight years of strife followed between his supporters and those of Murtagh (and on his death, those of Niall, brother of Celsus), who claimed the office. When Malachy finally restored order in 1137, he resigned and returned to Connor, divided that see and directed his half from Down. In 1139 he went to Rome (staying on the way at Clairvaux, where he met St. Bernard, who was to become his friend and biographer). Innocent II refused his request to be allowed to enter monastic life and made him papal legate to Ireland. He was successful in restoring ecclesiastical discipline, unified the Church in Ireland, and saw to the acceptance of the Roman over the Celtic liturgy. He died on Nov. 2 at Clairvaux on a later journey to Rome and was canonized by Pope Clement III, the first Irishman to be so honored by formal process. His so-called "prophecies of the popes," listing pontiffs from Celestine II (1143) to "the end of the world" under symbolic titles, were not "discovered" until 1595 (447 year after his death) and are considered spurious by scholars. F. D. Nov. 3.

MALAGRIDA, GABRIEL (1689–1761), missioner. Born on Sept. 18 (or Dec. 6) in Menaggio, Italy, he became a Jesuit in 1711, was sent to Brazil in 1721, and remained in the missions there, except for a return to Lisbon to be honored in 1749–51, until 1753, when he was recalled by dowager Queen Marianna. He was exiled to Setubal in 1756 when young King Joseph I banished the Jesuits. In 1758 he was falsely accused of a plot to kill the king, imprisoned for nearly three years, charged with heresy, and strangled to death at Lisbon, Portugal, on Sept. 21 by inquisition officials appointed by Prime Minister Pombal, his bitter enemy, in place of the regular judges.

MALARD, ST. (7th century). Bishop of Chartres, he attended the Council of Chalon-sur-Saône, France, in 650. F. D. Jan. 15.

MALCHUS, ST. (d. 260), martyr. *See* Alexander, St.

MALCHUS, ST. (d. 390?). Secretary to Pope Damasus, he attended a synod in 382 and worked on a revision of scripture. He was thought of as a possible successor to the papacy until unfounded rumors as to his virtue made him decide to leave Rome and seek refuge in a Syrian monastery. His biography was written by St. Jerome. F. D. Oct. 21.

MALCHUS, ST. (d. 1110), bishop. He became a Benedictine at Winchester, England, and was consecrated by St. Anselm as first bishop of Waterford, Ireland. F. D. Apr. 10.

MALCOLM I MAC DONALD (d. 954), king of Scotland. He succeeded Constantine I in 943, made a treaty with Edmund of West Saxony which gained Cumberland, but lost Northumbria in 954, and died in battle on the English-Scots border.

MALCOLM II (d. 1034), king of Scotland. He became king in 1005, succeeding his father, Kenneth II, by defeating and killing Kenneth III at Monzicvaird, Perthshire, and called his nation Scotia instead of Alban. He gained Lothian in 1018 by defeating Eadulf Cudel, and also gained control of Cambria north of the Solway. He acknowledged Canute of England in 1031 as his feudal overlord. He died on Nov. 25.

MALCOLM III CANMORE (d. 1093), king of Scotland. When Edward of Northumbria defeated Macbeth in 1054, Malcolm, son of Duncan, pursued the latter and defeated and slew him at Lumphanan, Scotland, in 1057, and was crowned king at Scone. Edgar Atheling of England fled to his court with his sisters, Margaret and Christina, and other Saxons after the battle of Hastings. Malcolm married Margaret, who had great influence on the government and the Church; together, they reformed abuses, rebuilt Iona, which had been devastated by the Danes, and set up new churches. Malcolm acknowledged the supremacy of the English kings in 1072 and 1091, but was slain in battle with William II near Alnwick, Northumberland, on Nov. 13.

MALCOLM IV (1141–1165), king of Scotland. Grandson of David I and called "the Maiden," he was crowned king at Scone in 1153. He was a weak monarch and lost Northumbria and Cumberland to Henry II of England in 1157, went with the English expedition to Toulouse in 1159, fought civil uprisings in 1160–64, and founded the abbey of Paisley. He died in Jedburgh, Scotland, on Dec. 9.

MALDONADO, JUAN (1533–1583), theologian. Born in Casas de Reina, Llerena, Spain, he took his doctorate in theology and taught at Salamanca. In 1558 he joined the Jesuits and was ordained in Rome in 1563. He then lectured at the Collège de Clermont in Paris until 1569, preached in Poitou and Poitiers, and resumed teaching from 1570 to 1576. He was

challenged for some of his utterances on the Immaculate Conception and purgatory, which were misunderstood, but was completely exonerated. He held several high posts in his Society, was appointed by Pope Gregory XIII to the commission to revise the Septuagint, and wrote an important commentary on the four gospels. He died in Rome on Jan. 5.

MALEBRANCHE, NICOLAS (1638–1715), philosopher. Born in Paris, on Aug. 6, he studied at Collège de La Marche and the Sorbonne and joined the Oratorians in 1660. His publication of *De la recherche de la verité* in 1674 marked him as a leading Cartesian. He developed the theory of occasionalism, stressed the dualism of mind and matter, and was attacked by Bossuet, Arnauld, Lamy, and others for his theory of grace and his explanation of pleasure and good. Other works include: *Conversations chrétiennes, Méditations chrétiennes et metaphysiques,* and *Traité de l'amour de Dieu.* He died in Paris on Oct. 13.

MALET, LUCAS. *See* Harrison, Mary St. Leger Kingsley.

MALHERBE, FRANÇOIS DE (1555–1628), poet. Born in Caen, Normandy, he studied at Paris, Basle, and Heidelberg, gave up law to serve Henri d'Angoulême, governor of Provence, and returned to Caen when Henri was killed. Complimentary odes to Henri IV and Marie de' Medici attracted royal attention and patronage in 1605. He ruled the literary world of Paris, purified the French language, set up exacting standards by pitiless criticism, and demanded polish and grace in the lyric. His own works include *Larmes de St. Pierre, Odes, Chansons, Stances,* and *Sonnets.* He died in Paris on Oct. 16.

MALLARD, ERNEST FRANÇOIS (1833–1894), mineralogist. Born in Châteauneuf-sur-Cher, France, on Feb. 4, he was a professor of mineralogy at École des Mines from 1872 until his death, did important research in the fields of crystallography and isomorphism, participated in the geological cartographing of France, and helped provide safer working conditions for miners by his investigations of gas and mine explosions. He was elected to the Academy of Science in 1890. He died in Paris on July 6. He contributed articles to scientific magazines and was the author of *Treatise on Geometrical and Physical Crystallography* (1879–84).

MALLEMORT, GÉRARD DE (d. 1260). Made archbishop of Bourges, France, in 1227, he founded monasteries, served as mediator between St. Louis and King Henry III of England, and defended Gascony against Simon de Montfort.

MALLINCKRODT, HERMANN VON (1821–1874), statesman. Born in Minden, Westphalia, on Feb. 5, he studied law at Berlin and Bonn, held judicial posts in the Paderborn district, and became a governor assessor in 1849. He was elected to the Prussian house of representatives in 1852, was appointed assistant in the ministry of the interior in 1859, government councilor for Düsseldorf in 1860, and elected to the North German Confederation diet in 1867 and the Prussian lower house in 1868. He was a leader of the Catholic Centre party, was strong in defending the Church, opposing the Austrian war of 1866, the federation of German states, and the Kulturkampf. He died in Berlin on May 26.

MALLINCKRODT, PAULINE (1817–1881), foundress. Born in Minden, Westphalia, on June 3, sister of Hermann, she established homes for the blind and for infants in Paderborn, and in 1849 founded the Congregation of the Sisters of Christian Charity (also known as Daughters of the Immaculate Conception) to teach the poor and care for the blind, of which she was first superior and which Pope Pius IX approved in 1863 and Pope Leo XIII confirmed in 1888. Forced into exile in 1873 by the Kulturkampf, she went to the United States and founded a provincial house in Wilkes Barre, Pennsylvania. She returned to set up a mother house near Brussels, visiting North and South America in later years. She died in Paderborn, Germany, on Apr. 30.

MALLOCK, WILLIAM HURRELL (1849–1923), novelist. Born in Cheriton Bishop, Devonshire, England, on Feb. 7, son of the local rector, William Mallock, and Margaret Froude, he was privately tutored and graduated from Oxford. In 1877 he published *The New Republic*, on contemporary religious and social thought, and satirizing Ruskin, Arnold, Pater, and other contemporaries. *The New Paul and Virginia* (1878) and *Is Life Worth Living?* (1879) followed. *The Old Order Changes* (1886) and *The Veil of the Temple* were popular novels; he also published poems, a commentary on Lucretius, and an attack on contemporary standards of wealth, *Social Equality* (1882). His interest in politics appears in *Labour and the Popular Welfare*, and *A Critical Examination of Socialism*; in religion, in *The Reconstruction of Belief*. His *Memoirs of Life and Literature* appeared in 1920. He became a convert during his last illness and died in Wincanton, England, on Apr. 2.

MALLONUS. *See* Mellonius, St.

MALLORY, STEPHEN RUSSELL (1813–1873). Son of an American engineer, he was born in Trinidad, West Indies, studied at Spring Hill, Alabama, was admitted to the Florida bar about 1839, served in the Seminole War, and was appointed collector of customs at Key West in 1845. He was elected to the United States Senate in 1851 and 1857, was chairman of the committee on naval affairs, resigned when Florida seceded, and became secretary of

the Confederate navy in 1861. He was arrested at the war's end when he fled with President Jefferson Davis, was imprisoned for ten months, and returned to law practice in Florida after his release. He died in Pensacola, Florida, on Nov. 9.

MALO, ST. (d. 621?), bishop. Born in Llancarfan, Wales, he became a monk there and was ordained. He migrated to Brittany and evangelized the area around the town now given his name, of which he became first bishop. He later settled near Saintes. He also is called Machutis and Maclou. F. D. Nov. 15.

MALONE, WILLIAM (1585–1655). Born in Dublin, Ireland, son of Simon, a merchant, he became a Jesuit at Rome in 1606, was sent as a missioner to Ireland, and recalled to Rome in 1635 to become rector of the Irish College. He was superior of the Jesuit mission in Ireland in 1647, but was captured and banished in 1649. He then was appointed rector of St. Gregory's College in Seville, Spain, where he remained until his death.

MALONEY, MARTIN (1848–1929), executive. Born in Ballingarry, Ireland, on Nov. 14, he was brought to the United States in 1854, worked in Pennsylvania mines, opened a plumbing shop in Scranton, and invented a gasoline burner for street lights which made him wealthy. He became president of the Pennsylvania Heat, Light, & Power Co., organized the United Gas Improvement Co., and was associated with other utilities organizations. His large charitable gifts helped to repair St. John Lateran, Rome, to build the church of St. Catherine, Spring Lake, New Jersey, and the Maloney Memorial Home for the Aged, Scranton, a chemical laboratory at Catholic University, and a medical clinic at the University of Pennsylvania. He was made a papal marquis by Leo XIII and a papal chamberlain by Pius X. He died in Philadelphia on May 8.

MALONEY, THOMAS J. (1859–1933), executive. Born in Covington, Kentucky, on July 12, he worked in the tobacco fields, became superintendent of manufacture for P. Lorillard Co., and vice-president when it merged with American Tobacco Co. in 1900, and president in 1911; he retired in 1924, was director of several corporations, and donated a million dollars to the diocese of Newark, New Jersey, and a quarter million to the Georgetown cancer research laboratory. He received two papal decorations and died in Teaneck, New Jersey, on Jan. 18.

MALORY, THOMAS (d. 1471). He probably was a knight of Newbold Revell, Warwickshire, England, in the service of the earl of Warwick. He failed to gain a pardon from Edward IV for his part in the War of the Roses, and transferred his property to his wife to avoid its confiscation. His *Morte d'Arthur*, published under that title by William Caxton, was probably based on a French compilation of eight or more separate romances, to which he gave a harmony, purpose, and dignity not present in earlier versions. His *Book of King Arthur and His Knights of the Round Table*, as he called his romance, is the most famous and popular of the Arthurian recensions; it also was the first work of size and importance in English prose, and had a decided influence on the development of the literary language.

MALOU, JULES EDOUARD (1810–1886), statesman. Born in Ypres, Belgium, on Oct. 19, he was minister of finance in 1844, formed a Catholic cabinet in 1846 with Count Barthélemy de Theux, served in the senate, led the moderate element after the Brussels riots of 1871, became strongly pro-clerical after 1878, and headed his government in 1884. His legislation in favor of Catholic schools led to new rioting, and he retired after two years. He died in Woluwe St. Lambert, Brabant, on July 11.

MALPIGHI, MARCELLO (1628–1694), anatomist. Born in Crevalcore, Italy, on Mar. 10, he received his degree in medicine at Bologna, occupied the chair of medicine there in 1656, was professor of theoretical medicine at Pisa from 1656 to 1659, and taught at Messina and again at Bologna. In 1692 he became physician to Pope Innocent XII and professor of medicine in the papal medical college, Rome, where he died on Nov. 29. He was the first to use the microscope in the study of anatomy; made important discoveries in the structure of the skin, kidneys, liver, and spleen; wrote a pioneer study of the embryology of the chick; and described the circulation of blood in the capillaries and the structure of the lungs. Among his works are *De pulmonibus, Anatome plantarum, De cerebro,* and *De lingua.* With Nehemiah Grew he laid the groundwork for the study of vegetable morphology.

MALRUBIUS, ST. (642?–722?). He became a monk at the monastery of St. Comgall, Bangor, Ireland, went to Scotland at twenty-nine, and founded a church and monastery at Applecross, from which he preached widely to the Picts for fifty years. Also known as Maolrubha, he is honored locally on Apr. 21.

MALRUBIUS, ST. (d. 1040?). A recluse in Merns, Scotland, he was slain by Norse invaders. F. D. Aug. 27.

MALTRET, CLAUDE (1621–1674). Born in Le Puy, France, on Oct. 3, he became a Jesuit in 1637, taught scripture, and was rector of Maontauban College in 1662 and of the Toulouse novitiate in 1672, serving there until his death on Jan. 3. He published critical editions of Procopius.

MALUS, ÉTIENNE LOUIS (1775–1812), physicist. Born in Paris on June 23, he studied at the Mézières military school, served in the army in Germany and Egypt, and then held governmental positions supervising fortifications in Antwerp and Strassburg. He became interested in optical research and in 1809 announced his discovery of the polarization of light by refraction, winning a prize of and membership in Académie des Sciences in 1810 for his work on double refraction of light in crystals. He died in Paris on Feb. 23.

MALVENDA, THOMAS (1566–1628). Born in Játiva, Valencia, Spain, he became a Dominican, served as assistant to Cardinal Baronius at Rome in 1600, revised the Dominican breviary, annotated Brasichelli's *Index expurgatorius,* and wrote annals of his order. He returned to Spain in 1608 and had completed a Latin version of the Old Testament through Ezechiel before his death on May 7.

MAMACHI, THOMAS MARIA (1713–1792), theologian. Born on Chios, he became a Dominican there, studied in Florence and Rome, was appointed professor of physics at the Sapienza in 1740, and in 1743 became professor of philosophy at the Propaganda. He was made prefect of the Casanatensian Library by Pope Benedict XIV, was director of the *Ecclesiastical Journal* from 1742 to 1785, became secretary of the Index in 1779 and master of the palace. He was involved in the dispute between the Jansenists and Jesuits, was a firm supporter of papal authority, wrote on Christian antiquities, and collaborated with Orsi on *De romani pontificis in synodos oecumenicas.* He died in Corneto, Italy, on Dec. 4.

MAMAS, ST. (d. 275?), martyr. According to SS. Basil and Gregory Nazianzen, he was a shepherd at Caesarea who suffered martyrdom under Aurelian. Eastern tradition says he was stoned to death as a boy, but the Roman Martyrology calls him the son of SS. Theodotus and Rufina and says he was slain in his old age. F. D. Aug. 17.

MAME, ALFRED HENRI AMAND (1811–1893), publisher. Born in Tours, France, on Aug. 17, son of Amand Mame, who had founded a printing firm there, he edited a series of classics from 1833 to 1845 and then put into effect his plan of combining all aspects of bookmaking and publishing, from the manufacture of paper to the distribution of the finished book, in one firm. By 1883 he was issuing three million books a year. He also introduced a profit-sharing system, a pension plan, and endowed schools for his workers. His son Paul (1833–1900), succeeded him. Alfred died in Tours on Apr. 12.

MAMELTA, ST. (d. 344?), martyr. She is said to have been a pagan priestess at Bethfarme, Persia, who was stoned and drowned after she became a Christian. F. D. Oct. 17.

MAMERTINUS, ST. (d. 462?). He directed

the monastery of SS. Cosmas and Damian in Auxerre, France. F. D. Mar. 30.

MAMERTUS, ST. (d. 475?), bishop. Brother of the poet Claudian, he became bishop of Vienne, France, in 461 and, after a series of misfortunes struck his diocese, introduced the penitential practice of rogation days, marked by psalm singing and processions, before the feast of the Ascension. F. D. May 11.

MAMILIAN, ST. (d. 460). Bishop of Palermo, Sicily, he is said to have been exiled to Tuscany by King Genseric. F. D. Sept. 15.

MAMMAEA, ST. (d. 287?), martyr. *See* Marcellus, St.

MANAHEN, ST. (1st century). Mentioned in the Acts of the Apostles (13:1) as a foster brother of Herod Antipas and a prophet, he is said to have died at Antioch. F. D. May 24.

MANCE, JEANNE (1606–1673). Born in Nogent-le-Roi, Champagne, France, daughter of Pierre, a king's lawyer, she went to Quebec in 1641, one of the first woman settlers in Canada. The next year she went to the new settlement of Montreal, used her home as a hospital, which was the beginning of the famous Hôtel Dieu in Montreal, and in 1644 built a hospital which she headed until 1661. In 1659 she went to France and brought back with her three Hospital Sisters of St. Joseph. Since then the Hôtel Dieu has been under the management of the Sisters of St. Joseph. She died in Montreal on June 19.

MANCINI, BL. CATHERINE (d. 1431). Born in Pisa, Italy, she was married at twelve and, on her husband's death, again at sixteen, widowed at twenty-four, and the mother of seven children, all of whom died young. She then made her house a hospital, attended the worst cases herself, became a Dominican tertiary, and eventually entered the Dominican convent of Santa Croce as Sr. Mary. (She is also known as Mary of Pisa). Having reformed this house, she moved on to set up a new community with an even stricter rule. Her cult was confirmed in 1855. F. D. Jan. 28.

MANCIUS, ST. (5th century?), martyr. A Roman, he was taken to Portugal and put to death at Evora by the traders who had enslaved him. F. D. Mar. 15.

MANDAL, ST. (d. 270?), martyr. *See* Basilides, St.

MANDEVILLE, JEAN DE. This is the pseudonym of Jean d'Outremeuse (1338–1400) of Liège, Flanders, for a travel account of the adventures of an imaginary English knight in the Orient from 1322 to 1356. *The voiage and travaille of Sir John Mandeville*, popular in the Middle Ages and later, is based on previous travel accounts by Albert of Aix, Odoric of Pordenone, and William of Boldensele. The author may have been Jean de Bourgogne, or Jean à la Barbe, called a doctor at Liège, but

these names may also be pseudonyms; even the name Mandeville is variously spelled Maundeville and Monteville.

MANECHILDIS, ST. (6th century?). Born in Perthois, France, one of seven daughters, all of whom are honored as saints in Champagne, she lived as a hermitess at Bienville on the Marne, devoting herself to the care of the poor and sick. She is also called Ménéhould. F. D. Oct. 14.

MANETTUS, ST. *See* Benedict dell' Antella, St.

MANEZ DE GUZMÁN, BL. (d. 1230?). Born in Calaruega, Burgos, Spain, son of Felix de Guzmán and Bl. Joan of Aza, and brother of St. Dominic, he was one of the original sixteen members of the Order of Preachers in 1216. He helped establish St. James at Paris and later was its prior, was chaplain to the convent at Prouille, and founded a convent at Madrid. His cult was approved in 1834. F. D. July 30.

MANGAN, JAMES CLARENCE (1803–1849), poet. Born in Dublin, Ireland, on May 1, he became a clerk, worked in the university library and then on the *Dublin University Magazine*, the *Nation*, and the *United Irishman*, and other journals, sometimes on the staff and sometimes as a contributor. He was unable to hold a position for long because of eccentricities in dress and alcoholism. His translations from the German and Gaelic (basing his poems on literal prose renderings by others), which scholars genuinely admired; serious critical essays as well as journalistic and humorous ones; and more than 800 poems expressing nostalgia for Ireland's past, hope for a cultural renaissance, and allegedly autobiographical sorrow over a lost love—these make up his literary output. He died in Dublin, on June 20, in the same year that Edgar Allan Poe died; the two have much in common, and it has been maintained by some that Poe read Mangan's work in magazine form.

MANIUS ACILIUS GLABRIO (d. 95), martyr. Consul in Rome in 91, of a family of which nine of the name held that office, he lived on an estate covering the Pincian Hill, was charged together with several senators of "introducing novelties," and forced to fight animals in the amphitheater at Diocletian's villa at Albanum. He was banished, but later was seized and executed for his religion.

MANN, THEODORE AUGUSTINE (1735–1809). Born in Yorkshire, England, on June 22, he went to Paris in 1754, became a convert in 1756, served in the Spanish army, but gave up his military career to enter the Chartreuse monastery in Nieuport, Belgium, where he was named prior in 1764. He left the order in 1777, but remained an abbé. He became secretary of the Brussels Academy in 1787, to which he had been elected long before, but left Belgium for Prague when the French invaded in 1794. He wrote on the Greek language, a history of Brussels, another of Marie Thérèse, a study of celestial bodies in relation to Newton's findings, and many papers on meteorology. He is said to have refused an offer by Emperor Joseph II of the see of Antwerp in order to continue his writing. He died in Prague (now Czechoslovakia) on Feb. 23.

MANNEA, ST. (d. 287?), martyr. *See* Marcellus, St.

MANNING, HENRY EDWARD (1808–1892), cardinal. Born in Totteridge, Hertfordshire, England, on July 15, son of a governor of the Bank of England, he studied at Oxford, spent a year in the colonial office, and returned to Oxford as a fellow of Merton College in 1832. He was ordained an Anglican minister, served in a Sussex parish until 1850 (the last seventeen as rector), married Caroline Sargent (she died in 1837), and was appointed archdeacon of Chichester in 1841. He became interested in the Oxford Movement and in 1851 became a convert and was ordained. In 1857 he founded the Oblates of St. Charles in Bayswater, London; he became superior there and was appointed provost of the Westminster provincial chapter. In 1865 he was appointed second archbishop of Westminster and devoted himself to Catholic education, poor relief, and the rights of the workers. He supported papal infallibility at the Vatican Council and was created a cardinal in 1875. He was named to the royal commissions on housing in 1885 and on education in 1886, founded the League of the Cross to promote temperance, and in 1889 mediated the London dock strike. He wrote widely, including *The Temporal Sovereignty of the Popes* (1860), *Four Great Evils of the Day* (1871), *The Catholic Church and Modern Society* (1880), and *Eternal Priesthood* (1883). He died in London on Jan. 14.

SHANE LESLIE, *Henry Edward Manning* (London, Burns, Oates, 1921); E. E. REYNOLDS, *Three Cardinals* (New York, Kenedy, 1958).

MANNONIUS, ST. (1st century), martyr. *See* Euphrasius, St.

MANNYNGE OF BRUNNE, ROBERT (14th century), poet. Born in Bourne, Lincolnshire, England, he became a Gilbertine canon at Sempringham in 1288, spent some time in Cambridge and the monastery of Brunne, and wrote *Handlyng Synne*, an adaptation of the French *Manuel des Peschiez* of William of Waddington, which presents narratives to illustrate the seven deadly sins, and a *Chronicle of England*, a modified translation of parts of Wace, Geoffrey of Monmouth, and Peter Langtoft. *Meditacyons of the Soper of Our Lord Jhesus* has also been attributed to him. He was living in Lincolnshire as late as 1338.

MANOGUE, PATRICK (1831–1895), bishop. Born in Desart, Kilkenny, Ireland, on Mar. 15, he studied at Callan, migrated to the United States, where he settled in New England, and then went to California where he became a miner. He studied at St. Mary's of the Lake, Chicago, and St. Sulpice, Paris, and was ordained there in 1861. He returned to California, engaged in missionary work among the Indians there and in Nevada, where he became pastor of Nevada City, and in 1881 was consecrated titular bishop of Ceramos and coadjutor of Grass Valley. He succeeded to that see in 1884, and when its boundaries were changed in 1886 and the episcopal see moved to Sacramento, California, he became its first bishop. He built a cathedral, acquired great influence among the miners, and settled several disputes between them and the mine owners. He died in Sacramento on Feb. 27.

MANRIQUE, GÓMEZ (1415?–1490?), author. Nephew of the marqués de Santillana, and uncle of Jorge Manrique, he played an important part in the military campaigns of John II, Henry IV, and Isabella II of Spain. His lyrical and satiric poems reveal both native and Italianate influences. He also wrote plays, of which the liturgical *Representación del nacimento de nuestro Señor* is the most significant.

MANRIQUE, JORGE (1440–1479), poet. Born in Paredes de Nava, Spain, son of Rodrigo, grand master of the Order of Santiago, he followed the military career of his father and his uncle Gómez and died fighting for Ferdinand and Isabella at the fortress of Garci-Muñoz, Cuenca. He wrote many lyric poems, but is chiefly known for *Coplas por la muerte de su padre* (1476), a memorial to his father and an effective elegy on the transitory in life, particularly of glory. Longfellow translated the *Coplas* in 1833.

MANSARD, FRANÇOIS (1598–1666), architect. Of Italian descent, he was born in Paris, France. He lost several commissions because of his perfectionism and abandoned other structures which he started (the church of Val de Grâce, Paris, for example) because he became dissatisfied with his early plans. He built Châteaux Bercy, Berny, and Fresnes, and, in Paris, Hôtels de Conti, de Toulouse, and Mazarin, and altered Hôtel Carnavalet. He or his grandnephew Jules Hardouin invented the "mansard" roof.

MANSARD, JULES. *See* Hardouin, Jules.

MANSI, GIOVANNI DOMENICO (1692–1769), archbishop. Born in Lucca, Italy, on Feb. 16, he joined the Congregation of Clerks Regular of the Mother of God in 1708 and remained in the mother house of the congregation until 1765, when he was appointed archbishop of Lucca. He published some ninety annotated editions of Calmet, Thomassin,

Baronius, Aeneas Silvius, and others (many of them hastily prepared). His collaboration with the French Encyclopedists on one of their projects cost him a cardinalate; his study of reserved cases was placed on the Index. His most important contribution is *Sacrorum Conciliorum*, on the councils (he completed fourteen of thirty-one volumes; the rest were published posthumously, from his notes). He died in Lucca on Sept. 27.

MANSUETUS, ST. (d. 350?). He became bishop of Toul, France, about 338. F. D. Sept. 3.

MANSUETUS, ST. (d. 483?), martyr. *See* Appian, St.

MANSUETUS, ST. (d. 484?), bishop and martyr. *See* Donatian, St.

MANSUETUS, ST. (5th century), martyr. He and St. Papinianus were African bishops slain by the Arian King Genseric. F. D. Nov. 28.

MANSUETUS, ST. (d. 690?), bishop. Born in Rome, he became bishop of Milan, Italy, about 627, and wrote against the Monothelites. F. D. Feb. 19.

MANTEGNA, ANDREA (1431–1506), painter. Born in Vicenza (or Padua), Italy, he studied under Francesco Squarcione, who adopted him, and early revealed his artistic inclination. His *Madonna in Glory*, painted for St. Sofia, Padua, in 1448 launched his career and he became one of the most important Renaissance painters of northern Italy. In 1460, Lodovico Gonzaga, marquess of Mantua, became his rather forgetful patron and he remained in Mantua, except when he was decorating the Belvedere chapel in the Vatican for Pope Innocent VIII, until his death there on Sept. 13. Among his greatest works are *The Triumph of Caesar, St. James, St. Sebastian, St. Euphemia, SS. Bernardino and Anthony, Holy Women at the Sepulcher, Agony in the Garden, Holy Family, Adoration of the Magi, Judith and the Head of Holofernes,* and other religious scenes and figures. He also was an outstanding engraver, though only a few of his copper plates are extant.

MANUCY, DOMINIC (1823–1885), bishop. Born in Mobile, Alabama, on Dec. 20, he studied at Spring Hill, was ordained in Mobile in 1850, and did parish work in that diocese until 1874, when he was named titular bishop of Dulma and vicar apostolic of Brownsville, Texas. He was transferred to Mobile in 1884, but retained the administration of Brownsville. Later in that year he resigned the see of Mobile, but was its administrator until 1885, when he was reappointed vicar apostolic of Brownsville and titular bishop of Maronea. He attended the third Plenary Council of Baltimore in 1884, and died in Mobile on Dec. 4.

MANUEL I (1469–1521), king of Portugal. He was born in Alcochete, Portugal, on May 31, succeeded John II as king in 1495, worked effectively with the Cortes, was a generous patron of arts and letters, and was so interested in exploration that he helped to fit out the expeditions of Vasco da Gama, Cabral, Cortereal, Almeida, and Albuquerque. He gained from the pope permission for the members of the Knights of the Order of Christ and of the Order of Santiago to marry, led several unsuccessful campaigns against the Moors in northern Africa, and was especially violent in his persecution of the Jews. He died in Lisbon on Dec. 13.

MANUEL, ST. (d. 362), martyr. *See* Ismael, St.

MANUEL CHYSOLORAS (d. 1415). Born in Constantinople, he went to Venice to seek aid for besieged Constantinople, became the first professor of Greek literature at Florence in 1396, taught at Milan and Padua, where he introduced Greek masterpieces to the Italian humanists, and later broke relations with many of them. In 1404 he was Emperor Manuel Palaeologus' ambassador to Venice, Rome, and England, and on his return to Constantinople worked to effect reunion between the Greek Church and Rome. He accompanied antipope John XXIII to the Council of Constance and died there on Apr. 15. He wrote several treatises, translated Plato's *Republic* into Latin, and wrote the first modern Greek grammar, *Erotemeta.*

MANUK, PETER (1676–1749), founder. Born on Feb. 7 in Sebaste, Lower Armenia, he entered Holy Cross cloister there in 1691, took the name Mechitar (the Comforter), but after he was ordained deacon left the cloister to travel for a year and a half (during which time he became interested in Western civilization) and returned to Sebaste. He submitted to Rome and was ordained in 1696 and went to Constantinople, where he became noted for his preaching and his advocacy of reunion of the Armenian Church with Rome. He was forced to flee when anti-Catholic feeling was aroused by the actions of Louis XIV's envoy, Count Ferrol, and fled to Venice. He built a church and convent in Modon in 1701 and there established the Mechitarist Order, which was approved in 1712 by Pope Clement XI, who appointed him abbot. In 1715 the Turks invaded Modon and destroyed the abbacy. Mechitar escaped to Venice and built a monastery on the island of San Lazzaro, where he remained until his death on Apr. 16. He established a printing press and wrote commentaries on the Bible and an Armenian grammar, dictionary, catechism, and a translation of the Bible into Armenian.

MANUTIUS, ALDUS (1450–1515), publisher. Born in Sermoneta, Italy, he received a humanistic scholar's education in Rome, Ferrara, and Mirandola, and in 1484 became tutor to Alberto and Lionello Pio, princes of Carpi.

In 1490, with the support of Prince Alberto, he planned a printing house in Venice to make available the most handsome and most accurate editions of the greatest Greek authors at the lowest possible cost. The publications of this Aldine Press (1494–1515) are world renowned, include first editions of many Latin and Greek classics, and are collectors' items. In 1500 he founded the New Academy or Aldine Academy of Hellenists to promote the study of Greek literature and its publication; it attracted such scholars as Erasmus and Linacre to Italy. In 1499 he married the daughter of Andrea Toresano of Asola, a printer, combined the two firms, and added the name Asolanus to his title pages. He originated many type fonts and was the first to use italics and small capital letters. He died in Venice on Feb. 3.

MANUTIUS, ALDUS (1547–1597), publisher. Born in Venice, Italy, son of Paulus, whom he succeeded as head of the Aldine Press in 1574, he worked in Bologna, Pisa, and Rome as professor of eloquence and wrote antiquarian treatises and a life of Cosimo de' Medici. On his death in Venice, the press was discontinued.

MANUTIUS, PAULUS (1512–1574), publisher. Born in Venice, Italy, son of Aldus, he took over the management of the Aldine Press in 1533, issued excellent editions of Latin classics, and moved the press to Rome in 1562 at the invitation of Pope Pius IV, but returned it to Venice in 1570. He also was a critic and wrote *De senatu romano*, *De civitate romana*, and on Roman antiquities.

MANZANILLO, JUAN DE (16th century). A Dominican, he was bishop of Caracas, Venezuela, and rebuilt the cathedral of Santa Anna after the city had been burned by the English under Francis Drake.

MANZI, BL. ANTONIO (1237?–1267). A citizen of Padua, Italy, he gave away his fortune, was reviled by his two sisters and the townspeople, and left the area to live in poverty. He was known as Antony the Pilgrim because of his costume, his habit of sleeping on the road, and his many devout journeys to Rome, Compostela, Cologne, and the Holy Land. F. D. Feb. 1.

MANZONI, ALESSANDRO (1785–1873), author. Born in Milan, Italy, on Mar. 7, he studied under the Somachi and Barnabites at Pavia, led a dissolute life in Milan, and in 1805 joined his mother (who had separated from his father in 1792) in Paris, where he became a friend of Fauriol and a follower of Voltairean precepts. He married Henriette Blondel in 1808, and when she became a Catholic in 1810 followed her back into the Church. They settled in Milan and he devoted himself to writing. He became a friend of Antonio Rosmini, an ardent advocate of Italian unification, and a defender of Catholicism. His greatest work is *The Betrothed* (*I Promessi Sposi*), published in 1827 and rewritten in 1840, one of the great romances of world literature. He also wrote poems on the chief feasts of the Church, *Il conte di Carmagnola* and *L'Adelchi* (tragedies), *Il cinque maggio* (an ode on Napoleon's death), and *Osservazioni sulla morale cattolica*. He died in Milan on May 22.

MAOLRUAIN, ST. (d. 792). He compiled the Tallaght Martyrology at the Irish monastery which he founded and ruled as abbot at Tallaght. F. D. July 7.

MAOLRUBHA. *See* Malrubius, St.

MAP, WALTER (1140?–1210?), author. Born near Hereford, England, of Welsh ancestry, he studied at Paris, became a clerk at Henry II's court in 1162, was a canon of Lincoln and held other benefices, was Henry's representative at the third Lateran Council in 1179, where he disputed with the Waldensians, became archdeacon of Oxford in 1197, and sought hard to become a bishop. He wrote Latin poems, but is best known for his *De nugis curialium*, a compendium of history, legend, jest, folklore, superstition, and didacticism. His narrative style, while appealing, is also diffuse, unselective, and sometimes highly strained. Much of *Courtiers' Trifles* is autobiographical (on university life, the council in Rome, Thomas à Becket, and Louis VII of France); much of it is more incredible than the similar accounts of marvels by his contemporary, Geoffrey of Monmouth; much of it is spoiled by his intense hostility toward Cistercians and Knights Templar.

MAPPALICUS, ST. (d. 250?), martyr. One of eighteen Christians who were tortured, sent into captivity in the mines, or allowed to die of starvation or disease in prison at Carthage during the persecution of Decius. They are memorialized by St. Cyprian. F. D. Apr. 17.

MAPRILIS, ST. (d. 300?), martyr. *See* Epictetus, St.

MARAMALDI, BL. GUY (d. 1391). Born in Naples, Italy, he became a Dominican, was widely known as preacher and theologian, established a friary at Ragusa, and served as inquisitor general for the kingdom of Naples. His cult was approved in 1612. F. D. June 25.

MARAN, PRUDENTIUS (1683–1762), scholar. Born on Oct. 14 in Sézanne, Marne, France, he studied at Paris, became a Benedictine at Meaux in 1703, and was sent to St. Germain-des-Prés, Paris, to collaborate on an edition of the works of St. Cyril of Jerusalem. He also edited works of SS. Justin, Cyprian, and Basil, and wrote on the divinity of Christ. In 1737 he went to Blancs-Manteaux, Paris, where he remained until his death on Apr. 2.

MARANA, ST. (5th century). *See* Cyra, St.

MARATTA, CARLO (1625–1713), painter. Born in Camerino, Ancona, Italy, on May 13, he studied under Andrea Sacchi in Rome, and in 1650 his commission by Pope Alexander VII to do a painting for the Lateran baptistery launched him on a successful art career. Famed for his portraits and religious paintings, he also was skilled as an architect. He was a member of the Academy of St. Luke in Rome, restored several of Raphael's frescoes in the Vatican, and in 1704 was knighted by Pope Clement XI and appointed painter in ordinary to King Louis XIV of France. He died in Rome on Dec. 15.

MARBEAU, EMMANUEL JULES MARIE (1844–1921), bishop. Born in Paris on Nov. 12, he was ordained in Orléans in 1874, became bishop of Meaux in 1910, and for remaining at his city during the battle of the Marne and directing its administration was decorated by the government. He died on May 31.

MARBODIUS (1035?–1123), bishop. Born in Angers, France, he studied under Rainuldus, taught at the cathedral school, and in 1067 was appointed head of the schools there. In 1096 he became bishop of Rennes, attended the Council of Tours in 1104, acted as administrator of Angers in 1109, and in 1123 resigned his bishopric to retire to the monastery of St. Aubin in Angers, where he died on Sept. 11. He wrote lives of saints, hymns, and letters, and on monasticism and gems.

MARBODUS (11th century), bishop. He studied under the canonist, Fulbert of Chartres, became bishop of Rennes, France, and with Bishop Ulger of Angers developed the cathedral school in the latter city which, two centuries later, became a university.

MARCA, PIERRE DE (1594–1662), archbishop. Born in Gan, Béarn, France, on Jan. 24, he studied at Auch and Toulouse, became councilor of the Pau parliament in 1615 and its president in 1621, and a member of the council of state at Paris in 1639. Ten years after his wife's death in 1641 he was ordained, and appointed bishop of Couserans by King Louis XIII. He did not take office until 1651, when he retracted the Gallican views in his *Concordia sacerdotii et imperii*, written at Richelieu's request. He was made archbishop of Toulouse in 1652, minister of state about 1658, and was active in combating Jansenism, but he defended King Louis XIV's arrest of Cardinal de Retz, archbishop of Paris. He was given the see of Paris when the cardinal died, but died himself three weeks later on Sept. 11.

MARCELLA, ST. (d. 202), martyr. See Plutarch, St.

MARCELLA, ST. (d. 410). On the death of her husband, this Roman matron began a life in imitation of the Eastern ascetics, and was soon able to form several communities within the capital. She was a regular correspondent with St. Jerome on spiritual matters. Although she had given away her fortune to the poor, the Goths demanded her non-existent wealth when they sacked Rome in 410. Her life was spared, but she died soon after. F. D. Jan. 31.

MARCELLIAN, ST. (d. 250), martyr. See Secundian, St.

MARCELLIAN, ST. (d. 287?), martyr. He and his brother Mark were deacons who were put to death at Rome during the persecution of Diocletian. Legend says they were encouraged in their faith and under torture by St. Sebastian. Their tomb in the catacombs of St. Balbina was discovered in 1902. F. D. June 18 (also, July 29).

MARCELLINA, ST. (d. 398?). Sister of St. Ambrose of Milan, she was consecrated to a religious life by Pope Liberius in 353, and lived a life of great austerity and holiness in Rome. Her brother addressed his discourse on the excellence of virginity to her and welcomed her advice in dealing with dedicated virgins in his diocese. F. D. July 17.

MARCELLINUS, ST. (d. 304), pope and martyr. Born in Rome, he succeeded St. Caius to the papacy on June 30, 296. A Donatist libel that he weakened during the persecution of Diocletian and offered sacrifice to the pagan gods, but recanted at a Council of Sinuessa, is now discredited; there was no such council. Whether he died as a martyr, as long believed, is not certain; he died in Rome on Oct. 25. F. D. Apr. 26.

MARCELLINUS, ST. (d. 250), martyr. See Cyriacus, St.

MARCELLINUS, ST. (3rd century). He is listed as the second or third bishop of Ravenna, Italy, where he ruled in mid-century. F. D. Oct. 5.

MARCELLINUS, ST. (d. 304), martyr. A priest, he and Peter, an exorcist, were beheaded in Rome during the persecution of Diocletian; Pope Damasus wrote an epitaph and Constantine built a church in their honor. F. D. June 2.

MARCELLINUS, ST. (d. 320), martyr. See Argeus, St.

MARCELLINUS, ST. (d. 374?), bishop. He came as a missioner to the Dauphiné, France, with two other African priests, SS. Domninus and Vincent, became bishop of Embrun, and suffered persecution and exile at the hands of the Arians. F. D. Apr. 20.

MARCELLINUS, ST. (d. 413), martyr. Tribunal secretary to Emperor Honorius, he was sent to Carthage to preside over a discussion between Catholic and Donatist bishops. When he decided against the latter and began with his brother Agrarius to enforce the edict with great severity, the two were seized and executed at Carthage. It was to Marcellinus that his friend St. Augustine dedicated the *City of God.* F. D. Apr. 6.

MARCELLINUS, ST. (d. 566?). A native of

Ancona, Italy, he became its bishop about 550. F. D. Jan. 9.

MARCELLINUS, ST. (d. 762?). He was an Anglo-Saxon who went with St. Willibrord to evangelize the Frisians. He worked for fifteen years in Friesland and Guelderland, and then joined St. Lebuin to help convert Saxon barbarians. He went to Rome with St. Boniface in 738, and died in Oldensee, Frisia. F. D. July 14.

MARCELLINUS OF CIVEZZA. See Ranise, Pietro.

MARCELLINUS COMES (d. 534?). A native of Illyria, he held high positions at the court of Emperor Justin I at Constantinople and became chancellor when Justinian succeeded to the throne. Marcellinus wrote *Annals* of the years 379 to 534, limited almost entirely to the East. His hostility to heretics shows strongly; the work contains some errors in chronology and lacks fullness.

MARCELLO, BENEDETTO (1696–1739), composer. Born in Venice, Italy, he studied music under Gasparini, took up law, was a member of the Council of Forty for fourteen years, and held office in Pola and Brescia. He wrote the libretto for Ruggieri's *Aruto in Sparta*, composed music for a paraphrase of the Psalms, the *Salve Regina*, and the *Miserere*, and left a manuscript study of musical theory. He died in Brescia, Italy.

MARCELLUS I, ST. (d. 309), pope. A Roman who succeeded St. Marcellinus to the papacy in May or June 308, he was banished by Maxentius and died in exile. There is no proof that he was a martyr, though he is sometimes so listed. F. D. Jan. 16.

MARCELLUS II (1501–1555), pope. Marcellus Cervini was born in Montepulciano, Tuscany, Italy, on May 6, studied at Siena and Rome, where he was appointed papal secretary by Paul III, was named bishop of Nicastro, became secretary of Cardinal Alessandro Farnese in 1538, and was created cardinal in 1539. He became administrator of Reggio in 1540 and of Gubbio in 1544, instituted sweeping reforms in both sees, and accompanied Farnese on a diplomatic mission to Charles V of Germany and Francis I of France in 1540. He was appointed one of the three presidents of the Council of Trent in 1545, became librarian of the Vatican in 1548, and on April 9, 1555, was elected pope, and was consecrated on April 10. He died three weeks later in Rome on May 1. Palestrina's *Missa Papae Marcelli* was dedicated to him.

MARCELLUS, ST. (d. 178?), martyr. A priest at Lyons, France, he fled the city during the persecution of Marcus Aurelius but was apprehended near Chalons-sur-Saône. When he refused to sacrifice to the pagan gods, he was buried to the waist and died three days later of exposure. F. D. Sept. 4.

MARCELLUS, ST. (d. 254), martyr. See Eusebius, St.

MARCELLUS, ST. (d. 274), martyr. See Anastasius, St.

MARCELLUS, ST. (d. 287?), martyr. A tribune, he was beheaded at Thmuis with his wife, Mannea; and sons, John, Serapion, and Peter; a bishop, Miletius; and twelve others, the entire Christian population of Oxyrynchus, Egypt. F. D. Aug. 27.

MARCELLUS, ST. (d. 298), martyr. A centurion in the Roman army at Tangier, he refused to join in a celebration of the emperor's birthday (an acknowledgment of deification), declared himself a Christian, and was put to death by the sword. F. D. Oct. 30.

MARCELLUS, ST. (d. 303?), martyr. See Sabinus, St.

MARCELLUS, ST. (d. 349), martyr. A priest in Nicomedia, he was hurled to his death by Arians during the reign of Constantius. F. D. Nov. 26.

MARCELLUS, ST. (d. 362), martyr. See Elpidius, St.

MARCELLUS, ST. (d. 389?), bishop and martyr. A judge in Cyprus, he became bishop of Apamoea, Syria, where he was killed by a mob while destroying a pagan shrine, probably at Aulona, on orders of Emperor Theodosius the Great. F. D. Aug. 14.

MARCELLUS, ST. (d. 430?), bishop. A native of Paris, he succeeded Prudentius, whose archdeacon he was, as bishop there. F. D. Nov. 1.

MARCELLUS, ST. (d. 474), bishop. Born in Avignon, Gaul, he succeeded his brother, St. Petronius, as bishop of Die, where he served for many years under great opposition from the Arians. F. D. Apr. 9.

MARCELLUS, ST. (d. 485?), abbot. Born in Apamea, Syria, he inherited a fortune, studied in Antioch and Ephesus, then became a monk at the monastery of Eirenaion, near Constantinople, and its third abbot. Under his direction it achieved great fame and influence. He signed the condemnation of Eutyches in 448 and objected to Patricius because of his Arianism. He is surnamed Akimetes, as his monks were called *Akoimetoi* ("not-resters") because the divine office was chanted twenty-four hours a day. F. D. Dec. 29.

MARCH, AUZIAS (1397?–1459), poet. Born in Valencia, Spain, he is said to have been a soldier in the Naples campaign of 1442. He wrote more than 100 love lyrics and elegies in the style and spirit of Petrarch and Dante; the object of his lines was Teresa Bou. March contributed much to the Catalan language and had a strong effect on later poets.

MARCHAND, JEAN BAPTISTE (1760–1825), missioner. Born in Verchères, Quebec,

Canada, on Feb. 25, he was ordained in 1786 and named second principal of the Sulpician seminary in Montreal two years later. In 1796 he was sent to the Huron Indians at present-day Sandwich, Ontario (opposite Detroit), where he remained until his death there on Apr. 14.

MARCHAND, BL. JOSEPH (d. 1835), martyr. Born in Passavant, France, he became a missioner and was sent from Paris to Annam, where he was tortured to death. He was beatified in 1900. F. D. Nov. 30.

MARCHANT, PETER (1585–1661), theologian. Born in Couvin, Liège, Flanders, he was a Franciscan in 1601, taught in several schools, and was elected definitor general of the order in 1625 and commissary general of the German, Belgian, Holland, British, and Irish provinces in 1639. In 1661 he was obliged to retract the support he had given Peter Walsh's supporters in Ireland in their opposition to the papal nuncio, Rinacini, and died soon after at Ghent, Flanders, on Nov. 11. He wrote on St. Joseph, Franciscan history, and many theological treatises, chief of which is his three-volume *Tribunal sacramentale*.

MARCHESI, POMPEO (1790–1858), sculptor. Born in Saltrio, Italy, on Aug. 7, he studied under Canova in Rome, and became professor of sculpture at the Academy in Milan. He executed the statue of St. Ambrose in Milan, *Mater Dolorosa* in the San Carlo church, a bust of Goethe in Frankfort, and statues of Charles Emmanuel III, Emperor Francis I of Austria, and Philibert Emanuel of Savoy. He died in Milan, Italy, on Feb. 6.

MARCHETTI-SELVAGGIANI, FRANCESCO (1871–1951), cardinal. Born in Rome on Oct. 1, he was a seminary classmate of Pope Pius XII, ordained in 1896, named titular archbishop of Seleucia de Isauria in 1918, and served as papal delegate to Washington and to Berne, Switzerland, and as nuncio to Venezuela and Austria. He was made a cardinal and bishop of Ostia and Frascatti in 1930 and served as archpriest of St. John Lateran, secretary of the Congregation of the Holy Office, and dean of the college of cardinals. He died in Vatican City on Jan. 13.

MARCHI, GIUSEPPE (1795–1860), archaeologist. Born in Tolmezzo, Italy, on Feb. 22, he joined the Jesuits in 1814, taught at several colleges, was ordained in 1833, and became professor of rhetoric at the Roman College. He was appointed prefect of the Kirscher Museum in 1838, conservator of the cemeteries in Rome in 1842, consultor of the Congregation of the Index in 1847, and in 1854 helped create the Lateran Museum, of which he became co-director. He died on Feb. 10 in Rome. He wrote several treatises on the catacombs and on early Christian art.

MARCIA, ST. (d. 285?), martyr. *See* Ariston, St.

MARCIAN (390?–457), emperor. Born in Thrace of a poor and obscure family, he joined the army, served with distinction against the Persians and Huns, and came to the attention of Aspar, who named him one of his choices as successor to the Eastern throne and a senator at Constantinople. Theodosius II died in 450 and was succeeded by his sister Pulcheria. She married Marcian, who was crowned by the patriarch on Aug. 25—the first time an emperor took office with a religious ceremony. He initiated a moderate policy, reformed tax laws, refused to continue paying the tribute demanded by Attila, aided cities in distress, and by his wise rule inaugurated a period of prosperity. In 451 he summoned the Council of Chalcedon, which denounced Eutychianism and the Robber Council of Ephesus, deposed Dioscurus of Alexandria, accepted the dogmatic *Tome* of Pope St. Leo I, and pronounced Constantinople second only to Rome among the sees of Christendom. This last canon was declared null and void by Leo, who approved the acts of the council which applied to matters of faith. In 452, with Western Emperor Valentinian III, Marcian promulgated laws to enforce the council's decrees. He successfully enforced the decrees in the area around Constantinople but failed in Syria and Egypt, where, after Pulcheria's death in 453, revolt broke out which continued throughout the rest of his reign. He died in Jan. in Constantinople.

MARCIAN, ST. (d. 120), bishop and martyr. He is said to have been first bishop of Tortona, Italy, and martyred forty-five years after his consecration, during the reign of Hadrian. F. D. Mar. 6.

MARCIAN, ST. (d. 127?). He served as the fourth bishop of Ravenna, Italy, from about 112 to about 127. F. D. May 22.

MARCIAN, ST. (d. 243), martyr. He was put to death at Iconium in Lycaonia. F. D. July 11.

MARCIAN, ST. (d. 250?), martyr. *See* Lucian, St.

MARCIAN, ST. (d. 255?), bishop and martyr. He probably was a papal legate to Syracuse, Sicily, and was thrown from a tower to his death. Discredited legend calls him a personal representative of St. Peter. F. D. June 14.

MARCIAN, ST. (d. 304?), martyr. *See* Abundius, St.

MARCIAN, ST. (d. 351), martyr. *See* Martyrius, St.

MARCIAN, ST. (d. 387?), hermit. A native of Cyrrhus, Syria, of a patrician family, he retired to the desert of Chalcis, between Antioch and the Euphrates, to live as a hermit; large numbers of disciples, including prelates, were attracted by his holiness. F. D. Nov. 2.

MARCIAN, ST. (4th century), martyr. He and

Nicander, said to have been Roman soldiers, were beheaded, probably at Durostorum, Bulgaria. Other accounts, highly embellished, give the place of their death as Alexandria in Egypt, Constanta in Romania, and Venafro in Italy. F. D. June 17.

MARCIAN, ST. (d. 471?). Spending his lifetime in Constantinople, this Roman relative of Emperor Theodosius was ordained in 455, became treasurer of St. Sophia, and was charged with heresy over his extreme austerities, but fully cleared. He built and repaired a number of churches and dispersed a fortune in charities. F. D. Jan. 10.

MARCIAN, ST. (d. 484?), martyr. *See* Aquilinus, St.

MARCIAN, ST. (5th century). A monk at the abbey of Auxerre, Gaul, under St. Mamertinus, to which he went to escape the Visigothic occupation of Bourges, he served as cowherd and aroused admiration for his great humility. F. D. Apr. 20.

MARCIAN, ST. (d. 730), martyr. *See* Julian, St.

MARCIAN, ST. (d. 757?), bishop. He directed the see of Pampeluna in Navarre, Spain, and attended the sixth Council of Toledo in 737. F. D. June 30.

MARCIAN, ST. (d. 1010). Born in Saigon (Vaucluse), France, he became abbot-founder of the Benedictine monastery of St. Eusebius of Apt. F. D. Aug. 25.

MARCIANA, ST. (d. 303?), martyr. Born in Mauritania, she was tortured and finally torn to death by animals in the arena at Caesarea in North Africa during the persecution of Diocletian. She may be identical with a St. Marciana, patron of Tortosa, Spain, who is said to have been put to death at Toledo. F. D. Jan. 9 (sometimes, July 12).

MARCIUS, ST. (d. 679). A Benedictine monk at Monte Cassino, Italy, he retired to a cave on Mondragone, where he died. He was mentioned by Pope St. Gregory the Great in his life of St. Benedict. F. D. Oct. 24.

MARCOLINO OF FORLÌ. *See* Amanni, Bl. Marcolino.

MARCONI, GUGLIELMO (1874–1937), physicist. Born in Bologna, Italy, on Apr. 25, he studied there and at Florence and Leghorn, became interested in physics and electricity as a boy, and was intrigued with the possibility of using electromagnetic waves to send messages through space. In 1895 he devised a transmitter which sent messages over a distance of a mile; he patented a system capable of transmitting several miles in 1896 in England; and in 1897 was able to send messages to ships twelve miles at sea. He formed Marconi's Wireless Telegraph and Signal Company, Ltd., in 1897, transmitted across the English Channel in 1898, and in 1901 across the Atlantic Ocean.

He perfected a magnetic detector in 1902, improved transmitting techniques, invented a directional antenna in 1905, the timed-spark system of generation of continuous waves in 1912, and in 1916–26 devoted himself to perfecting the transmission of beamed radio waves. He also worked on short-wave and ultra-short-wave transmission and multiplex transmission of voice and code. He served with the Italian military during World War I, and was a delegate to the Versailles peace conference in 1919. Marconi received many honors, among them the Nobel Prize for physics in 1909 and the Albert Medal of the Royal Society of Arts, and was made a member of the Italian senate by King Victor Emmanuel in 1909. He died in Rome on July 20.

MARCONI, BL. MARK DEI (1480–1510). Born in Milliarino, near Mantua, Italy, he became a Hieronymite at the monastery of St. Matthew there. His cult was approved in 1906. F. D. Feb. 24.

MARCOUF, ST. (6th century). A monk whose name was continued in that of a monastery near Avranches, France, he retired each Lent to an island which also is named for him.

MARCOUL, ST. (d. 558?). Born in Bayeux, Normandy, he was a preacher in the diocese of Coutances at thirty, then built a hermitage at Nanteuil on land given him by King Childebert. This became a great monastic center and SS. Criou, Domardus, and Helier were among his disciples. Marcoul (or Marculfus) was the patron of skin diseases, kings venerated his relics in the hope of receiving the gift of healing scrofula, and his shrine was popular until destroyed by the revolutionaries in 1793. F. D. May 1.

MARCOUX, JOSEPH (1791–1855), missioner. Born in Canada on Mar. 16, he was ordained in 1813 and spent his life as a missioner among the Indians at St. Regis and Caughnawaga. He wrote a French-Iroquois dictionary, an Iroquois grammar, and translated a life of Christ, prayers, and hymns for his people. He died on May 29.

MARCULFUS. *See* Marcouf, St.

MARCUS DIADOCHUS (4th century). He wrote a sermon against the Arians which was discovered and published at Basle, Switzerland, in 1694.

MARCUS EREMITA (5th century), author. Probably the superior of a laura in Ancyra, Galatia, he became a hermit as an old man in the desert east of Palestine. He wrote treatises on the ascetic and spiritual life and a treatise against the Nestorians and probably died before 451.

MARDARIUS, ST. (4th century), martyr. *See* Eustratius, St.

MARDONIUS, ST. (d. 303), martyr. He and St. Migdonius were court officials at Rome;

during the persecution of Diocletian the former was drowned and the latter burned to death. F. D. Dec. 23.

MARDONIUS, ST. (305?), martyr. *See* Eugene, St.

MAREAS, ST. (d. 342), bishop and martyr. *See* Abdiesus, St.

MARÉCHAL, AMBROSE (1764–1828), archbishop. Born in Ingres, France, on Aug. 28, he studied law and then for the priesthood at the Sulpician seminary in Orléans, was ordained in 1792, and fled the French Revolution to Baltimore, Maryland, the same year. He engaged in missionary work for seven years, taught theology at St. Mary's College and Georgetown, and in 1803 was recalled to France to teach. He returned to teaching in Baltimore in 1812, was appointed bishop of Philadelphia in 1816, which he declined, and coadjutor of Baltimore in 1817, and succeeded to the see as archbishop later the same year. He successfully abolished trusteeism in his see, completed its cathedral in 1821, and died in Baltimore on Jan. 29.

MARENCO, CARLO (1800–1846), dramatist. Born in Cassolo, Piedmont, Italy, he studied law and became a treasury official in Savona, where he died. He wrote several tragedies, inspired by Dante but highly sentimental in tone, including: *Pia de' Tolomei, Arnoldo da Brescia,* and *Conte Ugolino.*

MARENCO, LEOPOLDO (1831–1899), dramatist. Son of Carlo, he was born in Ceva, Italy, and also worked for the treasury. In 1860 he was appointed professor of Latin literature at Bologna; he later went to Milan until 1871. Among his verse plays, based on mediaeval and modern history, are: *Celeste, Tempeste alpine, Marcellina, Piccarda Donati,* and *Saffo.*

MARENZIO, LUCA (1550–1599), composer. Born in Coccaglia, Lombardy, he is noted for his madrigals and motets and also a mass. He died in Rome.

MARERI, BL. PHILIPPA (d. 1236). Born in Cicoli, Italy, to a landowning family which often played host to St. Francis of Assisi, she ran away to escape an arranged marriage, but was forgiven and allowed to live a life of retirement with a group which followed a rule based on that of St. Clare. Bl. Roger of Todi became spiritual adviser and Philippa abbess of a community devoted to poverty and prayer. F. D. Feb. 16.

MAREST, THOMAS (d. 1433). Curé of St. Nicolas, Coutances, France, from 1397, he wrote a manuscript account of the Hundred Years' War and its effect on his area.

MARGARET, ST. (d. 304?), martyr. Daughter of a pagan priest in Antioch, she was turned out of her home when her Christianity was discovered, and lived as a shepherdess. When she spurned the advances of a Roman official, he arrested her and had her tortured and beheaded. Even these details are legendary; later accretions to her story are fantastic. Her actual existence and martyrdom are not denied; she became one of the most widely venerated of Christian saints, and is a patron of childbirth. F. D. July 20.

MARGARET, ST. (d. 1192). Called of Hungarian ancestry in one old biography and of English in another, she made pilgrimages to the Holy Land, Montserrat in Spain, and Puy in France, then entered the Cistercian monastery at Sauve Bénite, France, where her shrine was known as that of Margaret of England. F. D. Feb. 3.

MARGARET, BL. (1207?–1225?), martyr. Born in Louvain, Flanders, she was a servant at the inn of a relative named Aubert. On the eve of the day Aubert and his wife were to become religious, they were murdered. When the bandits realized that Margaret was a witness, they carried her off and tried to force her to marry one of them. When she refused, they cut her throat. Her cult was approved in 1905. F. D. Sept. 2.

MARGARET (1283–1290), queen. Called "the Maid of Norway," she was the daughter of Eric II of Norway and Margaret, daughter of Alexander III of Scotland. The latter was killed in 1286 and the Scots nobility chose six regents to rule for his infant granddaughter. In 1289, King Edward I of England obtained a dispensation from Pope Nicholas IV to permit the marriage of Prince Edward and Margaret. The English king promised to respect the independence of Scotland, sent a ship to Norway for the princess, and escorted her and her father aboard. The girl died at one of the Orkney islands on her way to Scotland and was buried there. Ten years later a woman from Germany arrived in Norway, claiming that she was Margaret and that she had been kidnaped and sold into slavery. The story was widely believed, but she was captured by King Haakon V and burned in Bergen, Norway, as a witch in 1301. The populace was outraged and for a long time the so-called daughter of Eric was revered as a saint.

MARGARET, BL. (d. 1330). A native of Faenza, Italy, she became a Vallombrosan nun and second abbess of the convent of St. John the Evangelist near Florence. F. D. Aug. 26.

MARGARET, ST. (d. 1395?). Born in San Severino, Italy, she was married at fifteen to a husband whose abuse she bore patiently until his death. She devoted the rest of her life to prayer and penitence, and was called Margaret the Barefooted. F. D. Aug. 27.

MARGARET OF ANJOU (1430–1482), queen. Born probably in Pont à Mousson, France, on Mar. 23, daughter of René of

Anjou, she was married to Henry VI of England in 1445. She was the virtual ruler of England because of Henry's imbecility, and, when her rule was resisted by the duke of York, the War of the Roses broke out. Forced to flee to Scotland after defeat followed earlier successes, she returned with an army, won at Wakefield (1460) and St. Albans (1461), but was defeated by Edward IV, York's son, at Towton in 1461. Edward was proclaimed king, and in 1471 she was defeated at Tewkesbury and her son put to death. She was imprisoned for five years until Louis XI of France ransomed her in 1476, and then returned to France, where she died at Dampière on Aug. 25.

MARGARET OF AUSTRIA (1480–1530), princess. Daughter of Maximilian I of Austria and Mary of Burgundy, she was born in Brussels on Jan. 10, raised in the French court, and in 1496 was married to John of Asturias, heir of the Spanish crown, who died a year later. In 1501 she was married to Duke Philibert II of Savoy, who died three years later. In 1507 she was made regent of the Netherlands, centralized authority, repressed heresy, developed economic advances, and in 1529 negotiated with Louise of Savoy the Peace of Cambrai, also known as the Ladies' Peace. She died in Mechlin (Belgium) on Dec. 1.

MARGARET COLONNA, BL. (d. 1280). Daughter of Prince Odo Colonna, she refused offers of marriage and established a Poor Clare convent in a castle on the family estate in Palestrina, Italy. Her cult was confirmed by Pope Pius IX in 1847. F. D. Nov. 7.

MARGARET OF CORTONA, ST. (1247–1297). Daughter of a farming family in Laviano, Italy, she ran away from a stepmother and lived for nine years as the mistress of a wealthy cavalier, to whom she bore a son. After he was killed, she became penitent. The Franciscan Giunta Bevegnati became her confessor and helped her through three years of near-despair, intense mortification (of which he disapproved), and work in hospitals. After a brief period as a recluse she became a Franciscan tertiary in Cortona, opened a hospital with the assistance of the city council, and organized a group of women, the Poverelle, to work there, and another group to support it. After eight years with the sick and poor she was suddenly charged with immorality with friars and suffered from this scandal, even though all names were cleared. In her last years she enjoyed a happier international reputation for conversions and cures. Shes died in Cortona, Italy. F. D. Feb. 22.

FRANÇOIS MAURIAC, St. Margaret of Cortona (New York, Philosophical Library, 1948).

MARGARET OF HUNGARY, ST. (1242–1270). Daughter of King Béla IV, she became a Dominican novice at twelve in a royal convent built on an island in the Danube. Although she was a princess among nuns who were of noble descent, she objected to any special treatment and went out of her way to perform the most menial tasks and the most exacting labors on behalf of the squalid poor and most advanced hospital cases. The extent of her labors and fasting and hours of prayer brought on the fatigue of which she died on Jan. 18. F. D. Jan. 26.

MARGARET OF LORRAINE, BL. (1463–1521). Daughter of Duke Ferri of Lorraine, and niece of Margaret of Anjou, she was born in Vaudémont castle, Lorraine, and married Duke René of Alençon in 1488. After his death in 1492, she devoted herself to raising her three children and to works of charity. In 1513, when they were of age, she entered a convent at Montagne and later founded a Poor Clare convent at Argentan, Brittany, where in 1519 she became a nun and where she died on Nov. 2. Her cult was confirmed in 1921. F. D. Nov. 6.

MARGARET OF METOLA, BL. (1287?–1320). Abandoned as a blind orphan in a Città-di-Castello, Italy, church, she was brought up by various poor families, then was given over to a group of nuns, who found her holiness a rebuke to their disregard for their rule and who so calumniated her that she returned to the impoverished villagers. At fifteen she became a Dominican tertiary, took care of workers' children during the day, and taught them prayers, psalms, and the catechism. She died in Città-di-Castello, and her cult was confirmed in 1609. F. D. Apr. 13.

MARGARET MARY, ST. See Alacoque, St. Margaret Mary.

MARGARET OF PARMA (1522–1586). Illegitimate daughter of Emperor Charles V, she was born in Brussels, and married Alessandro de' Medici, duke of Florence, in 1536. He was murdered a year later, and in 1542 she married Ottavio Farnese, duke of Parma and Piacenza. She was named regent of the Netherlands by Philip II in 1559, with Granvelle as her adviser. Though she favored the populace, the policies of Granvelle triumphed and, when the Inquisition was introduced, the country rebelled in 1566. Margaret resigned in 1567 when Alva was sent into the nation to crush the revolt.

MARGARET OF RAVENNA, BL. (1442?–1505). Born in Russi, near Ravenna, Italy, she became blind as an infant and suffered from ill health through her life. She succeeded in directing a large group of men and women, married and single, living in the world but devoted to piety and prayer. It never became a permanent institute, but Ven. Jerome Maluselli, their spiritual adviser, developed the plan into the organization known as the Priests of the Good Jesus. F. D. Jan. 23.

MARGARET OF SAVOY, BL. (1382–1464). The daughter of Duke Amadeus of Savoy, she was born at Pinerolo, Italy, and in 1403 married Marquis Theodore of Montferrat. On his death in 1418, she devoted herself to good works, became a Dominican tertiary, and refused marriage to Philip Visconti of Milan. In 1426 she formed a Dominican community in Alba, Liguria, and became its first prioress. The last years of her life were darkened by baseless rumors of her over-strict discipline with her nuns and of favoring the Waldensian heresy. She died in Alba, Italy, on Nov. 23. Her cult was confirmed in 1669. F. D. Dec. 23.

MARGARET OF SCOTLAND, ST. (1050?–1093). Granddaughter of King Edmund of England and daughter of Edward the Exile, she married King Malcolm III of Scotland. She bettered the court and the country by aid to education and religion, lessened superstition, and removed many evils. Three of her six sons—Edgar, Alexander, and St. David—became kings after their father; one of her two daughters, Matilda (Maud), married Henry I of England. Her care of the sick and poor, ransoming of captives, and construction of hostels, refuges, and churches matched the ardor of her private fasts and devotions. She died in Edinburgh four days after her husband and her son Edward were slain on Nov. 12 during an attack by William II of England. She was canonized in 1250 and declared patroness of Scotland in 1673. F. D. June 10 (in Scotland, Nov. 16).

MARGARITONE D'AREZZO (1236?–1289), painter. Born in Arezzo, Italy, he painted in the late Byzantine tradition, though most of his contemporaries had begun to imitate Giotto. Frescoes in San Clemente, madonnas, and numerous portraits of St. Francis, simple in style, were completed in Arezzo, Siena, Florence, Pisa, and Castiglione.

MARGIL, ANTONIO (1657–1726), missioner. Born in Valencia, Spain, on Aug. 18, he joined the Franciscans there in 1673, was sent as a missionary to Mexico City in 1683, and spent the rest of his life preaching to the Indians of Central America. He was appointed guardian of the mission college of Guadalupe in 1706 and founded the missions of Guadalupe, Texas, in 1716. He died in Mexico City on Aug. 6 and is called the "Apostle of Guatemala."

MARGOTTI, CARLO (1891–1951), archbishop. Born in Ravenna, Italy, on Apr. 22, he was titular archbishop of Mesembria and apostolic delegate to Greece and Turkey in 1930–34, then became archbishop of Gorizia, labored to lessen the Yugoslav-Italian border riots, was arrested by Marshal Tito and sentenced to death in 1945, and released through Allied intervention. He died in Gorizia, Italy, on July 31.

MARGOTTI, GIACOMO (1823–1887). Born in San Remo, Italy, on May 11, he studied at the Ventimiglia seminary and took his doctorate at Genoa in 1845. In 1848 he helped found the daily *L'Armonia*, suppressed a year later by Cavour. Margotti then began *Il Piemonte*, which later resumed the name *L'Armonia*. In 1863, at the suggestion of Pope Pius IX, the paper became *L'Unità Cattolica*. In its columns he exerted great influence on Italian Catholics, so great that he once barely escaped assassination. He wrote several books on the history of his times and died on May 6.

MARI, ST. (2nd century), bishop. *See* Addai, St.

MARIA (d. 1395), queen of Hungary. Daughter of Louis I, she succeeded to the throne on her father's death in 1382. She was faced by internal dissension and after 1387 was only nominal ruler, when her husband Sigismund of Luxemburg, who succeeded to the throne on her death, took over the reins of government. Genuinely interested in Church matters, she was active in promoting better training for the clergy, and built several churches. She is also known as Marie of Anjou.

MARIA I (d. 1816), queen of Portugal. *See* John VI.

MARIA II (d. 1853), queen of Portugal. *See* Miguel.

MARIA OF AUSTRIA (1505–1558), queen. Daughter of Philip the Fair of Burgundy and Joan of Castile, sister of Charles V and Ferdinand I, she was born in Brussels, was married to Louis II of Hungary at seventeen and widowed at twenty-one. In 1530 she was appointed by Charles V as governor of the Netherlands, succeeding Margaret of Austria, and ruled firmly for twenty-four years. She was a patron of the arts, made a large collection of manuscripts, and on the abdication of Charles retired to Spain and died at Cigales.

MARIA DE LA CABEZA, BL. (d. 1175?). Born in Torrejon, Spain, she married St. Isidore the Farmer. Her cult was approved in 1697. F. D. Sept. 9.

MARIA CHRISTINA (1858–1929), queen. Born in Gross-Seelowitz, Austria, on July 21, daughter of Archduke Karl Ferdinand, she became abbess of a convent, but in 1879 was permitted to leave to be married to King Alfonzo XII of Spain. When he died in 1885 she acted as regent for their daughter Mercedes and then for a posthumous son, Alfonzo XIII, born in 1886. After his maturity in 1902 she lived in partial seclusion. She died in Madrid on Feb. 6.

MARIA GORETTI, ST. (1890–1902), martyr. Born in Ancona, Italy, on Oct. 16, she was the third of seven children of Luigi Goretti and Assunta Carlini. The family moved to Ferriere di Conca, near Anzio, where Luigi became the partner of a man named Serenelli, who lived in the same house and had a son, Alessandro. Maria was a beautiful child and quite mature for her age, which attracted the attention of Alessandro. On July 5, 1902, he attempted to attack her, threatening her with death if she refused him. Though she fought him off, he stabbed her fourteen times with a dagger, and she died of wounds the next day, after having forgiven her attacker. She was canonized as a martyr for purity on July 24, 1950, by Pope Pius XII. F. D. July 6.

MARÍA LUISA, BL. (1782–1824), queen. Daughter of King Charles IV of Spain and María Luisa of Parma, she was married to Louis of Parma in 1795. Napoleon named the latter the king of Etruria in 1801, but he died in 1803; María Luisa then became regent for their son Charles Louis. When Napoleon took over the kingdom in 1807, she retired to Spain, then took refuge in Parma, Nice, and Rome; she remained in a convent there in 1811–14. Her son was given Lucca by the Congress of Vienna, with his mother ruling as regent; her *Memoirs* were published in 1814. She was beatified in 1876.

MARIA MAMALA, BL. (d. 1453). A Spanish noblewoman, and wife of Henry de Guzmán, she entered the Poor Clares at Seville, Spain, after her husband's death. F. D. Mar. 31.

MARIA THERESA (1717–1780), queen. Daughter of Emperor Charles VI and Elizabeth of Brunswick-Wolfenbüttel, she was born in Vienna on May 13, married her cousin, Francis of Lorraine, in 1736, and on the death of her father in 1740 succeeded to the Hapsburg possessions as queen of Austria and Hungary. She was recognized as such by her Austrian subjects, but the objections of Prussia, where Frederick II was building Prussia into a rival of Austria, and other German states set off the War of the Austrian Succession which, on its settlement in 1748, left her undisputed ruler except for Silesia, which she was obliged to cede to Prussia. She granted equal rights to Francis; her husband was elected emperor in 1745; but she continued to dominate in the rule of the state. Because of Prussian rivalry, she and her minister Kaunitz reversed the usual Hapsburg policy, sought friendship and alliance with France, and in 1756 she embarked on the fruitless Seven Years' War, at the conclusion of which she finally was obliged to confirm the cession of Silesia. When Francis died in 1765 she made her son co-regent, and by the first partition of Poland in 1772 and subsequent accessions of land from Turkey and Poland added to the Hapsburg dominions. She devoted herself to unifying her realms with absolute authority vested in the crown, and cau-

tiously encouraged agricultural, administration, financial, and educational reforms, though she placed the state above all else. She died in Vienna on Nov. 29.

MARIALES, XANTES (1580?–1660). Born in Venice, Italy, he became a Dominican, studied in Spain, was ordained, taught at Venice and Padua, where he was regent for three terms, and was exiled twice by the senate for the vigor of his writings in defense of the papacy. He died in Venice.

MARIANA, JUAN DE (1536–1624), economist. Born in Talavera, Toledo, Spain, in Apr., he became a Jesuit in 1554, studied at Alcalá, was ordained in 1561 and went to Rome to teach theology, then to Sicily, and in 1569–74 occupied the chair of theology at Paris. Illness forced him to return to Spain, and he spent the rest of his life in Toledo, where he died on Feb. 16. He wrote *Historiae de rebus Hispaniae*, a monumental history of Spain in Latin, which he later translated into Spanish. In 1599 his *De rege et regis institutione*, in which he maintained that it is lawful to put despots to death under certain conditions, was published and though dedicated to King Philip III and accepted without objection in Spain, caused a sensation in France, where it was construed as favorable to the assassination of King Henry III and was denounced by the Sorbonne. Soon after the assassination of Henry IV in 1610 it was ordered publicly burned by parliament. In 1609 the publication of his *De monetae mutatione*, which opposed currency depreciation, led to his arrest on a charge of treason to the king and he was sentenced to imprisonment for life, which was mitigated to retirement to a Franciscan convent. In his later years he was among the group of Jesuits who wanted changes made in the Society, but he evidently was completely reconciled at his death. He also wrote *De ponderibus et mensuris*, biblical commentary, and prepared an edition of Isidore of Seville.

JOHN LAURES, *The Political Economy of Juan de Mariana* (New York, Fordham U., 1928).

MARIANI, DOMENICO (1863–1939), cardinal. Born in Posta, Italy, on Apr. 3, he was ordained, was created a cardinal in 1935, served as provost to the commision for administering papal estates and goods, and died in Vatican City on Apr. 23.

MARIANI, BL. RAYNERIUS (d. 1304). Born in Arezzo, Italy, he became a Franciscan laybrother and died at Borgo Sansepolcro. His cult was confirmed in 1802. F. D. Nov. 3.

MARIANUS, ST. (d. 259), martyr. *See* James, St.

MARIANUS, ST. (d. 283), martyr. *See* Diodorus, St.

MARIANUS, ST. (d. 515?). He became a recluse at Entreaigues, Berry, France, and was the subject of a biography by St. Gregory of Tours. F. D. Aug. 19.

MARIANUS (d. 1523), historian. Born in Florence, Italy, he became a Friar Minor and wrote *Fasciculus chronicarum*, containing a history of the Franciscans to 1486, based on primary sources; biographies of 150 women of the second Order of St. Francis; and accounts of his order's settlements in Italy. He died in Florence on July 20 while administering the sacraments to the victims of plague.

MARIANUS, ST., martyr. *See* Chrysanthus, St.

MARIANUS SCOTUS, BL. (1028–1082), historian. Born in Ireland, Moelbrigte became a monk in 1052, entered the Irish monastery of St. Martin in Cologne in 1056, and was ordained in 1059 at Würzburg. He became a hermit at Fulda in 1060, but in 1070 moved to Mainz, Germany, under his former abbot, Siegfried, and died there. He was the author of a *Chronicle* relating the history of the world to 1082, which influenced that of Florence of Worcester. F. D. Dec. 22.

MARIANUS SCOTUS, BL. (d. 1088). Muiredach mac Robartaigh was born in Donegal, Ireland, became a religious hermit of sorts, and, on his way to Rome in 1067 with several companions, became a Benedictine at Michelsburg, Germany. In 1078 he became founder-abbot of St. Peter's, Regensburg, where he was famed as a scribe. He wrote poems and theological studies of his own, as well as transcribing and distributing many works by others. The center attracted others from his homeland and became the mother of several famous monasteries in southern Germany. F. D. Feb. 9.

MARIE OF ANJOU, queen of Hungary. *See* Maria, queen of Hungary.

MARIE ANTOINETTE (1755–1793), queen. Born in Vienna on Nov. 2, daughter of Emperor Francis I and Maria Theresa of Austria, she was married to Louis, the French dauphin, in a diplomatic move to affirm the alliance between Austria and France, in 1770. After Louis became king in 1774, her frivolous extravagances, outspoken sympathy for Austria, and apparent unconcern for the misery of many of her subjects caused her to become a focus of discontent; she also was a victim of a violent campaign of calumny directed by many forces in and outside the court. When the French Revolution broke out, royalty was a major target. She and Louis XVI were captured at Varennes as they attempted to flee the country. Though a prisoner in the Tuileries, she corresponded with her brother, Leopold II of Austria, and when Austria declared war on France she is said to have supplied defense plans to her brother's generals. She was removed to the Temple, treated with considerable

brutality, charged with treason, and guillotined in Paris on Oct. 16.

MARIE DE FRANCE (12th century), poet. A native of Normandy, she was probably a member of the group of troubadours around Henry II and Queen Eleanor, and the author of fifteen narrative lays of the loves and adventures of Breton knights, the *Ysopet*, a collection of 103 fables translated into French from English, and the *Legend of the Purgatory of St. Patrick*.

MARIE DE L'INCARNATION, BL. (1566?–1618). Barbara Avrillot, daughter of a government official, was born in Paris on Feb. 1, educated at Longchamps, married at seventeen to Pierre Acarie, and became the mother of six children (four entered religious life). She engaged in much charitable work in Paris, brought the Carmelites from Spain to France and helped them open five convents, was counseled by St. Francis de Sales, and after the death of her husband in 1613 became a Carmelite laysister at Amiens, taking the name of Marie of the Incarnation. She enjoyed a number of supernatural gifts, died in Pointoise, France, and was beatified in 1791. F. D. Apr. 18.

MARIE DE L'INCARNATION, VEN. (1599–1672). Marie Guyard was born in Tours, France, on Oct. 28, married M. Martin, a silk manufacturer, when seventeen, was widowed two years later, and in 1629 joined the Ursulines in Tours. She went to Canada in 1639 and in 1641 laid the cornerstone of the first Ursuline convent in Quebec. She rebuilt it after it was destroyed by fire in 1650, and spent the rest of her life teaching Indians. Her *Lettres*, published in Paris, 1677–81, give a valuable picture of Quebec from 1639 to 1671. She died in Quebec on Apr. 30.

MARIE THÉRÈSE OF AUSTRIA (1638–1683), queen. Daughter of Philip IV of Spain, she was born in Madrid on Sept. 10, gave up all claims to the Spanish throne and was married to Louis XIV of France in 1660. Because of her husband's numerous affairs, she lived an unhappy life, which she sought to fill with works of piety. She died in Versailles, France, on July 10.

MARIGNOLLI, GIOVANNI DE (1290–1357), bishop. Born in Florence, Italy, he became a Franciscan there, taught theology at Bologna, and in 1338 was sent by Pope Benedict XII from Avignon to China. His group made the trip overland and arrived in Peking in 1341. He was well received at the Chinese court, toured the country for three years, visited the Dutch East Indies, and sailed home, arriving in Naples in 1353. In 1354 he was named bishop of Bisignano; Florence sent him as legate to Avignon in 1356; the next year he became councilor and court historian to Emperor Charles IV. His *Chronicon Bohemiae,* in which his Eastern adventures are recorded, was of great value to geographers.

MARILLAC, LOUISE DE. *See* Louise de Marillac, St.

MARINA. The Latin form of the Greek Pelagia, this name has been given to a number of holy women in pious legends, where she generally is described as a girl who disguised herself as a boy and lived a solitary life in a settlement of monastic caves. Her story is that of SS. Pelagia (Oct. 8), Euphrosyna (Jan. 1), and Margaret (July 20). The Roman Martyrology lists her as a martyr at Alexandria with both June 18 and July 17 as feast days.

MARINI, DOMENICO (1599–1669), archbishop. Born in Rome on Oct. 21, brother of Tommaso and Giovanni, he became a Dominican in 1615, studied at Salamanca and Alcalá, and on his return to Rome was assigned the chair of theology at the Minerva. He then taught in Toulouse and Paris, was recalled to Rome to become master of theology, and then prior of the Minerva, which he rebuilt. He was appointed archbishop of Avignon, France, in 1648, helped restore its university to its former importance, and died there on June 20.

MARINI, GIOVANNI BAPTISTA (1597–1669). Born on Nov. 28 in Rome, Italy, brother of Tommaso and Domenico, he became a Dominican in 1613, studied at Salamanca and Alcalá, and taught in Rome. He was named secretary of the Congregation of the Index in 1628, was embroiled in the controversy between the Dominicans and Jesuits over works listed on the Index, and in 1650 was elected general of his order, a position he held until his death in Rome on May 6.

MARINI, LEONARDO (1509–1573), archbishop. Born on Chios, he became a Dominican there, studied in Genoa, and in 1550 was made administrator of Mantua, Italy. Pope Julius III sent him as nuncio to Charles V of Spain in 1553 and in 1562 Pius IV appointed him metropolitan of Lanciano and sent him as legate to the Council of Trent. He served on commissions (1566–70) to prepare a new breviary, missal, and catechism and acted as papal emissary to the court of Maximilian II at the council's conclusion. Pope Pius V made him bishop of Alba and apostolic visitor to twenty-five dioceses to establish Tridentine reforms. In 1572, Pope Gregory XIII sent him to Spain and Portugal to renew their alliance against the Turks. He died in Rome on June 11.

MARINI, LUIGI GAETANO (1742–1815), scholar. Born in Sant' Orcangelo, Italy, on Dec. 18, he studied in San Marino, Rimini, Bologna, and Ravenna. He was in orders, though never ordained, went to Rome in 1764, and become coadjutor to the prefect of archives in 1772 and president of the Vatican Library and Museum. He went to Paris with the curial archives when Napoleon stole them in 1810, and was ready to accompany them on their return when he died on May 7. He wrote a standard treatise on papyri, *Acts and Monuments of the Arval Brothers* of ancient Rome, and on epigraphy, and classified some 5000 inscriptions in the Vatican.

MARINI, TOMMASO (d. 1636). Brother of Domenico and Giovanni, he became a Dominican in Rome and taught at the Minerva there. He was Provincial of the Holy Land, was socius of his order, and held numerous other offices, acting as secretary of three general chapters before his death in Naples.

MARINONI, BL. FRANCISCO JOHN (1490–1562). Born in Venice, he became a priest and served as chaplain and then superior of the hospital for incurables there. He became a canon in the cathedral and in 1528 resigned his canonry to become a Theatine, taking the name John. He accompanied St. Cajetan to Naples to found a Theatine house there, became famous for his preaching, helped St. Cajetan establish *montes pietatis* (pawnshops) for the poor, and refused the archbishopric of Naples when it was offered to him. His cult was authorized by Pope Clement XIII in 1762. F. D. Dec. 13.

MARINUS I (d. 884?), pope. The son of a priest, he was born in Gallese, Tuscany, Italy, and in 869, as a deacon, was sent by Pope Adrian II to preside over the eighth General Council in Constantinople. He was made bishop of Caere by John VIII, papal treasurer, and ambassador to Constantinople when the Photian schism began in 880. He was elected pope, on John's assassination, on Dec. 16, 882, renewed the condemnation of Photius, reinstated Formosus as bishop of Porto and absolved him of censure, tried to secure the support of Emperor Charles the Fat, and continued close negotiations with King Alfred of England. He died in Rome on May 15. He sometimes is called Martin II.

MARINUS II (d. 946), pope. A native of Rome and a cardinal, he was elected pope on Oct. 30, 942, through the influence of Alberic. His pontificate was uneventful, though he attempted reforms and encouraged the monastic movement. He died in Rome in May. He is sometimes called Martin III.

MARINUS, ST. (d. 262?), martyr. A Roman of a noble family in Caesarea in Palestine, he was about to become a centurion when he was denounced as a Christian by a rival and executed. F. D. Mar. 3.

MARINUS, ST. (d. 283). He is said to have been the son of a senator, who was tortured and beheaded in Rome. F. D. Dec. 26.

MARINUS, ST. (d. 290), martyr. He was

slain at Anazarbus, Cilicia, during the Diocletian persecution. F. D. Aug. 8.

MARINUS, ST. (4th century?). He is said to have been ordained a deacon by Bishop Gaudentius of Rimini and to have died as a hermit in the area now occupied by the republic of San Marino. F. D. Sept. 4.

MARINUS, ST. (d. 731), martyr. A Benedictine at Maurienne, Savoy, he became a hermit at Chandor, where he was slain by Saracens. F. D. Nov. 24.

MARINUS, BL. (d. 1170). He became Benedictine abbot of La Cava, Italy, in 1146, and in 1156 was mediator in the quarrel between Pope Eugene III and the kings of Sicily. F. D. Dec. 15.

MARIOTTE, EDME (1620?–1684), physicist. Born in Dijon, France, he was ordained and made prior of St. Martin's, near Dijon. He performed many experiments with heat, cold, light, sight, color, water, and the pendulum. He became widely known as an expert on hydrostatics, discovered the law of gases named after him, proved the laws of impact between bodies, and developed several valuable pieces of laboratory equipment. He published widely on his findings and an *Essay on Logic,* and died in Paris on May 12.

MARIQUE, PIERRE JOSEPH (1872–1957), educator. Born in Scilles, Belgium, on Jan. 24, and a graduate of the College of St. Servais in Liège, he taught in his homeland before coming to the United States in 1903. He served on the faculty of Seton Hall, City College, and Columbia, and was professor of education at Fordham from 1918 to 1946. He wrote a long-standard *History of Christian Education,* a *Philosophy of Education,* and numerous other professional items. He died in New York City on Apr. 10.

MARISCO, ADAM DE (d. 1257). Probably born in Somerset, England, he studied at Oxford under Robert Grosseteste, became rector of Wearmouth, Durham, about 1234, and joined the Friars Minor three years later. He was the first teacher at the famous Franciscan house at Oxford, helped organize the course of studies there, and was constantly consulted by the great of his time because of his great learning, for which he was called "Doctor Illustris." He was a friend of Simon de Montfort and supported him in his reforming interests.

MARISCOTTI, ST. CLARICE (1584?–1640). Born in Vignarello, Italy, and educated at Viterbo, she was forced by her aristocratic parents into a Franciscan convent, as Sr. Hyacintha. For ten years she violated the very essence of the Rule and kept the community in turmoil. Following a severe illness, she reformed, devoted herself to the care of the sick, poor and aged, begged to gain funds for two additional charitable establishments, and even

became a brilliant and successful mistress of novices. She was canonized in 1807. F. D. Jan. 30.

MARITAIN, RAÏSSA (1883–1960), author. Raïssa Oumansoff was born in Marioupol, Russia, of Jewish parents, emigrated to Paris with her parents when ten, was admitted to the Sorbonne when only sixteen, and there met Jacques Maritain and the group which was to make such an impact on French intellectual life in the early twentieth century: Charles Péguy, Ernest Psichari, Léon Bloy, Charles Rouault, Henri Massis, Georges Sorel, and Jean Cocteau. She and Jacques were married in 1904, became converts in 1906, and worked together until her death in Paris on Nov. 4. She wrote *The Prince of This World* (1936), *St. Thomas Aquinas, the Angel of the Schools* (1935), a juvenile, *Prayer and Intelligence,* with her husband, and two autobiographical volumes: *We Have Been Friends Together* (1942) and *Adventures in Grace* (1945).

MARIUS, ST. (d. 260?), martyr. A nobleman, he became a convert and traveled to Rome, being tortured and beheaded during the Claudian persecution for attempting to bury the ashes of other martyrs burned to death in the arena. His wife Martha and their sons, Abachum and Audifax, were slain with him. F. D. Jan. 19.

MARIUS, ST. (d. 555), abbot. Also called May and, erroneously, Maurus, he is believed to have been founder of the abbey of Bodon, France, to which he came from Paris. F. D. Jan. 27.

MARIUS MERCATOR (390?–451?), apologist. Probably a native of North Africa, he was the author of several influential treatises. While in Rome in 417 or 418 he wrote two anti-Pelagian works which he sent to St. Augustine, and while in Constantinople (429–48) his treatises against the Pelagians led to the condemnation of Julian of Eclanum and Caelestius at Ephesus in 431. He also wrote two treatises against the Nestorians and translated many Greek theological writings.

MARK, ST. (d. 336), pope. A native Roman, he became pope on Jan. 18, 336, built two basilicas on land donated by Constantine, and decreed that a new pope should be consecrated by the bishop of Ostia. He died in Rome. F. D. Oct. 7.

MARK, ST. (d. 74?), apostle. Probably of a Levitical family and the son of that Mary at whose house in Jerusalem the apostles stayed, he went in 44 with SS. Paul and Barnabas (a relative) to Antioch (Acts 12:25), Cyprus and Pamphylia (Acts 13:3,13), then to Jerusalem. In 50 he was again in Antioch, then in Cyprus, and in 61 in Rome, where he helped Paul during his first imprisonment (Col. 4:10) and apparently was a disciple of St. Peter (I Pet.

5:13), gathering material which he put into the second gospel. His authorship of this is attested by Papias, Irenaeus, Clement of Alexandria, Origen, Tertullian, Eusebius, and others. Its style is the Greek of everyday life, direct, matter-of-fact, vivid, but not stylized. It emphasizes the actions of Christ and His divine mission, power, and Person. He is said to have later become first bishop of Alexandria in Egypt. Although he is now identified with John surnamed Mark (Acts 12:25), they were given separate feasts; in the Eastern Church, the latter is called bishop of Byblos. The *Acta* of St. Mark, which call him a martyr, are not to be credited. F. D. Apr. 25.

MARK, ST. (d. 150?), martyr. He was put to death in Rome with St. Timothy and memorialized by Pope Pius I. F. D. Mar. 25.

MARK, ST. (d. 156?), bishop. He is said to have been the first bishop of Jerusalem not of Jewish birth, to have ruled the see for twenty years, and to have been a martyr. F. D. Oct. 22.

MARK, ST. (d. 269), martyr. *See* Lucius, St.

MARK, ST. (d. 287?), martyr. *See* Marcellian, St.

MARK, ST. (d. 303?), martyr. SS. Alexander, Alphius, Heliodorus, Neon, Nicon, Zosimus, and thirty soldiers were put to death at Antioch in Pisidia after they were converted by Mark, a shepherd. F. D. Sept. 28.

MARK, ST. (d. 305?), martyr. He and St. Stephen were put to death at Antioch in Pisidia during the reign of Galerius. F. D. Nov. 22.

MARK, ST. (d. 362?), bishop. Because he had attacked the pagans and destroyed a temple, the bishop of Arethusa, on Mt. Lebanon, was captured during the reign of Julian the Apostate and frightfully tortured. When freed and pardoned, he converted many who had witnessed his fortitude under suffering. F. D. Mar. 29.

MARK, ST. (5th century), bishop. *See* Priscus, St.

MARK, BL. (1426–1497). Born in Santa Maria di Montegallo, near Ascoli, Italy, he became a physician, married, then separated by mutual consent, his wife becoming a Poor Clare. He entered the Franciscans at Fabriano, then preached throughout Italy for forty years, practicing extreme mortification. To help the poor victims of usurers he set up a number of charitable pawnshops, known in Italy as *monti di pietà*. F. D. Mar. 20.

MARK, BL. (d. 1498). Born in Modena, Italy, he was a successful Franciscan preacher; his cult was approved in 1857. F. D. Sept. 23.

MARK OF GALILEE, ST. (d. 92), bishop and martyr. He was a missionary bishop to the Abruzzi area of Italy, where he was martyred. F. D. Apr. 28.

MARK OF LISBON. *See* Silva, Marcos da.

MARMAGGI, FRANCESCO (1876–1949),

cardinal. Born in Rome on Aug. 31, he was ordained in 1900, began a diplomatic career which saw him as papal nuncio to Romania and Poland, was named a cardinal in 1935, and became prefect of the Congregation of the Council in 1938. He died in Rome on Nov. 3.

MARNOCK, ST. (d. 625?), bishop. A monk with St. Columba on Iona, he became a missionary bishop in Scotland. Kilmarnock is named after him. F. D. Mar. 1 (also, Oct. 25).

MARO, ST. (d. 99?), martyr. *See* Eutyches, St.

MARO, ST. (d. 433). A Syrian solitary, whose model was St. Zebinus, he gave advice to St. John Chrysostom and numerous visitors who thronged to his hermitage. His body was later interred at a monastery near the source of the Orontes River, called Beit-Marun, which was to be associated with the beginnings of the Maronites. F. D. Feb. 14.

MAROLUS, ST. (d. 423). A Syrian, he became bishop of Milan, Italy, in 408. F. D. Apr. 23.

MARONI, PAUL (b. 1695), missioner. Born on Nov. 1, he became a Jesuit in Austria in 1712, was sent to Quito, Ecuador, in 1723, taught theology there, then served as a missioner among the Indians along the Napo and Aguarico rivers, where he founded several settlements and compiled a diary. His descriptions of his explorations and the maps he prepared were of value to geographers.

MAROTAS, ST. (d. 344), martyr. *See* Lazarus, St.

MAROVEUS, ST. (d. 650?). A Benedictine monk at Bobbio, he became abbot-founder of Precipiano, near Tortona, Italy. F. D. Oct. 22.

MARQUARD, ST. (d. 880), bishop and martyr. A Benedictine monk at New Corbie, Saxony, he was bishop of Hildesheim from 874 to 880, and was slain by pagan Norsemen, who trapped the army of Duke Bruno, near Ebsdorf. F. D. Feb. 2.

MARQUETTE, JACQUES (1637–1675), explorer. Born on June 10 in Laon, France, he studied in Nancy and Pont-à-Mousson, became a Jesuit in 1653, taught in Rheims, Charlesville, and Langres, was ordained, and in 1666 was sent on the Canadian mission. After some time in Three Rivers and Quebec he went to Sault Ste. Marie in 1668; when the Hurons deserted for fear of the Sioux, he followed them to Mackinac and founded St. Ignace in 1671. In 1673 he joined Louis Joliet on an exploring expedition and discovered the Mississippi River, which they descended from the mouth of the Wisconsin as far as the Arkansas River. On his return he continued teaching and instructing the Indians until his death, near what is now Ludington, Michigan, on May 19. His journal, published as *Voyage et découverte de quelques pays et nations de l'Amerique septen-*

trionale in 1681 is a valuable source for early American history.

AGNES REPPLIER, *Père Marquette* (Garden City, N. Y., Doubleday, 1929).

MARQUINA, EDUARDO (1879–1946), dramatist. Born in Barcelona, Spain, he studied law, became interested in the literary revolt of 1898, and became a journalist. He published four collections of poems before 1910, but became interested in the drama after the success of his *Doña María la brava* (1909). Other plays, many of which were a return to poetic drama, include *Las hijas del Cid, En Flandes se ha puesto el sol, Las flores de Aragón, El gran capitán, Fuente escondita,* and *En el nombre del padre.* He also wrote comedies (*Cuando florezcan los rosales*), novels, and biographies. He was elected to the Spanish Academy, was an officer in international literary associations, gave readings in Central and South America, and died in New York City on Nov. 21.

MARRYAT, FLORENCE (1838–1899), novelist. Born in Brighton, England, on July 9, daughter of the novelist Frederick Marryat (whose biography she wrote), she married Col. T. Ross Church in 1854 and went with him to India, where she began writing novels in 1865; she completed some ninety. On her return, she edited *London Society* from 1872 to 1876, appeared on the stage as actress, opera singer, and lecturer, and began a school of journalism. In 1881 she wrote a drama, *Her World,* in which she starred. Her second husband was Col. Francis Lean. She had become a convert some years before her death in London on Oct. 27.

MARSDEN, BL. WILLIAM (d. 1586), martyr. Born in Lancashire, England, he studied at Oxford, was ordained at Rheims, and was sent on the English mission. He was captured and executed on the Isle of Wight during the Elizabethan persecution, on the charge of being a priest. He was beatified in 1929. F. D. Apr. 25.

MARSHALL, THOMAS (1818–1877). Born in England, he graduated from Cambridge in 1840, became an Anglican clergyman, was influenced by the Tractarian movement, began writing on the early Church, and was converted in 1845. He was first inspector of Catholic schools in England from 1847 to 1860, when his hostile pamphlets on Protestant mission work caused a furore. He resigned and went on two lecture trips to the United States. His books include *Christian Missions, Christianity in China,* and similar titles. He died in Surbiton, Surrey, England, on Dec. 14.

MARSHALL, THOMAS. *See* Beche, Bl. John.

MARSIGLI, LUIGI FERDINANDO DE (1658–1730), geographer. Born in Bologna, Italy, on July 10, he served in the Venetian army and with the Austrian forces resisting the Turkish invasion of Hungary, was wounded and captured in 1683, and released the next year. During the War of the Spanish Succession, after the surrender of Breisach in 1703 by his superior, Count d'Arco (who was beheaded), Marsigli also was accused of surrendering without military reason and dropped from the army. During his travels he studied the flora and fauna of other countries, as well as their natural resources and physical characteristics, wrote on the Thracian and Danubian regions, and accumulated scientific collections which he gave to Bologna. He founded the Institute of Arts and Sciences in 1712, and a press, later run by the Dominicans, and became associated with the Paris Academy of Sciences and, when he visited London in 1727, the Royal Society. He died in Bologna, Italy, on Nov. 1.

MARSUPPINI, CARLO (1399?–1453). Born in Arezzo, Italy, he became a leading classicist, under the patronage of the Medici, lectured in Florence, served as apostolic secretary, and in 1444 became chancellor of the republic. He wrote Latin poems and translated part of the *Iliad.* He is best known as Carlo Aretino.

MARTANA, ST. (d. 254?), martyr. *See* Eusebius, St.

MARTÈNE, EDMOND (1654–1739), historian. Born in St. Jean de Losne, France, on Dec. 22, he became a Benedictine of St. Maur in 1672, studied at St. Germain, Paris, where he helped to prepare a new edition of the Fathers of the Church, and devoted his life to studies and writings on liturgy and history. These include a commentary on the Rule of St. Benedict, a history of Marmoutier, a biography of Claude Martin, and a continuation of d'Achery's *Spicilegium.* In 1708, with Ursin Durand, he visited 900 churches and abbeys in France and Belgium for a revised edition of *Gallia Christiana* and for the five-volume *Thesaurus novus anecdotorum* (1717). He died at St. Germain on June 20.

MARTHA, ST. (d. 80?). Sister of Lazarus and Mary, she lived with them in the house in Bethany which Christ often visited. Martha took care of serving Him, and has become the prototype of those seeking to live the active life; Mary, the symbol of the contemplative way. It was Martha who searched out Christ after the death of Lazarus. The story of the family's missionary voyage to France in later years is mere legend. F. D. July 29.

MARTHA, ST. (d. 252), martyr. She was put to death at Astorga, Spain, during the reign of Decius. F. D. Feb. 23.

MARTHA, ST. (d. 260?), martyr. *See* Marius, St.

MARTIAL, ST. (d. 150?), martyr. *See* Alexander, St.

MARTIAL, ST. (d. 250?), bishop. He is traditionally held to have been sent from Rome as a missioner to the Limousin and to have been bishop of Limoges, Gaul. Other biographical details, such as identification with the boy who supplied loaves and fishes at the time of Christ's miracle, are later fictions. Two of his missionary associates, Bl. Alpinian and Bl. Austriclinian, are honored with him on June 30.

MARTIAL, ST. (d. 300?), martyr. *See* Epictetus, St.

MARTIAL, ST. (d. 304), martyr. *See* Apodemius, St.; also, Faustus, St.

MARTIALL, JOHN (1534–1597). Born in Worcestershire, England, he studied at Winchester and Oxford, where he received his degree in law in 1556, taught at Winchester, and was forced to flee to France at Elizabeth's accession. He studied at Douai, took his degree in divinity in 1567, joined Allen at the newly founded English College there in 1568, then took a canonry at Lille, France, where he died on Apr. 3. He wrote *Treatise on the Cross* (1564) and a reply to an attack by the Calvinist James Calfhill.

MARTIANAY, JEAN (1647–1717), scholar. Born in St. Sever Cap, France, on Dec. 30, he became a Benedictine and an outstanding biblical scholar. He taught scripture at Arles, Bordeau, and Carcassone, edited the writings of St. Jerome, wrote a method of explaining scripture, a New Testament in French, and several polemical works, and died at St. Germain-des-Prés, Paris, on June 16.

MARTIGNY, JOSEPH ALEXANDRE (1808–1880), archaeologist. Born in Sauverny, Ain, France, on Apr. 22, he studied at the Belley seminary, was ordained and taught there, became a curate at Cressy, parish priest at Arbignieu, curé of Bagéle-Chatêl, and later a monsignor. His interest in archaeology led to the publication in 1865 of his monumental *Dictionnaire des antiquités chrétiennes*. He died in Belley, France, on Aug. 19.

MARTIN I, ST. (d. 655), pope and martyr. A native of Todi, Umbria, he served as nuncio to Constantinople for Pope Theodore I, whom he succeeded on July 21, 649. He immediately convened a council at the Lateran which condemned Monothelism, as well as the imperial decrees *Ecthesis* of Heraclius and *Typos* of Constans II. The latter had Martin forcibly deported to Constantinople in 653, imprisoned, condemned for treason, and in 654 exiled to Cherson, Crimea, where he died on Sept. 16 of ill treatment and starvation, the last of the popes to be venerated as a martyr. F. D. Nov. 12.

MARTIN II, pope. *See* Marinus I.

MARTIN III, pope. *See* Marinus II.

MARTIN IV (d. 1285), pope. Simon de Brie was born in Montpensier, Touraine, France, became canon and treasurer of St. Martin of Tours church, and was appointed chancellor of France by King Louis IX in 1260. He was created cardinal-priest in 1262 by Pope Urban VI and served as legate to France in 1261–68 and again in 1271–76. He was elected pope at Viterbo on Feb. 22, 1281, and crowned on Mar. 23 through the influence of Charles of Anjou, the second pope with the name Martin (he is called Martin IV because Popes Marinus I and II were known as Popes Martin II and III), and remained dependent on Charles throughout his pontificate. His excommunication of Charles's enemy, Greek Emperor Michael Palaeologus, resulted in a renewal of the Greek schism which had been healed at the Council of Lyons in 1274. When Sicily revolted against Charles, his excommunication of the Sicilian king, Peter III of Aragon, further alienated the Italian people. He never resided in Rome, and died in Perugia, Italy, on Mar. 28.

MARTIN V (1368–1431), pope. Oddone Colonna was born in Genazzano, near Rome, Italy, of a powerful Italian family, studied at Perugia, served Popes Urban VI and Boniface IX, and was administrator of the archdiocese of Palestrina from 1401 to 1405 and again in 1412. He was made cardinal-deacon in 1405, attended the Council of Pisa, and supported antipopes Alexander V and John XXIII against Pope Gregory XII. Though only a subdeacon, he was the choice of the delegates at the Council of Constance to effect the reconciliation of Christendom, and was elected pope on Nov. 11, 1417. He was ordained two days later, consecrated bishop the next day, and crowned on Nov. 21 at Constance. He quickly concluded concordats with Germany, France, England, and Spain. In 1419, John XXIII submitted to him, and, though Benedict XIII would not, his successor Clement VIII submitted in 1429, which ended the Western schism. Martin returned the papacy to Rome in 1420 (the year he proclaimed a crusade against the Hussites) by recognizing Joanna as lawful queen of Naples (whereupon her troops evacuated Rome) and reaching an agreement with Braccio di Montone, ruler over central Italy, regarding a division of provinces. He rebuilt Rome, practically in ruins, bringing in many Tuscan artists; was a vigorous opponent of the conciliar theory of Church government, which he denounced while reasserting papal supremacy; began plans for clerical reform; reestablished his dominion over the Papal States; but had difficulty with a powerful curia, the question of Gallican liberties, and peninsular politics. He died in Rome on Feb. 20.

MARTIN, ST. (2nd century), bishop. He is said to have been sent to Vienne, Gaul, about 132 as its third bishop. F. D. July 1.

MARTIN, ST. (d. 210?), bishop. He is listed

as tenth bishop of Trèves, Gaul, and may have been martyred. F. D. July 19.

MARTIN, ST. (d. 350?), bishop. He is listed as the seventh bishop of Tongres, Belgium, and long was honored as an evangelist of Brabant. F. D. June 21.

MARTIN, ST. (d. 400?). A follower of St. Martin of Tours, he became abbot-founder of the monastery of Saujon, France. F. D. Dec. 7.

MARTIN, ST. (d. 579?), archbishop. His origin is unknown, but he arrived in Spain, perhaps as a pilgrim, at a time when the Arians were strong, and converted King Theodomir and most of Galicia. He spurred a strict form of monasticism through northwestern Spain, became bishop of Dumium and of Braga, and wrote a collection of canons, a conduct book, a commentary on local superstitions, and other works. F. D. Mar. 20.

MARTIN, ST. (d. 580?). An Italian Benedictine at Monte Cassino, also known as Mark, who became a hermit in Campania, he was highly praised by St. Gregory the Great. F. D. Oct. 24.

MARTIN III, BL. (d. 1259). Abbot and prior general of the Camaldolese order from 1248, he compiled their new constitutions. F. D. Sept. 13.

MARTIN (1400?–1464?). Born in Liebnitz, Zips, Hungary, he studied at Cracow and Vienna, and became a Benedictine while on a journey to Italy in 1425. He attended the Council of Basle in 1428, was appointed prior of Schöttenkloster abbey, Vienna, abbot in 1446, and in 1451 visitor of the abbeys in the Salzburg diocese, with authority to institute reforms. He resigned about 1460 and died on July 28 (sometimes listed as July 29, 1470).

MARTIN, AUGUSTE MARIE (1803–1875), bishop. Born in St. Malo, France, on Feb. 1, he was ordained in Rennes in 1828, did parish work there, taught at Collège Royal in 1828–39, went to Vincennes, where he was vicar general of the see and twice its administrator, and in 1845 went to the United States. He labored in New Orleans, was vicar general in 1849–53, was appointed first vicar of the diocese of Natchitoches (later to be Alexandria), Louisiana, in 1853, attended the second Plenary Council of Baltimore in 1866, and was a strong supporter of papal infallibility at the Vatican Council in 1869–70. He died in Natchitoches on Sept. 29.

MARTIN, ENRICO (d. 1632), engineer. Possibly a Frenchman (though his birthplace and nationality are unknown), he was in 1607 given the task of draining the valley around Mexico City. Floods, corrosion, political disputes, and rival appointments of other superiors delayed the project; by 1629 it was still unfinished and the mouth of Martin's tunnel was in such poor shape that it could not divert waters from the canals leading from the lakes. Martin himself had been jailed; the day after his release, the tunnel collapsed and 30,000 were drowned in the floods. Martin never recovered from the charges hurled against him; his tunnel was converted into an open canal during the next century.

MARTIN, FÉLIX (1804–1886), antiquarian. Son of the mayor of Auray, Brittany, France, he was born there on Oct. 4, became a Jesuit in 1823, and taught for two years at St. Acheul until the college was closed in 1828 as a result of anti-religious government pressure. He then taught in Spain, Belgium, and Switzerland, where he was ordained in 1831, and in 1842 was sent to Montreal, Canada, to help in reestablishing his Society there. He was superior of Lower Canada in 1844, led in aiding victims of the typhoid epidemic of 1847, and in 1851 opened St. Mary's College, of which he was rector until 1857. He established the college archives, designed St. Patrick's church, and achieved wide recognition as an antiquarian by his research into Canadian history and his role in publishing the *Jesuit Relations*. He went to Rome to seek additional sources on the early missions and unearthed much unpublished material. He was recalled to France in 1861, became rector of Vannes College in 1862, and was spiritual director at five colleges in Poitiers, Paris, and Rouen from 1865 to 1882, when all were closed by the government. He died in Paris on Nov. 25.

MARTIN, GREGORY (d. 1582), translator. Born in Maxfield, Sussex, England, he studied at Oxford, left the university for religious reasons, and became tutor of the children of Thomas Howard, fourth duke of Norfolk, including the martyr Philip Howard, earl of Arundel. In 1570, Martin went to Douai, was ordained a Jesuit in Rome in 1573, and in 1576 helped to establish and set up the curriculum of the English College there. He went to Rheims when Douai College was transferred there in 1578. He was appointed head of the group (including Richard Bristowe, John Reynolds, and Thomas Worthington) which produced the Douai-Rheims version of the Vulgate. He also wrote criticism on the heretical corruption of scripture, poems, and the treatises *Of Schisme* and *Of Christian Peregrination*. He died in Rheims, France, on Oct. 28.

MARTIN, KONRAD (1812–1879), bishop. Born in Geismar, Saxony, on May 18, he studied at Munich, Halle, and Würzburg, received his doctorate in divinity from Münster in 1835, and was ordained at Cologne in 1836. He taught at Wipperfürth and Cologne, wrote a textbook on Catholicism in 1843 which was widely used in Prussia, and was appointed professor of theology at Bonn and inspector of seminaries that same year. In 1856 he became bishop of Paderborn, founded Bonifatius-Verein, of which he was president from 1859 to 1875 and which helped establish missionary centers, founded a minor seminary at Heiligenstadt, and attended the Vatican Council, where he helped word the final decree on papal infallibility, which he had championed. Because of his ecumenical work he was bitterly attacked by some government leaders, was imprisoned at Wesel in 1874, and declared by the state to be no longer a bishop. He escaped to Holland, was expelled by demand of Prussia, and went to Mont St. Guibert, near Brussels, Belgium, from where he secretly ruled his diocese and where he died on July 16. A prolific writer, he published in 1839 a pamphlet against Hermesianism, under the pseudonym Fridericus Lange, which caused a sensation; other writings include *The Chief Duties of Catholic Germany*, several pleas to German Protestants, *Deliberations of the Vatican Council*, and translations and studies of St. Thomas Aquinas.

MARTÍN, LUIS (1846–1906). Born in Melgar, near Burgos, Spain, he became a Jesuit at eighteen, taught rhetoric in Poyanne, France, and in 1877 became rector of Salamanca. He attained a reputation as a theologian, was assistant of his Society in Spain in 1891, and in 1892 became its twenty-fourth general, moving to Fiesole, Italy, where he died.

MARTÍN MANUEL, ST. (d. 1156), martyr. Born in Auranca, near Coimbra, Portugal, he was serving as priest in Soure when captured and so mistreated by the Moors that he died. F. D. Jan. 31.

MARTÍN, MARIE FRANÇOISE THÉRÈSE. See Thérèse of Lisieux, St.

MARTIN, PAULIN (1840–1890), scholar. Born in Lycam, Lot, France, on July 20, he studied at the Montfaucon, St. Sulpice, and the French seminary in Rome, where he was ordained in 1863 and received his doctorate in theology in 1868, specializing in the study of Semitic languages. After a decade as curate in Paris, he was appointed to the chair of scripture and oriental languages in the Institut Catholique there in 1878, a position he held until his death in Amélie-les-Bains, France, on Jan. 14. He wrote an introduction to the Bible and several studies of New Testament textual criticism.

MARTIN, BL. RICHARD (d. 1588), martyr. Born in Shropshire, England, and educated at Oxford, he was convicted of aiding priests during the Elizabethan persecution and was hanged with five others at Tyburn. He was beatified in 1929. F. D. Aug. 30.

MARTIN CID, ST. (d. 1152). Born in Zamora, Spain, he was abbot-founder of the Cistercian monastery of Val Paraiso, to which St. Bernard sent the first community. F. D. Oct. 8.

MARTIN OF COCHEM (1630–1712). Born in Cochem, Germany, he became a Capuchin, was ordained, taught theology, and found himself in an era devastated by the plague of 1666 and without pastoral guidance. He began to preach in simple fashion in the archdioceses of Trier and Ingelheim, made many converts, then turned to publishing popular treatises on the life of Christ, the history of the Church, sacraments, prayer, legends of the saints, homilies, and inspirational narratives. He died in Waghäusel, Germany, on Sept. 10.

MARTÍN Y GARCIA, LUIS (1846–1906). Born in Melgar de Fernamental, Burgos, Spain, on Aug. 19, he studied at the seminary there, became a Jesuit in 1864, and was ordained in 1876. He served as rector of the Salamanca seminary, which he rebuilt, superior of Deusto-Bilbao College, and provincial of Castile. He was elected twenty-fifth general of the Jesuits in 1892 and held that office until his death in Fiesole, Italy, on Apr. 18.

MARTÍN DE HINOJOSA, ST. (d. 1213), bishop. Born in Castile, Spain, he became a Cistercian, was founder-abbot of Huerta, near Soria, in 1164, served as bishop of Sigüenza from 1185 to 1192, then resigned to live as a monk. F. D. Sept. 3.

MARTÍN OF LEÓN (d. 1203). Born in Old Castile, Spain, he became an Augustinian at San Marcello, then served at St. Isidore's church in León. He wrote a number of biblical commentaries, and is honored locally on Jan. 11.

MARTIN STREBSKI (d. 1278), chronicler. A native of Troppau (Oppavia), he became a Dominican at Prague, Bohemia, chamberlain to Pope Clement IV in Rome, and archbishop of Gnesen, Poland, in 1278. He died in Bologna, Italy, while on the way to his see. He wrote *Chronica pontificum et imperatorum*, which was popular in the Middle Ages, but which consists of mere fable and legend. The third edition (1277) has the account of Pope Joan and is responsible for spreading this myth.

MARTIN OF TOURS, ST. (315?–397), bishop. Born in Sabaria, Pannonia (now Hungary), of pagan parents, he became a catechumen about 325, was educated at Pavia, and when fifteen was conscripted by the army. About 327, at Amiens, he cut his cloak in half to share it with a freezing beggar; as the result of a vision of Christ, approving his action by wearing the cloak, he was converted. Permitted to leave the army about 339, he was ordained an exorcist by St. Hilary, visited his parents in Lombardy, was scourged by the Arians, and became a recluse on an island in the Tyrrhenian Sea. In 361, when he learned that Hilary had returned to Gaul, he joined him at Poitiers and was a hermit for ten years, founding the first monastic community in Gaul, at Ligugé. In 370 or 371, despite his objections, he was consecrated bishop of Tours. While he devoted himself to spreading the faith and destroying paganism in his diocese, he lived the life of a monk, spending much time in meditation in a chapel outside the city. Many monks were attracted there and the great monastic center of Marmoutier was established. Martin was an unrelenting foe of Arianism and Priscillianism, but when he pleaded with Emperor Maximus to spare Priscillian (who had been justly condemned of heresy at the Council of Saragossa) from the death penalty, he was accused by Bishop Ithacius of Ossanova of being himself tainted by the heresy. Martin's objection to imperial intervention in ecclesiastical matters was at first successful, but, after he left, Ithacius persuaded Maximus to have Priscillian and several of his Spanish followers beheaded. This gave widespread support to the heresy. Maximus and Ithacius were censured by Pope St. Siricius for their part in the affair. Martin died in Candes, Touraine, on Nov. 8. His tomb immediately became a great pilgrimage center. His life, marked by unusual miracles, was recorded by Sulpicius Severus; St. Augustine used it as a base for his biography. F. D. Nov. 11.

MARTIN OF VALENCIA. *See* Boil, Juan Martino de.

MARTIN OF VERTOU, ST. (d. 601). Born of a Frankish family in Nantes, he was ordained deacon by St. Felix and went to Poitou, where he preached unsuccessfully. He founded the abbeys of Vertou and St. Jouin-de-Marnes and other monastic establishments, as well as a convent in Durieu, Gaul, where he died. Biographical details are often confused with those of St. Martin of Braga. F. D. Oct. 24.

MARTINA. Stories are told of a Martina who was martyred in Rome in the third century during the persecution of Severus. A church was built in her honor in the seventeenth century, and she has had Jan. 1 and Jan. 30 as feast days, but her existence is seriously doubted; the name may have been confused with that of St. Tatiana.

MARTINELLI, SEBASTIANO (1848–1918), cardinal. Born in Santa Anna, near Lucca, Italy, on Aug. 20, he became an Augustinian at fifteen, was ordained in 1871, taught theology, and was elected prior general in 1889 and in 1895. He was made archbishop of Ephesus in 1896, sent to the United States as second apostolic delegate, and was named a cardinal in 1901. He served on the canon-law commission from 1906 to 1917, was prefect of the Congregation of Rites in 1909, and died in Rome on July 4.

MARTINENGO, BL. MARIA MAGDALENA (1687–1737). Born of the noble da Barco family in Brescia, Italy, she became a Capuchin sister at eighteen, served as mistress of novices and, in 1732, as prioress. She was beatified in 1900. F. D. July 28.

MARTINET, BL. JULIAN (d. 1606). Born in Medinaceli, Spain, he worked as a tailor, tried twice to join the Franciscans, but was dismissed because of the extremes he wished to follow. His holy reputation finally won him entrance to the friary in Scalceda. As a laybrother, with the name of Julian of St. Augustine, he was allowed to pursue a life of the most extreme mortification. He was beatified in 1825. F. D. Apr. 8.

MARTINEZ, LUIS MARIA (1881–1956), archbishop. Born in Molina de Caballeros, Mexico, on June 9, he was ordained in 1904, taught at the Morelia seminary, and worked out an acceptable Church-state relationship during the presidency of his radical friend, Lazaro Cárdenas (1934–46), and his two successors. His social views were quite liberal and he offended the reactionaries by pleading for more use of the voting privilege, approving anti-polio injections, and full awareness of modernity. He became auxiliary bishop of Morelia in 1923, coadjutor in 1934, archbishop in 1937, and primate of Mexico in 1951. He died in Mexico City on Feb. 9.

MARTINI, ANTONIO (1720–1809), archbishop. Born in Prato, Tuscany, Italy, on Apr. 20, he was ordained, became head of a college in Turin, then accepted a pension from King Charles Emmanuel of Sardinia so that he could devote full time to a translation of the New Testament from the Greek, which he published in 1771, and of the Old Testament, on which he worked with Rabbi Terni. Pleased by the result, Pope Pius VI made him an archbishop in 1781. He died in Florence, Italy, on Dec. 31.

MARTINI, GIAMBATTISTA (1706–1784), composer. Born in Bologna, Italy, on Apr. 24, he studied under his father, Predieri, and Riccieri, and was choirmaster at San Francesco, Bologna, in 1725. He became a Franciscan in 1729, wrote two valuable treatises on music, *Storia della musica* and *Saggio di contrappunto*, composed in the Roman school, and died in Bologna on Oct. 4.

MARTINI, MARTINO (1614–1661), missioner. Born in Trent, Italy, he became a Jesuit in 1631, studied at the Roman College, and was sent to China, arriving in 1643. He returned to Rome in 1650 as procurator for the Chinese mission and published a complete geographical description of China; the first part of a projected history; and an account of the war with the Tatars—all of which attracted great attention. He translated ascetical and theological works (including the works of Suarez) into Chinese. He returned to China in 1658 and died at Hangtscheu on June 6.

MARTINI, SIMONE (1283?–1344?), painter.

Born in Siena, Italy, he studied under Duccio, painted a fresco of the *Virgin and Child* at Siena in 1315 which attracted great attention, and decorated the churches of St. Catherine, Pisa, San Domenico, Orvieto, St. Martin, Assisi, and Santa Maria Novella, Florence. His portraits of Petrarch's Laura, of the poet himself (who dedicated two sonnets to him), and of Gen. Fogliano are also famous. He died on Aug. 4 at Siena, Italy (or Avignon, France), as a member of the papal court. He also is known as Simone Memmi or Simone di Martino.

MARTINI OF SIENA (1439–1502), architect. Born in Siena, Italy, he served at the court of Urbino in 1476 and of Naples in 1491. He designed the church of Madonna del Calcinaio at Cortona in 1485 and translated Vitruvius into Italian.

MARTINIAN, ST., martyr. Nothing definite is known of his life, although he is held to be one of the earliest martyrs, but the legend which linked him with St. Processus as jailer of SS. Peter and Paul is unfounded. F. D. July 2.

MARTINIAN, ST. (d. 435?). Named bishop of Milan, Italy, in 423, he attended the Council of Ephesus, and wrote against the Nestorian heresy. F. D. Jan. 2.

MARTINIAN, ST. (d. 458), martyr. An armorer for a Vandal, he was ordered by his master to marry the slave Maxima, who had taken a vow of virginity and who converted him. Saturian and two other brothers of Martinian fled with Maxima, but were recaptured. On the Vandal's death Maxima was freed (and later entered a monastery where she died peacefully), but the brothers were sold to a Berber chief. Caught converting other slaves, they were tortured and dragged to death by horses. F. D. Oct. 16.

MARTINIAN THE HERMIT. Now believed to be a legendary figure, though once venerated at Constantinople, he was described as a Palestinian recluse during the reign of Constantius. When approached by a temptress named Zoe, he thrust his feet into a fire, an action which converted the woman.

MARTINOV, JOHN (1821–1894), scholar. Born in Russia on Oct. 7, he studied at St. Petersburg and became tutor for the family of Count Schouvalov. He became a convert, a step which exiled him from his native land, and in 1845 joined the Jesuits. He was a papal theologian at the Vatican Council, became a consultant on oriental rites to the College of Propaganda, and wrote voluminously for scholarly journals. His books include *Annus Ecclesiasticus Graeco-Slavonicus*, the eleventh volume of the Bollandist's *Acta Sanctorum* for Oct. He died on Apr. 26 at Cannes, France.

MARTINUS POLONUS (d. 1278), archbishop. Born in Troppau, Silesia, he was chaplain and confessor to Pope Clement IV, was named archbishop of Gnesen, Poland, in 1278, and wrote a history of the popes.

MARTINUZZI, GEORGE (1482–1551), cardinal. George Utjesenovic (his real name, though he preferred to be called Martinuzzi, his Italian mother's name) was born in Karmicac, Dalmatia, entered the service of Duke John Corvinus when eight, of Duchess Hedwig, widow of Count Stephen Zapolya, in 1503, and the following year entered a monastery near Ofen, where he was ordained. He was appointed prior of Czenstochau monastery in Poland, then of Sajolad monastery in Hungary, and there met John Zapolya, the Hungarian pretender and son of Duchess Hedwig, who had just been defeated at the battle of Kashau by King Ferdinand, in 1527, and followed Zapolya into exile in Poland. George helped Zapolya to raise an army which soundly defeated Ferdinand at Ravay in 1528, and became royal counselor and treasurer. In 1534, John appointed him bishop of Grosswardein (not papally approved until 1539), and on John's death in 1540 he became a guardian of the nine-day-old king, John Sigismund, and chief adviser to the child's mother, Isabella. Martinuzzi ruled the country and with the aid of Sultan Suleiman of Turkey resisted Ferdinand, who claimed Hungary. In 1551, he forced Isabella to sign a treaty with Ferdinand by which peace was restored, territory exchanged, and Martinuzzi became archbishop of Gran and a cardinal. When Ferdinand's general, Castaldo, convinced the king that Martinuzzi was betraying him by a secret agreement with the sultan, they decided to get rid of him and on Dec. 16 Martinuzzi was assassinated at Alvincy. In spite of his dedication to politics, the cardinal was deeply concerned over the advance of Protestantism and sought to stem it.

MARTIUS, ST. (d. 530?). Director of the abbey of Clermont, France, after earlier years as a hermit, he lived to be ninety and was highly praised by St. Gregory of Tours. F. D. Apr. 13.

MARTY, MARTIN (1834–1896), bishop. Born in Schwyz, Switzerland, on Jan. 11, he studied at Schwyz, Fribourg, and Einsiedeln, and in 1854 became a Benedictine. He was ordained in 1856, became a professor at Einsiedeln and in 1860 went to the United States, where he became prior of St. Meinrad's in 1865 and abbot in 1875. In 1879 he was appointed titular bishop of Tiberias and vicar apostolic of Dakota, became first bishop of Sioux Falls in 1889, was transferred to St. Cloud, Minnesota, in 1895, and administered Sioux Falls in 1895–96. He founded St. Meinrad's College in 1866, wrote a history of the Benedictines, and died in St. Cloud on Sept. 19.

MARTYRIUS, ST. (d. 351), martyr. A subdeacon, he was slain at Constantinople with Marcian, a choirboy, by the Arian patriarch, Macedonius. F. D. Oct. 25.

MARTYRIUS, ST. (d. 397), martyr. *See* Sisinius, St.

MARUCCHI, ORAZIO (1852–1931), archaeologist. Born in Rome, he became director of the Egyptian Museum of the Vatican and of the Christian Museum of the Lateran, and held chairs of Christian archaeology at the College of San Apollinaire and the University of Rome. He edited *Nuovo Bolletino di Archeologia Cristiana* and wrote widely on the catacombs, epigraphy, the ancient city, and a study of the sanctity of marriage as established by ancient monuments.

MARULIC, MARKO (1450–1524), poet. Born in Spalato, Croatia, he studied at Padua, entered a monastery in Spalato, and wrote in Latin on politics, history, and theology. His *De institutione bene vivendi* (1506) was followed by many poems in the Croatian vernacular, mystery plays (the first dramas of the region), and an epic on the *History of Judith*.

MARUTHAS, ST. (d. 415?), bishop. A bishop of the Syrian Church, whose see was located in Maiferkat, Mesopotamia, near the Persian border, he was influential in securing a measure of freedom for Christians when Yezdigerd became king of Persia in 399. He was a friend of St. John Chrysostom, was noted for his knowledge of medicine, collected the *Acta* of the martyrs of Sapor's persecution and the relics of many of those martyrs, and wrote several hymns in praise of them. F. D. Dec. 4.

MARY, VIRGIN (1st century). Daughter of Heli (Joachim) and Anne, names given in scriptural and other accounts, Mary was descended from royal (David) and priestly (Aaron) ancestry. Tradition holds that her parents were old and long childless, and that she was born in Jerusalem (though there are claims for Sepphoris and for Nazareth); her birthday has been celebrated, from before the seventh century, on Sept. 8. It is dogma that, inasmuch as she was to be the mother of the second Person of the Holy Trinity, her soul should be spotless; her unique gift, as the only human free from all stain of original sin from the moment of her conception, is acknowledged as her Immaculate Conception. This dogma was formally established in 1854 by Pope Pius IX, who established Dec. 8 as the feast of the Immaculate Conception. The name Mary (from the Hebrew Miriam, probably meaning "wished-for child") is honored on Sept. 12, the feast of the Holy Name of Mary, dating from the sixteenth century and established formally in 1683 by Pope Innocent XI. Tradition also holds that her parents presented her in the Temple, perhaps on her third birthday (but later in some accounts), on which occasion

Mary made a vow of perpetual virginity. The feast of the Presentation, which dates back to the sixth century, but was not firmly established until 1585 in the pontificate of Sixtus V, is Nov. 12. Legend says that she was brought up in the Temple, which is unlikely; she apparently visited its precincts regularly, since her family lived nearby and since she, as were her parents, was devoted to prayer. In the apocrypha she was fourteen when the high priest suggested that she marry (legally, she could have been considered for marriage at twelve and a half); she is said to have reminded him that she had taken a vow of virginity and the priest is said to have prayed for direction and to have been miraculously informed that Joseph should be her spouse. According to betrothal custom, the bride legally belonged to the bridegroom for about a year before the marriage was celebrated. The marriage was arranged by Joseph's parents, and, although Mary agreed to current social and religious pressures that she be married, she expected that her vow would be honored. Before the formal marriage of Mary and Joseph, the Angel Gabriel appeared to her and announced that she had been chosen to be, virginally, by divine request, the mother of the Redeemer. She chose to agree; the account is in Luke 1:26–38. The feast of the Annunciation, honored as early as the fourth century, is now observed on Mar. 25, a date probably agreed upon in the seventh century by Pope Sergius. In her delight to impart her news to her cousin Elizabeth, who, the angel had informed her, had also conceived, Mary went to the house of Zachary in Juda to visit her, and stayed for three months (until the birth of John the Baptist, according to some commentators). The visit was marked by Elizabeth's immediate acknowledgment of Mary as Mother of God and by Mary's response in the prayer now called the *Magnificat* (Luke 1:5–25; 39–56). The feast of the Visitation, kept since the thirteenth century, is July 2. The feast of the Motherhood of Mary, dating at least from the fifteenth century, was formally set as Oct. 11 by Pope Pius XI in 1931. On her return, Mary was obviously with child, and Joseph was perplexed, thought of ending the betrothal, but was informed by an angel as to the mystery of the Incarnation and even as to the name Jesus, and proceeded with the marriage (Matt. 1:19–25). In accordance with the decree of Caesar Augustus, Joseph and Mary traveled nearly sixty miles from Nazareth to Bethlehem for the census and payment of taxes, found the town overcrowded because of the number who had come to be enrolled, and took shelter in a rocky area usually reserved for animals. There Christ was born (Luke 2:1–20). The feast of the Nativity (celebrated before 336) is Dec. 25; the day and month were decided upon, apparently, in relation to Mar. 25, long held to be the identical date of Christ's conception as well as of His death. Eight days later He was circumcised, in a private home or in the synagogue; the feast of the Circumcision has been celebrated on Jan. 1 since the sixth century. After forty days, according to the law, Mary presented herself at the Temple for ritual purification, bringing a sacrificial gift of two pigeons; it was on this occasion that Simeon acknowledged the Redeemer, to whom he had been presented by His Mother, as did Anna the Prophetess (Luke 2:22–40). The feast of the Purification, dating from the fourth century, is Feb. 2; in the Eastern churches it is called Hypapante ("the Meeting"), stressing the presentation of the Child to God through Simeon. Mary and Joseph returned to Bethlehem, where the wise men from the East came at a later date to honor the Child. Because of increasing rumors about one who had been born "King of the Jews," Herod became fearful and ordered the execution of all males under the age of two, lest his alleged rival live. The feast of their martyrdom (feast of the Holy Innocents) has been kept since the fifth century on Dec. 28; they numbered between six and, at most, twenty-five. To escape the anger of Herod, Joseph and Mary were directed to take flight to Egypt, a ten-day journey away; they lived there for an unstated number of years amid an extremely large Jewish colony. They had returned to Nazareth before Christ was twelve. It was the family's custom to go to the Temple annually, and it was on such an occasion that Christ began his discussions with the learned doctors, remaining behind after his parents had returned home (Luke 2:41–52). Mary next appears in scripture at the marriage feast at Cana (John 2:1–12); there are references to her presence during His public mission and she long served the daily needs of her carpenter husband Joseph (who apparently died before Christ was thirty). Mary followed her Son through His Passion and was present at the crucifixion, when Christ commended her to St. John (John 19:25–27). The impact of the treatment of Christ by His enemies and by the sins of the world is commemorated in the feast of the Seven Dolors, held on Good Friday (from as early as the fifteenth century in Cologne) and also on Sept. 15 (through the custom established by the Servites). It is generally believed that Mary was present at the Resurrection (although this is not in scripture). She was present in the discussions about the early Church presided over by St. Peter in the "upper room" in Jerusalem, was with the apostles at Pentecost, and presumably witnessed the Ascension of Christ. There are no authentic documents as to her later life; she may have remained in Jerusalem; she may have gone to Ephesus with St. John and others; she may have wandered from place to place as persecution mounted. She is held to have died about the year 48. The belief that her body was assumed into heaven (on the contention that, since she had never been subject to sin, she could not be subject to one of its effects, corrosive death), as a unique foreshadowing of the resurrection of the bodies of all mankind, is one of the oldest traditions of the Church; Mary's Assumption was declared dogma by Pope Pius XII in 1950. The feast is celebrated on Aug. 15. Other feasts include Feb. 11 (Our Lady of Lourdes, commemorating the vision of St. Bernadette Soubirous); July 16 (Our Lady of Mt. Carmel, commemorating the gift of the scapular to St. Simon Stock); Aug. 5 (commemorating the dedication of the basilica of Santa Maria Maggiore, Rome); Sept. 24 (Our Lady of Ransom, commemorating the successful establishment of the Mercedarians by St. Peter Nolasco); and Oct. 7 (established after the battle of Lepanto to honor the devotion of the rosary).

HENRI DANIEL-ROPS, *The Book of Mary* (New York, Hawhorne, 1960); FULTON J. SHEEN, *The World's First Love* (Garden City, N. Y., Image Books, 1956).

MARY I (1516–1558), queen of England. Daughter of Henry VIII and Catherine of Aragon, Mary Tudor was born on Feb. 18 at Greenwich, England, recognized as the heir to the throne, and offered in marriage to several of the crowned heads of Europe. When Henry decided to divorce Catherine to marry Anne Boleyn, Mary was separated in 1531 from her mother, treated as illegitimate (Henry claimed his marriage to Catherine was invalid), and, after Elizabeth's birth, was obliged to sign an agreement in 1536 by which she declared her mother's marriage to Henry invalid, recognized Henry's ecclesiastical supremacy, and renounced the pope's authority. In 1544 her succession to the throne after Edward and his heirs was recognized. On the death of Henry in 1547, Edward VI ascended the throne and Mary left the court and resided at various manors. During this period she resisted the demands of the king's councilors to give up her Catholicism, whereupon Northumberland convinced Edward to name Lady Jane Grey as his successor. Mary's appeal to Emperor Charles V for aid almost resulted in war. When Edward died in 1553, Lord Northumberland attempted to have Lady Jane Grey proclaimed queen, but Mary received the country's support, Northumberland was arrested and later executed, and Mary was crowned queen. Parliament ratified her coronation, mass was restored, though Protestantism was allowed to continue, bishops deposed in the previous reigns were restored to their sees, and

Cranmer and Latimer were imprisoned in the Tower. In 1554 rebellion led by Sir Thomas Wyatt broke out when Mary announced her intention of marrying Philip of Spain, but was crushed and its leaders executed, among them Lady Jane Grey and Wyatt, though Mary spared Elizabeth, who seemingly was implicated. On July 25, 1554, she married Philip and the following December the interdict on England was lifted when parliament restored the supremacy of the pope and re-enacted the laws against heresy. Mary's government attempted to restore Catholicism and brought to trial and executed many of the leaders of the Protestant groups, among them Latimer, Ridley, Rogers, and Cranmer, a step which led to constant turmoil. In 1557 she joined Spain in a war against France which, though successful at first, resulted in the loss of Calais to the French the next year. She died in London on Nov. 17.

H. F. M. PRESCOTT, *Mary Tudor* (New York, Macmillan, 1953).

MARY, ST. (1st century). According to Acts 12:12, she was the mother of John surnamed Mark and it was to her house, where a meeting of the faithful was being held, that Peter went when he was released from Herod's prison by an angel in the year 41 (Acts 12:1–11). F. D. June 29.

MARY, ST. (1st century). *See* Martha, St. (d. 80?).

MARY, ST. (d. 254?), martyr. *See* Eusebius, St.

MARY, ST. (d. 304), martyr. *See* Saturninus, St.

MARY, ST. (4th century). The Christian slave of a Roman official, Tertullus, she was subjected to great torture during the persecution of Diocletian, but released at the demand of the spectators. She is listed as a martyr because of her sufferings. F. D. Nov. 1.

MARY, ST. (d. 730), martyr. *See* Julian, St.
MARY, ST. (d. 851), martyr. *See* Flora, St.
MARY, ST. (d. 1180?), martyr. *See* Bernard, St.

MARY OF THE ANGELS, BL. *See* Fontanella, Bl. Mary.

MARY OF BURGUNDY (1457–1482), duchess. Daughter of Charles the Bold, last duke of Burgundy, and Isabella de Bourbon, she was born in Brussels, Flanders, on Feb. 13. She lost Burgundy, Picardy, Artois, and Franche-Comté to Louis XI of France. She granted the Great Privilege of 1477 to her Flemish subjects to regain their support and in the same year became duchess of Burgundy when her father was killed in battle at Nancy. She married Archduke Maximilian, son of Emperor Frederick III of Germany in 1477. They had two children, Philip I of Spain, father of Charles V, and Margaret, duchess of Savoy. She died in

Brussels on Mar. 27 in a fall from a horse, and her lands were inherited by Philip.

MARY OF CEREVELLON, ST. (d. 1290). Born in Barcelona, Spain, she devoted herself to helping Christians enslaved by Moors. In 1265 she joined a community of women which became a third order regular of Our Lady of Ransom (Mercedarians), and became its first prioress. She was called Maria de Socós because of her good works and in Spain is the patroness of sailors. Her cult was confirmed in 1692. F. D. Sept. 19.

MARY CHRISTINA, BL. (1812–1836), queen. Born in Cagliari, Sardinia, daughter of King Victor Emmanuel of Savoy and Maria Teresa, niece of Emperor Joseph II, she married King Ferdinand II of the Two Sicilies in 1832. She was beatified in 1872. F. D. Jan. 31.

MARY OF CLEOPHAS, ST. (1st century). Mother of James the Less and Joseph (John 19:25), the wife of Cleophas, who (according to St. Jerome) may have been St. Joseph's brother, she was present at the crucifixion (Matt. 27:56; Mark 15:40–47) and with Mary Magdalen went to the tomb on the first Easter (Mark 16:1–9). F. D. Apr. 9.

MARY CROCIFISSA, ST. *See* Di Rosa, St. Paula.

MARY OF EGYPT (5th century). The life of St. Cyriacus by Cyril of Scythopolis tells of a woman who lived in a cave in the Jordanian desert, who claimed to have been a public entertainer and great sinner, who told her story to passing hermits, and who was found dead when they returned a year later. The story was developed into an elaborate mediaeval legend, and exists in many variants.

MARY EUPHRASIA, ST. *See* Pelletier, Rose Virginia.

MARY EVARISTA, SR. *See* Harks, Anna.

MARY FRANCES OF NAPLES, ST. *See* Gallo, St. Anna Maria.

MARY OF GUISE. *See* Guise, Marie de.

MARY OF LORRAINE. *See* Guise, Marie de.

MARY MAGDALEN, ST. (1st century). Probably from Magdala on the western shore of the Sea of Galilee near Tiberias, she is said in the writings of St. Gregory the Great and others to have been a notorious sinner before she met Christ. While He was dining at the house of a Pharisee, she came in, washed Christ's feet with her tears, dried them with her hair, and anointed them. When the Pharisee complained, Christ rebuked him and forgave Mary her sins. She then followed Him and His apostles on their missionary travels through Galilee. She also is traditionally considered to be the sister of Martha and Lazarus, whose home in Bethany Christ often visited. Christ dined with them on the day before His entry into Jerusalem, and Mary anointed His head and feet. This time, Judas and some of the apostles objected to the action as wasteful, but Christ defended her. She was with the Virgin Mary at the crucifixion and went to anoint Christ's body as it lay in the tomb, only to find the stone rolled back on Easter morning. Wandering in grief, she was the first human to see and be greeted by the risen Christ. According to Eastern tradition, she went to Ephesus with Mary and St. John and died there. A false but pious legend claims that she, Lazarus, Martha, and others came to Provence, France, and evangelized that area. F. D. July 22.

MARY OF MODENA (1685–1718), queen. Born in Modena, Italy, on Oct. 5, she was married by proxy to the duke of York (later James II) at the suggestion of Louis XIV, went to England in 1673, sought to have the penal laws against Catholics made less stringent, and was strongly opposed by religious leaders for entering politics. When her son, James Stuart, was born in 1688 he was defamed by extreme calumny; fears of a Catholic uprising were cleverly though crudely spread, and, combined with political hostility to James II, led to the "bloodless revolution." The royal family fled to France in 1688 after a three-year rule, and the child was recognized as James III by King Louis XIV. She died in St. Germain-en-Laye, France, on May 7.

MARY OF OIGNIES, BL. (d. 1213). Born in Nivelles, Brabant, she was married at fourteen, persuaded her husband to respect her vow of virginity, and with him took care of the lepers they took into their house turned hospital. She subjected herself to severe austerities, was particularly devoted to the Eucharist, had a number of supernatural gifts, and died as a recluse in Oignies (now Belgium). Her life was written by Cardinal James de Vitry. F. D. June 23.

MARY OF PISA. *See* Mancini, Bl. Catherine.

MARY SALOME, ST. (1st century). Wife of Zebedee and mother of St. James the Greater and St. John the Evangelist, she was one of those who served Christ during His public life and was present at the crucifixion, burial, and Resurrection. F. D. Oct. 22.

MARY OF SCOTLAND (1542–1587), queen. Born at Linlithgow palace, near Edinburgh, Scotland, on Dec. 7 or 8, daughter of James V of Scotland and Marie de Guise, she succeeded to the crown when her father died six days after her birth and was crowned in 1543 when nine months old, with the earl of Arran, James Hamilton II, as regent. When an attempt to marry her to Edward VI of England was unsuccessful, she was betrothed to the dauphin of France (later Francis II) in 1548, was raised and educated in France, and married Francis in 1558. When Mary Tudor died in 1558, she became the principal claimant to the English throne as next in succession to Henry VIII and his children; Catholics claimed Elizabeth was not eligible since the Church had never recognized Henry's marriage to Elizabeth's mother, Anne Boleyn. In 1559, Francis and she were crowned king and queen of France. In 1560 war broke out between the followers of John Knox and Marie de Guise, who had become regent in 1554. With the aid of French troops the regent defeated the Protestants, but she died in June, and when Francis died in Dec., Mary, now dowager queen of France, returned to Scotland to govern in person. She arrived in Aug. 1561, recognized the rights of the Protestants, subdued a rebellion in the north in 1562, and in 1563 began to press her claims to the throne of England as Elizabeth's successor. She married her cousin, Henry Stuart, Lord Darnley (great-grandson of Henry VII) in 1565, a marriage that caused a rebellion led by her illegitimate half-brother, the earl of Moray, and supported by Queen Elizabeth, because she and Darnley were Catholics. After the rebellion was suppressed, she tried to restore Catholicism in Scotland and to establish her absolute authority. In 1566 a group of malcontents, of whom her jealous and quarrelsome husband was one, formed a conspiracy and murdered her Italian secretary, David Rizzio. She escaped with Darnley, whom she reaccepted, to the protection of the earl of Bothwell in Edinburgh, and with his aid quelled the insurrection and forced Rizzio's murderers to flee to England. A son, James, was born to Mary and Darnley and in 1567 Darnley was murdered. Bothwell was suspected but was exonerated in a quick trial, and took Mary, practically a captive, to his castle. After divorcing his wife, he married Mary. In this act Mary herself was clearly foolish, but her complicity in the deaths of others (Darnley included) has never been established. Scotland rebelled against the pair; the lords defeated Mary's and Bothwell's army at Carberry Hill, caused him to flee Scotland (later, he died in Denmark), imprisoned Mary at Loch Leven castle, and forced her to abdicate in favor of her son (who became James VI), with Moray as regent. In 1568 she escaped and raised an army, but was defeated at Langside, near Glasgow, by Moray. She fled to England, where Elizabeth had promised her asylum. An unsuccessful Catholic revolt in 1569 led to her confinement in various castles (she was held at Sheffield from 1569 to 1583) for the rest of her life, during which she was the object of countless plots, uprisings, and intrigues. In 1572 a plan for Mary to divorce Bothwell and marry Thomas Howard, duke of Norfolk, who also had a strong claim to the English throne, was discovered and Norfolk was beheaded. In 1586 the Babington plot to murder Elizabeth was uncovered, and Mary was accused of being its director. No evidence could be found; Mary admitted that she had always sought to escape, but denied any orders to have Elizabeth killed. She was tried for treason, declared guilty, and beheaded at Fotheringay castle on Feb. 8.

MARY SOLEDAD. *See* Torres-Acosta, Bl. Emanuela.

MAS, ST. JOAQUINA DE VEDRUNA DE (1783–1854), foundress. Born near Barcelona, Spain, on Apr. 16, the fifth of eight children of Lorenzo de Vedruna and Teresa Vidal, she married Teodoro de Mas, a lawyer, in 1799. The family suffered during the Napoleonic war of 1808–13, but was reunited when Teodoro resigned his army commission; he died three years later. Joaquina served in a hospital in Vich while bringing up six children, became a Franciscan tertiary, and in 1820 under the direction of Fr. Esteban Fabregas planned a new teaching and nursing order. Revolution interrupted; Joaquina was imprisoned and exiled, but returned in 1823. Fr. Fabregas drew up the rule for her Carmelite Sisters of Charity in 1826 and she began work at Vich with six associates. Civil war, imprisonment, and dispersal interfered with their plans, but they took their solemn vows in 1844. Mother Joaquina was superior until she was paralyzed in 1851; she died three years later, of cholera, on Aug. 28. She was canonized in 1959 by Pope John XXIII. F. D. May 22.

MASACCIO, TOMMASO (1401–1428?), painter. Born in Castello San Giovanni, Val d'Arno, Italy, on Dec. 21, Tommaso di ser Giovanni di Simone dei Guidi studied under Masolino da Panicale and was influenced by Brunelleschi and Donatello. He did frescoes in the church of San Clemente, Rome, and in the Brancacci chapel, Florence, completing some of the work of his master; some of his own work was eventually finished by Filippino Lippi. Also notable is his altarpiece for the church of the Carmine, Pisa. Careless about dress and business, "Hulking Tom" (Masaccio) is believed to have died in Rome. His work is noted for its sense of perspective, knowledge of anatomy, and naturalistic presentation of form, emotion, and landscape.

MASCARON, JULES (1634–1703), bishop. Born in Marseilles, France, he joined the Congregation of the Oratory, preached to large audiences through France, was called to the court in 1666, and retained royal favor even though he harshly denounced sins in aristocratic circles. He became bishop of Tulle in 1671 and was transferred to Agen in 1679. His sermons were published in 1704. He died in Agen, France, on Nov. 20.

MASCOLI, BL. LORENZO DEI (1476–1535). Born in Villamagna in the Abruzzi, Italy, he became a Franciscan near Ortona, practiced extreme austerities, and was one of

the greatest preachers of his day. He died at Ortona, Italy, and his cult was confirmed in 1923. F. D. June 6.

MASO DI BANCO. *See* Giottino.

MASOLINO DA PANICALE (1383?–1447?), painter. Tommaso di Cristoforo di Fini was born in Panicale di Valdese, Italy, and known as Masolino da Panicale. He studied under Starnina and about 1415 executed the frescoes of the lives of SS. Ambrose and Catherine in the church of San Clemente, Rome. He settled in Florence in 1423 and painted frescoes in the Brancacci chapel; between 1428 and 1435 he did those of St. John the Baptist in Castiglione d' Olona. His work has delicacy and grace, something of the style of Giotto, and skill in the portraiture of women and of landscape backgrounds. His religious subjects ranged from a *Temptation of Adam and Eve* to a *Resurrection of Tabitha*; his crowds, particularly in his *Baptism of Christ*, show the effective detail of later genre paintings. Masaccio was his most celebrated pupil.

MASON, BL. JOHN (d. 1591), martyr. *See* Genings, Bl. Edmund.

MASON, RICHARD (1599–1678). A native of Wiltshire, England, he was professed as a Franciscan in 1629, ordained at Douai in 1633, and served successively as definitor, guardian, and visitor of Brabant. He was elected provincial in 1659, became domestic chaplain to Lord Arundell of Wardour in 1662, and remained in England until 1675 when he returned to Douai, France, where he died on Dec. 30. Known in religion as Father Angelus a S. Francisco, he wrote many devotional treatises, *Apologia pro Scoto Anglo*, and a collection of biographies of English Franciscans.

MASSAIA, LORENZO GUGLIELMO (1809–1889), cardinal. Born in Piova, Piedmont, Italy, on June 9, he studied at Collegio Reale in Asti, then at the diocesan seminary, and in 1825 joined the Capuchins, taking the name Guglielmo. After his ordination he became a lector in philosophy, noted for his preaching ability, and confessor of Victor Emmanuel and the duke of Genoa. In 1846 he was appointed first vicar apostolic to the Galla region of Abyssinia, and landed and worked in the disguise of a merchant. When, at his request, a vicar apostolic to the Copts was appointed, the action caused such opposition he was banished and fled to Europe in 1850, the first of the seven exiles into which he was forced during thirty-five years of mission activity, during which he built up a colony of 10,000 Catholics. He also translated the Bible and compiled a dictionary in Ethiopian. Ill health, brought on by earlier physical attacks, caused him to resign in 1880; he was appointed titular archbishop of Stauropolis later that year and in 1884 was created a cardinal. He died in Cremona, Italy, on Aug. 6.

MASSALENIS, BL. PIETRO DE (1375–1453). Born in Othoca, Sardinia, he became a Camaldolese at San Michele de Murano, Venice, in 1410, and was noted for his mysticism. F. D. Dec. 20.

MASSALIUS, ST. (1st century), martyr. *See* Euphrasius, St.

MASSÉ, ENEMOND (1574–1646), missioner. Born in Lyons, France, he became one of the first missionary Jesuits in New France. He and Fr. Biard established a mission at what is now Bar Harbor, Maine, but saw it destroyed by the English. He returned to Canada in 1625 and, except for the period after the fall of Quebec, he spent the rest of his life ministering to the Indians. He died in Sillery, Quebec, on May 12.

MASSEY, BL. RENÉ (d. 1792). A Benedictine monk of St. Maur, he took Julian as his name in religion, was stationed at St. Melania in Rennes when the French Revolution broke out, and was slain in Paris during the September massacres. He was beatified in 1926. F. D. Sept. 2.

MASSI, GENTILE (1378?–1427?), painter. Born probably in Fabriano, Italy, he designed an altarpiece in Venice and decorated the doges' palace there about 1411, decorated a chapel in Brescia, lived in Florence about 1419–23, and worked in Siena, Orvieto, and Rome. A *St. Francis, Adoration of the Magi,* and work in St. John Lateran are typical, marked by heavy use of gold and brilliant coloring.

MASSIAS, BL. JUAN DE (1585–1645). Born of impoverished, noble parents in Ribera, Estramadura, Spain, he was orphaned as a child and raised by an uncle for whom he worked as a shepherd. He served two years on a ranch in Peru, then became a Dominican laybrother at Lima, where he became porter. He was beatified in 1837. F. D. Sept. 18.

MASSILLON, JEAN BAPTISTE (1663–1742), bishop. Born in Hyères, Provence, France, on June 24, he studied at the college there and in Marseilles, entered the Oratorians in 1681, and taught at Pèzenas, Marseilles, Montbrison, and Vienne, where he was ordained in 1691. After his appointment as director of St. Magloire seminary in Paris in 1695 he developed into one of the greatest preachers of the day and frequently preached at the court of Louis XIV. Accused of a tendency toward Jansenism, he fell from the king's favor after 1704, though his preaching in the churches of Paris remained sensationally successful, and in 1715 he preached the king's funeral oration. In 1717 he was appointed bishop of Clermont, was made a member of the French Academy in 1718, and devoted himself to ecclesiastical reforms in his diocese (he held annual priests' synods from 1723 to 1742 at which he delivered conferences) and working for his flock, especially the poor. He died on Sept. 18 in Clermont, France.

MASSIMI, MASSIMO (1877–1954), cardinal. Born in Rome on Apr. 19, he was dean of the rota from 1925 to 1935, made a cardinal, placed in charge of drafting the canon code for Eastern churches, drafted the laws governing Vatican City, and served on the congregations for the Sacraments and for the Propagation of the Faith. He was prefect of the supreme tribunal of the apostolic signatura at the time of his death in Rome on Mar. 6.

MASSON, LOUIS FRANÇOIS RODRIGUE (1833–1903), governor. Born in Terrebonne, Quebec, Canada, he studied at Georgetown and St. Hyacinthe, Quebec, and was admitted to the bar in 1859. He served in the Canadian parliament as Conservative member for Terrebonne from 1867 to 1882, was minister of militia and defense in 1878–80, president of the council, and in 1884–87 served as lieutenant governor of the province. He was returned to the senate in 1882 and 1892 and also served as mayor of Terrebonne.

MASSOULIÉ, ANTOINE (1632–1706), theologian. Born in Toulouse, France, on Oct. 28, he joined the Dominicans as a youth, became noted for his knowledge of Greek and Hebrew, and as an outstanding scholar of the works of St. Thomas Aquinas and vigorous opponent of quietism. He wrote: *Divus Thomas sui interpres de divina motione, Traité de la véritable oraison,* and *Traité de l'amour de Dieu.* He died in Rome on Jan. 23.

MASSUET, RENÉ (1666–1716), patrologist. Born in St. Ouen de Mancelles, France, on Aug. 13, he became a Benedictine of St. Maur, studied in Orléans, taught at Bec, Caen, Fecamp, and Rome, and after 1703 was stationed at St. Germain-des-Prés, Paris, where he taught theology. He edited the writings of St. Irenaeus (1710) and the fifth volume of Mabillon's *Annales* of his order. He died in Paris on Jan. 11.

MASSYS, QUENTIN (1466?–1530), painter. Born in Louvain, Belgium, where he had a studio from 1495 to 1510, he was listed as a painter of the Guild of Antwerp in 1491, was twice married, and had sixteen children. His paintings are considered the last of the Flemish masterpieces prior to the triumph of the Italian school. Among his best works are: *Life of St. Anne,* a triptych, *Burial of Christ,* for the Antwerp cathedral, *Ecce Homo, Mater Dolorosa, Adoration of the Kings, Banker and His Wife,* and a portrait of Erasmus. All are marked by harmonious coloring, careful execution, and candid realism. He died in Antwerp, Belgium, between July 13 and Sept. 16.

MASTERS, RICHARD (d. 1534). *See* Barton, Elizabeth.

MASTRIUS, BARTHOLOMEW (1602–1673), theologian. Born in Meldola, Italy, he studied at Cesena, Bologna, Padua, and Rome, and became a lector. An authority on Duns Scotus, he engaged in heated disputations with other theologians, particularly Matthew Ferchi and John Ponce. He wrote treatises on philosophy and moral theology and commentaries on the *Sentences*. He died on Jan. 3.

MATERNUS, ST. (d. 307?), bishop. Appointed to the see of Milan, Italy, in 295 by popular acclaim, he suffered during the persecution of Diocletian, but was not slain. F. D. July 18.

MATERNUS, ST. (d. 325?), bishop. The first definitely known bishop of Cologne, he was one of three chosen by Emperor Constantine to judge the charges against St. Caecilian made by the Donatist bishops of Africa. Maternus was also present at the Council of Arles called by the emperor when the Donatists demanded a new trial after the unanimous vindication of Caecilian. Maternus may also have been bishop of Trèves, where he probably died. A discredited legend makes him son of the widow of Naim sent by St. Peter to evangelize the Gauls. F. D. Sept. 14.

MATHEW, THEOBALD (1790–1856). Born at Thomastown castle, Tipperary, Ireland, on Oct. 10, he studied at Kilkenny and Maynooth, joined the Capuchins in Dublin in 1808, and was ordained in 1814. After a year in Kilkenny, he went to Cork in 1816, where he spent the next twenty-four years founding schools and a library and working with the poor. In 1828 he was appointed provincial of Ireland, a position he held until 1851, and in 1838 founded the Cork Total Abstinence Society, which launched a temperance movement that swept Ireland and England. He was a leader in organizing relief from the famines of 1846–47, and in 1848–51 spread the temperance movement to the United States. He is called "the apostle of temperance"; more than 7,000,000 are reputed to have taken his pledge. He died in Queenstown, Cork, Ireland, on Dec. 8.

MATHIEU, FRANÇOIS DÉSIRÉ (1839–1908), cardinal. Born on May 27 in Einville, Meurthe et Moselle, France, he studied at the Nancy seminary and was ordained in 1863. After teaching in Pont à Mousson, where he served as curate and as chaplain to a convent, he was appointed bishop of Angers in 1893 and transferred to Toulouse in 1896. He was created cardinal in 1899 and engaged in diplomatic activities until his death in London while attending the Eucharistic Congress on Oct. 26. He wrote on the history of Lorraine, the concordat of 1801, and other works, and was made a member of the French Academy in 1907.

MATHIEU, OLIVER (1853–1929), archbishop. Born in Quebec, he studied at its seminary and at Laval and St. Thomas, Rome, was ordained, taught philosophy at Laval in 1878–99, then served as its rector to 1910. He was named archbishop of Regina, Saskatchewan, Canada, in 1911 and received English and French decorations. He died in Regina on Oct. 26.

MATHIS, MICHAEL AMBROSE (1885–1960), founder. Born in South Bend, Indiana, on Oct. 6, he joined the Congregation of Holy Cross in 1901, studied at Holy Cross seminary of Notre Dame, and was ordained in 1914. He received his doctorate in theology from Catholic University in 1920, taught scripture at Holy Cross College in Washington, D.C., from 1915 to 1924, then founded Holy Cross foreign mission seminary and served as its superior for seven years. He founded the *Bengalese*, its mission magazine, in 1917, serving as its editor until 1933, was co-founder, with Mother Anna Dengel, of the Medical Mission Sisters in 1925, and served on the Notre Dame University faculty from 1939 to 1941, when he became chaplain of St. Joseph's Hospital in South Bend. He was a leader in the liturgical movement in the United States and founder of Notre Dame's summer liturgy program, of which he was director from 1947. He died at Notre Dame on Mar. 10.

MATILDA, ST. (895?–968). Daughter of Count Dietrich of Westphalia and Reinhild of Denmark, in 913 she married Otto of Saxony, who became king six years later. He permitted his queen to dispense great charities, a custom which she continued after his death in 936 and which caused her sons Otto and Henry to turn on her for an accounting and on themselves in bitter civil war. In time she was able to follow a life of her own choice, built three convents and a monastery, and saw another son, St. Bruno, become archbishop of Cologne. She is also called Maud. F. D. Mar. 14.

MATILDA OF CANOSSA (1046–1114). When her father, Count Boniface II of Tuscany, was murdered in 1053, her mother, Beatrice, married Duke Gottfried of Lorraine. Mother and daughter were taken prisoners to Germany in 1055 by Emperor Henry III, but were returned in 1056. Matilda was married to her stepbrother, Gottfried of Lower Lorraine, but separated from him in 1071. She was ruler of the strategic territory of northern Italy and became a close friend of Gregory VII when he ascended the papal throne in 1073. After Gregory excommunicated Henry

IV in 1076, she was instrumental in arranging the reconciliation between them at her castle in Canossa. In 1077 she donated her dominions (though she was to remain ruler until her death) to the pope, the "donation of Matilda" or "patrimony of St. Peter" (reconfirmed in 1112). They were the nucleus of the future Papal States, but a source of dispute between pope and emperor until Frederick II recognized the Church's claim in 1213. She saw her lands devastated in 1082 when Henry's armies passed through her territory to attack the papacy. She led an army in support of Pope Victor III against antipope Wibert in 1087, but Henry's threats caused the Romans to desert Victor. In 1089 she married Duke Welf of Bavaria (Gottfried had died in 1076). In 1090, Henry invaded and devastated her territories and, though defeated at Canossa in 1091, won over Matilda's husband in 1095. In 1110, when King Henry V came to Italy, accord was established and he appointed her vice-regent of Liguria. She died near Modena, Italy, on July 24.

MATRONA, ST. (d. 300), martyr. *See* Alexandra, St.

MATRONA, ST., martyr. A servant in Thessalonica, she was beaten to death by her mistress because of her faith. Another of the name, born in Barcelona, Spain, was slain in Rome for aiding Christian prisoners there. A third, of Portuguese birth, died near Capua, Italy, of dysentery and was invoked by later sufferers. None of these stories is complete and none is dated. F. D. Mar. 15.

MATTEI, BL. CATHERINE (1486–1547). Born of poverty-stricken parents in Racconigi, Italy, she became a Dominican tertiary at twenty-eight and had numerous supernatural experiences, including the stigmata. Her cult was confirmed in 1810. F. D. Sept. 4.

MATTEO OF AQUASPARTA. *See* Bentivenghi, Matteo.

MATTEO OF GIRGENTI. *See* Gimarra, Bl. Matteo.

MATTEO DA SIENA. *See* Bartolo, Matteo di.

MATTEUCCI, CARLO (1811–1868), physicist. Born in Forlì, Romagna, Italy, on June 21, he studied at Bologna, where he received his doctorate, and L'École Polytechnique, Paris. In 1837 he taught physics at the college in Ravenna, when his fame spread was invited to the chair of physics at Pisa, and made his discoveries in the fields of electrophysiology and electrodynamics. He was made commissioner from Tuscany to Charles Albert in 1848, director of the Tuscany telegraph system in 1849, represented Tuscany at Turin in 1859, and became inspector general of the Italian kingdom's telegraph system in 1860, a member of the Italian senate and minister of pub-

lic instruction in 1862. He died in Ardenza, Italy, on July 25.

MATTHEW, ST. (1st century), apostle. Called Levi, he was the son of Alpheus, was born probably in Galilee, and served in the profitable though socially outcast trade of tax collector at Capharnaum. When Christ passed his office and called him (Mark 2:14), Matthew unhesitatingly became one of the twelve apostles. He was the author of the first of the four gospels, written between the years 40 and 50, probably in Aramaic for his fellow convert Jews in Palestine. The original seems to have been in existence in 120, when Papias wrote a commentary on it; it had, in the meantime, been translated into Greek (probably by 62). His record of Christ's life, miracles, death, and Resurrection, His relationship to the Old Law and foundation of the Church, make his Gospel the first defense of Christianity. Matthew's careful arrangement into formal divisions, fondness for numbers, and frequent references to coinage and treasure reveal his early activity. Legend makes him a martyr in the East. F. D. Sept. 12.

MATTHEW, ST. (d. 1003), martyr. *See* Benedict, St.

MATTHEW, BL. (d. 1134), cardinal. A priest at Rheims, France, he became a Benedictine at St. Martin-des-Champs in 1108 and its prior in 1117. He became cardinal-bishop of Albano in 1125 and papal legate to France and Germany in 1128. F. D. Dec. 25.

MATTHEW OF BEAUVAIS, ST. (d. 1098?), martyr. He served with Bishop Roger of Beauvais, France, became a crusader, and was taken prisoner and beheaded after he refused to comply with a Saracen order to renounce his faith. F. D. Mar. 27.

MATTHEW OF CRACOW (1335?–1410), bishop. Born in Cracow, he studied at Prague, taught theology and served as dean there, and in 1382 headed a delegation from the university to Pope Urban VI. In 1395 he became counselor of Ruprecht II and professor at Heidelberg, and its rector in 1396. When Ruprecht III became king of Rome in 1400 he acted on several diplomatic missions for him, was appointed bishop of Worms in 1404, and was Ruprecht's representative at the Council of Pisa in 1409, where he supported Pope Gregory XII. He wrote several theological treatises and commentaries, among them *De consolatione theologiae, De modo confitendi,* and *De corpore Christi.* He died in Pisa, Italy, on Mar. 5.

MATTHEW OF JANOW (d. 1394). Born in Bohemia, son of Wenzel of Janow, a knight, he studied at Prague and Paris, and in 1381 was appointed canon of the Prague cathedral, where he became a noted confessor. He was a fervent believer in frequent Communion but advocated removing relics and images from churches (he deplored the excessive importance attached to accidental external practices), though he retracted both views when they were condemned by the Synod of Prague in 1389. He collected several treatises under the title *Regulae veteris et novi testamenti*. He died in Prague, Bohemia, on Nov. 30.

MATTHEW OF MANTUA. *See* Carreri, Giovanni Francesco.

MATTHEW PARIS (1200?–1259), historian. A monk at St. Albans, England, from 1217, he was a close friend of King Haakon IV after a stay in Norway, and invited him to join the crusade with St. Louis of France. Matthew's *Chronica majora* is a summary of Roger of Wendover's history up to the year 1235, then becomes a valuable account of eyewitnessed or source-supported incidents to the year 1259. The work attacks royal ineptitude, the mendicant orders, the greed of the Roman court, and foreign intervention in domestic affairs. He also wrote a corrected chronicle for the period 1067–1253 and a life of Stephen Langton.

MATTHEW DE TERMINI, BL. (d. 1309). Born in Sicily, he studied law at Bologna, became chancellor to King Manfred, and, after being seriously wounded in battle, an Augustinian laybrother under the name of Augustine Novello. With Bl. Clement of Osimo he drew up the new constitutions of the Augustinians and brought them to Rome; Pope Nicholas IV made him a canonist, and Boniface VIII a legate to Siena. He was prior general from 1298 to 1300, then resigned to live as a hermit. F. D. May 19.

MATTHEW, TOBIE (1577–1655). Born in Salisbury, England, on Oct. 3, son of an Anglican minister of the same name who was to become archbishop of York, he studied at Oxford, was admitted to Gray's Inn in 1599, and became a member of parliament in 1601 and a member of Elizabeth's court. In 1604, while in Florence, he became a convert, in 1606 returned to England, and was imprisoned for six months for his faith. He left England for the Continent and in 1614 was ordained in Rome. He returned to England in 1617, stayed with an old friend, Francis Bacon, was exiled again from 1619 to 1622, and on his return was sent by the king to Madrid to arrange the marriage of Prince Charles and the Spanish Infanta. He was knighted by Charles (later King Charles I) in 1623 and remained in England until 1640, when the Civil War broke out and he fled to Ghent, Flanders, where he spent the rest of his life with the Jesuits, whom he probably joined, until his death on Oct. 13. He translated Bacon's essays into Italian and St. Augustine's *Confessions* and St. Teresa's autobiography into English.

MATTHEW OF WESTMINSTER. The name is mistakenly assigned to the author of the *Flores historiarum* by an unknown copyist. A chronicle from creation to 1326, this was written by Matthew Paris (to 1259), by monks of St. Albans (1259–65) and a group of unknown Westminster authors (1265–1325).

MATTHEWS, FRANCIS P. (1887–1952), executive. Born in Albion, Nebraska, on Mar. 15, he studied at Creighton University, became president of the National Thrift Assurance Co., the Securities Investment Corporation, and an Omaha bank. He served as general counsel for the Reconstruction Finance Corp. in Nebraska and Wyoming, was supreme knight of the Knights of Columbus in 1935–39, secretary of the navy in 1949–51, and ambassador to Ireland in 1951–52. He died in Omaha, Nebraska, on Oct. 18.

MATTHEWS, JAMES JOSEPH EDMUND (1871–1938), educator. Born in England on Jan. 22, he became a Benedictine in 1888, was ordained in 1896, was president of Ampleforth College in 1903–24, and abbot of Ampleforth from 1924 until his death there on Apr. 7.

MATTHIA DEI NAZAREI, BL. (d. 1300). The only child of Count Matelica, she was born in Matelica, March of Ancona, refused marriage, and became a nun at Santa Maria Maddalena convent there. She is reputed to have been abbess for forty years and died there on Dec. 28. Her cult was confirmed in 1756. F. D. Nov. 7.

MATTHIAS (1557–1619), emperor. Son of Emperor Maximilian II and Mary, daughter of Charles V, he was born in Vienna on Feb. 24, headed the government of the Netherlands in 1577 at the invitation of the Catholics there, but resigned in 1581. He became governor of Austria in 1593, put down the peasants' uprising of 1595, negotiated the Peace of Vienna in 1606 with Stephen Bocskay, leader of the Hungarians and Transylvanians rebelling against Matthias' brother Emperor Rudolf II, arranged peace with the Turks in 1606, and in 1608 forced Rudolf to let him rule Hungary, Austria, and Moravia. In 1611 a revolt in Bohemia led to his becoming king there against Rudolf, whose troops were ravaging the country, and in 1612 he succeeded as emperor on Rudolf's death. He pursued a vacillating course which alienated both Catholics and Protestants, depended heavily on Cardinal Melchior Khlesl, whom both sides distrusted, signed an unfavorable treaty with the Turks, who possessed Hungary in 1615, and in 1617 caused his cousin Ferdinand of Styria to be elected king of Bohemia and Hungary. He failed to take decisive action in the Bohemian revolt in 1618 even when Khlesl was kidnaped by Ferdinand and the other archdukes, not realizing its importance—it was the prelude to the Thirty Years' War—and died, amid the dissensions preceding that disaster, in Vienna on Mar. 20.

MATTHIAS, ST. (1st century), apostle. Chosen to succeed Judas Iscariot, he served widely in Judaea and Cappadocia, and is said to have been martyred at Colchis. Numerous popular stories exist, but all that is known with certainty appears in Acts 1:21–22. F. D. Feb. 24.

MATTHIAS, ST. (d. 120?). He was bishop of Jerusalem at a time when his people were dispersed by persecution. F. D. Jan. 30.

MATTHIAS CORVINUS (1440–1490), king. Born in Kolozsvar, Hungary, on Feb. 23, son of János Hunyady, he was early embroiled in the political feuds of his times. In 1456 he was accused of conspiracy against King Ladislaus V and arrested. Matthias' brother, Ladislaus, was executed, but, after King Ladislaus died, Matthias joined the court of the king of Bohemia, George Podiebrad, to whose daughter Catharine he was betrothed and whom he married in 1462. In 1458, Matthias was named king of Hungary and, after reaching an agreement with Emperor Frederick III, to whom a group of dissident Hungarians had offered the crown, he was crowned king in 1463. In 1467, Podiebrad was excommunicated by the pope and the next year Matthias led an expedition against the Bohemian king, who defeated Matthias before his death in 1471, when the Bohemians chose Wladislaw of Poland as king. Desultory warfare ensued from 1471 to 1476 between Frederick and Matthias, but in 1476 broke out in earnest; Matthias invaded Austria and captured Vienna in 1485. He had now established Hungary as a leading power, had ambitions as emperor of the Holy Roman Empire, and also dreamed of a crusade against the Turks, which never materialized, although his victories over the Turks kept them from overrunning Europe. He seized much church property and appointed his friends bishops. He introduced needed reforms in the army, the courts, and the fiscal administration, encouraged the arts and sciences, developed a library of 50,000 volumes, and was called "the Just" by his people. He died in Vienna on Apr. 6.

MATTHIAS, BL. MARIA DE (1805–1866), foundress. Born in Vallecorsa, Italy, she was encouraged by Ven. John Merlini, who became her spiritual director, to follow her inclination toward a life in religion. In 1834 she took charge of a school at Acuto and founded there a religious group which became the Sisters of the Adorers of the Precious Blood. In 1837 she was charged with conducting religious services, but was exonerated by her bishop. Her

houses and schools increased and the work was extended to include education of adult women and girls. By the time of her canonization in 1950 there were more than 400 establishments throughout the world. F. D. Aug. 20.

MATTHIAS OF NEUBURG (14th century), chronicler. Probably born in Neuburg, Baden, Germany, he studied law at Bologna, became solicitor at the Basle episcopal court, and was probably the author of a valuable Latin chronicle of the period from 1243 to 1355. He probably died in Strassburg, Alsace, between 1364 and 1370.

MATTIUZZI, BL. ODORIC (1286?–1331), missionary. Born in Villanova, Italy, of Czech parentage, he joined the Franciscans about 1300, was sent as a missioner to the East in 1318, and spent the next twelve years traveling through Asia. He spent three years in Peking, was the first European to enter Tibet, and on his return dictated an account of his travels which gained wide popularity when plagiarized in Mandeville's works. It has been published in many languages. Early stories credit him with many conversions in the East, but it may be that his chief purpose was to map the area for mission opportunities. Also known as Odoric of Pordenone, he died in Udine, Italy, and his cult was approved in 1755. F. D. Jan. 14.

MATURIN, BASIL WILLIAM (1847–1915). Born in Grangegorman, Dublin, Ireland, he studied at Trinity College, went as an Anglican curate in Peterstow, England, in 1870, became a Cowley Father, and went to St. Clement's, Philadelphia, Pennsylvania, in 1881. He became a convert in 1897, was ordained in 1898, worked in Westminster and Pimlico, and in 1913 became chaplain at Oxford. He was drowned when the *Lusitania* sank on May 7. He published several spiritual writings, sermons, and the autobiographical *Price of Unity*.

MATURINUS, ST. (d. 388). Legend says he was born in Larchant, Sens, of pagan parents whom he converted after his baptism, was ordained by St. Polycarp when twenty, was a successful missioner in his native region, and died in Rome. F. D. Nov. 1.

MATURUS, ST. (d. 177), martyr. *See* Pothinus, St.

MATZ, NICHOLAS CHRYSOSTOM (1850–1917), bishop. Born in Münster, Lorraine, on Apr. 6, he studied in Finstigen, France, and Mt. St. Mary of the West seminary, Cincinnati, Ohio, and was ordained in 1874. He did parish work in Colorado and Utah, became titular bishop of Telmissus and coadjutor bishop of Denver in 1887, and second bishop of Denver in 1889. Two colleges and many charitable institutions were built during his episcopate. He died in Denver, Colorado, on Aug. 9.

MAUBANT, BL. PIERRE (d. 1839), martyr. *See* Imbert, Bl. Laurence.

MAUD. *See* Matilda, St.

MAUDEZ. *See* Mawes, St.

MAUGHOLD, ST. (d. 498?), bishop. An Irish outlaw, he was converted by St. Patrick and barred from the country as part of his penance. He settled on the Isle of Man, where he became bishop and established several parishes. He is also called Maccaldus and Maccul. F. D. Apr. 27.

MAUGUILLE. *See* Madelgisilus, St.

MAUNOIR, BL. JULIAN (1606–1683). Born in Rennes, France, he became a Jesuit in 1625, studied Breton, and went to evangelize that backward and neglected area. He and a singing priest, Michael Le Nobletz, reclaimed the people by old and newly composed religious songs; the missioners also used colored pictures, plays, processions, and the simplest of "revivalist" techniques. During his forty-three years there he converted thousands, and the number of priests increased from two to more than 1000, facts which were later deplored by Renan. He was beatified in 1951. F. D. Jan. 28.

MAUNOURY, AUGUSTE FRANÇOIS (1811–1898), scholar. Born in Champsecret, Orne, France, on Oct. 30, he studied at the Séez seminary, was ordained, and taught classics, becoming an authority on ancient Greece. In 1852 he was appointed professor of rhetoric, continuing in that position until 1875, when he devoted himself to biblical studies. He was appointed canon of the cathedral in Séez, France, in 1877 and remained there until his death on Nov. 17. He published commentaries on the epistles and the Psalms and wrote *Chrestomathie* and a Greek grammar.

MAURA, ST. (d. 250?), martyr. *See* Fusca, St.

MAURA, ST. (d. 286), martyr. *See* Timothy, St.

MAURA, ST. (5th century). *See* Brigid, St.

MAURA, ST. (827–850?). Sister of Eutropius, bishop of Troyes, France, she was born there and devoted her life to prayer and charities. St. Prudentius has left a memorial oration. F. D. Sept. 21.

MAURICE, ST. (d. 287?), martyr. He was an officer, with Exuperius and Candidus, in the Theban Legion, of which a number were Christians from Egypt. It is unlikely that the entire unit of 6000 men was Christian, as many have maintained. While encamped at Octodurum (Martigny) on the Rhône River, Emperor Maximian ordered the army to sacrifice to the gods (or to attack Begaudae civilians, as some claim). Encouraged by Maurice, Christians in the Theban Legion refused and were put to death. Among them were SS. Adventor (at Turin), Alexander (at Bergamo), Gereon (at Cologne), Innocent, Octavius, and Solutor (at Turin), Ursus, Victor, another Victor (at Solothurn; F. D. Sept. 30), and Vitalis. The principal source of the story is St. Eucherius, bishop of Lyons in the first half of the fifth century, who wrote an account of these martyrs for Bishop Salvius. A shrine was built late in the fourth century at Agaunum (St. Maurice-en-Valois) for their relics. F. D. Sept. 22.

MAURICE, ST. (d. 329?), martyr. *See* Daniel, St.

MAURICE OF CORNOET, BL. (1114?–1191). Born in Loudéac, Brittany, he studied at Paris, became a Cistercian at Langonel in 1144, its abbot in 1147, and abbot-founder of Cornoet in 1177. He was a counselor to the kings of Brittany. His cult was approved by Pope Clement XI. F. D. Oct. 13.

MAURICE DE SULLY (d. 1196), bishop. Born in Sully-sur-Loire, France, he went to Paris in 1140, was ordained, taught theology, was archdeacon of Paris in 1159, and became its bishop in 1160. He was a close friend of King Louis VII, helped to build the cathedral of Notre Dame, served as one of the directors of the royal treasury in 1190 when the king was on crusade, and actively defended Thomas à Becket in his controversy with King Henry II of England. He spent his last year in retirement at St. Victor's, Paris, where he died on Sept. 11.

MAURICIUS, FLAVIUS TIBERIUS (539–602), emperor. A native of Cappadocia, and of an ancient Roman family, he made the army a career and earned the favor of Emperor Tiberius II for his successful expedition against the Persians. On his return he married Constantia, Tiberius' daughter, and was appointed successor to the throne, which he ascended almost at once on Tiberius' death in 578. He inaugurated a policy of economy at the court, continued the war with the Persians for another ten years, but, when he did nothing to protect Italy from barbarian invasion, the Italians called on the Franks for aid—a step which eventually led to the establishment of the Western emperors. When Pope Gregory I was elected in 590, he asked the emperor to annul the election, an action claimed by some as acknowledgment by Gregory of imperial right to veto papal elections. Their relations later deteriorated when Gregory led the resistance to the invading Lombards when the emperor offered no help. Gregory's opposition to the tyranny of Mauricius' exarch at Ravenna and the emperor's protection of the schismatic bishops of northern Italy and approval of Patriarch John IV of Constantinople's use of the title "oecumenical patriarch" helped widen the breach. Though Mauricius continued to buy off the Avars from their raids, he did not ransom some 12,000 captured Roman soldiers in 599 and they were massacred by the Avars. In 602 revolt broke out in the army, which elected Phocas emperor and marched on Constantinople. Mauricius fled, was captured at Chalcedon, and with his five sons murdered on Nov. 27.

MAURILIUS, ST. (d. 453?), bishop. Born in Milan, Italy, he migrated to Gaul where he became a follower of St. Martin of Tours, who ordained him, and about 423 became bishop of Angers. F. D. Sept. 13.

MAURILIUS, ST. (d. 580). He was bishop of Cahors, France, and a biblical scholar. F. D. Sept. 3.

MAURILIUS, ST. (d. 1067), bishop. Born in Rheims, France, he was master of the cathedral school at Halberstadt, became a Benedictine monk at Fécamp, Normandy, and abbot of St. Mary's, Florence. In 1055 he was made archbishop of Rouen and wrote strongly against Berengarius. F. D. Aug. 9.

MAURIN, PETER (1877–1949). Born in Oulet, Languedoc, France, on May 15, he studied and taught in Paris, worked on a French farm, went to the United States in 1911, studied while engaged in a variety of jobs, helped found the Catholic Worker Movement, and in 1933 joined Dorothy Day in New York City as co-founder of the *Catholic Worker*, a newspaper. He wrote much and preached on street corners on the need of social and economic reform, gathered some of his columns for *Easy Essays*, established thirteen farming communities, and died at one of them, Maryfarm, in Newburgh, New York, on May 15.

MAURONTIUS, ST. (634–701). The eldest son of SS. Adalbald and Rictrudis of Flanders, he served in the court of King Clovis II, and on the death of his father entered the monastery of Marchiennes, then built the Benedictine abbey of Breuil, near Douai, where he became abbot, and of which town he is the patron. F. D. May 5.

MAURONTIUS, ST. (d. 804?). He was abbot of the Benedictine monastery of St. Victor in Marseilles, France, and became bishop of that see in about 767. F. D. Oct. 21.

MAURUS, ST. (d. 117?), bishop and martyr. He and SS. Pantaleemon and Sergius are said to have been slain at Bisceglia on the Adriatic during the reign of Trajan. F. D. July 27.

MAURUS, ST. (d. 257), martyr. *See* Bonus, St.

MAURUS, ST., martyr. A priest at Rheims, Gaul, he and fifty of his flock were slain there during the persecution either of Valerian (about 260) or of Diocletian (about 300). F. D. Aug. 22.

MAURUS, ST. (d. 284?), martyr. Born in North Africa, he was slain in Rome during the reign of Numerian. F. D. Nov. 22.

MAURUS, ST. (3rd century), martyr. *See* Claudius, St.

MAURUS, ST. (d. 303?), martyr. He and St. Papias were soldiers put to death at Rome during the persecution of Maximian. F. D. Jan. 29.

MAURUS, ST. (d. 383). He became second bishop of Verdun, France, in 353. F. D. Nov. 8.

MAURUS, ST. (d. 580?). Son of a Roman noble, he was turned over to St. Benedict at twelve for instruction and care. When the latter retired to Monte Cassino in 525, St. Maurus may have succeeded him as superior of the monastery at Subiaco. A ninth-century manuscript tells of a Maurus who served in France during the reign of King Theodebert, but there is no proof that they were the same person. F. D. Jan. 15.

MAURUS, ST. (d. 600?). The twelfth bishop of Verona, Italy, he died as a hermit. F. D. Nov. 21.

MAURUS, ST. (d. 946), bishop. A native of Rome and nephew of Pope John IX, he was ordained, then became a Benedictine at Classe in Ravenna, its abbot in 926, and bishop of Cesena, Italy, in 934. F. D. Jan. 20.

MAURUS, BL. (d. 1070?), bishop. A Benedictine monk at Pannonhalma, Hungary, he became bishop of Pecs in 1036 and wrote several saints' lives. His cult was approved in 1848. F. D. Dec. 4.

MAURUS, SYLVESTER (1619–1687), theologian. Born in Spoleto, Italy, on Dec. 31, he joined the Jesuits in 1636, studied at Macerata College, was appointed to the chair of philosophy there, then to the chair of theology at the Roman College, and later was rector there. He died in Rome on Jan. 13. He wrote *Quaestionum philosophicarum* and *Opus theologicum*, and edited Aristotle's works.

MAURY, JEAN SIFFREIN (1746–1817), cardinal. Born in Valréas, Vaucluse, France, on June 26, he studied in Avignon and at the Collège de France, Paris, and was ordained in 1769. Appointed vicar general of Lombez, he attracted widespread attention by his panegyric on St. Louis in 1772, became royal preacher, and preached the Lenten sermons to the court in 1778. His panegyric on St. Vincent de Paul in 1784 led to his election to the French Academy. He became a deputy in 1789 and headed the Church and royalist party opposed to Mirabeau. When the assembly was dissolved in 1791 he was forced to flee to Coblenz, and the following year was appointed archbishop of Nicaea and represented Pope Pius VI at the election of Emperor Francis II at Frankfort. In 1794 he was created a cardinal and made archbishop of Montefiascone. He participated in the election of Pope Pius VII, opposed the concordat with Napoleon, but when it was signed returned to France. He then became a follower of Napoleon, whose divorce he supported, and was rewarded with the see of Paris in 1810. In 1814, when Napoleon was defeated, he was suspended by the pope and imprisoned for several months in Castel Sant' Angelo. Unable to return to France because of the Bourbons' opposition, he was reconciled with Pope Pius VII, who restored his cardinalcy. He died on May 10 in Rome.

MAUVIER. *See* Menele, St.

MAVILUS, ST. (d. 212), martyr. He was slain by wild beasts in an arena at Adrumetum, Africa, during the persecution of Caracalla. F. D. Jan. 4.

MAWES, ST. (6th century?). An Irishman, he lived as a hermit in Cornwall, England, then migrated to an island off the coast of Brittany, where he settled with disciples. He is also called Maudez. F. D. Nov. 18.

MAXELLINDIS, ST. (d. 670?), martyr. Born in Caudry, near Cambrai, France, she fled a marriage arranged by her family with Harduin of Solesmes because she had planned to become a nun. Harduin pursued her and stabbed her to death. F. D. Nov. 13.

MAXENTIA, ST. According to legend, she was the daughter of an Irish prince, who fled to Senlis, France, to avoid marriage. She lived there as a recluse until her suitor found her and, in a rage, beheaded her. F. D. Nov. 20.

MAXENTIOLUS, ST. (5th century). A follower of St. Martin of Tours, he became abbot-founder of a monastery at Cunault, Gaul. F. D. Dec. 17.

MAXENTIUS, ST. (d. 287?), martyr. *See* Constantius, St.

MAXENTIUS, ST. (448?–515). Born in Agde, Gaul, he became a monk at a monastery in Poitou, now named St. Maixent in his honor. As abbot there he was highly regarded by Clovis I and protected his people against barbarian raids. F. D. June 26.

MAXFIELD, BL. THOMAS (1590?–1616), martyr. Born in Staffordshire, England, when his father was under sentence of death for aiding priests, Thomas was later ordained at Douai and sent on the English mission in 1615. He was arrested in London and when he refused to take the Oath of Supremacy acknowledging King James was hanged, drawn, and quartered at Tyburn, in spite of the intercession of the Spanish ambassador. F. D. July 1.

MAXIMA, ST. (d. 302?), martyr. *See* Julia, St.

MAXIMA, ST. (d. 304), martyr. A Roman slave, she was scourged to death during the Diocletian persecution. F. D. Sept. 2.

MAXIMA, ST. (d. 304), martyr. *See* Donatilla, St.; also, Montanus, St.

MAXIMA, ST. (5th century). See Martinian, St.

MAXIMIAN, ST. (d. 290), martyr. *See* Lucian of Beauvais, St.

MAXIMIAN, ST. (d. 363), martyr. *See* Bonosus, St.

MAXIMIAN, ST. (d. 404), bishop. An African convert from Donatism, he became bishop of Bagae, Numidia, resigned when his nomination proved displeasing to the people, regained the basilica of Calvianum from the Donatists, but was injured when they threw him from a tower. He then sailed to Italy, where he died. F. D. Oct. 3.

MAXIMIAN, ST. (d. 556). He was appointed bishop of Ravenna, Italy, by Pope Vigilius in 546. F. D. Feb. 22.

MAXIMIAN, ST. (d. 594), bishop. Born in Sicily, he became a Benedictine monk at the abbey of St. Andrew in Rome, represented Popes Pelagius and Gregory the Great at Constantinople, and in 591 was appointed papal legate and bishop of Syracuse, Sicily, by the latter. F. D. June 9.

MAXIMILIAN I (1459–1519), emperor. Born in Neustadt, Germany, on Mar. 22, son of Emperor Frederick III and Leonora of Portugal, he married Mary of Burgundy in 1477, fought against Louis XI of France to defend his wife's inheritance of Burgundy and the Netherlands, and defeated Louis at Guinegate in 1749. When Mary died in 1482, many of the Netherlands states refused to recognize him as regent of his son Philip, and he was obliged to accept the treaty of Arras with Louis, by which his daughter Margaret was betrothed to the dauphin (the future Charles VIII), with Burgundy, Artois, and Flanders her dowry, and was forbidden the guardianship of Philip. The next few years he spent putting down a French-incited insurrection in the Netherlands; forced the return of Philip to him in 1485; was elected king of the Romans in 1486; and in 1490 married Anne of Brittany by proxy. On the death of Matthias Corvinus of Hungary in 1490, he claimed the throne of Hungary, drove the Hungarians from Austria, but in 1491 was obliged to give up his attempt on the crown by recognizing Ladislaus of Bohemia as king of Hungary, who in turn recognized Maximilian as successor if Ladislaus had no male heir. When Charles VIII married Anne in 1491, he warred on France and recovered Artois and Franche-Comté by the treaty of Senlis (1493), and on his father's death in 1493 succeeded him as emperor. He married Bianca Sforza, daughter of the duke of Milan, in 1494, and turned his attention to Italy. He joined Pope Julius II, Ferdinand of Spain, and Louis XII in the League of Cambrai in 1509 against Venice, and when Venice was reconciled with the pope joined the Holy League with England, Spain, Venice, and the pope against the French, who were defeated near Thérouanne in 1513. When Francis I became king of France, he defeated Maximilian, and forced the latter to give up Verona to the Venetians for 200,000 ducats. Maximilian established an imperial chamber of justice independent of the emperor, which he set up in 1495 to meet the diet's demand for reform when he requested money for his Italian campaign; he also proclaimed a perpetual land peace, levied a general tax, and established a standing army. In 1500 he permitted a council of regency, though he generally ignored it, and set up the Aulic council, a court of justice for Austria and the empire, against the imperial chamber. In 1499 he acknowledged the independence of Switzerland by the treaty of Bâle. He married his son Philip to Joanna of Castile, the infanta of Spain. He died on Jan. 12 at Wels, Upper Austria.

MAXIMILIAN II (1527–1576), emperor. Son of Emperor Ferdinand I and Anne, daughter of King Ladislaus of Hungary, he was born in Vienna on July 31, married Marie, daughter of Emperor Charles V, in 1548, was recognized as king of Bohemia in 1549, showed a tendency to Protestantism as a youth, but conformed to Catholicism after 1560. He was elected king of the Romans in 1562, later confirmed by the pope, was crowned king of Hungary in 1563, and succeeded his father as emperor in 1564. He engaged in war against the Turks, which was ended by a truce in 1568, allowed religious freedom in Austria and Hungary, though the Catholic Reformation made large gains in Germany, and in 1574 declared himself a candidate for the throne of Poland. He was elected by the senate, but Stephen Bathory was elected by the diet. He died in Regensburg, Bavaria, on Oct. 12, on the eve of invading Poland.

MAXIMILIAN (1832–1867), emperor of Mexico. Born in Venice, Italy, on July 6, Ferdinand Maximilian Joseph, archduke of Austria and brother of Emperor Francis Joseph, trained in the navy, was appointed its head in 1854, and married Carlota (born in Laeren, Belgium, on June 7, 1840), daughter of King Leopold I of Belgium, in 1857. Maximilian was made emperor of Mexico in 1864 by the French, who had been attempting to conquer Mexico. The opposition was led by Benito Juarez and when, at the end of the Civil War, the United States protested against the French occupation of Mexico, the French troops were withdrawn, and Maximilian's army was annihilated at Querétaro in 1867. He was court-martialed and shot at Querétaro, Mexico, on June 19. Carlota had returned to Europe in 1866 to secure aid for her husband, became insane when unsuc-

cessful, and was confined in a château at Meyssen, near Brussels, until her death there on Jan. 19, 1927.

MAXIMILIAN (d. 284?), bishop and martyr. Born in Cilli, Styria, he was educated from the age of seven by a priest, gave his wealth away, and went on pilgrimage to Rome. Pope St. Sixtus II sent him as a missionary to Noricum (the region between Styria and Bavaria), where he established his see at Lorch and reigned for twenty years before he was beheaded outside Cilli when he refused to sacrifice to the pagan gods. F. D. Oct. 12.

MAXIMILIAN, ST. (274–295), martyr. A North African conscript who refused to take a military oath, he was executed for impiety to the pagan gods. F. D. Mar. 12.

MAXIMILIAN I (1573–1651), elector. Surnamed "the Great," he was born in Munich, on Apr. 17, son of William V of Bavaria, was educated privately and at Ingolstadt, and became duke when his father abdicated in 1597, and reformed government, courts, and army. He occupied the Protestant stronghold of Donauwörth in 1607 and re-established Catholicism as its religion, an action which caused a group of Protestant princes to found in 1608 the Protestant Union led by Frederick IV of the Palatinate, whereupon he organized the Catholic League in 1609. When the Thirty Years' War broke out in 1619, during which Bavaria was devastated, he placed the league army at the disposal of Emperor Ferdinand II against the newly elected king of Bohemia, Frederick V, but signed a treaty of neutrality with the Protestant Union, occupying Upper Austria as security. After the victory of his forces under Tilly at White Mt. in 1620 and the occupation of the Rhenish Palatinate, Maximilian received the electoral vote forfeited by Frederick in 1623, and in 1628 was invested with the Upper Palatinate. He led those demanding the dismissal of the head of the imperial army, Albrecht Wallenstein, and forced Ferdinand's acquiescence in 1630, but was obliged to agree to the restoration of his command when the Swedes under Gustavus Adolphus defeated Tilly in 1631–32 and pillaged Munich. The devastation and destruction wreaked on Bavaria by the invading armies forced him to negotiate a separate armistice with France and Sweden at Ulm in 1647. He abrogated it at Ferdinand's instigation, but, when Bavaria was invaded and his forces defeated at Zusmarshausen in 1648, he was obliged to agree to the Treaty of Westphalia which incorporated the Upper Palatinate with Bavaria and recognized him and his descendants as electors. Throughout his reign, which was constantly beset by war, he fought to restore and spread Catholicism wherever he could, founded colleges and monasteries, and was known for his charities. He died in Ingolstadt, Germany, on Sept. 27.

MAXIMINUS, ST. (d. 347?), bishop. Born in Silly, Gaul, near Poitiers, he studied at Trèves and succeeded St. Agritius as its bishop. He gave asylum to St. Athanasius for two years and also to St. Paul, bishop of Constantinople. He was active against the Arians at several councils, and most outspoken against the heretical stand of Emperor Constans. He died in Trèves, Gaul. F. D. May 29.

MAXIMINUS, ST. (d. 363), martyr. See Juventinus, St.

MAXIMINUS, ST. (5th century?). Popular legend has called him one of the seventy-two disciples of Christ and the leader of a large group including SS. Mary Magdalen, Martha, and Lazarus which went to Provence. This story, however, is no older than the eleventh century. Maximinus may have been a fifth-century bishop of Aix, Gaul. F. D. June 8.

MAXIMINUS, ST. (d. 520?). He was first abbot of the monastery of Micy, near Orléans, France, founded by King Clovis. F. D. Dec. 15.

MAXIMUS, ST. (d. 195?). He succeeded St. Prosdocimus about 168 as bishop of Padua, Italy. F. D. Aug. 2.

MAXIMUS, ST. (2nd century), martyr. See Florus, St.

MAXIMUS, ST. (d. 250), martyr. A businessman in Ephesus (or in Lampsacus), he was tortured and stoned to death when he refused to sacrifice to Diana during the Decian persecution. F. D. Apr. 30.

MAXIMUS, ST. (d. 250?), martyr. He was a deacon, killed when he was thrown from a cliff at Aquila, southern Italy, of which he is patron, during the Decian persecution. F. D. Oct. 20.

MAXIMUS, ST. (d. 251), martyr. A Persian nobleman, he and St. Olympiades were beaten to death for their faith during the Decian persecution. F. D. Apr. 15.

MAXIMUS, ST. (d. 254?), martyr. See Eusebius, St.

MAXIMUS, ST. (d. 255?), martyr. He was put to death at Rome during the Valerian persecution. F. D. Nov. 19.

MAXIMUS, ST. (d. 260), martyr. See Cassius, St.

MAXIMUS, ST. (d. 267?), martyr. See Anatolianus, St.

MAXIMUS, ST. (d. 282), bishop. He was administrator of the patriarchate of Alexandria from 251 to 264 while St. Dionysius was in exile, then ruled the see until his death. On his orders, Paul of Samosata was exiled from Egypt. F. D. Dec. 27.

MAXIMUS, ST. (3rd century). Bishop of Nola, Italy, he lived in mountain hide-outs during the Decian persecution, suffered from exposure, and died of the effects of working under such conditions. F. D. Jan. 15.

MAXIMUS, ST. (3rd century), martyr. See Quiriacus, St.

MAXIMUS, ST. (d. 303), martyr. See Dadas, St.

MAXIMUS, ST. (d. 304), martyr. He probably was put to death at Coma in Campania, Italy, although the Roman Martyrology says his death was at Apamea, Phrygia. F. D. Oct. 30.

MAXIMUS, ST. (d. 304), martyr. See Fabius, St.

MAXIMUS, ST. (d. 310?), martyr. See Asclepiodotus, St.

MAXIMUS, ST. (d. 350?), bishop. Crippled from torture suffered during the Diocletian persecution, he lived to succeed St. Macarius as bishop of Jerusalem. He was misled by Arian friends to oppose St. Athanasius, but changed his position to firm support of Christian dogma. F. D. May 5.

MAXIMUS, ST. (d. 378). He became nineteenth bishop of Mainz, Germany, about 354, was persecuted by the Arians, and was noted as a scholar. F. D. Nov. 18.

MAXIMUS, ST. (d. 384?), martyr. He and his brother Victorinus were sent from Rome by Pope Damasus to preach in Gaul and seized and put to death near Évreux by pagans. F. D. May 25.

MAXIMUS, ST. (4th century), bishop. Appointed bishop of Naples, Italy, in 359, he was forced into exile and died abroad; because of this mistreatment he has been referred to as a martyr. F. D. June 10.

MAXIMUS, ST. (d. 460?), bishop. Born near Digne, Provence, he entered the monastery of Lérins and became its second abbot in 426; under his direction it became an outstanding spiritual center. Despite his objections, he was made bishop of Riez and consecrated by St. Hilary. F. D. Nov. 27.

MAXIMUS, ST. (d. 470?). He was abbot-founder of the monastery of Chinon, near Tours, France. F. D. Aug. 20.

MAXIMUS, ST. (d. 470?) He was bishop of Turin, Italy, and wrote homilies and ascetical works. F. D. June 25.

MAXIMUS, ST. (d. 484), martyr. See Liberatus, St.

MAXIMUS, ST. (d. 511). He was bishop of Pavia, Italy. F. D. Jan. 8.

MAXIMUS, ST. (6th century). He was a bishop of Verona, Italy. F. D. May 29.

MAXIMUS THE CONFESSOR, ST. (580?–662). Maximus Homologetes, a noble born in Constantinople, became secretary to Emperor Heraclitus, but resigned to become a monk at Chrysopolis, near Constantinople, and, later, its abbot. He aided the struggle against the Monothelites, defended Pope Honorius from charges of having held that heresy, and upheld the authority of the papacy. In 645 he debated

Pyrrhus so successfully in public that the latter went to Rome to abjure his former erroneous position, but in 648 Emperor Constans issued a decree favoring the heresy; Maximus was in Rome at the Lateran Council (649) which condemned it. Pope St. Martin I was exiled and martyred in 653 for opposing the imperial decree; Maximus took up the battle, was seized and brought to trial in Constantinople, maimed, and exiled to Thrace. For six years he suffered great hardships there with two friends, both named Anastasius, was brought back for another trial, again tortured, and sentenced to life imprisonment. He died at Chersoneus, near Batum on the Black Sea. One Athanasius preceded him in death; the other died in 666. Maximus was a prolific writer on theological, ascetical, and mystical subjects and left commentaries on scripture, a dialogue on the spiritual life, and a work on liturgical symbolism, *Mystagogia.* F. D. Aug. 13.

MAXWELL, WILLIAM (1676–1744). The fourteenth Lord Maxwell, fifth earl of Nithsdale, was born in Terregles, Scotland, succeeded his father in 1683, and followed the family in loyalty to the Stuart cause. He married Winifred, daughter of the first marquis of Powis, in 1699. In 1715 he joined the move to put James Francis Edward Stuart on the throne, was captured at Preston, and condemned to death, but managed to escape from the Tower of London with his wife's help. They spent the rest of their lives in poverty in Rome, still in attendance on James. William died there on Mar. 2; his widow, in May 1749.

MAYER, CHRISTIAN (1719–1783), astronomer. Born in Mederizenhi, Moravia, on Aug. 20, he joined the Jesuits in 1745, taught at Aschaffenburg, and later became professor of mathematics and physics at Heidelberg. He built an astronomical observatory at Schwetzingen and in 1755 built and became director of the Mannheim observatory. He wrote *Expositio de transitu Veneris* and *Observations de la comète de 1781.* He died at Heidelberg, Germany, on Apr. 16.

MAYER, RUPERT (1877–1945). Born in Stuttgart, Germany, he was ordained in 1899, became a Jesuit, and in 1906–12 gave missions in Germany, Switzerland, and Holland. He was assigned to Munich, where his preaching, charitable work, and sanctity attracted attention and caused him to be known as the "men's apostle" for his apostolic work. He was a chaplain in the German army during World War I, and was repeatedly arrested after Hitler came to power for his opposition to the Nazi regime. During an imprisonment at Sachsenhausen in 1939, his physical condition was so bad he was released by the Nazis and sent to the Benedictine monastery at Ettal. When the war ended, he returned to Munich, Germany, where he

died on the altar while preaching on Nov. 1.

MAYEUL. *See* Majolus, St.

MAYHEW, EDWARD (1569–1625). Born in Salisbury, England, he attended college in Rheims in 1583, was tonsured in 1590, ordained in Rome in 1595, and sent on the English mission. In 1607 he was received into the Benedictines by the last priest of the English Benedictines, thus continuing the congregation. In 1613 he retired to Dieulwart, Lorraine, served as prior of St. Lawrence's monastery there until 1620, was appointed one of the definitors to unite the English, Spanish, and Italian congregations engaged in missionary work in England in 1617, and was vicar of the nuns at Cambrai, Spanish Netherlands, from 1623 until his death on Sept. 14.

MAYNARD, THEODORE (1890–1956), author. Born in Madras, India, on Nov. 3, of Protestant missionaries, he was educated in England, worked in the United States in 1909–10, returned to England, and became a convert there. A free-lance journalist, he also worked for the government during World War I. He married Sara Casey of South Africa, a novelist and poet who became the mother of their seven children, and returned to the United States in 1920. He taught at Dominican College in California, St. John's University, Fordham, Georgetown, and Mt. St. Mary's, Maryland, and lectured widely until his health broke down in 1936. He wrote half a dozen volumes of poetry, several texts and anthologies, an autobiography, a survey of the Catholic Church in the United States, and biographies of de Soto, Xavier, Vincent de Paul, Mary Tudor, Queen Elizabeth, Orestes Brownson, Junipero Serra, Mother Cabrini, St. Benedict, and many other figures. Sara Maynard died in 1945, and in 1946 he married Kathleen Sheehan, spending his last years in Port Washington, New York, where he died on Oct. 18.

MAYNE, BL. CUTHBERT (1544–1577), martyr. Born in Youlson, Devonshire, England, he was raised as a Protestant by his uncle, a schismatic priest, and was ordained a minister. At Oxford he met Bl. Edmund Campion and Dr. Gregory Martin, at whose urging he became a convert in 1570. He fled, when their letters to him were intercepted, to Douai, where he was ordained in 1576 and sent back to England with Bl. John Payne. After a year in Cornwall, he was apprehended on the estate of Francis Tregian, tried, convicted of being a priest, and hanged, drawn, and quartered in Launceston, the first of the "seminary priests" to be martyred. He was beatified in 1886 and is the protomartyr of English seminaries. F. D. Nov. 29.

MAYOR, JOHN (1496–1550), historian. Born in Gleghornie, near Haddington, Scotland, he studied at Oxford and Cambridge, and received his doctorate in theology at Paris in 1505. He taught logic and theology at Paris (1505–18;

1525-30) and St. Andrew's (1518-25), and was provost of St. Salvator's from 1530 until his death there. Though he taught that the ecclesiastical authority of the Church was in the whole Church instead of the pope and advocated a national Scottish church, he remained Catholic. He wrote *Historia majoris Britanniae, tam Angliae quam Scotiae* and theological treatises.

MAYR, BEDA (1742-1794), philosopher. Born on Jan. 15 in Daiting, near Augsburg, Germany, he studied there and at Munich and Freiburg im Breisgau, joined the Benedictines in 1762, was ordained in 1766 and taught at Heiligenkreuz seminary, Donauwörth, where he was also prior for several years, except for four years as pastor of Mündling, until his death on Apr. 28. He was Kantian in his outlook and wrote on philosophy, theology, and mathematics, and twenty-one plays, and poetry.

MAYRON, FRANCIS (1280?-1327?), theologian. Probably born in Mayronnes, Basses-Alpes, France, he joined the Franciscans, studied under Duns Scotus at Paris, taught there for years, and may have introduced the test known as *Actus Sorbonicus* there. He wrote many theological treatises. He died in Piacenza, Italy, probably on July 26.

MAZARIN, JULES (1602-1661), cardinal. Born in Piscina, Abruzzi, on July 14, he was educated in Rome, went to the university of Alcalá as Jerome Colonna's chamberlain when seventeen, and on his return to Rome about 1622 received his doctorate. He served in Colonna's regiment in the Valtelline, negotiated to end the War of the Mantuan Succession in 1629 at Pope Urban VIII's request and the treaty of Turin between France and Savoy in 1632, was vice-legate at Avignon in 1634, nuncio at the French court in 1634-36, and in 1639 became a naturalized Frenchman and entered the king's service under Richelieu. As French ambassador, he settled the quarrel over Christine's regency in Savoy in 1640, was made a cardinal in 1641, and on Richelieu's death in 1642 succeeded him as minister. On Louis XIII's death in 1643 he became sole adviser and confidant of the regent, Anne of Austria, and soon became all-powerful. He continued Richelieu's policy of allying various German states against Austria, of securing the Rhine as France's border, and vigorously prosecuted the war with Spain. In 1648 he was able to secure the return of Alsace to France by the Treaty of Westphalia, which successfully ended the Thirty Years' War. At home, he alienated the nobles by building up the power of the crown and preventing access to the queen, by playing one group against another so that no one trusted him, and by his cynical plundering to amass an enormous personal fortune. In 1648 disagree-

ment between the crown and the Paris parliament led to revolt of the Fronde, which led to the expulsion of the queen, Louis XIV, and Mazarin from Paris in 1649. He was exiled in 1651, but during his exile promoted the formation of a royal party devoted to advancing the welfare of the realm through the monarch, returned to the court early in 1652, was obliged to retire to Sedan later in the year as part of the plan to reconcile parliament to the court, but returned early in 1653 as leader of the royal group with all his former power. He wielded as great influence over Louis XIV when he attained his majority as he had over Louis' mother, Anne. He effected a series of treaties with England, Sweden, Poland, and Brandenburg which returned the cities of northwest France and restored French influence in the Baltic, formed the League of the Rhine against Austria, and in 1659 signed the Treaty of Pyrenees with Spain by which France was ceded Roussilon and much of French Flanders, and Louis married Maria Theresa, daughter of King Philip IV. He died in Vincennes, France, on Mar. 9, probably the wealthiest man in Europe.

MAZENOD, CHARLES JOSEPH EUGENE DE (1782-1861), bishop. Born in Aix, Provence, France, on Aug. 1, he was obliged to flee to Italy during the French Revolution, and was ordained in 1811 at Amiens. He engaged in pastoral activities in Aix, became interested in missionary work, and in 1816 founded the institute which in 1826 was approved by Pope Leo XII as the Congregation of the Oblates of Mary Immaculate and of which he remained superior general until his death. In 1832 he was appointed titular bishop of Icosium and in 1837 bishop of Marseilles, where he restored ecclesiastical discipline and became noted for his defense of the papacy against the attacks of Gallicanists and civil authorities. He endorsed the dogma of the Immaculate Conception, was made a peer, and died in Marseilles, France, on May 21.

MAZOTA, ST. (8th century?). She is believed to have been the leader of a group of nineteen women who came from Ireland to found a religious community at Abernathy, Scotland. f. d. Dec. 23.

MAZZARELLO, ST. MARY DOMINICA (1837-1881), foundress. Born in Mornese, in Piedmont, Italy, she took care of relatives during a plague, which so weakened her that she had to become a dressmaker instead of working on their farm. She taught this trade to others, was active in the church sodality, and, when St. John Bosco was looking for someone to direct girls as he was working for boys, she was placed in charge, at thirty-five, of a building intended as a men's college. The villagers at first objected to the occupation of the school building, but later accepted Sr. Mary and the group which became the Daughters of Our Lady Help of Christians (Salesian Sisters). A dozen establishments soon grew up; the congregation spread to France, and sent teaching sisters to Argentina. She died at the mother house in Nizza Monferrato, Italy, and was canonized in 1951. F. D. May 14.

MAZZELLA, CAMILLO (1833–1900), cardinal. Born in Vitulano, Italy, on Feb. 10, he studied at the seminary in Benevento and was ordained in 1855. After two years as parish priest at Vitulano, he joined the Jesuits in 1857; when they were expelled from Italy in 1860, he went to Fourvières and taught theology. In 1867 he came to the United States and taught at Georgetown until 1869, when he was appointed professor and prefect of studies at Woodstock College. In 1878 he was appointed to the chair of theology at the Gregorian, Rome, and made prefect of studies. He was created cardinal-deacon in 1886, cardinal-priest in 1896, and in 1897 was appointed to the see of Palestrina, the first Jesuit to become a cardinal-bishop; he also served as president of the Academy of St. Thomas, and as prefect of the congregations of the Index, of Studies, and of Rites. He wrote *De religione et ecclesia, De virtutibus infusis, De Deo creante,* and *De gratia Christi.* He died in Rome on Mar. 26.

MAZZINGHI, BL. ANGELO AGOSTINO (1377–1438). Born in Florence, Italy, he joined the Carmelites there, and became prior at Frascati and Florence and provincial of Tuscany. He was widely esteemed as a preacher and revered as a model religious. He died on Aug. 15. His cult was confirmed in 1761. F. D. Aug. 18.

MAZZOLA, GIROLAMO. *See* Mazzuola, Girolamo.

MAZZOLINI, LODOVICO (1480–1528?), painter. Born in Ferrara, Italy, he probably studied under Panetti, married Vacchi's daughter in 1521, and became noted for his luminous coloring in *Christ in the Midst of the Scribes* and *Adoration of the Magi,* his masterpieces. He is sometimes called Il Ferrarese.

MAZZOLINI, SYLVESTRO (1460–1523), theologian. Born in Priero, Piedmont, Italy, he joined the Dominicans in 1475, taught at Bologna, Pavia, and Rome, and was appointed master of the Sacred College in 1515. He early challenged Martin Luther and his teachings and a long controversy between the two developed. Among his writings are *De juridica et irrefragabili veritate romanae ecclesiae romanique pontificis, Errata et argumenta M. Lutheri, summa summarum, quae Sylvestrina dicitur,* as well as treatises on the planets, history, and St. Thomas Aquinas. He died in Rome. He is also known as Sylvester Prierias.

MAZZONI, GUIDO (1450–1518), sculptor. Born in Modena, Italy, he worked in Naples in 1491, went to France with Charles VIII in 1495, and completed a number of *pietàs* for churches in Modena, Ferrara, and Naples, and a bronze bust of King Ferdinand. He is called Il Modanino.

MAZZONI, JACOPO (1548–1598), philosopher. Born in Cesena, Italy, he studied at Bologna and Padua, taught at Pisa, and was given a chair at Rome by Pope Gregory XIII. He was one of the founders of the Accademia della Crusca and wrote on Aristotle, Plato, Dante, and *De triplici hominum vita.*

MAZZUCHELLI, PIETRO FRANCESCO (1571?–1626), painter. Born in Moranzone, Italy, he painted altarpieces in Rome as a youth and after settling in Venice and studying Titian, Tintoretto, and Veronese, completely changed his style. Cardinal Borommeo became his patron. He established a school in Milan, was knighted by the duke of Savoy, and was killed in Piacenza in a fall from the scaffolding while painting the cupola of the cathedral. Outstanding works are *St. Michael Triumphant* in San Giovanni church, Como, and a *Flagellation.* He is known as Il Morazzone.

MAZZUCHELLI, SAMUEL CHARLES (1806–1864), missioner. Born in Milan, Italy, son of a prominent banker, he studied at Faenza and Rome, where he became a Dominican in 1823, and was sent to the United States in 1828. He was ordained in Cincinnati in 1830, spent three years on Mackinac Island, and in 1833 established Green Bay, Wisconsin, as the headquarters for his travels all over the midwestern section of the United States, ministering to the Indians, building churches, schools, convents, public buildings. He designed the first capital of Iowa in Iowa City. In 1843 he attempted unsuccessfully to convert Joseph Smith, the Mormon leader, was Bishop Loras' theologian at the fifth Provincial Council in Baltimore, and in 1844 visited Italy, where he wrote and issued his *Memoirs* (the English translation of which appeared in 1915). In 1845 he was founding president of Sinsinawa Mound College and founded the Dominican Congregation of the Most Holy Rosary in 1847. He served as chaplain of the first territorial legislature of Wisconsin, and was pastor in Benton, Wisconsin, when he died on Feb. 23.

MAZZUOLA, GIROLAMO FRANCESCO MARIA (1504–1540), painter. Born in Parma, Italy, on Jan. 11, "Il Parmigiano" was raised by his uncles after his father's death, became enthusiastic about Corregio's work, and attracted attention by his frescoes in the church of San Giovanni. He went to Rome in 1523, where he was influenced by Raphael's style, fled to Bologna in 1527 when Rome was sacked, and painted a series of altarpieces for St. Margaret's. He returned to Parma in 1531 and was commissioned by the Confraternity of the

Steccata to do a series of frescoes. His interest in alchemy led him to neglect his work and he was imprisoned in 1537 for failing to fulfill his contract. When released, he fled to Castel Maggiore, where he died on Aug. 24. He was a prolific worker, painting generally on religious themes. He was one of the first engravers of Italy, and is known also as Mazzola and Mazzuoli.

MC ANDREW, JAMES (1862–1922), general. Born in Hawley, Pennsylvania, he graduated from West Point, fought in Cuba and the Philippines during the Spanish-American War, and in 1917 was in command of the 18th Infantry Regiment of the 1st Division in France in World War I. He later helped to organize the war college at Langres, was chief of staff to Gen. John Pershing, and commandant of the General Staff College in Washington, D.C., where he died on Apr. 30.

MC AULIFFE, MAURICE FRANCIS (1875–1944), bishop. Born in Hartford, Connecticut, on June 17, he studied at Mt. St. Mary's College, Maryland, St. Sulpice seminary, Paris, and St. Willibrord's seminary, Eichstädtt, Germany, and was ordained in 1900. He taught at St. Thomas seminary, Hartford, was vice-president in 1906–22 and its president in 1922–34, was appointed titular bishop of Dercos and auxiliary of Hartford in 1925, and became bishop of the see in 1934. He died on Dec. 15.

MC CABE, EDWARD (1816–1885), cardinal. Born in Dublin, Ireland, on Feb. 14, he studied at Maynooth and was ordained in 1839. He served as curate in Clontarf and Dublin, declined appointment as bishop of Grahamstown, South Africa, in 1854 and served as parish priest in Dublin and Kingstown until 1877 when he became auxiliary bishop of Dublin. He succeeded Cardinal Cullen to the see as archbishop in 1879, was created cardinal in 1882, and died at Kingstown, Ireland, on Feb. 11. He was attacked through much of his term for his opposition to the Land League and other nationalist groups.

MC CABE, FRANCIS XAVIER (1872–1948), educator. Born in New Orleans on Feb. 6, he studied in Missouri seminaries and was ordained a Vincentian in 1896. He taught at St. Vincent's, Los Angeles, in 1896–1906, and was president of De Paul University in 1910–20, where he introduced co-education and established a law school. He became a pastor in New Orleans in 1928, then director of St. Mary's seminary, Perryville, and died in New Orleans on July 3.

MC CABE, WILLIAM BERNARD (1801–1891), author. Born in Dublin, Ireland, on Nov. 23, he worked on Dublin and London newspapers, became consul at London for the Uruguayan government in 1847–51, and wrote *Catholic History of England,* novels (*Adelaide, Agnes Arnold, Bertha, Florine*), and translations from German and Italian. He died on Dec. 14.

MC CARRAN, PATRICK ANTHONY (1876–1954), senator. Born in Reno, Nevada, on Aug. 8, he studied at Nevada, became a rancher, then took up law. He became a member of the state legislature in 1903, married Martha Weeks in that year, passed the bar in 1905, was a district attorney in 1906–9, associate justice of the state supreme court in 1912–18, president of the state bar association, and a power in Nevada politics for twenty-five years. In 1933 he began his career in the United States Senate, where he attacked the attempt to pack the supreme court, advocated the creation of the air force as a separate unit, and sponsored the 1938 bill for the creation of the Civil Aeronautics Authority. A Democrat, he frequently clashed with Presidents Roosevelt and Truman, particularly over foreign policy, attacking the abandonment of nationalist China, the refusal to accept Spain in the North Atlantic Treaty Organization and to build air bases there, and the tolerance of communist advice and direction. As a member of the committee on foreign co-operation, the senate judiciary committee, and the internal security subcommittee, he was a stormy and controversial figure. He was the sponsor of the McCarran-Walter Immigration and Naturalization Bill in 1952, which was passed over Truman's veto. He died in Hawthorne, Nevada, on Sept. 28.

MC CARTHY, DENIS ALOYSIUS (1870–1931), poet. Born in Carrick-on-Suir, Tipperary, Ireland, on July 25, he was educated there, went to the United States at fifteen, and married Ruphine Morris in Charlestown, Massachusetts, in 1901. He wrote for newspapers and magazines, edited the *North American Teacher,* was a Chautauqua lecturer, worked with the Knights of Columbus during World War I, and was associated with numerous educational and literary groups in and around Boston, Massachusetts. His volumes of verse include *A Round of Rimes* (1909), *Voices from Erin* (1910), *Heart Songs and Home Songs* (1916), *Songs of Sunrise* (1917), *Ould Father Toomey* (1927), and *The Harp of Life* (1929). He died on Aug. 18.

MC CARTHY, JOSEPH EDWARD (1877–1955), bishop. Born in Waterbury, Connecticut, on Nov. 14, he studied at Holy Cross, the Catholic University of America, and St. Sulpice, Paris, and was ordained in Paris in 1903. He became vice-president of St. Thomas preparatory seminary in Bloomfield, Connecticut, and in 1932 was appointed bishop of Portland, Maine. He died on Sept. 8.

MC CARTHY, JOSEPH R. (1909–1957),

senator. Born in Grand Chute, Wisconsin, on Nov. 14, of a farming family, he graduated in law from Marquette University, was admitted to the bar in 1935, and was elected circuit judge. In World War II he became a captain in the Marine Corps, fought in the Pacific area, and was elected to the United States Senate in 1946 and in 1952. From 1950 to 1954 he was an outspoken opponent of communism, of all who appeared in any way to have supported it, even of many individuals who occupied high government posts. As chairman of the committee on investigations in 1953 he aroused sharp and bitter differences of public opinion, and a senate censure, for abusive language and silence before an elections committee, came in 1954. He died of hepatitis in Bethesda, Maryland, on May 2 and was buried in Appleton, Wisconsin.

MC CARTHY, JUSTIN J. (1900–1959), bishop. Born in Sayre, Pennsylvania, on Nov. 26, he studied at Seton Hall and the North American College, Rome, where he was ordained in 1927, and then taught at Immaculate Conception seminary in Darlington, New Jersey, for the next twenty-six years, the last sixteen years as spiritual director. He was made a papal chamberlain in 1941, domestic prelate in 1949, and pastor in South Orange, New Jersey, in 1953. In 1954 he was appointed auxiliary bishop of Newark, and in 1957, second bishop of Camden. He died in Elizabeth, New Jersey, on Dec. 26.

MC CARTHY, BL. THADDEUS (d. 1497), bishop. Born in Munster, Ireland, he studied at Kilcrea and in 1482 was appointed bishop of Ross by Pope Sixtus IV. Hugh O'Driscoll, auxiliary of the previous bishop, drove him out in 1488, but the dispute was resolved in 1490 when Pope Innocent VIII declared Hugh bishop of Ross and gave Thaddeus the see of Cork and Cloyne. When his enemies barred his entry, he went to Rome, where Pope Alexander VI upheld him. He died at Ivrea, Italy, on the way home. His cult was confirmed in 1895. F. D. Oct. 25.

MC CLOSKEY, JOHN (1810–1885), cardinal. Born on Mar. 20, in Brooklyn, New York, he graduated from Mt. St. Mary's College, Maryland, in 1828, studied at the seminary there, and was ordained in 1834. After a period as chaplain at Bellevue Hospital in New York City he taught at the seminary in Nyack, studied at the Gregorian, Rome, from 1835 to 1837, became pastor of St. Joseph's New York, where he ended a revolt of the trustees, was appointed first president of St. John's College, Fordham, in 1841, and in 1843 was named bishop of Axiere and coadjutor of New York. He was appointed first bishop of Albany in 1847 and archbishop of New York in 1864. He attended the second and third plenary councils in Baltimore and the Vatican Council in 1870; although a believer in papal infallibility, he opposed its proclamation as inexpedient at that time. In 1875 he was named the first American cardinal by Pope Pius IX, dedicated St. Patrick's cathedral in 1879, and retired from active management of the archdiocese in 1884. He died in Poughkeepsie, New York, on Oct. 10.

JOHN M. FARLEY, *Life of John Cardinal McCloskey*, (New York, Longmans, 1918).

MC CLOSKEY, WILLIAM GEORGE (1823–1909), bishop. Born in Brooklyn, New York, on Nov. 10, he studied at Mt. St. Mary's College and seminary, Maryland, and was ordained in 1852. He was a parish priest, then returned to teach theology at the seminary. In 1859 he became first rector of the North American College in Rome. In 1868 he was appointed bishop of Louisville, Kentucky, built 100 churches and a seminary, and attended the Vatican Council in 1870 and the second and third plenary councils of Baltimore. He died in Louisville on Sept. 17.

MC COLE, C. JOHN (1905–1939), critic. Born in Sagola, Wisconsin, on Apr. 25, he studied at St. Norbert's and Notre Dame, taught there and at St. John's, Brooklyn, and lectured at many colleges in the metropolitan New York area. He served as chairman of the board of directors of the Catholic Poetry Society, and published *On Poetry* (with Andrew Smithberger) in 1930 and *Lucifer at Large* (1937) on contemporary literature. He died in New York City on Jan. 14.

MC CORMACK, JOHN (1884–1945), singer. Born in Athlone, Ireland, on June 14, he early gave evidence of his singing ability, studied at Summerhill College, won the gold medal for singing at the national Irish festival in 1902, and after a short tour in the United States went to Italy to study under Sabatini. He made his debut at Covent Garden, London, in *Cavalleria Rusticana* in 1907, in New York in *La Traviata* at the Manhattan Opera House in 1909, sang in opera in Chicago, Philadelphia, and New York's Metropolitan, and after 1913 appeared only on the concert stage, where he was enormously successful as a singer of ballads and Irish folk songs. He became an American citizen in 1919, was made a papal count in 1928, and died in Dublin on Sept. 16.

MC CORMICK, ANNE O'HARE (1882–1954), journalist. Born in Yorkshire, England, of American parents, Thomas and Teresa O'Hare, she was brought up in Columbus, Ohio, studied at St. Mary of the Springs, and began writing in 1922 as an associate editor of the *Catholic Universe-Bulletin* of Cleveland, for which her mother had written a column and poetry. She married Francis J. McCormick, a Dayton engineer, frequently accompanied him abroad, wrote a few articles for the New York *Times Magazine*, then began a regular column, "Abroad," in 1921. In 1936 she became the first woman to be appointed to that newspaper's editorial board, and in 1937 was the second woman to receive the Pulitzer Prize, for foreign correspondence. She wrote incisively and astutely on the period of Mussolini, Hitler, and Stalin, whose rise and fall she recorded, the United Nations, worsening relations with Asia, and the Korean War. She received a great number of honors and awards, honorary degrees from sixteen colleges, and the Laetare Medal in 1944. In 1946–48 she was a delegate to the United Nations Educational, Scientific and Cultural Organization Conferences. She was the author of *The Hammer and the Scythe* (1928), was elected to the National Institute of Arts and Letters, and died in New York City on May 29.

MC CORT, JOHN JOSEPH (1860–1936), bishop. Born in Philadelphia on Feb. 16, he studied at LaSalle and St. Charles Borromeo seminary there, and was ordained in Philadelphia in 1883. He taught mathematics and church history at St. Charles from 1883 until 1899, when he was appointed pastor of Our Mother of Saviour church, became a domestic prelate and vicar general in 1910, and in 1912 was consecrated titular bishop of Azotus and auxiliary of Philadelphia. He was appointed coadjutor of Altoona, Pennsylvania, in 1920, succeeded to that see later that year, and died in Altoona on Apr. 21.

MC DERMOTT, ARTHUR VINCENT (1888–1949), general. Born in Brooklyn, New York, on Aug. 27, he studied at Columbia and New York Law School, joined the national guard, served in the Mexican border campaign, and in World War I was wounded in Belgium, and climbed through the ranks from private to brigadier general. He married Genevieve Markey in 1919, became active in politics, and was deputy city controller in 1938. In the national guard he was judge advocate of the state forces by 1934. In 1940 he became director of selective service for New York. He died in New York City on Dec. 18.

MC DEVITT, PHILIP RICHARD (1858–1935), bishop. Born in Philadelphia on July 12, he graduated from LaSalle, studied at St. Charles Borromeo seminary, and was ordained in Philadelphia in 1885. He served as superintendent of Catholic schools in Philadelphia from 1899 to 1916, was made a domestic prelate in 1910, when he was also president of the American Catholic Historical Society, and in 1916 was appointed bishop of Harrisburg. He was named episcopal chairman of the Catholic press department of the National Catholic Welfare Conference in 1918,

and died in Harrisburg, Pennsylvania, on Nov. 11.

MC DONNELL, CHARLES EDWARD (1854–1921), bishop. Born in New York City on Feb. 1, he studied at St. Francis Xavier and the North American College, Rome, was ordained in 1878, and later received his doctorate in divinity. He completed five years of parish work in New York on his return, became secretary to Cardinal McCloskey in 1884 and Archbishop Corrigan in 1885, was chancellor of the see in 1885–92, was made a monsignor in 1890, and in 1892 was consecrated as second bishop of Brooklyn. He increased the number of national churches to care for increasing immigration, held two diocesan synods, and erected new parishes, two hospitals, and many charitable institutions. He died in Brooklyn on Aug. 8.

MC DONNELL, THOMAS J. (1894–1961), bishop. Born in New York City on Aug. 18, he studied at Cathedral College and Fordham, and St. Joseph's seminary, Yonkers, New York, and was ordained in 1919. He did pastoral work in New York, was director of the archdiocesan Society for the Propagation of the Faith in 1923–36, became national director in 1936, a position he held until 1950, was editor of *Good Work Magazine* in 1923–36, and in 1947 was consecrated titular bishop of Sela and auxiliary of New York. He was named coadjutor bishop of Wheeling, West Virginia, in 1951, and died there on Jan. 25.

MC EVAY, FERGUS PATRICK (1856–1911), archbishop. Born in Lindsay, Ontario, Canada, on Dec. 8, he was ordained in Kingston in 1882, became rector of cathedrals in Peterborough and Hamilton, was vicar general of the latter see, was named a monsignor, and in 1899 was consecrated bishop of London, Ontario. He was transferred to Toronto in 1908, began St. Augustine's seminary, attended the first National Council of Canada, and helped to found the Church Extension Society of his country. He died on May 10.

MC FADDEN, JAMES AUGUSTINE (1880–1952), bishop. Born in Cleveland, Ohio, on Dec. 24, he studied at St. Ignatius College and St. Mary's seminary there, and was ordained in Cleveland in 1905. He did parish work in Cleveland, was rector of the seminary in 1917–23, chancellor of the diocese in 1925, was made a domestic prelate in 1927, and was appointed titular bishop of Bida and auxiliary of Cleveland in 1932. He was appointed first bishop of Youngstown, Ohio, in 1943, and died on Nov. 16.

MC FARLAND, FRANCIS PATRICK (1819–1874), bishop. Born in Franklin, Pennsylvania, on Apr. 16, he studied at Mt. St. Mary's College, Maryland, taught there, and was ordained in New York in 1845. After teaching a year at Fordham he became pastor in Watertown and Utica, New York, was appointed vicar apostolic of Florida in 1857 but declined, and in 1858 was appointed third bishop of Hartford, Connecticut. He lived in Providence, Rhode Island, and attended the Vatican Council in 1869–70. His diocese was divided in 1872 and he then moved to Hartford, where he began the cathedral, and died on Oct. 12.

MC FAUL, JAMES AUGUSTINE (1850–1917), bishop. Born in Larne, Antrim, Ireland, on June 6, he was brought to the United States as an infant, studied at St. Vincent's, Pennsylvania, St. Francis Xavier, New York, and Seton Hall, and was ordained in 1877. He served in New Jersey parishes, became pastor of the cathedral in Trenton in 1890, and the bishop's secretary, and in 1892 vicar general. He was appointed bishop of that see in 1894, was especially interested in the immigrants and social-welfare work, and died in Trenton, New Jersey, on June 16.

MC GARRY, WILLIAM JAMES (1894–1941), educator. Born in Hamilton, Massachusetts, on Mar. 14, he became a Jesuit, was ordained in 1925, taught mathematics and philosophy at Fordham (1918–22) and Weston (1930–37), was president of Boston College in 1937–39, and became editor of *Theological Studies*. He wrote *The Biblical Commission, Anthropology and the Knowledge of God, The Mystical Body,* and *Paul and the Crucified*. He died in New York City on Sept. 23.

MC GAVICK, ALEXANDER JAMES (1863–1948), bishop. Born in Fox Lake, Illinois, on Aug. 22, he studied at St. Viator's College and seminary, was ordained in Chicago in 1887, became a pastor there in 1897, was named auxiliary bishop in 1898, and founded welfare and youth groups in that city. He helped to revitalize the National Catholic Welfare Conference, was named bishop of La Crosse, Wisconsin, in 1922, built a high school there, and continued to engage in welfare work. He died in La Crosse on Aug. 25.

MC GEE, THOMAS D'ARCY (1825–1868), editor. Born in Carlingford, Louth, Ireland, on Apr. 13, he emigrated to the United States in 1842, became an editor on the Boston *Pilot*, went back to Ireland in 1845 where he became an editor of *The Freeman's Journal* and *Nation* in Dublin, was arrested in 1848 for his activities in the Irish revolt and as secretary of the Irish Confederation but escaped to New York. There he established *The Nation*, became embroiled in disputes with Archbishop Hughes, and moved the paper to Boston, Buffalo, and back to New York as *The American Celt*. In 1857 he established *The New Era* in Montreal, was elected to the Canadian parliament, and was prominent in the establishment of the Dominion of Canada. He was assassinated by a Fenian in Ottawa, Canada, on Apr. 7. Among his writings were *History of the Irish Settlers in North America, Catholic History of North America, History of Ireland,* and *Poems.*

MC GILL, JOHN (1809–1872), bishop. Born in Philadelphia on Nov. 4, he graduated from St. Joseph's College in 1828, read law, and was admitted to the bar. He then studied at St. Thomas seminary, Kentucky, and St. Mary's seminary, Baltimore, and was ordained in 1835 in Bardstown. He served in Kentucky parishes, became assistant editor of the *Catholic Advocate* under Martin J. Spalding, who appointed him his vicar general, and in 1850 was named bishop of Richmond, Virginia. He built churches and schools, fought the Know-Nothing movement, was a supporter of the Confederacy in the Civil War, rebuilt his diocese after the war, and preached at the Vatican Council in 1869. Among his writings were *The True Church* (1862) and *Our Faith, Our Victory* (1865). He died in Richmond on Jan. 14.

MC GILLICUDDY, CORNELIUS (1862–1956), sportsman. Born in East Brookfield, Massachusetts, on Dec. 23, "Connie Mack" worked in a shoe factory, played baseball with a local team, and moved up the sports ladder through Meriden and Hartford to Washington, Buffalo, and Pittsburgh, where he was made manager in 1894. After a transfer to Milwaukee, he went to Philadelphia in 1901 when the new American League was formed. Between 1902 and 1931 his teams won nine league championships and five world's series. In 1939 he was selected by sports writers as one of the original thirteen figures to be permanently honored in the Baseball Hall of Fame at Cooperstown, New York, and was the only one living to attend the ceremony. He acquired complete control of the Philadelphia team in 1940 and transferred it to others in 1950. He died in Philadelphia on Feb. 8.

MC GINNIS, WILLIAM F. (1867–1932). Born in Brooklyn, New York, on Dec. 28, he studied at St. John's and the North American College, Rome, and was ordained in 1891. He did parish work on Long Island and was pastor in Westbury in 1904–19 and of St. Thomas Aquinas church, Brooklyn, from 1919 until his death there on May 16. He founded and served as president of the Catholic Truth Society, edited its journal, *Truth,* and was named a monsignor in 1926.

MC GIVNEY, MICHAEL JOSEPH (1852–1890). Born in Waterbury, Connecticut, on Aug. 12, he studied at St. Hyacinth, Canada, Niagara University, and St. Mary's, Baltimore, and was ordained in 1877. Assigned to St. Mary's parish in New Haven, Connecticut, he founded the Knights of Columbus there in 1882, and was its national chaplain until his death in Thomaston, Connecticut, on Aug. 14.

MC GIVNEY, PATRICK J. (d. 1928). Born in Waterbury, Connecticut, he studied at Niagara and at seminaries in Montreal and Boston, and was ordained in 1892. He was pastor of parishes in Connecticut, at Middletown, New Canaan, and Bridgeport, was named a monsignor, and served as supreme chaplain of the Knights of Columbus, of which his brother Michael had been a founder. He died in Paris on May 8.

MC GLOIN, FRANK (1846–1921), jurist. Born in Gort, Galway, Ireland, on Feb. 22, he was taken to New Orleans, Louisiana, as a child, studied at St. Mary's College in Missouri, fought in the Confederate army, and was admitted to the bar in 1866. He assisted Chief Justice White in his fight against state lotteries, became justice of the state court of appeals in 1880, was eidtor of the *Hibernian*, and wrote *The Conquest of Europe, The Light of Faith* (1905), and a novel, *The Story of Norodom*.

MC GLYNN, EDWARD (1837–1900). Born in New York City, on Sept. 27, he studied at the Propaganda in Rome, and was ordained there in 1860. He did parish work in New York and in 1866 became pastor of St. Stephen's. He became intensely interested in social reform, was attracted to the economic theories of Henry George, and became an enthusiastic supporter of George's single-tax (on land) theory. In 1886 his active campaigning for George in the mayoralty campaign brought him into conflict with Archbishop Corrigan. When he refused the archbishop's order not to speak at a campaign rally, he was suspended from his priestly duties and early in 1887 removed from his pastorate. When he refused to retract his land theories on the demand of the prefect of the Congregation of the Propaganda and then refused the pope's summons to Rome, he was excommunicated. He continued advocating his single-tax theories as president of the Anti-Poverty Society, but in 1892 was reinstated by the papal delegate to the United States, Msgr. Satolli, who declared his single-tax views were not contrary to Catholic teaching. He was received by the pope in 1893, was transferred to the pastorate of St. Mary's church in Newburgh, New York, in 1894, and died there on Jan. 7.

MC GOLRICK, JAMES (1841–1918), bishop. Born in Borrisokane, Tipperary, Ireland, on May 1, he studied at All Hallows, Dublin, was ordained there, and went to the United States in 1867. He was assistant pastor of the St. Paul cathedral in 1867, pastor of Immaculate Con-

ception church in 1868–89, and in 1889 was appointed first bishop of Duluth, Minnesota, where he remained until his death there on Jan. 23.

MC GOVERN, PATRICK ALOYSIUS ALPHONSUS (1872–1951), bishop. Born in Omaha, Nebraska, on Oct. 14, he studied at Creighton and Mt. St. Mary of the West seminary, Cincinnati, and was ordained in 1895. He was pastor of St. Philomena cathedral in Omaha in 1898–1907 and of St. Peter's church in 1907–12, then was appointed bishop of Cheyenne, Wyoming. He held a diocesan synod in 1913, and died on Nov. 8.

MC GOVERN, THOMAS (1832–1898), bishop. Born in Swanlinbar, Cavan, Ireland, he went to the United States, studied at St. Mary's, Maryland, and St. Charles Borromeo, Philadelphia, and was ordained in 1861. He did pastoral work in the Philadelphia diocese until 1887, when he was appointed second bishop of Harrisburg, Pennsylvania. He died there on July 25.

MC GRATH, JAMES (1835–1898). Born in Holy Cross, Tipperary, Ireland, on June 26, he studied at the University of Dublin, joined the Oblates of Mary Immaculate in 1855, and in 1856 was sent to Canada, where he studied at Ottawa, and was ordained in 1859. He engaged in missionary work in Ottawa and Texas, became noted for his missions in New York and New England, and in 1870 became pastor of St. John's parish and built Immaculate Conception church, where he introduced new ideas of parochial education with Grey Nuns from Canada in 1880. He was elected first provincial of the Oblate American province in 1883. He died in Albany, New York, on Jan. 12.

MC GRATH, JOSEPH (1882–1961), archbishop. Born in Kilkenny, Ireland, on Mar. 24, he studied at St. John's seminary, Waterford, and in France and Rome, and was ordained in 1908. He did diocesan work in Clifton, England, was transferred to Menevia, Wales, in 1920, became its bishop, and in 1940 was appointed archbishop of Cardiff, Wales, where he reigned until his death on Mar. 13.

MC GRATH, JOSEPH FRANCIS (1871–1950), bishop. Born in Kilmacow, Kilkenny, Ireland, on Mar. 1, he studied at St. Kieran's College, Kilkenny, and the Grand seminary, Montreal, and was ordained in 1895. He did parish work in Boston, Springfield, Portland, Scranton, Nesqually, and Seattle, and then went to Oregon. He was appointed bishop of Baker City, Oregon, in 1918, where he died on Apr. 12.

MC GRAW, JAMES J. (1874–1928), banker. Born in Leavenworth, Kansas, on Aug. 21, he settled in Tulsa, Oklahoma, where he was president of the Exchange National Bank from 1921 until his death. He also was president of a lumber company, was Republican national committeeman in 1916–20, and was in charge of all overseas disbursements of the Knights of Columbus in France during World War I. He was decorated by France and Belgium and died in Hot Springs, Arkansas, on Mar. 3.

MC GROARTY, JOHN STEVEN (1862–1944), poet. Born in Foster Township, Pennsylvania, on Aug. 20, he studied in Wilkes-Barre, married Ida Lubrecht in 1890, became treasurer of Luzerne County, studied law, and passed the bar in 1894. After two years he went to a Butte, Montana, law office, and in 1901 joined the staff of the Los Angeles *Times*. He became a campaigner for the preservation or restoration of the California missions (for which he was decorated by Pope Pius XI), and wrote *The Mission Play*, produced at San Gabriel for twenty years. He wrote other plays (*Osceola, La Golondrina, Babylon*), historical and travel sketches, and poems of California and Wyoming. He was named poet laureate of California in 1933, was elected congressman in 1934, received honorary degrees from California and Santa Clara, and died in Tujunga, Los Angeles, California, on Aug. 7.

MC GUINNESS, EUGENE JOSEPH (1889–1957), bishop. Born in Hallertown, Pennsylvania, on Sept. 6, he studied at St. Charles Borromeo seminary in Philadelphia, where he was ordained in 1915. He served in Philadelphia parishes, was executive secretary of the American Board of Catholic Missions in 1923–27, was appointed first vice-president of the Extension Society in 1925, was an associate editor of *Extension Magazine*, and was made a domestic prelate in 1929. He was consecrated bishop of Raleigh, North Carolina, in 1937, remained there until 1944, when he was named coadjutor of Oklahoma City and Tulsa, and succeeded to that see in 1948. He died on Dec. 27.

MC KAY, CLAUDE (1890–1948), author. Born in Sunny Vale, Jamaica, on Sept. 15, he wrote poems at an early age, published *Songs of Jamaica* in 1911, and went to the United States a year later. He studied at Tuskegee Normal Institute and Kansas State, worked as a waiter and porter, then joined the staff of the *Liberator* in New York (1919–22) and the *Dreadnought* in London, both revolutionary in tone. He was a spokesman for the American Workers party, but a trip to Russia disillusioned him. He published *Home to Harlem* (1928), *Banjo* (1929), *Gingertown* (1932), *Banana Bottom* (1933), and the autobiographical *A Long Way from Home* (1937). Poems include *Spring in New Hampshire* (1920) and *Harlem Shadows* (1922). Much of his early work is marked by extreme realism; other passages indicate that he was apparently exploited as champion of a somewhat undefined cause. His last work was *Harlem: Negro Metropolis*. He be-

came a convert in Chicago in 1944, worked for the Catholic Youth Organization and for Friendship House there, and died in Chicago on May 22.

MC KENNA, JOSEPH (1843–1926), jurist. Born in Philadelphia on Aug. 10, he studied for the priesthood, but gave up this career, and graduated from Benicia Collegiate Institute, California, in 1865. He was admitted to the bar the same year, served in the state legislature in 1875–76, ran unsuccessfully for Congress in 1876, 1878, and in 1880 but was elected in 1884 and served four terms. He was appointed United States circuit judge in 1892, attorney general of the United States in 1897, and eight months later associate justice of the United States Supreme Court, a position he held until his resignation in 1925. He died in Washington, D.C., on Nov. 21.

MC KEOUGH, MICHAEL J. (1892–1960), educator. Born in Green Bay, Wisconsin, on Sept. 18, he studied at St. Norbert's, became a Norbertine in 1912, and was ordained in 1914. He served as a chaplain in World War I, received his doctorate at Catholic University in 1926, and taught at St. Norbert's to 1932. He was principal of several boys' high schools in 1932–45, taught at Catholic University in 1945–51, was editor of the *Catholic Educational Review* in 1947–49, and became head of the education department at St. Norbert's in 1951 and dean in 1952. He died in Green Bay on June 5.

MC LAUGHLIN, THOMAS HENRY (1881–1947), bishop. Born in New York City, on July 15, he studied at St. Francis Xavier and Innsbruck, and was ordained in 1904. He served as a chaplain in Austria while studying for his doctorate in sacred theology at Innsbruck and on his return taught philosophy and theology at Seton Hall College and Immaculate Conception seminary in New Jersey. He became president of the college in 1922, a domestic prelate in 1923, rector of the seminary and vicar general of the Newark diocese in 1933, prothonotary apostolic in 1934, and in 1935 was consecrated titular bishop of Nisa and auxiliary of Newark. He was appointed first bishop of Paterson, New Jersey, in 1937, and died there on Mar. 17.

MC LOUGHLIN, JOHN (1784–1857). Born in La Rivière du Loup, Quebec, Canada, on Oct. 19, he studied in Canada and Scotland, became a doctor, but gave up practice to become a partner in the North-West Company. When it merged with the Hudson's Bay Company in 1821 he remained in charge at Fort William on Lake Superior; in 1824 he was chief factor at the headquarters in Fort Vancouver, Oregon Territory. He was a stern businessman, but noted for his justice and personal generosity. His rule was marked by an absence of

Indian wars and by good relations with all missionaries. He became a convert in 1842; fed, clothed, and supplied the immigrants to Oregon in 1843–45; resigned from the trading company in 1846; and founded Oregon City. A Methodist missionary group which he previously had aided brought suit against him, gained most of his property, and left him to die a pauper on Sept. 3.

MC MAHON, JAMES O'BRIEN (1903–1952), senator. Born in Norwalk, Connecticut, on Oct. 6, he graduated from Fordham and from the Yale Law School, became a judge in the Norwalk city court in 1933, and served as special assistant to the United States attorney general to 1935 and as assistant attorney general to 1939. He married Rosemary Turner in 1940, was elected to the United States Senate in 1944, and re-elected in 1950. He was chairman of the congressional joint committee on atomic energy, recommended expanded production for civil use apart from military control, wrote the McMahon Act for the control of atomic energy, served on foreign relations and interstate commerce committees, and was a champion of civil rights. He was generally called Brien McMahon. He died in Washington, D.C., on July 29.

MC MAHON, JOHN JOSEPH (1875–1932), bishop. Born in Hinsdale, New York, on Sept. 27, he studied at St. Bonaventure, New York, and the Propaganda, Rome, and was ordained in Rome in 1900. He did parish work in Buffalo diocese, was assistant superintendent of schools in 1904–6, chancellor and then vicar general, diocesan visitor to communities of nuns, and in 1928, was appointed bishop of Trenton, New Jersey. He died in Buffalo, New York, on Dec. 31.

MC MAHON, JOSEPH M. (1862–1939). Born in New York City on Nov. 18, he graduated from Manhattan in 1880 and was ordained in 1886. He served at St. Patrick's cathedral in 1886–1901, when he founded Our Lady of Lourdes parish, and served as head of the Cathedral Free Circulating Library until it was absorbed by the New York Public Library in 1902. He founded the Catholic Library Reading Circles (later merged with the Catholic Library Association) and helped organize the Catholic Summer School of America. He was made a domestic prelate in 1921, and died on Jan. 6.

MC MAHON, LAWRENCE STEPHEN (1835–1893), bishop. Born in St. Johns, New Brunswick, Canada, on Dec. 26, he was raised in Cambridge, Massachusetts, studied at Holy Cross and St. Mary's, Baltimore, and in Montreal, France, and Italy, and was ordained in Rome in 1860. He was chaplain of the 28th Massachusetts Regiment during the Civil War, then served as pastor in Bridgewater and New

Bedford, Massachusetts. He became vicar general of Providence, Rhode Island, in 1872, and in 1879 was consecrated fifth bishop of Hartford, Connecticut. He finished building St. Joseph's cathedral there and greatly expanded the number of parishes, churches, schools, and convents. He died in Lakeville, Connecticut, on Aug. 21.

MC MAHON, MARTIN THOMAS (1838–1903), jurist. Born in Laprairie, Canada, he was brought to the United States as an infant, graduated from Fordham in 1855, studied law in Buffalo, New York, and was admitted to the bar in California in 1861. He served during the Civil War, received the medal of honor, and retired as a major general. He was corporation counsel for New York City in 1866–67 and minister to Paraguay in 1868–69; then resumed his law practice in New York until 1881. He served as receiver of taxes, state assemblyman and senator, and in 1896 was elected judge of the court of general sessions in New York City, where he died on Apr. 21.

MC MASTER, JAMES ALPHONSUS (1820–1886), editor. Born in Duanesburg, New York, on Apr. 1, he studied at Union College but left in 1839, studied law, and probably attended Union Theological seminary. A convert in 1845, he transferred to Louvain, but decided he had no vocation for the priesthood, and returned to write for the New York *Tribune*. He bought the *Freeman's Journal* in 1848 and was its editor until his death in Brooklyn on Dec. 29. He quarreled violently with Bishop Hughes, former owner of the *Journal*, on Irish politics, with Orestes Brownson on philosophy, and was notoriously anti-abolitionist. In 1861 he was imprisoned and his paper suppressed for eleven months for his personal attacks on Abraham Lincoln and his administration. He died on Dec. 29.

MC MULLEN, JOHN (1832–1885), bishop. Born in Ballynahinch, Down, Ireland, on Jan. 8, he studied at St. Mary of the Lake, Chicago, and the Propaganda, Rome, and was ordained in 1858. He did parish work in the Chicago diocese from 1858 to 1881 (except for 1861–66, when he was rector of St. Mary of the Lake), became vicar general of the see in 1877, and was its administrator in 1879–80. He founded the *Catholic Monthly Magazine* in 1865. In 1881 he was consecrated first bishop of Davenport, Iowa, where he showed great interest in education, founded St. Ambrose College in 1882, and died on July 4.

MC NABB, VINCENT (1868–1943), theologian. Born in Portaferry, Down, Ireland, on July 8, the tenth of eleven children of a master mariner and a dressmaker, he studied at St. Malachy's, Belfast, and in Gloucestershire and at Louvain. He became a Dominican in 1885 and was ordained in 1891. He was stationed in

London slum areas and worked energetically for social reforms and for a "back-to-the-land movement." He deplored machinery, woman's suffrage, city life, and materialism. He was prior at Holy Cross, Leicester, and at Hawkesyard, Staffordshire, lectured on St. Thomas Aquinas at the University of London, wrote articles for *Blackfriars*, and engaged in violent controversy over theological interpretations of the Council of Trent with his Jesuit friend, Fr. de la Tille. He was equally at home living in the abject poverty he sought to change and arguing from public platforms in Hyde Park. He wrote some thirty books, including *Infallibility, Oxford Conferences on Prayer, Frontiers of Faith and Reason, The Catholic Church and Philosophy, The Church and the Land, Old Principles and the New Order, Francis Thompson and Other Essays, Path of Prayer*, biographies of SS. John Fisher and Elizabeth of Portugal, and a *Life of Christ*. He was decorated by the Belgian government for his contributions to war relief and was given the highest Dominican rank, Master of Sacred Theology. He died in London on June 17.

MC NAMARA, JOHN MICHAEL (1878–1960), bishop. Born in Baltimore on Aug. 12, he studied at Loyola College and St. Mary's seminary there, and was ordained in 1902. He did parish work in Maryland towns until 1911, when he was assigned to Washington, D.C., where he became founding pastor of St. Gabriel's in 1919. In 1927 he was appointed titular bishop of Eumenia and auxiliary of Baltimore, served as administrator of the see in 1947, and became auxiliary bishop of Washington in that same year when it became an independent diocese. He died in Washington on Nov. 26.

MC NEILL, JAMES (1869–1938), governor. Born in Glenarm, Antrim, Ireland, on Mar. 27 or 29, he studied in Dublin and at Cambridge, entered the civil service, and was in Bombay, India, from 1890 until his retirement in 1915. He returned to Ireland, worked with his brothers Charles and John for Irish independence, and was arrested after the 1916 rising in Dublin, although he had not been a member of any proscribed group. He then joined the forces of Eamon de Valera, and in 1922 helped to draft the constitution of the Free State. He was a high commissioner at London from 1923, in which year he married Josephine Aherne, and in 1928 became governor general. His title and office were not liked by the nationalists and he resigned in 1932, to be replaced by a president. He died in London on Dec. 12.

MC NEIRNY, FRANCIS (1828–1894), bishop. Born in New York City on Apr. 25, he studied at Montreal College and the Grand seminary there, and was ordained in New York in 1854. He did parish work in the New York archdiocese, was appointed chancellor in 1857,

secretary to Archbishop Hughes in 1859, and in 1871 was appointed titular bishop of Rhesaina and coadjutor of Albany, New York. He became administrator of that see in 1874, succeeded to it in 1877, and died there on Jan. 2.

MC NICHOLAS, JOHN TIMOTHY (1877–1950), archbishop. Born in Kiltimaugh, Mayo, Ireland, on Dec. 15, he was brought to the United States by his parents at the age of four, studied at St. Joseph's College, Philadelphia, St. Rose's priory, Springfield, Kentucky, St. Joseph's house of studies, Somerset, Ohio, and the Minerva, Rome. He became a Dominican in 1894 and was ordained in 1901 in Somerset, Ohio. He taught at St. Joseph's and the Dominican house of studies, Washington, D.C., until 1908, when he became national director of the Holy Name Society and editor of the *Holy Name Journal*. He served in these capacities, and was pastor of St. Catherine of Siena in New York in 1913–16, until 1917, when he was appointed assistant to the master general of his order in Rome. He was appointed bishop of Duluth, Minnesota, in 1918, was translated to Indianapolis in 1925 but never took possession of that see, and became archbishop of Cincinnati in 1925. He founded the Athenaeum of Ohio in 1928, was with the National Catholic Welfare Conference in 1929–35, and episcopal chairman of the National Legion of Decency in 1933–43. He died on Apr. 22.

MC NICHOLS, JOHN PATRICK (1875–1932), educator. Born in St. Louis, Missouri, on Feb. 24, he studied at the university there and at St. Stanislaus seminary in Missouri, became a Jesuit in 1891, and was ordained in 1906. He taught at Xavier (Cincinnati) and Champion (Prairie du Chien, Wisconsin) until 1915, was dean at Marquette in 1919–21, wrote textbooks in rhetoric, and was president of the University of Detroit from 1921 until his death at Ann Arbor, Michigan, on Apr. 26.

MC QUAID, BERNARD JOHN (1823–1909), bishop. Born in New York City on Dec. 15, he was raised by the Sisters of Charity when his father was murdered, studied at Chambly College, Quebec, and St. John's seminary, Fordham, and was ordained in 1848. He engaged in pastoral work, was appointed rector of St. Patrick's cathedral in Newark in 1853, and in 1866 vicar general of that diocese. He helped found Seton Hall College in 1857 and served as its president for ten years, and also as a chaplain in the Civil War. In 1868 he was appointed first bishop of Rochester, New York, opposed the definition of papal infallibility at the Vatican Council in 1870, and established a preparatory and major seminary and a school system (he was strongly in favor of Catholic-school education for Catholic children and repeatedly clashed with Archbishop Ireland and other bishops on this point). He died in Rochester on Jan. 18.

MC SHANE, DANIEL L. (1888–1927), missioner. Born in Columbus, Indiana, on Sept. 13, he studied at St. Joseph's, at St. Mary's seminary, Baltimore, and at Maryknoll, where in 1914 he was the first priest to be ordained in that order. He was sent to China in 1919, worked in the Kwangtung province, and died there at Loting of smallpox on June 4.

MC SHERRY, JAMES (1819–1869), jurist. Born in Liberty Town, Maryland, on July 29, he graduated from Mt. St. Mary's College, Emmitsburg, in 1838, was admitted to the bar in 1840, and practiced in Frederick until his death there on July 13. He wrote two novels and a *History of Maryland*.

MC SHERRY, JAMES (1842–1907), jurist. Son of James McSherry, he was born in Frederick, Maryland, studied at Mt. St. Mary's College, Emmitsburg, and was arrested and imprisoned for his Southern sympathies in 1861. He was admitted to the bar in 1864, was appointed chief justice of a circuit court in 1887, and chief justice of the court of appeals of Maryland in 1896, a position he occupied until his death in Frederick on Oct. 23.

MC SHERRY, RICHARD (1817–1885), physician. Born in Martinsburg, West Virginia, he studied at Georgetown and Maryland, and received his medical degree from the University of Pennsylvania in 1841 after serving in the army medical corps from 1838 to 1840. He was an assistant surgeon in the U. S. Navy from 1843 to 1856, when he began practicing in Baltimore. He was the first president of the Baltimore Academy of Medicine. He died in Baltimore on Oct. 7.

MEADE, JOHN. *See* Almeida, John.

MEAGHER, THOMAS FRANCIS (1823–1867), general. Born in Waterford, Ireland, on Aug. 3, he studied at Clongowes and Stonyhurst, became noted for his oratory, and became a follower of O'Connell, whose leadership he left in 1848. The same year he went to France, became involved in the rebellion there, was arrested, and sentenced to be hanged. When the sentence was commuted to life he was sent to the penal colony in Tasmania in 1849, escaped to New York in 1852, was admitted to the bar in 1855, and the next year founded the *Irish News*. He went to Central America on an exploring trip in 1857, joined the Union forces when the Civil War broke out, and was brigadier general of the Irish Brigade he organized. He was appointed territorial secretary of Montana in 1865 and was drowned at Fort Benton, Missouri, when he fell from a steamer while on a trip through his territory.

MECHITAR. *See* Manuk, Peter.

MECHTEL, JOHANN (1562–1635?), historian. Born in Pfalzel, Germany, he studied there and at Trier, was ordained about 1587, became pastor at Eltz, canon in Limburg in 1592, dean in 1604, but resigned and became canon in Trier. He was the author of the *Limburg Chronicle*. He died in Trier, Germany, sometime after 1631.

MECHTILDIS, ST. (1125–1160). Born in Bavaria, daughter of Count Berthold of Andechs, she studied and later became a Benedictine at the convent of Diessen, which had been founded by her parents. There she became abbess, and in 1153 went to the convent in Edelstetten, which the bishop of Augsburg asked her to reform; she met considerable opposition until the malcontents were expelled. She had numerous supernatural gifts. F. D. May 31.

MECHTILDIS, ST. (1241?–1298). Born in Helfta, Saxony, she was placed at seven, at her own request, in the Rodardsdorf convent, of which her sister, Gertrude von Hackeborn, later became abbess. She became a Benedictine nun at Helfta in 1258, served as mistress of novices, and had many mystical experiences, which were recorded by St. Gertrude the Great in *Liber specialis gratiae*. She died in Helfta. F. D. Nov. 19.

MECHTILDIS OF MAGDEBURG (1210?–1282), mystic. Born in Saxony of a noble family, she claimed to have visions at the age of twelve, became a Beguine at Magdeburg in 1230, living under Dominican direction and writing an account of her experience at the direction of her confessor. In 1270 she became a Cistercian nun at Helfta near Eisleben. Five volumes of her inspirations were written between 1250 and 1264, and a sixth was completed at Helfta; her style is colorful, poetic, and aphoristic. She died at Helfta, Saxony, on Oct. 8, and has been termed a saint by some writers.

MEDA, BL. FELICIA (1378–1444). Born in Milan, Italy, she became a Poor Clare at St. Ursula's convent there in 1400 and was elected abbess in 1425. In 1439 she was sent to Pesaro to found and serve as abbess of a Poor Clare convent. She died on Sept. 30. Her cult was approved in 1812. F. D. July 24.

MEDAILLE, JEAN PAUL (1618–1689), missioner. Born in Carcassonne, Aude, France, on Jan. 29, he joined the Jesuits in 1640, became noted as a teacher of rhetoric and philosophy, and for his eighteen successful years of missionary work in Velay, Auvergne, Languedoc, and Aveyron. In 1650 he founded the Congregation of the Sisters of St. Joseph at Le Puy for the Christian education of children. He died in Auch, France, on May 15.

MEDARD, ST. (470?–560?), bishop. Born in Salency, Picardy, he was ordained at thirty-three, attained fame as a preacher and missioner, and became bishop of Vermandois in 530. Other biographical details are legendary. F. D. June 8.

MEDERICUS, ST. (d. 700?). Born in Autun, France, he entered St. Martin's monastery at thirteen and later was its abbot. He was a recluse in his last years. He is also called Merry. F. D. Aug. 29.

MEDICES, HIERONYMUS (1569–1622), scholar. Born in Camerino, Umbria, Italy, he joined the Dominicans in Ancona, became a professor of philosophy at Bologna, general censor for the Inquisition in Mantua, received his doctorate in 1611, and in 1618 was stationed in Mantua, Italy, and probably died there. He arranged the *Summa Theologiae* in syllogistic form: *Summae theologiae S. Thomae Aquinatis doctoris angelici formalis explicatio* (1614–23).

MEDICI, COSIMO DE' (1389–1464), statesman. Surnamed "the Elder," son of Giovanni di Bicci de' Medici (1360–1429), who laid the foundation of the Medici wealth through his banking and commercial interests, he was born in Florence, Italy, on Sept. 27, succeeded his father as head of the family, and joined the Florentine republic against the Albizzi and Pazzi oligarchies. Exiled for a short time in 1433, the Medici returned more popular than ever, drove the Albizzi from the city, and when Cosimo secured control of the supreme council, he became actual ruler of Florence. In foreign affairs, he allied the family and Florence with the Sforza in Milan against the Rome-Venice alliance and maintained a policy of friendliness with Naples to secure Florence from attack; at home, he was a liberal patron of the arts and learning, built magnificent public buildings, founded an academy at Florence with Marsilio Ficino at its head, which introduced Greek learning to the West, acquired a large collection of manuscripts, which he donated to the Laurentian Library, and patronized Brunelleschi, Donatello, Ghiberti, and Luca della Robbia, among others. He died in Florence on Aug. 1 and was posthumously named *Pater Patriae* by the council for his services to the republic.

MEDICI, COSIMO I DE' (1519–1574). Surnamed "the Great," son of Giovanni de' Medici delle Bande Nere and Lorenzo the Magnificent's granddaughter, Maria Salviati, he was born on June 12, was recognized by the council as ruler of Florence when Alessandro de' Medici was murdered in 1537, ruthlessly suppressed all opposition, and proclaimed himself sole ruler and duke of Florence. He completely reorganized the administration and legal code, organized an army and navy, and married Eleonora da Toledo, a Spaniard, to cement his relations with Spain. He con-

quered Siena in 1555, received it as a fief from Spain in 1557, evidently embraced a life of vice when his wife died in 1562, and then married his mistress Camilla Martelli. He was crowned grand duke of Tuscany by Pope Pius V in 1570 in Rome. Cosimo was a liberal patron of the arts, a competent ruler, but cruel and ruthless to his enemies. He died in Castello, Italy, on Apr. 21.

MEDICI, LORENZO DE' (1449–1492). Son of Piero de' Medici (Il Gottoso) and grandson of Cosimo the Elder, he was born in Florence on Jan. 1, and on his father's death in 1469 became joint ruler with his brother Giuliano (b. 1453). In 1478 conspirators headed by the Pazzi and the Riario, the family of Pope Sixtus IV, assassinated Giuliano and wounded Lorenzo, who was attending mass in the cathedral. When the archbishop of Pisa, who was involved in the plot, was murdered by a vengeance-seeking mob, Lorenzo was excommunicated by the pope and war between Florence and Rome broke out. It lasted until 1484, when Sixtus' death and the election of Pope Innocent VIII, a friend of Lorenzo, ended the war and the excommunication. In the next few years under his rule Florence reached the peak of its Renaissance glory. He ruled justly and prudently, expended vast sums to encourage art and learning, founded the University of Pisa and the Greek academy at Florence, collected priceless Greek and Latin manuscripts, and spent large sums on public buildings. Although his life was frequently one of immorality, he was so characteristic of all that was finest in the Renaissance that he is surnamed "the Magnificent." The last years of his regime were disturbed by the rise of Savonarola, who gave him the last rites on his deathbed in Florence on Apr. 8. His poetry is notable for its reverence for learning and appreciation of the classics; outstanding are *La nencia da barberino, Caccia col Falcone, Ambra*, and his robust but coarse carnival songs. Among his children was Giovanni, who later became Pope Clement VII.

MEDICI, BL. ROLAND DE' (d. 1386). He lived as a shelterless recluse in the forests of Parma, Italy, for twenty-six years and died at Borgone. His cult was confirmed in 1852. F. D. Sept. 15.

MEDINA, BARTHOLOMEW (1527–1581), theologian. Born in Medina, Spain, he studied at Salamanca under Francisco Vittoria and became principal professor of theology at Salamanca and spent his entire life teaching there. He is said to have introduced and formulated the system of probabilism; he also wrote commentaries on St. Thomas Aquinas.

MEDINA, JUAN DE (1490–1547), theologian. Born in Medina de Pomar, Burgos, Spain, he entered St. Ildefonsus College, Alcalá, received his doctorate in philosophy and theology, and became canon and master of theology there. He became primary professor about 1526, a position he occupied the rest of his life. He wrote many theological treatises.

MEDINA, MIGUEL DE (1489–1578), theologian. Born in Belalcázar, Spain, he joined the Franciscans, studied at Alcalá, received his doctorate from Toledo, and was appointed to the chair of scripture at Alcalá in 1550. He was Philip II's representative at the Council of Trent in 1560, was appointed superior of St. John's of the Kings, Toledo, defended the *Commentaries* of John Ferus, and as a result was condemned by the Toledo Inquisition in 1573. His five years in prison resulted in illness that caused his release early in 1578; he died in Toledo, Spain, on May 1. He was completely exonerated by the supreme tribunal of the Inquisition shortly after. He wrote several theological treatises.

MEDINA SIDONIA, ALONZO PÉREZ DE GUZMÁN DE (1550–1615). Born on Sept. 10 in Spain, he succeeded his father as seventh duke of Medina Sidonia in 1555, and when his grandfather died in 1558 inherited one of the largest fortunes in Europe and became governor of Milan and captain general of Andalusia. In 1588 he was appointed commander in chief of the Spanish Armada, suffered disastrous defeat at the hands of the English, returning to Spain with but a third of his fleet, and was openly ridiculed. Despite this, his loss of Cadiz to the English in 1596, and the destruction of a squadron he commanded by the Dutch near Gibraltar in 1606, he retained royal favor until his death.

MEDOLLA, ANDREA (1522–1582), painter. Born in Sibenik (now Sebenico), Dalmatia, Andrea Schiavone studied in Venice under his godfather, Rocco Medulić, became acquainted with Pietro Aretino, Tintoretto, and Titian, in whose studio he worked and who praised his work highly, and painted for the great families of Italy. Among his masterpieces are *Jesus at Emmaeus with Luke and Cleophas, Pilate Washing His Hands, The Last Supper, Madonna and Child with SS. Francis and Jerome,* and *Jesus Bound between a Malefactor and Two Soldiers.* He completed a *Pietà, Holy Family, Adoration of the Shepherds,* and was one of the first to produce simple landscapes. He also was a noted engraver, the first to produce pictures on copper with nitric acid and probably the first to engrave with a dry needle. Among his noted engravings are *Curing of the Lame Man, Moses Saved by Pharao's Daughter,* and *Abduction of the Trojan Helen.* He died poverty-sticken in Venice, Italy. He is also known as Andrea Meldolla and Andreas Me-

dulić, the name Medolla (faulty) was acquired in his youth when he was so nicknamed for deficiencies in his drawing technique.

MEDRANO, FRANCISCO DE (1570–1607), poet. Born in Seville, Spain, he visited Rome, wrote neoclassic poetry, and is noted for his imitations of Horace, comparable to those of Fray Luis de León.

MEDULIC, ANDREAS. *See* Medolla, Andrea.

MEDWALL, HENRY (15th century), dramatist. Born in England, he was ordained, became chaplain to Cardinal Morton, and wrote two plays between 1490 and 1501. *Nature* is a typical morality play, with touches of realistic humor; *Fulgens and Lucres* (probably 1497) is the first English play to use characters from everyday life, not as types, but as representatives of the contemporary world; the plot is based on Bonaccorso's *De vera nobilitate*; the performance may have been at Morton's Lambeth palace in the capital.

MEEHAN, CHARLES PATRICK (1812–1890), author. Born in Dublin on July 12, he studied at the Irish College, Rome, was ordained in 1834, and returned to Ireland as parish priest in Rathdrum until his transfer to SS. Michael and John church in Dublin, where he stayed until his death on Mar. 14. He wrote historical works and biographies, translated Italian authors, and edited anthologies.

MEEHAN, THOMAS FRANCIS (1854–1942), historian. Born in Brooklyn, New York, on Sept. 19, he studied at St. Francis Xavier, was managing editor of the *Irish American* in 1874–1904, on the staff of the New York *Herald* in 1894–96, and New York correspondent for newspapers in Baltimore, Philadelphia, and Richmond. He was associated with the periodical *America* from its founding in 1909, contributed to *Catholic Builders of the United States,* was assistant managing editor of the Catholic Encyclopedia in 1906–8, and was president of the American Catholic Historical Society, supervising many of its publications and proceedings until his death in New York City on July 7.

MÉEN. *See* Magenulf, St.

MEERSCHAERT, THEOPHILE (1847–1924), bishop. Born in Russignies, Belgium, on Aug. 24, he studied at Renaix, Audenarde, and the American College in Louvain, and was ordained in Mechlin in 1871. He went to the United States in 1872, worked as a missionary in Mississippi, became rector of St. Mary's cathedral in Natchez in 1880, and vicar general of that see, and served as administrator in 1888. He was appointed titular bishop of Sidyma and first vicar apostolic of Oklahoma and Indian Territory in 1891, engaged in missionary activities to the Indians and white settlers in his area, and in 1905 was appointed first bishop of Oklahoma City. He was made an assistant at the pontifical throne in 1916, and died in Oklahoma City, Oklahoma, on Feb. 21.

MÈGE, ANTOINE JOSEPH (1625–1691). Born in Clermont, France, he joined the Benedictines in 1643, went to St. Denis abbey in 1659 to teach theology, and was appointed prior of Bethel monastery in 1681. He spent his last years at St. Germain-des-Prés, Paris, where he died on Apr. 15. He wrote a commentary on the Rule of St. Benedict, several ascetical treatises, and translated St. Ambrose's *On Virginity*.

MEGERLIN, JOHN ULRICH (1644–1709), apologist. Born in Messkirch, Baden, the eighth of nine children of a tavernkeeper, he studied at Ingolstadt and Salzburg, became a discalced Augustinian, taking the name Abraham, in 1662, and was ordained at Vienna in 1666. He became Leopold I's court preacher in 1677, prior in Vienna, Graz, and Rome, and later provincial. He published sermons, a commentary on Judas, and many collections of popular spiritual reflections. Some of his satire (*A Hundred Excellent Fools*, 1709) was influenced by Sebastian Brant; he himself influenced Jean Paul Richter and the poet Schiller. He is best known as Abraham a Sancta Clara.

MEGINHARD, BL. (d. 1059). A Benedictine monk in Hersfeld, Germany, he was abbot there in 1035, rebuilt it after a disastrous fire in 1037, and was known as a biblical scholar. F. D. Sept. 26.

MEIGNAN, GUILLAUME RENÉ (1817–1896), cardinal. Born in Chauvigné, France, on Apr. 12, he studied at Le Mans seminary and the Collège de Tessé, was ordained in 1840, continued his studies at Paris and Munich, and took up the study of scripture in Berlin. He received his doctorate in theology from the Sapienza in 1846, taught in Paris schools, was appointed professor of scripture at the Sorbonne in 1861, vicar general of Paris in 1863, and bishop of Châlons-sur-Marne in 1864. He was a leading opponent of Ernest Renan and an outstanding apologist. He was transferred to Arras in 1882, was appointed archbishop of Tours in 1884, and in 1892 was created a cardinal. He died in Tours, France, on Jan. 20.

MEILLEUR, JEAN BAPTISTE (1796–1878), educator. Born in St. Laurent, Quebec, Canada, on May 9, he studied at the Montreal Sulpician college, Middlebury, and medicine at Castletown, Vermont. He helped found Assumption College in Quebec, edited *L'Echo du pays* in 1834, when he was elected to the Canadian parliament, and was first superintendent of education for Lower Canada from 1842 to 1855. He became postmaster of Montreal in 1862. He wrote widely for periodicals, several textbooks, and a history of Canadian education, *Mémorial de l'éducation*. He died on Dec. 7.

MEINGE. *See* Memmius, St.

MEINGOLD (d. 892?). The name is possibly a combination of Meingaud, count of Wormsfeld, who was assassinated in 892 after years of feuds, and of Meingold, a holy hermit in the Huy area. Details of their lives may have become confused in a pious history of one called saint and venerated locally on Feb. 8.

MEINGOS, BL. (d. 1200?). He directed the Benedictine abbey of Weingarten, Swabia, during his last twelve years. F. D. Apr. 2.

MEINHARD, BL. (d. 1196), bishop. Sent to the Latvian mission, this Augustinian canon regular was consecrated in 1184 to direct the see of Yxkill, which later was transferred to Riga, Latvia. F. D. Apr. 12.

MEINRAD, ST. (d. 861). A priest at the Benedictine abbey at Reichenau, he taught near Zurich, then obtained permission in 829 to live as a solitary. For twenty-five years he lived in his hermitage near Einsiedeln, Switzerland, until two bandits, believing that he had a hidden material treasure, broke in on him and clubbed him to death. F. D. Jan. 21.

MEINULF. *See* Magenulf, St.

MEINWERK (d. 1036), bishop. Born in Saxony, he studied for the priesthood at Halberstadt and Hildesheim and was consecrated bishop of Paderborn by St. Willigis in 1009. He rebuilt the cathedral in Paderborn, made its school widely known, founded religious houses there and in Abdinghof, and served as adviser to Emperors Henry II and Conrad II. Although his cult was never confirmed, he long was honored on June 5.

MEISSONIER, JEAN LOUIS ERNEST (1815–1891), painter. Born in Lyons, France, on Feb. 21, he studied under Léon Cogniet in Paris and attracted attention with his book illustrations and etchings. He established a new school of genre painting with his minute and detailed paintings. In 1859 he began a series of gigantic historical canvases, particularly battle scenes, depicting great events of the First Empire which made him the most popular artist of his times. In later years he turned to Venetian scenes and architectural views. Among his best-known miniatures are *The Painter in His Studio*, *The Readers*, *The Smokers*, *The Bowling Party*, and *The Quarrel*; of his epic canvases, *1814*, *Desaix to the Army of the Rhine*, *1805*, *1807* (on which he worked fourteen years), and *Napoleon I with His Staff*. He died in Paris on Jan. 31.

MEL, ST. (d. 488?). He is said to have been

the son of St. Patrick's sister Darerca, and the brother of SS. Melchu, Muinis, and Rioch, all of whom became bishops while missioners in Ireland, near Ardagh. F. D. Feb. 6.

MELAINE, ST. (d. 530?), bishop. Born in Placet, Brittany, he was a monk when called to succeed St. Amand in the see of Rennes. He wiped out idolatry in his diocese, helped draw up the canons of the Council of Orléans in 511, and was highly revered by King Clovis. Also called Melanius, he died in Placet. F. D. Jan. 6.

MELAN, ST. (d. 550?). He was bishop of Viviers in Gaul from 519 until his death, some time after 549. F. D. June 15.

MELANIA THE ELDER, ST. (d. 400?). She was one of the first matrons of the patrician class to visit the Holy Land. F. D. June 8.

MELANIA THE YOUNGER, ST. (383?-439). Daughter of a Roman senator, and granddaughter of St. Melania the Elder, she married Pinian, son of prefect Valerius Severus, in 397, had two children who died, and thereafter directed a center of religious life at their villa. She devoted her great wealth to the poor and needy, and established churches and monasteries through the empire. About 410, at the invasion of the Goths, she and her husband fled to Tagaste, Numidia, where they founded two monasteries. In 417 they moved to Jerusalem, met St. Jerome and his group in Bethlehem, and again followed a prayerful life in separate monasteries. F. D. Dec. 31.

MELANIUS. *See* Melaine, St.; also, Mellonius, St.

MELANTIUS, ST. (d. 385?). Bishop of Rhinocolura, he was imprisoned and then banished from his see near the border of Egypt and Palestine for his opposition to Arianism. F. D. Jan. 16.

MELASIPPUS, ST. (d. 360), martyr. He and his wife Carina were tortured to death and their child Antoninus beheaded during the persecution of Julian the Apostate. F. D. Nov. 7.

MELCHER, JOSEPH (1806-1873), bishop. Born in Vienna, on Mar. 19, he studied at the Modena, Italy, seminary, was ordained there in 1830, was a chaplain at the ducal court in 1831, then went to the United States, where he did pastoral work in Little Rock and St. Louis. In 1855 he was appointed bishop of the new see of Quincy, Illinois, but declined the appointment, and in 1868 was appointed first bishop of Green Bay, Wisconsin. He reigned until his death there on Dec. 20.

MELCHERS, PAUL (1813-1895), cardinal. Born on Jan. 6 in Münster, Westphalia, he studied law at Bonn, practiced for several years in Münster, and then studied theology at Mu-

nich. He was ordained in 1841, served as parish priest in Haltren, was appointed rector of the diocesan seminary in 1851, vicar general in 1854, bishop of Osnabrück in 1857, and archbishop of Cologne in 1866. He opposed the definition of the dogma of papal infallibility at the Vatican Council in 1870, but energetically supported it when it was proclaimed. He opposed the Kulturkampf, was imprisoned for six months in 1873 for excommunicating two priests who had joined the Old Catholics, and was forced to flee from Germany in 1875. He sought refuge in Maastricht, Holland, and ruled his diocese from there until 1885, when he resigned his see and was created cardinal. He joined the Jesuits in 1892. He died in Rome on Dec. 14.

MELCHIADES, pope. *See* Miltiades, St.

MELCHIOR (1st century). *See* Balthasar.

MELÉNDEZ VALDÉS, JUAN (1754-1817), poet. Born in Ribera del Fresno, near Badajoz, Spain, on Mar. 11, he studied law at Salamanca, won the Spanish Academy prize in 1780 for his *Batilo*, and in 1781 was appointed to a chair of humanities at Salamanca. In 1784 he won a prize offered for a comedy by the city of Madrid with *Las bodas de Camacho el rico*. He published a collection of lyrical and pastoral poems in 1785, was appointed a judge in Saragossa in 1789, judicial chancellor in Valladolid in 1791, and fiscal of the supreme court in Madrid in 1797. When his friend the minister Jovellanos was defeated, he was forced to leave Madrid and eventually settled in Salamanca. He became attached to the French party in Spain, was appointed councilor of state by Joseph Bonaparte in 1808 and then minister of education, was forced to flee when the French were forced out of Spain in 1813, spent the next four years in exile in France, and died in Montpellier on May 24. He also wrote *La caida de Luzbel*, an epic on creation; romances (*La mañana de San Juan*); philosophical odes (*La presencia de Dios*, *La gloria de las artes*); pastoral poems; and a translation of the *Aeneid*. He was heavily influenced by Luis de León and Herrera and by the English Alexander Pope, Thomson, and Young.

MELETIUS, ST. (2nd century), martyr. *See* Susanna, St.

MELETIUS, ST. (d. 295?). As bishop of Pontus, Galatia-Cappadocia, he suffered during the persecution of Diocletian and was praised by the historian Eusebius. F. D. Dec. 4.

MELETIUS OF ANTIOCH, ST. (d. 381), bishop. Born in Melitene, Armenia, he became bishop of Sebaste in 358 or 359, but was driven into the desert, went to Beroea, Syria, of which he may have been bishop, then was elected bishop of Antioch as a compromise candidate in the conflict between Arians and Christians.

When he condemned the former he was banished by Emperor Constans; the result was a schism, with the Catholics of Antioch calling themselves Meletians or Eustathians in honor of the bishop to whom they gave allegiance. On the death of Constans, Meletius was recalled by Julian and returned to his strife-torn see, only to find that the opposing faction, led by Lucifer Cagliari, had consecrated Paulinus as bishop. The Council of Alexandria failed to resolve the dispute. Thereafter, Meletius was in power or exiled, welcomed or banished by emperors, in and out of favor with increasingly disparate groups. In 374, Pope Damasus recognized Paulinus as bishop, appointed him papal legate in the East; Jerome allowed himself to be consecrated presbyter by Paulinus. Cratian recalled all the exiled bishops and restored Meletius. The latter died at Constantinople while presiding over the second Ecumenical Council. SS. Gregory of Nyssa and John Chrysostom preached eulogies. F. D. Feb. 12.

MELEUSIPPUS. *See* Eleusippus.

MELI, GIOVANNI (1740–1815), poet. Born in Palermo, Sicily, on Mar. 4, he studied medicine, became a doctor, and in 1787 was appointed to the chair of chemistry at Palermo, a position he held for nineteen years. He became noted for his eclogues, odes, and sonnets in the Sicilian dialect. He died on Dec. 20.

MELITINA, ST. (2nd century), martyr A young girl, she was put to death at Marcianopolis, Thrace, during the reign of Antoninus Pius. F. D. Sept. 15.

MELITO, ST. (d. 180?), bishop. Author of an apology for Christianity addressed to Marcus Aurelius, he was bishop of Sardis, in Lydia, and wrote works praised by Eusebius and St. Jerome. He is sometimes confused with a similarly named martyr, hero of a Sardinian story. F. D. Apr. 1.

MELITO, ST. (d. 320), martyr. Youngest of the forty soldier-martyrs of Sebaste, Phrygia, he was put to death during the persecution of Licinius. The group had been exposed for three days and nights in a freezing lake; the survivors, including Melito, had their legs and arms broken and were then thrown into a furnace. F. D. Mar. 10.

MELLA, ST. (d. 780?). Mother of SS. Cannech and Tigernach, she became a nun after her husband's death, and was abbess of Doire-Melle in Leitrim, Ireland. F. D. Apr. 25.

MELLINI, BL. LUKE (d. 1460?). An Italian monk, he was appointed general of his order, the Celestines, by Pope Nicholas V. F. D. Aug. 24.

MELLITUS, ST. (d. 624), archbishop. Sent from Rome in 601 by Pope St. Gregory the Great to aid St. Augustine in England, he preached three years in Kent, became the first bishop of London, converted Sigebert, king of the East Saxons, and many others, was banished to France at his death, then recalled and made archbishop of Canterbury in 619. F. D. Apr. 24.

MELLONIUS, ST. (d. 314), bishop. Probably the first bishop of Rouen, France, legend had him a Welshman converted near Cardiff and sent by Pope St. Stephen I to preach to the Gauls. He is also called Mallonus and Melanius. F. D. Oct. 22.

MELORUS, ST. (6th century). When his father, Duke Melanius of Cornwall, England, was murdered, the seven-year-old boy was mutilated and sent to a monastery. The boy's exceptional spirituality disturbed his uncle, the murderer, who had Melorus assassinated at fourteen. F. D. Oct. 1.

MELOZZO DA FORLÌ (1438?–1494), painter. Born in Forlì, Italy, he came under the influence of Piero della Francesca, worked for Federigo da Montefeltro at the court of Urbino, was recommended by him to Pope Sixtus IV, became the pope's official painter, and with him opened the Academy of St. Luke. In 1477 he began the fresco in the Pinacoteca of the Vatican of *Platina Receiving the Keys of the Vatican from the Pope.* He was a pioneer in the use of foreshortening, particularly for vaultings. He died in Forlì.

MELZI, FRANCISCO (1490?–1568). Born in Milan, Italy, he became a friend of Leonardo da Vinci and inherited his manuscripts, books, and drawings, which he preserved. He is believed by some to have been a painter of note, but probably never progressed beyond the status of a gifted miniaturist.

MEMBRE, ZENOBIUS (1645–1687), missioner. Born in Bapaume, Pas de-Calais, France, he joined the Franciscans, was sent on the Canadian mission in 1675, and worked among the Illinois Indians. He accompanied La Salle on his descent of the Mississippi to the Gulf of Mexico in 1681, then returned to Europe, where he became superior of the monastery in Bapaume. In 1684 he accompanied La Salle on a colonizing expedition to Louisiana and, when the ship was blown off course, landed on the coast of Texas at Matagorda Bay, probably the first colonizing expedition in Texas, where they built a fort. He was killed there in an Indian massacre.

MEMLING, HANS (1430?–1494?), painter. Born in Mainz, Germany, of Dutch parents, he was a prosperous burgher in Bruges by 1480 and noted for his paintings. He was probably a pupil of Van der Weyden and became a leader of the early Netherlands school. He died in Bruges, Flanders, on Aug. 11. Among his outstanding works are a triptych with *The Marriage of St. Catherine* as the central panel and *The Martyrdom of St. John the Baptist* and *The Vision at Patmos* on the wings; portraits of the Moreel family, a diptych with the Virgin and Child, a diptych of Martin van Niuwenhove, the shrine of St. Ursula, all in St. John's hospital in Bruges; the triptych, *Adoration of the Magi* for Jean Floreins, *Christ Enthroned, Madonna and Child with Angels,* and an altarpiece of the *Passion* in the Lübeck cathedral.

MEMMI, SIMONE. *See* Martini, Simone.

MEMMIUS, ST. (d. 300?). He preached in Gaul during the latter half of the third century and was first bishop of Châlons-sur-Marne, France. Early legend had him sent there by St. Peter. He is also called Meinge and Menge. F. D. Aug. 5.

MEMNON, ST. (d. 300?), martyr. *See* Severus, St.

MEMORIAN. *See* Numerian, St.

MEMORIUS, ST. (d. 451), martyr. A deacon at Troyes, France, also known as Mesmin, he was sent with four companions by St. Lupus to beg Attila to spare the area; all were beheaded. The story is untrustworthy. F. D. Sept. 7.

MENA, JUAN DE (1411–1456), poet. Born in Cordova, Spain, he studied there and at Salamanca and Rome, became a member of the court of Juan II of Castile, and served as his Latin secretary and as royal historiographer. He wrote poems in the classical manner, notably *El labirinto de fortuna* (1444) and *La coronación,* and was influenced by Lucan, Vergil, and Dante. He was the first to translate the *Iliad* into Spanish. He died in Torrelaguna, Spain.

MENA, PEDRO DE (d. 1693), sculptor. Born in Adra, Spain, he studied there with his father and in Granada under Alonzo Cano. He completed statues of saints for the convent of El Angel, Granada, and in 1658–62 completed forty relief figures of saints for the cathedral in Málaga. He also did a *Madonna and Child with St. Joseph,* and a *Crucifixion* for Madrid churches, an equestrian statue of St. James for the Toledo cathedral, and several nudes.

MENAGE, GILLES DE (1613–1692), lexicographer. Born in Angers, France, he became a lawyer, then was ordained, and was stationed at Notre Dame, Paris. He wrote Latin poetry and *Dictonnaire étymologique, ou origines de la langue française* (1650–94) and *Origini della lingua italiana* (1669), valuable philological studies. His conversation and witticisms were published posthumously as *Menagiana.* He is believed by some to be the original of Vadius in Molière's *Femmes savantes.* He died in Paris on July 23.

MÉNARD, LÉON (1706–1767), author. Born in Tarrascon, France, he studied at Lyons and law at Toulouse, and was appointed counselor of the superior court in Nîmes. In 1744 he went to Paris, became a member of the Academy of Inscriptions, and devoted himself to writing the history of Nîmes, *Les amours de Callisthène et de Chariclée,* and *Moeurs et usages des Grecs.* He died in Paris on Oct. 1.

MÉNARD, NICOLAS HUGUES (1585–1644). Born in Paris, son of Catherine de' Medici's secretary, he joined the Benedictines in 1607, was professed in 1612, and in 1613 joined the St. Vannes' reform movement in Verdun which was to develop into the Congregation of St. Maur. He became a noted preacher in Paris, wrote several biographies, taught for sixteen years at Cluny, and was superior of St. Germain-des-Prés seminary, Paris, during his last years. He died on Jan. 21.

MÉNARD, RENÉ (1604–1661?), missioner. Born in Paris, he became a Jesuit and was sent on the Canadian mission in 1640. He worked among the Hurons and Iroquois, and in 1659 set out for the Far West, probably established a post at Keweenaw, in Wisconsin, and then left for Dakota country and was never heard from again.

MENDAÑA DE NEYRA, ALVARO DE (1541–1595), explorer. Born in Saragossa, Spain, he went to Lima, Peru, in 1558, where his uncle, Viceroy García de Castro, provided him with two ships in 1567 for a voyage of exploration in the Pacific. He discovered the Solomon Islands and returned in 1568. In 1595 he discovered and named the Marquesas, established a colony at Bahia Graciosa, but died at Santa Cruz, Solomon Islands, on Oct. 18. His wife completed the voyage and reached Manila in Feb. 1597.

MENDEL, GREGOR JOHANN (1822–1884). Born in Heinzendorf, Austrian Silesia, on July 22, he studied at Olmütz, joined the Augustinians in 1843, was ordained in 1847, and taught until 1851, when he went to the University of Vienna. In 1853 he returned to St. Thomas' abbey in Brünn, where he taught until 1868, when he was appointed abbot. In this position he became engaged in a dispute with the government which imposed a tax on the abbey which continued until his death. From his days as a novice he conducted an intensive series of experiments with peas and kept painstaking records over many years of the characteristics of many generations of the plants he bred. The results are known as Mendel's Law. Briefly stated it is that each characteristic is transmitted from parent to offspring, independent of any other characteristic; each parent contributes one predisposing factor for each characteristic; and where each pair of factors differ, one usually appears as a dominant characteristic and the other a recessive characteristic. In the offspring of pure-bred parents, the dominant characteristic will predominate. In the offspring of these hybrids (the third generation), one fourth will exhibit the recessive characteristic; one fourth, the dominant characteristic; and the other half, although hybrid, will also reveal the dominant characteristic (this is the Mendelian ratio). He published his findings in the journal of the Natural History Society of Brünn in two articles in 1865 and 1869, but their importance was not recognized until the turn of the century, when they were discovered almost simultaneously and publicized by a group of botanists, de Vries in Holland, Correns in Germany, and Tschermak in Austria. His experiments in heredity were the beginnings of the modern science of genetics. He died in Brünn, Austria, on Jan. 6.

MENDES DE SILVA, JOÃO (1420–1482). Born in Portugal, he spent ten years at a Hieronymite monastery in Spain, and joined the Franciscans in Italy when his sanctity and the miracles attributed to him attracted great attention. In 1469 he founded Notre Dame de la Paix convent in Milan, which became the center of a Franciscan reform that spread over Italy and whose members were called Amadeans or Amadists after his death. He died in Milan, is often called Blessed, and is known as Amadeus of Portugal.

MENDÍBURU, MANUEL DE (1805–1885), diplomat. Born in Lima, Peru, on Oct. 29, he studied at San Marcos del Rimac University, was appointed the consulate's amanuensis in 1819, served in the army in the Peruvian revolt, and was captured by the Spaniards. After his release he was sent on diplomatic missions to Brazil and Spain, and rose to the rank of brigadier general. He served as prefect of several departments, and was appointed director of the School of Arts and Trade in Lima in 1870. He served as secretary of the ministry of foreign affairs, war, and agriculture, in the chamber of deputies, as general in chief of the army, and vice-president of the constituent assembly. He spent several years as Peruvian ambassador to England, Bolivia, and Peru, wrote *Diccionario histórico-biográfico del Perú* (1874–85), and reorganized the library and national archives in Lima. He died on Jan. 21.

MENDIETA, JERÓNIMO (1525–1604), missionary. Born in Vitoria, Spain, he joined the Franciscans in Bilbao and in 1554 was sent to New Spain, where he soon achieved such a reputation that a provincial chapter voted to allow him to appoint the provincial officers. In 1569 he returned to Europe for a general chapter meeting, made suggestions regarding the government and administration of New Spain to Juan de Ovando, visitor of the Council of the Indies, went back to New Spain, despite some opposition, in 1573, served as guardian and superior of a succession of Franciscan

houses, and died in Mexico City on May 9. From 1571 to 1596 he wrote his monumental and fearless *Historia Eclesiastica Indiana* which was not printed until 1870.

MENDOZA, ANTONIO (1485?–1552), governor. Born in Granada, Spain, the count of Tendilla was a favorite at the court of Charles V and was appointed the first viceroy of New Spain, arriving in Mexico in 1535. He brought a printing press with him, printed *La escala de San Juan Climoca* in 1536, established a mint, built schools and hospitals, and founded a college. He introduced better agricultural and sheep-breeding methods, encouraged silk culture, and sent expeditions to Colorado and New Mexico. He bettered the conditions of the natives, although he was unable to stop their enslavement, as he had hoped to do. He became viceroy of Peru in 1550 and continued his just rule in that country.

MENDOZA, DIEGO HURTADE DE (1503?–1575), author. Born in Granada, Spain, he studied at Salamanca, was Charles V's ambassador to Venice in 1530, to England, and his representative at the Council of Trent in 1543. In 1547 he served as special ambassador to Rome and captain general of Siena, was exiled by Philip II to Granada from 1568 to 1571 because of his trouble with a noble of the court, and died in Madrid. He wrote distinguished poetry and prose, and his two outstanding works were *Lazarillo de Tormes* (though most authorities consider his authorship doubtful) and *Guerra de Granada*.

MENDOZA, FRANCISCO SARMIENTO DE (d. 1595), bishop. Born in Burgos, Spain, he studied at Salamanca, taught canon law there, served as auditor at Valladolid for six years and of the rota in Rome for twelve years, and was appointed bishop of Astorga in 1574. He was transferred to Jaen, Spain, in 1580, where he lived until his death. He wrote several treatises on canon law.

MENDOZA, JUAN GONZALEZ DE (1540?–1617), bishop. Born in Toledo, Spain, he served in the army, became a Benedictine, and was sent to China in 1580 by Philip II. There he gathered information on economics, politics, and national customs and later published his observations. He spent two years in Mexico, and after his return to Spain was made bishop of the Lipari Islands, then of Chiapas, and finally of Popayán, Colombia, where he died.

MENDOZA, PEDRO GONZALEZ DE (1428–1495), cardinal. Born in Guadalajara, Spain, on May 3, he became a member of the court of King Juan II of Castile in 1450, when he was also made canon of Toledo, was appointed bishop of Calahorra in 1453 and in 1467 of Siguenza, and was created cardinal in 1473. In that year he was appointed King

Henry IV of Castile's chancellor, and became Ferdinand's and Isabella's grand chancellor in 1474, a position he held until his death, and where he was in a position to support Columbus. He was appointed archbishop of Seville in 1474, administered the see of Osma in 1482–83, and in 1482 was appointed archbishop of Toledo and primate of Spain. He built Santa Cruz College in Valladolid for poor students, a hospital for foundlings in Toledo, and several churches. He died in Guadalajara on Jan. 11.

MÉNÉHOULD. *See* Manechildis, St.

MENELE, ST. (d. 720?). Born in Anjou, France, he became a Benedictine monk at Carméry, then restored and served as abbot of the monastery of Ménat, near Clermont, France. He is also called Mauvier. F. D. July 22.

MENENDEZ Y PELAYO, MARCELINO (1856–1912), critic. Born in Santander, Spain, on Nov. 3, he studied at Barcelona, was appointed to the chair of literature at Madrid at twenty-two, and three years later became a member of the Spanish Academy. He was a master of European languages and dominated scholarship in Spain at the end of the century. In 1898 he gave up his teaching post to become director of the Biblioteca Nacional and became director of the Academia de la Historia in 1910. He twice (1884, 1891) served as deputy in the Cortes. His critical work was extensive and influential: *Heterodoxes Españoles* (1880), on political and literary history since the Priscillian heresy; *Horacio en España* (1877); *Historia de las ideas esteticas* (1883–91), on aesthetic ideas in Europe as well as in Spain; *Ciencia española* (1887), on culture during and after the Inquisition. He also wrote poems, a study of the origins of the Spanish novel, and histories of mediaeval, mystical, and Latin-American poetry, and edited the plays of Calderón and of Lope de Vega, an anthology of Castilian poems, and a bibliography of Castilian writers. He died in Santander on May 19.

MENESES, ALEJO DE (1560–1617). An Augustinian, he was a missioner among the Nestorians of India, was made archbishop of Goa, and convened the Council of Diamper in 1599 to establish the Church along the Malabar coast. He was transferred to Braga, Portugal, as bishop, became president of the Council of Castile, and died in Madrid.

MENESES, OSORIO FRANCISCO (1630–1705), painter. Born in Seville, Spain, he was a pupil of Murillo, and became secretary and president of the Academy of Seville. Several of his works were so close to Murillo's style that they were considered for many years as originals from his master's brush. Of his own work, his *Prophet Elijah* and one on the *Order*

of St. Francis are outstanding. He probably died in Seville.

MENESTRIER, CLAUDE FRANÇOIS (1631–1705), antiquarian. Born in Lyons, France, on Mar. 9, he became a Jesuit and taught rhetoric there, and composed ballets and dramas for the visit of Louis XIV to the city in 1658 and for other such occasions. He also published widely on heraldry. From 1670 to 1695 he was stationed in Paris and preached in the surrounding area, composed Latin inscriptions for prints, and wrote on medals, portraits, tombs, and armor. He died in Paris on Jan. 21.

MENGARINI, GREGORIO (1811–1886), missioner. Born on July 21, in Rome, he joined the Jesuits in 1828, taught at Rome, Modena, and Reggio, studied at the Roman College, and was ordained in 1840 and sent to the United States. After a short stay at Georgetown, he was sent with Fr. DeSmet and others to Montana, where he ministered to the Flathead Indians until 1849. He went to Oregon for a year and then to California, where he helped establish Santa Clara mission (which was to grow into the present university) and spent the rest of his life as treasurer and vice-president. He died there on Sept. 23. He wrote a Salish, or Flathead, grammar and other linguistic studies.

MENGE. *See* Memmius, St.

MENGS, ANTHON RAFAEL (1728–1779), painter. Born in Aussig, Bohemia, on Mar. 12, he studied under his father, whom he accompanied to Rome in 1741, declined an appointment as painter of the elector of Saxony when sixteen, and returned to Rome, where he married and became a convert in 1748. His *Holy Family* attracted attention and he was appointed court painter at Dresden by King Augustus III of Poland and Saxony in 1749, returned to Rome in 1752, and worked for the duke of Northumberland among others. He became director of the Academy of Painting in 1754, painted a fresco on the dome of St. Eusebius in Rome, an altarpiece in Naples, and the fresco of *Apollo and the Muses* in Cardinal Albani's villa. In 1761 he went to Madrid as painter to King Charles III, returned to paint in the Vatican for Pope Clement XIV, and, after another period in Madrid, during which he did the *Apotheosis of Trajan* in the royal palace, returned to Rome, where he died on June 29.

MENIGNUS, ST. (d. 251), martyr. A dyer in Parium, Mysia, Asia Minor, he had his fingers chopped off when he tore down an edict against Christians, and was beheaded during the persecution of Decius. F. D. Mar. 15.

MENINGAUD, ST. (d. 794), bishop. He joined the Benedictines at Fritzlar in 738, served as abbot, became bishop of Würzburg,

Germany, about 754, and resigned in 787 to spend his last years at the abbey of Neustadt. F. D. Mar. 16.

MENNA, ST. (d. 395?). She lived in Lorraine and was a relative of St. Eucharius. F. D. Oct. 3.

MENNAS, ST. (3rd century?), martyr. According to legend, he was an Egyptian in the Roman army at Cotyaeum, Phrygia, when Diocletian's persecution broke out. He fled the army, lived as a recluse in the mountains, but proclaimed his Christianity during games in the amphitheater at Cotyaeum, whereupon he was tortured and beheaded. His cult spread over the East, he became one of the great warrior saints of the Middle Ages, and great myths and untrustworthy legends became attached to his name. F. D. Nov. 11.

MENNAS, ST. (4th century), martyr. According to legend, he was sent from Athens to Alexandria by Emperor Galerius to quiet the populace. On the successful completion of his mission, he publicly declared his Christianity and, with Eugraphus, began to preach. He was haled before Hermogenes, but his actions under torture so affected his judge that he also became a Christian. They were then beheaded. F. D. Dec. 10.

MENNAS, ST. (d. 552), patriarch. Born in Alexandria, he became a priest in Constantinople and in 536 was appointed its patriarch, in place of Anthimus, who had been papally deposed, and was consecrated by Pope St. Agapetus there. He vigorously condemned Origenism, but signed the decrees of Emperor Justinian anathematizing the Three Chapters. Pope Vigilius excommunicated Mennas and the other signers. The patriarch submitted, was soon reconciled but was excommunicated again in 551. He was once more reconciled shortly before his death on Aug. 24. F. D. Aug. 25.

MENNAS, ST. (6th century), hermit. A Greek from Asia Minor, he became a hermit in the Abruzzi, highly praised by St. Gregory the Great. F. D. Nov. 11.

MENOCHIO, GIOVANNI STEPHANO (1575-1655), scholar. Born in Padua, Italy, he joined the Jesuits in 1594, and taught sacred scripture and moral theology at Milan. He served as superior in Cremona, Milan, and Genoa, and became rector of the Roman college, provincial of the Milan and Rome provinces, assistant for Italy, and admonitor of two generals. He died in Rome on Feb. 4. He wrote profusely on biblical subjects, including the three-volume *Brevis explicatio sensus litteralis sacrae scripturae.*

MENODORA, ST. (d. 304?), martyr. During the persecutions of Diocletian and Maximian, she and her sisters Metrodora and Nymphodora refused to sacrifice to the pagan gods and were tortured and slain in Bithynia. F. D. Sept. 10.

MENSING, JOHN (d. 1541?), bishop. Born in Magdeburg, Saxony (or Zütphen, Holland), he became a Dominican in 1495, and studied at Wittenberg and Frankfort-im-Oder, where he received his doctorate. In 1522–24 he preached at Magdeburg cathedral, particularly against the reformers, and also at Dessau. He was professor at Frankfort in 1529, attended the Diet of Augsburg in 1530, was elected provincial of his order in 1534, and was appointed suffragan bishop of Halberstadt, Germany.

MENTELIN, JOHANNES (1410?–1478), publisher. A native of Schlettstadt, Germany, he became an illuminator at Strassburg, Alsace, where he joined the painters' and goldsmiths' guild. After training as a printer at Mainz, he established a printing establishment in Strassburg about 1460 and became one of the leading typographers of the fifteenth century. He died on Dec. 12.

MENZINI, BENEDETTO (1646–1704), poet. Born in Florence, he was ordained, taught at Florence and Prato, and in 1681 went to Rome to join the literary circle of Queen Christina of Sweden. At her death in 1689 he was given a canonry by Pope Innocent XII and taught rhetoric in Rome. He wrote on the release of Venice and capture of Budapest in *Canzoni eroiche e morali* and on other contemporary matters in *Academia Tusculana*; his *Paradiso terrestre* is a continuation of Tasso's *Mondo creato*; he also wrote elegies, pastorals, satires, and anacreontic lyrics. His *Arte poetica* was effective literary criticism. He died in Rome on Sept. 7.

MERCADÉ, EUSTACHE (15th century), dramatist. An official of the abbey of Corbie in 1414, he wrote the mystery play, *La Vie, la passion, et la vengeance de Jésus Christ.*

MERCATI, GIOVANNI (1866–1957), cardinal. Born in Gaida, Italy, on Dec. 18, he was ordained in 1889, and became Vatican librarian in 1919 to succeed Cardinal Ratti, who, when he became Pope Pius XI, made his friend a cardinal in 1926. He died in Vatican City on Aug. 22.

MERCIER, DÉSIRÉ JOSEPH (1851–1926), cardinal. Born in Braine l'Alleud, Belgium, on Nov. 21, he studied at Malines, Paris, and Leipzig, and was ordained in 1874. He taught philosophy at Malines in 1877–82, then held chairs in Thomistic philosophy in Rome and at Louvain. In 1906 he was made archbishop of Malines and in 1907 a cardinal. He had founded *Revue Néo-Scholastique* in 1894, and was its editor until 1906, founded the Institute of Philosophy, and published *Les Origines de la psychologie contemporaine* (1897). Because of his opposition to German brutality during the occupation of Belgium during World War I he was placed under house arrest. He continued to issue pastoral letters, which helped to unify the nation; after the war he was a leader in ecumenical congresses, worked for Christian reunion, and in 1920 founded the International Union of Social Studies. His philosophical position, expressed in several volumes, including *La Vie intérieure* (1918), met with considerable opposition. He died in Mechlin, Belgium, on Jan. 23.

MERCIER, LOUIS HONORÉ (1840–1894), statesman. Born in Iberville, Quebec, Canada, on Oct. 15, he was educated at Ste. Marie College in Montreal, was editor of *Le Courier* in St. Hyacintha (1862–64), was admitted to the bar in 1866, and entered politics as an opponent of confederation and a proponent of annexation with the United States. He was elected to the house of commons in 1873, helped found the Nationalist party in 1885, served in the Quebec assembly from 1879, and was premier at Quebec from 1887 to 1891. His law indemnifying the Jesuits for land previously confiscated by the government aroused controversy, but was approved by parliament. He died on Oct. 30 in Montreal.

MERCIER, LOUIS JOSEPH ALEXANDRE (1880–1953), educator. Born in Le Mans, France, on June 19, he was taken to Chicago, Illinois, in 1890, studied and taught at St. Ignatius College there, and did graduate work at Chicago and Columbia. He taught French in a Chicago school, at Wisconsin, married Zoe Lassagne, and in 1911 went to the Harvard School of Education. He published textbooks, was an interpreter with the British forces during the early years of World War I, returned to Harvard to defend Irving Babbitt in the quarrel of humanists, and wrote *Le mouvement humaniste* (1928) and *The Challenge of Humanism* (1933). He became associate editor of *Education* and *New Scholasticism*, received honorary degrees, and after his retirement from Harvard in 1946 taught comparative literature at Georgetown. He died in Chevy Chase, Maryland, on Mar. 12.

MERCOEUR, PHILIPPE EMMANUEL DE LORRAINE DE (1558–1602), governor. Head of the younger branch of the house of Lorraine, he was named governor of Brittany in 1582, revolted after the murder of the duc de Guise, and maintained the loyalty of the Bretons against the forces of Elizabeth I of England and Henry IV of France. He capitulated to France for a huge indemnity and married his daughter to Henry's son, the duke of Vendôme, who succeeded him as governor. He then fought against the Turks in Hungary and died at Nuremberg, Germany.

MERCURIA, ST. (d. 250), martyr. *See* Epimachus, St.

MERCURIALI, GERONIMO (1530–1606),

physician. Born in Forlì, Italy, on Sept. 30, he studied at Bologna and Padua, where he received his degree in medicine. He practiced in Forlì, then moved to Rome where his *De arte gymnastica* established him as a leading physician. In 1569 he was appointed to the chair of medicine at Padua, in 1587 at Bologna, and then at Pisa, where he remained until his retirement in 1605. He translated several medical classics, including a critical study of Hippocrates' works (1588). He died in Forlì on Sept. 30.

MERCURIALIS, ST. (d. 406?), bishop. He was the first to hold the Italian see of Forlì and was active in his opposition to the inroads of Arianism. F. D. May 23.

MERCURIAN, EVERARD (1514–1580). Born in Marcour, Luxembourg, he became a Jesuit in 1548, and in 1573 became the fourth general of his Society and first non-Spaniard to hold that position. He completed the Rule, drawing up a summary of the *Constitutions* from the writings of St. Ignatius Loyola, established the Maronite and English missions (sending Frs. Campion and Persons to Britain), and was in command of 5000 Jesuits at his death on Aug. 1.

MERCURIUS, ST. (d. 300?), martyr. He is said to have been one of a group of guards escorting Christians to their death at Lentini, Sicily, who were so impressed by their prisoners that they were converted and beheaded with them. F. D. Dec. 10.

MERCURIUS, ST., martyr. Unquestionably, he was an actual figure; legend, however, calls him a Scythian officer in a Roman army which repelled the barbarians attacking Rome. When he refused to join in sacrificing to the pagan gods after the victory, he was exiled to Caesarea, tortured, and beheaded. He long was venerated as one of the "warrior saints." F. D. Nov. 25.

MEREWENNA, ST. (d. 970?). She was abbess of the Benedictine convent at Rumsey, Hampshire, England, after its restoration by King Edgar. F. D. May 13.

MERIADOC, ST. (d. 886?). Possibly of Welsh origin, he seems to have built several churches in Cornwall, and then to have traveled to Brittany, where he may have been a regionary bishop. Legends about him are features of a miracle play in Cornish. F. D. June 7.

MERIADOC, ST. (d. 1302), bishop. Born in Brittany, he was a priest, then a hermit, and finally was called by the clergy of Vannes, France, to become bishop there. His reign was marked by great charity. F. D. June 7.

MERICI, ST. ANGELA (1470?–1540), foundress. She was born on Mar. 21 in Desenzano, Lombardy, was orphaned at ten and brought up at Salo by an uncle, became a Franciscan tertiary in her teens, and followed a life of extreme austerity. She was twenty-two when her uncle died, and she proceeded to work with other young women to educate the poor children of Desenzano and Brescia. On a pilgrimage to the Holy Land she became blind at Crete, but regained her sight on her return. In 1533 a dozen followers joined her in Brescia (from which she had been driven in 1512 by war) and on Nov. 25, 1535, the group, now numbering twenty-eight, consecrated themselves with her to St. Ursula. They studied and prayed together, though most of them lived in their own homes, and continued her original project of educating poor girls. St. Angela became the first superior of the new association, which was formally approved as the Company of St. Ursula by Pope Paul III in 1544. She was canonized in 1807.

MERIGHI, MICHELANGELO. *See* Caravaggio, Michelangelo.

MERMILLOD, GASPARD (1824–1892), cardinal. Born in Carouge, Switzerland, on Sept. 22, he studied at Fribourg, was ordained in 1847, served as curate in Geneva, where he founded two journals, became vicar general for the canton of Geneva in 1857, titular bishop of Hebron and auxiliary for Geneva in 1864, and administrator in 1871. When the pope appointed him vicar apostolic he was expelled from Switzerland by the city council and governed from France. Though appointed bishop, he failed to gain recognition from the canton until 1890, when he was created cardinal. He wrote ecclesiastical works and founded Union Catholique d'études sociales et économiques. He died in Rome on Feb. 23.

MÉRODE, FRÉDÉRIC FRANÇOIS XAVIER GHISLAIN DE (1820–1874), archbishop. Born in Brussels, grandnephew of Lafayette, he studied at Namur, Juilly, and the military academy in Brussels. He served with the army, was foreign attaché in Algeria, resigned in 1847, and was ordained in Rome in 1849. After a chaplaincy in Viterbo, he was placed in charge of the prisons of Rome by Pope Pius IX in 1850, introduced reforms which attracted wide attention, and then took charge in Perugia. In 1860 he helped establish a papal army, with himself as minister of war and Lamoricière as commander in chief. After defeats at Castelfidardo and Ancona, he devoted himself to civic improvements in Rome, but his outspoken criticism of the French caused his dismissal as minister. In 1866 he was appointed papal almoner and titular archbishop of Mylitene. He opposed the definition of papal infallibility at the Vatican Council in 1870, but accepted it after its definition. He died in Rome.

MERRY. *See* Medericus, St.; also, Mitrius, St.

MERRY DEL VAL, RAFAEL (1865–1930), cardinal. Born in London on Oct. 10, son of the secretary of the Spanish legation, of the same name, and Sophia de Zulueta, he studied at Namur, Brussels, and Ushaw. His theological work was completed at the Pontifical Academy and the Gregorian in Rome and he was ordained in 1888. He had various papal posts, was in 1896 secretary of the commission on Anglican orders, and in 1897 apostolic delegate to Canada to inquire into the school controversy. In 1900 he became titular archbishop of Nicaea; in 1903, secretary of the college of cardinals, secretary of state to Pope Pius X, and cardinal-priest. He opposed modernism in France, founded the Association of the Sacred Heart in Trastevere, was well known for his charities, and published *The Truth of Papal Claims* (1902). He served Benedict XV and Pius XI as secretary of the holy office and died in Rome on Feb. 26.

MERRYN. *See* Modwenna, St.

MERSENNE, MARIN (1588–1648), theologian. Born on Sept. 8 near Oizé, France, he studied at Le Mans and La Flèche, where he met Descartes, entered the Minims novitiate near Paris in 1611, taught philosophy at Nevers in 1614–20, then returned to Paris, where he died on Sept. 1. He engaged in scientific research, encouraged the scientists of his day, and became Descartes' closest friend and greatest defender. He wrote on theology, philosophy, mathematics, science, and translated several of Galileo's works.

MERULUS, ST. (6th century). *See* Antony, St.

MESCHLER, MORITZ (1830–1912), theologian. Born in Brig, Switzerland, on Sept. 16, he became a Jesuit in 1916, studied in Engleberg and at Bonn and Ratisbon, and was ordained in 1862. He served as master of novices for twenty-one years, was rector of several colleges, provincial three times, and assistant general for fourteen years. He wrote on the Holy Spirit, Sacred Heart, St. Joseph, the Virgin Mary, and Christ, and was well known for his *Meditations.*

MESMIN. *See* Memorius, St.

MESPELBRONN, JULIUS ECHTER VON (1545–1619), bishop. Born at the castle of Mespelbronn, Germany, he studied in Germany, and at Paris and the German College, Rome, where he was ordained. He became bishop of Würzburg in 1573, founded its Julius hospital in 1579, and in 1582 its university. He was effective in increasing converts in his diocese and in 1609 became a leading member of the Catholic League.

MESROP, ST. (d. 440), bishop. An Armenian, he was a monk under the direction of St. Nerses and then a missioner who worked with St. Isaac the Great on an alphabet and on translations of scripture from Greek and Syriac and of the liturgy. He did the same for Georgia, established schools in both countries, and continued preaching and teaching until he was past eighty. F. D. Feb. 19.

MESSALINA, ST. (3rd century), martyr. She is said to have been denounced as a Christian and beaten to death when she visited St. Felician in prison at Foligno, Italy. F. D. Jan. 19.

MESSINA, ANTONELLO DA (1430?–1497), painter. Born in Messina, Sicily, he became a pupil of Antonio Colantonio in Naples, determined to follow the Flemish masters in his painting, returned to Messina where he executed a triptych since destroyed, and went to Venice in 1473, where he did an altar screen for San Cassiano church, and became famed for his skill in oils and new coloring technique. He died in Messina.

MESSINGHAM, THOMAS (d. 1638?). Born in Meath, Ireland, he studied at the Irish College in Paris, taught there, and in 1621 was appointed rector. He was appointed prothonotary apostolic, honorary dean of St. Patrick's, Dublin, in 1624, but probably never returned to Ireland and died in Paris. He wrote *Florilegium insulae sanctorum*, on the Irish saints.

MESSMER, SEBASTIAN GEBHARD (1847–1930), archbishop. Born in Goldach, Switzerland, on Aug. 29, he studied at St. George's seminary, St. Gall, Innsbruck, and the Apollinaris, Rome, and was ordained in Innsbruck in 1871. He went to the United States in that year to teach theology at Seton Hall until 1889. He helped draft the decrees for and was secretary of the Plenary Council in Baltimore in 1884 and with Denis O'Connell edited its decrees for publication, taught canon law at Catholic University in 1889–91, and in 1891 was appointed bishop of Green Bay, Wisconsin. He was translated to Milwaukee and made an archbishop in 1903 and was appointed an assistant at the pontifical throne in 1906. He had great influence with the German-speaking Catholics of the Midwest, which he used to support America's efforts in World War I. He wrote canonical treatises and contributed to scholarly journals. He died in Goldach, on Aug. 4.

METASTATIO, PIETRO (1698–1782), dramatist. Born in Rome on Jan. 3, Pietro Bonaventura Trapassi was apprenticed to a goldsmith as a youth, and adopted by Gravina, a wealthy littérateur, who left him on his death in 1718 a fortune which he quickly dissipated. He took up law in Naples, became interested in poetry, and attracted great attention with his *Orti Esperidi* (1721), a successful musical drama. He became the protégé of the noted actress, Romanina, for whom he wrote *Didone abbandonata*, accompanied her on her tours, and in 1729, with her aid, was appointed court poet in Vienna. He devoted the rest of his life to writing scores of musical dramas (the fore-runners of opera), oratorios, cantatas and canzonas. He died in Vienna on Apr. 12. His melodramas were set to music by such composers as Gluck, Handel, Mozart, and Hasse; outstanding are *Attilio Regolo*, *Artaxerxes*, *Temistocle*, *Il re pastore*, and *Clemenza di Tito*.

METCALFE, EDWARD (1792–1847). Born in Yorkshire, England, he joined the Benedictines at Ampleforth in 1811, was ordained in 1816, served on missions at Kilvington, and in 1824 left Ampleforth to found a monastery at Prior Park, which shortly after 1830 was secularized. In 1831 he went to Wales, was transferred to Newport in 1836 and in 1847 to Bristol. He did considerable translation into Welsh. When plague broke out in Leeds, England, he offered his services and died there on May 7 of the plague.

METELLI, BL. MICHELINA (1300–1356). Born in Pesaro, Italy, she was married at twelve to Duke Malatesta of Rimini and widowed at twenty. When her young son died soon after, she gave up her social life, became a Franciscan tertiary, begged for the poor, took care of lepers, distributed her fortune to the poor, and lived in great austerity. Her cult was approved in 1737. F. D. June 20.

METELLUS, ST. (d. 305?), martyr. *See* Eugene, St.

METHAM, THOMAS (d. 1573). A native of Metham, Yorkshire, England, he was knighted in 1553 by Queen Mary, imprisoned with his second wife, Edith Palmes, in 1565 in York castle for his adherence to Catholicism, and died there eight years later.

METHODIUS I, ST. (d. 847), patriarch. Born in Sicily and educated in Syracuse, he became a monk at Constantinople, built a monastery on Chios, and returned to the Eastern capital, where in 815 he fought the Iconoclastic heresy of Emperor Leo the Armenian until he was exiled. He reported to Pope Paschal I, returned to Constantinople, and was imprisoned for seven years by Michael the Stammerer. He suffered under a third emperor, Theophilus, but on the latter's death in 842 he replaced the Iconoclast-supporter John as patriarch. His reign was marked by the definition of icons at the Synod of Constantinople, but marred by a quarrel with the monks under St. Theodore Studites, some of whose writings he had condemned. Methodius wrote a life of St. Theophanes and other biographies. F. D. June 14.

METHODIUS, ST. (d. 884), archbishop. Born in Thessalonica, he became governor of one of the Slav colonies in Opsikion province, but then a monk. With his brother Cyril he was sent in 861 by Photius to convert the Khazars in the Dnieper-Volga region. On his return he was elected abbot of an important monastery. In 863, again with his brother, he was sent by Photius to convert the Moravians, but, though successful, incurred the enmity of the German clergy and the ordination of their neophytes was refused by the German bishop of Passau. They went to Rome, bringing with them the alleged relics of Pope St. Clement, and were warmly received by Pope Adrian II, who praised their work and their use of the liturgy in Slavonic, and decreed that their neophytes were to be ordained. On the death of his brother, Methodius returned to Moravia, where at the request of Kosel, prince of Pannonia, he was made metropolitan of Sirmium and his ecclesiastical territory extended to Bulgaria. Despite papal approval, the German clergy continued to oppose him and had him imprisoned. Pope John VIII finally had him released after two years, but forbade him to use Slavonic in the liturgy. In Rome he convinced the pope of his orthodoxy and regained permission to use Slavonic, returned to Moravia, but had to spend the rest of his life fighting the German bloc. According to legend, he translated most of the Bible into Slavonic. He died on Apr. 6. The feast of SS. Cyril and Methodius, who are called Apostles of the Slavs, was extended to the Western Church by Pope Leo XIII in 1880. F. D. July 7.

METHODIUS OF OLYMPUS, ST. (d. 311?), bishop and martyr. St. Jerome says he was bishop of Olympus, Lycia, then of Tyre (which is doubtful), and was martyred at Chalcis in Greece. His writings include *The Resurrection* and *Banquet of the Ten Virgins* (which fell into the error of Millenarianism). F. D. Sept. 18.

METRANUS, ST. (d. 250?), martyr. He was put to death at Alexandria, Egypt, during the persecution of Decius. F. D. Jan. 31.

METRAS, ST. (d. 249), martyr. *See* Apollonia, St.

METRODORA, ST. (d. 304?). *See* Menodora, St.

METROPHANES, ST. (d. 325), bishop. He became bishop of Byzantium in 313, possibly its first, after the area became independent of the diocese of Heraclea. F. D. June 4.

METTERNICH, CLEMENS WENZEL NEPOMUK LOTHAR VON (1773–1859), diplomat. Born in Coblenz, Germany, on May 15, son of an Austrian diplomat, he studied at Strassburg and law at Mainz, was forced to leave at the outbreak of the French Revolution, and represented Westphalia at the coronations of Leopold II and of Francis II in 1792. He joined his father's diplomatic staff in Brussels, spent some time in England, and in 1795 married Countess von Kaunitz, acquiring vast estates and entrée to exclusive Austrian circles. He represented the Westphalian college of counts at the Congress of Bastadt from 1797

to 1799, was appointed Austrian envoy to Saxony in 1801, ambassador to Berlin in 1803, and in 1806, at Napoleon's request, to Paris. He urged Austria to oppose Napoleon and when war broke out between France and Austria in 1809 was imprisoned, but soon after was exchanged for several French diplomats. When Napoleon's victories caused Austria to sue for peace, Metternich became minister of state, then was minister of foreign affairs for the next forty years. The Treaty of Schönbrunn reduced Austria to a second-rate power, and Metternich resolved to restore her to her first-class status. Though signing an alliance in 1813 and professing friendship with Napoleon, he was able to placate Russia, and maintained neutrality in the war between France and Russia, meanwhile building up Austria's military strength. He was created a hereditary prince of the Austrian Empire and count of Daruvar in 1813. After Napoleon's disastrous invasion of Russia, he joined with Russia, Prussia, and Great Britain in the Quadruple Alliance, which eventually defeated Napoleon at Leipzig in 1814. He dominated the Congress of Vienna in 1814–15, at which he reestablished the position of Austria, instituted a European system which became known as the "concert of powers" designed to stabilize Europe and suppress any revolutionary tendencies, and was appointed state chancellor in 1821. The period 1815–48 became known as the "age of Metternich" and he was the chief arbiter of Europe. He labored to make Austria predominant in Italy, opposed German unity as he sought to make Austria supreme in the Germanic confederation, and checked French domination while preventing French ruin as he played France against Russia and Prussia to maintain the balance of power. He dominated the congresses of Aix-la-Chapelle in 1818, Karlsbad in 1819, Troppau in 1820, Laibach in 1821, and Verona in 1822. He was the guiding light of the Holy Alliance which became the symbol of reaction, and set up a system of censorship, espionage, and suppression of revolutionary movement which made him hated by liberals and revolutionists. His inability to understand the nature of nationalism, especially in Italy and Germany, eventually led to his downfall. In 1848 revolution broke out in Austria and Metternich was forced to resign. He fled to England, spent the next year and a half there and in the Netherlands, returned to Austria in 1851, and lived in retirement on his estate of Johannesberg. He died in Vienna on June 11. His *Memoirs* were published in 1880–84 and his collected letters in 1899.

MEUGANT, ST. (6th century). A follower of St. Illtyd, he lived as a hermit in Wales and died at Bardsey. He is also called Morgan. F. D. Sept. 26.

MEUNG, JEAN DE. *See* Jean Clopinel de Meung.

MEVENNUS. *See* Mewan, St.

MEWAN, ST. (d. 617?). Born in Gwent, Wales, and a relative of St. Samson, he followed the latter from Cornwall to Brittany and founded a monastery at Gaël, whose holy well later became a place of pilgrimage as the saint's name became associated with the cure of skin diseases. He is also called Maine and Mevennus. F. D. June 21.

MEYNELL, ALICE CHRISTIANA GERTRUDE (1847–1922), poet. Born in Barnes, England, on Sept. 22, daughter of Thomas and Christiana Weller Thompson, she became a convert about 1870. A meeting with Aubrey de Vere led to friendship with Tennyson; they encouraged her publication of *Preludes* in 1875. She married Wilfrid Meynell in 1877 and with him edited the *Pen* in 1880, which published and brought them into association with Browning, Rossetti, Ruskin, and Swinburne. From 1881 to 1898 they edited the *Weekly Register* and from 1883 to 1895 the monthly *Merry England*. Essays published in *Dublin Review* and the *Scots Observer* (edited by W. E. Henley) were gathered in *The Rhythm of Life* (1893). She became the friend of Coventry Patmore, Francis Thompson, and George Meredith, wrote a weekly article for the *Pall Mall Gazette*, and issued a second collection of essays, *The Colour of Life* (1896). *Poems, Other Poems*, and *Later Poems* appeared between 1893 and 1902; *A Father of Women* (1917) and *Last Poems* (1923) completed her poetical output. Other collections of essays were: *The Children, The Spirit of Place, Ceres' Runaway, Hearts of Controversy,* and *The Second Person Singular. John Ruskin* appeared in 1900. She wrote prefaces to many volumes by others and compiled such anthologies as *The Flower of the Mind* and *The School of Poetry.* She died in London on Nov. 27.

VIOLA MEYNELL, *Alice Meynell, A Memoir* (London, Cape, 1929).

MEZGER, FRANCIS (1632–1701), philosopher. Born in Ingolstadt, Bavaria, on Oct. 25, brother of Joseph and Paul, he joined the Benedictines, was ordained in 1657, and taught philosophy at Salzburg, Austria, from 1659 to 1668, serving as secretary of the university in 1661. He taught at various Benedictine monasteries until 1688, when he became master of novices and director of clerics at the Salzburg monastery, where he remained until his death on Dec. 11. He wrote philosophical treatises and translated others.

MEZGER, JOSEPH (1635–1683). Born in Eichstädt, Germany, on Sept. 5, brother of Francis and Paul, he joined the Benedictines, was ordained in 1659, became master of novices and sub-prior of the Salzburg monastery, Austria, in 1661, taught at Salzburg University until 1673, when he was made prior of the monastery, and was appointed vice-chancellor of the university in 1678. He died at St. Gall monastery, near Constance, Switzerland, on Oct. 26. He wrote a history of Salzburg and philosophical treatises.

MEZGER, PAUL (1637–1702), philosopher. Born in Eichstädt, Germany, on Nov. 23, brother of Francis and Joseph, he joined the Benedictines, was ordained in 1660, taught at the Salzburg gymnasium, was master of novices from 1664 to 1666, taught at Salzburg University (except for a year at Göttweig monastery) for the next thirty-two years, and was appointed vice-chancellor of the university in 1683. He died in Salzburg, Austria, on Apr. 12. He wrote philosophical, historical, and theological treatises.

MEZZOFANTI, GIUSEPPI (1774–1849), cardinal. Born in Bologna, Italy, on Sept. 19, he studied at the Scuole Pie, where he specialized in oriental languages. He was ordained in 1797 and appointed to the chair of Hebrew at Bologna. Dismissed when he refused to take the oath of allegiance to the Cisalpine Republic, he was appointed assistant librarian in 1803, and professor of Hebrew and Greek in 1804–8. He was appointed librarian in 1815, reoccupied the chair of oriental languages, was a member of the delegation which apologized to Pope Pius VII in 1831 for the city's rebellion, and accepted the pope's invitation to join his service. He was appointed domestic prelate, canon at Santa Maria Maggiore and St. Peter's, custodian of the Vatican Library in 1833, and prefect of the Congregation of Oriental Rites. In 1838 he was created cardinal, and served on the congregations of Propaganda, Rites, the Index, and the Examination of Bishops. He was hailed as the greatest polyglot of all times and is reputed to have spoken thirty-eight languages fluently and to have had a knowledge of thirty others. He died in Rome on Mar. 15.

MICHAEL, ST. (d. 820?), bishop. He was consecrated bishop of Synnada, by St. Tarasius of Constantinople, sent to Rome to inform Pope St. Leo III of the situation in the East, and banished to Galatia by Emperor Leo the Armenian for his staunch opposition to the Iconoclast heresy. F. D. May 23.

MICHAEL ATTALIATES (11th century), statesman. Arriving in Constantinople from Attalia after 1030, he rose to power in the imperial court, became chief justice, and in 1072 prepared a compendium of law for Emperor Michael Parapinakes. He founded a monastery and asylum for the poor in the capital, prepared its ordinances and a catalogue of its library, and wrote an eyewitness account of Byzantine history covering the years 1034–79.

MICHAEL OF CESENA (1270?–1342),

theologian. Michael Fuschi was born in Cesena, Italy, joined the Franciscans, studied at Paris and received his doctorate in theology, and taught at Bologna. He was elected minister general in 1316, opposed strenuously Pope John XXII's bull, *Quorundam exigit*, and became involved in the controversy over whether it was heretical to believe Christ and the apostles possessed earthly property. He was summoned to Avignon in 1327, re-elected general minister in 1328, and fled to Pisa with William of Occam and Bonagratia of Bergamo, where he denounced the pope and published the decree of Louis of Bavaria deposing the pope. He was condemned by a general chapter of his order in 1329 and expelled from the Franciscans and sentenced to life imprisonment in 1331. He was deserted by his followers in his last years and probably was repentant on his death in Munich, Bavaria, on Nov. 29.

MICHAEL OF CHERNIGOV, ST. (d. 1246), martyr. Duke of Chernigov, he fled when the Tatars attacked Kiev, Ukraine, but returned to plead for his people. The Tatar chieftain, Bati, attempted to get him to apostatize and, when he refused, tortured and beheaded him with Theodore, one of his nobles, on Sept. 20. F. D. Sept. 21.

MICHAEL DE SANCTIS, ST. See Sanctis, St. Miguel de.

MICHAEL SCOTUS (1175?–1234), mathematician. Probably a native of Scotland, he studied at the Durham cathedral school, Oxford, and Paris, where he became proficient in mathematics, taught at Bologna, and about 1200 joined the court of Frederick II in Palermo. He went to Toledo in 1209, where he studied astronomy and became adept in alchemy and magic, and returned to Palermo in 1220. He declined the archbishoprics of Cashel, Ireland, in 1223 and Canterbury (again in 1227). He wrote several treatises on astronomy and alchemy, *Liber physiognomiae* (which was widely reprinted), and translated Aristotle's *Ethics* and several of Averroes' commentaries. He is depicted as a magician in Dante's *Inferno*, Boccaccio's *Decameron*, and in Scott's *Lay of the Last Minstrel*.

MICHAEL WISNIOWIECKI (d. 1673), king of Poland. He succeeded John Casimir as king in 1669, and struggled without military success against major invasions by Cossacks, Tatars, and Turks.

MICHAUD, JOHN STEPHEN (1843–1908), bishop. Born in Burlington, Vermont, on Nov. 24, he studied in Montreal and at Holy Cross and St. Joseph's seminary, Troy, New York, and was ordained in 1873. He did parish work in Vermont until 1892, when he was consecrated titular bishop of Modra and coadjutor of Burlington. He became second occupant of that see in 1899, a position he held until his death on Dec. 22 in New York City. He wrote a *History of the Catholic Church in the New England States* (1899).

MICHAUD, JOSEPH FRANÇOIS (1767–1839), historian. Born in Albens, Savoy, he studied at Bourg, entered the publishing business in Lyons in 1786, became a journalist in Paris, and was arrested for his defense of the royal family in 1795, but escaped. He was later imprisoned for his criticism of Napoleon, founded and was editor of *Biographie universelle* in 1808 (which eventually appeared in fifty-two volumes from 1811–28), was elected to the French Academy in 1814, and became deputy editor of *La Quotidienne*. He wrote a *History of the Crusades* and was co-editor of the thirty-two-volume *Collection des mémoires*. He died in Passy, France, on Sept. 30.

MICHEL, GEORGE FRANCIS (1890–1938), liturgist. He was born in St. Paul, Minnesota, on June 26, studied at St. John's, Collegeville, became a Benedictine there in 1909, taking the name Virgil, and was ordained in 1916. After further study at Catholic and Columbia universities, he taught at St. John's from 1918 to 1924, studied at St. Anselm's, Rome and the Louvain, became interested in the liturgical movement, and on his return to St. John's in 1926 founded the liturgical magazine, *Orate Fratres* (now *Worship*), and the Liturgical Press. He soon became the leader of the liturgical movement in the United States and, except for the years 1930–33 among the Chippewa Indians in Minnesota, devoted his life to it, the Catholic social movement, and the revival of Thomism. He was a vigorous proponent of adult education, organized the first liturgical summer school at the Minnesota abbey, wrote *The Liturgy of the Church, Christian Social Reconstruction*, and *The Christian in the World*, and founded the Institute for Social Studies, of which he became director in 1935. He also was interested in the plight of the Indian, reorganized Indian missions in the Duluth and Crookston dioceses, and held an Indian congress in 1932. He died in Collegeville, Minnesota, on Nov. 26.

MICHEL, JEAN (d. 1501), dramatist. Author of the revised and enlarged mystery play of the Passion composed by Arnoul Gréban, and another on the Resurrection, he was probably the physician of Charles VIII's son and on the medical faculty at Angers, France; or he may have been another Jean Michael who was Charles VIII's physician and was appointed counselor in 1491 and died in 1495.

MICHEL OF NORTHGATE (14th century). He was an associate of St. Augustine of Canterbury, England, and in 1340 completed a translation of *La Somme des vices et des vertus*, written in 1279 by Frère Lorens for Philip II of France. Michel's English title is *Ayenbite* *of Inwit* (*Remorse of Conscience*); the work treats of the commandments, the Lord's Prayer, the gifts of the Holy Spirit, and the visions of the Apocalypse. It is an important linguistic monument in Kentish.

MICHELANGELO (1475–1564), artist. Born in Caprese, Italy, on Mar. 6, Michelangelo Buonarroti studied under the Ghirlandaio brothers, received additional training in Florence at the Medici palace in 1489–92, and studied sculpture under Bertoldo. He went to Bologna in 1494–95, worked as a sculptor in Florence in 1495, then went to Rome (1496–1501). Thereafter he lived alternately in Florence and Rome, settling permanently in Rome in 1534. He was a many-sided genius. Politian had introduced him to the literary world of Florence; he was a student of Dante, and wrote poetry himself; his sonnets are especially appealing. He was influenced by Savonarola and lived a comparatively austere life as a result, determinedly devoted to perfecting his creations. As a sculptor, which activity he seems to have preferred, he is noted for his early *Madonna Seated on a Step, Battle of the Centaurs, St. John in the Wilderness,* and *Pietà. Christ the Risen Saviour, David,* and the apostles for Santa Maria del Fiore stand out in his middle period. Later he completed the tomb of Pope Julius II, including the monumental *Moses.* As a painter he completed many religious figures and scenes, and the great cartoon of *The Battle of Pisa,* before he was called to Rome to work on a series of commissions for Popes Julius II, Leo X, Clement VII, and Paul III. He decorated the Sistine Chapel, beginning its ceiling in 1508, and spending nearly five years on its fresco of creation, the fall of man, and the coming of the Redeemer, with its supporting illustrations of prophets and sybils, the ancestry of the Virgin Mary, and the history of the human race up to the time of Noe. He completed his *Last Judgment* on the chapel's altar wall in 1535–41; the nudes were clothed by later workers. As an architect he completed the memorial chapel for the Medici family at the request of Clement VII, the façade of San Lorenzo, and was placed in charge of the fortifications of Florence in 1529. His most important structure was the basilica of St. Peter's, of which he was named chief architect in 1546 by Paul III. He carried out Bramante's plans, with some modifications, made a clay model of his own design for the upper dome, but lived to see only the drum completed. He died in Rome on Feb. 18, and was buried in Florence.

MICHELIS, EDWARD (1813–1855), theologian. Born in St. Mauritz on Feb. 6, he was ordained in 1836 and became private secretary of the archbishop of Cologne, with whom he was imprisoned in 1837. Released in 1841, he established the Sisters of Divine Providence and founded an orphanage in 1842, and was appointed professor of theology at Luxembourg seminary in 1845, a position he held until his death there on June 8. He founded *Münstersche Sonntagsblatt,* was editor-in-chief of *Das Luxemburger Wort,* and wrote theological treatises.

MICHELOZZO DI BARTOLOMMEO, MICHELOZZI (1395–1472), architect. Born in Florence, Italy, he became interested in architecture and worked with Donatello, who greatly influenced his work, and Ghiberti in their architectural projects. He came under the patronage of Cosimo de' Medici, who made him his court architect and art adviser, and with Brunelleschi was a leader in establishing the Renaissance style. He died in Florence. Among his outstanding works were the Riccardi palace in Florence, which he built for Cosimo de' Medici, the Medici chapel in Santa Croce church, the rebuilding of the convent of San Marco, the restoration of the Palazzo Vecchio, and a silver statue of St. John the Baptist.

MIDA. *See* Ida, Bl.

MIDAN, ST. (d. 610?). He lived in Anglesey, Wales, and is venerated there on Sept. 30.

MIDDENDORP, JAKOB (1537–1611), theologian. Born in Oldenzaal, or Ootmarsum, Holland, he studied in Zwolle and at Cologne, where he received his doctorate in philosophy and law and licentiate in theology. After teaching at several academies he returned to Cologne, where he became dean of St. Maria in 1580, twice rector of the university (1580–81 and 1602–4), dean of St. Andreas in 1596, canon of the cathedral chapter in 1601, and vice-chancellor of the university in 1602. He died in Cologne, Germany, on Jan. 13. He wrote theological treatises.

MIDDLEMORE, BL. HUMPHREY (d. 1535), martyr. One of three Carthusians who took over the direction of the Charterhouse in London after the execution of Bl. John Houghton, he and Bl. William Exmew (a Cambridge graduate and Prior John's confessor) and Bl. Sebastian Newdigate (a former member of Henry VIII's court) were imprisoned at Marshalsea, suspended by chains for two weeks, and executed at Tyburn for refusing to subscribe to the king's Act of Supremacy. They were beatified in 1886. F. D. June 19.

MIDDLETON, BL. ANTONY (d. 1590), martyr. Born in Yorkshire and ordained at Douai, he went to the English mission in 1586. Captured at a house in Clerkenwell, he was hanged in front of it and, when he preached for the crowd as he was pulled from the gibbet, was hacked to pieces. He was beatified in 1929. F. D. May 6.

MIÈGE, JEAN BAPTISTE (1815–1884),

bishop. Born in La Foret, Haute-Savoie, France, on Sept. 18, he studied at Conflans College, the Moutiers seminary, the Roman College, Rome, joined the Jesuits in 1836, and was ordained in 1847. He taught at St. Louis, did missionary work in the St. Louis archdiocese, and in 1850 was appointed titular bishop of Messene and first vicar apostolic of the Indian Territory east of the Rocky Mountains. He labored throughout his vast and sparsely settled territory and brought the Benedictines in to help as missionaries; in 1859 they established the priory which was the forerunner of St. Benedict's College, Atchison. The territory was divided into two vicariates in 1859, with Bishop Miége at the head of that designated the Kansas Territory. He consecrated his cathedral, attended the Vatican Council in 1869–70, toured South America to raise funds for his see, and resigned his vicariate in 1874. He was spiritual director at Woodstock from 1874 to 1884, except for 1877–80, when he was president of Detroit University, which he had founded in 1877. He died in Woodstock, Maryland, on July 21.

MIESZKO I (d. 992), king of Poland. Ruler of Posen about 962, he accepted the overlordship of the German emperor, paying yearly tribute and promising military support. He became a Christian in 963 and invited missioners to the country; a see was established at Posen, under the supervision of Magdeburg. His first wife, Dabrowska, sister of the king of Bohemia, and his second, Oda, helped him in building monasteries and convents. He later gained independence from Germany by declaring himself a vassal of the pope.

MIESZKO II (d. 1034), king of Poland. He succeeded his father, Boleslav Chobry, in 1025, but was attacked from all quarters, could not defend his military position, and lost his title as king when he reaccepted the overlordship of the German emperor. He is also called Mieczyslav. Revolution filled the subsequent interregnum until 1040.

MIESZKO III (d. 1202), king of Poland. He became king in 1173 and reigned so tyrannically that he was driven out four years later by the nobles. He returned to fight against Leznek I, claimed the crown from 1194 until he died in 1202, and passed on the leadership of rebellion to his son, Ladislas Laskonogi, who fought and claimed the throne as Ladislas III until 1206.

MIGAZZI, CHRISTOPHER ANTON (1714–1803), cardinal. A native of the Tyrol, he became a page in the household of the bishop of Passau when nine, studied at the German College, Rome, and returned to the Tyrol in 1736. He accompanied Cardinal Lamberg to the conclave of 1740, remained to study in Rome, was appointed auditor of the rota for Germany in 1745, negotiated several missions for Empress Maria Theresa, and was appointed coadjutor of Mechlin in 1751. He served as the empress' ambassador to Madrid, was appointed coadjutor of Waitzen in 1756, but before he could assume his duties was appointed archbishop of Vienna later in the same year. He was appointed administrator of Waitzen for life in 1761 and created cardinal. He became a leader in the struggle against the growing atheism, anti-clericalism, and the infringement of Church rights of the Aufklarung (Enlightenment) movement. When Joseph II succeeded to the Austrian throne he suppressed convents, interfered with religious orders, and trespassed continually in Church affairs, despite the cardinal's protests. Migazzi gained some minor concessions when Grand Duke Leopold of Tuscany succeeded Joseph in 1790. He died in Vienna on Apr. 14.

MIGDONIUS, ST. (d. 303), martyr. See Mardonius, St.

MIGNARD, PIERRE (1610–1695), painter. Born in Troyes, France, on Nov. 7, he studied painting at Bourges, Fontainebleau, and Paris with Simon Vouet. In 1635 he went to Rome and became famed for his portraits of Popes Urban VIII, Innocent X, Alexander VII, and Roman and Venetian nobles. He also became eminent in fresco painting and in religious painting; his madonnas were so popular they were called *mignardes*. In 1657 he was called back to France by Louis XIV, painted the king ten times, and members of the royal family and court. In 1664 he painted *Paradise* in the Val de Grâce church, possibly the largest fresco in the world and containing more than 200 life-size portraits. He became a close friend of Molière, Racine, Boileau, La Fontaine, and their circle, and the leader of the opposition to Le Brun, who was president of the Academy, which had been founded by Colbert. On the death of Le Brun in 1690 his differences were resolved and he was admitted to the Academy as president. Other works are *St. Luke Painting the Virgin*, *Visitation*, and *St. Cecelia*. He died in Paris on May 30.

MIGNE, JACQUES PAUL (1800–1875), publisher. Born in St. Flour, France, on Oct. 25, he studied theology at Orléans, was ordained in 1824, and became pastor of Puiseaux in 1825. He resigned when his bishop objected to a pamphlet he wrote, went to Paris, where he founded *L'Univers Religieux* (later *L'Univers*) in 1833, and edited it until 1836, when he devoted himself exclusively to the publishing house, L'Imprimerie Catholique, which he had founded, devoted to the publication of theological works at low prices for religious. He issued hundreds of works, most famous of which are the 221-volume *Patrologiae Latinae cursus completus* and the 166-volume *Patro-*

logiae Graecae cursus completus. Fire destroyed his plant and stock in 1868; he later was forbidden to continue publishing by the archbishop of Paris, who objected to his commercial practice and deprived him of his priestly functions. He died in Paris on Oct. 24.

MIGUEL (1802–1866), king of Portugal. Son of King John VI, he was born in Lisbon on Oct. 26, became regent of Maria II, daughter of Pedro IV, and in 1828 was asked by the Cortes to take the throne. Attacked by philosophical Liberals and supporters of the French Revolution, he was deposed in 1834 and driven from the country. Maria II became queen (until 1853), but had little to say in the new anti-clerical government. The Church was persecuted through the rest of the century, religious orders were suppressed, and property confiscated; education and religious instruction withered. Miguel died in Bronnbach, Baden, on Nov. 14.

MIKKELSEN, CANUTE (d. 1478). Dean of the church of Our Lady, Copenhagen, Denmark, he became rector of the University of Erfurt, Germany, in 1434 and bishop of Viborg, Denmark, in 1451. He was a diplomat and scholar and wrote Latin notes for the *Law of Jutland* and a treatise on the plague.

MILBURGA, ST. (d. 722?). Sister of SS. Mildred and Mildgytha and niece of King Wulfhere of Mercia, she established the Benedictine convent of Wenlock in Shropshire, England, and became its abbess. F. D. Feb. 23.

MILDE, VINZENZ EDUARD (1777–1853), archbishop. Born in Brünn, Moravia, he entered the minor seminary in Vienna in 1794, went on to ordination, and was appointed to the chair of pedagogics at the University of Vienna. He became court chaplain of Emperor Francis I, who named him bishop of Leitmeritz in 1823 and prince-archbishop of Vienna in 1831, the first commoner to occupy the see. When the revolution of 1848 broke, he was criticized by many of his clergy for his neutrality, but at an assembly of bishops in 1849 was named one of a committee of five to negotiate with the state in defense of the rights of the Church. He died in Vienna.

MILDGYTHA, ST. (d. 676?). Sister of SS. Mildred and Milburga, she became a Benedictine at Minster, where her mother St. Ermenburga was abbess, and later was abbess at a convent in Northumbria. F. D. Jan. 17.

MILDRED, ST. (d. 725?). The second daughter of Merewald and St. Ermenburga, and sister of SS. Milburga and Mildgytha, she was educated at a convent at Chelles, France, then returned to England to become a Benedictine at Minster on the Isle of Thanet, where she followed her mother as abbess. F. D. July 13.

MILES, GEORGE HENRY (1824–1871),

dramatist. Born in Baltimore, Maryland, on July 31, he graduated from Mt. St. Mary's in 1843, practiced law in Baltimore, but turned to literature when he had several short stories published, won a $1000 prize offered by Edwin Forrest for his tragedy, *The Arabian Prophet, Mahommed,* in 1850, and scored a dramatic success with his *Hernando de Soto* in 1852. He was appointed professor of English literature at Mt. St. Mary's in 1859, a position he held until he retired in 1867 to devote his full time to writing. He went to Spain in 1861 on a diplomatic mission, again in 1864, and died at his home near Emmitsburg on July 23. Among his plays were *Mary's Birthday, Señor Valiente,* and *The Seven Sisters;* he also wrote poetry and three novels.

MILES, RICHARD PIUS (1791–1860), bishop. Born in Prince George County, Maryland, on May 17, he studied at St. Rose of Lima priory, Springfield, Kentucky, joined the Dominicans in 1810, continued his studies at St. Thomas' College, and was ordained in 1816. He taught there and engaged in missionary work, went to Ohio in 1828, became superior of St. Rose's priory in 1833, of St. Joseph's priory in Ohio in 1836, and was elected provincial in 1837. Later that year he was appointed first bishop of the new diocese of Nashville, Tennessee, though not consecrated until a year later. He was one of the bishops selected to take the decrees of the fourth Provincial Council of Baltimore to Rome in 1840, toured Europe for aid for his see, founded St. Athanasius seminary in 1839, erected Seven Dolors cathedral in 1847, and died in Nashville on Feb. 21.

MILETIUS, ST. (d. 287?), martyr. *See* Marcellus, St.

MILETUS, VITUS (1549–1615), theologian. Vitus Müller was born in Gmünd, Swabia, studied at the German College, Rome, was ordained in 1575 when he received a doctorate in theology from Bologna, and was called to Mainz and Erfurt by their electors to aid in clerical reform and to help restore Catholicism. In 1582, 1601, and 1604 he brought the pallium from Rome for the new archbishops, became provost of St. Moritz, dean of the Liebfrauenstift, and received several canonrics. He wrote polemical and apologetic works and died in Mainz, Germany, on Sept. 11.

MILIANI, BL. CONRAD (1234–1289). Born in Ascoli Picano, Italy, of a noble family, he entered the Franciscans with Jerome Masci (later Pope Nicholas IV), and was professed and received his doctorate at Perugia with him. He then went to the African mission, had great success in Libya, returned to serve his boyhood friend, now a cardinal, and then taught theology at Paris. He was noted for his austerities, received several supernatural gifts, and was on his way to Rome when he fell ill and died at Ascoli, Italy. F. D. Apr. 19.

MILIC, JAN (d. 1374), reformer. Born in Kremsier, Moravia, he served as registrar and corrector of Charles IV's chancery, and was a priest, canon, and archdeacon in Prague. In 1363 he began bitterly denouncing the laxity of religious and laity, was imprisoned by the Inquisition in Rome for preaching that the Anti-Christ had arrived in 1367, but was released by Pope Urban V. He founded a refuge for women in Prague in 1372, was denounced by the clergy of Prague in 1373 for his preaching, and was exonerated by Pope Gregory XI in Avignon. He died in Avignon, France, on June 29.

MILLÁN DE LA COGOLLA. *See* Emilian, St. (d. 574).

MILLER, FERDINAND VON (1813–1887). Born in Fürstenfeldbruck, Bavaria, he studied bronze founding under his uncle Stiglmayr, then under Soyer and Blus in Paris, and, after visiting foundries in England and the Netherlands, returned to Munich, where he succeeded his uncle as inspector of the Munich bronze foundry. Under his management it gained a world-wide reputation for its artistry and excellence of casting, and cast statues for artisans all over the world. He was responsible for the Munich Exhibition of Art and Art Crafts in 1876.

MILLET, JEAN FRANÇOIS (1814–1875), painter. Born in Gruchy, near Gréville, La Manche, France, on Oct. 4, he worked in his father's fields as a youth, studied in Cherbourg, and in 1837 went to Paris, where he entered the studio of Paul Delaroche. His lack of success and disagreement with Delaroche caused him to return to Gréville in 1840, but in 1844 his *Milkwoman* and *Riding Lesson* caused much comment and launched him on his career when several noted artists (including Diaz and Rousseau) supported him. In 1848 the purchase of his *Winnower* by the minister of state, who also gave him a commission, allowed him to settle in Barbizon on the edge of Fontainebleau forest, where he spent the rest of his life. Millet's work is characterized by its truthful and symbolical portrayal of peasant life, is impressionistic in treatment, and noted for the pose of his figures (though he seldom used models), and the skillful unity of figures and landscape. Among his outstanding works are *Gleaners, Angelus, Sower, Man with the Hoe, Shepherd with Flock, Shepherdess, Harvesters Resting, Golden Age, Bathers, Mother Asking Alms,* and *Newborn Lamb*. He also was effective as an etcher. He died in Barbizon, France, on Jan. 20.

MILLET, PIERRE (1635–1708), missioner. Born in Bourges, France, on Nov. 19, he joined the Jesuits in Paris in 1655, studied and taught at La Flèche and Compiègne until 1664, and studied theology at Louis-le-Grand College in Paris until 1668, when he was sent on the Canadian mission. He worked among the Onondagas until 1672 and the Oneidas until 1685. He was chaplain at Fort Niagara and Catarakouy in 1688, was captured and tortured by the Iroquois in 1689, held captive for five years, during which he ministered to French captives and made many converts, and was freed to return to Quebec in 1694. He taught for a year at Quebec college, spent 1696–1703 in missionary work and returned to the college in 1704, where he remained until his death on Dec. 31.

MILNER, JOHN (1752–1826), bishop. Born in London on Oct. 14, he studied at Douai, was ordained in 1777, and in 1779 became pastor at Winchester, where he remained for twenty-three years. He was an ardent defender of the papacy, became embroiled in controversy with the sizable body of Catholics (some of whom organized the Catholic Committee in 1782, later known as the Cisalpine Club) who issued a *Protestation* in 1789 which was anti-papal in tone in an attempt to secure Catholic emancipation in England, and vehemently opposed the oath based on the *Protestation* which Prime Minister Pitt proposed all Catholics should take. He played a prominent role in modifying the oath in the Relief Bill of 1791, which relaxed some of the restrictions on Catholics and legalized the saying of mass. The controversy over his *History of Winchester* (1789) led him to write *Letters to a Prebendary* (1800) and *The End of Controversy* (which was not published until 1818). In 1803 he was consecrated titular bishop of Castabala and vicar apostolic of the Midland District, the stronghold of a Cisalpine group called the Staffordshire clergy, was appointed parliamentary agent for the Irish bishops seeking Catholic emancipation, and became embroiled in a bitter quarrel with the bishop of London over his criticism of the ecclesiastical rule of the London district. He wavered in his support of a plan giving the British crown the veto over bishops' appointments, finally opposing it when the Irish bishops condemned the veto in 1808. He led the opposition which led to the defeat of a government-sponsored bill for full Catholic emancipation in 1813, which contained several clauses opposed by the Church, and incurred the enmity of the lay Catholics on the Catholic Board who had supported the measure and who expelled him from the board. His trip to Rome on the matter led to a letter from the prefect of Propaganda in 1814, allowing Catholics to grant a limited veto to the crown. On his return his unbridled articles in the *Orthodox Journal* led to a prohibition against his further writing in it, though he continued publishing controversial pamphlets. He died in Wolverhampton, England, on Apr. 19.

MILNER, BL. RALPH (d. 1591), martyr. Born in Stacksteads, England, he lived at Winchester with his wife and eight children, became a convert, and was arrested the day he made his first Communion. His imprisonment was quite lenient and he was often at liberty, during which time he helped several priests. He was arrested for aiding Bl. Roger Dickenson, executed at Winchester with him, and beatified in 1929. F. D. July 7.

MILO CRISPIN (12th century), biographer. A monk at the Benedictine abbey of Bec, France, for many decades, he wrote lives of five of its abbots: Lanfranc, archbishop of Canterbury, Gulielmus de Bellomonte, Boso, Theobaldus, and Letardus.

MILO OF SÉLINCOURT, BL. (d. 1158), bishop. With a group of other hermits near Calais, France, he joined the Premonstratensians, and in 1123 became abbot of the monastery of Donmartin. In 1131 he was appointed bishop of Thérouanne. He was noted for his learning and was a strict disciplinarian. With St. Bernard he opposed the confused teachings of Gilbert de la Porrée on the Trinity and appeared against him at the councils of Paris and Rheims (1147–48). F. D. July 16.

MILTIADES, ST. (d. 314), pope. Said to have been a native of Africa, he became pope on July 2, 311. In 313, Constantine granted religious freedom to Christians and the Donatist schism arose in Africa. Miltiades is also known as Melchiades, under which name he is venerated in the Roman Martyrology, and as Milziadus. He was given the Lateran palace by Constantine's wife, and held a synod there condemning Donatus. He died on Jan. 11; he is honored on Dec. 10 as his feast day because of his sufferings on that day during the persecution of Maximian.

MILTIZ, KARL VON (1480?–1529). Born in Meissen, Germany, he was canon at Mainz, Trier, and Meissen, and about 1514 went to Rome, where he was appointed papal chamberlain and notary and became agent for the elector of Saxony and Duke George. In 1519 he was appointed papal nuncio to his elector and to negotiate with Martin Luther, with whom he held three unsuccessful meetings. He drowned near Gross Steinheim, Germany, on Nov. 20.

MIMMI, MARCELLO (1882–1961), cardinal. Born in Poggio di Castel San Pietro, near Bologna, Italy, on July 18, he studied at Bologna, was ordained in 1905, and served in the Italian army as chaplain during World War I. His organization of Catholic youths in Bologna in 1928 was felt to be a challenge to fascism. He was appointed bishop of Cremona in 1930, was archbishop of Bari in 1933–52, where he

founded Italy's first Boys' Town, and became archbishop of Naples in 1952. He was created a cardinal-bishop in 1953, appointed head of the Congregation of the Consistory in Rome in 1957, became president of the Pontifical Committee for Latin America, and died in Rome on March 6.

MINEAS, ST. (d. 250?), martyr. A soldier, he was slain during the Decian persecution for spreading Christianity in the army garrison at Florence, Italy. F. D. Oct. 25.

MINERVUS, ST. (3rd century), martyr. *See* Eleazar, St.

MING, JOHN JOSEPH (1838–1910), author. Born in Gyswyl, Unterwalden, Switzerland, on Sept. 20, he studied at the Benedictine college in Engelburg, became a Jesuit in Germany in 1856, studied at Aachen and Maria Laach, was ordained in 1868, became a preacher in Kreuzberg, and in 1871 taught theology at Görz, Austria. He came to the United States in 1872 and, after two years of pastoral activity, taught at various Catholic colleges, settling at St. Louis University, where he remained for twenty-one years, and became a pioneer in the Catholic sociological field. He died in Parma, Ohio, on June 17. He wrote on ethics, socialism, and the temporal power of the pope.

MINGUELLA Y ARNEDO, TORIBIO (1836–1920), bishop. Born in Egeo de Cornago, Spain, on Apr. 16, he studied at Tarragona, became a Discalced Augustinian at Monteagudo, was ordained, and was sent to the Philippines in 1858. He became secretary general and historian of the province, returned to Spain as rector of San Mullán, became bishop of Puerto Rico in 1894, of Siguenza, Spain, in 1897, and retired in 1916. He wrote on probability, on San Mullán, on Philippine missions, and palaeography, a Spanish-Tagal grammar, a history of the diocese of Siguenza, and other historical and biographical works. He died in Monteagudo, Spain, on Aug. 1.

MINKELERS, JEAN PIERRE (1748–1824). Born in Maastricht, Holland, he studied at Louvain, and taught natural philosophy there in 1772. In 1784, while a member of a committee investigating the best gas for balloons, he discovered illuminating gas. He resigned from Louvain in 1794 to become professor of physics and chemistry at the Central School in Maastricht, where he died on July 4.

MINO, MINO DI GIOVANNI DI (1431–1484), sculptor. Born in Poppi, Italy, he did a number of religious and secular portraits, but is chiefly known for his sculptures. He was a stonemason in Florence, studied under da Settignano, and often worked in Rome. He was engaged on the monument of Pope Paul II in 1473 and later completed commissions for Sixtus IV. Monuments appear in the church of

La Badia, Florence; busts in Florence and Fiesole; a tabernacle in Santa Maria, Trastevere; he did many altars, madonnas, and memorials in other centers. He is also known as Mino da Fiesole, and died in Florence, Italy, on July 11.

MIRA DE AMESCUA (1578?–1644), dramatist. Born in Guadix, Spain, he was ordained, became a canon in Guadix, and later moved to Madrid. He went to Naples with the count of Lemos and in 1619 was named chaplain to Cardinal-Prince Ferdinand of Austria. He wrote a number of plays, quite influential because of their technical skill; he often is compared with Alarcón.

MIRAEUS, AUBERT (1573–1640), historian. Born in Brussels on Nov. 30, he studied at Douai and Louvain, and became canon of the Antwerp cathedral and secretary to his uncle, the bishop of Antwerp, in 1608. In 1611 he was appointed almoner and librarian of Archduke Albert of Austria, became viceroy of the Netherlands, and, in 1624, vicar general of Antwerp and dean of the cathedral. He wrote some thirty-nine historical treatises and biographies and died in Antwerp, Flanders, on Oct. 19.

MIRANDA, BARTOLOME CARRANZA DE (d. 1576), archbishop. Born in Spain, he became a Dominican, was known as a theologian and canon lawyer, wrote *Summa conciliorum omnium* (1573), was censured for alleged heresy, tried before the Inquisition, and acquitted.

MIRANDOLA, GIOVANNI PICO DELLA. *See* Pico della Mirandola, Giovanni.

MIRIN, ST. (7th century?). Probably a disciple of St. Comgall and abbot of Bangor, he was an Irish missionary who labored in Scotland and died in Paisley where his shrine was greatly venerated. F. D. Sept. 15.

MIROCLES, ST. (d. 318). An archbishop of Milan, Italy, he was one of the originators of the Ambrosian liturgy. F. D. Dec. 3.

MISTRAL, GABRIELA (1889–1957), poet. This was the pen name of Lucilla Godoy y Alcayaga, who was born in Vicuna, Chile, on Apr. 7, of Basque and Indian parentage. She taught in a number of girls' schools from 1904 to 1914, when she won a national poetry contest; thereafter she wrote for magazines and newspapers. In 1922 she published *Sonnets on Death*; other volumes of poetry were *Desolation* (1922), *Tenderness* (1923), and *Tala* (1938). She delivered lectures in Mexico City, became head of the Letters and Arts Committee of the Institute for International Cooperation of the League of Nations, and came to the United States in 1930 to teach at Barnard, Vassar, and Middlebury colleges. She also served in the Chilean diplomatic service at Madrid, Lisbon, Nice, Rio de Janeiro, Naples,

and Los Angeles. In 1945, she was awarded the Nobel Prize for literature. During her last years she was active on behalf of the victims of the Spanish Civil War. She died on Jan. 9 at Hempstead, New York.

MISTRANGELO, ALFONSO MARIA (1852–1930), cardinal. Born in Savona, Italy, on Apr. 26, he became a Piarist in 1869 and in 1909 superior of his order. He was made archbishop of Florence in 1899 and a cardinal in 1915. He died in Florence, Italy, on Nov. 7.

MITCHEL, JOHN PURROY (1879–1918), mayor. Born in New York City, he studied at Fordham and Columbia, took his degree at New York Law School, and was admitted to the bar in 1901. He was special council for the city in 1906–7, commissioner of accounts in 1907–9, and rose to political fame by his prosecution of grafters. He was president of the board of aldermen in 1909–13, often served as acting mayor, was appointed collector of the port of New York by President Wilson in 1913, and was elected mayor of New York later that year. Defeated in a re-election attempt in 1917, he joined the army air service, and was killed while training at Gerstner Camp, Lake Charles, Louisiana, on July 6.

MITCHELL, JOHN (1870–1919), executive. Born in Braidwood, Illinois, on Feb. 4, he began working in the coal mines when twelve, joined the Knights of Labor in 1885, the United Mine Workers of America in 1890 when it was founded, and rose in the organization until he became president in 1898, a position he held until 1908. He was appointed chairman of the New York State Industrial Commission in 1915, and held this position until his death in New York City on Sept. 9. He wrote *Organized Labor* (1903) and *The Wage Earner and His Problems* (1913).

MITRIUS, ST. (d. 314), martyr. A Greek slave, also known as Merry, he was slain by his master in Provence. F. D. Nov. 13.

MITTARELLI, NICOLA GIACOMO (1707–1777), historian. Born in Venice on Sept. 2, he joined the Camaldolese with the name Gian Benedetto when fourteen, studied at Florence and Rome, and taught at San Michele di Murano monastery near Venice. He became archivist at San Parisio monastery in Treviso, abbot of San Michele in 1760, and was elected general of the order in 1765. In 1770 he returned to San Michele and remained there until his death on Aug. 4. He wrote the nine-volume *Annales* of his order and historical and theological treatises.

MIVART, ST. GEORGE JACKSON (1827–1900), biologist. Born in London on Nov. 30, he was educated at Harrow and King's College, London, and became a convert in 1844. During the next two years he studied at St. Mary's College, Oscott, became a student at Lincoln's

Inn in 1846, and was admitted to the bar in 1851 but did not practice. He became lecturer of comparative anatomy at St. Mary's Hospital Medical School in 1862 and was made a member of the Royal Society on Thomas Huxley's recommendation for his *On the Appendicular Skeleton of the Primates.* In 1871 he published *Genesis of Species,* which alienated Huxley and made him the leading opponent of Darwin and his theory of evolution, and proposed a theory which reconciled evolution and Catholicism. He became professor of biology at University College, Kensington, in 1874, received a doctorate in philosophy from Pope Pius IX in 1876, and in medicine from Louvain in 1884. Articles published in the *Nineteenth Century* from 1885 to 1890 were placed on the Index and, when repeated formal requests that he sign a profession of faith were ignored, he was excommunicated by Cardinal Vaughan. He lectured at Louvain from 1890 to 1893, was elected president of the Linnean Society in 1892, and died in London on Apr. 1. He was buried in unconsecrated ground, but his friends persuaded ecclesiastical authorities that the heterodoxy of his later years was caused by illness and he was reburied in a Kensal Green Catholic cemetery.

MOCHELLOC, ST. (d. 639?). He was venerated as patron of Kilmallock, Limerick, Ireland. F. D. Mar. 26.

MOCHOEMOC, ST. (d. 656?). Nephew of St. Ita, he was born in Munster, Ireland, became a monk at Bangor, and set up a community in Tipperary. F. D. Mar. 13.

MOCHTA, ST. (d. 535?), bishop. A Briton brought to Ireland as a child by his Christian parents, he became a follower of St. Patrick and supposedly went to Rome, where he was appointed bishop by Pope St. Leo I. It is more likely, however, he was made bishop of Louth by St. Patrick. F. D. Aug. 19.

MOCHUA. *See* Cuan, St.

MOCHUDA. *See* Carthach, St.

MOCHUMNA. *See* Machar, St.

MOCQUEREAU, ANDRÉ (1849–1930), scholar. Born in Tessoualle, France, on June 6, he studied in Paris, became a concert cellist, and in 1875 entered the Benedictines at Solesmes. His thirteen-volume *Paléographie musicale* (1889–1928) established the form of liturgical chant and was declared by Pope Pius X to be the model to be imitated. He wrote half a dozen other major studies on Gregorian and Ambrosian chant. He died in Solesmes, France, on Jan. 25.

MODAN, ST. (d. 550?). He is believed to have been a Scottish monk, who preached at Stirling and Falkirk, often retiring for contemplation in a mountainous retreat near Dumbarton, Scotland. F. D. Feb. 4.

MODANINO, IL. *See* Mazzoni, Guido.

MODERAN, ST. (d. 730). Born in Rennes, France, he became its bishop in 703, made a pilgrimage to Rome in 720, resigned his see, and became a Benedictine monk at Berceto, Parma. F. D. Oct. 22.

MODESTA, ST. (d. 304?), martyr. *See* Macedonius, St.

MODESTA, ST. (d. 680?). She was first abbess of the Benedictine abbey of Oehren at Trier, Germany. F. D. Nov. 4.

MODESTUS, ST. (2nd century?), martyr. He was put to death at Carthage, North Africa, and is revered as patron of Cartagena, Spain. F. D. Feb. 12.

MODESTUS, ST. (d. 300?), martyr. *See* St. Vitus.

MODESTUS, ST. (d. 303), martyr. *See* Florence, St.

MODESTUS, ST. (d. 304?), martyr. A native of Sardinia, he was a deacon when slain during the Diocletian persecution. F. D. Oct. 2.

MODESTUS, ST. (d. 489). He became bishop of Trèves, France, in 486. F. D. Feb. 24.

MODESTUS, ST. (d. 722?), bishop. He was a Benedictine monk at Salzburg, Austria, who became a regionary bishop in Carinthia and was most successful in converting that area. F. D. Feb. 5.

MODOALD, ST. (d. 640?), bishop. Brother of St. Severa and Bl. Iduberga, he became adviser to King Dagobert, who appointed him bishop of Trèves, France, in 622. He attended the Council of Rheims (625), founded several religious houses, and lashed with considerable effect against the evil state of the court. The name sometimes appears as Romoaldus. F. D. May 12.

MODOMNOC, ST. (6th century?). An Irish monk, he went to study in Wales under St. David, settled in Kilkenny, and may have become bishop of Ossory, Ireland. Because he was a beekeeper while abroad, a legend grew up that his bees followed him on his return and that he thus introduced them to Ireland. F. D. Feb. 13.

MODWENNA, ST. She possibly is a St. Monenna who lived in the middle of the seventh century and was a recluse on the island of Andresey in the Trent River, but the facts of her life are inextricably confused with those of the Irish Monine, said to have been the first abbot of Killeavy (d. 517?); Modwenna, who succeeded St. Hilda as abbess of Whitby (d. 695?); and Modwenna, abbess of Polesworth in Warwickshire (d. 900?). There are many other spellings, including Merryn.

MOELIAI, ST. (d. 493?). He was appointed by St. Patrick to direct the monastery of Nendrum, Ireland, where he trained SS. Colman and Finian. F. D. June 23.

MOELLER, HENRY (1849–1925), archbishop. Born in Cincinnati, Ohio, on Dec. 11, he studied at St. Francis Xavier there and the North American College, Rome, and was ordained in Rome in 1876. He taught at Mt. St. Mary's seminary, Cincinnati, was secretary to Bishop Chatard of Vincinnes and then of Archbishop Elder of Cincinnati, who appointed him chancellor in 1886, and in 1900 was appointed bishop of Columbus. He was named titular archbishop of Aeropolis and coadjutor of Cincinnati in 1903, succeeded to that see in 1904, was an active proponent of better educational facilities and standards, went to Rome with Bishop Schrembs in 1922 to defend successfully the activities of the National Catholic Welfare Conference, in which he was greatly interested, and in 1923 was made an assistant at the pontifical throne. He died in Cincinnati on Jan. 5.

MOGROBEJO, ST. TORIBIO ALFONSO DE (1538–1606), archbishop. Born in Mayorga, Spain, he was a lawyer, professor of law at Salamanca, then chief judge of the inquisitorial court at Granada. Still a layman, he was appointed in 1580 archbishop of the vacant see of Lima, Peru. In spite of his objections, he received holy orders in 1578, was consecrated in 1580, and sailed for Peru immediately. He visited all parts of his huge diocese, removed all who had been abusing the natives by extortion, injustice, or vicious example, met with tremendous opposition, but in time restored ecclesiastical discipline and a sense of justice in many areas. He learned the languages, heard complaints, dispensed charity, and confirmed St. Rose of Lima and, probably, Bl. Martin Porres and John Massias. In 1591 he established the first seminary in the New World at Lima. He died at Sana, near Lima, on Mar. 23, and was canonized in 1726. F. D. Apr. 27.

MÖHLER, JOHANN ADAM (1796–1838), theologian. Born in Igersheim, Württemberg, on Apr. 6, he studied at Tübingen and the Rottenburg seminary and was ordained in 1819. He became a tutor at Tübingen in 1821, professor in 1826, and received his doctorate in theology in 1828. He became the founder and leading Catholic exponent of the theological science of comparative symbolism and in 1832 published *Symbolik oder Darstellung der dogmatischen Gegansätze der Katholiken und Protestanten,* which caused great discussion and controversy among both Catholics and Protestants. He became professor of exegesis at Munich, was forced to retire because of ill health in 1836, was appointed dean of the Würzburg cathedral in 1838, but died on Apr. 12 at Munich, Germany, before occupying this position. Other writings include *Der Einheit in der Kirche oder das Prinzip des Katholismus* (somewhat marred by Febronianism) in 1825; studies on the Reformation, celibacy, and patristics, and biographical sketches of SS. Athanasius and Anselm of Canterbury.

MOHR, CHRISTIAN (1823–1888), sculptor. Born in Andernach, Germany, he settled in Cologne in 1845, and during the next forty years produced statues and sculptural decorations for the cathedral there as well as sculptures in the Düsseldorf assembly hall, Aachen (thirty-four figures of emperors), and Lübeck. He died in Cologne, Germany.

MOHR, JOSEPH (1834–1892). Born in Siegburg, Rhine, Germany, on Jan. 11, he was a priest who led the movement to restore pre-Reformation hymns to popularity among the German people. He wrote many hymn and prayer books. He died in Munich, Germany, on Feb. 7.

MOIGNO, FRANÇOIS NAPOLÉON MARIE (1804–1884), physicist. Born in Guémené, Morbihan, France, on Apr. 15, he studied at Ste. Anne d'Auray, became a Jesuit in 1822, studied theology at Montrouge, and was forced to flee to Switzerland when the revolution broke out in 1830. He taught mathematics at Ste. Geneviève in Paris in 1836, where he became well known for his preaching and scientific writings, left the Jesuits in 1843, and after a tour of Europe became chaplain of the Lycée Louis-le-Grand from 1848 to 1851. He became science editor of *Presse* in 1850 and *Pays* in 1851, and founded *Cosmos* in 1852 and *Les Mondes* in 1862. He died at St. Denis, France, on July 14. He wrote scientific and apologetical works and translated English and Italian scientific works into French.

MOLA, GASPARO. *See* Molo, Gasparo.

MOLAGGA, ST. (d. 664?). An Irishman, he studied under St. David of Wales and founded a monastery at Fermoy, Ireland. He is also known as Laicin. F. D. Jan. 20.

MOLAISSE. *See* Laserian, St.

MOLAY, JACQUES DE (1244?–1314). Born at Rahon, Jura, he was a Knight Templar at Beaune, grand master in 1298, and distinguished himself defending Palestine against the Saracens. When the Templars were driven out, he retired to Cyprus, where he planned a new campaign to recover the Holy Land. Summoned to France in 1306, he presented a plan for a crusade to Pope Clement V at Poitiers. He found King Philip the Fair intriguing to have the Templars suppressed, chiefly because he wanted their great wealth. The members of the order were vilified by calculated lies; Philip's agents gained confessions under torture, and the king controlled the grand inquisitor and three of his judges. Pope Clement V was asked to suppress the order officially. He sought first to have the Templars unite with the Hospitallers, but Philip did not approve. Clement launched an investigation of the knights' irregularities in other countries besides France, and found no evidence to support Philip's charges. Calumnies increased on the one hand; on the other, knights who appeared before the Council of Vienne insisted that their confessions had been forced from them under torture. A provincial council then was called by Philip's hireling churchmen, and fifty-four knights who appeared at Vienne were burned to death at Paris in 1307 on the charge of being lapsed heretics. Philip himself came before the Council of Vienne and demanded the suppression of the order; the pope and his councilors compromised: they said the charges raised against the Templars were not proved, but that it seemed prudent to dissolve the group. Their property was ordered given over to the Hospitallers, but Philip managed to have most of the wealth diverted to himself. When Jacques de Molay and the grand preceptor of Normandy, Geoffroy de Charnay, were tried, they raised serious objections to all charges through a trial which lasted seven years, but when they insisted that their former confessions had been forced from them they were declared to be heretics and burned at the stake in Paris on Mar. 18.

MOLÌ, GASPARO. *See* Molo, Gasparo.

MOLIÈRE (1622–1673), dramatist. Jean Baptiste Poquelin was born in Paris on Jan. 15, studied at Collège de Clermont and, probably, law in Orléans. He became valet to King Louis XIII about 1640, and when twenty-one, taking the name Molière, joined the Béjarts, a family of strolling players, attempted to open a theater in Paris, and, when it failed, toured the provinces. In 1653 he produced his first successful drama, *L'Etourdi*, in Lyons, and in 1658 opened a theater in Paris. When King Louis XIV attended and was delighted with the performance of his *Le Docteur amoureux*, the company's reputation was made. In 1659 he produced his highly successful *Les précieuses ridicules* and during the next fourteen years produced a steady stream of comedies, satires, and dramas. He was stricken while acting in his last play, *Le malade imaginaire*, in Paris and died on Feb. 17. His plays were notable for their comedy of intrigue, and manners, humorous dialogue, accurate and forceful delineation of human nature, and ridicule of hypocrisy and affectation. His range was wide, from farces like *Sganarelle* (1660), paraphrases of Terence (*L'École des maris*), comedy ballet (*Les fâcheux*), social comedy (*L'École des femmes*), to the deep anger of *Tartuffe*, which after its first production in 1664 was banned for almost five years. *Don Juan*, produced in 1665, also was forbidden, but King Louis adopted Molière's acting company as his own. Although his health began to fail, he produced in succession such masterpieces as *Le Médecin malgré lui*, *L'Avare*, *Amphitryon* (wittily de-

veloped from Plautus), *George Dandin*, *Le Misanthrope*, *Le bourgeois gentilhomme*, *Les femmes savantes*, and *Le malade imaginaire* (1673). His combination of wit and high seriousness affected French drama for a long period of time, though few writers matched it. In his personal life he suffered from constant criticism, from political and ecclesiastical leaders; many of his jibes offended churchmen in high places, but, although the archbishop of Paris forbade public recognition of his death, he was secretly buried in St. Joseph's cemetery.

MOLINA, ALONSO DE (1511?–1584), missioner. Born in Escalona, Toledo, Spain, he went to Mexico with his parents in 1523, became expert in the Nahuatl language, which he taught the first Franciscans who arrived in 1524, and became a Franciscan about 1534. He spent the rest of his life working among the Indians, serving as superior at Texcoco in 1555. He wrote philological and theological treatises and died in Mexico City.

MOLINA, ANTONIO DE (1560–1612?). Born in Villaneuva de los Infantes, Spain, he joined the Augustinian Hermits in 1575, became a superior of one of their houses, and taught theology. He left the Augustinians for the stricter Carthusians, became prior of their monastery at Miraflores, near Burgos, Spain, and died there on Sept. 21, possibly in 1619. He wrote ascetical works, chief of which was *Instruccion de sacerdotes*, which went into some twenty editions.

MOLINA, JUAN IGNACIO (1740–1829), naturalist. Born on July 20 in Guaraculen, Chile, he studied at Santiago, became a Jesuit at fifteen, was sent to Italy in 1767, and was ordained in Imola. He taught in Bologna, became interested in the natural sciences, founded a library in Talca, and published historical and geographical works on Chile. He died on Oct. 23 (or Sept. 12) in Bologna or Imola. Chile has named a town after him and several genera of plants are named after him in honor of his work in botany.

MOLINA, LUIS DE (1535–1600), theologian. Born in Cuenca, New Castile, Spain, he became a Jesuit at Alcalá when eighteen, studied there and at Coimbra, where he taught philosophy, and in 1570 went to Evorca, where he was professor of theology for the next twenty years. He returned to Cuenca to devote himself to writing in 1590, but was appointed to the chair of moral philosophy at the Jesuit college in Madrid, where he died on Oct. 12. Molina's principal work, on which he worked thirty years, *Concordia liberi arbitrii cum gratiae donis* (1588), caused great controversy when published, together with his *Appendix ad Concordiam* (1589). In it he presented a new logical metaphysical system, now known as Molinism, to reconcile the supremacy of God's grace, the cause of sanctification of the soul, and the fact that man is endowed with free will. His theory was attacked as a revival of Pelagianism, especially by the Dominicans. Molina was denounced to the Spanish Inquisition; Pope Clement VIII imposed silence on all disputants in 1594, and in 1598 instituted a Congregatio de auxiliis to settle the matter. Molinism was finally exonerated in 1607 by Pope Paul V. Its essential points were adopted by the Jesuits, but opposition by the Thomistic doctrine of grace, particularly supported by the Dominicans, has caused the controversy to continue. Molina also wrote *Commentaria in primum partem D. Thomae* (1592) and *De justitia et jure* (1593).

MOLINET, JEAN (d. 1507), poet. A canon of the collegiate church in Valenciennes, he was chronicler of the house of Burgundy and librarian to Margaret of Austria, and wrote troubadour verse of complicated rhythms on conventional themes. His prose translation of the *Roman de la rose* (1503), like his other work in that medium, is heavy with Latinisms.

MOLING, ST. (d. 697), bishop. Called by the historian Giraldus Cambrensis one of the four prophets of Ireland, he is said to have been born in Wexford, Ireland, of royal blood, to have become a monk at Glendalough, to have attracted wide respect for his austerity, and to have succeeded St. Aidan as bishop of Ferns, Leinster. He is also called Myllin. F. D. June 17.

MOLINOS, MIGUEL DE (1640–1696). Born in Municsa, Spain, on Dec. 21, he studied at Valencia, was ordained, went to Rome in 1662, soon became a celebrated confessor and spiritual director, and there developed the philosophy known as quietism. An extreme form of mysticism, it led to the recommendation of the abandonment of all conscious human effort, the sacraments, and prayer. His writings, especially *Guida spirituale* (1675), and theories became widely popular and influential. They were condemned as heretical in 1687 in Pope Innocent XI's bull *Coelestis Pastor* and all his works condemned; though Molinos publicly adjured them, he was sentenced to life imprisonment. He died in Rome on Dec. 28, receiving the sacraments on his deathbed.

MOLITOR, WILHELM (1819–1880), author. Born in Zweibrücken, Rhine Palatinate, on Aug. 24, he studied philosophy and law at Munich and Heidelberg and served in various state positions from 1843 to 1849, when he went to Bonn to study theology. He was ordained in 1851, became secretary of the bishop of Speyer, and in 1857 taught at the episcopal seminary. He was consultor in Rome in 1868 to assist in the preparatory work for the Vatican Council, a member of the Bavarian *Land-*

tag from 1875 to 1877, and founded several papers which headed the Catholic movement in the Palatinate. He wrote poetry (*Domlieder*), dramas (*Maria Magdalena; Des Kaisers Guenstling; Dramatische Spiele*), many novels, biographies, legal studies, and a treatise on Goethe's *Faust*. He died in Speyer, Germany, on Jan. 11.

MOLLOY, FRANCIS (d. 1684?), theologian. Born in King's County, Ireland, he joined the Franciscans, was appointed lecturer in philosophy at Klosterneuberg College, Austria, in 1642, to the chair of theology at Gratz in 1645, and professor at St. Isidore College in Rome in 1650, where he spent the rest of his life. He wrote several theological tracts, an Irish catechism, and the first printed Irish-Latin grammar. His name is sometimes listed as O'Molloy.

MOLLOY, GERALD (1834–1906), theologian. Born near Dublin on Sept. 10, he was educated at Castleknock and Maynooth, taught theology at the latter in 1857, was appointed professor of natural philosophy at the Catholic University of Ireland in 1874 and dean in 1883, a position he held until his death. He served as assistant commissioner of education in primary schools, was successively senator, fellow, member of the governing board, and vice-chancellor of the Royal University of Ireland, and a member of the board of intermediate education. He was interested in geology and electricity and lectured widely on natural science. He died at Aberdeen, Scotland, on Oct. 1. He published scientific and philosophical books and translations from Dante.

MOLLOY, THOMAS E. (1885–1956), bishop. Born in Nashua, New Hamphire, on Sept. 4, he studied at St. Anselm's College there, St. Francis College and St. John's seminary, Brooklyn, and the North American College, Rome, and was ordained in 1908. He did parish work in Brooklyn, was secretary to auxiliary Bishop Mundelein in 1909–15, and accompanied him to Chicago when he became archbishop of that see. He returned to Brooklyn in 1916, was spiritual director of Cathedral College, served as president of St. Joseph's College for women from 1916 to 1920, when he was appointed titular bishop of Lorea and auxiliary of Brooklyn. He became third bishop of Brooklyn in 1921, founded the Immaculate Conception seminary, Huntington, in 1930, and in 1951 was given the personal title of archbishop. He died in Brooklyn on Nov. 26.

MOLLUOG. *See* Moloc, St.

MOLO, GASPARO (17th century). Born in Breglio or Lugano, Italy, he became noted for his skill in producing medals and coins, was master of the mint in Florence in 1608, struck medals and coins for the courts of Florence and Mantua, and about 1623 went to Rome as die-cutter at the papal mint, where he remained for the rest of his life. His name is sometimes spelled Mola or Moli.

MOLOC, ST. (d. 572?), bishop. Said to have been born in Scotland and trained in Ireland by St. Brendan, he returned to Scotland to serve as a missionary bishop in Lismore, Ross, and the Hebrides, and died in Rossmarkie, Scotland. He is also called Molluog and Murlach. F. D. June 25.

MOLONY, THOMAS FRANCIS (1865–1949), jurist. Born in Dublin on Jan. 31, he studied at Trinity College. He passed the Irish bar in 1887 and the English in 1900, married Pauline Rispin in 1899, and became crown counsel for Carlow county in 1906 and Dublin county in 1907. He became solicitor general for Ireland in 1912, attorney general in 1913, judge of the court of appeal in 1915, and lord chief justice from 1918 to 1924, during a politically difficult period, when he had to defend martial law, sit in a court surrounded by barbed wire, and rely on the constant presence of armed guards. He then went to England, was made a baronet in 1925, chairman of a committee on the treatment of juvenile offenders, director of the national bank, and in 1931 vice-chancellor of Trinity. He died in Wimbledon, England, on Sept. 3.

MOLUA, ST. (d. 608). Born in Limerick, Ireland, he was a herder, then became a monk under St. Comgall at Bangor, where he was ordained. He founded more than 100 monasteries and is said to have submitted a most austere rule for them to Pope St. Gregory the Great. F. D. Aug. 4.

MOLYNEUX, CARYLL (1624–1699). He fought in the Royalist army during the English Civil War, succeeded to the family title as third viscount of Molyneux, was persecuted as a Catholic cavalier, but was made lord-lieutenant of Lancashire when James II ascended the throne. He was arrested on a charge of treason during the Lancashire Plot, but acquitted in 1694.

MOLYNEUX, THOMAS (d. 1681), martyr. Born probably in Alt Grange, Ince Blundell, Scotland, he became a Jesuit on the Continent, returned to England, was arrested at the time of the Titus Oates Plot, jailed at Morpeth, England, and died of ill treatment on Jan. 12.

MOMBRITIUS, BONINO (1424–1482?), philologian. Of a noble Milanese family, he studied at Ferrara, Italy, edited many writings of ancient Christian authors, collected records of the lives of saints in his *Sanctuarium*, and wrote poetry. He died between 1482 and 1502.

MOMMOLINUS, ST. (d. 686?), bishop. A native of Coutances, France, he became a Benedictine monk at Luxeuil, was sent to St. Omer in Artois, became superior of the old monastery (now St. Mommolin) there, moved to the new monastery in Sithiu, and in 660 succeeded St. Eligius as bishop of Noyon-Tournai. F. D. Oct. 16.

MONACO, LORENZO (1370?–1425), painter. Born in Siena or Florence, Italy, he became a Camaldolese monk, took his vows in 1391, and painted in the style of Gaddi. He completed many madonnas, scenes from the life of the Virgin Mary, *Adoration of the Kings*, and other deeply spiritual frescoes. Dom Lorenzo taught many monastic painters, including Filippo Lippi, and was an influence on Fra Angelico.

MONAGHAN, FRANCIS JOSEPH (1890–1942), bishop. Born in Newark, New Jersey, on Oct. 30, he studied at Seton Hall and the North American College, Rome, and was ordained in 1915. He did parish work in Jersey City, taught theology at Immaculate Conception seminary from 1926 to 1933, was president of Seton Hall in 1933–36, and was made a papal chamberlain in 1934. He was consecrated titular bishop of Mela and coadjutor of Ogdensburg, New York, in 1936, succeeded to the see in 1939, and died on Nov. 13.

MONAGHAN, JOHN JAMES JOSEPH (1856–1935), bishop. Born in Sumter, South Carolina, on May 23, he studied at St. Charles's, Maryland, and St. Mary's seminary, Baltimore, and was ordained in Charleston in 1880. He engaged in pastoral work in South Carolina, was chancellor of the Charleston diocese in 1887–88, assistant to the vicar general in 1888–97, and was consecrated bishop of Wilmington, Delaware, in 1897. He resigned in 1925 and was named titular bishop of Lydda, and died in Wilmington on Jan. 7.

MONAGHAN, JOHN PATRICK (1890–1961). Born in Dunamore, Tyrone, Ireland, on Feb. 12, he studied at St. Francis, Brooklyn, and St. Joseph's seminary, Yonkers, New York. After his ordination, he taught at Cathedral College, New York, wrote and lectured on the labor movement, was one of the founders and national chaplain of the Association of Catholic Trade Unionists and directed its labor schools. He was made a domestic prelate in 1957 and served as pastor in Staten Island and Manhattan for twenty-one years before his death in New York City on July 26.

MONALDO, ST. BUONFIGLIO (d. 1261), founder. He was one of seven Florentines who had joined the Confraternity of the Blessed Virgin (the Laudesi) in a particularly lax period in the city's history and who were inspired by a vision on the feast of the Assumption to take up a life of solitude and prayer. After nearly fifteen years of austerity at a hermitage on Monte Senario, they took the name, in 1240, of Servants of Mary, or Servites. Six were ordained, developed as mendicant friars under the direction of James of Poggibonsi and

Bishop Ardingo of Florence, and established many houses and foreign missions. Br. Buonfiglio served as its first prior general from 1240 to 1256 and died on Jan. 1; St. John Buonagiunta succeeded him; St. Bartholomew Amidei (Br. Hugh) established the order in Paris and St. Ricovero Ugoccione (Br. Sostenes) in Germany. SS. Benedict dell' Antella (Br. Amadeus) and Gerardino Sostegni (Br. Manettus) were ordained; St. Alexis Falconieri became a laybrother and was the only one to live to see the order approved by Pope Benedict XI in 1304. The "Seven Holy Founders" of the Servites were canonized in 1887 by Pope Leo XIII. F. D. Feb. 12.

MONAN, ST. (d. 874), martyr. A missioner in the Firth of Forth area in Scotland, he and a large number of Christians were slain by pagan Danes. F. D. Mar. 1.

MONAS, ST. (d. 249). He became bishop of Milan, Italy, in 193 and suffered through several persecutions during his fifty-six-year rule. F. D. Oct. 12.

MONCADA, FRANCISCO DE (1586–1635). Born at Valencia, Spain, on Dec. 29, son of the governor of Sardinia and Catalonia, and count of Osuna, he joined the army and in 1624 was appointed ambassador to the Viennese court by King Philip IV, and in 1629 to Brussels. In 1630 he was made commander in chief of the navy, of the army in 1632, and governor of Belgium in 1634 until the arrival of Prince Cardinal Ferdinand, whom he accompanied on an expedition into the duchy of Cleves. He was killed during the siege of Goch, Germany.

MONCAN. See Cuan, St.

MONDINO DEI LUCCI (1275?–1327?), anatomist. Probably born in Bologna, Italy, he was one of the first dissectionists and wrote a manual on systematic dissection, *Anatomia,* which was widely used in medical schools for the next three centuries. He died in Bologna. He is also known as Mundinus.

MONE, FRANZ (1796–1871), historian. Born in Mingolsheim, Baden, on May 12, he studied at Heidelberg, taught history there in 1817, was secretary of the library in 1818, professor in 1822, and head of the library in 1825. He was professor at Louvain from 1827 to 1831, became editor of the *Karlsruher Zeitung,* and, in 1835, director of the National Archives in Karlsruhe, a position he held until his retirement in 1868. He wrote widely on early history, *Urgeschichte des badischen Landes;* literary history, *Geschichte des Heidentums;* the three-volume *Lateinische Hymnen;* a history of Baden; twenty-one volumes of *Zeitschrift für die Geschichte des Oberrheins,* which he founded; and works on early drama. He died in Karlsruhe, Germany, on Mar. 12.

MONEGUNDIS, ST. (d. 570). On the death of her two daughters, she gained her husband's consent to shut herself in a cell at Chartres, France, her native city, and later at Tours, where she died. A group of women followed her example and the foundation became the convent of St. Pierre le Puellier. F. D. July 2.

MONER, BL. DALMATIUS (1291–1341). Born in Santa Columba, Spain, he studied at Montpellier, and at twenty-five became a Dominican in Gerona, Spain. He practiced great austerities and had unusual spiritual gifts. He died on Sept. 24, and his cult was confirmed in 1721. F. D. Sept. 26.

MONETA (d. 1240), theologian. Born in Cremona, Italy, he became a professor of theology at Bologna and an early follower of St. Dominic, whose order he joined in 1220. He wrote *Summa contra Catharos et Waldenses, Summa casuum conscientiae,* and a commentary on Aristotle's logic. He died in Bologna, Italy.

MONGE, GASPARD (1746–1818), mathematician. Born in Beaune, France, on May 10, he studied at Oratorian colleges there and at Lyons, became a physics teacher, and then studied at the practical school attached to the Mézières military school. There he developed a method of applying geometry to construction problems which is now known as descriptive geometry. He taught mathematics at Mézières in 1768 and physics in 1771, and in 1780 became a member of the Academy of Sciences, and was appointed to the chair of hydraulics at the Lycée in Paris. In 1781 he announced his discovery of the curves of curvature of a surface in a memoir for the Academy of Turin, left Mézières in 1783 to become examiner of naval candidates for École de Marine, served as minister of marine in 1792–93, was one of the leaders in the founding of L'École Polytechnique, where he taught and was an active supporter of the revolution and then Napoleon. He was appointed a member of the senate with the title of count of Pelusium, but was deprived of his honors and academic positions when Napoleon was exiled. In addition to the numerous articles he wrote *Traite élementaire de la statique* and *Géometrie descriptive.* He died in Paris on July 18.

MONICA, ST. (332–387). Born at Tagaste, in North Africa, she was married to Patricius, a personable but dissolute pagan. By her charity, forbearance, and prayers she converted him and his mother. Of their children, the eldest was St. Augustine, who was wayward as a philosopher and as an individual by the time of his father's death in 371. Monica fasted and prayed for him for fifteen years before he accepted Christianity at Milan. For eight months she lived with him, his son Adeodatus, and other associates at Cassiciacum, and soon after Easter, 387, when preparing for a return to Africa, she died at the port of Ostia, Italy.

Most of the information about her comes from Chapter 9 of her son's *Confessions*. F. D. May 4.

MONITOR, ST. (d. 490?). He was twelfth bishop of Orléans, France. F. D. Nov. 10.

MONROE, JAMES (1799–1870). Nephew of President James Monroe, he was born in Albermarle County, Virginia, on Sept. 10, graduated from West Point in 1815, served in the action against the Algerian pirates the same year, was an aid to Gen. Scott from 1817 to 1822, and resigned from the army in 1832. He entered politics in New York City, was a member of the board of aldermen from 1833 to 1835, of Congress from 1839 to 1841, and of the New York State legislature from 1850 to 1852, when he retired to private life. He died in Orange, New Jersey, on Sept. 7.

MONSABRÉ, JACQUES MARIE LOUIS (1827–1907). Born in Blois, France, on Dec. 10, he was ordained in 1851 and joined the Dominicans in 1855. In 1857 he preached the Lenten sermons at St. Nizier church, Lyons, the beginning of a famous preaching career, which led him all over France and Belgium and to London and Rome. He was preacher in Notre Dame for more than twenty years, where he was favorably compared to Boussuet and Lacordaire. He retired in 1903 and died in Le Havre, France, on Feb. 21.

MONSELL, WILLIAM (1812–1894). Born in Tervoe, Limerick, Ireland, on Sept. 21, he studied at Winchester and Oxford, succeeded to the family estates on his father's death in 1822, and represented Limerick in parliament from 1847 to 1874. He was a convert in 1850, privy councilor in 1855, vice-president of the board of trade in 1866, undersecretary of the colonies from 1868 to 1870, postmaster general from 1871 to 1873, and was raised to the peerage as Baron Emly in 1874. He died in Tervoe, on Apr. 20.

MONSTRELET, ENGUERRAND DE (1390?–1453), historian. Probably born in Monstrelet, France, he spent his life in the service of Duke Philip of Burgundy, count of Flanders. He was tax collector in 1436, bailiff of the Cambrai chapter from 1436 to 1440, provost of Cambrai from 1444 to 1446, and of Walincourt from 1445 until his death. He was present at an interview between Joan of Arc and Philip when she was captured before Compiègne, and was the author of a chronicle of European history covering the period from 1380 to 1444.

MONTAGNA, BARTOLOMMEO (1450?–1523), painter. Born in Orzinuovi, Italy, he settled in Vicenza in 1480, where he founded a school of painting; he also worked at Bassano, Padua, and Verona. His religious figures are severe in design, showing the influence of Bellini and Mantegna. Among the finest are frescoes in San Nazzaro, Verona, on the life of St. Blaise; altarpieces for San Sebastiano, Verona, and San Michele, Vicenza; and an *Ecce Homo* and numerous madonnas. He died in Vicenza, Italy, on Oct. 11.

MONTAIGNE, MICHEL EYQUEN DE (1533–1592), author. Born on Feb. 28 at Château de Montaigne near Bordeaux, France, son of the mayor of Bordeaux, he knew Latin at six, and studied at Guyenne and Bordeaux, and probably law at Toulouse. He became a judge in Bordeaux in 1554, counselor in Périgord, and a member of the Bordeaux parliament, and was at court in 1561–63. He married Françoise de la Chassaigne in 1565, sold his counselorship in 1570, and retired to his château, where from 1571 to 1580 he prepared the first collection of his *Essais*, which exerted wide influence. Editions appeared in 1582, 1587, and 1588, which contained new essays and rewritten versions of earlier ones. Previously, he had translated Raimond Sebond's *Theologia naturalis* (1568), had written the skeptical *Apologie de Raimond Sebond*, and in 1570 had edited the literary papers of his friend Étienne de la Boétie. He wrote a *Journal* of a trip through Europe in 1580–81, served as mayor of Bordeaux from 1581 to 1585, and, despite some of his philosophical remarks, died in the Church. His *Essais*, known to Shakespeare through their translation into English by Florio in 1603, had considerable effect on the development of English prose, and of European thought in general. They were controversial, graceful, often autobiographical reflections, epicurean and easygoing in tone. He died at his birthplace on Sept. 13.

MONTALEMBERT, CHARLES FORBES RENÉ DE TROYON DE (1810–1870). Born in London on May 29, son of Marc René de Montalembert and his English wife, he spent his youth in England, studied at the Collège Ste. Barbe in Paris, wrote for the newly founded (1829) *Le Correspondant*, traveled in Ireland in 1830, and late that year met and became associated with Lamennais and Lacordaire as editor of *L'Avenir*, in which position he became famous as an eloquent champion of the Church and of freedom for Ireland and Poland. In 1831 he succeeded to his father's peerage on the latter's death, was found guilty of operating a primary school in the famous Free School Case, in which he brilliantly pleaded the cause of religious freedom, and moved to Munich in 1832 when Pope Gregory XVI condemned *L'Avenir* in the encyclical *Mirari vos*. Montalembert submitted at once as he did the following year when the pope denounced his introduction to Mickiewicz's *Livre des pèlerins polonais*, and during the next few years pleaded in vain with Lamennais to do the same. He began contributing to Abbé Migne's *L'Univers*

Religieux and was instrumental in its continuance under Louis Veuillot. In 1836 he published *Vie de Ste. Elizabeth de Hongary* and married the daughter of Felix de Mérode, a descendant of the saint. In the house of peers, he became leader of the liberal Catholic party, defended the rights of the Church vigorously, and denounced European radicalism. He wrote *Du devoir des catholiques dans la question de la liberté d'enseignement* (1844) and was thanked by Pope Pius IX for his role in defending Catholicism in France. He was a member of the assembly in 1848; was elected to the legislature, where he debated with Victor Hugo, in 1849; supported Louis Napoleon in 1851, an action he later regretted; was elected to the French Academy in 1849; and served as a deputy in the assembly in 1852-57. He was managing editor of *Le Correspondant* in 1855 and developed it as liberal opposition to *L'Univers Religieux* of Veuillot, with whom he had broken. He visited England in 1855 and the next year published *L'Avenir politique de l'Angleterre* on British parilamentary institutions. His attacks on Napoleon III's government (he was the chief and often the only public opponent of the emperor) caused him to be sentenced to six months in prison in 1858 (a sentence remitted by the emperor), and his attacks on Napoleon's and Italian nationalists' actions against Pius IX further intensified the governmental enmity. In 1863 his speech at the Congress of Belgian Catholics in Mechlin in favor of modern democracy and the reconciliation of Catholic teaching and the religious freedom granted in modern democracies caused great controversy in Catholic circles. In 1869 he broke with *Le Correspondant*, which refused to publish an article containing an attack on *Civiltà Cattolica*, supporter of the view that older forms of government were better than modern ones, and in a widely circulated letter written a few days before his death he opposed papal infallibility. He died in Paris on Mar. 13. Among his other writings are the seven-volume *Les moines d'occident* (1860–77), *Une nation en deuil: la Pologne* (1861), *L' Église libre dans l'état libre* (1863) and *Le Pape et la Pologne* (1864). His *Speeches* and *Polemics* were also collected and published. *Catholic Interests in the Nineteenth Century, Constitutional Liberty*, studies of Pius IX and a biography of Lacoraire, and his *Monks of the West, from St. Benedict to St. Bernard* are among his titles translated into English.

MONTALVÁN, JUAN PÉREZ DE (1602–1638), author. A successful dramatist at seventeen, he took his doctorate in theology, joined the Congregation of St. Peter in Madrid, and at the suggestion of Lope de Vega composed *Orfeo en lengua castellana* (1624), along with eight narratives, *Sucesos y prodigios de amor.*

His prose *Vida y purgatorio de San Patricio* (1627) influenced Calderón's drama on St. Patrick's purgatory. Other stories and plays followed, notably the drama *Amantes de Teruel.*

MONTAÑES, JUAN MARTÍNEZ (1580?–1649), sculptor. Born in Seville or Alcalá la Real, Spain, he studied under Pablo de Rojas in Granada and settled in Seville, where he became noted for the realism of his statues. Outstanding are *Head and Hands of St. Ignatius* and *St. Francis Xavier* for the university in Seville; *St. Jerome* for St. Isidro del Campo monastery near Seville; the head of Philip IV for the equestrian statue in Madrid; the *Immaculate Conception* in Seville cathedral; *Christ Carrying the Cross*; *St. Bruno*; and *St. John the Evangelist.*

MONTAÑOL, BL. SEBASTIAN (d. 1616), martyr. A Spanish Dominican missioner, he was slain by Indians at Zacateca, Mexico, after he rebuked them for profaning the Eucharist. F. D. Dec. 10.

MONTANUS, ST. (d. 259), martyr. *See* Victoricus, St.

MONTANUS, ST. (d. 300?), martyr. A soldier, he was put to death on the island of Ponza, Italy, during the Diocletian persecution. F. D. June 17.

MONTANUS, ST. (d. 304), martyr. A priest in Sirmium, Dalmatia, he was put to death by drowning, with his wife Maxima, during the Diocletian persecution. F. D. Mar. 26.

MONTAULT, XAVIER BARBIER DE (1830–1901), archaeologist. Born in Loudun, France, on Feb. 6, he was raised by his uncle, the bishop of Angers, studied at St. Sulpice, the Sapienza, and the Roman College, but was obliged to return to France in 1857 because of ill health. He became historiographer of the diocese of Angers, founded a diocesan museum, was in Rome from 1871 to 1875 to study antiquities, and was theologian to the bishop of Angers at the Vatican Council. He wrote archaeological studies, many of which appeared in sixteen volumes of a sixty-volume project. He died in Blaslay, France, on Mar. 29.

MONTCALM DE ST. VÉRAN, LOUIS JOSEPH DE (1712–1759), general. Born in Candiac, near Nîmes, France, on Feb. 28, he entered the army at fifteen, served in France and the Netherlands during the War of the Austrian Succession, and was named colonel in 1743. In 1756 he was sent to Canada as commander in chief of the French army under Governor Vaudreuil. He soon opposed Vaudreuil, whom he fruitlessly denounced to the home authorities as dishonest and incompetent. He defeated the English at Fort Ontario in 1756, Fort William Henry in 1757, and Ticonderoga in 1758, but was killed in battle on Sept. 14 unsuccessfully defending Quebec.

MONTE CORVINO, GIOVANNI DI (1247?–1328?), archbishop. He was sent as papal legate to the khan of Persia in 1289, toured the coast of India in 1291–92, and reached Peking, China, sometime before 1305. Pope Clement V made him archbishop of Peking in 1307 and sent him three bishops in 1308; Giovanni developed several mission stations, including one at Amoy, China.

MONTEAGUDO, ANNA DE LOS ANGELOS (1602–1686). Born in Arepiqua, Peru, she became a Dominican at the convent of St. Catherine of Siena, where she was educated, was mistress of novices, lived a life modeled on that of St. Rose of Lima, and died at the convent on Jan. 10.

MONTEIRO, JUAN DE (16th century). He became first bishop of Colombo, Ceylon, in an area Christianized by the Franciscans, and converted Juan Dharmapala, grandson of the Cingalese king.

MONTEMARTI, BL. REGINALD (1292–1348). Born near Orvieto, Italy, he became a Dominican, preached in that area, and died at Piperno. His cult was approved in 1877. F. D. Apr. 9.

MONTEMAYOR, JORGE DE (1520?–1561), author. Born in Montemôr, Coimbra, Portugal, he was a royal musician and wrote in Spanish *La Diana enamorada*, a popular, autobiographical novel. It was imitated by Lope da Vega in *La Arcadia*, by Cervantes in *La Galatea*, and somewhat by Sir Philip Sidney in his *Arcadia*, and is the source of the Felix-Felismena episode in Shakespeare's *Two Gentlemen of Verona*. He also wrote *Cancionero*, a collection of lyric poems. He died in Turin, Italy, on Feb. 26.

MONTESINO, ANTONIO (d. 1545), missioner. A Dominican who made his profession at Salamanca, he was sent to New Spain in 1510, denounced the enslaving of the Indians in 1511, and was returned to Spain in 1512, where he successfully pleaded his cause to the king. In 1526 he accompanied a group of colonists which may have made a temporary settlement at New York, returned to San Domingo, traveled to Venezuela in 1528, and may have been martyred by West Indians.

MONTESINOS, LUIS DE (d. 1621), theologian. A Dominican who became known for his scholarship and clarity of presentation, he taught at several universities and was professor of Thomistic theology at Alcalá, Spain, for the last thirty years of his life. He wrote a commentary on St. Thomas Aquinas. He died on Oct. 7.

MONTESQUIEU, CHARLES LOUIS DE SECONDAT DE LA BRÉDE ET DE (1689–1755), philosopher. Born in Château de La Bréde, near Bordeaux, France, on January 18, Charles de Secondat studied at Juilly and law at Bordeaux, and was councilor of the Bordeaux parliament in 1714. In 1716 he inherited his uncle's title of baron of Montesquieu and the latter's position as president of the Bordeaux parliament, a position he held the next twelve years. His *Lettres persanes*, a satire on French society, the customs of his times, and the Church, published anonymously in 1721, caused a great stir and was enormously popular. He was elected to the French Academy in 1725, but a seldom-invoked rule prohibiting non-residents of Paris annulled his election until 1728, when he was admitted after moving to Paris. In 1734 his *Considérations sur les causes de la grandeur et décadence des Romains* attracted serious attention and in 1748 he published his greatest work, *L'Esprit des lois*, a comparative study of three types of government (republic, monarchy, and despotism), and his reflections on law, government, religion, customs, and the principles underlying each. He espoused freedom of religion, denounced slavery and torture, proposed the separation of the powers of government into executive, legislative, and judiciary, and advocated humane treatment of criminals. Its influence was enormous and was particularly felt in the United States, where Hamilton, Jay, Jefferson, and Madison reflected its teachings. Though placed on the Roman Index in 1752, it is one of the most important books of the eighteenth century and has had a tremendous effect on political thought. Montesquieu died on Jan. 10 in Paris.

MONTESSORI, MARIA (1870–1952), educator. Born in Charavelle, Ancona, Italy, on Aug. 31, she was the first woman to get her medical degree from the University of Rome (in 1894), devoted herself to teaching defective children, and in 1898 founded the Orthophrenic School, of which she was principal, to teach them. She then extended her educational theories to normal children in schools in Rome, opening the first of her *case dei bambini* (children's houses) in the slums of Rome in 1907. Although she encountered vigorous opposition from conservative educators, her success with all intellectual levels of children caused her system—based on teaching childen by providing them with chosen material, and, with no attempt at formal training, allowing their natural initiative to train them, with the teacher as a guide rather than an instructor—to be widely adopted. She lectured on her pedagogical methods at Rome in 1900–7, was appointed government inspector of schools in Italy in 1922, and was occupied in her later years in teaching her methods in England, India, Spain, and the Netherlands, where she died at Noordwijk on May 6. Her system of education is outlined in her *The Montessori Method* (1912), *The Advanced Montessori Method*

(1917), and *Education for a New World* (1946).

E. M. STANDING, *Maria Montessori* (Fresno, Calif., Academy Library Guild, 1957).

MONTEVERDE, CLAUDIO (1567–1643), composer. Born in Cremona, Italy, in May, he studied music under Ingegneri and published a book of canzonets when sixteen. He was appointed the duke of Mantua's choirmaster in 1602, maestro of San Marco, Venice, in 1613, and was ordained in 1633. He produced many choral compositions, madrigals, operas, cantatas, and ballets, and is called the father of instrumentation, famed for his use of new instrumental effects, unprepared discords, and unusual and daring combinations of musical instruments. His opera *Orfeo*, produced in 1608, is a landmark of musical history. Other titles include: *Arianna, Il combattimento di Tancredi e Clorinda, Proserpina rapita, Adone,* and *Il ritorno d'Ulisse.* He died in Venice on Nov. 29.

MONTFAUCON, BERNARD DE (1655–1741), scholar. Born in Château de Soulage, Aude, France, he entered the Académie des Cadets in Perpignan in 1672, served in the army, and in 1676 was professed as a Benedictine. After study at Sorèze, he spent eight years at La Grasse in Aude, was sent to Ste. Croix in Bordeaux and then to St. Germain-des-Prés in Paris. He helped prepare an edition of the Greek Fathers, was appointed curator of the numismatic collection at St. Germain in 1694, worked on an edition of St. Athanasius, and in 1698 visited Italian monasteries to study manuscripts. He was appointed procurator general in Rome, resigned to return to France in 1701, and spent the rest of his life in scholarly pursuits at St. Germain (where he died on Dec. 19). There he gathered a group of scholars called Bernardins, established a unique center of learning and research, founded the science of Greek palaeography, and was an indefatigable bibliographer and archaeologist. Among his outstanding works are a thirteen-volume edition of St. John Chrysostom's writings, an edition of Origen, *Palaeographia Graeca, Bibliotheca bibliothecarum manuscriptorum nova,* the ten-volume *L'Antiquite expliquée et représentée en figures,* and the five-volume *Monuments de la monarchie française.*

MONTFORT, LOUIS DE. *See* Louis of Montfort, St.

MONTGOLFIER, JACQUES ÉTIENNE (1745–1799). Born in Vidalon-les-Annonay, Ardèche, France, on Jan. 7, he studied mathematics at Paris, became an architect, abandoned this calling to run his father's paper mill with his brother, and pursued the study of physics, which had always intrigued him. He invented the *montgolfier,* a balloon filled with hot air, which he successfully sent aloft in 1783 and repeated the experiment later the same year at Versailles before Louis XVI and Benjamin Franklin among others. He died on Aug. 2 in Serrières, France.

MONTGOLFIER, JOSEPH MICHEL (1740–1810), inventor. Born in Vidalon-les-Annonay, Ardèche, France, on Aug. 26, he founded a paper-manufacturing firm with his brother, Jacques. He produced inventions to improve paper manufacturing and stereotyping, and a hydraulic ram, and became interested in the properties of heated air. He and his brother invented the first practical balloon and in 1783 successfully floated a balloon at Annonay by means of hot air, thus inaugurating lighter-than-air vehicles, and later actually ascended in a ballon with six other men at Lyons—a feat for which he was admitted to the Academy. His business was destroyed by the French Revolution, but he secured a governmental post and was named demonstrator of the Conservatory of Arts and Trades. He died in Balaruc-les-Bains, Hérault, France, on June 26. He wrote *Discours sur l'aérostat* and *Voyageurs aériens* with his brother, *Mémoires sur la machine aérostatique,* and *Notes sur le bélier hydraulique.*

MONTGOMERY, GEORGE THOMAS (1847–1907), bishop. Born in Davies County, Kentucky, on Dec. 30, he studied at St. Mary's seminary, Baltimore, where he was ordained in 1879, went to California, and became chancellor of San Francisco. In 1894 he was consecrated titular bishop of Tumi and coadjutor of Monterey and Los Angeles, to which he succeeded in 1896. He became noted for his insistence on Catholic education, his defense of the rights of the Indians, particularly the rights of Indian parents to give their children the education they desired, and of the rights of the Church and the responsibilities of Catholics as American citizens. He was appointed titular archbishop of Auximum and coadjutor of San Francisco in 1903, and died there on Jan. 10.

MONTJEU, PHILIBERT DE (d. 1439). He became bishop of Coutances, France, in 1424 and presided over the group of theologians sent by the Council of Basle to the Bohemians and Moravians to seek to reconcile them with the Church.

MONTMAGNY, CHARLES JACQUES HUAULT DE (17th century), governor. Born in France, he joined the Order of Malta in 1622, and fought the Moslems and African corsairs. He was appointed second governor of Canada, replacing Champlain, in 1636 and inaugurated a wise rule of building and colonizing, checked the power of the Iroquois with whom he concluded a treaty at Three Rivers, founded a school for Huron boys, and encouraged the conversion of the Indians. He ruled for three terms until 1648, when he returned to France. He then was sent to St. Christopher in the Antilles, where he died after 1651.

MONTMIRAIL, JOHN DE (1165–1217). Son of Lord Andrew of Montmirail and Ferté-Gaucher, he entered the army, became a member of the French court, and lived a life of luxury and dissipation. He changed his way of life on his thirtieth birthday, built a hospital for the sick poor, engaged in charitable work, lived a life of austerity and poverty, and after donating his wealth to the poor entered the Cistercian monastery of Longpont. He died on Sept. 2.

MONTMORENCY, ANNE DE (1493–1567). The first duke of Montmorency, he was born in Chantilly, France, on March 15, was educated with the future Francis I, appointed marshal in 1522, was captured with Francis at Pavia in 1525, and helped negotiate his release in 1526. He was appointed grand marshal of the royal house and governor of Languedoc, negotiated the treaty of Cambrai in 1529 which released Francis' sons held hostage by Charles V since 1526, and in 1530 inaugurated a new diplomatic policy of peace with the emperor and pope. When Francis' ambitions in Italy led to war with Charles in 1536, Montmorency inaugurated a scorched-earth policy in Provence which defeated the emperor's advance, and negotiated the treaty of peace between Charles and Francis in 1538. He was appointed constable in 1538, ousted in 1541 because of his policy of peace with the emperor, but was returned to favor after Francis' death by King Henry II in 1547 and made a duke and peer in 1551. He captured Metz from the Spanish in 1552, was defeated and captured at St. Quentin in 1557, but while in prison began the negotiations which resulted in the treaty of Cateau-Cambrésis in 1559 by which France obtained territory but renounced her claims in Italy and Savoy. Dismissed by Francis II, he was reinstated by Catherine de' Medici. He joined a triumvirate with the duke of Guise and the maréchal de St. André to save Catholicism in 1561 and was wounded and captured by the Huguenots at the battle of Dreux in 1562. He joined the Protestant Condé in 1563 to try to take Le Havre from the English, but warred against him when the second religious war broke out. He was killed in the battle of St. Denis, France, on Nov. 10. A generous patron of arts and letters, he was noted for his military prowess (and for his cruelty to his foes), and his unremitting efforts on behalf of his religion and of the aggrandizement of royal power.

MONTOR, ALEX FRANÇOIS ARTAUD DE (1772–1849), diplomat. Born in Paris on July 31, he was an exile during the French Revolution, served on diplomatic missions to the papacy for the royal princes, and was in Condé's army during the Champagne campaign. He was secretary of the French legation in Rome, chargé d'affaires in Florence in 1805, was recalled in 1807, and was censor during the last few years of the empire. He was secretary in the Vienna embassy at the restoration, and also in Rome, but retired in 1830 to devote himself to literary pursuits. He wrote histories of Pius VII, VIII, and IX, and of Leo XII, and translated Dante's *Divine Comedy*. He died in Paris on Nov. 12.

MONTORSOLI, GIOVANNI ANGELICO (1507–1563), architect. Born in Florence, Italy, he worked there and in Rome, Genoa, Bologna, Messina, and Paris. For a short period he was a member of the Servites and thereafter called himself Fra Giovanni. In 1522–25 he built or enlarged the Serra and Doria palaces, remodeled the interior of San Mateo, and in 1530–34 he worked with Michelangelo on the Medici chapel in Florence, where he carved the statue of St. Cosmas. He completed fountains in Messina, three chapels in its cathedral, and the church of San Lorenzo. He also designed the tomb (1561) in the chapter house of the Annunziata, where he was buried after his death in Florence.

MONTUCCI, ANTONIO (1762–1829), scholar. Born in Siena, Italy, he studied languages there and became a doctor of laws, went to England in 1789, and tutored families in London and Edinburgh. He issued editions of Alfieri's tragedies (1805–6) and Lorenzo de' Medici's poems, became interested in Chinese culture and language, published *De studiis sinicis* (1808), engaged in controversy with other Sinologists, went to Paris and Prussia, and completed work on his dictionary (29,000 Chinese characters) in 1825. In the meantime, Morrison and De Guignes had published their dictionaries, which could not be surpassed, and Montucci's was never printed. His books and manuscripts went to the Vatican Library on his return to Italy, where he died in Siena on Mar. 25.

MONTYON, ANTOINE JEAN BAPTISTE ROBERT AUGET DE (1733–1820). Born in Paris on Dec. 23, he became king's advocate at the court of Le Châtelet, a member of the council in 1758, master of petitions in 1760, and intendant of Auvergne in 1767, then of Provence, and later of La Rochelle. He was appointed councilor of state in 1775, left France when the Revolution broke out, returned in 1815, and died in Paris on Dec. 29. He was noted for his great charities and reputedly gave a fortune to the poor, established a series of prizes to reward scientific and literary achievements, notably the Montyon Prize of Virtue awarded by the French Academy, and was the author of *Eloge de Michel de l'Hôpital* and *Récherches et considérations sur la population de la France.*

MOODY, JOHN (1868–1958), economist. Born in Jersey City, New Jersey, on May 2, and educated in the Bayonne schools, he rose from errand boy to accountant with a wholesale firm, then was associated with a New York brokerage firm as a securities analyst. In 1900 he married Agnes Addison and founded his own *Manual of Railroad and Corporation Securities;* in 1905 he founded *Moody's Magazine* and in 1909 his *Analysis of Investments.* He opened his own investment service in New York, with branches abroad, wrote a number of volumes on capital, trusts, and management, and became a convert in 1931. He wrote *The Railroad Builders* (1919), *The Remaking of Europe* (1921), an autobiography, *The Long Road Home* (1933), popular theology, *Fast by the Road* (1942), and a biography, *John Henry Newman* (1945). He served as president of the Liturgical Arts Society, received an honorary degree from Boston College, and was knighted by Pope Pius XI. He died at La Jolla, California, on Feb. 16.

MOON, PARKER THOMAS (1892–1936), historian. Born in New York City on June 5, he graduated from Columbia in 1913, became a convert in 1914, and after further study at Columbia became an instructor in history. He became noted for his knowledge of contemporary history and international affairs, participated in the peace conference at Paris after World War I, and in 1919 resumed teaching at Columbia, where he became a professor in 1931. He became editor of the *Political Science Quarterly* and *Proceedings of the Academy of Political Science* in 1928, retaining this position until his death, was president of the American Catholic Historical Association in 1926 and the Catholic Association for International Peace in 1931–34, and died in New York City on June 11. He was a popular lecturer, and wrote numerous books, including a series of European history texts with Carlton Hayes, and *Imperialism and World Politics* (1926).

MOONEY, EDWARD FRANCIS (1882–1958), cardinal. Born in Mt. Savage, Maryland, on May 9, he studied at St. Charles's, Maryland, St. Mary's seminary, Baltimore, and the North American College, Rome, and was ordained in 1909. He taught at St. Mary's seminary, Cleveland, until 1916 when he became principal of the Cathedral Latin School. He held this position until 1922, when he was appointed pastor of St. Patrick's in Youngstown, and became spiritual director of the North American College, Rome, in 1923. He was appointed titular archbishop of Irenopolis and apostolic delegate to India in 1926, was apostolic delegate to Japan in 1931, and in 1933 was appointed archbishop of Rochester, New York. He was chairman of the administrative board of the National Catholic Welfare Conference in 1935–45, was promoted to Detroit, Michigan, as its first archbishop in 1937, was created a cardinal-priest in 1946, and died in Rome on Oct. 25.

MOOR, ANTONIS. *See* Moro, Antonio.

MOORE, ARTHUR (1849–1904). He was born in Liverpool, England, studied at Upshaw, was elected to the house of commons in 1874, and advocated home rule for Ireland, university education for Irish Catholics, better housing, and land reforms. He received the title of count from the pope in 1877, lost his seat in 1885, and spent the rest of his life in charitable activities, lecturing, and writing for newspapers. He established and endowed the Cistercian abbey at Roscrea, and died at Mooresfort, Tipperary, Ireland.

MOORE, EDWARD ROBERTS (1894–1952). Born in New York City on Jan. 9, he graduated from Fordham, where he also took his doctorate, St. John's seminary, Yonkers, and Catholic University. After ordination he served in St. Peter's, the oldest New York City parish, in 1919–23, and recorded his experiences in *Roman Collar* (1951). He was director of the social-action division of Catholic Charities in 1923–41, taught at the Fordham School of Social Service in 1924–38, worked with the Catholic Youth Organization, the New York province of Newman Clubs, the municipal slum clearance and low-cost housing units, and was a member of the city's Housing Authority in 1939–44. He had returned to St. Peter's as pastor in 1937, established a large lending library and discussion groups, and published a newspaper. He became a monsignor in 1941, wrote *Heart in Pilgrimage* (on Mother Seton) with Evelyn Eaton, and died in New York City on June 2.

MOORE, JOHN (1834–1901), bishop. Born in Castletown, Westmeath, Ireland, on July 27, he went to Charleston, South Carolina, in 1848, studied at St. John the Baptist seminary there, Courbrée College, France, and the Propaganda, Rome, and was ordained in Rome in 1860. He served as curate of the cathedral in Charleston during the Civil War, pastor of St. Patrick's church in 1865–77, was vicar general of the diocese from 1871, and in 1877 was consecrated second bishop of St. Augustine, Florida. He attended the third Plenary Council of Baltimore in 1884, was one of the two bishops who brought the council's decrees to Rome, and died in St. Augustine on July 30.

MOORE, MICHAEL (1640–1726). Born in Dublin, he studied at Nantes and Paris, taught at the Collège des Grassins, and on his return to Ireland was ordained in 1684. He was appointed vicar general of Dublin, provost of

Trinity College in 1689 by James II, was forced to resign in 1690 when his sermon in Christ Church cathedral offended James, and went to Paris. He became censor of books in Rome, rector and professor of philosophy at Cardinal Barbarigo's college in Montefiascone, rector of the university of Paris in 1701, principal of the Collège de Navarre and professor of philosophy, Greek, and Hebrew at the Collège de France. Blind the last few years of his life, he died in Paris on Aug. 22.

MOORE, THOMAS (1779–1852), poet. Born on May 28 in Dublin, he studied at Trinity College, studied law in London, though never admitted to the bar, and in 1801 published his first book of poems. He went to Bermuda in 1803 as registrar of the admiralty court, traveled through the United States and Canada, and returned to England in 1805. In 1819 he went to Europe to escape creditors when a deputy he had left in Bermuda absconded with £6000, but repaid the loss and returned in 1822. He wrote *Irish Melodies, Lalla Rookh* (1817), the satiric *Intercepted Letters* and *The Fudge Family,* and biographies of Edward Fitzgerald, Sheridan, and Byron (who left him his memoirs, which Moore destroyed), and the strange autobiography, *The Travels of an Irish Gentleman in Search of a Religion.* He is best known for the lyrics of such songs as *Believe Me if All Those Endearing Young Charms, Oft in the Stilly Night,* and *The Harp That Once through Tara's Halls.* He died in Devizes, England, on Feb. 26.

MOORHEAD, LOUIS D. (1892–1951), physician. Born in Chicago on Nov. 22, he studied at Loyola and Chicago universities and Rush Medical College. He was dean of the school of medicine at Loyola in 1918–41, taught surgery there in 1918–28, and was head of the department of surgery in 1928–41. He was chief of the medical board of the archdiocese of Chicago, a director of Catholic Charities, and personal physician to Cardinals Mundelein and Stritch. He served the health, police, and fire departments of Chicago and was a founder of the American Board of Surgery. He was honored by Italy and twice decorated by the papacy. He died in Chicago on Sept. 14.

MORA, FRANCIS (1827–1905), bishop. Born in Vich, Catalonia, Spain, on Nov. 25, he studied at the seminary there, went to California in 1855, and was ordained in Santa Barbara in 1856. He spent the next seventeen years in missionary work at San Juan Bautista mission, as superior of San Luis Obispo in 1861–66, and in 1873 was consecrated titular bishop of Mosynopolis and coadjutor of Monterey-Los Angeles. He succeeded to that see in 1878, resigned in 1896, and was appointed titular bishop of Hieropolis, and returned to his native land where he died in Sarriá, Spain, on Aug. 3.

MORA Y DEL RIO, JOSÉ (1854–1928), bishop. Born in Pajuacarari, Mexico, on Feb. 24, he studied in Zamora and Rome and was ordained in 1877. He was named bishop of Tehuantepec in 1893 and later of Leon, and in 1908 was consecrated archbishop and primate of Mexico. He instituted agricultural reforms and sought to better working conditions, but was arrested in 1927 and exiled during government persecution of the Church. He died in San Antonio, Texas, on Apr. 22.

MORAES, FRANCISCO DE (1500?–1572), novelist. Born in Braganza, Portugal, he was treasurer of the household of John III, served in Paris with the Portuguese ambassador in 1540–44, and was a knight commander of the Order of Christ. In 1544 he completed *Palmerín de Inglaterra* (published in France in 1548 and in a Portuguese version in 1567), the most significant narrative of chivalry after *Amadis de Gaul.* Even Cervantes, who condemned the extravagant exploits of earlier versions, praised its artistic unity and style. The story had great influence on the work of Vicente, Paravicino, and others; for centuries it was incorrectly attributed to Luís Hurtado de Toledo. Moraes was assassinated at Evora, Portugal.

MORALES, AMBROSIO (1513–1591), historian. Born in Cordova, Spain, he studied at Salamanca and Alcalá, was ordained, and became professor of belles-lettres at Alcalá. He was appointed chronicler of Castile in 1574, continued Ocampo's *Crónica general de España* to 1037, and wrote other historical treatises.

MORALES, CHRISTÓBAL (1512–1553), composer. Born in Seville, Spain, on Jan. 2, he was a member of the papal choir from 1535 to 1540, was influenced by the Dutch school, and stands with Vittoria as one of the greatest Spanish composers. He was particularly influential in his invention of contrapuntal devices, wrote polyphonic *Lamentations,* Gregorian *Magnificats,* and masses for four, five, and six voices. He died in Málaga, Spain, on June 14.

MORALES, BL. FRANCISCO DE (d. 1622), martyr. Born in Madrid, he became a Dominican and labored for twenty years at the mission in Satzuma, Japan. In 1608 he was at Fuximi and in 1614 went to Nagasaki, where he was burned alive with Bl. Charles Spinola and others. He was beatified in 1867. F. D. Sept. 10.

MORALES, JUAN BAUTISTA (1597?–1664), missionary. Born in Ecija, Andalusia, Spain, he joined the Dominicans, was sent to the Philippines on missionary work, and in 1633 to China, where he became embroiled in the dispute between Jesuits and Dominicans over acceptance of Chinese customs in matters of religion. He was sent to Rome in 1643 and secured a condemnation of the Jesuit methods by Pope Innocent X in 1645. When Alexander

VII rescinded the condemnation, Morales appealed the matter to Rome in 1661 (Clement IX decided against the Jesuits in 1669). He died in Fu-ning, China, on Sept. 17.

MORALES, LUIS DE (1509?–1586), painter. Born in Badajoz, Estremadura, Spain, he became famed for his religious paintings, characterized by harshness, melancholy, and vivid portrayals of saintly sufferings. They were extremely popular in Spain for their discerning and accurate reflection of the Spanish character, temperament, and faith. Among his chief works are *Ecce Homo, Mater Dolorosa, Virgin and Child, Holy Family, Christ at the Column,* and *Christ Carrying the Cross.* He died in Badajoz.

MORAN, PATRICK FRANCIS (1830–1911), cardinal. Born in Leighlinbridge, Carlow, Ireland, on Sept. 16, he studied at the Irish College, in Rome, and was ordained with special permission at twenty-three and received his doctorate in theology there. He served as vice-rector of the Irish College, taught Hebrew at the Propaganda, was vice-rector of the Scots College, became secretary to his uncle, Cardinal Cullen, in 1886, went with him to the Vatican Council, and founded the *Irish Ecclesiastical Record.* He was made titular bishop of Olba and coadjutor of Ossory, founded convents, industrial schools, and a library, developed St. Kiernan's College, and was an active champion of home rule. In 1884 he was transferred to Australia as third archbishop of Sydney. He became the first Australian cardinal in 1885, visited all the parishes of New Zealand in 1886 and those of New Holland later, and held three plenary synods in 1885, 1895, and 1905. He built St. Patrick's seminary, Manly, consecrated fourteen bishops, and dedicated more than 500 churches. Active in civic affairs, he labored for a strong Australian army and navy, pleaded for federation, and saw many laws favorable to workers introduced by the labor ministry. He wrote *Essay on the Origin of the Irish Church, History of the Catholic Archbishops of London, Letters of the Anglican Reformation, Reunion of Christendom and Its Critics, History of the Catholic Church in Australia,* and studies of Irish saints and of the Cromwellian persecution in Ireland. He died in Manly, near Sydney, on Aug. 16.

MORAND, ST. (d. 1115?). Born into the nobility in Worms, Germany, he was educated in its cathedral school, ordained, and after a pilgrimage to Compostela became a Benedictine at Cluny at the hands of St. Hugh the Great. About 1200 he was sent to Altkirch at the request of Count Frederick Pferz, who had restored the church of St. Christopher, to serve the people of Lower Alsace, where he labored with great success. He became a patron of vineyard workers. F. D. June 3.

MORATÍN, LEANDRO FERNANDEZ DE (1760–1828), dramatist. Born in Madrid on Mar. 10, he was apprenticed to a jeweler as a youth, and won two academy prizes for poetry in 1779 and 1782 which brought him to the attention of Jovellanos, who had him appointed secretary of Count Cabarrús' mission to Paris in 1787. On his return in 1789, Manuel Godoy, the prime minister, became his patron, and he began writing plays, the first of which, *El viejo y la niña,* was staged in 1790. He was forced to flee Spain in 1808 when Godoy fell, but returned when Joseph Bonaparte came to power and made him royal librarian. Forced to flee again when Bonaparte was ousted, he passed the rest of his life in exile and died in Paris on June 21. He is often referred to as "the Younger" to distinguish him from his father, Nicolás. Among his outstanding plays are *El sí de las niñas, El café, El barón,* and *La mojigata.* He also translated *Hamlet* and several of Molière's plays and wrote *Orígines del teatro español.*

MORATÍN, NICOLÁS FERNÁNDEZ DE (1737–1780). Born in Madrid, he became a lawyer, professor of poetry at the imperial college, and a leader in the movement to reform the Spanish theater. He wrote dramas in the French style, among them *Hormesinda,* an epic poem, *Las naves de Cortés destruidas,* and poems on hunting and bullfighting.

MORAZZONE, IL. *See* Mazzuchelli, Pietro.

MORBIOLI, BL. LUIGI (1433–1485). Born in Bologna, Italy, he married, but became notorious for his infidelity. In 1462, after a serious illness, he reformed, became a Carmelite tertiary, and devoted himself to teaching catechism and begging alms for the poor. He died in Bologna on Nov. 9, and his cult was confirmed in 1843. F. D. Nov. 16.

MORCELLI, STEFANO ANTONIO (1737–1822. Born on Jan. 17 in Chiari, Italy, he studied in Brescia, became a Jesuit in 1753, taught at Fermo, Ragusa, and the Roman College, and established an academy of archaeology at the Kircher Museum. He became Cardinal Albani's librarian when the Jesuits were suppressed in 1773, provost in Chiari in 1791, and was noted for his knowledge of ancient inscriptions about which he wrote several treatises. He died in Chiari, on Jan. 1.

MORE, HELEN (1606–1633). Born in Low Leyton, Essex, England, on Mar. 25, the great-great-granddaughter of St. Thomas More, she joined the Benedictines as Dame Gertrude at Cambrai, Flanders, in 1623. There she came under the direction of Dom Augustine Baker. She died in Cambrai on Aug. 17. Two spiritual books were published posthumously.

MORE, HENRY (1586–1661). Great-grandson of St. Thomas More, he studied at St. Omer, France, and Valladolid, Spain, joined the Jesuits, and was sent on the English mission. He was imprisoned in 1632 and 1640, was elected provincial in 1635, served twice as rector of St. Omer (1649–52 and 1657–60), and died in Watten, England. He wrote a history of the English Jesuits and a life of Christ.

MORE, BL. HUGH (1563–1588), martyr. Born in Grantham, Lincolnshire, England, he was educated at Oxford and Gray's Inn, became reconciled to the Church, and went to Rheims. On his return to England he was accused of having renounced Anglicanism and was hanged at Lincoln's Inn Fields, London, on Aug. 28 during the Elizabethan persecution. F. D. Sept. 1.

MORE, ST. THOMAS (1478–1535), martyr. Son of John More, lawyer and judge, he was born in London, England, on Feb. 6. At about twelve he was a page in the service of John Morton, archbishop of Canterbury and chancellor, who sent him to Oxford. He then studied law, thought of entering the Carthusians, entered parliament in 1504, and married Jane Holt in 1505. Their home soon became an intellectual center, filled with enthusiasm for mediaeval and Renaissance thought, and even a workshop for drama. More visited Louvain and Paris, was in 1510 elected an undersheriff of London, and in 1511, when his wife died, married a widow, Alice Middleton, within a month. He had been tutor to the young Henry VIII; now that he was king, Henry pressed More into service, sending him on diplomatic missions to Flanders and France, appointing him to the royal council in 1517, and knighting him in 1521. More served as high steward of the universities of Cambridge and Oxford and was several times consulted about the king's proposed divorce. In 1529 he succeeded Cardinal Wolsey as chancellor, an honor he accepted with grave misgivings. He refused to participate in the formal discussions on the king's marriage, a silence which irritated Henry. When the latter, as a condition of pardoning the northern clergy, required them to sign an oath declaring him the "supreme head of the church in England," More sought to resign, but was persuaded not to. When the question of dismissing Catherine of Aragon rose in parliament, More refused to sign the request to the pope which Henry sought. More openly opposed a series of measures against the Church and in 1532 tendered his resignation. He retired to his home in Chelsea for eighteen months, practically poverty-stricken by his loss of income, and devoted himself to writing. In 1534 he was ordered to recognize the child of Henry and Anne Boleyn as the lawful successor to the throne, by subscribing to an oath whose wording went beyond the Act of Succession in that it required acknowledgment of Henry's supremacy and repudiation of the pope. More refused

and was imprisoned in the Tower. In 1635 he was tried for treason for opposing the Act of Supremacy and within a week, on July 6, was beheaded. His English writings include poems, a life of Pico della Mirandola, a history of Richard III (based on Lancastrian sources, and a direct influence on Shakespeare's play), *Four Last Things* (1522), *Supplication of Souls* (1529), *Dialogue of Comfort* (1534), several major controversial works against Tyndale, Frith, and other heretics, letters, and prayers. His writings in Latin include translations from Lucian, occasional poems, *Vindication of Henry against Luther* (1523), *Treatise on the Passion* (1524), and *Utopia* (1515–16). The last is an account of an imaginary society ruled by reason, but without revelation, marked by obvious overtones of serious satire against current social, economic, and political weakness. The death of England's leading humanist shocked Europe and was a serious blow to the new scholarship. More was canonized in 1935. F. D. July 9.

R. W. CHAMBERS, *Thomas More* (London, Cape, 1953); E. E. REYNOLDS, *St. Thomas More* (Garden City, N.Y., Image Books, 1958).

MOREAU, LOUIS ZÉPHIRIN (d. 1901), bishop. Born in Canada, he was ordained, was stationed in Montreal, became secretary to Bishop Prince of St. Hyacinthe, Quebec, in 1852, and succeeded to that see in 1876. He dedicated its stone cathedral, installed its chapter in 1876, introduced the Marist brothers to his see, and founded a community, Soeurs de St. Joseph, to direct rural schools. He died on May 24.

MOREL, GALL (1803–1872), scholar. Born in St. Fiden, Switzerland, on Mar. 24, he studied there and in Einsiedeln monastery, Switzerland, and was ordained in 1826. He taught rhetoric there to 1832, became abbey librarian in 1835, a position he was to hold all his life, and served successively as choral director, prefect, rector of the abbey school, archivist, and sub-prior. He wrote some ten volumes of verse, built up the library, helped found the Swiss Society for Historical Research in 1840, and became an authority in aesthetics. He died in Einsiedeln on Dec. 16.

MORELL, JULIANA (1594–1653). Born in Barcelona, Spain, on Feb. 16, she studied there and at Avignon, France, became a Dominican at the convent of Ste. Praxède there, and took her vows in 1610. She was named prioress three times and remained there until her death on June 26. She wrote several spiritual tracts and was highly praised by Lope de Vega.

MORERI, LOUIS (1643–1680), scholar. Born in Bargemont, Fréjus, France, on Mar. 25, he studied at Draguignan, Aix, and Lyons. He was ordained, preached in Lyons for five years, and in 1673 became secretary of the bishop of Apt.

The next year his *Grand dictionnaire historique,* an encyclopedia of history and mythology, was published. He died in Paris on July 10.

MORETO Y CABAÑA, AGUSTÍN (1618–1669), dramatist. Born in Madrid, on Apr. 9, he studied at Alcalá, served briefly in the army, and had his first play produced in 1640. He took minor orders in 1642, but entered court circles through his friendship with Calderón and wrote a score of comedies—witty, clever in diction, and quietly humorous. He was ordained in 1657 and joined the household of the archbishop of Toledo. Among his seventy plays are *El desdén con el desdén* (the original of Molière's *Princesse d'Elide*), *El lindo don Diego, Los jueces de Castilla, San Franco de Sena,* and the historical *El valiente justiciero,* on Pedro the Cruel. He also wrote masques, farces, and dramas in other contemporary modes. He died in Toledo, Spain, on Oct. 28.

MORETTO DA BRESCIA. *See* Bonvicino, Alessandro.

MORGAGNI, GIOVANNI BATTISTA (1682–1771), anatomist. Born in Forlì, Italy, on Feb. 25, he studied at Bologna under Albertini and Valsalva, whose assistant in anatomy he became. He did several years of graduate work at Bologna, research at Pisa and Padua, and in 1706 began lecturing on anatomy, at Bologna. Publication of his *Adversaria anatomica* (1706) led to an appointment at Padua and then at Bologna as professor of anatomy. He specialized on the throat, did research in pulmonary diseases, related meningitis as a sequel to ear infection, and decided tuberculosis was contagious (causing laws to be passed in Rome and Naples segregating tuberculars), did research on the pulse and palpitation of the heart, and insisted there were no valid cures for cancer except an operation. His studies of disease and its effect on the body as revealed by postmortem examinations made him one of the greatest of pathological anatomists. He was elected to the English Royal Society in 1724, the Paris Academy of Sciences in 1731, the Russian Imperial Academy in 1735, and the Berlin Academy in 1754. His *De sedibus et causis morborum per anatomen indigatis* (1771) is regarded as the foundation of modern pathology. He died in Bologna, Italy, on Dec. 6.

MORGAN. *See* Meugant, St.

MORGHEN, RAFFAELLO (1758?–1833), engraver. Born in Portici, Italy, on June 19, he studied engraving under his father, Filippo, and in Rome under Volpato, and there assisted in engraving Raphael's paintings for the Vatican. He went to Florence, under the patronage of Grand Duke Ferdinand of Tuscany, in 1793, founded a school of engraving there, taught at its academy, and developed into a leading engraver. He was invited by Napoleon to Paris, where he received many honors and produced more than 250 plates. He died in Florence, Italy, on Apr. 8.

MORIARTY, DAVID (1812–1877), bishop. Born in Ardfert, Kerry, Ireland, he studied at Boulogne-sur-Mer, France, Maynooth, and Dunboyne. After ordination, he was appointed vice-president of the Irish College in Paris and, four years later, president of All Hallows in Dublin. He was appointed coadjutor of Kerry in 1854 and succeeded to the see in 1856. He died on Oct. 1.

MORICE, ADRIAN GABRIEL (1859–1938), missioner. Born in Mayenne, France, he was ordained, sent to Canada as a missioner, wrote a dictionary of the Dene or Carrier language and other Indian linguistic studies, and died in St. Boniface, Manitoba, on Apr. 21.

MORICUS, ST. (d. 1236). The fifth to join the Friars Minor, he is featured in St. Bonaventure's life of St. Francis of Assisi. F. D. Mar. 30.

MORIGI, MICHELANGELO. *See* Caravaggio, Michelangelo.

MORIN, JEAN (1591–1659), author. Born in Blois, France, he was raised a Calvinist, converted by Cardinal Duperron, and in 1618 joined the Paris Oratory. He was appointed superior of the oratory in Orléans, and in Angers, accompanied Queen Henrietta to England in 1625, returned to Paris in 1628, and remained there until his death on Feb. 28 except for a brief period in Rome in 1640 to work on reunion of the Greek Church with Rome. He was noted for his knowledge of the Bible and oriental languages, and wrote theological and historical studies.

MORIN, LEOPOLD FRÉDÉRIC GERMAIN (1861–1946), scholar. Born in Caen, France, on Nov. 6, he studied there and in Lisieux, became a Benedictine at Maredsous, Belgium, in 1881, and was ordained in 1886. He was interested in the Fathers of the Church, wrote widely for *Revue Bénédictine,* edited three volumes of *Anecdota Maredsolana,* two collections of unedited sermons by St. Augustine, and numerous works which he discovered: by Gottschalk, St. Clement of Rome, St. Jerome, Niceta of Remesiana, Arnobius the Younger, and others. His most significant edition was of the works of St. Caesarius of Arles; his best-known work, on which he labored for twenty years, has been translated as *The Ideal of the Monastic Life Found in the Apostolic Age.* He was honored by many learned societies and received honorary degrees from Oxford, Zurich, Budapest, and Fribourg. He lived at Munich from about 1920 to 1939, was transferred to Fribourg as war broke out, and died at Orselina-Locarno, Switzerland, on Feb. 13.

MORLEY, HENRY. *See* Parker, Henry.

MORLEY, SYLVANUS GRISWOLD (1883–1948). Born in Chester, Pennsylvania, on June 7, he studied at Pennsylvania Military College, became interested in archaeology, made field trips to the American Southwest in 1909, and moved to Santa Fe, New Mexico. He became a research fellow of the Carnegie Institution in 1915, worked in Mexico and Guatemala, wrote *Introduction to the Study of Maya Hieroglyphics, The Ancient Maya,* and other studies, and was an acknowledged authority on Maya and Yucatán cultures. He was a convert late in life, and died in Santa Fe on Sept. 2.

MORO, ANTONIO (1512?–1575?), painter. He was born in Utrecht, Holland, probably studied there under Jan van Scorel, became a member of St. Luke's Guild in Antwerp in 1547, and the following year received the patronage of Cardinal Granvelle of Arras. He traveled through Italy in 1550, rapidly rose in fame as a portraitist, and became court painter to the Hapsburgs. He painted the king, queen, and infanta of Portugal in Lisbon and Maximilian of Bohemia in Madrid, and returned to Rome in 1552. In 1553 he was in England, where he painted Mary Tudor and Elizabeth, returned to Holland in 1554, and became a property holder of means, using the name Morro van Dashorst, and executed several commissions for the duke of Alba. Other portraits include those of Jean d'Archel, Hubert Goltzius, his wife, Margaret of Parma, and the duke of Alba. He died in Antwerp, Flanders. He is also known as Antonis Mor or Moor.

MORO, IL. *See* Torbido, Francesco.

MOROC, ST. (9th century). He was abbot of Dunkeld, Scotland, and then bishop of Dunblane. F. D. Nov. 8.

MORONE, GIOVANNI (1509–1580), cardinal. He was born in Milan, Italy, on Jan. 25, son of the chancellor there. Pope Clement VII named him bishop of Modena in 1529, a move which led Cardinal Ippolito d'Este to occupy the see forcibly, on the grounds it had been promised to him; the dispute was not resolved until 1532. Morone served on papal missions to Milan in 1535, and the court of Ferdinand, king of the Romans, from 1536 to 1542, and represented the pope at Spiers in 1542. He was created a cardinal in that year, and with Cardinals Parisio and Pole was named to preside at the Council of Trent as the pope's representative. He was papal legate at Bologna in 1544 and was sent to the Diet of Augsburg in 1545. During the pontificate of Pope Paul IV, who was suspicious of his views, he was accused of heresy in 1557 and imprisoned until 1560, when Paul's successor, Pope Pius IV, reopened the case and declared him innocent. He presided over the final sessions of the Council of Trent, served on diplomatic missions to Genoa in 1575, at the Diet of Ratisbon in 1576, was made bishop of Ostia, directed the English

College in 1579–80, and with St. Ignatius helped found the German College in Rome. He died in Rome on Dec. 1.

MORONI, GAETANO (1802–1883). Born in Rome on Oct. 17, he was a barber's apprentice, served Mauro Cappellari as secretary before and after the latter was elected Pope Gregory XVI. He wrote more than 100,000 letters, built up a large personal library, and drew on his notes and books for his *Dizionario di erudizione storico-ecclesiastica.* He died in Rome on Nov. 3.

MORONI, GIOVANNI BATTISTA (1525?–1578), painter. Born in Bondo, Bergamo, Italy, he studied under Moretto da Brescia and became known for his forceful portraits and religious paintings. He died in Bergamo on Feb. 5. Among his outstanding works are *Portrait of a Lady, Portrait of a Man, The Tailor, Woman with Two Children, A Gentleman in Adoration before the Madonna.* His work was admired by Titian, and influenced that of Van Dyck.

MORRIS, JOHN (1826–1893). Born in Ootacamund, India, on July 4, he studied at Harrow, England, went to Trinity College in 1845 to become an Anglican minister, was converted to Catholicism in 1846, went to the English College in Rome, and was ordained. He served as canon in Northampton in 1850, vice-rector to Rome in 1853–56, and postulator for the English martyrs. He became Cardinal Wiseman's secretary, a Jesuit in 1867, rector of St. Ignatius, Malta, and held official posts in the English province of his Society. He wrote lives of Thomas à Becket and John Gerard, *Conditions of Catholics under James I,* and *Troubles of Our Catholic Forefathers.* He died in Wimbledon, England, on Oct. 22.

MORRIS, JOHN BAPTIST (1866–1946), bishop. Born in Hendersonville, Tennessee, on June 29, he studied at St. Mary's College, Kentucky, and the North American College, Rome, and was ordained in 1892. He became pastor of the Nashville cathedral, Bishop Rademacher's secretary and chancellor in 1894, vicar general of the see in 1900–6, and titular bishop of Acmonia and coadjutor of Little Rock, Arkansas, in 1906. He succeeded to that see in 1907, founded Little Rock College in 1908 and St. John's seminary in 1911, was made an assistant at the pontifical throne in 1931, and died on Oct. 22.

MORRIS, JOHN BRANDE (1812–1880). Born in Brentwood, Middlesex, England, on Sept. 4, he studied at Oxford and taught Hebrew at Exeter. He joined the Tractarian movement, became a convert in 1846, and was ordained in 1851. He taught at Prior Park, did parish work, and from 1880 until his death there on Apr. 9 was chaplain of the Misericordia nuns in Hammersmith, London. He translated selections from SS. Ephraem and John

Chrysostom before his conversion and wrote works of religious interest after.

MORRIS, MARTIN (1834-1909), jurist. Born in Washington, D.C., on Dec. 3, he studied at Georgetown, practiced law in Baltimore and Washington after 1863 in partnership with Richard T. Merrick and later with George E. Hamilton, and in 1871 was one of the founders of his university's law school. He died in Washington on Sept. 12.

MORRISROE, PATRICK (1869-1947), bishop. Born in Charlestown, Mayo, Ireland, he was ordained in 1894, taught English and the classics at Ballaghdereen College in 1895-96, and was dean at Maynooth from 1896 to 1911, when he was named bishop of Achonry, Sligo, Ireland.

MORSE, BL. HENRY (1595-1645), martyr. Born in Broome, Sussex, England, he studied at Cambridge and law at Gray's Inn, and became a convert at Douai. He was ordained in 1623, returned secretly to England in 1624, was imprisoned for three years, during which he made his novitiate under a Jesuit prisoner, and exiled to Flanders, where he served as a chaplain. From 1633 to 1641 he served in England again, as Cuthbert Claxton, worked actively during the plague of 1636-37, which he himself caught, and converted 560 according to statistics in the charges brought against him. He was again exiled, but returned in 1643, to be captured in Cumberland after eighteen months and hanged at Tyburn. The French, Spanish, and Portuguese ambassadors attended the execution as a sign of protest and redeemed his relics. He was beatified in 1929. F. D. Feb. 1. PHILIP CARAMAN, *Priest of the Plague: Henry Morse, S.J.* (New York, Farrar, 1957).

MORTON, JOHN (1420?-1500), cardinal. Born in Dorsetshire, England, he was educated at Oxford, ordained, and became an ecclesiastical lawyer in London. Cardinal Bourchier became his patron, and he obtained several lucrative preferments, all of which he lost after the Lancastrians' defeat in the Civil War in 1461. He was attainted and lived in exile at the court of Margaret of Anjou, returned to England in 1470, and after finally submitting to Edward IV had the attainder revoked, was appointed master of the rolls in 1473, archdeacon of Winchester and Chester in 1474 when he was sent on a mission to Hungary, and bishop of Ely in 1478. He was imprisoned during the reign of Richard III, escaped to Flanders, returned with Henry VII, whose principal counselor he became, in 1485, was made archbishop of Canterbury in 1486 and chancellor of England in 1487. He was created cardinal in 1493 and chancellor of Oxford in 1495. He was the source of information for the *History of Richard III* by Thomas More, who was a page in his household and who eulogized him in

Utopia. He died at Knowle, Kent, on Sept. 15.

MORTON, BL. ROBERT (d. 1588), martyr. Born in Bawtry, Yorkshire, England, he studied at Rheims and Rome and was ordained in 1587. Sent on the English mission, he was captured and hanged in London during the Elizabethan persecution for being a priest. He was beatified in 1929. F. D. Aug. 28.

MORWENNA, ST. (5th century). A holy woman of Cornwall, England, she is often confused with others of the same name or with such Irish saints as the sixth-century hermit Monnine. F. D. July 8.

MOSCHUS, JOHANNES (550?-619). He was probably born in Damascus, Syria, became a monk at St. Theodosius monastery in Jerusalem, stayed with a group of hermits in the Jordan Valley, then went to St. Sabas' laura near Bethlehem. About 578 he accompanied the future patriarch of Jerusalem, Sophronius, on a trip to Egypt, spent some ten years in the laura of Aeliatae on Mt. Sinai, visited monasteries near Jerusalem and the Dead Sea, went to Antioch in 604, returned to Egypt in 607, visited Cyprus, and in 614 went to Rome, where he died. He was surnamed "the Abstemious" and wrote *Pratum spirituale*, one of the earliest works on hagiography and a valuable source of information on early Eastern monastic practices.

MOSCICKI, MICHAEL (1898-1961), diplomat. Son of Ignace Moscicki, president of Poland in 1926-39, he became a research biologist at Kiev, Russia, served in the Polish diplomatic service in 1920-39 as plenipotentiary to Vienna, Tokyo, and Brussels, came to the United States in 1939 on the outbreak of World War II, and served as Free Poland's delegate to the Captive European Nations Assembly. He died in New York City on Mar. 4.

MOSES, ST. (d. 250?), martyr. He was slain in Africa, probably during the Decian persecution. F. D. Dec. 18.

MOSES, ST. (d. 251), martyr. A Roman priest, noted for his stand against Novatianism, he was one of the victims of Decius' persecution. He and St. Cyprian exchanged letters. F. D. Nov. 25.

MOSES, ST. (d. 372?), bishop. An Arab who lived in the area between Syria and Egypt, he was asked by Mavia, queen of the Saracens, who had been defeated by Rome, to preach to her people as a roving bishop. He is mentioned by Theodoret. F. D. Feb. 7.

MOSES, ST. (d. 400?). An Abyssinian slave of an Egyptian official, he was notoriously evil and widely known as a troublemaker. When he killed another slave, he fled from his home and formed a gang which terrorized the region for fifteen years. Taking flight into the desert of Skete, he was converted by the monks at Petra, joined them as a hermit, practiced extraordinary mortification, and became renowned for his supernatural gifts. When an old man he was ordained by the patriarch of Alexandria. He was sixty-five when he and six other monks were murdered by a roving band. F. D. Aug. 28.

MOSES OF CHORENE (5th century), author. A native of Choren or Chorni, Armenia, he studied in Edessa, Constantinople, Alexandria, Athens, and Rome, may have been a bishop, and probably aided Mesrop in an Armenian translation of the Bible.

MOSEUS, ST. (d. 250), martyr. *See* Ammonius, St.

MOTOLINIA, TORIBIO. *See* Paredes, Toribio.

MOUCHY, ANTOINE DE (1494–1574), theologian. Born in Ressons-sur-Matz, Picardy, he was appointed rector of the University of Paris in 1539, became professor at the Sorbonne, canon of Noyon, and was active against the Calvinists. He was at the Council of Trent in 1562 and the Synod of Rheims in 1564, edited a *Corpus juris canonici*, and wrote in defense of the mass. He died in Paris on May 8.

MOUFANG, FRANZ CHRISTOPH IGNAZ (1817–1890), theologian. He was born in Mainz, Germany, on Feb. 17, studied at Bonn and Munich and the Mainz seminary, and was ordained in 1839. After several pastoral positions he taught in Mainz in 1845, became regent and professor of the Mainz seminary in 1851, a canon in 1854, and aided in the preparatory work of the Vatican Council in 1868. He opposed the Kulturkampf, occupied a seat in the Hessian *Landtag* as his bishop's representative after 1863, and in 1871 became a member of the German *Reichstag*. He was elected administrator of the Mainz diocese in 1877 when the theological school of the seminary was closed, was made a domestic prelate in 1886, and resumed his post as regent when the theological school was reopened in 1887. He wrote theological treatises, reorganized and published the *Katholik*, which he co-edited from 1851 until his death in Mainz on Feb. 27, and wrote on the history of the catechism in Germany.

MOVEAN, ST. (5th century). A disciple of St. Patrick, he was abbot of Innis-Coosery, Down, Ireland; he may have been a hermit in Perthshire at the time of his death. F. D. July 22.

MOVERS, FRANZ KARL (1806–1856), scholar. Born in Koesfeld, Westphalia, Germany, on July 17, he studied at Münster and Bonn, specialized in oriental languages, and was ordained in 1829. He became pastor at Berkum in 1833 and taught exegesis at Breslau, Germany, from 1839 until his death on Sept. 28. He published exegetical theses and *Die Phönizier*, on the religion, history, and antiquities of the Phoenicians.

MOY DE SONS, KARL ERNST VON

(1799–1867), jurist. Born in Munich, Germany, on Aug. 10, he became an attorney in 1830, professor of law at Würtzburg in 1833, and at Munich in 1837. He was dropped from the faculty when he protested against Ludwig II's affair with Lola Montez, became a court official in Neuburg, and in 1851 professor of German law at Innsbruck, a position he retained until his retirement in 1863. He was president of the German Catholic General Assembly in 1864, but supported the concordat. He wrote histories of the Church in Germany, the papacy, matrimonial impediments, and Bavaria, and edited the first four volumes of *Archiv für katholisches Kirchenrecht* for Austria and Germany. He died in Innsbruck, Austria, on Aug. 1.

MOYA Y CONTRERAS, PEDRO DE (1520?–1591). Born in Cordova, Spain, he took his doctorate in canon law at Salamanca, became inquisitor at Saragossa and Murcia, and established the Inquisition in Mexico in 1571. He became archbishop of Mexico in 1573, viceroy of New Spain in 1584–85, presided at the third Provincial Council of Mexico in 1585, returned to Spain, and in 1591 became president of the Council of the Indies.

MOYE, VEN. JOHN MARTIN (1730–1793), founder. Born in Cutting, Lorraine, on Jan. 27, he studied at Pont-à-Mousson and Strassburg and the Metz seminary and was ordained in 1754. Appointed vicar of Metz, he directed a number of women in the establishment of schools for rural children, a group which in 1767 became the Sisters of Divine Providence. He was then appointed rector of the minor seminary of St. Dié, joined the Society of Foreign Missions at Paris in 1769, and went to China in 1773. In 1782 he founded the Christian Virgins, who followed the rule of the Sisters of Divine Providence and worked as catechists and nurses for the next 150 years in China. He returned to France in 1784 in ill health, directed the sisters, preached widely in Alsace and Lorraine, and went into exile at Trier in 1791 when the French Revolution broke out. After the French captured the city, he and the sisters worked with victims of typhoid, of which he died on May 4. He was declared Venerable by Pope Leo XIII in 1891.

MOYLAN, FRANCIS (1739–1815), bishop. He was born in Cork, Ireland, brother of Stephen, educated in Paris, received his doctorate in theology at Toulouse, and was ordained in 1761. After a period of pastoral work in Paris he returned to Cork as a pastor, was appointed bishop of Kerry in 1775, and transferred to Cork in 1787, where he remained until his death. He helped establish Maynooth College and was one of its first trustees.

MOYLAN, STEPHEN (1734–1811), general. Born in Cork, Ireland, brother of Francis, he was educated in Paris, engaged in the shipping business in Lisbon from 1765 to 1768, emigrated to the United States, and settled in Philadelphia. In 1771 he helped found the Friendly Sons of St. Patrick there and became its first president. He joined the Continental Army in 1775, became Washington's aide-de-camp and secretary in 1776, and was appointed quartermaster general. He resigned to raise a troop of cavalry, served with distinction, and was brevetted brigadier general in 1783. He became register and recorder of Chester County, Pennsylvania, in 1792, and was appointed state commissioner of loans in 1793. He died in Philadelphia on Apr. 13.

MOZART, JOHANN CHRYSOSTOM WOLFGANG AMADEUS (1756–1791), composer. Born in Salzburg, Austria, on Jan. 27, son of Leopold Mozart, musician and the court composer, he displayed his musical genius as a child when he began playing the piano at three and composing at four. He was taught music by his father, who took him and his sister Maria on a concert tour when he was seven. He wrote his first oratorio at eleven, had his first opera, *La finta semplice*, produced in Vienna in 1768, and when twelve was appointed concertmaster to the archbishop of Salzburg. He went on a triumphant tour of Italy in 1769–70, performed his famous feat of scoring Allegri's *Miserere* after hearing it twice in Rome, produced his opera *Mitridate* in Milan, was created Knight of the Golden Spur by the pope, and was acclaimed as the greatest living musical genius. He returned to Salzburg, where he remained, except for occasional trips, until 1777. He then went to Vienna, where he produced operas, symphonies, concerts, concertos, and quartets with astonishing rapidity. His musical fame grew, but his fortunes languished; the last years of his life were poverty-stricken; and when he died in Vienna on Dec. 5 he was buried in a pauper's grave. Among his outstanding operas are *The Marriage of Figaro* (1786), *Don Giovanni* (1787), *Così fan tutte* (1790), and *The Magic Flute* (1791). He also wrote forty-one symphonies, thirty string quartets, fifteen masses, as well as sonatas and concertos.

MOZZI, LUIGI (1746–1813). Born in Bergamo, Italy, on May 26, he became a Jesuit in 1763, a canon in Bergamo when the Society was suppressed in 1773, and examiner of candidates for the priesthood. He vigorously opposed Jansenism, was made an apostolic missionary by Pope Pius VI, rejoined the Jesuits when they were restored in Naples in 1804, and died near Milan, Italy, on June 24. He wrote theological works and translated others from French and English.

MRAK, IGNATIUS (1818–1901), bishop. Born in Hotovle, Austria, on Oct. 17, he studied at the Laibach seminary, was ordained in 1837, spent two years as tutor in Legnano, Italy, and in 1840 returned to Laibach, where he occupied various assistant positions until he emigrated to the United States in 1845. He worked on Indian missions in Michigan, was appointed vicar general, and in 1868 became 2nd bishop of Marquette. Ill health caused him to resign in 1879, he was made titular bishop of Antinoe, and when he recovered his health returned to the Indian missions in Michigan. He retired in 1899 and spent the rest of his life as chaplain at St. Mary's hospital in Marquette, Michigan, where he died on Jan. 2.

MUCHAR, ALBERT ANTON VON (1781–1849), historian. Born in Linez, Tyrol, on Nov. 22, he studied in Graz, joined the Benedictines in 1808, and was ordained. He studied oriental languages, became keeper of the archives in 1831, professor of oriental languages and the Bible at his monastery's seminary and in 1825 of philology at Graz, and took up the study of Austrian history, on which he wrote widely. He was elected to the Vienna Academy of Sciences in 1829, and helped found the Historical Society of Inner Austria. He died in Graz, Austria, on June 6.

MUCIUS, ST. (d. 250), martyr. *See* Parmenius, St.

MUCIUS, ST. (d. 304), martyr. A Roman, he was a priest at Constantinople, where he was beheaded during the persecution of Diocletian. F. D. May 13.

MUCIUS, ST. (d. 312), martyr. *See* Silvanus, St.

MÜHLBACHER, ENGELBERT (1843–1903), historian. Born in Gresten, Austria, on Oct. 4, he joined the Austin canons in 1862, was ordained in 1867, received his doctorate in theology from Innsbruck in 1874, and studied history at Vienna. He became a lecturer at Innsbruck in 1878, professor at Vienna in 1881, and took over the management of the *Regesta imperii* in 1895. He arranged the Austrian state archives and was a member of the Academy of Sciences. In 1892 he began editing Carlovingian documents for *Monumenta Germaniae Historica*, published *Deutsche Geschichte unter den Karolingern* (1896), and from 1897 edited *Mitteilungen des Instituts für österreichische Geschichtsforschung*. He died in Vienna on July 17.

MUIRCHU, ST. (7th century). An Irishman, he wrote biographies of SS. Brigid and Patrick. F. D. June 8.

MULDOON, PETER JAMES (1863–1927), bishop. Born in Columbia, California, on Oct. 10, he studied at St. Mary's in Kentucky and St. Mary's seminary, Baltimore, and was ordained in Brooklyn in 1886. He engaged in parish work in Chicago, was chancellor of the archdiocese and the archbishop's secretary in 1888–95, and pastor of St. Charles Borromeo church there for the next thirteen years. He was consecrated titular bishop of Tamasus and auxiliary bishop of Chicago in 1901, and in 1908 was appointed first bishop of Rockford, Illinois. He died in Rockford on Oct. 8.

MULHALL, MICHAEL GEORGE (1829–1900), statistician. Born in Dublin on Sept. 29, he studied at the Irish College in Rome, established the first English paper, the *Standard*, in South America at Buenos Aires in 1861, and had the first English book, *Handbook of the River Plate*, printed in Argentina in 1869. He died in Dublin on Dec. 13. He wrote numerous books on economics, notably *Dictionary of Statistics*. His wife, Marion McMorrough Mulhall, also an economist, completed several of his works and published many of her own.

MULHOLLAND, ST. CLAIR AUGUSTINE (1839–1910), general. Born in Lisburn, Antrim, Ireland, on Apr. 1, he was brought to the United States as a boy, served with distinction in the Civil War, was brevetted major general in 1864, and received the Congressional Medal of Honor. He was appointed chief of police of Philadelphia in 1868, and federal pension agent, and became an authority on penology. He died in Philadelphia on Feb. 17.

MULLANPHY, JOHN (1758–1833). Born near Enniskillen, Fermanagh, Ireland, he went to France in 1778, served in the Irish Brigade, returned to Ireland at the outbreak of the French Revolution, and in 1792 emigrated to the United States. After several years in Philadelphia, Baltimore, and Frankfort, Kentucky, he settled in St. Louis in 1804, where he became a real-estate investor. He fought in the War of 1812 and served under Andrew Jackson at New Orleans, made a fortune in cotton speculation during and after the war, and spent the last years of his life spending it for charitable purposes and as contributions to building churches, convents, and hospitals. He died in St. Louis on Aug. 29.

MULLANY, PATRICK FRANCIS (1847–1893), educator. Born near Killenaule, Ireland, on June 29, he was educated in Deerfield, Massachusetts, and Utica, New York. He became a Christian Brother in 1862, taking the name Azarias, taught at Albany, New York City, and Philadelphia, and at Rock Hill College, Maryland, where he was president from 1870 to 1886. His most important writings include *An Essay Contributing to a Philosophy of Literature* (1874), *Aristotle and the Christian Church* (1888), and *Phases of Thought and Criticism* (1892). Three volumes of essays on education and philosophy, delivered as lectures or published in journals, appeared posthumously. He died in Plattsburg, New York, on Aug. 20.

MULLEN, TOBIAS (1818–1900), bishop. Born in Tyrone, Ireland, on Mar. 4, he studied at Maynooth, went on the American mission in 1843, and was ordained in Pittsburgh in 1844. He did pastoral work there until he was consecrated bishop of Erie, Pennsylvania, in 1868. He founded the weekly, *Lake Shore Visitor*, which he also edited, inaugurated a wide building program, with particular attention paid to the needs of immigrants in his see, consecrated St. Peter's cathedral in 1893, resigned in 1899 and was appointed titular bishop of Germanicopolis, and died in Erie on Apr. 22.

MÜLLER, ADAM HEINRICH (1779–1829), economist. Born in Berlin, on June 30, he studied law at Göttingen, became referendary in Berlin, and in 1805 became a convert. He became co-editor of a periodical, *Phoebus*, in 1808, imperial commissioner in the Tyrol in 1813, and later governmental counselor. He participated in the Council of Vienna in 1815, and became Austrian consul general for Saxony in Leipzig, where he edited several periodicals. He was made a noble in 1826 as Ritter von Nittersdorf and appointed imperial counselor in 1827. He was an opponent of Liberalism, believed the reorganization of political institutions should be modeled on mediaeval feudalism, and was a vigorous opponent of Adam Smith and his economic individualism and theory of free trade. He wrote widely on economics and political theory and died in Vienna on Jan. 17.

MÜLLER, JOHANN (1436–1476), astronomer. Born in Königsberg, Germany, on June 6, he studied at Leipzig, went to Vienna in 1450 to study under the famous astronomer George of Peurbach, and became a lecturer at the university. He became associated with Peurbach and with him made numerous astronomical and mathematical studies. In 1461 he accompanied his patron, Cardinal Bessarion, to Italy, learned Greek to complete Peurbach's *Epitome* on Ptolemy's *Almagest*, continued his astronomical researches, collected Greek manuscripts, computed a calendar, and eclipses and dates of Easter for the next thirty years, and incurred the enmity of George of Trebizond when he revealed the errors of his commentaries on Ptolemy and Theon. In 1468 he went to Budapest as custodian of King Matthias Corvinus' library, but left in 1471 to settle in Nuremberg, where Bernhard Walther became his patron, pupil, and associate in founding an observatory and establishing a printing office. They published Peurbach's *Theoriae planetarum novae* and Müller's *Calendarium novum* and *Ephemerides*, in which he calculated the positions of the sun, moon, and planets and the eclipses from 1475 to 1506 (Columbus used it to reach America and predict the eclipse of Feb. 29, 1504). He was called to Rome by Pope Sixtus

IV in 1472 to assist in reforming the calendar, was appointed bishop of Ratisbon, though he probably never occupied his chair, and died in Rome on July 6. He invented many improved mathematical and astronomical instruments, introduced algebra into Germany, and advanced the knowledge of trigonometry; his observations of the great comet of 1472 (later named Halley's) are the foundation of the modern study of comets. He was known as Johannes de Monterigo, Johannes Germanus or Francus, and Regiomontanus.

MÜLLER, JOHANN (1801-1858), physiologist. Born in Coblentz, Germany, on July 14, he studied at Bonn, where he attracted attention by his prize-winning *De respiratione foetus*, and received his medical degree in 1822. He studied medicine for two years at Berlin and began teaching at Bonn in 1824. He was appointed professor of medicine at Berlin in 1832, edited *Archives of Anatomy and Physiology* from 1834 to 1840, and became rector of the university in 1847. He made great medical advances by his studies in reflex action, optical illusion, blood plasma, cartilage composition, the mechanism of sight and sound, and formulated the law of specific nerve energies. His name is given to the ducts of the preliminary fetal kidney. His *Handbuch der Physiologie des Menschen* helped to establish his fame as "father of modern physiology." He died in Berlin on Apr. 28.

MÜLLER, KARL (1818-1893), painter. Born in Darmstadt, Germany, on Oct. 29, he studied art in Italy from 1839 to 1843 after receiving a commission to do the frescoes of the Fürstenburg church in Remagen, and became a professor at Düsseldorf and a member of a school of German religious painters called "the Nazarenes." His *Crowning, Birth, Annunciation,* and *Visitation of Mary* in the Fürstenburg church are among his best paintings. He also is known for his altarpiece, *Christ with the Disciples at Emmaus,* in Bonn, and *Magnificat, Holy Family,* and *Immaculate Conception.* He died in Darmstadt on Oct. 29.

MULLOCK, JOHN T. (1807-1869), bishop. Born in Limerick, Ireland, he joined the Franciscans, studied at St. Bonaventure's, Seville, and St. Isidore's, Rome, where he was ordained in 1830. He was sent to Ireland for pastoral work, was appointed coadjutor bishop of St. John's, Newfoundland, in 1847, and succeeded to the see in 1850. He died there on Mar. 26. Among his writings are a life of St. Alphonsus Maria Liguori, a history of the Irish Franciscan province, and several translations.

MUMFORD, THOMAS. *See* Downes, Thomas.

MUMMOLUS, ST. (d. 678?). He was second abbot of the Benedictine monastery of Fleury, France. F. D. Aug. 8.

MUMMOLUS, ST. (d. 690?). An Irishman, he succeeded St. Fursey as abbot of Lagny, France. F. D. Nov. 18.

MUN, ST. (5th century), bishop. Called a nephew of St. Patrick, he was consecrated bishop of Longford, Ireland, by the latter, and became a hermit in his old age. F. D. Feb. 6.

MUN, ADRIEN ALBERT MARIE DE (1841-1914), sociologist. Born in Lumigny, France, on Feb. 23, he graduated from St. Cyr, served with the cavalry in Algeria and in the Franco-Prussian War, and was decorated. After witnessing in Paris the horrors under the commune, he devoted himself to social work. He was co-founder of Cercles catholiques d'ouvriers, to educate and legislate for the laboring classes, and published a journal. He resigned his commission in the army in 1875, was elected to the chamber of deputies, and was active in promoting legislation for old-age pensions, health insurance, shorter working hours, the banning of child labor, and limitations on the use of female labor. He was elected to the French Academy in 1897, and became in 1901 vice-president of the Popular Liberal party, a major force against socialism and anti-Catholicism. He died in Bordeaux, France, on Oct. 6.

MÜNCH-BELLINGHAUSEN, ELIGIUS FRANZ JOSEPH VON (1806-1871), dramatist. Born in Cracow, Poland, on Apr. 2, he studied at the Melk seminary and Vienna, and had his first drama, *Griseldis,* produced in 1835. He continued to write dramas, but also served as councilor in 1840, keeper of the court library in 1844, a member of parliament in 1861, and superintendent of the court theaters in 1867-70. Among his best-known dramas are *Der Sohn der Wildnis, Der Fechter von Ravenna,* and a translation of Shakespeare's *Coriolanus;* he also wrote short stories and poetry. He wrote under the pseudonym, Friedrich Halm. He died in Vienna on May 22.

MUNCHIN, ST. Called "the Wise," he is believed to have settled in Limerick, Ireland, and even to have become a bishop there, where he is venerated as patron. A Munchin did come there from Clare in the seventh century. F. D. Jan. 2.

MUNDELEIN, GEORGE WILLIAM (1872-1939), cardinal. Born in New York City on July 2, he studied at Manhattan College, St. Vincent seminary, Latrobe, Pennsylvania, and the Propaganda, Rome, where he was ordained in 1895. He became secretary to Bishop McDonnell of Brooklyn, served as chancellor of the diocese in 1897-1909, was made a domestic prelate in 1906, and auxiliary bishop of Brooklyn and titular bishop of Loryma in 1909. He was appointed archbishop of Chicago in 1915, greatly expanded the number of churches, schools, hospitals, and other institutions, founded the Quigley preparatory seminary, St.

Mary of the Lake seminary, and the Associated Catholic Charities (in 1917), and was created a cardinal in 1924. He was a friend of the needy and the working man, a vigorous supporter of social reform, a friend and adviser of President Franklin D. Roosevelt, and early opponent of nazism. He died in Chicago on Oct. 2.

MUNDEN, BL. JOHN (d. 1584), martyr. Born in Coltley, England, he was educated at Winchester and Oxford, became a teacher in Dorsetshire after he lost his fellowship for religious reasons, went to Rome, and was ordained at Rheims in 1582. Captured on his return to England and imprisoned in the Tower for a year, he was hanged at Tyburn on the charge of being a priest. F. D. Feb. 12.

MUNDINUS. See Mondino dei Lucci.

MUNDUS, ST. (d. 962?). He directed several monastic settlements in Scotland, including that at Carlyle. F. D. Apr. 15.

MUNDWILER, FINTAN (1835–1898). Born in Dietikon, Switzerland, on July 12, he studied at Einsiedeln, joined the Benedictines there in 1854, and was ordained in 1859. The following year he was sent to teach at the new St. Meinrad monastery in Indiana, engaged in missionary work in the area, was appointed prior of St. Meinrad's when it was made an abbey in 1869, and elected abbot in 1880. He established priories in Arkansas, Louisiana, and North Dakota and became first president of the Helvetico-American Congregation of Benedictines. He died at St. Meinrad's on Feb. 14.

MUNGO. See Kentigern, St.

MUNTANER, RAMON (1265–1336), historian. Born in Perelada, Catalonia, Spain, he was a soldier of fortune and minstrel for thirty years, serving with Roger de Flor in Sicily in 1300, as well as in Asia Minor. He was governor of Gallipoli and of Jerba. On his return to Spain he wrote a history of the princes of Aragon from James the Conqueror to Alfonso IV.

MÜNTZ, ENGÈNE (1845–1902), scholar. Born in Soulz-sous-Forêts, Alsace, on June 11, he studied law but abandoned it for the study of the history of art at L'École Française in Rome. He joined the faculty of L'École des Beaux-Arts in 1878, was professor of aesthetics from 1885 to 1892, and entered the Institute in 1893. Among his outstanding works are Les arts à la cour des papes, Précurseurs de la renaissance, Raphaël, Historie de l'art en Italie pendant la renaissance, Léonard de Vinci, Le Palais des papes à Avignon, and La Bibliotheque du Vatican. He died in Paris on Nov. 2.

MURA MC FEREDACH, ST. (d. 645?). Born in Donegal, Ireland, he was named abbot of the monastery of Fahan, Derry, Ireland, by St. Columba. F. D. Mar. 12.

MURATORI, LUIGI ANTONIO (1672–1760), scholar. Born in Vignola, near Modena,

Italy, he studied at its university and was ordained in 1694. He became connected with the Ambrosian Library in Milan in 1694 and was librarian and archivist of the Modena Library until his death on Jan. 23. He supported the Estes in their conflict with the pope over the ownership of Comachio in 1708 and became provost of St. Maria della Pomposa in 1716. His chief works include the four-volume Anecdota latina ex ambrosianae bibliothecae codicibus (1697–98, 1713), followed by Anecdota graeca; the twenty-eight-volume Rerum italicarum scriptores (1723–51); the six-volume Antiquitates italicae medii aevi (1738–42), which contained the oldest known list of New Testament books, written in the eighth century from a second-century list; the twelve-volume Annali d'Italia (1744–49); and several volumes of inscriptions. He also wrote treatises on philosophy, law, politics, and religion, particularly De ingeniorum moderatione in religionis negotio. Several of his religious works were vigorously challenged. He died in Modena, Italy, on Jan. 23.

MURDOCH, JOHN (1796–1865), bishop. He was second vicar apostolic of Scotland, with headquarters in Glasgow, and was consecrated titular bishop of Castabala.

MUREDACH, ST. (6th century?), bishop. Of the royal house of King Laoghaire, he is reputed to have been first bishop of Killala, Ireland, though he probably lived at a later date. He also is said to have died as a hermit on the island of Inismurray and is sometimes known as Murtagh. F. D. Aug. 12.

MURET, MARC ANTOINE (1526–1585). Born in Muret, Limousin, France, he studied at Poitiers, and taught there and at Bordeaux and Paris. Accused of heresy, he went to Toulouse about 1552, Lombardy, and in 1555 to Venice, where he taught. He entered the service of Cardinal Ippolito d'Este, accompanied him to Paris and in 1563 to Rome, where he spent the rest of his life teaching the classics. In 1566 he also became professor of civil law, was ordained in 1576, and died in Rome. He edited Horace, Terence, Cicero, Catullus, Tibullus, and Propertius, and wrote Variae lectiones, which Lambinus accused him of plagiarizing, and a commentary on Ronsard's Amours.

MURILLO, BARTOLOMÉ ESTEBAN (1617–1682), painter. Born in Seville, Spain, on Dec. 31, he was orphaned at ten and raised by his uncle, Juan Lagares. He studied painting under Juan del Castillo, painted cheap religious paintings for the Seville fair, went to Cadiz in 1640, and the next year to Madrid where Velásquez, the king's painter, became his patron. He returned to Seville in 1644, and the following year began the series of eleven portraits (including Death of St. Clare,

St. Francis of Assisi Supporting the Body of Christ) for the Franciscan monastery there, which established him as a painter. In 1660 he helped found the Academy of Seville and became its president. In 1681, while painting the Marriage of St. Catherine altarpiece in the Capuchin church in Cadiz, he fell from a scaffolding and died on Apr. 5 in Seville from the injuries. Murillo devoted himself almost exclusively to religious subjects. His paintings of the early period, known as those of the cold (frio) style, include the Franciscan sketches. In his warm (calido) style were the works of 1652–56, including Vision of St. Anthony and SS. Leander and Isidore. His Founding of Santa Maria Maggiore, Seville, began his work in estilo vaporoso (misty blendings of light and shade); in this manner are his more than fifteen Immaculate Conceptions. Other work includes his favorite Charity of Thomas of Villanova; the eight pictures he executed (1670–74) for the Caridad church of St. George (Miracle of the Loaves and Fishes, Return of the Prodigal, St. Peter Released from Prison); the twenty paintings (1676) for the Capuchin seminary, Seville; St. John of God, Holy Family, St. John on Patmos, Vision of St. Anthony of Padua, and Pouilleux, one of his few genre paintings; and an altarpiece on St. Catherine for the Capuchin church, Cadiz. His work is characterized by softness, splendor and harmony of color, tender and spiritual feeling, and idealism.

MURIS, JOHANNES DE (13th century). He was master of mathematics at Oxford, and wrote Speculum musicae between 1340 and 1350, the most scholarly account of musical theory, consonance, dissonance, modes, and intervals of his time.

MURIS, JULIANUS DE (14th century). He taught at the Sorbonne in Paris in 1321 and was its rector in 1350. He advocated counterpoint in his writings on musical theory, which include Musica practica, musica speculativa, Ars contrapuncti, and Libellus practicae centus mensurabilis.

MURITTA, ST. (d. 500?), martyr. See Eugenius, St.

MURLACH. See Moloc, St.

MURMELLIUS, JOHANNES (1480?–1517), scholar. Born in Roermond, Holland, he studied at Deventer, Cologne, and Münster, introduced the study of Greek in the Netherlands, and published poems and textbooks. He wrote a strong defense of the scholar Reuchlin.

MURNER, THOMAS (1475–1537), satirist. Born in Oberehnheim, Alsace, on Dec. 24, he joined the Franciscans when sixteen, was ordained, and during the following decades studied and taught at Paris, Cracow, Freiburg, where he received his doctorate in theology in 1506, and Basle, where he received his doctorate in law in 1518. He was at first sympathetic to Luther, when he believed he was attempting to reform the evils in the Church, but became one of his most violent opponents. He translated Henry VIII's book on the sacraments into German in 1522, visited England in 1523, and on his return to Strassburg was obliged to flee to Lucerne, where he became leader of the opposition to Zwingli. His controversial writings, nearly sixty in number, were marked by bitter, often coarse, wit, but were widely popular. After further wanderings he settled in Oberehnheim, where he served as pastor and died.

MURPHY, DENIS (1833–1896), historian. Born in Newmarket, Cork, Ireland, he studied in England, Germany, and Spain, became a Jesuit at sixteen, and taught at Clongowes Wood and University College, Dublin. He wrote an authoritative study of Cromwell in Ireland (1883), edited O'Clery's Life of Hugh Roe O'Donnell (1893) with a translation, and studies of Irish abbeys. He edited the Kildare Archaeological Journal and other such publications, published a textbook of Irish history, served as vice-president of the Royal Irish Academy, and received an honorary degree from the Royal University. He was completing a manuscript of the Irish martyrs from the reign of Henry VIII when he died in Dublin on May 18.

MURPHY, EDWARD (d. 1729), archbishop. Bishop of Kildare, Ireland, he was transferred to Dublin as archbishop in 1724, but was forced to live in refuge outside the city because of the stringent penal laws.

MURPHY, FRANCIS PARNELL (1877–1958), governor. Born in Winchester, New Hampshire, on Aug. 16, he studied at Dartmouth, became an executive in a shoe company, president of Radio Voice of New Hampshire, a member of the state legislature, and was twice governor of his state, the first Catholic to be elected to that office, in 1937–41. He received honorary degrees from Boston College and New Hampshire. He died in Nashua, New Hampshire, on Dec. 19.

MURPHY, FRANK (1890–1949), jurist. Born in Harbor Beach, Michigan, on Apr. 13, he studied at Michigan, did graduate work in law in London and Dublin, served as an army captain in World War I, then opened his law office in Detroit. There he became an assistant United States district attorney, municipal judge, and mayor, gaining a national reputation by his handling of a major and crippling industrial strike. He was governor general of the Philippines in 1933 and appointed first high commissioner there in 1935, a ten-year term; he resigned in 1937 to run for governor of Michigan at the request of Franklin D. Roosevelt and won a two-year term which was troubled by industrial unrest and the sit-down strikes. In 1939–40 he was attorney general in President Roosevelt's cabinet and was active in anti-trust actions against capital and labor monopolies. In 1940 he was appointed to the Supreme Court, where he was known as a member of the liberal faction. He died in Detroit on July 19.

MURPHY, FREDERICK E. (1872–1940), journalist. Born in Troy, Wisconsin, on Dec. 5, he graduated from Notre Dame in 1893, joined the staff of the *Minneapolis Tribune*, and became interested in writing on farm problems. A retirement to his own farm, caused by ill health in 1918, intensified his concern and, on his return to the *Tribune* as president and publisher in 1921, he became a leading spokesman for the western farmer. By the time of the depression of the 1930s he was recognized as a leading authority on American agriculture. He was a delegate to the World Wheat Conference in 1933, one of the permanent American representatives on the International Wheat Advisory Committee, and active as president of several firms. He died in New York City on Feb. 14.

MURPHY, HENRY V. (1888–1960), architect. A native of Hore Heads, New York, he graduated from the Pratt Institute School of Architecture, Brooklyn, and became a leading ecclesiastical architect, designing schools, churches and public buildings in the eastern United States. Among his achievements were St. John's University and Archbishop Molloy High School in Jamaica, New York. He died in Brooklyn on May 17.

MURPHY, JOHN BENJAMIN (1857–1916), surgeon. Born near Appleton, Wisconsin, on Dec. 21, he took his degree at Rush Medical College, Chicago, in 1879, served in that city, studied in Europe, and returned to revolutionize intestinal surgery. He did pioneer work with the gall bladder, developed a method of repairing injured blood vessels, adapted an Italian scheme for relaxing tubercular lungs, and experimented in joint diseases. He taught at Rush and Northwestern from 1884 to 1908 and was consulting surgeon in many Chicago hospitals. Notes on his clinical consultations were published and widely circulated. He served as president of the American Medical Association and other organizations, received the Laetare Medal from Notre Dame University in 1902, was given honorary degrees by Illinois and Sheffield, and was honored by England, France, Germany, and by Pope Benedict XV. He died on Mackinack Island, Michigan, on Aug. 11.

MURPHY, THOMAS EDWARD (1856–1933), educator. Born in New York City on Jan. 27, he studied at St. Francis Xavier, became a Jesuit in 1875, studied in Quebec and

at Woodstock, and was ordained in 1890. He was vice-president of Georgetown in 1891–93, president of St. Francis Xavier to 1900, stationed at Holy Cross to 1906, and its president to 1911. He then became rector of St. Ignatius' church, Brooklyn, where he died on Dec. 14.

MURPHY, WILLIAM FRANCIS (1885–1950), bishop. Born in Kalamazoo, Michigan, on May 11, he studied at St. Jerome and Assumption colleges, Ontario, Canada, and the Propaganda and Apollinaris in Rome, and was ordained in 1908. After further study in Rome he engaged in parish work in Ann Arbor, Marine City, and at the Detroit cathedral, and was founding pastor of St. David's in Detroit in 1921–38. He was made a domestic prelate in 1938, and was appointed first bishop of Saginaw, Michigan, in 1938. He died on Feb. 7.

MURRAY, DANIEL (1768–1852), archbishop. Born in Sheepwalk, Wicklow, Ireland, he studied in Dublin and at Salamanca, and was ordained in 1790. He was curate in Dublin and Arklow, from where he escaped with his life in the rebellion of 1798 to Dublin. In 1809 he was appointed coadjutor bishop of Dublin, served as president of Maynooth for a year, and in 1823 succeeded to the see of Dublin. He supported the Catholic Association and the Queen's colleges, but accepted Rome's decision against the latter's educational policies. He died in Dublin.

MURRAY, GILBERT (1866–1957), scholar. Born in Sydney, Australia, on Jan. 2, he studied in London and at Oxford, and in 1889 began to teach Greek at Glasgow. He published *History of Ancient Greek Literature* in 1897, and returned to Oxford to teach Greek there from 1899 until his retirement in 1936. He married Lady Mary Howard in 1889, issued editions of Euripides, and later made translations of all the Greek dramatists, many of which saw stage production. He also published *The Rise of the Greek Epic* (1907), *Four* (later titled *Five*) *Stages of Greek Religion* (1913); *Religio Grammatici* (1918), *Greek Studies* (1947), and *Hellenism and the Modern World* (1953). He was active in propaganda work during both world wars and was given the Order of Merit in 1941. He returned to the Church in which he had been baptized as a child a few weeks before his death in Oxford, England, on May 20.

MURRAY, JOHN GREGORY (1877–1956), archbishop. Born in Waterbury, Connecticut, on Feb. 26. he studied at Holy Cross, the North American College, Rome, and Louvain, where he was ordained in 1900. He taught Greek and Latin at St. Thomas seminary, Hartford, became chancellor of the diocese in 1903, and in 1919 was appointed titular bishop of Flavias and auxiliary of Hartford. He was transferred to Portland, Maine, in 1925, and in 1931 to St. Paul as archbishop. He died in St. Paul, Minnesota, on Oct. 11.

MURRAY, JOHN HUBERT PLUNKETT (1861–1940), governor. Born in Sydney, Australia, on Dec. 29, to Sir Terence and Agnes Edwards, he was educated there and at Brighton and Oxford, was called to the bar in 1886, and returned to Australia to practice as crown prosecutor and district court judge (1901–2). He became a convert, was commander of an infantry unit during the Boer War, and retired as a lieutenant colonel. In 1907 he was acting administrator of Papua, where he was chief justice until his death, and lieutenant governor from 1908 also to 1940. The territory was taken over by Australia in 1908, and Murray made an international reputation in dealing successfully with cannibals and the slave trade, ignorance and taxation, the copra trade and justice. He was knighted in 1925, held in high respect by the islanders, and died in Samarai, Papua, on Feb. 27.

MURRAY, JOHN O'KANE (1847–1885). Born in Antrim, Ireland, on Dec. 12, he was brought to New York in 1856, attended Fordham College, became a physician, and wrote a number of popular volumes on church history, saints' lives, Irish poetry, and English literature and history. He died in Chicago, Illinois, on July 30.

MURRAY, LAURENCE O. (1864–1926). Born in Steuben County, New York, he studied at Niagara and New York universities, was admitted to the bar in 1893, practiced law in New York City, and was appointed to the treasury department. He was deputy comptroller of currency in 1898–99 and comptroller in 1908–13. He was secretary of commerce in 1904–8 in the Theodore Roosevelt cabinet, and later became a banker. During World War I he served in the accounting section of the signal corps, as field secretary of the Knights of Columbus, and with the American Red Cross. He died in Elmira, New York, on June 10.

MURRAY, PATRICK (1811–1882), theologian. Born in Clones, Monaghan, Ireland, on Nov. 18, he studied at Maynooth, was ordained, served as curate in Dublin, was appointed professor at Maynooth in 1838, a position he held until his death there on Nov. 15, and became prefect of the Dunboyne Establishment in 1879. He wrote *De ecclesia Christi* (1861–66), *Essays, Chiefly Theological* (1850–53), and *De gratia* (1877).

MURRAY, PHILIP (1886–1952), labor leader. Born in Blantyre, Scotland, on May 25, he was taken to the United States in 1902, went through the sixth grade of school, worked in the mines of Pennsylvania, rising in favor with the miners, and became an American citizen in 1911. He joined the United Mine Workers of America in 1912, became president of District No. 5 in 1916, and was international vice-president in 1926–42. In 1940 he succeeded John L. Lewis as president of the Congress of Industrial Organizations and in 1942 became first president of the United Steel Workers of America after a break with Lewis. He was a member of the War Labor Board of Pennsylvania in 1917 under President Wilson and of the Bituminous Coal Production Commission in that same year; in 1921 he worked with President Harding to settle labor tension in the West Virginia mining areas. He quarreled with President Truman in 1945; delayed until 1948 acting on suggestions that he clear his union offices of communist sympathizers, a delay which caused considerable censure; gained extensive pension rights for his steel workers in 1949; and was the head of four million workers in the CIO. He died in San Francisco, California, on Nov. 9.

MURRAY, THOMAS C. (1873–1959), dramatist. Born in Macroon, Cork, Ireland, in Jan., he studied at St. Patrick's, Dublin, taught in Cork, and wrote for educational journals. He founded the Cork Little Theatre with Terence MacSwiney, Con O'Leary, and Daniel Corkery, which produced his first play, *Wheel of Fortune* (rewritten in 1917 as *Sovereign Love*) in 1908. In 1910 his *Birthright* was produced by the Abbey Theatre players in Dublin; productions in London and Boston followed. *Maurice Harte* appeared in 1912, highly praised by Yeats. Murray was headmaster at Inchicore from 1915 to 1932, was a founding member of the Irish Academy of Letters, and a member of the film censorship appeal board. Other plays, all dealing with contemporary Ireland, include *The Briery Gap* (1918), *Spring, Aftermath, Autumn Fire* (his most successful work), *The Pipe in the Fields, The Blind Wolf, A Flutter of Wings, Michaelmas Eve, A Stag at Bay, A Spot in the Sun,* and *Illumination* (1939; produced in 1946). A novel, *Spring Horizon,* appeared in 1937. He received an honorary degree from the National University of Ireland in 1950, and died in Dublin on Mar. 7.

MURRAY, THOMAS EDWARD (1891–1961. Born in Albany, New York, on June 20, he studied at St. Francis Xavier, New York, and mechanical engineering at Yale, became president of the family engineering firm when twenty-four, and patented some 200 inventions in the fields of welding and electricity. He was appointed receiver for the bankrupt Interborough Rapid Transit System in New York in 1932, became noted for his settlements of labor disputes during World War II, served as director of numerous industrial firms, and in 1950 was appointed a member of the

Atomic Energy Commission by President Truman. At the end of his seven-year term he became a consultant of the Joint Congressional Committee on Atomic Energy, was unsuccessful in his quest for the Democratic nomination for United States senator from New York in 1958, and urged the resumption of nuclear testing in 1960. He was twice honored by the pope for his charitable activities, was awarded the Laetare Medal from Notre Dame in 1952, and received honorary degrees from numerous colleges. He died in New York City on May 26.

MURTAGH. *See* Muredach, St.

MUSH, JOHN (1551?–1612?). Born in Yorkshire, England, he studied at Douai and Rome, was ordained in 1583 and sent on the English mission. He was confessor to Bl. Margaret Clitherow, who was martyred for sheltering him and another priest, and was captured in 1586, but escaped and continued his work in the north. He tried to reconcile the differences among the priests in Wisbech prison in 1595, came into controversy with Fr. Persons when he attempted to set up a priests' organization, and in 1602 appealed in Rome against the appointment of an archpriest and wrote *Declaratio motuum* to support his contentions. Accused of schism, he was acquitted and returned to England, where he acted as assistant to two archpriests and was chaplain to Lady Dormer. He wrote a biography of Margaret Clitherow and an account of the persecutions in northern England, and died in Wenge, Buckinghamshire.

MUSONIUS, ST. (d. 305?), martyr. *See* Eugene, St.

MUSOPHILUS. *See* Schwalbe, Benedict.

MUSSO, CORNELIUS (1511–1574). Born in Piacenza, Italy, he became a Friar Minor Conventual, a great preacher, and author of biblical commentaries and sermons. Appointed bishop of Bitonto, he attended the Council of Trent, gave the opening oration, and was active in the discussion of justification. He died in Rome.

MUSTIOLA, ST. (d. 273), martyr. A noble lady of Chiusi, Tuscany, she ministered to St. Irenaeus and other Christians who had been imprisoned by Turcius, a Roman officer. Turcius tried to force his attentions on her and, when spurned, tortured Irenaeus to death. When Mustiola denounced Turcius for his barbarism, he beat her to death. F. D. July 3.

MUSUROS, MARKOS (1470–1517), scholar. Born in Retimo, Crete, he studied at Florence under John Lascaris, became professor of Greek at Padua in 1503, lectured at Venice, became a member of the Aldine Academy, and helped prepare the Aldine editions of the Greek classics. He edited *Etymologicum magnum*, first Latin and Greek lexicon, established a Greek printing press in Rome in 1516, and was appointed bishop of Malvasia by Pope Leo, but died in Rome before occupying his see.

MUTIS, JOSÉ CELESTINO (1732–1808), naturalist. Born in Cadiz, Spain, on Apr. 6, he studied medicine at Seville and Madrid, where he became professor of anatomy and began practicing medicine in 1757. He accompanied the viceroy of New Granada to South America as personal physician in 1760, taught mathematics in Bogotá, and turned his attention to natural history. In 1772 he became a cleric, possibly a priest, and canon at Bogotá cathedral; in 1783 he was appointed head of a botanical expedition and, in 1790, director of the Royal Academy of Natural History in Santa Fe. He made valuable studies of the cinchona plant, laying out an entire plantation for his studies, and his collection of plants, drawings of plants, and flora and fauna of New Granada numbered in the thousands. He died in Bogotá, Colombia, on Sept. 2. Although he published only several articles in periodicals during his lifetime, his work on quinine, *El arcano de la quina*, was published in 1828 and his complete writings appeared in 1870.

MUZIANO, GIROLAMO (1528–1592), painter. Born in Acquafredda, near Brescia, Italy, he studied under Girolamo Romanino, went to Rome about 1550, and became so known for his landscape paintings he was called "Il giovane de' paesi" ("Young man of the landscapes"). His *Resurrection of Lazarus* won praise from Michelangelo and established him as an outstanding artist; Pope Gregory III appointed him superintendent of the Vatican, where he encouraged and developed the art of mosaics. His mosaics in the Gregorian chapel are considered among the finest of the modern era. He founded the Academy of St. Luke in Rome, where he died. Among his greatest paintings are *Christ Giving the Keys to St. Peter, St. Francis Receiving the Stigmata, Circumcision, Ascension,* and *St. Jerome Preaching to Monks in the Desert.*

MUZZARELLI, ALFONSO (1749–1813), theologian. Born in Ferrara, Italy, on Aug. 22, he joined the Jesuits in 1768, taught at Bologna and Imola, and when the Jesuits were suppressed in 1773 became director of the Collegio dei Nobili in Parma. He was appointed theologian of the Poenitentiara by Pope Pius VII, whom he followed into exile in 1809, and died in Paris on May 25. He wrote many theological and ascetical treatises.

MYRON, ST. (d. 250?), martyr. A priest at Cyzicus, Mycia, Asia Minor, he was slain while defending his church buildings. F. D. Aug. 17.

MYRON, ST. (250?–350?). He was a bishop in Crete, called a "wonder-worker." F. D. Aug. 8.

MYROPE, ST. (d. 251?), martyr. A native of the Greek island of Chios, she was scourged and imprisoned for having hidden the body of the martyred St. Isidore, and died from mistreatment. F. D. July 13.

MZEC, BL. JOHN MARY (d. 1887), martyr. A native of Uganda, Africa, who baptized many when they were facing death by persecution, he was beheaded in 1887 and beatified in 1912. F. D. Jan. 27.

N

NABOR, ST. (3rd century), martyr. *See* Basilides, St.

NABOR, ST. (3rd century), martyr. *See* Felix, St.

NACCHIANTE, GIACOMO (d. 1569), bishop. Born in Florence, Italy, he studied at Bologna, taught at St. Thomas of Minerva in Rome, and was appointed bishop of Chioggia in 1544. He attended the Council of Trent in 1546 and acted as Pope Pius IV's representative on several occasions. He wrote theological and scriptural studies and died in Chioggia, Italy, on May 6.

NÁDASDY, LADISLAUS (d. 1730). He became bishop of Csanád, Hungary, in 1710, after the area had been freed of a 136-year occupation by the Turks.

NAGAI, TAKASHI (1908–1951), physician. Born in Matsue, Japan, he studied medicine at Nagasaki, became a convert in 1934, two years after graduation, and by 1946 was full professor of physiotherapy at Nagasaki. He was an X-ray technician during World War II, and was poisoned by radiation when the A-bomb was dropped on Nagasaki, killing his wife. He wrote on her death, on the children who remained, *The Bells of Nagasaki, Psychology of an Atomic Battlefield*, and other works. He died in Urakami, Japan, on May 1.

NAGL, FRANZ XAVER (1855–1913), cardinal. Born in Vienna on Nov. 26, he studied in Krems, Seitenstettin, St. Pölten, and Rome, and was ordained in 1878. He taught exegesis in Vienna, was court chaplain, became rector of the church of Santa Maria dell' Anima Teutonicorum in Rome, and wrote its history. In 1902 he became bishop of Trieste-Capo d' Istria, in 1909 coadjutor bishop of Vienna, and in 1911 its prince-archbishop and cardinal. He died in Vienna on Feb. 4.

NAHUM, ST. (9th century). A convert of SS. Cyril and Methodius, he probably succeeded St. Clement of Okhrida as bishop of Velitsa. He is one of the seven Apostles of Bulgaria. F. D. July 17.

NAMASIUS, ST. (d. 559?). He was twenty-second bishop of Vienne, Gaul; his cult was confirmed in 1903. F. D. Nov. 17.

NAMATIUS, ST. (5th century). He was ninth bishop of Clermont, France, and in office in 462. F. D. Oct. 27.

NAMPHANION, ST. (d. 180?), martyr. He and several other Carthaginians were put to death at Madaura, Numidia. F. D. July 4.

NANINI, GIOVANNI MARIA (1540?–1607), composer. Born in Tivoli, Italy, he studied at Rome under Gaudio Mell, and opened in Rome the first public school of music headed by an Italian. Palestrina, whom he succeeded as maestro in Santa Maria Maggiore in 1579, was one of his assistants. Nanini became a member of the papal choir in 1577, wrote motets, madrigals, canzonets, and church music. In 1604 he became choirmaster of the Sistine Chapel, where his *Hodie nobis coelorum Rex* is still sung in Christmas services. He died in Rome on Mar. 11.

NANKER (d. 1341). He was bishop of Cracow, Poland, and was transferred to Breslau, Silesia, in 1326 by Pope John XXII after the Polish and German factions of the latter diocese had elected two candidates, Weit and Lutold. When King John of Bohemia seized a castle belonging to the cathedral chapter, the bishop excommunicated him, but was forced to flee to Neisse, Silesia, where he died.

NANNI, GIOVANNI (1432?–1502), historian. Born in Viterbo, Italy, he became a Dominican, served as master of the palace under Pope Alexander VI, and was a classical and oriental scholar of such Renaissance enthusiasm that he adopted the name Annius. He wrote a commentary on the Apocalypse, histories of the crusades, Turkey, the Etruscans, and a seventeen-volume *Antiquitatum variarum*, based on ancient texts which he accepted as genuine, but which scholars have proved to be spurious.

NANTERIUS, ST. (d. 1044?). He was abbot of the Benedictine monastery of St. Michel near Verdun, France. F. D. Oct. 30.

NANTEUIL, ROBERT (1630–1678), engraver. Born in Rheims, France, he became interested in engraving, received his doctorate in philosophy in 1645, went to Paris in 1648, and there began to engrave for a living. He was appointed royal engraver in 1658, opened an atelier, and was so successful he caused King Louis XIV to raise engravers to the same level as other artists. He left some 243 plates and was an expert crayon and pastel portraitist. He died in Paris.

NAPOLEON I (1769–1821), emperor. Son of Charles Bonaparte (or Buonoparte) and Maria Ramolino, he was born in Ajaccio, Corsica, on Aug. 15, and studied at military schools in Brienne and Paris. In 1793 he revealed his military ability by his recapture of Toulon from the English, advanced to the rank of general in 1794, was imprisoned when the Thermidorians gained control of the French government, but was soon released, and in 1795 put down a revolt in Paris. He married Josephine de Beauharnais in a civil ceremony in 1796, was put in charge of French forces in Italy late in March, and in 1797 defeated the Sardinians, drove the Austrians from Italy, and was acclaimed a military genius. He invaded Austria, forced it to sign the Peace of Compo Formio, ending Austrian domination of northern Italy, securing guaranties of the left bank of the Rhine, and acquiring the Austrian Netherlands for France. In 1798 he invaded and conquered Egypt in the first step of a plan to conquer the British Empire by capturing India, was cut off from the Continent by Nelson's naval victory at the mouth of the Nile, and, despite further victories over the Turks in Syria, was obliged to abandon the expedition late in 1799. He executed the *coup d'état* of 18 Brumarie (Nov. 9, 1799) which made him first consul and practically ended the Directory government. He invaded Italy to defeat the Austrians again at Merengo (1800), signed the Peace of Lunéville (1801), which ended the coalition against France, and the peace of Amiens with England in 1802. In July 1801 he had signed a concordat with Pope Pius VII, ending the schism and restoring Catholicism as the official religion of France. In Apr. 1802 he promulgated it, with the organic articles supposedly designed to regulate the administration of the Church in France, but in reality subjecting the Church to state control. He instituted widespread administrative, legal, and legislative reforms, reformed the financial structure and established the bank of France, proclaimed the civil code in 1804, and was proclaimed emperor of the French in 1804. He invited the pope to France to crown him emperor, but crowned himself when he took the crown from Pope Pius VII's hands; he was crowned king of Italy the following May 26. War broke out between France and England in 1803; a new coalition of England, Russia, Austria, and Sweden was formed against France in 1805; and Nelson's victory at Trafalgar ended all hopes of invasion of England. He turned on Austria, defeated the Austrians and Russians at Austerlitz, and dictated the Treaty of Pressburg. He abolished the Holy Roman Empire in 1806 and established the Confederation of the Rhine of the German states except Prussia and Austria, which caused Prussia to form a new coalition with Russia and England against him. He defeated the Prussians at Jena, and occupied Berlin, crushed the Russians at Friedland in 1807, and forced both to sign the Peace of Tilsit, depriving Prussia of half of its territories and making Russia and France secret allies. He was now master of Europe, England alone opposing him. In 1806 he had proclaimed the Berlin Decree and in 1807 the Milan Decree, which closed the ports of all Europe to England, inaugurating the "continental system" by which he hoped to bring England to terms by ending its vital maritime commerce. In 1806 he had hemmed in the Papal States by evicting the Bourbons from Naples and placing his brother, Joseph on the throne. When the pope refused to join his continental system by excluding England from papal dominions, Napoleon annexed the Papal States in 1809, whereupon Pope Pius VII excommunicated him. Napoleon abducted the pope in July 1809, and imprisoned him in France until his disastrous defeat in Russia caused him to effect a reconciliation in 1812; Pius did not return to Rome until May 1814. In 1807 the emperor invaded Spain and Portugal to bring the Iberian peninsula under his control in the trade war with England, and in 1808 he caused Ferdinand VII to renounce his claim to the Spanish throne and placed his brother, Joseph Bonaparte, on the throne. He set his relatives on thrones all over Europe: his brother-in-law, Murat, replaced Joseph as king of Naples; Eugène de Beauharnais ruled in Italy; Louis Bonaparte in Holland; Jerome Bonaparte in Westphalia; and Gen. Bernadotte became crown prince of Sweden. Revolutions broke out in Spain and Portugal and the ensuing Peninsula War drained France. England landed an army in Portugal in 1808 which reached Spain, but by the end of the year Napoleon had driven the English out. In April 1809 war again broke out with Austria, which he ended by the Treaty of Schönnbrunn six months later. He caused Paris diocesan authorities to declare his marriage to Josephine null and void on Jan. 9, 1810, married Marie Louise of Austria on Apr. 1, and denounced the cardinals and bishops who opposed him for his treatment of the pope and his new marriage. In 1810 he annexed Holland, and in 1812 invaded Russia because of the czar's refusal to enforce the continental system, occupied Moscow, and attempted to reach a truce with the Russians. They refused and, caught in the vigors of the Russian winter, he was forced into a disastrous retreat. In 1813 he signed a new concordat with the pope, which, though intended solely as the basis for further discussions, he proclaimed as law; Pius then disavowed his signature. Prussia entered an alliance with Russia and Austria declared war; France found itself facing a new coalition of these three and England and Sweden. Successful at first at the battle of Dresden, Napoleon was defeated at Leipzig in 1814, abdicated, and was exiled to the island of Elba. He escaped early in 1815, raised a fresh army, and threatened all Europe. He was completely defeated at Waterloo, once again abdicated, and was sent to the island of St. Helena as a prisoner of war. He was imprisoned there, writing his *Mémoires* and served by a Catholic chaplain, until his death on May 5.

NAPOLEON III (1808–1873), emperor. Charles Louis Napoleon Bonaparte, son of Louis Bonaparte, King of Holland and Napoleon I's brother, and Hortense Beauharnais, was born in Paris on Apr. 20. After Waterloo he lived in exile with his mother, who was separated from Louis, at Arenenburg, Switzerland, and Augsburg. He was educated by private tutors and studied military tactics. In 1830-31 he participated in the unsuccessful uprising in the Romagna against the pope; in 1832, the death of the duke of Reichstadt made him pretender to the French throne; he attempted coups in 1836 (was captured and exiled to New York) and in 1840 was captured, tried, and sentenced to life imprisonment, but in 1846 escaped to London. He returned to France when revolution broke out in 1848, was elected to the national assembly and with the aid of his counselors became president of the republic. In 1849 he dispatched an army to Rome to destroy the Roman Republic and restore the pope, though secretly sympathizing with the Italian nationalist movement. His *coup d'état* of Dec. 2, 1851, dissolved the constitution, and he was elected president for ten years. A year later he was proclaimed emperor. He allied France with England in the Crimean War (1853–56). In 1858 he reached an agreement with Cavour at Plombières that France would aid Piedmont in driving the Austrians from Italy, which would become a confederation under the King of Sardinia with the pope as honorary president. In the consequent war, French victories led to revolts against the pope, and he incurred the severe criticism of French Catholics. He signed the separate peace of Villa Franca in 1859, but had lost Catholic support and began to flirt with the radicals to overcome this loss. In 1863, he sent an army to Mexico to establish a French Catholic empire, an effort which resulted in disaster when Maximilian, his puppet emperor, was executed in 1867, and the United States, after the Civil War, threatened to intervene. In 1864 he agreed to withdraw French troops from Rome within two years over the bitter opposition of the pope. Having completed the withdrawal in 1866, he signed the Franco-Prussian agreement with Bismarck, who completely outmatched him. Napoleon dispatched the Antibes Legion to aid papal troops against Garibaldi's threats in 1867, and alienated some Italians and at the same time the pope when he refused its use against Victor Emmanuel. He was obliged to make great concessions to parliament in 1869, but triumphed once again when an 1870 plebiscite overwhelmingly supported him. In July war with Prussia broke out over the succession to the Spanish throne, and in Sept. his surrender at Sedan ended the empire. He was imprisoned by the Germans at Wilhelmshöhe until the conclusion of the peace, went to England on his release in 1871, and died at Chiselhurst, near London, on Jan. 9.

NAPPER, BL. GEORGE (1550–1610), martyr. Born in Holywell Manor, Oxford, England, he studied at Corpus Christi College, but was expelled after three years because of his religion. He was imprisoned in 1580, released in 1589 when he approved the royal supremacy, repented, went to Dousa, and was ordained in 1596. Sent on the English mission in 1603, he was arrested near Kirtlington and executed at Oxford for being a priest. He was beatified in 1929. F. D. Nov. 9.

NARCISSUS, ST. (1st century). *See* Ampliatus, St.

NARCISSUS, ST. (d. 215?), bishop. A Greek, he was appointed bishop of Jerusalem at an advanced age, attended the Council of Jerusalem where his support of Roman customs caused him to be calumniated, and went into hiding as a hermit. According to a letter written by his successor, Alexander, he lived almost 120 years. F. D. Oct. 29.

NARCISSUS, ST. (d. 260?), martyr. *See* Crescentio, St.

NARCISSUS, ST. (d. 307?), bishop and martyr. He is said to have been put to death at Gerona, Spain, with his deacon, St. Felix, during the Diocletian persecution. F. D. Mar. 18.

NARCISSUS, ST. (d. 320), martyr. *See* Argeus, St.

NARDI, JACOPO (1476–1563), author. Born in Florence, Italy, he early became embroiled in Florentine politics, a follower of Savanarola, and a member of the republican party, under which he held several governmental positions though he retained friendly relations with the Medici. He participated in the republican revolution in 1527, was expelled in 1530, and settled in Venice, where he died on Mar. 11. He wrote a history of Florence, two comedies, a biography, and translations of Livy and Cicero.

NARNUS, ST. (d. 75?). He is said to have

been the first bishop of Bergamo, Italy, and consecrated by St. Barnabas. F. D. Aug. 27.

NARSES, ST. (d. 344), martyr. *See* Lazarus, St.

NARTZALUS, ST. (d. 180), martyr. *See* Speratus, St.

NARUSZEWICZ, ADAM STANISLAW (1733–1796), bishop. Born in Pinsk, Lithuania, he became a Jesuit in 1748, studied in France, taught in Vilna, and became director of the Collegium Nobilium in Warsaw. After the suppression of the Jesuits he was named bishop of Smolensk and then of Lutsk. He wrote sentimental *Idylls*, a collection of *Satires*, biography, a *History of the Crimea* (1787), and the scholarly six-volume *History of the Polish Nation* (1780–86), based on archival material and touched by a note of warning to the nobility to abandon lawless and arbitrary ways. He died in Janow, Galicia.

NARVAEZ, PANFILO DE (1480?–1528), explorer. Born in Valladolid, Spain, he went to America as an army officer in 1498, served as lieutenant governor of Cuba, and in 1520 was sent to Mexico to force the submission of Cortés. He was captured and imprisoned at Vera Cruz for two years, returned to Spain, and in 1527 sailed with an expedition of colonists for Florida. He lost many of the party during stops at Santo Domingo and Santiago de Cuba, and in 1528 arrived in what is described as Tampa Bay. After landing, they were misled by Indian guides, set out across country, built boats to follow the gulf coast, and were swept out to sea and drowned south of the Mississippi delta. A few survivors reached Mexico.

NASALLI-ROCCA DI CORNELIANO, GIOVANNI BATTISTA (1872–1952), cardinal. Born in Italy, he was ordained, became archbishop of Bologna in 1921, and was created a cardinal in 1923. He died in Bologna on Mar. 13.

NATALIA, ST. (d. 304?). *See* Adrain, St.

NATALIA, ST. (d. 311?). She served the Christians imprisoned at Nicomedia during the persecution of Diocletian and died later at Constantinople. F. D. Dec. 1.

NATALIA, ST. (d. 852?), martyr. *See* Aurelius, St.

NATALIS, ST. (6th century). He worked with St. Columba in spreading monasticism through northern Ireland and served as abbot of Cill, Daunhinis, and Naile. F. D. Jan. 27.

NATALIS, ALEXANDRE (1639–1724), historian. Born in Rouen, France, on Jan. 19, he studied there and joined the Dominicans in 1655, studied and taught at Paris, and obtained his doctorate from the Sorbonne in 1675. Under the influence of Jean Baptiste Colbert, later archbishop of Rouen, he published twenty-four volumes on the history of

the Church to the Council of Trent, *Selecta historiae ecclesiasticae capita;* six volumes on the history of the Old Testament followed. Early praise of the church history by Pope Innocent XI in 1682 changed to official censure when later volumes caused the charge of Gallicanism to be raised. Innocent placed it on the Index in 1684; although Natalis accepted the censure, the work was not removed from the Index until 1734, when it was issued in corrected form by Fr. Roncaglia. Natalis also wrote the ten-volume *Theologia dogmatica et moralia*, sermons, a commentary on the gospels, a handbook for preachers, studies in the authorship of St. Thomas Aquinas, and editions of ecclesiastical documents. In 1704 he fell into Jansenism, but quickly withdrew from his error. He became provincial of the province of France in 1706 and died at Paris on Aug. 21. He is also known as Alexander Noël.

NATHALAN, ST. (d. 678), bishop. Born in the diocese of Aberdeen, Scotland, he abandoned the life of a noble to become a farmer, spending his free hours in contemplation. He fed the area during a famine and built churches at Tullicht and elsewhere. His cult was approved in 1898. F. D. Jan. 19.

NATHAN, GEORGE JEAN (1882–1958), critic. Born in Fort Wayne, Indiana, on Feb. 14, he studied at Cornell and Bologna, became drama critic for *Bohemian* and *Outing* in 1906, founded *Smart Set* in 1914 and *American Mercury* in 1924, with Henry L. Mencken, and later established *American Spectator*. In his lifetime he wrote vitriolic and demanding dramatic criticism for more than thirty journals; many were published in book form. He married Julie Haydon, an actress, in 1955 and became a convert shortly before his death in New York City on Apr. 8.

NATHANAEL (1st century), apostle. Mentioned in John 1:43–51 as a friend of Philip who brought him to Christ, Nathanael is generally considered to be the personal name of Bartholomew who is designated Bar-Tolmai (son of Tolmai) by the synoptic authors.

NATHY, ST. (d. 610?), bishop. A native of Sligo, Ireland, he was a disciple of St. Finnian of Clonard and became founder and abbot-bishop of a monastery at Anchory. His cult was confirmed in 1903. F. D. Aug. 9.

NAUROSE, BL. WILLIAM DE (1297–1369). Born in Toulouse, France, he joined the Hermits of St. Augustine there, was sent to the University of Paris, and preached widely in France, particularly on purgatory. His cult was confirmed in 1893. F. D. May 18.

NAUSEA, FREDERIC (1480?–1552), bishop. Born in Waischenfeld, Franconia, he was educated at Nuremberg, Pavia, Padua, and Siena. He attended several diets and conventions as secretary of the archbishop of Cologne, became pastor and canon in Frankfort-im-Main, but was forced to leave by the Lutherans. In 1526 he was preacher at the Mainz cathedral, became King Ferdinand's counselor and court preacher in 1534, coadjutor to the bishop of Vienna in 1538, and succeeded to the see in 1541. He worked vigorously for the reunion of the Protestant churches, was forbidden to attend the early meetings of the Council of Trent by the king, but participated in the reopening in 1551, and died there on Feb. 6. He was the author of several theological tracts.

NAVALIS, ST. (d. 305?), martyr. *See* Valentine, St.

NAVARETTE, BL. ALPHONSUS (d. 1617), martyr. Born in Vallodolid, Spain, he became a Dominican, was sent to the Philippines and, in 1611, to Japan. He became vicar provincial at Nagasaki, cared for the sick, rescued exposed infants, preached effectively, and converted many before a widespread persecution, which lasted from 1617 to 1632, began. He was beheaded at Omura, Japan, with a native catechist. He was beatified in 1867. F. D. June 1.

NAVARRETE, DOMINGO FERNÁNDEZ (1610?–1689), archbishop. Born in Peñafiel, Castile, Spain, he became a Dominican and in 1646 he was sent on missionary work to the Philippines. He arrived in 1648, taught theology at St. Thomas academy in Manila, and was sent to China in 1657, where he remained until he went to Rome in 1673 as prefect of the Dominican mission to dispute with the Jesuits over the use of Chinese customs in religion. He returned to Spain in 1677, was appointed archbishop of Santo Domingo, West Indies, and remained there until his death. He wrote several books on Chinese customs and language.

NAVARRETE, FRANCISCO MANUEL DE (1768–1809), poet. Born in Zamora, Mexico, he became a Franciscan, taught Latin at the University of Valladolid, and wrote pastoral poetry, published in Mexico in 1823 as *Entretenimientos poéticos.*

NAVARRETE, JUAN FERNÁNDEZ (1526–1579), painter. Born in Logroño, Spain, he became a deaf-mute at three (he is called *El mudo*) and when placed with the Hieronymite monks for education revealed his artistic ability. He probably studied under Becerra in Spain and Titian in Venice (he remained in Italy twenty years) and by the time he returned to Spain was highly regarded as an artist. He was appointed Philip II's painter in 1568 and commissioned to decorate the Escorial, where he painted most of his pictures. He greatly influenced the Madrid school and is often called the Spanish Titian. He died in Toledo, Spain, in Feb. or on Mar. 28. Among his chief works are *Holy Family, Nativity, Abraham and the Three Angels, Martyrdom of St. Paul,* and *Baptism of Christ.*

NAVARRETE, MARTÍN FERNÁNDEZ DE (1765–1844), historian. Born in Alvalos (Logroño), Spain, on Nov. 8, he studied at the seminary in Vergara, joined the navy when fifteen, but resigned because of ill health and in 1789 was commissioned by the minister of marine to gather the documents of Spain's maritime history. He rejoined the navy in 1792 when Spain went to war with France, and in 1796 was assigned to the marine department, where he established the hydrographic office. He became chief clerk in 1803, accountant of the supreme court of Almirantazgo in 1807, and resigned the following year when Joseph Bonaparte was placed on the throne of Spain. He became head of the hydrographic office in 1823, director of the Academy of History in 1824, served as senator several times, and was made a member of the marine division of the Royal Council of the Indies in 1834. He died in Madrid on Oct. 8. His most famous work is *Colección de los viajes y descubrimientos que hicieron por mar los españoles desde el fin del siglo xv,* a valuable source on Spanish explorations and discoveries, but his *Colección de documentos inéditos,* a history of the Spanish navy, a bibliography of Spanish maritime material, and a life of Cervantes are also highly regarded.

NAVARRO, BL. PAUL (1560–1612), martyr. Born in Laino, Italy, he became a Jesuit, served as a missioner in India, was rector of the Jesuit house at Amanguchi for twenty years, and, for his missionary activities in Nagasaki, Japan, was arrested and burned to death at Ximabara, Japan, on Nov. 1. He was one of the 205 martyrs of Japan beatified by Pope Pius IX in 1867. F. D. Sept. 10.

NAVARRUS. *See* Aspelcueta, Martin.

NAZARIUS, ST. (d. 68?), martyr. Possibly a legendary figure, he supposedly was the son of a pagan Roman army officer and a Christian mother, instructed at Rome by St. Peter, and beheaded at Milan, Italy, with St. Celsus during Nero's first persecution. F. D. July 28.

NAZARIUS, ST. (3rd century), martyr. *See* Basilides, St.

NAZARIUS, JOHN PAUL (1556–1645?), theologian. Born in Cremona, Italy, he joined the Dominicans as a youth, studied at Bologna, and taught at Dominican colleges throughout Italy, and in 1592 was sent to Prague to combat the spreading Protestantism. In 1596 he became regent of studies in Milan, was appointed by the pope to defend Catholic teaching on the mass against the Lutherans in Chiavenna in 1597, and in 1620 was sent on a diplomatic mission for Milan to Spain. He wrote theological treatises and died in Bologna, Italy.

NEALE, LEONARD (1746–1817), archbishop. Born near Port Tobacco, Maryland, on Oct. 15, he studied at St. Omer, Flanders, Bruges, and Liège, joined the Jesuits in 1767, and was ordained. When the Jesuits were suppressed in 1773 he engaged in pastoral work in England until 1779, then went to British Guiana as a missionary. Ill health forced him to return to the United States in 1783. He went to Philadelphia in 1793 as pastor of St. Mary's church, was appointed president of Georgetown in 1799, titular bishop of Gortyna and coadjutor of Baltimore, Maryland, in 1800, and succeeded to the see as its second archbishop in 1815, receiving the pallium in 1816. He died in Washington, D.C., on June 18.

NEBRIDIUS, ST. (6th century). He became bishop of Egara, Spain, near Barcelona, about 527. F. D. Feb. 9.

NEBRIJA, ANTONIO DE. See Jarava, Antonio Martínez de.

NECKERE, LEO RAYMOND DE (1800–1833), bishop. Born in Wevelghem, Belgium, on June 6, he studied at Roulers and the Ghent Lazarist seminary, went to the United States in response to a call for priests, studied at St. Thomas seminary, Kentucky, and St. Mary of the Barrens, Missouri, joined the Lazarists in 1820, and was ordained in 1822. He taught at St. Mary's, engaged in missionary work in Missouri and Louisiana, and was appointed vicar general of New Orleans in 1827 and its bishop in 1829. He died in New Orleans on Sept. 4 of the plague which he caught while ministering to the stricken.

NECTAN, ST. (6th century?). He was venerated during the Middle Ages at Hartland in Devonshire and in Cornwall, particularly by the English Augustinians. He was either a Welsh or an Irish missioner and may have died a martyr. He is also called Nighton. F. D. June 17.

NECTARIUS, ST. (d. 375). Bishop of Vienne, Gaul, he was active in preaching and writing against the Arians in the Dauphiné. F. D. May 5.

NECTARIUS, ST. (d. 397), patriarch. Son of a senator at Tarsus, he became praetor at Constantinople, and succeeded St. Gregory Nazianzen as eleventh bishop of that see in 381. His elevation was by popular demand, although at the time he had not yet been baptized. In 388 the Arians, whom he castigated, burned his house down; it was claimed, however, that he was too tolerant of the Novatians, and St. Gregory was not happy about his reign as bishop. He abolished the practice of public penance, preached on the martyr Theodore, died on Sept. 27, and was succeeded by St. John Chrysostom. F. D. Oct. 11.

NECTARIUS, ST. (d. 550?). He was bishop

of Autun, France, and a friend of St. Germanus of Paris. F. D. Sept. 13.

NÉEL, BL. JOHN PETER (1832–1862), martyr. A French missionary priest, he was tortured and beheaded at Kuy-tsheu, with Bl. Martin, a native catechist. They were beatified in 1909. F. D. Feb. 18.

NEHER, STEPHAN JAKOB (1829–1902), historian. Born in Ebnat, Württemberg, Germany, on July 24, he studied at Tübingen, was ordained, and engaged in pastoral activities in Dorfmerkingen, Zöbingen, and Nordhausen. He became a prolific writer of church history; his chief work was the three-volume *Kirchliche Geographie und Statistik* (1864–68). He died in Nordhausen, Germany, on Oct. 7.

NÉLATON, AUGUSTE (1807–1873), surgeon. Born in Paris on June 17, he studied medicine at Paris, devised several new operational techniques, and developed several new plastic operations. He became professor of clinical surgery at the university in 1851, was admitted to the Academy of Sciences in 1867, attended Napoleon III, and was made senator in 1868 in recognition of his contributions to French medicine. He wrote *Elements of Pathological Surgery* (1854–60), and died in Paris on Sept. 21.

NELSON, ELIJAH. See Neville, Edmund.

NELSON, BL. JOHN (d. 1578), martyr. Born in Skelton, England, he left for the Continent, was ordained at Douai, later became a Jesuit, was arrested as an underground priest, and hanged, drawn, and quartered at Tyburn for refusing to take Elizabeth's Oath of Supremacy. F. D. Feb. 3.

NEMESIAN, ST. (d. 257), bishop and martyr. During the persecution of Valerian he was condemned by the governor of Numidia to labor in the marble quarries of Sigum, northern Africa, where he died. A letter from St. Cyprian encouraging him and his fellow sufferers is extant. They were the following bishops of Numidia: Davitus, two named Felix, Jader, Litteus, Lucius, Polyanus, Victor, and many priests and lay people, most of whom died of ill treatment. F. D. Sept. 10.

NEMESIUS, ST. (d. 250), martyr. A native of Alexandria, he was tortured and burned at the stake during Decius' persecution. F. D. Dec. 19.

NEMESIUS, ST. (d. 260?), martyr. A Roman deacon, he was killed at Rome with his daughter Lucilla during the persecution of Valerian. F. D. Aug. 25 (also, Oct. 31; Dec. 8).

NENNIUS, ST. (6th century). An Irish follower of St. Finian of Clonard, he is called one of the "twelve apostles" of Ireland. F. D. Jan. 17.

NENNIUS (9th century), historian. He lived in Wales and wrote *Historia britonum*, which contains a physical description of the island and accounts of the Roman occupation, the inroads of the Picts and Scots, and the Saxon conquest. It is of more value as mythology than as history and is one of the sources of the Arthurian legend.

NENNOC, ST. (d. 467?). Daughter of Brychan of Brecknock, she is said to have followed St. Germanus from England to France and to have become abbess in Armorica. F. D. June 4.

NENNUS, ST. (7th century), abbot. He succeeded St. Enda in directing the monasteries on the Irish islands of Arran and Bute. F. D. June 14.

NEON, ST. (d. 254?), martyr. See Eusebius, St.

NEON, ST. (d. 303?), martyr. See Asterius, St.; also, Claudius, St.; Mark, St.

NEOPHYTUS, ST. (d. 257?), martyr. See Athanasius, St.

NEOPHYTUS, ST. (d. 310), martyr. A boy of less than fifteen, he was slain at Nicaea during the Diocletian persecution. F. D. Jan. 20.

NEOPOLUS, ST. (d. 300?), martyr. He was tortured to death at Alexandria, Egypt, during the Diocletian persecution. F. D. Aug. 15.

NEOT, ST. (d. 880?). Unreliable legends call him a Benedictine priest of Glastonbury, England, who became a hermit in Cornwall. F. D. July 31.

NÉRAZ, JOHN CLAUDIUS (1828–1894), bishop. Born in Anse, Rhone, France, on Jan. 12, he studied at St. Jodard seminary there, the Aix seminary, and the Grand seminary in Lyons, and was ordained in Galveston, Texas, in 1853. He engaged in missionary work in Texas, was appointed first vicar general of San Antonio in 1870, was administrator of the see in 1880–81, and in 1881 was appointed second bishop of San Antonio, Texas. He died there on Nov. 15.

NEREUS, ST. (1st century?), martyr. He and Achilleus were praetorian soldiers who were converted to Christianity and slain in Terracina, Italy. Pope Damasus wrote an epitaph for them in the late fourth century. F. D. May 12.

NERI, ANTONIO (d. 1614). A Florentine and a priest, he was known for his knowledge of chemistry and glassmaking and is the author of *L'arte vetraria*, a valuable work on glass manufacture.

NERI, PHILIP. See Philip Neri, St.

NERINCKX, CHARLES (1761–1824), missioner. Born in Herffelingen, Belgium, on Oct. 2, he studied at Enghien, Gheel, Louvain, and the Mechlin seminary, and was ordained in 1785. He became vicar of the Mechlin cathedral, pastor of Everberg-Meerbeke in 1794, and in 1797 was forced into hiding when the revolutionary government ordered his arrest. He came to the United States in 1804 and began missionary work in Kentucky in 1805. He re-fused the bishopric of New Orleans in 1809, founded the congregation of the Sisters of Loretto at the Foot of the Cross in 1812, made several trips to Belgium to raise funds and secure new missioners, and acquired an art collection which he presented to the Louisville diocese. He went to Missouri in 1824 and died in Ste. Geneviève there on Aug. 12.

NÉRON, BL. PIERRE FRANÇOIS (1818–1860), martyr. Born in Bornay, France, he joined the Society for Foreign Missions in 1846, was sent to Hong Kong, and was director of a seminary in West Tonkin, Indochina, when captured and beheaded. He was beatified in 1919. F. D. Nov. 3.

NERSES, ST. (d. 343), bishop. The bishop of Sahgerd, Persia, was beheaded with several companions, including his disciple Joseph, by Sapor II of Persia when they refused to sacrifice to the sun. F. D. Nov. 20.

NERSES I, ST. (d. 373), patriarch. Of royal Armenian descent, he lived in Caesarea, Cappodocia, married a princess, and on her death became chamberlain to King Arshak of Armenia. He later became a priest, was elected patriarch of Armenia in 353, encouraged monasteries, built hospitals, and inaugurated an ecclesiastical program so vigorous that it incurred the king's displeasure. When he condemned Arshak for the murder of the queen, he was exiled to Edessa. He returned in 369 when Pap became king, refused the king entrance to the church because of his dissolute life, and was poisoned at a banquet tendered him by the king. He was known as "the Great." F. D. Nov. 19.

NERSES KLAIETSI, ST. (d. 1173). Born in Hromkla, Cilicia, he was educated by his uncle, Katholikos Gregory II, and was ordained by his brother, Katholikos Gregory III, both of whom he followed as katholikos of Armenia in 1166. Both had been in favor of and in union with the papacy and Nerses followed their lead, although actual union was not confirmed until 1198 by Emperor Leo II, and worked for the reunion of the Orthodox Greeks and Rome. He worked unsuccessfully to unite the Greek and Armenian churches, and wrote poetry, hymns, spiritual works, and a history of Armenia, receiving the surname Schnorkhali ("the Gracious") because of the high quality of his writing. He died on Aug. 13. F. D. Aug. 3.

NERSES OF LAMBRON, ST. (1153–1198), archbishop. Born in Lambron, Cilicia, son of Prince Oschin II of Lambron and nephew of Patriarch Nerses IV, he was ordained in 1169, consecrated archbishop of Tarsus in 1176, and like his uncle, labored to unite the Greek and Armenian churches. His address at the Council of Hromkla in 1179 was so eloquent that reunion was voted, but it was not put into effect when its supporter, Emperor Manuel

Comnenus, died the next year. He was one of the twelve bishops who signed the agreement uniting the Church in Cilicia with Rome in return for Pope Celestine's recognition of Prince Leo II of Cilicia as king of Armenia in 1198. Nerses was an outstanding scholar, poet, linguist, and theologian. He wrote many hymns, scriptural commentaries, an explanation of the liturgy, and translated the Rule of St. Benedict and St. Gregory's *Dialogues* into Armenian, as well as biographical sketches of the desert fathers from the Coptic. F. D. July 17.

NERUCCI, BL. LAURENCE (d. 1420), martyr. Five years after the execution of John Hus in 1415, Pope Martin V called for a crusade and sent several preachers from Siena into Bohemia, among them Bl. Laurence Nerucci, and three fellow Servites: Augustine Cennini, Bartholomew Donati, and John Baptist Petrucci. When word spread that they were in a Prague monastery, a crowd attacked and burned them and sixty other friars living there to death. Their cult was approved in 1918. F. D. Aug. 31.

NESTABUS, ST. (d. 362?), martyr. *See* Eusebius, St.

NESTOR, ST. (d. 251), bishop and martyr. The bishop of Magydus in Pamphylia so encouraged his flock during the persecution of Decius that he was sent to Perge, Pamphylia, and there tortured and crucified. F. D. Feb. 26.

NESTOR, ST. (d. 304?), martyr. He was slain in Thessalonica, Greece, during the Diocletian persecution. F. D. Oct. 8.

NESTOR, ST. (d. 362), martyr. A young man in Gaza, Palestine, he was tortured during the reign of Julian the Apostate, dragged with others to execution, and left to die on the roadside. F. D. Sept. 8.

NESTOR, ST. (4th century), bishop and martyr. *See* Arcardius, St.

NETTER, BL. THOMAS (1375?–1430). Born in Saffron Walden, Essex, he joined the Carmelites in London, studied at Oxford, and was ordained in 1400. In 1409 he attended the Council of Pisa, where he reputedly supported Pope Alexander V's election, and on his return to England was most prominent in the struggle against Lollardism, participating in the trials of several of John Wyclif's followers (and writing *Doctrinale fidei* against them). He was elected prior provincial of the Carmelites in England in about 1415 and became confessor and councilor of King Henry V. He played an outstanding role at the Council of Constance in 1415, and at its conclusion was a member of the delegation to the king of Poland and the grand duke of Lithuania. His influence was such there that he is called the "apostle of Lithuania," though it is doubtful he converted the grand duke. He returned to England in 1420, became tutor of Henry VI in 1422 and accom-

panied him to France in 1430. He wrote several theological treatises, chief of which was *Doctrinale antiquitatum fidei ecclesiae catholicae*, which was not published until 1253. He died in Rouen, France. F. D. Nov. 2.

NETTO, JOSEPH SEBASTIAN (1841–1920), cardinal. Born in Lagos, Portugal, he was ordained, served as a parish priest in 1873, became a Franciscan in 1875, bishop of Angola and the Congo, Africa, in 1879, patriarch of Lisbon in 1883, and a cardinal in 1884. He resigned in 1907 to serve as a friar until 1910, when the revolution drove him into refuge near Seville, Spain, where he remained until his death.

NEUGART, TRUDPERT (1742–1825), historian. Born in Villingen, Baden, Germany, on Feb. 23, he studied at St. George and St. Blasien abbey schools, joined the Benedictines in 1759, and was ordained in 1765. He taught biblical languages at Freiburg in 1767, returned to St. Blasien in 1770, devoted himself to research, and became provost of Krozingen in 1793. When the abbey was secularized and its property assigned to Baden, he arranged for the resettlement of the monks in Austria near Klagenfurt. He died at St. Paul's monastery there on Dec. 15. He wrote a history of the diocese of Constance up to 1306, of St. Paul abbey, and a treatise on penance.

NEUMANN, JOHANN BALTHASAR (1687–1753), architect. Born in Eger, Hungary, he served in the French army as a youth, and became an architect of note, widely recognized as an outstanding proponent of the rococo style. He built espiscopal palaces and castles at Bruchsal, Coblenz, Werneck, Vienna, several churches, and restored the cathedrals at Speyer, Mainz, and Würzburg, Bavaria, where he died.

NEUMANN, VEN. JOHN NEPOMUCENE (1811–1860), bishop. Born in Prachatitz, Bohemia, on Mar. 28, he studied at the Budweis seminary and at Prague, went to New York, and was ordained there in 1836. He did missionary work in New York until 1840, when he joined the Redemptorists in Pittsburgh. He also worked as a missionary in Maryland, Virginia, and Ohio, where he became popular among the German populace, was appointed superior of his community in Pittsburgh in 1844, provincial in 1847, and in 1852 was consecrated bishop of Philadelphia. He launched a vigorous program of school building, established a preparatory seminary, and became known for his sanctity, charity, and spiritual writings and preaching. He died in Philadelphia on Jan. 5 and was declared Venerable in 1896.

NEUMAYR, FRANZ (1697–1765), author. Born in Munich, Germany, on Jan. 17, he joined the Jesuits in 1712, preached missions, directed the Latin sodality in Munich, and became a noted preacher at the cathedral in

Augsburg, Bavaria, from 1752 to 1763. He died there on May 1. He was a prolific author, wrote more than 100 books and pamphlets, and was famed for his religious plays collected in *Theatrum asceticum* and *Theatrum politicum*.

NÈVE, FELIX JEAN BAPTISTE JOSEPH (1816–1893), philologian. Born in Ath, Belgium, on June 13, he studied at the Catholic college in Lille, received his doctorate in philosophy from Louvain in 1838, and taught classics there from 1841 to 1877. One of the most distinguished orientalists of the nineteenth century, he introduced the study of Sanskrit in Belgium, translated many Sanskrit and Armenian works into French, and wrote a history of Louvain in the sixteenth and seventeenth centuries. He died at Louvain on May 23.

NEVILLE, EDMUND (1605–1647). Born in Hopcut, Lancashire, England, he studied at St. Omer and the English College in Rome, joined the Jesuits in 1626, and after a period in Ghent was sent on the English mission in 1637. He worked in Oxford and South Wales, often using the alias Sales, was arrested as a priest but released, and died in England on July 18. He wrote *Palm of Christian Fortitude* and a life of St. Augustine.

NEVILLE, EDMUND (1563–1648). Probably son of Sir John Neville of Leversedge, Yorkshire, England, he studied on the Continent, was ordained in 1608, became a Jesuit in 1609, and was sent on the English mission. He was captured and imprisoned, and died as a result of ill treatment as a prisoner. He worked as a missioner under the alias Elijah Nelson.

NEVILLE, EDWARD (d. 1538), martyr. Son of Baron Bergavenny, he served in the court of Henry VIII, fought in France, and was the king's standard-bearer in 1531. He was arrested in 1538 with Cardinal Pole's brother, charged with conspiracy and sent to the Tower, and beheaded in London a month later, on Dec. 8.

NEVILS, WILLIAM COLEMAN (1878–1955), educator. Born in Philadelphia on May 29, he studied at St. Joseph's College, became a Jesuit in 1896, taught in Boston and New York City high schools, and at St. Andrews and Holy Cross, and went to Georgetown in 1918. He served as dean, chancellor, and from 1928 to 1935 as president, and reorganized the school of foreign service. He received honorary degrees from Georgetown, Loyola (New Orleans), and St. Joseph's, was decorated by many governments, was pastor in New York City in 1935–42, and first president of the new Scranton University in 1942–47. He wrote *Miniatures of Georgetown* (1934) and *Moulders of Men* (1953), and edited *The Saving Sense* (1947). He died in Washington, D.C., on Oct. 12.

NEVOLO. *See* Novellone, Bl.

NEWDIGATE, BL. SEBASTIAN (d. 1535), martyr. Son of John Newdigate of Harefield Place, Middlesex, England, he studied at Cambridge, was attached to the court, and became privy councilor to Henry VIII. When his wife died in 1524 he became a Carthusian monk in the London charterhouse. He was arrested in 1535, refused to sign the Act of Supremacy, and was executed at Tyburn with Bl. William Exmew and Humphrey Middlemore. They were beatified in 1886. F. D. June 19.

NEWMAN, JOHN HENRY (1801–1890), cardinal. Born in London, on Feb. 21, son of a banker, he graduated from Oxford in 1820, acquired an Oriel fellowship in 1822, and in 1824 became an Anglican deacon. He became curate at St. Clement's, an Anglican priest in 1825, resigned his curateship in 1826 when he was appointed a tutor of Oriel College, and in 1828 became vicar of St. Mary's, the university church, a position he held the next fifteen years. He soon attracted attention with his sermons and writings. In 1832 he published *Arians of the Fourth Century*, the first volume of a projected but never-completed history of the Church councils, and in 1833, after hearing John Keble's sermon, *National Apostasy*, became a leader, with Keble, Froude, and Pusey, in the Oxford Movement concerned with reforming the Anglican church. He became one of the Tractarians who were engaged in publishing a series of studies of aspects of church history and doctrine, and wrote most of the earlier *Tracts for the Times*. In 1841 his publication of *Tract 90*, in which he demonstrated that the thirty-nine Articles were consistent with Catholicism, caused a sensation in Anglican circles; it was widely condemned for its Roman Catholic tendencies, and further publication of the tracts was banned by the bishop of Oxford. Newman resigned from St. Mary's in 1843 and retired to Littlemore, where he devoted himself, with a group of followers, to study, meditation, and the writing of *Essay on the Development of Christian Doctrine*. He became a convert on Oct. 9, 1845, leading many of the adherents of the Oxford Movement (which collapsed when he left) with him during the next few years. In 1846 he went to Rome, studied at the Propaganda, was ordained in 1847, and returned to England in 1848 to establish the English community of the Oratorians in Birmingham. In 1851 he was sued by an unfrocked priest, Giacinto Achilli, who had been delivering anti-Catholic lectures and whom Newman had exposed in a lecture. Newman was convicted of criminal libel, but the court costs of $60,000 were quickly oversubscribed by friends throughout the world. In 1851, also he was appointed rector of the Catholic University in Ireland, delivered the lectures there which comprise his *Idea of a University*

(1852), and in 1854 was formally installed as rector. He resigned in 1858, when the university failed to receive from the Irish bishops the support it merited, returned to the oratory in Birmingham, and opened a boys' school at Edgbaston in 1859. In 1864, following an exchange of letters with Charles Kingsley over a slurring remark the latter had made about Catholic priests, Newman wrote his *Apologia pro vita sua*, which attracted wide attention. He spent the next fifteen years writing and lecturing, and in 1879 was created a cardinal by Pope Leo XIII. He also wrote *The Present Position of Catholics in England, Second Spring, Callista* (a novel), *An Essay in Aid of a Grammar of Assent*, eight volumes of *Parochial and Plain Sermons, Discourses to Mixed Congregations, The Dream of Gerontius*, and other poems, including *Lead, Kindly Light*. He died in Birmingham, England, on Aug. 10.

WILFRID WARD, *The Life of John Henry Cardinal Newman* (New York, Longmans, 1912); JOHN MOODY, *John Henry Newman* (New York, Sheed, 1945).

NEWPORT, BL. RICHARD (d. 1612), martyr. A native of Harringworth, Northamptonshire, England, he studied and was ordained in Rome in 1597, entered the English underground mission in London, and was captured and exiled a number of times before being condemned to be hanged at Tyburn for his priesthood. F. D. May 30.

NEWTON, JOHN (1823–1895), general. Born in Norfolk, Virginia, on Aug. 23, he studied and taught at West Point, became a convert, was chief engineer of the Utah Expedition in 1858, and served with the Union army during the Civil War, attaining the rank of major general. In 1866 he supervised fortifications and improved waterways in New York City, and invented a steam drill and other devices to solve his engineering problems. He retired from the army in 1886, was city commissioner of public works until 1888, and then became president of the Panama Railroad Co. He died in New York City on May 1.

NEYROT, BL. ANTONY (d. 1460), martyr. Born in Rivoli, Italy, he became a Dominican at San Marco in Florence and was captured by the Moors while sailing for Sicily and made a slave in Tunis. There he became a Moslem, married, but repented, and publicly renounced his actions before the ruler. He was condemned to death and was stoned, hacked by swords, and thrown into a fire. He was beatified in 1767. F. D. Apr. 10.

NICANDER, ST. (d. 300?), martyr. *See* Hesychius, St.

NICANDER, ST. (d. 304?), martyr. An Egyptian doctor, he was put to death because he attended Christian captives during the Diocletian persecution. F. D. Mar. 15.

NICANDER, ST. (4th century), martyr. *See* Marcian, St.

NICANDER, ST., martyr. A bishop, he and St. Hermas, a priest, were slain at Myra in Asia Minor at an undetermined date. F. D. Nov. 4.

NICANOR, ST. (d. 76?). A Jew who was chosen deacon by the apostles (Acts 6:5), may have gone to Cyprus. A legend adds that he was martyred there during the persecution of Vespasian. F. D. Jan. 10.

NICARETE, ST. (d. 410?). A native of Nicomedia, she migrated to Constantinople where she was a friend of St. John Chrysostom. Because of her defense of him she was exiled. F. D. Dec. 27.

NICASIUS, ST. (d. 285?), martyr. A regionary bishop, he was slain with Quirinus, a priest, and Scubiculus, a deacon, while traveling from Paris to Rouen. St. Pientia, who buried the body of Nicasius, was then put to death. F. D. Oct. 11.

NICASIUS, ST. (5th century), bishop and martyr. He, his deacon, St. Florentius, his lector, St. Jucundus, and sister, St. Eutropia, were slain at Rheims, Gaul, of which he is listed as tenth bishop, by invading barbarians in 407 or 451. F. D. Dec. 14.

NICCOLA PISANO (1220?–1278), sculptor. Born in Pisa, Italy, he early attracted the attention of Frederick II of Swabia, who commissioned him to finish his castles in Naples, and became a well-known architect. In 1260 his marble pulpit for the baptistery in Pisa launched him on a second famous career as a sculptor, successfully combining classical and Gothic elements. Among his great sculptures are the pulpit of the Siena cathedral, the shrine of St. Dominic in a Bologna church, a fountain in Perugia, and sculptures in the Lucca cathedral; he designed the basilica of St. Anthony in Padua and the interior of Santa Trinitá in Florence. He died in Pisa.

NICCOLÒ DE FOLIGNO. *See* Liberatore, Niccolò di.

NICEPHORUS. Called a local saint in Istria and said to have suffered martyrdom in 260, he is now considered to be a pious fiction.

NICEPHORUS, ST. (d. 284), martyr. *See* Claudian, St.

NICEPHORUS, ST. (758–828), patriarch. Philosopher, musician, and statesman in the service of Constantine VI, he was secretary to the second Nicaean Council. Though a layman, he was elected patriarch of Constantinople to succeed St. Tarasius and swore to uphold the freedom to venerate icons, for which stand his father had been scourged and exiled. He was briefly out of favor with St. Theodore Studites, who condemned him for reinstating a priest who had permitted Constantine to contract a bigamous marriage. He spent his last fifteen years in exile after Emperor Leo I revived the Iconoclast heresy, dying on June 2 in a monastery on the Bosphorus. His writings include a defense of icons and two historical chronicles. F. D. Mar. 13.

NICÉRON, JEAN PIERRE (1685-1738), scholar. Born in Paris on Mar. 11, he studied at Collège Mazarin, joined the Barnabites in 1702, and taught at colleges in Loche and Montargis. In 1716 he went to Paris and worked on a massive biographical encyclopedia, *Mémoires pour servir à l'histoire des hommes illustres de la république des lettres*, which appeared in thirty-nine volumes from 1727 to 1740. He also translated several English works. He died in Paris on July 8.

NICETA OF REMESIANA, ST. (335?-415?), bishop. A missioner who preached in modern Romania and Yugoslavia, then called Dacia, he may have been the author of the hymn, *Te Deum*. He wrote on liturgical singing, faith, the creed, the Trinity, and the particularly appealing *Names and Titles of Our Savior;* these long were falsely attributed to Nicetius of Trier or Nicetas of Aquileia. He was highly praised by St. Jerome and by St. Paulinus of Nola, who wrote to him in verse. F. D. June 22.

NICETAS, ST. (d. 735?). Bishop of Apollonias, Bithynia, he was persecuted by Emperor Leo the Armenian and driven from his see during the Iconoclast heresy to Anatolia, where he died. F. D. Mar. 20.

NICETAS, ST. (d. 1107), bishop. Born in Kiev, Russia, he became a monk there, returning to monasticism after a brief and independent life as a recluse. He became bishop of Novgorod, Russia, in 1095. F. D. Jan. 31.

NICETAS OF CONSTANTINOPLE, ST. (d. 838?). A native of Paphlagonia and a patrician, he was a courtier at the court of Empress Irene, to whom he was related, was supposedly sent as one of her representatives to the second Ecumenical Council of Nicaea, and became prefect of Sicily. In 811 he entered a monastery at Constantinople, from which he was driven by Emperor Leo V when he refused to support the emperor's attack on icons. He eventually settled in Katisia, Paphlagonia, where he died. F. D. Oct. 6.

NICETAS THE GOTH, ST. (d. 375), martyr. Called "the Great" by the Greeks, he was converted by the Arian Ulfilas, who ordained him. In 372, King Athanaric of the eastern Goths launched a persecution and Nicetas, when he refused to worship an idol, was burned to death with other Christians of his area. F. D. Sept. 15.

NICETAS OF PEREASLAV, ST. (d. 1186), martyr. A tax collector near Rostov, Russia, he became a recluse, an extreme ascetic, lived for a while on a pillar, was known for his gift of healing, and died of a beating given him by outlaws. F. D. May 24.

NICETIUS, ST. (d. 566?), bishop. Born in Auvergne, Gaul, he became a monk and then abbot of his monastery, probably Limoges. In 532 he was appointed bishop of Trèves (the last Gallo-Roman bishop of that see), excommunicated Clotaire I for his crimes, and was exiled by the king. When Sigebert succeeded his father to the throne, Nicetius was restored to his see, participated in several synods, restored ecclesiastical discipline to his diocese, founded a school for the clergy, fought heresy, and was noted for his justice and charity. He probably died on Oct. 1. F. D. Dec. 5.

NICETIUS, ST. (d. 573), bishop. Of Burgundian descent, he was ordained, became a great preacher, saw to it that the boys of his parish learned to write, and was nominated by St. Sacerdos as bishop of Lyons, Gaul, in 553. F. D. Apr. 2.

NICETIUS, ST. (d. 611?), bishop. Probably the friend of Pope St. Gregory the Great and the host of St. Columban when the latter had to flee the hostility of King Thierry II, he restored the see of Besançon, Gaul, which had been destroyed by the Huns. He is also called Nizier. F. D. Feb. 8.

NICETUS, ST. (5th century). He is listed as fifteenth bishop of Vienne, Gaul, in 449. F. D. May 5.

NICHOLAS I, ST. (d. 867), pope. Of a distinguished Roman family, he served under Benedict III, whom he succeeded Apr. 24, 858, and immediately took actions which justified his surname, "the Great." He insisted on the indissolubility of the marriage bond when he denounced the second marriage of the emperor's nephew, King Lothaire II of Lorraine, as irregular and refused to withdraw from this stand in the face of an invasion of Rome. He also insisted on freedom of marriage when he compelled Charles the Bold to accept the marriage of his daughter to Baldwin of Flanders without the king's consent and forced the archbishop to recall her excommunication. In 861 he obliged Archbishop Hincmar of Rheims to restore Bishop Rothad of Soissons, causing the archbishop to acknowledge that the Holy See had full authority to intervene in important causes and to pass independent judgment. He twice excommunicated the powerful John, archbishop of Ravenna, for abuses of his office, forcing him to submit in both instances. He was involved in difficulties with Constantinople from the day he took office, involving the manipulation of the patriarchate there by Photius and Emperor Michael III, whom he excommunicated in 863, which was not resolved until the new emperor, Basil I, came to the throne and expelled Photius on the very day Nicholas died. He was also active in the missionary field, sending St. Anskar as papal legate to Scandinavia and through his missionaries and correspondence with King Boris (his letter to Boris, *Responsa Nicolai ad Consulta Bulgarorum*, is a landmark in papal rulings on matters of faith and liturgy) leading the Bulgars to Christianity. His pontificate restored the papacy to great prestige, emphasized its primacy (he unhesitatingly set aside decrees of councils which conflicted with Church law and teaching), reiterated the ascendancy of the Church over secular sovereigns in matters concerning the Church, and instituted reforms among the clergy and hierarchy. He became famous for his justice, his impatience with wrongdoing, his concern for the poor, and as a patron of literature and the arts. F. D. Nov. 13.

NICHOLAS II (d. 1061), pope. Born in Chevron, Savoy, Italy, Gerhard of Burgundy became a canon in Liège and, in 1046, bishop of Florence, where he introduced strict ecclesiastical reforms. In 1058, when Pope Stephen X died, John Mincius was named pope in a tumultuous election as Benedict X by the Tusculan party, despite Stephen's orders to postpone any election until Hildebrand arrived from Germany. In Dec. a group of protesting cardinals met at Siena, elected Gerhard as Pope Nicholas II, and deposed and drove out Benedict. Consecrated on Jan. 24, 1059, Nicholas called a synod in the Lateran that year which provided rules for the election of popes based on the free election by the cardinals of a man to be chosen from the Roman clergy unless a qualified man could not be found in their ranks, thus eliminating popular elections, and, though imperial confirmation was allowed, it was so only as a personal privilege granted by the pope. Concubinage, lay investiture, and simoniacal ordinations were also condemned. Nicholas concluded agreements with the Normans which provided powerful support for the papacy. He died in Florence, Italy, on July 27.

NICHOLAS III (1216?–1280), pope. Giovanni Gaetani Orsini was born in Rome, was early given administration of several Roman churches, and in 1244 was created cardinal-deacon by Pope Innocent IV, whom he accompanied on his flight to Lyons a month later. He attempted unsuccessfully to reconcile the Guelphs and Ghibellines of Florence in 1252, was selected by France and England in 1258 to ratify their peace treaty, and in 1261 helped elect Pope Urban IV, who appointed him protector of the Franciscans in 1263. He was elected pope at Viterbo on Nov. 25, 1277, and was consecrated on Dec. 26. His pontificate was noted for his efforts to free the papacy from secular interference; his curtailment of Charles of Anjou's power in central Italy by causing him, in 1278, to give up his title of senator and his office of imperial vicar of Tuscany; his strug-

gle to maintain Christianity in Hungary; fruitless efforts to restore peace between France and Castile; the renunciation of Rudolf of Hapsburg's claims to the Romagna; closer relations with the Byzantine court, though the efforts begun at the second Council of Lyons in 1274 to reunite the Eastern Church to Rome ultimately failed; and the nepotism he practiced to the advantage of the house of Orsini in high offices, though he personally lived an exemplary life of high moral purpose. He died in Soriano, near Viterbo, Italy, on Aug. 22.

NICHOLAS IV (d. 1292), pope. Girolamo Masci was born in Ascoli, Ancona, Italy, and early joined the Franciscans. In 1272 he journeyed to Constantinople to invite the Greeks to participate in the second Council of Lyons, was elected general of the Franciscans in 1274, and was created cardinal-priest in 1278. He was appointed bishop of Palestrina in 1281 and was elected the first Franciscan pope on Feb. 15, 1288, an honor he accepted only after a second election on Feb. 22. He crowned Charles II of Anjou king of Sicily and Naples, over Rudolf of Hapsburg's claims, in 1289, an action which led to an estrangement between Rudolf and the papacy, appealed in vain for a new crusade when the destruction of Acre in 1291 ended Christian power in the East, and founded the universities of Montpellier and Lisbon. He died in Rome on Apr. 4.

NICHOLAS V (1397–1455), pope. Tommaso Parentucelli was born in Sarzana, Liguria, Italy, on Nov. 15, studied at Bologna, tutored the Strozzi and Albizzi families in Florence, and received his master's degree in theology from Bologna in 1422. He became secretary of the bishop of Bologna, Cardinal Niccolò Albergati, an outstanding bibliophile, accompanied his patron on several diplomatic missions, and, though appointed his successor, was unable to occupy his see because of disorders in the city. He conducted diplomatic missions to Italy and Germany for Pope Eugene IV, was created cardinal in 1446, and elected pope on Mar. 6 (and consecrated on Mar. 19), 1447. He launched a program of beautifying Rome, the Trevi Fountain, the Vatican, and St. Peter's; encouraged the arts, literature, and scholarship; founded the Vatican Library; and inaugurated a period which has been called the "golden age of the humanists." In 1448 he signed the Concordat of Vienna with Frederick III, king of the Romans, by which the king recognized the pope's right to confirm bishops, accepted the submission of antipope Felix V in 1449 (and appointed him cardinal of Santa Sabina), brought about the dissolution of the Council of Basle, and proclaimed 1450 a jubilee year to celebrate the schism's end. He inaugurated great ecclesiastical and monastic reforms in France (through Cardinal D'Estouteville), Germany

(Nicholas of Cusa in the north and St. John Capistran in southern Germany and Poland), and Italy (Cardinal Bessarion), and in 1452 crowned Frederick III the first Hapsburg Holy Roman emperor (and last emperor to be crowned in Rome). In 1453 an uprising led by Stefano Porcaro was suppressed and its leader executed, and in 1453 Constantinople fell to the Turks. Despite his efforts to launch a crusade, his pleas fell on deaf ears. He died in Rome on Mar. 24.

NICHOLAS V (d. 1333), antipope. Pietro Rainalducci was born in Corbario, Italy, and joined the Franciscans in 1310. In 1328, Emperor Louis IV (the Bavarian), who had been excommunicated by Pope John XXII in 1324, declared John deposed and proclaimed Peter pope as Nicholas V. Peter was driven from Rome three months later, and was excommunicated by Pope John in 1329. He submitted in 1330, and was held in the papal palace in Avignon, France, until his death on Oct. 16.

NICHOLAS, ST. (d. 350?), bishop. Though born of wealthy parents in Parara in Asia Minor, he grew up as an orphan. Later, he gave away his possessions to the poor and sick, made a pilgrimage to Jerusalem, and on his return was elected bishop of Myra. He devoted himself to the conversion of sinners and the care of orphans, making numerous gifts to the latter. Many mediaeval legends have him arranging dowries for poor servant girls, or tossing bags of money into homes which faced starvation, or coming to the aid of lost sailors and penurious prisoners. The most popular story has him restore life to three murdered children who had been pickled in brine. In 1087 his relics were stolen by Italians and carried to Bari, which became a major shrine. By the thirteenth century his feast was a gift-giving day in many parts of Europe. The figure of Santa Claus is a non-Catholic creation, based on legends associated with Thor, the kindly god of fire in Germanic legend, who was associated with winter and the yule log, and who rode in a chariot drawn by goats named Cracker and Gnasher. Bishop Nicholas was chained in prison during the persecution of Diocletian, was released by Constantine, and served his diocese for several decades afterward. He died in Myra. He is patron of Russia and of Greece. F. D. Dec. 6.

NICHOLAS, ST. (925), patriarch. Often called "the Mystic" because he was a member of the secret council of the court, he was deposed as patriarch of Constantinople and exiled when he refused to permit Emperor Leo the Wise to marry a fourth time, a step forbidden by the Eastern Church. F. D. May 15.

NICHOLAS, ST. (1075–1094). He was a Greek who wandered through southern Italy as a holy pilgrim, attracting crowds by his simplicity, though often being treated roughly as a madman. He was canonized four years after his death by Pope Urban II. F. D. June 2.

NICHOLAS (d. 1159), geographer. Abbot of Thingeyre, he was the first to record Norse discoveries in America, and established that Leif the Lucky, son of Eric the Red, and the merchant Thorfinn Karlsefni made the only two known voyages to Vinland. He mapped Halluland as south of Greenland, with Markland and Vinland below them.

NICHOLAS, BL. (d. 1163?). He and his father became Cistercians at the hands of St. Bernard; Nicholas became abbot of the monastery of Vaucelles, France. F. D. May 31.

NICHOLAS, ST. (d. 1227), martyr. *See* Daniel, St.

NICHOLAS CHRYSOBERGES, ST. (d. 996). He was patriarch of Constantinople from 983 until his death. F. D. Dec. 16.

NICHOLAS OF CUSA (1400?–1464), cardinal. Born in Cues, near Trier, Germany, son of Johann Cryfts, he studied at Heidelberg, Padua, and Cologne, may have been Cardinal Orsini's secretary in 1425, was ordained in 1430, and was given several benefices. He attended the Council of Basle in 1431, where he supported Pope Eugene IV, was sent to Constantinople by the pope in 1437 to invite the emperor and archbishops to the Council of Florence, and in 1438 was appointed papal legate to plead the cause of Eugene before the courts of Europe. In 1449 he was created cardinal-priest by Pope Nicholas V, was appointed bishop of Brixen in the Tyrol in 1450, but was unable to occupy his see until 1452, went to northern Germany and the Netherlands as papal legate, and was highly successful in putting into effect the ecclesiastical and monastic reforms of Nicholas in 1451 and 1452. When he returned to Brixen, his efforts to reform his own diocese led to a struggle, which was to be lifelong, with Archduke Sigismund of Austria. He was imprisoned by Sigismund in 1460, but escaped to Rome, where Pope Pius II excommunicated the archduke and made Nicholas camerarius of the Sacred College. Among his writings are *De concordantia catholica* (outlining reforms for the Church and the Empire), *De auctoritate praesidendi in concilio generali* (in which he defended the supremacy of a council over the pope, a position he later modified), *De cribratione alchorani*, *De quaerendo Deum*, and *Reparatio calendarii*, all characterized by great independence and originality, mystic intuition and deep speculation. In his scientific writings he maintained that the earth was round, a star like other stars, and not the center of the universe. He died in Todi, Italy, on Aug. 11.

NICHOLAS VON FLÜE, ST. (1417–1487). Born near Sachseln, Switzerland, on the Flüeli, he fought in the army, became a captain, and later a judge and deputy. Happily married and the father of ten children, he decided when he was about fifty to become a hermit and retired to a cell at Ranft, near Sachseln. There he prayed twelve hours a day, gave advice willingly to a stream of daily visitors and even to the government, which adopted his suggestion that Fribourg and Soleure be accepted into the Swiss Confederation after independence had been won from Charles the Bold. Bruder Klaus, as he was widely called, was canonized in 1947. F. D. Mar. 22.

NICHOLAS OF FORCA PALENA, Bl. (1349–1449). A priest at Forca Palena in the Abruzzi, Italy, he founded a society of Hermits of St. Jerome at Naples, with other houses in Florence and Rome, which later was amalgamated with the Hieronymites founded by Bl. Peter of Pisa. Although his cult among the Hieronymites was confirmed in 1771, Pope Benedict XIV refused assent to his solemn beatification. F. D. Oct. 1.

NICHOLAS GIUSTINIANI (12th century). He became a Benedictine monk at San Niccolò del Lido, in Venice, in 1153, but was released from his vows in 1172 when all the male members of the Giustiniani family perished at sea. Nicholas then was married to Anna Michieli, daughter of the doge. After fathering six sons and three daughters, thus preserving the family name, he asked permission to return to his monastery in 1179. His wife entered a convent on the island of Aniano, which they had established. He is often listed as Blessed and honored on Nov. 21, though there has been no formal beatification.

NICHOLAS OF GORRAN (1232–1295?), scholar. Born in Gorran, France, he joined the Dominicans, served several times as prior of St. James in Paris, and became adviser and confessor of Philip IV of France. He was famed as a preacher and for his commentaries on the Bible, particularly on St. Paul and the Apocalypse.

NICHOLAS OF HUNGARY, BL. (d. 1369), martyr. *See* Antony of Saxony, Bl.

NICHOLAS OF KULM (14th century). A German priest, he established in 1372 the hospice of St. Andrew in Rome, which was united in 1431 with that set up by Johann Peters and which became the Anima, center for German nationals in the city.

NICHOLAS OF LYRA (1270–1340), exegete. Born in Lyra, Normandy, France, he joined the Franciscans, took his doctorate in theology at Paris, and taught at the Sorbonne where he joined the faculty in opposing Pope John XXII over the definition of the beatific vision. He was active in working for Jewish conversions and wrote several theological treatises, chief of which was the five-volume *Postillae perpetuae*

in universam sacram scripturam, the first printed biblical commentary. Of wide influence, it stressed the necessity of the literal interpretation of scripture, warning against the mystical and allegorical readings which had been forced upon it by too many earlier commentators. He died in Paris.

NICHOLAS MAC MAELISU (d. 1302). He became primate of Armagh, Ireland, in 1272, and in 1291 called an assembly of his fellow bishops at Tuam to consider ways of stopping secular interference.

NICHOLAS OF OSIMO (d. 1453). Born in Osimo, Italy, he received his doctorate in law from Bologna, joined the Observant Friars Minor, was instrumental in securing Observant independence from the Conventuals in 1440, was appointed visitator and then superior of the Holy Land, and died in Rome. He wrote several treatises on moral theology.

NICHOLAS PAGLIA, BL. (d. 1255). Born in Giovinazzo, Italy, he is said to have become a Dominican after he heard St. Dominic preach. He established monasteries at Perugia in 1233 and at Trani in 1254 and was prior provincial at Rome in 1230 and in 1255. His cult was confirmed in 1828. F. D. Feb. 14.

NICHOLAS POLITI, BL. (1117–1167). Born in Aderno, Sicily, he lived as a recluse on Mt. Etna for thirty years. His cult was approved by Pope Julius II. F. D. Aug. 17.

NICHOLAS OF STRASSBURG (14th century), mystic. Educated at Paris, he became a Dominican, lector in Cologne's Dominican academy, and in 1325 was sent as visitator to reform the German province by Pope John XXII. There he assumed the office of inquisitor, became involved in a dispute over Master Eckhardt, whom he favored, with the archbishop of Cologne, was excommunicated (a sentence lifted by the pope), in 1327 was definitor at a general chapter of his order, and in 1329 was vicar of the German Dominicans.

NICHOLAS STUDITES, ST. (d. 863). Born in Sydonia, Crete, he became a monk at the monastery of Studius, Constantinople when eighteen. The monks were banished during the persecutions of the Iconoclasts, and they continued to suffer imperial attacks until 842. In 858, St. Ignatius was replaced as patriarch of Constantinople by Photius, a political appointee of Emperor Michael III. Nicholas refused to recognize Photius, again went into exile, was captured, and brought back as a prisoner. When Michael died in 867, Emperor Basil, who succeeded him, restored Ignatius as patriarch and Nicholas as abbot of the Studites. The latter asked to be excused because of his extreme age and spent his last years in quiet prayer. He died at Studius. F. D. Feb. 4.

NICHOLAS OF TOLENTINE, ST. (1245–

1305). Born in Sant' Angelo, near Fermo, Italy, he became an Augustinian in 1263, and was ordained at Cingoli about 1270. He was a successful preacher and in 1274 was sent to Tolentino, a town of evil ways and a schismatic populace. He preached there for thirty years, treating the sick and poor with great tenderness and others with harsh though just strictures. He became famous as a confessor, won many converts, died in Tolentino, and was canonized in 1446. F. D. Sept. 10.

NICHOLS, VEN. GEORGE (1550?–1589), martyr. He studied at Oxford, taught at St. Paul's, London, went to Rheims and Rome, and was ordained at Laon in 1583. He was sent on the English mission, arrested in Oxford with Fr. Richard Yaxley, Humphrey Prichard, a Welsh tavern employee, and Thomas Belson. All four were tortured, imprisoned, and executed at Oxford on Oct. 19.

NICHOLSON, FRANCIS (1650–1731). Born in Manchester, England, he studied at Oxford, became an Anglican minister at Oxford and Canterbury, and was converted sometime after 1680. During James II's reign he worked for the sovereign, was forced to flee the uprising of 1688, and shortly after joined the Carthusians in Flanders. He returned to England in 1692, entered the service of Catharine of Braganza, the dowager queen, and accompanied her back to Portugal, where he remained until his death in Lisbon on Aug. 13.

NICKEL, GOSWIN (1582–1664). Born in Jülich, Germany, he became a Jesuit, and in 1652 was elected tenth general of his Society He inherited problems arising from Jansenism and from the quarrel over the Chinese rites reported on by Matteo Ricci. He died on July 31.

NICODEMUS (1st century). A Pharisee and a sanhedrist, and one of the ambassadors sent by Aristobulus to Pompey, according to Josephus, he is mentioned in John 3:1–21, where he has a lengthy discourse with Christ, in John 7:50–51, where he attempts to defend Christ before the Sanhedrim, and in John 19:39–42, where he helps Joseph of Arimethea bury Him in the sepulcher.

NICOLAI, JEAN (1594–1673), theologian. Born in Mouzay, France, he joined the Dominicans when twelve, was professed in 1612, studied at St. James in Paris, received his doctorate in theology from the Sorbonne in 1632, taught at several Dominican houses, and served on the committee to examine and bar from the Sorbonne Jansenist teachings. He wrote theological treatises, poetry, and political tracts, and prepared new editions of older theologians, mainly works on St. Thomas. He died in Paris on May 7.

NICOLAI, MICHAEL (15th century). A parish priest in Odense, Denmark, he wrote religious poetry, published in 1514, some of which was later used in Lutheran hymnbooks, and adapted a Rosary of the Virgin in 1496.

NICOLAS, ARMELLE (1606–1671). Born in Campenéac, Brittany, France, on Sept. 9, she became a servant-maid when twenty-two, served in various neighboring towns, and became so renowned for her humility, piety, and sanctity that she was called "la bonne Armelle" and held in the highest esteem. While porter at an Ursuline convent in Vannes she related her spiritual experiences to Sr. Jeanne de la Nativité, who included them in a later biography. Though honored after her death in Vannes on Oct. 24, she was never canonized.

NICOLAS, AUGUSTE (1807–1888), apologist. Born in Bordeaux, France, on Jan. 6, he became a lawyer, was justice of the peace in Bordeaux from 1841 to 1849, when he became assistant minister of public worship, was appointed general inspector of libraries in 1854, judge of the Seine tribunal in 1860, and councilor of the Paris court of appeals. He wrote popular works of apologetics, and died in Versailles on Jan. 18.

NICOLAS, BL. GILBERT (1463–1532). A native of Riom, France, he became a Franciscan Observant at La Rochelle. He was confessor to St. Joan of Valois and assisted her in founding the Order of the Annonciades, for which he secured papal approval in 1502. In 1517 he was elected and held for life the office of commissary general of the Observants. His cult was approved in 1647. Because of his devotion to Mary in the Annunciation, he was honored by Popes Alexander VI and Leo X; the latter gave him the name Gabriel Mary, under which name his cult was approved in 1647. F. D. Aug. 27.

NICOLAUS GERMANUS (15th century), cartographer. A German priest, he is known for his Cosmographia of Don Nicolò, a Latin translation of the Geography of Ptolemy, with revised maps in which he substituted for Ptolemy's flat projection his own Donis projection with new methods of delineating geographic units such as countries, lakes, and mountains.

NICOLAZIC, YVES (17th century). A simple villager in Auray, Brittany, he claimed in 1624 to have seen an apparition of St. Anne, who directed the rebuilding of a chapel there which had been destroyed 1000 years before. Bishop Rosmadec of Vannes approved the project, and the still-popular shrine was erected.

NICOLE, PIERRE (1625–1695), theologian. Born in Chartres, France, on Oct. 19, he studied at Paris, and in 1649–52 he taught at Port Royal (Racine was one of his pupils) and became a friend of Antoine Arnauld. He traveled to Germany in 1658, where he translated Pascal's Provinciales (he had helped Pascal in its writing) into Latin, and in 1676 had his application for ordination turned down by the bishop of Chartres. He was embroiled in numerous theological disputes thereafter, supported the Jansenists (many of his writings reveal this leaning), sided with Bossuet against the quietists, and took Mabillon's side in the discussion over monastic studies. He died in Paris on Nov. 16.

NICOLÒ DE TUDESCHI (1386–1445), bishop. Born in Catania, Sicily, he joined the Benedictines in 1400, studied at Bologna (where he received his doctorate in canon law in 1411), taught at Parma (1412–18) and Siena (1419–30), was appointed abbot of Maniacio in 1425, and taught at Bologna in 1431–32. He was called to Rome in 1433 as auditor of the rota and apostolic referendary, entered the services of the king of Sicily in 1434, and was appointed bishop of Palermo in 1435. He supported antipope Felix V, who named him a cardinal in 1440. He wrote widely on canon law and a tract supporting conciliar supremacy. He died in Palermo, Sicily, on Feb. 24.

NICOMEDES, ST. (d. 90?), martyr. He was probably a Roman priest. Legend says he was tortured and beaten to death for burying the body of St. Felicula. F. D. Sept. 15.

NICON, ST. (d. 250?), martyr. A Roman soldier who became a convert and a monk while in the Near East, he fled to Sicily with a number of followers and was put to death with them there (not in Palestine) during the persecution of Decius. F. D. Mar. 23.

NICON, ST. (d. 303?), martyr. See Mark, St.

NICOSTRATUS, ST. (d. 303), martyr. He is said to have been a Roman tribune who was put to death with Antiochus and other Christian soldiers at Caesarea in Palestine during the persecution of Diocletian. F. D. May 21.

NICOSTRATUS, ST. (d. 305?), martyr. See Castorius, St.

NIDER, JOHN (1380–1438), theologian. Born in Swabia, he joined the Dominicans, studied at Vienna and Cologne, where he was ordained, became noted for his preaching, and after attending the Council of Constance returned to Vienna in 1425 to teach at the university. In 1427 he was elected prior in Nuremberg. He became noted for his insistence on reform and in 1431 was appointed prior of the convent of strict observance in Basle. He was theologian at the Council of Basle and served as legate to the Bohemians in 1434 to effect a reconciliation. He favored continuing the Council of Basle in Germany after its dissolution by Pope Eugene IV, but submitted to the pope, returned to teaching at Vienna in 1436, and served as dean of the university twice before his death in Colmar, Alsace, on Aug. 13.

NIDGER, BL. (d. 829?), bishop. He was abbot of the Benedictine monastery of Otto-

beuren, Bavaria, before he became bishop of Augsburg in 822. F. D. Apr. 15.

NIEHEIM, DIETRICH VON (1339?–1418), historian. Born in the diocese of Paderborn, Germany, he studied law in Italy, but never received the doctorate, became a papal notary at Avignon, and served in the chancery office of several popes. Boniface IX made him bishop of Verden in 1395, but he never gained possession of his see. He was distressed by the beginnings of the Western schism, wrote tracts to end it, and declared his allegiance to Alexander V and John XXIII. He grew disillusioned about the latter, abandoned him, and wrote against him both in tracts and in his history of the Council of Constance (1414–16). Because historians are not in agreement about Dietrich's authorship of several proposals for ending the schism, the extent of his efforts have not been determined; if De necessitate reformationis and others are his, then he seems to have been one of the greatest forces in restoring unity to the Church. Admitted titles are an attack on Wyclif, guides for curial administration, a history of the papal chancery from 1380 on, and a non-extant geography. He died in Maastricht, Netherlands, on Mar. 22.

NIEREMBERG Y OTIN, JUAN EUSEBIO (1595–1658), theologian. Born in Madrid, of German parents, he studied at Alcalá and Salamanca, joined the Jesuits in 1614, continued his studies at Colegio de Huete, and was ordained in 1623. He taught at the Colegio Imperial in Madrid for nineteen years, was confessor to Philip II's granddaughter, the duchess of Mantua, and died in Madrid. He wrote more than seventy works, including treatises on grace, eternity, the Immaculate Conception, the widely popular De la afición de Jesús (1630), and an account of the natural history of the Indies (1635).

NIESSENBERGER, HANS (15th century), architect. Born in Graz, Styria, he worked on the cathedrals in Freiburg, Strassburg, and Milan, marked by late Gothic style, between 1471 and 1483.

NIEUWLAND, JULIUS ARTHUR (1878–1936), chemist. Born in Hansbeke, Belgium, on Feb. 14, he was brought to the United States as a child, graduated from Notre Dame in 1899, became a member of the Congregation of Holy Cross, and was ordained in 1903. He took his doctorate of philosophy at Catholic University in 1904, returned to teach chemistry and botany at Notre Dame, and in 1920–23 was dean of the college of science. He also served as curator of the botanical herbaria at the university. He received medals and honors for his research in synthetic rubber from 1906 to 1931, when he succeeded in producing that substance. His publication of Some Reactions on Acetylene led to the discovery of Lewisite,

the poison gas of World War I. He became
professor of chemistry in 1918, was editor of
American Midland Naturalist, which he had
founded in 1909, and died in Washington,
D.C., on June 11.

NIGER, PETER GEORGE (1434-1484?),
theologian. Born in Kaaden, Bohemia, he
studied at Salamanca and Montpellier, joined
the Dominicans in 1452, and finished his
studies at Leipzig and Bologna. He became
lector of theology in 1461, regent of studies in
Cologne in 1465, was elected prior of Eichstätt
about 1469, and after teaching at the Ratisbon
convent became professor of exegesis at Ingolstadt in 1478. He was appointed rector of the
new academy in Buda, Hungary, by King
Matthias Corvinus, and probably died there. He
wrote on logic and psychology and devoted
much time to preaching to Jews and engaging
rabbis in Talmudic controversy.

NIGHTON. *See* Nectan, St.

NIHUS, BARTHOLD (1590?-1657), bishop.
Born in Holtorf, Hanover (or Wolpe, Brunswick), on Feb. 7, he studied at Helmstedt and
Jena, became a convert in 1622, and entered
the House of Proselytes in Cologne, was ordained, and became its director. He became
provost of a Cistercian monastery in 1627,
abbot of the Premonstratensian monastery in
1629, from which he was forced by war to flee
in 1631, and canon of Holy Cross church,
Hildesheim. He served the papal nuncio, Fabio
Chigi (Pope Alexander VII) in 1645 at Münster, and Archbishop Schönborn of Mayence,
who appointed him suffragan bishop of Saxony
and Thuringia in 1655. He died in Erfurt, Germany, on Mar. 10. He wrote theological and
apologetic works.

NIKOLAUS OF DINKELSBÜHL (1360?-
1433), theologian. Born in Dinkelsbühl, Germany, he studied at Vienna, where he was to
teach for most of his life, became dean of the
faculty in 1397, and rector of the university and
canon of St. Stephen cathedral in 1405. He
represented Duke Albert V of Austria at the
Council of Constance (1414-18), helped examine witnesses in the trial of Hieronymus of
Prague, Bohemia, and in 1425 became confessor of Duke Albert V. He declined the
bishopric of Passau, helped draw up the reform
program for the Council of Basle in 1431, and
died in Mariazell, Styria, on Mar. 17.

NIKON, ST. (d. 998). Surnamed Metanoite
because he always began his sermons with this
Greek word meaning "repent," he was born in
Pontus, on the Black Sea in Asia Minor, became a monk at the monastery of Khrysopetro,
and after twelve years there was sent as a missionary to Crete, where he remained for
twenty years. He then went to Greece, where he
died in a monastery in Peloponnesus. F. D. Nov.
26.

NILAMMON, ST. (d. 404). A monk in
Egypt, he closed up his cell when he was
chosen a bishop, and died in prayer while his
consecrators waited. F. D. June 6.

NILAN, JOHN JOSEPH (1855-1934),
bishop. Born in Newburyport, Massachusetts,
on Aug. 1, he studied at St. Raphael College,
Nicolet, Canada, and St. Joseph's seminary,
Troy, New York, and was ordained in 1878.
He served in Massachusetts parishes, and was
pastor of St. Joseph's, Amesbury, from 1892 to
1910, when he was consecrated bishop of Hartford, Connecticut. He died there on Apr. 13.

NILLES, NIKOLAUS (1828-1907), theologian. Born in Rippweiler, Luxembourg, on June
21, he studied in Rome from 1847 to 1853,
was ordained, and worked as a parish priest
until 1858, when he became a Jesuit. He
taught canon law at Innsbruck, Austria, from
1859 until his death on Jan. 31, and was president of the seminary there from 1860 to 1875.
He wrote some fifty works on theology, asceticism, and the liturgy.

NILUS, ST. (d. 310?), bishop and martyr. *See*
Peleus, St.

NILUS THE ELDER, ST. (d. 430?). He
probably was an imperial official at Constantinople, who at an advanced age decided to live
the life of a recluse with his son Theodulus on
Mt. Sinai. He was a follower of St. John
Chrysostom and rebuked Emperor Arcadius
for banishing him. After he was ordained he
wrote many treatises on theological and scriptural themes as well as many still extant letters.
Some authorities believe there were two
Niluses, one of whom, the writer, also called
"the Wise," was a monk in Ancyra, Galatia.
F. D. Nov. 12.

NILUS THE YOUNGER, ST. (910?-1004).
A Greek born in Rossana, Italy, he spent his
youth recklessly, but after the death of a woman
with whom he lived and of their child, he
joined the Basilian monks of St. Adrian in
Calabria. He became their abbot, but had to flee
when the Saracens invaded in 981. He and his
monks were given refuge at Monte Cassino,
then at Vallelucio. In 996 they established a
monastery at Serperi. Nilus pleaded that the
antipope John XVI be shown mercy, although
he condemned his schism. The monastery of
Grottaferrata on Monte Carvo was built by his
monks under St. Bartholomew; it acknowledges
St. Nilus as founder-abbot and still follows the
Byzantine rite. He died in Frascati, Italy, on
Dec. 27. F. D. Sept. 26.

NINIAN, ST. (d. 432?), bishop. A Briton, he
studied at Rome where he was consecrated,
possibly by the pope, and then returned to
evangelize Britain. He established his see at
Whitborn, built a church and a monastery
which became the center of his missionary
activities among the Britons, with whom he

was most successful, and the Picts, whose conversions were not enduring. F. D. Sept. 16.

NINO, ST. (4th century). Reputed to have been a native of Cappadocia in Asia Minor (though other legends say Rome, Jerusalem, and even Gaul), she was captured and brought to Georgia (Iberia) as a slave. There her miracles so impressed all that even the king and queen were impressed, became Christians, supported her work, and had Constantine send missionaries to their country. The story has been embroidered with myths and legends, but probably is substantially true. Nino (called Christiana in the Roman Martyrology) supposedly spent the last years of her life as a recluse at Bodbe, Kakhetia, Georgia, Russia, where she died and was buried. She is venerated as the apostle of Georgia. F. D. Dec. 15.

NIRSCHL, JOSEPH (1823–1904), theologian. Born in Durchfurth, Lower Bavaria, on Feb. 24, he was ordained in 1851, received his doctorate in theology from Munich in 1854, became professor of church history at Passau in 1862 and at Würzburg in 1879, and was dean of the cathedral in 1892. He wrote several works on patristics and died in Würzburg, Germany, on Jan. 17.

NISSEN, ST. (5th century). Converted in Ireland by St. Patrick, he was given charge of the monastery of Montgarth, Wexford. F. D. July 25.

NITHARD (795?–843?), historian. Son of Charlemagne's daughter, Bertha, and Anghilbert, he supported Charles the Bald's claims against Lothair, served on an unsuccessful mission to Lothair in 840, fought with Charles at the battle of Fontenoy in 841, and was probably lay abbot of St. Riquier, where he was buried. He was the author of *De dissensionibus filiorum Ludovici Pii*, in which he describes the causes of the quarrel between Charles and Lothair, blaming the latter for the dissensions.

NITHARD, ST. (d. 845), martyr. A Benedictine, he went with St. Anskar from New Corbie to Sweden, where he was slain by pagans. F. D. Feb. 4.

NIVARD, ST. (d. 670). Brother-in-law of King Childeric II of Austrasia, he became archbishop of Rheims, France, and restored the abbey of Hautvilliers, Champagne, France, where he was buried. F. D. Sept. 1.

NIVARD (1100?–1150?). He was the youngest brother of St. Bernard, who joined him at the Cistercian monastery of Clairvaux and became master of novices at Vaucelles. His cult is not confirmed, though he is honored locally on Feb. 7.

NIZA, MARCOS DE (1495?–1558), missioner. Born in Nice, Savoy, he joined the Franciscans, went to America in 1531, and served as a missioner in Guatemala, Mexico, and Peru. In 1539 he was sent on an exploring trip which took him as far north as Arizona and New Mexico, and wrote a glowing description, *Descubrimiento de las siete ciudades*. A subsequent expedition led by Francisco Coronado in 1540 punctured the myth of towns with gold-lined streets; Fr. Marcos returned to Mexico City, where he remained as provincial of his order in New Spain until his death there on Mar. 25.

NIZIER. *See* Nicetius, St. (d. 611?).

NOAILLES, LOUIS ANTOINE DE (1651–1729), cardinal. Born on May 27, in the Château of Teyssière, Auvergne, France, son of the first duke of Noailles, he studied at the Collège du Plessis, Paris, received his doctorate from the Sorbonne in 1676, was appointed bishop of Cahors in 1679, and transferred to Châlons-sur-Marne the following year. He was appointed archbishop of Paris in 1695, instituted widespread ecclesiastical reforms, was created cardinal in 1700, and was appointed prior of Navarre in 1704 and head of the Sorbonne in 1710. He was attacked by the Jesuits for his alleged Jansenist leanings, which he denied, though he refused to accept Pope Clement XI's bull *Unigenitus* (1713), and in 1715 deprived the Jesuits in his see of their faculties. He finally accepted the bull in 1728 and restored the Jesuits' privileges. He died in Paris on May 4.

NOBILI, ROBERTO DE' (1577–1656), missioner. Born in Rome, Italy, he studied at the Roman College, became a Jesuit at Naples in 1596, was ordained in 1603, and was sent to India in 1604. He learned local languages, adopted Brahmin customs and dress to overcome native hostility, cut himself off from his fellow Europeans, and was remarkably successful in making 4000 converts in three southern Indian districts. Accused of allowing his converts to retain religious practices alien to Catholicism, he was severely censured but finally cleared. He was imprisoned at Madurai in 1640–41 because of anti-foreign feeling, but remained there after his release until 1654, when he was sent to Ceylon. After two years he was sent to Mylapore, India, where he died on Jan. 16. He translated many prayers and dogmatic works into Sanskrit and wrote a catechism in Tamil, and other religious works. VINCENT CRONIN, *A Pearl to India* (New York, Dutton, 1959).

NOBLE, DANIEL (1810–1885). Born on Jan. 14 of an old Yorkshire, England, family, he studied medicine in Preston and at St. Andrew's, was admitted to the Royal College of Surgeons, began to practice in Manchester in 1834, and became a specialist in mental diseases. He was president of the Manchester Phrenological Society, a fellow of the College of Physicians, wrote on the mind, nervous system, psychological medicine, mesmerism, and sanitary reform, and died in Manchester, England, on Jan. 12.

NOGARA, BARTOLOMEO (1868–1954), scholar. Born near Como, Italy, he was placed in charge of a papal museum in 1900 and by 1933 was director general of all Vatican City monuments, museums, galleries, and libraries. He was a member of 200 scientific societies, an authority on the Etruscans, and edited *Art Treasures of the Vatican*. He died in Rome on June 19.

NOLA, GIOVANNI MARLIANO DA (1488–1558?), sculptor. Born in Nola, Italy, he studied under Agnolo Fiore in Naples, and after further study in Rome returned to Naples, where he produced ecclesiastical sculptures, altarpieces, and tombs.

NOLASCO, PEDRO. *See* Peter Nolasco, St.

NOLENS, WILLEM HUBERT (1860–1931), economist. Born in Benlo, Holland, on Sept. 7, he was ordained, became a monsignor, was elected to the Dutch parliament in 1896, and was leader of the Catholic party. In 1909 he taught labor legislation at the Municipal University, Amsterdam, and later became president of the Labor Council, worked on labor legislation for the League of Nations at Geneva, and in 1923 was named minister of state. He died in The Hague on Aug. 27.

NOLL, JOHN FRANCIS (1875–1956), archbishop. Born in Fort Wayne, Indiana, on Jan. 25, he studied at St. Lawrence, Wisconsin, and Mt. St. Mary of the West seminary, Cincinnati, and was ordained in 1898. He served as pastor in New Haven and Hartford, Connecticut, and Huntington, Indiana, and in 1925 was consecrated bishop of Fort Wayne, Indiana. He founded and was editor of the weekly newspaper, *Our Sunday Visitor*, in 1912, and saw it become the largest Catholic weekly in the United States. He was treasurer of the American Board of Catholic Missions, chairman of the National Organization for Decent Literature, and in 1953 was given the personal title of archbishop. He died at Fort Wayne on July 31.

NOLLET, JEAN ANTOINE (1700–1770), physicist. Born in Pimpré, Oise, France, on Nov. 19, he studied at Clermont, Beauvais, and Paris, was ordained, and with Dufay and Réaumur began research in physics, particularly electricity. He gave a course in experimental physics in 1735 and in 1739 was given the new chair of physics at Turin and was elected to the Academy of Sciences. After lecturing at Bordeaux and Versailles, he was appointed professor at the Royal College of Navarre in 1753, and taught at the artillery school in Mézières in 1761. He was the first to note the significance of sharp points on electricity conductors, which later resulted in the development of lightning rods; experimented

with the osmosis of water into alcohol; and wrote widely. He died in Paris on Apr. 25.

NON, ST. (6th century). Possibly the wife of a Welsh chieftain named Sant, she was the mother of St. David of Wales. Both Alturnun in Cornwall and Dirinon in Brittany claim her grave. Biographical details remain obscure. F. D. Mar. 3.

NONNA, ST. (d. 374). Brought up a Christian, she married Gregory, a magistrate of Nazianzus in Cappadocia, whom she converted. Their children were SS. Gregory Nazianzen, Gorgonia, and Caesarius. F. D. Aug. 5.

NONNOSUS, ST. (d. 458?). A Benedictine at the monastery of Mt. Soracte, near Rome, he was praised by St. Gregory the Great. F. D. Sept. 2.

NONNOTTE, CLAUDE ADRIEN (1711–1793). Born in Besançon, France, on July 29, he became a Jesuit at nineteen, preached widely, and was famed for his *Examen critique ou réfutation du livre des moeurs* (1754), which irritated Voltaire. He also published *Dictionnaire philosophique de la religion* (1772) in answer to Voltaire's attacks on Christianity in *Dictionnaire philosophique*. He died in Besançon on July 29.

NONNUS, ST. (d. 458?). A monk at Tabennisi, Egypt, he became bishop of Edessa in 448, worked among the Arabs near Heliopolis, and helped to convert St. Pelagia. F. D. Dec. 2.

NONNUS (5th century). An inhabitant of Panopolis, Upper Egypt, he is known only for *Dionysiaca*, a poem on Bacchus, written when he was a pagan, and for his *Paraphrase of the Fourth Gospel*, composed after he became a Christian.

NORBERT, ST. (1080?–1134), founder. Born in Xanten, in the duchy of Cleves, near Wesel, Prussia, son of Heribert of Gennep and Hedwig of Guise, he lived a wasteful courtier's life, even after he received minor orders. During a hunting trip he was struck by lightning, determined to reform, and was ordained in 1115. Three years later he sold his estates and possessions, gave the money to the poor, and received permission from Pope Gelasius to become a preacher at large. Bl. Hugh of Fosses, chaplain of the archbishop of Cambrai, joined him and they went forward with plans for a new order. Though they failed to make more strict the rules of the canons at Laon, its bishop, Bartholomew, gave Norbert a grant of land in a valley called Prémonstré. The order of Premonstratensians began there in 1120 with thirteen associates; by the end of 1121 there were forty. They followed the Rule of St. Augustine, with additions, lived an austere life, and continued their attempts to reform the canons regular. Norbert's constitutions were approved by Pope Honorius II in 1125, by which time he had established eight abbeys and two convents. Theobald, count of Champagne, sought to join the order, but Norbert said that he did not seem to have a true vocation and suggested that he marry, carry on his ordinary duties, and follow certain religious rules and devotions. This may be the first example of a layman affiliated with a religious order as a kind of tertiary. In 1126, Norbert was chosen bishop of Magdeburg by Emperor Lothair, and, against great opposition, and three attempts at assassination, reformed a diocese which had fallen into careless and scandalous ways. In his last years he helped to win the support of Germany for Pope Innocent II against the schismatic claims of antipope Anacletus II, and also served as imperial chancellor. He died in Magdeburg, Saxony, and was canonized in 1582 by Pope Gregory XIII. F. D. June 6.

CORNELIUS J. KIRKFLEET, *History of St. Norbert* (St. Louis, Herder, 1916).

NORIS, HENRY (1631–1704), cardinal. Of English extraction, he was born in Verona, Italy, on Aug. 29, studied at Rimini under the Jesuits, and became a Hermit of St. Augustine. He taught at Pesaro and Perugia and was professor of church history at Padua from 1674 to 1692. He was permitted to publish *The History of Pelagianism* and a dissertation on the fifth General Council in 1673 after defending his orthodoxy before a special commission; was named a qualificator of the Holy Office by Pope Clement X; and became assistant librarian of the Vatican in 1692 and in 1695 a cardinal-priest. He was named librarian of the Vatican in 1700, a position he occupied until his death in Rome on Feb. 23. He wrote several other treatises; after his death he was accused of Jansenist leanings and his books put on a forbidden list by the Spanish Inquisition. Pope Benedict XIV ordered their removal in 1748, and declared the accusations to be groundless.

NORRIS, SYLVESTER (1570?–1630). Born in Somersetshire, England, he studied at Rheims and the English College in Rome, where he was ordained. He was sent on the English mission in 1596, often used the alias Newton Smith in his work, was imprisoned in Bridewell in 1605 for allegedly participating in the Gunpowder Plot, was banished in 1606, and returned to Rome where he became a Jesuit. He taught at various Jesuit colleges, was sent back on the English mission in 1611, and was appointed superior of the Hampshire area in 1621, where he remained until his death on Mar. 16. He wrote several controversial works.

NORTHCOTE, JAMES SPENCER (1821–1907). Born in Feniton Court, Devonshire, England, on May 26, he studied at Oxford, became an Anglican curate in 1844, and was a convert in 1846, a year after his wife became a Catholic. He taught at Prior Park College, and edited the periodical, *Rambler*, from 1852 to 1854. After his wife's death in 1853 he studied for the priesthood under John Henry Newman, whom he had met at Oxford, and was ordained in 1855. He was in parish work from 1857 to 1860, when he was appointed vice-president of Oscott College, was made president later that year, and resigned in 1876 because of ill health. He returned to parish work at Stone and at Stoke-upon-Trent, England, where he died on Mar. 3. With William Brownlow he wrote *Roma sotterranea*, a scholarly study of the catacombs.

NOSTRAINUS, ST. (d. 450?). His years as bishop of Naples, Italy, were marked by forceful opposition to Arianism and Pelagianism. F. D. Feb .14.

NOTBURGA, ST. (1264?–1313?). Born at Rattenberg in the Tyrol, of peasant parents, she became a kitchen maid in the household of Count Henry. Dismissed by Henry's wife, Ottilia, for giving table scraps to the poor instead of to the pigs, she worked for a farmer, but returned as Henry's housekeeper after the death of Ottilia. Her cult was confirmed in 1862 as patron of servants. F. D. Sept. 14.

NOTHELM, ST. (d. 740?), bishop. A priest in London, he became archbishop of Canterbury in 734, corresponded with St. Boniface, and provided much material for St. Bede's *Ecclesiastical History of England*. F. D. Oct. 17.

NORTHROP, HENRY PINCKNEY (1842–1916), bishop. Born in Charleston, South Carolina, on May 5, he studied at Georgetown, Mt. St. Mary's, Maryland, and the North American College, Rome, and was ordained in 1865. He did parish work in the Carolinas and in 1882 was consecrated titular bishop of Rosalia and vicar apostolic of North Carolina. He became fourth bishop of Charleston in 1883, but continued as vicar of North Carolina until 1888, labored to rebuild the cathedral and other churches destroyed by an 1886 earthquake, and dedicated St. John the Baptist cathedral in 1907. He died on June 7 in Charleston.

NORTON, CHRISTOPHER (d. 1570), martyr. Born in Norton Conyers, Yorkshire, England, of a distinguished Catholic family, he took part in the northern uprising of 1569 with his father and eight brothers, fled to Flanders when it failed, and was captured with his uncle. When he refused to apostatize he was hanged and quartered at Tyburn on May 27.

NORTON, RICHARD (16th century). Head of a large Catholic family at Norton Conyers, Yorkshire, England, he held positions of trust under Henry VIII and Edward VI, was governor of Norham castle under Mary, and sheriff of Yorkshire in 1568–69. He joined the Pilgrimage of Grace with his nine sons, was pardoned, joined the uprising of 1569, was declared a traitor, and escaped to Flanders. Four of his sons escaped with him; Christopher, the sixth, was captured and executed at Tyburn.

NOTHOMB, JEAN BAPTISTE (1805–1881), statesman. Born in Messancy, Luxembourg, on July 3, he studied law at Liège, received his doctorate in 1826, and practiced in Luxembourg and Brussels. He took part in the war for independence in 1830, was secretary of the committee drawing up a constitution, and was elected to the first Belgian legislature. He was secretary of foreign affairs from 1831 to 1836, minister of public works from 1837 to 1840, became minister of the interior in 1841, and in 1845 was minister plenipotentiary to Berlin. He spent the rest of his career in the diplomatic service, was made baron in 1852, wrote *Essai historique et politique sur la révolution belge* (1833), and died in Berlin on Sept. 16.

NOTKER (940?–1008), bishop. Born in Swabia and nephew of Emperor Otto I, he was a monk at St. Gall, Switzerland, became provost, and in 969 was appointed imperial chaplain in Italy and in 922 bishop of Liège, Flanders. He established the Liège schools which became famed for their teachers and pupils, and served in governmental positions under Otto III and Henry II. He died on Apr. 10.

NOTKER BABULUS, BL. (840–912). Born in Heiligau, Switzerland, he became a Benedictine at the abbey of St. Gall and, in spite of his stammering (*babulus*), developed a school of music, composing thirty-eight sequences, some hymns, a martyrology, and, perhaps, a metrical life of St. Gall. He also distinguished himself as librarian and guestmaster. He was beatified in 1512. F. D. Apr. 6.

NOTKER LABEO (950?–1022). Nephew of Ekkehard I, he was sent to St. Gall, Switzerland, became a monk there, and was noted for his knowledge of theology, philosophy, science, music, and poetry. He taught for many years and wrote a rhetoric, a manual for computing dates, and essays on logic and music. He also translated into German works by Boethius, Aristotle, and Vergil. His clear, highly poetic style made him one of the great stylists of early German literature and led him to be called Teutonicus by later critics.

NOTKER PHYSICUS (d. 975). A painter and hymn writer of the tenth century, he was a Benedictine at St. Gall from at least 956 to 965 and is probably the Notker Notarius who was a physician at the court of Emperor Otto I. He died on Nov. 12.

NOUNECHIOS (5th century). Bishop of Charadrus, Asia Minor, he attended the Coun-

cil of Chalcedon in 451, and signed the letter of the bishops of Isauria to Emperor Leo in 458 as bishop of Charadrus and Lamos.

NOURI, BL. FRANÇOIS (1598–1638), martyr. Born in Vendôme, France, he became a Capuchin at Le Mans and was ordained in 1625 as Fr. Agathangelus. He went to Syria and in 1633 to Egypt, where, joined by Fr. Cassian Lopez-Neto, he labored unsuccessfully to reunite the Coptic Church and the papacy. In 1638 they were sent to Abyssinia, where they were arrested, hanged by the cords of their habits, and stoned to death on orders of King Fasilidas. They were beatified in 1904. F. D. Aug. 7.

NOURRISSON, JEAN FELIX (1825–1899), philosopher. Born in Thiers, Puy-le-Dôme, France, on July 18, he studied at the college there and Collège Stanislas in Paris, where he became a professor in 1849. He was admitted to the bar in 1850, but turned to philosophy, received his doctorate in 1852, and held chairs of philosophy at Lycée du Rennes, Clermont-Ferrand, Lycée Napoléon, and Collège de France. He wrote on the Fathers of the Church, Bossuet, Leibniz, Pascal, Rousseau, Spinoza, Voltaire, and the thought of the French Revolution, and was admitted to the Académie des Sciences Morales et Politiques in 1870. He died in Paris on June 13.

NOVATUS, ST. (d. 151?). He is called the son of the Roman senator, St. Pudens, and brother of SS. Praxedes and Pudentiana. F. D. June 20.

NOVELLONE, BL. (d. 1280). Born in Faenza, Italy, he was a shoemaker who led a wastrel life until he was twenty-four. Illness made him serious and he became a Franciscan tertiary. He practiced great mortifications and, when his wife died, became a hermit at the Camaldolese monastery of San Maglorio, Faenza. He is also known as Nevolo. His cult was approved in 1817. F. D. Aug. 13.

NOYELLE, CHARLES DE (1615–1686). Born in Brussels, Belgium, on July 28, he became a Jesuit before he was twenty, was ordained, and in 1682 was unanimously elected twelfth general of his Society. His generalate was marked by increasing tension in France, where Louis XIV published the Declaration of the Clergy in 1682; although he prudentially attempted to support the papacy and still not offend the French government, he dissatisfied Pope Innocent XI, who forbade the reception of new members and threatened to suppress the order. Fr. de Noyelle died on Dec. 12.

NOYES, ALFRED (1880–1958), poet. Born in Wolverhampton, Staffordshire, England, on Sept. 16, he began writing at nine, attended Oxford, and published his first volume, *The Loom of Years*, in 1902. Six more volumes appeared before 1909: *The Flower of Old Japan, Poems, The Forest of Wild Thyme, Drake, Forty Singing Seamen,* and *The Enchanted Island.* Much of this was immediately popular, for he captured the flavor of the Tennysonian narrative. He married Garnett Daniels, an American, in 1907, taught at Princeton and Columbia from 1914 to 1923 (except for service in 1916 with the British foreign office), and was honored by his government and received honorary degrees from Yale and Glasgow. Old England is the material for *Tales of the Mermaid Tavern* (1913) and a play, *Robin Hood; The Wine Press* and *Lucifer's Feast* treat of World War I; *The Torchbearers,* of the march of science. His first wife died in 1926 and he married Mary Mayne Weld-Blundell in 1927. He also became a convert in 1927 and recorded his experience in his autobiography, *The Unknown God.* Other prose includes the critical volumes: *Some Aspects of Modern Poetry* (1924), *The Opalescent Parrot* (1929), and *Pageant of Letters* (1940); two novels, *The Sun Cure* and *No Other Man;* and critical biographies of Horace and Voltaire. *Orchard's Bay* (1939), *If Judgment Comes* (1941), and *Shadows on the Downs* (1941) were among his last volumes of poetry. He lectured or read in more than 1000 American communities and is particularly remembered for such ballads as *The Highwayman,* lilting lyrics like *The Barrel Organ,* and his long narratives and portrait poems. He died on the Isle of Wight on June 28.

NUGENT, FRANCIS (1569–1635). Born either in Brettoville or Moyrath, Ireland, of noble parents, he was sent to France, studied at Paris and Louvain, became a Capuchin in 1589, was ordained, and about 1594 was provincial in France and professor at Paris. He held numerous offices in Venice, Belgium, and Ireland, and founded monasteries in Paderborn, Mainz, Dublin, and Slane. Poor health caused his retirement in 1631 to Charleville, France, where he died.

NUGENT, JAMES (1822–1905). Born in Liverpool, England, on Mar. 3, he studied at Ushaw and the English College, Roma, and was ordained in Liverpool in 1846. He engaged in pastoral work in Blackburn and Wigan, and in 1849 was sent to Liverpool, where he opened the Catholic Institute in 1853. He was appointed chaplain of Walton prison in 1863 (serving until 1885), founded the Refuge for Homeless Boys in 1865, and two years later founded the *Northern Press* (it became the *Catholic Times* in 1872). He organized the League of the Cross to promote the temperance movement in 1872, established the Refuge for Fallen Women in Bevington Bush in 1891, became a monsignor in 1892, and founded the House of Providence, Liverpool,

for unmarried mothers in 1897. He died in Liverpool on June 27.

NUMAR, CHRISTOPHER (d. 1528), cardinal. Born in Forlì, Italy, he became a Friar Minor, studied at Bologna and Paris, and held several posts in his order. Pope Leo X made him a cardinal that same year. He became bishop of Alatri and Isernia in 1520 and of Riez, Provence, in 1526, apostolic legate to France, nuncio, and commissary for the construction of the Vatican basilica. He wrote theological and ascetical treatises, lost when Rome was sacked by the duke of Bourbon in 1527. After much mistreatment by the French, for which King Francis I apologized, he died in Ancona, Italy, on Mar. 23, and was buried in Rome.

NUMERIAN, ST. (d. 666?), bishop. Son of a senator in Trèves, Gaul, he was a Benedictine monk there, served in the abbey at Luxeuil, then returned to his birthplace as bishop. He is also known as Memorian. F. D. July 5.

NUMIDICUS, ST. (d. 252), martyr. He and other Africans were burned at the stake in Carthage during the Decian persecution; he was dragged out of the ashes and lived to be ordained by St. Cyprian. F. D. Aug. 9.

NUÑEZ, PEDRO (1492–1577), mathematician. Born in Alcacer-do-Sol, Portugal, he studied at Lisbon and Salamanca, was appointed inspector general at Goa, Portuguese India, in 1519, and returned to Portugal in 1529 to become royal cosmographer. He taught at Lisbon from 1541 until 1544, when he was appointed professor of mathematics at Coimbra, Portugal, a position he occupied for the next eighteen years, and died there. He was the inventor of the loxodromic line and of an instrument for measuring angles (named the *nonnius* in his honor), and wrote treatises on astronomy, navigation, geometry, and the projection of maps.

NUÑEZ DE VILLAVICENIO (1635–1700), painter. Born in Seville, Spain, he studied under Murillo there and with Matteo Preti on Malta, later returning to work with Murillo in Seville. Together they founded the Academy of Seville and Nuñez became his master's executor. He did historical, portrait, and genre work; *St. John the Evangelist* and *Children Playing with Dice* are among his best known.

NUNILO, ST. (d. 851), martyr. Native of Adahuesca, Spain, she and St. Alodia were daughters of a Christian mother and Mohammedan father, raised as Christians, and beheaded during the persecution of Abdur Rahman II. F. D. Oct. 22.

NUSSBAUM, JOHANN NEPOMUK VON (1829–1890). Born in Munich, Germany, on Sept. 2, he studied at the university there, and elsewhere in Europe, and was professor of surgery at Munich from 1860 until his death there thirty years later on Sept. 2. He made notable contributions in pelvic surgery and in introducing antisepsis in German clinics, and was the author of about 100 medical works.

NUSSBAUM, PAUL JOSEPH (1869–1935), bishop. Born in Philadelphia on Sept. 7, he became a Passionist in 1887 and was ordained in Brazil in 1894. He did mission work in Brazil and the United States, served as second consultor of the eastern province of his order in 1911, and in 1913 became first bishop of Corpus Christi, Texas. He resigned in 1920 and was appointed titular bishop of Gerasa, and in 1922 was appointed bishop of Marquette, Michigan, where he died on June 24.

NUTTER, BL. JOHN (d. 1584), martyr. Born near Burnley, England, and graduated in divinity from Oxford, he became a convert, went to Rheims, and was ordained there in 1582. Captured on his return to England and imprisoned in London for a year, he was hanged at Tyburn on the charge of being a priest. F. D. Feb. 12.

NUYENS, WILHELMUS (1823–1894), historian. Born in Avenhorn, Holland, on Aug. 18, he studied at Enkhuizen, became a doctor at Utrecht, and practiced medicine in Westwoud, Holland, where he died on Dec. 10. He published poetry, but is best known for his history of the influences of Catholic culture on Europe, that on the civil wars in Holland from 1559 to 1598, and a sequel on Church and state in the Netherlands from 1598 to 1625.

NYMPHA, ST. Although mentioned in the Roman Martyrology for Nov. 10, she remains an uncertain figure; legend says she was martyred at Porto, Italy, in the fourth century.

NYMPHODORA, ST. (d. 304?), martyr. *See* Menodora, St.

O

OAKELEY, FREDERICK (1802–1890). Born in Shrewsbury, England, on Sept. 5, he graduated from Oxford in 1824, was a fellow at Balliol, and became rector of Margaret chapel, London, in 1839. When he defended Newman's *Tract* 90 he was suspended by his bishop, joined Newman at Littlemore, became a convert in 1845, and was ordained in 1847. He was appointed canon of Westminster and spent the rest of his life there and as rector of St. John's, Islington, England, where he died on Jan. 30. He wrote several theological works and a biography of St. Augustine.

OBERMAIER, HUGO (1877–1946), paleontologist. Born in Ratisbon, Bavaria, he was ordained, taught at L'Institut de Paléontologie Humaine in Paris, and excavated with Breuil and the prince of Monaco a prehistoric home site at Castillo, Spain, from about 1913 to 1939. He was well known for his geological discoveries in the Pyrenees and the Cordillera Cantabrica and for his work in the painted cave at Pileta in southern Spain. At the outbreak of the civil war he went to Fribourg, Switzerland, where he died.

OBITIUS, ST. (d. 1204?). A knight in Brescia, Italy, he became a Benedictine laybrother after escaping death by drowning and experiencing visions. His cult was approved in 1900. F. D. Feb. 4.

OBRECHT, JAKOB (1430?–1506?), composer. Born in Utrecht, Netherlands, he became choirmaster of the cathedral there in 1465 and of Notre Dame, Antwerp, in 1492. Five masses were published in 1503; other work includes hymns and motets.

OBREGÓN, BERNARDINO (1540–1599), founder. Born in Las Huelgas, near Burgos, Spain, he became an army officer, retired to dedicate himself to the care of the Madrid sick, attracted others to him in this endeavor, and in 1567 received approval from the papal nuncio for the Order of Poor Infirmarians (later called Obregonians). Its members followed the Rule of the Third Order of St. Francis, and served in hospitals in Spain, Belgium, and the Indies; they were dispersed by the French Revolution. Obregón went to Lisbon in 1592 to found an orphanage for boys. He died in Madrid.

O'BRIEN, EDWARD CHARLES (1860–1927). Born in Fort Edward, New York, on Apr. 20, he studied at Georgetown, was disbursing officer for the House of Representatives in Washington in 1889, president of the division of docks in New York City in 1895–98, and from 1905 to 1909 minister to Paraguay and Uruguay. He died in Montevideo, Uruguay, on June 21.

O'BRIEN, EDWARD JOSEPH (1890–1941), critic. Born in Boston, Massachusetts, on Dec. 10, he attended Boston College and Harvard, but did not graduate from either, was assistant editor of *Poetry Journal* in 1912–15 and of *Poet Lore* in 1914–15, published two volumes of poetry, two plays, and several books of criticism, and lived abroad after 1922. He married the English novelist, Romer Wilson, and, on her death in 1930, Ruth Gorgel. In 1937 he became European story editor for Metro-Goldwyn-Mayer films. From 1915 until his death in Garrod's Cross, England, on Feb.

25, he issued an annual collection of *Best Short Stories*. He also edited four volumes of *Best British Short Stories* with John Cournos. He published other collections of fiction and *The Advance of the American Short Story*.

O'BRIEN, IGNATIUS JOHN (1857–1930), chancellor. Born in Cork, Ireland, on July 31, he studied there and for two years at the Catholic University in Dublin. He became a reporter on *Saunders' Newsletter* and the *Freeman's Journal*, studied law, and passed the bar in 1881. Success was slow until in 1887 he defended Canon Keller of Youghal in a case involving the seal of the confessional and gained his release through the court of appeals. He rose steadily, in 1911 became solicitor general for Ireland, in 1912 attorney general, and in 1913 lord chancellor. He was made a baronet in 1916, was replaced by a conservative in 1918, and left Ireland in protest against Sinn Fein extremists. He became Baron Shandon, took residence on the Isle of Wight, and became in 1923 a member of the English bar. He served in the house of lords until his death in London on Sept. 10.

O'BRIEN, MICHAEL JOSEPH (1870–1960), historian. Born in Fermoy, Cork, Ireland, he studied at St. Colman's there and later received an honorary doctorate from the National University of Ireland. He served in the accounting department of the Western Union Telegraph Co. in New York City from 1889 until his retirement in 1936. He wrote more than 20 books on the contribution of the Irish to the American army during the revolution, the Irish schoolmasters in the colonies, and Irish settlers in New England and New York. He was librarian of the Society of Friendly Sons of St. Patrick, historiographer of the American-Irish Historical Society, and a founder of the Catholic Writers Guild. He died in Yonkers, New York, on Nov. 11.

O'BRIEN, MORGAN JOSEPH (1852–1937), jurist. Born in New York City on Apr. 28, he studied at Fordham, St. Francis Xavier, and Columbia Law School, and began practicing law in New York. He became interested in politics, was elected to the state supreme court in 1887, and served in various New York courts until 1906, when he resumed his private law practice. He served as president of the New York Bar Association, helped reorganize the Equitable Life Assurance Society after the revelations of the investigation of insurance companies, and became a leading member of Tammany Hall, which he defied in 1936 to present a new charter for New York. He died in New York City on June 16.

O'BRIEN, TERENCE ALBERT (1600–1651), bishop. Born in Limerick, Ireland, he became a Dominican there, studied at Toledo from 1622 to 1630, and returned to Limerick. He was prior there and at Lorrha and in 1643 became provincial of Ireland. He was named coadjutor bishop of Emly in 1647, declared against Ormond in 1650, and urged resistance to the end at the siege of Limerick in 1651. When the city fell, he was court-martialed by the parliamentarians and executed on Oct. 31.

O'BRUADAIR, DAVID (1625?–1698), poet. Born in Barrymore, Cork (or Connello, Limerick), Ireland, he became noted for poetry characterized by vigor and grace. He wrote elegies, satires, and religious and political verse; many are valuable pictures of seventeenth-century Ireland. He also wrote a history of Ireland for the years 1641–48.

O'CALLAGHAN, EDMUND BAILEY (1797–1880), historian. Born in Mallow, Cork, Ireland, on Feb. 28, he studied medicine in Paris, migrated to Canada in 1823, and became editor·in 1834 of the *Vindicator*, periodical of the National Patriotic Movement. He was elected to parliament in 1836, participated in the revolt of 1837, and when it failed fled to the United States. He began practicing medicine in Albany in 1838, edited an industrial journal, the *Northern Light*, took up the study of Dutch when attracted by old New York records, and in 1846 published the first volume of *History of New Netherland*, New York's first serious history. He was appointed keeper of New York State's historical manuscripts in 1848, a position he held for twenty-two years, and in 1870 went to New York City to edit its municipal records, which he never was able to publish, and died there on May 29. He wrote many books on New York history, edited the eleven-volume *Documents Relating to the Colonial History of New York* (1855–61), and was the first to call attention to the treasures of the *Jesuit Relations*.

OCAMPO, SEBASTIAN DE (1465–1509?), explorer. An early Spanish settler in Hispaniola, he was dispatched in 1508 by the governor, Nicolás de Ovando, to explore Cuba, and proved it to be an island by sailing around it. He died after 1509.

O'CAROLAN, TORLOGH (1670–1738), poet. Born in County Meath, Ireland, and blinded from smallpox as a youth, he became famed for his ability with the harp and for the more than 200 poems he composed and set to music, among them *Ode to Whiskey* and *Receipt for Drinking*. Thomas Moore used many of O'Carolan's melodies as musical settings for his poems. He died in Ballyfarnon, Ireland, on Mar. 25.

OCCLEVE, THOMAS. *See* Hoccleve, Thomas.

OCEANUS, ST. (d. 310?), martyr. *See* Ammianus, St.

OCKENHEIM, JEAN D'. *See* Okeghem, Jean d'.

O'CONNELL, DANIEL (1775–1847), statesman. Called "the Liberator," he was born in Carhen, Kerry, Ireland, on Aug. 6, studied at Queenstown, St. Omer, and Douai, began his law course in London in 1794, and was admitted to the Irish bar in 1798. He led the movement to improve the lot of the Irish and the Church in Ireland, fought the existing union with England, organized local committees to work for Irish rights, bitterly opposed Sir Robert Peel, chief secretary for Ireland, and in 1815 was involved in a duel with a member of the Dublin Corporation, named D'Esterrc, and killed him. In 1823, with Sheil, he founded the Catholic Association to press emancipation claims and built it into a powerful, nationwide organization. It was suppressed by the government in 1825, but O'Connell changed its name to the New Catholic Association, which soon elected candidates to parliament. In 1828 he was named to the English parliament as member from Clare. Parliament's refusal to seat him because of his religion was a major cause of the Catholic Emancipation Act of 1829, opening all public offices except the chancellorship and lieutenancy of Ireland to Catholics. He was finally seated, joined the Whigs, became a brilliant orator and parliamentarian, and vigorously agitated for reform. He was successful in abolishing the payment of tithes to the established church, but resisted the poor law and the anti-rent movement as too radical. He was elected first Catholic lord mayor of Dublin since James II's time. When Peel became prime minister in that same year, 1841, O'Connell revived the Catholic Association as the Repeal Association, and in 1842–43 headed huge meetings to demand an end of the union. Arrested on Peel's orders on a charge of conspiracy and sedition in 1843, he was convicted in 1844 and sentenced to a year in prison, a sentence reversed by the house of lords. In ill health as a result of his stay in prison, he began to vacillate and his hold on the Irish people was broken. The revolutionary Young Irelanders, founded in 1840, seized control and, aided by the tragic potato famines of the forties completely collapsed his moderate movement. He died in Genoa, Italy, while on the way to Rome, on May 15.

O'CONNELL, DANIEL M. (1885–1958), editor. Born in Louisville, Kentucky, on Aug. 27, he studied at St. Mary's College, St. Louis, became a Jesuit in 1903, and was ordained in 1918. He taught and was dean (1924–30) at Xavier University, Cincinnati, Ohio, served as first secretary of the Jesuit Educational Association, was on the staff of *America*, and in 1934 founded Spiritual Book Associates, which he also directed. He later taught at Detroit and

West Baden, and edited writings by Cardinal Newman and other English texts. He died in West Baden, Indiana, on July 29.

O'CONNELL, DENIS JOSEPH (1849–1927), bishop. Born in Donoughmore, Cork, Ireland, about Jan. 28, he studied at St. Charles College, Maryland, and the Propaganda, Rome, and was ordained in 1877. He engaged in pastoral work in Richmond, Virginia, acted as secretary to Bishop George Conroy of Armagh on a papal mission to Canada, worked on the preparations for the third Plenary Council of Baltimore, and was appointed rector of the North American College, Rome, in 1885. After a decade in this position, during which he was made a domestic prelate in 1887, he served as vicar of Santa Maria church in Rome in 1895–1903. He was appointed rector of Catholic University, Washington, in 1903, serving in this capacity until 1908, when he was consecrated titular bishop of Sebaste and auxiliary bishop of San Francisco. He was appointed bishop of Richmond in 1912, resigned in 1926 and was named titular archbishop of Mariammc, and died in Richmond on Jan. 1.

O'CONNELL, EUGENE (1815–1891), bishop. Born in Kingscourt, Meath, Ireland, on June 18, he studied at the Navan seminary and St. Patrick's, Maynooth, and was ordained there in 1842. He taught at Navan seminary until 1851, when he was appointed head of Santa Inez College in California. He was appointed director of St. Thomas seminary in San Francisco in 1852, and in 1854 returned to Ireland as dean of All Hallows College. In 1861 he was consecrated titular bishop of Flaviopolis and vicar apostolic of Marysville, west of the Colorado River in the northwestern United States. In 1868 the vicariate was formed into the diocese of Grass Valley and he became its first bishop. He resigned in 1884 in ill health, was appointed titular bishop of Joppa, and died in Los Angeles on Dec. 4.

O'CONNELL, JOHN (1810–1858). The third son of Daniel O'Connell, he was born in Dublin on Dec. 24, became a member of parliament for Youghal in 1832, for Athlone in 1837, and for Kilkenny from 1841 to 1847. He wrote a *Repeal Dictionary* (1845), edited his father's speeches, wrote an autobiography, and retired from politics in 1857. He died in Kingstown, Ireland, on May 24.

O'CONNELL, WILLIAM HENRY (1859–1944), cardinal. Born in Lowell, Massachusetts, on Dec. 8, he graduated from Boston College in 1881, studied at St. Charles College, Maryland, and the North American College, Rome, and was ordained in 1884. He did parish work in the Boston archdiocese during the next decade, was appointed rector of the North American College in 1895, a domestic prelate in 1897, and bishop of Portland, Maine, in 1901. He went to Japan as papal envoy in 1905, became titular bishop of Constantia and coadjutor of Boston in 1906, and succeeded to the see in 1907. He held archdiocesan synods in 1909 and 1919, and was created cardinal-priest in 1911. He began an extensive building program with charitable gifts of considerable size which were made to the see and out of his own fortune. His *Letters* (covering the years 1876–1901) and *Recollections of Seventy Years* were published. He died in Boston on Apr. 22.

DOROTHY WAYMAN, *Cardinal O'Connell of Boston* (New York, Farrar, 1955).

O'CONNOR, DENIS (1841–1911), archbishop. Born in Pickering, Ontario, Canada, on Mar. 28, he became a Basilian, was ordained in 1863, taught and was superior of Assumption College, Sandwich, became bishop of London, Ontario, in 1890, and in 1899 was named third archbishop of Toronto. He developed new parishes, widened catechetical instruction, resigned in 1908 and was made titular archbishop of Laodicea, and died in Toronto on June 30.

O'CONNOR, JAMES FRANCIS THADDEUS (1886–1949), jurist. Born in Grand Forks, North Dakota, on Nov. 10, he studied at North Dakota and Yale, where he taught for three years, was admitted to the North Dakota bar in 1908, and served in the state legislature in 1915–19. He was defeated in a bid for the governorship in 1920 and for the United States Senate in 1922, moved to California, was a law associate of Sen. William McAdoo for five years, and again was an unsuccessful candidate for governor. President Franklin D. Roosevelt made him controller of currency in 1933–38; he later wrote of this in *Banks under Roosevelt*. He became a United States district judge in 1940 and was chairman of the Franklin D. Roosevelt Library Corporation. He died in Los Angeles on Sept. 28.

O'CONNOR, JOHN JOSEPH (1855–1927), bishop. Born in Newark, New Jersey, on June 11, he studied at Seton Hall, the North American College, Rome, and Louvain. He was ordained in 1877, taught philosophy at Seton Hall and the diocesan seminary in 1878–92, was appointed rector of the seminary and vicar general of Newark in 1892, was a pastor there for the next six years, and was named bishop of Newark in 1901. He died in South Orange, New Jersey, on May 20.

O'CONNOR, JOHN JOSEPH (1870–1952). Born in Clonmel, Ireland, on Dec. 5, he studied at Douai and in Rome, was ordained in 1895, stationed in Bradford, England, and was made a monsignor in 1937. He published sermons, a study of Savonarola, and *Father Brown on Chesterton*. He was a close friend of

G. K. Chesterton from 1904 on, was the model on which the character of Chesterton's fictional detective, Father Brown, was based, and converted the author in 1922. Fr. O'Connor died on Feb. 6.

O'CONNOR, MICHAEL (1810–1872), bishop. Born in Cobh, Cork, Ireland, on Sept. 27, he studied in France and at the Propaganda in Rome, and was ordained in Rome in 1833. He received his doctorate in divinity in 1834, taught at the Propaganda and the Irish College in Rome, returned to a curacy at Fermoy in Ireland, and about 1839 went to Philadelphia as rector of St. Charles Borromeo seminary. He became vicar general of the Pittsburgh diocese in 1841 and was appointed first bishop of Pittsburgh in 1843. He founded a diocesan paper, *The Catholic*, in 1844, and when the see was divided in 1853 became first bishop of Erie, the lesser of the two dioceses, but was recalled to Pittsburgh the following year by popular demand. He finished the cathedral in 1855, was allowed to resign in 1860 to become a Jesuit, and made his profession in Boston in 1862. He taught at Boston College in 1863, became socius to the Maryland provincial, and devoted the rest of his life to missionary work, particularly among the Negroes. He died in Woodstock, Maryland, on Oct. 18.

O'CONOR, CHARLES (1710–1791). Born in Belanagare, Roscommon, Ireland, he early became interested in manuscript records, which he built into the famous Stowe collection. He was one of the founders of the Roman Catholic Committee in 1757. His publication of *Dissertations on the History of Ireland* in 1753 led to correspondence with Samuel Johnson.

O'CONOR, CHARLES (1804–1884). Born in New York City on Jan. 22 of Irish immigrants, he was admitted to the bar in 1824, became well known as a successful attorney, and was a member of the New York State Constitutional Convention in 1846. He opposed slavery but supported states' rights, and was senior defense counsel in the trial of Jefferson Davis for treason in 1865. He helped expose the Boss Tweed ring in 1871–74, was nominated for president of the United States by a Democratic splinter party which refused to accept the nomination at Baltimore of Horace Greeley and convened in Louisiana in 1872. He did not take part in the campaign, but received 29,000 votes on the Straight-Out Democratic and Labor-Reform ballots in the November election which Ulysses S. Grant won. He was Samuel Tilden's counsel before the electoral commission in the disputed presidential election of 1876, retired in 1881, and died on Nantucket Island, Massachusetts, on May 12. He wrote *Peculation Triumphant* (1875) on his struggle with Tweed.

O'CONOR, HERBERT ROMULUS (1897–

864

1960), governor. Born in Baltimore, Maryland, on Nov. 17, he studied at Loyola and law at Maryland, and became active in politics. He was a state's attorney in 1924–34, state attorney general in 1935–39, and served two terms as governor from 1939 to 1946. He was elected to the United States Senate in 1946 and was chairman of the crime committee and the internal security subcommittee, where he was a vigorous opponent of communism. In 1953 he became counsel of the American Marine Institute in Washington, D.C., a position he held until his death in Baltimore on Mar. 4.

OCTAVIAN. *See* Victor IV, antipope.

OCTAVIAN, ST. (d. 484), martyr. He was an archdeacon at Carthage and one of the thousands slain there by the Arian Huneric, king of the Vandals. F. D. Mar. 22.

OCTAVIAN, BL. (1060?–1128?), bishop. Born near Besançon, France, brother of Pope Callixtus II, he became a Benedictine at the abbey of St. Peter in Pavia, and in 1129 was made bishop of Savona, Italy. His cult was approved in 1783. F. D. Aug. 6.

OCTAVIUS, ST. (d. 287?), martyr. *See* Maurice, St.

O'CULLENAN, GELASIUS (d. 1580), martyr. Born in Ballyshannon, Donegal, Ireland, he studied at Salamanca and Paris, received his doctorate from the Sorbonne, became a Cistercian monk, and was appointed abbot of Boyle, a monastery in Roscommon County, Ireland, which had been suppressed. He went to Dublin, where he is supposed to have had it restored, was imprisoned in Lough Key, and when he refused to conform was tortured and hanged outside Dublin on Nov. 21.

O'CURRY, EUGENE (1796–1862), scholar. Born in Dunaha, Clare, Ireland, son of a farmer, he was self-educated. He was an antiquarian for the Ordnance Survey of Ireland in 1834, catalogued the Irish manuscripts in the British Museum, and when the project was abandoned worked on Irish manuscripts in Trinity College, Dublin, and the Royal Irish Academy. With his brother-in-law, John O'Donovan, he helped found the Archaeological Society in 1840. He served on the council of the Celtic Society in 1853 and became first professor of Irish history and archaeology at the Catholic University in Dublin in 1855. His *Manuscript Materials of Ancient Irish History* (1860) and *Manners and Customs of the Ancient Irish* (1873) are valuable studies of Irish mediaeval life and customs. He also translated several Irish works and was one of the first to decipher the Brehon Laws. He died in Dublin on July 30.

ODA, ST. (d. 723?). She was a French princess, who married the duke of Aquitaine, and after his death distributed her wealth in caring for the poor and sick. She was honored at a shrine at Amay, near Liège, Belgium. F. D. Oct. 23.

O'DALY, DANIEL (1595–1662), diplomat. Born in Kerry, Ireland, he became a Dominican, studied at Burgos and Bordeaux, and after ordination returned to Tralee as parish priest. He taught theology at Louvain in 1627, went to Madrid in 1629, helped establish and became first rector of the Irish Dominican College in Lisbon, and set up a convent for refugee Irish Dominican nuns there in 1639. He served on diplomatic missions for King Philip of Spain and the queen of Portugal and helped to conclude a treaty between France and Portugal in 1655. He accepted the bishopric of Coimbra, Portugal, and presidency of the privy council in order to raise funds for his college, but died in Lisbon on June 30 before the appointive bull arrived. He wrote a history of the earls of Desmond.

O'DEA, EDWARD JOHN (1856–1932), bishop. Born in Boston, Massachusetts, on Nov. 23, he studied at St. Michael's, Oregon, St. Ignatius, San Francisco, and the Grand seminary, Montreal, and was ordained in Montreal in 1882. He did pastoral work in the Oregon City diocese, was secretary to Archbishop Gross in 1882–92, became pastor of a Portland parish, and in 1896 was consecrated third bishop of Nesqually. The see was transferred to Seattle in 1907, Bishop O'Dea was made an assistant at the pontifical throne in 1925, and he died in Seattle, Washington, on Dec. 25.

ODERISI, BL. PHILIP (d. 1285). A Benedictine monk at Fontavellana, Italy, he became bishop of Nocera, Italy, in 1254 and defended the Friars Minor. F. D. Sept. 18.

ODERISIUS, BL. (d. 1105), cardinal. Born in Marsi, Italy, he was educated and became a Benedictine at Monte Cassino. At about fifty-five he became cardinal-priest of St. Cyriacus, Termis, and in 1087 became abbot of Monte Cassino, Italy. He wrote much poetry. F. D. Dec. 2.

ODESCALCHI, CARLO (1786–1841), cardinal. Born in Rome on Mar. 5, he was ordained in 1808, became a member of Pope Pius VII's household, served on several papal missions, and was created cardinal and archbishop of Ferrara in 1823. He resigned the see in 1826, returned to Rome, and was appointed bishop of Sabina and prefect of several congregations. He resigned his cardinalate in 1839 to become a Jesuit, and died in Modena, Italy, on Aug. 17.

O'DEVANY, CORNELIUS (1532?–1612), bishop and martyr. A native of Ireland, he became a Franciscan in Donegal, was named bishop of Down and Connor in 1582, and imprisoned in Dublin castle in 1588 for two years on a charge of treason. Released for lack of evidence, he was rearrested in 1611 while administering confirmation and was hanged and quartered in Dublin on Feb. 11.

ODHRAN. *See* Otteran, St.

ODILIA, ST. (d. 720?). According to legend, she was born blind in Obernheim, Alsace, was cast out by her father, Adalric, an Alsatian lord, and raised in a convent near Besançon, where she was miraculously cured at twelve when she was baptized by St. Erhard. She founded a monastery at her father's castle of Hohenburg (now Odilienberg), Alsace, of which she became abbess, and, later, at nearby Niedermünster. Her monastery became a popular shrine during the Middle Ages. She is also known as Ottilia and Adilia. F. D. Dec. 13.

ODILO, BL. (10th century). He was a Benedictine monk at Gorze, Lorraine, who in 945 became abbot of Stavelot-Malmédy, raised its scholarly and disciplinary standards, and was alive there in 954. F. D. Oct. 15.

ODILO, ST. (962–1049). He became a monk at Cluny under St. Majolus, whose coadjutor he became in 991 and whom he succeeded 3 years later. During his administration a great number of daughter houses developed from Cluny. He is particularly remembered for gaining acceptance of the rule guaranteeing sanctuary to those who sought refuge within a church and for instituting the feast of All Souls Day (Nov. 2). He also wrote many sermons and poems on the Incarnation, Redemption, and Blessed Virgin. F. D. Jan. 1.

ODIN, JOHN MARY (1801–1870), archbishop. Born in Ambierle, Lôire, France, on Feb. 25, son of a farmer, he studied at the classical schools of Roanne and Verriere, L'Argentière and Alix colleges, and the Sulpician Seminary in Lyons, and in 1822 accompanied Bishop Dubourg to New Orleans. He was sent to the Barrens, Missouri, where he became a Lazarist, was ordained in 1824, and engaged in missionary work among the Arkansas Indians and taught at the Barrens seminary. He was Bishop Rosati's theologian at the second Provincial Council in Baltimore in 1833, was delegated to take its decrees to Rome, and spent two years in Europe raising funds for American missions. On his return he opened a school at Cape Girardeau, Missouri, and continued his pastoral and missionary activities until 1840, when he was sent to Texas as viceprefect. He became titular bishop of Clandiopolis and vicar apostolic of Texas in 1842, secured recognition of the Church's possessions by the new republic of Texas, made a trip to Europe in 1845 to secure more missionaries, and was appointed first bishop of Galveston in 1847. He invited religious orders into Texas, encouraged the opening of schools, and labored there until 1861, when he was appointed second archbishop of New Orleans. He went to

Rome in 1867, attended the Vatican Council, where he fell ill, and died on May 25 in his native Ambierle.

ODINGTON, WALTER (d. 1330?). A Benedictine monk, also known as Walter of Evesham from the Worcestershire monastery where he spent several years, he went to Oxford about 1316, where he produced astronomical, mathematical, and musical treatises, chief of which was *De speculatione musices*, on the theory of music, with some rules for composition.

ODO, ST. (801–880), bishop. A soldier, he entered the Benedictines at Corbie, where he taught the sons of Charles Martel and became abbot in 851. He was made bishop of Beauvais, France, in 861 and was successful in reforming the Church in northern France and as a peacemaker. F. D. Jan. 28.

ODO, ST. (d. 959), archbishop. Born in East Anglia of Danish parents, he became bishop of Ramsbury, Wessex, and was present at the battle of Brunanburh, where the Danes, Scots, and Northumbrians were defeated by King Athelstan. In 942 he was made archbishop of Canterbury, after he had received the Benedictine habit at Fleury. He was active in the legal reforms of Kings Edmund and Edgar, and played a conspicuous role in the monastic reforms of SS. Dunstan, Ethelwold, and Oswald. F. D. July 4.

ODO, BL. (1050–1113), bishop. Born in Orléans, France, he taught at Toul, was placed in charge of the cathedral school at Tournai, and attained a great reputation as a poet, rhetorician, astronomer, and philosopher. A follower of Boethius, he was successful in winning from nominalism many followers of Raimbert of Lille. About 1090 he read Augustine's work on free will, became interested in theology, gave away his wealth, and engaged in extreme austerities. He then retired from life as a canon and with a number of former students followed the Benedictine rule while living in the abandoned monastery of St. Martin. He was chosen bishop of Cambrai in 1105, but refused to be invested by Emperor Henry V. He devoted his last years to scholarship and died at Anchin, France. His writings include treatises on the canon of the mass, on original sin, on Christ as Messias, and a polyglot psalter. F. D. June 19.

ODO, ST. (d. 1122), bishop. Of a noble Spanish family, he was a soldier who became an archdeacon at Urgell, Spain, and who was appointed bishop there by Pope Urban II in 1105. F. D. July 7.

ODO OF BAYEUX (1036?–1097), bishop. Half-brother of William the Conqueror, he became bishop of Bayeux about 1049, accompanied William on the invasion of England, and ruled as a regent in 1067. He fell out of royal favor, was imprisoned for four years, and released before William's death; he rebelled against William II in 1088 and was exiled. He died in Palermo, Italy, on his way to the crusade.

ODO OF CHERITON (d. 1247). A preacher noted for his use of exempla or moralized fables in his sermons, he probably took his master's degree at Paris, is believed to have been a Cistercian or Praemonstratensian, and probably was the son of William of Cheriton, lord of the manor in Rochester, England, whose estates he inherited in 1233. His instructive narratives were collected in *Parabolae*; he also wrote *Sermones de sanctis* and tracts on the Passion and on penitence.

ODO OF CLUNY, ST. (879?–942), abbot. Born near Le Mans, France, he was at the court of William, duke of Aquitaine, was educated at Tours and Paris, and in 909 became a Benedictine at the monastery of Baume under Bl. Berno. In 924 he became abbot and in 927 succeeded Berno as second abbot of Cluny. In 931 he was authorized by Pope John XI to undertake the reform of the monasteries in northern France and Italy. In 936, Pope Leo VII called him to Rome to try to effect peace between the besieging Hugh of Provence and Alberic of Rome; success came in 942. He was the author of several treatises, a biography of St. Gerald of Aurillac, and an epic poem on the Redemption. He died at Tours, France. F. D. Nov. 18.

ODO OF GLANFEUIL (9th century). A monk of Glanfeuil abbey, St. Maur-sur-Loire, France, he became its abbot in 861 and of St. Maur des Fossés in 868. He issued a revised life of St. Maurus, allegedly written originally by Faustus of Monte Cassino, and also wrote *Miracula S. Mauri*.

ODO OF NOVARA, BL. (1105?–1200). Carthusian prior of the monastery of Geyrach in Slavonia, he was so interfered with by the bishop of the diocese that he went to Rome to ask permission to resign his post. He then became chaplain to a convent at Tagliacozzo, Italy, serving with exemplary devotion and patience through a long and severe illness until he was nearly 100. His cult was approved in 1859. F. D. Jan. 14.

O'DOHERTY, MICHAEL J. (1874–1949), archbishop. Born in Charlestown, Mayo, Ireland, on July 30, he served as president of the Irish College in Salamanca, Spain, and was named archbishop of Manila, the Philippines, in 1916. He died in Manila on Oct. 14.

O'DONAGHUE, DENIS (1848–1925), bishop. Born in Daviess County, Indiana, on Nov. 30, he studied at St. Meinrad's College, St. Thomas College, Bardstown, Kentucky, and the Grand seminary, Montreal, and was ordained in 1874. He did parish work in Indi-

anapolis, served as chancellor of the diocese of Vincennes in 1874–1900, and was rector of St. Patrick's, Indianapolis, in 1885–1910. He was consecrated titular bishop of Pomario and auxiliary of Indianapolis in 1900, and in 1910 was appointed bishop of Louisville. He resigned in 1924 and was named titular bishop of Lebedus, and died in Louisville, Kentucky, on Nov. 7.

O'DONNELL, CHARLES LEO (1884–1934), poet. Born in Greenfield, Indiana, on Nov. 15, he graduated from Notre Dame, became a member of the Congregation of Holy Cross, studied further in Washington, and was ordained and obtained his doctorate in philosophy in 1910. He taught English literature at Notre Dame until 1918, served as a chaplain with the Rainbow Division during World War I, then became provincial and in 1925 assistant superior general of his order. He was named president of Notre Dame in 1928, and built its law school. He wrote considerable criticism, published three volumes of poetry, *The Dead Musician* (1916), *Cloister* (1922), and *A Rime of the Rood* (1928), and edited *Notre Dame Verse*. He died in South Bend, Indiana, on June 4.

O'DONNELL, EDMUND (1542–1575), martyr. Born in Limerick, Ireland, he became a Jesuit at Rome in 1561, went to Flanders because of ill health, and in 1564 returned to Limerick, where he taught until 1568. Expelled by the English, he went to Lisbon, returned in 1574, was arrested, and, when he refused to apostatize, was hanged, drawn, and quartered at Cork on Mar. 16 He is often listed as Edmundus Daniell and is the first Jesuit executed during the Elizabethan persecutions.

O'DONNELL, PATRICK (1856–1927), cardinal. Born in Kilraine, Donegal, Ireland, on Nov. 28, he studied in Letterkenny and at Maynooth and Dunbayne and was ordained in 1880. He taught at Dunbayne, became bishop of Raphoe in 1888, and built churches and an industrial school at Killybegs and a seminary at Letterkenny. He became coadjutor of Armagh in 1922, archbishop of that see in 1924, and cardinal in 1925. He was strongly interested in Gaelic, tried to blend the Irish nationalists after the death of Parnell in 1901, was active in the Irish Convention in 1917–18, and helped to found the National University. He worked for peace after the partition was established, held a plenary synod at Maynooth in 1927, and died in Carlingford, Ireland, on Oct. 22.

O'DONOVAN, JOHN (1809–1861), archaeologist. Born in Atateemore, Kilkenny, Ireland, he studied in Dublin, and with Eugene O'Curry, his brother-in-law, became an authority on Irish antiquities and language. He worked on the Ordnance Survey of Ireland from 1830 to 1842, began in 1836 to catalogue the Irish manuscripts in Trinity College, and founded the Archaeological Society in 1840 with O'Curry. He was appointed professor of Celtic in Queen's College, Belfast, in 1856, translated many of the great Irish classics, wrote an Irish grammar, edited the *Annals of Ireland by the Four Masters*, and spent his last years working on the Brehon Laws. His letters, written while engaged on the survey, fill 103 volumes at the Royal Irish Academy. He died in Dublin on Dec. 9.

ODORIC OF PORDENONE. *See* Mattiuzzi, Bl. Odoric.

O'DUGAN, JOHN (d. 1372). He was the author of a collection of verses on the chief families in Ireland before the English came, which is of great historical value, and of several other poems on the kings and provinces of Ireland.

ODULF, ST. (d. 855?). Born in Oorshot, Brabant, he served as a priest there, became a canon at Utrecht, and was sent by St. Frederick to evangelize Friesland. He had great success, built a church and an Augustinian monastery in Stavoren, and worked there until his return to Utrecht as an old man. F. D. June 12.

ODUVALD, ST. (d. 698). He was a nobleman who became a monk at Melrose abbey, Scotland, and later its abbot. F. D. May 26.

O'DWYER, JOSEPH (1841–1898), physician. Born in Cleveland, Ohio, he studied at McGill and the College of Physicians in New York, became resident surgeon in the city hospital, and in 1872 joined the New York Foundling Hospital staff. He was a specialist in children's diseases, served as president of the American Pediatric Society, and introduced a successful method of aiding breathing in cases of suffocation caused by the closing of the larynx in cases of diphtheria. He died in New York City on Jan. 7.

O'DWYER, MICHAEL FRANCIS (1864–1940), governor. Born in Barronstown, Tipperary, Ireland, one of fourteen children, he studied at St. Stanislaus College and Oxford, entered the civil service in 1882, and went to India in 1885. He was director of records and agriculture in the Punjab, married Una Bord in 1896, was selected by Lord Curzon to help organize the Northwest Frontier Province, and was collector of revenue in 1901–8. He served as lieutenant governor there in 1912–19, was knighted in 1913, weathered the early agitation led by Annie Besant, the civil disobedience passivity of Ghandi, and the storm which rose after his approval of the action of Gen. Dyer in firing on a mob at Amristar. O'Dwyer served on the commission to reorganize the Indian army (1919–20), published *India as I Saw It* (1925), opposed the constitutional movements

of 1919 and 1935, sought to keep India within the empire, and was assassinated by a nationalist while he was making a speech in London on Mar. 13.

OECUMENIUS (10th century). Bishop of Trikka, Thessaly, about 990, he is the disputed author of commentaries on the Apocalypse, Acts, and Catholic and Pauline epistles found in a manuscript of the tenth or eleventh century.

OEDGRIM (d. 1158?). Bishop of Skara, Sweden, he attended the consecration of Lund cathedral in 1145, consecrated part of the present cathedral in 1151, and saw the Cistercians settle in his diocese.

OENGUS. *See* Aengus the Culdee, St.

OERTEL, ABRAHAM (1527–1598), cartographer. Born in Antwerp, Belgium, on Apr. 4, he became a map salesman in his youth and eventually one of the world's great cartographers, called the Ptolemy of his times. In 1564 (five years before Mercator) he published his eight-leaved map of the world. In 1570 appeared *Theatrum orbis terrarum*, the first modern world atlas, with seventy copper engravings, a geographical dictionary of ancient and modern names, and a catalogue of maps of some ninety-six cartographers who lived before him; revised and enlarged editions followed. King Philip II named him royal geographer in 1575. Other studies on geography and coins followed, including *Thesaurus geographicus* (1596). He is also known as Ortelius. He died in Antwerp on June 28.

OERTEL, JOHN JAMES MAXIMILIAN (1811–1882), journalist. Born in Ansbach, Bavaria, on Apr. 27, he studied at the University of Erlangen, was ordained a Lutheran minister, and came to New York in 1837. He was embroiled in denominational disputes, became a convert in 1840, and taught German at Fordham. He edited a German Catholic weekly in Cincinnati; founded the *Kirchenzeitung* in Baltimore in 1836, developed it into the leading German paper in the United States, and moved it to New York in 1851; and published *Altes und Neues* in 1869. He died in Jamaica, New York, on Aug. 21.

O'FARRELL, MICHAEL JOSEPH (1832–1894), bishop. Born in Limerick, Ireland, on Dec. 2, he studied at All Hallows College, Dublin, and St. Sulpice, Paris, became a Sulpician, and was ordained in Limerick in 1855. He was sent to Montreal to teach at the Grand seminary, left the Sulpicians, and became rector of St. Peter's, New York. He was consecrated first bishop of Trenton, New Jersey, in 1881, participated in the third Plenary Council of Baltimore in 1884, and died in Trenton on Apr. 2.

OFFA (d. 796), king. A Saxon, he succeeded to the throne of Mercia on the murder of his cousin Ethelbald by Beornraed in 757, spent the next fourteen years consolidating his kingdom, and then launched a series of successful wars against the Hestingi, West Saxons, and Welsh which established his domain as equal with Northumbria and Wessex. He induced Pope Hadrian I to establish the archbishopric of Lichfield in 788 to free him from Canterbury's domination, encouraged the spread of Christianity by generous donations to monasteries, and established diplomatic relations with Charlemagne. Except for his murder in 794, of King Ethelbert of East Anglia, whose kingdom he annexed, his reign was an enlightened one. He died on July 29.

O'FIHELY, MAURICE (1460?-1513), archbishop. Born in Clonfert, Galway, Ireland (or Baltimore, Cork), he studied at Oxford, where he became a Franciscan, and at Padua, where he was ordained and became professor of philosophy. He was proofreader for several Venetian printing houses. In 1506 he was appointed archbishop of Tuam, attended the Lateran Council in 1512, left for his see in 1513, but died on the way in Galway.

O'FLANAGAN, MICHAEL (1876-1942). Born in Roscommon County, Ireland, on Aug. 13, he was ordained in 1899, headed the Sinn Fein in 1918, and led the Irish independence movement against Great Britain. He died in Dublin on Aug. 7.

O'GALLAGHER, REDMOND (d. 1601), bishop. A leading churchman in Armagh, Ireland during the Reformation, he was appointed bishop of Derry in 1569, administrator of the province in 1575, and was so active in defense of the Church that he was slain in 1601.

OGERIUS, BL. (d. 1214). A Cistercian, he became abbot of Locedio, Vercelli, Italy, and wrote sermons on the doctrine of the Immaculate Conception. His cult was confirmed in 1875. He is also known as Ogler. F. D. Sept. 10.

OGGIONO, MARCO DA (1470?-1549?), painter. Born in Oggiono, near Milan, Italy, he became a pupil of Leonardo da Vinci and one of his chief copyists. He completed a series of notable frescoes for the church of Santa Maria della Grazie, Milan, before his death there (variously given as 1530, 1540, or 1549).

OGILVIE, BL. JOHN (1579?-1615), martyr. Born in Banffshire, Scotland, son of the baron of Drum-na-Keith and Lady Douglas of Lochleven, he became a convert from Calvinism at Louvain in 1596. He studied at Olmütz and Brünn, joined the Jesuits in 1600, and was ordained in 1610 at Paris. He had worked in Austria and France before he went to Scotland in 1613 as John Watson. He served the Catholics hidden in Edinburgh and Glasgow and won a number of converts. Betrayed, he was captured, tortured for months. and hanged in

Glasgow, Scotland, after he refused to abandon his faith. He was beatified in 1929. F. D. Mar. 10.

OGLER. See Ogerius, Bl.

OGMUND, ST. (d. 1121). Bishop of Holar, Iceland, and venerated as one of the apostles of Iceland, he was canonized in 1201. F. D. Mar. 8.

O'GORMAN, THOMAS (1843-1921), bishop. Born in Boston, on May 1, he studied at seminaries in Maximieux and Monthluel, France, and was ordained in St. Paul, Minnesota, in 1865. He engaged in pastoral work in Rochester, until 1878, when he joined the Paulists. He traveled with Paulist mission bands until 1882 when he returned to Faribault, Minnesota, as a pastor, was appointed first rector of St. Thomas College in St. Paul in 1885, to the chair of ecclesiastical history at Catholic University in 1890, and second bishop of Sioux Falls, South Dakota in 1896. He was sent to Rome in 1902 by President Roosevelt to help settle the "friar-land claims" in the Philippines, encouraged education in his see, founded Columbus College in Chamberlain, South Dakota, in 1909, and died in Sioux Falls on Sept. 18. He wrote A History of the Roman Catholic Church in the United States (1895).

O'GROWNEY, EUGENE (1863-1899). Born in Ballyfallon, Meath, Ireland, on Aug. 25, he studied in Navan and Maynooth, was ordained in 1888, and became professor of Gaelic at Maynooth in 1891. He became editor of the Gaelic Journal, helped found the Gaelic League in 1893, and was a leader in helping revive the language with his simple lessons in Irish in the Weekly Freeman. He died in Los Angeles, California, where he had been sent because of ill health, on Oct. 18.

O'HAGAN, JOHN (1822-1890), lawyer. Born in Newry, Down, Ireland, on Mar. 19, he graduated from Trinity College in 1842, was admitted to the bar, appointed a commissioner of education in 1861, and in 1869 was selected by Gladstone as first judicial head of the Irish Land Commission and a judge of the high court of justice. He died near Dublin on Nov. 10. He contributed articles and poetry to magazines and was the first English translator of the Chanson de Roland.

O'HAGAN, THOMAS (1812-1885), chancellor. Born in Belfast, Ireland, on May 29, he studied law, was admitted to the bar in 1836, was editor of the Newry Examiner from 1838 to 1841, and was admitted to the inner bar in 1849. He was appointed solicitor general for Ireland in 1860, attorney general in 1861, became a member of the Irish privy council, and was a member of parliament from 1863 to 1865. He was made justice of the common pleas in 1865, was lord chancellor of Ireland from 1868 to 1874 and in 1880-81. He was created first baron of Tullyhogue in 1870. He died on Feb. 1.

O'HAGAN, THOMAS (1855–1939), author. Born near Toronto, Ontario, Canada, on Mar. 6, he graduated from Ottawa in 1882, took his doctorate of philosophy at Syracuse, and also studied at Cornell, Wisconsin, Chicago, and in Europe. He taught in Canadian high schools from 1884 to 1893, organized a teachers' association, and also taught in the United States. He edited the Chicago diocesan newspaper, *New World*, in 1910–13. He wrote *Studies in Poetry, Canadian Essays, Genesis of Christian Art, Spain*, and other prose studies; his poems include *A Gate of Flowers* (1887), *In Dreamland, In the Heart of the Meadow, Songs of the Heroic Days*, and *Chap Book*. He died on Mar. 2.

O'HANLON, JOHN (1821–1905), historian. Born in Stradbally, Queen's, Ireland, he studied at Carlow College, went to the United States, was ordained in 1847, and served in the St. Louis diocese. In 1853 he returned to Ireland, did parish work in Dublin, and died there on Feb. 1. He wrote *Irish-American History of the United States*, biographies of St. Laurence O'Toole and St. Dympna, and prepared materials for a history of Queen's County.

O'HARA, EDWIN VINCENT (1881–1956), archbishop. Born in Lanesboro, Minnesota, on Sept. 6, he studied at St. Thomas College and St. Paul seminary, Catholic University, Washington, and L'Institut Catholique, Paris, and was ordained in St. Paul in 1905. He did pastoral work in the Oregon City (now Portland, Oregon) diocese, serving as assistant and then was pastor of St. Mary's cathedral in 1905–20, superintendent of schools in 1907–20, chairman of the industrial welfare committee of Oregon in 1914–18, of the Portland housing commission in 1915–20, and served as army chaplain during World War I. He was a pastor in Eugene, Oregon, in 1920–28, director of the rural life bureau of the National Catholic Welfare Conference in 1920–30, founded *St. Isidore's Plow* (later *Catholic Rural Life*) in 1921, and the National Catholic Rural Life Conference in 1923. He was appointed bishop of Great Falls, Montana, in 1930, and was chairman of the episcopal committee of the Confraternity of Christian Doctrine in 1935 and of the social action department of the National Catholic Welfare Conference in 1936–42. He was transferred to Kansas City, Missouri, in 1939, and was elected president of the International Catholic Rural Life Conference in 1951. He was made an archbishop in 1954. He wrote several books, including *Pioneer Catholic History of Oregon* (1909) and *The Church and the Country Community* (1927), and was a leader in catechetical work in the United States and in preparing a new

English version of the Bible. He died in Milan, Italy, on Sept. 11.

O'HARA, FRANK (1876–1938), educator. Born in Lanesboro, Minnesota, on Mar. 24, he taught economics at Catholic University, Washington, D.C., from 1909 to 1938, founded Columbus University in Washington in 1919, and died there on July 30.

O'HARA, JOHN FRANCIS (1888–1960), cardinal. Born in Ann Arbor, Michigan, on May 1, he studied at Collegio del Sagrado Corazon College in Montevideo, Uruguay (where his father was consul) and at Notre Dame, became a member of the Congregation of Holy Cross in 1911, and was ordained in 1916. After a year of further study at Catholic University and Pennsylvania, he began teaching at Notre Dame, established its College of Commerce and Latin-American exchange program, and was the university's president in 1934–39. He also conducted a news service which supplied seventy-five Spanish-American papers and was active in the National Foreign Trade Council. He attended the eighth Inter-American Congress at Lima, Peru, in 1938 for President Franklin D. Roosevelt, made a survey of South American school systems, and in 1939 headed a social-service commission in Venezuela at the invitation of President Contreras. He was appointed military delegate of the United States armed forces and titular bishop of Mylasa in 1939. He was named bishop of Buffalo, New York, in 1945, archbishop of Philadelphia in 1951, and cardinal in 1958. He created thirty parishes, built fifty-five new schools and fourteen high schools, and was actively interested in the education of the retarded. He died in Philadelphia on Aug. 28.

O'HARA, THEODORE (1822–1867), editor. Born in Danville, Kentucky, on Feb. 11, he graduated from St. Joseph's College in Bardstown in 1839, studied law, was admitted to the bar in 1842, and after a short period as clerk in the treasury department in Washington, became a reporter on the Frankfort *Yeoman*. He served in the Mexican War, joined a filibustering expedition to free Cuba in 1849–50, was an editor of the Louisville *Times* in 1852, and from 1856 to 1861 of the Mobile *Register*. He served in the Confederate army during the Civil War, became a cotton merchant in Georgia after the war, and died of malaria near Guerryton, Alabama, on June 6. He wrote the poem, *The Bivouac of the Dead*.

O'HARA, WILLIAM (1816–1899), bishop. Born in Dungiven, Derry, Ireland, on Apr. 14, he studied at Georgetown and the Propaganda, Rome, where he was ordained in 1842, and did parish work in Philadelphia. He taught at St. Charles Borromeo seminary there, became rector in 1856, vicar general of the diocese in 1860, and was pastor of St. Patrick's church from 1856 to 1868, when he was consecrated first bishop of Scranton. He built St. Thomas College and greatly increased the number of religious and religious institutions in his see. He died in Scranton, Pennsylvania, on Feb. 3.

O'HELY, PATRICK (d. 1579), bishop and martyr. A native of Connaught, Ireland, he became a Franciscan and studied at Alcalá and in Rome. In 1576 he was appointed bishop of Mayo, did not reach Ireland until 1579, when the country was under occupation, was seized in Limerick, and when he refused to acknowledge the total supremacy of Elizabeth was tortured and executed in Kilmallock in Sept.

O'HERLAHY, THOMAS (d. 1579). Consecrated bishop of Ross, Ireland, about 1560, he attended the Council of Trent and when he tried to enforce its decrees in Ireland had to flee. Captured and imprisoned in the Tower of London, he was released in custody of the lord of Muskery, was again imprisoned and released, and left his wealthy guardian's refuge for a life of austerity on a small farm. He died at seventy (or eighty) near Kilcrea Friary, Cork, Ireland.

O'HERN, CHARLES A. (1881-1925). Born in Lawrence, Kansas, on Dec. 31, he studied at St. Ignatius College, Chicago, the North American College and the Propaganda in Rome, and was ordained in 1906. He was appointed vice-rector of the North American College in 1907, rector in 1917, was named private chamberlain to Pius X in 1911 and to Benedict XV in 1914, domestic prelate in 1917, and died on May 13.

O'HERN, JOHN FRANCIS (1874-1933), bishop. Born in Olean, New York, on June 4, he studied at St. Andrew's and St. Bernard's seminaries, Rochester, and the Propaganda, Rome, and was ordained in 1901. He did parish work in Rochester, was appointed vicar general in 1923, made a domestic prelate in 1924, and apostolic administrator in 1927-28. He was appointed bishop of Rochester, New York, in 1929, and died there on May 22.

O'HIGGINS, AMBROSE BERNARD (1720?-1801), governor. Born in County Meath, Ireland, he studied at Cadiz and then migrated to South America, where he became a pedlar in Lima. He then turned to road building, joined the Spanish army engineer corps, advanced rapidly, was made count of Ballenar, and in 1788 governor general of Chile and marquis of Osorno. He governed with great ability and success and in 1796 was appointed viceroy of Peru, a position he held until his death in Lima, Peru, on Mar. 18.

O'HIGGINS, BERNARD (1776-1842). Natural son of Ambrose O'Higgins, he was born in Chillan, Chile, on Aug. 20, educated in England, but returned to Chile on his father's death in 1801. He joined Juan Martinez de Rosas in revolt against Spain in 1811 and replaced José Miguel Carrera (who had displaced Rosas in 1811) as leader of the revolutionary forces in 1813. Defeated at Rancagua in 1814 by the Spaniards, in large measure because of dissension among the revolutionist leaders, he fled to Argentina, where he joined forces with San Martín in the effort to free Chile. In 1817 his leadership led the revolutionists to victory over the royalist forces at Chasabuco in a battle which broke the Spaniards' control, and he was acclaimed dictator of Chile. He ruled well until 1823, when a revolution drove him from office and he fled to Peru. He lived there until his death in Lima on Oct. 24.

O'HIGGINS, KEVIN CHRISTOPHER (1892-1927). Born in Stradbally, Queen's, Ireland, on June 7, he studied at Clongowes Wood, Carlow, and Maynooth colleges, and the National University. He joined the Sinn Fein movement as a student, was jailed in 1917, and was a member of the revolutionary parliament in 1918 and assistant minister for local affairs in 1919. He defended the formation of the Irish Free State in 1921 and became minister for economic affairs. As minister for justice during the civil war of 1922 he approved the execution of seventy-seven republicans; this led to widespread resentment, culminating in the murder of his father in 1923 and his own assassination in Dublin on July 10. He had been working for the creation of an undivided Ireland within the British commonwealth.

OHLER, ALOYS KARL (1817-1889), educator. Born in Mainz, Germany, on Jan. 2, he studied at the gymnasium there, at Giessen, and was ordained in 1839. He engaged in pastoral work, was appointed director of the Catholic Teachers' Training College in Bensheim in 1852, and was made a canon of the Mainz cathedral in 1867 in charge of education at the diocesan seminary until it was closed by the Kulturkampf in 1878. He died in Mainz on Aug. 24. He wrote several influential treatises on education.

O'HURLEY, DERMOD (d. 1584), bishop and martyr. Born in Limerick, Ireland, he studied in Europe, taught at Louvain and Rheims, and then went to Rome. In 1581, though not a priest, he was appointed archbishop of Cashel and consecrated by Pope Gregory XIII. He returned to Ireland in 1583, was imprisoned in Dublin castle, tortured, and when he refused to renounce his religion was hanged in Dublin on June 19 (or 29).

O'HUSSEY, MAELBRIGHTE (d. 1614). A native of Clogher, Ulster, Ireland, he became a Franciscan, taught at Douai, and in 1607 taught theology at St. Anthony College, Louvain. He wrote poetry and was noted for his knowledge of Irish language, history, and customs. His *Christian Catechism* (1608) was the first book in Gaelic printed in Europe.

OJEDA, ALONSO DE (1466?–1515?), explorer. Born in Cuenca, Spain, of a noble family, he joined the household of the duke of Medina as a youth, and was patronized by the bishop of Burgos, through whose offices he accompanied Columbus on his second voyage to America. In 1499 he commanded three vessels on an exploratory voyage to South America, with Juan de la Cosa and Amerigo Vespucci as cartographers. He set out again in 1502, established a colony at Santa Cruz, but his cruelty caused a revolt and the colonists sent him back to Spain, where he was eventually exonerated. He was made governor of the territories of northern South America in 1508, had his colony at present-day Cartagena wiped out by Indians, but escaped with one companion, and founded San Sebastian de Uraba. On the way to Hispaniola for supplies he was shipwrecked, but managed to reach Cuba. He is believed to have died at Santo Domingo.

OKEGHEM, JEAN D' (1430?–1495), musician. Born probably in Termonde, E. Flanders, he became choir boy in the Antwerp cathedral, was ordained, and in 1453 became chief chanter, and later choirmaster, at the court of Charles VII, who appointed him treasurer of St. Martin's in Tours, France, a position he held until his death. He founded a new school of music (known as the second Netherland school) based on the principle he embodied in his compositions of free imitation by which each new voice was allowed to enter on any interval regardless of its distance from the original theme's initial note. Most of his music is lost, though his *Missa cujusvis toni* and *Cantiones sacrae* have survived. He is believed to have written a motet in canon form for thirty-six voices, but it has never been found. He is also known as Ockenheim.

OLAF, ST. (995–1030), king. Son of King Harold of Norway, Olaf Haraldsson, often called "the Fat," spent his youth as a pirate. In 1010 he was baptized at Rouen by Archbishop Robert, and in 1013 served King Ethelred in England against the Danes, returning with several priests who, after he deposed Earl Sweyn and became king in 1015, helped Christianize Norway. His rule was so harsh that he was forced to flee when his subjects, aided by Canute of England and Denmark, revolted. In an attempt to recapture his land he was killed in the battle of Stiklestad, Norway. Though not too popular during his lifetime, he was later regarded as a hero who had tried to unify and Christianize Norway. He was canonized in 1164 and is patron of Norway. F. D. July 29.

OLAF SKUTKONUNG (d. 1024), king of Sweden. Son of Eric the Conqueror, he was the first Christian ruler of Sweden, becoming

king in 993, brought in Anglo-Saxon laborers, and battled with St. Olaf of Norway.

OLAFSSÖN, THORLEIF (d. 1455). He was bishop of Viborg, Denmark, from 1430 to 1450, when he was transferred to Bergen, Norway. He was killed by Germans at the Munkalif convent there on Sept. 1.

OLAGUER. *See* Ollegarius, St.

OLÁH, NICOLAUS (1493–1568), archbishop. Born in Nagyszeben (Hermanstadt), Hungary, on Jan. 10, he studied in Várad, became a page at Wladislaw's court, and was ordained in 1516 or 1518. He was secretary to the bishop of Fünfkirchen, became canon of the Gran chapter, archdeacon of Komorn in 1522, and secretary to King Louis II in 1526, and later of Queen Maria. He joined the court of King Ferdinand I of Bohemia, became bishop of Agram and chancellor in 1543, bishop of Erlau in 1548, archbishop of Gran in 1553, and primate of Hungary. He was the leader of the counter-Reformation there, called several synods to reform the clergy, restore discipline, and establish schools, and had a great effect on religious life in the nation. He wrote several historical works, including *Hungary and Atilla*, and initiated the publication of a breviary and a return to the ringing of the Angelus. He died on Jan. 15 in Nagyszombat (Pozsony), Slovakia.

OLAV, ST. (d. 950?), king. A Swedish ruler, he was slain near Stockholm after rebellious followers ordered him to sacrifice to pagan gods. F. D. July 30.

OLDCORNE, BL. EDWARD (d. 1606), martyr. A native of York, England, he studied at Rheims and Rome, where he was ordained in 1587 and then accepted as a Jesuit, without any noviceship, and sent to England. He worked in Worcestershire under the name of Hall for seventeen years; was betrayed by a man named Littleton, racked five times in the attempt to elicit information which he did not have about the Gunpowder Plot, and hanged and hacked to death in York. Littleton, who publicly asked pardon for his crime, and Ralph Ashley, a Jesuit laybrother, were put to death at the same time. The two Jesuits were beatified in 1929. F. D. Apr. 7.

OLDEGAR. *See* Ollegarius, St.

OLDENBACH, FREDERICK LOUIS (1857–1933), meteorologist. Born in Rochester, New York, on Oct. 21, he studied at Canisius, became a Jesuit in 1881, was sent to Europe for study in the Netherlands and England, was ordained in 1892, and was assigned to teach at St. Ignatius College (now John Carroll University) in Cleveland, Ohio. He became interested in astronomy and meteorology, founded a meteorological observatory at the college in 1896, built the first ceraunograph in 1899, founded a seismological observatory in 1900, and his suggestion led to the formation of the Jesuit Seismological Service in 1909. He died in Cleveland on Mar. 15.

OLDHAM, HUGH (d. 1519), bishop. Born in Crumpsell (or Oldham), Lancashire, England, he studied at Oxford and Cambridge, was ordained, and became the countess of Richmond's chaplain. He was the recipient of many benefices and in 1504 was appointed bishop of Exeter. He founded the Manchester Grammar School in 1515, influenced the founding of Oxford's Corpus Christi College for the secular clergy rather than for order priests, and was a substantial benefactor. He became involved in a jurisdictional dispute with the abbot of Tavistock that became so bitter he was excommunicated, but Rome absolved him on his death on June 25.

OLDOINI, AGOSTINO (1612–1683), historian. Born on Jan. 6 in La Spezzia, Italy, he became a Jesuit in 1628, taught classics and philosophy in Perugia, and devoted his late years to historical and bibliographical writing, particularly a four-volume history of the popes. He died in Perugia, Italy, on Mar. 23.

O'LEARY, ARTHUR (1729–1802). Born in in Iveleary, Cork, Ireland, he became a Franciscan at St. Malo, France, where he studied, was ordained, and served as prison chaplain. He returned to Cork in 1771, became noted for his preaching and wit, and was chaplain of the Spanish embassy in London from 1789 until his death on Jan. 8.

O'LEARY, HENRY JOSEPH (1879–1938), archbishop. Born in Richibucto, New Brunswick, Canada, on Mar. 13, he was ordained, became bishop of Charlottstown in 1913, developed St. Dunstan's College, became archbishop of Edmonton in 1920, and died in Victoria, British Columbia, on Mar. 5.

O'LEARY, PETER (1839–1920). Born in Cluaindroichead, Cork, Ireland, he studied at Fermoy and Maynooth, was ordained and did parish work, became a canon in 1906, and wrote many books in Gaelic to keep the language alive during the period of English suppression. He also translated the New Testament, the *Imitation*, Aesop, and made modernizations of ancient myths. He died on Mar. 21.

O'LEARY, THOMAS MICHAEL (1875–1949), bishop. Born in Dover, New Hampshire, on Apr. 16, he studied at Mungret College, Limerick, Ireland, and the Grand seminary, Montreal, where he was ordained in 1897. He engaged in parish work in Manchester and Concord, and became chancellor of Manchester in 1904, secretary to Bishop Delany there, and in 1914 vicar general of the see. In 1921, he was consecrated bishop of Springfield, Massachusetts, and reigned until his death there on Oct. 10.

OLESNICKI, ZBIGNIEW (1389–1455), cardinal. He became bishop of Cracow, Poland, in 1423, was active as an opponent of the Hussites, and was made a cardinal in 1439 by antipope Felix V. He was chancellor of the university after the death of King Ladislas II in 1434 and raised it to a high intellectual level by adding great scholars from Poland and (a new policy) from outside the country. The cardinal threw his support to Pope Nicholas V after the Union of Florence. He died in Sandomir, Poland, on Apr. 1.

OLGA, ST. (879?–969). Married in 903 to Prince Igor I of Kiev, Russia, she was a cruel and barbarous woman (she scalded her husband's murderers to death in 945 and murdered hundreds of their followers) until she was baptized at Constantinople in 957. She then requested Emperor Otto I to send missionaries to Kiev. Although St. Adalbert of Magdeburg was sent and the queen exerted great efforts, the mission proved a failure, as did her attempt to convert her son, Svyatoslav. Christianity was introduced, however, by her grandson, St. Vladimir. F. D. July 11.

OLIER, JEAN JACQUES (1608–1657), founder. Born in Paris, France, on Sept. 20, he studied under the Jesuits in Lyons, at Harcourt College and the Sorbonne, and changed from a frivolous dilettante to a serious social worker when he joined the endeavors of St. Vincent de Paul. Encouraged by St. Francis de Sales, he was ordained in 1633. He continued working with St. Vincent, but became associated with the Oratorians under Fr. de Condren. In 1641, Olier entered into a community life with two other priests in a Paris suburb, Vaugirard, and later that year took over the parish of St. Sulpice, one of the largest but most run-down in France. He introduced wide reforms, taught vigorously, and built an orphanage, houses of shelter, and schools. In 1642 he founded the St. Sulpice seminary, which soon became a model training center. The great demand for his priests to found and direct seminaries in other dioceses, beginning with Nantes in 1648, led him to modify his original concept of St. Sulpice as a community of secular priests. In 1651 the Society of St. Sulpice (Sulpicians) was approved (papally, in 1664) and organized to provide priests for the direction of seminaries. He made many converts, denounced Cardinal Mazarin for his episcopal nominations, crusaded against dueling, and fought fiercely against Jansenism. He died in St. Sulpice on Apr. 2.

OLIVA, GIAN PAOLO (1600–1681). Born in Genoa, Italy, on Oct. 4, he became a Jesuit in 1616, was an outstanding palace preacher under four popes, became vicar general in 1661 with the right of succession (because of the advanced age of his predecessor, Goswin Nickel), and was elected eleventh general of his Society in 1664. He was active in encouraging missions, especially in Japan, and in lessening dissension among religious orders. His mission to Persia had great success at the start; he fostered learning and continued the growing struggle against Jansenism and theological errors. He died at Sant' Andrea Quirinale, Rome, on Nov. 26.

OLIVAINT, PIERRE (1816–1871), martyr. Born in Paris on Feb. 22, he studied at the College of Charlemagne and the Normal School, was converted in 1837, and taught at Grenoble and history at Bourbon College. He became a Jesuit in 1845, taught history at Brugelette College in Belgium, and was ordained. He returned to Paris in 1852 and was stationed at Vaugirard College, of which he became rector and where he taught until 1865, when he was appointed superior of the Paris house. He was arrested by the leaders of the Paris commune, dragged through the streets, and massacred with fifty-one others on Apr. 26.

OLIVE. She is the heroine of a pious legend, developed in miracle-play form, which describes her as a Christian girl of thirteen who was captured in Palermo by the Moslems, carried to Tunis, won a number of converts to Christianity, and was tortured and beheaded. She long was honored in the diocese of Carthage on June 10; oddly, the Mohammedans in Tunis also built a mosque in her honor.

OLIVER, GEORGE (1781–1861), antiquarian. Born in Newington, Surrey, England, on Feb. 9, he studied at Sedgley Park School and Stonyhurst College, where he taught for five years, and in 1806 was ordained. He was sent to a mission in Exeter in 1807 and spent the rest of his life there, well known for his archaeological studies and writings on Devonshire antiquities outstanding of which was *Monasticon Dioecesis Exoniensis* (1846). He died in Exeter, England, on Mar. 23.

OLIVERA, ANTÓNIO DE (d. 1641). Born in León, Spain, he became a Carmelite as Anthony of the Mother of God, taught philosophy at Alcalá, and prepared a three-volume course on elementary philosophy.

OLIVI, PIERRE JEAN (1248?–1298). Born in Sérignan, France, he became a Franciscan at Béziers when twelve, received his baccalaureate from Paris, and went to Rome, where he became a leader of those in favor of strict observance of the rule. The ensuing struggle between adherents of the strict and those of the lax observance of the rule rent the Franciscans for eight years. He was accused of heresy at the general chapter of 1282 at Strassburg, had several of his propositions censured, and his writings confiscated in 1283 but was exonerated at the general chapter in Montpellier in 1287. He was lector of theology in Florence and Montpellier, accused and exonerated again at the general chapter in 1292, and spent the

balance of his life in Narbonne, France, where he died on Mar. 14. The struggle raged after his death, when his disciples venerated him as a saint. His writings on speculative matters, exegesis, and observance of the Franciscan rule were condemned at general chapters in 1299, 1312, and 1319; his tomb was destroyed in 1318; and in 1326 Pope John XXII condemned his *Postilla in Apocalypsim*.

OLIVIER DE LA MARCHE (1426–1501), poet. Born in the Château de la Marche, Franche-Comté, France, he was knighted in 1465 by the count of Charolais (later Charles the Bold, duke of Burgundy), who appointed him bailiff in 1467, was taken prisoner at the battle of Nancy in 1477, and when freed entered the service of the duke's daughter Marie. He wrote *Mémoires*, prose accounts of tournaments, and poems, chief of which is *Le Chevalier délibéré*, considered both an autobiography and an allegorical life of Charles.

OLLÉ-LAPRUNE, LÉON (1839–1898), philosopher. He taught in several lower schools and from 1875 until his death in Paris on Feb. 19 taught philosophy in L'École Normale. He was noted for his studies in the role of the will in faith and as a leader in Catholic philosophical circles. He wrote *La Philosophie et le temps présent* (1890), *Prix de la vie* (1894), *La Vitalité chrétienne* (1901), and *La Raison et le rationalisme* (1907).

OLLEGARIUS, ST. (1060–1137), archbishop. Born in Barcelona, Spain, he became an Augustinian at fifteen, was prior of several houses in France, and in 1115 became administrator of Barcelona and archbishop when the see was transferred to Tarragona the next year. He attended the Lateran Council (1123), supported the new Knights Templars, preached a crusade against the Moors in Spain, and rebuilt much of the property they had destroyed. He is also called Olaguer and Oldegar. F. D. Mar. 6.

OLYMPIADES, ST. (d. 303), martyr. A Roman official, he was tortured to death at Almeria, Italy, during the persecution of Diocletian. F. D. Dec. 1.

OLYMPIADES, ST. (d. 251), martyr. See Maximus, St.

O'LOGHLEN, MICHAEL (1789–1846), jurist. A native of Ennis, Clare, Ireland, he studied at Trinity College, was admitted to the Dublin bar in 1811, and became a leading lawyer. He was appointed solicitor general of Ireland (the first Catholic since James II's time) in 1834, was a member of parliament, became attorney general in 1835, baron of the exchequer in 1836, and master of the rolls in 1837, a position he held until his death.

OLYMPIAS, ST. (361?–408?). Born in Constantinople of a noble family, she married Nebridius, prefect of the city, refused another marriage when he died, and became a deaconess with the approval of St. Nectarius, bishop of Constantinople. When St. John Chrysostom succeeded to the see, he accepted her and her disciples under his protection. After his exile in 404, her community was disbanded by the usurping bishop, Atticus, and she was subjected to great persecution which was assuaged to some extent by correspondence from St. John (some seventeen letters are extant). She died in exile in Nicomedia on July 25. F. D. Dec. 17.

OLYMPIUS, ST. (d. 257), martyr. *See* Symphronius, St.

OLYMPIUS, ST. (d. 343), bishop. He was so staunch as supporter of St. Athanasius and opponent of Arianism that he was removed from his see in Enos, Rumelia, by Emperor Constantius. F. D. June 12.

O'MEARA, KATHLEEN (1839–1888), author. Born in Dublin, Ireland, she moved to Paris with her parents about 1844. She published her first novel in 1867, wrote five more (*Narka* was the most popular), biographies of Frederic Ozanam and St. John Vianney, a series, *Bells of the Sanctuary*, and articles for English and American magazines. She died in Paris on Nov. 10.

OMER, ST. (595?–670?), bishop. Born near Coutances, France, he became a Benedictine monk at Luxeuil under St. Eustace, and about 637 was appointed bishop of the run-down diocese of Thérouanne. He founded Sithiu (later the town of St. Omer) and many other abbeys and restored his see to a flourishing state. He is also known as Audomarus. F. D. Sept. 9.

OÑATE, JUAN DE (1555?–1615?), explorer. Born in Guadalajara, Mexico, a city his father founded, he married the granddaughter of Cortés. In 1598, after considerable delay, he was allowed to journey from Zacatecas with 400 settlers, and Indians and cattle, and established San Juan, New Mexico. He made exploratory trips to Arizona and Kansas, but was relieved of his governorship in 1608. His expedition to New Mexico was recounted in a narrative poem by Gaspar de Villagrá.

ONCHO, ST. (d. 600?). An Irish poet, he made many pilgrimages, seeking relics and information about former holy men who had been associated with the monastery of Clonmore. F. D. Feb. 8.

O'NEILL, GEORGE (1863–1947). Born in Dungannon, Ireland, he studied in Tullabeg and the Royal and National universities, became a Jesuit in 1880, and after ordination was one of the founders of the publication, *Studies*. He went to Australia in 1922, taught history and languages at Corpus Christi College, Werribee, wrote several biographies, *Essays on Poetry*, scriptural commentaries (the Psalms and Job), and edited collections of poetry, scriptural readings, and an anthology of John Henry Newman. He retired in 1946

when his eyesight failed and died in Sydney, Australia, on July 19.

O'NEILL, HUGH (1540–1616). Son of Matthew O'Neill, he was raised in England, succeeded his brother Brian as baron of Dungannon in 1562 after an inter-family war between his father and Shane O'Neill resulted in Brian's and his father's death, and returned to Ireland in 1568. He joined the English expedition against the rebel earl of Desmond in 1580, was in parliament in 1585 as the second earl of Tyrone, and was played against other Irish chieftains by the British, who refused to return to grandfather's land. In 1594, when his brother joined the rebellion in Ireland, he was accused of aiding and sympathizing with the rebels and barely escaped imprisonment. He joined the rebellion in 1595, negotiated, with Hugh Roe O'Donnell, with Philip II of Spain for aid, and repeatedly defeated the English even while proclaiming his loyalty and attempting to negotiate with them for Catholic freedom in Ulster. A truce arranged by the earl of Essex in 1599 failed when Queen Elizabeth turned it down. In 1601, aid came from the Spaniards, but Lord Mountjoy defeated both the Irish and Spaniards at Kinsale. O'Neill escaped until 1603, when he surrendered and received a full pardon from King James I. He was driven from Ireland in 1607, attainted by the Irish parliament and his lands confiscated, and fled to Rome, where he died.

O'NEILL, OWEN ROE (1582–1649). Nephew of Hugh, second earl of Tyrone, he joined the Spanish army in Flanders in 1603, rose to the rank of colonel, and in 1640 led the defense of Arras against an overwhelming French army. In 1642 he led a force of Irish soldiers who had served in Europe home to the Irish rebellion which had broken out in 1641, was appointed commander of the rebel forces in Ulster, and won a momentous victory at Benburg in 1646 against great odds. Dissension among the Catholic leaders nullified the victory, and he died suddenly on Nov. 6 near Cavan shortly after the fall of Drogheda to Cromwell's forces.

ONESIMUS, ST. (1st century), martyr. A slave who had robbed his Phrygian master, Philemon, he was converted and baptized by St. Paul, who obtained pardon for his crime and made him a messenger (of the Epistles to Philemon and with Tychicus to the Colossians). He is sometimes confused with the bishop of Ephesus. F. D. Feb. 16.

ONESIMUS. Bishop of Ephesus sometime after the term of St. Timothy, he was one of the Christian crowd which in 107 hailed St. Ignatius of Antioch on his way to martyrdom in Rome. He is often confused with the Onesimus of St. Paul's epistle to Philemon.

ONESIPHORUS, ST. (d. 80?), martyr. He is

mentioned by St. Paul (II Tim. 4:19); tradition says he followed Paul and was torn to pieces by wild horses somewhere on the Hellespont during the reign of Domitian. Porphyrius, a member of his household, died with them. F. D. Sept. 6.

O'NIELL, CHARLES AUSTIN (1869–1951), jurist. Born in Franklin, Louisiana, he studied at the Christian Brothers College, Memphis, Tennessee, and law at Tulane, and was admitted to the bar in 1893. He became a district judge in 1908 and was named to the state supreme court in 1912. His interpretations of municipal zoning became nationwide precedents. He was presiding judge at the impeachment of Gov. Huey Long in 1929 until the proceedings were abandoned, outlasted attempts by the governor to remove him, and retired in 1949. He died in New Orleans on Mar. 8.

ONUPHRIUS, ST. (d. 400?), martyr. An abbot named Paphnutius found him wandering in the Thebaid, Egypt, covered with hair from head to foot. After a day's discussions Onuphrius died, having earlier told the abbot that he obviously had been sent to bless and bury him. His feast, June 12, was popular for centuries, particularly in the Coptic and Ethiopian rites. His story may be a pious fiction.

OPPENORDT, GILLES MARIE (1672–1742), artist. Born in Paris, he studied in Rome under Bernini and Borromini, and attracted the atttention of the French regent with his high altars for St. Germain-des-Prés and St. Sulpice in Paris in 1704. Among his works are the John the Baptist chapel in the Amiens cathedral and the Dominican novitiate church, Paris, and decorations in the Palais Royal and Hôtel du Grand Prieur de France. He died in Paris.

OPPORTUNA, ST. (d. 770?). Born in Normandy, she became a Benedictine nun and later abbess of Montreuil. She died shortly after her brother St. Chrodegang was murdered. F. D. Apr. 22.

OPTATIAN, ST. (d. 505?). He was bishop of Brescia, Italy, from about 451 until his death. F. D. July 14.

OPTATUS, ST. (d. 304), martyr. *See* Apodemius, St.

OPTATUS, ST. (d. 387?), bishop. A convert from paganism, the bishop of Milevis, Numidia, was the first to refute the Donatists in Africa. He wrote strenuously against them; his arguments are historically significant since they speak of the supremacy of the pope; the validity of the sacraments, whatever the moral character of those administering them; the necessity of baptism; and also refer to the parts of the sacrifice of the mass, prayers at baptism, differences in penance, and veneration of relics. F. D. June 4.

OPTATUS, ST. (d. 530?). He became bishop of Auxerre, France, about 529. F. D. Aug. 31.

O'QUEELY, MALACHIAS (d. 1645), archbishop. Born in Thomond, Ireland, he studied at Navarre College in Paris, was appointed vicar apostolic of Killaloe, and in 1631 archbishop of Tuam over the initial objections of his subjects. His reforms and religious zeal called forth the protests of the Protestant archbishop in 1641. In 1643 he attended the organization of the Catholic Confederation and was appointed to its supreme council; he later was president of Connaught. He was killed leading a force against the Convenanters at Balliodares, Ireland, on Oct. 27.

O'QUINN, JAMES (d. 1881). The first bishop of Brisbane, Australia, he was born in Rathbawn, Ireland, on Mar. 17, consecrated at Dublin in 1859 and arrived in his see, with five priests, in 1861. He organized the Queensland Immigration Society to bring ten shiploads of Irish settlers to the colony, but ran into great opposition; anti-Catholic feeling ran high and slogans appeared warning that Queensland was in danger of becoming Quinn's land. As a result, the government, which had supported his society, suppressed it in 1865. Bishop O'Quinn founded the Catholic newspaper, the *Australian*, in 1878 built orphanages, the cathedrals of St. Stephen, and fifty-two schools, and organized and personally visited all quarters of a diocese of nearly 700,000 square miles. He died in Brisbane on Aug. 18.

ORBELLIS, NICOLAS D' (1400?–1475), theologian. A native of France, he joined the Observantines and became professor of theology at Angers, France, famed for his knowledge of the writings and teaching of Duns Scotus. He died in Rome. His chief work was a commentary on Scotus' *Four Books of Sentences.*

ORCAGNA. *See* Cione, Andrea di.

ORDERICUS VITALIS (1075–1143?), historian. Born in Normandy, he was brought to England by his parents, but when ten was sent back to the monastery of St. Evroult, where he became a monk and spent the rest of his life, except for brief trips on the Continent and to England. He began a history of his abbey which grew into the thirteen-volume *Historia ecclesiastica,* of particular interest for the years 751–1141, including the Norman invasion of England and the first crusade. Though sometimes inaccurate, it is colorful and picturesque in detail and valuable for its inclusion of popular literature and song. He also wrote Latin poetry.

ORDOÑO I (d. 866), king of León. He became king in 850, and rebuilt the monastery of Sahagún, destroyed by the Moors when they overran his nation in 846.

ORDOÑO II (10th century), king of León. He had inherited Galicia from his father and joined it to León when he succeeded his brother García in 914. He defeated the Moors at San Esteban and was crushed by them at Valdejunquera, subdued the counts of Castile, and built the cathedral in León.

ORDOÑO, ST. (d. 1066), bishop. He was a Benedictine at the abbey of Sahagún, Spain, and became bishop of Astorga in 1062. F. D. Feb. 23.

O'REGAN, ANTHONY (1809–1866), bishop. Born in Lavalleyroe, Mayo, Ireland, he studied at Maynooth and was ordained in Tuam in 1834. He taught theology and scripture at St. Jarlath's College, Tuam, became its president in 1844, and then went to the United States in 1849 to be head of the St. Louis seminary. He was consecrated third bishop of Chicago in 1854, encountered great resistance from the clergy of the see, and resigned in 1858 and was appointed titular bishop of Dora. He died in London on Nov. 13.

OREGLIA DI SANTO STEFANO, LUIGI (1828–1913), cardinal. Born in Bebe Vaginena, Italy, he was ordained, became titular archbishop of Damietta in 1866, and was created a cardinal in 1873. He was a leading opponent of modernism, served as a member of the Roman curia, and died in Rome.

O'REILLY, BERNARD (1803–1856), bishop. Born in Cunnareen, Longford, Ireland, he came to the United States in 1825, studied at the Grand seminary, Montreal, and St. Mary's, Baltimore, and was ordained in Philadelphia in 1831. After serving in Brooklyn, he was sent to Rochester in 1832, where he remained until 1847, when he was appointed vicar general of Rochester and rector of the diocesan seminary. He was appointed titular bishop of Pompeiopolis and coadjutor of Hartford, Connecticut, in 1850 and succeeded to the see in 1852. During his episcopacy, he greatly expanded the number of clergy, schools, and churches in his diocese, and founded St. Mary's seminary, Providence, Rhode Island, in 1851. He died at sea on Jan. 23.

O'REILLY, BERNARD (1824–1894), bishop. Born in Ballymeg, Meath, Ireland, on Jan. 10, he was ordained, and was consecrated third bishop of Liverpool in 1873. He built twenty-two parishes in his twenty-one years in the see, and opened the diocesan seminary of St. Joseph at Upholland in 1883. He died in Liverpool, England, on Apr. 9.

O'REILLY, BERNARD (1820–1907), historian. Born in Mayo, Ireland, on Sept. 29, he went to Canada as a youth, studied at Laval University, and was ordained in 1843. He did parish work, became a Jesuit, taught at St. John's College, Fordham, in New York, and during the Civil War was chaplain of the Irish Brigade of the Army of the Potomac. He left the Jesuits after the war, joined the staff of the *New American Encyclopedia,* and contrib-

uted articles to the New York *Sun.* He was made a monsignor in 1887 in Rome. On his return he became chaplain at Mt. St. Vincent convent in New York City, where he remained until his death on Apr. 26. He wrote biographies of Popes Leo XIII and Pius IX and of Bishop John McHale.

O'REILLY, CHARLES JOSEPH (1862–1923), bishop. Born in Carlton, New Brunswick, Canada, on Jan. 4 (possibly in 1860), he studied at St. Joseph's College, Memramcook, and the Grand seminary, Montreal, and was ordained in Portland, Oregon, in 1890. He did pastoral work in the Oregon City archdiocese, served as editor of the *Catholic Sentinel,* and when the diocese of Baker, Oregon, was erected in 1903, became its first bishop. He was transferred to the see of Lincoln, Nebraska, in 1918, and died there on Feb. 4.

O'REILLY, EDMUND (1616–1669), archbishop. Born in Dublin, he was educated and ordained there in 1639, studied at Louvain, was prefect of its Irish College, vicar general on his return to Dublin in 1640, and administrator of the archdiocese from 1642 to 1648. He was imprisoned by the Puritans in 1653, expelled from Ireland, and went to the Lisle Irish College, where he was appointed archbishop of Armagh. He was unable to reach his see until 1659, was charged with favoring the Puritans against the Stuarts, and recalled to Rome in 1661, where he was exonerated but prevented from returning to Armagh by the British until 1665. He was arrested by the duke of Ormond when he refused to support Peter Walsh's Remonstrance and expelled to France, where he died in Saumur.

O'REILLY, EDMUND (1811–1878), theologian. Born in London on Apr. 30, he studied at Clongowes, Maynooth, and Rome, where he received his doctorate in divinity, was ordained in 1838, and taught theology at Maynooth until 1851. He then became a Jesuit in Naples, taught at St. Beuno's College in North Wales, was appointed professor of theology at the Catholic University of Dublin in 1855, and was provincial of Ireland from 1863 to 1870. He wrote *The Relations of the Church to Society,* was highly regarded by Cardinal Newman, and died in Dublin on Nov. 10.

O'REILLY, HUGH (1580–1653). He became bishop of Armagh, Ireland, in 1628. He summoned the bishops of Ulster to a synod at Kells in 1642 in which he declared lawful the war against the invading English; he convened a synod of clerical and civil leaders at Kilkenny later in 1642, where the Confederation of Kilkenny, of which he became head, was formed. Loyal to King Charles I, it assumed all functions of government and waged war against the Cromwell faction which had closed schools, seized property, and suppressed religion

877

throughout Catholic Ireland. He became general of the Irish forces after most of the Catholic leaders had been slain in battle, and died at an abbey on Trinity Island, Lough Erne, Ireland.

O'REILLY, JAMES (d. 1887), bishop-elect. Appointed first bishop of Wichita, Kansas, in 1887, he died on July 26 before his consecration.

O'REILLY, JAMES (1855–1934), bishop. Born in Lisgrea, Cavan, Ireland, on Oct. 10, he studied at All Hallows, Dublin, and was ordained in 1880. He went to the United States, served in Minnesota parishes, was pastor of St. Anthony of Padua in Minneapolis from 1886 to 1910, and in 1910 was consecrated bishop of Fargo, North Dakota, a position he held until his death there on Dec. 19.

O'REILLY, JOHN BOYLE (1844–1890), editor. Born in Drouth castle, Drogheda, Ireland, on June 24, he was an apprentice on the Drogheda *Argus* and the Preston, England, *Guardian,* served in the British army, returned to Ireland in 1863, and joined the Fenian movement. He was captured and charged with rebellion, but because of his youth was sentenced to twenty years in the penal colony of Australia. He escaped in 1869 in a whaler which took him to Massachusetts. He became editor of the Boston *Pilot* in 1870 and part owner in 1876. He wrote four volumes of poetry, a novel, *Moondyne,* based on his experiences in Australia, collaborated on another, *The King's Men,* and helped many young authors to get their start. He died in Hull, Massachusetts, on Aug. 10.

O'REILLY, MICHAEL (d. 1758). Bishop of Derry, Ireland, he became primate of Armagh in 1749, and spent much time hiding in the outlying areas to escape persecution. He wrote two catechisms, one in English and one in Irish.

O'REILLY, MICHAEL FRANCIS (1847–1917), scientist. Born in Cavan, Ireland, on Sept. 29, he studied in New York and Montreal, became a Christian brother, taught in St. Joseph's College, London, from 1870, and did graduate work at London University. He taught in Waterford, Ireland, in 1893–96, and at Manhattan College, New York, from 1896 until his death there on Jan. 20. He wrote on electricity, astronomy, and the rotation of the earth, and compiled the catalogue of the Latimer Clark Library for the American Institute of Electrical Engineers. He also compiled a bibliography of works on electricity and magnetism. He published under the name Brother Potamian.

O'REILLY, MYLES WILLIAM PATRICK (1825–1880). Born near Balbriggan, Dublin, Ireland, on Mar. 13, he studied at Ushaw College and at London, and returned to Ireland in 1847. He aided the formation of the Catholic University in Dublin, joined the Louth Rifles in 1854, and in 1859 organized and fought as a major with the Irish Brigade of the papal army until its surrender at Spoleto, Italy, in 1860. He was a member of parliament from Longford from 1862 to 1876 and assistant commissioner of intermediate education for Ireland from 1879 until his death in Dublin on Feb. 6.

O'REILLY, PATRICK THOMAS (1833–1892), bishop. Born in Kilnaleck, Ireland, on Dec. 24, he was brought to Boston in his youth, studied at St. Charles College, Maryland, and St. Mary's seminary, Baltimore, and was ordained in Boston in 1857. He did parish work in Worcester and Boston, and was pastor of St. John's in Worcester when he was appointed first bishop of Springfield, Massachusetts, in 1870. He died in Springfield on May 28.

O'REILLY, THOMAS CHARLES (1873–1938), bishop. Born in Cleveland, Ohio, on Feb. 22, he studied at John Carroll University there and the North American College and the Propaganda in Rome, and was ordained in Rome in 1898. He engaged in parish work in Cleveland, taught at St. Mary's seminary in 1901–10, was chancellor of the diocese in 1910–16 and vicar general in 1916–21, pastor of St. John the Evangelist cathedral in 1911–28, and vicar general of religious in 1922–28. He was consecrated bishop of Scranton, Pennsylvania, in 1928. He died in Miami Beach, Florida, on Mar. 25.

ORELLANA, FRANCISCO DE (1490?–1546?), explorer. Born in Trujillo, Spain, he went to Peru in 1535, and served with Pizarro in 1540–41, on the expedition to the Napo River. While scouting for Pizarro's main force, he left him, discovered the Amazon River, and explored it from the Andes to the Atlantic Ocean. He was given royal approval to conquer his newly discovered river area, but an expedition in 1544 was unsuccessful. He probably died in Venezuela.

ORENTIUS, ST. (d. 240?), martyr. He and his wife, Patientia, were put to death for their faith at Loret in northern Aragon, Spain. F. D. May 1.

ORENTIUS, ST. (d. 439?), bishop. He was called from his life as a hermit near Tarbes, France, by the people of Auch to serve as their bishop for forty years. F. D. May 1.

ORESME, NICOLE (d. 1382), bishop. Born in Bayeux, Normandy, he studied theology at Paris, was grand master of the Collège de Navarre in 1356, a canon of Rouen in 1362, dean of the chapter in 1364, and in 1377 was appointed bishop of Lisieux, where he remained until his death on July 11. He became a close friend and adviser of Charles V (though probably never his tutor, as often reported) and was famed for his works in economics, mathematics, and physics. His outstanding economic works are commentaries on Aristotle's politics, economics, and ethics and a *Treatise on Coins*. In mathematics his *Tractatus de latitudinibus formarum* preceded some of Descartes' work in analytic geometry and illustrated latitude, longitude, and rectangular co-ordinates; his demonstration of the law of space was identical with and an influence on Galileo's. His *Traité du ciel et du monde* (1377), in which he proved the earth moves, and not the heavens, contains conclusions later expounded by Copernicus.

ORESTES, ST. (4th century), martyr. *See* Eustratius, St.

ORESTES, ST. (d. 304), martyr. He was slain in Cappadocia during the Diocletian persecution. F. D. Nov. 9.

ORFANEL, BL. HYACINTH (1578–1622), martyr. Born in Llana, Valencia, Spain, he became a Dominican at Barcelona, was sent to Japan, and burned alive at Nagasaki after years of work in the missions. He was beatified in 1867. F. D. Sept. 10.

ORIANI, BARNABA (1752–1832), astronomer. Born in Garegnano, Italy, on July 17, he studied at San Alessandro College in Milan, became a Barnabite, and was ordained in 1775. He joined the Brera observatory staff in Milan in 1776, and became assistant astronomer in 1778 and director in 1802. His calculations of the orbit and a table of elements of Uranus published in 1785 attracted widespread attention and led to an offer of a professorship at Palermo, which he refused. He was appointed president of a commission to regulate the new system of weights and measures in the newly established republic of Lombardy, was appointed count and senator when it became a Napoleonic kingdom, and was one of those appointed to measure the arc of the meridians between the Rimini and Rome zeniths. He was a prolific contributor on astronomical subjects to the *Effemeridi di Milano* for more than fifty years and wrote several treatises on spherical trigonometry. He died in Milan, Italy, on Nov. 12.

ORICULUS, ST. (d. 430?), martyr. He was one of a group of Christians put to death by the Arian Vandals near Carthage in North Africa. F. D. Nov. 18.

ORIENTALIS (4th century). As bishop of Bordeaux, Gaul, he attended the Council of Arles in 314.

ORIENTIUS (5th century), poet. A native of Gaul, he evidently led a life of gaiety as a youth, was converted, and became a pastor at a period when Gaul was being invaded by the barbarians. He wrote the elegiac *Commonitorium*, 1036 verses describing the path, and the pitfalls, to heaven. He is believed by some to be the Orientius appointed bishop of Augusta Ausciorum (Auch) in 410, who acted as ambassador of King Theodoric I of the Goths to Roman generals Aetius and Litorius in 439.

ORIGEN (185?–254?), theologian. Born of Christian parents, probably in Alexandria, Origines Adamantius was the son of Leonidas, who suffered martyrdom during the persecution of the Christians in Alexandria in 202, a fate which Origen himself barely escaped. He studied under Pantaenus and Clement at the catechetical school in Alexandria, and was appointed its head by Bishop Demetrius in 203 to succeed Clement. He studied pagan philosophy and literature under Ammonius Saccas to gain wider knowledge and insights for his teaching, embraced a strict, ascetic way of life, and even castrated himself in the mistaken belief this would add to the purity of his life. From 218 to 230 he devoted himself to literary activities and teaching in Alexandria, though he visited Rome in 211, Palestine in 215, and Antioch about 218 during these years, and published his studies of the Bible, *Hexapla* and *Tetrapla*, in which he compared original Hebrew texts of the Old Testament and Greek versions in an attempt to secure a more reliable text, and provided commentaries on these texts. He became popular as a preacher and while in Palestine delivered lectures in churches in Jerusalem and Caesarea, actions disapproved by his bishop, Demetrius (Alexandrian ecclesiastical discipline forbade preaching by laymen), who recalled him to Alexandria in 216. About 230, while on the way to Greece, he was ordained in Caesarea by his friend Bishop Theoctistus. This step resulted in the actions taken by Demetrius at two synods, which expelled Origen from Alexandria and deprived him of his priesthood. Origen's appeal to Pope Fabian was denied and Demetrius' action upheld. Origen then settled in Caesarea in Palestine in 231, established a school which became famed for his teaching and scholarship, and devoted himself to preaching, traveling widely, and visiting Athens (237) and Arabia, where he was successful in refuting Bishop Beryllus' teaching that Christ's divine nature did not exist before His human nature. During the persecution of Maximian in 235–37 he took refuge in Caesarea in Cappadocia, and there wrote his stirring *Exhortation to Martyrdom* and *Prayer*. He was arrested in 250, on the outbreak of the Cedian persecution, imprisoned and subjected to great tortures, but was eventually released. He probably died at Tyre. Origen was one of the most prolific and influential of the early Christian writers. Besides his textual studies, he wrote exegetical treatises on the Bible which

were widely studied; *Scholia* (short, mainly grammatical, annotations); *Homilies*, among the oldest examples of Christian preaching and based on exegesis; and *Commentaries*, on most of the books of the Bible. In apologetics his most important work was *Contra Celsus*, in which he refuted Celsus' attacks on Christianity. He also wrote on dogma in *De principiis* (c. 228), the first systematic exposition of the teachings of the Church treating of God, heavenly spirits, man, and the world, ethics, and scripture; and *Stromata* (most of which is lost), in which he compared Christian teaching with that of the pagan philosophers, proving the truth of Christian teaching from the works of Plato, Aristotle, Numenius, and Cornutus. Origen himself has never been condemned by the Church and it is a matter of dispute among scholars whether his teaching, known as Origenism, has ever been condemned by an Ecumenical Council. Even during his lifetime some of his writings provoked great controversy, and local synods have denounced various aspects of his thought, notably the Synod of Constantinople in 543, which subscribed to Justinian's *Liber adversus Origenum*. Few of his original manuscripts have survived, and most of his teaching is known through reconstructions and translations, the exact authenticity of which is dubious. However, his views on the Trinity in *De principiis*, and on the body and soul of Christ, his doctrines on the pre-existence and destiny of souls, and his denial that the mortal body and the resurrection body are the same have been repeatedly denounced.
JEAN DANIELOU, *Origen* (New York, Sheed, 1955).

ORINGA, BL. (d. 1310). A pious servant, she gathered a group to serve under the Rule of St. Augustine and founded a convent at Castello di Santa Croce, Tuscany, Italy. She is also called Christiana. F. D. Jan. 4 (sometimes, Jan. 10).

ORIOL, ST. JOSEPH, (1650–1702). Born in Barcelona, Spain, he became a priest, gained a doctorate in theology, and worked as a tutor. He followed a course of extreme asceticism, lived on bread and water for twenty-six years, and was successful as a confessor and in his work with soldiers and with children. He had a number of supernatural gifts and was canonized in 1909. F. D. Mar. 23.

O'RIORDÁN, MICHAEL (1857–1919). Born in Limerick, Ireland, he studied at the Irish College, Propaganda, and Gregorian, in Rome, was ordained in 1883, served in Westminster, England, and Limerick, and from 1905 until his death in Rome on Aug. 27 was rector of the Irish College. He was made a monsignor, honored by Louvain, and wrote a life of St. Columbanus, among other works.

ORLANDINI, NICCOLÒ (1554–1606). Born in Florence, Italy, he became a Jesuit in 1572, was rector of the college in Nola, master of novices at Naples, and secretary to the general. He began a history of his Society, but had completed only the generalate of St. Ignatius when he died in Rome on May 17.

ORLANDUS DE LASSUS. *See* Lattre, Roland de.

ORONTIUS, ST. (d. 305), martyr. Born in Cimiez, France, he was put to death with his brother, St. Vincent, and St. Victor, at Puigcerda in the Spanish Pyrenees, where they had been preaching. F. D. Jan. 22.

O'RORKE, PATRICK (1837–1863). Born on Mar. 25 in Cavan, Ireland, he was brought to Rochester, New York, when a year old, graduated with honors from West Point in 1861, became colonel of the 104th New York Volunteers, and was killed during the Civil War in defense of Little Round Top at Gettysburg, Pennsylvania.

OROSIUS, PAULUS (b. 380?), historian. Born in Braga, Portugal, he became a priest and went to Africa in 413 or 414 to discuss Priscillianism with St. Augustine at Hippo. He then joined St. Jerome, whom he aided in the struggle against Pelagius and his heretical doctrines; attended the Council of Jerusalem in 415, where he denounced Pelagius and drew the condemnation of Bishop John of Jerusalem, a Pelagius sympathizer; returned to St. Augustine in 416; and set out for his native land. Because of Vandal victories in Spain, he returned to Hippo, where at Augustine's suggestion he wrote and in 418 completed *Historiarum adversus paganos*, the first Christian history, often read as a complement to Book 3 of the *City of God*. It was widely popular in the Middle Ages, was translated by Alfred the Great, and though hastily written is of value especially for details of the period after 378. Orosius also wrote *Commonitorium de errore Priscillianistarum et Origenestarum* and *Liber apologeticus contra Pelagium*.

OROZCO, BL. ALPHONSUS DE (1500–1591). Born in Oropesa, Spain, he studied at Talavera, Toledo, and Salamanca, and became a Hermit of St. Augustine in 1522 after hearing St. Thomas of Villanova preach. He served as prior at Seville and Valladolid and in 1556 became preacher at the court of King Philip II. He left many mystical writings and was beatified in 1881. F. D. Sept. 19.

OROZCO Y JIMINEZ, FRANCISCO (1865?–1936), bishop. Born in Zamora, Mexico, he studied in Rome at Colegio Pio Latino Americano and the Gregorian and was ordained in 1887. He taught theology at the Zamora seminary and at the University of Mexico, and became bishop of Chiapas in 1902 and archbishop of Guadalajara in 1912.

He went to Rome in 1914–16, returned to defend the Church against the limitations of the new constitution, was exiled in 1917, and, after returning, was again exiled in 1926 and 1932. He died in Guadalajara, Mexico, on Feb. 18.

ORSI, GIUSEPPE AGOSTINO FRAN-CESCO (1672–1761), cardinal. Born in Florence, Italy, on May 9, he became a Dominican in 1708, taking the name Giuseppe, and was master of studies at San Marco, Florence, professor of theology at St. Thomas College, Rome, in 1732, and later prior. He became Cardinal Neri Orsini's theologian in 1734, secretary of the Congregation of the Index in 1738, papal theologian in 1749, and cardinal in 1759. He wrote on baptism, grace, the papacy, and the twenty-volume *Storia ecclesiastica* (1747–61), covering the history of the Church through the sixth century. He died in Rome on June 12.

ORSIESIUS, ST. (d. 380?). A follower of St. Pachomius, he was placed in charge of the desert monastery of Khenoboski and later of the community at Tabennisi, in Egypt. His rule was so strict that many rebelled, and he retired in favor of St. Theodore. When the latter died, in 368, Orsiesius returned to office. An ascetical treatise, which contains an abridgment of his rule, was translated by St. Jerome. F. D. June 15.

ORSINI, GIAMBATTISTA (d. 1503), cardinal. Nephew of Cardinal Latino Orsini, he was ordained young, became a canon of St. Peter's, and was created a cardinal in 1483. He received, and ruled in absentia, the see of Taranto from Pope Innocent VIII in 1491, and ruled Romagna, the Marches, and Bologna as papal legate. He played a conspicuous role in the election of Pope Alexander VI in 1492, but, when he joined the duke of Bracciano in support of the Florentines and French against the pope, he was taken captive at the pope's orders and imprisoned in Castel Sant' Angelo, Rome, where he died on Feb. 22, reportedly of poison.

ORSINI, GIAN GAETANO (d. 1339?), cardinal. He was created a cardinal in 1316, and spent the years 1326–34 in Italy attempting to bring the papal territories back to papal allegiance. He placed Rome under an interdict when Louis of Bavaria was crowned there in 1327, and, when the emperor left, entered with King Robert of Naples and accepted the city's acknowledgment of papal suzerainty. He was forbidden to war against the Colonna by Pope John XXII, subdued Corneto and Viterbo in 1328–29, and returned to Avignon, France, in 1334, where he remained until his death, possibly on Aug. 27, 1335.

ORSINI, GIORDANO (d. 1438), cardinal. He was ordained young, became auditor of the rota, and in 1400 was appointed archbishop of Naples. He was created a cardinal in 1405, was appointed cardinal-bishop of Albano in 1412, participated in the Council of Pisa, and helped elect antipopes Alexander V and John XXIII, whom he served as envoy to Spain and legate to the Marches. He also participated in the Council of Constance, where he helped elect Pope Martin V in 1417 and served him as legate to attempt to negotiate peace between England and France. He was sent to Bohemia in 1426 to help combat the Hussites, was appointed cardinal-bishop of Sabina in 1431, acted as Pope Eugene IV's representative at the Council of Basel, founded an Augustinian monastery at Bracciano, and became dean of the college of cardinals. He died in Petricoli, Italy, on July 29.

ORSINI, LATINO (1411–1477), cardinal. Of the Roman branch of the Orsini family, he was ordained young, became bishop of Conza in 1438, archbishop of Trani in 1439, and was created a cardinal in 1448. He received the archbishopric of Bari in 1454, served as legate for the Marches, was named camerlengo of the college of cardinals in 1471, and in 1472 was appointed governor of the Papal States and commander in chief of the papal fleet warring on the Turks. Pope Sixtus IV also gave him the archdiocese of Taranto, which he ruled in absentia. He founded San Salvatore in Lauro monastery in Rome, and spent the later years of his life atoning for his worldly youth. His vast wealth was left, with the pope's permission, to his illegitimate son, Paul. He died on Aug. 11.

ORSINI, MATTEO ROSSO (d. 1305), cardinal. A Roman, he became legate of the Marches, fought against Peter de Vico's invasion of Italy, and was named archpriest of the Vatican basilica and cardinal protector of the Franciscans soon after his uncle, Cardinal Gaetano Orsini, was elected pope as Nicholas III in 1277. At the conclave in Viterbo to elect Nicholas' successor in 1280, he and his uncle, Cardinal Giordano Orsini, opposed the French choice, Simon de Brion, and were imprisoned by the French party, who elected Simon as Martin IV. The latter excommunicated the leader of the attack and put Viterbo under an interdict. Matteo was subsequently reconciled with Martin, supported Pope Boniface VIII in the latter's conflict with Philip the Fair of France, brought the pontiff back to Rome after the Anagni attack in 1303, and attended some thirteen conclaves from 1254 until his death in Perugia, Italy.

ORSINI, MATTEO (d. 1340?), cardinal. He became a Dominican, taught at Paris, Florence, and Rome, and was named provincial of the Rome province in 1322. He was appointed bishop of Girgenti, Sicily, in 1326, was transferred to the archdiocese of Liponto and created a cardinal-priest in 1327, and made cardinal-bishop of Sabina in 1338. He died probably on Aug. 18.

ORSINI, NAPOLEONE (1263–1342), cardinal. Brother of Pope Nicholas III, he was born in Rome, was ordained, appointed papal chamberlain by Honorius IV in 1285, and cardinal in 1288 and archpriest of St. Peter's. He served on diplomatic missions for Pope Boniface VIII to receive Orvieto's submission to the pope and as legate to Umbria, Spoleto, and Ancona, and for Pope Clement V between 1306 and 1309 to reconcile in the Papal States. In later years he became a supporter of the French kings, defended the Franciscan Spirituals, and sympathized with Louis of Bavaria against the pope. He died at Avignon, France, on Mar. 24.

ORSISIUS (4th century). An Egyptian monk, he became a disciple of Pachomius on the island of Tabenna in the Nile, was elected his successor in 348, but refused the office in favor of Theodore, whom he succeeded as hegumen about 380. He is said to be the author of *Doctrina de institutione monachorum*, which St. Jerome translated into Latin.

ORSUCCI, BL. ANGELUS (1573–1622), martyr. Born in Lucca, Italy, he became a Dominican, studied at Valencia, Spain, went to the Orient, was imprisoned at Omura for four years, and burned to death at Nagasaki, Japan. He was beatified in 1867. F. D. Sept. 10.

ORTEGA, BL. FRANCIS OF JESUS (d. 1632), martyr. Born in Villamediana, Spain, he became a Hermit of St. Augustine at Valladolid in 1614, went to Mexico in 1622, and then with Bl. Vincenzo Carvalho to Manila and Japan. He was burned alive at Nagasaki, and beatified in 1867. F. D. Sept. 3.

ORTELIUS. *See* Oertel, Abraham.

ORTLIEB (d. 1164). Bishop of Basle, Switzerland, he went with Emperor Conrad III on a crusade to Palestine, and with Frederick Barbarossa as he invaded papal territory in Italy; he had assumed the see of Fribourg in 1137.

ORTOLANO FERRARESE, L'. *See* Benvenuti, Giovanni Battista.

ORTYNSKY, STEPHEN SOTER (1866–1916), bishop. Born in Ortynyczi, Galicia, Austria, on Jan. 29, he received his doctorate in divinity at Cracow, was professed a monk of the Order of St. Basil the Great in 1889, and was ordained in 1891. He taught at the university in Lawrow, Galicia, became head of St. Paul monastery, Michaelovka, and was famed for his preaching ability and intense nationalism. In 1907 he was sent to the United States to minister to Catholics of the Greek rite as titular bishop of Daulia and auxiliary to the Latin bishops—the first Ukrainian Catholic bishop in the United States. He had marked success in keeping the Ruthenians and the Ukrainians in the Church, founded St. Mary of the Immaculate Conception church in Philadelphia in 1909, and in 1913 was appointed Greek Catholic bishop for the United States with St. Mary's his see cathedral. He founded a fraternal order for his people, Providence, and its organ, *Ameryka,* and died in Philadelphia, on Mar. 24.

ORY, MATTHIEU (1492–1557), theologian. Born in La Caune, France, he became a Dominican at eighteen, studied at the Sorbonne, and was appointed grand inquisitor of France in 1534, a position he held until his death in Paris. When St. Ignatius Loyola was denounced for the *Spiritual Exercises,* Ory condemned the accusers. He wrote several treatises on heresy, and died in Paris.

O'RYAN, JOHN (1874–1961), general. Born in New York City on Aug. 21, he studied at City College and law at New York University, practiced law in New York, joined the national guard, and in 1912, when he had risen to major general, joined the regular army. He graduated from the War College in 1914, commanded the 6th New York Division on the Mexican border in 1916, and in World War I led the 27th Division in France. He resumed his law practice after the war, was chief counsel of a senate investigating committee in 1923, served on the New York transit commission in 1921–26, and was police commissioner of the city in 1934. He pleaded for preparedness before World War II, was chairman of Fighting Funds for Finland in 1940, and wrote *The Modern Army in Action* and *The Story of the 27th Division.* He died in South Salem, New York, on Jan. 29.

OSANNA OF CATTARO. *See* Cosie, Bl. Catherine.

OSBALD (d. 799), king. When King Ethelbert of Northumbria was murdered in 796, Osbald was elected his successor by some of the rulers, but after a twenty-seven-day rule was forced to flee and took refuge at Lindisfarne, off the coast of Northumberland, England. There a letter from Alcuin urging him to become a monk and avoid murder and civil war caused him to go to the land of the Picts, where he became an abbot.

OSBERN (11th century), hagiographer. Born in Canterbury, England, he became a monk, prior of Christ Church, and was ordained by Archbishop Lanfranc. He wrote biographies of SS. Alphege, Dunstan, and Odo, and two treatises on music. He died between 1088 and 1093.

OSBURGA, ST. (d. 1016). Supposedly the first abbess of a convent founded at Coventry, England, by King Canute, though she may have lived earlier, she was especially revered in the fifteenth and sixteenth centuries. F. D. Mar. 30.

O'SHAUGHNESSY, EDITH COUES (1870–1939), author. Born in Columbia, South Carolina, to Elliot and Jeanie McKinney Coues, she studied in Baltimore and with private tutors, and in 1901 married Nelson O'Shaughnessy of the diplomatic service. As a result of her stay in Mexico, where her husband was chargé d'affaires, she wrote *A Diplomat's Wife in Mexico* (1916) and *Diplomatic Days in Mexico*. She accompanied her husband to posts in Germany, Russia, Vienna, and Roumania, and wrote *My Lorraine Journal, Alsace, Intimate Pages of Mexican History, Viennese Medley, Married Life, Other Ways and Other Flesh*, and a biography of Marie Adelaide of Luxembourg (1929). She died in New York City on Feb. 18.

O'SHEA, WILLIAM JAMES (1863–1939), educator. Born in New York City, on Oct. 10, he studied at City and Manhattan colleges, taught in the public-school system from 1887, and became a principal in 1901, district superintendent in 1906, and associate superintendent in 1918. He became superintendent of schools in 1924, helped to advance pension plans, retired in 1934, and died in New York City on Jan. 16.

OSMUND, ST. (d. 1099), bishop. Son of the count of Séez and of Isabella, half-sister of William the Conqueror, he came to England at the invasion, was made chancellor and, in 1078, bishop of Salisbury. He instituted in his cathedral the Norman practice of a chapter of canons regular instead of monks. He was one of the royal commissioners for the Domesday survey, supported King William II against St. Anselm in the controversy over investiture (later admitting his error), and established uniform liturgical services (the "Sarum use") in his diocese. He collected an extensive library, became a skilled bookbinder, and reputedly wrote a life of St. Aldhelm. He was canonized in 1457. F. D. Dec. 4.

OSSAT, ARNAUD D' (1537–1604), cardinal. Born in Larroque-Magnoac, Gascony, on July 20, son of a blacksmith, he studied at Auch, Paris, and law at Bourges. He became a lawyer in parliament and in 1572 secretary to the archbishop of Toulouse. In Rome when the prelate died in 1584, he remained there to work in the French embassy, became secretary to Cardinals d'Este and Joyeuse, was forced to flee when Cardinal de Guise was murdered in 1588, but returned the next year as agent of Henry III's widow. He acted for Henry IV in the negotiations which led to the king's reconciliation with the pope in 1595 and the restoration of peace in France. Appointed bishop of Rennes in 1596, he was created cardinal in 1598 and then bishop of

Bayeux, though he remained in Rome. He served on diplomatic missions to Venice and Florence in 1598, was chief adviser to the French ambassadors in Rome by Henry's orders, and instrumental in securing papal acquiescence to many of Henry's actions, such as the expulsion of the Jesuits, non-publication of the decrees of the Council of Trent, the Edict of Nantes, annulment of Henry's marriage to Margaret of Valois, and the defense of de Thou and Montaigne. His many diplomatic letters have been published. He died in Rome on Mar. 13.

OSTIENSIS, LEO MARSICANUS (1045–1115?), cardinal. Of an old Italian family, he became a Benedictine at Monte Cassino when fourteen, and was librarian and archivist and in charge of disputes involving the abbey. He was made cardinal-bishop by Pope Paschal II, defended the pope against Henry V, and wrote a valuable chronicle of Lower Italy for the period 529–1075, *Legenda sancti Benedicti longa*, unfinished at his death on May 22, and other treatises.

O'SULLIVAN BEARE, PHILIP (1590?–1660), author. A native of Ireland, he was sent to Spain in 1602, studied at Compostella, and served in the Spanish army. He wrote a biography of St. Patrick and a *Catholic History of Ireland* before his death in Spain.

O'SULLIVAN, JEREMIAH (1842–1896), bishop. Born in Kanturck, Cork, Ireland, on Feb. 6, he went to the United States in 1863, studied at St. Charles College and St. Mary's seminary, Maryland, and was ordained in Baltimore in 1868. He was consecrated fourth bishop of Mobile, Alabama, in 1885, and was occupied throughout his regime with the pressing financial burdens of his see caused by the Civil War. He died in Mobile on Aug. 10.

OSWALD, ST. (605?–642), king and martyr. When his father, Aethelfrith, was defeated and killed by Raedwald in 617, he fled from Northumbria to Scotland and was converted to Christianity while at Iona. In 634 he defeated the Welsh Caedwalla at Hexham. This gained him the throne of Northumbria, which he sought to evangelize, asking the Scots for missioners. He was married to Cyneburga, daughter of Cynegils, first Christian king of Wessex, and was slain in battle at Maserfield with the pagan King Penda of Mercia. F. D. Aug. 5.

OSWALD OF WORCESTER, ST. (d. 992), archbishop. Educated by his uncle, he became priest and dean at Winchester, then a Benedictine at Fleury, and returned to England to serve as bishop of Worcester. He founded houses at Westburg-on-Trym and Ramsey, and with SS. Dunstan and Ethelwold worked hard against clerical abuses and toward increasing monastic vocations. In 972 he became archbishop of York, retaining his other see as well. He died on Feb. 29. F. D. Feb. 28.

OSWIN, ST. (d. 651), English king and martyr. On the death in 633 of his father, King Osric of Deira (Northumbria), he was taken to Wessex, where he was educated and baptized by St. Aidan. He succeeded St. Oswald as king in 642 and reigned until he was treacherously murdered at Gilling, Yorkshire, by order of his cousin, King Oswy of Bernicia, with whom he had disagreed, but against whom he had refused to wage war. F. D. Aug. 20.

OSYTH, ST. (d. 675?), martyr. Said to have been daughter of the Mercian chieftain, Frithwald, she was raised at a Benedictine convent, probably in Aylesbury, and was married against her will to King Sighere of the East Saxons. When she wished to become a nun he gave her some land at Chich in Essex, where she built a monastery and was killed in a raid by Danish pirates. F. D. Oct. 7.

OTFRIED (800?–870?), poet. Born probably in Weissenburg, Alsace, he studied at St. Gall, at Fulda under Rabanus Maurus, and at the Benedictine abbey in Weissenburg, where he became prefect of the school and notary in 851. He spent most of his life writing *Evangelienbuch*, finished about 868, a 15,000-line German version of the life of Christ in strophic form. It is a monument of Old High German poetry as the first poem using rude rhyme instead of conventional alliteration. His sources include Rabanus, Alcuin, Bede, and SS. Augustine and Jerome.

OTGER, ST. (8th century). *See* Wiro, St.

OTHLO (1013–1072), biographer. Born in Freising, Germany, he studied in Tegernsee and Hersfeld, served under Bishop Meginhard of Würzburg, and became a Benedictine at Ratisbon in 1032. He was appointed dean and given charge of the monastery school in 1055, fled to Fulda in 1062 to escape the interference of Bishop Otto, and returned in 1067. He wrote biographies of SS. Wolfgang, Boniface, Alto, and Magnus, the autobiographical *Dialogus de suis tentationibus*, and theological treatises.

OTHMAR, ST. (d. 759). A Teuton priest, he was appointed abbot of the Benedictine monastery of St. Gall, Switzerland, and restored its buildings. He died in prison during unjust imprisonment by two neighboring nobles. F. D. Nov. 16.

OTILLIA. *See* Odilia, St.

O'TOOLE, GEORGE BARRY (1886–1944), author. Born in Toledo, Ohio, on Dec. 11, he studied at St. John's there, Columbia, and received two doctorates from the Propaganda, Rome. He was ordained in 1911, served as secretary to Bishop Schrembs of Toledo in 1911–15, became pastor at Bowling Green, taught philosophy at St. Vincent's, Latrobe, Pennsyl-vania, and served as an army chaplain in 1918–19. After the war he returned to St. Vincent's, taught biology at Seton Hall, and from 1925 to 1933 served as co-founder and rector of Fu Jen University in Peking. He became a monsignor in 1934 and returned to teach philosophy at Duquesne until 1937 and at Catholic University thereafter. He edited *China Monthly*, and wrote *The Case against Evolution* (1925), *An Enemy Sowed Cockle* (with Theodore McManus), *The Romans, Race: Nation: Person*, a logic textbook, and pamphlets on ethical medical problems. He died in Mar.

OTTERAN, ST. (d. 563), abbot. An abbot of Meath, Ireland, said to be a Briton, he was one of the twelve disciples who accompanied St. Columba to Iona, where he died shortly after. He is also known as Odhran. F. D. Oct. 27.

OTTO I (912–973), emperor. Eldest son of King Henry the Fowler and his second wife, Matilda, he was born on Nov. 23, probably served in his father's army, and succeeded to the crown of Germany in 936. He extended his rule over the entire Germanic world, instead of the Saxon area alone, both by war and marriages he arranged. He fought his brother Henry, his half-brother Thankmar, and later his son Ludolph and son-in-law Conrad of Lorraine. He balanced the strength of France and Burgundy, reduced Bavaria to a dependency, and in 951 crossed the Alps, subdued Berengarius II, married Queen Adelaide (who had called him to Italy), and ruled as king of the Lombards. In 955 he routed the Magyars at Lechfield, removing the Hungarian threat, then sought a strong alliance between Church and state. He aided the spread of the Church in the north, established the see of Magdeburg, and sent his son Ludolph (d. 957) to aid the papacy against Berengarius. He invaded Italy in 962, was crowned emperor by Pope John XII, promised to protect the Church and confirmed the rights and territories of the papacy, while the pope acknowledged that the emperor's confirmation was necessary for a papal election and swore fealty to the emperor. When John plotted with the emperor's enemies while Otto was fighting Berengarius, Otto returned to Rome, deposed the pope, and presided at a synod which chose Leo VIII in 963. The next year the Romans rebelled, a council declared Leo's election void, and John forced Leo to flee, but as Otto prepared to march on the city John was mysteriously murdered. The Romans elected Benedict V pope, but Otto restored Leo. He returned to Germany in 965, but returned to quell another revolt in 966 over the new pope, John XIII. He had his son Otto crowned emperor in 967, sought to control southern Italy, and when peace was restored received the homage of the rulers of Poland, Bohemia, and Denmark. Otto died suddenly in Memleben, Saxony, on May 7.

He is considered the founder of the Holy Roman Empire.

OTTO II (955–983), emperor. Son of Otto I and his second wife, Adelaide of Lombardy, he was born in Rome, chosen king of Germany in 961, and crowned joint emperor of the Holy Roman Empire by Pope John XIII in 967. In 972 he married Theophano, daughter of the Eastern emperor, Romanus, and in 973 became sole emperor on his father's death. He suppressed revolts by his cousin, Duke Henry II of Bavaria, whom he defeated in 976, crushed the attempt of King Harold III of Denmark in 974 to overthrow German rule, and forced King Boleslaus II of Bohemia to acknowledge his allegiance in 977. In 980 he forced King Lothair of France to renounce his claims to Lorraine. Going to Rome, he restored Pope Benedict VII, who had been attacked by Crescentius, then marched into Apulia (which he claimed through his marriage) to repulse the Saracens. He was defeated at Stilo in 982 by combined Saracen and Eastern forces and forced to give up Apulia and Calabria. This also led to revolts in northern Europe and Bohemia, Church gains were erased, and the empire was badly shaken. After arranging the election of his son Otto as king in 983, he went to Rome to select John XIV as pope, contracted malaria, and died there on Dec. 7.

OTTO III (980–1002), emperor. Son of Otto II and Theophano, he was crowned king of Germany in 983, kidnaped by Duke Henry II of Bavaria, who, deposed by Otto II in 976, had designs on the throne, and returned in 984. After an expedition against the Bohemians and the Wends, he was declared of age in 995, recognized as king of the Lombards when he crossed to Italy in 996, and crowned Holy Roman emperor by his cousin Bruno, then Pope Gregory V. When Gregory was driven from Rome by Crescentius, Otto returned in 998, restored the pope, and beheaded Crescentius and his leaders. In 999, Otto chose his tutor, Gerbert of Aurillac, to be Pope Sylvester II, took residence in Rome, and tried to restore the city to its former position as capital of a universal empire. The populace remained hostile and in 1001 Otto was forced to flee. While launching a counterattack, he died at Paterno, Italy, on Jan. 23.

OTTO IV (1174?–1218), emperor. The second son of Duke Henry the Lion of Bavaria and Matilda, daughter of King Henry II of England, he was born probably in Argenton, France, on May 10, and educated at the court of his uncle, King Richard I of England. When Emperor Henry VI died, Otto was chosen king of Germany at Cologne in 1198 over the Hohenstaufen candidate, Duke Philip of Swabia. Pope Innocent III recognized Otto as emperor in 1200 when Philip seized the see of Mainz,

and Otto recognized the pope's temporal possessions and rights. Philip was assassinated in 1208; Otto married his dead enemy's daughter; reconciliation was effected between the warring forces; and Otto was elected king—an election recognized by the pope when Otto acknowledged the pope's territorial claims in Italy and the right of appeal to the pope in ecclesiastical affairs. He was crowned emperor of the Holy Roman Empire in 1209, but in 1210 differences arose with Pope Innocent III. When Otto claimed Sicily and invaded Apulia, he was excommunicated. He completed his conquest of southern Italy, but when a rebellion of German princes, aided by King Philip Augustus of France, broke out, Otto was ousted as emperor. An assemblage of nobles at Nuremberg chose King Frederick of Naples and Sicily, who, supported by the pope, became Emperor Frederick II in 1212. When Otto's army, though aided by King John of England, was destroyed by the French at Bouvines in 1214, his cause came to an end. He retired to Brunswick and died at Harzburg, Germany, on May 19, absolved of his excommunication.

OTTO, ST. (d. 1139), bishop. Born in Swabia, he was ordained while quite young and served from 1090 under Emperor Henry IV, who made him chancellor about 1101. He endeavored to reconcile the emperor and pope and refused to accept the bishopric of Bamberg, when nominated for it by Henry in 1103, until he went to Rome and was consecrated by Pope Paschal II in 1106. He recovered much church property, finished his cathedral and built churches, schools, and some twenty monasteries. At the request of Boleslaus III of Poland, he went to Pomerania in 1124 and was most successful there in missionary activities. He died on June 30 and was canonized in 1189. F. D. July 2.

OTTO, ST. (d. 1220), martyr. *See* Berard, St.

OTTO OF FREISING (1111?–1158), bishop. Son of St. Leopold IV of Austria and Agnes, daughter of Henry IV, he was made provost of canons at Klosterneuburg, near Vienna, when a child, studied at Paris, became a Cistercian at Morimond on the way home about 1134, and was made abbot in 1137 or 1138 and bishop of Freising later the same year. He inaugurated ecclesiastical reforms, encouraged learning, and restored the Church to a position of prestige and influence. He was instrumental in reconciling Frederick and Henry the Lion, restored peace between the emperor and pope, and in 1147 accompanied his half-brother Conrad III on an unsuccessful crusade to the Holy Land and had the force under his command destroyed. He died on Sept. 22 while attending a general chapter at Morimond monastery, Champagne, France. He wrote a universal history, emphasizing the conflict between good and evil, and an unfinished history of Emperor Frederick.

OTTO OF PASSAU (14th century). A native of Flanders, he became a Franciscan in Cologne and wrote the popular *Die vierundzwanzig Alten oder der guldin Tron der minnenden Seelen* (1386), in which the twenty-four ancients of Apoc. 4:4 speak epigrams selected from scripture, the Fathers, scholastics, mystics, and selected pagan authors.

OTTO OF ST. BLASIEN (d. 1223), historian. Probably the abbot of St. Blasien in the Black Forest, Baden, he wrote a chronicle of the years 1146 to 1209 as a supplement to the annals of Otto of Freising. He died at his abbey on July 23.

OTTOCAR I (d. 1230), king of Bohemia. He became duke in 1197 and king in 1198, receiving the title from Philip the Swabian and also the right to invest the bishops of Prague. In 1221 he ceded his judicial control of the clergy to the ecclesiastical courts, though he retained the power to direct their secular efforts.

OTTOCAR II (1230?–1278), king of Bohemia. Son of Wenceslas I, he became king in 1253, two years after he had captured Austria; he added Styria in 1254 after war with Hungary. He then absorbed Carinthia and Carniola and was considered too powerful to be considered as king of Germany, though he sought that crown. Rudolf I became king of Germany, took Ottocar's added territories from him, and in 1275 imposed an imperial ban against him. Revolt forced Ottocar to accept Rudolf's terms. Though he regained Bohemia and Moravia, he fought Rudolf again and was slain in battle in Lower Austria.

OUARDON. *See* Hardoin, St.

OUEN, ST. (610–684), bishop. Son of St. Authaire, he was born in Sancy, near Soissons, France, served at the court of King Clotaire II, and was made chancellor by Clotaire's successor, Dagobert I. He built a monastery at Rebais in 636, to which he sought to retire, but the king refused permission; King Clovis II later granted it. Ouen was ordained and in 641 was consecrated bishop of Rouen. He fought simony, encouraged learning, founded several monasteries, and tried to eliminate paganism in his diocese. He attended the Synod of Châlons-sur-Marne in 644 and, always close to the court, became the trusted adviser of King Thierry III. He died at Clichy, France, as he was returning from a political mission to Cologne. He is also known as Audoenus and Owen. F. D. Aug. 24.

OUDACIUS. *See* Eddogwy, St.

OURSLER, FULTON (1893–1952), author. Born in Baltimore, Maryland, on Jan. 22, he studied law briefly, worked on the Baltimore *American* in 1910–12, chiefly as music and dramatic critics, moved to New York City, edited two magazines there, and began free-

lance writing. He was editor in chief of Macfadden publications, including *Liberty* and ten monthly magazines, from 1931 to 1942, during which time he evolved the plan of publishing condensed fiction. In 1925 he married Grace Perkins, an actress, who was his co-author for the play, *The Walking Gentleman*. He also wrote *The Spider* and *All the King's Men*. He also wrote more than fifteen novels, half of them detective stories under the pseudonym Anthony Abbot. After a trip to Jerusalem, described in *A Skeptic in the Holy Land* (1936), he became a convert, and was a frequent guest on the "Catholic Hour" radio program. *The Happy Grotto* (1949), a reporter's estimate of Lourdes, followed. His most popular books were *The Greatest Story Ever Told* and *The Greatest Book Ever Written*. From 1944 until his death in Pleasantville, New York, on May 24, he was senior editor of *Reader's Digest*.

OUTREMEUSE, JEAN D' (1338–1400). *See* Mandeville, Jean de.

OUTRILLE. *See* Austregisilus, St.

OVERBECK, FRIEDRICH (1789–1869), painter. Born in Lübeck, Germany, on July 3, he studied in Vienna and in 1810 went to Rome, where, with Philip Veit, Schadow, and others, he founded a romantic school of painting. As professor in St. Luke's Academy, Rome, he helped spread pre-Raphaelite influence. His group set out to revive German religious painting, lived at the Franciscan monastery of St. Isidore, and because of their simple and austere way of life came to be called the Nazarites. He completed the *Miracle of the Roses* for the Portiuncula in Assisi and frescoes illustrating *Jerusalem Delivered* for the Roman villa of Prince Massimo and a series on Joseph in Egypt for Consul General Bartholdi. He died in Rome on Nov. 12.

OVERBERG, BERNHARD HEINRICH (1754–1826), educator. Born in Höckel, near Osnabrück, Germany, on May 1, he was a peddler, studied in Rheine and Münster, and was ordained in 1779. From curate in Everswinkel he became director of the new normal school in Münster, devoted himself to improving teaching methods and curricula, and wrote widely. He became confessor to Princess Gallitzin in 1789, influenced school legislation in Germany, served on the school commission, as regent of the seminary in 1809, and as consistorial chancellor in 1816. He died in Münster, Germany, on Nov. 9.

OVIEDO, MATTHEW D' (17th century). A Spanish Franciscan, he was appointed archbishop of Dublin in 1600, landed in Ireland, but was unable to set foot in Dublin because of political and religious turmoil, ruled his diocese through three vicars general, and resigned it in 1611, when he returned to Spain.

OWEN. *See* Eoghan, St.; also, Hywyn, St.; Ouen, St.

OWEN, BL. NICHOLAS (d. 1606), martyr. Of unknown birthplace, he was probably a carpenter, and was a Jesuit laybrother in 1580. Imprisoned for openly affirming his belief in the innocence of Edmund Campion, he served Jesuit priests for the next two decades, is believed to have aided Fr. John Gerard in his escape from the Tower of London, and to have constructed secret hiding places for priests in mansions all over England. He was captured in Worcestershire, subjected to incredible tortures to force him to reveal the places he had built and the persons he had aided, and died from the tortures sometime between March 3 and Nov. 12 in the Tower in London. F. D. Mar. 12.

OXENFORD, JOHN (1812–1877), dramatist. Born in London on Aug. 12, he worked in a London law office, and early evinced great interest in literature and the theater. His first play was written in 1835 (eventually he wrote some sixty-eight plays); he wrote librettos for operas, and translated works of Goethe, Molière, Boyardo, and Calderón into English. He was dramatic critic of the London *Times* for the last two decades of his life, wrote numerous magazine and newspaper articles, and was a convert in 1875. He died in London on Feb. 21.

OXENHAM, HENRY NUTCOMBE (1829–1888). Born in Harrow, England, on Nov. 15, son of a minister teaching at Harrow, he studied there and at Oxford, and became an Anglican minister. He held several benefices, became a convert, studied for the priesthood at St. Edmund's College, but left after receiving minor orders, and devoted himself to working for reunion of the Anglican church to Rome. He opposed the doctrine of papal infallibility even after the Vatican Council but, though a friend of Döllinger, remained in the Church. He died at Kensington, England, on Mar. 23. He was the author of several books, among them *Catholic Eschatology*.

OYE. *See* Authaire, St.

OZANAM, ANTOINE FRÉDÉRIC (1813–1853). Born in Milan, Italy, on April 23, he studied law at Paris, and achieved great prominence with a pamphlet against the Saint-Simonians in 1831. He went to Paris to study, became associated with Chateaubriand, Lacordaire, and Ampère there, and in 1833 was one of the group that founded the St. Vincent de Paul Society. He was appointed a judge in Lyons in 1836 the year he received his doctorate in law and returned to Paris in 1838 to get his doctorate in letters. He became professor of commercial law at Lyons, taught at Stanislaus College in 1839, and in 1844 was professor at the Sorbonne. Ill in his late years, he traveled to Spain and Italy for his health, and died in Marseilles, France, on Sept. 8. He twice won the Grand Prix Cobert of the Academy of Inscriptions. He published *La Civilisation chrétienne chez les Francs* (1849), *Poètes franciscains en Italie au XIIIe siècle*, *Études germaniques* (1847), and an edition of documents on the history of Italy. He was one of the most influential Catholic thinkers of the century.

OZANAM, JACQUES (1640–1717), mathematician. Born in Bouligneux, France, he studied theology, but preferred mathematics (he published his first treatise when fifteen) and on his father's death taught mathematics in Lyons. In 1670 he published trigonometric and logarithmic tables whose accuracy attracted wide attention. He moved to Paris, where he lived by tutoring, continued to publish works on mathematics, was elected to the Academy of Sciences in 1701, and died in Paris on Apr. 3.

P

PABIALI, ST. (5th century). *See* Brychan.

PABO, ST. (d. 510?). Son of a border chieftain, he went from Scotland to Wales, where he founded the monastery of Llanbabon, Anglesey. F. D. Nov. 9.

PABU. *See* Tudwal, St.

PACCA, BARTOLOMMEO (1756–1844), cardinal. Born in Benevento, Italy, on Dec. 27, he studied in Rome, and in 1785 was appointed papal nuncio at Cologne by Pius VI. He met opposition from the elector-bishops in Germany (then in the throes of Febronianism), prevented the adoption of a new concordat, went as nuncio to Portugal in 1794, and was created cardinal in 1801. He was made prosecretary of state by Pius VII in 1808, incurred the enmity of the French, accompanied Pope Pius VII when Napoleon had the pontiff kidnaped, was imprisoned in Fenestrelle, and deported to Uzès. He rejoined the pope later in 1814 in Rome and began to re-establish religious orders wherever possible. At the Congress of Vienna his continuingly severe attitude toward Napoleon ended his diplomatic activity. He served Pope Leo XII as pro-datary, was cardinal-legate of Velletri, served on various congregations, and vigorously opposed the Carbonari. A generous patron of the arts, he financed excavations at Ostia and corresponded with writers, artists, and scientists. He died in Rome on Feb. 19.

PACE, EDWARD ALOYSIUS (1861–1938),

psychologist. Born in Starke, Florida, on July 3, he studied at St. Charles, Maryland, and the North American and Urban colleges in Rome. He was ordained in 1885 and received his doctorate in theology in 1886. He became chancellor of St. Augustine, Florida, studied psychology at Louvain and Paris, and after receiving his doctorate in psychology at Leipzig in 1891 returned to teach at Catholic University, Washington. He spent the rest of his years there, serving as dean three times and as vice-rector in 1924–35. He was co-founder and first editor of the *Catholic Educational Review* in 1911, was made a monsignor in 1920, became first editor of *Studies in Psychology and Psychiatry* in 1926, was a founder and first president of the American Catholic Philosophical Association, and played an active role in the publication of the *Catholic Encyclopedia*. He was chairman of the American Council of Education in 1925–26, an editor of *New Scholasticism* in 1927–36, and author of hundreds of articles on psychology, theology, philosophy, and education. He died in Washington, D.C., on Apr. 26.

PACHECO, BL. ALFONSO (1550–1583), martyr. Born in Minayá, Castile, he became a Jesuit in 1566 and was sent to Goa, Portuguese India, where he was ordained. He was killed with Bl. Rudolph Aquaviva at Cuncolim, India, and was beatified in 1893. F. D. July 27.

PACHECO, BL. FRANCISCO (1566–1626), martyr. Born in Ponte da Lima, Portugal, he became a Jesuit, was sent to Macao in 1592, was ordained, labored there and in Japan, and served as provincial, vicar general, and diocesan administrator. He and eight others were burned to death at Nagasaki, Japan, and were beatified in 1867. F. D. June 20.

PACHOMIUS, ST. (d. 311?), martyr. *See* Hesychius, St.

PACHOMIUS, ST. (292?–348). Born in the Upper Thebaid, Egypt, he was drafted as a soldier, was treated with kindness by Christians during a harsh training period, and after his release was converted and baptized. He lived in the desert with the hermit Palaemon, but eventually built a monastery of his own at Tabennisi, on the banks of the Nile. His brother John was the first of more than 100 followers; between 318 and 336 he founded six other monasteries, and a convent for his sister and her friends. By the time of his death he was directing several thousand men in nine centers, for whom he outlined a cenobitic rule, recommended active work in trades, arranged degrees of exercises in accord with each hermit's austerity, and read scripture as a lector. Both SS. Jerome and Benedict borrowed suggestions from Pachomius' rule. He died on May 15. F. D. May 9.

PACHTLER, GEORGE MICHAEL (1825–

1889), educator. Born in Mergentheim, Württemberg, on Sept. 14, he studied at Tübingen, was ordained in 1848, and after further studies at Munich taught in Ellwangen. He became a Jesuit in 1856, taught at Feldkirch, Austria, served as a military chaplain with the Tyrolese, and when the Jesuits were expelled from Germany in 1872 spent his last years in Austria and Holland, and died in Exaten, Holland, on Aug. 12. He was the first editor of *Stimmen aus Maria-Laach* and wrote books on Church and state, the Vatican Council, the Jesuit *Ratio studiorum*, and educational problems, especially in *Die Reform unserer Gymnasien* and in four volumes of *Monumenta Germaniae paedagogica*, which he edited.

PACIAN, ST. (d. 390?), bishop. A writer on a great variety of topics, though only a few pages on baptism, penance, and the papacy, and some letters against the Novatian heresy remain, he became bishop of Barcelona, Spain, in 365. F. D. Mar. 9.

PACIFICO OF SAN SEVERINO. *See* Divini, St. Charles Antony.

PACIFICUS (d. 1234?). William of Lisciano was born probably in Ascoli, Italy, became a poet at the court of Frederick II of Sicily, and was so impressed by the preaching of St. Francis of Assisi in 1212 that he joined the new order and took the name Pacificus. He was sent to France in 1217 and was first provincial of the Friars Minor there, was with Francis when the saint received the stigmata in 1226, and in 1227 had the Poor Clares of Siena entrusted to his care by the papal bull, *Magna sicut*. He is said to have been sent back to France by Bro. Elias and to have died there in Lens.

PACIOLI, LUCAS (1450?–1509?), mathematician. Born in Borgo San Sepolcro, Tuscany, Italy, he became a Franciscan and taught in Perugia, Rome, Naples, Pisa, and Venice. He wrote mathematical treatises, notably *Summa de arithmetica* (1494), which introduced double-entry bookkeeping and the theory of probability, and *Divina proportioni* (1509), with plates by Leonardo da Vinci, which used letters for numerical quantities, and an edition of Euclid. He is sometimes known as Luca di Borgo or de Burgo.

PACIFICUS OF CERANO. *See* Ramota, Pacifico.

PADARN. *See* Paternus, St. (5th century).

PADEREWSKI, IGNACE JAN (1860–1941), president. Born in Kurilovka, Poland (then Russia) on Nov. 6, he revealed musical ability at an early age and was giving piano recitals at twelve. He studied in Berlin, gained fame in Vienna and Paris in 1887–89, visited the United States in 1891 and 1902, and gave concert tours throughout Europe from 1892 to 1914. For the next four years he organized the Polish Legion in America, sent 18,000 men

overseas, and at the end of World War I returned to Poland to serve as premier and minister of foreign affairs. He attended the Versailles peace negotiations and accepted the compromise of the Polish corridor; in 1919, when
the Allies announced that his country had only
a twenty-five-year mandate over East Galicia,
the Pilsudski government fell and Paderewski
resigned. He had given nearly $3,000,000 to
Poland and was now forced to return to the
concert stage after three years of complete absence from the piano. He again toured the
Continent and the United States, continued to
donate extensively to charity, returned to Poland
in 1939 to condemn Hitler in a radio address,
and, after the flight of President Moszicki to
Romania, became president of the Polish government-in-exile in 1940. He made his headquarters in California, but often returned to
Europe; he established a hospital in Edinburgh
for Polish war veterans. He was internationally
honored and received many honorary degrees;
his early autobiography, *My Story* (1937), was
written with Mary Lawton as co-author. He
died in New York City on June 29.

PADILLA, JUAN DE (d. 1544?), martyr. A
member of the Andalusian province of the
Friars Minor, he was sent to Mexico about
1528, and championed the rights of the Indians while an army chaplain. He was a missioner from 1531 to 1540, was founder and
first superior of Tzapotitlán, Tuchpán, and
Tulantcingo monasteries, and went with Coronado to the Upper Rio Grande in search of
the fabled seven cities in 1540 and to central
Kansas in 1542. When Coronado returned to
Mexico he remained to preach to the Indians,
and was murdered, with his party of nine, by
other Indians about Nov. 30, somewhere in
the American Southwest. He is the first martyr
on United States soil.

PADOVANINO, IL. *See* Varotari, Alessandro.

PADUINUS, ST. (d. 703?). Prior of the Benedictine abbey of St. Vincent, Le Mans, France,
he became first abbot of the nearby monastery
of St. Mary. He is also called Pavin. F. D.
Nov. 15.

PAEON, ST. (d. 165?), martyr. *See* Justin
Martyr, St.

PAGANO, MARIO (1748–1799). Born in
Brienza, Salerno, Italy, on Dec. 8, he lectured
at Naples, where he practiced law, was imprisoned in 1768 for his writings on Roman legislation, exonerated of charges of irreligion, and
became professor of law in 1787. He wrote the
constitution for Naples when the French established a republic there in 1799, fought
against the monarchists, and was imprisoned
and executed in Naples on Oct. 29 when the
monarchy was restored, despite a promised pardon. He wrote two plays, *Gerbino* and *Aga-
memnon*, while in prison.

PAGANUS, BL. (d. 1274), martyr. A Dominican, he succeeded St. Peter of Verna as inquisitor general and, similarly, was murdered by
heretics. F. D. Dec. 26.

PAGE, VEN. ANTHONY (1571–1593),
martyr. Born in Harrow-on-the-Hill, Middlesex,
England, he studied at Oxford, went to the
English college at Rheims in 1584, and was
ordained there in 1591. He was sent on the
English mission, was arrested, and hanged,
drawn, and quartered for his priesthood at York
on Apr. 20 or 30.

PAGE, BL. FRANCIS (d. 1602), martyr.
Born in Antwerp, Flanders, of English parents,
he became a convert, was ordained at Douai in
1600, and sent on the English mission. Betrayed, he was imprisoned, became a Jesuit in
prison, and was executed at Tyburn. He was
beatified in 1929. F. D. Apr. 20.

PAGHOLO, BARTOLOMMEO. *See* Bartolommeo, Fra.

PAGI, ANTOINE (1624–1699), historian.
Born in Rognes, Bouches-du-Rhone, France,
on Mar. 31, he studied at Aix and became a
Franciscan at Arles. He was elected to the first
of four terms as provincial in 1653, and devoted himself to correcting Baronius' *Annales
ecclesiastici*. Although he finished *Critica historico-chronologica in Annales ecclesiasticos
Baronii*, only the first of its four volumes was
published (1689) before his death in Aix,
France, on June 5; the rest were edited and
published by his nephew François in 1705.

PAGI, FRANÇOIS (1654–1721), historian.
Born on Sept. 7 in Lambese, Provence, France,
he studied at Toulon under the Oratorians,
became a Franciscan, served three terms as provincial, and helped his uncle, Antoine, in correcting Baronius' *Annales ecclesiastici*, edited
Antoine's *Critica historico-chronologica*, and
wrote a history of the popes to 1447. He died
in Orange, France, on Jan. 21.

PAGNINO, SANTES (1470–1541), philologist. Born in Lucca, Tuscany, Italy, he became
a Dominican at Fiesole when sixteen, studied
under Savonarola, and became proficient in
oriental languages. He went to Rome at the
call of Pope Leo X to teach in the free school
for oriental languages, to Avignon in 1521,
and to Lyons, France, in 1524, where he built
a hospital for the plague victims, became a
citizen, and died on Aug. 24. He translated the
Bible from Greek and Hebrew, wrote scriptural
commentaries, and *Thesaurus linguae sanctae*
(1529).

PAILLOT, BL. CLOTILDE (1739–1794),
martyr. Born in Bavay, France, she became an
Ursuline nun in 1756. She was superior of the
Ursuline convent at Valenciennes in 1794 when
the nuns were arrested for illegally reopening
the convent, and eleven of them guillotined,
five on Oct. 17 and six, including Bl. Clotilde,

on Oct. 22. They were beatified in 1920 by Pope Benedict XV and are known as the Ursuline Martyrs of Valenciennes. F. D. Oct. 17.

PAINE, JOHN. *See* Payne, Bl. John.

PAIR. *See* Paternus, St. (d. 570?).

PALAEMON, ST. (d. 325). He became a recluse in the Upper Thebaid, Egypt, during the Diocletian persecution, and was joined there by St. Pachomius and other early cenobitic monks. He died in Tabenna, Egypt. F. D. Jan. 11.

PALAFOX Y MENDOZA, JUAN DE (1600–1659), archbishop. Born in Fitero, Navarre, Spain, on June 24, he studied at Salamanca, was appointed to the council of war, and resigned to study for the priesthood. He was ordained in 1629, became a royal almoner, and was named bishop of Puebla de los Angeles, Mexico, in 1639. There he engaged in bitter jurisdictional disputes with the Franciscans, Dominicans, Augustinians, and Jesuits. His attacks became so severe that he was forced to flee from Puebla. His most serious conflict, with the Jesuits, was resolved in his favor in 1648 by Pope Innocent X, and he was transferred to Osma, Spain, where he died on Oct. 1.

PALATIAS, ST. (d. 302), martyr. She and her slave Laurentia, who had converted her, were put to death at Fermo, Italy, during the Diocletian persecution. F. D. Oct. 8.

PALEOTTI, GABRIELE (1522–1597), cardinal. Born in Bologna, Italy, on Oct. 4, he received his doctorate in civil and canon law in 1546, taught civil law, and became a canon of the cathedral in 1549. He gave up teaching in 1555, became auditor of the rota in 1556, was a representative of Pope Pius IV at the Council of Trent, and was created cardinal in 1565. In 1567 he was appointed bishop of Bologna (and its first archbishop when it was made an archdiocese in 1582) and was most active in putting the Tridentine reforms into effect there. He was made cardinal-bishop of Albano in 1589, and of Sabina in 1591. He died in Rome on July 22. He wrote several theological treatises, works on the administration of a diocese, and kept a journal of the proceedings at Trent, a valuable source of information on the council.

PALESTRINA, GIOVANNI PIERLUIGI DA (1525?–1594), composer. Giovanni Pierluigi was born in Palestrina, Italy, probably on Dec. 17, was a chorister in the cathedral there, and in 1537 was in the choir school of Santa Maria Maggiore in Rome. He became organist of the cathedral in Palestrina in 1544, was appointed choirmaster at St. Peter's in 1551 by Pope Julius III, to whom he dedicated his first book of masses, *Misse Ecce Sacerdos* (1554), and in 1555 was a singer in the Sistine Chapel. On his accession to the papal throne in 1555, Paul IV revived the rule that only single men could be members of the papal choir

and pensioned off Palestrina and two other married men; later in the year Palestrina became choirmaster at St. John Lateran, a position he held until 1560. In 1560 he became choirmaster at Santa Maria Maggiore, declined an offer from Emperor Maximilian in 1568 to head the court musical establishment in Vienna, and in 1570 was reappointed choirmaster of St. Peter's. Pope Gregory XIII appointed him, with Annabale Zoilo, in 1577 to revise and "purify" the Gregorian chant, an almost impossible task which they were forced to abandon a few years later, and in 1578 gave him the title of master of music at St. Peter's. Unofficially, he directed some musical activities at the Oratory of his friend, St. Philip Neri. In 1580, on the death of his wife, he petitioned the pope for permission to become a priest, took minor orders, but abandoned his plan and remarried in 1581. He spent the rest of his life composing music and caring for his business interests and those of his wife. Palestrina early dedicated himself to harmonizing music with Catholic devotion and liturgy. He produced nearly 100 masses, almost 600 motets, and other liturgical compositions, psalms, hymns, offertories, litanies, magnificats, lamentations, and secular madrigals. Among his greatest works are the following masses: *Assumpta est Maria, Papae Marcelli, Pro defunctis, Brevis, Johannes, Laudate Dominum, Te Deum, Repleatur os meum, L'Homme Armé, Hexacord, Iste confessor;* motets: *Stabat Mater, Sicut cervus, Super flamina Babylonis, Ave Maria, Salve Regina, Exultebo Domine, Dum complerentur;* the spiritual madrigal, *Song of Solomon,* in twenty-nine motets; and the secular madrigal settings of Petrarch's *Virgine bella.* His *Improperia,* first sung in 1561, is still performed in St. Peter's on Good Friday. He died in Rome on Feb. 2.

HENRY COATES, *Palestrina* (New York, Dutton, 1938).

PALEY, FREDERICK APTHORP (1815–1888), scholar. Born in Easingwold, England, on Jan. 14, he studied at Shrewsbury and Cambridge, was attracted to the Oxford Movement, and for this was in 1846 expelled from St. John's, Cambridge. He became a convert that year and spent the next fourteen years as a tutor. He again taught at Cambridge from 1860 to 1874, and then at the Catholic University of Kensington until 1877. He wrote a study of architecture and edited and prepared commentaries on the works of Aeschylus, Aristophanes, Euripides, Homer, Ovid, Pindar, Martial, and Sophocles. He died in Bournemouth, England, on Dec. 9.

PALLADIO, ANDREA (1518–1580), architect. He was born in Vicenza, Italy, was given the name Palladio (after the goddess Pallas) by his patron, the poet Gian Trissino, became a sculptor's apprentice, and turned to architecture. Most of his structures were town palaces in Vicenza; outstanding are the basilica and Villa Capra (known as the Rotonda) there; Villa Giacomelli, Treviso; and San Giorgio Maggiore and Il Redentore, Venice. His *Il antichità di Roma* and *I quattro libri dell' architettura* had long-lasting influence. In England, spread by Inigo Jones's importation of his classic designs, his architectural style proved so popular that Palladian was the prevalent architecture of seventeenth-century England; it spread to the United States as Georgian and was adopted by Thomas Jefferson for the University of Virginia buildings. Palladio died in Venice, Italy, on Aug. 19.

PALLADIUS (368–431?). Born in Galatia, he became a monk on the Mount of Olives at twenty, remained three years, then visited the monastic communities in Egypt, where he met Didymus the Blind (who had known St. Anthony) and became a disciple of Evagrius of Pontus in the Nitrian desert. When the latter died in 399, Palladius returned to Asia Minor, visiting St. Jerome in Bethlehem and Rufinus of Aquileia and Melania in Jerusalem along the way. He was made bishop in Bithynia (possibly of Helenopolis, by St. John Chrysostom), was imprisoned for eleven months about 403 for his support of John, and went to Rome in 405 to plead the patriarch's cause before the pope. He was imprisoned on his return to Constantinople as a member of Honorius' (emperor in the West) delegation to Arcadius (emperor in the East) to plead for St. John, and banished to Upper Egypt. He was at Ancyra in 412, changed his see for that of Aspuna, Galatia, in 417, and in 420 wrote *Historia Lausiaca*, an account of monasticism in Egypt and Palestine told through biographies and stories and an invaluable study of the lives and teachings of the first monks. He also wrote a life of St. John Chrysostom. Although he was accused of Origenism by SS. Jerome and Epiphanius, the charges are groundless. He died sometime before 431.

PALLADIUS, ST. (d. 432), bishop. Consecrated by Pope Celestine I in 431, he went to Ireland, landing at Leinster. Though he made some converts and founded three churches, he left after less than a year for Scotland, where he died soon after. F. D. July 7.

PALLADIUS, ST. (d. 661), bishop. Founder of several monasteries, and abbot at St. Germanus in Auxerre, Gaul, he became bishop there in 622. F. D. Apr. 10.

PALLAVICINO, PIETRO SFORZA (1607–1667), cardinal. Born of a noble Parma family on Nov. 28, he became a priest, took doctorates in philosophy and theology, and was papally appointed to several congregations. In 1637 he became a Jesuit, teaching philosophy and theol-

ogy at the Roman College from 1639 to 1651. He resigned to write a history of the Council of Trent on the pope's order, to refute Paolo Sarpi's account. He was created cardinal in 1657 by Alexander VII. He wrote poems and a tragedy, a refutation of attacks on the Jesuits, a study of confession, an edition of the works of Giovanni Ciampoli, and the four-volume *Assertiones theologicae*. He died on June 5.

PALLEN, CONDÉ BENOIST (1858–1929), author. Born in St. Louis, Missouri, on Dec. 5, he studied at Georgetown and St. Louis, where he took his doctorate in 1885, and became editor of *Church Progress* and *Catholic World* (1887–97). He was managing editor of the *Catholic Encyclopedia* in 1905–13 and president of its publishing firm in 1913–20. He wrote *Philosophy of Literature* (1897), *What Is Liberalism?* (1899), *Collected Poems* (1915), *Education of Boys* (1917), *Crucible Island* (1919), and *As Man to Man* (1927). He died in New York City on May 26.

PALLOTTI, BL. VINCENT (1795–1850), founder. Born in Rome, on Apr. 21, son of a grocer, he was ordained at twenty-three. He taught theology at the Sapienza, became friendly with St. Caspar del Bufalo and Cardinal Wiseman, and then entered parish work. He was attached to a church where he suffered ten years of scandalous insult from the other curates. In 1835, the Society of Catholic Apostolate, which he had long been planning, took shape. For a time it was called the Pious Society of Missions. He brought together priests and brothers, not under vows, with an associated institute of nuns, and an affiliate of the laity, working actively for the faith in ways which Pope Pius XI said made him a forerunner of Catholic Action. He also set up schools for the working classes, held night courses, introduced prayers after the Epiphany for the return of the Eastern Church, was well known for his charity and widely sought out as a confessor. These last actions are seen even in his death, for he caught a chill while hearing confessions in a cold church in Rome after he had given away his overcoat. F. D. Jan. 22.

PALMA, JACOPO (1544–1628), painter. Born in Venice, Italy, he studied the work of Titian and Tintoretto, whom he imitated, and was facile in coloring but was criticized for careless execution. Among his best works are *Madonna with Saints*, *Last Judgment*, and *Crucifixion of St. Andrew*. He is called "Il Giovane" (the Younger) to distinguish him from his granduncle, Jacopo Palma, "Il Vecchio" (the Elder). He died in Venice.

PALMA, JACOPO NIGRETI (1480?–1528), painter. Born in Serinalta, near Bergamo, Italy, he studied under Giovanni Bellini and developed as Master of a school noted for idyllic landscapes, brilliant coloring and lighting, and striking portraiture, particularly of women. Among his best works are his favorite "holy conversations" of the Holy Family or madonna with saints; the altar triptych in Santa Maria Formosa, Venice, of SS. Barbara, Anthony of the Desert, and Sebastian; and other religious figures and scenes. He died in Venice, Italy, on July 30.

PALMATIUS, ST. (3rd century), martyr. *See* Calepodius, St.

PALMER, GRETTA (1905–1953), author. Born in St. Louis, Missouri, on Sept. 13, she studied at Vassar, was on the staff of *The New Yorker* and the New York *World-Telegram*, began free-lancing in 1934, served as a war correspondent in World War II, and remained in the Far East to write feature articles on postwar conditions. She became a convert in 1946, wrote numerous magazine articles, a syndicated column for Catholic magazines, and several books, best known of which were God's *Underground* (1949) and *God's Underground in Asia* (1952). She died in New York City on Aug. 15.

PALMER, WILLIAM (1811–1879). Born in Mixbury, Oxfordshire, England, on July 12, he studied at Rugby and Oxford, became an Anglican deacon, and was a tutor at Durham and Oxford from 1834 to 1843. In 1840 and 1842 he went to Russia to try to persuade the Orthodox Church to acknowledge that of England as a branch of the Catholic Church. In 1855 he became a convert in Rome, where he remained until his death on Apr. 4. He wrote on Christian symbolism and a commentary on Daniel.

PALMIERI, DOMENICO (1829–1909), theologian. Born in Piacenza, Italy, on July 4, he studied there, was ordained and became a Jesuit in 1852, and taught scripture and oriental languages at Maastricht, Holland, from 1880 to 1887 and philosophy at the Roman College for the next sixteen years. He wrote on the Immaculate Conception, original sin, penance, matrimony, grace, and the papacy; several books refuting the work of Loisy; and commentaries on the *Divine Comedy* and books of the Bible. He died in Rome on May 29.

PALMIERI, LUIGI (1807–1896), physicist. Born in Faicchio, Benevento, Italy, on Apr. 22, he studied in Caiazzo and at Naples, where he received his degree in architecture. He taught at several secondary schools, became professor of physics at the Royal Naval School in Naples in 1845, and in 1847 at the university there. He joined the staff of the Mt. Vesuvius observatory in 1848, became its director in 1854, was made director of the physical observatory of Naples, was honored with the new chair of meteorological and terrestrial physics at the university, and was elected to many learned societies. He published on his observa-

tions, particularly of the 1872 eruption of Vesuvius, made modifications in existing scientific equipment, developed a sensitive seismometer, and invented a pluviometer. He died in Naples, Italy, on Sept. 9.

PALOTINUS, ST. (4th century), martyr. *See* Dominus, St.

PALOU, FRANCISCO (1722?–1789?), missioner. Born in Palma, Majorca, he became a Friar Minor there, and studied under Junípero Serra, with whom he went to Mexico in 1740. He taught at San Fernando College, Mexico City, and worked among the Indians of the Sierra Gorda and San Sabás (now Texas) regions until 1759, when he was recalled to San Fernando College. In 1767 he was sent to Lower California with Fr. Serra and other Franciscans, and in 1769 succeeded Serra as superior of the lower missions and came into conflict with Gov. Barri over the rights of the Indians. When his missions were turned over to the Dominicans in 1773 he went to Upper California. He was a member of the exploring party which discovered San Francisco Bay in 1774, founded Mission Dolores in 1776, and remained in the San Francisco area until 1784, when he succeeded Fr. Serra as superior of the California missions. He returned to San Fernando in 1785 and became its guardian in 1786, a position he held until his death. He wrote *Noticias*, the source history of the California missions from 1767 to 1784, and a life of Fr. Serra.

PALUDE, PETER DE (1275?–1342), archbishop. Born in Varambon, Savoy, he became a Dominican in Lyons and studied in Paris. He was definitor from France at two general chapters, papal delegate to Flanders in 1318, where he failed to arrange peace with France, and was on a committee which examined the work of Petrus Olivi. In 1329 he was appointed patriarch of Jerusalem and went to Egypt, where he failed to convince the sultan to surrender the Holy Land. In 1332 he presided at a council called by King Philip of France to discuss the beatific vision and Pope John XXII's opinion of it. He wrote commentaries on the Bible and the *Sentences* of Peter Lombard and a concordance to the *Summa* of St. Thomas.

PAMBO, ST. (d. 390?). A disciple of St. Anthony, he was one of the founders of a group of monasteries in the Nitrian desert of Egypt. He practiced severe physical mortifications and devoted himself to manual labor and long periods of prayer and meditation. He particularly stressed the need of silence and the fruitlessness of empty talk. His reputation for great wisdom drew many visitors, among them Rufinus and SS. Athanasius and Melania the Elder. F. D. July 18.

PAMÈLE, JACQUES DE JOIGNY DE (1536–1587), theologian. Born in Bruges,

Flanders, on May 13, he studied at Boneffe abbey and Paris, became a canon at St. Donatien, Bruges, in 1561, and was ordained in 1562. He helped to prepare the Index (1571) and after expulsion by the Calvinists went to Douai. He was appointed bishop of St. Omer, but died at Mons, Belgium, on Sept. 19 before he took office. He wrote theological treatises, a liturgical commentary on the twelfth-century *Ordo*, and a catalogue of biblical commentaries, and edited the works of St. Cyprian, Tertullian, and Rhabanus Maurus.

PAMMACHIUS, ST. (d. 410). A Roman senator, he married Paulina, daughter of St. Paula, in 385. He was a close friend of St. Jerome, with whom he carried on a vigorous correspondence. In 397, on the death of his wife, he devoted himself and his wealth to the poor and the sick. With St. Fabiola, he built a hospice at Porto for pilgrims, the first such in the West. He attempted unsuccessfully to moderate the bitterness of the controversy between St. Jerome and Rufinus and his attempts to return the inhabitants of his Numidican estates from Donatism to the Church drew a letter of thanks from St. Augustine. The site of his house in Rome is now occupied by the Church of SS. John and Paul. F. D. Aug. 30.

PAMPHILUS, ST. (d. 309), martyr. Born in Berytus, Phoenicia, he studied there and at Alexandria, was ordained at Caesarea in Palestine, and remained there to amass a great library, establish a school, and direct a group of scripture scholars. One of his students was the historian Eusebius, who had such regard for his master that he added the name Pamphili to his own and wrote an elaborate, now-lost biography of him. Pamphilus was tortured and imprisoned in 308 for refusing to sacrifice to the pagan gods. Another governor later ordered Pamphilus, Paul of Jamnia, Seleucus, and Valens, a deacon, beheaded. Porphyrius, a brilliant young scholar, and Julian, a catechumen, were burned to death, and Theodulus, an aged servant of the governor, was crucified. F. D. June 1.

PAMPHILUS, ST. (d. 400?). A Greek, he was consecrated bishop of Capua, Italy, by Pope Siricius. F. D. Sept. 7.

PAMPHILUS, ST. (d. 700?). He was bishop of Sulmona and Corfinium in the Abruzzi district of Italy. He aroused opposition because he rose at midnight on Sundays, sang the office, said mass, distributed alms, and invited the poor to breakfast. He was denounced as an Arian for this to Pope Sergius; the latter approved his practice and sent him a large gift for his poor. F. D. Apr. 28.

PANACREA, ST. (1378–1383). Born in Quarona, Italy, she was saying her prayers as a child of five when killed by her stepmother. Her cult was approved in 1867. F. D. May 1.

PANATTIERI, BL. MARIA MAGDALEN DEI (1443–1503). Born in Trino, Piedmont, she became a Dominican tertiary in her own home, modeled her life on that of St. Catherine of Siena, and devoted her life to charitable works, prayer, and conferences. Her cult was approved by Pope Leo XIII. F. D. Oct. 13.

PANCHARIUS, ST. (d. 303), martyr. A Roman senator, he was put to death at Nicomedia during the reign of Maximinian. F. D. Mar. 19.

PANCHARIUS, ST. (d. 356?). Bishop of Besançon, France, he had great difficulty with the Arian officials appointed by Emperor Constantius. F. D. July 22.

PANCRAS, ST. (d. 90?), bishop and martyr. A native of Antioch and said to have been converted by St. Peter, he was sent to Taormina in Sicily as bishop, and later stoned to death there by a band of outlaws. F. D. Apr. 3.

PANCRAS, ST. (d. 304?), martyr. Executed at Rome during the Diocletian persecution, he was buried in the cemetery of Calepodius, which was given his name, and honored by a basilica built about 500 by Pope Symmachus. Relics were sent to England by Pope Vitalian, St. Augustine named the first church in Canterbury after Pancras, and his cult spread through England. The name, with fictionalized action, appears in Cardinal Wiseman's novel, *Fabiola*. F. D. May 12.

PANDULPH (d. 1226), bishop. Born in Rome, he became a subdeacon in Pope Innocent III's household, was sent to England in 1211 to secure the king's acceptance of Stephen Langton as archbishop of Canterbury, and when the mission failed returned to Rome. In 1213 he was again papal envoy to England and accepted homage of King John as a fief of the Holy See. He became the king's adviser and was rewarded with the see of Norwich (though he was not consecrated until 1222). He excommunicated the barons, and suspended Langton, when they refused to accept the papal bull annulling Magna Charta, and returned to Rome when a new papal legate arrived in England. He went to England again as legate in 1218, and from 1219 to 1221 ruled during the minority of Henry III. The opposition of Langton, now cardinal, caused his recall in 1221, and he lived in Rome until his death on Sept. 16.

PANIGAROLA, FRANCESCO (1548–1594), bishop. Born in Milan, Italy, on Feb. 6, he studied law at Pavia and Bologna, and after a youth of dissipation became a Friar Minor at Florence in 1567. He was a successful preacher in Rome, converted many Calvinists, and raised funds for Franciscan churches and buildings in Antwerp, Turin, and major Italian cities. He was appointed coadjutor of Ferrara in 1586, was transferred to Asti in 1587, and named assistant to Cardinal Cajetan, papal legate to France. He wrote theological treatises and biblical commentaries and died in Asti, Italy, on May 31.

PANNARTZ, ARNOLD (d. 1476?), printer. Probably a native of Prague, Bohemia, he became a cleric at Cologne, and associated with Konrad Sweynheym when the two were called to Subiaco, in 1464, to establish the first known printing press in Italy. They printed four books there in a new type, roman, and in 1467 went to Rome where they published some forty-six books in the next six years. Though Pope Sixtus IV aided them when their books failed to sell, they separated in 1473. Pannartz printed twelve more books before his death.

PANTAENUS, ST. (d. 216?). Probably born in Sicily, he was a convert from stoicism and became head of the catechetical school at Alexandria, Egypt, which he raised to a position of eminence; Clement of Alexandria was one of his pupils about 180. Eusebius reports that he died as a missioner in India (probably an error for Ethiopia). F. D. July 7.

PANTAGATHUS, ST. (475–540), bishop. An attendant of King Clovis, he left the court to study for the priesthood, and later was given the see of Vienne, France. F. D. Apr. 17.

PANTALEEMON, ST. (d. 117?), martyr. See Maurus, St.

PANTALEON, ST. (d. 305?), martyr. Legend makes him the son of a pagan father, Eustorgius, and a Christian mother, Eubula, and a physician in the service of Emperor Galerius Maximian at Nicomedia. Although his faith lapsed, he was brought back by a Christian friend named Hermolaus. During the Diocletian persecution he was betrayed by fellow doctors and beheaded. He is known for his treatment of the sick without asking for fees, which gave rise to his name, Greek for "all-compassionate." F. D. July 27.

PANVINIO, ONOFRIO (1530–1568), historian. Born in Verona, Italy, on Feb. 23, he became an Augustinian Hermit at eleven, studied in Rome, and was appointed to the Vatican Library in 1556. He spent several years visiting libraries in Italy and Germany, wrote historical, theological, and archaeological works, and was among the first to apply criticism to history, confirming his statements by checking coins, medals, and inscriptions. He died in Palermo, Italy, on Apr. 7.

PANZANI, GREGORIO (d. 1662), bishop. Obliged to leave the Oratorians because of ill health, he became a secular priest in Arezzo, Italy, and in 1634 was sent on a secret mission to England by Cardinal Barberini to report on the condition of Catholics there, to reconcile the serious differences between the secular and order priests, and to act informally as papal agent to the government. On his return

he became a judge in the civil courts and in 1640 was named bishop of Mileto, Italy.

PAPAS, ST. (d. 300?), martyr. He was put to death in Lycaonia in Asia Minor during the Diocletian persecution. F. D. Mar. 16.

PAPENBROECK, DANIEL VON (1628–1714), scholar. Born in Antwerp, Flanders, he joined the Jesuits in 1646, was assigned in 1659 to work with Frs. Bolland and Henschen on the preparation of the monumental *Acta sanctorum* and devoted fifty-five years to the project. He ran into great difficulties; his denial that the Carmelites could date their order back to the prophet Elias met a barrage of thirty pamphlets, a complete condemnation of all volumes published to 1695 by the Spanish Inquisition, and an attack in Rome which led to his catalogue of the popes also being placed on the Index, in 1700. His assistant, Fr. Conrad Jannick, received papal assurance in 1697 that the Spanish condemnation was not universal; serious illness, however, and cataracts left him blind for five years. After an operation in 1702 he worked again for seven years on the *Acta* and during his last five completed a history of Antwerp to the year 1700. He died there on June 28.

PAPHNUTIUS, ST. (d. 303?), martyr. He was one of a group slain in Egypt during the Diocletian persecution. F. D. Sept. 24.

PAPHNUTIUS, ST. (d. 350?), bishop. An Egyptian, he joined St. Antony as a monk in 311 and became bishop in the Upper Thebaid. During the persecution of Maximian he was tortured and lost an eye. He played a prominent role at the Council of Nicaea (325) where he advocated permitting the marriage of the clergy before ordination. He was a forceful opponent of Arianism, brought Maximus, bishop of Jerusalem, back to Catholicism at the Council of Tyre (335), and was a close friend of St. Athanasius and Emperor Constantine. F. D. Sept. 11.

PAPHNUTIUS (4th century). Called "the Buffalo" because of his love of solitude, he was an anchorite in the desert of Skene, Egypt, became abbot of his community, and was ninety when Cassian visited him in 395.

PAPIANUS, ST. (5th century), martyr. See Mansuetus, St.

PAPIAS, ST. (d. 120?). He was bishop of Hierapolis, Phrygia, a friend of St. Polycarp, and a voluminous writer, though only fragments remain. F. D. Feb. 22.

PAPIAS, ST. (d. 120?), martyr. See Astius, St.
PAPIAS, ST. (d. 250?), martyr. See Claudian, St.
PAPIAS, ST. (d. 284), martyr. See Claudian, St.
PAPIAS, ST. (d. 303?), martyr. He was put to death, probably in Sicily, during the persecution of Diocletian. F. D. June 28.

PAPINI, GIOVANNI (1881–1956), author. Born in Florence, Italy, on Jan. 9, he was brought up by his father, an atheist and revolutionary, educated in Florence schools, and taught and was a librarian for several years. He founded *Leonardo*, a review to which he contributed articles of pragmatic outlook, published several pessimistic studies of philosophy, and was co-founder of *La Voce* in 1908 and of *Lacerba* in 1913. He wrote for other journals in Italy and France, was co-founder of *Le Vrai Italie* in 1918, continued to produce philosophical novels, and published three volumes of poems. He became a convert in 1920, when he also issued his *Life of Christ*. *Laborers in the Vineyard*, *St. Augustine*, *Dante Vivo*, and the commentary of an imaginary pope on current social questions, *The Letters of Pope Celestine VI*, followed. His work met with mixed critical and scholarly reactions; his last book, a study of Satan which denied the justice of God, was placed on the Index. Papini recanted before his death in Florence, on July 8.

PAPINI, NICHOLAS (1751?–1834), historian. Born in San Giovanni Valdarno, Italy, he became a Conventual, taught at Modena, and held several offices in his order at Assisi and Rome from 1800 to 1809. He wrote on the Franciscans and a life of St. Francis and died in Terni, Italy, on Dec. 16.

PAPOUL. *See* Papulus, St.

PAPULUS, ST. (d. 300?), martyr. A missioner with St. Saturninus in southern France, he was slain during the Diocletian persecution, and revered at a shrine in Toulouse. He is also known as Papoul. F. D. Nov. 3.

PAPYLUS, ST., martyr. *See* Carpus, St.

PARA DU PHANJAS, FRANÇOIS (1724–1797). Born in Phanja Champsaur Castle, Basses-Alpes, France, he became a Jesuit in 1740, and taught and wrote philosophy, physics, and mathematics while at Besançon. His philosophy reveals the influence of Condillac and Malebranche. He died in Paris.

PARACELSUS, PHILIPPUS AUREOLUS (1493?–1541), physician. Theophrastus Bombastus von Hohenheim was born in Sihlbrücke, Schwyz, Switzerland, on Nov. 10, son of a physician, studied under his father and Joannes Trithemius, abbot of Sponheim, and Sigmund Fugger at Schwaz, traveled throughout Europe studying medicine, and became a doctor. He became city physician and professor of physic and surgery at Basle in 1526, was driven from the city by his egotism and dissension with other members of the faculty, and spent the next decade wandering over Europe, winning renown for his knowledge of medicine, alchemy, and metallurgy, though incurring the enmity of many of the learned men of his time. He finally settled in Salzburg, Austria, where he died on Sept. 24. Often called the father of modern materia medica, he was a pioneer in many areas of medical science, denounced many of the current, fallacious medical theories of his times, and opposed the widely held humoral theory of medicine. He opposed indiscriminate purging and bleeding, preferring specific remedies, introduced the use of many new medicines (arsenic, mercury, iron, opium, sulphur), and wrote numerous medical and occult works. His works were collected in a ten-volume edition at Basle in 1589–91, and several were translated into English (*One Hundred and Fourteen Experiments and Cures*, *Elixir of Life*, and *The Philosophers' Stone*). He is the subject of Robert Browning's *Paracelsus*, and of many legends associated with his popular reputation as a magician. He died in Salzburg, Austria, on Sept. 24.

PARAMON, ST. (d. 250), martyr. He is one of 375 Christians put to death during the Decian persecution and venerated in the Eastern Churches. F. D. Nov. 29.

PARDIES, IGNACE GASTON (1636–1673). Born in Pau, France, on Sept. 5, he became a Jesuit in 1652, taught at the College of Louis le Grand, Paris, and wrote on comets, light, optics, the construction of sundials, and a text on geometry. He died on Apr. 22 in Paris of a fever contracted while caring for the inmates of a prison.

PARDO BAZÁN, EMILIA. *See* Quiroga, Emilia.

PARDULPHUS, ST. (658?–738?). Born in Sardent, France, he was a recluse and became Benedictine abbot of Guerét. F. D. Oct. 6.

PARÉ, AMBROISE (1517?–1590), surgeon. Born in Bourg-Hersent, Maine, France, he was apprenticed to a barber as a youth and became barber-surgeon at the Hôtel Dieu in Paris in 1529. After studying surgery in Paris under Sylvius, he became Marshal Rohan's field surgeon, Henry II's surgeon in 1552, a member of the Collège de St. Cosme in 1554, and in 1563 chamberlain and surgeon of King Charles IX. He pioneered in new methods of treating gunshot wounds, abandoning the boiling-oil treatment widely practiced, substituted ligature of arteries for cauterization, and developed the operation of herniotomy for strangulated hernia of the groin. He also introduced new methods in obstetrics and popularized the use of artificial limbs and eyes. He died on Dec. 20. The story that he was a Huguenot and spared from death in the St. Bartholomew's massacre in 1573 by royal command has been disproved.

PAREDES, TORIBIO (d. 1568), missioner. Born in Benavente, Spain, he became a Franciscan, taking the name of his birthplace, and went to Mexico with the first Franciscan mission. There he changed his name to Motolinia, the Indian name for "poor." He also worked in Guatemala and Nicaragua, was superior of several houses and provincial of Santo Evangelico, helped found Puebla, Mexico, and is reputed to have baptized 400,000 Indians. He wrote a history of the Indians and a letter to Emperor Charles V in 1555, violently attacking Bartolomé de las Casas for his social theories. He died in Mexico City on Aug. 10.

PAREDES Y FLORES, ST. MARIANA DE (1618–1645). Born of Spanish descent in Quito, Ecuador (then Peru), she was brought up by a married sister, in whose home she remained as a recluse. Her austerities were of the most extreme nature, and at twenty-six she offered herself as a victim for the sins of the city in the hope that tragedies would end; earthquakes and plague ceased, and she died as a last victim of the epidemic. She was beatified in 1950 by Pope Pius XII. F. D. May 26.

PARÉGORIUS. Said to have been put to death about 260 by Lollian, governor of Licia, for destroying idols, he is the hero of a pious legend.

PAREGRUS, ST. (d. 297), martyr. See Hipparchus, St.

PAREJA, FRANCISCO (d. 1628), missioner. Born in Aufion, Spain, he became a Franciscan and in 1593 was sent to St. Augustine, Florida. He worked with the Indians and wrote catechisms for the Timuquanan tribe, one of which, published in 1612, was the first book in an Indian language published in the United States; he also wrote a Timuquanan grammar. After 1613 he went to Mexico, where he died on Jan. 25.

PARENT, ÉTIENNE (1801–1874), journalist. Born in Beauport, Quebec, Canada, he studied at the seminary there and at Nicolet and at twenty-one became editor of *Le Canadien*. After three years he took up the study of law, passed the bar in 1828, became translator and librarian in the assembly, and returned to *Le Canadien* as editor from 1831 to 1842. His demands for reform resulted in imprisonment in 1837–38 and to his election to the assembly in 1842. He was clerk of the executive council (1842–47), assistant secretary for Lower Canada (1847–67), and then assistant secretary of state. He was a potent force in the intellectual revival of his country and wrote much on economics, religion, philosophy, and the working class. He died in Ottawa on Dec. 22.

PARIS, ST. (d. 346). He is said to have been a Greek who became bishop of Teano, near Naples, Italy. F. D. Aug. 5.

PARIS, ALEXIS PAULIN (1800–1881), philologist. Born in Avenay, Marne, France, on Mar. 25, he studied at Rheims, became a clerk and later assistant librarian at the Bibliothèque Nationale, and engaged in research in mediaeval literature. He was elected to the Academy of Inscriptions and Belles-Lettres in 1837, became an editor of *Histoire littéraire de la France*, and in 1853, and accepted a chair of mediaeval literature created for him at the Collège de France where he remained until his resignation in 1872. He wrote a critical study of his library's manuscripts; edited *chansons de geste*, Arthurian narratives, and early drama; did historical studies, including an account of Marco Polo; and translated Byron and defended Byronism in *Apologie de l'école romantique*. He died on Feb. 13.

PARIS, GASTON BRUNO PAULIN (1839–1903), philologist. Born in Avenay, Marne, France, on Aug. 9, he studied at Collège Rollin, and at Göttingen, Bonn, École des Chartes, and Paris, where he received his doctorate in literature in 1865. He founded *Revue Critique* that year, taught in a private school, became professor of languages at the École des Hautes Études and later head of department, and in 1872, when with Paul Meyer he founded *Romania*, he succeeded his father as professor of mediaeval literature at the Collège de France. He was appointed director in 1895, named to the French Academy in 1896, and wrote with thoroughness and great influence on mediaeval poetry, legends, romances, and linguistics. In 1902 he became editor of *Journal des Savants*. He died in Cannes, France, on Mar. 5, having returned to Catholicism some years earlier.

PARISIO, ST. (1160–1267). Born in Treviso, Italy, he became a Camaldolese at twelve, was ordained, and in 1190 became chaplain of the convent of St. Christina, at Traviso, serving for seventy-seven years. F. D. June 11.

PARKER, HENRY (1476–1556), poet. Son of Sir William Parker, one of the advisers of Richard III, and of Alice Lovel, he entered the service of Henry VIII, whom he initially defended against Pope Clement VII. He was ambassador to Archduke Ferdinand (and sent back to London serious warning about the spread and direction of Lutheranism), and was the friend and defender of Princess Mary. He wrote poetry, appearing in anthologies under his title of eighth Lord Morley.

PARKINSON, ANTHONY (1667–1728), historian. A native of England, he became professor of philosophy at Douai in 1692, was sent to the English mission in 1695, was head of the Franciscans in Warwick (1698–1701), Birmingham (1701–10), and definitor of the province (1707–10). He was nominal guardian of Oxford (1710–13) and twice provincial (1713–16; 1722–25). He compiled a study of the Friars Minor in England and died on Jan. 30.

PARLATORE, FILIPPO (1816–1877), botanist. Born in Palermo, Sicily, on Aug. 8, he studied medicine there, practiced for a time and became an assistant professor of anatomy, but abandoned it for botany and travel throughout Europe. At the third congress of Italian naturalists in Florence in 1841 he proposed the establishment of a general herbarium. Grand

Duke Leopold put the plan into effect, and appointed him professor of botany at the museum of natural sciences and director of its botanical garden, a position he held for more than thirty years. He made trips to study the flora of Mont Blanc in 1849 and Scandinavia in 1851, on which he issued reports. He published on botanical subjects; his monument is *Flora Italiana* (1848–74), of which volumes 6–10 were completed from his notes by T. Caruel. He died in Florence, Italy, on Sept. 9.

PARMENAS, ST. (d. 98?), martyr. One of the seven deacons ordained by the apostles (Acts 6:5), he is said to have been martyred at Philippi, in Macedonia, during the persecution of Trajan. F. D. Jan. 23.

PARMENIUS, ST. (d. 250), martyr. He was beheaded near Babylon during the persecution of Decius. Two other priests, Chrysotelus and Helimenas, and two deacons, Luke and Mucius, were executed with him. F. D. Apr. 22.

PARMENTIER, ANDRÉ (1780–1830), horticulturist. Born in Enghien, Belgium, on July 3, he studied at Louvain and became a landscape gardener. He came to New York in 1824, where he established a botanical nursery in Brooklyn and became the earliest famous professional landscape gardener in the United States, laying out gardens all along the Atlantic coast. He died in Brooklyn on Nov. 26. His daughter, Adèle Bayer, carried on the business until 1832 when she sold it and with her mother devoted herself to charitable work, especially to aiding the Indian missions and among seamen. She died in Brooklyn on Jan. 22, 1892.

PARMENTIER, ANTOINE AUGUSTIN (1737–1813). Born in Montdidier, France, on Aug. 17, he became a pharmacist in Paris, joined the Hanoverian army in 1757, and added to his medical knowledge while several times a prisoner. He became pharmacist at the Hôtel des Invalides, Paris, in 1774, introduced the potato to France, improved maize and chestnut cultivation, was a provisioner during the revolution, and about 1803 was named inspector general of health. He wrote on horticulture and died in Paris on Dec. 13.

PARMIGIANO, IL. *See* Mazzuola, Girolamo.

PARRENIN, DOMINIQUE (1665–1741), missionary. Born in Russey, France, on Sept. 1, he became a Jesuit in 1685 and was sent to China in 1697. At Peking his great knowledge favorably impressed Emperor K'ang-hi. When Yong-tching succeeded his father in 1723, he reversed the policy toward Christians and might have extirpated the faith in China had it not been for the influence of Fr. Parrenin. He found the missioner's services indispensable when dealing with Russian and Portuguese diplomats. Parrenin helped prepare maps of China, translated scientific articles into Tatar-Manchu, and wrote to Europe to correct many errors

about the history and scientific achievements of China. He died in Peking, China, on Sept. 29.

PARSCH, PIUS (1884–1954), liturgist. Born in Olmütz, Moravia, on May 18, he studied at Klosterneuburg, Austria, was ordained in 1909, and did parish work in Vienna. He returned to Klosterneuburg to teach pastoral theology in 1909, served as a chaplain in World War I, became interested in the liturgy and initiated a program of liturgical missions. He began writing on the subject, had his first book published in English in 1916, *The Liturgy of the Mass*, and in the next three decades became the leader of the liturgical movement. Among his works published in English are *The Breviary Explained* (1952) and *The Church's Year of Grace* (five volumes, 1953–59). He died in Klosterneuburg.

PARSONS, WILFRID (1887–1958), editor. Born in Philadelphia, Pennsylvania, on Mar. 17, he became a Jesuit in 1903, took his doctorate at Louvain in 1910, taught at Boston College and Holy Cross, was ordained in 1918, and spent two years in advanced study at the Gregorian University, Rome. On his return he taught theology at Woodstock College, was editor of the weekly journal *America* from 1925 to 1936, and founded the quarterly *Thought*. From 1936 to 1940 he taught political philosophy at Georgetown, served as dean of its graduate school, and reorganized its library. In his last years he held the chair of political science at Catholic University. His books include *The Pope and Italy*, *Church and State*, *Mexican Martyrdom*, *Which Way Democracy*, *Early Catholic Americana*, and *The First Freedom*. He died in Washington, D.C., on Oct. 28.

PARTHENIUS, ST. (3rd century), martyr. *See* Calocerus, St.

PARUTA, PAOLO (1540–1598), diplomat, historian. Born in Venice, Italy, on May 14, he accompanied the Venetian ambassador to Maximilian II's court in 1562 and became historiographer of the republic. A member of the Morosini group which took over the government in 1582, he became a senator, governor of Brescia in 1590, ambassador to Rome in 1592, procurator of St. Mark in 1596. He wrote a history of the war which ended with the battle of Lepanto; a history of Venice from 1513 to 1551; *Della perfezione della vita politica*, a dialogue influenced by Machiavelli and opposed to Bellarmine; and published his diplomatic dispatches from Rome. He died in Venice, Italy, on Dec. 6.

PASCAL, BLAISE (1623–1662), scientist. Born in Clermont-Ferrand, France, on Jan. 19, he was educated by his father in Paris, became interested in mathematics, and when not yet seventeen wrote a book on the conic sections, which, though never published, was the forerunner of modern treatment of the subject. In it he presented his proposition of the mystic hexagon from which he deduced more than 400 corollaries; a résumé was published in 1640, *Essai sur les coniques*. At eighteen he invented a calculating machine, and soon was hailed for such contributions as the theory of probability and the allied theory of combinatorial analysis (which he and Fermat created in correspondence), his great advances in the field of differential calculus, his invention of the arithmetical triangle (Pascal's triangle), and his theorems and solutions to problems involving the cycloid. He spent much time at Port Royal, but, though sympathetic with much of its teaching and many of its proponents, he was never actually a member of the group there. In 1647 he published *Nouvelles expériences sur le vide*. His experiments of 1648 with the barometer on the Puy de Dôme in Auvergne and later on a Paris tower in which he showed the height of mercury in a barometer decreased the higher the barometer is carried, and a treatise written sometime before 1651 (published in 1663) on the equilibrium of confined liquids, make him one of the founders of the science of hydrodynamics. He also propounded Pascal's law (the law of pressure) that pressure applied to a confined liquid at any point is transmitted undiminished in all directions through the fluid, to act upon every part of the confining vessel at right angles to its interior surface and equally upon equal areas. While in Rouen, where his father was intendant of Normandy, he was attracted to Jansenism and became greatly interested in the Port Royal group when his sister Jacqueline entered the convent there in 1651. In 1654 he renounced the world, lived ascetically, and practically beggared himself with his charitable donations. In 1656–57 his *Les Provinciales, ou Lettres ecrites . . . à un provincial (Provincial Letters)*, under the pseudonym Louis de Montalte, written to defend his friend, Antoine Arnaud, against Jesuit charges of Jansenism, were hailed as an eloquent defense of Jansenism, became wildly popular, and are considered among the finest examples of the use of irony in literature. It was quickly taken up by those believing in merely personal morality and by the Church's enemies as an attack on her teachings. The letters are the source of many distortions and untruths bruited as facts by enemies of the Society since. Plagued by ill health the latter years of his life, he planned to write a great apologetical work, but died in Paris on Aug. 19 before doing so. Eight years after his death, his *Pensées sur la religion et sur quelques autres sujets* were issued by Port Royal in an incomplete and altered edition. In the *Pensées*, Pascal decides that man's reasoning powers cannot solve his difficulties and answer the problems of

the universe and that only through faith and revelation can man ever attain such knowledge. Based on an outline for the apologia for Christianity he had planned, together with his notes and meditations, this work is now recognized as a strong defense of orthodox Christianity; it was not until 1844 that a scholarly edition (Faugère's) appeared.

PASCHAL (d. 692), antipope. On the death of Pope Conon in 687, Paschal, a Roman archdeacon, and Theodore, Roman archpriest, were each elected pope by small groups of Roman clergy and residents. When Pope St. Servius was elected by the great majority, Theodore submitted at once. Paschal had bribed Exarch John of Ravenna to support his claim, but John withdrew his support as soon as Sergius was elected. Paschal was sent to a monastery, where he died five years later.

PASCHAL I (d. 824), pope. Son of Bonosus, a Roman, he studied in the Lateran and was appointed superior of the monastery of St. Stephen, which cared for pilgrims to Rome. He was chosen pope on the death of Stephen IV and took office the next day, Jan. 25, 817. That year he received a pact from Emperor Louis the Pious promising to respect papal territory and jurisdiction. In 823, Louis' son, Lothair, came to Rome to be consecrated by the pope; while there, he broke the pact by presiding in a case which favored a group of nobles opposing the papacy. After his departure, two pro-Frankish officials of the papal court, who had testified at the trial, were found blinded and killed. The pope was accused of ordering the murder, but denied under oath any such complicity. When Louis sent investigators, Paschal declared that the dead officials had been traitors, and refused to surrender the servants who had committed the deed. The action led to the subsequent Constitution of Lothair, which heavily restricted the judicial and police powers of the papacy in Italy. Paschal also was unsuccessful in his attempt to end the Iconoclast heresy led by Emperor Leo the Armenian, although he encouraged SS. Nicephorus and Theodore Studites in Constantinople and found refuge for large numbers of Grecian exiles who came to Rome. He died on Feb. 11.

PASCHAL II (d. 1118), pope. A native of Bieda, near Viterbo, Italy, Rainerius became a monk at Cluny and when twenty was sent on monastery business to Rome, where he joined Pope Gregory VII's court and was created a cardinal-priest. He was elected pope, over his protests, on Aug. 13, 1099, and ordained the following day. Henry IV continued his struggle with the papacy, but antipope Clement III died in 1100, and, though a new antipope, Sylvester IV, was elected, the Diet of Mainz deposed Henry IV in Dec. 1105 and his son ascended the throne early the next year as

Henry V. When Henry IV died in 1106, his son announced he intended to follow his father's policies and the investiture dispute broke out anew. Paschal denounced lay investiture at synods at Guastalla in 1106 and Troyes in 1107, concluded an agreement with King Henry I of England by which the king gave up the right of investiture and in return the bishops offered homage to the king as vassals, and in 1107, on a trip to France, reconciled King Philip to the Church and sought his aid against the emperor. In 1110, Henry V invaded Italy and imprisoned Paschal and forced him to sign the concordat of Sutri by which the pope renounced his rights of investiture. Paschal crowned Henry emperor at Rome on Apr. 13 and Sylvester IV submitted to Paschal, but at the Lateran Council of 1112 declared the concordat had been extorted and denounced it. Henry temporarily acquiesced, but in 1117 invaded Rome and drove Paschal from the city. Paschal returned in 1118 and died there on Jan. 21.

PASCHAL III (d. 1168), antipope. Guido of Cremona was elected to succeed Cardinal Octavian (antipope Victor IV), at the insistence of Reginald of Dassel, on Apr. 21, 1164. The imperial group electing him consisted of two cardinals, two German bishops, and a Roman prefect. He canonized Charlemagne in 1165 at the demand of Frederick Barbarossa, an action which the Church never approved, and crowned Barbarossa a second time in Rome in 1167. He died in Rome on Sept. 20.

PASCHARIUS, ST. (d. 680?). Bishop of Nantes, Gaul, he founded the abbey of Aindre in the Loire estuary. F. D. July 10.

PASCHASIA, ST. (d. 178?), martyr. She is said to have been put to death near Dijon, Gaul. F. D. Jan. 9.

PASCHASIUS, ST. (d. 312?). He is listed as the eleventh bishop of Vienne in Gaul. F. D. Feb. 22.

PASCHASIUS, ST. (d. 437), martyr. *See* Arcadius, St.

PASCHASIUS, ST. (d. 512?). He was a deacon in Rome who, in good faith, became a follower of antipope Laurence. He wrote on theology. F. D. May 31.

PASCHASIUS RADBERTUS, ST. (d. 860?). Abandoned at a convent gate in Soissons, France, he was educated at St. Peter's there, and became a Benedictine monk at Corbie under SS. Adalhard and Wala, whose lives he wrote. He also wrote several scripture commentaries and the significant *De corpore et sanguine Christi*. In 822 he helped to set up New Corbie in Westphalia, where he was abbot in 844–851. F. D. Apr. 26.

PASCUAL, BL. PEDRO (1227–1300), bishop and martyr. Born in Valencia, Spain, he studied at Paris and was ordained when twenty-four. He taught theology at Barcelona, was tutor of

Sancho, son of James I of Aragon, who was made archbishop of Toledo with Bl. Peter as administrator. In 1296 he was appointed bishop of Jáen, which was governed by the Moors. He insisted on preaching to the infidels and ransoming captives, and was imprisoned in Granada, Spain. He used the money sent to ransom him to save others, remained in prison, and died of ill-treatment. His cult was confirmed in 1673 by Pope Clement X. F. D. Dec. 6.

PASICRATES, ST. (d. 302?), martyr. A Roman legionnaire, he and St. Valentio were executed at Durostorum (now Silistria), Bulgaria, when their faith was discovered. F. D. May 25.

PASQUINI, BERNARDO (1637–1710), composer. Born in Massa di Valnevola, Florence, Tuscany, Italy, on Dec. 7, he became organist at Santa Maria Maggiore, Rome, wrote many toccatas and suites for harpsichord, ten operas, and eight oratorios. He had an influence on the development of the sonata and on the work of Respighi. He died in Rome on Nov. 21.

PASSAGLIA, CARLO (1812–1887). Born in Lucca, Italy, on May 9, he became a Jesuit in 1827, taught at the Gregorian, left the Society in 1859, and was appointed to a chair at the Sapienza by Pope Pius IX. In 1861 he wrote *Pro causa italica*, which advised the pope to give up his temporal power; it was placed on the Index and he fled to Turin. He edited several newspapers, marked by anti-clerical petulance, and taught theology in Turin, although he had been deprived of his priestly privileges. He was reconciled to the Church shortly before his death on Mar. 12 at Turin, Italy.

PASSIGNANO, IL. *See* Cresti, Domenico.

PASSIONEI, BL. BENEDICT DE' (1560–1625). Born in Urbino, Italy, he became a lawyer, then in 1584 a Capuchin friar at Fano. He served with St. Laurence of Brindisi in Austria and Bohemia, and was beatified in 1867. F. D. Apr. 30.

PASSIONEI, DOMENICO (1682–1761), cardinal. Born in Fossombrone, Italy, on Dec. 2, he studied at the Clementine College and the Sapienza in Rome, was ordained, and served on papal missions to Paris in 1706, The Hague in 1708, Utrecht in 1712, Baden in 1714, and Turin. He was inquisitor at Malta from 1717 to 1719, nuncio to Switzerland in 1721, to Vienna in 1730, became secretary of Propaganda, and in 1738 of briefs. He was created a cardinal, and in 1755 was appointed librarian of the Church. He amassed a personal library of more than 30,000 volumes, carried on a correspondence with foreign scholars, and showed Jansenistic tendencies (he encouraged the publication of Arnaud's works). He died on July 5.

PASTEUR, LOUIS (1822–1895), bacteriologist. Born on Dec. 27 in Dôle, Jura, France, son of a poor tanner, he was an indifferent scholar at the Arbois Collège Communal, went to Paris in 1838, but returned home in ill health. He received a bachelor's degree from the Royal College at Besançon in 1840, taught there, entered the École Normale in 1843, and in 1848 received his doctorate in chemistry from the Sorbonne. His thesis, which attracted great attention, proved that the different reaction of two apparently similar tartaric acids was caused because each had different crystals. He became professor of physics at the lycée in Dijon in 1848, of chemistry at Strassburg in 1849, and received the Legion of Honor medal for producing racemic acid from ordinary commercial acid. He was appointed professor and dean of the new faculté des sciences at Lille in 1854, director of scientific studies at École Normale Superieure in 1857, and professor of geology and chemistry at the École des Beaux Arts in 1863. For his research on polarization of light he won the Rumford Medal of the Royal Society of London in 1856. After years of studying fermentation and putrefaction, he proved that these phenomena were caused by minute organisms which also caused milk to sour; in 1864 he declared that these organisms came from similar organisms in the air and were not spontaneously generated, as had been believed. In 1865 he went to southern France at the request of the government to study silkworm diseases and succeeded in isolating two bacilli causing their death, a discovery which saved the silk industry. His findings were established in 1877; in 1868 he had discovered a method of preventing contagion in farm stock, and checked anthrax in cattle in 1879 and cholera in chickens in 1880. He was professor of chemistry at the Sorbonne from 1867 to 1889, was elected to the Academy of Medicine in 1873, continued his germ studies, gave his attention to childbed fever, discovered streptococcus and staphylococci, and in 1885 inoculated and cured for the first time a child bitten by a rabid dog. He received awards from many governments and honorary degrees, received the Copley Medal in 1874, was elected to the French Academy in 1881, made life secretary of the Academy of Sciences in 1887, director of the Pasteur Institute on its founding in 1886, and received all the degrees of the Legion of Honor. He died in Villeneuve l'Étang near Sèvres, France, on Sept. 28.

PASTOR, ST. (d. 160?). He was a priest in Rome, possibly the brother of Pope St. Pius I. F. D. July 26.

PASTOR, ST. (d. 304?), martyr. See Justus, St.

PASTOR, ST. (d. 311?), martyr. He, St. Victorinus, and other Christians were put to death at Nicomedia during the Diocletian persecution. F. D. Mar. 29.

PASTOR, LUDWIG VON (1854–1928), historian. Born on Jan. 3 in Aachen, Germany, he was raised a Catholic by his mother after the death of his Protestant father, studied at Louvain, Vienna, Bonn, Berlin, Prague, and Rome, and became lecturer at Innsbruck in 1880, and professor of church history in 1887. He was appointed director of the Austrian Historical Institute in Rome in 1901, was Austrian envoy to the Holy See in 1921–28, and died at Innsbruck, Austria, on Sept. 30. He wrote numerous historical works, chief of which was his monumental thirty-eight-volume *History of the Popes* (1915–52).

PASTURE, ROGER DE LA. *See* Van der Weyden, Rogier.

PATAPIUS, ST. (7th century). A monk in Egypt, he became a recluse near Constantinople. F. D. Dec. 8.

PATENSON, BL. WILLIAM (d. 1592), martyr. Born in Durham, England, he was ordained at Rheims in 1587, entered the English underground mission the next year, and was arrested in London in 1591. While in prison he converted six criminals who shared his cell. All were executed, Fr. Patenson with particular brutality. He was beatified in 1929. F. D. Jan. 22.

PATER. (d. 1115), bishop. Bishop of Poitiers, France, he was a member of the ecclesiastical council which excommunicated King Philip I of France for his divorce; he also condemned the tyranny of William, Count of Poitou, who eventually exiled him. One of the other council members was Bl. Robert of Arbrissel, whom he helped to establish the abbey of Fontrevault. His cult was never sanctioned officially.

PATERIUS, ST. (d. 606), bishop. A monk at Rome, he was raised to the see of Brescia, Italy, by Pope St. Gregory the Great and wrote biblical commentaries. F. D. Feb. 21.

PATERNIAN, ST. (d. 470?), bishop. A St. Paternian is said to have lived through the last years of the Diocletian persecution, hiding in the mountains until he could return to Fano, Italy, to become its bishop. However, he is believed to be identical with the bishop who lived nearly a century and a half later and took charge of the diocese of Bologna, Italy, in 450. F. D. July 12.

PATERNUS, ST. (2nd century). Born in Bilbao, Spain, he was an early bishop, perhaps the first, of Auch, France. F. D. Sept. 28.

PATERNUS, ST. (d. 255?). An Egyptian, he was arrested while on a pilgrimage to Rome, thrown into a dungeon, and allowed to die. F. D. Aug. 21.

PATERNUS, ST. (5th century), bishop. Said to have been an Irish hermit, he founded a monastery in Ceredigion, Cardiganshire, Wales, where he served as abbot and bishop for twenty-one years. Fable associated him with King

Arthur, and a mix-up of biographies confused him with the bishop of Vannes of the same name. He is also called Padarn. F. D. Apr. 15.

PATERNUS, ST. (5th century), bishop. Consecrated bishop of Vannes, Brittany, about 465, and sometimes called Pern, he is often identified with a Welsh bishop of the same name. F. D. Apr. 15.

PATERNUS, ST. (d. 570?), bishop. Born in Poitiers, Gaul, he became monk at Ansion, Poitou, a hermit with St. Scubilio, near Coutances, Normandy, and, later, abbot of the large group which followed them. He became bishop of Avranches at seventy and served for thirteen years; he is also known as Pair. F. D. Apr. 16.

PATERNUS, ST. (d. 726). Born in Brittany, he was a Benedictine monk at Cessier, near Avranches, then at St. Pierre near Sens, Gaul, where he was murdered as he sought to reform some malefactors. F. D. Nov. 12.

PATERNUS, ST. (d. 1058). A Scot, he entered the Benedictine abbey of Abdinghof in Paderborn, Westphalia, became a solitary there, and was burned to death in his cell when the town was destroyed by fire. F. D. Apr. 10.

PATIENS, ST. (2nd century). The fourth bishop of Metz, he is venerated as patron of the see. F. D. Jan. 8.

PATIENS, ST. (d. 491?), bishop. Made archbishop of Lyons, Gaul, about 450, he was known for his charities, his church-building, and his aid to victims of the Goths' invasion of Burgundy. He fought Arianism, which was prevalent in Lyons, was highly praised by Sidonius Apollinaris, and directed one of his priests, Constantius, to write a life of St. Germanus of Auxerre. F. D. Sept. 11.

PATIENTIA, ST. (d. 240?), martyr. See Orentius, St.

PATMORE, COVENTRY KERSEY DIGHTON (1823–1896), poet. Born in Woodford Green, Essex, England, on July 23, son of an eccentric writer, Peter George Patmore, he fled to France after a duel, had his first poetry published at his father's expense in 1844, and withdrew it when the critics proved hostile. To save him from poverty, Richard Monckton Milnes secured an assistant librarianship in the British Museum for him in 1846. In 1850 his poem, The Seasons, was published in the pre-Raphaelite journal, the Germ, and as a result he met Ruskin (who had been taught Greek by Patmore's first wife, Emily Augusta Andrews, whom he married in 1847), Browning, Tennyson, and the Rossettis. His Tamerton Church Tower (1853) was well received and The Angel in the House (1854; to which The Espousals, Faithful Forever, and The Victories of Love were added before 1863), which exalted the sanctity of marriage, was very successful. After Emily's death in 1862, he became a Catholic

in Rome, partly through the influence of Aubrey de Vere, married Marianne Caroline Byles in 1864, and retired from his library post to an estate he bought in East Grinstead. In 1877, To The Unknown Eros (thoughts on love, death, and immortality, and reflecting the spiritual changes following his conversion) appeared and in 1878, Amelia. Critical essays were collected in Principle in Art (1889), Religio Poetae (1893), and Rod, Root, and Flower (1895). After the death of his second wife in 1880 he married Harriet Robson in 1881 and retired to Lymington, England, where he died on Nov. 26. His poetry was uneven, now extremely sentimental, and now matching that of the best of Tennyson and of the Spanish mystics; his criticism is effectively epigrammatical and marked by philosophical soundness.

BASIL CHAMPNEYS, Memoirs and Correspondence of Coventry Patmore (London, 1900); OSBERT BURDETT, The Idea of Coventry Patmore (London, Milford, 1921).

PATRICIA, ST. (d. 304?), martyr. See Macedonius, St.

PATRICIA, ST. (d. 665?). A legendary figure supposedly related to the imperial family at Constantinople, she fled to Rome to escape an arranged marriage, became a nun, returned briefly to give her wealth to the poor, and went back to Italy. She died in Naples, Italy, of which she became a patron. F. D. Aug. 25.

PATRICIAN, ST. (5th century). A bishop in Scotland, he was driven out by barbarians and lived thereafter on the Isle of Man. F. D. Oct. 14.

PATRICK, ST. (d. 450?). Called Patrick the Elder, he is said to have been related to St. Patrick of Ireland. F. D. Aug. 24.

PATRICK, ST. (389?–461?), archbishop. Of Romano-British origin, he may have been born near Dunbarton, Scotland, or in Cumberland, England, the son of Calpurnius, a town official, and was carried to pagan Ireland as a slave shortly after the beginning of the fifth century. After six years he escaped, probably to Gaul, and came back to Britain at about twenty-two. He may have studied at Lérins off the coast of France, in 412–15, and spent fifteen years in Auxerre, Gaul, where he may have been ordained, and may have been consecrated bishop by St. Germanus in 432 after some twenty years on the Continent. Landing, it is believed, in Ulster, he toured the island, gained many converts in Meath, Leitrim, and Munster, suffered from the attacks of hostile druids and chieftains, and eventually won most of the island to Christianity and consecrated enough bishops to hold a synod at Armagh toward the end of his life. The date and place of his death are uncertain, though Saul, on Strangford Lough, Downpatrick, Ireland, is a possibility. He wrote Con-

fessio (a statement of his labors which contains autobiographical material) and a *Letter to the Soldiers of Coroticus,* denouncing the slaughter of a group of Irish Christians by raiding Welshmen, also Christians, under Coroticus. Few saints have had more legends attached to them than the apostle of Ireland. F. D. Mar. 17. JOHN HEALY, *Life and Work of St. Patrick* (Dublin, Gill, 1905); JOHN MACNEILL, *St. Patrick, Apostle of Ireland* (London, Sheed, 1934); PAUL GALLICO, *The Steadfast Man* (Garden City, N.Y., Doubleday, 1958).

PATRIZI, BL. ANTONIO DE' (d. 1311). Born in Siena, Italy, he joined the Hermits of St. Augustine at Monte Ciano and became superior of the group. His cult was approved in 1804. F. D. Apr. 27.

PATRIZZI, FRANCESCO (1529–1597), philosopher. Born in Dalmatia, he was appointed to the chair of philosophy in Rome about 1592, secured Pope Clement VIII as patron, and taught the philosophy of Plato. He was a vigorous opponent of Aristotelianism. He wrote *Discussiones peripateticae* (1571) and *Paralleli militari* (1594).

PATRIZI, FRANCIS XAVIER (1797–1881). Born in Rome on June 19, he became a Jesuit in 1814, was ordained in 1824, and was professor of scripture and Hebrew in the Roman College. He fled to England during the revolution of 1848, taught there and at Louvain, and returned to teach in Rome until the revolution of 1870 ended his work. He retired to the German-Hungarian College in Rome, where he died on Apr. 23. He wrote twenty-one exegetical and theological treatises, including *De interpretatione scriptuarum sacrarum* (1844) and *De evangeliis* (1853).

PATROBAS, ST. (1st century). He and St. Philologus are hailed by St. Paul in Rom. 16:14–18. F. D. Nov. 4.

PATROCLUS, ST. (d. 259?), martyr. Two widely separated manuscripts detail the staunchness of this respected citizen of Troyes, Gaul, whom Aurelian (either the Roman emperor or a local governor) ordered drowned, then, when that failed, beheaded for his religious beliefs. F. D. Jan. 21.

PATTO, ST. (d. 788), bishop. He went from Britain to become abbot of a monastery in Saxony, and later became bishop of Werden. F. D. Mar. 30.

PAUL I, ST. (d. 767), pope. Educated in Rome, where he was ordained, he served on diplomatic missions for his brother, Pope Stephen II (III), one of which led to Lombard King Desiderius' promise to restore several papal cities. On Apr. 26, 757, he was elected Stephen's successor, and was consecrated on May 29. He maintained friendly relations with Pepin, though at first he was unsuccessful in enlisting his aid to force Desiderius to keep his promise.

Paul resisted the attempted encroachments of Byzantine forces and finally concluded a peaceful settlement with Desiderius as to boundaries in 765. He opposed the iconoclasm of Emperor Constantine Copronymus, and died in Rome. F. D. June 28.

PAUL II (1417–1471), pope. Born in Venice, Italy, on Feb. 23, Pietro Barbo was destined for a business career, but abandoned it for the religious life when his uncle, Eugene IV, was elected pope in 1431. He became archdeacon of Bologna, bishop of Cervia and of Vicenza, and in 1440 was created a cardinal. He was a leading figure in the pontificates of Popes Nicholas V and Callistus III, but fell out of favor with Pope Pius II. He was elected his successor on Aug. 30, 1464, and was consecrated on Sept. 16. He denounced the paganism of the humanists in Rome and suppressed the College of Apostolic Abbreviators in 1466 and the Roman Academy, members of which, led by Pomponius Laetus and Bartolomeo Sacchi (Platina), had concocted a plot against the pope's life, which was discovered and led to their imprisonment. He unsuccessfully attempted a crusade against the Turks, whose capture of Negropont in Greece in 1470 shocked Europe, and was likewise unsuccessful in an attempt to reunite the Russian Orthodox Church to Rome. He became embroiled in a quarrel with King George Podiebrad of Bohemia over the Hussites and with King Louis XI of France over the pragmatic sanction. He engaged on a building program in Rome, granted the privilege of wearing red birettas to cardinals, encouraged the arts and especially printing, and ordered the celebration of a jubilee every twenty-fifth year. Although Paul delighted in pomp and display, it is now agreed the charges of excessive luxury long leveled at him are not true, but were a result of the distortions promulgated in Platina's inaccurate and spiteful biography of Paul. He died in Rome on July 26.

PAUL III (1468–1549), pope. Alessandro Farnese was born in Rome (or Camino) on Feb. 29, studied in Rome, Pavia, and Florence at Lorenzo de' Medici's palace, and was made a cardinal by Pope Alexander VI when twenty-five. He led a worldly life and had several illegitimate children until he was appointed bishop of Parma in 1509, when he completely changed his way of life. He was ordained in 1519, sorrowfully watched his son, Pier Luigi, join the emperor's forces and participate in the sack of Rome in 1527, but helped to remove his excommunication. He became bishop of Ostia in 1529, and on Oct. 13, 1534, was elected pope and was consecrated on Nov. 3. He began his pontificate with a display of nepotism by appointing several teen-aged grandsons cardinals and his son, Pier Luigi, cardinal and secretary of state. His appointment of his son as duke of Parma and Piacenza in 1544 ended in Pier's assassination in 1547. In 1536 his plea for a general council was ignored when Francis I and the Protestant princes opposed it. In England, Henry VIII executed John Fisher and Thomas More and moved toward complete independence of the papacy; in 1538, Paul excommunicated Henry and placed England under an interdict. He was neutral in the quarrel between Francis I and Charles V, and in 1538 succeeded in negotiating a truce by the Treaty of Nice, giving Charles Milan and Francis Savoy and Piedmont—a step which broke the alliance of 1536 between Francis and the Turks for an invasion of Italy. Paul began appointing men of great ability to the college of cardinals—Jacopo Sadoleto, Reginald Pole, Gasparo Contarini, Gian Pietro Carafa—and instituted reforms of the papal court, the clergy, and the religious orders. He was increasingly occupied with the spread of Protestantism in Germany, approved Ignatius Loyola's new order in 1540, reorganized the Inquisition in 1542, instituted the Index in 1543, and in 1545 convoked the Council of Trent. The council was delayed by the outbreak of war between France and the empire, but, when the war was ended by the Treaty of Crepy in 1544, was again called and finally began work on Dec. 15, 1545. Disagreements broke out between Emperor Charles V and the pope, and in 1547 Paul ordered the council moved to Bologna to get it out of imperial territory into that of the Papal States. When adherents of the emperor refused to leave Trent, Paul prorogued the council indefinitely. During his pontificate he forbade the enslavement of Indians, rebuked Francis I for his cruelty to Protestants, and was a great patron of the arts. He commissioned Michelangelo to paint the ceiling of the Sistine Chapel and made him director of the building of St. Peter's in 1547. Paul died in the Quirinal, Rome, on Nov. 10.

PAUL IV (1476–1559), pope. Born in Benevento, Italy, on June 28, Giovanni Pietro Caraffa became bishop of Chieti, resigned to become a member of the papal court, was sent to England on a diplomatic mission for Pope Leo in 1513, was nuncio to Spain in 1515, despite his dislike of the Spanish, and in 1524 gave up his benefices to join the Theatines and became general. Forced to flee to Venice when Rome was sacked in 1527, the Theatines were recalled by Pope Paul III to draw up a plan for the reform of the papal court, and in 1536 Caraffa was created a cardinal. He was appointed archbishop of Naples, was a leader in ecclesiastical reform, reorganized the Inquisition in Italy, and on May 23, 1555, despite strenuous Spanish opposition, was elected pope and consecrated on May 26. His appointment

of members of his family to high office—in particular, his nephew, Carlo Caraffa, as cardinal secretary of state—proved unfortunate, though he deprived them of their offices in 1559 when he discovered their perfidies. In 1555, Paul allied himself with the French against Spain, but was decisively defeated and forced to make peace with Philip II at Cava in 1557. He intensified the efforts of the Inquisition, instituted harsh reform measures, and even accused Cardinals Morone, whom he imprisoned, and Pole of heresy, recalling the latter from England. He died in Rome on Aug. 18.

PAUL, ST. (d. 67?), apostle and martyr. The biography of St. Paul is in the Acts of the Apostles by St. Luke. There it is recorded that Saul of Tarsus, formerly a persecutor of Christians, was struck blind to the ground while he was journeying to Damascus and censured by the voice of Christ (Acts 9:3–18). Thereafter he was an earnest preacher of Christianity. Through the sponsorship of Barnabas he was accepted by the disciples in Jerusalem. He returned to Tarsus, was rejoined by Barnabas, and preached in Antioch and Syria. He went again to Jerusalem in 44, was ordained with Barnabas, and went to Cyprus, where they converted the proconsul Sergius Paulus and exposed Elymas. He went to Perga, then to Antioch in Pisidia, Iconium, and Lystra, healed a cripple, was stoned, and fled to Derbe. With Barnabas he went to Antioch in Syria, to Jerusalem for a third time about 49, and attended the meeting when the question of accepting Gentile converts was settled (Gal. 2). Between 49 and 52, with Silas, he traveled from Derbe to Lystra, gained Timothy as a disciple, proceeded through Phrygia, Galatia, and Thessalonica, and stopped in Philippi, and was joined by St. Luke through part of that journey. Paul was imprisoned in Philippi with Silas, escaped miraculously, proceeded to Athens, and talked there on "the unknown God." He returned to Jerusalem from Corinth about 52, went to Antioch, and from 52 to 56 journeyed through Galatia, Macedonia, and Achaia, probably spending three winters at Ephesus. When he visited the Temple in Jerusalem he was seized, transported to Caesarea, and imprisoned for two years. As a Roman citizen he demanded to be tried before the emperor, and was sent by ship to Rome. He went by way of Myra and Crete, was shipwrecked on Malta, reached Rome, was tried, and after a long term in prison was released. He then went to Spain, the Near East, Macedonia, and Nicopolis in 65–66, returned to Rome, was recaptured, and was beheaded, perhaps on the Ostian Way. His epistles were written on questions of ecclesiastical discipline and practice, to correct false doctrine and explain the Church's position, and to encourage or to admonish the faithful in various parts of the Mediterranean world. The epistle to the Romans was written from Corinth in 57 or 58; I Corinthians, from Ephesus in early 57; II Corinthians, probably from Philippi in 57; Galatians, from Ephesus about 54; Colossians, Philemon, Ephesians, and Philippians, apparently from Rome in the spring of 63; I and II Thessalonians, from Corinth in 51–52, his earliest writings. He also wrote two pastoral epistles to Timothy and one to Titus. The epistle to the Hebrews is attributed to varied authorship and is dated from 60 to 96. St. Paul shares June 29 with St. Peter as his feast day.

JUSTO PÉREZ DE URBEL, *St. Paul, the Apostle of the Gentiles* (Westminster, Md., Newman, 1956); DANIEL-ROPS, *Saint Paul, Apostle of Nations* (Chicago, Fides, 1953).

PAUL, ST. (2nd century), martyr. *See* Catus, St.

PAUL, ST. (d. 244?), martyr. *See* Crescens, St.

PAUL, ST. (d. 251), martyr. *See* Peter, St.

PAUL, ST. (d. 270?), martyr. *See* Juliana, St.

PAUL, ST. (d. 272), martyr. *See* Reverianus, St.

PAUL, ST. (d. 290), bishop and martyr. Consecrated at Rome, he was sent with SS. Dionysius and Saturninus to evangelize Gaul; they were put to death near Narbonne. Legend has falsely identified him with the Sergius Paulus converted by St. Paul (Acts 13). F. D. Mar. 22.

PAUL, ST. (d. 303), martyr. *See* Aquilinus, St.

PAUL, ST. (d. 305?), martyr. *See* Heraclius, St.

PAUL, ST. (d. 309), martyr. *See* Pamphilus, St.

PAUL I, ST. (d. 350?), patriarch. Born in Thessalonica, he was made a deacon by Bishop Alexander of Constantinople, whom he succeeded as patriarch in about 336. He was exiled three times (to Pontus, Trèves, and Mesopotamia) by the Arians, with the support of Emperor Constantius. Two rival bishops, Macedonius and Eusebius of Nicomedia, claimed his see, with the emperor favoring the former. Transferred to a dungeon in Cucusus, Armenia, he was starved there and then strangled. F. D. June 7.

PAUL, ST. (d. 362?). *See* John, St.

PAUL, ST. (d. 405?), bishop. A native of Rheims, France, he became a hermit near Arles during the barbarian invasions, then was chosen bishop of the now-extinct diocese of Trois-Châteaux in Dauphiné. F. D. Feb. 1.

PAUL, ST. (d. 649?), bishop. He was a French courtier who became a hermit, a Benedictine at the monastery of Tholey, where he directed the school, and about 630 was made bishop of Verdun by King Dagobert. F. D. Feb. 8.

PAUL IV, ST. (d. 784), patriarch. A native of Salamis, Cyprus, he became patriarch of Constantinople in 780 and advocated the restoration of icons when Empress Irene became regent. In 784 he entered the monastery of Florus, whence he pleaded for a council to condemn Iconoclasm; it was held three years after his death. F. D. Aug. 28.

PAUL, ST. (d. 840). Bishop of Prusa, he was banished from his see in Bithynia during the Iconoclastic heresy and died an exile in Egypt. F. D. Mar. 7.

PAUL, ST. (d. 851), martyr. A deacon at Cordova, Spain, and a member of the community of St. Zoilus there, he was active in caring for Christians imprisoned by Moors, who seized and beheaded him. F. D. July 20.

PAUL, ST. (d. 856), martyr. *See* Elias, St.

PAUL, FATHER. *See* Wattson, Lewis Thomas.

PAUL AURELIAN, ST. (d. 573?), bishop. Born in Wales and a fellow student with St. David, he became a hermit, a priest, then traveled with twelve companions to Brittany, where he established a monastery on the Island of Batz, later becoming bishop of León in the area. F. D. Mar. 12.

PAUL OF THE CROSS, ST. (1694–1775), founder. Born in Ovada, Italy, on Jan. 3, Paolo Francesco Danei began at fifteen a life of austerity with his brother Giovanni Battista and others, was in the army for a year, and returned to his life of prayer. In 1720 a vision of the Virgin Mary directed him to form an order preaching the passion of Christ; after seven years of difficulties, he and his brother set up a house at Monte Argentaro with papal permission. They lost a number of novices because of the severity of their rule, but it was approved with modifications in 1741 by Pope Benedict XIV, and the Passionists (as the Barefooted Clerks of the Holy Cross and Passion were known) began to spread through Italy. Paul of the Cross, as he was called, preached with great success, possessed a large number of supernatural gifts, and worked to create an affiliate of nuns. His institute received final approbation in 1769 from Pope Clement XIV. He died in Rome on Oct. 18, and was canonized in 1867. F. D. Apr. 28.

CHARLES ALMERAS, *St. Paul of the Cross* (Garden City, N.Y., Hanover, 1960).

PAUL OF CYPRUS, ST. (d. 777), martyr. During the suppression of icons by Emperor Constantine Copronymus, Paul was tortured and burned to death when he refused to desecrate a crucifix. F. D. Mar. 17.

PAUL OF GAZA, ST. (d. 308), martyr. He was beheaded in Gaza, Palestine, during the persecution of Maximian II. F. D. July 25.

PAUL THE HERMIT, ST. (229?–342). Born in Egypt, he went into the desert at twenty-two during the Decian persecution rather than endanger friends who had given him haven, and lived in a cave for ninety years, relying on nearby palm trees for food and clothing. The life of "the first hermit" was written by St. Jerome. F. D. Jan. 10.

PAUL OF JAMNIA, ST. (d. 309), martyr. *See* Pamphilus, St.

PAUL OF LATROS, ST. (d. 956). Son of an army officer, he was born near Pergamos, near Smyrna, Turkey, became a monk at Karia on Mt. Olympus, and then a hermit on Mt. Latros. His holiness attracted so many disciples that he retired to the island of Samos, but was followed by enthusiasts, and finally acceded to the request of the Mt. Latros monks to return. F. D. Dec. 15.

PAUL OF MIDDELBURG (1446–1534), bishop. Born in Middelburg, Holland, he studied at Louvain, was canon at Middelburg and later deprived of that post, accepted a chair in science at Padua in 1480, and became physician to the duke of Urbino, who endowed him with the Benedictine abbey of Castel Durante in 1488. Pope Alexander VI made him bishop of Fossombrone in 1494. His work on calendar reform caused him to be invited to the fifth Lateran Council. He died in Rome on Dec. 13.

PAUL OF NARBONNE, ST. (d. 290?). He was one of a number of missioners sent to evangelize Gaul, two of whom, SS. Dionysius and Saturninus, were martyred. F. D. Mar. 22.

PAUL OF ST. CLARE, BL. (d. 1622). *See* Franco, Bl. Apollinaris.

PAUL DE SANTA MARIA (1351?–1435), archbishop. Solomon Ha-Levi was born of Jewish parents in Burgos, Spain, and became a wealthy and influential scholar and rabbi. He was a convert in 1390, studied at Paris, where he took his doctorate in theology, and became bishop of Cartagena in 1405 and archbishop of Burgos in 1415. He was appointed chancellor by King Henry of Castile in 1416, was one of the governing council after Henry's death, and tutor to young King John II. He died in Burgos, on Aug. 29 and was succeeded as bishop by his son Alfonso.

PAUL THE SIMPLE, ST. (d. 339?). He was an Egyptian who, when he discovered the infidelity of his wife, left their farm at sixty and joined St. Antony in the desert, proving the strength of his desire for the new life by exceptional humility. F. D. Mar. 7.

PAULA, ST. (d. 273?), martyr. A native of Nicomedia in the Near East, she visited St. Lucillian and other Christians imprisoned at Byzantium, and was tortured and beheaded there. F. D. June 3.

PAULA, ST. (d. 305), martyr. *See* Cyriacus, St.; also, Heraclius, St.

PAULA, ST. (347–404). Patron of widows, she was admired for her virtuous married life. At her husband's death, when she was thirty-two, she gave her wealth to the poor and, at the suggestion of St. Marcella, began a life of austerity. After the death of her eldest daughter, St. Blesilla, she left Rome with another daughter, St. Eustochium, on a pilgrimage to Bethlehem, where she settled in the desert under the spiritual direction of St. Jerome. There they built a monastery for men, a convent for women, and a church. The communities were self-supporting and devoted to solitary contemplation. Paula also studied Hebrew, and later devoted her time to the care of St. Jerome. Another daughter, Paulina, married St. Pammachius; her only son, Toxotius, married Laetia, a convert from paganism, and their child, Paula the Younger, succeeded her grandmother as superior of the desert communities. Paula died in Jerusalem. F. D. Jan. 26.

PAULA, ST. (1443–1514). Born in Montaldo, near Mantua, Italy, she became a Poor Clare in Mantua at fifteen, served as abbess three times, and had a number of mystical experiences. Her cult was approved in 1906. F. D. Oct. 29.

PAULI, JOHANNES (1455?–1530?). Master of arts at Strassburg, Alsace, before he became a Franciscan, he then preached at Thann in 1479, went to Oppenheim in 1481, was guardian at Berne in 1504 and at Strassburg from 1506 to 1510, preached from other centers, and died in Thann, Alsace. He wrote the collection of humorous German folk stories, *Schimpf und Ernst*, which influenced Hans Sachs and later poets, and published scriptural studies by others and a *Ship of Fools*.

PAULILLUS, ST. (d. 303), martyr. *See* Anastasius, St.

PAULILLUS, ST. (d. 437), martyr. *See* Arcadius, St.

PAULINA, ST. (d. 254?), martyr. *See* Eusebius, St.

PAULINA, ST. (d. 302), martyr. *See* Artemius, St.

PAULINUS, ST. (d. 303), martyr. *See* Felicissimus, St.

PAULINUS, ST. (d. 358), bishop. A native of Gascony, he was educated at Poitiers and was a follower of St. Maximinus, whom he succeeded as bishop of Trèves in 349. He met St. Athanasius at Trèves during the latter's exile and warmly supported him at the Synod of Arles in 353. His opposition to Emperor Constantius' support of Arianism resulted in his exile to Phrygia, where he died. F. D. Aug. 31.

PAULINUS (d. 365). He became bishop of Lucca, Italy, about 355; local legend calls him a first-century martyr sent there by St. Peter, later honored on July 12.

PAULINUS (5th century), biographer. Received into the deaconate at Milan, Italy, sometime after 375, he was secretary to St. Ambrose and wrote his friend's biography at the request of St. Augustine. He also was active against the Pelagian heresy, on which he wrote to Pope Zosimus about 416.

PAULINUS, ST. (d. 505?). Disciple of St. Iltyd, he is believed to have been abbot-founder of the monastery of Whitland, Wales, where SS. David and Teilo followed him. F. D. Nov. 23.

PAULINUS, ST. (d. 545). He became bishop of Brescia, Italy, about 524. F. D. Apr. 29.

PAULINUS, ST. (584?–644), archbishop. A Roman monk sent to Britain in 601 by Pope Gregory I, with SS. Mellitus and Justus, to aid St. Augustine, he worked in Kent, where he was consecrated bishop in 625. He accompanied Ethelburga, daughter of King Ethelbert of Kent, as her guardian, when she married pagan King Edwin of Northumbria. In 627 he baptized Edwin at York, where he established his see, and made a large number of other converts. He was forced to flee to Kent with Ethelburga and her children when the Mercians defeated Edwin at Hatfield in 634. He administered the vacant see of Rochester until his death there ten years later. F. D. Oct. 10.

PAULINUS, ST. (726?–804), patriarch. Born near Friuli, Italy, to a farming family, he became a priest and scholar, and was appointed patriarch of Aquileia in 776 and represented Charlemagne at all Church councils. He called a synod at Friuli after 791 to suppress the Adoptionist heresy, being spread by Bishop Felix of Urgel, that Christ was man and no more than the adopted son of God. He preached widely to the pagans of Carinthia and Styria and sent missioners to the Huns and other conquered tribes. He wrote widely on prayer, Communion, the Incarnation, and against the contemporary practice of mass baptisms of unprepared barbarians. F. D. Jan. 28.

PAULINUS, ST. (d. 826). This bishop of Sinigaglia, Italy, became patron of that diocese after his death. F. D. May 4.

PAULINUS, ST. (d. 843), bishop. An Englishman, he was returning from the Holy Land in 835 when the people of Capua, Italy, asked him to be their bishop. He was driven out by a Saracen invasion and died in Sicopolis. F. D. Oct. 10.

PAULINUS OF NOLA, ST. (354?–431), bishop. Born near Bordeaux, Pontius Meropius Anicius Paulinus, son of the Roman prefect of Gaul, studied rhetoric under the poet Ausonius, became a distinguished lawyer, and held several public offices in Italy. His work also took him to Gaul and Spain, where he married Therasia. He and his brother were baptized by St. Delphinus; in 390 he moved from Aquitaine to his wife's estate in Spain, where they had a son who died after a few days. Paplinus and Therasia then gave much of their property to the poor and began a life of austerity. In 393 he was suddenly made a priest by the bishop of Barcelona; settled at Nola, near Naples; gave away most of his Aquitaine property, against the violent opposition of relatives; and was treated with coldness by Pope Siricius and the Roman court because of the manner of his ordination. His charities were extensive; he built a hostel for travelers after his own house became overcrowded by the poor, a chapel near the tomb of St. Felix, and an aqueduct. In 410 he was chosen by the populace as their bishop and ruled his see well. He was in correspondence with SS. Augustine and Jerome, the host of SS. Melania the Elder and Nicetas of Remesiana, and the friend of SS. Martin of Tours and Ambrose. His last years before his death at Nola were saddened by the invasion of Campania by Alaric. Of his writings, fifty-one letters, a few prose fragments, and thirty-two poems (including the first Christian wedding song) remain. F. D. June 22.

PAULINUS OF PELLA (5th century), poet. Of a Bordelaise family, son of a government official, and probably the grandson of the poet Ausonius, he was born in Pella, Macedonia, lived in Carthage as a boy, and then returned to Bordeaux, where at eighty-three he wrote a poetic autobiography, *Eucharisticon Deo sub ephemeridis meae textu*, which gives an excellent picture of the period.

PAULINUS A. S. BARTHOLOMAEO. *See* Wesdin, Philip.

PAULUS DIACONUS (720?–799?), historian. Born in Friuli, Italy, he probably was educated at the court of King Rachis at Pavia, went to that of Duke Achis at Benevento in 763, was a monk at Monte Cassino, Italy, and in 782 a member of Charlemagne's entourage. He returned to Monte Cassino after 787 and probably died there on Apr. 13. He wrote *Historia Romana*, an extension of Eutropius, with six late books covering the period to Justinian; *De gestis Langobardorum*, for the period 586–744; a commentary on the Rule of St. Benedict; and a collection of homilies.

PAULUS SONCINAS. *See* Barbus, Paulus.

PAULUS VENETUS (1368?–1428), theologian. Born in Udine, Italy, he became a Hermit of the Order of St. Augustine at Venice, studied at Oxford in 1390, and at Padua, where he lectured for some twenty-five years. He wrote *Logica duplex*, widely used as a textbook in the fifteenth and sixteenth centuries, and a treatise on the Immaculate Conception. He died in Venice, Italy, on June 15.

PAUSILIPPUS, ST. (d. 130), martyr. He was put to death at Constantinople with St. Theodore during the reign of Hadrian. F. D. Apr. 15.

PAUSIS, ST. (d. 303), martyr. *See* Agapius, St.

PAVILLON, NICHOLAS (1597–1677), bishop. Born in Paris, he joined the St. Lazare community and became so well known for his charity and preaching that Richelieu made him bishop of Alet in 1640. Although devoted in his work, he became so concerned about it that he defied correction by Pope Alexander VII and King Louis XIV in 1664. He became tainted with Jansenism and his *Rituel d'Alet* (1666) was condemned by Pope Clement IX.

PAVIN. *See* Paduinus, St.

PAVONI, BL. ANTONIO (1326–1374), martyr. Born in Savigliano, Italy, he entered the Dominican priory there, became inquisitor general for Piedmont and Liguria, and was ambushed and killed by seven men after preaching a sermon at Bricherasio. F. D. Apr. 9.

PAVONI, BL. LODOVICO (1784–1849), founder. Born in Brescia, Italy, he became a Dominican priest in 1807, did parish work, and became pastor of St. Barnabas in his home city in 1818. There, in spite of hostility on the part of the Josephinists, he managed to set up an elementary school of printing design and music for boys. After a cholera epidemic in 1836 demanded more of his time, he was given added charge of an orphanage and a school for the deaf and dumb. In 1847 his long-planned hope for a group of priests and lay-brothers to work in the trades became a reality, and the Congregation of the Sons of Mary Immaculate was officially founded. Two years later, Austria shelled Brescia, his buildings fell with the city, and he died a few days after the attack at Saiano, near Brescia. He was beatified in 1947. F. D. Apr. 1.

PAYERAS, MARIANO (1739–1823), missioner. Born in Inca, Majorca, he became a Franciscan at Parma in 1784, was sent to Mexico in 1793, and ministered to the Indians in Monterey and California. He was president of the missions from 1815 to 1820 and vicar of the bishop of Sonora, and later visited all twenty existing missions in California. He was honored for his labors and exploratory reports by the Spanish monarch in 1819. He died on Apr. 28.

PAYNE, BL. JOHN (d. 1582), martyr. Born in Peterborough, England, he was ordained at Douai in 1576, and worked on the English mission for two years in Essex and London, with secret headquarters at the home of Lady Petre in Ingatestone. Arrested, freed, and banished, he returned in 1579. He was later betrayed, imprisoned for months in the Tower, and tortured and hanged at Chelmsford, England. He was beatified in 1886. F. D. Apr. 2.

PÁZMÁNY, PETER (1570–1637), cardinal. Born in Grosswardein, Hungary, of Calvinist nobility, he studied at Nagyvarad and Kolozs-var, and became a convert in 1583 and a Jesuit in 1587. He studied in Rome under Bellarmine, taught at Gratz, returned to Hungary in 1601, and wrote against Stephen Magyary, who had declared that Catholicism was the cause of Hungary's ruin, and against Peter Alvinczy, Pázmány became provost of Turócz, was named bishop of Nyitra, archbishop of Esztergom in 1616, and cardinal-primate of Hungary in 1629. An outstanding preacher, he published his sermons in 1636, which long were used as models; he also wrote *Hodoegus: Guide to God's Truth* (1613), a prayer book, and a translation of the *Imitation of Christ*. He put the decrees of the Council of Trent into effect, introduced the *Missale Romanum*, enforced clerical celibacy, built schools, a college at Pozsony, the Catholic University of Budapest, and seminaries, including the Pazmaneum in Vienna for Hungarian students (1623), and instituted regular conferences for the hierarchy. He helped to raise Ferdinand II to the throne, established peace between Hungary and Transylvania in 1622, helped to gain religious freedom for Protestants, and worked for close co-operation between Hungary and Austria. He died on Mar. 19.

PAZ Y FIGUEROA, MARIA ANTONIA DE SAN JOSÉ DE (1730–1799). Born in Santiago del Estero, Argentina, she formed a group of religious companions when she was fifteen, worked with the Sisters of Pious Sermons, preached widely and with success, established a retreat house in Buenos Aires in 1780, founded an asylum for magdalens, and died on Mar. 6.

PEACOCK, REGINALD. *See* Pecock, Reginald.

PEARSE, PADRAIC H. (1879–1916), educator. Born in Dublin on Nov. 10, son of James Pearse, an English sculptor, he was educated there, founded the New Ireland Literary Society, graduated from the Royal University and Catholic University College, and began teaching at the latter at twenty-four. He edited the Gaelic League's *Sword of Light*, founded St. Edna's School for boys in 1908 to perpetuate Gaelic culture, and soon developed St. Ita's School for girls. His passion play was produced in 1911 by the Abbey Theatre; *Songs of Slumber and Sorrow* (poems in Gaelic) was published; and in 1913 he visited the United States. During that year he helped to organize a revolutionary army, the Irish Republican Brotherhood, worked secretly with Thomas MacDonagh and Joseph Plunkett, and signed the republican proclamation on Apr. 24 declaring Ireland's independence. Pearse was elected president and commander in chief; Dublin was shelled heavily, and after a week of fighting, Pearse was obliged to surrender. He was executed in Dublin on May 3.

PECHAM, JOHN (1240–1292), archbishop. Born in Patcham, Sussex, England, he studied at Lewes monastery and at Paris, and joined the Franciscans about 1250. He taught at Oxford, became provincial of England, and in 1276 went to Rome. He was appointed archbishop of Canterbury in 1279, vigorously instituted ecclesiastical reforms and combated Averroism, and was made apostolic protector of his order. He died on Dec. 6. He wrote theological tracts, a life of St. Anthony of Padua, and some poetry. His name is also spelled Peckham.

PECKHAM, JOHN. *See* Pecham, John.

PECOCK, REGINALD (1395?–1460?), bishop. Born in northern Wales, he went to Oxford, taught at Exeter College, was ordained in 1421, and became master of Whittington College, London, and rector of St. Michael's in Riola in 1431. He was appointed bishop of St. Asaph in 1444, criticized the bishops as "pulpit-brawlers" like the friars, and was transferred to Chichester in 1450. He wrote *The Book or Rule of Christian Religion* and *Donet* (1440?), *The Repressor of Over Much Blaming of the Clergy* (1455), and *Book of Faith* (1456), important monuments of fifteenth-century English prose, but open to correction because of their lack of precision in his discussion of Lollard errors. Pecock was made privy councilor, approved Richard of York as protector, and fell out of favor as that faction declined in power. In 1457 he was declared guilty of heresy by a commission appointed by Archbishop Bourchier and sentenced illegally. Although he abjured and thus escaped the stake, he appealed to Pope Callistus III, who ordered his restitution. Bourchier refused to accept the pope's bulls, and when Callistus died another trial was ordered in 1459 by Pope Pius II. Pecock had resigned his see of his own volition and no judicial action was taken; he was, however, confined to Thorney abbey, Cambridgeshire, England, where he probably died. His name is also spelled Peacock.

PECTORIUS. His name appears at the end of a long poem in Greek, inscribed on a marble tablet, and discovered at Autun, France, in 1839. The epigraph refers to transubstantiation, the communion of saints, prayers for the dead, the symbolism of the fish, and could have been composed as early as the second or as late as the sixth century.

PEDRO II (1174–1213), king of Aragon. Son of Alfonso II, he became king in 1196, opposed the Albigensian views of Count Raymond of Toulouse, and went to Rome in 1204, where he declared himself a vassal of the pope. When the fury of the Albigensian crusade mounted, he joined his vassals against Simon de Montfort and was killed at the battle of Muret, France, on Sept. 12 or 13.

PEDRO III (1239?–1285), king of Aragon and Sicily. Son of James I of Aragon, he became king in 1276, married Constance, daughter of Manfred and granddaughter of Emperor Frederick II, and in 1282 led a fleet against Sicily, defeated Charles of Anjou there, and ruled as King Pedro I of Sicily from 1282 to 1285. While the action expanded Aragonese power, it made the aristocracy, burghers, and clerics hostile. Pedro refused to continue Sicily as a vassal of the Papal States and withstood a French fleet sent against him by the papacy. In Spain the nobles forced Pedro to sign the General Privilege in 1283, which defined their rights and established annual meetings of the Cortes. He died in Villafranca de Panedés, near Barcelona, Spain, on Nov. 10 or 11.

PEDRO IV (1319?–1387), king of Aragon. Born in Balaquer, Spain, on Sept. 5, the son of Alfonso IV and called "the Ceremonious," he recovered the Balearic Islands in 1343, fought a fruitless war against Genoa, and gradually lost power to the nobles, who restrained him by demanding full obedience to the General Privilege of 1283. He defeated the nobles in 1348, however, destroyed that charter of liberties by slashing it to shreds with his sword, and also limited the powers of clergy, burghers, and peasants. He fought Pedro the Cruel of Castile in 1357–61, conquered Sicily in 1377, and died in Barcelona, Spain, on Jan. 5.

PEDRO I (1320–1367), king of Portugal. Born in Coimbra, Portugal, on Apr. 8, he went to war against his father, Alfonso IV, allied himself with Pedro the Cruel of Castile to take vengeance on the murderers of his mistress, Inés de Castro (killed in 1355 with Alfonso's approval), and after 1357 ruled as a violent but popular despot. He held the nobles in subjection, limited the banking activity of the Jews, was notoriously immoral, but introduced successful laws for navigation, agriculture, and lessening of Church grievances. His son Ferdinand I (1345–1383) continued his father's government policies and imitated his immoralities, joined John of Gaunt in his claim on the crown of Castile, was undone by his mistress, Leonor Telles, and was so crushed by Castile that Portugal almost lost its sovereignty. He died in Estremoz, Portugal, on Apr. 8.

PEDRO II (1648–1706), king of Portugal. He was born in Lisbon, Portugal, on Apr. 26, son of John IV, became regent in 1667 when his imbecile brother Alfonso VI (who had been named king in 1656) was deposed, became king in 1683 when Alfonso died, learned that gold had been discovered in Brazil, and suffered a partition of Portugal when a British-Spanish army occupied Madrid. He regained from the papacy the right of Portugal to nominate bishops for sees in the Far East. He died in Alcántara, Spain, on Dec. 9.

PEDRO III (d. 1786), king of Portugal. *See* John VI, king of Portugal.

PEDRO IV (1798–1834), king of Portugal. Born in Lisbon, Portugal, on Oct. 12, son of John VI, he was taken to Brazil in 1807, became regent there when his father returned to Europe in 1820, declared Brazil independent in 1822, and became its first emperor as Pedro I; Portugal recognized Brazil's independence in 1825. His rule was arbitrary and depended too much on the Portuguese aristocracy; the Brazilians forced him to abdicate in 1831 in favor of his son, Emperor Pedro II. Pedro had become King Pedro IV of Portugal in 1826, but gave the throne over to his daughter, Maria II. When his brother Miguel would not let her rule in 1834, Pedro returned to Portugal, forced Miguel into exile, and saw Maria crowned two days before he died in Lisbon on Sept. 24.

PEDRO DE CORDOVA (1460?–1525). Born in Cordova, Andalusia, Spain, he studied at Salamanca, became a Dominican there, and in 1510 was sent to Santo Domingo, where he founded the Santa Cruz province and became the first inquisitor in America. He was known for his defense of the Indians and wrote one of the first catechisms printed in the New World for the Indians (1544). He died on Santo Domingo.

PEDRO DE LA CADIRETA, BL. (d. 1277), martyr. Born in Moya, Spain, he became a Dominican friar and was stoned to death at Urgell by heretics. F. D. Dec. 20.

PEDROG. *See* Petroc, St.

PEGA, ST. (d. 719?). Sister of St. Guthlac, she lived in retirement at the edge of Peterborough Fen, England, at a place now called Peakirk. She died in Rome while on a pilgrimage. F. D. Jan. 8.

PEGASIUS, ST. (d. 345), martyr. *See* Acindynus, St.

PEIS, ST. FRANCIS IGNATIUS VINCENT (1701–1781). Born in Laconi, Sardinia, the second of nine children, he became a Capuchin at Buoncammino, Cagliari, when he was twenty. Bro. Ignatius worked as a beggar, then for fifteen years as a weaver. In 1741 he began forty years of seeking alms, educating the ignorant, curing the sick, and ending feuds. He was canonized in 1951 by Pope Pius XII. F. D. May 11.

PELAGIA, ST. (d. 311?), martyr. She was a fifteen-year-old Christian in Antioch, who threw herself from a rooftop to protect her virginity when a squad of soldiers entered her house to arrest her. Her action was praised in a homily by St. John Chrysostom; St. Augustine, however, completely opposed such an action at the beginning of his *City of God*. F. D. June 9.

PELAGIA, ST. (d. 320), martyr. *See* Januarius, St.

PELAGIA, ST. (d. 361), martyr. *See* Domiarius, St.

PELAGIA. *See* Marina, St.

PELAGIA OF TARSUS. The heroine of a pious legend, she is said to have become a Christian when she ran away from an engagement to the son of Diocletian; when her fiancé found out, he committed suicide. The emperor ordered her brought before him, found her so beautiful he offered marriage, and ordered her burned to death when she refused.

PELAGIUS I (d. 561), pope. Born in Rome, son of the vicar of one of the two districts into which Rome was then divided, he accompanied Pope Agapetus I to Constantinople and was appointed nuncio by Agapitus just before his death there in 536. He returned to Rome when Pope Silverius was driven from the city by Belisarius, agent of Empress Theodora, and on Vigilius' accession to the papal throne in 537 became a trusted adviser of Emperor Justinian. Pelagius participated in the Synod of Constantinople in 543 which condemned Origenism, then returned to Rome, where he was Justinian's representative when Vigilius was forced to go to Constantinople in 545 to condemn the Three Chapters of Theodore of Mopsuestia and others. When Totila, king of the Goths, defeated Belisarius and captured Rome in 546, Pelagius prevailed upon the victor to spare the inhabitants. Totila sent him to Constantinople to negotiate a peace with Justinian, who refused. The struggle raged until Totila's death and that of his successor left Rome firmly in the hands of the emperor. In 551 Pelagius was imprisoned for supporting Vigilius when the pope opposed the ratification of Justinian's condemnation of the Three Chapters at the fifth General Council of Constantinople in 553. When Vigilius confirmed the council's decrees in his *Constitutum* of 554, Pelagius refused to accept, but eventually supported Vigilius, returned to the emperor's favor, accompanied Vigilius on his return trip, and was with him when he died at Syracuse in 555. He was elected Vigilius' successor on Apr. 16, 556. Opposed by many of the Western bishops for his confirmation of the Council of Constantinople's decrees, he labored unsuccessfully to heal the schism caused by the Three Chapters controversy in Italy, but was successful in Gaul. He restored order in Italy by using Justinian's pragmatic sanction of 554, which confirmed the temporal power of the papacy and firmly established the pope's temporal dominions. He also took vigorous action to eliminate simony, instituted widespread ecclesiastical reforms, and worked to alleviate the distress of the Goth invasions and wars. He died in Rome on Mar. 4.

PELAGIUS II (d. 590), pope. Born in Rome, son of Winigild, a Goth, he was elected pope on Nov. 26, 579, during the Lombard siege of Rome and persuaded the Lombards to withdraw. He sent to Constantinople for imperial aid in resisting the barbarian invasions and, when the emperor was unable to help, turned to the Franks for aid, for the first time in the history of the papacy, in 580 or 581—a move of great future significance. His entire pontificate was plagued by Lombard attacks. He attempted unsuccessfully to end the schism in Italy caused by Vigilius' condemnation of the Three Chapters, protested the use of the title of "ecumenical patriarch" by John, patriarch of Constantinople, and rejoiced in the elimination of Arianism in Spain when the Visigoths there were converted to Christianity. He died of the plague in Rome on Feb 7.

PELAGIUS, ST. (d. 283?), martyr. A boy, he was slain in Istria, Italy, during the reign of Numerian and is venerated as patron of Constance, Switzerland. F. D. Aug. 28.

PELAGIUS, ST. (4th century). A bishop in Laodicea, he was exiled for his activity by Arian Emperor Valens. Recalled by Gratian, he attended the Council of Constantinople in 381. F. D. Mar. 25.

PELAGIUS, ST. (912?–925), martyr. As a boy of ten he was left at Cordova, Spain, as a hostage for his uncle, who failed to ransom him. After three years he was tortured to death by the Moors when he refused to renounce his faith. His story is the basis of a long poem (962) by Hroswitha of Gandersheim. F. D. June 26.

PELAGIUS, ST. (d. 950?), martyr. *See* Arsenius, St.

PELARGUS. *See* Stork, Ambrose.

PELAYO, ALVARO (1280?–1352), bishop. A Spaniard, he studied law at Bologna, Italy, became a Franciscan in 1304, studied under Duns Scotus, and tutored the children of Don Pedro, regent of Portugal. He was confessor to Pope John XXII at Avignon, was made a bishop in 1233, and in 1235 given the see of Sylves, Portugal, and made apostolic nuncio. He wrote *De planctu ecclesiae* on ecclesiastical abuses and rights. He died at Seville, Spain, on Jan. 25.

PELERIN, FELIX (1843–1926), educator. Born on Apr. 10, he became a Christian brother, taking the name Fabrician, and taught in secondary schools in New York City and Providence and philosophy at Manhattan College. He served as president of St. John's College, Washington, and St. Mary's College, Oakland, California, and was librarian at Manhattan at the time of his death in New York City on Sept. 26.

PELEUS, ST. (d. 310?), bishop and martyr. An Egyptian bishop, he was condemned to the quarries of Palestine with a group of other Christians during the persecution of Maximian. He and Nilus, another Egyptian bishop, Elias, a priest, and an unknown Egyptian layman were later burned alive, probably at Phunon, near Petra, Palestine. F. D. Sept. 19.

PELINGOTTO, BL. GIOVANNI (1240–1304). Born to a wealthy merchant family in Urbino, Italy, he became a Franciscan tertiary, living a life of prayer and austerity at home; in his later years he was active in caring for the sick, poor, and beggars. His cult was confirmed in 1918. F. D. June 1.

PELINUS, ST. (d. 361), martyr. He was put to death at Confinium, near Samnium, Italy, during the reign of Julian the Apostate. F. D. Dec. 5.

PELISSON-FONTANIER, PAUL (1624–1693). Born in Béziers, France, he studied at Montauban, law at Toulouse, became Nicolas Fouquet's secretary in 1652, was admitted to the French Academy for his *Histoire de l'Academie française* (1653), and named master of accounts in 1659 and counselor of the king in 1660. He was imprisoned in the Bastille in 1661 for his loyalty to the deposed Fouquet, but was named royal historian by King Louis XIV on his release in 1666. He became a convert in 1670, became a subdeacon, and received Guieont abbey and the administration of the funds of other monasteries. He wrote a life of Louis XIV, a defense of Fouquet (while he was in prison), and a treatise on the Eucharist. He died in Versailles, France, on Feb. 7.

PELLEGRINETTI, ERMENEGILDO (1876–1943), cardinal. Born in Camaiore, Italy, on Mar. 22, one of eleven children, he was educated at the seminary in Lucca, served Bishop Achille Ratti as secretary, and when the latter became Pope Pius XI was named nuncio to Yugoslavia and titular archbishop of Adana in 1922. He arranged a concordat with the Vatican and returned to Rome to be made a cardinal in 1937. He died in Rome on Mar. 29.

PELLEGRINO. *See* Laziozi, St. Pellegrino.

PELLEGRINO DA BOLOGNA. *See* Tibaldi, Pellagrino.

PELLETIER, BERTRAND (1761–1797), chemist. Born in Bayonne, France, he made important chemical discoveries especially regarding phosphorus, became a professor of the Polytechnic School in Paris in 1795, and was elected to the Institute. His collected works were published as *Memoirs and Observations* (1798).

PELLETIER, PIERRE JOSEPH (1788–1842), chemist. Born in Paris on Mar. 22, the son of the chemist, Bertrand, he became a follower of Lavoisier and studied medicine. He was the discoverer of strychnine and published a description of his researches in 1818. In 1820, with Caventoy, he discovered quinine, for which he was awarded the Montyon Prize of the Paris Academy of Science in 1827. He became a professor at the École de Pharmacie, a director in 1832, and was elected to the Academy of Sciences in 1840. Several alkaloids (including pelletierine) were named after him. He died in Paris on July 19.

PELLETIER, ST. ROSE VIRGINIA (1796–1868), foundress. Mother Mary of St. Euphrasia was born on the island of Noirmoutier, Brittany, and went to school in Tours, where in 1814 she became a novice in the convent of Our Lady of Charity of the Refuge, an institute founded in 1641 by St. John Eudes. In 1825 she became superior, opened a branch at Angers, and struggled to have her various foundations under a central authority rather than separate existence under diocesan bishops. She succeeded, and the Institute of Our Lady of Charity of the Good Shepherd received papal approval in 1835. She was canonized in 1940 by Pope Pius XII. F. D. Apr. 24.

PELLICER, ANTHONY DOMINIC (1824–1880), bishop. Born in St. Augustine, Florida, on Dec. 7, he studied at Spring Hill College, and St. Vincent de Paul seminary, New Orleans, and was ordained in Mobile in 1850. He did parish work there, was vicar general in 1867–74, and was appointed first bishop of San Antonio, Texas, in 1874. He died there on Apr. 14.

PELLICO, SILVIO (1788–1854). Born in Saluzzio, Piedmont, Italy, on June 24, son of a government employee, he became a French teacher in Milan in 1808, was discharged by the Austrian authorities, and taught privately. He became a friend of several outstanding Italian authors, among them Manzoni, and in 1819 his *Francesca da Rimini*, a tragedy (later translated by Byron), was produced to great acclaim. In 1819 he became an editor of *Il Conciliatore*, a periodical founded by Count Lambertenghi; its policy of opposing foreign intervention in Italy led to its suppression by the Austrians. In 1820 he was arrested as an alleged member of the Carbonari and sentenced to death. Instead he was given fifteen years of hard labor and released in 1830, broken in health. He wrote *Le mie Prigioni* (1832; a widely popular diary of his prison years); twelve tragedies, lyric poetry of romantic outlook, other poems on patriotic and mediaeval themes, a translation of Byron's *Manfred*, and a collection of letters. He died in retirement at Turin, Italy, on Jan. 31.

PELLISSIER, GUILLAUME (1490?–1568), bishop. Born in Melgueil, Languedoc, France, he studied law and theology, became a canon in 1527, and coadjutor of his uncle, the bishop of Maguelonne, whom he succeeded in 1529. He served on several diplomatic missions for King Francis I, and helped arrange peace with Charles V in 1529 and the marriage of Henry II and Catherine de' Medici in 1533. In 1536 he translated his see to Montpellier, became ambassador to Venice, bought many manuscripts, was arrested and charged with heresy by the parliament of Toulouse, exonerated, and devoted himself to combating Protestantism. When the Protestants destroyed his cathedral in 1567, he fled to the castle of Montferraud, France, where he died.

PELOUZE, THÉOPHILE JULES (1807–1867), chemist. Born in Valognes, France, on Feb. 26, he studied pharmacy, became professor at Lille in 1830, assayer to the mint in 1833, and taught at L'École Polytechnique, Paris, and the Collège de France to 1851. He worked with Liebig in Germany in 1836 on chemical studies, became a member of the Academy of Sciences in 1837, president of the mint commission in 1848, and a member of the Paris municipal commission in 1849. He isolated tannic acid, discovered that beet root and cane sugar are the same, isolated the class of salts called nitrosulphates, introduced sodium sulphate in glass manufacture, made studies of enamel, the effect of sunlight on glass, and determined the weight of several elements. He died in Paris on May 31.

PELTRIE, MADELEINE DE LA (1603–1671). Madeleine Chauvigny was born in Caen, France, married Charles de la Peltrie against her will in 1620, and when he died five years later devoted her life and fortune to charitable projects. In 1639 she accompanied Marie de l'Incarnation to Quebec, went to Montreal in 1642 but returned to Quebec a year and a half later, and, though never professed, led the life of a religious under Marie. She died in Quebec on Nov. 18.

PEÑA, FRANCISCO (1540?–1612). Born in Villaroya de los Pinares, Spain, he studied law at Valencia, was appointed auditor of the rota for Spain by Philip II, and was on the commission which published *Corpus juris canonici* in 1582. He also wrote theological treatises and biographies.

PEÑALVER Y CARDENAS, LUIS IGNATIUS (1749–1810), archbishop. Born in Havana, Cuba, on Apr. 3, he studied there at St. Ignatius College and St. Jerome University, and was ordained in Havana in 1772. He was appointed vicar general of Santiago in 1773, and served there until 1793 when he became titular bishop of Tricca and administrator of Louisiana and the Two Floridas. He traveled through the entire territory later defined in the Louisiana Purchase, bitterly censured its inhabitants for their ignorance and lack of spirituality, and in 1801 was named archbishop of

Guatemala. He resigned this see in 1806 and returned to Havana, where he died on July 17.

PENDLETON, HENRY (d. 1557). Born in Manchester, England, he preached against Lutheranism during the reign of Henry VIII, became a conformist under Edward VI, and became a Protestant minister at Blymhill, Staffordshire. He returned to Catholicism in 1553, served as chaplain to Bishop Bonner, and wrote several homilies. He died in London in Sept.

PENNA, FRANCESCO ORAZIO DELLA (1681-1745). Born in Italy, he became a Capuchin, went to Tibet, and translated into Tibetan Bellarmine's *Christian Doctrine* and Thurlot's *Treasure of Christian Doctrine*, and several Tibetan works into Italian. He compiled the first Tibetan dictionary, with 35,000 listings. He died at Patan, Nepal.

PENNI, GIANFRANCESCO (1488?-1528?), painter. Born in Florence, Italy, he became a pupil of Raphael and worked with him in the Farnesina, the Loggie and Sala di Constantino in the Vatican, and elsewhere. Although he made an excellent copy of the *Entombment*, his original work was not striking. He became Raphael's legatee and executor.

PEPIN I OF LANDEN (d. 639). He joined with Bishop Arnulf of Metz to aid Clotaire II to overthrow Brunhilda, and with Arnulf was appointed mayor of the palace by Clotaire to help his son Dagobert I to rule Austrasia. When Dagobert succeeded his father in 629 he dispensed with the services of Pepin, who withdrew to Aquitaine. He returned to Austrasia on Dagobert's death in 638 and ruled in Sigebert's name until his death. The marriage of Pepin's and Arnulf's children founded the Carolingian dynasty in France. His name is sometimes spelled Pippin.

PEPIN II OF HERISTAL (d. 714), king. Son of Adalgiselus and Bertha, daughter of Pepin I, and father of Charles Martel, he became mayor of the palace of Austrasia in 676 and leader of the nobles opposed to Ebroin and Neustria. Pepin's victory at Tertry in 687 ended the Merovingian reign. He warred on the Frisians, and defeated their forces under Duke Radborn; many of the Frisians then turned Christian. At the time of his death on Dec. 16 at Jupille, all Gaul except Aquitaine was under his rule.

PEPIN THE SHORT (714-768), king. Son of Charles Martel and father of Charlemagne, he, with his older brother Carloman, was educated by the monks of St. Denis. When his father died in 741, he became ruler of Burgundy, Neustria, and Provence, and Carloman of the rest of Charles's realms. Strong opposition developed from Griffon, his stepbrother, and the dukes of the Aquitania and Alamannia. When war broke out the brothers agreed in 743 on Childeric III, a Merovingian, as king. In 747,

Carloman retired to a monastery, and in 751 Pepin, with the pope's consent, deposed Childeric, was elected king of the Franks at Soissons, and consecrated by St. Boniface in Pope Zachary's name. This co-operation between temporal and spiritual authority was to have far-reaching effects. In 754, Pope Stephen IV recrowned Pepin and his two sons, Carloman and Charlemagne, and requested the aid of Pepin against the Lombards. The king accepted the title of *patricius* and protector of the Holy See, restored papal territories by a successful war (754-56) against the Lombards under King Aistulf, and recognized the territorial claims of the pope. He extended his territory by defeating the Arabs at Septimania and conquering Aquitania, unified the kingdom and at least defended its borders against Saxon and Bavarian raids, and helped to extend the spiritual jurisdiction of the Church, though he always insisted on the supremacy of the Frankish king. He died at St. Denis, France, on Sept. 24.

PERBOYRE, BL. JEAN GABRIEL (1802-1840), martyr. Born in Puech, France, he joined the Lazarists (Vincentians) in 1818 and was ordained in 1826. He taught theology until 1832, when he became assistant director of the novitiate at Paris. In 1835, when his brother died in China, he asked to be sent to Honan. In 1839, while stationed at Hupeh, China, he was captured, tortured, and strangled to death. He was beatified in 1889. F. D. Sept. 11.

PERCHE, NAPOLEON JOSEPH (1805-1883), bishop. Born in Angers, France, on Jan. 10, he taught philosophy at eighteen, studied at the Beaupréau seminary, and was ordained there when twenty-four. He served in French parishes until 1837, when he went to the United States at the invitation of Bishop Flaget of Bardstown. He then went to New Orleans, Louisiana, as almoner of the Ursulines, a post he held for twenty-eight years, founded *Le Propagateur Catholique* in 1842, mainly to support Archbishop Blanc in his controversy with the wardens of the cathedral over who was to select the curates, and edited it until 1857, when ill health caused him to resign. He was named titular bishop of Abdera and coadjutor of Archbishop Odin in 1870 and later in the year succeeded as third archbishop of New Orleans. He died in New Orleans on Dec. 27.

PERCY, JOHN (1569-1641). Born in Holmeside, Durham, England, on Sept. 27, he was a convert at fourteen, studied at Rheims and at the English College, Rome, and in 1594 became a Jesuit in Belgium. He was sent to England in 1596, captured on his way by the Dutch, tortured, and delivered in London as a prisoner. He escaped, joined Fr. Gerard, was arrested in Harrowden in 1605, and banished to Belgium at the intercession of the Spanish ambassador. He became superior of the Jesuits in

Belgium, taught scripture at Louvain, returned to England, was again captured, and sentenced to death in 1610. Still in prison in 1622, he was chosen by King James I to debate the Catholic position with Archbishop Laud and other Anglican leaders. This led to several major conversions; he was released in 1625, ordered banished in 1635, but managed to remain in London until his death on Dec. 3. He often used the alias John Fisher.

PERCY, BL. THOMAS (1528–1572), martyr. Son of Sir Thomas Percy, who was hanged at Tyburn as one of the leaders of the Pilgrimage of Grace, he became earl of Northumberland in 1557. During Queen Mary's reign he served her on the Scottish border, and in 1558 married Anne Somerset, daughter of the earl of Worcester, by whom he had four children. In 1568, Mary Queen of Scots took refuge at Carlisle in Yorkshire and he became one of her leading supporters. Ordered with Charles Neville, earl of Westmoreland, to appear before Queen Elizabeth, he refused, and the two began what came to be known as the Rising of the North. Received by most of the people of northern England, who were still Catholic at heart, with great enthusiasm, they were defeated by Elizabeth's troops under the earl of Sussex, who wreaked bloody vengeance on the people and towns that had supported the uprising. Bl. Thomas fled to Scotland, was captured by the earl of Moray, imprisoned for nearly three years, and then surrendered to Elizabeth by Moray's successor, the earl of Mar, for £2000. Brought to York, he was offered his freedom if he would apostatize, refused, and was beheaded on Aug. 22. He was beatified in 1896. F. D. Aug. 26.

M. M. MERRICK, *Thomas Percy* (London, 1949).

PEREGRINUS, ST. (d. 120?), martyr. *See* Astius, St.

PEREGRINUS, ST. (d. 192), martyr. *See* Eusebius, St.

PEREGRINUS, ST. (d. 261?), bishop and martyr. Said to have been the first bishop of Auxerre, France, he was sent to Gaul by Pope Sixtus II, preached successfully in Marseilles and Lyons, and was beheaded at Entrains after he interfered with the dedication of a temple to Jupiter and attacked idolatry. F. D. May 16.

PEREGRINUS, ST. (d. 300?), martyr. *See* Irenaeus, St.

PEREGRINUS, ST. (d. 304?), martyr. Born in Rome, he became the first bishop of Auxerre, Gaul, and was slain during the Diocletian persecution. F. D. May 16.

PEREGRINUS, BL. (d. 1240). Born in Falcrone, Italy, he was a student at Bologna in 1220 when he heard St. Francis of Assisi preach. He joined the friars as a laybrother at San Severino. F. D. Sept. 6.

PEREGRINUS, ST. (d. 1250?) *See* Evangelist, Bl.

PEREGRINUS, ST. (d. 1291). He was a Camaldolese monk who served as abbot of Santa Maria dell' Isola and as prior of Camaldoli, Italy. F. D. June 3.

PEREGRINUS. *See* Cetheus, St.

PEREIRA, BENEDICT (1535?–1610), theologian. Born in Ruzafa, Spain, he became a Jesuit in 1552, taught in Rome, and wrote biblical commentaries, notably on Genesis, Daniel, and St. John. He died in Rome on Mar. 6.

PEREIRA, BL. NUÑEZ ALVAREZ DE (1360–1431). Born near Lisbon, Portugal, he married at seventeen, was appointed a military commander in 1383 by King John I, and with him defeated the Castilian army and established Portugal as independent. When his wife died in 1422, he served as a Carmelite laybrother in a friary he had founded at Lisbon, and died there on Nov. 1. His cult was approved in 1918. F. D. Nov. 6.

PÉREZ, JUAN (d. 1512?). Of a noble Spanish family, he became Queen Isabella's accountant and, after he became a Franciscan, her confessor. He retired from the court to La Rábida in Andalusia, became its guardian, and when Columbus came there in 1484 or 1485 joined Fr. Antonio de Marchena in accepting his description of the earth. Fr. Pérez persuaded the queen to support the explorer just as he was about to leave for France, blessed the fleet as it sailed, accompanied Columbus on his second voyage, and said the first mass in the New World on Dec. 8, 1493, at Point Conception, Haiti. He then became guardian of the Franciscan monastery at Santo Domingo, Haiti. What happened to him after that is not known, though he was definitely reported dead by 1513.

PÉREZ DE HITA, GINÉS (16th century). Born in Murcia, Spain, he fought against the Moors and wrote *Guerras civiles de Granada* (1595–1604), a fictional account of the struggle between Moors at Granada and on the victory of Ferdinand V over the Moors at Vega.

PERFECTUS, ST. (d. 851), martyr. A priest at Cordova, Spain, he was put to death by the Moors. F. D. Apr. 18.

PERGOLESI, GIOVANNI BATTISTA (1710–1736), composer. Born in Naples, Italy, on Jan. 3, he studied music at its conservatory, attracted attention with his religious drama, *San Guglielmo d'Aquitania*, while a student, and wrote plays for the secular stage. He composed a mass of thanksgiving after a Naples earthquake, other masses, an intermezzo (*La serva padrona*, 1731), and is best known for his *Stabat Mater*, written shortly before his death at Pozzuoli, Italy, on Mar. 16.

PERMANEDER, FRANZ MICHAEL (1794–1862), canonist. Born in Traunstein, Bavaria, on Aug. 12, he studied at Landshut and was ordained in 1818. He became professor of canon law and church history at the Freising Lyceum in 1834 and at Munich in 1847. He wrote theological treatises and died at Ratisbon, Bavaria, on Oct. 10.

PERN. *See* Paternus, St. (5th century).

PERNTER, JOSEF MARIA (1848–1908), physicist. Born in Neumarkt, Tyrol, on Mar. 15, he studied at Innsbruck, became a Jesuit, and taught physics in Kalocsa and Kalksburg. He left the Society in 1877 because of ill health, took his doctorate in physics at Vienna, and in 1878 joined the staff of the Central Meterological Institute. He also was professor at Innsbruck in 1890 and at Vienna in 1897. As director of the Institute he extended its work in seismology and weather forecasting, supplying advance weather data to telegraph offices for distribution. He wrote on atmospheric conditions and an influential defense of science and faith. He died in Arco, Italy, on Dec. 20.

PEROSI, CARLO (1868–1930), cardinal. Born in Tortona, Italy, he was ordained in 1891 and brought to serve at the Vatican basilica in 1903 by Pope Pius X. He became consultor to the Congregation of the Council and was a member of the tribunal of the Apostolic Penitentiary and of the Consistorial Congregation. In 1915 he became a consultor to the Congregation of the Holy Office and a canon of St. Mary Major. He was made a cardinal in 1926 and secretary of the Consistorial Congregation in 1928. He died in Vatican City on Feb. 22.

PEROSI, LORENZO (1872–1956), composer. Born in Tortona, Italy, on Dec. 20, he studied at the Milan conservatory and in Regensburg, was ordained, and became choirmaster in Imola in 1895, at St. Mark's, Venice, in 1897, and then of the pontifical chorus of the Sistine Chapel. His trilogy, *La passione di Cristo*, was produced in 1897. He also wrote *La transfigurazione, La risurrezione de Lazaro, Il natale del Redentore, Moses, In patris memoriam,* twenty-five masses, and pieces for organ and orchestra. He died in Rome on Oct. 12.

PERPETUA, ST. (d. 80?). A Roman matron, she is said to have been converted by St. Peter and to have converted her husband and her son St. Nazarius. F. D. Aug. 4.

PERPETUA, ST. (d. 203), martyr. Vivia, or Vibia, Perpetua was a young wife and mother, daughter of a Carthaginian pagan, who refused to sacrifice to the gods during the persecution of Severus, was imprisoned, exposed in the public games to wild beasts, and then stabbed by gladiators. F. D. Mar. 5.

PERPETUUS, ST. (d. 494?). He was bishop of Tours, France, for thirty years, rebuilt the basilica of St. Martin, and died under the pressure of the inroads of Arian ideas and Gothic barbarians. His so-called will is a seventeenth-century forgery. F. D. Apr. 8.

PERRAN. *See* Piran.

PERRAUD, ADOLPHE (1828–1906), cardinal. Born in Lyons, France, on Feb. 7, he studied in the École Normale, taught in the Angers *lycée*, joined the reorganized Oratorians in 1852, and was ordained in 1855. He became professor of history at the St. Lô minor seminary, was called to Paris because of his preaching ability, visited Ireland in 1860, was appointed professor of ecclesiastical history at the Sorbonne in 1866 and to the committee of higher education in 1870, and was a chaplain in Gen. MacMahon's army. He was made bishop of Autun in 1874, elected to the French Academy in 1882, served as superior of the oratory from 1884 to 1901, and created cardinal in 1893. He wrote historical and theological works, a study of Richelieu, and elegiac and Lenten sermons. He died on Feb. 18.

PERRAULT, CHARLES (1628–1703), author. Born in Paris on Jan. 12, he became a lawyer, and was appointed controller general of the king's buildings. He persuaded Colbert to establish a pension fund for writers and scholars, helped found the Academy of Sciences and re-establish the Academy of Painting, became life secretary of the Academy of Inscriptions and Belles Lettres when it was founded in 1663, and was elected to the French Academy in 1671. He died in Paris on May 16. He was one of the leaders of the "Moderns" against Bossuet, Fénelon, and Boileau of the "Ancients," a controversy started by his introduction to *Le siècle de Louis le Grand* and his four-volume *Parallèle des anciens et des modernes* (1688–98), wrote poetry, and is also known for *Contes de ma Mère l'Oye*, a collection of fairy tales which included retellings of Cinderella, Little Red Riding Hood, Tom Thumb, and Puss in Boots. He also wrote *Mémoires*.

PERRAULT, CLAUDE (1613–1688), architect. Brother of Charles, he was born in Paris on Sept. 25, studied for his medical degree at Paris, and was noted as an anatomist. He was one of the first members of the Academy of Sciences and achieved success in chemistry, physics, and zoology. In 1665 he won a competition for the design for the east façade of the Louvre, the Colonnade, the building of which occupied his next fifteen years. He translated Vitruvius with a commentary (1673) and designed an arch on Rue St. Antoine, the observatory, and several churches in Paris, where he died on Oct. 9.

PERREUX. *See* Petroc, St.

PERREYVE, HENRI (1831–1865). Born in Paris on Apr. 11, he studied at the Collège St. Louis, was ordained in 1858, and became associated with Fr. Pététol and the group trying to re-establish the Oratorians, chaplain to the Lycée St. Louis in 1860, and professor of ecclesiastical history at the Sorbonne in 1861. He wrote meditations on scripture and other ascetical works and died in Paris on June 18.

PERRONE, GIOVANNI (1794–1876), theologian. Born in Chieri, Italy, on Mar. 11, he received his doctorate in theology at Turin, became a Jesuit in 1815, taught theology at Orvieto and the Roman College (1833–48), was exiled for three years when the republic came into power, and returned in 1851. He then held the chair of dogma at the Roman College, except for a period as rector at Ferrara, for the rest of his teaching career. He combated the position of Georg Hermes, was active in promoting the dogma of the Immaculate Conception, and wrote more than forty works, including the long-popular nine-volume *Praelectiones theologicae*. He died in Rome on Aug. 28.

PERRY, STEPHEN JOSEPH (1833–1889), astronomer. Born in London on Aug. 26, he studied at Douai, became a Jesuit in 1853, and studied at St. Acheul, Stonyhurst, and mathematics in London and Paris. In 1860 he was put in charge of the observatory and taught physics and mathematics at Stonyhurst, went to St. Beuno's in Wales in 1863, and was ordained in 1866. He then returned to Stonyhurst, where the observatory became noted for its studies in meteorology and solar physics. He engaged in magnetic surveys of France and Belgium from 1868 to 1871, made numerous trips all over the world to observe solar eclipses, in 1874 and 1882 to Kerguelen in the Indian Ocean and Madagascar to observe a transit of Venus, and died on Dec. 27 in the Salut Islands, off the coast of French Guiana, while on an expedition to study a solar eclipse.

PERSEVERANDA, ST. (726?). She is said to have gone from Spain to Poitiers, France, with her two sisters, to have founded a convent there, and to have died in Poitou while in flight from a notorious pirate. She is also called Pezaine. F. D. June 26.

PERSICO, IGNATIUS (1823–1896), cardinal. Born in Naples, Italy, on Jan. 30, he became a Capuchin in 1839, was ordained in 1846, and was sent as a missioner to India, where he became assistant to Bishop Hartmann and helped to establish the Bombay *Catholic Examiner* in 1850. During the Goanese schism in 1853 he went to Rome and London to explain the situation to the pope and to gain English recognition of Catholic rights. He was made titular bishop of Gratianopolis in 1854, visitor of the vicariate of Agra in 1854, administrator in 1855, and then its vicar apostolic in 1856. Ill health caused him to return to Italy in 1860. He was sent to the United States in 1866, attended the Council of Baltimore, was appointed bishop of Savannah in 1870 but was

obliged to resign because of ill health in 1872, and made titular bishop of Bolina in 1874. He was apostolic delegate to Canada in 1874, to Malabar in 1874, and was appointed bishop of Aquino, Italy, in 1878. He resigned the see in 1887 and was appointed titular archbishop of Tamiathis in 1887, and was apostolic delegate to Ireland. He was created cardinal-priest in 1893, and died in Rome on Dec. 7.

PERUGINO, IL. *See* Vannucci, Pietro de Christoforo.

PERUZZI, BALDASSARE (1481–1536), painter. Born in Volterra, Italy, on Mar. 7, he was a painter in his youth, went to Rome in 1508, worked with Raphael on the frescoes of the Villa Farnesina, under Bramante in St. Peter's, and later became superintendent of the work about 1520 and made a design, never executed, for completing St. Peter's. He designed many buildings, palaces, and villas throughout Italy; the Palazzo Massimo, built in Rome about 1530, and his fresco, *Judgment of Paris* in the Villa Belcaro, are considered his masterpieces. He died in Rome on Jan. 6.

PESCH, TILMANN (1836–1899), philosopher. Born in Cologne, Germany, on Feb. 1, he became a Jesuit in 1852, studied at Paderborn, Bonn, and Maria-Laach, and taught in this last in 1867–69. After seven years of missionary labors in Germany he taught philosophy at Blyenbeck from 1876 to 1884, then retired to write and continue missionary activity. He wrote treatises on the scholarly and popular level, among them *Christliche Lebensphilosophie* and *Das Religiöse Leben*. He died in Valkenburg, Holland, on Oct. 18.

PESCHGES, JOHN HUBERT (1881–1944), bishop. Born in West Newton, Minnesota, on May 11, he studied at St. John's University, and St. Paul's seminary, and was ordained in Winona in 1905. He did parish and missionary work in the Winona diocese, became vice-president of St. Mary's College, Winona, in 1913 and was president from 1918 to 1933. While pastor of St. Augustine's church in Austin, he was appointed bishop of Crookston, Minnesota, in 1938, and died there on Oct. 30.

PÉTAIN, HENRI PHILIPPE (1856–1951), general. Born in Cauchy la Tour, France, on May 24, he studied at St. Cyr and École de Guerre, became an army officer, achieved success with artillery in World War I, restored morale to the French army, and was the general who led the heroic defense of Verdun. He was named a marshal in 1918. He served as ambassador to Spain in 1939–40. In the latter year, when France was overrun by German forces and a provisional government set up at Vichy by former premier Laval, Pétain was made head of state, ordered collaboration with the conquerors, and directed a continuation of military action against the Free French forces under Charles de Gaulle. Although his government was recognized by the United States, he ordered Adm. Darlan's fleet to oppose the Allied landing in North Africa and branded Darlan a traitor when cease-fire orders came from his flagship. Feelings ran high: some felt that Pétain had been tricked into his position; others that he was senile and an irresponsible figurehead; others that he was vain beyond patriotism. When the Allies invaded France, Pétain was carried off to Germany; he was returned in 1945, brought to trial as a traitor, stripped of his distinctions and property, and ordered shot. De Gaulle was influential in having the penalty commuted to life imprisonment, and he died as a prisoner on Isle d'Yeu, off Brittany, on July 23.

PÉTAU, DENIS (1583–1652), theologian. Born in Orléans, France, he studied there and at Paris, taught philosophy in Bourges in 1602–5, and became a Jesuit. He taught at Rheims and La Flèche and was professor of theology at Paris from 1621 to 1643 and librarian from 1623. He wrote on history, philosophy, dogma, patristics, and chronology; important works include *De theologicis dogmatibus* (1644–50), *De doctrina temporum* (1627), *Tabulae chronologicae* (1628), *Rationarum temporum* (1633; a history of the world), *De Incarnatione Verbi*, and translations, particularly of St. Epiphanius (1622). He died in Paris on Dec. 11. He is also known as Dionysius Petavius.

PETAVIUS, DIONYSIUS. *See* Pétau, Denis.

PETER, ST. (d. 64?), pope and martyr. Born in Bethsaida, Simon, son of John, he was a fisherman who lived in Capharnauum on Lake Genesareth with his brother Andrew. Andrew, who had gone to the Jordan River to hear John the Baptist preach, introduced Simon to Christ, who renamed him Cephas (in Aramaic; Petros in Greek), a word meaning "rock." Peter was the first to acknowledge the Redeemer as "the Son of the living God," after which he was named head of the Church and was promised full authority over it (Matt. 16:13–20). He was involved in the miracle of the great catch of fish (Luke 5:1–11), was present at the Transfiguration (Matt. 17), at the Agony in the Garden (Matt. 26:36–46); all four evangelists (for example, Luke 22:31–62) have recorded his denial of Christ at His capture. Peter became a firm leader of the followers of Christ (John 21:15–19), presided over the early Church in the "upper room" in Jerusalem and presided at the selection of a successor to Judas (Acts 1:15–26; 2:14–36). He directed the disciples in baptizing those who flocked to hear them, performed his first miracle when he cured a man lame from birth, confirmed those whom Philip the Deacon had baptized, and crushed the magician Simon Magus. In the Acts of the Apostles

there are further details. He also converted the centurion Cornelius, was rebuked by St. Paul for making concessions to customs of the old law (Gal. 2), and was captured and imprisoned by Herod Agrippa I about 43, and released by an angel. He may have served as bishop of Antioch as early as 47. He then went to Rome, where he ruled as first bishop until his death, by crucifixion (according to Tertullian) with his head downward (a detail added by Origen), during the reign of Nero (54–68) in the arena of Nero's gardens at the foot of Vatican hill. He was buried nearby. Recent excavations under the main altar of St. Peter's have unearthed what is now generally agreed is the apostle's tomb. Human bones found in this tomb are now under intensive study in an attempt to ascertain if they are those of St. Peter. F. D. (with St. Paul) June 29. Peter's first epistle was written in 63; the second, close to the time of his death.

WILLIAM THOMAS WALSH, *St. Peter the Apostle* (Garden City, N.Y., Image Books, 1959).

PETER (d. 1046), king of Hungary. Son of the doge of Venice and the sister of St. Stephen, he succeeded to the throne in 1038, brought in German and Italian favorites, and aroused such hostility among the Hungarians that he was driven from the throne in 1041. For the next few years his brother-in-law Aba Samú occupied the throne, but Peter drove Aba Samú out. Peter himself was overthrown by a pagan uprising under Vatha in 1046, which massacred the Christians and destroyed their churches.

PETER, ST. (d. 251), martyr. When he refused to sacrifice to the pagan gods during the persecution of Decius, he was tortured and beheaded at Lampsacus, Mysia, on the Hellespont. SS. Andrew, Paul, and Dionysia are said to have been put to death at Troas, Cyzigus, shortly after, by the same official. F. D. May 15.

PETER, ST. (d. 260?), martyr. *See* Julian, St.

PETER, ST. (d. 269), martyr. *See* Lucius, St.

PETER, ST. (d. 303), martyr. *See* Gorgonius, St.

PETER, ST. (d. 309), Egyptian martyr. *See* Leucius, St.

PETER, ST. (d. 350?), bishop. Patron of Braga, Portugal, he is said to have been its first bishop, to have cured the local king's daughter of leprosy, and to have been martyred after he baptized her. F. D. Apr. 26.

PETER, ST. (5th century), martyr. *See* Aprhrodisius, St.

PETER, ST. (d. 610?). He was secretary to Pope St. Gregory the Great and is the patron of Salassola, Italy. The pope dedicated his *Dialogues* to him. F. D. Mar. 12.

PETER, ST. (d. 735?). He was bishop of Pavia, Italy. F. D. May 7.

PETER, ST. (d. 743), martyr. He was a scribe

at Majuma, Palestine, and was put to death there during an Arab persecution. F. D. Feb. 21.

PETER, ST. (d. 851), martyr. A priest in Cordova, Spain, he was beheaded by the Moorish governor after he had criticized Mohammed. With him died Habentius, a monk at St. Christopher; Jeremias, founder of the monastery of Tábanos; Sabinian and Wistremundus, monks at St. Zoilus; and Wallabonsus, a deacon. F. D. June 7.

PETER, ST. (d. 855), martyr. *See* Amator, St.

PETER, ST. (d. 900?), martyr. *See* Andrew, St.

PETER, ST. (d. 1060?). Born in Carsoli, Italy, he became a well-known preacher in Anagni, Tivoli, and Subiaco. He died in Trevi, Italy, and was canonized in 1215. F. D. Aug. 25.

PETER, ST. (d. 1109), bishop. A French Benedictine, he settled in Spain, followed the Cluniac observance, and became archbishop of Toledo and, in 1101, bishop of Osma. F. D. Aug. 2.

PETER, BL. (d. 1136). Born and educated in England, he set out on a pilgrimage to Rome with St. Stephen Harding. On their return, Stephen remained at Molesme. Peter later returned to this center, became a Benedictine priest, and was widely known as a preacher. In his last years he was chaplain at the convent at Juilly-les-Nonnais, France, where St. Bernard's sister, St. Humbelina, was prioress. F. D. June 23.

PETER, BL. (d. 1208). In 1195 he became the ninth abbot of the Benedictine monastery of Cava, Italy. He was beatified in 1928. F. D. Mar. 13.

PETER, ST. (d. 1220), martyr. *See* Berard, St.

PETER, BL. (1442–1490). Born in Mogliano, Italy, he studied law at Perugia, and in 1467 became a Franciscan Observant. He was the preaching companion of St. James della Marca and was vicar provincial of the Franciscan province of the Marches three times and of Rome once. He served as adviser to the duke of Camerino and was the confidant of his daughter, Bl. Baptista Varani. He died on July 25 and his cult was approved in 1760. F. D. July 30.

PETER, BL. (d. 1627), martyr. *See* Bertrán, Bl. Louis.

PETER, SARAH (1800–1877). Born in Chillicothe, Ohio, on May 10, daughter of Thomas Worthington, governor of that state, she married Edward King in 1816 and was widowed in 1836. She married William Peter, British consul in Philadelphia, in 1844, founded the School of Design for Women there, and returned to Cincinnati at his death in 1853. She became a Catholic in 1855, devoted herself to charity, helped establish foundations for several religious orders, and served as a nurse during the Civil War. She died in Cincinnati, Ohio, on Feb. 6.

PETER ACOTANTO, BL. (d. 1180?). Born in Venice, he devoted his life to caring for the sick and became a recluse in his last few years. His cult was approved by Pope Clement VIII. F. D. Sept. 23.

PETER OF ALCÁNTARA, ST. (1499–1562), mystic. Pedro Garavito was born in Alcántara, Spain, son of the governor, studied law at Salamanca, became a Franciscan Observant at sixteen, and was ordained in 1524. He held offices in his order at Robredillo, Plasencia, Lapa, and Estremadura. When he was defeated at the provincial chapter in Plasencia in 1540 in his attempt to impose stricter rules, he resigned and lived as a hermit with Friar Martin of St. Mary on a mountain near Lisbon. In 1554 he secured papal permission to build a friary near Pedrosa, where he installed the strictest rule in 1555. The monks there became known as Alcantarines and in 1561 were made into the province of St. Joseph under the Observants, which drew much censure from the Conventuals. In 1560 he met St. Teresa at Avila, became her confessor, and encouraged her in reforming the Carmelites. His life was one of great austerity and penance and was marked by supernatural occurrences. His *Treatise on Prayer and Meditation* was widely used by St. Francis de Sales. He died in Arenas, Spain, on Oct. 18 and was canonized in 1669. F.D. Oct. 19.

PETER OF ALEXANDRIA, ST. (d. 311), bishop and martyr. Born in Alexandria, Egypt, he became head of the catechetical school there, and was renowned for his knowledge of scripture. He became patriarch of Alexandria in 300, promulgated decrees for receiving relapsed heretics back to the Church, excommunicated Bishop Meletius of Lycopolis for remaining in schism, and fought the rising errors of Origen and Arius. He was forced into hiding during the Diocletian persecution, ruling his see from exile. When he returned to Alexandria, he was seized and put to death there. F. D. Nov. 26.

PETER APSELAMUS. *See* Peter Balsam, St.

PETER OF AQUILA (d. 1361), bishop. Born in Aquila, Abruzzi, Italy, he joined the Friars Minor and became provincial of Tuscany. He was appointed confessor of Queen Joan I of Naples in 1334, inquisitor of Florence, bishop of San Angelo de Lombardi in 1347, and was transferred to Trivento the following year. He wrote commentaries on the *Sentences* of Duns Scotus, and was surnamed Scotellus for his knowledge of Scotus' works. He died in Trivento, Italy.

PETER ARMENGOL, BL. (1238?–1304). Member of a noble Catalonian family, he is said in an extravagant story to have become an outlaw, almost killing his father in an ambush, whereupon he joined the Mercedarians. He twice went from Spain to Africa to redeem captives; held as a hostage, he was hanged, but found to be alive by another missioner who had been delayed. He continued his work of rescuing Christians from the Moors for ten more years. He died near Tarragona, Spain. F. D. Apr. 27.

PETER OF THE ASSUMPTION, BL. (d. 1617), martyr. Born in Cuerva, near Toledo, Spain, he was sent to Japan in 1601 with fifty Franciscans whom he directed at a friary in Nagasaki. He was beheaded there for his faith, and was beatified in 1867. F. D. May 22.

PETER OF ATROA, ST. (773–837). Born near Ephesus, Asia Minor, and christened Theophylact, he became a monk in Phrygia at eighteen, taking the name Peter, and was superior of the monastery of St. Zachary near Atroa when he was thirty-two. Persecution by the Iconoclasts drove him into exile on two occasions, once for fifteen years. F. D. Jan. 1.

PETER OF AUVERGNE (d. 1310?), theologian. A canon of Paris and probably a student of St. Thomas Aquinas, he was appointed rector of the university by the papal legate in 1279 and elected to that office in 1296. He wrote theological treatises and was thought by some authorities to have written a supplement to St. Thomas' *Summa.*

PETER OF AVILA, BL. (1562–1622), martyr. Born in Palomares, Castile, Spain, he became a Franciscan, went to the Philippines and to Japan in 1617 with Bl. Louis Sotelo, and was burned alive in Nagasaki, Japan. He was beatified in 1867. F. D. Sept. 10.

PETER BALSAM, ST. (d. 311?), martyr. A native of Eleutheropolis, he was buried alive in Palestine. Eusebius calls him Peter Absalamus and says that he was burned to death on Jan. 11. A St. Peter Apselamus (or Balsamus) was crucified in Aulana, near Hebron, about 291. F. D. Jan. 3.

PETER BAPTIST, ST. (1545–1597), martyr. Born near Avila, Spain, he became a Franciscan in 1567, served in Mexico and the Philippines, and was executed with twenty-six other Christians in Japan. The victims of the mass martyrdom were publicly and scornfully put on exhibition in various villages before they were crucified and speared to death. Among them were Frs. Martin de Aguirre, Francis Blanco, and Philip de las Casas; a Franciscan laybrother, Francis of St. Michael; Gonsalo Garcia, an Indian convert who had become a Franciscan; Caius Francis, a Japanese soldier and Franciscan tertiary; Francis of Miako, a native doctor and Franciscan tertiary; Leo Karasuma, the first Korean to become a Franciscan tertiary; and three altar boys named Antony Deynan, Louis Ibarki, and Thomas Kasak. The group was canonized in 1862. F. D. Feb. 5.

PETER BECCHETTI (13th century). *See* John Bechetti.

PETER OF BERGAMO. *See* Almadura, Pietro.

PETER OF BLOIS (1135?–1208?), diplomat. Born in Blois, France, he studied at Tours, probably under John of Salisbury at Paris, law at Bologna, and returned to France to teach. In 1167 he went to Sicily as tutor to King William II and counselor to his queen, left in 1169 and traveled in France, and went to England about 1173 and entered the service of King Henry II, becoming his chief counselor. He was the archbishop of Canterbury's chancellor from 1176 to 1189, was sent to Rome in 1177 to plead against the monks of that diocese, and again in 1187. After Henry's death he served as secretary to Queen Eleanor of Aquitaine until 1195. He wrote historically important letters, ascetical treatises, scriptural commentaries, a continuation of the history of Croyland monastery, attacks on the morals of the English clergy and the lack of faith among the leading crusaders, and a history of Catholicism which Pope Alexander III sent to the sultan of Iconium.

PETER CANISIUS. *See* Canisius, St. Peter.

PETER OF CANTERBURY, ST. (d. 606). A Benedictine, he was sent from Rome by Pope St. Gregory the Great on the first mission to England, became abbot of the monastery of SS. Peter and Paul at Canterbury, and was drowned near Boulogne while on a mission to France. F. D. Jan. 6.

PETER OF CASTELNAU, BL. (d. 1208), martyr. Born near Montpellier, France, he became in 1199 archdeacon at Maguelone. He became a Cistercian about 1202 and was appointed inquisitor of the Albigensians in 1203 by Pope Innocent III. He was assassinated by a lance at the instigation of Raymund VI of Toulouse. F. D. Jan. 15.

PETER CELLENSIS (d. 1183), bishop. Born in Champagne, France, he studied at St. Martin-des-Champs, Paris, became a Benedictine, and was made abbot of La Celle in 1150 and of St. Remy's, Rheims, in 1162. He was appointed bishop of Chartres, France, in 1181 and died there on Feb. 20. Sermons, a biblical commentary, and a study of conscience are among his publications.

PETER OF CHAVANON, ST. (1003–1080). Born in Langeac, France, he became a secular priest there, then founded a monastery of Augustinian canons regular at Pébrac in Auvergne and became its first provost. He died on Sept. 9. F. D. Sept. 11.

PETER CHRYSOLOGUS, ST. (406–450?), Doctor of the Church. Born in Imola, Italy, he studied there under Bishop Cornelius, who ordained him. About 433, according to legend, at the insistence of Pope St. Sixtus III he was elected archbishop of Ravenna and devoted himself to eradicating paganism and reforming his diocese. He achieved a great reputation for his eloquence in preaching (*chrysologus* means "the golden-voiced"), and many of his homilies are still extant. He died in Imola on Dec. 2, and was declared a Doctor of the Church by Pope Benedict XIII in 1729. F. D. Dec. 4.

PETER COMESTOR (d. 1178?). A priest at Notre Dame in Troyes, France, he became dean of the chapter about 1148, was a member of the chapter of Notre Dame in Paris in 1160 and shortly after became chancellor, and was put in charge of the theological school in 1164. Toward the end of his life he retired to St. Victor abbey, Paris, became a canon, and died there. He was widely regarded as a great scholar, wrote commentaries and allegories on scripture and *Historia scholastica,* a sacred history which enjoyed great vogue for three centuries.

PETER OF DAMASCUS, ST. (d. 750?), martyr. A bishop in Damascus, he was maimed, blinded, tied to a cross, and beheaded by Arabs for preaching against Mohammedanism. F. D. Oct. 4.

PETER DAMIAN, ST. (1007–1072), bishop, Doctor of the Church. Born in Ravenna, Italy, he was mistreated by a brother as a young orphan, and rescued by another brother who sent him to Parma to be educated. He became a Benedictine at Fonte Avellana after a time as teacher, ascetic, and apostle to the poor. He continued his austere customs in the monastery, but illness turned him to the intense study of scripture. He became abbot, unwillingly, in 1043, founded five hermitages, and was appointed bishop of Ostia and a cardinal by Pope Stephen IX in 1057. Relieved of his diocese by Alexander II, he returned to the life of a monk and wrote considerable Latin poetry and numerous tracts which demanded closer attention to penance and humility on the part of clerics and attention to the letter of the vow of poverty. He fought simony, clerical marriage, monastic wandering, and was forerunner of the Hildebrandine reforms. He died in Faenza, Italy, on his return from a papal mission. He was declared a Doctor of the Church in 1828. F. D. Feb. 23.

O. J. BLUM, *St. Peter Damian* (Washington, D.C., Catholic Univ., 1947).

PETER GONZALEZ, BL. (1190–1246). Born in Asturga, Spain, he was appointed a canon by his uncle, a bishop, then became a Dominican, effective as a preacher and as confessor to King Ferdinand III. He reformed much of the court, preached a crusade against the Moors, and obtained kind treatment for captives after the taking of Seville and Cordova. He then preached through Galicia, paying particular attention to mariners, by whom he was later to be venerated as St. Elmo. He died at Tuy, Spain, in 1741. His cult was confirmed by Pope Benedict XIV. F. D. Apr. 14.

PETER OF GUBBIO, BL. (d. 1250?). A member of the Ghisengi family, he became provincial of the Brictinian Hermits of St. Augustine, and was venerated at a shrine in Gubbio, Italy. F. D. Mar. 23.

PETER THE HERMIT (1050?–1115). Born in Amiens, France, he became a hermit, and allegedly went to the Holy Land, where he suffered the indignities heaped on pilgrims, and returned convinced that he was to be a great leader. He was one of very many who preached the crusade proclaimed in 1095 by Pope Urban II at the Council of Clermont. He led a group to Turkey which was annihilated near Nicaea while he was absent in Constantinople, handed the remaining force over to Godfrey of Bouillon, and later served as one of the envoys to King Kerbûga of Mosul. On his return he founded Neumoutier monastery, at Huy, Flanders, where he died on July 8. He long was venerated by a popular cult.

PETER HOSDENC (d. 1197), theologian. Born probably in Gisberoi, France, he studied and taught in Rheims, became a canon and cantor of its cathedral, and is often called Petrus Cantor. He taught theology at the Paris cathedral school in 1170, was cantor there in 1180, acted as papal judge at Troyes in 1188 and at Compiègne in 1196 and 1197, and was elected dean of the cathedral chapter in Rheims in 1196. He died at Long Pont abbey, near Laon, France, on Sept. 22 while on his way to the new post. He wrote scriptural commentaries, with valuable notes on the gospels and the Apocalypse, and *Summa de sacramentis,* with important details on mediaeval penance.

PETER IGNEUS, BL. (d. 1089), bishop. A monk of the order of Vallombrosa, he was made cardinal bishop of Albano, Italy, by Pope Gregory VII and became his legate to France and Germany. F. D. Feb. 8.

PETER LOMBARD (1100?–1160?), theologian. Born in Lumello (or Novara), Italy, he studied at Bologna, Rheims under St. Bernard, and Paris where he heard Abelard, whose writings had great influence on him. He was teaching at the cathedral school of Notre Dame in 1145–50 when he wrote *Sententiarum Libri IV.* This *Book of Sentences,* which earned him the title *magister,* was compiled from scripture and the Fathers of the Church (especially St. Augustine), Gratian's *Decretum,* and the work of Abelard, Alger of Liège, and Ivo of Chartres. It discussed the corpus of Christian doctrine in the form of questions and answers in which traditional dogma and theories were systematically arranged and controversies and opinions of the period summarized in the questions. It became the most famous theological work of the Middle Ages, the essential text for every university, and a work which called forth commentaries by all theologians of consequence. He also wrote commentaries on St. Paul and the Psalms and a series of sermons. He was appointed archbishop of Paris in 1158 or 1159, but resigned within a year or so and died sometime between 1160 and 1164.

PETER OF LUXEMBOURG, BL. (1369–1387), cardinal. Born in Lorraine of a noble family, he was orphaned at four, was taken to Paris, and in 1380–81 was held hostage for his older brother's ransom. Clement VII, antipope at Avignon, nominated him as bishop of Metz at fourteen, and as cardinal at sixteen, though he was only a deacon. He made many reforms, but because of political conditions joined Clement at Avignon, where his charity and austerities were widely recognized. He died at Villeneuve, France, and was beatified in 1527. F. D. July 2.

PETER MARTINEZ, ST. (d. 1000?), archbishop. Also known as Peter of Monzonzo, he was born in Spanish Galicia, became a Benedictine at St. Mary of Monzonzo abbey about 950, later was abbot of St. Martin de Antealtares in Compostella, Spain, and about 986 became archbishop of that city. He played a heroic part in the reconquest of Spain, and is one of those to whom the authorship of the *Salve Regina* is attributed. F. D. Sept. 10.

PETER DE MONTBOISSIER (1092?–1156). Born in Auvergne, France, he became a Benedictine monk at Cluny in 1109, prior of Vézelay at twenty, and in 1122 abbot of Cluny. St. Bernard of Clairvaux accused Cluny of general laxness. Peter met this charge by instituting spiritual, intellectual, and financial reforms which led to Cluny becoming again the greatest abbey in Europe. He gave Abelard sanctuary at Cluny, caused the pope to lighten his sentence, and reconciled him and St. Bernard. He corresponded widely, wrote against the Petrobrusian heresy, was a theological writer of distinction, composed poems and hymns (of which *Caelum, gaude, terra, plaude,* is best known) and had Latin translations of the Koran and Arabian astronomical works made. He died on Christmas Day. His cult has never been formally approved, but his feast is observed in the diocese of Arras on Dec. 29.

PETER OF MONZONZO. *See* Peter Martinez, St.

PETER OF MT. ATHOS, ST. (8th century?). He is said to have been the first Christian recluse to settle in the region of Mt. Athos in Macedonia and to have lived there for fifty years. Other biographical details are legendary. F. D. June 12.

PETER NOLASCO, ST. (1189?–1258), founder. With the Dominican St. Raymond of Peñafort, his spiritual director, he worked long and compassionately for the great number of Christians who had been tyrannized or enslaved by the Moors. At some time between 1222 and 1234 he proposed the organization of the Order of Our Lady of Ransom (Mercedarians), which is said to have been developed

from plans of St. Raymond. They are called co-founders, and the latter preached at Peter's vow ceremony. Pope Gregory IX approved the foundation, and King James of Aragon lent his earnest support. Members of the order traveled throughout the Moorish world, with Peter quite a successful convert-maker in Spain and Africa, although he was imprisoned in Algiers. He died in Barcelona, Spain, on Dec. 25, and was canonized in 1628. F. D. Jan. 28.

PETER ORSEOLO, ST. (928–987). At twenty he commanded a fleet against the pirates of the Adriatic; at forty-eight he replaced the slain Peter Candiani as doge of Venice after a civil uprising in which much of the city was burned. Some say he was responsible for the murder and for the fire; others point to his restoration of the ruins, his settlement of the claims of his predecessor's widow, and his reputation for holiness and competent statesmanship. Two years later, probably with his wife's consent, he retired to a private hermitage at the Benedictine abbey of Cuxa, France, where he spent the rest of his days in strict asceticism. F. D. Jan. 10.

PETER PAPPACARBONE, ST. (d. 1123), bishop. Born in Salerno, Italy, he entered the Benedictine monastery of Cava, which had been founded by his uncle, St. Alferius. In 1062 he went to Cluny, and in 1079 was recalled and made first bishop of Policastro, but was released with permission after a few months and became abbot at Cava, Italy. In time he was able to introduce the strict Cluniac reforms, which attracted large numbers of vocations; Peter himself accepted over 3000. F. D. Mar. 4.

PETER PARENZI, ST. (d. 1199), martyr. Born in Rome, he was papally appointed governor of Orvieto, Italy, in 1199 to put an end to the Catharist heresy, but was seized and viciously put to death because of his strictures. F. D. May 22.

PETER OF POITIERS (12th century). A disciple of Peter Abelard, he defended his master in a letter to St. Bernard and was driven into the mountains near Cévennes. He lived there in isolation, complaining in angry letters to the bishop of Mende, violently attacking the Carthusians, insisting that Abelard was not guilty of formal heresy, and professing his own adherence to Catholic dogma. He is also known as Pierre Bérenger.

PETER OF POITIERS (1130?–1215), theologian. Born in Poitiers, France, he studied at Paris, where he became professor of theology and taught for thirty-eight years. In 1169 he succeeded Peter Comestor in the chair of scholastic theology; he became chancellor, and in 1191 was appointed by Pope Celestine III arbiter of a dispute between St. Eloi and St. Victor abbeys. In 1179 he published a synopsis of his popular and clever lectures; he also wrote scriptural commentaries. He died in Paris.

PETER REGALATUS, ST. (1392–1456). Born in Valladolid, Spain, he became a Franciscan at thirteen, reformed several communities, paid zealous attention to the rule, and lived an extremely austere life. He died at Aguilar on Mar. 30. F. D. May 13 (sometimes, Mar. 30).

PETER OF SASSOFERRATO, BL. (d. 1231), martyr. *See* John of Perugia, Bl.

PETER OF SEBASTE, ST. (340?–391), bishop. Youngest of ten children of SS. Basil the Elder and Emmilia, he was the brother of SS. Basil, Gregory of Nyssa, and Macrina, and the grandson of St. Macrina the Elder. He was brought up in religious studies by his sister, then joined his brother Basil in a monastery in Armenia. Peter succeeded him as superior in 362, was ordained in 370, and became bishop of Sebaste ten years later. He was particularly active against the Arians, attended the Council of Constantinople (381), and was long commemorated for his charity, humility, and philosophical and oratorical brilliance. F. D. Jan. 9.

PETER OF SIENA, BL. (d. 1321), martyr. *See* Thomas of Tolentino, Bl.

PETER OF TARENTAISE, ST. (1102–1175), archbishop. Born near Vienne, France, he joined the Cistercians at the abbey of Bonnevaux at twelve; his two brothers and father followed him later. At thirty he was abbot of a new house at Tamié, between Geneva and Savoy; there he built a hospice. He succeeded the deposed archbishop of Tarentaise in 1142 and thoroughly reformed an area which had fallen to pieces, even finding it necessary to replace a corrupt clergy, which he did by bringing in Augustinian canons regular. After thirteen years of personal attention to ecclesiastical and charitable needs, he disappeared, living as a laybrother at a Cistercian abbey in Switzerland until found and ordered back to his see. From it he went to preach in Italy and France against Emperor Frederick Barbarossa's support of the antipope, Victor, throwing the weight of his order on the side of the true pope, Alexander III. He died at Besançon, France, on his return from a futile attempt to reconcile Kings Louis VII of France and Henry II of England, although peace followed at his death. He was canonized in 1191. F. D. May 8.

PETER TECELANO, BL. (d. 1289). A combmaker in Tuscany, he became a Franciscan laybrother after the death of his wife and was known as a mystic. His cult was approved in 1802. F. D. Dec. 11.

PETER THOMAS, ST. (1305–1366). Born in Salles, France, he became a Carmelite, rising to the office of procurator general in 1342, directing the order from Avignon. He became a papal diplomat, negotiating with the Italian city-states, presiding as bishop at Milan at the coronation of Emperor Charles IV as king of Italy, and journeying into Serbia and Hungary. He was appointed bishop of Patti and Lipari in 1354, of Coron in 1359, archbishop of Candia in 1363, and titular Latin patriarch of Constantinople in 1364. In 1359 he led a military expedition to Constantinople as papal legate, and in 1365 led a disastrous military force against the pagan, Alexandria. Severely wounded, he died shortly after, on Jan. 6, in Cyprus. His cult was approved in 1608. F. D. Jan. 28.

PETER OF TREIA, BL. (d. 1304). Born in Montecchio, he received his habit from St. Francis of Assisi, was ordained, and worked at Torano and elsewhere in Italy with Bl. Conrad of Offida. His cult was approved in 1793. F. D. Feb. 17.

PETER OF VERONA, ST. (1205?–1252), martyr. Born in Verona, Italy, he studied at Bologna, and became a Dominican at the hands of St. Dominic. He preached with astonishing success in Lombardy, bringing many into the Church, and in 1234 Pope Gregory IX appointed him inquisitor general for all of northern Italy. He continued to be successful until he was assassinated on Apr. 6, while on his way north from Como. His companion, Bro. Dominic, also beaten, died a few days later; their murderer, Carino, repented and became a Dominican laybrother at Forlì. The murder was a popular theme for Fra Angelico and many other painters. F. D. Apr. 29.

PETER VINCIOLI, ST. (d. 1007). Born near Perugia, Italy, of a noble family, he founded the Benedictine abbey of St. Peter there and became its first abbot. F. D. July 10.

PETERS, JOHANN (14th century). A German officer in the papal guard, he, with his wife, erected a shelter for German pilgrims in 1350, which was developed into Santa Maria dell' Anima in 1386. The present church was built early in the sixteenth century, shortly after the founding of Anima College for priests.

PETERSON, JOHN BERTRAM (1871–1944), bishop. Born in Salem, Massachusetts, on July 15, he studied at St. Anselm's College, New Hampshire, St. John's seminary, Brighton, and was ordained in 1899. After further study at Catholic University, Paris, and the French School of History, Rome, he taught at St. John's seminary in 1901–12 and was rector in 1912–26. He served on diocesan committees, was made a domestic prelate in 1915, and was consecrated titular bishop of Hippo and auxiliary of Boston in 1927. He was appointed bishop of Manchester, New Hampshire, in 1932, and died on Mar. 15.

PETERSSEN, GERLAC (1377?–1411). Born

in Deventer, Holland, he joined the Brethren of the Common Life as a manuscript copyist, followed Florent Radewyn to his new monastery of regular canons at Windhejheim in 1386, remained there as a simple clerk until 1403, and wrote several spiritual treatises. The theory that Thomas à Kempis used many of his ideas in *Imitation of Christ* has long since been disproved.

PETIT-DIDIER, JEAN JOSEPH (1664–1758), theologian. Born in St. Nicholas-du-Port, Lorraine, on Oct. 23, brother of Matthieu, he became a Jesuit in 1683 and taught at Strassburg in 1694–1701 and at Pont-à-Mousson in 1704–8. He was spiritual director of Duchess Elizabeth Charlotte of Lorraine in 1730, but returned to the Jesuit house in St. Nicholas, where he remained until his death on Aug. 10 in Pont-à-Mousson. He wrote a study of justice and the law, a refutation of Jansenism, and on SS. Francis Xavier and John Francis Regis.

PETIT-DIDIER, MATTHIEU (1659–1728), theologian. Born in St. Nicholas-du-Port, Lorraine, on Dec. 18, he studied at Nancy, became a Benedictine in 1675, professor of theology at St. Mihiel in 1682, and abbot of Senones in 1715. He was elected president of his congregation in 1723, made titular bishop of Acra in 1725, and wrote theological treatises and a study of papal infallibility (1724) banned by the Jansenists. He died in Senones, Lorraine, on July (or June) 15.

PETITOT, HENRI (1880–1934), scholar. Born in Armentières, France, on Aug. 2, he studied there, became a Dominican, was ordained, served in the army during World War I, and was stationed in Amiens and Nancy houses, returning to Nancy as prior. After 1927 he was at St. Honoré, Paris, where he died on Oct. 4. He wrote *Introduction à la philosophie traditionelle ou classique*, studies of Pascal and Mère Marie de Jésus, biographies of SS. Thomas Aquinas, Joan of Arc, and Thérèse of Liseux, and on mystical theology: *La Doctrine ascétique de mystique intégrale* and *L'Introduction a la sainteté*.

PETRARCH (1304–1374), poet. Francesco di Petracco was born in Arezzo, Italy, on July 20, son of Ser Petracco, a friend of Dante and a notary at the Florentine court of the Riformagione who was expelled from Florence in 1302, as a White Guelph, to Arezzo, to Pisa in 1310, and then Avignon in 1313. Francesco studied the humanities under Convennole of Prato at Carpentras from 1315 to 1319, law at Montpellier and Bologna, and returned to Avignon on his father's death in 1326 and took minor orders. He gave up law for literature, embarked on the fashionable life of Avignon, and in 1327 saw Laura (probably the wife of Hugues de Sade), who was to be the

inspiration of so much of his poetry. He entered the service of Cardinal Colonna, was made a canon, traveled in Europe in 1330–37, and settled in Vaucluse, Italy. He began a Latin history of Rome, which he abandoned to write *Africa*, a Latin epic on the Punic wars. The fame of his learning and genius spread, and sovereigns competed to bring him to their courts. In 1341 he received the laurel crown of poet from the Roman senate, spent the next few years traveling through Italy in search of manuscripts (he discovered several of Cicero's and Quintilian's), and formed close friendships with Boccaccio and with Cola d' Rienzi, whom he accompanied on an embassy from the Romans to Pope Clement VI to persuade the pontiff to return to Rome. In 1348 his patron, Cardinal Colonna, and Laura both died of the plague. He was in the service of Lord Visconti of Milan from 1350 to 1360, serving on diplomatic missions to the German emperor, Venice, and the French king. He retired to Arqua, north of Padua, Italy, in 1370, and died there on July 19. Although his Latin works (which he felt represented his greatest work) are outstanding, he achieved his greatest fame in his Italian verse, particularly in *Trionfi*, and *Canzoniere*, which contains remarkably exquisite and finished sonnets, madrigals, and songs. Among his other works are *Carmen, bucolicum, Epistolae metricae, De contemptu mundi, De vita solitaria, De viris illustribus, De ocio religiosorum*, and letters.

PETRE, EDWARD (1631–1699). Born in London, he studied at St. Omer, joined the Jesuits in 1671, was imprisoned for a year in Newgate at the time of the Titus Oates Plot, succeeded to his title on his brother's death in 1679, and in 1680 was arrested when he was appointed Catholic rector of the London district. He was freed in 1683, and two years later became confessor of King James II, who made him a clerk of the closet. His influence over the king made Petre extremely unpopular, and James's request in 1685 to Pope Innocent XI to appoint Petre a bishop (and in 1686, a cardinal) led to much acrimonious correspondence when the pope refused. In 1687 the king's appointment of Petre as privy councilor aroused violent opposition, and he was the subject of libelous attacks. He was forced to flee abroad when the revolution broke out in 1688, and became rector of St. Omer, France, in 1693.

PETROC, ST. (6th century). Possibly the son of a Welsh chieftain who studied in Ireland, he settled at Lanwethinoc (later called Padstow) Cornwall, with Bishop Wethinoc, possibly for thirty years, then traveled to the Holy Land and perhaps the Far East, returned and set up a chapel and mill at Bodmin for a number of fellow hermits. There are an amazing number of fantastic legends, including one in which Petroc (also called Pedrog and Perreux) tamed a dragon which was suffering from a splinter in his eye. F. D. June 4.

PETRONAX, ST. (d. 747?). Born in Brescia, Italy, he visited the tomb of St. Benedict in 717, met a number of hermits living amid the ruins of the monastery destroyed by the Lombards, stayed as their superior, and with gifts from the duke of Beneventum and three popes rebuilt Monte Cassino, SS. Willibald and Sturmius were both there during his long rule. F. D. May 6.

PETRONI, BL. PEDRO (1311–1361). Born in Siena, Italy, he became a Carthusian at the monastery of Maggiano at seventeen, received numerous supernatural gifts, and was instrumental in bringing about the spiritual reformation of Boccaccio, as the latter affirms in letter to Petrarch. F. D. May 29.

PETRONILA (d. 1162), queen of Aragon. Daughter of Ramiro II, she was betrothed almost at birth to Ramón Berenguer IV, count of Catalonia, and became queen in 1137.

PETRONILLA, ST. (d. 251?), martyr. Born in Rome, she is said to have been slain when she refused to marry Flaccus, a nobleman; an early Roman fresco portrays her martyrdom; legends and gnostic apocrypha erroneously called her the daughter of St. Peter the Apostle. F. D. May 31.

PETRONILLA, BL. (d. 1355). Descended from the counts of Troyes, she became the first abbess of the convent of Poor Clares at Le Moncel, France, and was their patron until the order was dispersed during the French Revolution. F. D. May 14.

PETRONILLA OF CHEMILLÉ (1115–1149). She was the first abbess of the powerful double monastery of Fontevrault, France, founded by St. Robert d'Arbrissel, and having a community of 3000 nuns at the time of his death in 1117.

PETRONIUS, ST. (d. 445?), bishop. Probably the son of a Roman official in Gaul, he was made bishop of Bologna, Italy, about 432 and is said to have built the monastery of St. Stephen there. F. D. Oct. 4.

PETRONIUS, ST. (d. 450?). He was bishop of Verona, Italy, in the mid-fifth century. F. D. Sept. 6.

PETRONIUS, ST. (d. 463?). Son of a senator at Avignon, he was bishop of Dié, France, from about 456 to 463. F. D. Jan. 10.

PETRUCCI, BL. GIOVANNI BATISTA (d. 1420), martyr. *See* Cennini, Bl. Agostino.

PETRUCCI, OTTAVIANO DE' (1466–1539), printer. Born in Fossombrone, Italy, on June 18, he studied printing, secured a twenty-year patent from the city of Venice in 1498 for the development of printing music from movable type, and turned his shop over

to two colleagues, Amadeo Scotti and Niccolò da Rafael, in 1511. He operated a music press in Fossombrone from 1513 to 1523, and received a fifteen-year license to print from the Papal States. He perfected the process of printing mensural and polyphonic music from movable type. He died in Fossombrone on May 7.

PETRUS ALFONSUS (1062–1110). Moses Sephardi, a Jew in Huesca, Aragon, Spain, became physician to King Alfonso I, who was his godfather when Sephardi was converted. He wrote a justification of his conversion in 1106 in the form of twelve dialogues between a Christian and a Jew and *Disciplina clericalis*, both of which have frequently been translated.

PETRUS AUREOLI (1280–1322?), archbishop. A Franciscan at Toulouse, France, probably his native city, he taught theology there and at Paris, and became provincial of Aquitaine in 1319 and archbishop of Aix in 1321. He wrote sermons, commentaries on Peter Lombard and St. Bernard, and introduction to scripture, and a defense of the doctrine of the Immaculate Conception. In philosophy he was an anti-Thomist and a forerunner of Occam.

PETRUS CANTOR. *See* Peter Hosdenc.

PETRUS DIACONUS (6th century). A Scythian monk, he went to Rome in 519 to appeal to Pope Hormisdas over the Theopaschite controversy about which he wrote *De incarnatione et gratia*.

PETRUS DIACONUS (d. 605?). He was a follower of Gregory the Great whose questioning led the pope to write his *Dialogues*.

PETRUS DIACONUS (d. 960?). Also surnamed Subdiaconus, he was a monk at Monte Cassino, became subdeacon of St. Januarius in Naples, Italy, and wrote the lives of several saints and continued a history of the Naples diocese.

PETRUS DIACONUS (1107?–1140). Born in Rome, a descendant of the counts of Tusculum, he was sent to Monte Cassino in 1115, became a monk, and left to follow Abbot Oderisius to Atina about 1127. He returned in 1137, became Emperor Lothair II's chaplain and secretary when he appeared before him on the abbey's business, and on his return became librarian and archivist. He wrote several historical works, continued the history of Monte Cassino from 1075 to 1138, and forged the *Passion of St. Placidus* under the name of Gordian.

PETRUS DE NATALIBUS (d. 1400?). A native of Venice, Italy, he became bishop of Equilio in 1370, and was the author of a long-popular *Legends of the Saints*.

PEUERBACH, GEORGE VON (1423–1461), astronomer. Born in Peuerbach, Austria, on May 30, he received his master's degree in philosophy from Vienna about 1440, lectured on astronomy at Ferrera while on a trip to Italy in 1448, refused professorships at Bologna and Padua, and returned in 1450 to lecture at Vienna, where he died on Apr. 8. He is generally considered the founder of Western astronomical observation, provided the first transition from the duodecimal to the decimal system in his revision of Ptolemy's *Amalgest,* and wrote a score of astronomical treatises, chief of which was *Theoricae novae planetarum,* which became the basic text in the study of astronomy until Copernicus' time.

PEUTINGER, KONRAD (1465–1547), antiquarian. Born in Augsburg, Germany, on Oct. 14, he studied at Padua, Bologna, and Florence, became interested in antiquities while in Rome, returned to Germany in 1490, and became a syndic in Augsburg in 1497. He became a counselor of Emperor Maximilian, for whom he carried out several diplomatic missions, notably negotiations with the Hungarians in 1506 and with the Venetians in 1512, encouraged the arts and literature, and built up an outstanding collection of manuscripts, statues, coins, and inscriptions. He represented Augsburg at the Diet of Worms in 1521, was at first sympathetic to Luther, but changed his view and retired from the diet in opposition to attempts to establish Protestantism. He published a history of the Goths by Jordanes and of the Langobards by Paulus Diaconus, and issued *Romanae vestustatis fragmenta* (1505), a collection of Roman inscriptions. He was made a patrician in 1528 and a noble a short time before his death in Augsburg on Dec. 28.

PEYTO, WILLIAM (d. 1558?), cardinal. Born in Warwickshire, England, he studied at Cambridge, became a Franciscan, and was confessor to Princess Mary. He was provincial of England, was imprisoned in 1532 when he denounced Henry VIII's divorce to the king's face, and went to Europe after his release. He was appointed bishop of Salisbury in 1543 by Pope Paul III, but never occupied his see, resigning in 1553 and retiring to a monastery in Chelsea. He was created cardinal in 1557. He died either in France or, according to Franciscan tradition, in London of injuries suffered when he was stoned by a mob.

PEZ, BERNHARD (1683–1735), historian. Born in Ybbs, Austria, on Feb. 22, he studied in Vienna and Krems, and became a Benedictine in 1699 at the Melk monastery, where he taught in 1704 and was ordained in 1708. He became librarian there in 1713, and in 1715–17 visited his order's houses in Austria, Bavaria, and Swabia in search of manuscripts, and in 1728 went to France for the same purpose. He compiled *Thesaurus anecdotorum novissimus* and *Bibliotheca ascetica,* edited the homilies of Gottfried von Admont, and wrote a defense of

his order. He died in Melk, Hungary, on Mar. 27.

PEZ, HIERONYMUS (1685–1762). Born in Ybbs, Austria, on Oct. 14, he became a Benedictine in 1703, was ordained in 1711, was an assistant to his brother, Bernhard, and succeeded him as librarian at Melk, Hungary, where he died on Oct. 14. His chief works were the collections of sources of Austrian history, *Scriptores rerum Austriacarum,* and a history of St. Leopold.

PEZAINÉ. *See* Perseveranda, St.

PFALZ-NEUBERG, FRANZ LUDWIG (d. 1732). Brother of Count Palatine Wolfgang, he became bishop of Worms and bishop of Breslau, Silesia, in 1683. He also was grand master of the German Knights, provost of Ellwangen, and elector of Trèves and of Mainz. He separated the civil and ecclesiastical courts in Breslau, defined the extent of jurisdiction of the consistory and vicar general, and tried to keep the diocese together when the death of the last duke of Liegnitz-Brieg-Wolhau led to a claim by King Charles XII of Sweden to church land and buildings.

PFANNER, FRANZ (1825–1909), missioner. Born in Langen, Austria, he was ordained in 1850, served as a curate, was chaplain to the Sisters of Mercy in Agram, and became a Trappist in 1864. He reorganized the Tre Fontane monastery in Rome in 1866, established a Trappist foundation in Mariastern, Bosnia, in 1869, of which he became abbot, and in 1880 went to Cape Colony, South Africa. He settled at Dunbrody, and then established Marianhill monastery, Natal, and founded the Sisters of the Precious Blood in 1885 to teach Kafir girls; the order was papally approved in 1907. He established seven mission stations, was first abbot of Marianhill in 1885–93 and spent the rest of his life in the mission at Emmaus, South Africa, where he died on May 24.

PFEFFERKORN, JOHANNES (1469?–1521?). Probably a native of Nuremberg, Germany, he was a Jew who became a convert in 1505, but went to extremes in his writings, his attempts to have all Jewish writings destroyed, and his violent controversy wih Jacob Reuchlin. He died in Cologne, Germany, before 1524.

PFISTER, ADOLF (1810–1878), educator. Born in Hechingen, Germany, on Sept. 26, he studied there and in the Strassburg seminary, and was ordained in 1833. He served as curate and pastor in several communities and became school inspector in Ehingen in 1851. He founded and edited *Rottenburger Kirchenblatt* (1857–60), edited *Katholisches Schulwochenblatt* from 1860 under various titles (as *Magazin für Pedagogik* from 1868 to 1872), and with Hermann Rolfus edited *Real-Encyclopädie des Erziehungs- und Unterrichtswesens* *nach katholischen Principien* (1863–66). He wrote educational treatises and translated Thomas à Kempis before his death in Ober-Dischingen, Würtemberg, on Apr. 29.

PFISTER, ALBRECHT (1420?–1470?), printer. A German wood engraver, he presumably worked for Gutenberg and later founded a press in Bamberg, where he printed Boner's *Edelstein* (1461), *The Book of the Four Histories, Belial,* and *Biblia pauperum* (1462). For a time the invention of printing from movable type was attributed to him.

PFLUG, JULIUS VON (1499–1564), bishop. Born in Eythra, near Leipzig, he studied at Leipzig, Padua, and Bologna, where he received his doctorate in 1521. He held several benefices, and was dean of the cathedral in Meissen and provost of the collegiate church in Zeitz. In 1534 at Leipzig and in 1539 in Meissen he participated in councils which sought to reconcile Catholocism and Protestanism. He was elected bishop of Naumburg in 1541, but John Frederick, pro-Lutheran elector of Saxony, installed Nicholas von Amsdorf. Pflug did not occupy his see until 1547, but by then almost all its occupants changed their faith and all but one of its priests had married; he made as many concessions as possible, but was unable to regain the area. He helped to draw up the Interim of Augsburg, appeared briefly at the Council of Trent in 1551, and died at Zeitz, Germany, on Sept. 3, the last Catholic bishop of Naumburg-Zeitz.

PHAEBADIUS, ST. (d. 392?). A bishop of Agen, France, he worked with St. Hilary of Poitiers to check Arianism in southern Gaul, presided at a number of councils, and was highly praised by St. Jerome. F. D. Apr. 25.

PHAL. *See* Fidolus, St.

PHARAILDIS, ST. (d. 740?). So many legends grew up about this popular Belgian saint, called Varelde, Verylde, or Veerle in Flanders, that her actual career is obscured. She had secretly promised to remain a virgin, but was married for wealth by her parents, and honored her vow through several unhappy years. F. D. Jan. 4.

PHARNACIUS, ST. (d. 304?), martyr. *See* Cyriac, St.

PHELAN, JAMES DUVAL (1861–1930), senator. Born in San Francisco, California, on Apr. 20, he studied at St. Ignatius and law at the University of California, practiced in San Francisco, and became a leader in Democratic politics. He was mayor of San Francisco for three terms in 1897–1902, reformed the city charter, and was chairman of the relief and reconstruction committee following the earthquake of 1906. He went to Europe for the state department in 1913, was United States senator from California in 1915–21, and served as a regent of the University of California. Santa

Clara give him an honorary doctorate. He died in San José, California, on Aug. 7.

PHELAN, MARIE GERARD (1872–1960), educator. Born in Kilkenny, Ireland, on Jan. 29, she became a member of the Religious of the Sacred Heart in 1893, served as headmistress in a Liverpool, England, convent, and went to New York in 1907 to assist Mother Marie Joseph Butler in establishing Marymount College at Tarrytown. She served as dean and as president there, was superior and provincial of the North American province of her institute, and in 1946 was elected superior general of all the religious of the institute throughout the world. Under her direction, twenty-eight new schools and colleges were established, including Marymount in New York City. She died in New York City on Mar. 22.

PHELAN, RICHARD (1828–1904), bishop. Born in Sralee, Kilkenny, Ireland, on Jan. 1, he studied at St. Kieran's, went to the United States in 1844, continued his studies at St. Mary's, Baltimore, and was ordained in 1854 in Pittsburgh. He served in various posts in the diocese, became vicar general, and in 1885 was appointed titular bishop of Cibyra and coadjutor of Pittsburgh. He succeeded to the see in 1889 and in the fifteen years of his reign proved himself an able administrator and a friend of the thousands of foreign-born immigrants who flooded his diocese seeking work in the coal mines and steel industry. He died in Idlewood, Pennsylvania, on Dec. 20.

PHIALA, ST. (5th century), martyr. *See* Fingar, St.

PHILADELPHUS, ST. (d. 251), martyr. *See* Alphius, St.

PHILASTRIUS, ST. (d. 387?), bishop. A Spaniard, he traveled widely through the Roman world. He strenuously opposed Auxentius, the Arian, at Milan, met St. Augustine and St. Ambrose there about 384, and became bishop of Brescia, Italy. He wrote a *Catalogue of Heresies* as a guide for his parishioners, much of it based on a lost work by Hippolytus. F. D. July 18.

PHILEAS, ST. (d. 304), bishop and martyr. An Egyptian convert, he became bishop of Thmuis, was imprisoned, converted Philoromus, the imperial treasurer, by the example of his fortitude under questioning, and was beheaded with his new convert. Eusebius records his trial and death. F. D. Feb. 4.

PHILEAS, ST. (d. 311?), martyr. *See* Hesychius, St.

PHILEMON, ST. (d. 1st century), martyr. A wealthy citizen of Colossae, Phrygia, he was a close friend of St. Paul, who converted him. He was the recipient of the short epistle to Philemon, in which Paul asked him to forgive his runaway slave, Onesimus, who, after fleeing to Rome, had come under the apostle's spiritual direction. According to tradition, he freed the slave and later was stoned to death with his wife, Apphia, in Colossae. F. D. Nov. 22.

PHILEMON, ST. (d. 305?), martyr. *See* Apollonius, St.

PHILETUS, ST. (d. 121?), martyr. He is said to have been a Roman senator, put to death in Illyria with SS. Amphilochius, Cronidas, Lydia, Macedo, and Theoprepius during the reign of Hadrian. F. D. Mar. 27.

PHILIBERT, ST. (608?–685?). Born in Gascony, he was sent to be educated at the court of King Dagobert I by his father Philibaud, bishop in Aire. When twenty he became a monk at Rébais and succeeded St. Aile as abbot. He visited many Columbanian monasteries and in 654 founded a monastery for men at Jumièges and for women at Pavilly. When he denounced Ebroin, mayor of the palace, for his tyranny he was imprisoned at Rouen and then exiled. He later founded the monasteries of Noirmoutier and Quinçay. F. D. Aug. 20.

PHILIP I (1478–1506), king of Castile. Son of Emperor Maximilian I and Mary of Burgundy, and called "the Handsome," he was born in Bruges, Flanders, on July 22, became titular duke of Burgundy and ruler of the Spanish Netherlands in 1482, and on his marriage to Joanna, daughter of Ferdinand (of Aragon) and Isabella (of Castile) in 1496, became king of Castile in 1504 when Isabella died. He died in Spain on Sept. 25. Emperors Charles V and Ferdinand I were his sons. He is sometimes called Philip I of Spain.

PHILIP I (1052–1108), king of France. Son of Henry I and Anne of Russia, he ascended the throne of France on the death of his father in 1060 with Count Baldwin of Flanders as regent. He was declared of age in 1066, and enlarged his dominions by his seizure of Corbie in 1074 and the gift of Gâtinois for his promise to keep hands off in the dynastic struggle in Anjou. He opposed the union of Normandy with England and supported William Curthouse against William the Conqueror and William Rufus. Philip lived a life of lax morals, practiced simony, opposed the reforms of Pope Gregory VII, and, when he married Bertrade, daughter of Simon of Montfort, and wife of Count Fulk of Anjou, who was still alive, in 1092, he was excommunicated by Pope Urban II. He repeatedly defied the Holy See until 1104 when he finally made peace with Pope Paschal II. He was unsuccessful in extending the royal authority, and in the last years of his life his son Louis VI ran the government. He died on July 29.

PHILIP II (1165–1223), king of France. Also known as Philip Augustus, son of Louis VII and Adela, daughter of Count Theobald II of Champagne, he was born in Gonesse, France, on Aug. 21, ruled for his father in 1179, and

succeeded him in 1180. He fought against an alliance of Burgundy, Champagne, and Flanders in 1181–85, acquired Amiens, Artois, and much of Vermandois in 1185, and made peace with Burgundy in 1186. He aided the sons of Henry II of England in their revolt against their father, and secured territory from Henry in 1189 when he also agreed to join the English king on a crusade. On the death of his first wife Isabella in 1189 or 1190, he married Ingeborg of Denmark, and in 1196 put her aside to marry Agnes, daughter of Duke Bertold IV of Meran. He was excommunicated by Pope Innocent III and France was placed under an interdict in 1199. He submitted to the Holy See in 1200 and recognized Ingeborg as his wife, though he held her in prison until 1213. When Henry died in 1190, he joined Richard I of England on a crusade, quarreled with him, and after the siege of Acre returned to France because of ill health in 1191. He joined Emperor Henry VI against Richard but in five years of warfare (1194–99) was forced to surrender most of the territory he had acquired. When Richard died in 1199 and John ascended the throne of England, Philip seized the opportunity to support John's nephew, Duke Arthur I of Brittany, and forced John to cede to him Normandy, Brittany, Anjou, Maine, and Touraine in 1206. In 1213, Emperor Otto IV formed a coalition with King John of England, Renaud of Dammartin, and Ferdinand of Flanders against Philip, who defeated their forces at Bouvines in 1214 and established the military might of France. In 1213 he also prepared to invade England at the request of Pope Innocent III, who had excommunicated John, but abandoned the project when John submitted to the Pope and Philip's fleet was defeated. Philip greatly strengthened the monarchy, increased the territorial boundaries of his country, reformed the administration of justice, the financial structure of the country, the army, and was a staunch defender of the rights of the Church. He died in Mantes, France, on July 14.

PHILIP III (1245–1285), king of France. Surnamed "the Bold," son of Louis IX and Margaret, daughter of Count Raymond Bérenger IV of Provence, he was born in Poissy, France, on Apr. 3, married Isabella of Aragon in 1262, went on the crusade in 1269, and on his father's death in 1270 became king. When Isabella died he married Marie, daughter of Henry III of Brabant, in 1274; added Poitou, Auvergne, and Toulouse to France by a treaty with England in 1279; and united Navarre to France by the marriage of his son, Philip IV, to Jeanne of Navarre in 1284. In 1284 he began a war against Peter of Aragon with the encouragement of Pope Martin IV, who had declared Peter deposed and had offered Philip's son Charles the crown of Aragon. Philip was forced to abandon his expedition, and died on the march home at Perpignan on Oct. 5. Although a weak monarch influenced by others, he increased the royal authority in France and French territories.

PHILIP IV (1268–1350), king of France. Surnamed le Bel ("the Fair"), son of Philip III and Isabella of Aragon, he married Jeanne of Navarre in 1284, uniting Navarre to France, and succeeded to the throne on his father's death in 1285. He became embroiled in a bitter series of disputes with Pope Boniface VIII. In an attempt to bolster the crown's revenues he ordered a continuation of the temporary taxation on the clergy permitted to finance the Albigensian and Aragonese crusades. Boniface denounced the action by the bull *Clericis laicos* in 1296, but was forced to capitulate to Philip to save papal income when the king forbade the export of precious metals. Philip had Bishop Bernard Saisset of Pamiers arrested in 1301 and called the first States-General in French history in 1302–3 to defend his action. Boniface issued the bull *Unam sanctam* in 1302; in retaliation, Philip had Boniface forcibly seized by Guillaume de Nogaret in 1303 at Anagni. Boniface was soon released, but died shortly after. In 1305, Philip succeeded in having Bertrand de Got, a Frenchman, elected as Pope Clement V, who moved the papacy to Avignon in 1309, thus beginning the "Babylonian captivity" of the popes. In his quest for revenue Philip persecuted the Jews, the Italian bankers (the Lombards), and in 1307, on the pretense of reforming the Church, dissolved the Knights Templars, diverted their wealth to his treasury and executed hundreds of knights, including their general. In the political sphere he seized on transgressions of several of the subjects of Edward I of England to invade and subjugate Guienne in 1294–96. Philip defeated the English king when Edward came to the defense of his domains, and Edward made a truce in 1297; Philip was obliged to return most of his conquests by the treaty of peace with Edward in 1303. In 1297, Philip invaded and conquered Flanders, but the Flemings revolted and decisively defeated him at Courtrai, Flanders, in 1302. He died in Fontainebleau, France, on Nov. 29.

PHILIP V (1294?–1322), king of France. Surnamed "the Tall," son of Philip IV and Jeanne of Navarre, he married Jeanne, daughter of Count Otto IV of Burgundy, in 1307, became regent for the posthumous son of his brother Louis X, and succeeded to the throne in 1316 on the child's death at the age of four days. He unsuccessfully attempted to provide uniform weights and currency, made some administrative and army reforms, and frequently convoked assemblies to approve his measures. In

1321 he launched a persecution of lepers and Jews on the rumor they were to put into effect a Moslem plot to destroy the Christians by poisoning wells throughout the country. He died at Longchamps, Paris, on Jan. 2.

PHILIP VI (1293–1350), king of France. Son of Charles of Valois, and grandson of Philip III, he married Jeanne, daughter of Robert II of Burgundy, in 1313, succeeded his cousin Charles IV in 1328 as king, reinstated the count of Flanders, who had been deposed by a rebellion, by his victory over Jakob van Artevelde at Cassel in 1328, and became involved in a war with Edward III of England, who claimed the French throne (Edward's mother was Isabella of France), and in 1336 invaded France. Philip's forces were disastrously routed at Crécy in 1346, and when the English captured Calais in 1347 he negotiated a truce which lasted during his lifetime. He resorted to heavy taxes and loans to finance the war, debased the currency, and sold privileges to the provincial assemblies. He added Montpellier and Dauphiné to the French domains by purchase, and saw his kingdom ravaged by the Black Plague toward the end of his reign. He died in Nogent-le-Roi, France, on Aug. 12.

PHILIP I (d. 1598), king of Portugal. He was placed on the throne of Portugal in 1580 by Philip II of Spain. He ruled adequately, but the nation was torn by Spanish intervention and suffered politically as the Protestant powers became powerful.

PHILIP II (d. 1621), king of Portugal. He succeeded Philip I as king in 1598 and was also dominated by Spain. Colonies in the East fell into the hands of Britain and Holland, and the Dutch also seized part of Brazil during his reign.

PHILIP III (d. 1640), king of Portugal. He became king in 1621, proved to be a spendthrift, and, with his chief minister, Olivares, reduced the already few liberties of the Spanish-dominated nation. He expelled the papal nuncio, increased taxes, invited the Jews to return (for financial reasons), and so alienated the populace that they turned to the duke of Braganza for release from the yoke of a ruler imposed on them by Spain.

PHILIP I, king of Spain. *See* Philip I, king of Castile.

PHILIP II (1527–1598), king of Spain. Son of Emperor Charles V and Isabella of Portugal, he was born in Valladolid, Spain, on May 21, studied widely, was a patron of the arts, was well liked at home, but had little diplomatic success abroad. In 1543 he was married to Mary of Portugal, a cousin; she died in 1545 and Charles arranged his son's marriage to Mary of England, eleven years older than Philip, to gain an ally against France. In 1556, when Charles gave up the Spanish crown, Philip became king of Spain, Naples, Milan, Sicily, the Netherlands, and other territories. France broke its treaty with Spain and joined Pope Paul IV in an attempt to remove Spanish power from Italy. A Spanish force under the duke of Alva defeated the French army of the duke of Guise in the Papal States. Spain then defeated France at St. Quentin and Gravelines, and imposed peace in 1559. Queen Mary died in 1558 and Philip married Elizabeth of Valois in 1559. He faced a three-year revolt (1567–70) by the Moriscoes when he ordered them to change their language and costume, and moved them into inner Spain. When the Portuguese succession seemed to run out and the aged Cardinal Henry took over the kingship, Philip stepped in, conquered the country quickly, and established a union which lasted until 1640. To end the Turkish domination of the Mediterranean he joined the Holy League with Pope Pius V and Venice; its fleet, led by Philip's half-brother, Don Juan, defeated the Turks in the battle of Lepanto (1571); a Spanish treaty with Turkey followed in 1578. When Philip's aunt, Margaret of Parma, whom he had appointed regent of the Netherlands, could not control the nobility or keep religious rebellion in check, Philip sent the duke of Alva to conquer and rule the country. When Alva was recalled in 1573, the defeated William of Orange rose again to try to establish independence. William was assassinated in 1584, but the northern provinces remained free. Elizabeth's accession to the English throne had imperiled Philip's empire. The two were natural enemies, since she was considered protectress of Protestantism by the continental world and since Philip's major concern was the restoration of Catholicism. When Mary Queen of Scots was executed, Philip decided to move directly against England. In 1588 he sent an armada across the channel, but it was almost completely destroyed in a storm; remnants of the fleet were easy victims to English vessels; ships from the colonies were thereafter the prey of English freebooters. Philip was pious and earnest, but austere and ruthless; he was not always aware of the pace at which the world was moving, and maintained a disastrous policy toward France. He died in the Escorial, near Madrid on Sept. 18.

WILLIAM THOMAS WALSH, *Philip II* (New York, McMullen, 1937).

PHILIP III (1578–1621), king of Spain. Son of Philip II and Anne of Austria (daughter of Maximilian II), he became king in 1598 and was deeply interested in the activities of the Church. Hundreds of monasteries were established during his reign. Agriculture and industry continued to decline, wool raising increased, huge estates grew up, and the court became extremely corrupt under the direction of the king's favorite, the duke of Lerma. War with the English ended in 1605; peace with the Dutch lasted from 1609 to 1621; the Moors were finally expelled from Spain in 1609. Late in his reign the nation was swept into the Thirty Years' War. He died in Madrid on Mar. 31.

PHILIP IV (1605–1665), king of Spain. Son of Philip III, he was born in Valladolid on Apr. 8, became king in 1621 and left the rule of the kingdom in the hands of his chief minister, Gaspar de Guzmán (1587–1645), count of Olivares and duke of Santander, who introduced administrative reforms and increased centralization of royal power. War with France in 1622 proved disastrous; failure to summon the Cortes and the imposition of heavy taxes led to rebellion and the formation of the Catalan Republic (1640–52). This came to an end when Barcelona submitted, but by an agreement in 1659 the Catalans gained many lost privileges. French successes continued; the Spanish army was badly beaten at Rocroi in 1643 and Olivares fell from power; Naples revolted in 1647–48; and the French brought Spanish military hopes to an end in the battle of the Dunes in 1658. By the Treaty of the Pyrenees (1659), Spain ceded fortifications in Flanders and Artois, other territory, and agreed to the marriage of Louis XIV and Philip's daughter, Maria Teresa. He died on Sept. 7.

PHILIP V (1683–1746), king of Spain. Born in Versailles, France, on Dec. 19, Philip of Anjou, grandson of Louis XIV of France, was named by the childless Charles II to be his successor and ascended the throne in 1700. The War of the Spanish Succession broke out a year later; France announced in 1704 that Archduke Charles of Austria should be considered king of Spain. The British captured Gibraltar in 1704; Charles captured Barcelona in 1705 and won the allegiance of Catalonia and Valencia; the Portuguese seized Madrid in 1706, but were driven back; and Britain seized Minorca in 1709. Philip had growing success and in 1713, by the Treaty of Utrecht, was acknowledged as king by England and Holland, on the guarantee that Spain and France would not unite. Spain also ceded Sicily to Victor Amadeus of Savoy. In a treaty with Austria in 1714, Spain gave up control of the Netherlands and Luxembourg and holdings in Italy. Philip, in spite of his promise, hoped to gain the French crown. He married Elisabetta Farnese in 1714 and regained power in Italy through skillful marriages and reliance on Alberoni as his minister; he captured Sardinia in 1717 and Sicily in 1718. By the Treaty of The Hague (1720) Philip gave Sardinia to Savoy and Sicily to Austria, and gained the Austrian promise of the succession in Parma, Piacenza, and Tuscany to Charles, eldest son of Elisabetta and himself, and the agreement of the emperor to relinquish all claims to Spain. In 1724 he gave up the throne to Louis I, his son by his first wife, Marie Louise of Savoy (d. 1714); Louis died after a year, and Philip returned to power. In 1733–38, Spain joined France in the War of the Polish Succession, and invaded Lombardy, Naples, and Sicily. By the Treaty of Vienna (1738) his son Charles gave up the Parmese and other duchies he had inherited in 1731. Spain fought England in 1739–41, and joined France in the War of the Austrian Succession in 1740–48. Philip died in Madrid on July 9.

PHILIP, ST. (d. 80?), apostle and martyr. Born in Bethsaida, Galilee, he may have been a follower of St. John the Baptist before he was selected by Christ. It was Philip who spoke of the Messias to Nathanael, was present at the miracle of the loaves, and was singled out for a special reply of Our Lord before His Passion. He later preached in Asia Minor and is believed to have been crucified at Hierapolis during the persecution of Domitian. F. D. May 1.

PHILIP, ST. (d. 150?), martyr. *See* Felix, St.

PHILIP, ST. (d. 180?). Bishop of Gortyna, he worked earnestly in Crete against the Marcionite heresy and wrote a now-lost work against Gnosticism. F. D. Apr. 11.

PHILIP, ST. (d. 270?), martyr. Bishop of Fermo, Italy, he was slain there. F. D. Oct. 22.

PHILIP, ST. He is the father of St. Eugenia in the legend of that third-century martyr.

PHILIP, ST. (d. 301?), martyr. *See* Straton, St.

PHILIP, ST. (d. 304), bishop and martyr. Bishop of Heraclea, near Constantinople, he, Severus, a priest, and his deacons, Hermes and Eusebius, were tortured and burned to death at Adrianopolis during the persecution of Diocletian when they refused to surrender the sacred books. F. D. Oct. 22.

PHILIP, ST. (d. 578?). He was bishop of Vienne, France, from about 560 until his death. F. D. Feb. 3.

PHILIP BENIZI, ST. (1233–1285). Born in Florence, Italy, on Aug. 15, he studied at Paris and at Padua, where he received his doctorate in medicine at nineteen. He practiced medicine for a year, but in 1254 he joined the Servites (Order of the Servants of Mary), was sent to their house in Siena in 1258, and was ordained there. He became known as a zealous preacher and was made superior of several friaries. In 1267, over his protests, he was elected fifth prior general of the order. Proposed by Cardinal Ottobuoni in 1268 as the successor of Pope Clement IV, he fled to the mountains, where he remained in a cave until a pope was elected. He was present at the second General Council of Lyons in 1274, and in 1279 he reconciled the differences of the Guelphs and Ghibellines. During those years he established new foundations in Italy and Germany, was most active in reconciling and converting many to the Church, and attracted many outstanding men to the Servites. He died at Todi, Italy, on Aug. 22 and was canonized in 1671. F. D. Aug. 23.

PHILIP BERRUYER, BL. (d. 1260). Nephew of St. William of Bourges, he followed his uncle as archbishop of Bourges, France. F. D. Jan. 9.

PHILIP OF THE BLESSED TRINITY (1603–1671), theologian. Born in Malaucene, France, he became a Discalced Carmelite at Lyons in 1521, studied in Rome, and in 1629 was sent to Goa, Portuguese India. He returned to Rome in 1638 and after a period in France was twice elected general of his order. He wrote several theological treatises and died in Naples, Italy, on Feb. 28.

PHILIP THE DEACON, ST. (1st century). One of the seven deacons ordained by the apostles (Acts 6:5–8), he may have been a Greek or a native of Caesarea. He preached in Samaria, and baptized Simon Magus and, on the road to Gaza, the eunuch of Queen Candace of Ethiopia. St. Paul visited him and his four daughters in Caesarea (Acts 21: 8–9). Tradition makes him bishop of Tralles in Lydia. F. D. June 6.

PHILIP OF JESUS (d. 1597), martyr. Born in Mexico City, he became a Franciscan, left the order to become a merchant in the Philippines, and asked for readmittance to the order in 1590. On his way back to Mexico he was captured by Japanese in 1596 and crucified in Nagasaki, Japan. F. D. Feb. 5.

PHILIP NERI, ST. (1515–1595), founder. Born in Florence, Italy, on July 22, he was educated there by the Dominicans, and at about eighteen went to Rome where he lived an ascetic life for two years while serving as a tutor. He studied theology for three years, then abandoned formal study to talk directly to the people on the streets and in the market areas. The city was especially corrupt at the time— most ecclesiastical appointees were mere politicians who showed no interest in church matters or human needs. St. Philip converted many of the common people, his own good nature and sense of humor serving him well. In 1548 he founded a group of laymen who worked in the hospitals, took care of convalescents and pilgrims, and spread the popularity of the Forty Hours' Devotion. His confessor, Fr. Persiano Rossa, suggested that Philip return to his studies and become a priest; he did so and was ordained in 1551. He became widely known as a confessor, had remarkable success with converts, and introduced the practice of informal spiritual conferences for his penitents. When the groups became too large, he received the assistance of other priests, who came popularly to be called Oratorians because they called the group to the oratory for prayer. The name was used for a group of five young priests who worked with him at the church of San Giovanni and followed spiritual exercises under his direction. The society of Oratorians was formally approved in 1575 by Pope Gregory XIII. As superior, Philip was busier than ever: building the new church of Santa Maria in Vallicella, directing his associates, giving counsel to a somewhat respiritualized college of cardinals, and astonishing many by the rapture of his devotions. He died in Rome, and was canonized in 1622. F. D. May 26.

THEODORE MAYNARD, *Mystic in Motley* (Milwaukee, Bruce, 1946); LOUIS PONNELLE and L. BORDET, *St. Philip Neri and the Roman Society of His Times*, trans. R. F. Kerr (London, Sheed, 1932).

PHILIP OF SWABIA (1177?–1208), king of Germany. Son of Frederick Barbarossa and brother of Emperor Henry VI, he became bishop of Würzburg, Bavaria, in 1191, resigned his see in 1192, and became duke of Swabia in 1196. He agreed to support the Hohenstaufen request that he become king in 1198, but three months later a minority faction declared for Otto IV. Philip was supported by the imperial princes and Philip Augustus of France; Otto, by Guelph leaders, Richard I of England, and in 1201 by Pope Innocent III. Three years later Philip began to win battles, captured Cologne in 1206, and was arranging to negotiate with the Papal States when he was assassinated in Bamberg, Germany, on June 21.

PHILIP OF ZELL, ST. (d. 770?). An Anglo-Saxon priest, he settled near Worms, Germany, as a hermit on his return from a pilgrimage, and was often consulted by King Pepin and others. In time, Philip was joined by Horskolf, another priest, and they built a church as their disciples increased. F. D. May 3.

PHILIPPA, ST. (d. 220), martyr. *See* Dionysius, St.

PHILIPPA OF HAINAULT (1314?–1369), queen. Daughter of William the Good of Holland and Hainault, she was married to King Edward III of England, her cousin, in 1328, and gave him allies for his war with France and troops to help in the defeat of the Scots forces at Neville' Cross in 1346. She was popular with the English people, was the patron of the historian Froissart, and molded close trade relations between England and Flanders. She died in Windsor castle, England, on Aug. 15.

PHILIPPE DE THUAN (12th century), poet. Of a Norman family, he lived near Caen, France, went to England, and wrote an elaborate collection of beast fables, *Li Bestiare* or *Physiologus*, which had an effect on language and later poetic symbolism rather than on the development of poetic craftsmanship. He also wrote *Li Cumpoz* or *Computus. Livre des créatures*, of which *Li Bestiaire* is a part, reflects the Church year and was written about 1115.

PHILIPS, PETER (16th century), musician. Born in England in the 1560s, he left during the religious controversies, traveled through Europe, and became Duke Albert's organist in Antwerp. He was ordained, held canonries at Bethune and then Soignes in 1612, and wrote numerous masses, motets, and madrigals. Some of his collections are *Cantiones sacrae, Les rossignols spirituels*, and *Gemmulae sacrae*. He died in Brussels, Flanders, between 1633 and 1640.

PHILLIMORE, JOHN SWINNERTON (1873–1926), poet. Born in Boconnoc, Cornwall, England, on Feb. 26, he studied at Oxford where he won numerous awards, lectured and tutored there in 1895–99, and then accepted the chair of Greek at Glasgow. He had already completed (with S. G. Owen) *Musa clauda*, translations of Latin elegies, and a translation from the Russian of Lermontov's novel A *Hero of Nowadays*, and contributed to *Essays in Liberalism*. He published verse translations of three plays by Sophocles (1902), edited Propertius and Statius, and was given the chair of humanities in 1906. He became a convert that year. He edited Philostratus, and wrote on the classical influence on English literature, allegory, criticism, and the problems of translation, Thomas More, Horace, Lucian, and Latin hymns (of which he compiled an anthology). His *Poems* appeared in 1902; he added to them in *Things New and Old* (1918). He also wrote for scholarly journals and for the *New Witness* and *G. K.'s Weekly*. He died in Sheffield, England, on Nov. 16.

PHILLIP, ROBERT (d. 1647). Of a Scots family, he was ordained in Rome, arrested and tried in Edinburgh for saying mass, and, although condemned to death, was in 1613 banished to France. He became an Oratorian, was Queen Henrietta Maria's confessor in England in 1628, and when he served as her emissary to secure papal aid for King Charles was charged with being a spy. He was released at Richelieu's request, but imprisoned in the Tower in 1641, then released when the queen interceded. He went to Europe with the royal party in 1642 and died in Paris on Jan. 4.

PHILLIPPS, AMBROSE LISLE MARCH (1809–1878). Born in Garendon Park, Leicestershire, England, he studied in private schools near Gloucester and Birmingham, became a convert at sixteen, attended Cambridge with Kenelm Digby, but was unable to finish because of ill health. He spent some time in Italy, returned to England, founded Catholic missions and helped to build the Cistercian monastery of Mt. St. Bernard. With George Spencer he in 1828 founded the Association of Universal Prayer for the Conversion of England, engaged in correspondence with all the leaders of the subsequent Oxford Movement, and in 1857 founded the Association for Promoting the Unity of Christendom, with some 9000 members, many of them Anglican clergymen. Archbishop Manning opposed the latter group and arranged for papal condemnation in 1864. Phillipps took the name De Lisle in 1862 when he inherited the estates of that family. He resigned from the condemned association, remained on friendly terms with Manning, wrote many apologetical pamphlets, and died in Garendon on Mar. 5.

PHILLIPS, CHARLES (1880–1933), author. Born in New Richmond, Wisconsin, on Nov. 20, he studied at De La Salle, Toronto, entered journalism, and in 1901 was managing editor of the *Northwestern Chronicle* (St. Paul). He edited *New Century* (Washington) in 1903–6, *Republican Voice* (New Richmond) in 1906–7, and the *Monitor* (San Francisco) to 1915. Meanwhile, he had taken his degree at St. Mary's, Oakland, and later studied at Catholic University and Oxford. He served with the Knights of Columbus and the Red Cross during World War I, directed relief work in Poland in 1919–22, and wrote *The New Poland* (1923). He taught literature at Notre Dame from 1924 on, was associate editor of *Catholic World*, founded and edited *Pan*, and wrote poems (*Back Home, High in the Tower*), plays (*The Divine Friend, The Shepherd of the Valley*), a novel (*The Doctor's Wooing*), and biographies of Lincoln and Paderewski. He died in South Bend, Indiana, on Dec. 29.

PHILLIPS, GEORGE (1804–1872), canonist. Born in Königsberg, Germany, on Sept. 6, son of an English merchant, he studied law at Berlin and Göttingen, taking his degree at the latter in 1824 and becoming professor at Berlin in 1827. He was a convert in 1828 and was appointed counsel of the Bavarian ministry of the interior in 1833. He was professor of history and law at Munich from 1834 to 1847, founded *Historischpolitische Blätter* with Guido Görres in 1838, was elected to the national assembly in 1848, and appointed to the chair of German law at Innsbruck in 1850, and at Vienna in 1851, where he remained until his death on Sept. 6. He wrote treatises on German and canon law.

PHILO, ST. (d. 150?). *See* Agathopus, St.

PHILOCALUS, ST. (4th century), martyr. *See* Dominus, St.

PHILOGONIUS, ST. (d. 324), bishop. A lawyer at Antioch, he was married and had a daughter when in 319 he became bishop of the see there. He was one of the first to denounce Arianism and was imprisoned for a time during the persecution of Maximinus and Licinius. A panegyric preached by St. John Chrysostom is extant. F. D. Dec. 20.

PHILOLOGUS, ST. (1st century). *See* Patrobas, St.

PHILOMENA. Her cult, authorized by Pope Gregory XVI in 1837, began with the discovery of the skeleton of a young girl and of a small vial with a residue believed to be blood in the catacomb of St. Priscilla in Rome in 1802. An inscription on a tablet near the tomb was translated "Peace be with thee, Philomena." When the remains were translated to the church of Mugnano del Cardinale, in the diocese of Nola, her devotion became widespread and she was honored on Aug. 11. However, in 1961, because she had been venerated because of popular fervor rather than liturgical fact, the Church removed her name, from the calendar of saints.

PHILOMENA, ST. (d. 500?). She is honored in the region of San Severino, Ancona, Italy. F. D. July 5.

PHILOMENUS, ST. (d. 275), martyr. He was put to death at Ancyra, Galatia, during the reign of Aurelian. F. D. Nov. 29.

PHILONELLA, ST. (1st century). She and Zenais, perhaps her sister, were natives of Tarsus and related to St. Paul. F. D. Oct. 11.

PHILOROMUS, ST. (d. 304), martyr. *See* Phileas, St.

PHILOTERUS, ST. (d. 303), martyr. He is said to have been a noble, slain at Nicomedia during the Diocletian persecution. F. D. May 19.

PHILOTHEUS, ST. (d. 297), martyr. *See* Hipparchus, St.

PHILPOT, GLYN WARREN (1884–1937), painter. Born in London on Oct. 5, he sketched at an early age, had a year and a half of schooling, went to Lambeth Art School for two years of training, and at eighteen went to France. He painted at Rouen and Paris, studied Titian and Goya in the Louvre, and remained a traditional craftsman in spite of contemporary trends. He became a convert in 1906, lived in London, painted *Manuelito* on a trip to Spain, produced portraits to earn a living, then went to live in Spain in 1910. *Zarzarossa* followed: *The Marble Worker* won an American prize; he visited the United States and Venice and returned to England during World War I. He was elected royal artist in 1923, went to Paris in 1931, changed his style, and lost many followers. One-man shows, including water colors, attracted attention. Increasing heart strain slowed him down, and he died suddenly in London on Dec. 16.

PHILPOTT, BL. CLEMENT (d. 1540), martyr. *See* Brindholm, Bl. Edmund.

PHLEGON, ST. (1st century), bishop and martyr. Known to St. Paul (Rom. 16:14), he

931

became bishop of Hyrcania, and was put to death by Jewish opposition. F. D. Apr. 8.

PHOCAS, ST. (d. 117), bishop and martyr. The bishop of Sinope on the Black Sea was put to death during the reign of Trajan. F. D. July 14.

PHOCAS, ST. (d. 320?), martyr. Said to have been suffocated to death at Antioch, he may have become confused with the second-century bishop of Sinope. F. D. Mar. 5.

PHOCAS THE GARDENER, ST. (d. 303?), martyr. A native of Sinope on the Black Sea, he devoted himself to gardening as he lived a life of prayer and austerity as a hermit. He was beheaded during Diocletian's persecution by a group of soldiers to whom he had given shelter and lodging. St. Asterius, bishop of Amasea, delivered a panegyric on him in 400 which is still extant, in which he says St. Phocas was venerated by sailors, many of whom he aided. F. D. Sept. 22 (also, July 23).

PHOEBE, ST. (1st century). She was a deaconess at Cenchrae, near Corinth and evidently (Rom. 16:1–3) the bearer of St. Paul's epistle to the Romans, written about 57, to Italy. The legend that she was St. Paul's wife is unfounded. F. D. Sept. 3.

PHOTINA. Legend has it that she was the Samaritan woman who talked with Christ at the well (John 4:1–42), and has her convert Nero's daughter Domnina and 100 servants before she was martyred in Rome. The story has no basis in fact.

PHOTINUS, ST. (d. 305?), martyr. See Anicetus, St.

PHOTINUS. See Pothinus, St.

PIA, ST. (2nd century), martyr. See Catus, St.

PIANCIANI, GIAMBATTISTA (1784–1862), physicist. Born in Spoleto, Italy, on Oct. 27, he became a Jesuit in 1805, taught physics in various schools, and was appointed professor at the Roman College, where he taught for twenty-four years. He was forced to flee from Rome during the revolution of 1848 and came to the United States, where he taught at Georgetown in 1849–50. He returned to Rome in 1851, and taught at the Roman College and Collegio Filosofico, of which he was appointed president in 1860 and where he died on Mar. 23. He wrote on electricity and magnetism.

PIANO CARPINE, GIOVANNI DA (1182–1252?), archbishop. Born in Pian di Carpine, near Perugia, Italy, he became a Franciscan, accompanied Caesar of Spires on a missionary journey to Germany in 1221, and became provincial in Saxony and in Spain. In 1246 he was sent by Pope Innocent IV to the court of the Great Khan, covered some 3000 miles to Karâkorum, Mongolia, in 100 days, and wrote the first account of the countries and peoples he had visited, *Liber Tatarorum* (*Travels in Ta-*

tary, Tibet and China). He acted as papal legate to St. Louis in France, and on his return was appointed archbishop of Antivari, Dalmatia. He is sometimes called Carpini.

PIATON, ST. (d. 286?), martyr. Born in Benevento, Italy, he was sent to Gaul and was probably slain at Tournai during the persecution of Maximian. F. D. Oct. 1.

PIAZZA, ADEODATO GIOVANNI (1884–1957), cardinal. Born in Vigo di Cadore, northern Italy, he became a Discalced Carmelite, was ordained in 1908, and taught for several years. He was made bishop of Benevento in 1930, patriarch of Venice in 1935, cardinal in 1935, and cardinal-bishop in 1937. He served as a member of the curia, was secretary of the Congregation of the Consistory, and died in Rome on Nov. 30.

PIAZZI, GIUSEPPE (1746–1826), astronomer. Born in Ponte, Valtellina, Italy, on July 16, he became a Theatine in Milan, studied in Milan, Turin, Rome, and Genoa, and taught at Genoa and Malta. He became professor of theology in Rome in 1779, of higher mathematics at Palermo Academy in 1780, and the next year secured a grant from the viceroy of Sicily to found and direct an observatory which began observations in 1792. He discovered the first known planetoid, Ceres, in 1801, published catalogues of the fixed stars in 1803 and 1814, was commissioned to reform Sicily's weights and measures in 1812, and in 1817 was placed in charge of the government observatory at Naples, where he died on July 22. He wrote on astronomy, the aberration of light, and the length of the tropical year.

PIBUSH, BL. JOHN (d. 1601), martyr. Born in Thirsk, Yorkshire, England, he was ordained at Rheims in 1587, served the English underground mission until 1593, was captured, escaped, and recaptured. He suffered from mistreatment and tuberculosis in a London prison during his last five years and was executed on the charge of priesthood. He was beatified in 1929. F. D. Feb. 18.

PICARD, JEAN (1620–1682), astronomer. Born in La Flêche, France, on July 21, he became a priest, was appointed prior of Rillé in Anjou, and studied astronomy under Gassendi, whom he succeeded as professor of astronomy at the Collège de France in 1655. He made the first accurate measurement of a degree of the earth's meridian, from Mahoisine to Sourdon, near Amiens, in 1669–70. His work helped Newton calculate the force of gravitation. He introduced new methods and inventions, among them the transit instrument, micrometer, and pendulum clock, and was the first to use the telescope in the measurement of angles. He helped found the Paris observatory, was an early member of the French Academy, and in 1679 established *Connaisance des temps* and published its first five annual volumes. He died in Paris on Oct. 12.

PICCOLOMINI, ALESSANDRO (1508–1578), bishop. Born in Siena, Italy, on June 13, he wrote several comedies and licentious poetry in his early years, translated Ovid, Homer, and Aristotle, and wrote on philosophy, astronomy, and calendar reform. In 1540 he became professor of philosophy at Padua and in 1574 was named titular bishop of Patrae and coadjutor of Siena, but died on Mar. 12 before taking office.

PICCOLOMINI, BL. AMBROSIO (d. 1347?). He and Bl. Antonio de' Patrizi and Bernardo Tolomei founded the Benedictine abbey of Montoliveto Maggiore, near Siena, Italy. F. D. Aug. 21.

PICCOLOMINI, FRANCIS (1582–1651). Born in Siena, Italy, he became a Jesuit at eighteen, taught philosophy at the Roman College, and in 1649 became the eighth general of his Society. He died on June 17.

PICCOLOMINI, BL. GIACOMO (1259–1305). Born in Siena, Italy, he became a Servite laybrother at fourteen, and was noted for his devotion to prayer and the most menial tasks. F. D. Apr. 16.

PICCOLOMINI-AMMANNATI, JACOPO (1422–1479), cardinal. Born near Lucca, Italy, he studied in Florence, became Cardinal Capranica's private secretary in 1450, and secretary of briefs under Popes Callistus III and Pius II. He was appointed bishop of Pavia in 1460 and a cardinal in 1461. He disagreed with Popes Paul II (who imprisoned him on conspiracy charges) and Sixtus IV, and in 1470 was transferred to Lucca and named papal delegate to Umbria. He was a patron of the arts, wrote a continuation of Pius II's *Commentarii*, and died in San Lorenzo, Italy, on Sept. 10.

PICENARDI, BL. ELISABETTA (1428–1468). Born in Mantua, Italy, she became a Servite tertiary with her sister, later being joined by several other young women whose spiritual life she directed. She was beatified in 1804. F. D. Feb. 20.

PICHLER, ANTONIO (1697–1779), engraver. Born in Brixen, Tyrol, on Apr. 12, son of a physician, he gave up his work as a merchant to study goldsmithing and gem engraving in Naples and Rome, where he died on Sept. 14. He was also known as Johann Anton.

PICHLER, GIOVANNI (1734–1791), painter. Born in Naples on Jan. 1, he studied under his father, Antonio, and Corvi, completed a series of historical paintings for the Franciscans in Orioli and the Augustinians in Bracciano, contemporary portraits, and skillfully engraved gems. He died in Rome on Jan. 25. Like his father, he also was known as Johann Anton. His half-brother Giuseppe, also called Johann Joseph (1760–1820), was

his student and painted portraits and classical miniatures.

PICHLER, LUIGI (1773–1854). Born in Rome on Jan. 31, the son of Antonio Pichler's second marriage, he studied art under De Angelis and gem cutting under his half-brother Giovanni, and developed as a great cameo engraver. Two of his achievements were copies of 500 gems in the Vienna Cabinet in 1818 for presentation by the Emperor to the pope and copies of his brother's and father's intaglios, to which he added his own, for the city of Vienna. He died in Rome on Mar. 13.

PICHLER, VITUS (1670–1736), canonist. Born in Grossberghofen, Germany, on May 24, he was ordained a parish priest and in 1696 became a Jesuit. He was professor of philosophy at Brigue and Dillingen, theology at Augsburg, and canon law at Ingolstadt. He wrote against Lutheranism, on papal infallibility, and canon-law texts. He died in Munich, Bavaria, where he was prefect of higher studies, on Feb. 15.

PICKERING, BL. THOMAS (1621–1679), martyr. Born in Westmoreland, England, he became a Benedictine laybrother at Douai and was sent to serve in the royal chapel at London. During the Titus Oates hysteria he was seized and hanged at Tyburn. He was beatified in 1929. F. D. May 9.

PICO DELLA MIRANDOLA, GIOVANNI (1463–1494), scholar. Born in the family castle of Mirandola, Modena, Italy, he gave up his share of the family wealth to study canon law at Bologna and philosophy and languages in universities in France and Italy. He became renowned for his learning and brilliance, piety and good manners, and on his return to Rome in 1486 offered to dispute with anyone on any of 900 theses, was forbidden to do so, and his book containing the theses interdicted. He was cleared of the charge of heresy by Pope Alexander VI in 1493. He left Rome in 1487, traveled through Italy, using Florence as his center, published a mystical exposition of creation in *Hepatplus* (1489), planned a complete exposition of the Church against her enemies of which only the section *In astrologiam* was completed, and for a time was deeply influenced by Savonarola. Toward the end of his life he disposed of his inheritance and planned to become a missionary preacher, but died in Florence, Italy, on Nov. 17 before effecting his aim. He was admired as an outstanding and typical humanist by St. Thomas More.

PICO DELLA MIRANDOLA, GIOVANNI FRANCESCO (1469–1533), philosopher. Nephew of Giovanni Pico della Mirandola, he was murdered with his son, Albert, during an inter-family war by his nephew Galeotto II, who had captured the family castle of Mirandola in the duchy of Modena, Italy. He wrote a life of his uncle which Thomas More translated.

PICONIO, BERNADINE A (1633–1709), theologian. Henri Bernardine de Picquigny was born and educated at Picquigny, Picardy, became a Capuchin in 1649, became a professor of theology, and wrote *Triplex expositio epistolarum sancti Pauli*. He died in Paris on Dec. 8.

PICQUET, FRANÇOIS (1708–1781), missioner. Born in Bourg, Bresse, France, on Dec. 4, he studied at the Lyons seminary and St. Sulpice in Paris, where he was ordained in 1734 as a Sulpician after he had received his doctorate from the Sorbonne. He was sent to Canada later the same year, ministered to the Algonquins and Iroquois, and became so influential he was able to secure their neutrality in the French and English War of 1743–48. He founded Fort Presentation (which developed into Ogdensburg, New York) in 1749 and made it and Oka centers for Catholic Indians. He went to France in 1753 to discuss ways of strengthening the colony and on his return led the Indians against the British from 1754 to 1760, even though a price was set on his head. On his return to France he engaged in pastoral work in Paris until 1772, was canon at Bourg cathedral, and died in Verjon, France.

PIDAL, PEDRO JOSÉ (1800–1865), prime minister. Born in Spain of Austrian descent, he served in the army, as a senator, president of the Cortes, held several ministerial posts, and was prime minister. He was a member of the Royal Spanish Academy of Language director of the Academy of History, and president of the Academy of Moral and Political Sciences. Queen Isabella II made him marquis de Pidal in 1848.

PIDAL Y MON, ALEJANDRO (1847–1913). Son of Pedro, he was a deputy in the Spanish Cortes and became its president and minister of public works. He was a member of the Royal Spanish Academy of Language (and its director from 1907 to 1913), the Academy of History, the Academy of Moral and Political Sciences, and the Madrid Academy of Jurisprudence, serving as its president in 1895–98.

PIDAL Y MON, LUIS (1842–1913), ambassador. Son of Pedro, he was a deputy and secretary in the Spanish Cortes, president of the senate, president of the council of state, minister of public works, and ambassador to the Vatican. He was a member of the Royal Academy of Moral and Political Sciences and the Royal Spanish Academy of Language.

PIE, LOUIS EDOUARD DÉSIRÉ (1815–1880), cardinal. Born in Pontgouin, France, on Sept. 26, he studied in Chartres and St. Sulpice, Paris, was ordained in 1839, and became vicar general of Chartres in 1844 and bishop of Poitiers in 1849. He established new missions and parishes, helped to restore provincial synods, aided the building of the Sacred Heart national shrine in Montmartre, fought modernist errors, censured Napoleon III strongly on occasion, and championed the dogma of papal infallibility after its approval by the Vatican Council. In 1879 he was created a cardinal-priest. He died in Angoulême, France, on May 17.

PIECK, ST. NICHOLAS (d. 1572), martyr. A Franciscan friar, he was guardian of the house at Gorkum, near Dordrecht, Holland, and made the conversion of Calvinists his lifework. In June 1572 he and others were seized when anti-Spanish Calvinist forces occupied the town, cruelly treated, and offered their lives if they would dishonor the Eucharist. In spite of an order from the prince of Orange directing their release, he was hanged with Nicholas Poppel, Leonard van Wechel, and fifteen others. The martyrs of Gorkum were canonized in 1867. F. D. July 9.

PIEDCOURT, BL. MARIE ANN (d. 1794), martyr. *See* Lidoin, Bl. Marie.

PIEL, PETER (1835–1904), musician. Born in Kessewick, Germany, on Aug. 12, he studied in Kampen, Netherlands, and became professor of music at the Boppard seminary there in 1868, a position he held until his death on Aug. 21. He composed masses, motets, madrigals, and antiphons in the classical manner, was a leader in the movement to reform church music, and teacher of great influence. He was made royal director of music in 1887 and wrote *Harmonielehre*, which became a widely used text of liturgical music.

PIENTIA, ST. (d. 285?), martyr. *See* Nicasius, St.

PIERIUS, ST. (d. 309?). Head of the catechetical school in Alexandria, Egypt, where St. Pamphilus was his disciple, he gained the name "Origen the Younger" for his preaching and writing, some of which is marked by Origen's errors. He was praised by Eusebius and St. Jerome, suffered during the Diocletian persecution but was not martyred, and died in Rome after 309. F. D. Nov. 4.

PIERLEONI, PIETRO. *See* Anacletus II, antipope.

PIERLUIGI, GIOVANNI. *See* Palestrina, Giovanni Pierluigi da.

PIERO DELLA FRANCESCA. *See* Franceschi, Piero de'.

PIERO DI SAN SEPOLCRO. *See* Franceschi, Piero de'.

PIEROZZI, ST. ANTONIO (1389–1459), archbishop. Antoninus was born in Florence, Italy, on Mar. 1, became a Dominican at Fiesole at sixteen after he had heard Bl. John Dominici preach and had followed his spiritual direction for a year. He directed many houses as prior or superior. Antoninus was widely known as a canonist, attended the Council of Florence, and became archbishop of that see in 1446. Humble, to the point of directing a palace with only six attendants, and exceptionally charitable, he was active and bitter in his attacks on usury and sorcery, was sought out by the state government and by the papacy as a diplomat, reformed the Roman curia, and exhausted himself by personal care of the victims of pestilence, famine, earthquakes, and storms which struck the city during the last decade of his life. The "people's prelate" died on May 2. He was canonized in 1523. F. D. May 10.

PIERRE DE MARICOURT (13th century). Born in Maricourt, Somme, France, he was a physician, sometimes called "the Pilgrim," probably a crusader, and fought with the army of Charles of Anjou at the siege of Lucera, Italy, in 1269. He wrote an influential study of the laws of magnetism, *Epistola de magnete*.

PIERRE DE MONTREUIL (d. 1266), architect. He was principal architect to King Louis IX of France, for whom in 1245–48 he built the Sainte Chapelle; he also built the refectory and lady chapel at St. Germain-des-Prés and a chapel at Vincennes.

PIERRON, JEAN (b. 1631), missioner. Born in Dun-sur-Meuse, France, on Sept. 28, he became a Jesuit in 1650, taught in Rheims, Verdun, and Metz, and in 1667 was sent to Canada. He ministered to the Iroquois and Mohawks, taught by using paintings, had success with converts, and returned to France in 1678.

PIERSON, PHILIPPE (1642–1688), missioner. Born in Ath, Belgium, he became a Jesuit in 1670, studied at Louvain, Lille, and Douai, taught at Armentières and Bethune, and was sent to Canada in 1666. He taught at Quebec, was ordained in 1669, and spent the rest of his life among the Huron and Sioux Indians of the Lake Superior region. He died in Lorette, Quebec.

PIERSON, BL. WALTER (d. 1537), martyr. See Beer, Bl. Richard.

PIETRO DA CORTONA. See Berrettini, Pietro.

PIFFL, FREDERICK (1864–1932), cardinal. Born in Landskron, Bohemia, on Oct. 15, he studied at Klosterneuburg monastery, was ordained in 1888, and after parish work was recalled to teach theology and serve as provost of his monastery. He became archbishop of Vienna in 1913 and a cardinal in 1914, and was particularly interested in the progress of liturgical music at the Vienna Academy. He died in Vienna on Apr. 20.

PIGGHE, ALBERT (1490?–1542), theologian. Born in Kampen, Flanders, he studied at Louvain under Adrian of Utrecht and at Cologne, where he took his doctorate in theology in 1517, went to Spain with Adrian, and then to Rome when his teacher became pope. He served on diplomatic missions for Adrian VI and two successors, was appointed provost of St. John's, Utrecht, in 1535, and disputed at Ratisbon in 1541. He wrote theological treatises, some with dubious theories, controversial works against Henry VIII and Protestants, and tracts on astronomy, including one on calendar reform. He died in Utrecht, Flanders, on Dec. 26.

PIGMENIUS, ST. (d. 362), martyr. A priest, he was put to death in Rome by drowning in the Tiber during the persecution of Julian the Apostate. F. D. Mar. 24.

PIGNATELLI, GENNARO GRANITO (1851–1948), cardinal. Born in Naples on Apr. 10, the prince of Belmonte and count of Copertino studied in Mondragone and the Naples seminary and was ordained in 1879. He was counselor to the nuncio at Paris, became titular archbishop of Edessa in 1899, was papal nuncio to Vienna, and in 1911 was made a cardinal. He became bishop of Albano in 1914, bishop of Ostia in 1930, and prefect of the Congregation of the Ceremonial. He died in Vatican City on Feb. 16.

PIGNATELLI, ST. JOSEPH (1737–1811). Born in Saragossa, Spain, he joined the Jesuits in Tarragona at sixteen, was ordained in 1763, and in 1767 went to Corsica and later to Ferrara, Italy, when his Society was expelled from Spain by King Charles III. When Pope Clement XIV suppressed the Jesuits in 1773, he became a secular priest and spent the next twenty years at Bologna in study and in aiding his more unfortunate fellow exiles. In 1797 he joined a group of Russian Jesuits (who had not been suppressed) in the realm of the duke of Parma, established a quasi-novitiate at Colorno in 1799, and in 1804 was appointed provincial of the re-established province of the Society in the kingdom of Naples. When the French invaded Naples in 1804, and dispersed the Society there, Joseph went to Rome, where he was appointed provincial for Italy. He labored to restore the Society (which took place in 1814) so valiantly that at his beatification ceremonies Pope Pius XI called him "the restorer of the Jesuits." He died in Rome on Nov. 11, and was canonized in 1954. F. D. Nov. 28.

PIHRING, ENRICUS (1606?–1678?). A native of Sigarthin, near Passau, Bavaria, he became a Jesuit at twenty-two, taught at Dillingen for twelve years, and wrote studies of canon law.

PIKE, VEN. WILLIAM (d. 1591), martyr. Born in Dorsetshire, England, he became a joiner, lived at West Marley, was arrested, and while a prisoner in Dorchester was converted by Ven. Thomas Pilchard. He was executed at Dorchester, probably on Dec. 22.

PILCHARD, VEN. THOMAS (1557–1587), martyr. Born in Battle, Sussex, England, he studied at Oxford and Rheims, was ordained at Laon in 1583, sent to England, captured and banished, but again returned. While imprisoned for his priesthood he made thirty conversions of other prisoners, and was violently tortured as a result. He was hanged, drawn, and quartered at Dorchester on Mar. 21.

PILGRIM (d. 991), bishop. A Benedictine at Niederaltaich monastery, Bavaria, he was named bishop of Passau in 971, was active in converting the Hungarians, held three synods, and was the author of the "forgeries of Lorch," a collection of documents he fabricated to prove that Passau should be raised to an archdiocese and he receive the pallium. He died on May 20. He is mentioned in the *Niebelungenlied*.

PILIGRIM (d. 1036). He became archbishop of Cologne, Germany, in 1021, accompanied Henry II and Conrad II on their expeditions to Italy, and gained the title of imperial chancellor of Italy for himself and his successors.

PINCHON, ST. GUILLAUME (d. 1234), bishop. Born in Brittany, he became canon and bishop of St. Brieuc in 1220, shortly after his ordination. When he defended the rights of the Church against temporal encroachment he was banished to Poitiers, France. He was canonized in 1253. F. D. July 29.

PINDEMONTE, IPPOLITO (1753–1823), poet. Born in Verona, Italy, on Nov. 13, of a noble family, he studied at Collegio di San Carlo, Modena, became a member of the Order of Malta (but resigned about 1783), traveled through Europe, and returned to Verona in 1791 to devote himself to writing. He died there on Nov. 18. Among his chief works were *Poesie* (1785), *Prose campestri* (1795), *Sepolcri*, and a translation of the *Odyssey* on which he worked fifteen years. He was greatly influenced by Thomas Gray and James Macpherson; his story, *Abaritte*, is an imitation of Johnson's *Rasselas*.

PIÑEDA, JUAN DE (1558–1637), theologian. Born in Seville, Spain, he became a Jesuit in 1572 and taught in Seville, Cordova, and Madrid. He became rector at Seville, consultor to the Inquisition, in which capacity he visited many Spanish libraries to examine their books, and in 1612 published the *Index librorum prohibitorum*. He wrote biblical commentaries (on Job, Canticles, and Ecclesiastes), a study of Solomon, and a controversial interpretation of Pliny. He died in Seville on Jan. 27.

PINGRÉ, ALEXANDRE GUY (1711–1796), astronomer. Born in Paris on Sept. 11, he studied at the Augustinian college in Senlis, where he entered that order at sixteen, and taught theology there in 1735. In 1737 he was rebuked by the bishop of Pamiers and in 1745 removed from his position for his Jansenistic tendencies and his objection to the papal bull *Unigenitus*. By 1747 he had abandoned his erroneous views and in 1749 was named professor of astronomy at the Rouen Academy, was made corresponding secretary of the Academy of Sciences, librarian of Ste. Geneviève, chancellor of the university, and built an observatory at Ste. Geneviève where he labored for some forty years. He compiled the first nautical almanac for 1754, calculated the eclipses for ten centuries B.C., traveled to the Pacific (1760) and Haiti (1769) to observe the transit of Venus, and published several astronomical studies. He died on May 1.

PINI, BL. MICHAEL (1445?–1552). Born in Florence, Italy, he was a favored courtier of Lorenzo de' Medici, became a Camaldolese in 1502, was ordained, and lived in a walled hermitage in Florence until death. F. D. Jan. 27.

PINIAN, ST. (d. 432). *See* Melania the Younger, St.

PINNA DA ENCARNAÇAO, MATTHEUS (1687–1764), theologian. Born in Rio de Janeiro, Brazil, on Aug. 23, he became a Benedictine there in 1703, studied in Bahia, and was ordained in 1708. He taught theology, was abbot of Nossa Senhora de Montserrate in Rio in 1726, was banished from the monastery by the governor of Brazil in 1727, and escaped to Portugal, where he lived at court. He had his abbey restored in 1729, was elected provincial abbot in 1732, re-elected abbot in Rio in 1739, in Bahia in 1746, and refused re-election as provincial abbot in 1752, when he retired. He died in Rio de Janeiro on Dec. 18. He wrote a treatise on grace, had several volumes of sermons published, and a six-volume *Theologia scholastica dogmatica*.

PINOT, BL. NOEL (1747–1794), martyr. A priest who served at a hospital for incurables and then as curate in Louroux-Béconnais, France, he was forced to continue his work secretly after arrest and trial by a revolutionary tribunal. His whereabouts was betrayed by a friend and he was captured while preparing for mass and guillotined twelve days later, still wearing his priestly vestments. He was beatified in 1926. F. D. Feb. 21.

PINTEN, JOSEPH G. (1867–1945), bishop. Born in Rockland, Michigan, on Oct. 3, he studied at St. Francis seminary, Milwaukee, and the Propaganda, Rome, and was ordained in Rome in 1890. He did parish work in Michigan, was vicar general of Marquette and Sault Ste. Marie in 1916–21, and was appointed bishop of Superior, Wisconsin, in 1921. He was transferred to Grand Rapids in 1926, and retired in 1940. He died on Nov. 6.

PINTO, FERNÃO MENDES (1509?–1583). Born in Montemor-o-Velho, Portugal, he became a page of the duke of Coimbra, went to the East Indies in 1537, where he spent the next twenty-one years traveling throughout the Far East, and wrote *Peregrinaçao*, a vivid and imaginative description of his adventures, frequently reprinted and translated. He died in Almada, Portugal, on July 8.

PINTURICCHIO (1454?–1513), painter. Bernardino di Betto was born in Verona, Italy, studied under Fiorenzo di Lorenzo, and became famous for his decorative frescoes and panel pictures in Perugia, Rome, and Siena. He was tagged with the name Pinturicchio ("the Dauber"). He worked with Perugino, who greatly influenced him, on the frescoes in the Sistine Chapel in 1480, decorated the Borgia apartments in the Vatican for Pope Alexander VI, executed the frescoes in Santa Maria del Popolo, painted the life of St. Bernardino in the Ara Coeli in Rome, and in 1501 did the frescoes for the Blessed Sacrament chapel in Santa Maria Maggiore in Spello. His masterpiece is considered to be the ten scenes from the life of Pope Pius II which Cardinal Piccolomini commissioned him to paint for the Piccolomini Library in Siena in 1502. He died in Siena, Italy, on Dec. 11.

PINYTUS, ST. (2nd century). He was a bishop in Crete about 180. F. D. Oct. 10.

PINZÓN, MARTÍN ALONSO (1440?–1493), navigator. Born in Palos de Moguer, Spain, of a seafaring family, he became a pilot, and sailed to Africa under a French navigator, Cousin, who had him dropped from the Dieppe service for mutinous conduct on the voyage. On his return to Spain he met Columbus, supported his claims to Isabella, contributed to the expedition, built the three ships, and raised the crews. He accompanied Columbus as commander of the *Pinta* (his brother Francisco Martín was pilot and another brother, Vincente, commanded the *Niña*). He twice deserted Columbus' fleet, the first time off the Cuban coast in the hope of being the first to discover the new world (he was the first to see Haiti), and then on his return off the Azores in an attempt to reach Spain before Columbus could make his report. The king refused to see him and he soon died of the effects of his voyage.

PINZÓN, VICENTE YAÑEZ (1460–1524?), navigator. A brother of Martín, he was born in Palos de Moguer, Spain, was commander of the *Niña* on Columbus' expedition, rescued the explorer when the *Santa Maria* was driven ashore off Santo Domingo in Dec. 1492, helped quell a mutiny on the *Santa Maria*, and was loyal to Columbus. In 1499 he set out with his own flotilla, discovered the mouth of the Amazon River and sailed across the Caribbean and the Gulf of Mexico. He accompanied Juan Díaz de Solís on a voyage to the southern part of South America in 1508, was probably ennobled by Charles V, and disappeared from history after 1523.

PIOMBO, SEBASTIANO DEL. *See* Luciani, Sebastiano.

PIONIUS, ST. (d. 250?), martyr. A priest in Smyrna (now Izmir, Turkey), who had converted many, he was seized during the persecution of Decius, tortured extremely, and finally burned to death when he refused to sacrifice to the gods even after his own bishop had weakened. Eusebius included an eyewitness report in his *Ecclesiastical History*. F. D. Feb. 1.

PIOR, ST. (d. 395). An Egyptian hermit, he was an early disciple of St. Antony of the Desert. F. D. Jan. 17.

PIPERION, ST. (d. 254?), martyr. *See* Candidus, St.

PIPPI, GIULIO. *See* Giulio Romano.

PIPPIN. *See* Pepin.

PIRAN, ST. (6th century). Founder of a hermitage in Cornwall, he was patron of the tin miners there and honored on Mar. 5 and on May 11. He has erroneously been identified with St. Kieran. He is also known as Perran.

PIRANESI, GIOVANNI BATTISTA (1720–1778), engraver. Born in Venice, Italy, he studied drawing under his uncle Lucchesi, and went to Rome in 1738, where he studied architecture under Valeriani and engraving under Vasi and opened a print shop, and became famed for his etchings of antiquities. He etched thousands of copper plates executed in a bold, powerful manner, some of the finest of which were in his *Architectura Romana* (208 plates), *Magnificenza dei Romana* and *Antique Statues, Vases and Busts*. He died in Rome on Nov. 9.

PIRKHEIMER, WILLIBALD (1470–1530). Born in Eichstätt, Germany, on Dec. 5, son of a lawyer, he studied at Padua and Pavia, was a Nuremberg town councilor from 1498 to 1523, and a leading humanist. He led a local unit in the Swiss war of 1499, wrote a historical account of it, was appointed imperial councilor by Maximilian, defended Reuchlin against the Cologne theologians, attacked Johann Eck, and sided with Luther early in his career. He was named in the bull of excommunication of 1520, but was absolved in 1521 when he formally denounced Luther's teachings as heretical. He attacked Protestantism with force after hearing of the persecutions to which his sister Charitas (1466–1532) was subjected at the Poor Clare convent in Nuremberg, of which she had been abbess from 1503, and where their sister Clara and two of his daughters were nuns. He had dedicated a translation of Plutarch to Charitas, one of St.

Fulgentius to her and Clara, and also issued translations of Euclid, Lucian, Plato, Xenophon, and the Church Fathers into Latin. He died in Nuremberg, Germany, on Dec. 22.

PIRMINUS, ST. (d. 753), bishop. A monk of southern Aragon, Spain, he fled the Moors and settled in the Rhineland, where he founded the Benedictine monasteries of Reichenau (of which he was first abbot), Murbach in Gaul, and Amorbach in Franconia. He was a regional missionary bishop (but not of the see of Meaux, as the Roman Martyrology states) and the author of *Dicta Pirmini*, a popular catechism. F. D. Nov. 3.

PIROTTI, ST. POMPILIO (1710–1756). Born at Montecalvo, Italy, he joined the Piarists, was ordained, and taught for several years in Apulia. He was then appointed missioner apostolic in Emilia and Venetia. Expelled from Naples by the King, he was recalled to continue his work when the populace clamored for him. He died in Campo, near Lecce, Italy, and was canonized in 1934. F. D. July 15.

PISANO, ANDREA (1270?–1348?), sculptor. Born in Pisa, Italy, and also called Andrea da Pontedera, he was at first a goldsmith, then studied under Giovanni Pisano, and after a period in Venice, where he did several statues for St. Mark's façade, went to Florence, where he executed the first bronze door (on the south side) for the San Giovanni baptistery. He succeeded Giotto as head of the work on the Florence cathedral and campanile (Giotto's Tower) for which he executed several bas-reliefs designed by Giotto, and spent his last years in Orvieto working on the façade of the cathedral, of which he had been appointed architect in 1347. He is considered the founder of the Florentine school of sculpture. He died in Florence.

PISANO, GIOVANNI (1240?–1320?), sculptor. Born in Pisa, Italy, son of Niccola Pisano, he assisted his father on the Siena cathedral pulpit and the Perugia fountain, executed pulpits for Sant' Andrea in Pistoia and the Pisa cathedral (his outstanding achievements), the tomb of Emperor Henry VII's wife, Margarita, in 1313, Pope Urban IV's monument at Perugia, and several madonnas. Also noted as an architect, his outstanding work in this field was the Canto Santo cloisters in Pisa, the façade of the cathedral in Siena, and Santa Maria della Spina in Pisa, the first church in Italy built in the Gothic style.

PISANO, NICCOLA. *See* Niccola Pisano.

PISANO, VITTORE (1380?–1456?), painter. Born sometime between 1380 and 1397, in Pisa, Italy, he studied under Gentile da Fabriano, whom he assisted on the ducal palace in Venice and who greatly influenced him, and became noted for his frescoes, bird and animal paintings, and his portraits. He enjoyed great popularity, was patronized by King Alfonso of Naples, the Estes, and the duke of Ferrara, among others, and painted frescoes in the Lateran, Pavia's Castello, Florence, Verona, and Venice, though only the *Annunciation* in St. Fermo, Verona, and *St. George Mounting His Horse* in St. Anastasia, Verona, have survived. Of his paintings, characterized by their detail and draftsmanship, few remain, notably *Portrait of a Lady* and *The Miraculous Stag Appearing to St. Eustace.* He was particularly noted for his medals, some of whose subjects were Lionello d'Este, Francesco Sforza, and Vittorino da Feltre. He is also known as Pisanello.

PISANELLO. *See* Pisano, Vittore.

PISE, CHARLES CONSTANTINE (1801–1866). Born in Annapolis, Maryland, on Nov. 22, he studied at Georgetown, became a Jesuit in 1815, but left in 1820 and went to Rome, where he was ordained in 1825. He taught at Mt. St. Mary's College, Emmitsburg, Maryland, and was a curate in Baltimore and Washington. He was first Catholic chaplain to the United States Senate in 1832, was stationed in New York City from 1834 to 1849, and from then until his death on May 26 was pastor of St. Charles Borromeo, Brooklyn. He wrote a five-volume *History of the Catholic Church* (1827–30), *Christianity and the Church*, poems, and a play, and founded *The Catholic Expositor and Literary Magazine* (1841).

PISONNAULT, PIERRE ADOLPHE (1815–1883), bishop. Born in St. Philippe, Quebec, Canada, on Nov. 23, he studied in Montreal and St. Sulpice, Paris, and was ordained there in 1840. He was consecrated bishop of London, Ontario, in 1856; the see was transferred to Sandwich in 1859. He resigned in 1866, and died in Montreal on Jan. 30.

PISTORIUS, JOHANN (1546–1608). Born in Nidda, Hesse, on Feb. 14, son of a Protestant minister, he studied at Marburg and Wittenberg, received his doctorate in medicine, was appointed court physician to Margrave Karl II of Baden-Durlach in 1575, and privy councilor of James III of Baden-Hochberg in 1584. He became a convert in 1588, was ordained in Freiburg in 1591, and served as vicar general of Constance, imperial councilor, and confessor to Emperor Rudolph II. He wrote controversial works, including *Anatomia Lutheri*, and historical and philosophical treatises, and died in Freiburg, Germany, on July 18.

PITAVAL, JOHN BAPTIST (1858–1928), archbishop. Born in St. Genis-Terrenoire, France, on Feb. 10, he studied at the Lyons seminary, went to the United States in 1881, finished his studies at St. Charles, Maryland, and was ordained in Sante Fe in 1881. He did missionary work in the western United States, was consecrated titular bishop of Sora and auxiliary of Santa Fe, New Mexico, in 1902, administered the see in 1908, and was appointed its archbishop in 1909. He resigned in 1918 and was appointed titular archbishop of Amida, and died in Denver, Colorado, on May 23.

PITHOU, PIERRE (1539–1596). Born in Troyes, France, on Nov. 1, he studied at Paris, Bourges, and Valence, was admitted to the bar in Paris in 1560, left when the religious conflict broke into warfare, later went to Sedan, where he wrote a code of law for the duc de Bouillion, and Basle, returned to France in 1570, and became a Catholic in 1573. He supported Henry IV, defended the rights of the French bishops to absolve the king without papal sanction, and in 1594 published *Les libertés de l'église gallicane*, an eighty-three-article codification of Gallican beliefs which had great influence, cited as law as late as 1768 and published as late as an 1824 edition. He was appointed procurator general of the Parliament of Paris by Henry IV, but soon resigned to devote himself to writing. He edited Petronius, Quintillian, Salvian, and others, and died in Nogent-sur-Seine, France, on Nov. 1.

PITONI, JOSEPH (1657–1743), composer. Born in Rieti, Italy, on Mar. 18, he studied music in Rome as a child, was head of the choir at Monte Rotondo at sixteen and of the Assisi choir in 1674, and returned to Rome in 1677 to become choirmaster of several churches. He was appointed director of St. John Lateran in 1708, and choirmaster of St. Peter's in 1719, a position he held until his death in Rome on Feb. 1, and wrote numerous musical compositions.

PITRA, JEAN BAPTISTE FRANÇOIS (1812–1889), cardinal. Born in Champforgeuil, France, on Aug. 1, he studied in Autun, was ordained in 1836, and taught rhetoric in the seminary there until 1841. He attracted attention by deciphering a third-century inscription found in Autun, became a Benedictine in 1841, and was prior of St. Germain in 1843. In Paris he was a collaborator of Abbé Migne on *Cursus patrologiae*, and in 1859–60 was sent on a visit to Russian libraries and the Basilian monasteries of Galicia by Pope Pius IX. He returned to Rome in 1861, supervised a new edition of Greek-rite liturgical books, and in 1863 was created cardinal. He was appointed librarian of the Vatican in 1869, supervised the cataloguing of its manuscripts, was named cardinal-bishop of Frascati in 1879, transferred to the see of Porto and Santa Rufina in 1884, and was protector of several congregations, including the Cistercians and Eudists. He wrote on Greek canon law and

hymnography; a history of the Bollandists' *Acta sanctorum; Spicilegium Solesmense*, unpublished works of early Christian writers, and two supplements; other historical and archaeological works; biographies of St. Léger and Paul Liebermann; and edited collections of Byzantine hymns. He died in Rome on Feb. 9.

PITTS, JOHN (1560–1616). Born in Alton, Hampshire, England, on Oct. 17, he studied at Winchester, Oxford, and the English College in Rome, and was ordained in 1588. He taught in Rheims, took his doctorate in divinity at Ingolstadt, was a canon in Verdun, confessor and almoner of the duchess of Cleves for twelve years, and dean of Liverdun, Lorraine, where he died on Oct. 17. He published *De illustribus scriptoribus* and other parts of *Relationum historicarum de rebus Angliae*, based on often erroneous biographical entries by Bishop Bale.

PIUS I, ST. (d. 155), pope. Son of Rufinus and brother of Hermas who wrote *The Shepherd*, he was a native of Aquileia, Italy, and may have been a slave. He became pope in 140, vigorously fought Valentinianism and Gnosticism, and excommunicated Marcion, a Gnostic preacher, who then formed his own church. There is no evidence that he was a martyr, though he was so venerated for some time. F. D. July 11.

PIUS II (1405–1464), pope. Aeneas Silvius de' Piccolomini was born in Corsignano (later renamed Pienza in his honor), Italy, on Oct. 18. He studied at Siena, where he became known for his sensual life, then at Florence, became secretary to Bishop Domenico Capranica of Fermo in 1431, and accompanied him to the Council of Basle in 1431–35. During this period he served on diplomatic missions for several bishops, among them to England and Scotland for Cardinal Albergati, and in 1436, though a layman, occupied a seat on the council. When it was transferred to Florence, he exercised great influence, supported the council against Pope Eugene IV, and helped elect Amadeus of Savoy antipope Felix V. He became Felix's secretary, participated in the Diet of Frankfort on Main in 1442, gained a reputation as a humanist, and met and became secretary to Frederick III of Germany, who appointed him poet laureate and used him on diplomatic missions. In 1445 he submitted to Pope Eugene and abandoned his wastrel life. He was ordained subdeacon in 1446, made bishop of Trieste in 1447–50 and bishop of Siena in 1450, negotiated the concordat of Aschaffenburg, and was created a cardinal and a prince of the empire in 1456. He was elected pope on Aug. 19, 1458, and crowned on Sept. 3. In 1459 he preached a crusade against the Turks (who had captured Constantinople in 1453), which was to be the goal of his entire pontificate, but received little support from the temporal princes. In 1460 he issued his bull *Execrabilis*, condemning all appeals from the pope to an ecumenical council. He was faced with a revival of Gallicanism in France when he refused to support King Louis XI's choice of René of Anjou as king of Naples and backed Ferdinand in 1461, and difficulties in Germany when he became embroiled in arguments with Archbishop Diether of Mainz, who was backing King George Podiebrad of Bavaria's attempts to depose Emperor Frederick III, whom Pius supported—an argument which continued indecisively until Pius' death. In 1464 Pius started on a crusade, but was stricken with fever and died at Ancona, Italy, on Aug. 15. Pius was a voluminous author and wrote poetry, plays, fiction, orations, and history, often under the name Aeneas Silvius. Among his best-known works are *Miseriae curialium* (1473), Latin poems which influenced contemporary English satire; *Pii II Commentarii rerum memorabilium*, his autobiography, the only one left by any pope; *Cosmographiae in Asiae et Europae . . . descriptione* (1503); and *Historica Bohemica* (1532).

PIUS III (1439–1503), pope. Francesco Todeschini Piccolomini was born in Siena, Italy, on May 29, nephew of Pope Pius II, who raised him. He received his doctorate in canon law at Perugia, and was created cardinal-deacon and appointed archbishop of Siena in 1460. He acted as legate to the March of Ancona and Germany, became cardinal-protector of Germany, and was known for his piety. He was elected pope on Sept. 22, 1503, was crowned on Oct. 8, but died in Rome on Oct. 18.

PIUS IV (1499–1565), pope. Giovanni Angelo de' Medici (no relation to the famous Medici family) was born in Milan, Italy, on Mar. 31, son of a notary, studied at Pavia and Bologna, where he received his doctorate, went to Rome in 1527, was appointed prothonotary by Pope Clement VII, and during Pope Paul III's pontificate helped rule several cities in the Papal States. He was ordained in 1545, became archbishop of Ragusa in 1546, was created a cardinal in 1549, and was appointed legate in Romagna and commander of the papal troops by Pope Julius III. On Dec. 25, 1559, he was elected pope, and was crowned on Jan. 6, 1560. He appointed his nephew, St. Charles Borromeo, then twenty-two, as his cardinal-secretary of state, tried the Carafas for murder and had four of them executed (among them, Cardinal Carlo Carafa and his brother, Duke Giovanni of Paliano; a sentence which Pope St. Pius V was to declare unjust), and embarked on a program of building in Rome which led to the imposition of unpopular taxes on the populace. He issued a bull reconvening the Council of Trent later the same year,

brought it to a successful conclusion in 1563, and confirmed all its decrees with the bull *Benedictus Deus* in 1564. Though decidedly in favor of reform, he relaxed the rigor of his predecessor's rule, was a liberal patron of the arts (saw the Belvedere court completed and commissioned the building of the Casino Pio IV, the Porta Pia, and Santa Maria degli Angeli), founded the pontifical printing press, and witnessed the beginning of the French religious wars in 1562. He escaped an assassination attempt in 1564, and died in Rome on Dec. 9. Although he evidently had three illegitimate children prior to 1542, his personal life after his ordination was blameless.

PIUS V, ST. (1504–1572), pope. Born in Bosco, Switzerland, on Jan. 17, Antonio Michael Ghislieri became a Dominican at fourteen in Voghera, was ordained in 1528, taught theology and served as master of novices and superior, was made bishop of Nepi and Sutri and inquisitor general for Lombardy in 1556, and cardinal in 1557. Named bishop of Mondovi in 1559, he restored war-torn Piedmont, and succeeded Pope Pius IV on Jan. 7 (crowned on Jan. 17), 1566. As pope, he gave large sums to the poor and sick (including all funds donated for his coronation), reformed the curia, tightened laws to keep the clergy in their own dioceses, removed legendary references from the new breviary (1568) and missal (1570), and saw to it that the new catechism was spread abroad in all vernaculars. He declared Thomas Aquinas a Doctor of the Church, excommunicated Queen Elizabeth of England, and sent a fleet under Don Juan of Austria and Marcantonio Colonna to defeat the Turkish fleet at Lepanto in 1571 and stem the Moslem tide. Personally, he was a man who lived by his monastic rule, tending the sick himself, fasting to great lengths, devoted to prayer, instituting the feast of the Holy Rosary and approving an office to Mary. He died in Rome on May 1 and was canonized in 1712. F. D. May 5.

PIUS VI (1717–1799), pope. Giovanni Angelico Braschi was born in Cesena, Italy, on Dec. 27, studied at the Jesuit college there and law at Ferrara, was engaged to be married, but decided to enter the priesthood though he was not ordained until he was thirty-seven. He became secretary to Pope Benedict XIV and canon of St. Peter's in 1755 and papal treasurer in 1766, and was created a cardinal by Pope Clement XIV in 1773. On Feb. 15, 1775, he was elected pope, and was crowned on Feb. 22. He immediately proclaimed a jubilee year, launched a program of public works, drained the Pontine marshes, and encouraged scholarship and the arts. His pontificate was troubled by the rise of state interference in Church affairs, particularly in Austria and

France. In 1782 he went to Vienna in an unsuccessful attempt to persuade Emperor Joseph II to abandon his claim to complete ecclesiastical authority in his realms. In 1784, Pius reluctantly signed a concordat granting Joseph many of his demands, including the right to name the bishops of Milan and Mantua. In Tuscany, Joseph's brother, Grand Duke Leopold II, denied papal supremacy and at the Synod of Pistoia in 1786 sanctioned the teachings of Quesnel and Jansenism; eighty-five of the synod's propositions were denounced in the bull *Auctorem fidei* in 1794. In the Two Sicilies, Ferdinand IV repudiated the 700-year-old papal suzerainty and claimed the right to nominate all ecclesiastical benefices; when the pope refused to accept his nominees for bishops, more than half the sees were empty by 1791, but a temporary truce was agreed upon and more than sixty vacant sees filled. In France the anti-Church measures of the French Revolution culminated in the Civil Constitution of the Clergy promulgated in 1790, which Pius denounced in 1791, forbidding all priests to subscribe to it. In retaliation, France annexed Avignon and Venaissin, papal territories. When the French attaché, Jean Hugon de Basseville, who had been propagating revolutionary propaganda in Rome, was murdered there in 1793, and Pius protested Louis XVI's execution and sided with the anti-French alliance, Napoleon's armies invaded the Papal States, forcing Pius to accept the truce of Bologna in 1796 and the Treaty of Tolentino in 1797 by which he ceded Avignon, Venaissin, Ferrara, Bologna, and the Romagna to France, paid millions of francs in reparations, and surrendered hundreds of art masterpieces to Napoleon. In Aug. 1797 an abortive revolution in Rome, wherein the French general, Duphot, was killed, led to the occupation of Rome by the French and their proclamation of the Roman republic on Feb. 15, 1798. Pius was taken prisoner, held in various cities, and finally taken to Valance, France, where he died on Aug. 29, after reigning twenty-four years, the longest pontificate since that of Peter.

PIUS VII (1740–1823), pope. Barnaba Chiaramonti was born in Cesena, Italy, on Aug. 14, educated at the college for nobles at Ravenna, and at sixteen became a Benedictine at Santa Maria del Monte monastery near Cesena. After ordination he taught at Parma and Rome, and was appointed abbot of San Callisto monastery in Rome by Pope Pius VI, a friend of the family. He was appointed bishop of Tivoli in 1782, and was created a cardinal and bishop of Imola in 1785. He was elected pope on Mar. 14, 1800 (and crowned on Mar. 21) at a conclave in Venice. He created Ercole Consalvi cardinal-secretary of state, set about reforming the administration of the Papal States, and in 1801

signed a concordat with Napoleon which re-established the Church in France and set up a new hierarchy in return for great concessions on the pope's part. When Napoleon published the concordat in 1802, he also published the seventy-seven Organic Articles which further restricted the Church in France, despite vigorous papal objections. In 1804, Pius went to Paris to crown Napoleon emperor (actually, Napoleon placed the crown on his own head in Notre Dame). Differences arose between pope and emperor (Pius refused to annul the marriage of Napoleon's brother, Jerome, to Miss Patterson, and refused Napoleon's demands he expel all subjects of nations at war with France and participate in the continental blockade against England), and in 1808 the French army occupied Rome, whereupon Pius became a voluntary captive. He was forced to change secretaries of state several times at French insistence, but late in 1808 he refused to expel Cardinal Pacca, then secretary of state; whereupon Napoleon, in 1809, proclaimed the annexation of the Papal States to the empire. On Feb. 10, Pius excommunicated Napoleon, who arrested the pope and imprisoned him in Savona and later at Fontainebleau. When Pius refused to confirm Napoleon's bishops, the emperor subjected the Church to every indignity, and convened a national council in Bordeaux in 1811. Weakened by ill treatment and illness, Pius agreed to Napoleon's demands, and in Jan. 1813 signed a new concordat, agreeing to the French annexation of the Papal States and the decrees of the national council. Two months later, Pius declared the concordat null and void, since he had been forced to sign it by violence. He was freed after Napoleon's defeat at Laon in 1814, and returned to Rome in May. He set about rebuilding the Church, reinstituted the Inquisition, issued a decree of amnesty, and re-established the Society of Jesus. Obliged to leave Rome on Mar. 22, when Murat threatened during the days of Napoleon's escape, he returned the following June and remained there until his death. In 1815 the Congress of Vienna restored the Papal States to the pope. He negotiated a new concordat with Louis XVIII abrogating the Organic Articles, but Gallican opposition was so strong it was never ratified. Concordats were negotiated with Bavaria in 1817 and Prussia in 1821, but a revolution in Spain in 1820 led to numerous anti-Church laws, and, when Pius refused to accept the anti-papal Canon Villanueva as Spanish ambassador to Rome, relations were broken off in 1823. The suppression of the revolt later the same year resulted in the repeal of the anti-Catholic laws by King Ferdinand VII. Despite the ill-treatment he had received from Napoleon, he gave the emperor's family haven in Rome after Napoleon was exiled and intervened with the British government to secure better treatment for him on St. Helena. The rest of his pontificate he devoted to reconstructing the Papal States, reviving the Church throughout Europe, patronizing the arts and learning, instituting a building program in Rome, and expanding world-wide missionary activities. He died in Rome on Aug. 20.

PIUS VIII (1761–1830), pope. Francesco Xaverio Castiglione was born in Cingoli, Italy, on Nov. 20, and studied at the Jesuit school in Osimo and at Bologna and Rome. After ordination he became vicar general of Anagni, later of Cingoli, then provost of the cathedral there. He was appointed bishop of Montalto in 1800, was transferred to Cesena and was imprisoned by the French when he refused to take the oath of allegiance to the king of Italy. He was created a cardinal in 1816, appointed bishop of Frascati in 1822, and was elected pope on Mar. 31, 1829, and crowned on Apr. 5. In ill health at his election, he reigned only twenty months and died in Rome on Nov. 30. During his brief pontificate he issued the bull, *Litteris altero abhinc*, regulating mixed marriages in Prussia.

PIUS IX (1792–1878), pope. Giovanni Maria Mastai-Ferretti was born in Sinigaglia, Italy, on May 13, and studied at the Piarist college in Volterra and Rome, which he was forced to leave because of the political unrest in 1810. He returned to the Roman seminary in 1814, was ordained in 1819, served as spiritual director of an orphan asylum, and in 1823 was sent to Chile as auditor to the apostolic delegate. He became director of San Michele hospital and canon of Santa Maria on his return in 1825, and in 1827 was appointed archbishop of Spoleto, which in 1831 he saved from attack by a band of revolutionaries. He was transferred to the diocese of Imola in 1832, created a cardinal in 1840, and on June 16, 1846, was elected pope and crowned on June 21. He began a moderately liberal policy of governing the Papal States, granted an amnesty to all political prisoners, and in the next two years inaugurated a series of widespread political reforms. In 1848 he granted a constitution, but when he refused to consider war with Austria, for which the Italian nationalists were clamoring, his prime minister, Pellegrino Rossi, was assassinated, and he was besieged in the Quirinal. He escaped to Gaeta and revolutionary forces took over Rome, proclaiming a republic in 1849. In June, French troops restored order and Pius returned in Apr. 1850. When Austria was defeated at Magenta in 1859 and forced to withdraw her troops from the papal legations, revolts broke out in several Romagna cities. In 1860, Piedmontese forces under Victor Emmanuel II defeated the papal army at Castelfidardo and Ancona and annexed all papal territory except Rome. Pius excommunicated Victor Emmanuel, but in 1864 an agreement was reached by which Piedmont agreed not to annex any more papal territory and Napoleon III withdrew French troops from Rome. When French forces were defeated at Sedan in 1870, Piedmontese troops attacked Rome and on Sept. 20 occupied Rome, ending the temporal power of the pope, who refused to recognize the new kingdom or accept any offers of remuneration, and declared himself a prisoner. Throughout his pontificate, Pius encountered great difficulties in Europe. A concordat negotiated with Austria in 1855 was rendered ineffective by agitation raised against it and abolished in 1870 by Austria, which took over the management of ecclesiastical matters in 1874; in Germany, anti-Church feeling culminated in the Kulturkampf which began in 1873; Russia, which launched a violent anti-Catholic campaign after the Polish revolt of 1863, broke off relations with the papacy in 1866; the denunciations of Swiss outrages in Pius' encyclical letter of 1873 led to the expulsion of the papal nuncio in 1874; and only in Spain did a satisfactory situation exist with the concordat of 1851 as amended in 1859, and in Portugal with the concordat of 1857. Pius established the English hierarchy in 1850, and the Dutch in 1853, proclaimed the dogma of the Immaculate Conception by the bull *Ineffabilis Deus* in 1854, and issued the encyclical *Quanta cura*, accompanied by the *Syllabus of Errors*, in 1864, denouncing naturalism, communism, socialism, indifferentism, liberalism, and freemasonry. In 1869 he convoked the Vatican Council, which proclaimed the dogma of papal infallibility in 1870. In 1875 he consecrated the world to the Sacred Heart, and three years later, on Feb. 7, he died in Rome after the longest papal reign in history.

E. E. Y. HALES, *Pio Nono* (Garden City, N.Y., Image Books, 1962).

PIUS X, ST. (1835–1914), pope. Guiseppe Sarto was born in Riese, Italy, second of ten children of the municipal courier. He was educated locally and in 1850 entered the seminary at Padua, where he was ordained in 1858. For the next seventeen years he engaged in pastoral work in Tombolo and Salzano, where he became pastor. He was diocesan chancellor of Treviso from 1875 to 1884. He then was appointed bishop of Mantua, a run-down diocese which he revived so successfully that in 1893 he was appointed cardinal and patriarch of Venice, although he was unable to direct his see until 1894, because the Italian government claimed the right to nominate the patriarch. He was elected pope on Aug. 4, 1903, and crowned on Aug. 9. The great struggle of his pontificate was against modernism, called the "synthesis of all heresies," which he examined and denounced in the decree, *Lamentabili sane exitu,* and the encyclical, *Pascendi dominici gregis.* He began the task of codifying canon law, set up a commission to revise the Vulgate, instituted reforms in seminary rules and training, reorganized the offices and congregations of the Holy See, ordered a revision of the breviary and the psalter and a reform of liturgical music, and encouraged frequent reception of Holy Communion, especially by children. He also urged Italian Catholics to take a more active role in politics. In 1905, France renounced the concordat of 1801 and offered a choice between governmental control of ecclesiastical affairs or confiscation of church property. When Pius unequivocally rejected the former, France broke off relations and passed anti-Church laws. Pius died on Aug. 20, shortly after the outbreak of World War I. He was canonized in 1954, the first pope to be canonized in nearly 300 years. F. D. Sept. 3.

KATHERINE BURTON, *The Great Mantle* (New York, Longmans, 1951).

PIUS XI (1857–1939), pope. Ambrosio Damien Achille Ratti was born in Desio, Italy, on May 31, and educated at seminaries in Seviso and Milan and the Lombard College, the Gregorian University, and the Academy of St. Thomas in Rome. He was ordained, stationed briefly in a small parish, and transferred to the cathedral in Milan. At twenty-five he became professor of theology and sacred eloquence at the seminary there and a member of the staff of the Ambrosiana Library, which he thoroughly reorganized. On the one hand, he published many scholarly articles, volumes on the development of the Church in Lombardy, on the Milanese Missal, on St. Charles Borromeo, and editions of the letters of Pius II and fragments of Vergil and Juvenal, and *Liber diurnus,* the oldest known register of the papal chancery. On the other hand, he was most active with the downtrodden chimney sweeps, with the new German colony in Milan, and as a convent chaplain. He also found time both to make a detailed study of the effects of Marxism in an industrial city and to exercise with the members of the Italian Alpine Club, climbing both the Matterhorn and Mont Blanc. In 1914 he was appointed director of the Vatican Library, which he also modernized and completely revised. In 1918 he was made apostolic visitor to Poland, the Baltic nations, and, later, to Russia; he was the first papal nuncio to Poland on its restoration as a nation, and apostolic commissioner in Upper Silesia before the plebiscite vote in the Oppeln area. It was while he was in the north that he saw at first hand the effects of communism, and that he worked actively with refugees. He returned to Rome in 1921, was made a cardinal on June 13, and elevated as archbishop of Milan on Sept. 8. He

was elected pope on Feb. 6, 1922, and crowned on Feb. 12. During his reign he restored much of St. Peter's, reinforced the catacombs, built the Oriental Institute, the Institute of Christian Archeology, the Russian and Ruthenian colleges, the Ateneo Lateranense, and the office buildings, workshops, post office, and hospital in Vatican City. His greatest political achievement was the Lateran Treaty with Italy, signed on Feb. 11, 1929, after three years of negotiations, which released the pope from virtual imprisonment since 1870, created Vatican City as a state, and arranged a concordat. During his pontificate, SS. Margaret Mary Alacoque, Albertus Magnus, Robert Bellarmine, John Bosco, Peter Canisius, John Eudes, John Fisher, Thomas More, Thérèse Martin, Bernadette Soubirous, and John Vianney were canonized; 200 victims of the Elizabethan persecution in England, were beatified; and the feast of Christ the King was instituted. Among the pope's major encyclicals were: *Quadragesimo anno,* on the fortieth anniversary of Leo XIII's letter on capital and labor; *Casti connubii,* on Christian marriage and family life; *Vigilanti cura,* on motion pictures; *Mens nostra,* on retreats and spiritual exercises; *Ad salutem,* on St. Augustine; *Rerum omnium,* on St. Francis de Sales; *Studiorum ducem,* on St. Thomas Aquinas and Thomism as the basis of Christian philosophy. Two others, *Non abbiamo* and *Mit brennender Sorge* attacked fascism and national socialism in Italy and Germany, the rise of which disturbed the last years of his life and led to World War II. He died on Feb. 10, seven months before Poland was attacked.

PHILIP HUGHES, *Pope Pius the Eleventh* (London, Sheed, 1938); ZSOLT ARADI, *Pius XI: The Pope and the Man* (Garden City, New York, Hanover, 1958).

PIUS XII (1876–1958), pope. Eugenio Pacelli was born in Rome on Mar. 2, studied at the Capranica, Gregorian, and law at the Sapienza, and was ordained in 1899. He joined the staff of the papal secretariat of state in 1901, and taught at the Apollinare and law at the Accademia dei Nobili Ecclesiastici. He became secretary of the Commission for the Code of Canon Law and consultor of the Holy Office in 1912, secretary of Extraordinary Ecclesiastical Affairs in 1914 when he negotiated a concordat with Serbia, and was appointed titular archbishop of Sardes and nuncio to Bavaria in 1917, when he presented Benedict XV's peace proposals to Kaiser Wilhelm II. He was named first papal nuncio to Berlin in 1920, negotiated a concordat with Bavaria in 1925, Prussia in 1929, and Austria in 1934, was created cardinal late in 1929, and was appointed papal secretary of state in 1930. He fought fascism and nazism, was papal legate to the Eucharistic congresses in Buenos Aires in 1934, and in Budapest in 1938, and to Lourdes in 1935, visited the United States in 1936, and on Mar. 2, 1939, was elected pope and was crowned on Mar. 12. Devoted to the promotion of peace throughout the world, he was faced by the outbreak of World War II only seven months after his election. He labored to lessen its horrors and to alleviate suffering and distress throughout the world, and at its end to secure a just and lasting peace. After the war his pontificate was faced by the spread of communism and persecutions of the Church. He repeatedly denounced communism as incompatible with Catholicism and human rights and dignity. Throughout his pontificate he insisted on the rights and duties of the individual, the fundamental role of the family in human society, and the need of the Church to continue and broaden its apostolate. He constantly sought to solve contemporary problems by bringing spiritual principles to bear on them, and encouraged wider participation of the laity in spiritual affairs by his teaching on the Mystical Body, the modification of the Eucharistic fast, the celebration of evening mass, the use of the vernacular in the administration of some of the sacraments, a revised Holy Week liturgy, and the institution of new feasts. In 1939 and 1940 he permitted traditional native customs to be employed in religious ceremonies where such customs in no way affected the religious aspect of the ceremony in China, Korea, and India, thus settling a controversy which had raged since the eighteenth-century Jesuit missionaries had followed this practice in China; he founded the Pontificate Institute for Sacerdotal Vocations in 1941; and proclaimed 1950 a holy year. On Nov. 1 he defined the doctrine of the Assumption of the Virgin Mary, and proclaimed Dec. 1953–Dec. 1954 a Marian Year. During his reign he issued a great number of encyclicals, allocutions, briefs, and addresses. Among the most important of his forty-one encyclicals are: *Summi pontificatus* (1939), on the function of the church in the modern world; *Mystici corporis Christi* (1943), on the mystical body of Christ; *Divino afflante Spiritu* (1943), on the study of the Bible; *Mediator Dei* (1947), on the liturgy; and *Humani generis* (1950), denouncing several modern errors such as extreme theories of evolution, historicism, indifferentism, warning against attempts to distort Catholic truths, and stressing the necessity of Church teaching. Some of the other subjects denouncing several modern errors such as ex- *eunte octavo*, 1940, *Fidei donum*, 1957, and *Evangelii praecones*, 1951); communist persecution of the Church (*Orientales ecclesias*, 1947); peace and social disorders (*Optatissima pax*, 1947); sacred music (*Musicae sacrae*, 1955); radio, motion pictures, and televison

(*Miranda prorsus*, 1957); on crises in Hungary (*Luctuosissimi eventus*, 1956), the Middle East (*Laetamur admodum*, 1956), Palestine (*In multiplicibus curis*, 1948), and China (*Ad apostolorum principis*, 1958); the Sacred Heart (*Haurietis aquas*, 1956); and St. Bernard (*Doctor mellifluus*, 1953). He was widely venerated for his sanctity and asceticism and is reputed to have experienced supernatural visions. He canonized thirty-three saints during his pontificate, among them: Pope Pius X, Mother Frances Cabrini, first citizen of the United States to be so honored, Catherine Labouré, Margaret of Hungary, Louis Marie Grignon de Montfort, and Maria Goretti, and beatified 164. He was particularly noted for his audiences and is reputed to have received some 10,000,000 persons in audiences during his pontificate. He died at Castel Gandolfo, Italy, on Oct. 9.

ALDEN HATCH and SEAMUS WALSHE, *Crown of Glory* (New York, Hawthorne, 1958).

PIZARRO, FRANCISCO (1471?–1541), explorer. Born in Trujillo, Estremadura, Spain, illegitimate son of Gonzalo Pizarro, a Spanish officer, he was neglected and uneducated, went to the New World soon after its discovery, accompanied Alonzade Ojeda on his expedition from Hispaniola to Urabá in 1510, and was in charge of the colony for a short period. He was with Balboa when the Pacific Ocean was discovered in 1513, settled at Panama in 1519, and in 1522 and 1526, with Hernando de Luque, a priest, and Diego de Almagro, a soldier, led expeditions south of the equator which revealed to them the long-sought southern Inca Empire. When the governor of Panama refused to aid him, Pizarro returned to Spain in 1528; Charles V made him governor of the province of New Castile with the authority of a viceroy. In 1531 he set out from Panama with 180 men and twenty-seven horses and in the next five years, against overwhelming odds, conquered the Inca Empire and acquired great hoards of treasure. In 1537 he and Diego de Almagro had a controversy over the boundaries of their respective territories and the following year he defeated Almagro in battle and executed his adversary. Pizarro himself was assassinated by Almagro's followers on June 6 in Lima, Peru.

PIZZICOLLI, CIRIACO (1391?–1455?). Born in Ancona, Italy, he collected manuscripts and ancient artifacts throughout the Orient and the Mediterranean basin, copied inscriptions at Morea, Greece, and became an authority on epigraphy. Two volumes of inscriptions were published centuries after his death at Cremona, Italy.

PLACENTINI, BL. ARCHANGELO (1390?–1460). Born in Calafatimi, Sicily, he lived as a hermit, went to Alcamo to reorganize a hospice for the poor, and when Pope Martin V suppressed the hermitages of Sicily became a Friar Minor of the Observance at Palermo. He helped promote the new branch throughout Sicily and became minister provincial of the Sicilian Observants. He died on Apr. 10. His cult was confirmed by Pope Gregory XVI in 1836. F. D. July 30.

PLACID, ST. (d. 550?), martyr. Son of the patrician Tertullus, he was placed under St. Benedict's care as a child and probably went with the latter to Monte Cassino (said to have been donated by Tertullus). The Roman Martyrology says that he, two brothers and a sister, and thirty-three others were martyred by pirates at Messina, where he had founded the monastery of St. John. There was an earlier Placid who was martyred in Messina, but St. Benedict's disciple probably was never in Sicily except in the legendary biography by Peter the Deacon, invented in the mid-twelfth century. F. D. Oct. 4.

PLACID, ST. (d. 650?), martyr. A wealthy landowner, he gave land for the establishment of the Benedictine abbey of Dissentis in Switzerland, which St. Sigisbert founded and ruled as abbot. Placid, who became a monk under him, was murdered when he sought to protect the rights of the foundation. F. D. July 11.

PLACID, ST. (d. 1248). Born in Rodi, Italy, he became a Cistercian at Corno, withdrew to Ocre as a hermit, then founded the monastery of Santo Spirito in the Abruzzi, of which he became superior. F. D. June 12.

PLACIDA VIEL, BL. See Viel, Victoria Eulalia Jacqueline.

PLACIDIA, ST. (d. 460?). She is venerated at Verona, Italy, and has sometimes, erroneously, been identified as daughter of Valentinian III. F. D. Oct. 11.

PLACIDIA. See Galla Placidia.

PLAGENS, JOSEPH CASIMIR (1880–1943), bishop. Born in Detroit, Michigan, on Jan. 29, he studied at the University of Detroit and St. Mary's seminary, Baltimore, and was ordained in 1903. He served as pastor in Port Austin and Detroit, was made a domestic prelate in 1923, and was consecrated titular bishop of Rhodiapolis and auxiliary of Detroit in 1924 while a pastor (1919–35). He was vicar general of the diocese in 1924–35, and was appointed bishop of Marquette and Sault Sainte Marie in 1935. He was transferred to Grand Rapids, Michigan, in 1940, and died there on Mar. 31.

PLANTIN, CHRISTOPHE (1514–1589), publisher. Born near Tours, France, he learned printing and bookbinding under Robert Macé II in Caen from 1535 to 1540, spent some time in Paris, and in 1549 began a bindery in Antwerp, Belgium, which soon became famous. He founded a press and publishing house in 1555, was obliged to leave Antwerp in 1562 when charged with associating with heretics, returned the next year when he disproved the charges (though modern research was to reveal his association with the Familists, a mystical heretical sect, and his printing of several heretical works), and published an eight-volume *Biblia polyglotta* (1569–73). He was appointed royal architypographer in 1573, with the privilege of printing all liturgical books in Philip II's domains and received the exclusive license for liturgical formularies from Rome (a license the firm was to hold for 200 years). He left his business to his sons-in-law in 1583 to establish a bookstore and press to serve the new University of Leyden, but returned to Antwerp in 1585 to work until his death there on July 1. Plantin published more than 1600 tastefully chosen and designed books; his publishing firm endured until 1867, when it was bought by the government for a museum.

PLASDEN, BL. POLYDORE (d. 1591), martyr. Born in London, he studied at Rheims and Rome, where he was ordained in 1588. Sent on the English mission, he was captured with Bl. Edmund Genings, charged with being a priest, and hanged, drawn, and quartered at Tyburn. He was beatified in 1929. F. D. Dec. 10.

PLASSMAN, THOMAS BERNARD (1879–1959), educator. Born in Avenwedde bei Guetersloh, Westphalia, Germany, on Mar. 19, he came to the United States at fifteen, graduated from St. Francis Solanus College, Illinois, and became a Franciscan at Paterson, New Jersey, in 1898. He obtained his doctoral degree from Catholic University and, after ordination in 1906, pursued oriental and biblical studies at Rome, Bonn, Louvain, and in Palestine. He was a contributor to the *Catholic Encyclopedia*, wrote several spiritual books, served on the editorial board of the Confraternity revision of the Bible, as president of the Catholic Biblical Association and of the Catholic Historical Association, was founder and president for thirty-eight years of the Franciscan Educational Conference, and was active in the formation of the Franciscan Institute. From 1920 to 1949 he was president of St. Bonaventure College, which he saw grow from 300 to 2200 students; from 1949 to 1952 he was provincial of the New York Franciscan province; in 1952 he became rector of the seminary of Christ the King. He served on many educational committees, state and national, and received several honorary degrees. He died in Olean, New York, on Feb. 13.

PLATEAU, JOSEPH ANTOINE (1801–1883), physicist. Born in Brussels, Belgium, on Oct. 14, he studied there and at Liège, where he received his doctorate in physical and mathematical science in 1829. He became professor of physics at Ghent and did research on the varying effects of light and color on the retina. He became blind in 1843, gave up teaching, but continued his experiments with the assistance of his son Félix and son-in-law Van der Mensbruyghe. He completed investigations on surface tension and on the properties of liquids, which were published in 1873. He died in Ghent, Belgium, on Sept. 15.

PLATINA. *See* Sacchi, Bartolommeo de.

PLATO, ST. (d. 306?), martyr. Brother of St. Antiochus, he was put to death at Ancyra, Galatia. F. D. July 22.

PLATO, ST. (734?-814). At twenty-four he became a monk at Symboleon on Mt. Olympus in Bithynia, rising to abbot in 770; he later became abbot of Sakkudion, which he turned over to his nephew, St. Theodore Studites, after twelve years. He was imprisoned and banished when he opposed the divorce of Emperor Constantine Porphyrogenitus, was released by Michael I in 811, but was bedridden until his death in Constantinople. F. D. Apr. 4.

PLATONIS, ST. (d. 308). She founded a convent at Nisibis, Mesopotamia; the Roman Martyrology erroneously lists her as a martyr. F. D. Apr. 6.

PLEASINGTON, WILLIAM. *See* Blesington, Bl. John.

PLECHELM, ST. (d. 730?), bishop. Born in Northumbria, he went with SS. Wiro and Otger to the Low Countries as a missionary bishop. F. D. July 15.

PLEGMUND, ST. (d. 914), archbishop. A native of Mercia, he became a hermit on an island near Chester, England, a member of King Alfred's court, and was appointed archbishop of Canterbury in 890 and consecrated by Pope Formosus in Rome. He was in Rome again in 908, probably to secure Pope Sergius III's approval of his reign as archbishop, since Formosus' ordinations were condemned in 895 and again in 905. He died probably in Canterbury, England, where he is buried in the cathedral. F. D. Aug. 2.

PLESSIS, JOSEPH OCTAVE (1763-1822), archbishop. Born in Montreal, on Mar. 3, he studied there and in Quebec, became secretary to Bishop Briand in 1783, and was ordained in 1786. He was named coadjutor of Quebec in 1797 and succeeded to the see in 1806. He was instrumental in reducing the antagonism between the Protestant government and his people, rallied French Canadians to the government in the War of 1812 against the Americans, was appointed to the legislative council, secured governmental recognition of his episcopacy and approval of the creation of several vicariates, and was active in defending the rights of the Church and the French in Canada. He was instrumental in reorganizing Nicolet College and founding St. Hyacinthe College, and became an archbishop in 1819

when Quebec was made an archdiocese. He died in Quebec on Dec. 4.

PLOWDEN, CHARLES (1743-1821). Born in Plowden, Shropshire, England, he was educated at St. Omer, became a Jesuit in 1759, and was ordained in Rome in 1770. He was at the English College, Bruges, until his society was suppressed in 1773, was imprisoned for several months, then returned to England as chaplain at Lulworth castle. He helped found Stonyhurst College in 1794, became master of novices at Hodder, provincial, rector of Stonyhurst in 1817, and died in Jougne, France, on June 13. He wrote a score of polemical tracts and carried on a lifelong correspondence with Bishop Carroll of Baltimore.

PLOWDEN, EDMUND (1518-1585), lawyer. Born in Plowden, Shropshire, England, he studied at Cambridge and Oxford, law in the Middle Temple in 1538, and qualified as a physician in 1552. He was a member of parliament in 1553-55, inherited the Plowden estates in 1557, became treasurer of Middle Temple in 1561, and lectured there and at New Inn. He frequently and successfully defended Catholics in the courts, including Bishop Bonner, though he lost his offices under Queen Elizabeth. He wrote in favor of the succession of Mary Stuart, and published commentaries on contemporary law. He died in London, Feb. 6.

PLOWDEN, FRANCIS (1749-1819). Born in Plowden, Shropshire, England, on June 8, he was educated at St. Omer, became a Jesuit in 1766, taught in Bruges, and when the Jesuits were suppressed in 1773, since he had not been ordained, was released from his vows and married. He returned to England, studied law, but because of his religion was not admitted to the bar until 1792. His lack of tact made him a center of controversy for the rest of his life. His brother Robert attacked his *Jura Anglorum* (1792), though it was praised by Oxford; His *Historical Review of the State of Ireland* (1803) displeased the government and *Ireland since the Union* (1811) led to a suit by the government and a fine of £5000 for libel. He fled to Paris to avoid paying it and died there on Jan. 4. He wrote on usury, contemporary politics, and Catholic Emancipation.

PLOWDEN, ROBERT (1740-1823). Brother of Charles and Francis, he was born in Shropshire, England, on Jan. 27, became a Jesuit in 1756, was ordained in 1763, was director of the Carmelite nuns at Hoogstraet, Holland, and was stationed in Arlington, England, from 1777 to 1787 and in Bristol, where he directed missions to 1815. He was chaplain to the Fitzherbert family at Swynnerton to 1820, then retired to Wappenbury, England, where he died on June 27.

PLOWDEN, THOMAS (1594–1664). Born in Oxfordshire, England, grandson of Edmund Plowden, he became a Jesuit in 1617 on the Continent, was sent to England in 1622 and captured in London in 1628. Released, he spent his life in the English mission field, often hiding under the name Salisbury. He died in London on Feb. 13.

PLOWDEN, THOMAS PERCY (1672–1745). Born in Shiplake, Oxfordshire, England, he became a Jesuit in 1693, was rector of the English College in Rome in 1731, superior at Ghent in 1735, and rector of St. Omer in 1739–45. He died in Watten, England, on Sept. 21.

PLUMIER, CHARLES (1646–1704), botanist. Born in Marseilles, France, on Apr. 20, he became a Franciscan Minim at sixteen, and studied botany at the Trinità dei Monti monastery in Rome under Boccone and on his return to France under Joseph de Tournefort. In 1689 he accompanied Surian on a government expedition to the French West Indies, was made royal botanist on his return, and headed expeditions to the West Indies and Central America in 1693 and 1695. He died in Puerto de Santa Maria, near Cadiz, Spain, on Nov. 20. Plumier wrote voluminously, left some 6000 drawings of plants, birds, and fish, and had the genus *Plumeria* named in his honor by Linnaeus and Tournefort. Among his works are: *Description des plantes de l'Amérique* (1693); *Nova plantarum americanarum genera* (1703), which described some 700 species of 100 genera (which Linnaeus took into his system without change); and *Filicetum Americanum* (1703).

PLUMTREE, BL. THOMAS (d. 1570), English martyr. Born in Lincolnshire, England, and graduated from Oxford in 1546, he became pastor at Stubton, a teacher, and a chaplain with the insurgent forces in the North during the reign of Queen Elizabeth. When the rebellion failed, he was captured and hanged as a warning in Durham to all those who sought to help Roman Catholics. He was beatified in 1886. F. D. Feb. 4.

PLUNKETT, CHRISTOPHER J. (1867–1939). Born in Dublin on July 1, he studied at Blackrock College and the Royal University, Dublin, and in France, became a member of the Congregation of the Holy Ghost, and was ordained in 1893. He taught at Duquesne, Pittsburgh, Pennsylvania, established the first Catholic parish for Negroes in Philadelphia (1912) and in New York (St. Mark's, 1931), served in the Puerto Rico missions, and in 1933 became American provincial of his order. He died in New York City on Aug. 17.

PLUNKETT, GEORGE NOBLE (1851–1948), author. Born in Ireland on Dec. 3, he studied in France, Italy, England, and Trinity College, Dublin, and became interested in the preservation of Irish culture and antiquities, serving as officer in numerous societies. He was vice-president of the Irish Academy in 1907–14, was a member of parliament in 1917–27, and became minister for foreign affairs and for fine arts in the new Irish cabinet after home rule was granted. He wrote on Botticelli and other art figures, published *Arrows*, a book of poems, and edited with E. J. Hogan *The Jacobite War in Ireland*. He died in Dublin on Mar. 12.

PLUNKETT, JOSEPH MARY (1887–1916), poet. Born in Dublin, he studied at Belvedere and Stonyhurst, suffered much from ill health and spent his winters on the Continent, returned to edit the *Irish Review* for Thomas MacDonagh from 1911 to 1914. With the latter, Padraic Pearse, and Roger Casement he was a partner in founding the Irish theater in 1914. His only book of poems was *The Circle and the Sword* (1911). He died in Dublin during the Easter Rebellion.

PLUNKETT, BL. OLIVER (1629–1681), bishop and martyr. Born at Loughcrew, County Meath, Ireland, of a titled family, he fought for the cause of Charles I and for Irish freedom. He then studied at the Benedictine abbey of St. Mary's, Dublin, and at the Irish College in Rome, where he was ordained in 1654. He became theologian in the College of the Propagation of the Faith, consultor of the Sacred Congregation of the Index, and procurator for the Irish bishops until 1669, when he was consecrated at Ghent as archbishop of Armagh. He spent four years in reorganizing his diocese, which had suffered from the prolonged absences of his persecuted predecessors. In 1673, renewed persecution sent him into hiding and caused other Irish bishops to flee; in 1678 all priests and bishops who had remained were ordered expelled. In Dec. 1679, the archbishop was imprisoned in Dublin castle on the false charge of conspiring to bring about armed rebellion. Only a single witness, an apostate priest, appeared at the trial, and the charge was dropped. However, Plunkett was removed to Newgate prison in London, where he was held for nine months. There he became a Benedictine Oblate at the hands of Dom Maurus Corker, superior of the English province, also a prisoner. In 1681, at a travesty of a trial, he was declared guilty of high treason, for alleged complicity in the Titus Oates Plot, and hanged, drawn, and quartered at Tyburn on July 1, the last Catholic to be martyred there. He was beatified in 1920. F. D. July 11. ALICE CURTAYNE, *The Trial of Oliver Plunkett* (New York, Sheed, 1953).

PLUTARCH, ST. (d. 202), martyr. Brother of Bishop Heraclas of Alexandria, Egypt, both of whom had been converted by Origen when they were students in his catechetical school, he was seized early in the decade-long persecution of Septimius Severus. Origen accompanied Plutarch to his place of execution in Alexandria; other students—Heraclides, Hero, and Serenus—were also slain. Marcella and her daughter Potomioena were scalded to death; their executioner, Basilides, became a convert and was beheaded. Herais, a young girl, was burned to death and Rhais and another Serenus were killed in the same general persecution. F. D. June 28.

PODIUS, ST. (d. 1002), bishop. Son of the margrave of Tuscany, he became a canon in Florence, and was made bishop of Florence in 990. F. D. May 28.

POEMEN, ST. (d. 450?), abbot. With several brothers, he went into the Egyptian desert of Skete to live as a hermit, but in 408 was forced to flee before Berber raids. At Terenuthis, in the ruins of a pagan temple, they founded a community of hermits, governed in turn by Poemen and Anubis, his brother. Poemen practiced great austerities, insisted on solitude, and exhorted frequent communion. On the death of Anubis he was made sole abbot and became famed for his wisdom. He died in the Thebais desert of Egypt as one of the most famous of the early fathers. F. D. Aug. 27.

POGGIO BRACCIOLINI, GIOVANNI FRANCESCO (1380–1459), scholar. Born in Terranuova, Italy, he was educated at Florence, and went to Rome in 1402 where he became one of Pope Boniface IX's apostolic secretaries, a position he held under the four succeeding pontiffs. In 1415 he discovered a manuscript in the library of Cluny containing several of Cicero's discourses, the first of a series of many such discoveries he made during his lifetime. Among the others were Lucretius' *De natura rerum*, the complete text of Quintilian's *Institutio oratoria* at St. Gall's, Statius' *Silvae*, Tacitus' *Germania*, and an incomplete Petronius. He was Pope Martin V's secretary in 1423, took up the study of archaeology, and from 1453 to 1458 was chancellor of Florence. He died there on Oct. 10. He was a prolific writer on a variety of subjects; among his books are a description of Roman ruins, *De varietate fortunae*; a dialogue on avarice, *De miseriis humanae condicionis*; and a history of Florence. He compiled *Facetiae* (1474), a collection of scurrilous anecdotes, and translated Lucian and Xenophon. He frequently engaged in vituperative controversies with such humanists as Lorenzo Valla and Francesco Filelfo.

POHLE, JOSEPH (1852–1916), theologian. Born in Niederspay, Germany, on Mar. 19, he studied at Trier and the Gregorian, Rome, was ordained in 1887, taught philosophy, theology, and apologetics in Switzerland, at Leeds and Fulda, Catholic University in Washington,

Münster, and Breslau. He was made a monsignor in 1913, was rector at Breslau in 1915–16, wrote a biography of Angelo Secchi, who had taught him astonomy, a treatise on providence, and the twelve-volume *Lehrbuch der Dogmatik*. He wrote for many journals, edited the *Philosophisches Jahrbuch* of the Görres Society, and died in Breslau, Germany, on Feb. 21.

POINSOT, JOHN (1589–1644), theologian. Born in Lisbon, Portugal, on June 9, he studied at Coimbra and Louvain and became a Dominican about 1612 at Madrid. He taught theology at the monastery and university of Alcalá and attracted many scholars by his brilliance. In 1643 he was appointed royal confessor by Philip IV. He wrote expositions of the teaching of St. Thomas Aquinas, a summary of Christian doctrine, and a *Treatise on a Happy Death*. He is also known as John of St. Thomas. He died in Fraga, Spain, on June 17.

POLDING, JOHN BEDE (1794–1877), archbishop. Born in Liverpool, England, on Oct. 18, he studied at St. Gregory's monastery, joined the Benedictines in 1810, and was ordained in 1819. He did parish work, became sub-prior of his monastery, and in 1833 was appointed vicar apostolic of Madras and titular bishop of Hiero-Caesarea, but declined because of his health. He was appointed bishop of the new vicariate of New South Wales in 1834, went to Rome in 1841 to petition successfully for the establishment of a hierarchy in Australia, and the following year was appointed first archbishop of Sydney and primate of Australia. He served on a diplomatic mission to Malta and was appointed an assistant to the pontifical throne the same year, held synods in Sydney and Melbourne in 1844 and 1859, and founded Sydney's Universal College of St. John and St. Mary's College in Lyndhurst. He died in Sydney on Mar. 16.

POLE, BL. MARGARET (1471?–1541), martyr. Niece of Kings Edward IV and Richard III of England and daughter of the duke of Clarence, she was born at Farley castle, near Bath, England, on Aug. 14, and married Sir Reginald Pole of Buckinghamshire about 1491, by whom she had five children. Widowed by the time Henry VIII took the throne, she was made countess of Salisbury, governess to Princess Mary, and given back her estates. Although Henry called her the saintliest woman in the realm, he took everything away again when she refused to approve of Anne Boleyn. When her son, who was to be Cardinal Reginald Pole, wrote against the Act of Supremacy, Henry swore to wipe out the family. She was imprisoned for two years in the Tower, where she almost froze to death, was never tried, and was beheaded in the Tower at seventy after a servile parliament passed a bill of attainder. F. D. May 28.

POLE, REGINALD (1500–1558), cardinal. Born in Stouton castle, Staffordshire, England, on Mar. 3, son of Sir Richard Pole and Margaret Plantagenet, he was educated at the Charterhouse in Sheen and Oxford, and received numerous benefices when but a youth. In 1521 he went to Padua for further study, visited Rome in 1526, and when the matter of King Henry VIII's attempted divorce became critical was allowed to continue his studies at Paris, though required by the king to press the university for a statement favorable to the divorce. He was recalled to England by Henry, was offered the archbishopric of York but declined, and in 1531 lost the favor of the king when he wrote a private document pleading with the king to desist from his course. He returned to Padua in 1532. He attempted to mediate between Henry and Rome, but in 1536 his *Pro ecclesiasticae unitatis defensione* controverted Henry's claim to be the head of the Church in England. Later in that year he refused Henry's summons to return to England, accepted Pope Paul III's appointment to a commission to reform the Church, and in Dec. was created a cardinal, though still a layman. In 1538 he attempted unsuccessfully to organize a league against Henry, who was systematically destroying the Pole family, (Pole's mother and brother were executed by Henry and the cardinal was attainted), was appointed legate in 1539 to rule Viterbo, and in 1542 was one of the three legates appointed to preside over the Council of Trent (which began in Dec. 1545). He was a prominent candidate for the papacy in the conclave of 1549, and in 1553, on the death of King Edward VI, he was appointed legate to England. He formally absolved parliament of the guilt of schism on Nov. 30, 1554, and worked with Queen Mary to restore the Church in England. He summoned a synod in 1555, was appointed archbishop of Canterbury on Cranmer's execution in 1556, was ordained later in the year, and two days later consecrated archbishop. His last year was saddened by the action of Pope Paul IV, who canceled Pole's legation in 1557 (war had broken out between the pope, who made an alliance with France, and Philip II, who, as Mary's husband, was trying to draw England into the conflict on Spain's side) and suspected Pole (without justification) of heretical leanings. Pole died in London on Nov. 17.

POLENI, GIOVANNI (1683–1761), engineer. Born in Venice, on Aug. 23, he became professor of astronomy at Padua when twenty-five and occupied the chair of physics in 1715 and of mathematics in 1719. He became an authority in hydraulic engineering, was put in charge of flood control of the Lombardy River,

and in 1748 was commissioned by Pope Benedict XIV to report on the repairs necessary for St. Peter's cupola. He was elected to the Paris Academy of Sciences in 1739 (as well as those of Berlin, London, and St. Petersburg), and was also elected a magistrate of Padua, Italy, where he died on Nov. 14. He wrote several scientific and antiquarian treatises.

POLIDORO DA CARAVAGGIO. *See* Caldara, Polidoro.

POLIGNAC, MELCHIOR DE (1661–1742), cardinal. Born in Le Puy, France, on Oct. 11, he studied at Collège de Clermont and the Sorbonne, and became French ambassador to Poland in 1693. When the election of the prince de Conti as successor to King John Sobieski of Poland failed to materialize, Polignac was blamed and recalled to his abbey of Bon Port by Louis XIV. In 1706 he was sent to Rome to settle difficulties with Pope Clement XI, was made a cardinal in 1713, but was banished to Flanders for political reasons in 1718. He was soon back in favor, was named archbishop of Auch in 1724, and was sent to Rome to represent France in 1724–32 and to clarify the difficulties arising from the promulgation of the bull *Unigenitus*. He had succeeded Bossuet as a member of the French Academy in 1704, wrote *Anti-Lucretius*, a poem in imitation of Vergil, and was interested in antiquarianism. He died in Paris on Apr. 3.

POLIT, MANUEL MARÍA (1862–1932), archbishop. Born in Quito, Ecuador, he studied in France and England, returned to Ecuador in 1881, practiced law, and taught at the Central University, Quito. In 1891 he became a priest, and wrote historical studies, and *The Family of St. Teresa in America*. He was named bishop of Cuenca, Ecuador, in 1907, and was archbishop of Quito at the time of his death there on Oct. 1.

POLITI, LANCELOT (1483–1553), archbishop. Born in Siena, Italy, he studied at the Siena academy, received his doctorate in civil and canon law at sixteen, and taught there in 1508. He joined the Dominicans in 1513 (with the name Ambrosius Catharinus), developed into a strenuous opponent of Protestantism, and played a prominent role in the Council of Trent. He was appointed bishop of Minori in 1546, archbishop of Conza in 1552, and died in Naples on the way to Rome.

POLITIAN. *See* Ambrogini, Angelo de'.

POLIUS, ST. (3rd century), martyr. *See* Eutychius, St.

POLLAJUOLO, ANTONIO (1429?–1498), painter. Born in Florence, Italy, he studied under his father, a noted goldsmith, painting under Uccello, sculpture under Donatello, and worked as a goldsmith in Ghiberti's studio. He became head of one of Florence's leading workshops and is reported to have been one of the first artists to study anatomy by dissection. His paintings were noted for their vitality, action and anatomical knowledge, especially in his nudes. He collaborated with his brother Piero on several altarpieces, notably *Martyrdom of St. Sebastian* and the embroideries for the San Giovanni baptistery; painted *Communion of Mary Magdalen, David, Labors of Hercules, Apollo and Daphne, Holy Family, Tobias and the Angel, Hercules and Nessus,* portraits, and carved the tomb of Pope Sixtus IV (1489), a monument of Pope Innocent VIII in St. Peter's, and a bas-relief of the nativity in collaboration with Betti. He died in Rome on Feb. 4.

POLLAJUOLO, PIERO BENCI (1443–1496), painter. Born in Florence, Italy, he studied under his brother Antonio, and under Castagno, Uccello, and Baldovinetti, collaborated with Antonio on several altarpieces, and painted several of his own, *Coronation of the Virgin, Prudence, Tobias and the Angel, Annunciation,* and portraits, including that of Galeazzo Sforza. He died in Rome.

POLLIO, ST. (d. 304), martyr. A lector at Cibalis in the Pannonian area of modern Yugoslavia, he led the Christians there after the death of their bishop and was himself burned to death during the Diocletian persecution. F. D. Apr. 28.

PÖLLNITZ, KARL LUDWIG VON (1692–1775). A wanderer through Europe, whose vagabondage reduced him to poverty, he served in the army in Spain, was made reader and director of the Berlin theater by Frederick the Great, wrote gossipy comments on courtiers and court life, published witty and observant memoirs (1734), and twice shifted from Catholicism to Calvinism, returning to the Church shortly before his death.

POLO, GASPAR GIL (1530?–1591), poet. Born in Valencia, Spain, he became coadjutor to the president of the upper financial chamber in 1572 and was sent to Barcelona in 1580 by Philip II to supervise the royal patrimony. He wrote *Canto de Turia* and *Diana enamorada,* a continuation of Montemayor's *Diana;* Polo's *Diana* was translated into English (1583) by Bartholomew Young. He died in Barcelona, Spain.

POLO, MARCO (1254–1324), explorer. A native of Venice, son of Nicolò Polo, a Venetian merchant engaged in commerce with the East with his brother Maffeo, he accompanied his father and uncle in 1271 on a trip to unexplored China. They left from Acre, crossed Armenia to Baghdad, Persia to Balkh, the Pamirs to Kashgar, thence to Lob Nor via Khotan and Cherchen, and then crossed the Gobi Desert to Peking, which they reached in 1275. They were kindly received by Kublai Khan and Marco entered his service, going on missions to Shansi, Shensi, Szechuen, and Yunnan provinces, Tibet, and northern Burma. He served as governor of Yangchow for three years, visited and made notes on the far-flung areas affected by the khan's rule, as far north as Karakorum and south to Cochin China and the southern Indian states, and with his father and uncle acquired great riches. In 1292 the Polos left China as escorts for the Mongol bride (the lady Cocacin) sent by the Kublai Khan for the Khan Arghon of Persia, going by sea across the Indian Ocean, since the overland route was war threatened. They traveled from Fukien (probably Changchow), were detained in Sumatra and southern India, and delivered the bride in Persia two years later. They arrived back in Venice via Tabriz, Trebizond, Constantinople, and Negropont in 1295. In 1298, Marco was captured at the battle of Curzola while commanding a Venetian galley against the Genoese, and was imprisoned for a year in Genoa. While in prison he dictated in French to a fellow prisoner, Rusticiano of Pisa, his *Travels,* which were an immediate sensation and became world famous. Polo was the greatest traveler of the Middle Ages and the first European to travel across continental Asia and write an account of the fabulous kingdoms he visited. Though much of his material is based on fantastic travelers' tales, much also is factual and an invaluable source of knowledge and insight into the countries and peoples of the East. He died in Venice, Italy, on Jan. 9.

POLO DE MEDINA, SALVADOR JACINTO (1607?–1660?), poet. Born in Murcia, Spain, he became secretary to the bishop of Lugo about 1637, and wrote satirical and other verse, collected in 1664. His chief titles are *Academias del jardin, Buen humor de las musas Apolo y Dafne,* and *Pan y Siringa* (all published in 1630); *Hospital de incurables* (1636), a prose imitation of Quevedo's *Suenos;* and the influential critical treatise *A Lelio, gobierno moral* (1657).

POLYANUS, ST. (d. 257), bishop and martyr. See Nemesian, St.

POLYCARP, ST. (d. 156), bishop and martyr. One of the apostolic fathers, he preserved the Christian tradition as a disciple of St. John, who consecrated him bishop, and passed it on to Papias and St. Irenaeus. He wrote two letters to the Philippians, one requesting news of St. Ignatius of Antioch, and one about the necessity of firmness in the face of heresy (perhaps that of Marcion). Eusebius reports that he was eighty-six when he was captured and burned and speared to death in Smyrna, on Feb. 23, during the persecution of Marcus Aurelius. A genuine *Martyrdom of St. Polycarp,* probably the oldest formal example of acts of the martyrs, exists, but a life by Pionius is legendary. F. D. Jan. 26.

POLYCHRONIUS, ST. (d. 250), bishop and martyr. The bishop of Babylon was beaten to death during the persecution of Decius. F. D. Feb. 17.

POLYCHRONIUS, ST. (4th century), martyr. A priest who attended the Council of Nicaea in 325, he was slain by Arians while celebrating mass. F. D. Dec. 6.

POLYEUCTUS, ST. (d. 259), martyr. A Roman officer of Greek descent, he was converted to Christianity, and tortured and beheaded at Meletene, Armenia, during the persecution of either Decius or Valerian. Additional biographical details are pious accretions. He was the model for the hero of Corneille's drama, *Polyeucte* (1642). F. D. Feb. 13.

POLYXENA, ST. (1st century). *See* Xantippa, St.

POMBAL, SEBASTIÃO JOSÉ DE CARVALHO E MELLO (1699–1782), statesman. Born in Soure, near Coimbra, Portugal, on May 13, he was educated at Coimbra. He was appointed minister to London in 1739 and to Vienna in 1745, was recalled by King John V in 1750, but, after John's death later the same year, was named secretary of state for foreign affairs by King Joseph in 1751, and first minister and count of Oeras in 1759. He soon became the most influential person in the kingdom, which he practically ruled. He proclaimed a policy of royal absolutism, suppressed an alleged uprising of the nobility, after an attempt on the king's life in 1758, by public torture and death of the duke of Aveiro and members of the Tavora family in 1759, made the Inquisition a department of government, and ruthlessly suppressed all opposition. He confiscated the property of the Portuguese Jesuits and deported them to the Papal States in 1759, attempted to have the Society suppressed, expelled the papal nuncio and broke off relations with Rome in 1760 when Pope Clement XIII refused to accede to his wishes, and in effect set up a Portuguese church with himself as head. He was appointed marquis of Pombal in 1770, admitted a nuncio to Portugal the same year, and in 1773 Pope Clement XIV suppressed the Society in an attempt to end the schism. Pombal abolished Indian slavery, reformed the government and the military, continued Portugal's political friendship with England, and encouraged agriculture, commerce, and manufacture. When King Joseph died in 1777, he was forced into retirement and exiled to his castle by the new ruler, Queen Maria I. He died in Pombal, Portugal, on Aug. 8.

POMPEIUS, ST. (d. 120?), martyr. *See* Astius, St.

POMPEIUS, ST. (d. 250), martyr. *See* Africanus, St.

POMPEIUS, ST. (d. 290?). He was bishop of Pavia, Italy. F. D. Dec. 14.

POMPILI, BASILIO (1858–1931), cardinal. Born in Spoleto, Italy, on Apr. 16, he studied at the Vatican and Pontifical seminaries, was ordained in 1880, and was appointed to the Congregation of the Council, the Penitentiary, and the rota. He was a chief consultant to Pope Pius X's commission for the codification of canon law, was named a cardinal in 1911, vicar general of Rome in 1913, and cardinal-bishop of Valletri in 1917. He died in Rome on May 5.

POMPONAZZI, PIETRO (1462–1525), philosopher. Born in Mantua, Italy, he taught at Padua, Ferrara, and Bologna, and became an outstanding Aristotelian and the leader of the anti-Averroists. He was accused of heresy for the views he presented in *Tractatus de immortalitate animae* (1516) and defended in *Apologia* (1517) and the bitter *Defensorium* (1519). He had questioned whether the soul survives the body and presented the thesis that the mortality of the soul might be a better basis for morality than the concept of rewards and punishment in the life hereafter. He retracted these views when pressed by Pope Leo X. He also wrote *De incantationibus* (1520) and *De fato* (1523), and died in Bologna, Italy.

POMPONIUS, ST. (d. 536). Appointed bishop of Naples, Italy, in 508, he had to spend most of his years opposing Arianism. F. D. Apr. 30.

POMPOSA, ST. (d. 835), martyr. A nun at Penamelaria, Spain, she was beheaded at nearby Cordova by the Moors. F. D. Sept. 19.

PONCE, JOHN (1603–1670), theologian. Born in Cork, Ireland, he went to Belgium and joined the Franciscans, studied at Louvain, Cologne, and St. Isidore's College in Rome, and taught at St. Isidore's, Lyons, and Paris. He became head of the Ludovisian college in Rome and superior at St. Isidore's, and was a vigorous supporter of the Irish Confederate Catholics. He wrote theological treatises, chief of which were *Commentarii theologici* (1661), *Cursus philosophae* (1643) and *Integer cursus theologiae* (1652), and helped Luke Wadding edit the works of Duns Scotus. He died in Paris.

PONCE DE LEON, JUAN (1460?–1521), explorer. Born in San Servas, Campos, Spain, he was a page in Pedro de Guzmán's household, tutored the Infante Fernando, served against the Moors in Granada, and in 1493 was a member of Columbus' second voyage. He was an aide of Gov. Nicolás Ovando during the revolt on San Domingo in 1502–4, explored Puerto Rico in 1508, and conquered it and was appointed its governor in 1509. He was removed from office in favor of Diego Columbus' prior claim in 1512, but meanwhile had acquired a fortune from his governorship. He set out in 1513 to discover the fabled treasure and fountain of youth reportedly on the island of Bimini north of San Domingo and explored the east and west coasts of Florida. He secured a grant from King Ferdinand for settling Florida in 1514, led an expedition against the Caribs south of Puerto Rico in 1515, and returned to Puerto Rico where he stayed until 1521, when he led an expedition to Florida, was wounded in an encounter with the Indians, and died of his wounds.

PONCET, JOSEPH ANTHONY DE LA RIVIÈRE (1610–1675), missioner. Born in Paris on May 7, he joined the Jesuits in 1629, studied at Clermont, Rome, and Rouen, taught at Orléans from 1631 to 1634, and in 1638 accompanied Marie de l'Incarnation to Canada. He worked among the Hurons and Algonquins until 1657, when he was returned to France because of an ecclesiastical dispute. He was appointed French penitentiary at Loreto, Italy, and then went to Martinique, where he died on June 18.

PONGRACZ, BL. STEPHEN (1582–1619), martyr. A Croatian, born in Alvinez, he became a Jesuit at Brünn, taught at Laibach and Klagenfurt, was professor of theology at Graz in 1611–15, and was tortured and slain by Calvinists at Kashan, Hungary, with several others. He was beatified in 1905. F. D. Sept. 8.

PONTADERA, ANDREA DA. See Andrea Pisano.

PONTE, LORENZO DA (1749–1838), librettist. Born Emmanuel Conegliano in Ceneda, Italy, on Mar. 10, of Jewish parents, he was converted with them when fourteen and adopted the name of the bishop of the diocese. The latter educated him; after five years of study at the Ceneda seminary, Da Ponte then taught at Treviso, went to Vienna where he was appointed poet of the Imperial Theater by Joseph II, and composed the libretti of Mozart's *Le Nozze de Figaro, Don Giovanni,* and *Così fan tutte.* Obliged to leave Vienna, on Joseph's death, he went to Trieste, then London and New York in 1805. He failed in an attempt to popularize opera in the latter city and taught Italian at Columbia University. He died in New York City on Aug. 17.

PONTIAN, ST. (d. 236?), pope and martyr. A Roman, he succeeded St. Urban I to the papacy on July 21, 230, and called a synod at Rome in 232 which confirmed the judgments of two Alexandrian synods held the previous year to condemn Origen's teachings. He was exiled by Emperor Maximinus to the mines of Sardinia, where he died of ill-treatment. Before his death he met the antipope, Hippolytus, also in exile, and reconciled him with the Church, thus ending his schism. Pontian re-

signed his office on Sept. 28, 235, and probably died a year later. F. D. Nov. 19.

PONTIAN, ST. (d. 169), martyr. He was put to death at Spoleto, Italy, during the reign of Marcus Aurelius. F. D. Jan. 19.

PONTIAN, ST. (d. 192), martyr. See Eusebius, St.

PONTIAN, ST. (d. 259?), martyr. He and four others were slain in Rome during the reign of Valerian. F. D. Dec. 2.

PONTIAN, ST. (d. 302?), martyr. He and SS. Praetextatus and Trason were slain at Rome for aiding Christians awaiting death during the Diocletian persecution. F. D. Dec. 11.

PONTICUS, ST. (d. 177), martyr. See Pothinus, St.

PONTIUS, ST. (d. 258?), martyr. Bishop of Milan, Italy, he was put to death at Cimiez, near Nice, France. F. D. May 14.

PONTIUS, ST. (d. 260?). He was a deacon who accompanied St. Cyprian, bishop of Carthage, into exile and who wrote a panegyric of the martyr. F. D. Mar. 8.

PONTIUS, BL. (d. 1140). Born in Balmey, France, he was a canon at Lyons, founded a charterhouse at Meyriat, his paternal estate, joined the Carthusians, and became bishop of Belley in 1121. F. D. Dec. 13.

PONTIUS CARBONELL (1250?–1320?). Born in Barcelona, Spain, he became a Franciscan, was stationed in Barcelona, and was teacher and confessor to St. Louis, bishop of Toulouse, during his imprisonment there. In 1314 he was sent by Jaime II to his brother, King Frederick II of Sicily, to plead that no protection be given to the Fraticelli. He wrote commentaries on scripture.

PONTIUS OF FAUCIGNY, ST. (d. 1178). Born in Savoy, France, of a noble family, he became a canon regular of Abondance abbey in Chablais and in 1144 abbot-founder of the monastery of St. Sixtus. In 1172 he was made abbot of Abondance, resigned soon after, and retired to St. Sixtus, where he died. His cult was confirmed in 1806. F. D. Nov. 26.

PONTORMO, JACOPO DA. See Carucci, Jacopo.

PONZIANO, FRANCES. See Frances of Rome, St.

POORE, RICHARD. See Ricardus Anglicus.

POPE, ALEXANDER (1688–1744), poet. Born in London on May 21, son of a merchant, he was educated at home, sometimes by underground priests from the Continent, and in art by a maternal aunt. He was barred from professional life by current penal laws against Catholics (which eventually forced his father to dispose of his business); he also was handicapped by a deforming bone disease, which kept him frail and in poor health through his life. He began to write at an early age, published his *Pastorals* (1709) in an anthology, an expected piece of apprentice work, and in 1711 issued his *Essay on Criticism*, a plea for soundness in criticism and an announcement of his traditional respect for Horace, Boileau, and the classical outlook. He published *Rape of the Lock* in 1712 (revised and enlarged in 1714), a poem which used the elaborate machinery of the epic to report on the insignificant theft of a lock of hair; the incident, however, had caused an unfortunate taking of sides in the tightly knit, Catholic village of Binfield, and John Caryll, formerly of the state department, had asked Pope to end the social warfare. In London, which Pope was legally allowed only to visit, he became interested in politics, favored the Tories, and wrote *Windsor Forest* (1713) in praise of their peace efforts. The resultant attacks by libelous writers directed by Addison, as Whig party paymaster, led to an estrangement between the two men. Pope was friendly with Swift, John Arbuthnot, John Gay, William Congreve, and other literary figures, wrote translations of Homer's *Iliad* and *Odyssey*, which brought him a good income, and edited (without the scholarly knowledge he should have had) the plays of Shakespeare. Richard Bentley attacked his Homer (chiefly because he differed as to methods of translation, but also because of the unsoundness of some interpretation) and Lewis Theobald attacked his edition of Shakespeare for its scholarly shortcomings. Satires and moral epistles, imitating Horace in form, but directed against current social, economic, political, and philosophical abuses, and marked by considerable imagination, humor, epigrammatic flavor, and technical polish, followed in quantity. Many of them were related to what he planned as a long philosophical discourse on human conduct and which became the incomplete *Essay on Man*; Pope's heavy reliance on the work of Bolingbroke, a deist, led him into many carelessly expressed statements. Before and after this Pope wrote his two versions of the *Dunciad*, a poem planned as early as 1714 when he was a member of the Scriblerus Club with Swift and others. It is a scathing attack on literary mediocrity and incompetence; although, in keeping with other eighteenth-century poets, he named writers and their work, his poem is not a personal diatribe against persons with whom he could not get along. Lewis Theobald, the chief dunce (person who misuses his intellect) in the first version of the *Dunciad* (with some passages of personal spite), was logically replaced by Colley Cibber as king of the dunces in the final draft of the poem. Cibber, a second-rate poet laureate, represented everything in literature and criticism to which Pope and his fellow critics fundamentally objected. Pope's other major work includes the highly autobiographical *Epistle to Dr. Arbuthnot* and *Epistle to Augustus* and the somewhat romantically sentimental *Eloisa to Abelard*. Many occasional poems in patterns other than the heroic couplet (of which he was a master) and prose criticism, and a large body of correspondence, also remain. He died in England at Twickenham, an estate on the Thames to which he had gone in 1719, on May 30.

ROBERT K. ROOT, *The Poetical Career of Alexander Pope* (Princeton, Princeton U., 1939); EDITH SITWELL, *Alexander Pope* (New York, Cosmopolitan, 1930).

POPE-HENNESSY, UNA (1876–1949), author. Daughter of Sir Arthur Birch, and born in England, she became a convert, married Gen. Ladislaus Pope-Hennessy in 1910, and was named a Dame Commander of the British Empire for her work during World War I. While with her husband at the British embassy in Washington, D.C., she wrote *Three English Women* in America, and of her stay in Leningrad, *The Closed City*. She wrote biographies of Walter Scott, Agnes Strickland, Dickens, Charles Kingsley, and other studies. She died in London on Aug. 16.

POPPEL, ST. NICHOLAS (d. 1572), martyr. *See* Pieck, St. Nicholas.

POPPO, ST. (978–1048). After a military career he made pilgrimages to Rome and Jerusalem, became a Benedictine monk at St. Thierry in 1006, restored the monasteries at Beaulieu and St. Vannes, and served as abbot at Stavelot-Malmédy and as adviser to Emperor St. Henry II. Under Poppo's rule discipline was bettered at Hautmont, Marchiennes, St. Maximinus, and elsewhere. F. D. Jan. 25.

POQUELIN, JEAN BAPTISTE. *See* Molière.

PORCARIUS, ST. (d. 732?), martyr. He was the second of this name to be abbot of Lérins, France, which at this time had more than 500 monks and novices. Warned of an impending attack by Saracens, he sent off the young students and religious in the only boat available and warned the rest to prepare for martyrdom. All were slain except four who were carried into slavery. F. D. Aug. 11.

PORDENONE, GIOVANNI. *See* Sachis, Giovanni de.

PORMORT, VEN. THOMAS (1559?–1592), martyr. Born in Hull, England, he studied at Cambridge, fled to Rheims, was ordained at Rome in 1587, and served as prefect of studies at the Swiss College in Milan in 1590. He was sent on the English mission, was twice captured in 1591, and was tortured, convicted as a priest, and hanged in London on Feb. 20.

PORPHYRY, ST. (d. 80?), martyr. *See* Onesiphorus, St.

PORPHYRY, ST. (d. 171), martyr. He was

put to death at Ephesus during the reign of Aurelian. F. D. Nov. 4.

PORPHYRY, ST. (d. 309), martyr. A servant of St. Pamphilus, he demanded that the martyred St. Elias and his four companions be given decent burial, whereupon he was seized, racked, burned, and beheaded at Caesarea in Palestine. F. D. Feb. 16.

PORPHYRY, ST. (d. 362). He is said to have been an actor and horse trader, who was attacking baptism in a burlesque presented before Julian the Apostate, when he suddenly declared his belief and was slain on the spot. F. D. Sept. 15.

PORPHYRY, ST. (353–420), bishop. A Greek who lived a life of seclusion, first in the Egyptian desert and then in Palestine, he made frequent pilgrimages to the places of Christ's Passion. At forty he was ordained, continued his austerities, and in 396 was acclaimed bishop of Gaza and entrusted with the relic of the holy cross. His destruction of pagan temples and attempts to drive out idolatrous customs proved successful, but riots almost cost him his life. F. D. Feb. 26.

PORRAS, BL. RAPHAELA (1850–1925), foundress. Daughter of the mayor of Pedro Abad, near Cordova, Spain, she and her elder sister Dolores sought to become nuns. After several disappointing experiences, they and a group of fourteen were transferred to Madrid, where Raphaela founded the congregation of the Handmaids of the Sacred Heart, to educate children and to assist in the retreat movement. In 1877, Sister Raphaela was elected mother general, but varied interpretations of administration, led by Dolores, caused internal conflict. In 1893, Raphaela resigned her post and went to Rome to serve obscurely as housekeeper in a Roman convent until her death. She was beatified in 1952. The congregation today has foundations in several countries, including the United States. F. D. Jan. 6.

PORRECTA, SERAFINA. *See* Capponi, Serafina.

PORRES, BL. MARTIN DE (1579–1639). Born in Lima, Peru, the illegitimate son of a Spanish knight, Juan de Porres, and a Panamanian woman, he was apprenticed to a barber-surgeon at twelve, but at fifteen became a Dominican laybrother in Lima. He devoted himself to the sick, the poor, and the African slaves in the city. He was noted for his practical nature as well as holy practices, established an orphanage and foundling hospital, and was a friend of St. Rose of Lima and Bl. John Massias. He died in Lima on Nov. 3 and was beatified in 1837. In the United States he is patron of those engaged in the work of interracial justice. F. D. Nov. 5.

PORRO, BL. GIOVÁNNI ANGELO (d. 1506). Born in Milan, Italy, he joined the Serv-

ants of Mary (Servites) and was sent to Monte Senario, became master of novices at Florence, and served in Milan and Cavacurta. His cult was approved in 1737. F. D. Oct. 24.

PORRO Y REINADO, FRANCISCO (1738–1814), bishop. Born in Cadiz, Spain, he joined the Order of Minims, served as its general, and in 1801 was appointed bishop of Louisiana and the Two Floridas but never set foot in his see. He was translated to Tarazona, Spain, in 1803, and died there on Jan. 3.

PORTA, CARLO (1775–1821), poet. Born in Milan, Italy, he studied at Monza and at Milan, became a treasury official in Venice and Milan and a governmental official under the Cisalpine Republic. He became a romanticist, a follower of Manzoni and Grossi, and was noted for his use of the Milanese dialect in his poetry. He died in Milan on Jan. 5.

PORTA, GIACOMO DELLA (1542–1604), architect. Born at Porlezza, Italy, on Lake Lugano, he studied under Michelangelo, sculpture under Il Gobbo, worked under Vignola, whom he succeeded as architect of St. Peter's, and finished the cupola in 1590 or 1592. He finished Vignola's plans for Il Gesù, built San Giovanni de' Fiorentini from Sansovino's designs, constructed the interior of the Sapienza which Michelangelo had designed, and finished the Farnese palace in Rome. He designed the Villa Aldobrandini, the Annunziata in Genoa, and was the sculptor of the fountains on the Piazza Mattei and at the Capitol.

PORTER, FRANCIS (1622–1702), historian. Born in Kingston, Ireland, he became a Franciscan in Rome, taught theology and history at St. Isidore's College, and became theologian and historiographer to King James II of England. He published a refutation of Protestant principles in 1679, a plea for the termination of penal laws throughout Europe, a compendium of the ecclesiastical annals of Ireland (1690), and theological, scriptural, and other controversial treatises. He died in Rome on Apr. 7.

PORTER, GEORGE (1825–1889), archbishop. Born in Exeter, England, he studied at Stonyhurst, joined the Jesuits in 1841, taught at Stonyhurst, of which he was prefect of studies in 1849, and St. Francis Xavier's, Liverpool, studied theology at St. Beuno's, Wales, and was ordained in 1856. After further study in Rome, he taught at Stonyhurst and Liesse in France, occupied the chair of theology at St. Beuno's, and was appointed rector at Liverpool. He was sent to London in 1871, became master of novices in 1873, rector of the Farm Street church in 1881, assistant to the general at Fiesole, and in 1886 was appointed archbishop of Bombay, India, where he died on Sept. 28.

PORTIANUS, ST. (d. 533). A slave, he became abbot of the monastery of Miranda, Auvergne, France, and succeeded in forcing King Thierry of Austrasia to release captives. F. D. Nov. 24.

PORTIER, MICHAEL (1795–1859), bishop. Born in Montbrison, Loire, France, on Sept. 7, he studied at the Lyons seminary, went to the United States in 1807, finished his studies at St. Mary's seminary, Baltimore, and was ordained in 1818 in St. Louis. He engaged in missionary activities, became vicar general of New Orleans, was appointed vicar apostolic of the Floridas and Alabama in 1825, and was consecrated titular bishop of Oleno in 1826. He visited France in 1829 in quest of missionaries and financial aid, encouraged the founding of Spring Hill College in 1830, consecrated his cathedral in 1850, and in 1859 became first bishop of Mobile when his vicariate was changed to a diocese. He died in Mobile, Alabama, on May 14.

POSADAS, BL. FRANCISCO DE (1644–1713). Born in Cordova, Spain, he became a Dominican in 1663, was famed as a preacher, and devoted his last forty years to missions in southwestern Spain. Among his writings are the *Triumph of Chastity* and a biography of St. Dominic. He died at Aracoeli, Spain, and was beatified in 1818. F. D. Sept. 20.

POSSENTI, ST. FRANCISCO (1838–1862). Eleventh child of a lawyer in Assisi, Italy, and educated by the Jesuits at Spoleto, he became a Passionist at Morroville in 1856 and took the name Bro. Gabriel of Our Lady of Sorrows. After a dutiful life of penance and self-effacement, he died of tuberculosis at Isola. He was beatified in 1920. F. D. Feb. 27.

POSSESSOR, ST. (d. 485?), bishop. A judge in Verdun, Gaul, he became its bishop in 470 and suffered much with his flock from barbarian invasions. F. D. May 11.

POSSEVINO, ANTONIO (1533?–1611), diplomat. Born in Mantua, Italy, he went to Rome when sixteen, became Cardinal Ercole Gonzaga's secretary, and in 1559 joined the Jesuits. He was ordained in 1561, was a successful preacher in France where he brought many Calvinists back to Catholicism, became rector of Avignon and Lyons colleges, and in 1573 secretary of the Society's general. He served as papal legate to Sweden in 1577 to receive King John III into the Church, returned as vicar apostolic to Scandinavia in 1578, was papal legate in 1581 in an unsuccessful attempt to reunite Russia with Rome, and nuncio to Poland in 1582. He preached widely in northern Europe, helped reconcile the Ruthenians, and in 1587 began teaching at Padua, where Francis de Sales was one of his pupils. He returned to Rome in 1591, was expelled by the Spanish party for his role in securing recognition of Henry IV as king of France, and devoted the rest of his life to writing and collecting books. He died in Ferrara, Italy, on Feb. 26.

POSSIDIUS, ST. (d. 440?), bishop. He was appointed bishop of Calama, Numidia, about 397, suffered mistreatment at the hands of the Donatists, and fought the Pelagians, especially at the Council of Milevum (416). After the destruction of Calama by the Vandals under Genseric, he went to Hippo and was present at the death of St. Augustine. He then went into exile, and may have died in Italy. His life of Augustine, under whom he had studied, supplements the *Confessions* and contains a bibliography of that saint's writings. F. D. May 16.

POSTEL, ST. JULIA FRANCES CATHERINE (1756–1846), foundress. Born at Barfleur, France, on Nov. 28, she attended the Benedictine convent at Valognes, and opened a school for girls at Barfleur when she was eighteen. This was closed by the revolutionists, and she became an underground agent for her religion. She established a secret chapel in her home; when it became too dangerous to reserve the Eucharist there, she was allowed to carry it on her person and to administer it to the dying when no priest was available. After the concordat of 1801, she helped restore religion by her teaching, then went to Cherbourg in 1805, began teaching again, and with the encouragement of a local priest, Fr. Cabart, founded the Sisters of the Christian Schools of Mercy with three other teachers in 1807, and took the name Sr. Mary Magdalen. In 1811 the Sisters of Providence returned to Cherbourg and she decided to move her community elsewhere. After great hardships the group was able to settle at Tamersville in 1815, but in 1830 she obtained the abbey of St. Sauveur le Vicomte, France, and from then on the congregation flourished. She died there. She was canonized in 1925. F. D. July 16.

POSTGATE, VEN. NICHOLAS (1596?–1679), martyr. Born in Kirkdale House, Egton, Yorkshire, England, he studied at Douai, was ordained in 1628, and was sent on the English mission in 1630. He was captured near Whitby, tried and condemned as a priest, and executed at York on Aug. 7.

POTAMIA, ST. (d. 302), martyr. *See* Felix, St.

POTAMIAN, BRO. *See* O'Reilly, Michael Francis.

POTAMIOENA THE ELDER, ST. (d. 202), martyr. *See* Plutarch, St.

POTAMIOENA THE YOUNGER, ST. (d. 304?), martyr. She was put to death for her faith at Alexandria during the Diocletian persecution. F. D. June 7.

POTAMION, ST. (d. 340?), bishop and martyr. Bishop of Heraclea, Egypt, he was tortured so viciously during the persecution of Maximinus Daza in 310 that he was crippled and partly blinded. He lived, however, to attend the councils of Nicaea (325) and Tyre (335), where he supported St. Athanasius. During the persecution of the Arian Emperor Constantius he was so badly clubbed that he died shortly after his arrest. F. D. May 18.

POTENTIAN, ST. (d. 300?), martyr. *See* Sabinian, St.

POTHIER, ROBERT JOSEPH (1699–1772), jurist. Born in Orléans, France, on Jan. 9, son of a judge, he became a successful lawyer, and in 1750 a judge of the petty court in Orléans and professor of law at the university there. His legal writings influenced the framers of the Code Napoleon. Among his works are the three-volume arrangement of Roman law texts, *Pandectae Justinianae* (1748–52), and studies of marriage and the civil law. He died in Orléans on Mar. 2.

POTHINUS, ST. (d. 177), bishop and martyr. The bishop of Lyons (also called Photinus), at least ninety years of age, and some forty-seven other Christians living there and in Vienne, were publicly scorned, then insulted and stoned, and finally brought to trial, tortured to almost incredible extremes, and put to death during the persecution of Marcus Aurelius. The account of their martyrdom (sometimes attributed to St. Irenaeus) which Eusebius used is one of the earliest and fullest such narratives. The group included a physician named Alexander; Attalus; Biblis; Maturus, only recently a catechumen; Ponticus, aged fifteen; Sanctus, a deacon; and Vettius Epagathus, their defense attorney. There were forty-eight of "the martyrs of Lyons." F. D. June 2.

POUGET, JEAN FRANÇOIS ALBERT DU (1817–1904), anthropologist. The marquis de Nadaillac spent his early life in French government service, and was prefect of Basses-Pyrenées in 1871 and of Indre-et-Loire in 1877. He devoted his later years to anthropology, conducted extensive explorations of the caves of southern France, became an outstanding authority on their primitive paintings, and was noted for his knowledge of prehistoric America. He wrote on prehistoric man and epochs, cave drawings, and the declining birth rate. He died in Rougemon, France, on Oct. 1.

POUNDE, THOMAS (1538?–1612?). Born in Beaumond, Hampshire, England, on May 29, he studied at Winchester College, was admitted to Lincoln's Inn in 1559, was esquire to Elizabeth I about 1560, and left the court in 1569 when publicly insulted by the queen. He became a convert, worked to convert others, and was made a Jesuit laybrother in 1578. He was imprisoned in the Tower of London in 1581 for his proselytizing and spent the next

30 years in and out of prisons. He died at Beaumond on Feb. 26.

POUSSIN, NICOLAS (1594–1666), painter. Born in Les Andelys, France, he went to Paris in 1612 with Varin, a painter, under whom he studied, but returned to his home in ill-health and poverty. He went to Rome in 1624, acquired a reputation for his admiration of the ancients and the authenticity of his portraits, and painted *Triumph of Flora, Rape of the Sabines*, and the first series of the *Seven Sacraments* for Cassiano del Pozo. In 1640 he was called to Paris to work for Richelieu and the king, but returned to Rome in 1643, embittered by the jealousies and intrigues of the court and French painters. His canvases, especially his landscapes, have strong color appeal, remained indubitably French despite their Italian place of composition, and had great influence on Claud Lorrain and others. His best-known works include: *Woman Taken in Adultery, Last Supper, Vision of St. Paul, Martyrdom of St. Erasmus, Diogenes, Moses Taken from the River, Childhood of Jupiter*, and *Four Seasons*. He died in Rome on Nov. 19.

POWEL, BL. PHILIP (1594–1646), martyr. Born in Tralon, Brecknockshire, England, on Feb. 2, he studied law under Dom Augustine Baker and at the Temple in London, and became a Benedictine at Douai. He was ordained in 1618, was sent on the English mission in 1622, working in Somerset and Devon. He was a military chaplain during the civil war, was captured off South Wales, and brought to London. He was condemned as a priest and hanged, drawn, and quartered at Tyburn. F. D. June 30.

POWELL, BL. EDWARD (1478?–1540), martyr. Born in Wales, he became a fellow of Oriel College, Oxford, and a canon at Salisbury. He wrote several treatises against Luther and was one of the counselors chosen by Catherine of Aragon to defend her against Henry VIII's divorce suit. He wrote a book defending the marriage, preached eloquently in its favor, and in 1534 was jailed at Dorchester. He was kept in solitary confinement for six years and then hanged, drawn, and quartered at Smithfield, London, for refusing to acknowledge Henry's spiritual supremacy. He was beatified in 1886. F. D. July 30.

POWER, MICHAEL (1804–1847), bishop. Born in Halifax, Nova Scotia, Canada, on Oct. 17, he was ordained, served as vicar general of Montreal, and in 1842 was consecrated first bishop of Toronto, Ontario. He laid the cornerstone of the cathedral, presided over the council of public instruction, was active in increasing Catholic educational opportunities, and died on Oct. 1 while tending the stricken during a typhus epidemic.

POWYS, ELIZABETH MYERS (1912–

1947), author. Born in Manchester, England, on Dec. 23, she became a secretary in London, wrote a novel at fifteen, and suffered a breakdown in health at twenty-five. While she was hospitalized she wrote short stories, and published her first novel, *A Well Full of Leaves* (1943), which won the Tom Gallon Prize. She married Littleton Powys that year, then published *The Basilisk of St. James* and *Mrs. Christopher*. Her short stories, *Good Beds: Men Only*, were published posthumously, as were her *Letters*. She died in Sherborne, England, on May 24.

POYNTER, WILLIAM (1762–1827), bishop. Born in Petersfield, England, on May 20, he studied at Douai, was ordained in 1786, and stayed on as professor and prefect of studies. When the college was closed during the French Revolution, he returned to England in 1795, helped found St. Edmund's College, and was its president from 1801 to 1813. He was made coadjutor of London in 1803, became vicar apostolic in 1812, and in 1814 went to Rome to protest the attacks made on him by Bishop Milner (who was ordered to desist by the pope). He was successful in negotiating with the French government for the return of the Douai colleges to the Church, but the bulk of the cash settlement was confiscated by the British government. He died in London on Nov. 26.

POZZO, ANDREAS (1642–1709), painter. Born in Trent, Italy, he early became interested in painting, joined the Jesuits as a lay-brother when twenty-four, and was noted for his mastery of perspective. Among his outstanding works were the frescoes on the ceiling and dome of S. Ignazio in Rome, in St. Bartolommeo in Modena, the Cassinese abbey in Arezzo, the altar of the Jesuit church in Venice, and the St. Ignatius altar in the Gesù in Rome. He died in Vienna.

PRADES, JEAN MARTIN DE (1720?–1782), theologian. Born in Castelsarrasin, France, he studied at St. Sulpice, and ignited a violent controversy when in 1751 he presented his doctoral thesis on certitude at Paris. It was censured by the university and the archbishop of Paris, and condemned by Pope Benedict XIV. He fled to Holland, published his *Apology* (1752), was appointed lector, on Voltaire's recommendation, of Frederick of Prussia, who gave him two canonries, and moved to Berlin. He signed a formula of recantation in 1754, and became archdeacon of the Glogau chapter, in Germany, where he remained for the rest of his life. He wrote several other works which contain dubious theological doctrines.

PRAEJECTUS, ST. (d. 676), bishop. Known also as Prix, Prest, and Preils, he studied under St. Genesius, bishop of Auvergne, and suc-

ceeded to the see of Clermont about 666. He set up numerous church establishments, including hospitals, and was known as an authority on history and music. After an alleged conspiracy against King Childeric II, for which Hector of Marseilles was put to death, Praejectus was libeled as the real enemy of the monarch and waylaid near Clermont, Gaul, by a group of assassins who slew St. Amarin by mistake and then stabbed the bishop to death. F. D. Jan. 25.

PRAESIDIUS, ST. (d. 484?), martyr. *See* Donatian, St.

PRAETEXTATUS, ST. (d. 302?), martyr. *See* Pontian, St.

PRAETEXTATUS, ST. (d. 586), bishop and martyr. Appointed bishop of Rouen, Gaul, about 549, he suffered from the political turmoil of the time, particularly from the hostility of Fredegunda, mistress of King Chilperic, who murdered the latter's brother and sons and, perhaps, Chilperic himself to assure the throne for her own son, Clotaire II. The bishop censured her constantly, was sent into exile after a trial (quite falsely, according to St. Gregory of Tours), and, on his return, was stabbed to death in his church at Rouen by a royal assassin. He died on Apr. 14. F. D. Feb. 24.

PRAGMATIUS, ST. (d. 520?). As bishop of Autun, France, he saw his diocese afflicted by war between the sons of Clovis. F. D. Nov. 22.

PRAT, FERDINAND (1857–1938), theologian. Born in Lafretoire, France, on Feb. 10, he studied there, became a Jesuit in 1873, and taught at Toulouse and in Beirut, Syria. He was ordained in 1887, published biblical studies, taught in France and Belgium, and was appointed in 1925 to devote all his time to scholarship. He was a consultor to the Pontifical Biblical Commission, editor of *Études Bibliques*, and wrote *The Bible and History, The Ten Commandments, Origen, Theologian and Exegete, The Theology of St. Paul,* and *The Theology of St. John.* He is best known for his monumental *Jesus Christ, His Life, His Doctrine, and His Work.* He died in Toulouse, France, on Aug. 4.

PRAT, GUILLAUME DE (d. 1560). He became bishop of Clermont, France, in 1528, founded Clermont College at Paris, and was a delegate of King Francis I at the Council of Trent.

PRAXEAS (2nd century). A native of Asia, he was imprisoned for several months for his faith, was in Rome sometime between 190 and 198, and according to Tertullian persuaded Pope Zephyrinus to recall a letter the pope had written which declared that Montanus and Prisca had prophetic gifts. He taught in Carthage, was accused of monarchianism by Tertullian, in his treatise, *Adversus Praxean*, recanted, and was a leader of the anti-Montanist group.

PRAXEDES, ST. That she was buried near St. Prudentia in the cemetery of Priscilla, Rome, is all the information known. Legend calls her daughter of a Roman senator, Pudens, and sister of St. Prudentia, who aided Christians during the reign of Marcus Aurelius. F. D. July 21.

PRAY, GEORGE (1723–1801), historian. Born in Ersekujvár, Hungary, on Sept. 11, he studied at Pozsony, joined the Jesuits in 1745, and continued his studies at St. Ann's in Vienna and Nagy-Szombat. He was ordained in 1754 and taught at Rozsnyó, the Theresianum in Vienna, Győr, Nagy-Szombat, and Buda. He became imperial historiographer in Gran when the Jesuits were suppressed in 1773, librarian in Pest in 1777, a canon in Grosswardein in 1790, represented the chapter in the Hungarian *Reichstag*, and was appointed abbot of Tormowa. He wrote major historical treatises, ranks with Stephan Katona as founder of scientific historical writing in Hungary, and died in Pest, Hungary, on Sept. 23.

PRECIPIANO, HUMBERT GUILLAUME DE (1626–1711), archbishop. Born in Besançon, France, he studied at Constance, Besançon and Louvain, received his licentiate in law and doctorate in philosophy from Dôle, and became dean of the Besançon chapter, commendatory abbot of Bellevaux, and ecclesiastical councilor of the Dôle court. He was Burgundy's plenipotentiary at the Diet of Ratisbon in 1667, went to Madrid in 1672 as head councilor for Burgundy and Netherlands affairs, was consecrated bishop of Bruges in 1683, where he vigorously fought Jansenism, and in 1690 became archbishop of Mechlin, where he continued his struggle against Jansenism. He also became involved in a controversy with the procurator general of the area, whom he excommunicated, over infringement of Church rights—a dispute which was settled by Philip V. He died in Brussels, Belgium, on June 7.

PRÉMARE, JOSEPH HENRI MARIE DE (1666–1736), missioner. Born in Cherbourg, France, on July 17, he joined the Jesuits in 1683, and was sent as a missioner to China in 1698. He was imprisoned in Canton in 1724 when Christianity was proscribed by the emperor, and was banished to Macao, where he died on Sept. 17. He wrote *Notitia linguae sinicae*, a Chinese grammar, and translated several Chinese works.

PRENDERGAST, EDMOND FRANCIS (1843–1918), archbishop. Born in Clonmel, Ireland, on May 3, he went to the United States in 1859, studied at St. Charles Borromeo seminary, Philadelphia, was ordained in 1865, did pastoral work, and was vicar general of that see in 1895–97. He was consecrated titular bishop of Scilium and auxiliary in 1897, and succeeded to the see in 1911 as archbishop.

A number of charitable institutions, Misericordia Hospital, and West Philadelphia Catholic High School were built during his reign. He died in Philadelphia on Feb. 26.

PRESTON, THOMAS (d. 1640). An Englishman, he studied at the English College in Rome, was ordained, and in 1590 became a Benedictine. In 1603 he was sent on the English mission, was arrested for his priesthood, and was expelled from England in 1614. He participated in a conference in Rheims to unite the English congregation, Monte Cassino and Valladolid English monks, and then returned to England, where he was arrested, held in various prisons, and died in Clink prison on Apr. 5. He wrote several books under the alias of Roger Widdrington, supporting King James I's Oath of Allegiance, but later denounced his position and submitted to Rome.

PRESTON, THOMAS SCOTT (1824–1891). Born in Hartford, Connecticut, on July 23, he studied at Trinity College there and General Theological seminary in New York, was ordained an Episcopalian minister in 1847 and served in Episcopalian churches. He became a convert in 1849, studied at Fordham, was ordained in 1850, and served at St. Patrick's cathedral and a parish in Yonkers. In 1853 he was appointed secretary to Archbishop Hughes, chancellor in 1855, became pastor of St. Ann's in 1862, vicar general in 1873, founded the Sisters of the Divine Compassion in 1873 and administered the diocese for a time in 1890. He was appointed a domestic prelate in 1881 and prothonotary apostolic in 1888. He wrote fifteen historical and devotional books and died in New York City on Nov. 4.

PRIBER, CHRISTIAN (18th century), missioner. Born in France, he became a Jesuit, worked with Cherokee Indians in Tennessee, compiled a dictionary and grammar of their language, adopted many of their customs, and was made secretary of a federation whose plans of government he drew up. The English sent an expedition from South Carolina to arrest him, fearing his influence with French allies, but the Indians would not surrender him. He was captured in Alabama in 1741 and died sometime afterward as an English prisoner in Frederica, Georgia.

PRICE, JOHN (1861–1926). Born in England, he was ordained, and became the English member of the rota and in 1922 a member of the supreme council of the Council for the Propagation of the Faith. He wrote *Is the Pope Independent?* He died in Darlington, England, on Apr. 28.

PRICE, THOMAS FREDERICK (1860–1919), founder. Born in Wilmington, North Carolina, on Aug. 19, he studied at St. Charles College, Maryland, and St. Mary's seminary, Baltimore, and was ordained in 1886. He did missionary work in North Carolina, founded and edited *Truth* in 1897, established an orphanage in Raleigh in 1898, and founded the *Orphan Boy*, and in 1902 began the Regina Apostolorum, a training center for missionary priests in Raleigh. In 1904 he met Fr. James Anthony Walsh, and in 1911 the two received papal approval of the Catholic Foreign Mission Society of America (Maryknoll Fathers). In 1918 he led the first group of four Maryknoll priests to China and established a mission at Yeungkong in southern China; he died the following year on Sept. 12 in Hong Kong.

PRICHARD, VEN. HUMPHREY (d. 1589), martyr. *See* Nichols, Ven. George.

PRIDEAUX, THOMAS (1525?–1592?), poet. Born in Devonshire, England, he went into exile because of his faith and in 1574, probably in Madrid, married Helen, daughter of Thomas More's friend, John Clement. He wrote a long elegy for Stephen Gardiner, bishop of Winchester, and the more secular poem, *Lamentation of Dido.*

PRIERIAS, SYLVESTER. *See* Mazzolini, Sylvester.

PRILIDIAN, ST. (d. 250?), martyr. *See* Babylas, St.

PRIMADICCI, JAMES (d. 1460). Born in Bologna, Italy, he became a Franciscan and favored the strict-observance group. In 1437, Pope Eugene IV named him head of a mission which was successful in reuniting the Armenian Church with Rome and in 1444 he was sent to the exarchate of Ravenna, and elsewhere in Italy, to raise support for a crusade. In 1445 he went to the East as commissary and in 1446–49 served as vicar general of the Cismontane branches of the Observants. He died in Bologna.

PRIMALDI, BL. ANTONIO (d. 1480), martyr. An aged artisan in Otranto, Italy, he was hacked to death with 800 others by the pillaging Turks under Mohammed II when he rallied his fellow townsmen to choose death rather than apostasy. His cult was approved in 1771. F. D. Aug. 14.

PRIMITIVUS, ST. (d. 120?), martyr. *See* Getulius, St.

PRIMITIVUS, ST. (d. 300?), martyr. *See* Facundus, St.

PRIMITIVUS, ST. (d. 304), martyr. *See* Apodemius, St.

PRIMUS, ST. (d. 297?), martyr. *See* Felician, St.

PRIMUS, ST. (d. 320), martyr. *See* Cyrinus, St.

PRIMUS, ST. (d. 362), martyr. *See* Donatus, St.

PRIN, BL. JEAN REINÉ (d. 1794), martyr. An Ursuline nun, she took the name Sr. Laurentina, and was guillotined at Valenciennes, France, during the French Revolution. She was beatified in 1920. F. D. Oct. 17.

PRINCE, JOHN CHARLES (1804–1860), bishop. Born in Canada, he was ordained, became titular bishop of Martyropolis and co-adjutor bishop of Montreal in 1845, and in 1852 became first bishop of St. Hyacinthe, Quebec. He built a new cathedral chapel after the old one burned down, and founded twenty parishes. He died on May 5.

PRINCIPIUS, ST. (d. 505?). Elder brother of St. Remigius, he became bishop of Soissons, France. F. D. Sept. 25.

PRIOR, ST. (295?–395?). He was one of the first followers of St. Antony in the Egyptian desert. F. D. June 17.

PRISCA, ST. (d. 270?), martyr. She was slain in Rome and is honored by a church built on the Aventine there. F. D. Jan. 18.

PRISCA. *See* Priscilla, St.

PRISCIAN, ST. (d. 304?), martyr. *See* Carponius, St.

PRISCIAN (6th century), grammarian. Probably a native of Caesarea, Priscianus Caesariensis taught at Constantinople and wrote *Institutiones grammaticae*, the best-known Latin grammar of antiquity and the basis of Rabanus Maurus' work in the Middle Ages; a translation of the *Periegesis of Dionysius*; a book on the versification of the *Aeneid*; poems and books on coins and numbers; and a panegyric on Emperor Anastasius I he delivered about 512.

PRISCILLA, ST. (d. 98?), martyr. She probably was the wife of the martyred Manius Acilius Glabrio, mother of St. Pudens, and host to St. Peter the Apostle at her Roman villa, beneath which is a major catacomb named after her. There is a reference to the family in Suetonius. She is also called Prisca, but the question of accurate identification remains a confusing problem. F. D. Jan. 16.

PRISCILLA, ST. (1st century). *See* Aquila, St.

PRISCILLIAN, ST. (d. 362), martyr. *See* Priscus, St.

PRISCUS, ST. (d. 66?), martyr. He is said to have been sent by St. Peter to Capua, Italy, as bishop and to have been put to death by Nero. F. D. Sept. 1.

PRISCUS, ST. (d. 260), martyr. *See* Alexander, St.

PRISCUS, ST. (d. 272?), martyr. He and another leading citizen, Cottus, fled from Besançon, Gaul, but were captured and beheaded with other Christians at Auxerre during the reign of Aurelian. He is also known as Prix. F. D. May 26.

PRISCUS, ST. (d. 362), martyr. He was a priest put to death at Rome with St. Priscillian, also a cleric, and St. Benedicta, a laywoman. F. D. Jan. 4.

PRISCUS, ST. (5th century). A bishop in northern Africa, he was cast adrift with eleven priests in a rudderless boat, landed in Italy, and became bishop of Capua. The others became bishops elsewhere: Adjutor, Augustus, Canion, Castrensis, Elpidius, Heraclius, Mark, Rosius, Secundinus, Tammarus, and Vindonius. F. D. Sept. 1.

PRIVATUS, ST. (d. 223), martyr. A Roman citizen, he was scourged to death during the reign of Alexander Severus. F. D. Sept. 28.

PRIVATUS, ST. (d. 266), martyr. Bishop of Gévaudon (Mende), Gaul, he was seized by invading barbarians and beaten to death when he refused to reveal the hiding place of his people. F. D. Aug. 21.

PRIX. See Praejectus, St.; also, Priscus, St. (d. 272?).

PRO, MIGUEL (1891–1927). Born in Guadalupe, near Zacatecas, Mexico, on July 13, he joined the Jesuits in 1911, was professed in 1913, and was forced to flee to the United States in 1914 when revolution broke out in Mexico and the novitiate at which he was studying at El Llano was overrun by Venustiano's anti-religious forces. Later in the year he was sent to Granada, Spain, and studied there until 1920 when he was sent to teach at Granada de Nicaragua. In 1922–24 he resumed his studies in Sarriá, Spain, and then went to Enghien, Belgium, where he was ordained in 1925. Despite the reign of religious persecution pursued by Elías Calles in Mexico, he returned to his native land in 1926, defied governmental orders forbidding religious practices and rites, and ministered to the spiritual needs of thousands. He was arrested in 1927 and accused of participating in a plot to assassinate the Mexican president, Álvaro Obregón. Although the true instigator of the plot confessed and was executed, Fr. Pro was arbitrarily shot to death by the police in Mexico City on Nov. 22.

PROBA, FALTONIA (4th century), poet. Daughter of Petronius Probianius, consul in 322, she married Claudius Celcinus Adalphius, Roman prefect in 351, was converted to Christianity, and wrote a poem based on the Old Testament and the gospel life of Christ.

PROBUS, ST. (d. 175?). He came from Rome to become bishop of Ravenna, Italy. F. D. Nov. 10.

PROBUS, ST. (d. 304), martyr. See Tarachus, St.

PROBUS, ST. (d. 437), martyr. See Arcadius, St.

PROBUS, ST. (d. 571?). He was bishop of Rieti, Italy. F. D. Mar. 15.

PROBUS, ST. (6th century). He was bishop of Verona, Italy, about 591. F. D. Jan. 12.

PROCESSUS, ST., martyr. Always linked with St. Martinian, he was venerated in Rome as one of the earliest martyrs. The legend which made them the jailers of SS. Peter and Paul is totally unfounded. F. D. July 2.

PROCHORUS, ST. (1st century), martyr. He was one of the seven deacons ordained by the apostles; traditionally, he is said to have been bishop of Nicomedia and to have been put to death at Antioch. F. D. Apr. 9.

PROCLUS, ST. (d. 115), martyr. See Hilarion, St.

PROCLUS, ST. (d. 446?), archbishop. A native of Constantinople, he was a disciple of St. John Chrysostom and became secretary to Archbishop Atticus, who ordained him. Appointed bishop of Cyzicus, he never took office because of the opposition of the people there; in 434 he was elected patriarch of Constantinople. His episcopate was characterized by his gentle administration and mild attitude toward heretics, particularly the Nestorians, though he firmly adhered to traditional teaching and in his most famous work, *Tome to the Armenians*, condemned the writings of Theodore of Mopsuestia, which were Nestorian in outlook. He died on July 24. F. D. Oct. 24.

PROCOPIUS, ST. (d. 303), martyr. Born at Jerusalem, he was a reader in the church at Scythopolis and became the first victim of the persecution of Diocletian. When ordered to sacrifice to the gods or to the emperor, he refused and was beheaded. Incredible legends, completely discredited, have grown up around his name. F. D. July 8.

PROCOPIUS, ST. (d. 750?). See Basil, St.

PROCOPIUS, ST. (980?–1053). Born in Bohemia, he studied at Prague, was ordained, became a hermit, and then founded the Basilian abbey of Sazaba in Prague, where he served as abbot. F. D. July 4.

PROCTER, ADELAIDE ANNE (1825–1864), poet. Born in London on Oct. 30, daughter of Bryan Waller Procter, a poet, she began writing poetry as a child. She became a convert in 1851, a contributor (under the name Mary Berwick) of poems to *Household Words*, edited by Charles Dickens, in 1853, and *All the Year Round*. They were collected in *Legends and Lyrics* and became very popular. She edited *Victoria Regia* in 1861, became interested in charitable works and women's suffrage, and died in London on Feb. 2.

PROCULUS, ST. (2nd century), martyr. See Florus, St.

PROCULUS, ST. (d. 304?), martyr. Believed to have been a Roman officer, he was crucified in Bologna, Italy, in the reign of Maximian and was long venerated as patron of that city. It is possible that he and St. Proculus of Pozzuoli and St. Proculus of Ravenna are one and the same. F. D. June 1.

PROCULUS, ST. (d. 305?), martyr. *See* Januarius, St.

PROCULUS, ST. (d. 310), bishop and martyr. Bishop of Terni, Italy, he was put to death during the reign of Maxentius. F. D. Apr. 14.

PROCULUS, ST. (d. 320?). He was bishop of Verona, Italy, who suffered under but outlived the Diocletian persecution. F. D. Dec. 9.

PROCULUS, ST. (d. 542), bishop and martyr. Born in Bologna, Italy, he became its bishop in 540 and was put to death with many of his flock by Totila the Goth. He and the fourth-century soldier of the same name were enshrined in the Benedictine basilica of San Procolo. St. Proculus, bishop of Terni (or Narni), honored on Dec. 1, is probably identical with this bishop of Bologna. F. D. June 1.

PROCULUS, ST. (8th century), martyr. Bishop of Autun, France, he was slain after 717 by invading Huns. F. D. Dec. 1.

PROSCHKO, FRANZ ISIDOR (1816–1891), author. Born in Hohenfurt, Bohemia, on Apr. 2, he worked in governmental bureaus and wrote the two-volume *Der Jesuits* (1857), *Die Nadel* (1858), *Pugatschew* (1860), and *Ausgewählte erzählungen und Gedichte* (1873). He died in Vienna on Feb. 6.

PROSDOCE, ST. (4th century), martyr. *See* Domnina, St.

PROSDOCIMUS, ST. (d. 100?). He was the first bishop of Padua, Italy. F. D. Nov. 7.

PROSKE, KARL (1794–1861). Born in Grobing, Upper Silesia, he took his medical degree at Halle, became court physician at Oppeln, was an army surgeon in 1813–15, and in 1821 gave up medicine for the priesthood. He was ordained in Ratisbon in 1826, collected church music, and was made canon and choirmaster of the Ratisbon cathedral in 1830. He continued to collect and transcribe hundreds of musical scores; he published the four-volume *Musica divina* (1853–62) and *Selectus novus missae* (1857–61) before he died in Ratisbon, Germany, on Dec. 20.

PROSPER, ST. (d. 453). He was bishop of Orléans, France. F. D. July 29.

PROSPER, ST. (390?–465). A layman in Aquitaine, he moved to Marseilles in Gaul, where in 428 he joined Hilary in supporting St. Augustine's views on predestination, grace, and free will in opposition to the semi-Pelagianism which was associated with the writings of St. John Cassian. He also wrote a number of poems, the longest of which was *Those without Grace*, and a prose *Chronicle* of universal history, which ended with the 455 capture of Rome by the Vandals. Prosper later became secretary of Pope St. Leo the Great and died in Rome. F. D. June 25.

PROSPER, ST. (d. 466?), bishop. He is said to have directed the see of Reggio in Emilia (not Calabria), Italy, for twenty-two years, a reign noted by his exceptional charities. F. D. June 25.

PROTASE, ST., martyr. *See* Gervase, St.

PROTASIUS, ST. (d. 352). He became bishop of Milan, Italy, in 331 and defended St. Athanasius against the Arians, especially at the Synod of Sardica (343). F. D. Nov. 24.

PROTERIUS, ST. (d. 457), patriarch and martyr. When the Council of Chalcedon condemned the heretic Dioscorus in 451, Proterius replaced him as patriarch of Alexandria. The Monothelite followers of Eutyches turned to Eleurus after the death of Dioscorus, tried to take over Alexandria and the church, and stabbed Proterius to death within the sanctuary on Good Friday. F. D. Feb. 28.

PROTHADIUS, ST. (d. 624). He succeeded St. Nicetius as bishop of Besançon, France. F. D. Feb. 10.

PROTOGENES, ST. (4th century), bishop. A Syrian priest, he was banished by Emperor Valens, recalled by Theodosius, and made bishop of Carrhae (now Haran, Turkey). F. D. May 6.

PROTUS, ST. (d. 303), martyr. A priest, he and his deacon, St. Januarius, were missioners on Sardinia when captured and beheaded at Porto Torres during the Diocletian persecution. F. D. Oct. 25.

PROTUS, ST. (d. 304?), martyr. *See* Cantius, St.

PROTUS, ST., martyr. According to legend, he and his brother Hyacinth were Romans and servants in the house of Basilla, martyred in Rome. Another legend has them slaves of Eugenia, daughter of an Egyptian prefect, who fled to Rome and were martyred with her and Basilla, whom she had converted. Their remains were found on the Salernian Way in 1845. F. D. Sept. 11.

PROTUS VINCENTIUS (4th century). He was second bishop of Capua, Italy, papal legate at the Council of Nicaea (325), in attendance at the Council of Sardica (343), and a strong opponent of Arianism. At Arles in 353 he sided with Constantius and voted for the deposition of St. Athanasius, a step which he publicly renounced at Rimini.

PROUT, FR. *See* Mahony, Francis Sylvester.

PROVANCHER, LÉON ABEL (1820–1892), naturalist. Born on Mar. 10 in Bécancourt, Quebec, he studied at Nicolet, was ordained in 1844, and engaged in pastoral work for the next twenty-five years. Always interested in natural history, he founded the *Naturaliste Canadien* in 1868, and spent the rest of his life as its editor (until 1888) and in research on Canadian flora and fauna. He died in Cap Rouge, Quebec, on Mar. 23. Among his writings were *Flore du Canada*

(1862) and the three-volume *Faune entomologique du Canada* (1877–90).

PROVINUS, ST. (d. 420?), bishop. A Gaul, he served under St. Ambrose at Milan and as coadjutor to St. Felix, bishop of Como, Italy, whom he succeeded in 391. F. D. Mar. 8.

PRUDENTIUS, ST. (d. 700?), bishop. Born in Armentia, Spain, he was ordained after several years of life as a hermit, and became bishop of Tarazona, Aragon, of which he is now the patron. F. D. Apr. 28.

PRUDENTIUS (d. 861), bishop. Born in Spain, Galindo probably fled the Saracen persecutions as a youth, went to Gaul where he changed his name, studied at the Palatine school, and about 847 became bishop of Troyes. In 849 he became involved in a dispute with Hincmar, archbishop of Rheims, and defended the theory of double predestination and that Christ died only for those saved. He wrote *De praedestinatione contra Johannem Scotum* in 851 and *Epistola tractoria ad Wenilonem* in 856 in defense of his theory. He died in Troyes, France, on Apr. 6, a date celebrated there as his feast day, though he is not recognized as a saint elsewhere. He wrote a life of the Virgin Mary, some poetry, and *Annales Bertiani*, a trustworthy history of the western Franks from 853 to 861.

PRUDENTIUS, AURELIUS CLEMENS (348–405?), poet. Born in the Tarraconensis, Spain, he practiced law, served as provincial governor twice, became a member of the emperor's court, but retired to pursue an ascetic and religious way of life. He probably died in Spain sometime after 405. Among his works are the *Cathemerinon*, a collection of hymns; *Peri Stephanon*, a collection of narratives of martyrs; *Apotheosis*, on the Trinity; *Hamartigenia*, on sin's origin; *Psychomachia*, an allegorical poem; *Dittochaeon*, on biblical events; and *Contra Symmachum*.

PRZEMYSLAV (d. 1296), king of Poland. He was elected king in 1290, crowned in 1295 with papal approval, and murdered shortly thereafter.

PSALMODIUS, ST. (d. 690?). A follower of St. Brendan, he went from Ireland to France and became a hermit at Limoges. He is also called Sauman. F. D. June 14.

PSAUME, NICHOLAS (1518–1575), bishop. Born in Chaumont-sur-Aire, France, he studied at the Norbertine abbey in Verdun, Paris, Orléans and Poitiers, joined the Norbertines, was ordained in 1540, and received his doctorate in theology from Paris. He became abbot of St. Paul's, Verdun, represented the Norbertines at the Council of Trent in 1546, and was consecrated bishop of Verdun in 1548. He attended the Council of Trent in 1551–52, led the attack on abuses, edited the council's canons in 1552, and was in attendance when it reconvened in 1562. He edited French ecclesiastical law to conform with Tridentine decrees and helped found a Jesuit college in Verdun, France. He died there on Aug. 10.

PSELLUS, MICHAEL (1018?–1078?), statesman. Born in Constantinople, he became a lawyer, a judge at Philadelphia, imperial secretary to Emperor Michael V, and taught at the academy at Constantinople, where he was highly regarded as philosopher and Platonist. He gave up teaching when appointed Constantine IX's secretary of state, entered the Olympos monastery in 1054, but was obliged to return to Constantinople when he quarreled with the monks. He was imperial ambassador to Isaac Comnenos when Isaac defeated the imperial army near Nicaea in 1057, joined him when he entered Constantinople as Isaac I, served under Constantine X from 1059 to 1067, and was Michael VII's chief minister of state until his death. He preached the panegyric for Patriarch John VIII (Xiphilinos). under whom he had studied and whom he had followed to Olympos, and wrote on a wide variety of subjects. Among his outstanding works were a commentary on Aristotle, treatises on anatomy and medicine, a law compendium, poems, a history from 976 to 1077, and some 500 letters.

PSICHARI, ERNEST (1883–1914). Son of Jean Psichari, a professor at Paris, and Noémi, daughter of Ernest Renan, he began his career as a poet, became a soldier, and wrote a defense of the military life. A somewhat autobiographical study, *Le Voyage du centurion* (1912), followed. He became a convert in 1913 and was planning to become a Dominican when he was recalled to the army as a lieutenant. He died in battle at St. Vincent Rossignol, Belgium, on Aug. 22.

PTOLEMY, ST. (1st century). He is known as a disciple of St. Peter, who sent him as bishop to Nepi, Tuscany, where he was put to death. F. D. Aug. 24.

PTOLEMY, ST. (d. 165?), martyr. He was put to death at Rome during the reign of Antoninus Pius for instructing a woman in Christianity; when Lucius and another man objected to the sentence, they also were slain. They are honored by St. Justin Martyr. F. D. Oct. 19.

PTOLEMY, ST. (d. 249), martyr. *See* Ammon, St.

PUBLIA, ST. (d. 370?). A native of Syria, she gathered a group of religious women in her house at Antioch when she was widowed. She is supposed to have been ordered put to death by Julian the Apostate in 362 when he took offense at a hymn they were singing, but the sentence was deferred and she died in Persia. F. D. Oct. 9.

PUBLIUS, ST. (d. 112?). He is traditionally identified as a citizen of Malta who befriended St. Paul (Acts 28:7) and later bishop of the island; other accounts list him as bishop of Athens and a martyr there during the persecution of Trajan. F. D. Jan. 21.

PUBLIUS, ST. (2nd century), martyr. *See* Aurelius, St.

PUBLIUS, ST. (d. 304), martyr. *See* Apodemius, St.

PUBLIUS, ST. (d. 380?). A senator's son, he gave up his wealth, became a hermit in the Euphrates region, and eventually superior of two large groups of anchorites, one Greek and one Syrian. He is recorded by Theodoret. F. D. Jan. 25.

PUCCI, BL. ANTONIO (1819–1892). Born at Poggiole, Italy, and christened Eustace, he became a Servite at Florence in 1837, was ordained in 1843, and became a parish priest at the resort town of Viareggio. He was noted for his charity, his work during two epidemics, the establishment of a home for sick children, and initial work of the Holy Childhood Society. He was beatified in 1952. F. D. Jan. 14.

PUCCI-FRANCESCHI, BL. BARTOLOMMEO (d. 1330). A wealthy citizen of Montepulciano, Italy, he became a Franciscan priest there, receiving many supernatural gifts before his death, at a very advanced age, on May 6. His cult was confirmed in 1880. F. D. May 23.

PUCCINI, GIACOMO (d. 1712), composer. Born in Lucca, he became choirmaster of that Italian republic, wrote much ecclesiastical music, taught Guglielmi, and was the first of a long line of composers and musical historians, including his great-great-grandson, the composer of operas.

PUCCINI, GIACOMO ANTONIO (1858–1924), composer. Born in Lucca, Italy, on June 22, of a family long and widely known in music, he studied at the Milan conservatory under Ponchielli. His first opera (in one act) was *Il villi*, performed in 1884; *Edgar* and *Manon Lescaut* followed. His greatest successes were *La Bohème* (1896) and *Tosca* (1900). *Madame Butterfly* (1904) and *The Girl of the Golden West* (1910), both based on plays by the American dramatist, David Belasco, did not then have the same appeal; *La Rondine* (1917) proved a failure. Three one-acters, *Il tabarro*, *Suor Angelica*, and *Gianni Schicchi*, were produced in 1917; *Turandot* was completed by Franco Alfano and produced posthumously in 1926. Puccini died in Brussels of a heart attack, following an operation for cancer of the throat, on Nov. 29.

PUDENS. *See* Pudentiana.

PUDENTIANA. Also called Potentiana, she long was called the saintly daughter of Pudens, a Roman senator of the first century. Her name, however, seems to have come into existence as the result of a scribal error listing a grant of land for a church (*ecclesia pudentiana*) given by a Christian named Pudens, who may have been the same as the Pudens mentioned in II Tim. 4:21.

PUGET, PIERRE (1622–1694), sculptor. Born in Marseilles, France, on Oct. 31, he studied shipbuilding as a youth, became a cabinetmaker's helper in Florence, and studied painting in Rome under Pietro da Cortona. He engaged in shipbuilding in France in 1643, and beginning in 1653 painted altarpieces in Aix and Marseilles. In 1655 he gave up painting for sculpture, went to Genoa in 1660 to buy marble for Fouquet, and there executed many of his works noted for their anatomical mastery, power, and accurate modeling. He returned to France in 1669 at Colbert's invitation and became known as the "Michelangelo of France." Among his outstanding sculptures are *Milo of Crotona*, *Perseus and Andromeda*, the bas-relief, *Alexander* and *Diogenes*, a statue of St. Sebastian, the *Caryatides* for the Toulon Hôtel de Ville. He died in Marseilles on Dec. 2.

PUGH, GEORGE ELLIS (1822–1876), senator. Born in Cincinnati, Ohio, on Nov. 28, he graduated from Miami University, Ohio, in 1843 and was admitted to the bar. He served in the Mexican War, in the Ohio house of representatives in 1848–49, was Cincinnati city solicitor in 1850, state attorney general in 1852–54, and Ohio's first United States senator from 1855 to 1861. He became a convert about this time, was defeated in subsequent elections, and died in Cincinnati on July 19.

PUGIN, AUGUSTUS WELBY NORTHMORE (1812–1852), architect. Born in London on Mar. 1, he studied under his father there and in Normandy. He designed furniture for Windsor castle, scenery for the operatic production of *Kenilworth*, and stage machinery for the Drury Lane Theatre in London. In 1831 he opened an architectural supply shop, which failed; his first wife died in childbirth in 1832; and in 1833 he married Louisa Burton. He became a convert in 1834 and his wife followed in 1839. He designed the chapel and decorated the new college at Oscott (1838) and taught ecclesiastical antiquities there until 1844. He built a fifteenth-century-style house at Laverstock, near Salisbury, called St. Marie's Grange, and another, St. Augustine's Grange, later at Ramsgate; restored many cathedrals and colleges, and built numerous parish churches, chapels, convents, and monasteries; and wrote on church decoration, ancient houses, metal work, plain song, and Gothic architecture. He became insane in his last year, and died in Ramsgate, England, on Sept. 14.

PUISEUX, VICTOR ALEXANDRE (1820–1883), astronomer. Born in Argenteuil, Seine-et-Oise, France, on Apr. 16, he studied at Collège Rollin in Paris, entered L'École Normale in 1837, became associate professor in mathematics in 1840, and received his doctorate in mathematics in 1841. He taught at Rennes, went to Besançon in 1845, returned to L'École Normale in 1849, and lectured at the Sorbonne and Collège de France. He was assistant astronomer at the Paris observatory from 1855 to 1859, and in 1857 occupied the chair of astronomy at the Sorbonne, a position he held until a few months before his death. He was co-editor of *Annales scientifiques de l'école normale supérieure* in 1864, edited *Connaissance des temps* and was a member of the Bureau des Longitudes from 1868 to 1872, was elected to the French Academy in 1871, and was editor in chief of a new edition of Laplace's works. He died in Frontenay, France, on Sept. 9.

PULASKI, CASIMIR (1748–1779), general. Born in Winary, Podolia, Poland, on Mar. 4, son of Count Joseph Pulaski, he studied law, served in the guard of Duke Charles of Courland, and in 1768 joined the uprising led by the Confederation of Barr formed by his father to free Poland from foreign domination through Stanislaus II. He was at first successful, but his forces were finally crushed and in 1772 he was forced to flee to Turkey and in 1775 to France. There he offered his sword to Benjamin Franklin to aid the American colonists in their revolt against England. He joined Washington in Boston in 1777, fought gallantly, though often unsuccessfully, through the revolution at the head of Pulaski's Legion, was wounded during the siege of Savannah, Georgia, and died from the wound aboard the *Wasp* in Savannah harbor on Oct. 11.

PULCHERIA, ST. (399–453), empress. Granddaughter of Theodosius the Great and daughter of Emperor Arcadius, she was born on Jan. 19. The senate in 414 named her Augusta and regent of her brother Theodosius II, whose education was entrusted to her. At her direction he married Athenias (christened Eudocia), but declared his wife to be Augusta. Conflict developed: Pulcheria supported the Catholics and Athenias supported Nestorius. Pulcheria was banished; when Athenias was exiled to Jerusalem in 441 for infidelity, Pulcheria returned. When Theodosius died in 450, Pulcheria was proclaimed empress, married an army officer, Marcian, had him proclaimed emperor, and the two ruled the empire. In 451 they sponsored the Council of Chalcedon, which denounced Monophytism. She built many churches and helped establish a university at Constantinople. F. D. Sept. 10.

PULCI, LUIGI (1432–1484), poet. Born in Florence, Italy, on Aug. 15, he wrote *Morgante maggiore* (1481), a romantic poem of the

travels of members of Charlemagne's court, which became quite popular, and other poems. He died in Padua, Italy.

PURCELL, JOHN BAPTIST (1800–1883), archbishop. Born in Mallow, Ireland, on Feb. 26, he studied at St. Patrick's College there, came to the United States when eighteen, taught at Asbury College in Baltimore, tutored, and entered Mt. St. Mary's seminary in 1820. He went to St. Sulpice seminaries in Issy in 1823 and then in Paris, where he was ordained in 1826. He returned to Mt. St. Mary's as a professor in 1826, became its president in 1829, and in 1833 was appointed second bishop of Cincinnati, Ohio. There he was faced with the problems raised by the waves of German immigrants, built a new cathedral and seminary, and after a series of disputations with Alexander Campbell, a minister who accused the Church of being the enemy of culture and Americanism, was overwhelmed by the number of converts which resulted. He went to Europe in 1835, 1838, and 1843 to recruit clergy for his fast-growing see, which became an archdiocese in 1850. He founded St. Francis Xavier College and Mt. St. Mary of the West in Cincinnati in 1848, quieted a Know-Nothing mob preparing to burn his cathedral in 1853, strongly supported the Union during the Civil War, preached at the second Council of Baltimore in 1866, and attended the Vatican Council, where he opposed as inopportune the definition of the dogma of papal infallibility, though he accepted its proclamation. His last years were weighted down by a financial disaster in 1879, caused by the collapse of a diocesan savings fund managed by his brother Edward. He retired from active duty as archbishop in 1880, and died at St. Martin's, Ohio, on July 4.

PURICELLI, BL. JULIANA (1427–1501). Born in Busto-Arizio, Italy, she became an Augustinian nun and joined Bl. Catherine da Pallanza at Sacra Monte sopra Varese, Italy, where she died. Her cult was approved in 1769. F. D. Aug. 14.

PÜRSTINGER, BERTHOLD (1465–1543), bishop. Born in Salzburg, Austria, he was a canon lawyer, served the archbishop of Salzburg, and in 1508 was appointed bishop of Chiemsee. He attended councils at Salzburg (1512) and Mühldorf (1522), defended rebellious peasants in his diocese against charges of treason, retired to a monastery in 1526 after the initial success of Lutheranism, and about 1529 went to Saalfelden, Germany, where he built a hospital and church and died on July 19. He wrote an elaborate and able theology (1528, in German; 1531, in Latin), a treatise on the mass, a listing of contemporary clerical abuses, and a defense of the Eucharist against reformer polemicists.

PUSICIUS, ST. (d. 341), martyr. *See* Simeon Barsabae, St.

PUSTET, FRIEDRICH (1798–1882), publisher. Born in Passau, Germany, on Mar. 25, he studied bookbinding with his father, Anton, opened a bookstore in Passau in 1819, established a press in 1822, and built a paper mill in 1836. He published a variety of titles, but specialized in theology, liturgical works, and church music. He retired and took over a Munich textbook firm in 1862, which he controlled until 1874. He died on Mar. 5. His sons Friedrich (1831–1902) and Karl (1839–1910) were in 1860 placed in charge of liturgical and vernacular publications; Klemens (1833–1898) inherited the paper factory.

PUTEANUS, ERYCIUS (1574–1646). Born in Venloo, Limbourg, on Nov. 4, he studied at Dordrecht, Cologne, and Louvain, and went to Italy in 1597, where Cardinal Borromeo secured for him a professorship at the Palatine School in Milan in 1600. He was appointed King Philip IV's historiographer in 1603, accepted the chair of ancient history in Louvain in 1606, a position he held for the rest of his life, and was appointed Archduke Albert's honorary chancellor in 1612. He died in Louvain, Flanders, on Sept. 17.

PUTZER, JOSEPH (1836–1904), theologian. Born in Rodaneck, Tyrol, on Mar. 4, he joined the Congregation of the Most Holy Redeemer in 1856, was ordained in 1859, and was sent to the United States in 1876. He was at St. Alphonsus' seminary in Baltimore from 1880, engaged in pastoral activities until 1884, and was made superior of St. Mary's in Buffalo. In 1887 he was appointed to the chair of moral theology at St. Mary's, Ilchester, Maryland, and remained there until his death on May 15. He revised Fr. Konings' *Commentarium in facultates apostolicas* and wrote theological treatises.

PUVIS DE CHAVENNES, PIERRE CECILE (1824–1898), painter. Born in Lyons, France, on Dec. 14, he studied at Lyons and the Lycée Henri IV in Paris. He intended to follow his father's profession of mining engineer, but after a visit to Italy in 1847 determined to become a painter. He studied under Henry Scheffer, Delacroix, and Thomas Couture, exhibited a *Pietà* at the Salon of 1852, and opened a studio which he maintained until 1897. By the time his *Return from the Hunt* was shown in the Salon in 1859, he was regarded as a leading painter and soon became famed for his murals. In 1864–65 he painted a series of panels for the Amiens Museum (among them, *Woman Weeping over the Ruins of Her Home, Woman Spinning, Labor Rest* and *Ave picardia nutrix*). Among his outstanding works are the series on Ste. Geneviève's life in the Pantheon in Paris; the decorative paintings for the Lyons Museum (*Vision of the Antique, Sacred Grove, The Rhône* and *The Saône*); *Science, Arts, and Letters* in the Sorbonne; the decorations for the Hôtel de Ville in Paris (notably *Winter* and *Summer*); and nine panels, *Muses Welcoming the Genius of Enlightenment* for the Boston Public Library. He died in Paris on Oct. 24.

PYRKER, JOHANN LADISLAUS VON OBERWART (1772–1847), archbishop. Born in Lángh, Hungary, on Nov. 2, he studied at Stuhlweissenburg and Fünfkirchen, became a Cistercian in 1792, and was ordained in 1796. He served as prior and abbot of the house at Lilienfeld and as parish priest, was appointed bishop of Zips in 1818, patriarch of Aquileia and primate of Dalmatia with his see at Venice in 1820, and archbishop of Erlau in 1827. He built up a notable art collection, which became the nucleus of the Hungarian National Museum, and wrote dramatic works and epic poems. He died in Vienna on Dec. 2.

Q

QUADRAGESIMUS, ST. (d. 590?). A shepherd and archdeacon at Policastro, Italy, he was cited by St. Gregory the Great. F. D. Oct. 26.

QUADRATUS, ST. (d. 130?), bishop. He is believed to have succeeded St. Publius as bishop of Athens, and may be the apologist referred to by Eusebius and St. Jerome as writing a now-lost explanation of Christianity, supported by evidence of Christ's miracles, to Emperor Hadrian in 124 or 125. Another bishop, who preached in Asia Minor, and is honored on Aug. 21, may be the same person. F. D. May 26.

QUADRATUS, ST. (d. 257), martyr. Im-

prisoned for years in Nicomedia, and elsewhere, he was put to death in Herbipolis during the persecution of Valerian. F. D. May 7.

QUADRATUS, ST. (d. 304?), martyr. A bishop in Anatolia, he was put to death with SS. Emmanuel, Theodosius, and forty other Christians during the persecution of Diocletian. F. D. Mar. 26.

QUADRELLI, ST. ALBERT (d. 1179), bishop. Born in Rivolta d'Adda, near Cremona, Italy, he was a pastor there for twenty-five years before becoming bishop of Lodi in 1168. F. D. July 4.

QUARESIMI, FRANCESCO (1583–1650). Born in Lodi, Italy, on Apr. 4, he studied at Mantua, became a Franciscan and taught theology and philosophy there, and was guardian and minister of his province. He became guardian and vice-commissary apostolic in Aleppo, Syria, in 1616, commissary apostolic of the East in 1618, and was twice imprisoned by the Turks. After a visit to Europe in 1620, he returned to the East as papal commissary at Aleppo from 1627 to 1629, when he reported to the papacy on the Eastern churches. He traveled through the Middle East and Europe, was guardian of St. Angelo in Milan in 1637, served as definitor and procurator general of his order from 1645 to 1648, and died in Milan, Italy, on Oct. 25. He wrote many treatises, chief of which are *Elucidatio terrae sanctae* and *Jerosolymae afflictae*.

QUARTER, WILLIAM (1806–1848), bishop. Born in Killure, Offaly, Ireland, on Jan. 21, he studied at Maynooth, went to Quebec in 1822, then to Mt. St. Mary's, Maryland, and was ordained in New York in 1829. He engaged in pastoral work in New York, where he became pastor of St. Mary's in 1833, and in 1843 was appointed first bishop of Chicago. He established St. Mary of the Lake seminary in 1845, was active among immigrants, and began the first diocesan theological conferences in the country. He died in Chicago on Apr. 10.

QUARTILLOSA, ST. (d. 259), martyr. *See* Victoricus, St.

QUARTUS, ST. (1st century). A follower of the apostles, he greeted the Christians in Rome (Rom. 16:23) and may have been a bishop. F. D. Nov. 3.

QUARTUS, ST. (d. 258), martyr. *See* Sixtus II, St.

QUEIPO DE LLANO, GONZALO (1875–1951), general. Born in Tordesillas, Spain, on Feb. 5, he became an army officer, and was the general in charge of the nationalist forces which captured Málaga in 1937 and held Seville during the civil war of 1938; he made many broadcasts to the nation and was known as the "radio general." A monarchist, he was often out of favor with Generalissimo Franco, but was given the title of marquis in 1950. He died in Seville, Spain, on Mar. 9.

QUELEN, HYACINTHE LOUIS DE (1778–1839), archbishop. Born in Paris on Oct. 8, he studied at Collège de Navarre and was ordained in 1807. After a year as vicar general of St. Brieuc, he became Cardinal Fesch's secretary, vicar general of Paris, and coadjutor to the archbishop of Paris, succeeding to the see in 1821. He was elected to the French Academy in 1824, accused of royalist leanings, and during the revolution of 1830 was driven from his palace. He died in Paris on Dec. 31.

QUENTIN. *See* Quintinus, St.; also, Quintius, St. (d. 570?).

QUERCIA, JACOPO DELLA (1374–1438),

sculptor. Born near Siena, Italy, son of a goldsmith under whom he studied, he was forced to leave Siena about 1400 because of political disturbances and went to Florence, where he became noted for his sculptures. His masterpieces are the Fonte Gaia in Siena, on which he worked ten years and for which he is sometimes called Jacopo della Fonte, and the central doorway of San Petronio in Bologna. He died on Oct. 20.

QUERINI, ANGELO MARIA (1680–1755), cardinal. Born in Venice on Mar. 30, he became a Benedictine in 1696, professor of scripture at Florence in 1705, and in 1718 was appointed to the commission to revise the Greek liturgical books. He became bishop of Corfu in 1723, was transferred to Brescia in 1728, and then created a cardinal. In 1730 he headed the Vatican Library, was appointed prefect of the Congregation of the Index, became involved in a dispute with Muratori over the number of holy days, which was silenced by the pope in 1750, and over the patriarchate of Aquileia, which caused him to leave Rome in 1751. He wrote histories of the Greek church and papacy, on the liturgy, and edited Cardinal Pole's correspondence. He died in Brescia, Italy, on Jan. 6.

QUESNEL, PASQUIER (1634–1719). Born in Paris on July 14, he studied at the Sorbonne, joined the Oratorians in 1657, and was assigned to teach young students. He published *Abrégé de la morale de l'Évangile* (reflections on the four evangelists which was to be developed as *Réflexions morales*) for his students and in 1675 published an edition of the works of St. Leo the Great which was condemned and placed on the Index in 1676 for the Gallican tone of its notes. In 1681 he was transferred to Orléans because of his Jansenist views and in 1684 was obliged to leave the Oratorians when he refused to subscribe to a formula drawn up by the Oratory against Jansenism. He joined Antoine Arnauld in Brussels (after whose death in 1694 he assumed the leadership of the Jansenists), published *La Nouveau Testament en français avec des réflexions morales sur chaque verset*, popularly known as *Réflexions morales* (1687–92), which became one of the most controversial books of its times, and numerous tracts supporting his heretical tendencies, and in 1703 was imprisoned at Philip V's orders by Archbishop Humbert of Mechlin. He escaped to Amsterdam and continued to defend the views expressed in *Réflexions morales*, which was condemned by Pope Clement XI in 1708 and by the bull *Unigenitus*, which condemned 101 propositions, particularly on grace, in 1713. Quesnel never accepted the condemnation, though he requested and was granted the last sacraments on his deathbed. In his dying profession of

966

faith he appealed to a future general council to judge *Unigenitus* and vindicate him. He died in Amsterdam, Flanders, on Dec. 2.

QUEVEDO, JUAN DE (d. 1519), bishop. Born in Bejori, Old Castile, Spain, he was appointed bishop of Santa Maria de la Antiqua (Darien), in 1513, the first American mainland bishop. He was accused of neglect of duty by Las Casas, but in 1518 returned to Spain, where he asked King Charles to impose restrictions on imperial governors to protect the natives and proposed a plan for educating the natives. He died in Barcelona, Spain, on Dec. 24.

QUEZON, MANUEL (1878–1944), president. Born in Baler, Tayabas, the Philippines, on Aug. 19, he went to school there, joined the rebels against the American army of occupation in 1898, and returned to study law at Santo Tomás in 1902. He served as prosecuting attorney in Mindoro and Tayabas provinces, was a member of the assembly in 1906–9, went to Washington, D.C., as resident commissioner, and edited *Filipino People*, a journal seeking Philippine independence. He was president of the Philippine senate in 1916. He successfully opposed the Hare-Haws-Cutting bill of 1933 to defer independence and approved, with reservations, the Tydings-McDuffie Act of 1934 which set a future date for freedom. The Philippine constitution was adopted by plebiscite and Quezon became first president in 1935. Conservative in policy and interested in social reform, he began to assume more and more duties to speed up needed changes; he introduced new taxes, women's suffrage, and the nationalization of mines. In 1939 all factions agreed to support him in his attempt to better conditions; in 1940 he abolished political parties, but was still approved by the majority. He was re-elected president in 1941, two weeks before the Japanese invasion. He went to Australia at the request of Gen. MacArthur, and then to the United States, where he set up his government in exile. President Franklin D. Roosevelt signed a bill extending Quezon's term of office and promising total independence when the Japanese occupation ended or in 1946, whichever came first. Quezon's health began to fail sharply, and he died of tuberculosis at Saranac Lake, New York, on Aug. 1.

QUIGLEY, JAMES EDWARD (1854–1915), bishop. Born in Oshawa, Ontario, Canada, on Oct. 15, he was brought to the United States by his parents when a child, graduated from St. Joseph's College, Buffalo, in 1872, studied at Our Lady of Angels seminary there, and at Innsbruck, and the Propaganda in Rome, where he received his doctorate and was ordained in Rome in 1879. He served as pastor of churches in Attica and Buffalo, New York, and in 1897 was consecrated bishop of Buffalo, where he became a prominent figure in the labor movement through his encouragement of trade unionism. He was appointed archbishop of Chicago in 1903, expanded his clergy and religious buildings, fought socialism, encouraged the founding of the Catholic Church Extension Society under Fr. Francis Kelly, and founded Cathedral College. He died in Buffalo on July 10.

QUIGLEY, THOMAS J. (1905–1960), educator. Born in Pittsburgh, Pennsylvania, on Mar. 4, he studied at Duquesne and St. Vincent seminary, Pennsylvania, was ordained in 1931, became superintendent of schools in Pittsburgh in 1939, served as president of the National Catholic Music Educators Association and editor of its *Musart*, and died in Pittsburgh on Dec. 26.

QUIN, MICHAEL JOSEPH (1796–1843), editor. Born in Thurles, Tipperary, Ireland, he became a member of the London bar and a journalist. He wrote an account of a trip to Spain for the *Morning Herald* in 1823, was editor of the *Monthly Review* from 1825 to 1832, edited the *Catholic Journal* for a year, founded the *Dublin Review* in 1836, and edited the *Tablet* in 1842, and wrote several travel books. He died in Boulogne-sur-Mer, France, on Feb. 19.

QUINIDIUS, ST. (d. 579). He was called from his life as a hermit to become bishop of Vaison in Provence. F. D. Feb. 15.

QUINLAN, JOHN (1826–1883), bishop. Born in Cloyne, Cork, Ireland, on Oct. 19, he went to the United States in 1844, studied at Mt. St. Mary's, Maryland, and was ordained in Cincinnati in 1853. He did missionary and pastoral work in the Cincinnati archdiocese, was rector of Mt. St. Mary of the West seminary in 1854–59, and was consecrated second bishop of Mobile, Alabama, in 1859. He labored to repair the damage caused his see by the Civil War and to enlarge Catholic activities there, and died in Mobile on Mar. 9.

QUINN, DANIEL JOSEPH (1864–1940), educator. Born in New York City on May 12, he became a Jesuit in 1888, was ordained in 1899, served as president of Fordham University in 1906–11, and then engaged in parish work. He died in New York City on Mar. 9.

QUINN, EDEL (1907–1944). Born in Greenane, Ireland, on Sept. 14, she joined the Legion of Mary in 1927, became a leader in its work and missionary activities, and in 1936 went to Africa where she established and spread the Legion especially among the natives. She died in Nairobi, Kenya, on May 12.

QUINOÑES, FRANCIS (1482?–1540), cardinal. Born in León, Spain, son of the count of Luna, he served as a page in Cardinal Ximenes' household, and when sixteen joined the Friars Minor. He became confessor to Charles V, was elected commissary general of the Ultramon-

tane Franciscans in 1521, was minister general
from 1523 to 1527, was instrumental in persuading Charles V to set Pope Clement VII
free in 1527, and helped negotiate the treaties
of Barcelona in 1528 and of Cambrai in 1529.
He was created a cardinal in 1528, was bishop
of Coria, Spain, from 1530 to 1533, served as
Pope Paul III's ambassador to King Ferdinand
I of Hungary in 1536, administered Acerno
for a time in 1539, and helped reform the
Roman breviary. He died in Veroli, Italy, on
Nov. 5.

QUINTA, ST. (d. 249), Egyptian martyr. *See*
Apollonia, St.

QUINTA. *See* Cointha, St.

QUINTANA, AUGUSTÍN (1660?–1734),
missioner. Born in Antequera, Oaxaca, Mexico,
he joined the Dominicans there in 1688 and
spent the next twenty-eight years ministering
to the Mixe Indians in southern Oaxaca. He
was then appointed superior at Zacavila, but
ill-health caused his retirement to Antequera,
where he died. He wrote a grammar of the
Mixe language.

QUINTIAN, ST. (d. 430?), martyr. *See*
Julian, St.

QUINTIAN, ST. (d. 527?). He went from
Africa to Gaul during the Arian Vandal perse-
cution, became bishop of Rodez, was driven
out by the Arian Visigoths, and succeeded St.
Euphrasius as bishop of Clermont, Gaul. F. D.
Nov. 13.

QUINTILIAN, ST. (d. 303), martyr. *See*
Dadas, St.

QUINTILIAN, ST. (d. 304), martyr. *See*
Apodemius, St.

QUINTINUS, ST. (d. 287), martyr. According to legend, he was a Roman who went with
St. Lucian of Beauvais as missioner to Gaul.
He was so successful around Amiens that he
was imprisoned and beheaded at the town on
the Somme now called St. Quentin, by which
name he is also known. F. D. Oct. 31.

QUINTIUS, ST. (d. 570?). Born in Tours,
Gaul, he became an official in the Frankish
court, and was murdered near Montressor on
orders from the queen (probably Fredegunde),
with whom he refused to have an affair. He is
also known as Quentin. F. D. Oct. 4.

QUINTUS, ST. (d. 255?), martyr. He, St.
Simplicius, and others were put to death in
Africa during the Decian persecution. F. D.
Dec. 18.

QUINTUS, ST. (d. 484?), martyr. *See*
Aquilinus, St.

QUINZANI, BL. STEPHANA (1457–1530).
Born near Brescia, Italy, she became a Dominican tertiary at fifteen, founded a convent near
Soncino, and devoted herself to nursing the
sick and caring for the poor. She is said to have
received the stigmata. She was beatified in
1740. F. D. Jan. 2.

QUIRIACUS, ST. (3rd century), martyr.
Bishop of Ostia, Italy, he, St. Maximus, a
priest, St. Archelaus, a deacon, and a body of
Christian soldiers were said to have been put
to death during the reign of Alexander Severus
between 235 and 255. F. D. Aug. 23.

QUIRIACUS, ST. (d. 550?). A Greek, he
lived until he was past 100 as a recluse in
numerous Palestine lauras. F. D. Sept. 29.

QUIRICUS (d. 304?), martyr. *See* Julitta, St.

QUIRINUS, ST. (d. 269?), martyr. He was
put to death in Rome during the reign of
Claudian II. F. D. Mar. 25.

QUIRINUS, ST. (d. 285?), martyr. *See*
Nicasius, St.

QUIRINUS, ST. (d. 308), bishop and martyr.
The bishop of Siscia (modern Sisak, Croatia)
was tortured, sent up to a larger city in Hungary for trial, and put to death by drowning.
His death during the Diocletian persecution
was praised by St. Jerome and by Prudentius.
F. D. June 4.

QUIROGA, EMILIA PARDO BAZÁN
(1852–1921), novelist. Born in Coruña, Spain,
on Sept. 16, Emilia Bazán married Juan
Quiroga in 1868, traveled on the Continent,
wrote on the work of Benedict Feyjóo and the
Christian epic poets, some plays, the romantic
San Francisco de Assisi, and realistic, sometimes naturalistic, fiction in the style of Zola.
She was a leader in the feminist movement,
founded the review, *Nuevo teatro crítico*, and
died in Madrid on May 15.

QUITERIA, ST. (5th century), martyr. She
is said to have been the daughter of a Galician
prince, who fled to escape an arranged marriage with a pagan and an order to give up
her faith, was traced to Aire, Gascony, and
beheaded there. Both France and Portugal
claimed to have her relics. F. D. May 22.

QUODVULTDEUS, ST. (d. 450?). He was
bishop of Carthage in North Africa, banished
in 439 to Italy, where he died in Naples. F. D.
Feb. 19.

R

RABANUS MAURUS, BL. (784?–856), archbishop. Born in Mainz, Germany, he studied
at the monastery at Fulda, under Abbot Ban-

gulf, and made such progress that he was advanced to Tours, to learn from Alcuin. On his
return to Fulda, as a Benedictine monk, he

worked in the library Charlemagne had established there, mastered Hebrew, Greek, and Syriac, synopsized the early Church Fathers in preparation for work on the scriptures, and directed the abbey school. Famine, plague, and building programs interrupted his labors for ten years, but he was ordained in 814, became a teacher under abbot Egilius, and abbot himself in 822. He wrote a great number of homilies, a martyrology, a number of poems, including *Veni Creator Spiritus*, numerous attacks on heresies, and regulations for making Church laws better obeyed, so strict that an angry plot against him almost cost him his life. He served the papacy well by attending a succession of synods and councils, built several monasteries, and at seventy-one was made archbishop of Mainz. This meant no change in his devotion to learning, to the instruction of the clergy, care of the poor and famine-stricken, or his own stringent way of fasting. He died in Winkel, near Mainz. His biography was written by his disciple Rudolf. F. D. Feb. 4.

RABATA, BL. ALOYSIUS (1430?-1490). He became a Carmelite friar at Trapani, Sicily, and later was prior at Randazzo, where he repaired roads, begged for alms, and was noted for his fasting and humility. He died of a blow on the head from an assailant whom he refused to identify. F. D. May. 11.

RABBULAS (d. 435), bishop. Son of a heathen priest and Christian mother, he was converted by Eusebius and Acacius, became a monk and a disciple of Theodore of Mopsuetia, with whom he later quarreled, and in 412 was appointed bishop of Edessa. He denounced Nestorius and his teaching, but subscribed to a denunciation of St. Cyril's teaching as heretical at the Council of Ephesus, though he later became Cyril's greatest supporter in the fight against Nestorianism. He wrote several treatises and is considered by some authorities to be the author of the *Peshitto*.

RABELAIS, FRANÇOIS (1495?-1553), author. Born in Chinon, Touraine, France, son of an apothecary or a tavernkeeper, he probably studied at the convents of Seuilly and La Baumette where the du Bellay brothers and Geoffrey d'Estissac were schoolmates, became a Franciscan at Fontenay le Comte monastery sometime before 1519, where he was ordained and attained a rank which enabled him to sign deeds for the community. He made himself master of Greek and Latin, and in 1524 left to become a Benedictine at Maillezais. In 1530 he left to be a secular priest, studied medicine at Montpellier, became physician at the Hôtel Dieu in Lyons in 1532. In 1533 he published *Pantagruel*, satirizing all classes of society, particularly monks, which was condemned later in the year by the Sorbonne, and *Gargantua* in 1535. In 1534 he accompanied

Cardinal du Bellay, as physician, to Rome, and obtained an indult from Pope Paul III in 1536 which absolved him from ecclesiastical censure and allowed him to pursue his medical studies and to leave conventual life. He became a canon of St. Maur, received his doctorate from Montpellier in 1537, and went to Italy in 1540 as physician and to collect manuscripts for Guillaume du Bellay, governor of Piedmont. He returned to France later in the year to answer charges of betraying diplomatic confidences, went back to Turin, and remained in du Bellay's service until the latter's death in 1543. Francis I issued a license for the publication of the second book of *Pantagruel* in 1546; Rabelais was physician to the town of Metz in 1546-47, went to Rome in 1547, and wrote *Sciomachie*, an account of the Roman festival to celebrate the birth of the second son of Henry II and Catherine de' Medici. In 1550, Cardinal du Bellay secured for him the benefices of St. Martin du Meudon and St. Christoph du Jambet in France, which he held until he resigned it in 1553. He published the third and last book of *Pantagruel* in 1552; it was censured by the Sorbonne and its sale suppressed by parliament, but the suspension was lifted on the king's return. A fourth book of *Pantagruel*, over the authorship of which controversy still rages, was published posthumously in 1562. The five volumes of *La Vie de Gargantua et de Pantagruel* are a gigantic satire of the history of civilization, touching on all human institutions. In it he employs a rich, picturesque, vulgar vocabulary, coarse humor, great learning and eloquence. He died, probably in Paris, on Apr. 9.

D. B. WYNDHAM LEWIS, *François Villon* (New York, Coward, 1928).

RACHO, ST. (d. 660). Also called Ragnobert, he is listed as the first Frankish bishop of Autun, France. F. D. Jan. 25.

RACINE, ANTOINE (1822-1893), bishop. Born in St. Ambrose, Quebec, Canada, on Jan. 26, he studied at the Quebec seminary, was ordained in 1844, and was consecrated first bishop of Sherbrooke in 1874. He died there on July 17.

RACINE, DOMINIQUE (d. 1888). He was consecrated in 1878 as first bishop of Chicoutimi, Quebec, Canada, and died on Jan. 28.

RACINE, JEAN (1639-1699), dramatist. Born in La Ferté-Milon, France, on Dec. 21, he was orphaned when four, entered the college of Beauvais in 1655, where he passed three years at Port Royal and imbibed the Jansenism prevalent there, and the Collège d'Harcourt in 1658, where he met La Fontaine and Boileau. He led a dissipated life which caused his relatives to send him to his uncle, Abbé Sesvrin, in Uzès. He returned to Paris in 1663, achieved fame with two odes, and in 1664 had his first tragedy, *La Thébaide*, produced. He wrote steadily until 1677, when the failure of *Phèdre* and theatrical quarrels caused him to abandon the stage. He married, quarreled seriously with Molière and Corneille but later admitted his errors, was elected to the French Academy in 1673, was appointed royal historiographer in 1677, and wrote histories of Port Royal and of France under Louis XIV. In 1689 he wrote *Esther*, at Mme. de Maintenon's request, and in 1691 *Athalie*. His style has simple elegance, logic, precision, and polish. He considered love in all its aspects, excelling in the portrayal of his heroines. Among his greatest works are *Andromaque* (1667), *Les plaideurs*, his only comedy, *Britannicus, Bérénice, Bajazet, Mithridate,* and *Iphigénie* (1674). He died in Paris on Apr. 21.

RADBERT. *See* Paschasius Radbertus.

RADBOD, ST. (d. 918), bishop. The great-grandson of the last pagan king of Friesland, he became a Benedictine monk and in 900 bishop of Utrecht, ruling also as abbot, and wrote hymns and poems. When the Danes invaded, he moved to Deventer, Flanders, where he died. F. D. Nov. 29.

RADCLIFFE, JAMES (1689–1716). Born in London on June 28 of an old Northumberland, England, family, he was educated in France, became third earl of Derwentwater at his father's death in 1705, joined the cause of James Stuart, son of King James II of England in 1715, was captured at Preston, and beheaded on Tower Hill in London on Feb. 24. His forfeited estates were given to Greenwich Hospital.

RADEGUND, ST. (518–587). She was the daughter of pagan King Berthaire of Thuringia, who was murdered by his brother Hermenfrid. With the booty that Frankish King Clotaire of Neustria acquired when he defeated Hermenfrid was twelve-year-old Radegund, whom he educated as a Christian and married six years later. She bore his cruelty and infidelities patiently until he murdered her brother. She then retired from the world and became a nun at Saix. About 557 she built the double monastery of the Holy Cross at Poitiers, one of the first of its kind and a great center of learning. For the ceremony there celebrating the acquisition of a portion of the true cross Venantius Fortunatus composed the hymn, *Vexilla regis prodeunt*; he also wrote a biography of Radegund, who died in Poitiers, Gaul. F. D. Aug. 13.

RADEMACHER, JOSEPH (1840–1900), bishop. Born in Westphalia, Michigan, on Dec. 3, he studied at St. Vincent's, Pennsylvania, and was ordained in Fort Wayne in 1863. He did pastoral work there until 1883, when he was appointed bishop of Nashville, Tennessee. He was transferred to Fort Wayne in 1893,

suffered a mental breakdown in 1898, and died in Fort Wayne, Indiana, on Jan. 12.

RADER, MATTHEW (1561–1634). Born in Innichen, Tyrol, he became a Jesuit at twenty, taught for the next two decades, and then devoted himself to writing and scholarly works. He died in Munich, Germany, on Dec. 22. He wrote *Bavaria sancta* (1615–27), *Bavaria pia* (1628), published editions of Martial and Quintus Curtius, the acts of the eighth Ecumenical Council, and the works of St. John Climacus.

RADEWYNS, FLORENS (1350?–1400), founder. Born in Leyderdam, Holland, he studied at Prague, became a canon in Utrecht, and was converted from a frivolous life by Gerard Groote, whose disciple he became. He was ordained, went to Deventer where he received a benefice, and worked under Groote, with whom he established the Brethren of the Common Life. He taught Thomas à Kempis, who wrote his biography, was noted for his knowledge of the Bible and his austerities, and died at Deventer, Holland, on Mar. 25.

RADOWITZ, JOSEPH MARIA VON (1797–1853), diplomat. Born in Blankenburg, Germany, on Feb. 6, of a Hungarian family long settled in Germany, he served in the French army, as an officer in the service of the elector of Hesse in 1815–23, and then joined the Prussian army, where he rose to the rank of general. He became professor of mathematics at the Cassel military school and subsequently teacher to Prince Albert. An opponent of Liberalism, he helped found the *Politisches Wochenblatt* in 1831 and for his writings was removed from Berlin by the king in 1835. He was Prussian minister plenipotentiary at the Frankfort diet in 1836, a close adviser of Frederick William IV when he became king in 1840, and Prussian ambassador to Karlsruhe, Stuttgart, and Darmstadt in 1842. He became a leader of the move to unify Germany by reforming the confederation under Prussian domination, advocated war to unify the German people and strengthen Germany among the European nations, proposed social reform to secure the support of the working classes, and advised a constitutional form of government subordinate to the crown. When Metternich was overthrown in 1848 and Frederick William appointed a liberal ministry, he retired from the government, but was elected to the Parliament of Frankfort, where he again worked for confederation. In 1849 he helped elect Frederick William IV emperor, who again made him one of his chief advisers. He was appointed minister of foreign affairs in 1850, but retired six weeks later when threatened war between Prussia and Austria was averted. He was ambassador extraordinary to England in 1851, retired later in the year, returned to Berlin as military adviser in 1852, and died there on Dec. 25.

RADULF, ST. (d. 866), archbishop. Son of Count Radulf of Cahors, he was educated by Bertrand, abbot of Solignac. He was Benedictine abbot of St. Medard, Soissons, and other monasteries before he became bishop of Bourges, France, in 840. He studied the Fathers of the Church, developed learning, took an active part in many synods, and protected the hospices for the poor. From his own wealth he established religious foundations at Berri, at Quercy, and in the Limousin. He also wrote a summary of canon law for the clergy of his archdiocese. He is also called Raoul. F. D. June 21.

RADULPH OF RIVO (d. 1403), historian. Born in Breda, Dutch Brabant, he studied in Italy, Paris, and Orléans, was invested with the deanery of Tongres in 1371 (though he did not take possession until 1383), studied at Cologne and in 1397 served as rector there. Replaced by a sub-dean in Tongres in 1390, he resumed his office there in 1398, was active in the reform of the liturgy, and died in Tongres, Belgium, on Nov. 3. He wrote historical works and on the breviary and the mass.

RAFFEIX, PIERRE (1633–1724), missioner. Born in Clermont, France, he became a Jesuit in 1653, was sent on the Canadian mission in 1663, established Caughnawaga, near Montreal, for converted Iroquois in 1668, and spent the next twelve years among the Cayugas and Senecas. He also served as procurator to the mission in Quebec, where he died. He executed several excellent maps of New France.

RAGNOBERT. *See* Racho, St.; also, Rambert.

RAGONESI, FRANCESCO (1850–1931), cardinal. Born in Bagnaia, Italy, he was ordained and served as apostolic delegate to Colombia in 1904–12 and as papal nuncio to Spain in 1919–21. He became a cardinal-priest in 1921, was prefect of the tribunal of the Apostolic Segnatura, and died in Poggia Acaiano, Tuscany, Italy, on Sept. 14.

RAGUENEAU, PAUL (1608–1680), missioner. Born in Paris on Mar. 18, he became a Jesuit in 1626, was sent on the Canadian mission in 1636, and labored under Jean de Brébeuf. He was appointed superior of the mission to the Hurons in 1645 and worked with them until the Iroquois practically annihilated them; he led the remnants to Quebec. He was appointed superior of the Canadian missions and vice-rector of Quebec College in 1650, was removed to Three Rivers in 1656, and was made superior to the Iroquois mission in 1657. He barely escaped martyrdom when several of his companions were martyred before his eyes, helped the French in Iroquois country escape a massacre plot by leading them safely to Quebec

in 1658, accompanied Bishop Laval to France in 1662, became procurator of the missions, and died in Paris on Sept. 8. He wrote the *Relations* of 1648–52 and was the first to mention Niagara Falls.

RAIBOLINI, FRANCESCO (1450?–1517), painter. Born in Bologna, Italy, son of a carpenter, he was a goldsmith until he was forty, serving under a Frenchman named Duc, from whom he took the name Francia. In 1483 and several times thereafter he was steward of the goldsmith's guild. He also designed medals, worked in niello, and was master of the mint to Giavanni Bentivoglio and later to Pope Julius II. He made jewelry, designed armor, and created the type for the 1501 Aldine edition of Vergil. All these tasks, demanding great attention to detail, had effects on his painting, in which he became interested when Lorenzo Costa established his studio in Francia's house. He completed many religious portraits and scenes (*Baptism of Christ; Virgin Enthroned; Annunciation; Assumption; Virgin in a Rose Garden*); the reredos in San Giacomo Maggiore, Bentivoglio, and the Felicini in Bologna. His work is lyrical and highly ornamented, often with touches suggesting music, forceful and balanced. He died on Jan. 5 in Bologna.

RAIBOLINI, GIACOMO (1485–1557), painter. Eldest son of Francesco, he worked with his brother Giulio (1487–1543) on many churches in Bologna, Italy. Although he was the better craftsman, though far inferior to his father, he and Giulio signed their work jointly, as J. J. Francia.

RAICH, JOHANN MICHAEL (1832–1907), theologian. Born in Ottobeuren, Bavaria, on Jan. 17, he studied at the German College, Rome, where he was ordained in 1858, became Bishop von Ketteler's secretary at Mainz in 1859, a cathedral prebend in 1867, and accompanied the bishop to the Vatican Council. He was appointed cathedral canon in 1890, became editor of *Der Katholik* in 1891 and cathedral dean in 1900, and died in Mainz, Germany, on Mar. 28. He wrote theological and literary works and edited others.

RAIMONDI, MARCANTONIO (1480?–1534?), engraver. Born in Bologna, Italy, he studied niello and gold line engraving under Francia, the goldsmith, and began his career by copying plates of Dürer so accurately that Dürer objected. Raphael was so taken with his engraving of Michelangelo's cartoon, *The Climbers*, which Raimondi did in Rome in 1510, that he selected him to engrave his works. He devoted himself almost exclusively to engraving the works of Raphael and his friends. His engravings of Romano's illustrations for Arentino's *Sonnetti lussuriosi* were so licentious he was imprisoned by Pope Clement VII, but was released through the intercession of Cardinal de' Medici. He engraved some 600 plates, among them *Adam and Eve, Massacre of the Innocents, Judgment of Paris, Lucretia* after Raphael, *Martyrdom of St. Lawrence* after Bandinelli, and *Hercules and Antaeus* after Romano. He died in Bologna, to which he had fled in 1527 after the sack of Rome.

RAINALD OF DASSEL (1115?–1167), archbishop. Son of Count Rainald I, the Saxon, he studied at the Hildesheim cathedral school, and became a member of the chapter there and provost in 1148, and of the Münster chapter in 1154. He served on a diplomatic mission from Frederick I to Pope Eugene III in 1153, was appointed chancellor by the emperor in 1156, and inaugurated a policy of imperial supremacy over Italy and the papacy. He was appointed archbishop of Cologne in 1159, supported antipope Victor IV, but in a series of diplomatic missions to France, England, Genoa, and Pisa failed to win support for the antipope. He was excommunicated by Pope Alexander III in 1163, succeeded in electing antipope Paschal III on Victor's death in 1164, though the lawful pope's adherents in Germany continued to gain, and died in Tusculum, Italy, on Aug. 14 of plague while leading a contingent of imperial troops.

RAINERIUS MARIANI, BL. (d. 1304). Born in Arezzo, Italy, he became a Friar Minor and had a notably holy career. He died on Nov. 1, and his cult was confirmed in 1802. F. D. Nov. 12.

RAINERO, ST. (d. 1160). After a wasteful life in Pisa, Italy, he met Alberto Leccapecore, a monk, reformed his ways, and became a penitential pilgrim and then a hermit under the direction of the monasteries of St. Andrew and of St. Vitus in Pisa, where he died. An extravagant biography was written by Canon Benincasa, a close friend. F. D. June 17.

RAINUZZI, BL. GIOVANNI (d. 1330?). He was a Benedictine monk at the monastery of St. Margaret in Todi, Italy, so widely known for his charities that he was called John the Almsgiver. F. D. June 8.

RÂLE, SEBASTIAN (1657–1724), missioner. Born in Pontarlier, France, on Jan. 4, he became a Jesuit in 1675, studied and taught at Carpentras, Nîmes, and Lyons. In 1689, he went on the Canadian mission and worked among the Abenaki Indians on the Kennebec River, for thirty years. He was accused by the English colonists of inciting Abenaki raids on their villages, and during Queen Anne's War had his headquarters at Norridgewock, Maine, destroyed in 1705. When peace was established by the Treaty of Utrecht in 1713, he rebuilt the village, but in 1721 hostilities broke out between the Abenakis and the colonists when the Indians accused the English of trespassing

on their land. Fr. Râle was killed in a surprise attack on Norridgewock on Aug. 23. He wrote an Abenaki dictionary and wrote two letters of the Jesuit *Relations*. His name is sometimes spelled Rasle.

RALPH, BL. (d. 1152). An Englishman, he became a monk at Clairvaux under St. Benedict, who sent him as abbot-founder of Vaucelles, near Cambrai, France. F. D. Dec. 30.

RALPH, BL. (d. 1241). A Cistercian monk, he became abbot of Thoronet in 1209 and in 1216 was appointed bishop of Sisteron, France. F. D. Apr. 14.

RALPH DE DICETO (1120–1202), historian. Probably born in France, he studied at Paris, became an archdeacon in Middlesex, England, in 1152, and dean of St. Paul's, London, in 1180. He sided with King Henry II early in the quarrel with Becket, but was sympathetic toward St. Thomas at the Council of Northampton in 1164. Two chronicles, *Abbreviationes chronicorum* and *Ymagines historiarum* (the second based in part on the history of Robert de Monte), drew on contemporary documents for their account of the events of the last half of the century. He died on Nov. 22.

RAM, PIERRE FRANÇOIS XAVIER DE (1804–1865), historian. Born in Louvain, Belgium, on Sept. 2, he studied at Mechlin seminary, was ordained in 1827, and became diocesan archivist, professor at the seminary, a leading hagiographer, and was active in combating the anti-Catholicism of King William I. He published an edition of Butler's *Lives of the Saints* (1828–35), and in 1834 was appointed first rector of the Catholic University of Louvain, where he died on May 14. He is credited with more than 200 works, among them *Synodicon Belgicum* (1828–58), a collection of unpublished documents on church history.

RAMBALDONI, VITTORINO DE'. *See* Vittorino da Feltre.

RAMBERT (d. 680?). An influential noble in the court of Thierry III of Austrasia, he was exiled and slain in the Jura Mountains on orders of Ebroin, mayor of the imperial palace. He also is called Ragnobert and honored locally as a saint on June 13.

RAMEAU, JEAN PHILIPPE (1683–1764), composer. Born in Dijon, France, on Sept. 25, he studied music under his father, organist of Dijon cathedral. He went to Milan in 1701, joined a group of itinerant actors, and between 1702 and 1722 was organist at Clermont, Paris, Dijon, and Lyons; in 1722 he settled in Paris. He wrote *Traité de l'harmonie* (1722), *Nouveau système de musique theorique* (1726), and *Generation harmonique* (1737), in which he presented the first real systematization of harmony, suggested inversions of chords, established a principle of chord progression by a "fundamental bass" not identical with the real bass of the music, evolved the system of chord building by thirds and presented his scientific-musical ideas which became the foundation of present-day musical theory. He began to write operas at fifty and his first attempt was *Hippolyte et Aricie* (1733), which caused great controversy over its innovations. He composed some twenty-four operas and ballets, chief of which were *Castor et Pollux* (1737), *Dardanus* (1739), and *Zoroastre* (1749). He also composed for the harpsichord and wrote church motets. He died in Paris on Sept. 12.

RAMENGHI, BARTOLOMMEO (1484–1542), painter. Born in Bagnacavallo, Italy, a name by which he often was called, he studied under Francesco Francia at Florence, assisted Raphael in decorating the Vatican, and in his late work was influenced by Dosso Dossi. He directed an art school in Bologna and produced considerable religious painting, including *Christ Crucified* and *Madonna with Saints*. He died in Bologna, Italy, in Aug.

RAMIRO I (d. 1063), king of Aragon. Son of Sancho the Great, he inherited the kingdom of Aragon from his father in 1035 when Spain was redivided.

RAMIRO II (12th century), king of Aragon. Brother of Alfonso I, he was a monk who was permitted to leave his monastery to marry, was king of Aragon in 1134, produced an heir, Petronila, to carry on the dynasty, and returned to his monastery in 1137.

RAMIRUS, ST. (6th century?), martyr. He was prior at St. Claudius at León, Spain, and was massacred with the entire monastic community by Arian Visigoths. St. Vincent, their abbot, had been slain two days before. This occurred in either 554 or 630. F. D. Mar. 13.

RAMÓN LULL, BL. (1232?–1315), martyr. Born in Palma, Majorca, he served as a pleasure-loving courtier with King James of Aragon. He became tutor to Prince James, was appointed grand seneschal by the king, and in 1257 married Blanca Picany. Despite his marriage and their two children, he continued his dissolute life until 1263, when he suddenly reformed and became a Franciscan tertiary. Imbued with a desire to convert the Moors, he studied Arabic for nine years and Mohammedan philosophy, toured Europe seeking support for his missionary aims, founded the short-lived Blessed Trinity College on Majorca in 1276 to put into effect his idea of a missionary college which would teach the language and culture of the mission peoples, and in 1291 went to Tunis. He was imprisoned in 1292 for his preaching and on his release taught Arabic metaphysics at Paris. He returned to Africa in 1306, was again deported, and on a third visit in 1315 was stoned. He died of his injuries the next day, June 26, in Bougie, Tunis. Bl. Ramón wrote more than 300 treatises, many in Arabic, on philosophy, music, astronomy, navigation, law, mathematics, and theology. Chief of his writings was *Arbre de philosophia de amor*; he also wrote mystical poetry of the highest order, and *Blanquerna*, the first novel written in Catalan. A bull of Pope Gregory XI dated 1376, condemning some of Bl. Ramón's writings, was declared spurious in 1419. Tradition had Bl. Ramón beatified by Pope Leo X in the sixteenth century; he was formally beatified in 1847 by Pope Pius IX. F. D. Sept. 5.

E. ALLISON PEERS, *Ramón Lull* (New York, Macmillan, 1929).

RAMOTA, BL. PACIFICO (1424–1482). Born in Cerano, Piedmont, Italy, he was orphaned when young, joined the Franciscans of the Strict Observance in 1445, gained fame as a preacher, founded Vigevano near Novara, and in 1475 wrote a long-influential treatise on moral theology. Pope Sixtus IV twice sent him to Sardinia, first to correct irregularities, then to preach a crusade. He died there at Sassari and his cult was confirmed in 1745. F. D. June 8.

RAMPOLLA, MARIANO (1843–1913), cardinal. Born in Polizzi, Sicily, on Aug. 17, he studied at Collegio Capranica and the Accademia dei Nobili in Rome, was ordained, and in 1875 was named councilor to the papal nuncio in Madrid. On his return he became secretary for Eastern affairs and in 1880 secretary for ecclesiastical affairs. He became nuncio to Madrid and titular archbishop of Heracles in 1882, and suggested the pope as mediator between Spain and Germany in the quarrel over the Carolina Islands in 1885. He was created a cardinal in 1887 and papal secretary of state. His position was a difficult one, in that he was forced to attack the Crispi premiership in Italy over the penal laws against the clergy, and in that he antagonized Germany and Austria when he sought to strengthen French ties with the Vatican. He resigned his office at the election of Pope Pius X, retired to study archaeology, and died in Rome on Dec. 16.

RAMUSIO, GIAMBATTISTA (1485–1557). Born in Treviso, Italy, he was Venetian ambassador to France, Switzerland, and Rome, served the Council of Ten in Venice as secretary, and compiled collections of travel accounts, *Delle navigationi e viaggi* (1550, 1559, 1566), many of which have bearing on American history.

RANCÉ, JEAN-ARMAND LE BOUTHILLIER DE (1626–1700). Born in Paris on Jan. 9, son of Denis, lord of Rancé, he received several benefices, including the abbacy of La Trappe and a Notre Dame of Paris canonry, in 1637, and was ordained in 1651. On receiving his inheritance on the death of his father in 1652, he followed a worldly career. He was elected to the general assembly of the French clergy in 1655, and became chaplain to the duke of Orléans in 1656. In 1660 he reformed his life, received permission from the king to be the regular abbot of La Trappe in 1663, and instituted widespread reforms in the abbey. His austerities caused his opponents to accuse him of Jansenism, which he disproved repeatedly by his attacks on that heresy. Ill-health caused him to resign as abbot in 1695, and he died at La Trappe on Oct. 27. He wrote several spiritual books.

RANDALL, JAMES RYDER (1839–1908), journalist. Born in Baltimore, Maryland, he studied at Georgetown, but did not graduate because of illness. After a trip to South America he worked in a printing shop, moved to New Orleans in 1859, and taught literature at Poydras College in 1860. In 1861 he wrote the Civil War song, *Maryland, My Maryland*. Unable to fight for the Confederacy because of his health, he became an editor on the Augusta, Georgia, *Constitutionalist*. He spent the rest of his life as a journalist, and died in Augusta on Jan. 14.

RANDOALD, ST. (d. 677?), martyr. A Benedictine monk of the monastery of Granfel, Grisons, Switzerland, he was slain with Abbot Germanus by soldiers for remonstrating against the ducal oppression of the poor in the Moutier Valley. F. D. Feb. 21.

RANISE, PIETRO (1822–1906), historian. Born in Civezza, Liguria, Italy, on May 24, he became a Friar Minor in 1838, taking the name Marcellinus of Civezza, and, after study at Tivoli and Lucca, was ordained in 1845. He taught until 1854; two years later he began his lifework of recording the history of Franciscan missions. He worked at Recco, Prato, and Rome; wrote on the popes in Italy, the legends of St. Francis, and Franciscan bibliography; and was definitor general of his order from 1881 to 1899. He then retired to Leghorn, Italy, where he died on Mar. 27.

RANULF DE GLANVILLE (d. 1190), judge. Born in Stratford, Suffolk, England, of Norman descent, he held offices in several counties, and was sheriff of York from 1163 to 1189, and of Lancashire from 1173. In the latter capacity he led a force against the rebellious sons of Henry II, who had joined with the Scots and French, and he captured King William the Lion of Scotland at Alnwick. In 1176, Ranulf was a justice itinerant and in 1180 chief justiciar. He was executor of Henry's will in 1189, accompanied Richard I on the crusade, to which he contributed a large sum of money, and died at Acre, Palestine. He built a leper hospital at Somerton and shares with his nephew Hubert Walter the reputed authorship

of *Tractus de legibus*, the first known work on English law.

RANULPHUS, ST. (d. 700?), martyr. Father of St. Hadulph, bishop of Arras-Cambrai, he was put to death in Thélus, near Arras, Gaul. F. D. May 27.

RANUZZI, BL. JEROME (d. 1455). Born in Sant' Angelo, Vado, Italy, he became a Servite, studied at Bologna, was ordained, and taught at several Servite houses. He became the adviser of Frederick of Montefeltro, duke of Urbino, and was surnamed "the angel of good counsel" because of his wisdom and spirituality. His cult was confirmed in 1775. F. D. Dec. 11.

RAOUL. *See* Radulf, St.

RAOUL GLABER (d. 1050?). Born in Burgundy before 1000, he was forced by his uncle to enter the monastery of St. Léger de Champeaux, from which he was expelled, drifted from one monastery to another, restored or originated inscriptions on altars at St. Germain, wrote a life of Abbot William of Dijon and a *Chronicle* covering the years 900–1045. He had little sense of chronology, none of geography, gave trivial and superstitious occurrences the same weight as important events, and unconsciously reveals a low state of customs and culture. He died in Cluny, France.

RAPHAEL (1483–1520), painter. Raphael Santi (Sanzio) was born in Urbino, Italy, on Apr. 6, son of Giovanni Santi, a painter at the court of Duke Federico II at Monteféltro. He studied painting under his father and Timoteo Viti, joined Perugino's studio in Perugia in 1499, and soon began to help execute some of his master's paintings. About 1500 he began to paint independently and to attract attention with his paintings for churches in Città di Castello, notably the *Crucifixion* for San Domenico and *Sposalezio* for San Francesco, and *Madonna Enthroned with Saints* for San Antonio, Perugia. In 1504 he went to Florence, where he was influenced by the techniques of Signorelli, da Vinci, Michelangelo, and Fra Bartolommeo, with whom he became a close friend, there painted his *Coronation of the Virgin*, and began a serious study of perspective and the human figure, using nudes and anatomical studies of corpses and skeletons. He spent the next few years painting in Florence, Perugia, Siena (where he helped Pinturicchio with sketches for the Piccolomini frescoes), and Urbino, and during this Florentine period of his career became famous for his madonnas. In 1508 he settled in Rome, was patronized by Pope Julius II, Agostino Chigi, and Bindo Altoviti, redecorated the Vatican Stanze, and executed paintings for many churches in the city. He was appointed chief architect of St. Peter's on Bramante's death in 1514, and conservator of antique buildings and inspector of all excavations in and around Rome in 1515.

In this position he prepared a survey of ancient Rome and presented a report to Pope Leo X in 1518, pleading for the preservation of ancient buildings. His work is characterized by its expression of passion and character, and noted for its composition, harmony, scope of design, and soaring beauty, and the spiritual beauty of his feminine figures. Among his masterpieces are *Transfiguration* and the Vatican Stanze: the allegorical female figures of *Theology, Poetry, Science* and *Law; Triumph of Religion, School of Athens, Flaying of Marsyas,* and *Temptation of Eve; Deliverance of St. Peter, Repulse of Attila from Rome by Leo I,* and *Miracle of Bolsena; Battle of Ostia, Incendio del Borgo;* and the so-called *Raphael's Bible* of fifty-two biblical subjects, executed by his students. Others are *Madonna di San Sisto,* an altarpiece for Piacenza's San Sisto; *Entombment,* for the Perugia cathedral; *Ansidei Madonna* for San Fiorenzi, Florence; *Adoration of the Trinity* in San Severo, Perugia; *Holy Family, Adoration of the Magi, Madonna del Gran Duca, Madonna del Pesce, Madonna del Giardino, Madonna del Cardinello;* and the *Cowper Madonna,* and the celebrated cartoons, ten designs for the tapestry of the pope's chapel. He was also an accomplished architect, designed the Pandolfini palace in Florence, and prepared a design for St. Peter's which was never executed. Raphael was one of the most prolific of the great artists, partly attributable to his practice of sketching paintings, allowing his assistants to fill them in and then finishing them himself. He died in Rome on Apr. 6.

RAPHAELA, MARY. *See* Porras, Bl. Raphaela.

RAPIN, RENÉ (1621–1687), poet. Born in Tours, France, he became a Jesuit in 1639, taught rhetoric, and wrote widely. Among his works are *Eclogae sacrae* (1659), *Histoire du jansénisme, Mémoires sur l'eglise, L'Ésprit du christianisme,* and *La Perfection du christianisme.* His *Of Gardens* (1665) was translated into English and his *Observations sur les poèmes d'Horace et de Virgile* and *Réflexions sur la poétique d'Aristotle* were most influential as criticism. He died in Paris.

RAPPE, LOUIS AMADEUS (1801–1877), bishop. Born in Andrehem, France, on Feb. 2, he studied at Boulogne College, was ordained in Arras in 1829, and in 1840 went to the United States. He engaged in missionary activity in the Cincinnati diocese and in 1847 was consecrated first bishop of Cleveland, Ohio. He encouraged Catholic education and charitable work in his diocese, established a diocesan seminary in 1848 and two short-lived colleges (St. John's in Cleveland and St. Louis in Louisville), held five diocesan synods, and finished his cathedral in 1852. He resigned his see in

1870 and did missionary work in Vermont until his death in St. Albans there on Sept. 8.

RÄSS, ANDREAS (1794–1887), bishop. Born in Sigolsheim, Alsace, on Apr. 6, he studied at Schlettstadt, Nancy, and the Mainz seminary, and was ordained in 1816. In 1821 he founded *Katholik* in Mainz, with Nicholas Weis, and during the next two decades translated and published many works, among them Butler's *Lives of the Saints* and the eighteen-volume *Bibliothek der katholischen Kanzelberedsamkeit* (1829–36). He received his doctorate in theology from Würzburg in 1822, became professor and director of the Mainz seminary in 1825, then of Molsheim, and in 1829 superior of the Strassburg seminary. Appointed coadjutor of Strassburg in 1840, he succeeded to the see in 1842. He was a fervent adherent of papal infallibility at the Vatican Council, alienated the Alsatians in 1874 when he told the German *Reichstag* that Alsace-Lorraine Catholics accepted the treaty of Frankfort, and died in Strassburg, Alsace, on Nov. 17. He was the author of several works, chief of which was the thirteen-volume *Die Convertiten seit der Reformation* (1866–80).

RASYPHUS, ST. (5th century), martyr. He and St. Ravennus were Britons who fled to northern France to escape invading armies, lived as hermits, and were slain there by pagans at Macé. F. D. July 23.

RATTBORNE, JOSEPH (1807–1842). Born in Lincoln, England, on May 11, he studied at Ushaw and St. Edmund's Old Hall, was ordained in 1830, and later in the year went to the mission at Chowes, where he spent the rest of his life until his death on Aug. 12. He published a series of pamphlets on controversial subjects under the pseudonym Alethphilos.

RATHERIUS OF VERONA (887–974), bishop. Of a noble Liège family, he became a Benedictine monk at Lobbes, accompanied Abbot Hilduin to Italy in 926, was appointed bishop of Verona in 931, but resigned after two years when a quarrel with the king caused his imprisonment in Como. He escaped to Provence in 939, returned to Lobbes in 944, but in 946 returned to Italy, was a prisoner of Berengarius for a time, and then regained his see. He was forced to flee again in 948, was a member of the invading army of Ludolph of Swabia, and when unable to regain Verona returned to Lobbes in 952. He taught at the cathedral school of Cologne, whose archbishop appointed him bishop of Liège in 953. Driven from his see by a revolt in 955, he retired to Aulne abbey, had Verona restored to him by Emperor Otto in 962, was forced to leave once again in 968, went to Lobbes in 968, and caused such trouble that Bishop Notker of Liège sent him to the monastery at Aulne, near Liège, Flanders. There he died on Apr. 25.

RATHO, BL. (d. 953). The Graf von Andechs was a Bavarian count who fought against the Hungarian invaders, made a pilgrimage to Rome and Jerusalem in 948, and in 951 completed a church and the monastery of Wörth on an island in the Amper River, Bavaria. He died there as a Benedictine. He also is known as Rago, Rapato, and Rasso. F. D. May 17.

RATISBONNE, MARIA ALPHONSE (1814–1884). Born in Strassburg, Alsace, on May 1, he studied law at Paris, became a member of his uncle's banking firm, and on his return from a trip to the Orient was converted in 1842. He helped his brother, Maria Theodor, found the Sisterhood of Our Lady of Sion in 1843, was ordained and joined the Jesuits in 1847, but left the Society to bring the Sisterhood to Jerusalem in 1855. He built the convent of St. John at Ain Karin in 1860, and spent the rest of his life there working for the conversion of Jews and Mohammedans. He died on May 6.

RATISBONNE, MARIA THEODOR (1802–1884). Born on Dec. 28 in Strassburg, Alsace, he studied at the Royal College and became a Jewish leader there. He became a convert in 1826, was ordained in 1830, and did pastoral work in Strassburg until 1840, when he became assistant director of the Confraternity of Notre Dame in Paris. In 1843 he founded, with his brother, Maria Alphonse, the Sisterhood of Our Lady of Sion, which opened several houses for the Christian education of Jewish children. He spent the rest of his life working to convert Jews, was made prothonotary apostolic by Pope Leo XIII, and died in Paris on Jan. 10. He wrote several books, among them a life of St. Bernard.

RATRAMNUS (9th century). A Benedictine monk at Corbie, Picardy, France, he wrote several important theological treatises, among them *De corpore et sanguine Domini* written at the request of Emperor Charles the Bald, which was placed on the Index in 1559 but removed in 1900; *Contra Graecorum opposita Romanam Ecclesiam infamantium*, which he wrote in 868 at the request of the Rheims province bishops to refute Photius who had attacked Catholic teaching; and *De praedestinatione*. He died sometime after 868.

RATZINGER, GEORG (1844–1899). Born in Rickering, Bavaria, on Apr. 3, he studied at Munich, was ordained in 1867 and took his doctorate at Munich in 1868. He did pastoral work in Berchtesgaden, Landshut, and Günzelhafen, was editor of *Fränkisches Volksblatt* (1870–71) and *Volksfreund* (1874–76), a member of the Bavarian diet in 1875–77 and 1893, and the imperial *Reichstag* in 1877–78 and 1898, and was active in politics, first with

the Centre party and later the Peasant Union party. He wrote on political theory and history, and died in Munich, Bavaria, on Dec. 3.

RAUSCHER, JOSEPH OTHMAR (1797–1875), cardinal. Born in Vienna on Oct. 6, he studied there, was ordained, became a curate at Hütteldorf, and taught canon law at Salzburg. In 1849 he was appointed prince-bishop of Sekkau, played a prominent role in the meeting of the Austrian bishops in 1849 which marked the revival of the Austrian episcopate, and in 1852 was named imperial plenipotentiary to draw up and negotiate the concordat between Austria and the papacy which was finally signed in 1855. He was appointed archbishop of Vienna in the midst of the negotiations in 1853, and was created a cardinal in 1855. When anti-Church sentiment broke out in 1866 after Austria's disastrous war with Prussia, Rauscher unsuccessfully led the resistance to the new laws, inimical to the Church, which were passed, but was instrumental in preventing the extremes of the Kulturkampf in Germany, and continued his fight for Church rights through the rest of his life. He was a leader of those opposed to the definition of the dogma of papal infallibility at the Vatican Council as inopportune, but accepted the council's decrees, and vigorously opposed the absorption of the Papal States in Italy in 1870. He died in Vienna on Nov. 24.

RAVAILLE, ANTOINE (1605–1676), theologian. Born in Albi, Languedoc, France, he became a Dominican in 1624, taught theology at Dominican schools and from 1671 to 1676 at the university of Toulouse, and was provincial of Occitania from 1653 to 1657. Also known as Antonio Reginald, he wrote several works on grace, chief of which was *De mente concilii Tridentini circa gratiam* (1706). He died in Toulouse, France, on Apr. 12.

RAVALLI, ANTONIO (1811–1884), missioner. Born in Italy, he joined the Jesuits in 1833 and in 1843 went to America in response to a plea from Fr. de Smet for missionaries. He spent his life among the Indians in Washington, Montana, and Idaho, and died at St. Mary's mission, Montana, where he had spent his last eighteen years, on Oct. 2.

RAVASCHIERI, BL. BALTHASAR (1420?–1492). A native of Chiari, Italy, he joined the Friars Minor of the Observance, preached successfully with Bl. Bernardino of Feltre, and despite his ill-health was a popular confessor. He died on Oct. 17 in Binasco, Italy, and his cult was confirmed in 1930. F. D. Oct. 25.

RAVENNUS, ST. (5th century), martyr. *See* Rasyphus, St.

RAVESTEYN, JOSSE (1506?–1570), theologian. Born in Tielt, Flanders, he studied at Louvain, taught there, and was president of Houterle College from 1540 to 1553. He was rector of Louvain in 1545 and 1550, received his doctorate in theology in 1546, was active in the Council of Trent where he represented Louvain, and was made provost of Walcourt about 1558. He became director of a group of nuns in the Louvain hospital in 1559 and held that position until his death. He wrote theological works, and was responsible for the condemnation of the teachings of Baius.

RAVIGNAN, GUSTAVE FRANÇOIS XAVIER DE LA CROIX DE (1795-1858). Born in Bayonne, France, on Dec. 1, he served in the Spanish campaign of 1814 as lieutenant of cavalry, was admitted to the bar on his return, elected a king's counsel in 1817, and a deputy attorney general in 1821. He entered the Sulpician seminary at Issy in 1822, joined the Jesuits later the same year, and was ordained in 1828. He taught theology at St. Acheul's and Brieg, Switzerland, and in 1835 was acclaimed for his Lenten sermons in the Amiens cathedral. His preaching at Notre Dame and subsequently in Belgium, Rome, and London was equally successful. He was superior of the Jesuits at Bordeaux in 1837 42 and in Paris in 1848-51. He became the target of the anti-Jesuit forces in France, was accused and completely vindicated of charges of conspiring with the anti-religious government, and in 1844 wrote a defense of the society, *De l'existence et de l'institut des Jésuites*. He became embroiled in a disagreement with Archbishop Affre of Paris over the disbandment of the French Jesuits in 1844, and in 1855 preached the Lenten sermons before Napoleon III in the Tuileries. He died in Paris on Feb. 26.

RAWES, HENRY AUGUSTUS (1826-1885), founder. Born in Easington, England, on Dec. 11, he studied at Cambridge, became an Anglican minister, held several curacies, and became warden of the Soho House of Charity in 1854. He was a convert in 1856, became a member of the Oblates of St. Charles, and was ordained in 1857. He engaged in pastoral activity, became prefect of studies at St. Charles's College, and was elected superior of his congregation in 1880, a position he held until his death in Brighton, England, on Apr. 24. He was the founder of the Society of Servants of the Holy Ghost and a confraternity named after St. John. He wrote *Sursum* (1864), *Septem* (1869), and *The Beloved Disciple* (1872).

RAWLINS, BL. ALEXANDER (d. 1595), martyr. A native of Gloucester, England, he twice was imprisoned in London for his faith, went to the Continent on his release, was ordained in 1590 at Rheims, and sent on the English mission in 1590. He was hanged, drawn, and quartered at York, with Bl. Henry Walpole, on the charge of being a priest. He was beatified in 1929. F. D. Apr. 7.

RAYMBAULT, CHARLES (1602-1643),

missioner. A Frenchman, he joined the Jesuits in 1621 in Rouen, became procurator of the Canadian mission and in 1640 went to Quebec. He worked among the Nipissing and Algonquin Indians, and with Fr. Jogues among the Sauteux. He died in Quebec, the first Jesuit to die in Canada.

RAYMOND MARTINI (1220?-1284?), theologian. Born in Subirats, Catalonia, he became a Dominican, an expert in oriental languages, censor of Jewish writings for Jaime I of Aragon, and preached to the Moors in Spain and Tunis. On his return to Spain in 1269 he devoted himself to teaching oriental languages and writing polemics against the Jews, chief of which was *Pugio fidei Christianae*. He died sometime after July 1284.

RAYMOND OF SABUNDE (d. 1437), theologian. Born in Barcelona, Spain, he taught philosophy, theology, and medicine at Toulouse and wrote *Theologia naturalis*, widely popular in the sixteenth century for its treatment of nature and revelation, and translated into French by Montaigne. Raymond also was known as a mystic.

RAYMOND IV OF SAINT-GILLES (1043?-1105). Son of Raymond III, he became count of Rouergue, Nîmes, and Narbonne in 1066, and on the death of his brother, William IV, in 1088, of Toulouse, and thus one of the most powerful lords in France. After a visit from Pope Urban II in 1095, he raised an army to join the crusade to the Holy Lands in 1096. His troops pillaged in Durazzo and fought the imperial troops while he was in Constantinople, where he refused to swear allegiance to Emperor Alexius as had Bohemond and Godfrey of Bouillon. He became a bitter rival of Bohemond, the Norman leader, broke with him when they quarreled over Bohemond's seizure of Antioch, and in 1099 captured Jerusalem. He refused the kingship of Jerusalem, went to Constantinople to seek Alexius' aid against Bohemond (who was threatening Raymond's city of Laodicea), and joined the crusade of William IX of Aquitaine. The army was destroyed by the Turks, he was imprisoned by Tancred (acting as regent for Bohemond) at Tarsus in 1102, and on his release captured Tripoli in 1103, established a county for his family, and died there.

RAYMUND, ST. (d. 1126), bishop. Born in Durban, France, he became an Augustinian canon regular at Pamiers and in 1104 was made second bishop of Barbastro, Spain, after it was regained from the Moors. F. D. June 21.

RAYMUND OF CAPUA, BL. (1330-1399). Raymund delle Vigne was born in Capua, Italy, became a Dominican, and held offices at Rome, Florence, and Siena. He met St. Catherine of Siena and in 1376 was appointed her spiritual director. They worked to help victims of a plague, to begin a new crusade, and, when Florence and the Tuscan League rebelled against the pope, sought peace and the pope's return to Rome. When the Western schism began, Pope Urban VI sent Raymund to France to win Emperor Charles V from Clement VII. Twice he was turned back from his mission, for which Catherine bitterly assailed him. When she died in 1380 he was elected master general of the Dominicans and in his remaining nineteen years labored so effectively to reinvigorate the order that he is often called its second founder. He wrote biographies of SS. Catherine (1395) and Agnes of Montepulciano and a commentary on the *Magnificat*. He died in Nuremberg, Germany, and was beatified in 1899. F. D. Oct. 5.

RAYMUND OF FITERO, ST. (d. 1163). Born in Aragon, Spain, he was a canon at the cathedral of Tarazona, became a Cistercian at the monastery of Scala Dei, France, and founded Fitero in Navarre. In 1158, with another monk who had once been a knight, Diego Velasquez, he bargained with King Sancho of Castile to give them the town of Calatrava, which was about to be attacked by the Moors. With the assistance of a large army raised with the help of the archbishop of Toledo, they marched to defend the city. When the Moors did not attack, Abbot Raymund formed the military order of the Knights of Calatrava from the best of the new soldiers. They lived under Benedictine rule, but fought actively against the infidel. His cult was approved in 1719. F. D. Feb. 6.

RAYMUND NONNATUS, ST. (1204–1240), cardinal. Born in Portello, Catalonia, Spain, he gained his name from the fact that his mother died in childbirth and he was taken from her body after her death. He became a Mercedarian at Barcelona and within a few years succeeded St. Peter Nolasco as chief ransomer of the order. Sent to Algiers to rescue Christian captives, he exhausted his funds and then offered himself as a hostage for others. He was tortured for eight months before he was ransomed. Back in Spain, he was made a cardinal by Pope Gregory IX, but died at Cardona, Spain, while on his way to Rome. He was canonized in 1657. F. D. Aug. 31.

RAYMUND OF PEÑAFORT, ST. (1175–1275), canonist. Born in Villafranca, Catalonia, he taught philosophy in Barcelona at twenty, became a doctor of canon law, and in 1219 an associate of Bishop Berengarius. In 1222 he became a Dominican, for which order he prepared a compendium of problems of conscience, roamed Spain preaching to Moors and to Christians who had returned from slavery, and led prayers for the war which was to free his country. He shares with St. Peter

Nolasco the honor of organizing the Order of Our Lady of Ransom (Mercedarians) for the rescue of prisoners. Called to Rome in 1230 by Gregory IX to become his confessor, he spent three years there collecting papal decretals uttered since 1150, which codification became a cornerstone of canon law until the revision of 1917. Back in Spain, he took up his work as confessor and preacher, and from 1238 to 1240 was master general of his order. In his last thirty-four years he was active in the conversion of thousands, introduced the study of Hebrew and Arabic to several Dominican centers, encouraged St. Thomas Aquinas to write his *Summa contra Gentiles*, and set up several monasteries in North Africa. He died in Barcelona, Spain, on Jan. 6, and was canonized in 1601. F. D. Jan. 23.

RAYMUND OF TOULOUSE, ST. (d. 1118). Born at Toulouse, France, he was a member of the choir in the church of St. Sernin there. After his wife's death he devoted himself to charitable works and then became a canon at St. Sernin's. He died on July 3 and was buried in an almshouse he had founded. His cult was approved in 1652. F. D. July 8.

RAYMUNDUS JORDANUS (15th century). A French Canon Regular of St. Augustine, he wrote under the pseudonym Idiota, was prior of the Augustinian house at Uzès, France, and became abbot of Selles-sur-Cher, where he died. He wrote treatises on the religious life, the Virgin Mary, *Oculus mysticus*, and *Contemplationes de amore divino*. Some scholars, including Bellarmine, have maintained that his work is that of a tenth-century unknown.

RAYNALD, ST. (d. 1225), bishop. Born in Umbria, he became a Benedictine at Fontavellana, and was made bishop of Nocera, Italy, in 1222. F. D. Feb. 9.

RAYNALD DE BAR (d. 1151). He became abbot of Cîteaux, France, in 1133, compiled the first collection of Cistercian statutes, and helped to unite the Benedictine centers at Obazine and Savigny with Cîteaux. F. D. Dec. 16.

RAYNALDI, ODORICO (1595–1671), scholar. Born in Treviso, Italy, he studied at Padua and Parma, became an Oratorian at Rome, and served two terms as superior. He was in charge of the continuation of Baronius' annals for the years 1198–1565, a task on which he worked for thirty-one years. He died in Rome on Jan. 22.

RAYNAUD, THÉOPHILE (1583–1663), theologian. Born in Sospello, France, on Nov. 15, he became a Jesuit in 1602, and taught at Avignon, Lyons, and Rome. Almost 100 works are credited to him, which were collected in nineteen volumes and published in 1865. He died in Lyons, France, on Oct. 31.

RAYNERIUS, ST. (d. 1077). He was bishop of Aquila, in the Abruzzi, Italy. F. D. Dec. 30.

RAYNERIUS, ST. (d. 1180). A Benedictine at Fontavellana, Italy, he became bishop of Cagli in 1156 and archbishop of Spalato (now in Jugoslavia) in 1175. When he defended ecclesiastical immunity, some of the citizens murdered him. F. D. Aug. 4.

RAYNERIUS, BL. (d. 1586?). Born in Sansepolcro, Italy, he became a Capuchin friar after his wife died. He died at Todi, and his cult was confirmed by Pope Pius VII. F. D. Nov. 5.

RAYNOUARD, FRANÇOIS JUSTE MARIE (1761–1836), poet. Born in Brignoles, France, on Sept. 8, he studied law and was admitted to the bar at Aix, was an enthusiastic supporter of the French Revolution and a member of the Girondins in the assembly, but when his ardor cooled was imprisoned in 1793. On his release he returned to Aix and became a lawyer. He wrote plays and poetry, for which he was elected to the French Academy in 1807, served in the legislature from 1806 to 1814, retired from politics when Napoleon fell, and became a member of the Academy of Inscriptions and Belles Lettres in 1815. Among his works are *Socrate au temple d'Aglaure* (1802), the plays *Eléonore de Bavière*, *Les templiers* (1805), *Les états de Blois* (1809), and studies of the troubadours and their language. He died in Passy, Paris, on Oct. 27.

REDEMPTA, ST. (6th century). *See* Romula, St.

REDEMPTUS, ST. (d. 586), bishop. A friend of St. Gregory the Great, he was appointed bishop of Ferentini, south of Rome. F. D. Apr. 8.

REDEMPTUS OF THE CROSS, BL. *See* Berthelot, Bl. Pierre.

REDFORD, SEBASTIAN (1701–1763). A native of England and born on Apr. 27, he studied at St. Omer, Watten, and Liège, became a Jesuit, and was chaplain to several English families. He wrote *The Nature of Church Reformation Fully Considered*, which caused such a stir that excise officers seized the undistributed copies. He died on Jan. 2.

REDI, ST. ANNA MARIA (1747–1770). Born in Arezzo, Italy, she became a Discalced Carmelite at Florence in 1765 and followed a rigid rule of self-sacrifice. She was canonized as St. Teresa Margaret in 1934. F. D. Mar. 11.

REDI, FRANCESCO (1626–1698), poet. Born in Arezzo, Italy, on Feb. 18, he studied medicine and received his degree, was a member of the Colonna household for five years, and in 1654 went to Florence as physician to Grand Duke Ferdinand II and then to Cosimo III. He helped prepare the *Vocabolario* of the Crusca, taught in the Florence Studio, and was an early member of the Arcadia. He died

in Pisa, Italy, on Mar. 1. He wrote medical works and poems, chief of which were *Bacco in Toscana* and *Arianna inferma*.

REDING, AUGUSTINE (1625–1692). Born in Lichtensteig, Switzerland, on Aug. 10, he studied at Einsiedeln, where he joined the Benedictines in 1641, was ordained in 1649, and became master of novices. He received his doctorate in theology from Freiburg in 1654, taught at the Salzburg Benedictine university in that year, was prior of Einsiedeln in 1658, and was elected prince-abbot in 1670. He wrote numerous theological treatises, and died at Einsiedeln, Switzerland, on Mar. 13.

REDING, BL. THOMAS (d. 1537), martyr. *See* Beer, Bl. Richard.

REEVE, ARTHUR BENJAMIN (1881–1936), author. Born in Patchogue, New York, he graduated from Princeton in 1903, studied at New York Law School, but devoted himself to writing instead of law. He was assistant editor of *Public Opinion* in 1906, editor of *Our Own Times* to 1910, and then on the staff of *Survey*. He wrote more than forty novels, many of them mysteries centering about the popular character, Craig Kennedy, and a nonfictional study of post-World War I racketeering, *The Golden Age of Crime* (1931). He and his wife (Margaret Wilson Reeve) became converts in 1926. He died in Trenton, New Jersey, on Aug. 9.

REGIMBALD, ST. (d. 1039), bishop. A Benedictine monk at the abbey of SS. Ulric and Afra at Augsburg, Bavaria, he went to Ebersberg in 1015 and in 1022 became abbot of Lorsch. He founded the latter's daughter-abbey of Heiligenberg and was named bishop of Speyer, Bavaria, in 1032. F. D. Oct. 13.

REGINA, ST., martyr. She was an actual martyr at Autun, France. Legend has her the daughter of a pagan, Clement, and tortured and beheaded during the second century when she refused to marry the proconsul Olybrius. F. D. Sept. 7.

REGINALD (d. 1135). Probably a Benedictine monk at Winchester, England, he became the first bishop of Stavenger, Norway. With money which King Sigurd Jorsalafarer gave him for permission to set aside Queen Malmfrid and marry a favorite named Cecilia, the bishop began a cathedral. He was hanged by King Harald Gille for allegedly concealing royal treasure.

REGINALD, ANTONIN. *See* Ravaille, Antoine.

REGINALD OF ORLÉANS, BL. (1183–1220). Born in St. Gilles, Languedoc, France, he taught canon law at Paris in 1206–11 and in 1212 was dean at St. Aignan in Orléans. He met and joined St. Dominic in Rome in 1218 and established houses at Bologna and at Paris, winning many members for the new order. He died in Paris. His cult was confirmed in 1875. F. D. Feb. 17.

REGINALD OF PIPERNO (1230?–1290?), theologian. Born in Piperno, Italy, he became a Dominican at Naples, confessor of St. Thomas Aquinas about 1260, and his constant companion, preaching his funeral sermon in 1274. He began teaching at Naples in 1272 and after Thomas' death succeeded him in the chair of philosophy there. He collected Thomas' works, among them four *Opuscula* he copied down from the saint's lectures.

REGINO OF PRÜM (d. 915). Born probably in Altrip, Germany, he joined the Benedictines, became abbot of Prüm in 892, and labored to repair the ravages of Norman raids. In 899 he was driven from the abbey by Richarius, and resigned his office when he retired to Trier, where he aided Archbishop Ratbod in his ecclesiastical reforms and rebuilt St. Martin's abbey. He died in Trier, Germany. He wrote a chronicle and on liturgical singing and ecclesiastical discipline.

REGIOMONTANUS. *See* Müller, Johann.

RÉGIS, JEAN BAPTISTE (1663?–1738), cartographer. Born in Istres, Provence, France, on June 11 (or Jan. 29, 1664), he became a Jesuit in 1679 (or 1683) and was sent on the Chinese mission in 1698. In 1701 he was one of three priests assigned to prepare a comprehensive map of China by Emperor K'ang-hi. In 1708 he prepared a map of the Great Wall of China, and with various priests worked from 1709 to 1717 on the general map of China which was published in France in 1735. He also translated from the Chinese, and died in Peking on Nov. 24.

REGIS, ST. JOHN FRANCIS (1597–1640). Born in Fontcouverte, France, he was educated at Béziers, became a Jesuit in 1615, was ordained in 1631, and served in the Languedoc, Vivaris, and Velay areas. In Montpellier he worked in hospitals and prisons and won many converts and lapsed Catholics by his preaching. In southeastern France he was equally successful, especially in areas which had been without spiritual direction for twenty years and in others where poverty and savagery went hand in hand. He roamed the mountain passes and forests at all hours and in all weather, serving hundreds. By the time he had a church in Le Puy in 1636 he had a congregation of 5000, with lay groups active in the care of prisoners, the sick, and magdalens. Because he was so successful in reforming these last penitents, he was frequently beaten and suffered much vilification, but his converts persisted in their new life. He died on Dec. 31 of exhaustion and pleurisy in La Louvesc, France, which became a shrine. He was canonized in 1737. F. D. June 16.

RÉGIS, PIERRE SYLVAIN (1632–1707),

philosopher. Born in La Salvetat de Blanquefort, France, he studied at the Sorbonne, where he became a follower of Descartes' philosophy, and taught it at Toulouse, Aigues Mortes, and Paris until about 1680, when the teaching of Cartesianism was forbidden. He was elected to the Academy of Sciences in 1699, was a leading opponent of Malebranche's idealism, and prepared a systematization of Cartesian philosophy in *Cours de philosophie* (1690). He died in Paris.

REGNAULT, HENRI VICTOR (1810–1878), scientist. Born in Aachen, Germany, on July 21, he was orphaned at eight, worked in Paris as a clerk, studied at L'École Polytechnique, graduated from the School of Mines, and taught there. He was admitted to the Academy of Sciences in 1840, was appointed to the chair of physics at the Collège de France in 1841, chief engineer of mines for his researches in steam and its properties in 1847, and in 1854 director of the Sèvres porcelain works. He received the Rumford Medal and, in 1869, the Copley Medal of the London Royal Society, and was made a Commander of the Legion of Honor in 1863. His researches into the vapor tensions of volatile liquids, on the specific heat of liquids, gases, and solids, his determination of the coefficients of expansion of air and other gases, and his inventions give him an honored place among scientists. The scientific law that at constant pressure the specific heat of gas is constant bears his name. He devised Regnault's hygrometer, and wrote several chemical treatises. He died in Paris on Jan. 19.

REGNIER, MATHURIN (1573–1613), poet. Born in Chartres, France, he entered holy orders, went to Rome as Cardinal de Joyeuse's secretary, returned in 1604, and was made a canon of Chartres in 1609. He wrote sixteen satires against the follies of contemporary society.

REGULA, ST. (3rd century). *See* Felix, St.

REGULUS, ST. (d. 250?), bishop. A Greek, he is said to have accompanied St. Dionysius to France, and perhaps was bishop of Arles before he presided at Senlis. F. D. Mar. 30.

REGULUS, ST. (d. 545?), martyr. Driven from northern Africa by the Arians, he landed in Tuscany, where he was put to death by King Totila. F. D. Sept. 1.

REGULUS, ST. (d. 698), bishop. A Benedictine monk at Rebais, France, he succeeded St. Nivard in 673 as archbishop of Rheims and in 680 founded the abbey of Orbais. F. D. Sept. 3.

REICHENSPERGER, AUGUST (1808–1895). Born in Coblenz, Germany, on Mar. 22, he studied at Bonn, Heidelberg, and Berlin, entered the Prussian civil service, became counsel in the land courts of Cologne and

Trier, chamber president in 1848 when he helped found the Borromaeus Society, and counsel of appeal in Cologne in 1849. He served in the Frankfort parliament, Prussian national assembly, and Erfurt parliament, was a member of the Prussian second chamber in 1851–63, co-founder of the Centre (Catholic) party, and from 1871 to 1884 was a member of the *Reichstag*. He was a frequent contributor to periodicals on art, criticism, history, and politics. He died in Cologne, Germany, on July 16.

REICHENSPERGER, PETER (1810–1892), parliamentarian. Born in Coblenz, Germany, on May 28, he studied at Bonn and Heidelberg, became a lawyer in Coblenz in 1843, counselor of the court of appeal in Cologne in 1850, and of the Berlin supreme court in 1859. He was active with his brother August in the Prussian and Erfurt parliaments, the Prussian second chamber, the constituent North German *Reichstag*, and from 1871 to his death was a member of the German *Reichstag*. He was a proponent of constitutional monarchy, helped found the Centre party, and fought for Church rights. He died in Berlin on Dec. 31.

REID, CHRISTIAN. *See* Tiernan, Frances.

REID, RICHARD (1896–1961), editor. Born in Winchester, Massachusetts, on Jan. 21, he graduated from Holy Cross and did further study at Columbia and Fordham, served with the infantry in World War I, and taught at Xavier High School in New York City on his return. He then entered journalism, worked for the *Daily Chronicle* and *Daily Herald* in Augusta, Georgia, in 1920–21, became executive secretary of the Georgia Catholic Laymen's Association, and edited its *Bulletin* so successfully that he was acknowledged widely as a major force in the lessening of religious bigotry. He married Katherine O'Leary in 1923, was admitted to the Georgia bar in 1929, and practiced in Georgia until 1940, when he returned to New York City as editor of the *Catholic News*. He served on the executive board of the National Council of Catholic Men in 1929–40 and was its counsel in 1937–40, was president of the Catholic Press Association in 1932–34, a lecturer at Notre Dame in 1937–40, and a trustee or adviser or associate of many major Catholic projects in the United States. He was honored three times by the papacy, received honorary degrees from Holy Cross, Spring Hill, Dayton, Manhattan, Fordham, St. Bonaventure, and Iona, and was given the Laetare Medal in 1936 and the Hoey Medal for his work in interracial justice in 1946. He wrote *The Morality of the Newspaper* (1937) and, with Fr. Edward Moffett, *Three Days to Eternity* (1957). He died in New Rochelle, New York, on Jan. 24.

REIFFENSTUEL, JOHANN GEORG (1641–1703), theologian. Born in Kaltenbrunn, Bavaria, on July 2, he became a Franciscan in 1658, taught philosophy at Freising, Landshut, and Munich from 1665 to 1680, when he was appointed guardian of the Weilheim convent, was definitor of his province in 1677, and taught canon law at Freising until ill-health forced him to retire. He wrote a moral theology text, and died in Freising, Germany, on Oct. 5.

REIG Y CASANOVA, ENRICO (1859–1927), cardinal. Born in Valencia, Spain, he was ordained and was made bishop of Valencia in 1914 and a cardinal in 1922. He died in Toledo, Spain, on Aug. 25.

REILLY, JOSEPH JOHN (1881–1951), critic. Born in Springfield, Massachusetts, on Jan. 16, he studied at Holy Cross, Columbia, taught at Fordham in 1904–7 and City College to 1910, took his doctorate at Yale, and was chief examiner for the Massachusetts civil service commission in 1912–21 and superintendent of schools in Ware in 1921–26. He married Anna Walsh in 1922. He was a member of the English department at Hunter College from 1926 until his death in New York City on Jan. 23. He also was librarian there in 1928–48. He wrote several critical studies and collections, including *Lowell as Critic, Newman as Man of Letters, Dear Prue's People,* and *Of Books and Men,* edited anthologies, and taught in the Fordham summer school.

REINELDIS, ST. (d. 680), martyr. She is said to have been the daughter of Count Witger and St. Amalberga, and sister of St. Gudula, who became a nun and was murdered at Saintes, France, together with two clerics, by raiding barbarians. F. D. July 16.

REINHARD, BL. (d. 1170?). A Benedictine, he directed the school at Stavelot-Malmédy, and about 1130 became the first abbot of the monastery of Reinhausen, Saxony. F. D. Mar. 7.

REINMAR OF HAGENAU (1160?–1210?), poet. A German poet from Hagenau, Alsace, he was probably on Duke Leopold's crusade in 1190 and was a member of the Austrian court in 1195, where he was acknowledged one of the greatest of minnesingers. Walter von Vogelweide may have been his student.

REINOLD, ST. (d. 960?). A Benedictine in the monastery of St. Pantaleon in Cologne, Germany, he was placed in charge of building. When he worked harder than the stonemasons, the laborers killed him with their hammers and hid his body, later recovered, near the Rhine. He later became patron of stonemasons. Other details cannot be separated from legend, especially since he appears as the youngest of four sons in William Caxton's romantic poem, *Aymon*. F. D. Jan. 7.

REISACH, CARL VON (1800–1869), cardinal. Born in Roth, Germany, on July 7, he studied at Neuburg, Munich, Heidelberg, Göttingen, and Lanshut, where he received his doctorate in jurisprudence. He studied for the priesthood at Innsbruck and the German College in Rome, was ordained in 1828, received his doctorate in theology in 1829, and was appointed rector at the Propaganda by Pope Pius VII. He was appointed bishop of Eichstätt, Bavaria, in 1836, coadjutor of Munich-Freising in 1841, and succeeded to that see as archbishop in 1847. When his defense of Church rights made him unpopular with the government, he was created cardinal-priest in Rome by Pope Pius IX, became president of the Congregation of Ecclesiastico-Political Affairs, consultor of several congregations, and minister of education for the Papal States. He was appointed cardinal-bishop of Ostia in 1868, and died in Contamine, France, on Dec. 22.

REISCH, GREGOR (1467?–1525). Born in Balingen, Württemberg, Germany, he studied at Freiburg and Baden, and joined the Carthusians. He became prior of Klein-Basel in 1500 and of Freiburg, Germany, in 1503, a position he held until his death there on May 9, and was confessor of Emperor Maximilian I. He wrote *Margarita philosophica* (1503), a popular encyclopedia, and helped Erasmus with his edition of St. Jerome.

RELINDIS, ST. (d. 750?). Educated at Valenciennes, France, she was appointed abbess of the Benedictine convent of Eyck by St. Boniface. She is also called Renula. F. D. Feb. 6.

REMACLUS, ST. (d. 663?), bishop. He seems to have been a native of Aquitaine, France, who became a Benedictine monk, was ordained, and appointed by St. Eligius as first abbot of Solignac, near Limoges, and later of Cugnon, Luxembourg. About 648 he founded the twin abbeys of Stavelot and Malmédy, and from about 652 to 664 apparently was a missionary bishop. He died at Stavelot. F. D. Sept. 3.

REMBERT, ST. (d. 888), archbishop. Born near Bruges, Flanders, he became a monk at the monastery of Torhout. As assistant and successor to St. Anskar, archbishop of Hamburg-Bremen he wrote the latter's biography and zealously imitated him in his missionary work in redeeming Christians captured by the Norsemen and Slavs, and in the direction of the Church throughout Scandinavia. F. D. Feb. 4.

REMIGIUS, ST. (437?–530?), bishop. Son of Count Emilius of Laon and St. Celina, he was elected bishop of Rheims, France, in 459 when only twenty-two and a layman. He was later ordained and baptized Clovis, his two sisters, and thousands of his soldiers after the victory over the Alemanni, about 497. He was the leader at the conference at Lyons which

denounced Arianism. He died on Jan. 13. F. D. Oct. 1.

REMIGIUS, ST. (d. 772?), bishop. Illegitimate son of Charles Martel, he became bishop of Rouen, France, in 755, and labored for the introduction of the Roman rite and chant to Gaul. F. D. Jan. 19.

REMIGIUS, BL. (d. 783), bishop. Son of Duke Hugh of Alsace, he became abbot of the Benedictine monastery of Münster and, in 776, bishop of Strassburg. F. D. Mar. 20.

REMIGIUS, ST. (d. 875), bishop. He served as royal chaplain before being appointed archbishop of Lyons, France. He attacked Gottschalk's theory of predestination, but defended the latter when he was attacked by Hincmar of Rheims. F. D. Oct. 28.

REMIGIUS OF AUXERRE (d. 908). After studying under Dunchad of Rheims he became a noted teacher at St. Germain, Auxerre, Paris (where he may have been the first doctor to teach publicly), and Rheims, and wrote glossaries on the Bible and Boethius' *Opuscula sacra*, and *Ennarationes in psalmos*. He is also known as Remi.

RENATUS, ST. (d. 422?). He is listed as bishop of Augers, Gaul, and of Sorrento, Italy; the reference may be to two distinct persons. F. D. Nov. 12.

RENAUDOT, EUSEBIUS (1648–1720). Born in Paris on July 22, he became an Oratorian in 1666. Obliged to leave because of ill-health, he became an outstanding orientalist and liturgical writer, and a friend and adviser of Louis XIV. He was an adherent of Bossuet, was accused of Jansenist leanings toward the end of his life, and wrote several treatises against the Calvinists. He was made a member of the French Academy in 1689 and of the Academy of Inscriptions in 1691. Among his writings were *History of the Patriarchs of Alexandria* (1713) and *Collection of Oriental Liturgies* (1716). He died in Paris on Sept. 1.

RENAUDOT, THÉOPHRASTE (1586–1653). Born in Loudun, France, he joined the faculty of medicine at Montpellier in 1606, was appointed king's physician in 1612, became interested in the plight of the needy, and established an office to help them receive aid and secure jobs in 1617, and in 1618 was named commissioner general of the poor. He became a convert in 1628, founded the first French newspaper, *Gazette de France*, in 1631, and instituted a free medical clinic for the poor in 1640, a step which incurred great hostility from the Paris medical faculty. Defeated in its attempts to forbid him from practicing, the faculty renewed its attacks after the deaths of his friends, Richelieu and Louis XIII, and he was forbidden to practice by parliament in 1644. He devoted the rest of his life to journalism until his death in Paris on Oct. 25. He was the author of *La présence des absents* (1642) and several biographies.

RENÉ THE GOOD (1409–1480), king. Count of Provence, duke of Anjou, and titular king of Naples, he was born in Angers, France, on Jan. 16, son of Louis II of Anjou and Provence. He married Isabelle of Lorraine in 1431 and succeeded to that duchy after the death of his father-in-law, Charles, but was defeated and imprisoned by another claimant, the count of Vaudemont. He purchased his freedom and the duchy in 1437 by a huge ransom, invaded Italy to lay claim to Naples, was prevented from doing so by Alfonso V of Aragon, and returned to Provence. His court at Aix became a cultural center, where he supported the dying art of the troubador poets. His son became king of Aragon and his daughter Margaret married Henry VI of England. He died in Aix, France, on July 10.

RENI, GUIDO. *See* Guido Reni.

RENOUF, PETER LE PAGE (1822–1897), scholar. Born in Guernsey on Aug. 23, he studied at Elizabeth College there and Oxford, and became a convert in 1842. He left Oxford to travel on the Continent in 1846–55, then became professor of ancient history at Catholic University of Dublin in 1855–64. He married Ludovika la Roche in 1857. He was strongly opposed to the doctrine of papal infallibility (his essay on Pope Honorius was placed on the Index), but accepted the Vatican Council pronouncement in 1870. He became inspector of schools, and in 1885–91 was named keeper of Egyptian and Assyrian antiquities in the British Museum. He became president of the Society of Biblical Archaeology in 1887, wrote a grammar of the Egyptian language and *The Religion of Ancient Egypt*, was knighted in 1896, and died in London on Oct. 14.

RENTY, GASTON JEAN BAPTISTE DE (1611–1649). Son of the baron of Renty, he was born near Bayeux, Normandy, France, studied at Collège de Navarre, Caen, and the College of the Nobles in Paris, served in the army, and became a member of the court. In 1638 he gave up his career to devote himself to aiding the needy and teaching Christian doctrine, helped found Frères Cordonniers, a society of shoemakers and tailors who donated a part of their earnings to the poor, and died on Apr. 24.

RENULA. *See* Relindis, St.

REPARATA, ST. (3rd century), martyr. According to legend, she was a twelve-year-old beheaded at Caesarea in Palestine during the reign of Decius for refusing to sacrifice to the gods. F. D. Oct. 8.

REPINGTON, PHILIP (d. 1424), cardinal. He studied at Oxford, became an Augustinian canon in Leicester, was excommunicated in 1382 for his Wyclifism but restored when he recanted later the same year, and in 1394 became abbot of his monastery. He was chancellor of Oxford in 1397 and from 1400 to 1402, became Henry IV's confessor, and in 1404 was appointed bishop of Lincoln. He was created cardinal by Pope Gregory XII in 1408, and reinstated by the Council of Constance when the Council of Pisa in 1409 deposed Gregory and annulled his acts, but resigned his bishopric in 1419.

REPOSITUS, ST. (d. 303?), martyr. *See* Honoratus, St.

REPPLIER, AGNES (1885–1950), author. Born in Philadelphia, Pennsylvania, on Apr. 1, she was educated there (and wrote of her experiences in *In Our Convent Days*, 1905), and began to contribute stories and essays to the *Catholic World* and *Atlantic Monthly*, encouraged by Fr. Isaac Hecker and Thomas Bailey Aldrich. Collections of her early work appeared in *Books and Men* (1888), *Points of View, Essays in Miniature, Essays in Idleness*, and *Varia. The Happy Half Century* (1908), chiefly autobiographical, and *Counter Currents* (1916), chiefly critical, followed. The informal, personal essay gradually declined as an art form after World War I, and in 1929 Miss Repplier turned to biographical writing: *Père Marquette, Mère Marie of the Ursulines*, and *Junípero Serra*. Her last essays appeared in *In Pursuit of Laughter* (1937); *Eight Decades* (1937) was a graceful autobiography. She was given honorary degrees by Yale, Princeton, Columbia, Pennsylvania, and Marquette universities, and received the gold medal of the American Academy of Arts and Letters and in 1911 the Laetare Medal. She died in Philadelphia on Dec. 15.

RESE, FREDERICK (1791–1871), bishop. Born in Weinenburg, Hanover, Germany, on Feb. 6, he was orphaned when a child, became a tailor, joined the army in 1813 and fought at Waterloo, studied at the Propaganda in Rome, and was ordained in 1822. He went to Africa as a missionary, was forced to return to Germany because of ill-health in 1824, and then went to the United States, where he was the first German priest in the then Northwest Territory. He went to Germany in 1829 to get missionaries and financial aid, and caused the Leopoldine Society of Vienna to be founded to aid German churches and schools in the United States. He became vicar general for Michigan-Wisconsin in 1830, was administrator of Cincinnati in 1832, and in 1833 was appointed first bishop of Detroit. He established St. Philip's College at Hamtramck in 1837, suffered a mental breakdown in 1837, and, after Bishop Lefevere was appointed his coadjutor in 1841, spent the rest of his life seeking to restore his health in Europe. He died in Hildesheim, Germany, on Dec. 30. His name was sometimes spelled Reze.

RESINELLI, ROBERTO DEI (d. 1377). An Augustinian, he was bishop of Forlìmpopoli, Italy, and saw his city attacked and destroyed by Cardinal Albornoz during the papal war with the Ordelaffi of Forlì. Resinelli transferred the see and the relics of St. Rufillus to Bertinoro, Italy.

RESPIGHI, LORENZO (1824–1890), astronomer. Born in Cortemaggiore, Piacenza, Italy, on Oct. 7, he studied at Parma and Bologna, taught at the latter university, and in 1851 was appointed professor of astronomy there. He was appointed director of the Bologna observatory in 1855, discovered three comets, and became known for his work in astronomy and meteorology. He was forced to leave the university and observatory in 1865 when he refused to take an oath of subjection to King Victor Emmanuel II, became an astronomer at the Vatican observatory in Rome, and in 1866 became its director and professor of physics at the Sapienza. He made the first systematic observations of protuberances on the sun, discovered new means of measuring the diameter of the sun and compiled a catalogue of the declinations of some 2534 boreal stars, and in 1871 went on a British expedition to the Indies to observe the solar eclipse. He died in Rome on Dec. 10.

RESPIGHI, OTTORINO (1879–1936), composer. Born in Bologna, Italy, on July 9, he studied with his father and others, including Giuseppe Martucci, then went to St. Petersburg to work under Rimsky-Korsakov and to Berlin to study under Max Bruch. He was a concert violinist in 1903–8, taught in Berlin in 1908–9, and in 1913 went to Rome to teach composition at Liceo de S. Cecelia; he became its rector in 1924. He completed a concerto for piano and orchestra in 1902; operas include *Belfagor, Maria Egiziaca, La fiamma,* and *The Sunken Bell* (based on a drama by Gerhardt Hauptmann); other work includes sonatas, concerti, *Antique Suite, Church Windows,* and *The Birds.* He is best known, perhaps, for his *Fountains of Rome* (1917), *Pines of Rome,* and *Festivals of Rome.* Much of his work was introduced to American audiences by Arturo Toscanini. Respighi died in Rome on Apr. 18 and was buried in Bologna, Italy.

RESTITUTA, ST. (d. 271?), martyr. She is said to have been a Roman who was beheaded with Cyril and others at Sora in Campania, Italy, during the persecution of Aurelian. F. D. May 27.

RESTITUTA, ST. (3rd century), martyr. She was put to death at Carthage in Africa during the persecution of Valerian (255) or of Diocletian (304). F. D. May 17.

RESTITUTUS, ST. (1st century), martyr. *See* Crispulus, St.

RESTITUTUS, ST. (d. 299?), martyr. He was put to death in Rome during the Diocletian persecution. F. D. May 29.

RESTITUTUS, ST. (d. 305?), martyr. *See* Donatus, St.

RESTITUTUS, ST. He was a bishop of Carthage, North Africa, about whom St. Augustine preached a memorial sermon. F. D. Dec. 9.

RESTREPO, BERNARDO HERRERA (1845–1928), archbishop. Born in France and educated in Italy, he went to Colombia, where in 1888 was named archbishop of Bogotá, and primate of Colombia. He died in Bogotá on Jan. 2.

RETHEL, ALFRED (1816–1859), painter. Born in Aachen, Germany, on May 15, he studied under Bastine and Schadow. Among his outstanding works were portraits of Charles V, Maximilian I, and Maximilian II in the Frankfort imperial hall, the cycle of frescoes of the life of Charlemagne for the Aachen Rathaus from 1846 to 1851, a series of drawings illustrating *Dance of Death, Hannibal Crossing the Alps,* and *Nemesis Pursuing a Murderer.* He died in Düsseldorf, Germany, on Dec. 1.

RETZ, FRANCIS (1673–1750). Born in Prague (then Austria), he was ordained a Jesuit, and in 1730 was unanimously elected fifteenth general of his Society. He died on Nov. 19.

RETZ, JEAN FRANÇOIS PAUL DE GONDI DE (1614–1679), cardinal. Born in the Château de Montmirail in Oct., he spent his youth in riotous living to defeat his family's plan to make him a churchman. He sided with the count de Soissons in his intrigues against Richelieu, but when the count was killed in the battle of La Marfée in 1641 he turned his attention to an ecclesiastic career. He was appointed coadjutor to his uncle, the archbishop of Paris, in 1643, and titular archbishop of Corinth in 1644, and became a popular preacher. He opposed Mazarin, but when the prince de Condé revolted against the king he became a member of the royal party; Louis XIV secured a cardinalcy for him in 1651. When Condé was defeated, Mazarin returned from exile and caused de Retz to be arrested in 1652 and imprisoned. He succeeded to the see of Paris in 1654, but, when he realized he would not be allowed to rule, resigned it in 1662 in exchange for several benefices. When transferred to Nantes, he escaped to Rome, where Pope Innocent X insisted he retain his archbishopric and whence he ruled his see. He was active in an attempt to restore the Stuarts, resigned his see in 1662 when Louis XIV, after Mazarin's death, refused to allow him to return to Paris, and was given the abbey of St. Denis in exchange. He sided with Louis in several disputes between the king and Pope Alexander VII, became embroiled in 1665–66 in the dispute between the pope and the Sorbonne when he tried to convince the pope that two French anti-infallibilist teachings were not heretical, and represented Louis XIV several times in Rome. He spent the declining years of his life writing his *Memoirs*. He died in Paris on Aug. 24.

REUCHLIN, JOHANNES (1455–1522), scholar. Born in Pforzheim, Baden, Germany, on Feb. 22, he studied at Freiburg, Paris, and Basle, where he received his master's in 1477, taught Latin and Greek, became bachelor of jurisprudence in Orléans in 1479, and licentiate of law in Poitiers in 1481. He became counsel and secretary of Count Eberhard of Württemberg and assessor of the high court about 1484, was forced to flee to Heidelberg when Eberhard VI succeeded as count, and became counsel to the elector there. When Eberhard VI was deposed, he returned to Stuttgart, served as imperial judge of the Swabian Confederation from 1502 to 1512, and became professor of Greek and Hebrew at Ingolstadt in 1520 and of Tübingen in 1521. He became involved in the controversy regarding the destruction of all Jewish books advocated by Johann Pfefferkorn when he advised Emperor Maximilian that only those Jewish books calumniating Christianity should be destroyed. He wrote *Augenspiegel* (1511) to answer the opposition this decision occasioned. He wrote two Latin comedies (*Sergius* and *Henno*), took the lead in spreading the study of Hebrew in Germany, and wrote *Rudimenta linguae hebraicae* (1506), the first Hebrew grammer written by a Christian, *De accentibus et orthographia hebraeorum* (1518), and *De arte cabbalistica*, and prepared an edition of the penitential psalms. He died in Liebenzell, Germany, on June 30.

REUMONT, ALFRED VON (1808–1887), diplomat. Born in Aachen, Germany, on Aug. 15, he studied at Bonn and Heidelberg, tutored in Florence, and in 1829 became secretary to the Prussian ambassador there. He received his doctorate in philosophy from Erlangen in 1833, worked in the foreign office in Berlin, was secretary of the Prussian legations in Florence and Rome from 1836 to 1843, returned to the foreign office, and acted as secretary to King Frederick William IV, who ennobled him in 1846. He was counsel to the Prussian legation in Rome in 1846 and ambassador to Tuscany in 1851, after which he retired to devote himself to writing. He issued a score of books, including biographies of Andrea del Sarto, Cellini, Lorenzo de' Medici, and Michelangelo. He died in Aachen on Apr. 27.

REUSENS, EDMOND (1831–1903), ar-chaeologist. Born in Wijneghem, Holland, on Apr. 25, he was ordained in 1854, studied at Louvain, and was librarian there from 1859 until 1896. With Msgr. de Ram, he founded *Analectes pour servir à l'historie ecclésiastique de la Belgique* in 1864, taught Christian archaeology from 1864 to 1900, and became professor of palaeography in 1881. He was appointed to the royal commission of monuments in 1884, of history in 1900, and died at Louvain, Belgium, on Dec. 24. He wrote *Eléments d'archéologie chrétienne* (1871–75) and other studies.

REVAI, NICHOLAS (1750–1807), poet. Born in Szent Miklós, Hungary, he became a Piarist at seventeen, taught literature for several years, and in 1802 became professor of philology at Pest. Original elegies and imitations of classical writers were published in 1778 and 1787; he is best known for his studies of Magyar grammer in *Antiquitates literaturae hungaricae* (1803) and *Elaboratior grammatica hungarica* (1803–6).

REVERIANUS, ST. (d. 272), martyr. A bishop, he went from Italy with a priest, Paul, to preach in the area around Autun, Gaul, where they were put to death during the reign of Aurelian. F. D. June 1.

REVERMANN, THEODORE H. (1877–1941), bishop. Born in Louisville, Kentucky, on Aug. 9, he studied at St. Meinrad, Indiana, Canisius, Innsbruck, and the Gregorian, Rome, and was ordained in Innsbruck in 1901. He taught at Preston Park seminary in Louisville, was a pastor in Jefferstown in 1904–21 and in Louisville in 1921 to 1926, when he was appointed bishop of Superior, Wisconsin. He died on July 18.

REVOCATUS, ST. (d. 203), martyr. Imprisoned, scourged, and thrown to the wild beasts in the public games at Carthage, during the persecution of Serevus, he had refused with St. Perpetua and others to sacrifice to the pagan gods. F. D. Mar. 5.

REY, ANTHONY (1807–1847). Born in Lyons, France, on Mar. 19, he studied at Fribourg, became a Jesuit in 1827, and after teaching at Fribourg and Sion for a time went to the United States in 1840 as professor of philosophy at Georgetown. He did pastoral work in Philadelphia, became vice-president of Georgetown in 1845, an army chaplain in 1846, and was killed in Ceralvo, Mexico, on Jan. 19 by a band of Mexican guerrillas.

REY, MARK. *See* Fidelis of Sigmaringen, St.

REYES, GABRIEL M. (1892–1952), archbishop. Born in Kalibo, Panay, Philippines, he studied and was ordained at Jaro in 1915, became bishop of Cebu in 1932, and in 1934 became the first Filipino archbishop of the islands. He was a heroic leader from a mountain refuge of the resistance movement against the Japanese occupation army during World War II. He died in Washington, D.C., on Oct. 10.

REYNOLDS, IGNATIUS ALOYSIUS (1798–1855), bishop. Born in Bardstown, Kentucky, on Aug. 22, he studied at St. Thomas seminary there and St. Mary's seminary, Baltimore, and was ordained in 1823. He taught at St. Joseph's College, Bardstown, of which he became president, and St. Thomas seminary until 1830, when he engaged in missionary activities, serving also as superior of the Sisters of Charity of Nazareth in 1833–34. He was vicar general of Bardstown in 1841–44, and in 1844 was consecrated bishop of Charleston, South Carolina, where he died on Mar. 6. He edited the *Works* of Bishop John England of Charleston (1849).

REYNOLDS, BL. RICHARD (1490?–1535), martyr. Born in Devon, England, and a graduate of Cambridge, he studied there for the priesthood, became university preacher, and in 1513 became a Bridgettine monk at Syon abbey. His sanctity and learning were particularly praised by Cardinal Pole, but he was rounded up with others and imprisoned when he refused to subscribe to the Act of Supremacy which Henry VIII said put him in charge of the Church. He was hanged at Tyburn, after he had been forced to witness the exceptional brutality with which four others before him were treated. He was beatified in 1886. F. D. May 4.

REYNOLDS, THOMAS. *See* Green, Bl. Thomas.

REYNOLDS, WILLIAM (1544?–1594). Born in Pinhorn, England, he studied at Winchester and Oxford, became a convert in 1575, studied further at Douai and Rheims, and was ordained in 1580. He taught at Rheims, worked on the Rheims translation of the Bible, and became chaplain of the Beguines in Antwerp, Belgium, where he died on Aug. 24. His name is also spelled Rainolds or Raynolds.

RHAIS, ST. (d. 202), martyr. *See* Plutarch, St.

RHEINBERGER, JOSEPH GABRIEL (1839–1901), composer. Born in Vaduz, Lichtenstein, on Mar. 17, he studied organ at the Munich conservatory and under Franz Lachner, and in 1859 was appointed professor at the conservatory, a position he held until shortly before his death there on Nov. 25. He became organist at the court church, conductor of the Munich Oratorio Society, inspector of the Royal Academy of Music in 1867, royal court conductor in 1877, and was ennobled. He wrote some 200 musical compositions, among them twenty sonatas for the organ, twelve masses, motets, oratorios (*Christo-*

forus and *Montfort*), operas, and cantatas (*The Star of Bethlehem*).

RHETICUS, ST. (d. 334), bishop. A Gallo-Roman, he became bishop of Autun, Gaul, about 310 and attended the Lateran synod in 313 which condemned Donatism. F. D. July 20.

RHIPSIME, ST. (d. 312?), martyr. Although she lived and was martyred, details of her life are legendary. She is called a member of a community of virgins at Rome and one whose beauty attracted the attention of Emperor Diocletian. She, Gaiana, who directed the group, and others fled to Alexandria, then to Armenia, where Rhipsime was sought by King Tiridates. When she refused him, he had her burned alive; Gaiana and her companions were also slain. F. D. Sept. 30.

RHO, GIACOMO (1593–1638), missioner. Born in Milan, Italy, he became a Jesuit at twenty, was ordained, and in 1617 was sent to China. He was commissioned by the emperor in 1631 to reform the Chinese calendar and worked at this task until his death in Peking on Apr. 27.

RHODE, PAUL PETER (1871–1945), bishop. Born in Neustadt, Germany, on Sept. 18, he was brought to the United States by his widowed mother in 1879, studied at St. Mary's, Kentucky, and St. Ignatius, Chicago, and St. Francis seminary, Milwaukee, and was ordained in 1894. He did parish work in Chicago until 1908, when he was consecrated titular bishop of Barca and auxiliary of Chicago. He was vicar general of the archdiocese from 1909 to 1915, when he was appointed bishop of Green Bay, Wisconsin, and reigned there until his death on Mar. 3.

RHODES, ALEXANDRE DE (1591–1660), missioner. Born in Avignon, France, on Mar. 15, he joined the Jesuits in 1612 and was sent to Cochin China in 1624. He went to Tonkin in 1627 and was most successful in convert work until 1630, when an outbreak of religious persecution caused him to leave. He was recalled to Rome, was sent as a missioner to Persia, and died there in Ispahan on Nov. 5.

RHODES, MARY (19th century). Educated in Baltimore, Maryland, she opened a school near St. Charles's church, Bardstown, Kentucky. Two companions joined her, and under the direction of Fr. Charles Nerinckx and with the approval of Bishop Flaget, they and two others took the religious habit in 1812 as Sisters of Loretto at the Foot of the Cross. Anne Rhodes became the first superior; when she died late in 1812 she was succeeded by Mary. Devoted to teaching, the order spread through southern and midwestern United States; it received final papal approval in 1907.

RHODO (2nd century), author. A native of Asia, he studied under Tatian in Rome and wrote several Christian works, two of which are quoted in Eusebius: a work against the Marcionites and a treatise on the creation of the world.

RHODOPIANUS, ST. (4th century), martyr. *See* Diodorus, St.

RHYNDACENSUS. *See* Lascaris, Janus.

RIBADENEIRA, PEDRO DE (1526–1611). Born in Toledo, Spain, on Nov. 1, he became a page of Cardinal Farnese in Rome, became a Jesuit there in 1540, studied at Paris, Louvain, and Padua, taught rhetoric in 1549 at a new Jesuit college in Palermo, and in 1552 was appointed to the German College by St. Ignatius. He was ordained in 1553, preached and worked to secure recognition of the Jesuits in the Low Countries, and ministered to Mary Tudor in London in 1559. He returned to Italy in 1560, became provincial of Tuscany, commissary general in Sicily, visitor of Lombardy, assistant for Spain and Portugal, and in 1573 was ordered to Toledo to recover from the poor health he was to endure the rest of his life. He wrote a life of St. Ignatius (1572) which became very popular, *Flos sanctorum*, and *Historia eclesiástica del Cisma*. He died in Toledo on Sept. 22.

RIBAS, ANDRÉS PÉREZ DE (1576–1655), missioner. Born in Cordova, Spain, he became a Jesuit in 1602 and was sent immediately to Mexico, where he completed his novitiate in 1604 and was sent to work among the Indians of northern Sinaloa. He became superior of that area, helped convert the Yaquis of Sonora, and returned to Mexico City, where he taught and became provincial. He visited Rome in 1643 and on his return devoted himself to writing *Historia de los triunfos de nuestra santa fé* (1645), a history of Jesuit missions in Mexico. He died in Mexico on Mar. 26.

RIBERA, BL. JUAN DE (1532–1611), archbishop. Son of the Duke of Alcalá, he studied at Salamanca (where he later taught theology), was ordained in 1557, became bishop of Badajoz, Spain, and archbishop of Valencia in 1568. He founded and endowed the College of Corpus Christi and in his personal life was a holy man, patient in long illness; politically, he was extremely severe toward the Moors, deporting them from Valencia as economic enemies of the state. He was beatified in 1796. F. D. Jan. 6.

RIBERA, JUSEPE DE (1590?–1652?), painter. Born in Játiba, Spain, on Jan. 12, he studied painting in Valencia under Francisco Ribalta, visited Rome, where he studied Raphael's works, and Parma, where he studied and was greatly influenced by the works of Caravaggio, and settled in Naples in 1616. He was noted for the power and precision of his drawing, unusual coloring, and realistic scenes of martyrdom. He was elected to the Academy of St. Luke in Rome in 1626, was patronized by the Spanish viceroy, the duke of Ossuna, for whom he painted his famous *Immaculate Conception* at the Augustinian monastery in Salamanca, and was knighted by Pope Innocent X in 1644. He was also famous for his etchings, notably *Don Juan on Horseback* and the *Drunken Silenus with Satyrs*. Among his principal works are *Martyrdom of St. Bartholomew, Martyrdom of St. Sebastian, St. Agnes, St. Jerome, Descent from the Cross, Adoration of the Shepherds, Venus and Adonis,* and *Silenus and the Satyrs*. He was widely known as Lo Spagnoletto ("Little Spaniard"). He died in Naples, Italy.

RIBERT, ST. (7th century). He was abbot of the Benedictine monastery at St. Valéry-sur-Somme, France, and may have been a regionary bishop in Normandy. F. D. Sept. 15.

RICARDUS ANGLICUS (13th century). An English priest, and probably a graduate of Paris, he was rector of the law school at Bologna in 1226, wrote *Ordo judiciaris,* and pioneered in scientific judicial procedure. Some believe he is the same as Bishop Richard Poore (d. 1237).

RICCARDI, NICHOLAS (1585–1639), theologian. Born in Genoa, Italy, he studied at the Pincian Academy in Spain, where he became a Dominican. He went to Rome in 1621, taught theology and was regent of studies at the Minerva, and was appointed master of the sacred palace in 1629 and pontifical preacher. He wrote a history of the Council of Trent, biblical commentaries, and sermons. He died in Rome on May 30.

RICCI, ALEXANDRINA DEI. *See* Catherine dei Ricci, St.

RICCI, LORENZO (1703–1775). Born in Florence, Italy, on Aug. 2, he studied at Cicognini College, became a Jesuit in 1718, taught at Siena and the Roman College, and was professed in 1736. He was appointed secretary of the Jesuits in 1755 and was elected general in 1758. During his generalship the Society was suppressed in one country after another and in 1773 was entirely suppressed by Pope Clement XIV. He was imprisoned in the Castle of Sant' Angelo, Rome, where he died on Nov. 24.

RICCI, MATTEO (1552–1610), missioner. Born in Macerata, Italy, on Oct. 8, he studied there, went to Rome for law, and joined the Jesuits in 1571. He was sent to India in 1577, was ordained in 1579, and after teaching at Cochin and Goa was sent to China in 1583. He established a mission at Chao-k'ing, near Canton, was forced to leave in 1589, and moved to Shao-chow in northern Kwangtung. Here he abandoned his previous practice of dressing and living as a bonze, and adopted Chinese manners, customs, and dress. In 1595 he moved to Nan-ch'ang, and in 1598 to Nanking. He was summoned to Peking in 1601 by the emperor, Wan-li, presented at the court (though not to the emperor), entered the imperial service as astronomer and mathematician, and was allowed to reside in Peking until his death there on May 11. Ricci was the first missioner to establish Catholicism in China and laid the foundation for future efforts there. He and the Jesuits were severely criticized by the Dominicans for his tolerance of Chinese beliefs and customs allegedly alien and inimical to Christianity. The controversy raged for almost a century after his death. In 1704 a committee of cardinals in Rome decreed that all the Chinese practices allowed by the Jesuits to new Chinese converts must be repudiated; a direct result of the decree was a formal prohibition in 1717 by the Chinese emperor of Christianity in China. Not until 1939 was Ricci finally vindicated, when a papal decree permitted tolerance of such practices as recognition of the regard in which Confucius was held by the Chinese and their reverence for their ancestors. He wrote a history of his mission, a catechism, which led Emperor K'ang Hi to allow the preaching of the gospel in 1692, and translated Chinese classics into Latin and Euclid and the Gregorian calendar into Chinese.

VINCENT CRONIN, *The Wise Man from the West* (Garden City, N.Y., Image Books, 1957).

RICCI, SCIPIONE DE (1741–1810), bishop. Born in Florence, Italy, he was ordained in 1766, served as auditor to the papal nuncio at Florence, and in 1780 became bishop of Pistoia and Prato. He introduced many reforms, but went to extremes. Led by Peter Leopold, grand duke of Tuscany, he convoked a synod at Pistoia in 1786, the acts of which were completely Gallican and Jansenist in intent. The synod was denounced by a papal commission in 1790, and Ricci was forced to resign his see and take flight. Pope Pius V also condemned the propositions of the Pistoian synod in 1794; Ricci was captured and imprisoned, retracted his statements, and was released in 1805 by Pius VII.

RICCIARELLI, DANIELE DA. *See* Volterra, Daniele da.

RICCIO, ANDREA BRIOSCO (1470?–1532). Born in Padua, Italy, he designed Santa Guistine there; in sculpture he created a bronze paschal candelabrum for San Antonio, Padua, and the marble tomb of Girolamo della Torre in San Fermo, Verona.

RICCIO, DOMENICO (1494–1567), painter. Born in Verona, Italy, he was a pupil of Caroto, and was influenced by Titian, Torbido, and Michelangelo. He was successful in handling color and light, made a name as a pic-

torial artist, and is best known for his *Vision of the Madonna* altarpiece, *Coronation Procession of Charles V*, and landscapes, and busts of popes, all in Verona. He is called Brusasorci, as was his son Felice (1540–1605).

RICCIOLI, GIOVANNI BATTISTA (1598–1671), astronomer. Born in Ferrara, Italy, on Apr. 17, he joined the Jesuits in 1614, became a professor at Parma and Bologna, and then devoted himself to the study of astronomy. In 1651 he published *Almagestum novum*, in which he presented his theory that the sun and certain planets revolved around the earth and that other planets were satellites of the sun, and rejected the Copernican theory. He made a detailed study of the moon, worked out more exact measurements of the earth, and observed Saturn's rings. He wrote mathematical, astronomical, and geographical treatises, including *Astronomia reformata* (1665). He died in Bologna, Italy, on June 25.

RICE, EDMUND IGNATIUS (1762–1844), founder. Born in Callan, Ireland, he worked in his uncle's export house in Waterford and became owner on his death, and noted for his piety and charity. In 1800 he disposed of the business, opened a school in Waterford in 1802, and soon had schools in several neighboring towns. He and his associates drew up a rule, pronounced vows before the bishop of Waterford in 1808, applied for papal approbation in 1817, and had the new congregation, Fratres Monachi (the Institute of the Brothers of the Christian School of Ireland), approved by Pope Pius VII in 1820. Br. Ignatius was elected superior general, a position he held until his resignation in 1838, when he retired. Before his death in Waterford, Ireland, on Aug. 29 he saw eleven communities of his institute established in Ireland, and eleven more in England; it is now found throughout the world.

RICE, JOHN JOSEPH (1871–1938), bishop. Born in Leicester, Massachusetts, on Dec. 6, he studied at Holy Cross, Laval, Montreal, and the Propaganda, Rome, and was ordained in 1894. He did parish work in Springfield and in Maine, missionary work among the Indians of northern Maine, taught at St. John's seminary, Brighton, and was its rector in 1894–1910, and was consecrated bishop of Burlington, Vermont, in 1910. He died there on Mar. 31.

RICH, HUGH (d. 1534). *See* Barton, Elizabeth.

RICHARD I (1157–1199), king. Son of King Henry II of England and Eleanor of Aquitaine, he was born probably in Oxford, England, on Sept. 8, was invested with the duchy of Aquitaine in 1169, and in 1173 joined Geoffrey of Brittany and his brother Henry in a revolt against their father. He was defeated by the king and pardoned, crushed a revolt by the count of Toulouse in 1175, and, when he refused Aquitaine's homage to Henry as heir apparent, became embroiled in a war with his brother which ended with the latter's death in 1183. In 1188 he and Philip II of France warred on and defeated his father, and in 1189, on his father's death, he succeeded to the throne of England, the duchy of Normandy, and the country of Anjou. In 1190 he and Philip went on the third crusade, but he soon quarreled with Philip. After he captured Cyprus in 1191 (where he married Berengaria, daughter of King Sancho VI of Navarre), and after victories at Acre (where he massacred 2000 Saracen prisoners and insulted Leopold of Austria) and Arsuf in 1191 and Jaffa in 1192, he signed a treaty with Saladin late in 1192. He set out for England, where his younger brother, John, was reported allied with Philip and seeking to overthrow him. On the way home he was captured by Duke Leopold of Austria, who surrendered him early in 1193 to Emperor Henry VI, who forced him to pay a ransom for his release. He arrived in England in 1194, put down John's insubordination, and, after appointing Hubert Walter to govern, returned to the Continent to defeat Philip at Gisors in 1195. In 1199 he became embroiled in a dispute with the viscount of Limoges, and died on Apr. 6 from a wound sustained while leading an assault on the castle of Chalus near Limoges, France. He is also known as Richard the Lion-Hearted (Coeur de Lion).

RICHARD, ST. (d. 720). Father of SS. Willibald, Winebald, and Walburga, he left Wessex, England, with his two sons for a pilgrimage to French shrines and to Rome. He died at Lucca, Italy, whose citizens called him an English king, and showed great devotion, particularly in the twelfth century. F. D. Feb. 7.

RICHARD, ST. (12th century), bishop. Said to have been an Englishman, he attended the third Lateran Council in 1179, and may have been made bishop of Andria, Italy, by Adrian IV. He long was erroneously listed as a fifth-century bishop in the period of Attila. F. D. June 9.

RICHARD (15th century). Of unknown origin, he was a Friar Minor who came to France from Jerusalem in 1428 and preached so fervently that he acquired a great following. He was forced to leave Paris when denounced by the theological faculty of the university (probably because he favored King Charles VII of France—Paris was then occupied by the English), and went to Orléans and then to Troyes, where he met Joan of Arc and became her confessor. He broke with Joan over his defense of Catherine de la Rochelle, whom Joan disliked, was at Joan's trial in 1431, and

later in the same year was interdicted by the Poitiers inquisitor from preaching. He disappeared after this.

RICHARD, CHARLES LOUIS (1711–1794), theologian. Born in Blainville-sur-l'Eau, Lorraine, in Apr., he became a Dominican at sixteen, studied at Paris, and received his doctorate in theology from the Sorbonne. He became noted for his preaching and defense of Catholicism, was forced to flee to Belgium when the French Revolution broke out, but was captured and executed at Mons, Belgium, on Aug. 16 for a work he wrote comparing the crucifixion of Christ to the execution of King Louis XVI. He also wrote *Bibliothèque sacrée* (1760) and *Analyses des conciles* (1772–77).

RICHARD DE BURY (1287–1345), bishop. Born in Bury St. Edmunds, England, on Jan. 24, son of Sir Richard Aungerville and called de Bury after his birthplace, he studied at Oxford, joined the Benedictines, became tutor of Prince Edward, and, when the latter became King Edward III in 1327, was appointed bishop of Durham in 1333. He became chancellor of England in 1334, treasurer in 1336, and served on diplomatic missions for the king, notably to Pope John XII, Scotland, and France. He founded Durham College (now Trinity) at Oxford and bequeathed to it his extensive library. He died in Auckland, Durham, on Apr. 24. He was a generous patron of literature, an avid bibliophile, and wrote *Epistolae familiarum, Orationes ad principes*, and *Philobiblon*, his experiences as a book collector, which was not printed until 1473.

RICHARD OF CIRENCESTER (1335?–1400?), historian. A Benedictine monk of Westminster, he made a pilgrimage to Jerusalem in 1391 and wrote a chronicle of the period from 447 to 1066, *Speculum historiale de gestis regum Angliae*. He is also reputed to have written *De officiis* and *Super symbolum majus et minus*. His name was used by Charles Bertram in the forgery of *De situ Britanniae*, the manuscript of which Bertram claimed to have discovered in 1747.

RICHARD OF CORNWALL (13th century). A Franciscan who studied at Oxford and Paris, he accompanied Haymo of Faversham to Rome to oppose Brother Elias, was driven from his lecturing at Oxford in 1250, and went to Paris. He returned to Oxford in 1255 as regent-master of friars, and was severely criticized by Roger Bacon for his teaching. He wrote several commentaries. Some consider him to be the same as Richard Rufus.

RICHARD OF INGWORTH (d. 1240?). A Franciscan priest, he accompanied Agnellus to England in 1224 and founded the first Franciscan houses in London, Oxford, and Northampton. He was custodian in Cambridge, acting vicar of the English province in 1230, and served as provincial minister in Ireland. In 1239 he went on a pilgrimage to the Holy Land and died on the way.

RICHARD OF MIDDLETON (d. 1307?). Probably born in Middleton Stoney, Oxfordshire, or Middleton, Cheyney, Northamptonshire, he studied at Oxford and at Paris. He joined the Franciscans, was appointed to examine the doctrines of Peter Olivus in 1278, was tutor to two of the sons of Charles II in Naples in 1286, accompanied them into captivity when Peter of Aragon defeated Charles, and was released with them in 1295. He was a student of hypnotism and wrote about it in *Quodlibeta*, in which he discussed auto-suggestion and mental telepathy, wrote theological treatises, and is considered by some to be one of the Four Masters who wrote the exposition on the Rule of St. Francis.

RICHARD RUFUS. *See* Richard of Cornwall.

RICHARD OF ST. ANNE, BL. (d. 1622). *See* Franco, Bl. Apollinaris.

RICHARD OF ST. VICTOR (d. 1173). A native of Scotland, he became a monk at St. Victor in Paris, and studied under the mystic, Hugh of St. Victor, whose disciple he became and whose principles he developed in his own writings. He became sub-prior of St. Victor's in 1159, prior in 1164, and in 1165 sheltered St. Thomas of Canterbury when Thomas was forced to flee from England. His major works are *Benjamin major* and *Benjamin minor* in which he describes the six stages of mystical contemplation, treatises on the Trinity, on the attributes of the three divine Persons, and *Tractatus exceptionum*, on secular learning, which he felt was worthless.

RICHARD DE LA VERGNE, FRANÇOIS MARIE BENJAMIN (1819–1908), cardinal. Born in Nantes, France, on Mar. 1, he studied at St. Sulpice, Paris, was ordained in 1844, was secretary of the bishop of Nantes in 1849, and became vicar general in 1850–69. He was appointed bishop of Belley in 1871, coadjutor to the archbishop of Paris in 1875, succeeded to the see in 1886, and was created cardinal in 1889. He was sympathetic to the monarchists and formed the Union de la France Chrétienne, a monarchist group opposed to Pope Leo XIII's *Ralliement* to the French republic, which was dissolved at the pope's request. He fought modernism, and for a time was driven from his palace by the government for his vigorous opposition to church and state separation legislation in 1906. He died in Paris on Jan. 28.

RICHARD DE WYCH, ST. (1197?–1253), bishop. Born in Droitwich, Worcestershire, England, he was educated at Oxford under Grosseteste, and at Paris and Bologna, where he became a doctor of canon law. In 1235 he became chancellor of Oxford, then chancellor to St. Edmund Rich, archbishop of Canterbury, until the latter retired to the Continent. He was ordained at Orléans in 1243, returned to England as a parish priest, was made chancellor to St. Boniface at Canterbury, and, in 1244, bishop of Chichester. King Henry III refused to acknowledge him and fought him as he had St. Edmund, seized all ecclesiastical funds, and only bowed under a papal threat of excommunication. He continued to oppose the king over the penalties he gave priests guilty of extortion or immorality, exhausted his fortune in charities, and died near Dover, England, after preaching for a crusade. He was canonized in 1262. F. D. Apr. 3.

RICHARDIS, ST. (d. 895?), empress. Daughter of the count of Alsace, she married Charles the Fat at twenty-two. When he accused her of infidelity, she appeared before the imperial assembly and cleared herself by the ordeal by fire. She then left the court, lived for a while at the convent at Hohenburg, and then at Andlau, which she had founded. F. D. Sept. 18.

RICHARDSON, BL. WILLIAM (d. 1603), martyr. Born near Sheffield, England, he studied at Valladolid, Spain, was ordained at Seville in 1594, entered the English underground mission as Mr. Anderson, was captured, and executed at Tyburn on the charge of being a priest. He was the last of the Elizabethan martyrs and was beatified in 1929. F. D. Feb. 17.

RICHARIUS, ST. (d. 645?). Born in Celles, France, he protected two Irish missioners from the pagans near Amiens, was converted by them, and became a priest. He was a successful preacher, influenced SS. Adalbald and Rictrudis, ransomed many captives, built an abbey at Celles, and became a hermit in his last years. He is also known as Riquier. F. D. Apr. 26.

RICHELIEU, ARMAND JEAN DU PLESSIS DE (1585–1642), cardinal. Born in Paris on Sept. 9, he was educated at Navarre and Lisieux, appointed bishop of Luçon by King Henry IV in 1607, and elected by the Poitou clergy to the States General in 1614. He became almoner of Anne of Austria in 1615, and in 1616 was appointed, through Marie de' Medici's influence, a secretary of state by King Louis XIII. He was exiled to Blos, with Marie in 1617 when Concini, her favorite, was murdered, and to Avignon in 1618 (where he wrote *Instruction du Chretien*), but returned to power when Marie de' Medici escaped from Blois in 1618 and he was appointed to negotiate between mother and son. He was recalled to his position as secretary of state by Louis in 1619, was created a cardinal by Pope Gregory XV in 1622, and when Louis and his mother were reconciled was named a member of the king's council and chief minister in 1624. He incurred the jealousy of Marie when he established himself as the most powerful figure in France, which he practically ruled for the rest of his life. He had two basic policies: the establishment of the royal authority as supreme in France, and of France as the dominating European power. To realize the first he sought to destroy the power of the nobility and crush the Huguenots. He achieved this by an edict in 1626 which destroyed all fortified castles not needed for the defense of France against invasion and by thwarting the conspiracy of the king's brother, Gaston of Orléans, by arresting his governor, Marshal D'Ornano, who died in prison, and by executing Gaston's friend, Henri de Talleyrand, marquis of Chablais and Vendôme. Gaston led another rebellion in 1639, which was crushed when his sole powerful supporter, Duke Henri de Montmorency, governor of Languedoc, was defeated and executed for treason with Marillac in 1632. In 1630, Richelieu faced disaster when Marie de' Medici and Anne of Austria were reconciled and prevailed on Louis to dismiss the cardinal. However, Richelieu retained his hold on Louis, who decided for him; Marie was banished from Paris and in 1631 fled to the Netherlands. He then eliminated the Huguenot threat by his campaign against the duc de Rohan, culminating in the capture of La Rochelle and the peace of Alain in 1629. Early in his administration he aided the Netherlands and German Protestant princes against the emperor, despite intense Catholic opposition. When Emperor Ferdinand was triumphant in 1629, a united Germany faced France, whereupon Richelieu in 1631 subsidized Gustavus IV Adolphus and set the Swedish ruler against Germany. In 1635 he formed an alliance with Sweden and Bernhard of Saxe-Weimar, and declared war on the emperor. France's entry into the Thirty Years' War, which lasted the rest of his life and was not concluded until the Treaty of Westphalia in 1648, confirmed Richelieu's policies when French successes were recognized in agreements which established the Bourbons as the prevailing European dynasty. Richelieu was a liberal patron of the arts, rebuilt the Sorbonne, and in 1635 founded the French Academy. Among his writings were his *Mémoires* and *Testament politique*. He died in Paris on Dec. 4.

HILAIRE BELLOC, *Richelieu* (Philadelphia, Lippincott, 1929).

RICHER (10th century). Son of a knight at the court of Louis IV d'Outre-Mer, he became a monk at St. Rémi, Rheims, where Archbishop Gerbert commissioned him to write a history of France as a continuation of Hincmar's annals. The manuscript remained in obscurity until discovered and published in 1833. It is a major source of information for the period from about 880 to the tenth century and presents the first definite statement of the concept of French nationalism.

RICHER, EDMOND (1560–1631), theologian. Born in Chaource, Aube, France, he became a doctor of theology at the Sorbonne, taught literature and philosophy at the college of Cardinal Lemoine, and in 1594 was its director. In 1595 he became an active opponent of the Jesuits, who in turn attacked his *De ecclesiastica et politica potestate* (1611), and he lost his office. He was called before the Inquisition in Rome, imprisoned in Paris on his return, but was released after retractation and named canon of Paris.

RICHTER, HENRY JOSEPH (1838–1916), bishop. Born in Neuenkirchen, Oldenburg, Germany, on Apr. 9, he went to the United States in 1854, studied at St. Joseph's, Kentucky, Xavier College and Mt. St. Mary's seminary, Cincinnati, Ohio, and the North American College, Rome, where he was ordained in 1865. He was vice-president and taught at the Cincinnati seminary in 1865–70, was rector at St. Laurence and chaplain at Mt. St. Vincent, and in 1883 became first bishop of Grand Rapids, Michigan. He died there on Dec. 26.

RICKABY, JOSEPH (1845–1932), philosopher. Born in Everingham, Yorkshire, England, on Nov. 20, he studied at Stonyhurst, became a Jesuit in 1862, was chaplain at Campion Hall, Oxford, in 1897–99 and 1900–24, and spent his last years at St. Bueno's College, Wales. He also taught at Oscott College, published his talks to undergraduates as *The Lord My Light*, and also wrote *Moral Theology, The Moral Teaching of St. Thomas, Political and Moral Essays, Free Will and Four English Philosophers, Notes on St. Paul, Of God and His Creatures*, and *Old Man's Jottings*. He died at St. Bueno's on Dec. 18.

RICOLDO DA MONTE DI CROCE (1243?–1320). Born in Florence, Italy, he became a Dominican in 1267, taught in Tuscany from 1272 to 1288, went on pilgrimage to the Holy Land, and then as a missionary to Persia and the Far East. He returned to Florence shortly before 1302, and died there on Oct. 31. He wrote a description of his travels, *Itinerarium*, a treatise against Mohammedanism, *Contra legem saracenorum*, other treatises, and began a translation of the Koran.

RICONICO, BARTOLOMMEO (d. 1401?), historian. Born in Pisa, Italy, and known as Bartholomew of Pisa, he studied at Bologna, became a Friar Minor, preached, and served as lector at Padua, Pisa, Siena, and Florence. His *De conformitate vitae B. P. Francisci ad vitam domini nostri Jesu Christi*, which made a pious comparison between Christ and St. Francis, was written between 1385 and 1399, and first published in 1510. It was lauded by many, and as widely attacked on the grounds that it forced the comparison and continued too many extravagant legends. It was the special target of Lutherans and of Jansenists in later years. He also wrote a life of the Virgin Mary, an exposition of the Franciscan Rule, and Lenten sermons. Some of his writings were long attributed to Bartholomew of San Concordio and by Bartolommeo Albisi.

RICTIOVARUS. Although the name appears in many writings as that of a Roman prefect who put a great number of early Christians to death and was himself converted by St. Lucy and martyred in northern Italy, he probably is a pious fiction.

RICTRUDIS, ST. (d. 688). Born in Gascony, she married St. Adalbald, a Frankish courtier serving King Clovis, and settled at Ostrevant, Flanders. The four children they had in a widely talked-about happy marriage were SS. Adalsindis, Clotsindis, Eusebia, and Maurontius. After her husband's murder by some of her own relatives, she managed to avoid another marriage which Clovis II was arranging, and gained permission to found and enter a double monastery at Marchiennes, Flanders. F. D. May 12.

RIDDER, HERMAN (1851–1915), publisher. Born in New York City on Mar. 5, he was an errand boy and insurance agent before he established the weekly *Katholisches Volksblatt* in 1878 and the *Catholic News* in 1886. He was treasurer, manager of the daily *Staats-Zeitung* from 1890 to 1907, then became its president, and directed its sympathies toward Germany at the start of World War I. He was active in Democratic politics and a bitter foe of Tammany Hall. He was treasurer of the national Democratic committee in 1908, a director of the Associated Press in 1900–15 (and treasurer in 1907–9), president of the American Newspaper Publishers' Association in 1907–11), vice-president of the Hudson-Fulton commemorative celebration, and manager of the New York state board of charities. He died on Nov. 1.

RIDEL, FÉLIX CLAIR (d. 1884), bishop. Appointed vicar apostolic of Korea in 1870, he was unable even to send missionaries to his persecuted territory until 1876, though a dictionary and grammar were published a year earlier. He entered the country in 1877, was imprisoned and released, and returned to China with Fr. Deguette at the insistence of the French government.

RIDOLFI, FORTUNATUS (1777–1850). Born in Zenano, Italy, on Nov. 8, he studied at Monza, served in the army of the Cisalpine Republic in 1799, became a Barnabite, taught in Cremona and elsewhere until the French suppressed religious orders, and took refuge in Brixen. He aided the victims of the famine in Lombardy, and established several oratories. He died on Apr. 8.

RIEMENSCHNEIDER, TILLMANN (1468?–1531), sculptor. Born in Osterode, Harz, Germany, he joined the Guild of St. Luke in Würzburg in 1483 and became one of the foremost German sculptors of the Renaissance. He was city architect in 1505–7, councilor in 1509, and burgomaster in 1520, was imprisoned in 1525 for his participation in a peasants' uprising, and spent the rest of his life in retirement. Among his chief works were the tomb of Emperor Henry II and his wife, Kunigunde, in the Bamberg cathedral, his carvings and statues, especially *Adam and Eve*, for the Marien Kapelle in Würzburg, the madonna of the Neumünsterkirche, the tabernacle and cross of the Würzburg cathedral, and many wood carvings.

RIENZI, COLA DI (1313–1354). Probably born in Rome and believed by some authorities to be the natural son of Emperor Henry VII, he received a classical education at Anagni and became a notary in Rome, where the anarchy then prevailing led him to conceive a plan to restore order by ending the power of the barons and establishing a popular government with Rome as the capital of a united Italy. He was sent by the Roman party to Avignon in 1343 to request Pope Clement VI to return to Rome, was made a papal notary, and in 1347 was granted dictatorial power and named tribune by the people. At first successful and favored by the pope, who named him rector, he soon became inflated with his own power, lived a life of luxury, and alienated the people and his supporters by excessive taxation. He was driven from Rome by the end of the year, took refuge with the Spiritual Franciscans of Monte Maiella, and in 1350 went to Prague, where he tried to convince Emperor Charles IV that he had been sent by the Holy Spirit. He was thrown into prison, sent to the pope in Avignon in 1352, but through his friend Petrarch's intercession, was freed. Pope Innocent VI sent him with Cardinal Albornoz to Rome in 1354 to help restore order, with the title of "senator." His cruelty, luxurious living, and the high taxes he imposed led to a revolt, and on Oct. 8 he was slain in Rome by the populace. His life is the basis of Wagner's opera, *Rienzi*.

RIFFEL, CASPAR (1807–1856), historian. Born in Büdesheim, Germany, on Jan. 19, he studied at Mainz, Bonn, and Tübingen, was ordained in 1830, and engaged in pastoral work. He taught theology at Giessen in 1835, raised a storm of controversy from Protestants when the first volume of his history of the

Church, with its uncomplimentary description of the Reformation, was published in 1841, and was pensioned by the Hessian government in 1842. He then went to Mainz, Germany, was appointed professor of history in the seminary in 1851, and died there on Dec. 15.

RIGBY, BL. JOHN (1570?–1600), martyr. Born near Wigan, Lancashire, England, he became a servant to a Protestant family, attended Anglican services to conform to state law, repented, and won back many, including his father, to the Catholic faith. Denounced for this as a renegade, he was hanged, drawn, and quartered in Southwark, England. He was beatified in 1929. F. D. June 21.

RIGBY, NICHOLAS (1800–1886). Born in Walton, England, he studied at Ushaw, was ordained in 1826, engaged in pastoral work, settled in Ugthorpe where he built a college, retired in 1884, and died there on Sept. 7. He wrote a study of scripture and controversial pamphlets.

RIGGS, THOMAS LAWRAWSON (1888–1943), author. Born in New London, Connecticut, on June 28, he graduated from Yale in 1910, took a graduate degree at Harvard, and returned to teach at Yale from 1912 to 1917. He went abroad with a medical unit in World War I, became a lieutenant of infantry, and after the war studied in Yonkers and Hartford seminaries. He was ordained in 1922, served as administrator of an East Haven parish and as chaplain of the Yale Catholic Club until 1938, was prominent in other church activities, and was chaplain of the More Club from 1938 to 1943, when he founded the St. Thomas More Association at Yale and built its chapel. He wrote *The Book of Kildare* (poems, 1911), *Saving Angel*, and many translations. He died in New Haven, Connecticut, on Apr. 26.

RIGHI, BL. GIOVANNI BATTISTA (1469–1539). Born in Fabriano, Italy, this Franciscan priest worked for the sick and lived under such rigorous asceticism that his life matched that of the desert fathers. His cult was approved in 1903. F. D. Mar. 11.

RIGO, ST. *See* Henry of Treviso, Bl.

RIGOBERT, ST. (d. 745?), archbishop. As abbot of Orbais, France, he fell into disfavor with Charles Martel, probably after he became archbishop of Rheims. He returned after exile and devoted his last years to contemplative prayer. F. D. Jan. 4.

RINALDUCCI, BL. SIMON (d. 1322). Born in Todi, Italy, he became an Augustinian in 1280 and served as prior of several houses before becoming provincial of Umbria. His cult was approved in 1833. F. D. Apr. 20.

RINIERI. *See* Rizzerio, Bl.

RINUCCINI, GIOVANNI BATTISTA (1592–1653), archbishop. Born in Rome, nephew of Cardinal Ottavo, he studied at Rome, Bologna, Perugia, and Pisa, where he received his doctorate when twenty-two, and was ordained. He became an advocate in Rome and in 1625 was appointed archbishop of Fermo, Italy, where he remained until 1645, when he was appointed nuncio to Ireland. Unsuccessful in his attempts to unite the dissident elements involved in the Irish struggle against England, he returned to his diocese in 1649 and remained there until his death.

RIO, ALEXIS-FRANÇOIS (1797–1874), critic. Born on the island of Arz, Morbihan, France, on May 20, he studied at Vannes, taught, went to Paris, and became secretary in the ministry of foreign affairs in 1828. He spent three years in England, where he came into close contact with the pre-Raphaelites, and by his writings helped to restore the art of the Middle Ages to a respected position in the history of art. He wrote *Essai sur l'histoire de l'esprit humain dans l'antiquité* (1828–30), *L'Art chrétien* (1861–67), *Epilogue à l'art chrétien* (1872), and *L'idéal antique et l'idéal chrétien* (1873). He died in Paris on June 17.

RIOCH, ST. (d. 480?). Called a nephew of St. Patrick, he became abbot of Innisboffin, Longford, Ireland. F. D. Aug. 1.

RIOJA, FRANCISCO DE (1583–1659), poet. Born in Seville, Spain, he became a canon at the cathedral there and a member of the Inquisition. He wrote considerable poetry in the Castilian tongue and died in Madrid.

RIORDAN, PATRICK WILLIAM (1841–1914), archbishop. Born in Chatham, New Brunswick, Canada, on Aug. 27, he graduated from Notre Dame in 1858, studied at St. Mary's of the Lake, Chicago, St. Sulpice, Paris, with the first class at the North American College, Rome, and Louvain where he earned his doctorate in theology, and was ordained in Mechlin, Belgium, in 1865. He taught at St. Mary's in Chicago and did pastoral work there, and in 1883 was named titular archbishop of Cabesa and coadjutor of San Francisco. He succeeded to that see in 1884, built St. Mary's cathedral and numerous churches, schools, and religious institutions, founded St. Patrick's seminary in 1898, helped settle the Pious Fund claims against Mexico before the International Arbitration Court at The Hague in 1902, and was obliged to rebuild his diocese after the San Francisco earthquake of 1906. He died in San Francisco on Dec. 27.

RIPALDA, JUAN MARTÍNEZ DE (1594–1648), theologian. Born in Pamplona, Navarre, Spain, he became a Jesuit in 1609, taught at Monforte, Salamanca, and Madrid, became censor of the Inquisition, and confessor to de Olivares, with whom he left in exile. He wrote widely, on grace, will, creation, the maternity of Mary, and against Baius. He died in Madrid on Apr. 26.

RIPON, GEORGE FREDERICK SAMUEL ROBINSON, MARQUESS OF (1827–1909), diplomat. Son of the prime minister of England, he was born in London on Oct. 24 and privately educated. He became a member of the House of Commons in 1852 as a Liberal, succeeded to his father's titles as second earl of Ripon and viscount Goderich on the latter's death in 1859, entered the House of Lords, and was a member of each Liberal administration for the next fifty years. He was secretary of state for war in 1859–61 and 1863–66, undersecretary of state for India in 1861–63, and secretary in 1866. He served as lord president of the council in 1868–73, was chairman of the commission which settled the *Alabama* claims with the United States in 1873 (for which service he was made marquess of Ripon), and from 1871 to 1874 was grand master of the Masons. He resigned this position in 1874 to enter the Catholic Church, and retired from public life. He re-entered public affairs as governor general and viceroy of India from 1880 to 1884, in which position he encouraged the development of Indian self-government, was first lord of the admiralty in 1886, secretary for the colonies from 1892 to 1895, and lord privy seal from 1905 to his resignation in 1908. He died on July 9, near Ripon, England.

RIQUIER. *See* Richarius, St.

RISBY, RICHARD (1490–1534), martyr. Born in Reading, England, he studied at Winchester, became a fellow at New College, Oxford, resigned in 1513 to join the Franciscans, and became warden of the Observant friary at Canterbury. He was executed at Tyburn on Apr. 20 after twice refusing a pardon if he would acknowledge the king's supremacy over the Church.

RISHANGER, WILLIAM (1250?–1312?), historian. Born in Rishangles, Suffolk, England, he joined the Benedictines in 1271 and is known for his history of the Barons' War, *Narratio de bellis apud Lewes et Evesham,* and a history of the reign of Edward I. He died sometime after 1312.

RISHTON, EDWARD (1550–1585). Born in Ste. Ménehould, Lorraine, he studied at Oxford, became a convert in 1573, and was the first Englishman to matriculate at Douai. He was ordained in 1576, returned to England in 1580, was arrested and condemned to death in 1581, but exiled instead. He went to Pont-à-Mousson to study and fled to escape the plague to Ste. Ménehould, where he died on June 29.

RITA OF CASCIA, ST. (1381–1457). Born in Roccaporena, near Spoleto, Italy, she was married to a brutal and dissolute husband, although she had wished to become an Augustinian nun. After eighteen years of sorrow, she was widowed when her husband was killed in a brawl. Their two sons sought to continue the vendetta, but Rita persuaded them to avoid vengeance. They did, but contracted a fatal illness. She was then free to enter the Augustinian convent in Cascia, Italy, taking vows in 1413. She devoted herself intensely to the care of others and to prayer for those negligent in their religious duties. In spite of years of serious illness, she never lessened her austerities until her death in Cascia. She was canonized in 1900 and is called "the saint of desperate cases" throughout the Spanish world. F. D. May 22.

RITTER, JOSEPH IGNATIUS (1787–1857), historian. Born in Schweinitz, Silesia, on Apr. 12, he studied at Breslau, was ordained in 1811, and was assigned to pastoral work. In 1823 he was appointed professor of church history at Bonn, where he met and was influenced by Hermes, became professor at Breslau in 1830, and in 1840 was appointed administrator of the diocese, where his actions dissipated any suspicion of Hermesianism. He wrote *Handbuch der Kirchengeschichte* (1826–33) and other historical studies, and died in Breslau, Germany, on Jan. 5.

RIZAL, JOSÉ MERCADO (1861–1896). Born in Calamba, Luzon, Philippine Islands, on June 19, he studied at the Ateneo in Manila and at Madrid, where he received his medical degree in 1884 and his doctorate in philosophy in 1885. He studied law at Heidelberg, studied further at Paris, Berlin, and Leipzig, and published a novel in Berlin, *Noli me tangere* (1886), a diatribe against the Spanish administration and religious orders in the islands, which was extremely popular. He returned to the Philippines in 1887, but was forced to leave because of his book and spent the next four years in Japan, the United States, England, France, and Belgium. In 1891 he went to Hong Kong where he practiced medicine for a year, and then returned to Manila, whence the government deported him to Mindanao for his revolutionary agitation. In 1896 he went to Spain, was arrested, returned to Manila, and after a dubious trial was sentenced to be shot as a revolutionary instigator. He was executed on Dec. 30. While awaiting execution, he returned to the Church. The province of Rizal in the Philippines was named after him and he is hailed as a national hero in the Philippines.

RIZZERIO, BL. (d. 1260). Entering religious life after he heard St. Francis of Assisi preach in 1222, he was ordained a Franciscan, became provincial, and died when quite young. He is incorrectly called Rinieri in the *Fioretti.* His cult was confirmed in 1836. F. D. Feb. 7.

RIZZIO, DAVID (1533?–1566). Born in Turin, Italy, he was in the entourage of the Piedmontese ambassador to Scotland in 1561, entered the service of Mary, Queen of Scots, as a musician in 1564, and became her private foreign secretary and confidant. Lord Darnley, jealous of his influence over the queen and fearing he was her lover, organized a conspiracy of Scottish lords against him, which murdered him in Holyrood castle, Edinburgh, on Mar. 9.

ROBBIA, ANDREA DELLA (1431–1528), sculptor. Born in Florence, Italy, he studied under his uncle, Luca, and became his assistant. Among his outstanding works were the marble altar of S. Maria delle Grazie church in Arezzo, the medallions on the Foundling Hospital in Florence, and the decorated ceiling of the cathedral in Pistoia. He developed the use of enameled clay for use in friezes, fountains, and altarpieces.

ROBBIA, LUCA DELLA (1400?–1482), sculptor. Born in Florence, Italy, he probably studied under Ghiberti, and about 1446 perfected the known processes of enameling into a new secret process which produced brilliant coloring, especially blues, in a hard, durable, bright glaze. He applied his process to fine decorative reliefs and figures of clay which attracted immediate attention, and established a school of glazed terra-cotta sculpture which the Robbia family maintained for the next century and a half. Among his outstanding works are the madonna in Urbino, the crucifix and ceiling of San Miniato in Florence, Bishop Federighi's tomb at Santa Trinity, and the tabernacle at Impruneta. He died in Florence on Sept. 22.

ROBERT I (865?–923), king of France. He was the son of Count Robert the Strong of Anjou and brother of Eudes, who became king of the West Franks in 888. He did not claim Eudes' crown on his brother's death in 898, continued to recognize the reign of Charles III, and fought against Norman invasions in northern France. In 921, with a group of Frankish nobles, he rebelled against Charles III, drove the king into Lorraine, and in 922 was chosen king at Rheims in opposition to Charles. He was killed at the battle of Soissons, France, on June 15. He often is not included in the recognized line of French kings.

ROBERT II (970?–1031), king of France. Called "the Pious," he was born in Orléans, France, son of Hugh Capet, studied under Gerbert (later Pope Sylvester II), and was crowned co-ruler by his father in 987. He married Rosala, widow of Count Arnold II of Flanders, in 988, but repudiated her in 989. He succeeded to the throne in 996, married Bertha of Burgundy, widow of Eudes I of Blois, that year, and was excommunicated by

Pope Gregory V. He submitted in 1002 and married Constance. In 1010 he took Bertha to Rome, but when the pope again refused to recognize their marriage returned to Constance. He made the eldest of the four sons of this marriage, Hugh (1007–25), his co-ruler in 1017, and after Hugh's death in 1025 was faced by a revolt of the younger sons. Robert died in Melun, France, on July 20. He is sometimes called Robert I, since the reign of Robert (865?–923) is often not recognized in the line of the kings of France.

ROBERT DE BRUCE (1274–1329), king of Scotland. Grandson of Robert I de Bruce, he was born on July 11, probably at Ayrshire, Scotland. He swore allegiance to Edward I of England in 1296 and 1297 and alternately fought against him or (as in 1299, when he was one of the four regents of Edward Baliol) stood high in his favor. In 1306, during a conference in the Franciscan church at Dumfries with his enemy, John "Red" Comyn, Bruce stabbed him; his associates killed the wounded man and also slew Comyn's brother. Bruce then was crowned king at Scone, was defeated at Methven and Dalry, and was forced into exile on the island of Rachrine, off the coast of Antrim, Ireland. The English broke into St. Duthlac's in Rosshire and seized his wife, Isabella of Mar, and daughter Marjory; many of Bruce's followers were slain, their property taken, and Bruce himself was declared excommunicated by the papal legate. In 1307 he invaded Scotland and within two years regained almost all of his kingdom. In 1312 the English invaded, but the army of 100,000 under Edward III was routed at Bannockburn and 30,000 slain. In 1317, Bruce went to Ireland on behalf of his brother Edward, and defeated an English army under the baron of Clare. He returned to invade England, defeated Edward again, in Yorkshire, and signed a peace in 1323 which lasted thirteen years. Edward III attacked in 1327, but Bruce again won and had his claim to the throne recognized and the nation acknowledged as independent. Bruce, a victim of leprosy, died at Cardross Castle, Scotland, on June 7.

ROBERT II (1316–1390), king of Scotland. Son of Walter and Marjory, daughter of King Robert de Bruce, he was born on Mar. 2, fought at the Scots defeat at Halidon Hill (1333), became regent with Morey in 1334, was removed by King Edward III of England, but returned as regent in 1338, and recaptured Edinburgh in 1341. When David II, his uncle, died, he became king (the first of the house of Stuart) in 1371. Frequent border raids disturbed the peace. England finally invaded by force in 1385 under Richard II. Robert then invaded England in 1388, but was too old to campaign vigorously; the estates made his son Robert guardian in 1389. He died in Dundonald, Ayrshire, Scotland, on May 15.

ROBERT III (1340?-1406), king of Scotland. Son of Robert II, he succeeded to the crown in 1390. He continued to suffer from war with England; Henry IV invaded Scotland in 1400 and Archibald Douglas led a force into England in 1402. One son, Robert, was slain by the duke of Albany; a second, James, was captured and imprisoned by Henry. King Robert thereafter fell into a melancholy mood which hastened his death at Rothesay, Bute, Scotland, on Apr. 4.

ROBERT, ST. (d. 1159), abbot. Born in Gargrave, Yorkshire, England, he was ordained and, after a period of parish work, became a Benedictine at Whitby. In 1132 he founded the strict monastery of Fountains Abbey, which adopted the Cistercian Rule. In 1138 he set up the Cistercian monastery of Newminster, where he became abbot; later, he founded houses at Pipewell, Roche, and Sawley, and wrote a now-lost commentary on the Psalms. F. D. June 7.

ROBERT OF ARBRISSEL (1047?-1117?). Born in Arbrissel (now Arbressec), Brittany, he studied at Paris, was ordained, returned to Rennes, where he became vicar, in 1089, and devoted himself to ecclesiastical reforms. The death of his patron, Bishop Sylvester de la Guerche, in 1093 caused him to flee to Angers to escape the enemies he had made by his reforms, and in 1095 he became a hermit in the forest of Craon. In 1096 he became founding abbot of the La Roé monastery at the request of the many followers who had been attracted by his asceticism, and later the same year was appointed "preacher" by Pope Urban II. His eloquence attracted huge crowds everywhere, and in 1099 he founded the double monastery of Fontevrault to accommodate the many postulants La Roé could not accept. He attended the Council of Poitiers in 1100, where he supported the excommunication of Philip of France, and of Nantes in 1110, and died at Orsan, France, after a chapter he had called in 1116 set up a permanent organization for his monks.

ROBERT DE BRUCE VI (1210-1295). Son of Robert de Bruce V and Isabel, niece of Scots King William the Lion, he was recognized as heir apparent of Scotland in 1238-41, succeeded his father as lord of Annandale, served as an English justiciar, inherited his mother's estates in 1251, and was a regent in Scotland in 1255. He fought for Henry III of England against the barons, became Henry's chief justice in 1268, and returned to Scotland in 1272. He recognized Margaret in 1284 as successor to the crown, but claimed it himself in 1286. He accepted Margaret's marriage to Edward, prince of Wales, and to union with England in 1290,

regretted this and prepared to fight in 1292. Edward I of England decided against his claim in favor of John Baliol in 1292. He died at Lochmaben castle, Scotland.

ROBERT OF COURÇON (d. 1218), cardinal. Born in Kedleston, England, he studied at Oxford, Rome, and Paris, where he became chancellor in 1211, and was created cardinal in 1212. He was appointed to preach the crusade in 1213, and headed a commission in 1215 to investigate errors at Paris resulting from the introduction of Arabian translations of Aristotle in the university, which led to the prohibition of Aristotle's treatises and summaries of them. He campaigned against heresy in France, and accompanied the crusaders as Pope Honorius III's legate to Egypt, where he died during the siege of Damietta, Egypt.

ROBERT OF COURTENAY (d. 1228), emperor. He succeeded his father, Peter of Courtenay, as emperor of Constantinople in 1221. He twice was defeated in 1224, had his territory reduced almost to the city limits, and later was driven out of the capital by a Burgundian knight, and died in Achaia, Greece.

ROBERT OF GENEVA (1342-1394), antipope. Born in Geneva, Switzerland, son of Count Amadeus III, he was appointed prothonotary in 1359, bishop of Therouanne in 1361, archbishop of Cambrai in 1368, and was created cardinal in 1371. He served as papal legate to Upper Italy from 1376 to 1378, where he earned the title "executioner of Cesena" for his reputed massacre of 4000 rebels there. On Sept. 20, 1378, the French cardinals who opposed Pope Urban VI reconsidered and elected Robert, who took the name Clement VII, the first antipope of the great Western schism. He set up court at Avignon, France, where, supported by the French, he remained until his death on Sept. 16.

ROBERT GRUTHUYSEN, BL. (d. 1157), Born in Bruges, Belgium, he became a Benedictine at Clairvaux, was abbot of Dunes in 1139, and succeeded St. Bernard as abbot of Clairvaux in 1153. F. D. Apr. 29.

ROBERT GUISCARD (1016?-1085). Born near Coutances, France, eldest son of Tancred, seigneur of Hauteville, he went to Italy in 1046 as a soldier of fortune (Guiscard means "sly") under his brother Drogo, count of the Normans. In 1051 he entered the service of his brother Humphrey, when the latter succeeded the assassinated Drogo, and in 1057 he succeeded Humphrey as head of the Normans. He began a campaign to wrest all southern Italy from Byzantine control and in 1059 was created duke of Apulia and Calabria (which he had conquered) and lord of Sicily by Pope Nicholas II in return for his promise to protect the papacy. In 1071 and 1072 he captured Bari, Byzantine's Italian capital, and

Palermo. He was excommunicated in 1074 for an attack on a papal fief, but in 1080 was reconciled to Gregory VII when he came to the latter's support during the dispute with Emperor Henry IV. In 1081, Robert and his son Bohemond launched an invasion of the Byzantine Empire which progressed successfully until Feb., when the Venetian fleet and Alexius Comnenus defeated the Normans. On land, Robert had almost reached Constantinople when he was recalled to rescue Rome and Gregory VII from the hands of Henry and antipope Clement III. He then returned to the Near East, recovered Corfu, off the coast of Greece, which Bohemond had lost, and had just disembarked on Cephalonia when he died on July 17.

ROBERT OF JUMIÈGES (d. 1055?), archbishop. A native of Normandy, Robert Champart became a monk at St. Ouen in Rouen, was made prior, and in 1037 was elected abbot of Jumièges, where he aided St. Edward the Confessor. When the latter became king of England in 1043, Robert returned to England with him and was named bishop of London in 1044, and became head of the Norman party and a principal adviser of the king. He was appointed archbishop of Canterbury in 1051 over the opposition of the English clergy, was forced to flee to Rome in 1052 when his opponent, Godwin, head of the Saxon party, returned from exile, and was outlawed by the witenagemot. Though the pope reinstated him, he was never able to regain his see, and probably died at Jumièges, Normandy, on May 26.

ROBERT DE KETENE (12th century), scholar. An Englishman, he traveled through the Near East, where he learned Arabic, became archdeacon at Pamplona, Spain, and for Peter the Venerable of Cluny made the first translation of the Koran (printed in 1543) and other writings.

ROBERT OF LUZARCHES (13th century), architect. Born in Luzarches, France, he probably worked on Notre Dame cathedral, was royally commissioned to beautify Paris, and is best known as the architect of Notre Dame in Amiens, France, which he began in 1220.

ROBERT OF MELUN (1100?–1167), bishop. An Englishman, he studied at Melun, France, under Hugh of St. Victor and Abelard, taught philosophy, and had as pupils John of Salisbury and Thomas à Becket, through whose influence he was appointed bishop of Hereford in 1163. He died in Hereford, England. He wrote several theological treatises, among them a *Summa sententiarum*.

ROBERT OF MOLESMES, ST. (1024?–1110), founder. Born near Troyes, France, he became a Benedictine monk at Moutier-la-Celle at fifteen, its prior, then abbot at St.

Michael of Tonnerre, where he was unable to better discipline. He left to direct some hermits in a forest near Collan, but also met opposition there. With a small and serious core, including SS. Alberic and Stephen Harding, he moved in 1098 to Cîteaux (Cistercium) near Dijon and began a new foundation, of which he became abbot. This was the beginning of the Cistercian order. He later returned to Molesmes, which now humbly accepted his direction during his last ten years. He died there on Mar. 21, and was canonized in 1222. F. D. Apr. 29.

ROBERT DE MONTE (1100?–1186), historian. An Englishman, born in Torigni-sur-Vire, France, he was abbot of Mont-St.-Michel in 1154–86, and continued the chronicles of William of Jumièges and Sigebert of Gemblours.

ROBERT, PULLEN (1100?–1147?), cardinal. Of English parentage, he studied in England as a youth, was archdeacon of Rochester in 1134, went to Paris about 1135, became famed for his scholarly achievements and teaching (John of Salisbury was one of his pupils), and was an associate of St. Bernard who wrote asking him to aid Pope Eugenius III, Bernard's pupil, who became pope in 1145. He then returned to Oxford, where he taught and helped develop the Oxford schools. He went to Rome about 1143, was created a cardinal by Pope Celestine II, and was appointed chancellor by Pope Lucius II about 1145. He was an opponent of Abelard's teachings, and wrote *Sententiarum Theologicarum*, which became a popular textbook.

ROBERT OF SALENTINO, BL. (1272–1341). A Benedictine monk and disciple of Pietro del Morone in Umbria, Italy, he founded fourteen monasteries of the hermits of St. Damian which Pietro had founded before he became Pope Celestine V. F. D. July 18.

ROBERT OF SHREWSBURY (12th century). An Englishman, he was abbot of Shrewsbury before 1160 and wrote a *Life of St. Wenefred.*

ROBERT DE TURLANDE, ST. (d. 1067). Founder of the Benedictine monastery of Chaise-Dieu in Auvergne, France, he was a canon in the church of St. Julian, Brioude, until he decided to become a hermit. He and a penitent knight named Stephen had so many followers that they set up a formal house, with 300 monks, from which came many later establishments. F. D. Apr. 17.

ROBERTS, BL. JOHN (1577–1610), martyr. Born in Trawfynydd, Merionethshire, Wales, he studied at Oxford, but left in 1598 to study law. While in Europe he became a convert, and in 1599 a Benedictine at Valladolid. In 1602 he set out for England, was arrested shortly after his arrival, and deported. He returned, became famed for his work among the plague-stricken in London, and during the next seven years was arrested five times, but was released, exiled, or escaped each time. During 1606, when he had been banished to France, he helped found, with Dom Augustine Bradshaw, a monastery for the English monks of Valladolid at Douai. He returned to England early in 1610, was arrested, convicted of being a priest, and hanged, drawn, and quartered at Tyburn. He was beatified in 1929. F. D. Dec. 10.

ROBERTSON, JAMES BURTON (1800–1877), historian. Born in London on Nov. 15, he was raised in the West Indies, where his father had property, attended St. Edmund's College, studied law, and was admitted to the bar in 1829. He abandoned law to study philosophy in France, lived in Germany from 1837 to 1854, where he translated several German works, and in 1855 was appointed professor of history at the Catholic University in Dublin by John Henry Newman. He wrote historical works, including *Lectures on Various Subjects* (1858) and *Lectures on Edmund Burke* (1868), and some poetry. He died in Dublin on Feb. 14.

ROBINSON, VEN. CHRISTOPHER (d. 1598), martyr. Born in Woodside, Cumberland, England, he studied at Rheims and was ordained in 1592. Sent on the English mission, he wrote an eyewitness account of the martyrdom of John Boste, labored in Cumberland and Westmoreland, was arrested and condemned as a priest acting secretly, and was hanged at Carlisle on Aug. 19.

ROBINSON, HENRY MORTON (1898–1961), author. Born in Boston, Massachusetts, on Sept. 7, he served in the navy during World War I, studied at Columbia, taught there in 1924–27, and published *Children of Morningside*, a novel in verse, in 1927. He wrote magazine stories and articles, was an editor of *Reader's Digest* in 1935–45, was co-author of *A Skeleton Key to Finnegan's Wake* (1944), and wrote such popular fiction as *The Cardinal* (1950) and *Water of Life* (1960). He died in New York City on Jan. 13.

ROBINSON, BL. JOHN (d. 1588), martyr. Born in Ferrensby, Yorkshire, England, he married, and on the death of his wife went to Rheims, France, and was ordained in 1585. Sent on the English mission, he was seized in London, tried as a priest during the Elizabethan persecution, and hanged, drawn, and quartered at Ipswich. He was beatified in 1929. F. D. Oct. 1.

ROBINSON, PASCHAL (1870–1948), archbishop. Born in Dublin, he was taken to the United States as an infant, studied law, became a newspaperman, and was an associate editor of *North American Review* in 1892–96.

He became a Franciscan in 1896, was ordained in Rome in 1901, taught theology at Catholic University to 1919, and represented the Vatican at the peace conference at Versailles in that year. He was named archbishop of Tyana in 1927 and went to Ireland in 1929 as the first papal nuncio in 300 years. He died in Dublin on Aug. 27.

ROBINSON, WILLIAM CALLYHAN(1834–1911), jurist. Born in Norwich, Connecticut, on July 26, he studied at Wesleyan, Dartmouth, and the Episcopal Theological seminary, became an Episcopalian minister, and served in churches in Pittston and Scranton, Pennsylvania. He became a convert in 1863, was admitted to the bar in 1864, and from 1869 to 1895 was professor of law at Yale. He was judge of the New Haven city court in 1869–71, of the court of common pleas in 1874–76, and was a member of the state legislature in 1874. He was appointed a professor at the Catholic University in 1895, reorganized the school of social sciences, and was dean of the law school until his death in Washington, D.C., on Nov. 6.

ROBUSTI, JACOPO. *See* Tintoretto.

ROCABERTI, JUAN TOMAS DE (1624?–1699), archbishop. Born in Perelada, Spain, he studied at Gerona, where he joined the Dominicans, and taught theology at Valencia. He became provincial of Aragon in 1666, was elected general of the Dominicans in 1670, appointed first archbishop of Valencia in 1676, governor of Valencia by Charles II, and in 1695 became inquisitor general of Spain, noted for his energetic defense of papal supremacy. He died in Madrid on June 13. His chief works were the twenty-one-volume *Bibliotheca maxima pontifica* (1697–99), and *De romani pontificis auctoritate* (1693).

ROCCA, ANGELO (1545–1620), theologian. Born in Arecevia (formerly Rocca), Italy, he was admitted to the Augustinian monastery in Camerino when seven, and studied at Perugia, Rome, Venice, and Padua, where he received his doctorate in theology in 1577. He became secretary to the Augustinian superior general in 1579, headed the Vatican printing press in 1585, and was in charge of proposed new editions of the Bible and the works of the Fathers. He was appointed sacristan of the papal chapel in 1595, titular bishop of Tagaste in 1605, and in 1614 founded the Angelica Library in Rome, where he died on Apr. 8. He wrote theological works, and edited the works of Egidio Colonna and Augustinus Triumphus.

ROCH, ST. (1295–1378?). Born probably in Montpellier, France, he served the plague-stricken in Rome and devoted himself through life to the care of the sick. He is a patron invoked against pestilence and is known in Italy as Rocco and in Spain as Roque. F. D. Aug. 16.

ROCHAMBEAU, JEAN BAPTISTE DONA-TIEN DE VIMEUR DE (1725–1807), general. Born in Vendôme, France, on July 1, he joined the army at seventeen, distinguished himself in the War of the Austrian Succession, the Minorca expedition in 1756, and the Seven Years' War, and succeeded his father as governor of Vendôme in 1749. In 1780 he was appointed lieutenant general and placed in charge of 6000 French troops sent to America to aid the colonists against the British. Count de Rochambeau served under Washington, participated in the siege of Yorktown, returned to France, and in 1791 was appointed a marshal. He commanded an army against the Austrians in 1792, resigned later in the year, barely escaped the guillotine when he fell out of favor with the Terrorists and was imprisoned, but later had his rank restored by Napoleon. He spent his last years writing his *Memoirs*, which were published in 1809, two years after his death in Thore, France, on May 10.

ROCHE, BL. ALAIN DE LA (1428–1475). Born in Brittany, he became a Dominican, studied at Paris, taught for sixteen years in France, Belgium, Holland, and Germany, and preached zealously on devotion to the rosary. He is also known as Alanus de Rupe. F. D. Sept. 8.

ROCHE, EDWARD PATRICK (1874–1950), archbishop. Born in Placentia, Canada, he studied at All Hallows, Dublin, Ireland, served as a parish priest in the fishing village of Topsail, Newfoundland, became a monsignor in 1914, and archbishop of St. John's, Newfoundland, in 1915. He died in St. John's on Sept. 23.

ROCHE, BL. JOHN (d. 1588), martyr. *See* Ward, Bl. Margaret.

ROCHECHOUART, GABRIELLE DE (1670–1704). Sister of Mme. de Montespan and friend of Mme. de Maintenon, she became abbess of Fontevrault, France, developed the abbey school, and translated the complete works of Plato from the Latin of Ficino.

ROCHEFOUCAULD, BL. FRANÇOIS JOSEPH DE LA (d. 1792), martyr. *See* Du Lau, Bl. Jean.

ROCHEFOUCAULD, BL. PIERRE LOUIS DE LA (d. 1792), martyr. *See* Du Lau, Bl. Jean.

ROCHESTER, BL. JOHN (d. 1537), martyr. He and another Carthusian, Bl. William Walworth, went to Hull, England, when a renegade was placed in charge of the London Charterhouse, were eventually arrested, refused to subscribe to the Act of Supremacy which made Henry VIII head of the Church, and were executed at York, England. He was beatified in 1886. F. D. May 11.

ROCHETTE, DÉSIRÉ RAOUL (1789–1854), archaeologist. Born in St. Amand, France, on Mar. 9, he studied at L'École Normale Supérieure, taught at Louis-le-Grand in 1810, at L'École Normale, and succeeded Guizot as professor of history at the Sorbonne in 1815. He was elected to the Academy of Inscriptions in 1816, and was appointed censor in 1820, a move which aroused such hostility among the students that his courses were suspended. He occupied the chair of archaeology in 1824, was elected to the Academy of Fine Arts in 1838, and became its perpetual secretary in 1839. He wrote many archaeological treatises, among them *Cours d'archéologie* (1828) and *Peintures antiques* (1836), and died in Paris on June 3. He is often called Raoul-Rochette.

ROCK, DANIEL (1799–1871), liturgist. Born in Liverpool, England, on Aug. 31, he studied at St. Edmund's and the English College, Rome, where he was ordained in 1824. He served in London, then became a private chaplain to the earl of Shrewsbury. He became a member of the Adelphi, an association of priests formed to secure restoration of the hierarchy, in 1840, was elected a canon of Southwark in 1852, and shortly after gave up his pastoral activities to pursue archaeological studies. He wrote *Hierugia, or the Holy Sacrifice of the Mass* (1833), *The Liturgy of the Mass* (1832), and the three-volume *The Church of Our Fathers* (1849–54). He died in London on Nov. 28.

ROCKNE, KNUTE KENNETH (1888–1931), athlete. Born in Voss, Norway, he was taken to the United States as a child of five, graduated from the University of Notre Dame in 1914, and became its assistant football coach. He was head coach from 1918 to his death in an airplane crash near Bazaar, Kansas, on Mar. 31. His teams were undefeated in 1919, 1920, 1924, 1929, and 1930; they were victorious in 105 out of 122 games. He became a convert in 1925.

ROCKWELL, JOSEPH HORACE (1862–1927), educator. Born in Boston, he studied at Boston College and Woodstock, was ordained a Jesuit in 1895, taught, served as president of St. Francis Xavier College, New York, and in 1926 was made procurator of the new province of New England. He died in Boston on Aug. 1.

RODAN. *See* Ruadan, St.

RODAT, EMILIE DE. *See* Emily de Rodat, St.

RODERIC. *See* Rudericus, St.

RODINGUS, ST. (d. 690?). An Irish monk, he was ordained, preached in Germany, and entered the Benedictine abbey of Tholey, near Trèves, France. He became abbot-founder of Wasloi, later renamed Beaulieu. He is also called Rouin. F. D. Sept. 17.

RODRIGO DIAZ DE BIVAR (1040?–1099). Born in Burgos, Spain, he commanded the army of King Sancho II of Castile, helped him defeat his royal brother Alfonso VI of León and his sister Elvira and was called *campeador* (champion) by the Spaniards and *seid* or *cid* by the Moors. Sancho was slain while attacking the capital of his sister Urraca. Alfonso soon exiled Rodrigo, who then went into the service of the Moorish king of Saragossa, often fighting against the Spanish Christians. He then turned to fight the Moors alone, besieging and capturing Valencia in 1094 and setting himself up as lord there. He died after an army he had sent to rescue a relative was crushed near Alcira. Many legendary details were added to these bald facts; by 1140 *Poema del Cid* had been written in his honor (some 3700 lines are extant); extravagant elaborations followed. The legendary figure appears in Corneille's tragedy (*Le Cid*) and Massenet's opera.

RODRIGO JIMÉNEZ DE RADA (d. 1247), archbishop. Born in Spain, he was ordained, was a royal counselor, fought at the battle of Las Navas de Tolosa, built the cathedral of Toledo, of which see he became archbishop in 1210, consolidated its primacy, and built the first general schools.

RODRIGUES FERREIRA, ALEXANDRE (1756–1815), naturalist, explorer. Born in Bahia, Brazil, he studied at Coimbra in Portugal, taught natural history there, and in 1778 became cataloguer at the Museo da Ajuda in Lisbon. The government appointed him head of an exploring expedition to Brazil in 1783, and he spent the next nine years exploring the people, flora, and fauna of the interior. In 1792 he was appointed director of the Gabinete de Historia Natural and of the Jardin Botanico in Lisbon, Portugal, a position he held until his death there.

RODRÍGUEZ, ALONSO (1526–1616). Born in Valladolid, Spain, he joined the Jesuits when twenty, taught at Monterey, was master of novices for twelve years (Francis Suarez was one of his novices), rector of Monterey for seventeen years, and spiritual director at Cordova for eleven years. He wrote *The Practice of Christian and Religious Perfection* (1609), which was widely translated, and died in Seville, Spain, on Feb. 21.

RODRÍGUEZ, BL. ALONSO (d. 1628), martyr. See Gonzalez, Bl. Roque.

RODRÍGUEZ, ALPHONSUS. See Alphonsus Rodriguez.

RODRÍGUEZ, JOÃO (1558–1633), missioner. Born in Alcochete, Portugal, he joined the Jesuits in 1576, was sent as a missionary to Japan in 1583, became a favorite of the emperor, and labored to open Japan to Westerners. He died in Japan. He wrote a Japanese-Portuguese dictionary (1603), and *Arte da lingoa de Japan* (1604), a Japanese grammar.

RODRÍGUEZ, BL. PEDRO (d. 1242). He, Damian Vaz, and six Portuguese companions, all Knights of St. John of Santiago, were murdered by Moors at Tavira, Portugal, during a military truce. They are honored locally on June 11.

RODRON, ST. (d. 888), martyr. See Ageranus, St.

ROE, BL. ALBAN BARTHOLOMEW (1583?–1642), martyr. Born near Bury St. Edmunds, England, he was educated at Cambridge, was converted there, studied at Douai, and became a Benedictine monk in Lorraine. As Dom Alban, he was captured in England in 1627 and spent most of his remaining years in prison. He translated St. John Fisher's work on prayer, encouraged Bl. Thomas Green (Reynolds) in his last days, and was executed with the latter at Tyburn because of his priesthood. He was beatified in 1929. F. D. Jan. 21. BEDE CAMM, *Nine Martyr Monks* (London, Burns, Oates, 1931).

ROGATIAN, ST. (d. 256), martyr. A priest, he probably was put to death at Carthage, North Africa, with a layman named Felicissimus; they were praised by St. Cyprian. F. D. Oct. 26.

ROGATIAN, ST. (3rd century), martyr. See Donatian, St.

ROGATIAN, ST. (d. 304), martyr. See Saturninus, St.

ROGATUS, ST. (d. 484), martyr. See Liberatus, St.

ROGELLUS, ST. (d. 852), martyr. A monk, he and a young follower (listed as Servus Dei) were slain at Cordova, Spain, when they denounced Mohammedanism. F. D. Sept. 16.

ROGER (d. 1179), bishop. The son of the earl of Gloucester was educated with Prince Henry (later King Henry II), was ordained, and in 1163 was appointed bishop of Worcester, England. He was one of the bishops sent to Rome to enter the king's complaint against Thomas à Becket, but his loyalty to the archbishop of Canterbury and his refusal to join the bishops' condemnation of St. Thomas caused him to fall from royal favor. He joined Thomas in the latter's exile in 1167, denounced the king at Falaise in 1170, but was soon reconciled. After Thomas' murder, he staved off a threatened interdict of England by his appeal to the pope, acted on several diplomatic missions for Pope Alexander III, and died in Tours, France, on Aug 9.

ROGER, BL. JAMES (d. 1539). See Whiting, Bl. Richard.

ROGER BACON (1214?–1294), philosopher, scientist. Born near Ilchester, Somerset, England, he was at Oxford about 1230 and went to Paris before 1236. He lectured at Paris, became interested in physical and natural science, returned to England about 1251, joined the Franciscans, and in 1257 was sent to Paris, but was obliged to retire from academic work because of ill health. During the next decade he wrote *De speculis, De mirabile potestate artis et naturae, Metaphysica, De multiplicatione specierum,* and *De computo.* In 1266, Pope Clement IV requested him to write a general treatise on the sciences. He planned and began work on an exhaustive encyclopedia of the sciences, *Communia naturalium,* but in 1267 put it aside to write the less pretentious *Opus majus,* which he finished in 1268. In 1277 his works were condemned by a Franciscan council, possibly because of his intemperate attacks on many of his contemporaries, and he was imprisoned until 1292. On his release he began *Compendium studii theologiae,* but died, probably on June 11 at Oxford, before its completion. Among his other writings are *Quaestiones* on Aristotle's *Physics* and *Metaphysics, Opus minus, Opus tertium,* a Greek grammar, and a Hebrew grammar which he began but never finished. Bacon is often considered the forerunner of modern scientific method. The basic factors in his scientific approach were mathematics and experimentation. He may have invented a telescope and microscope, and possibly was the first person to observe spiral nebula through a reflecting telescope and cells through a microscope.

ROGER OF BRUGES. *See* Van der Weyden, Rogier.

ROGER OF ELLANT, BL. (d. 1160). He became a Cistercian at Lorroy, France, founded the monastery of Ellant, where he became abbot, and devoted his life to the care of the sick. F. D. Jan. 4.

ROGER OF HOVEDEN (d. 1201?), historian. Born in Hoveden (now Howden), Yorkshire, England, he became a professor of theology at Oxford, a member of King Henry II's court in 1173, a king's clerk, and served on several diplomatic missions for the king. He was a justice in 1189, probably retired from public life after Henry's death, and reputedly became a priest in Howden, where he devoted himself to writing in Latin a *History of England* from 732 to 1201 which is an important source of information for the last quarter of the twelfth century.

ROGER LE FORT (1277?–1367), archbishop. Born in the district of Limousin, France, he was a subdeacon when he was chosen archbishop of Orléans in 1321. In 1328 he went to Limoges and in 1343 to Bourges. There he popularized the feast of the Immaculate Conception and, at his death, left his wealth for the education of poor boys. Honored on Mar. 1, he was never officially beatified.

ROGER OF TODI, BL. (d. 1237). Ruggiero da Todi received the religious habit at the hands of St. Francis of Assisi and became spiritual counselor at the convent of Poor Clares in Rieti, Italy, of which Bl. Philippa Mareri was superior. F. D. Jan. 14.

ROGER OF WENDOVER (d. 1236?), historian. Born in Wendover, Buckinghamshire, England, he joined the Benedictines, became prior of Belvoir, but was deposed and went to St. Albans abbey, where he wrote *Flores historiarum,* a chronicle from creation to 1235, a valuable source of knowledge for the opening decades of the thirteenth century.

ROGGE, CONRAD (d. 1501). A learned humanist, he studied at Perugia, Italy, became bishop of Strengnäs, Sweden, in 1479, built the cathedral choir, founded a hospital for infirm priests, and founded a charterhouse, Svartsjö, and printed a revised breviary.

ROGGERI, ST. TEOBALDO (d. 1150). Born in Vico, Italy, he left his comfortable home in Liguria and became a cobbler's apprentice in Alba and later a loader of grain sacks and other merchandise. He became sexton of the church of St. Laurence, gave most of his meager income to the poor, and lived in the most simple and austere manner. He became a patron of shoemakers and porters. F. D. June 1.

ROHAULT DE FLEURY, CHARLES (1801–1875), architect. Born in Paris on July 23, he studied science at L'École Polytechnique, but in 1825 decided on architecture as a career, designed buildings in Paris, including the Museum of Natural History in 1830, and wrote *Manuel des lois du bâtiment* (1862). He also wrote on Christian archaeology. He died in Paris on Aug. 11.

ROHLMAN, HENRY P. (1876–1957), archbishop. Born in Appelhulsen, Westphalia, Germany, on Mar. 17, he studied at St. Lawrence College, Wisconsin, Columbia College, Dubuque, and the Grand seminary, Montreal, and was ordained in Montreal in 1901. He served as curate and pastor in Dubuque and Waterloo, with a period as business manager of Loras College in 1917–24, and in 1927 was consecrated bishop of Davenport, Iowa. He was appointed titular archbishop of Macra and coadjutor archbishop of Dubuque in 1944, and succeeded to that see in 1946. He resigned in 1955 and was appointed titular archbishop of Cotrada. He died in Dubuque, Iowa, on Sept. 13.

ROHRBACHER, RENÉ FRANÇOIS (1789–1856), historian. Born in Langatte, France, on Sept. 27, he studied at Sarrebourg and Phalsebourg, taught at the latter, entered the Nancy seminary, and was ordained in 1812. He did pastoral and missionary work, joined the Congregation of St. Peter, founded by Felicité and

Jean de La Mennais, in 1827, and taught its novices until 1835. He taught at the Nancy seminary, spent his last years in Paris, and died there on Jan. 17. He wrote several historical works, chief of which is the twenty-nine-volume *Histoire universelle de l'église catholique* (1842–49).

ROJAS, BL. SIMON DE (d. 1624). Born in Valladolid, Spain, he became a Trinitarian, served as superior of the order, became famous for his mission work, and was confessor to the court of Philip III and tutor to his children. He was beatified in 1766. F. D. Sept. 28.

ROJAS Y ZORRILLA, FRANCISCO DE (1607–1648?), dramatist. Born in Toledo, Spain, on Oct. 4, he probably studied at the university there, joined the army, and by 1632 was well known for his plays in verse. He created the *comedia de figurón*, in which his characters' most ridiculous aspects are presented in a play, and was widely imitated by French and Spanish playwrights. He received the Order of Santiago in 1644. Among his more than sixty pieces, his best known are *Del rey abajo ninguno*, *Entre bobos anda el juego* and *Casarse por vengarse*, on which Le Sage's *Gil Blas* is believed to have been based. He died in Madrid on Jan. 23.

ROKEWODE, JOHN GAGE (1786–1842), antiquarian. Born on Sept. 13, son of Sir Thomas Gage of Hengrave, he studied at Stonyhurst, was admitted to the bar, but never practiced, and devoted himself to the study of antiquities. He was director of the Society of Antiquaries from 1829 to 1842, became a member of the Royal Society, and wrote books and articles on Suffolk antiquities. He died in Lancashire, England, on Oct. 14.

ROLFUS, HERMANN (1821–1896), educator. Born in Freiburg, Germany, on May 24, he studied there and was ordained in 1844. He served as a parish priest, received a doctorate in theology from Freiburg in 1867, and was active in Catholic educational circles in Germany. With Adolf Pfister he edited *Real-Encyclopädie der Erziehungs- und Unterrichtswesens nach katholischen Principen* and *Süddeutsches katholisches Schulwochenblatt*. He died in Bühl, Germany, on Oct. 27.

ROLLE, RICHARD (1300?–1349?), mystic. Born in Thornton, England, he went to Oxford, left when he was nineteen, and became a hermit on the estate of a squire, John of Dalton, whose sons he had known at the university. Rolle lived as a contemplative, and often wrote for others in that area, and incurred the enmity of some of the clergy because he preached bitter attacks on those who failed to live up to their calling. He wrote the prose *De emendatione vitae* (*Form of Living*) for another recluse, Margaret Kirby of Ainderby, whom he directed, and also a commentary on the Psalms. He did a translation of the Psalms; another commentary on them (heavily indebted to Peter Lombard); the English poem, *Pricke of Conscience*, some 9600 lines of censure on contemporary failings, clerical abuses, and disregard of the sacramental nature of penance (its theology is based on that of Robert Grosseteste); and such ascetical writings as *De incendium amoris*, long popular in the realm of English mysticism. Some of his writings have been attributed, erroneously, to John Wyclif, but the latter has a distinct style, and was in rebellion against dogma, which Rolle was not. Rolle was widely venerated after his death at Hampole, England, on Sept. 29; the Cistercian nuns of the area wrote a service for a proposed feast on Jan. 20; the popular cult, never formally approved, did not lead to beatification.

ROLLIN, CHARLES (1661–1741), scholar. Born in Paris in Jan., he studied for the priesthood and was tonsured, but never ordained. He became professor at Collège de Plessis in 1687, at Collège Royal in 1688, and rector of the University of Paris in 1694. He revived the study of Greek and reformed the education system. He was appointed principal of Collège Beauvais in 1696, a position he held until his dismissal in 1722 for his opposition to the bull *Unigenitus*, and became a member of the Academy of Inscriptions in 1701. After his dismissal he devoted himself to writing until his death in Paris. Among his works were *Traité des études* (1726–31), the twelve-volume *Histoire ancienne* (1730–38), and the unfinished *Histoire romaine*.

ROLPH, THOMAS (1800–1858), physician. Born in England, he studied medicine, and practiced in Crutchedfriars, where he engaged in controversy with the Anglican rector over tithes. He went to Canada in 1832, where he served as emigration agent, but returned to England in 1839 and wrote several books on emigration. He died in Portsmouth, England, on Feb. 17.

ROMAEUS, BL. (d. 1380). A fellow pilgrim of Bl. Avertanus, he died near Lucca, Italy, of the plague a week after the latter. F. D. Feb. 25.

ROMANÇON, BL. PAUL (1805–1862), educator. Born in Thuret, France, on June 13, he became a Christian Brother in 1820 and was professed as Br. Benildus in 1821. He was in charge of the community and school at Billom, and in 1841 was sent to direct a new school and the community at Saugues, France, where he spent the rest of his life as an outstanding teacher. He was beatified in 1948. F. D. Aug. 13.

ROMANUS (9th century), pope. Born in Gallese, Italy, near Cività Castellana, he became cardinal of St. Peter ad Vincula, and pope in Aug. 897. He reigned only four months, recognized Lambert as emperor, annulled all Pope Stephen VI's acts regarding Formosus, and was driven from the papal throne in Nov. Where and when he died are not known.

ROMANUS, ST. (1st century), bishop and martyr. Said to have been a disciple of St. Peter, he was sent as bishop of Nepi, Tuscany, where he was put to death. F. D. Aug. 24.

ROMANUS, ST. (d. 258), martyr. Called Ostiarius (doorkeeper), he is said to have been a soldier beheaded in Rome the day before St. Laurence, who had instructed him in prison, was executed. F. D. Aug. 9.

ROMANUS, ST. (d. 297), martyr. *See* Hipparchus, St.

ROMANUS, ST. (d. 304), martyr. A native of Palestine, he was a deacon at Caesarea and at Antioch. Seen encouraging Christians to stand fast during the Diocletian persecution, he was tortured and strangled. Barula, a seven-year-old boy, is said to have been scourged and beheaded with him. F. D. Nov. 18.

ROMANUS, ST. (d. 385). He was a successful missioner among the pagans in the Gironde River region of France and died at Blaye. F. D. Nov. 24.

ROMANUS, ST. (d. 460?). At thirty-five he became a recluse in the Jura Mountains, France, but was soon joined by his brother, sister, and a large number of others. With St. Lupicinus he established the monasteries of Condat and Leuconne, and for their sister the convent of La Beaume. F. D. Feb. 28.

ROMANUS, ST. (d. 550?). A monk in a monastery near Monte Subiaco, Italy, he helped St. Benedict to establish his hermitage and brought him food. Legend says that he died in Auxerre, Gaul, after the Vandals had overrun Italy. F. D. May 22.

ROMANUS, ST. (d. 640?), bishop. He left the court of Clotaire II, became bishop of Rouen, France, about 630, erased the remnants of idolatry in his see, and was known for his work with prisoners condemned to death. F. D. Oct. 23.

ROMANUS. *See* Boris, St.

ROMANUS THE MELODIST, ST. (d. 540?). A Jew of Syrian descent, he became a deacon at Beirut, Syria, and a priest at Constantinople, where he is reputed to have composed 1000 hymns, of which some eighty are extant. F. D. Oct. 1.

ROMARIC, ST. (d. 653). A Merovingian nobleman at the court of Clotaire II, he was converted by St. Amatus, became a monk at Luxeuil, Gaul, and with St. Amatus founded on his estate at Habendum the monastery of Remiremont (named after him) in 620. In 623 he succeeded Amatus as abbot. In 653 he went to Metz to protest to Grimoald and his supporters against their plan to prevent Dagobert

from succeeding to the Austrasian throne. F. D. Dec. 8.

ROMBAULD. *See* Rumold, St.

ROMERO, JUAN (1559–1630), missioner. Born in Machena, Andalusia, Spain, he became a Jesuit in 1580, was sent to Peru in 1590, and was superior of the Tucuman missions in northern Argentina from 1593 to 1598. After a period in Rome as procurator, he returned to South America in 1610 and served as superior and rector of Jesuit colleges in Buenos Aires, Santiago del Estero, Argentina, and Santiago, Chile, and became first vice-provincial of Chile, where he died at Santiago on Mar. 31.

ROMOALDUS. *See* Modoald, St.

ROMUALD, ST. (950?–1027), founder. After a wasted youth in the ducal family of the Onesti of Ravenna, Italy, he witnessed his father kill a relative in a duel and retired in sorrow to a nearby monastery, where he angered a number of the monks because of his intense zeal. He then retired to a hermitage under the direction of Marinus; together, they influenced St. Peter Orsoleo, doge of Venice, and Romuald's father, Sergius, to give up the world and enter religious life. He wrote a commentary on the Psalms, suffered from scandalous lies, but persisted in his preaching and established a number of major monasteries. The most famous was at Camaldoli in Tuscany, set up in 1012, where he developed the rule of the new Camoldolese Benedictines. He died at Val di Castro, Italy, on June 19 and was canonized in 1595. St. Peter Damian wrote his biography. F. D. Feb. 7.

ROMULA, ST. (6th century). *See* Herunda, St.

ROMULUS, ST. (d. 90?), bishop and martyr. According to legend, he was a Roman converted by St. Peter, who appointed him first bishop of Fiesole, Italy, and a martyr there with Carissimus, Dulcissimus, and Crescentius during the Diocletian persecution. F. D. July 6.

ROMULUS, ST. (d. 112?), martyr. An official in the court of Trajan, he objected to the cruelty shown Christians and was seized and put to death. F. D. Sept. 5.

ROMULUS, ST. (d. 303), martyr. *See* Agapius, St.

ROMULUS, ST. (d. 304), martyr. *See* Donatus, St.

ROMULUS, ST. (d. 450?), bishop. *See* Conindrus, St.

ROMULUS, ST. (7th century). He was bishop of Genoa, Italy, in 641 and died sometime later at Matuziano; the town was later renamed St. Remo in his honor. F. D. Oct. 13.

RONALD, ST. (d. 1158). A chieftain in Orkney, Scotland, he built the cathedral of St. Magnus at Kirkwall, was slain by rebels, and was venerated as a martyr. F. D. Aug. 20.

RONAN. *See* Ruadan, St.

RONCI, BL. FRANCISCO (1223–1294). Born in Abri, Italy, he became a follower of St. Peter Celestine, and was with him at the Benedictine houses of Orfente and Morrone. In 1285 he became the first general of the Celestines and may have become a cardinal a month before his death in Oct. F. D. June 4.

RONSARD, PIERRE DE (1524–1585), poet. Born at the Château de la Poissonnière, near Vendôme, France, on Sept. 2 (or 11), he studied at Navarre College, Paris, and began a diplomatic career as page of Francis I's son, the duke of Orléans, and then of King James V of Scotland, where he lived for three years. He retired from court life in 1541 because of deafness and spent the next seven years in study at Collège de Coquerat. He became fascinated with poetry, led a conscious attempt to revolutionize French poetry, and with a group of young poets formed the *Plèiade*. He experimented with all classical forms except drama, became a master of the sonnet, wrote poems of love and nature, and was hailed as the greatest French lyric poet before the nineteenth century. He enriched the vocabulary, invented new meters, introduced harmony in French verse, and proscribed the hiatus. Ill the last ten years of his life, he spent those years at the priory of Saint-Cosme-en l'Isle, near Tours, France, where he died on Dec. 27. Outstanding among his works are *Les amours de Cassandre* (1550), *Odes* (1551–52), *Les hymnes* (1556), *Poèmes* (1560–73), *Discours des miseres de ce temps* (1560), *Remonstrance au peuple de France* (1563), and an unfinished epic, *La Franciade* (1572).

ROOTHAAN, JOHANN PHILIPP (1785–1853), theologian. Born in Amsterdam, Holland, on Nov. 23, he studied there under Jakob van Lennep, and in 1804 became a Jesuit in Dünaburg, White Russia, the only surviving Jesuit province. He taught there from 1806 to 1809, studied theology at Polotsk, and was ordained in 1812. He taught in Pusza, Orsa, and, when the Jesuits were expelled from Russia in 1820, in Brieg, Switzerland. He was appointed rector of the college of Turin, and in 1829 was elected twenty-first general of the Jesuits. He prepared a new edition of the *Exercises* of St. Ignatius, the widespread use of which he renewed in the Society, published a revised order of studies in 1832, laid special stress on home and foreign missions, and greatly increased the membership of the Society during his generalship. He died in Rome on May 8.

ROPER, MARGARET (1504–1544). Eldest daughter of St. Thomas More, she was born in London, well educated in classics and philosophy, married William Roper, an attorney, in 1521, and lived in her father's homes in the capital. She translated More's *Precatio domin-ica* as *A Devout Treatise upon the Paternoster*, visited her father when he was a prisoner in the Tower, agreed to the Oath of Succession and tried to persuade him to accept it, and was partner in a touching and warming correspondence with him. She was highly respected by Erasmus and other scholars.

E. E. REYNOLDS, *Margaret Roper* (New York, Kenedy, 1960).

ROPER, WILLIAM (1496?–1578), biographer. Son of John Roper, he studied law at Lincoln's Inn, became a member of Thomas More's household about 1518, and in 1521 married More's daughter Margaret. He became a Lutheran adherent about this time, was brought before Wolsey and censured, but returned to the Church. He was appointed prothonotary in 1524, succeeded to his father's estates, and was admitted to the bar in 1525. He was imprisoned for aiding a Catholic in 1542, served in parliament during the reigns of Henry VIII, Edward VI, and Mary, and was again charged with aiding Catholics in 1568 and 1569, imprisoned in the Tower, but released. He wrote *The Lyfe of Sir Thomas Moore, Knighte*, valuable as a monument in the history of English prose, but inaccurate in many details, since he wrote much of it from hearsay years after More's death in 1535 and was not present on many of the occasions described. He died in Canterbury on Jan. 4.

ROPERT, GULSTAN FRANCIS (1839–1903), bishop. Born in Kerfago, Morbihan, France, on Aug. 30, he joined the Society of the Sacred Hearts of Jesus and Mary, studied at its seminary in Paris, and was ordained in 1866. He did missionary work in the Hawaiian Islands, was appointed provincial of his Society in Hawaii in 1878, and was appointed titular bishop of Panopolis and vicar apostolic of Hawaii in 1892. He died in Honolulu on Jan. 4.

ROQUE, BL. PIERRE RENÉ (1758–1796), martyr. Born in Vannes, Brittany, he was ordained a Vincentian in 1782, served as professor of theology in his native town, was forced underground at the start of the French Revolution, and was eventually captured and guillotined in Vannes. He was beatified in 1934. F. D. Mar. 1.

ROQUE. *See* Roch, St.

ROSA, SALVATORE (1615–1673), painter. Born in Renella, Italy, on June 20, he was given lessons in drawing by an uncle and his father, who had studied under Spagnoletto, was sent to a college in Naples to study for the priesthood, but left to wander about southern Italy with a band of brigands sketching the area and people he encountered. On his father's death in 1632 he took up painting seriously to support his family, attracted the attention of Lanfranco and Falcone, who aided him, and in 1635 went to Rome, where he gained the patronage of Cardinal Brancaccio. About this time he gained a reputation for his witty, satirical poetry. He gained more attention with his painting, *Prometheus*, was invited to Florence in 1640 by the grand duke, worked for the Medici, but returned to Rome in 1649 and spent the rest of his life between Naples and Rome, where he died on Mar. 15. His work is noted for its vigor, grandeur of design, effective chiaroscuro, wild, desolate scenery, and pervasive air of melancholy. Among his masterpieces are *Conspiracy of Cataline*, *St. Paul in the Desert*, *Resurrection of Christ*, *Landscape with Figures*, *Shade of Samuel Appearing to Saul*, *Storm at Sea*, and self-portraits. He also executed several etchings. Among his satiric poems are *Painting, Babylon, Music, Poetry, War,* and *Envy*. He is also known as Renella or Arenella from his birthplace.

ROSALIA, ST. (d. 1160?). According to local tradition, she was born on Sicily and went at an early age to become an anchoress in a cave on Mt. Coschina; later she moved to a grotto on Mt. Pellegrino, near Palermo, where she died. F. D. Sept. 4 (also, July 15).

ROSATI, JOSEPH (1789–1843), bishop. Born in Sora, Naples, Italy, on Jan. 12, he studied at the diocesan seminary, entered the Congregation of the Mission (the Lazarists) in Rome in 1807, and was ordained in Rome in 1811. After working as a missionary in the Papal States until 1815, he went to the United States in 1816, taught theology at St. Thomas' seminary in Bardstown, Kentucky, and in 1818 went to Missouri with a group of missionaries and opened St. Mary's seminary at Perryville. In 1820 he became superior of his congregation in the United States, was appointed titular bishop of Tenagra and vicar apostolic of Mississippi and Alabama in 1822, and in 1823 was appointed coadjutor of Louisiana and the Floridas. When Louisiana was divided into the sees of New Orleans and St. Louis in 1826, he was instructed to occupy the New Orleans see, but in 1827, as he wished, he was made bishop of St. Louis (though he continued to administer New Orleans as well until 1830). He built St. Louis cathedral, was appointed apostolic delegate to negotiate an agreement between Haiti and the Holy See in 1842, and was appointed an assistant at the apostolic throne in 1843. He died in Rome on Sept. 25.

ROSCARROCK, NICHOLAS (1549?–1634), antiquarian. Born in Cornwall, England, tortured in the Tower for his religious beliefs during imprisonments between 1580 and 1599, he spent his last years in the service of Sir William Howard of Cumberland (later honored by Sir Walter Scott as "Belted Will"). He also wrote numerous dedicatory and religious poems.

ROSE, ST. (1234–1252). Born of poor parents in Viterbo, Italy, she began to preach on the streets there when but twelve, attacking the Ghibellines and denouncing Emperor Frederick II, who had been harassing the pope. After two years the emperor's supporters demanded her death, but she was banished from the city and went with her parents to Soriano. She died in Viterbo, and was canonized in 1457. F. D. Sept. 4.

ROSE OF LIMA, ST. (1586–1617). Born of Spanish parents in Lima, Peru, she was christened Isabella de Santa Maria de Flores and took, from her earliest childhood, St. Catherine of Siena as her model, imitating her life in every detail. She was noted for her beauty and her parents wished her to marry, but she refused, became a Dominican tertiary, and lived the life of a recluse in a small shack in her garden, practicing extreme mortification and penance. She experienced such extraordinary mystical gifts and visions that a commission of priests and doctors examined her, and pronounced her experiences supernatural. As the rumors of her holiness spread the garden became the spiritual goal of the city. When earthquakes struck near Lima, her prayers were credited with averting a like catastrophe in the city. In 1614, however, her austerities so affected her health that she accepted the offer of Don Gonzalo de Massa, a government official, to live in his home. She died there on Aug. 24. She was canonized in 1671, the first American born saint, and is patron of the New World. F. D. Aug. 30.

SHEILA KAYE-SMITH, *Quartet in Heaven* (Garden City, N.Y., Image Books, 1962).

ROSECRANS, SYLVESTER HORTON (1827–1878), bishop. Born in Homer, Ohio, on Feb. 5, he studied at Kenyon, became a convert in 1845, transferred to Fordham, studied at Mt. St. Mary of the West, Cincinnati, and the Propaganda in Rome, and was ordained in 1852. He taught at Mt. St. Mary seminary, became associate editor of the *Catholic Telegraph*, president of Mt. St. Mary of the West College in 1859, was consecrated auxiliary of Cincinnati and titular bishop of Pompeiopolis in 1862, and in 1868 became first bishop of the diocese of Columbus, Ohio. He founded St. Aloysius seminary in Columbus, and died there on Oct. 21.

ROSECRANS, WILLIAM STARKE (1819–1898), general. Born in Kingston, Ohio, on Sept. 6, he graduated from West Point in 1842, served briefly in the engineers' corps, and returned to teach at West Point in 1843–47. He became a convert in 1845. He resigned from the army in 1854, engaged in private enterprises until the outbreak of the Civil War, became a volunteer aide-de-camp to Gen. McClellan, rose to brigadier general of regulars, commanded successfully in various departments and battles, but in 1863 was decisively defeated at the battle of Chickamauga and soon after was relieved of all command. He resigned from the army in 1867, was minister to Mexico in 1868–69, and became involved in railroad interests and business there and in California from 1869 to 1881. He served in Congress from 1881 to 1885 as representative from California, was register of the federal treasury from 1885 to 1893, and was restored to the rank of brigadier general on the retired list by an act of Congress in 1889. He died near Redondo, California, on Mar. 11.

ROSENDO. *See* Rudesind, St.

ROSIUS, ST. (5th century), bishop. *See* Priscus, St.

ROSKOVÁNYI, AUGUST (1807–1892), bishop. Born in Szenna, Ung, Hungary, on Dec. 7, he studied at the Piarist college in Kis-Szeben, the Pest seminary, and the Augustineum in Vienna. He was ordained in 1831, engaged in pastoral activities, became a canon at Eger in 1836, received the abbey of Saár in 1839, became prefect of studies at Eger, and rector of the seminary in 1841. He was appointed auxiliary bishop in 1847, capitular vicar in 1850, bishop of Waitzen in 1851, and of Neutra in 1859. Among his theological treatises are the fourteen-volume *Monumenta catholica* (1847), seven-volume *Coelibatus et breviarium* (1867), sixteen-volume *Romanus pontifex tamquam primas ecclesiae* (1867) and the twelve-volume *Beata Virgo Maria in suo conceptu immaculata* (1873–74). He died on Feb. 24.

ROSMADEC, SEBASTIEN DE (17th century). He was bishop of Vannes at the time of the apparition of St. Anne of Yves Nicolazic, at Auray, France, and approved the reconstruction of the shrine there which had first been erected in the seventh century.

ROSMINI-SERBATI, ANTONIO (1797–1855), philosopher. Born in Rovereto, Austrian Tyrol, on Mar. 24, he was ordained in 1821, and received his doctorate in theology at Padua in 1822. In 1828, after a meeting with Abbé John Loewenbruck, he founded the Institute of Charity (the Rosminians), a religious society for training priests and teachers, at Monte Calvario near Domodossola. Encouraged by the pope, he began expounding his philosophical theories in opposition to the sensationalistic philosophy of the time and in 1829 published his *Nuovo saggio sull' origine delle idee* (*Origin of Ideas*). In 1835 several English missions were turned over to him by the pope; in 1838 the institute's constitutions were approved by Pope Gregory XVI and Rosmini was appointed provost general for life. His *Trattato della coscienza morale* (1839) touched off a controversy with the Jesuits, which Gregory XVI

quieted by enjoining silence on the disputants in 1843. He acted as envoy for Piedmont to enlist the pope's support of King Charles Albert against the Austrians in 1848, was one of those appointed by Pius IX to consider the definition of the dogma of the Immaculate Conception, and accompanied the pope into exile in Gaeta at the outbreak of the revolution in Rome. In 1849 his *Costituzione secondo la giustizia sociale* and *Cinque piaghe della santa chiesa* (both 1848) were condemned and placed on the Index. He submitted and retired to Stresa. When further attacks were launched on his works Pope Pius IX, in 1854, ordered all his works to be examined by the Index, which declared they could be read; whereupon the pope enjoined silence on all parties. Rosmini died the following year in Stresa, Italy, on July 1. In 1876 his unfinished and posthumously published *Teosofia* caused the controversy to flare up again, and it intensified after the death of Pius IX in 1878. In 1887 a decree of the Inquisition condemned forty propositions (from his teaching in ontology, natural philosophy, the soul, the Trinity, the Eucharist, the supernatural order, and the beatific vision), a condemnation Pope Leo XIII approved in 1889.

ROSS, JOHN ELLIOT (1884–1946), author. Born in Baltimore, Maryland, he studied at Loyola there, and at George Washington and Catholic universities. He became a Paulist, was ordained in 1912, received his doctorate in theology in Rome, and was stationed in Chicago. After two years he was chaplain of Catholic students at the University of Texas (1914–23), lecturing widely in the area. After a year of teaching at Catholic University he became chaplain of Catholic students at Columbia (1925–29), at Iowa (1929), and at Illinois (1930–31); he also served on the faculty of the last two institutions. Thereafter he devoted much of his time and effort to the work of the National Council of Christians and Jews. He wrote *Consumers and Wage Earners* (1912), *Co-operative Plenty*, *The Right to Work*, *Christian Ethics*, *Indulgences as a Social Factor in the Middle Ages*, *How Catholics See Protestants* (1928), collections of sermons, ethical commentaries, and a work on Newman, *Faith That Conquers Fear*. He was joint author of *The Religions of Democracy*. He died in New York City on Sept. 18.

ROSSELINO, ANTONIO. *See* Gambarelli, Antonio.

ROSSELLI, COSIMO (1439–1507), painter. Born in Florence, Italy, he became noted for his frescoes and was one of the artists commissioned by Pope Sixtus IV to decorate the Sistine Chapel. Among his pupils were Fra Bartolommeo and Piero di Cosimo. Among his outstanding works are *Last Supper* in the Sistine Chapel, *Miracle-Working Chalice* in Sant' Ambrogio, Florence, *Madonna and Child*, *Madonna in Adoration*, and *Coronation of the Virgin*. He died in Florence.

ROSSELLO, ST. JOSEPHA (1811–1880), foundress. Born in Albisola Marina, Italy, daughter of a potter, she became a Franciscan tertiary at sixteen, a servant at nineteen, and in 1837 with three companions founded the Daughters of Our Lady of Pity to teach poor children. She became superior of the community in 1840 and expanded its aims to care for wayward women. At her death the community had sixty-eight convents; it has since spread to South America. She was canonized in 1949. F. D. Dec. 7.

ROSSI, BERNARDO (1687–1775), theologian. Born in Cividale del Friuli, Italy, on Jan. 8, he became a Dominican in 1704, studied at Florence and Venice, where he taught for fifteen years, served as vicar general of his province twice, and was a member of the Venetian embassy to Louis XV in 1722. He gave up teaching in 1730 to devote himself to writing, prepared a new, twenty-four-volume edition of the works of St. Thomas Aquinas (1745–60), and wrote numerous dissertations on the saint and his writings, and *De peccato originali* (1757). He died in Venice, Italy, on Feb. 2.

ROSSI, CESARE DE. *See* Lawrence of Brindisi, St.

ROSSI, ST. GIOVANNI BATTISTA (1698–1764). Born in Voltaggio, near Genoa, Italy, he studied at Rome, was ordained in 1721, and served there, devoted to work in the hospitals and in St. Galla, a refuge for the poor, preaching and teaching homeless wanderers, marketmen, and cattle drovers. In 1731 he became a curate at the church of Santa Maria near the Aventine, where he gained a great reputation as confessor and preacher. He was canonized in 1881. F. D. May 23.

ROSSI, GIOVANNI BATTISTA DE (1822–1894), archaeologist. Born in Rome, Italy, on Feb. 23, he studied philosophy at the Collegio Romano and law at the Sapienza, where he took his doctor's degree in 1844. He catalogued many manuscripts in the Vatican Library, toured the catacombs with Fr. Marchi, S.J., and from 1844 to 1879 he made detailed tours of Europe, studying literature and culture, museums and libraries, monuments and scholarship at first hand. He wrote widely on inscriptions and documents; edited the monthly *Bulletino di archaeologia cristiana*; prepared a nine-volume edition of the epigraphist, Bartolommeo Borghesi; and wrote the four-volume *La Rome sotteranea cristiana*, with plates, and with Louis Duchesne the *Martyrologium Hieronymianum*. De Rossi's brother Michele Stefano, a geologist, assisted him in his work on

and prepared detailed plans of the Roman catacombs. Giovanni died in Rome on Sept. 20.

ROSSI, PELLEGRINO (1787–1848), diplomat. Born in Carrari, Italy, on July 13, he studied at Pavia and Bologna, where he practiced law. He was an adherent of Italian unity, joined the Carbonari, was appointed commissioner general of the central Italian provinces by Murat, king of Naples, but was forced to flee to France when Murat was defeated at Tolentino in 1815, and then to Geneva. Despite his Catholicism, he became professor of law at the university in 1819, was elected to the Geneva cantonal council, and drew up a constitution approved by the Swiss federal diet in 1832, but which was rejected by the communes. In 1833 he was appointed to the chair of political economy at the Collège de France, and was made a peer of France in 1839 and an officer of the Legion of Honor in 1841. He entered the diplomatic service in 1845, became ambassador to the Vatican, withdrew to private life when Louis Philippe fell in the revolution of 1848, was appointed minister of justice by the pope in the Fabbri ministry, and when the latter fell was appointed president of the pope's first constitutional government. A moderate, in accord with Pope Pius IX's ideas of government, he was hated by both conservatives and radicals and was assassinated in Rome on Nov. 15 while on his way to present his proposals to the legislative assembly. He wrote *Cours d'économie politique*, *Traité de droit pénal*, and collaborated on *Annales de législation et d'économie politique*.

ROSSI, RAFFAELE CARLO (1876–1948), cardinal. Born in Pisa, Italy, on Oct. 28, he became a Carmelite at twenty, was ordained in 1901, and was bishop of Volterra in 1920–23. He was secretary of the Consistorial Congregation from 1923 on, worked on the concordat with Italy in 1926, held other papal offices, and in 1930 was created a cardinal and titular bishop of Thessalonica. He died in Bassano del Grappa, Italy, on Sept. 17.

ROSSINI, GIOACCHINO ANTONIO (1792–1868), composer. Born in Pesaro, Italy, on Feb. 29, he had learned piano and voice by the age of ten, played horn in the theater in Bologna with his father, a trumpeter, and also earned a living as an accompanist. His first operas, in one or two acts, were produced at Venice and Bologna in 1810–12; most of them were imitative, as was *Tancredi* (1813), his first success. Best known are his *Barber of Seville* (1816), *Otello*, tragic in its original form but quickly revised to have a happy ending, *Cinderella* (1817), *Ermione* (1819), and *Zelmira* (1821). He became a witty and much sought-after man about town, climaxing a notorious early career by stealing the mistress of Barbaja, impressario of the Naples opera, for whom he worked. This was Isabella Colbran, who sang in his productions, was the object of a cantata written in 1819, and to whom he was married by the archbishop of Bologna in 1822. He then went to Vienna, composed cantatas for Prince Metternich, *Semiramide* (1823) at Venice, a cantata in London (1824) for the death of Lord Byron, and *The Journey to Rheims* (1825) and others while in Paris. While there he was director of the Théâtre Italien, was embroiled in long lawsuits over copyright to his own work, held various imperial posts, and enjoyed a large income. *William Tell*, his thirty-eighth opera, was produced in 1829. His private life was still notorious; his new mistress was Olympe Pélissier, acquired in 1832; he married her fifteen years later, two years after the death of his first wife. In his last years he suffered from despondency, to the point of mental collapse, recovered, recast earlier work, then lapsed into idleness. Some piano compositions followed, before his death in Passy, France, on Nov. 13.

ROSSOW, HELENA VON. *See* Hroswitha.

ROSTOCK, SEBASTIAN VON (1607–1671), bishop. Born in Grottkau, Silesia, on Aug. 24, he studied at Neisse and Olmütz, was ordained in 1633, and did pastoral work in Neisse. He was deported to Stettin when the Swiss captured the city, released, ennobled by the emperor, and returned to Neisse as pastor. In 1649 he was transferred to Breslau, was appointed vicar general in 1653, was instrumental in returning more than 600 churches to Catholic hands under the terms of the peace of Westphalia, devoted himself to reforming the clergy and rebuilding the church in his area, and became bishop of Breslau, Germany, in 1664. He died there on June 9.

ROSULA, ST. (d. 258?), martyr. *See* Crescentian, St.

ROSWEYDE, HÉRIBERT (1569–1629), scholar. Born in Utrecht, Flanders, on Jan. 21, he became a Jesuit in 1588, taught philosophy at Douai, and did considerable research in France and Flanders on church history and the lives of the saints. He began to copy original hagiographical texts and this project developed into the *Acta sanctorum* of the Bollandists which was announced in 1607; Cardinal Bellarmine estimated that it would take 200 years to complete; the Benedictine, Antony de Winghe, and others made a great amount of source material available to him. He was relieved of none of his regular tasks (as his followers were), but spent much time on the publication of translations and editions that he uncovered, including biographies of the desert fathers (1615) and a history of the Church. His notes and library were turned over to Fr. John van Bolland after his death in Antwerp, Flanders, on Oct. 5.

ROSWINDA, BL. (8th century). *See* Einhildis, St.

ROSWITHA. *See* Hroswitha.

ROTH, HEINRICH (1620–1668), missioner. Born in Augsburg, Germany, on Dec. 18, he became a Jesuit in 1639, was assigned to the Ethiopian mission, acted as Portuguese interpreter near Goa, was sent as an ambassador to one of the native princes, established a mission at Agra, and became an authority on Indian religions and customs. In 1662 he used the overland route through Kabul to return to Europe to seek additional missionaries, returned in 1664, and remained in Agra, India, until his death there on June 20. He pioneered in the study of Sanskrit, wrote a Sanskrit grammar, a description of the Sanskrit alphabet, and accounts of travel and conditions in the Far East.

ROTHE, DAVID (1573–1650), bishop. Born in Kilkenny, Ireland, he studied at Douai and Salamanca, where he received his doctorate in law, was ordained in 1600, taught theology in Rome from 1601 to 1609, and was Archbishop Lombard's secretary. He was appointed viceprimate of Armagh, Ireland, and prothonotary apostolic in 1609, held synods in 1614 and 1618, and became bishop of Ossory in 1618. He joined the Confederates in 1642, welcomed the papal nuncio, Giovanni Rinuccini, when he arrived in 1645, but in 1648 denounced the validity of the nuncio's censures and supported the action of the supreme council. He was driven from Ossory by Cromwell's supporters in 1650, but was allowed to return and died there on Apr. 20.

ROTRUDIS, ST. (d. 869?). She is believed to have been a sister, or daughter, of Charlemagne, and was buried at the Benedictine abbey of St. Bertin in St. Omer, France. F. D. June 22.

ROUALT, GEORGES (1871–1958), artist. Born in Paris on May 27, he had little formal schooling, was apprenticed to a stained-glass craftsman (the effects are obvious in his later paintings), and later studied at the Beaux-Arts School under Gustave Moreau. He worked slowly, sold his first canvas when he was past forty, would not sign others until they had rested for fifty years, and once destroyed 300 canvases with which he was dissatisfied. He was noted for heads of clowns, satiric sketches of judges, angry commentaries on the falseness of society, and particularly sad faces of Christ. He became a convert in mid-life and died in Paris on Feb. 13.

ROUIN. *See* Rodingus, St.

ROULEAU, RAYMOND MARIE (1866–1931), cardinal. Born in Isle Verte, Quebec, on Apr. 6, he studied at the Rimouski seminary, and the Dominican college in Corbara, Corsica. He became a Dominican in 1886, was ordained in 1892, and served as master of novices at St. Hyacinthe, Quebec, in 1894, as prior in Ottawa, in 1900, and as provincial of Canada in 1919. He was consecrated bishop of Valleyfield in 1923, became archbishop of Quebec in 1926, and was named a cardinal in 1927. He died in Quebec on May 31.

ROUQUETTE, ADRIEN (1813–1887), missioner. Born in New Orleans, Louisiana, he studied law and literature in Paris, Nantes, and Rennes, became editor of *Le Propagateur Catholique* in New Orleans in 1842, was ordained in 1845, and engaged in pastoral activities in New Orleans. In 1859 he became a missioner to the Choctaw Indians and spent the rest of his life ministering to them.

ROURE, MARIE DE, DUCHESSE D'AIGUILLON (1604–1675). Marie de Vignerot de Pontcourlay married Antoine de Roure, marquis de Combalet, in 1620, and, when he was killed in battle two years later, entered the Carmelite convent in Paris. When her uncle, Richelieu, became premier to Louis XIII she was recalled and placed in the service of Marie de' Medici and in charge of the cardinal's charities. She established La Salpêtrière, the first general hospital in Paris, and the Collège des Bon Enfants; paid the passage of the first missionary bishops to China and of the Jesuits and Ursulines to Canada; and contributed heavily to the work of St. Vincent de Paul. After her uncle's death she published his works, completed the Sorbonne, and established the Hôtel Richelieu (now the Bibliothèque National). She also was patroness of Corneille (who dedicated *Le Cid* to her), Scarron, Scudéry, Voiture, and Molière.

ROUSSEAU, JEAN BAPTISTE (1670–1741), poet. Born in Paris on Apr. 16, son of a shoemaker, he studied at Collège Louis le Grand, wrote his first play, *Le Café*, in 1694, and became noted for his odes, epigrams, and satires which made him many enemies. He became secretary to Marshal Tallard, French ambassador to London, about 1698, was admitted to the Academy of Inscriptions in 1700, and in 1710 was accused of libel and banished for life for his *Couplets infâmes*, licentious satires against La Motte and Saurin, in 1712. He spent the rest of his life in Switzerland, Austria, and Belgium, vainly seeking to have the court's decision rescinded, and died in La Genette, near Brussels, on May 17.

ROUTHIER, ADOLPHE (1839–1920), judge. Born in St. Placide, Quebec, Canada, on May 8, he studied at Laval, was admitted to the bar in 1861, taught at Laval, was judge of the superior court of Lower Canada, in 1873–1904, and chief justice in 1904–6, and president of the court of admiralty. He was knighted in 1911, honored by Popes Pius IX and Leo XIII, and wrote prose and poetry,

including the national anthem, *O Canada*, as Jean Picquefort. He died in St. Irénée, Quebec, on June 19.

ROUXEL, GUSTAVE AUGUSTIN (1840–1908), bishop. Born in Redon, France, on Feb. 2, he studied at the Eudist college there, the Rennes seminary, went to the United States and finished his studies at the New Orleans diocesan seminary, and was ordained there in 1868. He did pastoral and missionary work in the diocese, was appointed vicar general in 1878, was administrator in 1887–88, and in 1899 was appointed titular bishop of Curium and auxiliary of New Orleans. He administered the see while it was vacant in 1905–6, and died in New Orleans, Louisiana, on Mar. 17.

ROVEZZANO, BENEDETTO DA. *See* Gratini, Benedetto.

ROWLANDS, RICHARD. *See* Verstegan, Richard.

ROWSHAM, STEPHEN (d. 1587), martyr. Born in Oxfordshire, England, he studied at Oxford, became an Anglican minister about 1578, was a convert in 1581, studied at Rheims, and was ordained in 1582. He was sent on the English mission at once, captured almost immediately, and imprisoned until 1585 when he was banished from England. He returned the following year, was captured in Gloucestershire, and executed there in Mar.

ROY, CAMILLE JOSEPH (1870–1943), author. Born in Berthier-en-bas, Quebec, on Oct. 22, sixteenth of twenty children, he studied in the seminary there, received his doctorate from Laval, and did further work at L'Institut Catholique and the Sorbonne, Paris. He taught at the seminary from 1892 to 1898, was ordained in 1894, became professor of French literature at Laval in 1918 and of Canadian literature in 1927, and served four terms as rector. Pope Pius XI made him a monsignor in 1925. As a lecturer and writer he opposed the romantic and symbolist schools; he also worked for the preservation of the French language in Canada, and was a co-founder of the Société du Parler Français. His writings include: *Essais sur la littérature canadienne* (1907), *Nos origines littéraires*, *Études et croquis*, and an estimate of French literature from Mme. de Staël to Émile Faguet, one of his teachers in Paris. He lectured widely in Canada and France, received honorary degrees from Ottawa and Toronto and the gold medal of the French Academy in 1925, was made an officer of the Legion of Honor, and was a fellow of the Royal Society of Canada (and its president in 1928–29). He died in Quebec on June 24.

ROY, PERCY ALBERT (1889–1949), educator. Born in New Orleans, Louisiana, on Jan. 8, he studied at Immaculate Conception College, Woodstock, and St. Louis, taught in Louisiana schools, and was president of Loyola of the South in 1939–45. He then became pastor of St. Ann's, West Palm Beach, Florida, where he died on July 1.

ROYE, BL. FRANÇOIS DE (d. 1572), martyr. Born in Brussels, Belgium, he became a Franciscan at Gorkum, Holland, was ordained there, and soon after was seized by a group of Calvinists, and tortured and hanged at Briel, Holland. He was beatified in 1867. F. D. July 9.

ROYER-COLLARD, PIERRE PAUL (1763–1845), philosopher. Born in Sompuis, Marne, France, on June 21, he studied at Chaumont, became a lawyer in Paris, and although sympathetic to the French Revolution withdrew to La Marne in 1793. In 1797 he was a member of the council of 500, where he demanded freedom for Catholicism in France, became a royalist sympathizer secretly working for the restoration of the Bourbons, and retired from public life during the consulate to devote himself to philosophy. He was appointed to the chair of philosophy in the Sorbonne in 1811 and taught there until 1815, when he returned to public life as a member of the chamber of deputies almost continuously until 1839. He was elected president of the commission of public instruction in 1815, was admitted to the French Academy in 1827, and in 1828 was elected president of the chamber of deputies. He presented the address of 221 deputies to Charles X in 1830 protesting the king's arbitrary actions, and resigned from the chamber in 1842 to spend his last years in retirement. He died in Châteauvieux on Sept. 4. In philosophy he opposed the eighteenth-century sensationalism of Condillac, was instrumental in introducing the teaching of Thomas Reid into France, and was the founder and leader of the Doctrinaires. Among his followers were Cousin, Guizot, Remusot, and Jouffroy.

ROYO, BL. JOACHIM (d. 1747), martyr. Born in Asco, Catalonia, Spain, he became a Dominican in 1697, was sent to the China missions in 1712 to work with Bl. Pedro Sanz, was ordained, and became vicar apostolic of Fu-kien in 1730. He was captured in 1746 and strangled in prison. He was beatified in 1893. F. D. May 26.

RUADAN, ST. (5th century), bishop. He is said to have been consecrated in Ireland by St. Patrick and to have been a missioner in Cornwall and Brittany. The name is also spelled Rodan, Ronan, Ruman, and Rumon. F. D. June 1.

RUADAN, ST. (d. 584?). Born in Leinster, Ireland, he was a disciple of St. Finian and founded the monastery of Lothran, Tipperary, where he directed 150 monks. He is also called Rodan. F. D. Apr. 15.

RUBENS, PETER PAUL (1577–1640), painter. Born in Siegen, Westphalia, Germany, on June 29, he accompanied his mother to Antwerp when his father died in 1588, was educated there, and became a page in the household of the Countess van Labaing at Audenarde. He then studied art under Tobias Verhaecht (or vander Haegt), and from 1592 to 1596 worked under Adam van Noort. After further study under Otto Vaenius (or van Veen), he was named master by the Antwerp guild of painters in 1598. He joined the household of Duke Vincenzo Gonzaga of Mantua in Italy in 1600, spent the next eight years in Mantua and Rome (with a year, 1603, in Madrid), and during this period executed several of his masterpieces—all showing Italian influence, but typically Rubens—among them, *Baptism of Christ* for the Jesuits in Mantua, *Transfiguration, Circumcision* at Genoa's St. Ambrogio, three altarpieces for Santa Croce in Gerusalemme, and *Virgin in a Glory of Angels* for Santa Maria in Valicella, Rome. He returned to Antwerp in 1608 on his mother's death, built a house which he lavishly decorated, was named painter-in-ordinary to Archduke Albrecht and Infanta Isabella, regents of the Netherlands, in 1609, and married Isabella Brant later the same year. In this period he painted *Adoration of the Magi* for the municipality, *Raising of the Cross* (1611) for St. Walpurgis church, and in 1614 *Descent from the Cross*, and thirty-nine ceiling panels for St. Charles's church in Antwerp, which was destroyed by fire in 1718. In 1622 he was invited to Paris to decorate the Luxembourg by Marie de' Medici, and did a series of twenty-four pictures of her life which his assistants executed and which he finished in 1625, and *The Assumption of the Blessed Virgin* for the Antwerp cathedral in 1626. On the death of Albrecht and the termination of the truce between Spain and the Netherlands in 1621, Infanta Isabella entrusted Rubens with several diplomatic missions. In 1628 he went to Madrid, met Velásquez, copied Titian's masterpieces (later revealing their influence on his own work), and painted the royal family and five portraits of Philip IV, who knighted him. He went from there to England on the same mission which he successfully concluded, was knighted by King Charles I in 1630, prepared designs for the Whitehall banquet hall ceiling, and painted *Blessings of Peace*. He returned to Antwerp in 1630, married Helena Fourment (his first wife had died in 1626), and was named court painter by the new governor, Archduke Ferdinand. His paintings are characterized by their vigor of composition, technical skill, magnificent coloring and lighting, and fine decorative sense. He also did hundreds of drawings. Some of his greatest works are *Massacre of the Innocents, Nativity, Descent of the Holy Ghost, Conversion of Saul, Ma-*

donna Surrounded by Children, The Way to Golgotha, Crucifixion of Peter, Perseus and Andromeda, Rape of the Sabines, Battle of the Amazons, Venus in the Smithy of Vulcan, Triumph of Henry IV, Return from Work, Kirmess, and *Judgment of Paris.* He died in Antwerp, Flanders, on May 30.

RUDERICUS, ST. (d. 857), martyr. A priest at Cabra, Spain, he was severely beaten by his brothers, one of whom, a Moslem, announced that the insensible man had renounced Christianity. When he regained his senses, Rudericus fled, was caught and imprisoned as an apostate, and later beheaded. He is also called Roderic. F. D. Mar. 13.

RÜDESHEIM, RUDOLF VON. *See* Rudolf of Rüdesheim.

RUDESIND, ST. (907–977), bishop. Born of a noble Spanish family, he was publicly chosen bishop of Dumium at eighteen and, when his wastrel brother Sisnand, bishop of Compostella, was imprisoned for neglect of duty, he took over that see as well. He led a victorious army against the Norsemen at home and the Moors in Portugal during the king's absence, then was deposed by his brother, who had broken out of prison, and retired to a monastery. He built several others under the Benedictine rule, became abbot at Celanova, and was canonized in 1195. He is also called Rosendo. F. D. Mar. 1.

RUDOLF II (1552–1612), emperor. Son of Emperor Maximilian II and Marie, daughter of Emperor Charles V, he was born in Vienna on July 18, was educated in Spain, was crowned king of Hungary in 1572, of Bohemia in 1575, and succeeded his father as emperor in 1576. He was intensely devoted to the Church, but showed little ability to rule. A revolt in Hungary in 1604 was settled by the peace of Vienna in 1606, negotiated by his brother Matthias after the Hapsburg family had declared Rudolf incapable of ruling. Matthias forced Rudolf to let him assume the rule of Austria, Hungary, and Moravia in 1608. When revolution broke out in Bohemia, Rudolf was forced to grant religious freedom to the Protestant nobles there by the *Majestätsbrief* of 1609, and in 1611 to grant the throne of Bohemia to Matthias. He was a collector of art, greatly interested in alchemy, chemistry, astronomy and astrology, and patronized Tycho Brahe and Kepler. Rudolf died in Prague, Bohemia, on Jan. 20.

RUDOLF I (1218–1291), emperor. Son of Count Albert IV of Hapsburg and Countess Hedwig of Kiburg, Rudolf of Hapsburg was born in Limburg, Belgium, on May 1, and inherited the family possessions on the death of his father in 1239. He supported Emperor Frederick II and Conrad IV in their struggles with the papacy and was excommunicated by

Pope Innocent IV in 1254. When the Hohenstaufen fell he expanded his holdings, became the most powerful ruler in Germany, and in 1273 was elected emperor and German king over the opposition of King Ottacar II of Bohemia. He won the support of Pope Gregory X when he renounced his claims to papal territory and agreed to lead a crusade, and in 1276 launched a war against Ottacar which ended with the latter's death in battle in 1278 and gave him dominion over Ottacar's Austrian holdings. He inaugurated a period of peace, encouraged commerce, strengthened the central government, entered into a series of agreements with the princes and cities, and established the Hapsburg dynasty by investing his sons Albert and Rudolf with the duchies of Austria and Styria in 1282. He was successful in his disputes with Count Philip I of Burgundy in 1281, Archbishop Siegfried, metropolitan of Cologne (whose defeat by the duke of Brabant in 1288 ended his ambitions), Duke Otto IV of Upper Burgundy in 1289, and the house of Wettin in 1289, but failed in his attempt in 1291 to have his son elected king of the Germans. He died in Speyer, Germany, on July 15.

RUDOLF, ST. (d. 1066?). A Benedictine monk at Fontavellana, Italy, under St. Peter Damian, he became bishop of Gubbio in 1061. F. D. Oct. 17.

RUDOLF VON EMS (13th century), poet. A German in the service of the counts of Montfort, he was a friend of King Conräd IV, whom he accompanied to Italy about 1254, and is known for his narrative poetry, especially *Der gute Gerhard, Barlaam und Josaphat, Alexander,* and *Welchronik.*

RUDOLF OF FULDA (d. 862), historian. He became a Benedictine at Fulda, where he studied under Rabanus Maurus, was a member of the court of Louis the Pious, probably accompanied Rabanus to Mainz when he was made archbishop, and returned in his old age to Fulda, Germany, where he died in Mar. He continued Einhard's *Annales Fuldenses* from 838 to 862, wrote lives of St. Lioba and Rabanus Maurus, and *Miracula sanctorum in Fuldenses.*

RUDOLF OF RÜDESHEIM (1402?–1482), bishop. Born in Rüdesheim, Germany, he studied at Heidelberg and in Italy, where he received his doctorate in ecclesiastical law, became auditor of the rota, and served on diplomatic missions for Popes Pius II and Paul II and Emperor Frederick III. He served as papal legate to Bohemia, and effectively opposed the Hussite king, George of Podiebrad. He was appointed bishop of Lavant, Carinthia, in 1463 and was transferred to Breslau, Silesia, in 1468. He redeemed mortgaged church property and held two synods to seek to remove prevalent

abuses, and helped negotiate the peace of
Olmütz in 1479. He died in Breslau, Germany,
in Mar.

RUECKERS, HANS (d. 1640). A native of
Amsterdam, Holland, he was a member of the
Guild of St. Luke there and noted as an organ
builder. He built the predecessor of the pianoforte, a spinet with two keyboards, and founded
a firm of piano manufacturers which later
moved to Brussels.

RUFFI, ST. PETER CAMBIAN DE (d.
1365), martyr. A Dominican inquisitor, he was
sent to Piedmont and Lombardy in 1351 to
check the Waldensian heretics in Italy. They
waylaid and killed him. His cult was approved
in 1856. F. D. Feb. 2.

RUFFINI, PAOLO (1765–1822), mathematician. Born in Valentano, Italy, on Sept. 3, he
took degrees in medicine and mathematics at
Modena, where he received his medical degree.
He was appointed professor of analysis there
when twenty-three, of mathematics in 1791, a
member of the legislature in Milan in 1796, but
lost his university position when he refused to
take the republican oath imposed by the invading French. He was reinstated in 1799, became
professor of mathematics at a military school
in 1806 when Modena lost its rank as a university, and in 1814 returned, on its restoration, as rector and professor. He died at Modena, Italy, on May 10. He wrote treatises on
the impossibility of solving the quintic equation algebraically and the impossibility of the
quadrature of the circle, *Memoria sul tifo
contagioso, Dell' immortalitá dell' anima*, and
anticipated Horner's method in equations by
some fifteen years.

RUFILLUS, ST. (d. 382). He is said to have
been the first bishop of Forlimpopoli, in Emilia,
Italy. F. D. July 18.

RUFINA, ST. (d. 257?), martyr. According to
legend, she was the daughter of Asterius, a
Roman senator, and sister of St. Secunda.
When their fiancés apostatized during the persecution of Valerian, the two girls fled, but
were caught, tortured, and beheaded when
they refused to deny their faith. F. D. July
10.

RUFINA, ST. (d. 270?), martyr. *See* Theodotus, St.

RUFINA, ST. (d. 287?), martyr. *See* Justa, St.

RUFINUS, ST. (d. 250?), martyr. *See* Macarius, St.

RUFINUS, ST. (d. 287?), martyr. He and St.
Valerius were missioners in Gaul who were tor-
tured and beheaded at Soissons during the
Diocletian persecution. F. D. June 14.

RUFINUS, ST. (5th century). He was bishop
of Capua, Italy. F. D. Aug. 26.

RUFINUS, ST. (d. 675), martyr. He and his
brother Wulfhade were put to death by their
pagan father, the king of Mercia, England,

when he learned they had been baptized. F. D.
July 24.

RUFINUS OF AQUILEIA (345?–410?).
Born near Aquileia, Italy, of Christian parents,
he was baptized when twenty-five, became a
monk, and in 377 went to Egypt with Melania,
where he spent six years among the hermits
and became an admirer of Origen. He then
migrated to Palestine, where he built a monastery on Mt. Olivet, broke with Jerome during
the Origenist controversy, but was later reconciled to the saint, and in 397 returned to Italy
with Melania. There he began translating
Origen's works, revived the Origen controversy
with Jerome, which led to their final break
when Jerome violently attacked him and
Rufinus answered with his *Apology* and also
his *Apology to Pope Anastasius*. He died in
Sicily. In addition to his translations of Origen,
he also translated works of St. Basil, Gregory of
Nazianzus, Eusebius' *Church History*, wrote a
commentary on the *Benedictions of the Patriarchs* and *Exposition of the Creed*. He is sometimes known as Rufinus Tyrannius.

RUFUS, ST. (d. 90?). St. Paul welcomed him
at Rome (Rom. 16:13) and he is traditionally
referred to as a bishop in the East. F. D.
Nov. 21.

RUFUS, ST. (1st century?), martyr. A follower of St. Apollinaris of Ravenna, he is said
to have been slain as bishop of Capua, Italy.
F. D. Aug. 27.

RUFUS, ST. (d. 107?), martyr. A citizen of
Antioch (or possibly Philippi), he, with his
companion Zosimus, was thrown to the beasts
in the arena in Rome two days before the
martyrdom of St. Ignatius of Antioch, who had
been brought to Rome with them. The incident is mentioned in a letter by St. Polycarp
of Smyrna. F. D. Dec. 18.

RUFUS, ST. (d. 200). He is said to have been
the first bishop of Avignon, France. F. D.
Nov. 12.

RUFUS, ST. (d. 295), martyr. *See* Carpophorus, St.

RUFUS, ST. (d. 304), martyr. He and his
family were slain at Rome during the Diocletian persecution. F. D. Nov. 28.

RUFUS, ST. (d. 400?). He was bishop of
Metz, France, from about 370. A Rufus of
Metz was involved in the Priscillianist contro-
versy. F. D. Nov. 7.

RUGG, BL. JOHN (d. 1539), martyr. *See*
Cook, Bl. Hugh.

RUINART, THIERRY (1657–1709), historian. Born in Rheims, France, on June 10, he
became a Maurist in 1674, joined Mabillon at
St. Germain-des-Prés, near Paris, to aid in his
work, and soon became recognized as an outstanding church historian. He devoted his life
to scholarship and writing, and died at the
abbey of Hautvillers, near Rheims, on Sept. 27.

Among his writings were *Acta primorum martyrum sincera et selecta* (1689), *Historia persecutionis Vandalicae* (1694), volumes 8–9, with Mabillon, of *Acta sanctorum* (1700–1), and an edition of Gregory of Tours.

RUIZ, BL. MANOEL (1804–1860), martyr. Born in Santander, Spain, he was the superior of the Franciscan monastery in Damascus when anti-Christian riots broke out in 1860. He, seven other friars, and three laymen were murdered when they refused to become Moslems. The martyrs of Damascus were beatified in 1926. F. D. July 11.

RUIZ DE ALARCÓN Y MENDOZA, JUAN DE (1580–1639), dramatist. Born in Mexico City, he studied at Salamanca, Spain, spent three years in Seville practicing law, became a close friend of Cervantes, and settled in Madrid in 1611. He began to write for the stage, was successful at first, but incurred the enmity of Lope de Vega and his followers, and faded into obscurity. Among his plays are *Las paredes oyen, El examen de maridos* and *La verdad sospechosa* (upon which Corneille's *Le Menteur* is based). He died in Madrid on Aug. 4.

RUIZ DE MONTOYA, ANTONIO (1585–1652), missioner. Born in Lima, Peru, on June 13, he became a Jesuit in 1606, when he accompanied his provincial to Paraguay where he was to labor for the next thirty years. With Frs. Cataldino and Mazeta he founded the Guayra Reductions and in 1620 was made superior of the twenty-six reductions on the Parana, Uruguay, and Tape rivers, to which he added thirteen. In 1631 he moved some 15,000 Christians threatened by Brazilian slave hunters from Guayara to Paraguay, and in 1637 protested the slavers' depredations to Philip IV, who granted the reductions special privileges and protection. He died in Lima on Apr. 11. He wrote *Tesoro de la lengua guaraní, Arte y vocabulario de la lengua guaraní,* and *Catecismo de la lengua guaraní,* and a history of the reductions, *Conquista espiritual en las provincias del Paraguay.* He is reported to have personally baptized more than 100,000 Indians.

RUIZ DE MONTOYA, DIEGO (1562–1632), theologian. Born in Seville, Spain, he became a Jesuit in 1572 and taught at Granada, Baeza, Seville, and Cordova, of which he served as rector from the time of his profession in 1592 until his death in Seville on Mar. 15. He wrote theological treatises, chief of which were *Doctrina Christiana* and *De Trinitate* (1625).

RUIZ Y RODRIGUEZ, MANUEL DA-MATA (1875–1940), archbishop. Born in Corralillo, Cuba, he was ordained, became archbishop of Havana in 1925, and died there on Jan. 3.

RUMAN. *See* Ruadan, St.

RUMBOLD. *See* Rumold, St.

RUMOHR, KARL FRIEDRICH (1785–1843), critic. A native of Dresden, Germany, he early became interested in art, studied under the painter Fiorillo, made trips to Italy in 1804 (when he became a convert), 1816, and 1826, and became an authority on the history of art. His chief works are the three-volume *Italienische Forschungen* (1826–31), *Hans Holbein, Zur Geschichte und Theorie der Formschneidekunst,* and *Geist der Kochkunst.* He died in Dresden.

RUMOLD, ST. (d. 775), bishop and martyr. Probably an Anglo-Saxon Benedictine monk, though possibly from Ireland, he was consecrated regionary bishop and worked under St. Willibrord on missionary trips to Holland and Brabant, until he was murdered near Molines (Mechlin), Flanders. Legend has listed him as bishop of Dublin. He is also called Rombault, Rombaut, and Rumbold. F. D. July 3.

RUMON. *See* Ruadan, St.

RUMSIK, JOHANN (d. 1314), canonist. A German Dominican, he became a lector at Freiburg and compiled a *Summa confessorum,* which became the basis of a larger canonical study by Bartholomew of San Concordio.

RUMWOLD, ST. (7th century?). According to legend, he was a son of King Alchfrid of Northumbria and St. Cyneburga, who pronounced his profession of faith after his baptism at the age of three days and then died. F. D. Nov. 3.

RUPERT (1352–1410), emperor. Son of Rupert II, elector palatine of the Rhine, and Beatric, daughter of King Peter II of Sicily, he was born in Amberg, Germany, on May 5, and succeeded his father in 1398. When Wenceslaus I was deposed in 1400, Rupert then was elected emperor. He was defeated on his invasion of Italy in 1401–2 by Gian Galeazzo Visconti, to whom Wenceslaus had sold Milan, was recognized by Pope Boniface IX in 1403, and was steadfast in his support of the legitimate Roman line of popes. He was refused recognition as emperor when he sent envoys to support the cause of Pope Gregoy XII at the Council of Pisa in 1409, had little control over the nobles and cities of his dominions, and was faced throughout his reign by the specter of Wenceslaus, who refused to relinquish his imperial claims. He died at Landskron, near Oppenheim, Germany, on May 18.

RUPERT, ST. (d. 710?), bishop. Of Frankish descent, he was bishop of Worms before he became a missioner to Bavaria and converted Duke Theodo and hundreds of others. He was aided by SS. Thuniald, Gislar, and Vitalis in his preaching and in building a church, monastery, and school at Juvavum, Austria, which he renamed Salzburg, and where he served as first bishop and died. He is also known as Hrodbert. F. D. Mar. 29.

RUPERT, ST. (9th century). *See* Bertha, St.
RUSSELL, CHARLES (1832–1900), jurist.
Born in Newry, Ireland, on Nov. 10, he studied
in Belfast and St. Vincent's, Castleknock. He
was called to the Irish bar in 1854 and practiced in Down and Antrim. He went to Lincoln's Inn, London, in 1856, married Ellen
Mulholland in 1858, and was called to the English bar in 1859. He served as a member of
parliament in 1880–94, was twice attorney
general in Gladstone's ministry (1886 and
1892–94), spoke strongly for attention to Irish
grievances, and was chief counsel for Parnell
in 1888–89. He served on the committee ar-
bitrating the Bering Sea dispute with the
United States in 1893 and made important
contributions to the definition of international
law, and in 1899 was successful as arbitrator in
the boundary dispute between British Guiana
and Venezuela. He was made lord of appeal in
1894 and raised to the peerage as Baron Russell of Killowen, was appointed first Catholic
lord chief justice of England since the Reformation, and represented Great Britain on the
Venezuelan Boundaries Commission in 1899.
He received honorary degrees from Trinity
College, Dublin, Laval, Edinburgh, and Cambridge. He died in Kensington, London, on
Aug. 10.
RUSSELL, CHARLES WILLIAM (1812–
1880). Born in Killough, Ireland, on May 14,
he studied at Downpatrick and Maynooth, was
ordained in 1835, and taught at Maynooth. He
corresponded with the Tractarians at Oxford
and had a major influence on Newman. He
was appointed first vicar apostolic of Ceylon in
1842, but refused, returned to Maynooth in
1845, and in 1857 became its president. He
was joint editor of the eight-volume *Report on
the Carte Manscripts in the Bodlein Library*
and a collection of Irish state papers during
James I's reign, and wrote a life of Cardinal
Mezzofanti. He died in Dublin on Feb. 26.
RUSSELL, FRANCIS XAVIER JOSEPH
(1867–1946), judge. Born in London on July
2, son of Baron Charles Russell of Killowen,
he studied at Beaufort and Oxford, was called
to the bar in 1893, and married Mary Emily
Ritchie in 1900. He practiced in privy-council
cases, became associated with Sir Charles
Swinfen, and in 1918 began to plead in chancery. He became a chancery judge in 1919,
was appointed to the court of appeal in 1928,
and received a life peerage in 1929. He usually
limited himself to legal cases, but spoke
strongly in the House of Lords in 1937 against
extending the causes of divorce and against the
limited education bill of 1944. In 1928 he became a fellow of Oriel College and president
of the Thomas More Society. He died in Tad-
worth, England, on Dec. 20.
RUSSELL, PATRICK (d. 1692), archbishop.

Born in Dublin, he became its archbishop in
1683, held several provincial and diocesan
synods, reorganized the cathedral chapter, but
was seized and imprisoned after the battle of
the Boyne, and died in prison.
RUSSELL, RICHARD (1630–1693), bishop.
Born in Berkshire, England, he studied at Lisbon, Douai, and Paris, where he was ordained.
He became procurator in Lisbon in 1655, chaplain to the Portuguese ambassador in England
in 1657, and in 1660 secretary to the queen.
He helped in the negotiations over Charles
II's marriage to Catherine of Braganza in 1661,
was with the infanta on her trip to England,
and in 1671 was appointed bishop of Porta-
legre. In 1682 he was transferred to Vizéu,
Portugal, where he died on Nov. 15.
RUSSELL, WILLIAM THOMAS B. (1863–
1927), bishop. Born in Baltimore, Maryland,
on Oct. 20, he studied at St. Charles College
and St. Mary's seminary in Maryland, and the
North American College, Rome, and was ordained in Baltimore in 1889. He was pastor in
Hyattsville, Maryland, until 1894, when he became Cardinal Gibbons' secretary, and served
in this capacity until 1908, when he became
rector of St. Patrick's in Washington, D.C. He
was made a domestic prelate in 1911, and was
consecrated bishop of Charleston, South Carolina, in 1917. He was a member of the administrative board of the National Catholic
War Council, first chairman of the press division of the National Catholic Welfare Conference, and died in Charleston on Mar.
18.
RUSTICUS, ST. (d. 258?), martyr. *See*
Dionysius, St.
RUSTICUS, ST. (d. 290?), martyr. *See*
Firmus, St.
RUSTICUS, ST. (d. 446). He became bishop
of Clermont, Auvergne, Gaul, in 426. F. D.
Sept. 24.
RUSTICUS, ST. (d. 461?), bishop. Born in
Marseilles or Narbonnaise, Gaul, son of Bishop
Bonosus, he became a well-known preacher in
Rome, abandoned this career to become a
monk at Lérins, was ordained, and in 427 was
made bishop of Narbonne. He wanted to give
up his see because of the spread of Arianism
resulting from the Goth siege of Narbonne, but
was dissuaded from doing so by Pope St. Leo
I. He had correspondence with Leo and St.
Jerome, some of which is extant, attended the
Synod of Arles in 451 at which the bishops of
Gaul approved Leo's letter, *Epistola dogmatica*,
to Flavian of Constantinople, and his denunciation of Nestorianism, and built a cathedral
at Narbonne. F. D. Oct. 26.
RUSTICUS, ST. (d. 484), martyr. *See* Liberatus, St.
RUSTICUS, ST. (d. 574). Bishop of Trèves,
Gaul, he was deposed by St. Goas and spent

his last years in penance at the latter's monastery. F. D. Oct. 14.

RUSTICUS, BL. (d. 1092). In 1076 he was chosen third abbot general of the Vallombrosan order. F. D. Mar. 12.

RUTH, GEORGE HERMAN (1895–1948), athlete. Born in February in Baltimore, Maryland, he was raised as an orphan at St. Mary's Industrial School there. He became a baseball player, was dubbed "Babe" by his fans, and became one of the greatest of all baseball players. He established records as a Boston Red Sox pitcher, but gained greater fame for his batting prowess with the New York Yankees, with whom he played in 1920–35. Among his more than fifty records were those for most home runs (714) and most in one season (60). He died in New York City on August 16.

RUTH, MARY ANSELMA (1874–1957), educator. Born in Bavaria, she was brought to Brooklyn, New York, as a child, educated there, and became a Dominican sister in 1891. She studied at New Rochelle and took her doctorate at Fordham in 1922. She did mission work in Puerto Rico, was sub-prioress, mistress of novices, and superior of various convents of her order. She was mother general of the congregation from 1943 until her death in Amityville, New York, on Jan. 12. She became the first president of Molloy College in 1955.

RUTILIUS, ST. (d. 250), martyr. A native of northern Africa, he fled persecution, but later boldly declared himself a Christian and was burned to death. F. D. Aug. 2.

RUTTER, HENRY (1755–1838). Henry Banister was born in Lancashire, England, on Feb. 26, studied at Douai, was ordained, and became professor at St. Omer's College in 1781. On his return to England he spent the years from 1817 to 1834 in Yealand, Lancashire, and then moved to Dodding Green, where he died on Sept. 17. He wrote *Evangelical Harmony* and scriptural exegesis.

RUYSBROECK, BL. JOHN (1293–1381), mystic. Born in Ruysbroeck, Belgium, he studied in nearby Brussels, where he was ordained at twenty-four. In 1343 he, his uncle, and a canon of St. Gudule's went to live as hermits at Groenendael; after six years they formed their own community of Augustinian canons, with John as prior. He devoted his life to contemplation, had many supernatural experiences, and wrote such treatises on mysticism and sanctity as *The Kingdom of God's Lovers*, *Spiritual Espousals*, and *Spiritual Tabernacle*. He died in Groenendael, Flanders. F. D. Dec. 2.

RUYSCH, JOHN (1460?–1533), cartographer. Born in Utrecht, Netherlands, he was ordained, then became a Benedictine in 1492. He studied astronomy and painting, and went to Rome in 1508 where he helped Raphael in his paintings in the Vatican and published his map *Nova et universalior orbis cogniti tabula*, showing Spanish and Portuguese discoveries in the New World. On a trip to Portugal he was appointed astronomer of the fleet by the king, then returned to his monastery in Cologne, Germany, where he died.

RYAN, ABRAM JOSEPH (1838–1886), poet. Born in Hagerstown, Maryland, on Feb. 5, he studied at Niagara and the Vincentian novitiate in Germantown, Pennsylvania. He was ordained in 1861 and served as a chaplain in the Confederate army during the Civil War. After the war he served in Biloxi, Nashville, Knoxville, and Macon parishes, lectured widely, and wrote poetry, notably *The Conquered Banner*, which earned him the title "poet of the Confederacy." He edited *Pacificator* and *Banner of the South* in Augusta, Georgia, and the *Star* in New Orleans. His poems were collected in 1879. He died in Louisville, Kentucky, on Apr. 22.

RYAN, EDWARD FRANCIS (1878–1956), bishop. Born in Lynn, Massachusetts, on Mar. 10, he studied at Boston College and the North American College, Rome, and was ordained in 1905. He engaged in pastoral work and was pastor of Holy Name Church, West Roxbury, when he was appointed bishop of Burlington, Vermont, in 1944. He died on Nov. 3.

RYAN, GEORGE JOSEPH (1872–1949), educator. Born in New York City on July 7, he studied at St. Francis College, entered business, and became president of a Long Island City bank and of the Queens Chamber of Commerce. In 1918 he was appointed to the board of education, serving as its president from 1922 to 1936, and undertaking an elaborate building program and establishing its bureau of child guidance. He was honored by the Vatican, France, Belgium, Spain, Portugal, and Italy, and received honorary degrees from Fordham and Bologna. He served as a member of the state board of regents until his death in Flushing, New York, on Oct. 4.

RYAN, JAMES (1848–1923), bishop. Born near Thurles, Tipperary, Ireland, on June 17, he was taken at seven by his parents to Louisville, Kentucky. He studied at St. Thomas and St. Joseph colleges, the Preston Park seminary, and was ordained in Louisville in 1871. He taught, served in mission areas around Peoria, and became bishop of Alton, Illinois, in 1888. He died there on July 2.

RYAN, JOHN DENIS (1864–1933), executive. Born in Hancock, Michigan, on Oct. 10, he became an oil salesman in Pennsylvania, banker in Montana, and in 1906 became president of the Anaconda Copper Mining Co. He also helped direct the International Smelting Co. and American Brass Co. and several mining companies in South America. He was on the council of the Red Cross during World War I, served as chairman of the aircraft board under President Wilson, and assistant secretary of war. He returned to private industry after the war, was noted for his philanthropy, and was papally decorated in 1933. He died in New York City on Feb. 11.

RYAN, PATRICK JOHN (1831–1911), archbishop. Born in Cloneyharp, near Thurles, Ireland, on Feb. 20, he graduated from St. Patrick's, Carlow, in 1852, went to the United States, studied at St. Louis University, and was ordained in St. Louis in 1853. He served as curate at the cathedral and as rector at several churches, became a noted preacher, and converted many Confederate soldiers. He was Bishop Kenrick's theologian at the second Plenary Council of Baltimore in 1866, became vicar general of St. Louis, preached Lenten sermons in Rome in 1868, and in 1872 was consecrated titular bishop of Tricomia and coadjutor of St. Louis. He preached and lectured widely, was made titular archbishop of Salamis in 1884, and later in the same year was appointed sixth bishop (and second archbishop) of Philadelphia. During his reign the number of churches and schools was tripled. He took great interest in Negro and Indian missionary activity, was appointed to the Federal Indian commission by President Theodore Roosevelt, was a popular orator (he opened the Republican party's convention in 1900) and lecturer, and helped lessen anti-Catholic sentiment in the United States. He was editor of the *American Catholic Quarterly Review* from 1890 until his death in Philadelphia on Feb. 11.

RYAN, STEPHEN VINCENT (1825–1896), bishop. Born near Almonte, Ontario, Canada, on Jan. 1 (though 1826 and Perth are possible), he studied at St. Charles Borromeo seminary in Philadelphia, and, after he joined the Congregation of the Mission in 1844, at St. Mary's seminary of the Barrens, Missouri, and was ordained in St. Louis in 1849. He taught at St. Mary's until 1851, and at St. Vincent's College, Cape Girardeau, Missouri, where he was also rector, until 1857, when he was elected visitor general of his congregation in the United States. He was appointed second bishop of Buffalo in 1868, and engaged in numerous disputes with Bishop McQuaid of Rochester over Ryan's support of Archbishop Ireland in backing of Sylvester Malone as regent of the University of New York State against Bishop McQuaid, the archbishop's position on education, and the boundaries of the two neighboring sees. He founded the diocesan paper *Catholic Union* (now *Catholic Union and Times*) in 1872, and was noted as a controversialist in defense of the Church's position. He died in Buffalo, New York, on Apr. 10.

RYAN, THOMAS FORTUNE (1851–1928), financier. Born in Nelson County, Virginia, on Oct. 17, he worked in Baltimore and New York, and in 1874 bought a seat on the stock exchange. In association with William C. Whitney he financed street-car and lighting projects in New York City, Chicago, and other cities, and bought coal mines and railroad property in Ohio, Virginia, and West Virginia. He then invested in diamond fields in the Belgian Congo, controlled the tobacco market in the United States, helped to avert a national financial crisis in 1905, gained a controlling interest in the Equitable Life Assurance Society (which he later sold to J. P. Morgan), and became a director of more than thirty corporations. He was interested in politics as a Democratic leader, in Renaissance art, and in Catholic charities. He died in New York City on Nov. 23.

RYAN, VINCENT J. (1884–1951), bishop. Born in Arlington, Wisconsin, on July 1, he studied at St. Francis seminary, Milwaukee, and the St. Paul (Minnesota) seminary, and was ordained in 1912. He was chancellor of the Fargo, North Dakota, diocese in 1912–34, its administrator in 1935, and vicar general in 1939–40. He had become pastor of St. Anthony's church in 1918 and retained his pastorate until 1940, when he was appointed bishop of Bismarck, North Dakota. He was active in social work, president of the National Catholic Rural Life Conference in 1939–41, wrote numerous sociological studies, and died on Nov. 10.

RYCKEL, DENYS. *See* Van Leeuw, Denys.

RYDER, HENRY IGNATIUS DUDLEY (1837–1907). Born on Jan. 3, son of an Anglican clergyman who had followed Newman into the Catholic Church, he became a pupil of Newman at the Oratory about 1849, joined the Oratorians in 1856, and was ordained in 1863. He had a lifelong association with Newman, whom he succeeded as superior of the Birmingham Oratory in 1890. He died in Birmingham, England, on Oct. 7.

RYKEN, THEODORE JAMES (1797–1871), founder. Born in Elshout, Holland, on Aug. 30, he was orphaned when a child, was attracted to catechetical work, and in 1822 became Le Sage-ten-Broek's secretary. After a pilgrimage to Rome in 1826, when Pope Leo XII decorated him for his work in a cholera plague in Groningen, he joined the Trappists in 1827, left to come to the United States in 1831, and returned to Europe in 1834 to establish a teaching institute to provide teachers for American Catholics. In 1839 he established the Xaverian Brothers in Bruges, and served as superior general as Brother Francis Xavier until his resignation in 1860. He died in Bruges, Belgium.

S

SÁ MANOEL DE (1530–1596), theologian. Born in Villa do Conde, Portugal, he studied at Coimbra, became a Jesuit at fifteen, and taught at Coimbra and Gandia, where he tutored Francis Borgia. In 1557 he became a professor at the Roman College, was appointed to the committee preparing a new edition of the Septuagint, and engaged in missionary activity in northern Italy. He wrote theological treatises, chief of which were *Scholia quatuor evangelia* and *Notationes in totam scripturam sacram*. He died in Arona, Italy, on Dec. 30.

SÁ MEM DE (1500?–1572), governor. Born in Coimbra, Portugal, he was governor general of Brazil from about 1557, drove the French out of the Guanabara bay area in 1567, established Rio de Janeiro, and worked with Fr. Manuel de Nobrega on behalf of the natives. He died in Bahia, Brazil, on Mar. 2.

SÁ DE MIRANDA, FRANCISCO DE (1485?–1558), poet. Born in Coimbra, Portugal, he studied law in Lisbon, traveled in Spain and Italy, and dedicated himself to a life of literary production. He wrote six eclogues in Spanish and two in Portuguese, some pastorals, much poetry in the Petrarcan tradition, and two classical comedies: *Estrangeiros* and *Vilhalpandos*.

SAAVEDRA Y FAJARDO, DIEGO DE (1584–1648), diplomat. Born in Algezares, Murcia, Spain, he took his law degree at Salamanca, served as secretary to Cardinal Borja, Spanish ambassador to Rome, succeeded him, and carried out the policy of King Philip IV on diplomatic missions to Italy, Germany, and Switzerland. Important works include: *Idea de un príncipe* (1640), written in opposition to Machiavellianism; *República literaria* (1655), a utopian fantasy in the manner of Lucian; *Locuras de Europa*, a dialogue on peace among nations; and a study of Ferdinand the Catholic. He died in Madrid.

SAAVEDRA RAMÍREZ DE BAQUEDANO, ANGEL DE (1791–1865), poet. Born in Cordova, Spain, on Mar. 10, the son of the duke de Rivas, he entered the Seminario de Nobles in 1802, and served in the army from 1809 to 1813, when he retired to Seville to engage in literary activities. He was a member of the Cortes from 1820 to 1823, was active in the revolutionary movement, and was forced to flee when Ferdinand VII revoked the constitution in 1823. He lived in England, Italy, Malta, and France until 1834, when Ferdinand's death allowed him to return to Spain, and he fell heir to the dukedom of Rivas. He became minister of the interior in 1836 and served as ambassador to Naples in 1844–49, to France in 1849, and as president of the council of state in 1863. He wrote an epic, *El moro exposito* (1834); the tragedy, *Don Álvaro* (1835), which inspired the libretto of Verdi's *La forza del destino*; and *Romances históricos* (1841), a series of historical ballads. He died in Madrid on June 22.

SABADEL, ARMAND (1850–1914), theologian. Born in Langogne, France, on Nov. 16, he became a Capuchin in 1873, was ordained in 1875 as Fr. Pie, taught theology at Crest, went to Rome as secretary of his definitor general, and served as theologian to five papal congregations. He wrote lives of Bl. Crispin of Viterbo and Philomène de Ste. Colombe, edited *Diurnal de Marie* (a collection of hymns), and was editor of *Analecta*. He was named titular bishop of Corinth in 1911 and died in Rome on May 4.

SABAS, ST. (d. 272), martyr. Said to have been a Goth serving as an officer in Rome, and put to death there with seventy other Christians during the persecution of Aurelian, he may be identical with the St. Sabas who died exactly a century later. F. D. Apr. 24.

SABAS, ST. (d. 309), martyr. *See* Isaias, St.

SABAS, ST. (d. 372), martyr. A Goth, he served a priest named Sansala as lector, and was put to death with some fifty others after torture near Bucharest, Romania. F. D. Apr. 12.

SABAS, ST. (439–532). Born in Mutalaska, Cappadocia, son of an army officer, he ran away at eight to a nearby monastery. In 456 he went to Palestine, where he lived five years as a disciple of St. Euthymius and later as a desert solitary near Jericho. He attracted so many disciples that he founded a laura in 483, was ordained in 491, and in 493 was appointed archimandrite over all the hermit monks of Jerusalem. When friction arose between him and some of his subjects he left, but returned on orders from Elias, patriarch of Jerusalem. An opponent of Eutychianism, he went to Constantinople in 511 to persuade Emperor Anastasius to give up his support of the heresy and his interference with the Catholic bishops, but was unsuccessful. He visited Elias in exile, was with him at his death, then in 531 was again in Constantinople seeking redress from Emperor Justinian for Palestinians who had suffered damages during a Samaritan uprising. Sabas is regarded as one of the founders of Eastern monasticism. He died in Laura Mar Saba, near Jerusalem. F. D. Dec. 5.

SABAS. *See* Sava, St.

SABBATIUS, ST. (d. 277?), martyr. *See* Dorymedon, St.

SABEL, ST. (d. 362), martyr. *See* Ismael, St.

SABINA, ST. (d. 119?), martyr. Legend calls her a widow converted by her Syrian servant, Serapia, both of whom were slain during the reign of Hadrian. F. D. July 29.

SABINA, ST. (d. 127?), martyr. She has been honored in Rome, where a church is dedicated to her, from the earliest times. F. D. Aug. 29.

SABINA, ST. (d. 275?). She is said to have been the sister of St. Sabinian of Troyes, Gaul, and is venerated with him on Aug. 29.

SABINIAN, ST. (d. 300?), martyr. He is said to have been first bishop of Sens, Gaul, succeeded by St. Potentian, both of whom were put to death in that area. F. D. Dec. 31.

SABINIAN, ST. (d. 851), martyr. *See* Peter, St.

SABINIANUS (d. 606), pope. Born in Blera, Tuscany, Italy, he acted as Pope St. Gregory I's apostolic nuncio to Constantinople in 593, returned to Rome in 597, was elected Gregory's successor, and was consecrated on Sept. 13, 604. He was accused of selling wheat from the Church's granaries when famine threatened as the result of Lombard invasions. He died in Rome on Feb. 22.

SABINUS, ST. (d. 287), martyr. Born a noble in Egypt, he was put to death by drowning in the Nile during the Diocletian persecution. F. D. Mar. 13.

SABINUS, ST. (d. 303?), bishop and martyr. An Italian bishop (variously claimed by Assisi, Chiusi, Faenza, and Spoleto), he was tortured and beaten to death at Spoleto during Diocletian's persecution when he refused to sacrifice to a statue of Jupiter. Also tortured and martyred were two of his deacons, Marcellus and Exuperantius, the governor, Venustian, and the latter's family. F. D. Dec. 30.

SABINUS, ST. (d. 420), bishop. Friend of St. Ambrose, he was bishop of Piacenza, Italy, and served at the Council of Aquileia (381) which attacked Arianism, and at the Council of Milan (390) against Jovinian. As a deacon he had represented Pope Damasus at Antioch during the Meletian schism. F. D. Jan. 17.

SABINUS, ST. (5th century?), martyr. He and his brother Cyprian were put to death at La Bresse in Poitou, France (not at Brescia, Italy). A fifth-century St. Sabinus, a martyr near Poitiers, is said to have been a follower of St. Germanus of Auxere. F. D. July 11.

SABINUS, ST. (515?–566), bishop. Born in Apulia, Italy, he was the friend of St. Benedict and Pope Agapitus I, represented the latter against the heretic Anthimus in the court of Justinian and at a council in 536, and was bishop of Canosa. In his last years he was blind. F. D. Feb. 9.

SABRAN, LOUIS DE (1652–1732). Born in Paris on Mar. 1, he studied at St. Omer, became a Jesuit, and was one of King James II's chaplains in 1685. He was imprisoned in 1688 at the outbreak of the revolution in England, but escaped, became visitor of the Neapolitan Jesuits, and in 1699 was appointed president of the Liège episcopal seminary over the bitter opposition of the Jansenists. About 1708 he was appointed provincial, was rector of St. Omer from 1712 to 1715, and then became spiritual director of the English College in Rome, a position he held until his death there on Jan. 22.

SACCHI, BARTOLOMMEO DE (1421–1481). Also known as Platina, he was born in Piadena, near Cremona, Italy, was a soldier and a tutor, and in 1457 went to Florence to study Greek. In 1462 he was a member of Cardinal Francesco Gonzaga's household in Rome, was appointed to the College of Abbreviators by Pope Pius II in 1464, and was imprisoned when he denounced Paul II for removing him from that office because he belonged to the Academy of Pomponius Lactus. He was again imprisoned in 1468 on charges of heresy and plotting against the pope's life, and acquitted and released in 1469. He gained the vengeance he threatened in *Vitae pontificum* (1479), which falsely presented Paul II as opposed to science, and which is partisan and erroneous in other particulars; however, it is the first systematic history of the popes. Sacchi was appointed Vatican librarian in 1472 by Pope Sixtus IV, who made him prefect of the Vatican and commissioned him to collect the principal privileges of the Roman Church. He died in Rome.

SACCHONI, RAINERIO (d. 1263). Born in Piacenza, Italy, he was a member of the heretical Cathari for seventeen years and became one of their bishops. He was brought back to the Church by the preaching of a Catholic missionary, probably St. Peter Martyr, and joined the Dominicans. Assigned to mission work in northern Italy, he became inquisitor for Lombardy and Ancona, and incurred the bitter enmity of the heretics there, who had him exiled. He was recalled to Rome by Pope Urban IV in 1262.

SACERDOS, ST. (d. 551). He became bishop of Lyons, France, in 544, presided at the Council of Orléans in 549, and was adviser to King Childebert. His name is also given as Sadroc, Sardot, Sardou, Serdon, and Serdot. F. D. Sept. 12.

SACERDOS, ST. (d. 560?). He is believed to have been bishop of Saguntum, Spain. F. D. May 5.

SACERDOS, ST. (670–720?), bishop. Born near Sarlat, Périgord, France, he became a Benedictine monk and founded and was abbot of Calabre before he became bishop of Limoges. F. D. May 4.

SACHIS, GIOVANNI ANTONIO DE (1484?-1539), painter. He was born in Pordenone, Friuli, Italy, and became noted for the frescoes and altarpieces he painted for churches and villas around Pordenone and in Venice, Treviso, Mantua, Cremona, and Genoa. Among his outstanding works were *Glory of S. Lorenzo Giustiniani, Calling of S. Matthew,* and the frescoes in the Cremona and Treviso cathedrals. He died in Ferrara, Italy, in Jan. He is also known as Pordenone, Corticellis, Curticello, Regillo, and Licinio.

SADLER, THOMAS VINCENT FAUSTUS (1604-1680?). An English convert at seventeen, he joined the Benedictines, was professed in 1622, and engaged in missionary activities in England, where he was also chaplain to the Seldon and Tichborne families. He wrote several spiritual books, most popular of which was a prayerbook, *The Daily Exercise of the Devout Christian.* He died in Dieulward, Flanders, on Jan. 19.

SADLIER, ANNA TERESA (1854-1932), author. Born in Montreal, Canada, daughter of James and Mary Madden Sadlier, she studied in convent schools, mastered several languages, and began to write at eighteen. She published forty books and 200 short stories during her lifetime, from *Seven Years and Mair* (1878) through such adventure-filled narratives as *The Monk's Pardon, Carmelita, Master Gerard, The Pilkington Heir, Gerald de Lacey's Daughter,* and *Ethan Allen's Daughter* (1917). She also wrote stories for children and translated the *Sayings* of St. Alphonsus Liguori and other works from the French, German, and Italian. She died in Ottawa, Ontario, Canada, where she had lived from 1903.

SADLIER, MARY ANNE MADDEN (1820-1903), novelist. Born in Cootehill, Cavan, Ireland, on Dec. 31, she migrated to Canada in 1844 and married James Sadlier of the American publishing firm in 1846, moved to New York in 1860, and after her husband's death in 1869 returned to Canada. Always interested in writing, she wrote some sixty popular novels, with Irish backgrounds, including *The Red Hand of Ulster, The Confederate Chieftains, Willy Burke, Eleanor Preston,* and *The Old House by the Boyne.* She died in Montreal on Apr. 5.

SADOC, BL. (d. 1260), martyr. Possibly a Hungarian, he became a Dominican, was sent to Sandomir, Poland, where he founded a priory, and is believed to have been slain with the community of forty-eight he directed when the Tatars overran the area. Their cult was confirmed by Pope Pius VII. F. D. June 2.

SADOLETO, JACOPO (1477-1547), cardi-

nal. Born in Modena, Italy, he attracted the attention of Cardinal Caraffa (later Pope Paul IV) in Rome and became Pope Leo X's secretary. He was appointed bishop of Carpentras in 1517 and a member of a commission to study Church reforms in 1536 by Pope Paul III, who created him a cardinal later the same year, and with Cardinal Contarini drew up *Consilium de emendanda ecclesia.* He was a legate to Francis I in 1542 in an unsuccessful attempt to reconcile him with Charles V, and died on Oct. 18 in Rome, where he had been a close adviser of Pope Paul III. He wrote theological works, notably *De liberis recte instituendis* (1533), *Phaedrus, sive de laudibus philosophiae* (1538), and *Latin Poems* (1548).

SADOTH, ST. (d. 342?), bishop and martyr. Deacon to Bishop Simeon Barsabae of Seleucia-Ctesiphon, he succeeded the latter after his martyrdom during the persecution of King Sapor II of Persia, was himself captured, racked, and left in chains after some 120 Christians were executed for refusing to worship the sun. After five months of torture and imprisonment, eight others were slain, and the bishop was taken to Beit-Lapat, Persia, and beheaded there. F. D. Feb. 20.

SADROC. *See* Sacerdos, St. (d. 720).

SADWEN, ST. (6th century). He was the brother of St. Illtyd of Wales and a follower of St. Cadfan. F. D. Nov. 29.

SAENS. *See* Sidonius, St.

SAGAR, ST. (d. 175?), martyr. Bishop of Laodicea, Phrygia, he was put to death in the reign of Marcus Aurelius. F. D. Oct. 6.

SAGARD, THÉODAT GABRIEL (17th century), missioner. A French Recollect laybrother, he was sent to Canada in 1623, worked among the Hurons, and was called back to France in 1624, where he bitterly denounced the traders for their evil influence over the Indians to the duc de Montmorency, viceroy of New France—a report which led to Richelieu's appointment of the Jesuits as missionaries to Canada in 1625. Late in his life (1686) he wrote a history of Canada and Recollect missions there.

SAHAGÚN, BERNARDINO DE (1499?-1590), historian. Born in Spain, he became a Franciscan, was sent to Mexico, and wrote an elaborate *History of Ancient Mexico,* on the Aztecs and the Spanish conquest, which was unpublished until 1829 (by Carlos de Bustamente) and not translated into English until 1932.

SAILER, JOHANN MICHAEL (1751-1832), bishop. Born in Aresing, Bavaria, on Oct. 17, he became a Jesuit in 1770, continued his studies at Ingolstadt when the Society was suppressed in 1773, and was ordained in 1775. He tutored, then taught at Ingolstadt in 1780, turned to literary work when the study of theology was abolished there the next year, and in 1784 was appointed professor at Dillingen. He was driven from there by opposing professors in 1794, was appointed professor at Ingolstadt in 1799, was appointed canon of Ratisbon in 1821, coadjutor bishop in 1822, and succeeded to that see in 1829. He was a staunch defender of Church rights and papal supremacy and an opponent of positivism, instituted widespread reforms, converted many, and wrote profusely; his works were collected in forty volumes (1830–41). He died in Ratisbon, Bavaria, on May 20.

SAINCTES, CLAUDE DE (1525–1591). Born in Perche, France, he joined the Canons Regular at fifteen, studied at Navarre College in Paris, where he received his doctorate in theology in 1555, attended the Conference of Poissy in 1561, and represented the University of Paris at the Council of Trent. He vigorously fought Protestant teaching, became a leading controversialist and preacher, and in 1575 was appointed bishop of Évreux. He was forced to flee for his support of the Catholic League when the royalists captured Évreux, but was captured, and when approval of the murder of Henry III was found in his writings he was sentenced to death for treason. Henry IV commuted his sentence to life imprisonment and he died several weeks later at Château de Crèvecoeur, France. He also wrote *Traité de l'ancien naturel des français* (1567), wherein he declared French kings were obliged to eradicate heretics.

SAINTE-CLAIRE DEVILLE, CHARLES (1814–1876), geologist. Born in St. Thomas, West Indies, on Feb. 26, he studied at L'École des Mines in Paris, and volcanic activity in the Antilles and at Vesuvius and Stromboli, concluding that volcanic disturbances are caused by sea water coming into contact with hot rocks through earth fissures. He became a member of the Academy of Sciences in 1857, an officer of Legion of Honor in 1862, inspector general of the meteorological service in 1872, and professor at Collège de France in 1875. He was also president of the observatory in Montsouris, one of a chain of observatories he established in France and Algiers. He died in Paris on Oct. 10.

SAINTE-CLAIRE, HENRI ÉTIENNE (1818–1881), chemist. Born in St. Thomas, West Indies, on Mar. 11, brother of Charles, he studied in Paris, where he built his own laboratory, organized the faculty of science at Besançon in 1844, and was professor and dean there until 1851, when he went to L'École Normale Superieure. He became a professor at the Sorbonne in 1853 and a member of the Academy of Sciences in 1861. His researches led him to the discovery of the theory of dis-

sociation, and his work on the metallurgy of aluminum resulted in the first commercial process of manufacturing it. He also pioneered in the use of petroleum as fuel, discovered toluene and the anhydride of nitric acid, and with Debray made important researches on platinum. He died in Boulogne, France, on July 1.

SAINT-COSME, JEAN FRANÇOIS BUISSON DE (1667–1707), missioner. Born in Quebec, he studied at the Missions Etrangères seminary there, was ordained in 1690, and labored in Nova Scotia and Illinois. About 1699 he established a mission at Natchez, Mississippi, but in 1704 left it to work with the Indians along the Mississippi River, where he was killed, with four companions, by the Shetimasha Indians.

ST. JOHN, AMBROSE (1815–1875). Born in Bletsoe, England, he studied at Oxford, where his lifelong friendship with John Henry Newman began, became a curate in 1841, studied with Newman at Littlemore, became a convert in 1845, and was ordained in Rome with the future cardinal in 1847. They joined the Oratorians and went to Birmingham, England, in 1847, where St. John remained until his death on May 24. Newman acknowledged in the *Apologia* his indebtedness to St. John.

SAINT-PALAIS, JACQUES MAURICE LANDES DE (1811–1877), bishop. Born in La Salvetat, Hérault, France, on Nov. 15, he studied at St. Nicholas du Chartonet and St. Sulpice, Paris, was ordained in 1836, went to the United States, and did missionary work. He was appointed vicar general of Vincennes, Indiana, and superior of St. Charles seminary there in 1847, administered the see in 1848, and was appointed its fourth bishop later the same year. He died at St. Mary-of-the-Woods, Indiana, on June 28.

SAINT-SEVERIN. *See* Bonald, Louis Gabriel Ambroise.

SAINT-SIMON, LOUIS DE ROUVROY DE (1675–1755). He was born on Jan. 16, served in the army, which he left in 1702 to join the court of Louis XIV, though not in the king's favor, became a supporter of the duke of Orléans, inclined toward Jansenism, and was a friend of Fénelon. He became a member of the council of regency for young Louis XV in 1715, and served as ambassador to Madrid in 1721 in an unsuccessful attempt to arrange the marriage of the latter and the infanta. He retired to his estate near Chartres in 1723. His *Mémoires*, written from about 1699 to 1751, are a valuable source of information about the events and characters of King Louis XIV's reign, though often inaccurate, particularly in religious matters. He died in Paris on Mar. 2.

SAINT-VALLIER, JEAN BAPTISTE DE

(1653–1727), bishop. Born in Grenoble, France, on Nov. 14, he studied at the seminary there and the Sorbonne, where he received his doctorate in theology. He became almoner of Louis XIV, was noted at court for his piety and charity, refused the bishoprics of Tours and Marseilles, and in 1684 was appointed vicar general and second bishop of Quebec. He brought many religious orders to Canada to expand missionary activities among the Indians, held synods in 1690, 1694, 1698, and 1700, instituted reforms among the religious, and built churches, schools, hospitals, convents, and parishes. He frequently quarreled with the civil governors, especially Frontenac, and had several disagreements with his predecessor, Laval, over his reorganization of the dioceses, which eliminated the seminary from any share in its direction and his expenditures. He was captured by the English on the return trip from Rome in 1704, imprisoned for five years, and did not return to Quebec until 1713. He died there on Dec. 26.

SAINT-VICTOR, ACHARD DE (1100–1172), bishop. Of a noble Norman (or English) family, he studied at St. Victor's, Paris, entered the cloister there, and in 1155 was elected its second abbot. He was elected bishop by the canons of Séez, but, despite the approval of Pope Adrian IV, the election was reversed by Henry II in favor of his own candidate, Frogier. Despite this and his close friendship with Thomas à Becket, he was friendly to the king and in 1162 was godfather of Henry's daughter Elinor. He was made bishop of Avranches in 1162, founded the abbey of the Holy Trinity at Lucerne, Switzerland, in 1164, and died and was buried there.

SALA, GEORGE AUGUSTUS HENRY (1828–1895), journalist. Born in London on Nov. 24, of a theatrical family, he was at various times a book illustrator, etcher, and engraver, attracted Charles Dickens' attention, and became a contributor to *Household Words* and *All the Year Round*. He was a special correspondent to Russia and in 1857 joined the *Daily Telegraph* as world correspondent. He founded *Sala's Journal*, became a convert, and published *Twice round the Clock* (1859), *The Baddington Peerage* (1860), *Rome and Venice* (1869), and *Life and Adventures* (1895). He died in Brighton, England, on Dec. 8.

SALAMON, LOUIS SIFFREN JOSEPH (1759–1829), bishop. Born in Carpentras, France, on Oct. 22, he studied at Avignon and became auditor of the rota. He resigned to return to Paris and a position in the parliament, which he held until it was abolished in 1790, and was appointed internuncio to Louis XVI's court. He was imprisoned during the Reign of Terror, twice escaped death, acted as vicar apostolic when he was released, and was ap-

pointed administrator of the Normandy diocese in 1801. He was appointed bishop of Orthozia by Pope Pius VII, and of St. Cloud, France, in 1820, where he died on June 11.

SALAZAR, DOMINGO DE (1512–1594), archbishop. Born in La Bastida, Spain, he became a Dominican, and was sent to Mexico, where he received his master's degree in theology and taught. He then worked among the Indians of Guajaca and Florida, but was later sent back to Mexico, where he became prior and then vice-provincial. When he returned to Spain he was imprisoned on false charges, released by Philip II, who appointed him bishop of the Philippines, and arrived in Manila in 1581. He devoted himself to the welfare of the Filipinos, returned to Spain to plead, successfully, for better treatment of the natives in 1591, and was appointed first archbishop of the metropolitan see of Manila. He died in Madrid on Dec. 4 before the bull appointing him arrived.

SALBERGA, ST. (d. 665?). Cured of blindness as a child by St. Eustace, she married very young, was widowed after two months, and was induced by her parents to marry a nobleman named Blandinus, by whom she had five children. By mutual consent they separated, St. Blandinus becoming a hermit. Salberga went first to Poulangey, which she had endowed, and then founded the convent of St. John the Baptist at Laon, France, in 650, where she died. F. D. Sept. 22.

SALES, FRANCIS DE. *See* Francis de Sales, St.

SALES, BL. JAMES (1556–1593), martyr. Born in Auvergne, France, he became a Jesuit novice at Billom when he was seventeen and the first graduate of the University of Pont-à-Mousson. After further studies at Paris, he was sent into Aubenas to conduct a series of debates with the Calvinist ministers and to preach there. During a Huguenot raid he and Bl. William Saultemouche, a laybrother, were tried by a mock court, then shot by arrows, stabbed, and beaten to death. F. D. Feb. 7.

SALES, RAOUL DE ROUSSY DE (1896–1942), journalist. Born in Paris on Mar. 5, he wrote literary and musical criticism for newspapers on both sides of the channel, worked with the Red Cross during World War I, and was assistant general secretary to the League of Red Cross Societies from 1922 to 1931. In 1932–36 he went to New York as correspondent of several newspapers, became chief diplomatic correspondent for the Havas Agency, with offices in Washington, D.C., in 1937, and president of the Association of Foreign News Correspondents. He married an American, Reine Tracy, wrote for the New York *Times*, and published *The Making of Tomorrow* and editions of letters from the French people (*They*

Speak for a Nation) and selections of Hitler's plans (*My New Order*) and other war propaganda. He was chancellor of the Free French delegation in the United States at his death in New York City on Mar. 5.

SALIMBENE DEGLI ADAMI (1221–1288?), historian. Born in Parma, Italy, on Oct. 9, he joined the Franciscans in 1238 over the violent opposition of his father, and was stationed in monasteries in Florence, Parma, Ravenna, Reggio, and Montefalcone, at which last he probably died. He is noted for his *Monumenta historica*, a chronicle of the years 1167–1287.

SALLUSTIA, ST. (d. 251), martyr. *See* Caerealis, St.

SALMERON, ALFONSO (1515–1585). Born in Toledo, Spain, on Sept. 8, he studied at Alcalá and Paris, where he met St. Ignatius and was one of the band of seven who founded the Society of Jesus in Montmartre in 1534. He accompanied Ignatius to Rome in 1537, was ordained, and devoted himself to the poor of Siena. In 1542 he went to Ireland as apostolic nuncio, and on his return to Rome later the same year became noted for his preaching. He was theologian, with Laynez, of Pope Paul III in 1546 at the Council of Trent, received his doctorate from Bologna in 1549, and was appointed professor at Ingolstadt by Duke William IV of Bavaria. On the duke's death in 1550 he returned to Verona, helped Ignatius draw up the Society's constitutions and establish the Jesuit college in Naples in 1551, then returned to the recently reopened Council of Trent as Pope Julian III's theologian. He spent 1555–56 in Germany, Poland, and Belgium, was appointed first provincial of Naples in 1558, vicar general in 1561, and in 1562, again with Laynez, was Pius IV's theologian at the resumed Council of Trent. The rest of his life was spent in preaching and writing; chief among his works were sixteen volumes of scriptural commentaries. He died in Naples, Italy, on Feb. 13.

SALMON, BL. PATRICK (d. 1594), martyr. A servant of Bl. Thomas Bosgrave, he was hanged with his master at Dorchester, England, for having abetted a priest, and beatified in 1929. F. D. July 4.

SALOME (1st century). Wife of Zebedee and mother of John and James (Matt. 20:20), she followed Christ (Matt. 27:56), and probably is the Salome present at the crucifixion (Matt. 27:56; Mark 15:40) and at the tomb the morning of the Resurrection (Mark 15:40; 16:1). She is considered by some authorities to be the sister of the Virgin Mary mentioned in John 19:25.

SALOMEA, BL. (1202?–1268). Daughter of King Leszek of Poland, she was betrothed to Prince Coloman of Hungary when three, mar-

ried when thirteen, became a Franciscan tertiary, and was widowed in 1225. She founded a convent of Poor Clares at Zawichost, which was transferred to Skala, became a nun there in 1240, and later was elected abbess. Her cult was approved by Pope Clement X. F. D. Nov. 17.

SALOMONE, BL. JACOPO (1231–1314). Born in Venice, Italy, of a noble family, he became a Dominican at seventeen, served as prior at several houses, and devoted himself to prayer, care of the poor, and great austerities. He had a great many supernatural gifts, and gained a reputation for extraordinary patience as a victim of cancer. He died in Forlì, Italy; his cult was approved in 1526. F. D. May 31.

SALONIUS, ST. (3rd century). He was first bishop of Genoa, Italy, often listed as Salomon or Solomon by scribal error. F. D. Sept. 28.

SALPOINTE, JOHN BAPTIST (1825–1898), archbishop. Born in St. Maurice de Poinsat, Puy-de-Dôme, France, on Feb. 21 or 22, he studied at the seminary in Clermont-Ferrand and was ordained in 1851. He did parish work, taught at the Clermont-Ferrand preparatory seminary in 1855–59, and then went to the United States, where he engaged in missionary activities in the Santa Fe diocese. He was appointed vicar general of the see in 1860 and in 1869 was consecrated titular bishop of Doryla and vicar apostolic of Arizona, in which position he fought the government's practice of placing Catholic Indians under Protestant missionaries. He was made titular archbishop of Anazarbus and coadjutor of Santa Fe, New Mexico, in 1884, succeeded to that see in 1885, and reigned until 1894, when he resigned and was appointed titular archbishop of Constantia (Tomi). He died in Tucson, Arizona, on July 15.

SALT, BL. ROBERT (d. 1537), martyr. *See* Beer, Bl. Richard.

SALUTARIS, ST. (d. 500?), martyr. *See* Eugenius, St.

SALUTATI, LINO COLUCCIO DI PIERO (1331–1406), scholar. Born in Tuscany, Italy, on Feb. 13, he studied at Bologna, became secretary to Pope Urban IV, and in 1375 was appointed chancellor of the republic of Florence, a position he held until his death on May 4. He was prominent in Florentine scholarly circles, corresponded widely with the leading humanists of his time, among them Petrarch, and collected old manuscripts, acquiring copies of Catullus, Cato, Germanicus, Pompeius, and Maximanus, among others. He also wrote several treatises, and translated parts of Dante's *Divine Comedy* into Latin verse.

SALVATIERRA, JUAN MARIA (1648–1717), missioner. Born in Milan, Italy, on Nov. 15, he studied at the Jesuit college in

Parma, joined the Society, and in 1675 was sent to Mexico. He taught at Puebla, and in 1680 was given permission to work among the Tarumari Indians of Chihuahua. He worked there until he was appointed visitor of Jesuit missions in 1690, was inspired by Fr. Eusebio Kino to go to southern California in 1697, founded several missions (Our Lady of Loreto at Concepcion Bay in Oct. 1697), and explored the region. He was appointed provincial of Mexico in 1704, returned to his missions in 1707, and died at Guadalajara, Mexico, on July 17.

SALVATOR OF HORTA, ST. (1520–1567). Born in Santa Columba, Spain, he became a Franciscan laybrother, served as a cook in monasteries in Tortosa and Horta, practiced severe austerities, and died on Sardinia. He was canonized in 1938. F. D. Mar. 18.

SALVI, GIOVANNI BATTISTA (1605–1685), painter. Born in Sassoferrato, Italy, he studied painting under his father, Tarquinio Salvi, Dominichino, and the Caracci, at Naples, and later moved to Rome, where he spent most of his life and died. He is noted for his paintings of the Virgin Mary, best known of which is *Our Lady of the Rosary with St. Dominic and St. Catherine* in Santa Sabina, Rome. Others are *Madonna with Angels, Assumption of the Blessed Virgin, Virgin of Sorrows,* and *Infant Jesus Asleep on His Mother's Knees.*

SALVIAN THE PRESBYTER (5th century). Born probably in Trèves, Gaul, which was overrun four times by barbarians during a life which spanned most of the century, he married, but his wife entered a convent when he went to Lérins, where he seems to have been ordained. He taught rhetoric there to SS. Caesarius, Hilary, and Honoratus, among others. He wrote on the Church, the sacraments, scriptural commentaries, homilies, letters, and the particularly important *The Present Judgment* and *The Governance of God,* which laid bare the greed and injustice of his day, particularly among officials and the landed aristocracy.

SALVIATI, BL. ELISABETH (d. 1519). She directed the Camaldolese convent of St. John the Evangelist at Boldrone, Italy; her cult seems to have been approved by Pope Urban VIII. F. D. Feb. 11.

SALVINUS, ST. (d. 562). He was bishop of Verona, Italy. F. D. Oct. 12.

SALVIUS, ST. (d. 584), bishop. A French lawyer, he became a monk, was chosen abbot, and then lived as a hermit. In 574 he was made bishop of Albi, Gaul, continued his austerities, and was known for his great charities. With St. Gregory of Tours he corrected a lapse from orthodoxy of King Chilperic of Soissons. Salvius died while attending the sick during an epidemic. F. D. Sept. 10.

SALVIUS, ST. (6th century). He is listed as a hermit living in Normandy, but may be identical with St. Salvius, bishop of Albi. F. D. Oct. 28.

SALVIUS, ST. (d. 625?), bishop. Also called Sauve, he was bishop of Amiens, France, during the reign of Theodoric II, but further details of his life have been confused with those of St. Salvius of Albi and of Salvius of Africa, a martyr commemorated by St. Augustine. F. D. Jan. 11.

SALVIUS, ST. (d. 768?), bishop and martyr. A missionary bishop who had great success with converts in a single year, he, with his companion, St. Superius (so named because his body was found buried in a pit above that of Salvius), is said to have been murdered by the son of an official in Valenciennes, France. F. D. June 26.

SALZMANN, JOSEPH (1819–1874). Born in Münzbach, Austria, on Aug. 17, he was ordained in 1842, worked in the diocese of Linz as a parish priest, and in 1847 volunteered to go to the United States. He became a pastor in Milwaukee, was involved in bitter disputes with atheists of his parish, and in 1856 was successful in raising funds to open a seminary at St. Francis, Wisconsin. He also founded the first Catholic normal school in the United States and Pio Nono College. He died in St. Francis on Jan. 17.

SAMBIN. *See* Similian, St.

SAMBURGA, JOSEPH ANTON (1752–1815), theologian. Born in Walldorf, Germany, on June 9, of Italian parents, he studied at the Augustinian monastic school at Wiesloch and Heidelberg, finished his studies in Italy, and was ordained in Como in 1774. He was a chaplain, a court preacher at Mannheim in 1785, and taught Prince Louis (later King Louis I of Bavaria) and the other children of the elector of Bavaria, Duke Maximilian Joseph, in 1806, and wrote theological treatises. He died in Nymphenburg, Germany, on Jan. or June 5.

SAMONAS, ST. (4th century), martyr. *See* Gurias, St.

SAMSON, ST. (5th century). Surnamed Xenodochius ("the Hospitable"), he founded and supported a hospital for the poor in Constantinople. When it burned down, after his death, it was rebuilt by Emperor Justinian. F. D. June 27.

SAMSON, ST. (485?–565?), bishop. Son of Amon of Dyfed and Anna of Gwent, he was born in Glamorgan, Wales, and educated by St. Illtyd. After ordination by St. Dyfrig he retired to a small community on the island of Caldey off the coast of Pembrokeshire and became abbot. He visited Ireland and on his return retired to live as a hermit. He was again made abbot of a monastery and was consecrated bishop by St. Dubricius. After this he traveled through Cornwall, founding churches and monasteries and evangelizing, then went to Brittany, making missionary trips throughout the country, including Paris. King Childbert is supposed to have nominated him bishop of Dol. He also visited Sicily and the Channel Islands. He died at the monastery he had founded in Dol, Brittany. F. D. July 28.

SAMSON (1135–1211). Born in Tottington, England, he received his master's degree at Paris, taught in Bury, went to Rome in 1160 as representative of the monks of St. Edmunds to protest an agreement between their Abbot Hugh and King Henry II. He was imprisoned on his return, became a monk himself in 1166, and in 1182 was elected abbot on the death of Hugh, a position he filled until his death at St. Edmunds thirty years later. He was appointed a judge in ecclesiastical cases by Pope Lucius III, served on the royal council as a baron, and successfully resisted William of Longchamp's attempts to restrict the Benedictines. He is portrayed in Carlyle's *Past and Present* as an excellent example of a mediaeval churchman.

SAMUEL, ST. (d. 309). *See* Elias, St.

SAMUEL, ST. (d. 1227), martyr. *See* Daniel, St.

SAMUEL O'HAINGLY (d. 1121), bishop. Nephew of Donat O'Haingly and a Benedictine monk at St. Alban's, he was consecrated at Winchester in 1096 by St. Anselm as the fourth bishop of Dublin. St. Anselm censured him for removing the monks from the cathedral and establishing a secular canonry.

SANABRIA Y MARTÍNEZ, VICTOR M. (1899–1952), archbishop. Born in San Rafael, Costa Rica, on Jan. 17, he was ordained in Rome in 1921. He wrote history, biography, and on canon law, became bishop of Alijuela, was named archbishop of San Jose in 1940, and played a prominent role in settling the rebellion of 1948. He died in Costa Rica on June 8.

SANCHA, ST. (1180?–1229). Daughter of King Sancho I of Portugal, she brought the Dominicans and Franciscans to her area and founded the Augustinian convent of Cellas, which she transferred to Cistercian rule and entered as a nun. Her cult was approved in 1705. F. D. Mar. 13.

SÁNCHEZ, ALONZO (1547–1593). Born in Mondejar, Spain, he joined the Jesuits in 1565, taught at Navalcarnero College, and became its rector. In 1579 he went on the Mexican mission, became rector of the seminary there, and in 1501 was one of the first groups of Jesuits sent to the Philippine Islands. He acted as Bishop Salazar's counselor, made several trips to China, and in 1586 was sent to Madrid to plead with Philip II to retain the islands. He then proceeded to Rome, where he convinced the Jesuit general to keep the Jesuits in the Philippines, was appointed visitor of several Spanish provinces, and died at Alcalá, Spain, on May 27. He wrote an account of Christianity in China.

SÁNCHEZ, ALONZO COELLO (1515–1590), painter. Born in Benifaro, Valencia, Spain, he studied painting under and became a follower of Antonio Moro. In 1552 he entered the service of Don Juan of Portugal, and on Juan's death was appointed Moro's successor as court painter by Philip II of Spain. He did altarpieces for the Escorial, but is more famous for his portaits, particularly those of Padre Siguenza, Ignatius Loyola, Gregory XIII, and Philip II, whom he painted many times. He died in Madrid. He is also known as Alonzo Sanchez Coello, his Portuguese mother's name.

SÁNCHEZ, JOSÉ BERNARDO (1778–1833), missioner. Born in Robledillo, Spain, on Sept. 7, he joined the Franciscans in 1794 and was sent to Mexico in 1803. After a short stay at San Fernando College, he was sent to California in 1804, and spent the rest of his life in various California missions. He was president of the missions and vicar of the bishop from 1827 to 1831, and died at San Gabriel mission on Jan. 15.

SANCHEZ, THOMAS (1550–1610). Born in Cordova, Spain, he joined the Jesuits in 1567, served for a time as master of novices at Granada College, and devoted the rest of his life to writing. His chief works are *Disputationes de sancti matrimonii sacramento* (1602), some editions of which have been placed on the Index because of changes made in the text by editors after Sanchez' death, and *Opus morale in praecepta decalogi*, which suffered the same fate. He died in Granada, Spain, on May 19.

SANCHO I RAMIREZ (1045?–1094), king of Aragon and Navarre. Son of Ramiro I of Navarre, he became king of Aragon in 1063 and was joint ruler of Navarre, with Alfonso VI of Castile, after Sancho III's murder in 1054. He became sole ruler of Navarre in 1076 on the death of Sancho V, and died at the siege of Huesca, Spain.

SANCHO I, king of Castile. *See* Sancho III, king of Navarre.

SANCHO II (d. 1072), king of Castile. Son of Ferdinand I of Castile, he succeeded his father as king in 1065, fought his brothers and sisters who had inherited Spanish territories from their father, conquered León from his brother Alfonso VI, and then Galicia and Toro, and was assassinated while besieging Zamora, Spain.

SANCHO III (12th century), king of Castile. Son of Alfonso VII, he became king in 1157 but faced difficulty when his brother, Ferdinand II, became king of León and a strong power by his marriage to Urraca of Portugal. Sancho stepped down after a year's rule.

SANCHO IV (1258?–1295), king of Castile and León. He deposed his father, Alfonso X, in 1282 and faced a civil war directed by his older brother's sons and supported by Alfonso III of Aragon. Later, he defeated the Moors and captured Tarifa in 1292.

SANCHO III (965?–1035), king of Navarre, Castile, and León. Called "the Great" and also known as Sancho Garces III, he succeeded his father, García Sanchez, as king of Navarre, in 1000, made the country independent of Carlovingian rule, succeeded to the crown of Castile by his marriage, and conquered that country and most of León to unite Spain for a short time. He captured Calahorra and in 1008 Ribagorza and Sobrarbe from the Moors, called the synods of Leyra and Pamplona, and was active in church affairs. He weakened the unity of Spain he had achieved by dividing his holdings among his four sons on his death.

SANCHO V (d. 1076), king of Navarre. He succeeded García III in 1054 and was murdered by his brothers.

SANCHO VI (d. 1094), king of Navarre. Son of García Ramirez and called "the Wise," he became king in 1050, fortified the country, remained undefeated in battle, and was influential as a statesman and patron of learning.

SANCHO VIII (d. 1234), king of Navarre. Son of Sancho VII, and called "the Strong," he became king in 1194, took over church revenues, granting major privileges in return, gave his palaces and other property to the see of Pamplona, and led an expedition against the Moors in North Africa. During his absence Castile and Aragon invaded and seized the provinces of Alava and Guipuzcoa. He won the decisive battle of Las Navas de Tolosa in 1212 against the Moors, and died in retirement.

SANCHO I (1154–1211), king of Portugal. He succeeded Alfonso Henriques in 1185, lost the territory south of the Tagus River to the Moors, but built towns and opened up new areas and was known as "the Peopler." He endowed bishoprics and abbeys and generously supported the Hospitallers of Aviz and of San Thiago. He fell under the domination of a fortune teller and fought the clergy so vigorously that the country was placed under interdict. He distributed too much territory to his supporters and was forced to demand much of it back to gain income for the administration of the realm. He imprisoned the bishop of Coimbra, refused to grant military immunity to the clergy, and constantly interfered with rights and privileges. He made some concessions to aroused leaders before his death.

SANCHO II (d. 1246), king of Portugal. See Alfonso III.

SANCHO. See Sanctius, St.

SANCHO DE AVILA (1546–1625), bishop. Born in Avila, Old Castile, Spain, he studied and was ordained at Salamanca and became, successively, bishop of Murcia, Jaen, Siguenza in 1615, and Plasencia in 1622. He wrote sermons, lives of SS. Augustine and Thomas, and a treatise on the veneration of relics. He also served as a confessor of St. Teresa. He died in Plasencia, Spain, on Dec. 6 or 7.

SANCHO GARCIA I (d. 925), king of Navarre. Surnamed Abarca, he succeeded Fortun García in 905, was victorious against the Moors and drove them from his borders, and extended his holdings to Najera.

SANCTES, BL. (d. 1392). Born in Cori, Italy, he became an Augustinian and had success as a missioner. His cult was approved by Pope Leo XIII. F. D. Oct. 5.

SANCTIAN, ST. (d. 273), martyr. See Augustine, St.

SANCTINUS, ST. (d. 300?). Called first bishop of Meaux, France, he probably is identical with the bishop of Verdun of the same name, but is listed in the Roman Martyrology under Sept. 22.

SANCTIS, ST. MIGUEL DE (1591–1625). Born in Vich, Spanish Catalonia, he joined the Trinitarians at Barcelona in 1603 and transferred to their discalced group at Saragossa in 1607. He was later ordained, served twice as superior at Valladolid, and had several supernatural gifts. He was canonized in 1862. F. D. Apr. 10 (sometimes, July 5).

SANCTIUS, ST. (d. 851), martyr. Born in Albi, France, he was carried off to Cordova as a Moorish prisoner of war, became a military cadet, then declared for Christianity, and was put to death by impalement. He is also known as Sancho. F. D. June 5.

SANCTUS, ST. (d. 177), martyr. See Pothinus, St.

SANDEO, FELINO MARIA (1444–1503), bishop. Born in Felina, Italy, he taught canon law at Ferrara from 1466 to 1474, at Pisa for the next ten years, and in 1484 was appointed auditor of the sacred palace at Rome. He was appointed bishop of Penna and Atri in 1495, coadjutor of Lucca later that year, and succeeded to the latter see in 1499. He wrote theological treatises, and died in Lucca, probably in Oct.

SANDER, ANTON (1586–1664), historian. Born in Antwerp, Belgium, he studied at Douai and Louvain, and was ordained in Ghent. He was engaged in parish work, became Cardinal de la Cueva's secretary and almoner in 1625, and canon, and in 1654 penitentiary, at Ypres. He resigned in 1657 to devote himself to writing, and died in Afflighem, Belgium, on Jan. 10. Among his books are *Flandria illustrata, Elogia cardinalium sanctitate* (1625),

Bibliotheca belgica manuscripta (1641–43), and *Chorographia sacra Brabantiae* (1659).

SANDERS, NICHOLAS (1530?–1581), historian. Born in Charlwood, Surrey, England, he studied at Winchester and Oxford, became an ally of Cardinal Pole in the cardinal's attempt to reform Oxford, and was forced to flee from England on Elizabeth's accession. He was ordained in Rome, where he received his doctorate of divinity, was Cardinal Hosius' theologian at the Council of Trent, accompanied the cardinal on missions to Poland, Prussia, and Lithuania, and in 1565 became professor of theology at Louvain. His learning and ability made him leader of the English exiles; in 1567 he, with Thomas Harding and Thomas Peacock, was given authority by Pope Pius V to receive back into the Church Englishmen who had lapsed into heresy. He became Pope Gregory XIII's consultor on English affairs in 1572, worked to secure the restoration of Catholicism to England, went to Spain in 1573 to secure Philip II's support, and in 1579 was sent as papal agent to Ireland with Spanish troops to join the Desmond Fitzgeralds in a revolt against the government. When the revolt was suppressed, he led a fugitive's life until he died in Ireland, probably of exhaustion. Among his writings were *De origine ac progressu schismatis anglicani* (1585); a prime source of information on the state of Catholics in Elizabeth's England, *De visibili monarchia ecclesiae* (1571); and several treatises replying by Jewel's *Apologie: The Supper of the Lord* (1565), *A Treatise of Images* (1566), and *The Rock of the Church* (1567).

SANDILA, ST. (d. 855?), martyr. He was slain at Cordova, Spain, during the Moorish persecution. F. D. Sept. 3.

SANDS, BENJAMIN F. (1812–1883), admiral. Born in Baltimore, Maryland, on Feb. 11, he was appointed a midshipman in 1828, worked on coastal surveys from 1834 to 1841, became a lieutenant in 1840, worked at the naval observatory from 1844 to 1847, took part in the Mexican War, and became a convert in 1850. He was advanced to commander in 1855, served as chief of the bureau of construction in 1858–61, commanded several ships blockading the southern states during the Civil War, was made commodore in 1866, superintendent of the naval observatory in 1867–74, and was appointed rear admiral in 1871. He retired in 1874, and died in Washington, D.C., on June 30. His autobiography, *From Reefer to Rear Admiral*, was published by his son in 1899 from notes he left.

SANDS, JAMES HOBAN (1845–1911), admiral. Born in Washington, D.C., on July 12, son of Adm. Benjamin F. Sands, he graduated from the Naval Academy in 1863, served on ships blockading the South during the Civil War, commanded the West Indies fleet after the war, and served as head of the Brooklyn, Boston, Philadelphia, and Washington navy yards. He was appointed a rear admiral in 1902, superintendent of the Naval Academy in 1906–7, retired in 1907, and died in Washington, D.C., on Oct. 26.

SANDS, WILLIAM FRANKLIN (1874–1946), diplomat. Born in Washington, D.C., on July 29, he studied in Switzerland and Austria, took his law degree at Georgetown, and entered the diplomatic service in 1896. He was second secretary in Tokyo until 1899, and with the legation in Korea until he was expelled by the Japanese in 1904. He then served in Central America, married Edith Keating in 1909, represented American business firms in Ecuador and London from 1911 to 1916, and worked for the relief of German and Austrian prisoners in Russia during and after World War I. He then set up a diplomatic training school within the American state department, held the chair of diplomacy in Georgetown's Foreign Service School, and wrote *Undiplomatic Memories* (1930) and *Our Jungle Diplomacy* (1944). He died on June 17.

SANDYS, VEN. JOHN (d. 1586), martyr. Born in Chester, England, he studied in Rheims, was ordained there in 1584, was sent on the English missions, and was captured and brutally executed at Gloucester on Aug. 11.

SAN GALLO, ANTONIO DA, THE ELDER (1455–1534), architect. Born in Florence, Italy, he went with his brother Giuliano to Rome in 1480 and became a noted architect and military engineer. He was appointed to fortify several castles by Pope Alexander, was chief engineer of fortifications in Florence, and also painted: frescoes in the church of the Madonna di San Biagio, Montepulciano, and the portico of the Servi in Florence. He died in Florence on Dec. 27.

SAN GALLO, ANTONIO PICCONI DA, THE YOUNGER (1483–1546), architect. Antonio Coroliano was born in Mugello, Italy, took the surname of his uncles Giuliano and Antonio, studied under Bramante in Rome, succeeded him in the building of St. Peter's, and worked under Popes Leo X, Clement VII, and Paul III for the next forty-one years. In 1536 he succeeded Raphael as architect of St. Peter's for which he prepared an elaborate plan later rejected by Michelangelo, and built and prepared plans for many churches and buildings. He was also an outstanding military engineer and built fortifications for numerous cities. Among his masterpieces are the Palazzo Farnese, completed after his death, Santo Spirito church in Borgo, and the Palazzo Sacchetti. He finished with his brother Battista the Villa Madama from Raphael's plans and the church of the Madonno di Loreto which his Uncle Giuliano had begun, and designed the Sala Regia and the Pauline chapel in the Vatican. He died in Terni, Italy, on Oct. 3.

SAN GALLO, GIULIANO DA (1445?–1516), architect. Born in Florence, Italy, son of a wood-carver, Giuliano Giamberti studied under Francione in Florence, went to Rome to study architecture in 1480, worked on the San Marco palace, and returned to Florence when the city went to war with Naples, and was put in charge of the harbor fortifications of Ostia in 1483. He entered the service of the Medici family, was patronized by Lorenzo, who gave him the surname San Gallo when he built the hermitage of San Agostino there, returned to Rome on Lorenzo's death in 1492, and then accompanied Cardinal della Rovere to France. He was taken prisoner during the war against the Pisans, was appointed architect to St. Peter's in 1503, returned to Florence in 1511 because of ill health, and died there on Oct. 20. Among his masterpieces are the Gondi and Strozzi palaces, the Madonna delle Carceri church in Prato, the villa at Poggio a Cajano, the sacristy of Santo Spirito, and the restored ceiling of Santa Maria Maggiore.

SANMICHELI, MICHELE (1484–1559), architect. Born in Verona, Italy, he worked with Bramante in Rome, then with Michelangelo and Sansovino, and with San Gallo on fortifications in central Italy; he is said to have been the first to employ bastions. He built city gates for Venice and Verona, the Pompeii and other palaces in Verona, and the Grimani and Mocenigo palaces in Venice. He wrote a study of classical architecture.

SANNAZARO, JACOPO (1485–1530), poet. Born in Naples, Italy, on July 28, he studied under Potanus in Naples, fought for and accompanied his patron, King Frederick of Naples, into exile in Tours when he was driven out in 1501 by King Louis XII of France, returned to Italy on the former's death in 1504, and died in Rome in Aug. As a youth he wrote *Arcadia* (1504), which was highly successful and greatly influenced Italian prose, but his main reputation is built on his Latin poetry, chief of which were *Eclogae piscatoriae*, *Salices*, and *De partu virginis*. He also wrote Italian verse patterned on Petrarch. During his stay in Tours he discovered a manuscript of previously unknown Latin poetry, including fragments of Ovid's *Halieutica*, the *Cynegetica* of Grattius Faliscus, and work by other Latin poets.

SANSEDONI, BL. AMBROSE (1220–1286). Born in Siena, Italy, he became a Dominican at seventeen and was sent to Cologne to study with St. Thomas Aquinas under St. Albertus Magnus. He taught theology at Paris for three years, then preached widely through Europe, winning many sinners, halting a heresy in Bohemia, and serving as peacemaker between Manfred of Siena and the papacy. His cult was confirmed in 1622. He is also known as Ambrose of Siena. F. D. Mar. 20.

SAN SEPOLCRO, PIERO DI. *See* Franceschi, Piero de'.

SANSEVERINO, GAETANO (1811–1865), philosopher. Born in Naples, Italy, he studied at the Nola seminary, was ordained, became a canon of the Naples cathedral, taught at the seminary, then at the university, and later was scrittore at the National Library. He founded *La Scienza e la Fede* in 1840, and spent his life seeking to restore scholastic philosophy in the centers of learning in Italy as the true Christian philosophy. He wrote the five-volume *Philosophia christiana cum antiqua et nova comparata* (1862), *La dottrina di S. Tommaso* (1853), and *I principali sistemi della filosofia del criterio* (1850–53). He died in Naples on Nov. 16.

SANSOVINO, ANDREA CONTUCCI DEL. *See* Contucci, Andrea.

SANSOVINO, JACOPO (1486–1570), sculptor. Jacopo Tatti was born in Florence, Italy, on July 2 and became an apprentice of Andrea Sansovino, whose surname he took. He spent his youth as a sculptor in Florence, went to Rome where he studied architecture, worked under Bramante, and was patronized by Pope Julius II. In 1527 he moved to Venice, where he constructed public and private buildings in the classic Roman style. Among his achievements in Venice were the Library of St. Mark, the Cornaro palace, the mint, San Giorgio de' Greci church, the statues of Mars and Neptune in the doge's palace, and the Loggia of St. Mark's. A statue of St. James, Florence, Madonna del Prato in San Agostino church, Rome, and a marble relief in the St. Anthony chapel, Padua, also are memorable. He died in Venice on Sept. 27.

SANTA CRUZ, ALVARO DE BAZÁN DE (1526–1588), admiral. Born in Granada, Spain, he commanded a division of the allied fleet under Don Juan of Austria at the battle of Lepanto, later defeated the Portuguese pretender at Terceira in 1583, and suggested and helped construct and organize the Spanish Armada of Philip II. He died at Lisbon before its disastrous expedition against England.

SANTA MARÍA, PABLO DE (d. 1456), archbishop. A converted rabbi, he was archbishop of Burgos, Spain, from 1396 to 1435, counselor to King John II, and wrote *Scrutinium scripturarum*, published in 1474. His son, Alonso de Cartagena, also wrote widely and succeeded him as archbishop from 1435 to 1456, and was outstanding as a member of the Council of Basle.

SANTA RITTA DURÂO, JOSÉ DE (1737–

1784), poet. Born near Marianna, Brazil, he studied at the Jesuit college in Rio de Janeiro and at Coimbra, and became an Augustinian at Leira. He was stationed in Rome, and went to Coimbra about 1778 to teach theology and serve as prior. He wrote *Caramurú*, an epic account of the discovery and settlement of Bahía by Diego Alvares.

SANTI, GIOVANNI (1435?–1494), painter. Father of the painter Raphael, he was born in Colbordolo, Urbino, Italy, was a merchant, studied under Piero della Francesca, and seems to have worked for Melozzo da Forlì. He became court painter to the duke of Urbina, designed several altarpieces and madonnas, an *Annunciation,* and a *St. Jerome.*

SANTI, RAPHAEL. *See* Raphael.

SANTILLANA, IÑIGO LÓPEZ DE MENDOZA DE (1398–1458), poet. Heavily influenced by the Italian Renaissance and imitative of Dante, Petrarch, and Boccaccio, he was the first to write sonnets in Spanish, wrote a dialogue (*Comedieta, de Ponza*), a dramatic poem (*Dialógo de Bias contra fortuna*), songs called *serranillas,* and other poetry.

SANTILLANA, JUANA INÉS DE ASBAJE Y RAMÍREZ DE (1648?–1695), poet. Born in San Miguel de Nepantla, Mexico, she became a nun at sixteen, taking the name Juana de la Cruz, and wrote lyric poetry and short religious plays, showing the influence of Góngora and Calderón. Two volumes were published in her lifetime; a third, *Fama y orbas póstumas* (1700), referred to her on the title page as the "tenth Muse" of Mexico.

SANTINI, GIOVANNI SANTE GASPERO (1787–1877), astronomer. Born in Caprese, Italy, on Jan. 30, he studied at Prato, Pisa, and Milan. He became assistant to the director of the Padua observatory in 1806, was appointed to the chair of astronomy at the university in 1813, director of the observatory in 1814, served as rector in 1824 and 1856, and was director of mathematical studies from 1845 to 1872. He built the Padua observatory into a world-famous institution, catalogued the stars between declination $+10°$ and $-10°$ from 1847 to 1857, did important research on comets, and calculated the orbital disturbances from 1832 to 1852 caused by the comet of Biela. He died in Padua, Italy, on June 26.

SANTLEY, SIR CHARLES (1834–1922). Born in Liverpool, England, on Feb. 28, son of William, an organist, and Margaret Fletcher Santley, he was educated at Liverpool Institute, sang with the Philharmonic Society at fifteen, and soon became a soloist. He studied singing in Milan under Gaetano Nava in 1855–57, was trained in acting, and became a baritone in operatic productions in the British Isles, the Continent, and the United States.

He became a convert in 1880, toured Africa, Australasia, and Canada between 1898 and 1903, received the gold medal of the Royce Philharmonic Society, and published on the art of singing and *Reminiscences* (1909). He was knighted in 1907. He died in London on Sept. 22.

SANTORINI, GIOVANNI (1681–1737), anatomist. Born in Florence, Italy, he studied medicine at Pisa, and practiced and taught at Florence, where he became professor of anatomy. He pioneered in obstetrics, and discovered the veins leading from the sinuses, tubercules of the larynx, and the fissures in the external ear.

SANTOS, JOÃO DOS (d. 1622), missioner. Born in Evora, Portugal, he became a Dominican, was sent to Africa in 1586, spent the next eleven years in Tete, Querimba, and Sofala, where he was commissary of the Bulla da Cruzada, and in 1597 was sent to India. He returned to Europe in 1606, but came back to India in 1617 and remained there until his death in Goa. He wrote *Ethiopia Oriental,* which describes the Portuguese occupation of Africa and the native Bantus.

SANUTO, MARINO (1466–1536), explorer. Born in Venice, Italy, on May 22, he entered the service of the merchants there, became a member of the council in 1486, a senator in 1498, and a searcher in foreign areas for their interests, but also showed interest in possibilities of converting the natives of far places. His *Liber secretorum fidelium crucis super terrae sanctae recuperatione,* dedicated to the pope, is a handbook for crusaders, and a detailed account of the geography, trade routes, and ethnography of the Near East. He also wrote lives of the doges, a history of the war between Venice and Ferrara, and a diary. He died on Apr. 4.

SANZ, BL. PEDRO (d. 1747), bishop and martyr. Born in Asco, Catalonia, he joined the Dominicans in 1697, and went to the Philippines in 1712 and to China in 1713. He labored in Fu-kien province, becoming vicar apostolic and bishop in 1730. He was carried in chains to Foochow, left to starve in prison for a year, tortured, and beheaded. Four other Dominican priests from Spain—John Alcober, Francis Diaz, Joaquim Royo, and Francis Serrano—were also slain. They were beatified in 1892. F. D. May 26.

SAPIEHA, ADAM STEFAN (1867–1951), cardinal. Born in Krasiczyn, Austria, on May 14, he was ordained in 1893, served as prefect of the Lwow seminary for six years, and received his doctorate in Rome in 1899. He was stationed at the Vatican from 1905 to 1911, when he was named bishop of Cracow. He became archbishop of Warsaw in 1925 and a cardinal in 1946. He was active in relief work for refugees in both world wars, developed libraries, hospitals, co-operatives, and charitable institutions in both dioceses. He suffered abusive treatment by Hans Frank, Nazi governor, during the German occupation, and was robbed of his property and all welfare agencies by the Communists in 1950. With Archbishop (later Cardinal) Stefan Wyszynski he led the battle against communism. He died in Cracow, Poland, on July 23.

SAPOR, ST. (d. 339), bishop and martyr. He was tortured and died of his wounds during the persecution by King Sapor II of Persia. Isaac, another bishop, was stoned to death, and Abraham, Mahanes, and Simeon were slain at the same time. F. D. Nov. 30.

SARBELIUS, ST. (d. 101), martyr. He was pagan high priest of Edessa, Mesopotamia, was converted with his sister Barbea, and tortured and slain there during the persecution of Trajan. F. D. Jan. 29.

SARBIEWSKI, MATHIAS CASIMIR (1595–1645), poet. Born near Plonsk, Poland, on Feb. 24, he joined the Jesuits in 1612, studied at Vilna, Polotsk, and Rome, and was ordained in 1623. He taught at Vilna from 1626 to 1635, when he became King Ladislas' preacher and confidant, and was named to help revise the hymns of the breviary by Pope Urban VIII. He died on Apr. 2. He wrote prose, notably *De Deo uno et trino tractatus*, *De angelis*, and *De acuto et arguto*, but is better known for his Latin poetry—religious, patriotic, and on nature, often in the style of Horace, to whose poetry he was devoted and indebted.

SARIC, IVAN (1871–1960), archbishop. Born in Travnik in the archdiocese of Sarajevo, Bosnia, on Sept. 27, he was ordained in 1894, made a bishop in 1908, and in 1922 appointed archbishop of Serajevo. He was forced to flee to Austria in 1945 when the Tito forces gained control of Yugoslavia, and died in Madrid, where he had lived for several years.

SARKANDER, BL. JOHN (1576–1620), martyr. Born in Silesia, he studied at Prague and was ordained. In his parish at Holleschau he rescued 250 heretics with the help of Baron von Lobkovitz but thereby aroused the hostility of the Hussite Bitowsky von Bystritz. During the Thirty Years' War he went to Cracow, then returned to his parish and saved it from destruction by appealing to the faith of the invading Polish soldiers. Bystritz thereupon charged him with having invited the Poles into the area, had him tried, and commanded him to inform his judges what information he had learned from Lobkovitz as a penitent. John protested his patriotism and refused to break the sacramental seal of confession. He was racked, branded, made a living

torch, and died a month later from his tortures. He was beatified in 1859. F. D. Mar. 17.

SARMATA, ST. (d. 357), martyr. An Egyptian, he was a monastic follower of St. Antony of the desert and slain at his place of seclusion by marauding Arabs. F. D. Oct. 11.

SARNELLI, VEN. GENNARO MARIA (1702–1744). Born in Naples, Italy, on Sept. 12, son of Baron Angelo Sarnelli, he studied law, entered the seminary at twenty-six, and was ordained in 1732. He became a member of the Propaganda of Naples, a group of secular priests dedicated to apostolic work. In 1733 he joined St. Alphonsus at Scala in founding the Congregation of the Most Holy Redeemer. Together they gave missions along the Amalfi coast until Januarius became ill in 1735. Nine years later he was able to resume his missionary endeavors, worked with the poor and abandoned, attacked those in high places who were responsible for crime and vice, and led a crusade against immorality. He died in Naples on June 30. He was declared Venerable in 1874.

SARSFIELD, PATRICK (1650?–1693), soldier. Born in Lucan, Ireland, he served in the duke of Monmouth's regiment, but later in the king's army against the duke, and was wounded at the battle of Sedgemoor. He supported King James II in 1688, conducted his campaign in Ireland in 1689 and subdued Connaught for the king, captured and headed the defense of Limerick, for which James made him earl of Lucan, and served under St. Ruth, with whom he violently disagreed, in the 1691 campaign. He was forced to surrender at the second siege of Limerick, which led to the Treaty of Limerick, joined the Irish Brigade in France, and died at Huy, Belgium, on July 19 from wounds received in battle.

SARTO, ANDREA DEL. See Andrea del Sarto.

SASANDA, BL. LUIS (d. 1624), martyr. Son of Bl. Michael Sasanda, who had been martyred at Yeddo, Japan, he became a Franciscan in Mexico, was ordained in Manila in 1622, went to Japan with Bl. Louis Sotelo, and was burned to death at Simabura on Aug. 25 with Bl. Louis and 3 others. He was beatified in 1867. F. D. June 1.

SASSOFERRATO, GIOVANNI DA. See Salvi, Giovanni Battista.

SATOLLI, FRANCESCO (1839–1910), cardinal. Born in Marsciano, Italy, on July 21, he studied at the Perugia seminary, was ordained in 1862, received his doctorate at the Sapienza, and taught at the Perugia seminary in 1864. He was pastor in Marsciano and Montecassino, professor at the Propaganda and the Roman seminary in 1882, rector of the Greek College in 1884, president of the Academi dei Nobili Ecclesiastici in 1886, and archbishop of Le-

panto in 1888. He attended the centenary of
the American hierarchy in Baltimore in 1889,
returned to the United States in 1892 to help
solve several educational problems, and in
1893 was appointed the first apostolic delegate
to the United States. He was created a cardinal-
priest in 1895, returned to Rome in 1896 as
prefect of the Congregation of Studies and
archpriest of the Lateran, and in 1903 was
appointed cardinal-bishop of Frascati. He wrote
several theological works, including commentaries on St. Thomas. He died in Rome on
Jan. 8.

SATOR, ST. (d. 303?), martyr. *See* Honoratus, St.

SATURIAN, ST. (d. 458), martyr. *See* Martinian, St.

SATURNINUS, ST. (1st century), martyr.
See Euphrasius, St.

SATURNINUS, ST. (d. 120?), martyr. *See*
Astius, St.

SATURNINUS, ST. (2nd century), martyr.
See Catus, St.

SATURNINUS, ST. (d. 203), martyr. Spiritual tutor and biographer of the early imprisonment of St. Perpetua and four others, he
was scourged and then killed by a leopard in
the public games at Carthage during the persecution of Severus, when he refused to sacrifice
to the pagan gods. F. D. Mar. 6.

SATURNINUS, ST. (d. 250?), martyr. He
and SS. Thyrsus and Victor were put to death
in Egypt, probably during the persecution of
Decius. F. D. Jan. 31.

SATURNINUS, ST. (d. 250), martyr. *See*
Theodulus, St.

SATURNINUS, ST. (d. 258?), martyr. *See*
Antony, St.

SATURNINUS, ST. (d. 273), martyr. *See*
Craton, St.

SATURNINUS, ST. (d. 290?), martyr. *See*
Paul of Narbonne, St.

SATURNINUS, ST. (3rd century?), bishop
and martyr. He is said to have been sent by
Pope St. Clement to evangelize Spanish
Navarre and Toulouse, Gaul, of which city he
became first bishop, and so successful with converts that pagan priests had him dragged to
death by a bull. F. D. Nov. 29.

SATURNINUS, ST. (d. 300?), martyr. *See*
Epictetus, St.

SATURNINUS, ST. (d. 303), martyr. He was
slain at Cagliari, Sardinia, during the Diocletian persecution. F. D. Oct. 30.

SATURNINUS, ST. (d. 304), martyr. A priest
who was seized while saying mass at the home
of St. Emeritus in Abitina, Africa, he was
taken in chains to Carthage, to be tortured
and left to die in prison with nearly fifty of
his parishioners during the Diocletian persecution. They included his sons Felix, Hilarion,
and Saturninus the Younger, a lector; his

daughter Mary; Davitus and Felix, senators;
Ampelius, Rogatian, Thelica, and Victoria. F. D.
Feb. 11.

SATURNINUS, ST. (d. 304), martyr. He was
put to death at Alexandria, Egypt, during the
Diocletian persecution. F. D. May 2.

SATURNINUS, ST. (d. 304), martyr. *See*
Apodemius, St.

SATURNINUS, ST. (d. 309?), martyr. Said
to have been a Roman priest from Carthage,
he was tortured and beheaded at Rome with
Sisinius, a deacon, during Diocletian's persecution. F. D. Nov. 29.

SATURNINUS, ST. (d. 356). He was bishop
of Verona, Italy. F. D. Apr. 7.

SATURNINUS, ST. (d. 434?), martyr. *See*
Felix, St.

SATURNINUS THE YOUNGER, ST. (d.
304), martyr. *See* Saturninus, St. (Feb. 11).

SATURUS, ST. (5th century). Master of the
household under the Arian Vandal King
Huneric, he was stripped of his possessions
when it was revealed that he was a Christian,
and forced to live as a beggar. F. D. Mar. 29.

SATYRUS, ST. (d. 267), martyr. An Arab
convert, he was put to death in either Achaia
or Antioch. F. D. Jan. 12.

SATYRUS, ST. (d. 379?). Elder brother of
St. Ambrose, he was probably born at Trèves,
France, moved to Rome with the family about
354 when his father died, and became a lawyer.
When Ambrose became bishop of Milan in
374, Satyrus accompanied him to administer
the temporal affairs of the diocese, which he
did efficiently and with justice. He died in
Milan, and was eulogized by Ambrose in his
famous funeral sermon "On the Death of a
Brother." F. D. Sept. 17.

SAULI, ST. ALEXANDER (1534–1592),
bishop. Born in Milan, Italy, he joined the
Barnabites when seventeen, studied at Pavia,
and was ordained in 1556. He taught at Pavia,
became the bishop's theologian and so successful a preacher he was invited to preach in
the cathedral at Milan by St. Charles Borromeo and became spiritual adviser to the latter and to Cardinal Sfondrati (later Pope
Gregory XIV). In 1567 he was elected provost general of his congregation and resisted
Cardinal Borromeo's efforts to unite a group of
Humiliati friars with the Barnabites. In 1570
he was appointed bishop of Aleria, Corsica,
where he ruled for twenty years, raising the
see from a hopeless state to one of flourishing
spiritual activity. Gregory XIV transferred
him to Pavia, despite his objections, in 1591.
He died in Calozza, Italy, and was canonized
in 1904. F. D. Oct. 11.

SAULTEMOUCHE, BL. WILLIAM (d.
1539), martyr. A servant at the Jesuit college
at Billom, France, he became a laybrother and
later accompanied Bl. James Salès on a preach-

ing mission into the Huguenot stronghold of
Aubenas, France. An attack on the town resulted in the public execution of both men
after two days of brutal treatment. F. D. Feb. 7.

SAUMAN. See Psalmodius, St.

SAUVAGE, GEORGE (d. 1951). Born in
St. Remy du Piren, France, he studied at the
Angelica and at Poitiers, was ordained a member of the Congregation of Holy Cross in
1899, and taught psychology at Angers to 1903
and in Washington, D.C., to 1914. He served
as liaison officer with the French and English
armies during World War I, then became procurator general of his order in Rome from 1919
until his retirement in ill health in 1947. He
was a consultor of several papal congregations. He died in Notre Dame, Indiana, on
Mar. 8.

SAUVE, PAUL (1908–1960), premier. He
studied law in Quebec and was elected to its
legislative assembly at twenty-three. He became
speaker in 1937, served in World War II, and
in 1946 became a member of Premier Duplessis' cabinet. On the death of Duplessis in
1959, he was elected premier and head of the
Union Nationale Party, but died four months
later, on Jan. 2, at St. Eustache, Canada.

SAUVE. See Salvius, St.

SAVA, ST. (1174–1237), archbishop. Son of
Stephen I of Serbia, he became a monk at
Mt. Athos when he was seventeen, and was
joined there by his father when the latter was
deposed five years later. The two then established the monastery of Khilandari, of which
Sava (also called Sabas) became abbot. He
trained the novices, translated a psalter into
Serbian, and returned to his homeland after
civil war ended in 1207, bringing several monks
with him to educate and convert the nation.
He established the monastery of Studenitsa and
frequently retired there for contemplation, but
was called to Constantinople in 1219. Returning, he continued to reform the lives of his
people, and presided in 1222 at the second
coronation of his brother, Stephen II, as king.
He died in Tirnovo, Bulgaria, while returning
from a mission in the Near East. Nationalism
influenced many ecclesiastical moves, but there
is nothing to prove the contention of a few historians that St. Sava led the orthodox schism
from Rome; he is still the Catholic patron of
Serbia. F. D. Jan. 14.

SAVAGE, COURTENAY (1890–1946), author. Born in New York City on July 20, he
studied in private schools and writing at Columbia, wrote short stories, articles, and fourteen
plays, and entered public-relations work. He
became a convert in 1937, devoted himself to
Catholic radio and theater work, founded the
Catholic Actors Guild in Chicago, and worked
for the National Catholic Welfare Council.
He had his *Home Is the Hero* (on Robert

Louis Stevenson), *They All Want Something,*
and *The Little Dog Laughed* produced on
Broadway, and later wrote a fictional account
of St. Christopher, *The Wayfarer's Friend*. He
died in Rome on Aug. 23.

SAVARIC (d. 1205), bishop. Cousin of
Emperor Henry VI, he became archdeacon of
Canterbury, England, in 1175; of Northampton, in 1180. He joined the crusaders in 1191,
was elected bishop of Bath while on the crusade, and was ordained in 1192 in Rome. Pope
Celestine III's consent to joining Glastonbury
abbey to the see of Bath was opposed by the
monks of the abbey in 1196, and by King
Richard I, and set off a dispute which was not
resolved until Savaric seized the abbey by
force in 1199 and a second appeal by the
monks was dismissed by Pope Innocent III in
1202 and Savaric declared abbot. He was instrumental in securing a charter for the city of
Wells from King John. He died in Rome.

SAVARY DES BRUSLONS, JACQUES
(1657–1716). Son of Jacques Savary, he became inspector general of the Paris customs
house in 1686, compiled lists of dutiable materials and rules concerning trade in France
and elsewhere, and with his brother Louis
Philémon Savary prepared *Dictionaire du commerce* (published in 1723 and in an English
translation in 1774). Louis (1654–1727), was
a canon of the chapter of St. Maur and French
agent for the house of Mantua; he had nearly
completed a supplementary volume at the time
of his death.

SAVIGNY, KARL FRIEDRICH (1814–
1875), diplomat. Born in Berlin on Sept. 19,
son of Friedrich Karl, privy councilor of the
court of appeals, and a Catholic mother, Kunigunde Brentano, he studied in Berlin, Rome,
Naples, Munich, and Paris, and rose through
the diplomatic ranks from 1836 to 1848. In
1849 he became councilor of legations and a
member of the ministry of foreign affairs; the
next year Prussian ambassador at Karlsruhe; in
1859, at Dresden; in 1862, at Brussels. From
1864 to 1868 he was minister at the Diet of
the German Confederation at Frankfort; then
worked with Bismarck, after the Austro-Prussian War, in making peace with the southern
German states; presided at the meetings for
drafting a constitution for the northern states;
and was a plenipotentiary at the *Reichstag*
which decided the national constitution. From
1867 on he was a leader of the Catholic faction
in various parliamentary assemblages, and in
1871 helped to begin the Centre party. He
died in Frankfort-on-Main, Germany, on
Feb. 11.

SAVINA, ST. (d. 311). During the persecution of Diocletian she visited the Christians
imprisoned in Milan, Italy, and saw to their
burial after execution. F. D. Jan. 30.

SAVINIAN, ST. (d. 303?), martyr. *See* Honoratus, St.

SAVINUS, ST. (d. 870), English martyr. *See* Theodore, St.

SAVIO, ST. DOMINIC (1842–1857). Born in Riva, Italy, to a peasant family, he entered the oratory of St. Francis de Sales in Turin at twelve, and was directed by St. John Bosco, who later wrote his biography. There he formed the Company of the Immaculate Conception, performed the most menial tasks, prayed at great length for those in need, especially the English, and lived an exemplary life. He was sent home to Mondino, Italy, when taken ill of inflammation of the lungs, and died there. He was canonized in 1954 by Pope Pius XII. F. D. Mar. 9.

SAVONAROLA, GIROLAMO (1452–1498). Born in Ferrara, Italy, on Sept. 2, destined at first for a medical career, he joined the Dominicans in Bologna about 1474, spent six years there and in 1482 was sent as a missionary to northern Italian cities. At first unsuccessful as a preacher, he achieved complete oratorical confidence while preaching at Brescia in 1486 on the Apocalypse and soon became noted all over Italy for his fiery sermons. In 1489 he began preaching at San Marco's in Florence, and in 1490 began his attacks on corruption in government and in the Church. Elected prior of San Marco later that year, he reformed it rigorously, refused to pay homage to Florence's leader, Lorenzo de' Medici, denounced his rule, and predicted his death. His influence rapidly rose and in 1494 he led the resistance against Lorenzo's son, Piero, who was overthrown, and King Charles VIII of France, who was forced to reduce his exorbitant demands on Florence. When Charles left the city in 1495, Savonarola became the virtual ruler, instituted tax reforms, aided the poor, reformed the courts, put into effect a republican form of government, and changed Florence from a lax, corrupt, pleasure-loving city to an ascetic, practically monastic community, often by extreme censorship and violent methods. Among those he denounced were Pope Alexander VI and the corrupt papal court. In 1495 he was summoned to Rome three times to explain his denunciations, each time refusing despite the threat of an interdict on Florence. He was excommunicated in 1497, but refused to acknowledge the validity of the bull of excommunication by declaring that he was divinely inspired and that Alexander was no true pope since he had been simoniacally elected. When a plot to restore Piero de' Medici was uncovered, several of the ringleaders were executed, and Savonarola's popularity began to wane when he refused to interfere with the executions of several well-liked men. Prohibited from preaching and

again summoned to Rome, he ignored both orders, and when his party, the Piagnoni, resumed power in 1498, he began preaching in his usual vein. When the Piagnoni went out of power, Alexander demanded he be tried either by the Florentines or in Rome. His stubbornness cost him the favor of the populace; he took refuge in St. Mark's, but was arrested, subjected to torture for six weeks, and on May 23, after receiving absolution, was hanged and burned at the stake in Florence. He wrote *Il trionfo della croce, Dialogo della verita, Compendium revelationum, Trattato circa il reggimento di Firenze*, treatises on Aristotle and Thomas Aquinas, poems, and sermons. MICHAEL DE LA BEDOYERE, *The Meddlesome Friar and The Wayward Pope* (Garden City, N.Y., Hanover House, 1958).

SAXE, JEAN DE. *See* Johannes Danko; also, Counnot, Jean de.

SAXO GRAMMATICUS (1150?–1220?), historian. Born probably at Zealand, Denmark, he may have been a cleric and studied at Paris. He was secretary to Archbishop Absalon of Lund, at whose suggestion he wrote *Gesta Danorum* (or *Historia Danica*), a history of Denmark from earliest times to 1187, valuable to historians and one of the sources of the story of Shakespeare's *Hamlet*.

SAZAN, ST. (d. 400?). *See* Aizan, St.

SBARRETTI, DONATO (1856–1939), cardinal. Born in Montefranche, Italy, on Nov. 12, he was ordained in 1879, became bishop of Havana in 1900, apostolic delegate to Canada in 1902–10, cardinal-priest in 1916, and cardinal-bishop of Sabina and Poggio Mirteto in 1928. He was secretary of the Congregation of the Holy Office from 1930 until his death in Vatican City on Apr. 1.

SCACCIA, PROSPERO (1857–1932), archbishop. Born in Citta della Pieve, Italy, on May 30, he was ordained, became a papal assistant bishop of Tivoli in 1903, archbishop of Siena in 1905, and chancellor of the theological college there. He died in Siena, Italy, on Sept. 28.

SCALIGER, JULIUS CAESAR (1484–1558), scholar. Born on Apr. 23, in Riva, on Lake Garda, Italy, he followed a military career, studied medicine, went to France as the bishop of Agen's physician in 1526, and took the name of Jules César de l'Escale de Bordonis when he became a French citizen. He became an ardent Ciceronian, quarreled violently with Erasmus in *Oratio pro Cicerone* (1531), wrote widely on poetry and Latin authors, and issued a systematic treatise on poetry, *Poetices* (1561), which had an important effect on future literary forms. He was greatly interested in botany and urged a classification of plants according to their unique characteristics. He also wrote *De comicis di-*

mensionibus (1539), *De causis linguae latinae* (1540), translations of Aristotle's *Natural History* and Hippocrates' *Insomniae*, and commentaries on their medical and botanical writings. He died in Agen, France, on Oct. 21.

SCALIMOLI, ANDREA (17th century), theologian. Born in Castellaneta, Apulia, Italy, he joined the Franciscans, took as his name in religion Andrea di Castellana, and served as provincial of his province. He engaged in missionary work in Moldavia, Wallachia, and Transylvania, and was prefect apostolic in Hungary and visitor of Franciscan missions in Russia. His experiences in the latter posts were related in *Missionarius apostolicus* (1644).

SCAMMACCA, BL. BERNARDO (d. 1486). Born in Catania, Sicily, he lived a dissolute life, became seriously injured, joined the Dominicans after his recovery, and devoted himself to years of penance. He died on Feb. 9. His cult was approved in 1825. F. D. Feb. 16.

SCAMMON, ELLAKIM PARKER (1816–1894), educator. Born in Whitefield, Maine, on Dec. 27, he graduated from West Point in 1837, taught mathematics there, served in the Seminole and Mexican wars, and became a convert in 1846. He was a member of the topographical corps surveying the Great Lakes from 1847 to 1854, left the army in 1856, taught at St. Mary's and Polytechnic colleges in Cincinnati, Ohio, then served in the Civil War, becoming a brigadier general in 1862. He was consul at Prince Edward Island from 1866 to 1871, became professor of mathematics at Seton Hall College, New Jersey, in 1875, retired in 1882, and died in New York City on Dec. 7.

SCANLAN, LAWRENCE (1843–1915), bishop. Born in Ballytarsna, Tipperary, Ireland, on Sept. 29, he studied at St. Patrick's College, Thurles, and All Hallows seminary, Dublin, and was ordained in Dublin in 1868. He went to San Francisco, engaged in pastoral and missionary activities in California, Nevada, and Utah, was appointed vicar of Utah and Nevada in 1873, and in 1887 was appointed titular bishop of Larandum and first vicar apostolic of Utah. He was named first bishop of the new diocese of Salt Lake City in 1891, labored to build up his see, established All Hallows College there in 1895, and dedicated St. Mary Magdalene cathedral in 1909. He died in Salt Lake City, Utah, on May 10.

SCANNABECCHI, FILIPPO (1352?–1410), painter. A Bolognese painter, he became noted for his paintings of madonnas and is often known as Lippo dalle Madonne because of this.

SCANNELL, RICHARD (1845–1916), bishop. Born in Cork, Ireland, on May 12, he studied at All Hallows, was ordained in 1871, went to the United States, and became curate and pastor in Nashville, Tennessee, parishes.

He was administrator of that diocese in 1880–83, became first bishop of Concordia, Kansas, in 1887, and was transferred to Omaha, Nebraska, in 1891. He died on Jan. 8.

SCANNELL, THOMAS BARTHOLOMEW (1854–1917), theologian. Born in London on July 8, he studied in Ware, London, and the English College, Rome, was ordained in 1878, and returned to teach at St. Edmund's College and serve in Weybridge and Southwark parishes. He collaborated on *A Manual of Catholic Theology* and revised the *Catholic Dictionary*. He died in Brighton, England, on Feb. 17.

SCAPINELLI DI LEGUINO, RAPHAEL (1858–1933), cardinal. Born in Modena, Italy, on Apr. 25, he was ordained in 1881, taught in the Reggio seminary, became secretary to the papal nuncio to Lisbon, and in 1907 was named apostolic delegate to Madrid. He was consultor or secretary on several papal commissions and congregations, was nuncio to Vienna in 1912–16, created a cardinal in 1915, and named apostolic datary in 1930. He died in Vatican City on Sept. 17.

SCARAMELLI, GIOVANNI BATTISTA (1687–1752), author. Born in Rome on Nov. 24, he became a Jesuit in 1706, spent the next fifteen years preaching, and then devoted himself to writing such spiritual and ascetical works as *Vita di Suor Maria Crocifissa* (1750), *Discerni mento de spiriti* (1753), *Direttorio ascetico* (1752), and *Il direttorio mistico* (1754). He died in Macerata, Italy, on Jan. 11.

SCARAMPI, PIERFRANCESCO (1596–1656). Born in Monferrato, Italy, he gave up an army career desired by his family, and in 1636 became an Oratorian. In 1643 he was sent as Pope Urban VIII's envoy to the supreme council of the Confederation in Ireland, where he became so popular with the Irish that they offered him the see of Tuam, but he declined. He returned to Rome in 1645, and died there on Oct. 14 of the plague he had caught while ministering to the sick.

SCARISBRICK, EDWARD (1639–1709). Born near Ormskirk, England, he was educated at St. Omer, returned to England, became a Jesuit at Watten in 1660, was stationed at Liège in 1671 and St. Omer in 1675, and again went to England, where he became chaplain to King James II. He taught at the Jesuit house in Ghent in 1693, wrote *Catholic Loyalty* (1688) and other titles, and died in Lancashire, England, on Feb. 19.

SCARLATTI, ALESSANDRO (1659–1725), composer. Born in Palermo, Sicily, on May 2, he probably studied under Carissimi, and became maestro to Queen Christina in Rome when his first opera, *Gli epuivoci nell' sembiante*, performed in 1679, attracted her attention. In 1684 he became choirmaster to the viceroy in Naples, where he remained until 1702, when he went to Florence and was patronized by the duke of Tuscany's son. He returned to Rome to become assistant maestro at Santa Maria Maggiore, a member of the Arcadian Academy in 1706, and principal maestro at Santa Maria in 1707. He returned to Naples in 1708, became choirmaster of the royal chapel in 1713, and, except for the years 1718–21 in Rome, spent most of the rest of his life there. He was a prolific composer, wrote more than 100 operas, including *Pompeo* (1684), *Teodore* (1693), *Laodicea e Berenice* (1701), *Il Ciro* (1712), and *Il Tigrane* (1715); some 200 masses, *Tu es Petrus* and *Missa ad usum cappelae pontificiae*; several oratorios, *Agar ed Ismaele* and *La Vergine addolorata*; and many motets and shorter pieces. He did much to develop and elaborate orchestral music and originated the classical style of the eighteenth century. He died in Naples, Italy, on Oct. 24.

SCARLATTI, GIUSEPPE DOMENICO (1685–1757), composer. Son of Alessandro, he was born in Naples on Oct. 26, studied under his father and Gasparmi, entered the service of Queen Casimire of Poland in 1709, was maestro of St. Peter's in Rome in 1715–19, musician at the Lisbon court in 1721–25, music master of the princess of the Asturias at Madrid after 1729, visited Dublin and London in 1740–42, and returned in 1745 to Naples, where he died. He was considered the greatest harpsichordist of his day and defeated Handel in a competition in 1708. He composed some sixty sonatas for the harpsichord which so influenced digital technique that he was called the "father of piano forte playing."

SCARPAZZA, VITTORE. *See* Carpaccio, Vittore.

SCARPETTI, ANGELO. *See* Angelus de Borgo San Sepolcro, St.

SCARRON, PAUL (1610–1660), author. Born in Paris on July 4, he graduated from the Sorbonne, was tonsured when nineteen, and became a member of the bishop of Le Mans' household. He accompanied the bishop to Rome in 1635, was made a canon in St. Julian's cathedral in 1636 (though not a priest), but resigned to marry Mlle. Françoise d'Aubigné, the future Mme. de Maintenon, in 1652. He was noted for his comedies and was so successful with his burlesque verse in *Le Typhon* (1642) and *Le Virgile travesti* (1648–52) that he raised it to a recognized literary form. Outstanding works include *Roman comique*; comedies such as *Le Marquis ridicule* (1656), *Jodelet, Les trois Dorothées*, and *Le Gardien de soi-même*; and *Nouvelles magicomiques* (1659), many of whose plots and characters were adapted by Molière and Beaumarchais. His travesties were widely imitated in England

by Charles Cotton, Richard Flecknoe, and others. He died in Paris on Oct. 7.

SCHADOW, FRIEDRICH WILHELM VON (1789–1862), painter. Son of the sculptor Johann Gottfried Schadow, he was born in Berlin on Sept. 6, went to Rome in 1810, studied under Overbeck, and became a member of the Nazarite band of pre-Raphaelites and a convert. In 1819 he taught at the Berlin Academy and in 1826 was director of the Düsseldorf Academy of Painting, a position he held until 1859. He built the academy into an outstanding art center, and is considered the founder of the Old Düsseldorf school. His religious paintings were extremely popular and noted for their realism, color, and form: *The Wise and Foolish Virgins*, *Christ and His Disciples at Emmaus*, *Ascension of the Virgin*, *Four Evangelists*, and *Queen of Heaven*. He died in Düsseldorf, Germany, on Mar. 19.

SCHAEPMAN, HERMAN (1844–1903), poet. Born in Tubbergen, Holland, on Mar. 2, he studied at Oldenzall College and Kuilenberg and Ryzenburg seminaries, was ordained in 1867, and received his doctorate in divinity in Rome in 1869. He taught at Ryzenburg in 1870, was co-founder of the periodical, *De Wachter*, in 1871, and was the first priest to be elected to the States General. He fought for Catholic emancipation in Holland, was noted for his poetry, *De Paus* (1866), *De Pers*, *De eeuw en haar koning, Napoleon* (1873) and *Aya Sofia* (1886), and was made a domestic prelate and then prothonotary apostolic by Pope Leo XIII. He died in Rome on Jan. 21.

SCHALL VON BELL, JOHANN ADAM (1591–1666), missioner. Born in Cologne, Germany, he studied in Rome, became a Jesuit in 1611, and in 1618 was sent to China. He was obliged to remain in Macao because of warfare in China until 1622, when he began his activities in Shen-si. In 1630 he went to Peking to work on the reform of the Chinese calendar and prepared a series of more than 100 textbooks on astronomy, mathematics, and allied subjects to help educate the Chinese in the sciences necessary for an understanding of astronomy. The task was completed in 1638 and its success allowed him and other missionaries throughout China to intensify their apostolic efforts. He came into great favor with Emperor Ts'ung-cheng (who conferred on him the rank of mandarin, despite his objections, in 1634) and later with Emperor Shun-chi (who appointed him president of the board of mathematics). In 1650 he dedicated the first Christian church in Peking, and in 1657 he was given imperial permission to preach Christianity throughout China; he is said to have won 100,000 converts. Shun-chi died in 1662, and two years later Fr. Schall was imprisoned;

he was sentenced to death by the regents in 1665, but when an earthquake shook Peking, he was released and returned to his church. He died in Peking on Aug. 15.

SCHANNAT, JOHANN FRIEDRICH (1683–1739), historian. Born in Luxembourg, on July 23, he studied at Louvain, bcame a lawyer, studied for the priesthood, and was ordained. He was commissioned by various abbots and bishops to write histories of their sees and abbeys, and in 1735 was sent to Italy by the archbishop of Prague to write a history of the councils of the Church. Among his works are the eleven-volume *Conciliae Germaniae* (1759–90), which Joseph Hartzheim continued, *Historia Fuldensis* (1729) and *Eiflia illustrata* (1825–55). He died in Heidelberg, Germany, on Mar. 6.

SCHATZGEYER, CASPAR (1463?–1527). Born in Landshut, Germany, he became a Franciscan, was provincial at Strassburg, and in 1523 became inquisitor for Germany. He was very active against the reformers, helped to save Bavaria for the Church, and wrote more than twenty books on monasticism, grace, marriage, purgatory, and the mass. He died in Munich, Germany, on Sept. 18.

SCHÄUFELIN, HANS LEONHARD (1490–1540), painter. Born in Nuremberg, Germany, he studied under and became the assistant of Dürer. He did an illuminated psalter for Count von Ottingen; woodcuts for Emperor Maximilian's *Theuerdank*; *St. Jerome* and other paintings; frescoes in the town hall and the Ziegler altar in St. George's church, both in Nordlingen, where he became a magistrate in 1515. He died in Nuremberg.

SCHÄZLER, CONSTANTINE VON (1827–1880), theologian. Born in Ratisbon, Germany, on May 7, he studied at Erlangen, law at Munich and Heidelberg, and then became an army officer. He left the army, received his doctorate in law from Erlangen, practiced law, and became a convert in 1850. He studied theology at Louvain, became a Jesuit in 1851, and was ordained in 1856. He left the Jesuits in 1857, received his doctorate in theology from Munich in 1859, became a tutor at the Osnabrück seminary in 1861, taught at Freiburg in 1862, and was archepiscopal councilor in 1866. He was Bishop Fessler's theologian at the Vatican Council, moved to Rome in 1873 where he was made a domestic prelate in 1874, and reentered the Jesuits just before his death in Interlaken, Switzerland, on Sept. 19.

SCHEDEL, HARTMANN (1440–1514), historian. Born in Nuremberg, Germany, on Feb. 13, he studied at Leipzig and Padua, where he received his doctorate in medicine in 1466, and became a physician in Nördlingen, Amberg, and Nuremberg, where he lived from 1481 until his death on Nov. 28. He wrote several books,

chief of which were *Liber chronicarum* (1493), a world chronicle, and *Liber antiquitatum* (1504), a collection of inscriptions.

SCHEEBEN, MATTHIAS JOSEPH (1835–1888), author. Born in Meckenheim, Germany, on Mar. 1, he studied at the Gregorian in Rome, was ordained in 1858, taught at the Cologne seminary from 1860 to 1875, founded the Cologne *Pastoralblatt* in 1867, edited *Das ökumenische Concil*, and wrote several books on grace, most popular of which was *Die Herrlichkeiten der göttlichen gnade*. He died in Cologne, Germany, on July 21.

SCHEFFLER, JOHANNES (1624–1677), poet. Born in Breslau, son of a Polish nobleman, he took his degree in medicine at Padua and became court physician to the prince of Oels, Silesia. He became a convert in 1653, taking the confirmation name Angelus Silesius, under which he later wrote. He was ordained in 1661, wrote some 200 religious poems (*Heilige Seelenlust*), a long epigrammatic poem, *The Cherubic Pilgrim*, and fifty-five controversial tracts on Protestantism, some of which were collected in his two-volume *Ecclesiologia*. He died in Breslau on June 9.

SCHEFFMACHER, JOHN JAMES (1668–1733), theologian. Born in Kientzheim, Alsace, on Apr. 27, he became a Jesuit and after ordination was noted as a preacher. He taught theology at Strassburg, where he was appointed to the chair of apologetics in 1715 and served as rector in 1728–31. He wrote the popular *Lettres d'un docteur allemand* and *Lettres d'un théologien*. He died in Strassburg, Alsace, on Aug. 18.

SCHEINER, CHRISTOPH (1575–1650), astronomer. Born in Wald, Swabia, on July 25, he became a Jesuit in 1595, studied mathematics at Ingolstadt, taught at Dillingen, and in 1610 returned to Ingolstadt, where he began his astronomical studies which were to include some 2000 observations of the sun. In 1611 he discovered, described, and made continuous observations of sunspots which involved him in a dispute with Galileo, who claimed prior discovery. In 1616 he went to Innsbruck, where his studies of the eye revealed the retina as the seat of vision, became rector of the Jesuit college in Neisse, Silesia, in 1626, and then professor of mathematics in Rome. He later returned to Neisse, where he died on July 18. He wrote numerous treatises on the sun and its properties, chief of which was the *Rosa Ursinus* (1626–30) containing his observations on the sun and describing his methods. He also invented a pantograph and produced a more perfect helioscope.

SCHELBLE, JOHANN NEPOMUK (1789–1837), composer. Born in Hüfingen, Germany, on May 16, he became an opera singer at Stuttgart at eighteen and taught at a music school there. He went to Vienna, where he met Beethoven in 1814, to Berlin in 1818, where he was befriended by Clemens Brentano, and later that year founded the Society of St. Cecilia to popularize classical music in Frankfort-on-Main. He remained there, directing concerts until 1836, when ill health caused him to return to his native town, where he died on Aug. 6. He wrote a mass and other compositions.

SCHELSTRATE, EMMANUEL (1649–1692), theologian. Born in Antwerp, Brabant, he was a canon at its cathedral, was appointed assistant librarian of the Vatican Library by Pope Innocent IX, and became a leading proponent of the theory of papal supremacy and an authority on church history. Among his numerous writings is *Antiquitas illustrata circa concilia generalia et provincialia* (1678). He died in Rome on Apr. 6.

SCHENKL, MAURUS VON (1749–1816), theologian. Born in Auerbach, Bavaria, on Jan. 4, he studied in Amberg, became a Benedictine in 1768, and was ordained in 1772. He was pastor in Gelgenbach, taught at Weltenburg from 1778 until 1783, when he became librarian, taught at Prüfening, and at the Amberg lyceum in 1790. He served as rector there from 1794 to 1798, and as regent until 1808, was appointed spiritual adviser to the king in 1804, and died in Amberg, Germany, on June 14. He wrote *Juris ecclesiastici statu Germaniae maxime* (1785), *Ethica christiana universalis* (1800–1), and *Theologiae pastoralis systema* (1815–25).

SCHENUTE, ST. (334?–452?). Born in Schenalolet, Akhym, Egypt, he became a monk at a double monastery ruled over by his uncle, Bgol, whom he succeeded in 388 as abbot. He accompanied St. Cyril of Alexandria as archimandrite to the Council of Ephesus in 431. He introduced vows to monastic life and combined some features of the cenobitic with the anchoretic way of life. He is said to have ruled over 2200 monks and 1800 nuns at his monastery in Atripe, Egypt, which made him the most powerful abbot of the country and one of its major figures. He was a leader in the development of communal monastic life and a strict disciplinarian who emphasized the austerity of monastic life, instituted certain practices akin to present-day monastic vows, but discouraged study and undisciplined penances. He lived to be 118, and was born no earlier than 332 and died no later than 466. He is also called Schnudi and Sinuthius. F. D. July 1.

SCHER, PHILIP GEORGE (1880–1953), bishop. Born in Belleville, Illinois, on Feb. 22, he studied at the Josephinum, Columbus, Ohio, and the Propaganda, Rome, and was ordained in 1904. He taught at the Josephinum, did parish work in California, became vicar

general of Monterey-Fresno in 1931, and administered the see from then until 1933, when he was appointed its bishop. He died in Fresno, California, on Jan. 3.

SCHERER, GEORG (1540–1605), educator. Born in Schwaz, Tyrol, he became a Jesuit in 1559, was ordained, was court preacher to Archduke Matthias from 1577 to 1600, rector of the Jesuit college in Vienna in 1590, was transferred to Linz, Austria, in 1594, and died there on Nov. 30. He was a vigorous controversialist, and was noted for his conversions.

SCHERER-BOCCARD, THEODORE VON (1816–1885), journalist. Born in Dornach, Switzerland, on May 12, he studied in Solothurn and Fribourg, took up journalism on his return to Solothurn, and founded the newspaper, *Die Schildwache am Jura*, in 1836. He entered politics in 1838 when he became a member of the Swiss council, was forced to flee to France in 1841 for his political activities, and later the same year founded in Lucerne the *Staatszeitung der katholischen Schweiz*, which became the leading Catholic Conservative party paper. He became secretary of the Sonderbund's president in 1845, and founded *Katholische Annalen* in 1847 as the journal of the Academy of St. Charles Borromeo, a society of Swiss scholars, which he had founded in 1844, both of which were ended by the war of the Sonderbund. He was made a Roman count by Pope Pius IX in 1852, helped found the Swiss Pius Association in 1857, of which he was president until his death, and headed the Society for Home Missions founded in 1863. He added Boccard to his name in 1868 when he married Marie Louise von Boccard. He wrote historical and apologetic treatises and was one of the editors of the *Archiv für schweizerische Reformationsgeschichte* (1869–75). He died in Solothurn, Switzerland, on Feb. 6.

SCHERVIER, FRANCES (1819–1876), foundress. Born in Aachen, Germany, on Jan. 3, she began working for the sick and poor at an early age, joined a charitable group devoted to such work in 1840, and in 1845 united with four other women in a foundation known as Sisters of the Poor of St. Francis. She was superior, established an infirmary in Aachen during a smallpox epidemic, cared for cholera victims, and by 1850 had set up a hospital for incurables and several relief kitchens and home-nursing centers. The constitutions of the order were approved by the bishop of Cologne and by the pope; more homes and hospitals were opened in other parts of Germany, and in 1855 a group of six sisters was sent to Cincinnati, Ohio, to establish a hospital.

SCHIAVONE, ANDREA. *See* Medolla, Andrea.

SCHILLING, MARY (1856–1940), educator. Born in St. Louis, she became a School Sister of Notre Dame, taking the name Mother Mary Stanislaus Kostka, founded Mt. Mary College, Milwaukee, was commissary general of her congregation from 1917 to 1935, and died in Elm Grove, Wisconsin, on Mar. 11.

SCHINNER, AUGUSTIN FRANCIS (1863–1937), bishop. Born in Milwaukee, Wisconsin, on May 1, he studied at St. Francis seminary, was ordained in 1886, and taught there until 1893. He was secretary to the archbishop and vicar general of the archdiocese of Milwaukee until 1905, when he was consecrated bishop of Superior. He resigned in 1913, but was appointed first bishop of Spokane, Washington, in 1914, resigning because of age in 1925. He died in Milwaukee on Feb. 7.

SCHINNER, MATTHAEUS (1470?–1522), cardinal. Born in Mühlbach, Switzerland, son of the lord of Montigny, he was parish priest in Aernen in 1496, became dean of the Sion cathedral, and bishop of Sion in 1499. He was leader of the Swiss cantons in their alliance with the popes to drive the French from Italy, was appointed bishop of Novara and created a cardinal in 1511, and was named papal legate for Italy and Germany in 1512. He commanded a Swiss-Venetian army which drove the French from Milan and, when Louis XII recaptured Milan, defeated the French in the battle of Novara in 1513, a feat which caused the duke of Milan to make him margrave of Vigevano. In 1515 he was defeated at the battle of Marignano, spent the next three years unsuccessfully trying to ally England, Spain, and the pope against France, and in 1516 was driven from Sion into exile in Zurich. He helped elect Charles V emperor in 1519, was appointed bishop of Catania, Sicily, in 1520, and again led an army against Francis I for Milan in 1521. He was appointed administrator of the Papal States by Adrian VI, and died of the plague in Rome on Oct. 1.

SCHLARMAN, JOSEPH H. (1879–1951), archbishop. Born in Breese Township, Illinois, on Feb. 23, he studied at Quincy and Innsbruck, was ordained in 1904, and took his doctorate at the Gregorian, Rome, in 1907. He was a curate in Belleville, Illinois, in 1907–9, chancellor to 1930, bishop of Peoria in 1930, and raised to archbishop in 1951. He served as chairman of the state's prison-reform commission in 1936–37, was president of the National Catholic Rural Life Conference in 1943–44, wrote *Mexico, Land of Volcanoes*, was greatly interested in Mexico and Central America, and was engaged in founding a seminary for Mexican students at the time of his death in Peoria, Illinois, on Nov. 10.

SCHLEGEL, FRIEDRICH VON (1772–1829), scholar. Born in Hanover, Germany, on Mar. 10, he studied law at Göttingen and art and literature at Leipzig, and with his brother August Wilhelm founded in 1798 the *Athenäum*, a critical review, which in its two years of existence was the organ of the romantic school. He became a tutor in Jena and married Jakob Mendelssohn's daughter, Mme. Dorothea Veit, who divorced her husband to marry him in 1800, went to Paris in 1802 as editor of the magazine *Europa*, and became a convert in 1808. He became Archduke Charles' secretary in Vienna in 1809, bitterly opposed Napoleon, and lectured on modern history in Vienna in 1811. He was councilor of the Austrian legation to the federal diet from 1815 to 1818, accompanied Metternich on a trip to Italy, edited the magazine *Concordia* in 1820–23, and spent the remainder of his life writing and lecturing. He wrote numerous books on philosophy, notably *Ueber die Sprache und Weisheit der Inder* (1808) and *Die Geschichte der alten und neuen Literatur* (1815); *History of Ancient and Modern Literature* (1815), lectures on *The Philosophy of History* (1835), and *Lectures on the Philosophy of Life* (1828) were published in English. He also wrote poetry, *Poetisches Tagebuch* (1805–6) and *Gedichte* (1809); *Luzinde* (1799), a novel; and *Alarkos* (1802), a tragedy. He died in Dresden, Germany, on Jan. 12.

SCHLEGEL, THEODORE (d. 1529), martyr. When the bishop of Chur, Switzerland, fled at the outset of the Reformation in 1524, the see was directed by his administrator, Abbot Theodore, who was publicly beheaded on Jan. 1.

SCHLÖR, ALOYSIUS (1805–1852), author. Born in Vienna on June 17, he studied there, was ordained in 1828, became chaplain at Altlerchenfeld, prefect of studies at the Vienna seminary in 1831, and received his doctorate in theology in 1832. He was Emperor Ferdinand's confessor in 1834–37, engaged in missionary work, and became spiritual director of the seminary in Graz, Austria, where he became noted for his retreats and where he remained until his death on Nov. 2. He wrote numerous spiritual works, including *Jesu mein Verlangen*.

SCHLOSSER, JOHN FREDERICK HENRY (1780–1851), jurist. Born in Frankfort-on-Main, Germany, on Dec. 30, he studied law at Jena, received his doctorate in jurisprudence in 1803, practiced law in Frankfort, was appointed counsel of the municipal court in 1806, and director of the lyceum in 1812. He became a convert in 1814, represented Frankfort at the Congress of Vienna, was a champion of Catholic rights, and spent the later years of his life in charitable works and encouraging the arts (including the publication of *Monumenta Germaniae*). He wrote several books and collaborated with Goethe in *Aus meinem Leben*. He died in Frankfort on Jan. 22.

SCHMALZGRUEBER, FRANZ XAVER (1663–1735), canonist. Born in Griesbach, Bavaria, on Oct. 9, he became a Jesuit in 1679, studied at Ingolstadt, and received his doctorate in theology and canon law. He taught at numerous seminaries and colleges (at Dillingen and Ingolstadt from 1703 to 1716), was chancellor of Dillingen, served as Jesuit book censor in Rome for two years, and was prefect of studies at Munich. He wrote *Jus Ecclesiasticum Universum* and other studies in canon law, and died in Dillingen, Germany, on Nov. 7.

SCHMID, CHRISTOPH VON (1768–1845), author. Born in Dinkelsbühl, Bavaria, on Aug. 15, he studied at Dillingen, was ordained in 1791, and spent the next five years in pastoral activity. In 1796 he was named director of the school in Thannhausen, and then served as parish priest at Oberstadion from 1816 until 1826, when he was appointed canon of the cathedral in Augsburg, Germany, where he remained until his death. Early in his career he began to write successful stories for children which were widely translated.

SCHMIDT, AUSTIN GUILFORD (1883–1960). Born in Cincinnati, Ohio, on July 24, he studied at Xavier and St. Louis, became a Jesuit, and was ordained in 1917. He took his doctorate at Michigan in 1923, taught at St. Louis in 1919–26, was appointed dean of the Loyola University Graduate School, Chicago, in 1928, and became director of the Loyola University Press. He died in West Baden, Indiana, on July 22.

SCHMIDT, FRIEDRICH VON (1825–1891), architect. Born in Frickenhofen, Germany, he studied at Stuttgart and in 1845 became a member of the guild building the cathedral in Cologne. He spent almost fifteen years on it, becoming a master workman in 1848, received his certificate as architect in 1856, and helped design the towers of the cathedral. He became a convert in 1858, went to Milan to restore San Ambrogio cathedral, to Vienna in 1859, where he became cathedral architect in 1862 and chief architect in 1865, and in 1888 was made a baron by the emperor. He designed churches and public buildings throughout Germany and Austria, and is particularly known for his restoration of St. Stephen's cathedral in Vienna, its city hall, and the church in Fünfhaus. He died in Vienna.

SCHMIDT, WILHELM (1868–1954), historian. Born in Hörde, Germany, on Feb. 16, he studied at Berlin and Vienna, joined the Society of the Divine Word in 1890, and taught at Vienna. He founded the Anthropological Institute in Mölding, of which he became director, taught at Freiburg after 1938, and was interested in the sociology and ethnol-

ogy of the Far East. His books include *The Origin and Growth of Religion* (1931), *High Gods in North America* (1933), and *Primitive Revelation* (1939).

SCHNEEMANN, GERARD (1829–1885), theologian. Born in Wesel, Germany, on Feb. 12, he abandoned the study of law to enter the Münster seminary, became a Jesuit in 1851, and was ordained in 1856. He taught at Bonn, Aachen, and Maria Laach, contributed to scholarly journals, edited *Stimmen aus Maria-Laach* from 1871 to 1877, wrote several treatises, notably a refutation of Döllinger's writings, *Studien über die Honoriusfräge* (1864), and collaborated on *Acta et decreta sacrorum conciliorum recentiorum*. He died in Kerkrade, Holland, on Nov. 20.

SCHNELLER, JOSEPH (d. 1860). He was third pastor of the earliest church in Brooklyn, New York, St. Paul's, founded the *Weekly Register and Catholic Diary* in 1833, and was a violent controversialist with opponents of the Church in the metropolitan area.

SCHOENBERG, MATTHIAS VON (1732–1792), author. Born in Ehingen, Germany, on Nov. 9, he became a Jesuit in 1750, headed Eleemosyna Aurea, a society founded to provide popularly written books on the faith, from 1766 to 1772, became ecclesiastical councilor to the elector of Bavaria when the Jesuits were suppressed in 1773, and devoted his life to writing some forty books and brochures on religion. He died in Munich, Germany, on Apr. 20.

SCHÖFFER, PETER (1425?–1503), publisher. Born in Gernsheim, Germany, he took minor orders, was a manuscript copyist in Paris in 1451, appeared as a witness in 1455 for Johannes Fust (whose daughter he married) in his suit against Gutenberg (he probably was a printer for either or both of them), and became Fust's partner in his publishing and printing establishment. In 1456 he left Fust to establish his own firm, issuing works on civil law, canon law, and theology. Probably its outstanding product was the psalters of 1457 and 1459, which are believed to have been prepared by Gutenberg. He died in Mainz, Germany.

SCHÖFFLER, BL. AUGUSTUS (1822–1851), martyr. Born in Mittelbronn, Lorraine, he joined the Society of Foreign Missions in Paris, was sent to Tonkin in 1848, and was beheaded at Annam, Indochina, on May 1 for his missionary work. He was beatified in 1900. F. D. Nov. 6.

SCHOLASTICA, ST. (d. 543). Sister of St. Benedict, she apparently was abbess of a double monastery she founded about five miles south of Monte Cassino. She was devoted to prayer, and met her brother once a year for long ascetic discussions; nothing else is known of her except an account of her last days in the *Dialogues* of St. Gregory. F. D. Feb. 10.

SCHOLLINER, HERMAN (1722–1795), theologian. Born in Freising, Bavaria, on Jan. 15, he became a Benedictine in 1738, studied at Erfurt and Salzburg, and was head of the Benedictine house of studies in Bavaria from 1752 to 1757. He was elected to the Bavarian Academy of Sciences in 1759, was professor at Salzburg in 1759–66, prior of his monastery in 1772, and taught at Ingolstadt from 1776 until 1780, when he became provost at Welchenberg, where he died on July 16. He wrote numerous theological and historical tracts.

SCHOLS, CHARLES MATHIEU (1849–1897), scientist. Born in Maastricht, Holland, on Mar. 28, he received his degree in civil engineering from the polytechnic school in Delft, taught at the Royal Military Academy of Breda, and in 1878 taught geodesy at Delft. He became noted for his mathematical and geodetic treatises, was elected to the Royal Academy of Sciences in 1880, was made secretary of the royal surveying committee in 1881, and supervised the government's geographical survey of 1886. He died in Delft, Holland, on Mar. 28.

SCHOLZ, JOHN MARTIN AUGUSTINE (1794–1852), scholar. Born in Kapsdorf, Germany, on Feb. 8, he studied at Breslau, Freiburg, where he received his doctorate in theology in 1817, and Paris, where he studied oriental languages under Silvestre de Sacy. He traveled through Europe and the Holy Land in 1821, and taught exegesis at Bonn from 1823, when he was ordained, and wrote exegetical and travel books, and edited *Novum Testamentum Graece*. He died in Bonn, Germany, on Oct. 20.

SCHONBORN, JOHANN PHILIPP VON (1605–1673), archbishop. Born in Eschbach, Germany, on Aug. 6, he became a cleric at the Würzburg cathedral when sixteen, and at Mainz in 1625, cathedral canon at Würzburg in 1629 and at Worms in 1630, and provost at Würzburg in 1635. He was appointed bishop of Würzburg in 1642, ordained in 1645, appointed archbishop of Mainz in 1647, and bishop of Worms in 1663. His reign was devoted to repairing the ravages of the Thirty Years' War, improving and increasing the clergy, and effecting widespread reforms. He died in Würzburg, Germany, on Feb. 12.

SCHONGAUER, MARTIN (1445?–1491), painter. Born in Colmar, Alsace, son of a Bavarian goldsmith, he is known to have studied at Leipzig, took up painting (greatly influenced by the work of Rogier van der Weyden) and then engraving. The only work definitely identified as his is the altarpiece of St. Martin's church in Colmar, *Madonna of the Rose Arbor*. A *Nativity*, *Annunciation*, and *Virgin* and *St. Anthony Adoring the Christ Child* also are attributed to him. He executed more than 100 plates, all of religious subjects, notable for their minute detail and delicate line. Among his best plates are the *Wise and Foolish Virgins* and *Passion* series, *Adoration of the Magi*, and *Temptation of St. Anthony*. He is often called Martin Schön because of the beauty of his work. He died in Breisbach, Germany, on Feb. 2.

SCHÖNINGH, FERDINAND FRIEDRICH JOSEPH (1815–1883), publisher. Born in Meppen, Hanover, Germany, on Mar. 16, he entered the book business as an apprentice in 1831, opened a book and art store in 1847 in Paderborn, founded the periodicals *Westfälisches Kirchenblatt* and *Westfälische Volksblatt* in 1848 and 1849, and in 1849 founded a publishing house which became noted for its scientific, literary, and theological works. It also added three periodicals, *Chrysologus* (1860), *Blätter für kirchliche Wissenschaft und Praxis* (1867), and *Gymnasium* (1883), before its founder died in Paderborn, Germany, on Aug. 18.

SCHOPPE, KASPAR (1576–1649), scholar. Born in Neumarkt, the Palatinate, Germany, he studied at Heidelberg, Altdorf, and Ingolstadt, and became a convert in 1598. He wrote strong attacks on Joseph Justus Scaliger and King James I of England in bitter contemporary controversies; *De arte critica*; editions of Varro and Symmachus; rhetorical studies; and *Poemata varia*. He also is called Scioppius.

SCHORLEMER-ALST, BURGHARD VON (1825–1895). Born in Heringhausen, Westphalia, Germany, on Oct. 21, he studied at the Royal Saxon Military Academy in Dresden, served in the Prussian army, which he left to marry Countess Droste zu Vischering in 1852, became interested in the peasants' conditions, and in 1862 published a pamphlet, *Die Lage des Bauernstandes in Westfalen*, proposing the formation of peasant unions. He became a member of the Prussian agricultural board in 1863, manager of the central agricultural union in 1862, founded two agricultural schools, and in 1870 was elected to the lower house of the Prussian diet, of which he was a member until 1889. He was a chairman of the Centre party in 1875–89, fought Bismarck's Kulturkampf, and worked unceasingly to better the conditions of the farming class through the Westphalian Peasant Union founded in 1871. He was made a member of the council of state in 1884, a life member of the upper house of the Prussian diet in 1891, and was honored by the pope, who made him privy chamberlain. He died in Alst, near Burgsteinfurt, Germany, on Mar. 17.

SCHOTIN, ST. (6th century). He left Ireland to become a disciple of St. David of Wales, returned and founded a school for boys in Kilkenny, and lived as a hermit on Mt. Mairge. F. D. Jan. 6.

SCHOTT, GASPAR (1608–1666), physicist. Born in Königshofen, Germany, on Feb. 5, he became a Jesuit in 1627, taught at the Jesuit college in Palermo, Italy, studied in Rome, returned to Germany in 1657, and taught at Augsburg until his death there on May 22. He wrote on science, mathematics, and magic, including *Magia universalis naturae et artis* (1657–59) and *Cursus mathematicus*.

SCHRADER, CLEMENT (1820–1875), theologian. Born in Itzüm, Hanover, Germany, in Nov., he studied at the German College in Rome, where he was prefect of studies, joined the Jesuits in 1848, taught at the Roman College and at Vienna, helped edit the periodical, *Der Papst und die modernen Ideen* in 1864–67, and then was appointed to the commission to prepare for the Vatican Council. When he refused to take the oath to the Austrian government he was ousted as professor at the University of Vienna in 1869, whereupon he was appointed professor of theology at the Catholic University in Poitiers, France, where he remained until his death on Feb. 23. He wrote theological treatises, including *De unitate romana, De Deo creante* and *De triplici ordine.*

SCHRAM, DOMINIC (1722–1797), theologian. Born in Bamberg, Germany, on Oct. 24, he joined the Benedictines in 1743, was ordained in 1748, taught at the monastery in Banz, Germany, until 1782, when he became prior of the Michelsberg monastery, and in 1787 returned to Banz, where he remained until his death there on Sept. 21. He wrote *Compendium theologiae* (1768), *Institutiones theologiae mysticae* (1774), and the eighteen-volume *Analysis operum sacrorum patrum et scriptorum ecclesiasticorum* (1780–96).

SCHRANK, FRANZ PAULA VON (1747–1835), naturalist. Born in Varnbach, Austria, on Aug. 21, he studied in Passau, became a Jesuit when fifteen, studied at Vienna, Oedenburg, Raab, and Tyrnau, and taught at the college in Linz in 1769. When the Jesuits were suppressed in 1773, he went to Vienna, where he was ordained in 1774 and received his doctorate in theology two years later. He taught mathematics in Amberg and rhetoric in Burghausen, where he became interested in agriculture. In 1784 he was appointed professor of botany at Ingolstadt, where he served several times as rector, and in 1809 he was elected a member of the Munich Academy of Sciences and director of the botanical garden, a position he held until his death in Munich, Germany, on Dec. 22. He wrote some 200 articles and forty books, including *Bayerische flora* (1789), *Primitiae florae salisburgensis*

(1792), *Flora monacensis* (1811–20) with 400 color plates, and *Plantae rariores horti academici monacensis* (1819) with 100 color plates.

SCHRAUDOLPH, JOHANN (1808–1879), painter. Born in Oberstdorf, Germany, he studied under Schlotthauer in Munich, Cornelius, and Heinrich Hess, became a popular painter of devotional pictures, and is best known for his frescoes in the Speyer cathedral and on the life of St. Boniface in the basilica in Munich. He died on May 31.

SCHREIBER, CHRISTIAN KARL AUGUST (1872–1933), bishop. Born in Somborn, Germany, on Aug. 3, he studied at the Gregorian, Rome, was ordained in 1898, taught at Fulda, and in 1921 was made bishop of Meissen. When the concordat between Germany and the Vatican was signed in 1929 he became the first Catholic bishop of Berlin since the Reformation. He died in Berlin on Sept. 2.

SCHREMBS, JOSEPH (1866–1945), archbishop. Born in Wuzelhofen, near Ratisbon, Bavaria, Germany, on Mar. 12, he migrated to the United States in 1877, studied at St. Vincent's College, Pennsylvania, Laval University, and the Grand seminary, Montreal, and was ordained in Grand Rapids, Michigan, in 1889. He engaged in pastoral work in Michigan, was appointed vicar general of Grand Rapids in 1903, and was made a domestic prelate in 1906. He was appointed titular bishop of Sophene and auxiliary of Grand Rapids in 1911, became first bishop of Toledo later the same year, and was appointed bishop of Cleveland in 1921. He was a member of the National Catholic War Council and the administrative committee of the National Catholic Welfare Conference, was president and protector of the Priests' Eucharistic League, and was made an archbishop in 1929. He died on Nov. 2 in Cleveland.

SCHRIECK, LOUISE VANDER (1813–1886). Born in Bergen op Zoom, Holland, on Nov. 14, and baptized Josephine, she studied under the Sisters of Notre Dame de Namur, devoted herself to charitable work, joined the Notre Dame sisters in 1837, and was professed in 1839. She was sent to the United States with seven other nuns in 1840 when the first foundation of the community outside Belgium was established in Cincinnati, Ohio, was named superior in 1845, superior-provincial of the area east of the Rocky Mountains in 1848, and held that position until her death in Cincinnati on Dec. 3, founding twenty-six convents and increasing the number of her nuns to some 800, most of them devoted to teaching.

SCHUBERT, FRANZ PETER (1797–1828), composer. Born in the Himmelpfortgrund, a suburb of Vienna, Austria, on Jan. 31, son of a schoolmaster, he was taught music as a child by his father and by Michael Holzer, organist of the Liechtenthal church, where he was first soprano at ten. He entered the Imperial and Royal seminary, Vienna's chief music school, as a choirboy in the royal chapel in 1808, and soon impressed his teachers, Antonio Salieri and Wenzel Ruzicka, with his amazing aptitude. He began composing music with a *Fantasy* for pianoforte in 1810, but left the school to become a teacher in his father's school in 1813, continued with private lessons from Salieri, wrote his first opera (*Des Teufels Lustschloss*) and *Mass in F* in 1814, and in 1815 wrote *Erlkönig* and *Mass in G.* In 1816 he gave up teaching to devote himself exclusively to composing, had his first work performed publicly in 1818, an overture played at a Vienna hotel. In that same year he became music master for the family of Count Johann Esterházy in Hungary, but quickly returned to Vienna. Two operas, *Die Zwillingsbrüder* and *Die Zauberharfe*, were performed in 1820, and in 1821 his first published work, *Erlkönig*, appeared by private subscription and was a great success. The next three years were years of disappointment (though of great productivity), during which several of his operas were turned down or quickly withdrawn, but in 1825 his works began to gain wider acceptance and his income, which was always to be small, prospered. During the next three years he turned out in great profusion some of his finest work. He was refused a conductorship at the Vienna opera in 1826 when he would not alter one of his songs, gave the only public concert of his works in the spring of 1828, was stricken with typhoid, and died on Nov. 19 in Vienna. Schubert's music is noted for its warm spontaneousness, fresh, poetic quality, and imagination. He worked at great speed, seldom revising. Among his principal works are *Symphony in B Minor* (called the *Unfinished Symphony*), *Symphony in C Major* (1828), *Alfonso und Estrella, Fierabras*, and *Rosamunde, Salve Regina, Stabat Mater, Tantum Ergo*, and *Magnificat*. He wrote more than 600 songs, among them *Ave Maria* and *Gretchen am Spinnrade*; the cycles *Müllerlieder, Winterreise, Schwanengesang*; the Scot songs, Shakespeare songs, and those he wrote to Goethe's and Schiller's poems. He wrote twenty piano sonatas, eight symphonies, six masses, and a large body of chamber music, such as *Moments musicaux* and the *Trout* quintet, besides his operas.

SCHULER, ANTHONY JOSEPH (1869–1944), bishop. Born in St. Mary's, Pennsylvania, on Sept. 30, he became a Jesuit in 1886, studied at St. Stanislaus seminary, St. Louis University, and Woodstock, and was ordained in 1901. He taught at Sacred Heart (now Regis) College, Denver, was its president in 1903–6, taught at St. Stanislaus in 1906–7, did parish work in Texas and Colorado, and

in 1915 was consecrated first bishop of El Paso, Texas. He built St. Patrick's cathedral, and died in El Paso on June 5.

SCHULTE, KARL JOSEF (1871–1941), cardinal. Born in Valbert, Westphalia, on Sept. 14, he became editor of *Bischofliche Hirtenbriefe* in 1912, archbishop of Cologne in 1920, and a cardinal in 1921. He was an outstanding opponent of the Nazi regime before and during World War II. He died in Cologne, Germany, on Mar. 11.

SCHUSTER, ALFREDO LUDOVICO ILDEFONSO (1880–1954), cardinal. Born in Rome on Jan. 18, of Swiss ancestry, he became a Benedictine in 1898, studied at the International College, Rome, was ordained in 1904, and continued his studies until 1914. He was procurator general of his order at Monte Cassino, abbot of St. Paul outside the Walls, and president of the Pontifical Oriental Institute. He was president of the pontifical commission for sacred art in Italy in 1924, visitor of seminaries, and wrote on art, architecture, history, and liturgy. In 1929 he was made archbishop of Milan and a cardinal and became an outspoken defender of moral, political, and social rights and an active enemy of communism. He died in the Venegono seminary on Aug. 30.

SCHWAB, FELIX (17th century), composer. Born in Altdorf Weingarten, Württemberg, Germany, he became a Franciscan monk, was ordained in 1656, and became musical director at a Constance monastery, then guardian at Weingarten. He published three volumes of masses and other choral music between 1634 and 1656.

SCHWALBE, BENEDICT (d. 1521). A learned Benedictine monk (also called Chelidonius and Musophilus) at the abbey of St. Abidius, Nuremberg, Germany, he wrote Latin verses for Dürer's *Apocalypse, Passion of Christ*, and *Life of Mary*, as well as poems on the monastery and its abbots. He died on Sept. 8 as abbot of the monastery of the Virgin Mary in Vienna.

SCHWANE, JOSEPH (1824–1892), theologian. Born in Dorsten, Westphalia, Germany, on Apr. 2, he studied there, at Recklinghausen and Münster, and was ordained in 1847. After further studies at Bonn and Tübingen, he became director of von Galen's institute in Münster in 1849, taught at Münster from 1853 until his death, and was made a domestic prelate in 1890. He died at Münster, Germany, on June 6. He wrote theological treatises and a history of dogmatics.

SCHWANN, THEODOR (1810–1882), physiologist. Born in Neuss, Germany, on Dec. 7, he studied at Bonn, Würzburg, and Berlin, became an assistant in the Berlin Anatomical Museum, professor of anatomy at Louvain in

1838, and of physiology and comparative anatomy at Liège in 1848, a position he held until his retirement in 1880. He early discovered the nerve sheath now called Schwann's envelope, with Johannes Müller discovered and described pepsin in gastric juice (1836), proved in 1837 the cellular make-up of animals and plants and that animal cells proceed partly from tissues, recognized the living nature of yeast in 1839, proved the falsity of the spontaneous-generation theory, and revealed the nature and function of the gall in digestion when he produced the first gastric fistula in 1844. His work on the cellular composition of plants and animals revolutionized the study of biology and medicine. He died in Cologne, Germany, on Jan. 11.

SCHWANTHALER, LUDWIG VON (1802–1848), sculptor. Born in Munich, Germany, on Aug. 26, he turned to painting in the classical manner, taught sculpture at Munich Academy in 1835, and was the founder of the modern classical school of sculpture. His devotion to themes of national interest coincided with the growth of nationalism, and he was so overwhelmed with commissions that he left much of their execution in the hands of his assistants and in many cases produced his works too quickly. His later work was decidedly romantic. Best known are his twelve bronze figures of Bavarian princes for the Königslav throne room, the statue of *Bavaria* in the Munich Hall of Fame, monuments to Jean Paul Richter, Mozart, Goethe, statues of emperors, Shakespeare, and a bronze *Dancing Girl* at Wiesbaden, and decorations for the palace of King Ludwig I at Munich, where he died on Nov. 15.

SCHWARTZ, ANTON MARIA (d. 1929), founder. An Austrian priest, he founded the Pious Workers of St. Joseph Calasanctius at Vienna in 1889, a group devoted to works of charity, care of workers, teaching catechism, directing oratories, distribution of Catholic literature, and adoration of the Eucharist. Fr. Schwartz wrote biographies and a prayer book for workers, and his group opened three colleges.

SCHWARZ, BERTHOLD (14th century?). Said to have been born in Freiburg, Germany, he was a Franciscan monk and was erroneously credited with the discovery of gunpowder by Felix Hemmelin in his *De nobilitate et rusticitate dialogus* (c. 1450). He is commonly credited, however, with making the first bronze cannons in his Venetian workshop.

SCHWARZENBERG, FRIEDRICH (1809–1885), cardinal. Born in Vienna on Apr. 6, son of Prince Joseph John Schwarzenberg, he studied at Salzburg and the seminary in Vienna, received his doctorate in theology, and was ordained in 1833. He became a curate in the cathedral parish, in 1835 was elected prince-archbishop of Salzburg by the metropolitan chapter, and was created a cardinal in 1842. He initiated clerical reforms, convened the first synod in 175 years in 1848, and presided over a meeting of the Austrian bishops in 1849–50 which presented the Church's demands to the Austrian government and marked the beginning of a genuine Austrian episcopate. He was appointed archbishop of Prague in 1850, presided at a meeting of Austrian bishops in 1856 to carry out the concordat which had just been signed, but when the concordat was annulled in 1868 became embroiled in the struggle against the oppressive measures passed by the *Reichstag* against the Church. He died in Vienna on Mar. 27.

SCHWEBACH, JAMES (1847–1921), bishop. Born in Platen, Luxembourg, on Aug. 15, he studied at Diekirch College, went to the United States in 1864, continued his studies at St. Francis seminary, Milwaukee, and was ordained in St. Paul in 1870. He served as pastor of St. Mary's in La Crosse, Wisconsin, for twenty-two years from 1870, was appointed vicar general of La Crosse in 1882, administered the diocese in 1891, and was consecrated its bishop in 1892. He died on June 6 in La Crosse.

SCHWERTNER, AUGUSTUS JOHN (1870–1939), bishop. Born in Canton, Ohio, on Dec. 23, he studied at Canisius and St. Mary's seminary, Cleveland, and was ordained in Cleveland in 1897. He served as curate in Youngstown, and pastor in Milan, Rockport, and Lima from 1897 to 1913, when he was appointed chancellor of Toledo. He occupied this position in 1913–21, became a domestic prelate in 1916, and in 1921 was appointed bishop of Wichita, Kansas. He died in Wichita on Oct. 2.

SCHWIND, MORITZ VON (1804–1871), painter. Born in Vienna on Jan. 21, he studied at Ludwig Schnorr von Caroldfeld's studio, spent some time in Rome and Carlsruhe, and in 1827 came to Munich, where he was greatly influenced by Cornelius and became a leading romanticist. Among his best works are the frescoes of the life of St. Elizabeth in Wartburg castle, the decorations in the Treck room of Ludwig II's castle in Munich, sixty water colors of Charlemagne for Hohenschwangau castle, *Knight Kurt's Bridal Procession* in the Kunsthalle, Carlsruhe, a fresco of *The Magic Flute* in the Vienna Opera House, *Singer's Contest, Symphony, Cinderella* and other legends, and many amusing etchings and humorous sketches. He died in Munich, Germany, on Feb. 8.

SCHYNSE, AUGUST (1857–1891), explorer. Born in Wallhausen, Germany, he studied at Bonn and the seminary in Speyer, was ordained in 1880, and in 1882 was sent to Africa. He reported on his mission to the Congo in *Zwei Jahre am Kongo* (1889). He went to East Africa in 1888, traveled from there to the coast with Stanley and Emin Pasha, and went with the latter to Victoria and Uganda; these explorations were recorded in *Mit Stanley und Emin Pascha durch Deutsch Ost-Afrika* (1890).

SCIOPPIUS. *See* Schoppe, Kaspar.

SCOPELLI, ST. JANE (1428–1491). Born in Reggio d'Emilia, Italy, she was refused permission by her parents to become a nun, but on their death founded the Carmelite convent of Our Lady of the People at Reggio and became its prioress. Her cult was approved in 1771. F. D. July 9.

SCORAILLE, RAOUL DE (1842–1921). Born in Périgueux, France, on Jan. 24, he studied in Sarlat and Paris, became a Jesuit in 1860, was ordained in 1874, and taught philosophy at Vals. He was editorial director of *Études* after 1888, superior of the Toulouse province, rector of Gemert, Holland, and author of a biography of Suarez. He died in Toulouse, France, on July 11.

SCOTIVOLI, ST. BENVENUTO (d. 1282), bishop. Born in Ancona, Italy, he studied law at Bologna, Italy, was ordained and made administrator of Osimo, became a Franciscan, and was consecrated bishop of Osimo in 1264. He was canonized less than four years after his death by Pope Martin IV. F. D. Mar. 22.

SCOTT, CUTHBERT (d. 1564), bishop. Vice-chancellor of the University of Cambridge and a noted theologian, he was appointed bishop of Chester, England, in 1556, was one of four bishops who defended Catholic dogma at the conference at Westminster early in Elizabeth's reign, was imprisoned in the Tower, escaped to the Continent when released on bail, and died at Louvain, Belgium, on Oct. 9.

SCOTT, VEN. MONTFORT (d. 1591), martyr. Born in Norfolk, England, he went to Douai in 1574 as one of its earliest theology students, was ordained a deacon, returned to England in 1576, was captured, and freed. He returned to Douai in 1577, was ordained, and went back to England. He labored in Kent, Yorkshire, and elsewhere until 1584, when he was captured, imprisoned for seven years, released and immediately rearrested, and put to death in London on July 2.

SCOTT, BL. WILLIAM (d. 1612), martyr. Born in Chigwell, Essex, England, he became a convert while a law student at Cambridge and a Benedictine at Sahagún, Spain, in 1604. Back in London he saw the martyrdom of Bl. John Roberts, the Benedictine who had converted him, but was able to serve in the underground mission for a year, as Fr. Maurus, before he was captured and deported. This happened at least once more before the penalty was changed to death, and he was hanged at Tyburn for his priesthood. He was beatified in 1929. F. D. May 30.

SCRYVEN, BL. THOMAS (d. 1537), martyr. *See* Beer, Bl. Richard.

SCUBICULUS, ST. (d. 285?), martyr. *See* Nicasius, St.

SCUBILIO, ST. (6th century). He was an associate of St. Paternus in founding Mont-St.-Michel, France.

SEACHNALL. *See* Secundinus, St. (d. 447).

SEARLE, GEORGE (1839–1918), astronomer. Born in London on June 27, he was educated in Brookline, Massachusetts, and at Harvard, and became a convert in 1862. He was assistant at the Dudley observatory, Albany, New York, where he discovered the asteroid Pandora, taught mathematics at Annapolis, and became an assistant at the Harvard observatory in 1866. He became a Paulist in 1868 and was superior general in 1904. He taught at Catholic University, published popular studies, and died in New York City on July 7.

SEBALD, ST. (d. 770?). Patron of Nuremberg, Bavaria, he lived as a hermit in the Reichswald and probably was a fellow Benedictine monk with SS. Willibald and Winebald on their missions. F. D. Aug. 19.

SEBASTIAN (1554–1578), king of Portugal. Posthumous son of Infante John of Portugal, he succeeded his grandfather John III under the regency of his uncle, Cardinal Henry, but was under the control of his grandfather's widow from 1557 on. He gave a fleet to the French king to suppress the Huguenots, then in 1578 he turned to the conquest of North Africa. Without sufficient manpower or financial support he failed; his army was annihilated and he was slain at the battle of Alcacer, Morocco, on Aug. 4. Rumors grew that he had not been killed, and four pretenders appeared in the next twenty years who claimed the throne. Calderón and Zorrilla used his story in their writings.

SEBASTIAN, ST. (d. 288?), martyr. Pious legend has it that he joined the Roman army, pleaded with Christian prisoners to be firm in their faith under persecution, and won numerous converts, including the prefect of Rome himself. When Diocletian, who had made him a captain of his guard, discovered he was actually a Christian, Sebastian was ordered shot to death by archers. Such details, and others, inspired much later art. All that is factually known is that he had a holy reputation at Milan before the time of St. Ambrose, probably was a martyr, and was buried in the catacombs in Rome. F. D. Jan. 20.

SEBASTIANA, ST. (1st century), martyr. Converted by St. Paul, she was beheaded at Heraclea, Thrace, during the reign of Domitian. F. D. Sept. 16.

SEBASTIANO DEL PIOMBO. *See* Luciani, Sebastiano.

SEBBE, ST. (d. 694?), king. In 664 he became king of the East Saxons, with Sighere, adhered to Christianity in spite of the latter's apostasy, and after a peaceful reign of thirty years gave up his crown to live in London as a monk. F. D. Sept. 1.

SECCHI, PIETRO ANGELO (1818–1878), astronomer. Born in Reggio, Emilia, Italy, on June 18, he studied there, became a Jesuit in 1833, studied further at the Roman College, and taught physics there in 1839 and at the Jesuit college in Loreto in 1841. He was ordained in 1847, taught at Stonyhurst in England and Georgetown in Washington, D.C., returned to England in 1849, and in 1850 became director of the Roman College observatory, which he rebuilt in 1852. He published *Memorie del Collegio Romano* (1859), in which he verified 10,000 double stars; made studies of Mars, Saturn, and Jupiter and the latter's four moons, which he published in *Il quadro fisico del sistema solare* (1859); devoted years to a study of the sun, traveling to Spain in 1860 and Sicily in 1870 to observe eclipses; discovered the five Secchi types of stars; pioneered in classifying stars in a system which became the basis of later astronomers' classifications; and invented the heliospectroscope, star spectroscope, and telespectroscope. He also made effective studies in meteorology, pioneered in weather forecasting, inventing the meteorograph to record all the forces which affect weather (atmospheric pressure, temperature, wind velocity). His *Dell' unità delle forze fisiche* (1864), in which he attributed all natural processes to kinetic energy and synthesized the knowledge of earlier natural sciences, was widely popular. He also wrote *Catalogo delle stelle* (1867), *Le Soleil* (1870), *Fisica solare* (1869), *Le Stelle* (1877). He died in Rome on Feb. 26.

SECHNALL. *See* Secundinus, St. (d. 447?).

SECUNDA, ST. (d. 180), martyr. *See* Speratus, St.

SECUNDA, ST. (d. 257?), martyr. *See* Rufina, St.

SECUNDA, ST. (d. 304), martyr. *See* Donatilla, St.

SECUNDIAN, ST. (d. 250), martyr. A government official, he was put to death near Civitavecchia, Italy, with SS. Marcellian and Verian during the Decian persecution. F. D. Aug. 9.

SECUNDIAN, ST. (d. 304), martyr. *See* Donatus, St.

SECUNDILLA, ST. (d. 305?), martyr. *See* Heraclius, St.

SECUNDINA, ST. (d. 250?), martyr. She was scourged to death near Rome during the Decian persecution. F. D. Jan. 15.

SECUNDINUS, ST. (d. 259), martyr. *See* Agapius, St.

SECUNDINUS, ST. (d. 306?), martyr. He was put to death at Cordova, Spain, during the Diocletian persecution. F. D. May 21.

SECUNDINUS, ST. (d. 434?), martyr. *See* Felix, St.

SECUNDINUS, ST. (375?–447?), bishop. With Auxilius and Iserninus he was sent from Gaul in 439 to help St. Patrick in Ireland, where he became first bishop of Dunslaughlin in Meath, then assistant bishop of Armagh. He composed the first Latin hymn written in Ireland. He is also known as Sechnall and Seachnall. F. D. Nov. 27.

SECUNDINUS, ST. (5th century), bishop. *See* Auxilius, St.; also, Priscus, St.

SECUNDULUS, ST. (d. 203), martyr. Captured during the persecution of Severus, he died in prison at Carthage, North Africa, shortly before SS. Perpetua and Felicity were martyred for refusing to sacrifice to the pagan gods. F. D. Mar. 6.

SECUNDUS, ST. (1st century). *See* Caecilius, St.

SECUNDUS, ST. (d. 119). An officer in the imperial army, he was beheaded at Asti, Italy, during the reign of Hadrian. F. D. Mar. 29.

SECUNDUS, ST. (d. 250?), martyr. *See* Epictetus, St.

SECUNDUS, ST. (d. 295?), martyr. *See* Carpophorus, St.

SECUNDUS, ST. (d. 303), martyr. *See* Anastasius, St.

SECUNDUS, ST. (d. 357), martyr. A priest at Alexandria, he was slain with a great many persons when the Arian George of Cappadocia was placed in charge of the see which rightly belonged to St. Athanasius. F. D. May 21.

SECUNDUS, JOANNES. *See* Everaerts, Jan Nicolai.

SECURUS, ST. (d. 450?), martyr. *See* Januarius, St.

SEDBERGH, ADAM (d. 1537), martyr. Cistercian abbot of Jervaulx, Yorkshire, England, he was among the many whom Henry VIII ordered hanged in June for the support they gave to those who undertook the pilgrimage of grace.

SEDGWICK, THOMAS (d. 1573). Rector in Edwarton, Suffolk, England, in 1552, he received his doctorate in divinity from Oxford in 1554, served as rector in several posts, and in 1557 became a professor at Cambridge. He received a rectorship and vicariate in 1558, lost his posts when Elizabeth I ascended the throne, and in 1570 was probably in a Yorkshire prison, where he remained until his death.

SEDULIUS, CAELIUS (5th century), poet. He was a layman who moved from Italy to Achaia, where he wrote Christian poetry, chief of which were *Carmen paschale*, a summary of the Bible, and two hymns. He is also mentioned in Isidore of Seville's *De viris illustribus*.

SEDULIUS SCOTUS (9th century), author. An Irish teacher at Liège during Emperor Lothair's reign (840–55), he gained fame as a scribe and poet. His most important works are *De rectoribus christianis*, a treatise for the instruction of Christian rulers, *Collecteana in omnes beati Pauli epistolas*, a commentary on Porphyry's *Isagoge*, and almost 100 poems. He probably spent his last days in Milan, but the place and date of his death are unknown. The Irish form of his name is Siadhal or Shiel.

SEELOS, FRANCIS X. (1819–1867), missioner. Born in Füssen, Bavaria, on Jan. 11, he studied at Augsburg and Munich, joined the Congregation of the Most Holy Redeemer, and in 1843 went to Baltimore, Maryland, where he was ordained in 1844. He became superior in Pittsburgh, in 1851, and in 1860 returned to Baltimore, where he was spiritual director of professed Redemptorists. He declined the bishopric of Pittsburgh in 1860, spent his last years in missionary work, and died in New Orleans, Louisiana, on Oct. 4.

SEEP, JOSEPH (1838–1928). Born in Voerden, Germany, on May 7, he was taken to the United States in 1849, became a cigar maker and cotton buyer in Kentucky, and in 1859 moved to Titusville, Pennsylvania, when petroleum was discovered there, and became an associate of John D. Rockefeller, Sr., in the new oil business. He owned thirty-seven offices across the country for the purchase of oil, was associated with the Standard Oil Co. and the South Penn Co., and became a director of other business and banking houses. He was decorated by the papacy for his charities. He died in Titusville on Apr. 1.

SEFRIED (12th century). He was first abbot of the monastery of Aldersbach, Bavaria, which was transferred to the Cistercians in 1146 by Bishop Egilbert of Passau, and helped to start its library.

SEGHERS, CHARLES JOHN (1839–1886), bishop. Born in Ghent, Belgium, on Dec. 26, he studied at the American seminary in Louvain, was ordained in 1863, and later that year was sent to Vancouver Island. He was appointed bishop in 1873, established numerous missions in Alaska, and in 1878 was appointed coadjutor of Oregon City, succeeding to that see in 1880. He returned to his first see in 1884 as archbishop and was murdered on Nov. 28 on a trip to Alaska by a mentally unbalanced companion. He is often called the "apostle of Alaska."

SEGHERS, DANIEL (1590–1661), painter. Born in Antwerp, Belgium, where he studied under Jan Brueghel, he was a member of the painters' guild in 1611, decorated homes, including that of Amelia of Solms, and was in popular demand for working with such contemporaries as Rubens, Brouwer, and Schut, surrounding their madonnas, landscapes, and historical scenes with sharp and decorative floral borders. His name sometimes appears as Zegers. He died in Amsterdam, Holland.

SEGNERI, PAOLO (1624–1694). Born in Nettuno, Italy, on Mar. 21, he studied at the Roman College, became a Jesuit in 1637, was ordained in 1653, and from 1665 to 1692 gave popular missions in Italy. Pope Innocent XII was so impressed by a sermon preached before him that he made Segneri theologian of the Penitentiaria. He published numerous theological works, chief of which were *Il penitente instruito*, *Il confessore instruito*, and *La Manna dell' anima*. He died in Rome on Dec. 9.

SÉGUR, LOUIS GASTON DE (1820–1881), author. Born in Paris on Apr. 15, he entered the diplomatic service as attaché in the Rome embassy in 1842 but left the following year to enter St. Sulpice. He was ordained in 1847, worked among the poor, was imprisoned in Paris, was appointed auditor of the rota for France in 1852, but was forced to retire in 1856 when stricken with blindness. He devoted himself to social and vocational work, founded the St. Francis de Sales Association in 1858, and wrote pamphlets explaining in popular style the doctrines of the Church. He died in Paris on June 9.

SÉGUR, SOPHIE ROSTOPCHINE DE (1797–1874). Daughter of Gen. Rostopchine, who fired the city of Moscow to turn Napoleon back in 1812, she married Comte Eugène de Ségur of the French army, and wrote short novels, chiefly juveniles, for *Bibliothèque Rose*; these include *Pauvre Blaise* (1862), *Les vacances* (1865), and *Le mauvais génie* (1867).

SEGURA Y SAENZ, PEDRO (1880–1957), cardinal. Born in Burgos, Spain, he was an uncompromising opponent of all non-Catholics and much contemporary culture, was expelled from the country in 1931, returned in 1935, and became archbishop of Seville in 1937. He died in Madrid on Apr. 8.

SEIDENBUSCH, RUPERT (1830–1895), bishop. Born in Munich, Bavaria, Germany, on Oct. 13 (or 30), he went to the United States, studied at St. Vincent's College and seminary, Beatty, Pennsylvania, became a Benedictine in 1850, and was ordained in 1852. He spent the next decade in missionary work in New Jersey and Pennsylvania, was elected prior of St. Vincent's in 1862, and first abbot of St. Louis-on-the-Lake, Collegeville, Minnesota, in 1866. He resigned his abbacy in 1875 when he was appointed titular bishop of Halia and vicar apostolic of northern Minnesota. He resigned his vicarship in 1888, and died in Richmond, Virginia, on June 2.

SEIDL, JOHANN GABRIEL (1804–1875),

poet. Born in Vienna, on June 21, he studied law there, tutored privately, and in 1829 became a teacher at the Cilli gymnasium. He returned to Vienna in 1840 as keeper of the imperial cabinet of medals and antiques, acted as book censor until 1848, and in 1851 was appointed to the Academy of Sciences. He was made imperial treasurer in 1856, ministerial counsel in 1866, and in 1874 received the title of aulic councilor. He wrote some sixty novels, collections of legends, drama, and poetry. Outstanding are *Bifolien*, a collection of his poetry, *Flinserln*, and the Austrian national anthem. He died in Vienna on July 17.

SEINE. *See* Sequanus, St.

SEITZ, ALEXANDER MAXIMILIAN (1811–1888), painter. Born in Munich, Germany, he studied under Cornelius, did frescoes for the church of All Saints, then went to Rome, where he worked with Overbeck on the frescoes for Castel Gandolfo, and with his son Ludwig completed Overbeck's frescoes for the Diakovar cathedral. He became famed for his *Mater amabilis, St. Anthony and St. Benedict, Rest during the Flight to Egypt* and the fresco of the *Prodigal Son* in the Trinità de' Monti in Rome, where he died.

SELEUCUS, ST. (d. 300?), martyr. *See* Hieronides, St.

SELEUCUS, ST. (d. 309), martyr. A Palestinian, he was beheaded at Caesarea after the executioners heard him praise the courage of St. Porphyry under torture. F. D. Feb. 16.

SELGAS Y CARRASCO, JOSÉ (1824–1882), author. Born in Lorca, Murcia, Spain, he studied at San Fulgencio seminary, was obliged to leave because of his family's straitened financial situation, and went to Madrid where he secured a governmental position, and became a journalist. He was a member of the Conservative party, secretary of Prime Minister Martínez Campos, and was elected to the Spanish Academy. *La primavera* and *El estio* represent his best poetry and *Dos rivales* and *Una madre* his outstanding novels. He died in Madrid on Feb. 5.

SELVAGGIO, GIULIO LORENZO (1728–1772), archaeologist. Born in Naples, Italy, on Aug. 10, he was ordained in 1752, became censor of books for Naples, and was appointed professor of canon law in 1764. On his death in Naples in Nov., he left the six-volume *Antiquitatum ecclesiasticarum institutiones* which his friend, Canon Kalephati, finished and published (1772–76). He also wrote *Institutionum canonicarum* (1770).

SEMMELWEIS, IGNAZ PHILIPP (1818–1865), physician. Born in Ofen, Hungary, on July 1, he studied medicine at Vienna and Pest, received his medical degree at Vienna in 1844, and in 1846 became an assistant at the first obstetrical clinic there. In 1847 his observations led him to declare that the high mortality rate among mothers was caused by infection from examining physicians; he proved his theory by reducing such infections from ten per cent to one per cent in two years by ordering antisepsis. His discovery of the cause of puerperal fever established him as the pioneer in antiseptic treatment, a predecessor of Lister. He became head physician at St. Roch's hospital in Pest in 1851 and professor of obstetrics in 1852. He suffered a mental breakdown in 1865 and died in Vienna on Aug. 13.

SEMMES, RAPHAEL (1809–1877), admiral. Born in Charles County, Maryland, on Sept. 27, he was appointed a midshipman in 1826, took a leave of absence in 1832 to study law, was admitted to the bar in 1834, and returned to the navy in 1835, rising to commander in 1855. He served with land forces in the Mexican War, and then in the lighthouse service and became secretary of the lighthouse board in 1858. At the outbreak of the Civil War he resigned from the navy, was appointed commander in the Confederate navy (and rose to the rank of rear admiral), and commanded the *Sumter* and in 1862 the famous *Alabama,* which wreaked heavy losses on Union shipping. When the *Alabama* was sunk off the coast of France in 1864, he escaped to England and then back to Virginia, where he helped in the defense of Richmond, commanded the James River squadron, and received the rank of brigadier general. After the war he taught at Louisiana State University in 1866, became editor of the *Memphis Daily Bulletin,* and practiced law in Mobile, Alabama. He wrote *Service Afloat and Ashore during the Mexican War* (1851), *The Cruise of the Alabama and Sumter* (1864), and *Memoirs of Service Afloat during the War between the States* (1869). He died at Point Clear, Alabama, on Aug. 30.

SEMOLEI, IL. *See* Franco, Giovanni Battista.

SEMPLE, HENRY CHURCHILL (1853–1925). Born in Montgomery, Alabama, on Oct. 18, he studied at Mt. St. Mary's, Maryland, and the American College, Rome, became a Jesuit in 1876, and was ordained in 1879. He taught literature at Spring Hill and Georgetown, was president of Immaculate Conception College, New Orleans, in 1895–99, and wrote *Anglican Ordinations,* a biography of St. John Berchmans, and spiritual readings. He died on June 27.

SEÑA, BALTHASAR (1580?–1614), missioner. Born in Barcelona, Spain, he became a Jesuit in 1608, went to Paraguay in 1610 with Fr. Juan Romero, was ordained there, and spent his life with the Guaraní and Itatine Indians. He defended them against slave traders, wrote an Itatine dictionary, and died in Guarambaré, Paraguay, on July 19.

SENACH, ST. (6th century). He was a disciple of St. Finian, whom he succeeded at Clonard, Ireland. F. D. Aug. 3.

SENAN, ST. (d. 560). Born in Munster, Ireland, he became a monk at Kilmanagh in Ossory, journeyed to Rome, returned by way of Wales where he met St. David, and founded several monasteries before he died at his last settlement on Scattery Island in the Shannon River. Details are confusing, since some twenty or more Irish saints of this name are listed. F. D. Mar. 8.

SEÑAN, JOSÉ FRANCISCO DE PAULA (1760–1823), missioner. Born in Barcelona, Spain, on Mar. 3, he joined the Franciscans in 1774, was sent to San Fernando College in Mexico City in 1784, and in 1787 to California, where he remained at San Carlos mission until 1795. After a visit to Mexico to report on the California missions he returned to California in 1798 and spent the rest of his life at San Buenaventura mission, where he died on Aug. 24. He was president of the missions from 1812 to 1815 and from 1819 until his death.

SENATOR, ST. (d. 475?), bishop. He was sent as a priest, with St. Abundius, to represent Pope St. Leo I at the Council of Chalcedon which considered the Monophysite heresy; he also was papal legate to a synod in Milan, Italy, where he succeeded St. Benignus as bishop about 472. F. D. May 28.

SENEFELDER, ALOYS (1771–1834), inventor. Born in Prague, Silesia, on Nov. 6, son of an actor, he studied at Munich and law at Ingolstadt, was forced to leave in 1791 on the death of his father, tried acting, and then began to write plays. Trying to devise a method to print his own plays, he discovered in 1796 a method of printing from limestone which was the beginning of lithography. He was appointed director of the royal lithographic office in Munich in 1809, improved his processes, received numerous honors, and died in Munich, Germany, on Feb. 26. He wrote an account of his invention which was published in English as *A Complete Course of Lithography* (1819).

SENNEN, ST. (d. 303?), martyr. *See* Abdon, St.

SENOCH, ST. (d. 576). Born of pagan parents in Poitou, Gaul, he became a Christian, and a hermit who attracted many disciples and was praised by St. Gregory of Tours, his contemporary. F. D. Oct. 24.

SENORINA, ST. (d. 982). She was brought up by an aunt, Godina, abbess of the Benedictine convent of St. John of Venaria, whom she succeeded, moving the community to Basto, near Braga, Spain. F. D. Apr. 22.

SEPTIMUS, ST. (d. 303?), martyr. *See* Honoratus, St.

SEPTIMUS, ST. (d. 484), martyr. *See* Liberatus, St.

SEPULVEDA, JUAN GINES DE (1490?–1574), historian. Born near Cordova, Spain, he studied at Alcalá, lived in Italy until 1536, returned to Spain, where he became chaplain to Charles V and tutor to Philip II. He wrote controversial pamphlets against Luther, a life of Cardinal Albornoz, attacked Las Casas on the slavery question, and wrote histories of the reign of Charles V and of the achievements of Spain in Mexico and the New World.

SEQUANUS, ST. (d. 580?). Born in Mesmont, Burgundy, he lived as a hermit at Verrey-sous-Drée, was ordained, and became a monk at Réomé. He later founded a monastery in Segestre, around which grew up the town of St. Seine, France. F. D. Sept. 19.

SERAFINI, CAMILLO (1864–1952), governor. Born in Rome, he was in 1929 appointed governor of Vatican City by Pope Pius XI, modernized its municipal organization, and, as an avid numismatist, classified 1500 coins found near the site of St. Peter's tomb. He died in Vatican City on Mar. 21.

SERAFINI, GIULIO (1867–1938), cardinal. Born in Bolsena, Italy, on Oct. 18, he was ordained, became a noted scholar and educator, was created a cardinal-priest in 1930, served as prefect of the Congregation of the Council, and died in Vatican City on July 16.

SERAPHINA, ST. (d. 1253). Born in San Geminiano, Italy, she became a paralytic as a girl, and, after her parents died, only one devoted friend would heal her repulsive sores. Her patience during her short but extreme sufferings was astonishing. Ghirlandajo painted her portrait, with white violets covering the wooden planks of her deathbed. She is also called Santa Fina. F. D. Mar. 12.

SERAPHINO, ST. (1540–1604). Born in Montegranaro, Italy, of humble parentage, he worked as a shepherd, was badly treated by his brother on their parents' death, and became a Capuchin laybrother in 1556 at Ascoli Piceno. He died on Oct. 12 and was canonized in 1767. F. D. Oct. 13.

SERAPIA, ST. (d. 119?), martyr. *See* Sabina, St.

SERAPION, ST. (d. 195?), martyr. An Easterner, he was put to death during the persecution of Septimius Severus, probably in Macedonia. F. D. July 13.

SERAPION, ST. (d. 211). Bishop of Antioch from 199 to 211, he is known for three theological works mentioned by Eusebius, a letter against Montanism, a treatise addressed to Domninus (who had abandoned Christianity), and a work warning that the Docetic gospel was erroneous. F. D. Oct. 30.

SERAPION, ST. (d. 249), martyr. *See* Apollonia, St.

SERAPION, ST. (d. 252), martyr. He was thrown off a high roof in Alexandria, Egypt, by a mob during Decius' persecution. F. D. Nov. 14.

SERAPION, ST. (d. 284), martyr. *See* Claudian, St.

SERAPION, ST. (d. 300?), martyr. *See* Hieronides, St.

SERAPION, ST. (d. 310), martyr. *See* Theodore, St.

SERAPION, ST. (d. 370?), bishop. After teaching in Alexandria he became a hermit under St. Antony, then became bishop of Thmuis in Lower Egypt, and wrote and fought against the Arians and Manichaeans. Because of his labors against heresy and his support of St. Athanasius he was banished by Emperor Constantius. F. D. Mar. 21.

SERAPION, BL. (d. 1240), martyr. Said to have been an Englishman, he fought the Moors in Spain under Alfonso IX of Castile and then joined the Mercedarians. While in Algiers ransoming Christian slaves, he was held as hostage, angered the Moors by his preaching, and was crucified. His cult was approved in 1728 by Pope Benedict XIII. F. D. Nov. 14.

SEREDI, JUSTINIAN (d. 1945), cardinal. Archbishop of Esztergom and primate of Hungary, he was seized as a hostage by German officials during the occupation of his country during World War II. He died in mid-April at sixty-one.

SERENICUS, ST. (d. 669). Natives of Spoleto, Italy, he and his brother Serinus are said to have become Benedictines in Rome and, later, hermits in France. Disciples surrounded them; although Serenicus lived in separate seclusion along the Sarthe River, he had to form a monastery for his many followers. Serenus outlived him, at Saulges. F. D. May 7.

SERENUS, ST. (d. 202), martyr. *See* Plutarch, St.

SERENUS, ST. (d. 606). He was bishop of Marseilles, Gaul. St. Gregory wrote him letters asking for care of Roman missionaries traveling to England; on other occasions, Gregory reprimanded him for his iconoclasm. F. D. Aug. 9.

SERENUS, ST. (d. 680). *See* Serenicus, St.

SERENUS THE GARDENER, ST. (d. 302?), martyr. A Greek, he became a hermit at Sirmium (Mitrovika, Yugoslavia), was captured and tried after he had told the wife of an imperial guardsman to leave his garden, identified as a Christian, and beheaded. Many others were martyred in that area during the same persecution. The name is also spelled Sirenus. F. D. Feb. 23.

SERF, ST. (6th century?), bishop. Tradition makes him apostle of the Orkney Islands. He died and was buried at Culross, Scotland. He is also known as Servanus. F. D. July 1.

SERGEANT, JOHN (1623–1710). Born in Barrow-upon-Humber, Lincolnshire, England, he graduated from Cambridge in 1643. He served as secretary to Bishop Morton of Durham, became a convert, studied at the English College in Lisbon, was ordained in 1650, taught there, and in 1652 was appointed procurator and prefect of studies. He went on the English mission in 1653, but returned to Lisbon in 1654 and was elected canon in 1655. During the next two decades he engaged in controversy with Anglican ministers, was in contact with the privy council during the Titus Oates Plot, and several times escaped arrest disguised as a physician under the aliases of Dodd, Holland, and Smith. He wrote some fifty controversial treatises.

SERGIUS I, ST. (d. 701), pope. Son of a Syrian merchant, he was born in Palermo, Sicily, and educated and ordained at Rome. On Dec. 15, 687, he was elected pope, after Paschal and Theodore both claimed the throne but were restrained by Exarch John, who supported Sergius and levied a tribute after his election. In 693, Sergius refused to recognize the acts of the Council of Trullanum called by Emperor Justinian II, which claimed to legislate for the entire Church. Justinian thereupon sent Exarch Zachary of Ravenna to bring the pope to Constantinople and force him to approve the synod; the people of Rome and Ravenna revolted and forced the exarch to seek the pope's protection. Sergius vigorously encouraged the liturgy and its music and introduced the *Agnus Dei* into the mass. He received and baptized Caedwalla, king of the West Saxons, in 689, consecrated St. Willibrord in 695, and maintained contact with the English monks who were responsible for the missionary activity in Germany and Friesland. He died in Rome. F. D. Sept. 8.

SERGIUS II (d. 847), pope. Of a noble Roman family, he was educated in the Schola Cantorum, ordained cardinal-priest by Pope Paschal, and became archpriest under Pope Gregory IV, whom he succeeded in a disputed election in Jan. 844. When he imprisoned his opponent, a deacon named John, in a monastery, the Emperor Lothair, whose consent to Sergius' consecration had not been obtained, sent his son Louis at the head of an army to examine the election. Sergius satisfied Louis as to its validity, crowned him king, and appointed Louis' adviser, Bishop Drogo of Metz, legate to France and Germany. While he was pope the Saracens invaded to the walls of Rome, and pillaged St. Peter's and St. Paul's basilica. He died on Jan. 27.

SERGIUS III (d. 911), pope. Born in Rome, son of a noble, Benedict, he was a member of the group opposed to Pope Formosus, who appointed him bishop of Caere (allegedly so he could not become bishop of Rome). When Formosus died, he was an unsuccessful candidate for the papal throne, and joined Count

Alberic in Spoleto. When Pope Benedict IV died in 903, a dispute among several factions arose. When one of them chose Leo V of Ardea pope, a priest named Christopher murdered him and claimed the papal throne. Sergius was put forward as a candidate by Theodora (wife of the powerful Theophylact), imprisoned Christopher, was elected pope, and was consecrated on Jan. 29, 904. The Theophylacts (Theodora and her daughters Theodora the younger and the infamous Marozia, all notorious) ruled Rome during his pontificate and by some authorities Marozia is said to have been Sergius' mistress and the father of her son who was to become Pope John XI. Sergius restored the Lateran basilica, opposed Photius' errors, encouraged monastic life (Cluny was founded during his pontificate), and confirmed the establishment of several English sees. He died in Rome on Apr. 14.

SERGIUS IV (d. 1012), pope. Peter, nicknamed *Bucca Porci* ("Pig's Snout"), was the son of a Roman shoemaker and in 1004 became bishop of Albano. He was elected pope in 1009, consecrated on July 31, and took the name Sergius. He sided with the German party against John Crescentius, aided the poor, and was highly venerated. He died in Rome on May 12.

SERGIUS, ST. (d. 117?), martyr. *See* Maurus, St.

SERGIUS, ST. (d. 303?), martyr. Reported to have been an officer of the Roman army in Syria, he was stripped of his rank by Emperor Maximian when he refused, with his subaltern, Bacchus, to sacrifice to Jupiter, and was paraded through the streets in women's dress. Bacchus died of scourging, and Sergius was beheaded after extended tortures. F. D. Oct. 7.

SERGIUS, ST. (d. 304), martyr. He was put to death in Cappadocia during the Diocletian persecution. F. D. Feb. 24.

SERGIUS, ST. (d. 796), martyr. Sacristan at the monastery of St. Sabas near the Dead Sea, he was able to hide the few sacred vessels the settlement possessed before Arab marauders invaded it, beheaded him, and put John, Patricius, and about twenty others to death by suffocation. F. D. Mar. 20.

SERGIUS, ST. (14th century?). A Greek, he founded the monastery of Valamo in Lake Ladoga, Finland, with St. Germanus, where they worked to evangelize the Karelians. The date for this has been given as 1329 and also as late tenth century. F. D. June 28.

SERGIUS OF RADONEZH, ST. (1315?–1392). Born near Rostov, Russia, he was christened Bartholomew and when but a boy fled with his parents, to escape enemy attacks, to Radonezh, near Moscow. The family lost everything in their flight and became peasant farmers. After the death of his parents, he and

his brother Stephen, in 1335 became hermits at Makovka. When Stephen went to a monastery in Moscow, his brother continued alone. He attracted many disciples as his reputation grew and the monastery of the Holy Trinity was founded. He became abbot and was ordained, taking the name Sergius. When a quarrel developed in 1354 over the form of monastic life to be followed, Sergius left, but when the monastery went into decline he came back at the request of Metropolitan Alexis of Moscow. His prestige grew, and it was due to his advice that Prince Dmitry Donskoy of Moscow decided to oppose the Tatars and gained a momentous victory at Kulikovo Polye in 1380. He traveled widely, helping to promote peace in Russia and establishing new monasteries. F. D. Sept. 25.

SERIPANDO, GIROLAMO (1493–1563), theologian. Born in Troja, Apulia, Italy, on May 6, he declined a career in law to become an Augustinian when fourteen. He studied at Viterbo and Rome, lectured at Siena in 1515, and taught theology at Bologna in 1517. He served as vicar general from 1532 to 1534, became famed for his sermons, and was elected superior general in 1539. He attended the Council of Trent in 1546, was Pope Paul III's legate to the emperor and the king of France, declined the bishopric of Aquila, and resigned the generalship in 1551 to retire to a convent. In 1553 he emerged from retirement to act as legate from Naples to Charles V, was appointed archbishop of Salerno, and in 1561 was created a cardinal and a second papal legate at the Council of Trent, where he succeeded Cardinal Gonzaga as president. He wrote theological treatises, and died in Trent, Italy, on Mar. 17.

SERLO (d 1104). A Norman, he became a Benedictine at Mont-St.-Michel, went to England, and increased the number of monks at the abbey at Gloucester from two to more than 100 in his thirty years as abbot. Although he did some writing, it cannot be distinguished with certainty from that by others of the same name; his greatest contribution was a defense of the Church against King William II. He is sometimes called Blessed and honored on Mar. 3.

SEROUX D'AGINCOURT, JEAN BAPTISTE LOUIS GEORGE (1730–1814), archaeologist. Born in Beauvais, France, on Apr. 5. he served in the army, was appointed collector of taxes by Louis XV, and became interested in archaeology and an expert on early Christian art. He died in Rome on Sept. 24, leaving unfinished his *Histoire de l'art par les monuments* (1825).

SERPIERI, ALESSANDRO (1823–1885), astronomer. Born in San Giovanni, Italy, on Oct. 31, he studied at the Scolopians' college in Urbino, joined the order in 1838, and continued his studies at Ximenian College where he taught mathematics and astronomy when twenty. In 1846 he taught at Urbino college, then at the university, and in 1848 was ordained. He established an observatory at Urbino in 1850, and became noted for his observations of shooting stars and his studies in the field of seismology, in which he introduced the concept of the seismic radiant. He was appointed rector of the college in 1857 and taught there until 1884 when the secularization of the college led to his resignation. He became rector of the Collegio della Badia Fiesolana. He wrote a study of the earthquakes of 1873 and 1875 and works on electricity and physics. He died in Fiesole, Italy, on Feb. 22.

SERRA, JUNÍPERO (1713–1784), missionary. Born in Petra, Majorca, on Nov. 24, Miguel José Serra joined the Franciscans in 1730, when he took the name Junípero, became lector of philosophy at St. Francis friary in Pama, and was ordained in 1737. He received his dtocorate in theology at Pama, was appointed to the Duns Scotus chair of philosophy there in 1743, and in 1749 was sent, with Francisco Palou, to Mexico. He taught at San Fernando College in Mexico City, spent nine years among the Pame Indians of the Sierra Gorda, and was recalled to Mexico City in 1759. He became famed for his impassioned sermons, and in 1767 was appointed superior of a group of Franciscans assigned to replace the Jesuits among the Indians of Lower California. He was sent to Upper California in 1769 with Gaspar de Portola's expedition, and during the next fifteen years established twenty-one missions on the California coast and was the guiding force in the settlement of California. He frequently clashed with the military and civil authorities over their treatment of the Indians, and in 1773 drew up his famous *Representación* for Viceroy Bucareli in Mexico City in which he defended his views. He died at San Carlos mission near Monterey, California, on Aug. 28. He wrote numerous letters and a *Diario*, which was published more than a century after his death, and is reported to have baptized more than 6000 and confirmed more than 5000 Indians.

OMER ENGLEBERT, *The Last of the Conquistadors* (New York, Harcourt, 1957).

SERRANO, BL. FRANCISCO (d. 1648), martyr. Born in Spain, he was sent to China as a Dominican missioner, was arrested with Bl. Pedro Diaz, and while a prisoner at Fu-kien was elected titular bishop of Tipasa. Francisco Diaz, another Dominican, was strangled with him. They were beatified in 1893. F. D. Oct. 20.

SERRANO, BL. FRANCISCO (d. 1747), martyr. *See* Sanz, Bl. Pedro.

SERVAIS. *See* Servatius, St.

SERVANDUS, ST. (d. 305?), martyr. *See* Germanus, St.

SERVANUS. *See* Serf, St.

SERVATUS, ST. (d. 384), bishop. Possibly of Armenian origin, he attended the councils of Sardica and Rimini, worked in the Low Countries as bishop of Tongres, and died of fever, probably at Maastricht. He is also called Servais. F. D. May 13.

SERVILIAN, ST. (d. 117?), martyr. He and St. Sulpicius, who were converted by St. Flavia Domitilla, were beheaded for their faith during the reign of Trajan. F. D. Apr. 20.

SERVULUS, ST. (d. 434?), martyr. *See* Felix, St.

SERVULUS, ST. (d. 590?). According to St. Gregory the Great, he was a crippled beggar in Rome who lived a life of great piety and humility. F. D. Dec. 23.

SERVUS, ST. (d. 484), martyr. *See* Liberatus, St.

SERVUSDEI, ST. (d. 850), martyr. *See* Gumesindus, St.

SESTINI, BENEDICT (1816–1890), astronomer. Born in Florence, Italy, on Mar. 20, he became a Jesuit in 1836, studied at the Roman College, was appointed assistant to the director of the Roman observatory, and was ordained in 1844. He was appointed to the chair of higher mathematics at the Roman College, and in 1848 fled the revolution to the United States, where he taught at Georgetown until 1869 and then was stationed at Woodstock. In 1866 he founded the American edition of *Messenger of the Sacred Heart*, which he edited until 1885, and he was also director of the American branch of the Apostleship of Prayer and the League of the Sacred Heart. Ill health caused his retirement in 1884 to the novitiate at Frederick, Maryland, where he remained until his death on Jan. 17. He wrote mathematics textbooks, included in his *Memoirs of the Roman College*, a *Catalogue of Star-Colors*, the first over-all study of its kind, and made a series of sunspot drawings which were published in 1847.

SESTO, CESARE DA. *See* Cesare da Sesto.

SETHRIDA, ST. (d. 660?). Stepdaughter of Anna, king of the East Angles, she, with her stepsister, St. Ethelburga, became a Benedictine nun at the abbey of Faremoutier in France, and served as abbess on the death of St. Fara, the foundress. F. D. July 7 (also, Jan. 10).

SETON, VEN. ELIZABETH ANN BAYLEY (1774–1821), foundress. Born in New York City on Aug. 28, daughter of Richard Bayley, professor of anatomy at Columbia, and stepsister of Archbishop James Roosevelt Bayley of Baltimore, Elizabeth Bayley was educated by her father, and married William Magee Seton in 1794. She was interested in charitable work and in 1797 helped found the Society for the

Relief of Poor Widows with Small Children. She was widowed with five children when her husband died in 1803 at Leghorn, Italy (where she had brought him for his health), and on her return to New York in 1805 became a convert, a step which caused her family and friends to ostracize her. In 1808, Fr. Dubourg, rector of St. Mary's seminary, Baltimore, invited her to open a school in Baltimore, where she adopted a religious costume and life. In 1809, with four companions, she founded a religious community, the Sisters of St. Joseph, and a school for poor children, near Emmitsburg, Maryland (the beginning of the Catholic parochial-school system in the United States). She took private vows before Archbishop Carroll, who in 1812 approved the rule of the new community of which she was elected superior. She and eighteen sisters took their vows on July 19, 1813, and the first American religious society, the Sisters of Charity in the United States, was founded. The order spread rapidly and by the time of her death in Emmitsburg on Jan. 4 had twenty communities. She was declared Venerable by Pope John XXIII in 1959.

ANNABELLE M. MELVILLE, *Elizabeth Bayley Seton* (New York, Scribner, 1951).

SETON, ROBERT (1839–1927), archbishop. Born in Pisa, Italy, on Aug. 28, grandson of Mother Seton, he studied at Mt. St. Mary's, Maryland, Bonn, and the Propaganda in Rome in 1857, was the first student at the North American College in 1859, and then attended the Academia Ecclesiastici dei Nobili. He was ordained in 1865, was made a papal chamberlain in 1866, a prothonotary apostolic (the first American to receive this honor) in 1867, and became first chaplain at St. Elizabeth's convent near Madison, New Jersey, where he remained until he was named pastor of St. Joseph's, Jersey City, in 1876. He held this position until he returned to Rome in 1902 (where he was to remain for the next twelve years as an unofficial "ambassador" between the American people and the papacy, and New York *Times* correspondent), declined the archbishopric of Chicago in 1903, but later the same year was appointed titular archbishop of Heliopolis. He returned to Emmitsburg in 1914, and later returned to St. Elizabeth's College. He wrote *Memories of Many Years, The Dignity of Labor*, and *Roman Essays*, and edited many of Mother Seton's writings, including her *Memoirs, Letters*, and *Journal*. He died in Convent Station, New Jersey, on Mar. 22.

SETON, WILLIAM (1835–1905), author. Born in New York City on Jan. 28, grandson of Mother Seton, he studied at Fordham, Mt. St. Mary's, Maryland, and Bonn, and was admitted to the bar in New York. He fought in the Union army during the Civil War, was wounded twice at Antietam, and devoted himself to writing. He wrote widely on evolution (and did much to popularize the subject), scientific subjects (which he simplified for popular consumption), and historical fiction. Among his writings are *Romance of the Charter Oak* (1871), *The Pride of Lexington* (1873), and *A Glimpse of Organic Life* (1897). He died in New York City on Mar. 15.

SEVERA, ST. (d. 680?). Sister of St. Modoald, she became first abbess of the convent of St. Gemma at Villeneuve, near Bourges, France. F. D. July 20.

SEVERA, ST. (d. 750?). She was abbess of the Benedictine convent of Oehren at Trèves, France. F. D. July 20.

SEVERIAN, ST. (d. 305?), martyr. *See* Carpophorus, St.

SEVERIAN, ST. (d. 322), martyr. A senator in Sebaste, North Africa, he became a convert after witnessing the death of forty martyrs there during the persecution of Licinius, was seized, and tortured to death with iron rakes. F. D. Sept. 9.

SEVERIAN, ST. (d. 453), bishop and martyr. One of the many who opposed the Monophysite heresy, the bishop of Scythopolis was hunted down and put to death during the persecution which Emperor Theodosius II spread through Asia Minor after the fourth General Council at Chalcedon had condemned Eutyches and his imperially supported group. F. D. Feb. 21.

SEVERIAN (5th century), bishop. Bishop of Gabala, Syria, he came to Constantinople about 400 and achieved fame as a preacher when invited by St. John Chrysostom to preach. In the controversy between Empress Eudoxia he sided with the empress and when John went to Asia in 401 he plotted against him. He was ordered to leave by John on his return, but a truce was reached at Eudoxia's insistence, which was broken when Severian signed Theophilus of Alexandria's lampoon against John sent to Pope Innocent. When he preached that Chrysostom's exile was justified, he was driven from Constantinople by the people and joined forces with Acacius of Beroea and Antiochus of Ptolemais against John. They attempted to have the emperor permanently exile Chrysostom, incited an attack on him in 404, and consecrated Chrysostom's enemy, Porphyrius, bishop of Antioch when Flavian died. After this incident he is lost to history. Several of his sermons and homilies are still extant, and he is known to have written several biblical commentaries.

SEVERINUS (d. 640), pope. A Roman, he was elected successor of Pope Honorius on Oct. 15, 638, but Emperor Heraclius refused confirmation of his election when Severinus refused to sign the Monothelite *Ecthesis*. He remained steadfast, although the Lateran palace was sacked by Exarch Isaac to secure his assent, and was finally consecrated on May 28, 640. He anathemized the *Ecthesis* immediately, and died soon after in Rome on Aug. 2.

SEVERINUS, ST. (d. 170), martyr. *See* Exuperius, St.

SEVERINUS, ST. (d. 295?), martyr. *See* Carpophorus, St.

SEVERINUS, ST. (d. 300?). He was bishop of Trèves, France. F. D. Dec. 21.

SEVERINUS, ST. (d. 403?). As bishop of Cologne, Germany, he was active as an opponent of Arianism. F. D. Oct. 23.

SEVERINUS, ST. (420?), bishop. He was noted for his vigorous opposition to Arianism and evidently was bishop of Trèves, France, before he went to Bordeaux about 405. The Roman Martyrology erroneously lists him as bishop of Cologne. F. D. Oct. 23.

SEVERINUS, ST. (d. 480?). From the Near East, where he may have been of noble Roman descent, he went as a missioner to Noricum (Austria). The vices of that region astounded him and he prophesied the destruction of Astura, which was overrun by Huns soon after. He preached penance so earnestly that he reformed thousands, devoted many hours to the sick, poor, and captives, and established several monasteries. His chief follower, and biographer, was Eugippius. After his death his followers founded San Severino, near Naples, in his memory. F. D. Jan. 8.

SEVERINUS, ST. (d. 507), abbot. A Burgundian, he became a monk and, later, abbot at the monastery of Agaunum, and venerated, after his death, on Feb. 11. Details are questionable, however, since Agaunum was not in existence until 515.

SEVERINUS, ST. (d. 550?), bishop. Brother of St. Victorinus, he was appointed by Pope Vigilius as bishop of Septempeda (now called San Severino) in Ancona, Italy. F. D. June 8.

SEVERUS, ST. (d. 300?), martyr. A priest in Bizya, Thrace, he was beheaded there with the centurion Memnon; thirty-seven soldiers were put to the flames on this occasion. F. D. Aug. 20.

SEVERUS, ST. (d. 304), martyr. *See* Philip, St.

SEVERUS, ST. (d. 305?), martyr. *See* Carpophorus, St.

SEVERUS, ST. (d. 309), martyr. *See* Leucius, St.

SEVERUS, ST. (d. 348?). A native of Ravenna, Italy, he became its bishop in 283. F. D. Feb. 1.

SEVERUS, ST. (d. 409). He was bishop of Naples, Italy, and called a wonder-worker. F. D. Apr. 29.

SEVERUS, ST. (d. 450?), martyr. *See* Januarius, St.

SEVERUS, ST. (d. 455?), bishop. Born in Gaul, he worked with SS. Germanus of Auxerre

and Lupus of Troyes, went to England with the former to preach against the Pelagian heresy, also labored in Germany along the lower Moselle, and in 446 became bishop of Trèves, Gaul. F. D. Oct. 15.

SEVERUS, ST. (d. 483?), martyr. *See* Appian, St.

SEVERUS, ST. (5th century). A priest, allegedly from the Far East, who preached in Vienne, France, he was alive after 445. F. D. Aug. 5.

SEVERUS, ST. (d. 633), martyr. He was bishop of Barcelona, Spain, and tortured to death by the Arian Visigoths. F. D. Nov. 6.

SEVERUS, ST. (d. 690?), bishop. A priest, he became monk, abbot, and bishop of Avranches, then resigned his French see to return to the monastery. F. D. Feb. 1.

SEVERUS, BL. (d. 1067). A Benedictine at Brevnov, he was bishop of Prague, Bohemia, from 1031 until his death. F. D. Dec. 9.

SEVERUS SANCTUS ENDELECHUS (4th century). Probably of Gallic descent, he taught in the forum of Mars in Rome and was a friend of St. Paulinus of Nola, whose panegyric of Theodosius he inspired and which was dedicated to him. He wrote *De morte bonum*, a poem depicting an incident in which a miracle helped convert two pagans to Christianity.

SÉVIGNÉ, MARIE DE RABUTIN-CHANTAL DE (1626–1695), author. Granddaughter of St. Jane Frances de Chantal, she was born in Paris on Feb. 5, was orphaned at seven, and raised by her uncle, Abbé Christoph de Coulanges. She married the Marquis Henri de Sévigné in 1644, was widowed with two children when he was killed in a duel in 1651, and lived the next few years at the court. In 1677 she took up residence at Hôtel de Carnavalet, where she was to spend most of the rest of her life. She wrote more than 1500 letters, which give a brilliant picture of the court, the people frequenting it, and her times. Written with charm, picturesqueness, light irony, and wit, they are an outstanding part of seventeenth-century literature. She died on Apr. 17 at Grignan, France.

SEXBURGA, ST. (d. 699?). The daughter of Anna, king of the East Angles, and sister of SS. Etheldreda, Ethelburga, and Withburga, and half-sister of St. Sephrida, she married King Erconbert of Kent, by whom she had four children, two of them saints: Ercongota and Erminilda. When her husband died in 664, after twenty-four years of marriage, she retired to the convent of Minster, which she had founded, then went to Ely, England, where she was chosen abbess. F. D. July 6.

SEXTON, THOMAS (1848–1932). Born in Ballygannon, Waterford, Ireland, he was educated there, worked as a railroad clerk, at nineteen wrote for the *Nation* in Dublin, became a member of the Home Rule League, supported Parnell, and served in parliament from 1880 to 1896. He backed agrarian reform, was jailed with Parnell, became high sheriff of Dublin in 1887 and lord mayor in 1888–89. He opposed Parnell after 1892, edited the *Freeman's Journal* from that year until 1912, was on the Irish railways commission from 1906 to 1910, and retired from politics after the 1916 uprising to run a bakery and an insurance group. He died in Dublin on Nov. 1.

SEXTUS JULIUS AFRICANUS (3rd century), historian. Born in Libya, he lived in Emmaus, Jerusalem, from 195 to past 240, traveled widely in Asia Minor, and wrote a history of the world from the creation to the year 221.

SEZIN, ST. (d. 529?), bishop. A Briton, he preached in Ireland during the period of St. Patrick, then founded a monastery at Guic-Sezni, Brittany. F. D. Mar. 6.

SFONDRATI, CELESTINO (1644–1696), cardinal. Born in Milan, Italy, on Jan. 10, he studied at Rorschach school, joined the Benedictines in 1660, taught at Kempten, and was ordained in 1668. He became master of novices at his monastery at St. Gall, and taught canon law at the university of Salzburg from 1679 to 1682, when he was appointed vicar general by the abbot of St. Gall. He was made bishop of Novara in 1686, but never occupied his see because of his election as prince-abbot of St. Gall the following year. He was a leader in the fight against Gallicanism, was created a cardinal-priest in 1695, published theological treatises, and died the following year in Rome on Jan. 10.

SFORZA, BL. SERAPHINA (1432?–1478). Daughter of Guido, count of Urbino, she was orphaned as a child and raised at Rome by her uncle, Prince Colonna. When sixteen, she married Alexander Sforza, duke of Pesaro, who treated her cruelly; in 1457 their disagreements became so violent that he expelled her from his house. She went to a convent of the Poor Clares and eventually became a member of that order. Her cult was approved by Pope Benedict XIV in 1754. F. D. Sept. 9.

SHANAHAN, JEREMIAH FRANCIS (1834–1886), bishop. Born in Silver Lake, Susquehanna, Pennsylvania, on July 13, he studied at St. Joseph's, Binghamton, New York, and St. Charles Borromeo, Philadelphia, was ordained in 1859, was head of the Philadelphia preparatory seminary from 1859, and in 1868 was consecrated first bishop of Harrisburg, Pennsylvania, where he remained until his death there on Sept. 24.

SHANAHAN, JOHN WALTER (1846–1916), bishop. Born in Silver Lake, Susquehanna, Pennsylvania, on Jan. 3, he studied at St. Joseph's College, Binghamton, New York,

and St. Charles Borromeo seminary, Philadelphia, and was ordained in 1869. He did parish work, became superintendent of schools in the Philadelphia archdiocese, and in 1899 was appointed bishop of Harrisburg, Pennsylvania, where he reigned until his death there on Feb. 19.

SHANDON, IGNATIUS JOHN O'BRIEN (1857–1930), jurist. Born in Cork on July 30, he attended the Catholic University of Ireland, was admitted to the Irish bar in 1881 and the English in 1899, and was a bencher in 1907 and sergeant-at-law in 1910. He became solicitor general for Ireland in 1911, attorney general in 1912, and lord chancellor in 1913–18. He was created a baronet in 1916 and a baron in 1918. He died in London on Sept. 10.

SHANLEY, JOHN (1852–1909), bishop. Born in Albion, New York, on Jan. 4, he studied at St. Vincent's, Missouri, St. John's, Minnesota, and the Propaganda, Rome, where he was ordained in 1874. He did pastoral work in the St. Paul archdiocese for the next fifteen years, was consecrated first bishop of Jamestown, North Dakota (changed to Fargo in 1897), in 1889 founded the diocesan *Bulletin*, and died in Fargo on July 16 after greatly increasing the number of religious, churches, and schools in his see.

SHARPE, JAMES (1577–1630). Born in York, England, he became a convert as a youth, studied at the English College, Valladolid, Spain, and was ordained in 1604. He returned to England in 1606, was deported for his priesthood, and became a Jesuit in 1608. He was professor of scripture at Louvain, returned to England about 1611, and worked as a missioner, sometimes using the alias Pollard, until his death in Lincoln.

SHARPLES, JAMES (d. 1850), bishop. Born in England, he was ordained, became rector of St. Alban's, Blackburn, and in 1843 was named titular bishop of Samaria and coadjutor to Bishop Brown of Lancashire. He built St. John's church in Salford, later the cathedral for the diocese, and consecrated it in 1848. He died there on Aug. 16.

SHATTOCK, SAMUEL GEORGE (1852–1924), pathologist. Born in London on Nov. 3, son of Samuel Chapman and Jane Brown Betty, he changed his name to Shattock in 1882. He studied at University College, qualified as a physician in 1874, and taught pathology at St. Thomas' Hospital. He reorganized its pathological museum and that of the Royal College of Surgeons, and edited the *Transactions and Proceedings* of the Royal Society of Medicine, to which he contributed 150 articles. His influence on modern pathological science was great, and he was an authority on morbid anatomy, bacteria virulence, and the microbic origin of cancer. His *Thoughts on Religion* was published in 1926. He died in Wimbledon, England, on May 11.

SHAUGNESSY, GERALD (1887–1950), bishop. Born in Everett, Massachusetts, on May 19, he studied at All Hallows College, Salt Lake City, the Marist college and seminary, Washington, D.C., and Catholic University, and was ordained a Marist in 1920. He taught at the Marist college in 1920–23, Notre Dame seminary, New Orleans, in 1923–24, served with mission bands in 1924–28, and was again at the Marist college in 1929–30. He became master of the second novitiate of the Marists in 1932, and in 1933 was appointed bishop of Seattle, Washington, convened a diocesan synod in 1938, wrote and translated several books, and died on May 18, in Seattle.

SHAUGHNESSY, THOMAS GEORGE (1853–1923). Born in Milwaukee, Wisconsin, on Oct. 6, son of a police officer, he studied in that city, worked for the Milwaukee and St. Paul Railway, and studied law. William Van Horne made him general storekeeper of the line and, when in 1882 he became general manager of the Canadian Pacific, brought Shaughnessy to Montreal as general purchasing agent. He became a British citizen, assistant general manager in 1885, vice-president in 1891, and in 1899 succeeded Van Horne as president. He built a fleet of passenger vessels for the Atlantic trade and by his shrewdness weathered the economic crisis of 1913 and kept the Canadian Pacific a private venture. In 1918 he resigned as president and became chairman of the board of directors. He was knighted in 1901, received an honorary degree from Trinity College, Dublin, in 1911, was made baron in 1916. He died in Montreal, Canada, on Dec. 10.

SHAW, JOHN WILLIAM (1863–1934), bishop. Born in Mobile, Alabama, on Dec. 12, he studied at St. Finian's seminary, Navan, Ireland, and the Propaganda and the North American College, Rome, and was ordained in 1888. He was assigned to the cathedral in Mobile, engaged in pastoral work, was appointed rector of the cathedral in 1891, and was chancellor of Mobile in 1891–1910. In 1910 he was appointed titular bishop of Castabala and auxiliary of San Antonio, Texas, administered the see in 1910–11, and succeeded to it in 1911. He was made an assistant at the pontifical throne in 1916 and in 1918 became archbishop of New Orleans, Louisiana. He founded Notre Dame seminary in 1923, established the archdiocesan paper, *Catholic Action of the South*, and died in New Orleans, on Nov. 2.

SHEA, AMBROSE (1815–1905), diplomat. Born in St. John's, Newfoundland, on Sept. 17, he worked as a journalist from 1837 to 1845 and then went into business. He was elected

to the Newfoundland assembly in 1848, where he remained (except for 1869) until 1886, was speaker in 1855–60, and in 1864 was a delegate from Newfoundland to the Quebec conference on confederation. He was knighted in 1883, represented Newfoundland at a fisheries exhibition in London in 1883, and was instrumental in extending the treaty with the United States in 1885. He was appointed governor of the Bahama Islands in 1887 and revitalized the colony's commercial life, resigned in 1895, and retired to London, where he lived until his death on July 30.

SHEA, JOHN DAWSON GILMARY (1824–1892), historian. Born in New York on July 22, he worked for a Spanish merchant, studied law, and was admitted to the bar in 1846. He became a Jesuit in 1848, studied at Fordham, and St. Mary's, Montreal, but in 1852 left the Society. He became interested in American history, wrote *Discovery and Exploration of the Mississippi Valley* in 1852, and when it received favorable reviews was launched on a career of historical writing which was to produce almost 250 books. He edited the *Historical Magazine* in 1859–65, was one of the founders of the American Catholic Historical Society in 1887, was editor of Frank Leslie's magazines, of Sadlier's *Catholic Directory and Almanac*, and after 1889 of the *Catholic News*. He wrote *History of the Catholic Missions among the Indian Tribes of the United States* (1854), many pamphlets on early explorers in America, and six grammars and dictionaries of Indian languages. He also wrote the four-volume *History of the Catholic Church in the United States* (1886–92), the pioneer work of its kind, *The Hierarchy of the Catholic Church in the United States*, a life of Pope Pius IX, and several textbooks. He received honorary degrees from St. Francis Xavier, Fordham, and Georgetown, and the Laetare Medal in 1883. He died in Elizabeth, New Jersey, on Feb. 22.

SHEEHAN, PATRICK AUGUSTINE (1852–1913), novelist. Born in Mallow, Ireland, he studied in Fermoy and at Maynooth, was ordained in 1875, and was a curate in Plymouth and Exeter, England, Mallow, and Queenstown. In 1895 he was transferred to Doneraile and became canon there in 1905. His first novel, *Geoffrey Austin, Student*, appeared in 1895, followed by *The Triumph of Failure*, *Luke Delmege*, *My New Curate*, and *The Blindness of Dr. Gray*, popular studies of Irish pastoral life. He also wrote literary commentary, a volume of poems, and six other novels. He died in Doneraile, Ireland, on Dec. 5.

SHEIL, RICHARD LALOR (1791–1851), dramatist. Born in Drumdowney, Kilkenny, Ireland, on Aug. 17, he studied at Stonyhurst and Trinity College, Dublin, and law in London, and was admitted to the Irish bar in 1814.

He wrote several successful plays, became interested in politics, opposed O'Connell's policies on home rule, but later joined the Irish leader and became a prominent member of the Catholic Association. When the Catholic Relief Bill of 1829 opened parliament to Catholics, he was elected to the House of Commons in 1834 and served for eighteen years as a member of the Whig party. He became vice-president of the board of trade and a member of the privy council in 1839, was the lawyer for Daniel O'Connell's son, John, at the trials of 1844, master of the mint in 1846, and British minister to the court of Tuscany at Florence in 1850. Among his plays were *Adelaide, The Apostate,* and *Evadne;* his *Sketches of the Irish Bar* appeared after his death in Florence, Italy, on May 25.

SHELLEY, BL. EDWARD (d. 1588), martyr. A gentleman from Warminghurst, Sussex, England, he was hanged at Tyburn with Ven. Richard Flower and four others for aiding priests during the Elizabethan persecution. He was beatified in 1929. F. D. Aug. 30.

SHELLEY, RICHARD (d. 1586). Born in Chapham, Sussex, England, son of John Shelley and brother of Edward, he was a member of the entourage of his uncle, Sir Richard Shelley, the last grand prior of England, in Europe. He was arrested in 1580, for hiding priests, released and sent to the Continent in 1582, returned to England in 1583, and presented a petition to parliament on behalf of English Catholics, for which he was imprisoned in Marshalsea prison, London, where he died sometime in Mar.

SHENUTE. *See* Schenute, St.

SHEPHERD, JOHN (1512?–1563?), composer. An Englishman, he studied music at St. Paul's music school under Thomas Mulliner, was organist at Magdalen College, Oxford, from 1542 to 1547, received a fellowship at Magdalen in 1549, was a member of Queen Mary's Chapel Royal from 1553 to 1558, and probably received his doctorate in music from Oxford in 1554. He wrote *Esurientes,* a *Magnificat,* and masses and motets.

SHERIDAN, PHILIP HENRY (1831–1888), general. Born in Albany, New York, on Mar. 6, he graduated from West Point in 1853, and served in several Indian campaigns. During the Civil War he rose to the rank of major general, and became one of the great cavalry commanders of the war, serving in Ohio, Tennessee, and Virginia campaigns. He commanded the Army of the Shenandoah in 1864 and was at Appomattox. He was appointed military commander of the fifth military district (Louisiana and Texas) in 1867, where his rigorous rule caused President Johnson to recall him, and appoint him to the department of the Missouri for 16 years. He led a campaign

against the Indians in 1868–69. He was appointed lieutenant general in 1869, visited Europe in 1870–71 where he witnessed several of the battles of the Franco-Prussian War, and in 1875 was sent back to Louisiana. He succeeded Gen. Sherman as commander-in-chief of the army in 1883, and in 1888 was confirmed as general of the army. He died in Nonquitt, Massachusetts, on Aug. 5.

SHERMAN, ELEANOR BOYLE EWING (1824–1888). Born in Lancaster, Ohio, on Oct. 4, daughter of Thomas and Marie Ewing, she was educated at Visitation Convent, Washington, D.C., and in 1850 married William Tecumseh Sherman, who had been adopted by her parents. She published a memorial of her father in 1872, was a friend of Fr. Peter DeSmet, and in her last years promoted the work of Catholic missions among the Indians. She died in New York City on Nov. 28.

SHERSON, MARTIN (1563–1588), martyr. Born in Yorkshire, England, he studied at Oxford, the English colleges in Rheims and Rome, and was ordained in Laon in 1586. He was sent to England two months later, was imprisoned in Marshalsea prison later the same year, and died there sometime in Mar. or later.

SHERT, BL. JOHN (d. 1582), martyr. Born in Shert Hall, Cheshire, England, and a graduate of Oxford, he taught in London, became a convert, studied at Douai and Rome, was ordained in 1576, and sent to the English mission in 1579. He was hanged, drawn, and quartered at Tyburn on Nov. 21 after being forced to watch the similar execution of Bl. Thomas Ford. He was beatified in 1886. F. D. May 28.

SHERWIN, BL. RALPH (d. 1581), martyr. Born in Rodsley, Derbyshire, England, he studied at Oxford and became recognized as a classical scholar of distinction. In 1575 he became a Catholic, studied at Douai and Rome, was ordained in 1577, and in 1580 was sent on the English mission. Within three months he was arrested, was offered a bishopric if he would apostatize, and, when he refused, was hanged, drawn, and quartered at Tyburn with Bl. Edmund Campion and Alexander Briant. He was beatified in 1886. F. D. Dec. 1.

SHERWOOD, BL. THOMAS (1551?–1578), martyr. Arrested in London for having attended mass and tortured in an attempt to discover where he was imprisoned in the Tower's dungeon and after six months hanged at Tyburn for refusing to take Elizabeth's Oath of Supremacy. His mother, captured with him, died later, after fourteen years in prison. He was beatified in 1886. F. D. Feb. 7.

SHERWOOD, WILLIAM (d. 1482), bishop. An English ecclesiastic, he was appointed bishop of Meath, Ireland, in 1460, came into conflict with Thomas Fitzgerald, deputy of the lord lieutenant of Ireland, who accused him of causing several of the deputy's followers to be murdered; King Edward IV upheld Fitzgerald. The bishop was himself appointed deputy in 1475, but was so unpopular he was removed in 1477. He was chancellor of Ireland from 1475 to 1481, and died in Dublin on Dec. 3.

SHIEL. *See* Sedulius Scotus.

SHIELDS, JAMES (1806?-1879), general. Born in Altmore, Tyrone, Ireland, on May 16, he migrated to the United States in 1826, studied law, which he began to practice in Illinois in 1832, fought in the Black Hawk War, was elected to the state legislature in 1836, and became state auditor in 1839, state supreme court judge in 1843, and commissioner of the general land office in 1845. He served in the Mexican War, was wounded and brevetted major general, and in 1848, when he left the army, was appointed governor of Oregon Territory. He resigned this office to be Democratic senator from Illinois from 1849 to 1855, moved to Minnesota, where he was one of that state's first federal senators in 1858-59, then engaged in mining in California and Mexico for two years. He served in the Union army as brigadier general of volunteers from 1861 to 1862 when his defeat by Gen. "Stonewall" Jackson at Port Republic caused him to resign the next year. He took up the practice of law briefly in California, served as state railroad commissioner, was a member of the Missouri state legislature in 1874-79, state adjutant general in 1877, and was appointed in 1879 to fill a vacancy in the United States Senate. He died in Ottumwa, Iowa, on June 1.

SHIELDS, THOMAS EDWARD (1862-1921), educator. Born in Mendota, Minnesota, on May 9, he studied at St. Francis, Milwaukee, and at the seminary in St. Paul, was ordained in 1891, and took his doctorate in biology at Johns Hopkins in 1895. He taught and did parish work in St. Paul, and was on the faculty of Catholic University from 1902 until his death in Washington, D.C., on Feb. 15. He taught psychology and education, founded the summer school for sisters in 1911 and was its first dean, and founded the Sisters' College and the *Catholic Educational Review* in that year. He published many texts and wrote, among other titles, *The Making and Unmaking of a Dullard* and *Psychology of Education.*

SHIPMAN, ANDREW JACKSON (1857-1915). Born in Springvale, Virginia, on Oct. 15, he studied at Georgetown, became a convert, edited the Vienna *Times,* and was assistant manager of a coal company in Ohio. In 1884 he was with the customs service in New York City, studied law, and began working for Slavonic immigrants. He became an authority on Church law, was a member of the board of regents of the University of the State of New York, an adviser to the Syrian Catholics, author of *The Mass According to the Greek Rite,* and a member of the New York constitutional convention of 1915. He died in New York on Oct. 17.

SHIRLEY, JAMES (1596-1666), dramatist. Born in London on Sept. 18, he studied at the Merchant Taylors School, Oxford, and Cambridge, took Anglican orders in 1619, and served in a parish near St. Albans until his conversion. He then taught in St. Albans until 1625, when he went to London to begin work in the theater. He had written poems as early as 1616; he now became a popular playwright, producing *Love's Tricks, The Traitor, Hyde Park, The Gamester, The Royal Master, The Maid's Revenge,* and more than twenty-five others between 1631 and 1642. He was in Dublin in 1636-37 when the London stage was closed by the plague, and wrote *St. Patrick for Ireland* there. In 1642-44 he fought for the Loyalists under the duke of Newcastle; when the king's fortune changed, and with the theaters closed, he taught at Whitefriars, London, and published textbooks on English and Latin grammar. In 1646 he began writing plays again: *The Triumph of Beauty* and *The Contentions of Ajax and Ulysses* were followed by *The Cardinal* (1652) and eight others. His work follows the manner of John Fletcher, for whom he worked, and that of his friends, Philip Massinger and John Ford. His sources are continental, as were theirs; his characters, often adaptations; but the development was original, as were the effective craftsmanship, reliance on striking scenes, contemporary satire, and poetic fervor. *The Gamester,* in particular, was often revived (by Garrick and others), and Charles Lamb highly praised his contribution to the stage. Shirley died in London, shortly after he was driven from his home by the great fire, on Oct. 29.

SHORTER, DORA SIGERSON (d. 1918), poet. Born in Dublin, she published *The Lady's Slipper, The Song of Earl Roderick,* and ten other volumes, including *Collected Poems* (1907), with a preface by George Meredith. She contributed to the ballad revival in Ireland and married Clement Shorter. She died on Jan. 6.

SIADHAL. Of the several men of this name, one was abbot of Kildare, Ireland, and died in 828; another attended a council in Rome in 721; best known was the scholar who flourished from 840 to 860 and who is commonly called Sedulius Scotus.

SIAGRIUS. *See* Syagrius, St.

SIARDUS, ST. (d. 1230). He became abbot

of the Premonstratensian monastery of Marien-gaarden, Frisia, in 1196. F. D. Nov. 13.

SIBBEL, JOSEPH (1850–1907), sculptor. Born in Dülmen, Germany, on June 7, he studied wood carving under Friedrich Ewertz and clay modeling in Münster, emigrated to the United States in 1873, worked with a group of ecclesiastical sculptors in Cincinnati, established a studio in New York, and became famed for his ecclesiastical sculptures. Outstanding are the statue of St. Patrick in the cathedral in New York, *Our Lady Comforter of the Afflicted* and *Death of St. Joseph* in St. Francis Xavier church, St. Louis, and SS. Isaac Jogues, Katherine Tekakwitha, Rose of Lima, and Turibius in St. Joseph's seminary, Yonkers, New York. He died in New York City on July 10.

SIBILIA, ENRICO (1861–1948), cardinal. Born in Anagni, Italy, on Mar. 17, he was ordained in 1884, entered the papal diplomatic service, and was nuncio to Colombia, Brazil, and Chile, to Santiago, Spain, in 1908, and named titular bishop of Side. He was nuncio to Austria from 1923 to 1935, arranged the concordat with the Vatican, and was named a cardinal in 1935. He died in Rome on Aug. 4.

SIBOUR, MARIE DOMINIQUE AUGUSTE (1792–1857). Born in St. Paul-Trois-Châteaux, Drôme, France, on Aug. 4, he studied at Avignon and Paris, was ordained in Rome in 1818, and named canon of the Nîmes cathedral in 1822. He was appointed administrator of Nîmes in 1837, bishop of Digne in 1839, and in 1848 archbishop of Paris, where he held a provincial council in 1849 and a diocesan synod in 1850. He introduced the Roman rite in Paris, was named a senator in 1852 by Napoleon III, at whose marriage he officiated in 1853, and was assassinated by an interdicted priest, Jean Verger, in Paris on Jan. 3.

SIBYLLINA OF PAVIA. *See* Biscossi, Sibyllina.

SICARD (d. 1215), bishop. He succeeded Offredus as bishop of Cremona, Italy, in 1185, performed papal diplomatic missions, and is known for his *Chronicon*, a chronicle of world history to 1213 especially important for historians for its information on Frederick I's crusade, and such ecclesiastical writings as *Mitrale* and *Summa canonum*.

SIDGREAVES, WALTER (1837–1919), astronomer. Born in Grimsbargh, Preston, England, on Oct. 4, he became a Jesuit at seventeen, taught at Beaumont and in Malta, then was stationed at the Stonyhurst observatory, which he outfitted. He was one of the first to study terrestrial magnetism, worked with Fr. Perry on a magnetic survey of France, and observed the transit of Venus in 1874 for his

government. He specialized in stellar spectroscopy, won prizes at international expositions for his photographs, and was made a fellow of the Royal Astronomical Society in 1891. He died at Stonyhurst, England, on June 12.

SIDONIUS, ST. (d. 690?). He went from Ireland to Jumièges, France, and was appointed by St. Ouen the first abbot of a Benedictine monastery (later called Saint Saëns after him) near Rouen. F. D. Nov. 14.

SIDONIUS APOLLINARIS, ST. (430?–479?), bishop. Caius Sollius Apollinaris was born in Lyons, Gaul, on Nov. 5, became a soldier, married Papianilla, daughter of Emperor Avitus, by whom he had four children, and lived for several years at the court in Rome. When Avitus was overthrown, he supported various candidates for emperor, served as prefect of Rome in 468, then returned to Auvergne and became a gentleman farmer, carrying on a large correspondence with other gentlemen in southern Gaul; many of these letters are still extant and are valuable historical sources. Later he was senator and prefect of Rome under Emperor Anthemius but resigned, returned home, and unwillingly was made bishop of Avernum (Clermont). He soon became recognized as an ecclesiastical authority, abandoned his leisurely and worldly way of life, lived humbly, and cared for the poor. During a great famine he provided for thousands. He is said to have instituted rogation days as days of prayer against the incursions of the Goths, who troubled his see for the rest of his life. He led the opposition of the inhabitants of Clermont to Visigothic King Euric and was exiled to Carcassone when the city finally fell. He later returned to Clermont, Gaul, where he died. He was an outstanding orator, famous as a poet (twenty-four of his poems are extant), and wrote panegyrics on several emperors. F. D. Aug. 21.

SIDRONIUS, ST. (d. 270?), martyr. He was put to death at Rome during the persecution of Aurelian; another of the name is venerated locally at Sens, France. Biographical details are confused and untrustworthy. F. D. July 11.

SIENI, CYRIL (d. 1799?). Born in Catalonia, Spain, he became a Capuchin, and was appointed vicar general of New Orleans in 1772, where he incurred the enmity of the Capuchin superior, Dagobert, and the governor, Unzaga, when he attempted to impose ecclesiastical reforms. He was appointed titular bishop of Tricali and auxiliary of Santiago, within whose jurisdiction Louisiana fell. His efforts at reform failed and in 1793 he was ordered back to Spain, but was still in Havana, Cuba, in 1799.

SIENKIEWICZ, HENRYK (1846–1916), novelist. Born in Wola, Poland, on May 4, he studied philosophy at Warsaw, became editor of the newspaper *Slowo* in 1869, and wrote his first novel *Na Marne* (*In Vain*) in

1870. He traveled to North and Central America in 1876, and returned to write a series of nationalistic novels on the grandeur of Poland's past: *With Fire and Sword* (1890), *The Deluge* (1891) and *Pan Michael* (1893). He is best known for his *Quo Vadis?* (1895), on the beginning of Christianity in Italy. Other works translated into English include *Without Dogma, Yanko the Musician, The Knights of the Cross,* and *The Third Woman*. He also wrote accounts of his travels to America and Africa. He won the Nobel Prize for literature in 1905 and died in Vevey, Switzerland on Nov. 14 while working for war relief for Polish victims of World War I.

SIEPEL, IGNAZ (1876–1932), chancellor. Born in Vienna on July 19, he studied at its university, was ordained in 1899, and taught theology at Salzburg in 1909 and at Vienna in 1917. He became minister of public welfare in 1918, headed the Christian Socialist party, and in 1922 was named chancellor. Msgr. Siepel secured an international loan to prevent national bankruptcy, and resigned in 1924. He again was chancellor in 1926–29, resigned when his dual position as government official and churchman was criticized, and for two months in 1930 was minister of foreign affairs. He died in Pernitz, Austria, on Aug. 2.

SIFFRED, ST. Born in Albano, Italy, he became a monk at Lérins, France, and bishop of Carpentras, Provence. He died either in 540 or 660. F. D. Nov. 27.

SIFRARD, ST. (d. 888), martyr. See Ageranus, St.

SIGEBERT, ST. (d. 635). King of East Anglia, he was baptized in Gaul and introduced Christianity into his kingdom with SS. Felix and Fursey. He became a Benedictine monk, but was taken from the cloister by his subjects when Penda of Mercia invaded East Anglia, and fell in battle. F. D. Sept. 27.

SIGEBERT III, ST. (631–656), king. Son of King Dagobert I of France, he was educated by Bl. Pepin of Landen, and ascended to the throne of Austrasia at his father's death in 638, while his brother Clovis ruled the rest of the kingdom. He was active in his charitable concern for hospitals and churches and established twelve monasteries, including Malmédy. F. D. Feb. 1.

SIGEBERT OF GEMBLOUX (1035?–1112), historian. Born near Gembloux, Namur, Belgium, he was educated at Gembloux abbey, became a monk there, taught at St. Vincent, Metz, and about 1070 returned to Gembloux where he became head of the abbey school, a position he held until his death on Nov. 5. He wrote *Chronicon sive chronographia*, a survey of world history, *De scriptoribus ecclesiasticis*, a catalogue of 171 ecclesiastical writers, biographies, a poem on the Theban legion,

and three treatises defending the imperial position and the rights of temporal princes against papal claims.

SIGFRID, ST. (d. 690), abbot. A follower of St. Benedict Biscop at Wearmouth, England, he was a deacon when elected coadjutor-abbot of that monastery on the death of St. Esterwine in 688. F. D. Aug. 22.

SIGFRID, ST. (d. 1030?). Born probably in Northumbria, England, he was a bishop at the court of King Olaf Tryggvasson of Norway from 977 to 1000 and worked as a missionary bishop in Westergötland from 1002 to 1008. He then went to Vexiö, Sweden, where he preached to the heathens until his death. He was canonized by Pope Adrian IV. F. D. Feb. 15.

SIGHARD, BL. (d. 1162). A Cistercian monk at Jouy, he founded the monastery of Bonlieu, near Bordeaux, France, and became its first abbot. F. D. Apr. 5.

SIGIRANUS, ST. (d. 655?). Born in Berry, France, he was a cupbearer of Clotaire II, broke his engagement to a nobleman's daughter, and became a monk in Tours, where his father was bishop. Imprisoned for a time as a madman because of the recklessness with which he distributed his estate, he went on pilgrimage to Rome and on his return became abbot-founder of Méobecq and then Longoretum (afterward called St. Cyran). He was also known as Cyran. F. D. Dec. 5.

SIGISBERT, ST. (d. 650?), abbot. See Placid, St.

SIGISMUND (1368–1437), emperor. Born in Nuremberg, Germany, on Feb. 15, second son of Emperor Charles IV, he was betrothed to Maria, daughter of King Louis of Hungary and Poland, and, though unpopular with the Hungarians, succeeded to the throne of Hungary on Louis' death in 1387. When Murad I's victory at Kossovo in 1389 threatened Europe, he gathered a crusading army from all over Europe, was crushingly defeated by Bajazet I at Nicopolis in 1596, but was saved by an Osmanli attack on the Turks. He then supported a revolt of the nobles against his brother Wenceslaus' governors in Bohemia. When Wenceslaus was deposed as emperor in 1400, he appointed Sigismund imperial vicar for Germany and governor of Bohemia, but the accord between them ended when Wenceslaus refused to agree to Sigismund's accession of the Bohemian throne. He quickly suppressed a revolt in 1403 which proclaimed him deposed in favor of Ladislas of Naples. When Emperor Rupert of Germany died in 1410, Sigismund was elected, as was Jost of Moravia by a rival group. Since Wenceslaus had never waived his title, there were now three emperors. When Jost died, Wenceslaus withdrew and Sigismund was elected emperor in 1411. He prevailed upon antipope John XXIII to call the Council of Constance in 1414, became its president and a leader in the deposition of John, though unsuccessful in persuading Benedict XIII to abdicate. He issued a safe conduct to John Hus, but repudiated it and had him burned at the stake as a heretic in 1415. In that year also he transferred Brandenburg to Frederick of Hohenzollern, who became Margrave Frederick I of Brandenburg. When Wenceslaus died in 1419, violent opposition to Sigismund's succession to the throne of Bohemia led to the Hussite revolt, and when Sigismund persuaded Pope Martin V to proclaim a crusade, bitter religious wars, leading to the Thirty Years' War, followed. Defeated by Zizka in 1420 and 1422, he was deposed by an assembly in 1421, when the throne was offered to a Polish prince. Hussite raids into imperial territory in 1423 and new Turkish invasions caused him to negotiate unsuccessfully in 1429. In 1431 the disaster at Domazlice caused him to renew negotiations, the Council of Basle was convoked, and he had himself crowned king of Lombardy. In 1433, after two years' negotiations in Italy with Pope Eugene IV, the pontiff crowned him emperor, and accord between the moderate Hussites and the Church was reached. Civil war in Bohemia, the extremists' defeat at Lipan in 1434, and the signing of the compact in Iglau led to his acceptance as king of Bohemia in 1436. He died in Znaim, Bohemia, on Dec. 9.

SIGISMUND I (1467–1548), king of Poland. Son of King Casimir IV of Poland and Elizabeth of Austria, he was born on Jan. 1, successfully ruled Glogau as prince and Silesia as governor, was elected grand duke of Lithuania in 1505, and became king of Poland in 1506. He redeemed mortgaged royal estates, ceded more and more power to the nobles, abolished serfdom, and fought successfully against Russians, Tatars, and Wallachians. When the Teutonic Knights were secularized and went over to Lutheranism, Poland recognized their territory as a Protestant state in 1525, but gained Prussia as a fief in return. Sigismund encouraged religious reforms, particularly of an extremely corrupt clergy; many of these reforms were successful after 1530. Toward the end of his reign, Russia made some inroads and captured Smolensk. Sigismund died at Cracow, Poland, on Apr. 1.

SIGISMUND II (1520–1572), king of Poland. Born on Aug. 1, he succeeded his father, Sigismund I, in 1548, opposed demands that he abolish the celibacy of the clergy, and fought the attempt (abandoned in 1570) to set up a national church. He reorganized the ecclesiastical courts, worked out a compromise with Protestant factions, and eventually saw the adoption of reform measures proposed at the Council of Trent. Vernacular literature (including translations of scripture) flourished. In 1569 he brought Poland, Ruthenia, and Lithuania together by the Union of Lublin. The Jagiello dynasty ended with the death of Sigismund (often called Augustus) in Knyszyn, Poland, on July 14. The archbishop of Gnesen ruled as regent for two years; the nobles then elected Henry of Valois their king; Henry left after five months to become king of France.

SIGISMUND III (1566–1632), king of Poland and Sweden. Son of John III of Sweden and Princess Catherine of Poland, he was elected king of Poland in 1587 with the help of John Zamoyski and allied himself with the Catholic faction in Europe by his marriage to Anne of Hapsburg. He established a firm and stable government, strengthened the work of the counter-Reformation by building schools, which he staffed with Jesuits, who also became popular preachers, and helped to effect a reunion of the Ruthenian clergy with Rome. He was liberal with territorial grants, promising Swedish holdings in Estonia and Livonia to Poland and Polish lands to Austria (for which he was impeached by the Polish diet in 1592). He inherited the Swedish crown in 1594, refused to support the national religion, Protestantism, brought in the Polish army in 1598 to defend his position, and was defeated by Protestant forces at Stangebro. He was deposed in 1604 and replaced by Charles IX, but never ceded his claim. His attempt to limit the power of the Polish diet and to make Catholicism prevail in Poland led to a revolt led by Zebrzydowski. Sigismund also tried to prevail upon Russia to accept Catholicism, but failed. He fought with Austria and against Sweden in the Thirty Years' War, and against the Tatars, who attacked Poland, and moved the capital from Cracow to Warsaw, where he died.

SIGNORELLI, LUCA (1441–1523), painter. Born in Cortona, Italy, he studied painting under Piero de' Franceschi, probably spent his youth in Florence, and was greatly influenced by Donatello's sculpture. He was a civic official of some importance in Cortona in 1479, was elected a burgher of Città di Castello in 1488, and was a delegate from Cortona to Florence in 1508 and 1512. His work is noted for its austerity, intense energy, realism, splendor of conception, and mastery of anatomy. Outstanding works are the frescoes at Monte Oliveto near Siena, those of the *Last Judgment* in the Orvieto cathedral, a *Madonna and Child* which influenced Michelangelo, *Pan*, and his paintings in the Perugia cathedral. He executed several paintings for Pope Julius II in the Vatican, but these were later destroyed to make way for some of Raphael's work. He died in Cortona.

SIGOLENA, ST. (d. 769?). Daughter of a noble in Aquitaine, she became a Benedictine nun at the convent of Troclar in southern France after her husband's death, and was later its abbess. F. D. July 24.

SIGOLINUS, ST. (d. 670?). He was abbot of the Benedictine monastery of Stavelot-Malmédy, Belgium. F. D. Oct. 29.

SIGRADA, ST. (d. 678?). When her husband died she became a Benedictine nun at St. Marianus, Soissons, France; she died shortly after her sons, SS. Leodegarius and Warinus, were put to death. F. D. Aug. 8.

SIKORSKI, WLADISLAW (1881–1943), premier. Born in Tyszow Narodovy, Austrian Galicia, on May 20, he studied engineering at Lwow, engaged in the underground freedom movement during World War I, and became an aide to Marshal Pilsudski with the Polish Legion in Austria. During the Ukraine campaign of 1919 and the Polish-Russian war of 1920 he commanded an army corps; he repulsed Gen. Budenny at Warsaw. He served as chief of staff in 1921–22, and became prime minister and minister of the interior on the assassination of President Narvkowitz. He was premier in 1923, minister of war in 1924–25, and was dismissed after his disagreement with Pilsudski in 1928. He went to France, advocated the French-Polish alliance and warned against the new Germany, and in 1939 became commander of the Polish Legion in France and premier of the government in exile. He was killed in an airplane crash at Gibraltar on July 4, with his daughter, Sophia Lesniowska, Gen. Tadeusz, chief of the Polish general staff, and other military leaders.

SILAS, ST. (1st century). He and Judas were sent to Antioch, with Paul and Barnabas, to deliver the letter of the Council of Jerusalem to the Gentile converts in Syria (Acts 15:22; 18:5). He then went with Paul to Syria, Cilicia, and Macedonia, and was beaten and imprisoned at Philippi. He stayed with Timothy at Beria, came with him to join Paul at Corinth, and died in Macedonia. He may have been St. Peter's secretary, Silvanus (I Pet. 5:12; II Cor. 1:19; II Thess. 1:1); legend makes him the first bishop of Corinth. F. D. July 13.

SILICIUS. *See* Guijeno, Juan Martínez.

SILVA, BL. AMADEUS DA (1420?–1482). Brother of Bl. Beatrice, he joined the Hieronymites in Portugal in 1442, and about 1452 transferred to the Franciscans at Udeba, Lombardy, as a laybrother. He was ordained in 1459, was sent to reform the friars at Marignano, and was so successful that others who began to show more respect for the rule were called Amadeists. He died in Milan, Italy. F. D. Aug. 10.

SILVA, BL. BEATRICE DA (1424–1490), foundress. Born in Portugal, daughter of the count of Viana and sister of Bl. Amadeus, she was reared in the household of Princess Isabel, whom she accompanied to Spain when the latter married John II of Castile. Disturbed by the jealousy of the ladies of the court, she entered the Cistercian convent at Toledo and in 1484 founded the Congregation of the Immaculate Conception, which followed the Benedictine rule. After her death the Conceptionists followed the rule of St. Clare. Her cult was confirmed in 1926. F. D. Aug. 18.

SILVA, MARCOS DA (d. 1591), bishop. Born in Lisbon, Portugal, he wrote the biographical *Chronicles of the Friars Minor* (1556–68), edited a grammar of the Bicol language of the Philippines, and was appointed bishop of Oporto. He is also known as Mark of Lisbon.

SILVANUS, ST. (d. 150?), martyr. He was put to death by drowning in the Tiber at Rome during the persecution of Antoninus when he refused to sacrifice to the pagan gods. Legend has incorrectly made him and six others the sons of St. Felicitas and given rise to the story of the Seven Brothers. F. D. July 10.

SILVANUS, ST. (d. 311?), bishop and martyr. The bishop of Gaza, Palestine, was seized in the reign of Maximinus and sent to the copper mines near Petra, Arabia. He was considered useless because of his age and was beheaded there with forty other aged Christian prisoners. F. D. May 29 (sometimes, May 4).

SILVANUS, ST. (d. 312), bishop and martyr. The bishop of Emesa, Phoenicia, was put to death with Luke, a deacon, and Mucius, a lector, during the persecution of Maximian. F. D. Feb. 6.

SILVANUS, ST. (4th century). He left the stage to become a monk at Tabennisi under St. Pachomius, who had to excommunicate him twenty years later when he grew lax; repentance followed and he returned to his life of solitude. F. D. May 15.

SILVANUS, ST. (d. 450?). A monk at Constantinople, he became bishop of Troas, Phrygia. F. D. Dec. 2.

SILVANUS. *See* Silas, St.

SILVERIUS, ST. (d. 537), pope and martyr. Born in Frosinone, Campania, Italy, the son of Pope Hormisdas, he was a subdeacon in Rome in Apr. 536, when Pope Agapitus I died. The Ostrogothic King Theodehad hurriedly made him bishop and asked his acceptance as pope, in a move to prevent the election of an Eastern candidate. He became pope on June 1 or 8 and incurred the hatred of Empress Theodora and the Byzantines when he refused to recognize the Monophysite patriarchs Anthimus and Severus. When the Ostrogothic army laid waste to part of Rome, Silverius invited the Byzantine leader, Belisarius, into the city. A forged letter blamed the pope for the devastation; he was kidnaped and carried off to Asia Minor. Belisarius, on orders from the empress, proclaimed Vigilius as pope in Mar. 537. Emperor Justinian ordered the return of Silverius, but the pope was seized in Mar. on landing in Italy, carried on orders of Vigilius to an island near Naples, and left to starve to death; others say he was murdered. He was deposed on Nov. 11 and died on Dec. 2. F. D. June 20.

SILVESTER, FRANCIS (1474?–1526). Born in Ferrara, Italy, he became a Dominican at fourteen, received his master's in theology in 1516, and served as prior in Ferrara and Bologna. In 1519 he was elected vicar general of the Lombard congregation, became regent of the Bologna college in 1521, was appointed vicar general of his order by Pope Clement VII, and in 1525 was elected master general of the Dominicans. He wrote theological treatises, chief of which was a commentary on the *Summa contra Gentiles* of St. Thomas Aquinas. He died in Rennes, France, on Sept. 19.

SILVIN, ST. (d. 720?), bishop. Brought up in the French court, he studied and was ordained in Rome, returned as bishop to the northern part of France, preaching widely, redeemed captives, and served the poor for forty years. He became a Benedictine monk at Auchy-les-Moines, France, where he died. F. D. Feb. 17.

SILVINUS, ST. (d. 444). He became bishop of Brescia, Italy, when a very old man. F. D. Sept. 28.

SILVINUS, ST. (d. 550?). He was bishop of Verona, Italy. F. D. Sept. 12.

SILVINUS, ST. (8th century). He became bishop of Cremona, Italy, in 733.

SIMBERT, ST. (d. 809?), bishop. He studied at the abbey of Murbach, near Colmar, Alsace, and became a Benedictine monk there and its abbot. He retained his abbacy when made bishop of Augsburg in 778, and was active as a reformer. He was canonized by Pope Nicholas V. F. D. Oct. 13.

SIMEON, ST. (1st century). A resident of Jerusalem, he had his wish that he might see the Messias before he died fulfilled when he saw Jesus brought to the Temple by Mary and Joseph. When he held the Child in his arms he gave utterance to the prayer, *Nunc Dimittis* (Luke 2:25–35). F. D. Oct. 8.

SIMEON, ST. (d. 107?), bishop and martyr. Son of Cleophas, he was a cousin of Christ, one of His disciples, and the successor of St. James as bishop of Jerusalem, serving there before and after the burning of the city. He escaped several persecutions but, when over 100 years old, was captured, tortured, and crucified under that of Trajan. F. D. Feb. 18.

SIMEON, ST. (d. 339), martyr. *See* Sapor, St.

SIMEON, ST. (d. 1016). This Armenian her-mit left his cell to make pilgrimages to Jerusalem, Rome, Compostella, and elsewhere in Europe. He spent his last years at the Benedictine monastery of Padolirone, near Padua, Italy. He was canonized by Pope Benedict VIII. F. D. July 26.

SIMEON, ST. (d. 1035). A native of Syracuse, Sicily, he studied at Constantinople, and became a hermit on Mt. Sinai and later at Trèves, France. His life of penance and austerity commanded great respect, though some stoned his cell at the rumor that he was a magician. He was one of the first to be canonized formally, in 1042. F. D. June 1.

SIMEON, BL. (d. 1141). He was abbot of the Benedictine abbey of La Cava, Italy, from 1124 and highly thought of by Pope Innocent II. His cult was confirmed in 1928. F. D. Nov. 16.

SIMEON, JOSEPH. *See* Lobb, Emmanuel.

SIMEON BARSABAE, ST. (d. 341), bishop and martyr. The bishop of Seleucia-Ctesiphon was one of more than 100 Christians beheaded or otherwise put to death during the persecution of King Sapor II of Persia for refusing to worship the sun. These included two priests, Abdechalas and Ananias; Pusicius, a royal overseer, and his daughter; and Usthazanes, a royal tutor. F. D. Apr. 21.

SIMEON OF DURHAM (1138?), historian. After studying at the Benedictine monastery at Jarrow, England, he was professed at Durham (to where it was moved in 1074) about 1085, and is known for his *Historia ecclesiae Dunelmensis*, a history of the Durham church to 1096 and *Historia Anglorum et Dacorum*, a chronicle of English history to 1129. He died between 1130 and 1138.

SIMEON METAPHRASTES (d. 1000?). He wrote a collection of legends of the saints, probably compiled at the request of Emperor Constantine VII Porphyrogenitus. Though his feast was celebrated on Nov. 28 in the Byzantine church, his cult has never been recognized in Rome.

SIMEON SALUS, ST. (d. 589?). He lived in the Sinai desert near the Dead Sea for almost thirty years, then at Emesa, Syria, practicing such extreme austerities that he was called *salus*, mad. F. D. July 1.

SIMEON STYLITES, ST. (390–459). Son of a Cilician shepherd, he decided at thirteen to devote his life to prayer. He spent two years in a monastery, then went to one which was stricter, but his austerities there were so extreme he was dismissed. He then found an open hermitage, where he chained himself to a rock. Crowds interfered with his life, so he built a pillar about ten feet high, and less than six feet broad. He lived in such seclusion for twenty years until his death, his last pillar (*stylos*) being more than sixty feet high. From his elevation he preached twice a day, exhorting great crowds to avoid blasphemy and injustice and to pray for the dead. Theodoret and other eyewitnesses attest to the humility and genuine devotion of the saint, to the fact that he fasted completely every Lent for forty years, and to the great number of converts he made. F. D. Jan. 5.

SIMEON STYLITES THE YOUNGER, ST. (517?–592?). Born in Antioch, he was five when his father died. He entered the community of St. John Stylites and at seven began to live on a pillar, remaining there for sixty-eight years. When he was twenty, because of the crowds attracted by his holiness and wisdom he moved to a pillar in a more inaccessible place, the Hill of Wonders, near Antioch. At thirty, he established a monastery for his disciples and was ordained at thirty-three. He said mass on his pillar and great crowds came to listen to his preaching and prophecies. F. D. Sept. 3.

SIMEON OF TRENT, ST. (d. 1475). A child of two and a half, he was killed at Easter time and his body thrown into a canal. Popular anger blamed the murder on the Jews of the city of Trent, but such attribution is seriously to be questioned. F. D. Mar. 24.

SIMILIAN, ST. (d. 310). The bishop of Nantes in Gaul was highly praised by St. Gregory the Great. He is also called Sambin. F. D. June 16.

SIMITRIUS, ST. (d. 159?), martyr. He and twenty-two others were captured while attending mass in the church of St. Praxedes in Rome, and beheaded. F. D. May 26.

SIMON, ST. (1st century), apostle. Surnamed the Cananean—that is, "the Zealot"—because of his devotion to the Jewish law, he was one of the original twelve followers of Christ. According to tradition he preached in Egypt, then went with St. Jude to Persia, where they suffered martyrdom. F. D. Oct. 28.

SIMON, BL. (d. 1215). A Cistercian lay-brother and mystic at Aulne, near Liège, Flanders, he was invited to Rome by Pope Innocent III. F. D. Nov. 6.

SIMON, BL. (d. 1482). Born in Lipnicza, Poland, he studied at Cracow and in 1453, after hearing St. John Capistran preach, joined the Friars Minor. He became an outstanding preacher, and served as master of novices, guardian, and provincial of his order. He died in Cracow, Poland, on July 18 of the plague he had caught while caring for the stricken. He was beatified in 1685. F. D. July 20.

SIMON, YVES RENE MARIE (1903–1961), philosopher. Born in Cherbourg, France, on Mar. 14, he studied at the University of Paris, received his Ph. D. from the Institut Catholique de Paris, where he was a pupil of Jacques Maritain, in 1929, and was professor of phi-

losophy at the University of Lille in 1930–38. He came to the United States, taught philosophy at Notre Dame in 1938–48, and then at the University of Chicago until his death at Notre Dame on May 11. He was an authority on St. Thomas Aquinas and on the nature of liberty, authority and free will, and wrote numerous treatises, among them *Ontology du Connaître, Nature and Functions of Authority* (1942), *Community of the Free* (1947), and *Philosophy of Democratic Government* (1951).

SIMON OF CRAMAUD (1360?–1422), cardinal. Born near Rochechouart, France, he studied law at Orléans, became a noted canonist, and was appointed bishop of Agen in 1382. He was transferred to Béziers the following year, to Poitiers in 1385, was named to Sens in 1390 but never occupied the see, and in 1391 became titular patriarch of Alexandria and administrator of Avignon. He was appointed archbishop of Rheims in 1409, served as president of the Council of Pisa (1409), where he proclaimed the deposition of Gregory XII and Benedict XIII and helped elect Alexander V, and was created a cardinal and administrator of Poitiers in 1413. He was a sturdy supporter of the temporal authority, for which he is often called a forerunner of Gallicanism, and at the Council of Constance helped establish a papal election plan which allowed certain national representatives to vote. He died in Poitiers, France, on Dec. 14.

SIMON OF CREMONA (d. 1390), theologian. A noted Augustinian preacher, he was most successful in northern Italy, where he died in Padua.

SIMON OF CRÉPY, ST. (d. 1082). Count of Crépy, Valois, he was raised at the court of William the Conqueror, fought against Philip I of France, resisted the wishes of the count of Auvergne and William that he marry their daughters, and became a Benedictine monk at the abbey of St. Claude at Condat. He became active in diplomatic matters, helping settle disputes between St. Hugh of Cluny and the king of France, between William and his sons, and was successful in 1080 in negotiating peace among Norman leaders at the expressed direction of Pope St. Gregory VII. F. D. Sept. 30.

SIMON OF GHENT (14th century). Bishop of Salisbury, England, from 1297 to 1315, he is one of several who has been called the author of the *Ancren Riwle*, a thirteenth-century handbook for use by a group of women who retired to live as anchoresses.

SIMON IV DE MONTFORT (1160?–1218). Son of Simon de Montfort and Alicia, daughter of the earl of Leicester, he succeeded his father as baron de Montfort in 1181, married Alice de Montmorency in 1190, and in 1199 went on the crusade with Thibaud de Champagne to the Holy Land. He succeeded to the earldom of Leicester about 1204 on the death of his uncle and inherited vast estates in England, which were seized in 1207 by King John for an alleged debt. In 1208 he was appointed commander of the French forces in the crusade against the Albigenses, whom he defeated in a campaign notorious for its cruelty, remained in southern France after Carcassonne was captured in 1209, was invested with the viscounties of Beziers and Carcassonne, and in 1211 attacked and overran the territories of Raymond VI of Toulouse. He defeated Raymond and Peter II of Aragon at the battle of Muret in 1213, and was proclaimed count of Toulouse and duke of Narbonne by his crusaders in 1215 and confirmed by the pope later the same year. In 1215, through the pope's insistence, he regained his estates in England from King John, who intermittently recognized his earldom of Leicester. In 1217 revolt broke out in Provence and centered in Toulouse. Simon laid siege to the city, and on June 25 was killed during an attack.

SIMON STOCK, ST. (d. 1265). Born in Aylesford, Kent, he left a hermitage to make a pilgrimage to Jerusalem, where he joined the early Carmelites, returning to England after the Moslems drove them out. As superior general he made a number of foundations in the British Isles and on the Continent, established houses at the universities of Cambridge, Oxford, Paris, and Bologna, revised the rule (approved by Pope Innocent IV in 1237) to organize the alms-seeking methods of an order which now was to become mendicant. He died at Bordeaux. It was he who popularized the wearing of the brown scapular in honor of the Virgin Mary, but the genuineness of the vision which directed this has been strenuously challenged. He has never been formally canonized, but is honored in parts of England and by the Carmelite order on May 16.

SIMON OF SUDBURY (d. 1381), archbishop. Born in Sudbury, Suffolk, England, he received his degree in law at Paris, became Pope Innocent VI's chaplain, and in 1356 was sent to England as nuncio. After serving as chancellor of Salisbury, he became bishop of London in 1361, helped conduct negotiations with John of Gaunt in France in 1372-73, and succeeded to the archbishopric of Canterbury in 1375. London's Bishop Courtenay's insistence caused him to summon Wyclif before the bishops in 1377, but Wyclif's influential supporters caused Simon to free him without condemnation. He was made lord chancellor in 1380, and was murdered in the Tower of London on June 14 by a mob which decapitated him during the peasants' uprising of 1381.

SIMON OF TOURNAI (12th century), philosopher. A professor at the university of Paris

in 1184, he was noted for his lectures on philosophy and theology. His use of the Arab translations of Aristotle and other philosophers caused enmity among the conservative group of the university, but his works, notably *Summa theologica, Quaestiones, Sermones,* and *Expositio in symbolum s. Athanasii,* are orthodox.

SIMONE DI MARTINI. *See* Martini, Simone.

SIMONE DA ORSENIGO (14th century). A native of Orsenigo, Como, Italy, he was one of the master architects who worked on the Milan cathedral.

SIMPLICIAN, ST. (d. 400), bishop. A friend and admired adviser of St. Ambrose, whom he succeeded as bishop of Milan in 397, he also was a confidant of St. Augustine and greatly influenced the latter's decision to become a Catholic. Although he died in May, he is honored by the Augustinians on Aug. 13.

SIMPLICIUS, ST. (d. 483), pope. A native of Tivoli, Italy, he became pope on Mar. 3, 468, defended the action of the Council of Chalcedon against the Monophysite heresy, and devoted himself to caring for the victims of the invasion of Italy by the Heruli, whose leader Odoacer occupied Rome and deposed the last emperor, Romulus Augustus, in 476, thus ending the Roman Empire. The pontificate of Simplicius was further disturbed by the promulgation of Emperor Zeno's *Henoticon* in 482, although its full effects were not felt until after the pope's death. F. D. Mar. 10.

SIMPLICIUS, ST. (d. 161?), martyr. He and his sons Constantius and Victorian were put to death in Rome during the reign of Marcus Aurelius. F. D. Aug. 26.

SIMPLICIUS, ST. (d. 255?), martyr. *See* Quintus, St.

SIMPLICIUS, ST. (3rd century), martyr. *See* Calepodius, St.

SIMPLICIUS, ST. (d. 304), martyr. He was buried alive, on Sardinia, during the Diocletian persecution. F. D. May 15.

SIMPLICIUS, ST. (d. 304?), martyr. *See* Beatrice, St.

SIMPLICIUS, ST. (d. 305?), martyr. *See* Castorius, St.

SIMPLICIUS, ST. (4th century?), bishop. One bishop of this name is mentioned by St. Athanasius as present at the Council of Sardica in 347; apparently a second succeeded Bishop Egemonius to the Gallic see of Autun in 390. Legends which became attached to the name are listed by St. Gregory of Tours. F. D. June 24.

SIMPLICIUS, ST. (d. 477), bishop. He ruled his see of Bourges, France, effectively in spite of struggles with the Arian Visigoths and powerful aristocrats. He died on Mar. 1. F. D. June 16.

SIMPLICIUS, ST. (d. 535?). He was bishop of Verona, Italy. F. D. Nov. 20.

SIMPLICIUS, ST. (d. 570?). He was third abbot of Monte Cassino, Italy, and a disciple of St. Benedict. F. D. Oct. 22.

SIMPSON, RICHARD (1820–1876). A graduate of Oxford, he was ordained an Anglican clergyman, but became a convert in 1845. He edited the *Rambler* and founded the *Home and Foreign Review* in 1862 with Sir John Acton; this was discontinued in 1864 because of ecclesiastical opposition. He helped Gladstone write his hostile pamphlet, *Vaticanism*, published an edition of Edmund Campion and studies of Shakespeare, and died near Rome on Apr. 5.

SINCERO, LUIGI (1870–1936), cardinal. Born in Italy, he was ordained in 1892, taught in the Vercelli seminary, and went to Rome as auditor of the rota. He was made a cardinal in 1923, cardinal-bishop of Palestrina and chancellor of the Pontifical University in 1933, and president of the commission for the codification of oriental canon law in 1934. He died in Rome on Feb. 7.

SINCHEALL, ST. (5th century). A follower of St. Patrick, he was abbot-founder of a monastery and school at Killeigh, Offaly, Ireland, where he directed 150 monks. F. D. Mar. 26.

SINDIMIUS, ST. (d. 303), martyr. *See* Anastasius, St.

SINDULPHUS, ST. (d. 669?). He was thirty-first bishop of Vienne, Gaul. F. D. Dec. 10.

SINIBALDI, GUITTONCINO (1270–1336). Born in Pistoja, Italy, he studied law there and at Bologna, supported the Ghibilline faction in his native city and left when the Guelphs triumphed, taught law at Treviso, Siena, Florence, Perugia, and Naples, published his notes on the Justinian Code, wrote sonnets to Selvaggia di Vergiolesi, an ideal lady matching the Beatrice of Dante, and was a friend of the greater poet. He is also known as Cino da Pistoja.

SIONITA, GABRIEL (1577–1648), scholar. Born in Edden, Lebanon, he went to Rome at seven, studied Latin, Syriac, and Hebrew, and was taken to Paris by Savary de Brèves, former French ambassador to Turkey, who wished to issue a polyglot bible. Sionita was given a chair in Semitic languages at the Sorbonne, received his doctorate in 1620, and was ordained in 1622. With John Hesronita, another Maronite, he published a Latin translation of the Arabic psalter in 1614; in 1616 he alone issued an Arabic grammar. Other translations and editions followed, but work on the polyglot was slow, partly because of insufficient funds, and partly because of Sionita's dilatory workmanship. Cardinal Richelieu had him imprisoned in 1640, released him after three months, and

gained a promise of serious attention, which Sionita kept. He corrected the Arabic and Syriac texts and prepared a revised translation into Latin of all books except Ruth. He died in Paris.

SIRE, DOMINIQUE (1827–1917). Born in St. Jory, France, on Mar. 12, he studied at St. Sulpice, was ordained in 1851, and taught at the seminaries of Le Puy and St. Sulpice. He served as a delegate to arrange exchange of prisoners during the Paris Commune, prepared the translations of the papal bull *Ineffabilis* on the Immaculate Conception, and died in St. Jory on Dec. 11.

SIRENUS. *See* Serenus the Gardener.

SIRICIUS, ST. (d. 399), pope. A Roman deacon, he succeeded Pope Damasus in Dec. 384. He denounced Jovinian, who had questioned the virginity of Mary, supported St. Martin of Tours, and excommunicated Felix of Trèves for his part in the execution of the heretic Priscillian. His letter to Bishop Himerius of Tarragona in 385, the earliest complete decree extant, asserted the validity of Arian baptism and the necessity for clerical celibacy—the first known decree on the matter from Rome. He died in Rome. F. D. Nov. 26.

SIRICIUS, ST. (d. 434?), martyr. *See* Felix, St.

SIRLETO, GUGLIELMO (1514–1585), cardinal. Born in Guardavelle, Calabria, Italy, son of a physician, he became a friend of Cardinal Cervino (later Pope Marcellus II), for whom he prepared a memorandum on the questions discussed at the Council of Trent, was appointed custodian at the Vatican Library in 1549, prepared a catalogue of its Greek manuscripts and a new edition of the Vulgate, and was appointed prothonotary by Pope Paul IV. He taught in Rome, served as adviser to the cardinal-legates at the Council of Trent, was created a cardinal in 1565, was appointed bishop of San Marco in 1566 and of Squillace in 1568, and in 1570 was made librarian of the Vatican Library. He helped prepare the Roman catechism and a new edition of the Roman Martyrology, and headed the commission for the reform of the Roman breviary. He died in Rome on Oct. 6.

SIRMOND, JACQUES (1559–1651), scholar. Born in Riom, Puy-de-Dôme, France, in Oct., he became a Jesuit in 1576, taught classics in Paris in 1581, and from 1590 to 1606 was secretary to the general, Aquaviva, in Rome. He returned to France in 1608, and two years later published the first of the many Greek and Latin Christian authors he was to edit. He became Louis XIII's confessor in 1637. He edited the capitularies of Charles the Bald and the early French councils, and the works of Sidonius Apollinaris, Theodoret of Cyrus,

Ennodius, Hincmar of Rheims, and others. He died in Paris on Oct. 7.

SISEBUTUS, ST. (d. 1082). He developed the Benedictine abbey of Cardena, Spain, near Burgos, with great success. He gave refuge there to the Cid (Rodrigo Diaz de Vivar), the patriot who was to be perpetuated in the Spanish epic. F. D. Mar. 15.

SISENANDUS, ST. (d. 851), martyr. Born in Badajoz, Spain, he was a deacon at Cordova when beheaded in a Moorish persecution. F. D. July 16.

SISINIUS, ST. (d. 309?), martyr. *See* Saturninus, St.

SISINIUS, ST. (d. 397), martyr. He was a deacon who went from Cappadocia with Martyrius, a lector, to evangelize the Tyrol at the request of St. Vigilius, bishop of Trent. They gained many converts, built a church, and were beaten to death when attempting to aid Christians who were being forced to attend a pagan festival. Alexander, younger brother of Martyrius, was burned alive. F. D. May 29.

SISINIUS, ST. (4th century). Bishop of Cyzicus, Asia Minor, he outlived torture during the Diocletian persecution and was present at the Council of Nicaea (325). F. D. Nov. 23.

SISINNIUS (d. 708), pope. A native of Syria, he probably was consecrated on Jan. 15, 708, and died three weeks later on Feb. 4.

SISOES, ST. (d. 429?). He lived a life of austerity in the Egyptian desert for sixty-two years, following the example of St. Antony, and attracted many disciples. F. D. July 6.

SITJAR, BUENAVENTURA (1739–1808), missioner. Born in Porrera, Majorca, Balearic Islands, on Dec. 9, he joined the Franciscans in 1758, was ordained, and was sent to San Fernando College in Mexico City. He went to California in 1770 and was appointed first missionary by Junípero Serra when he arrived there in 1771. He spent the rest of his life working among the Indians, baptizing some 3400. He wrote a grammar of the Telame language. He died at the mission of San Antonio, California, on Sept. 3.

SITRIC II (11th century), king. King of the Danes in Dublin, he seems to have followed his subjects into the Church in 1038. He built the cathedral of the Holy Trinity (seized in Elizabeth's day and renamed Christ Church), helped to organize parishes, and saw Donatus appointed first bishop of the see.

SIVIARD, ST. (d. 729?). He succeeded his father as abbot of the Benedictine monastery of St. Calais, France. F. D. Mar. 1.

SIXTUS I, ST. (d. 125), pope. A Roman, he succeeded St. Alexander I to the papacy in 115. Nothing is known of his decade of service. F. D. Apr. 3.

SIXTUS II, ST. (d. 258), pope and martyr. Possibly a Greek, he was elected pope on Aug.

30, 257. During the persecution of Valerian, Sixtus was seized while preaching at mass in the catacomb of Praetextatus in Rome, condemned, and beheaded with his deacons, SS. Agapitus and Felicissimus. Also taken and martyred were St. Quartus and four subdeacons, SS. Januarius, Magnus, Stephen, and Vincent. F. D. Aug. 6.

SIXTUS III, ST. (d. 440), pope. A leading cleric in Rome, he succeeded Pope St. Celestine on July 31, 432. He fought Pelagianism and Nestorianism, but because of his conciliatory efforts was accused of sympathy toward the adherents of those heresies. He built several basilicas, including St. Mary Major and St. Peter in Chains. F. D. Aug. 19.

SIXTUS IV (1414–1484), pope. Francesco de la Rovere was born in Savona, Italy, on July 21, became a Franciscan, studied at Pavia, Padua, and Bologna, and was ordained. He lectured at Padua, Bologna, Pavia, Siena, and Florence was appointed minister general of his order in 1464, and in 1467 was created a cardinal. He was elected pope on Aug. 9, 1471, and was consecrated on Aug. 25. He tried unsuccessfully to continue the crusade against the Turks and sent Cardinal Caraffa on an unsuccessful expedition against them, denounced the pragmatic sanction in France (especially Louis XI's decree of 1475 requiring royal permission for the publication of papal documents in France), and continued efforts to reunite the Russian church to Rome. He involved himself in Italian politics and diplomacy, became embroiled in the disturbances in Florence, where his nephew and the Pazzi attempted to overthrow the Medici, and, when Florence took vengeance on the conspirators, placed the city under interdict and waged war against it in 1478–80. He conspired with the Venetians in their attack on Ferrara, which he wanted for his nephew, and was finally forced to make peace with the princes allied against him. He was a generous patron of the arts (he built the Sistine Chapel and bridge, founded the Sistine choir, was the second founder of the Vatican Library, commissioned paintings on a prodigal scale, and patronized writers, scholars, musicians, and artists lavishly), encouraged the monastic orders, formally annulled the decrees of the Council of Constance, attempted to suppress the abuses of the Spanish Inquisition which he had authorized in 1478, and opposed the Waldenses with great vigor. He was guilty of flagrant nepotism; simony flourished; taxes were ruinous; and his appointments of unworthy men to high office sowed the seeds of scandals which burdened the papacy for the next half century. He died in Rome on Aug. 12.

SIXTUS V (1521–1590), pope. Felice Peretti was born in Grottamare, Italy, on Dec. 13, entered the Friars Minor at Montalto when nine, entered the order, continued his education at Ferrara and Bologna, and was ordained in Siena in 1547. He became noted for his preaching and as a reformer, served as rector in Siena, Naples, and Venice, and in 1557 became inquisitor at Venice. His severity caused his recall to Rome in 1560. He taught at the Sapienza, became procurator and vicar general of his order, and in 1565 accompanied Cardinal Buoncompagni (later Pope Gregory XIII) to Spain to hear charges of heresy against the archbishop of Toledo. He was appointed bishop of Sant' Agata dei Goti, Naples, in 1566, became Pope Pius V's confessor, and was created a cardinal-priest in 1570, taking the name Montalto. He was transferred to the see of Fermo in 1571, and during the reign of Pope Gregory XIII, with whom he had been at odds since their trip to Spain in 1565, lived in retirement, devoting himself to editing the works of St. Ambrose. On the death of Gregory in 1585, he was elected pope on Apr. 24, 1585, and was consecrated on May 1. During his pontificate he exterminated the bands of outlaws which had terrorized the Papal States, reorganized and replenished the Vatican treasury, launched a tremendous building program, built the Aqua Felice aqueduct and drained the Pontine marshes, instituted ecclesiastical reforms, fixed the number of cardinals at seventy, and reorganized the papal curia. In 1587 he entered an alliance with Philip II of Spain to conquer England, but their plans were ended by the defeat of the Spanish Armada in 1588. He built the new Lateran palace and the Vatican Library, and died in the Quirinal palace in Rome on Aug. 27.

SIXTUS, ST. (d. 300?). Appointed bishop of Rheims, France, in 290, he moved there from Soissons. F. D. Sept. 1.

SKARGA, PETER (1536–1612). Born in Grojec, Poland, he studied at Cracow and Warsaw, tutored in Vienna in 1557, was ordained there in 1564, and became a canon of the Lemberg cathedral. He became a Jesuit in 1568, went to Rome, and on his return to Poland taught at Pultusk and Wilna. He was a close friend of King Stephen Báthory, who appointed him rector of the Wilna academy, became superior in Cracow in 1584 and founded the Brotherhood of Mercy there, was appointed court preacher by Sigismund III in 1588, a position he held the rest of his life, and in 1596 was largely instrumental in effecting the return of the Ruthenian Church to Rome. He was emissary in a fruitless mission to the nobles in their revolt against Sigismund, and died in Cracow, Poland, on Sept. 27. He wrote theological works, a history of the Church, popular lives of the saints, *On the Unity of the Church of God*, and collections of sermons.

SKELTON, JOHN (1460?–1529), poet. Born probably in Norfolk, England, he studied at Cambridge, Oxford, and Louvain, and became tutor of the later King Henry VIII. He was named poet laureate in 1493, having already attained fame for his Latin work and having been praised by Erasmus as the greatest of the English writers. Skelton was ordained in 1498, became rector of Diss, and lived there at least from 1504 to 1523. He wrote a number of short poems; *The Bouge of Court*, a satiric portrait of court life; *Philip Sparrow*, an amusing elegy on the death of a child's pet; *Elinor Rumming*, a violent portrait of drunkenness; *Magnificence*, a morality play; and three angry portraits of the world of Cardinal Wolsey: *Speak, Parrot, Colin Clout*, and *Why Come Ye Not to Court?* (1521–23). These poems also attacked the wasteful policies of Henry, domestic and foreign, and after the appearance of the last, Skelton took sanctuary in Westminster. He may have been the tutor of Henry Howard, had some slight influence on Edmund Spenser, and in the twentieth century his brisk rhymes have been imitated by Robert Graves. Much false biography has resulted from the appearance, after his death at Westminster on June 21, of the scurrilous *Merrie Tales of Skelton*.

SKEVINGTON, THOMAS (d. 1533), bishop. Abbot of Beaulieu, Hampshire, England, he completed the cathedral of Bangor, Wales, and added an episcopal residence and the bells which were sold by the sixteenth-century Anglican bishop, Arthur Bulkeley.

SKINNER, RICHARD DANA (1893–1941), critic. Born in Detroit, Michigan, on Apr. 21, he graduated from Harvard in 1915, having married Margaret Hill in 1913. He was on the staff of the Boston *Herald* until 1917, when he joined the aviation corps; he rose to the rank of captain, and was decorated by the American, French, and Italian governments. He edited a trade paper, wrote advertising, and became partner in an industrial advisory firm after World War I. In 1924–34 he was drama critic of *Commonweal* and, in 1935–36, associate editor of the *North American Review* (founded by his great-grandfather, Richard Henry Dana). He published *Our Changing Theatre* (1931), *Eugene O'Neill—A Poet's Quest* (1935), and *Seven Kinds of Inflation* (1937). He died in New York City on Nov. 6.

SKODA, JOSEF (1805–1881), physician. Born in Pilsen, Bohemia, on Dec. 10, he studied at Vienna, where he received his doctorate in medicine in 1831, worked in the Vienna General Hospital, was appointed city physician for the poor in 1839, head of a new department for consumptives there the next year, and, in 1846, professor of medical clinics. He revived the percussion diagnosis method which had fallen into disuse, became famed as a diagnostician, and established a separate section of his department for skin diseases which gave great impetus to the study of dermatology. He died in Vienna on June 13.

SKRBENSKY-HRISTE, LEON DE (1863–1938), cardinal. Born in Hansdorf, Austria-Hungary, he was ordained, became archbishop of Prague in 1899 and privy councilor to Emperor Franz Josef, was created a cardinal in 1901, and lived in seclusion after an automobile injury in 1920. He died in Niederlangendorf, Czechoslovakia, on Dec. 24.

SLADE, BL. JOHN (d. 1583), martyr. Born in Manston, Dorsetshire, England, he was educated at Oxford and became a teacher. He was arrested and hanged, drawn, and quartered in Winchester for denying the supremacy of Queen Elizabeth in spiritual matters. He was beatified in 1929. F. D. Oct. 30.

SLAVIN, ROBERT JOSEPH (1907–1961), educator. Born in Dorchester, Massachusetts, on Mar. 19, he studied at Providence College, St. Thomas Aquinas, River Forest, Illinois, and Immaculate Conception, Washington, D.C. He joined the Dominicans in 1926, was ordained in 1934, taught philosophy at Catholic University, Washington, in 1936–47, and in 1947 was appointed president of Providence College, a position he held until his death there on Apr. 24.

SLOANE, THOMAS O'CONOR (1851–1940), editor. Born in New York City on Nov. 24, he studied at St. Francis Xavier and Columbia, taught science at Seton Hall in 1888–89, invented a self-recording photometer and other devices, served on the staff of *Scientific American, Youth's Companion,* and other journals, edited *Amazing Stories,* wrote a dozen volumes on liquid air, india rubber, chemistry, and popular science, and translated Johannes Jörgensen's *St. Francis of Assisi.* He was a member of the New Jersey board of education in 1905–11. He died in South Orange, New Jersey, on Aug. 7.

SLOMŠEK, ANTON MARTIN (1800–1862). Bishop of Maribor, Jugoslavia, he became famous for his efforts to educate the people of his native Slovenia. He reformed the schools, introduced new textbooks, many of which he wrote, founded the weekly, *Drobtinice,* and in 1851, established *Druzba sr. Mohora* to spread Catholicism by the wide distribution of Catholic literature. He died on Sept. 24.

SLOTANUS, JOHN. See Van der Slooten, Johann.

SLUTER, CLAUX (d. 1405?), sculptor. Born in Holland, he entered the service of Philip the Bold of Burgundy, and worked at Dijon and at the Carthusian monastery of Champmol, which Philip founded in 1383. He completed realistic statues of Philip and Duchess Mar-

guerite, St. John, St. Catherine, a fountain of Moses and five other prophets, and the tomb of Philip; his nephew, Claux de Werne, completed the latter in 1411.

SLYTHURST, THOMAS (d. 1560). Born in Berkshire, England, he received his degree from Oxford, was rector of Chalfont St. Peter for ten years from 1545, and of Chalfont St. Giles in 1555, and became first president of Trinity College, Oxford. When Cardinal Pole was elected chancellor, Slythurst was appointed to a committee to regulate theological exercises, and died in the Tower of London.

SMARAGDUS, ST. (d. 304?), martyr. *See* Cyriacus, St.

SMARAGDUS, ST. (d. 843). Born in Languedoc, France, he became a Benedictine at Aniane, Herault, taking the name Ardo, and was taught by Abbot St. Benedict. He was given charge of the monastery schools, succeeded Benedict in 814, and wrote a life of the latter in 822. He died at the monastery. F. D. Mar. 7.

SMITH, ALFRED EMANUEL (1873–1944), governor. He was born in New York City's Lower East Side on Dec. 20, and in 1903 was elected to the state assembly and served for twelve years, becoming Democratic leader in 1911 and speaker in 1913. He was elected sheriff of New York county in 1915 and became president of the New York City board of aldermen in 1918. He was elected governor of New York in 1918, was defeated for re-election by Nathan Miller in 1920, but re-elected in 1922, 1924, and 1926. His terms as governor were notable for their able administration and progressive social legislation in the fields of housing, education, hospitals, workmen's compensation, as well as the public development of natural resources and the building of roads, parkways, and parks. In 1928 he was Democratic nominee for United States president, the first Catholic ever nominated. He was overwhelmingly defeated by Herbert Hoover in a campaign marred by the injection of religious bigotry. He devoted the remainder of his life to business, religious, and civic activities. He actively re-entered politics only once thereafter, to break publicly with Franklin D. Roosevelt over New Deal policies.

A. E. SMITH, *Up to Now* (New York, Viking, 1928); EMILY SMITH and HAWTHORNE DANIEL, *The Happy Warrior* (Garden City, N.Y., Doubleday, 1956).

SMITH, ALPHONSE JOHN (1883–1935), bishop. Born in Madison, Indiana, on Nov. 14, he studied at St. Mary's College, Kansas, and the North American College, Rome, and was ordained in 1908. He was assistant pastor at the cathedral in Indianapolis from then until 1921, when he became pastor of St. Joan of Arc church there, and in 1924 was consecrated bishop of Nashville, Tennessee. He died on Dec. 16.

SMITH, GEORGE D. (1879–1960), author. Born in Weymouth, England, he joined the Canons Lateran, studied at St. Edmund's, and was ordained in 1897. He was prior at Bodmin in 1900–11, became titular abbot of Leicester in 1914, taught theology at St. Edmund's for thirty-four years (1918–52), became editor of the *Clergy Review*, a position he held until his death, and in 1946–51 served as abbot of his order in Rome. He wrote on Christ, the Virgin Mary, the sacraments, and *Teachings of the Catholic Church* (1940). He died at St. Leonard's-on-Sea, England, on Nov. 11.

SMITH, JAMES (1790?–1866), journalist. Born in Skolland, Shetland Islands, he studied law at Edinburgh, was a supreme court solicitor there, and became a convert. He founded the *Edinburgh Catholic Magazine* in 1832 and when he went to London in 1838 continued its publication (without Edinburgh in the title), began the *Catholic Directory*, edited the *Dublin Review* in 1837, and was a prominent defender of Catholicism in England. He died in Jan.

SMITH, MATTHEW J. W. (1891–1960), editor. Born in Altoona, Pennsylvania, on June 9, he worked four years for the local *Tribune* and then on the *Pueblo* (Colorado) *Chieftain*. He studied at St. Thomas seminary, Denver, became editor of the *Denver Catholic Register* in 1913, and developed a successful paper from which a national edition and then a chain of thirty-three diocesan papers grew. He was ordained in 1923, was made a monsignor in 1933, founded a school of journalism in Denver, and was honored by the Spanish government. He died in Denver, Colorado, on June 15.

SMITH, RICHARD (1500–1563). A native of Worcestershire, England, he studied at Oxford, and was appointed first regius professor of divinity by Henry VIII in 1536. He became master of Whittington College, rector of St. Dunstan's, principal of St. Alban's, and reputedly abjured papal authority in 1547. If so, he quickly repudiated his abjuration, for he was deprived of his professorship and arrested. On his release he became a professor of divinity at Louvain, recovered his preferments when Mary ascended the throne, and was prominent in the trials of Cranmer, Ridley, and Latimer, preaching at the execution of the latter two. He lost all under Elizabeth, was imprisoned, but escaped to Douai, where Philip II appointed him dean of St. Peter's church. He became chancellor and professor when Douai University was founded in 1562, and died there on July 9. He wrote on the mass and refutations of Beza, Calvin, and Melanchthon.

SMITH, RICHARD (1568–1655), bishop.

Born in Hanworth, Lincolnshire, England, in Nov., he studied at Oxford, where he became a convert, went to the English College in Rome in 1586, and was ordained in 1592. He received his doctorate in theology at Valladolid, taught at the English College, became a professor at Seville in 1598, and was sent on the English mission in 1603. He represented the secular clergy in the archpriest controversy in Rome against Fr. Persons, became superior of the English secular priests at Arras College, Paris, in 1613, and was appointed vicar apostolic to England and bishop of Chalcedon in 1625. He engaged in controversy with the regulars over his claim to the rights of an ordinary, which was decided against him in 1627 when Pope Urban VIII ruled he was not an ordinary, and was ordered arrested by the government in 1628. He was forced to flee to France in 1631, lived with Richelieu in Paris until the cardinal's death in 1642, and spent the rest of his life until his death in Paris on Mar. 18 at the convent of the English Augustinian nuns.

SMITH, THOMAS KILBY (1820–1887), general. Born in Boston on Sept. 23, he was educated at a military academy in Cincinnati, Ohio, studied law under Chief Justice Chase, and in 1853 was appointed special agent of the post office department. He was appointed marshal of southern Ohio, and served in the Union army during the Civil War, rising to the rank of major general, and was put in charge of the department of southern Alabama and Florida. He was appointed United States consul in Panama in 1866, engaged in journalism in New York, and became a convert. He died in New York City on Dec. 14.

SMITH, WALTER BEDELL (1895–1961), general. Born in Indianapolis, Indiana, on Oct. 5, he was interested in the army as a youth, joining the National Guard when 15, served in the regular army from 1917 when he fought in World War I, and, though he had never attended any military school, rose to the rank of lieutenant general as chief of staff to General Dwight Eisenhower in World War II. He received the German surrender in 1945, served as ambassador to Russia in 1946–49, returned to the United States to lead the 1st Army, and in 1950 became director of the Central Intelligence Agency. He became Undersecretary of State in 1953, returned the following year to private industry, and died in Washington, D.C., on Aug. 9. He wrote *Eisenhower's Six Great Decisions* (1946) and *My Three Years in Moscow* (1950).

SMITS, WILLIAM (1704–1770). Born in Kevelaer in the duchy of Geldern, he became a Friar Minor in Belgium, taught scripture, and published a series of exegetical studies from 1732 to 1744. From then until 1767 he published thirteen books of an annotated translation of the Bible, undertaken at the suggestion of Archbishop Thomas Philip of Mechlin. He was appointed head of the Franciscan biblical institute at Antwerp in 1765 and died on Dec. 1.

SMYTH, TIMOTHY CLEMENT (1810–1865), bishop. Born in Finlea, Clare, Ireland, on Jan. 24, he studied at Trinity College, Dublin, and Mt. Melleray, where he joined the Cistercians in 1838, and was ordained in Waterford in 1841. He was sent to the United States, founded New Melleray monastery, near Dubuque, Iowa, in 1849, and in 1857 was appointed titular bishop of Thanasis and coadjutor of Dubuque. He succeeded to the see in 1858, was administrator of Chicago in 1858–59, and died in Dubuque on Sept. 22.

SNOW, VEN. PETER (d. 1598), martyr. Born near Ripon, England, he escaped to Rheims in 1589 and was ordained there in 1591. Sent on the English mission, he avoided arrest until May 1598, when he was captured near York with Ralph Grimston, condemned for being a priest, and executed at York on June 15.

SOBIESKI, JOHN. See John III Sobieski.

SOCRATES, ST. (d. 220), martyr. See Dionysius, St.

SOCRATES, ST. (d. 275), martyr. See Dionysius, St.

SOCRATES, ST. (d. 304?), martyr. He and St. Stephen are reputed to have been British Christians who were followers of St. Amphibalus and were martyred in Britain during the Diocletian persecution, although Abretania, in Asia Minor, or possibly Bithynia, is more likely. F. D. Sept. 17.

SOCRATES (5th century), historian. Born in Constantinople about 379, he studied under Helladius and Ammonius, was probably a lawyer, and is famed as the author of *Historia ecclesiae*, a continuation of Eusebius' work covering the years 306–439. It is characterized by its objectivity and fair-mindedness, though marred by the author's weakness for accepting dubious material as fact and his inaccuracies regarding the Church in the West. He died sometime after 440.

SODELBIA, ST. (6th century). See Eithene, St.

SODOMA, IL. See Bazzi, Giovanni Antonio.

SOIRON, BL. CATHERINE (d. 1794), martyr. She and her sister Thérèse were porters in the Carmelite convent of Compiègne, France; they were executed with that entire community of nuns in Paris during the French Revolution. F. D. July 17.

SOIRON, BL. THÉRÈSE (d. 1794), martyr. See Soiron, Bl. Catherine.

SOLA, ST. (d. 794). An Anglo-Saxon monk, he was ordained by St. Boniface, whom he had followed to Germany, and lived as a hermit near Fulda and then near Eichstätt, Germany, where he attracted many disciples and founded the Benedictine abbey of Solnhofen. F. D. Dec. 3.

SOLANGE, ST. (d. 880). Born of a poor family of vineyard workers near Bourges, France, she became a shepherdess whose beauty attracted the lustful attention of a noble in Poitiers. He kidnaped her, but when she leaped from the horse on which he was carrying her off, he pursued and killed her. The sources of the story are questionable, however. F. D. May 10.

SOLANO, ST. FRANCISCO (1549–1610). Born at Montilla, Spain, on Mar. 10, he joined the Franciscans in 1569 and was ordained in 1576. He became an effective preacher and convert-maker, and, when he requested a missionary assignment, was sent to Peru. For twenty years he devoted himself untiringly to the welfare of the Indians and Spanish colonists, learning the dialects and customs of many tribes. He was made custodian of Franciscan houses in Argentina and Paraguay, and then guardian of the Lima friary. In Lima, Trujillo, and other towns the effectiveness of his preaching was astounding and he was called "the wonder-worker of the New World." He died in Lima, Peru, and was canonized in 1726. F. D. July 14.

SOLARI, ANDREA (1460?–1515), painter. Born in Milan, Italy, brother of Cristoforo Solari, he studied painting in Venice under Giovanni Bellini, who greatly influenced his early work, and later in Milan under Leonardo da Vinci, whose style he closely imitated. He is noted for the coloring, modeling, and brightness of tone in his later works. Among his chief works are *Descent from the Cross, Madonna with a Child, Holy Family with St. Jerome, Salome with the Head of John the Baptist, Repose on the Flight to Egypt, Ecce Homo,* and an unfinished *Assumption of the Virgin* and frescoes in the castle of Cardinal Georges d'Amboise at Gaillon, France.

SOLARI, ANTONIO (1382–1445), painter. Son of a Bohemian blacksmith whose trade he pursued as a youth, he became interested in painting, attracted the favor of Queen Joanna of Naples, and became the leading painter and head of a school there. His outstanding work is a series of twenty frescoes in a monastery near San Severino, representing the life of St. Benedict. He was nicknamed Il Zingaro ("The Gypsy").

SOLARI, CRISTOFORO (1450?–1525?), sculptor. Born in Milan, Italy, he accompanied his brother, Andrea, to Venice in 1490, took up sculpture, and on his return to Milan in 1498 entered the service of Ludovico Sforza. When the Sforzas were overthrown he went to Rome, but returned to Milan, where in 1503 he was in charge of the building of the cathedral. His outstanding works are the tomb of Sforza's wife, of which only the figures of Beatrice d'Este and Ludovico survive, several statues in the Milan cathedral, and the cupola of Santa Maria della Passione in Milan. He is often called Il Gobbo ("The Hunchback"). He died in Milan.

SOLARI, GUINIFORTE (1429–1481), architect. A native of Milan, Italy, he became one of the architects of the Certosa, of which his father, Giovanni (1400–1480), was superintendent, in 1465, designed several Milanese churches, and was one of the architects of the Sforza's fortified castle.

SOLEMNUS, ST. (d. 511?). He became bishop of Chartres, Gaul, about 490, and attended the baptism of Clovis. F. D. Sept. 25.

SOLINA, ST. (d. 290), martyr. A young Gascon girl, she fled to Chartres to avoid being married to a pagan, and was beheaded there. F. D. Oct. 17.

SOLOCHON, ST. (d. 305). He and three other Egyptian soldiers were beaten to death at Chalcedon, Asia Minor, during the reign of Maximian when their faith became known. F. D. May 17.

SOLOMON I, ST. (d. 434), king. Born in Cornwall, England, and married to St. Gwen, he ruled Brittany until his death at the hands of heathen rebels. F. D. June 25.

SOLOMON III (d. 874), king. He defended Brittany against the Franks and Norsemen and against civil insurrection. When he was assassinated on June 25 by enemies, the Bretons acclaimed him a saint and martyr.

SOLOMON (d. 1074), king of Hungary. Son of Andrew I, he was supported by the German faction for the throne of Hungary on the death of his uncle Béla I in 1063, but was overthrown by his cousin Géza I in 1074.

SOLOMON, ST. (d. 857), martyr. A Christian who was captured during the Moorish occupation of Spain, he was charged with apostasy, imprisoned, and beheaded with St. Roderick at Cordova. F. D. Mar. 13.

SOLUTOR, ST. (d. 287?), martyr. See Maurice, St.

SOLUTOR, ST. (d. 297), martyr. See Adventor, St.

SOLUTOR, ST. (d. 305?), martyr. See Valentine, St.

SOMERS, BL. THOMAS (d. 1610), martyr. Born in Skelsmergh, Westmoreland, England, he became a schoolmaster, then went to Douai, where he was ordained. Sent on the English mission, where he used the name of Wilson, he was captured, convicted of being a priest, and hanged, drawn, and quartered at Tyburn with Bl. John Roberts. He was beatified in 1929. F. D. Dec. 10.

SOMERSET, THOMAS (1530?–1587). Son of the earl of Worcester, he was imprisoned in the Fleet prison in London from 1562 to 1572 for translating and printing a sermon by the archbishop of Rheims, was rearrested on a charge of treason in 1587, and imprisoned in the Tower of London, where he died on May 27.

SOMMA, BONAVENTURA (1893–1960), composer. He was the director of the St. Cecilia choir in Rome for thirty-four years (1926–60), took it on tour through Canada and the United States in 1955, and wrote symphonic compositions for orchestra and choir, violin and piano, and organ. He died in Rome on Oct. 23.

SONATI, BARTOLOMMEO (d. 1420), martyr. See Cennini, Bl. Agostino.

SONIS, GASTON DE (1825–1887), general. Born in Pointe-à-Pitre, Guadaloupe, West Indies, he studied at St. Cyr and Saumur, France, became an army officer, was seriously wounded in the Franco-Prussian War, and rose to the rank of general. He tendered his resignation in 1880 in protest against the government's decree dispersing religious orders and spent the rest of his life in Paris as a Carmelite tertiary.

SONNIUS, FRANCISCUS (1506–1576), bishop. Born in Zon, Brabant, on Aug. 12, Francis Van de Velde studied at Bois-le-Duc and Louvain, was ordained, received his doctorate in theology in 1539, and after pastoral work in Meerbeck and Louvain became a professor of theology at Louvain in 1544. He changed his name to Sonnius, attended several sessions of the Council of Trent, participated in the religious disputation in Worms in 1557, and was sent by Philip II on a diplomatic mission affecting the Church in Belgium. He was appointed bishop of Bois-le-Duc in 1566 and first bishop of Antwerp in 1569, where he held two diocesan synods. He wrote against Calvinism and a textbook in dogmatics, and died in Antwerp, Belgium, on June 30.

SOPHIA, ST. She is listed in the Roman Martyrology under Sept. 30 as the mother of Faith, Hope, and Charity, who died while praying at their tomb three days after their legendary death in 138.

SOPHIA, ST. (d. 200?), martyr. See Irene, St.

SOPHIA, ST. (d. 250?), martyr. She was put to death in Fermo, Italy, during the persecution of Decius. F. D. Apr. 30.

SOPHRONIUS (5th century). Bishop of Constantina (or Tella), Osrhoene, he was anti-Monophysite with pro-Nestorian sympathies, attended a synod in Antioch in 445, and the Robber Council of Ephesus in 449, where he was accused of sorcery. The case was referred to the bishop of Edessa and he was evidently cleared, for he attended the Council of Chalcedon in 451 where he apparently joined in anathematizing Nestorius.

SOPHRONIUS, ST. (6th century). He is

said to have been bishop of Cyprus. F. D.
Dec. 8.

SOPHRONIUS, ST. (d. 638?), patriarch.
Born in Damascus, Syria, he probably traveled
through Syria and Egypt before he became a
recluse in 580 with John Moschus in sanctu-
aries directed by SS. Sabas and Theodius. He
became patriarch of Jerusalem after 620,
fought the Monothelite heresy, and sent his
associate Stephen to Rome to have the papacy
take a strong stand against it. Honorius took no
action, but Pope Martin I eventually condemned the heresy at the Lateran Council
of 649. Sophronius wrote a number of doctrinal treatises, biographies, homilies, and
poems before the Saracens overran his see. F. D.
Mar. 11.

SORBAIT, PAUL DE (1624–1691), physician. Born in Hainault, Belgium, he studied at
Paderborn and Padua, where he received his
medical degree, and practiced in Rome, Cologne, and Arnheim. In 1652 he became a
member of the faculty at Vienna, a professor
in 1655, and court physician to dowager
Empress Eleonora in 1658. In 1679, he was
appointed chief supervisor of sanitary conditions by Emperor Leopold I, who ennobled
him, and headed a company of students during
the Turkish siege of 1683. He wrote numerous
medical works, and died in Vienna on Apr. 19.

SORDO DEL BAROZZO, IL. See Baglione,
Giovanni.

SORETH, BL. JOHN (1405?–1471). Born in
Caen, France, he became a Carmelite at sixteen, was ordained, and studied at Paris. In
1440 he became prior provincial of the French
Carmelites and settled a dispute between the
mendicant friars and the University of Paris,
as well as a schism in the Carmelite province
in Germany. In 1451 he was elected prior general of his order and served in that capacity
until his death. He labored to introduce reforms, but was only moderately successful.
About 1452 he permitted nuns to join the
order and set up convents for them throughout
Europe. He probably introduced the third order
of Carmelites and in 1455 at Liège drew up a
rule for tertiaries which is the basis of the present rule. He died on July 25 at Angers, France,
and his cult was approved in 1865. F. D. July 30.

SORIN, EDWARD (1814–1893), educator.
Born in Ahuillé, France, on Feb. 6, he studied
at the diocesan seminary and was ordained in
1838. He joined the Congregation of Holy
Cross in 1840, and was sent to the United
States to establish the congregation in 1841 in
the Vincennes diocese. After a short period at
St. Peter's near Vincennes, he was granted a
parcel of land near South Bend, Indiana, by
the bishop to found a college in 1842, and in
1844 received a state charter and built the first
building of the University of Notre Dame. Fr.

Sorin was its first president, a position he held
until 1865. He introduced the Sisters of Holy
Cross to the United States in 1843, founded
Ave Maria in 1865, and three years later was
appointed superior general of his congregation,
a position he held until his death at Notre
Dame, Indiana, on Oct. 31. It was at his suggestion that the Laetare Medal award was instituted in 1883.

SOSIPATER, ST. (2nd century). A relative
and follower of St. Paul (Rom. 16:21), he
made several journeys with him and is traditionally said to have gone later to Corfu. F. D.
June 25.

SOSIUS, ST. (d. 305?), martyr. See Januarius,
St.

SOSTEGNI, ST. GERARDINO (13th century), founder. See Monaldo, St. Buonfiglio.

SOSTHENES, ST. (1st century). He was in
charge of a synagogue at Corinth (Acts 18:17)
and is said to have been the first bishop of
Colophon in Asia Minor. F. D. Nov. 28.

SOSTHENES, ST. (d. 307), martyr. He and
St. Victor were directed to torture St. Euphemia
at Chalcedon, but were converted by her courage, and were themselves martyred. F. D.
Sept. 10.

SOTELO, BL. LUIS (d. 1624), martyr. Born
in Seville, Spain, he became a Franciscan at
Salamanca, and after ordination went to the
Philippines and in 1603 to Japan. Arrested and
sent back to Spain in 1613, he returned to
Japan in 1622 and was arrested and burned to
death at Ximabura. Louis Baba, a native catechist, who went to Spain and back with him
and who became a Franciscan while imprisoned
at Omura, was killed with him. They were
beatified in 1867. F. D. Aug. 25.

SOTER, ST. (d. 175), pope. Born in Fondi,
Italy, he succeeded St. Anicetus to the papacy
in 166, opposed the Montanist heresy, and
wrote a *Letter to the Corinthians* in reply to
one sent by St. Dionysius. No record of his
death as a martyr is extant. F. D. Apr. 22.

SOTERIS, ST. (d. 304), martyr. An ancestor
of St. Ambrose, she was tortured (perhaps as
early as the persecution of Decius) and beaten
and beheaded (fifty years later) under Diocletian. F. D. Feb. 10.

SOTO, DOMINGO (1494–1560), theologian.
Born in Segovia, Spain, he studied there, at
Alcalá and Paris, taught at San Ildefonso College, Alcalá, about 1520, became a leader of
the moderate realists in the dispute with the
nominalists and in 1524 joined the Dominicans in Burgos. He taught at St. Paul's there
until 1532, when he was appointed to the
chair of theology at Salamanca. In 1545 he resigned to accept Charles V's appointment as
imperial theologian to the Council of Trent,
where he also represented his order, became
Charles' confessor in 1547, declined the bish-

opric of Segovia, and returned to Salamanca in 1550 as prior. He was appointed to the principal chair of theology at Salamanca in 1552, which he held until his resignation in 1556, and died at Salamanca, Spain, on Nov. 15. He wrote *Summulae* (1529) on Aristotle's *Physics*, *De natura et gratia* (1547), and *De justitia et jure* (1556).

SOUBIRAN, BL. MARIE TERESA DE (1835–1889), foundress. Born in Castelnaudary, France, she was christened Sophia Teresa Augustina Marie, at nineteen joined a community of laywomen living in community under temporary vows at Ghent, and returned to her native town to establish a *béguinage* and become its superior in 1854. After ten years she founded the Society of Mary Auxiliatrix at Toulouse. With the help of Fr. Paul Ginhac she drew up a rule approved by the pope in 1868, and the Society began to spread, especially in large cities where they devoted themselves to helping working girls. After a period of exile in England because of the Franco-Prussian War, the Society experienced difficulties because of too rapid expansion and Mother Marie Teresa resigned. In 1874, due to the machinations of one who had invalidly joined the order and become mother general, she was even expelled from the Society. After being refused by several communities, she was accepted in 1877 by the nuns of Our Lady of Charity convent at Paris, where she remained until her death on June 7. She was beatified in 1946. F. D. Oct. 20.

SOUBIROUS, MARIE BERNARDE. *See* Bernadette of Lourdes, St.

SOURDIS, FRANÇOIS DE (d. 1628). He became archbishop of Bordeaux, France, in 1599, drained the neighboring marshes, built a Carthusian monastery, introduced a number of new religious congregations, aided the Jesuit College of the Madeleine, and was a court counselor during the youth of Louis XIII.

SOUSA, LUIZ DE (1555–1632), author. Born in Portugal, he studied at Coimbra, joined the Order of Malta, fought against the Moors in the Mediterranean, and was taken prisoner. On his return, he devoted himself from 1584 to 1599 to literary pursuits, interrupted by further military service; he became a Dominican in 1613. His chief writings include a history of the reign of James III and *Historia de S. Domingos*.

SOUTHERNE, VEN. WILLIAM (d. 1618), martyr. He studied at Douai, was ordained there, returned to Baswich, England, to serve Catholics in that area, was arrested while saying mass, condemned as a priest, imprisoned at Stafford, and hanged at Newcastle on Apr. 30.

SOUTHWELL, NATHANIEL BACON. *See* Bacon, Nathaniel.

SOUTHWELL, BL. ROBERT (1561–1595), martyr and poet. Born in Horsham St. Faith,

Norfolk, England, he studied at Douai and Paris, and began his training as a Jesuit at seventeen in Rome. He taught at the English College there, was ordained in 1584, and returned to England as a missioner in 1586 with Fr. Henry Garnet. The following year he became secret chaplain at the London home of Anne, countess of Arundel, whose husband, Bl. Philip, had already been imprisoned, and directed his spiritual activities from there for five years. Captured at Harrow, he was imprisoned in the Tower, tortured nearly a dozen times, condemned as a priest, and hanged at Tyburn. At Arundel House he wrote *Mary Magdalen's Funeral Tears* and *Epistle of Comfort*, both homilitic prose tracts, and a large number of poems (including *The Burning Babe*) in a skillful lyric style that is compressed, highly metaphorical, and moving. F. D. Feb. 21. CHRISTOPHER DEVLIN, *The Life of Robert Southwell* (New York, Farrar, 1956).

SOUTHWORTH, BL. JOHN (1592–1654), martyr. Born in Lancashire, England, he studied at Douai, was ordained in 1618, and entered England in 1619 to serve the Catholics of the London area until 1623. He then was a chaplain in Belgium, but returned to Lancashire, was arrested in 1627, ordered out of the country, but apparently stayed, only to be arrested in 1632. He was given freedom to live in the city, served heroically through the plague of 1636, but was frequently arrested thereafter on the charge of preaching his religion, and finally executed at Tyburn when he refused to disavow his priesthood. He was beatified in 1929. F. D. June 28.

SOUVAY, CHARLES LÉON (1870–1939), educator. Born in Saulxures-sur-Moselotte, France, on Dec. 15, he became a Vincentian (Congregation of the Missions) in 1893, was ordained in 1896, and taught at Kenrick seminary, St. Louis, from 1903 to 1932, where he was rector (1926–30). He became assistant superior in 1933, and died in Paris on Dec. 19.

SOZOMEN, SALAMINIUS HERMIAS (400?–447?), historian. Born in Bethelia, Palestine, of a Christian family, he studied under the monks there as a youth, settled in Constantinople early in the fifth century, and practiced law. There he conceived the project of writing a history of the Church to continue Eusebius' study from 323 to 439, and began it about 443. Although completed only to the year 425, *Historia ecclesiae*, written in Greek, is a valuable source of early church history, especially in the fields of monasticism and missionary work, though it has been criticized for its dependence on Socrates' history, inadequate treatment of the Western Church, and lack of grasp of the significance of major historical developments.

SOZON, ST., martyr. A legendary shepherd

in Cilicia, he supposedly broke off the hand of a golden image, distributed the pieces to the poor, and was burned at the stake. F. D. Sept. 7.

SPADAFORA, BL. DOMINIC (d. 1521). Born in Messina, Sicily, he became a Dominican at Palermo, was ordained, and spent several years teaching at Padua. After preaching at Palermo, he served at Rome as aide to Fr. Joachim Torriano, master general of the Dominicans, and in 1493 took charge of the shrine of Our Lady of Grace near Monte Cerignone. Except for several long missionary trips, he spent the rest of his life there until his death on Dec. 21. His cult was confirmed in 1921. F. D. Oct. 3.

SPAGNI, ANDREA (1716–1788), educator. Born in Florence, Italy, on Aug. 8, he became a Jesuit in 1731, taught mathematics at the Roman College, and was an assistant at the observatory. He wrote on philosophy and theology; *De miraculis* (1777) is a compendium of the literature on miracles. He died in Rome on Sept. 16.

SPAGNOLETTO, LO. *See* Ribera, Giuseppe.

SPALDING, JOHN LANCASTER (1840–1916), archbishop. Born in Lebanon, Kentucky, on June 2, he studied at St. Mary's College, Kentucky, Mt. St. Mary's, Maryland, and the American College, Louvain, where he was ordained in 1863. After further study at the Belgian College in Rome, he returned to the United States in 1865, engaged in pastoral work in Kentucky, became chancellor of the Louisville diocese, and was Archbishop François Blanchet's theologian at the second Plenary Council of Baltimore in 1866. He was in New York from 1872 to 1877, writing the biography of his uncle, Martin J. Spalding, archbishop of Baltimore, and in pastoral work, and was appointed first bishop of Peoria, Illinois, in 1876. He became a noted orator and publicist of the Church, a vigorous advocate of the Catholic parochial-school system and an American Catholic University, and served on President Roosevelt's Anthracite Coal Strike Commission in 1902. Ill health caused him to resign as bishop of Peoria in 1908, whereupon Pope St. Pius X appointed him titular archbishop of Scythopolis. He lived in retirement until his death in Peoria on Aug. 25.

SPALDING, MARTIN JOHN (1810–1872), archbishop. Born in Rolling Fork, Kentucky, on May 23, he graduated from St. Mary's College near Lebanon in 1826, studied at Bardstown seminary and the Propaganda, Rome, and was ordained in Rome in 1834. He became pastor of the Bardstown cathedral, taught at the seminary there, and was appointed rector of St. Joseph's College in 1838. He resigned in 1840 to devote himself to pastoral work and lecturing, for which he became famed through-

out the United States and Canada, was named vicar general of Louisville in 1844, titular bishop of Lengone and coadjutor in 1848, and succeeded to the see in 1850. He built a cathedral in 1852, went to England the same year to lend encouragement and financial aid to John Henry Newman, who had just been fined in the suit brought against him by Achilli, and in 1855 led the resistance to the Know-Nothing attacks which had led to a massacre of Catholic German and Irish immigrants in Louisville. He was an editor of the *Metropolitan*, edited the *Catholic Advocate* for several years, and in 1858 helped found its successor, the Louisville *Guardian*. With Bishop Lefevere of Detroit he helped establish the American College at Louvain in 1857, and was a leading proponent for a North American College in Rome and an American Catholic University. A southerner in sympathies, he fought any attempt to have the Church take a stand for either side in the Civil War, and in 1864 was appointed archbishop of Baltimore. He was active at the second Plenary Council there in 1866, labored to rehabilitate the Church in the South after the Civil War and in charitable activities, participated in the Vatican Council in 1870 as a member of the Commission on Faith and Postulata, was a strong supporter of the definition of papal infallibility, and died in Baltimore, Maryland, on Feb. 7. He wrote numerous books, among them *A History of the Protestant Reformation* (1860), a biography of Bishop Flaget, and, with Fr. John McGill, *General Evidences of Catholicity* (1847).

SPALLANZANI, LAZZARO (1729–1799), scientist. Born in Scandiano, Modena, Italy, on Jan. 10, he studied at Reggio and Bologna, became interested in science, took up law, and was ordained. He taught at Reggio in 1754, and in 1760 at Modena, where his work on natural science attracted attention. He became professor of natural history at Pavia in 1768, founded and built up its museum with collections from his expeditions, made a trip to Turkey for scientific observations, and studied the volcanoes of Vesuvius, Sicily, and the Lipari Islands. He laid the foundations of experimental zoology, and his most important scientific research was in regeneration and digestion, where he discovered the action of saliva. His experiments disproved Needham's theory of spontaneous generation. He wrote *Dissertazioni di fisica animale e vegetale* (1780), was honored by many learned societies, and died in Pavia, Italy, on Feb. 12.

SPANUOLO, BL. BAPTISTA (1448–1516). Born in Mantua, Italy, of a Spanish father and Brescian mother, he became a Carmelite at Ferrara in 1464, effected many reforms, and became prior general in 1513. He wrote more than 50,000 lines of Latin poetry against paganism, on papal abuses, the feasts of the Church, and the Virgin Mary, and had a major influence on the English poet, Alexander Barclay. He is often called Baptista Mantuanus. He died in Mantua. F. D. Mar. 20.

SPEARMAN, FRANK HAMILTON (1859–1937), author. Born in Buffalo, New York, he studied at Lawrence College in Wisconsin, became a convert in 1884, married Eugenie Lonergan, and became a banker. He began writing railroad stories (*The Nerve of Foley* and *Held for Orders*); novels (*Dr. Bryson, The Daughter of a Magnate,* and *The Close of the Day*); and a serious study of American transportation, *The Strategy of Great Railroads.* He then turned to the western scene; his most popular novel, *Whispering Smith* (1909), was filmed in 1915, as were many of his early stories. *Nan of Music Mountain* also became a popular motion picture. *Laramie Holds the Range* and *Gunlock Ranch* followed; *The Marriage Verdict* (1923) and *Merrilie Dawes* drew on his banking experience. *Selwood of Sleepy Cat, Spanish Lover,* and *Carmen of the Rancho* were historical tales. He received honorary degrees from Notre Dame, Santa Clara, and Loyola (Los Angeles) and the Laetare Medal in 1935, two years before his death in Hollywood, California, on Dec. 29.

SPECKBACHER, JOSEF (1767–1820). Born in Gnadenwald, near Hall, Tyrol, on July 13, son of a peasant and uneducated, he worked in the salt mines at Hall as a youth, and joined the army in 1797 in the war against France. He opposed the cession of the Tyrol to Bavaria in 1806, and in 1809 led the Tyrolese forces in their fight for freedom against the French. Defeated later in the year at Melleck and Mt. Isel, he fled into the mountains, and the next year escaped to Vienna. He returned to the Tyrol in 1813 at the head of the Tyrolese volunteers in the Austrian army, and in 1814 was able to return peacefully to his farm. He died in Hall on Mar. 28.

SPEDALIERI, NICOLA (1740–1795), theologian. Born in Bronte, Catania, Sicily, on Dec. 6, he studied at the Monreale seminary on the island, was ordained, and taught philosophy. He went to Rome about 1773, spent the next ten years in study, received a benefice at the Vatican basilica in 1784, and wrote several works, notably *I diritti dell' uomo* (1791), which was praised by Pope Pius VI. It aroused great controversy for its thesis that political sovereignty emanates from the people, and was banned by several absolutist governments. He also wrote *Confutazione di Gibbon* (1784), *Ragionamento sopra l'arte di governare* (1779), and *Ragionamente sull' influenza della religione cristiana sulla società civile.* He died in Rome on Nov. 26.

SPEE, FRIEDRICH VON (1591–1635),

poet. Born in Kaiserswerth, on the Rhine, on Feb. 25, he studied at Cologne, became a Jesuit in 1610, studied and taught at Trier, Fulda, Würzburg, Speyer, Worms, and Mainz, and was ordained in 1622. He taught at Paderborn in 1624–26 and during the next nine years at Speyer, Wesel, Trier, and Cologne. He moved to Trier in 1633, was outstanding in his care of the wounded during the siege of that German city in 1635, and died there on Aug. 7 of an infection caught while tending the wounded. He wrote several books of poetry and *Cautio criminalis* (1631), which describes and condemns the abuses and horrors of witchcraft trials.

SPEED, BL. JOHN (d. 1594), martyr. A layman who harbored priests in Durham, England, during the Elizabethan persecution and who was executed there on Feb. 4, he was beatified in 1929. F. D. July 24.

SPENCER, GEORGE (1799–1864). Born in London on Dec. 21, son of the earl of Spencer, he studied at Eton and Cambridge, became an Anglican minister in 1824, chaplain to the bishop of Chester, and rector in Brington. He became a convert in 1830, studied in Rome, was ordained there in 1832, returned to England, and engaged in pastoral work in West Bromwich. He taught at Oscott in 1839, joined the Passionists in 1846, was professed in 1848 as Fr. Ignatius of St. Paul, and spent the rest of his life in missionary activities in England. He died in Carstairs, Scotland, on Oct. 1.

SPENSER, JOHN (1601–1671). Born in Lincolnshire, England, he studied at Cambridge, where he became a convert, and in 1627 joined the Jesuits. In 1657 he participated in a much-publicized conference with two Anglican ministers, which he described in *Schism Unmasked* (1658). He wrote other books of a controversial nature, was chaplain to the earl of Shrewsbury, and died in Grafton, England. He sometimes used the names of Hatcliffe and Tyrrwhit as aliases.

SPENSER, VEN. WILLIAM (d. 1589), martyr. Born in Ghisburn, Yorkshire, England, he studied at Oxford, became a fellow there, was converted in 1582, went to Rheims, and was ordained in 1583. He was sent to England in 1584, brought his father and uncle (William Horn, later a priest) back to the Church, served Catholic prisoners at York castle, and was hanged at York, for being a priest, on Sept. 24. Ven. Robert Hardesty, who had hidden him, was executed with him.

SPERANDEA, ST. (d. 1276). Related to St. Ubald of Gubbio, she became Benedictine abbess at Cingoli, Ancola, Italy, and is venerated as its patron. F. D. Sept. 11.

SPERATUS, ST. (d. 180), martyr. He and eleven others were put to death by the sword (but not tortured) at Scillium (Tunisia) on orders of Vigellius Saturninus, proconsul of Africa; the report of their death comprises the first *Acts* of martyrs in that Roman province. The others were SS. Aquilinus, Cittinus, Donata, Felix, Generosa, Januaria, Laetantius, Nartzalus, Secunda, Vestia, and Veturius. F. D. July 17.

SPES, ST. (d. 513). He was abbot of the monastery of Campi, Italy. Blind for forty years, he regained his sight shortly before his death. F. D. Mar. 28.

SPEUSIPPUS. *See* Eleusippus.

SPEYER, WENDELIN VON. *See* Johann von Speyer.

SPIESS, CASSIAN (1866–1905), bishop. Born in Sankt Jacob, Austria, on July 12, he was ordained a Benedictine, sent to German East Africa, and made first vicar apostolic of southern Zanzibar in 1902. He and two Benedictine nuns and two laybrothers were killed by natives.

SPILLMANN, JOSEPH (1842–1905), author. Born in Zug, Switzerland, he studied at Feldkirch, became a Jesuit in 1862, served as a medical aide in the Franco-Prussian War, and went to England after the suppression of his Society in France, and was ordained in 1874. He wrote for *Stimmen aus Maria-Laach* and *Katholische Missionen,* editing the latter in 1880–90, wrote popular stories for juveniles (later collected as *Wolken und Sonnenschein*), longer romances in the tradition of Scott and Dickens, and poetry. He died in Luxembourg on Feb. 20.

SPINA, ALFONSO DE (d. 1491?), bishop. A Jewish convert to Catholicism, he became a Franciscan, served as superior of the Friars Minor house of studies in Salamanca for years, and became famed for his preaching and scholarship. He was made bishop of Thermopylae, Greece, in 1491, and wrote several works, chief of which was *Fortalitium fidei* (1458).

SPINA, BARTOLOMMEO (1475?–1546), theologian. Born in Pisa, Italy, he became a Dominican there about 1494, taught in various Dominican schools, engaged in a controversy with Cardinal Cajetan in 1518, served as prior-provincial of the Holy Land, and was appointed to the chair of theology at Padua in 1536. He became Master of the Sacred Palace in 1542, a position he held until his death in Rome, and in 1546 condemned Ambrose Catharinus as a heretic. He wrote theological treatises.

SPINELLO ARETINO, LUCA (1333?–1410), painter. Born probably in Aretino, Italy, he studied under Jacopo di Casentino and was influenced by Giotto. He decorated churches in Florence and Pisa, and palaces in Siena, and did frescoes in Arezzo and Casentino.

SPINOLA, BL. CHARLES (d. 1622), martyr. An Italian Jesuit, he labored as a missionary for eighteen years in Japan and was burned to death with a group of Christians at Nagasaki. Among those executed with him were Bl. Sebastian Kimura, the first Japanese priest, Bl. Isabel Fernandez, a Spanish widow who was condemned for sheltering Bl. Charles, and her four-year-old son, Ignatius. They were among the 205 beatified by Pope Pius IX in 1867 as the martyrs of Japan. F. D. Sept. 10.

SPINOLA, CHRISTOPHER ROYAS DE (1526–1695), bishop. Born near Roermond, Netherlands, of a noble Spanish family, he studied at Cologne, where he became a Franciscan, and taught theology and philosophy. He was appointed provincial in Spain, accompanied Emperor Leopold's wife, Margaret Theresa, to Vienna, and acted as one of his diplomatic representatives there. He was appointed titular bishop of Knin in 1668, attempted to reconcile several of the Protestant princes to Rome, and in 1683 submitted a plan of reunion to a group of Protestant theologians which was tabled by Pope Innocent III because of his too-liberal concessions. He was appointed bishop of Wiener-Neustadt in 1686 and in 1691 head of a group to seek ecclesiastical unity in Austria-Hungary. He died in Wiener-Neustadt, Austria, on Mar. 12.

SPINULUS, ST. (8th century). A Benedictine monk at Moyen-Moutier, France, he became abbot founder of the abbey of Bégon-Celle (now St. Blasien), France. F. D. Nov. 5.

SPIRIDION, ST. (4th century), bishop. A married shepherd of Cyprus, he became bishop of Tremithus and, though unschooled, was famed for his knowledge of scripture and firm opposition to Arianism. According to the Roman Martyrology he was tortured, lost an eye, and was sent to work in the mines during the persecution of Galerius Maximian. F. D. Dec. 14.

SPONDE, HENRI DE (1568–1643), bishop. Born in Mauléon, Basses-Pyrénées, France, on Jan. 6, he studied at Orthez, was in the entourage of the ambassador to Scotland, studied law on his return, and in 1589 became a jurist at the Tours parliament. He became a convert in 1595, went to Rome in 1600 with Cardinal de Sourdis, and was ordained in 1606. He was appointed reviser of penitentiary briefs by Pope Paul V, and in 1625 became bishop of Pamiers, a position he held until illness caused his resignation in 1639. He wrote theological treatises, an abridgment of Baronius' *Annals,* and a continuation of the *Annals* from 1197 to 1639. He died in Toulouse, France, on May 18.

SPONTINI, GASPARO LUIGI PACIFICO (1774–1851), composer. Born in Maiolati, Anaconda, Italy, on Nov. 14, he studied music under local teachers at Jesi, and under Sala and Tritto in Naples, went to Rome in 1796, and began writing operas. He became court composer in Palermo in 1800, moved to Paris in

1803, secured Empress Josephine as a patroness, was appointed conductor of Italian opera at the Odéon in 1810, and went to Berlin as chief choirmaster in 1820. He was elected to the Institute in Paris in 1838, went to Rome in 1842, was appointed count of St. Andrea in 1844 by Pope Gregory XVI, retired to his native town in 1850, and died there on Jan. 24. Among his outstanding operas are *La vestale* (1807), *Fernando Cortez* (1809), *Olympie* (1819; revised in 1826), and *Agnes von Hohenstaufen* (1829; revised in 1837). He also composed the music for Thomas Moore's *Lalla Rookh* (1821).

SPORER, PATRITIUS (d. 1683), theologian. Born in Passau, Bavaria, he became a Friar Minor there in 1637, taught theology as a probabilist and follower of Duns Scotus, became the bishop of Passau's theologian, and wrote theological treatises, chief of which was the three-volume *Theologia moralis decalogis et sacramentalis* (1681). He died in Passau on May 29.

SPORTELLI, VEN. CAESAR (1702–1750). Born in Nola, Italy, on Mar. 29, he became a lawyer, joined St. Alphonsus's new institute at thirty-three, was ordained, and worked closely with him for priests, religious, and sinners with great zeal. He was the saint's constant companion, founded the house of Mater Domini, Caposele, and that at Pagani, where Alphonsus died. Caesar died in Pagani, Italy. The cause of his beatification was introduced in 1899.

SPROTT, VEN. THOMAS (d. 1600), martyr. Born in Skelsmergh, Westmoreland, England, he was ordained at Douai in 1596, was sent on the English mission, was captured in Lincoln, and executed there on July 11 for having a breviary in his possession. He also is listed as Thomas Spratt.

SQUIERS, HERBERT GOLDSMITH (1859–1911), diplomat. Born in Madoc, Canada, of American parents, on Apr. 20, he studied at Canadaigua Academy in New York and Minnesota Military Academy, and became an army lieutenant in 1877. He served as military instructor at Fordham in 1885–90, and resigned from the army in 1891. He was appointed second secretary at the Berlin embassy in 1894, first secretary in Peking in 1898, and became a convert in that year. He was chief of staff in Peking during the Boxer uprising in 1900, was minister to Cuba in 1902–5, and to Panama from 1906 until ill health forced him to resign in 1910. He died in London on Oct. 19.

STACHYS, ST. (1st century). A friend of St. Paul (Rom. 16:9), he is believed to have been consecrated bishop of Byzantium by St. Andrew. F. D. Oct. 21.

STADLER, JOHN EVANGELIST (1804–1868), hagiographer. Born in Parkstetten, Ger-

many, on Dec. 24, he studied at Landshut, where he became proficient in oriental and modern languages, and was ordained in 1827. He received his doctorate in theology from the Munich Georgianum in 1829, taught at Munich in 1831, went to the Georgianum in 1832, and became canon in 1838 and dean at Augsburg cathedral in 1858. He began *Vollständiges Heiligen-Lexikon* (1858–62), a popular collection of lives of the saints, but died on Dec. 30 in Augsburg, Germany, while writing the third of the five-volume set.

STANFIELD, WILLIAM CLARKSON (1793–1867), painter. Born on Dec. 3 in Sunderland, England, he became a sailor in 1812, but was injured in 1816. He began painting under the encouragement of Douglas Jerrold and Frederick Marryat, the novelist, and when pictures he exhibited at the Society of British Artists in 1824 and 1827 were favorably received began painting seriously. Though self-taught, he became a leader of the English realists, and a Royal Academician in 1835. His sea paintings, including *Battle of Trafalgar*, were particularly popular. He died on Mar. 13.

STANG, WILLIAM (1854–1907), bishop. Born in Langenbrücken, Baden, Germany, on Aug. 21, he studied in Germany and Belgium, was ordained at Louvain in 1878, and went to Providence, Rhode Island, where he was curate at the cathedral, and later to Cranston. He was chancellor of the diocese for ten years, in 1895 was named vice-rector of the American College at Louvain and in 1898 professor of moral theology there. He returned to Providence in 1899 and in 1904 was made first bishop of Fall River, Massachusetts. He wrote philosophical and theological works, a biography of Luther, a history of the Reformation, a study of the Huguenots, a business guide for priests, and a study of socialism. He died in Rochester, Minnesota, on Feb. 2.

STANISLAS I LESZCZYNSKI (1677–1766), king of Poland. When Charles XII of Sweden deposed Augustus II, elector of Saxony, as king of Poland, the nobility elected Stanislas in 1704, at Charles's direction. Civil war resulted; Russia invaded; Charles was defeated at Poltava; the new king fled to Sweden in 1709 and then to France; and Augustus returned to rule as Russia wished. When Augustus died, Stanislas returned as king in 1733, was forced out by Russia after a year, gave up the throne in 1736, and retired to France.

STANISLAS II PONIATOWSKI (1732–1798), king of Poland. A Polish noble, he was a diplomat at the court of Catherine the Great of Russia at St. Petersburg. He was elected king of Poland in 1764 through her influence, saw the first partition of Poland in 1772, introduced a constitution in 1791, but could not control national dissatisfaction with Russian domination. A second partition in 1793 led to rebellion under Tadeusz Kosciusko, who was defeated in 1794. Stanislas abdicated in 1795 and returned to Russia; the third partition destroyed independence.

STANISLAUS KOSTKA, MOTHER MARY, *See* Schilling, Mary.

STANISLAUS KOSTKA, ST. (1550–1568). Born in Rostkovo, Poland, about Aug. 28, son of a senator, he was sent to the Jesuit college at Vienna when fourteen. Despite bitter opposition from his father, he determined to become a Jesuit and ran away to Dillingen, Germany, to seek out St. Peter Canisius. The latter sent him to Rome, where St. Francis Borgia admitted him in 1567. He died less than a year later, on Dec. 8, in Rome, but had impressed all by his humility and innocence. He was canonized in 1726. F. D. Nov. 13 (also, Aug. 15).

STANISLAUS SZCZEPANOWSKI, ST. (1030–1079), bishop and martyr. Born in Szczepanow, near Cracow, Poland, on July 26, he was educated at Gnesen, became a canon at the cathedral of Cracow, and bishop there in 1072. When he censured King Boleslaus II for his savagery and injustice, the monarch promised to reform; instead he kidnaped a noble's wife, and brought upon himself the punishment of excommunication. Boleslaus then angrily invaded the bishop's chapel in a Cracow suburb and slew him, as he was saying mass, whereupon Pope St. Gregory VII placed the country under an interdict; the king later fled to Hungary. Stanislaus, patron of Cracow, was canonized in 1253. F. D. May 7.

STANSEL, VALENTIN (1621–1705), astronomer. Born in Olmütz, Moravia, he became a Jesuit in 1637, taught at Olmütz and Prague, and was ordained. He went to Portugal, where he taught astronomy at Evora, then was sent to Brazil, where he taught moral theology and later was superior of the San Salvador seminary in Bahia. He made extensive astronomical observations, particularly of comets, and published widely. He died in Bahia, Brazil, on Dec. 18.

STANYHURST, RICHARD (1547–1618), author. Born in Dublin, son of the speaker of the Irish house of commons, he studied at Oxford and law in London, and in 1569 or 1570 accompanied Bl. Edmund Campion on a visit to Ireland. On the death of his wife, Janet Barnewall, in 1579 he went to the Netherlands, and there became a convert. He went to Spain as adviser on English affairs, and when his second wife, Helen Cockley, died in 1602, studied for the priesthood, was ordained, and became Archduke Albert's chaplain. He wrote a history of Ireland, a biography of St. Patrick, *Hebdomada Mariana* (1609) and *Hebdomada Eucharistica*, and translated Vergil's *Aeneid* into

English hexameters (1582). He died in Brussels.

STAPF, JOSEPH AMBROSE (1785–1844), theologian. Born in Fliess, Tyrol, Austria, on Aug. 15, he received his doctorate in theology from Innsbruck, taught there in 1821 and at the Brixen seminary, where he was cathedral canon, in 1823. He wrote several theological treatises, chief of which were the four-volume *Theologia moralis in compendium redacta* (1827–30), which became official Austrian seminaries' textbook in 1830, and *Erziehungslehre im Geiste der katholischen Kirche* (1832). He died in Brixen, northern Italy, on Jan. 10.

STAPHYLUS, FRIEDRICH (1512–1564), theologian. Born in Osnabrück, Germany, on Aug. 27, he was orphaned early and raised by an uncle in Danzig, and studied at Cracow, Padua, and Wittenberg. He became a tutor to the count of Eberstein's family on Melanchthon's recommendation, taught theology at Königsberg in 1546, became involved in a theological dispute with William Gnapheus, and, though elected first rector in 1547, resigned in 1548. On his return he became involved in further religious disputes until, in 1552, he became a convert and joined the household of the bishop of Breslau. He was appointed to the imperial council by Ferdinand I in 1555, was one of the Catholic collocutors at the Disputation of Worms in 1557, and was appointed professor of theology at Ingolstadt in 1560 when the pope issued a papal dispensation, since he was married, for him to receive his doctorate in theology and canon law. He was active in the Catholic movement in Bavaria and Austria, was curator of the University of Ingolstadt, was author of several reforms drawn up for Pope Pius IV for the Council of Trent, and was ennobled by the emperor. He died in Ingolstadt, Germany, on Mar. 5.

STAPLETON, THEOBALD (17th century). An Irish priest from Kilkenny, he published *Catechismus seu doctrina christiana latino-hibernica* (1639), the first book which employed Roman type to print Irish.

STAPLETON, THOMAS (1535–1598). Born in Henfield, Sussex, England, in July, he studied at Winchester and Oxford, where he became a fellow in 1553, left England when Elizabeth I ascended the throne, and continued his studies at Louvain and Paris. He returned to England, received the prebend of Woodhorne in Chichester cathedral in 1558, was deprived of it in 1563 when he refused to denounce papal authority, returned to Louvain, and in 1568 became an associate of Cardinal Allen at Douai and helped found the English College there. He became professor of divinity, a canon of St. Anatus, received his doctorate of divinity in 1571, and in 1584 became a

Jesuit. He left the Society shortly after to return to Douai, was appointed professor of scripture at Louvain in 1590, and then dean of Hilverenbeeck. He was made prothonotary apostolic in 1597, wrote many controversial works against the attacks on the Church in England and in defense of the faith which were collected and published in Paris in 1620, and translated Bede's *Ecclesiastical History* and Hosius' *Express Word of God*. He died in Louvain, Belgium, on Oct. 12.

STARIHA, JOHN (1845–1915), bishop. Born in Semic, Krain, Austria, on May 12, he studied there, and St. Francis seminary, Milwaukee, and was ordained in 1869. He engaged in pastoral work in Saulte-Ste.-Marie and Marquette diocese until 1871, when he joined the St. Paul diocese, was vicar general in 1897–1902, and was consecrated first bishop of Lead, South Dakota (the see was transferred to Rapid City in 1930), in 1902. He resigned in 1909 and was appointed titular bishop of Antipatris, and died in Laibach, Austria, on Nov. 28.

STAROWOLSKI, SIMON (1585–1656), author. Born in Stara Wola, Poland, he studied at Louvain and Cracow, and taught philosophy at Cracow. He became Chodkiewicz' secretary, tutored noblemen's sons, and was ordained in 1639. He became a canon in Cracow, administered the see for a period in 1655, and died there. He wrote some sixty books, notably *The True Knights, Lament of the Dying Mother, Poland,* and *Scriptorum Polonicorum Hecatontas*.

STARR, ELIZA ALLEN (1824–1901), educator. Born in Deerfield, Massachusetts, on Aug. 29, she studied art in Boston, tutored in Mississippi, taught in Brooklyn and Philadelphia, became a convert in 1854, and moved to Chicago in 1856. She instituted a series of annual art lectures, opened a studio, and in 1871 went to St. Mary's College, South Bend, Indiana, to organize an art department. She wrote *Pilgrims and Shrines, Patron Saints, Christian Art in Our Own Age,* and *Songs of a Lifetime*. She received the Laetare Medal in 1885, the first woman to be so honored. She died in Durand, Illinois, on Sept. 8.

STATTLER, BENEDICT (1728–1797), theologian. Born in Kötzting, Bavaria, on Jan. 30, he became a Jesuit in 1745, and taught at Solothurn, Innsbruck, and Ingolstadt, where he occupied the chair of theology even after the Jesuits were suppressed in 1773. Forced to stop teaching when former Jesuits were forbidden to teach in Bavaria in 1783, he engaged in parish work, and then became a member of the Munich electoral committee on censures. He wrote *Anti-Kant* (1788), a refutation of Kant's *Critique,* and *Demonstratio evangelica* (1770). He died in Munich, Germany, on Aug. 21.

STAUDENMAIER, FRANZ ANTON (1800–

1856), theologian. Born in Donzdorf, Württemberg, Germany, on Sept. 11, he studied at Tübingen and the Rottenburg seminary, and was ordained in 1827. He taught at the Tübingen seminary in 1828, dogmatic theology at Giessen in 1830 and Freiburg im Breisgau in 1837, and in 1843 was made a cathedral canon. He helped to found *Jahrbücher für Theologie* and, in 1839, *Zeitschrift für Theologie*. He wrote *Der Geist des Christenthums* (1835), the unfinished *Die Philosophie des Christenthums oder Metaphysik* (1844–52), and *Encyklopädie der theologischen* (1834). He died in Freiburg, Germany, on Jan. 19.

STAUPITZ, JOHANN VON (1460?–1524). Born in Motterwitz, Germany, he studied at Leipzig, became an Augustinian, prior at Tübingen in 1498, and doctor of theology in 1500. After a period as prior in Munich, he was elected vicar general of the German congregation in 1503, became professor and first dean of the theological faculty at Wittenburg, and in 1512 resigned to move to southern Germany. In 1518 he was assigned the task of remonstrating with Martin Luther and, when he sent Luther's explanation of indulgences to Rome and released Luther from obedience to his order, he was accused of Lutheran tendencies. In 1520 the situation was cleared; he resigned his vicar generalship, became a Benedictine in 1522, and was appointed abbot of St. Peter's, Salzburg, Austria. He died there on Dec. 28.

STEARNS, FRANK WATERMAN (1856–1939), merchant. Born in Boston, Massachusetts, on Nov. 8, he graduated from Amherst in 1878, and in 1880 joined his father in the R. H. Stearns & Co. retail dry-goods store in Boston which he developed during his years as president and chairman of the board. He early supported Calvin Coolidge in politics and helped him become governor of Massachusetts and later president of the United States. He became a convert late in life and died in Boston on Mar. 6.

STEEN, CORNELIS CORNELISSEN VAN DEN (1567–1637), scholar. Born in Bocholt, Flemish Limburg, on Dec. 18, he studied at Maastricht, Cologne, Douai, and Louvain, became a Jesuit in 1592, and was ordained in 1595. He was professor of scripture and Hebrew at Louvain until 1616 when he was transferred to a similar position in Rome. His lifetime work was a series of commentaries on the entire Catholic canon of scripture, except Job and the Psalms, which explained literal and figurative meanings and cited the Fathers of the Church and later interpreters. He is known as Cornelius a Lapide on the Latin title pages of his work. He died in Rome on Mar. 12.

STEFANESCHI, GIACOMO GAETANI

(1270?–1343), cardinal. Born in Rome, he studied at Rome and Paris, taught there, and returned to Rome, where he studied law. He was made a canon of St. Peter's, auditor of the rota, and was created a cardinal-deacon in 1295, though he was never ordained a priest. He was sent to Bologna in 1296 as Pope Boniface VIII's legate, and wrote, among other works, *Opus metricum,* a poetic life of Pope Celestine V. He died in Avignon, France, on June 23.

STEFFANI, AGOSTINO (1654–1728), composer. Born in Castelfranco, Treviso, Italy, on July 25, he was brought from a Venice choir to the court of the elector in Munich when twelve, became court musician, director of court music, and organist in 1675. He was ordained about 1680, and became choirmaster at the Hanover court in 1688. He visited the German courts on a diplomatic mission in 1696, Brussels in 1698, and later that year joined the Palatine elector's court in Düsseldorf. He was appointed titular bishop of Spizza in 1706, was elected honorary president for life of the Academy of Ancient Music in London in 1724, and wrote some eighteen operas, more than 100 chamber duets, and numerous religious pieces, notably a *Stabat Mater* and *Psalmodia vespertina.* He died in Frankfort, Germany, on Feb. 12.

STEIN, EDITH (1891–1942), author. Born of Jewish parents in Breslau, Germany, on Oct. 12, she studied at the university there and at Göttingen. She taught in Breslau schools, received her doctorate in philosophy from Freiburg in 1916, and became assistant to and a follower of Edward Husserl, the phenomenologist. She became a convert in 1922, taught at a Dominican convent in Speyer in 1922–32, and became known for her translations of St. Thomas Aquinas and Cardinal Newman. In 1932 she became a lecturer at the Educational Institute at Münster, lost her position because of her Jewish ancestry when the Nazis came to power in 1933 and in 1934 became a Carmelite nun at Cologne, taking the name Benedicta of the Cross. She was transferred to the Carmelite convent in Echt, Holland, in 1938 to protect her from the Nazis, but was arrested in 1942 when the Germans overran Holland, was deported to Auschwitz, Germany, and put to death in the gas chambers about Aug. 10. She wrote religious meditations and on philosophy and education. Her works were collected and published after her death; *The Science of the Cross* (1960), a study of St. John of the Cross, and a selection of *Writings* (1956) have been translated into English.

STEINLE, EDUARD VON (1810–1886), painter. Born in Vienna, on July 2, he studied painting, and was greatly influenced by Kupelweiser, Overbeck, and Cornelius of the pre-

Raphaelites. After several trips to Rome, he settled in Frankfort, where he received commissions to paint in Rheineck castle and the Hall of the Emperors, and taught at the Städel Art Institute there in 1850. Among his outstanding works were his paintings in St. Aegidius, Münster, the church of Our Lady, Aachen, the angels in the Cologne cathedral choir, and the frescoes of the development of civilization in the Wallraf-Richartz Museum, Cologne. Among his individual canvases are *Sibyl, Lorelei, Warder of the Tower, Madonna Holding the Child, Visitation,* and *Mary Magdalen Seeking Christ.* He also did book illustrations for *Parsifal,* Shakespeare, and the writings of his friend Brentano. He died in Frankfort, Germany, on Sept. 19.

STEINS, WALTER BISSCHOP (d. 1881), bishop. A Jesuit, he went to India in 1859, became vicar apostolic of Bombay, India, in 1861, was transferred to the vicariate of Western Bengal in 1867, and in 1879 was named bishop of Auckland, New Zealand, where he died on Sept. 1.

STENO, NICOLAUS (1638–1686), anatomist. Niels Stensen was born in Copenhagen, Denmark, on Jan. 11, son of a Lutheran goldsmith in whose shop he worked as a youth, studied at the universities of Copenhagen and Leyden, where he received his doctorate in medicine in 1664 *in absentia,* and soon became known for his skill in anatomical dissections. He wrote *Disputatio de glandulis oris* (1660) to prove his discovery of the parotid salivary gland called *ductus stenonianus* (a discovery claimed by a former teacher, Gerard Blasius) and *Observationes anatomicae* (1662) describing his further discoveries in the glandular system. He went to Italy in 1666, where he was patronized by Grand Duke Ferdinand II of Florence, and became anatomist at Santa Maria Nuova hospital, and became a convert in 1667. He returned to Denmark in 1672 to fill a specially created position, royal anatomist, at the University of Denmark, since he was prevented from becoming a professor by his religion. He returned to Florence in 1674 to become tutor to Ferdinand's son, was ordained in 1675, and in 1677 was appointed vicar apostolic to Hanover and titular bishop of Titiopolis. He was appointed auxiliary bishop of Münster in 1680, where he labored to reform the clergy and the spiritual life of his people, was vicar apostolic to Hamburg in 1683–85 and died in Schwerin, Germany, on Nov. 25. Steno made many important discoveries in anatomy, revealed the existence and function of numerous glands, the structure of muscles and sinews, studied the nature and functions of heart, brain, and reproductive organs, and pioneered in crystallography, geology, and palaeontology. His scientific works, including treatises on the anatomy of the brain and on muscles and glands, were not published until 1910; he also wrote theological treatises, notably *Epistola de propria conversione* (1677).

STENSEN, NIELS. *See* Steno, Nicolaus.

STEPHANAS (1st century). *See* Achacius.

STEPHEN I, ST. (d. 257), pope. A Roman by birth, he became pope on May 12, 254. Little is known of his pontificate except that it was marred by a violent dispute with St. Cyprian and the African bishops who had declared baptism administered by heretics invalid. Stephen ruled such baptism valid and refused to receive delegates from the African synod supporting Cyprian. Although he threatened them with excommunication, he never invoked this action. Tradition says he was beheaded while saying mass in the catacombs, but no proof exists. F. D. Aug. 2.

STEPHEN II (d. 752). A native Roman, and a priest, he was elected successor to Pope St. Zachary on Mar. 23, but was stricken with apoplexy and died two days later. He was never consecrated or ordained, and, since these steps were the usual marks of the beginning of a pontificate, he often is omitted from lists of the popes.

STEPHEN II [III] (d. 757), pope. A native Roman, who had been orphaned when a youth and brought up in the Lateran palace, he was unanimously elected and consecrated pope on Mar. 26, 752. His pontificate was troubled by the Lombards when King Aistulf violated a forty-year truce he had made with the pope and levied a tribute on the Romans. Stephen's appeal for aid to Emperor Constantine Copronymus in Constantinople went unheeded, and he had to go to Gaul to seek Pepin's aid —the first pope to cross the Alps. He crowned Pepin king of the Franks in 754 and received promises of help. Pepin invaded Italy in 754 and forced Aistulf to restore Ravenna and other cities, but, when the Frankish king returned to Gaul, Aistulf marched on Rome and besieged the city early in 756. Pepin returned again, subdued Aistulf, made Stephen the first pope-king, and originated the Papal States, giving the pope the exarchate of Ravenna and the Pentapolis in the celebrated Act of Donation. When Aistulf died, Stephen supported Duke Desiderius of Istria for the Lombard throne against Aistulf's brother, Ratchis, who had become a monk at Monte Cassino in 749, and was successful in having him crowned king. Stephen was then faced with a revolt by the archbishop of Ravenna, whom he had appointed governor, which he quelled by imprisoning the archbishop. Stephen died in Rome on Apr. 26.

STEPHEN III [IV] (720?–772), pope. A Sicilian and a Benedictine monk of St. Chry-

sogonus, he was elected pope on Aug. 1, and consecrated on Aug. 7, 768, more than a year after the death of Pope St. Paul I, whose close friend he had been, and after two antipopes who had been illegally elected to the chair of Peter, Constantine II and Philip, were deposed. As a result of this scandal the Lateran Council of 769, which cruelly abused Constantine, who had been blinded on orders of the deacon Christophorus, decreed that only cardinals could be chosen popes in the future, and laymen were forbidden to be present at the election. Stephen also sanctioned the use of images by condemning the decrees issued by Emperor Constantine Copronymus at a Council at Constantinople in 753, which had decreed the use of icons was heretical. Stephen died in Rome on Jan. 24.

STEPHEN IV [V] (d. 817), pope. A Roman by birth and of the noble Colonna family, he was raised in the Lateran palace, and on June 22, 816, was elected pope and consecrated at once. He made the Romans take an oath of fealty to Emperor Louis the Pious, went to Rheims to crown him, and improved relations between the Holy See and the emperor. Stephen died in Rome within six months, on Jan. 24.

STEPHEN V [VI] (d. 891), pope. Born in Rome of a noble family, he was educated by Bishop Zachary, the Vatican librarian, created cardinal by Pope Marinus I, and in Sept. 885 was elected pope, without the consent of Emperor Charles the Fat, who later assented. Stephen helped relieve a famine by using his father's wealth, crowned Count Guido III of Spoleto emperor after the death of Charles the Fat, and recognized Louis the Blind as king of Provence. He persuaded Emperor Leo the Wise to drive Photius into exile from Constantinople, but was unsuccessful in his attempt to get armed forces from the emperor to resist Saracen attacks. He died in Rome on Sept. 14.

STEPHEN VI [VII] (d. 897), pope. A Roman, son of a priest named John, he became bishop of Anagni, and in May 896 was elected bishop of Anagni, and in May 896 was elected pope by the Spoleto faction led by Emperor Lambert's mother, Ageltruda. She caused Stephen to exhume the body of Pope Formosus and hold a trial over the body; Stephen annulled Formosus' ordinations, pronounced excommunication on the dead pope, and had his body thrown into the Tiber. Stephen himself was imprisoned by an angry Roman mob and strangled to death in prison in Aug.

STEPHEN VII [VIII] (d. 931), pope. A Roman, son of Teudemund, and a cardinal-priest when elected pope in Dec. 928, through the influence of the powerful Marozia, he died in Rome in Feb., possibly by assassination.

STEPHEN VIII [IX] (d. 942), pope. A

Roman, he became a cardinal-priest, was elected pope on July 14, 939, and was probably subject to Prince Alberic of the Romans, who repulsed an attack of King Hugo on Rome during Stephen's brief pontificate. He died in Rome in Oct.

STEPHEN IX [X] (d. 1058), pope. Frederick, brother of Godfrey, duke of Lorraine, was son of Duke Gozelon of Lower Lorraine and Junca, daughter of King Berengarius II of Italy. He became a canon at Liège, and was appointed chancellor and librarian by his cousin, Pope Leo IX, about 1051. He was one of Leo's legates to Constantinople in 1054 when the schism between Rome and the Eastern Church became final, became a monk at Monte Cassino in 1055 to avoid Emperor Henry III the Black, and in 1057 became abbot there. He was created a cardinal-priest by Pope Victor II and on Aug. 3, 1057, succeeded him as pope. He energetically pushed the ecclesiastical reforms of his predecessor, but died in Rome on Mar. 29, a few months after his consecration.

STEPHEN (1097?–1154), king of England. Son of Count Stephen Henry of Blois and Adela, daughter of William the Conqueror, he was born in Blois, France, became king of England in 1135 and was accepted by Normandy and by Pope Innocent II, but not by Matilda, daughter of Henry I of England, whom he had previously acknowledged as successor to the crown. He fought David I of Scotland, Matilda's uncle, crushed leading nobles by seizing their estates, and upset Church relations by attacking the bishops of Ely, Lincoln, and Salisbury. He was defeated and captured in 1141 by Earl Robert of Gloucester, Matilda's half-brother, and was deposed by a Church council, but regained the crown in 1142. Civil war followed until 1153; his feud with the papacy (1147–51) resulted in an interdict in 1148. He fought an invasion by Henry of Anjou, sought to place his son Eustace on the throne, and, when the latter died, bowed to Henry, gave up the right of succession, and died on Oct. 25 at Feversham abbey, which he had founded and to which he retired.

STEPHEN, ST. (975–1038), king of Hungary. Born in Gran, son of Géza, chief of the Magyars, he was named Vaik, but was baptized by St. Adalbert of Prague at the same time as his father and given the name Stephen. When twenty he married Gisela, sister of Henry, duke of Bavaria, and in 997 succeeded his father. He had to suppress a series of revolts by rival pagan nobles opposed to his policy of Christianization, but consolidated his position, and sent St. Anastasius to Rome to secure the approval of Pope Sylvester II to the establishment of a hierarchy, with Anastasius as first archbishop, and also approval

of his own kingship. The pope approved both requests and Stephen became the first king of Hungary in 1001, wearing a crown the pope sent him by Anastasius. The nation was then divided into episcopal sees, more Magyar clergy became available, and Stephen founded monasteries and abbeys (including the famous Benedictine abbey of Pannonhalma) and established a system of tithes to support building and aid the poor. He fought crime and superstition, welded the Magyars into a strong national group, abolished tribes, set up a system of counties, and made the nobles vassals of the crown. In 1031 his son Emeric died, and the rest of his lifetime was embittered by family disputes over the succession; some of his nephews even conspired against his life. He died on Aug. 15 and was buried at Szekesfehervar, but in 1083 Pope St. Gregory VII directed that his relics be enshrined in the church of Our Lady at Buda; Stephen and Emeric were canonized at that time. Stephen is the national hero and spiritual patron of Hungary. His incorrupted right hand is treasured as a sacred relic; his crown, insignia of Hungarian sovereignty, was taken into custody by the United States after World War II. F. D. Sept. 2 (in Hungary, Aug. 20).

STEPHEN II (d. 1131), king of Hungary. Son of Coloman, he succeeded his father as king in 1114, warred unsuccessfully against Poland, Austria, and Russia, abdicated in 1131, and retired to a monastery, where he died.

STEPHEN V (1239–1272), king of Hungary. Son of King Béla IV, he was ruler of the duchy of Styria in 1254–59, was married to Elizabeth, a Cuman, by his father in 1255 for political reasons, and lost his duchy to Ottocar II of Bohemia in 1260. He revolted in 1262 and forced his father to divide the realms with him, and in 1268 invaded and proclaimed himself king of Bulgaria. On the death of Béla in 1270 he succeeded to the throne of Hungary, faced widespread opposition for his supposed pagan leanings, brought on by Elizabeth's influence, and in 1271 at Mosony defeated the dissidents who had united with Ottocar II of Bohemia. He made the Bohemian king restore his conquests in western Hungary, and died on Aug. 6 while on an expedition against the kidnapers of his son Ladislaus.

STEPHEN, ST. (d. 35?), martyr. A learned Jew, possibly educated at Alexandria, he was converted to Christianity and was chosen the first of seven deacons by the apostles (Acts 6:1–5). He was accused of blasphemy by the elders of a group of synagogues, dragged before the Sanhedrin where he made an eloquent defense (Acts 7:2–53), and hurried off to the outskirts of Jerusalem, stripped, and stoned to death: the first Christian martyr. Among the willing witnesses was Saul of Tarsus. F. D. Dec. 26 (also, Aug. 3).

STEPHEN, ST. (1st century), bishop and martyr. According to a seventeenth-century legend, he was the first bishop of Reggio, Italy, sent there by St. Paul and put to death during the persecution of Nero. F. D. July 5.

STEPHEN, ST. (d. 258), martyr. *See* Sixtus II, St.

STEPHEN, ST. (d. 300?), martyr. *See* Eutychius, St.

STEPHEN, ST. (d. 304?), martyr. *See* Socrates, St.

STEPHEN, ST. (d. 305?), martyr. *See* Mark, St.

STEPHEN, ST. (d. 481), patriarch and martyr. He opposed the Monophysite heretics at Antioch so firmly that they seized and drowned him in the Orontes River. F. D. Apr. 25.

STEPHEN, ST. (d. 512). Bishop of Lyons, Gaul, he was successful in converting many Burgundian Arians. F. D. Feb. 13.

STEPHEN, ST. (d. 760?), bishop. A native of Cappadocia, Asia Minor, he became bishop of Surosh (now Sudak) in the Crimea, was exiled for his opposition to Iconoclasm during the persecution of Emperor Leo III, was restored in 740 by Emperor Constantine V, and became a noted and successful missionary preacher to the Slavs, Khazars, and Varangians of neighboring areas. F. D. Dec. 15.

STEPHEN, ST. (d. 1075?), bishop. A Benedictine monk at New Corbie in Saxony, he was sent to Sweden as a missionary bishop, had considerable success with the pagans, though his work was not lasting, and may have died as a martyr at Uppsala or Norrala, Sweden. F. D. June 2.

STEPHEN, BL. (d. 1144), cardinal. He was a Cistercian monk at Clairvaux, France, when he was made bishop of Palestrina, Italy, in 1141 and a cardinal. F. D. Mar. 17.

STEPHEN, BL. (d. 1209), martyr. Cistercian abbot of St. Gilles in Languedoc, France, he and a monk, Hildebrand, were slain by Albigensian heretics. F. D. Apr. 11.

STEPHEN, ST. (d. 1396), bishop. A monk at Rostov, Russia, he was sent to preach in an area southwest of the Urals, learning and translating scripture and liturgy into the Zyriane language, for which he invented an alphabet. After twelve years or more he was made a bishop of Perm in 1383, fought the Strigolnik heresy, and died in Moscow. F. D. Apr. 26.

STEPHEN OF AUTUN (d. 1139?), bishop. Born in Bangé, Anjou, France, son of Lord Gaucerannus, he was bishop of Bangé in 1112, attended a synod in Tournus in 1115, and had the diocese of Autun placed under his protection by Pope Paschal II in 1116. He began building his cathedral, which was consecrated in 1131, in 1120, participated in the crowning of Louis VI's son, Philip, in 1129, and in 1136 resigned his see to enter the monastery at Cluny, where he died. He was noted for his learning and wrote *De sacramento altaris*.

STEPHEN BÁTHORY (1533–1586), king of Poland. Born in Hungary, he married Anna, sister of the last of the Jagellons of Poland. He was elected prince of Transylvania in 1571 and king of Poland in 1575, introduced reforms, and waged war for years with Ivan the Terrible of Russia which gained Livonia for Poland. He spent the last years of his life preparing for an unrealized war against the Turks.

STEPHEN DU BOURG, ST. (d. 1118). He was a canon at Valence, France, joined St. Bruno as one of the first Carthusians at Grande Chartreuse, and in 1116 was founder-abbot of the charterhouse at Meyria. F. D. Jan. 4.

STEPHEN OF BOURBON (d. 1261). Born in Belleville, France, he studied at the cathedral in Mâcon and at Paris, became a Dominican about 1220, and was a noted preacher and inquisitor in several districts of eastern and southern France. He wrote *De septem donus Spiritus Sancti* and *Anecdotes historiques, légendes et apologues*.

STEPHEN OF CAIAZZO, ST. (935–1023), bishop. Born in Macerata, Italy, he studied at Capua, became Benedictine abbot of San Salvatore Maggiore, and in 979 was named bishop of Caiazzo, Italy, of which he is patron. F. D. Oct. 29.

STEPHEN OF CARDEÑA, ST. (d. 872), martyr. Abbot of the Benedictine monastery of Cardeña, near Burgos, Spain, he was slain by Saracens with 200 of his community. Their cult was approved in 1603. F. D. Aug. 6.

STEPHEN OF CHATILLON, ST. (d. 1208), bishop. Born in Lyons, France, he became a Carthusian at Portes, was its prior in 1196, and in 1203 was named bishop of Dié. His cult was approved in 1907. F. D. Sept. 7.

STEPHEN HARDING, ST. (d. 1134), founder. Born and educated in Sherborne, Dorsetshire, England, he went on a pilgrimage to Rome and on his way home joined some hermits living in the Burgundian forest near Molesme. After some years, when discipline lessened, he left in 1098 with St. Robert, abbot of the monastery, St. Alberic its prior, and twenty monks for the more isolated area at Cîteaux, and on forest land given them by Lord Rainald of Beaune founded a new abbey. Stephen became sub-prior and moved up when Alberic became abbot on Robert's return to Molesme. Alberic died in 1109; Stephen succeeded him and made the Rule of St. Benedict, which they had been following, even more rigorous. Vocations fell off as a result, but the new Cistercian order gained new life when thirty men led by Bernard asked to be admitted; after this, houses were established at Pontigny, Morimond, and Clairvaux; by 1119 there were six others. Stephen then drew up the rule which organized the Cistercians as an order. He resigned in 1133 because of old age and increasing blindness, and died at the abbey. He was canonized in 1623. F. D. Apr. 17.

JOHN D. DALGAIRNS, *Life of St. Stephen Harding*, rev. H. Thurston (Westminster, Md., Newman, 1946).

STEPHEN OF LIÈGE, BL. (d. 1061). He served as canon at St. Denis, Liège, Flanders, became a Benedictine at St. Vannes in Verdun, later returning to found and serve as abbot of the monastery of St. Laurence in his native city. F. D. Jan. 13.

STEPHEN DEL LUPO, ST. (d. 1191). A Benedictine monk at San Liberatore de Majella, he was founder-abbot of San Pietro at Vallebona, near Manopello, Italy. F. D. July 19.

STEPHEN OF MURET, ST. (1046–1124), founder. Born in Thiers, France, he was educated at Benevento, Italy, then founded a monastery near Limoges, France, with a rule like that of the Carthusians and Camaldolese. The group, which he directed for forty-six years, was administered by laybrothers. After his death the community moved to Grandmont and became known as the Order of Grandmont. It began to decline after two generations, and disappeared in the eighteenth century. He died in Muret, near Limoges, and was canonized in 1189 by Pope Clement III. F. D. Feb. 8.

STEPHEN OF NARBONNE (d. 1242), martyr. A Franciscan, he was appointed inquisitor at Toulouse, France, and was murdered with eleven associates in Avignonet, France, by Albigensians. F. D. May 28.

STEPHEN OF OBAZINE, ST. (d. 1154). A hermit, he established a number of refuges near Tulle, France, and, later, a convent for 150 nuns. Both groups followed extreme austerities. In 1142 he became a Cistercian, and was made abbot. F. D. Mar. 8.

STEPHEN PECHERSKY, ST. (d. 1094), bishop. He succeeded St. Theodosius as abbot of the monastery of Caves in Kiev, Russia, in 1074, was displaced and founded a new community at Klov, and became bishop of Vladimir in 1091. F. D. Apr. 27.

STEPHEN OF RIETI, ST. (d. 560?). Abbot of a monastery in Italy, he was praised for his patience in a homily of St. Gregory the Great. F. D. Feb. 13.

STEPHEN OF TOURNAI (1128–1203), bishop. Born in Orléans, France, he joined the Order of Canons Regular there about 1150, studied law at Bologna, and was elected abbot of St. Euverte in Orléans in 1167 and of Ste. Geneviève in Paris in 1177, which he rebuilt, adding a monastic school. He was appointed bishop of Tournai in 1192, and died there in Sept. He wrote *Summa in decretum Gratiani*.

STEPHEN THE YOUNGER, ST. (714–764), martyr. Born in Constantinople, he entered the monastery of St. Auxentius near Chalcedon at fifteen, became its abbot fifteen years later, and afterward resigned to live as a hermit. When he refused to support Constantine Copronymus' Iconoclasm, the emperor burned the monastery and imprisoned him, exiled him to Proconessus for two years, and then brought him back to Constantinople. There he was tortured and stoned to death by a mob when he refused to support the heresy. SS. Andrew, Basil, and 300 monks were slain with him. F. D. Nov. 28.

STEPHENS, HENRY ROBERT (1665–1723), theologian. Born in Liège, Belgium, on Aug. 5, of English parents, he became a Jesuit in 1683, and spent the next twenty years at the Liège seminary as professor of theology and superior. He vigorously combatted the Jansenists in Belgium and wrote several treatises answering their attacks. He died in Liège on June 15.

STEPHENS, THOMAS (1549?–1619), missioner. Born in Bushton, Wiltshire, England, he studied at Winchester and Oxford, but did not graduate, and became a Jesuit in Rome in 1575 at the Roman College. He sailed from Lisbon to Portuguese India in 1579 (a detailed account of his voyage has been printed), became spiritual coadjutor of Goa in 1578–79, and was rector of Salsette College. He spent the rest of his life ministering to the Brahmin Catholics of Salsette. He learned Sanskrit, Canarese (vernacular Malabar), and Hindustani, published grammars (his *Arte de lingua Canarin* was the first Indian grammar by a European), wrote *The Christian Purânna*, a catechism, and numerous letters (some are included in Hakluyt's *Voyages*), several of which to his father and brother are reputed to have led to the founding of the East India Company because of the glowing trade potentials in India he painted. He died in Goa, Portuguese India.

STEPINAC, ALOJZIJE (1898–1960), cardinal. Born in Krasic, Austria-Hungary, on May 8, of a wealthy farming family, he completed high school in 1916, fought during World War I, was wounded and captured by the Italians, and joined the Yugoslav volunteer corps to fight for Croatian freedom. He rose to lieutenant by 1919, studied at the University of Zagreb, and in 1924 went to the German-Hungarian College in Rome. He received degrees in philosophy and theology from the Gregorian, was ordained in 1930, and assigned to the chancery in Zagreb. He became titular archbishop of Nicopsis and coadjutor there in 1934 and succeeded Archbishop Bauer in that see in 1937. He developed Catholic Action, warning against growing political evils, and when war broke out helped to direct relief of refugees, both Christians and Jews, defying the Nazi regime by his attacks on German tactics and racial theories. After Tito rose to power, the archbishop was arrested in 1946 and charged with collaborating with the Croatian underground, serving as their military vicar, and hiding their archives. Although he produced documents to support his position and to contradict these charges and the additional one that he had imposed conversions on Orthodox Church members, Stepinac was sentenced to sixteen years at hard labor, chiefly for vague "crimes against the state." After five years he was released, but confined to a small rectory in Krasic, and forbidden to act as a bishop. He was named cardinal in 1952 by Pope Pius XII and spent his last years serving his parishioners in an unheated church. He caught pneumonia, which complicated recovery from a rare type of blood poisoning, and died in Krasic (now Yugoslavia), on Feb. 10.

STERCATIUS, ST. (4th century), martyr. *See* Victor, St.

STEUCHO, AGOSTINO (1496–1549), bishop. Born in Gubbio, Umbria, Italy, he joined the Canons Regular of the Lateran there when seventeen, became director of Cardinal Grimani's library in Venice in 1525, prior of the Reggio canons in 1530, and then of the Gubbio canons, and in 1538 was appointed bishop of Kisamos, Crete. He became head of the Vatican Library later the same year, was sent as legate of Pope Paul III to the Council of Trent in 1547 at Bologna, and died in Venice, Italy, on the return trip. He wrote numerous exegetical works which were edited by Ambrogio Morando and published in 1578.

STEVENSON, JOSEPH (1806–1895), historian. Born in Berwick-on-Tweed, Scotland, on Nov. 27, he studied at Durham and Glasgow, worked in the government archive office, and in 1831 joined the staff of the British Museum. On the death of his son he became an Anglican minister, served as librarian at the Durham cathedral in 1841–48, and was rector of Leighton Buzzard in 1849–63. He became an editor of the Public Records Office in 1857, a convert in 1863, and entered the Oscott seminary in 1869 when his wife died. He was ordained in 1872, became a Jesuit in 1877, but left after his novitiate to continue his historical researches. He edited many series of classical authors for various societies, wrote reports for the Historical Manuscript Commission, worked on the Roman Transcripts Series of the British Record Office, and recommended publications of chronicles in what became the famous Rolls Series. He died in London on Feb. 8.

STEVIN, SIMON (1548–1620), scientist.

Born in Bruges, Belgium, he was a bookkeeper in Antwerp, and settled in the Netherlands in the employ of Stadtholder Maurice of Nassau, who appointed him director of finances, inspector of dikes, and quartermaster general. He became a leading mathematician with great influence in the world of finance on the publication of his *Tafelen van Interest* (1582); wrote *De Thiende* (1585), a pioneering work on calculus; *De Beghinselen der Weeghconst* (1586), his best-known work on mechanics, which set forth for the first time the theorems of the hydrostatic paradox, the equilibrium of bodies on an inclined plane, and the parallelogram of forces; and *Vita politica* (1590), a treatise on the duties of citizens. He died in Leyden, Netherlands.

STIFTER, ADALBERT (1805–1868), poet. Born in Oberplan, Bohemia, on Oct. 23, he studied at Vienna, tutored, and achieved success with the publication in the 1840s of his story, *Der Condor*. He was forced to flee the uprisings in Vienna in 1848 and settled in Linz, where he became a member of the school board in 1850. A romanticist, he became popular for his poetry: *Bunte Steine, Der Nachsommer, Witiko,* and *Der Hochwald*. He died in Linz, Austria, on Oct. 28.

STILLA, BL. (d. 1140?). Born in Abenberg, near Nuremberg, Bavaria, daughter of Count Wolfgang II, she built the church of St. Peter, took a vow of virginity, and lived at home as a nun. Her cult was confirmed in 1927. F. D. July 19.

STÖCKL, ALBERT (1823–1895), theologian. Born in Freuchtlingen, Bavaria, on Mar. 15, he studied in Eichstätt and was ordained in 1848. After a period as rector, he taught philosophy at the lyceum in 1850 and received his doctorate in philosophy from Würzburg in 1855. He taught at the Münster Academy in 1862, resigned in 1871 to become a parish priest in Eichstätt, where he was made a cathedral canon the next year, and was a member of the lower house of the *Reichstag* in 1878–81. He was a leader in the revival of interest in Thomism, and wrote, among other titles, *Lehrbuch der Philosophie* (1868), *Grundriss der Aesthetik* (1871), and *Grundriss der Geschichte der Philosophie* (1894). He died in Eichstätt, Germany, on Nov. 15.

STOCKLEY, WILLIAM (1859–1943), critic. Born in Templeogue, Dublin, Ireland, he studied at Trinity College, Dublin, went to Canada, and taught at the universities of New Brunswick (1886–1902) and Ottawa (1902–3). He became a convert in 1894. In 1905, after two years as headmaster of a school in Halifax, he became professor of literature at University College, Cork; he retired in 1930. He was alderman in Cork in 1920–29, university deputy to the dail in 1921–23, and a member of the first government of De Valera, until disagreement forced his withdrawal from political life. He wrote on Shakespeare, Burke, Wordsworth, Tennyson, *Newman, Education, and Ireland,* and *Studies in Irish Biography.*

STODDARD, CHARLES WARREN (1843–1909), author. Born in Rochester, New York, on Aug. 7, he attended a nearby academy in 1857–58, worked in a bookshop in California, studied at the prep school of the College of California for a year, and in 1864 went to the Hawaiian Islands to recover his health. There he met Fr. Damien of Molokai, on his return wrote for the *Californian,* had his *Poems,* edited by Bret Harte, published in 1867, and became a convert in that year. He made several trips to the South Sea islands, published *South-Sea Idylls* in 1873, and in that year became roving correspondent of the San Francisco *Chronicle,* traveling over Europe (serving for a short time as Mark Twain's secretary in London), the Holy Land, and Hawaii during the next decade. In 1885 he became a professor of English at Notre Dame, and lectured at the Catholic University from 1889 to 1892, but was obliged to resign both positions because of ill-health. He returned to California in 1905, and died in Monterey on Apr. 23. He wrote *The Lepers of Molokai* (1885), *In the Footprints of the Padres, Hawaiian Life, The Island of Tranquil Delights, For the Pleasure of His Company* (his only novel), and *A Troubled Heart,* the story of his conversion. His *Poems* were collected in 1917.

STOEGER, JOHANN BAPTIST (1810–1883). Born in Enrersfeld, Austria, on Oct. 4, he became a Benedictine laybrother in 1840 and served as a cook and baker through the rest of a life marked by exceptional piety. The cause of his canonization was introduced in 1915.

STOKES, FREDERICK WILFRID SCOTT (1860–1927), engineer. Born in Worcestershire, England, on Apr. 9, he was educated at St. Francis Xavier's, Liverpool, and Catholic University College, Kensington. He became an engineer, designed bridges and railway structures, and in 1885 joined the firm of Ransomes & Rapier in Ipswich. He became managing director in 1897 and chairman in 1907. He married Irene Ionides in 1900. He developed cement-making rotary kilns, improved his firm's portable cranes and shipyard and dam sluices, and invented an artillery mortar which bears his name. He served in such government posts as the ministry of munitions and the industrial reconstruction council, was president of the British Engineers' Association, and was decorated by the Egyptian and British governments. He died in Ruthin, Wales, on Feb. 7.

STOLBERG, FRIEDRICH LEOPOLD (1750–1819), diplomat, author. Born in Bramstedt, Holstein, on Nov. 7, he was raised in Copenhagen, where he met and was deeply influenced by Friedrich Klopstock, studied law at Halle and Göttingen where, with his brother, he became a member of a literary group. He traveled through Switzerland with Count von Haugwitz and Goethe in 1775, entered the service of the Protestant bishop of Lübeck in 1777, represented him at the Danish court, and became chief administrator at Eutin in 1781 and magistrate at Neuenburg in 1785. In 1789 he was appointed Danish ambassador to Berlin, president of his bishop's board of ecclesiastical administration in 1791, was Danish ambassador to Russia in 1797. He became a convert in 1800, resigned his various posts, was subjected to bitter attacks, and finally in 1816 retired to Sondermühlen, near Osnabrück, Germany, where he died on Dec. 5. He wrote poetry, novels, biographies, and meditations, chief of which were *Ballads* (1779), *Lambics* (1784), *The Island* (1788), *Geschichte der Religion Jesu Christi,* and translated works by Homer, Plato, and St. Augustine.

STOLZ, ALBAN ISIDOR (1808–1883), theologian. Born in Bühl, Baden, Germany, on Feb. 3, he studied in Rastatt and law and theology at Freiburg. He lost his faith there, entered Heidelberg in 1830 to study philology, and, having regained his faith, entered the Freiburg seminary in 1832, and was ordained in 1833. He worked in various parishes, became an instructor at the Brushal gymnasium in 1841 and at the Freiburg theological college in 1843, received his doctorate in theology in 1845, and became professor of theology at the university in 1847. He was rector of the university in 1849–50, founded the Catholic Journeymen's Association in Freiburg in 1851, introduced and was director of the St. Vincent de Paul Society there, and in 1868 became archepiscopal spiritual counselor. He wrote theological works, notably *Erziehungskunst* (1873) but it was in the popularization of religious subjects that he became famed throughout Germany. Among his most popular works were *Legende oder der Christliche Sternhimmel* (1851–60), *Die heilige Elisabeth* (1865), *Spanisches für die gebildete Welt* (1908), and *Besuch bei Sem, Chem und Japhet* (1857). He died in Freiburg, Germany, on Oct. 16.

STOLZENHAGEN, BENEDICT (1381–1465), theologian. Born near Jüterbock, Brandenburg, Germany, he became a Cistercian at Paradies, Poland, taking the name Jacobus, and received his doctorate and taught theology at Cracow. He left the Cistercians for the stricter Carthusians in 1441, taught canon law at Erfurt, became rector in 1456, and died there. He wrote eighty treatises on the soul, indulgences, clerical shortcomings, and moral theology.

STONE, JAMES KENT (1840–1921). Born in Boston, Massachusetts, on Nov. 10, he took his degree at Harvard, studied at Göttingen, fought during the Civil War, and became an Episcopal minister (as his father had been) in 1866. He was president of Kenyon and Hobart colleges, where he also taught classics. He became a convert in 1869, was ordained in 1872, became a Paulist, and in 1878 a Passionist as Fr. Fidelis. He spent three years in Rome and twelve in South America, where he was provincial, returned to preach at Harvard and, in 1901, to direct its summer school, and again served in South America from 1908 to 1914. He returned to Chicago, went to California in ill health, and died there on Oct. 14. He wrote *The Invitation Heeded*.

STONE, BL. JOHN (d. 1539?), martyr. An Augustinian friar and theological scholar, he was imprisoned at Canterbury, England, for refusing to accept Henry VIII as the head of the Church, and hanged there sometime after mid-December 1538. F. D. May 12.

STONE, MARMADUKE (1748–1834), educator. Born in Draycot, England, on Nov. 28, he studied at St. Omer, became a Jesuit in 1767, and master and in 1790 president of Liège academy, which in 1794 was transferred to Stonyhurst, England, when threatened by the French revolutionists. In 1803 he was made provincial (through his reunion with the Russian Jesuits), retired from Stonyhurst in 1827, and died in St. Helens, England, on Aug. 21.

STONE, MARY JEAN (1853–1908), author. Born in Brighton, Sussex, England, she studied in Paris and Aschaffenburg, and became a convert while in Germany. She wrote *Mary the First, Queen of England* (1901), and *Reformation and Renaissance* (1904), and died in Battle, England, on May 3.

STONNES, JAMES (1513–1586?). Ordained in Durham, England, in 1539, he spent his life secretly ministering to the Catholics in Durham and Lancashire. He was arrested in 1585 in Newpark, Lancashire, imprisoned in New Fleet, Manchester, when he refused to acknowledge the royal supremacy, and probably died there.

STOREY, BL. JOHN (1504?–1571), martyr. Born in northern England, he studied canon and civil law at Oxford, became the university's first professor of civil law, entered public practice, married, and became a member of parliament. He attacked the Act of Uniformity and liturgical changes made by the advisers of the child-king, Edward VI, was imprisoned, and then went to Louvain. During the reign of Mary Tudor he was chancellor of the dioceses of Cambridge and Oxford, and represented the queen at the trial of Cranmer, the Anglican

bishop. He opposed Elizabeth's Act of Supremacy while in parliament at the beginning of her reign, was imprisoned, escaped to Louvain, was kidnaped and brought back to face trial and excessively brutal execution at Tyburn. Some historians, following John Foxe, claim that Storey was the most vicious of Mary's agents in bringing heretics to death; evidence is available, however, to show that he brought an end to the practice of burning at the stake, and that he was not the monster pictured by his enemies. F. D. June 1.

STORK, AMBROSE (1488?–1557), theologian. Born in Nidda, Hesse, he became a Dominican in Freiburg, attended the Diet of Worms in 1540, and was theologian to the archbishop of Trèves at the Council of Trent in 1546 and in 1561. He wrote, using the name Pelargus, on the Anabaptists and Iconoclasts and a treatise on the mass against Oescalampadius.

STOSS, VEIT (1438?–1533), artist. Born in Nuremberg, Germany, he became famed as a wood carver. Among his outstanding works are the *Death and Assumption of the Blessed Virgin* for the high altar of the Marienkirche, Cracow (where he had a workshop and lived from 1477 to 1496), *Annunciation* in St. Lawrence's Church, the altar in St. Aegidius, Nuremberg, and the tomb of King Casimir IV in the Cracow cathedral. He died in Nuremberg.

STRADIVARI, ANTONIO (1644–1737), violinmaker. Born in Cremona (or one of the nearby villages), Italy, he began making violins while a pupil of Nicholas Amati in the latter's workshop from 1667 to 1679, set himself up in 1680, and began to produce his world-famous violins. His finest work was produced from 1700 to 1725, and he made about 1000 violins (more than 500 are still extant), fifty cellos, and a dozen violas. He died in Cremona on Dec. 18 or 19.

STRAIN, JOHN (1810–1883), archbishop. Born in Edinburgh, Scotland, on Dec. 8, he studied at Aquhorties seminary and the Scots College, Rome, was ordained in 1833, engaged in pastoral work at Dalbeattie from 1834 to 1857, became president of Blairs College, Aberdeen, in 1858, and in 1864 was appointed vicar apostolic of the eastern district of Scotland and bishop of Abila. He was one of those mainly responsible for the restoration of the Scots hierarchy in 1878, and was appointed first archbishop of St. Andrews and Edinburgh in 1881. He died in Edinburgh on July 2.

STRAMBI, ST. VINCENZO (1745–1824), bishop. Born in Civitavecchia, Italy, he was ordained in 1767, became a Passionist in 1768, was made provincial in 1781, and bishop of Macerata and Tolentino in 1801. When he refused to take the oath of allegiance to Napoleon in 1808 he was expelled from his see. He returned in 1813, only to have Napoleon make Macerata his headquarters in his abortive attempt to regain power. The bishop pleaded successfully with both the French and Austrians to spare his people after the defeat of Murat. At the death of Pope Pius VII, he resigned his see and became adviser to Pope Leo XII. He died on Jan. 1 and was canonized in 1950. F. D. Sept. 25.

STRANSHAM, BL. EDWARD (1554?–1586), martyr. Also known as Transham and as Edmund Barber, he was born near Oxford, England, educated there and at Douai, and ordained at Soissons in 1580. He served in the underground mission in England for two years, returned to Rheims with twelve converts, became ill with consumption, then went back to face persecution. He was arrested for saying mass and hanged at Tyburn. F. D. Jan. 21.

STRASSMAIER, JOHANN NEPOMUK (1846–1920), scholar. Born in Hagenberg, Bavaria, on May 15, he studied there and in Metten, became a Jesuit and studied at Maria Laach, served with an ambulance unit in the Franco-Prussian War, and completed his studies in Wales. He was ordained in 1876, began working on Assyrian texts in the British Museum, and published six significant studies of inscriptions, including those of Cambyses and Darius. With Fr. Joseph Epping he worked eight years on the Babylonian calendar tablets, which led to the publication of *Astronomisches aus Babylon*. He died in London on May 15.

STRATA, BL. MARIA VICTORIA (1562–1617), foundress. Born in Genoa, Italy, Maria Victoria Fornari married Angelo Strata in 1579 and was widowed within a decade. After educating her six children, she founded, in 1604, an order of nuns devoted to Mary (who reputedly appeared to her in several visions) in the mystery of the annunciation, called the Blue Anonciades of Genoa. She died on Dec. 15. F. D. Sept. 12.

STRATON, ST. (d. 300?), martyr. *See* Hieronides, St.

STRATON, ST. (d. 301?), martyr. He and SS. Philip and Eutychian were so active in making converts at Nicomedia and attacking theatrical obscenities that they were burned at the stake there with St. Cyprian. F. D. Aug. 17.

STRATONICUS, ST. (d. 315), martyr. *See* Hermylus, St.

STREBER, FRANZ IGNAZ VON (1758–1841), numismatist. Born in Reisbach, Lower Bavaria, on Feb. 11, he was ordained and made court chaplain in 1783. He was appointed curator of the elector's cabinet of coins, spent years writing and arranging the Palatinal and Bavarian collections of the Wittelsbach line, and wrote several numismatic treatises. He

was appointed auxiliary bishop of Munich in 1821 and cathedral provost in 1822. He died in Munich, Germany, on Apr. 26.

STREBER, FRANZ SERAPH (1805–1864), numismatist. Nephew of Franz Ignaz, he was born in Deutenkofen, Lower Bavaria, on Feb. 26, received his doctorate in theology at Erlangen in 1830, taught archaeology at Munich in 1835, and was appointed curator of the royal cabinet of coins in 1841. He was twice rector of Munich, was elected to the Academy of Munich in 1854. He prepared a catalogue of some 18,000 Greek coins and published *Numismata nonnulla graeca* in 1834. He died in Munich, Germany, on Nov. 21.

STREBER, HERMANN (1839–1896). Son of Franz Seraph, he was born in Munich on Sept. 27, studied at its university and the Freising seminary, and was ordained in 1864. He taught at Wilhelmsgymnasium, received his doctorate in theology in Rome in 1869, and was dismissed from his teaching post the following year for his support of the dogma of papal infallibility. After pastoral work, he became connected editorially with the new edition of *Kirchenlexikon*, on which he worked until ill-health caused his retirement in 1892. He died in Tölz, Germany, on Aug. 9.

STREMONIE. *See* Austremonius, St.

STREPAR, BL. JAMES (d. 1409), archbishop. Member of a noble Polish family in Galicia and a senator, he joined the Franciscans at Lwow, became prior of the friary there, and vigorously defended the mendicant friars against the attacks of the regular clergy. He was most successful in preaching to the dissident Orthodox (he headed a group of Franciscans and Dominicans known as the Company of Christ's Itinerants), and in 1392 was appointed to the see of Galich where he built many schools, churches, hospitals, and religious houses. He died at Lwow, Galicia, on June 1 (possibly in 1411) and his cult was confirmed in 1791. F. D. Oct. 21.

STRITCH, SAMUEL ALPHONSUS (1887–1958), cardinal. Born in Nashville, Tennessee, on Aug. 17, he studied at St. Gregory's, Cincinnati, and the North American College, Rome. He was ordained in 1910, did parish work in the Nashville diocese in 1909–16, was secretary to Bishop Byrne in 1916–19, and was chancellor of the diocese in 1911–21, also serving as diocesan superintendent of schools from 1915. He was made a domestic prelate in 1921, and was consecrated bishop of Toledo in 1921. He built a new cathedral, was appointed archbishop of Milwaukee in 1930, and archbishop of Chicago in 1939. He was deeply interested in liturgical music and banned from his sees familiar popular songs for weddings and funerals. He also attacked materialism, worked for higher motion-picture standards, better social conditions for the Negroes and Puerto Ricans in urban centers, and better labor conditions, and developed Catholic charities and the Catholic Youth Organization. He became chairman of the administrative council of the National Catholic Welfare Conference in 1945, and was created a cardinal in 1946. He had just been given charge of the mission work of the Church as pro-prefect of the Congregation of Propaganda (on Mar. 1) when he died of blood poisoning in Rome on May 27.

STROSSMAYER, JOSEPH GEORG (1815–1905), bishop. Born in Essék, Croatia, on Feb. 4, he studied at the Diakovár and Budapest seminaries, was ordained in 1838, and served as vicar at Peterwardein. He received his doctorate in theology from the Augustineum, Vienna, in 1842, taught at Djakovo, became court chaplain in 1847, and professor at the university of Vienna. He was appointed bishop of Djakovo and apostolic administrator of Belgrade-Semendria in 1849 and fought vigorously for separation of the Croat Church from Hungarian ecclesiastical direction. He represented Croatia-Slavonia in the Vienna *Reichsrat* in 1860 and advocated a federalist Austria with Croatia-Slavonia-Dalmatia a member. He pursued this even after the Croat-Hungarian compromise of 1868–73. He was a vigorous opponent of papal infallibility at the Vatican Council and did not publish the decrees of the council in his diocese until late in 1872. He built a new cathedral and seminary, founded Zagreb University, actively promoted Slavic cultural unity as the road to the political unity of Serbs, Slovenes, Croats, and Bulgars, and attempted to reunite the Orthodox Church to Rome by using Slavic in the liturgy. He received the pallium from Pope Leo XIII in 1898. He wrote *Monumenta slavorum meridionalium* (1863). He died on Apr. 8.

STUART, HENRY BENEDICT MARIA CLEMENT (1725–1807), cardinal. Grandson of King James II of England, son of James Stuart, the first Pretender, and brother of Charles Edward the Pretender, he was born in Rome on Mar. 11, was created a cardinal in 1747, and was ordained the following year, and made an archpriest of the Vatican basilica. He was made titular archbishop of Corinth in 1759, cardinal-bishop of Frascati, where he founded a seminary, in 1761, and was impoverished when his French benefices and property were seized during the French Revolution. He fled to Venice in 1799, was granted a pension by George III of England, and returned to Frascati in 1800. He became bishop of Ostia and Velletri, and died in Frascati, Italy, on July 13.

STUART, HENRY LONGAN (1875–1928),

author. Born in London, he studied at Ratcliffe College, was a rancher in Colorado, served with the royal artillery during World War I, with the Italian liaison staff, and on the military mission to Paris in 1919. He did newspaper work in London, Paris, Boston, and New York, joined the editorial staff of *Commonweal*, and wrote the novels *Weeping Cross* (1908, in the tradition of Hawthorne) and *Fenella* (1911, on Pearl Craigie, an American novelist). He also translated Claudel, Herriot, and Julian Green. He died in New York City on Aug. 26.

STUART, JAMES FRANCIS EDWARD (1688–1766), prince. Born in St. James's Palace, London, on June 10, son of King James II and Mary of Modena, he was sent to France with his mother in December when it was evident his father's overthrow was imminent, and when James died in 1701 was proclaimed heir to the English throne as James III, though the Stuarts had been excluded from the throne by the English Act of Succession of 1701. He was attainted in 1702, accompanied French forces on an abortive attempt to invade Scotland in 1706, and served in the French army. He was forced to leave France by the Treaty of Utrecht in 1713, and went to Scotland in 1715 to support the Jacobite revolt headed by the earl of Mar, but the rebellion failed. He settled in Rome, married Princess Clementina Sobieski, daughter of Prince John Sobieski of Poland, in 1719, was pensioned by Pope Benedict XIII in 1727, was the center of numerous plans to regain the English throne, but when his son, Charles Edward, failed in the rebellion of 1745, abandoned all hope of succession. He died in Rome on Jan. 1.

STUART, JANET ERSKINE (1857–1914), educator and poet. Born on Nov. 11 in Cottesmore, Rutland, England, youngest of thirteen children of Canon Andrew Stuart, the Anglican rector there, and Mary Noel, she became a convert in 1879 and entered the Society of the Sacred Heart at Roehampton in 1882. She made her final vows in 1889, served as mistress of novices and superior there, as superior vicar of England, and in 1911 became superior general of her society, succeeding Mother Digby, whose secretary or associate she had been for twenty-nine years. She founded convents at Aberdeen, Bonchurch, and Tunbridge Wells, and colleges at Newcastle and St. Charles, visited all parts of the world, and returned from Japan by way of the United States. Her particular concern was education, as is clear from her *Education of Catholic Girls* (1911). Other writings include *Highways and Byways in the Spiritual Life* (1923), *Prayer in Faith* (1936), *The Society of the Sacred Heart* (1915), and *Poems* (1924). She died in Roehampton, England, on Oct. 21.

STUART, JOHN PATRICK CRICHTON (1847-1900), archaeologist. Born in Mt. Stuart, Isle of Bute, on Sept. 12, he became third marquess of Bute at his father's death in 1848, studied at Harrow and Oxford, was influenced by Newman, and became a convert in 1868. His father had developed the port of Cardiff, Wales; John became a grower of grapes on his Welsh estates from 1877, became mayor of Cardiff in 1890, and president of University College there. He was interested in local history and literature, restored castles, unearthed monastery ruins, and wrote on Wallace, Robert I, and Scots antiquities. He was rector of St. Andrews in 1892–98 and a major benefactor of that university, provost of Rothesay in 1896–99, and received three honorary degrees. He restored Rothesay and Falkland castles, St. Andrews and Pluscarden priories, Greyfriars, Elgin, and St. Blase's chapel, Bute, and other structures. He was interested in Coptic liturgy, made an English translation of the breviary, edited the *Altus* of St. Columba, published works of other scholars on mediaeval history and archaeology, and served as president of the British Archaeological Society. He was owner of the *Scottish Review* from 1880 on. He died in Dumfries, Scotland, on Oct. 9.

STURMIUS, ST. (d. 779). Born in Bavaria, he was educated by St. Wigbert at the abbey of Fritzlar and became the first German Benedictine. After ordination he did mission work in Westphalia, and in 744 founded the monastery of Fulda, of which St. Boniface appointed him first abbot and where he built up a great school. On a trip to Monte Cassino and Rome he secured independence from episcopal control for Fulda from Pope St. Zachary. St. Lull, bishop of Mainz, later claimed jurisdiction over Fulda, and Sturmius was exiled for two years by Pepin but later restored to his abbacy. He died in Fulda, Germany, and was canonized in 1139. F. D. Dec. 17.

STURZO, LUIGI (1871–1959), statesman. Born in Caltagirone, Sicily, on Nov. 26, he entered the local seminary at twelve, was ordained in 1894, and continued his studies at the Gregorian, Rome, where he received his doctorate in theology. He taught at the Caltagirone seminary, founded a weekly newspaper in 1897 and a daily in Palermo in 1899. He was elected vice-mayor of Caltagirone (the clergy were forbidden by law to hold higher office) in 1905, a position he held for fifteen years, reorganized the school and farming system, developed a water supply, and built workers' homes. In 1919 he founded the Popular party (later developed as the Christian Democratic party), which defended labor unions, woman suffrage, income taxes, and free education. This work had the approval of Pope Benedict XV and marked the return of Italian Catholics to political life for the first time since the seizure of the Papal States. Alcide de Gaspari and Mario Scelba, both later to be premiers of Italy, worked with Sturzo. Devoted to applying Christian principles to government and social and economic problems, he was a vigorous opponent of Benito Mussolini, and, when the latter took over the government in 1925, Sturzo was forced into a twenty-one-year exile. He lived in England, France, and the United States, and lectured and wrote widely. He returned to his homeland in 1946 after publishing fourteen books, was a leader in the successful fight against the Communists when they threatened to win the 1948 election, and became the conscience of the victorious Christian Democratic party constantly fighting statism and urging the party to a higher vision. He was made a life member of the senate in 1952, the first priest so honored, and died in Rome on Aug. 8. He wrote on politics, economics, religion, theology, and sociology. among his best-known works are *Church and State, Italy and Fascism, Spiritual Problems of Our Times, Man in Society and History,* and *Nationalism and Internationalism.*

STYRIACUS, ST. (d. 315?), martyr. *See* Agapius, St.

SUARDI, BARTOLOMMEO (1460?–1529), painter. Called Il Bramantino, he was brought up and studied in Milan, was influenced by Foppa, and later became the assistant of Bramante. He was an engineer at Milan in 1523 and later served as court architect to Duke Francis Borgia. Paintings include *St. Martin, Adoration of the Magi, Flight into Egypt, Ecce Homo,* and madonnas.

SUAREZ, AMMANUEL HERNANDEZ (1895–1954). Born in Asturias, Spain, on Nov. 5, he became a Dominican and was head of his order from 1946 until his death near Perpignan, France, on June 30.

SUAREZ, FRANCISCO (1548–1617), theologian. Born in Granada, Spain, on Jan. 5, he was educated at Salamanca, became a Jesuit in 1564, was ordained in 1572, and taught at Avila, Segovia, Valladolid, Alcalá, Salamanca, and Rome. He received his doctorate at Evorta, was appointed principal professor of theology at Coimbra by Philip II in 1597 (and taught there until 1616), and was recognized as an outstanding philosophical jurist. His works refute the contemporary interpretations of the theory of the divine right of kings; his *De Defensio catholicae fidei,* written in 1613 at Pope Paul V's request against James I's Oath of Allegiance, was bitterly denounced by that monarch, who had it publicly burned by the hangman. He is often called the last of the scholastic philosophers, founded a school of his own. Suarism, which taught a congruism midway between Molina and the predestinarian teachings of the Dominicans, and a mitigated realism midway between Duns Scotus and William of Occam. He also taught that the same doctrine may be held by both science and faith, and his political doctrine that earthly power is held by the body of men from whom kings and rulers receive it (which was based on the Catholic doctrine that all men are equal before God) is considered a basic Catholic teaching on democracy. He wrote numerous other theological works. He died in Lisbon, Portugal, on Sept. 25.

SUAU, PIERRE (1861–1916), historian. Born in Guadeloupe on June 7, he was educated at Toulouse and Angers, became a Jesuit in 1878, served on the editorial staff of *Études*, and wrote on his Society, Spain, Madagascar, and a life of St. Francis Borgia. He died on Aug. 15.

SUCCESSUS, ST. (2nd century), martyr. *See* Catus, St.

SUCCESSUS, ST. (d. 304), martyr. *See* Apodemius, St.

SUGAR, VEN. JOHN (1558–1604), martyr. Born in Wombourn, Staffordshire, England, he studied at Oxford, left without taking his degree, may have been a minister at Cannock, but was ordained at Douai in 1601, and returned to the English mission. He was arrested in 1603 in Rowington, imprisoned for a year, and hanged at Warwick on July 16 for being a priest.

SUGER (1081?–1151), abbot. Probably born in St. Denis, France, he was sent as a student to the abbey there in 1091 with the future King Louis VI, also studied at St. Benoît-sur-Loire, near Orléans, became secretary of Abbot Adam of St. Denis in 1106, provost of Berneval in 1107 and of Toury in 1109. In 1118 he was Louis' representative at the court of Gelasius II in southern France, and in 1121–22 to Pope Callistus II in Rome. He was elected abbot of St. Denis in 1122, was ordained on his return to the abbey, and attended the Lateran Council in 1123. He became an adviser of Louis VI and Louis VII, reformed his abbey in 1127, and as regent of France from 1147 to 1149 when King Louis VII was on the second crusade built up the royal power, encouraged trade and commerce, and initiated reforms in the administration of justice. He was in the midst of raising an army for the crusades when he died at St. Denis. He wrote biographies of Louis the Fat and Louis VII and other treatises.

SUHARD, EMMANUEL (1874–1949), cardinal. Born in Brittany, France, on Apr. 5, he studied and was ordained in Rome, and returned to teach in the provincial seminary. He was named bishop of Bayeux-Liseux, served as archbishop of Rheims for ten years, and in 1935 was made a cardinal. He became archbishop of Paris in 1940, working quietly during the occupation, protecting underground Catholic Action, supporting the secretly published newspaper, *Témoignage Chrétien*, and directing the flow of Jewish refugees, resistance leaders, and other sought-after figures. He was strongly censured by those who did not know of his hidden labors and who objected to his seeming lack of hostility toward the invaders. He worked incessantly to revitalize clergy and people, visited his parishioners everywhere, established the Mission de Paris and the Centre Intellectuel des Catholiques Français, and advanced intellectual life and bettered the parish community. His pastoral letters on Providence, property, the family, *The Meaning of God, Growth or Decline*, and the worker-priest became world renowned and influential. His writings were collected in *The Church Today* (1953). He died in Paris on May 30.

SUIDAS (10th century). Probably an ecclesiastic in Constantinople, he wrote a Greek lexicon or encyclopedia of biography from the classical period to the middle of the tenth century, particularly valuable for its literary material.

SULAGA, JOHN (d. 1555), martyr. A monk in a Chaldean monastery, he was sent to Rome in 1551 and consecrated bishop by Pope Julius III. On his return he consecrated two metropolitans and three bishops, but was opposed by the Nestorian patriarch Simeon Denha, imprisoned, and put to death.

SULLIVAN, ALEXANDER MARTIN (1830–1884), journalist. Born in Bantry, Ireland, he became a journalist, editor and owner of the *Nation, Weekly News*, and *Zozimus*, was imprisoned for his political activities in 1868, elected a member of parliament in 1874, and admitted to the Irish bar in 1876. He was made queen's counsel in 1881, defended many Irish patriots, and was active in the temperance movement. He died in Dublin on Oct. 17.

SULLIVAN, PETER JOHN (1821–1883), general. Born in Cork, Ireland, on Mar. 15, he was brought to the United States by his parents in 1823, studied at the University of Pennsylvania, served in the Mexican War, and became a stenographer in the United States Senate. He was admitted to the bar in Ohio in 1848, became a brigadier general of volunteers in the Union army during the Civil War, was United States minister to Colombia from 1865 to 1869, and died in Cincinnati, Ohio, on Mar. 2.

SULPICIUS, ST. (d. 117?), martyr. *See* Servilian, St.

SULPICIUS, ST. (d. 591), bishop. Appointed bishop of Bourges, France, in 584, he attended the Council of Mâcon the following year, and was held in high respect in the area. He is sometimes confused with Sulpicius Pius of Bourges, who lived at a later date, and with the historian Sulpicius Severus. F. D. Jan. 29.

SULPICIUS II, ST. (d. 647), bishop. A Merovingian biography written a few years after his death records his successful opposition to a local tyrant appointed by King Dagobert, his consecration as bishop of Bourges, France, in 624, attendance at the Council of Clichy in 627, and conversion of the entire city of Bourges by the fame of his works of prayer, fasting, and widespread charity. F. D. Jan. 17.

SULPICIUS, ST. (d. 843), martyr. He became bishop of Bayeux, Normandy, in about 838 and was slain by invading Norsemen at Livry, near Versailles. F. D. Sept. 4.

SULPICIUS SEVERUS (360?–420?). A native of Aquitania, he was educated at Bordeaux, became a lawyer, married but soon lost his wife, and about 390 was baptized, gave up his wealth, and retired to Primuliacum. He may have become a priest and may, in his last years, have fallen into and out of Pelagianism. His *Chronicles* are a history of the Old Testament and of early Christian persecutions; he also wrote a life of St. Martin of Tours, whom he knew personally. For a while he was identified with St. Sulpicius Severus, Archbishop of Bourges.

SUMMERS, WALTER G. (1889–1938), psychologist. Born in New York City on Mar. 27, he was ordained a Jesuit, taught psychology at Fordham after 1931, and invented an electric lie-detecting apparatus which was widely used in police and psychiatric work. He died in New York City on Sept. 24.

SUNAMAN, ST. (d. 1040?), martyr. He and SS. Unaman and Winaman, nephews of the English missioner St. Sigfrid, were slain by pagans in Scandinavia. F. D. Feb. 15.

SUNNIVA (10th century?). According to legend which seems to be a variant of St. Ursula's story, she was the daughter of an Irish king, who fled by sea with her brother Alban and a number of women. They were shipwrecked on the island of Selje, off Norway, lived in caves, and when an armed group arrived from the mainland it found that the visitors had been entombed by a landslide. Another version has them killed by the Norse mainlanders.

SUPERIUS, ST. (d. 768?), martyr. *See* Salvius, St.

SURANUS, ST. (d. 580?). St. Gregory the Great records how this abbot of the monastery in Sora, near Caserta, Italy, was slain in anger by Lombard hordes who took him prisoner for his wealth, only to find that what the abbey possessed had been exhausted in the care and feeding of refugees. F. D. Jan. 24.

SURIUS, LAURENTIUS (1522–1578), author. Born in Lubeck, Germany, he studied at Frankfort-im-Oder and Cologne, where he met Peter Canisius, became a convert, and in 1542 a Carthusian. He wrote a history of Church councils, a collection of lives of saints, translated Tauler and Ruysbroeck, completed the *Institutiones* of Florentius of Haarlem, and edited a new edition of Charlemagne's *Homiliarium*. He died on May 23.

SURREY, LORD. *See* Howard, Henry.

SUSANNA, ST. (2nd century). She and a number of other soldiers' wives were said to have been put to death with their children in Galatia. St. Meletius, who commanded the military unit, is listed in the Roman Martyrology as dying with 252 others, long honored on May 24, but the story is suspect as no more than a pious legend.

SUSANNA, ST. (d. 293), martyr. *See* Archelais, St.

SUSANNA, ST. (d. 295), martyr. Called the daughter of a priest, Gabinius, and a niece of Pope St. Caius, she is said to have been chosen by Emperor Diocletian as a bride for his son-in-law, Maximian. She refused, and converted her uncles, Claudius and Maximus, both agents of the emperor. The new Christians were burned alive at Cumae; Susanna and her father were beheaded. The entire story is probably no more than a pious legend. F. D. Aug. 11.

SUSANNA, ST. (d. 362), martyr. Daughter of a pagan priest and his Jewish wife, she became a convert after their death, served as a deaconess at Eleutheropolis, and was put to death during the reign of Julian the Apostate. F. D. Sept. 19.

SUSO, BL. HENRY (1295?–1365), mystic. Born on Mar. 21 near Constance, Switzerland, Henry von Berg (who early adopted his mother's name, Suso) entered the Dominican priory there at thirteen, was professed, and sent to Cologne for higher studies. There he studied under Johann Eckhart from 1314 to 1318; Suso defended his teacher's writings against charges of heresy in his own *Little Book of Truth*. Suso engaged in extreme mortifications for ten years, then at forty began a career as preacher. He worked successfully to reform women's convents, and was a popular and influential speaker in Alsace, Switzerland, and the Low Countries. His mystical life had begun when he was eighteen, when he made himself the "Servant of Eternal Wisdom." His *Book of Eternal Wisdom* became one of the most influential treatises of the mystical life. He suffered many humiliations, was falsely charged with theft, sacrilege, poisoning, heresy, and adultery. He broke down under the succession of distresses, climaxed when his sister ran away from her convent. He was able to bring her back as a penitent and was completely exonerated of all libels. He became prior, probably of Diessenhofen, in 1343, removed his monastery's debt, and in 1348 was sent to the Dominican house in Ulm, Germany, where he died on Jan. 25. He was beatified in 1831. F. D. Mar. 2.

SUTTON, RICHARD (d. 1524). Son of Sir William Sutton of Leicestershire, England, he studied law, was admitted to the Inner Temple, and was a privy councilor in 1498. In 1509 he founded and endowed Brasenose College at Oxford; he also was generous in his donations to various religious and educational institutions, and was knighted by King Henry VIII. He died in Sept. or Oct.

SUTTON, BL. ROBERT (d. 1587), martyr. Born in Burton-on-Trent, England, he studied at Oxford, became Anglican rector at Lutterworth, Leicestershire, in 1571, was converted by his younger brother, William, and fled to Douai with his brother Abraham in 1575. He later taught in London and was hanged at Clerkenwell for having been reconciled with Catholicism. F. D. Oct. 5.

SUZANNI, BL. PHILIP (d. 1306). Born in Piacenza, Italy, he became an Augustinian there and established a reputation for his devotion to prayer. His cult was approved in 1756. F. D. May 24.

SVEINSSON, JON (1857-1944), author. Born in Modruvellir, Iceland, on Nov. 16, he was sent to school in Denmark, became a convert about 1870, became a Jesuit at Amiens, France, in 1878, and went to Belgium when his Society was suppressed by the government. He was ordained in England in 1891, built a leper hospital at Reykjavik, Iceland, and published eight autobiographical books on the character of "Nonni." He also published *Iceland Flowers, Journey through Iceland,* and *The Island of Fire.* He was long stationed in Holland, served French prisoners in Austria during World War I, and was seized and interned in Cologne, Germany, where he died on Nov. 1.

SVERKER (d. 1150), king of Sweden. After a century of battles between Goths and Swedes, who alternated rulers, the two peoples found mutual accord under Sverker, who became king in 1134. Christianity flourished and many sees, including Uppsala (1163), and monasteries were founded.

SWALLOWELL, BL. GEORGE (d. 1594), martyr. Born near Durham, England, he became a Protestant minister and teacher, and was executed at Darlington on July 26 after his conversion. He was beatified in 1929. F. D. July 24.

SWART, CLAUDIUS CLAUSSÖN (b. 1388), cartographer. Born in Salling, Fünen, Denmark, on Sept. 14, he apparently was a priest, went to Rome and was active in the

humanist movement, made detailed studies of Ptolemy, and was the first to make a map of northwestern Europe, including Greenland. He is believed to have visited both Greenland and Iceland. He is also known as Claudius Clavus.

SWEELINCK, JAN PIETERSZOON (1562?-1621), composer. Born in Deventer, Holland, in May, to Pieter and Elsken Sweling Swybertzoom, he lived as a youth in Amsterdam, where his father became organist. He studied under the latter and at Haarlem, became organist at the Old Church, Amsterdam, in 1577, and remained there until his death on Oct. 16. He composed sixty-eight instrumental and 254 vocal pieces of music, and taught many famous organists. Using counterpoint, his compositions (both formal and popularly humorous) were in the madrigal, motet, chanson, and villanella forms; other compositions include dances, toccatas, choral variations, and a *Regina coeli* and *Te Deum.*

SWEENY, JOHN (1821-1901), bishop. Born in Clones, Monaghan, Ireland, he was brought to Canada by his parents in 1828, studied at St. Andrew's and the Quebec seminary, and after ordination was assigned to missionary work. He served in Chatham and Barachois parishes, was vicar general of New Brunswick, and succeeded to the see of St. John, New Brunswick, in 1860. He attended the Vatican Council of 1870, consecrated the cathedral in 1885, and retired in 1901. He died on Mar. 25.

SWETCHINE, SOPHIE JEANNE SOYMANOF (1782-1857), author. Born in Moscow, Russia, on Nov. 22, she married Gen. Swetchine at seventeen and became a member of the court. She became a convert at thirty-three, was forced to leave Russia when her husband was accused of complicity in a court plot, and moved to Paris in 1816 where she opened a salon which became famous. She died in Paris on Sept. 12. Her letters were published posthumously.

SWETHIN, ST. (d. 870), martyr. *See* Theodore, St.

SWEYNHEIM, KONRAD (d. 1477), printer. Born in Schwanheim, Frankfort, Germany, he was ordained, and at the invitation of Cardinal John Turrecremata established a printing press with Arnold Pannartz at the abbey of Subiaco in 1464. They moved their press to the Massimi palace, Rome, in 1467, and published Donatus (1464), works by Cicero, Lactanctius, and other classics and Fathers of the Church. Sweynheim is believed to have been the type founder and compositor, while Pannartz did the printing. The former's dies reveal the first steps toward casting Latin chraracters in modern syle; he also cast the first Greek type. The printing venture was not successful and the partnership was dissolved in 1472. Sweynheim became a canon at St. Victor's, Mainz, was supported by Pope Sixtus IV, and in his last years engraved several maps on copper, notably the *Cosmography* of Ptolemy (1478). He died in Rome.

SWITHBERT, ST. (647–713), bishop. Born in Northumbria, he studied in Ireland under St. Egbert, and in 690 joined the group of eleven Benedictines who set out under St. Willibrord to convert Friesland. After great success he returned to England to seek more missioners and to be consecrated by St. Wilfrid. More converts followed his travels along the Rhine, but he had to retire when the Saxons invaded, and in 710 he founded a monastery at Kaiserswerth, Germany, where he died. F. D. Mar. 1.

SWITHBERT THE YOUNGER, ST. (d. 807), bishop. An English monk, he went on a mission to Germany and was appointed bishop of Werden, Westphalia. F. D. Apr. 30.

SWITHRED. *See* Feologeld.

SWITHUN, ST. (d. 862), bishop. Born in Wessex, England, he studied at Winchester, was ordained, became chaplain to King Egbert of West Saxony, and taught Prince Ethelwulf. As king, the latter made Swithun bishop of Winchester in 852. He died on July 2. He is widely known from the never-explained old saw that, if it rains on his feast day (July 15), it will rain for forty days after.

SYAGRIUS, ST. (d. 600), bishop. A Gallo-Roman by birth, he became bishop of Autun about 560 and directed his French see in a time of great political and ecclesiastical disagreement. St. Augustine and his missioners stayed with him on their way to England. F. D. Aug. 27.

SYAGRIUS, ST. (d. 787?), bishop. A monk at Lérins, France, he became founder and abbot of the Benedictine monastery of St. Pons in Cimiez, Provence. He became bishop of Nice in 777. F. D. May 23.

SYKES, VEN. EDMUND (d. 1587), martyr. Born in Leeds, England, he was ordained at Rheims in 1581, returned to his native Yorkshire in 1582 to labor in the underground missions, and was arrested and banished in 1585. He returned to England in 1586, was betrayed by his brother after six months of missionary work, condemned as a priest, and hanged at York on Mar. 23.

SYLVANUS, ST. (3rd century), martyr. A Syrian bishop, he was sent to the mines as a slave and slain in Palestine sometime before the reign of Maximian. F. D. Nov. 5.

SYLVANUS, ST. (d. 311?), bishop and martyr. The bishop of Emesa, Syria, was thrown with several Phoenician companions to the wild beasts of the arena during the reign of Maximinus. F. D. Feb. 6.

SYLVANUS, ST. (4th century), martyr. *See* Bianor, St.

SYLVANUS, ST. (d. 950?), martyr. *See* Arsenius, St.

SYLVESTER I, ST. (d. 335), pope. Son of a Roman, Rufinus, he succeeded to the papacy on Jan. 31, 314. The Council of Arles was held shortly after, and in 325 the first Ecumenical Council at Nicaea. He was represented at both councils, which condemned Donatism and Arianism respectively. An old, now discredited, tradition says he cured Constantine of leprosy by baptizing him and in return received great concessions and territories (Donation of Constantine). F. D. Dec. 31.

SYLVESTER II (d. 1003), pope. Born in Aurillac, Auvergne, France, Gerbert studied at the monastery there, and at Barcelona, Cordova, and Seville, taught at the Rheims cathedral school, and in 983 received Bobbio abbey from Emperor Otto II, but left it to develop the Rheims school as an outstanding center of learning. He supported Hugh Capet's successful claim to the crown, and in 991 was elected archbishop of Rheims by a synod which had deposed Arnulph, natural son of King Lothair, whom Capet had helped acquire the see. Because of opposition to his reign, Pope John XV sent two legates to examine the matter, and in 995 they declared Arnulph's deposition invalid and Gerbert's election void. Gerbert became teacher to Emperor Otto III, accompanied the emperor to Rome for his coronation, and in 998 was appointed archbishop of Ravenna, Italy. On Feb. 18, 999, he was elected pope (the first Frenchman to be so honored), took the name Sylvester, and was consecrated on Apr. 2. He inaugurated ecclesiastical reforms, especially against simony and concubinage, confirmed Arnulph's archbishopric, established ecclesiastical metropolitans for Poland and Hungary, recognized the ruler of Hungary, St. Stephen, as king, and forced King Robert of France to put aside Bertha for his lawful wife. He invented the pendulum clock, introduced Arabic numbers into western Europe, wrote treatises on mathematical, philosophical, and theological subjects, and was so learned he was regarded as a sorcerer. Forced to flee an uprising in Rome in 1001, he soon returned, and remained there until his death on May 12.

SYLVESTER III (11th century), pope. The Roman John, bishop of Sabina, was elected as Pope Sylvester III by the adversaries of Pope Benedict IX in Feb. 1044. He and his adherents were driven from Rome by Benedict in April, but in 1045 he resumed his claims when Benedict, who had resigned to live privately the dissolute life he had always practiced, attempted to depose Pope Gregory VI. King Henry III ended the conflict by driving out

Sylvester and Benedict, and caused Gregory to resign. The Council of Sutri in 1046 declared all three to be deposed and elected Suidger, bishop of Bamberg, pope as Clement II. Sylvester died on Mar. 3. Although listed as a pope in *Annuario Pontificio*, he is often considered an antipope.

SYLVESTER IV (d. 1111), antipope. When antipope Albert died in 1102, the adherents of Emperor Henry IV, who had fought with Popes Urban II and Paschal II over the question of investitures, selected Maginulf, a Roman, as antipope Sylvester IV on Nov. 18, 1105. Never widely supported, he lost all backing when Henry died in 1106.

SYLVESTER, ST. (d. 525?). He became bishop of Châlons-sur-Saône, Gaul, about 484 and was praised by St. Gregory of Tours. F. D. Nov. 20.

SYLVESTER, BERNARD (12th century), philosopher. Probably a pupil of Thierry of Chartres, he wrote *De mundi universitate* between 1145 and 1153, which has strong Neo-Platonist and Neo-Pythagorean tendencies.

SYLVESTER OF GOZZOLINI, ST. (1177–1267), founder. Born in Osimo, Italy, of the noble Gozzolini family, he studied law at Bologna and Padua and then became a secular priest at Osimo. In 1227 he gave up his benefice, became a hermit, and attracted many disciples. In 1231 he built a monastery in Montefano and founded a new congregation (popularly called the Blue Benedictines), approved in 1247 by Pope Innocent IV, which spread rapidly and which he ruled until his death. He was canonized by Pope Clement VIII in 1598. F. D. Nov. 26.

SYLVIUS, FRANCIS (1581–1649), theologian. Born in Braine-le-Comte, Hainault, Belgium, he studied at Mons, Louvain, and Douai, and received his doctorate in theology in 1610. He taught at Douai in 1613, became director of the seminary, canon of St. Amat's in 1618, dean in 1622, and vice-chancellor of the university. He actively opposed the attempts of the Louvain theologians to inculcate Jansenism in 1648, and wrote a commentary on St. Thomas Aquinas' *Summa* which was favorably compared with Cajetan's. He wrote commentaries on the Bible, against Jansenism, and *Enchiridion theologiae pastoralis*, which became the preferred textbook on theology for French and Belgian seminarians. He died in Douai, France, on Feb. 22.

SYMEON METAPHRASTES (10th century), author. Probably the same as Simeon Magister the Logothete (secretary of state), he was a favorite of Emperor Constantine VII and the outstanding compiler of the legends of saints in the Byzantine Church. His *Menology* (translated into Latin as *Vita ss. priscorum patrum* in 1556–58) has been compared

to Jacobus de Voragine's *Golden Legend*. He was also the author of a chronicle, collections of maxims of SS. Basil and Macarius of Egypt, prayers, poems, and nine letters. He is regarded as a saint in the Orthodox Church and honored on Nov. 28.

SYMMACHUS, ST. (d. 514), pope. A native of Sardinia, the son of Fortunatus, he became archdeacon under Pope Anastasius II, whom he succeeded on Nov. 22, 498. He was immediately faced with an antipope, Laurence, who had been elected by a minority of the clergy of Byzantine leanings and who was supported by Emperor Anastasius of Constantinople. Both claimants appealed to Theodoric, the Gothic king at Ravenna, who ruled that Symmachus had been lawfully elected. However, his pontificate was repeatedly disturbed by this conflict. He aided the victims of barbarian raids and Arian persecutions, helped the poor, and built several new basilicas. F. D. July 19.

SYMPHORIAN, ST. (d. 180?), martyr. A native of Autun, Gaul, and a member of a senatorial family, he was beaten, imprisoned, and beheaded during the reign of Marcus Aurelius because he had scorned a statue of the goddess Cybele. F. D. Aug. 22.

SYMPHORIAN, ST. (d. 305?), martyr. See Castorius, St.

SYMPHOROSA, ST. (d. 135?), martyr. The widow of the martyred St. Getulius was ordered by Emperor Hadrian to sacrifice to the gods; when she refused, she was tortured and thrown into the Anio River. Legend has given her seven sons, supposed to have been slain with her, each in a different manner. While Crescens, Eugenius, Julian, Justin, Nemesius, Primativus, and Stacteus were martyrs, they were not her children, were not related to each other, and died at different times and places. F. D. July 18.

SYMPHOROSA, ST. (d. 285?), martyr. See Ariston, St.

SYMPHRONIUS, ST. (d. 257), martyr. He was a slave who helped to convert the Roman tribune Olympius, his wife Exuperia, and their son Theodulus. They were burned to death in Rome during the persecution of Valerian. F. D. July 26.

SYNCLETICA, ST. (d. 400?), hermit. Daughter of wealthy Macedonian parents living in Alexandria, Egypt, she and her blind sister became recluses after the rest of their family died. She taught many women who came to her refuge for advice and was widely revered for her humility and patience before her death of cancer at the age of eighty-four. F. D. Jan. 5.

SYNESIUS, ST. (d. 275), martyr. A lector at Rome, he was put to death during the reign of Aurelian. F. D. Dec. 12.

SYNTYCHE, ST. (1st century). She was a supporter of Christianity at Philippi, mentioned by St. Paul (Phil. 4:2–3). F. D. July 22.

SYRUS, ST. He is said to have been the first bishop of Pavia, Italy, in the second or third century, but not earlier. F. D. Dec. 9.

SYRUS, ST. (380?). A priest at San Remo, Italy, he became bishop of Genoa about 324 and is now its chief patron. F. D. June 29 (also, July 7).

SZÁNTÓ, STEPHEN (1541–1612). Born in Raab, Hungary, he studied at Vienna and the German College in Rome, became a Jesuit there, and was ordained. He returned to Vienna in 1566, taught successively at Nagy-Szombát, Vienna, and Graz. He was partly successful in establishing the Hungarian College in Rome, was sent to Transylvania as a missioner in 1579, and when the Jesuits were expelled from Transylvania went to Séllye. He wrote a Hungarian catechism, translated the New Testament, and prepared the Hungarian section of Celepino's dictionary. He died in Olmütz, now Czechoslovakia.

SZARZYNSKI, STANISLAS (18th century), composer. Born in Poland, he became a Cistercian monk, composed two concerti, *Jesu spes mea* and *Pariendo non gravaris*, *Mass of the Seven Dolors of Mary*, motets, and sonatas for violin and organ, all between 1692 and 1713.

SZENTIVÁNYI, MARTIN (1633–1708). Born in Szentiván, Hungary, on Oct. 20, he became a Jesuit in 1653, taught at Vienna for five years and mathematics and theology at Nagy-Szombát for sixteen years, and was chancellor of the university for twelve years. He also was governor of the Vienna Pasmaneum and the Nagy-Szombát academy, and wrote theological treatises. He died in Nagy-Szombát (Trnava, Hungary, on Mar. 5.

SZUJSKI, JOSEPH (1835–1883), author. Born in Tarnow, Poland, he studied there and at Cracow and Vienna, founded the *Polish Review* in 1866, became professor of history at Cracow in 1869, and was rector until 1879, when he was made a peer. He became secretary of the Cracow Academy of Sciences, which he helped to established in 1872, and a member of the Austrian house of lords in 1881. He wrote poetry (*The Defence of Czestochowa* and *The Servant of the Tombs*), drama (*Wallas, Hedwige, and George Lubomirski*), a history of Poland, studies on literature, Lucian, and Marcus Aurelius, and translated works by Aeschylus and Aristophanes. He died in Cracow, Poland.

SZYMONOWICZ, SIMON (1558–1629), poet. Born in Lemberg, (now Lwow), Poland, he studied there and in Cracow, France and the Netherlands, and on his return became a private tutor. He was noted as a humanist and for his Latin and Polish poetry, outstanding of which were *Flagellum Livoris* and *Aelinopaean*, and, in Polish, his *Idylls*.

T

TABB, JOHN BANNISTER (1845–1909), poet. Born near Richmond, Virginia, on Mar. 22, he was privately educated, served in the Confederate navy during the Civil War, and was captured and met Sidney Lanier while in prison. At the end of the war he was unsuccessful in a musical career, taught at St. Paul's school in Baltimore, and in 1872 became a convert. He studied for the priesthood in St. Charles' seminary in Baltimore, was ordained in 1884, and taught English at St. Charles' until he became blind shortly before his death. He was widely known for his short, aphoristic lyrics, many in the manner employed by Emily Dickinson; volumes appeared as *Poems* (1894), *Lyrics* (1897), *Child Verse* (1899), and *Later Lyrics* (1902). Some have been published posthumously. He died in Ellicott City, Maryland, on Nov. 19.

TACCI, GIOVANNI (1864–1928), cardinal. Born in Mogliano, Italy, he entered the papal diplomatic service after ordination, and was apostolic delegate to Constantinople in 1904–7 and nuncio to Belgium. He was stationed in the Vatican from 1916 to 1920, when he became a cardinal, titular archbishop of Nicaea, and secretary of the Congregation of the Eastern Church. He died in Rome on June 30.

TACHÉ, ALEXANDRE ANTONIN (1823–1894), archbishop. Born in Fraserville, Quebec, Canada, on July 23, he studied at St. Hyacinthe College and the Montreal seminary, and there joined the Oblates of Mary Immaculate. In 1845 he was sent as a missionary to the Red River region of western Canada, and was ordained in St. Boniface later the same year. In 1850 he was appointed coadjutor of Bishop Provencher, vicar apostolic, of the vicariate of St. Boniface, which comprised the territory west of the Great Lakes and north to the Pole, was consecrated titular bishop of Arath in Marseilles in 1851, and succeeded to the see of St. Boniface (made a diocese in 1847) in 1853. He established missions throughout northwest Canada, was successful in having a new vicariate apostolic, Athabasca-Mackenzie, set up from the northern part of his diocese in 1862, and concentrated his efforts on Assiniboia (now Manitoba). In 1869 he went to Rome to attend the Vatican Council, but was requested to return home by the Canadian government when a revolt led by Louis Riel broke out in western Canada. It was caused by the sale of land to the newly formed dominion of Canada without the consent of the French, who constituted half of the population and who were threatened with being dispossessed from their farms. He was successful in convincing the leaders, with whom he was in complete sympathy, to give up their revolt and gained a partial amnesty in 1874. He became archbishop when his see, St. Boniface, was raised to that stature in 1871, and devoted himself to building up his see. In 1889 the separate school system, which had been guaranteed by the provincial constitution, was abolished and Taché spent the rest of his life fighting for its restoration. He died in St. Boniface, Manitoba, on June 22.

TACHÉ, ÉTIENNE PASCAL (1795–1865), premier. Born in St. Thomas, Quebec, Canada, on Sept. 5, he served in the War of 1812 against the Americans, studied medicine in Philadelphia, became a noted physician in Canada, and after vigorously opposing the union uniting Upper and Lower Canada, was elected to its first legislative assembly in 1841 and again in 1844. He became adjutant general of militia in 1846, chief commissioner of public works in 1848, and served continuously in the cabinet from 1848 to 1856. He was knighted in 1858, appointed aide-de-camp to Queen Victoria in 1860, formed the Taché-MacDonald ministry in 1856 and in 1864, served as speaker, and was president of the convention which led to confederation. He died in St. Thomas on July 29.

TAIGI, BL. ANNA MARIA (1769–1837). Anna Gesualda was born in Siena, Italy, on May 29, moved to Rome, was a domestic and factory worker from the age of thirteen, to aid her impoverished family, and married Domenico Taigi, a servant, in 1790. She lived a pious life, bringing up five children, making clothes for the poor and working with the sick, and received numerous supernatural gifts. Fr. Angelo, a Servite, and Cardinal Pedicini were her spiritual advisers. She was beatified in 1920. F. D. June 9.

TAKACH, BASIL (1879–1948), bishop. Born in Vuckovoje, Hungary, on Oct. 27, he studied at the Greek Catholic seminary at Uzhorod, and was ordained in 1902. He engaged in pastoral activities in the Muncak diocese until 1911, when he became controller of the see's treasury, and was spiritual director of the diocesan seminary in Uzhorod in 1919–24. He was appointed in 1924 titular bishop of Zela and first bishop of the Byzantine rite exarchate of Pittsburgh, where he died on May 13.

TALARICAN, ST. (8th century?), bishop. Probably born in Scotland, he was made bishop of Sodor and the western islands of Scotland in 720 by Pope Gregory II; many churches of the area were dedicated in his honor. Also known as Tarkin, his name appears in Kiltarlity (Inverness-shire), and various St. Tarkin's wells. F. D. Oct. 30.

TALBOT, JAMES (1726–1790), bishop. Brother of the fourteenth earl of Shrewsbury, he studied at Douai, was ordained, and in 1759 was appointed coadjutor to Bishop Challoner. He was arrested in 1769 and 1771 for saying mass in England (the last priest to be so indicted), acquitted in each case for lack of evidence, and in 1781 succeeded Bishop Challoner as vicar apostolic of the London District, a position he retained until his death in Hammersmith. He founded an academy in Hertfordshire which developed into St. Edmund's College.

TALBOT, JOHN (1535?–1607?). Son of Sir John Talbot of Grafton, Worcestershire, England, and father of the ninth earl of Shrewsbury, he became a member of Lincoln's Inn in 1556. From 1580 until his death he was constantly harassed for his Catholicism, imprisoned many times, and subjected to numerous fines for his recusancy. He was arrested in 1605 and accused of complicity in the Gunpowder Plot, but exonerated.

TALBOT, PETER (1620–1680), archbishop. Born in Dublin, he became a Jesuit in Portugal, he was ordained, and taught theology at Antwerp. He served on diplomatic missions for the exiled Charles II of England, who had set up a court in Antwerp and who was received into the Church privately by Talbot. When Charles returned to England, Talbot resigned from the Jesuits, became a member of the court and the queen's almoner, but was forced to return to Europe when accused of a plot to assassinate the duke of Ormond. He was appointed archbishop of Dublin in 1669, held a diocesan synod in 1670, became involved in a controversy with Archbishop Oliver Plunkett of Armagh over the primatial authority, and actively sought to secure relief from the king for Irish Catholics. He was banished from Ireland in 1673 when further persecutions were loosed on the Irish Catholics, and lived in Paris until 1675, when he was allowed to return to England, and in 1677 to Ireland. He was arrested in 1678 on a charge of fomenting rebellion, imprisoned in Dublin castle, and died there two years later, early in Nov. He wrote ecclesiastical treatises, chief of which was the eight-volume *Treatise on the Nature of Catholic Faith and Heresy* (1658).

TALBOT, THOMAS JOSEPH (1727–1795). Brother of Bishop James Talbot, he was born on Feb. 14, studied and was ordained at Douai, did parish work in Brockhampton after 1754, and when the Jesuits were expelled from France became president of St. Omer's College in 1762. In 1766 he became titular bishop of Acon and coadjutor of the Midland District in England, succeeding to that rule in 1778. He worked peacefully for the end of penal laws against Catholics and was in part responsible for the beginning of Oscott College. He died in Hotwells, near Bristol, England, on Apr. 24.

TALIDA, ST. (4th century). She was in charge of a convent at Antinoë, Egypt, in which she lived for eighty years. F. D. Jan. 5.

TALLIS, THOMAS (1505?–1585), composer. Born in England, possibly Leicestershire, he became a chorister at St. Paul's cathedral in London, was appointed organist of Waltham abbey in 1536, and lost this position when the abbey was dissolved in 1540. He became a gentleman in the royal chapel in 1542 and, despite his Catholicism, which he refused to abandon, held the post even during the reigns of Henry VIII, Edward VI, and Elizabeth. He became famed for his musical compositions, and with William Byrd was given the lifelong monopoly for printing music in England in 1575. His *Salve intemerata*, a mass, *Spem in alium non habui*, a forty-part motet, and *Lamentations* are his principal compositions. He died on Nov. 23 in Greenwich, England.

TALON, JEAN BAPTISTE (1625–1691). Born in Châlons-sur-Marne, France, he studied at Clermont College in Paris, took up military administration, was a war commissary in Turenne's army in Flanders in 1654, intendant of Hainaut in 1655, and in 1663 was appointed intendant of Canada. He inaugurated a far-sighted plan for developing Canada (marred by his strife with Bishop Laval over supplying liquor to the Indians), participated in an expedition against the Iroquois in 1666, reorganized the courts and disposition of the settlers, encouraged exploration, agriculture, and commerce, and increased French claims in North America enormously. He returned to France in 1670, was made count d'Orsainville by Louis XIV in 1675, and vigorously supported the Stuarts in their claim to the English throne. He died in Versailles, France, on Nov. 23.

TALON, NICOLAS (1605–1691), historian. Born in Moulins, France, on Aug. 31, he became a Jesuit in 1621, was ordained, and became noted for his preaching, for his missionary work in the prisons and hospitals of Paris, and as chaplain to the French army in Flanders. He wrote biographies of St. Francis de Sales and St. Francis Borgia, the funeral oration of Louis XIII, and the four-volume *Histoire sainte* (1640), a popular but unreliable Bible history. He died in Paris on Mar. 29.

TALON, PIERRE (b. 1676), explorer. Born in Quebec, Canada, of a French family, he went with his parents to Louisiana in 1684, and when the Spaniards occupied the country went to Mexico City, where he became part of the viceroy's retinue. He became a Spanish marine and when his ship was captured enrolled in the French marines. Back in Brest, France, he described the peoples and territory of the southern United States for French authorities, and possibly crossed the Mississippi before La Salle's discovery. He died in France.

TAMBURINI, MICHELANGELO (1648–1730). Born in Modena, Italy, he became a Jesuit at seventeen, taught philosophy and theology, was theologian to Cardinal Renaud d'Este, and became provincial at Venice, secretary and vicar to Thyrsus Gonzalez, Jesuit general, and in 1706 the fourteenth general of his Society. He quieted the discussions over Chinese rites, developed the mission in Paraguay (sending seventy-seven missioners there in a single year), but saw his order harshly treated in France under Louis XIV and the regent. Fr. Tamburini died on Feb. 28.

TAMBURINI, THOMAS (1591–1675), theologian. Born in Caltanisetta, Sicily, on Mar. 6, he became a Jesuit at fifteen, taught and was rector at several Jesuit colleges, and wrote on the mass and the sacraments, *De bulla cruciata*, and *Juris divini exposito*. Though accused of laxity, he wrote a strong defense of the position he took in his treatises on penance and confession. He died in Palermo, Sicily, on Oct. 10. He also wrote *Methodus expeditae confessionis*, *Explicatio decalogi*, and *De sacrificio missae*.

TAMISIER, MARIE MARTHE BAPTISTINE (1834–1910). Born in Tours, France, on Nov. 1, she studied at the Sacred Heart school in Marmoutier, and promoted devotion to the Blessed Sacrament throughout France. With the encouragement and support of Bishop Richard of Belley she began to promote pilgrimages to shrines noted for their Eucharistic miracles, a movement which led to the beginning of International Eucharistic congresses. She died in Tours on June 20.

TAMMARUS, ST. (5th century), bishop. *See* Priscus, St.

TANCO, ST. (d. 808), bishop. Said to be an Irish monk who became attached to the abbey of Amalbarich in Saxony, he succeeded St. Patto as abbot and then as bishop of Werden, Saxony. Legend has it that he was killed while preaching against paganism in Flanders. F. D. Feb. 15.

TANCRED (1072?–1112), prince. Son of Marquess Odo and Emma, daughter of Robert Guiscard, he entered the service of Bohemund on the first crusade (1096), defeated the Greek troops at the Vardar in 1097, and refused to take an oath of loyalty to the Byzantine Emperor Alexis Comnenus until forced to by Bohemund. He captured Tarsus, but was obliged to surrender it to Baldwin, and helped take Antioch in 1098 and Jerusalem in 1099.

He was prince of Galilee, acted as regent of Antioch when Bohemund was a captive of the Turks in 1100–3, took over the government of Edessa when Baldwin II of Jerusalem was captured at Harran in 1104, and became regent of Antioch again when Bohemund returned to Europe in the fall. During the next few years he extended his holdings by conquests in Cilicia and northern Syria, and defied Bohemund's cession of Antioch to Alexius by the Treaty of Durazzo in 1108, but was obliged to restore Edessa to Baldwin when the latter was released. He became prince of Antioch on Bohemund's death in 1110. His adventures, many of them legendary, form the basis of Tasso's *Gerusalemme liberata*. Tancred died in Antioch on Dec. 12.

TANEY, ROGER BROOKE (1777–1865), jurist. Born in Calvert County, Maryland, on Mar. 17, he graduated from Dickinson College, studied law, and was admitted to the bar in 1799. He served in the Maryland general assembly in 1799–1800, was defeated for re-election in 1800 and 1802, and moved to Frederick in 1801. In 1811 he successfully defended Gen. James Wilkinson, commander in chief of the army, against charges of co-conspiracy with Aaron Burr in treason. He lost a bid for the House of Representatives in 1812, served in the Maryland senate in 1816–21, successfully defended Jacob Gruber, a Methodist minister, against charges of inciting slaves to insurrection in 1819, moved to Baltimore in 1823, and became a leader of the bar there and a supporter of Andrew Jackson. He was attorney general of Maryland in 1827–31, attorney general of the United States in 1831–33, and in 1833 was appointed secretary of the treasury by President Jackson. His nomination was rejected by the senate in 1834, the first time a cabinet nomination by the president had been rejected, and he resigned. He was nominated for associate justice of the United States Supreme Court in 1835, but the nomination was held up by the senate; when Chief Justice John Marshall died late that year, he was nominated as his successor. After strong opposition he was confirmed in 1836 as the fifth chief justice of the supreme court and the first Catholic to hold the post. He held the chief justiceship the rest of his life, and during his incumbency upheld states' rights in numerous decisions. His most discussed decision was in the Dred Scott Case (1857) in which he declared that a Negro "had no rights which the white man was bound to respect," that a slave was merely property, and that Congress could not exclude slavery from territories, a ruling which caused great controversy. He died in Washington, D.C., on Oct. 12.

CARL B. SWISHER, *Roger B. Taney* (New York, Macmillan, 1935).

TANGUAY, CYPRIEN (1819–1902), genealogist. Born in Quebec, he studied in the seminary there, was ordained in 1843, and spent the next decade in pastoral work, mainly at Rimouski. He was appointed to the statistics department in 1867 and sent to France to study archives, became an original fellow of the Royal Society of Canada, and compiled the seven-volume *Dictionnaire généalogique des familles canadiennes françaises* (1871–90) and a chronological list of Canadian clergy. He was made a monsignor in 1887.

TANNER, ADAM (1571–1632), theologian. Born in Innsbruck, Tyrol, Austria, he became a Jesuit in 1589, taught Hebrew and theology, and in 1601, with Fr. Gretser, participated on the Catholic side of the religious debate in Ratisbon. He was appointed to the chair of scholastic theology at Ingolstadt in 1603 and became a leading proponent of the Catholic position against Protestant attacks. He was appointed professor at the university of Vienna in 1618, and then chancellor of the university of Prague. Obliged to flee when King Gustavus Adolphus advanced into Austria, he died at Unken, Austria, on May 25. He wrote theological and controversial works, including *Universa theologia scholastica* (1626–27), *Anatomiae confessionis augustanae* (1613), and *Defensionis ecclesiae libertatis* (1607).

TANNER, CONRAD (1752–1825). Born in Arth, Schwyz, Switzerland, on Dec. 28, he studied at Einsiedeln, became a Benedictine in 1772, and was ordained in 1777. He taught in Bellinzona and Einsiedeln, became librarian of his abbey in 1787, and was forced to flee to Tyrol when the revolution broke out. After years of pastoral work he was called back to Einsiedeln, Switzerland, was master of novices, abbot in 1808, and died there on Apr. 7. He wrote the five-volume *Betrachtungen zur sittlichen* (1804–8), and *Bildung des Geistlichen* (1807).

TANNER, EDMUND (1526?–1579), bishop. Born probably in Calverstown, Kildare, Ireland, he was in Rome and probably a priest in 1565, became a Jesuit, taught at the Roman College, and in 1567 went to Dillingen, where he received his doctorate in divinity. He left the Jesuits because of ill-health, was appointed bishop of Cork and Cloyne in 1574, returned to Ireland in 1575, was imprisoned, but soon released, and spent the rest of his life traveling about Ireland as commissary-apostolic. He died in Ossory, Ireland, on June 4, although another report claims that he died of torture in Dublin castle.

TANNER, MATTHIAS (1630–1692). Born in Pilsen, Bohemia, on Feb. 28, he became a Jesuit in 1646, taught at Prague, and was provincial of the Bohemian province for six years. He wrote two books on Jesuit martyrs and heroes and an explanation of the mass before his death in Prague, Bohemia, on Feb. 8.

TAPARELLI, BL. AIMO (1395-1495). Born in Savigliano, Piedmont, Italy, he married, and later joined the Dominicans and taught at Turin. He was an effective preacher and became chaplain to Bl. Amadeus, duke of Savoy. In 1466 he was appointed an official of the Inquisition, to replace one who had been murdered at Cevere; later he was inquisitor general in Upper Lombardy and Liguria, where he served for thirty years. He died on Aug. 15 and his cult was confirmed in 1856. F. D. Aug. 18.

TAPARELLI D'AZEGLIO, PROSPERO ALOYSIUS (1793-1862), philosopher. Born in Turin, Italy, on Nov. 24, son of the Sardinian ambassador to the Papal States about 1815, he studied in Senis, Turin, and Paris, and in 1814 became a Jesuit. He was appointed first rector of the Roman College on its restoration to the Jesuits by Leo XII in 1824, taught philosophy at Palermo for sixteen years, and was on the editorial staff of *Civiltá Cattolica* for many years. He wrote numerous treatises, chief of which were *Saggio teoretico di diretto naturale appogiato sul fatto*, propounding the theory that civil governments originated from the authority granted them by the heads of family groups; an abridgment of this work, which was extremely popular, *Elementary Course in Natural Right*; and *Esame critico deggli ordini rappresentativi nella societá moderna*. He also invented a musical instrument he called the violicembolo which Liszt praised and called the symphonium. He died in Rome on Sept. 20.

TARABOTTI, HELENA (1605-1652), author. A native of Venice, Italy, she was placed in the convent of Santa Ana when eleven and spent her life there. She wrote treatises on the spiritual life which attracted attention, among them *La luce monacale* and *Paradiso monacale*.

TARACHUS, ST. (239?-304), martyr. Born in Claudiopolis, Isauria, and also called Tharacus, he was a retired officer of the Roman army when he was arrested in Cilicia with SS. Probus, a Roman citizen, and Andronicus, a young plebeian, during the persecution of Diocletian and Maximian. They were questioned and tortured three times in Tarsus, Mopsuestia, and Anazarbus. On their refusal to sacrifice to the pagan gods they were beheaded. F. D. Oct. 11.

TARASIUS, ST. (d. 806), patriarch. A layman who was serving as secretary in the imperial court, he was chosen patriarch of Constantinople against his wishes in 784. Following the decisions of the seventh Ecumenical Council at Nicaea, he was able to restore icons in the churches of the East, to reduce simony, and follow a personally ascetic life. When Constantine VI set aside his wife to marry a palace servant, Tarasius opposed him, though St. Theodore Studites and others claimed that the mere refusal to approve bigamy was too mild. Tarasius suffered from royal hostility, but two reigns later was able to live in peace. He is also known as Tharasius. F. D. Feb. 25.

TARBULA, ST. (d. 345), martyr. Sister of Bishop Simeon, who also was martyred by King Sapor II of Persia, she was accused of witchcraft and sawed to death on May 5. F. D. Apr. 22.

TARDINI, DOMENICO (1888-1961), cardinal. Born in Rome on Feb. 29, he studied at the Pontifical seminary there, was ordained in 1912, taught theology at the Pontifical Lateran Athenerm, and in 1920 became a member of the curia. He became undersecretary of the Congregation for Extraordinary Ecclesiastical Affairs in 1929 and secretary in 1937, declined the offer of a cardinalate from Pope Pius XII in 1953, and was appointed archbishop of Milan. In 1958 he was named secretary of state and created cardinal by Pope John XXIII, with whom he had worked closely on diplomatic matters for years. He died in Rome on July 30.

TARISEL, PIERRE (1442?-1510). He became famed as a master mason, was brought to Noyon in 1475 to save the crumbling cathedral, to Arras in 1477 to do work for the king, and in 1483 was appointed master mason of Amiens. Between 1497 and 1503 he saved the cathedral from collapse by rebuilding portions of it and an ingenious use of iron bands to brace it. He probably died in Amiens, France, in Aug.

TARKIN. *See* Talarican, St.

TARQUINI, CAMILLUS (1810-1874), cardinal. Born in Marta, Italy, on Sept. 27, he became a Jesuit in 1837, taught canon law at the Roman College, and published *Juris ecclesiastici publici institutiones* (1862). He also became a leading authority on Etruscan antiquities and wrote an Etruscan grammar and dictionary. He was elected president of the historical section of the Accademia de' Quiriti, and in 1873 was created a cardinal by Pope Pius IX. He died in Rome on Feb. 15.

TARSICIA, ST. (d. 600?). Sister of St. Ferreol and granddaughter of King Clotaire II, she became a recluse near Rodez, France. F. D. Jan. 15

TARSICIUS, ST. (d. 255?), martyr. While carrying the Holy Eucharist, he was beset by a mob on the Appian Way in Rome and stoned to death. Pope Damasus wrote a poem about the incident; Cardinal Nicholas Wiseman elaborated it in his novel, *Fabiola*. F. D. Aug. 15.

TARSILLA, ST. (d. 550?). Paternal aunt of St. Gregory the Great, she lived a life of great holiness with her sister Emiliana. Both experienced visions which were reported by St.

Gregory in his *Dialogues*. Emiliana died a few days after Tarsilla (sometimes spelled Tharsilla) on Jan. 5. F. D. Dec. 24.

TARTAGLIA, NICOLÒ (1500?–1557), mathematician. Born in Brescia, Italy, Nicolò Fontana was orphaned when six, was given the nickname Tartaglia ("the Stammerer") when a soldier's blow in 1512 caused him to stammer, assumed that name, taught himself as a practical engineer, and in 1521 began teaching in Verona. He went to Venice in 1534, proved the soundness of his methods by defeating Antonio del Fiore in a mathematical contest in 1535, and achieved fame solving the cubic equation in 1541. He became embroiled in a bitter controversy with Cardau when the latter inserted Tartaglia's solution of cubic equations in his *Ars magna* (1545). He taught at Brescia in 1548, but returned to Venice after a year and a half, and remained there until his death on Dec. 13. He pioneered in the application of mathematics to artillery by studying projectile curves, and also studied fortifications and methods for raising sunken ships. He wrote numerous mathematical treatises, and made the first Italian translation of Euclid.

TARTINI, GIUSEPPE (1692–1770), composer. Born in Pirano, Italy, on Apr. 12, he studied law at Padua, became interested in music and the violin, was forced to flee to Assisi when accused of abducting a relative of Cardinal Cornaro whom he had secretly married, and there studied under Pedro Boemo. He returned to Padua later, became solo violinist and orchestra conductor at the cathedral there in 1721, a position he held, except for two years in Count Kinsky's service in Prague, the rest of his life. He established one of the most famous violin schools in Padua in 1728 (some of his pupils were Bini, Nardini, Pasqualino, Pugnani, and Viotti), wrote a great number of violin compositions and a *Miserere*, and made the combination tone (or third tone) the basis of a new system of harmony which he described in *Trattato di musica* in 1754. He died in Padua, Italy, on Feb. 16.

TASCHEREAU, ELZÉAR ALEXANDRE (1820–1898), cardinal. Born in St. Marie de la Beauce, Quebec, Canada, on Feb. 17, he graduated from the Quebec seminary in 1836, studied in Rome, and was ordained on his return in 1842. He became a professor at the seminary in Quebec, a member of its council, helped found Laval University in 1852, went to the French seminary in Rome in 1854, and received his doctorate in canon law in 1856. He was superior of the seminary from 1860 to 1866, served as Archbishop Baillargeon's theologian at the Vatican Council, and in 1871 was appointed archbishop of Quebec. He increased the number of religious and institutions in his archdioceses, founded the Sacred Heart Hospi-

tal, and in 1886 was created the first Canadian cardinal. He died in Quebec on Apr. 12.

TASCHEREAU, HENRI ELZÉAR (1836–1909), jurist. Born in Ste. Marie de la Beauce, Quebec, Canada, on Oct. 7, he studied in the Quebec seminary, was called to the bar in 1857, and practiced in Quebec. He served in the assembly in 1861–67, was named judge of the provincial superior court in 1871, of the supreme court of Canada in 1878–1902, and was chief justice from 1902 until 1906, when he retired. He was knighted in 1902, was appointed to the imperial privy council in 1904, and published widely on civil procedure and Canadian criminal law. He died in Montreal on Oct. 12.

TASSACH, ST. (d. 470?), bishop. A disciple of St. Patrick, he became abbot-bishop of the monastery in Elphin, Roscommon, Ireland, of which location he is now venerated as patron. He is also known as Asicus. F. D. Apr. 27.

TASSACH, ST. (d. 495?), bishop. A disciple of St. Patrick, to whom he gave the last sacraments, he was the first to be raised to the see of Raholp, Down, Ireland. He is also known as Asicus. F. D. Apr. 14.

TASSÉ, JOSEPH (1848–1895), author. Born in Montreal, Canada, on Oct. 23, he studied at Bourget College, became editor of the periodical *Le Canada* in Ottawa when nineteen, of Montreal's *La Minerve* from 1869 to 1872, was elected to the house of commons in 1878 and 1882, and was appointed to the senate in 1891. He wrote several books, chief of which was *Les Canadiens de l'ouest* (1878), and died on Jan. 17.

TASSILO, BL. (8th century). Duke of Bavaria and founder of many Benedictine abbeys, he later joined the order at Jumièges, France, and died in Lorsch, Hesse, after 794. F. D. Dec. 13.

TASSIN, RENÉ PROSPER (1697–1777), historian. Born in Lonlay, France, he joined the Benedictines at Jumièges in 1718, and collaborated with Dom Toustain on an edition of Theodore the Studite's works. When a dispute broke out between the chapters of St. Ouen and Rouen, they undertook a historical defense, the six-volume *Nouveau traité de diplomatique* (1750–65), which Tassin finished when Toustain died while writing the second volume. Tassin also wrote *Histoire littéraire de la congregation de Saint-Maur* (1770). He died in Paris.

TASSO, TORQUATO (1544–1595), poet. Born on Mar. 11 in Sorrento, Italy, of a noble family and son of a poet, he was educated at the court of the dukes of Urbino, Venice, and Padua, became interested in poetry, and wrote *Rinaldo* when twenty. He joined the household of Cardinal Luigi d'Este, whom he accompanied to France in 1570, where he met Ronsard and other poets, and on his return entered the service of Duke Alphonso II of Ferrara, brother of the cardinal, and in 1574 taught at Padua. About 1575 he entered a tragic period of his life, believed by some to have been caused by a hopeless love for the duke's sister, Leonora, by others because of religious scruples caused by his earlier lax way of living. Whatever the cause, he fell into the duke's disfavor, and was twice committed to an insane asylum, the second time from 1579 to 1586. On his release he went from one court to another, finally settling at Sant' Onofrio convent in Rome, under the protection of Pope Clement VIII, where he died in Apr. He wrote lyrics, dialogues, a pastoral verse drama, *Aminta* (1573), and his greatest poem, *Gerusalemme liberate* (1575), an epical treatment of the third crusade; other long poems were *Il Torrismondo* (1587) and *Gerusalemme conquistata* (1593), a revision of the earlier epic. *Jerusalem Delivered* is narrated by the crusader Gillaume de Tyre; there are four chief love stories, reflections on the power and dignity, as well as the weakness, of man, and strong religious fervor.

TASSONI, ALESSANDRO (1565–1635), poet. Born in Modena, Italy, he became secretary to Cardinal Ascanio Colonna in Rome, and spent most of his life in the service of various Italian princes, principally Charles Emmanuel I of Savoy and Francisco I of Modena. He became known for his criticism (his *Considerations on Petrarch*, published in 1609 caused great controversy because of its severity toward Petrarch) and poetry, chief of which was the mock-heroic poem, *Secchia rapita* (*The Rape of the Bucket*, 1622), which ridiculed the Italian civil wars between neighboring cities. He also wrote *Pensieri diversi* (1612). He died in Modena.

TATIAN, ST. (d. 284?), martyr. He was deacon to St. Hilary, bishop of Aquileid, Italy, and was slain there with him during the reign of Numerian. F. D. Mar. 16.

TATIAN, ST. (d. 362), martyr. *See* Macedonius, St.

TATIANA, ST. (d. 230?), martyr. Listed in the Roman Martyrology as put to death in Rome during the persecution of Alexander Severus, she is honored in the Greek Church with two other martyrs, Euthasia and Mertios. F. D. Jan. 12.

TATIANUS DULAS, ST. (d. 310?), martyr. He was tortured and put to death at Zephyrium, Cilicia, after refusing to sacrifice to Apollo. F. D. June 15.

TATION, ST. (d. 304?), martyr. He was beheaded at Claudiopolis, Bithynia, during the Diocletian persecution. F. D. Aug. 24.

TATTI, JACOPO. *See* Sansovino, Jacopo.

TATWIN, ST. (d. 734), bishop. A Benedictine monk in Worcestershire, England, he suc-

ceeded St. Brithwald in 731 as bishop of Canterbury. F. D. July 30.

TAULER, JOHANN (1300?–1361), mystic. Born in Strassburg, Alsace, he became a Dominican, in 1315, studied in Strassburg and Cologne, where he became a disciple of Meister Eckhart and probably met Henry Suso, and after a period at St. James' college in Paris returned to Strassburg. He went to Basle in 1338, when Strassburg was put under an interdict, and there became a member of the Friends of God, a popular mystic movement devoted to spreading Eckhart's teaching. He returned to Strassburg about 1347, achieved great popularity by his aid to the sick during the Black Plague of 1348, and became noted for his sermons of great intellectual appeal toward strengthening the spiritual life (eighty-four were collected and published in 1498; some sixty-seven more were added in later editions, but his authorship of many of these is suspect). He died in Strassburg on June 16.

TAUNTON, ETHELRED (1857–1907), author. Born in Rugeley, Staffordshire, England, on Oct. 17, he studied at Downside, joined the Congregation of the Oblates, and was ordained in 1883. He left the Oblates in 1886, engaged in pastoral work, was partially paralyzed by a fall, spent some time in Bruges where he founded *St. Luke's Magazine*, and died in London on May 9. He wrote histories of the Jesuits and Benedictines in England, biographies, and *History of Church Music*.

TAURINUS, ST. (d. 412?). He was bishop of Évreux, Normandy. F. D. Aug. 11.

TAVANTI, JACOPO (d. 1607). An Italian Servite, he wrote *Ager dominicus*, a biblical commentary in twenty-five volumes.

TAVELLI, ST. GIOVANNI (d. 1446), bishop. Born in Tossignano, near Imola, Italy, he studied at Bologna, then joined a lay nursing congregation, the Jesuats. He wrote a biography of the founder, several devotional treatises, and translated spiritual works, including parts of the Bible, into Italian. He was chosen bishop of Ferrara in 1431 and in 1438 assisted Pope Eugene IV at the Council of Ferrara, convoked to effect a union of the Latin and Byzantine churches. His cult was approved in 1748 by Pope Benedict XIV. F. D. July 24.

TAVERA, JUAN (d. 1545), cardinal. Born in Spain, he served at court, founded the general hospital of San Juan Bautista, outside Toledo, was made archbishop of that see from 1534, and was created a cardinal.

TAVERNER, JOHN (1475?–1536?), composer. Born in Norfolk, England, he was organist at the church in Boston in 1500–25, and was appointed choirmaster at Cardinal College, Oxford, by Wolsey, where he remained until 1530. He composed eight masses (including the *Western Wynde Mass*), magnificats, and motets; sacred music includes *Gaude Maria Virgo, Mater Christi*; other hymns are *In Trouble and Adversity* and *O Give Thanks*. He died in Boston, England. He sometimes is confused with a John Taverner who was an agent of Thomas Cromwell.

TAVIGLI, NICHOLAS. *See* Tavilic, Bl. Nicholas.

TAVILIC, BL. NICHOLAS (d. 1391), martyr. Born in Sibenik, Dalmatia, he became a Friar Minor at Rivotorto, Italy, and worked on the Franciscan missions for twenty years, especially among the Paterines in Bosnia, and then in Palestine, where he was hacked to death by Mohammedans. His cult was confirmed in 1888 by Pope Leo XIII. F. D. Dec. 5. His name is sometimes spelled Tavigli.

TAXTER, JOHN DE (d. 1265?), historian. Professed a Benedictine at Bury St. Edmund's, England, about 1244, he wrote a chronicle from creation to 1263, valuable for contemporary information.

TAYLOR, FRANCES MARGARET (1832–1900), foundress. Daughter of a Lincolnshire, England, minister, she was born on Jan. 20, engaged in charitable work in her father's parish, was one of Florence Nightingale's nurses in the Crimean War in 1854, and became a convert. On her return to London, she founded the Poor Servants of the Mother of God, in 1808 and became superior general of the congregation, as Mother Mary Magdalen, a position she held until her death in London on June 9; the congregation was approved by Pope Leo XIII in 1885. She was also editor of *The Lamp* for a time, helped in the founding of *The Month* and *The Messenger of the Sacred Heart*, and wrote biographies and spiritual works.

TAYLOR, VEN. HUGH (d. 1585), martyr. Born in Durham, England, he went to Rheims in 1582, was ordained there in 1585, and sent on the English mission. He was the first to be executed under the 1585 law of Elizabeth I outlawing priests. He was hanged, drawn, and quartered at York on Nov. 25. Marmaduke Bowes of Angram Grange, near Cleveland, was executed on Nov. 26 for having harbored him.

TAYLOR, VINCENT GEORGE (1877–1959). Born in Norfolk, Virginia, on Sept. 19, he studied at Belmont abbey, North Carolina, became a Benedictine in 1897, and was ordained in 1902. He did parish and missionary work in North Carolina, was elected abbot-ordinary of Belmont abbey in 1924, and died on Nov. 5.

TEBALDEO, ANTONIO (1463–1537), poet. Born in Ferrara, Italy, Antonio Tebaldi was a tutor to Isabella d'Este and a member of the court of Pope Leo X. He changed his name when he entered the life of the academies, and

wrote artificial and highly figurative Italian pastorals and lyrics, Latin epigrams and poems, and a redaction of Poliziano's play, *Orfeo*. He died in Rome.

TEDESCHINI, FEDERICO (1873–1959), cardinal. Born in Antrodoco, Italy, on Oct. 12, he studied at the Pontifical seminary, was ordained in 1896, and became a clerk in the papal secretariat of state. He was appointed chancellor of apostolic briefs by Pope St. Pius X in 1907, was substitute secretary of state from 1914 until 1921 when he was appointed apostolic nuncio to Madrid and titular archbishop of Lepanto. He served in this capacity until 1935, when he was created a cardinal. He became archpriest of St. Peter's basilica, cardinal datary in charge of papal bulls, papal legate to the Marian Congress in Peru in 1954, and died in Rome on Nov. 2.

TEGWIN. *See* Tudy, St.

TEILHARD DE CHARDIN, PIERRE (1881–1955), paleontologist. Born in Clermont-Ferrand, France, he studied at a school near Lyons, became a Jesuit in 1899, was ordained in 1912, served in World War I and was decorated for gallantry, and took his doctorate at the Sorbonne. He did research in geology and paleontology in China from 1923 to 1945, was a discoverer of the fossilized "Peking man," and later became an associate with an anthropological research foundation in New York City. He developed a controversial theory of evolution reconciling science and religion and propounded his ideas in a number of works, chief of which are *The Phenomenon of Man* (1959) and *The Divine Milieu* (1960). He died in New York City on Apr. 10.

TEILO, ST. (6th century), bishop. Born near Penally, Pembrokeshire, Wales, he studied under St. Dubricius, met St. David, and when the yellow plague began ravaging Wales in 547 went to Brittany. On his return he settled at the monastery of Llandeilo Fawr, Wales. F. D. Feb. 9.

TEIXERA, PEDRO (d. 1640), explorer. Born in Portugal, he went to Brazil, and commanded the expedition which explored the Amazon River in 1637–38. He discovered the Rio Negro, claimed the Napo River for Portugal, and pushed through the upper reaches of the Amazon to Quito, Ecuador. An account of his travels was published by the Jesuit, Cristóbal de Acuña, who made the return trip to Brazil with him.

TELEMACHUS. *See* Almachius, St.

TELESIO, BERNARDINO (1509–1588), philosopher. Born in Cosenza, near Naples, Italy, he studied at Milan, Rome, and Padua, was patronized by Pope Paul IV in Rome, and founded the Academia Cosentina at Cosenza when he returned. He became the leader of the anti-Aristoteleans and criticized the Aristoteleans for relying too heavily on reason and not enough on the senses. He died in Cosenza.

TELESPHORUS, ST. (d. 136?), pope and martyr. A Greek, he began his pontificate in 125 and was put to death during the persecution of Hadrian. F. D. Jan. 5.

TÉLLEZ, GABRIEL (1571–1648), dramatist. Born in Madrid he studied at Alcalá de Henares, became a Mercedarian in 1601, was ordained before 1610, became superior at Trujillo in 1619, and in 1624 published *Los cigarreles de Toledo*, a collection of poems, plays, and stories in the fashion of Boccaccio's *Decameron*, and under the name Tirso de Molina. He wrote more than 300 plays, chief of which is *El burlador de Sevilla y convidado de piedra* (1630), which introduced the character of Don Juan to literature. Other plays, religious, historical, folk, psychological, include: *La prudemcia en la mujer, El condenado por desconfiado, Marta la piadosa, Los amantes de Teruel,* and *El vergozoso en palacio*. He stopped writing about 1625 after being censured by the Council of Castile for his overrealistic presentation of vice, became historiographer of his order in 1637, and prior of Soria, Aragón, in 1645, and died there on Mar. 21.

TELLO (d. 773). Appointed bishop of Chur, Switzerland, in 758, he began its romanesque cathedral, decorated by Dürer and Holbein paintings at a later date.

TEMPEL, WILHELM (1821–1889), astronomer. Born in Cunnersdorf, Saxony, Germany, on Dec. 4, he studied lithography, went to Copenhagen where he became interested in literature, and in about 1850 settled in Venice, where he practiced lithography. There he married and became a convert, took up astronomy, though he had no scientific training, and in 1859 discovered a comet and a nebula. He was unsuccessful in an attempt to enter the imperial observatory in Paris because of Leverrier's opposition, moved to Marseilles in 1860 as assistant astronomer to Benjamin Valz, but was forced to abandon this position after a few months, and resumed his trade of lithography. He continued his astronomical observations during the next ten years, discovered numerous comets and planets, obtained a position in the Milan observatory in 1871, and in 1874 became director of the Arcetri observatory near Florence, where his work on nebulae attracted international attention. He died in Arcetri, Italy, on Mar. 16.

TENCIN, PIERRE GUERIN DE (1680–1758), cardinal. Born in Grenoble, France, on Aug. 22, he studied at Grenoble and the Sorbonne, became prior there in 1702, and received his doctorate in 1705. He became vicar general of Sens, was Cardinal de Rohan's conclavist in Rome in 1721, remained there as French chargé d'affaires, and in 1724 was appointed archbishop of Embrun. He was an active opponent of Jansenism, was created cardinal in 1739, acted as French ambassador to Rome, was appointed archbishop of Lyons in 1740, and resigned his ambassadorship to occupy his see in 1742. He was appointed Louis XV's minister of state later the same year, retired to Lyons, France, in 1752, and died there on Mar. 2.

TENENAN, ST. (d. 635?), bishop. A Briton, he crossed to Brittany, where he was a hermit before his elevation to the see of León, Spain. F. D. July 16.

TENIERS, DAVID, THE ELDER (1582–1649), painter. Born in Antwerp, Flanders, son of a mercer, he studied painting under Rubens and with Elsheimer in Italy, and returned to Antwerp in 1606, where he became noted for his landscapes, rural scenes of peasants at work and at play, and historical paintings. Among his most famous works are *Dutch Kitchen, Peasants Carousing in Front of a Tavern, Playing at Bowls,* and *Temptation of St. Anthony*. He died in Antwerp.

TENIERS, DAVID (1610–1690), painter. Born in Antwerp, Flanders, on Dec. 15 and called "the Younger," he studied with his father, and possibly under Rubens or Brouwer, and achieved a perfection of style and mastery of technique which stamped him a master of genre painting. He became a member of the painters' guild in Antwerp, a master in 1633, married Anna, daughter of Jan Breughel, in 1637, and was patronized by Archduke William, for whom he was court painter and bought additions to his art collection, and by Don Juan of Austria. About 1643 he bought Dry Toren near Brussels and lived the life of a manor lord, became head of the Antwerp painters' guild in 1645, and founded the Academy at Brussels in 1663. He is famous for his beautifully colored scenes of peasant life, of which he painted some 800. Among his outstanding works are *Prodigal Son, Merry Repast, The Smokers, Marriage Festival, Village Festival, The Artist and His Family, Flemish Tap-Room,* and *Peasants' Dance*. He died in Brussels.

TENNEY, SARAH BROWNSON (1839–1876), author. Born in Chelsea, Massachusetts, daughter of Orestes Brownson, she wrote literary criticism for her father's *Review;* three novels, *Marian Elwood* (1863), *At Anchor,* and *Heremore Brandon;* and a life of Prince Demetrius Gallitzen (1873). She married William J. Tenney in 1873, and died in Elizabeth, New Jersey, on Oct. 30.

TENNEY, WILLIAM JEWETT (1814–1883), editor. Born in Newport, Rhode Island, he graduated from Yale in 1832, studied medicine, but abandoned it for law and was admitted to the bar. The date of his conversion is unknown. He worked on the *Journal of*

Commerce (1841–43), wrote editorials for the *Evening Post* (1847–48), and became an editor for D. Appleton & Co. in 1853, a position he held until his death. In 1861 he began editing *Appleton's Annual Cyclopaedia*, was collector of the port of Elizabeth, New Jersey, during President Buchanan's administration, and married Orestes Brownson's daughter in 1873. He wrote a military history of the Civil War and collaborated on Jefferson Davis' *Rise and Fall of the Confederate Government*. He died in Newark, New Jersey, on Sept. 20.

TENORIO, PEDRO (d. 1399), archbishop. Born in Spain, he was ordained, was an influential figure in the courts of Henry II, John I, and Henry III, became archbishop of Toledo in 1376, restored many public buildings at his own expense, and founded Villafranca del Puente, a hospital.

TERENCE, ST. (1st century), bishop and marytr. Listed as bishop of Iconium (Galatia?), he and the Tertius mentioned by St. Paul (Rom. 16:22) may have been the same person. F. D. June 21.

TERENCE, ST. (d. 250), martyr. *See* Africanus, St.

TERENTIAN, ST. (d. 118), martyr. Bishop of Todi, Italy, he was tortured and beheaded during the reign of Hadrian. F. D. Sept. 1.

TERESA, ST. (d. 1250). Eldest of three daughters of King Sancho I of Portugal, she married her cousin Alfonso IX, king of León, had several children, and then was separated from him when the marriage was declared invalid by the papacy. She made a Cistercian convent of the lax Benedictine monastery on her estate near Coimbra and built up the property to care for 300 nuns. She traveled as an extern and even aided Alfonso's second wife, Berengaria, in establishing peace and arranging the succession to the throne of León for their respective children. Her cult was approved in 1705 by Pope Clement XI. F. D. June 17.

TERESA OF AVILA, ST. (1515–1582), foundress. Born in Avila, Castile, Spain, on Mar. 28, one of nine children of her father's second wife, Teresa de Cepeda y Ahumada, she was early attracted to the religious life. Early in 1531 she was sent to the Augustinian convent at Avila as a student, but was forced to leave late the following year because of illness. Despite her father's initial opposition, she decided to become a nun and became a Carmelite at Avila in 1536 and was professed in 1537. The following year she again became ill and left the convent, returning in 1540, and did not regain her health again until 1541. During 1555–56 she began to experience visions and hear voices and went through a period tormented by the fear they were inspired by the devil. After several years of spiritual desolation and direction by unsatisfactory spiritual advisers, she met St.

Peter of Alcántara in 1557, who declared her supernatural experiences were of divine origin. In 1562 she founded the monastery of St. Joseph of Avila, in the face of bitter opposition, to provide a convent for nuns wishing to lead a more spiritual life than that possible under the lax regard for the rule so prevalent at the time. Strict enclosure, silence, austerity, coarse clothing, sandals (hence the name of "discalced"—unshod), and perpetual abstinence were the features of this first monastery of the Discalced Carmelites. For the next five years she remained at St. Joseph's, but in 1567, after a visit from Fr. P. Rubeo (Rossi), prior general of the Carmelites, during which he approved St. Joseph's and gave her permission to establish other convents with the same rule, she founded a second convent at Medino del Campo (eventually she set up fifteen others). There she met a young friar who wished to follow her reform, John Yepes (St. John of the Cross), and in 1568 and 1569 founded her first monastery for men at Duruelo; thereafter, she left to St. John the task of establishing men's monasteries while she traveled tirelessly from one end of Spain to the other, founding convents and preaching her reforms. By now the word of what she was doing had swept Europe and again great opposition to her reforms arose, culminating in a general chapter of the Carmelites at Piacenza in 1575, at which Fr. Rubeo agreed to severe restrictions on the reforming group. Five years of constant strife followed, which rent the Carmelites. The reformed group was constantly harassed and persecuted (St. John of the Cross was actually imprisoned and fifty nuns of the Incarnation convent in Avila were excommunicated) until finally, in 1580, as the result of the intercession of King Philip II, Pope Gregory XIII issued a bull recognizing the Discalced Reform as a separate province, which became operative at the chapter of Alcalá, with Fr. P. Gracián as provincial of the Discalceds. Two years later, on Oct. 4 (Oct. 15 by the new Gregorian calendar), she died in Alba de Tormes, where she is buried. St. Teresa was a practical, hardheaded woman who never hesitated to criticize those in authority when she knew they were in the wrong. She also was possessed both of great idealism and a sense of humor. Few have so united the contemplative and the active life. She was one of the greatest mystics, experiencing the whole range of supernatural experiences, which, by order of her confessors, she duly recorded. Her *Autobiography* (1565), *Exclamations of the Soul to God* (1569), *Way of Perfection* (1573), and *Interior Castle* (1577) are among the great spiritual classics. She was canonized in 1622 by Pope Gregory XV. F. D. Oct. 12.

Complete Works of St. Teresa, ed. and trans. by E. Allison Peers (London, Sheed, 1944);

MARCELLE AUCLAIR, *Teresa of Avila* (Garden City, N.Y., Image Books, 1959).

TERILL, ANTHONY (1623–1676), theologian. Anthony Bonville was born in Canford, Dorsetshire, England, became a convert at fifteen, and went to the English College at St. Omer, taking the name Terill. He continued his studies at the English College in Rome, was ordained in 1647, and became a Jesuit that year. He became penitentiary at Loreto, professor of philosophy at Florence, then at Parma, and finally at the English College in Liège, Belgium, where he served as rector for three years and where he died on Oct. 11. He wrote theological studies.

TERNAN, ST. (5th century?), bishop. Said to have been a native of Scotland, consecrated by Palladius in 432, he may have been a missioner to the Picts; other fragmentary information dates him a century later, and calls him a monk at the abbey of Culross. F. D. June 12.

TERNATIUS, ST. (d. 680?). He was eleventh bishop of Besançon, France. F. D. Aug. 8.

TERRASSON, ANDRÉ (1669–1723). Born in Lyons, France, he joined the Oratorians, became noted as a speaker, and preached the Lenten sermons of 1717 before Louis XIV at the court of Lorraine and at Notre Dame in Paris, where he died on Apr. 25. He was accused of Jansenist tendencies. His lectures were collected and published in 1726.

TERRASSON, GASPARD (1680–1752). Brother of André, he was born in Lyons, France, in Oct., joined the Oratorians, delivered the funeral oration of Louis XIV's son and preached the Lenten sermons at Notre Dame in Paris. He was an ardent Jansenist, vigorously opposed the bull *Unigenitus*, anonymously published *Lettres sur la justice chrétienne*, condemned by the Paris theology faculty in 1734, and was obliged to leave the Oratorians. He moved to Auxerre, where in 1735 he was arrested for his Jansenist activities and imprisoned for eight years. He published a retraction (questioned by some authorities), and died in Paris on Jan. 2.

TERREBOTTI, SANTUCCIA (d. 1305). Born in Gubbio, Italy, she decided with her husband to enter religious life after the death of their young daughter. She became abbess of a Benedictine community which moved to Rome and took the name of Servants of Mary. Her cult was never formally approved, although she was venerated locally on Mar. 21.

TERRIEN, JEAN BAPTISTE (1832–1902), theologian. Born in St. Laurent-des-Autels, Maine-et-Loire, France, on Aug. 26, he became a Jesuit in Angers in 1854, and taught theology at Laval seminary in 1864–80, at St. Helier, Jersey, in 1880–88, and at the Catholic Institute in Paris in 1891–94. He wrote theological treatises, chief of which is the four-

volume *La Mère de Dieu et la Mère des hommes* (1900–2). He died in Bellevue, near Paris, on Dec. 5.

TERRY, RICHARD RUNCIMAN (1865–1938), musician. Born in Ellington, Northumberland, England, on Jan. 3, he went to Oxford and Cambridge, left without his degree, and taught music at Elstow School, near Bedford. He was organist in Antigua for three years, returned to England in 1893, became a convert, and in 1896 was appointed musical director at Downside. He developed the choir at that Benedictine abbey, unearthed the liturgical music of such sixteenth-century composers as William Byrd, edited the Catholic hymnal, helped to revive Tudor music and earlier secular and liturgical music, and continued his research into Tudor polyphony when named choirmaster of Westminster cathedral, London, in 1901. He wrote on plain song, hymns, and carols, had considerable effect on young musicians, received an honorary degree at Durham in 1911, was knighted in 1922, and died in London on Apr. 18.

TERTIUS, ST. (1st century). *See* Terence, St.

TERTIUS, ST. (d. 484), martyr. *See* Dionysia, St.

TERTULLA, ST. (d. 259), martyr. *See* Agapius, St.

TERTULLIAN, ST. (d. 490?). He is listed as the eighth bishop of Bologna, Italy. F. D. Apr. 27.

TERTULLINUS, ST. (d. 257), martyr. A priest, he was slain at Rome during the reign of Valerian, two days after his ordination. F. D. Aug. 4.

TESSIER, GASTON (1887–1960). Born in France, he became interested in the labor movement at an early age. He was a resistance leader during World War II, president of the French Confederation of Christian Workers and of the International Federation of Christian Trade Unions, from 1943 until his death, and fought attempts on the part of the communist-dominated World Federation of Trade Unions to absorb and direct the labor movement. He died in Paris on Aug. 8.

TESTA, BL. CHERUBINUS (1449–1479). He was an Augustinian friar-hermit at Avigliana, Italy, whose cult was approved by Pope Pius IX. F. D. Dec. 17.

TETRICUS, ST. (d. 572), bishop. Son of St. Gregory, bishop of Langres, France, and uncle of St. Gregory of Tours, he succeeded his father to the see about 540. F. D. Mar. 20.

TETRICUS, ST. (d. 707), bishop. Abbot of the Benedictine abbey of St. Germanus and popularly acclaimed as bishop of Auxerre, France, he met his death when a hostile archdeacon stabbed him in sleep. F. D. Apr. 12.

TETTA, ST. (d. 772?). She was abbess of the

Benedictine convent in Dorsetshire, England, where she ruled over 500 nuns; she sent many sisters, including SS. Lioba and Thecla, to Germany to help St. Boniface. F. D. Sept. 28.

TETZEL, JOHANN (1465–1519). Born in Pirna, Meissen, Germany, he graduated from Leipzig in 1487 and shortly after became a Dominican. He was transferred to Poland in 1497, became prior of Glogau in Silesia, and in 1509 was appointed inquisitor for Poland. He returned to Leipzig, became inquisitor for Saxony, preached throughout Germany from 1503 to 1510 as indulgence preacher for the Teutonic Knights of Livonia, and in 1516 became indulgence preacher to aid in the building of St. Peter's in Rome. In 1517 his preaching at Jüterborg, near Wittenberg, led to Martin Luther's publication of his ninety-five theses on Oct. 31. The following year Tetzel published several replies to Luther's theses and sermons, notably his *Vorlegung*, received his doctorate in theology, and, when his health broke, returned to the Leipzig priory late in 1518. He was censured early the next year by Charles von Miltitz, the papal envoy, and died in Leipzig on Aug. 11. Although Tetzel's preaching of indulgences is subject to the severest criticism for its teaching regarding indulgences for the dead, and is considered the immediate cause for the publication of Luther's theses, Tetzel himself never merited the abuses which were heaped on his head. His moral character has been completely cleared by modern historians. He clearly recognized that Luther's attacks were against fundamental Catholic teaching and authority, and labored ceaselessly to combat Luther's views.

TEUTONICUS. *See* Notker Labeo.

TEUZZO, BL. (d. 1072?). A Benedictine monk at St. Mary's (La Badia), Florence, he lived as a hermit for fifty years; he also supported St. John Gualbert in his attack on simony. F. D. Aug. 9.

THADDEUS. *See* Jude, St.

THAIS. Legend describes her as an Egyptian courtesan who had been raised a Christian, brought back to the faith by St. Paphnutius (or St. Bessarion or St. Serapion), immured in a cell for three penitential years, and eventually allowed to become a nun. She was honored as a saint on Oct. 8.

THALASSIUS, ST. (5th century). He lived in a cave at Tillima, Syria, first with his disciple Limnaeus, and then alone. St. Theodoret, bishop of Cyrrhus, who visited him, recounts his piety. F. D. Feb. 22.

THALASSIUS (5th century). Consecrated bishop of Angers, France, in 453, he prepared a compendium of canon law and history of the decisions of the councils held in his see.

THALBERG, SIGISMOND (1812–1871), composer. Born in Geneva, Switzerland, on

Jan. 7 or Feb. 7, illegitimate son of Prince Moritz Dietrichstein, he studied at the Polytechnic Institute in Vienna, where his musical aptitude was discovered and encouraged by Mittag, and under Sechter and Hummel. In 1826 he gave his first piano concert in Prince Metternich's salon, toured Europe in 1830, was appointed imperial soloist in 1834, gave concerts in Europe, the United States, and Brazil, and also composed some 100 musical numbers, including two operas, *Florinda* (1851) and *Christian di Suezia* (1855). He died in Posilipio, Italy, on Apr. 27.

THALELAEUS, ST. (d. 284?), martyr. Believed to have come from Lebanon, he practiced medicine in Anazarbus, showing great attention and charity to the poor. He was beheaded with Alexander, Asterius, and others at Aegae, Cilicia, during the persecution of Numerian. F. D. May 20.

THALELAEUS, ST. (d. 450?), hermit. Born in Cilicia, he became a recluse near a pagan shrine at Gabala, later living in an outdoor cage. In his sixty years of this attention-commanding life he gained many converts. F. D. Feb. 27.

THALHOFER, VALENTIN (1825–1891), theologian. Born in Unterroth, Germany, on Jan. 21, he studied at Dillingen and Munich, where he received his doctorate in theology in 1848, and was ordained. He was prefect at the Dillingen lyceum from 1863 to 1876, director of priests at the Georgianum, and professor at Munich and, in 1877, at Eichstätt, where he was also cathedral dean and in 1879 cathedral provost. He wrote theological works, chief of which was *Handbuch der Liturgik*, and edited the eighty-volume *Library of the Fathers* (1869–88). He died in Unterroth on Sept. 17.

THALUS, ST. (d. 300?), martyr. He and St. Trophimus were crucified at Laodicea, Syria, during the Diocletian persecution. F. D. Mar. 11.

THAMEL, ST. (d. 125?), martyr. A pagan priest, he was converted, and was slain with his sister and four or five others in the East during the reign of Hadrian. F. D. Sept. 4.

THANGMAR (d. 1022?). He became a notary, then librarian, and finally head of the cathedral school in Hildesheim, Germany, and dean there. He taught Emperor Henry II and Bishop Bernward of Hildesheim. He accompanied the bishop to Rome in 1000 and acted as his ambassador to the imperial court on several diplomatic missions. He wrote *Vita Bernwardi* (1022), a valuable picture of life in the eleventh century.

THARACUS. *See* Tarachus, St.

THARASIUS. *See* Tarasius, St.

THARSILLA, ST. *See* Tarsilla, St.

THAYER, JOHN (1758–1815), missioner. Born in Boston, Massachusetts, on May 15, he graduated from Yale in 1779, became a licensed Congregationalist minister (though not ordained), and was chaplain to John Hancock's company in Boston during the revolution. He went to Europe after the war, was converted in Rome in 1783, studied at the College of Navarre and St. Sulpice in Paris, and was ordained in 1787, the first native New Englander to become a priest. He wrote an account of his conversion (1787), spent two years on the London mission, returned to Boston in 1790, and in 1791 was put in charge of the Catholics in Boston by Bishop John Carroll. His difficult temperament and tactlessness caused great friction, and after 1792 he left to engage in roving missionary activities, settling in Alexandria, Virginia in 1793. Forced to leave because of his excessive zeal and anti-slavery views, he wandered about the states, settling in Kentucky in 1797 as assistant to Fr. Stephen Badin. In 1803 he went to Limerick, Ireland, where he remained until his death on Feb. 5.

THEA, ST. (d. 308), martyr. *See* Valentina, St.

THÉAU. *See* Tillo, St.

THÉBAUD, AUGUSTUS (1807–1885), educator. Born in Nantes, France, on Nov. 20, he studied at the Nantes seminary, was ordained in 1832, engaged in pastoral work, and in 1835 became a Jesuit in Rome. He continued his studies at the Roman College and at the Sorbonne, volunteered for the United States in 1838, became professor of chemistry at St. Mary's College in Kentucky, rector of the college in 1846, and later that year became first Jesuit president of St. John's College, Fordham, New York from 1846 to 1851, and again from 1860 to 1863. He was pastor of St. Joseph's church in Troy, New York, in 1859–60, 1863–69, and 1873–74, spent the intervening years teaching and in pastoral activity in Montreal and Jersey City, and in 1875 was made professor at St. Francis Xavier College in New York, where he died on Dec. 17. He wrote *The Church and the Gentile World* (1878), *The Church and the Moral World* (1881), *The Irish Race in the Past and Present* (1873), his memoirs, and two novels.

THECLA, ST. (1st century). According to a second-century romance, the *Acts of Paul and Thecla*, she was a native of Iconium who, after hearing St. Paul preach, resolved to be a virgin, was subjected to great torture, escaped to follow the apostle, garbed in boy's dress, and died as a hermit in Seleucia. She was widely venerated during the Middle Ages on Sept. 23.

THECLA, ST. (1st century?), martyr. *See* Dorothy, St.

THECLA, ST. (d. 293), martyr. *See* Archelais, St.

THECLA, ST. (3rd century), martyr. *See* Boniface, St.

THECLA, ST. (d. 306), martyr. A Palestinian, he was exposed to wild beasts in the amphitheater at Caesarea. When not killed, he was offered his freedom if he would sacrifice to the pagan gods, but refused and was thrown into the sea with St. Agapius. F. D. Aug. 19.

THECLA, ST. (d. 790?). A Benedictine nun at Wimborne abbey in England, she was sent to Germany on the mission led by St. Lioba. St. Boniface made her abbess of Ochsenfürt and later of Kitzingen. F. D. Oct. 15.

THEGAN OF TRÈVES (d. 850?), historian. Assistant bishop of Trèves, Gaul, and a friend of Walafrid Strabo, he wrote *Vita Ludovici imperatoris*, a rather unsatisfactory life of Louis the Pious; its fuller annular account for 814–35 is probably the work of another author. He may be identical with Theganbert, provost of the monastery of St. Cassius, Bonn.

THELICA, ST. (d. 304), martyr. *See* Saturninus, St.

THEMISTOCLES, ST. (d. 253), martyr. A shepherd in Myra, Licia, he was beheaded when he refused to reveal the hiding place of a fellow Christian. F. D. Dec. 21.

THÉNARD, LOUIS JACQUES (1777–1857), chemist. Born in Louptière, Aube, France, on May 4, he went to Paris as a youth to study chemistry under Vauquelin, taught chemistry at L'Ecole Polytechnique in 1798 and Collège de France in 1802, and became a member of the Academy of Sciences in 1810. He was made dean of the Faculté des Sciences in 1821, a baron in 1825, and chancellor of the university. He worked closely with Gay-Lussac for many years, and the two discovered boron and proved that oxymuriatic acid is a simple substance. Thénard discovered hydrogen peroxide and cobalt ultramarine (Thénard's blue), wrote numerous scientific papers, and in 1813 published the four-volume *Traité élementaire de chimie*, which was a standard French chemistry text for the next twenty-five years and was widely translated. He died in Paris on June 21.

THENEVA, ST. (7th century). Mother of St. Kentigern, she is with him joint patron of Glasgow, Scotland. F. D. July 18.

THEOBALD I (d. 1253), king of Navarre. Thibault de Champagne was chosen to succeed his uncle, Sancho VII, in 1234, enjoyed a peaceful reign, and was a patron of troubadour poets and poetry.

THEOBALD II (d. 1270), king of Navarre. Son of Theobald I, he became king in 1253, married Isabel, daughter of St. Louis of France, with whom he went to Tunis on crusade, and died at Trapani, Sicily, on his return.

THEOBALD, ST. (d. 1001). He was archbishop of Vienne, France, from 970 until his death. His cult was confirmed in 1903. The name is also spelled Thibaud. F. D. May 21.

THEOBALD, ST. (1017–1066). Son of Count

Arnoul of Champagne, France, he became a soldier, attained his father's permission to retire at eighteen to a life of contemplation, and moved to a forest retreat in Luxembourg. He was joined by a nobleman named Walter; they performed menial labor for the people of the area, fled to undertake a series of pilgrimages when their reputation for holiness began to interfere with their program of prayer, and finally settled at Salanigo, near Vicenza, Italy. After Walter's death, Theobald intensified his austerities, and was professed as a Camaldolese before his last painful illness. He was canonized in 1073 by Pope Alexander II. F. D. June 30.

THEOBALD (d. 1161), archbishop. Of Norman descent, he joined the Benedictines at Bec, became prior in 1127, abbot in 1137, and was elected archbishop of Canterbury in 1138. He attended the second Lateran Council, introduced civil law to England, founded a law school at Canterbury, and came into conflict with Bishop Henry of Winchester, who as papal legate appointed St. William of York as achbishop, which Theobald opposed. About 1150, Theobald was appointed legate, defied King Stephen, who had forbidden all English bishops to attend a papally summoned council in Rheims, and was banished by the king and had his property seized. The pope put England under an interdict (disregarded except in Canterbury); archbishop and king were reconciled in 1148. Theobald was again forced to flee when he refused to crown Stephen's son Eustace, helped reconcile Stephen and Henry of Anjou by the Treaty of Wallingford (which recognized Stephen as king and established that Henry was to succeed him), and when Stephen died in 1154 crowned Henry II. He encouraged young men to take up scholarship and statesmanship, and brought many into his household, among them Thomas à Becket. He died on Apr. 18 in Canterbury.

THEOBALD, ST. (d. 1247). Son of Bouchard of Montmorency, he was born at Marley, France, served in the court of King Philip Augustus II, and became a Cistercian at the abbey of Vaux-de-Cernay in 1220 and its abbot in 1235. He died on Dec. 8. F. D. July 27.

THEOCTISTA, ST. According to legend, she was a woman of Lesbos, carried off by Arabs to Paros, where she escaped and lived as a recluse for thirty years. F. D. Nov. 10.

THEODARD, ST. (d. 670?), bishop. A follower of St. Remaclus at the Benedictine abbey of Malmédy-Stavelot, France, he succeeded him in 653 as abbot and in 662 as bishop of Tongres-Maastricht. He was murdered by robbers on his way to Childeric II of Austrasia to protest the seizure of Church lands by a group of nobles. F. D. Sept. 10.

THEODARD, ST. (d. 893), archbishop. Born in Montauriol, France, and educated at the Benedictine abbey there and in the law at Toulouse, he was ordained and became secretary to Archbishop Sigebold of Narbonne. He succeeded him, rebuilt the cathedral, fed the famine-stricken, redeemed captives from the Moors, and restored spiritual life. When his health broke under the intensity of his labors, he retired to die at Montauriol. He is also known as Audard. F. D. May 1.

THEODEMAR, ST. (d. 1152). Born in Bremen, Germany, he is said to have been a Premonstratensian missioner among the Wends with St. Vicelinus. F. D. May 17.

THEODEMIR, ST. (d. 851), martyr. A monk, he was slain at Cordova, Spain, during the persecution of Abderrahman II. F. D. July 25.

THEODICHILDIS, ST. (7th century). She was the first abbess of the Benedictine foundation at Jouarre in Meaux, France, to which she came in 660 from the convent at Faremoutiers. F. D. June 28.

THEODMARUS. See Thiemo, St.

THEODOLUS, ST. (d. 840?). Born in Besançon, France, he was chaplain to Charlemagne, Benedictine abbot of Agaunum, and bishop of Sion in the Valais. F. D. Aug. 17.

THEODORA, ST. (d. 132), martyr. Sister of St. Hermes, she was put to death in Rome a few months after his martyrdom. F. D. Apr. 1.

THEODORA, ST. (d. 304), martyr. She was rescued from a brothel in Alexandria, Egypt, by St. Didymus, and was slain with him. F. D. Apr. 28.

THEODORA, ST. (d. 305?). A Roman matron of considerable wealth, she was particularly charitable toward the Christian martyrs during the Diocletian persecution, of which she herself died a victim. F. D. Sept. 17.

THEODORA OF ALEXANDRIA, ST. Legend calls her the sinful wife of Gregory, prefect of Egypt, who repented and fled to a desert monastery. F. D. Sept. 11.

THEODORE I (d. 649), pope. A Greek of Jerusalem and son of a bishop, he became pope on Nov. 24, 642. He vigorously opposed Monothelitism, which was to plague his pontificate; refused to recognize Paul as patriarch of Constantinople, since his predecessor, Pyrrhus, had been illegally deposed; and attempted unsuccessfully to win back Pyrrhus and Paul, both of whom he was forced to excommunicate in 648 and 649 respectively. His actions against Monothelitism were approved by the bishops of Cyprus, Palestine, and Africa, but Emperor Constans II refused to withdraw the *Ecthesis*, merely issuing the *Type*, at Paul's instigation, forbidding discussion of the doctrine of one or two wills in Christ, a step which was denounced by the West. Theodore died in Rome on May 14.

THEODORE (7th century), antipope. See Paschal, antipope.

THEODORE II (d. 897), pope. A Roman and son of Photius, he was elected pope sometime in Dec. 897, but died after a pontificate of only twenty days. During his brief pontificate he recognized the validity of Pope Formosus' orders, reinstated the clerics degraded by Pope Stephen VII, and had Formosus' body reburied in St. Peter's.

THEODORE, ST. (d. 130?). *See* Pausilippus, St.

THEODORE, ST. (d. 220), martyr. *See* Dionysius, St.

THEODORE, ST. (d. 258?), martyr. *See* Antony, St.

THEODORE, ST. (d. 302), martyr. *See* Zeno, St.

THEODORE, ST. (d. 310), bishop and martyr. The bishop of Pentapolis, his deacon Irenaeus, and two lectors, Ammonius and Serapion, were tortured in Libya and had their tongues cut out during the reign of Gallienus. F. D. Mar. 26.

THEODORE, ST. (d. 310?), bishop. A skilled copyist of manuscripts, he was put to death in his see of Cyrene, North Africa, when he refused to surrender copies of scripture. F. D. July 4.

THEODORE, ST. (d. 310?), martyr. *See* Ammianus, St.; also, Asclepiodotus, St.

THEODORE, ST. (d. 311?), martyr. *See* Faustus, St.

THEODORE, ST. (d. 319), martyr. *See* Theodore Tiro, St.

THEODORE, ST. (314?–368). Born in the Upper Thebaid, Egypt, he became a disciple of St. Pachomius of Tabenna, was ordained, and succeeded him as abbot about 347. He is called "the Sanctified." F. D. Apr. 27 (in the East, May 16).

THEODORE, ST. (d. 370), martyr. He, St. Urban, and eighty other priests were burned to death on a ship off Africa on orders of the Arian Emperor Valens, after they had pleaded for leniency toward Catholics. F. D. Sept. 5.

THEODORE, ST. (d. 575?). Born in Arcisia, Dauphiné, France, he was a follower of St. Caesarius of Arles, became abbot in Vienne, founded several monasteries, and later lived as a hermit in a walled-up cell in the church of St. Lawrence, Vienne. He is also called Theuderius. F. D. Oct. 29.

THEODORE, ST. (6th century). A sacristan in the basilica of St. Peter's, Rome, he was praised by St. Gregory the Great. F. D. Dec. 26.

THEODORE, ST. (d. 778). Appointed bishop of Pavia, Italy, in 743, he was frequently exiled by the Arian forces of the heretical Lombard kings. F. D. May 20.

THEODORE, ST. (d. 841). He and his brother Theophanes were natives of Kerak, Moab (now in Transjordan), and became monks of the laura of St. Sabas in Jerusalem. He became a priest and was sent by his patriarch to protest Leo the Armenian's iconoclasm. Leo had verses cut in the cheeks of the brothers (they were called "the Graphi" thereafter) and banished them. On Leo's death they returned to Constantinople, but suffered exile again when Theophilus became emperor in 829. Theodore died in Apamca, Bithynia, from the ill-treatment he had received. On the death of Theophilus, Theophanes was made bishop of Nicaea, where he died on Oct. 11, 845. F. D. Dec. 27.

THEODORE, ST. (d. 870), martyr. He was slain at the Benedictine abbey of Croyland, England, by invading Danes; with him died Askega, the prior; Swethin, the sub-prior, and Agamund, Egdred, Elfgete, Grimkeld, Savinus, Ulrick, and others. F. D. Apr. 9.

THEODORE, ST. (d. 1246), martyr. *See* Michael of Chernigov, St.

THEODORE, ST., martyr. *See* Drusus, St.

THEODORE THE BLACK, ST. (d. 1299). Duke of Yaroslav and Smolensk, Russia, he helped extend Christianity, built several churches, ruled wisely, and fought against the Tatar onslaughts. He became a monk a few days before his death. F. D. Sept. 19.

THEODORE OF CANTERBURY, ST. (602?–690), archbishop. Born in Tarsus, Cilicia, he studied at Athens and became a Basilian monk at Rome. At sixty-six he was appointed seventh archbishop of Canterbury by Pope St. Vitalian on the recommendation of St. Adrian. On his arrival with Adrian in 669 he toured England, filled vacant sees, restored discipline, opened schools, and adjusted conflicting claims between SS. Wilfrid and Chad over York. In 673 he called the first provincial synod at Hertford, where the date for Easter was fixed, and was the first archbishop to be acknowledged as the leader of the Church in England. In 678 he created the sees of Hereford, Lindsey, and Worcester, and allowed King Egfrid, whom Wilfrid had condemned for not allowing his wife to enter a convent, to appoint the new bishops. The king refused to accept the pope's order allowing Wilfrid to appoint suffragan bishops; Theodore seems not have opposed the monarch on this, but later was reconciled with Wilfrid. In 680, Theodore called a provincial council at Hatfield which affirmed the bishops' adherence to the tenets of the five ecumenical councils. The extent of his authorship of *The Penitential of Theodore* is confused; this collection of decisions in cases of conscience became the basis of the penitential system in the West. His twenty-one years as metropolitan were characterized by administrative zeal and rewarded by success which raised the Church to a higher level than it had yet attained in England. He died in Canterbury, England. F. D. Sept. 19.

THEODORE OF EGYPT, ST. (4th century). He was a follower of St. Ammonius and lived as a monk in the Egyptian desert. F. D. Jan. 7.

THEODORE OF EMDEN (d. 1572), martyr. A Dutch Franciscan, he was confessor to the Franciscan nuns at Gorkum, Holland, seized by Calvinists there, and hanged at Briel. F. D. July 9.

THEODORE OF GAZA (d. 1478). Born in Thessalonica, Greece, he fled Turkish rule in Constantinople in 1429, and settled in Italy. He taught Greek at Siena, Ferrara, and Rome, was a member of Nicholas V's court for a period, and was a considerable influence in the humanist movement through the academy he founded at Ferrara, his translations of Aristotle's works into Latin, and his expositions on Aristotle's treatises on natural science.

THEODORE OF HERACLEA, ST. (4th century), martyr. Believed to have been a general in the army of Licinius and governor of Pontus and the surrounding area, and tortured and beheaded after it was discovered that he was a Christian, he is often pictured in early art as fighting a dragon from horseback. He is sometimes confused with St. Theodore of Amasea, also a soldier. F. D. Feb. 7.

THEODORE OF MOPSUESTIA (350?–428), bishop. Born in Antioch, he received a classical education at the school of Libanius, a pagan rhetorician, and there met St. John Chrysostom, whom he followed, when eighteen, to the school of Diodorus and Carterius, where he embraced an ascetic way of life. He returned to a worldly life briefly, but then reaccepted monastic life and became famed for his knowledge of scripture. He was ordained sometime between 383 and 386, was active against the Arians, Origenists, and Apollinarists, and an opponent of Julian the Apostate, and about 392 left Antioch to rejoin Diodorus, who probably was instrumental in having him named bishop of Mopsuestia, Cilicia, later the same year. He attended the Synod of Constantinople in 394, defended Chrysostom, and, though friendly with several prominent Pelagians, joined in the condemnation of Pelagianism at a synod in Cilicia. He died in Mopsuestia. Theodore was widely recognized as an outstanding theologian and wrote exegetical commentaries on most books of the Bible, and theological treatises, among them, *De sacramentis, De fide, De Incarnatione, Contra Eunomium, Contra magicam artem, Contra allegoristas*, and *De assumente et assumpto*. Although completely orthodox during his lifetime, he was assailed after his death when many of his writings were adopted by the Nestorians. Emperor Justinian anathematized the Three Chapters (as Theodore's writings, several of Theodoret's, and a letter of Ibas came to be called) in 544 in an attempt to bring the Monophysites back to the Church, an action which many bishops pointed out was to condemn the Council of Chalcedon. When the fifth General Council, held in Constantinople in 553 despite the fact Vigilius had withdrawn his permission, placed Theodore's person and writings under anathema, Vigilius was forced to approve the synod's decree—a step which led to several schisms in the West, notably at Aquileia and Milan.

THEODORE OF SKION, ST. (d. 613), bishop. Born in Galicia, he lived in austere solitude in the mountains, had many supernatural gifts, was ordained, and founded several monasteries. He was made bishop of Anastasiopolis by Emperor Maurice between 582 and 590, but was permitted to retire to his hermitage after ten years. F. D. Apr. 22.

THEODORE STUDITES, ST. (759–826), abbot. A native of Constantinople and nephew of St. Plato, abbot of Symboleon on Mt. Olympus, Bithynia, he was ordained in 787 and in 794 succeeded his uncle Plato as abbot of Succudium, near Constantinople, which his family had founded. When he protested, in 796, against an adulterous second marriage of Emperor Constantine VI, he was exiled to Thessalonica, but recalled when Constantine's mother Irene deposed her son in 797. In 799 he moved his monastery within the walls of the city and was given charge of the Studios, a famous monastery founded in 463 which had been neglected. He transformed it into a powerful monastery, with more than 1000 monks, a center of Eastern monastic revival whose influence spread over Russia, Bulgaria, Serbia, and even to Mt. Athos. In 809, when he and other monks objected to the appointment of Nicephorus, a layman, as patriarch of Constantinople and the reinstatement of Joseph, a priest who had blessed Constantine VI's second marriage, they were imprisoned and then banished and the monks of the Studios dispersed. The breach was healed in 811 when he was freed on the death of Emperor Nicephorus I and joined with Patriarch Nicephorus in denouncing Emperor Leo V the Armenian's Iconoclastic leanings—an action which led to his banishment in 813 to Mysia and later to Bonita, Anatolia. From there he wrote several letters to Pope St. Paschal I in which he emphasized the primacy of the bishop of Rome. He spent three years at Bonita, subjected to beatings and tortures, and was then sent to Smyrna, where he was in the custody of an Iconoclast archbishop who wanted him beheaded. When Leo was murdered in 820, Emperor Michael the Stammerer restored the exiles. When they refused to support his ban on icons, he barred them from their former offices. Theodore then left the city, visited monasteries in Bithynia, and was joined by many of his monks at a monastery on Akrita, where he died. He wrote voluminously on monastic life and the veneration of images, and sermons, hymns, and letters. F. D. Nov. 11.

THEODORE TIRO, ST. (d. 306), martyr. According to legend, he was a recruit (*tiro*) in the Roman army in Pontus on the Black Sea when he refused to join in idolatrous worship. Freed, he set fire to the temple of Cybele at Euchaita and was tortured and burned alive. He is greatly venerated in the East with SS. George and Demetrios, the three "warrior saints." F. D. Nov. 9. He may, however, be identical with a Theodore who was a general in the army of Licinius, who was said to have been crucified at Heraclea, Thrace, in 319. F. D. Feb. 7.

THEODORE TRICHINAS, ST. (d. 330?). Clad only in a hair shirt, he lived a life of solitary austerity near Constantinople. F. D. Apr. 20.

THEODORET, ST. (d. 362), martyr. A priest at Antioch, Syria, he refused to surrender the sacred church vessels to the prefect Julian (uncle of Emperor Julian the Apostate) and was tortured and beheaded. F. D. Oct. 23.

THEODORET (393?–457?), bishop. Born in Antioch, Syria, he entered a monastery as a youth and at twenty-three gave his fortune to the poor and became a monk at Nicerte. He remained there until about 423 when he was made bishop of Cyrus, Syria, against his wishes. He governed his see with great wisdom, became famed as a preacher, fought paganism and heresy, and was noted for his conversions, particularly among the Marcionites. Prominent in the Antiochene school of theology, he was a close friend of Nestorius, and repeatedly defended him, refusing to admit that Nestorius taught the heretical doctrine of two persons in Christ. He soon became involved in bitter controversy with St. Cyril of Alexandria in the Christological dispute between Nestorius and Cyril, and at the Council of Ephesus in 431 he voted with Nestorius, John of Antioch, and their group for the deposition of Cyril and the anathema against him, and reiterated his stand at synods in Tarsus and Antioch later the same year. He probably drew up the conciliatory declaration of faith about 433 which Cyril accepted and which led to the reconciliation of John of Antioch with Cyril. He entered the fray again in 437 against Cyril when the latter denounced Diodorus of Tarsus and Theodore of Mopsuestia as instigators of the Nestorian heresy. Dioscorus, who had succeeded Cyril as patriarch of Alexandria in 444, secured an imperial edict in 448 forbidding Theodoret from leaving his see, and accused him of Nestorianism. When Theodoret convinced Patriarch Flavian to denounce Eutyches, Dioscurus and Eutyches caused Theodoret to be deposed at the Synod of Ephesus (the Robber Council) in 449 and ordered to the Nicerte monastery by imperial decree. Theodoret appealed to Rome, and Pope Leo declared the deposition invalid and restored him to his see in 450. He was summoned to the Council of Chalcedon in 451 by Emperor Marcian and reluctantly agreed to the anathema of Nestorius, after which he probably abandoned his Nestorian views. It is uncertain whether his remaining years were spent in Cyrus or the Nicerte monastery, though they probably were in the peaceful administration of his diocese. Theodoret wrote commentaries on the Bible, history, 200 valuable letters, and *De divina providentia*, *Historia ecclesiastica* (from 325 to 429), *Eranistes*, against the Monophysites, and *Graecarum affectionum curatio*, on Christian apologetics. His writings against St. Cyril were condemned during the Three Chapters controversy of Justinian and by the Council of Constantinople in 553, but he has never been condemned by the Church.

THEODORIC (d. 1102), antipope. Bishop of Rufina, he was elected in 1100, by the imperial faction supporting Henry IV to succeed antipope Clement III in opposition to Pope Paschal II. He soon submitted to the pope.

THEODORIC, ST. (d. 533?). Born near Rheims, Gaul, he was married against his will and persuaded his wife to agree to separate. He became a priest under St. Remigius and founded a religious community at Mont d'Or near Rheims. He was noted for his conversions and his persuasion of fallen-away Catholics, among them his own father, to return to the Church. He also is known as Thierry and as Theodericus. F. D. July 1.

THEODORIC II, ST. (d. 1022), bishop. A Benedictine monk at St. Pierre-le-Vif, in Sens, France, he became a court counselor and bishop of Orléans. F. D. Jan. 27.

THEODORIC, BL. (d. 1087). He studied at Mauberge, France, became a Benedictine at Lobbes, and in 1055 was abbot of St. Hubert. He successfully introduced the Cluniac reform there and in other abbeys of the Ardennes region. F. D. Oct. 25.

THEODORIC OF CHARTRES (d. 1150?), philosopher. Born in France, he probably studied at Chartres, was head of the school there in 1121, and then taught at Paris, where John of Salisbury was one of his pupils. He defended the classics against the Cornificians, was interested in the natural sciences, and was a Platonist who taught the Platonic explanation of reality and the ultrarealistic theory of universals. He was a teacher in Chartres, France, in 1141, and died there.

THEODORUS LECTOR (6th century), historian. A lector at St. Sophia church in Constantinople, he wrote *Historia tripartita*, excerpts from the writings of Socrates, Sozomen, and Theodoret, and a history of the period from Theodosius II's death to Justin I which has disappeared.

THEODOSIA, ST. (d. 300), martyr. *See* Alexandra, St.

THEODOSIA, ST. (d. 308), martyr. An eighteen-year-old native of Tyre, she was seized in Caesarea while inspiring Christians who had refused to sacrifice to idols, and put to death by drowning during the persecution of Maximian. F. D. Apr. 2.

THEODOSIA, ST. (d. 361), martyr. *See* Domitius, St.

THEODOSIUS, ST. (d. 269), martyr. *See* Lucius, St.

THEODOSIUS, ST. (d. 304?), martyr. *See* Quadratus, St.

THEODOSIUS, ST. (d. 516), bishop. He directed the see of Auxerre, France, from about 507 until his death. F. D. July 17.

THEODOSIUS, ST. (d. 1074), abbot. Born to a well-to-do family, he worked with the laborers on his father's farm despite his parents' protests. In 1032 he joined the monks at the Caves of Kiev, Russia, succeeded Barlaam as abbot, and aided in the formal establishment of monasticism in Russia. He put the community under formal discipline, stressed the need for corporal works as well as prayer and mortification, and urged his monks to participate in the life of the people around them. He was canonized by the bishops of Kiev in 1108. F. D. July 9.

THEODOSIUS THE CENOBIARCH, ST. (423–529). Born in Garissus, Macedonia, he became a lector, then set out for Jerusalem, visited St. Simeon Stylites, took charge of a church near Bethlehem for a brief period, then retired to a nearby cave for a life of solitude. Thereafter he built a monastery near the Dead Sea, with three hostels for the sick, the aged, and the insane, and three churches for the Greeks and Armenians, the Persians and Arabs, and for the Slavs. By this time there were several hundred monks under his direction and as many patients. The patriarch of Jerusalem gave St. Sabas charge of the hermits, and placed Theodosius over all those living a community life. When Emperor Anastasius supported Eutyches, Theodosius preached throughout Jerusalem, pleading for opposition to the Monophysite heresy; imperial bribery, forgery, and banishment failed to break his zeal. F. D. Jan. 11.

THEODOSIUS FLORENTINI (1808–1865). Born in Münster, Grisons, Switzerland, on May 23, he became a Capuchin in 1825, was ordained in 1830, became a lecturer in philosophy, and in 1838 guardian at Baden. He was forced to leave Switzerland for Alsace in 1844 because of his vigorous defense of Church

rights, but returned later in the year and founded the Franciscan Sisters of the Holy Cross in Altorf and in 1852 the Sisters of Mercy in Ingenbohl. He engaged in educational and social work, refounded Maria-Hilf zu Schwyx College, which had been closed, encouraged mission activities in Switzerland by founding a series of home missions and the Pius Society, and helped spread Catholic literature by setting up an organization to print and distribute Catholic material. He became superior at Chur in 1845, definitor in 1857, and vicar general of the Chur diocese in 1860. He died in Heiden, Switzerland on Feb. 15.

THEODOSIUS I THE GREAT (346?–395), emperor. Flavius Theodosius was born in Spain, son of Gen. Comes Theodosius, accompanied his father on the latter's expedition to Britain in 368–69, defeated the Sarmatians in 374, and was military governor of Moesia in 375–76. When his father was executed in 376 (probably at Emperor Valens' order), he retired to Spain. Valens was killed in the battle of Adrianople in 378, and Emperor Gratian appointed Theodosius augustus of the East in 379. He was baptized in 380, and with Gratian issued the edict, *De fide catholica,* condemning Arianism, and making communion with the Holy See the test of orthodoxy. He called the first Council of Constantinople in 381, which proclaimed the Nicene Creed and anathematized other doctrines as heretical, reorganized the army, and waged a successful campaign against the Visigoths, permitting them to settle in specified areas in the empire and securing their services as soldiers. In 383 he named his son Arcadius emperor in the East, and, when Maximus revolted in Britain and Gratian was murdered in the same year, was obliged to accept Maximus as his colleague with the understanding that Maximus would allow Gratian's brother, Valentinian II, to reign in Italy. When Maximus invaded Italy in 387, Valentinian fled to Theodosius, who, the following year, marched against Maximus and defeated him near Aquileia on July 28. When Maximus and his son were murdered, Theodosius bestowed on Valentinian all the lands his father had ruled. In 390 occurred his massacre of 7000 rebellious people in Thessalonica, which led to St. Ambrose's edict forbidding Theodosius to enter the church and the emperor's acceptance of eight months of penance to expiate his crime. In 392, Arbogast, Valentinian's tutor, caused his pupil's murder and set up Eugenius as Western emperor. Theodosius marched against Eugenius and on Sept. 5–9, 394, defeated Eugenius' forces, which fought under the old pagan banners, some thirty-five miles from Aquileia. Eugenius was murdered by his own troops, Arbogast committed suicide, and Theodosius became sole emperor of the Roman

Empire, now entirely Christian. He had his son Honorius proclaimed emperor in the West under Stillicho's guardianship, and then retired to Milan, Italy, where he died on Jan. 17. Theodosius' reign was notable for the close connection between the Church and state which was to have far-reaching future effects. He forced Arian bishops to relinquish their sees to orthodox bishops and practically wiped out Arianism. He was equally severe toward Manichaeism and other heresies, and in 392 he issued an edict decrying pagan rites and forbade the restoral of the altar of victory in the Roman senate.

THEODOTA, ST. (d. 304?), martyr. A noblewoman of Nicaea, she is said in legend to have refused to marry the prefect Leucatius, who denounced her; when she refused to sacrifice to the pagan gods, she was burned to death. F. D. Aug. 2.

THEODOTA, ST. (d. 318?), martyr. A penitent prostitute at Philippopolis, Thrace, she was tortured and stoned to death when she refused to sacrifice to Apollo. F. D. Sept. 29.

THEODOTA, ST. (d. 735?), martyr. She was put to death at Constantinople for hiding icons from the officers of Emperor Leo the Isaurian. F. D. July 17.

THEODOTUS, ST. (d. 270?), martyr. He, his wife Rufina, and Ammia, the foster mother of their daughter St. Mammas, were put to death in Cappadocia during the reign of Aurelian. F. D. Aug. 31.

THEODOTUS, ST. (d. 325?), bishop. He suffered imprisonment for his faith while directing his see of Cyrenia, Cyprus, during the persecution of Licinius. F. D. May 6.

THEODOTUS, ST. (d. 334). He was bishop of Laodicea, a friend of the historian Eusebius, and involved in Arian association, although he accepted the Nicene Creed. F. D. Nov. 2.

THEODOTUS, ST. (d. 484?), martyr. See Aquilinus, St.

THEODOTUS. He is the hero of a pious legend, an innkeeper who recovered the bodies of seven Christian girls who were drowned, and was himself beheaded, during the fourth-century Diocletian persecution. The story has it that he had promised relics to a priest named Fronto who was building a new church; Fronto made the guards drunk and escaped with the corpse of Theodotus, about which he set up a shrine. They were honored on May 18.

THEODULF, ST. (d. 776). He was the third abbot-bishop of the Benedictine monastery at Lobbes, near Liège, Flanders. F. D. June 24.

THEODULF (760?–821), bishop. Born in Spain, he became a member of Charlemagne's court in 794, was noted for his learning, and about 798 was appointed bishop of Orléans and of several abbeys. He instituted reforms in his diocese, went on a diplomatic mission for Charlemagne, described in his poem *Versus contra judices*, and participated in the theological dispute over the Trinity. He wrote *De spiritu sancto* and *De ordine baptismi* at the emperor's request and also was noted for his poetry, which gives colorful pictures of the times. He wrote *Versus contra judices* on the Frankish legal system, and a hymn for Palm Sunday, *Gloria, laus et honor*. He fell into disfavor during Louis the Pious' reign, was accused of participating in King Bernard of Italy's conspiracy, and was exiled to Angers, France, in 818, where he died on Dec. 18.

THEODULUS, ST. (d. 113?), martyr. See Alexander, St.

THEODULUS, ST. (d. 135?), martyr. See Hypatus, St.

THEODULUS, ST. (d. 140), martyr. See Cyriacus, St.

THEODULUS, ST. (d. 250), martyr. During the persecution of Decius, ten Christians on Crete were tortured and beheaded when they refused to sacrifice to the gods. They are known as the Ten Martyrs of Crete and included SS. Agathopus, Basilides, Cleomenes, Eunician, Euporus, Evaristus, Gelasius, Saturninus, and Zoticus.

THEODULUS, ST. (d. 257), martyr. See Symphronius, St.

THEODULUS, ST. (d. 303), martyr. See Agathopedes.

THEODULUS, ST. (d. 309), martyr. An aged servant of Firmilian, governor of Palestine, he visited St. Elias and his four Egyptian companions in prison in Caesarea before their death and was angrily condemned by his master to death by crucifixion. F. D. Feb. 17.

THEODULUS, ST. (d. 362), martyr. See Macedonius, St.

THEOFRID, ST. (d. 690?). A Benedictine monk at Luxeuil, France, he became abbot of Corbie in 662 and a regionary bishop. F. D. Jan. 26.

THEOFRID, ST. (d. 728). Born in Orange, France, he was Benedictine abbot of Carmery-en-Velay (later called St. Chaffre after him) and died of ill-treatment by invading Saracens; as a result he was venerated as a martyr. F. D. Oct. 19.

THEOGENES, ST. (d. 258), bishop and martyr. Bishop of Hippo Regius, in North Africa, he was slain there with thirty-six others during the persecution of Valerian; another record sets the scene of martyrdom at Laodicea in Phrygia. F. D. Jan. 25.

THEOGENES, ST. (d. 320), martyr. See Cyrinus, St.

THEOGER, BL. (d. 1120), bishop. An Alsatian, he was a canon in Mainz, Germany, became a Benedictine monk at Hirschau, prior of Raichenbach, and abbot of St. Georgen. He was consecrated bishop of Metz in 1118, but soon retired to Cluny. F. D. Apr. 29.

THEOGONIUS, ST. (d. 304), martyr. *See* Bassa, St.

THEONAS, ST. (d. 284), martyr. *See* Theopemptus, St.

THEONAS, ST. (d. 300). He became bishop of Alexandria, Egypt, in 281, developed the influence of the catechetical school there, and was a firm opponent of Sabellianism. F. D. Aug. 23.

THEONESTUS, ST. (d. 425), martyr. Slain at Altino, Italy, by invading Vandals, he probably was a native of that place; he also has been called bishop of Philippi, Macedonia, driven from his see by the Arians, sent by the pope to Mainz, Germany, and murdered as he fled before the Vandals. F. D. Oct. 30.

THEONILLA, ST. (d. 303?), martyr. *See* Asterius, St.; also, Claudius, St.

THEOPEMPTUS, ST. (d. 284), bishop and martyr. He was slain in his see city of Nicomedia, with St. Theonas, whom he had converted. F. D. Jan. 3.

THEOPHANES, ST. (d. 810?), martyr. An imperial officer, he was tortured to death at Constantinople because of his opposition to the Iconoclasm of Emperor Leo the Armenian. F. D. Dec. 4.

THEOPHANES, ST. (d. 817). Born in Constantinople, he served there at the court of Constantine V, then built two monasteries: on Mt. Sigriana, where he became abbot, and on the island of Kalonymos. In 787 he attended the second Council of Nicaea, which approved the veneration of icons. Emperor Leo declared against them in 814, but failed to persuade Theophanes to defend him and had the abbot scourged, imprisoned, and banished to the island of Samothrace, where he died as a result of mistreatment. He wrote a chronicle covering the years 284–813; his biography was written by St. Methodius. F. D. Mar. 12.

THEOPHANES, ST. (d. 845), bishop. *See* Theodore, St.

THEOPHANES KERAMEUS (d. 1152). Archbishop of Rossano, Calabria, from 1129 to 1152, he is noted for his sermons and homiletic writings, written in Greek and exceptionally lucid and natural.

THEOPHILA, ST. (d. 303), martyr. *See* Agapes, St.

THEOPHILUS (1st century). Called a Christian and an imperial official of the Roman administration, St. Luke addressed to him his gospel and the Acts of the Apostles (Luke 1:3; Acts 1:1). Since his name means "beloved of God," some authorities believe he is a fictitious person symbolizing the Gentile Christian.

THEOPHILUS, ST. (d. 181). An Eastern philosopher, he was converted and became bishop of Antioch, Syria, and well known as an apologist. F. D. Oct. 13.

THEOPHILUS, ST. (d. 195?), bishop. He ruled the see of Caesarea, Palestine, during the early quarrel over the dating of Easter. F. D. Mar. 5.

THEOPHILUS (2nd century). Bishop of Antioch, Syria, in the last quarter of the second century, he was a convert from paganism. He wrote *Ad Autolycum*, a Christian apologetical work, commentaries, catechisms, a history, and refutations of Marcion and Hermogenes.

THEOPHILUS, ST. (d. 249), martyr. *See* Ammon, St.

THEOPHILUS, ST. (d. 250), martyr. *See* Caesarius, St.; also, Macarius, St.

THEOPHILUS, ST. (d. 302?), martyr. He and St. Trophimus were beheaded in Rome during the Diocletian persecution. F. D. July 23.

THEOPHILUS, ST. (d. 304), martyr. A lawyer, he is said to have been put to death at Caesarea in Cappadocia during the Diocletian persecution. F. D. Feb. 6.

THEOPHILUS (d. 412), patriarch. Uncle of St. Cyril, he was elected patriarch of Constantinople in 385. In 390 his destruction of several pagan temples in Alexandria set off a riot, which he quelled by destroying the famous temple of Serapis and erecting a Christian church on its site. He attempted unsuccessfully in 391 or 392 to end the schism at Antioch, was sympathetic to the Origenists, sided with Johannes and Rufinus in the quarrel with Epiphanius and Jerome, banished Bishop Paulus, an opponent of Origen, and admonished Jerome for his friendly relations with Paulus. About 399 he quarreled with archpresbyter Isidore, a friend of the Origenists, and turned against them, and then against the monks of Nitria when Isidore sought refuge with them. In 401 he condemned Origenism at the Synod of Alexandria, led a force of soldiers against the Nitria monks as Origenists, and destroyed their habitations. Some of them, the so-called "four tall brothers," escaped to Constantinople, and complained to the emperor who in 402 ordered Theophilus to appear at a synod over which St. John Chrysostom presided and apologize to the "brothers." Theophilus tried, instead, to have Chrysostom condemn them; when he refused, Theophilus, in collaboration with Empress Eudoxia, had trumped-up charges brought against Chrysostom in 403 and had him exiled. An uprising caused the empress to recall Chrysostom, and Theophilus was forced to flee. He was reconciled with the monks at the Synod of the Oak. He wrote a book against Origen, and several of his Easter letters are still extant.

THEOPHILUS, ST. (d. 430?). He succeeded St. Gaudentius as bishop of Brescia, Italy. F. D. Apr. 27.

THEOPHILUS, ST. (d. 750?). Born in Bulgaria, he became a monk in Asia Minor at a monastery which followed the Benedictine Rule and was persecuted and exiled by Emperor Leo the Isaurian during the Iconoclast heresy. F. D. Oct. 2.

THEOPHILUS, ST. (d. 789), martyr. Admiral of the Christian fleet at Cyprus, he was captured when the Saracens overran the islands, imprisoned for a year, then beheaded after torture. F. D. July 22.

THEOPHILUS THE PENITENT. The hero of a Latin play by the tenth-century dramatist, Hrosvitha of Gandesheim, this legendary figure is a precursor of the Faust theme. Deposed from his position as administrator by a new bishop, Theophilus makes a pact with Satan, renounces Christ and His mother, and regains his post. Remorse leads to repentance, he is forgiven through Mary, publicly confesses his shame, and has the miraculously returned pact burned by the bishop. He was sometimes listed as an actual saint.

THEOPHORUS. See Ignatius of Antioch.

THEOPHYLACT, ST. (d. 845), bishop. An Asian, he was educated by St. Tarasius at Constantinople and by St. Michael the Confessor. The former made him a bishop of Nicomedia and he distinguished himself by his work for the poor, blind, and insane, and by defending the Church against the Iconoclasts at a council called by St. Nicephorus, and so angered Emperor Leo V that he was imprisoned for thirty years in Caria, Asia Minor, where he died. F. D. Mar. 7.

THEOPISTUS, ST. (d. 118), martyr. See Eustace, St.

THEOPREPIUS, ST. (d. 121?), martyr. See Philetus, St.

THEOTICUS, ST. (d. 311?), martyr. See Arianus, St.

THEOTIMUS, ST. (d. 407), bishop. From his home on the Black Sea he became an apostle to the barbarians along the lower Danube and bishop of Tomi. He was a defender of Origen against St. Epiphanius. F. D. Apr. 20.

THEOTOCOPULI, DOMENICO. See Greco, El.

THEOTONIUS, ST. (1086-1166). Born in Ganfeo, Spain, he was educated at Coimbra, ordained, and stationed at Viseu, where he gained a reputation both for his work among the poor and his condemnation of the scandalous life of the queen. After a pilgrimage he joined the Augustinian canons regular at Coimbra, Portugal, serving as prior and abbot during his last thirty years. He persuaded the new king, Alphonsus, to release his Mozarabic captives. F. D. Feb. 18.

THÉRÈSE OF LISIEUX, ST. (1873-1897). Daughter of Louis Martin, a watchmaker, and Zélie Guérin, Marie Françoise Thérèse was born on Jan. 2 in Alençon, France, the youngest of nine children. At five, when her mother died, the family moved to Lisieux, where she was raised by her older sisters and an aunt. Her sister Pauline joined the Carmelites when Thérèse was nine; another sister entered the order five years later. When Thérèse tried to follow, she was refused permission, but after a year was admitted to the Carmel at Lisieux. She was professed in 1890 and took the name Thérèse of the Child Jesus. She became mistress of novices and led a quiet life of prayer, meditation, and patient acceptance of suffering. In 1894 the prioress, Mother Agnes (her sister Pauline), ordered her to write the story of her childhood, which she finished in 1896. In 1897, on the order of the new prioress, Mother Marie de Gonzague, she added an account of her life in the convent which she had written for her sister Marie. The whole is her autobiography, *The Story of a Soul*, which became one of the most widely read spiritual works. The first printed versions were too carefully edited by her sister Pauline; the entire original manuscript was not released until 1956. Thérèse died in Liseux of tuberculosis on Sept. 30. A popular cult sprang up quickly for the "Little Flower," as she was called, and Pope Pius XI canonized her in 1925. She was declared co-patron with St. Francis Xavier of missions and missionaries in 1927, and in 1944 was named co-patron of France with Joan of Arc. F. D. Oct. 3.

Autobiography, trans. Ronald Knox (New York, Kenedy, 1958); JOHN BEEVERS, *Storm of Glory* (Garden City, N.Y., Image Books, 1955).

THESPESIUS, ST. (d. 230?), martyr. He was put to death in Cappadocia during the persecution of Alexander Severus. F. D. June 1.

THESPESIUS, ST. (d. 235), martyr. See Anatolius, St.

THETGO. See Tudy, St.

THEUTGER. See Deochar, St.

THIBAUD. See Theobald, St.

THIBAUT IV DE CHAMPAGNE (1201-1253), king. Born in Troyes, France, son of Thibaut III, count of Champagne, and Blanche, sister of King Sancho VII of Navarre, he inherited his father's title only after repulsing the claims of his uncle, the count of Brenne, and those of Queen Alice of Cyprus. He supported the nobles against Blanche of Castile during Louis IX's minority, but after quarreling with them joined the queen. In 1234 he succeeded Sancho as king of Navarre, joined Gregory IX's crusade in 1239, was defeated at Gaza, Palestine, in 1240, and returned to Europe. He is praised for *Poésies du roi de Navarre*, particularly his four crusade songs, and hailed by Dante and Petrarch. He died in Pampeluna, Spain, on July 8.

THIEMO, ST. (d. 1102), bishop and martyr. A member of the family of the counts of Meglin, Bavaria, he became a Benedictine at Niederaltaich abbey, where he achieved fame as a painter and metalworker. In 1077 he became abbot of St. Peter's, Salzburg, Austria, and in 1090 was made its archbishop. Imprisoned and exiled for his support of Pope Gregory VII, he joined the crusading army, was captured and tortured at Ascalon, and put to death at Corozain when he refused to become a Moslem. He is also called Theodmarus. F. D. Sept. 28.

THIENTO, BL. (d. 955), martyr. Abbot of the Benedictine monastery of Wessobrunn, Bavaria, he was slain with six of his community by invading Hungarians. F. D. Aug. 10.

THIERRY. *See* Theodoric, St. (d. 533?).

THIERRY OF FREIBURG (13th century). A Dominican, he was elected superior general of Germany in 1293, taught at Paris in 1297, and was appointed vicar of the German province of his order in 1310. He wrote treatises on theology, metaphysics, and cosmology, chief of which was *De fride* (1304), in which he described the rays of a rainbow.

THIERS, LOUIS ADOLPHE (1797–1877), statesman, historian. Born in Marseilles, France, on Apr. 16, he studied there, law at Aix, was admitted to the bar in 1818, and in 1821 went to Paris. He became assistant editor of *Constitutionnel*, a Liberal journal, opposed Charles X's government, and achieved widespread recognition with his ten-volume *Histoire de la révolution française* (1823–27). In 1830 he helped found *National*, a newspaper which helped cause the downfall of the Bourbons, was elected deputy from Aix and vigorously supported Louis Philippe, helped drive Charles from the throne in the July revolution of 1830, was secretary of finances in 1830–31, and in 1832 was appointed minister of the interior, and became president of the council. He filled several cabinet posts in the next few years, was elected to the French Academy in 1834, resigned from the government in 1836 when he was minister of foreign affairs, headed the opposition in 1838, and again became chief minister of foreign affairs in 1840, but his anti-English policies forced him to resign later the same year. He was a leading member of the constituent and legislative assemblies of 1848–51, and a leader of the February revolution of 1848, did not oppose Napoleon III for president in 1848, but withdrew his support when he became emperor, and was arrested by Napoleon and forced into exile in 1851–52. On his return to France he retired from public life to finish the twenty-volume *Histoire du consulat et de l'Empire* (1845–62). He returned as a deputy in 1863, became leader of the antiimperialists, and opposed the war with Prussia in 1870. He was elected to the national assembly (by twenty-six constituencies), negotiated the Treaty of Frankfort with Germany in Mar. 1871, and suppressed the insurrection of the commune. He was elected first president of the Third Republic on Aug. 30. He aroused violent dislikes by his arbitrary rule, though he was mainly instrumental in causing France to rise from the disaster of the Franco-Prussian War, and resigned in May, 1873, when a measure curbing executive powers was passed. He held his seat in the assembly until 1876, when he occupied a seat in the chamber of deputies until his death in St. Germain-en-Laye, near Paris, on Sept. 3. His sixteen-volume *Discours parlementaires* was published posthumously.

THIJM, JOSEPH ALBERT ALBERDINGK (1820–1889), author. Born in Amsterdam, Holland, on July 8, he studied there, embarked on a business career, but abandoned it to pursue literature. He became art critic of the *Spectator* in 1842, a disciple of Bilderdijk, and soon was recognized for his poetry and art knowledge, and as a leader of the Catholic revival in the Netherlands. He was active in seeking the restoration of the hierarchy there, edited the periodical, *Dietsche Warande*, from 1855 to 1886, and wrote pamphlets on the Church. He died in Amsterdam on Mar. 17.

THIJM, PETER PAUL MARIA ALBERDINGK (1827–1904). Brother of Joseph, he was born in Amsterdam, Holland, on Oct. 21, graduated from the athenaeum there in 1857, became a history teacher in Maastricht, and professor at Louvain in 1870, and established there a chair of Dutch literature. He was active in the Catholic revival movement in the Netherlands, a member of groups devoted to Flemish culture, served as president of the Flemish Academy, and wrote several books. He died at Louvain, Belgium, on Feb. 1.

THILL, FRANK AUGUSTINE (1893–1957), bishop. Born in Dayton, Ohio, on Oct. 12, he studied at Dayton, Mt. St. Mary of the West seminary, Cincinnati, and the Angelicum, Rome, and was ordained in Cincinnati in 1920. He was one of the organizers of the Catholic Students' Mission Crusade in 1918, serving as secretary-treasurer until 1935 and executor-counselor from then until his death, was made a papal chamberlain in 1928, was chancellor of the Cincinnati archdiocese in 1935–38, became a domestic prelate in 1937, and was consecrated bishop of Concordia in 1938. He was transferred to Salina, Kansas, in 1944, and served there until his death on May 21.

THIMELBY, RICHARD (1614–1672), missioner. Born in Lincolnshire, England, he became a Jesuit in 1632, taught theology at Liège, Flanders, for sixteen years, and was sent on the English mission where he worked under the alias Ashby. He was appointed master of novices in Ghent in 1666, rector of St. Omer's, Flanders, in 1672, and died there on Jan. 7.

THIRION, JULIEN (1852–1918), scientist. Born in Sclayn, Belgium, he studied at Namur, became a Jesuit at twenty, taught science at Louvain, wrote on optics and mathematics, and was editor of the *Annales* of the Société Scientifique de Bruxelles and of *Revue des questions scientifiques*. He died on Feb. 23.

THIRKELD, BL. RICHARD (d. 1583). Born in the diocese of Durham, England, he went to Oxford, also studied at Douai and Rheims, was ordained late in life in 1579, served the English underground mission in Yorkshire, was followed after his visits to prisoners aroused suspicion, captured, and brutally executed at York for his priesthood. He was beatified in 1886. F. D. May 29.

THÖLDE, JOHANNES (17th century), chemist. Born in Frankenhausen, Germany, he wrote *Cursus triumphalis antimonii* (1604) on the use of antimony in fevers, which became an influential tract. He pretended that his chemical publications were no more than translations from a "German monk," Basilius Valentinus, whose name he created.

THOMAIS, ST. (d. 476). The wife of a fisherman at Alexandria, Egypt, she fought off attempted rape by her father-in-law, who then murdered her. F. D. Apr. 14.

THOMAS, ST. (1st century), apostle. Surnamed "Didymus," the twin, he was born probably in Galilee and became one of the twelve apostles, though where and when are not known. He was present at Lazarus' resurrection and at the Last Supper, and is particularly remembered for his skepticism and his later fullhearted acknowledgment of the Resurrection of Christ (John 20:24–29). Eusebius says that Thomas later preached in Parthia, and very ancient tradition says he suffered martyrdom in southern India. F. D. Dec. 21.

THOMAS, ST. (d. 720?), abbot. Born in Maurienne, Savoy, he became a Benedictine, lived as a hermit at Farfa, near Rome, and as abbot restored the monastery there with the help of the duke of Spoleto. F. D. Dec. 10.

THOMAS, BL. (d. 1337). Born in Costacciaro, Italy, near Gubbio, he joined the Camaldolese at Sitria, then sought a stricter life of solitude and moved to a cave on Monte Cupo. F. D. Mar. 25.

THOMAS, CHARLES LOUIS AMBROISE (1811–1896), composer. Born in Metz, France, on Aug. 5, son of a musician, he entered the Paris conservatory in 1828, won prizes and, in 1832, the Grand Prix de Rome. He studied under Kalkbrenner, Barbereau, and Lesueur, gained attention with his compositions, had his *La double echelle* produced by the Opéra Comique in 1837, and, in 1838, *Le Perru-*

quier de la Régence followed by a succession of operas during the next two decades. He was appointed to the Institute in 1851, became professor of composition at the conservatory in 1852, and in 1871 was appointed director, a position he held until his death in Paris on Feb. 12. Among his works are *Hamlet* (1868), *Françoise de Rimini* (1877), *Messe solennele* (1857), *Marche religieuse* (1865), and *Mignon* (1866), which in 1894 gained him the grand cross of the Legion of Honor (to which he had been elected in 1845) on the occasion of its thousandth performance.

THOMAS OF ANTIOCH, ST. (d. 782). He was a Syrian monk who lived near Antioch and is honored as a mediator against plague. F. D. Nov. 18.

THOMAS AQUINAS, ST. (1225–1274), theologian and Doctor of the Church. Born in the castle of Roccasecca, near Aquino, Italy, he was placed by his parents as an oblate in the Benedictine monastery of Monte Cassino from 1230 to 1239, studied at the newly founded University of Naples, and became a Dominican, over his family's strong opposition, in 1245 at Paris. He remained there for three years, studying under Albertus Magnus, accompanied the latter to Cologne, was ordained in 1250, returned to Paris in 1252, and became master of theology. He was a commentator on the gospels and on Peter Lombard until 1256, when he received his license to teach. He taught at Paris until 1259, receiving his doctorate in 1257, aided St. Albert at the general chapter of their order at Valenciennes in 1259 which established the system of studies adopted by the Dominicans, then lectured at Anagni, Orvieto, Rome, Viterbo, and other Italian cities. As a result of his meeting at Orvieto with William of Moerbeke, who had translated Aristotle, Thomas became interested in commenting on the Greek philosopher. After nine years he returned to Paris, in 1268, and became entangled in the struggles between the order priests and seculars and with the Augustinians over the support given Averroes. In 1272 he established a new house of studies at Naples. Pope Gregory X sent him in 1274 to attend the Council of Lyons, but he died on the way. Most of his writing was completed in his last twenty years. It includes his early commentaries on the *Sentences* of Peter Lombard (1254–56); on Boethius' *De Trinitate* and *De hebdomadibus*; on *De divinis nominibus* of Dionysius the Pseudo-Areopagite; on the anonymous *Liber de causis*; and on the major works of Aristotle (including the *Physics, Metaphysics, Nichomachaean Ethics, Politics,* and *The Soul*). St. Thomas also wrote on truth, the power of God, evil, spiritual creatures, the soul, being and essence, the eternity of the world, the unity of the intellect, and a defense of religious orders. The manual of Christian belief, *Summa contra Gentiles*, was written about 1260, and the monumental *Summa theologiae*, projected to synthesize all Christian thought, was prepared in 1265–72. *Compendium theologiae* followed in 1273. Except for the limitations of thirteenth-century science, what St. Thomas had to say about God and man, creation and purpose, mind and matter, will, the soul, knowledge, human conduct, motives, habits, acts, grace, and faith remains fundamental in Catholic thinking and has been papally approved as such. He labored to present these basic beliefs in an orderly fashion, distinguishing carefully between revelation and reason, theology and philosophy, and the conclusions drawn from a reservoir of world thought, both pagan and Christian. St. Thomas died at the Cistercian monastery in Fossa Nuova, Italy. He was canonized in 1323 by Pope John XXII; Pius V declared him a Doctor of the Church in 1567; Leo XIII declared him master of all scholastic doctors in 1879 and the universal patron of universities, colleges, and schools in 1880. F. D. Mar. 7.

G. K. CHESTERTON, *Saint Thomas Aquinas* (Garden City, N.Y., Image Books, 1956); MARTIN CYRIL D'ARCY, *Thomas Aquinas* (Boston, Little, Brown, 1930); JACQUES MARITAIN, *Angelic Doctor* (New York, Dial, 1931); ETIENNE GILSON, *The Christian Philosophy of St. Thomas* (New York, Random, 1956).

THOMAS OF BAYEUX (d. 1100), archbishop. A protégé of Odo of Bayeux, he was appointed archbishop of York in 1070 and was immediately embroiled in a dispute with Lanfranc when he refused to acknowledge the jurisdiction of Westminster. Lanfranc refused to consecrate him, but was persuaded to do so by the king. Thomas went to Rome to appeal his case to the pope, who referred the case to a council of English bishops, which decided in Lanfranc's favor.

THOMAS À BECKET, ST. (1118–1170), archbishop and martyr. Born in London of wealthy parents of Norman descent, he studied at Merton priory, law in London, and went on to Paris. He became a business apprentice, and in 1144 entered the household of Archbishop Theobald of Canterbury. He was sent on missions to Rome and in 1154 was appointed archdeacon. In 1155 he became chancellor to King Henry II. He soon became, after Henry, the most powerful person in the realm, widely known for his sumptuous style of living. In 1159 he went with Henry's military expedition to Toulouse. Despite vigorous objections, the king appointed him archbishop of Canterbury in 1162 to fill the vacancy caused by Theobald's death in 1161. He resigned his chancellorship, was ordained the day before his consecration, and adopted a contrastingly austere way of life. He also made it clear that he would not be the king's pawn. A major clash came when Henry sought to usurp ecclesiastical privileges which had been granted to the papacy since the Norman invasion. In 1164, Thomas momentarily approved the Constitutions of Clarendon, which denied to the clergy the right to be tried in ecclesiastical courts, to appeal directly to Rome, and to excommunicate a tenant-in-chief without the king's consent. Later that year a council at Northampton denounced him and he fled to France to present his case to Pope Alexander III. Thomas had been hotheaded, and had also failed to support his own bishops; the king was equally stubborn; the pope proved unwilling to offend a strong monarch. Excommunications and recriminations followed; the king confiscated the property of Thomas' friends and threatened vengeance against the Cistercians, at whose abbey in Pontigny Thomas stayed. There he spent six years in quiet prayer, until July 1170, when King Louis of France helped to effect a meeting of Henry and Thomas at Montmartre. The men were personally reconciled, although the basic disagreement remained unresolved. Thomas returned to Canterbury, but his refusal to remove all censures was reported abroad to Henry. The king's angry retort led four knights to sail for England and to murder Thomas within his cathedral. He was immediately acclaimed as a martyr and in 1173 was declared a saint by Pope Innocent III. Henry did public penance at his tomb and Canterbury soon became a major shrine, the goal of pilgrims, including Chaucer's literary creations, for some 350 years, until it was destroyed at the time of a quarrel between another King Henry (VIII) and another chancellor named Thomas (More). F. D. Dec. 29.

T. S. ELIOT's *Murder in the Cathedral* (1935) a dramatic account of his martyrdom. ALFRED DUGGAN, *My Life for My Sheep* (Garden City, N.Y., Image Books, 1957).

THOMAS OF BECKINGTON (1390?–1465), bishop. Born in Beckington, Somerset, England, he studied at Winchester and Oxford, was ordained, and became archdeacon of Buckingham, canon at Wells, and in 1423 dean of the Arches. He acquired great influence with King Henry VI, served on diplomatic missions, was appointed lord privy seal in 1442, and bishop of Bath and Wells in 1443. He died in Wells, England, on Jan. 14.

THOMAS OF BIVILLE, ST. (1187–1257). Thomas Hélye was born in Biville, Normandy, became a teacher and catechist there, studied at Paris, where he was ordained, became pastor of St. Maurice, and was famous throughout Normandy for his preaching. A story that he was chaplain to St. Louis IX is unfounded.

His cult was confirmed in 1859. F. D. Oct. 19.

THOMAS OF BRADWARDINE (1290?-1349), archbishop. Born in Chichester, England, he studied at Oxford, and in 1325 was one of the proctors involved in the dispute between the university and the archdeacon of Oxford. He became famed as a theologian and for his lectures on theology, became chaplain of Richard de Bury, bishop of Durham, in 1335, and chancellor of St. Paul's cathedral. He accompanied Edward III on trips to Europe as chaplain, was one of the peace commissioners to King Philip, and in 1348 was elected archbishop of Canterbury by the chapter. The king objected, but when his candidate, John Ufford, died, consented, and Thomas was consecrated at Avignon in 1349. He contracted the plague on his return to England and died in London on Aug. 26. He had great theological knowledge (Chaucer coupled him with St. Thomas Aquinas and Boethius), and wrote theological treatises, chief of which was *De causa Dei contra Pelagium*, and mathematical works, among them *De proportionibus* (1495) and *Geometrica speculativa* (1530).

THOMAS OF CANTELUPE, ST. (1218?-1282), bishop. Born in Hambleden, England, son of Baron William of Cantelupe, he was educated by his uncle, the bishop of Worcester, who sent him to Oxford when he was nineteen. Shortly after, he joined his brother, Hugh, in Paris and accompanied his father to the thirteenth General Council at Lyons in 1245, where he was probably ordained and became chaplain to Pope Innocent IV. After further studies at Orléans and Paris he returned to Oxford and became chancellor in 1262. He supported the barons in their struggle against Henry III and in 1264 went to Amiens to present their case to St. Louis. When Henry was defeated at Lewes, Thomas became chancellor of England in 1265 for a short time, but was dismissed after the death of Simon de Montfort. After a period in Paris (1265-72) he returned to Oxford in 1274, continued to hold a plurality of benefices (he had received permission to do so from Pope Innocent IV), and in 1275 was chosen bishop of Hereford (he is also known as Thomas of Hereford), a see which had deteriorated greatly, but which he restored. His last years were clouded by a dispute with John Peckham, archbishop of Canterbury, who excommunicated him in 1282. He appealed to Pope Martin IV in person at Orvieto and was cordially received by the pope. While awaiting at Montefiascone, Italy, a settlement of the case, he was taken ill and died on Aug. 25. He was canonized in 1320. F. D. Oct. 3.

THOMAS OF CANTIMPRÉ (1201-1272), theologian. Born in Leuw St. Pierre, near Brussels, he studied at Liège, joined the Canons Regular of St. Augustine in Cantimpré at sixteen, was ordained, and in 1232 joined the Dominicans in Louvain. He studied under Albert the Great in Cologne and at Paris, became professor of theology at Louvain in 1240, and then engaged in successful missionary activity throughout Germany, France, and Belgium. He wrote *De natura rerum* and *Bonum universale de apibus*. He died on May 15.

THOMAS OF CELANO (1200?-1255?). Born in Celano, Abruzzi, Italy, he became one of the earliest followers of St. Francis of Assisi, joined the Franciscans in 1215, and accompanied Caesar of Speyer to Germany in 1221. In 1222 he became custos in Cologne, Mayence, Speyer, and Worms, vicar of the German province, and returned to Italy in 1223 and became St. Francis' companion. He wrote the first life of St. Francis immediately after the saint's canonization in 1228, and between 1244 and 1247 wrote a second life. He also wrote on the miracles of St. Francis, a life of St. Clare, and the *Dies irae*.

THOMAS OF CORI, BL. (1655-1729). Born in Cori, Italy, he became a Franciscan in 1677, was ordained and served as a master of novices, then gained permission to retire to the friary at Civitella, where he preached to the bandits in the mountains about Subiaco. He was beatified in 1785. F. D. Jan. 19.

THOMAS OF DOVER (d. 1295). A Benedictine monk at St. Martin's priory, Dover, England, he was a feeble old man when French raiders found him ill in bed, the only person left in the settlement. When he refused to disclose the hiding place of church valuables, he was murdered. Canonization proceedings were begun in 1382, but never completed; he is honored locally on Aug. 2.

THOMAS OF ECCLESTON (13th century), historian. He became a Friar Minor about 1232, studied at Oxford between 1230 and 1240, was stationed in London, and wrote *De adventu fratrum minorum in Angliam*, which chronicles the work of the Franciscans from their arrival in 1224 under the leadership of Agnellus of Pisa to 1258.

THOMAS OF ERCELDOUNE (1220?-1297?), poet. Also called Thomas the Rhymer and Thomas Learmont, he was born in Scotland. He wrote a series of poetic legends; many prophecies, popular in Scotland, also were attributed to him.

THOMAS OF FOLIGNO, BL. (d. 1369), martyr. See Antony of Saxony, Bl.

THOMAS OF HEREFORD, ST. See Thomas of Cantelupe, St.

THOMAS ILLYRICUS, BL. (15th century). A native of Osimo, Italy, he became a Franciscan and retired to a forest solitude near Arcachon, France. When he found on the beach a wooden statue of Mary and Jesus, apparently an oriental carving of the thirteenth century, he erected a shrine for it. Pius IX, who visited the permanent church in 1870, gave papal approval to the devotion.

THOMAS À JESU. *See* Avila, Diez Sanchez de.

THOMAS OF JESUS. *See* Andrada, Thomas de.

THOMAS OF JORZ (d. 1310), cardinal. Probably an Englishman, he became a Dominican in England, master of theology at Oxford, prior of the Dominicans there, and was provincial of England from 1296 to 1303. He became an adviser to King Edward, and his confessor, and while on a royal diplomatic mission to Lyons in 1305 was created cardinal. While on a trip to King Henry VII of Germany as legate for Pope Clement V, he died in Grenoble, France, on Dec. 13. He wrote theological works, including a commentary on the *Sentences*.

THOMAS À KEMPIS (1380?–1471), author. Thomas Haemerken was born in Kempen, near Düsseldorf, Germany, in 1379 or 1380, son of a blacksmith, studied in Deventer under Florentius Radewyn, and in 1399 joined the Augustinian Brothers of the Common Life at Agnetenberg in Zwolle, where he was professed in 1407. He was ordained in 1413, and was sub-prior in 1425 and again in 1448. He spent his life at convents in Zwolle and Lunenkerk, near Harlingen, where the brothers moved in 1429–32 while Utrecht was under an interdict, as a copyist, and writing biographies of Gerhard Groot, of his first disciples, of Florentius Radewyn, tracts on the monastic life, spiritual works, sermons, hymns, and letters. He died at Agnetenberg, near Zwolle, Netherlands, on July 25. The most famous work attributed to him is *The Imitation of Christ* (1486), which scholars now generally agree was written by him. His name is also spelled Hammerken, Hemerken, or Hämmerlein.

THOMAS O'CONOR (d. 1201). He became bishop of Armagh, Ireland, in 1181. When Bishop John Comyn of Dublin persuaded Pope Lucius III to bar O'Conor and all succeeding primates of Ireland from visiting certain provinces and from holding courts within the diocese of Dublin, a long and bitter controversy was begun.

THOMAS OF STRASBURG (d. 1357). Born at Strassburg or Hagenau, Alsace, he became an Augustinian, taught, and in 1341 went to Paris, where he became famed for his lectures. He was a follower of the teachings of Giles of Rome and opposed those of Henry of Ghent. He was elected general of the Augustinians in 1345, a position he held until his death, revised the constitutions of his order, founded a *studium generale* in Verona in 1351, and wrote

a commentary on Peter the Lombard's *Sentences*.

THOMAS OF TOLENTINO, BL. (d. 1321), martyr. Becoming a Franciscan in Italy, he went to the Armenian missions, gained papal and royal assistance during several return trips to Europe, pushed on to Persia, then set out for China. When his ship was driven to Salsette Island, near Bombay, he was captured by Moslems, tortured, and beheaded with two other Franciscans, Bl. James of Padua and Peter of Siena, and a layman, Bl. Demetrius of Tiflis. They were beatified in 1894. F. D. Apr. 9.

THOMAS OF VILLANOVA, ST. (1488–1555), bishop. Son of Alonzo Tomás García and Lucía Martínez Castellanos, he was born in Fuentellana, Castile, Spain, near Villanueva from which he received his name), studied at Alcalá, became an Augustinian in 1516, and was ordained in 1518. He was prior at Salamanca, Burgos, and Valladolid, provincial of Andalusia and Castile, and in 1533 sent the first Augustinian missioners to America. Nominated by Emperor Charles V, whose chaplain he was, for the see of Granada, he declined the honor but in 1544 was appointed archbishop of Valladolid, a see vacant for ninety years. He continued to follow the way of life of a monk, devoted himself to helping the poor, established orphanages for unwanted babies, and preached widely and effectively. He labored zealously among the Moors, sought to restore clerical discipline, and, though he did not attend the Council of Trent, used his influence with the Spanish bishops there to promote the internal reform of the Church. He died in Valencia, Spain, on Sept. 8 and was canonized in 1658. F. D. Sept. 22.

THOMAS OF WALDEN. *See* Netter, Thomas.

THOMASSIN, LOUIS (1619–1695), theologian. Born in Aix-en-Provence, France, on Aug. 28, he joined the Oratorians when thirteen, taught, became professor of literature at Saumur, and then at St. Magloire seminary in Paris, where he remained until his death on Dec. 24. He wrote theological treatises, chief of which are *Ancienne et nouvelle discipline de l'église* (1678–79), *Dogmatum theologicorum* (1680–89) and *Traité dogmatique et historique* (1705).

THOMIAN, ST. (d. 660). He became archbishop of Armagh, Ireland, in 623. F. D. Jan. 10.

THOMPSON, DIANA CALVERT (1811–1896). Born in Humsden, Hertfordshire, England, she married Edward Thompson, became a convert with her husband in 1846, and devoted herself to writing. Her best-known work is her biography of St. Charles Borromeo. She died in Cheltenham, England, on Aug. 21.

THOMPSON, EDWARD HEALY (1813–

1891), author. Born in Oakham, Rutlandshire, England, he studied in Oakham and at Cambridge, and became an Anglican minister. He became a convert in 1846, wrote biographies and spiritual works, edited the Clifford Tracts, and died at Cheltenham, England, on May 21.

THOMPSON, FRANCIS (1859–1907), poet. Born in Preston, Lancashire, England, on Dec. 16, son of a doctor, he entered St. Cuthbert's College at Ushaw in 1870 to study for the priesthood. He abandoned this in 1877 on the advice of his counselors, studied medicine from 1878 to 1884 at Owens College, where he acquired the drug habit, and in 1885 went to London, broken in health, and worked at various positions until he collapsed in the slums as a drug addict. In 1887 he sent some poetry and an essay to Wilfrid Meynell, co-editor of the magazine *Merry England*. Meynell read the manuscripts a year later, published them, sought out and found their author, and placed Thompson in a London hospital. He then sent him to the care of the Canons Regular in Storrington where he was cured of his addiction. Thompson returned to London in 1890, spent 1892–95 at the Capuchin monastery in Pantasaph, Wales, and returned to London in 1896, where he remained until his death there on Nov. 13. His *Hound of Heaven* is considered one of the greatest religious lyrics. During his lifetime he published *Poems* (1893), *Sister Songs* (1895), and *New Poems* (1897); he also wrote a biography of St. Ignatius and a collection of essays, including one on the poet Shelley. His works were collected in a three-volume edition by Wilfrid Meynell in 1913; recently discovered critical reviews have been compiled in two volumes by Fr. Terence L. Connolly, S.J., who has also edited additional poems and plays.

THOMPSON, BL. JAMES (d. 1582), martyr. Born in York, England, he went to Rheims to become a priest. In 1581 he was obliged to return to England because of ill health, but labored there as Mr. Hudson until he was arrested and hanged at Knavesmire in York. He was beatified in 1895. F. D. Nov. 28.

THOMPSON, JOHN SPARROW DAVID (1844–1894), premier. Born in Halifax, Nova Scotia, on Nov. 10, son of a government official, he studied there and was admitted to the bar in 1865. He became a convert in 1870, was elected an alderman in Halifax in 1871, to the assembly in 1877, became attorney general in 1878, and premier of Nova Scotia in 1882. He became a judge of the supreme court the same year, minister of justice of Canada, in 1885, and went to Washington as adviser of the British government with the fisheries commission, for which he was knighted by Queen Victoria. He became Canada's first Catholic premier in 1892, served on the Bering Sea Commission at Paris in 1893, was appointed to Great Britain's privy council, and died suddenly on a visit to Windsor castle in England on Dec. 12.

THONISSEN, JEAN JOSEPH (1817–1891), penologist. Born in Hasselt, Limbourg, Belgium, on Jan. 21, he entered government service, became interested in penal law, but was dismissed by the Liberal government in 1848. He was appointed to the chair of criminal law at Louvain that year, devoted himself to writing and to seeking the abolition of the death penalty, and in 1863 was elected to the parliament. He adopted many tenets of Liberalism, which he abandoned after they were papally censured in Pius IX's *Syllabus of Errors*. In 1872 the king invited him to form a ministry, but he was unable to do so when his own party refused to support him. He became minister in 1884, labored to reform penal procedure and to put the new school law into effect, but was forced to retire because of ill-health in 1887. He wrote biographies of Leopold I and Félix de Mérode, a history of socialism, the centenary volume for the Royal Academy of Belgium, of which he was a member, and the first section of an unfinished history of penal law covering India, Egypt, Judaea, Athens, and the empire of the Franks. He died in Louvain, Belgium, on Aug. 17.

THORFINN, ST. (d. 1285), bishop. A holy man from Trondhjem, Norway, he may have been canon of the cathedral of Nidaros and a Cistercian at the abbey of Tautra before he became bishop of Hamar. Opposition to King Eric's attempt to presume on ecclesiastical privileges led to exile for several clerics, and Bishop Thorfinn, shipwrecked in flight, finally reached a Flemish abbey near Bruges. There he died, commemorated by a poem written by one of the monks, Walter de Muda. F. D. Jan. 8.

THORING, MATHIAS (d. 1469). A Renaissance classical scholar, he wrote *Replicae*, published at Basle by Conrad of Leonberg.

THORLAC THORHALLSSON (1133–1193), bishop. Born in Iceland, he was ordained in 1151, spent the next ten years studying in Paris and Lincoln, founded an Augustinian monastery of which he was abbot, and in 1178 became bishop of Skalholt. Despite great opposition, he introduced widespread ecclesiastical reforms and erased simony and incontinency among his clergy before he died on Dec. 23. His cult has never been officially confirmed.

THORNE, BL. JOHN (d. 1539), martyr. *See* Whiting, Bl. Richard.

THOROLD, ALGAR LABOUCHERE (1866–1936), author. Born in England, he went to Eton and Oxford, became a convert in 1882, and in 1894 married Theresa Mansel. He was on the staff of *Truth* in 1912–17, worked in the propaganda division of the war office in

1917–18, was a member of the British delegation to the peace conference at Versailles, and became first press attaché to the British embassy in Paris in 1920. In 1926–34 he was editor of the *Dublin Review*. He wrote *Catholic Mysticism, Six Masters in Disillusion*, and a biography of Henry Labouchere, and translated selections from Bl. Angela of Foligno, St. Catherine of Siena, and others.

THOU, JACQUES AUGUSTE DE (1553–1617), diplomat. Born in Paris on Oct. 8, son of Christoph de Thou, first president of the Paris parliament, he studied at Paris and Valence, where he met Joseph Scaliger, became a canon at Notre Dame in 1571, and accompanied Paul de Foix on the latter's diplomatic mission to Italy in 1572. He went to Guienne in 1581 and there met Henry of Navarre, became master of petitions in the Paris parliament in 1584 and councilor of state in 1588, and helped reconcile Henry III and Henry of Navarre. He opposed the league, entered Navarre's service on Henry III's death, in 1589, became grand master of the royal library in 1593, helped prepare the Edict of Nantes in 1598, and assisted at the Conference of Fontainebleu in 1600 and the treaties of Ste. Menehould (1614) and Loudun (1616). He espoused Gallican ideas in France and prevented the publication of the decrees of the Council of Trent in France. He is best known for his *Historia sui temporis* (1604–20), covering the period 1546–1607, which was placed on the Index in 1609, and his memoirs, *Commentarius de vita sua* (1620), covering the period 1553–1601. He died in Paris on May 7.

THOU, NICOLAS DE (1528–1598), bishop. Uncle of Jacques Auguste, he was born in Paris, became a canon of Notre Dame in 1547, and was appointed bishop of Chartres in 1573. Sympathetic to Henry of Navarre, he opposed the Catholic League, and joined the French bishops in 1591 who condemned Gregory XIV's excommunication of Henry. He assisted at Henry's abjuration in St. Denis in 1593, and, as the representative of the archbishop of Rheims, anointed Henry king in 1594. He died in Villebon, France, on Nov. 5.

THRASEAS, ST. (d. 170?), martyr. Bishop of Eumenia, Phrygia, he opposed the Montanist heresy, and became a martyr at Smyrna. F. D. Oct. 5.

THUGUT, JOHANN AMADEUS FRANZ DE PAULA (1736–1818), diplomat. Born in Linz, Austria, on Mar. 31, son of an army official, he studied at the Oriental Academy, Vienna, and became a translator at the Austrian embassy in Constantinople in 1754, secretary of the state chancery (where he acted as a French agent), and in 1769 chargé d'affaires. He was ennobled in 1771, appointed internuncio at Constantinople, and under Prince Kaunitz negotiated Turkey's cession of Bukovina to Austria in 1775, for which he was made a baron. He was Maria Theresa's intermediary in her negotiations with Frederick the Great in 1778, was ambassador to Warsaw in 1780–83 and to Naples in 1787–89, accompanied the allied army which invaded France in 1792, and was appointed chancellor in 1794. His policy was so devoted to Austrian interests that he alienated Austria's allies. Austrian defeats in Italy in 1796–97 and the peace of Campo Formio forced on Austria by Napoleon and giving Belgium to France led to increased demands for his removal. When the defeat of Hohenlinden in 1800 made his position untenable, he resigned, and retired from public life. He died in Vienna on May 28.

THULIS, VEN. JOHN (1568?–1616?), martyr. Born in Upholland, Lancashire, England, he studied at Rheims, was ordained in Rome in 1590, and returned to England in 1592. He was imprisoned in Cambridgeshire, wrote in favor of the institution of the archpriest and later opposed it, worked in Lancashire, was again captured, escaped, and was recaptured, and executed on Mar. 18 at Lancaster with Roger Wrenno, a weaver, and three thieves whom he had converted.

THUN-HOHENSTEIN, LEO (1811–1888), statesman. Born at the family castle of Tetschen, Bohemia, on Apr. 7, Count Leo studied at Prague and became a member of the Bohemian diet. He served in Galicia in 1846, and in 1848 was appointed president of the administrative board and actual ruler of Bohemia. He was captured and imprisoned in Prague when the revolution came, but was freed and helped the military put down the revolt. He was appointed minister of worship and education in 1849, reorganized the educational system, and was instrumental in negotiating a concordat with the papacy in 1852. When Austria became a constitutional monarchy in 1860, his post was abolished, but in 1861 the emperor appointed him to a life membership in the upper house of the legislature. He helped draft the declaration of 1868 and the fundamental articles of 1871. During his several terms in the Bohemian diet he led the Federalist party, was a vigorous proponent of Bohemian autonomy, and founded the party's chief paper, *Vaterland*. He had a lifelong interest in the revival of the Czech language and literature, and published a treatise on Bohemian literature in 1842. He died in Vienna on Dec. 17.

THURSTON, HERBERT (1856–1939), author. Born in London, he studied at Mt. St. Mary's, Stonyhurst, and the University of London, became a Jesuit, and was ordained in 1890. He was stationed in London, contributed to journals, and wrote widely. Titles include

Life of St. Hugh of Lincoln, The War and the Prophets, The Memory of Our Dead, Modern Spiritualism, Christian Science, No Popery, and *Superstition.* He was co-editor with Bishop Ward of the Westminster Library, and from 1926 until his death worked on a revision of Butler's *Lives of the Saints.* He lectured widely against spiritualism and was equally the foe of superstitious practices, extravagant claims in hagiography, false devotions, and pietistic writing. He died in London on Nov. 6.

THWING, JOHN. *See* Twenge, St. John.

THWING, BL. THOMAS (1635–1680), martyr. Born in Heworth, Yorkshire, England, he studied at Douai, was ordained in 1664, and sent to the English mission. He served as chaplain to his relative, Sir Miles Stapleton, and directed a school; in 1677 he became chaplain at the Institute of Mary at Dolebank, where three of his sisters were nuns. He was arrested with his uncle, Sir Thomas Gascoigne, during the hysteria over the Titus Oates Plot, and hanged, drawn, and quartered at York. He was beatified in 1929. F. D. Oct. 23.

THYRAUS, HERMANN (1532–1591), educator. Born in Neuss, Germany, he studied at Cologne and the German College, Rome, became a Jesuit in 1556, taught theology, at Ingolstadt and Trier, served as rector of the latter university in 1565–70, provincial of the Rhine province in 1571–78, and rector of the college in Mainz, Germany, until his death there on Oct. 26. He wrote volumes of sermons, *Confessio Augustana,* anti-Lutheran controversy; *Liber de religionis libertate,* attributed to him, probably was by his brother Peter.

THYRSUS, ST. (2nd century), martyr. *See* Andochius, St.

THYRSUS, ST. (d. 250?), martyr. *See* Saturninus, St.

THYRSUS, ST. (d. 251), martyr. Put to death at Apollonia in Phrygia with SS. Leucius and Callinicus, he is patron of Sisteron in southern France. F. D. Jan. 28.

TIBALDI, PELLEGRINO (1527?–1592?), painter. Pellegrino di Tibaldi de' Pellegrini was born in Bologna, Italy, son of a stonemason, studied under Bagna Cavello, and went to Rome where he studied Michelangelo's works and helped on the decoration of Castle Sant' Angelo and Trinità de' Monti. He became famed for his decorative works in Cardinal Poggi's villa in Rome and his palace in Bologna, many of whose subjects illustrated the *Odyssey.* In 1586 he was invited by Philip II to decorate the Escorial in Spain, and spent nine years there. He became architect of the Milan cathedral on his return and designed the church of San Fedele. Other works are *St. John Preaching in the Wilderness, Presentation in the Temple,* the ceiling of the library in Madrid, and *The Marriage of St. Catherine.* He died in Milan, Italy. He is also known as Pellegrino da Bologna.

TIBBA, ST. (7th century). *See* Kyneburga, St.

TIBERIUS, ST. (d. 303), martyr. *See* Florence, St.

TIBURTIUS, ST. (d. 288?), martyr. Unreliable sources call him a subdeacon at Rome who was beheaded there at the time of St. Sebastian. F. D. Aug. 11.

TIBURTIUS, ST. *See* Cecilia, St.

TICHBORNE, CHIDIOCK (1558?–1586), poet. He was executed in London for his part in an unsuccessful attempt to rescue Mary Queen of Scots; his father had been imprisoned because of expressed sympathies for Spain; an uncle died in prison as a religious martyr; a nephew, Fr. William Tichborne, was executed in 1601. Chidiock is remembered for *The Untimely End,* a poem once erroneously attributed to Walter Ralegh.

TICHBORNE, VEN. NICHOLAS (d. 1601), martyr. Born in Hartley Mauditt, Hampshire, England, he was sought out in 1592, finally captured in 1597, gave evidence against his family, and was released. However, he effected the release of his brother Thomas from the Gatehouse, London, in 1598, and was taken and executed at Tyburn on Aug. 24. Thomas Hackshot of Mursley, Buckinghamshire, was hanged with him, on the same charge.

TIEF, FRANCIS JOSEPH (1881–1938), bishop. Born in Greenwich, Connecticut, on Mar. 7, he studied at Niagara University and St. Bonaventure College, New York, and was ordained in 1908. He did parish work in Kansas, was vicar general of the Kansas City see in 1916–20, and was appointed bishop of Concordia, Kansas, in 1920. He resigned in 1938 and was appointed titular bishop of Nisa, and died on June 11.

TIEFFENTALLER, JOSEPH (1710–1785), missioner. Born in Bozen, Tyrol, on Aug. 27, he became a Jesuit in 1729, was sent to the Far East as a missionary in 1740, and became famed for his linguistic and scholarly achievements. When the Jesuits were suppressed in 1773, he remained in India, died in Lucknow on July 5, and was buried in Agra. Among his writings were *Descriptio Indiae,* a book of maps of the Ganges basin, histories of the Hindus and of India, and linguistic studies of Parsee.

TIEPOLO, GIOVANNI BATTISTA (1696?–1769?), painter. Born in Venice on Apr. 5, son of a sea captain, he studied under Lazzarini and was greatly influenced by the works of Paolo Veronese. In 1721 he married Cecelia, sister of the painter Guardi. He achieved fame for his paintings in northern Italy, particularly those in the doge's palace and Santa Maria della Pietà in Venice. In 1750 he went to Würzburg, where he spent three years painting frescoes depicting Frederick Barbarossa's life and the altarpieces, *Ascension of the Virgin* and *Fall of the Angels*, in the archbishop's palace. On his return, he was elected president of the Academy of Padua, and about 1763 accepted the invitation of King Charles III of Spain to execute a series of frescoes for the royal palace in Madrid. His paintings are noted for their delicacy, color, turbulent movement, inventiveness, and fantasy of subject matter. Outstanding are *Spain and Her Provinces*, *Christ in the Garden of Olives*, *Madonna in Glory*, *Crowning with Thorns*, *Holy Family with St. Gaetano*, and *Sacrifice of Abraham*. He died in Madrid on Mar. 27.

TIERNAN, FRANCES CHRISTINE (1846–1920), novelist. Born in Salisbury, North Carolina, daughter of Charles and Elizabeth Caldwell Fisher, she wrote forty novels between 1870 and 1915 and received the Laetare Medal in 1909. *The Land of the Sky* praised her native state; *Under the Southern Cross* was a defense of secession and the Confederate cause; other popular titles were *A Daughter of Bohemia*, *The Picture of Las Cruces*, and *The Wargrave Trust*. Her mother was a Catholic and Frances became a convert when young; she married James Marquis Tiernan in 1887 and went with him to Mexico; at his death in 1898 she returned to Salisbury, where she died on Mar. 24. She wrote under the name of Christian Reid.

TIERNEY, MARK ALOYSIUS (1795–1862), antiquarian. Born in Brighton, England, in Sept., he studied at Baddesley Green and St. Edmund's College, where he was ordained in 1818, and taught there. He did parish work in London and Sussex after 1819, and became well known for his historical and antiquarian studies. He was elected a fellow of the Society of Antiquaries in 1833, of the Royal Society in 1841, became the first canon penitentiary of Southwark after the hierarchy was restored, was second editor of the *Dublin Review*, and edited and revised five volumes of Dodd's *Church History of England* (1839–43). In 1842 he became the duke of Norfolk's chaplain at Arundel, England, where he died on Feb. 19.

TIERNEY, MICHAEL (1839–1908), bishop. Born in Cahir, Tipperary, Ireland, on Sept. 29, he went to the United States, studied at St. Thomas, Bardstown, Kentucky, Montreal, and St. Joseph's, Troy, and was ordained in Troy in 1866. He served as pastor in New England, Stamford, and Hartford, Connecticut, parishes and supervised the erection of the cathedral in the latter city. He became chancellor there and was consecrated sixth bishop of Hartford in 1894. He built many charitable institutions

and hospitals and founded St. Thomas' seminary in 1898. He died in Hartford on Oct. 5.

TIERNEY, RICHARD HENRY (1872–1928), editor. Born in New York City on Sept. 2, he studied at St. Francis Xavier, became a Jesuit in 1892, did further study at Woodstock and Linz, Austria, and was ordained in 1907. He taught at Gonzaga (Washington, D.C.), Holy Cross, and Woodstock, and in 1913 was appointed to the staff of the weekly, *America*. He was its editor in 1914–25, edited *Catholic Mind*, and wrote widely on educational, historical and psychological subjects. He died in New York City on Feb. 10.

TIGERNACH, ST. (d. 549), bishop. Said to have been the godchild of St. Brigid, and educated in Scotland, he may have been a monk at Clones as well as a bishop of Clogher, but accounts are not too clear. He also is called Tierney and Tierry. F. D. Apr. 4.

TIGHERNACH O'BRAEIN (d. 1088). A native of Connaught, Ireland, he became abbot of Roscommon and Clonmacnoise, and wrote one of the earliest Irish annals, which relates events both in Ireland and on the Continent.

TIGRIDIA. *See* Trigidia, St.

TIGRIS, ST. (5th century). Sister of St. Patrick (and often identified with Darerca), she married Gollit and was the mother of SS. Loman of Trim, Munis of Forgney, Broccaid of Emlagh, Broccen of Breaghwy, and Mugenoc of All Duimi Gluin, all bishops.

TIGRIUS, ST. (d. 406?). He was a priest at Constantinople, who, with Eutropius, a lector, was tortured by torches after the senate building was destroyed by fire following the banishment of St. John Chrysostom. Originally a slave, he seems to have been banished to Mesopotamia when no information was elicited. F. D. Jan. 12.

TIHEN, J. HENRY (1861–1940), bishop. Born in Oldenburg, Indiana, on July 14, he graduated from St. Benedict's College, Kansas, in 1881, studied at St. Francis seminary, Wisconsin, and was ordained in St. Louis in 1886. After engaging in parish work in St. Louis, he was rector of the Wichita cathedral from 1889 to 1911, was appointed chancellor in 1895, vicar general and a domestic prelate in 1907, and was consecrated bishop of Lincoln, Nebraska, in 1911. He was transferred to Denver in 1917, resigned in 1931 and was appointed titular bishop of Bosana, and died in Wichita, Kansas, on Jan. 14.

TILBERT, ST. (d. 789). A Benedictine, he was eighth bishop of Hexham, England, from 781 until his death. F. D. Sept. 7.

TILLEMONT, LOUIS SÉBASTIEN LE NAIN DE (1637–1698), historian. Born in Paris on Nov. 30, he studied at Port Royal under Nicole and at Beauvais with Canon Hermant, and was ordained in 1676. When the Port Royal community was dissolved in 1679, he retired to his estate at Tillemont, Paris, where he remained until his death on Jan. 10. Among his histories were the six-volume *Histoire des empereurs pendant les six premiers siècles de l'église* and the sixteen-volume *Mémoires pour servir a l'histoire ecclésiastique des six premiers siècles,* and a collection on notes on St. Louis.

TILLO, ST. (d. 702?). A Saxon, brought to the Low Countries as a slave, he was ransomed by St. Eligius, baptized, and became a student at the abbey of Solignac. Ordained, he became evangelizer of the area about Courtrai, and in his old age a recluse. He is also known as Théau, Tilman, Hillonius, and other names. F. D. Jan. 7.

TILLY, JOHANN TSERCLAES (1559–1632), general. Born in the château of Tilly, Brabant, in Feb., he was educated in Cologne, and about 1574 became a soldier in the Netherlands under Alessandro Farnese. He participated in Parma's siege of Antwerp, and in 1590 was appointed governor of Dun and Villefranche by the duke of Lorraine. He declined the offer of Henry IV to join the French army in 1594, joined the Austrian forces under Emperor Rudolf II fighting the Turks in Hungary in 1600, became colonel of the imperial army in 1602, headed a Walloon regiment in the assault on Budapest, was appointed general of artillery in 1604, and field marshal of the imperial forces in 1605. He entered the service of Duke Maximilian I of Bavaria, the leader of the Catholic League, as head of the Bavarian army in 1610, became commander in chief of the army of the league at the outbreak of the Thirty Years' War in 1618, and by his victory at Weisser Berg (White Mountain), near Prague, on Nov. 8, 1620, ended the Bohemian revolt. He was made a count for his victory in 1622 at Höchst where he practically destroyed the army of Christian of Brunswick; his victory at Stadtlohn in 1623 ended Christian's and Mansfeld's opposition; in 1626 his victory over King Christian IV of Denmark at Lütter-am-Barenberge in Brunswick ended the Dane's campaign. In 1630, Wallenstein was dismissed as head of the reduced imperial forces and Tilly was made their commander. In 1631 his armies besieged and captured Magdeburg, which was subjected to sacking and the torch on May 10; in July, he attacked Gustavus II Adolphus of Sweden's forces at Werben and was repulsed; in September they met at Breitenfeld, near Leipzig, and Tilly was defeated; in April 1632, Gustavus annihilated Tilly's forces near Rain on the Lech River. Tilly died of wounds received there on Apr. 30 in Ingolstadt, Bavaria.

TILMAN. See Tillo, St.

TIMMERMANS, FELIX (1886–1947), au-

thor. Born in Lier, Belgium, he followed the family trade of lacemaking, tried painting, and drifted into writing, which soon became an enthusiasm. His first book of short stories (*Dusk of Death*) appeared in 1910. *Pallieter* (1924), *Droll Peter* (1930), *The Triptych of the Three Kings* (1936) followed; he is best known for his novels, *Boerenpsalm,* on Flemish peasant life, and *The Perfect Joy of St. Francis.* He died in Lier.

TIMOLAUS, ST. (d. 303), martyr. See Agapius, St.

TIMON, ST. (1st century). One of the first deacons to be appointed by the apostles themselves, he is recorded only in Acts 6:5. F. D. Apr. 19.

TIMON, JOHN (1797–1867), bishop. Born in Conewago, Pennsylvania, on Feb. 12, he studied at St. Mary's, Baltimore, Maryland, and St. Mary's seminary, Missouri, joined the Lazarists in 1823, and was ordained in 1826. He was a missioner in Texas, Missouri, Arkansas, and Illinois, taught at St. Mary's, Missouri, and in 1835 was appointed first visitor of the American Lazarists. He became first bishop of Buffalo, New York, in 1847, labored among the workers on the Erie and Genesee canals and with the families of immigrants who settled the farms of the western part of the state, abolished trusteeism in his see, and built many churches. He died in Buffalo on Apr. 16.

TIMOTHY, ST. (d. 97?), bishop and martyr. The disciple of St. Paul was born, probably in Lycaonia, of a Gentile father and a Jewish mother who became a convert. He replaced Barnabas as Paul's companion and traveled to the Near East and Greece. He visited Thessalonica for the apostle and brought back news on which Paul based his epistle; he is mentioned in I Cor. 16:10 after a similar visitation to Corinth. The two men seem to have been imprisoned together in Caesarea and in Rome. Released, Paul went back to the East and Timothy stayed at Ephesus, whose first bishop he became, according to tradition. He is said to have been stoned to death there when he opposed a pagan festival. F. D. Jan. 24.

TIMOTHY, ST. (d. 150?), martyr. See Mark, St.

TIMOTHY, ST. (d. 250?), martyr. A deacon in Africa, he was burned to death during the Decian persecution. F. D. Dec. 19.

TIMOTHY, ST. (d. 286), martyr. A lector at Fenapeis, Egypt, and married only three weeks to St. Maura, he refused to turn over the sacred books to the governor during the Diocletian persecution. They both were tortured to extremes, then nailed to a wall, where they hung for nine days before death. F. D. May 3.

TIMOTHY, ST. (d. 290?), martyr. See Apollinaris, St.

TIMOTHY, ST. (3rd century), martyr. *See* Eutychius, St.

TIMOTHY, ST. (d. 304), bishop and martyr. The bishop of Gaza, Palestine, was burned alive there during the persecution of Diocletian. F. D. Aug. 19.

TIMOTHY, ST. (d. 311), martyr. A priest from Antioch, Syria, he was tortured and beheaded at Rome during the Diocletian persecution. F. D. Aug. 22.

TIMOTHY, ST. (d. 345?), martyr. *See* Diogenes, St.

TIMOTHY, ST. (d. 362), bishop and martyr. Because of his outspoken direction of the see of Prussa in Bithynia, he was put to death by Julian the Apostate. F. D. June 10.

TIMOTHY, BL. (1414–1504). Born in Montecchio, near Aquila, Italy, he became a Franciscan Observant and was known for his supernatural gifts. His cult was confirmed in 1870. F. D. Aug. 26.

TINCKER, MARY AGNES (1833–1907), author. Born in Ellsworth, Maine, on July 18, she taught, became a convert at twenty, served as a nurse during the Civil War, and spent the years 1873–87 in Italy. She wrote such novels as *The House of Yorke* (1872), *Grapes and Thorns* (1874), *Six Sunny Months* (1878), *Signor Monaldini's Niece* (1879), and *Autumn Leaves* (1898). She died in Boston, Massachusetts, on Dec. 4.

TINEL, EDGAR (1854–1912), composer. Born in Sinay, Belgium, on Mar. 27, he studied at the Brussels conservatory, won prizes for piano compositions as early as 1873, and became director of the Institute for Sacred Music at Mechlin in 1882. His cantata, *Klokke Roeland*, won the Grand Prix in 1877; his oratorio *Franciscus* (1888) finally established him. He became inspector of music schools in 1889, professor of counterpoint at the Brussels conservatory in 1896, and wrote *Mass of the Holy Virgin of Lourdes*, an *Alleluia* and *Te Deum*, the opera *Katharina* (1909), motets, songs, and a scholarly study of Gregorian chant. He died in Brussels on Oct. 28.

TINTORETTO (1518–1594), painter. Jacopo Robusti was born in Venice, Italy, on Sept. 29, son of a dyer (when his name, "little dyer"), studied under Titian, and attracted great attention with his *Worship of the Golden Calf* and *Last Judgment* for Santa Maria dell' Orto church about 1560. He then won a contest from Veronese and Zuccaro and others to decorate the Scuola di San Roccò, Venice, and worked intermittently from 1564 to about 1587 on more than sixty scenes on the Passion, and glorifying Venetian saints for it (one of these paintings is his enormous *Crucifixion* with some eighty figures). He also did paintings and portraits for the ducal palace and other buildings and for churches in the Venice area.

Tintoretto early vowed to combine Titian's color and Michelangelo's design in his work, and his best work is noted for its mastery of anatomy, use of light and shade, composition, and richness of tone. He was often called "Il Furioso" for the intensity with which he worked and the speed of his painting. Among his masterpieces are *Abraham's Sacrifice, Marriage at Cana, St. George and the Dragon, Miracle of the Loaves and Fishes, Resurrection, Miracle of St. Mark, Last Supper, Finding of the Body of St. Mark, Marriage of St. Catherine, Two Brothers,* and *Paradise*. He died in Venice on May 31.

TIRABOSCHI, GIROLAMO (1731–1794), scholar. Born near Bergamo, Italy, he became a Jesuit, taught at the Brera in Milan in 1766, was appointed librarian of the Biblioteca Estense by Duke Francesco III of Modena in 1770, and wrote the thirteen-volume *Storia della letteratura italiana* (1772–83), from Etruscan times to 1700, and *Biblioteca Modense*. He died on June 3.

TIRSO DE MOLINA. *See* Téllez, Gabriel.

TISIO, BENVENUTO (1481–1559), painter. Born in Garofalo, Italy, Tisio (or Tisi) studied under Panetti and Costa, went to Cremona in 1495, where he studied under Baccaccino, and in 1509 went to Rome, where he was greatly influenced by Raphael. He executed paintings for churches and palaces in Ferrara, Bologna, and Rome, and became blind in 1550. His early work is notable for its charm and idyllic approach to rural life, and his later paintings reveal definite traces of Raphael's influence. Among his outstanding works are the frescoes of Prince Borso d'Este's life in the Schifanója palace, *Adoration of the Magi, Resurrection of Lazarus,* the frescoes of SS. Peter and Paul in the cathedral, *St. Nicholas Reviving the Birds, Massacre of the Innocents, Madonna Enthroned, Bacchus,* and *Sacrifice to Ceres*. He died in Ferrara, Italy, on Sept. 6. He is sometimes called Il Garofalo.

TISSOT, JAMES (1836–1902), painter. Born in Nantes, France, on Oct. 15, he studied at the Academy of Fine Arts in Paris, and under Ingres and Flandrin. He exhibited in the Salon from 1859 to 1870, took part in the Franco-Prussian War, and was forced to flee to England in 1871 when the commune took over the government. He became well known as a portrait painter and illustrator, became interested in religious art, and spent a decade in the Holy Land painting a series of 865 water colors on the life of Christ, which introduced a new, modern concept of religious art. Other work includes a series of water colors, *La femme à Paris, Meeting between Faust and Marguerite, Mavourneen, La Filense;* a group of aquarelles of life in London; and illustrations for the Old Testament. He died in Buillon, France, on Aug. 3.

TITEIMANS, BL. FRANCIS (d. 1537). He studied at Louvain, Belgium, became a Capuchin, and worked as a hospital aid at St. James, Rome, where he died. F. D. Oct. 4.

TITIAN, ST. (d. 536). Said to have come from Germany, he became bishop of Brescia, Italy. F. D. Mar. 3.

TITIAN, ST. (d. 650). He was bishop of Oderzo, near Venice, Italy, for thirty years. F. D. Jan. 16.

TITIAN (1477?–1576), painter. Tiziano Vecelli (or Vecellio) was born in Pieve di Cadore, Italy, and was sent to Venice when about ten to study under Sebastiano Zuccato, and later under Giovanni Bellini. He worked with Giorgione in 1507–8 decorating the Fondaco de' Tedeschi in Venice, and about 1511 went to Padua to paint at the Scuola di San Antonio. He succeeded Bellini as painter to the doges in 1516, and in 1518 completed *Assumption of the Madonna* for the church of the Frari in Ferrara which was sensationally popular. From this time to the end of his life he was deluged with commissions and patronized by the d'Estes, Gonzagas, Medici, Charles III, and Philip II. He returned to Venice in 1523, where he married in 1525 a lady known only as Cecilia, was summoned to Bologna in 1532 to do the portrait of Emperor Charles V, who appointed him court painter, as did Philip II, and in 1533 was made a count palatine by the emperor. He was ousted from his position and sued in 1538 by the Venetian government for neglect of his official duties, but was restored when he finished *Barbarossa's Victory at Spoleto* for the town hall. In 1546 he went to Rome, where he painted Pope Paul III and met Michelangelo, to Germany in 1548 and 1550–51, where he painted Charles and many of the royalty, and in 1566 was elected to the Florentine Academy. Titian is famous for his rich, golden, transparent coloring and unsurpassed for his brush work. So prodigious was his output (he painted almost to the end of his ninety-nine-year life) that only a few of his masterpieces can be listed here: *Assumption of the Virgin, Entombment, Martyrdom of St. Peter, Worship of Venus, Noli me tangere, Virgin with the Rabbit, Bacchus and Ariadne, Presentation of the Blessed Virgin, Rape of Europa, Gypsy Madonna, Venus Blindfolding Cupid, Madonna with Cherries, Tribute Money, Sacred and Profane Love,* an uncompleted *pietà,* and portraits of Ippolito de' Medici, the archbishop of Milan, Alfonso d'Este, Aretino, Charles V, *Magdalen, Venus of Urbino,* and *La Bella di Tiziano.* He died of the plague in Venice, Italy, on Aug. 27.

TITUS, ST. (1st century), bishop. Convert and secretary of St. Paul, he traveled with his master to Jerusalem to discuss the Mosaic law, then he went on to Ephesus and Corinth (as is clear from I and II Cor.). He was left in Crete as bishop to carry on the work begun by Paul, and the latter's epistle gives him instruction about spiritual discipline and the qualities for good bishops. The so-called Acts of Titus are fiction. Pope Pius IX assigned Feb. 6. as his feast day.

TITUS (4th century), bishop. A literalist in scriptural interpretation, and praised by St. Jerome, he was bishop of Bostra, wrote *Contra Manichaeos,* was involved in controversy with Julian the Apostate, attended the Council of Antioch in 363, and probably died during the reign of Valens.

TITUS, ST. (5th century), martyr. A deacon, he was slain during the sack of Rome by the Goths while tending the starving poor. F. D. Aug. 16.

TITUS, ST. *See* Dismas, St.

TOALDO, GIUSEPPE (1719–1797), physicist. Born in Pianezze, Italy, he studied at the Padua seminary, where he edited the works of Galileo (1744), was ordained, taught mathematics there, became pastor of Montegalda in 1754, and was appointed to the chair of astronomy at Padua in 1762. He did research in atmospheric electricity, helped popularize the use of lightning rods with his *Della maniera di difendere gli edificii dal fumine* (1772), and was elected to the London Royal Society for his scientific achievements. He also wrote treatises on gnomonics (measurement of time by sundials) and the influence of the stars, and *Compendium of Spherics and Geography* (1773). He died in Padua, Italy.

TOBIAS, ST. (d. 315?), martyr. *See* Agapius, St.

TOBIAS (14th century), founder. He was the leader of a group of laymen at Mechlin, Brabant, who worked with the plague-stricken, buried the dead (becoming known as Cellites, from *cella,* grave), and were highly praised by Pope Gregory XI. Later, they took as their patron St. Alexius of Syria, who also had engaged in hospital work. In 1469, when a rule had been adopted and a home established at Aix-la-Chapelle, Fr. Dominicus Brock and five brothers took their solemn vows. The Alexian Brothers are now established in Belgium, England, Germany and the United States.

TOBIN, AGNES (1863–1939), poet. Born in San Francisco, daughter of Richard Tobin, she graduated from convent school, lived in Italy, and in London and Sussex near the Meynells, and returned to California in 1924. She translated much of Petrarch, the Italian sonnets of Milton, a version of Racine's *Phèdre* for Mrs. Patrick Campbell, and wrote poetry of her own which was hailed by Yeats, Pound, and Edmund Gosse; Alice Maynell described her in *The Shepherdess* and Joseph Conrad dedicated *Under Western Eyes* to her. She died in San Francisco.

TOBIN, DANIEL J. (1875?–1955), union leader. Born in Ireland, he went to the United States, became a teamster in Boston, was a friend of Samuel Gompers, and rose to power in the International Brotherhood of Teamsters Union of the American Federation of Labor. He was president of the union from 1907 to 1952, by which date it had a membership of 1,250,000. He was treasurer of the American Federation of Labor in 1917–28, vice-president from 1933, and continued as a member of the executive council of the Federation after his retirement as president of the Teamsters. He died in Indianapolis, Indiana, on Nov. 14.

TOBIN, MAURICE JOSEPH (1901–1953), governor. Born in Roxbury, Massachusetts, on May 22, he was unable to finish high school for economic reasons, worked in a leather factory and as a telephone mechanic, became active in politics at nineteen, and was elected to the Boston school committee in 1931. He became a political protégé of James M. Curley, but defeated him for mayor of Boston in 1937 and 1941, and introduced an austerity budget to an almost bankrupt city. He was governor of Massachusetts in 1944–46 and introduced a fair employment law and other social welfare benefits, but was defeated for re-election. In 1948 he became secretary of labor in President Truman's cabinet and was an active opponent of the Taft-Hartley law. He died in Scituate, Massachusetts, on July 19.

TOBIN, RICHARD M. (1866–1952), executive. Born in San Francisco on Apr. 9, he became director of the Hibernia Bank there in 1906, its secretary-treasurer at twenty-three, as the city rose again after the earthquake-fire which destroyed it, and in 1933 its president. He served in the navy during World War I, became naval attaché to the embassy in Rome and at the 1919 peace conference at Versailles, and was minister to the Netherlands in 1923–29. He was made a Knight of Malta in 1931 and was the first American to be named to the Utrecht Academy. He died in San Francisco on Jan. 23.

TOCQUEVILLE, CHARLES ALEXIS HENRI MAURICE CLÉREL DE (1805–1859), statesman, author. Born in Paris, on July 29, he studied in Metz and law at Paris, and in 1827 became a judge in Versailles. In 1831 he visited the United States with Gustave de Beaumont to study its penal system, and on his return wrote his four-volume *La démocratie en Amérique* (1835–40), an enthusiastic account of the American political

system, which led to his election to the Academy of Moral and Political Sciences in 1838 and the French Academy in 1841. He was elected to the chamber of deputies in 1839, to the constituent assembly in 1848, served as minister of foreign affairs for several months in 1849, and was forced from public life by Napoleon III's *coup d'état* of 1851. He devoted the rest of his life to writing *L'ancien régime et la révolution* (1856). He also wrote *Du système pénitentiaire aux États-Unis* (1833) with de Beaumont, which was awarded the Prix Monthyon by the French Academy. He died in Cannes, France, on Apr. 16.

TOEBBE, AUGUSTUS MARIE (1829–1884), bishop. Born in Meppen, Hanover, Germany, on Jan. 15, he studied at Mt. St. Mary of the West seminary in Cincinnati, Ohio, was ordained in 1854 and did pastoral work in that city, and was theologian at the first Plenary Council of Baltimore in 1852. He was appointed second bishop of Covington, Kentucky, in 1870, saw a large increase in the number of parishes, and died there on May 2.

TOLEDO, FRANCISCO DE (1515?–1584), viceroy. He served under Charles V and Philip II, and in 1569 was appointed viceroy of Peru. He reorganized the government and the finances of the colony, forced the great estate owners to submit to his rule as the crown's representative, introduced the Inquisition to Peru, and promulgated the governmental regulations known as the *Libro de tasas* laws. His administration was besmirched by the execution of Tupac Amaru, the last Inca, in 1571 when trouble broke out between the Spaniards and Incas. When he returned to Spain in 1581 he was charged with misappropriating public funds and censured by the king for his execution of Amaru. He died in Seville, Spain, in Sept.

TOLEDO, FRANCISCO (1532–1596), cardinal. Born in Cordova, Spain, on Oct. 4, he studied at Valencia and Salamanca, taught philosophy at the latter, was ordained, and became a Jesuit in 1558. He went to Rome in 1559, taught at the Roman College, where he became prefect of studies, and served as theologian of the Penitentiary for twenty-four years. He accompanied Commendore on the latter's mission to Emperor Maximilian and King Sigismund of Poland, served on diplomatic missions for popes to Bavaria, Germany, Poland, Vienna, and Louvain (where he received Baius' abjuration), and was largely responsible for Henry IV's reconciliation to the Church. He was created a cardinal by Pope Clement VIII in 1593, and died in Rome on Sept. 14. He wrote such philosophical and theological works as *Commentaria cum quaestionibus in universam Aristotelis logicam* (1572), *Commentaria de physica auscultatione* (1573), *De* *anima* (1574), which was used as a text at Salamanca, the four-volume *In Summam theologiae S. Thomae Aquinatis enarratio*, and *Summa casuum sive instructio sacerdotum* (1599).

TOLOMEI, BL. BONAVENTURA (d. 1348). He went from a life of piety to one of vice and sacrilege, repented, became a Dominican, and died in Siena, Italy, while serving the victims of plague. F. D. Dec. 27.

TOLOMEI, BL. GIOVANNI (1272–1348), founder. Born in Siena, Italy, he was educated by his uncle, a Dominican friar, and became a doctor of laws at the local university. He held several government positions, including that of mayor, but resigned and in 1313 withdrew to Chiusuri with two friends, Ambrose Piccolomini and Patrick Patrizi, to follow the solitary life. Summoned before Pope John XXII on charges of unorthodox belief, they were exonerated, but directed to follow one of the approved monastic orders. They chose the Benedictines, called their hermitage Monte Oliveto, and so established the Congregation of Montoliveto in 1319. Their Benedictine group was successful, new monasteries were founded, and in 1344 they received papal approval from Clement VI. When a plague broke out in Siena, Italy, in 1348, Br. Bernard (as John was then known) and eighty of his monks who were caring for the stricken became its victims. His cult was confirmed in 1644. F. D. Aug. 21.

TOLOMEI, GIOVANNI BATTISTA (1653–1726), cardinal. Born in Camberaia, Italy, on Dec. 3, he studied at Florence, law at Pisa, and became a Jesuit in 1673 in Rome. He was elected procurator general of his Society in 1683–85, then became professor of philosophy and later of theology at the Roman College. He became rector there and then of the German College, was consultor for the congregations of the Index, of Indulgences, and of Rites, and was on the commission to examine bishops. He was created a cardinal in 1712 by Pope Clement XI, whose theological adviser he became. Among his writings were *Philosophia mentis et sensuum* (1696) and *De primatu beati Petri*. He died at the Roman College on Jan. 19.

TOMÁS DE BERLANGA (d. 1551), bishop. Born in Berlanga, Spain, he became a Dominican at Salamanca in 1508 and served as prior on Santo Domingo, which became a separate province in 1528 through his efforts. He was first provincial, but soon was transferred to Panama, made bishop, and directed by the Spanish government to arbitrate between Pizarro and Almagro. No success was possible, however, since Pizarro sent Almagro into Chile, thus preventing a meeting of the three men. He made a report on the geography and eth-

nography of Peru, built a convent at Lima, transferred gifts made to himself to hospitals in Panama and Nicaragua, returned to his native town in 1537, and died there on Aug. 8.

TOMÁS, ST. CATERINA (1533–1574). Born in Valdemuzza, Majorca, she was orphaned at seven, suffered under drudgery and hostility in the home of an uncle, and became an Augustinian at Palma at twenty. She was subject to many supernatural trials and also experienced ecstasies for days at a time. She was canonized in 1930. F. D. Apr. 1.

TOMITANO, MARTINO. *See* Bernardino da Feltre.

TOMMASI, BL. GIUSEPPE MARIA (1649–1713), cardinal. Son of the duke of Palermo and of Rosalia Traino, both of whom later entered religious life, as did four of his sisters, he was born in Alicati, Sicily, on Sept. 12, and entered the Theatine novitiate at Palermo at fifteen. After 1673 he was stationed at San Silvestro in Rome, studying scripture, Hebrew, and Greek philosophy. He wrote scholarly treatises on the Psalms and on liturgy. In 1697, Pope Innocent XII called him to the Vatican, where he worked for reforms among religious orders and continued his interest in theology and music and relief of the poor. He became a cardinal shortly after Clement XI, whose confessor he had been, became pope. He died in Rome, and was beatified in 1803. F. D. Jan. 1.

TOMMASO DI STEFANO. *See* Giottino.

TONGIORGI, SALVATORE (1820–1865), philosopher. Born in Rome on Dec. 25, he became a Jesuit at seventeen, taught at Reggio and Forlì, and in 1853 became professor of philosophy at the Roman College. He was appointed assistant to the provincial of the Roman province in 1864, and died in Rome the next year on Nov. 12. His three-volume *Institutiones philosophicae* (1861) was widely used as a textbook.

TOOTELL, HUGH (1671?–1743), historian. Born in Durston-in-Broughton, Lancashire, England, he studied at Douai and St. Gregory's seminary in Paris, was ordained, and returned to England as chaplain of the Molyneux family in 1695. After several trips to the Continent, he settled in Harvington Hall, Worcestershire, in 1722, became chaplain in 1726, and remained there until his death on Feb. 27. He wrote numerous works on church history, chief of which was his three-volume *Church History of England from 1500 to 1688* (1737–42). He often wrote under the name of Charles Dodd.

TORBIDO, FRANCESCO (16th century), painter. Born in Verona, Italy, about 1486, he studied under Giorgione in Venice and Liberale, was adopted by the latter and settled in Verona, and executed frescoes for the cathedral and churches in and around his native city. He is often called Il Moro.

TORELLI, LUIGIA (1500?-1559?), foundress. The countess of Guastalla was married and widowed twice by the time she was twenty-five. She became embroiled with members of her family over her inheritance, sold her estates, and in 1536 became an Angelical, a congregation (approved by Pope Paul III in 1534) she had founded and endowed, and took the name Paola Maria. The congregation was under the direction of St. Antonio Zaccaria, founder of the Banabites with whom she worked in the rehabilitation of women. When Pope Paul III ordered the Angelicals cloistered in 1557, she established another community in Milan, the Daughters of Mary (also called Guastallines), devoted to the care of orphans. She died on Oct. 29 (perhaps as late as 1569).

TORELLO, BL. (1201-1281). Born in Poppi, Italy, and given to dissipation in his earlier years, he suddenly reformed, gave away his fortune, and became a recluse, living outside the town for fifty years and following a life of the most extreme asceticism. F. D. Mar. 16.

TORNIELLI, BL. BONAVENTURA (1411?-1491). Born in Forlì, Italy, he became a Servite in 1448, preached through Tuscany and Venice at the request of Pope Sixtus VI, and was made vicar general of the order in 1488. His cult was confirmed in 1911. F. D. Mar. 31.

TORNIELLI, GIROLAMO FRANCESCO (1693-1752), author. Born in Cameri, Italy, on Feb. 1, he became a Jesuit, taught, for a time, and in 1733 began a popular preaching career which earned him the surname Metastasio. He also wrote hymns set to popular tunes. He died in Bologna, Italy, on Apr. 6 (or May 12).

TORQUATUS, ST. (1st century). *See* Caecilius, St.

TORQUEMADA, TOMÁS DE (1420-1498). Born in Valladolid, Spain, nephew of Cardinal Juan de Torquemada, he became a Dominican in Valladolid, was prior of Santa Cruz monastery, Segovia, for twenty-two years, confessor to the Infanta Isabella, and when she became queen of Castile in 1474 was one of her closest advisers. He was appointed assistant inquisitor in 1482, and the following year chief inquisitor of Castile and Aragon. He established courts in the major cities, a high council, held a general assembly of inquisitors in 1484, and set up an extremely harsh system of rules which he rigorously enforced. He was responsible for having the Jews expelled from Spain in 1492, and is estimated to have executed about 2000 persons for heresy. He retired to Avila, Spain, where he died on Sept. 16.

TORRES, FRANCISCO (1509?-1584). Born

in Herrera, Palencia, Spain, he studied at Salamanca, went to Rome in the households of Cardinals Salviati and Seripando, attended the Council of Trent in 1562, and became a Jesuit in 1567. He taught at the Roman College, helped revise the Sixtine Vulgate, wrote numerous treatises, and translated several of the Greek Fathers. He died in Rome on Nov. 21.

TORRES-ACOSTA, BL. EMANUELA (1826-1887), foundress. Born in Madrid, Spain, she was invited with six other women in 1851, by Michael Martinez y Sanz, a Servite tertiary, to attend the sick in Madrid. In 1856 he split the group and made Mary Soledad, the name she took, superioress at Madrid. Despite difficulties, the Handmaids of Mary Serving the Sick received diocesan approval in 1861, distinguished themselves in a cholera outbreak in 1865, and soon spread throughout Spain. The first overseas foundation was opened in Cuba in 1875. She was beatified in 1950. F. D. Oct. 11.

TORRES NAHARRO, BARTOLOMÉ DE (1480-1530?), dramatist. Born in Torres de Miguel Sexmero, Spain, he served in the army, studied at Salamanca, and was ordained. He went to Rome about 1511, became chaplain to Fabricio Colonna, his patron, was banished for *Tinelaria*, a satirical comedy on court life, and settled in Naples. His plays were published in *Propaladia* (1517), with a preface on dramatic theory; they include the comedies *Trofea*, *Himenea* (called the first "cloak and sword" play in Spanish literature), *Serafina*, and *Soldadesca*. He adhered to the five-act tradition, paid strict attention to plot, and had some influence on the theater. He also wrote ballads, epistles, and sonnets. He probably died in Spain.

TORRICELLI, EVANGELISTA (1608-1647), physicist. Born in Faenza, Italy, on Oct. 15, he studied there, went to Rome in 1626, and became a student of Benedetto Castelli, favorite pupil of Galileo, to whom Castelli recommended him in 1641. He remained in Florence at the request of the grand duke, succeeded Galileo as professor of mathematics at the university, and provided the solutions for many problems in mathematics and physics, among them ascertaining the cycloid's area, discovering a method of producing a high vacuum (Torricellian vacuum), and the law regulating the flow of a liquid out of the orifice of a vessel. In 1643 he invented the barometer. He died in Florence, Italy, on Oct. 25.

TORRUBIA, JOSÉ (d. 1768). Born in Granada, Spain, he joined St. Peter of Alcántara's order (the Alcantarines) there, was sent to the Philippines as secretary to Commissioner-General Foguéras, and was imprisoned by the religious orders which objected to the commissioner's reforms. After returning to Spain, he went to Rome, where he left his order to become a Franciscan, was sent to the Philippines, traveled through Asia and America, and returned to Spain in 1750. He wrote ecclesiastical works, a book on the natural history of Spain, and *Disertacion historico-politico-geográfica de las islas Filipinas* (1736). He died in the monastery of Ara Coeli, Rome.

TORTHRED, ST. (d. 870?), martyr. *See* Beocca, St.

TOSCANELLI, PAOLO DAL POZZO (1397–1482), cosmographer. Born in Florence, Italy, son of a physician, he studied at Padua, where he met his lifelong friend, Nicholas of Cusa, received his doctorate in medicine in 1524, then returned to Florence where he spent the rest of his life, except for short trips to Tuscany, Todi, and Rome. He soon became the leading mathematician, astronomer and cosmographer of his times, observed the orbits of the comets of 1443, 1449–50, 1457, and 1472, and Halley's comet of 1456, and built the gnomon on Santa Maria del Fiore cathedral in 1468 to settle the altitudes of the solstices. His letter of 1474 to Canon Ferdam Martins of Lisbon outlining his scheme for a western ocean crossing to China influenced Christopher Columbus, who had correspondence with him and reportedly used Toscanelli's map on his voyage of discovery to America. He wrote such treatises as *Prospettiva* and *Meteorologia agricola* and a translation of Ptolemy's geography. He died in Florence on May 10.

TOSCANINI, ARTURO (1867–1957), musician. Born in Parma, Italy, on Mar. 25, he studied at its conservatory, conducted one of his own compositions at seventeen, became a cellist with leading orchestras, and a conductor at nineteen while in Rio de Janeiro. He returned to conduct in Italy and at thirty-one was leader at La Scala. He conducted the premiere of Puccini's *Girl of the Golden West* at the Metropolitan Opera House in New York and concerts in the United States during World War I, was decorated for bravery (he directed an army band during an Italian battle against the Austrians), and was active in welfare work through 1918. He conducted the New York Philharmonic from 1926 to 1936, the Palestine Symphony in Tel Aviv in 1936, and again in 1938, and the National Broadcasting Company Symphony in 1937–40, which he then took on a tour of South America. He returned to the New York Philharmonic in 1942, was guest conductor elsewhere, did a great deal of war-relief work, and in 1950 toured the United States with the N.B.C. Symphony. His 1954 season was his last; his health had failed, though he had managed to complete a great number of re-

cordings. He died in New York City on Jan. 16.

TOSELLI, FLOVIANO (1701–1768). Born in Bologna, Italy, he became a Capuchin in 1717, taking the name Bernard or Bernardine, compiled a bibliography of Franciscan writings (1747), and wrote treatises on philosophy and dogmatic theology in the Scotist tradition.

TOSI, EUGENIO (1864–1929), cardinal. Born in Busto Arsizio, Italy, he was ordained, was named archbishop of Milan and a cardinal in 1922, and died in his see city on Jan. 7.

TOSTADO, ALONSO (1400?–1455), bishop. Born in Madrigal, Castile, he studied at Salamanca, participated in the Council of Basle, and was accused of heresy in 1443. He wrote *Defensorium* against his critics (among them Torquemada), in which he challenged the authority of the pope, was appointed grand chancellor of Castile on his return to Spain, and in 1499 became bishop of Avila. He wrote commentaries on the historical books of the Bible and on the history by Eusebius. He died at Bonilla de la Sierra, near Avila, Spain, on Sept. 3. He is also known as Alphonsus Abulensis.

TOSTI, LUIGI (1811–1897), historian. Born in Naples, Italy, on Feb. 13, he was placed under his uncle's care in Monte Cassino in 1819 when his father died, studied at Rome, and was ordained in 1833. He returned to Monte Cassino, where he taught for the next twenty years. He was a vigorous supporter of Pope Pius IX's plan for Italy, was imprisoned in 1844 on a charge of conspiracy, and forbidden to publish his projected *L'Ateneo italiano*, a review dedicated to supporting the pope as head of the *Risorgimento*, and was released only on Pope Pius IX's personal intervention. He fought to exempt Monte Cassino and other monasteries from Italian spoliation laws, refused a professorship at Pisa, and was appointed assistant archivist at the Vatican by Pope Leo XIII. He was designated by the pope to negotiate with the Italian government for the restoration of St. Paul's to the Benedictines, but was unsuccessful, as he also was in his attempt in 1896 to effect the reunion of the Anglican church to Rome through his friend, Gladstone. He wrote *Storia della badia di Monte Cassino* (1842), *Storia della lega Lombard*, *Storia del concilio di Constanza*, *Storia dell' origine dello scisma greco*, *La contessa Matilde* (1859), and *Ricordi biblici*. He died in Monte Cassino, Italy, on Sept. 24.

TOTNAN, ST. (d. 689), martyr. *See* Kilian, St.

TOUCHET, ARTURO (1848–1926), cardinal. Born in Bayeux, France, on Nov. 13, he was ordained, was in 1909 placed in charge of investigating the charges against Joan of Arc preliminary to her canonization, became bishop of Orléans, and in 1922, was made a cardinal. He died in Orléans, France, on Sept. 23.

TOUCHET, GEORGE ANSELM (d. 1689?). Son of the second earl of Castlehaven, he was born in Stalbridge, Dorset, England, was professed a Benedictine in 1643 with the name Anselm, was sent as a missionary to southern England, and became Queen Catherine of Braganza's chaplain in 1671 at Somerset House, where he remained until his banishment in 1675. Parliament forbade his succession to the earldom in 1678. He wrote *Historical Collections out of Several Grave Protestant Historians concerning the Changes in Religion* (1674).

TOURNEFORT, JOSEPH PITTON DE (1656–1708), botanist. Born in Aix, Provence, France, on June 5, he studied at the Jesuit college there and theology at Aix, but left in 1677 to study medicine at Montpellier and Barcelona, and made scientific trips to Spain and the Pyrenées. He was appointed professor at the Jardin des Plantes in Paris in 1688, was elected to the Academy in 1692, and became a doctor of medicine in 1698. He traveled to Asia Minor and Greece in 1700–2, collected more than 1300 species of plants, and wrote *Relation d'un voyage du Levant* (published in 1717). He was appointed professor of medicine at the Collège de France in 1702, and he died in Paris on Dec. 28. He founded a system of classifying plants based on the form of the corolla, which he explained in his three-volume *Élements de botanique* (1694; 451 plates), revised in the three-volume *Institutiones rei herbariae* (1700; 476 plates), but the system was generally discarded after the middle of the eighteenth century. A genus of some 120 species of the *Borraginaceae* family was named *Tournefortia* by Linnaeus. He also wrote *Histoire des plantes qui naissent aux environs de Paris* (1698). He died in Paris on Dec. 28.

TOURNÉLY, HONORÉ (1658–1729), theologian. Born in Antibes, Provence, France, on Aug. 28, he studied at the Sorbonne, where he received his doctorate in 1686, and in 1688 went to Douai to teach theology. In 1692 he was appointed professor of theology at the Sorbonne, a position he held for twenty-four years, became a canon of Sainte Chapelle, and was given the abbey of Plainpied. Though always a defender of Gallicanism, he was a vigorous opponent of the Jansenists and fought to have *Unigenitus* accepted by the French clergy on its publication in 1713. When Louis XIV died in 1715, the Jansenists gained control of the theology faculty at the Sorbonne, expunged *Unigenitus* from its registers, and expelled him with other supporters of the papal bull. He was reinstated in 1721 through the intervention of the duke of Orléans, who

was then regent, and retired in 1725. He published his lectures under the general title of *Praelectiones theologicae*, treating the Trinity, the Church, grace, the sacraments, and the Incarnation. He died in Paris on Dec. 26.

TOURNON, CHARLES THOMAS MAILLARD DE (1668–1710), cardinal. Born in Turin, Italy, on Dec. 21, he studied at the Propaganda in Rome, and was ordained. He was appointed patriarch of Antioch and papal legate to India and China in 1701 to take charge of the missions there and eliminate the "Chinese rites" among the native Christians. He reached India in 1703, went to China in 1705, was denounced by the emperor for attempting to abolish the native rites, and when he ordered the missionaries to abolish the rites under threat of excommunication, was imprisoned in Macao. He was created a cardinal in 1707, but died in prison on June 8.

TOURON, ANTOINE (1686–1775), author. Born in Graulhet, France, on Sept. 5, he became a Dominican, taught theology in Toulouse, and then devoted his life to writing some thirty biographical and historical works on the Dominicans, including a biography of St. Thomas Aquinas. He died in Paris on Sept. 2.

TOUSTAIN, CHARLES FRANÇOIS (1700–1754). Born in Repas, Séez, France, on Oct. 13, he joined the Benedictines of St. Maur in Jumièges in 1718, studied at Fécamp abbey and Bonne Nouvelle monastery in Rouen, became an outstanding linguist, and was ordained in 1729. He served at St. Ouen in Rouen, St. Germain-des-Prés and Blancs Manteaux, became noted for his asceticism and scholarship, which was tinged with Jansenism, and died at St. Denis, Paris, on July 1. He collaborated with Tassin on the six-volume *Nouveau traité de diplomatique* (1750–65) and an unpublished edition of the works of St. Theodore Studites; he wrote, among other books, *La Vérité persecutée par l'erreur* (1733).

TOUTTÉE, ANTOINE AUGUSTIN (1677–1718), scholar. Born in Riom, Puy-de-Dôme, France, on Dec. 13, he studied with the Oratorians there, joined the Benedictines of St. Maur at Vendôme in 1698, and was ordained in 1702. He taught at Vendôme, St. Benoît-sur-Loire, and St. Denis during the next decade, and in 1712 retired to St. Germain-des-Prés, Paris, to devote himself to preparing an edition of the works of St. Cyril of Jerusalem. He died there on Dec. 25.

TRACEY, JAMES FRANCIS (1854–1925), jurist. Born in Albany, New York, on May 30, he studied at Georgetown and the Albany Law School, taught at the latter from 1890 to 1905, then became associate justice of the supreme court of the Philippine Islands. He died on Sept. 20.

TRACY, ALEXANDRE DE PROUVILLE

DE (1603–1670), viceroy. He joined the army as a youth and rose to the rank of lieutenant general. He was appointed viceroy of New France by King Louis XIV in 1665, waged a successful campaign against the Mohawks in 1666, and negotiated a peace with the Iroquois. He died in France.

TRANQUILLINUS, ST. (d. 286), martyr. Legend associates him with the death of St. Sebastian. F. D. July 6.

TRASON, ST. (d. 302?), martyr. *See* Pontian, St.

TRAVERSARI, AMBROSIO (1386–1439), abbot. Born in Portico, Italy, on Sept. 16, he became a Camaldolese monk at fourteen at St. Mary of the Angels monastery in Florence, where he remained until 1431 when Pope Eugene IV appointed him abbot-general of his order. He put into effect much-needed reforms and was later appointed to reform the Vallombrosans. He accompanied the pope on the latter's flight from Rome in 1434, and in 1435 was sent as papal envoy to the Council of Basle. He was active in 1438 and 1439 in attempting to reunite the Eastern Church with Rome, was praised by Eastern Emperor John VII, and helped draw up the reunion agreement in 1439. A typical Renaissance scholar, he knew Greek, Latin, and Hebrew thoroughly, translated many of the Greek Fathers, and was noted for his learning. He died on Oct. 20, has a popular cult among the Camaldolese, as Bl. Ambrose of Camaldoli, but has never been officially beatified.

TREDWAY, LETTICE MARY (1595–1677). Born in Buckley Park, Northhamptonshire, England, she joined the Canonesses Regular of the Lateran at Beaulieu in 1616, and in 1634, with Fr. Carre (Miles Pinkney), founded in Paris a convent for canonesses who were English, and was its first abbess until 1675. She also helped to found St. Gregory seminary to train priests for the English mission. She died in Oct.

TREGIAN, FRANCIS (1548–1608), poet. Born in Cornwall of a family related to Elizabeth Woodville, Queen Elizabeth's grandmother, he was a courtier at Elizabeth's court, then retired to his home near Truro. Here, in 1577, he had his property seized for harboring Bl. Cuthbert Mayne, and was himself imprisoned for twenty-eight years. In 1602 he was freed by James I, went to Douai, to Madrid, and later to Lisbon, where he took care of Irish refugees until his death there on Sept. 25. His poems, written in prison, exist only in manuscript.

TREMBLAY, FRANÇOIS LECLERC DU (1577–1683). Born in Paris, on Nov. 4, he was in the army and became a Capuchin friar in 1599, taking the name Joseph. He became secretary to Cardinal Richelieu in 1611, his con-

fidant in domestic diplomacy, and his envoy on foreign missions. So powerful that he was known as "His Gray Eminence," Fr. Joseph was a shrewd diplomat, and lived a life of extremes, matching his times. He became provincial of his order in 1613, sent missioners to India and Canada, wrote religious tracts, preached a crusade against the Turks, and wrote the Latin poem, *Le Turciad*. He is inevitably associated with Richelieu's policies especially that of containing the Hapsburgs, and, in his zeal for the Church, he tried to force Catholicism on many of the Protestant opposition in France. He died in Rueil, France, on Dec. 18.

TREMORUS, ST. (6th century). Infant son of St. Triphina (who entered a convent after his death and is honored on Jan. 29), he was murdered at Carhaix, Brittany, by his stepfather, Count Conmore. F. D. Nov. 7.

TRÉSEL, BL. MARIE (d. 1794), martyr. *See* Lidoin, Bl. Marie.

TRICASSIN, CHARLES JOSEPH (d. 1681), theologian. Born in Troyes, France, he became a Capuchin, and was noted for his writings on the Augustinian doctrine of grace, which were violently attacked by the Jansenists: *De praedestinatione hominum ad gloriam* (1669), *De indifferenti lapsi hominis arbitrio* (1673), and *De necessaria ad salutem gratia omnibus et singulis data* (1673).

TRIESNECKER, FRANCIS A PAULA (1745–1817), astronomer. Born in Kirchberg, Lower Austria, on Apr. 2, he became a Jesuit at sixteen, studied at Vienna and Tyrnau, and taught at several Jesuit colleges. When the Society was suppressed he went to Graz, where he was ordained. He was appointed assistant director at the Vienna observatory and in 1792 became director, a position he held the rest of his life. He was editor of the periodical, *Ephemerides*, and from 1787 to 1806 published in it his observations of the heavenly bodies and his *Tabulae Mercurii, Martis, Veneris, Solares*. He wrote treatises for other astronomical journals, measured the triangulation of Lower Austria and Galicia, and in 1802 published *Novae motuum lunarium tabulae*. He died in Vienna on Jan. 29.

TRIGIDIA, ST. (d. 925?). Daughter of Count Sancho García of Castile, she became abbess of the Benedictine convent at Ona, near Burgos, which her father built for her. The name also appears as Tigridia. F. D. Nov. 22.

TRILLO, ST. (6th century). Son of a Breton chieftain, he became a missioner to Wales with St. Cadfan. F. D. June 15.

TRIPHINA, ST. (d. 306?), martyr. *See* Agatho, St.

TRIPHINA, ST. (6th century). *See* Tremorus, St.

TRIPHYLLIUS, ST. (d. 370?), bishop. A native of Cyprus, he studied law in Beirut, Syria, then became a follower of St. Spiridion. As bishop of Niocosia he attended the Council of Sardica with Spiridion in 347; they were outspoken in their opposition to Arianism and support of Athanasius. Triphyllius wrote a poetic life of Spiridion and philosophical studies which St. Jerome admired. F. D. June 13.

TRIPOS, ST. (d. d. 270?), martyr. *See* Basilides, St.

TRISSINO, GIOVANNI GIORGIO (1478–1550), poet. Born in Vicenza, Italy, on July 8, he studied under Demetrius Chalcondylas in Milan and Niccolò Leoniceno in Ferrara. He became a leading humanist, was banished from Vicenza in 1509 when his family supported Maximilian, and in 1515 wrote his tragedy *Sofonisba*, in blank verse and the first modern classical tragedy. He was Pope Leo X's nuncio to Germany in the same year, served as Pope Clement VII's ambassador, and was made a count palatine by Emperor Charles V in 1532. He lived in Venice and Padua until 1545. His conversations in Florence inspired Machiavelli's *Dialogo*; his own dialogue, *Il castellano*, proposed an Italian, rather than district, grammar and had considerable influence in establishing a national language; he also wrote an epic poem, *L'Italia liberata dai Goti* (1547–48). He died in Rome on Dec. 8.

TRITHEIM, JOHANNES (1462–1516), scholar. Born in Trittenheim on the Moselle, Germany, on Feb. 1, he studied classics at Würzburg, became a Benedictine at Sponheim in 1482, and, though not yet ordained, was elected abbot in 1484. Under his guidance the abbey achieved a wide reputation for scholarship and for its library. Dissatisfaction among the monks over his strict discipline caused him to resign after twenty-three years as abbot. He retired to the monastery of St. James in Würzburg, Bavaria, in 1506, became abbot, and remained there the rest of his life, except for a short period at the imperial court in 1508, until his death on Dec. 13. He wrote ascetical works, collected in *Opera pia et spiritualia* (1604), church history, sermons for monks, and *De luminaribus Germaniae* (1495). He also invented a popular shorthand system, which he outlined in *Stenographia* (published in 1606). His name is sometimes written Trithemius.

TRIVET, NICHOLAS (1258?–1328), author. Son of a judge, he was born in Norfolk, England, became a Dominican in London, studied at Oxford and Paris, became prior in London, and taught at Oxford. He wrote *Annales sex regum Angliae*, a chronicle of the Angevin kings of England from 1136 to 1307, and a commentary on St. Augustine's *City of God*.

TROADIUS, ST. (d. 250), martyr. He was slain at Neo-Caesarea, Pontus, during the reign of Decius. F. D. Dec. 28.

TROBEC, JAMES (1838–1921), bishop. Born in Billichgraz, Carniola, Austria, on July 10, he went to the United States, where he studied at St. Vincent's college and seminary, Beatty, Pennsylvania, and was ordained in St. Paul in 1865. He engaged in pastoral work there until 1897 when he was appointed bishop of St. Cloud, Minnesota. He resigned in 1914 and was named titular bishop of Lycopolis, and died in St. Cloud on Dec. 15.

TROJAN, ST. (d. 533). He succeeded St. Vivian as bishop of Saintes, France. The name is also spelled Troyen. F. D. Nov. 30.

TROLOPP, FRANCIS. *See* Feval, Paul Henri Corentin.

TROND. *See* Trudo, St.

TROPHIMUS, ST. (1st century). A Gentile from Ephesus, he accompanied St. Paul on his third missionary journey (Acts 20:4), and provoked a protest when Paul brought him into the temple at Jerusalem (Acts 21:26–32). He is also mentioned in II Tim. 4:20. F. D. Dec. 29.

TROPHIMUS, ST. (d. 277?), martyr. *See* Dorymedon, St.

TROPHIMUS, ST. (3rd century?), bishop. According to St. Gregory, he was one of the six bishops sent from Rome with St. Dionysius in the middle of the third century to evangelize Gaul, and became first bishop of Arles. F. D. Dec. 29.

TROPHIMUS, ST. (d. 300?), martyr. *See* Thalus, St.

TROPHIMUS, ST. (d. 302?), martyr. *See* Theophilus, St.

TROPHIMUS, ST. (d. 304?), martyr. *See* Eucarpius, St.

TROTEMAN, JOCELIN (d. 1242), bishop. Probably born in Wells, Somerset, England, and known also as Jocelin of Wells, he had acquired several benefices by 1203 when he was a king's justiciar. He was elected bishop of Bath in 1206, left England because of the interdict of 1208, returned in 1213 when King John submitted to the pope, and was present at the signing of Magna Charta as a king's counselor. He and the bishop of Winchester anointed young Henry III after John's death in 1216 and helped expel the French and restore the king's possessions. In 1218 he settled a dispute between his diocese and the abbey of Glastonbury and became bishop of Bath and Wells. He founded St. John's Hospital in Wells and rebuilt the cathedral, where he was buried on his death, Nov. 19.

TROY, JOHN THOMAS (1739–1823), archbishop. Born in Blanchardstown, near Dublin, Ireland, on May 10, he became a Dominican in 1757, studied at St. Clement's,

Rome, became prior there in 1772, and in 1776 was appointed bishop of Ossory. He corrected abuses in the diocese, suppressed the gangs which were attacking landlords (he acted in support of authority, although he opposed excessive rents), and in 1781–82 served as administrator of Armagh. He became archbishop of Dublin in 1786. He supported union, but opposed those who engaged in active violence, excommunicated those who joined in the rebellion of 1798, accepted in 1799 the government veto on ecclesiastical appointments, helped found Maynooth, and began the pro-cathedral. He died in Dublin on May 11.

TROYEN. *See* Trojan.

TRUCHSESS VON WALDBURG, OTTO (1514–1573), cardinal. Born in Castle Scheer, Swabia, on Feb. 26, he studied at Tübingen, Padua, Pavia, and Bologna, where he received his doctorate in theology, received numerous canonries as a youth, and in 1541 became an imperial councilor. He was appointed a papal chamberlain, bishop of Augsburg in 1543, mediated a dispute between the emperor and pope, and was created a cardinal in 1544. He instituted widespread reforms, founded the University of Dillingen in 1549 and the seminary there in 1555, and was appointed head of the Inquisition in Rome in 1555 and cardinal-bishop of Albano in 1562. He died in Rome on Apr. 2.

TRUDO, ST. (d. 690?). Of Frankish parentage, he was educated at the cathedral school of Metz, Gaul, where he was ordained by St. Clodulf. He returned as a missionary to his native Hasbaye, Brabant, where he built a Benedictine monastery on his estate, about 660, and a convent near Bruges. He is also called Trond. F. D. Nov. 23.

TRUEBA, ANTONIO DE (1821–1899), poet. Born in Montellana, Biscay, Spain, he went to Madrid in 1836, and published two books of poetry: *El libro de los cantares* (1852) and *El libro de los montañas* (1868). His collections of short narratives on the Basque country were effective, but his historical novels (such as *El Cid campeador*) failed. He was appointed historiographer of Biscay by Queen Isabella II, and died in Bilbao, Spain, on Mar. 10.

TRUMWIN, ST. (7th century), bishop. He was bishop of the Picts from 681 to 685, with the monastery of Abercorn as his see. After the English were defeated, Trumwin sent his monks to several monasteries in the south and retired to Whitby, England, where he died. F. D. Feb. 10.

TRYPHENA, ST. (1st century). She and St. Tryphosa, from Iconium, Lycaonia, were converts of St. Paul (Rom. 16:12). F. D. Nov. 10.

TRYPHON, ST. (3rd century). According to legend, he was a native of Phrygia who was a gooseherd as a boy and was martyred in Nicaea during the Decian persecution. F. D. Nov. 10.

TRYPHON, ST. (d. 484?), martyr. *See* Aquilinus, St.

TRYPHONIA, ST. (3rd century), martyr. A widow, she was put to death in Rome. F. D. Oct. 18.

TRYPHOSA, ST. (1st century). *See* Tryphenia, St.

TSCHIDERER ZU GLEIFHEIM, JOHANN NEPOMUK VON (1777–1860), bishop. Born in Bozen (now Bolzano), Italy, on Feb. 15, he was ordained in 1800, was appointed a notary public while pursuing further studies in Rome, engaged in pastoral work, and then became a professor of theology at the Trent seminary. He was parish priest at Sarnthal, and then at Meran from 1810 to 1826, when he was appointed pro-vicar of Trent. He became bishop of Heliopolis and vicar general of Voralberg in 1832, and in 1835 bishop of Trent, Italy, a position he filled until his death there on Dec. 3.

TSCHUPICK, JOHN NEPOMUK (1729–1784), preacher. Born in Vienna on Apr. 7 (or 12), he became a Jesuit in 1744, taught rhetoric, and in 1763 was appointed preacher at the Vienna cathedral, famed for his sermons, which were collected in ten volumes (1785–87). He died in Vienna on July 20.

TSU-CHANG, JOSEPH WAN (1908–1961), bishop. Born in Hengchow, China, on Feb. 8, he was ordained in 1934 as a Franciscan, and in 1952 was consecrated bishop of Hengchow. He was imprisoned by the Chinese Communists in 1955 when he refused to join them in establishing a schismatic church, and died in an unidentified prison.

TUDE. *See* Antidius, St.

TUDINUS. *See* Tudy, St.

TUDNO, ST. (6th century). His name is given to the Welsh locality of Llandudno, Carnavon. F. D. June 5.

TUDO, ST. (d. 664). He succeeded St. Colman as bishop of Lindisfarne off the coast of Northumberland, England, and died of plague after a year. F. D Oct. 21.

TUDWAL, ST. (d. 564?), bishop. Probably a Welshman, he migrated with his family and followers to Brittany where his cousin, Deroc, was king of Dummonia, settled in Lan Pabu, León, established several monasteries, was consecrated bishop, and retired to the monastery of Treher (now Tréguier), France, which calls him its first bishop. He is known as Pabu (Father) in Brittany. F. D. Dec. 1.

TUDY, ST. (5th century). A follower of St. Maudez and associate of St. Corentin, he left a hermitage to become abbot of Landevennec, Brittany, then crossed to the mission in Cornwall, England. He is also called Tegwin, Thetgo, and Tudinus. F. D. May 9.

TUIGG, JOHN (1821–1889), bishop. Born in Donaghmore, Cork, Ireland, on Feb. 19, he studied in Dublin, and St. Michael's, Pittsburgh, Pennsylvania, and was ordained in Pittsburgh in 1850. He became the bishop of Pittsburgh's secretary, founded several parishes, and in 1869 was appointed vicar of the eastern area of the see. When Pittsburgh was divided into the two dioceses of Pittsburgh and Allegheny City in 1876, he was appointed bishop of Pittsburgh. He was faced with numerous financial difficulties resulting from the depression of 1873 and great bitterness over the division of the see. In 1877 he was appointed administrator of the see of Allegheny City, which became vacant as a result of Bishop Domenec's resignation. The see of Allegheny City was suppressed in 1889 and its territory included in the see of Pittsburgh, five months before Bishop Tuigg's death in Altoona, Pennsylvania, on Dec. 7.

TULASNE, LOUIS RENÉ (1815–1885), botanist. Born in Azay-le-Rideau, Indre-et-Loire, France, on Sept. 12, he studied law at Poitiers, but became interested in botany and joined Auguste de Saint-Hilaire's expedition to Brazil. He was appointed assistant naturalist at the Paris Museum of Natural History in 1842 (a position he held until his retirement in 1872), was elected to the French Academy, and died at Hyères, France, on Dec. 22. He did extensive research on fungi (several species are named after him) and with his brother Charles wrote on his findings.

TUMULTY, JOSEPH PATRICK (1879–1954). Born in Jersey City, New Jersey, on May 5, he studied at St. Peter's, passed the bar in 1902, practiced in his state, and became a member of its assembly in 1907. He at first opposed the rising Woodrow Wilson, then fought the party bosses who sought to oppose Wilson's bid for the governorship. When Wilson was elected president in 1912, Tumulty served as his secretary from 1912 to 1921, handling appointments, dealing with the press, and acting as a sounding board for the president's views. Generally, they worked hand in hand, though there were two quarrels: the first came when Tumulty expressed disapproval of Wilson's second marriage; the second caused a complete breach. Tumulty wrote to Robert Lansing, secretary of state, that Wilson was so ill during his postwar tours of the country that he should be declared incompetent and the government placed in the hands of Vice-President Thomas Marshall. Tumulty then returned to law practice in partnership with his son. He wrote *Woodrow Wilson as I Know Him* and *In the White House Looking Glass*. He died in Olney, Maryland, on Apr. 8.

TUNSTAL, BL. THOMAS (d. 1616), martyr. Born at Whinfell, Westmoreland, England, he studied at Douai, was ordained in 1609, and sent on the English mission in 1610. He was arrested shortly after his arrival and spent the rest of his life in various prisons, becoming a Benedictine during one imprisonment. He was hanged in Norwich, England, for his priesthood, and beatified in 1929. F. D. July 13.

TUNSTALL, CUTHBERT (1474–1559), bishop. Born in Hackforth, Yorkshire, England, he studied at Oxford, Cambridge, and Padua, became Archbishop Warham's chancellor in 1511, rector of Harrow-on-the-Hill, canon of Lincoln in 1514, and archdeacon of Chester in 1515, when he accompanied Thomas More on a diplomatic mission to Charles V in Brussels and met Erasmus. He became master of the rolls in 1516, dean of Salisbury in 1521, was appointed bishop of London in 1522, lord privy seal in 1523, and became one of Queen Catherine's counselors in the divorce action brought by Henry VIII. In 1530 he was translated to Durham, accepted the King's claim to supremacy over the Church, and in 1537 was appointed president of the Council of the North. He acted on several diplomatic missions to France for Henry, but after Henry's death became more vigorous in his opposition to the reform measures. When he refused to deny transubstantiation he was imprisoned in the Tower in 1551 and deprived of his bishopric in 1552, but had it restored when Mary ascended the throne in 1553. He ruled peacefully during Mary's reign, but vigorously resisted Elizabeth's anti-Catholic measures, refused to take the Oath of Supremacy, and when he refused to consecrate Matthew Parker archbishop of Canterbury was deprived of his see in 1559 and imprisoned in Lambeth palace, London, where he died on Nov. 18. Among his theological treatises are *De veritate corporis et sanguinis domini nostri Jesu Christi in Eucharistia* (1554), *De arte supputandi* (1522), and *Compendium ethicorum Aristotelis* (1554).

TUNSTALL, CUTHBERT. See Constable, Cuthbert.

TUNSTED, SIMON (d. 1369). Born in Norwich, England, he joined the Greyfriars there, received his doctorate in theology, was warden of the Norwich Franciscan house, became regent master of the Oxford Minorities in 1351, and in 1360 became English provincial superior. He wrote a commentary on Aristotle's *Meteora* and is usually considered the author of *Quatuor principalia musicae*, a treatise on music. He died in Bruisyard, Suffolk.

TURA, COSIMO (1430?–1495), artist. Born in Ferrara, Italy, he studied at Padua under Squarcione, was influenced by Donatello and Mantagna, and created a *Pietà, Annunciation,*

Crucifixion, Dead Christ Upheld by Angels, panels of saints, and a *Madonna* altarpiece.

TURIAF, ST. (d. 750). He succeeded St. Samson as bishop of Dol in Brittany. F. D. July 13.

TURIBIUS, ST. *See* Mogrobejo, St. Toribio Alfonso de.

TURIBIUS, ST. (d. 450?), bishop of Astorga. Active against the Priscillianists as bishop of Astorga, Spain, he exchanged important letters with Pope St. Leo the Great, and did much to check the spread of the new heresy. F. D. Apr. 16.

TURIBIUS, ST. (d. 528?). Founder of the abbey of Liébana in Asturias, Spain, he became its abbot and may later have been a bishop. F. D. Apr. 16.

TURKETIL, ST. (887–975). Nephew of King Edred of England and royal chancellor, he became a Benedictine monk and abbot at Croyland, where he established a school. F. D. July 11.

TURNBULL, WILLIAM (d. 1454), bishop. He was consecrated bishop of Glasgow, Scotland, in 1447 and in 1450 obtained from Pope Nicholas V the charter for the university of that city.

TURNÈBE, ADRIEN (1512–1565), scholar. Born in Andely, Normandy, France, he studied at Paris, taught at Toulouse in 1533, Greek at Paris in 1547, and Greek philosophy in 1561, and served as one of the supervisors of Greek works for the royal printing press from 1552 to 1555. He was attracted to Protestantism, but probably died a Catholic in Paris on June 12. He was highly regarded as a classical scholar; translated Greek authors into Latin, among them Aeschylus, Aristotle, Plutarch, and Theophrastus; and wrote commentaries on the classics, poems, and treatises which were collected and published in 1600.

TURNER, BL. ANTONY (d. 1679), martyr. Born in Leicestershire, England, son of a Protestant minister, he graduated from Cambridge, became a convert, studied in Rome, and joined the Jesuits in Watten when twenty-four. He was sent to England and labored in the Worcester area for eighteen years before he was hanged and quartered at Tyburn for alleged conspiracy in the Titus Oates Plot. He was beatified in 1929. F. D. June 20.

TURNER, WILLIAM (1871–1936), bishop. Born in Kilmallock, Limerick, Ireland, on Apr. 8, he studied at Mungret and the Royal University, the North American and Urban colleges, Rome, and was ordained in 1893. He spent another year studying at L'Institut Catholique, Paris, was assigned to St. Paul, Minnesota, and taught at St. Thomas College, the St. Paul seminary, and Catholic University, where he was librarian from 1907 to 1919. He edited the *Catholic Universe Bulletin* (1911–19), was associate editor of the *Catholic Historical Review* (1915–18), and editor of the *American Ecclesiastical Review* (1914–19), and in 1919 was appointed bishop of Buffalo, New York. He enlarged every area of his see, was particularly active in charitable work, and died in Buffalo on July 10. He wrote *History of Philosophy* and *Lessons in Logic.*

TURNINUS, ST. (8th century). *See* Fredegand, St.

TURPIN (d. 800), archbishop. A monk of St. Denis, Paris, he was appointed archbishop of Rheims by Charlemagne about 753. He was long considered to be the author of *Historia Karoli magni et Rotholandi,* celebrating Charlemagne's deeds, but modern scholarship calls this a twelfth-century compilation of legends. He built up the library of the Rheims cathedral, and died on Sept. 2.

TURRIANI, BL. ANTONIO (d. 1694). Born in Milan, Italy, he became a physician at Padua, practiced at Milan, then joined the Augustinian Hermits. His cult was confirmed in 1759. F. D. July 24.

TURZO, JOHANN (d. 1520). A Hungarian, he was coadjutor to Bishop Roth of Breslau, Silesia, whom he succeeded in 1506. He held synods to improve spiritual life, aided the schools of his diocese, and was active as a humanist.

TUTILO, ST. (d. 915?). Educated at the Benedictine monastery of St. Gall, he was placed in charge of the school there, and was a poet, tutor, craftsman, and musician. He was particularly influential in developing liturgical tropes and, with Bl. Notker Valbulus, in writing sequences. F. D. Mar. 28.

TUTO, BL. (d. 815). In 764 he founded the Benedictine abbey of Ottobeuren, Bavaria, and became its first abbot. F. D. Nov. 19.

TUTO, BL. (d. 930), bishop. A Benedictine monk at the abbey of St. Emmeram in Ratisbon, Germany, he became its abbot, then bishop there. He also served as secretary to Emperor Arnold. F. D. May 14.

TWENGE, ST. JOHN (1319–1379). Born in Bridlington, England, he studied at Oxford and was prior of St. Augustine's, Bridlington, for seventeen years until his death there on Oct. 10. He was canonized by Pope Boniface IX in 1401, is known as St. John of Bridlington, and was a patron of women in difficult labor. F. D. Oct. 21.

TWIKETAL (d. 975). According to unreliable sources, he was born in England of royal descent, became a cleric, was chancellor for Kings Athelstan, Edward, and Edred, became a monk in Croyland abbey, which he restored in 946, and became its abbot. He died in July.

TWINGER, JACOB (1346–1420), historian. Born in Königshofen, Alsace, and also known as Jacob von Königshofen, he was ordained in

1382, became pastor in Drusenheim, notary apostolic in 1394, and canon and archivist in Strassburg in 1395. He wrote *Chronicles of Strassburg*, one of the first universal histories in German and a valuable source of the events of 1382–1415. He died in Strassburg, Alsace, on Dec. 27.

TYCHICUS, ST. (1st century), bishop. A disciple of St. Paul (Col. 4:7–8 and Eph. 6:21–22), he is said to have been named bishop of Paphos in Cyprus. F. D. Apr. 29.

TYCHON, ST. (5th century), bishop. In the direction of his see of Amanthus (now Limassol) in Cyprus, he was active against the pagan worship of Aphrodite. He became patron of winegrowers and his shrine long was famous. F. D. June 16.

TYDFIL, ST. (d. 480?). A Welsh girl, she was slain by barbarian marauders in Glamorgan, Wales. F. D. Aug. 23.

TYLDEN, THOMAS (1624–1688). Born in Addington, Kent, England, he studied at Oxford and Cambridge, became a convert about 1641, went to Lisbon, was ordained, and taught philosophy and theology in the English College there from 1650 to 1655, when he became its president. He received his doctorate in divinity in 1660, went to England as chaplain of Princess Catherine of Braganza, was charged with conspiracy in the murder of Sir Edmund Godfrey during the Titus Oates Plot hysteria, and fled to Paris. Later cleared, he returned as the queen's chaplain and almoner. He wrote controversial works under the name of Thomas Godden and died in London on Dec. 1.

TYLER, WILLIAM (1806–1849), bishop. Born in Derby, Vermont, on June 5, he was converted with his parents about 1821, studied under Bishop Fenwick and at a seminary in Montreal, and was ordained in 1829. He was assigned to the cathedral in Boston, did missionary work throughout New England, and in 1844 was consecrated first bishop of the newly erected see of Hartford, Connecticut. Because of the small number of Catholics there, he moved the seat of the see to Providence, Rhode Island, was a leader in the temperance movement, and died in Providence on June 18.

TYRANNIO, ST. (d. 310), bishop and martyr. Bishop of Tyre, he was imprisoned and tortured at Antioch, and, when he refused to sacrifice to the pagan gods, was put to death by drowning. F. D. Feb. 20.

TYRIE, JAMES (1543–1597), theologian. Born in Drumkilbo, Perthshire, Scotland, he studied at St. Andrews, accompanied Edmund Hay to Rome in 1562 and became a Jesuit there, and in 1567 taught at Clermont College, Paris. He engaged John Knox in controversy, helped prepare Acquaviva's *Ratio studiorum*, became rector of Clermont, and headed the Scots Jesuit mission in 1590. He became professor at Pont-à-Mousson and head of the Scots College later that year, assistant for France and Germany in Rome in 1592, advised Pope Clement VIII on Scottish affairs, and helped re-establish the Scottish hospital there. He died in Rome on May 27.

TYRRELL, WILLIAM GEORGE (1866–1947). Born in Naini Tal, India, on Aug. 17, he was educated in Germany and at Balliol, and entered the foreign office in 1889. He was secretary to Lord Sanderson in the state department in 1896–1903 and of the committee on imperial defense for a year, went briefly to Rome, then served as Viscount Grey's private secretary from 1907 to 1915. He had a breakdown when two sons were killed in World War I, recovered, worked on the committee evaluating the League of Nations and in the foreign-office intelligence department, and attended the Versailles peace conference. He accompanied Lord Grey to Washington, became adviser to Lord Curzon, particularly at the Lausanne Conference, and supported Ramsay MacDonald's moves toward close association with France, particularly in containing Germany. In 1925 he became permanent undersecretary of state, went to Paris as ambassador in 1928–34, then retired from the service. He had married Mary Ann Urquhart in 1890, received numerous honors from his government, became Baron Tyrrell of Avon in 1929, was made an honorary fellow of Balliol, and received honorary degrees from Oxford and Dublin. In 1925 he became president of the British Board of Film Censors, a position he held until his death in London on Mar. 14.

TYSILIO, ST. (7th century?), abbot. Son of a Welsh prince, he became a monk at Meifod, Montgomeryshire, Wales, under Abbot Gwyddfarch, whom he succeeded. Driven from Meifod by his older brother's widow, who wanted him to marry her, he sailed to Brittany in 617 with several monks and founded Suliac, where he died. F. D. Nov. 8.

U

UBAGHS, CASIMIR (1800–1875), philosopher. Born in Berg-lez-Fauquemont, France, on Nov. 26, he taught philosophy at the Rolduc seminary and in 1830 at Louvain, where he became the leader of the ontologico-traditionalist school. He wrote treatises expounding his theories which were widely popular, was ordered to correct five propositions in his writings by the Index in 1843, and in 1846 became editor of *Revue Catholique*, the official journal of ontologism. He and his group were vigorously opposed by other scholars, and in 1864 a series of propositions in his ontological works was condemned by the Congregation of the Index. He retired from public life, and died at Louvain, Belgium, on Feb. 15.

UBALD ADIMARI, BL. (1246–1315). One of the dissipated leaders of the Ghibelline gangs in Florence, he heard a sermon by St. Philip Benizi when he was thirty, joined the latter as a Servite priest, and devoted the rest of his life to preaching and penance. He was beatified in 1821. F. D. Apr. 9.

UBALD BALDASSINI, ST. (1100?–1160), bishop. Born in Gubbio, Italy, and orphaned when young, he was educated by his bishop-uncle, ordained, and made dean of the cathedral. He had some success in reforming the canons, was chosen bishop of Perugia in 1126, refused the honor, but was made bishop of Gubbio in 1128. He diverted Frederick Barbarossa from sacking his diocese, although the emperor had just ruined Spoleto. He was canonized in 1192. F. D. May 16.

UBERTINO OF CASALE (1259–1330?). Born in Casale, Italy, he became a Franciscan at Genoa in 1273, studied at Paris for nine years, and in 1287 settled in Florence, where he lectured at Santa Croce and devoted himself to preaching. He became a leader of the Spirituals in Tuscany, denounced the government of the Franciscans and several popes for refusing to accept the Spirituals' definition of Franciscan poverty, and in 1305 was forbidden to preach and banished to the La Verno convent by Pope Benedict XI. While there, he wrote *Arbor vitae crucifixae Jesu Christi*, in which he denounced the leaders of the Church, including the pope and head of the Franciscans. In 1307 he became chaplain to Cardinal Napoleone Orsini, former protector of the Ancona Spirituals, who deputed him to absolve Siena from the ecclesiastical censure its populace had incurred. He was summoned to Avignon to settle the dispute within his order, which had reached bitter proportions, demanded the formation of a new reform order, and denounced papal decisions on the question of Franciscan poverty. The bull *Exivi de paradiso* (1312) settled the latter point, and he was denied permission to form a reform group. He retired from public life to Avignon in 1313, and received permission from Pope John XXII to enter the Benedictine abbey at Gembloux in 1317. He became involved in the dispute of the Franciscans and Dominicans over the poverty of Christ and the apostles (which led to Michael of Cesena's schism), wrote a thesis on the subject for Pope John XXII, which the pope accepted, and then returned to Cardinal Orsini's service, where he continued to write on the matter after the settlement of 1322–23. He was denounced as a heretic and excommunicated in 1325, but escaped arrest by fleeing to Germany and the protection of Louis IV of Bavaria, and then disappeared from history.

UCCELLO, PAOLO (1396?–1475), painter. Paolo di Dono was born in Florence, Italy, apprenticed to Lorenzo Ghiberti, with whom he probably worked on the gates of the baptistery, studied geometry under Manetti, became interested in painting, and was noted for his realism and command of linear perspective. He did an equestrian portrait of Sir John Hawkwood, a portrait group of himself, Giotto, Donatello, Manetti, and Brunelleschi, and *Battle of San Romano*. He acquired the nickname Il Uccello because of his bird paintings. He died in Florence on Dec. 10.

UGHELLI, FERDINANDO (1595–1670), historian. Born in Florence, Italy, on Mar. 21, he became a Cistercian there, studied at the Gregorian in Rome, became abbot of Settimo, Florence, and in 1638 of Tre Fontane, Rome, a position he held until his death there on May 19. He became so famed as a historian that Pope Alexander VII granted him an annual pension to defray his research expenses, was a consultor of the Index, and Cardinal Carlo de' Medici's theologian. Among his outstanding works are the nine-volume *Italia sacra sive de episcopus Italiae* (1643–62) and a study of the Cistercians.

UGOCCIONE, ST. RICOVERO (13th century), founder. *See* Monaldo, St. Buonfiglio.

UGOLINO OF MONTE GIORGIO. *See* Boniscambi, Ugolino.

UHTRED (1315?–1396), theologian. Born in Boldon, North Durham, England, he became a Benedictine at Durham about 1332, went to London in 1337, Durham College in 1340, and received his doctorate at Oxford in 1357. He was four times prior of Finchale abbey (1367, 1379, 1386, and 1392), was one of the delegates sent with Wyclif to Bruges by King Edward III in 1374 to discuss the problem of canonical provision in England, participated in a council later in the year to decide whether the king was obliged to recognize the papal suzerainty King John had granted to Pope Innocent III (he asserted the pope's right, but voted against it), and was sub-prior of Durham abbey in 1381. He died in Finchale abbey, England, on Jan. 24. He wrote several theological treatises. His name is sometimes spelled Utred or Owtred.

UJEJSKI, CORNELIUS (1823–1897), poet. Born in Beremiany, Galicia, he studied at Lemberg, and wrote *Maraton* (1843). His *Choral*, written on the occasion of the murder of thousands of Galician noblemen in 1846 by peasants incited by the Austrian government, established his fame as a poet and became Poland's national hymn. He published two volumes of poetry, *Skargi Jeremiego* (1847) and *Melodye Biblijne* (1852), and died in Cholojewie.

ULENBERG, KASPAR (1549–1617), author. Born in Lippstadt, Westphalia, Germany, he studied at Soest, Brunswick, and Wittenberg, taught in Lunden, and went to Cologne, where in 1572 he became a convert. He studied philosophy at Cologne, taught at the Laurentianum gymnasium there, and was ordained in 1575. He did parish work in Kaiserswerth and Cologne, became regent of the Laurentianum in 1593, a position he held for twenty-two years, and was rector of the university in 1610–12. He wrote theological treatises, *Historia de vita* (1622), *Die Psalmen* (1582), and a widely used German translation of the Bible. He died in Cologne, Germany, on Feb. 16.

ULFILAS (311?–383?), bishop. Born in Dacia, traditionally believed to Christian parents captured by the Goths, he was educated and became a lector there, and in 341 was consecrated bishop of the West Goths by Eusebius of Nicomedia at Antioch. He worked for seven years in the area north of the Danube, was driven out by pagan leaders, and settled south of that river, at Moesia, for thirty years. He knew Latin, Greek, and Gothic, preached and wrote in all three languages, and completed a Gothic translation of the Bible; most of the New Testament version is extant.

ULFRID, ST. (d. 1029), martyr. An English missioner to Germany and Sweden, he was slain after he destroyed a pagan idol. F. D. Jan. 18.

ULLATHORNE, WILLIAM BERNARD (1806–1889), bishop. Born in Pocklington, Yorkshire, England, on May 7, he went to sea as a cabin boy in 1819, and on his return became a Benedictine at Downside in 1823, was professed and took the name Bernard in 1825, attended Ampleforth and Ushaw colleges, and was ordained at the latter in 1831. He volunteered for the Australian mission in 1832, went there in 1833 as vicar general of Mauritius, and remained there until 1835, when Bishop Polding arrived as vicar apostolic of Australia. On his return to England, he agitated for the abolition of the transportation of criminals to Australia, wrote a treatise on the colony, and in 1838 returned there with several missionaries he had secured. He returned to England two years later, was appointed vicar apostolic of the Western District of England and titular bishop of Hetalona in 1843, and in 1845 was transferred to the Central District, where he spent the rest of his life. He was sent to Rome by his fellow English bishops in 1848 to secure the restoration of the English hierarchy and on its proclamation by Pope Pius IX was appointed bishop of Birmingham. He built up his diocese, encouraged new religious congregations, among them Cardinal Newman's Oratorians at Edgbaston, and established a seminary at Olton in 1873. He attended the Vatican Council in 1870, resigned his see in 1888, was given the title of archbishop of Cabasa, and retired to Oscott College, near Birmingham, England, where he died on Mar. 21. His *Autobiography* and *Letters* appeared in 1892.

ULLERSTON, RICHARD (d. 1423). Born in Lancaster, England, he was ordained in 1383, was a fellow at Queen's College, Oxford (where he received his doctorate in divinity in 1394), from 1391 to 1403, became chancellor in 1408, and wrote several treaties and a plan for ecclesiastical reform for Bishop Salisbury in 1408.

ULLOA, ANTONIO DE (1716–1795), scientist. Born in Seville, Spain, on Jan. 12, he joined the navy in 1733, spent 1735–45 on an expedition of the French Academy to Peru to measure a degree of the meridian at the equator, and on his way home was captured by the British and taken prisoner to England, where he became a fellow of the Royal Society. On his return to Spain he worked on several scientific commissions, served as governor of Louisiana in 1766–68, and was appointed lieutenant general of the navy in 1779. He was one of the founders of the observatory at Cadiz, established the first museum of natural history and the first metallurgical laboratory in Spain, and wrote on his work in the Americas. He died near Cadiz, Spain, on July 5.

ULLOA, FRANCISCO DE (d. 1540?), explorer. A captain under Hernando Cortés in Mexico, he was dispatched by the latter, against the viceroy's orders, in 1539 to explore the gulf of California, sailed to the head of the gulf in 1539, and proved Lower California to be a peninsula. According to some authorities, he was forced to return to New Spain in 1540 when his supplies ran out, and was killed by a soldier there; another version is that he disappeared with one of the ships.

ULPHIA, ST. (d. 750?). A solitary at St. Acheul under the spiritual direction of St. Domitius, she formed a community at Amiens Gaul, after his death, but later returned to her hermitage. F. D. Jan. 31.

ULRIC, ST. (890–973), bishop. Born in Augsburg, Germany, he was educated at St. Gall, Switzerland, and returned to his native city to serve under his uncle, St. Adalbero, and to succeed him as bishop in 923. He devoted himself to relieving the sufferings of those who had been left desolate by the Magyar invasion, and in his last years he retired to St. Gall. He was canonized by Pope John XV in 993, the first recorded papal canonization. F. D. July 4.

ULRIC OF ZELL, ST. (1020?–1093), abbot. Born in Ratisbon, Germany, he was a court page before becoming archdeacon and provost of the cathedral under his uncle, Notker, bishop of Freising. After a pilgrimage to Rome and Jerusalem, he became a Benedictine at Cluny in 1061, was ordained, served as chaplain to the nuns at Marcigny, as prior of Peterlingen, and then founded the monastery at Rüggersburg. When he opposed Bishop Burchard of Lausanne, who was supporting Emperor Henry V against the pope, he was recalled, founded and was prior of the monastery of Zell in the Black Forest, and also established a convent at Bollschweil. His *Consuetudines cluniacenses* deals with liturgy and the direction of novices and of monasteries. He became blind in 1073 and died in Augsburg, Germany, on July 10. F. D. July 14.

ULRICH IV (d. 1177). Ruler of Tarasp in the Tyrol, he called Benedictine monks from Ottobeuren to the rebuilt monastery of Schuls; this became an abbey before he transferred it in 1146 to Vintschgau and, in 1150, to Burgeis, later called Marienberg. Ulrich became a Benedictine about 1164 and died at Marienberg, Germany, on Dec. 14.

ULRICH OF RICHENTHAL (d. 1438?). Born in Constance, Switzerland, he compiled an accurate and valuable chronicle of the events of the Council of Constance in 1414–18.

ULRICH VON TÜRHEIM (13th century), poet. A Swabian, he wrote a long narrative poem on the legend of Tristram and Iseult, relying on a previous romance by Gottfried von Strassburg, usually dated 1240, and a version of Wolfram von Eschenbach's *Willehalm*, which he called *Der starke Rennewart* (1250).

ULRICK, ST. (d. 870), martyr. See Theodore, St.

ULTAN, ST. (d. 657), bishop. He supposedly was bishop of Ardbraccan, Ireland, although there are several saints of this name. He is also said to have collected the writings of St. Brigid. F. D. Sept. 4.

ULTAN, ST. (d. 686?), abbot. He and his brothers, SS. Foillan and Fursey, went from Ireland to found the abbey of Burgh castle in Yarmouth, England. On his return from a pilgrimage to Rome, Ultan became abbot of monasteries at Fosses and Péronne, France. F. D. May 2.

UNAMAN, ST. (d. 1040?), martyr. See Sunaman, St.

UNDSET, SIGRID (1882–1949), novelist. Born in Kalundberg, Norway, on May 20, she was brought up in Oslo, where she became an office worker, from 1898 to 1908, after the death of her father. Her first novel, *Frau Marta Oulie* (1907), was written in diary form; *Happy Youth* (1908), *Jenny* (1911), and *Spring* (1914) followed, dealing with family life in the contemporary world, loneliness, and the questioning of authority. She dipped into history for *Viga-Ljot and Vidgis* (1909). She married Anders Svarstad, a divorced artist, in 1912; they had three children; she was separated from him in 1924 before she became a convert in 1925. She had explored the Catholicism of mediaeval Norway for her trilogy, *Kristin Lavransdatter* (*The Bridal Wreath*, *The Mistress of Husaby*, and *The Cross*), in 1920–22. Another psychological and historical series, *Olav Audunsson*, followed in 1925–27, and led to the Nobel Prize for literature in 1927. Later work includes *Gymnadenin* (1929), *The Burning Bush* (1930), *Ida Elisabeth* (1932), and *The Faithful Wife* (1936), on the Europe between wars and human existence in general, *The Longest Years* (1934), an autobiography, and *Saga of Saints* (1935), on mediaeval life in Norway. *Madame Dorothea* (1939) dealt with eighteenth-century Norway; *Stages on the Road* and *Men, Women and Places* were biographical essays. Her books were banned by the Nazis and she escaped to America in 1941, after radio service for a time with the government in exile. Her last work includes *Return to the Future* (1942) and *Happy Days in Norway* (1943), collections of old legends, and *Catherine of Siena* (1954). She was given an honorary degree by Smith College, returned to Norway in 1945 and was decorated by King Haakon VII, and died in Lillehammer, Norway, on June 10.

UNNI, ST. (d. 936). A Benedictine from New Corbie, Saxony, he became ninth bishop of Bremen, Germany, in 918. He had missionary success in Denmark and Sweden, and died at Birka, Sweden. F. D. Sept. 17.

URBAN I, ST. (d. 230), pope. Son of Pontianus, and a Roman, he was elected pope in 222, and was buried in the cemetery of St. Callistus on the Appian Way, possibly after

being put to death during the persecution of
Alexander Severus. His pontificate was disturbed by the continued schism of Hippolytus
and his followers. Another Urban, a martyr,
was buried in the nearby cemetery of Praetextatus. It is possible that the pope was not
martyred and that the two names were confused. F. D. May 23.

URBAN II, BL. (1042–1099), pope. Odo of
Lagery was born in Châtillons-sur-Marne,
France, of the family of the counts of Semur,
and studied at Rheims under St. Bruno, founder
of the Carthusians, who became his adviser
when he was pope. He became archdeacon
there and in 1070 a Benedictine at Cluny. He
was appointed grand prior by St. Hugh and in
1078 was created cardinal-bishop of Ostia. On
Mar. 12, 1088, at Terracina in Campania, he
was elected pope by acclamation, but for the
next four years was obliged to struggle with
antipope Clement III (Guibert), who was supported by Emperor Henry IV. In 1095, at a
synod at Piacenza, he reiterated the Gregorian
decrees regarding clerical celibacy, lay investitures, and simony. Later that year at Clermont,
as a result of a plea from Emperor Alexius I
of Byzantine, he preached the first crusade,
which was launched in 1097 and resulted in
the capture of Jerusalem in 1099. In 1097, also,
Emperor Henry IV finally left Italy and in 1098
Guibert's party left Rome. In 1099 he called a
council at Bari to close the breach between
Rome and Constantinople, which, though unsuccessful in its main purpose, settled other
problems. His pontificate was marked by his
struggles with secular kings (he reaffirmed the
excommunication of Henry IV, excommunicated King Philip I of France, and was dissuaded by St. Anselm from doing the same to
William Rufus of England), continued reforms in the Church, and the beginning of
great intellectual movements (St. Anselm laid
the foundations of scholasticism; St. Ivo of
Chartres systematized canon law; and the
abbeys of Cîteaux and Fontevrault were
founded). He was beatified in 1881. F. D. July
29.

URBAN III (d. 1187), pope. Uberto Crivelli
was born, at a date unknown, in Milan, Italy,
of a noble Milanese family which was severely
mistreated by the Emperor Frederick Barbarossa, was created cardinal in 1182 by Pope
Lucius II, and appointed in 1185 archbishop of
Milan. To prevent any interference in the election by the emperor, he was elected pope on
Nov. 25, 1185, the very day Lucius died, and
was consecrated on Dec. 1 at Verona. He at
once became involved in the disputes of his
predecessors with the emperor over the latter's
violation of Church rights, refused to crown
the emperor's son, Henry, and, when the patriarch of Aquileia did, he excommunicated the

patriarch and all participating bishops, and
then consecrated Fulmar archbishop of Trier,
though Frederick had already granted investiture to Rudolf. Frederick cut off Urban's communications to the German bishops, sent
Henry to lay waste to the Papal States, and
caused the German bishops at the Diet of
Gelnhausen in 1187 to urge the pope to modify his stand. Urban was on his way to Venice
to announce the emperor's excommunication
when he died in Ferrara, Italy, on Oct.
20.

URBAN IV (d. 1264), pope. Jacques Panta-
léon was born in Troyes, Champagne, France,
studied at the cathedral school there, received
his doctorate in canon law from Paris, became
a canon at Laon, archdeacon of Liège, attended
the Council of Lyons in 1245, and was sent on
a diplomatic mission to Germany in 1247 by
Pope Innocent IV. He became archdeacon of
Laon in 1249, was appointed bishop of Verdun
in 1253, patriarch of Jerusalem in 1255, and on
Aug. 29, 1261, was elected pope at Viterbo,
and was consecrated on Sept. 4. Among the
outstanding acts of his pontificate were his appointment of fourteen new cardinals, seven of
whom were French (there were but eight cardinals at the time of his election); the restoration of papal finances on a sound basis; his successful efforts to restore the prestige and
influence of the papacy; his establishment of a
powerful new Guelph party to oppose the
Ghibellines; and Roman recognition of his
rule (though he never entered Rome). He
spent much of his regime attempting to remove
Sicily from Hohenstaufen control by opposing
Manfred, who had assumed the crown of Sicily,
but died before his choice for the crown,
Charles of Anjou, was able to launch an expedition to Sicily. His recognition of Charles was
to have repercussions in later centuries in the
frequent wars between France and Italy. He
instituted the feast of Corpus Christi in 1264.
He died in Perugia, Italy, on Oct. 2.

URBAN V, BL. (1310–1370), pope. Guillaume de Grimoard was born in Grisac, Languedoc, France, educated at Montpellier and
Toulouse, became a Benedictine at Chirac,
where he was ordained, took his doctorate at
Paris, and taught there and at Avignon, Montpellier, and Toulouse. He became abbot of St.
Germain, Auxerre, in 1352, served the papacy
on diplomatic missions, and in 1361 was made
abbot of St. Victor, Marseilles. He was serving
as legate to Queen Joanna at Naples when he
learned that he had been elected pope on Sept.
28, 1362, returned to Avignon, and was consecrated on Nov. 6. He tried, but with only
slight success, to restore peace to Europe. He
made peace with Barnabo Visconti in 1364,
failed to suppress the *condottieri* (marauding
soldiers) in France and Italy, but had better

success in his attempt to launch a crusade against the Turks in 1367. In 1367, after Cardinal Albornoz had restored order in the Papal States, Urban moved the papacy from Avignon (where it had been for forty-nine years) to Rome. In 1368, German Emperor Charles IV visited him there; the pope crowned his consort as empress, but nothing further came of the meeting except Charles's promise to respect the rights of the Church in Germany. In 1369 the Greek Emperor John V Palaeologus came to Rome and abjured his schism, but was unable to bring his people back to the Church with him. Later that year war broke out between France and England, Perugia erupted into revolt, unrest surged through Italy, and when disorders shook Rome Urban returned to Avignon in France, in spite of warnings from St. Bridget, where he died less than three months later. His cult was confirmed in 1870. F. D. Dec. 19.

URBAN VI (1318?–1389), pope. Bartolommeo Prignano was born in Naples, Italy, went to Avignon as a youth, and in 1364 was appointed archbishop of Acerenza. He was transferred to Bari in 1377, was made head of the papal chancery, and on Apr. 8 was elected pope (and consecrated on Apr. 18), the last pope not a cardinal to be elected. Intent on ecclesiastical reform, he tactlessly alienated most of the cardinals. On Sept. 20, 1378, at Fondi, after having previously declared Urban illegally elected (the election had taken place with a mob threatening violence if the cardinals did not elect an Italian), the disaffected cardinals elected Robert of Geneva antipope Clement VII, which began a schism that was to last until 1417. Christendom was torn in two, with western Europe (except England and her possessions) recognizing Clement, and most of Germany, Poland, Hungary, Flanders, and Italy (except Naples) recognizing Urban. But Queen Joanna of Naples quickly declared for Clement and was deposed by Urban, who recognized Charles of Durazzo as her successor. He soon fell out with Charles, alienated most of the cardinals remaining loyal to him by his violence and intemperance, and appointed fourteen new cardinals. When he discovered a plot among several of his older cardinals to depose him, he imprisoned them, subjected them to torture, and executed them. He then excommunicated the king and queen of Naples for aiding the conspirators, thereupon setting off a war between the Papal States and Naples. He died in Rome on Oct. 15, possibly by poisoning.

URBAN VII (1521–1590), pope. Giovanni Baptista Castagna was born in Rome on Aug. 4, received his doctorate in civil and canon law from Bologna, accompanied his uncle, Cardinal Girolamo Verallo, on a papal mission to France,

and in 1553 was appointed archbishop of Rossano and ordained priest later the same month. He served as governor of Fano in 1555, then of Perugia and Umbria, participated in the Council of Trent in 1562–63, and was papal nuncio to Philip II of Spain from 1565 to 1572. He resigned the see of Rossano in 1573, went to Venice as papal nuncio, became governor of Bologna in 1577, and was Pope Gregory XII's legate to the peace negotiations between Philip II and the United Provinces in Cologne the following year. He was created a cardinal in 1583, appointed legate of Bologna in 1584, and in 1586 inquisitor general. He was elected pope on Sept. 15, 1590, but was never consecrated, as he died on Sept. 27 in Rome.

URBAN VIII (1568–1644), pope. Maffeo Barberini was born in Florence, Italy, on Apr. 5, was brought up in Rome by his uncle Francesco, studied at the Collegio Romano and Pisa, where he received his doctorate in law, and became abbreviator apostolic and referendary of the Segnatura di Giustizia. He served as governor of Fano for Pope Clement VIII in 1592, papal legate to France in 1601, was appointed archbishop of Nazareth in 1604, and then nuncio to King Henry IV in Paris. He was created a cardinal in 1606, was transferred to the see of Spoleto in 1608, was legate to Bologna in 1617 and prefect of the Segnatura di Giustizia, and on Aug. 6, 1623, was elected pope, and was consecrated on Sept. 29. He pursued a policy of attempting to control the Hapsburgs, traditional menace to Italy and Rome, supported Richelieu's foreign policy, though this meant opposition to Catholic Austria, and failed to support Emperor Ferdinand II's war against the Protestant Gustavus Adolphus as forcefully as many wished. He actively encouraged missionary activities and orders, forbade Indian slavery in Paraguay, Brazil, and the West Indies by a 1639 bull, sent legates to England in a fruitless attempt to restore Catholicism, appointed a committee in 1629 to reform the breviary and approved their not too popular changes in 1631, and condemned Jansen's *Augustinus* in 1642. He added Urbino to the papal territories in 1626, became involved in a discreditable war with Odoardo Farnese, duke of Parma, in 1641, when he took possession of Farnese's Castro and excommunicated him in 1642, but, when Tuscany, Modena, and Venice joined the duke in 1643, was obliged to sue for peace in 1644. A patron of literature and the arts, he built the papal residence at Castel Gandolfo and the Barberini palace, founded the Barberini Library (which was incorporated into the Vatican Library in 1902), and the Vatican seminary, and consecrated St. Peter's on Nov. 18, 1626. His pontificate was marred by his excessive nepotism and the second condemnation of Galileo by the Inquisition in 1633. He died in Rome on July 29.

URBAN, ST. (1st century). *See* Ampliatus, St.

URBAN, ST. (d. 250?), martyr. *See* Babylas, St.

URBAN, ST. (d. 285?), martyr. *See* Ariston, St.

URBAN, ST. (d. 304), martyr. *See* Apodemius, St.

URBAN, ST. (d. 356?). He was bishop of Teano, Campania. F. D. Dec. 7.

URBAN, ST. (d. 370), martyr. *See* Theodore, St.

URBAN, ST. (d. 390?). He became bishop of Langres in 374 and is honored in Burgundy as a patron of vineyard workers. F. D. Apr. 2.

URBAN, ST. (5th century), bishop. *See* Crescens, St.

URBAN, ST. (d. 940?). He directed the Benedictine monastery of Peñalba, Spain, and worked with St. Gennadius to effect a monastic revival in Astorga. F. D. Apr. 6.

URBICIUS, ST. (6th century). After the death of his companion, St. Liphardus, whom he joined as a recluse at Meung-sur-Loire, France, he became abbot of the monastery founded there. F. D. June 3.

URCISCENUS, ST. (d. 216?). He became seventh bishop of Pavia, Italy, about 183. F. D. June 21.

URRÁBURU, JUAN JOSÉ (1844–1904), philosopher. Born in Ceanuri, Biscay, Spain, on May 23, he became a Jesuit at Guipúzcoa in 1860, and taught theology at Poyanne, France, and the Gregorian, Rome, from 1878 to 1886. He was rector of Valladolid in 1887–90, of Colegio Maximo Oña in 1891–97, and of the Salamanca seminary in 1898–1902. He wrote theological works, including the eight-volume *Institutiones philosophiae* (1890–1900) and the five-volume *Compendium philosophiae scholasticae* (1902–4). He died in Burgos, Spain, on Aug. 13.

URRACA (d. 1126), queen of Castile. Daughter of Alfonso VI, she became queen in 1109, fought against (though sometimes at the side of) her husband, Alfonso I of Aragon, and eventually joined in full-scale attack upon him, with the help of her son by a former marriage, later Alfonso VII.

URSICINUS, ST. (1st century), martyr. He was put to death at Ravenna, Italy; biographical details are untrustworthy. F. D. June 19.

URSICINUS, ST. (d. 380?). He is listed as the fourth bishop of Sens, active against Arianism in Gaul. F. D. July 24.

URSICINUS, ST. (4th century). He was bishop of Brescia, Italy, and attended the 347 Council of Sardica. F. D. Dec. 1.

URSICINUS, ST. (d. 585?). He was bishop of Cahors, France, often spoken of by St. Gregory of Tours. F. D. Dec. 20.

URSICINUS, ST. (d. 625?). Probably an Irishman, he followed St. Columban to Metz, Gaul, and became founder-abbot of a community of monks at what is now St. Ursanne, Switzerland. F. D. Dec. 20.

URSICINUS, ST. (d. 760). Benedictine abbot of Disentis, Switzerland, he was bishop of Chur from 754 to 758, then resigned to become a hermit. F. D. Oct. 2.

URSICIUS, ST. (d. 304), martyr. He was a tribune in the imperial army, beheaded at Nicomedia during the Diocletian persecution. F. D. Aug. 14.

URSINUS, ST. (3rd century). He was the first bishop of Bourges in Gaul; fictional legends made him a disciple sent to Europe by Christ. F. D. Nov. 9.

URSINUS (7th century). He was bishop of Ceneda, near Venice, Italy, and attended the Council of Rome in 680 which discussed the Monothelite heresy.

URSMAR, ST. (d. 713), bishop. Builder of several churches and of monasteries at Aulne and Wallers during the evangelization of Flanders, he became abbot of the Benedictine center of Lobbes, Flanders, around 690. He may have been bishop of Lobbes before this date. F. D. Apr. 19.

USUARD (d. 875?). A member of the Benedictines at St. Germain-des-Prés abbey in Paris, he went to Spain in 858 and wrote an account of his trip. Charles the Bald appointed him to compile *Martyrologium*, based to a large extent on Ado's *Martyrology*, which became famous in the Middle Ages.

URSULA, ST., martyr. Legend calls her the daughter of a Christian king in Britain, who was ordered to marry a pagan, gained a delay of three years, went on a pilgrimage to Rome with 11,000 associates and ladies in waiting, and on their return all were slain at Cologne by the Huns when Ursula refused to marry their chief. They long were honored on Oct. 21, but Pope Benedict XV intended to remove the story from the Roman Martyrology. The fiction actually developed after the finding of the bones of martyrs in a Cologne basilica in the late fourth or early fifth century. The incredible number of the legendary royal entourage grew from an ignorant reading of the inscription XI MM VV (eleven virgin martyrs) on a tomb; the name Ursula was that of an eight-year-old girl buried nearby.

URSULINA, BL. (1375–1410). Born in Parma, Italy, she claimed that she had supernatural directives to go to Avignon to heal the great Western schism. With two companions and her mother, the young girl pleaded several times with Clement VII, but his court scoffed at her, terming her a sorcerer. She died after a pilgrimage to the Holy Land. F. D. Apr. 7.

URSUS, ST. (d. 286?), martyr. *See* Victor, St.

URSUS, ST. (d. 287?), martyr. *See* Maurice, St.

URSUS, ST. (d. 396). He was bishop of Ravenna, Italy. F. D. Apr. 13.

URSUS, ST. (d. 508), bishop. A hermit living outside the church of St. Amator at Auxerre, Gaul, he was made bishop of that city in his old age. F. D. July 30.

USTHAZANES, ST. (d. 341), martyr. *See* Simeon Barsabae, St.

UTTO, BL. (750?-820). He founded and was abbot of the Benedictine monastery of Metten, Bavaria. His cult was approved in 1909. F. D. Oct. 3.

V

VACARIUS (1120-1200?), canonist. Born in northern Italy, he was brought to England by Thomas à Becket, whom he served as counsel in a dispute between the latter and Archbishop Theobald of Winchester. The case was decided in Becket's favor in 1146. Vacarius preached throughout England in 1149, prepared a compendium of Justinian's *Digest* and *Codex* which was widely used as a textbook, and later taught at Oxford. In 1154 he became legal counsel to Archbishop Roger de Pont l'Évêque of York, received a prebendary at Southwell (which he passed to his nephew in 1191), and was prior of Thurgarton in 1198. Pope Innocent III empowered him to preach the crusade in northern England. Vacarius also wrote *Summa de assumpto homine* and *Summa de matrimonio.*

VACHON, ALEXANDRE (1885-1953), archbishop. Born in St. Raymond, Quebec, on Aug. 16, he was educated in Quebec, and at Laval, Harvard, and Massachusetts Institute of Technology. He became a leading chemist and biologist, was a member of several scientific academies, and director of the National Research Council and the Fisheries Board of Canada. He was ordained in 1910, became titular archbishop of Acrida and coadjutor of Ottawa in 1939, succeeded as archbishop of Ottawa in 1940, and died in Dallas, Texas, on Mar. 30.

VAFFARD, FRANÇOIS (1655-1726). Born in Blois, France, he became a Discalced Augustinian under the name Ange de Ste. Rosalie. He published an elaborate genealogy of French kings and courtiers, completed by his collaborator, Fr. Simplicien. He died in Paris.

VAILLANT DE GUESLIS, FRANCOIS (1646-1718), missioner. Born in Orléans, France, on July 20, he became a Jesuit in 1665, was sent to Canada in 1670, and was ordained in Quebec in 1675. He labored among the Mohawks from 1679 to 1684, was in Quebec from 1685 to 1702 (except for 1692-96 in Montreal, where he was superior), served as ambassador to Gov. Thomas Dongan of New York in 1688, worked among the Senecas in 1702-5, and served in Montreal from 1709 to 1715. He returned to France, and died in Moulins on Sept. 24.

VAISE, ST. (d. 500). A wealthy citizen of Saintes, France, he was murdered by his relatives because he distributed all his possessions to the poor. F. D. Apr. 16.

VALDÉS, ALFONSO DE (1500?-1532), chancellor. Born in Cuenca, Castile, Spain, he became a member of Emperor Charles V's entourage, accompanied him on his coronation at Aachen in 1520 and to the Diet of Worms in 1521, became secretary of the imperial chancery in 1522, and in 1529 published *Lactantius*, a violent attack on Pope Clement VII. He was denounced to the Inquisition by the papal nuncio in Madrid, but was exonerated at the emperor's wish, negotiated with Melanchthon at the Diet of Augsburg in 1530, and died in Vienna in Oct. An ardent humanist, he was a fervent disciple of Erasmus, whose ideas he spread in Spain.

VALENS, ST. (d. 309), martyr. *See* Pamphilus, St.

VALENS, ST. (d. 531). He became bishop of Verona, Italy, in 524. F. D. July 26.

VALENTINA, ST. (d. 308), martyr. A Christian in Caesarea during the persecution of Maximinus II, she protested the torture of St. Thea to Firmilian, governor of Palestine, who promptly put her to torture and then burned the two girls to death. F. D. July 25.

VALENTINE (d. 827), pope. Born in Rome, he was appointed archdeacon by Pope Paschal I, elected pope in Aug. 827, and died in Rome a month later.

VALENTINE, ST. (d. 269?), martyr. A priest who was beheaded at Rome during the persecution of Claudius the Goth, he was buried on the Flaminian Way at a site later occupied by a basilica and catacomb. It is possible that his life and that of Bishop Valentine are identical. F. D. Feb. 14.

VALENTINE, ST. (3rd century). He was bishop of Genoa, Italy, from about 295 to about 307. F. D. May 2.

VALENTINE, ST. (3rd century), bishop. He was decapitated on the Flaminian Way at the present site of Terni, sixty miles from Rome, probably during the persecution of Emperor Claudian. It is possible the people of his see, Interamna, selected the same feast day, Feb. 14, to commemorate him as that honoring the Valentine who died in Rome, or that the two were one and the same person.

VALENTINE, ST. (d. 304?), martyr. A priest, he was put to death at Viterbo, Italy, with his deacon Hilary during the Diocletian persecution. F. D. Nov. 3.

VALENTINE, ST. (d. 305?), bishop and martyr. Bishop of Tongres (or of Trèves), Gaul, he was put to death during the Diocletian persecution. F. D. July 16.

VALENTINE, ST. (d. 305?), martyr. He and SS. Felician and Victorinus (F. D. Nov. 11), Solutor and Victor (F. D. Nov. 13), Agricola, Concordius, and Navalis (F. D. Dec. 16) were said to have been martyred at Ravenna, Italy, during the Diocletian persecution. St. Peter Chrysologus, however, says that St. Apollinaris was the only Ravenna martyr. The names associated with St. Valentine were long venerated there.

VALENTINE, ST. (4th century). He was fourth bishop of Strassburg, Alsace. F. D. Sept. 2.

VALENTINE, ST. (d. 470?), bishop. An abbot, he became a bishop serving the missions in Rhaetia, and died at Mais in the Tyrol. F. D. Jan. 7.

VALENTINE, ST. (d. 715?), martyr. *See* Engratia, St.

VALENTINI, BL. HELENA (1396?–1458). Born in Undine, Italy, and married at fifteen to Antonio dei Cavalcanti, she became an Augustinian tertiary when her husband died twenty-five years later, and devoted her last years to continuing charities and austerities. Her cult was approved in 1848. F. D. Apr. 23.

VALENTINIAN I (321–375), emperor. Born in Cibalis (Mikanovici), Pannonia, he joined the army, rose to high rank under Julian and Jovian, becoming a tribune, about 360, was in Julian's company in Antioch, and in 363 was exiled to Gaul when he refused to pay tribute to idols. He was proclaimed emperor by the army on Feb. 26, 364, and appointed his brother emperor in the East. He constructed a chain of fortresses along the Rhine and Danube frontiers, was engaged in spasmodic war against the Burgundians and Alemanni in Gaul from 365 until he signed a peace treaty with Macrianus in 374, sent his general, Theodosius, to drive the Picts and Scots from Britain, and established the province of Valentia there in 368. An able and energetic ruler, he reduced taxes and encouraged education. In 374 he went to Ilyricum to deal with the Quadi and Sarmatians, was stricken with apoplexy, and

died at Bregetio (near Bratislava, Czechoslovakia), on Nov. 17.

VALENTINIAN II (371–392), emperor. Flavius Valentinianus was born in Vienne, Gaul, son of Emperor Valentinian I and his second wife, Justina. On the death of his father in 375 he was proclaimed by the army co-ruler with his brother Gratian, who recognized him as ruler of Italy, Africa, and Illyricum. During his minority he lived in Milan with his mother Justina, who led the Arian party which was routed by St. Ambrose. When Maximus, who had murdered Gratian in 383, invaded Italy in 387, Valentinian fled for aid to Theodosius, emperor of the East, who restored him in 388. He renounced his Arian leanings and invited Ambrose to Vienne to baptize him, but was assassinated there on May 15, probably by Arbogast, his Frankish general, before this could be accomplished. St. Ambrose delivered his funeral oration, *De obitu Valentiniani consolatio*, in which he discussed baptism of desire.

VALENTINIAN III (419–455), emperor. Son of Constantius III and Galla Placidia, Theodosius' daughter, and nephew of Emperor Honorius, he was born in Ravenna, Italy, on July 3, and in 425 was named emperor of the West by his uncle, Theodosius II, with his mother as regent. During his reign the empire suffered a serious decline. Africa was lost by Boniface to the Vandals under Huneric in 439; Aetius, who had great influence over Valentinian, gave way to the Visigoths in Gaul and engaged in a civil war with Boniface; and in 446 Britain was evacuated. Late in the reign, Attila and his Huns invaded Gaul and, though defeated by Aetius in 451 on the Catalaunian Plains near Châlons-sur-Marne, invaded Italy in 452 and was dissuaded from sacking Rome by Pope St. Leo I, after Valentinian had fled. In 454 he murdered Aetius and was murdered in turn in Rome on Mar. 16 by the senator, Petronius Maximus, whose wife he reportedly dishonored. During his reign Valentinian promulgated several decrees denouncing various heretical sects, particularly the Manichaeans, strongly supported Pope St. Leo I as supreme head of the Church, and at Leo's request called the Council of Chalcedon in 451.

VALENTINIAN, ST. (d. 500?). He was bishop of Salerno, Italy. F. D. Nov. 3.

VALENTIO, ST. (d. 302?), martyr. *See* Pasicrates, St.

VALERIA, ST. (2nd century?), martyr. She and St. Vitalis, her soldier husband, were put to death near Milan, Italy, probably during the reign of Marcus Aurelius. He is the titular saint of the basilica at Ravenna. F. D. Apr. 28.

VALERIAN, ST. (d. 178), martyr. A companion of St. Pothinus, he escaped when the saint was martyred at Lyons, Gaul, but was ap-

prehended at Tournus, near Autun, and beheaded. F. D. Sept. 15.

VALERIAN, ST. (d. 190?), martyr. *See*
Cecelia, St.

VALERIAN, ST. (d. 300?), martyr. *See*
Hieronides, St.

VALERIAN, ST. (d. 305?), martyr. *See*
Donatus, St.

VALERIAN, ST. (d. 321?), martyr. *See*
Julian, St.

VALERIAN, ST. (d. 350?). Bishop of Auxerre,
France, he was an active opponent of Arianism.
F. D. May 13.

VALERIAN, ST. (d. 389). He became bishop
of Aquileia, Italy, in 369 and spent twenty
years combating the Arianism shared by his
predecessor. F. D. Nov. 27.

VALERIAN, ST. (d. 457), bishop and martyr. Bishop of Abbenza in Africa, he refused to
surrender the sacred vessels of his church during the persecution of Arian King Genseric,
and was driven from the city. More than eighty
years old, he died of exposure. F. D. Dec. 15.

VALERIAN, ST. (d. 460?), bishop. A monk
on the island of Lérins, he was called to the
mainland as bishop of Cimiez, Gaul. F. D.
July 23.

VALERIAN, ST. (5th century), bishop. *See*
Crescens, St.

VALERIUS, ST. (2nd century), martyr. He
is said to have been the husband of St. Cecilia
and put to death at Rome with his brother
Tiburtius and Maximus, an official, but the
story is questionable. F. D. Apr. 14.

VALERIUS, ST. (d. 287?), martyr. *See* Rufinus, St.

VALERIUS, ST. (d. 315), bishop. He was exiled during the Diocletian persecution, but returned to serve as bishop of Saragossa, Spain.
St. Vincent of Saragossa served under him as
deacon. F. D. Jan. 28.

VALERIUS, ST. (d. 320?), bishop. An unreliable account had him consecrated by St. Peter
in the first century; it is now believed that he
lived three centuries later, as bishop of Trèves,
Gaul. F. D. Jan. 29.

VALERIUS, ST. (d. 453?), bishop. A hermit,
he was carried from his solitary life and acclaimed bishop of Sorrento, Italy, by the populace. F. D. Jan. 16.

VALERIUS, ST. (5th century). He was bishop
of Antibes, Gaul, about 450. F. D. Feb. 19.

VALERIUS, ST. (d. 695). Born in Astorga,
Spain, he became a monk and abbot at the
monastery of San Pedro de Montes. He wrote
ascetical works. F. D. Feb. 21.

VALERIUS, ST. (7th century). *See* Lambert,
St.

VALÉRY. *See* Walaricus, St.

VALFRÉ, BL. SEBASTIAN (1629–1710).
Born in Piedmont, Italy, he became an Oratorian at Turin in 1651. He instructed a lay

confraternity, served as master of novices, and
in 1661 became superior. He was an untiring
preacher and confessor, converted many on his
missions, and took active care of those in hospitals and in prison, even after he was nearly
eighty. He was beatified in 1834. F. D. Jan. 30.

VALLARSI, DOMINIC (1702–1771), scholar.
Born in Verona, Italy, on Nov. 13, he studied
there, was ordained, and devoted himself to
archaeological studies and the writings of the
early Fathers. He was appointed reviser for
oriental languages by Pope Benedict XIV, published an eleven-volume edition of the *Works*
of St. Jerome (1734–42), an incomplete edition of Rufinus' *Works* (1745), and helped in
Scipio Maffei's revision of the Maurist edition
of St. Hilary's *Works* (1730). He died in
Verona on Aug. 14.

VALLE, PIETRO DELLE (1586–1652).
Born in Rome on Apr. 2, he became a soldier
in the papal service, fought against the Barbary
states in 1611, and in 1614 went on a pilgrimage to the Holy Land which was to last more
than eleven years and led him through Egypt,
Arabia, Persia, and India. On his return to
Rome in 1626 he was appointed a papal chamberlain by Pope Urban VIII, and wrote a series
of letters to a friend in Naples, describing his
adventures, which were collected and published
as *Viaggi in Turchia, Persia, et India*. He died
in Rome on Apr. 21.

**VALLÉE-POUSSIN, CHARLES LOUIS JO-
SEPH XAVIER DE LA** (1827–1903), mineralogist. Born in Namur, Belgium, he studied
at Collège Notre Dame de la Paix there and
mathematics at Paris, and in 1863 was appointed professor of geology and mineralogy
at Louvain. He became noted for his studies of
crystalline rocks and the formation of the
Meuse Valley, was appointed to the Royal
Academy of Belgium in 1885, and was vice-
president of the council preparing the geological map of Belgium in 1903. He died in Brussels, Belgium.

VALLGORNERA, THOMAS DE (1595?–
1665), theologian. Born in Catalonia, Spain,
he became a Dominican in Barcelona, where
he was vice-general about 1642, and wrote
Mystica theologia D. Thomae (1662), which
had many editions. He died on Sept. 15.

VALOIS, HENRI DE (1603–1676), scholar.
Born in Paris on Sept. 10, he studied at Verdun, Clermont College, and law at Bourges,
and practiced law in Paris. He published editions of such Greek ecclesiastical historians as
Eusebius, Constantine, Socrates, Sozomen, and
Theodorus, which were praised for their critical
and philological annotations. He died in Paris
on May 7.

VALROGER, HYACINTHE DE (1814–
1876). Born in Caen, France, on Jan. 6, he
studied medicine, then was ordained in 1837.

He became director of the Bayeux minor seminary, titular canon of the cathedral there in 1847, and became an Oratorian in 1852. He taught theology at Bayeux, was assistant general, and wrote theological and philosophical treatises. He died on Oct. 10.

VALVERDE, VINCENT DE (d. 1541), bishop. Born in Oropesa, Spain, he became a Dominican in 1524, accompanied Pizarro in 1529 on the latter's conquest of Peru, and was named bishop of Cuzco, the city of the Peruvian kings, in 1537, and protector of the natives. He was constantly involved in disputes with the military as he tried to defend the Indians, attempted to settle the feud between Pizarro and Almagro, and when the former was assassinated was forced to flee to Panama. He was killed on the way there by Indians on the island of Puná, near Guayaquil, Ecuador, on Oct. 31.

VAN ASCHE, PETER, ST. (d. 1572), martyr. Born in Asche, near Brussels, he became a Franciscan laybrother at Gorkum, Holland, and was hanged by Calvinists at Briel, Holland. F. D. July 9.

VAN BENEDEN, PIERRE JOSEPH (1809–1894), naturalist. Born in Mechlin, Belgium, on Dec. 19, he studied medicine, was appointed curator of the natural history museum at Louvain in 1831, and was professor of zoology at the Catholic University there from 1836 until his death. He became an expert on marine invertebrates, established the first laboratory and aquarium for the study of marine life in 1843, and did major research in the life history of parasitic worms. He became president of the Royal Academy of Belgium in 1881, and died in Louvain, Belgium, on Jan. 8.

VAN BOLLAND, JOHN (1596–1665), scholar. Born in Tirlemont, Limburg, he became a Jesuit and taught literature at Ruremonde, Malines, Brussels, and Antwerp. Asked by his Belgian superior to evaluate the work on the *Acta sanctorum* left uncompleted at his death by Heribert Rosweyde, Fr. Bolland offered to complete the work, modifying it to include evaluations of accuracy and elaborate notes. After five years he was relieved of all other tasks and given an assistant, Fr. Godfrey Henschen, who displayed such erudition and accuracy in preparing the calendar of February that Bolland held up the proofs of his January volume. They worked jointly on this, and it appeared in two volumes in 1643, establishing the methods adopted for later work. February was published in three volumes in 1658; Fr. Daniel von Papenbroeck joined them in 1659, and from July 1660 to Dec. 1662 they toured the major cities of Europe. The volumes for March did not appear until 1668; Bolland had died three years before, on Sept. 12, in Antwerp. The work of the Bollandists, as the organization devoted to the preparation and accreditation of material on the lives of saints is called, continues.

VAN BOMMEL, CORNELIUS RICHARD ANTON (1790–1852), bishop. Born in Leyden, Holland, on Apr. 5, he studied at Münster and was ordained in 1816, returning to establish a college at Hageveld. This was closed by royal decree in 1825, and van Bommel was a major force in the agitation which led King William to agree to a concordat with Leo XII. In 1829 he was made bishop of Liège, a see vacant for twenty years, where he reorganized the educational system and gave support to the beginnings of its Catholic university. He died on Apr. 7.

VAN BUREN, WILLIAM HOLME (1819–1883), surgeon. Born in Philadelphia on Apr. 5, he studied at Yale, medicine at the University of Pennsylvania and Paris, and received his medical degree from Pennsylvania in 1840. He served in the army, on the medical faculty of New York University after 1845, was appointed professor of anatomy in 1852, and resigned in 1865. He was professor of surgery at Bellevue from 1866 until his death in New York City on Mar. 25. He wrote *Contributions to Practical Surgery* (1865) and *Lectures on Diseases of the Rectum* (1870), was president of the Pathological Society, and vice-president of the New York Academy of Medicine.

VAN CALCKER, JAN JOOST. See Joest, Jan.

VAN CLEEF, JAN (1646–1716), painter. Born in Guelderland, Flanders, he studied under Primo Gentile and Gaspard de Craeyer and at the latter's death completed church art and tapestries begun for Louis XIV. His subjects were religious, marked by effective portraiture. His *Nuns Giving Aid during the Plague, Immaculate Conception, Assumption,* and *Magdalen* are his best-known canvases. He died in Ghent, Flanders, on Dec. 18.

VAN CLEEF, JOOST (1518?–1556), painter. Son of the elder William van Cleef, who also was a member of the Antwerp Academy, he imitated the Italian style, was successful with portraits, and worked in France, England, Germany, and Spain. Many altarpieces exist in Flemish churches; much other work was retouched and ruined during the madness of his last years.

VAN CLEEF, MARTIN (1520–1570), painter. Son of the younger William van Cleef, he studied under Franz Floris, completed landscapes, turned to figures, and achieved success in genre painting, often working with his brother Henry. He was a member of the Antwerp Academy.

VANDAL, ALBERT (1853–1910), historian. Born in Paris on July 7, he became an auditor of the council of state, but left government service to study at L'École Libre des Sciences Politiques under Albert Sorel, whom he succeeded as professor of diplomatic history. He became an expert on the first empire and wrote *L'Avènement de Bonaparte, Louis XV et Elisabeth de Russie,* and *Napoléon et Alexandre I,* for which he was elected to the French Academy in 1897. He died in Paris on Aug. 30.

VAN DEN BROEK, THEODORE J. (1783–1851), missioner. Born in Amsterdam, Holland, on Nov. 5, he studied there, was ordained in Germany in 1808, and became a Dominican in 1817. He did parish work in Alkmaar, went to the United States as a missionary in 1832, served in Baltimore, Cincinnati, Kentucky, Ohio, and Wisconsin, where he ministered to the Menominee and Winnebago Indians from 1836 (except for a period in 1847–48 when he went to Holland to secure immigrants) until his death at Little Chute, Wisconsin, on Nov. 5.

VAN DEN BUNDERE, JOANNES (1482–1557), theologian. Born in Ghent, Flanders, he became a Dominican there about 1500, studied further at Louvain, and from 1517 almost to his death taught philosophy and theology at Ghent. He served as prior three times and was inquisitor general of Tournai. His writings were controversial volumes on Lutheranism, Calvinism, and the Mennonites. He died in Ghent on Jan. 8. He is also known as Joannes Bunderius.

VAN DER BOSCH, PETER (1686–1736), scholar. Born in Brussels on Oct. 19, he graduated from the university there and became a Jesuit in 1705, studied at Mechlin, Rome, and Louvain, and was ordained in 1719. In 1721 he was assigned to the Bollandist project, *Acta Sanctorum,* and worked on the volumes for July and August. He died on Nov. 14.

VAN DER SANDT, MAXIMILIAN (1578–1656). Born in Amsterdam, Holland, on Apr. 17, he joined the Jesuits in 1597, taught at Würzburg and Mainz, became superior of the seminary at Würzburg, and wrote theological and philosophical works. He died in Cologne, Germany, on June 21.

VAN DER SLOOTEN, JOHANN (d. 1560), author. Born in Geffen, Brabant, Belgium, he joined the Dominicans about 1525, taught at Cologne, received his doctorate in theology in 1554, and was appointed prior in Cologne and papal inquisitor of Cologne and the Rhineland. He wrote theological treatises, notably *Disputationum adversus haereticos* (1558) and *De retinenda fide orthodoxa et catholica* (1560), and died in Cologne, Germany, on July 9. He also is known as John Slotanus.

VAN DER WEYDEN, ROGIER (1400?–1464), painter. Born in Tournai, France, Roger de la Pasture studied goldsmithing, was apprenticed to Robert Campin in 1427, became a master painter admitted to the Guild of St. Luke in 1432, and in 1435 was painter-in-ordinary to the city of Brussels. He visited Italy in 1449, was impressed by the Italian masters, and executed several commissions, but retained his Flemish style and is considered the founder of the Brabant school. His paintings, noted for their religious fervor, tinged with sadness, were extremely popular even in his own lifetime. Outstanding are the triptych, *The Seven Sacraments;* the polyptych, *Last Judgment; Adoration of the Magi, Nativity,* and *Joys and Sorrows of Our Lady of Pity.* He died in Brussels. He is also known as Roger of Bruges, Roger of Brussels, or Roger Weyden.

VAN DE VELDE, JAMES OLIVER (1795–1855), bishop. Born near Termonde, Belgium, on Apr. 3, he was privately educated and at the Mechlin seminary, taught in Puers and Mechlin, and in 1817 went to the United States, where he studied at Georgetown, became a Jesuit, and in 1827 was ordained. He engaged in chaplain and missionary activities until 1831, went to St. Louis University, and became its vice-president in 1833 and president in 1840–43. He was vice-provincial of Missouri in 1843–48, procurator in 1848, when he was appointed bishop of Chicago, and was consecrated in 1849. He encountered opposition to his appointment among the clergy, was emissary of the decrees of the Council of Baltimore to Rome in 1852, and in 1853 was transferred to Natchez. He was administrator of Chicago in 1853–54 and of Quincy, Illinois, in 1853–55, and died of yellow fever in Natchez, Mississippi, on Nov. 13.

VAN DE VELDE, PETER (1505?–1580), painter. Pieter de Kempeneer (Pedro Campaña in Spanish) was born in Brussels, spent his youth in Italy studying the works of Raphael, and then went to Spain, where he settled in Seville from 1537 to 1562. In 1537 he joined with Luis de Vargas and Torregiano in establishing a school of the arts there which was to grow into the Academy of Seville. He returned to Brussels in 1563, became director of the tapestry works and engineer under the duke of Alva, and remained there until his death. Outstanding works are the altarpiece, *Descent from the Cross, Purification of the Virgin,* and *Resurrection.*

VAN DE VEN, CORNELIUS (1865–1922), bishop. Born in Oirschot, Holland, on June 16, he studied at the Bois-le-Duc seminary, Holland, was ordained in 1890, went to the United States in that year, and was attached to the New Orleans diocese. He served as pastor in Louisiana cities until 1904, when he was appointed bishop of Natchitoches, and in 1910 of Alexandria, when the see was moved there. He died on May 8 in Shreveport, Louisiana.

VAN DE VYVER, AUGUSTINE (1844–

1911), bishop. Born in Haesdonck, East Flanders, Belgium, on Dec. 1, he studied at the American College in Louvain, was ordained in 1870, and went to the United States, where he spent the next decade in parish work in Virginia. He was appointed vicar general of Richmond, Virginia, in 1881, and its sixth bishop in 1889. He built the cathedral of the Sacred Heart, expanded the educational and charitable facilities of the diocese, and died in Richmond on Oct. 16.

VAN DYCK, ANTOON (1599–1641), painter. Born in Antwerp, Flanders, on Mar. 22, he studied there under Hendrick van Balen and in Rubens' studio and progressed so rapidly that at nineteen he was admitted to the Guild of St. Luke. He worked at the court of King James I of England for a year, then went to Italy for five, returning to Antwerp in 1626. He traveled to other European cities before a second commissioned visit to England in 1632; King Charles I knighted him and gave him an annual pension. He painted some thirty-six portraits of the monarch, and many of Queen Henrietta, their children, and the English aristocracy. He traveled frequently between London, Antwerp, and Paris, completing vivid portraits and striking etchings. His best work, of more than 900 paintings, includes *Crucifixion, Deposition, Adoration of the Shepherds, St. Augustine in Ecstasy, St. Martin Dividing His Cloak*; his Flemish realism was effectively softened as a result of his study of Italian masters. He died in London on Dec. 9.

VANE, THOMAS (17th century). He received his doctorate in divinity, at Cambridge, became an Anglican minister, and was appointed King Charles I's chaplain. He became a convert, went to Paris where he received his medical degree, practiced medicine, and wrote the story of his conversion, *A Lost Sheep Returned Home* (1643).

VAN EST, WILLEM HESSELS (1542–1613). Born in Gorkum, Holland, he studied at Utrecht and Louvain, teaching philosophy at the latter and studying scripture under the controversial Baius. In 1582 he became professor of theology at Douai, a position he retained until his death there on Sept. 20. He was rector of the diocesan seminary and was chancellor of the university for his last eighteen years. He was drawn into the quarrel of the universities which supported Baius against the refutation by Lessius; Est possibly wrote the condemnation of Lessius. While his opinion on grace and free will are open to clarification, he is learned and careful in his elaborate study of the Pauline and Catholic epistles.

VAN EYCK, HUBERT (1366?–1426), painter. Born in Maaseyck, Flanders, he was painting as early as 1413, moved to Ghent in 1424, and was for a time in the service of Duke William IV of Bavaria-Hainault. With his brother Jan he is known as the founder of the school of Bruges. He died in Ghent, Flanders, on Sept. 18.

VAN EYCK, JAN (1380?–1441), painter. Younger brother of Hubert, he was born in Maaseyck, near Liège, Flanders, was active as a painter in Antwerp and Cambrai between 1420 and 1422, and was in the service of Jean Sans Merci at The Hague in 1425. He later was in the service of Philip the Good at Bruges and Lille, for whom he made a diplomatic mission to Portugal in 1428–29. He married about 1433 and settled in Bruges. Critics have not determined whether he or Hubert van Eyck is the author of the many religious paintings they left; nor have they agreed which part each played in creating the great altarpiece, *The Adoration of the Lamb*, which reveals so much of mediaeval allegory, history, theology, and apocalyptic knowledge. The work reveals both the old and new styles of painting, great realism, details of nature, contemporary life, carefully designed interiors, and over 200 figures. Other joint work includes: *Portrait of an Old Man, The Man with the Pinks*, and many madonnas. Jan alone is credited with *Consecration of Thomas à Becket, St. Barbara*, and contemporary portraits. Jan died in Bruges, Flanders, on July 9.

VAN EYCKEN, JEAN BAPTISTE (1809–1853), painter. Born in Brussels, Belgium, on Sept. 16, he devoted himself to painting after his father's death in 1829, became a member of the Academy of Belgium in 1830, and was named professor of drawing in 1839 after winning several prizes. He completed *Captive Christians* and fourteen illustrations of the passion of Christ for La Chapelle; a series of murals on the beatitudes; and the popular *Divine Pity* and *Abundance*. He died in Schaerbeek on Dec. 19.

VANGEON, HENRI (1895–1944), author. Born in Bray-sur-Seine, France, he studied at Sens, drifted into atheism, joined anticlerical literary groups, went to Paris in 1893 to study medicine, took his degree in 1901 and practiced in Bray until 1909. He had written poetry, continued his interest in literature, moved to Orsay in 1909, and founded *Nouvelle Revue Française*, to which he contributed many essays on the arts. During World War I he returned to the Church, changed his name to Ghéon, wrote the story of his conversion, and after the war wrote, produced, and often acted in over fifty plays in the style of earlier miracles. Produced throughout Europe by members of the Compagnons de Notre Dame, a group he founded in 1925, they were widely translated; four (*The Marvellous History of St. Bernard, The Comedian, The Marriage of St. Francis,* and *Christmas on the Village Square)* appeared in English. He also wrote lives of such saints as the Curé d'Ars, Thérèse of Lisieux, Margaret Mary, John Bosco, Vincent Ferrer, and a three-volume novel, *Le Jeux de l'enfer et du ciel*, on John Vianney.

VAN HOORNAER, BL. JOHANNES (d. 1572), martyr. Born in Cologne, Germany, he became a Dominican, and was a parish priest at Horner, near Gorkum, Holland. When he learned that the Franciscan community there had been imprisoned by a Calvinist mob, he went to give them aid, and was seized, and tortured and hanged with them at Breil, Holland. He was beatified in 1867. F. D. July 9.

VAN HOVE, PETER (d. 1793). Born in Rethy, Flanders, he became a Friar Minor, studied at the Franciscan biblical institute at Antwerp, and succeeded his teacher, William Smits, its founder, as head in 1770. He continued the latter's Flemish translation of the Vulgate and wrote scriptural commentaries and a defense of infallibility. He died in Antwerp, Flanders.

VAN KALCKER, JAN STEPHANUS (1499?-1546), painter. Born in the duchy of Cleves before 1510, he began studying under Titian in 1536 and made brilliantly accurate copies of his master and others. He prepared plates for Andrea Vesalius' *De corporis humani Fabrici* (1543) and for Giorgio Vasari's *Lives of the Most Excellent Painters* (1550). He died in Naples, Italy.

VAN LEEUW, DENYS (1403-1471), theologian. Born in Ryckel, Limberg, Flanders, he studied at Zwolle and Cologne, and entered the charterhouse of Roermond in 1423. He wrote commentaries on scripture and on the works of Boethius, Peter Lombard, John Climacus, and Dionysius the Aereopagite, by whom he was greatly influenced. He also translated Cassian, wrote treatises on theology, ecclesiastical discipline, homilies, and a tract against Mohammedanism; titles include *Summa fidei orthodoxae, De meditatione*, and *De doctrina vitae christianae*. His piety, mystical experiences, and scholarship made his monastery famous. In 1451-52 he went with Nicholas of Cusa to Germany to preach a crusade; he was procurator of his monastery in 1459, spent 1466-69 building a monastery at Bois-le-Duc, and then returned to Roermond, Flanders, where he died on Mar. 21. His works have been called a summary of the scholastic teaching of the Middle Ages and he has been termed the last of the schoolmen. Though SS. Francis de Sales and Alphonsus Liguori refer to him as Blessed, he has never been beatified. He is also known as Dionysius the Carthusian, Denys Ryckel, and Denis the Carthusian.

VANNA. *See* Jane of Orvieto, St.

VANNE. *See* Vitonus, St.

VANNI, ANDREA (1320-1414), painter. Born in Siena, Italy, he served in governing that city, where he was advised by St. Catherine, was ambassador to the pope at Avignon and Naples, and became an artist. With his brother Simone, Bortolo di Fredi, and Taddeo di Bartolo he was a minor leader in early Sienese art. A *Crucifixion*, several madonnas, a *St. Sebastian*, and other religious paintings were completed in Siena and Naples.

VANNI, FRANCESCO (1565-1609), painter. Born in Siena, Italy, he studied painting under Salimbene and Passarotti and Raphael's works under de' Vecchi in Rome, was unsuccessful in interesting the Sienese in his work, and moved to Parma and Bologna, where he came under the influence of the Umbrian painter, Baroccio. He went to Rome at Pope Clement VIII's commission to paint what was to be his masterpiece, *Simon Magus Rebuked by St. Peter*, as the altar picture for St. Peter's. He painted for other Italian churches, made some architectural contributions, and died in Siena.

VANNUCCI, PIETRO DI CHRISTOFORO (1446-1524), painter. Born in Città della Pieve, Italy, Il Perugino studied in Perugia under Fiorenzo di Lorenzo and went to Florence in 1472 to study with Verrocchio as a fellow pupil of Leonardo da Vinci. In 1475 he executed the frescoes for the Palazzo Pubblico, Perugia, and then the fresco *St. Sebastian* for a nearby church. In 1480, Pope Sixtus IV commissioned him to do four frescoes for the Sistine Chapel, of which only *Christ Giving the Keys to St. Peter* remains. From 1486 to 1491 most of his work was done in Florence; he then went to Rome and other cities; from 1496 to the end of his life he worked near or in Perugia. He was a prolific but inferior painter in his later years, but for his earlier achievements is called the greatest painter of the Umbrian school. He completed several madonnas, *Annunciation, Adoration of the Infant Christ, Crucifixion, Pietà*, altarpieces of *The Ascension* for San Pietro, Perugia, and *Madonna and Saints* for the Pavia Certosa, and frescoes for the audience hall of the Perugia Cambio. He died in Fontignano, Italy, in Feb. of a plague.

VANNUTELLI, SERAFINO (1834-1915), cardinal. Born in Genazzano, Italy, on Nov. 26, he studied at the Capranica, was ordained at Rome in 1860, taught at the Pontifical seminary there, and became apostolic delegate to Mexico, Ecuador, Colombia, Peru, and Central America. He was papal nuncio at Brussels from 1865 to 1879, was named titular archbishop of Nicaea in 1869, and nuncio at Vienna from 1879 to 1884. He became a cardinal in 1893, archbishop of Bologna, bishop of Frascati, prefect of the Congregation of Bishops and Regulars, and in 1899 grand penitentiary. Age and weak eyes forced him to ask for relief, and he was rotated to the see of Porto. He died in Rome on Aug. 19.

VANNUTELLI, VINCENZO (1836–1930), cardinal. Born in Genazzano, Italy, on Dec. 5, he studied at the Gregorian and Apollinaire in Rome, was ordained in 1860, and taught theology at the Vatican seminary. He served as papal nuncio to Belgium in 1866, undersecretary of state to Pope Pius IX in 1875, and auditor of the rota in 1878. He was consecrated titular archbishop of Sardes in 1880 and made apostolic delegate to Constantinople, went as nuncio to Portugal in 1883, and in 1889 became a cardinal-priest. He was made cardinal-bishop of Palestrina and Ostia in 1900. He died in Vatican City on July 9.

VAN ORLEY, BERNAERT (1491?–1542), painter. Born in Brussels, he studied under his father, Valentyn (1466–1530?), under Raphael in Rome, settled in Brussels in 1515, and became official painter to the regent of the Netherlands, Margaret of Austria, in 1518, and her successor, Mary of Hungary, in 1530. He knew and was influenced by Dürer, who painted his portrait. He flirted with Lutheranism but returned to Catholicism after public penance and died in Brussels on Jan. 6. Among his chief works are an altarpiece at Furnes of scenes from the lives of SS. Thomas and Matthias, tapestries for the Vatican designed from sketches by Raphael, stained glass, and religious paintings such as *Death of the Virgin* and *Flight into Egypt*.

VANOT, BL. MARIE LOUISE (d. 1794), martyr. An Ursuline sister, under the name Natalie, she was guillotined with others of her community at Valenciennes, France, during the French Revolution. She was beatified in 1920. F. D. Oct. 17.

VAN ROEY, JOSEPH (1874–1961), cardinal. Born in Vorsselaer, Antwerp, Belgium, on Jan. 18, he studied at Herenthals College and the Malines seminary, and was ordained in 1897. After receiving his degree from Louvain, he taught there in 1901, became vicar general of Malines in 1907, and archbishop of that see and primate of Belgium in 1926, and a cardinal in 1927. He was noted for work in Catholic Action, founded the International Union for Social Questions, strongly opposed the Nazis during the German occupation of Belgium in World War II, and died in Mechlin, Belgium, on Aug. 6.

VAN ROSSUM, WILLEM MARINUS (1854–1932), cardinal. Born in Zwolle, Netherlands, on Sept. 3, he studied in Culenburg, joined the Redemptorists in 1873, and was ordained in 1879. He taught at various monasteries, was sent to Rome in 1895, and became Consultor of the Holy Office the following year. He was created a cardinal-bishop in 1911, was papal delegate to the Eucharistic Congress in Vienna in 1912, became president of the Biblical Commission in 1914, and prepared the encyclical *Spiritus Paraclitus* on the Church's teaching regarding scripture. He was appointed great penitentiary of the Holy Roman Church in 1915, prefect of propaganda in 1918, when he was consecrated a bishop, and devoted the rest of his life to spreading the Church's missionary activities over the world on a planned basis, and centralized in Rome, with emphasis on the necessity of building native clergy. He wrote *De essentia sacramenti ordinis* (1914). He died in Maastricht, Netherlands, on Aug. 30.

VAN SCOREL, JAN (1495–1562), painter. Born near Schoorl, Holland, he studied in Haarlem, under Jacob Cornelius in Amsterdam, Jan Mabuse in Utrecht, and Dürer in Nuremberg. He made a trip to the Holy Land, returned by way of Rome, where he was made supervisor of the Vatican gallery by Pope Adrian VI, and on his arrival in Utrecht was ordained and became a canon there. He did several altarpieces, *Mary Magdalen, Baptism of Christ*, and many portraits, including groups of crusaders. He was a pioneer in introducing the Italian Renaissance influence to the Low Countries.

VARANI, BL. CAMILLA (d. 1527). Daughter of the lord of Camerino, she became a Poor Clare at Urbino, Italy, in 1481, taking the name Baptista, and experienced a number of visions which she recorded in *The Sufferings of the Agonizing Heart of Jesus*. She was transferred to a new convent at Camerino, Italy, which her father built, and continued to receive supernatural gifts, which she reported in a letter to Bl. Mark of Montegallo. Her cult was confirmed in 1843. F. D. June 7.

VARGAS, LUÍS DE (1502–1568), painter. Born in Seville, Spain, he studied there and was greatly influenced by the works of Campaña, then went to Italy, where he stayed for twenty-eight years. He is noted for such religious paintings as *Purification of the Virgin, La Gamba*, and *Christ Bearing the Cross*. He died in Seville.

VARGAS Y MEXIA, FRANCISCO DE (d. 1566), diplomat. Born in Madrid, he studied law at Alcalá, became attorney general of the Council of Castile, went to the Council of Trent in 1545 as Charles V's representative, was Spanish ambassador to Venice from 1552 to 1559, and after 1559 to the Roman curia. He prepared several theological papers for the Council of Trent at the request of Pope Pius IV in 1563, was appointed state councilor on his return to Spain, but soon resigned to enter the Hieronymite monastery of La Cisla, where he died.

VAROLIO, COSTANZO (1543?–1575),

physician. Born in Bologna, Italy, he studied and later taught at its university, became physician to Pope Gregory XIII at Rome, wrote *De nervis opticis* (1573), and made studies of the human brain (the anatomical designation *pons Varloii* bears his name).

VAROTARI, ALESSANDRO (1590–1650), painter. Born in Padua, Italy, he imitated Veronese and Titian, completed frescoes for the church of San Andrea, Bergamo, a *Marriage at Cana* and *St. Liberatus*, in Venice. He also worked in Padua, and is often called Il Padovanino.

VARUS, ST. (4th century?), martyr. A Roman soldier in Upper Egypt who was guarding seven monks in prison, he took the place of one who had died, and was tortured and hanged. F. D. Oct. 19.

VASARI, GIORGIO (1511–1574), critic. Born in Arezzo, Italy, on July 30, he studied stained-glass painting under Guglielmo da Marcillo, went to Florence at thirteen, studied under Michelangelo, Andrea del Sarto, and Baccio Bandinelli, and was patronized by the Medici. He studied Raphael's works in Rome in 1531, returned to Florence in 1541, and was in the service of Cosimo de' Medici from 1553 until his death. However, his great claim to fame is his authorship of the *Lives of the Outstanding Italian Architects, Painters, and Sculptors* (1550), a collection of biographies of artists and criticisms of their works, which is a colorful and valuable source of information, but marred by inaccuracies. Among his own paintings, the wall and ceiling paintings of the great hall in the Palazzo Vecchio in Florence, frescoes on the cupola of the cathedral there, and murals in the Sala Regia in the Vatican are outstanding. He died in Florence, Italy, on June 27.

VASQUEZ, GABRIEL (1549?–1604), theologian. Born in Villaescusa de Haro, Cuenca, Spain, he studied at Alcalá, joined the Jesuits in 1569, taught at Ocana, Madrid, and Alcalá, spent six years at the Roman College, then returned to Alcalá to teach philosophy for the rest of his life. He achieved an outstanding reputation as a theologian, particularly well versed in the works of SS. Augustine and Thomas Aquinas, was a rival of Suárez, and wrote theological works, including *De cultu adorationis* (1594) and the eight-volume *Commentarium ac disputationum in S. Thomae* (1598–1615). He died in Alcalá, Spain, on Sept. 23.

VASS, JOSEPH (1877–1930). Born in Sárvár, Hungary, on Apr. 25, he studied at Budapest and the German College, Rome, where he was ordained. He did parish work, was chaplain at the University of Budapest, and in 1919 began teaching theology there. Msgr. Vass was a leader of the Christian National party, or-

ganized the Catholic People's Association, and was elected to the first national assembly after the collapse of the Communist regime. He was minister of food, of education, and of social welfare and labor from 1922 until his death in Budapest on Sept. 8.

VATABLE, FRANÇOIS (d. 1547). Born in Gamaches, Picardy, France, he was rector of Bramet in Valois in 1530 when King Francis I appointed him to the chair of Hebrew of the newly founded Collège de France. His lectures were so popular he is credited with restoring the study of Hebrew in France. He was later appointed abbot of Bellozane, translated Aristotle's *Meterologica* (1548) and *Parva naturalia* (1619) into Latin, and died in Paris on Mar. 16. His name is sometimes spelled Watebled, Gastebled, or Ouatebled.

VAUDREUIL, PHILIPPE DE RIGAUD DE (1640?–1725), governor. Born in Languedoc, France, he served in the army in 1659–76, achieving the rank of colonel, was sent to Canada in 1687 as head of a marine unit, defended Montreal against the Iroquois in 1689, and Quebec against Phips in 1690. He was appointed governor of Montreal in 1698, and became governor general of Canada in 1703, a position he held until his death in Quebec on Oct. 10. He was an able administrator, fortified Quebec, Montreal, built Fort Niagara, and encouraged commerce and agriculture.

VAUDREUIL DE CAVAGNAL, PIERRE FRANÇOIS DE RIGAUD DE (1704–1778), governor. The son of Philippe, he was born in Quebec on Nov. 22, served in the army, rising to the rank of major, was appointed governor of Three Rivers in 1733, governor of Louisiana from 1742 to 1753, then was appointed governor general of Canada. During his rule the Seven Years' War broke out, and when Wolfe attacked Quebec in 1760 his interference in military matters hindered Montcalm's defense of the city. He retreated to Montreal when Quebec fell and on Sept. 8, 1760, surrendered the city and Canada to England. He was arrested on his return to France, and, though acquitted in 1761 of dishonesty, is generally held responsible for the fall of New France. He died in Paris on Aug. 4.

VAUGHAN, BERNARD JOHN (1847–1922). Born in Courtfield, Herefordshire, England, on Sept. 20, brother of Herbert and John Vaughan, he studied at Stonyhurst, which had been given to the Jesuits by his great-grandfather, Thomas Weld. He became a Jesuit in 1866, taught at Beaumont, and was ordained in 1880. He did parish work in Manchester in 1883–99, attaining fame as preacher and debater. Transferred to London, he continued to attract attention by his sermons, widely quoted by the press, and published in several collections. He preached in America (1910–13), China and Japan (1913), and Africa (1922). He worked for poor relief and social reform, and built an orphanage in Whitechapel. He was a chaplain with the British army during World War I. He published *Society, Sin, and the Saviour* (1907), based on his sermons, *Socialism from the Christian Standpoint, The Roman Claims, Loaves and Fishes, What of Today?* and many studies of socialism. He died in Roehampton, England, on Oct. 31.

VAUGHAN, HERBERT (1832–1903), cardinal. Born in Gloucester, England, on Apr. 15, he studied at Stonyhurst, Brugelette in Belgium, Downside abbey and the Roman College, and was ordained in Lucca in 1854. He became vice-president of St. Edmund's College, Ware, England, in 1855, and was involved in the controversy between the Oblates of St. Charles, which he had joined, and the canons, which resulted in Rome's decision which led to the Oblates leaving St. Edmund's. In 1863–65 he toured the United States and South America to raise funds for St. Joseph's College for foreign missions which he founded in 1866 at Mill Hill, near London, bought the London *Tablet* in 1868, was its editor for three years, then traveled through the United States in 1871–72 to study missionary needs there. He was appointed bishop of Salford in 1872, labored to increase the supply of secular priests by building St. Bede's college and seminary, built Catholic orphanages to recover orphans from general and Protestant workhouses, increased educational facilities, instituted annual diocesan synods, and reorganized and revitalized the diocese. With Bishop Clifford of Clifton he represented the English hierarchy in its dispute with the religious orders over jurisdiction and the rights of the bishops, was appointed third archbishop of Westminster in 1892, and was created a cardinal and primate of England in 1893. He established Oscott as a central seminary, withdrew in 1894 the prohibition against Catholics attending Cambridge and Oxford, instituted a commission in 1896 to investigate Anglican claims to the validity of their orders which led to Pope Leo XIII's bull *Apostolicae sedis*, upholding the commission's reports that Anglican orders were invalid, and in 1895 began building Westminster cathedral, which opened its doors in 1903. He retired to St. Joseph's College early in 1903 because of ill-health, and died there on June 19.

J. G. SNEAD-COX, *Life of Herbert Vaughan*, 2 vols. (London, 1910).

VAUGHAN, JOHN STEPHEN (1853–1925), bishop. Brother of Bernard and Herbert, he was born in Courtfield, Ross, England, studied at Downside, St. Gregory's, Monte

Cassino, Bruges, and the English College, Rome, and was ordained in 1876. He worked three years in Australia, then did parish work in London. He organized lectures on Catholicism in many London areas in 1890–1903, became a domestic prelate in 1896 and a canon of Westminster in 1898. He lived in Rome in 1904–7, preached in Canada and the United States, was named titular bishop of Sebastopolis and auxiliary of Salford, England, in 1909, was stationed in Manchester, and in 1912 became rector of St. Bede's College there, serving two terms. He wrote *Concerning the Holy Bible, Dangers of the Day, Faith and Folly, Happiness and Reality, Life after Death, The Purpose of the Papacy*, and collections of sermons and ascetical works.

VAUGHAN, ROGER WILLIAM BEDE (1834–1883), archbishop. Brother of Herbert Vaughan, he was born in Courtfield, Herefordshire, England, on Jan. 9, studied at Downside, where he joined the Benedictines in 1851, and in 1855 went to Rome, where he was ordained in 1859. He returned to Downside in 1860, taught philosophy there in 1861, and was prior of St. Michael's in Belmont from 1862 until 1872, when he was appointed titular archbishop of Nazianzen and coadjutor to Archbishop Polding of Sydney, Australia, succeeding to that see in 1877. He died while on a visit to England, where he was seeking priests for his see, at Ince-Blundell Hall, Lancashire, on Aug. 17.

VAUX, THOMAS (1510–1566), poet. Educated at Cambridge, England, the second Baron Vaux served Cardinal Wolsey and Henry VIII abroad and became a member of the House of Lords in 1531. After 1536 he remained out of office until the time of Queen Mary. His poems, long erroneously attributed to a Nicholas Vaux, appeared in numerous anthologies after his death, especially *The Paradyse of Daynty Devises* (1576).

VAUXELLES, BLAISE (1651–1729). Born in Limoges, France, on July 5, he became a Discalced Carmelite in 1671, taking the name Honoratus a Sancta Maria, was sent to Malta, served as sub-prior, and returned to France. He taught theology and philosophy, served as provincial and visitor general, and wrote widely to combat Jansenism, Gallicanism, quietism, and rationalism. His best-known works include *A Treatise on Indulgences, On Contemplation, The Motives and Practice of Divine Love*, a study of the orders of knighthood, a life of St. John of the Cross, and *Réflexions sur les règles et l'usage de la critique*. He died in Lille, France.

VAVASOUR, THOMAS (1536?–1585), physician. An Englishman, he studied medicine in Venice, where he received his medical degree, returned to England, and practiced at

York. He allowed mass to be said in his home there, was accused of sheltering Bl. Edmund Campion in 1572, and was imprisoned in Hull castle in 1574. On his release in 1579 he again allowed mass to be said, was imprisoned, and again released when he signed the Oath of Supremacy, but was returned to Hull castle in York as a recusant, and died there on May 2.

VAVASSEUR, FRANÇOIS (1605–1681). Born in Paray-le-Monial, France, on Dec. 8, he joined the Jesuits in 1621, taught theology and scripture at Bourges and Paris, and actively participated in the Jansenist controversy. He wrote several scholarly works, among them *Theurgicon* (1644), and *Elegiarum liber* (1656), *Cornelius Jansenius Iprensis suspectus* (1650), and *De epigrammate* (1669). He died in Paris on Dec. 16.

VAZ, BL. DAMIAN (d. 1242). *See* Rodríguez, Bl. Peter.

VAZ, LUIS JOSEPH (1651–1711), missioner. Born in Goa, India, of native Christian parents, he studied at St. Thomas College there, was ordained in 1676, engaged in missionary activities in Portuguese territory, and was superior of the Kanara mission in 1681. He became an Oratorian in 1684, and in 1687 he went to Ceylon, where he was the only Catholic priest for the next ten years. He worked to establish a native Church, wrote catechisms in Singhalese and Tamil, was the friend of the king of Kandy, and, despite the bitter animosity of the Dutch, and imprisonment by them on the charge of being a spy, made many converts. By the time of his death in Kandy, Ceylon, on Jan. 16, there were 75,000 Catholics on the island, a feat of conversion which earned him the title of "Apostle of Ceylon."

VECCHIETTA, LORENZO DI PIETRO (1412?–1480), painter. Born in Castiglione di Val d'Orcia, Italy, he studied painting under Taddeo Bartoli and Giacomo della Quercia and sculpture under Donatello, and became one of the most important figures of the later Sienese school. He did frescoes in the Santa Maria Hospital and the baptistery of San Giovanni in Siena and *Assumption of the Virgin* in the cathedral. Of his sculpture, the *Risen Christ* for the Siena cathedral high altar is his most important. He died in his native village. He is often called Il Vecchietta.

VECHEL, BL. LEONARDUS (d. 1572), martyr. Born in Bois-le-Duc, Holland, he studied at Louvain, was ordained, and became parish priest at Gorkum, where he was seized with others by a Calvinist mob, and tortured, hanged, and mutilated at Briel, Holland. He was beatified in 1868. F. D. July 9.

VEDAST, ST. (d. 539), bishop. He was serving in the diocese of Toul, France, when King Clovis I sought a priest to prepare him for baptism. He then aided St. Remigius in the conversion of the Franks, was consecrated bishop of Arras in 499, and began work in a see where Christianity did not exist. After forty years of his zealous efforts, religion flourished. F. D. Feb. 6.

VEERLE. *See* Pharaildis, St.

VEGA, ANDREAS DE (d. 1560?), theologian. Born in Segovia, Old Castile, Spain, he studied at Salamanca, taught theology there, then joined the Franciscan Observantines. He taught at the Observantine monastery, was sent to the Council of Trent as a theologian by Emperor Charles V, and actively participated in discussions on the scriptures and justification. He wrote theological treatises, chief of which are *De justificatione* (1546) and *Tridentini decreti de justificatione* (1548). He died in Salamanca, Spain.

VEGA CARPIO, LOPE FÉLIX DE (1562–1635), dramatist. Born in Madrid, he studied at the Theatine college there, early evinced an interest in writing (completing a play when fourteen), and entered the service of Bishop Jerónimo Manrique, who sent him to the University of Alcalá in 1577–81. He went on an expedition to the Azores in 1582 and was secretary to the Marqués de las Navas in 1583–87. He sailed with the Spanish armada against England, and, after a short period in Valencia, married Isabel de Urbina, sister of Philip II's herald, in 1590, and became a member of the duke of Alva's household until 1595. He was forced to flee from Madrid to Valencia when he wounded a rival in a duel in 1596, and after the death of his wife in 1597 he traveled throughout Spain and became its leading playwright. He was notorious for his amorous affairs, became the marquis de Malpica's secretary, married Juana del Guardo in 1598, and moved to Madrid about 1610, where Juana died in 1613. He then turned to a clerical life and was ordained in 1614, continued writing, but did not reform his moral conduct. He received a doctorate in theology from Pope Urban VIII in 1627, and died in Madrid on Aug. 27. He was one of the most prolific writers of all times (often writing a play in a day). He wrote over 2000 plays, 1500 *comedias* (of which some 500 are extant) and 500 *autos, loas,* and *entremeses,* noted for their vivid imagination and dramatic characterizations, and a great body of verse: *Arcadia, Corona trágica* (on the life of Mary Queen of Scots), *Pastores de Belén,* and *Dragontea* (against Sir Francis Drake). Among his works which have been translated into English are *The Beautiful Deformed, The Father Outwitted, The Greatest Alcade, The King, Star of Seville, The Constant Prince, The Sheep Well,* and a novel, *The Pilgrim.*

HUGO A. RENNERT, *Life of Lope de Vega* (New

York, Stechert, 1937); JAMES FITZMAURICE-KELLY, *Lope de Vega and the Spanish Drama* (London, Oxford, 1902).

VEGA Y VARGAS, GARCIA LASO DE LA (1539–1617?), historian. Born in Cuzco, Peru, on Apr. 12, son of an officer who fought under Cortés and Pizarro, and an Inca princess, he traveled through Inca territory to gather material for a history of his mother's people. He was called to Spain in 1559 by Philip II, who feared his increasing popularity with the native population. There he served under John of Austria against the Moors at Granada, wrote *Historia de la Florida* about 1584 on the expedition of de Soto, and from 1600 to 1616 worked on *Comentarios reales*, a history of the Incas and of the conquest of Peru. The work is especially valuable for its firsthand reports of life in South America. He died in Cordova, Spain.

VEGA Y VARGAS, SEBASTIAN GARCI-LASO DE LA (d. 1559), governor. Born in Badajoz, Spain, he served in Mexico under Cortés, in Guatemala under de Alvarado, and in Peru under Pizarro. He was named governor of Cuzco, Peru, in 1548, worked successfully to better the condition of the natives, who regarded him highly, married an Inca princess, and died in Cuzco.

VEGHE, JOHANNES (1435?–1504). Born in Münster, Westphalia, Germany, he studied at Cologne, and in 1451 joined the Brethren of the Common Life in Münster. He became first rector of their house in Rostock in 1469 and rector of Münster in 1475, a position he resigned because of ill-health in 1481. He then became confessor of the Sisters of Niesink in Münster, where he remained until his death on Sept. 21. He wrote several religious works—among them *Geistliche Jagd, Geistliches Blumenbett, Marientrost, Weingarten der Seele*—and had a series of sermons published.

VEGIO, MAFFEO (1406–1458), author. Born in Lodi, Italy, he studied at Pavia, and taught poetry and law there for ten years. He was ordained, was appointed secretary of papal briefs, apostolic datary, and a canon at St. Peter's by Pope Eugene IV. He later joined the Augustinians, wrote numerous books (among them *De educatione*) on the education of children, which had great influence, and died in Rome. Among his poetical works are *De morte Astyanactis, Velleris aurei*, a supplement to the *Aeneid*, and epigrams.

VEHE, MICHAEL (d. 1559), bishop. Born in Bierbarach, Germany, he joined the Dominicans there, studied at Heidelberg, where he received his doctorate in theology in 1513, and was appointed regent of the Dominican house of studies in Heidelberg in 1515. He became theologian to Cardinal Albert of Mainz, was active in combating Protestantism, wrote treatises refuting the reformers, and was appointed bishop of Halberstadt in 1559. He died two months later in April at Halle, Germany.

VEIT, PHILIPP (1793–1877), painter. Born in Berlin on Feb. 13, grandson of Moses Mendelssohn and stepson of Friedrich von Schlegel, he became a convert in 1810, went to Dresden the following year to study drawing under Matthai, and in 1811 went to Vienna to study portrait painting. After fighting in the war in 1813, he went to Rome in 1815, studied under Overbeck and Cornelius, was a disciple of the Nazarene group, and in 1830 settled in Frankfort, where he was director, until 1843, of the Städel Institute, which he developed as an important center of romantic art. He moved to Mainz, Germany, in 1854, and was director of the art gallery there until his death on Dec. 18. Among his outstanding works are *Christianity Bringing the Fine Arts into Germany, Seven Fruitful Years, Two Marys at the Grave, Crowning of the Virgin, Triumph of Religion, Scenes from Dante's Paradise, Temple, Assumption of the Virgin*, and portraits of Charlemagne, Frederick II, Otto I, and Henry VII in Frankfort's Hall of Emperors.

VEITH, JOHANN EMANUEL (1787–1876). Born of Jewish parents in Kuttenplan, Bohemia, he studied philosophy at Prague and medicine at Vienna where he received his medical degree in 1808, was director of a veterinarian's school, and in 1817 became a convert. He joined the Redemptorists a month after his ordination in 1821, became famed as a preacher at Maria Stiegen in 1821–30 and at the cathedral of St. Stephen in 1831–45, and from then until 1863, when he became deaf and blind and was forced to retire, as part-time preacher. He published a score of books containing his sermons, prayers, and homilies. He died in Vienna on Nov. 6.

VELÁSQUEZ, DIEGO RODRÍQUEZ DE SILVA Y (1599–1660), painter. Born in Seville, Spain, and baptized on June 6, son of Juan Rodríquez de Silva and Géronima Velásquez, whose name he took, he studied under Herrara el Viejar and Pachecho, married the latter's daughter in 1618, was patronized by Philip IV, and about 1623 was appointed court painter and moved to Madrid in 1624. He traveled in Italy in 1629–31, and again in 1649–51, when Philip IV delegated him to found an art museum in Spain and sent him to Italy to secure statuary for it. He was a royal official in 1652–60, and in 1659 was awarded the Cross of Santiago by the king, one of the highest honors of the kingdom. He was famous for his landscapes, historical and genre subjects, and portraits, all notable for their force, realism, and masterly and bold execution. Among his best-known works are *Adoration of the Shepherds, Joseph's Coat, Forge of Vulcan, Las*

Meniñas, Venus and Cupid, Coronation of the Virgin, St. John the Evangelist, Lot and His Daughters, Surrender of Breda, and *Crucifixion*. Equally famous are his portraits, particularly those of Philip IV (of whom he painted some forty, Innocent X, Prince Baltasar Carlos, the duke of Olivares, Adm. Pulido Pareja, and the series of dwarfs and jesters. He died in Madrid on Aug. 6.

VELLEICUS, ST. (8th century). An Englishman, he went to Germany with St. Swithbert and became abbot of the Benedictine monastery of Kaiserswerth, on the Rhine River. F. D. Aug. 29.

VELLOSO, JOSÉ MARIANO DA CONCECÇAO (1742–1811). Born in Mariana, Brazil, he wrote *Flora fluminese* and other botanical studies.

VENANTIUS, ST. (d. 255?), bishop and martyr. He was put to death at Spalato in Dalmatia. F. D. Apr. 1.

VENANTIUS. Said to have been a seventeen-year-old martyr at Camerino, Italy, in the mid-third century, he is probably to be identified with St. Venantius, bishop of Salona, Dalmatia.

VENANTIUS, ST. (d. 544). A convert from Arianism, he became a monk at Viviers, Gaul, and, later, bishop, there. F. D. Aug. 5.

VENANTIUS HONORIUS CLEMENTIANUS FORTUNATUS, ST. (535?–605?), poet. Born near Treviso, Italy, he was educated in Ravenna, and in 565 went to Germany. His journey is recorded in poems, congratulating bishops, signalizing church construction, humorously describing a trip on the Moselle, honoring the marriage of King Sigebert and Brunehild at Metz in 566, and praising her subsequent conversion from Arianism. Similar poems mark his journey across France to Paris, where he wrote of the recitation of the office to orchestral accompaniment on the eve of a feast, praised King Caribert, and made a pilgrimage to the tomb of St. Martin at Tours. He lived at Poitiers for twenty years after 567, where he was ordained and became the friend and adviser of St. Radegund (wife of King Clotaire I) and her adopted daughter Agnes at their convent. When Radegund received in 569 from Emperor Justin a relic of the cross, Venantius Fortunatus wrote his famous and still-used hymns, *Vexilla regis prodeunt* and *Pange lingua*. He wrote an elegy for Radegund's cousin, Amalafried, who died at Constantinople in the imperial service; and another for Queen Galeswintha, Brunehild's sister, put to death by her husband Chilperic about 569. He published his poems at the suggestion of Gregory of Tours, went to the court of Austrasia, came to know SS. Felix of Nantes and Leontius of Bordeaux, and around 600 succeeded Plato as bishop of Poitiers. He wrote a long poem on St. Martin, and lyricized prose

biographies of SS. Hilary of Poitiers, Marcellus and Germanus of Paris, Paternus of Avranches, and Radegund (who died about 587). Other poems, marked by descriptive digressions, make valuable reference to contemporary Merovingian figures, history, and thought, and give details of cooking, family life, the condition of women, buildings, and works of art. They heavily influenced the use of allegory, tenderness and refinement, mastery of form, affected language, and deliberate obscurity of much subsequent French poetry. He died in Poitiers, Gaul. F. D. Dec. 14.

VÉNARD, BL. JOHN THÉOPHANE (1829–1861), French martyr. Born in Poitiers, France, on Nov. 21, he studied at the seminary there, joined the Society of Foreign Missions at Paris in 1851, was ordained in 1852, and sent to Hong Kong. From 1854 to 1860 he served the persecuted Christians in Tonkin, where he was captured, chained in a cage, and beheaded at Ke Cho on Feb. 2. He was beatified in 1900. F. D. Nov. 6.

VENERANDUS, ST. (d. 275), martyr. A leading citizen of Troyes, Gaul, he was slain during the reign of Aurelian. F. D. Nov. 14.

VENERANDUS, ST. (d. 423), bishop. Born of a senatorial family in Clermont, Auvergne, he was raised to direct its see. F. D. Dec. 24.

VENERINI, BL. ROSA (1656–1728). Born in Viterbo, Italy, she began to teach religion to the women of her neighborhood; in 1685, under the direction of Fr. Ignatius Martinelli, S.J., she opened a free school. In 1692 she went to organize the school system of the diocese of Monte Fiascone at the invitation of Cardinal Barbarigo. A number of schools were set up in other areas, sometimes in spite of great opposition, and in 1713 she began one in Rome. Her teachers were organized as a religious institute, the Venerini Sisters, after her death. She was beatified in 1952 by Pope Pius XII. F. D. May 7.

VENERIUS, ST. (d. 409), bishop. A deacon serving St. Ambrose, he succeeded St. Simplician as bishop of Milan in 400. F. D. May 4.

VENERIUS, ST. He spent his life as a hermit on the island of Tino, off Genoa, in the seventh or ninth century. F. D. Sept. 13.

VENTURA, BL. (12th century). Born in Spello, Italy, near Assisi, he joined the Cruciferi, built a hospice on his family's land, and ruled its abbey under the Benedictine rule. F. D. May 3.

VENTURA, BL. (1278?–1348). Born in Valdiseve, Italy, he was an unschooled wool-carder until the age of forty, when he became a Camaldolese laybrother at Santa Maria degli Angeli in Florence. He was sought out by the entire community for his exceptional spiritual knowledge. F. D. June 9.

VENTURA DI RAULICA, GIOACCHINO

(1792–1861), philosopher. Born in Palermo, Sicily, on Dec. 8, he joined the Jesuits in 1808, and, when the Society was suppressed there in 1817, the Theatines. After ordination, he attracted attention by his preaching, was appointed professor of canon law at the Sapienza by Pope Leo XII about 1824, and served as superior general of the Theatines from 1830 to 1833. He became famed for his championship of liberty and as leader of the moderate party of reformers, defended the Sicilian revolution in 1848, and proposed an Italian confederation under the pope. When Pope Pius IX was exiled to Gaeta, he recognized the Roman republic as commissioner from Sicily, supported separation of Church and state in Italy, and opposed French intervention in Italian affairs. He went to Paris in 1851, tried in vain to bring Lamennais back to the Church, preached at the Madeleine, and delivered the Lenten sermons in the Tuileries before Napoleon III. He wrote *La Raison philosophique et la raison catholique* (1852), *Le Pouvoir politique chrétien*, and *Philosophie chrétienne* (1861). He died in Versailles, France, on Aug. 2.

VENTURINO OF BERGAMO (1304–1346). Born in Bergamo, Italy, on Apr. 9, he joined the Dominicans there in 1310, and became famed for his preaching. He led a pilgrimage of some 30,000 converts to Rome in 1335, which led to the condemnation of such pilgrimages by his master general, and was imprisoned in Avignon in 1335–43, when he sought an audience with Pope Benedict XII, who feared he was trying to seize the papal throne. He was freed by Pope Clement VI, who commissioned him to preach a crusade in 1344. He died in Smyrna, Turkey, on Mar. 28.

VENUSTI, RAFFAELE (d. 1543). Born in Tirano, Valtellina, Italy, he joined the Congregation of Lateran Canons Regular of S. Salvatore and was noted for his theological writings against Lutheranism and Calvinism. His fame was such that both King Henry VIII and Emperor Charles V asked him to write a treatise on the former's attempted divorce. He died in Venice.

VENUSTIAN, ST. (d. 303?), martyr. *See* Sabinus, St.

VENUSTUS, ST. (3rd century), martyr. *See* Heliodorus, St.

VENUSTUS, ST. (d. 362?), martyr. *See* Faustinus, St.

VERANUS, ST. (d. 480?). Son of St. Eucherius of Lyons, he became a monk at Lérins and then bishop of Vence, Gaul. A fifth-century bishop, honored on Nov. 11, is probably the same person. F. D. Sept. 10.

VERANUS, ST. (d. 590). Born in Vaucluse, France, he became bishop of Cavaillon, France. F. D. Oct. 19.

VERBIEST, FERDINAND (1623–1688), missioner. Born in Pitthem, Belgium, on Oct. 9, he joined the Jesuits in 1641, studied at Seville, was ordained, and in 1658 was sent to China as a missioner. He began his work in Shen-si, was sent to Peking in 1660 as assistant to Fr. Adam Schall, with whom he was imprisoned when Christian persecutions erupted in 1664, and succeeded him as astronomer. In 1668 he bested the mandarin who had unleashed the persecution in a test of astronomical knowledge, was appointed head of the bureau of mathematics, and was able to reactivate the Christian missions by securing an end of persecution in 1669. He became influential with the Emperor K'ang-hi, for whom he constructed numerous astronomical instruments and who studied under him and made him a mandarin. He was appointed vice-provincial of China in 1677, advocated strenuously the necessity of a native clergy, saying mass and administering the sacraments in Chinese, and when the attack on Jesuit methods of religious instruction in China was launched in Rome by Fr. Navarrete, he submitted a defense which led to a letter of commendation to him by Pope Innocent XI in 1681. He wrote treatises in Chinese, including instructions on the construction and use of his astronomical instruments, notes on his astronomical observations, and translated the missal into Chinese. He died in Peking on Jan. 28.

VERCELLONE, CARLO (d. 1869), scholar. Born in Biella, Milan, Italy, he joined the Barnabites in Genoa in 1829, studied at Turin and Rome, and taught at Turin, Alessandria, Perugia, and Parma. He was appointed president of the Barnabite college in Rome in 1847, became procurator of his order. was elected general, while retaining his college presidency, and served until his death in Rome on Jan. 19. He was highly regarded for his biblical scholarship, edited the Vatican edition of the Bible prepared by Cardinal Mai in 1857, prepared a new edition of the New Testament in 1859, was co-editor of the first two volumes of the *Bibliorum sacrorum graecus codex vaticanus* (1868–81), and wrote *Variae lectiones Vulgatae* (1860–64), studies on the Vulgate text.

VERDA, ST. (d. 344), martyr. *See* Daniel, St.

VERDAGUER, JACINTO (1845–1902), poet. Born in Riudeperas, Barcelona, Spain, on Apr. 17, he won first prize in a poetry contest in 1861, was ordained in 1870, and became noted for his poetry, chief of which is the epic, *La Atlantica* (1877); among his other works are *Canigó*, *Idilis y cants mistichs*, and *Oda a Barcelona*. He died in Vallvidrera, Spain, on June 10.

VERDAGUER, PEDRO (1835–1911), bishop. Born in San Pedro de Torello, Catalonia, Spain, on Dec. 10, he studied at the Vich and

Barcelona seminaries, went to the United States, and finished his studies at St. Vincent's seminary, Cape Girardeau, Missouri, and was ordained in San Francisco in 1862. He did pastoral work in the Monterey-Los Angeles diocese, and in 1890 was appointed titular bishop of Aulon and vicar apostolic of Brownsville, Texas. He was consecrated in Barcelona, and died on Oct. 28 on his way from Santa Maria to Mercedes, Texas.

VERDE, ALESSANDRO (1865-1958), cardinal. Born in Sant' Antimo, Italy, on Mar. 27, he was ordained in 1888, and took his doctorate in theology at the Pontifical seminary, Rome, where he also taught. From 1909 until his death he was associated with the procedure of canonization, notably in the cases of Joan of Arc and Mother Xavier Cabrini. He was a canon of St. Peter's basilica in 1915 and became secretary of the Congregation of Rites and a cardinal in 1925. He died in Rome on Mar. 29.

VERDI, GIUSEPPE FORTUNINO FRANCESCO (1813-1901), composer. Born in Roncole, Italy, on Oct. 10, he studied under Pietro Baistrocchi, organist at the church, whom he succeeded at ten years of age, and later Ferdinando Provesi, of San Bartolomeo collegiate church, and wrote his first symphony in 1828. He went to Milan in 1832, studied under Vincenzo Lavigna, was appointed conductor of the Busseto municipal orchestra and organist of San Bartolomeo church in 1835, married Margherita, daughter of his benefactor, Antonio Barezzi, in 1836, and had his first opera, *Oberto, Conte di San Bonifacio*, produced in Milan in 1839. His *Un giorno di regno* (1840) was a failure, but the success of *Nabucodonosor* (1842) launched him on a career which in the next half-century resulted in a series of operas. He actively supported the revolutionary movement in 1848, married Giuseppina Strepponi (his first wife had died in 1840), a singer with whom he had lived for several years, in 1859, was elected a deputy to parliament in 1860, serving infrequently until 1865, and, though appointed senator in 1875, refused on religious grounds to act with an anti-Catholic government. Among his outstanding operas are *I Lombardi* (1843), *Ernani* (1844), *Macbeth* (1847), *Rigoletto* (1851), *Il Trovatore* (1853), *La Traviata* (1853), *Les vêpres siciliennes* (1855), *La forza del destino* (1862), *Aida* (1871), *Otello* (1887), and *Falstaff* (1893); of his religious music *Ave Maria, Laudi alla Virgine, Stabat Mater* (1896), *Te Deum* (1895), and a *Requiem Mass* (1874) in honor of Manzoni are outstanding. He died in Milan, Italy, on Jan. 27.

VERDIANA, BL. (d. 1240?). Born in Tuscany, and a housekeeper at twelve, she went on a pilgrimage to Spain and on her return joined a number of her fellow pilgrims as a recluse

in a hermitage they built for her. There she lived for thirty-four years, probably as a Vallombrosan nun. The name is also spelled Veridiana. Her cult was approved in 1533. F. D. Feb. 16.

VERDIER, JEAN PIERRE (1864-1940), cardinal. Born in Lacroix-Barrez, Aveyron, France, on Feb. 19, he studied at the Rodez seminary, joined the Sulpicians, finished his studies in Rome, and was ordained in 1887. He became director of Périgueux's major seminary in 1889, at Lyons in 1892, of St. Sulpice, Paris, in 1905, superior of L'Institut Catholique, Paris, in 1912, and visitor of Sulpician seminaries in the United States and Canada in 1923. He was elected superior general of the Sulpicians in 1929, became archbishop of Paris, and was created a cardinal by Pope Pius XI. He was a strong believer in Catholic Action, was interested in the social problems confronting France, and labored to improve his clergy. He was papal legate to Czechoslovakia in 1935, attended the Eucharistic Congress in Algiers in 1939, and died in Paris on Apr. 9. He wrote several books and was co-editor of *Revue Pratique d'Apologétique*.

VERECUNDUS, ST. (d. 522). He was bishop of Verona, Italy. F. D. Oct. 22.

VERECUNDUS (d. 552). Bishop of Junca, Byzacena, Africa, he attended the Council of Constantinople in 551, supported the Three Chapters and Pope Vigilius there, and with Primasius of Hadrumeta excommunicated Theodore Askidas and deposed Mennas, patriarch of Constantinople, for their actions. He followed Vigilius on the pope's flight to Chalcedon and died soon after. He wrote commentaries on the Old Testament, poems, and a collection of documents on the Council of Chalcedon.

VEREMUND, ST. (d. 1092). Born in Navarre, Spain, he entered the Benedictine abbey at Hirache at an early age, serving under his uncle, Bl. Munius, whom he succeeded as abbot. His monastery became one of the most influential in Spain. He was especially attentive to the needs of the poor, gained papal support for the Mozarabic liturgy, and increased devotion to Mary and the Holy Child with the enthusiastic co-operation of King Sancho Ramirez. F. D. Mar. 8.

VERENA, ST. (3rd century). Legend calls her a native of Egypt who came to Switzerland seeking a relative, possibly St. Victor, who had been in the massacred Theban Legion. She is supposed to have lived as a recluse in a cave near Zurich, Switzerland. F. D. Sept. 1.

VERGANI, PAOLO (1753-1820?), economist. Born in Piedmont, Italy, he studied canon and civil law, was ordained, and went to Rome, where he became a canon of St. John Lateran. He wrote treatises on criminology, chief of which was *Trattado sulla pena de morte* (1780), was appointed assessor general of finances, inspector of agriculture, and wrote on financial aspects of the Papal States. When the Lateran chapter was dispersed in 1811 he went to Paris, where he taught Italian and wrote *La legislation de Napoleon le grand* (1812) and *Essai historique* (1814). He died in Paris.

VERGERIO, PIER PAOLO (1370–1444?). Born in Capodistria, Trieste, on July 23, he studied at Bologna, Padua, and Florence, and taught at the first two universities. He was in Rome in 1406 and secretary to Popes Innocent VII and Gregory XII, became canon of Ravenna, participated in the Council of Constance in 1414, and was one of a delegation headed by Emperor Sigismund, who in 1415 attempted to secure Benedict VIII's renunciation of his claims to the papal throne. After 1417 he became Sigismund's secretary, was one of the orators at the Hussite disputation in Prague in 1420, and wrote several theological works, though he never advanced beyond minor orders. He died in Budapest, Hungary, on July 8.

VERGIL, POLYDORE (1470?–1555?). Born in Urbino, Italy, he studied at Bologna and Padua, became the duke of Urbino's secretary, chamberlain to Pope Alexander VI, and in 1501 went to England as collector of papal revenue. In 1505 he was commissioned to write a history of England (*Anglicae historicae*), published in 1533) by King Henry VII, who granted him several preferments, and in 1510 he became a naturalized English citizen. He was deprived of his position as collector by Cardinal Wolsey, with whom he quarreled and who had him imprisoned on a charge of libel, returned to Italy in the reign of Edward VI, and probably died in his native town. He also wrote *Proverbiorum libellus* (1498) and *De inventoribus rerum* (1499).

VERIAN, ST. (d. 250), martyr. *See* Secundian, St.

VERING, FRIEDRICH HEINRICH (1833–1896), canonist. Born in Liesborn, Westphalia, on Mar. 9, he studied in Paderborn, law at Bonn and Heidelberg, became professor at the latter in 1862, professor of canon law at the new Czernowitz University at Bukowina, Austria, in 1875, and of canon law at the German University in Prague in 1879, a position he held until his death there on Mar. 30. He wrote several textbooks on canon law.

VERISSIMUS, ST. (d. 302?), martyr. *See* Julia, St.

VERNAGALLI, BL. DOMINIC (d. 1218). Born in Pisa, Italy, he became a Camaldolese at the abbey of St. Michael there and built its hospital. He was beatified in 1854. F. D. Apr. 20.

VERNAZZA, TOMMASINA (1497–1587).

Born in Genoa, Italy, she became a canoness regular at St. Maria delle Grazie there, which she entered at thirteen, taking the name Battistina, served as prioress and treasurer, and wrote spiritual colloquies, homilies, and poems. She probably wrote a life of St. Catherine of Genoa, whose disciple and goddaughter she was. She died in Genoa.

VERNE, JULES (1828–1905), novelist. Born in Nantes, France, on Feb. 8, he studied there and law at Paris but became interested in writing for the stage, writing *Les pailles rompues* (1850) and *Onze jours de siège*. In 1863 the successful publication of *Five Weeks in a Balloon* led to a career of writing imaginative scientific fiction which made him widely popular. Many of his descriptions and scientific devices which seemed fantastic at the time have become twentieth-century commonplaces. Among his greatest successes are *Around the World in Eighty Days, Twenty Thousand Leagues under the Sea, The Mysterious Island, Michael Strogoff, A Journey to the Center of the Earth*, and *A Trip to the Moon*, all of which have been translated into English. He died in Amiens, France, on Mar. 24.

VERNIER, PIERRE (1580?–1637). Born in Ornans, Franche-Comté, France, he became castellan of the castle there, treasurer and councilor of Burgundy, and interested in mathematics and especially the uses of the quadrant. He invented the vernier, a device by which a fixed scale of measurement to very small fractions can be read on sextants, barometers, and other graduated instruments. He died in Ornans, France, on Sept. 14.

VERNON, GRENVILLE (1883–1941), critic. Born in Providence, Rhode Island, on July 22, he graduated from Harvard in 1905, did journalism work in New York City, was editor for Dial Press, wrote a novel, *Image in the Path*, plays, including *The Dictator's Wife*, compiled a collection of American folk songs, and married Valentine d'Orn. He was music critic of the New York *Times* in 1908 and of the *Herald Tribune* from 1909 to 1921. He wrote on music for *Commonweal* from 1926 to 1941, succeeding Richard Dana Skinner as dramatic critic on that weekly shortly before his death in New York City on Nov. 30.

VEROLOT, BL. JULETTE (d. 1794), martyr. Born in Troyes, France, she became a Carmelite nun at Compiègne, the last to be professed there before the French Revolution. She was seized and guillotined there five years later with the rest of her community. She was beatified in 1906. F. D. July 17.

VÉRON, FRANÇOIS (1575?–1649), controversialist. Born in Paris, he joined the Jesuits, taught at several colleges, then left the Society. He preached through Béarn, Champagne, Lorraine, Normandy, and other areas of France attracting large crowds and making many converts. He used a method of controversy which he taught at Collège de France, St. Lazaire, and St. Sulpice and which was most successful, though attracting opposition from some Catholic sources and causing his work on the primacy of the Church to be placed on the Index. He was an opponent of the Jansenists, and wrote *La Méthode nouvelle*, *L'épitomé de toutes les controverses de religion en ce siècle*, and *Règle de la foi catholique*. He died in Carenton, France.

VERONESE, PAOLO (1528–1588), painter. Paolo Cagliari, or Caliari, was born in Verona, Italy, son of the sculptor Gabriele, studied with his father, then turned to painting under the direction of Antonio Badile, whose daughter he married. He worked at Verona, Mantua, and Castelfranco, and went to Venice in 1555 to decorate the ceiling and paint an altarpiece for the church of San Sebastiano. His historical paintings in a castle near Vicenza attracted the attention of Titian, for whom he worked in decorating the library of St. Mark. He completed his *Marriage at Cana* in 1562, portrayed the martyrdom of St. Sebastian and of SS. Marcellus and Marcellinus, and gained fame by his *Mystical Marriage of St. Catherine*, *Vision of St. Helena*, *Family of Darius before Alexander*, and portrait of St. Paul. He was fond of decoration, brilliant color, and lavish background; paid little attention to historic detail (introducing forks in scenes from apostolic times, Swiss guards in Old Testament settings, and animal pets at the edges of religious compositions—for which he was censured by the Inquisition); and had a masterly sense of composition, grace, and beauty. He died in Venice on Apr. 19. Two sons, Gabriele (b. 1568) and Carletto (b. 1570), also became painters.

VERONICA, ST. (1st century). According to legend, she was the woman who wiped the face of Christ when He fell on the way to Calvary, an image of His face becoming imprinted on the cloth. A veil, said to be this relic, has been venerated at St. Peter's, Rome, since the eighth century, but no marks are now apparent. Actually, the name of the woman is not known; Veronica may have been developed from the words *vera icon* (true image), but even this is hypothesis. F. D. July 12.

VERONICA, ST. (d. 1727). *See* Giuliani, St. Ursula.

VERONICA OF BINASCO, BL. (1445–1497). Born near Milan, Italy, she entered the Augustinian convent of St. Martha there and devoted her life to prayer. F. D. Jan. 13.

VEROT, JEAN MARCEL PIERRE AUGUSTE (1805–1876), bishop. Born in Le Puy, Haute-Loire, France, on May 23, he studied at St. Sulpice, Paris, was ordained in 1828, and joined the Sulpicians in 1829. He was sent to Baltimore in 1830 and taught at St. Mary's college and seminary until 1853. He did pastoral work until 1858, when he was consecrated titular bishop of Danaba and vicar apostolic of Florida. He labored to rebuild and reinvigorate his rundown see, to which he encouraged immigration. In 1861 he preached a sermon, "A Tract for the Times: Slavery and Abolition," which, though condemning the slave trade, defended slavery; it was widely circulated and suppressed by Secretary of War Seward in Baltimore. Verot was transferred to Savannah, Georgia, in 1861, as its third bishop, and after the Civil War struggled to restore that badly damaged diocese; he was concurrently vicar of Florida. He attended the Vatican Council in 1870, where he vigorously opposed the proclamation of the dogma of papal infallibility, though he accepted it as soon as it was passed. He was administrator of the vicariate of Florida in 1861–70 and was transferred in 1870 to St. Augustine, Florida, as the see's first bishop, and died there on June 10.

VERRAZANO, GIOVANNI DA (1480?–1527?), explorer. Born in Val di Greve, Italy, he entered the naval service of Francis I of France and became well known for his privateering activities, especially against Spanish treasure ships. In 1524 he was sent by Francis on an exploratory voyage to the New World. A letter of his, the authenticity of which has been questioned, describes New York harbor, the Hudson River, and the New England coast. He may have been killed by Indians on a trip to the West Indies in 1526; it is also claimed that he was captured off the coast of Cadiz in 1527 and executed as a pirate at Puerto del Pico, Spain, in Nov., under the name of Juan Florin, at the order of Emperor Charles V.

VERREAU, HOSPICE ANTHELME (1828–1901). Born in L'Islet, Quebec, Canada, on Sept. 6, he studied at the Quebec seminary, where he was ordained, taught at Ste. Thérèse College, and became principal of the new Jacques Cartier Normal School in 1857, a position he held until his death. He became known for his historical writings, and in 1873 was commissioned by the Canadian government to search European archives for Canadian material. He died in Montreal.

VERRI, PIETRO (1728–1797), economist. Born in Milan, Italy, in Dec., he studied at Monza, Rome, and Parma, served in the Austrian army as a youth, and on his return devoted himself to the study of economics. He favored breaking up large landed estates, was a supporter of the theory of demand and supply, was a member of the Milan council of economy in 1765, president of the chamber of counts in 1780, helped found the Società del Caffè, and wrote several political and economic works. He died in Milan on June 29.

VERROCCHIO, ANDREA DEL (1435–1488), sculptor. Born in Florence, Italy, Andrea di Michele di Francesco de' Cioni studied under Giuliano Verrocchio, a goldsmith, whose name he took, and sculpture under Donatello. Of his painting, only *Baptism of Christ* in the Uffizi, Florence, is ascribed to him with certainty, though *Tobias and the Angel* and *Madonna and Angels* are probably his. Outstanding among his sculpture are the bronze *Incredulity of St. Thomas*, the equestrian statue of Bartolommeo Colleoni in Venice, *David* in Florence, *Boy with a Dolphin*, the mausoleum of Giovanni and Piero de' Medici in San Lorenzo, Florence, the monument to Cardinal Forteguerra in the Pistoia cathedral, and *Beheading John the Baptist*, one of the reliefs of the silver altar frontal of the Florentine baptistery. Leonardo da Vinci, Perugino, Botticini, and Lorenzo di Credi were among his pupils and helpers. He was one of the first sculptors to use casts from living and dead subjects. He died in Venice.

VERSERESKUL, AUXENTIUS (17th century). He was bishop at Armenierstadt, Transylvania, who converted the Armenian emigrants who had settled the city in 1700 from Eutychianism to Catholicism in the Armenian rite.

VERSTEGAN, RICHARD (1550?–1640?), author. Born in London of Dutch extraction, he studied at Oxford under his grandfather's name, Rowlands, and, when unable to secure a degree because of his Catholicism, returned to his ancestral land and settled in Antwerp in 1576. His publication of *Theatrum crudelitatis haereticorum* in Paris in 1583 honored contemporary martyrs and caused the English ambassador to France to enter a diplomatic protest, which led to Verstegan's imprisonment in 1587. He was freed through the intercession of Cardinal Allen, became corresponding agent in Rome for the cardinal, English Catholics, and Jesuits, and wrote prayer books and controversial tracts. In 1595 he received the monopoly for printing English manuals, helped write and publish *Dolman's Conference*, and translated the hymns in the *Primer* of 1599. His *Restitution of Decayed Intelligence* (1605) had great influence on the antiquarian Camden's *Britannia;* it also contained such stories as the Pied Piper, later used by Robert Browning. He published epigrams and several poems, and his letters to Robert Persons are historically significant. He died in Antwerp, Netherlands.

VERTIN, JOHN (1844–1899), bishop. Born in Doblice, Carniola, Austria, on July 17, he studied at Rudolfswert, went to America when nineteen, finished his theological studies at St.

Francis, Wisconsin, and was ordained in 1866. He served in various administrative posts and as a missioner in northern Michigan until 1879, when he was appointed third bishop of Marquette, Wisconsin. He died in Marquette on Feb. 26.

VERTOT, RENÉ AUBERT DE (1655–1735), historian. Born in Benetot, Normandy, France, on Nov. 25, he studied at the Rouen seminary, left to join the Capuchins and then the Premonstratensian canons at Valsery, and served as pastor in Normandy. He wrote *Histoire de la conjuration de Portugal* (1690), *Histoire des revolutions de Suède* (1695), the three-volume *Histoire des revolutions de la republique romaine* (1719), and the four-volume *Histoire des chevaliers hospitaliers de Saint-Jean de Jérusalem* (1726). He was elected to the Academy of Inscriptions in 1703, and died in Paris on June 15.

VERULUS, ST. (d. 434?), martyr. *See* Felix, St.

VERUS, ST. (4th century). He attended a synod at Arles, Gaul, in 314 as bishop of Vienne, France. F. D. Aug. 1.

VERUS, ST. (4th century). He is listed as the third bishop of Salerno, Italy. F. D. Aug. 1.

VERYLDE. *See* Pharaildis.

VERZERI, BL. TERESA (1801–1852), foundress. Born in Bergamo, Italy, on July 31, she began a school for girls with four of her sisters and her widowed mother, serving under simple vows and a rule prepared by Canon Joseph Benaglio. She also planned more schools, recreational centers for women, and retreats, her aims matching those of St. Madeleine Sophie Barat. But the group, Daughters of the Sacred Heart, was given separate papal approval in 1841. Bl. Ludovico Pavoni obtained a mother house for them in Brescia and served as their chaplain. Teresa died of cholera in Brescia, Italy. She was beatified in 1946. F. D. Mar. 3.

VESALIUS, ANDREAS (1514–1564), anatomist. Born in Brussels, Belgium, on Dec. 31, son of Charles V's court apothecary, he studied at Louvain, Cologne, Paris, Venice, and Padua, where he received his medical degree in 1537 and taught anatomy and surgery until 1541. He also lectured in Louvain, Venice, Basle, Pisa, and Bologna, published *Tabulae anatomicae* (1538) and *De fabrica humani corporis* (1543), and was appointed Charles V's physician in 1544. He retained this position on the accession of Philip II in 1555, went on a pilgrimage to the Holy Land in 1564, and died on his way home when shipwrecked on the island of Zante in Oct. He brought a new concept to the study of the human body, revealed numerous errors in Galen's work, particularly his *Anatomy* (he believed Galen had never dissected a human body), and was bitterly attacked during his lifetime by Galen's supporters.

VESPASIANO DA BISTICCI (1421–1498). Born in Florence, Italy, he became an outstanding book collector, advised Cosimo de' Medici in the creation of the Laurentian Library in Florence, spent fourteen years collecting books for the duke of Urbino's library, and left a valuable collection of some 300 biographies of fifteenth-century humanists.

VESPUCCI, AMERIGO (1451–1512), explorer. Born in Florence, Italy, on Mar. 9, he was educated by his uncle, a Dominican friar, early showing an aptitude for astronomy and cosmography, served as a clerk in the Medici commercial house in Florence, moved to Spain (where he met Columbus) as an agent of the Medici about 1490, and went on four exploratory expeditions to the New World in 1497–98 (according to his own account, the no-longer extant *Quattro giornate*, thus making him the first discoverer of North America, though this date is now believed to be false), 1499–1500, 1501–2, and 1503–4. He became a Spanish citizen in 1505, was appointed a navigator in 1508, and held this position until his death in Seville, Spain, on Feb. 22. He wrote several letters, one of which geographer Martin Waldseemüller (Hylacomylus) included in his *Cosmographiae introductio* (1507), in which he suggested naming the new continent America in honor of Amerigo.

VESTIA, ST. (d. 180), martyr. *See* Speratus, St.

VETANCOURT, AUGUSTÍN DE (1620–1700), historian. Born in Mexico City, he became a Franciscan at Puebla, was a student of Aztec antiquities, published *Arte de lengua mexicana* (1673), *Teatro mexicano descripción breve de los sucesos ejemplares, históricos, políticos, militares y religiosos*, based on Torquemada, and became commissary general of his order in the Indies.

VETTER, CONRAD 1547–1622). Born in Engen, Baden, he was ordained, became prefect of music at the Hall collegiate church for nobles, and in 1576 joined the Jesuits in Munich. He became famed as a preacher at Munich and Ratisbon, noted for his conversions, and wrote books and pamphlets characterized by coarseness but tremendously popular. He died in Munich, Germany, on Oct. 11.

VETTIUS EPAGATHUS, ST. (d. 177), martyr. *See* Pothinus, St.

VETURIUS, ST. (d. 180), martyr. *See* Speratus, St.

VEUILLOT, LOUIS (1813–1883), journalist. Born in Boynes, Loiret, France, on Oct. 11, he worked for an attorney in Paris, became interested in writing, an editor of a Rouen newspaper, *Echo de Rouen*, of one in Périgueux, and of *La Paix* in Paris. He joined the staff of

L'Univers Religieux, which he built into a leading Catholic journal. He spent a month in prison for his defense of a Catholic priest in 1844, was criticized by many of the hierarchy for the violence of his positions, opposed Napoleon III's war with Austria in 1859, and in 1860 saw *L'Univers* suppressed by the government when it printed Pope Pius IX's *Nullis certe*. He began *L'Univers* again in 1867, denounced the imperialism of Napoleon III and the attempts to deprive the pope of the Papal States, was a zealous supporter of the ultramontane party, and vigorously supported the doctrine of papal infallibility at the Vatican Council. Among his chief works are poems, literary criticism, and *Les libre penseurs* (1848), *La Vie de notre seigneur Jésus Christ* (1864), *Paris pendant les deux sièges* (1871), and his *Correspondance* in seven volumes (1884). His newspaper writings were collected in the twenty-two-volume *Mélanges religieux, historiques, politiques et littéraires* (1856–1909). He died in Paris on Apr. 7.

VEUSTER, JOSEPH DE (1840–1888), missioner. Born in Tremeloo, Belgium, on Jan. 3, he studied at the College of Braine-le-Comte, and was professed as a member of the Fathers of the Sacred Hearts of Jesus and Mary (the Picpus Fathers), taking the name Damien, in 1860. He was sent to Hawaii in 1864, ordained that year in Honolulu, and became active in the mission field. In 1873, with the permission of his bishop, he became resident chaplain to the leper colony on Molokai, hitherto without even regular medical supervision. Fr. Damien cared for their spiritual and physical needs, helped them build houses, dressed their sores, buried their dead, and after twelve years found himself a victim of the disease. In his last three years he was aided by two priests and two laybrothers, but became helpless and died on Mar. 28. One of the first memorials to him was the vindication of his character written by Robert Louis Stevenson (1905).
JOHN FARROW, *Damien the Leper* (Garden City, N.Y., Image Books, 1954).

VEZZOSI, ANTONIO FRANCESCO (1708–1783), scholar. Born in Arezzo, Italy, on Oct. 4, he joined the Theatines in 1731, and taught philosophy at the Rimini seminary in 1736 and at San Andrea della Valle in Rome in 1742. He edited the eleven-volume *Works* of Cardinal Tommasi (1749–69), was appointed professor of church history at the Sapienza in 1753, was elected general of the Theatines, and wrote *I scrittori de' Chierici regolari detti Teatini* (1780). He died in Rome on May 29.

VIADANA, LUDOVICO. *See* Grossi, Ludovico.

VIADER, JOSÉ (b. 1765), missioner. Born

in Gallimes, Catalonia, Spain, on Aug. 27, he became a Franciscan at Barcelona in 1788, was sent to Mexico in 1795, and to California in 1796. He served as assistant to Fr. Magin Catala at Santa Clara until 1833, resisted the interference of colonists and government officials, and returned to Spain.

VIALAR, ST. ANNE MARGUERITE ADELAIDE EMELIE DE (1797–1856), foundress. Daughter of Baron James de Vialar and his wife Antoinette, she was born in Gaillac, Languedoc, France, and educated at Paris. She was fifteen when her mother died, and was estranged from her father when he tried to arrange a marriage for her and when she persisted in caring for the sick and poor in her own wing of the family residence. At twenty-one she inherited her grandfather's fortune and bought a house in the neighborhood, entered it with eleven postulants, and prepared to organize the Congregation of Sisters of St. Joseph of the Apparition to care for the poor and sick and to educate young children, both in France and in the foreign missions. Their rule was approved by Archbishop de Gualy of Albi, when he accepted the profession of a group of eighteen in 1835. The order spread to Algeria, Tunis, Malta, the Balkans, became the first group of nuns in the Holy Land in modern times, and went out to Greece, Burma, and Australia; there were forty settlements in the lifetime of the foundress. She died on Aug. 24, and was canonized in 1951. F. D. June 17.

VIANNEY, ST. JEAN BAPTISTE (1786–1859). Born at Dardilly, France, on May 8, he began to study for the priesthood at twenty and experienced great difficulties in his studies. In 1809 he was drafted into the army, resumed his studies in 1811, but continued to have such difficulties that it was recommended he be dropped, was rescued by his friend and teacher, Abbé Balley, and was finally ordained in 1815. He was appointed in 1818 parish priest of Ars, where he spent the rest of his life. He set to work reforming the people of the parish, who had fallen into a state of indifference. In 1824, Catherine Lassagne and Benedicta Lardet, at his encouragement, opened a free school for girls which in 1827 became La Providence, a shelter for orphans and homeless children. He also set up a shrine to St. Philomena (no longer recognized by the Church), to whose cult he was devoted. Ars became a place of pilgrimage as his reputation as a spiritual guide spread and he became famed as a confessor, spending sixteen to eighteen hours a day in the confessional. He was gifted with an uncanny insight into men's minds and souls. He was under great strain because of the unusual attention he received, was often scorned because of his lack of advanced training, was rejected for higher posts

by his superiors, and suffered from manifestations which were declared to be diabolical attacks. He continued his lifework at Ars, refusing belated honors, and died there on Aug. 4. He was canonized in 1925 by Pope Pius XI, who in 1929 proclaimed him patron of parish priests. F. D. Aug. 8 (formerly, Aug. 9).
FRANCIS TROCHU, *Curé d'Ars* (New York, Kenedy, 1928); HENRI GHÉON, *The Secret of the Curé d'Ars* (New York, Sheed, 1929).

VIATOR, ST. (378?). Once listed as a first-century bishop of Brescia, Italy, he probably was the bishop of Bergamo from 344 to 378. F. D. Dec. 14.

VIATOR, ST. (d. 390?). He was a companion of St. Justus, archbishop of Lyons, Gaul, and became a hermit with him. F. D. Oct. 21.

VICARI, HERMANN VON (1773–1868), archbishop. Born in Aulendorf, Upper Swabia, Germany, on May 13, he studied law at Vienna, and was ordained in 1797. He became a member of the Constance episcopal curia, a cathedral canon at Freiburg when the see of Constance was suppressed in 1802, vice-general in 1827, and cathedral dean in 1830. He was appointed auxiliary bishop of Freiburg and titular bishop of Macra in 1832, served as diocesan administrator in 1836 and 1842, and was made archbishop of Freiburg in 1842. He fought against Josephinism, was at one time imprisoned in his palace for his resistance to the government, encouraged learning, and reinvigorated Catholic life in his diocese. He died in Freiburg, Germany, on Apr. 14.

VICELIN, ST. (1086?–1154), bishop. Born in Hameln, he studied at the cathedral school at Paderborn, Prussia, possibly also at Laon, France, and became canon of the cathedral and head of the school at Bremen. After his ordination by St. Norbert he worked as a missionary among the Wends in Holstein, first at Lübeck, then at Wippenthorp. He founded monasteries in Neumünster, Högersdorf, and Segeberg, and was most successful in his missionary efforts until pirates sacked the area. In 1149 he was appointed bishop of Staargard (now Oldenburg), over the opposition of Frederick Barbarossa, but probably was kept from occupying his see. He was stricken with paralysis in 1152 and remained at Neuminster abbey, Lorraine, until his death there. F. D. Dec. 12.

VICENTE, GIL (1470?–1537?), dramatist. Born in Barcellos, Portugal, he studied law, and in 1502 produced at court his first play, *Visitacao*, celebrating the birth of John III. He became a leading playwright, and is considered the founder of Portuguese drama. He wrote some forty-two *autos*, tragedies, comedias, and farces (showing Spanish influence, but definitely of original merit)—fourteen in Portuguese, ten in Spanish. Outstanding are *The*

Judge of Beyra, the *Portuguese Fidalgo,* and the trilogy *Auto of the Ship of Purgatory, Auto of the Ship of the Inferno,* and *Auto of the Ship of Glory* (1517–19).

VICENZA, JOHN DE (15th century), founder. He founded the Portuguese Boni Homines, or Secular Canons of St. John the Evangelist (not related to the English institute of the same name) at Villar de Frades and absorbed the Secular Canons of St. George of Venice. The order had charge of hospitals in Portugal, and did missionary work in India and Ethiopia. John de Vicenza became bishop of Lamego, Portugal.

VICI, BL. ANTONIO (1381?–1461). Born in Stroncone, Italy, he became a Franciscan laybrother at twelve; at twenty-six he assisted Bl. Thomas of Florence in training novices at Fiesole and from 1421 to 1431 worked with the latter on a papal mission through Siena and Corsica which sought to suppress the heretical Fraticelli. His last thirty years were spent in retirement and severe austerity in retreats near Assisi, Italy. He is also known as Anthony of Stroncone. His cult was confirmed in 1687. F. D. Feb. 7.

VICO, ANTONIO (1847–1929), cardinal. Born in Agugliana, Italy, he was ordained, served as papal nuncio to Spain in 1907, was named bishop of Porto and Santa Rufina, became a cardinal in 1911, and was prefect of the Congregation of Rites. He died on Feb. 25.

VICO, FRANCESCO DE (1805–1848), astronomer. Born in Macerata, Italy, on May 19, he joined the Jesuits in Rome, taught mathematics and astronomy at the Roman College, and in 1839 was appointed director of its observatory, which he built into one of Europe's leading observatories. Forced to leave Rome by the revolution in 1848, he went to Georgetown in Washington, D.C., as director of its newly founded observatory. He set the length of the day as 23 hours, 21 minutes, 22 seconds, wrote articles for the *Memorie* of the Roman College from 1836 to 1847, *The Discovery of Six Comets, The Rotation Period of the Planet Venus,* was a charter member of the Italian Society of Science, and won scientific awards, including the Lalande Medal of the French Academy. He also wrote musical compositions, chief of which is his *Lamentations.* He died in London on Nov. 15.

VICTOR I, ST. (d. 199), pope. A native of Africa, he reigned from 189. During his pontificate a serious controversy arose over the dating of Easter. St. Jerome states that he was the first to use Latin in the liturgy. His pontificate was also disturbed by the teaching in Rome by Theodotus that Christ was no more than a man endowed with supernatural powers by the Holy Spirit. Victor is said to have died a martyr, but there is no evidence. F. D. July 28.

VICTOR II (1018?–1057), pope. Son of Count Hartwig and Countess Baliza, Gebhard, count of Dollnstein-Hirschberg, was born in Swabia, was appointed bishop of Eichstätt by Emperor Henry III, a distant relative, through the influence of his uncle, Bishop Gebhard III of Ratisbon, and though only twenty-four at the time proved himself an outstanding administrator and an excellent bishop. As count of Calvi, Tollenstein, and Hirschberg, he soon established himself as one of the emperor's most influential advisers, accompanied him to Rome for the latter's crowning in 1046, participated in the negotiations between pope and emperor at Ratisbon and Bamberg in 1052, and became regent of Bavaria for the three-year-old Henry IV in 1053. Through the influence of Hildebrand and the support of the emperor, he was elected and consecrated pope on Apr. 16, 1055 (retaining his bishopric of Eichstätt). He persuaded the emperor to restore the papal lands he had seized, and Spoleto and Camerino, reconciled him with Duchess Beatrice of Tuscany, supported ecclesiastical reform, and convoked a synod in Florence in 1055 which condemned simony and incontinence, which Victor fought throughout his pontificate. He caused King Ferdinand of Spain to recognize Henry III as emperor, attended the emperor when the latter died in 1056, acted as Henry IV's regent, and had the six-year-old boy enthroned at Aachen. He died at Arezzo, Italy, on July 28 while on a trip to settle a jurisdictional dispute between the bishops of Arezzo and Siena.

VICTOR III, BL. (1027?–1087), pope. Born in Benevento, Italy, Daufar, only son of Duke Dauferius Benevento, he became a monk at La Cava, persisted in his vocation despite family interference, and went to St. Sophia, Benevento, and other monasteries. He helped to negotiate a peace with the Normans for Pope St. Leo IX in 1053, was at the court of Victor II of Florence for a time, and became a Benedictine at Monte Cassino in 1054. Elected abbot in 1057, he rebuilt Monte Cassino and made it one of the greatest centers of learning and scholarship in Europe. He was sent to Constantinople as papal legate, but returned before reaching there when he learned of the pope's death and in 1059 was made cardinal-priest. He served as papal vicar for Campania, Apulia, and Calabria, was Gregory VII's intermediary with the Normans, and with Hugh of Cluny attempted a reconciliation between Emperor Henry IV and the pope in 1083. On Gregory's death, despite his own dilatory tactics which delayed the election a year, he was elected pope, given the name Victor, and forcibly vested on May 24, 1086, but promptly retired to Monte Cassino. Consecrated on May 9, 1087, he shuttled between Rome and the monastery until his death four months later at Monte Cassino. His brief reign was marked by civil strife, the continuing quarrel over lay investiture, and the struggle with the antipope Clement III (Guibert of Ravenna), whom he excommunicated at the Council of Benevento just before his death. His cult was confirmed in 1727 and reapproved in 1887 by Pope Leo XIII. F. D. Sept. 16.

VICTOR IV (12th century), antipope. On the death of antipope Anacletus II, Cardinal Gregory Conti was proclaimed pope as Victor IV by Roger of Sicily and the Pierleoni family in Mar. 1138. Through the influence of St. Bernard he was reconciled to Pope Innocent II, to whom he freely submitted on May 29 and renounced his office.

VICTOR IV (V) (d. 1164), antipope. Of the Roman family of the counts of Tusculum, Octavian of Monticello, Tivoli, was created a cardinal in 1138, supported Emperor Frederick Barbarossa, and on Sept. 7, 1159, was elected pope as Victor IV by a small (four or five) group of dissident cardinals in opposition to the chancellor Rolando, who had been elected Pope Alexander III. When a synod convoked by Frederick at Pavia in 1160 confirmed Victor, the pope excommunicated the emperor. Victor never achieved any real support outside of Germany, and died in Lucca, Italy, on Apr. 20.

VICTOR, ST. (d. 176?), martyr. He was put to death with his wife Corona in Syria. F. D. May 14.

VICTOR, ST. (d. 250?), martyr. See Saturninus, St.

VICTOR, ST. (d. 257), bishop and martyr. See Nemesian, St.

VICTOR, ST. (d. 258?), martyr. See Antony, St.; also, Crescentian, St.

VICTOR, ST. (d. 284), martyr. See Claudian, St.

VICTOR, ST. (d. 286?), martyr. He is one of a group of 300 members of the Theban Legion, put to death at Xanten on the Rhine River for their Christianity, and honored on Oct. 10. Another St. Victor is honored with St. Ursus, both members of the Theban Legion, at Soleur, Switzerland, on Sept. 30.

VICTOR, ST. (d. 290?), martyr. Legend says he was an officer in the Roman army at Marseilles, who was tortured and beheaded during the persecution of Maximian. His prison guards, Alexander, Felician, and Longinus, whom he converted, were slain with him. F. D. July 21.

VICTOR, ST. (d. 300?), martyr. He was slain at Braga, Portugal, during the Diocletian persecution. F. D. Apr. 12.

VICTOR, ST. (d. 304), martyr. He was put to death at Merida, Spain. SS. Antinogenes and Stercatius, listed as his brothers, were more

likely fellow martyrs with St. Theozonus of Sebaste in Armenia. F. D. July 24.

VICTOR, ST. (d. 305), martyr. See Orontius, St.; also, Valentine, St.

VICTOR, ST. (d. 310), martyr. See Sosthenes, St.

VICTOR, ST. (d. 375). He ruled as bishop of Piacenza, Italy, from about 332 until his death and was active as an opponent of Arianism. F. D. Dec. 7.

VICTOR, ST. (4th century), martyr. See Ambicus, St.; also, Domninus, St.; Marcellinus, St.

VICTOR, ST. (d. 505?). Bishop of Vita, Byzacena, Africa, he is the author of *Historia persecutionis Africanae provinciae*, a valuable contemporary account of the Arian Vandals' persecution of the orthodox Christians of northern Africa, which contains several documents of the times available in no other source. He died in exile on Sardinia. F. D. Aug. 23.

VICTOR (d. 569?). Bishop of Tunnunum in northern Africa, he was a fervent supporter of the Three Chapters, and, when he refused to heed Justinian I's edict of 544 condemning them, was imprisoned and exiled to the Balearic Islands and later to Egypt. His continued resistance led to his imprisonment in a Constantinople monastery, where he probably died. He wrote a chronicle of the world from creation to 566 and *De poenitentia*, long ascribed to St. Ambrose.

VICTOR, ST. (6th century), bishop. He was bishop of Capua, Italy, from 541 to 554, was highly respected for his learning, wrote theological treatises, among them *De cyclo paschali* (550) and *Capitula de resurrectione Domini*, commentaries on the Bible, and edited the *Codex fuldensis*, one of the oldest known manuscripts of the Vulgate, in which he substituted a harmony of the gospels in place of the four individual gospels. F. D. Oct. 17.

VICTOR (7th century). He became bishop of Carthage, North Africa, in 635, apparently the last to rule the see until the eleventh century.

VICTOR THE HERMIT, ST. (d. 610?). Born in the diocese of Troyes, France, this priest became a recluse at Arcis-sur-Aube, and was honored in a panegyric by St. Bernard, who seems to have drawn on local legends. He is also known as Vittré. F. D. Feb. 26.

VICTOR MAURUS, ST. (d. 303?), martyr. Believed to have been from Mauritania and an imperial guardsman, he was tortured as an old man and beheaded for his faith at Milan, Italy, during the persecution of Maximian. F. D. May 8.

VICTORIA, ST. (d. 250?), martyr. See Anatolia, St.

VICTORIA, ST. (d. 304), martyr. *See* Acisclus, St.; also, Saturninus, St.

VICTORIA, TOMÁS LUIZ DE (1540?–1611?), composer. Born in Avila, Castile, Spain, and often called Tommaso Ludovico da Vittoria, he went to Rome, studied under Escobedo and Morales in the papal chapel, became a master himself at the German College in 1573, and at Sant' Apollinare in 1575. He returned to Spain in 1589 and lived in Madrid until his death there on Aug. 27. He wrote motets, psalms, antiphons, and masses, particularly a *Requiem* (1605) for the Princess Maria.

VICTORIAN, ST. (d. 161?), martyr. *See* Simplicius, St.

VICTORIAN, ST. (d. 484), martyr. A wealthy citizen of Carthage, and proconsul there, he was tortured and slain during the persecution of the Christians by the Arian king of the Vandals, Huneric. Four others died with him. F. D. Mar. 23.

VICTORIAN, ST. (d. 558). Born in Italy, he served at monasteries in France and Spain, becoming abbot of Asan in Aragon. His vigorous and devout career is eulogized in a poem by Venantius Fortunatus. F. D. Jan. 12.

VICTORICUS, ST. (d. 259), martyr. A Carthaginian priest, he was imprisoned for months during the persecution of Solon, and then beheaded. A deacon named Flavian, Julian, Lucius, Montanus, Quartillosa, and the latter's husband and son were put to death with him. F. D. Feb. 24.

VICTORICUS, ST. (d. 287?), martyr. *See* Fuscian, St.

VICTORINUS, ST. (d. 99?), martyr. *See* Eutyches, St.; also, Maro, St.

VICTORINUS, ST. (d. 260), martyr. *See* Cassius, St.

VICTORINUS, ST. (d. 267?), martyr. *See* Anatolianus, St.

VICTORINUS, ST. (d. 284), martyr. *See* Claudian, St.

VICTORINUS, ST. (d. 303?), bishop and martyr. A Greek, he became bishop of Pettau, in Styria, Upper Pannonia, where he was put to death. He wrote commentaries on the Bible, and fought several heresies, though he himself was seemingly inclined toward Millenarianism. F. D. Nov. 2.

VICTORINUS, ST. (d. 305?), martyr. *See* Carpophorus, St.; also, Valentine, St.

VICTORINUS, ST. (d. 311?), martyr. *See* Pastor, St.

VICTORINUS, ST. (d. 384?), martyr. *See* Maximus, St.

VICTORINUS, ST. (d. 450?), martyr. *See* Januarius, St.

VICTORINUS, ST. (d. 543), hermit. He lived a solitary life near Ancona, Italy, with his brother, St. Severino. F. D. June 8.

VICTORINUS, ST. (d. 644). He became bishop of Como, Italy, in 628 and opposed the Lombard spread of Arianism. F. D. Sept. 5.

VICTORINUS, GAIUS MARIUS (4th century), philosopher. Born in Africa about 300, he went to Rome, where he became famed as a teacher, became a convert sometime before 361, and wrote treatises on grammar, philosophy, and theology (most of which have disappeared), commentaries on the Bible, and translations of Cicero, Aristotle, Origen, and Porphyry Chief works are *Ars grammatica*, *Liber de definitionibus*, *De syllogismis hypotheticis*, *Adversus Arium*, *De homoousio recipendo*, and *De Trinitate*.

VICTORIUS, ST. (d. 300?), martyr. *See* Claudius, St.

VICTORIUS, ST. (d. 490?). A disciple of St. Martin of Tours, he was made bishop of Le Mans. Gaul, about 453. F. D. Sept. 1.

VICTRICIUS, ST. (330?–407?), bishop. Born probably near the Scheldt River as the son of a Roman legionnaire, he became a soldier at seventeen, a convert to Christianity, and, when he refused to bear arms any longer, was tried and dismissed from the army. He became bishop of Rouen about 380 or 386; about 396 he was invited to Britain to settle differences between bishops there. Although accused of heresy by political opponents, he was exonerated and praised by Pope St. Innocent I. Victricius introduced monasticism at Rouen, Gaul, established many religious centers, and wrote *The Praise of the Saints*. F. D. Aug. 7.

VIDA, MARCO GIROLAMO (1490?–1566), poet. Born in Cremona, Italy, he studied at Mantua, Padua, and Bologna, and became a priest. He went to Rome, where he became a canon of the Lateran and was patronized by Pope Leo X, became noted for the elegant Latin of his poetry, and in 1527 published *De arte poetica*, describing the humanist concept of poetry. He was appointed prior of St. Sylvester at Frascati by Pope Leo X to allow him to write an epic poem on Christ, and in 1535 published *Christias*, on the life of Christ and the founding and spread of Christianity. His chief other poems are *Bombices* (on silkworms) and *Scacchiae ludus* (on chess). Pope Clement VII appointed him apostolic prothonotary and in 1562 bishop of Alba, Italy, where he died on Sept. 27.

VIDAL Y BARRAQUER, FRANÇOIS D'ASSISE (1868–1943), cardinal. Born in Cambrils, Spain, he was ordained in 1899, named titular bishop of Pentacomia in 1913, administrator of Solsona in 1914, archbishop of Tarragona in 1919, and cardinal-priest in 1921. He opposed the falangists and the Franco government and left Spain in 1937 to live in Italy. He died in Fribourg, Switzerland, on Sept. 14.

VIDAL, PEIRE (13th century), poet. Son of

a furrier in Toulouse, France, he became a troubadour in the courts of France and Spain, was in the service of Viscount Barral of Marseilles, lived for a while in the Near East, may have gone on the crusades with the marquis of Montferrat, and may have served at the court of the king of Hungary. He died very early in the thirteenth century.

VIEIRA, ANTONIO (1608–1697), diplomat. Born in Lisbon, Portugal, on Feb. 6, he was brought to Brazil as a child, joined the Jesuits in Bahia in 1623, and was ordained in 1635. He became noted for his patriotic sermons during the Dutch war with Brazil in 1638–40, was one of those sent to Portugal in 1641 to assure the new King John IV of Brazil's loyalty after Portugal's successful revolt against Spain in 1640, and became a trusted adviser of the king, the infante's teacher, court preacher, and a member of the royal council. He denounced the Portuguese Inquisition, worked in the navy and war departments, where he helped plan the defensive war against Spain, reorganized the exchequer and the Brazilian Trade Company, and encouraged the restoration of Portugal's commerce. He served on diplomatic missions to Paris, The Hague, London, and Rome, then returned in 1652 to the Maranhão and Tocantins Indians in Brazil. He incurred the hatred of the slaveowners and traders for his denunciations of their excesses and cruelties to the Indians, successfully pleaded for the Indians at Lisbon in 1654, and returned to Brazil the next year. He worked among the Indians until 1661, when the slaveowners succeeded in having him recalled to Portugal. There he found an unfriendly King Alfonso II and enemies at court, who denounced him to the Inquisition for alleged doctrinal errors. He was imprisoned from 1665 to 1667, when the new King Pedro II reversed the Inquisition's decision. He spent 1669–75 in Rome, was Pope Clement X's preacher and a close friend of Christina of Sweden, returned to Brazil in 1681, and there faced another series of false accusations, including a charge of murder, all of which were disproved although several years after his death in Bahia, where he had become provincial, on July 18. His sermons were published in sixteen volumes, his letters in three volumes, and he also wrote *Historia do Futuro* (1718).

VIEL, FRANÇOIS ÉTIENNE BERNAR ALEXANDRE (1736–1821). Born in New Orleans on Oct. 31, son of a French physician who immigrated to Louisiana, he was sent in 1747 to study at the Oratorians' Royal Academy in Juilly, France, joined the Oratorians, and was ordained, the first native-born Louisianan to become a priest. He taught at Soissons and Le Mans, returned to the academy in Juilly in 1760, and became rector in 1776. He

returned to Louisiana when the French Revolution closed Oratorian institutions in 1792, served as parish priest of the Attakapas for the next twenty years, and returned to France in 1812 to help re-establish his order and teach at Juilly, where he died on Dec. 16. He translated several works from French to Latin (he was noted for his Latin verse), including Fénelon's *Télémaque* and *Le Voyage de la Grande Chartreuse.*

VIEL, NICOLAS (d. 1625), martyr. A French priest who was sent to Canada in 1623, he devoted himself to the Hurons, and was drowned by a group of Hurons in Rivière des Prairies on a trip back to Quebec.

VIEL, BL. VICTORIA EULALIA JACQUELINE (1815–1877). Born in Val-Vacher, Normandy, the eighth child of a farming family, she entered the convent of the Sisterhood of Christian Schools at seventeen as Sr. Placida. She trained under Mother Mary Postel, the foundress, became mistress of novices, and in 1846 was chosen as the second superior of the order. During her term she built many orphanages, nurseries, schools for the poor, and opened more than fifty new convents. She was beatified in 1951. F. D. Mar. 4.

VIERTHALER, FRANZ MICHAEL (1758–1827), educator. Born in Mauerkirchen, Upper Austria, on Sept. 25, he studied law at Salzburg, taught in the Virgilian College for Nobles there in 1783, and attracted favorable attention with the publication of the first of his seven-volume *Philosophische Geschichte der Menschheit* (1787–1819). He was appointed director of the Salzburg seminary for teachers in 1790, and became a leading educator, advocating practical training in teaching, broadening the teaching of natural sciences, and opposing corporal punishment of pupils. He became court librarian in 1796, was editor of the *Salzburger Staatszeitung* in 1799–1806 and of the *Salzburger Literaturzeitung* in 1800–2, and was appointed supervisor of the public schools in the duchy of Salzburg in 1803. He was appointed director of the orphan asylum in Vienna in 1807, and died there on Oct. 3. He wrote several pedagogical treatises, chief of which was *Elemente der Methodik und Pädagogik* (1791).

VIETE, FRANÇOIS (1540–1603), mathematician. Born in Fontenay-le-Comte, Poitou, France, he studied law at Poitiers, became a leading lawyer (including Mary Stuart as a client), lost his practice as a result of the religious wars, and tutored and served the Huguenot faction at La Rochelle. He later was a lawyer in Paris, a parliamentary councilor at Rennes, and wrote widely on the interrelationship of algebra and geometry and trigonometry. He popularized the use of letters as symbols in mathematics. He returned to the

Church before his death in Paris on Dec. 13. His *Opera mathematica* was published in Leyden, Holland, in 1646.

VIGER, DENIS BENJAMIN (1774-1861), journalist. Born in Montreal, Canada, on Aug. 19, he studied at the Sulpician College there, became a member of the bar, and was elected to parliament in 1808, 1810, 1814, and 1827. He went to London in 1828 and 1830 to defend French Canadian interests before the English parliament, was a member of the upper house in 1830, and of the Canadian parliament after the union of the provinces, in 1841 and 1845. As a member of the Liberal party he helped found the newspapers *La Minerva* and *L'Aurore des Canadas*, and wrote articles on Canadian politics. He died in Montreal on Feb. 13.

VIGER, JACQUES (1787-1858), historian. Born in Montreal, Canada, he studied at the Sulpician College there, served in the War of 1812 against the Americans, was elected first mayor of Montreal in 1833, became a leading archaeologist, compiling the twenty-eight-volume *Sabretache* of maps, portraits, and documents, and founded the Historical Society of Montreal. He died there on Dec. 12.

VIGILIUS (d. 555), pope. A native of Rome, he became a deacon, and was chosen by Pope Boniface II as his successor in 531, but opposition to the plan of a pope naming his successor caused Boniface to withdraw his nomination. He served as papal representative at Constantinople for Pope Agapetus I, became an ally of Empress Theodora, who desired his support of Monophysitism and who provided funds to aid him in his quest for the papacy, and in 536 returned to Rome at hearing of Pope Agapetus' death. When he found that Silverius had been elected pope he enlisted the support of Belisarius, commander of the Byzantine forces in Rome, and was declared elected pope, and consecrated on Mar. 29, 537. Silverius was exiled on the island of Palmaria and, on his death of mistreatment there, Vigilius was recognized as pope by the Roman clergy. He soon denounced the Monophysite heresy and in letters to Emperor Justinian and Patriarch Menas of Constantinople he supported Ephesus and Chalcedon. In 544 he was faced with the Three Chapters controversy, when Justinian's edict condemning the Three Chapters was construed in the West as a condemnation of the decrees of the Council of Chalcedon. When Vigilius refused to support the decree, he was brought to Constantinople by Justinian's men in 546 or early 547, and finally, after seven years' imprisonment in Constantinople, acknowledged the decrees. He died at Syracuse, Sicily, on the return journey on June 7.

VIGILIUS, ST. (d. 405), bishop and martyr.

Born in Trent, Italy (of which he is patron), and educated at Athens, he became bishop of his native city in 385, fought usury, dispensed charity, and converted many pagans. When three of his missioners, including St. Alexander, were slain, he eulogized them in letters to SS. Simplician and John Chrysostom. Vigilius was stoned to death when he overthrew a statue of Saturn in Rendena, Italy. F. D. June 26.

VIGILIUS (5th century). Bishop of Tapsus, Byzacena, Africa, he is known to have attended Vandal King Huneric's council in Carthage in 484 and to have written treatises against the heretics, notably *Contra Arianos*, *Contra Sabellianos*, and *Contra Eutychetem*, but was not the author of *Quicumque* long attributed to him. It is believed he went to Constantinople when the Vandals exiled Catholic bishops from Africa.

VIGILIUS, ST. (6th century). He was bishop of Brescia, Lombardy, as late as 506. F. D. Sept. 26.

VIGILIUS, ST. (d. 685), bishop and martyr. He succeeded St. Palladius as bishop of Auxerre, France, in 662 and was put to death near Compiègne on orders of Waraton, mayor of the palace. F. D. Mar. 11.

VIGNE, RAYMUND DELLE. *See* Raymund of Capua, Bl.

VIGNOLA, GIACOMO BAROCCHIO DA (1507-1573), architect. Giacomo Barocchio (or Barozzio) was born in Vignola, Italy, on Oct. 1, studied under Michelangelo, and given patronage by Pope Julius, who appointed him papal architect in 1550 and commissioned him to construct the Villa Giulia. In 1564 he succeeded Michelangelo as architect of St. Peter's and carried on his work. Other works are the Farnese castle in Viterbo, the Jesuit church (the Gèsu) and Sant' Andrea church in Rome and the Church of the Angels in Assisi. He wrote two influential books on architecture; *Regole delle cinque ordini d'architettura* (1563) is still used. He died in Rome on July 7.

VIGOR, ST. (d. 537?), bishop. Born in Artois, France, he was educated by St. Vedast in Assisi. He wrote two influential books on arjections, and in 513 became bishop of Bayeux and erased the last vestiges of paganism in his see. F. D. Nov. 1.

VIGOR, SIMON (1515?-1575), bishop. Born in Évreux, Normandy, France, son of a court physician, he studied at Paris and Navarre College, became rector of the University of Paris in 1540, received his doctorate in theology in 1545, and was appointed penitentiary of Évreux. He became a leading controversialist for the Catholic cause, was a theologian from the Sorbonne at the Council of Trent in 1563, became pastor of St. Paul de Paris, the royal parish, and in 1572 was appointed bishop of Narbonne. He died in Carcassonne, France, on Nov. 1.

VIGOUROUX, FULCRAIN GRÉGOIRE (1837–1915), scholar. Born in Nant d'Aveyron, France, on Feb. 13, he studied in Rodez and Paris, was ordained in 1861, and became a Sulpician. He taught philosophy in Autun and Issy and exegesis at the seminary and L'Institut Catholique in Paris. He was editor of the five-volume *Dictionnaire de la Bible* (1895–1913) and, with Bacuez, wrote *Manuel des sciences bibliques*. He wrote on saints' lives and rationalism, scripture and archaeology, prepared an eight-volume polyglot bible, and in 1903 was named consultor of the Vatican Biblical Commission. He died in Issy, France, on Feb. 21.

VIGRI, CATHERINE DE. *See* Catherine de Vigri, St.

VILLAGRAN, FRANCISCO DE (1507?–1563), governor. Born in Astorga, León, Spain, he served Valdivia in Peru and on the conquest of Chile in 1540–45, became governor when Valdivia was slain about 1554, was replaced in 1557 and restored in 1561, and extended Spanish imperialism beyond the Andes.

VILLALOBOS, FRANCISCO LÓPEZ DE (1473?–1549?), physician. Born in Toledo, Spain, of a Jewish family, he became a doctor, a convert, and court physician to Ferdinand and to Charles V. He also wrote *Tratado de los tres grandes vicios*, some poetry, and a translation of the *Amphitruo* of Plautus.

VILLANI, GIOVANNI (1275?–1348), historian. A wealthy Florentine merchant, he became influential in civic affairs as a Guelph, served on the staff of the mint, was one of the hostages given to Ferrara in 1341 as security for the purchase price of Lucca, and as a member of the Peruzzi company was imprisoned when its bank failed in 1346. He is known for his history of Florence from the earliest times to 1348. It was continued by his brother Matteo and by the latter's son, Filippo. He died of the plague in Florence.

VILLANOVANUS, ARNALDUS (1235–1313?), physician. Named after his native town, which may have been Villanueva, Catalonia, Spain, or Villeneuve-Loubet, Grasse, France, he studied under John Casamila in Barcelona, taught medicine at Barcelona, Montpellier, and Paris, and became so noted for his knowledge of alchemy and pharmacology that he treated Popes Innocent V, Boniface VIII, Benedict XI and Clement V, and at various times was personal physician to Pedro III and James II of Aragon and Frederick II of Sicily. He was banished by the Inquisition in Spain and in Paris for his often-heretical writings, which contain numerous theological errors, but did much to instil scientific method in medi-

cine and pharmacology. He died at sea near Genoa, Italy.

VILLANUS, ST. (d. 1237), bishop. Born in Gubbio, Italy, he became a Benedictine monk at Fonte Vellana, and was appointed bishop of Gubbio in 1206. F. D. May 7.

VILLEFRANCHE, JACQUES MELCHIOR (1829–1904), author. Born in Couzon-sur-Sâone, France, on Dec. 17, he studied in Largentière, entered the telegraph service as a youth, and served in it until 1875, when he left to edit *Journal de l'Ain*, and to write. He wrote *Pius IX* (1847), *Vie de Dom Bosco* (1887), *Histoire de Napoléon III* (1896), and several novels, most popular of which is *Cinéas* (1869). He died in Bourg, France, on May 10.

VILLEHARDOUIN, GEOFFROI DE. *See* Geoffrey de Villhardouin.

VILLENEUVE, JEAN MARIE RODRIGUE (1883–1947), cardinal. Born in Montreal on Nov. 2, he joined the Oblates of Mary Immaculate in 1901, and was ordained in 1907. He served as master of novices from 1920 to 1930, when he was appointed first bishop of Gravelbourg, Saskatchewan, and was elected archbishop of Quebec on Dec. 28, 1931. He launched a broad program of Catholic Action, was active in social movements, especially labor and colonization, built a new seminary, was active in raising the standards of higher education in Canada, and supported Canadian participation in World War I despite the general opposition of the French populace. He was created a cardinal in 1933, and died near Los Angeles, California, on Jan. 17.

VILLENEUVE, BL. ROSELINE DE (d. 1329). Daughter of Baron des Arcs, she became a Carthusian nun at Bertrand at twenty-five, prioress of Celle Roubaud in Provence, and had supernatural gifts. Her cult was confirmed in 1851. F. D. Jan. 17.

VILLENEUVE-BARCEMENT, JEAN PAUL ALBAN DE (1784–1850). Born in St. Auban, Var, France, on Aug. 8, he became a councilor of state in 1828, refused to take the oath to Louis Philippe's government in 1830, served as deputy in 1830–31 and 1840–48, and in 1832 was appointed royal commissary in the Var. He was active in promoting social-reform laws to care for paupers and orphans, fought to limit child labor, for a living wage and legal protection for laborers, and against exploitation of the poor by the wealthy. He wrote *Économie politique chrétienne* (1834), *Histoire de l'économie politique* (1841), and *Le Livre des affligés* (1841), and was appointed a member of the Académie des Sciences Morales in 1848. He died in Paris on June 8.

VILLERMÉ, LOUIS RENÉ (1782–1863), economist. Born in Paris on Mar. 10, he studied medicine but was soon attracted to social studies. He wrote treatises on the evils of the penal system, founded the *Annales d'Hygiene,* and wrote on child labor and health hazards in industry. He was elected to the Académie des Sciences Morales about 1833. Chief of his works are *Table de l'état physique et moral des ouvriers* (1840), *Les associations ouvrières* (1849), and *Les cités ouvrières* (1850). He died in Paris on Nov. 16.

VILLICUS, ST. (d. 568). He was bishop of Metz, Gaul, from 543 until his death. F. D. Apr. 17.

VIMIN, ST. (6th century). He is said to have been a Scottish bishop, who founded the monastery of Holywood. F. D. Jan. 21.

VINCENT, ST. (d. 192), martyr. *See* Eusebius, St.

VINCENT, ST. (d. 258), martyr. *See* Sixtus II, St.

VINCENT, ST. (d. 292?), martyr. He is said to have been a deacon in Gascony, beheaded at Agen for interfering with a Druid feast. F. D. June 9.

VINCENT, ST. (d. 303), bishop and martyr. The first bishop of Bevagna, in Umbria, Italy, he was put to death during the persecution of Diocletian. F. D. June 6.

VINCENT, ST. (d. 304), martyr. He is said to have been put to death at Collioure, Languedoc, Gaul, during the Diocletian persecution. F. D. Apr. 19.

VINCENT, ST. (d. 305), martyr. *See* Orontius, St.

VINCENT, ST. (d. 380), bishop. An African who succeeded St. Domninus as bishop of Digne, France, he is patron of that city and diocese. F. D. Jan. 22.

VINCENT, ST. (5th century?), martyr. He was first bishop of Dax, Gascony, and was slain with St. Laetus, his deacon, also of Xaintes. The Roman Martyrology erroneously listed them as martyrs in the neighborhood of Toledo, Spain. F. D. Sept. 1.

VINCENT, ST. (d. 546?), bishop. He was appointed bishop of Troyes, France, about ten years before his death. F. D. Feb. 4.

VINCENT, ST. (d. 554?), martyr. He was abbot of the monastery of St. Claudius in León, Spain, and was slain by Arians with his prior, St. Ramirus. The event may have occurred as late as 630. F. D. Sept. 11.

VINCENT, ST. (6th century?), martyr. *See* Ramirus, St.

VINCENT, BL. (d. 1504). Born in Aquila, Italy, he became a Franciscan laybrother and was noted for his supernatural gifts. His cult was approved in 1785. F. D. Aug. 7.

VINCENT, LOUIS HUGUES (1872–1960), archaeologist. Born in St. Alban de Varaize, France, on Aug. 31, he became a Dominican at Lyons, and was sent in 1891 to study at St. Étienne, Jerusalem. He worked there with Fr. Lagrange and spent his last fifty years teaching at L'École Biblique in Jerusalem. He wrote on Palestinian archaeology; *Jérusalem nouvelle* (1914–22), on the period of Christian beginning to the era of the crusades; *Jérusalem de l'ancien testament* (1954–56); and, with Fr. Abel, a series of treatises on the shrines of the area. He died in Jerusalem on Dec. 30.

VINCENT OF BEAUVAIS (1190?–1264?). After joining the Dominicans in Paris about 1218, he spent his life at the monastery of Royaumont, near Paris, most of it devoted to writing a monumental Latin encyclopedia of human knowledge, which drew on some 450 authors, *Speculum majus.* He wrote three of its parts: *Nature,* following the order of the six days of creation in Genesis; *Instruction,* covering knowledge from the liberal to mechanic arts; and *History,* the story of man since Adam; a fourth part, *Morals,* is of unknown authorship. He was tutor to Louis IX's sons.

VINCENT THE DEACON, ST. (d. 304), martyr. Born in Huesca, Spain, he served St. Valerius as a deacon before he was put to death at Valencia during the Diocletian persecution. He is a patron of vineyard workers. F. D. Jan. 22.

VINCENT FERRER, ST. (1350?–1419). Born in Valencia, Spain, on Jan. 23, he became a Dominican at seventeen, taught philosophy at the University of Lérida at twenty-one, and was then sent to preach through Spain, France, Switzerland, the Netherlands, and northern Italy. His success with sinners and converts was great, he cleared many cities of vice, and mended many major quarrels. His greatest achievement was bringing the great Western schism to an end. St. Vincent had supported Clement VII, who ruled at Avignon, over Urban VI of Rome, and he became confessor to Clement's successor, Peter de Luna, who took the name Benedict XIII. He left the French papal court when he could not arrange a meeting or compromise between the rival pontiffs. The situation prevailed from 1378 to 1414, when Benedict XIII refused to resign, as two others did, to permit a new election. On Vincent's advice, King Ferdinand deposed Peter de Luna, and the scandalous quarrel came to an end. Although weakened by age, Vincent spoke with vigor and influence up to his death at seventy in Vannes, Brittany. He was canonized in 1455. F. D. Apr. 5.

H. GHÉON, *St. Vincent Ferrer,* trans. F. Sheed (New York, Sheed, 1939).

VINCENT OF LÉRINS, ST. (d. 450?). Possibly a soldier during an era of barbarian invasions, he became a monk at the abbey of Lérins, off the coast of France. Ordained, he wrote his *Commonitories* about 434, soon after the Council of Ephesus (431); they were brief memoranda on the tradition, orthodoxy, and universality of the Church; on faith, divine authority, contemporary heresy; on progress which respects the orbit within which a doctrine grows; on the work of councils, and the spiritual supremacy of the pope. A Vincent was attacked by Prosper of Aquitaine and others for alleged semi-Pelagian views on grace and free will, but there is no evidence that this Vincent of Lérins is the person referred to. F. D. May 24.

VINCENT MADELGARIUS, ST. (615?-687?). Born in Strepy les Binche, Hainault, he married, about 635, St. Waldetrudis (their four children—Landericus, Dentelinus, Madalberta, and Aldetrudis—became saints). He probably went to Ireland on a mission for King Dagobert I, brought back several missionary monks, and about 643 entered a Benedictine monastery and his wife became a nun. He took the name Vincent and founded Haumont in 653; later, he established Soignies, Belgium, where he died on July 14. F. D. Sept. 20.

VINCENT DE PAUL, ST. (1580?-1660), founder. He was born in Pouy, Gascony, of a peasant family, studied at Dax, Saragossa, and Toulouse, and was ordained at twenty. In 1605 he is said to have been captured by pirates and enslaved for two years in Barbary. On his escape he continued his studies in Rome, then became a chaplain to Queen Margaret of Valois in Paris. In 1611 he met St. Pierre de Bérulle, founder of the Oratorians, which Vincent joined, who recommended him as tutor to the children of Philippe Emmanuel de Gondi, count of Joigny. His work with the poor and his sermons at Folleville and as pastor at Châtillon-les-Dombes attracted attention. In 1618 he met St. Francis de Sales at Paris and was appointed ecclesiastical superior of the Visitation; in 1619 he became chaplain to the galley slaves waiting to be shipped from the capital. In 1625 he founded a congregation of missionaries, endowed by the de Gondis and devoted to the evangelization of country people, whose low spiritual state he had deplored since 1612, as well as to the inspiriting of a lazy clergy. The Congregation of the Missions (sometimes called Lazarists from the name of one of their early houses, St. Lazare, or Vincentians, after their founder) soon spread through Europe. Vincent also established parish confraternities to help the poor and from them, in 1633, with St. Louise de Marillac, he founded the Sisters of Charity. He established hospitals, wrote a series of spiritual rules for clerics and laity, directed the setting up of foundling homes, and labored to better the education of priests by opening new seminaries. He ransomed more than 1000 Christian slaves in northern Africa, became influential with Anne of Austria, regent until Louis XIV became king, opposed Jansenism, and sought to relieve distress during the civil war unleashed by Cardinal Mazarin's policies, which he had opposed. Though seriously ill in his last years, he continued his work until his death in Paris on Sept. 27. He was canonized by Pope Clement XII in 1737 and declared patron of all charitable groups by Pope Leo XIII. F. D. July 19.

JEAN CALVET, *St. Vincent de Paul*, trans. L. C. Sheppard (New York, McKay, 1951); THEODORE MAYNARD, *Apostle of Charity* (New York, Dial, 1939).

VINCENT OF ST. JOSEPH, BL. (1596-1622), martyr. Born in Ayamonte, Seville, Spain, he went to Mexico, became a Franciscan laybrother in 1615, and went to the Philippines in 1618 and to Japan in 1619. He was arrested and caged for two years, then burned to death at Nagasaki. He was beatified in 1867. F. D. Sept. 10.

VINCENT OF SARAGOSSA, ST. (d. 304), martyr. Born in Huesca, Spain, and taught and ordained by St. Valerius, he was seized with his master during a persecution. Valerius was exiled, but Vincent was subjected to extended and fatal tortures at Valencia, Spain, by Dacian, the Roman governor. His sufferings were described by St. Leo and Prudentius and praised by St. Augustine. F. D. Jan. 22.

VINCENZA. *See* Gerosa, St. Catherine.

VINCI, LEONARDO DA. *See* Leonardo da Vinci.

VINCIOLI, BL. ALESSANDRO (d. 1363), bishop. Born in Perugia, Italy, he became an adviser to Pope John XXII, was appointed bishop of Nocera, and died at Sassoferrato, Italy. F. D. May 3.

VINDEMIALIS, ST. (d. 485?), martyr. *See* Eugene, St.

VINDICIAN, ST. (632?-712), bishop. Born in Bullecourt, France, he became bishop of Cambrai about 669 and was successful in conversions and the establishment of monasteries. He was outspoken in condemning evil, including that of King Thierry for his apparent complacency over the murder of St. Leger. F. D. Mar. 11.

VINDONIUS, ST. (5th century), bishop. *See* Priscus, St.

VIOLLET-LE-DUC, EUGÈNE EMMANUEL (1814-1879), architect. Born in Paris on Jan. 27, he studied architecture under Leclère and at Collège Bourbon, and in 1840 was appointed inspector at Ste. Chapelle. He was appointed inspector general of ancient buildings in France in 1853 and professor at L'École des Beaux-Arts in 1863. He became the leading proponent of the Gothic revival in France and internationally known for his restoration of historic French buildings. Among his better-known restorations are the Ste. Chapelle and Notre Dame in Paris with J. B.

Lassus in 1845–55, the cathedrals of Amiens and Laon, the château of Pierrefonds, and the walls of Carcassonne. He commanded a corps of engineers during the siege of Paris in 1870–71, was elected deputy in 1874, and wrote numerous books, chief of which are the ten-volume *Dictionnaire raisonné de l'architecture française du XI au XVI siècle* (1854–69), *Dictionnaire raisonné du mobilier français, Histoire d'un hôtel de ville et d'une cathédrale, L'Art russe,* as well as numerous monograms on the various structures he restored. He died in Lausanne, Switzerland, on Sept. 17.

VIOTTI, GIOVANNI BATTISTA (1753–1824), violinist. Born in Fontanetto, Piedmont, Italy, on May 23, he studied the violin under Giovannini and then with Pugnani in Turin, accompanied the latter on a tour in 1780–81, and made his successful public debut in Paris in 1782. He became a member of Marie Antoinette's court in 1784, fled to London from the French Revolution in 1792, and became leader at the King's Theatre. He was compelled to leave London in 1798, when falsely accused of conspiring against the French Directory, went to Germany until allowed to return to England in 1801, had an unsuccessful career as a wine merchant in London, returned to his musical career in 1813, and became director of the French Opera from 1819 to 1821, but returned to London where he died on Mar. 3. He composed some twenty-nine violin concertos and much chamber music.

VIRGIL, ST. (d. 610?), archbishop. Born in Gascony and educated on Lérins, near Cannes, Gaul, he became a monk there and was vicar apostolic for Pope St. Gregory the Great to the kingdom of Childebert II, and as archbishop of Arles probably consecrated St. Augustine as bishop of Canterbury. F. D. Mar. 5.

VIRGIL, ST. (d. 784), bishop. An Irish monk, he went to Palestine in 743, spent two years in France, was made abbot of St. Peter's at Salzburg, Austria, and archbishop of that city about 765. He rebuilt the cathedral, sent missioners to Carinthia, and became known as the Apostle of the Slovenes. He was canonized in 1233 by Pope Gregory IX. F. D. Nov. 27.

VISCHER, PETER (1455–1529), sculptor. Born in Nuremberg, Germany, he began his career as an assistant to his father, a bronze founder, and eventually set up his own establishment in Nuremberg. He executed the sepulcher monument to St. Sebaldus in Nuremberg, on which he labored from 1505 to 1519, statues of Theodoric and Arthur in Innsbruck for Emperor Maximilian I in 1413, the tomb of Archbishop Ernst in Magdeburg and the three memorial tablets of the bishop of Bamberg. Five sons—Peter (1487?–1528), Her-

mann (1486?–1516), Paul, Jakob, and Hans—worked with him and much of his work, particularly of his later period, was executed either with them or possibly by them. Peter died in Nuremberg on Jan. 7.

VISCONTI, GIOVANNI BATTISTA (1712–1784), archaeologist. Born in Sarzana, Italy, he lived in Rome, succeeded Winckelmann as prefect of antiquities, and collected examples of antique art for the Vatican at the request of Popes Clement XIV and Pius VI. His son Ennio Quirino Visconti (1751–1818) helped him in the selection of engravings for the first volume of *Museo Pio-Clementino*.

VISCONTI, IGNATIUS (1682–1755). Born in Milan, Italy, he became a Jesuit, was ordained. and in 1751 became sixteenth general of his Society. He had difficulties in Martinique, where Fr. Antoine de la Valette was accused of trading, recalled to explain the situation, and later sent back to his mission; tension also increased in Portugal under pressures from Pombal. Fr. Visconti died on May 4.

VISDELOU, CLAUDE DE (1656–1737), bishop. Born in Château de Bienassis, Pléneuf, Brittany, France, on Aug. 12, he joined the Jesuits in 1673, and in 1687 was sent to China. He became known for his wide knowledge of Chinese culture and literature, was the only Jesuit in favor of the prohibition of the "Chinese rites" in 1705, and was appointed vicar apostolic of Kwei-chou and titular bishop of Claudiopolis by the papal legate to China. When his superiors opposed the appointment on the grounds that he had no papal dispensation to accept such a position, he was secretly consecrated bishop in Macao in 1709, and then retired to the French Capuchin monastery in Pondicherry, India, where he remained until his death on Nov. 11. He devoted his retirement to studying Chinese literature and writing on Chinese subjects.

VISSIA, ST. (d. 250?), martyr. She was slain at Fermo, Italy, during the Decian persecution. F. D. Apr. 12.

VIT. VINCENZO DE (1810–1892), scholar. Born in Mestrina, Italy, on July 10, he studied at Padua, was ordained in 1836, and was appointed librarian of the Accademia dei Concordia in Rovigo and canon of the cathedral in 1844. He entered Rosmini's Institute of Charity in Stresa, and devoted himself to a revision of Forcellini's *Lexicon totius latinitatis,* which was completed in 1879. His own Works appeared in eleven volumes in 1875–92. He died at Domo d'Ossola, Italy, on Aug. 17.

VITALIAN, ST. (d. 672), pope. Born in Segni, Italy, he began his pontificate on July 30, 557. It was disturbed by the strength of the Monothelite heresy in the East and by Emperor Constans II, but marked happily by the end of the quarrel between the English and Irish bishops over the Easter feast. Vitalian conferred with St. Benedict Biscop in Rome and sent SS. Adrian and Theodore of Tarsus to England to strengthen the Church there. F. D. Jan. 27.

VITALIAN, ST. (d. 776). He was bishop of Osimo, Italy; another of the same name was bishop of Capua at an indefinite date. F. D. July 16.

VITALINI, BONIFAZIO (1320?–1388?), jurist. Born in Mantua, Italy, he studied law at Padua, practiced criminal law in Mantua, then was ordained. He was appointed rector of San Martinio de' Tribesi in Mantua in 1350, professor at Avignon in 1352, prothonotary apostolic, fiscal of the Roman curia, and auditor of the sacred palace. He wrote *Super maleficiis* (1505) and a commentary on the Clementines (1522), and died in Avignon, France, sometime after 1388.

VITALIS, ST. (d. 150), martyr. *See* Alexander, St.

VITALIS, ST. (2nd century?), martyr. *See* Valeria, St.

VITALIS, ST. (d. 250), martyr. *See* Caesarius, St.; also, Epictetus, St.

VITALIS, ST. (d. 285?), martyr. *See* Ariston, St.

VITALIS, ST. (d. 287?), martyr. *See* Maurice, St.

VITALIS, ST. (d. 303?), martyr. *See* Honoratus, St.

VITALIS, ST. (d. 304?), martyr. Legend calls him a slave whose courage under torture so impressed his master, Agricola, that the latter became a convert. Both were slain at Bologna, Italy, probably during the persecution of Diocletian. F. D. Nov. 4.

VITALIS OF SAVIGNY, BL. (1063?–1122). Chaplain of Count Robert of Mortain, half-brother of William the Conqueror, he left his service to live as a hermit for seventeen years. In 1112 he founded the abbey of Savigny in Normandy (from which many monasteries in France and England were founded), traveled widely, achieved fame as a great preacher, and died on a visit to England. F. D. Sept. 16 (sometimes, Jan. 7).

VITELLESCHI, MUZIO (1563–1645). Born in Rome on Dec. 2, he joined the Jesuits in 1583, taught, was appointed rector of the English College in 1593, served as provincial of the Rome and Naples provinces, and in 1615 was elected general of the Jesuits. He extended the missionary activities of his Society, was involved in disputes with France over the supremacy of the pope, and established the English mission as a province. He died in Rome on Feb. 9.

VITI, TIMOTEO (1467–1524), painter. Born

in Ferrara, Italy, he studied with Francia at Bologna in 1490–95 and with Costa, settled in Urbino, where the duke became his patron and where he served as chief magistrate, and taught Raphael. The effective line, balance, and charm of Raphael often caused confusion as to authorship; *Madonna with Two Saints*, formerly attributed to the pupil, is Viti's. The latter also did an *Annunciation, St. Margaret, St. Apollonia,* and the altarpiece in the Urbino cathedral. He broke from his own teachers and showed more individualism after 1504 in a Magdalen in the Pinatoteca, Bologna, and altarpieces in Cagli and the cathedral in Gubbio.

VITONUS, ST. (d. 525?), bishop. Also known as Vanne, he was appointed bishop of Verdun, France, about 500 after his aged uncle, St. Euspicius, refused the see from Clovis, and in the twenty-five years of his episcopate he is reputed to have made his diocese entirely Catholic. He is also said to have founded a college outside Verdun which became Benedictine in 952, was renamed St. Vanne, and in 1600 became the center of the Congregation of St. Vanne and St. Hydulphe. F. D. Nov. 9.

VITORES, ST. (d. 950?), martyr. He was a priest at Cerezo, near Burgos, Spain, who was beheaded by the Moors to whom he was preaching. F. D. Aug. 26.

VITTORIA, FRANCISCO DI. *See* Francis of Vittoria.

VITTORIA, TOMMASO LUDOVICO DA. *See* Victoria, Tomás Luiz de.

VITTORINO DA FELTRE (1378–1446), educator. Born in Feltre, Italy, Vittorino de' Rambaldoni studied and received his doctorate at Padua, became known for his knowledge of mathematics and Greek, and then opened a private school in Padua. He was appointed to the chair of rhetoric at the University of Padua in 1422, resigned, and opened a school at Venice in 1423, and a school at the Mantuan court in 1425, which became famed for its excellence. Among his students were George of Trebizond and Theodore Gaza. He died in Mantua, Italy.

VITTRÉ. *See* Victor the Hermit.

VITUS, ST. (d. 300?), martyr. He, his tutor, Modestus, and his nurse, Crescentia, were slain at Lucania, Italy. A great number of legends grew up, especially in France and Germany, where alleged relics of St. Vitus were taken. He came to be regarded as protector against epilepsy, madness, bites from snakes and dogs, nervous diseases, and was a patron of actors and dancers. The origin of such devotion may be that strolling players were accustomed to rest in chapels dedicated to him. F. D. June 15.

VIVA, DOMENICO (1648–1726), author. Born in Lecce, Italy, on Oct. 19, he joined the

Jesuits in 1663, taught the humanities, Greek, philosophy and theology, became rector of the College of Naples in 1711, then served as provincial of the Naples province. He wrote several treatises, chief of which was *Trutina theologica damnatarum thesium* (1708). He died on July 5.

VIVALDI, ANTONIO (1675?-1741), composer. Born in Venice, he studied violin with his father, was ordained, served in Darmstadt, and in 1713 was appointed director of the Conservatorio della Pietà, Venice. He produced thirty-nine operas there and wrote many sonatas and concerti for the violin. Many formerly unknown works were unearthed in the twentieth century. He died in Vienna and was buried on July 28.

VIVALDO, BL. (d. 1300). A native of San Gemignano, Italy, he was a Franciscan tertiary who nursed St. Bartolo through twenty years of leprosy, then lived as a hermit in Tuscany. F. D. May 11.

VIVARINI, ALVISE (1446?-1503?), painter. Son of Antonio, he studied painting under his uncle, Bortolommeo, worked with Bellini either as a pupil or studio foreman, and was granted the title of depentor by the grand council in 1492. Among his works are a polytych in the Franciscan monastery of Montefiorentino, *St. Ambrose Enthroned* in the Frari church in Venice, *Madonna and Saints*, and *Resurrection* in San Giovanni in Bragora. Among his pupils were Cima, Lotto, Montegna, and Bonsignori.

VIVARINI, ANTONIO (1415?-1476?), painter. Probably born in Murano, Italy, and often called Antonio da Murano, he was probably influenced by Gentile da Fabriano and Pisanello, and studied with Giovanni da Murano, with whom he established a workshop in Murano. They frequently worked together on paintings. After Giovanni died about 1447, Antonio worked in partnership with his brother Bartolommeo in 1450-59. Antonio is considered the founder of the Murano school of painting and was the first of the Vivarini family of painters. Outstanding works are *Adoration of the Magi* and the Parenzo cathedral altarpiece, and with Giovanni, *Madonna Enthroned*. He died probably in Vienna sometime between 1476 and 1484.

VIVARINI, BARTOLOMMEO (1432?-1499), painter. Born probably in Murano, Italy, brother of Antonio, he entered a partnership with his brother in 1450 and painted with him (notably *Madonna and Child with Saints* and *Glory of St. Peter*). They dissolved the partnership and Bartolommeo went on to paint *Enthroned Virgin*, *Virgin of Mercy*, *St. Augustine*, *Virgin and Child*, *St. Mary Magdalene*, and *St. John Capistran*. He was one of the first painters to do oil paintings in

Venice. He is also known as Bartolommeo da Murano.

VIVENTIOLUS, ST. (d. 524), archbishop. He was a monk at the monastery of St. Oyend who was asked to become archbishop of Lyons, France. F. D. July 12.

VIVENTIUS, ST. (d. 400?). A Samaritan, he became a priest, traveled across Europe, served St. Hilary of Poitiers, and spent his last years as a hermit in France. F. D. Jan. 13.

VIVES, JUAN LUIS (1492-1540), philosopher. Born in Valencia, Spain, on Mar. 6, he was forced to leave Spain because of the Inquisition in 1509, studied at Paris, and settled in Bruges in 1512. He became tutor to Guillaume de Croy, nineteen-year-old cardinal and archbishop of Toledo, in 1517, taught at Louvain in 1519, and in 1523 joined the faculty of Corpus Christi College, Oxford, at Henry VII's invitation and was tutor to Princess Mary. He was arrested and expelled from England for his defense of Catherine of Aragon, returned to Louvain where he was a colleague of Erasmus, and aroused the hostility of the authorities for a commentary on the *City of God*, in which he dismissed earlier annotaters, and returned to Bruges. His most significant works are *Introductio ad sapientiam* (1524), *Ad animi exercitationem in Deum commentatiunculae*, *Exercitatio linquae latinae* (1538), *De disciplinis*, and *De institutione feminae Christianae* (1523). His *De subventione pauperum* (1526) was a plan for public relief which was actually put into practice in Paris in 1525. He died in Bruges, Flanders, on May 6.

VIVES Y TUTO, JOSE CALASANZIO (1854-1913), cardinal. Born in San Andres de Llevaneras, Spain, on Feb. 15, he studied in Mataro, became a Capuchin in 1869 in Guatemala, escaped to California during civil war, and because of ill-health was not ordained until 1876, in Toulouse. During the persecution of 1880 he withdrew to Spain, worked to unite long-separated factions of his order, and was called to Rome in 1887. He became consultor of the holy office, general definitor of the Capuchins, a cardinal in 1899, and prefect of the Congregation of Religious in 1908. He wrote theological and ascetical works, attacked modernism, and was confessor to Pope Pius X. He died in Rome on Sept. 7.

VIVIAN, ST. (d. 460?). As bishop of Saintes, Gaul, he held his see together during a Visigoth invasion of western France. F. D. Aug. 28.

VLADIMIR I, ST. (956?-1015). Grandson of St. Olga and illegitimate son of Sviastoslav, grand duke of Kiev, and his mistress, Malushka, he was given Novgorod to rule by his father. Civil war broke out between his half-brothers Yaropolk and Oleg; Yaropolk made himself ruler by defeating and killing Oleg, and, when he captured Novgorod, Vladimir was forced to flee to Scandinavia in 977. Vladimir returned with an army, captured Novgorod, and defeated and slew Yaropolk at Rodno in 980; Vladimir was now sole ruler of Russia, notorious for his barbarism and immorality. After his conquest of Kherson in the Crimea in 988, he became impressed by the progress of Christianity and approached Eastern Emperor Basil II about marrying the emperor's daughter Anne. He was converted, reformed his life, and married Anne. On his return to Kiev, he invited Greek missionaries to Russia, led his people to Christianity, borrowed canonical features from the West, and built schools and churches. His later years were troubled by rebellions led by the sons of his first marriages, although two sons by Anne, SS. Romanus (Boris) and David (Gleb), became martyrs. In 1014 he was obliged to march against his rebellious son Yaroslav in Novgorod, fell ill on the way, and died at Beresyx, Russia, He is patron of the Russian Catholics. F. D. July 15.

VODALUS, ST. (d. 720?). A Gaelic missioner, he crossed to the Continent, preaching through France until he settled into a life of solitary contemplation near Soissons, Gaul. F. D. Feb. 5.

VOGLER, GEORG JOSEPH (1749–1814), composer. Born in Würzburg, Germany, on June 15, son of a violinmaker, he studied law at Bamberg, music under Martini in Bologna and Francesco Vallotti in Padua, and theology in Rome, where he was ordained in 1773. He was made apostolic prothonotary and chamberlain to the pope, became court chaplain at Mannheim in 1775, established a music school there, and wrote musical treatises. He became chief choirmaster in Munich in 1783, chapelmaster of the king of Sweden at Stockholm from 1786 to 1789, and established a school there, and court conductor of Grand Duke Louis I at Darmstadt in 1807, where he established his most successful musical school. He composed opera, organ music, and church music, and was widely known as Abbé Vogler as he traveled over Europe, conducting, giving organ concerts, and demonstrating his unusual organ-like invention, the orchestrion. He was particularly famed for his teaching ability and numbered among his pupils Kornacher, Gänsbacher, Meyerbeer, and Weber. He is the abbé of Robert Browning's poem, *Abt Vogler*. Among his operas are *La Kermesse* (1783), *Castore e Polluce* (1787), and *Samori* (1804). He died in Darmstadt, Germany, on May 6.

VOGLIA, BL. CHIARITO (d. 1348). In 1342 he founded an Augustinian convent in Florence, Italy, which his wife entered and where he worked as a servant until he became a plague victim. F. D. May 25.

VOGÜÉ, CHARLES JEAN MELCHIOR DE (1829–1916), archaeologist. Born in Paris on Oct. 18, he served in the French diplomatic service, resigned in 1852 to travel in the Near East, and was named ambassador to Constantinople in 1871 and to Vienna in 1875. He was elected to the French Academy in 1891. He wrote on Russian goldwork, the churches of the Holy Land, the temple of Jerusalem, Syrian science, and *Une famille vivaroise*, an autobiography. He was president of the Agricultural Society of France, cofounder of L'Oeuvre des Écoles d'Orient, of which he became president in 1900, and was active in Red Cross and other charitable and social work. He died in Paris on Nov. 9.

VOGÜÉ, EUGÈNE MARIE MELCHIOR DE (1848–1910), author. Born in Nice, France, on Feb. 25, he studied at Versailles and law at Grenoble, served and was wounded in the Franco-Prussian war, and entered the diplomatic service at its conclusion. He was attaché in Constantinople in 1873, in Egypt in 1875, and in St. Petersburg from 1878 until 1882, when he resigned to devote himself to literature. He was elected to the French Academy in 1888, was a member of the chamber of deputies from 1893 to 1896, and died in Paris on Feb. 24. Among his books are *Le Roman russe* (1886), which greatly influenced French literature by introducing and popularizing Russian novelists in France, *Questions contemporaines* (1892), *Devant le siècle* (1896), and *Sous l'horizon* (1904).

VOLK, WILHELM (1804–1869), author. Born in Halberstadt, Germany, on Jan. 25, he studied there and at Magdeburg, law at Göttingen and Berlin, practiced in Magdeburg, and in 1838 was appointed government councilor at Erfurt. He became a convert in 1855 and retired from public life in 1858. He wrote *Simeon, Wanderungen und Heimkehr eines christlichen Forschers* (1862–63), biographies of SS. Brigitta, Francis de Sales, and Matilda, and translated from the Latin, Spanish, Italian, and Swedish. He died in Erfurt, Germany, on Mar. 17. He often used the pseudonym Ludwig Clarus.

VOLKER, BL. (d. 1132), martyr. A Benedictine monk from Siegburg, Germany, he was put to death while preaching the gospel to the Obotrites. F. D. Mar. 7.

VOLTA, ALESSANDRO (1745–1827), physicist. Born in Como, Lombardy, Italy, on Feb. 18, he was early attracted to the study of electricity, and in 1769 elicited much favorable comment with his *De vi attractiva ignis electrici*. He became professor of physics in the Como gymnasium in 1774, was appointed to the chair of physics at the university of Pavia in 1779, and became famous for his work in electricity. He invented an electric condenser, a working model of an electrophorus in 1775, the voltaic cell (the volt is named in his honor), and in 1800 described his greatest discovery, the voltaic pile (or battery), an apparatus which generated a current of electricity by the contact of different substances. In 1801, in Paris, he exhibited his experiment on contact electricity to Napoleon, who made him a senator of Lombardy, was appointed director of the philosophical faculty at Padua in 1815, and retired in 1819 to Como, Italy, where he died on Mar. 5. His treatises on electricity were collected in 1816.

VOLTERRA, DANIELE DA (1509–1566), painter. Daniele da Ricciarelli was born in Volterra, Italy, worked in the studios of Bazzi and Baldassare Peruzzi in Siena, went to Rome where he was befriended by and became a devoted follower of Michelangelo, was patronized by Pope Paul III, who appointed him superintendent of the Vatican works, and after he lost this position when Paul died in 1549 devoted himself to sculpture. He helped decorate the Farnese and Belvedere palaces in Rome, but is best known for his paintings, chief of which are *Descent from the Cross*, *Massacre of the Innocents*, and *David Killing Goliath*. His work closely resembles that of Michelangelo, with whose work some of his was often confused. He is sometimes called *Il Braccatoni* ("the Breeches Maker") because Pope Paul IV commissioned him to drape some of the nudes in Michelangelo's *Last Judgment*. He died in Rome.

VOLUSIAN, ST. (d. 496), bishop. Consecrated bishop of Tours, France, in 488, he was driven from his see by the Visigoths and died in exile. A legend that he was executed by his persecutors resulted in his being listed as a martyr. F. D. Jan. 18.

VONDEL, JOOST VAN DEN (1587–1679), dramatist. Born in Cologne, Germany, on Nov. 17, of Dutch parents, he returned with them to Amsterdam when he was about eight, had his first poem published in 1605, studied foreign languages, and became an accountant in the public loan office. He was a convert about 1620, and wrote *The Pasha* (1612) and other dramas, chiefly on biblical and classical themes; lyrics from the plays also gained him a reputation as a poet. His masterpiece, *Lucifer* (1654), has often been compared to Milton's *Paradise Lost*, because of the resemblance of theme; other work includes *Palamedes*, *De Kruisbergh*, *Peter en Pauwels*, *Maria Stuart*, *Salmonens*, *Leeuwendalers*, *Hecuba*, *Electra*, and *Iphegenia in Aulis*. He died in Antwerp, Flanders, on Feb. 5.

VONIER, ANSCAR (1875–1938), author. Born in Ringschnaitt, Württemberg, Germany, he studied in France and at Sant' Anselmo,

Rome, where he became a Benedictine and taught, then went to England, where he remained for the rest of his life. He and his monks rebuilt the ancient abbey of Buckfast (dating back to the era of St. Petroc) by their own manual effort, the sale of honey, and donations from far and wide. Besides restoring the Norman-Gothic structure to its pre-Reformation beauty, Abbot Vonier wrote *The Human Soul* (1913), *The Personality of Christ*, *The Christian Mind*, *The Divine Motherhood*, *A Key to the Doctrine of the Eucharist*, *The Angels*, *Death and Judgment*, *Christ the King of Glory*, *The People of God*, and *The Art of Christ*, among other titles. He died at Buckfast, Devonshire, England, on Dec. 26.

VÖRÖSMARTY, MIHÁLY (1800–1855), poet. Born in Nyék, Hungary, on Dec. 1, he studied law, wrote for *Aurora*, and developed as one of the great nineteenth-century poetic exponents of nationalism. He wrote *The Call*; the epics *Zalan's Flight* (1825), *Erlan*, and *Two Neighboring Castles*; and translated the works of Shakespeare. He was an ardent supporter of Kossuth, served in parliament, but suffered much after the war of independence. He died in Pest, Hungary, on Nov. 19.

VOTUS, ST. (d. 750?), hermit. *See* John of Atarés, St.

VRATANIA, SIMEON (17th century). A monk, he led a group of emigrant Wallachians from Serbia to Zagreb, Croatia, about 1600, was given the monastery of St. Michael on Mt. Marzha near Ivanitz, and in 1611 was appointed bishop of all Catholic Serbs.

VRAU, PHILIBERT (1829–1905). Born in Lille, France, on Nov. 19, he studied at the municipal college there, abandoned his religion on his graduation but returned to the Church in 1854, and devoted himself to working with his brother-in-law, Camille Féron-Vrau in social work among the laboring classes. He established nocturnal adoration of the Blessed Sacrament in Lille in 1857, was instrumental in starting Eucharistic congresses, the first of which was held in Lille, and was active in many religious societies. He died in Lille on May 16.

VRIE, THEODORIC (15th century). A member of the Order of Hermits of St. Augustine and a lector in sacred theology in Saxony, he is an eyewitness chronicler of the Council of Constance, which he described in *De consolatione*.

VULPIAN, ST. (d. 304?), martyr. A Syrian, he was put to death by drowning at Tyre, Phoenicia, during the Diocletian persecution. F. D. Apr. 3.

VYEVAIN, BL. (d. 1285). He was archbishop of York, England. F. D. Aug. 26.

W

WAAGEN, WILHELM HEINRICH (1841–1900), geologist. Born in Munich, Germany, on June 23, he received his doctorate in philosophy from Munich, became an instructor in paleontology there, tutored Princess Theresa and Prince Arnulf of Bavaria, and spent 1870–75 working on a geological survey of India. He became an instructor at Vienna in 1877, taught geology in Prague in 1879, and paleontology at Vienna in 1890. He was an editor of the periodical *Geognostisch-paläontologische Beiträge* while in Munich, and in 1894–1900 was editor of *Beiträge zur Paläontologie*, and wrote numerous geological treatises. He died in Vienna on Mar. 24.

WAAL, ANTON MARIA DE (1837–1917), archaeologist. Born in Emmerich, Prussia, on May 4, he studied there and in Münster, was ordained in 1862, taught in Gaesdonk, and did parish work in Rome. In 1870 he was chaplain with the papal army. He became a monsignor, published widely on Roman antiquities, was honored by Austria and Prussia, and in 1915 directed the excavation of St. Sebastian on the Appian Way. He also wrote three novels (*Valeria, Katakombenbilder*, and *Judas Ende*), plays, and poems. He died in Rome on Feb. 23.

WACE, ROBERT (1100?–1174), poet. Born on Jersey of a noble family, he studied at Caen and Paris, became a reader to King Henry I on his return to Caen about 1130, began writing poetry, and sometime between 1160 and 1170 was canon of Bayeux, Normandy, where he died. Among his writings are the 15,000-line *Brut* (*Geste des Bretons*) for Queen Eleanor of England in 1155, *Roman de Rou* (*Geste des Normanz*), dedicated to Henry in 1160, on the dukes of Normandy, which contains a well-known description of the battle of Hastings, and lives of St. Nicholas and St. Margaret. The *Brut* developed the Arthurian legend; his version stands between those of Geoffrey of Monmouth and Layamon. Wace pictured Arthur as the leader of the colorful world of chivalrous adventure, used the device of the round table for the first time in English literature, and amplified the account of the death of the king and his departure to Avalon.

WACCAR, ST. (d. 755), martyr. He was a German Benedictine who was slain at Dokkum with St. Boniface. F. D. June 5.

WÄCHTER, EBERHARD (1762–1852), painter. Born in Stuttgart, Germany, on Feb. 29, he studied painting in Paris (under Regnault, David, and Gros) and in Rome, where he became a convert and a member of the romantic school of painters. He went to Vienna in 1798, illustrated books, painted, and founded the Brotherhood of Painters, which led to formation of the Nazarene school in Rome. Among his paintings are *Child Jesus on the Lamb, Job and His Friends, Mater dolorosa, Caritas, Cimon in Prison*, and *Ulysses and the Sirens*. He died in Stuttgart, Germany, on Aug. 14.

WADDING, LUKE (1588–1657), historian. Born in Waterford, Ireland, on Oct. 16, he studied at the Irish College in Lisbon, joined the Franciscans at the Immaculate Conception convent in Matozinhos, was sent for further studies to Leyria, Lisbon, and Coimbra, and was ordained in 1613. He continued his studies at Salamanca, taught theology at St. Francis College, and in 1618 was appointed theologian to Philip III's commission to Rome to promote the doctrine of the Immaculate Conception. He conceived the idea of collecting and publishing the writings of the great Franciscans of all times. His annotated edition of St. Francis' writing in 1623 was the beginning of a writing and editing career, which culminated in a complete edition of the writings of Duns Scotus (sixteen volumes, 1639) and his biography of the Subtle Doctor (1644), and his eight-volume uncompleted *Annales ordinis minorum* (1625–54), the history of the Franciscans to 1540. He founded the Irish Franciscan College of St. Isidore's (of which he was guardian four terms) in Rome in 1625, the Ludovisian College there for Irish secular priests in 1628, and a novitiate for St. Isidore's in Capranica in 1656. He was appointed procurator of the Franciscans in 1630 and 1632, procurator and agent for the Irish Supreme Council of the Confederates in 1642, was active in securing support for the Irish revolutionists, became vice-commissary of the Franciscans in the Roman curia in 1645 and commissary in 1648, consultor of the congregations of the Index, Rites, and Propaganda, and was a member of the commission appointed by Pope Urban VIII to reform the breviary and other liturgical books. He was reportedly offered numerous bishoprics but declined them all. He also wrote *De Hebraicae linguae origine*, which he used as an introduction to Marius a Calasio's Hebrew concordance, which he published by establishing a Hebrew press at Ara convent in Coeli; edited and published Angelo del Paz' biblical commentaries; revised and edited Ciacconius' *Lives of the Popes and Cardinals*; and wrote biographies and theo-

logical treatises. He died in Rome on Nov.
18.

WADDING, MICHAEL (1591–1644), missioner. Born in Waterford, Ireland, he studied
at the Irish seminary at Salamanca, joined the
Jesuits in 1609, was sent to the Mexican mission, where he labored among the Indians,
taught in several colleges in Mexico, and died
there on Dec. 18. He wrote *Practica de la teo-
logica mistica* (1681) under the name Godinez,
which he adopted in Mexico.

WADHAMS, EDGAR PHILIP (1817–1891),
bishop. Born in Lewis, New York, on May 17,
he studied at Middletown College, Connecticut, and General Theological seminary, New
York, and became an Episcopalian deacon. He
was converted in 1846, studied at St. Mary's
seminary, Baltimore, and was ordained in Albany in 1850. He became rector of the Albany
cathedral and vicar general of that diocese, and
in 1872, when the new diocese of Ogdensburg
was established, was appointed its first bishop.
He attended the third Plenary Council of Baltimore in 1884, held three diocesan synods, enlarged his cathedral, doubled the number of
clergy and churches in his diocese, and died in
Ogdensburg, New York, on Dec. 5.

WAGGAMAN, MARY TERESA MC KEE
(1846–1931), author. Born in Baltimore, she
was educated in Maryland and New York, married Dr. Samuel Waggaman in 1870, became
the mother of eleven children, and in 1894
began a long career in juvenile literature. She
wrote poetry and short stories, but is chiefly remembered for her juvenile narratives: *Carroll
Dare, The Strong Arm of Avalon, White Eagle,
Buddy, Carmelita, The Secret of Pomonoke,
Lorimer Light, Nan Nobody, Shipmates,* and
The Trevelyan Twins. She died in Washington,
D.C., on July 30.

WAGNER, ROBERT FERDINAND (1877–
1953), senator. Born in Nastetten, Germany,
on June 8, he was brought to the United States
at the age of eight, and graduated from City
College and New York Law School. He served
in the state assembly in 1904–8, the state senate in 1909–18, and as floor leader the last five
years. He sponsored bills for better working
conditions, widows' pensions, larger compensation, and worked with Gov. Smith to put
through nearly sixty measures of social reform.
In 1918 he was raised to the bench of the state
supreme court. He was Democratic senator
from New York from 1927 to 1949, when illness forced his resignation. During that time,
particularly under the Roosevelt administra-
tions, he was chairman of the National Labor
Board (1933–34), sponsored the National
Labor Relations Act of 1935, the first social
security act, housing and slum-clearance proposals, and the anti-lynching bill. He helped to
create the Reconstruction Finance Corpora-

tion, was a leader in labor legislation, and
served as chairman of the American Palestine
Committee, and on such senate committees as
Banking and Currency and Foreign Affairs. He
became a convert in 1946. He died in New
York City on May 4.

WALARICUS, ST. (d. 620?). A monk at
Autumo, at Auxerre, France, and at Luxeuil,
where he finally settled under St. Columban,
until the latter's expulsion by King Theodoric,
he preached in northern France, then retired
to found and rule over the monastery of Len-
cone near the mouth of the Somme. He is also
known as Valéry. F. D. Apr. 1.

WALBERT, ST. (d. 678?). Duke of Lorraine, he became the husband of St. Bertilia
and the father of SS. Aldegundis and Waldetrudis. F. D. May 11.

WALBURGA, ST. (d. 779). Daughter of
Richard, a West Saxon chieftain, she was born
in Devonshire, England, became a Benedictine
at Wimborne in Dorset, went to the German
mission with St. Lioba in 748, and shared
the direction of the double monastery of
Heidenheim with her brother Winebald. At his
death she was appointed abbess of both houses
by her brother St. Willibald, bishop of Eichstätt, and died there. She is believed to have
studied medicine, and a watery fluid from
rocks on which her relics rest has resulted in
many cures. She was honored on May 1 (Wal-
purgisnacht), probably to offset the pagan regard for the earth goddess Walborg. She is
also called Falbourg. F. D. Feb. 25.

WALDEBERT, ST. (665?). A Frankish noble
and officer, he became a monk at Luxeuil,
France, lived with permission as a solitary
nearby, succeeded St. Eustace as abbot in 628,
introduced the Benedictine rule, separated the
monastery from episcopal control, and gave it
his own estates. F. D. May 2.

WALDETRUDIS, ST. (d. 688?). Daughter
of SS. Walbert and Bertilia, she married St.
Vincent Madelgar. After the birth of their
fourth child, he entered the abbey of Haut-
mond, and two years later she dedicated herself
to a life of prayer, eventually founding a convent about which grew up the city of Mons,
Belgium. Their children were SS. Landericus,
Dentelinus, Aldetrudis, and Madelberta. The
last two succeeded St. Aldegundis, sister of
Waldetrudis, as abbess of Mauberge. F. D.
Apr. 9.

WALDSEEMÜLLER, MARTIN (1470?–
1522?), cartographer. Born in Freiburg, Germany, he studied theology at its university, became interested in cartography and geography
as a youth, and in 1507 published a map of the
world, *Universalis cosmographia,* containing the
first mention of the name America and showing
South America as an island, and *Cosmographiae
introductio,* which contains an explanation of

the use of the name America (suggesting the New World be so named) and a Latin translation of the four voyages of Amerigo Vespucci. In 1511 he produced the *Carta itineraria Europae,* the first printed wall map of Europe, helped prepare the 1513 edition of Ptolemy's *Geography* which is regarded as the first modern atlas, was appointed canon of St. Dié in Lorraine in 1514, and in 1516 produced his *Carta marina navigatoria.* He often used the Greek spelling of his name, Illacomilus, in signing his maps. He died in St. Dié.

WALEMBERT, BL. (1084–1141). A native of Furness, Belgium, he founded the Augustinian abbey of Mont St. Martin near Cambrai, of which he was first superior. F. D. Dec. 31.

WALENBURCH, ADRIAN VON (d. 1669), bishop. Born in Rotterdam, Netherlands, he studied in France with his brother Peter, received his doctorate in civil and canon law, and on his return to Rotterdam studied theology. He became a member of the duke of Pfalz-Neuburg's court at Düsseldorf, went to Cologne in 1646, became a cathedral canon the following year, and in 1661 was appointed auxiliary bishop, vicar general and titular bishop of Adrianople. With Peter he wrote theological treatises and engaged in controversy with leading Protestant theologians. He died in Mainz (or Wiesbaden), Germany, on Sept. 11 or 14.

WALENBURCH, PETER VON (d. 1675), bishop. Born in Rotterdam, Netherlands, he went to France with his brother Adrian, received his doctorate in canon and civil law, and returned to Rotterdam to study theology. He went with Adrian to the court of the duke of Pfalz-Neuburg in Düsseldorf, became a canon at the cathedral churches of St. Peter and St. Victor in Mainz, and was appointed auxiliary bishop and titular bishop of Mysia in 1658. He worked with Leibniz on the latter's plan for reunion, and in 1669 was appointed his brother's successor as auxiliary bishop of Cologne, Germany, where he died on Dec. 21. He was the main author of the numerous controversial tracts the two brothers wrote, engaged in frequent controversies with outstanding Protestant divines, and was successful in conversion work, notably of Landgrave Ernst of Hesse-Rheinfels in 1652.

WALFRID, ST. (d. 765?). Galfrido della Gherardesca was born in Pisa, Italy, married, and had several children before he decided to lead a monastic life. He and a son, with two friends, built the abbey of Palazzuolo, near Monte Verde, Italy, following the Benedictine rule, and were soon joined by more than fifty others; his wife, Thesia, and daughter became nuns at a nearby convent. Walfrid, who served as abbot for ten years, was canonized in 1861. F.D. Feb. 15.

WALKER, FRANK COMERFORD (1886–1959), jurist. Born in Plymouth, Pennsylvania, on May 30, he was taken to Montana at the age of three and grew up in Butte. He studied at Gonzaga in Spokane, Washington, and law at Notre Dame, graduated in 1909, and passed the Montana bar in that same year. He was an assistant district attorney in 1909–12, was elected to the state legislature, married Hallie Boucher, and became a partner with his brother in a law firm. He was equally successful in business, directed a chain of motion-picture theaters, and continued his interest in politics. He contributed heavily to the gubernatorial and presidential campaigns of Franklin Delano Roosevelt, whom he had met in 1920, was among the president's closest advisers after 1933, and became head of the National Emergency Council and in 1935 director of the Works Relief Program. He was postmaster general in 1940–45 and chairman of the Democratic National Committee in 1943–44. He died in New York City on Sept. 13.

WALKER, JAMES JOHN (1881–1946), mayor. Born in New York City, on June 19, he was a politician and song writer, was mayor of New York City from 1926 through the prohibition era and its attendant crime, and resigned in 1932 when his administration was ordered investigated by the state. He went to Paris, later returned, and died in New York City on Dec. 18.

WALKER, JOHN (1732–1807), lexicographer. Born in Colney Hatch, Middlesex, England, on Mar. 18, he became an actor for David Garrick in London and in the theater in Dublin, left the stage in 1768, opened a school at Kensington with James Usher in 1769, and became a convert. The school closed after two years and Walker went on speaking tours, then began work on his *Critical Pronouncing Dictionary and Expositor of the English Language* (1791), long a standard work, and still of literary and critical value. He also prepared a rhyming dictionary, a rhetorical grammar, school texts, and handbooks on elocution. He died in London on Aug. 1.

WALL, BL. JOHN (1620–1679), martyr. Born in Lancashire, England, he studied at Douai and was ordained at Rome in 1645. He became a Franciscan (as Fr. Joachim of St. Anne) in 1651 at Douai and in 1656 returned to England. He served the Catholics of Worcestershire for almost twenty-two years before he was arrested and charged with being a priest. Although exonerated of alleged conspiracy in the Titus Oates Plot, he was ordered to renounce his religion, refused, and was hanged, drawn, and quartered at Redhill, Worcester, the only English martyr there. He was beatified in 1929. F. D. Aug. 26.

WALLABONSUS, ST. (d. 851), martyr. *See* Peter, St.

WALLACE, WILLIAM (1270?–1305). Son of Sir Malcolm Wallace, he was probably born in Elderslie, Renfrewshire, Scotland, led the Scots revolt against the English sheriffs who were placed in key positions throughout his nation, formed a large and powerful army, attacked Scone, besieged Dundee, and in 1297 won a major victory at Stirling Bridge. He soon captured Edinburgh and other major centers and within the month had invaded England. In 1298, Edward I defeated him at Falkirk, slew 10,000 Scots, and Wallace fled to France, and probably to Rome. He disappeared from history in 1299–1303, returned to Scotland in 1304 with a price on his head, was captured in 1305, near Glasgow, and hanged, drawn, and quartered in London as a rebel on Aug. 23.

WALLENSTEIN, ALBRECHT WENZEL EUSEBIUS VON (1583–1634), general. Born of noble Protestant parents in Herrmanic, Bohemia, on Sept. 15, he studied at the Jesuit College at Olmütz, where he became a convert, and at Altdorf, Bologna, and Padua. He served in the army of Emperor Rudolf II against the Turks in Hungary, participated in the siege of Gran in 1606, and returned to Bohemia later in 1606. He married Lucretia Nikossie von Landeck in 1610, and on her death in 1614 inherited her vast estates in Moravia and her great wealth. When the Thirty Years' War broke out in Bohemia in 1618, he joined the imperial (Catholic) forces, and in 1620 played a major role in the brilliant victory at White Mountain, near Prague, which placed Bohemia under Archduke Ferdinand of Austria's domination, and received his family's land and other grants from the emperor, which he formed into Friedland. He was made an imperial count palatine in 1622, a prince of the empire in 1623, and in 1625 duke of Friedland. In 1626 he raised an army and joined the forces of Emperor Maximilian, defeated Mansfeld at Dessau in 1626, invaded and conquered Hungary, and in 1627 cleared Silesia of the remnants of Mansfeld's army. He bought the duchy of Sagan from the emperor, joined Tilly in the struggle against Christian IV, occupied the duchy of Mecklenburg, which was awarded to him, and in 1628 suffered a serious reverse when he failed to capture the free city of Stratsund (which he hoped would gain the emperor sea power by the conquest of the Hanseatic League) despite a siege of several months. His policy of bringing all the nobles into subjection to the crown had aroused the bitter enmity of the princes, who in 1630 persuaded the emperor to relieve him of his command. He turned over his army to Tilly, but in 1632, after Tilly's death, the conquest of Bohemia by the Saxons, and Gustavus Adolphus'

advance on Munich, the emperor returned him to supreme command of the army. He captured Prague, drove the Saxons from Bohemia, and was defeated by Gustavus Adolphus' army at Lützen, Saxony, at which the Swedish king was killed. When he failed to follow up this opening by attacking the Swedish forces, he was relieved of his command in 1634 by Ferdinand, when the emperor decided he was negotiating a separate peace which would have made him head of a unified Germany. He was accused of treason, fled to Eger, Bohemia, where he hoped to resume negotiations with the Swedes under Duke Bernhard, and was murdered there on Feb. 25 by one of his officers, Col. Butler, in the pay of the emperor.

WALLON, HENRI ALEXANDRE (1812–1904), historian. Born in Valenciennes, Nord, France, on Dec. 23, he became a fellow at the Lycée Louis le Grand, then a professor, was appointed master of conferences at the École Normale in 1840, and six years later became Guizot's assistant at the Sorbonne. He entered public life in 1847 as assistant deputy at the constituent assembly, represented Nord in the legislative assembly in 1849, but resigned and became professor of history at the Sorbonne in 1850. He was elected permanent secretary of the Academy of Inscriptions, to the national assembly in 1871, was minister of public education in 1875–76, was appointed senator with life tenure in 1878, and served as dean of the Paris faculty of letters from 1876 to 1887. He wrote studies of the French Revolution, biographies of Joan of Arc and St. Louis, and a critical study of Renan's life of Christ. He died in Paris.

WALMESLEY, CHARLES (1722–1797), bishop. Born in Wigan, Lancashire, England, on Jan. 13, he studied at St. Gregory's College, Douai, joined the Benedictines in Paris in 1739, received his doctorate from the Sorbonne, and became noted for his knowledge of astronomy and mathematics. He was prior of St. Edmund's, Paris, in 1749–53, became procurator of the English Benedictines in 1754 in Rome and in 1756 was made coadjutor to Bishop York, vicar apostolic of the western district, and titular bishop of Rama. He administered the vicariate when Bishop York retired in 1763 and succeeded to it when the bishop died in 1770. He vigorously opposed the actions of the Catholic Committee in 1789, consecrated John Carroll the first American bishop in 1790, and wrote astronomical and mathematical treatises and the popular *General History of the Christian Church*, under the pseudonym of Pastorini. He died in Bath, England, on Nov. 25.

WALPOLE, BL. HENRY (1558–1595), martyr. Born in Docking, Norfolk, England, he left Cambridge without a degree, witnessed the execution of Edmund Campion (which he commemorated in print), and went to Rheims in 1582. He became a Jesuit at Rome in 1584, was ordained in 1588, served as a chaplain in Flanders, and assisted Robert Persons in establishing seminaries in Spain. In 1593 he landed in England, was captured in York, and imprisoned in the Tower. Two years later, after many trials, forced confessions, and frequent torture, he was hanged, drawn, and quartered in York. A number of poems written during his imprisonment survive. He was beatified in 1929. F. D. Apr. 7.

WALPURGIS. *See* Walburga, St.

WALSH, EDWARD (1805–1850), poet. Born in Londonderry, Ireland, he taught in Millstreet and Tourin, had his poems published in the *Nation,* and became an assistant editor on the Dublin *Monitor* in 1843. He published *Reliques of Irish Jacobite Poetry* (1844) and *Irish Popular Songs* (1847), was obliged to accept a teaching position in the Spike Island prison and in 1849 at the Cork workhouse, and died in Cork, Ireland, on Aug. 6.

WALSH, FRANCIS AUGUSTINE (1884–1938), educator. Born in Cincinnati, Ohio, on Mar. 21, he studied at Xavier University, St. Mary's seminary, Cincinnati, and the Gregorian, Rome, and was ordained in 1907. He did parish work in Cincinnati, taught at the seminary in 1911–22, except for a period as chaplain in World War I, and taught at Mt. St. Joseph, Ohio, and at Xavier in 1920–23. He went to Catholic University in 1923, became a Benedictine, taught philosophy there from 1924 until his death, was regent of its seminary, and also taught ethics at Trinity College, Washington. He was active in the cause of Negro education, was chaplain at Howard University, directed the school of apologetics at Catholic University, out of which developed the Confraternity of Christian Doctrine (he was its director in 1933–38), and wrote *Religion and Liturgy* (1933), *The Priest of God* (1937), *Integral Philosophy* (1937), and a missal with Fr. Lasance. He edited the *Placidian* in 1923–29 and became editor of *New Scholasticism* in 1937. He died in Washington, D.C.

WALSH, FRANCIS PATRICK (1864–1939), jurist. Born in St. Louis, Missouri, on July 20, he worked at various jobs as a boy, studied law, was admitted to the Missouri bar in 1889, and became an outstanding trial lawyer and member of the Democratic party in St. Louis. He led a reform group which elected Joseph W. Folk governor in 1904, sponsored a program of progressive legislation which attracted nationwide attention, supported Woodrow Wilson for president in 1912, and in 1913 was appointed chairman of the new Commission on Industrial Relations by Wilson. He resigned in 1918 to become co-chairman of the

National War Labor Board. He worked vigorously for Irish freedom after World War I as chairman of the American Commission for Irish Independence and counsel for the Irish Republic, and was active in civil-liberties cases, notably the Preparedness Day bombing case in San Francisco in 1916, in which he was Tom Mooney's counsel, and the Sacco-Vanzetti case. He became one of the outstanding labor lawyers in the United States, was appointed chairman of the New York State Power Authority in 1931 by Franklin D. Roosevelt, for whom he organized the National Progressive League in the 1932 presidential campaign, was elected first president of the National Lawyers Guild in 1936, and died in New York City on May 2.

WALSH, JAMES ANTHONY (1867–1936), founder. Born in Cambridge, Massachusetts, on Feb. 24, he studied at Boston College, Harvard, and St. John's seminary, Boston, and was ordained in 1892. He engaged in pastoral work, became interested in the missions, was appointed director of the Boston branch of the Society for the Propagation of the Faith in 1903, and in 1906 was co-founder of the Catholic Foreign Mission Bureau, which in 1907 began to publish *The Field Afar,* a magazine devoted to missionary activities. In 1911 he and Fr. Thomas Frederick Price received papal approval for the founding of the Catholic Foreign Mission Society which became famed as the Maryknoll Fathers. They sent their first group of priests to China under Fr. Price in 1918 and by the time of Bishop Walsh's death at Maryknoll on Apr. 14 had missions all over the Far East. He was elected first superior in 1929 when a permanent constitution was adopted, and was appointed titular bishop of Siene in 1933.

WALSH, JAMES JOSEPH (1865–1942), author. Born in Archbald, Pennsylvania, on Apr. 12, he graduated from St. John's (Fordham) and took his master's degree there, became a Jesuit in 1885, but resigned after six years because of poor health. He took his medical degree at Pennsylvania in 1895, did further study in Paris and Vienna, served as correspondent to the international medical congress in Russia, and returned in 1897 to practice in New York City. He was professor and dean of the Fordham medical school in 1905–13, taught physiological psychology at Cathedral College, lectured, and wrote widely. He married in 1915, received the Laetare Medal in 1916, and continued to publish a series of volumes under the imprint of the Fordham University Press, the name under which he published his books. These include: *Catholic Churchmen in Science* (1906), *Makers of Modern Medicine, The Popes and Science, Education: How Old the New, The Thirteenth the Greatest of Cen-*

turies, *Health through Will Power, The World's Debt to the Irish, Laughter and Health, The Church and Healing, A Golden Treasury of Mediaeval Literature, High Points of Mediaeval Culture, The Century of Columbus,* and other popular studies. He was active in many Catholic organizations, was on the original board of the Catholic Book Club, and was twice honored by the papacy. He died in New York City on Feb. 28.

WALSH, JOHN (1830–1898), bishop. Born in Mooncoin, Kilkenny, Ireland, on May 24, he was ordained in 1854, did parish work in Canada, and was consecrated bishop of Sandwich, Ontario, in 1867. He had the see city retransferred to London, Ontario, in 1869, began a new cathedral in 1881, and was made archbishop of Toronto in 1889. He died there on July 31.

WALSH, LOUIS J. (1880–1942), author. Born in Maghera, Derry, Ireland, he studied at St. Columba's, Derry, and University College, Dublin, became a lawyer in 1905, and married Mary McKenna in 1908. His office was sacked and he was imprisoned in 1920–21 during the British occupation of Ireland; in 1922 he was appointed a district judge, and was the first to conduct cases entirely in Gaelic. He wrote on rural life in Ulster in *Twilight Reveries, Our Own Wee Town, Old Friends, The Grand Audit Night,* and other titles; on his own career in *Tales of a Country Attorney;* and a satire on bigotry, *The Pope in Killybuck.*

WALSH, LOUIS SEBASTIAN (1858–1924), bishop. Born in Salem, Massachusetts, on Jan. 22, he studied at Holy Cross, the Grand seminary, Montreal, St. Sulpice, Paris, and the Apolinaris and the Minerva in Rome, where he was ordained in 1882. After parish work he taught at St. John's seminary, Boston, in 1884–97, then became supervisor of schools for the archdiocese of Boston. He held this position until 1906, when he was consecrated bishop of Portland, Maine. He helped found the New England Catholic Historical Society and the Catholic Education Association of America, served as president of the school section of the latter, and wrote several books. He died on May 12 in Portland.

WALSH, MICHAEL (1897–1938), poet. Born in Ben-of-Fore, Westmeath, Ireland, he studied at Mungret, suffered from ill-health most of his life, wrote for many Irish magazines, and published three volumes of poetry: *Brown Earth and Green, Heart Remembers Morning,* and *Red on the Holly.* His lyrics rely heavily on the natural surroundings of his birthplace and religious devotion. He died on Dec. 1.

WALSH, PATRICK (1840–1900), journalist. Born in Ballingary, Limerick, Ireland, on Jan.

1, he was brought to Charleston, South Carolina, in 1852, worked as a printer, attended Georgetown from 1859 to 1861, and then joined his state's militia as a lieutenant. From 1862 until his death he edited the *Constitutionalist* at Atlanta, Georgia, as well as serving on the *Pacificator* (1864), *Banner of the South* (1867), and *Chronicle and Sentinel,* which he purchased in 1877. He served as general manager of the Associated Press in the South, in the state legislature (1872–76), and became United States senator in 1894. He died in Atlanta, Georgia, on Mar. 19.

WALSH, PETER (1608?–1688). Born in Mooretown, Kildare, Ireland, he studied at the Irish College of St. Anthony in Louvain, where he joined the Franciscans and was ordained, and returned to Kilkenny. There he became involved in the political situation on the side of the Ormondist party, opposed the papal nuncio, Rinuccini, and became chaplain of the Munster army. He was in London in 1660, was appointed agent of the Irish bishops in 1661, worked actively for the acceptance by the Irish of the Remonstrance, and, when it was opposed by the Irish clergy at a synod in Dublin in 1666 for its attitude to the pope and papal supremacy, he broke with the Church to head a group of heretics known as the Velasians. He was excommunicated by a general chapter of the Franciscans at Valladolid in 1670 and, though Velasianism was practically non-existent by 1671, he continued his position until shortly before his death, when he was reconciled with the Church. He died in London on Mar. 15.

WALSH, ROBERT (1784–1859), author. Born in Baltimore, Maryland, on Aug. 30, he graduated from Georgetown in 1801, studied law, traveled in Europe, and was admitted to the bar in 1808. He settled in Philadelphia, edited the *American Register* in 1809–10, founded the first American quarterly, *American Review of History and Politics,* in 1811, the *National Gazette and Literary Register* in 1820 (and edited it until 1836), edited the *Museum of Foreign Literature* in 1822–23, and established the *American Quarterly Review* in 1827. He was professor of English at the University of Pennsylvania from 1818 to 1828 and a trustee from 1828 to 1833, moved to Paris in 1837, and was appointed American consul general there in 1844. He was known for his political essays, especially *A Letter on the Genius and Disposition of the French Government* (1810) and *An Appeal from the Judgments of Great Britain Respecting the United States* (1815), contributed articles to literary journals and encyclopedias, and in 1836 published *Didactics: Social, Literary and Political,* a collections of essays. He died in Paris on Feb. 7.

WALSH, THOMAS (1777–1849), bishop.

Born in London in Oct., son of an Irish merchant, he studied at St. Omer's and Old Hall Green, became secretary of Bishop Stapleton of the Midland District in 1801, was ordained, and in 1804 became spiritual moderator at Sedgley Park School. He served as president of Oscott from 1818 to 1826, was appointed coadjutor of Bishop Milner and titular bishop of Cambysopalis in 1825, and succeeded him as vicar apostolic of the Midland District in 1826. He was translated to the London District in 1848, and died there on Feb. 18.

WALSH, THOMAS (1875–1928), author. Born in Brooklyn, New York, on Oct. 14, he graduated from St. Francis Xavier College, Georgetown, and Columbia, became a freelance writer, and interested himself in Hispanic literature and culture. He was decorated by Spain and South American nations, was elected to the Royal Academy of Seville, and received honorary doctorates from Georgetown and Notre Dame. He became associate editor of *Commonweal*, edited *The Hispanic Anthology* (1920), *The Catholic Anthology* (1927), and the poems of Rubén Dario, and published his own poetry in *The Prison Ships* (1909), *The Pilgrim Kings* (1915), *Gardens Overseas* (1917), and *Don Folquet* (1920). He died in Brooklyn on Oct. 29.

WALSH, THOMAS JOSEPH (1873–1952), bishop. Born in Parker's Landing, Pennsylvania, on Dec. 6, he studied at St. Bonaventure's and the Apollinaris, Rome, and was ordained in 1900. He did parish work in Buffalo, was secretary to Bishops Colton and Quigley in 1900–15, and chancellor of the diocese from 1900 to 1918, when he was appointed bishop of Trenton, New Jersey. He was transferred to Newark in 1928, and became that see's first archbishop in 1937. He died in South Orange, New Jersey, on June 6.

WALSH, WILLIAM (1512?–1577), bishop. Born in Dunboyne, Meath, Ireland, he joined the Cistercians at their Bective monastery, studied at Oxford, and was forced to go to Europe when Bective was confiscated in 1537. He became Cardinal Pole's chaplain in Rome, transferred to the Canons Regular of St. Augustine, and was appointed prior of the suppressed monasteries of Duleek and Colpe. He accompanied Cardinal Pole, now papal legate, back to England in 1544, was appointed bishop of Meath by the cardinal to replace Bishop Staples in 1545, resisted Elizabeth's innovations in the liturgy, and in 1560 was imprisoned when he refused to take the Oath of Supremacy. In 1564 his appointment by the legate was declared void in Rome, but he was reappointed by the pope. He was imprisoned in Dublin castle in 1565 when he again refused the Oath of Supremacy, escaped to France in 1572, and then went to Spain, where he died in the Cis-

tercian monastery in Alcalá de Henares on Jan. 4.

WALSH, WILLIAM J. (1841–1921), archbishop. Born in Dublin on Jan. 30, he studied at its Catholic University under Newman and at Maynooth and Dunboyne. He taught theology from 1867 to 1878, became vice-president of Maynooth in 1878 and later its president, and supported Gladstone's land bill. He became archbishop of Dublin and primate of Ireland in 1885, acted on behalf of Parnell at his trial and as labor mediator, and wrote on Catholic education in royal colleges, Gregorian music, and bimetalism. He was the first chancellor of the National University, and was a strong supporter of the republican leaders from 1918 until his death in Dublin on Apr. 9.

WALSH, WILLIAM THOMAS (1891–1949), author. Born in Waterbury, Connecticut, on Sept. 11, he studied at Yale, worked on Waterbury, Philadelphia and Hartford newspapers, was head of the department of English at Roxbury School, Cheshire, from 1919 to 1933, and professor of English at Manhattanville College, New York City, from 1933 to 1947 when he retired to devote himself to writing. He married Helen Sherwood in 1914. He wrote short stories, a novel, *Out of the Whirlwind* (1935), a play, *Shekels* (1937), *Lyric Poems* (1939), essays. *Characters of the Inquisition* (1940) and *Our Lady of Fatima* (1947), his most popular work. He is also known for his biographies, *Isabella of Spain* (1930), *Philip II* (1937), *St. Teresa of Avila* (1943), *St. Peter the Apostle* (1948), and *Saints in Action* (1961). He was awarded the Laetare Medal in 1941, was honored by the Spanish government, and received an honorary degree from Fordham. He died in White Plains, New York, on Feb. 22.

WALSINGHAM, THOMAS (d. 1422?), historian. Probably born in Walsingham, Norfolk, England, he studied at St. Albans abbey, became a Benedictine monk there, was in charge of the scriptorium, and was appointed superior of Wymondham priory in 1394, a position he held until 1409 when he returned to Walsingham, where he died. His chronicles, leading sources of information for the fourteenth century, are *Chronica majora* (before 1388); *Chronicon Angliae*, covering the period 1328–88; *Gesta abbatum*; *Historia anglicana*, for the period 1272–1422; *Ypodigma Neustriae*, a history of the dukes of Normandy; and a history of St. Albans from 1272 to 1393.

WALSTAN, ST. (d. 1016). Born in Bawburgh, England, he gave away his inheritance, and became a servant and farm laborer, devoted to the poor and to prayer. His shrine was very popular up to the time of its destruction during the reign of Henry VIII. F. D. May 30.

WALTER, ST. (d. 1070). Born in Aquitaine,

France, he studied and became an Augustinian at Dorat under Bl. Isaac; for his last thirty-eight years he was abbot of L'Esterp, France, with a wide reputation for success with sinners. F. D. May 11.

WALTER, ST. (d. 1150). An Englishman, he became abbot of the Benedictine monastery of Fontenelle, France. F. D. June 4.

WALTER, FERDINAND (1794–1879), jurist. Born in Wetzlar, Hesse, Germany, on Nov. 30, he studied in Mülheim and Cologne, fought against Napoleon in the Russian army, received his law degree at Heidelberg in 1817, and taught there. In 1819 he was appointed to the University of Bonn and taught there until blindness forced his resignation in 1875. He was a vigorous defender of Church rights, served in the Prussian national assembly in 1848 and the first chamber of deputies in 1849, but is particularly known for his juristic writings. Among his chief works are *Lehrbuch des Kirchenrechts* (1822), *Corpus juris Germanici antiqui* (1824), *Juristische Encyclopädie* (1856), and *Fontes juris ecclesiastici antiqui et hodierni* (1862). He died in Bonn, Germany, on Dec. 13.

WALTER OF CHÂTILLON (13th century), poet. Born in Lille, France, Walter de Insulis studied in Paris under Étienne of Beauvais, settled in Châtillon, taking its name, where he was head of the schools, left to study law at Bologna, and served as secretary to Archbishops Henry and William of Rheims. He wrote the *Alexandreid*, a Latin poem describing Alexander's exploits, and theological treatises. He probably died of the plague in Amiens early in the thirteenth century.

WALTER OF EVESHAM. *See* Odington, Walter.

WALTER DE INSULIS. *See* Walter of Châtillon.

WALTER OF MERTON (d. 1277), bishop. Probably born in Merton, Surrey, England, he became a priest, prothonotary of the chancery in 1258, was prebendary of St. Paul's in London in 1259 and of Exeter in 1262, was appointed chancellor by Henry III in 1261, and in that same year founded Merton College, which he endowed. He lost his chancellorship in 1263, but regained it in 1271 when he was justiciar, and in 1274 was made bishop of Rochester. He died on Oct. 27 while crossing the Medway River in England.

WALTER OF MORTAGNE (d. 1174), theologian. Born in Mortagne, Flanders, he studied at Tournai, taught at St. Geneviève, Paris, from 1136 until 1144, when he left for Laon and there became bishop. He wrote theological treatises, notably on the Trinity, and was considered the leader of the indifferentists in the field of philosophy. He died in Laon, France.

WALTER OF PONTOISE, ST. (d. 1099). Born in Picardy, France, he taught philosophy and rhetoric before he became a Benedictine at Rebais in Brie. He was unwillingly appointed prior of Pontoise, withdrew to solitude several times, but was ordered to serve by Pope St. Gregory VII. Because of his vigorous attacks on the evil lives of many of the clergy, he was beaten, imprisoned, and otherwise the victim of persecution. F. D. Apr. 8.

WALTER OF ST. VICTOR (12th century), theologian. Prior of St. Victor monastery, near Paris, about 1175, he wrote *Contra quatour labyrinthos Franciae* (c. 1179), an attack on the dialectical method in theology and directed particularly against Peter Abelard, Peter Lombard, Peter of Poitiers, and Gilbert de la Porrée. He died sometime after 1180.

WALTER VON DER VOGELWEIDE (1170?–1230?), poet. Born near Bozen, Tyrol (or in Switzerland or Bavaria), he studied under Reinmar von Hagenau in Austria, joined the Austrian court, and received patronage from Duke Frederick of Vienna and Leopold VII in 1180–98. He then served Duke Philip of Swabia in 1208, Landgrave Hermann of Thuringia, and was influenced by St. Elizabeth of Hungary. He introduced folk touches, ethical observations, and genuine patriotic and love themes into court poetry, and contributed much to the development of the German lyric. He probably died in Würzburg, Germany, where he had been given an estate sometime after 1220 by Frederick II, for whom he wrote *Kreuzlied*. He may have gone on the crusade of 1227–28.

WALTER OF WINTERBURN (d. 1305), cardinal. A native of England, he joined the Dominicans, became King Edward I's spiritual director, was provincial of England from 1290 to 1298, and in 1304 was created a cardinal by Pope Benedict XI. He wrote treatises, chief of which was *Questiones theologicae*. He died in Genoa, Italy, on Aug. 26, while on his way from the conclave of 1305 to visit Pope Clement V in France.

WALTHEOF, ST. (d. 1160?). After the death of his father, Simon, earl of Huntington, his mother, Maud, married St. David I of Scotland. Waltheof was educated at the royal court, where he became a close friend of St. Aelred, then joined the Augustinian canons at Nostell, Yorkshire, England. He became prior of Kirkham, then became a Cistercian at Wardon, Bedfordshire, and abbot of Melrose. In 1154 he was chosen archbishop of St. Andrew's, but declined the post. F. D. Aug. 3.

WALTMAN, BL. (d. 1138). One of the companions of St. Norbert when he went to Antwerp, Brabant, to crush the heresy of Tanchelm, he remained there as abbot of the Premonstratensian monastery of St. Michael's, which the local clergy gave to the order in gratitude. F. D. Apr. 11 .

WALTO, BL. (d. 1156). Also known as Balto, he was abbot of the Benedictine monastery of Wessobrünn, Bavaria. F. D. Dec. 27.

WALWORTH, CLARENCE AUGUSTUS (1820–1900). Born in Plattsburg, New York, on May 30, he graduated from Union College in 1838, was admitted to the bar in 1841, but gave up his law practice to study for the ministry at General Theological seminary in New York. After three years he left and in 1845 became a convert, taking the name Alban Alphonsus at confirmation. With Isaac Hecker and James McMaster, he joined the Redemptorists in 1846 at St. Trond College in Belgium and after further study at Wittenberg was ordained in 1848. When the Redemptorists opened an American province he was sent to the United States in 1851 and became a successful preacher of missions. In 1858, Frs. Hecker, Walworth, and three others were released from their vows as Redemptorists and founded the Congregation of St. Paul (the Paulist Fathers). Before the constitutions of the new group were approved by the New York archbishop, which approval marked the actual founding of the Paulists, Walworth withdrew from the group in a dispute over the form of the vows to be taken. He returned in 1861, but overwork on the missions caused him to resign in 1865. He spent from 1866 until his death on Sept. 19 as pastor of St. Mary's in Albany. A leader in the temperance movement, he also wrote several books.

WALWORTH, BL. WILLIAM (d. 1537), martyr. *See* Rochester, Bl. John.

WANDELBERT (9th century). A native Frenchman, he was born in 813, was a monk at Prüm, Flanders, in 839 and wrote a life of St. Goar, a martyrology in verse, and a treatise on the mass. He died sometime after 850.

WANDREGISILUS, ST. (d. 668). Born near Verdun, he served in the Austrasian court. About 626 he and his wife agreed to separate and enter the religious life. He became a Benedictine at St. Baudry in Montfaucon, France, lived as a hermit at St. Usanne, then went to the abbeys of St. Columban at Bobbio and Roumain-Moûtier. There he was ordained by St. Ouen, after which he founded the great abbey of Fontenelle, Gaul. He is also known as Wandrille. F. D. July 22.

WANDRILLE. *See* Wandregisilus, St.

WANG, ERIK A. (1859–1913). Born in Kongsvinger, Norway, on Aug. 29, he became a convert when young, studied in Denmark, Belgium, and at the Propaganda in Rome, and was ordained in 1882. He was stationed at Christiana and Tromsö until 1899, then became rector at Bergen. He edited the journal *St. Olav* and served as secretary to Msgr. Fel-

lize, prefect apostolic. He died in Bergen, Norway.

WANG, FRANCIS X. (1920–1957). A young Chinese Jesuit trained in Hopei, he died at Shanghai shortly after being released from a communist prison where he had been confined and tortured for four years.

WANG WEN-CHENG, PAUL (1882–1961), bishop. Born in Kian-Yun, China, he was ordained in 1911, and consecrated bishop in 1930. He served in the see of Shunking until his death in China on Jan. 28.

WANGNERECK, HEINRICH (1595–1664), theologian. Born in Munich, Germany, in July, he joined the Jesuits in Landsberg at sixteen, taught philosophy and theology at Dillingen, became noted as a teacher and preacher, wrote a score of theological treatises, and served as chancellor of the university for twenty-four years. He was superior at Lindau from 1655 until 1660, when he returned to Dillingen, Germany. He died there on Nov. 11.

WANINGUS, ST. (d. 683?). Appointed governor of an area in Normandy by the Merovingian Clotaire III, he gave up courtly idleness and wealth and with St. Wandregisilus established an abbey at Fontenelle and the church of the Holy Trinity in the valley of Fécamp. F. D. Jan. 9.

WARCOP, BL. THOMAS (d. 1597), martyr. A Yorkshire gentleman, he was condemned for aiding and sheltering priests, with one of whom, Bl. William Andleby, he was hanged at York, England. He was beatified in 1929. F. D. July 4.

WARD, ARTEMUS. *See* Browne, Charles Farrar.

WARD, BERNARD NICHOLAS (1857–1920), author. Born in Old Hall, Hertfordshire, England, on Feb. 4, he studied at St. Edmund's, Old Hall, and Oscott, was ordained in 1882, served as master of Old Hall in 1882–85, established a new mission at Willesden in 1885–88, taught at Oscott in 1888–90, and was vice-president and then president (1893–1916) of St. Edmund's. He became a domestic prelate in 1895, canon of Westminster in 1903, and published *History of St. Edmund's* (1893), *Commentary on St. Luke, Life of St. Edmund of Canterbury, Catholic London a Century Ago, The Dawn of the Catholic Revival* (1909), *The Eve of Catholic Emancipation* (1911–12), and *The Sequel to Catholic Emancipation* (1915). He was appointed first bishop of Brentwood, England, in 1917, and died there on Jan. 21.

WARD, FELIX (1854–1927). Born in Limerick, Ireland, he was brought to the United States in his youth, became a Passionist at Pittsburgh, and was ordained in 1878. He wrote a history of his order, of which he became provincial, and died in Hoboken, New Jersey, on June 9.

WARD, HUGH (1590?–1635), hagiographer. Born in Donegal, Ireland, he went to Spain in 1607, studied at Salamanca, met Luke Wadding, and became a Franciscan in 1616. After ordination he taught philosophy at Paris and at St. Anthony's College, Louvain, where he became rector in 1626. He developed a circle of archaeological scholars there, searched Europe for documents relating to Irish saints, and with Fr. Patrick Fleming and Bro. Michael O'Clery gathered materials for *Thesaurus antiquitatum hibernicarum,* a project developed after his death at Louvain, Flanders, on Nov. 8. He wrote on Irish names and martyrs, and on SS. Patrick and Rumold, as well as Latin epigrams and hymns.

WARD, JAMES HARMAN (1806–1861). Born in Hartford, Connecticut, he studied at Vermont Military Academy and Trinity College in Hartford, was appointed a midshipman in 1823, became a convert, taught at the Naval Academy, and wrote *Manual of Naval Tactics* (1858) and *Steam for Millions.* When the Civil War broke out he was put in charge of the Potomac flotilla in 1861, and was killed in an attack on Matthias Point, Virginia, on June 27, the first Union naval officer to die in the war.

WARD, JOHN CHAMBERLAIN (1873–1929), bishop. Born in West View, Ohio, on May 25, he studied at St. Meinrad's seminary, Indiana, and was ordained in 1884, did parish work in Leavenworth, Kansas, until 1910, was appointed bishop of Kansas City, Kansas, in 1910, and died there on Apr. 29.

WARD, BL. MARGARET (d. 1588), martyr. Born in Congleton, Cheshire, she, with her Irish servant, Bl. John Roche (alias Neale), helped Fr. Richard Watson escape from Bridewell prison. When they refused to disclose the priest's hide-out, they were hanged, drawn, and quartered at Tyburn. They were beatified in 1929. F. D. Aug. 30.

WARD, MARY (1585–1645), foundress. Born on Jan. 23 in Yorkshire, England, she joined the Poor Clares in St. Omer as a lay sister in 1606, founded a house for Englishwomen at Gravelines in 1607, and in 1609 formed a group of her followers into a religious community in St. Omer devoted to founding schools. The community incurred much disfavor for its innovations (no enclosure, no choir, no religious habit, freedom from diocesan supervision), and, though it spread to Flanders, Bavaria, Austria, and Italy and had numerous influential supporters, was suppressed in 1630 when she applied to the papacy for formal approbation. Encouraged by Pope Urban VIII, she reconstituted her congregation, returned to England in 1639, and in 1642 established her

group at Heworth, near York, where she died on Jan. 23. The rule of this institute had its rule approved by Pope Clement XI in 1703, and as the Institute of Mary by Pope Pius IX in 1877.

WARD, THOMAS (1652–1708). Born in Danby castle, near Guisborough, Yorkshire, England, on Apr. 13, he possibly was educated at Cambridge, tutored, and became a convert. He served in the papal guard against the Turks, returned to England in 1688, and wrote controversial works, chief of which are *England's Reformation* (1710) and *Errata to the Protestant Bible* (1688). He died in St. Germain-des-Prés, Paris.

WARD, WILFRID PHILIP (1856–1916), editor. Born in Ware, Hertfordshire, England, on Jan. 2, son of William George Ward and brother of Bernard, he studied at Ushaw, the Gregorian in Rome, and at London. He married Josephine Mary Hope-Scott in 1887, taught philosophy at Ushaw in 1890, was a member of the royal commission on Irish university education in 1891, examiner in philosophy at the Royal University of Ireland in 1891–92, and in 1906 became editor of the *Dublin Review.* He wrote apologetical works: *The Wish to Believe* (1882), *The Clothes of Religion* (1886), *Witnesses to the Unseen* (1893); collections of essays: *Problems and Persons* (1903), *Ten Personal Studies* (1908), and *Men and Matters* (1914); and biographies of his father, Cardinals Newman and Wiseman, and a memoir of Aubrey de Vere. He was a co-founder of the Synthetic Society (1896–1908) which discussed philosophy and religion. He died in Hampstead, England, on Apr. 9.

WARD, WILLIAM. *See* Webster, Bl. William.

WARD, WILLIAM GEORGE (1812–1882), author. Born in London, on Mar. 21, he studied at Winchester and Oxford and became a fellow at Balliol College. He became an Anglican minister, taught mathematics at Balliol, and was an influential figure in the religious revival at the university. At first an opponent of the Oxford Movement, he became an enthusiastic follower of John Henry Newman and the Tractarians in 1838 and on the publication of *Tract 90* strongly defended Newman in two pamphlets. His support of the Tractarian movement caused him to lose his teaching positions. His *The Ideal of a Christian Church* appeared in 1844, was severely censured by convocation for its Catholic tinge, and early in 1845 he was deprived of his university degrees. In Sept. he became a convert, taught moral philosophy at Old Hall in 1846, dogmatic philosophy at St. Edmund's in 1852–58, became editor of the *Dublin Review* in 1863, and in the fifteen years of his editorship made it a leading Catholic periodical. He was an uncompromising controversalist, a vigorous supporter of papal infallibility, opposed liberalism and modernism in the Church, and was co-founder of the Metaphysical Society in 1869. He also wrote *On Nature and Grace*, a theological treatise (1858). He died in Hampstead, England, on July 6.

WARDE, MARY FRANCIS XAVIER (1810–1884). Born in Mountrath, Queen's County, Ireland, she joined the Sisters of Mercy in 1828, was appointed superior of the Carlow convent in 1837, founded the convent of Naas in 1839 and of Weyford in 1840, and in 1843 went to Pittsburgh, Pennsylvania, to establish a foundation there. She opened houses in Chicago in 1846, Loretto, Pennsylvania, in 1848, and Providence, Rhode Island, in 1850. By the time of her death in Manchester, New Hampshire, on Sept. 17, she had opened convents and schools from coast to coast.

WARHAM, WILLIAM (1450?–1532), archbishop. Born in Church Oakley, Hampshire, England, he studied at Winchester and Oxford, became a fellow at the latter in 1475, received his doctorate in law in 1488, became an advocate in the London ecclesiastical courts, and in 1490 was appointed head of Oxford's civil law school. Widely recognized for his legal abilities, he served on diplomatic missions during which he obtained numerous ecclesiastical benefices, became master of the rolls in 1494, resigned to become keeper of the great seal, and in 1501 was elected bishop of London (consecrated in 1502). He was nominated archbishop of Canterbury by the pope in 1503, appointed chancellor of England in 1504, chancellor of Oxford in 1506, and crowned Henry VIII and Catherine of Aragon in 1509. He had great influence during the early part of Henry's reign, but was obliged to resign the chancellorship in 1515 because of his opposition to Henry's French policy and the rise of Wolsey, who succeeded him. He became involved in a dispute with the cardinal in 1518 when as papal legate Wolsey infringed on Warham's rights as metropolitan. In the question of the king's divorce he worked to conciliate all parties. He acted as assessor for Wolsey in 1527 to investigate the validity of Henry's marriage to Catherine, was appointed the queen's counsel, though offering her no assistance, and in 1530 signed Henry's petition to the pope for the divorce. He supported Henry's initial moves to seize control of the Church in England, but in 1532 changed his position and protested the king's and parliament's actions against the pope and his own ecclesiastical authority. He died in Hackington, England, on Aug. 22.

WARTENBERG, FRANZ WILHELM VON (1593–1661), cardinal. Son of Duke Ferdinand of Bavaria and Marie Pettenbeckin, he was born in Munich on Mar. 1, studied at Ingolstadt and the German College in Rome, became president of Elector Ferdinand of Cologne's council in 1621, a member of the Ratisbon diet in 1622, and bishop of Osnabrück in 1625. When he occupied the see in 1628, he re-established Catholicism in his largely Protestant diocese, was elected bishop of Verden in 1630 and of Minden in 1631, was forced to surrender the see of Osnabrück to Swedish conquerors in 1633, and was ordained a priest and consecrated a bishop while in exile in 1636. He was appointed coadjutor-bishop of Ratisbon while in Rome in 1641, vicar apostolic of Bremen in 1645, and succeeded to the see of Ratisbon in 1650. He was obliged to surrender Verden, Minden, and Bremen to the Protestants by the Treaty of Westphalia, was created a cardinal in 1661, and died in Ratisbon, Germany on Dec. 1.

WARWICK, RICHARD BEAUCHAMP, EARL OF. *See* Beauchamp, Richard.

WATERSON, BL. EDWARD (d. 1593), martyr. Born in London, he journeyed to Turkey, became a convert at the English College, Rome, studied at Rheims, and was ordained in 1592. When he slipped into England he was captured at Newcastle, and hanged, drawn, and quartered because of his priesthood. He was beatified in 1929. F. D. Jan. 7.

WATERTON, CHARLES (1782–1865), naturalist. Born in Walton Hall, near Wakefield, Yorkshire, England, he studied at Stonyhurst, and in 1804 went to Georgetown, British Guiana, to oversee his uncle's estates. He spent 1812–28 exploring Guiana and studying its tropical fauna. He returned to England in 1829, where he remained the rest of his life except for trips to Europe and the United States. He wrote *Wanderings in South America* and an *Autobiography*, and died at Walton Hall, where he had created a wildlife sanctuary.

WATKINSON, BL. ROBERT (1579?–1602), martyr. Born in Hemingborough, Yorkshire, England, he studied at Douai and Rome, was ordained at Arras in 1602, and entered the English mission that year under the alias of John Wilson. He was arrested in London at twenty-three and executed at Tyburn for his priesthood. F. D. Apr. 20.

WATTEAU, JEAN ANTOINE (1684–1721), painter. Born in Valenciennes, France, on Oct. 10, he studied under Guérin, went to Paris in 1702, where he worked under both Gillot and Audran, director of the Luxembourg. He attracted the attention and patronage of the art collector, de Crozat, and in 1717 was admitted to the French Academy when his *Embarkation for Cythera* was the sensation of the season. He became noted for his paintings of picnics, festivals, balls, military encampments, pastoral scenes (for which he was called "Le Peintre des fêtes galantes"), which introduced a new era in French art, typified by fanciful, graceful canvases touched by diffused lighting. He died in Nogent-sur-Marne, France, on July 18.

WATTERSON, JOHN AMBROSE (1844–1899), bishop. Born in Bairdstown, Pennsylvania, on May 27, he studied at Mt. St. Mary's, Maryland, was ordained in 1868, taught at Mt. St. Mary's until 1877, and was its rector until 1880, when he was appointed bishop of Columbus, Ohio. He died there on Apr. 17.

WATTSON, LEWIS THOMAS (1863–1940), founder. Born in Millington, Maryland, on Jan. 16, he studied at the General Theological seminary, New York, and after his graduation in 1885 became rector of St. John's Episcopal church in Kingston, New York. He left in 1895 to assume a pastorate in Omaha, Nebraska, became a novitiate in the Episcopal Order of the Holy Cross in Maryland in 1898, and was professed as a friar, taking the name Paul. He built a monastery in Graymoor, near Garrison, New York, in 1900, and later that year received his first member of the Society of the Atonement, as he called his new order. He founded *The Lamp* in 1903, launched the Church Unity Octave in 1908, and in 1909 brought seventeen of his Society into the Catholic Church en bloc by special dispensation of Pope Pius X. These included a group of nuns led by Sr. Mary Lurana White, who, encouraged by Fr. Paul, had founded a nun's community at Graymoor in 1898. Fr. Paul entered St. Joseph's seminary, Yonkers, New York, and in 1910 was ordained. He was subjected to numerous court suits against the property he and Sr. Lurana held, which were settled when they made payments to the plaintiffs. He built St. Christopher's Inn for homeless men, promoted his octave of prayer, and in 1916 had it extended to the universal Church by Pope Benedict XVI as The Chair of Unity Octave. He established the Graymoor Press in 1921, a major seminary in Washington, D.C., in 1925, launched the "Ave Maria Hour" on radio in 1935, and saw his order spread to three continents by the time of his death at Graymoor on Feb. 8.

WAUCHOPE, ROBERT (d. 1551). When Archbishop Cromer was deposed in 1539 on suspicion of heresy, Wauchope became primate of Armagh, Ireland. He was a noted theologian and was present at the Council of Trent.

WAVRIN, JEHAN DE (1394?–1474?), historian. The seigneur de Forestal was a French chronicler, whose *Recueil des croniques et anciennes istories de la Grant Bretaigne* recorded the actual and legendary history of England to 1471.

WAY, BL. WILLIAM (1561–1588), martyr.

Born in Exeter, England, he was educated and ordained (1586) at Rheims and sent on the English mission. He was arrested under the name Flower, condemned as a priest, and hanged, drawn, and quartered at Kingston-on-Thames during the Elizabethan persecution. He was beatified in 1929. F. D. Sept. 23.

WAYNFLETE, WILLIAM (1395?–1486), bishop. Born in Wainfleet, England, he studied at Winchester and Oxford, was ordained in 1426, and became Master of Winchester School in 1429, and a fellow of Eton College in 1440 and its provost in 1443. He was named bishop of Winchester in 1447, and developed a school of philosophy and theology at Oxford in 1448 which became Magdalen College in 1458. He was a member of the king's council, was an intermediary with the rebel Jack Cade, fell out of favor with the Yorkists as a result, but was able to break with them when he was named chancellor by King Henry VI in 1456. He caused the trial and deposition of Bishop Pecocke of Chichester for his Lollard tendencies in 1457, was forced to resign his chancellorship in 1460 when the duke of York's forces were victorious in the War of the Roses, and when the duke was proclaimed king as Edward IV in 1461 was forced into hiding. He was pardoned by Edward the following year, but joined the revolt which freed Henry VI in 1470, crowned Henry king, but when the Lancastrian forces were defeated at Barnet and Tewkesbury, sued for a pardon and took an oath of loyalty to Edward. He remained loyal to Edward and Richard III, and founded a school at Wainfleet in 1484, and died at his palace in South Waltham, Hampshire, on Aug. 11.

WEALE, WILLIAM HENRY JAMES (1832–1917), critic. Born in London on Mar. 8, he was educated there at King's College, became a convert in 1849, married Helena Walton, and settled in Bruges in 1855. He wrote a guidebook on Belgian and Rhenish archaeology, and studies of Flemish art, early bookbinding, manuscript illustration, heraldry, the city of Bruges, and the antiquities of Flanders. He classified the Flemish art in the South Kensington Museum of London in 1872 and in 1890 became keeper of the National Art Library. He was an associate of the Royal Academy of Belgium and was decorated by King Leopold. He died in London on Apr. 26.

WEATHERS, WILLIAM (1814–1895), bishop. Born in Wales on Nov. 12, he studied at Baddesley and Old Hall, and was ordained at the latter in 1838. He was its vice-president and procurator in 1843–51 and president to 1868, and reorganized the college. In 1869 he was appointed rector of the Hammersmith seminary, a position he held until it was closed in 1892. He was elected a canon of Westminster in 1851, was theologian for the English bishops in preparations for the Vatican Council in 1868, was elevated to domestic prelate in 1869, and three years later was named auxiliary to Archbishop Manning and titular bishop of Amycla. He retired to Islesworth, Middlesex, as chaplain to the Sisters of Chanty, and died there on Mar. 4.

WEBB, BENJAMIN JOSEPH (1814–1897), journalist. Born in Bardstown, Kentucky, he studied at St. Joseph's College there, became a printer, and worked for the Louisville *Journal*. In 1836 he began publishing the Bardstown *Catholic Advocate*, moved it to Louisville in 1841, and returned as manager in 1847. Bishop Spalding, one of its editors, persuaded him to publish the Louisville *Catholic Guardian* from 1858 to 1862, after his successful attack on the Know-Nothing movement in *Letters of a Kentucky Catholic*. He was a regular contributor to the *Catholic Advocate* after its revival in 1869, author of *The Centenary of Catholicity in Kentucky* (1884), and state senator from 1867 to 1875. He died in Louisville on Aug. 2.

WEBBE, SAMUEL (1740–1816), composer. Born probably in London, he was apprenticed to a cabinetmaker when eleven, and then became a music copyist for Welcker in Soho, who secured organ lessons for him from Barbandt, organist of the Bavarian ambassador's chapel. He began composing in 1763, won the Catch Club prize for *O That I Had Wings* (1766), and composed other catches, glees, and songs, for which he won twenty-seven medals during his lifetime. He became secretary to the Catch Club in 1794, librarian of the Glee Club in 1787, served as organist of the Sardinian embassy from 1776 to 1795, and published a *Collection of Motets* (1792) and *A Collection of Masses for Small Choirs* (1792), which was widely used, and nine books of glees. He died in London on May 25.

WEBER, ANSELM (1862–1921), missioner. Born in New Salem, Michigan, on Nov. 10, he was educated at St. Francis College, Cincinnati, Ohio, became a Friar Minor in 1882, was ordained in 1889, taught in Cincinnati, and in 1898 was sent to serve the Navajos in Arizona. He began a school at St. Michael's, had the Indian reservations extended, gained some helpful legislation on their behalf, and worked throughout Arizona and New Mexico. He wrote a Navajo dictionary and catechism and was preparing a grammar when he died in Rochester, Minnesota, on Mar. 7.

WEBER, CARL MARIA FRIEDRICH ERNST VON (1786–1826), composer. Born in Eutin, Lower Saxony, on Nov. 18, son of an impoverished nobleman who was director of a traveling dramatic company and gave him some musical training, he studied under Michael Haydn in Salzburg in 1798, and Johann Kal-

cher in Munich, composed his first opera, *Das Waldmädchen*, in 1800 when just past thirteen, and in 1803 was in Vienna, where he studied under Abbé Vogler. He was appointed choirmaster of the Breslau City Theatre, in 1804–6, joined the household of Duke Eugene of Würtemberg in 1806, became private secretary to Eugene's brother, Duke Ludwig, who made him music teacher of his children, and matched the duke's dissipations. In 1810, the duke's brother, King Frederic of Würtemberg, exiled Weber for selling exemptions from military service, an unjust charge. He gave a series of concerts until 1813, when he became Kapellmeister of the Prague National Theatre. In 1816 he was appointed conductor of the Dresden Royal Opera House, and there became a founder of the German romantic school of music. He died in London on June 5 while supervising the production of his opera, *Oberon*. He composed a huge body of work: operas, two symphonies, piano concertos, chamber and orchestral music, and a few liturgical works, including two masses. His operas are *Peter Schmoll und seine Nachbarn* (1803), *Turandot, Rübezahl* (unfinished, 1805), *Silvana* (1810), *Abu Hassan* (1811), *Preciosa* (1821), *Der Freischütz* (1821), *Euryanthe* (1823), and the unfinished *Die drei Pintos* which Mahler completed and produced in 1888. He is also known for four piano sonatas in C, A flat, D minor, and E minor, concertos in F minor (*Concertstrück*), C, and E flat.

WEBER, FRIEDRICH WILHELM (1813–1894), poet. Born in Alhausen, Westphalia, on Dec. 24, he studied in Paderborn and took his doctorate in medicine at Greifswalk. He practiced medicine at Driburg for a quarter of a century, served as a member of the Centre party in the Prussian house of deputies, and in 1887 moved to Nieheim, where he died on Apr. 5. He wrote much poetry, chief of which were *Dreizehnlinden* (1878), *Gedichte* (1881), *Goliath* (1892), and *Herbstblätter* (1895).

WEBER, HEINRICH (1834–1898), historian. Born in Euerdorf, Würzburg, Germany, on June 21, he studied at the Würzburg seminary, in Bamberg, and at Würzburg, and was ordained in 1857. He did parish work, taught in the Würzburg gymnasium in 1865, and in 1871–98 taught at the Bamberg lyceum. He remained until his death there on Jan. 18. He wrote historical treatises, pamphlets, and biographies, chief of which was *Geschichte der gelehrten Schulen in Hochstift Bamberg, 1007–1803* (1880–82). He died in Bamberg, Germany, on Jan. 18.

WEBER, JOHANN CHRYSANTH (1798–1858). He was born in Lienz, Tyrol, on Oct. 26, studied at Innsbruck, joined the Benedictines in Marienberg, taking the name Beda, continued his studies at Brixen, and was ordained in 1824. He taught in Meran from 1828 to 1848, when he was elected deputy to the national parliament in Frankfort. He became pastor there, founded the newspaper, *Das Frankfurter katholische Kirchenblatt* in 1853, wrote political and ecclesiastical treatises, was appointed canon of Limburg, episcopal commissary and a member of the diocesan court, and died in Frankfort, Germany, on Feb. 28.

WEBERN, ANTON VON (1883–1945), composer. Born in Vienna on Dec. 3, he studied and took his doctorate in philosophy there in 1906, and was a pupil and ardent follower of Arnold Schönberg. He had been interested in mediaeval polyphony, but with Schönberg and Alban Berg struck out in strikingly modern fashion. He conducted in Germany, Prague, and Vienna (notably for Schönberg's Society for Private Performances, in 1918), established a choir, then retired to Mödling to write and teach. He adopted and sought to popularize Schönberg's theories opposing the "tonality" of Western music. Webern went further than his master in developing the latter's twelve-tone serial techniques. His work was banned by the Nazis and he was ordered not to teach, taking a position as proofreader in Vienna to keep alive. He moved to Salzburg near the end of World War II and was accidentally shot and killed by an occupation-force soldier while walking in his garden at Mittersill on Sept. 15. He wrote ten choral settings of Stefan George (1908–9), pieces for orchestra, and for violin and piano, and the expressionistic *Marcia funebra*, pieces for cello, and songs (to words by Rainier Maria Rilke and others). He also wrote cantatas, variations for orchestra, and chamber music (particularly in 1927–38), and five canons based on prayers from the breviary, and three *Spiritual Folk Sons*.

WEBLEY, VEN. HENRY (d. 1588), martyr. *See* Dean, Bl. William.

WEBLEY, VEN. THOMAS (d. 1585), martyr. A dyer in Gloucester, England, he was arrested with Bl. Thomas Alfield for distributing Dr. Allen's *True and Modest Defence*, was imprisoned in the Tower, tortured, and hanged at Tyburn on July 6.

WEBSTER, BL. AUGUSTINE (d. 1535), martyr. Trained at Sheen, England, he was prior of the Charterhouse at Axholme, and was consulting with the Carthusians in London when, attending Bl. John Houghton on a visit to Thomas Cromwell, he was seized and imprisoned in the Tower. At a later trial he refused to subscribe to Henry VIII's Act of Supremacy and was treated most savagely before and after being hanged at Tyburn. He was beatified in 1886. F. D. May 4.

WEBSTER, BL. WILLIAM (d. 1641), martyr. Also known as William Ward, he was born in Thornby, Westmoreland, England, went to Douai in 1604, was ordained in 1608, and sent on the English mission. Twenty of his next thirty-three years were spent in prisons. When he refused to leave London, after the parliamentary decree of Apr. 7, 1641 banishing all priests under pain of death, he was captured and hanged at Tyburn. F. D. July 26.

WECHEL, ST. LEONARD VAN (d. 1572), martyr. *See* Pieck, St. Nicholas.

WEDERIG (11th century). He was a Benedictine who converted six wastrel knights who banded together after their reform to build the abbey of Afflighem near Alost, Brabant, on land given in 1084 by the Countess Adela.

WEEDALL, HENRY (1788–1859), educator. Born in London on Sept. 8, he studied at Sedgley Park and Oscott, and was ordained in 1814. He became prefect of studies at Oscott in 1816, vice-president in 1818, and president in 1826. He became Bishop Thomas Walsh's vicar general in 1828, was appointed vicar apostolic of the northern district and titular bishop of Abydos in 1840, but declined the honor, and was rector at Leamington from 1843 to 1848. He then became vicar general of the central district under Bishop Ullathorne, and in 1852 first provost of the Birmingham chapter. He returned to Oscott in 1853, was made a domestic prelate in 1854, and died at Oscott, England, on Nov. 7.

WEGG-PROSSER, FRANCIS RICHARD HAGGIT (1824–1911). Francis Haggit was born in Newnham Courtney, Oxfordshire, England, studied at Eton and Oxford, adopted the name Wegg-Prosser when he inherited his great-uncle's estates near Hereford in 1849, and served in parliament from 1847 to 1852, when he became a convert. He built a church on his estate which became pro-cathedral for the diocese of Newport and a novitiate for the Benedictines, and was active in church organizations. He died on his estate on Aug. 16.

WEHRLE, VINCENT DE PAUL (1855–1941), bishop. Born in Berg, St. Gall, Switzerland, on Dec. 19, he studied at the diocesan seminary there and at Einsiedeln, where he joined the Benedictines in 1875, and after his ordination in 1882 was sent to the United States. He served as a missionary in Arkansas, Indiana, and the Dakotas, founding parishes, missions, and the priory of St. Gall in 1884 and Assumption abbey at Richardton, North Dakota, in 1901, of which he was elected abbot in 1903. He was appointed first bishop of Bismarck, North Dakota, in 1910, retired in 1939 and was named titular bishop of Teos, and died on Nov. 2.

WEIS, NICOLAUS VON (1796–1869), bishop. Born in Rimlingen, Lorraine, on Mar. 8, he studied at the Mainz seminary, was ordained in 1818, taught at the seminary for two years, and then did parish work. He was canon of the cathedral in 1822–37, during which time he and Andreas Rass translated ecclesiastical works, prepared a twenty-four-volume German edition of Butler's *Lives of the Saints* (1821–27), founded the review, *Der Katholik*, in 1821, of which he was editor from 1827 to 1841, and was dean of the cathedral from 1837 to 1842, when he was appointed bishop of Speyer, Germany. He died there on Dec. 13.

WEISLINGER, JOHANN NIKOLAUS (1691–1755), author. Born in Püttlingen, Lorraine, he studied in Strassburg and at Heidelberg, was ordained in 1726, became parish priest at Waldulm, and was at Kappel-Rodeck from 1730 to 1750. He achieved recognition as a controversialist and wrote *Friss Vogel oder stirb* (1723), among other polemics. He died in Kappel-Rodeck, Baden, on Aug. 29.

WEISS, JOHANN BAPTIST (1820–1899), historian. Born in Ettenheim, Baden, Germany, on July 17, he studied at Freiburg, Tübingen, Heidelberg, and Munich, taught English and French in Freiburg, and in 1848 was appointed lecturer in history at its university. He became editor of *Freiburger Zeitung* in 1850, professor of Austrian history at Graz in 1853, and taught there until 1891. He wrote, among other historical works, a thirty-two-volume history of the world to the Congress of Vienna. He died in Graz, Austria, on Mar. 8.

WEITENAUER, IGNATIUS (1709–1783). Born in Ingolstadt, Bavaria, Germany, on Nov. 1, he became a Jesuit in 1724, was ordained, and taught at several Jesuit colleges, chiefly at Eichstädt for eleven years, and in 1753 became professor of philosophy and oriental languages at Innsbruck, where he wrote biblical and linguistic treatises. When his Society was suppressed in 1773, he continued his writing at the Cistercian abbey of Salsmansweiler in Salem, Württemberg, and died there on Feb. 4. Among his outstanding works are *Biblia sacra* (1773), *Lexicon biblicum* (1758), *Hexaglotton geminum*; he also translated the *Bible* into German and edited the nineteen-volume *Subsidia eloquentiae sacrae* (1764–69).

WELBOURN, BL. THOMAS (d. 1605), martyr. Born in Yorkshire, England, he became a teacher, was convicted of making Catholic converts, and was hanged, drawn, and quartered at York. He was beatified in 1929. F. D. Aug. 1.

WELCH, THOMAS ANTHONY (1884–1959), bishop. Born in Faribault, Minnesota, on Nov. 2, he studied at St. Paul College and seminary, and was ordained there in 1909. He was secretary to Archbishop Ireland from 1909 to 1918 and to Archbishop Dowling from 1919 to 1922, was chancellor of St. Paul in 1919–24

and vicar general in 1924–25, was made a domestic prelate in 1924, and was appointed bishop of Duluth, Minnesota, in 1925. He died on Sept. 9.

WELD, FREDERICK ALOYSIUS (1823–1891), governor. Born in Chideok Manor, Dorset, England, he studied at Stonyhurst and Fribourg, went to New Zealand in 1843, and thoroughly explored the country. He became a member of the house of representatives there in 1853, a member of the executive council in 1854, and minister of native affairs in 1860. He became premier and chief secretary in 1864 and a proponent of home rule for the colony. He retired from public life in 1866 because of ill-health and returned briefly to England. He served as governor of West Australia from 1869 to 1875, of Tasmania from 1875 to 1880, and of Singapore and the Straits Settlements from 1880 to 1887. He was given high honors by the British government and make a knight of the Roman Order by Pope Pius IX, retired to Chideok Manor in 1887, and died there.

WELD, THOMAS (1750–1810). Born in Lulworth, England, he studied at St. Omer, Bruges, became noted for his charity to French refugees, and in 1794 gave Stonyhurst Hall and some thirty acres to the exiled Jesuit community from St. Omer, marking the founding of Stonyhurst College in England. He also supported the Trappist monastery at Mt. Melleray, Ireland, and the English Poor Clares, who had been forced to flee from Gravelines. He died at Stonyhurst.

WELD, THOMAS (1773–1837), cardinal. Son of Thomas Weld of Lulworth, he was born in London on Jan. 22, continued his father's charitable activities, and was a staunch defender of Bishop Milner. On the death of his wife he studied for the priesthood, was ordained in 1821, and was consecrated titular bishop of Amycla and coadjutor of the Upper Canada vicariate in 1826, but never reached Canada because of ill-health which forced him to resign his vicariate. He was created a cardinal in 1830.

WELLS, BL. SWITHIN (1536–1591), martyr. Born near Twyford, England, he served as a schoolmaster until jailed in 1586 on suspicion of aiding the Babington plot. He apparently had been converted three years before. Released, he traveled to Rome in the service of the earl of Southampton and returned to work for the Catholic underground in England. Topcliffe's spies surprised Fr. Edmund Genings saying mass at the Wells home in 1591, and the two were hanged. His name is also spelled Swithun. F. D. Dec. 10.

WELONSKI, CASIMIR (1833?–1915). Stationed at the cathedral in Plotsk, Poland, he became rector of the seminary there and later became a Piarist as Fr. Justinus. He was prior general of his order and died in Czestochowa, Poland.

WELSER, BARTHOLOMEUS (1488–1561), merchant. Born in Augsburg, Germany, he worked for his father, a prosperous merchant, until the latter's death in 1518, when, with his brother Anton, he founded Wesler & Co. The firm was granted exclusive trading rights in Venezuela in 1528 by Charles V, to whom they repeatedly extended loans and who made Bartholomeus a noble in 1532, and held the monopoly there until 1556 when the Spanish crown reclaimed the country. He served on the privy council from 1548 to 1556, retired from the business in 1553, and died in Amberg, Swabia.

WELSH, MARTIN STANISLAUS (1876–1961). Born in Cambridge, Massachusetts, on June 4, he studied at Boston College and St. John's seminary, Boston, joined the Dominicans, and was ordained in 1906. After further study in Rome, he taught at the Dominican House of Studies, Washington, D.C., and was then named president of Aquinas College, Columbus, Ohio. After fourteen years in this position, he was transferred to Providence College where he taught mathematics for thirty years, serving as vice-president in 1923–31. He wrote theological treatises and on canon law, spent the last years of his life as chaplain for the Dominican sisters in Plainville, and died in Natick, Massachusetts, on June 21.

WELTE, BENEDICT (1805–1885), scholar. Born in Ratzenried, Württemberg, Germany, on Nov. 25, he studied at Tübingen and Bonn, was ordained at twenty-eight, and became a professor of Old Testament exegesis at Tübingen in 1840. He finished Herbst's *Historisch-kritische Einleitung* (1840–44) writing the third volume himself, translated an Armenian biography of St. Mesrob, the book of Job in 1849, and with Heinrich Wetzer edited the twelve-volume *Kirchenlexikon*, an encyclopedia of Catholicism. He became canon of the Rottenburg cathedral in 1857, and died on May 27.

WENCESLAS (d. 1305), king of Poland. Son of the king of Bohemia, he was elected king about 1300. Challenged by the Piast faction, he was forced to abdicate, and returned to Bohemia.

WENCESLAUS (1361–1419), emperor, German king. Son of Emperor Charles IV and Anna, daughter of Duke Henry II of Schweidnitz, he was born in Nuremberg, Germany, on Feb. 26, was crowned king of Bohemia as Wenceslaus IV in 1363, invested with Brandenburg in 1373, and at his father's instigation was elected king of the Germans and emperor in 1376. He became actual ruler on his father's death in 1378, inherited Luxembourg in 1383, and helped secure the throne of Hungary for his half-brother Sigismund in 1387. Faced by widespread dissension in Germany, he devoted himself to Bohemia after 1389. He became involved in a dispute with his nobles and hierarchy (especially with the archbishop of Prague, whose vicar general, St. John of Nepomuk, he had killed when his plans for a new Bohemian bishopric in 1396 had been opposed) and was imprisoned in 1393–94, but released at the demand of his German princes. His attempt with Charles VI of France to induce Pope Boniface IX and antipope Benedict XIII to resign so a newly elected pope would end the schism, and his neglect of German affairs, his alliance with France, his sale of Milan to Gian Galeazzo Visconti, and his prolonged absences in Bohemia caused four electors to meet and declare him deposed in 1400; in his place they elected Rupert III count palatinate of the Rhine. In 1402 he fought with Sigismund, who held him in captivity for a year and a half, during which he resigned the crown of Bohemia. When Sigismund returned to Hungary in 1404, Wenceslaus resumed the throne of Bohemia, renounced his right to the German throne in 1410, and faced religious difficulties in his domains. He was favorably disposed to John Hus, attempted to persuade antipope John XXIII not to act against Hus, and twice (1411, 1413) attempted to mediate in Hus's favor. He persuaded Hus to leave Prague when the reformer was excommunicated and the city threatened with an interdict in 1412, did little to suppress the religious outbursts which erupted after Hus's execution at Constance in 1415, and died of apoplexy in Prague on Aug. 16 when rioting broke out there.

WENCESLAUS IV, king of Bohemia. *See* Wenceslaus, emperor.

WENCESLAUS, ST. (907?–935). Born near Prague, Bohemia, son of Duke Ratislav and Drahomira, he was raised and educated by his grandmother, St. Ludmila. On the death of his father in battle against the Magyars, the anti-Christian faction in Bohemia, encouraged by Drahomira, attempted to gain control and murdered Ludmila. Despite this opposition, Wenceslaus became duke, exiled his mother, and inaugurated a rule marked by patience and justice. Politically, he placed his duchy under the protection of Germany and in 926 acknowledged his vassalage to King Henry I. His Christian, pro-Germany policy, coupled with his strict measures against his opposition, led to the rise of a powerful party of Czech nobles which his brother Boleslav joined. Wenceslaus was murdered at Alt-Bunzlau, Bohemia, by his brother and other malcontents. Although he was acclaimed as a martyr in the Roman Martyrology, his death seems to have been due to politics. He is a patron of Bohemia and Slovakia and honored on Sept. 28.

WENDEL, JOSEF (1901–1960), cardinal. Born in Blieskastel, Saar, Germany, on May 2, he studied at the Speyer seminary and the German College, Rome, received doctorates in philosophy and theology, and was ordained in 1927. He held parish posts, was director of Catholic Charities in Speyer, became coadjutor bishop there in 1941, and succeeded to the see in 1943. He was particularly active on behalf of refugees, rebuilt 120 churches destroyed during the war, and spoke in many areas outside Germany on behalf of its citizens in the postwar period. In 1952 he was named ninth archbishop of Munich and seventieth bishop of Freising; he labored for better housing conditions and served as vicar of Catholics in the German armed forces. He was created a cardinal in 1953, organized the 1960 Eucharistic Congress in Munich which attracted a million pilgrims, and died in Munich, Germany, on Dec. 31.

WENDELIN OF SPEYER. *See* Johann von Speyer.

WENRICH OF TRIER (11th century). A canon at Verdun and then located at Trier, Gaul, he was the author of a letter in 1081 to Pope Gregory VII in which he defended Henry IV and condemned Gregory's actions against the emperor. That he was bishop of Gembloux is doubtful.

WERBURGA, ST. (d. 700?). Daughter of King Wulfhere of Mercia and St. Ermenilda, she escaped the threat of a regally arranged marriage and eventually was allowed to enter religious life at Ely, England, under the instruction of St. Etheldreda. Later, she was in charge of convents at Hanbury, Threckingham, and Weedon. F. D. Feb. 3.

WERENFRID, ST. (d. 780?). He went from England to join St. Willibrord on the Frisian mission and died at Arnheim, Netherlands. F. D. Aug. 14.

WERINUS. *See* Gerinus, St.

WERNER, FRIEDRICH LUDWIG ZACHARIAS (1768–1823). Born in Königsberg, Prussia, on Nov. 18, he studied at the university there, was a clerk in the war department, married and was divorced three times, but in 1810 became a convert in Rome. He studied for the priesthood at the Aschaffenburg seminary, where he was ordained in 1814, participated in the Congress of Vienna, and in 1817 joined the household of Archbishop von Hohenwarth of Vienna in 1817. He joined the Redemptorists in 1821, but was obliged to leave because of ill-health. An impressive preacher (his sermons were collected in 1840), he was also noted for his poetry, particularly for his tragedies, *Der Vierundzwanzigster Febnear* (1804) and *Die Mutter der Makkabäer*. He died in Vienna on Feb. 17.

WERNZ, FRANCIS XAVER (1842–1914). Born in Rottweill, Württemberg, on Dec. 4, he became a Jesuit in 1852, taught canon law at the Gregorian in Rome in 1883 and became its rector in 1904, and was elected twenty-fifth general of the Society of Jesus in 1906. He was consultor to several congregations, and was a member of the committee for codifying canon law. During his generalate the Society expanded all over the world despite charges that the order was not loyal to the papacy and was guilty of modernism. He died in Rome on Aug. 19.

WESDIN, PHILIP (1748–1806), missioner. Born in Hoff, Austria, on Apr. 25, he became a Carmelite, taking the name Philip a S. Bartholomaeo, and in 1774 was sent to Malabar. He learned Sanskrit, became vicar general, and returned to Rome in 1789. After a period in Vienna from 1798 to 1800, he became prefect of studies at the Propaganda in Rome, and remained there until his death on Jan. 7. He wrote the first printed Sanskrit grammar, and on the Church in the Orient, Brahminism, linquistics, and scripture.

WESSEL GOESPORT (1420–1489), theologian. Born in Gröningen, Holland, he studied with the Brethren of the Common Life, whom he joined, at Zwolle and at Cologne. He taught at Heidelberg in 1456–57, went to Paris in 1458, where he supported nominalism, and was forced to leave in 1473 when Louis XI issued his decree against nominalism. After a period at Venice and Basle, he returned about 1479 to Holland, and lived at Zwolle and Gröningen, where he died on Oct. 4. Although a layman, he wrote widely on theological subjects: his *Farrago rerum theologicarum* (1521) had a preface by Luther who, with many Protestants, considered him a forerunner of the Reformation. Some of his writings were placed on the Index in the sixteenth century, but there is no question of his basic Catholic beliefs. He is also known as Gansfort Wessel, Harmenss Gansfort or Goesevoyrd.

WESTCOTT, SEBASTIAN (1524–1583?). A chorister at St. Paul's Cathedral, London, he became organist there in 1550, a position he held for the next thirty-three years. The musical plays and pageants he produced were extremely popular and he composed several liturgical works during Queen Mary's reign. He was dismissed in 1559 when he refused to sign the articles of supremacy, but was reinstated by Queen Elizabeth I, imprisoned again in 1577 as a Catholic recusant, and again released at the queen's request in 1578, and died sometime after 1583.

WESTON, WILLIAM (1550?–1615), missioner. Born in Maidstone, England, he studied at Oxford, Paris, and Douai, was ordained, joined the Jesuits in Rome in 1575, and made his novitiate in Spain. He was sent as a missionary to England in 1584, was arrested in

1586, and imprisoned at Wisbech in 1588–98. He was moved to the Tower in 1599, and was exiled from England in 1603. He went at first to Seville, then to Valladolid, Spain, where he became rector and where he died on June 9.

WETTERLÉ, ÉMILE (1861–1931), journalist. Born in Colmar, Alsace, on Apr. 2, he was ordained in 1889, became a leader in Alsace in the pro-French movement, founded the *Alsatian Courier*, and served in the *Reichstag* from 1898 to 1914. Although often condemned and imprisoned for political activity by German authorities, he founded the Alsatian National party in 1910, served France during World War I, and was a member of the French chamber of deputies in 1919–24. He then became canonic counselor to the French embassy to the Vatican. He died in Ouchy, Switzerland, on July 24.

WETZER, HEINRICH JOSEPH (1801–1853), orientalist. Born in Anzefahr, Hesse-Kassel, Germany, on Mar. 19, he studied at Marburg, Tübingen, Freiburg, where he received his doctorate in theology and philosophy in 1824, and Paris. He taught oriental philology at Freiburg in 1830, became librarian there in 1850, and with Benedict Welte edited the twelve-volume *Kirchenlexikon*, an encyclopedia of Catholicism. He died in Freiburg, Germany, on Nov. 5. He also began a study of fourth-century Arianism.

WEYDEN, ROGER. *See* Van der Weyden, Roger.

WHELAN, JAMES (1822–1878), bishop. Born in Kilkenny, Ireland, and baptized on June 8, he went to the United States, studied at St. Rose convent, Springfield, Kentucky, and St. Joseph's priory, Somerset, Ohio, became a Dominican in 1839, and was ordained in Somerset in 1846. He taught at St. Joseph's, was sub-prior in 1848–50, and president in 1851–54, and served as provincial of the Dominicans in the United States in 1854–58. He was appointed titular bishop of Marcopolis and coadjutor of Nashville, Tennessee, in 1859, succeeded to the see the following year, and reigned until 1864, when he resigned and was appointed titular bishop of Diocletianapolis. He died in Zanesville, Ohio, on Feb. 18.

WHELAN, RICHARD VINCENT (1809–1874), bishop. Born in Baltimore on Jan. 28, he studied at Mt. St. Mary's, Maryland, and St. Sulpice, Paris, and was ordained in 1831. He did parish work in Richmond, Virginia, in 1831–40, was consecrated its second bishop in 1841, founded St. Vincent's seminary and college there and was its president until it closed in 1846. In 1850 he was transferred to Wheeling, West Virginia, as its first bishop. He built a cathedral, diocesan seminary, and St. Vincent's College, attended the first and second plenary councils of Baltimore and the Vatican Council of 1869–70, and died in Baltimore on July 7.

WHIPPLE, AMIEL WEEKS (1816–1863), general. Born in Greenwich, Massachusetts, in Oct. or Nov., he studied at Amherst and the Military Academy at West Point. He graduated in 1841 as second lieutenant of artillery, transferred to the engineers, helped survey the boundary between the United States and Canada and Mexico, and the railroad route to the Pacific. He became a captain in 1855, a convert in 1857, and served under Gen. McDowell and Gen. McClellan as chief engineer during the Civil War. He was brigadier general in charge of the Virginia side of the Washington defense system in 1862, was wounded at the battle of Chancellorsville, and died in Washington, D.C., on May 7 shortly after being raised to the rank of major general.

WHITBREAD, BL. THOMAS (d. 1679), martyr. A native of Essex, England, he studied at St. Omer and became a Jesuit at Watten in 1635. He returned to England after ordination, teaching and publishing a number of pamphlets. He was provincial at the time of his arrest during the Titus Oates Plot, and was hanged and quartered with four other priests at Tyburn on the charge of conspiring to kill Charles II. He was beatified in 1929. F. D. June 20.

WHITE, ANDREW (1579–1656), missioner. Born in London, he studied at St. Alban's in Valladolid, the English College in Seville, and Douai, where he was ordained about 1605. He was sent on the English mission in 1606 and was seized and banished. He joined the Jesuits at Louvain in 1607, taught theology at Louvain and Liège, where he became prefect of studies, engaged in occasional mission work in England in 1625–28, and in 1629 returned there and was active in Hampshire. He became interested in the plans of George Calvert, first baron of Baltimore, to establish a Catholic colony in America, and in 1633 joined the expedition to settle Maryland. He worked with the colonists and among the Indians until 1644, when a group of insurgents led by William Claiborne attacked Jesuit settlements, seized Fr. White, and sent him in chains to London. He was tried for treason for his priesthood, acquitted on his plea he had been brought to England forcibly, but banished. He went to the Netherlands, but returned to England in a few months, attempted in vain to return to Maryland, and spent the rest of his life in missionary activities in England and as a chaplain to a noble Hampshire family. Fr. White played an important role in the founding of Maryland. He wrote *Declaratio coloniae domini baronis de Baltimore* to attract colonists for the new colony, *Relatio itineris in Marilandiam*, also written in English as *A Briefe Re-*

lation of the Voyage unto Maryland, and prepared a grammar, dictionary, and catechism for the Indians in their native tongue. He died, probably in London, on Dec. 27.

WHITE, CHARLES DANIEL (1879–1955), bishop. Born in Grand Rapids, Michigan, on Jan. 5, he was educated at St. Francis seminary, Wisconsin, and the Propaganda, Rome, and was ordained in Rome in 1910. He was a curate at St. Andrew's cathedral and taught at St. Joseph's seminary in Grand Rapids in 1911–19, was rector there from 1919, and made a domestic prelate in 1925, and was consecrated bishop of Spokane, Washington, in 1927. He died on Sept. 25.

WHITE, CHARLES IGNATIUS (1807–1878), editor. Born in Baltimore, Maryland, on Feb. 1, he studied at Mt. St. Mary's, Emmitsburg, St. Mary's College, Baltimore, and St. Sulpice, Paris, where he was ordained in 1830. On his return he engaged in pastoral work in Baltimore and the surrounding area and taught moral theology in St. Mary's seminary in 1843–45. He edited the *Annual Catholic Almanac* from 1834 to 1857, founded the *Religious Cabinet* (later, the *United States Catholic Magazine and Metropolitan Magazine*) in 1842, and edited the diocesan weekly *Catholic Mirror*, which he had helped found in 1849, from 1850 to 1855. He became rector at St. Matthew's church in Washington, D.C., in 1857, a position he held until his death there on April 1. He founded a school and church, an infant asylum, and a home for aged Negroes, and also translated several French works.

WHITE, EDWARD DOUGLASS (1825–1921), judge. Born in Lafourche, Louisiana, on Nov. 3, son of Governor Edward White. He studied at Mt. St. Mary's, Maryland, Loyola, New Orleans, and Georgetown. He served with the Confederate army, was captured and paroled in 1863, and admitted to the Louisiana bar in 1868. He was elected state senator in 1874, and was state supreme-court justice in 1877–90, United States senator in 1891–94, and was appointed associate justice of the supreme court in 1894 by President Cleveland, and chief justice in 1910 by President Taft. He wrote opinions on 700 cases, was basically a conservative, revealed a deep knowledge of civil law (from his state experience); a major decision established minimum wages for railroad employees. He was awarded the Laetare Medal in 1914. He died in Washington, D.C., on May 19.

WHITE, BL. EUSTACE (d. 1591), martyr. A native of Louth, Lincolnshire, England, he was converted, studied at Rheims, and was ordained at Rome in 1588. Sent on the English mission, he was arrested at Blandford three years later, tortured for six weeks during the Elizabethan persecution, and hanged, drawn,

and quartered at Tyburn. He was beatified in 1929. F. D. Dec. 10.

WHITE, STEPHEN (1574–1646), educator. Born in Clonmel, Ireland, he studied at Trinity College, Dublin, and the Irish College in Salamanca, Spain, where he joined the Jesuits in 1596. He taught there until 1606, when he went to Ingolstadt to teach, and then to Dillingen. He became noted in Germany for his knowledge of Irish history, returned to Ireland, taught at the Jesuit college in Dublin, and when it was confiscated by the government spent the rest of his life teaching in Waterford and Lismore. He died in Galway, Ireland.

WHITE, STEPHEN MALLORY (1853–1901), senator. Born in San Francisco, California, on Jan. 19, he studied at St. Ignatius (San Francisco) and Santa Clara colleges, studied law, and was admitted to the bar in 1874. He was district attorney of Los Angeles County in 1883–84, state senator in 1889–91, and was elected to the United States Senate in 1893 where he opposed imperialism, big business, and political "bossism" and was in favor of free coinage of silver. He died in Los Angeles on Feb. 21.

WHITE, THOMAS (1593–1676). Born in Essex, England, he studied at St. Omer, Valladolid, and Douai, was ordained in 1617, continued his studies at the Sorbonne, and then returned to Douai, where he taught theology. He was appointed president of the English College in Lisbon in 1630, resigned to return to England in 1633, and devoted himself to writing. He was assailed for some of his theological and political teaching, was censured by the Inquisition in 1655 and 1657, and made his submission to the Holy See. He died in London on July 6.

WHITESIDE, THOMAS (1857–1921), bishop. Born in Lancashire, England, on Apr. 17, he was ordained in Rome in 1885, became rector of St. Joseph's seminary, Upholland, and in 1894 became fourth bishop of Liverpool. He was made an archbishop in 1911, and died in Liverpool on Jan. 28.

WHITFIELD, JAMES (1770–1834), archbishop. Born in Liverpool, England, on Nov. 3, he studied at the Sulpician seminary in Lyons, France, and was ordained in 1809. He did parish work until 1817, when he went to Baltimore, working especially among the Negroes. He was appointed titular bishop of Apollonia and coadjutor of Baltimore in 1828, and was consecrated its archbishop in that year. He opened the first Provincial Council of Baltimore in 1829, a synod in 1831, and convened the second Provincial Council in 1833. He died on Oct. 19 in Baltimore.

WHITING, BL. RICHARD (1460?–1539), martyr. Born in Wrington, Somerset, England, he studied at Cambridge, was ordained in 1501, and in 1525 became last abbot of Benedictine Glastonbury. In 1534 he and his monks took the oath of supremacy, but in 1539 he refused to surrender his monastery to Henry VIII's agents, was arrested, convicted without trial of treason, and hanged, drawn, and quartered at Glastonbury on Nov. 15, with Bl. John Thorne, treasurer of the abbey church, and Roger James, youngest of the community. They were beatified in 1895. F. D. Dec. 1.

WHITTY, ROBERT (1817–1895). Born in Pouldarrig, Wexford, Ireland, on Sept. 1, he studied at Maynooth, was ordained in 1840 in London, became provost of the metropolitan chapter, and in 1850 was appointed Bishop Wiseman's vicar general. He became a Jesuit in Verona in 1857, lecturer in canon law at St. Beuno's College, Wales, was elected provincial of Scotland, and then served as assistant to the general of his Society. He died on Sept. 1.

WIBALD (1098–1158). Born near Stavelot, Belgium, he studied at the monastic schools there and at Liège, joined the Benedictines at Waulsort in 1117, where he became head of the monastic school, went to Stavelot, and in 1130 was elected abbot of Stavelot and Malmédy, and in 1146, of Corvey, Fishbeck, and Kemnade. He restored discipline to Corvey, built Stavelot into one of the greatest monasteries of the times, became councilor to Emperors Lothair and Conrad III, and labored to keep peace between pope and emperor. He was appointed abbot of Monte Cassino by Lothair in 1137, but resigned after a month's reign, when Roger of Sicily threatened to destroy the monastery. He was Conrad III's envoy to the pope, tutored the emperor's son in 1147–49, and served on diplomatic missions for Frederick Barbarossa. He died on his way back from one of these missions to Constantinople in Bitolia, Paphlagonia, on July 19, reportedly poisoned by the Greeks. He wrote hundreds of letters which give an excellent picture of his era.

WIBORADA, ST. (d. 926), martyr. Born in Klingnau, Aargau, Switzerland, she joined her brother Hatto, a priest, as housekeeper, turned their house into a hospital, and, when he became a Benedictine at St. Gall, worked as a bookbinder for the abbey library. Later, as a recluse, she attracted many by her spiritual life, and was slain by invading Hungarian barbarians; through her gift of prophecy, the monks were able to escape. She was canonized in 1047. F. D. May 2.

WICHMANS, FRANCIS (1596–1661). Born in Antwerp, Holland, he joined the Augustinians in Tangerloo, Belgium, in 1612, was ordained in 1620, and graduated from Louvain. He became a parish priest at Mierlo in 1630 and at Tilburg in 1632, served as dean of Helmond and then of Hilvarenbeek, and in 1642

was named coadjutator of Tangerloo abbey and in 1644 its abbot. He fought anti-Catholic legislation and wrote widely.

WICTERP, ST. (d. 749), bishop. Also known as Wiko, he helped to establish the monasteries of Füssen, Kempten, and Wessobrün in Germany, served as abbot of Ellwangen, and became tenth bishop of Augsburg, Germany. F. D. Apr. 18.

WIDMER, JOSEPH (1779–1844), theologian. Born in Hohenraim, Lucerne, Switzerland, on Aug. 15, he studied at Lucerne and Landshut, was ordained, taught philosophy in 1804 and theology in 1819, at the Lucerne lyceum, until he was removed by the government in 1833. He became provost of the collegiate chapter of Beromünster, Switzerland, in 1841, and remained there until his death on Dec. 10. He wrote theological treatises, and edited the works of Sailer, Geiger, and Gügler.

WIDMERPOOL, BL. ROBERT (d. 1588), martyr. Born in Widmerpool, Nottinghamshire, England, he was educated at Oxford, became a teacher, and tutored the sons of the earl of Northumberland. He was arrested for sheltering a priest, and hanged, drawn, and quartered near Canterbury. He was beatified in 1929. F. D. Oct. 1.

WIDUKIND OF CORBIE (10th century), historian. A Saxon at the abbey of Corbie in Germany, he wrote the historically valuable chronicle, *Res gestae saxonicae sive annalium libri tres*, telling the story of the Saxons from the Roman Empire to the reign of Otto.

WIEST, STEPHAN (1748–1797), theologian. Born in Teisbach, Lower Bavaria, on Mar. 7, he studied in Landshut, joined the Cistercians at their Aldersbach monastery in 1767, and was ordained in 1772. After further study at Ingolstadt, he taught mathematics, philosophy, and theology at Aldersbach from 1774 to 1781, when he became a professor at Ingolstadt, served as its rector in 1787–88, and returned to Aldersbach, Bavaria, in 1794, where he remained until his death on Apr. 10. He wrote several theological treatises.

WIGBERT, ST. (d. 746?). An English monk, he was invited by St. Boniface to help convert the Germans and to serve as abbot of the Benedictine monastery of Fritzlar. He also was at Ohrdruf, Thuringia, then returned to his earlier abbey where he practiced most rigorous penances and fasts until his death. F. D. Aug. 13.

WIGBOD (8th century). He wrote several theological works, of which only *Quaestiones in octateuchum*, a Latin commentary on the Octateuch written at Charlemagne's request, is extant.

WIGGER, WINAND MICHAEL (1841–1901), bishop. Born in New York City on Dec. 9, he studied at St. Francis Xavier, Fordham, Seton Hall seminary, and Collegio Brignole-Sale, Genoa, and was ordained in Genoa in 1865. After receiving his doctorate in divinity at the Sapienza in Rome in 1866, he returned to New Jersey where he spent the next years as pastor in Madison, Orange, and Summit until 1881, when he was consecrated third bishop of Newark. He was an active proponent of Catholic education at the Third Plenary Council of Baltimore in 1884, worked zealously to aid immigrants, and built a cathedral and numerous schools and churches. He died in Newark, New Jersey, on Jan. 5.

WIGLEY, GEORGE J. (d. 1866), journalist. Born in Rome, he became an architect there, but went to Paris where he became a journalist, an associate of Frederico Ozanam, and one of the group which founded the Society of St. Vincent de Paul. He moved to London and in 1844 helped to found the English branch of the Society, and in 1860 to set up the charitable Peter's Pence Association. He died in Rome on Jan. 20.

WIHO. *See* Wicterp, St.

WILBERFORCE, HENRY WILLIAM (1807–1873). Born in Clapham, England, on Sept. 22, son of William, the noted philanthropist, he studied under Newman at Oxford, law at Lincoln's Inn, and became an Anglican clergyman in 1834. He served as curate at several English villages and in 1850 became a convert. He was editor of the *Catholic Standard* (later the *Weekly Register*) from 1854 to 1863. He died in Stroud, Gloucestershire, on Apr. 23.

WILBERFORCE, ROBERT ISAAC (1802–1857). Born in Clapham, England, on Dec. 19, son of William Wilberforce, the noted statesman and philanthropist, he studied at Oxford, was elected a fellow at Oriel in 1826, took Anglican orders, and was a leading Tractarian. He served as rector in Kent and Yorkshire, became canon of York cathedral in 1841, and in 1854 became a convert in Paris. He entered the Accademia in Rome to study for the priesthood, but died in Albano, Italy, on Feb. 3 after advancing only to minor orders. He wrote a five-volume *Life of William Wilberforce* (1838), with his brother Samuel, Anglican bishop of Oxford, and *The Five Empires* (1840) and *History of Erastianism* (1851).

WILCOX, BL. ROBERT (1558–1588), martyr. Born in Chester, England, he studied at Rheims, France, where he was ordained in 1585. In 1586 he was sent on the English mission, worked in Kent, was captured in Marshalsea and hanged, drawn, and quartered at Canterbury for being a Catholic priest. He was beatified in 1929. F. D. Oct. 1.

WILD, JOHANN (1495–1554). Born in Swabia, he became a Franciscan, studied at Cologne, was appointed professor of rhetoric and literature in 1528, and soon achieved fame for his preaching in Mainz. He was elected definitor of his province in 1540, became preacher at the cathedral, a position he held until his death, and was mainly instrumental in keeping Mainz Catholic. He convinced Albert of Brandenburg to spare the cathedral when he captured Mainz in 1552, wrote numerous commentaries on the Old Testament, and died in Mainz, Germany, on Sept. 8.

WILDE, OSCAR O'FLAHERTIE (1856–1900), author. Born in Dublin on Oct. 15, he studied at Trinity College there and Oxford, published poems, and became the center of an aesthetic cult satirized by W. S. Gilbert in *Patience*. He wrote stories (*The Happy Prince*) and *The Picture of Dorian Gray* (1891). He married Constance Lloyd in 1884 and had two sons, toured the United States as a lecturer, and was successful in the theater with *Lady Windermere's Fan* (1892), *A Woman of No Importance* (1893), *An Ideal Husband* (1895), and *The Importance of Being Earnest* (1899), all marked by his epigrammatic wit. In 1895 he lost a suit for criminal libel initiated against the marquess of Queensbury, was charged with perversion in a case involving Lord Alfred Douglas, and given a two-year sentence. He wrote the autobiographical *De profundis* in prison, went to Paris in 1897, wrote the *Ballad of Reading Gaol*, and became a convert shortly before his death in Paris on Nov. 30.

WILFRID, ST. (634–709), bishop. A native of Northumbria, possibly born in Ripon, he was sent by Queen Eanfled (wife of Northumbria's King Oswy) to become a monk at Lindisfarne at fourteen. In 653 he accompanied St. Benet Biscop to Lyons, refused marriage to the bishop's niece and a governorship, went to Rome to study, and returned to Lyons, where he witnessed the execution of the bishop and was almost executed himself. He returned to England in 660 or 661, was appointed abbot of Ripon by King Alcfrid of Deira who had recently built it, and promptly installed the Roman usage and the Rule of St. Benedict, and was ordained. He worked valiantly to supplant Celtic usage by that of Rome and succeeded at the Conference of Whitby in 664, the year he was appointed bishop of York by Alcfrid. He went to France to be consecrated, was delayed, and on his return in 666 found St. Chad had been appointed bishop of York by King Oswy of Northumbria; he retired to Ripon rather than contest the see. Archbishop Theodore of Canterbury removed Chad in 669 for irregularities in his election and restored Wilfrid to his see. He became embroiled in a dispute with Oswy's successor, Egfrid, when he supported Queen Etheldteda when she left her husband and became a nun. In 678, Theodore, as metropolitan, and encouraged by Egfrid, broke up Wilfrid's diocese into four sees; Wilfrid appealed in person to Pope St. Agatho (the first recorded appeal from an English bishop to Rome), who ordered Wilfrid restored. When the bishop returned to England in 680 and showed the pope's order to Egfrid, the latter imprisoned him; on his release nine months later, he went to Sussex where he was most successful in missionary activities and founded a monastery at Selsey. In 686, at the request of Theodore, who had realized his error in deposing Wilfrid, Wilfrid was recalled by Egfrid's successor, Aldfrid, who banished him in 691 when they disagreed, again over the question of the split dioceses, and he retired to Mercia, where he administered the see of Lichfield for several years. In 703 he was ordered by the new archbishop of Canterbury, St. Bertwald, at Aldfrid's instigation to accept the division, and when he refused was deprived of all his possessions and tenure. He again appealed in person to Rome and Pope John VI upheld him and ordered all concerned to settle the matter. Aldfrid refused to obey the order but, on his deathbed, withdrew his opposition. In 706, at a council in Yorkshire presided over by Bertwald, a compromise was reached restoring Ripon and Hexham to Wilfrid, and peace was finally restored. He died on a visitation to St. Andrew's monastery in Oundle in Northamptonshire. F. D. Oct. 12.

ELEANOR SHIPLEY DUCKETT, *Anglo-Saxon Saints and Scholars* (New York, Macmillan, 1947).

WILFRID II (d. 744), bishop. Educated at Whitby, England, under St. Hilda, he became chaplain and coadjutor to St. John of Beverley and succeeded him as bishop of York. Wilfrid also retired, as did John, to a monastery, probably Ripon. F. D. Apr. 29.

WILGEFORTIS. A creature of legend, she appears as one of nine sisters born to the wife of a pagan king in Portugal. Despite her vow of virginity, her father promised her in marriage to the king of Sicily. In response to prayer, she suddenly grew a beard and mustache, and the Sicilian king lost interest. At this, her father killed her. The narrative has many variants; she is known as Uncumber in England, Kümmernis in Germany, and Livrade in France.

WILHELM V (1548–1626). Born in Munich, Germany, on Sept. 29, son of Duke Albrecht V of Bavaria, he studied at Ingolstadt, and became duke in 1579. He led such a devout life he was named "the Pious," fought as a leader of the counter-Reformation, saving Bavaria for the Church, and in 1597 resigned his dukedom to spend the rest of his life in

devotional practices. He died in Schleissheim on Feb. 7.

WILHELM, JOSEPH (1845–1920), theologian. Born in Montzen, Belgium, he studied at Liège and the German College and Gregorian in Rome, was ordained in 1870, taught philosophy for nine years, and did parish work in Shoreham and Battle, England, until 1911. He then went to Aachen, Germany, where he died on Feb. 4. He was editor of the International Catholic Library, was co-author with T. B. Scannell of *Manual of Dogmatic Theology*, and collaborated on the *Catholic Dictionary*.

WILHELM OF HERLE (14th century), painter. Born in Herle, Limburg, Holland, he became a prominent painter and the leader of a school of artists active in Cologne for two decades at the end of the fourteenth century. His work includes *Madonna with the Bean Blossom*, *Christ on the Cross*, *St. Veronica*, and *Madonna with the Pea Blossom*.

WILLAERT, ADRIAN (1490–1562), composer. Born at Bruges, Belgium (or Roulers, Netherlands), he went to Paris to study law, then music theory under Josquin des Prés or Jean Moulin, went to Rome in 1516, and after a short period in Ferrara entered the service of King Louis II of Bohemia and Hungary. He became choirmaster of St. Mark's, Venice, in 1527, introduced antiphonal singing, founded the Venetian singing school where Zarlino and Cyprian de Rore were pupils, and composed motets, madrigals, hymns, psalms, and masses. He died in Venice, Italy, on Dec. 8.

WILLEHAD, ST. (d. 789), bishop. Born in Northumbria, England, he probably was educated at York, where he became a friend of Alcuin. In 766, after his ordination, he went to Friesland as a missioner; in 780, Charlemagne sent him to preach to the Saxons. When they rose against the Franks in 782 he was forced to flee. After a visit to Rome and two years at Echternach, he returned to Saxony, which had been reconquered by Charlemagne, and in 787 was appointed bishop of the Saxons with his see at Bremen. F. D. Nov. 8.

WILLEHAD, ST. (1483–1572), martyr. A native of Denmark, he became a Franciscan, was exiled at the advent of Lutheranism, lived at the monastery of Gorkum, Holland, and was slain by a Protestant mob at Briel, Holland, with eighteen companions. F. D. July 9.

WILLGING, JOSEPH CLEMENT (1884–1959), bishop. Born in Dubuque, Iowa, on Sept. 6, he graduated from Loras in 1905, studied at St. Mary's seminary, Baltimore, and was ordained in Dubuque in 1908. He was principal of St. Aloysisus Institute, Helena, Montana, in 1909–10, taught at Carroll College, and was chancellor of Helena from 1914 to 1927. He was made a papal chamberlain in 1921, was a pastor in Butte from 1927 to 1942, was made a domestic prelate in 1939, and served as vicar general of Helena from 1939 until his appointment as first bishop of Pueblo, Colorado, in 1941. He was made an assistant at the pontifical throne in 1958, and died in Denver, Colorado, on Mar. 3.

WILLIAM I (1027?–1087), king of England. Called "the Conqueror," the illegitimate son of Robert I, duke of Normandy, and Arletta, daughter of a tanner, he was born in Falaise, Normandy, and recognized as Robert's successor by the Norman dukes on Robert's death in 1035. He escaped many attempts on his life during his youth, put down an uprising, with the help of King Henry I of France, of the nobles at the battle of Val-ès-Dunes in 1047, supported Henry in his war with Count Geoffrey Martel of Anjou, and visited England in 1051, when he claimed he received recognition from Edward the Confessor as the successor to the English throne. In 1053 he married Matilda of Flanders (against papal opposition, but with Lanfranc's aid secured papal approval for the marriage in 1059). His growing power brought him into conflict with Henry, who invaded his domains in 1054 and in 1058, but William repulsed him on both occasions. In 1064, Harold, earl of Wessex, was shipwrecked on the French coast and turned over to William, who released the earl after securing his promise to support William's claim to the English throne. When Edward the Confessor died in 1066, Harold repudiated his pledge and was crowned king. William, with the approval of Pope Alexander II, invaded England, defeated and slew Harold at Hastings on Oct. 14, and was crowned king of England at Westminster. He put down several uprisings in the next few years, put down the rebellion of the earls of Norfolk and Hereford in 1074, and repulsed the Danes in 1075. He redistributed land and great estates to many of his followers, deposed Stigand and appointed Lanfranc archbishop of Canterbury, and approved the latter's widespread ecclesiastical reforms (though there were some clashes when the king attempted to interfere in Church affairs), established order in the country, and strengthened central authority, proclaiming in 1086 the loyalty to the king superseded that of any lesser lord. He directed a complete survey of his kingdom, collected in 1085 in the *Domesday Book.* He died in Rouen, France, on Sept. 9 from injuries suffered in a riding accident.

WILLIAM II (1056?–1100), king of England. Called Rufus (for his ruddy complexion), the third son of William the Conqueror and Matilda of Flanders, was born in Normandy, fought on the side of his father against his brother, Robert of Normandy, in 1079, and became king on William's death in 1087. He crushed a revolt led by Bishop Odo of Bayeux in 1088, invaded Normandy in 1091, gained partial allegiance, turned to Scotland, and won homage from Malcolm III. He quarreled with the papacy over Archbishop Anselm in 1097, and gained a reputation for extreme cruelty, avarice, and perversion. He became more warlike, fought again with his brother Robert, invaded Wales, attacked Maine in France, and was shot to death by an arrow in New Forest, England, on Aug. 2. The clergy at Winchester refused to give him Christian burial, but were overruled by Henry, bishop of Winchester, the king's cousin.

WILLIAM (1143–1214), king. Called "the Lion," the second son of Henry of Scotland, succeeded his brother, Malcolm IV, as king in 1165, and made an alliance with Louis VII of France in 1168. With Henry II's three sons and French support he invaded England in 1174, was captured at Alnwick, and was released by a treaty which subjugated Scotland to England. He founded many monasteries, including Arbroath, quarreled with Pope Alexander III over the see of St. Andrews, established a Church independent of England and subject directly to Rome in 1188, and ransomed his nation for a huge sum paid to Richard I of England. He spent his remaining years consolidating his kingdom, subduing some of the highland lords, and enforcing criminal law. He died in Stirling, Scotland.

WILLIAM, ST. (d. 1042?). A Benedictine in the monastery of Santagún, in León, Spain, he was driven out by a Saracen attack in 988 and settled in Peñacorada, where he built another monastery. F. D. Mar. 20.

WILLIAM, ST. (d. 1067), bishop. An Anglo-Saxon priest, he became chaplain to King Canute, who made him bishop of Roeskilde. He remained in Denmark, preached to the pagans, and severely censured King Sweyn Estridsen for his unchristian actions; later, they became friendly and William's rule was smoother. F. D. Sept. 2.

WILLIAM ARNAUD, ST. (d. 1242), martyr. He and two other Dominicans, who had been commissioned by Pope Gregory IX to combat the Albigensian heresy in the Toulouse district of France, were driven out of a number of cities, then tricked by a promise of refuge in a castle in Avignonet, France. There they were attacked by a military patrol which entered the building after dark, and assassinated with two Franciscans, Stephen and Raymund, two Benedictines, and five others. Their cult was confirmed in 1856. F. D. May 29.

WILLIAM OF AUVERGNE (d. 1249), bishop. Born in Aurillac, Auvergne, France, he studied at Paris, taught there, and in 1228 became bishop of Paris. He was a leader in the movement to adapt Aristotle's teaching to Christian philosophy, fought Manichaeism as revered by the Cathari, and refuted the doctrine of an eternal world as propounded by the Arabs. He wrote theological and philosophical treatises, among them *De moribus, De sacramentis, De Trinitate, De anima,* and *De universo.* He died in Paris.

WILLIAM OF AUXERRE (13th century), theologian. After studying at the University of Paris under Prevostin of Cremona, he taught there (John of Treviso was a pupil) and became archdeacon of Beauvais. He was one of the theologians selected by Pope Gregory IX in 1231 to prepare a new edition of the works of Aristotle to replace inaccurate and condemned translations, and wrote *Summa aurea.*

WILLIAM CALCULUS OF JUMIÉGES (d. 1090). He became a Benedictine monk at Jumièges, France, where he remained until his death, and wrote *Historia Normannorum,* a history of the Normans from 837 to 1137. He wrote the first seven books to 1087 (the first four of which were taken from the Norman history by Dudon of St. Quentin and corrected); the eighth book, to 1137, was added by an anonymous author.

WILLIAM OF CHAMPEAUX (1070?-1121), theologian. Born in Champeaux, France, he studied under Anselm of Laon, taught at the Paris cathedral school, and in 1108 was forced to retire to the abbey of St. Victor because of Abelard's criticisms of his teaching on universals. He opened the monastic school there in 1109, became bishop of Châlons-sur-Marne in 1113, and remained there until his death. He is regarded as the founder of scholastic realism and was an outstanding champion of orthodoxy. He was a friend of St. Bernard, possibly his teacher, and wrote several theological treatises, among them *De origine animae* and *Liber sententiarum.*

WILLIAM THE CLERK (13th century), poet. A Norman clerk, he wrote *Bestiaire divin, Besant de Dieu, Joies Notre Dame,* and *Vie de Tobie.*

WILLIAM OF CONCHES (1100?-1154?), scholastic. Born in Conches, Normandy, he became a pupil of Bernard of Chartres, taught theology at Paris, was Henry Plantagenet's tutor in 1122, and became one of the earliest Christian philosophers to study the physical sciences as taught by the Arabians. He was a student of cosmology and psychology, and wrote *Dragmaticon, Magna de naturis philosophia,* a commentary on Boethius' *Consolations of Philosophy,* and glosses on Plato's *Timaeus.*

WILLIAM THE CONQUEROR. *See* William I, king of England.

WILLIAM OF DIGULLEVILLE (14th century), poet. A Cistercian monk at Châlis abbey, France, he wrote three long and popular allegorical poems: *Pèlerinage de vie humaine, Pèlerinage de l'âme,* and *Pèlerinage de Jesus Christ.*

WILLIAM OF DIJON, ST. (962-1031). Son of Count Robert of Volpiano, he was born on the island of Giuglio in Lake Orta, Piedmont, Italy, he was entered in the Benedictine abbey of Locedio at seven, entered Cluny in 987, and was sent to reform St. Saturnin priory in 938. He was appointed abbot of St. Benignus at Dijon and ordained in 990, devoted himself to reforming monasteries in Burgundy, Lorraine, and Normandy, and eventually ruled over some forty monasteries. He built a church at Bénigne, established schools in many of the monasteries, and rebuilt the monastery of Fécamp, France, where he died. He is also known as William of St. Benignus. F. D. Jan. 1.

WILLIAM DE DONJEON, ST. (d. 1209), archbishop. Born in Nevers, France, he was a canon at Soissons and at Paris, then joined the Cistercians at Grandmont, becoming abbot at Fontaine-Jean and at Châlis. He was elected bishop of Bourges in 1200. He blended his life of austerity and the demands of a public career, becoming widely known as a confessor, a man who seldom relied on the civil arm for the punishment of criminals, but on persuasion instead, as a calm mediator of several ecclesiastical disputes, and as the converter of many Albigensians. He was canonized in 1218 by Pope Honorius III. F. D. Jan. 10.

WILLIAM DURANDUS (1237?-1296), bishop. Born in Puimisson, Provence, he studied law at Bologna, taught at Modena, was ordained a subdeacon in Rome by Pope Clement IV, who gave him canonries in France, and became secretary to Gregory X. He attended the second Council of Lyons in 1274, was absentee dean of Chartres, papal governor of Romagna, and leader of the attack which destroyed the stronghold of Guy of Montefeltro. In 1286 he was elected bishop of Mende, but his see was administered by his nephew for five years. He took over the see from 1291 to 1295, returned to Italy as governor of Romagna and Ancona, and died in Rome on Nov. 1. He wrote an elaborate treatment of the Roman rite, *Rationale divinorum officiorum,* with mystical and allegorical interpretations which influenced the next several centuries. He also wrote several works of canon law.

WILLIAM DURANDUS (d. 1328), bishop. Known as the younger, and often confused with his uncle, he was archdeacon at Mende, administered the diocese for his uncle in 1286-91, and was named its bishop in 1296 by Pope

Boniface VIII. He attended the Council of Vienne in 1311–12, headed a papal embassy to the Turks in 1326, and died in Cyprus on his return. He wrote on the process of general councils, a work which also attacked contemporary abuses and corruption.

WILLIAM OF ESKILSOÉ, ST. (1125?–1203). Born in St. Germain, France, he became a canon in Paris. When his reputation for discipline reached Denmark he was sought out by Saxo Grammaticus at the request of the bishop of Roeskilde to reform Danish monasticism. He was successful as abbot of Eskilsoë, Denmark, for thirty years, and established the monastery of St. Thomas in Zeeland. He died in Eskilsoë, and was canonized in 1224. F. D. Apr. 6.

WILLIAM OF FENOLI, BL. (d. 1205?). He was a Carthusian laybrother at the Charterhouse Casularum in Lombardy. His cult was confirmed by Pope Pius IX in 1860. F. D. Dec. 19.

WILLIAM FIRMATUS, ST. (d. 1090?). A soldier, then a doctor in Tours, France, he also became a canon at St. Venantius, though a layman. He then gave up his practice and wealth and lived in several hermitages, which he left twice for pilgrimages to Jerusalem. F. D. Apr. 24.

WILLIAM FITZHERBERT, ST. (d. 1154), archbishop. Nephew of King Stephen of England, he was royally appointed archbishop of York in 1140, but violently opposed by the Cistercians in England and those under St. Bernard at Clairvaux. A papal letter (a suspect document) supported him, but when Eugene III, a Cistercian, became pope, William was suspended and went to Sicily. His relatives attacked Fountains abbey, burned its farm lands, and mutilated Archdeacon Walter of York, who had first questioned the validity of his appointment. The pope deposed William in 1147 and replaced him with Henry Murdac, abbot of Fountains. The former archbishop then retired to Winchester for six years of penitence and austerity. When St. Bernard, Abbot Henry, and Pope Eugene all died in 1153, William went to Rome and regained his see from Pope Anastasius IV. When he returned to York in 1154, great crowds came to welcome him and a bridge broke under their weight. William promised to make restitution to Fountains abbey, but died in York within two months, probably by poisoning. Because no one was injured in the bridge accident attributed by his followers to William's prayers, and because of other happenings at his tomb, he was canonized in 1227 by Pope Honorius III. F. D. June 8.

WILLIAM OF GELLONE, ST. (755–812). Son of Thierry, count of Toulouse, he became a favorite courtier with Charlemagne, fought against the Moslems as duke of Aquitaine, then built a double monastery at Gellone. His sisters entered the convent there and he became a Benedictine monk under St. Benedict of Aniane. Many legendary details of his life appear in the mediaeval romances of *Aliscans* and *La Prise d'Orange*. He was canonized in 1066. F. D. May 28.

WILLIAM GIFFARD (d. 1129), bishop. A Norman, he was canon and dean in Rouen, chancellor to William I, William II, and Henry I of England, and in 1100, although only a deacon, was named bishop of Winchester. St. Anselm, returning from the Vatican Council of 1099 which opposed the investiture of non-priests, refused to consecrate him; a struggle with the king began and, when William was being consecrated by Gerard of York, the bishop-elect suddenly refused to continue the ceremony, since he had not been ordained, was exiled, and his property confiscated. He left with St. Anselm in 1103 for the Continent, returned after two years, sought to have Anselm reinstated, and when the latter was allowed back in 1107 was ordained and consecrated that same year. He regained Henry's confidence, frequently acted on his behalf, and completed the Domesday survey of Winchester. As bishop he established the Canons Regular of St. Augustine in Southwark, brought the first settlement of Cistercians to England, giving them a home at Waverley, and worked closely with the Benedictines in his see. He died in Winchester, England, on Jan. 25.

WILLIAM OF HIRSCHAU, BL. (d. 1091). A monk at St. Emmerau, Ratisbon, Bavaria, he restored the Benedictine abbey of Hirschau, Württemberg, where he became abbot, adopted the observance of Cluny, and was greatly concerned with improving the spiritual and material condition of the serfs. He reestablished the monastic school, built a large scriptorium, and helped develop the institution of laybrothers. He was learned in astronomy, music, mathematics, poetry, wrote scholarly treatises, and founded seven new abbeys. F. D. July 4.

WILLIAM OF MALEVAL, ST. (d. 1157). A French soldier who sought to make up for a dissipated youth, he made a series of pilgrimages between 1145 and 1153 before he became a recluse in Tuscany. He lived for a while at monasteries in Pisa and on Monte Pruno, but found the monks lax in their exceptions to the rule, and retired to a cave in 1155. After his death, his disciple Albert and a doctor named Renaldo built a hermitage at his grave and originated the Guilelmites, or Hermits of St. William. F. D. Feb. 10.

WILLIAM OF MALMESBURY (1095?–1143?), historian. Born probably in Somersetshire, England, he became a monk at Malmesbury, where he had been educated and where he became librarian. He wrote *Gesta regum Anglorum*, a history of English kings from the Saxon invasion to 1128; *Gesta pontificum*, an account of the bishops and chief monasteries in England to 1123, which exerted great influence on subsequent English ecclesiastical historians; *Historia novella*, bringing *Gesta regum* up to 1142; a history of Glastonbury abbey (where he probably spent some time), and a life of St. Dunstan. Much of his work is noted for its accuracy and critical judgment. He died in Analmesbury, England.

WILLIAM OF MOERBEKE (1215?–1286), bishop. An outstanding scholar, he translated the works of Aristotle at the request of St. Thomas Aquinas, Hero of Alexandria's *Catoptrics*, Proclus' *Theological Elements*, and works by Archimedes, Ptolemy, and others. He was a member of the pontifical court in Viterbo in 1268, attended the Council of Lyons in 1274, and was appointed bishop of Corinth, Greece, in 1277, remaining there until his death.

WILLIAM OF MONTE VERGINE. See William of Vercelli, St.

WILLIAM OF NANGUIS (d. 1303?), historian. Probably a native of Nancy, France, he became a Benedictine monk, was stationed at St. Denis abbey in Paris, and wrote a chronicle from creation to 1300, based on Sigbertus of Gemblours' chronicle to 1113 and not particularly reliable after that date. It was continued to 1368 by an unknown St. Denis monk and by Johannes of Venette. He also wrote biographies of Louis VIII, Louis IX, and Philip III, based on earlier lives, and *Chronicon abbreviatum regum Francorum*, an abridged version of his chronicle for the years 845–1300.

WILLIAM OF NEWBURGH (1136?–1198?), historian. Born in Bridlington, Yorkshire, England, he was entered in the Augustinian priory at Newburgh, West Riding, Yorkshire, as a child, became a canon, and spent the rest of his life there. He wrote *Historia rerum anglicarum*, a valuable history of England from the beginning of the Norman conquest in 1066 to 1198, a chief authority for the reign of Henry II, and a blistering attack on Geoffrey of Monmouth for his imaginative *History of the British Kings*.

WILLIAM OF NORWICH, ST. (d. 1144). He was a tanner's apprentice of twelve, whose tortured body was found in a sack in the woods near Norwich, England. Popular frenzy fostered by William of Turbeville, blamed the murder on the Jews, but such attribution is now discredited. F. D. Mar. 24.

WILLIAM OF OCKHAM (1280?–1349?), philosopher. Born in Ockham, Surrey, England, he studied at Oxford under John Duns Scotus, joined the Franciscans, and about

1310 went to Paris where he taught after 1320. He resigned in 1323 to work for the imperial party against Pope John XXII and was imprisoned in Avignon in 1328, but escaped to Pisa, where he lived under imperial protection, and then to the court of Louis of Bavaria. He wrote *Opus nonaginta dierum* in 1330 attacking a papal decree against the Franciscans, and about 1338 accused Pope John XXII of numerous heresies. With Marsilius of Padua at Louis' court he became a leading proponent of the absolute authority of the state, a vigorous opponent of papal temporal authority, and an agitator for the reform and simplification of scholastic philosophy. He opposed many basic doctrines of Thomism (the distinction between essence and existence, active and passive intellect, and the existence of intentional species), and was skeptical of Thomas' rationalism, declaring that certain facts can be apprehended only by faith and not by reason (for example, immortality). He proposed a theory of universals which led to his being labeled a "terminist," which held that logic deals with terms representing mental images rather than with realities. His demands for reform and his vigorous protests against many subtleties, and even the basic tenets, of scholastic philosophy caused him to be labeled "the first Protestant," but he always acknowledged the Church's authority in spiritual matters. He died probably in Munich, Germany.

WILLIAM PERAULT (d. 1270?). Born in Perault, France, he studied at Paris, joined the Dominicans there, and then was stationed at Lyons, where he administered the vacant see so successfully from 1245 to 1267 that he is often falsely called the archbishop of Lyons. He was noted for his preaching and theological treatises, chief of which are *Summa de virtutibus et vitiis* and *De eruditione seu de institutione religiosorum*. He died in Lyons between 1260 and 1275.

WILLIAM PINCHON, ST. (d. 1234), bishop. Born in Brittany, and ordained by Bishop Josselm, whom he succeeded as bishop of St. Brieuc in 1220, he was banished by Peter Mauclerc, duke of Brittany, for defending the rights of the Church, lived at Poitiers, and returned in 1230. He was canonized in 1247. F. D. July 29.

WILLIAM OF POITIERS (1020?–1087?), historian. Born in Préaux, Normandy, France, he studied at Poitiers, became a knight, was ordained, and became William the Conqueror's chaplain and archdeacon of the Lisieux cathedral. He wrote William's life in *Gesta Guilelmi*, a portion of which is still extant, and was noted for scholarship and poetry.

WILLIAM OF RAMSEY (12th–13th century). Born in Ramsey, England, he became a monk at Crowland abbey and wrote several lives of saints, among them of SS. Fremund, Edmund the King, Birinus, and Waltheof.

WILLIAM OF RUBRUCK (1200?–1256?), missioner. Born in Rubrouc, France, he became a close friend of King Louis IX, whom he accompanied on his crusade in 1248, and in 1253 was sent by the king, with two friars, to convert the Tatars to Christianity and to win them as allies against the Saracens. He eventually reached the court of the khan at Karakorum, and returned to Europe two years later. He wrote a description of his travels which gave Europe its first true description of China and its inhabitants, and proved that the Caspian was an inland sea. He died sometime after 1256. He is also called William of Ruysbroek, Ruysbrock, or Rubruquis.

WILLIAM OF ST. AMOUR (d. 1273?), theologian. A native of Burgundy, France, he became a professor at the university of Paris about 1250, headed the seculars in their controversy with the mendicants at the university, and bitterly attacked the mendicants in *De periculis novissimorum temporum* (1256), and *Liber de antichristo* (1266), which led to his banishment from France and denunciation by Alexander IV. He returned to the university in 1263, and remained there until his death.

WILLIAM OF ST. BENIGNUS, ST. *See* William of Dijon, St.

WILLIAM OF ST. THIERRY (1085?–1148?), theologian. Born in Liège, Belgium, he studied at St. Nicaise monastery in Rheims, where he joined the Benedictines, and in 1119 was made abbot of St. Thierry. He attended the first general Benedictine chapter in 1140 at St. Médard, resigned his abbacy in 1135, and retired to the Cistercian abbey in Signy, near Rheims, France, where he died on Sept. 8. A close friend of St. Bernard (his correspondence is extant), he wrote *De vita solitaria, De Deo contemplando, Speculum fidei, Enigma fidei*, several commentaries, and the beginning chapters of a biography of St. Bernard. He was the first to call attention to Abelard's errors in his *Disputatio adversus Petrum Abelardum* and *Disputatio catalicorum Patrum adversus dogmata Petri Abelardi* in reply to Abelard's *De erroribus Guillelmi de Conchis*.

WILLIAM OF SENS (12th century), architect. Probably born in Sens, France, he worked from 1174 to 1178 or 1179 rebuilding the fire-gutted choir of Canterbury cathedral, returned to France after being injured in a fall, and died a few years later.

WILLIAM OF SHOREHAM (14th century). Born in Shoreham, Kent, England, and the vicar of Chart Sutton from 1313, he wrote the earliest known English version of the complete psalter (in the Mercian dialect) and religious poems.

WILLIAM TEMPIER, BL. (d. 1197), bishop. Superior of the monastery of St. Hilaire de la Celle, France, he was chosen in 1184 as bishop of Poitiers, and distinguished himself as an opponent of simony and secular interference. F. D. Mar. 27.

WILLIAM OF TURBEVILLE (1095?–1174), bishop. He studied at the Benedictine cathedral priory in Norwich, England, joined the Benedictines there, taught, and later was prior. He helped spread the now-discredited story of Godwin Sturt that his twelve-year-old nephew, William, had been murdered by the Norwich Jews in 1144, was elected bishop of Norwich in 1146, and promoted the cult of William, building a chapel for his body in 1168. He was a firm supporter of Thomas à Becket in the latter's disputes with Henry II. The bishop died in Norwich in Jan.

WILLIAM OF TYRE (1130?–1187?), archbishop. Born probably in Palestine of French or English ancestry, he studied in France, became a cleric and archdeacon of Tyre about 1160, served on a diplomatic mission for King Amalric to Emperor Manuel Comnenus in 1168, and tutored the future King Baldwin IV of Jerusalem as a prince. He was chancellor in 1170–74, was appointed archbishop of Tyre in 1175, went to Europe in 1178 to launch a new crusade when Saladin threatened, and attended the Lateran Council in 1179. He was defeated in his bid for the patriarchate of Jerusalem by Heraclius, and went to Rome in 1182 or 1183 to appeal against the latter's appointment and his excommunication by the patriarch, and is reported by unreliable sources to have been poisoned in Rome by two followers of Heraclius some time before 1187. He wrote *Historia rerum in partibus transmarinis gestarum*, a history of the crusades and the kingdom of Jerusalem from 1095 to 1184, which is a major source of information for the period 1144–84, *Gesta orientalium principum*, and a history of the Lateran Council.

WILLIAM OF VERCELLI, ST. (1085–1142), founder. Born in Vercelli, Italy, he was brought up as an orphan, became a hermit on Monte Vergine, Italy, after a pilgrimage to Compostella, and attracted so many followers that a monastery was built. By 1119 his followers were united in the Benedictine congregation, the Hermits of Monte Vergine (Williamites), which he headed. The austerity of his rule led to dissension among his monks; to restore peace he left, and was taken under the protection of Roger I of Naples, who built a monastery for him in Salerno. He founded monasteries throughout Naples, and died at the Guglielmo monastery, near Nusco, Italy. He is also called William of Monte Vergine. F. D. June 25.

WILLIAM OF WAINFLEET. *See* Waynflete, William.

WILLIAM THE WALLOON (d. 1089). Elected abbot of St. Arnoul in Metz, Lorraine, in 1050, he was known for his knowledge of the works of SS. Augustine and Jerome, was also elected abbot of St. Remi in 1073, when Pope Gregory VII demanded of Archbishop Manasses of Rheims an outstanding abbot, but resigned later the same year because of the archbishop's continued repressive attitude to the abbey. In 1085 he accepted the bishopric of Metz from Emperor Henry IV, who had driven out Bishop Herimann illegally, but publicly apologized to the bishop and resigned in 1086. He retired to the abbey in Gorze, was restored as abbot of St. Arnoul by Bishop Herimann, and probably died there on Dec. 22.

WILLIAM OF WARE (13th century). Born in Ware, Hertfordshire, England, he joined the Franciscans as a youth, probably studied at Oxford, and spent some time at the London convent, but spent most of his life at Paris. There he studied under Alexander of Hales, became a master, and probably taught Duns Scotus. He was noted for his knowledge of philosophy and wrote several theological treatises.

WILLIAM OF WYKEHAM (1324–1404), bishop. Born in Wickham, Hampshire, England, he studied at a Winchester school, was secretary of the constable of Winchester castle, and in 1326 became King Edward III's architect and surveyor. He rebuilt Windsor castle, received numerous preferments and benefices from the king, and was ordained in 1362. Edward appointed him lord privy seal in 1364, bishop of Winchester in 1366, and in 1367 chancellor of England, in which position he practically ruled England. He was obliged to resign in 1372 when the war in France went badly, and devoted himself to ecclesiastical works. He became involved in a bitter dispute with John of Gaunt, who charged him with mismanagement of his see in 1376, and had his temporalities seized by Edward. Pardoned when King Richard II ascended the throne, he devoted himself to the founding of New College at Oxford, which he dedicated in 1386. He served again as chancellor in 1389–91, founded St. Mary's in Winchester, one of England's greatest public schools, in 1394, rebuilt the nave of his cathedral, and died in his palace at South Waltham, Hampshire, on Sept. 27.

WILLIAMS, JOHN JOSEPH (1822–1907), archbishop. Born in Boston on Apr. 27, he studied at the Sulpician college in Montreal and St. Sulpice, Paris, where he was ordained in 1845. He was stationed at the cathedral in Boston, was named rector in 1855, vicar general of the diocese in 1857, titular bishop of Tripoli and coadjutor of Boston, succeeded to the see in 1866, and became Boston's first archbishop when Boston was made a metropolitan see in 1875. He dedicated Holy Cross cathedral in 1875, established St. John's seminary in 1884, built charitable institutions, schools, and churches, founded the first conference of St. Vincent de Paul Society in New England, was one of the founders of the North American College in Rome, and attended the Vatican Council and the second and third councils of Baltimore. He died in Boston on Aug. 30 after a reign of forty years.

WILLIAMS, JOSEPH JOHN (1875–1940), anthropologist. Born in Boston, Massachusetts, on Dec. 1, he studied at Boston College, became a Jesuit, and was ordained in 1907. He served on the staff of *America* in 1909–11, did mission work in Jamaica, British West Indies, in 1912–17, and on his return was stationed at Woodstock, Holy Cross, and Boston colleges. He wrote *Keep the Gate* (1932) and other spiritual readings, but is best known for his ethnological studies: *Voodoos and Obeahs*, *Psychic Phenomena of Jamaica*, and *Whence the Black Irish of Jamaica?* He died at Lenox, Massachusetts, on Oct. 28.

WILLIAMS, MICHAEL (1877–1950), editor. Born in Halifax, Nova Scotia, on Feb. 5, he studied in New Brunswick, moved to Boston, and after several jobs began free-lance writing under the enthusiastic sponsorship of Philip Hale. Williams entered journalism, worked for the Boston *Post*, moved to New York, was on the staff of the *World* and *Evening Telegram*, and in 1904 went to Texas when weak lungs incapacitated him. He went to San Francisco, and became city editor of the *Examiner* the day before the earthquake. He shifted between the two coasts, worked for a brief period with Upton Sinclair in his Englewood, New Jersey, utopia; he also was joint author, with Sinclair, of *Good Health*. In 1912 he reaccepted Catholicism, covered the Mexican War for the International News Service, continued to free-lance, and in 1918 published his autobiography, *The Book of the High Romance*. He worked for United Welfare Organizations and the National Catholic War Council in World War I, wrote *American Catholics in the War* (1921), and in 1924 came again to New York, this time to found the weekly, *Commonweal*, which he edited until 1935. He also wrote *Catholicism and the Modern Mind*, *The Shadow of the Pope*, and *The Catholic Church in Action*. He died in Hartford, Connecticut, on Oct. 12.

WILLIBALD, ST. (700?–786), bishop. Born in the English kingdom of the West Saxons and educated at the monastery of Waltham, Hampshire, he went about 721 on a pilgrimage to Rome and the Holy Land. His is the first recorded trip by an English pilgrim to that part of the world and the first known English travel book. On his return he stayed for ten years at Monte Cassino, where he served St. Petronax in several Benedictine posts. Pope Gregory III then sent him to Germany, where he was ordained by his cousin, St. Boniface, and worked successfully in Thuringia. Boniface also consecrated him bishop of Eichstätt. He built a double monastery at Heidenheim, where his brother St. Winebald ruled the monks and his sister St. Walburga, the nuns. He was canonized in 938 by Pope Leo VII. F. D. July 7 (sometimes, June 7).

WILLIBERT (d. 889). He became archbishop of Cologne, Germany, in 870 and helped Ludwig the German to overcome Charles the Bald; the archbishopric thereby became part of the empire.

WILLIBRORD, ST. (658–739), bishop. Born in Northumbria, he was sent at seven to the monastery of Ripon under St. Wilfrid, and from 678 to 690 studied in Ireland with SS. Egbert and Wigbert. Ordained in 688, he was sent with eleven other Englishmen to Friesland. After great missionary success he was papally consecrated bishop of Utrecht in 695, under the name Clement. He founded the Benedictine abbey of Echternach, Luxembourg, but in 715 was obliged to withdraw from much of Upper Friesland when Duke Radbod reconquered the area. On the latter's death in 719 he was restored to his see. Called the "Apostle of the Frisians," he established the faith in the Netherlands, inaugurated an era of great English spiritual influence there, and prepared the way for St. Boniface. He died at Esternach. F. D. Nov. 7.

WILLIGIS, ST. (d. 1011), archbishop. Born in Schöningen, Germany, he was a canon of Hildesheim when Emperor Otto II sought him out because of his brilliant competence. He served as chaplain, tutor to Otto III, and in 971 as chancellor. He became archbishop of Mainz about 973, was made vicar apostolic of Germany by Pope Boniface II, crowned Emperors Otto III in 983 and Henry II in 1002, spread the faith through Scandinavia, and found as much time for prayer, scriptural study, personal care of the poor, and church building as for international statesmanship. F. D. Feb. 23.

WILLIRAM (d. 1085). Born near Worms in Franconia, Germany, he studied under Lanfranc and at Paris, became scholastic of the Bamberg cathedral chapter, and then a monk at a monastery in Fulda. In 1048 he became abbot at the Benedictine abbey at Ebersberg, Bavaria, a position he held until his death

there. He was the author of a popular German translation of the *Song of Songs*.

WILLOCK, EDWARD FRANCIS (1916–1960), editor. Born in South Boston, Massachusetts, on Apr. 22, he founded and edited, with Carol Jackson, the magazine *Integrity*, devoted to the lay apostolate, and in 1949 established Marycrest, in Pearl River, New York, a community devoted to Catholic life. He did free-lance writing and cartooning, published *Ye Gods* (1948) and *The Willock Book*, and died in Pearl River on Dec. 18.

WILMART, ANDRÉ (1876–1941), scholar. Born in Orléans, France, on Jan. 28, he studied there and at the Sorbonne, entered St. Sulpice in 1897, but after two years became a Benedictine at Solesmes, and, after the suppression of his order there in 1901, went to England. After ordination he made major studies in liturgy (*The Missal of Bobbio*), patristics (a number of editions), and early devotional literature (*Auteurs spirituels et textes dévots du moyen age latin*), writing more than 400 essays and pamphlets. Invited to the Vatican Library in 1929, he prepared a two-volume catalogue of the manuscripts given by Queen Christina of Sweden (*Analecta reginensia*), went to Paris in 1940, and was cataloguing Latin manuscripts in the Bibliothèque Nationale there when he died on Apr. 21.

WILMERS, WILHELM (1817–1899), theologian. Born in Broke, Westphalia, on Jan. 30, he joined the Jesuits in Brieg, Switzerland, in 1834, but was forced to leave the country when his Society was expelled in 1847, and was ordained in Ay, France, in 1848. He taught at Issenheim, Louvain, Cologne, Bonn, Aachen, and Maria-Laach, and in 1860 was Cardinal Geissel's theologian at a provincial council in Cologne and Bishop Meurin's theologian at the Vatican Council in 1870. He joined the theological faculty of Poitiers in 1876, taught at St. Helier in 1880 and on the Isle of Jersey, and then retired to write. Among his treatises are *Geschichte der Religion* (1856) and *Handbuch der Religion* (1871). He died at Roermond, Holland, on May 9.

WILTON, RICHARD (d. 1239). An English Trinitarian, he wrote commentaries on Peter Lombard's *Sentences*, and on Genesis and Jeremias, and treatises on current heresies, the immortality of the soul, and divine grace. He was probably never archbishop of Armagh or a cardinal as reported by Oldoinus.

WILTRUDIS, ST. (d. 986?). Wife of Berthold, duke of Bavaria, she became a nun after her husband's death about 947. In 976 she founded an abbey of Benedictine nuns called Bergen and became its abbess. F. D. Jan. 6

WIMMER, BONIFACE (1809–1887). Born

in Thalmassing, Bavaria, on Jan. 14, he studied at Ratisbon, Munich, and the Gregorian, Rome, where he was ordained in 1831. He joined the Benedictines at Metten abbey in 1833, and in 1846 went to the United States to aid German immigrants, and founded St. Vincent archabbey, college, and seminary in Beatty, Pennsylvania. He was appointed first abbot of the monastery in 1855, provided priests for parishes throughout the country, and was instrumental in founding abbeys. He died at St. Joseph's on Dec. 8.

WIMPFELING, JAKOB (1450–1528), theologian. Born in Schlettstadt, Alsace, on July 25, he studied at Freiburg, Erfurt, and Heidelberg, taught at the latter in 1471, and was preacher at the Speyer cathedral in 1483. In 1496 he published his *Isidoneus germanicus*, in which he advocated wider reading, even among pagan authors, greater attention to science, and opposed scholasticism. He became professor at Heidelberg in 1498, published *Adolescentia* in 1500, stressing firm moral training for the young, and in 1513 retired to his native village. He supported Luther, attempting to have his excommunication lifted, but was reconciled to the Church in 1521. He tried to persuade Luther and Zwingli to accept the Church's teaching, but was ridiculed by their adherents. Among his other writings are *Germanie* (1501) and *Epitome rerum germanicarum*, a history of the Germans. He died in Schlettstadt on Nov. 17.

WIMPINA, KONRAD (1465?–1531), theologian. Born in Buchen, Baden, Franconia, Germany, he studied at Leipzig, taught philosophy there, was rector in 1494, dean in 1494–95, and was ordained in 1495. He received his doctorate in theology in 1503, and in 1505 was appointed first rector of the new Frankfort-on-Oder University by Elector Joachim I of Brandenburg. He composed the theses debated by Johann Tetzel at Frankfort in 1518, frequently debated against Luther's doctrines, and published *Ana cephalaeosis* (1528), a refutation of Luther's teaching. He was the elector's theologian at the Diet of Augsburg in 1530 and one of the three Catholic theologians appointed to dispute with the Lutherans, and one of the composers of *Christlichen Unterricht gegen die Bekannthus M. Luther* against Luther's seventeen Swabian articles. He also wrote *Ars epistolandi* (1486) and *Tractatus de philosophorum* (1493). He died in Amorbach, Lower Franconia, on May 17.

WINAMAN, ST. (d. 1040?), martyr. *See* Sunaman, St.

WINCKELMANN, JOHANN JOACHIM (1717–1768), archaeologist. Born in Stendal, Prussia, son of a mechanic, he studied at Halle in 1738, became private librarian to Count Bünau near Dresden in 1748, became inter-ested in art, and in 1755 wrote *Gedanken über die Nachahmung*, on antique art, which attracted great attention. A convert in 1754, he went to Rome, became acquainted with the artists and literati there, particularly Raphael Mengs, who exerted great influence on him, made an intensive study of the art and antiquities of the city and southern Italy, and was soon recognized as an outstanding archaeologist and antiquarian. He became Cardinal Albani's adviser and librarian in 1759 and catalogued Baron von Stosch's collection of gems in Florence. He became antiquary of the apostolic chamber in 1763, and in 1764 published *Geschichte der Kunst des Altertums*, generally regarded as the first literary guide to the art of antiquity. He published the two-volume *Monumenti antichi inediti* (1767), and was murdered in Trieste by an Italian named Arcangeli for some gold coins he had shown him.

WINDISCHMANN, FRIEDRICH HEINRICH HUGO (1811–1861), orientalist. Born in Aschaffenburg, Germany, on Dec. 13, son of the philosopher Karl, he studied philosophy and oriental languages at Bonn, Munich, and in Rome, received his doctorate in theology at Munich in 1836, and was ordained in 1837. He became secretary to the archbishop of Munich, vicar of the cathedral, professor at Freising in 1838, canon of the cathedral in 1839, and vicar general of Munich in 1846. A member of the Bavarian Academy of Sciences from 1842, he was noted as one of the great orientalists of the nineteenth century, vigorously defended Church rights, and died in Munich, Germany, on Aug. 23.

WINDISCHMANN, KARL JOSEPH HIERONYMUS (1775–1839), philosopher. Born in Bonn, Germany, on Apr. 23, he studied at Mainz and medicine at Würzburg and Vienna, and began his medical practice in Mainz in 1797. He was appointed court physician of the elector of Mainz in 1801, taught philosophy at Aschaffenburg in 1803, and was professor of medicine and philosophy at the University of Bonn in 1818. He actively opposed Hermesianism at the university, and drew up a report for Roman authorities in 1834–35 which was largely responsible for its condemnation. An outstanding Christian philosopher, he was influenced by Schelling and Hegel. He wrote numerous philosophical and medical treatises, chief of which were *Die Philosophie im Fortgang der Weltgeschichte* (1827–34) and *Ueber Etwas* (1824), and edited von Schlegel's *Philosophische Vorlesungen*. He died in Bonn on Apr. 23.

WINDLE, BERTRAM COGHILL ALAN (1858–1929). Born in Mayfield, England, on May 8, he studied at Dublin, where he took his doctorates in science and medicine, taught anatomy and anthropology at Birmingham and archaeology at University College, Cork, becoming president there. He later taught at St. Michael's, Toronto, wrote widely on science, and died in Toronto, Canada, on Feb. 14.

WINDTHORST, LUDWIG (1812–1891), statesman. Born in Kaldenhof, Germany, on Jan. 17, he studied at Göttingen and Heidelberg, became a lawyer in Osnabrück, was appointed president of the Catholic state board for schools and churches of Hanover in 1842, and was elected to the Hanover diet in 1848. He became a leader of the legislature, supported the movement for a national confederation by joining the Great Germany party, and in 1851 was elected first Catholic president of the diet. He served as minister of justice for a short period in 1851, was in parliament from 1853 to 1862, was again king's minister until 1865, and in 1867 became a member of the *Reichstag* and Prussian *Landtag* (Hanover had become a Prussian province in 1866 and the North German Confederation had been formed in 1867). He was elected leader of the Centre party in 1874, assumed the leadership of the German Catholics, and was soon the chief opponent of Bismarck, with whom he had previously clashed repeatedly, when the chancellor put into effect the anti-Catholic policies of the Kulturkampf. By the mid-1850's he had built the party into such a formidable force that Bismarck was forced to abandon the Kulturkampf. He founded the Peoples Union for Catholic Germany in 1890, and died in Berlin on Mar. 14.

WINEBALD, ST. (d. 761). Brother of SS. Willibald and Walburga, he went on a pilgrimage to the Holy Land, fell ill on the way, and remained to study at Rome for seven years. After a period in his native England, he returned to Rome, where he met St. Boniface. After ordination, he became a missioner in Thuringia and later abbot of a double monastery built at Heidenheim by Williband, then bishop of Eichstätt, Germany, for him and his sister Walburga. F. D. Dec. 18.

WINEFRED, ST. (d. 650?), martyr. Definitely a historical figure, she probably was born in Wales. In legend, when she repulsed the amorous advances of Caradoc, a chieftain who pursued her to the door of a church, he beheaded her. Where her head fell a spring appeared, which was called the holy well (Holywell) and became a famous shrine until it was destroyed by Henry VIII. In another legend she was the niece of St. Beuno, who restored her to life, later becoming a nun in Denbighshire and abbess of the double monastery at Gwytherin. F. D. Nov. 3.

WINGHAM, THOMAS (1846–1893), musician. Born in London on Jan. 5, he became organist at St. Michael's church there when ten, entered the London Academy of Music in 1863, became organist of All Saints in Paddington in 1864, and studied at the Royal Academy of Music. He taught piano there in 1871, and then was musical director at the Brompton oratory in 1882, a position he held until his death in London on Mar. 24. He composed symphonies, masses, overtures, and other musical works.

WINKELMANN, CHRISTIAN HERMAN (1883–1946), bishop. Born in St. Louis, Missouri, on Sept. 12, he studied at St. Francis Solanus College, Quincy, Illinois, and Kenrick seminary, Missouri, and was ordained in 1907. He did parish work in the St. Louis archdiocese, was appointed titular bishop of Sita and auxiliary of St. Louis in 1933, became bishop of Wichita, Kansas, in 1939, and died there on Nov. 18.

WINNOC, ST. (d. 717?). Probably a Briton of royal blood, he was raised in Brittany and became a monk at St. Sithiu. With three Benedictines he was sent to evangelize the Morini, and founded a monastery at Wormhout (near Dunkirk), of which he was first abbot. F. D. Nov. 6.

WINSLOW, JAKOB BENIGNUS (1669–1760), anatomist. Born in Odense, Denmark, on Apr. 27, he studied there and at the University of Copenhagen, received his medical degree in 1694, went to Paris in 1698 to continue his studies under Duverney, and became a convert in 1699. He became professor of surgery in 1721, regent of the medical faculty in 1728, and in 1743 was appointed professor of anatomy and surgery at the Jardin du Roi in Paris. In 1745 he built and directed an anatomical theatre. A vigorous opponent of the Jansenists, who opposed his every promotion at the Sorbonne, he became widely recognized as an outstanding physician, numbering King Louis XII among his patients, and the leading anatomist of his times. He was made a member of the Academy of Sciences in 1708, and his *Exposition anatomique de la structure du corps humain* (1732) was widely used. He died in Paris on Apr. 3.

WINWALOE, ST. (6th century). Born in Brittany of English exiles, he entered a monastery on Lauré under Abbot Budoc. Later he founded Landévennec near Brest with the help of a local prince. F. D. Mar. 3. There may have been another saint of this name, born in Britain, perhaps of Welsh ancestry, who became a follower of St. Samson. The name is also spelled Gwenno, Valois, and Wingalolus.

WINZET, NINIAN (1518–1592). Born in Renfrew, Scotland, he probably was educated at Glasgow, was ordained in 1540, and became master of the Linlithgow grammar school about 1551. He became provost of St. Michael collegiate church, engaged in a public dispute with

John Knox in 1559, and lost his positions when he refused to accept Protestantism in 1560. He probably was Queen Mary's confessor for a time, was a leader in the struggle against Protestantism with his *Certane tractatis* (1562), and was forced to flee to France when the Protestants triumphed. He was at the University of Paris from 1565 to 1570, where he was proctor for the English nation, went to England in 1571 in the service of Bishop Leslie, Mary's ambassador in England, but returned to France when Leslie was imprisoned. He was appointed abbot of St. James's Benedictine Scots monastery in Ratisbon, Bavaria, in 1577, rebuilt its reputation, and died there on Sept. 21. He wrote controversial and theological works, among them *Last Blast of the Trompet of Gode's Worde, Flagellum sectariorum,* and *Velitatio in Georgium Buchananum* (1581).

WIOMAD, ST. (d. 790?). He was Benedictine abbot of Mettlach and about 750 became bishop of Trèves, France. F. D. Nov. 8.

WIREKER, NIGEL (d. 1200?), poet. A monk at Christ Church, Canterbury, England, he was precentor there in 1186–93. He wrote a satire on contemporary vanity and discontent, *Speculum stultorum,* in which a monk named Brunellus the Ass seeks out the physician Galen to cure him of imagined maladies; the satire is directed against current methods of teaching, theological warfare, and the multiplication of religious orders. Brunellus has just invited Galen to join an order to outdo all orders, when the ass's master, Bernard, puts Brunellus in his place. Chaucer refers to the narrative. Wireker has also been identified with the Nigellus de Longo Campo who wrote *Miracula S. Mariae Virginis, Passio S. Laurentii,* and other poems.

WIRNT VON GRAFENBERG (13th century), poet. A Bavarian nobleman, he wrote between 1202–5 the Middle High German epic, *Wigalois (Guinglain le Galois),* on the adventures of the son of Gawain; it was based on the French poem, *Li bel inconnu,* of Renaud de Beaujeu.

WIRO, ST. (d. 739?), bishop. With SS. Plechelm, another Benedictine priest, and Otger, a deacon, he went to Rome from England, was made a regionary bishop with Plechelm, and sent to evangelize the Low Countries. F. D. May 8.

WIRT, WIGAND (1460?–1519), theologian. Born in Frankfort, Germany, he joined the Dominicans there, and became prior at Stuttgart and then of Steyer. From 1494 he was engaged in a series of controversies when he attacked John Trithemius' doctrine of the Immaculate Conception in the latter's *De laudibus S. Annae,* which was settled in 1495, but renewed in a disputation with the Observantine John Spengler in 1501, and then with Fr. Conrad Hensel, in whose favor the bishop of Strassburg decided. Popes Sixtus IV and Alexander VI forbade the contending parties to charge each other with heresy. Wirt's attack on the Observantines in *Dialogus apologeticus* was banned by the archbishop of Mainz in 1506, and in 1512 Rome decided against Wirt when he again accused his opponents of spreading heresy. He died in Speyer, Germany, on June 30.

WISEMAN, NICHOLAS PATRICK STEPHEN (1802–1865), cardinal. Born in Seville, Spain, of Anglo-Irish parents, on Aug. 2, he studied at Ushaw College and the English College, Rome, and was ordained in 1825. He was appointed curator of Arabic manuscripts in the Vatican and professor of oriental languages in the Roman University in 1825, rector of the English College in 1838, a position he held for twelve years, visited England and delivered a series of lectures there in 1835–36 that attracted widespread attention, and in 1836 founded, with Michael Quin and Daniel O'Connell, the *Dublin Review.* He was appointed coadjutor to Bishop Walsh, vicar apostolic of the Central District, and bishop of Melipotamus and president of Oscott College in 1840, and encouraged the Oxford Movement and the converts from it, confirming Newman after the latter's conversion. In 1847 he was appointed pro-vicar apostolic of the London district (vicar apostolic in 1849), and became active in promoting missions and retreats, reviving religious orders, directing convert work, and giving aid to the poor. In 1850 he was created a cardinal by Pope Pius IX and archbishop of Westminster when the English hierarchy was restored, an action arousing great hostility among the English. He helped allay English fears that this was a step of "papal aggression" with his *Appeal to the English People* and by his conciliatory approach and the great esteem in which he was held. His latter years were clouded by his disagreement with his coadjutor, Bishop George Errington (who was relieved of his coadjutorship by papal decree in 1860), his difficulties with the metropolitan chapter, of which he became provost in 1856, over his founding of the Oblates of St. Charles, and the controversy over Catholic students at Oxford and Cambridge. Though at first sympathetic to the idea which Newman vigorously supported, Wiseman later forbade such attendance. Among his writings are *Horae Syriacae* (1827), *Lectures on the Catholic Church* (1836), *The Real Presence* (1836), and the novel *Fabiola* (1854). He died in London on Feb. 16.

WILFRID WARD, *The Life and Times of Cardinal Wiseman* (2 vols., London, 1897); E. E. REYNOLDS, *Three Cardinals* (New York, Kenedy, 1958).

WISHART, ROBERT (d. 1316), bishop. Consecrated bishop of Glasgow in 1270, he became a guardian of the realm on the death of King Alexander III in 1286, supported Edward I in 1290, but returned to the Scots cause about 1299. He worked with Bruce and Wallace, crowned the former in 1306, was captured at Methuen by the British, and released in 1314.

WISTREMUNDUS, ST. (d. 851), martyr. *See* Peter, St.

WITHBURGA, ST. (d. 743). Youngest daughter of King Anna of East Anglia, she retired on the death of her father in battle to a Benedictine convent she founded at Dereham in Norfolk, England. She died on Mar. 17. F. D. July 8.

WITT, FRANCIS XAVIER (1834–1888), composer. Born in Walderbach, Upper Palatinate, Bavaria, on Feb. 9, son of a teacher, he was taught music as a child, studied at Ratisbon, where he joined the cathedral choir and was influenced by Joseph Schrems, and was ordained in 1856. After pastoral work, he taught Gregorian chant at the Ratisbon seminary in 1859, was choirmaster at St. Emmeran church in 1862, and in 1866 founded *Fliegende Blätter für Kirchenmusik*, a journal devoted to improving and reforming church music. In 1868 he founded *Musica Sacra*, devoted to the role of music in the liturgy, and the St. Cecilia Society for those interested in liturgical music (serving as its president until his death). He became pastor of Schatzhofen in 1873, resigned because of ill-health in 1875, and then retired to Landshut, Bavaria, where he died on Dec. 2. He composed litanies, motets, and a score of masses.

WITTIKUND, BL. (d. 804?). He was a duke of Westphalia at war with Charlemagne, who, according to legend, saw a vision on Christmas night and became converted and baptized. F. D. Jan. 7.

WITTMANN, GEORGE MICHAEL (1760–1833), bishop. Born near Pleistein, Bavaria, on Jan. 23, he studied at Amberg and Heidelberg, was ordained in 1782, did parish work, and in 1788 taught in the Ratisbon seminary. He was rector there in 1802, pastor of the cathedral in 1804, auxiliary bishop of Ratisbon and titular bishop of Comana in 1829, vicar general in 1830, and was nominated for the bishopric of Ratisbon, Bavaria, but died there on Mar. 8 before he was preconized. He wrote theological treatises and helped in a translation of the New Testament.

WITTMANN, PATRIZIUS (1818–1883), editor. Born in Ellwangen, Württemberg, Germany, on Jan. 4, he studied in Ehinger and Tübingen. He joined the staff of *Sion* in Augsburg, published *Die Herrlichkeit der Kirche* and received his doctorate in philosophy in 1841, and moved to Augsburg as the editor of *Sion*. He founded several other periodicals, *Stadtund Landbote* (later *Neue Augsburger Zeitung*) and *Sendbote*, and wrote *Allgemeine Geschichte der katholischen Missionen* (1846–50). He died in Munich, Germany, on Oct. 3.

WITZEL, GEORG (1501–1573), theologian. Born in Vacha, Hesse, Germany, he studied at Erfurt and Wittenberg, and was ordained in 1520. He became vicar of Vacha, was attracted to Lutheranism, left the Church and married in 1524, and became a Lutheran minister. His *Pro defensione bonorum operum* (1532), under the pseudonym Agricola Phaqus, caused a furore and in 1533 he returned to the Church with his *Apologia*. In 1539 he proposed reunion with a public disputation at Leipzig, but was forced to flee when his efforts failed. He went to Berlin and then to Fulda, where his strenuous defense of the Church forced him to flee again. He wrote more than 100 treatises, among them *Methodus concordiae* (1537) and *Typus prioris Ecclesiae* (1539). He died in Mainz, Germany, on Feb. 16.

WIVINA, ST. (d. 1170?). Born in Oisy, Flanders, she refused marriage and when twenty-three became a hermitess near Brussels and was founder and first abbess of the Benedictine convent of Grand Bigard. F. D. Dec. 17 .

WIZO (8th century). An Anglo-Saxon, he went to Gaul in 782 with Alcuin, became a tutor in Charlemagne's court, and succeeded Alcuin in 796 as master of the palace school. Alcuin, who called him Candidus, names him in the dedication of his commentary on Ecclesiastes.

WLADISLAW II (1455–1516), king of Hungary and Bohemia. Son of King Casimir IV of Poland and Elizabeth, daughter of Albert II of Austria, he was elected to the Bohemian throne in 1471, and proved incapable of uniting the country against the powerful nobles. He was elected king of Hungary in 1490 on the death of Matthias Corvinus and by his weakness and inability soon undid most of the reforms and gains of his predecessor. His policy of close co-operation with the Hapsburgs (he arranged several dynastic marriages between his family and the Hapsburgs) caused the nobles, headed by Prince Stephen Zápolya of Transylvania, to unite against him, rendering his army useless by cutting off his revenue. In 1514 a peasant revolt was bloodily suppressed by John Zápolya. He died on Mar. 13.

WLADISLAW I, king of Hungary. *See* Ladislas VI, king of Poland.

WLADISLAW II, king of Hungary. *See* Wladislaw II, king of Hungary and Bohemia.

WLADISLAW. *See* Ladislas.

WOHLGEMUTH, MICHAEL (1434–1519), painter. Born in Nuremberg, Germany, he studied under Hans Pleydenwurff, who greatly influenced his technique, and established a workshop of his own which became famous throughout Europe. He painted altarpieces in Zwickau and Crailsheim churches; other work includes *Last Judgment* in the Nuremberg Town House and a *Votive Offering with St. Jerome*. He also did highly esteemed wood and copper engravings, and numbered Albert Dürer among his pupils. He died in Nuremberg.

WOLFF, GEORGE DERING (1822–1894), editor. Born in Martinsburg, West Virginia, on Aug. 25, he studied at Marshall College, was admitted to the bar, and became a minister of the German Reformed Church and a follower of John Williamson Nevin. In 1871 he became a convert, was editor of the Baltimore *Catholic Mirror* in 1872, and Philadelphia *Catholic Standard* from 1873 until his death in Norristown, Pennsylvania, on Jan. 29. He helped found the *American Catholic Quarterly Review* in 1876, and was on its staff until his death.

WOLFGANG, ST. (930?–994), bishop. A native of Swabia, he studied at Reichenau and Würzburg, taught at Trier, and in 864 became a Benedictine monk at Einsiedeln, Switzerland. He was headmaster of the abbey school which he developed, was ordained in 971, and was appointed bishop of Ratisbon, Bavaria, in 972. He strengthened ecclesiastical discipline, bettered education, restored monasteries, among them St. Emmeran, and became prominent in secular affairs, accompanying the emperor to several diets. He was tutor to Henry, son of the duke of Bavaria and later emperor, and was called the "great almoner" because of his generosity to the poor. His offices brought him no personal wealth, for he continued to follow his monastic rule. He died in Puppingen, Austria, and was canonized by Pope Leo IX in 1052. F. D. Oct. 31.

WOLFHARD. *See* Gualfardus, St.

WOLFHELM, BL. (1020?–1091). Educated at Cologne, he became a Benedictine monk at the abbey of St. Maximinus, then at St. Pantaleon, and served as abbot of Gladbach, Siegburg, and Brauweiler. He wrote on the Eucharist, on scripture, and on monastic discipline. F. D. Apr. 22.

WOLFRAM VON ESCHENBACH (1170?–1220?), poet. Born in Eschenbach, Bavaria, he was a knight who spent most of his life traveling from court to court, was patronized by Landgrave Hermann of Thuringia after 1203, and was Germany's greatest minnesinger. He probably died in Wehlenberg, Middle Franconia, Bavaria, where he had a small estate. He is the author of *Parzival*, written between 1200 and 1216 and considered the outstanding court epic of mediaeval Germany; the unfinished epic, *Titurel*; *Willehalm*, also unfinished; and lyric poems. He is a character in Wagner's *Tannhäuser*.

WOLOWSKI, LOUIS FRANÇOIS MICHEL REYMOND (1810–1876), economist. Born in Warsaw, Poland, on Aug. 31, he was secretary of the revolutionary Polish legation at Paris in 1830, settled there when the revolution was put down, and became a French citizen in 1836. He established *Revue de Legislation et de Jurisprudence* in 1834, taught industrial law at the Conservatory of Arts and Crafts from 1839 to 1872, and was elected to the assembly in 1846, to the Académie des Sciences Morales in 1855, to the national assembly in 1871, and a senator for life in 1875. He wrote economic treatises, favored free trade and state control of children and women's laboring conditions in industry, and helped found *Crédit Foncier*, to aid the farmer. He died in Gisors, France, on Aug. 14.

WOLSEY, THOMAS (1475?–1530), cardinal. Born in Ipswich, England, he studied at Oxford, became a fellow of Magdalen about 1497, received numerous benefices, became chaplain to the archbishop of Canterbury, and in 1503 chaplain and financial aid to Sir Richard Nanfan, who brought his ability to the attention of King Henry VII. He became a court chaplain in 1506, was employed by the king on diplomatic missions, especially one to Emperor Maximilian in 1508, and became master of the rolls. He was named dean of Lincoln in 1509, almoner and privy councilor at the accession of Henry VIII, and in 1511 became a canon of Windsor and began to exercise increasing influence at court. He accompanied Henry and organized the army for the campaign to France in 1513, was appointed bishop of Tournay (he never occupied the see and later surrendered it), and in 1514 became bishop of Lincoln. Later that year he was named archbishop of York, was created a cardinal in 1515 and chancellor of England. He was given the see of Bath and Wells *in commendam* in 1518. He consistently promoted a policy of alliance with France, but when Emperor Maximilian died in 1519 he inaugurated a policy of neutrality between Charles V of Spain and Francis I of France; when war between them broke out, he acted as mediator, signing a secret treaty with Charles against France at Henry's insistence. He aspired to the papacy on Pope Leo X's death in 1521 and again in 1523 on Pope Adrian VI's death, but was defeated both times, due in no small measure to lack of support from Charles. Pope Clement VII made him life papal legate to England in 1523 and gave him the see of Durham. When Charles threatened to dominate Europe after defeating Francis at Pavia in 1525, Wolsey persuaded Henry to resume his French alliance. Meanwhile, his personal pomp, extravagances, and heavy taxation had roused great resentment against him. He had been interested in

education, made gifts to the universities, and founded Cardinal College at Oxford (later called Henry VIII College and finally Christ Church). When Henry decided to cast off Catherine for Ann Boleyn, he acted on the king's behalf, though at first opposed, and went to Rome to persuade the pope to grant the king's wishes, learning on his return that the king had secretly sent another embassy. With Cardinal Campeggio he was appointed, as legate, to try the case in England, alienated Ann Boleyn by the protracted delays (manipulated deliberately by Campeggio), and, when the court referred the case to Rome in 1529, found his influence at an end. He was deprived of his chancellorship, had his possessions confiscated, and was ordered exiled. He retired to Esher, was pardoned, and had his possessions restored in 1530, and then retired to Cawood in York, where he ably ruled his diocese. He was arrested on a charge of treason and died at Leicester abbey on Nov. 29 while on his way to London for trial.
CHARLES W. FERGUSON, *Naked to Mine Enemies* (Boston, Little, Brown, 1958); HILAIRE BELLOC, *Wolsey* (Philadelphia, Lippincott, 1930).

WOLSKI, MARCIN. *See* Bielski, Marcin.

WOOD, JAMES FREDERICK (1813–1883), archbishop. Born in Philadelphia on Apr. 27, he studied at a private school and probably at an English academy, and became a bank clerk in Cincinnati after the family moved there in 1827. He became a convert in 1836, continued his studies at the Irish College and the Propaganda in Rome, and was ordained in Rome in 1844. After serving at the cathedral in Cincinnati he became pastor of St. Patrick's church there in 1854, and in 1857 was appointed titular bishop of Antigonia and coadjutor of Philadelphia. He succeeded to that see in 1860, denounced secret Catholic societies and the Fenians, and excommunicated Catholics belonging to the notorious Molly Maguire gang. He completed his cathedral in 1864, built up a parochial-school system, and actively supported the North American College in Rome, of which he served as treasurer of the board. He was appointed assistant at the pontifical throne in 1862, supported the dogma of papal infallibility at the Vatican Council, and in 1875 became Philadelphia's first archbishop when the diocese was made a metropolitan see. He died in Philadelphia on June 20.

WOOD, THOMAS (1499?–1588?). One of Queen Mary's chaplains, he was deprived of his numerous benefices, among them prebendary of Canterbury and several vicariates, in 1559, imprisoned for his priesthood in Marshalsea and Fleet prisons and the Tower of London from 1560, and died in Wisbech castle, England, sometime before 1588.

WOODFEN, BL. NICHOLAS (d. 1586),

martyr. An English priest, he served in the underground mission from 1580 to 1585 during the Elizabethan persecution, but was captured and hanged at Tyburn. He is also named Devereux and Wheeler in contemporary records. F. D. Jan. 21.

WOODHEAD, ABRAHAM (1609?–1678), controversialist. Born in Almonbury, Yorkshire, England, he studied at Oxford, where he became fellow in 1633 and proctor in 1641, became a convert in 1645 and the duke of Buckingham's tutor, and in 1654 formed a community with a group of friends in Hoxton. His Oxford fellowship, of which he had been deprived in 1648, was restored in 1660, but he soon gave it up to return to Hoxton, England, where he remained until his death on May 4. He wrote *Ancient Church Government* (1662–85) and *Guide in Controversies* (1667), and translated St. Teresa's *Life* and St. Augustine's *Confessions*.

WOODHOUSE, BL. THOMAS (d. 1573), martyr. He was a parish priest in Lincolnshire, England, who was arrested for his religious activity and imprisoned in 1561 until death; while in jail he became a Jesuit. He was hanged, drawn, and quartered at Tyburn, and was beatified in 1886. F. D. June 19.

WOODLOCK, THOMAS FRANCIS (1866–1945), editor. Born in Dublin, on Sept. 1, he studied at Beaumont and at London University, served as a broker's clerk, and joined his father and brother in the family's brokerage house. He went to New York in 1892, worked for the Dow-Jones News Service, specializing in railroad investments, and in 1902–5 was editor of the *Wall Street Journal*. He was a partner in a brokerage firm on the New York Stock Exchange from 1905 to 1918, worked thereafter for various corporations, was director of two railroads, and in 1925 was chosen by President Coolidge to serve on the Interstate Commerce Commission. He resigned in 1930 to return to the *Wall Street Journal*, for which he wrote a regular column, "Thinking It Over." He wrote books on American railroads, published *The Catholic Pattern* in 1942, and was awarded the Laetare Medal in 1943. He died in New York City on Aug. 25. His *Thinking It Over*, a collection of columns dealing with contemporary philosophy, history, and government, was published posthumously.

WOODS, JULIAN EDMUND TENISON (1832–1889), geologist. Born in London on Nov. 15, he studied in Newington, was on the staff of the London *Times* for a short period, and joined the Passionists in 1850. Forced to leave because of ill-health, he taught at Mont Bel College in France, went to Tasmania in 1854 as assistant director of Catholic schools for Bishop Wilson of Hobart Town, became assistant editor of the Adelaide *Times*, and was ordained in Adelaide in 1857. He became pastor at Penola, where he founded the Sisters of St. Joseph of the Sacred Heart and became secretary of Bishop Shal of Adelaide in 1866, founded the Brothers in 1869, and from 1870 to 1881 engaged in missionary activities in New South Wales, Queensland, and Tasmania. In 1883 he went to Malacca, Java, Siam, China, Japan, and southern Australia to observe their mineral resources, prepared a report for the British government on sources of coal in the Far East, and became an expert on the geology of the area. He wrote books and reports on the geology and zoology of Australia, Malaya, and the Philippines, was a fellow of the Geographical Society of London from 1859, and president of the Linnean Society of New South Wales in 1880. *Geological Observations in South Australia* (1862), *North Australia and Its Physical Geography* (1887), *Anatomy and Life History of Mollusca* (1888), and *Desert Sand Stone of Australia* (1889) are the titles of some of his writings. He died in Sydney, Australia, on Oct. 7.

WORDE, WYNKIN DE (d. 1534?), publisher. Born probably in Lorraine, he went to England in 1477 as an assistant to the printer, William Caxton. He was in charge of the latter's printing plant until Caxton's death and succeeded him in the venture. He developed the art of type cutting, introduced Roman letters, imported engravings from the Continent, and contributed greatly to the development of English taste by his publication of some 400 different works.

WÖRNDLE, AUGUST (1829–1902), painter. Brother of Edmund, he was born in Vienna on June 22, studied under Klieber and Joseph von Führich and at the Academy of Fine Arts in Vienna, went to Italy in 1853, where he studied under Cornelius and Overbeck in Rome. He worked with the former on the cartoons for the Campo Santo in Berlin, worked on a series of frescoes of the stations of the cross for the Innsbruck cemetery and Wörgle parish church with his brother Edmund in 1861–68, and then settled in Vienna. He taught at the Maria Theresa Academy in Vienna from 1872 to 1898 and was private tutor for the Archdukes Francis Ferdinand and Otto. Among his works are *Three Magi*, *The Liberation of Vienna From the Turks*, *Battle of Springes*, and frescoes for St. Anastasius church in Vienna, the chapel of the castle of Ambras, and the Salzburg cathedral. He died in Vienna on Apr. 26.

WÖRNDLE, EDMUND (1827–1906), painter. Born in Vienna, Austria, on July 28, he studied at the Schossen abbey school and then the Academy of Fine Arts in Vienna from 1846 to 1853. After a trip through the Holy Land and Italy in 1855–58 he devoted himself to painting in the romantic style, producing re-

ligious paintings and Tyrolean landscapes and historical scenes. Among his outstanding works are a series of sketches and oil paintings of the Holy Land, *Christ at Jacob's Well*, *Samson as the Lion Killer*, and, with his brother August, their *Parzival* series. He founded the Society of Ecclesiastical Art of the Tyrol, and died in Innsbruck, Austria, on Aug. 3.

WÖRNDLE, PHILIP VON (1755–1818), soldier. Born in Hötting-Innsbruck, Tyrol, on July 9, he studied at Innsbruck, where he received his doctorate in law in 1779, became a judge of the manor court of the abbey of Wilten, and an advocate. In 1796 he joined, as captain, a university company formed to resist the French, and by 1809 had risen to Tyrolese undercommissary and head of the Puster Valley defenses. He moved to Austria in 1810, fought against the French to liberate southern Tyrol, and in 1813 became provincial commissioner. He died in Linz, Austria, on Aug. 2.

WORSLEY, EDWARD (1605–1676). Born in Lancashire, England, he probably studied at Oxford, where he may have taken Anglican orders, became a Jesuit in 1626, was ordained in 1641, and taught philosophy at Liège. He was rector there in 1658–62, became procurator at Antwerp, and died there on Sept. 2. He wrote several ecclesiastical treatises.

WORTHINGTON, THOMAS (1549–1627). Born in Blainscough Hall, near Wigan, Lancashire, England, he studied at Oxford and Douai, and was ordained in 1577. He remained there to teach, went to England in 1580, was arrested and imprisoned in the Tower of London in 1584, and was banished to Normandy in 1585. He taught at Rheims, in 1587 became chaplain to Sir William Stanley's regiment, was appointed president of Douai in 1599, incurred the hostility of the secular clergy by his friendliness with the Jesuits, and was accused of inadequately training priests for the missions. He was summoned to Rome in 1613, replaced as president, and appointed as an apostolic notary on the Index. He returned to the English mission in 1616, was made titular archdeacon of Nottinghamshire and Derbyshire, and joined the Jesuits a few months before his death at Biddulph Hall in Staffordshire. He wrote ecclesiastical works, among them *The Rosarie of our Ladie* (1600) and *A Catalogue of Martyrs in Englande* (1608).

WOUTERS, ST. ANDREW (d. 1572). He was a parish priest at Heinot, Holland, who was imprisoned at Briel by the Calvinists and hanged as one of the martyrs of Gorkum. He was canonized in 1867. F. D. July 9.

WOUTERS, G. HENRY (1802–1872), historian. Born in Oostham, Limburg, Netherlands, on May 3, he taught at the University of Liège from 1829 to 1871, and wrote *Historiae ecclesiasticae compendium* (1842) and *Dissertationes* *in selecta historiae ecclesiasticae capita* (1868–72). He died on Jan. 5.

WRENNO, VEN. ROGER (d. 1616?), martyr. *See* Thulis, Ven. John.

WRIGHT, BL. PETER (d. 1651), martyr. Born in Slipton, Northamptonshire, he was converted at Liège, studied for the priesthood at Ghent and Rome, and became a Jesuit in 1629. Chaplain to the English forces in Flanders under Sir Henry Gage, with whom he returned to England and whom he accompanied during the Civil War, he was captured in 1650, and hanged, drawn, and quartered in London during the persecution of Oliver Cromwell. F. D. May 19.

WRIGHT, WILLIAM (1562–1639). Born in York, England, he was ordained, taught philosophy at Graz and Vienna, and in 1605 was sent on the English mission. He became chaplain to the Gage family in Suffolk, and was imprisoned in the Tower for his priesthood in 1607. He ministered to the stricken in the London plague, escaped to Leicestershire, where he established several missions, and after 1612 devoted himself to writing a dozen books and translations. He died on Jan. 18.

WULFEN, FRANZ XAVER VON (1728–1805), botanist. Born in Belgrade, Serbia, on Nov. 5, he studied at Kaschau, became a Jesuit in 1745, and taught at Vienna, Laibach, and in 1764, when the Jesuits were suppressed in Austria, at Klagenfurt, Germany, where he remained until his death on Mar. 17. He was highly regarded for his knowledge of the flora of the eastern Alps, where he discovered many new species of plants, and of mineralogy, for which he was elected to numerous scientific societies. The genus *Wulfenia* and the mineral wulfenite were named in his honor.

WULFHADE, ST. (d. 675), martyr. *See* Rufinus, St.

WULFRAM, ST. (d. 703?), archbishop. Born in Milly, France, son of Fulbert, a high court official, he served at the court of Theodoric III of Neustria, became a priest and was appointed to the see of Sens, France, for a short period while the rightful archbishop was banished, then prepared at the abbey of Fontenelle for missionary work among the Frisians. There he fought the practice of human sacrifice and made many converts. He returned to Fontenelle late in life and died there. F. D. Mar. 20.

WULFRIC (d. 1154). Born in Compton Martin, England, he was ordained, but became more interested in hunting and idleness than in parochial tasks. He reformed and became a recluse at Haselbury-Plucknett in Somersetshire, where he lived in extreme austerity. He was never canonized and was not a Cistercian, but was venerated after his death by many pilgrims and honored on Feb. 20.

WULFSTAN (10th century), poet. He was an English monk at Winchester, and is called the author of a Latin poem on the miracles of St. Swithin.

WULFSTAN, ST. (1008?–1095), bishop. Born in Warwickshire, England, he studied at Evesham and Peterborough, was ordained, then became a novice at the monastery in Worcester of which he later became prior. He was appointed bishop of Worcester in 1062 and distinguished himself by suppressing the vicious trade which sent the unsuspecting in Bristol's streets off to Ireland as slaves. He retained his see after the conquest of William I, who came to respect him, became a deputy to Lanfranc, and worked piously to lessen public discontent over the extremes of some of the conquerors. He was canonized in 1203. F. D. Jan. 19.

WULSIN, ST. (d. 1005), bishop. A Benedictine follower of St. Dunstan, he became superior of Westminster in 958, abbot in 980, and bishop of Sherborne, England, in 993. F. D. Jan. 8.

WUST, PETER (1884–1940), philosopher. Born in Rissenthal, Saar, Germany, on Aug. 28, he studied at Berlin and Strassburg, taught English and German in a number of municipal gymnasia, and took his doctorate at Bonn. He wrote on metaphysics, and the intellectual life in Germany. In 1930 he was appointed to the philosophy faculty at Münster, Germany, where he remained until his death on Apr. 3. His chief other writings include *Crisis in the West*, popularized by E. I. Watkin, *Ungewissheit und Wagnis*, and his autobiography, *Gestalten und Gedanken* (1940).

WYART, THÉOPHILE LOUIS HENRI (1839–1904). Born in Bouchain, Nord, France, on Oct. 12, he studied at the Cambrai seminaries, taught at Tourcoing College, served in the papal army from 1860 to 1870, and then in the French army during the Franco-Prussian War. He joined the Trappists at the end of the war, taking the name Sebastian, was ordained in 1877, received his doctorate in theology in 1880, became prior and in 1883 abbot of St. Marie du Mont monastery, and in 1887 vicar general of the Rancé congregation and abbot of Septfons. He labored for years to effect a reunion of the three congregations of Trappists, the Ancient Reform of Our Lady of La Trappe, the New Reform of Our Lady of La Trappe, and the Congregation of Belgium. In 1892 they merged and he was elected first general of the Order of the Reformed Cistercians of Our Lady of La Trappe (Our Lady of La Trappe was dropped from the title in 1902). He recovered Cîteaux in 1898 and made it the mother house of the order, and in 1899 resigned the abbacy of Septfons to become its abbot. He died in Rome on Aug. 18.

WYNHOVEN, PETER M. H. (1884–1944). Born in Venray, Holland, on Dec. 31, he studied there and at Kenrick seminary, St. Louis, Missouri, and was ordained in 1909. He did parish work in Louisiana, was vice-chancellor of New Orleans in 1933–40, became a monsignor in 1934, edited *Catholic Action of the South*, a weekly, and was president of the Catholic Press Association. He also published *The Sincere Seeker, Wild Wisdom*, and sermons. He served on state and national labor- and industrial-relations boards. He also founded Hope Haven, an industrial school for boys, orphanages, an institute for the deaf, social-welfare centers, a free labor bureau, and Associated Catholic Charities. He died on Sept. 13.

WYNNE, JOHN J. (1859–1948), editor. Born in New York City on Sept. 30, he studied at St. Francis Xavier, became a Jesuit at seventeen, and was ordained in 1890. He taught at St. Francis and at Boston College, directed the Apostleship of Prayer from 1892–1907 and was editor of the *Messenger of the Sacred Heart* in 1892–1902, and in 1909 became founder and first editor of the weekly, *America*. He then was in charge of the shrine of Our Lady of Martyrs at Auriesville, New York, worked for the cause of the Jesuit missionaries (who were

canonized in 1930), and wrote *The Jesuit Martyrs of North America*, and the material for the cause of Kateri Tekakwitha. He also was interested in the Belgian missions in the Congo, wrote successfully to prevent the expulsion of Augustinian and Franciscan missioners from the Philippines, organized the League of Daily Mass, and edited the encyclicals of Pope Leo XIII. In 1905 he formed the editorial board of the Catholic Encyclopedia, and in 1911–12 served as editor of that project, which resulted in the publication of seventeen volumes and a later dictionary. He died in New York City on Nov. 30.

WYNNE, ROBERT J. (1851–1922). Born in New York City on Nov. 18, he was Washington correspondent of the Cincinnati *Gazette* in 1880–92, private secretary to Secretary of the Treasury John G. Carlisle in 1893–96, correspondent of the New York *Times* in 1896–1902, and served as assistant postmaster general in 1902–4. Theodore Roosevelt appointed him postmaster general for 1904–5, and he was consul general in London from 1905 until he retired to private business in 1910. He died on Mar. 11.

X

XAINCTONGE, VEN. ANNE DE (1567–1621), foundress. Born in Dijon, France, on Nov. 21, daughter of a councilor, she planned an uncloistered order serving the educational needs of women. With the help of the Jesuits at the college in Dijon she persisted against strong opposition and with Claudine de Boisset and others founded a convent for her Sisters of St. Ursula of the Blessed Virgin in Dôle, Franche-Comté, then held by Spain in 1606. Her order spread through France and Switzerland, but all documents were destroyed during the French Revolution, and her process was not established until 1900 when she was declared venerable. She died at Dôle on June 8.

XANTIPPA, ST. (1st century). She and Polyxena were disciples of the apostles. F. D. Sept. 23.

XAVIER, FRANCIS. *See* Francis Xavier.

XIMÉNES, DIDACUS (d. 1560), theologian. Born in Spain, he studied at Salamanca, where he received his licentiate in law, was rector of the College of Cuenca there, joined the Dominicans in 1543, became assistant to the archbishop of Toledo in 1559, and wrote several theological treatises.

XIMENEZ DE CISNEROS, FRANCISCO (1436–1517), cardinal. Born in Torrelaguna, New Castile, Spain, he studied at Salamanca and Rome, received his degree in canon and

civil law, and became a consistorial advocate in Rome. When he claimed the benefice of Uzeda he was imprisoned for six years by Archbishop Carillo of Toledo, who had other plans for it; on his release in 1480 he became grand vicar of the diocese of Siguenza. He resigned to join the Franciscans in 1484, became noted for his preaching and austerities, was appointed Queen Isabella's confessor and was elected provincial of Castile, both in 1492, and in 1495 was appointed archbishop of Toledo, a position which automatically made him chancellor of Castile. He instituted ecclesiastical reforms, was known for his charity to the poor, and was recognized as a generous patron of learning. He began the first polyglot bible, which was completed in 1517, and founded the University of Alcalá. He served as regent in 1506–7 between the death of Philip I and the arrival of Ferdinand V from Italy, and in 1507 was created a cardinal and appointed grand inquisitor of Castile and León. He made reforms in the operation of the Inquisition, and financed and led an expedition against the Moors which captured Oran in 1509. He persuaded King Ferdinand to send an army to Italy to relieve Pope Julius II, who had been attacked by the French; by 1512 the Spanish army had driven out the French. Ximénez supported the pope against the actions of the schismatic Synod of

Pisa, which in 1511 had declared the pope deposed. On the death of Ferdinand in 1516 he served as regent, inaugurated governmental, financial, and military reforms, attempted to eliminate slavery in the New World, encouraging missionary activity there, and joined forces with Francis I of France to defeat the attempts of Jean d'Abret to recover Navarre. He died in Roa, near Valladolid, Spain, on Nov. 8.

XYSTUS. *See* Sixtus.

Y

YAXLEY, VEN. RICHARD (d. 1589), martyr. Son of William Yaxley of Boston, Lincolnshire, England, he went to Rheims in 1582 and was ordained in 1585. The following year he was sent on the English mission, was captured at Oxford with George Nichols, tortured, and executed there on Oct. 19.

YAZDANDOCTA (4th century). A wealthy Persian woman, she is said to have bought white robes and food for a final meal to the 120 martyrs who were put to death at Seleucia on Apr. 6, 345, on orders of King Sapor II; she also saw to their honorable burial.

YEO, MARGARET ROUTLEDGE (1877–1941), author. Born in Canterbury, England, to Charles and Dorothy Blomfield Routledge, she was educated privately there and at Lausanne, married Eric Yeo in 1906, and became a convert in 1916. She was interested in archaeology, wrote three collections of short stories, then produced several novels: *Salt* (1927), *King of Shadows*, *Wild Parsley*, *Uncertain Glory*, and *Full Circle* (1933). She then turned to biography and completed lives of St. Francis Xavier, Don Juan of Austria, St. Charles Borromeo, and others.

YEPES, JUAN DE. *See* John of the Cross, St.

YERGENS, HENRY (1870–1961), educator. Born in Philadelphia, Pennsylvania, he became a Christian Brother and spent seventy-two years as teacher and administrator. He became president of St. Thomas College, Scranton, Pennsylvania, in 1932, doubled its enrollment, and in 1938 secured university status for it. He became inspector of Christian Brothers' schools in the Middle Atlantic states and Ohio in 1940, a post he held until his retirement in 1958. He died in Ammendale, Maryland, on Jan. 8.

YMAR, ST. (d. 830?), martyr. A Benedictine monk at Reculver, Kent, England, he was slain by invading Danes. F. D. Nov. 12.

YON, PIETRO ALESSANDRO (1886–1943), composer. Born in Settimo Vittone, Italy, on Aug. 8, he went to the United States in 1907. He had studied at conservatories in Milan, Turin, and Rome, and was substitute organist at the Vatican in 1905–7 (and again in 1919–21). He became organist and choirmaster at St. Vincent Ferrer in New York City (1907–19 and 1921–26) and at St. Patrick's cathedral in 1927. He wrote more than seventy compositions, including thirteen masses and the oratorio, *The Triumph of St. Patrick* (1934). He died in Huntington, New York, on Nov. 22.

YOUNG, JOHN B. (1854–1928). Born in Alsace on Oct. 30, he became a Jesuit, was ordained in 1879, and was associated with St. Francis Xavier church in New York City, where as organist he developed a boys' *a capella* choir and worked with Pietro Yon and other organists in reforming church music. He died in Monroe, New York, on Sept. 26.

YOUNG, JOSUE MOODY (1808–1866), bishop. Born in Shapleigh, Maine, on Oct. 29, he became a convert in 1828, studied at Mt. St. Mary's, Maryland, and was ordained in 1838. He did pastoral work in Cincinnati until 1853 when he was appointed bishop of Pittsburgh; he was transferred to Erie, Pennsylvania, as its second bishop before his consecration. The discovery of oil in his diocese caused its population to increase suddenly and called for great efforts on the part of the bishop of provide churches and schools for the burgeoning Catholic populace. He died in Erie on Sept. 18.

YOUVILLE, BL. MARGUÉRITE D' (1701–1771), foundress. Marie Marguérite Dufrost de LaJemmerais was born in Varennes, Quebec, on Oct. 15, studied under the Ursulines in Quebec, married François d'Youville in 1722, and was widowed in 1730. She engaged in trade to support herself and her three children, devoted herself to charitable works as a Lady of Charity of the Confraternity of the Holy Family, and in 1737, with three companions, took the initial vows that founded the Grey Nuns; a formal declaration followed in 1745. In 1747 she was appointed directress of the General Hospital in Montreal, and with her companions took it over, and in 1755 Bishop Pontbriand of Quebec confirmed the Rule of the Grey Nuns with Mother d'Youville as superior. After her death on Dec. 23 in Montreal the Greys Nuns spread through Canada and the United States, China, Africa, and South America, and are particularly known for their schools, hospitals, and orphanages, and their work among the Arctic Indians and Eskimos. She was beatified by Pope John XXIII in 1959.

YRCHARD, ST. (5th century). A Scot, consecrated bishop by St. Ternan, he became a missioner among the Picts. F. D. Aug. 24.

YRIEIX, ST. *See* Aredius, St.

YSAMBERT, NICOLAS (1565?–1642), theologian. Born in Orléans, France, possibly in 1569, he studied at the Sorbonne, taught there, and in 1616 was appointed to a new chair of theology to study Catholic-Protestant controversy. He brought about the condemnation of Marc Antonio de Dominis, apostate bishop of Spalato, fought Gallicanism, and wrote a commentary on the *Summa* of St. Thomas Aquinas. He died in Paris on May 14.

Z

ZABARELLA, FRANCESCO (1360–1417), cardinal. Born in Padua, Italy, on Aug. 10, he studied law under Giovanni di Lignano at Bologna, and Florence, and taught at the latter and at Padua from 1385 to 1410. He became vicar of the bishop of Florence in 1385, archpriest of the Padua cathedral in 1398, and participated in several diplomatic missions for the Paduan government. He supported Venice when it annexed Padua in 1406, was councilor of the Venetian legate at the Council of Pisa in 1409, was appointed bishop of Florence in 1410 by antipope John XXIII, and created a cardinal the next year. He was an active supporter of John at the Council of Rome (1412–13) and the Council of Constance (1414), remained as John's representative when John fled in 1415, and persuaded him to resign in April. He attempted fruitlessly to persuade Jerome of Prague and Jean Petit to sign a modified retraction, and died at Constance, Switzerland, on Sept. 26. He never rose above minor orders.

ZACCARIA, ST. ANTONIO MARIA (1502–1539), founder. Born at Cremona, Italy, he studied medicine at Padua, graduated at twenty-two, and was ordained in 1528. At Milan in 1530, he founded the Clerks Regular of St. Paul (Barnabites) at St. Barnabas church. The order, approved by Pope Clement VII in 1533, labored to reform the Church. Worn out by his efforts, in which he tried to imitate St. Paul, he died at thirty-seven. He was canonized by Pope Leo XII in 1897. F. D. July 5.

ZACCARIA, FRANCESCO ANTONIO (1714–1795), theologian. Born in Venice, Italy, on Mar. 27, he became a Jesuit in Austria in 1731, taught at Görz, and was ordained at Rome in 1740. After parish work he became librarian at Modena in 1754, was removed in 1768 when he defended the papacy, and moved to Rome as librarian of the Jesuit house there. Pensioned by Popes Clement XIII and XIV and Pius VI to allow him freedom to write, he produced more than 150 works on theology, history, and canon law, including the twenty-two-volume *Raccolta di dissertazioni di storia ecclesia* (1792–97), the thirteen-volume *Thesaurus theologicus*, and *Bibliotheca antica e moderna di storia litteraria*. He also edited the periodical, *Storia litteraria d'Italia*, from 1750 to 1757, taught church history at the Sapienza, and was director of the Accademia dei Nobili Ecclesiastici. He died in Rome on Oct. 10.

ZACCONI, LUDOVICO (1555–1627), musician. Born in Pesaro, Italy, on June 11, he became an Augustinian at Venice, was ordained, and in 1565 was choirmaster at the Venice Augustinian church, then in the service of the duke of Bavaria (1592), and of Archduke Charles at Vienna (1596). He wrote a treatise on musical theory which discusses the method of presenting polyphony and outlines sixteenth-century music in its totality. He died in Pesaro, Italy, on Mar. 23.

ZACHAEUS, ST. (d. 116?). He is said to have been fourth bishop of Jerusalem. F. D. Aug. 23.

ZACHAEUS, ST. (d. 303), martyr. *See* Alphaeus, St.

ZACHARIAS CHRYSPOLITANUS (d. 1155?). Born in Besançon, France, he was master of the cathedral school there, became a Premonstratensian in Laon, and published a critical harmony of the gospels, based on that of Ammonius of Alexandria, and quoting heavily from the Fathers of the Church, Alcuin, and Remigius of Auxerre.

ZACHARY, ST. (d. 752), pope. Born in San Severino, Italy, of a Greek family, he crowded into his ten-year pontificate, which began on Dec. 10, 741, a successful peace treaty with the Lombard leaders, Liutprand and Rachis; active support of the German mission under St. Boniface, whom he made archbishop of Mainz; approval of Pepin the Short's claim to kingship, and had him anointed by his legate Boniface in 751; translations of the *Dialogues* of St. Gregory; restoration of Monte Cassino under St. Petronax; and rescue of slaves in the Roman markets and of nuns driven from Constantinople by the Iconoclasts. In his last years he lost Ravenna to the Lombard Aistulf and failed to make headway with the Eastern emperor. F. D. Mar. 22.

ZACHARY, ST. (1st century). St. Luke says that he was the father of St. John the Baptist, was a priest under the Old Law, was married to Elizabeth of the house of Aaron and the cousin of the Virgin Mary, that they were childless in their old age, that the angel Gabriel appeared to him in the Temple to foretell the birth of his son, and that, when he expressed doubt, he was struck dumb until the circumcision of John. Early Church Fathers held that he was murdered in the Temple on Herod's orders for refusing to tell where John was to be found. F. D. Nov. 5.

ZACHARY, ST. (d. 106?), bishop and martyr. He is said to have been the second to direct the see of Vienne, in Gaul, and put to death during the persecution of Trajan. F. D. May 26.

ZÁDORI, JÁNOS (1831–1887). Born in Katlócz, Neutra, Hungary, on Mar. 6, he studied at Vienna, was ordained in 1854, served as chaplain at Balassa-Gyarmat until 1864, when he became a professor of dogmatic theology at the Gran seminary, Hungary, and remained there until his death on Dec. 30. He was appointed a domestic prelate by Pope Leo XIII, edited *Uj magyar Sion*, a theological journal, from 1870 to 1886, and wrote theological, travel, devotional, and biographical works.

ZAHM, JOHN AUGUSTINE (1851–1921), scientist. Born in Lexington, Ohio, on June 11, he studied at Notre Dame, became a member of the Congregation of Holy Cross in 1871, and was ordained in 1875. He taught at Notre Dame where he held several offices, was vice-president in 1885–92, and was American provincial from 1898 to 1906. He established the congregation's house of studies, Holy Cross College in Washington, D.C., on a permanent basis, and developed the Dante and South American collections at his university's library, wrote on evolution, *Evolution and Dogma* (1896), and *Scientific Theory and Catholic Doctrine* (1896), and on expeditions to the Andes, and was a member of the Roosevelt expedition to South America in 1913–14. He died in Munich, Germany, on Nov. 10.

ZALLINGER ZUM THURN, JACOB ANTON (1735–1813), canonist, philosopher. Born in Bozen, Tyrol, on July 26, he studied at Innsbruck and Munich, joined the Jesuits in 1753, and was ordained in 1765. He taught philosophy at Munich, Dillingen, and Innsbruck, and canon law at Augsburg (1777–1807). He was in Rome in 1805–6 as papal councilor for German affairs, and died in Bozen on Jan. 11. He wrote on canon law and philosophy, against Kant and in favor of Newton.

ZALLWEIN, GREGOR (1712–1766), canonist. Born in Oberviechtach, Upper Palatinate, on Oct. 20, he studied at Ratisbon and Freising, became a Benedictine in 1733, and was ordained in 1737. After studies in canon law at Salzburg, Austria, he became master of novices at the abbey of Wessobrunn in 1739, prior in

1744, professor at the Strassburg seminary and in 1749 at the Benedictine university in Salzburg, where he remained until his death on Aug. 6 or 9. He wrote several canonical works.

ZALUSKI, JOSEF ANDRZEJ (1702–1774), bishop. Born in Poland, he was ordained, became canon of Plock, served as a canonist, and on the death of Augustus III supported Stanislas Leszczynski. He fled with the latter to Lorraine, held benefices there, and soon returned to Poland as bishop of Kiev. He built up a collection of 250,000 volumes, which he made into a public library and left to the nation at his death; in 1795 the Russians transferred it to St. Petersburg, where it became the core of the imperial library. He wrote widely in history and bibliography.

ZALVIDEA, JOSÉ MARIA DE (1780–1846), missioner. Born in Bilbao, Vizcaya, Spain, on Mar. 2, he joined the Franciscans in 1798, was sent to the College of San Fernando in Mexico in 1804, and the following year to California. He spent the rest of his life ministering to the Indians, and died at Mission San Luis Rey, California.

ZAMA, ST. (d. 268?). He is listed as the first known bishop of Bologna, Italy, and is said to have been consecrated by Pope Dionysius about 260. F. D. Jan. 24.

ZAMBDAS, ST. (d. 304?). He is called the thirty-seventh bishop of Jerusalem; his name was associated with the story of the massacre of the Theban Legion. F. D. Feb. 19.

ZAMBONI, GIUSEPPE (1776–1846), physicist. Born in Venice, Italy, in June, he studied at the Verona seminary, was ordained, taught physics at the lyceum there, and invented the Zamboni pile, a motor activated by the reaction of discs coated with zinc and manganese binoxide. He also developed an electrical clock. He died in Venice on July 25.

ZAMORA, ALFONSO DE (d. 1531). A Jewish rabbi, he became a convert in 1506, and revised the Hebrew text and translated the Chaldee paraphase for Cardinal Ximenes' polyglot bible.

ZAMPIERI, DOMENICO (1581–1641), painter. Also known as Domenichino, he was born in Bologna, Italy, on Oct. 21, studied in the Caracci Academy, and traveled through Italy studying paintings. In Rome he decorated the palace of Cardinal Agucchi, added frescoes to that of Cardinal Farnese, and worked in the Basilian abbey of Grotta Ferrata, Villa Frascati, and the churches of San Gregorio, San Andrea della Valle, and San Silvestro. Outstanding were *Condemnation of Adam and Eve, St. George and the Dragon*, and *Communion of St. Jerome* (1614). He was effective in the use of color and of background landscape, variety of facial characterization, and subordinate detail. He opened a school in Rome, but hostility and jealousy toward a shoemaker's son who had won a prize with a painting completed in early youth exploded about him and he retired to Bologna. After a brief period as painter and architect of the pontifical treasury under Gregory XV, he left to open another school at Naples. There his paintings were slashed by his enemies and his mind gave way, as the result of being poisoned, some charge. He died in Naples, Italy, on Apr. 16.

ZANELLA, GIACOMO (1820–1888), poet. Born in Chiampo, Italy, on Sept. 9, he was ordained, taught, and in his poems reveals the blend of science and nature often found in nineteenth-century romanticism. His lyrics are also marked by patriotic fervor and religious devotion; some are pleas for reconciliation of Church and state in his nation. He was appointed professor of Italian literature at Padua in 1866, was rector there in 1871–72, and died in Vicenza, Italy, on May 17.

ZANITAS, ST. (d. 344), martyr. *See* Lazarus, St.

ZÄNGERLE, ROMAN SEBASTIAN (1771–1848), bishop. Born in Ober-Kirchberg, Germany, on Jan. 20, he studied and became a Benedictine at Wiblingen in 1788 and was ordained in 1793. He taught oriental languages and scripture at several monasteries and at Cracow, Prague, and Vienna. He was dispensed from his religious vows in 1821, became a canon in Vienna, bishop of Seckau in 1824, and administrator of Leoben. He worked to remove the laxities which had spread in the two dioceses during the twelve years they had been without a bishop. He died in Seckau, Austria, on Apr. 27.

ZANTEDESCHI, FRANCESCO (1797–1873), physicist. An Italian priest who taught physics at the Venice lyceum and at Padua, he made numerous discoveries. He produced electric currents in a closed circuit with a magnet in 1820–30, before Faraday; discerned magnetic action on steel needles by ultraviolet light in 1838; and wrote on the repulsion of flames by a strong magnetic field. He wrote more than 350 scientific notes and articles and died in Padua, Italy, on Mar. 29.

ZARDETTI, JOHN JOSEPH FREDERICK OTTO (1847–1902), bishop. Born in Rohrschach, St. Gall, Switzerland on Jan. 24, he studied at Innsbruck and Stella Matutina College, Austria, and St. George seminary in St. Gall, and was ordained in 1870. He taught at St. Gall until 1876, became a cathedral canon there, taught at St. Francis seminary, Milwaukee, Wisconsin, in 1881–86, and was vicar general of the Northern Minnesota vicariate in 1886–89. He was appointed bishop of St. Cloud, Minnesota, in 1889, and reigned there until he was made archbishop of Bucharest,

Romania, in 1894. He resigned this see late that year, and was appointed titular archbishop of Mocissus in 1895 and consultor of the Congregation of Ecclesiastical Affairs in 1897, and died in Rome on May 10.

ZAREMBA, ALEXANDER (1857–1907). He was ordained in Poland, taught scripture at the seminary in Plotsk, became a monsignor, and edited the periodical, *Encyklopedia Koscrelna.*

ZARLINO, GUISEPPE (1517–1590), musician. Born in Chioggia, Italy, on Mar. 22, he left the Franciscan seminary after ordination as a deacon in 1541 to study music under Adrian Willaert in Venice. He was choirmaster at St. Mark's there from 1565 until his death on Feb. 14, composing masses and madrigals. He was made canon of Chioggia in 1582. He also wrote three treatises on musical theory, including *Sopplimenti musicali* (1588), which established the basis of modern major and minor scales and suggested dividing octaves into twelve semi-tones.

ZASIUS, ULRIC (1461–1536), jurist. Born in Constance, Switzerland, he studied at Tübingen, became episcopal notary in Constance, town clerk in Baden and Freiburg, and headmaster of the Freiburg Latin school. After law study at Freiburg he became professor of law there in 1506, imperial councilor, and wrote legal works. He was a friend of Erasmus and was initially attracted to Luther's teachings, but repudiated him in 1521. He died in Freiburg, Germany, on Nov. 24.

ZDISLAVA BERKA, BL. (d. 1252). Born in the diocese of Litomerici, Bavaria, and married to a noble of her family's choice, she became the mother of four children. Her husband proved unkind, although she was finally able to devote some of their wealth to the poor and the refugees from the Tartar invasion. Eventually she founded the Dominican priory of St. Laurence near her castle, received Communion daily (most unusual at that time), and by the example of her holy death brought about the reform of her husband. She was beatified in 1907. F. D. Jan. 1.

ZEBINAS, ST. (d. 297), martyr. *See* Antoninus, St.

ZEBINUS, ST. (5th century). He was the spiritual director of SS. Maro and Polychronius in rigorous early monasticism in Persia. F. D. Feb. 23.

ZEFFERINI, BL. HUGOLINO (d. 1470?). He was an Augustinian hermit, whose relics were venerated at Cortona, Italy. His cult was approved in 1804. F. D. Mar. 22.

ZEGERS, NICHOLAS TACITUS (d. 1559). Born in Diest (or Brussels), Flanders, he studied at Louvain, became a Franciscan at Cologne, and in 1536 became professor of biblical exegesis at the Franciscan house in Louvain. He retired in 1548 to write biblical commentaries, a New Testament concordance, and a Flemish catechism. He died in Louvain on Aug. 25.

ZELL, KARL (1793–1873). Born in Mannheim, Germany, on Apr. 8, he studied at Heidelberg, Göttingen, and Breslau, taught in Rastall in 1814 and philosophy at Freiburg in 1821, represented that university in the Baden diet in 1831–35, and as ministerial councilor instituted a complete reform of the Baden educational system. He became professor of archaeology at Heidelberg in 1848, served in the diet as an elected deputy in 1848–55, and was president of the Catholic Congress in Münster in 1852 and Vienna in 1853. He was Archbishop Vikari's aide in his struggles with the liberal government of Baden and fought vigorously for Church rights. He wrote literary and historical criticism and died in Freiburg, Germany, on Jan. 24.

ZELL, ULRICH (d. 1507), printer. Born in Hanau-im-Main, Prussia, he worked in the print shop of Fust and Schöffer in Mainz, went to Cologne about 1462, and opened the first press there. He printed textbooks, a Bible, and St. Augustine's *De doctrina christiana.*

ZENAIS, ST. (1st century). *See* Philonilla, St.

ZENAS, ST. (d. 304?), martyr. *See* Zeno, St.
ZENO, ST. (2nd century), martyr. *See* Eudoxius, St.
ZENO, ST. (d. 249), martyr. *See* Ammon, St.
ZENO, ST. (d. 300?). He was a spokesman of more than 10,000 Christians, who were working as slaves building the baths of Diocletian in Rome, and who were ordered put to death in a brutal massacre. F. D. July 9.
ZENO, ST. (d. 302), martyr. He and his sons Concordius and Theodore were put to death at Nicomedia during the Diocletian persecution. F. D. Sept. 2.
ZENO, ST. (d. 303), martyr. A Roman soldier stationed at Nicomedia, he was beaten and beheaded there during a pagan festival in the reign of Diocletian. F. D. Dec. 22.
ZENO, ST. (d. 303?), martyr. *See* Chariton, St.
ZENO, ST. (d. 304?), martyr. He freed the slaves on his estate in Philadelphia near the Dead Sea, gave up his wealth to the poor, was seized with a single servant, Zenas, and put to death with him during the persecution of Diocletian. F. D. June 23.
ZENO, ST. (d. 362?), martyr. *See* Eusebius, St.
ZENO, ST. (d. 371), bishop. Born probably in Africa, he became bishop of Verona, Italy, in 362, crushed much of the Arianism in his diocese, encouraged great charities, and was

spiritual director of a group of women dedicated to the religious life yet living in their own homes. F. D. Apr. 12.
ZENO, ST. (d. 399?), bishop. A cousin of the martyr St. Eusebius (F. D. Sept. 8), he survived the persecution of Julian the Apostate and became bishop of Gaza, Palestine. F. D. Dec. 26.
ZENOBIA, ST. (d. 310?), martyr. *See* Zenobius, St.
ZENOBIUS, ST. (d. 310?), martyr. A doctor and priest in Sidon, he was torn to pieces at Antioch during the Diocletian persecution. He probably is identical with St. Zenobius, physician-bishop of Aegae (Alexandretta), who was put to death with his sister Zenobia, and honored on Oct. 30. F. D. Oct. 29.
ZENOBIUS, ST. (310–390?), bishop. Friend of St. Ambrose, he went to Constantinople as the legate of Pope Damasus, and returned to become bishop of Florence, Italy. F. D. May 25.
ZEPEDAS, FRANCISCO. *See* Cepeda, Francisco.
ZEPHYRINUS, ST. (d. 217?), pope. A Roman of humble origin, he became pope in 199 and chose Callistus, who was to be his successor, as deacon and adviser. His reign was disturbed by the Montanist heresy, which Tertullian and Hippolytus embraced in 203. Although he is listed as a martyr, there is no indication that he so suffered. F. D. Aug. 26.
ZETICUS, ST. (d. 250), martyr. He was put to death in Crete during the persecution of Decius. F. D. Dec. 23.
ZEUSS, JOHANN KASPAR (1806–1856), philologian. Born in Vogtendorf, Upper Franconia, Germany, on July 22, he studied in Bamberg and at Munich, taught in that city and in 1837 in Speyer. In 1847 he became professor of history at Munich and later taught in Bamberg, but ill-health forced him to resign in 1855. He was dedicated to the study of Old Irish and the relationship of languages, and published the authoritative *Grammatica celtica* in 1853. He died in Vogtendorf on Nov. 10.
ZIEGELBAUER, MAGNOALD (1689–1750), historian. Born in Ellwangen, Swabia, Germany, he joined the Benedictines at Zwiefalten in 1707, was ordained in 1713, and taught theology at the abbey. He was transferred to Reichenau, taught theology at Göttweig in 1732–33, and in 1747 became secretary of the scholarly society, Societas Incognitorum, in Olmütz, Moravia, where he retired to devote himself to writing and died on Jan. 14. Chief of his many historical treatises is a four-volume literary history of the Benedictines.
ZIEGLER, GREGORIUS THOMAS (1770–1852), bishop. Born in Kirchheim, Germany,

on Mar. 7, he joined the Benedictines in 1788, was ordained in 1793, and became prior of Wiblingen in 1802. He went to Poland in 1806 when the monastery was suppressed, taught at Cracow, was professor of church history in the Linz lyceum in 1809–15, and of theology at Vienna from 1815 until 1822, when he became bishop of the newly established diocese of Tiniec. He was made bishop of Linz, Austria, in 1827, and died there on Apr. 15.

ZIERIKZEE, CORNELIUS VAN (1405?–1462). Born in Zierikzee, Zeeland, Holland, he joined the Franciscans of the Strict Observance when twenty, was sent to Scotland in 1447, founded numerous houses and successfully established his order, returned to Antwerp, Belgium, in 1462, and died there on Feb. 21.

ZIGLIARA, FRANCESCO (1833–1893), cardinal. Born in Bonifacio, Corsica, on Oct. 29, he became a Dominican at Rome at eighteen, taking the name Tommaso Maria, studied there and at Perugia, and was ordained in 1856. He taught philosophy in Rome, Corbara, and the Viterbo seminary, then at the Minerva and French colleges in Rome. He was made a cardinal in 1879, became prefect of the Congregation of Studies, and served on several other congregations. A leading Thomist, he was co-president of the Academy of St. Thomas Aquinas, supervised the preparation of the Leonine edition of St. Thomas' works, and wrote a *Summa philosophica*, and on the sacraments, the union of body and soul, the Index, and SS. Thomas and Bonaventure. He died in Rome on May 11.

ZIMMER, PATRICK BENEDICT (1752–1820), theologian. Born in Abtsgmund, Württemberg, Germany, on Feb. 22, he studied at Ellwangen and Dillingen, was ordained in 1775, and became a professor of theology at Dillingen in 1783. He became pastor at Steinheim in 1791, professor of theology at Ingolstadt in 1799, followed the university to Landshut in 1800, became professor of exegesis in 1807, and rector of the university in 1819 and also deputy in the Bavarian parliament. He died in Steinheim, Germany, on Oct. 16.

ZINGARELLI, NICOLÒ ANTONIO (1752–1837), composer. Born near Naples, Italy, on Apr. 4, he studied under Fedele Fenaroli and Speranza at Loreto, had his opera *Montesuma* produced at San Carlo in 1781, and in 1785 produced *Alsinda* in Milan. He became choirmaster of the Milan cathedral in 1792, at Loreto from 1794 to 1804, and then of the Sistine Chapel, Rome. He was imprisoned in Paris for refusing to play a *Te Deum* in St. Peter's for Napoleon in 1811, but was soon released, to become director of

Collegio di Musica in Naples in 1813, and choirmaster of the cathedral there in 1816. He produced hundreds of musical pieces, including operas: *Il mercato di Monfregoso* (1792), *Giulietta e Romeo* (1796), his best, and *Berenice* (1811); oratorios: *La Gerusalemme distrutta* (1794), *Il trionfo di Davide* (1788), and *La fuga in Egitto* (1837); and masses, including his own requiem. He died in Torre del Greco, Italy, on May 5.

ZINGERLE, PIUS (1801–1881), scholar. Born in Meran, Tyrol, on Mar. 17, he studied there and at Innsbruck, became a Benedictine at Marienberg in 1820, and was ordained in 1824. He did parish work, taught in the Meran gymnasium, was its director in 1852, and in 1862 became professor of oriental languages at the Sapienza, Rome. He returned to Marienberg, Germany, in ill-health in 1865 and taught theology and was sub-prior there until his death on Jan. 10. He translated Greek and Syrian texts, notably of St. Ephraem, into German, and wrote ascetical works and two volumes of poems.

ZITA, ST. (1218–1278). Born in Monte Sangrati, near Lucca, Italy, she became the servant of a wool dealer at the age of twelve, giving away food and clothing to the poor, working so dutifully that other servants slandered her, but succeeding in quieting the anger of her master over her charities. She remained with the Fatinelli family until her death, having been relieved of manual labor in her last years, but continuing to visit the sick, the poor, and prisoners. She was canonized in 1696 and is the patroness of domestics. F. D. Apr. 27.

ZOATHAN, ST. See Dismas, St.

ZOE, ST. (d. 135?), martyr. See Hesperus.

ZOE, ST. (d. 140), martyr. See Cyriacus, St.

ZOE, ST. (d. 286), martyr. Wife of an imperial official at Rome, she was put to death there. F. D. July 5.

ZOEGA, GEORG (1755–1809), archaeologist. Born in Daler, Schleswig, on Dec. 20, he studied in Altona and at Göttingen and Leipzig, became interested in archaeology while traveling in Italy, studied numismatics in Vienna, catalogued Stefano Borgia's coin collection, and gained a patron when Stefano became a cardinal and also in Pope Pius VI, who granted him a pension. He became a Catholic in 1783, was appointed interpreter of modern languages at the Propaganda, Danish consul general to Rome in 1798, professor at Kiel in 1802, and was elected to the academies of science of Rome and Vienna in 1806. He is considered, with Winckelmann and Visconti, the founder of scientific archaeology. He wrote on Egyptian rulers, the origin of obliks, Coptic manuscripts, and Roman antiquities. He also completed, with Blöndal, the first modern

Icelandic-Danish dictionary. He died in Rome on Feb. 10.

ZOEN (13th century). Bishop of Avignon, France, and papal legate to France, he presided at the Council of Albi, called in 1254 by St. Louis, to suppress the Albigensian heresy and reform the clergy.

ZOILUS, ST. (d. 298?), martyr. *See* Clement, St.

ZOILUS, ST. (d. 304?), martyr. He and a number of other Christians are believed to have been slain at Cordova, Spain, during the Diocletian persecution. His name is that of an actual martyr; other names, however, appear on other lists, of different times and places. F. D. June 27.

ZOLA, BL. GIOVANNI BATTISTA (1576–1626), martyr. Born in Brescia, Italy, he became a Jesuit in 1595, went to India in 1602, and labored in the missions of Japan from 1606 until banishment to China in 1614. He soon returned to Japan, however, and was captured and burned to death at Nagasaki. With him died John Kinsako, a native of Japan, who had become a Jesuit novice. They were beatified in 1867. F. D. June 20.

ZOLKIEWSKI, STANISLAUS (1547–1620), chancellor. Born in Turynka, Russia, he studied at Lemberg, fought under King Stephen Báthory against Ivan the Terrible, and was castellan of Lemberg in 1593. He supported Sigismund III, who seldom heeded his advice, in several rebellions, won a major victory at Guzow, and though he opposed war with the Muscovites as unjust was ordered to take an outnumbered army into Russia. He captured Moscow in 1610 with only 6000 troops, but Sigismund refused to ratify the peace terms by which Prince Wladislaw was to become tsar. Zolkiewski was appointed grand hetman in 1613, spent his last years fighting the Turks, and was killed at Cecora on Oct. 6 when the Turks destroyed his army.

ZONARAS, JOANNES (12th century), historian. Commander of Emperor Alexius Comnenus' bodyguard, he became first secretary of the chancery, but left Constantinople to become a monk on Hagia Glykeria. He wrote a universal history to the year 1118, drawn heavily from Dio Cassius, and commentaries on the canons of the apostles, the canonical letters of the fathers of the third and fourth centuries, and the Eastern synods.

ZONGHI, GIOVANNI MARIA (1847–1941), archbishop. Born in Italy, on Aug. 3, he was ordained, served in the curia of Pope Pius IX, was a recorder at the Vatican Council of 1870, private secretary to Pius XI, president of the Pontifical Ecclesiastical Academy, and in 1914 was made titular archbishop of Colosse by Benedict XV. He died in Fabriano, Italy, on Aug. 8.

ZORRILLA DE SAN MARTÍN, JUAN (1855–1931), poet. Born in Montevideo, Uruguay, on Dec. 28, he studied at its university and the College of the Immaculate Conception in Argentina, and in 1877 founded the Catholic periodical *El Bien Público*. He became a judge in 1878, served as a deputy in 1887–90, was minister to Spain, and taught aesthetics at Montevideo. His poetry appeared as *Notas de un himno* (1876), *La leyenda patria*, *Tabaré*, and *La profecía de Ezequiel* (1921). He died in Montevideo on Nov. 3.

ZOSIMA, ST. (d. 273?), martyr. *See* Bonosa, St.

ZOSIMUS, ST. (d. 418), pope. Born in Greece, he succeeded Pope St. Innocent I on Mar. 18, 417. His brief rule was marked by a controversy with the African bishops, among them St. Augustine, over their condemnation of Caelestius, whose Pelagian supporters came to Rome and misled the pontiff. When he discovered their deceit he wrote *Epistola tractoria* in strong condemnation of Pelagianism. F. D. Dec. 26.

ZOSIMUS, ST. (d. 107?), martyr. *See* Rufus, St.

ZOSIMUS, ST. (d. 110), martyr. He was put to death in Spoleto, Italy, during the reign of Trajan. F. D. June 19.

ZOSIMUS, ST. (d. 263?), martyr. *See* Heraclius, St.

ZOSIMUS, ST. (d. 303?), martyr. *See* Mark, St.

ZOSIMUS, ST. (5th century). He lived in a refuge on the banks of the Jordan in Palestine and is said to have been the biographer of St. Mary of Egypt. F .D. Apr. 4.

ZOSIMUS, ST. (6th century). A hermit in Palestine, he was known as "the wonderworker." F. D. Nov. 30.

ZOSIMUS, ST. (571?–660?), bishop. Placed in the monastery of Santa Lucia, near Syracuse, Sicily, at the age of seven, he often ran away, but later chose a cloistered life and in time became abbot and, in 649, bishop of his native city of Syracuse. F. D. Mar. 30.

ZOSIMUS, ST., martyr. *See* Drusus, St.

ZOTICUS, ST. (d. 120), martyr. *See* Amantius, St.

ZOTICUS, ST. (d. 204), bishop and martyr. The bishop of Comana, Cappadocia, fought the Montanist heresy and was put to death. F. D. July 21.

ZOTICUS, ST. (d. 250), martyr. *See* Theodulus, St.

ZOTICUS, ST. (3rd century), martyr. *See* Agathonicus, St.

ZOTICUS, ST. (d. 303?), martyr. *See* Caius, St.

ZOTICUS, ST. (d. 350?). A Roman priest, he went to Constantinople, built a hospital for the poor and orphans, and was persecuted by Arian Constantius. F. D. Dec. 31.

ZRINYI, MIKLÓS (1508–1566). He became ban of Croatia in 1542, fought to defend his land against Turkish invasion, participated in Charles V's siege of Vienna, and was killed at Szigetvár, Hungary, on Sept. 7, defending that fortress against overwhelming Turkish forces.

ZRINYI, MIKLÓS (1620–1664), poet. Grandson of Miklós Zrinyi (1508–66), who was a general and the ban of Croatia, he was born in Scákvár, Hungary, on Jan. 5. He also served as ban of Croatia, after 1647, and led the Hungarian forces against invading Turks. He was one of the first to use the Hungarian language for poetry, wrote lyrics, an epic on the sixteenth-century defense of Szigetvár, and a prose study of political power in the tradition of Machiavelli. He was killed in a hunting accident on Nov. 18.

ZUMÁRRAGA, JUAN DE (1468–1548), archbishop. Born in Durango, Spain, he became a Franciscan, was a judge in witchcraft trials in the Basque provinces, and in 1528 went to Mexico as protector of the Indians and first bishop, though not yet consecrated. He came into conflict with the civil authorities, particularly Nino de Guzmán, over the torture, enslavement, and widespread exploitation of the Indians and the murder of followers of Cortés, who had returned to Spain. Zumárraga placed Mexico City under an interdict and excommunicated the auditors, Matienzo and Delgadillo, after the flight of Guzmán. When Cortés returned, they were sent to Spain in irons and honest replacements sent to Mexico. Zumárraga was recalled to Spain in 1532, cleared himself of charges spread by Delgadillo, was consecrated in 1533, and returned to Mexico in 1534. He became involved in controversy over the validity of mass baptism administered by the Franciscans (decided in his favor by Pope Paul III in 1537) and over privileges granted missionaries of his order, a dispute settled by compromise. He secured a suspension of the new laws of Las Casas regulating relations between the Indians and colonists until the emperor modified them in 1545 to protect both colonist and Indian. He founded hospitals, a school for Indian girls, and Colegio de Santa Cruz de Tlaltelolco for the education of Indians, and brought the first press to the New World. In 1546 he was named first archbishop of Mexico, but died in Mexico on June 3, a month before the bull of appointment was sent.

ZUMÁRRAGA, BL. THOMAS (1575–1622), martyr. Born in Vitoria, Spain, he became a Dominican, was sent to the missions in Japan, captured and imprisoned for three years at Suzata (Omura), and burned to death there with other martyrs. He was beatified in 1867. F. D. Sept. 12.

ZUÑIGA, BL. PEDRO (1585–1622), martyr. Born in Seville, Spain, he went to Mexico, where his father was viceroy, became a Dominican in Spain, and after ordination was sent to the East. He was in the Philippines in 1612 and in Japan in 1620. He was burned alive at Nagasaki with Bl. Luiz Flores. Joachim Firaiama-Diaz, captain of the ship carrying the party to Japan, was beheaded with his crew on the same day. They were beatified in 1867. F. D. Aug. 19.

ZURBARÁN, FRANCISCO DE (1598–1662?), painter. Born in Fuente de Cantos, Estramadura, Spain, in Nov., he studied under Juan de las Roelas in Seville and attracted attention with his paintings of St. Peter Nolasco for the Mercenarios Descalozos' monastery in Seville. He soon was in great demand, became royal painter to Philip III, and did a series of paintings of St. Bonaventure, an altarpiece for St. Thomas Aquinas College, thirteen pictures for the Hieronymite monastery of Guadelupe, portraits of St. Jerome, and of religious founders for the Castellon Capuchin convent, and the *Labors of Hercules*, commissioned by Philip IV in 1650 for the palace of Buen Retiro in Madrid. Often called "the Spanish Caravaggio," he is noted for his rich coloring, fidelity to nature, and vigor and power. He died probably in Madrid.

ZURITA Y CASTRO, JERÓNIMO (1512–1580). Born in Saragossa, Spain, on Dec. 4, he became an inquisitorial secretary in 1547, director of the Inquisition in Aragon in 1548, and published work on the kings of Aragon and the Normans in Sicily, as well as a six-volume *Anales de la corona de Aragón* (1562–80). He died on Nov. 3.

ZURLA, GIACINTO PLACIDO (1769–1843), cardinal. Born in Legnano, Italy, on Apr. 2, he became a Camaldolese at San Michele di Murano, Venice, at eighteen, taught philosophy and theology, became interested in geography, and served as librarian. He was elected definitor of his order in 1809, acted as rector when Napoleon suppressed the college in Venice in 1810, and in 1814 taught at a nearby seminary. He went to Rome in 1821, was prefect of studies at Collegio Urbano, and in 1823 became cardinal. He was cardinal-vicar to Popes Leo XII, Pius VIII, and Gregory XVI, a member of several congregations, and noted for the energy of his reform activity. He published studies of the map prepared by a fellow Camaldolese, Fra Mauro (1806), and of the journeys of Marco Polo (1818–19). He died in Palermo, Sicily, on Oct. 29.

ZWIRNER, ERNST FRIEDRICH (1802–1861), architect. Born in Jakobswalde, Silesia, on Feb. 28, he studied at the Royal Academy Architecture, Breslau, and the University of

Berlin, worked under Schinkel in Berlin, and in 1833 was appointed architect of the Cologne cathedral, which he restored, and prepared plans for its completion. He also designed numerous churches and castles and died in Cologne, Germany, on Sept. 22.

ZWŸSEN, JAN (d. 1877). He was archbishop of Utrecht, Holland, and vicar apostolic of 's Hertogenbosch (Bois-le-Duc), a diocese where he was born, and held a synod there in 1865 to reorganize the Church in Holland. When religious freedom was allowed after over 200 years, he became bishop in 1868.

ZYBURA, JOHN STANISLAUS (1875–1943). Born in Subkau, Poland, on July 21, he studied in Cleveland, Ohio, and the North American College, Rome, and was ordained in 1898. He was stationed in Ohio parishes, but was stricken with tuberculosis in 1915. He retired from active duty that year and died in a Colorado Springs sanitarium on Oct. 7. He translated widely from the Italian, German, and Latin during his long illness, wrote *Contemporary Godlessness* (1924), and edited *Present-Day Thinkers and the New Scholasticism*.

SPELEOLOGISTS: St. Benedict
STENOGRAPHERS: St. Cassian; St. Genesius
STONECUTTERS: St. Clement
STONEMASONS: St. Barbara; St. Stephen
STUDENTS: St. Catherine of Alexandria; St. Thomas Aquinas
SURGEONS: SS. Cosmas and Damian
SWORDSMITHS: St. Maurice
TAILORS: St. Homobonus
TANNERS: SS. Crispin and Crispinian; St. Simon
TAX COLLECTORS: St. Matthew
TEACHERS: St. Catherine of Alexandria; St. Gregory the Great; St. John Baptist de la Salle
TELEGRAPH AND TELEPHONE WORKERS: St. Gabriel
TELEVISION WORKERS: St. Gabriel
TERTIARIES: St. Elizabeth of Hungary; St. Louis of France

THEOLOGIANS: St. Alphonsus Liguori; St. Augustine
THROAT: St. Blaise
TRAVELERS: St. Anthony of Padua; St. Christopher; St. Nicholas of Myra; St. Raphael
UNIVERSAL CHURCH: St. Joseph
UNIVERSITIES: Bl. Contardo Ferrini
VOCATIONS: St. Alphonsus
WATCHMEN: St. Peter of Alcantara
WEAVERS: St. Anastasia; St. Anastasius; St. Paul the Hermit
WHEELWRIGHTS: St. Catherine of Alexandria
WINEGROWERS: St. Vincent
WINE MERCHANTS: St. Amand
WOMEN IN LABOR: St. Anne
WORKINGMEN: St. Joseph
WRITERS: St. Francis de Sales; St. Lucy
YACHTSMEN: St. Adjutor
YOUTH: St. Aloysius Gonzaga; St. Gabriel Possenti; St. John Berchmans

THE SAINTS: PATRONS OF PLACES

ALSACE: St. Odila
ANDALUSIA: Bl. John of Avila
ANTIOCH: St. Barnabas
ARGENTINA: Our Lady of Lujan
ARMENIA: St. Gregory the Illuminator; St. Bartholomew
ASIA MINOR: St. John the Evangelist
AUSTRALIA: Our Lady Help of Christians
AUSTRIA: St. Severino
BAVARIA: St. Kilian
BELGIUM: St. Joseph
BOHEMIA: St. Ludmilla; St. Wenceslaus
BRAZIL: Immaculate Conception; St. Peter of Alcantara
CANADA: St. Anne; St. Joseph
CEYLON: St. Lawrence
CHILE: Our Lady of Mt. Carmel; St. James
CHINA: St. Joseph
COLOMBIA: St. Louis Bertrand; St. Peter Claver
CORSICA: Immaculate Conception; St. Alexander Sauli
CRETE: St. Titus
CYPRUS: St. Barnabas
CZECHOSLOVAKIA: St. John Nepomucene; St. Procopius; St. Wenceslaus
DOMINICAN REPUBLIC: Our Lady of High Grace; St. Dominic
EAST INDIES: St. Francis Xavier; St. Thomas the Apostle
ENGLAND: St. Augustine of Canterbury; St. George; St. Gregory the Great
ETHIOPIA: St. Frumentius
FINLAND: St. Henry
FRANCE: Our Lady of the Assumption; St. Denis; St. Joan of Arc, St. Martin of Tours; St. Remigius; St. Thérèse of Lisieux
GAUL: St. Irenaeus
GEORGIA (RUSSIA): St. Nino
GERMANY: St. Boniface; St. Michael; St. Peter Canisius; St. Suitbert
GREECE: St. Andrew; St. Nicholas of Myra
HOLLAND: St. Plechelm; St. Willibrord
HUNGARY: Bl. Astricus; St. Gerard; St. Stephen
INDIA: Our Lady of the Assumption
IRELAND: St. Brigid; St. Columba; St. Patrick

ITALY: St. Bernardine of Siena; St. Catherine of Siena; St. Francis of Assisi
JAPAN: St. Francis Xavier; St. Peter Baptist
LITHUANIA: St. Casimir; Bl. Cunegunda
MEXICO: Our Lady of Guadelupe; St. Martin de Valencia and Companions
MONACO: St. Devota
MORAVIA: SS. Cyril and Methodius
NEW ZEALAND: Our Lady Help of Christians
NORTH AMERICAS (CANADA AND UNITED STATES): St. Isaac Jogues and Companions
NORWAY: St. Olaf
PARAGUAY: Our Lady of the Assumption
PERSIA: St. Maruthas
PERU: St. Joseph
PHILIPPINES: Sacred Heart of Mary
POLAND: St. Casimir; Bl. Cunegunda; St. Hyacinth; St. Stanislas
PORTUGAL: Immaculate Conception; St. Antony of Portugal; St. Christian; St. Francis Borgia; St. George; St. Vincent
PRUSSIA: St. Adalbert; St. Bruno of Querfurt
ROUMANIA: St. Nicetas
ROME: St. Philip Neri
RUSSIA: St. Andrew; St. Nicholas of Myra; St. Thérèse of Lisieux
RUTHENIA: St. Bruno
SARDINIA: St. Ephesus
SAXONY: St. Willihad
SCOTLAND: St. Andrew; St. Columba; St. Palladius
SILESIA: St. Hedwig
SLOVAKIA: Our Lady of Sorrows
SOUTH AFRICA: Our Lady of the Assumption
SOUTH AMERICA: St. Rose of Lima
SPAIN: St. Euphrasius; St. Felix; St. James; Bl. John of Avila; St. Teresa of Avila
SWEDEN: St. Anskar; St. Sigfrid
SWITZERLAND: St. Andeol
UNITED STATES: Immaculate Conception
URUGUAY: Our Lady of Lujan
WALES: St. David
WEST INDIES: St. Gertrude
YUGOSLAVIA (CARINTHIA): St. Virgil

THE SAINTS: SYMBOLS IN ART

St. Agatha: tongs, veil
St. Agnes: lamb
St. Ambrose: bees, dove, ox, pen
St. Andrew: transverse cross
St. Angela Merici: ladder, cloak
St. Anne: door
St. Anthony of Egypt: bell, hog
St. Anthony of Padua: Christ Child, bread, book, lily
St. Augustine of Hippo: dove, child, shell, pen
St. Barbara: tower, palm, chalice, cannon
St. Barnabas: stones, ax, lance
St. Bartholomew: knife, flayed skin
St. Benedict: broken cup, raven, bell, crosier, bush
St. Bernardine of Siena: chrism
St. Bernard of Clairvaux: pen, bees
St. Blaise: wax taper, iron comb
St. Bonaventure: ciborium, cardinal's hat
St. Boniface: oak, ax, book, fox, scourge, fountain, raven, sword
St. Bruno: chalice
St. Catherine of Alexandria: wheel, lamb, sword
St. Catherine di Ricci: ring, crown, crucifix
St. Catherine of Siena: stigmata, cross, ring, lily
St. Cecilia: organ
St. Charles Borromeo: Eucharist
St. Christopher: giant, torrent, tree, Christ Child
St. Clare of Assisi: monstrance
St. Colette: lamb, birds
SS. Cosmas and Damian: phial, box of ointment
St. Cyril of Alexandria: pen
St. Cyril of Jerusalem: purse, book
St. Dominic: rosary, star
St. Dorothy: flowers, fruit
St. Edmund: arrow, sword
St. Elizabeth of Hungary: flowers, bread, pitcher
St. Francis of Assisi: deer, wolf, birds, fish, stigmata
St. Francis Xavier: crucifix, bell, ship
St. Geneviève: bread, keys, herd, candle
St. George: dragon
St. Gertrude: crown, taper, lily
SS. Gervase and Protase: scourge, club, sword

St. Giles: crosier, hind, hermitage
St. Helena: cross
St. Hilary: stick, pen, child
St. Ignatius Loyola: Eucharist, chasuble, book
St. Isidore: bees, pen
St. James the Greater: pilgrim's staff, shell, key, sword
St. James the Less: square rule, halberd, club
St. Jerome: lion
St. John Berchmans: cross, rosary
St. John Chrysostom: bees, dove, pen
St. John Climacus: ladder
St. John of God: alms, heart, crown of thorns
St. John the Baptist: lamb, skin of animal
St. John the Evangelist: eagle, chalice, kettle, armor
St. Josaphat: chalice, crown, winged deacon
St. Joseph: lily, rod, plane, carpenter's square
St. Jude: sword, square rule, club
St. Justin Martyr: ax, sword
St. Lawrence: cross, gridiron
St. Leander of Seville: pen
St. Liborius: pebbles, peacock
St. Longinus: lance
St. Louis IX of France: crown of thorns, nails
St. Lucy: cord, eyes
St. Luke: ox, book, brush, palette
St. Margaret: dragon
St. Mark: lion, book
St. Martha: holy water sprinkler, dragon
St. Mathias: lance
St. Matilda: purse, alms
St. Matthew: winged man, purse, lance
St. Maurus: scales, spade, crutch
St. Meinrad: two ravens
St. Michael: scales, banner, sword, dragon
St. Monica: sash, tears
St. Nicholas: boy in boat
St. Patrick: cross, harp, serpent, baptismal font, shamrock
St. Paul: sword
St. Peter: keys, boat, cock
St. Philip the Apostle: column
St. Philip Neri: altar, chasuble, vial
St. Rita: rose
St. Roch: angel, dog, bread
St. Rose of Lima: crown of thorns, anchor, city
St. Sebastian: arrows, crown

SS. Sergius and Bacchus: military garb, palm

St. Simon: saw, cross

St. Simon Stock: scapular

St. Teresa of Avila: heart, arrow, book

St. Thérèse of Lisieux: roses entwining a crucifix

St. Thomas the Apostle: lance, ax

St. Thomas Aquinas: chalice, monstrance, dove, ox

St. Ursula: ship, clock, arrow

St. Vincent: gridiron, boat

St. Vincent de Paul: children

St. Vincent Ferrer: pulpit, cardinal's hat, trumpet, captives

CHRONOLOGICAL CHART
OF POPES AND WORLD RULERS

Century	THE PAPACY	ROMAN EMPIRE
1st	St. Peter, 29–67	Augustus, 27 B.C.–A.D. 14
		Tiberius, 14–37
		Caligula, 37–41
		Claudius, 41–54
		Nero, 54–68
	St. Linus, 67–76	Galba, 68–69
		Otho, 69
		Vitellius, 69
	St. Cletus, 76–88	Vespasian, 69–79
	St. Clement, 88–97	Titus, 79–81
		Domitian, 81–96
2nd	St. Evaristus, 97–105	Nerva, 96–98
	St. Alexander I, 105–115	Trajan, 98–117
	St. Sixtus I, 115–125	Hadrian, 117–138
	St. Telesphorus, 125–136	
	St. Hyginus, 136–140	
	St. Pius I, 140–155	Antoninus Pius, 138–161
	St. Anicetus, 155–166	
	St. Soter, 166–175	Marcus Aurelius, 161–180
	St. Eleutherius, 175–189	Lucius Aurelius Verus, 161–169
	St. Victor I, 189–199	
		Commodus, 180–192
		Pertinax, 193
		Didius Julian, 193
3rd	St. Zephyrinus, 199–217	Septimus Severus, 193–211
	St. Callistus I, 217–222	Caracalla, 211–217
	[St. Hippolytus, antipope, 217–235]	Geta, 211–212
		Macrina, 217–218
		Heliogabalus, 218–222
	St. Urban I, 222–230	Alexander Severus, 222–235
	St. Pontianus, 230–235	Maximin, 235–238
	St. Anterus, 235–236	Gordian I, 237–238
	St. Fabian, 236–250	Popienus, 238
		Balbinus, 238
		Gordian III, 238–244
		Philippus, 244–249
		Decius, 249–251
	St. Cornelius, 251–253	Gallus, 251–253
	[Novatian, antipope, 251]	Aemelian, 252–253
	St. Lucius I, 253–254	Valerian, 253–259
	St. Stephen I, 254–257	Gallien, 259–268
	St. Sixtus II, 257–258	Claudius II, 268–270
	St. Dionysius, 259–268	Aurelian, 270–275
	St. Felix I, 269–274	Tacitus, 275–276
	St. Eutychianus, 275–283	Probus, 276–282
		Carus, 281–283

	THE PAPACY	EAST	WEST
4th	St. Caius, 283–296	Dioceltian, 284–305	Maximian (Maximianus Herculius), 286–305
	St. Marcellinus, 296–304	Galerius, 305–311	Constantius, 305–306
	St. Eusebius, 309	Licinius, 311–324	Severus, 306–307
	St. Miltiades, 311–314	Constantine I, 311–324	Maxentius, 311–324
	St. Sylvester I, 314–335	Constantine I, 324–337	
	St. Mark, 336	(emperor of East and West)	
	St. Julius I, 337–352	Constantius II, 337–350	Constantine II, 337–340
			Constans I, 337–350
		Constantius II, 350–361	
		Julian the Apostate, 361–363	
		Jovian, 363–364	
	Liberius, 352–366	(emperors of East and West)	
	[Felix II, antipope, 355–365]	Valens, 364–378	Valentinian I, 364–372
	St. Damasus I, 366–384	Theodosius the Great, 379–392	Gratian, 375–383
	[Ursinus, antipope, 366–367]	Maximus, 383–388	Valentinian II, 375–392
	St. Siricius, 384–399	Theodosius the Great, 392–392	
		(emperor of East and West)	
5th	St. Anastasius I, 399–401	Theodosius the Great, 392–395	Theodosius the Great, 379–395
	St. Innocent I, 401–417		Eugenius, 392–394
	St. Zozimus, 417–418	Arcardius, 395–408	Honorius, 395–423
	St. Boniface I, 418–422	Theodosius II, 408–450	Valentinian III, 425–454
	[Eulalius, antipope, 418–419]		Petronius, 455
	St. Celestine I, 422–432		Avitus, 455–457
	St. Sixtus III, 432–440	Marcian, 450–457	Majorian, 457–461
	St. Leo I, 440–461	Leo I, 457–474	Severus, 461–465

Century	THE PAPACY	EAST	WEST	FRANCE
	St. Hilarus, 461–468 St. Simplicius, 468–483		Anthemius, 467–472 Olybrius, 472 Glycerius, 473–474 Julius Nepos, 473–475 Romulus Augustulus, 475–476	
		Leo II, 474–474 Zeno, 474–491		
6th	St. Felix III (II), 483–492 St. Gelasius I, 492–496 Anastasius II, 496–498 St. Symmachus, 498–514 [Lawrence, antipope, 501–505] St. Hormisdas, 514–523 St. John I, 523–526 St. Felix IV (III), 526–530 Boniface II, 530–532 [Dioscorus, antipope, 530] John II, 533–535 St. Agapetus I, 535–536 St. Silverius, 536–537 Vigilius, 537–555 Pelagius I, 556–561	Anastasius I, 491–515 Justin I, 518–527 Justinian, 527–565		
7th	John III, 561–574 Benedict I, 575–579 Pelagius II, 579–590 St. Gregory I, 590–604 Sabinianus, 604–606 Boniface III, 607 St. Boniface IV, 608–615 St. Deusdedit (or Adeodatus I), 615–618 Boniface V, 619–625 Honorius I, 625–638 Severinus, 640 John IV, 640–642	Justin II, 565–578 Tiberius, 578–582 Maurice, 582–602 Phocas, 602–610 Heraclius I, 610–641 Constantine III, 641		
	Theodore I, 642–649 St. Martin I, 649–655 St. Eugene I, 654–657 St. Vitalian, 657–672 Adeodatus II, 672–676 Donus, 676–678 St. Agatho, 678–681 St. Leo II, 682–683 St. Benedict II, 684–685 John V, 685–686 Conon, 686–687 [Theodore, antipope, 687] [Paschal, antipope, 687] St. Sergius I, 687–701	Heracleonas, 641 Constans II, 641–668 Constantine IV, 668–685 Justinian II, 685–695; 705–711		Pepin of Heristal, 676–714
8th	John VI, 701–705 John VII, 705–707 Sisinnius, 708 Constantine, 708–715 St. Gregory II, 715–731 St. Gregory III, 731–741 St. Zachary, 741–752 Stephen III (II), 752–757 St. Paul I, 757–767 [Constantine, antipope, 767–769] [Philip, antipope, 768] Stephen IV (III), 768–772 Adrian I, 772–795	Leontius, 695–698 Tiberius III, 698–705 Philippicus, 711–713 Anastasius II, 713–715 Theodosius III, 715–717 Leo III the Isaurian, 717–741 Constantine V, 741–775 Leo IV the Khazar, 775–780 Constantine VI, 780–797		Charles Martel, 714–741 Pepin, 751–768 Charlemagne, 768–814

Century	THE PAPACY	EASTERN ROMAN EMPIRE	HOLY ROMAN EMPIRE	FRANCE	ENGLAND
9th	St. Leo III, 795–816	Irene, 797–802 Nicephoras I, 802–811 Michael I, 811–813	Charlemagne (Charles the Great), 800–814		
	Stephen V (IV), 816–817 St. Paschal I, 817–824 Eugene II, 824–827 Valentine, 827 Gregory IV, 827–844 [John, antipope, 844] Sergius II, 844–847 St. Leo IV, 847–855 Benedict III, 855–858 [Anastasius, antipope, 855] St. Nicholas I, 858–867 Adrian II, 867–872 John VIII, 872–882 Marinus I, 882–884 St. Adrian III, 884–885 Stephen VI (V), 885–891 Formosus, 891–896 Boniface VI, 896 Stephen VII (VI), 896–897 Romanus, 897 Theodore II, 897	Leo V, 813–820 Michael II, 820–829 Theophilus, 829–842 Michael III, 842–867 Basil I the Macedonian, 867–886 Leo VI, 896–912 [Alexander, 912–913]	Louis I the Pious, 814–840 Lothair, 840–855 Louis II the German, 855–875 Charles II the Bald, 875–877 Charles III the Fat, 881–887 Guy of Spoleto, 891–894 Lambert of Spoleto, 894–898 Arnulf of Carinthia, 896–899	Louis I, the Pious, 814–840 Lothaire, 840–855 Louis II, 855–875 Charles the Bald, 843–877 Charles the Fat, 844–887 Louis II, 877–879 Louis III, 879–882 Carloman, 879–884 Eudes, 888–898	Egbert, 828–839 Ethelwuff, 839–858 Ethelbald, 858–860 Ethelbert, 860–866 Ethelred I, 866–871 Alfred, 871–899
10th	John IX, 898–900 Benedict IV, 900–903 Leo V, 903 [Christopher, antipope, 903–904] Sergius III, 904–911 Anastasius III, 911–913 Lando, 913–914 John X, 914–928 Leo VI, 928 Stephen VIII (VII), 928–931 John XI, 931–935 Leo VII, 936–939 Stephen IX (VIII), 939–942 Marinus II, 942–946 Agapetus II, 946–955 John XII, 955–964 Leo VIII, 963–965 Benedict V, 964–966 John XIII, 965–972 Benedict VI, 973–974 [Boniface VII, antipope, 974; 984–985] Benedict VII, 974–983	Constantine VII, 912–959 [Romanus I, 919–944] Romanus II, 959–963 Basil II, 963–1025 Constantine VIII, 963–1028 [Nicephoras II Phocas, 963–969] [John I Tzimisces, 969–976]	Louis of Provence, 901 Berenger (of Friuli), 915 Henri I, the Fowler, 919–936 Otto I, 936–973 Otto II, 973–983	Robert I, 922–923 Charles the Simple, 893–923 Louis IV, L'Outremer, 936–954 Lothaire, 954–986 Louis V, 986–987 Hugh Capet, 987–996	Edward the Elder, 899–924 Athelstan, 924–940 Edmund I, 940–946 Edred, 946–955 Edwy, 955–959 Edgar, 959–975 Edward the Martyr, 975–979

POLAND	HUNGARY	SCOTLAND

Kenneth MacAlpine,
834–860

Grig, 860–863
Constantine I, 863–879

Aedh, 879–900

Constantine II,
900–943

Malcolm I, 943–954

Mieszko I, 962–992

Duke Géza,
970–997

Culren, 967–971?

Kenneth II, 971–995

Century	THE PAPACY	EASTERN ROMAN EMPIRE	HOLY ROMAN EMPIRE	FRANCE	ENGLAND

11th	John XIV, 983–984
	John XV, 985–996
	Gregory V,
	    996–999
	[John XVI,
	    antipope,
	    997–998]
	Sylvester II,
	    999–1003
	John XVII, 1003
	John XVIII,
	    1004–1009
	Sergius IV,
	    1009–1012
	Benedict VIII,
	    1012–1024
	[Gregory, anti-
	    pope, 1012]
	John XIX,
	    1024–1032
	
	Benedict IX,
	    1032–1044
	    (also 1045;
	    1047–1048)
	Sylvester III, 1045
	Benedict IX, 1045
	Gregory VI,
	    1045–1046
	Clement II,
	    1046–1047
	Benedict IX,
	    1047–1048
	Damasus II, 1048
	St. Leo IX,
	    1049–1054
	Victor II,
	    1055–1057
	Stephen X (IX),
	    1057–1058
	[Benedict X,
	    antipope,
	    1058–1059]
	Nicholas II,
	    1059–1061
	Alexander II,
	    1061–1073
	[Honorius II,
	    antipope,
	    1061–1072]
	St. Gregory VII,
	    1073–1085
	[Clement III,
	    antipope,
	    1084–1100]
	Bl. Victor III,
	    1086–1087
	Bl. Urban II,
	    1088–1099
		Zoe, 1028–1042
		[Romanus III,
		    1028–1034]
		[Michael IV,
		    1034–1041]
		[Michael V,
		    1041–1042]
		
		Zoe, 1042–1050
		Theodora,
		    1042–1056
		[Constantine IX,
		    1042–1055]
		
		Michael VI
		    Stratioticus,
		    1056–1057
		Isaac I Comnenus,
		    1057–1059
		Constantine X
		    Ducas,
		    1059–1067
		Michael VII
		    Ducas,
		    1067–1078
		[Romanus IV,
		    1067–1071]
		Nicephorus III
		    Botoniates,
		    1078–1081
			Otto III, 983–1002
			
			St. Henry II,
			    1002–1024
			
			Conrad II,
			    1024–1039
			
			Henry III,
			    1039–1056
			
			Henry IV,
			    1056–1106
				Robert I, 996–1031
				
				Henry I,
				    1031–1060
				
				Philip I,
				    1060–1108
					Ethelred the Un-
					    ready, 979–1016
					
					Edmund Ironside,
					    1016
					Canute, 1016–1035
					
					Harold I,
					    1035–1040
					Hardicanute,
					    1040–1042
					
					Edward the
					    Confessor,
					    1042–1066
					
					Harold II, 1066
					
					William I,
					    1066–1087
					
					William II,
					    1087–1100

12th	Paschal II,
	    1099–1118
	[Theodoric,
	    antipope,
	    1100–1102]
	[Albert, anti-
	    pope, 1102]
	[Sylvester IV,
	    antipope,
	    1105–1111]
	Gelasius II,
	    1118–1119
	[Gregory VIII,
	    antipope,
	    1118–1121]
		Alexius I,
		    1081–1118
		John II, 1118–1143
			Henry V,
			    1106–1125
				Louis VI,
				    1108–1137
					Henry I,
					    1100–1135

SPAIN	POLAND	HUNGARY	SCOTLAND
	Boleslav I, 992–1025	St. Stephen I, 997–1038	Kenneth III, 997–1005?
Sancho the Great, Castile & Navarre, 1000–1035	Miezko II, 1025–1034		Malcolm II, 1005–1034
		Peter, 1038–1046 [Aba Samú, 1038–1046]	
Ramiro I, Aragon, 1035–1063 Ferdinand I, Castile & León, 1035–1065 García, Navarre, 1035–1054	Casimir I, 1040–1058		Duncan, 1034–1040 Macbeth, 1040–1057
		Andrew I, 1047–1060	
Sancho Ramirez, Aragon, 1063–1094; Navarre, 1076–1094 Alfonso VI, Castile, 1072–1109; León, 1065–1109 Sancho V, Navarre, 1054–1076	Boleslav II, 1058–1079	Béla I, 1060–1063 Solomon, 1063–1074	Malcolm III, 1058–1093
	Ladislas I, 1081–1102	Géza I, 1074–1077 St. Ladislaus I, 1077–1095	
Pedro I, Aragon & Navarre, 1094–1104		Coloman, 1095–1114	Donald Bane, 1094–1097 Edgar, 1097–1107 Alexander I, 1107–1124
Alfonso I, Aragon & Navarre, 1104–1134 Ramiro II, Aragon, 1134–1137 Urraca, Castile & León, 1109–1126	Boleslav III, 1102–1138		
		Stephen II, 1114–1131	

Century	THE PAPACY	EAST ROMAN EMPIRE	HOLY ROMAN EMPIRE	FRANCE	ENGLAND
	Callistus II, 1119–1124				
	Honorius II, 1124–1130		Lothair II, 1125–1137		
	[Celestine II, antipope, 1124]				
	Innocent II, 1130–1143	Manuel I, 1143–1180			Stephen, 1135–1154
	[Anacletus II, antipope, 1130–1138]		Conrad III, 1137–1152	Louis VII, 1137–1180	
	[Victor IV, antipope, 1138]				
	Celestine II, 1143–1144				
	Lucius II, 1144–1145				
	Bl. Eugene III, 1145–1153		Frederick I Barbarossa, 1152–1190		
	Anastasius IV, 1153–1154				Henry II, 1154–1189
	Adrian IV, 1154–1159				
	Alexander III, 1159–1181				
	[Victor IV, antipope, 1159–1164]				
	[Paschal III, antipope, 1164–1168]				
	[Callistus III, antipope, 1168–1178]				
	[Innocent III, antipope, 1179–1180]	Alexius II, 1180–1183		Philip II Augustus, 1180–1223	
	Lucius III, 1181–1185	Andronicus, 1183–1185			
	Urban III, 1185–1187	Isaac II, 1185–1195			
	Gregory VIII, 1187				
	Clement III, 1187–1191		Henry VI, 1190–1197		Richard I, 1189–1199
	Celestine III, 1191–1198		Philip of Swabia, 1197–1208		
13th	Innocent III, 1198–1216	Alexius III, 1195–1203	Otto IV, 1198–1212		
	Honorius III, 1216–1227	Isaac II, 1203–1204 Alexius IV, 1203–1204	Frederick II, 1212–1250	Louis VIII, 1223–1226	John, 1199–1216 Henry III, 1216–1272
	Gregory IX, 1227–1241	Alexius V Ducas, 1204		St. Louis IX, 1226–1270	
	Celestine IV, 1241				
	Innocent IV, 1243–1254				
	Alexander IV, 1254–1261		Conrad IV, 1250–1254		
	Urban IV, 1261–1264				
	Clement IV, 1265–1268				
	Bl. Gregory X, 1271–1276		Rudolf I, 1273–1291		
	Bl. Innocent V, 1276			Philip III, 1270–1285	Edward I, 1272–1307
	Adrian V, 1276				
	John XXI, 1276–1277				
	Nicholas III, 1277–1280				
	Martin IV, 1281–1285				
	Honorius IV, 1285–1287				
	Nicholas IV, 1288–1292		Adolf, 1292–1298	Philip IV, the Fair, 1285–1314	

SPAIN	POLAND	HUNGARY	SCOTLAND	PORTUGAL
			David I, 1124–1153	
		Béla II, 1131–1141		
Petronila, Aragon, 1137–1162				Alfonso Henriques, 1139–1185
Alfonso VII, Castile & León, 1126–1157	Ladislas II, 1139–1146			
Sancho III, Castile, 1157–1158		Géza II, 1141–1161		
García Ramirez, Navarre, 1134–1150				
	Boleslav IV, 1146–1173		Malcolm IV, 1153–1165	
Alfonso II, Aragon, 1162–1196		Stephen III, 1162–1172		
Alfonso VIII, Castile, 1158–1214		Béla III, 1173–1196		
Ferdinand II, León, 1157–1188	Miezko III, 1173–1177; 1194–1202		William, 1165–1214	
Sancho VII, Navarre, 1150–1194	Casimir II, 1177–1194			
				Sancho I, 1185–1211
Pedro II, Aragon, 1196–1213		Emeric, 1196–1204		
Alfonso IX, León, 1188–1230	Ladislas III, 1202–1206	Ladislaus III, 1204–1205		
Sancho VIII, Navarre, 1194–1234	Leszek I, 1206–1227	Andrew II, 1205–1235	Alexander II, 1214–1249	Alfonso I, 1211–1223
	Boleslav V, 1227–1279	Béla IV, 1235–1270		Sancho II, 1223–1245
James I, Aragon, 1213–1276				
Henry I, Castile, 1214–1217				Alfonso III, 1245–1279
Ferdinand III, Castile, 1217–1252; León, 1230–1252			Alexander III, 1249–1286	
Teobaldo I, Navarre, 1234–1253				
Pedro III, Aragon, 1276–1285; Sicily, 1282–1285		Stephen V, 1270–1272		
Alfonso X, Castile & León, 1252–1284		Ladislaus IV, 1272–1290		
Teobaldo II, Navarre, 1253–1270				
Henry I, Navarre, 1270–1274	Leszek II, 1279–1288			Diniz, 1279–1325
Alfonso III, Aragon, 1285–1291			Margaret of Norway, 1286–1290	
Sancho IV, Castile & León, 1284–1295	Henry Probus, 1288–1290	Andrew III, 1290–1301		
Juana, Navarre, 1274–1305	Przemyslav, 1290–1296		John Baliol, 1292–1296	

Century	THE PAPACY	HOLY ROMAN EMPIRE	FRANCE	ENGLAND	SPAIN
	St. Celestine V, 1294–1296				James II, Aragon & Sicily, 1291–1327
14th	Boniface VIII, 1294–1303	Albert I, 1298–1308			Ferdinand IV, Castile, 1295–1312
	Bl. Benedict XI, 1303–1304	Henry VII, 1308–1314	Louis X, 1314–1316		
	Clement V, 1305–1314		John I, 1316	Edward II, 1307–1327	
	John XXII, 1316–1334	Louis of Bavaria, 1314–1347	Philip V, 1316–1322	Edward III, 1327–1377	
	[Nicholas V, antipope, 1330–1333]		Charles IV, 1322–1328		Alfonso IV, Aragon, 1327–1336
	Benedict XII, 1334–1342		Philip VI, 1328–1350		Alfonso XI, Castile, 1312–1350
	Clement VI, 1342–1352				
	Innocent VI, 1352–1362	Charles IV, 1347–1378			Pedro IV, Aragon, 1336–1387
	Bl. Urban V, 1362–1370		John II, 1350–1364		Pedro the Cruel, Castile, 1350–1369
	Gregory XI, 1370–1378		Charles V, 1364–1380	Richard II, 1377–1399	Henry II, Castile, 1369–1379
	Urban VI, 1378–1389	Wenceslaus, 1378–1400	Charles VI, 1380–1422	Henry IV, 1399–1413	John I, Aragon, 1387–1395
15th	Boniface IX, 1389–1404	Rupert, 1400–1410			John I, Castile, 1379–1390
	Innocent VII, 1404–1406				
	Gregory XII, 1406–1415	Sigismund, 1410–1437			Martin, Aragon & Sicily, 1395–1410
	[Clement VII, antipope, 1378–1394]				Henry III, Castile, 1390–1406
	[Benedict XIII, antipope, 1394–1423]				
	[Alexander V, antipope, 1409–1410]				Ferdinand I, Aragon & Sicily, 1412–1416
	[John XXIII, antipope, 1410–1415]			Henry V, 1413–1422	Alfonso V, Aragon, Sicily, & Naples, 1416–1458
	Martin V, 1417–1431		Charles VII, 1422–1461	Henry VI, 1422–1461	John II, Castile, 1406–1454
	Eugene IV, 1431–1447	Albert II, 1438–1439			John II, Aragon & Sicily, 1458–1479
	[Felix V, antipope, 1440–1449]	Frederick III, 1440–1493			Henry IV, Castile, 1454–1474
	Nicholas V, 1447–1455				
	Callistus III, 1455–1458			Edward IV, 1461–1483	
	Pius II, 1458–1464		Louis XI, 1461–1483	Edward V, 1483	
	Paul II, 1464–1471		Charles VIII, 1483–1498	Richard III, 1483–1485	Ferdinand II, Aragon, 1479–1516
	Sixtus IV, 1471–1484				Isabella, Castile, 1474–1504
	Innocent VIII, 1484–1492	Maximilian I, 1493–1519		Henry VII, 1485–1509	
16th	Alexander VI, 1492–1503		Louis XII, 1498–1515	Henry VIII, 1509–1547	Charles I (Emperor Charles V), 1516–1556
	Pius III, 1503		Francis I, 1515–1547		
	Julius II, 1503–1513				
	Leo X, 1513–1521	Charles V, 1519–1556			
	Adrian VI, 1522–1523				
	Clement VII, 1523–1524				
	Paul III, 1534–1549				
	Julius III, 1550–1555			Edward VI, 1547–1553	
	Marcellus II, 1555		Henry II, 1547–1559	Mary I, 1553–1558	

POLAND	HUNGARY	SCOTLAND	PORTUGAL
Wenceslas, 1300–1305 Ladislas IV, 1305–1333	Charles I (Robert of Anjou) 1308–1342 [Wenceslaus] [Otto of Ba- varia]	Robert I, 1306–1329 David Bruce, 1329–1370	Alfonso IV, 1325–1357
Casimir III, 1333–1370	Louis I the Great, 1342–1382		Pedro I, 1357–1367 Ferdinand I, 1367–1383
Louis I of Hungary, 1370–1382 Sigismund, 1382–1384 Hedwig (Jadwiga), 1384–1399 Ladislas V (Jagello), 1386–1434	Maria of Anjou, 1382–1385 Charles II, 1385–1386; of Naples, 1381–1385 Sigismund, 1387–1437	Robert II, 1370–1390 Robert III, 1390–1406 James I, 1406–1437	John I, 1385–1433
Ladislas VI, 1434–1444 Casimir IV, 1447–1492	Albert, 1438–1439 Wladislaw I, 1442–1444; as Ladislas VI of Poland, 1434–1444 [John Hunyady (regent), 1444–1453] Ladislaus V, 1444–1457; of Bohemia, 1453–1457 Matthias I Cor- vinus, 1458–1490	James II, 1437–1460 James III, 1460–1488 James IV, 1488–1513	Edward, 1433–1438 Alfonso V, 1438–1481 John II, 1481–1495 Emanuel, 1495–1521
John Albert, 1492–1501 Alexander, 1501–1505 Sigismund I, 1506–1548	Wladislaw II, 1490–1516 Louis II, 1516–1526; of Bohemia, 1509–1526 After 1526 the throne of Hun- gary was claimed by the Haps- burgs.	James V, 1513–1542 Mary Stuart, 1542–1567	John III, 1521–1557 Sebastian, 1557–1578
Sigismund II, 1548–1572		James VI, 1567–1625	

Century	THE PAPACY	HOLY ROMAN EMPIRE	FRANCE	ENGLAND	SPAIN
	Paul IV, 1555–1559	Ferdinand I, 1558–1564	Francis II, 1559–1560	Elizabeth I, 1558–1603	Philip II, 1556–1598
	Pius IV, 1559–1565	Maximilian II, 1564–1576	Charles IX, 1560–1574		
	St. Pius V, 1566–1572	Rudolf II, 1576–1612	Henry III, 1574–1589		
	Gregory XIII, 1572–1585		Henry IV, 1589–1610		
	Sixtus V, 1585–1590				
	Urban VII, 1590				
	Gregory XIV, 1590–1591				
	Innocent IX, 1591				
17th	Clement VIII, 1592–1605		Louis XIII, 1610–1643	James I, 1603–1625	Philip III, 1598–1621
	Leo XI, 1605	Matthias, 1612–1619		Charles I, 1625–1649	Philip IV, 1621–1665
	Paul V, 1605–1621	Ferdinand II, 1619–1637			
	Gregory XV, 1621–1623	Ferdinand III, 1637–1657			
	Urban VIII, 1623–1644	Leopold I, 1658–1705	Louis XIV, 1643–1715		
	Innocent X, 1644–1655			Oliver Cromwell, 1653–1658	
	Alexander VII, 1655–1667			Richard Cromwell, 1658–1659	Charles II, 1665–1700
	Clement IX, 1667–1669			Charles II, 1660–1685	
	Clement X, 1670–1676			James II, 1685–1688	
	Innocent XI, 1676–1689			Mary II, 1689–1694	
	Alexander VIII, 1689–1691			William III, 1689–1702	
18th	Innocent XII, 1691–1700			Anne, 1702–1714	
	Clement XI, 1700–1721	Joseph I, 1705–1711	Louis XV, 1715–1774	George I, 1714–1727	Philip V of Anjou, 1700–1724; 1724–1746
	Innocent XIII, 1721–1724	Charles VI, 1711–1740		George II, 1727–1760	Louis I, 1724
	Benedict XIII, 1724–1730	Charles VII of Bavaria, 1740–1745			
	Clement XII, 1730–1740	Francis I, 1745–1765			Ferdinand VI, 1746–1759
	Benedict XIV, 1740–1758			George III, 1760–1820	Charles III, 1759–1788
	Clement XIII, 1758–1769	Joseph II, 1765–1790			
	Clement XIV, 1769–1774				
19th	Pius VI, 1775–1799	Leopold II, 1790–1792	Louis XVI, 1774–1793		Charles IV, 1788–1807
	Pius VII, 1800–1823	Francis II, 1792–1806	Louis XVII, 1793–1795	George IV, 1820–1830	Joseph Napoleon, 1807–1814
	Leo XII, 1823–1829		Napoleon, 1799–1814		Ferdinand VII, 1814–1833
	Pius VIII, 1829–1830		Louis XVIII, 1814–1824	William IV, 1830–1837	
			Charles X, 1824–1830		
				Victoria, 1837–1901	Isabella II, 1833–1868
					Amadeo, 1871–1873
	Gregory XVI, 1831–1846		Louis Philippe, 1830–1848		Alfonso XII, 1874–1885
			Napoleon III, 1848–1870		
			Adolphe Thiers, 1871–1873		
	Pius IX, 1846–1878		Patrice M. Mac-Mahon, 1873–1879		

POLAND	AUSTRIA	PORTUGAL	UNITED STATES OF AMERICA
	Ferdinand I, 1558–1564		
	Maximilian II, 1564–1576		
	Rudolph II, 1572–1608; of Bohemia, 1575–1611	Henry, 1578–1580 Philip I, 1580–1598	
Stephen Bathory, 1576–1586			
Sigismund III, 1587–1632			
		Philip II, 1598–1621 Philip III, 1621–1640	
	Matthias II, 1608–1619; of Bohemia, 1611–1619	John IV, 1640–1656	
	Ferdinand II, 1619–1635		
Ladislas IV (VII), 1632–1648	Ferdinand III, 1635–1657		
John II Casimir, 1648–1668	Leopold I, 1658–1705	Alfonso VI, 1656–1667	
Michael Wisniowiecki, 1669–1673			
John III Sobieski, 1674–1696			
		Pedro II, 1683–1706	
		John V, 1706–1750	
Augustus II of Saxony, 1697–1733	Joseph I, 1705–1711		
Stanislas Lesczynski, 1704–1709; 1733–1736	Charles III (Emperor Charles VI), 1711–1740		
Augustus III, 1734–1763	Maria Theresa, 1740–1780		
		Joseph I, 1750–1777 Maria I, 1777–1816	
Stanislas II Poniatowski, 1764–1795	Joseph II, 1780–1790	Pedro III, 1777–1786	
			George Washington, 1789–1797
	Leopold II, 1790–1792		John Adams, 1797–1801
	Francis I, 1792–1835		Thomas Jefferson, 1801–1809
			James Madison, 1809–1817
		John VI, 1816–1826	James Monroe, 1817–1825
		Pedro IV, 1826–1828	John Quincy Adams, 1825–1829
		Miguel, 1828–1834	Andrew Jackson, 1829–1837
	Francis Joseph 1867–1916		Martin Van Buren, 1837–1841
			William Henry Harrison, 1841
			John Tyler, 1841–1845
		Maria II, 1834–1853	James K. Polk, 1845–1849
			Zachary Taylor, 1849–1850
			Millard Fillmore, 1850–1853
			Franklin Pierce, 1853–1857
			James Buchanan, 1857–1861
		Pedro V, 1853–1861	Abraham Lincoln, 1861–1865
		Louis I, 1861–1889	

Century	THE PAPACY	FRANCE	ENGLAND	SPAIN
20th	Leo XIII, 1878–1903	Jules Grévy, 1879–1887 Marie François Sadi-Carnot, 1887–1894 Jean Casimir-Périer, 1894–1895 Félix Faure, 1895–1899 Émile Loubet, 1899–1906 Armand Fallières, 1903–1913	Edward VII, 1901–1910	Alfonso XIII, 1886–1931
	St. Pius X, 1903–1914	Raymond Poincaré, 1913–1920 Paul Deschanel, 1920 Alexandre Millerand, 1920–1924	George V, 1910–1936	
	Benedict XV, 1914–1922 Pius XI, 1922–1939	Gaston Doumergue, 1924–1931 Paul Doumer, 1931–1932 Albert Lebrun 1932–1940 Henri Philippe Pétain, 1940–1944	Edward VIII, 1936	Alcalá Zamora, 1931–1936
	Pius XII, 1939–1958	Charles de Gaulle, 1945–1946 Georges Bidault, 1946–1947 Félix Gouin, 1946 Vincent Auriol, 1947–1954 Rene Coty, 1954–1958	George VI, 1936–1952 Elizabeth II, 1952–	Manuel Azaña, 1936 Francisco Franco, 1938–
	John XXIII, 1958–	Charles de Gaulle, 1959–		

POLAND	AUSTRIA	PORTUGAL	UNITED STATES OF AMERICA
		Carlos I, 1889–1908	Andrew Johnson, 1865–1869
			Ulysses S. Grant, 1869–1877
			Rutherford B. Hayes, 1877–1881
			James A. Garfield, 1881
			Chester A. Arthur, 1881–1885
			Grover Cleveland, 1885–1889; 1893–1897
			Benjamin Harrison, 1889–1893
			William McKinley, 1897–1901
		Manuel II, 1908–1910	Theodore Roosevelt, 1901–1909
		Theophilo Braga, 1910	William Howard Taft, 1909–1913
		Manuel de Arriaga, 1911–1915	Woodrow Wilson, 1913–1921
Ignace Paderewski, 1919–1921		Pimento de Castro, 1915	
Gabriel Narutowicz, 1922		Bernardino Machado, 1915–1917; 1925–1926	
Stanislas Wojchie-chowski, 1922–1926	Charles I, 1916–1918	Sidonio Paës, 1917–1918	Warren Gamaliel Harding, 1921–1923
Ignace Moscicki, 1926–1939	Michael Hainisch, 1920–1928	Antonio José de Al-meida, 1919–1923	Calvin Coolidge, 1923–1929
		Teixera Gomes, 1923–1925	Herbert Hoover, 1929–1933
	William Miklas, 1928–1938	Gomes da Costa, 1926	Franklin Delano Roose-velt, 1933–1945
		Antonio de Fragoso Carmona, 1928–1933	Harry S. Truman, 1945–1953
		Antonio de Oliveira Salazar, 1933–	
			Dwight David Eisenhower, 1953–1961
	Adolf Schaerf, 1957–		John Fitzgerald Kennedy, 1961–